More Than Just a [Textbook]

Now You and Your Students Can
Stay Connected
at Glencoe.com

Internet Resources

Step 1 Connect to **History** **ONLINE** at <u>glencoe.com</u>.

Step 2 Connect to online resources by using **QuickPass** codes. You can connect directly to the chapter you want.

Student **QuickPass**

Key in chapter number

Enter Student code TAJ0862c1 to access these resources:

- Online Student Edition
- Test Practice
- Multi-language Glossary
- Interactive Maps
- Workbooks
- Section Spotlight Videos
- Study Central™ and Study-to-Go™
- . . . and more

Teacher **QuickPass**

Key in chapter number

Enter Teacher code TAJ0879c1T to access all the student materials as well as to a wealth of special Web resources.

PHOTOLIBRARY.COM/INDEX OPEN; (BKGD)RYAN MCVAY/GETTY IMAGES

The American Journey

Features and Benefits

Dynamic Instructional Structure — presents clear and comprehensive coverage of American history.
- National Geographic co-authorship ensures that the **Reference Atlas**, **Geography Skills Handbook**, and every in-text map is accurate to the last detail.
- Each engaging section introduction includes **Reading Guide**, **Content and Academic Vocabulary**, and a motivating **American Diary** feature.
- Essential Questions for each section help students organize important concepts and make it easier to understand patterns and relationships.
- The **Visual Summary** at the end of each chapter presents the major concepts in a concise manner, complete with photographs.

Strong Reading Strand — encourages active reading and learning for students of all reading levels.
- **Main Idea** and **History and You** at the beginning of each main heading give students a focus and a reason for reading, and **Reading Checks** assess comprehension.
- The **Reading History** feature at the beginning of each unit allows students to learn and practice new content-area reading skills.
- The **Reading Essentials and Note-Taking Guide** ancillary combines a concise version of the text, at a lower reading level, with a two-column note-taking guide.

Differentiated Instruction — makes *The American Journey* accessible to students at all learning levels.
- **Differentiated Instruction** activities and strategies can be found in the **Teacher Wraparound Edition**, the **Unit Resource** ancillaries, and online at **glencoe.com**.
- **Reading and Study Skills Foldables®** are 3-D kinesthetic exercises that help students organize and process key concepts as they read.
- *The American Journey* in **Graphic Novel** is one of many motivating tools for differentiating instruction and engaging learners in history.

Standardized Test Preparation — gives students the opportunity to practice for state and national exams.
- **Chapter Assessments** are now in standardized test format to provide truly useful standardized test preparation.
- Prescriptive prompts on each chapter assessment page guide students to the pages where they can revisit the material.

Motivational Activities and Features — get students excited about American history.
- The **National Geographic Geography and History** features show students how geography and history are intertwined.
- The **TIME Notebook** features make connections between events and people in American history and students' lives.
- **America's Literature** and **You Decide** features help develop critical thinking skills using primary sources.

Teacher Resources — provide convenient strategies to help both new and experienced teachers.
- The **Teacher Wraparound Edition** now contains the **Brackets and Letters System**, identifying reading, differentiated instruction, writing support, critical thinking, and skill practice activities and strategies at the *exact* point-of-use.
- *TeacherWorks Plus*™ CD contains the Interactive Teacher Edition, all ancillaries and transparencies, *editable* blackline masters, and the most powerful easy-to-use lesson planner in the business.

Technology — provides time-saving aids to help you reduce preparation time and engage students creatively.
- *StudentWorks*™ *Plus* CD includes the Interactive Student Edition, all student workbooks, and *full audio of the entire text* in English, with a Spanish audio summary.
- *ExamView®* Assessment Suite CD-ROM allows you to make customized tests using a huge databank of questions, including DBQs, that can be modified for students at all levels.
- *The American Journey* at **glencoe.com** provides chapter-based, interactive activities and Web-based resources that will engage your students.
- *Study Central*™ is an online, section-based homework helper that offers additional content, skills practice, and vocabulary development.
- *Study-To-Go*™ provides content and vocabulary review activities for portable electronic devices.
- *Presentation Plus! With MindJogger CheckPoint* CD contains a PowerPoint® presentation of the textbook, all program transparencies, and the Interactive MindJogger quiz game.
- *The American Journey* Section Spotlight Video Program offers interesting and diverse content extension for each section.

Consultants & Reviewers

Academic Consultants

Laura Belmonte, Ph.D.
Associate Professor of
History
Oklahoma State University
Stillwater, Oklahoma

David Berger, Ph.D.
Broeklundian Professor of
History
Yeshiva University
New York, New York

Keith S. Bohannon, Ph.D.
Professor of History
University of West Georgia
Carrollton, Georgia

David Canton, Ph.D.
Jacob & Hilda Blaustein
Assistant Professor of
History
Connecticut College
New London, Connecticut

Jaime Cardenas, Jr., Ph.D.
Associate Professor of
History
Seattle Central Community
College
Seattle, Washington

Jeffrey A. Davis, Ph.D.
Associate Professor of
History
Bloomsburg University of
Pennsylvania
Bloomsburg, Pennsylvania

Allison Gough, Ph.D.
Assistant Professor of History
Hawaii Pacific University
Honolulu, Hawaii

Melissa Klapper, Ph.D.
Associate Professor of
History
Rowan University
Glassboro, New Jersey

Daniel Lewis, Ph.D.
Professor of History
California State Polytechnic
University
Pomona, California

Teacher Reviewers

Lysa Augustin
Davis Hills Middle School
Huntsville, Alabama

John Brandt
Cumberland County Middle
School
Cumberland, Virginia

Joanne Cogan
Fairgrounds Middle School
Nashua, New Hampshire

Stephanie Doyle
Breckinridge Middle School
Roanoke, Virginia

Teresa Gallup
York Suburban Middle
School
York, Pennsylvania

Tina Gersdorf
Jefferson Middle School
Champaign, Illinois

Michael Gordon
Barrington Middle School
Barrington, Illinois

Dawn Grindley
Westlake Middle School
Thornwood, New York

Chris Hartlieb
Highland Middle School
Highland, Illinois

Susan Hawes
Elm Middle School
Elmwood Park, Illinois

Thomas Joice
Clark Middle School
Vincennes, Indiana

Tom Kish
Zimmerman Middle School
Zimmerman, Minnesota

Steven Miller
Blue Ridge Middle School
Purcellville, Virginia

Lisa Ray
Chapin Middle School
Chapin, South Carolina

Terry Robinson
Alden Middle School
Alden, New York

Kathleen Shaeper
Allegany-Limestone Middle
School
Allegany, New York

Karan Stubbs
Bixby Middle School
Bixby, Oklahoma

Stephanie Sumick
Thompson Middle School
Middletown, New Jersey

Laura Tabachnick
Academy School
Brattleboro, Vermont

Lynn Voorhees
Creekside Middle School
Carmel, Indiana

Marjorie White
Brentwood Middle School
North Charleston, South
Carolina

Susan Yurkovic
Brownsburg West Middle
School
Brownsburg, Indiana

Contents

NATIONAL GEOGRAPHIC Reference Atlas

Unit 1

The Americas: Worlds Meet 1

Reading History Identifying the Main Idea. 2

Unit 2

Creating a Nation..... 116

Unit 3

Launching the Republic ..246

Contents

Unit 6

Reshaping the Nation.. 546

Unit 7

Reform and Empire. . . . 636

Contents

Unit 10

America in a Modern Era 936

Appendix

Features

LINKING PAST TO PRESENT

NATIONAL GEOGRAPHIC GEOGRAPHY & HISTORY

America's LITERATURE

Economics & History

People IN HISTORY

Primary Sources
INTERPRETING
POLITICAL CARTOONS

TIME NOTEBOOK

Chance & Error in History

Skills Handbook

Critical Thinking Skills

Social Studies Skills

1 Learn It!

2 Practice It!

3 Apply It!

Documents of American History

Primary Source Quotes

Primary Source Quotes

Maps

Maps In Motion Maps, charts, and graphs with this logo have been enhanced by InMotion graphics in the StudentWorks™ Plus CD-ROM and the Presentation Plus! CD-ROM. These InMotion graphics allow students to interact with layers of data and listen to audio components.

Charts, Graphs, & Diagrams

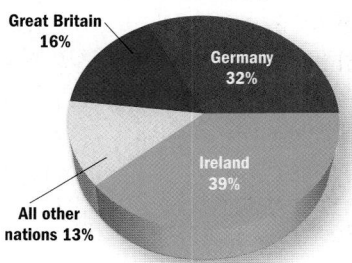

**Sources of U.S. Immigration,
1841–1860**

Great Britain 16%

Germany 32%

Ireland 39%

All other nations 13%

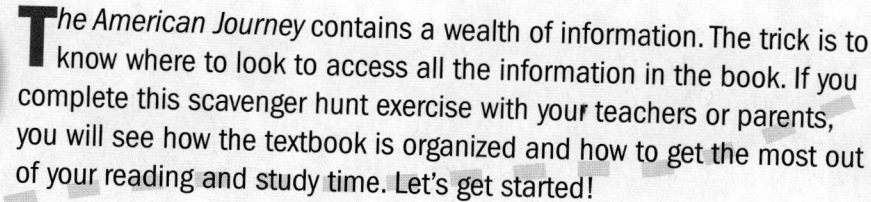

Scavenger Hunt

The American Journey contains a wealth of information. The trick is to know where to look to access all the information in the book. If you complete this scavenger hunt exercise with your teachers or parents, you will see how the textbook is organized and how to get the most out of your reading and study time. Let's get started!

1 How many units and how many chapters are in this book? 10 units, 31 chapters

2 Where would you look to quickly find facts about each state, including the capital and the year it was admitted into the Union? in the United States Facts spread in the Reference Atlas

3 You want to read the Declaration of Independence. How will you find it? in the Table of Contents and the Index

4 What time period does Chapter 16 cover? 1861–1865, the Civil War

5 In Chapter 4, what information will the *Foldables* activity help you organize? information about the growth of the colonies

6 What Reading History skill will you practice in Unit 2? Making Connections

7 Where can you find the Essential Questions for each chapter? on each Chapter Opener, on each Section Opener and Section Review, and in the Chapter Assessment

8 What is the History Online Web Activity for Chapter 12? California missions

9 Where in the back of the book can you quickly find the meaning of important vocabulary words such as *sodbuster*? in the English-Spanish Glossary

10 Where can you learn about and practice critical thinking and social studies skills? in the Skills Handbook, which is part of the Appendix

The Illinois Constitution

Illinois has had four constitutions since it became a state in 1818. The current Illinois Constitution was ratified (approved) by the voters in 1970. The following information is a summary of the 1970 Constitution. Locate the full text of the Illinois Constitution in your public or school library. You can also find it on the Internet in the state publication *Illinois Handbook of Government* at www.cyberdriveillinois.com.

Preamble

Like the U.S. Constitution, the Illinois Constitution has a preamble, or introduction. The preamble, which explains the purpose of the Constitution, is given below:

> *We, the People of the State of Illinois—grateful to Almighty God for the civil, political and religious liberty which He has permitted us to enjoy and seeking His blessing upon our endeavors—in order to provide for the health, safety and welfare of the people; maintain a representative and orderly government; eliminate poverty and inequality; assure legal, social and economic justice; provide opportunity for the fullest development of the individual; insure domestic tranquility; provide for the common defense; and secure the blessings of freedom and liberty to ourselves and our posterity—do ordain and establish this Constitution for the State of Illinois.*

The Articles

Following the preamble, there are fourteen articles, or parts, of the Illinois Constitution. The articles are listed in the table at the right.

Article I contains a Bill of Rights. The Bill of Rights has 24 sections, each guaranteeing specific rights. Many of these rights are the same as those found in the U.S. Constitution, but some additional rights are guaranteed by the Illinois Constitution. For example, Sections 18 and 19 of Article I specifically forbid discrimination on the basis of sex or physical or mental handicaps.

Just as the U.S. Constitution provides for a separation of powers within the federal government, **Article II** of the Illinois Constitution provides for the separation of the state government's power into legislative, executive, and judicial branches.

Article III gives the qualifications for suffrage (the right to vote) in Illinois. To be eligible to vote in an election, a person must be a U.S. citizen, at least 18 years old, and have been a resident of Illinois for at least thirty days preceding the election. A person who has been "convicted of a felony or otherwise under sentence in a correctional institution or jail" loses the right to vote until his or her sentence is complete.

Outline of the Illinois Constitution

Preamble	
Article I	Bill of Rights
Article II	The Powers of the State
Article III	Suffrage and Elections
Article IV	The Legislature
Article V	The Executive
Article VI	The Judiciary
Article VII	Local Government
Article VIII	Finance
Article IX	Revenue
Article X	Education
Article XI	Environment
Article XII	Militia
Article XIII	General Provisions
Article XIV	Constitutional Revision

Legislative Branch

Article IV gives rules for the legislative branch of government. The legislative branch is known as the General Assembly. Like the U.S. Congress, the General Assembly is a bicameral (two-house) legislature, consisting of a senate and a house of representatives.

Illinois is divided into 59 legislative districts. Each legislative district is further divided into two representative districts. Every ten years, the General Assembly is required to redistrict, or divide the state into new districts, after new census information becomes available. The Illinois Constitution requires that districts be "compact, contiguous [next to each other], and substantially equal in population."

Each legislative district elects one state senator, and each representative district elects one state representative. As a result, there are 59 senators and 118 representatives in the General Assembly. To be a member of the Illinois General Assembly, a person must be a U.S. citizen, at least 21 years old, and reside in the district being represented for at least two years prior to his or her election.

The main duty of the General Assembly is to make laws for the state of Illinois. A bill (proposed law) may begin in either the Senate or the House of Representatives. For a bill to pass, it must be approved by a majority of the members of each house.

After a bill is passed, it must be sent to the governor within 30 days. If the governor signs (approves) the bill, it becomes a law. If the governor vetoes (rejects) the bill, it cannot become a law unless the General Assembly overrides the veto. To override a veto, three-fifths of the members of both houses must vote to pass the bill.

The Illinois state government has a system of checks and balances, like the federal government. The governor's veto power is one check that the executive branch has on the legislative branch. The legislative branch also has ways to check the executive branch. The Senate must approve the governor's nominations for state offices. The House of Representatives has the power to impeach (charge with misconduct) members of the executive and judicial branches. The Senate tries impeachment cases. A two-thirds vote of the senators is required to convict and remove an official from office.

▲ Downtown Springfield, Illinois, in 1869 includes Lincoln and Herndon's law office, where Abraham Lincoln served as a licensed attorney.

▲ Abraham Lincoln Home, National Historic Site in Springfield

Executive Branch

Article V provides rules for the executive branch of government. The main duty of the executive branch is to carry out the laws passed by the General Assembly. The executive branch has six elected officers, as shown in the chart at the right. To be eligible for any of these offices, a person must be a U.S. citizen, at least 25 years old, and a resident of Illinois for the three years preceding his or her election. Elected officers of the executive branch serve four-year terms.

The governor and lieutenant governor must be from the same political party, but the other elected officers can be from another party. If the governor dies or is unable to serve for some other reason, the order of succession to the office is the Lieutenant Governor, the Attorney General, and then the Secretary of State.

Many of the governor's powers are similar to those of the president of the United States. There are some differences, however. The president nominates federal judges, but judges in Illinois are not nominated by the governor. The governor has the power to reduce or veto any item in an appropriations bill (a bill that spends money) while approving the rest of the bill. This is called a line-item veto and is a power that the president does not have. The president must either sign or veto an entire bill.

In addition to the six elected officers, there are other officers in the executive branch. These officers are called appointed officers. They are named by the governor, but their nominations must be approved by the Illinois Senate.

Judicial Branch

Article VI gives the rules for the judicial branch. The main duty of this branch is to interpret the laws and decide if people have followed the laws. Like the federal court system, the Illinois court system has three types of courts: a Supreme Court, an Appellate Court, and circuit courts.

Circuit courts have original jurisdiction in most matters, which means that they are the first courts to hear most cases. Circuit judges are elected and serve 6-year terms. Associate judges are appointed by the circuit judges and serve 4-year terms.

Selected Duties of Elected Officers of the Executive Branch

Governor
- Chief executive officer of the state
- Nominates state officials
- Makes annual reports to the General Assembly and proposes budgets for the state
- Grants reprieves, commutations, and pardons
- Signs or vetoes bills
- May call special sessions of the General Assembly

Lieutenant Governor
- Becomes governor if the governor dies or is unable to serve
- Performs duties delegated by the governor or prescribed by law

Attorney General
- Chief legal officer of the state
- Coordinates law enforcement activities within the state

Secretary of State
- Maintains the official records of the General Assembly and the executive branch
- Keeps the Great Seal of the State of Illinois

Comptroller
- Chief fiscal (financial) officer of the state
- Maintains the state's financial records
- Reviews and orders payments of the state's bills

Treasurer
- Safeguards and invests the state's monies
- Disburses monies as ordered by the comptroller

▲ Old State Capitol built in Springfield in 1837

The Appellate Court hears appeals from circuit courts. Appellate Court judges are elected and serve 10-year terms.

The Supreme Court has seven judges, called justices. They are elected and serve 10-year terms. The Supreme Court hears appeals from the Appellate Court and appeals from circuit courts when a death sentence is involved. The Supreme Court may also exercise original jurisdiction (hear a case for the first time) in cases relating to revenue, mandamus (ordering a public official to carry out his or her duties), prohibition (forbidding a court from trying a case that should be tried in another court), or habeas corpus (bringing a person before a court to determine if he or she is being legally held in custody).

Illinois is divided into five judicial districts for the selection of Supreme and Appellate Court judges. To be a judge in Illinois, a person must be a U.S. citizen, a licensed attorney of the state, and a resident of the district or circuit in which he or she is elected.

Articles VII–XIV

Article VII gives rules for local governments. Units of local government in Illinois include counties, townships, special districts, and municipalities (cities, villages, and incorporated towns). Local governments have limited powers. They may pass ordinances (local laws), and they may tax and borrow money. When there is a conflict between state and local governments, the state government's powers are greater.

Article VIII says that public funds (money) can only be used for public purposes. It also explains how public funds are to be budgeted, spent, and audited. The governor's office prepares a budget, which estimates how much money will be available and proposes how the money should be spent. However, the General Assembly actually decides how the money will be spent.

Article IX indicates how revenue (money) can be collected through taxes. Illinois has a non-graduated income tax. This means that there is a flat rate on all incomes. The personal property tax was eliminated in 1979, but there is still a tax on real estate property. Some entities, such as local governments and certain non-profit organizations, are exempt from this tax. Article IX also gives rules relating to state debts.

▲ Northern Cardinal, state bird of Illinois

Article X states that education in public schools through the secondary (high school) level shall be free. The state's education program is the responsibility of the State Board of Education.

Article XI says that people have the right to a "healthful environment." This article gives the General Assembly the power to make laws to insure a healthy environment in Illinois.

Article XII states that "the State militia consists of all able-bodied persons residing in the State except those exempted by law." The governor is the commander-in-chief of the state militia. He may use the militia to "enforce the laws, suppress insurrection or repel invasion."

Article XIII contains general provisions, including rules for people serving in state offices in Illinois. For example, a person convicted of "a felony, bribery, perjury, or other infamous crimes" cannot hold a public office in Illinois. This article also states that the General Assembly may spend public funds for public transportation.

Article XIV gives the rules for revising the Illinois Constitution. At least once every twenty years, the voters in the state must decide if a convention should be called to revise the Constitution. The General Assembly may also suggest amendments to the Constitution. Revisions and amendments must be approved by the voters. When amendments are made to the Illinois Constitution, the changes are made to the articles themselves, not added at the end like amendments to the U.S. Constitution.

Article XIV also states that a "vote of three-fifths of the members elected to each house of the General Assembly shall be required to request Congress to call a Federal Constitutional Convention, to ratify a proposed amendment to the Constitution of the United States, or to call a State Convention to ratify a proposed amendment to the Constitution of the United States."

▲ Cave-in-Rock
painting by Karl Bodmer

▲ Ulysses S. Grant Home
State Historic Site in Galena

How can I Test My Knowledge of the U.S. and Illinois Constitutions?

Pages IL36–IL59 of this text include a section called Constitution Test Practice. Each page contains five questions to test your understanding of the U.S. and Illinois Constitutions and flag etiquette. You should plan to complete one page each week to help build your knowledge.

Plan to spend a few minutes each day working on the test question for that day, unless your teacher asks you to do otherwise. All questions are multiple-choice questions. Some include visuals, such as documents, maps, charts, and graphs, that you will need to interpret in order to answer the questions. If you have difficulty with any question, you can refer to the Illinois Constitution Summary on pages IL28–IL33 or the U.S. Constitution on pages 214–223.

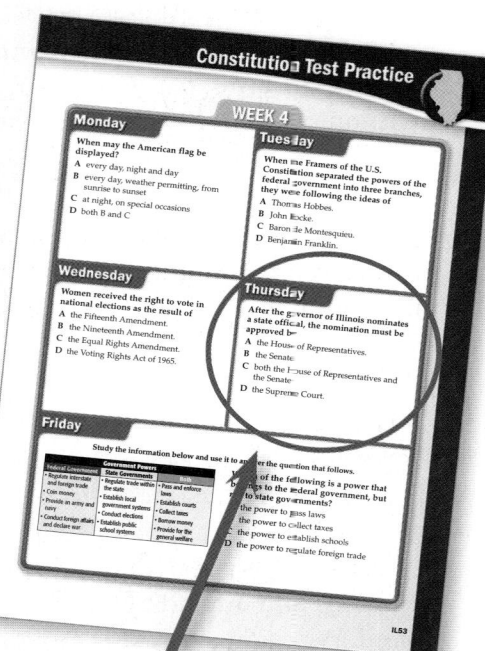

Thursday

After the governor of Illinois nominates a state official, the nomination must be approved by

A the House of Representatives.

B the Senate.

C both the House of Representatives and the Senate.

D the Supreme Court.

How does my textbook help me prepare for tests?

Your textbook contains many opportunities for you to get ready for tests every day. Take advantage of these so you don't need to cram before you take a test.

- The **sections** contain many maps and charts and other features with corresponding questions that allow you to practice interpreting text and visuals.

- The **section reviews** at the end of each section allow for further practice in evaluating, analyzing, and interpreting information and visuals.

- Answering the **Essential Questions** helps you focus on the main ideas of each section.

- The **Standardized Test Practice** questions in each chapter assessment help you prepare for multiple-choice test formats.

TEST-TAKING TIPS

- Go to bed early the night before the test.
- Read each question carefully and think about ways to solve it before you try to answer the question.
- Relax. Most people get nervous when taking a test. It's natural. Just do your best.
- Answer questions you are sure about first. If you do not know the answer, skip it and go back to that question later.
- Make sure to look at any visuals that are part of the question before you select your answer.

Constitution Test Practice

WEEK 1

Monday

What is the term of office of the president of the United States?

A two years

(B) four years

C six years

D eight years

Tuesday

The United States Constitution created a system of government that divided powers between the national government and the states. This system is known as

A republicanism.

(B) federalism.

C separation of powers.

D popular sovereignty.

Wednesday

Study the information below and use it to answer the question that follows.

We hold these truths to be self-evident, that all men are created equal, that they are endowed by their Creator with certain unalienable rights, that among these are Life, Liberty, and the pursuit of Happiness.

That to secure these rights, Governments are instituted among Men, deriving their just powers from the consent of the governed. . . .

—*Declaration of Independence*

According to the Declaration of Independence, governments derive their powers from

A God.

B the King of Great Britain.

C Congress.

(D) the people.

Thursday

Who is the chief executive officer of the state of Illinois?

(A) the governor

B the lieutenant governor

C the attorney general

D the secretary of state

Friday

An amendment to the Illinois Constitution may be proposed by

A the attorney general.

B the governor.

C the Supreme Court.

(D) the General Assembly.

WEEK 2

Monday

The justices of the Illinois Supreme Court are

A nominated by the governor.

B approved by the House of Representatives.

C approved by the Senate.

(D) elected by the people.

Tuesday

If the Illinois governor dies or is otherwise unable to serve, the order of succession is

(A) lieutenant governor, attorney general, secretary of state.

B lieutenant governor, secretary of state, attorney general.

C attorney general, lieutenant governor, secretary of state.

D secretary of state, lieutenant governor, attorney general.

Wednesday

Which of the following are the two primary functions of the United States Congress?

(A) to make the nation's laws and to control government spending

B to make the nation's laws and to negotiate treaties

C to make the nation's laws and to carry out those laws

D to make the nation's laws and to hear and rule on cases

Thursday

Which of the following amendments to the U.S. Constitution was repealed?

A the Twelfth Amendment

(B) the Eighteenth Amendment

C the Twenty-First Amendment

D the Twenty-Fifth Amendment

Friday

Study the picture below and use it to answer the question that follows.

When should the American flag be flown at half-mast?

(A) to mourn the death of a public official

B on national and state holidays

C to signal distress

D at night

Constitution Test Practice

WEEK 3

Monday

When was the Declaration of Independence approved?

A July 2, 1776

B July 4, 1776

C May 10, 1775

C September 17, 1787

Tuesday

According to the U.S. Constitution, the president can veto a bill passed by Congress, but Congress can override the veto by a vote of two-thirds of the members of both houses. This is an example of

A judicial review.

B checks and balances.

C amendments.

D federalism.

Wednesday

Study the information below and use it to answer the question that follows.

Legislative Branch

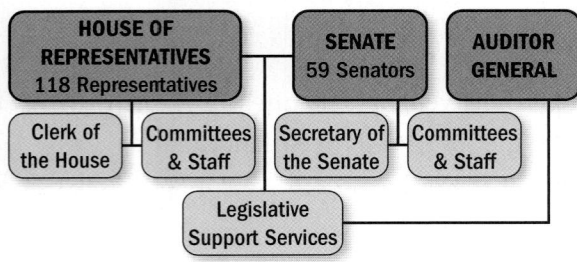

The chart illustrates the fact that the Illinois General Assembly

A is part of the executive branch of government.

B is part of the judicial branch of government.

C is a bicameral legislature.

D can appoint Supreme Court justices.

Thursday

If there is a tie vote in the U.S. Senate, who casts the deciding vote?

A the president of the United States

B the vice president of the United States

C the speaker of the House of Representatives

D the chief justice of the U.S. Supreme Court

Friday

If the governor of Illinois vetoes a bill, can it still become a law?

A Yes, by a three-fifths vote of both houses of the General Assembly.

B Yes, by a unanimous vote of both houses of the General Assembly.

C Yes, but only if the General Assembly makes the changes recommended by the governor.

D No, the bill cannot become a law.

WEEK 4

Monday

When may the American flag be displayed?

A every day, night and day

B every day, weather permitting, from sunrise to sunset

C at night, on special occasions

D both B and C

Tuesday

When the Framers of the U.S. Constitution separated the powers of the federal government into three branches, they were following the ideas of

A Thomas Hobbes.

B John Locke.

C Baron de Montesquieu.

D Benjamin Franklin.

Wednesday

Women received the right to vote in national elections as the result of

A the Fifteenth Amendment.

B the Nineteenth Amendment.

C the Equal Rights Amendment.

D the Voting Rights Act of 1965.

Thursday

After the governor of Illinois nominates a state official, the nomination must be approved by

A the House of Representatives.

B the Senate.

C both the House of Representatives and the Senate.

D the Supreme Court.

Friday

Study the information below and use it to answer the question that follows.

Government Powers

Federal Government	State Governments	Both
• Regulate interstate and foreign trade	• Regulate trade within the state	• Pass and enforce laws
• Coin money	• Establish local government systems	• Establish courts
• Provide an army and navy	• Conduct elections	• Collect taxes
• Conduct foreign affairs and declare war	• Establish public school systems	• Borrow money
		• Provide for the general welfare

Which of the following is a power that belongs to the federal government, but *not* to state governments?

A the power to pass laws

B the power to collect taxes

C the power to establish schools

D the power to regulate foreign trade

WEEK 5

Monday

What power does the governor of Illinois have that the president of the United States does not have?

A the power to veto bills

B the power to nominate judges

C the power to grant pardons

(D) the line-item veto

Tuesday

Who was the main author of the Declaration of Independence?

A John Adams

(B) Thomas Jefferson

C Benjamin Franklin

D George Washington

Wednesday

Study the information below and use it to answer the question that follows.

[The Congress shall have the Power] To make all Laws which shall be necessary and proper for carrying into Execution the foregoing Powers, and all other Powers vested by this Constitution in the Government of the United States, or in any Department or Officer thereof.

—The Constitution of the United States, Article I, Section 8

The powers assumed by Congress as a result of this clause are called

A expressed powers.

B reserved powers.

(C) implied powers.

D concurrent powers.

Thursday

Who is the chief legal officer of the state of Illinois?

A the governor

B the lieutenant governor

(C) the attorney general

D the chief justice of the Illinois Supreme Court

Friday

As a result of *Marbury* v. *Madison,* which branch of government has the right to determine when a law violates the U.S. Constitution?

A executive branch

B legislative branch

(C) judicial branch

D state governments

WEEK 6

Monday

The main duty of the executive branch of Illinois government is to

A make laws for the state of Illinois.

B carry out the laws of the state of Illinois.

C interpret the laws and decide if people have followed the laws.

D check the power of the legislative branch.

Tuesday

Racial segregation in public schools came to an end as the result of

A passage of the Fourteenth Amendment.

B passage of the Civil Rights Act of 1964.

C *Plessy v. Ferguson.*

D *Brown v. Board of Education.*

Wednesday

If the Illinois flag is flown with the American flag, where should the Illinois flag be flown?

A above the American flag

B below the American flag

C to the right of the American flag

D none of the above

Thursday

The strongest criticism of the U.S. Constitution by Anti-Federalists was that

A it lacked a bill of rights.

B it gave too much power to the states.

C it gave too many freedoms to individuals.

D it did not create a national government that was strong enough.

Friday

Study the information below and use it to answer the question that follows.

Circuit Courts shall have original jurisdiction of all justiciable matters except when the Supreme Court has original and exclusive jurisdiction. . . .

—Constitution of the State of Illinois, Article VI, Section 9

When the Illinois Constitution states that circuit courts have original jurisdiction in most matters, it means that

A circuit courts are the first courts to hear most cases.

B circuit courts are the final authority in most matters.

C circuit courts hear appeals from lower courts.

D decisions by circuit courts cannot be appealed.

WEEK 7

Monday

After a bill is passed by the Illinois General Assembly, it must be sent to the governor within

A 24 hours.

B 10 days.

C 30 days.

D 60 days.

Tuesday

Who was the first person to sign the Declaration of Independence?

A Thomas Jefferson

B Richard Henry Lee

C John Hancock

D Patrick Henry

Wednesday

Study the information below and use it to answer the question that follows.

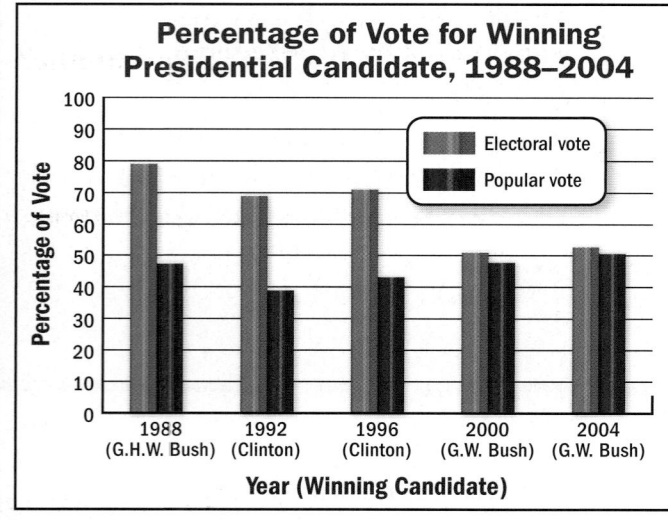

Percentage of Vote for Winning Presidential Candidate, 1988–2004

Legend: Electoral vote, Popular vote

Year (Winning Candidate): 1988 (G.H.W. Bush), 1992 (Clinton), 1996 (Clinton), 2000 (G.W. Bush), 2004 (G.W. Bush)

In past presidential elections it has been common for the popluar vote total to be different from the electoral vote total. To be elected president of the United States, a candidate must receive

A a majority of the popular vote.

B two-thirds of the electoral vote.

C a majority of the electoral vote.

D both A and C

Thursday

The Illinois Supreme Court has how many judges?

A 7

B 9

C 10

D 12

Friday

Which part of the U.S. Bill of Rights protects the rights of states by saying that powers not specifically given to the federal government are "reserved to the States respectively, or to the people"?

A the First Amendment

B the Fifth Amendment

C the Tenth Amendment

D the Twelfth Amendment

Constitution Test Practice

WEEK 8

Monday

Which of the following was *not* an issue during the Constitutional Convention?

A how many representatives each state should have in Congress

B how to count enslaved people for taxation and representation

C whether the slave trade should be allowed to continue

(D) whether enslaved people should be given the right to vote

Tuesday

The main duty of the legislative branch of Illinois government is to

(A) make laws for the state of Illinois.

B carry out the laws of the state of Illinois.

C interpret the laws and decide if people have followed the laws.

D check the power of the executive branch.

Wednesday

The Twelfth Amendment to the U.S. Constitution changed the method of electing the president by

(A) requiring that electors cast separate ballots for president and vice president.

B requiring that electors vote for two people for president.

C limiting the number of times that a president can be elected.

D allowing citizens living in Washington, D.C., to vote for president and vice president.

Thursday

Amendments to the Illinois Constitution are found

A at the end of the Constitution.

B at the beginning of the Constitution.

C after the preamble but before the articles.

(D) in the articles to which they pertain.

Friday

Study the information below and use it to answer the question that follows.

He [King George III] has combined with others to subject us to a jurisdiction foreign to our constitution, and unacknowledged by our laws; giving his Assent to their acts of pretended legislation. . . .

For imposing taxes on us without our Consent. . . .

—*The Declaration of Independence*

One of the grievances listed in the Declaration of Independence was "imposing taxes on us without our Consent." This grievance is often referred to as

A a boycott.

B a writ of assistance.

C quartering.

(D) taxation without representation.

WEEK 9

Monday

To be eligible to vote in Illinois, a person must be a U.S. citizen,

(A) at least 18 years old, and a resident of Illinois for at least 30 days before the election.

B at least 18 years old, and a resident of Illinois for at least six months before the election.

C at least 18 years old, and a resident of Illinois for at least one year before the election.

D at least 21 years old, and a resident of Illinois for at least 30 days before the election.

Tuesday

According to the U.S. Constitution, treaties with other nations must be approved by

A the president.

(B) the Senate.

C the House of Representatives.

D both B and C

Wednesday

Study the information below and use it to answer the question that follows.

No Bill of Attainder or ex post facto Law may be passed.
—*The Constitution of the United States, Article I, Section 9*

What is an ex post facto law?

A a law requiring that a prisoner be brought before a court to determine if he or she is being legally held in custody.

B a law that punishes a person without a jury trial.

(C) a law that makes an act a crime after the act has been committed.

D a law that orders a public official to carry out his or her duties.

Thursday

The American flag should never

A be flown upside down.

B be flown at half mast.

(C) touch the ground or floor beneath it.

D be flown at night.

Friday

What is the name of the legislative branch of government in Illinois?

A the Congress

(B) the General Assembly

C the Supreme Court

D the attorney general's office

Constitution Test Practice

WEEK 10

Monday

The Sixteenth Amendment to the U.S. Constitution created the

(A) federal income tax.

B state income tax.

C sales tax.

D all of the above

Tuesday

When the Declaration of Independence mentions the "unalienable rights" of life, liberty, and the pursuit of happiness, it is drawing on the ideas of

A Thomas Hobbes.

(B) John Locke.

C Baron de Montesquieu.

D Benjamin Franklin.

Wednesday

The main duty of the judicial branch of Illinois government is to

A make laws for the state of Illinois.

B carry out the laws of the state of Illinois.

(C) interpret the laws and decide if people have followed the laws.

D check the power of the legislative branch.

Thursday

What is the president's cabinet?

A the president's advisors

B the electors who vote for president and vice president

C the heads of the executive departments

(D) both A and C

Friday

Study the information below and use it to answer the question that follows.

Selected Legislative Districts of Illinois
(2001 Reapportionment)

Effingham, Jasper, Clay, Richland, Marion 107, 54, 108, Clinton, St. Clair, Washington, Jefferson, Wayne, Edwards, Monroe 116, 58, White, Perry 115, Hamilton, Randolph, Franklin 117, Jackson, Williamson, Saline, Gallatin, 59, 118, Union, Johnson, Pope, Hardin, Alexander, Pulaski, Massac

LEGEND
99 Representative District
50 Legislative (Senatorial) District

Each legislative district in Illinois is divided into

(A) two representative districts.

B three representative districts.

C four representative districts.

D five representative districts.

Constitution Test Practice

WEEK 11

Monday

According to the Declaration of Independence, governments exist to

A wage war.

(B) protect people's rights.

C control people.

D make people happy.

Tuesday

The Bill of Rights in the Illinois Constitution is

A the first ten amendments to the Illinois Constitution.

(B) the first article of the Illinois Constitution.

C the last article of the Illinois Constitution.

D the preamble to the Illinois Constitution.

Wednesday

Study the information below and use it to answer the question that follows.

The House of Representatives shall be composed of Members chosen every second Year by the People of the several States. . . . Representatives and direct Taxes shall be apportioned among the several States which may be included within this Union, according to their respective Numbers. . . .

The Senate of the United States shall be composed of two Senators from each State, chosen by the Legislature thereof, for six Years; and each Senator shall have one Vote. . . .

These excerpts from Article 1, Sections 2 and 3, of the United States Constitution illustrate

A the Virginia Plan.

B the New Jersey Plan.

(C) the Great Compromise.

D the Three-Fifths Compromise.

Thursday

In Illinois, the Appellate Court hears appeals from

(A) circuit courts.

B the Supreme Court.

C circuit courts, but only when the death sentence is involved.

D federal district courts.

Friday

What does the United States Constitution say about political parties?

A It establishes the two-party system.

B It protects the rights of people to create third parties.

C It outlaws political parties.

(D) It says nothing about political parties.

WEEK 12

Monday

The original purpose of the Convention that created the U.S. Constitution was

(A) to revise the Articles of Confederation.

B   to abolish slavery.

C   to create a strong national government.

D   to declare independence from Great Britain.

Tuesday

The Illinois Constitution is divided into how many articles?

A   7

B   10

(C) 14

D   24

Wednesday

The Illinois General Assembly has how many members?

A   59

B   118

(C) 177

D   435

Thursday

To be a U.S. senator, a person must be

A   25 years old and a citizen of the United States for 7 years.

B   25 years old and a citizen of the United States for 9 years.

(C) 30 years old and a citizen of the United States for 9 years.

D   35 years old and a citizen of the United States for 14 years.

Friday

Study the information below and use it to answer the question that follows.

When may the American flag be flown upside down?

A   to mourn the death of a public official

B   on national and state holidays

(C) to signal distress

D   never

Constitution Test Practice

WEEK 13

Monday

In the Illinois Constitution, which of the following is *not* included among crime victim's rights?

A the right to be protected from the accused

B the privilege of the writ of habeas corpus

C the right to restitution

D the right to make a statement to the court at sentencing

Tuesday

The Constitutional Convention was held

A in Philadelphia in 1776.

B in Philadelphia in 1787.

C in New York in 1776.

D in New York in 1787.

Wednesday

Study the information below and use it to answer the question that follows.

A tax on or measured by income shall be at a non-graduated rate. At any one time there may be no more than one such tax imposed by the State for State purposes on individuals and one such tax so imposed on corporations.

—The Constitution of the State of Illinois, Article IX, Section 3

The non-graduated tax is

A a flat rate tax.

B a tax that has different rates based on income.

C a tax that is required to graduate.

D a tax on personal property.

Thursday

According to the Declaration of Independence, if a government does not protect people's rights, the people have the right to

A alter it.

B abolish it.

C form a new government.

D all of the above

Friday

How many articles are there in the United States Constitution?

A 7

B 10

C 14

D 24

WEEK 14

Monday

When a flag becomes old and tattered, it should be

(A) destroyed by burning.

B buried.

C carefully preserved.

D none of the above

Tuesday

The elected officers of the executive branch in Illinois serve terms of

A two years.

(B) four years.

C six years.

D ten years.

Wednesday

The first plan of government for the United States was

A the Declaration of Independence.

(B) the Articles of Confederation.

C the U.S. Constitution.

D none of the above

Thursday

If citizens of Illinois meet the qualifications to vote,

A they can never lose the right to vote.

(B) they can be denied the right to vote if they are convicted of a felony.

C they can only lose the right to vote if they move to another state.

D they do not need to register in order to vote.

Friday

Study the information below and use it to answer the question that follows.

. . . We think they [people of African ancestry] are . . . not included, and were not intended to be included, under the word "citizens" in the Constitution, and can therefore claim none of the rights and privileges which that instrument provides for and secures to citizens of the United States. . . .

—Chief Justice Roger B. Taney, speaking for the majority, Dred Scott v. Sandford *(1857)*

The *Dred Scott* decision meant that

A slavery was unconstitutional.

B enslaved African Americans had the same rights as other Americans.

C enslaved African Americans had the right to be free if they had lived in a free state at any time.

(D) enslaved African Americans were not protected by the U.S. Constitution.

Constitution Test Practice

WEEK 15

Monday

To be eligible to run for governor in the state of Illinois, a person must be a U.S. citizen,

A   at least 21 years old, and a resident of Illinois for at least two years.

B   at least 25 years old, and a resident of Illinois for at least two years.

C   at least 25 years old, and a resident of Illinois for at least three years.

D   at least 35 years old, and a resident of Illinois for at least three years.

Tuesday

The first ten amendments to the U.S. Constitution are called the

A   Preamble.

B   Articles.

C   Bill of Rights.

D   Civil War amendments.

Wednesday

Study the information below and use it to answer the question that follows.

Judicial Branch

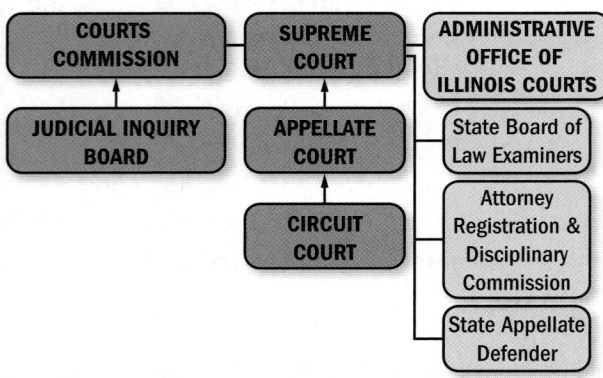

The Illinois court system has how many types of courts?

A   one

B   two

C   three

D   four

Thursday

Powers that belong *only* to the federal government are called

A   enumerated powers.

B   reserved powers.

C   concurrent powers.

D   both A and B

Friday

The Declaration of Independence included all of the following *except*

A   a list of rights that the colonists believed they should have.

B   a list of grievances that the colonists held against the king and Parliament.

C   the reasons for forming a new government.

D   a description of the structure of the new government.

WEEK 16

Monday

Who is often called the Father of the Constitution?

A Thomas Jefferson
B Benjamin Franklin
C James Madison
D George Washington

Tuesday

When is a star added to the American flag?

A when a war is won
B when a president dies
C when a state is added to the Union
D Stars are never added to the American flag.

Wednesday

The Declaration of Independence was written during

A the First Continental Congress.
B the Second Continental Congress.
C the Confederation Congress.
D the Constitutional Convention.

Thursday

To be a judge in Illinois, a person must be a U.S. citizen,

A at least 25 years old, and a resident of the state for at least three years.
B at least 25 years old, and a resident of the district or circuit in which he or she is elected.
C a licensed attorney of the state, and a resident of the state for at least three years.
D a licensed attorney of the state, and a resident of the district or circuit in which he or she is elected.

Friday

Study the information below and use it to answer the question that follows.

The Privilege of the Writ of Habeas Corpus shall not be suspended, unless when in Cases of Rebellion or Invasion the public Safety may require it.

—*U.S. Constitution, Article I, Section 9*

What is a writ of habeas corpus?

A a court order requiring that a prisoner be brought before a court to determine if he or she is being legally held in custody
B a court order that forbids a court to try a case that should be tried in another court
C a court order requiring a public official to carry out his or her duties
D a court order that punishes a person without a jury trial

Constitution Test Practice

WEEK 17

Monday

How many amendments have been added to the U.S. Constitution?

A 10

B 17

C 27

D 50

Tuesday

Who is the commander-in-chief of the Illinois state militia?

A the governor of Illinois

B the attorney general of Illinois

C the secretary of state of Illinois

D the comptroller of the state of Illinois

Wednesday

Study the information below and use it to answer the question that follows.

No person shall be elected to the office of the President more than twice, and no person who had held the office of President, or acted as President, for more than two years of a term to which some other person was elected President shall be elected to the office of the President more than once.

—The Constitution of the United States, Amendment XXII

What is the maximum number of years that a person can serve as president of the United States?

A 4 years

B 6 years

C 8 years

D 10 years

Thursday

Illinois is divided into how many judicial districts?

A 5

B 10

C 59

D 118

Friday

Powers that are shared by federal and state governments are called

A enumerated powers.

B reserved powers.

C concurrent powers.

D delegated powers.

WEEK 18

Monday

How many senators are there in the United States Senate?

A 50

(B) 100

C 435

D 440

Tuesday

The Illinois Supreme Court hears appeals from

A the Appellate Court.

B circuit courts when a death sentence is involved.

C federal district courts.

(D) both A and B

Wednesday

As commander-in-chief, the president of the United States can

(A) send troops to other parts of the world for up to 60 days without congressional approval.

B send troops to other parts of the world for up to a year without congressional approval.

C declare war.

D both A and C

Thursday

Which of the following Illinois officials must be from the same political party?

(A) the governor and lieutenant governor

B the governor, lieutenant governor, and attorney general

C the governor, lieutenant governor, attorney general, and secretary of state

D all of the elected executive branch officers

Friday

Study the information below and use it to answer the question that follows.

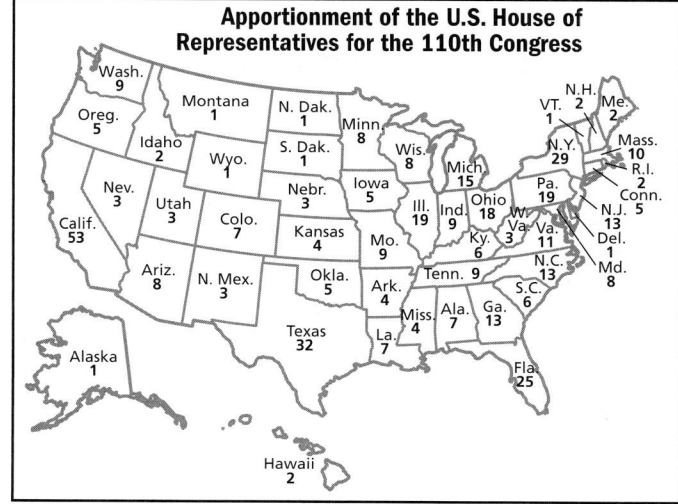

Apportionment of the U.S. House of Representatives for the 110th Congress

The number of representatives in the U.S. House of Representatives

A is the same for all states.

B is based on the population of each state at the time it was admitted to the Union.

(C) is based on the population of each state at the time of the latest census.

D is based on the geographic size of each state.

Constitution Test Practice

WEEK 19

Monday

Which of the following crimes would keep a person from holding public office in Illinois?

A felonies

B bribery

C perjury

(D) all of the above

Tuesday

How many voting members are there in the U.S. House of Representatives?

A 50

B 100

(C) 435

D 440

Wednesday

Study the information below and use it to answer the question that follows.

The Governor may reduce or veto any item of appropriations in a bill presented to him. Portions of a bill not reduced or vetoed shall become law.

—*The Constitution of the State of Illinois, Article IV*

An appropriations bill is a bill that

A approves the governor's nominations.

B approves associate judges of the circuit courts.

(C) spends money.

D defines appropriate behavior for public officials.

Thursday

What happens if no one candidate for president receives a majority of the electoral votes?

A The candidate who receives the majority of the popular votes becomes president.

(B) The House of Representatives elects the president.

C The Supreme Court elects the president.

D Each state must reallocate its votes based on the popular vote.

Friday

Federal courts include all of the following *except*

A the Supreme Court.

B appeals courts.

C district courts.

(D) small claims courts.

WEEK 20

Monday

The term of office for a U.S. senator is

A 2 years.

B 4 years.

C 6 years.

D 10 years.

Tuesday

In Illinois, state senators are elected from

A legislative districts.

B representative districts.

C judicial districts.

D both A and B

Wednesday

To be a member of the U.S. House of Representatives, a person must be

A 25 years old and a citizen of the United States for 7 years.

B 25 years old and a citizen of the United States for 9 years.

C 30 years old and a citizen of the United States for 9 years.

D 35 years old and a citizen of the United States for 14 years.

Thursday

Which amendment to the U.S. Constitution outlawed slavery in the United States?

A the Fifth Amendment

B the Thirteenth Amendment

C the Eighteenth Amendment

D the Twenty-Fourth Amendment

Friday

Study the picture below and use it to answer the question that follows.

In the current American flag, the stripes represent

A the number of states in the Union.

B the thirteen original colonies.

C both A and B

D neither A nor B

Constitution Test Practice

WEEK 21

Monday

Who is the leader of the U.S. House of Representatives?

A the Speaker of the House
B the vice president
C the president pro tempore
D both B and C

Tuesday

Who decides how public funds will be spent in Illinois?

A the governor
B the General Assembly
C the comptroller
D the treasurer

Wednesday

Study the information below and use it to answer the question that follows.

You have the right to remain silent. Anything you say can be used against you in a court of law. You have the right to have an attorney present now and during any future questioning. If you cannot afford an attorney, one will be appointed to you free of charge if you wish.

People who are in police custody must be told their rights to ensure that they do not unknowingly incriminate, or provide evidence against, themselves. This protection is guaranteed by

A the First Amendment.
B the Fourth Amendment.
C the Fifth Amendment.
D the Tenth Amendment.

Thursday

Who has the power to impeach members of the executive and judicial branches in Illinois?

A the governor
B the House of Representatives
C the Senate
D the Supreme Court

Friday

To run for president of the United States, a person must be a citizen of the United States by birth,

A at least 30 years old, and a resident of the United States for 9 years.
B at least 30 years old, and a resident of the United States for 14 years.
C at least 35 years old, and a resident of the United States for 9 years.
D at least 35 years old, and a resident of the United States for 14 years.

WEEK 22

Monday

What is the name of the legislative branch of the United States government?

(A) the Congress

B   the Supreme Court

C   the White House

D   the Cabinet

Tuesday

Who may preside over the United States Senate?

A   the speaker of the Senate

(B) the vice president

C   the minority leader

D   the chief justice of the Supreme Court

Wednesday

What is the "supreme Law of the Land" according to the U.S. Constitution?

A   laws passed by Congress

B   laws passed by Congress and treaties of the United States

(C) the U.S. Constitution, laws passed by Congress, and treaties of the United States

D   the U.S. Constitution and the state constitutions

Thursday

Illinois currently has which of the following taxes?

(A) income tax

B   personal property tax

C   homestead tax

D   recreation tax

Friday

Study the information below and use it to answer the question that follows.

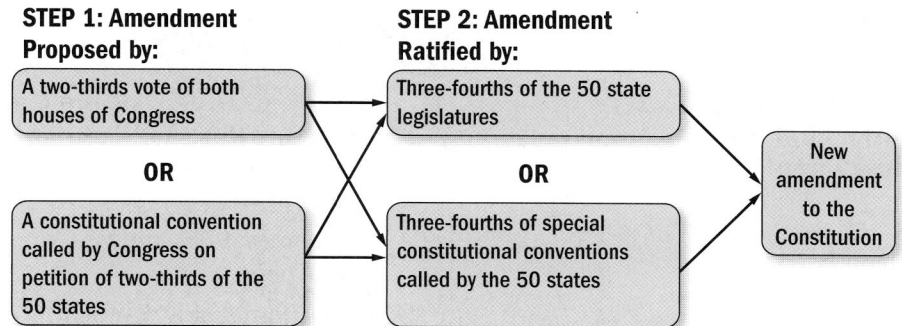

STEP 1: Amendment Proposed by:

A two-thirds vote of both houses of Congress

OR

A constitutional convention called by Congress on petition of two-thirds of the 50 states

STEP 2: Amendment Ratified by:

Three-fourths of the 50 state legislatures

OR

Three-fourths of special constitutional conventions called by the 50 states

New amendment to the Constitution

Amendments to the United States Constitution can be proposed by

(A) a two-thirds vote of both houses of Congress.

B   three-fourths of the 50 state legislatures.

C   three-fourths of the state constitutional conventions.

D   two-thirds of the original 13 states.

Constitution Test Practice

WEEK 23

Monday

Who is the chief fiscal officer of the state of Illinois?

A the governor

B the attorney general

C the comptroller

D the treasurer

Tuesday

The term of office for a member of the U.S. House of Representatives is

A 2 years.

B 4 years.

C 6 years.

D 10 years.

Wednesday

Study the information below and use it to answer the question that follows.

Number of Elected Officials in Illinois

U.S. Senators	2
U.S. Representatives	9
State Senators	59
State Representatives	118

Based on the table, how many electors will Illinois have in the Electoral College?

A 2

B 9

C 11

D 59

Thursday

What amendment to the U.S. Constitution guarantees freedom of religion?

A the First Amendment

B the Second Amendment

C the Fifth Amendment

D the Sixth Amendment

Friday

What happens to a bill if the president does not sign it within ten days, excluding Sundays, after he receives it?

A It becomes a law unless Congress has adjourned.

B It is automatically vetoed.

C It goes to the Senate to be reconsidered.

D It goes to the Supreme Court for approval.

WEEK 24

Monday

At the federal level, appropriations bills

(A) must originate in the House of Representatives.

B must originate in the Senate.

C may originate in either the House of Representatives or the Senate.

D must be submitted by the president.

Tuesday

When was the current Illinois Constitution approved?

A 1818

B 1870

(C) 1970

D 1979

Wednesday

Can a presidential veto be overridden?

A Yes, by a majority vote of both houses of Congress

(B) Yes, by a two-thirds vote of both houses of Congress

C Yes, by a three-fifths vote of both houses of Congress

D No, a presidential veto cannot be overridden

Thursday

What is the name of the national anthem of the United States?

A "America the Beautiful"

B "O! Say Can You See"

(C) "The Star-Spangled Banner"

D "By the Dawn's Early Light"

Friday

Study the information below and use it to answer the question that follows.

The President, Vice President and all civil Officers of the United States, shall be removed from Office on Impeachment for, and Conviction of, Treason, Bribery, or other high Crimes and Misdemeanors.

—*The Constitution of the United States, Article II, Section 4*

When the president of the United States is impeached,

A the Senate has the power of impeachment.

B the House of Representatives tries the president.

(C) the chief justice of the Supreme Court presides at the trial.

D the verdict is decided by popular vote.

Focus on Illinois

Correlation to the Illinois Learning Standards for Social Sciences

Standards	Student Edition Pages	Teacher Edition Pages
STATE GOAL 14: Understand political systems, with an emphasis on the United States.		
14A. Understand and explain basic Principles of the United States government.	186, 252, 264	185, 206
14.A.3 Describe how responsibilities are shared and limited by the United States and Illinois Constitutions and significant court decisions.	206, 207, 215–220, 221–225, 226–228, 266, 267, 270, 279, 322, 323, 324, 796, 798	IL28–IL33, IL85–IL88, 187, 188, 206, 279, 324, 327
14B. Understand the structures and functions of the political systems of Illinois, the United States and other nations.	215–220, 221–225, 226–228, 276, 842	IL28–IL33, 185, 190, 200, 204, 208, 210, 340
14.B.3 Identify and compare the basic political systems of Illinois and the United States as prescribed in their constitutions.	215–220	IL28–IL33, IL85–IL88, 188
14C. Understand election processes and responsibilities of citizens.	226–228, 336, 348, 456	IL28–IL33, IL85–IL88, 60, 198, 339, 751
14.C.3 Compare historical issues involving rights, roles and status of individuals in relation to municipalities, states and the nation.	99, 100, 101, 103, 122, 124, 125, 142, 152, 201, 449, 450, 451, 453, 454, 455, 486, 487, 493, 495, 496, 497, 522, 524, 539, 540, 727, 745, 746, 747, 874–879, 894–898, 990–997	122, 124, 255, 424, 426, 427, 428, 434, 435, 436, 437, 438, 449, 453, 456, 458, 459, 460, 461, 745, 886, 897, 898
14D. Understand the roles and influences of individuals and interest groups in the political systems of Illinois, the United States and other nations.	226–228, 320, 804, 910, 918	IL28–IL33, IL85–IL88, 200, 251, 264, 265, 266, 270, 271, 353, 643
14.D.3 Describe roles and influences of individuals, groups and media in shaping current Illinois and United States public policy (e.g., general public opinion, special interest groups, formal parties, media).	226–228, 666, 667, 726, 744, 745, 747, 759, 760, 764, 880–883, 990–997, 1000–1006	IL28–IL33, IL85–IL88, 253, 296, 353, 439, 643, 669, 686, 987
14E. Understand United States foreign policy as it relates to other nations and international issues.	372, 678, 778, 958, 970	260, 262, 263, 291, 320, 325, 357, 372, 375, 383, 672, 673, 675, 677, 679, 682, 688, 689, 693, 696, 712, 731, 803, 811, 849, 857, 859, 867, 904, 905, 908, 915, 940, 941, 944, 946, 947, 955, 961, 962
14.E.3 Compare the basic principles of the United States and its international interests (e.g., territory, environment, trade, use of technology).	260, 262, 263, 287, 288, 289, 290, 291, 293, 295, 296, 298, 325, 326, 674–677, 678–683, 684–689, 690–696, 712–717, 718–723, 728–732, 804–807, 808–813, 820–827, 828–832, 842–849, 856–859, 904–909, 910–915, 926–932, 942–947, 970–975, 976–981, 982–989	260, 290, 291, 325, 357, 373, 375, 383, 672, 673, 675, 677, 679, 680, 682, 688, 689, 693, 694, 696, 831, 832, 857, 859, 908, 915, 943
14F. Understand the development of United States political ideas and traditions.	194, 215–220, 221–225, 948	IL28–IL33, IL85–IL88, 66, 68, 98, 99, 100, 337
14.F.3a Analyze historical influences on the development of political ideas and practices as enumerated in the Declaration of Independence, the United States Constitution, the Bill of Rights and the Illinois Constitution.	61, 66, 68, 69, 79, 99, 100, 101, 103, 124, 125, 139, 140, 141, 142, 205, 206, 207, 210, 215–220, 518	IL28–IL33, IL85–IL88, 66, 68, 98, 99, 141, 205, 210
14.F.3b Describe how United States political ideas and traditions were instituted in the Constitution and the Bill of Rights.	205, 206, 207, 210, 215–220, 230–241, 253, 254, 255, 257, 418	116A, 184, 185, 194, 205, 206, 210, 254, 257
STATE GOAL 15: Understand economic systems, with an emphasis on the United States.		
15A. Understand how different economic systems operate in the exchange, production, distribution and consumption of goods and services.	388, 393, 592, 593, 602, 603, 754, 755, 757, 775, 782, 850–851, 862–863, 958–959	50, 52, 302, 306, 307, 314, 386, 398, 403, 413, 538, 595, 755, 1001
15.A.3a Explain how market prices signal producers about what, how and how much to produce.	393, 592, 593, 775, 782, 850–851	94, 308, 314, 387, 539, 575, 755, 775
15.A.3b Explain the relationship between productivity and wages.	602, 603, 754, 755, 757, 781, 783, 862–863	603, 755, 862
15.A.3c Describe the relationship between consumer purchases and businesses paying for productive resources.	595, 596, 597, 772, 958–959	597, 772
15.A.3d Describe the causes of unemployment (e.g., seasonal fluctuation in demand, changing jobs, changing skill requirements, national spending).	605, 606, 772, 773, 774, 775, 814, 962	605, 770, 771
15B. Understand that scarcity necessitates choices by consumers.	307, 352, 504, 949	352, 504, 952
15.B.3a Describe the "market clearing price" of a good or service.	814	814–815
15.B.3b Explain the effects of choice and competition on individuals and the economy as a whole.	307, 352, 504, 949	308, 949

Standards	Student Edition Pages	Teacher Edition Pages
15C. Understand that scarcity necessitates choices by producers.	308, 393, 555, 556, 586, 587	361, 555–556
15.C.3 Identify and explain the effects of various incentives to produce a good or service.	308, 393, 555, 556, 586, 587	393, 355–356
15D. Understand trade as an exchange of goods or services.	34, 72, 88, 358, 400, 947, 972, 985, 1000–1001	72, 341
15.D.3a Explain the effects of increasing and declining imports and exports to an individual and to the nation's economy as a whole.	100, 287, 288, 290, 291, 307, 309, 341, 680, 775, 776, 958–959, 982–989	94, 290, 299, 323
15.D.3b Explain how comparative advantage forms the basis for specialization and trade among nations.	947, 972, 985, 1000–1001	947, 1000
15.D.3c Explain how workers can affect their productivity through training and by using tools, machinery and technology.	306, 307, 312, 389, 392, 393, 400, 401, 402, 403, 592, 593, 755, 756, 816, 850, 862	93, 302, 306, 389, 390, 395, 743
15E. Understand the impact of government policies and decisions on production and consumption in the economy.	260, 304, 474, 642, 690, 860, 948, 958	350, 351, 679
15.E.3a Identify the types of taxes levied by differing levels of governments (e.g., income tax, sales tax, property tax).	122, 123, 124, 125, 257, 260, 261, 660, 796, 797, 815	124, 125, 538, 660
15.E.3b Explain how laws and government policies (e.g., property rights, contract enforcement, standard weights/measurements) establish rules that help a market economy function effectively.	534, 599, 752, 753, 781, 782, 783, 850–855, 970–975	350, 351, 770
STATE GOAL 16: Understand events, trends, individuals and movements shaping the history of Illinois, the United States and other nations.		
HISTORICAL ERAS **Local, State and United States History (US)**		
• Early history in the Americas to 1620	16–22, 34–41	5, 16–22
• Colonial history and settlement to 1763	58–61, 64–69, 72–75, 76–82, 88–95, 98–103, 104–107, 108–112, 122–125	58–61, 64–69, 72–75, 88–95, 96–103, 104–112, 122
• The American Revolution and early national period to 1820s	132–137, 138–142, 152–159, 160–165, 168–173, 174–178, 186–193, 194–201, 204–210, 252–257, 260–263, 264–270, 276–279, 280–285, 286–290, 294–298	123–125, 126–129, 132–137, 138–142, 152–159, 160–165, 168–173, 174–178, 186–193, 194–201, 204–210, 252–257, 260–263, 264–270, 276–279, 294–299
• National expansion from 1815 to 1850	304–309, 312–317	280–285, 312–317, 358–363, 366–371, 372–377, 378–382
• The Civil War and Reconstruction from 1850 to 1877	462–466, 474–479, 480–487, 490–497, 498–505, 506–512, 518–521, 522–527, 528–531, 534–540	448–451, 452–455, 456–461, 474–479, 480–487, 490–497, 498–505, 506–512, 518–521, 522–527, 528–531, 534–540
• Development of the industrial United States from 1865 to 1914	584–587, 588–593, 594–599, 602–606	582–583, 584–587, 588–593, 594–599, 602–606, 610–611, 612–617, 620–625, 626–632
• The emergence of the United States as a world power from 1890 to 1920	674–677, 678–683, 684–689, 690–696, 718–723, 728–732	674–677, 678–683, 684–689, 690–696, 702–703, 704–709, 712–717, 718–723, 724–727
• Prosperity, depression, the New Deal and World War II from 1920 to 1945	754–757, 772–777, 778–783, 786–791, 794–798, 804–807, 808–813, 814–819, 820–827, 828–832	770–771, 772–777, 778–783, 786–791, 794–798, 802–803, 804–807, 808–813, 814–819, 820–827, 828–832
• Post World War II and the Cold War from 1945 to 1968	842–849, 850–855, 856–859, 860–866, 904–909, 910–915, 918–923	840–841, 842–849, 850–855, 856–859, 860–866, 902–903, 904–909, 910–915, 918–920
• Contemporary United States from 1968 to present	894–898, 926–932, 942–947, 948–955, 958–962, 970–975, 976–981, 982–989, 990–997, 1000–1006	921–923, 926–932, 940–941, 942–947, 948–955, 958–962, 968–969, 970–975, 976–981, 982
16A. Apply the skills of historical analysis and interpretation.	56, 76, 104, 202, 276, 452, 562, 518, 698, 704, 728, 746, 808, 926	7, 11, 12, 21, 36, 38, 40, 59, 60, 79, 82, 103, 110, 123, 127, 134, 139, 143, 153, 165, 169, 170, 188, 197, 246A, 268, 283, 291, 315, 343, 345, 360, 368, 369, 373, 391, 402, 411, 419, 437, 453, 467, 477, 483, 493, 494, 501, 510, 523, 535, 536, 565, 568, 569, 603, 604, 613, 614, 621, 622, 627, 646, 652, 654, 668, 705, 715, 719, 722, 726, 727, 746, 775, 779, 789, 795, 797, 821, 824, 827, 844, 845, 852, 859, 876, 885, 905, 909, 913, 921, 929, 954, 977, 985, 994, 997
16.A.3a Describe how historians use models for organizing historical interpretation (e.g., biographies, political events, issues and conflicts).	47, 62, 102, 202, 698, 704, 746	14, 134
16.A.3b Make inferences about historical events and eras using historical maps and other historical sources.	11, 16, 18–19, 31, 32, 124, 134–135, 358, 498, 828	11, 35, 38, 140, 353, 363, 381, 390, 429, 477, 537, 667, 709, 862
16.A.3c Identify the differences between historical fact and interpretation.	35, 38, 41, 122, 127, 128, 129, 132, 294, 366, 462, 490, 675, 686, 689, 880–882	38, 53, 59, 91, 94, 127, 465, 492, 708, 713, 715, 806, 816, 822, 830, 899

Focus on Illinois

Standards	Student Edition Pages	Teacher Edition Pages
16B. Understand the development of significant political events.	73, 75, 122–125, 132–137, 138–142, 152–159, 160–165, 168–173, 188, 189, 197, 198, 199, 200, 201, 264–270, 278, 674–677, 678–683, 684–689, 712–717, 718–723, 728–732, 828, 856–859, 860–866, 942–947	123, 124, 127, 129, 133, 138, 139, 141
16.B.3a (US) Describe how different groups competed for power within the colonies and how that competition led to the development of political institutions during the early national period.	73, 75, 188, 189, 197, 198, 199, 200, 201, 264–270, 278	184, 209, 251, 264, 265, 266, 270, 271
16.B.3b (US) Explain how and why the colonies fought for their independence and how the colonists' ideas are reflected in the Declaration of Independence and the United States Constitution.	122–125, 132–137, 138–142, 152–159, 160–165, 168–173, 174–178, 204–210	120, 121–123, 124–126, 127, 128, 132, 133–135, 137, 139, 143, 150, 151, 152, 156, 158, 162, 163, 170–173, 174–176, 178, 184
16.B.3c (US) Describe the way the Constitution has changed over time as a result of amendments and Supreme Court decisions.	210, 254, 255, 277, 278, 279, 324, 326, 458, 459, 461, 509, 521, 524, 525, 527, 539, 642, 647, 654, 655, 660, 759, 761, 762	251, 254, 524, 526, 664, 874, 876
16.B.3d (US) Describe ways in which the United States developed as a world political power.	674–677, 678–683, 684–689, 712–717, 718–723, 728–732, 828, 856–859, 860–866, 942–947	700, 701, 712–717, 718–723, 728–732, 828, 856–859
16C. Understand the development of economic systems.	45, 47, 48, 50, 51, 52, 58–61, 79, 80, 81, 82, 90, 91, 92, 93, 100, 195, 196, 197, 307, 308, 309, 388, 395, 396, 398, 399, 402, 403, 588, 612–617, 754–757, 762, 796, 797, 798, 851, 852, 865–866	50, 82, 90, 304, 307, 350, 398, 399, 402, 403, 588, 865–866
16.C.3a (US) Describe economic motivations that attracted Europeans and others to the Americas, 1500–1750.	45, 47, 48, 50, 51, 52, 54, 55, 58–61, 79, 80, 81, 82, 84, 90, 91, 92, 93, 99, 100	27, 45, 49, 50, 52, 53, 56, 61, 83
16.C.3b (US) Explain relationships among the American economy and slavery, immigration, industrialization, labor and urbanization, 1700–present.	45, 47, 48, 50, 51, 52, 58–61, 79, 80, 81, 82, 90, 91, 92, 93, 99, 100, 195, 196, 197, 307, 308, 309, 388, 395, 396, 398, 399, 402, 403, 588, 612–617, 754–757, 762, 796, 797, 798, 851, 852, 865–866	57, 82, 83, 88, 304, 308, 309, 327, 386, 398, 402, 446, 431, 604, 607, 614, 745, 747, 797, 851
16.C.3c (US) Describe how economic developments and government policies after 1865 affected the country's economic institutions including corporations, banks and organized labor.	596, 597, 598, 599, 645, 647, 656, 657, 658, 661, 746, 747, 775, 777, 780, 781, 783, 797, 980–981	607, 645, 783, 797, 851
16D. Understand Illinois, United States and world social history.	448, 856, 874, 894	IL28–IL33, IL81–IL85, 448, 856
16.D.3a (US) Describe characteristics of different kinds of communities in various sections of America during the colonial/frontier periods and the 19th century.	72–75, 76–82, 88–95, 305, 308, 309, 379, 380, 406, 407, 408, 409, 410, 418, 419, 420, 552, 553, 554, 567, 568, 571, 613, 615, 616	58, 64, 72, 73, 74, 75, 76, 80, 82, 83, 89, 553
16.D.3b (US) Describe characteristics of different kinds of families in America during the colonial/frontier periods and the 19th century.	317, 342, 366, 400, 408, 409, 412, 563, 564	59, 67, 80, 83, 89, 100, 102
16E. Understand Illinois, United States and world environmental history.	89, 90, 92, 93, 94, 95, 313, 314, 316, 390, 392, 393, 565, 782, 787–788, 620–625, 1002–1003, 1006	IL81–IL85, 94, 95, 313, 314, 316, 390, 392, 393, 565, 620–625, 782, 787–788
16.E.3a (US) Describe how early settlers in Illinois and the United States adapted to, used and changed the environment prior to 1818.	89, 90, 92, 93, 94, 95, 313, 314, 316	IL81–IL85, 94, 95, 313, 314, 316
16.E.3b (US) Describe how the largely rural population of the United States adapted, used and changed the environment after 1818.	390, 392, 393, 565, 782, 787–788	356, 358, 788
16.E.3c (US) Describe the impact of urbanization and suburbanization, 1850–present, on the environment.	397, 398, 399, 616, 656, 620–625, 1002–1003, 1006	386, 396, 398, 610, 623, 865
STATE GOAL 17: Understand world geography and the effects of geography on society, with an emphasis on the United States.		
17A. Locate, describe and explain places, regions and features on the Earth.	Ref16–Ref31, 480, 910	14, 20, 21, 35, 50, 81, 89, 123, 154, 191, 283, 316, 341, 362, 401, 449, 483, 510, 557, 561, 679, 691, 706, 720, 805, 824, 844, 857, 945
17.A.3a Explain how people use geographic markers and boundaries to analyze and navigate the Earth (e.g., hemispheres, meridians, continents, bodies of water).	Ref17–Ref29, 31, 33, 34, 35, 36, 37, 40, 41, 44, 46, 51, 52, 77	35, 36, 76, 123
17.A.3b Explain how to make and use geographic representations to provide and enhance spatial information including maps, graphs, charts, models, aerial photographs, satellite images.	Ref18–Ref29, 5, 15	14, 20, 35, 39, 46, 73, 81, 93, 111, 156, 196, 253, 356, 359, 370, 373, 380, 395, 449, 454, 500, 537, 564, 568, 575, 579, 613, 621, 653, 676, 685, 705, 921, 988
17B. Analyze and explain characteristics and interactions of the Earth's physical systems.	Ref17, Ref29, 856	IL80–IL81, 856
17.B.3a Explain how physical processes including climate, plate tectonics, erosion, soil formation, water cycle, and circulation patterns in the ocean shape patterns in the environment and influence availability and quality of natural resources.	7, 8	IL80–IL81, 5, 18, 86, 93
17.B.3b Explain how changes in components of an ecosystem affect the system overall.	1000, 1002	23, 788, 1004

Standards	Student Edition Pages	Teacher Edition Pages
17C. Understand relationships between geographic factors and society.	Ref16–Ref17, 64, 104, 280, 462, 942, 982	IL80–IL81, 12, 17, 18, 20, 77, 89, 92, 94, 95
17.C.3a Explain how human activity is affected by geographic factors.	6, 7, 8, 9, 11–12, 16–17, 18, 19, 20, 21, 22, 24–25, 56, 76, 168, 175, 176, 189, 190, 191, 193, 281, 282, 305, 306, 307, 308, 309, 358–363, 367, 371, 374, 375, 376, 377, 378, 379, 380, 381, 382, 401, 402, 403, 448, 449, 450, 451, 475, 476, 477, 477, 479, 499, 502, 503, 505, 507, 508, 509, 510, 511, 553, 554, 621, 622, 624, 625, 679, 680, 681, 683, 705, 706, 708, 787, 788, 791, 904–907	4, 8, 12, 15, 17, 18, 20, 26, 40, 57, 77, 86, 89, 92, 94, 95, 123, 162, 170, 191, 305, 341, 357, 379, 380, 393, 396, 398, 505, 538, 550, 561, 563, 598, 862
17.C.3b Explain how patterns of resources are used throughout the world.	306, 553, 595, 597, 676, 946, 951–952, 955	20, 86, 538, 550, 595, 621, 1002
17.C.3c Analyze how human processes influence settlement patterns including migration and population growth.	6, 7, 8, 9, 13, 16, 17, 18, 19, 20, 21, 22, 24–25, 67, 189, 190, 191, 312, 313, 314, 315, 316, 317, 342, 343, 344, 345, 346, 347, 374, 377, 379, 380, 381, 382, 398, 399, 528, 567, 568, 571, 612, 613, 616, 620–625, 725, 788, 789, 790, 791, 828, 865–866, 1006	21, 302, 312, 313, 315, 380, 396, 550, 613, 621, 748, 749, 818
17D. Understand the historical significance of geography.	Ref17, 108, 260, 286, 394, 456, 462, 718, 820, 842	62, 63, 180, 181, 258, 259, 432, 433, 450, 510, 542, 543, 564, 569, 572, 573, 710, 711, 731, 748, 749, 862, 868, 869, 1008, 1009
17.D.3a Explain how and why spatial patterns of settlement change over time.	8, 67, 89, 92, 93, 94, 109, 111, 112, 190, 191, 281, 283, 284, 285, 312, 313, 314, 315, 317, 342, 343, 344, 345, 346, 347, 358–363, 367, 373, 374, 553, 554, 555, 557, 563, 564, 565, 567, 568, 571, 865–866, 1006	21, 313, 315, 316, 347, 356, 357, 360, 374, 380, 381, 398, 554, 556, 568, 613, 748–749, 818
17.D.3b Explain how interactions of geographic factors have shaped present conditions.	281, 283, 284, 285, 659, 661, 884–891, 904–909, 990–997	IL80–IL81, 53, 396, 564, 569
STATE GOAL 18: Understand social systems, with an emphasis on the United States.		
18A. Compare characteristics of culture as reflected in language, literature, the arts, traditions and institutions.	12, 13, 15, 21, 22, 29, 30, 33, 103, 205, 297, 298, 409, 410, 411, 412, 419, 420, 421, 435, 436, 438, 626–632, 759, 760, 761, 764, 783, 796, 798, 866, 886	19, 20, 65, 74, 89, 630, 761
18.A.3 Explain how language, literature, the arts, architecture and traditions contribute to the development and transmission of culture.	12, 13, 15, 21, 22, 29, 30, 33, 103, 205, 297, 298, 409, 410, 411, 412, 419, 420, 421, 435, 436, 438, 626–632, 759, 760, 761, 764, 783, 796, 798, 866	30, 31, 37, 92, 135, 343, 374, 399, 409, 410, 412, 421, 436, 562, 610, 611, 625, 627, 629, 630, 632, 687, 766–767, 758, 760, 764, 791, 864, 865, 866, 867
18B. Understand the roles and interactions of individuals and groups in society.	13, 14, 15, 42, 47, 48, 49, 72, 347, 349, 351, 369, 370, 424, 425, 426, 427, 428, 429, 430, 431, 449, 450, 492, 493, 501, 502, 503, 528, 536, 539, 540, 575, 576, 585, 587, 604, 605, 762, 763, 804–807, 814–819, 842–849, 880, 918–923	9, 22, 44, 47, 65, 120, 126, 128, 129, 188, 367, 370, 408
18.B.3a Analyze how individuals and groups interact with and within institutions (e.g., educational, military).	13, 14, 15, 42, 47, 48, 49, 50, 100, 101, 102, 103, 105, 106, 108, 133, 134, 136, 137, 161, 162, 163, 168, 174, 339, 340, 341, 344, 345, 347, 349, 351, 369, 370, 424, 425, 426, 427, 428, 429, 430, 431, 449, 450, 451, 453, 455, 459, 460, 461, 475, 477, 478, 479, 492, 493, 501, 502, 503, 528, 536, 539, 540, 575, 576, 585, 587, 604, 605, 606, 627, 628, 629, 651, 652, 653, 654, 655, 684, 706, 708, 709, 716, 717, 762, 763, 804–807, 814–819, 842–849, 918–923	22, 27, 44, 47, 75, 120, 128, 155, 157, 261, 410, 416, 419, 426, 434, 436, 458, 461, 516, 629, 640, 663, 872, 877, 879, 886, 919, 920, 928, 933
18.B.3b Explain how social institutions contribute to the development and transmission of culture.	66, 69, 103, 418, 419, 420, 421, 528, 531, 620, 626–632, 976	75, 419, 436, 640, 763
18C. Understand how social systems form and develop over time.	132, 378, 424, 425, 426, 427, 428, 429, 430, 431, 434–438, 510, 577, 578, 651, 652, 654, 662–668, 794, 874–879, 884–891, 894–898, 990	11, 22, 86, 100, 103, 382, 387, 408, 412, 562, 847, 866
18.C.3a Describe ways in which a diverse U.S. population has developed and maintained common beliefs (e.g., life, liberty and the pursuit of happiness; the Constitution and the Bill of Rights).	132, 139, 140, 141, 142, 154, 155, 156, 157, 159, 378, 424, 425, 426, 427, 428, 429, 430, 431, 434–438, 486, 487, 501, 507, 509, 510, 577, 578, 651, 652, 654, 662–668, 794, 874–879, 883, 884–891, 894–898	160, 410, 416, 417, 424, 425, 427, 435, 436, 486, 651, 652, 654, 666, 765, 852, 875, 877, 879, 885, 886, 890, 897, 928
18.C.3b Explain how diverse groups have contributed to U.S. social systems over time.	398, 399, 409, 410, 411, 412, 424, 425, 426, 427, 428, 429, 430, 431, 434–438, 520, 522, 612, 644, 646, 647, 651, 652, 653, 654, 655, 662–668, 725, 726, 814–819, 874–879, 884–891, 894–898, 990	381, 386, 398, 399, 424, 425, 435, 493, 562, 579, 610, 626, 652, 763, 819, 879, 886, 890, 895, 897

Focus on Illinois

Illinois Social Science Performance Descriptors

14.A Understand and explain basic principles of the United States government.

*Stage F	Stage G	Stage H
1. Define the concept of "consent of the governed." 2. Explain the importance of having a written constitution for a government. 3. Summarize the main points in constitutional documents (e.g., Declaration of Independence, Northwest Ordinance, Preamble of the United States Constitution). 4. Identify the basic similarities and differences between the Illinois and United States Constitutions. 5. Name the courts and judicial officials established to operate within the local, state, and federal governments. 6. Distinguish between the characteristics of a limited and unlimited government.	1. Compare and contrast responsibilities shared between the state and federal governments. 2. Identify the rights and principles of limited government found within the Declaration of Independence. 3. Classify the type of courts and judicial officials established to operate within the local, state, and federal governments. 4. Describe the role of the courts in judicial review.	1. Evaluate the rights and responsibilities of the individual within the family, social groups, community, or nation. 2. Categorize programs and services provided by governments into local, state, and federal levels. 3. Compare the similarities and differences in the state of Illinois and the national government's attempts to protect individual rights and still promote the common good. 4. Explain the influence of the Supreme Court and significant court decisions on the rights and responsibilities of citizens (e.g., defining, expanding, and limiting individual rights). 5. Analyze the efforts of our court system to take into account the rights of both those accused of crimes and their victims.

14.B Understand the structures and functions of the political systems of Illinois, the United States and other nations.

Stage F	Stage G	Stage H
1. Describe the characteristics of a two-house legislature. 2. Explain the reasons for having the system of checks and balances as part of the organization of the federal government. 3. Define the roles and responsibilities of top officials in Illinois State government (e.g., Governor, Sec. of State). 4. Explain the distributed and shared powers of the local, state, and federal government.	1. Describe the impact of the federal government's system of checks and balances (e.g., the results of a presidential veto). 2. Analyze historical examples of the system of checks and balances according to the respective branches of the federal government. 3. Compare similarities and differences in the powers of the Governor of the State of Illinois and the President of the United States to resolve conflicts and crises. 4. Formulate a conclusion about the use of power by state or national governmental executives. 5. Describe the organization of the Illinois General Assembly. 6. Define "jurisdiction" as it applies to a court system.	1. Compare the powers and responsibilities of the members of the House of Representatives and Senate within the United States Congress. 2. Explain the advantages and disadvantages of our federal system's separation of powers. 3. Differentiate among the powers, limitations, and responsibilities of the state government of Illinois and the federal government. 4. Distinguish between the powers and responsibilities of our state and federal courts as outlined in our state and national constitutions. 5. Illustrate the organization of the three branches of the state government of Illinois. 6. Justify why the Illinois Constitution cannot violate the United States Constitution.

*Performance descriptors are statements of how students can demonstrate the knowledge and skills they acquire.

The stages F, G, and H performance descriptors are for middle/junior high school.

14.C Understand election processes and responsibilities of citizens.

Stage F	Stage G	Stage H
1. Create a list of ideas that would encourage more civic responsibility among people. 2. Explain the role of a citizen in choosing leaders. 3. Illustrate how people are elected to all levels of our government. 4. Analyze historical events involving the extension or denial of political and electoral rights of various citizens or groups of people.	1. Describe the requirements for candidates for local, state, and national offices. 2. Compare the platforms of two or more political parties during an election to determine differences. 3. Explain the position on a particular issue of a candidate for political office.	1. Describe responsibilities that citizens share during an election. 2. Compare/contrast the historical positions of political parties in elections. 3. Compare historical examples of issues in local, state, or national elections affecting the civil rights of various groups. 4. Describe how voting barriers have been removed to allow greater participation in elections (e.g., common people gaining the right to vote, minority voting status). 5. Analyze an example of a government denying voting rights to individuals or groups. 6. Describe the election process at local, state, and national levels (e.g., campaigns, primaries, conventions).

14.D Understand the roles and influences of individuals and interest groups in the political systems of Illinois, the United States and other nations.

Stage F	Stage G	Stage H
1. Summarize an individual group's motivation for participating in the shaping of public policy. 2. Analyze actions taken by governments to improve lives of people. 3. Analyze ways in which the media is used by political parties and interest groups to influence public opinion. 4. Explain how political parties and interest groups affect legislation. 5. Describe an historical event or period in which political parties influenced public policy.	1. Explain the importance of an individual's responsibility to maintain a democratic, civil society. 2. Evaluate the benefits of highly involved citizens to a society. 3. Identify the reasons for public opinion polls sponsored by political parties, public interest groups, and the media. 4. Describe methods of communication that individuals, groups, and the media use to present information to the public. 5. Interpret political cartoons in terms of captions and images to persuade people to accept political positions on various issues.	1. Summarize the actions of an individual or group's effort to influence current public policy in their community, state, or nation. 2. Compare and contrast the roles and influence of various individuals, groups, and media in shaping current public policy issues in their community, state, or nation. 3. Measure political interest or activity in a civic or social cause. 4. Predict how technology and social change will impact the conduct of political parties.

14.E Understand United States foreign policy as it relates to other nations and international issues.

Stage F	Stage G	Stage H
1. Identify a political tradition or custom that had its origin in another country (e.g., representative government). 2. Describe the leadership role of the United States in international organizations (e.g., the United Nations, NATO, IMF). 3. Explain the costs and benefits of an historical treaty the United States has signed with another nation or international organization.	1. Review the principles the United States has traditionally held in joining international organizations (e.g., the interests and benefits of world peace, open trade over closed markets). 2. Explain an historical event in which the United States played a leading role. 3. Analyze an event or issue that links the people of Illinois to another nation (e.g., issues or negotiations over trade, immigration of ethnic groups).	1. Identify situations in which United States diplomacy favors one nation over another (e.g., trade military protection). 2. Compare the interests of the United States and other nations in making foreign policy decisions (e.g., defense, trade, environmental protection, communications). 3. Compare/contrast the ideals and interests of the United States in participating in international organizations. 4. Analyze cases of changing diplomatic relations between the United States and other people or nations (e.g., changing relations with Native American tribes, changing relations with the Soviet Union during and after World War II). 5. Predict the effects of technology on foreign policy decision-making.

14.F Understand the development of United States political ideas and traditions.

Stage F	Stage G	Stage H
1. Give examples of events where people have had to fight to win their equality. 2. Illustrate conflicts over the rights and freedom of competing individuals or groups (e.g., a novel about two families from the north and south during the Civil War). 3. Compare the arguments of competing public interest groups on constitutional rights.	1. Provide an argument justifying the need for civil rights for citizens of any nation. 2. Summarize the historical development of the concept of individual liberty (e.g., Colonial America to contemporary political interest groups). 3. Analyze the causes and effects of when national interests have called for the limitation or restriction of civil rights (e.g., internment of Japanese Americans during World War II).	1. Summarize the historical influences on the development of political ideas and practices as listed in the Declaration of Independence, the United States Constitution, the Bill of Rights, and the Illinois Constitution. 2. Give examples of how United States political ideas and traditions have either included or denied additional amendments respecting or extending the rights of its citizens. 3. Analyze an influential U.S. Supreme Court case decision and the impact it had in promoting or limiting civil rights. 4. Compare arguments for expanding or limiting freedoms and protection for citizens outlined in the Bill of Rights.

15.A Understand how different economic systems operate in the exchange, production, distribution and consumption of goods and services.

Stage F	Stage G	Stage H
1. Define productivity. 2. Demonstrate how productivity increases through the use of technology. 3. Demonstrate how education and training improve skills and increase productivity. 4. Explain that in a market economy, producers make the goods and services consumers want.	1. Explain that consumer demand determines what producers will produce in a market economy. 2. Identify the productive resources households sell to businesses and the payments received for those resources. 3. Identify the goods and services businesses sell to households and the payments received for those goods and services. 4. Identify times when students or adults are consumers and when students or adults are producers.	1. Explain how the price of productive resources in a market economy would influence producer decisions about how, how much, and what to produce. 2. Analyze the relationship between productivity and wages. 3. Demonstrate the circular flow of interaction among households, businesses, and government in the economy. 4. Describe the role of financial institutions in the economy. 5. Identify the causes of unemployment. 6. Define GDP.

15.B Understand that scarcity necessitates choices by consumers.

Stage F	Stage G	Stage H
1. Explain that a market exists whenever buyers and sellers exchange goods and services. 2. Identify examples of people acting as consumers and as producers. 3. Illustrate the law of demand. 4. Explain that prices are determined through the buying and selling decisions made by buyers and sellers. 5. Explain that competition takes place when there are many buyers and sellers of similar products. 6. Identify markets where there is competition among sellers. 7. Identify examples of competition among buyers.	1. Explain why people are both consumers and producers. 2. Identify markets where buyers and sellers meet face-to-face and markets in which buyers and sellers never meet directly. 3. Explain the benefits to consumers of competition among sellers. 4. Analyze the impact on prices of competition among buyers.	1. Explain why, as the market price of a good or service goes up, the quantity demanded by consumers goes down. 2. Determine the market clearing price when given data about the supply and demand for a product. 3. Predict how the change in price of one good or service can lead to changes in prices of other goods and services. 4. Explain how prices help allocate scarce goods and services in a market economy. 5. Explain why shortages and surpluses occur in a market economy and provide real-world examples of each.

15.C Understand that scarcity necessitates choices by producers.

Stage F	Stage G	Stage H
1. Explain how price is an incentive to buyers and sellers.	1. Analyze how changes in price affect producer behavior.	1. Provide examples of how changes in incentives encourage people to change their economic behavior in predictable ways.
2. Analyze the effect of price changes on buyers and sellers.	2. Identify non-price incentives to which people respond in the economy.	2. Provide examples of how the same incentive will bring about differing responses from differing people.
3. Explain that there are incentives other than price that affect people's behavior in the economy.	3. Explain why people's response to an incentive may vary because of differing values.	3. Explain why, as the market price of a good or service goes up, the quantity supplied also goes up.
4. Provide examples of positive incentives (rewards) that affect economic behavior.	4. Predict the impact on supply of a good or service when non-price determinants change (e.g., number of producers; cost of production).	
5. Provide examples of negative incentives (penalties) that affect economic behavior.		
6. Define the law of supply.		

15.D Understand trade as an exchange of goods or services.

Stage F	Stage G	Stage H
1. Define imports.	1. Identify exports produced in the local community or state.	1. Provide an example of comparative advantage in the school or community.
2. Define exports.	2. Explain why countries benefit when they exchange goods and services.	2. Explain why comparative advantage leads to specialization and trade.
3. Provide examples of economic specialization.	3. Explain how specialization usually increases productivity in an economy.	3. Identify barriers to trade and their impact, and explain why nations create barriers to trade.
4. Identify technologies that exist today that did not exist in the past (e.g., 10 to 20 years ago).	4. Provide examples of how specialization increases interdependence among consumers and producers.	4. Analyze the impact of an increase or decrease in imports on jobs and consumers in the U.S.
	5. Explain how technological changes have led to new and improved products.	5. Analyze the impact of an increase or decrease in exports on jobs and consumers in the U.S.
	6. Explain how people's incomes reflect choices they have made about education, training, skill development, and careers.	6. Identify new technologies over time and explain their impact on the economy.

15.E Understand the impact of government policies and decisions on production and consumption in the economy.

Stage F	Stage G	Stage H
1. Describe the differences between income tax, sales tax, and property tax. 2. Identify what people would give up if governments had no power to tax. 3. Identify what goods and services various levels of government provide. 4. Identify to which level of government certain taxes are paid.	1. Identify laws and government policies that protect property rights, enforce contracts, and maintain competition. 2. Explain why there is a role for government in the economy. 3. Explain how laws and government policies affecting the economy have changed over time.	1. Identify examples of proportional, progressive, and regressive taxes in the economy. 2. Evaluate the fairness and efficiency of each kind of tax. 3. Analyze the benefits and costs to individuals and businesses of government policies that affect the economy. 4. Identify the main sources of revenue for federal and for state governments. 5. Explain how laws and government policies affecting the economy establish rules to help a market economy function effectively.

16.A Apply the skills of historical analysis and interpretation.

Stage F	Stage G	Stage H
1. Distinguish between the important and insignificant details contained in an historical source. 2. Organize a series of historic maps of a region or place into an historical atlas. 3. Place a series of events from the past that are listed on a chronology or timeline and categorize them according to political, economic, environmental, or social importance. 4. Identify the times when significant events intersected using a series of chronologies organized into political, economic, environmental, and social history. 5. Compare two different interpretations of an historical figure. 6. Compare the account of an historic person or event in a textbook with an account of the person or event in another secondary source. 7. Locate on the World Wide Web multiple sources pertaining to a significant historic person or event. 8. Compare the value of primary and secondary sources.	1. Place events from a chronology on multiple tier timelines that are organized according to political, economic, environmental, and social history. 2. Organize a series of related historical events for depiction on a periodization chart. 3. Describe life during a specific period using multiple tier timelines, periodization charts, graphs, and charts with data organized by category. 4. Provide an example of two different interpretations of a significant event. 5. Explain how a significant historical event can have many causes.	1. Define the concept of a "watershed" event in history. 2. Explain why a primary source may not necessarily provide an accurate description of an historical event. 3. Identify the point of view of the author as found in a primary source document. 4. Identify any inconsistencies of an author as found in a primary source document. 5. Assess the value of posed and candid photographs as primary sources.

Focus on Illinois

16.B Understand the development of significant political events (U.S.).

Stage F	Stage G	Stage H
1. Organize a series of political events covering the span of American history, c1500–present, into a periodization chart. 2. Describe both the ideas and actions of significant political figures, events, or processes that affected the formation and development of modern political parties. 3. Interpret the actions and consequences of a significant figure in United States political history (e.g., Thomas Jefferson, Abraham Lincoln, Woodrow Wilson, Franklin D. Roosevelt). 4. Interpret the causes that led to the development of a particular political organization or institution (e.g., modern political parties, interest groups, Electoral College).	1. Identify the major periods in United States political history from colonial to contemporary times. 2. Summarize ideas that influenced the development of representative democracy as reflected in the Declaration of Independence and the Constitution of the United States. 3. Describe significant events that fostered the development of representative democracy after the adoption of the United States Constitution (e.g., amendments, supreme court rulings, legislation). 4. Compare and contrast the contributions of individuals or political groups who had a significant impact on the course of local, state, and national history.	1. Evaluate the consequences of constitutional change and continuity over time. 2. Summarize the significant events that occurred during the development of the Supreme Court of the United States. 3. Describe the contributions of individuals or groups who had a significant impact on the course of judicial history. 4. Describe the significant events and contributions of individuals or groups in the development of United States diplomatic history.

16.C Understand the development of economic systems (U.S.).

Stage F	Stage G	Stage H
1. Explain how significant economic events in the past have altered individual choices and influenced Untied States history. 2. Summarize the impact of significant economic events of earlier periods of United States history on contemporary economic structure. 3. Evaluate how an individual's ideas, inventions, or entrepreneurship (e.g., Thomas Edison, George Washington Carver, Henry Ford) affected the economy then and now. 4. Predict how technological advances may affect the United States economic system. 5. Analyze how a significant economic event (e.g., industrialization, the Great Depression, and the rise of computer technology) has influenced the development of the United States economic system.	1. Identify the major periods in United States economic history from colonial to contemporary times. 2. Describe the impact of trade from 1500–1750 on the political, social, and economic lives, and the environment of Native Americans and European colonists. 3. Describe how changes in science and technology affected the exchange of goods and services over time among the people in colonial America. 4. Explain how changes in economic activity during an earlier period influenced subsequent historical events (e.g., increase in the labor supply and unionization, depression and the New Deal).	1. Describe the impact of trade on political, social, economic, and environmental developments in a place or region of the United States, 1865–present. 2. Explain how changes in science and technology affected the exchange of goods and services, economic institutions, and the movement of people among different regions of the United States, 1865–present. 3. Explain how entrepreneurs organized their businesses and influenced government to limit competition and maximize profits. 4. Describe the economic causes of conflict in United States History since 1865 (e.g., Indian Wars, Civil War, urban unrest). 5. Describe significant people, ideas, and events in the rise of organized labor from 1865–1914.

16.D Understand Illinois, United States and world social history (U.S).

Stage F	Stage G	Stage H
1. Predict the impact that a controversial figure's ideas on changing social conditions had on contemporary interest groups.	**1.** Describe the changes and continuity in various interest groups' (e.g., workers, business persons, politicians) perception of social status over time.	**1.** Analyze the changing roles and status of men, women, and children from the colonial period through the 19th Century.
2. Analyze the issues of social status and social role in the past and present.	**2.** Compare and contrast family life in the early American period with another time period.	**2.** Compare the importance of people's customs and traditions during the historical development of a geographic region during the colonial/frontier periods and the 19th Century.
3. Describe the changes in family from one period to another.	**3.** Describe the significance of social factors such as status, role, customs, traditions, norms, and values during a turning point in United States social history.	
4. Trace the development of a significant social institution over time (e.g., Boy Scouts, Girl Scouts, NAACP).	**4.** Analyze the significance of cultural diversity in the social history of the United States.	**3.** Describe family life of select groups of people during the colonial/frontier periods and the 19th Century.

16.E Understand Illinois, United States and world environmental history (U.S.).

Stage F	Stage G	Stage H
1. Organize a series of environmental events covering the span of American history, c1500–present, into a periodization chart.	**1.** Identify turning points in United States environmental history.	**1.** Analyze the social, political, and economic effects on the abandoned environment of a significant migration of people from one region to another.
2. Describe how the environmental history of a place or region of the United States region has changed over time using a variety of geographic tools, including an historical atlas.	**2.** Describe the development of transportation and communication networks (e.g., river travel, pony express, internet).	**2.** Describe the demographic distribution of people before and after a significant migration in United States history.
3. Describe how the people of a specific region of the United States gained control over rivers or other principal physical features of their environment.	**3.** Explain how the environment affected economic and social developments of people in a specific region of the United States (e.g., Jamestown, "Wild West," natural disasters).	**3.** Describe the effects on the environment of the dispersion of European colonists in North America after 1500CE.
4. Describe how the competition between or among different groups of people for the same land affected the environment.	**4.** Explain how the environment affected economic and social developments of a specific cultural group after 1500.	**4.** Describe how major migrations have affected the cultural features of cities and rural communities in the United States.
5. Assess the effects of a significant invention or technological innovation on the physical and cultural environment on a place or region (e.g., plow, automobile, power plants).	**5.** Explain how the environment, economy, and society can be affected by the dependence of a region on a single crop or mode of production.	**5.** Assess the effect of the industrial revolution on the physical environment in the United States.
		6. Assess the effects on the environment of the historic process of suburbanization and rural depopulation.
		7. Assess the effects of a significant past natural environmental disaster on the physical and cultural features of the landscape of a place or region in the United States.

Focus on Illinois

17.A Locate, describe and explain places, regions and features on the Earth.

Stage F	Stage G	Stage H
1. Demonstrate understanding of the location of various physical and human features in Illinois, the United States, and the world by sketching a map from memory of different features.	**1.** Compare sketch maps with atlas maps to determine the accuracy of physical and cultural features (e.g., political/physical maps of Canada, the United States, and Europe).	**1.** Translate a mental map into sketch form to illustrate relative location of, size of, and distances between geographic features (e.g., cities mountains, rivers).
2. Interpret aerial photographs or satellite-produced images to locate and identify physical and human features (e.g., mountain ranges, rivers, vegetation regions, cities, dams, reservoirs).	**2.** Develop maps and flowcharts showing major patterns of movement of people and commodities (e.g., international trade in petroleum, countries that produce and those that consume resources, cartograms, population pyramids).	**2.** Demonstrate understanding of how to display spatial information by constructing maps, graphs, diagrams, and charts to display spatial information (e.g., choropleth maps, climographs, population pyramids).
3. Identify, using only a mental map, the countries through which a person would pass as they travel along a straight line route between two major cities (e.g., Paris to Moscow, Cairo to Nairobi).	**3.** Explain the purposes and distinguishing characteristics of selected map projections, globes, aerial photos, and satellite images.	**3.** Analyze patterns of movement in space and time (e.g., hurricane tracks over several seasons, the spread of influenza throughout the world).
4. Construct a choropleth map that shows the spatial distribution of the data (e.g., corn production in Illinois).	**4.** Demonstrate understanding of the spatial distribution of various phenomena by using latitude and longitude to plot data on a base map of the United States or the world (e.g., location of professional sports teams in the U.S. or the world).	**4.** Describe the location of places using the global system of time zones.
5. Explain how major countries in the world are connected and interrelate (e.g., trade, political alliances, humanitarian concerns).		**5.** Demonstrate understanding of world time zones by determining the date and time in selected cities around the world in reference to Springfield, Illinois.
6. Understand how parallels of latitude can be used to determine north-south direction and distance, and how meridians of longitude can be used to determine east-west direction and distance on a map or globe.		

17.B Analyze and explain characteristics and interactions of the Earth's physical systems.

Stage F	Stage G	Stage H
1. Identify the causes and nature of changes in environmental stress zones (fragile environments) (e.g., the rain forests of Brazil, taiga, north slope of Alaska).	1. Explain how Earth-Sun relationships affect Earth's energy balance (e.g., heating of soil and water at different seasons of the year, differential heating at different latitudes).	1. Analyze climographs for selected places and suggest reasons for similarities and differences in climates.
2. Describe the physical environment of the students' own region and the physical processes that act on it (e.g., weather, tectonic forces, wave action, freezing and thawing, gravity, soil building processes).	2. Identify and describe different climates in terms of precipitation and temperature and the types of plants and animals associated with each using pictures, maps, and graphs.	2. Hypothesize about the future effects of the use of technology on Earth's physical systems (e.g., climate, soil, air, water).
3. Describe ecosystems from local to global scales and the difference between them using photographs and other media as illustrations.	3. Analyze maps to determine the relationship among climate, natural vegetation, and natural resources.	3. Analyze the causes and effects of changes over time in physical landscapes (e.g., forest cover, water distribution, temperature fluctuations) as shown on maps, graphs, and satellite produced images.
4. Explain how and why ecosystems differ from place to place as a consequence of differences in soils, climates, and human and natural disturbances.	4. Predict the effects of an extreme weather phenomenon on the physical environment (e.g., a hurricane's impact on a coastal ecosystem).	4. Predict the potential outcomes of the continued movement of Earth's tectonic plates (e.g., continental drift, earthquakes, volcanic activity).

17.C Understand relationships between geographic factors and society.

Stage F	Stage G	Stage H
1. Compare the natural hazards that occur in Illinois with those occurring in other states to determine their intensity and effect on people.	1. Explain the different patterns in population density using geographic tools (e.g., pyramids, maps).	1. Explain the patterns of natural resource distribution (e.g., petroleum, timber) in various regions of the United States and the world.
2. Explain the concentrations of urban settlement centers with high population density using maps of Illinois and the United States.	2. Identify human induced changes in landforms, climate, natural vegetation, and resources of their local community, state of Illinois, nation, and the world.	2. Identify reasons related to the natural environment that influence the location of certain human activities (e.g., corn production in Illinois, rice in Southeast Asia).
3. Evaluate effects of technological change on transportation, communications, and resource use in Illinois, the United States, and the world.	3. Analyze physical and human environments in Illinois and the United States to determine ways that people adapt to and modify their environment.	3. Analyze rapidly growing urban centers to determine the impact of urban sprawl on the physical and human environment.
4. Identify ways that human behavior could be changed to solve specific environmental problems (e.g., outline a plan to reduce litter and stream pollution).	4. Formulate several hypotheses about relationships among resources, manufacturing and service industries, transportation, and population densities in different regions of the United States and the world.	4. Explain how human induced alterations of the environment have resulted in human migration (e.g., "Okies" from the Dust Bowl to California, the expanding Sahara).
	5. Predict the effects of an extreme weather phenomenon on human populations in different regions of the United States and the world (e.g., hurricanes, flooding, tornadoes).	5. Rank natural hazards based on the degree of impact on people and the physical environment (e.g., loss of life, destruction of property, economic impact, alteration of ecosystems).
	6. Identify social, political, and economic factors that attract people to, and repel people from, urban centers.	

17.D Understand the historical significance of geography.

Stage F	Stage G	Stage H
1. Explain how technological developments have influenced the migration of people to and within the United States over time. 2. Analyze selected historical events to determine how they influenced the migration of people throughout the world. 3. Hypothesize about relationships between physical features and the occurrence of human activities of a particular place and how these activities changed over the years. 4. Analyze how physical features have both posed barriers and provided avenues to settlement in Illinois and the United States.	1. Describe instances of how places can be changed or destroyed as a result of natural processes. 2. Describe how humans have adapted to environmental changes caused by natural processes. 3. Explain how human characteristics of a place are influenced by acculturation (e.g., Spanish culture in Middle and South America and the United States Southwest, Hindu and Muslim culture in Southeast Asia). 4. Explain how an environmental change in one part of the world can affect places in other parts of the world over periods of time.	1. Describe how legacies of the past have affected past and present human characteristics of places (e.g., wealth and poverty, exploitation, colonialism and independence). 2. Explain, in terms of "push-pull" factors, the major population movements that have occurred in the past and may occur among places and regions. 3. Analyze maps of human settlement and routes traveled in the past to determine the relationship between where people lived and their movements.

18.A Compare characteristics of culture as reflected in language, literature, the arts, traditions and institutions.

Stage F	Stage G	Stage H
1. Compare and contrast two or more cultures in terms of expressions of those cultures. 2. Compare a culture with one's own through the use of written, auditory, or visual materials. 3. Compare cultural differences/similarities from other parts of the world in terms of their language, literature, and arts. 4. Explain how social scientists analyze expressive culture and social discourse. 5. Identify what cultural relativism means. 6. Give an example of ethnocentrism. 7. Describe culture shock.	1. Describe what is studied within the field of anthropology. 2. Describe how a culture is reflected in its art, music, and/or architecture and institutions. 3. Explain how technology and the media have impacted expressive culture. 4. Analyze examples of patterns within literature, art, music, and/or architecture being transmitted from place to place.	1. Predict how technology/media will impact culture during the student's lifetime. 2. Analyze immigration patterns to see how American cultures have been shaped. 3. Identify various cultures that have combined to create a larger, multicultural American society. 4. Define the concept of the global community. 5. Draw conclusions about how the media creates and/or reinforces societal norms. 6. Evaluate the role of the humanities (e.g., literature, art, music, architecture) in a culture.

18.B Understand the roles and interactions of individuals and groups in society.

Stage F	Stage G	Stage H
1. Compare and contrast the concepts of conformity and deviance. **2.** Examine how the media portrays conformity and deviance. **3.** Identify examples of how an individual internalizes group norms. **4.** Compare formal and informal means of social control. **5.** Analyze the effectiveness of a national or local social institution in addressing a social problem (e.g., DARE, MADD).	**1.** Describe what is studied within the field of sociology. **2.** Describe what is studied within the field of psychology. **3.** Identify examples of how social, political, and economic institutions work together. **4.** Analyze the reasons why social institutions change over time. **5.** Identify how an individual may influence institutional or group behavior. **6.** Analyze the roles that various public and private institutions play as agents of socialization (e.g., schools).	**1.** Describe how interaction among people brings about social change (e.g., natives and colonizers, Peace Corps volunteers). **2.** Explain how changing topics of self and groups (e.g., minorities, women, children, adolescents) have affected the roles of social institutions. **3.** Explain how the changing concept of social institutions affects groups in society (e.g., minorities, women, children, adolescents). **4.** Describe how such groups as social clubs, schools, and churches influence the preservation and transmission of culture.

18.C Understand how social systems form and develop over time.

Stage F	Stage G	Stage H
1. Define subsistence strategy. **2.** Differentiate among pre-industrial, industrial, and postindustrial societies. **3.** Describe how the change from hunter-gatherer to settled society affected social roles. **4.** Explain how changes in the mode of production in a society affect educational, governmental, religious, and economic institutions.	**1.** Define the concept of diversity. **2.** Assess the impact that commonly held beliefs have had on social groups in the United States over time. **3.** Describe the contributions of significant individuals and groups to the common belief system of the United States. **4.** Describe how citizens and government can cooperate or have cooperated to solve an important social problem. **5.** Predict what social problems will become more pressing in the future.	**1.** Explain how diverse groups have enriched United States culture. **2.** Analyze how the ideals of the Founders have influenced the development of multicultural society in the United States. **3.** Explain the impact of prejudice on the operation of United States social, political, and economic institutions over time. **4.** Define cultural exchange and provide examples of cultural exchange between two groups.

Symbols of Illinois

State Flower

In 1908 the purple violet or native violet was approved as the Illinois state flower by the state legislature. The violet is found throughout eastern North America. Its edible purple flowers bloom from mid- to late spring and are sometimes used to make candies and jellies.

State Tree

The grand white oak was chosen as the Illinois state tree by a special poll of 900,000 schoolchildren in 1973. This tree is most abundant in North Central and Middle Atlantic states. The white oak usually grows to heights of 60 to 80 feet, but in dense woods it can reach a height of 150 feet. Its strong wood is one used for making furniture and hardwood flooring.

State Bird

The distinctive cardinal has been the Illinois state bird since 1929. This bird can be seen in the state's forests and fields throughout the year. The males are bright red, while the females are a more muted reddish brown. Both have heavy bills and crested heads.

State Mineral

Illinois is the leading United States producer of fluorite, which became the state mineral in 1965. Fluorite is transparent and glassy and can contain a variety of colors from a darker purple to light pink and white. The mineral is used in the manufacturing of steel, enamels, glass, and several chemicals.

State Seal

The State Seal of Illinois was first adopted in 1818 when Illinois gained statehood. Since then there have been several basic changes to the design. On the current seal, the eagle holds a red banner that displays the state motto, "State sovereignty, National Union." This motto means that Illinois governs itself under the government of the United States. Also on the seal is a shield bearing thirteen stars and stripes which represent the original thirteen states. The year of statehood and the year the design was adopted are recorded on the boulder.

State Flag

Illinois has had two official state flags. In 1915 the General Assembly had approved a design that featured the State Seal of Illinois on a square white background. Wanting to make it clear to those who were not familiar with the seal that it was the state's flag, the design was modified in 1969. The new flag is a white rectangle bearing the state seal and the added state name.

State Animal

The white-tailed deer was unofficially selected as the state animal by Illinois schoolchildren in 1980, and officially by the legislature in 1982. Midwestern settlers and Native Americans relied on the white-tailed deer for food, and on its hide for clothing and shelter. The coat of the deer is reddish brown in the summer and grayish brown in the winter. Its white tail, which is raised as a warning of danger, gives the species its name.

Illinois Counties

1. Jo Daviess
2. Stephenson
3. Winnebago
4. Boone
5. McHenry
6. Lake
7. Carroll
8. Ogle
9. Dekalb
10. Kane
11. Cook
12. Dupage
13. Will
14. Kendall
15. La Salle
16. Lee
17. Whiteside
18. Rock Island
19. Henry
20. Bureau
21. Grundy
22. Kankakee
23. Livingston
24. Putnam
25. Marshall
26. Stark
27. Knox

28. Mercer
29. Henderson
30. Warren
31. Peoria
32. Woodford
33. Ford
34. Iroquois
35. Vermillion
36. Champaign
37. McLean
38. Tazewell
39. Fulton
40. McDonough
41. Hancock
42. Adams
43. Brown
44. Schuyler
45. Mason
46. Logan
47. De Witt
48. Piatt
49. Douglas
50. Edgar
51. Coles
52. Moultrie
53. Macon
54. Sangamon

55. Menard
56. Cass
57. Pike
58. Scott
59. Morgan
60. Christian
61. Shelby
62. Cumberland
63. Clark
64. Crawford
65. Jasper
66. Effingham
67. Fayette
68. Montgomery
69. Macoupin
70. Greene
71. Calhoun
72. Jersey
73. Madison
74. Bond
75. Marion
76. Clay
77. Richland
78. Lawrence
79. Wabash
80. Edwards
81. Wayne

82. Jefferson
83. Washington
84. Clinton
85. St. Clair
86. Monroe
87. Randolph
88. Perry
89. Franklin
90. Hamilton
91. White
92. Gallatin
93. Saline
94. Williamson
95. Jackson
96. Union
97. Johnson
98. Pope
99. Hardin
100. Massac
101. Pulaski
102. Alexander

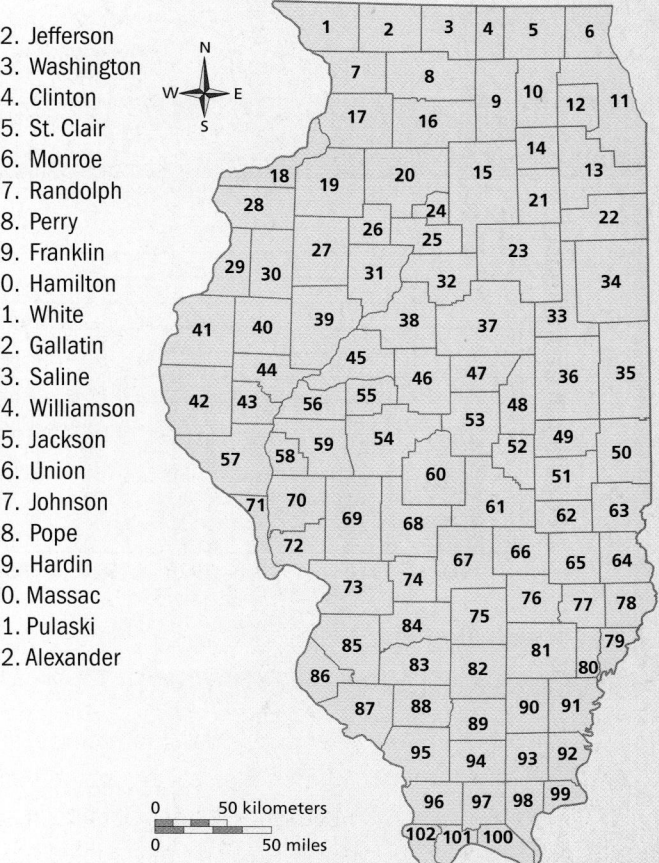

0   50 kilometers

0   50 miles

Albers Equal Area projection

Illinois's People

Comparing the Population of Illinois and the United States

	Illinois	United States
Population, 2006	12,831,970	299,398,484
Population, percent change, 2000 to 2005	3.3%	6.4%
Persons under 18 years old	25.4%	24.8%
Persons 65 years old and over	12.0%	12.4%
Females	50.9%	50.7%
Males	49.1%	49.3%
Whites	79.4%	80.2%
African Americans	15.1%	12.8%
Persons of Hispanic or Latino origins	14.3%	14.4%
Native Americans	0.3%	0.2%
Asian Americans	4.1%	4.3%

Note: Data on race are from those reporting only one race.
Source: *American Community Survey*, U.S. Census Bureau.

Population 1900–2010

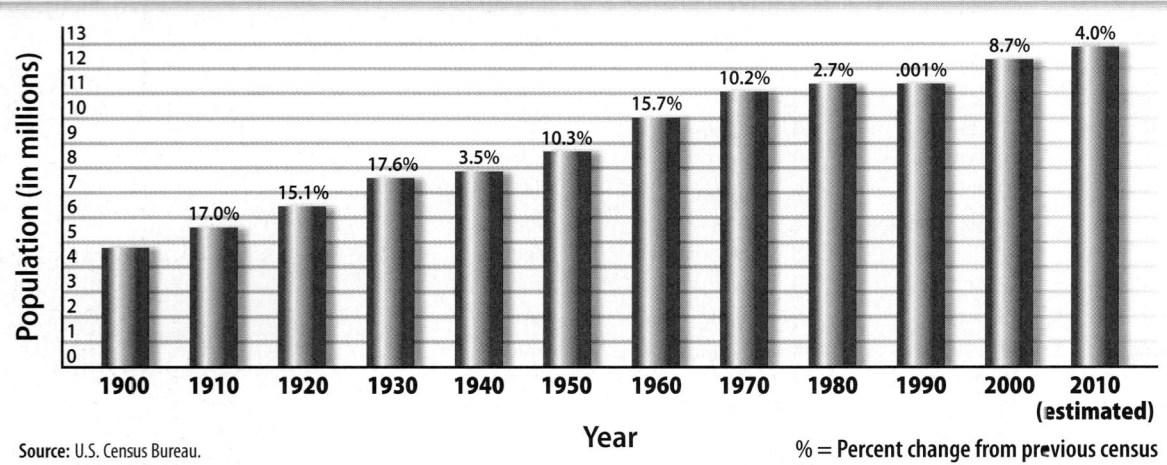

Source: U.S. Census Bureau.

% = Percent change from previous census

Illinois's Economy

Employment by Industry, 2006

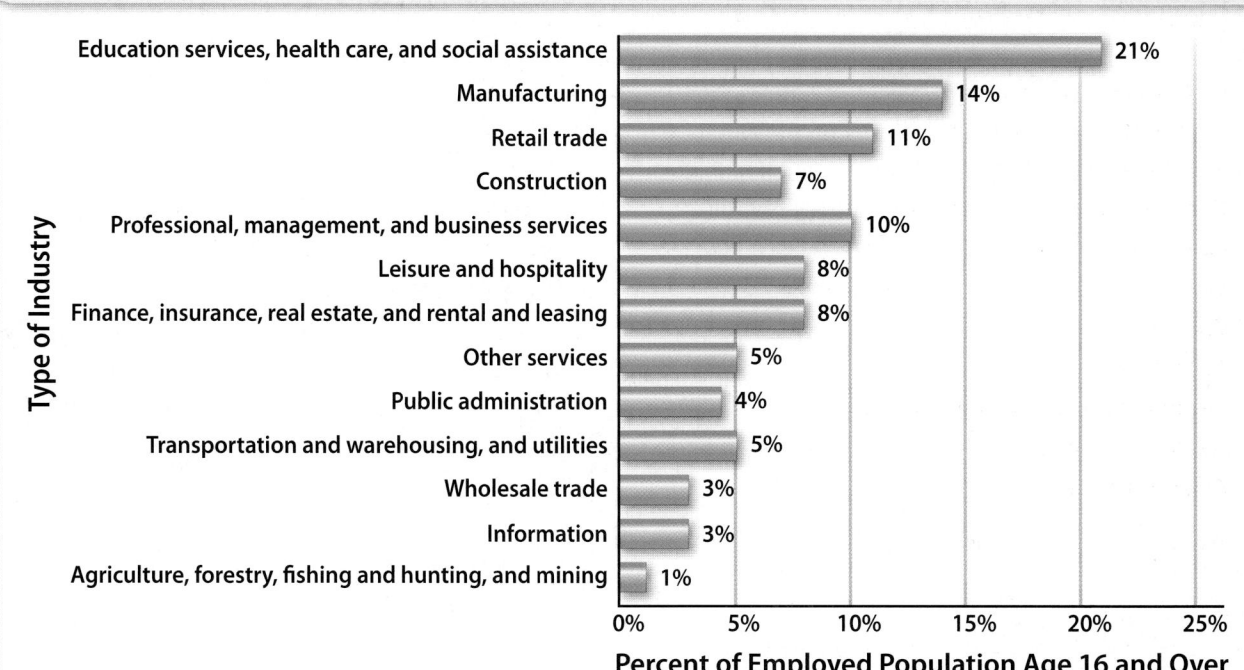

Type of Industry	Percent
Education services, health care, and social assistance	21%
Manufacturing	14%
Retail trade	11%
Construction	7%
Professional, management, and business services	10%
Leisure and hospitality	8%
Finance, insurance, real estate, and rental and leasing	8%
Other services	5%
Public administration	4%
Transportation and warehousing, and utilities	5%
Wholesale trade	3%
Information	3%
Agriculture, forestry, fishing and hunting, and mining	1%

Percent of Employed Population Age 16 and Over

Source: American Community Survey, U.S. Census Bureau.

Illinois Top 10 Leading Farm Products, 2006

Products	Total value (in millions of dollars)
Corn	$3,564
Soybeans	$2,646
Hogs	$978
Cattle and Calves	$603
Dairy Products	$296
Wheat	$124
Fruits & Vegetables	$92

Source: U.S. Department of Agriculture.

Illinois Employers by Number of Employees, 2004

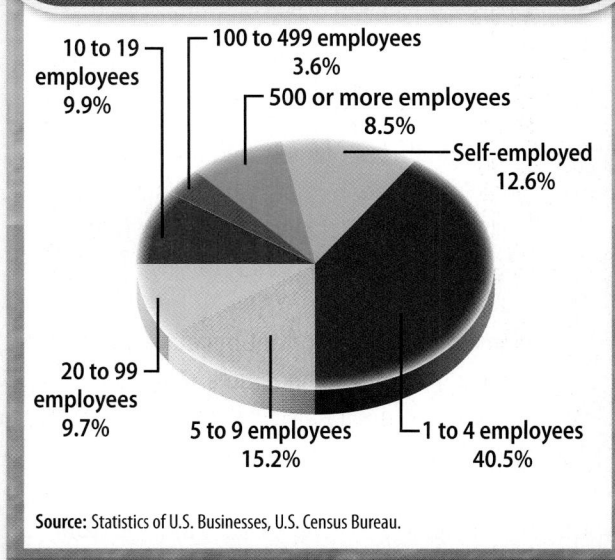

- 10 to 19 employees 9.9%
- 100 to 499 employees 3.6%
- 500 or more employees 8.5%
- Self-employed 12.6%
- 1 to 4 employees 40.5%
- 5 to 9 employees 15.2%
- 20 to 99 employees 9.7%

Source: Statistics of U.S. Businesses, U.S. Census Bureau.

The Geography of Illinois

Physical Geography

Illinois is in the part of the United States referred to as the Midwest. Like Ohio, Michigan, Indiana, Wisconsin, and Minnesota, it borders on the Great Lakes. The western and southern boundaries of Illinois are formed by the Ohio River and the Mississippi River. Illinois' overall area of 56,400 square miles (146,076 sq. km) ranks twenty-fourth of the fifty states.

Landforms Millions of years ago, the Illinois climate was extremely cold. Water was trapped in huge sheets of ice called glaciers that stretched from the North Pole into North America. Some of these thick, heavy sheets of ice moved slowly over Illinois, grinding the land flat.

Today, low plains cover about 90 percent of the state. The northwestern corner of the state has a somewhat higher elevation than the rest of the state. There you find the highest spot in Illinois, Charles Mound, which reaches 1,235 feet (405 m).

The southern portion of the Illinois plains that is called the Till Plains. It has rich, black soil perfect for growing crops. A band of hills called the Shawnee Hills reaches across Illinois south of the Till Plains. These hills are covered by trees and are now a national forest. Toward the southwest corner of the state, lower hills are separated by lowland areas.

Bodies of Water Illinois has many bodies of water which have been important in its development. These include Lake Michigan, the Illinois River, and the Mississippi River. The Ohio River also forms part of it's southern border.

Lake Michigan is important because it connects Illinois not only to the other states of the Midwest, but to eastern states such as New York. In the 1950s, the government made improvements to the St. Lawrence River to make it possible for oceangoing ships to move along its length. Ships could then go from

Illinois to the Atlantic Ocean and beyond. The lake also supplies water to more than 5 million people.

The Mississippi River is vital because it connects Illinois to the southern United States and the Gulf of Mexico. Since the 1800s the people of Illinois have used the river for transportation and to trade goods.

Some bodies of water in Illinois were made by humans. In the 1800s, people built the Illinois and Michigan Canal to connect the Chicago and Des Plaines rivers to the Illinois River and then the Mississippi River. The canal helped to provide a continuous waterway from Lake Michigan to the south. Because people travel on and tend to settle along waterways, the canal contributed to the growth of Chicago and the settlement of Illinois.

Climate The climate of Illinois also helped shape people's lives and where they live. Summers are hot—sometimes reaching 100°f (38°c) and winters are cold and snowy with temperature ranges dropping to 20 to 30 degrees below zero (–29° to –35°).

Ample rainfall led to the growth of tall grass prairies on the state's flat land and rich soils. Today, the prairies have been replaced by fields of corn and soybeans.

People and the Environment

The people of Illinois continue to make the best use of their state's natural resources. The rich soils of Illinois made it an inviting place to live in the 1800s, when most Americans were farmers. Thousands of people moved to the state from other parts of the country. In addition, southern Illinois has rich seams of coal. Mining has been a way of life in this area for many decades.

As in any state, the people who settled Illinois made an impact on the environment. Human activities have affected the land and water alike. Prairie land has been cleared and replaced with crops. Most of the state's forests were cut down to make way for farms and cities.

The rise of industry in Illinois also had its impact on the environment. Busy factories poured out smoke that polluted the air. Today, some companies dump chemicals and other harmful substances into waterways, harming the fish and plants living in them. Correcting these environmental issues to maintain the strong state economy is a high priority of the people and government of Illinois.

The History of Illinois

Native Americans and the French

Long before becoming part of the United States, the area of Illinois was home to Native Americans. The first Native Americans to settle there lived in small groups and supplied food to their people by hunting and gathering. Eventually, they began to grow corn, beans, and squash. Rich soil along rivers helped them grow an abundance of food and their villages grew very large.

By the 1600s, Native Americans lived in several different groups in the area. The Sac and Fox lived in the north, the Potawatomi and Ottawa settled near Lake Michigan, the Illinois lived in central Illinois, and the Cahokia set up villages in the far south.

The first Europeans to reach Illinois were the French. They had set up trading posts around the Great Lakes, where they traded with Native Americans for furs to be sold in Europe.

In 1673 two explorers—Jacques Marquette and Louis Jolliet—set out to explore the far-reaching Mississippi River. On the way, they passed through Illinois, claiming it for France. It remained in French hands until the mid-1700s.

France and Great Britain fought several wars for control of North America. The Treaty of Paris in 1763, following the final French defeat, stripped France of all territories east and west of the Mississippi River. As a result, Illinois passed into the control of the British.

Frenchmen Marquette and Jolliet explore the Mississippi River

Focus on Illinois

An 1832 view of Chicago which was established at Wolf's Point

Illinois in the United States

When the original thirteen British colonies won their independence, Illinois became a territory of the United States of America. The area that is now Ohio, Michigan, Indiana, Illinois, Wisconsin, and Minnesota was designated by the Northwest Ordinance of 1787. This document established boundaries and temporary territory governments there. It also stated that once the population of a territory in this large area had grown to a certain number, it could enter the union as a state.

Life On the Frontier Illinois fur trading continued to be important in Illinois. In 1779 an African American named Jean-Baptist-Point Du Sable founded a trading post where Chicago now stands. Its location along the shores of Lake Michigan made it an excellent site for trade.

Over time, the territory grew, as large numbers of settlers streamed into Illinois. Many cleared land and built farms, growing crops such as corn and other grains in Illinois' fertile soil.

Statehood and Conflict

On December 3, 1818, Illinois became the twenty-first state of the United States. Illinois entered the Union as a free state, which caused some conflict. Slavery was not legal in Illinois, but the state still had strong ties to the southern states that allowed slavery. Many Illinois settlers had come from the South, and the state's farmers sent their harvests south on the Mississippi River to be sold. A growing number of new settlers came from the North, though, and they opposed the spread of slavery.

The question of the spread of slavery became a major national issue in the 1850s. Democrat Stephen A. Douglas was a senator from Illinois. In 1854 he helped convince Congress to pass a law allowing people in new territories to choose whether to have slavery.

People in Illinois who opposed this idea began forming a new political party called the Republican Party. In 1858 the Republicans chose young lawyer Abraham Lincoln to oppose Douglas in his bid for reelection to the Senate. Douglas won, but Lincoln had become well-known and well-respected through his debates with Douglas throughout the campaign. Two years later, Republicans chose Lincoln to run as their candidate for president. He faced Douglas again, but this time Lincoln won.

Illinois in the Civil War

People in the South feared that Lincoln—a Northerner—would try to end slavery in the United States. To protect the policy of slavery, eleven states left the union and tried to form a new nation. The Civil War followed. Illinois sent about 250,000 men to fight in this war, which lasted from 1861 to 1865.

In the end, the North won the Civil War, thus restoring the Union. During the Civil War, President Lincoln had declared the end of slavery in the rebellious states. Later, slavery was banned across the whole country.

Near the end of the war, President Lincoln was shot and killed by John Wilkes Booth. Thousands of Americans honored Lincoln by standing along the railroad tracks as his funeral train carried his body back to Springfield, Illinois, for burial.

The Late 1800s

After the Civil War, new industries sprang up in Illinois, in addition to the already strong agriculture business. Companies built vast networks of railroad lines throughout the country. Many lines met in Chicago, which became a vital transportation center. The city used this advantage to become a center of the meatpacking industry. Railroads spurred other industries, such as the new iron and steel companies that were formed to make rails and engines. George Pullman's company in Illinois built railroad cars. The state's rich coal mines supplied much-needed fuel for the country, and the coal was also transported by trains.

In addition, railroads allowed Illinois agricultural products to be shipped east and west across the country. Other industries served the nation's farmers. Cyrus McCormick and John Deere made farm equipment in Illinois factories. Montgomery Ward and Sears, Roebuck established companies that sold goods to farmers by mail order.

The Growth of Cities The rise of these industries in the late 1800s and early 1900s attracted workers, and Illinois cities grew quickly.

Railroads were an important transit system in Illinois in the early 1900s

Mower wheels were manufactured at the McCormick Reaper Works in the early 1900s

Thousands of immigrants lived in crowded apartments with little sanitation, and groups of United States reformers called for new laws to help them. Other socially concerned people such as Jane Addams set up centers called settlement houses. There they taught immigrants to speak English and helped them adapt to American life.

Working conditions in the new factories were harsh. Workers—often children kept out of school—labored for long hours, six or seven days a week. Wages were low, and workers could be injured or even killed on the job.

Many people left farms, but thousands of workers came from other countries, attracted by the growing American economy. The population of Illinois nearly tripled between 1860 and 1900.

Many Illinois cities grew in this period, but none as much as Chicago. By 1890, it had a million people and was the second largest city in the nation. Chicago's growth is even more remarkable considering that it survived major disasters. In 1871 a fire destroyed much of the city. The people of Chicago rebounded, however, and simply rebuilt their homes and businesses.

Industry and Workers The change to an industrial economy and rapid growth brought Illinois some problems as well as benefits. Cities were at times crowded and unpleasant places to live, and factory owners and workers often clashed. Booming cities strained government resources in the late 1800s and early 1900s. City officials needed to provide more water and sewage systems and to build more streets and schools.

Labor Unions Some workers tried to form labor unions, hoping to force factory owners to make changes. The goal of the unions was to help workers bargain for better working conditions and better wages. The government and business owners sometimes responded harshly to the workers, however. When they went on strike—refusing to work—companies sometimes responded with violence.

Still, the Illinois government did take some action to help workers. New laws required workplaces to meet safety standards and limited the number of hours that children could work. Then, in the 1930s, the U.S. Congress passed new laws making it easier for workers to form unions. As a result, unions became strong in the factories and coal mines of Illinois.

Modern Illinois

In the last half of the 1900s, Illinois changed greatly. The cities increased their populations and people continued to move into the state and settle. The state's people are more diverse than ever, and the economy has changed.

Today Illinois' population is nearly 13 million people, making Illinois the fifth-most- populous state. About one in eight people are African Americans, and about one in seven are Latino. Four percent of the population are Asian American. Of the total population, nearly 14 percent were born in another country, showing that Illinois has a strong economy that attracts workers from all over the world.

A diverse crowd of Chicago Cubs fans celebrate a play-off win

The Government of Illinois

The Structure of State Government

Illinois is a democratic republic. In a democracy, power rests with the people. In a republic, day-to-day decisions are carried out by officials whom the people elect. The Illinois government has three branches, as does the national government.

The main responsibility of the state legislative branch, called the General Assembly, is to enact, to amend or to repeal laws as necessary. The General Assembly has two houses—the Senate and the House of Representatives. Both have the power to introduce a bill that might become a law, and both must agree on a law to pass it.

The primary duty of the executive branch is to carry out the laws made by the legislative branch. The executive branch has six elected officials: the Governor, Lieutenant Governor, Attorney General, Secretary of State, Treasurer, and Comptroller. Other officers in the executive branch are appointed.

Before it becomes a law, the governor must sign a bill that the General Assembly has approved. If he or she refuses to sign it, it may be returned to the General Assembly for revision or for another vote by the legislature which may overturn the veto.

The judicial branch interprets the laws and decides if the people have followed the law. The Illinois court system consists of a Supreme Court, appellate Court, and Circuit Courts. The Circuit Courts are the first courts to hear most cases. People who feel their rights were violated in a trial can appeal to an appellate court or even to the state Supreme Court. Its decisions are final.

Illinois Capital Cities

Kaskaskia, a city founded by the French settlers in the early 1700s, was the first capital city of the state of Illinois. The state's first capitol building in Kaskaskia was a small, two-story brick building.

Vandalia became the second capital city in 1820, two years after Illinois became a state. Three capitol buildings were built in Vandalia. The first was destroyed by fire, so another was built in 1824. Vandalia residents built yet a third capitol building in 1836, in an attempt to keep their city as the state capital.

The State Capitol Building at Springfield, Illinois

The capital city, however, was moved to Springfield, a more central location, in 1839. The government built a fifth capitol building in Springfield in 1853, but outgrew this location. Construction on a sixth capitol building (the present capitol) was begun in 1868 and took about 20 years to complete.

The Constitutions of Illinois

A constitution sets forth the structure of a government and the powers and responsibilities of its different branches. Illinois has had four constitutions. The first state constitution was approved in 1818. It set up the three branches of government and described the powers of each. The constitution outlined the rights of citizens and banned slavery.

A new constitution approved in 1848 made the judicial branch more independent of the legislature. Then another new constitution was adopted in 1870 which made minor changes.

The Constitution of 1970 In 1970, Illinois adopted its fourth and existing constitution. This constitution made several changes to the previous version. Under the new document, the General Assembly was required to meet each year. The new framework also mandated that the candidates for governor and lieutenant governor run as a team. The

document strengthened human rights. An important change in this constitution told employers that they could not treat people unfairly on the basis of race, color, creed, national ancestry, or gender. In addition. it gave the governor the power to cut the amount of money that the legislature voted to spend on a project. Finally, the new constitution gave more power to local governments.

The Rights of the People The people of Illinois enjoy certain rights. Some rights are guaranteed by the U.S. Constitution. Soon after the U.S. Constitution was adopted, some amendments, or changes, were added. These ten amendments—the Bill of Rights—spell out the rights of all Americans. The First Amendment, for instance, says that Congress cannot limit the freedom of speech.

The Illinois constitution recognizes certain rights as well. Some—like freedom of speech—are similar to those in the federal Bill of Rights. The Preamble to the Illinois Constitution specifically promises "efforts to provide for the health, safety and welfare of the people; [to] maintain a representative and orderly government, among other endeavors."

Over the years, the courts have been called upon to define what, exactly, some constitutional rights mean. For instance, in 1964 the U.S. Supreme Court heard the case of *Escobedo v. Illinois*. In this case, the Court ruled that a person who is in custody for questioning by the police must be given the opportunity to speak to a lawyer. Denying that right to a person in custody violates the person's constitutional rights. This was an important Court decision because it changed police policy, not just in Illinois, but across the country.

Illinois Government and Its People

Over the years, different groups have competed for political power in Illinois. Sometimes geography divided people. In the 1800s, people in different regions of the state wanted to make sure that their area benefited most from government actions. Members of the state legislature often disagreed. Another struggle for power was between people who lived in cities and those in rural areas. Each group wanted the government to respond to its concerns.

The state's different regions have generally had different political ties. Chicago has long been dominated by the Democratic Party. Its suburbs along with northern and central Illinois tend to vote Republican. Southern counties support either party, depending on the issues and candidates.

Though they have differences, the people of Illinois also work together. State officials do their best to make policies that will benefit the people living in all parts of the state.

Dedicated individuals have also had an impact on Illinois government. In the late 1800s, Florence Kelley published a report that detailed the harsh working conditions that factory workers faced. This report led the state government to pass new laws aimed at improving workplace safety.

Ida B. Wells-Barnett was another reformer who lived in Chicago. Wells-Barnett wrote about and campaigned for equal rights for African Americans. She also worked to make the criminal justice system more fair.

Illinois Governor Rod Blagojevich greets students

Illinois Leaders Today As in the past, state leaders guide the government of Illinois. Rod R. Blagojevich won his second term as governor of Illinois in 2006. His goals were to create more jobs, improve education, and to broaden access to health care.

Twenty-one people represent Illinois in Congress. Nineteen serve in the House of Representatives. The longest to serve was Dennis Hastert, who had officiated for many years as Speaker of the House before he retired in 2008.

The two senators from Illinois are Richard Durbin and Barack Obama. Durbin holds the second-highest position in the Democratic Party within the Senate. Elected in 2004, Obama became only the fifth African American U.S. senator in history. He also campaigned as a presidential candidate in the 2008 election.

Major Interest Groups Special interest groups play an important part in shaping today's government policy. Some groups are committed to common social goals. The members of AARP, for example, are people fifty years old or older. Their concern is the welfare of the aging population. Other groups share government policy goals. These groups try to influence state lawmakers to address their particular concerns when legislators consider new laws.

Other interest groups focus on economic issues. Businesses join together to try to pass laws that will benefit their profitability. Labor unions also send representatives to the state capitol to influence lawmakers.

The people of Illinois today are concerned primarily about the same issues that other Americans are. These include local and national security, the economy, and taxes.

Some issues, however, are strongly felt in Illinois. In particular, many people have claimed in recent years that electricity rates are too high. A large majority of people in the state think more money is needed to fund public schools. In addition, the governor's push to provide more state funding for health care has been heavily debated in the state legislature.

Focus on Illinois

Legislative Branch

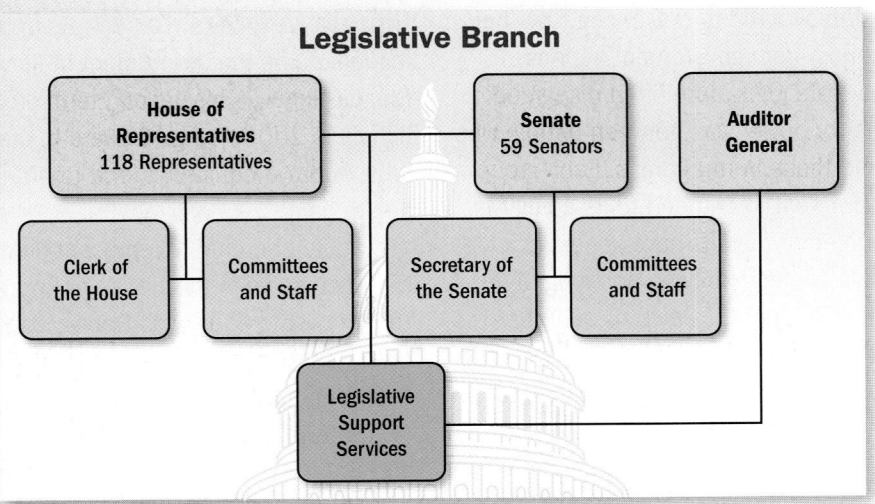

- House of Representatives — 118 Representatives
- Senate — 59 Senators
- Auditor General
- Clerk of the House
- Committees and Staff
- Secretary of the Senate
- Committees and Staff
- Legislative Support Services

Executive Branch

- Secretary Of State
- Treasurer
- Governor
- Lieutenant Governor
- Comptroller
- Attorney General
- Departments
- State Board of Elections
- Bureau of the Budget
- Education
- Civil Administrative Code Departments
- Department of Military Affairs
- Other Agencies, Boards, and Authorities

Judicial Branch

- Courts Commission
- Supreme Court
- Administrative Office of Illinois Courts
- Judicial Inquiry Board
- Appellate Court
- State Board of Law Examiners
- Attorney Registration and Disciplinary Commission
- Circuit Court
- State Appellate Defender

Funding the Government

The state funds its programs through taxes and other fees. Income taxes provide one-fifth of all Illinois government income. Another one-fifth comes from sales taxes, which people pay when they buy goods at a store, and from road taxes. The single biggest source of state government income, though, is money sent to the state from the federal government.

The biggest areas of Illinois state spending are assistance to poorer people and to education. These two areas make up almost half of all state spending. The state also spends money on health care, police protection and the courts, roadways, and other programs.

U.S. Senators Obama and Durbin with Congressional candidate L. Tammy Duckworth

The American Economic System

A Free Enterprise System

The United States has a free enterprise economic system. Freedom to choose is a key value underlying the American economy.

In any economy, people combine land, labor, and capital to produce goods and services. Land includes all natural resources, from trees to coal. Labor is the work of humans. Capital includes money and the ability of people to figure out how to combine these resources. Goods are products that are created in factories or grown on farms. Services are actions people perform for others, such as financial and banking services or teaching.

In some other countries the government controls the economy. In the United States, individuals and businesses own the three factors of production. They decide how to use their resources to supply goods and services. The people who start companies take a risk. There is a chance that others might not buy the things they are selling. If so, the business owner will lose money. Why would people take that risk? They do so hoping to gain a reward—profits. Profits are the earnings a business owner receives after

paying all expenses. In the United States, business owners have the right to keep their profits, which is the heart of the free enterprise system.

The Market in Action A free enterprise economy is also called a market economy, because the key decisions are made by individuals in markets. Markets include everything from the corner store where you buy a bottle of fruit juice, to the exchange that occurs when someone buys goods online, or even stocks bought and sold on stock exchanges.

Supply and demand drive markets. Supply is the total amount of a good or service that all companies that produce it can supply. Demand is the desire that all consumers have for that good or service. These forces work together to set prices.

Producers want high prices so they can make more profit. As prices rise, though, fewer consumers want to buy the good or service. Supply, then, is high at high prices and low at low prices, but demand is the opposite. Demand is high at low prices and low when prices are high. These forces balance each other until the two sides arrive at a price that satisfies both.

Focus on Illinois

Economic Growth and Productivity

Economists look for growth and productivity in measuring the health of an economy. Growth compares the value of goods and services produced from one year to the next. If that value rises, the economy is said to be growing.

Productivity looks at the number of resources used to produce goods and services. Using fewer resources to produce the same amount of output is more efficient. A producer who uses fewer resources can set lower prices and still earn profits. As you have read, profits are the reward business owners receive for taking risks. Economists generally conclude that if profits are growing, an economy is probably thriving.

Economists also look at wages. These are the payments workers receive for their labor. If workers' wages go up, they can purchase more goods and services. That encourages businesses to produce more, leading them to hire more workers. This situation has the effect of increasing wages across the whole economy.

Government's Role in the Economy

In some countries, the government plays a very large role in the nation's economy. Government officials, not individuals, decide what to produce.

In the United States, though, individuals make most economic decisions. Still, the government does play a part. It sets policies that require people to act fairly and competitively in the marketplace. For instance, there are laws to stop business owners from making false claims in advertisements. Laws also require consumers to complete payments when they have agreed to buy something.

In addition, the government also makes sure that businesses are competing with each other. Laws prevent one company from controlling any one good or service. Competition leads to better goods and services and it also leads to lower prices. By making sure that businesses compete, the government helps consumers.

The Economy of Illinois

Illinois Energy Sources

Coal is an important energy resource in Illinois. In fact, coal sits under nearly two-thirds of the state's land. Coal mines in the state contribute about $1 billion annually to the state's economy.

Illinois also has twelve nuclear power plants that generate energy, more nuclear plants than any other state. Scattered across the state, these plants produce electricity that is used in homes and businesses.

The People of Illinois

Another important resource of Illinois is its workers. The workforce of Illinois is highly skilled and well educated. Nearly nine in ten people 25 years old or older have a high school diploma. Nearly three in ten have a college degree or more advanced degree. Both of these figures are higher than the national averages.

One reason for this level of education is that state and local governments invest in their schools. Illinois ranks ninth among all states in the amount it spends per pupil in its elementary and secondary schools. About 8 percent of the state budget goes to the state's colleges and universities, which, again, is higher than the national average.

Of course, workers also learn on the job. The skills they gain as they work help them work more productively, in turn helping businesses to grow. Nearly half of all workers in the state are professional or highly trained.

The backbone of the Illinois economy has historically been agriculture

Illinois Industries

Manufacturing remains an important part of the state's economy. Factories in Illinois produce nearly 15 percent of the state's goods. Companies have for decades made a variety of earth-moving equipment, tools, and machinery. Food processing is a major industry in the state. As in the past, the excellent transportation network brings the raw materials from the nation's farms to be turned into food for consumers across the country.

High-technology industries have become an important part of the Illinois economy in recent decades. Some companies make parts that go into computers, while others produce medicines or do complex biotechnical research.

Printing and publishing are major industries in the state. Chicago also is a center of finance, and major insurance companies make their homes in Illinois as well.

Illinois also supports a strong tourist industry. For example, more than 1.4 million people came to the state from other countries in one recent year, and many more people come from other states. Housing and feeding these tourists creates more jobs for the people of Illinois and brings more profits to fuel the state's economy.

Of course, farming continues to play a major role in the Illinois economy. More than 80 per cent of the state's land area is occupied by farms. Farms produce more soybeans than any other state and usually rank first or second in corn production. Pork and beef, dairy products, and grains are other important agricultural products.

Illinois in the World Economy

This is the century of global trade. Some countries do not have enough of some resources to produce goods. Others have the natural resources but not the skilled workers to use them. Each nation specializes, producing what it is good at. As a result, nations produce more of some goods than they need to meet the demand of their people. They also produce less of other goods that their people want. Trade solves this problem. People in one country sell the extra units of the goods they produce to people in another country. Goods sold abroad are exports. Countries also buy from other countries the goods they do not make but want. Those goods are imports.

Illinois is now part of a global economy. Businesses in the state ship their goods around the world—and the people of Illinois buy goods from other lands. Illinois enjoys a strong position in world trade. Its airports and ports are well suited to handling the movement of goods and people. With its manufacturing companies that export earth-moving equipment, medicines, and computer parts, Illinois ranks sixth among all states in the value of its exports. Nearly 500,000 people in Illinois have jobs related to exporting.

In *Curriculum for Social Studies: Expectations of Excellence,* the National Council for the Social Studies (NCSS) identified 10 themes that serve as organizing strands for the social studies curriculum at every school level. These themes are interrelated and draw from all of the social science disciplines. Each theme provides student performance expectations in the areas of knowledge, processes, and attitudes. *The American Journey* content addresses the 10 NCSS themes.

Theme and Performance Expectation	Student Pages
I. *Culture* The study of culture helps students understand similarities and differences within groups of people. By studying a culture's beliefs, values, and traditions, students begin to gain a perspective that helps them relate to different groups. In the middle grades, students begin to examine aspects of culture and how culture influences human behavior.	
A. Compare similarities and differences in the ways groups, societies, and cultures meet human needs and concerns.	9, 10–15, 17–22, 24, 84, 85, 374, 387, 403, 407–412, 415, 567, 571, 613–616, 617, 737, 841, 900
B. Explain how information and experiences may be interpreted by people from diverse cultural perspectives and frames of reference.	24, 38, 43, 374, 375, 406–412, 415, 419–421, 566–571, 615, 617, 634, 635
C. Explain and give examples of how language, literature, the arts, architecture, other artifacts, traditions, beliefs, values, and behaviors contribute to the development and transmission of culture.	4–5, 9, 17–22, 29, 30, 31, 374, 381, 398–399, 407–409, 412, 421, 567, 571, 613, 615–617, 629, 630, 631, 632, 635, 685, 759–761, 787, 791
D. Explain why individuals and groups respond differently to their physical and social environments and/or changes to them on the basis of shared assumptions, values, and beliefs.	8–9, 10–15, 18–19, 24, 25, 44–47, 367, 371, 398–399, 406–412, 419, 421, 570–571, 613, 615–617
E. Articulate the implications of cultural diversity, as well as cohesion, within and across groups.	25, 85, 367–368, 372–377, 387, 398–399, 406–412, 557, 569, 570, 571, 613, 615–617, 634
II. *Time, Continuity, and Change* Understanding time, continuity, and change involves being knowledgeable about what things were like in the past and how things change and develop over time. Knowing how to read and reconstruct the past helps students gain a historical perspective. In the middle grades, students will continue to increase their knowledge of the past and of historical concepts. Students will also begin to learn how individual experiences, social values, and cultural traditions influence interpretations of the past.	
A. Demonstrate an understanding that different scholars may describe the same event or situation in different ways but must provide reasons or evidence for their views.	10, 35, 38, 140, 266, 364–365, 428–429, 447, 448–451, 461, 502, 529, 530, 536–537, 613, 629–630, 666, 686, 689, 698–699, 746–747, 759–761, 762–764, 890–891, 897–898, 916–917, 919–920, 921–922, 928–930
B. Identify and use key concepts such as chronology, causality, change, conflict, and complexity to explain, analyze, and show connections among patterns of historical change and continuity.	9, 59–60, 82, 98–103, 114, 115, 165, 169, 173, 182, 254, 270, 285, 288, 298, 305, 307, 314–315, 321, 325, 337–339, 347, 358, 366, 368–369, 384, 385, 387, 397, 399, 402, 411, 425, 435, 455, 456–461, 462, 466, 480, 483, 527, 531, 539, 540, 557, 609, 612, 614–615, 632, 634, 651, 655, 661, 677, 685–687, 689, 717, 751, 752–753, 755, 757, 759, 761–763, 764, 772, 777, 805, 807, 828, 856, 866, 874, 879, 888–889, 894–898, 912–913, 921–922, 948–955, 967, 977–979, 980, 997
C. Identify and describe selected historical periods and patterns of change within and across cultures, such as the rise of civilizations, the development of transportation systems, the growth and breakdown of colonial systems, and others.	7, 8, 9, 13–14, 15, 56–57, 99, 100–103, 104–107, 303, 312–317, 338, 339, 357, 389–391, 454–455, 535, 539–540, 583, 611, 626–632, 699, 745–746, 747, 758–764, 884–891, 895, 921–922
D. Identify and use processes important to reconstructing and reinterpreting the past, such as using a variety of sources, providing, validating, and weighing evidence for claims, checking credibility of sources, and searching for causality.	25, 36, 115, 461, 544, 685–686, 689, 769

Theme and Performance Expectation	Student Pages
E. Develop critical sensitivities such as empathy and skepticism regarding attitudes, values, and behaviors of people in different historical contexts.	70–71, 91, 130–131, 341, 382, 399, 404–405, 415, 420, 431, 441, 452, 453, 455, 488–489, 539–540, 558–559, 663–665, 744–747, 759–761, 762–764, 766–767, 787, 788–790, 825–827, 884, 886, 887, 891, 892–893, 898, 915, 932
F. Use knowledge of facts and concepts drawn from history, along with methods of historical inquiry, to inform decision-making about and action-taking on public issues.	273, 414, 441, 460–461, 539–540, 671, 688–689, 746–747, 751, 753, 891, 923, 997
III. People, Places, and Environments The study of people, places, and environments will help students as they create their spatial views and geographic perspective of the world. Students begin to make informed and critical decisions about the relationship between humans and their environment. In the middle school years, students can relate their personal experiences to happenings in other environments. These experiences will help students increase their abstract thought when analyzing human behavior in relation to physical and cultural environments.	
A. Elaborate mental maps of locales, regions, and the world that demonstrate understanding of relative location, direction, size, and shape.	7, 41, 169–173, 281, 283–285, 296, 347, 359, 367, 371, 463–464, 480–487, 554–555
B. Create, interpret, use, and distinguish various representations of the earth such as maps, globes, and photographs.	20, 25, 40, 50, 156, 190, 262, 283, 291, 296, 306, 308, 324, 329, 344, 360, 370, 374, 376, 379, 389, 415, 426, 449, 450, 454, 458, 465, 482, 484, 485, 503, 510, 511, 554, 562, 568, 586, 604, 653, 676, 681, 686, 695, 707, 720, 730, 781, 789, 822, 824, 830, 844, 847, 857, 875, 908, 911, 928, 961, 978, 980, 988
C. Use appropriate resources, data sources, and geographic tools such as aerial photographs, satellite images, geographic information systems (GIS), map projections, and cartography to generate, manipulate, and interpret information such as atlases, databases, grid systems, charts, graphs, and maps.	25, 32, 36, 67, 74, 78, 91, 110–111, 115, 124, 134, 156, 158, 171, 190, 213, 262, 277, 291, 296, 308, 313, 324, 343, 344, 360, 370, 373, 374, 376, 379, 395, 397, 401, 407, 414, 415, 449, 450, 454, 458, 465, 475, 476, 482, 484, 485, 500, 503, 507, 510, 511, 519, 525, 535, 537, 539, 553, 554, 556, 562, 568, 575, 576, 585, 586, 604, 621, 634, 643, 653, 657, 659, 660, 681, 686, 695, 707, 713, 720, 729, 730, 755, 756, 762, 773, 775, 779, 780, 781, 789, 795, 809, 812, 822, 824, 825, 830, 844, 847, 854, 857, 875, 881, 895, 900, 908, 911, 928, 929, 959, 961, 978, 980, 983, 986–987, 988, 994, 1001, 1002–1003, 1004
D. Estimate distance, calculate scale, and distinguish other geographic relationships such as population density and spatial distribution patterns.	77, 306, 308, 313, 373, 395, 407, 465, 621, 875, 900, 1005
E. Locate and describe varying landforms and geographic features, such as mountains, plateaus, islands, rain forests, deserts, and oceans, and explain their relationship within the ecosystem.	7, 8, 285, 382, 553, 788–789
F. Describe physical system changes such as seasons, climate and weather, and the water cycle and identify geographic patterns associated with them.	8, 557, 788–789
G. Describe how people create places that reflect cultural values and ideals as they build neighborhoods, parks, shopping centers, and the like.	382, 397–398, 399, 553, 624–625, 659
H. Examine, interpret, and analyze physical and cultural patterns and their interactions, such as land use, settlement patterns, cultural transmission of customs and ideas, and ecosystem changes.	7–9, 13, 15, 24, 25, 67, 79–80, 89–90, 190, 191, 261, 262, 281, 285, 313–314, 317, 328, 359, 361, 362, 363, 367, 369–370, 371, 379, 381–382, 385, 395, 397–399, 463–466, 481, 553–554, 557, 587, 611, 634, 679, 683, 725, 746, 788–789
I. Describe ways that historical events have been influenced by, and have influenced, physical and human geographic factors in local, regional, national, and global settings.	8–9, 13, 34–41, 74, 89–90, 93, 94, 169–173, 261–263, 280–285, 306, 307–308, 309, 316, 317, 359–363, 366–371, 379–380, 381–382, 392–393, 394–399, 463–466, 480–487, 551, 552–557, 580, 587, 608, 678–683, 788–789, 811, 829–832, 905, 909, 960
J. Observe and speculate about social and economic effects of environmental changes and crises resulting from phenomena such as floods, storms, and drought.	18, 397–398, 644, 787–788, 789, 996, 997
K. Propose, compare, and evaluate alternative uses of land and resources in communities, nations, and the world.	397–398, 1003

Theme and Performance Expectation	Student Pages
IV. *Individual Development and Identity* People and culture influence a person's identity. Examining the different forms of human behavior improve one's understanding of social relationships and the development of personal identity. The study of human behavior helps students become aware of how social processes influence a person's identity. In the middle years, issues of personal identity become important as students begin to view themselves in relation to others.	
A. Relate personal changes to social, cultural, and historical contexts.	73–75, 164–165, 381–382, 424–431, 490–497, 567
B. Describe personal connections to place—as associated with community, nation, and world.	145, 156, 162, 305, 309, 317, 321, 322, 329, 360, 361, 363, 369, 381–382, 425–426, 431, 490–497, 515, 621, 622
C. Describe the ways family, gender, ethnicity, nationality, and institutional affiliations contribute to personal identity.	73–75, 95, 102, 164–165, 305, 321, 381–382, 396, 397, 399, 415, 424–431, 490–497, 950–951
D. Relate such factors as physical endowment and capabilities, learning, motivation, personality, perception, and behavior to individual development.	75, 109–112, 162, 197, 278, 360, 361, 363, 426, 427, 428, 429, 492–493, 508–509, 570, 596, 666, 667, 852–853, 878, 972–973
E. Identify and describe ways regional, ethnic, and national cultures influence individuals' daily lives.	110–112, 396–397, 415, 424–431, 457, 490–497, 580, 663, 664, 665
F. Identify and describe the influence of perception, attitudes, values, and beliefs on personal identity.	322–324, 326, 381–382, 424–431, 490–497
G. Identify and interpret examples of stereotyping, conformity, and altruism.	396, 397, 399, 426–427, 431, 512, 617, 663, 664, 665, 762, 764, 825–827
H. Work independently and cooperatively to accomplish goals.	24, 25, 54, 55, 84, 85, 114, 115, 144, 145, 182, 183, 212, 213, 272, 273, 300, 301, 328, 329, 354, 355, 384, 385, 414, 415, 440, 441, 468–469, 470, 471, 514, 515, 544, 545, 580, 581, 608, 609, 634, 635, 670, 671, 700, 701, 736, 737, 768, 769, 800, 801, 834, 835, 870, 871, 900, 901, 934, 935, 966, 967, 1010, 1011
V. *Individuals, Groups, and Institutions* Institutions, such as schools, governments, and churches, influence people and often reflect a society's values. Because of the vital role that institutions play in people's lives, it is important that students know how institutions develop, what controls and influences them, and how humans react to them. Middle school students will gain experience by studying how institutions change over time. They should also be able to use their understanding to suggest ways how institutions can work for the common good.	
A. Demonstrate an understanding of concepts such as role, status, and social class in describing the interactions of individuals and social groups.	12, 21–22, 24, 47, 49, 54, 77, 80, 81, 82, 94, 344, 345, 419, 420, 421, 438, 487, 523, 577, 578, 602–606, 651–654, 655, 670
B. Analyze group and institutional influences on people, events, and elements of culture.	12, 13, 65, 82, 102, 127–129, 133–137, 153, 154, 158, 159, 162, 164–165, 175, 178, 195–196, 342–347, 360, 378–380, 381–382, 417, 419, 421, 434–438, 518–521, 544, 575–578, 602–606, 651–655, 670
C. Describe the various forms institutions take and the interactions of people with institutions.	46, 47, 65, 77, 78, 79, 80, 81–82, 102, 349, 381–382, 437–438, 520, 529, 544, 574–578, 602–605, 652–653, 655, 670
D. Identify and analyze examples of tensions between expressions of individuality and group or institutional efforts to promote social conformity.	49, 52, 65, 81–82, 84, 144, 164–165, 195–196, 201, 344–347, 349, 352, 379, 381–382, 396, 434–438
E. Identify and describe examples of tensions between belief systems and government policies and laws.	75, 80–81, 127–129, 144, 153, 154, 159, 177, 195–197, 201, 322, 323, 324, 340, 341, 343–344, 350, 352, 382, 396, 434–438, 486–487, 525–527, 650–655, 670
F. Describe the role of institutions in furthering both continuity and change.	21–22, 82, 102, 133, 137, 177–178, 194–201, 343–344, 381–382, 417, 418–421, 440, 470, 486–487, 529, 575–578, 604–606, 650–655
G. Apply knowledge of how groups and institutions work to meet individual needs and promote the common good.	84, 133, 137, 144, 178, 197–201, 212, 378–382, 417, 418–421, 424–431, 437–438, 486–487, 520, 529, 575–578, 604–606, 652–653, 654–655

Theme and Performance Expectation	Student Pages
VI. *Power, Authority, and Governance* Studying structures of power, authority, and governance and their functions in the United States and around the world is important for developing a notion of civic responsibility. Students will identify the purpose and characteristics of various types of government and how people try to resolve conflicts. Students will also examine the relationship between individual rights and responsibilities. During the middle school years, students apply what they have learned about rights and responsibilities in more complex contexts.	
A. Examine persistent issues involving the rights, roles, and status of the individual in relation to the general welfare.	66, 67, 68, 187–188, 193, 212, 254, 268, 269, 396–397, 451, 477–478, 517, 646–647, 796–797, 848–849
B. Describe the purpose of government and how its powers are acquired, used, and justified.	68, 100–101, 139–142, 144, 145, 188–193, 212, 253, 255–257, 269, 270, 272, 277–279, 298, 448–451, 459, 474–479, 504, 642–647, 670, 713–714, 715–717, 780–783, 786–791, 848, 880–883
C. Analyze and explain ideas and governmental mechanisms to meet needs and wants of citizens, regulate territory, manage conflict, and establish order and security.	21–22, 61, 68, 99–100, 139, 141–142, 144, 145, 188–193, 212, 254, 261, 262, 263, 264–270, 272, 277–279, 294–298, 382, 448–451, 474–479, 504, 534, 544, 645–647, 713–714, 715–717, 736, 780–783, 786–791, 848–849, 880–883
D. Describe the ways nations and organizations respond to forces of unity and diversity affecting order and security.	78, 84, 112, 139, 140, 141–142, 144, 187–193, 261, 262, 263, 265–270, 272, 298, 448–451, 474–479, 544, 713–714, 715–717, 736, 780–783, 786–791, 794–798
E. Identify and describe the basic features of the political system in the United States and identify representative leaders from various levels and branches of government.	207–208, 210, 212, 253, 255, 257, 274–275, 279, 798, 848, 949, 996
F. Explain conditions, actions, and motivations that contribute to conflict and cooperation within and among nations.	30, 32, 105, 106, 108–112, 139–142, 144, 150–151, 182, 261, 262, 263, 264–270, 272, 286–293, 296, 298, 325–326, 328, 343–347, 359, 363, 367–368, 369–371, 372–377, 448–451, 474–479, 564–565, 643–644, 646, 679–681, 682, 683, 684–689, 715–717, 736, 772–777, 843–847, 856–859
G. Describe and analyze the role of technology in communications, transportation, information processing, weapons development, or other areas as it contributes to or helps resolve conflicts.	30, 389–392, 393, 555–557, 581, 584–587, 589–590, 625, 704–709, 714–715, 717, 944–945
H. Explain and apply concepts such as power, role, status, justice, and influence to the examination of persistent issues and social problems.	47, 253, 254, 255, 257, 269, 396, 397, 476, 643–644, 646–647, 779, 780, 783, 794–798, 848–849, 883
I. Give examples and explain how governments attempt to achieve their stated ideals at home and abroad.	30, 99–100, 138–142, 144, 145, 150–151, 186–193, 212, 253, 255, 261, 278–279, 325, 326, 328, 382, 448–451, 474–479, 674–677, 693–694, 715–717, 772–777, 842–849, 880–883
VII. *Production, Distribution, and Consumption* Societies try to meet people's needs and wants by trying to answer the basic economic questions: What is to be produced? How should goods be produced? How should goods and services be distributed? How should land, labor, capital, and management be allocated? By studying how needs and wants are met, students learn how trade and government economic policies develop. In the middle grades, students increase their knowledge of economic concepts, principles, and reasoning.	
A. Give and explain examples of ways that economic systems structure choices about how goods and services are to be produced and distributed.	61, 89–95, 114, 304–309, 350–351, 389–390, 391, 392–393, 401, 414, 514, 538, 561, 563, 595, 598–599, 657–658, 661, 670, 726, 754–757, 768, 776–777, 815–816, 817, 851, 981
B. Describe the role that supply and demand, prices, incentives, and profits play in determining what is produced and distributed in a competitive market system.	93, 306, 307, 308–309, 350–351, 360–361, 391, 392–393, 402, 408, 561, 565, 575, 595–599, 661, 676–677, 726, 754–757, 775, 815–816, 817, 851
C. Explain the difference between private and public goods and services.	777
D. Describe a range of examples of the various institutions that make up economic systems such as households, business firms, banks, government agencies, labor unions, and corporations.	114, 257, 308–309, 349, 350, 396, 563, 564, 595–596, 599, 604–605, 606, 608, 657–658, 725, 773–777, 778, 780–781, 815–816, 851, 983
E. Describe the role of specialization and exchange in the economic process.	114, 360–361, 391, 661, 675–677

Theme and Performance Expectation	Student Pages
F. Explain and illustrate how values and beliefs influence different economic decisions.	84, 90, 91, 93, 94, 95, 114, 348–352, 401–402, 491–492, 494–495, 564, 599, 608, 658–659, 661, 675–677, 725, 851, 981
G. Differentiate among various forms of exchange and money.	92, 164, 189, 192, 360, 381, 497, 593, 756, 757, 773, 774, 775, 777
H. Compare basic economic systems according to who determines what is produced, distributed, and consumed.	99, 100, 304, 307, 360–361, 389, 391, 403, 597–599, 608, 745
I. Use economic concepts to help explain historical and current developments and issues in local, national, or global contexts.	89–95, 99, 100, 182, 256, 257, 272, 288, 290, 304–309, 340, 350–351, 352, 355, 359–363, 388–393, 401–402, 477, 491–492, 494–495, 497, 556–557, 561, 580, 595, 598, 599, 659–661, 674–677, 700, 754–757, 772–777, 786–791, 851, 960, 983, 989, 1002–1003
J. Use economic reasoning to compare different proposals for dealing with a contemporary social issue such as unemployment, acid rain, or high quality education.	497, 851, 1003–1004

VIII. Science, Technology, and Society

The study of science, technology, and society is ever changing. It raises questions about who will benefit from it and how fundamental values and beliefs can be preserved in a technology-driven society. By the middle grades, students research the complex relationships among technology, human values, and behavior. Students will learn how technology and science have brought about change and how they have often challenged accepted societal beliefs.

A. Examine and describe the influence of culture on scientific and technological choices and advancement, such as in transportation, medicine, and warfare.	37, 313–315, 316, 317, 389–392, 393, 400–403, 414, 555–557, 584–587, 589–593, 621, 624–625, 704–709
B. Show through specific examples how science and technology have changed people's perceptions of the social and natural world, such as in their relationship to the land, animal life, family life, and economic wants, needs, and security.	7, 37, 54, 315, 392–393, 401–403, 414, 588–593, 608, 609, 620–625, 631–632
C. Describe examples in which values, beliefs, and attitudes have been influenced by new scientific and technological knowledge, such as the invention of the printing press, conceptions of the universe, applications of atomic energy, and genetic discoveries.	30–31, 100, 401–403, 414, 589, 590, 909, 1001
D. Explain the need for laws and policies to govern scientific and technological applications, such as the safety and well-being of workers and consumers and the regulation of utilities, radio, and television.	395, 396, 397, 603, 646–647, 658, 796, 950
E. Seek reasonable and ethical solutions to problems that arise when scientific advancements and social norms or values come into conflict.	402, 412, 593, 625, 634

IX. Global Connections

As countries grow more interdependent, understanding global connections among world societies becomes important. Students will analyze emerging global issues in many different fields. They will also investigate relationships among the different cultures of the world. In the middle years, students analyze the interactions among states and countries and respond to global events and changes.

A. Describe instances in which language, art, music, belief systems, and other cultural elements can facilitate global understanding or cause misunderstanding.	178, 367–368, 408–409, 730, 805–806, 843, 857, 911–912, 915, 943–944, 962, 989, 992
B. Analyze examples of conflict, cooperation, and interdependence among groups, societies, and nations.	18, 19, 21–22, 49, 50, 52, 105–106, 109–112, 144, 145, 182, 286–293, 359, 367–371, 487, 665, 673, 690–696, 718–723, 728–732, 804–807, 820–827, 828–832, 834, 845–847, 856–859, 910–915, 945–946, 960–962, 979–980, 993, 994, 1001
C. Describe and analyze the effects of changing technologies on the global community.	60, 692–693, 704–709, 810, 829, 831–832, 945, 960, 1001
D. Explore the causes, consequences, and possible solutions to persistent, contemporary, and emerging global issues, such as health, security, resource allocation, economic development, and environmental quality.	50–52, 692–693, 696, 700, 728–732, 914, 943–944, 960, 1003, 1004, 1005, 1006
E. Describe and explain the relationships and tensions between national sovereignty and global interests in such matters as territory, natural resources, trade, use of technology, and welfare of people.	50, 52, 287–290, 293, 384, 665, 691, 693–696, 728–732, 908–909, 915, 945

Theme and Performance Expectation	Student Pages
F. Demonstrate understanding of concerns, standards, issues, and conflicts related to universal human rights.	91, 691, 695–696, 729–730, 809, 810, 825–827, 845–846, 955, 960–961, 980, 986
G. Identify and describe the roles of international and multinational organizations.	718–723, 730–732, 805, 808–810, 813, 820–827, 834, 843

X. *Civic Ideals and Practices*
Understanding civic ideals and practices is crucial to complete participation in society and is the main purpose of social studies. Students will learn about civic participation and the role of the citizen within his or her community, country, and world. By the middle grades, students will broaden their understanding to analyze and evaluate relationships between civic ideals and practices.

A. Examine the origins and continuing influence of key ideals of the democratic republican form of government, such as individual human dignity, liberty, justice, equality, and the rule of law.	61, 65–69, 75, 79, 100–101, 103, 120–121, 122–125, 141, 144, 150–151, 205–206, 207, 210, 212, 254, 255, 273, 419, 421, 522–527, 643, 855, 873, 875–879, 900
B. Identify and interpret sources and examples of the rights and responsibilities of citizens.	79, 123–125, 141, 144, 183, 205, 208, 210, 212, 254, 255, 273, 419, 421, 440, 522–527, 663, 666–668, 745, 875, 876, 877–879
C. Locate, access, analyze, organize, and apply information about selected public issues—recognizing and explaining multiple points of view.	65, 66, 68, 69, 123–125, 140, 209–210, 254, 256, 257, 266, 273, 322–323, 326, 328, 364–365, 419, 420, 428–429, 461, 468–469, 497, 502, 523–524, 526–527, 530, 643, 651, 659, 698–699, 745, 875–876, 916–917, 995, 996
D. Practice forms of civic discussion and participation consistent with the ideals of citizens in a democratic republic.	69, 103, 145, 183, 210, 212, 213, 254, 257, 267, 270, 273, 431, 494–495, 497, 524, 530, 643, 651, 745
E. Explain and analyze various forms of citizen action that influence public policy decisions.	125, 129, 144, 399, 419–420, 646–647, 651, 666, 667, 877–879, 884–891, 919, 928–929, 930
F. Identify and explain the roles of formal and informal political actors in influencing and shaping public policy and decision-making.	103, 197–201, 204–210, 253, 265–266, 322, 323, 419–420, 522–527, 646–647, 664, 665, 666, 667, 875–879
G. Analyze the influence of diverse forms of public opinion on the development of public policy and decision-making.	209–210, 265–266, 399, 419–420, 494–495, 497, 664–665
H. Analyze the effectiveness of selected public policies and citizen behaviors in realizing the stated ideals of a democratic republican form of government.	150–151, 183, 522–527, 651, 652, 653, 654, 670
I. Explain the relationship between policy statements and action plans used to address issues of public concern.	419, 420, 524–525, 875–879
J. Examine strategies designed to strengthen the "common good," which consider a range of options for citizen action.	254, 421, 524–525, 646

Using the Teacher Wraparound Edition

To Teachers:

Welcome to the Teacher Wraparound Edition of *The American Journey*. We have created this teacher edition based on input from experienced teachers and educational consultants. Our goal is to provide you with teaching strategies and activities that are labeled for you at point-of-use. The following pages will show the structure of the Teacher Wraparound Edition.

Student-Based Instruction

Point-of-Use
Strategies and activities apply directly to student content.

Differentiated Instruction
Leveled activities and options for differentiated instruction help meet the needs of all your students, including English language learners.

Review and Reinforcement
Reading and critical thinking skills are reinforced throughout the lesson.

Assessment and Intervention
- Chapter Assessments provide standardized test practice.
- Assessments gauge student mastery of content.
- Additional resources provide intervention options.

Planning and Teaching the Unit

Planning pages appear at the beginning of each unit.

Pacing Chart

Provides time management suggestions for teaching the unit

Author Note

Highlights author's ideas for teaching the unit

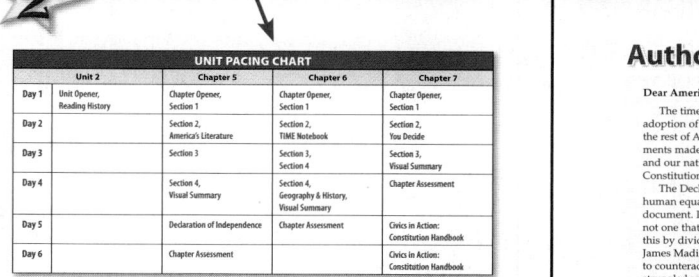

Teacher to Teacher

Includes activities from the classrooms of successful teachers

Unit Objectives

Identifies student learning expectations for the unit

Introducing the Unit

Stimulates discussion about unit themes

Why It Matters

Provides relevant questions and activities that address unit themes

Connect to Past Learning

Activates prior knowledge and links themes from previous units

Using the Teacher Wraparound Edition

Planning the Chapter

Chapter Planning Guides provide a snapshot of the scope of resources available to enhance and extend learning in each chapter.

Leveled Activities

Organizes resources by appropriate ability levels

Incorporating Resources

Utilizes a structured lesson plan to incorporate additional resources

*Spanish Resources

Indicates resources for English language learners

Teaching With Technology

Explains how to incorporate different Glencoe technology resources in the classroom

Online and Downloadable Learning

Engages students and caregivers with online and downloadable content

Additional Resources

Identifies supplemental resources for the chapter

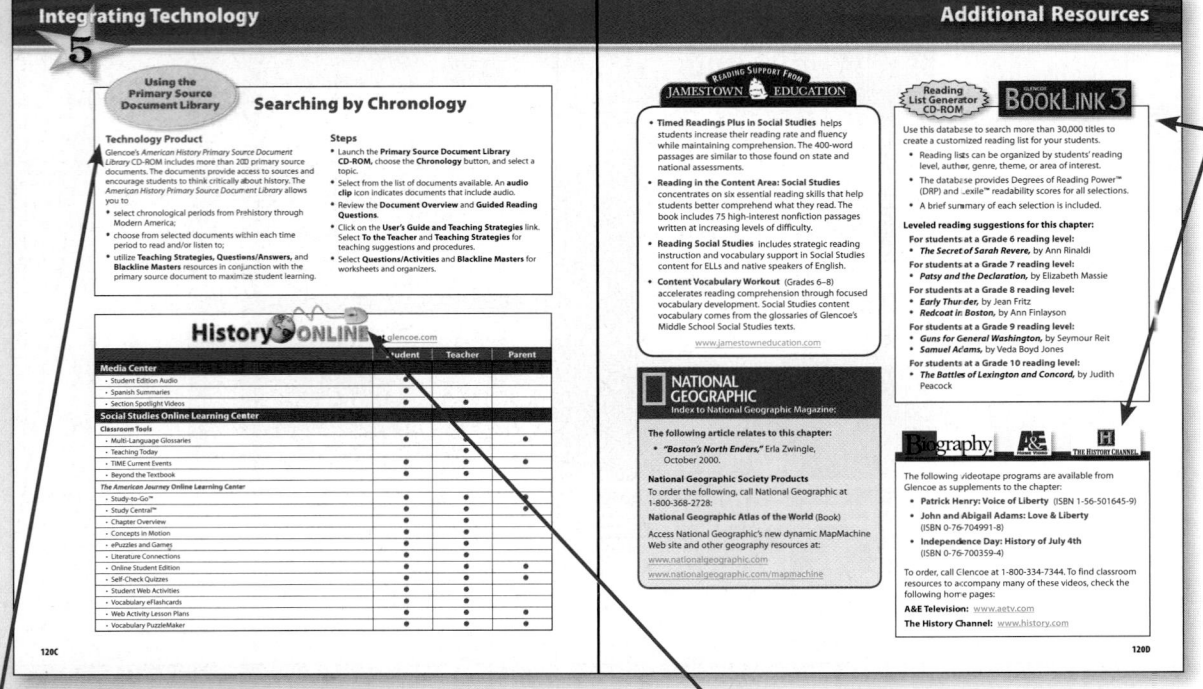

Teaching the Chapter

Preview chapter themes and concepts at the beginning of each chapter.

Chapter Objectives

Identifies student learning expectations for the chapter

Motivating Activities

Activates prior knowledge and makes connections between history and students' lives today

Time Line Activities

Reinforces sequencing and visual literacy skills

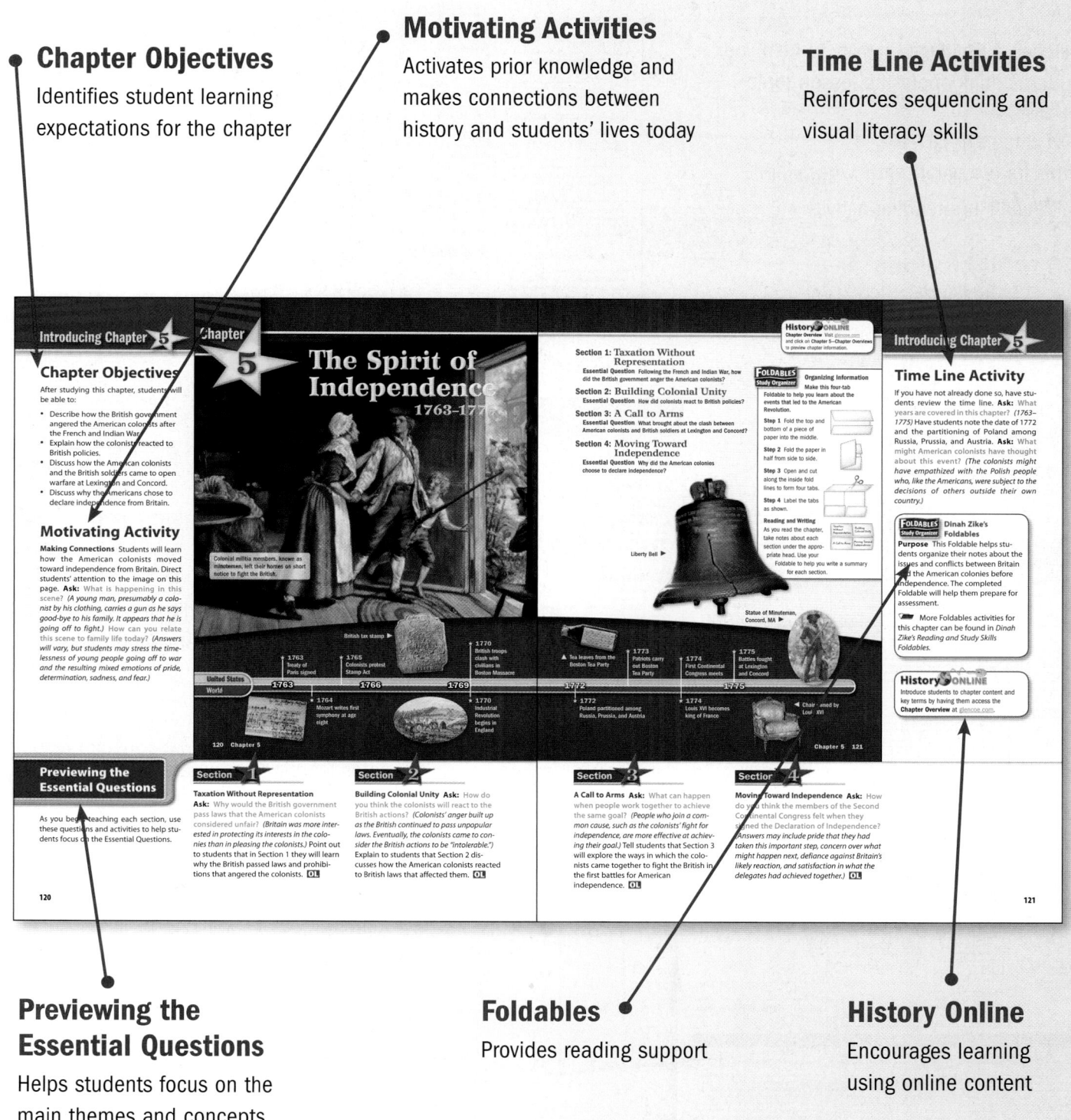

Previewing the Essential Questions

Helps students focus on the main themes and concepts found in each section

Foldables

Provides reading support

History Online

Encourages learning using online content

Lesson Structure

Each lesson in *The American Journey* is presented in a structured lesson plan: Focus, Teach, Assess, and Close.

FOCUS •

Includes a Bellringer activity to help your students think about the lesson topic

Reading Guide •

Provides answers to the Student Edition's pre-reading activity

Spotlight Video •

Engages students with the content using a short section-based video

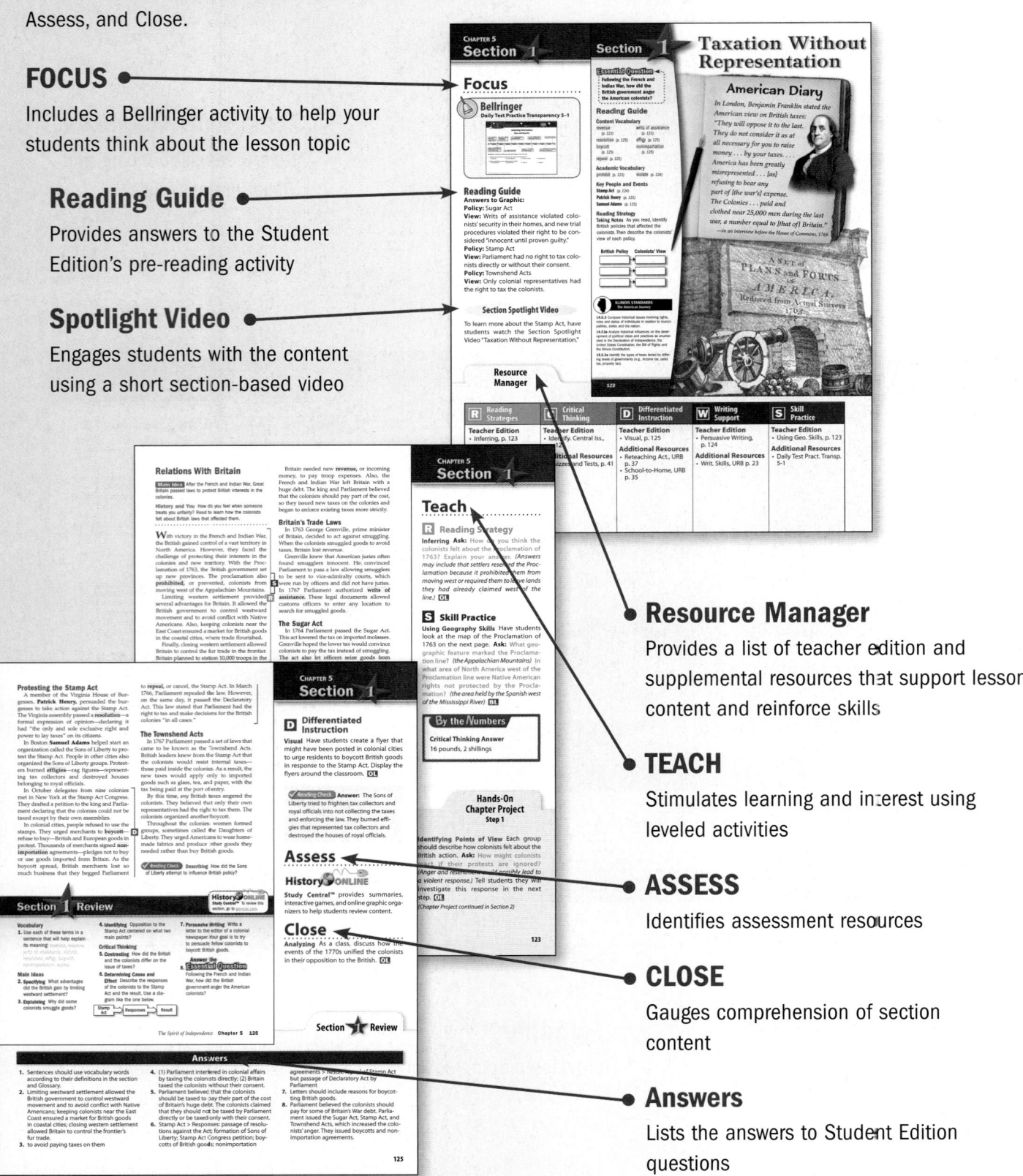

Resource Manager

Provides a list of teacher edition and supplemental resources that support lesson content and reinforce skills

TEACH

Stimulates learning and interest using leveled activities

ASSESS

Identifies assessment resources

CLOSE

Gauges comprehension of section content

Answers

Lists the answers to Student Edition questions

Understanding the Letters and Brackets

Letters*

The letters on the reduced Student Edition page identify the type of strategy or activity. See the key below to learn about the different types of strategies and activities.

Brackets

Brackets on the reduced Student Edition page correspond to teaching strategies and activities in the Teacher Wraparound Edition. As you teach the section, the brackets show you exactly where to teach these strategies and activities.

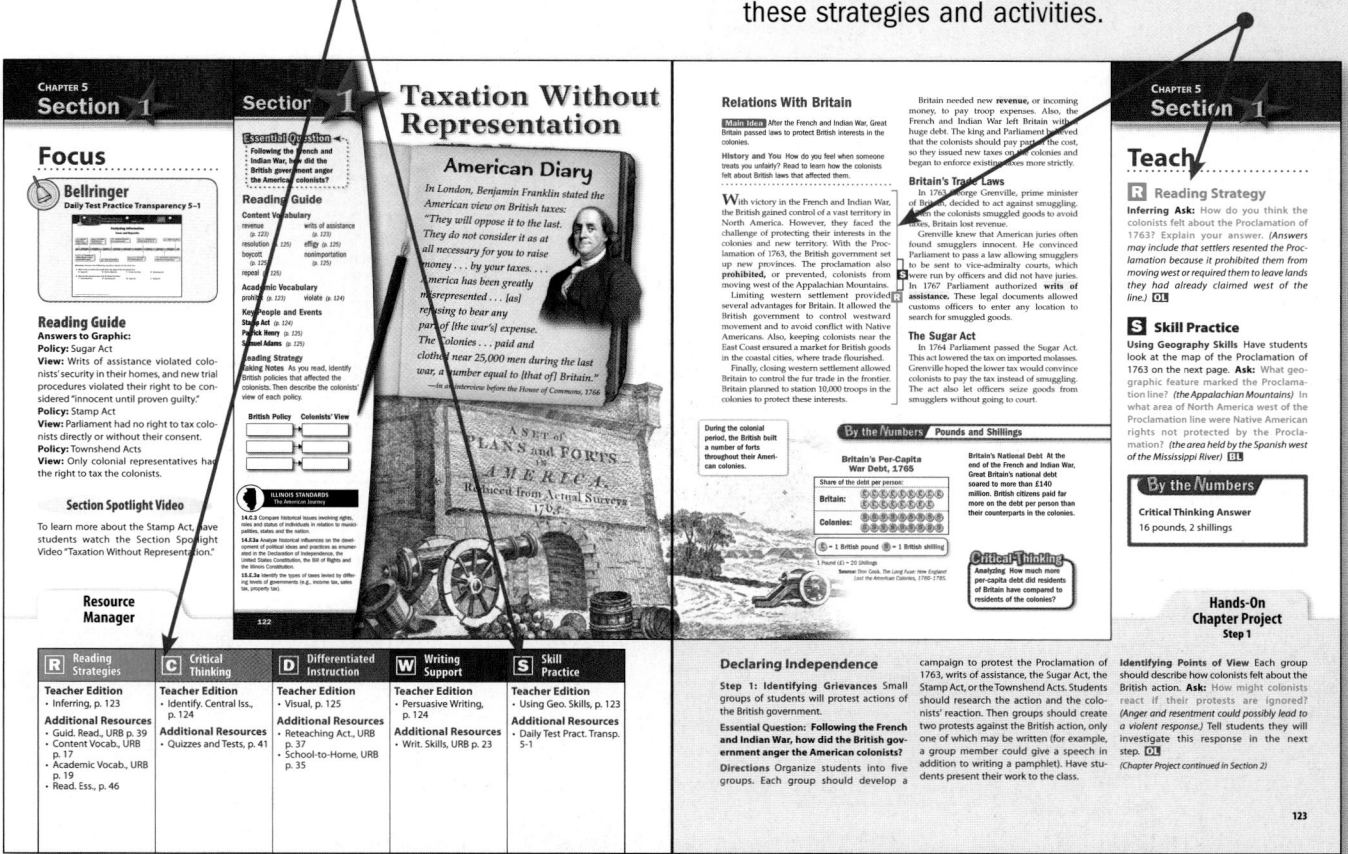

KEY for Using the Teacher Wraparound Edition

R **Reading Strategies** activities help you teach reading skills and vocabulary.

C **Critical Thinking** strategies help students apply and extend what they have learned.

D **Differentiated Instruction** activities provide differentiated instruction for students learning to speak English, along with suggestions for teaching various types of learners.

S **Skill Practice** strategies help students practice historical analysis and geography skills.

W **Writing Support** activities provide writing opportunities to help students comprehend the text.

* Letters are followed by a number when there is more than one of the same type of strategy or activity on the page.

Hands-On Chapter Projects

Extend student learning with unique and interactive Hands-On Chapter Projects. These activities allow students to take principles and put them to practical use. Projects progress through each section and culminate in a wrap-up discussion. Students conceptualize, plan, and execute their vision in a hands-on approach that makes history come alive.

Essential Question

Activities rooted in the Section-based Essential Question create connections to major themes.

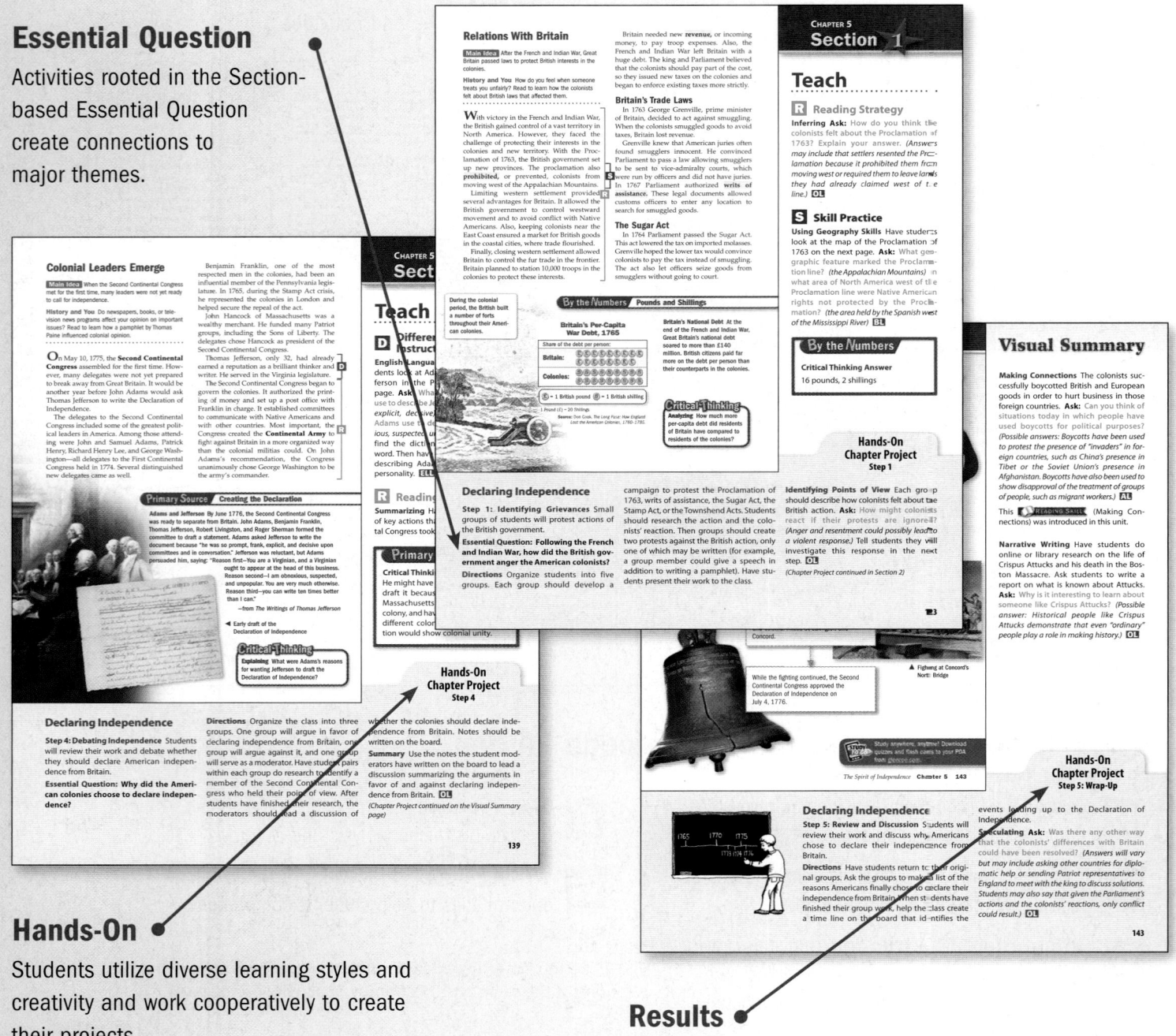

Hands-On

Students utilize diverse learning styles and creativity and work cooperatively to create their projects.

Results

The Hands-On Chapter Project culminates in an interactive discussion where students synthesize what they have learned and draw conclusions.

Differentiated Instruction

Each section of the Teacher Wraparound Edition of *The American Journey* provides differentiated instruction activities to meet the diverse needs of every student.

Additional Resources

Provides suggestions for incorporating additional resources based on students' different learning abilities

Differentiated Activities

Innovative ideas meet each student's interests and learning styles through point-of-use activities

Leveled Activities

Extends instruction beyond the text by suggesting activities related to content on the page

Dynamic Features

Use these creative features to explore historical events and themes.

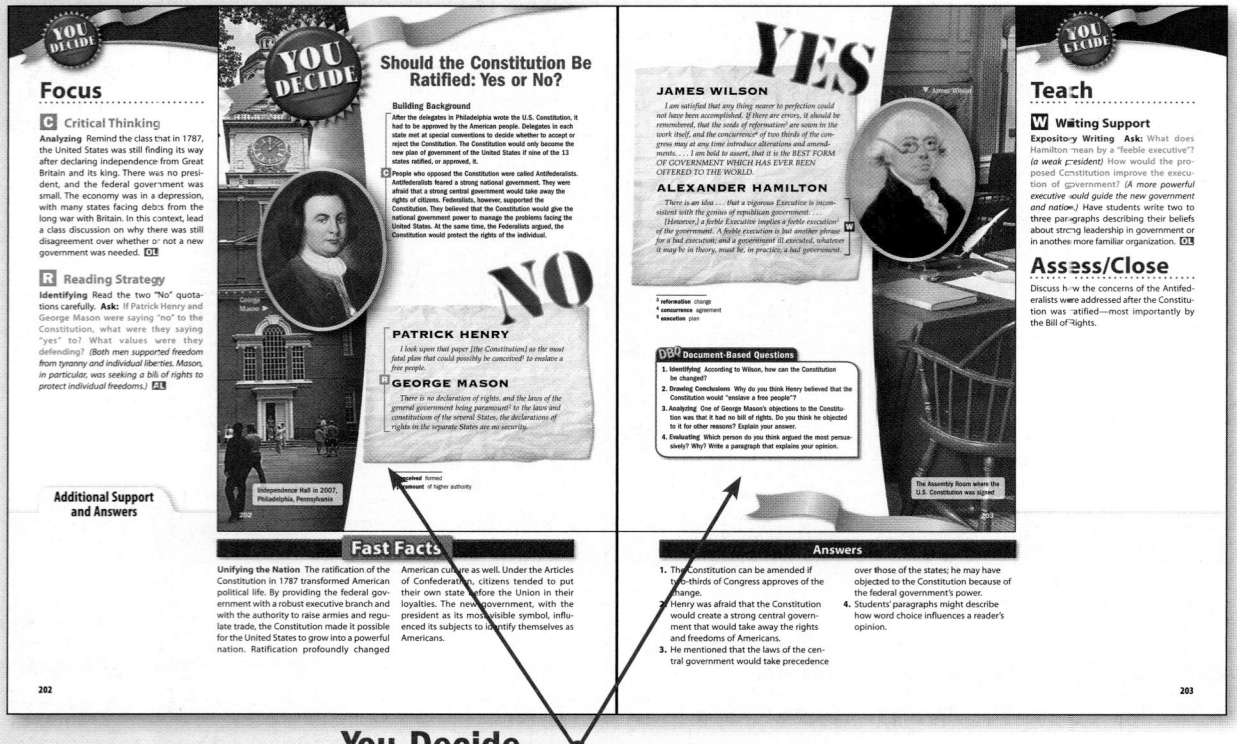

You Decide

Teaches students to analyze different points-of-view about historical decisions and issues

Additional Reading

Supplemental reading suggestions provide fun and varied opportunities for students to connect with history.

Chapter Summary and Assessment

Visual Summary

Summary activities help students to synthesize major chapter themes.

Chapter Assessment

Answers incorporate analysis and identify potential student pitfalls, challenges, distracters, and test-taking strategies.

Review the Essential Questions

Requires students to synthesize what they have learned

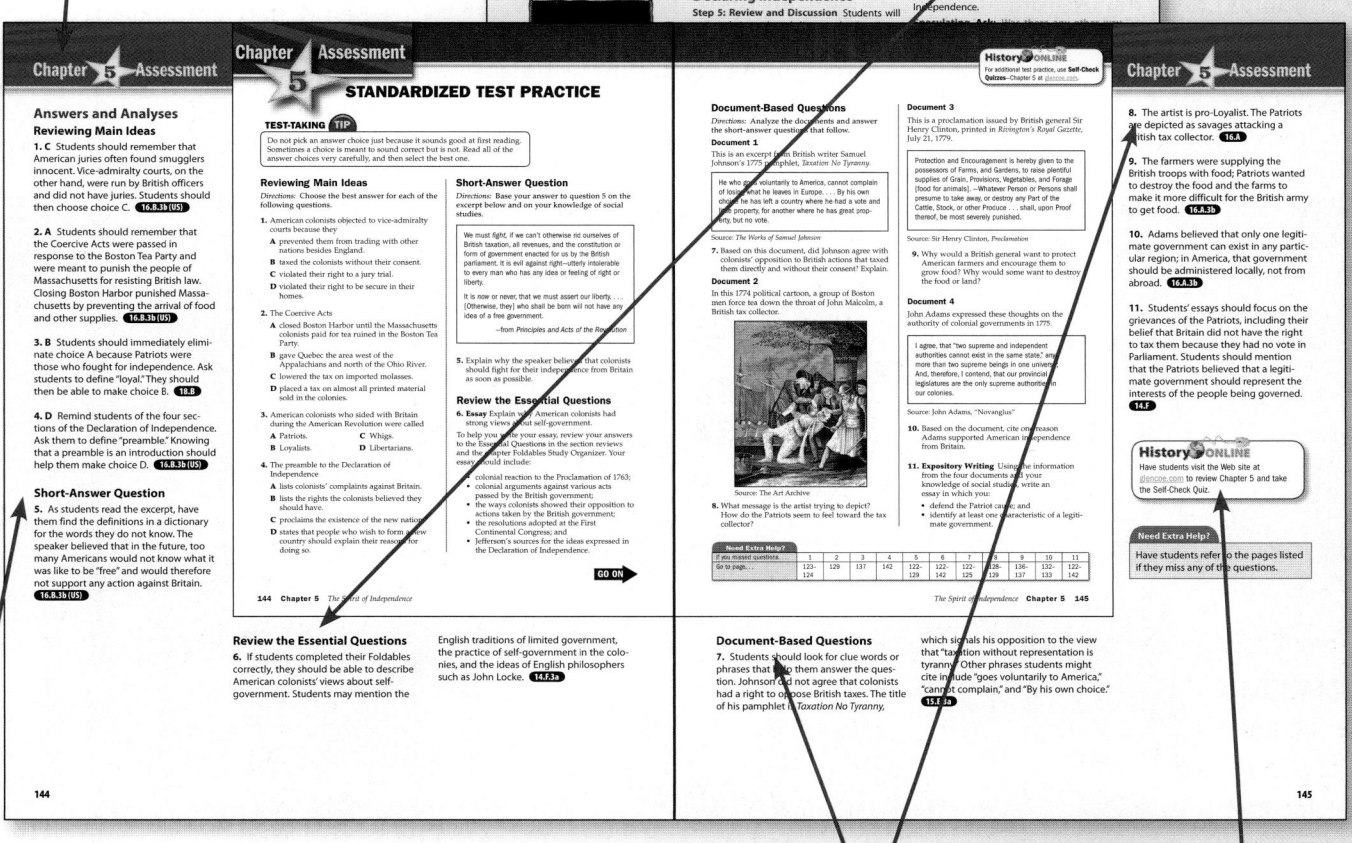

Short-Answer Question

Assesses students' ability to write accurately and concisely.

Document-Based Questions

Provides answers and analysis to document and graphic assessment

History Online

Provides additional assessment opportunities

Academic Vocabulary

How Can I Help My Students Learn Academic Vocabulary?

What Is Academic English?

Academic English is the language used in academics, business, and courts of law. It is the type of English used in textbooks, and contains linguistic features associated with academic disciplines like social studies. Proficiency in reading and using academic English is especially related to long-term success in all parts of life.

By reinforcing academic English, teachers can help learners to access authentic, academic texts—not simplified texts that dummy down the content. In this way, they can provide information that will help build their students' background knowledge rapidly.

What Is Academic Vocabulary?

Academic vocabulary is based on academic English. By the time children have completed elementary school, they must have acquired the knowledge needed to understand academic vocabulary. How many words should they acquire to be able to access their textbooks? A basic 2,000-word vocabulary of high-frequency words makes up 87% of the vocabulary of academic texts. Eight hundred other academic words comprise an additional 8% of the words. Three percent of the remaining words are technical words. The remaining 2% are low-frequency words. There may be as many as 123,000 low-frequency words in academic texts.

Why Should Students Learn Academic Vocabulary?

English learners who have a basic 2,000-word vocabulary are ready to acquire most general words found in their texts.

Knowledge of academic words and general words can significantly boost a student's comprehension level of academic texts. Students who learn and practice these words before they graduate from high school are likely to master academic material with more confidence and speed. They waste less time and effort in guessing words or

consulting dictionaries than those who only know the basic 2,000 words that characterize general conversation.

How Do I Include Academic Vocabulary and Academic English in My Teaching?

Teachers can provide students with academic vocabulary and help students understand the academic English of their text.

To develop academic English, learners must have already acquired basic proficiency in the grammar of everyday English.

Academic English should be taught within contexts that make sense. In terms of instruction, teaching academic English includes providing students with access to core curriculum—in this case Social Studies.

Academic English arises in part from social practices in which academic English is used. The acquisition of academic vocabulary and grammar is necessary to advance the development of academic English.

Tips for Teaching Academic Vocabulary:

✔ **Expose Students to Academic Vocabulary**
You do not need to call attention to words students are learning because they will acquire them subconsciously.

✔ **Do Not Correct Students' Mistakes When Using the Vocabulary Words**
All vocabulary understanding and spelling errors will disappear once the student reads more.

✔ **Help Students Decode the Words Themselves** Once they learn the alphabet, they should be able to decode words. Decoding each word they don't recognize will help them more than trying to focus on sentence structure. Once they can recognize the words, they can read "authentic" texts.

✔ **Do Not Ignore the English Learner in This Process** They can learn academic vocabulary before they are completely fluent in oral English.

✔ **Helping Students Build Academic Vocabulary Leads to Broader Learning** Students who have mastered the basic academic vocabulary are ready to continue acquiring words from the rest of the groups. To help determine which words are in the 2,000-word basic group, refer to *West's General Service List of English Words,* 1953. The list is designed to serve as a guide for teachers and as a checklist and goal list for students.

Guidelines for Teaching Academic Vocabulary

1. Direct and planned instruction	4. Practice
2. Models—that have increasingly difficult language	5. Motivation
3. Attention to form—pointing out linguistic features of words	6. Instructional feedback
	7. Assessment—on a regular basis

Classroom Activity

Writing About Modern America
Give students a brief writing assignment. Ask them to write a short essay about one of the topics listed below in the left column. Have students use as many of the academic vocabulary words in the right column as they can in their essay. When completed, ask student volunteers to share their writing. Note what academic vocabulary words they use.

Topic	Academic Vocabulary
The challenges of reducing poverty in America	sufficient
	minimum
	medical
	income
Recent technological advances	innovate
	technology
	media
	potential
	data
	transmit

Meeting the Diverse Needs of Our Students

by Douglas Fisher, Ph.D.

Today's classroom contains students from a variety of backgrounds with a variety of learning styles, strengths, and challenges. As teachers we are facing the challenge of helping students reach their educational potential. With careful planning, you can address the needs of all students in the social studies classroom. The basis for this planning is universal access. When classrooms are planned with universal access in mind, fewer students require specific accommodations.

What Is a Universal Access Design for Learning?

Universal design was first conceived in architectural studies

when business people, engineers, and architects began making considerations for physical access to buildings. The idea was to plan the environment in advance to ensure that everyone had access. As a result, the environment would not have to be changed later for people with physical disabilities, people pushing strollers, workers who had injuries, or others for whom the environment would be difficult to negotiate. The Center for Universal Design at www.design.ncsu.edu/cud defines Universal Design as:

The design of products and environments to be usable by all people, to the greatest extent possible, without the need for adaptation or specialized design.

Universal Design and Access in Education

Researchers, teachers, and parents in education have expanded the development of built-in adaptations and inclusive accommodations from architectural space to the educational experience, especially in the area of curriculum.

In 1998, the National Center to Improve the Tools of Educators (NCITE),

with the partnership of the Center for Applied Special Technology (CAST), proposed an expanded definition of universal design focused on education:

In terms of learning, universal design means the design of instructional materials and activities that allows the learning goals to be achievable by individuals with wide differences in their abilities to see, hear, speak, move, read, write, understand English, attend, organize, engage, and remember.

How Does Universal Design Work in Education?

Universal design and access, as they apply to education and schooling, suggest the following:

✓ **Inclusive Classroom Participation**
Curriculum should be designed with all students and their needs in mind. The Glencoe/McGraw-Hill social studies texts and materials were designed with a wide range of students in mind. For example, understanding that English learners and students who struggle with reading would be using this textbook, vocabulary is specifically taught and reinforced. Similarly, the teacher-support materials provide multiple instructional points to be used depending on the needs of the students in the class. Further, the text is written such that main ideas are identified for all learners. Activating prior knowledge is also taken into consideration

by the text. Connections between what students know and think about are made within the text.

✔ **Maximum Text Readability** In universally designed classrooms that provide access for all students, texts use direct language, clear noun-verb agreements, and clear construct-based wording. In addition to these factors, the Glencoe Social Studies text uses embedded definitions for difficult terms, provides for specific instruction in reading skills, uses a number of visual representations, and includes note-taking guides.

✔ **Adaptable and Accommodating** The content in this textbook can be easily translated, read aloud, or otherwise changed to meet the needs of students in the classroom. The section and end-of-chapter assessments provide students with multiple ways of demonstrating their content knowledge while also ensuring that they have practice with thinking in terms of multiple-choice questions. Critical thinking and analysis skills are also practiced.

How Is Differentiated Instruction the Key to Universal Access?

To differentiate instruction, teachers must acknowledge student differences in background knowledge and current reading, writing, and English language skills. They must also consider student learning styles and preferences, interests, and needs, and react accordingly. There are a number of general guidelines for differentiating instruction in the classroom to reach all students, including:

✔ **Link Assessment With Instruction** Assessments should occur before, during, and after instruction to ensure that the curriculum is aligned with what students do and do not know. Using assessments in this way allows you to plan instruction for whole groups, small groups, and individual students. Backward planning, where you establish the assessment before you begin instruction, is also important.

✔ **Clarify Key Concepts and Generalizations** Students need to know what is essential and how this information can be used in their future learning. In addition, students need to develop a sense of the **Big Ideas**—ideas that transcend time and place.

✔ **Emphasize Critical and Creative Thinking** The content, process, and products used or assigned in the classroom should require that students think about what they are learning. While some students may require support, additional motivation, varied tasks, materials, or equipment, the overall focus on critical and creative thinking allows for all students to participate in the lesson.

✔ **Include Teacher- and Student-Selected Tasks** A differentiated classroom includes both teacher- and student-selected activities and tasks. At some points in the lesson or day, the teacher must provide instruction and assign learning activities. In other parts of the lesson, students should be provided choices in how they engage with the content. This balance increases motivation, engagement, and learning.

How Do I Support Individual Students?

The vast majority of students will thrive in a classroom based on universal access and differentiated instruction. However, wise teachers recognize that no single option will work for all students and that there may be students who require unique systems of support to be successful.

Classroom Activity

Display a map of imperialism in Africa around 1914. Discuss with students the map's general information and have them list each country under the European power that controlled it.

To differentiate this activity:
- Have students imagine they are living in the early 1900s. Have them write a letter to a British newspaper about colonial rule in Africa.
- Have students record the number of African countries under European rule. Have them take the data and create a bar graph that shows which European powers were the most active colonizers at the time.
- Have students compose a song or poem about European rule in Africa, from an African's point of view.
- Have students choose a country of modern Africa to research. Have them write a three-page paper discussing how that country was affected by colonialism and how it has changed since the days of European rule.

Tips For Instruction

The following tips for instruction can support your efforts to help all students reach their maximum potential.

- ✔ Survey students to discover their individual differences. Use interest inventories of their unique talents so you can encourage contributions in the classroom.
- ✔ Be a model for respecting others. Adolescents crave social acceptance. The student with learning differences is especially sensitive to correction and criticism, particularly when it comes from a teacher. Your behavior will set the tone for how students treat one another.
- ✔ Expand opportunities for success. Provide a variety of instructional activities that reinforce skills and concepts.
- ✔ Establish measurable objectives and decide how you can best help students who meet them.
- ✔ Celebrate successes and make note of and praise "work in progress."
- ✔ Keep it simple. Point out problem areas if doing so can help a student effect change. Avoid overwhelming students with too many goals at one time.
- ✔ Assign cooperative group projects that challenge all students

to contribute to solving a problem or creating a product.

How Do I Reach Students With Learning Disabilities?

- ✔ Provide support and structure. Clearly specify rules, assignments, and responsibilities.
- ✔ Practice skills frequently. Use games and drills to help maintain student interest.
- ✔ Incorporate many modalities into the learning process. Provide opportunities to say, hear, write, read, and act out important concepts and information.
- ✔ Link new skills and concepts to those already mastered.
- ✔ If possible, allow students to record answers on audiotape.
- ✔ Allow extra time to complete assessments and assignments.
- ✔ Let students demonstrate proficiency with alternative presentations, including oral reports, role plays, art projects, and musical presentations.
- ✔ Provide outlines, notes, or tape recordings of lecture material.
- ✔ Pair students with peer helpers, and provide class time for pair interaction.

How Do I Reach Students With Behavioral Challenges?

- ✔ Provide a structured environment with clear-cut schedules, rules, seat assignments, and safety procedures.
- ✔ Reinforce appropriate behavior and model it for students.

- ✔ Cue distracted students back to the task through verbal signals and teacher proximity.
- ✔ Set goals that can be achieved in the short term. Work for long-term improvement in the big areas.

How Do I Reach Students With Physical Challenges?

- ✔ Openly discuss with the student any uncertainties you have about when to offer aid.
- ✔ Ask parents or therapists and students what special devices or procedures are needed and whether any special safety precautions need to be taken.
- ✔ Welcome students with physical challenges into all activities, including field trips, special events, and projects.
- ✔ Provide information to assist class members and adults in their understanding of support needed.

How Do I Reach Students with Visual Impairments?

- ✔ Facilitate independence. Modify assignments as needed.
- ✔ Teach classmates how and when to serve as visual guides.
- ✔ Limit unnecessary noise in the classroom if it distracts the student with visual impairments.
- ✔ Provide tactile models whenever possible.
- ✔ Foster a spirit of inclusion. Describe people and events as they occur in the classroom. Remind classmates that the student with visual impairments cannot interpret gestures and other forms of nonverbal communication.
- ✔ Provide taped lectures and reading assignments for use outside the classroom.
- ✔ Team the student with a sighted peer for written work.

How Do I Reach Students With Hearing Impairments?

✓ Seat students where they can see your lip movements easily and where they can avoid any visual distractions.
✓ Avoid standing with your back to the window or light source.
✓ Use an overhead projector so you can maintain eye contact while writing information for students.
✓ Seat students where they can see speakers.
✓ Write all assignments on the board, or hand out written instructions.
✓ If the student has a manual interpreter, allow both student and interpreter to select the most favorable seating arrangements.
✓ Teach students to look directly at each other when they speak.

How Do I Reach English Learners?

✓ Remember, students' ability to speak English does not reflect their academic abilities.
✓ Try to incorporate the students' cultural experience into your instruction. The help of a bilingual aide may be effective.
✓ Avoid any references in your instruction that could be construed as cultural stereotypes.
✓ Preteach important vocabulary and concepts.
✓ Encourage students to preview text before they begin reading, noting headings.
✓ Remind students not to ignore graphic organizers, photographs, and maps since there is much information in these visuals.
✓ Use memorabilia and photographs whenever possible to build background knowledge and understanding. An example of this would be coins in a foreign currency or a raw cotton ball to reinforce its importance in history.

How Do I Reach Gifted Students?

✓ Make arrangements for students to take selected subjects early and to work on independent projects.
✓ Ask "what if" questions to develop high-level thinking skills. Establish an environment safe for risk taking in your classroom.
✓ Emphasize concepts, theories, ideas, relationships, and generalizations about the content.
✓ Promote interest in the past by inviting students to make connections to the present.
✓ Let students express themselves in alternate ways such as creative writing, acting, debates, simulations, drawing, or music.
✓ Provide students with a catalog of helpful resources, listing such things as agencies that provide free and inexpensive materials, appropriate community services

and programs, and community experts who might be called upon to speak to your students.
✓ Assign extension projects that allow students to solve real-life problems related to their communities.

Douglas Fisher is a professor at San Diego State University, San Diego, CA.

Classroom Activity

Students respond eagerly to a subject when they can relate it to their own experiences. With the growing number of students who come from other world regions, explaining geography through a global theme (such as volcanoes) can give them a worldwide as well as a regional perspective. To develop this awareness, display a large world map. Have students use the library or the Internet to research the latitude and longitude of 15 major volcanoes around the world. Ask them to mark these locations on the map and answer the following questions:
• What patterns do you see in volcanic activity?
• What causes volcanic activity?
• Where in the world are volcanoes most active?
As a follow-up, suggest students go to http://volcano.und.nodak.edu/vwdocs/kids/legends.html to find legends about the origins of some of the world's volcanoes. Encourage students to share what they find with the class.

Backward Mapping

How Can My Instruction Help Students Succeed in a Standards-Based System?

by Emily M. Schell, Ed.D.

Content standards articulate what students should know and be able to do in every social studies classroom. Effective instructional planning based in the standards and maximizing available resources is essential for meaningful teaching and learning of social studies. Planning instruction with educational goals in mind makes for the most effective teaching.

How Do I Map My Curriculum?

Mapping the curriculum from beginning to end, and from the end to the beginning—backward mapping—makes for solid instruction. Mapping out the curriculum allows teachers to achieve several goals. These goals include a better understanding of the standards and content-specific objectives, organization and pacing of the curriculum, and focused assessment related to specific goals and objectives.

✔ **Begin the Process of Curriculum Mapping** To begin, teachers analyze the body of content standards for one grade level. They then compare and contrast these standards to additional sources of information that support effective teaching and learning at that grade level and in that subject area. This process works best with same-grade colleagues who bring varying perspectives and expertise to teaching this subject. As a result of this collaboration, strengths and weaknesses of the standards become apparent. Teachers will have a better understanding of the standards and identify concerns and questions for follow-up while mapping.

✔ **Analyze the Organization of the Standards-Based Content** Most social studies teachers agree with researchers that history is best taught in chronological order. However, some grade-level standards either do not or cannot present the content in chronological order. Rich discussions about themes and concepts tend to emerge, and teachers identify meaningful methods for presenting complex and overlapping information. In this way students will see the connections that transcend chronology.

✔ **Identify the Content and Order of Teaching** A plan is developed to present certain content first, then second, then third and so on. Folding in content that is either missing from the standards or essential in building background knowledge with students enters the curriculum map as well. Outside resources brought into the classroom are good supplements.

✔ **Separate Overlapping Units** Identify areas of instruction for the topics, themes, big ideas, or concepts. It is at this stage that backward planning is introduced for the development of instructional units, which will support the grade-level curriculum map. The instruction must support the planned assessment.

✔ **Map Curriculum at Each Grade Level** Curriculum planning should be shared among grade levels. Teachers will have a better understanding of what knowledge and skills students bring to their coursework if they take into consideration what has been learned previously.

How Do I Use Backward Mapping?

After a year-long course of study is mapped out, each unit must be further developed through backward mapping. You will start with the end in mind—knowing your curricular goals and objectives at the outset, which are often found in the content standards and articulated in the curriculum maps.

Once goals have been determined, teachers develop assessments that will show progress toward those goals and objectives. In the final step of this backward mapping process, teachers determine meaningful teaching and learning strategies and identify useful resources that support the assessment.

To use backward mapping in developing your units of instruction, consider the following steps:

Step One: Know Your Targets

First, identify exactly what students must know and do in this unit. Analyze content standards and any other resources that support curricular goals and objectives for this unit. As you plan, ask yourself:

- ✔ What do I want my students to know as a result of this unit?
- ✔ What skills will students develop during the course of this unit?
- ✔ How do I describe these goals clearly and concisely to my students so they understand where we should be at the end of this unit?
- ✔ What essential knowledge will students need to access to make sense of this information?
- ✔ Do my instructional goals align with strategies identified in the curriculum map?
- ✔ Have I introduced any Big Ideas that are pertinent to this content?

Step Two: Identify and Develop Assessments

- ✔ Second, consider the multiple forms of formal and informal assessments that will help you determine to what degree each student has achieved the stated goals and objectives seen in Step One. Some assessments are embedded throughout the instructional unit, while others come at the end of the unit. Some assessments are performance-based, while others are not. Some are authentic applications of information and skills, while others require the formal recall of information. Ask yourself:
- ✔ What do I want to know and see from each student?
- ✔ What are the best methods for students to demonstrate what they know and can do based on the goals and objectives?
- ✔ How many assessments do I need to determine what students know and can do?
- ✔ How will I balance informal and formal assessments?
- ✔ How will I assess students with diverse learning styles, skills, and abilities?
- ✔ How can I prepare and support students?
- ✔ How will these assessments promote student progress in social studies?
- ✔ At what time(s) during the unit will I administer these assessments?

Step Three: Develop Meaningful Instruction

After the assessments for the unit have been determined, consider the meaningful and effective teaching strategies that will support learning and student achievement on assessments. While developing lesson plans for instruction, ask yourself:

- ✔ How will students learn what they are expected to know?
- ✔ How will I engage students in the studies of this unit?
- ✔ In what ways might students relate or connect to this information?
- ✔ What research-based strategies will be most effective with my students and in these studies?
- ✔ How will I differentiate my instruction to meet the diverse needs of my students?
- ✔ How will I scaffold or provide access to the curriculum for my English learners?
- ✔ What vocabulary requires attention in this unit?
- ✔ How much time will I have to effectively teach this unit?
- ✔ How will I use the textbook and other resources to support the goals and objectives for this unit?
- ✔ What lessons will I develop?
- ✔ In what sequence will I teach these lessons during this unit?
- ✔ How will these lessons support the assessments from Step Two?

Step Four: Locate and Manage Resources

Effective teaching and learning of social studies requires the use of multiple forms of text and varied resources. Consider what you have available in your classroom, including your textbook, and identify resources you will add in order to teach this unit successfully. Ask yourself:

- ✔ What parts of the textbook are required for the lessons determined in Step Three?
- ✔ What ancillary materials are needed for the lessons in this unit?
- ✔ What Web sites will I recommend to students to support these lessons?
- ✔ Do I need to contact guest speakers or obtain outside resources?
- ✔ What literature resources are available to support this unit?

Emily Schell is Visiting Professor, San Diego State University; and Social Studies Education Director, SDSU City Heights Educational Collaborative, San Diego, CA

REFERENCE ATLAS

NATIONAL
GEOGRAPHIC

ATLAS KEY

SYMBOL KEY

⊥⊥⊥⊥ Canal	∘ Depression	� Below sea level
·········· Claimed boundary	+ Elevation	⟅⟆ Dry salt lake
▓▓▓▓ International boundary	⊛ National capital	⟅⟆ Lake
	• • Towns	≪ Rivers

Lava

Sand

⟜⟝ Swamp

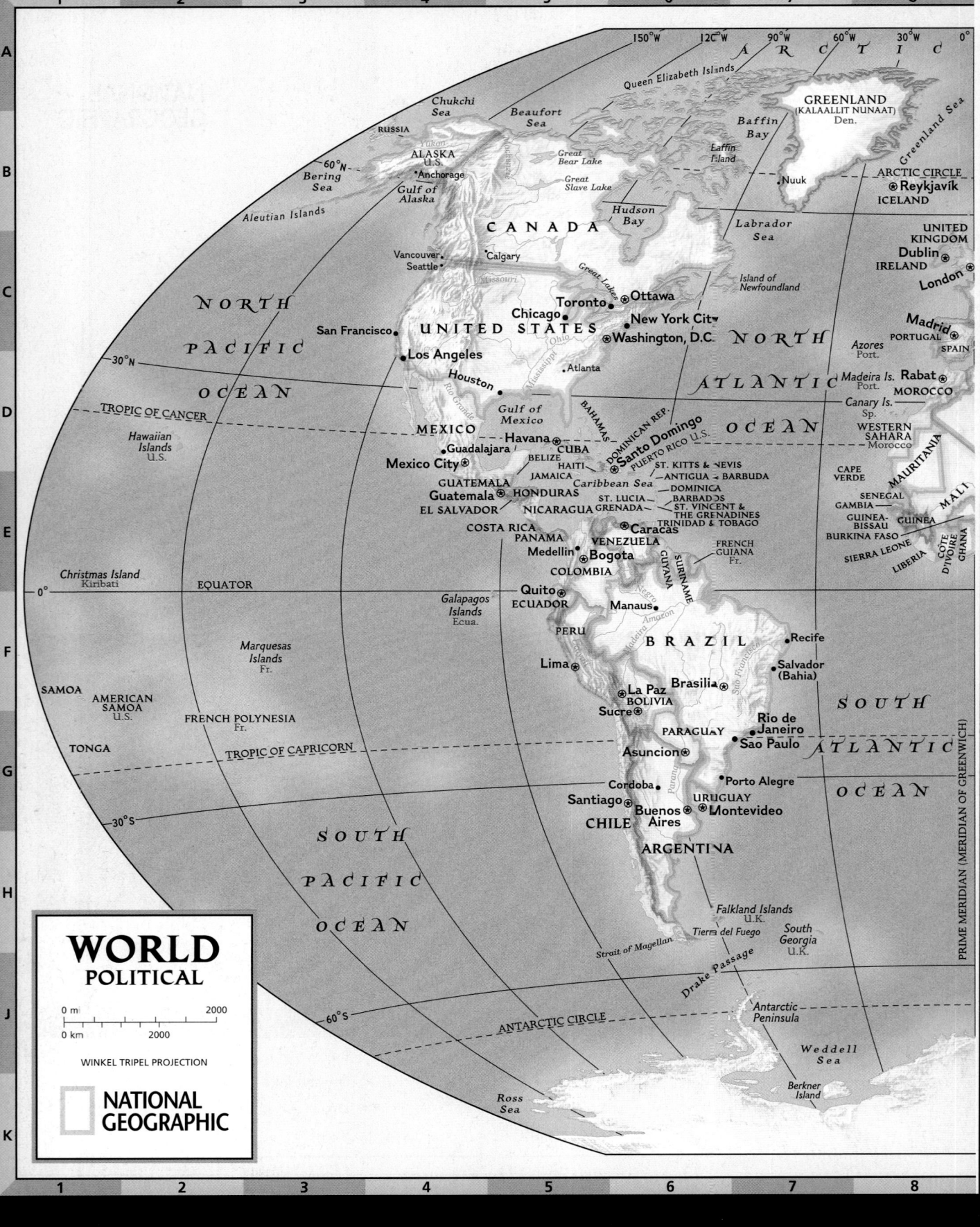

WORLD
POLITICAL

0 mi   2000
0 km   2000

WINKEL TRIPEL PROJECTION

NATIONAL GEOGRAPHIC

9 · **10** · **11** · **12** · **13** · **14** · **15** · **16**

A
B
C
D
E
F
G
H
J
K

Norwegian Sea *O C E A N* Franz Josef Land · Severnaya Zemlya · New Siberian Islands · East Siberian Sea

Svalbard Nor. · Barents Sea · Novaya Zemlya · Kara Sea · Laptev Sea

30°E · 60°E · 90°E · 120°E · 150°E

NORWAY · SWEDEN · FINLAND · R U S S I A · Ob · Yenisey · Lena · Yakutsk · 60°N · Bering Sea

Oslo · St. Petersburg · Yekaterinburg · Omsk · Novosibirsk · Lake Baikal · Sea of Okhotsk · Kamchatka Peninsula

DENMARK · NETH. · EST. · LATVIA · LITH. · Moscow · Samara · Volga · Ural · Irtysh · Astana · Ob · Sakhalin

GERMANY · BELARUS · POLAND · Kyiv (Kiev) · UKRAINE · KAZAKHSTAN · Ulaanbaatar · MONGOLIA · Harbin · Hokkaido · Sapporo · Honshu

Paris · BELG. · CZECH REP. · SLOVAKIA · MOLD. · Aral Sea · Almaty · Bishkek · Shenyang · NORTH KOREA · P'yŏngyang · JAPAN · Tokyo

SWITZ. · AUST. · HUNG. · ROMANIA · AZERBAIJAN · Tashkent · KYRGYZSTAN · Beijing · SOUTH KOREA · Seoul · Osaka

FRANCE · CROAT. · B&H · SERB. · BULGARIA · GEORGIA · ARMENIA · UZBEKISTAN · TURKMENISTAN · Dushanbe · C H I N A · Tianjin · Kyushu

ITALY · Rome · ALBANIA · MACED. · GREECE · TURKEY · Ashkhabad · Tehran · TAJIKISTAN · Islamabad · Chengdu · Shanghai · N O R T H

Mediterranean Sea · CYPRUS · SYRIA · IRAN · AFGHANISTAN · Lahore · NEPAL · Wuhan · 30°N · P A C I F I C

Algiers · TUNISIA · LEBANON · ISRAEL · IRAQ · Baghdad · JORDAN · KUWAIT · PAKISTAN · Delhi · BHUTAN · Guangzhou · Taipei · The People's Republic of China claims Taiwan as its 23rd province. · O C E A N

Tripoli · Cairo · BAHRAIN · QATAR · Riyadh · New Delhi · Dhaka · BANGLADESH · TAIWAN · Hong Kong · Philippine Sea

ALGERIA · LIBYA · EGYPT · Red Sea · SAUDI ARABIA · U.A.E. · Karachi · Masqat · Kolkata (Calcutta) · MYANMAR (BURMA) · Hanoi · Hainan · South China Sea · NORTHERN MARIANA ISLANDS U.S.

NIGER · CHAD · ERITREA · Khartoum · SUDAN · OMAN · Sanaa · YEMEN · Mumbai (Bombay) · INDIA · Nay Pyi Taw · LAOS · VIETNAM · Luzon · Manila · MARSHALL ISLANDS

Niamey · N'Djamena · Arabian Sea · Hyderabad · Bay of Bengal · THAILAND · Bangkok · CAMBODIA · PHILIPPINES

NIGERIA · Lagos · CENTRAL AFRICAN REPUBLIC · DJIBOUTI · Socotra Yemen · Bengaluru (Bangalore) · Chennai (Madras) · Phnom Penh · Ho Chi Minh City · PALAU · FEDERATED STATES OF MICRONESIA

EQ. GUINEA · CAMEROON · Bangui · DEM. REP. OF THE CONGO · UGANDA · KENYA · Colombo · SRI LANKA · BRUNEI · Mindanao · KIRIBATI

GABON · CONGO · Brazzaville · Kinshasa · RWANDA · BURUNDI · Nairobi · SEYCHELLES · MALDIVES · EQUATOR · Kuala Lumpur · MALAYSIA · Borneo · NAURU

SAO TOME & PRINCIPE · CABINDA Ang. · Luanda · TANZANIA · Dodoma · Dar es Salaam · COMOROS · SINGAPORE · Sumatra · I N D O N E S I A · New Guinea · PAPUA NEW GUINEA · SOLOMON ISLANDS · TUVALU

ANGOLA · ZAMBIA · Lusaka · MALAWI · Jakarta · Java · Surabaya · Celebes · Port Moresby · FIJI ISLANDS

NAMIBIA · Harare · ZIMBABWE · Antananarivo · MAURITIUS · I N D I A N · EAST TIMOR (TIMOR-LESTE) · Arafura Sea · Darwin · Coral Sea · VANUATU

Windhoek · BOTSWANA · MOZAMBIQUE · MADAGASCAR · Reunion Fr. · O C E A N · New Caledonia Fr.

Gaborone · Tshwane (Pretoria) · Maputo · SWAZILAND · AUSTRALIA · SOUTH PACIFIC OCEAN

SOUTH AFRICA · Bloemfontein · LESOTHO · Perth · Brisbane · North Island

Cape Town · Sydney · Canberra · Tasman Sea · Auckland

Kerguelen Islands Fr. · Melbourne · Darling · Murray · Tasmania · NEW ZEALAND · Wellington · South Island

60°S

A N T A R C T I C A · Ross Sea

ABBREVIATIONS

AUST.	....	AUSTRIA
B.&H.	....	BOSNIA &
		HERZEGOVINA
BELG.	....	BELGIUM
CROAT.	....	CROATIA
CZECH REP.	....	CZECH REPUBLIC
DEM. REP.	....	DEMOCRATIC
OF THE		REPUBLIC OF
CONGO		THE CONGO
EQ. GUINEA	....	EQUATORIAL GUINEA
EST.	....	ESTONIA
HUNG.	....	HUNGARY
LITH.	....	LITHUANIA
MACED.	....	MACEDONIA
MOLD.	....	MOLDOVA
NETH.	....	NETHERLANDS
SERB.	....	SERBIA
MONT.	....	MONTENEGRO
SLOV.	....	SLOVENIA
SWITZ.	....	SWITZERLAND
U.A.E.	....	UNITED ARAB EMIRATES

NORTH AMERICA

POLITICAL

0 mi   1000

0 km   1000

AZIMUTHAL EQUIDISTANT PROJECTION

NATIONAL GEOGRAPHIC

1. BAJA CALIFORNIA
2. BAJA CALIFORNIA SUR
3. SONORA
4. CHIHUAHUA
5. SINALOA
6. DURANGO
7. COAHUILA
8. NUEVO LEON
9. ZACATECAS
10. TAMAULIPAS
11. NAYARIT
12. AGUASCALIENTES
13. SAN LUIS POTOSI
14. JALISCO
15. GUANAJUATO
16. QUERETARO
17. HIDALGO
18. COLIMA
19. MICHOACAN
20. MEXICO
21. DISTRITO FEDERAL
22. TLAXCALA
23. MORELOS
24. PUEBLA
25. VERACRUZ
26. GUERRERO
27. OAXACA
28. TABASCO
29. CHIAPAS
30. CAMPECHE
31. QUINTANA ROO
32. YUCATAN

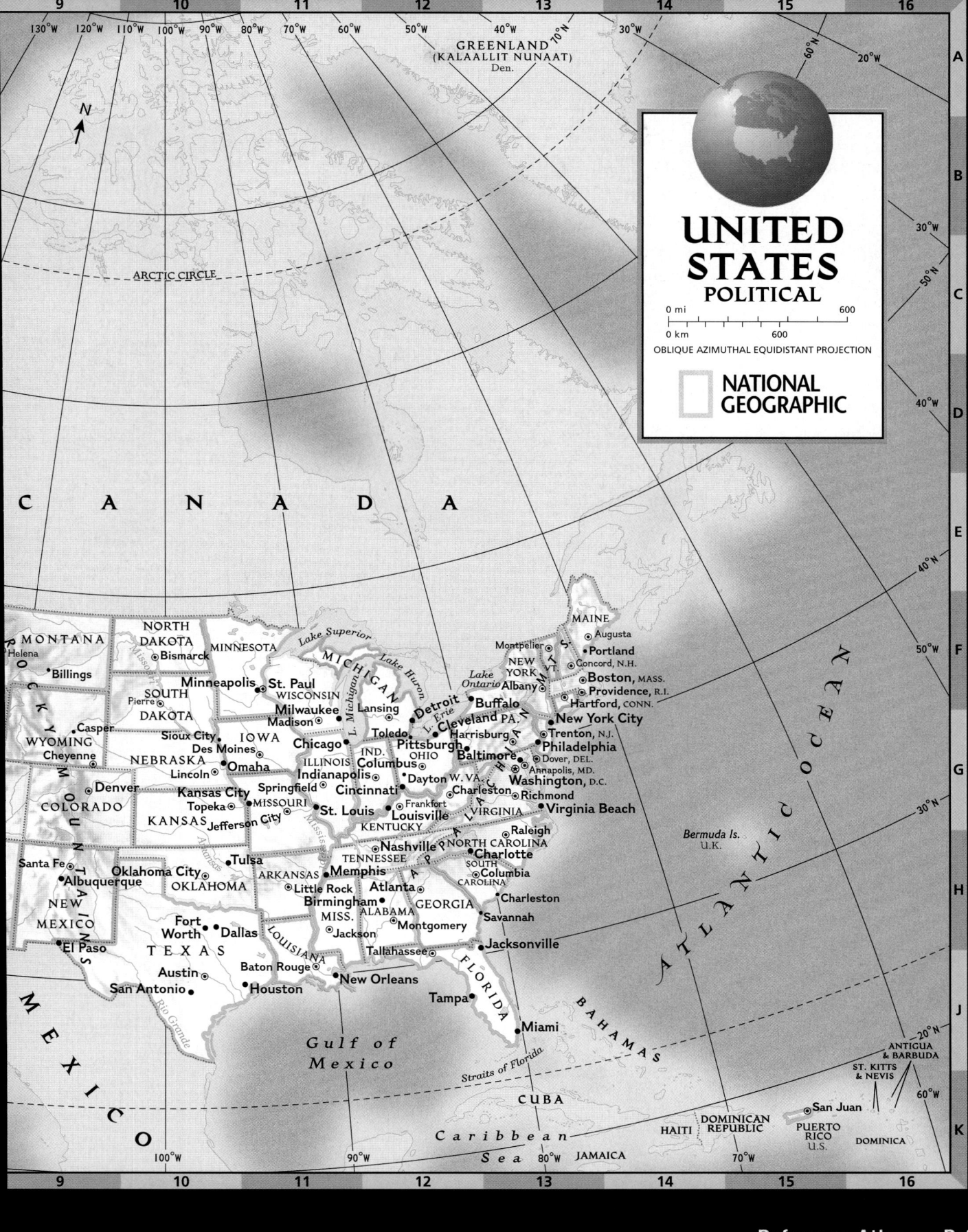

UNITED
STATES
POLITICAL

0 mi   600
0 km   600

OBLIQUE AZIMUTHAL EQUIDISTANT PROJECTION

NATIONAL GEOGRAPHIC

GREENLAND
(KALAALLIT NUNAAT)
Den.

ARCTIC CIRCLE

C A N A D A

MONTANA
Helena
•Billings

NORTH
DAKOTA
•Bismarck

MINNESOTA

Lake Superior

MICHIGAN

Lake Huron

MAINE

Augusta

Montpelier   •Portland
                Concord, N.H.

NEW
YORK   •Boston, MASS.
Albany   •Providence, R.I.
            Hartford, CONN.

SOUTH
DAKOTA
Pierre•

Minneapolis• •St. Paul
WISCONSIN
     Milwaukee•
Madison•   Lansing•

Detroit• Buffalo•
Cleveland•
Toledo•   Erie   PA.   New York City
Pittsburgh•   •Trenton, N.J.
                        •Philadelphia

WYOMING
Cheyenne•

Sioux City•
     IOWA
Des Moines•

Chicago•
ILLINOIS

L. Michigan

IND.
Columbus•
OHIO
Dayton• W. VA.

Harrisburg•
Baltimore•
         •Dover, DEL.
Annapolis, MD.
Washington, D.C.

Denver•
COLORADO

NEBRASKA
Lincoln• Omaha•

Kansas City•
Topeka•
MISSOURI
Jefferson City•

Springfield•
St. Louis•

Indianapolis•
Cincinnati•

Frankfort•
Louisville•
KENTUCKY

Charleston•

Richmond•
         •Virginia Beach

Santa Fe•
•Albuquerque

NEW
MEXICO

KANSAS

Tulsa•
Oklahoma City•
OKLAHOMA

Arkansas

ARKANSAS
•Little Rock

TENNESSEE
Memphis•

Nashville•

VIRGINIA

•Raleigh
NORTH CAROLINA
•Charlotte
SOUTH
CAROLINA
•Columbia

El Paso•

Fort
Worth• •Dallas
TEXAS
LOUISIANA

Austin•
San Antonio•

Jackson•
MISS.

Atlanta•
Birmingham•
ALABAMA   GEORGIA
•Montgomery

Baton Rouge•
•New Orleans

Tallahassee•

Charleston•

Savannah•

Jacksonville•

M E X I C O

Rio Grande

Houston•

Tampa•

FLORIDA

•Miami

Gulf of
Mexico

Straits of Florida

CUBA

BAHAMAS

Caribbean
Sea

JAMAICA

HAITI

DOMINICAN
REPUBLIC

•San Juan
PUERTO
RICO
U.S.

DOMINICA

ANTIGUA
& BARBUDA
ST. KITTS
& NEVIS

ATLANTIC OCEAN

Bermuda Is.
U.K.

APPALACHIAN

ROCKY MOUNTAINS

N

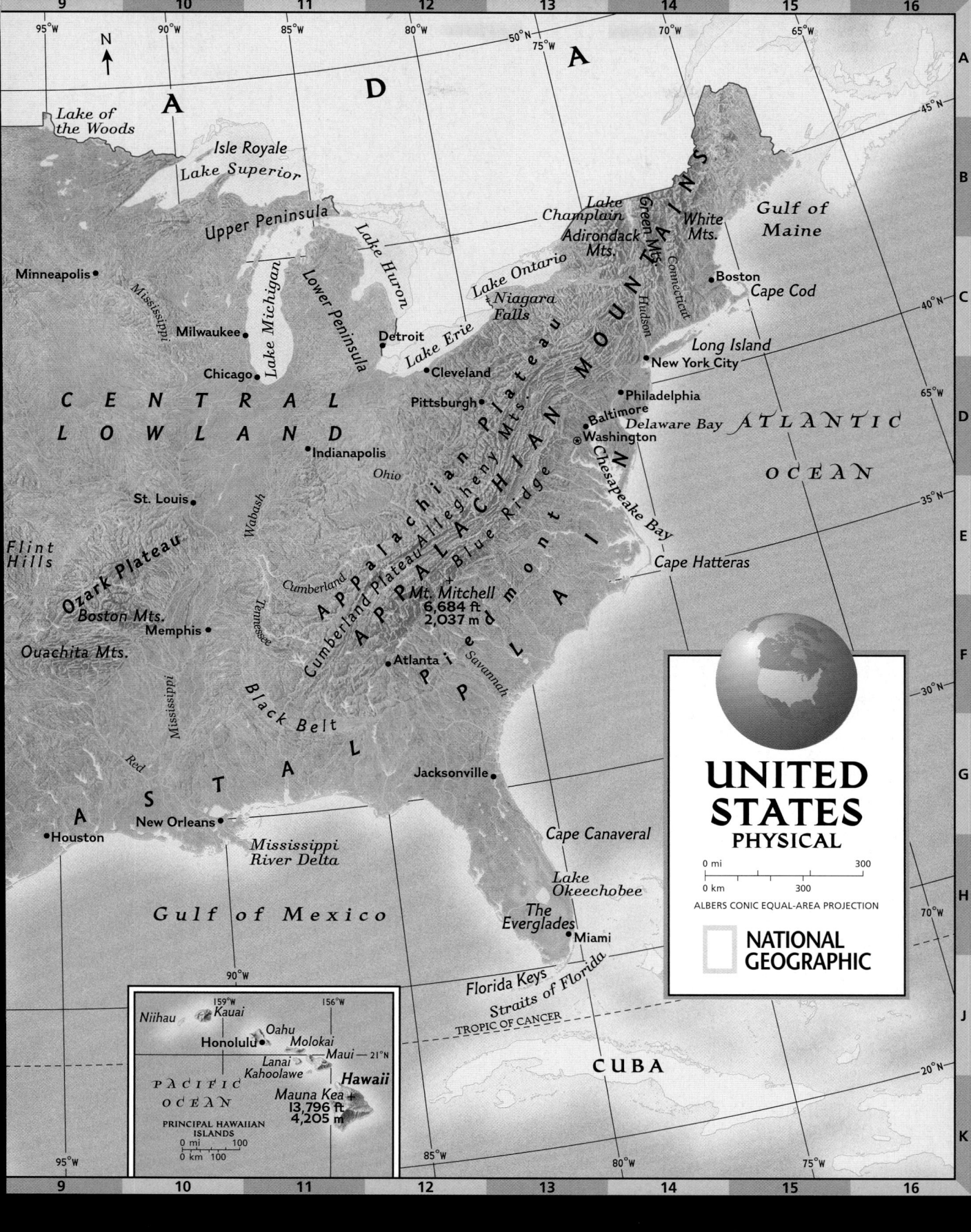

9   10   11   12   13   14   15   16

95°W   90°W   85°W   80°W   75°W   70°W   65°W

N

Lake of the Woods

C A N A D A

Isle Royale
Lake Superior
Upper Peninsula

Minneapolis •

Mississippi

Lower Peninsula

Lake Michigan

Lake Huron

• Milwaukee

Chicago •

Detroit •

Lake Erie

Cleveland •

Lake Ontario
Niagara Falls

Lake Champlain
Adirondack Mts.

Green Mts.

White Mts.

Gulf of Maine

• Boston
Cape Cod

Connecticut

Hudson

Long Island
• New York City

C E N T R A L
L O W L A N D

• Indianapolis

Ohio

Pittsburgh •

Appalachian Plateau
Allegheny Mts.

A P P A L A C H I A N   M O U N T A I N S

• Philadelphia

Baltimore •
Washington ⊛

Delaware Bay

Chesapeake Bay

ATLANTIC

OCEAN

St. Louis •

Wabash

Cumberland Plateau

Blue Ridge

Cumberland

Tennessee

Piedmont

Cape Hatteras

Flint Hills

Ozark Plateau

Boston Mts.

Memphis •

Ouachita Mts.

Mt. Mitchell
6,684 ft
2,037 m

Atlanta •

Savannah

Mississippi

Black Belt

Red

C O A S T A L   P L A I N

Jacksonville •

• Houston

New Orleans •

Mississippi River Delta

Cape Canaveral

Lake Okeechobee

The Everglades
• Miami

Gulf of Mexico

Florida Keys
Straits of Florida
TROPIC OF CANCER

C U B A

UNITED
STATES
PHYSICAL

0 mi   300
0 km   300
ALBERS CONIC EQUAL-AREA PROJECTION

NATIONAL
GEOGRAPHIC

159°W   156°W
Kauai
Niihau

Honolulu •   *Oahu* *Molokai*
Lanai *Maui* — 21°N
Kahoolawe   *Hawaii*

PACIFIC
OCEAN

Mauna Kea +
13,796 ft
4,205 m

PRINCIPAL HAWAIIAN
ISLANDS

0 mi   100
0 km   100

95°W   90°W   85°W   80°W   75°W

50°N
75°W
45°N
40°N
65°W
35°N
30°N
70°W
20°N

A New Nation, 1787

BRITISH NORTH AMERICA

Claimed by U.S. and Great Britain

Claimed by U.S. and Great Britain

Claimed by N.H. and N.Y.

Part of Mass.

NORTHWEST TERRITORY
Ceded by Va. to U.S. 1784

Ceded by Mass. to U.S. 1785

Ceded by Conn. to U.S. 1786 & 1800

Awarded to Pa. from Conn. 1782

Ceded by Mass. to N.Y. 1786

NEW HAMPSHIRE
MASSACHUSETTS
RHODE ISLAND
CONNECTICUT
New York City (1787-1790)
PA.
NEW JERSEY
MD.   DELAWARE

Ceded by New York to U.S. 1782

SPANISH

NORTH

AMERICA

SPANISH LOUISIANA

Mississippi

Missouri

Arkansas

Wabash

Ohio

UNITED
STATES

VIRGINIA

Claimed by Virginia

NORTH CAROLINA

Claimed by North Carolina

ALTA CALIFORNIA

Colorado

Gila

Ceded by S.C. to Ga. 1787

Claimed by Georgia

SOUTH CAROLINA

GEORGIA

Claimed by Ga., Spain and U.S.

BAJA CALIFORNIA

WESTERN INTERIOR PROVINCES

Rio Grande

EASTERN INTERIOR PROVINCES

SPANISH FLORIDA

Original 13 states
Land still claimed by states 1787
U.S. territory
British territory
Spanish territory
- - - Disputed boundary

Coming of Age, 1821

BRITISH NORTH AMERICA

Claimed by U.S. and Great Britain

Columbia

U.S.-British treaty line of 1818

RED RIVER BASIN To U.S. 1818

MAINE
1820

OREGON COUNTRY
U.S.-British agreement to joint occupation in 1818

Snake

Adams-Onis Treaty line of 1819

MICHIGAN TERRITORY

Mississippi

UNORGANIZED

TERRITORY

Missouri

INDIANA
1816

Ohio

Washington

ALTA CALIFORNIA

ILLINOIS
1818

Wabash

MISSOURI
1821

MEXICO

Arkansas

ARKANSAS TERRITORY

Red

MISSISSIPPI
1817

ALABAMA
1819

Rio Grande

TEXAS

LOUISIANA
1812

FLORIDA
To U.S.
1819

UNITED STATES
TERRITORIAL GROWTH

NATIONAL GEOGRAPHIC

Expanding West of the Mississippi, 1803

BRITISH NORTH AMERICA

Claimed by U.S. and Great Britain

OREGON COUNTRY
Claimed by Great Britain, Russia, Spain, and United States

Claimed by U.S. and Great Britain

VERMONT 1791

Mississippi

INDIANA

Missouri

TERRITORY

NEW SPAIN (SPANISH MEXICO)

LOUISIANA PURCHASE
Purchased by U.S. in 1803 from France

OHIO 1803

Philadelphia (1790-1800)

Washington (new capital 1800)

Arkansas

Ohio

Wabash

KENTUCKY 1792

TENNESSEE 1796

Red

Rio Grande

Claimed by U.S. and Spain

Ceded by Georgia to U.S. 1802

MISSISSIPPI TERR.

BAJA CALIFORNIA

SPANISH FLORIDA

Claimed by U.S. and Spain

States previously in the Union

States newly admitted

Coast to Coast, 1850 and beyond

BRITISH NORTH AMERICA

Treaty line of 1846

Treaty line of 1842

Treaty line of 1842

WASHINGTON 1889

MONTANA 1889

NORTH DAKOTA 1889

MINNESOTA 1858

OREGON TERRITORY
Added to U.S. in 1846

MINNESOTA TERRITORY

OREGON 1859

Snake

IDAHO 1890

SOUTH DAKOTA 1889

WISCONSIN 1848

MICHIGAN 1837

NEVADA 1864

WYOMING 1890

Missouri

UNORGANIZED

IOWA 1846

UTAH TERRITORY

NEBRASKA 1867

TERRITORY

CALIFORNIA 1850

UTAH 1896

COLORADO 1876

Arkansas

KANSAS 1861

Wabash

Ohio

W. VA. 1863

Washington

Colorado

ARIZONA 1912

NEW MEXICO TERRITORY

OKLAHOMA 1907

Red

ARKANSAS 1836

Gila

GADSDEN PURCHASE
To U.S. 1853

NEW MEXICO 1912

Mississippi

Rio Grande

TEXAS 1845

FLORIDA 1845

RUSSIA

ALASKA 1959
Purchased by U.S. 1867

MEXICO

HAWAII 1959
Annexed by U.S. 1898

States admitted after 1850

Grid references (top and bottom)

1   2   3   4   5   6   7   8

Grid references (sides)

A   B   C   D   E   F   G   H   J   K

10°E   20°E   30°E   40°E

40°N

30°N

EUROPE

Black Sea

Sea of Marmara

Istanbul

ANATOLIA

Ankara

TURKEY

Tunis

TUNISIA

Tripoli

Taurus Mountains

Aleppo

CYPRUS

SYRIA

LEBANON

Beirut

Damascus

ISRAEL

Jerusalem

Syrian Desert

Amman

Alexandria

Cairo

JORDAN

El Giza

Sinai Pen.

See inset below

Mediterranean Sea

LIBYA

EGYPT

Nile R.

Hejaz

Aswan High Dam

SAHARA

Boundary claimed by Sudan

Red Sea

SUDAN

AFRICA

30°E

30°N

Khartoum

Eastern Mediterranean Area

30°E

N

TURKEY

Aleppo

CYPRUS

SYRIA

LEBANON

Beirut

Damascus

Mediterranean Sea

Sea of Galilee

Golan Heights

Jordan River

Tel Aviv–Jaffa

West Bank

Jerusalem

Amman

Suez Canal

Gaza Strip

Dead Sea

ISRAEL

JORDAN

El Giza

Cairo

EGYPT

SAUDI ARABIA

Nile River

Gulf of Suez

Gulf of Aqaba

30°N

0 mi   100

0 km   100

Red Sea

MIDDLE EAST

PHYSICAL / POLITICAL

0 mi ——————— 500

0 km ——————— 500

AZIMUTHAL EQUIDISTANT PROJECTION

NATIONAL GEOGRAPHIC

United States Facts

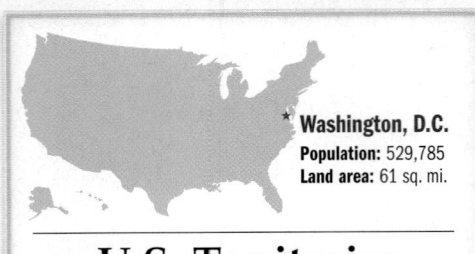

Washington, D.C.
Population: 529,785
Land area: 61 sq. mi.

U.S. Territories

Puerto Rico
Population: 3,987,837
Land area: 3,425 sq. mi.

Guam
Population: 180,692
Land area: 209 sq. mi.

U.S. Virgin Islands
Population: 107,560
Land area: 134 sq. mi.

American Samoa
Population: 57,066
Land area: 77 sq. mi.

The states are listed in the order they were admitted to the Union.

Population figures are based on the U.S. Bureau of the Census projections for July 2010. House of Representatives figures from the 2000 census are from the Clerk of the House of Representatives. States are not drawn to scale.

1 Delaware
Year Admitted: 1787
Population: 884,342
Land area: 1,955 sq. mi.
Representatives: 1
Dover

2 Pennsylvania
Year Admitted: 1787
Population: 12,584,487
Land area: 44,820 sq. mi.
Representatives: 19
Harrisburg

3 New Jersey
Year Admitted: 1787
Population: 9,018,231
Land area: 7,419 sq. mi.
Representatives: 13
Trenton

9 New Hampshire
Year Admitted: 1788
Population: 1,385,560
Land area: 8,969 sq. mi.
Representatives: 2
Concord

10 Virginia
Year Admitted: 1788
Population: 8,010,245
Land area: 39,598 sq. mi.
Representatives: 11
Richmond

11 New York
Year Admitted: 1788
Population: 19,443,672
Land area: 47,224 sq. mi.
Representatives: 29
Albany

17 Ohio
Year Admitted: 1803
Population: 11,576,181
Land area: 40,953 sq. mi.
Representatives: 18
Columbus

18 Louisiana
Year Admitted: 1812
Population: 4,612,679
Land area: 43,566 sq. mi.
Representatives: 7
Baton Rouge

19 Indiana
Year Admitted: 1816
Population: 6,392,139
Land area: 35,870 sq. mi.
Representatives: 9
Indianapolis

24 Missouri
Year Admitted: 1821
Population: 5,922,078
Land area: 68,898 sq. mi.
Representatives: 9
Jefferson City

25 Arkansas
Year Admitted: 1836
Population: 2,875,039
Land area: 52,075 sq. mi.
Representatives: 4
Little Rock

26 Michigan
Year Admitted: 1837
Population: 10,428,683
Land area: 56,809 sq. mi.
Representatives: 15
Lansing

27 Florida
Year Admitted: 1845
Population: 19,251,691
Land area: 53,997 sq. mi.
Representatives: 25
Tallahassee

28 Texas
Year Admitted: 1845
Population: 24,648,888
Land area: 261,914 sq. mi.
Representatives: 32
Austin

33 Oregon
Year Admitted: 1859
Population: 3,790,996
Land area: 96,003 sq. mi.
Representatives: 5
Salem

34 Kansas
Year Admitted: 1861
Population: 2,805,470
Land area: 81,823 sq. mi.
Representatives: 4
Topeka

35 West Virginia
Year Admitted: 1863
Population: 1,829,141
Land area: 24,087 sq. mi.
Representatives: 3
Charleston

36 Nevada
Year Admitted: 1864
Population: 2,690,531
Land area: 109,806 sq. mi.
Representatives: 3
Carson City

37 Nebraska
Year Admitted: 1867
Population: 1,768,997
Land area: 76,878 sq. mi.
Representatives: 3
Lincoln

42 Washington
Year Admitted: 1889
Population: 6,541,963
Land area: 66,582 sq. mi.
Representatives: 9
Olympia

43 Idaho
Year Admitted: 1890
Population: 1,517,291
Land area: 82,751 sq. mi.
Representatives: 2
Boise

44 Wyoming
Year Admitted: 1890
Population: 519,886
Land area: 97,105 sq. mi.
Representatives: 1
Cheyenne

45 Utah
Year Admitted: 1896
Population: 2,595,013
Land area: 82,168 sq. mi.
Representatives: 3
Salt Lake City

46 Oklahoma
Year Admitted: 1907
Population: 3,591,516
Land area: 68,679 sq. mi.
Representatives: 5
Oklahoma City

4 Georgia
Year Admitted: 1788
Population: 9,589,080
Land area: 57,919 sq. mi.
Representatives: 13

★ Atlanta

5 Connecticut
Year Admitted: 1788
Population: 3,577,490
Land area: 4,845 sq. mi.
Representatives: 5

★ Hartford

6 Massachusetts
Year Admitted: 1788
Population: 6,649,441
Land area: 7,838 sq. mi.
Representatives: 10

Boston ★

7 Maryland
Year Admitted: 1788
Population: 5,904,970
Land area: 9,775 sq. mi.
Representatives: 8

Annapolis ★

8 South Carolina
Year Admitted: 1788
Population: 4,446,704
Land area: 30,111 sq. mi.
Representatives: 6

Columbia
★

12 North Carolina
Year Admitted: 1789
Population: 9,345,823
Land area: 48,718 sq. mi.
Representatives: 13

★
Raleigh

13 Rhode Island
Year Admitted: 1790
Population: 1,116,652
Land area: 1,045 sq. mi.
Representatives: 2

★ Providence

14 Vermont
Year Admitted: 1791
Population: 652,512
Land area: 9,249 sq. mi.
Representatives: 1

★ Montpelier

15 Kentucky
Year Admitted: 1792
Population: 4,265,117
Land area: 39,732 sq. mi.
Representatives: 6

Frankfort ★

16 Tennessee
Year Admitted: 1796
Population: 6,230,852
Land area: 41,220 sq. mi.
Representatives: 9

★ Nashville

20 Mississippi
Year Admitted: 1817
Population: 2,971,412
Land area: 46,914 sq. mi.
Representatives: 4

★ Jackson

21 Illinois
Year Admitted: 1818
Population: 12,916,894
Land area: 55,593 sq. mi.
Representatives: 19

★ Springfield

22 Alabama
Year Admitted: 1819
Population: 4,596,330
Land area: 50,750 sq. mi.
Representatives: 7

Montgomery
★

23 Maine
Year Admitted: 1820
Population: 1,357,134
Land area: 30,865 sq. mi.
Representatives: 2

★ Augusta

29 Iowa
Year Admitted: 1846
Population: 3,009,907
Land area: 55,875 sq. mi.
Representatives: 5

Des Moines
★

30 Wisconsin
Year Admitted: 1848
Population: 5,727,426
Land area: 54,314 sq. mi.
Representatives: 8

Madison
★

31 California
Year Admitted: 1850
Population: 38,067,134
Land area: 155,973 sq. mi.
Representatives: 53

Sacramento ★

32 Minnesota
Year Admitted: 1858
Population: 5,420,636
Land area: 79,617 sq. mi.
Representatives: 8

Saint Paul
★

38 Colorado
Year Admitted: 1876
Population: 4,831,554
Land area: 103,730 sq. mi.
Representatives: 7

Denver ★

39 North Dakota
Year Admitted: 1889
Population: 636,623
Land area: 68,994 sq. mi.
Representatives: 1

Bismarck
★

40 South Dakota
Year Admitted: 1889
Population: 786,399
Land area: 75,898 sq. mi.
Representatives: 1

Pierre
★

41 Montana
Year Admitted: 1889
Population: 968,598
Land area: 145,556 sq. mi.
Representatives: 1

★ Helena

47 New Mexico
Year Admitted: 1912
Population: 1,980,225
Land area: 121,365 sq. mi.
Representatives: 3

★
Santa Fe

48 Arizona
Year Admitted: 1912
Population: 6,637,381
Land area: 113,642 sq. mi.
Representatives: 8

Phoenix
★

49 Alaska
Year Admitted: 1959
Population: 694,109
Land area: 570,374 sq. mi.
Representatives: 1

Juneau ★

50 Hawaii
Year Admitted: 1959
Population: 1,340,674
Land area: 6,432 sq. mi.
Representatives: 2

Honolulu

NATIONAL GEOGRAPHIC
Geography Skills Handbook

Focus

Understanding the Five Themes of Geography Use what your students know about their school to make a connection with the five themes of geography. As each theme is read aloud, write it on the board for students to see. **Ask:** How could you describe the location of our school? List student answers on the board. Then have students describe the physical and human characteristics that make the school unique. Continue until you have two or three student descriptions for each of the five themes of geography. **OL**

How Do I Study Geography?

Geographers have created these broad categories and standards as tools to help you understand the relationships among people, places, and environments.

🌐 5 Themes of Geography
🌐 6 Essential Elements
🌐 18 Geography Standards

5
Themes of Geography

1 Location

Location describes where something is. Absolute location describes a place's exact position on the Earth's surface. Relative location expresses where a place is in relation to another place.

2 Place

Place describes the physical and human characteristics that make a location unique.

3 Regions

Regions are areas that share common characteristics.

4 Movement

Movement explains how and why people and things move and are connected.

5 Human-Environment Interaction

Human-Environment Interaction describes the relationship between people and their environment.

Ref 16   Geography Skills Handbook

Additional Support

Fast Facts

Origin of Geography The first written document to use the word *geography* in the title was by Eratosthenes. He was a Greek scholar who lived from ca. 276 B.C. to 194 B.C. He was also the first to map the world using parallels and meridians.

American Geography The first textbook on American geography was published in 1784. It was called *Geography Made Easy* and was written by Jedidiah Morse. The inventor of Morse Code, Samuel Morse, was Jedidiah's oldest son.

Astrogeology With the advent of space travel, scientists have been able to study the geology of asteroids, planets, and moons. Rocks have been collected from the moon and brought back to the Earth for study. Unmanned spacecraft have analyzed soil samples from the planet Mars.

6
Essential Elements

18
Geography Standards

I. The World in Spatial Terms
Geographers look to see where a place is located. Location acts as a starting point to answer "Where Is It?" The location of a place helps you orient yourself as to where you are.

1 How to use maps and other tools

2 How to use mental maps to organize information

3 How to analyze the spatial organization of people, places, and environments

II. Places and Regions
Place describes physical characteristics such as landforms, climate, and plant or animal life. It might also describe human characteristics, including language and way of life. Places can also be organized into regions. **Regions** are places united by one or more characteristics.

4 The physical and human characteristics of places

5 How people create regions to interpret Earth's complexity

6 How culture and experience influence people's perceptions of places and regions

III. Physical Systems
Geographers study how physical systems, such as hurricanes, volcanoes, and glaciers, shape the surface of the Earth. They also look at how plants and animals depend upon one another and their surroundings for their survival.

7 The physical processes that shape Earth's surface

8 The distribution of ecosystems on Earth's surface

9 The characteristics, distribution, and migration of human populations

IV. Human Systems
People shape the world in which they live. They settle in certain places but not in others. An ongoing theme in geography is the movement of people, ideas, and goods.

10 The complexity of Earth's cultural mosaics

11 The patterns and networks of economic interdependence

12 The patterns of human settlement

13 The forces of cooperation and conflict

V. Environment and Society
How does the relationship between people and their natural surroundings influence the way people live? Geographers study how people use the environment and how their actions affect the environment.

14 How human actions modify the physical environment

15 How physical systems affect human systems

16 The meaning, use, and distribution of resources

VI. The Uses of Geography
Knowledge of geography helps us understand the relationships among people, places, and environments over time. Applying geographic skills helps you understand the past and prepare for the future.

17 How to apply geography to interpret the past

18 How to apply geography to interpret the present and plan for the future

Geography Skills Handbook   Ref 17

Teach

Questioning Remind students that asking questions is an important learning tool. Point out to students that they can begin to understand how the first essential element, *The World in Spatial Terms*, applies to a geographic location by asking, "Where is it?" **Ask:** What questions will help us learn more about the second essential element, *Places and Regions?* *(Possible answers: What is the climate of this area? What language is spoken here? How is the way of life of the people who live here similar across the region?)* What questions will help us learn about the third essential element, *Physical Systems?* *(Possible answers: What weather patterns are common in this area? Have landforms been affected by weather? Has the landscape been shaped by volcanoes or earthquakes? Was this region shaped by glaciers?)* Continue to have students develop questions for the remaining essential elements of geography. **OL**

Activity: Using the Six Essential Elements

Human Systems Ask: What are some ways that human systems have influenced the region in which you live? Explain that the way people have shaped this region has changed over time. Organize students into groups, and assign each group a point in time in the history of your area. You might choose to assign groups to the era before European contact, a point early in European colonization, and different periods up to and including the present. Have each group develop six to eight questions about its time period based on the six essential elements of geography. Questions might cover topics such as how people provided food or found work, who moved in or out of the area, and how the natural surroundings affected the people who lived in the region. Direct students to appropriate reference materials, including local history sources, encyclopedias, almanacs, atlases, and reliable online information sources, to find answers to their questions. When finished, have each group prepare an oral report on its historical period. Reports can be given chronologically as a class presentation on the history of your region. **AL**

Teach

Comparing and Contrasting Discuss the difference between globes and maps with students, showing them examples of each. **Ask:** Why might you use a globe? *(to see a true representation of the Earth, to see the relative distances between continents, to get an accurate representation of the size and shape of landmasses)* Why might you use a map? *(to get driving directions, to see different types of information represented on special-purpose maps, to see a small area in great detail)* **OL**

Additional Support and Answers

Globes and Maps

What Is a Globe? ▶
A **globe** is a round model of the Earth that shows its shape, lands, and directions as they truly relate to one another.

◀ What Is a Map?
A **map** is a flat drawing of all or part of the Earth's surface. Cartographers, or mapmakers, use mathematical formulas to transfer information from the round globe to a flat map.

Globes and Maps ▶
Globes and maps serve different purposes, and each has advantages and disadvantages.

	Advantages	Disadvantages
Globes	• Represent true land shape, distances, and directions	• Cannot show detailed information • Difficult to carry
Maps	• Show small areas in great detail • Display different types of information, such as population densities or natural resources • Transport easily	• Distort, or change, the accuracy of shapes and distances

Ref 18 Geography Skills Handbook

Activity: Understanding Map Projections

Predicting Consequences Bring several oranges or grapefruits to class. Have small groups of students draw the continents on the fruit, so that the fruit looks as much like a globe as possible. **Ask:** What do you think will happen if you try to turn this round representation into a flat represen-tation? Ask students to suggest ways to peel the fruit so that the peel will lie flat. Then have them carefully peel the fruit and lay it flat. **Ask:** How has flattening the peel distorted the accuracy of the "globe"? *(Distances are no longer accurate; there is extra space between landforms.)* **Ask:** What have you learned about the difficulty of representing the round Earth on a flat map? *(Students will recognize that it is difficult to represent a round object on a flat surface.)* **BL**

Map Projections

When the Earth's surface is flattened on a map, big gaps open up. Mapmakers stretch parts of the Earth to show either the correct shapes of places or their correct sizes. Mapmakers have developed different projections, or ways of showing the Earth on a flat piece of paper. Below are different map projections.

Goode's Interrupted Equal-Area Projection ▼

A map with this projection shows continents close to their true shapes and sizes. This projection is helpful to compare land area among continents.

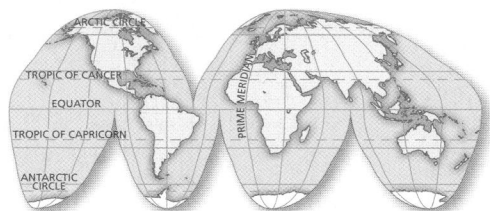

Mercator Projection ▼

The Mercator projection shows land shapes fairly accurately but not size or distance. Areas that are located far from the Equator are quite distorted. The Mercator projection shows true directions, however, making it useful for sea travel.

Robinson Projection ▼

The Robinson projection has minor distortions. Continents and oceans are close to their sizes and shapes, but the North and South Poles appear flattened.

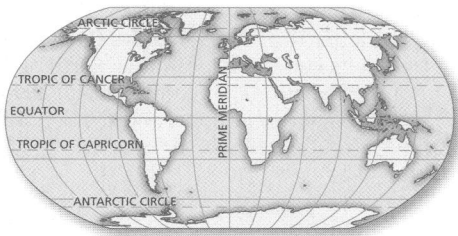

Winkel Tripel Projection ▼

This projection gives a good overall view of the continents' shapes and sizes. Land areas are not as distorted near the poles as they are in the Robinson projection.

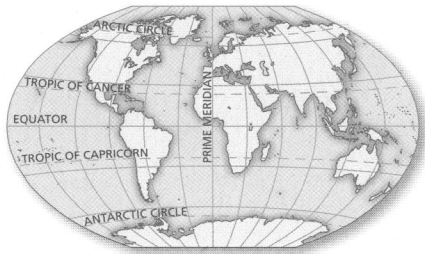

Skills Practice

1 **Comparing and Contrasting** Explain the similarities and differences between globes and maps.

2 **Describing** Why do map projections distort some parts of the Earth?

Geography Skills Handbook   **Ref 19**

Teach

Analyzing Information Ask: What is a map projection? *(a way of showing the Earth)* Locate Greenland on each of the map projections on this page. **Ask:** How does the depiction of Greenland change, based on the map projection? *(Goode's: appears on two different sections of the map; Robinson and Winkel Tripel: similar in shape and size, appears smaller than South America; Mercator: very large, even larger than Africa)* **OL**

Answers

1. Both globes and maps represent the Earth's surface. A globe is more accurate than a map because it is a model of the Earth's shape, depicting the true shape of lands, and representing directions as they truly relate to one another. Maps are flat representations of the Earth that can show small areas in great detail.

2. A map projection distorts some parts of the Earth because when the round Earth is depicted on a flat map, gaps develop. Mapmakers stretch parts of the Earth's surface to fill the gaps.

Teach

Drawing Conclusions Remind students that lines of latitude and longitude form an imaginary global grid over the surface of the Earth. **Ask:** Which lines run east to west? *(latitude)* Is the Equator a line of latitude or longitude? *(latitude)* What is 75°N called? *(the Arctic Circle)* Where is the Equator? *(at 0° latitude)* Where is the Prime Meridian? *(0° longitude)* Where is the International Date Line? *(180° longitude)* How can latitude and longitude be used to determine absolute location? *(Identifying the latitude and longitude of a place pinpoints it on a map.)* How can latitude and longitude be used to determine relative location? *(Relative location gives a place's location in relationship to another place. For example, you can say that North America is west of Europe.)* **OL**

Additional Support and Answers

Location

To locate places on Earth, geographers use a system of imaginary lines that crisscross the globe. These lines are called *latitude* and *longitude*.

Latitude ▶

- Lines of **latitude** are imaginary circles that run east to west around the globe. They are known as *parallels*. These parallels divide the globe into units called degrees.
- The **Equator** circles the middle of the Earth like a belt. It is located halfway between the North and South Poles. The Equator is 0° latitude.
- The letter *N* or *S* that follows the degree symbol tells you if the location is north or south of the Equator. The North Pole, for example, is 90°N (north) latitude, and the South Pole is 90°S (south) latitude.

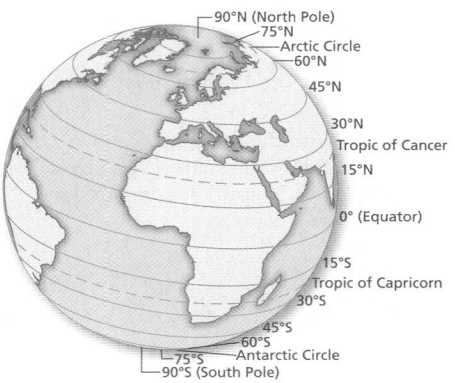

◀ Longitude

- Lines of **longitude,** also known as *meridians*, run from the North Pole to the South Pole. The **Prime Meridian** (also called the Meridian of Greenwich) is 0° longitude and runs through Greenwich, England.
- The letter *E* or *W* that follows the degree symbol tells you if the location is east or west of the Prime Meridian.
- On the opposite side of the Earth is the 180° meridian, also known as the International Date Line.

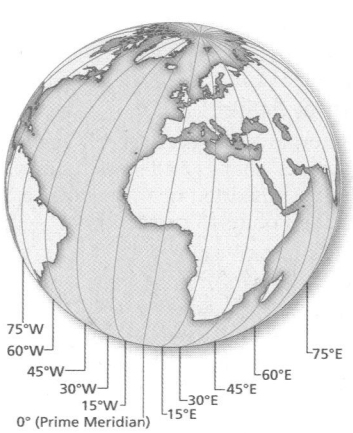

Absolute Location ▶

A place's exact location can be identified when you use both latitude and longitude. For example, Tokyo, Japan, is 36°N latitude and 140°E longitude.

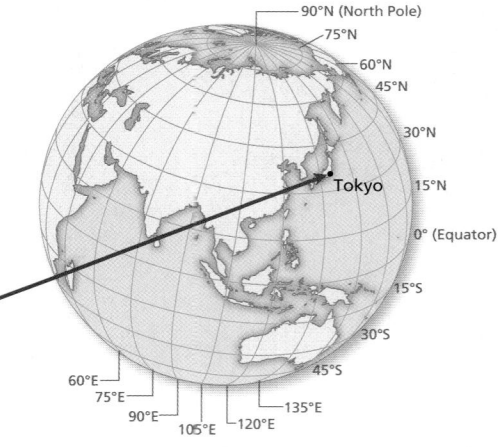

Ref 20   Geography Skills Handbook

Activity: Using a Gazetteer

Identifying Absolute Location Organize the class into groups. Have students in each group study the World: Political map in the National Geographic World Atlas and identify 10 different cities on the map. **Ask:** What is the absolute location of each of these cities? Students may have to estimate the degrees for many of the cities. Have them record the location in degrees of latitude and longitude for each city. Remind students to include the cardinal directions of north, south, east, and west. Show the class a gazetteer and, if possible, distribute copies of relevant pages to the students. Explain that a gazetteer is a geographic index or dictionary. Have students check their locations against the latitude and longitude listed in the gazetteer. To extend the activity, ask groups to use the information in the gazetteer to create a quiz. Have the groups use latitude and longitude to give either the absolute or relative location for a total of 10 cities and geographic features. Remind students to create an answer key. Then have groups exchange quizzes to test their knowledge of latitude and longitude. **OL**

Hemispheres

The Equator divides the Earth into Northern and Southern Hemispheres. Everything north of the Equator is in the Northern Hemisphere. Everything south of the Equator is in the Southern Hemisphere.

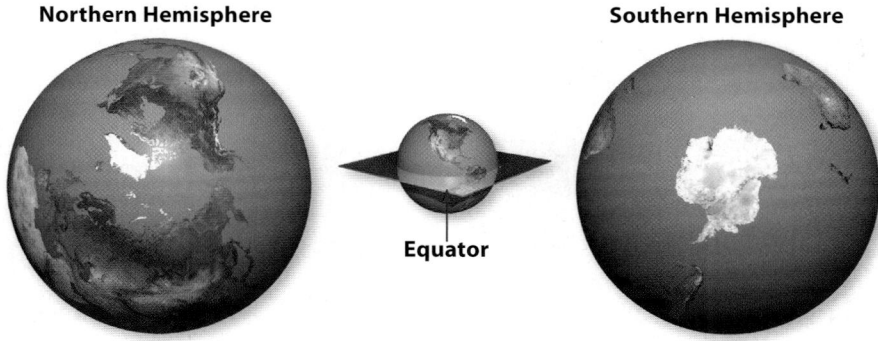

Northern Hemisphere   **Southern Hemisphere**

Equator

The Prime Meridian divides the Earth into Eastern and Western Hemispheres. Everything east of the Prime Meridian for 180 degrees is in the Eastern Hemisphere. Everything west of the Prime Meridian for 180 degrees is in the Western Hemisphere.

Western Hemisphere   **Eastern Hemisphere**

Prime Meridian

Skills Practice

1 **Identifying** What country is located at 30°S and 120°E?

2 **Analyzing Visuals** In which hemispheres is Europe located?

Geography Skills Handbook   **Ref 21**

Teach

Locating Tell students that the word part *hemi* means "half." This will help them remember that a hemisphere is a half of the Earth. **Ask:** *What are the four hemispheres depicted on this page?* (Northern, Southern, Eastern, Western) Have students look at each hemisphere and state what geographic regions or continents are visible.

Using a globe, test students' understanding of hemispheres by giving examples of places around the world and asking in which hemispheres those places are located. Examples: **Ask:** *In which hemispheres is New York City located? (the Northern and Western Hemispheres) What continent is in both the Northern and Western Hemispheres? (North America) In which hemispheres is the Nile River located? (the Eastern and Northern Hemispheres)* **BL**

Answers

1. Australia
2. the Eastern and Northern Hemispheres

Teach

Reading a Map Review the parts of a map as indicated on this page. **Ask:** What type of map is this? How do you know? *(Political/historical; you can tell from the title.)* How can you determine if Paris or Lyon is the capital of France? *(Note the symbol for capitals.)* Is Bulgaria east or west of Italy? How can you tell? *(It is east. You can tell by using the compass rose.)* **BL**

Extending the Activity Have students turn to the first page of the National Geographic Reference Atlas in the front of the textbook. Direct students to the Atlas Key and the Symbol Key. Have students review the maps in the Reference Atlas and note the parts of a map. Tell them to also look for features indicated by the Atlas Key and Symbol Key. You might want to point out that cartographers use different styles and sizes of fonts when labeling particular features. Have students compare how oceans, seas, rivers, and lakes are labeled on the maps. **OL**

Additional Support and Answers

Parts of a Map

In addition to latitude and longitude, maps feature other important tools to help you interpret the information they contain.

Title
The title tells you what information the map is showing.

Cities
Cities are symbolized by a solid circle (●). This symbol is found in the key and on the map.

World War II in Europe and Africa

Compass Rose
The compass rose is a symbol that tells you where the cardinal directions—north, south, east, and west—are positioned.

Boundary Lines
Boundary lines show the extent of an area's territory or political influence.

Major Axis powers
Greatest extent of Axis control
Allied or Ally-controlled
Neutral nations

Key
The key explains the symbols, colors, and lines on the map. The key is also called a *legend*.

Scale Bar
A measuring line, often called a scale bar, helps you figure distance on the map. The map scale shows the relationship between map measurements and actual distances on the Earth.

Capitals
Capitals are symbolized by a star (✪). This symbol is found in the key and on the map.

Ref 22   Geography Skills Handbook

Activity: Creating a Map

Mapping a Continent Provide students with outline maps of different continents. Tell students they will practice identifying parts of a map by creating one of their own. **Ask:** What features should you include on your maps? *(Title, key, scale bar, boundary lines, capital cities, other cities, and a compass rose; students may choose to include physical features as well.)* Direct students to use the appropriate political and physical maps in the National Geographic Reference Atlas for their continents. Have them draw boundaries and cities on their maps, create a key, include a compass rose, and represent the map's scale. When finished, have students who have worked on the same continents work together to discuss their maps, revising them as needed. **OL**

Using Scale

All maps are drawn to a certain scale. The scale of a map is the size of the map compared to the size of the actual land surface. Thus, the scale of a map varies with the size of the area shown.

Small-Scale Maps ▼

A small-scale map like this shows a large land area but little detail.

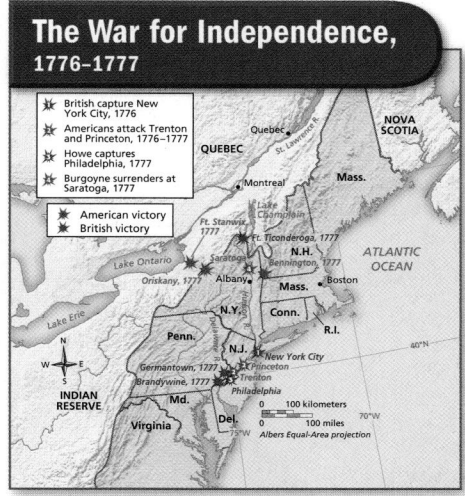

The War for Independence, 1776–1777

Large-Scale Maps ▼

A large-scale map like this shows a small land area with a great amount of detail.

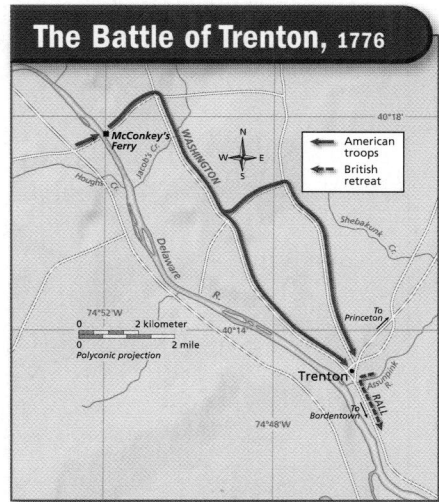

The Battle of Trenton, 1776

How Do I Use a Scale Bar?

A scale bar helps you determine actual distances that are represented on a map. First, measure the distance between two points on a map with a ruler. Then, check your measurement against the scale bar to find out how many kilometers or miles are represented by that length.

```
0    300 kilometers
0         300 miles
```

On the scale bar above, about ½ of an inch equals 300 miles. A little more than ½ of a centimeter is equal to 300 kilometers.

Skills Practice

1 **Defining** What is scale?

2 **Contrasting** What is the difference between a small-scale map and a large-scale map?

3 **Identifying** What are the four cardinal directions?

4 **Describing** Would you use a small-scale or a large-scale map to plan a car trip across the United States? Why?

Geography Skills Handbook   Ref 23

Teach

Reading Maps Ask: How does the physical map of South Asia differ from the political map of South Asia? *(The physical map does not identify the different countries by color; more geographic features are shown; elevation is indicated by color.)*

Have students think about the uses of physical maps. **Ask:** What important information is given on the physical map of South Asia? *(the locations of landforms such as mountains and plateaus; the locations of deserts and rivers; the elevations of the highest mountain peaks)* What physical features form natural boundaries between India and countries to the north? *(mountain ranges and the Thar Desert)* **OL**

Additional Support and Answers

Types of Maps
General Purpose Maps

Maps are amazingly useful tools. You can use them to show information and to make connections between seemingly unrelated topics. Geographers use many different types of maps. Maps that show a wide range of information about an area are called **general purpose maps.** Two of the most common general purpose maps are physical maps and political maps.

Physical Maps ▼

Physical maps call out landforms and water features. The map key explains what each color and symbol stands for.

South Asia: Physical

Physical maps use color and shadings to show **relief,** or how flat or rugged the land surface is.

Colors are used to show **elevation,** the height of an area above sea level.

Elevations
13,100 ft. (4,000 m)
6,500 ft. (2,000 m)
1,600 ft. (500 m)
650 ft. (200 m)
0 ft. (0 m)
Below sea level
▲ Mountain peak

Ref 24   Geography Skills Handbook

Fast Facts

Marco Polo Polo traveled from Europe to Asia in the late 1200s. His account of his time in Asia promoted interest in faraway places. This increased the sale and circulation of world maps. The geographic information he recorded was used by Columbus in his attempt to sail to Asia.

Amerigo Vespucci Vespucci was an Italian navigator, explorer, and acquaintance of Christopher Columbus. Vespucci left a series of documents about his voyages. The humanist Martin Waldseemüller suggested in 1507 that the lands be named America in Vespucci's honor.

Political Maps ▼

Political maps show the names and political boundaries of states and countries, along with human-made features such as cities or transportation routes.

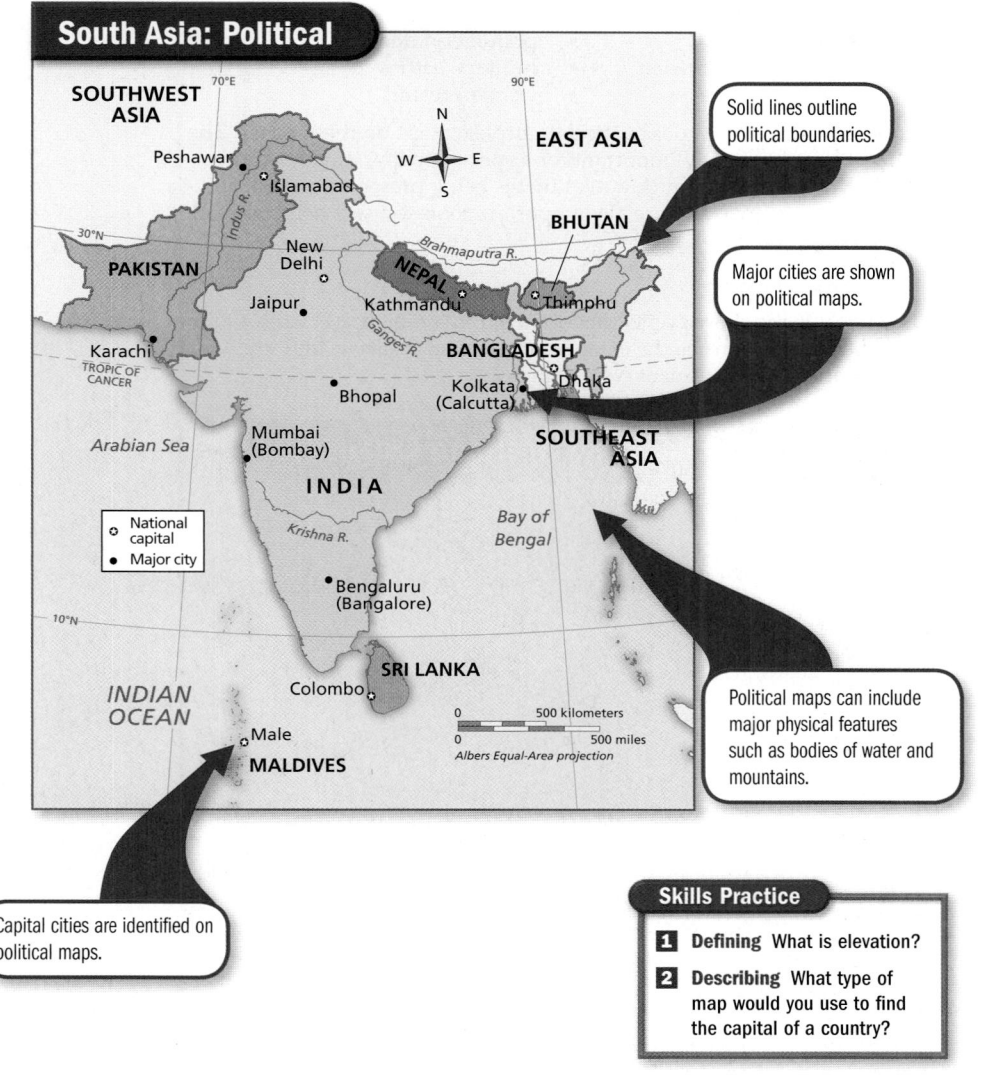

South Asia: Political

Solid lines outline political boundaries.

Major cities are shown on political maps.

Political maps can include major physical features such as bodies of water and mountains.

Capital cities are identified on political maps.

Skills Practice

1 Defining What is elevation?

2 Describing What type of map would you use to find the capital of a country?

Geography Skills Handbook   **Ref 25**

Teach
. . . .

Making Inferences Mapmakers often update maps. **Ask:** *What are some reasons that a political map would need to be revised? (because a national border changes or a capital city is relocated)* Have students use encyclopedias to research the histories of India, Pakistan, and Bangladesh. Have students create a chart listing the reasons a political map of South Asia would have changed over time. **OL**

Answers

1. Elevation is the height of an area above sea level.

2. A political map shows the capitals of countries.

Teach

Categorizing Assign each student a unit of the textbook. **Ask:** What types of maps are found in your unit? Direct them to create a table in their notebooks with the following headings: Political Maps, Physical Maps, Special Purpose Maps. Then tell them to survey the unit, identifying the types of maps and listing their titles and page numbers in the appropriate places in their tables. **OL**

Analyzing Information Ask: What does the map of the Louisiana Purchase and westward expansion show? *(the extent of the United States in 1803, the area of the Louisiana Purchase, and the exploration of lands to the west)* How do you know? *(The map title and the map key give us that information.)* What other information does the map include? *(cities and forts that were important in the area, and major bodies of water)* **OL**

Additional Support and Answers

Types of Maps

Special Purpose Maps

Some maps are made to present specific types of information. These are called **thematic** or **special purpose maps.** These maps usually show specific topics in detail. Special purpose maps may include information about:

- climate
- historical expansion
- natural resources
- population density
- military battles
- election results

Look at some of the types of special purpose maps on these pages. The map's title is especially important for a special purpose map because it tells you the type of information that is being presented. Colors and symbols in the map key are also important tools to use when you read these types of maps.

Historical Maps ▼

Historical maps show events that occurred in a region over time. On the map below, you can see the extent of the United States in 1803 and what other parts of the continent were being explored.

Louisiana Purchase and Westward Expansion

- United States, 1803
- Lewis and Clark
- Lewis and Clark return
- Pike
- ■ Fort

Lambert Azimuthal Equal-Area projection

Activity: Using Special Purpose Maps

Building a Map Library Ask: What kinds of special purpose maps might exist for our region? *(Answers will vary but might include maps of bike trails, maps of parks, and so on.)* Direct students to appropriate reference materials, such as encyclopedias, world almanacs, and atlases, as a starting point to find some special purpose maps. Then help them brainstorm a list of places to contact to try to collect additional examples of spe- cial purpose maps. Students may contact the local chamber of commerce, local hiking or biking groups, historical societies, and other organizations. As students collect examples of local special purpose maps, create a classroom display titled Maps of Our Region. Have students create a caption for each map in the display that describes its intended purpose. **OL**

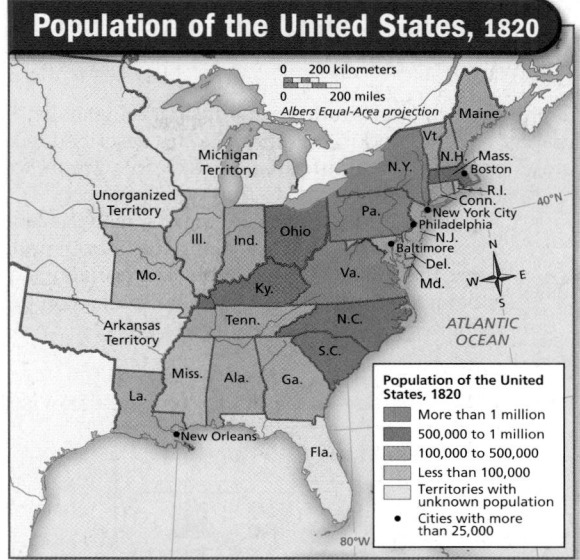

Population Density Maps ▶

Population is not evenly spread across the usable land. Population density is the average number of people that live in a square mile or square kilometer. Population density maps use colors that are explained in a key to indicate how many people live in a given area.

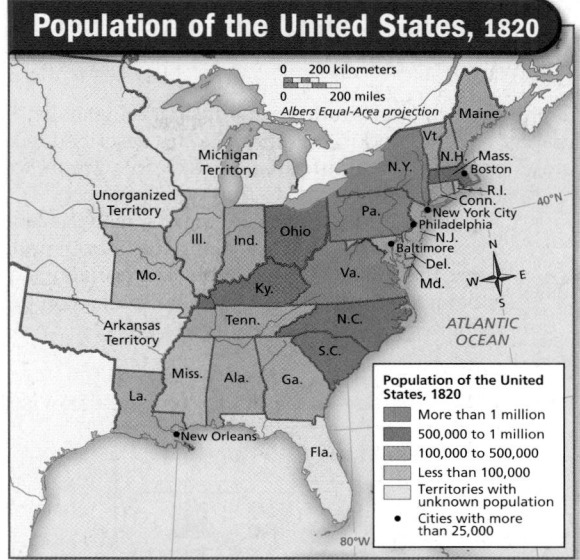

Population of the United States, 1820

0   200 kilometers
0   200 miles
Albers Equal-Area projection

Population of the United States, 1820
- More than 1 million
- 500,000 to 1 million
- 100,000 to 500,000
- Less than 100,000
- Territories with unknown population
- • Cities with more than 25,000

The Battle of Gettysburg, Day 3

- Confederate troops
- Union troops
- ← Confederate troop movements

0   1 kilometer
0   1 mile
Albers Equal-Area projection

◀ Military Maps

Military maps show the areas where battles occurred, troop movements, who controlled various sites, and who won the battles. Color-coded arrows and symbols shown in the key help you determine the sequence of events. It is also important to notice the geographical features near the battle site and how they could affect military strategy. On larger military maps, battle sites are often symbolized by a burst shell or a star.

Skills Practice

1 **Identifying** What type of special purpose map might show battles during World War II?

2 **Contrasting** What is the difference between a general purpose map and a special purpose map?

Geography Skills Handbook   Ref 27

Teach

Synthesizing Have students create a fill-in-the-blank quiz on types of maps, map features, and geography terms discussed in the Geography Skills Handbook. Their fill-in-the-blank statements should follow this format: The _____ of a map gives you important information about what the map is showing. *(title)* Ask student to write 10 fill-in-the-blank statements. Remind students to create an answer key on a separate sheet of paper. When students have finished the assignment, have them trade with a partner. After partners have completed their quizzes, have them hand the quizzes back to be scored. **ELL**

Answers

1. A historical map would show World War II battles.

2. A general purpose map shows a wide range of information about an area; a special purpose map shows specific topics about an area in detail.

Teach

Analyzing Information Bar graphs, circle graphs, and line graphs are used to compare information visually. **Ask:** What could you learn from the circle graph if the percentages were not included? *(You would not be able to learn exact percentages, but the breakdown still allows you to see the relative size of the immigrant groups during that time period.)* **OL**

Synthesizing Have students select one of the visuals from these two pages and write a paragraph that explains the information in the visual. Follow up with a class discussion on the advantages and disadvantages of both methods of presenting information. **OL**

Additional Support and Answers

Graphs, Charts, and Diagrams

Graphs

Graphs present and summarize information visually. The types of graphs you will find in this textbook are described below. Each part of a graph provides useful information. To read a graph, follow these steps:
- Read the graph's title to find out its subject.
- To understand bar and line graphs, read the labels along the **axes**—the horizontal line along the bottom and the vertical line along the left side of the graph. The horizontal axis tells you what is being measured. The vertical axis tells you the unit of measurement being used.

Bar Graphs ▼

Bar graphs use bars or wide lines to compare data visually.

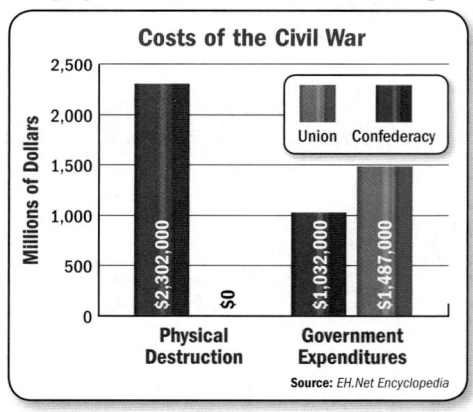

Costs of the Civil War

Source: EH.Net Encyclopedia

Circle Graphs ▼

You can use circle graphs when you want to show how the whole of something is divided into its parts. Because of their shape, circle graphs are often called *pie graphs*. Each slice represents a part or percentage of the whole pie. The complete circle represents a whole group—or 100 percent.

Line Graphs ▼

Line graphs help show changes over a period of time. The amounts being measured are plotted on the grid above each year and then are connected by a line.

Population of Virginia City, Nevada

*Estimate according to various Nevada historical sources.
Source: Nevada State Library and Archives, 2007

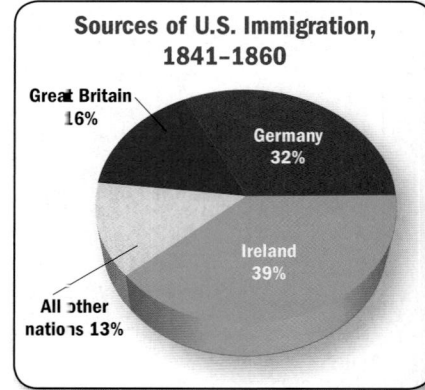

Sources of U.S. Immigration, 1841–1860

Great Britain 16%
Germany 32%
Ireland 39%
All other nations 13%

Activity: Using Graphs, Charts, and Diagrams

Speculating Ask: What types of graphs, charts, and diagrams do you think might be most commonly used in this textbook? *(Answers will vary.)* Create a chart on the board with the following across the top: Bar Graph, Circle Graph, Line Graph, Chart, Diagram. Have students copy the chart into their notebooks. Assign each student a chapter of the textbook, and have them write the title of each chart, graph, or diagram they find in the chapter in the appropriate column. When students have finished, create a tally of the numbers of each type of graphic that they found, using the chart on the board. Discuss with students the types of information that tend to be presented in each type of graph and in charts and diagrams. Finally, have students suggest what type of graph would best present the information in your chart. **OL**

Charts

Charts present related facts and numbers in an organized way. One type of chart is a table. A table arranges data, especially numbers, in rows and columns for easy reference. Charts can also be used to summarize ideas or main points of broader topics. This allows you to review material and compare main ideas easily.

Army Salaries (monthly)

Rank	Civil War	World War II 1942	Vietnam War 1965	Iraq War 2007
Private	*$13	$50	$85	$1203 – 1543.20
Corporal	$14	$66	$210	$1699.50
Sergeant	$17	$78	$261	$1854 – 2339.10
Sergeant Major	$21	$138	$486	$4110

*Until 1864, African Americans in the Civil War were paid only $7.00 per month.

Source: *Bureau of Economic Analysis*; Princeton Review; www.militaryfactory.com

Diagrams

Diagrams are drawings that show steps in a process, point out the parts of an object, or explain how something works.

The USS *Maine*

1 Torpedo tubes are devices to launch torpedoes.
2 Steam boilers power the engines.
3 Munitions were stored in the magazine.
4 Cowls provided fresh air below deck.

Skills Practice

1 Identifying What percentage does the whole circle in a circle graph represent?

2 Analyzing Information What type of graph would best show the number of Republicans and Democrats in the U.S. House of Representatives?

Geography Skills Handbook   Ref 29

Teach

Kinesthetic Have students use clay to make a model landscape showing some of the features described on these pages. Suggest that students paint the model after the clay dries to make it look more realistic. **BL**

Verbal/Linguistic The terms geographers use to describe the Earth come from many different languages. To illustrate this, have students locate the term *mesa*. Point out that geographers use the Spanish word, which means "table," to describe flat-topped, steep-sided hills. Other foreign terms American geographers use include *tsunami*, a Japanese word meaning "overflowing wave," and *fjord*, a Norwegian word meaning "long, narrow bay." **ELL**

Additional Support

Geographic Dictionary

As you read about the history of the United States, you will encounter the terms listed below. Many of the terms are pictured in the diagram.

absolute location exact location of a place on the Earth described by global coordinates

basin area of land drained by a given river and its branches; area of land surrounded by lands of higher elevations

bay part of a large body of water that extends into a shoreline, generally smaller than a gulf

canyon deep and narrow valley with steep walls

cape point of land that extends into a river, lake, or ocean

channel wide strait or waterway between two landmasses that lie close to each other; deep part of a river or other waterway

cliff steep, high wall of rock, earth, or ice

continent one of the seven large landmasses on the Earth

cultural feature characteristic that humans have created in a place, such as language, religion, housing, and settlement pattern

delta flat, low-lying land built up from soil carried downstream by a river and deposited at its mouth

divide stretch of high land that separates river systems

downstream direction in which a river or stream flows from its source to its mouth

elevation height of land above sea level

Equator imaginary line that runs around the Earth halfway between the North and South Poles; used as the starting point to measure degrees of north and south latitude

glacier large, thick body of slowly moving ice

gulf part of a large body of water that extends into a shoreline, generally larger and more deeply indented than a bay

harbor a sheltered place along a shoreline where ships can anchor safely

highland elevated land area such as a hill, mountain, or plateau

hill elevated land with sloping sides and rounded summit; generally smaller than a mountain

island land area, smaller than a continent, completely surrounded by water

isthmus narrow stretch of land connecting two larger land areas

lake a large inland body of water

latitude distance north or south of the Equator, measured in degrees

longitude distance east or west of the Prime Meridian, measured in degrees

lowland land, usually level, at a low elevation

map drawing of the Earth shown on a flat surface

meridian one of many lines on the global grid running from the North Pole to the South Pole; used to measure degrees of longitude

Ref 30 Geography Skills Handbook

Activity: Cooperative Learning Activity

Map Quiz Organize the class into two teams. Provide one team with a U.S. map and the other team with a map of your state. Assign each team the following task: Locate every major body of water in your assigned area. Record your findings, including (1) the name of each major body of water; (2) its relative and absolute location; and (3) the type of feature it is—lake, river, bay, and so on. When each team has completed its task, have them create a map quiz based on their work. The teams should then trade maps and challenge one another with their quizzes. **OL**

Mountain range · Source of river · Channel · Lake · Hills · Mouth of river · River · Downstream · Upstream · Plain · Tributary · Lowland · Basin · Canyon · Desert · Plateau · Highland · Glacier

mesa broad, flat-topped landform with steep sides; smaller than a plateau

mountain land with steep sides that rises sharply (1,000 feet or more) from surrounding land; generally larger and more rugged than a hill

mountain peak pointed top of a mountain

mountain range a series of connected mountains

mouth (of a river) place where a stream or river flows into a larger body of water

ocean one of the four major bodies of salt water that surround the continents

ocean current stream of either cold or warm water that moves in a definite direction through an ocean

parallel one of many lines on the global grid that circle the Earth north and south of the Equator; used to measure degrees of latitude

peninsula body of land jutting into a lake or ocean, surrounded on three sides by water

physical feature characteristic of a place occurring naturally, such as a landform, body of water, climate pattern, or resource

plain area of level land, usually at a low elevation and often covered with grasses

plateau large area of flat or rolling land at a high elevation, about 300 to 3,000 feet (90 to 900 m) high

Prime Meridian line of the global grid running from the North Pole to the South Pole at Greenwich, England; starting point for measuring degrees of east and west longitude

relief changes in elevation over a given area of land

river large natural stream of water that runs through land

sea large body of water completely surrounded by land

seacoast land lying next to a sea or ocean

sea level position on land level with surface of nearby ocean or sea

sound body of water between a coastline and one or more islands off the coast

source (of a river) place where a river or stream begins, often in highlands

strait narrow stretch of water joining two larger bodies of water

tributary small river or stream that flows into a larger river or stream; a branch of the river

upstream direction opposite the flow of a river; toward the source of a river or stream

valley area of low land between hills or mountains

volcano mountain created as ash or liquid rock erupts from inside the Earth

Geography Skills Handbook   Ref 31

Assess

Visual/Spatial Provide students with an outline map of the United States and some colored pencils. Have students use a different color to label each of the following: Appalachian Mountains, Great Lakes, Mississippi River, Atlantic Ocean, Pacific Ocean, Rocky Mountains, Great Plains, and the Gulf of Mexico. Have students think about how these features might affect European settlement patterns in North America. **OL**

Close

Drawing Conclusions Discuss how a region's physical geography influences settlement patterns and economic development. **OL**

Activity: Connecting Past and Present

Analyzing Information Have students use atlases and other resources to plan a cross-country trip through the United States. Direct them to choose a definite starting point and destination, and plot the route between the two points. Have them calculate the approximate distance of the journey and how long the journey might take. Students should also list points of interest along the way. Allow time for students to share their itineraries. Discuss how the journey would have been different at various times in America's history, such as in the colonial era, during the expansion into the West, on the transcontinental railroad, and so on. **OL**

UNIT PACING CHART

	Unit 1	Chapter 1	Chapter 2	Chapter 3	Chapter 4
Day 1	Unit Opener, Reading History	Chapter Opener, Section 1	Chapter Opener, Section 1	Chapter Opener, Section 1	Chapter Opener, Section 1
Day 2		Section 2	Section 2	Geography & History, Section 2	TIME Notebook, Section 2
Day 3		Section 3, Visual Summary	Section 3	America's Literature, Section 3	Section 3, Section 4, Visual Summary
Day 4		Chapter Assessment	Section 4, Visual Summary	Section 4, Visual Summary	Chapter Assessment
Day 5			Chapter Assessment	Chapter Assessment	

Teacher to Teacher

Terry Robinson
Alden Middle School
Alden, NY

Creating a Travel Brochure Tell students that they work for a small American advertising company in 1750. Representatives from the English colonies have chosen their company to develop a brochure that encourages people to settle in America. The brochure should highlight interesting facts and features about the New England Colonies, the Middle Colonies, and the Southern Colonies. Provide students with a sheet of 11" x 17" paper. Have them fold the paper to make three columns, one for each region. In each column, students should list:

• the names of the colonies in that region;

• at least two important leaders of the region;

• concise descriptions about the region's climate, resources, and employment opportunities;

• interesting facts to attract settlers.

Students' brochures should be colorfully decorated with an attractive design. You may want to show students examples of travel brochures to help them create their own. Display the brochures throughout the classroom. Have students identify the brochure that appeals to them the most and explain why.

Author Note

Dear American History Teacher,

This unit covers an enormous span of early American history. It will introduce your students to a vast and mostly unknown time period—the story of the first great migrations of peoples into the Americas and the remarkable ancient civilizations they created. Christopher Columbus is often described in the West as the "discoverer" of America, but the America he "discovered" was, in fact, a highly populated world of great diversity and accomplishment.

You will want your students to learn about these "pre-Columbian" civilizations. You will also want students to understand how Europeans explored the Americas and established their own civilizations. In much of the Americas, the encounters between the Europeans and the Native Americans (whom Europeans—not understanding where they were—called "Indians") were catastrophic. Native Americans were subjected to brutal military conquest. More importantly, however, they were exposed to deadly infectious diseases carried to the Americas unknowingly by Europeans. The Spanish and Portuguese conquest of Central and South America was as much a result of great outbreaks of disease as of military prowess.

In the lands that now make up the United States, the early European settlements were smaller and, at least at first, less deadly to the Native Americans living nearby. The civilization that emerged along the eastern coast of North America was substantially European to be sure, but it also absorbed many of the products, customs, and even languages of Native American groups. Settlements varied as a result of the different types of people who migrated to them, as did the climates and available economic resources. The American colonies that eventually became the first states of the United States were ostensibly British. There were people from other places as well, including France, Spain, and the many Africans who were forcibly shipped to America and sold into slavery.

Even in these early years, great differences were emerging among the regions of North America. Substantial contrasts were developing as well between the American colonies and Great Britain. These differences were noticeably more visible as a result of a great imperial war in the middle 1700s that inflamed North America.

Alan Brinkley

Unit Objectives

After studying this unit, students will be able to:

- Explain how people arrived in the Americas, and describe the cultural contributions of the Native Americans.
- Classify the explorers and their areas of exploration, and evaluate the impact of European exploration on Native American culture.
- Describe the founding of the European colonies in America.
- Discuss economic and cultural aspects of colonial life and explain the causes of the French and Indian War.

Introducing the Unit

Speculating As students prepare to study the unit, ask them to think about what life could be like if the British had not colonized America. **Ask:** How would your lives be different if the colonies had been developed by another country or not at all? *(Students could note that we might speak a different language, or that the area that is the United States might have been divided into different countries.)* Discuss with students that they will learn about how the colonies were established and how the new American society developed. **OL**

Unit 1

The Americas: Worlds Meet
Beginnings to 1770

Chapter 1
. . . .
The First Americans
Prehistory to 1492

Chapter 2
. . . .
Exploring the Americas
1400–1625

Chapter 3
. . . .
Colonial America
1587–1770

Chapter 4
. . . .
Growth of the Thirteen Colonies
1607–1770

Walnut carved Pilgrim bowl, 1608

Activity: Why It Matters

Why Study Early Explorers? Tell students that they can expect to learn about explorers who traveled to previously unknown places. **Ask:** Are there any areas that still need to be explored? *(Students might* *answer the ocean depths or outer space.)* As they study this unit, have students write about the benefits of exploring unknown places in their notebooks. **OL**

"All the land so far discovered is a bee-hive of people."

—Bartolomé de Las Casas

The Landing of the Pilgrims by Samuel Bartoll

Connect to Past Learning

The Americas: Worlds Meet Students should have some knowledge of early explorers like Christopher Columbus and early arrivals to the colonies, such as the Pilgrims. In this unit, they will learn about the first immigrants who came to America long before written history. They will learn how the English established colonies in America in the 1600s and 1700s. These colonies eventually gave birth to a distinctly new society and culture.

More About the Image

Visual Literacy Although Plymouth Rock is associated with the Pilgrims, there is no mention in sources from the 1600s of landing on a rock. However, the rock in the painting shows the date, December 22, when the exploring party came ashore at Plymouth. Pilgrims first began to appear in art in the early 1800s as the heroes of the newly independent nation. Artists depicted the landing of the Pilgrims in two ways: some suggested that the land was unoccupied and available for the Pilgrims' use, and others reflected the reality that Native Americans already occupied the land. Notice that in this painting, Native Americans can be seen watching the Pilgrims' arrival.

Why **Identifying the Main Idea** Is Important

Being able to identify the main idea (or the most important idea in a reading) and the supporting details (the facts and examples that explain the main idea) is important for reading comprehension. Breaking progressively more complex readings into smaller pieces will help students' understanding and will, in turn, help them organize their writing.

Learn It!

Copy several articles from *USA Today* or your local newspaper and bring them to class.

Divide students into groups of three or four, and distribute one article to each group. Ask that each group select one "secretary" to write down its findings and one "presenter"; then give groups a set amount of time to review their articles and identify the main idea and at least two supporting ideas. When time is up, ask each presenter to share the group's results with the class.

Use the exercise to show a real-world application of how determining the main idea and supporting details can make any reading less intimidating. **OL**

Practice It!

A main idea and two supporting details are given in the paragraph. Students should list the following:

Main Idea: Most people in New England lived in well-organized towns.

Supporting Detail: The meetinghouse, in the town's center, was used for church services and town meetings.

Supporting Detail: Cows grazed and the citizen army trained on a piece of land called the *green* or *common*. **OL**

Reading History

READING SKILL **Identifying the Main Idea**

Learn It!

Main ideas are the most important ideas in a paragraph, section, or chapter. Facts and examples that explain the main idea are the supporting details.

> **Main Idea**
> Maya traders transported goods along Mexico's coast.
>
> **Supporting Detail**
> The Maya traded many goods.
>
> **Supporting Detail**
> The traders visited a large area.

> —*from Chapter 1, p. 12*
> Maya traders also transported goods up and down Mexico's east coast. Their canoes carried jade statues, turquoise jewelry, cacao beans for making chocolate, and other goods to traders throughout a large area.

Practice It!

Read the paragraph and write the main idea and details on another sheet of paper.

> —*from Chapter 4, p. 89*
> Most people in New England lived in well-organized towns. The meetinghouse stood in the center of the town. This building was used for both church services and town meetings. The meetinghouse faced a piece of land called the *green* or *common*. Here cows grazed and the citizen army trained. Farmers lived in the town and worked in fields on its outskirts.

> **Main Idea**
> _____
>
> **Supporting Detail**
> _____
> _____
>
> **Supporting Detail**
> _____
> _____

2 **Unit 1** *The Americas: Worlds Meet*

Reading Strategy **Determining Importance**

Identifying the Main Idea Learning to determine the importance of ideas presented in paragraphs, sections, and chapters is vital to students' understanding of the material and their success in studying and writing for years to come. Assign students a subsection in one of the chapters in this unit, and have them identify the main idea and supporting details for each paragraph and then for the section as a whole. Discuss strategies for finding the main idea, such as looking in the first or last sentence of the paragraph. **BL**

Academic Vocabulary Preview

Listed below are the academic vocabulary words and their definitions that you will come across as you study Unit 1. Practice It! will help you study the words and definitions.

Academic Vocabulary	Definition	Practice It!
Chapter 1 The First Americans		
source (SAWRS) *p. 8*	to supply	**Identify** *the term from Chapter 1 that best completes the sentences.* **1.** Ancient civilizations created _____ systems for communication. **2.** Scientific measures can provide an _____ on the age of artifacts. **3.** The Inca built paved roads to _____ outposts of their empire.
estimate (EHS · tuh · muht) *p. 9*	approximate number	
complex (KAHM · PLEHKS) *p. 11*	complicated; highly detailed	
link (LIHNK) *p. 13*	to join or connect	
channel (CHA · nuhl) *p. 17*	a trench	
structure (STRUHK · chuhr) *p. 17*	a building	
Chapter 2 Exploring the Americas		
acquire (uh · KWYUHR) *p. 31*	to come into possession of	**Identify** *the term from Chapter 2 that best matches the underlined term or terms.* **4.** Some empires became wealthy after choosing to <u>establish</u> a tax on traded goods. **5.** The <u>planet Earth</u> is divided into two hemispheres. **6.** Europeans sailed to North America to <u>map</u> its coastline.
impose (ihm · POHZ) *p. 32*	to establish or apply by authority	
devote (dih · VOHT) *p. 39*	to give time, money, or effort to a cause	
alter (AWL · tuhr) *p. 40*	to change	
grant (GRANT) *p. 43*	special privilege	
found (FAUND) *p. 46*	to establish or set up	
globe (GLOHB) *p. 51*	the planet Earth	
chart (CHAHRT) *p. 51*	to map	
Chapter 3 Colonial America		

expand (ihk · SPAND) *p. 61*	to increase or grow	**Choose** *the word that best matches the meaning of each vocabulary term from Chapter 3 listed below.*
		
		7. expand
		  a. end
		  b. grow
		  c. give
		
		8. function
		  a. operate
		  b. discuss
		  c. provide

policy (PAH · luh · see) *p. 68*	a plan of action	
ethnic (EHTH · nihk) *p. 74*	sharing a common culture	
function (FUHNK · shuhn) *p. 75*	to operate	
estate (ih · STAYT) *p. 77*	a piece of land	
Chapter 4 Growth of the Thirteen Colonies		
rely (rih · LY) *p. 89*	to depend on	**Choose** *terms from Chapter 4 to complete the paragraph.* Settlers in New England had to _____ on children to help grow food. In Southern Colonies, tobacco was a _____ crop. Farmers' _____ for success was greater in Southern Colonies due to a milder climate and rich soil.
principal (PRIHN · suh · puhl) *p. 93*	most important	
successor (suhk · SEH · suhr) *p. 99*	one who follows another in order	
convert (kuhn · VUHRT) *p. 105*	to change religious beliefs	
design (dih · ZYN) *p. 106*	to plan	
prospect (PRAH · SPEHKT) *p. 110*	a chance for success	

Academic Vocabulary Preview

Before students begin the Practice It! activities, ask them to say each word aloud as a class. Remind students to use the phonetic spellings next to the words to help them say the words.

To further help students remember the definitions of the words, have them find the words in the unit. Students should read the sentences where they are found and try to use context clues to develop their own definition. Then, students should compare their definitions with those found in the chart to see if they are accurate. **OL**

Practice It!

Answers
1. complex
2. estimate
3. link
4. impose
5. globe
6. chart
7. b
8. a

Completion: rely, principal, prospect

Reading Strategy   Read to Write

Persuasive Writing In persuasive writing, it is important that the writer's main point be clear and that it be backed up with strong supporting details. The essay as a whole must have a main idea with supporting details but so must each subsection, or paragraph, of the essay. Have students choose an issue in this unit about which they have an opinion (*"I am for..."* or *"I am against..."*). In preparing their persuasive writing, have students first create an outline breaking down the writing as a whole and then each paragraph into a main point and two or three details to support that point. **OL**

Chapter Planning Guide

Key to Ability Levels
BL Below level   **AL** Above level
OL On level   **ELL** English Language Learners

Key to Teaching Resources
Print Material   DVD
CD-ROM   Transparency

BL	OL	AL	ELL		Resources	Chapter Opener	Section 1	Section 2	Section 3	Chapter Assess
					FOCUS					
BL	OL	AL	ELL	🖨	Daily Test Practice Transparencies		1–1	1–2	1–3	
					TEACH					
	OL	AL		📁	Geography and History Activity, URB				p. 31	
BL	OL		ELL	📁	Time Line Skills Activity, URB			p. 34		
BL	OL	AL	ELL	📁	Writing Skills Activity, URB				p. 23	
BL	OL	AL	ELL	📁	Content Vocabulary Activity, URB		p. 17	p. 17	p. 17	
BL	OL	AL	ELL	📁	Academic Vocabulary Activity, URB		p. 19	p. 19	p. 19	
BL	OL		ELL	📁	Social Studies Skills Activity, URB		p. 25			
BL	OL	AL	ELL	📁	Differentiated Instruction Activity, URB			p. 27		
BL	OL	AL	ELL	📁	Critical Thinking Skills Activity, URB				p. 29	
BL	OL	AL	ELL	📁	Linking Past and Present Activity, URB		p. 33			
	OL	AL		📁	Primary Source Readings, URB			p. 21		
BL	OL	AL	ELL	📁	School-to-Home Connection Activity, URB		p. 35	p. 35	p. 35	
BL	OL		ELL	📁	Guided Reading Activity, URB*		p. 39	p. 40	p. 41	
		AL		📁	Enrichment Activity, URB		p. 11			
BL	OL		ELL	📁	Reading Essentials and Note-Taking Guide*		p. 1	p. 4	p. 7	
BL	OL	AL	ELL	🖨	Lesson Transparencies		1A	1B	1C	
	OL			📁	American Biographies				p. 1	
BL	OL	AL	ELL	📁	Outline Map Resource Book	pp. 31, 33				
	OL	AL		🖨	American Art and Architecture Transparencies, Strategies, and Activities				1 2	

Note: Please refer to the *Unit Resource Book: The Americas: Worlds Meet* for this chapter's materials.

* Also available in Spanish

Levels					Resources	Chapter Opener	Section 1	Section 2	Section 3	Chapter Assess
BL	OL	AL	ELL		**TEACH** *(continued)*					
BL	OL	AL	ELL	📁	**NGS US Desk Map**		✓	✓	✓	
BL	OL	AL	ELL	📁	**American Literature Library**		✓	✓	✓	
BL	OL	AL	ELL	📁	**Writer's Guidebook**		✓	✓	✓	
	OL	AL		💿	**American History Primary Source Document Library CD-ROM**		✓	✓	✓	✓
BL	OL	AL	ELL	💿	**American Music Hits Through History**	✓	✓	✓	✓	
BL	OL	AL	ELL	💿	**StudentWorks™ Plus CD**	✓	✓	✓	✓	✓
	OL	AL		🎒	**Section Spotlight Videos**		✓	✓	✓	
BL	OL	AL	ELL	📽	**Writing Process Transparencies**		✓	✓	✓	✓
BL	OL	AL	ELL	💿	**Presentation Plus! With MindJogger CheckPoint CD**	✓	✓	✓	✓	✓
BL	OL	AL	ELL		**ASSESS**					
BL	OL	AL	ELL	📁	**Quizzes and Tests**		p. 1	p. 2	p. 3	pp. 5, 7, 9
BL	OL	AL	ELL	📁	**Authentic Assessment With Rubrics**		p. 1			
BL	OL	AL	ELL	📁	**Standardized Test Practice**					p. 1
BL	OL	AL	ELL	💿	***ExamView® Assessment Suite* CD-ROM***		1–1	1–2	1–3	Ch. 1
BL	OL	AL	ELL		**CLOSE**					
BL			ELL	📁	**Reteaching Activity, URB***		p. 37	p. 37	p. 37	p. 37
BL	OL		ELL	📁	**Reading and Study Skills Foldables® Activity**	p. 50	p. 50	p. 50	p. 50	p. 50
BL	OL	AL	ELL	📁	***The American Journey* in Graphic Novel**					p. 1
BL			ELL	📁	**Reading Strategies and Activities for the Social Studies Classroom**		✓	✓	✓	
BL	OL	AL	ELL	📽	**Graphic Organizer Transparencies & Strategies**		✓	✓	✓	

TeacherWorks ^{Plus}
All-In-One Planner and Resource Center

- Interactive Lesson Planner
- Interactive Teacher Edition
- Fully editable blackline masters
- Section Spotlight Videos Launch
- Differentiated Lesson Plans
- Printable reports of daily assignments
- Standards Tracking System

Professional Development Resources

- Strategies for Success
- Building Academic Vocabulary
- Success With English Learners DVD
- Differentiated Instruction Strategies DVD
- Teaching Literacy Strategies in Social Studies DVD
- Assessment DVD
- Standards-Based Instruction DVD

1

Online Crossword Puzzles

Using PuzzleMaker™ 3.1

Technology Product

Glencoe's Vocabulary PuzzleMaker™ 3.1 lets you create your own puzzles based on the glossary for classroom use. The PuzzleMaker allows you to

- create crossword puzzles based on vocabulary that is specific to what is taught in the classroom;
- create online (LAN-based, or local area network-based) or paper crossword puzzles.

Objectives

Completing the crossword puzzles helps students to

- recall vocabulary terms based on puzzle clues;
- reinforce their understanding of the vocabulary.

Steps

- Download, install, and run PuzzleMaker™ 3.1 from glencoe.com. Click on **Create a new puzzle.**
- Select the appropriate database.
- The *PuzzleMaker Wizard* will help you select a puzzle type and grid type.
- Make selections from the list. Indicate whether you want the words selected randomly or manually.
- Select the language and words you wish to use for the puzzle. Click **Finish.**
- Save your puzzle with PuzzlePlayer™ 3.1, or print copies for your students to complete.
- Use PuzzlePlayer™ 3.1 to review the puzzles.

History ONLINE at glencoe.com

	Student	Teacher	Parent
Media Center			
• Student Edition Audio	●		
• Spanish Summaries	●		
• Section Spotlight Videos	●	●	
Social Studies Online Learning Center			
Classroom Tools			
• Multi-Language Glossaries	●	●	●
• Teaching Today		●	
• TIME Current Events	●	●	●
• Beyond the Textbook	●	●	
***The American Journey* Online Learning Center**			
• Study-to-Go™	●	●	●
• Study Central™	●	●	●
• Chapter Overview	●	●	
• Concepts in Motion	●	●	
• ePuzzles and Games	●	●	
• Literature Connections	●	●	
• Online Student Edition	●	●	●
• Self-Check Quizzes	●	●	●
• Student Web Activities	●	●	
• Vocabulary eFlashcards	●	●	
• Web Activity Lesson Plans	●	●	●
• Vocabulary PuzzleMaker	●	●	●

READING SUPPORT FROM JAMESTOWN EDUCATION

- **Timed Readings Plus in Social Studies** helps students increase their reading rate and fluency while maintaining comprehension. The 400-word passages are similar to those found on state and national assessments.

- **Reading in the Content Area: Social Studies** concentrates on six essential reading skills that help students better comprehend what they read. The book includes 75 high-interest nonfiction passages written at increasing levels of difficulty.

- **Reading Social Studies** includes strategic reading instruction and vocabulary support in Social Studies content for ELLs and native speakers of English.

- **Content Vocabulary Workout** (Grades 6–8) accelerates reading comprehension through focused vocabulary development. Social Studies content vocabulary comes from the glossaries of Glencoe's Middle School Social Studies texts.

www.jamestowneducation.com

NATIONAL GEOGRAPHIC

Index to National Geographic Magazine:

The following articles relate to this chapter:

- *"The Unexpected Canyon,"* Virginia Morell, January 2006.
- *"Pyramid of Death,"* A.R. Williams, October 2006.

National Geographic Society Products

To order the following, call National Geographic at 1-800-368-2728:

National Geographic Atlas of the World (Book)

Access National Geographic's new dynamic MapMachine Web site and other geography resources at:

www.nationalgeographic.com

www.nationalgeographic.com/mapmachine

Reading List Generator CD-ROM / GLENCOE BOOKLINK 3

Use this database to search more than 30,000 titles to create a customized reading list for your students.

- Reading lists can be organized by students' reading level, author, genre, theme, or area of interest.
- The database provides Degrees of Reading Power™ (DRP) and Lexile™ readability scores for all selections.
- A brief summary of each selection is included.

Leveled reading suggestions for this chapter:

For students at a Grade 6 reading level:
- *Ikwa of the Mound-Builder Indians,* by Margaret Zehmer

For students at a Grade 7 reading level:
- *The Charm of the Bear Claw Necklace,* by Margaret Zehmer
- *Heart of a Jaguar,* by Marc Talbert

For students at a Grade 8 reading level:
- *California Indian Days,* by Diana Noonan & Keith Olsen

For students at a Grade 9 reading level:
- *Montezuma and the Fall of the Aztecs,* by Eric A. Kimmel
- *Who Came First?: New Clues to Prehistoric Americans,* by Patricia Lauber

For students at a Grade 10 reading level:
- *The Incas,* by Barbara L. Beck
- *The Maya: Indians of Central America,* by Sonia Bleeker

The following videotape programs are available from Glencoe as supplements to the chapter:

- **The Aztec Empire** (ISBN 0-76-700542-2)
- **The Pueblo Cliffdwellers** (ISBN 0-76-700613-5)
- **The Secret Mounds of Prehistoric America** (ISBN 1-56-501681-5)

To order, call Glencoe at 1-800-334-7344. To find classroom resources to accompany many of these videos, check the following home pages:

A&E Television: www.aetv.com

The History Channel: www.history.com

Chapter Objectives

After studying this chapter, students will be able to:

- Describe how agriculture changed the lives of early people.
- Relate how the early civilizations of Mexico and Central America developed socially, politically, and economically.
- Discuss how the way of life of the Native Americans of North America related to their environment.

Motivating Activity

Comparing and Contrasting Students will learn that civilizations of the early Americas, such as the Maya, developed forms of writing like petroglyphs and hieroglyphics to communicate. These peoples created societies that flourished long before Europeans arrived in the Americas. **Ask:** How do you think writing today compares to writing used by the first Americans? *(Writing today still uses symbols to represent things, ideas, and sounds. However, it is no longer necessary to use pictures; therefore, communication can be easier and faster.)* **Ask:** Can you think of any means of communication today that use pictures? *(Icons are used in computer programs and on cell phone screens. Signs, such as directional signs in airports, also make use of pictures.)* **OL**

Previewing the Essential Questions

As you begin teaching each section, use these questions and activities to help students focus on the Essential Questions.

Chapter 1
The First Americans
Prehistory to 1492

Petroglyphs are carvings or inscriptions on rock. These petroglyphs in southern Utah were created by several cultures.

◄ Maya plaque

Americas		
★ c. 28,000 B.C. Asian hunters enter North America	**★ c. 1500 B.C.** Olmec civilization develops in Mexico	**★ c. A.D. 700** Maya Empire reaches its peak

★ c. A.D. 1000 ★ Leif Eriksson discovers Newfoundland

Prehistory — 900

World	
★ c. 10,000 B.C. Last Ice Age ends	**★ c. 215 B.C.** Great Wall of China built

4   Chapter 1

Section 1

Migration to the Americas Ask: How could farming improve the lives of people who were hunters and gatherers? *(Farming could provide a steady source of food, which could allow people to spend time on other activities.)* Point out to students that in Section 1 they will learn why some early Americans moved from hunting and gathering to farming. **OL**

Section 2

Cities and Empires Ask: What might be necessary for a civilization to develop? *(systems for writing, counting, and tracking time; the ability to produce enough food to support many people; effective transportation and trading systems)* Explain to students that Section 2 discusses the development of the Olmec, Maya, Aztec, and Inca civilizations. **OL**

Section 1: Migration to the Americas
Essential Question How did agriculture change the lives of early people?

Section 2: Cities and Empires
Essential Question How did the early civilizations of Mexico and Central America develop socially, politically, and economically?

Section 3: North American Peoples
Essential Question How was the way of life of the Native Americans of North America related to their environment?

History ONLINE
Chapter Overview Visit glencoe.com and click on **Chapter 1—Chapter Overviews** to preview chapter information.

FOLDABLES Study Organizer

Organizing Information Make this Foldable to help organize what you learn about the first Americans.

Step 1 Fold a sheet of paper in half from side to side.

Step 2 Turn the paper and fold it into thirds. Cut the top layer only to make three equal tabs.

Step 3 Draw and label your Foldable as shown.

Reading and Writing On the front of the Foldable, diagram early migratory routes; label sites of the Mound Builders; show the empires of the Aztec, Inca, and other ancient civilizations; and include other visual information about the people of the Americas.

◀ Aztec serpent ▶

▼ Anasazi mortar, A.D. 1200

Introducing Chapter ★ 1

Time Line Activity

If you have not already done so, have students review the time line. Remind students that "c." represents "circa." This is an abbreviation that identifies that an event occurred around a certain time but not necessarily that specific year. **Ask:** What years are covered in this chapter? What were some of the civilizations that existed in the Americas during that time? *(c. 28,000 B.C.–c. A.D. 1400; Olmec, Maya, Anasazi, Hohokam, Aztec, and Inca civilizations)* Have students refer to the "World" section of the time line to identify civilizations in the rest of the world during the years covered. *(China, Europe, West Africa)*

FOLDABLES Study Organizer Dinah Zike's **Foldables®**
Purpose This Foldable helps students organize visual information about the people of the Americas. The completed Foldable will help them prepare for assessment.

▱ More Foldables activities for this chapter can be found in *Dinah Zike's Reading and Study Skills Foldables.*

History ONLINE
Introduce students to chapter content and key terms by having them access the **Chapter Overview** at glencoe.com.

★ **C. A.D. 1130** Drought strikes Anasazi communities

★ **C. A.D. 1300** Hohokam civilization begins to decline

★ **A.D. 1325** Aztec establish Tenochtitlán

★ **C. A.D. 1400** Inca Empire begins to expand

| 1100 | 1300 | 1500 |

★ **A.D. 1095** The Crusades begin

★ **A.D. 1215** England's King John signs Magna Carta

★ **A.D. 1312** Mansa Mūsā begins rule of West African kingdom of Mali

★ **A.D. 1368** Ming dynasty begins in China

Chapter 1   5

Section ★ 3

North American Peoples Ask: How might climate affect a civilization's way of life? *(Housing, clothing, farming, and hunting would be affected by climate.)* Tell students that Section 3 will explore the ways that Native Americans of North America developed lifestyles that were well suited to their environments. **OL**

Focus

Bellringer
Daily Test Practice Transparency 1–1

Reading Guide
Answers to Graphic:
1. in search of grains and fruit;
2. to hunt animals that were used for food, clothing, weapons, and shelter

Section Spotlight Video

To learn more about the Ice Age land bridge, have students watch the Section Spotlight Video "Early Peoples."

Resource Manager

Essential Question
How did agriculture change the lives of early people?

Reading Guide

Content Vocabulary
archaeology (p. 7)   maize (p. 9)
artifact (p. 7)   carbon dating (p. 9)
nomad (p. 8)   culture (p. 9)
migration (p. 8)

Academic Vocabulary
source (p. 8)   estimate (p. 9)

Key People and Events
Ice Age (p. 7)

Reading Strategy
Taking Notes As you read, identify reasons early peoples migrated from place to place.

Reasons Early Peoples Migrated
1.
2.

ILLINOIS STANDARDS
The American Journey

17.C.3a Explain how human activity is affected by geographic factors.

17.C.3c Analyze how human processes influence settlement patterns including migration and population growth.

Migration to the Americas

American Diary

In 1974 at Meadowcroft, Pennsylvania, archaeologist James Adovasio and his team made an amazing discovery. Digging through soil and rock, they found fire pits, bones, shells, and stone tools. This evidence seemed to show that humans had been living there more than 14,000 years ago. For Adovasio, this "meant that people had been . . . in western Pennsylvania some four thousand years before any human being was supposed to have set foot anywhere in this hemisphere."

—from The First Americans

R Reading Strategies	C Critical Thinking	D Differentiated Instruction	W Writing Support	S Skill Practice
Teacher Edition • Previewing, p. 7	**Teacher Edition** • Analyz. Information, p. 9	**Teacher Edition** • Naturalist, p. 7	**Teacher Edition** • Narrative Writing, p. 8	**Teacher Edition** • Visual Literacy, p. 8
Additional Resources • Guid. Read., URB p. 39 • Content Vocab., URB p. 17 • Academic Vocab., URB p. 19 • Read. Ess., p. 1	**Additional Resources** • Quizzes and Tests, p. 1 • Authentic Assess., p. 1 • Link. Past & Pres., URB p. 33	**Additional Resources** • School-to-Home, URB p. 35 • Reteaching Act., URB p. 37	**Additional Resources** • Enrichment Act., URB p. 11	**Additional Resources** • Daily Test Pract. Transp. 1-1 • Lesson Transp. 1A • Soc. Stud. Skills, URB p. 25

The Journey From Asia

Main Idea The first Americans were hunters and gatherers who came from Asia and spread throughout the Americas.

History and You Do you know if any prehistoric mammals, such as giant woolly mammoths or saber-toothed tigers, lived in your area? Read to find out why early peoples migrated to the Americas.

Recent archaeological finds such as those in Meadowcroft suggest that the first Americans arrived thousands of years ago, much earlier than once believed. By A.D. 1500, millions of Native Americans, belonging to more than 2,000 different groups, lived on the two continents of North America and South America.

When Europeans arrived in the Americas in the late 1400s, they found Native Americans living there. The Europeans wondered where these peoples had come from and how they happened to settle in the Americas. Some believed the Native Americans had come from Atlantis, an island that supposedly sank beneath the Atlantic Ocean.

Modern scientists are still trying to determine how the first people came to the Americas. Experts in **archaeology**, the study of ancient peoples, continue to piece together the story of the first Americans.

Archaeologists learn about the past from **artifacts**—the tools, weapons, baskets, and carvings of early peoples. Their discoveries show that many early peoples may have come across a land that later sank into the sea. This land was not the mythical Atlantis, however, but a strip of land called Beringia that once joined Asia and the Americas.

Crossing the Land Bridge

During its long history, Earth has gone through several ice ages. These are periods of extreme cold. Huge ice sheets, or glaciers, formed and covered much of Earth in the ice ages. The most recent **Ice Age** began 100,000 years ago and ended about 12,000 years ago. The lower sea level during this period exposed a strip of land that would have run from Siberia in northeastern Asia to what is now Alaska, the westernmost part of the Americas. That land bridge, Beringia, now lies under the Bering Strait.

If You Were There / Early Toolmakers

A Way to Survive As an early American, you moved from place to place in search of food and shelter. One of your most important advances was creating tools, which made hunting, gathering, building shelter, and making clothing much easier. You may have made tools from bone or antler. Most tools were made from stone. As technology advanced, you began making specific tools, such as food choppers, meat scrapers, and spear points.

Antler or bone tool found at Meadowcroft ▼

◄ Spear point from Meadowcroft

Critical Thinking
Making Inferences Why do you think you would have chosen stones to make tools?

Early Americans left evidence of their culture at Meadowcroft Rockshelter, near Pittsburgh, Pennsylvania.

Social Studies Skills Activity, URB p. 25

Teach

R Reading Strategy

Previewing Have students preview the section by scanning the main headings and the subheadings. **Ask:** What do you think this section will be about? *(migration, farming, and cultures of early Americans, methods used to learn about the past)* **BL**

D Differentiated Instruction

Naturalist Have students research to learn more about archaeology. Ask them to write a report describing the work, tools of the trade, and examples of artifacts archaeologists have discovered. **AL**

If You Were There

Critical Thinking Answer Stones were readily available, durable, and easy to shape.

Skills Practice Ask: Why might early Americans have made tools in different shapes? *(Tools were made to fit tasks, such as points for spears or longer edges for chopping and scraping.)* **OL**

Differentiated Instruction

Reading a Time Line

Objective: To learn how to read a time line to understand the relationships between events

Focus: Ask students why chronological order is important on a time line.

Teach: Have students study the time lines and answer the questions.

Assess: Students should use the self-assessment checklist.

Close: Discuss how a time line allows you to quickly identify when events occurred.

Differentiated Instruction Strategies

BL Direct students to list the major steps in creating a time line.

AL Have students create a time line that shows events of their own lives on the top and events in the U.S. on the bottom.

ELL Ask students to point to the different parts of a time line to identify the following concepts: "time span," "key event," "time interval."

S Skill Practice

Visual Literacy Have students look at the drawing of the hunters and read the sentence. **Ask:** How could early Americans hunt large animals such as mammoths and mastodons? (*Armed with spears, groups of hunters worked together to stalk the herds, charge at the animals, and hurl their weapons.*) **OL**

W Writing Support

Narrative Writing Have students take the role of an early American hunter. Ask them to write a story about the hunt as they would tell it to their families upon their return home. **OL**

Prehistoric Migrations to the Americas

Map Skills Answer
Rocky Mountains, Andes Mountains

Map Skills Practice
Ask: The glacier in North America extended south to about what latitude line? (*40°N*) **OL**

✓ Reading Check **Answer:** Archaeologists study tools, weapons, crafts, and artwork of early peoples in order to learn about the past.

Hands-On Chapter Project
Step 1

Creating a Museum Exhibition

Step 1: Creating a Pictorial Display Groups of students will prepare a display of images about Ice Age migrations and early villages.
Essential Question: How did agriculture change the lives of early people?
Directions Organize students into four groups. Explain that they are archaeologists.

Prehistoric Migrations to the Americas ☐ NATIONAL GEOGRAPHIC

◄ Prehistoric people may have come over the Bering Land Bridge. But they might also have arrived by boat, sailing along the eastern and western coasts of the Americas.

◄ Hunters learned to work together to bring down large animals.

Map Skills

Movement Along what major mountain ranges did the migration routes flow?

Searching for Hunting Grounds

The early Americans were **nomads**, people who moved from place to place. They ate grains and fruits but depended on hunting for much of their food. While on a hunt, they crossed Beringia into what is now Alaska and Canada.

The crossing of the land bridge was a **migration**, a movement of a large number of people into a new homeland. As the centuries passed, many people traveled from Asia either on foot across the land bridge or in boats. They spread out across the Americas, going as far east as the Atlantic Ocean and as far south as the tip of South America.

Hunting for Food

Native American legends tell of giant beasts that roamed Earth in ancient times. When the first Americans arrived from Asia, they did indeed find huge mammals. There were the saber-toothed tiger, the woolly mammoth, and the mastodon. The mammoth and mastodon resembled modern elephants in shape but had shaggy fur and long tusks.

Early Americans were skilled at hunting these beasts. Armed with spears, bands of hunters stalked herds of bison, mastodons, or mammoths and then charged at the animals, hurling their weapons. A single mammoth provided tons of meat, enough to feed a group of people for months. The hunters and their families used every part of the animal. They made the skin into clothing, carved the bones into weapons and tools, and may have used the long ribs to build shelters.

About 15,000 years ago, the Earth's temperatures began to rise. As the great glaciers melted and the oceans rose, Beringia was submerged again. The Americas were cut off from Asia. At the same time, the hunters of America faced a new challenge. The mammoths and other large animals began to die out, either from being overhunted or because of changes in the environment. Early Americans had to find other **sources**, or supplies, of food.

✓ Reading Check **Explaining** How do archaeologists learn about the past?

8 **Chapter 1** *The First Americans*

A museum has asked them to create an exhibition about early American cultures. Assign each group one of these topics: (1) the Ice Age, (2) hunting, (3) farming, (4) early villages. Instruct students to do research about their group's topic. They should collect facts, pictures, maps, and diagrams. Together, the group should discuss the research and decide what images to include in a display. Group members should prepare the images for display and include informative captions. Have the groups assemble their displays in the classroom. Explain that they will add displays to the exhibition in the next two sections.
Determining Cause and Effect As a class, discuss how the lives of early people changed over time. **Ask:** What factors contributed to these changes? **OL**
(Chapter Project continued in Section 2)

Settling Down

Main Idea Agriculture changed the way of life for early Americans.

History and You Think about the crops grown in your state or region. Read to find out about the foods that early Americans learned to grow.

. . . .

As the large animals disappeared, early Americans turned to other food sources. They hunted smaller game, caught fish, and gathered berries and grains. They also began to farm.

Planting Seeds and Farming

About 9,000 years ago, people living in what is now Mexico learned to plant and raise **maize,** an early form of corn. They also planted pumpkins, beans, and squash. Their harvests provided a steady, reliable source of food, so they no longer had to move from place to place. Farming also allowed people to spend time on activities other than finding food. This resulted in an improvement in the lives of early Americans.

Establishing Unique Cultures

Some early Americans remained nomadic hunters. Many others, however, knowing they would have a reliable food supply, began to settle down. Scientists have discovered villages that date from about 5,000 years ago. Using a method called **carbon dating,** scientists can measure the amount of radioactive carbon in an artifact made from bone or wood or another substance that was once alive. The amount of carbon provides an **estimate,** or approximate number, of the artifact's age.

The early Americans who settled down built permanent shelters from clay, stone, or wood. They made pottery and cloth. By studying and dating artifacts from these villages, scientists know that agriculture changed the lives of early Americans. These early Americans also developed common customs and beliefs. Over time, the groups of people living in the Americas developed their own **cultures,** or ways of life. **C**

✔**Reading Check** **Explaining** What is carbon dating? How does it work?

C Critical Thinking

Analyzing Information Ask: What is culture? *(the way of life of a group of people who share similar beliefs and customs)* **Ask:** What are some characteristics that people in the same culture group might share? *(Answers may include language, religion, clothing styles, musical forms, celebrations, and types of leisure activities.)* **OL**

✔**Reading Check** **Answer:** a method for estimating an artifact's age; measures amount of radioactive carbon in an artifact made from bone, wood, or other substance that was once alive

Assess

. . . .

History ONLINE

Study Central™ provides summaries, interactive games, and online graphic organizers to help students review content.

Close

. . . .

Discussing As a class, discuss ways that early Americans benefited from having a steady, reliable food source. **OL**

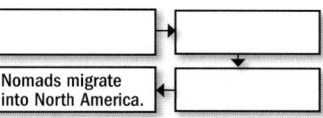
Section 1 Review

History ONLINE
Study Central™ To review this section, go to glencoe.com.

Vocabulary

1. Use each of these terms in a sentence that will help explain its meaning: archaeology, artifact, nomad, migration, source, maize, carbon dating, estimate, culture.

Main Ideas

2. Explaining How did early peoples arrive in the Americas?

3. Describing Describe the changes that early Americans underwent as the large animals disappeared.

Critical Thinking

4. Determining Cause and Effect How do you think the first Americans discovered that they could grow their own plants?

5. Sequencing Use a diagram like the one below to describe the sequence of events that resulted in the migration of nomads into North America from Asia.

```
┌──────────┐     ┌──────────┐
│          │ ──→ │          │
└──────────┘     └──────────┘
                      │
                      ↓
┌──────────────────┐ ┌──────────┐
│ Nomads migrate   │←│          │
│ into North       │ └──────────┘
│ America.         │
└──────────────────┘
```

6. Expository Writing Write a short essay describing the elements of culture of the early Americans and the elements of culture for American society today.

Answer the
7. Essential Question
How did agriculture change the lives of early people?

The First Americans **Chapter 1** 9

Section 1 Review

Answers

1. Sentences should use vocabulary words as they are defined in the section and Glossary.

2. Early peoples may have arrived in the Americas by crossing the land bridge at Beringia or by boat.

3. As the large animals disappeared, early Americans hunted smaller animals, fished, and gathered berries and grains. They also began to farm crops, such as maize, beans, and squash. Farming allowed villages and cultures to develop.

4. Answers should refer to observations and experiments early Americans must have made.

5. Ice Age begins > sea level drops > Beringia land bridge exposed

6. Essays should discuss how early peoples settled down into villages with permanent shelters, allowing the development of cultures, and then compare that with American culture today.

7. The earliest Americans came in search of animals to hunt. As the large animals disappeared, hunting was replaced by farming. Agriculture provided a reliable food source, allowing people to settle down into permanent communities. They were able to improve their lives because they could spend time on activities other than finding food. Over time, they developed their own cultures.

Section 2

Focus

Bellringer
Daily Test Practice Transparency 1–2

Reading Guide
Answers to Graphic:
Olmec: produced enough food to sustain cities, sculpted large stone monuments, built stone pavements and drainage systems; **Maya:** built large cities and stone pyramids; developed a calendar, hieroglyphic writing, and a number system; developed trade routes; **Aztec:** built Tenochtitlán on an island in a lake; built a large empire

Section Spotlight Video

To learn more about the Maya, watch the Section Spotlight Video "Cities and Empires."

Resource Manager

Essential Question
How did the early civilizations of Mexico and Central America develop socially, politically, and economically?

Reading Guide

Content Vocabulary

civilization (p. 11)	Quechua (p. 15)
theocracy (p. 12)	quipu (p. 15)
hieroglyphics (p. 12)	terrace (p. 15)

Academic Vocabulary

complex (p. 11)	link (p. 13)

Key People and Events
Olmec (p. 11)
Maya (p. 11)
Aztec (p. 13)
Inca (p. 14)

Reading Strategy
Taking Notes As you read, summarize the accomplishments of the Olmec, Maya, and Aztec.

ILLINOIS STANDARDS
The American Journey

16.A.3b Make inferences about historical events and eras using historical maps and other historical sources.

18.B.3a Analyze how individuals and groups interact with and within institutions (e.g., educational, military).

Cities and Empires

American Diary

Stories of "lost" cities led American explorer John Lloyd Stephens to southern Mexico in 1840. Stephens followed a steep mountain trail to a flat area covered with trees. Suddenly through openings in the trees, he "saw the front of a large building richly ornamented with . . . figures . . . curious and elegant." Stephens knew this palace had been built by a very advanced people.

—from Incidents of Travel in Central America Chiapas and Yucatán

The Maya built this great palace in the city of Palenque sometime during the A.D. 600s or 700s.

R Reading Strategies	C Critical Thinking	D Differentiated Instruction	W Writing Support	S Skill Practice
Teacher Edition • Deter. Import., p. 11 • Making Connect., p. 12 • Making Connect., p. 13 **Additional Resources** • Guid. Read., URB p. 40 • Cont. Vocab., URB p. 17 • Acad. Vocab., URB p. 19 • Read. Ess., p. 4	**Teacher Edition** • Predict. Consequences, p. 14 **Additional Resources** • Quizzes and Tests, p. 2	**Teacher Edition** • Visual/Spatial, p. 15 **Additional Resources** • Differ. Inst., URB p. 27 • School-to-Home, URB p. 35 • Reteaching, URB p. 37	**Teacher Edition** • Expository Writing, p. 12 **Additional Resources** • Pri. Source Read., URB p. 21	**Teacher Edition** • Using Geo. Skills, p. 14 **Additional Resources** • Daily Test Pract. Transp., 1-2 • Lesson Transp. 1B • Time Line Skills, URB p. 34

The Olmec, Maya, and Aztec

Main Idea The Olmec, Maya, and Aztec civilizations of Mexico and Central America flourished long before the arrival of Europeans.

History and You Do you use an electronic calendar to keep organized? Read to find out about the calendars and other accomplishments of early American civilizations.

Stephens had come across the ruins of Palenque (puh•LEHNG•kay), an early Maya city. Although it was small, Palenque was an extraordinary place. Its structures, carved from the gray granite of the mountaintop, were wonders of design and craftsmanship.

Long before the Europeans arrived in the early 1500s, several great **civilizations,** or highly developed societies, arose in what is now Mexico and Central America. These civilizations built enormous cities in thick jungles and on mountaintops that were hard to reach. They also developed **complex,** or highly detailed, systems for writing, counting, and tracking time.

Among the largest and most advanced of these early civilizations were the Olmec, the Maya, and the Aztec. Each of these civilizations spread out over hundreds of miles, included millions of people, and thrived for several centuries.

The Olmec

The **Olmec** flourished between 1500 B.C. and 300 B.C. along the Gulf Coast of what are now Mexico, Guatemala, and Honduras. Olmec farmers produced enough food to sustain cities containing thousands of people. Olmec workers sculpted large stone monuments and built stone pavements and drainage systems. For reasons not fully understood, the Olmec civilization declined and then collapsed.

The Maya

The **Maya** built their civilization in the steamy rain forests of present-day Mexico, Guatemala, Honduras, and Belize. They planted maize, beans, sweet potatoes, and other vegetables to feed their large population, which may have reached 2 million people.

By the Numbers / Maya Mathematics

0	1	2	3	4
5	6	7	8	9
10	11	12	13	14
15	16	17	18	19

Number System The Maya used a system of dots and bars to represent their system of numbers. A dot represented a value of one, and a bar represented five. A shell-like figure stood for zero. To add two numbers together, the symbols for each number were combined to make a new single number.

$$5 + 6 = 11$$

Critical Thinking

Inferring What does a sophisticated counting system reveal about the interests of the Maya?

Primary Source Reading Activity, URB p. 21

Teach

R Reading Strategy

Determining Importance Ask: Why would a system of writing be important to a civilization? *(It provides a way to transfer knowledge between people and to future generations; it is more precise than oral communication which can change as it is spoken from person to person.)* **OL**

By the Numbers

Critical Thinking Answer Students might suggest that the Maya wanted written records to track time or measure quantities of goods or supplies.

Skills Practice Ask students to write their ages and birth dates using Maya symbols. Have a few students write simple math equations on the board using the symbols and solve them as a class. **OL**

Differentiated Instruction

Native American Prophecies

Objective: To analyze Maya and Aztec sources and make inferences about what they prophesied

Focus: Ask students if they have ever wished they could predict the future.

Teach: Have students read the chant and song and decide what is being predicted.

Assess: Request that students point out specific words in the song and chant that indicate certain images.

Close: Discuss whether students think that the Native Americans' prophecies came true.

Differentiated Instruction Strategies

BL Have students discuss favorite songs or poems and what they mean.

AL Tell students to research the role of belief in the supernatural in Native American religions and prepare a presentation for the class.

ELL Ask students to explain in their own words what "prophecy" means.

W Writing Support

Expository Writing Have students research to learn more about Maya pyramids and temples. Ask them to write a report that explains how they were built and what their purpose was. Students should conclude by describing the role of the remains of these structures in Central America's tourism industry today. **AL**

W Writing Support

Expository Writing Have students research to learn more about Maya pyramids and temples. Ask them to write a report that explains how they were built and what their purpose was. Students should conclude by describing the role of the remains of these structures in Central America's tourism industry today. **AL**

R Reading Strategy

Making Connections Have students find the physical map of Mexico and Central America in the Reference Atlas. Ask them to describe the land's elevation that made it difficult for Maya traders to transport their goods over long distances on land *(Students should describe the land as mountainous.)* **OL**

History ONLINE

Objectives and answers to the Student Web Activity can be found at glencoe.com under the Web Activity Lesson Plan for this chapter.

Additional Support

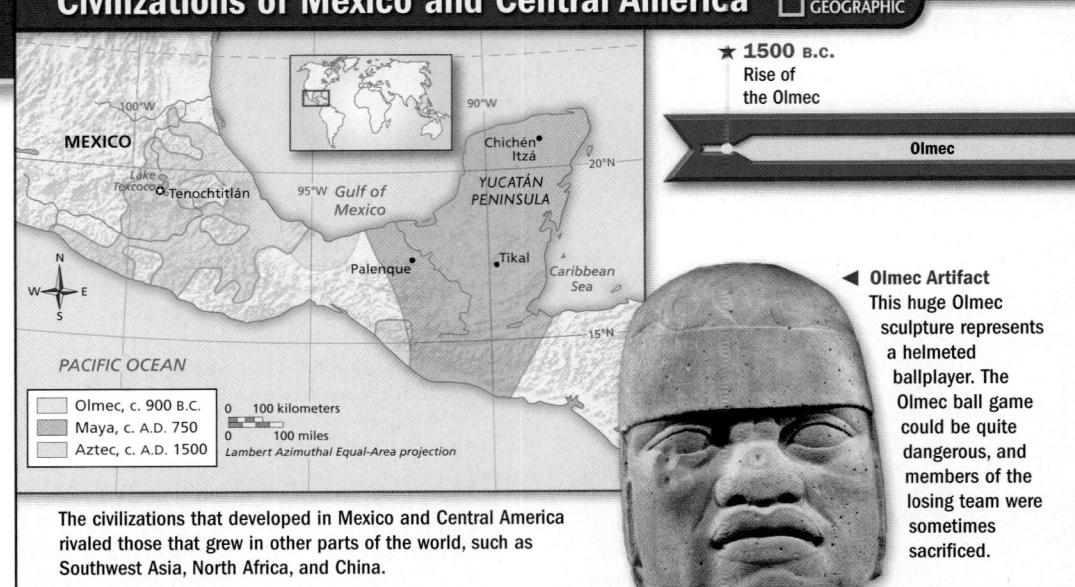

Civilizations of Mexico and Central America NATIONAL GEOGRAPHIC

★ **1500 B.C.** Rise of the Olmec

Olmec

◀ **Olmec Artifact** This huge Olmec sculpture represents a helmeted ballplayer. The Olmec ball game could be quite dangerous, and members of the losing team were sometimes sacrificed.

The civilizations that developed in Mexico and Central America rivaled those that grew in other parts of the world, such as Southwest Asia, North Africa, and China.

By A.D. 300, the Maya had built many large cities in the area. Each city had at least one stone pyramid. Some pyramids reached about 200 feet (61 m)—the height of a 20-story building. Steps ran up the pyramid sides to a temple on top.

The temples on top of the pyramids were religious and governmental centers. Here, priests performed rituals dedicated to the Maya gods. The Maya believed the gods controlled everything that happened on Earth. Because only priests knew the gods' wishes, the priests held great power in Maya society. Maya civilization was a **theocracy,** a society ruled by religious leaders.

Maya priests believed that the gods were visible in the stars, sun, and moon. They used their knowledge of astronomy to predict eclipses and to develop a 365-day calendar. Their desire to measure time increased their knowledge of mathematics. The Maya also developed a form of writing called **hieroglyphics.** Hieroglyphics uses symbols or pictures to represent things, ideas, and sounds.

Maya Transport and Trade

The Maya did not have wheeled vehicles or horses and carried goods overland on their backs. Maya traders traveled on a network of roads that were carved out of the jungle. Farmers brought maize and vegetables to outdoor markets in the cities and traded for cotton cloth, pottery, deer meat, and salt.

Maya traders also transported goods up and down Mexico's east coast. Their canoes carried jade statues, turquoise jewelry, cacao beans for making chocolate, and other goods to traders throughout a large area.

Decline of the Maya

Around A.D. 900, the Maya civilization in the lowlands began to decline. By 1100, the great cities were almost ghost towns. No one knows what caused the decline. Perhaps the soil became too exhausted by erosion and fire to produce enough food for the people.

History ONLINE

Student Web Activity Visit glencoe.com and complete the Chapter 1 Web Activity about the Maya.

Activity: Collaborative Learning

Verbal/Linguistic Maya hieroglyphic writing was complex. It used pictures of real objects and symbols to represent words and sounds. The Maya wrote books on paper made from tree bark that were folded like an accordion. Organize students into small groups. Instruct each group to create its own language system using pictures and symbols. Then ask the groups to use their writing systems to create brief stories folded into accordion books. When finished, the groups should trade their systems and books with another group. Students should work with their groups to decode the stories and then read the stories to the class. **OL**

★ 300 B.C.

★ A.D. 300
Maya build
large cities

★ 1100
Maya cities
abandoned

★ 1325
Aztec establish
Tenochtitlán

★ 1521
Spanish conquer Aztec

Maya

Aztec

Aztec Calendar The Aztec
calendar stone used
pictures to measure
days and months. ▶

◀ Maya Writing Maya
hieroglyphic writing
was the only true
system of writing
developed in the
Americas before
the 1400s.

DBQ Document-Based Questions

Speculating Choose one of these pictures.
Describe the image, and explain what you think
was its purpose.

The Maya civilization collapsed, but descendants of the Maya still live in parts of Mexico and Central America today.

The Aztec

Centuries after the fall of the Maya, a group of hunters called the **Aztec** wandered through central Mexico, searching for a permanent home. In 1325 they came upon an island in Lake Texcoco (tehs•KOH•koh), today part of Mexico City. There the Aztec saw a sign: an eagle with a snake in its beak sitting on a cactus. According to Aztec legend, this sign from their god meant their journey had ended and that this island was to be their home.

Tenochtitlán

On this island emerged Tenochtitlán (tay•NAWCH•teet•LAHN), one of the greatest cities in the Americas. Its construction was a miracle of engineering and human labor. Directed by priests and nobles, workers toiled day and night. They pulled soil from the bottom of the lake to make causeways, or bridges

of earth, **linking**—or connecting—the island and the shore. They filled parts of the lake with earth so they could grow crops.

In time the Aztec capital expanded to the mainland around the lake. At its height Tenochtitlán was the largest city in the Americas and one of the largest in the world. Tenochtitlán was also a center of trade, attracting thousands of merchants to its outdoor marketplaces.

Aztec War and Religion

The Aztec civilization grew into a military empire. In the 1400s, the Aztec army marched through central and southern Mexico, conquering nearly all rival communities. Conquered people were forced to work as slaves in Aztec cities and villages.

Like the Maya, the Aztec organized their society around their religion. The Aztec believed that human sacrifices were necessary to keep the gods pleased and to ensure abundant harvests. They made sacrifices of thousands of prisoners of war.

The First Americans **Chapter 1** **13**

R Reading Strategy

Making Connections A sign is something that conveys meaning and may include an object, a mark, or even a gesture. Like the Aztec, we interpret the meaning of signs. (Put your hand up, palm toward the class.) **Ask:** What meaning do you get from this sign? *(stop)* **BL**

DBQ Document-Based Questions

Answer
Olmec artifact: fierce appearance and helmet suggest reverence for athletic feats; **Mayan writing:** spear and dead animal suggest story about successful hunt; **Aztec calendar stone:** round shape suggests a way to track the repeating cycle of days and months

**Differentiated
Instruction**

Leveled Activities

**BL Guided Reading Activity,
URB p. 40**

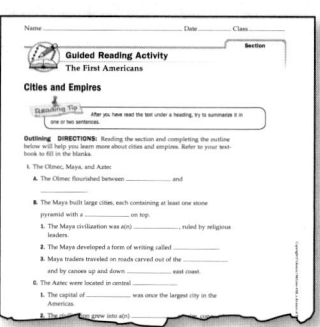

**OL Time Line Skills Activity,
URB p. 34**

ELL Reading Essentials, p. 4

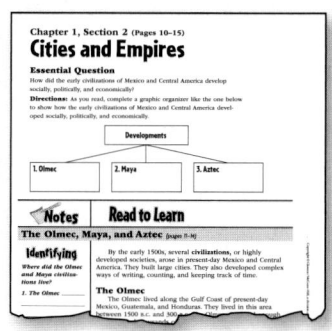

The Inca Empire ☐ NATIONAL GEOGRAPHIC

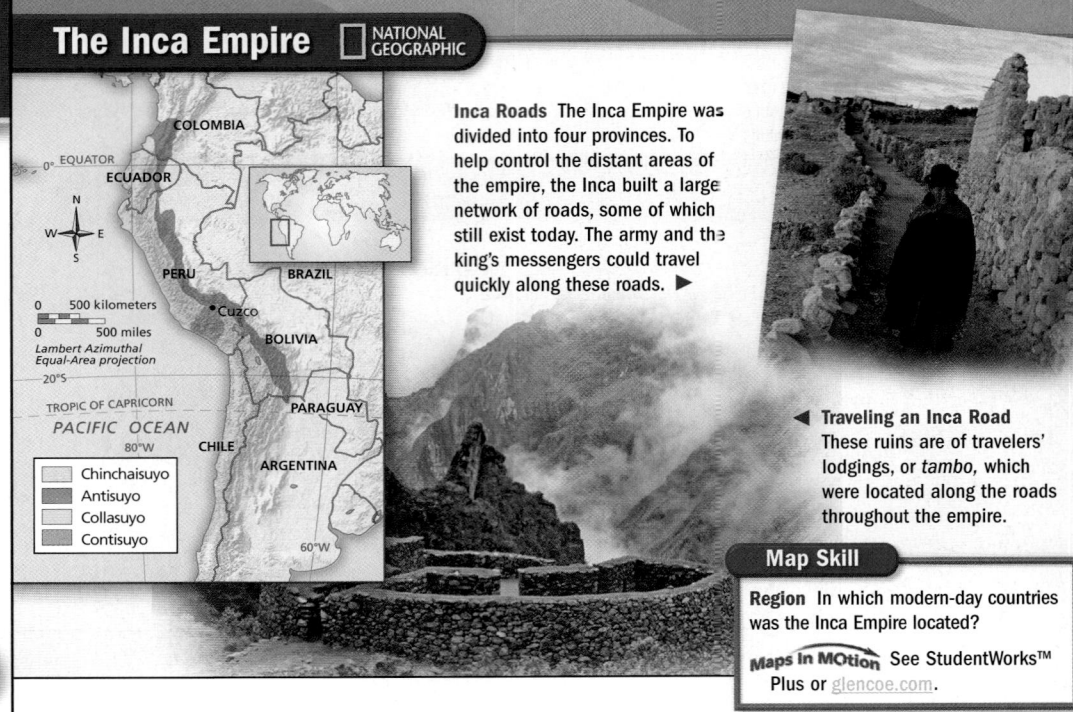

Inca Roads The Inca Empire was divided into four provinces. To help control the distant areas of the empire, the Inca built a large network of roads, some of which still exist today. The army and the king's messengers could travel quickly along these roads. ▶

COLOMBIA
0° EQUATOR
ECUADOR
PERU
•Cuzco
BRAZIL
BOLIVIA
PARAGUAY
TROPIC OF CAPRICORN
PACIFIC OCEAN
80°W
CHILE
ARGENTINA
0   500 kilometers
0   500 miles
Lambert Azimuthal
Equal-Area projection
20°S
60°W

Chinchaisuyo
Antisuyo
Collasuyo
Contisuyo

◀ Traveling an Inca Road These ruins are of travelers' lodgings, or *tambo*, which were located along the roads throughout the empire.

Map Skill

Region In which modern-day countries was the Inca Empire located?

Maps in MOtion See StudentWorks™ Plus or glencoe.com.

S Skill Practice

Using Geography Skills Using the world map in the Reference Atlas, have students locate and identify Rome, Italy. **BL**

C Critical Thinking

Predicting Consequences Ask: What problems might develop in an empire built on conquest? *(Conquered peoples might feel bitter and might revolt or find secret ways to resist conquerors.)* **OL**

The Inca Empire ☐ NATIONAL GEOGRAPHIC

Map Skills Answer

Colombia, Ecuador, Peru, Bolivia, Chile, Argentina

✔Reading Check **Answer:** It was the largest city in the Americas and one of the largest in the world. It was also a center of trade.

Hands-On Chapter Project
Step 2

Creating a Museum Exhibition

Step 2: Making Model Artifacts Students will create models of artifacts from early civilizations.

Essential Question: How did the early civilizations of Mexico and Central

A Great City Remembered

The first Europeans to see the Aztec capital were awed by its splendor. In 1519 Hernán Cortés led 550 Spanish soldiers into Tenochtitlán. Cortés wrote:

PRIMARY SOURCE

"There are forty towers at the least, all of stout construction and very lofty. . . . The workmanship both in wood and stone could not be bettered anywhere."
—Hernán Cortés, *Five Letters*

Bernal Díaz del Castillo, one of the soldiers, marveled at the "great stone towers and temples and buildings that rose straight up out of the water." Tenochtitlán, he explained, was a city of water. Some of the Spanish soldiers thought that Tenochtitlán was more magnificent than Rome and the other great European capitals of the time.

✔Reading Check **Describing** Why was Tenochtitlán important?

The Inca

Main Idea The Inca in South America developed a well-organized empire with a structured society.

History and You How do you keep track of your school records? Read to learn about the Inca's record-keeping system.

. . . .

Another great American civilization developed in the western highlands of South America. The empire of the Inca was the largest of the early American civilizations.

Around 1200, the **Inca** people founded their capital city of Cuzco (KOOS•koh). In 1438 the Inca emperor named Pachacuti (PAH•chah•KOO•tee) came to the throne. Through conquest, Pachacuti and his son, Topa Inca, built a large empire. It stretched from north to south for more than 3,000 miles (4,828 km), from present-day Colombia to northern Argentina and Chile.

America develop socially, politically, and economically?

Directions Assign each group one of the civilizations in this section. Group members should create displays by finding pictures and information about artifacts from their civilization. They should decide which artifacts to include in their display or create

models of the artifacts. Captions should include the approximate age of the artifact, its purpose, and the civilization that made it.

Making Inferences As a class, discuss what the artifacts reveal about the development of each civilization socially, politically, and economically. **OL**

(Chapter Project continued in Section 3)

The Inca state was built on war, and the Inca army was powerful. All men between 25 and 50 years old could be drafted to serve in the army for up to five years. Their weapons included clubs, spears, and spiked copper balls on ropes. Using slings, Inca soldiers could throw stones 30 yards (27 m).

Residents of conquered areas who did not resist were allowed to participate in the growing empire's government. Those who resisted or rebelled were dealt with harshly. Many people preferred to accept the terms offered by the Inca rather than go to war with the powerful Inca armies.

Life in the Empire

At its height, the Inca Empire had a population of more than 9 million, including many conquered peoples. To control this large empire, the Inca built at least 10,000 miles (16,093 km) of stone-paved roads that ran over rugged mountains, across deserts, and through dense jungles. Rope bridges, made from grass, crossed deep canyons and rivers.

Runners carried messages to and from the emperor and linked, or connected, outposts of the empire to Cuzco. The Inca language, **Quechua** (KEH•chuh•wuh), became the official language for the entire empire.

Although the Inca did not have a system of writing, they developed a system of record keeping with string called **quipus** (KEE•poos). Using various lengths and colors of string knotted in special patterns, the quipus were used to record information about resources such as grain supplies.

To farm their mountainous lands, the Inca cut **terraces,** or broad platforms, into steep slopes. They built stone walls on the terraces to hold the soil and plants in place. Inca farmers grew maize, squash, tomatoes, peanuts, chili peppers, cotton, and potatoes. **D**

All Inca land belonged to the emperor, who was believed to be a descendant of the sun god. To please the sun god, the Inca made magnificent gold jewelry and temple ornaments. The Inca also built cities devoted to religious ceremonies, including Machu Picchu, a site hidden high up in the Andes.

✔ **Reading Check** Explaining How did the Inca farm steep slopes?

History ONLINE
Study Central™ To review this section, go to glencoe.com.

Section 2 Review

Vocabulary

1. Write a short paragraph in which you use all of the following vocabulary terms: civilization, complex, theocracy, hieroglyphics, link, Quechua, quipu, terrace.

Main Ideas

2. **Describing** Describe the development of Tenochtitlán, and explain why the first Europeans to view the city were amazed by it.

3. **Explaining** How did the Inca build and govern their vast empire?

Critical Thinking

4. **Making Inferences** How does trade help enrich a civilization? Provide examples in your answer.

5. **Categorizing** Use a diagram like the one below to describe the role of religion in these early American civilizations.

Role of Religion
- Maya:
- Aztec:
- Inca:

6. **Persuasive Writing** Create a poster encouraging tourists to visit the ruins of an early American civilization. Use the images and text to describe the people and history of your chosen site.

Answer the
7. **Essential Question**
How did the early civilizations of Mexico and Central America develop socially, politically, and economically?

D Differentiated Instruction

Visual/Spatial Have students sketch terraces on a steep slope, or show them a picture of terraces at Machu Picchu. **Ask:** How do terraces change the landscape? *(Flat areas are carved on slopes.)* **Ask:** How might terraces affect the flow of rainwater and protect crops? *(Flat areas slow the flow of water down the slope, preventing the rushing water from washing the crops out of the ground.)* **OL**

✔ **Reading Check** **Answer:** They cut terraces into the slopes and built stone walls on the terraces to hold the soil and plants in place.

Assess
. . . .

History ONLINE

Study Central™ provides summaries, interactive games, and online graphic organizers to help students review content.

Close
. . . .

Summarizing As a class, review the social, political, and economic characteristics of each civilization described in this section. **OL**

Section 2 Review

Answers

1. Paragraphs should reflect an understanding of the terms.
2. It was built on an island, with causeways to the mainland and parts of the lake filled in to grow crops; Europeans were amazed by the great towers and buildings that seemed to rise out of the water.
3. empire built through conquest; Inca allowed conquered peoples to participate in government and built a large road system to help control the empire

4. Possible response: Trade fosters the exchange of goods, ideas, technology, and culture. Students might include examples of how trade influences language and art.
5. Maya: gods controlled everything; priests ruled because only they knew gods' wishes; Aztec: organized society around religion; sacrificed humans to please gods; Inca: emperor believed to be descended from sun god; made gold items to please sun god; built cities devoted to religious ceremonies.

6. Posters should present accurate information about an early American civilization, its history, and its historic location.
7. Possible response: built large cities; developed systems for writing, counting, and tracking time; built drainage systems, pyramids, roads, and bridges; grew vegetables and made products; traded with distant peoples; organized their governments and societies around religion; created large empires

Focus

Section 3

North American Peoples

Bellringer
Daily Test Practice Transparency 1–3

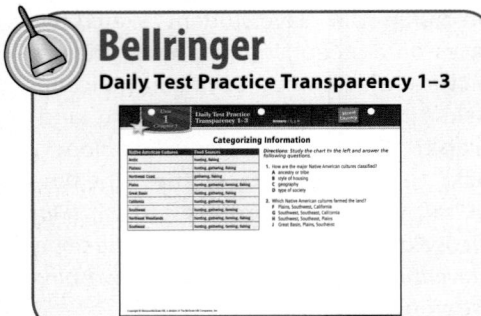

Reading Guide
Answers to Graphic:
Southwest: Hohokam, Anasazi, Hopi, Acoma, Zuni, Apache, Navajo; **Ohio Valley:** Mound Builders (Adena, Hopewell, Mississippians, Natchez); **North:** Inuit; **West:** Tlingit, Haida, Chinook, Nez Perce, Yakima, Pomo, Ute, Shoshone; **Great Plains:** Comanche, Dakota; **East:** Algonquian, Iroquois (Onondaga, Seneca, Mohawk, Oneida, Cayuga), Cherokee, Tuscarora; **Southeast:** Creek, Chickasaw, Cherokee

Section Spotlight Video

To learn more about the Native American settlement at Cahokia, watch the Section Spotlight Video "North American Peoples."

Resource Manager

Essential Question ◄
How was the way of life of the Native Americans of North America related to their environment?

Reading Guide

Content Vocabulary
pueblo (p. 17)   clan (p. 22)
federation (p. 21)

Academic Vocabulary
channel (p. 17)   structure (p. 17)

Key People and Events
Mound Builders (p. 18)
Iroquois (p. 21)

Reading Strategy
Taking Notes As you read, identify the Native American peoples who lived in the different areas of North America.

ILLINOIS STANDARDS
The American Journey

17.C.3a Explain how human activity is affected by geographic factors.
17.C.3c Analyze how human processes influence settlement patterns including migration and population growth.
18.A.3 Explain how language, literature, the arts, architecture and traditions contribute to the development and transmission of culture.

16

American Diary

In a Comanche story, Humpback, a powerful being, kept all of the buffalo for himself in a corral. Coyote, an animal known for his tricks, changed himself into a little dog and befriended Humpback's son. At night, Coyote slipped into the corral, barking loudly and stampeding the buffalo away. Humpback's son cried, "'Where is my little dog?' 'That was no dog,' Humpback said sadly. 'That was Coyote the Trickster. He has turned loose all our buffalo.'"

—from Dee Brown's Folktales of The Native American

R Reading Strategies	C Critical Thinking	D Differentiated Instruction	W Writing Support	S Skill Practice
Teacher Edition • Ident. the Main Idea, p. 19 • Academic Vocab., p. 22 **Additional Resources** • Guid. Read., URB p. 41 • Content Vocab., URB p. 17 • Academic Vocab., URB p. 19 • Read. Ess., p. 7	**Teacher Edition** • Ident. Cent. Issues, p. 17 • Analyzing Information, p. 18 • Contrasting, p. 20 **Additional Resources** • Quizzes and Tests, p. 3 • Crit. Think. Skills, URB p. 29	**Teacher Edition** • Kinesthetic, p. 17 • Gifted and Talented, p. 21 **Additional Resources** • Reteaching Act., URB p. 37 • School-to-Home, URB p. 35	**Teacher Edition** • Descriptive Writing, p. 18 • Expository Writing, p. 18 **Additional Resources** • Writ. Skills, URB p. 23	**Teacher Edition** • Using Geog. Skills, p. 20 **Additional Resources** • Daily Test Pract. Transp. 1-3 • Lesson Transp. 1C • Geo. & Hist., URB p. 31

Early Native Americans

Main Idea The Hohokam, the Anasazi, and the Mound Builders were among the most advanced of early North American civilizations.

History and You Has your area ever experienced a drought? How did the drought affect you? Read to learn how droughts may have caused the decline of a Native American civilization in the Southwest.

The Comanche were only one of many Native American cultures that rose and flourished in North America long before Europeans arrived in the 1500s. Among the most advanced of these earliest Native American cultures were the Hohokam and Anasazi of the Southwest and the Mound Builders of the Ohio River valley.

The Hohokam

The dry, hot desert of what is now Arizona was home to the Hohokam people. They may have come from Mexico about 300 B.C. The Hohokam culture flourished from about A.D. 300 to 1300 in an area bordered by the Gila and Salt River valleys.

The Hohokam were experts at squeezing every drop of available water from the sun-baked soil. Their way of life depended on the irrigation **channels,** or trenches, they dug to carry river water into their fields. In addition to hundreds of miles of irrigation channels, the Hohokam left behind pottery, carved stone, and shells etched with acid. The shells came from trade with coastal peoples.

The Anasazi

The Anasazi (AH•nuh•SAH•zee) lived around the same time as the Hohokam, roughly A.D. 1 to 1300, in the area known as the Four Corners. (This is the meeting place of the states currently known as Utah, Colorado, Arizona, and New Mexico.) There they built great stone dwellings that the Spanish explorers later called **pueblos** (PWEH•blohs), or villages. Pueblo Bonito, one of the most spectacular of the Anasazi pueblos, can still be seen in New Mexico. The huge semicircular **structure,** or building, of stone and sun-dried earth resembles an apartment building. It is four stories high and has hundreds of rooms. Archaeologists have found traces of a complex road system linking Pueblo Bonito with other villages. This suggests that Pueblo Bonito was an important trade or religious center for the Anasazi people.

Teach

C Critical Thinking

Identifying Central Issues Ask: What physical feature made it possible for the Hohokam to survive in the desert region? *(the Gila and Salt Rivers, which provided water for drinking and irrigating crops)* **OL**

D Differentiated Instruction

Kinesthetic Ask students to create a mural, a case display, or some other exhibit about the pueblos built by the Anasazi. Discuss how these structures might have been used by their inhabitants. **OL**

Primary Source

Critical Thinking Answer Possible answer: Native Americans hunted animals common to their region, gathered nearby plants for food, made shelters and clothing from available materials, and drank from streams and lakes in their area.

Primary Source / Buffalo Robe

For centuries, the Comanche and other Native American groups hunted herds of buffalo that used to wander on the Great Plains in what is now the central United States.

Using the Buffalo Sacred to the Native American peoples of the Plains, the buffalo provided many of the people's basic needs. Buffalo meat served as food, bones were made into tools and weapons, and skins were used to make shelters and clothing. Painted buffalo skins were often made into robes.

Critical Thinking

Explaining How do you think Native Americans such as the Comanche depended on the environment?

Differentiated Instruction

Leveled Activities

W₁ Writing Support

Descriptive Writing Have students take the role of an Anasazi leader. The Anasazi are looking for a new home. Ask students to write a description of the environment where they would like to live and how they would survive in that environment. *(Students might describe climate, soil fertility for farming, water sources, available building materials, and forests and grasslands that might have supported animals and edible plants.)* **OL**

W₂ Writing Support

Expository Writing Ask students to write an encyclopedia entry about the Mound Builders. Have students exchange entries and edit each other's work. **OL**

C Critical Thinking

Analyzing Information Ask: Why might these items found in the mounds suggest a widespread pattern of trade? *(The items were not common to that area and were likely from other regions.)* **AL**

Hands-On Chapter Project
Step 3

The Anasazi also built dwellings in the walls of steep cliffs. Cliff dwellings were easy to defend and offered protection from winter weather. Mesa Verde (MAY•suh VUHR•dee) in Colorado, one of the largest cliff dwellings, held several thousand inhabitants.

In about 1300 the Anasazi began leaving the pueblos and cliff dwellings to settle in smaller communities. Their large villages may have been abandoned because of droughts, long periods of little rainfall, during which their crops died.

The Mound Builders

The early cultures of Mexico and Central America appear to have influenced people living in lands to the north. In central North America, prehistoric Native Americans built thousands of mounds of earth that resembled the stone pyramids of the Maya and the Aztec. Some of the mounds contained burial chambers. Some were topped with temples, as in the Maya and Aztec cultures.

The mounds dotted the landscape from what is now known as Pennsylvania to the Mississippi River valley. Archaeologists think that the first mounds were built about 1000 B.C. They were not the work of a single group but of many different peoples, who are referred to as the **Mound Builders.**

Among the earliest Mound Builders were the Adena, hunters and gatherers who flourished in the Ohio Valley by 800 B.C. They were followed by the Hopewell people, who lived between 200 B.C. and A.D. 500. Farmers and traders, the Hopewell built huge burial mounds in the shapes of birds, bears, and snakes. Archaeologists have found freshwater pearls, shells, cloth, and copper in the mounds, indicating a widespread pattern of trade.

Cahokia

The largest settlement of the Mound Builders was Cahokia (kuh•HOH•kee•uh) in what is today Illinois. A people called the

Selected Sites of the Mound Builders [NATIONAL GEOGRAPHIC]

Adena Culture The Great Serpent Mound in southern Ohio (below) is an example of the earthen mounds built by the Adena people. At nearly a quarter mile long, it is the largest serpent effigy mound in the United States. An effigy mound is one made in the shape of a living creature. ▼

Lake Superior
90°W
80°W
Lake Michigan
Lake Huron
Lake Ontario
Lake Erie
40°N
0 100 kilometers
0 100 miles
Lambert Azimuthal Equal-Area projection
Cahokia
Missouri River
Ohio River
Serpent Mound
Kings Mounds
Spiro Mounds
Moundville
ATLANTIC OCEAN
30°N
Adena site
Hopewell site
Mississippian site

Creating a Museum Exhibition

Step 3: Creating a Mural Students will create a mural showing early Native American life.

Essential Question: How was the way of life of the Native Americans of North America related to their environment?

Directions Have each group choose a different Native American culture from this section. Supply large sheets of paper and art supplies. Group members should collect pictures and facts about

the environment and daily lives of the people. Using the research, each group should create a mural that illustrates how the people adapted to their environment. Group members should plan different scenes, sketch and color them, and write informative captions for each scene.

Analyzing As a class, identify the elements of the environment shown in each mural. Analyze how the Native Americans in each scene are adapting to their environment. **OL**

(Chapter Project continued on the Visual Summary page)

Mississippians built Cahokia after A.D. 900. The city may have had 16,000 or more residents. The largest mound in Cahokia, the Monks Mound, rises nearly 100 feet (30 m).

Cahokia resembled the great cities of Mexico, even though it was nearly 2,000 miles (3,200 km) away. The great pyramid-shaped mound dominated the city. A temple crowned the summit. Perhaps priests studied the heavens from the temple, or the priest-ruler may have lived there. A legend of the Natchez people, descendants of the Mississippians, hints of a direct link to Mexico:

R

PRIMARY SOURCE

"Before we came into this land, we lived yonder under the sun; [the speaker pointed southwest toward Mexico]. . . . Our nation extended itself along the great water [the Gulf of Mexico], where the large river [the Mississippi] loses itself."

—Natchez legend

✓ **Reading Check** **Explaining** How did the Mound Builders appear to be related to the Maya and Aztec cultures?

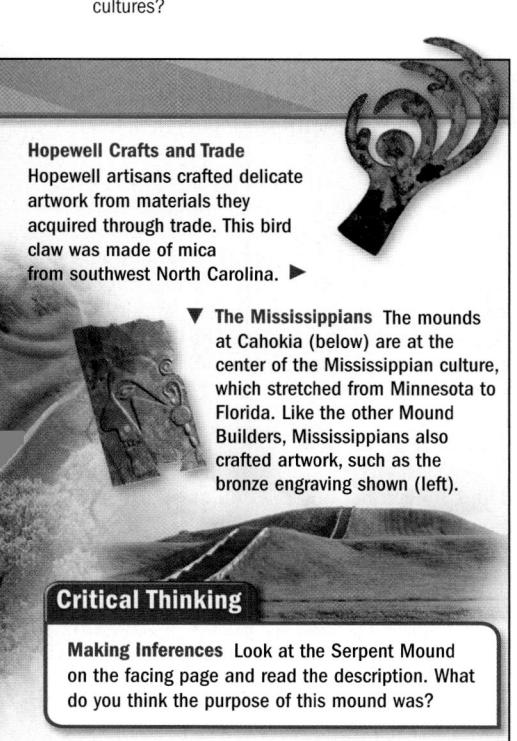

Hopewell Crafts and Trade
Hopewell artisans crafted delicate artwork from materials they acquired through trade. This bird claw was made of mica from southwest North Carolina. ▶

▼ **The Mississippians** The mounds at Cahokia (below) are at the center of the Mississippian culture, which stretched from Minnesota to Florida. Like the other Mound Builders, Mississippians also crafted artwork, such as the bronze engraving shown (left).

Critical Thinking

Making Inferences Look at the Serpent Mound on the facing page and read the description. What do you think the purpose of this mound was?

Other Native North Americans

Main Idea The early inhabitants of North America developed ways of life that were well suited to their environments.

History and You How has the climate in the area where you live affected the way that houses are built? Read to learn how Native Americans adapted to the climates of North America.

. . . .

The civilizations of the Hohokam, the Anasazi, and the Mound Builders eventually faded away. A number of other Native American cultures arose to take their place. Around the time that Europeans began arriving, North America was home to many different societies.

Peoples of the North

The people who settled in the northernmost part of North America, in the lands around the Arctic Ocean, are called the Inuit. Some scientists think the Inuit were the last migrants to cross the land bridge that connected Asia with North America.

The Inuit had many skills that helped them survive in the cold Arctic climate. They may have brought some of these skills from Siberia, which was probably their original home. In the winter the Inuit built igloos, low-lying structures of snow blocks, which protected them from severe weather.

Their clothing of furs and sealskins was warm and waterproof. The Inuit were hunters and fishers. In the coastal waters, they pursued whales, seals, and walruses in small, skin-covered boats. On land they hunted caribou, large deerlike animals that lived in the far north. The Inuit made clothing from caribou skins and burned seal oil in lamps.

Peoples of the West

North America's West Coast had a mild climate and dependable food sources. These conditions created a favorable environment for many different groups.

The First Americans **Chapter 1** **19**

R **Reading Strategy**

Identifying the Main Idea Draw a fishbone diagram on the board. **Ask:** What is the main idea of this paragraph? *(Cahokia resembled the great cities of Mexico.)* Write it on the body of the fish. **Ask:** What are the supporting details? *(pyramid-shaped mound, temple on top, Natchez legend suggests link to Mexico)* Write these on the fish's diagonal bones. **BL**

This **READING SKILL** (Identifying the Main Idea) was introduced in this unit.

✓ **Reading Check** **Answer:** The mounds they built resembled the stone pyramids of the Maya and Aztec. Some mounds were topped with temples, as in Maya and Aztec cultures.

Selected Sites of the Mound Builders

Critical Thinking Answer

Possible answer: It may have been used for religious ceremonies or for burial.

Additional Support

Activity: Connecting Past and Present

Comparing and Contrasting Have students select a Native American group from this section, such as the Inuit, and research how members of the group live today. For example, what type of clothing do they wear? In what type of housing do they live? How do they make a living? Then have students prepare a report that describes what they have discovered, comparing and contrasting the information with what they have learned from the textbook about the group's lifestyle in early history. **OL**

S Skill Practice

Using Geography Skills As students read these passages, ask them to locate on the map the various Native American peoples described in the text. Have students also look at the physical map of the United States in the Reference Atlas. **Ask:** *Which Native American peoples lived in mountainous areas? (Cherokee, Shoshone, Cheyenne, Pawnee, Anaszi, Ute, Navajo, Zuni, Apache)* **OL**

C Critical Thinking

Contrasting Ask: *How did the Ute and the Hopi differ in the kinds of shelters they built and the way they obtained food? (Ute built temporary shelters of branches and reeds and traveled in search of food. Hopi built adobe homes and farmed.) What might explain these differences in way of life? (The Great Basin was too rocky to farm, so the Ute could not settle in one place like the Hopi. Both peoples used materials available in their environment to build shelters.)* **OL**

Additional Support

Teacher Tip

Making a Chart Suggest that students think about the chart categories before doing their research. Then they will know what facts to look for.

Native American Cultures

NATIONAL GEOGRAPHIC

Differing Cultures Native American groups across North America developed their own unique ways of life. Styles of lodging and crafts varied from people to people.

The peoples of the northwestern coast, such as the Tlingit (TLIHNG•kuht), Haida, and Chinook, depended on the forest and the sea. They built wooden houses and made canoes, cloth, and baskets from tree bark. They fished for their main food, salmon, along the coast and in rivers such as the Columbia. They preserved the salmon by smoking it over fires.

S Salmon was also important for the people of the plateau region, the area between the Cascade Mountains and the Rocky Mountains. The Nez Perce (NEHZ PUHRS) and **C** Yakima peoples fished the rivers, hunted deer in forests, and gathered roots and berries. The Native Americans of the plateau region lived in earthen houses.

A great variety of cultures lived in what is now California. Along the northern coast, Native Americans fished for their food. In the more barren environment of the southern deserts, nomadic groups collected roots and seeds. In the central valley of California, the Pomo gathered acorns and pounded them into flour.

In the Great Basin region, between the Sierra Nevada and the Rocky Mountains, the soil was too hard and rocky for farming. Peoples such as the Ute (YOOT) and Shoshone (shuh•SHOH•N) traveled in search of food. They ate small game, pine nuts, juniper berries, roots, and some insects. The Great Basin peoples created temporary shelters from branches and reeds.

Peoples of the Southwest

Descendants of the Anasazi formed the Hopi, the Acoma, and the Zuni peoples of the Southwest. They built their homes from sundried mud bricks called adobe. They raised corn or maize as their basic food. They also grew beans, squash, melons, pumpkins, and fruit. Their trade network spread throughout the Southwest and into Mexico.

Activity: Interdisciplinary Connection

Health Early Native Americans gathered plants for more than just food. They used almost 3,000 different plants as medicine. For example, the Cherokee used bloodroot to cure coughs. By experimenting and observing results, Native Americans learned which plants promoted health and healing. Have students research to identify plants used as medicine by early Native Americans as well as to learn which plants are still used as medicines today. Have them summarize their findings in a chart using these categories: plant names, Native American groups who used them, early uses, and uses today. Point out that plant medicines are another way that Native Americans used their environment. **OL**

Southwest Pottery The peoples of the Southwest created beautiful pottery from the same clay with which they built their homes. Pots were used to store water and food. ▶

Buffalo Skin Bag The Native Americans of the Plains used the skins of the buffalo they hunted to make a number of everyday items. This buffalo skin bag shows a horse and rider. ▶

◀ Longhouses People of the East lived in bark-covered longhouses. Each building could shelter several families.

Northwest Artifact This ladle in the form of a bird was used by Native Americans in the Northwest at large parties called potlatches. Potlatches celebrated events such as births, deaths, and weddings. ▼

Map Skill

Region Identify some of the peoples who lived in the Great Plains region of North America.

Maps in MOtion See StudentWorks™ Plus or glencoe.com.

D Differentiated Instruction

Gifted and Talented Ask students to research how tepees were made and then build models of a tepee. Students can share their work with the class to demonstrate how tepees were suitable for nomadic peoples. **AL**

Native American Cultures NATIONAL GEOGRAPHIC

Map Skills Answer

Answers may include Ojibwa, Dakota, Omaha, Pawnee, Kiowa, Osage, Apache, and Comanche

Map Skills Practice

Refer students to the United States political map in the Reference Atlas. Have them use longitude and latitude lines and physical features to help them generally locate their state on the map of Native American cultures. **Ask:** Which Native American cultures lived in our state? *(Answers will depend on the state where students live.)* **OL**

In the 1500s, two new peoples settled in the region—the Apache and the Navajo. Unlike other peoples of the Southwest, these new groups were hunters and gatherers. They hunted deer and other game. In time, the Navajo settled in villages and built square houses called hogans. In addition to hunting, they began to grow maize and beans. They also began raising sheep in the 1600s.

Peoples of the Plains

The peoples of the Great Plains were nomadic. Their villages were temporary, lasting only for a growing season or two. When the people moved from place to place, they dragged their homes—cone-shaped skin tents called tepees—behind them. The men hunted antelope, deer, and buffalo. The women planted maize, squash, and beans.

When the Spanish brought horses to Mexico in the 1500s, some got loose and made their way north. Native Americans captured and tamed the wild horses. The Comanche,

the Dakota, and other Plains peoples became skilled riders. They hunted and fought on horseback, using spears, bows and arrows, and clubs while riding.

Peoples of the East

The peoples who lived in the woodlands of eastern North America formed complex societies. The many Algonquian groups were linked by similar languages. The **Iroquois** (IHR•uh•KWAH) and Cherokee had formal law codes and formed **federations**, governments that linked different groups.

The Iroquois lived near Canada in what is now northern New York State. There were five Iroquois groups or nations: the Onondaga (AH•nuhn•DAW•guh), the Seneca, the Mohawk, the Oneida, and the Cayuga.

These groups often warred with each other. Finally, in the 1500s, these five groups established the Great Peace, an alliance that was joined in 1715 by the Tuscarora peoples. This alliance was called the Iroquois League.

The First Americans **Chapter 1** **21**

Differentiated Instruction

Critical Thinking Skills Activity, URB p. 29

Critical Thinking Skills Activity
The First Americans

Analyzing Visual Information

Learning the Skill

Native American Population Density in North America, 1500

Analyzing Visual Information

Objective: To learn about Native American population density in North America

Focus: Ask students to define population density.

Teach: Tell students to use the map to complete the activity.

Assess: Have students summarize the patterns they observe on the map.

Close: Discuss how a high population density might affect a food supply.

Differentiated Instruction Strategies

BL Have students color their maps to show different population densities.

AL Ask students to identify which group might be considered more powerful based on their population density.

ELL Write the definition of "population density" on the chalkboard so students can refer to it.

Section 3

R Reading Strategy

Academic Vocabulary Ask: What is a clan? *(a group of related families)* Have students describe the benefits of being a member of a clan. *(Students may cite benefits such as protection from rival clans and the continuation of clan culture and traditions.)* **ELL**

✓ **Reading Check** **Answer:** They hunted and also fought on horseback.

Assess

History ONLINE

Study Central™ provides summaries, interactive games, and online graphic organizers to help students review content.

Close

Determining Cause and Effect As a class, discuss ways in which the environment shaped the lives of Native Americans in North America. **OL**

Section 3 Review

The League created a constitution. At first the constitution was represented symbolically through art. Later, after the arrival of the Europeans, it was written down.

The Iroquois constitution established the Grand Council, a group of leaders who met regularly to settle disputes among the various peoples. Although Grand Council members were men, women played an important part in choosing delegates to the council. The different members of the Iroquois League were organized according to **clans,** or groups of related families. The women in each clan chose a clan mother. These clan mothers then chose the male members of the Grand Council.

The Iroquois constitution describes the Iroquois people's desire for peace:

PRIMARY SOURCE

"I am Dekanawidah and with the Five Nations' Confederate Lords I plant the Tree of Great Peace. . . . Roots have spread out from the Tree of the Great Peace, one to the north, one to the east, one to the south and one to the west."

—Dekanawidah, Iroquois Constitution

Peoples of the Southeast

The Southeast was also a woodlands area but with a warmer climate than the eastern woodlands. The Creek, Chickasaw, and Cherokee were among the region's Native American peoples.

The Creek lived in loosely knit farming communities in what is now Georgia and Alabama. There they grew corn, tobacco, squash, and other crops. The Chickasaw, most of whom lived farther west in what is now Mississippi, farmed the fertile river bottomlands. The Cherokee farmed in the mountains of Georgia and the Carolinas.

Wherever they lived in North America, the first Americans developed ways of life that were well suited to their environments. In the 1500s, however, the Native Americans would meet a new people with vastly different beliefs, cultures, and ways of life. These newcomers were the Europeans, and their arrival would change the Native Americans' world forever.

✓ **Reading Check** **Describing** How did the peoples of the Great Plains use horses?

Section 3 Review

History ONLINE
Study Central™ To review this section, go to glencoe.com.

Vocabulary

1. Use each of these terms in a sentence that will help explain its meaning: channel, pueblo, structure, federation, clan.

Main Ideas

2. **Describing** Describe the cliff dwellings of the Anasazi and explain the advantages those dwellings offered.

3. **Explaining** What was the significance of the Iroquois League?

Critical Thinking

4. **Making Connections** What evidence suggests that the Mound Builders were influenced by other cultures?

5. **Contrasting** Use a diagram like the one below to show how the ways of life of Native American cultures differed by comparing their regions and forms of shelter.

Inuit	Hopi	Dakota
Region:	Region:	Region:
Shelter:	Shelter:	Shelter:

6. **Descriptive Writing** Choose one of the Native American peoples of North America and write two or three paragraphs describing a typical day in the life of a member of that group. Be sure to include details about the environment and the way of life of the group.

Answer the Essential Question

7. How was the way of life of the Native Americans of North America related to their environment?

Answers

1. Sentences should demonstrate an understanding of the terms.
2. The Anasazi built dwellings in the steep walls of cliffs in the Southwest. These dwellings were easy to defend and offered protection from winter weather.
3. The Iroquois League was a federation of Iroquois nations who agreed to exist peacefully. The league created a constitution, which was written down in later years.
4. Mounds resembled pyramids, some topped with temples as in Maya and Aztec culture; items found in mounds suggested trade with other cultures.
5. **Inuit:** far North, igloos; **Hopi:** Southwest, adobe; **Dakota:** Great Plains, tepees
6. Students' paragraphs should include accurate details about the way of life of a Native American group discussed in the section.
7. Possible response: Native Americans adapted to their environment. They built shelters using materials from their surroundings. They took advantage of available food sources. They fished nearby rivers, hunted animals of their region, gathered wild plants, and grew crops if their land was fertile.

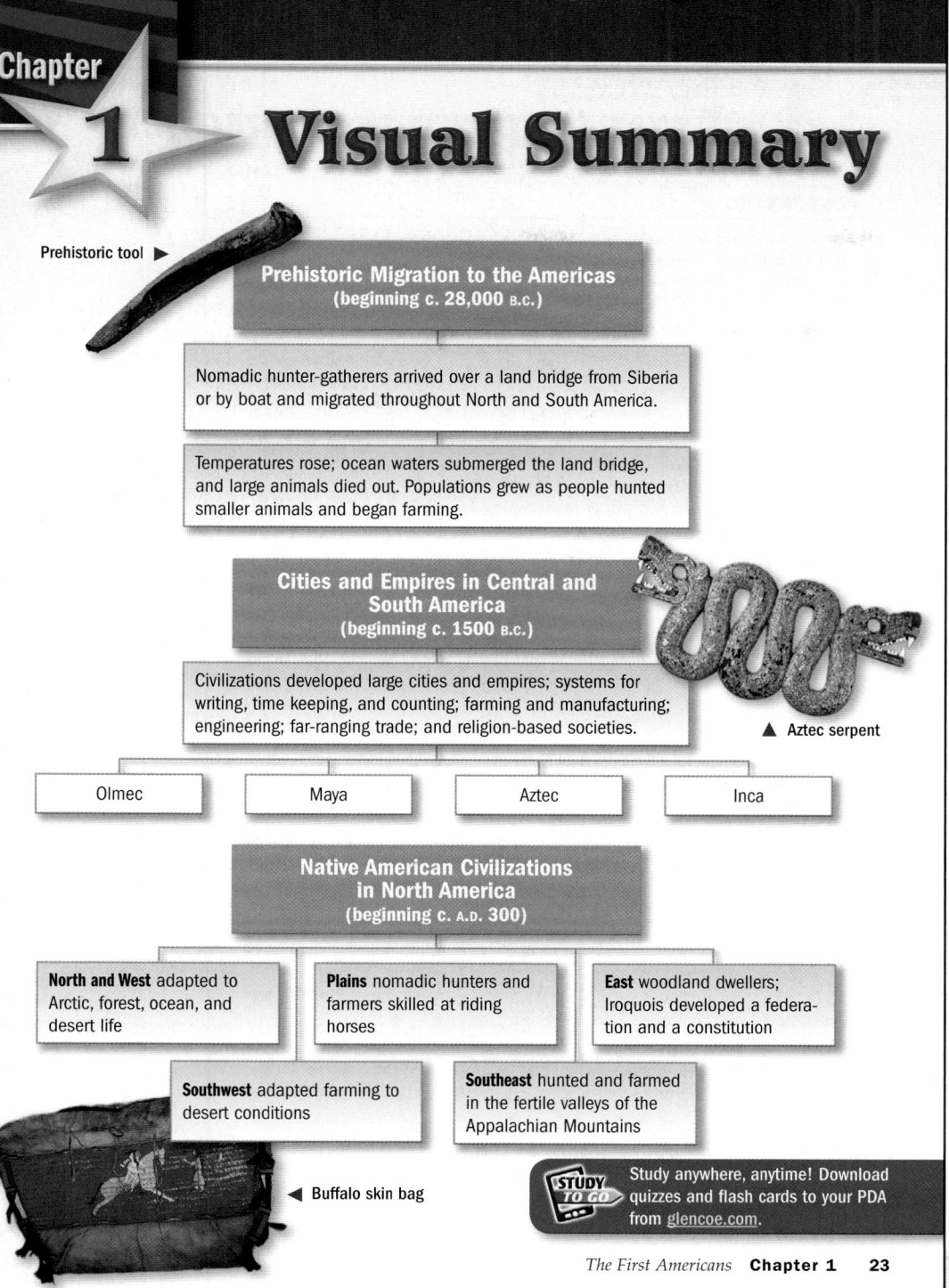

◀ Prehistoric tool

Prehistoric Migration to the Americas
(beginning c. 28,000 B.C.)

Nomadic hunter-gatherers arrived over a land bridge from Siberia or by boat and migrated throughout North and South America.

Temperatures rose; ocean waters submerged the land bridge, and large animals died out. Populations grew as people hunted smaller animals and began farming.

Cities and Empires in Central and South America
(beginning c. 1500 B.C.)

Civilizations developed large cities and empires; systems for writing, time keeping, and counting; farming and manufacturing; engineering; far-ranging trade; and religion-based societies.

▲ Aztec serpent

| Olmec | Maya | Aztec | Inca |

Native American Civilizations in North America
(beginning c. A.D. 300)

North and West adapted to Arctic, forest, ocean, and desert life

Plains nomadic hunters and farmers skilled at riding horses

East woodland dwellers; Iroquois developed a federation and a constitution

Southwest adapted farming to desert conditions

Southeast hunted and farmed in the fertile valleys of the Appalachian Mountains

◀ Buffalo skin bag

STUDY TO GO Study anywhere, anytime! Download quizzes and flash cards to your PDA from glencoe.com.

The First Americans **Chapter 1** 23

Visual Summary

Identifying Points of View Remind students that the military empire established by the Aztec forced conquered people into slavery. The Aztec also made human sacrifices of their prisoners of war. **Ask:** How do you think the Aztec justified their behavior? *(The Aztecs possibly believed that by conquering their rivals, they could use the enslaved people as sources of labor in cities and villages. In addition, because the Aztec believed that human sacrifices were necessary for religious purposes, they would consider the sacrifices justified.)* What might the enslaved people or prisoners of war have felt? *(anger, fear, hatred)* **OL**

Making Inferences Ask: Native American cultures in North America were well suited to their surrounding environments. What, however, might be the danger in this? *(If the environment changed, their culture or way of life could be negatively affected. For example, if moist, fertile land dried up, farming would become more difficult.)* What would the Native Americans need to do then? *(They would have to move elsewhere or adapt to the new environment.)* **OL**

Hands-On Chapter Project
Step 4: Wrap-Up

Creating a Museum Exhibition

Step 4: Presenting the Exhibition Students will prepare and give a presentation to museum visitors.

Directions Have the groups complete the exhibit by organizing the displays and murals and then creating signs to explain what visitors will see. Students may also create a map that outlines the displays and gives additional information about the topics covered. Invite other classes and guests to tour the museum. Have the visitors proceed together from one display to the next. As visitors reach each exhibit, students should be available to answer questions.

Analyzing Discuss the role of museums in a society. **Ask:** What purposes do museums serve? *(preserve artifacts and historical knowledge, educate visitors, create interest in preservation)* After visitors have left, ask students: What did people gain from visiting the classroom museum? *(Answers may include information, enrichment, enjoyment, and an interest in learning more.)* **OL**

Answers and Analyses

Reviewing Main Ideas

1. C Remind students to think about the effects of the Ice Age. Sea levels dropped which exposed a land bridge from Asia to present-day Alaska. **17.C.3a**

2. B Students should immediately eliminate choice C. Tobacco would not be the most important crop because it supplies no nutrition. Remind them of the definition of "maize"—an early form of corn. They might then recognize that B is the correct answer. **17.C.3c**

3. A Students might be familiar with the word "theology." Ask them what the word means (*the study of God and religion*). Students should then be able to select choice A. **18.B.3a**

4. C Tell students that they do not have to remember the key facts about all three groups to answer this question. If the facts from one of the choices fit one of the groups, then that is the correct answer. **17.D.3a**

Short-Answer Question

5. Students should identify passages in the excerpt where women are discussed. Although Grand Council members were men, women chose the delegates to the Council, and women were first to rebuke a leader for wrongdoing. **18.B.3a**

STANDARDIZED TEST PRACTICE

TEST-TAKING TIP

Answer the questions you know first, and go back to those for which you need more time.

Reviewing Main Ideas

Directions: Choose the best answer for each of the following questions.

1. Archaeologists believe that the Americas were first populated by people who

  A sailed ships from Europe and landed in what is now Greenland.

  B crossed into South America from Antarctica.

  C crossed a land bridge that connected northeastern Asia to what is now Alaska.

  D None of the above; evidence indicates that humans have always lived in the Americas.

2. The most important agricultural product grown by early Americans was probably

  A wheat.   **C** tobacco.

  B maize.   **D** rice.

3. Maya civilization can best be described as a society ruled by religious leaders, or a

  A theocracy.   **C** dictatorship.

  B democracy.   **D** kingdom.

4. The Creek, Chickasaw, and Cherokee peoples

  A fished for salmon, their main food source, along North America's West Coast.

  B are considered by most scientists to be the last migrants to cross Beringia into the Americas.

  C lived in farming communities throughout southeastern North America.

  D built thousands of mounds of earth, much like those of the Maya and the Aztec.

Short-Answer Question

Directions: Base your answers to question 5 on the excerpt below and on your knowledge of social studies.

If a Lord of the Confederacy should seek to establish any authority independent of the jurisdiction of the Confederacy of the Great Peace, which is the Five Nations, he shall be warned three times in open council, first by the women relatives, second by the men relatives and finally by the Lords of the Confederacy of the Nation to which he belongs. If the offending Lord is still [unwilling to change] he shall be dismissed by the War Chief of his nation for refusing to conform to the laws of the Great Peace. His nation shall then install the candidate nominated by the female name holders of his family.

—The Iroquois Constitution

5. What does this excerpt indicate about the role of women in Iroquois society?

Review the Essential Questions

6. Essay Compare the cultures of Native Americans of Mexico and Central America with the woodland Indians of eastern North America.

To help you write your essay, review your answers to the Essential Questions in the section reviews and the chapter Foldables Study Organizer. Your essay should include information about:

- the development of agriculture;
- the physical environment; and
- the customs and culture of various Native American peoples.

GO ON

Review the Essential Questions

6. If students completed their Foldables correctly, they should be able to compare different cultures of the Americas. Students' answers might focus on cultural differences such as types of government (theocracy, clans, federation), economies (agriculture, hunting, fishing, gathering), and types of communities (cities, villages, nomadic existence). **18.A**

History ONLINE
For additional test practice, use **Self-Check Quizzes**—Chapter 1 at glencoe.com.

Chapter 1 Assessment

Document-Based Questions

Directions: Analyze the documents and answer the short-answer questions that follow.

Document 1

The following map shows two possible routes early Native Americans might have taken to move from Asia into the Americas.

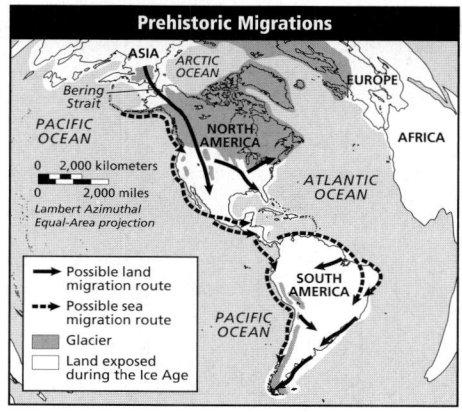

Prehistoric Migrations

ASIA · ARCTIC OCEAN · EUROPE
Bering Strait
PACIFIC OCEAN · NORTH AMERICA · AFRICA
0   2,000 kilometers
0   2,000 miles
Lambert Azimuthal Equal-Area projection
ATLANTIC OCEAN
SOUTH AMERICA
PACIFIC OCEAN

→ Possible land migration route
⇢ Possible sea migration route
▨ Glacier
☐ Land exposed during the Ice Age

7. How might the information on this map help explain the presence of early Native Americans in South America before they arrived in what is now the United States?

Document 2

In this excerpt from *The Conquest of New Spain,* Spanish conquistador Bernal Díaz del Castillo describes the manner of Aztec sacrifices.

> They strike open the wretched Indian's chest with flint knives and hastily tear out the palpitating [beating] heart which, with the blood, they present to the idols in whose name they have performed the sacrifice.

Source: *The Conquest of New Spain*

8. What do you think was the author's feeling about this Aztec ritual? Explain.

Document 3

A cacique chief expressed these thoughts to conquistador Hernando de Soto, who had summoned the chief to him.

> It is not my custom to visit any one, but rather all, of whom I have ever heard, have come to visit me, to serve and obey me, and pay me tribute, either voluntarily or by force: if you desire to see me, come where I am; if for peace, I will receive you with special goodwill; if for war, I will await you in my town; but neither for you, nor for any man, will I set back one foot.

Source: Edward Gaylord Bourne, "Account of Elvas"

9. Based on this document, describe the chief's position.

Document 4

The following illustration depicts a Pueblo Indian using a digging stick to plant corn seeds.

10. What might this illustration tell you about the lifestyle of the Pueblo Indians?

11. Expository Writing Using the information from the five documents and your knowledge of social studies, write an essay in which you:

- identify some ways Native Americans adapted to their environments; and

- explain why not all Native American cultures developed similarly.

8. Remind students that point of view can be revealed in the author's choice of words. The word "wretched" suggests sympathy for the victim. The words "hastily tear" paint a violent picture. "Palpitating" reminds the reader that the victim was alive during the ordeal. These words indicate that the author was appalled at the spectacle. **18.B.3a**

9. Have students consider the meaning of the key phrase "set back one foot" *(retreat)*. The chief is used to being the authority whom other people serve. He will not take orders from the conquistadors or retreat from them. **18.B.3a**

10. Pueblo Indians were not nomadic; they were farmers who settled in one place. Direct students' attention to the digging tool. This tool with a footrest suggests that since the Native Americans had a reliable food source, they had time to create inventions. **18.A.3**

11. Essays should identify elements of the environment, such as climate, soil fertility, game animals, landforms, and sources of water for irrigating and fishing. Native Americans adapted by taking advantage of the available resources for food, clothing, and shelter. These adaptations helped shape the way cultures developed. **16.E.3a (US)**

History ONLINE
Have students visit the Web site at glencoe.com to review Chapter 1 and take the Self-Check Quiz.

Need Extra Help?											
If You Missed Questions. . .	1	2	3	4	5	6	7	8	9	10	11
Go to Page. . .	7–8	9	12	22	21-22	10-22	7–8	13	14–15	20-21	6-22

Document-Based Questions

7. Have students identify on the map the methods used to reach South America and the United States. Discuss how these methods affect the time it takes to get there.

Traveling by boat is faster than walking. Early people could have reached South America by boat long before groups could have traveled the vast distance from Asia to North America on foot. **16.A.3b**

Need Extra Help?

Have students refer to the pages listed if they miss any of the questions.

Chapter Planning Guide

| Levels | | | | | Resources | Chapter Opener | Section 1 | Section 2 | Section 3 | Chapter Assess | Chapter Assess |
BL	OL	AL	ELL								
FOCUS											
BL	OL	AL	ELL		Daily Test Practice Transparencies		2–1	2–2	2–3	2–4	
TEACH											
	OL	AL			Geography and History Activity, URB					p. 59	
BL	OL		ELL		Time Line Skills Activity, URB				p. 62		
BL	OL	AL	ELL		Writing Skills Activity, URB		p. 51				
BL	OL	AL	ELL		Content Vocabulary Activity, URB		p. 45	p. 45	p. 45	p. 45	
BL			ELL		Academic Vocabulary Activity, URB		p. 47	p. 47	p. 47	p. 47	
	OL	AL			Citizenship and Decision-Making Skills Activity, URB					p. 3	
BL			ELL		Social Studies Skills Activity, URB				p. 53		
BL	OL	AL	ELL		Differentiated Instruction Activity, URB		p. 55				
BL	OL	AL	ELL		Critical Thinking Skills Activity, URB		p. 57				
BL	OL	AL	ELL		Linking Past and Present Activity, URB				p. 61		
	OL	AL			Primary Source Readings, URB				p. 49		
BL	OL	AL	ELL		School-to-Home Connection Activity, URB		p. 63	p. 63	p. 63	p. 63	
BL	OL		ELL		Guided Reading Activity, URB*		p. 67	p. 68	p. 69	p. 70	
BL	OL		ELL		Reading Essentials and Note-Taking Guide*		p. 10	p. 13	p. 16	p. 19	
BL	OL	AL	ELL		Lesson Transparencies		2A	2A, 2B	2B, 2C		
	OL				American Biographies			p. 2	p. 3		
BL	OL	AL	ELL		Outline Map Resource Book	pp. 23, 26, 30, 31, 35, 44, 48, 54					

Note: Please refer to the *Unit Resource Book: The Americas: Worlds Meet* for this chapter's materials.

* Also available in Spanish

Levels					Resources	Chapter Opener	Section 1	Section 2	Section 3	Chapter Assess	Chapter Assess
BL	OL	AL	ELL								
TEACH *(continued)*											
BL	OL	AL	ELL	📁	NGS US Desk Map		✓	✓	✓	✓	
BL	OL	AL	ELL	📁	American Literature Library		✓	✓	✓	✓	
BL	OL	AL	ELL	📁	Writer's Guidebook		✓	✓	✓	✓	
	OL	AL		💿	American History Primary Source Document Library CD-ROM		✓	✓	✓	✓	✓
BL	OL	AL	ELL	💿	American Music: Hits Through History	✓	✓	✓	✓	✓	
BL	OL	AL	ELL	💿	StudentWorks™ Plus CD	✓	✓	✓	✓	✓	✓
BL	OL	AL	ELL	🖥	Section Spotlight Videos		✓	✓	✓	✓	
BL	OL	AL	ELL	🖨	Writing Process Transparencies		✓	✓	✓	✓	✓
BL	OL	AL	ELL	💿	Presentation Plus! With MindJogger CheckPoint CD	✓	✓	✓	✓	✓	✓
ASSESS											
BL	OL	AL	ELL	📁	Quizzes and Tests		p. 11	p. 12	p. 13	p. 14	pp. 15, 17, 19
BL	OL	AL	ELL	📁	Authentic Assessment With Rubrics			p. 2			
BL	OL	AL	ELL	📁	Standardized Test Practice						p. 3
BL	OL	AL	ELL	💿	*ExamView® Assessment Suite* CD-ROM*		2–1	2–2	2–3	2–4	Ch. 2
CLOSE											
BL			ELL	📁	Reteaching Activity, URB*		p. 65	p. 65	p. 65	p. 65	p. 65
BL	OL		ELL	📁	Reading and Study Skills Foldables Activity	p. 52	p. 52	p. 52	p. 52	p. 52	p. 52
BL	OL	AL	ELL	📁	*The American Journey* in Graphic Novel						p. 9
BL			ELL	📁	Reading Strategies and Activities for the Social Studies Classroom		✓	✓	✓	✓	

Teacher Works *Plus*
All-In-One Planner and Resource Center

- Interactive Lesson Planner
- Interactive Teacher Edition
- Fully editable blackline masters
- Section Spotlight Videos Launch
- Differentiated Lesson Plans
- Printable reports of daily assignments
- Standards Tracking System

Professional Development Resources

- Strategies for Success
- Building Academic Vocabulary
- Success With English Learners DVD
- Differentiated Instruction Strategies DVD
- Teaching Literacy Strategies in Social Studies DVD
- Assessment DVD
- Standards-Based Instruction DVD

Integrating Technology

2

Using TechCONNECT™

Researching Famous People

Technology Product

CyberScout is a convenient and dynamic search engine that provides several easy ways to locate information outside the McGraw-Hill Learning Network. CyberScout searches only Web sites that have been reviewed by teachers, so the information students find is always appropriate and accurate.

Objective

Encourage students to research global and historical issues using CyberScout.

- Enable students to exercise research and study skills.
- Give students the opportunity to practice writing skills.

Steps

- Choose **CyberScout** from the **References menu.**
- Click a **subject area link** to narrow the search.
- The CyberScout page displays a set of results.
- Click the **Browse Famous People button.**
- Click a **name.**
- The CyberScout page displays a set of results.
- Click the **link** to a Web site of interest.
- Students will be redirected to the Web site.
- Students navigate the Web site to acquire information about a topic.
- Have students write a report about what they have learned.

History ONLINE at glencoe.com

	Student	Teacher	Parent
Media Center			
• Student Edition Audio	●		
• Spanish Summaries	●		
• Section Spotlight Videos	●	●	
Social Studies Online Learning Center			
Classroom Tools			
• Multi-Language Glossaries	●	●	●
• Teaching Today		●	
• TIME Current Events	●	●	●
• Beyond the Textbook	●	●	
***The American Journey* Online Learning Center**			
• Study-to-Go™	●	●	●
• Study Central™	●	●	●
• Chapter Overview	●	●	
• Concepts in Motion	●	●	
• ePuzzles and Games	●	●	
• Literature Connections	●	●	
• Online Student Edition	●	●	●
• Self-Check Quizzes	●	●	●
• Student Web Activities	●	●	
• Vocabulary eFlashcards	●	●	
• Web Activity Lesson Plans	●	●	●
• Vocabulary PuzzleMaker	●	●	●

- **Timed Readings Plus in Social Studies** helps students increase their reading rate and fluency while maintaining comprehension. The 400-word passages are similar to those found on state and national assessments.

- **Reading in the Content Area: Social Studies** concentrates on six essential reading skills that help students better comprehend what they read. The book includes 75 high-interest nonfiction passages written at increasing levels of difficulty.

- **Reading Social Studies** includes strategic reading instruction and vocabulary support in Social Studies content for ELLs and native speakers of English.

- **Content Vocabulary Workout** (Grades 6–8) accelerates reading comprehension through focused vocabulary development. Social Studies content vocabulary comes from the glossaries of Glencoe's Middle School Social Studies texts.

www.jamestowneducation.com

NATIONAL GEOGRAPHIC
Index to National Geographic Magazine:

The following articles relate to this chapter:

- *"In Search of Vikings,"* Priitt J. Vesilind, May 2000.

- *"Marco Polo, Parts I–III,"* Mike Edwards, May, June, July 2001.

National Geographic Society Products

To order the following, call National Geographic at 1-800-368-2728:

National Geographic Atlas of the World (Book).

Access National Geographic's new dynamic MapMachine Web site and other geography resources at:

www.nationalgeographic.com

www.nationalgeographic.com/mapmachine

Use this database to search more than 30,000 titles to create a customized reading list for your students.

- Reading lists can be organized by students' reading level, author, genre, theme, or area of interest.

- The database provides Degrees of Reading Power™ (DRP) and Lexile™ readability scores for all selections.

- A brief summary of each selection is included.

Leveled reading suggestions for this chapter:

For students at a Grade 6 reading level:
- *The World's Greatest Explorers,* William Scheller
- *Cultures Collide: Native Americans and Europeans, 1492–1700,* Ann Rossi

For students at a Grade 7 reading level:
- *Exploration and Conquest: The Americas After Columbus: 1500–1620,* Betsy Maestro
- *Hernando de Soto and the Spanish Search for Gold in World History,* Ann Graham Gaines

For students at a Grade 8 reading level:
- *The Age of Exploration,* Sarah Flowers
- *The Travels of Marco Polo,* Mary Hull

For students at a Grade 9 reading level:
- *The Age of Discovery: 1492–1815,* John Haywood
- *The Renaissance,* Paul Johnson

For students at a Grade 10 reading level:
- *Machu Picchu,* Amy Allison

The following videotape programs are available from Glencoe as supplements to the chapter:

- **Christopher Columbus: Explorer of the New World** (ISBN 1-56-501667-X)

- **The Aztec Empire** (ISBN 0-76-700542-2)

To order, call Glencoe at 1-800-334-7344. To find classroom resources to accompany many of these videos, check the following home pages:

A&E Television: www.aetv.com

The History Channel: www.history.com

Chapter Objectives

After studying this chapter, students will be able to:

- Describe the events and technological advances that supported European exploration.
- Explain why Spain and Portugal wanted to find a sea route to Asia.
- Understand the ways in which Spain's conquests affected the economic and social development of the Americas.
- Discuss why European nations established colonies in North America.

Motivating Activity

Identifying Central Issues Henry Hudson was one of the explorers sent by the Netherlands and, later, England to find a Northwest Passage to Asia. It was important to find this route because sailing around South America or Africa was time-consuming and expensive. During his last voyage in 1611, Hudson's starved and diseased crew mutinied. They sent him and others off into a boat on Hudson Bay. Hudson was never heard from again. **Ask:** Do you think finding a direct route to Asia was worth the loss of human life? Have students list modern explorers, such as astronauts, who have risked their lives. As they read the chapter, have students compare the risks each of the explorers took with the benefits that were earned.

Previewing the Essential Questions

As you begin teaching each section, use these questions and activities to help students focus on the Essential Questions.

Chapter 2
Exploring the Americas
1400–1625

Henry Hudson landing in North America

◀ Inca noble

Americas
World

c. 1438 ★
The Inca leader Pachacuti begins to build an empire

1492 ★
Christopher Columbus reaches America

★ 1497
John Cabot sails to Newfoundland

1400   1450   1500

1429 ★
Joan of Arc defeats the English at Orléans

★ c. 1456
Johannes Gutenberg uses movable metal type in printing

★ c. 1500
Songhai Empire rises in Africa

Section 1

A Changing World Ask: How can technology aid explorers? *(Technological advances can help with orientation, prediction, transportation, and communication of knowledge.)* Point out to students that in Section 1, they will learn about the events and technological advances that paved the way for European exploration. **OL**

Section 2

Early Exploration Ask: Why would it be more efficient to travel by sea than by land from Europe to Asia? *(A sea route would bypass Arab merchants, who charged for passage. It also would avoid mountain and desert travel.)* Point out to students that Section 2 discusses early European exploration in pursuit of a sea route to Asia. **OL**

Section 1: A Changing World
Essential Question What events and technological advances paved the way for European exploration?

Section 2: Early Exploration
Essential Question Why did Spain and Portugal want to find a sea route to Asia?

Section 3: Spain in America
Essential Question How did Spain's conquests affect the economic and social development of the Americas?

Section 4: Exploring North America
Essential Question Why did European nations establish colonies in North America?

History ONLINE
Chapter Overview Visit glencoe.com and click on **Chapter 2—Chapter Overviews** to preview chapter information.

FOLDABLES
Study Organizer

Organizing Information
Make this Foldable to help you organize what you learn about the exploration of the Americas.

Step 1 Place three sheets of paper about 1 inch apart.

Step 2 Fold the paper to form five equal tabs.

Step 3 Staple the sheets and label each tab as shown.

Reading and Writing
As you read the chapter, list important people, places, and facts under the appropriate tabs of the Foldable.

Exploring the Americas
A Changing World
Early Exploration
Spain in America
Exploring North America

◄ Juan de Oñate

★ **1519**
Cortés brings horses to North America

★ **1598**
Juan de Oñate founds province of New Mexico

★ **1609**
Henry Hudson explores the Hudson River area

1550

1600

★ **1517**
Martin Luther promotes Church reform

★ **1522**
Magellan's crew completes first voyage around the world

★ **1588**
England defeats Spanish Armada

Chapter 2   27

Introducing Chapter 2

Time Line Activity

If you have not already done so, have students review the time line. Remind them to read time lines from left to right.
Ask: Which event occurred first: the English defeat at Orléans or the first voyage around the world? *(the English defeat at Orléans)*

FOLDABLES
Study Organizer
Dinah Zike's Foldables

Purpose This Foldable helps students organize facts about the early European exploration of the Americas. The completed Foldable will help them prepare for assessment.

More Foldables activities for this chapter can be found in the *Dinah Zike's Reading and Study Skills Foldables*.

History ONLINE
Introduce students to chapter content and key terms by having them access the **Chapter Overview** at glencoe.com.

Section 3

Spain in America Ask: How might the conquest of a country influence its culture and economy? *(It might affect its language, religions, and trade relationships with other countries.)* Tell students that Section 3 will explore the impact of Spain's conquests on the people who lived in the Americas. **OL**

Section 4

Exploring North America Ask: What are the advantages for a country to have colonies? *(Answers might include trade opportunities, resources, and places for people to move.)* Explain to students that in Section 4, they will learn why European nations were eager to colonize North America. **OL**

Focus

Section ★ 1

A Changing World

Bellringer
Daily Test Practice Transparency 2–1

Reading Guide
Answers to Graphic:
printing press (provided more people with access to information), more accurate maps, better navigation tools (astrolabe, magnetic compass), improved ship design

Section Spotlight Video

Have students watch the Section Spotlight Video "A Changing World" to learn more about the Renaissance.

Resource Manager

Essential Question
What events and technological advances paved the way for European exploration?

Reading Guide

Content Vocabulary

classical (p. 30)   pilgrimage (p. 33)
technology (p. 31)   mosque (p. 33)
astrolabe (p. 31)   Quran (p. 33)

Academic Vocabulary

acquire (p. 31)   impose (p. 32)

Key People and Events

Crusades (p. 29)
Marco Polo (p. 29)
Renaissance (p. 30)
Mansa Mūsā (p. 33)

Reading Strategy
Taking Notes As you read, use a diagram like the one below to identify the advances in technology that paved the way for European voyages of exploration.

Technological Advances

ILLINOIS STANDARDS
The American Journey

16.A.3b Make inferences about historical events and eras using historical maps and other historical sources.

17.A Locate, describe and explain places, regions and features on the Earth.

17.A.3a Explain how people use geographic markers and boundaries to analyze and navigate the Earth (e.g., hemispheres, meridians, continents, bodies of water).

18.A.3 Explain how language, literature, the arts, architecture and traditions contribute to the development and transmission of culture.

American Diary

In 1271 Marco Polo set off from Italy on a great journey to China. Polo crossed the Gobi, a desert area north of China, about which he wrote: "The length of this Desert is so great that 'tis said it would take a year and more to ride from one end of it to the other. And here, where its breadth is least [narrowest], it takes a month to cross it. 'Tis all composed of hills and valleys of sand, and not a thing to eat is to be found on it."

—from The Travels of Marco Polo

Camels still cross the vast deserts of Asia today.

R Reading Strategies	**C** Critical Thinking	**D** Differentiated Instruction	**W** Writing Support	**S** Skill Practice
Teacher Edition • Summarizing, p. 30 • Outlining, p. 32 **Additional Resources** • Guid. Read., URB p. 67 • Content. Vocab., URB p. 45 • Academic Vocab., URB p. 47 • Read. Ess., p. 10	**Teacher Edition** • Analyzing Information, p. 30 • Deter. Cause & Effect, p. 31 **Additional Resources** • Quizzes and Tests, p. 11 • Crit. Think. Skills, URB p. 57	**Teacher Edition** • Visual/Spatial, p. 29 • ELL, p. 30 • Logical/Math., p. 32 **Additional Resources** • Reteach, URB p. 65 • School-to-Home, URB p. 63 • Differ. Inst., URB p. 55	**Teacher Edition** • Descriptive Writing, p. 33 **Additional Resources** • Writ. Skills, URB p. 51	**Teacher Edition** • Using Geo. Skills, p. 29 **Additional Resources** • Daily Test Pract. Transp. 2-1 • Lesson Transp., 2A

New Ideas and Nations

Main Idea The Renaissance began in the Italian city-states and spread throughout Europe.

History and You What do you know about the ancient civilizations of Greece and Rome? Read to learn about the renewed interest in classical learning during the Renaissance.

By the time Marco Polo returned from China, European interest in Asia had begun to grow. For centuries after the Roman Empire fell, the people of western Europe were isolated from the rest of the world. Dominated by the Catholic Church, their world was divided into a number of small kingdoms and city-states.

Meanwhile, the religion of Islam swept across the Middle East and Africa. European Christians feared losing access to the Holy Land—the birthplace of Christianity, in what is now Israel. In 1095 the Europeans launched the first of nine expeditions, known as the **Crusades,** to regain control of their holy sites from the Muslims.

The Crusades brought western Europeans into contact with the Middle East. Arab merchants sold spices, sugar, silk, and other goods from China and India to Europeans. As a result, European interest in Asia grew.

That interest grew even more after **Marco Polo** returned from China. In 1296 he began writing an account of his trip. He described Asia's marvels in his book *Travels,* which was widely read in Europe. Little did Marco Polo realize that 200 years later, *Travels* would inspire Christopher Columbus to sail in the opposite direction to reach the East.

The Growth of Trade

Merchants knew they could make a fortune selling goods from Asia. Wealthy Europeans clamored for spices from the East. They also wanted perfumes, silks, and precious stones.

Merchants first bought goods from Arab traders in the Middle East. These merchants then sent the goods overland by caravan to the Mediterranean Sea. From there the goods were sent by ship to Italian ports. The cities of Venice, Genoa, and Pisa prospered as centers of the growing trade. Arab merchants, however, charged high prices for their goods. Europeans began looking for a route to the East that bypassed the Arab merchants.

If You Were There / A Young Explorer

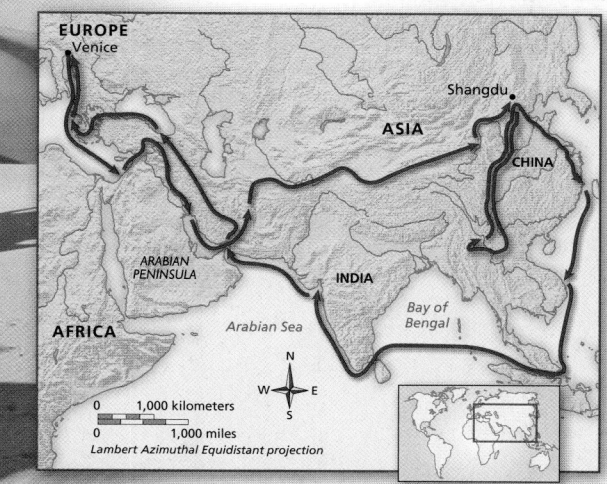

En Route Only 17 years old when his trip began, Marco Polo journeyed with his father and uncle, both Venetian merchants. If you were with them, you would have traveled on camels for more than three years. You also would have crossed almost 7,000 miles (11,265 km) of mountains and deserts before reaching your final destination: the fabled court of Kublai Khan (KOO-bluh KAHN), the Mongol emperor of China.

Critical Thinking
Explaining How would you have traveled to China? How long would it have taken to reach your destination?

▲ Map of Marco Polo's journey to China

Teach

S Skill Practice

Using Geography Skills Ask students to study the map depicting Marco Polo's route to China and back home. **Ask:** How did Polo's homeward voyage differ from his voyage to China? *(The homeward route was mostly by sea; the route to China included mountain and desert travel.)* Why do you think Polo traveled a different route home? *(The sea route probably would have been easier. Students also might suggest that he wanted to explore a new area.)* **OL**

D Differentiated Instruction

Visual/Spatial Have students draw or paint a scene depicting a Renaissance Italian port with ships that have returned from Asia. Ask them to include clues about the economic importance of the port and to make sure viewers can identify some of the traded goods. **BL**

If You Were There

Critical Thinking Answer
by boat and overland by camel; more than three years

Differentiated Instruction

Critical Thinking Activity, p. 57

Determining Cause and Effect

Objective: To understand cause-and-effect relationships

Focus: Ask students to define *cause* and *effect* and give examples from daily life.

Teach: Have students read each passage and record each cause and effect.

Assess: Assess each answer for accuracy, and discuss why incorrect answers are wrong.

Close: Ask students how they can determine cause-and-effect relationships as they read.

Differentiated Instruction Strategies

BL Write sentences that reflect examples of cause and effect.

AL Ask students to find newspaper articles that demonstrate cause and effect.

ELL Ask students to list words that signal cause-and-effect relationships.

C Critical Thinking

Analyzing Information Ask: Why did the use of the experimental approach lead to great advances in knowledge? *(Instead of relying on untested—and often unfounded—beliefs, it encouraged scientists to test these beliefs and theories scientifically.)* **OL**

D Differentiated Instruction

English Language Learners Write "rebirth" on the board. **Ask:** If we know what "birth" means, what does putting "re-" in front of the word do to its meaning? *(Re- means "again" or "anew.")* **ELL**

R Reading Strategy

Summarizing Ask: What resulted from the emergence of nation-states? *(Answers may include the establishment of national laws, courts, taxes, and armies, as well as an expansion of trade and overseas exploration.)* **BL**

✓ Reading Check **Answer:** spices, sugar, silk, perfumes, and precious stones

Additional Support

The Growth of Ideas

In the 1300s a powerful new spirit emerged in the Italian city-states and spread throughout Europe. Banking and the expansion of trade with Asia made Italian merchants wealthy. These citizens wanted to improve their knowledge of past civilizations and of the world. They studied the **classical**—ancient Greek and Roman—works with new interest. Taking a more experimental approach to science, many thinkers tested new and old theories and evaluated the results.

Many authors began to write about the individual and the universe. Artists studied the sculpture and architecture of the classical world. They particularly admired the harmony and balance in Greek art.

The Renaissance

This period of intellectual and artistic creativity was known as the **Renaissance** (REH•nuh•SAHNTS). The word means "rebirth" in French and refers to the renewed interest in classical Greek and Roman learning. The Renaissance spread throughout Europe over the next two centuries. It changed the way Europeans thought about themselves and the world. It also paved the way for an age of exploration and discovery.

Powerful Nations Emerge

During the Renaissance, merchants and bankers sought greater profits through foreign trade. They wanted to buy goods directly from the East. The development of nation-states in western Europe helped expand trade and interest in overseas exploration.

For years Europe was a patchwork of small states. By the 1400s, however, a new type of centralized state began to emerge in western Europe. Strong monarchs came to power in Spain, Portugal, England, and France. They began to establish national laws, courts, taxes, and armies to replace those of the local lords. These ambitious monarchs sought ways to increase trade and make their countries stronger and wealthier.

✓ Reading Check **Identifying** What goods did wealthy Europeans desire from the East?

LINKING PAST TO PRESENT — Navigation Tools

THEN "Land ho!" The tools that early explorers used to sail the uncharted seas were much different from the instruments used today. Early navigation tools such as the astrolabe could help determine a ship's approximate latitude by noting the locations of the stars.

NOW Today, navigation satellites do the work of an astrolabe—and much more. The NAVSTAR Global Positioning System (GPS) is a network of satellites launched by the United States. From space, the GPS can track the location of a ship or some other object on Earth within a few meters of its actual position.

▼ Astrolabe

Activity: Interdisciplinary Connection

Art Discuss the Renaissance and how it influenced painting, sculpture, and architecture. Ask an art teacher to bring in photographs of Renaissance art and architecture and discuss them with the class. **Ask:** How can art reflect the values of a society? *(Students might suggest that art demonstrates a society's willingness to explore, its current knowledge, its beliefs, and so on.)* Tell students to work in small groups and choose a contemporary painting or building. Have them discuss how that creation reflects the values of society today.* **AL**

Technology's Impact

Main Idea Technology produced better means of navigation and paved the way for European voyages of exploration.

History and You Have you ridden in a vehicle with an onboard navigation system? Read to learn how the astrolabe and compass improved navigation in the 1400s.
. . . .

Advances in **technology**—the use of scientific knowledge for practical purposes—paved the way for European voyages of exploration. In the 1450s the introduction of the printing press made it much easier to print books. Now more people had access to books and to new information. Many Europeans read Marco Polo's *Travels* when it appeared in printed form in 1477.

Better Maps and Instruments

Most early maps were inaccurate because they were drawn from the often-mistaken impressions of traders and travelers. Little by

Hikers can use a handheld GPS receiver to stay on course in the wilderness.

Critical Thinking

1. **Explaining** How have the tools used for navigation changed since the late 1400s?
2. **Analyzing** What major technological advancements have allowed improvements in navigation?

little, cartographers, or mapmakers, improved their skills. Using reports of explorers and information from Arab geographers, mapmakers made more accurate land and sea maps. These maps showed the directions of ocean currents. They also showed lines of latitude, which measured the distance north and south of the Equator.

Better instruments were developed for navigating the seas. Sailors could determine their latitude while at sea with an **astrolabe.** This instrument measured the positions of stars. Europeans also **acquired** the magnetic compass. A Chinese invention, the compass began to be widely used in Europe and the Middle East in the 1200s. The compass allowed sailors to determine their direction when they were far from land.

Better Ships

Advances in ship design allowed shipbuilders to build sailing vessels that were capable of long ocean voyages. The stern rudder and the triangular sail made it possible for ships to sail into the wind. Both of these new features came from the Arabs.

Then, in the late 1400s, the Portuguese developed the three-masted caravel. It was the first and most famous ship of the European age of exploration. The caravel sailed faster than earlier ships and carried more cargo and food supplies. It also could float in shallow water. This feature allowed sailors to explore inlets and to sail their ships up to the beach if they needed to make repairs. A Venetian sailor called the caravels "the best ships that sailed the seas."

By the mid-1400s, the Italian ports faced increased competition for foreign trade. As a result, a new era of exploration was launched. Powerful countries such as Portugal and Spain began searching for sea routes to Asia. Portugal began its explorations by sending ships down the west coast of Africa, an area Europeans had never visited before.

Reading Check **Explaining** How did the caravel affect overseas exploration in the 1400s?

Exploring the Americas **Chapter 2** **31**

C Critical Thinking

Determining Cause and Effect **Ask:** In what ways would access to Polo's *Travels* have influenced readers when it first appeared in print? (*Answers might include the idea that the book inspired Columbus and that some readers might learn about Asia for the first time.*) **AL**

LINKING PAST TO PRESENT

Critical Thinking Answers

1. Students might answer that today's tools are more accurate, but some are less self-contained and rely on satellites and computers to transmit information to them.

2. Answers may include electricity, computers, satellites, rockets, and global positioning systems.

Reading Check **Answer:** It traveled faster and allowed explorers to carry more cargo and food supplies than earlier ships did. It also could float in shallow water, making it possible to explore inlets.

Differentiated Instruction

Leveled Activities

R Reading Strategy

Outlining Have students make an outline as they read about the African kingdoms. Ask them to write the subheads and then add supporting details beneath each subhead as they read. **BL**

D Differentiated Instruction

Logical/Mathematical Ask: *For how many years did Ghana develop and flourish as an important trading empire? (from approximately A.D. 400 to 1076, or 676 years)* How does this time span compare with the age of the United States? *(Students might be surprised to learn that the United States is less than 240 years old; it has been a country for less than half the time that Ghana flourished.)* **OL**

African Trading Kingdoms
NATIONAL GEOGRAPHIC

Map Skills Answer
Mali

Hands-On Chapter Project
Step 1

Creating a Historical Calendar

Step 1: Gathering Facts and Creative Ideas Students will list people, technological developments, and events that represent the early exploration and colonization of the Americas to create a 12-month calendar.

African Trading Kingdoms
NATIONAL GEOGRAPHIC

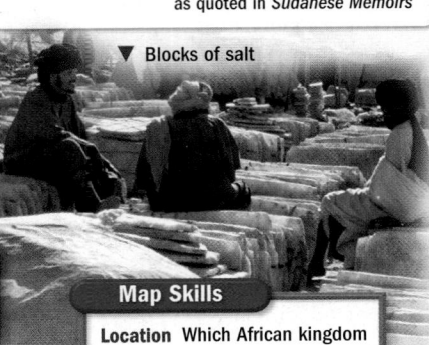

"In the sands of that country is gold, treasure inexpressible. . . . Merchants trade with salt for it, taking the salt on camels from the salt mines. . . . When they reach Ghana they weigh their salt and sell it against a certain unit of weight of gold."

—Abū Hāmid al-Gharnātī, as quoted in *Sudanese Memoirs*

▼ Blocks of salt

Map Skills
Location Which African kingdom extended farthest to the west?

African Kingdoms

R

Main Idea Ghana, Mali, and Songhai were among the most powerful empires in Africa.

History and You What items are valued today because they are rare? Read to find out how rare items, such as salt, drove the economies of early African kingdoms.

Powerful kingdoms flourished in Africa south of the Sahara between A.D. 400 and A.D. 1600. Africans mined gold, copper, and iron ore. Trade with Islamic societies in North Africa brought wealth as well as Islamic ideas and customs to the West African kingdoms.

City-states on the east coast of Africa also benefited from trade. Arab traders from the Middle East brought cotton, silk, and porcelain from India and China. They exchanged these goods for ivory and metals from the African interior.

The Portuguese sailed south along the western coast of Africa in the mid-1400s. They set up trading posts along the coastline. From these posts, they traded for gold and for enslaved people.

Ghana—A Trading Empire

Between A.D. 400 and A.D. 1100, a vast trading empire called Ghana emerged in West Africa. Well located between the salt mines of the Sahara and the gold mines to the south, Ghana prospered from the taxes **imposed**, or placed, on trade.

Caravans with gold, ivory, and slaves from Ghana crossed the Sahara to North Africa, **D** where Muslim traders loaded caravans with salt, cloth, and brass and headed back to Ghana. Trading contacts led many West Africans to become Muslims.

In 1076 people from North Africa, called Almoravids, attacked Ghana and disrupted its trade routes. While Ghana fought the Almoravids, new trade routes and gold mines opened up to the east, bypassing Ghana. Ghana then began to decline, and new states emerged in the region.

Essential Question: What events and technological advances paved the way for European exploration?

Directions Organize students into small groups. Explain that each group will be creating a 12-month calendar that depicts the early exploration and colonization of the Americas. Ask each group to make a list of approximately 15 people, technological developments, or events that they feel are particularly important to American exploration or colonization.

Summarizing Ask each group to explain why each explorer, technological development, or event they chose furthered European exploration or colonization.

(Chapter Project continued in Section 2)

Mali—A Powerful Kingdom

Mali, one of the new states, grew into a powerful kingdom. The people of Mali developed their own trade routes across the desert to North Africa. By the late 1200s, Mali's territory included the former kingdom of Ghana. The country was mainly agricultural, but gold mines enriched the kingdom.

Mali's greatest king, **Mansa Mūsā,** ruled from 1312 to 1337. He was described at the time as "the most powerful, the richest, the most fortunate, the most feared by his enemies, and the most able to do good to those around him." Mūsā made his kingdom famous.

In 1324 Mūsā, who was a Muslim, made a grand pilgrimage to the Muslim holy city of Makkah (Mecca) in western Saudi Arabia. A **pilgrimage** is a journey to a holy place. Arab writers reported that Mūsā traveled with a huge military escort. Ahead of him marched 500 royal servants who carried gold to distribute along the way.

Mūsā returned to Mali with an Arab architect who built great **mosques,** Muslim houses of worship, in the capital of Timbuktu. Under Mansa Mūsā, Timbuktu became an important center of Islamic art and learning.

The Songhai Empire

Some years later the Songhai (SAWNG•hy) people, who lived along the Niger River, rose up against Mali rule. They built a navy to control the Niger and in 1468 captured Timbuktu. Askìya Muhammad brought the Songhai Empire to the height of its power. Askìya strengthened his country and encouraged trade with Europe and Asia.

Plan of Government

Askìya introduced laws based on the teachings of the holy book of Islam, the **Quran.** Askìya also developed a sophisticated plan for his country's government. He divided Songhai into five provinces. To each province he appointed a governor, a tax collector, a court of judges, and a trade inspector. Everyone used the same weights and measures and followed the same legal system. In the late 1500s the North African kingdom of Morocco attacked the Songhai gold-trading centers. Using guns and cannons, the Moroccans easily defeated the empire.

Reading Check Explaining What goods did African kingdoms use for trading? What did they trade for?

History ONLINE
Study Central™ To review this section, go to glencoe.com.

Section 1 Review

Vocabulary

1. Use each of these terms in a sentence that will help explain its meaning: classical, technology, astrolabe, acquire, impose, pilgrimage, mosque, Quran.

Main Ideas

2. Identifying Why did interest in trade with the East increase during the Renaissance?

3. Describing How were maps improved to help sailors?

4. Discussing How did Timbuktu, in Mali, become an Islamic cultural center?

Critical Thinking

5. Organizing Use a diagram like the following to show the exchange of goods and ideas between North Africa and Ghana.

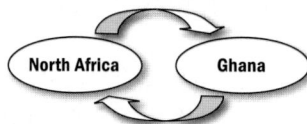

6. Persuasive Writing Take on the role of Marco Polo. Write one paragraph for the back cover that will make readers want to buy your book, *Travels*.

Answer the
7. Essential Question What events and technological advances paved the way for European exploration?

Exploring the Americas **Chapter 2** **33**

W Writing Support

Descriptive Writing Have students write an account of Mūsā's journey to Makkah from the point of view of a member of his military escort. The description should include an explanation for why the trip was made, details about the escort, events that occurred along the way, and what Mūsā did while he was in Makkah. **OL**

Reading Check **Answer:** gold, copper, iron ore, ivory, and slaves; cotton, silk, and porcelain from India and China, as well as for salt, cloth, and brass from North Africa

Assess

History ONLINE

Study Central™ provides summaries, interactive games, and online graphic organizers to help students review content.

Close

Explaining Have students explain how events and technological advances allowed European exploration to expand. **OL**

Section ⭐ Review

Answers

1. Students will use each term in a sentence that helps explain its meaning.

2. Merchants and bankers desired wealth, people wanted goods from the East, and monarchs of new nations wanted to show strength and wealth.

3. Maps became more accurate, showed the directions of ocean currents, and identified lines of latitude.

4. Mali's king, Mansa Mūsā, was a Muslim and returned from a pilgrimage to Makkah to build mosques and make Timbuktu a center of Islamic art and learning.

5. North Africa to Ghana: salt, cloth, brass, Islam; Ghana to North Africa: gold, ivory, slaves

6. Students will write paragraphs to persuade people to buy the book.

7. European interest in Asia due to growth of trade and Crusades, increased wealth, rise of nation-states, printing press, improved maps and navigation instruments, advances in ship design, and a desire for gold and slaves from western Africa.

Focus

Bellringer
Daily Test Practice Transparency 2–2

Reading Guide
Answers to Graphic:
Sponsored by Portugal: Dias, da Gama, Cabral, Vespucci
Sponsored by Spain: Columbus, Balboa, Vespucci, Magellan

Section Spotlight Video

Have students watch the Section Spotlight Video "Early Exploration" to learn more about Christopher Columbus.

Resource Manager

Essential Question
Why did Spain and Portugal want to find a sea route to Asia?

Reading Guide

Content Vocabulary
saga (p. 38)   strait (p. 41)
line of demarcation   circumnavigate
  (p. 41)   (p. 41)

Academic Vocabulary
devote (p. 39)   alter (p. 40)

Key People and Events
Henry the Navigator (p. 35)
Bartholomeu Dias (p. 36)
Vasco da Gama (p. 37)
Christopher Columbus (p. 38)
Amerigo Vespucci (p. 41)
Ferdinand Magellan (p. 41)

Reading Strategy
Taking Notes As you read, use a diagram like the one below to identify the explorers discussed in this section who were sponsored by Portugal and Spain.

```
            Explorers
           /         \
  Sponsored by    Sponsored by
   Portugal          Spain
```

ILLINOIS STANDARDS
The American Journey

15.D Understand trade as an exchange of goods or services.
16.A.3c Identify the differences between historical fact and interpretation.
17.A.3a Explain how people use geographic markers and boundaries to analyze and navigate the Earth (e.g., hemispheres, meridians, continents, bodies of water).

Early Exploration

American Diary

In 1492 Christopher Columbus led 90 sailors on a voyage into the unknown. As the voyage dragged on, the sailors grew quarrelsome. Columbus wrote:
"I am told . . . that if I persist in going onward, the best course of action will be to throw me into the sea some night."
Then, on the morning of October 12, a cannon fired from the ship Pinta, *indicating that land had been sighted. At dawn, Columbus left his ship, the* Santa María, *and went ashore.*

—from **The Log of Christopher Columbus**

Christopher Columbus lands on the Caribbean island that he named San Salvador.

R Reading Strategies	C Critical Thinking	D Differentiated Instruction	W Writing Support	S Skill Practice
Teacher Edition • Act. Prior Knowl., p. 36 • Making Connect., p. 37 • Questioning, p. 38 • Using Context Clues, p. 39 **Additional Resources** • Guid. Read., URB p. 68 • Content Vocab., URB p. 45 • Aca. Vocab., URB p. 47	**Teacher Edition** • Identify. Cent. Issues, p. 35 • Predict. Consequen., p. 41 **Additional Resources** • Quizzes and Tests, p. 12	**Teacher Edition** • Logical/Math., p. 37 • Intrapersonal, p. 38 **Additional Resources** • Reteach, URB p. 65 • School-to-Home, URB p. 63	**Teacher Edition** • Narrative Writing, p. 37 • Expository Writing, p. 40	**Teacher Edition** • Using Geo. Skills, p. 35 • Creating a Time Line, p. 41 **Additional Resources** • Daily Test Pract. Transp. 2-2 • Lesson Transp., 2A, 2B • Authentic Assess., p. 2

Seeking New Trade Routes

Main Idea Portugal took the lead in finding a sea route to India.

History and You What do you consider a long trip? A few hours on an airplane or a few days in a car? Read to learn about the long sea voyages that Portuguese ships made to find a sea route to India.

Columbus believed he had arrived in the Indies—islands located southeast of China. Unfortunately, Columbus was wrong. The maps that Columbus and the first European explorers used did not include the Americas. They showed three continents—Europe, Asia, and Africa—merged in a gigantic landmass bordered by oceans. Some explorers thought that the Western (Atlantic) and Eastern (Pacific) Oceans ran together to form what they called the Ocean Sea. No one realized that another huge landmass was missing from the maps. They also did not realize that the oceans were as large as they are.

Columbus sailed for Spain, but Portugal was the first European power to explore the boundaries of the known world. Because Portugal lacked a Mediterranean port, it could

not share in the trade between Asia and Europe. The country's rulers wanted to find a new route to China and India.

The Portuguese also hoped to find a more direct way to get West African gold. The gold traveled by caravan across the desert to North Africa and then by ship across the Mediterranean. Portuguese traders needed a better route.

Early Portuguese Voyages

Prince Henry of Portugal helped lay the groundwork for the era of exploration that was beginning. In about 1420, he set up a center for exploration at Sarges, on the southwestern tip of Portugal, "where endeth land and where beginneth sea."

Known as **Henry the Navigator,** the prince never intended to become an explorer himself. Instead, he planned the voyages and then analyzed the reports that his crews brought home. At Sarges, Prince Henry began his "school of navigation." There, astronomers, geographers, and mathematicians shared their knowledge with Portuguese sailors and shipbuilders. When each new voyage brought back new information, Henry's expert mapmakers updated the charts.

Teach

S Skill Practice

Using Geography Skills Ask students to draw a map showing how Columbus and other early European explorers would have depicted the known oceans and Europe, Asia, and Africa. (*The map may show one huge landmass—Europe, Asia, and Africa—bordered by the Western and Eastern Oceans. A variant might show the oceans merged into the Ocean Sea.*) **OL**

C Critical Thinking

Identifying Central Issues Ask: What types of knowledge did Henry the Navigator realize were important for exploration? *(information about astronomy, geography, mathematics, cartography, and navigation)* **BL**

If You Were There

Critical Thinking Answer
Answers might include courage, physical strength, stamina, and an ability to work in harsh conditions.

If You Were There / Ship's Boy on the *Santa María*

Life Aboard Ship Your day begins with prayers on deck. A single hot meal for the day is prepared over an open fire in the deck's sandbox. Your meal usually consists of salted meat or fresh fish, with dried peas and cheese. As a ship's boy, your major job is letting the crew know when it is time to do their chores. You do so by turning the sandglass every half-hour and calling out, "One glass is gone, and now the second flows!" After eight turns of the glass, or four hours, a new boy comes on deck to call the time. When you are off duty, you sleep anywhere on the deck that you can find shelter.

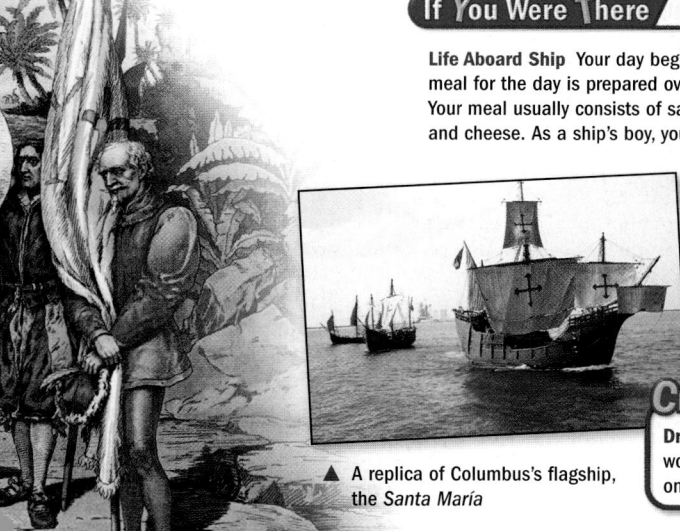

▲ A replica of Columbus's flagship, the *Santa María*

Critical-Thinking

Drawing Conclusions What qualities would you need to be a crew member on the *Santa María*?

Differentiated Instruction

Exploring the Americas

Authentic Assessment Activity, p. 2

Objective: To create a map of early European exploration using modern reference points

Focus: Ask students which explorers they will include on their maps and why each was important.

Teach: Have students research and create a map showing the explorers' routes using modern reference points.

Assess: Use the rubric to assess the accuracy of the map.

Close: Discuss what students have learned about map-making and early explorers' routes.

Differentiated Instruction Strategies

BL Have students describe verbally each route the explorer took.

AL Ask students to research what college classes they would take to become a cartographer.

ELL Ask students to label the modern reference points in English and their native languages.

R Reading Strategy

Activating Prior Knowledge Ask: Why did the Portuguese not want to travel overland to Asia? *(They wanted to bypass Arab merchants and their high prices.)* **OL**

Early Portuguese Exploration

NATIONAL GEOGRAPHIC

Critical Thinking Answer

All of the effects could lead to conflicts.

Critical Thinking Practice

Ask: How could increased knowledge about another region lead to future conflict? *(Knowledge that an area has desirable natural resources could lead to conflict.)* **AL**

History ONLINE

Objectives and answers to the Student Web Activity can be found at glencoe.com under the Web Activity Lesson Plan.

Early Portuguese Exploration

NATIONAL GEOGRAPHIC

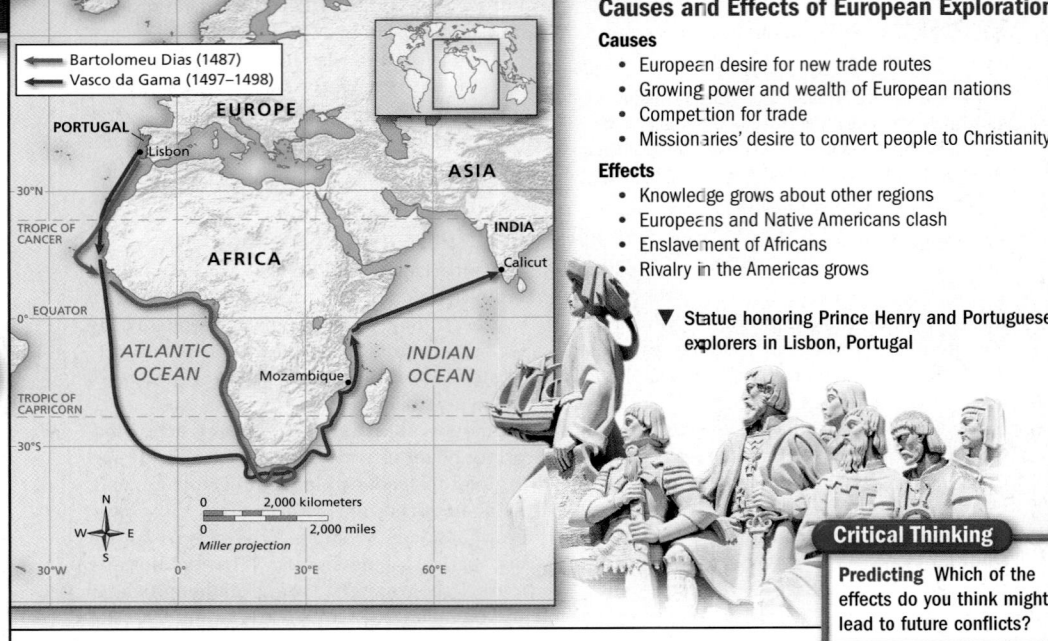

Bartolomeu Dias (1487)
Vasco da Gama (1497–1498)

Causes and Effects of European Exploration

Causes
- European desire for new trade routes
- Growing power and wealth of European nations
- Competition for trade
- Missionaries' desire to convert people to Christianity

Effects
- Knowledge grows about other regions
- Europeans and Native Americans clash
- Enslavement of Africans
- Rivalry in the Americas grows

▼ Statue honoring Prince Henry and Portuguese explorers in Lisbon, Portugal

Critical Thinking

Predicting Which of the effects do you think might lead to future conflicts?

As Portuguese ships moved south along the coast of West Africa, they traded for gold and ivory and established a number of trading posts in the region. Because of its abundance of gold, the area came to be known as the Gold Coast. In the mid-1400s Portuguese traders began buying enslaved people there as well.

King John II of Portugal launched new efforts to realize the Portuguese dream of a trading empire in Asia. If the Portuguese could find a sea route around Africa, they could trade directly with India and China. In the 1480s the king urged Portuguese sea captains to explore farther south along the African coast.

Bartholomeu Dias

In 1487 King John sent **Bartholomeu Dias** to explore the southernmost part of Africa and from there to sail northeast into the Indian Ocean. Dias set out from Lisbon with two small caravels and a slower supply ship. The expedition was also assigned some of Portugal's best pilots. They sailed for days.

After passing the mouth of the Orange River in South Africa, Dias ran into a fierce storm that lasted nearly two weeks. The strong winds carried him southward, off course, and out of sight of land. When the winds finally died down, Dias steered east and then north until he found land again. Dias realized that he had sailed past the southernmost point of Africa, called a cape because it projects into the sea.

Dias charted a course back home. On the return journey, Dias passed the cape again. He wrote that he had been around the "Cape of Storms." On learning of Dias's discovery, King John renamed this southern tip of land.

History ONLINE

Student Web Activity Visit glencoe.com and complete the Chapter 2 Web Activity about Prince Henry the Navigator.

Hands-On Chapter Project
Step 2

Creating a Historical Calendar

Step 2: Choosing the Calendar's Images Each group will search for images that represent the people, technological developments, and events for its calendar.

Essential Question: Why did Spain and Portugal want to find a sea route to Asia?

Directions Show students several examples of visually attractive calendars. Then have students search online or use library sources for images of the people, technological developments, and events they have chosen. Ask students to choose one image or a group of images for each month. Students should keep notes to remind them what each image depicts.

Analyzing Have students identify the images that are similar among all the European nations. Ask each group to identify which images they found that refer to Spain and Portugal's search for a sea route to Asia.

(Chapter Project continued in Section 3)

He called it the Cape of Good Hope. The king hoped that the passage around Africa might lead to a new route to India.

Vasco da Gama

The first Portuguese voyages to India were made years later. In July 1497, after much preparation, **Vasco da Gama** set out from Portugal with four ships. Da Gama did little coast hugging of Africa. Instead, his ships made a huge semicircular sweep through the Atlantic Ocean. At one point during the voyage, da Gama was closer to what is today Brazil than he was to Africa. It is said that da Gama made this unusual maneuver to reach currents that would help him round the Cape of Good Hope safely. During that huge sweep of the Atlantic, da Gama was out of sight of land for 96 days.

After rounding the Cape on November 22, da Gama visited cities along the coast of East Africa. Along the way, he met an Arab pilot who knew the Indian Ocean well. With the pilot's help, da Gama sailed on to India. He reached the port of Calicut in May 1498, completing the long-awaited eastern sea route to Asia.

The Portuguese Trading Empire

Events moved quickly after that. Less than six months after da Gama's return home, a fleet of 13 ships left Lisbon bound for the East. In command of this fleet was Pedro Álvares Cabral. With him were several captains, including Bartholomeu Dias. Cabral followed da Gama's route. His course, however, swung so wide around Africa that he reached Brazil, where he explored some of the coastline. Cabral claimed the land for his king and sent one of his ships back to Portugal with the good news while he continued on to India. Cabral gave Portugal a stake in the Americas.

Cabral returned home from India with cargoes of spices, porcelain, and other goods. Other Portuguese fleets repeated Cabral's success, and Portugal established its first permanent forts in India. Portuguese fleets began to make annual voyages to India. Their cargoes made the Portuguese capital of Lisbon the marketplace of Europe.

✓ **Reading Check** **Analyzing** What was the significance of the voyages of Dias and da Gama?

The Caravel

A Ship for Explorers Caravels ranged in length from 75 to 90 feet (23 to 27 m) and were suited for sailing along shallow coastlines. They were not, however, well suited for very long voyages, as they could not carry enough crew and supplies. Caravels were usually rigged with three or four masts, employing both square and triangular sails.

> **Critical Thinking**
>
> **Explaining** How did the caravel's lateen sails help sailors?

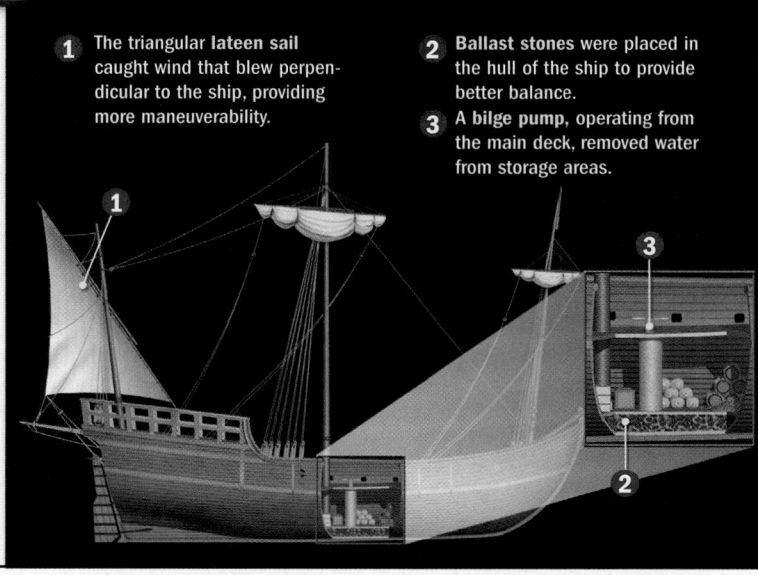

1 The triangular **lateen sail** caught wind that blew perpendicular to the ship, providing more maneuverability.

2 **Ballast stones** were placed in the hull of the ship to provide better balance.

3 A **bilge pump**, operating from the main deck, removed water from storage areas.

Technology Connection

D Differentiated Instruction

Intrapersonal Ask students how they might have felt if they were Christopher Columbus and were about to set out on the first voyage westward to Asia. Have students write journal entries in which they take the role of Columbus and tell their private thoughts about their excitement and fears. Advise them to draw on their knowledge of the technology available to Columbus as he planned his voyage. **OL**

R Reading Strategy

Questioning Have students read the bracketed text. **Ask:** Why is the word "discover" surrounded by quotation marks? *(The text above the bracketed material explains that the Vikings found America before the Europeans did. The quotation marks are used to signal that the word is not used literally.)* **OL**

Primary Source

Critical Thinking Answer
Eriksson found grapes there, which were used to make wine.

Additional Support

Teacher Tip

Collaborative Learning Doing research can sometimes isolate students, or cause some to feel like they do all the work. You can help groups work more effectively by delegating specific responsibilities among all members of the group.

Primary Source — The Vikings

The Vikings in America The Vikings established a settlement that is now called L'Anse aux Meadows in Newfoundland. When Leif Eriksson and his crew arrived in North America, they were persuaded to stay by the lush meadows, thick forests, and streams filled with fish. A wandering crew member also discovered groves of wild grapes. When they departed for home, the Viking ships were full of timber, a rare item in Greenland, and grapes stored as wine or raisins.

Viking coins ▶

"It is said, that their after-boat was filled with grapes. A cargo sufficient for the ship was cut, and when the spring came, they made their ship ready, and sailed away; and from its products Leif [Eriksson] gave the land a name, and called it Wineland [Vinland]. They sailed out to sea, and had fair winds until they sighted Greenland."

—from *Original Narratives of Early American History*

▼ Viking ship

Viking bracelet ▶

Critical Thinking
Speculating Why do you think Leif Eriksson gave the land he found the name "Vinland"?

Columbus Crosses the Atlantic

Main Idea After Christopher Columbus reached the Americas, Spain and Portugal divided the world's unexplored regions.

History and You Do you like traveling to new places? Read to learn about the European exploration of the Americas.

. . . .

Christopher **Columbus** had a different plan for reaching Asia. He planned to get there by sailing west. Born in Genoa, Italy, in 1451, Columbus became a sailor for Portugal. He had traveled as far north as the Arctic Circle and as far south as the Gold Coast.

In the 1400s most educated people believed the world was round. A more difficult matter was determining its size. Columbus was among those who based their estimates of the Earth's size on the work of Ptolemy, an ancient Greek astronomer. Columbus believed Asia was about 2,760 miles (4,441 km) from Europe—a voyage of about two months by ship. Ptolemy, however, underestimated the size of the world.

The Viking Voyages

Several centuries before Columbus, northern Europeans called Vikings had sailed to North America. In the A.D. 800s and 900s, Viking ships visited Iceland and Greenland and established settlements. According to Norse **sagas,** or traditional stories, a Viking sailor named Leif Eriksson explored a land west of Greenland about the year A.D. 1000. It was known as Vinland. Other Norse sagas describe failed attempts by the Vikings to settle in Vinland, which historians believe was North America. Archaeologists have found the remains of a Viking settlement in Newfoundland. No one is sure what other parts of North America the Vikings explored.

The Viking voyages to other lands were not well-known. Europeans did not "discover" the Americas until Columbus made his great voyage.

Activity: Collaborative Learning

Verbal/Linguistic Ask: What is a Viking saga? *(a traditional story told by the Vikings)* Find excerpts from translations of Viking sagas on the Internet or at the library, and distribute copies in class. Have students read them and discuss what information the Vikings included about themselves in their writings. Then ask the class to form small groups. The groups should research to learn more about Leif Eriksson's explorations and then write a page about him that might be included in a saga. Each group will read its saga aloud to the class. **OL**

Spain Backs Columbus

For most of the 1400s, Spanish monarchs **devoted,** or committed, their energy to driving the Muslims out of Spain. The last Muslim kingdom in Spain fell in 1492. King Ferdinand and Queen Isabella of Spain could then focus on other goals. The Spanish were watching the seafaring and trading successes of neighboring Portugal with envy. They, too, wanted the riches of Asian trade.

Columbus needed a sponsor to finance his project of a westward voyage to Asia. He visited many European courts looking for support. After years of frustration, he finally found a sponsor in Spain.

Queen Isabella, a devout Christian, was finally persuaded by her husband's minister of finance to support the expedition for two reasons. First, Columbus promised to bring Christianity to any lands he found. Second, if he found a way to Asia, Spain would become wealthy through the trade that would open up. The queen promised Columbus a share of any riches gained from lands he discovered on his way to Asia.

Columbus's First Voyage

On August 3, 1492, Columbus set out from Palos, Spain. He had two small ships, the *Niña* and the *Pinta,* and a larger one, the *Santa María.* Columbus served as captain of the *Santa María,* his flagship. The three ships carried about 90 sailors and a six-month supply of provisions. The small fleet stopped at the Canary Islands off the coast of West Africa for repairs and to stock up on supplies. Columbus then set out on the difficult voyage westward across unknown and mysterious stretches of the Atlantic Ocean.

The ships had good winds, but after a month at sea the sailors began to worry. Columbus, however, was determined.

R Reading Strategy

Using Context Clues Remind students that they can use clues to find the meaning of an unfamiliar word from the surrounding text. **Ask:** What does "provisions" mean? (*Necessary supplies, such as food and water, arranged for ahead of time. Clues in the text are* "six-month supply" *and* "stock up on supplies.") **ELL**

People IN HISTORY

Critical Thinking Answers

1. arriving in India, obtaining rewards, achieving high rank, and ruling the lands he discovered
2. Students may respond that Queen Isabella wanted to convert the Native Americans to Christianity. She wanted settlers to interact with Native Americans so that they could influence them.

People IN HISTORY

Isabella
Queen of Spain

Queen Isabella was a devout Christian, and her beliefs were reflected in many aspects of her rule. She insisted that Columbus treat the Native Americans fairly and ordered Columbus to release several Native Americans that he brought back as slaves. Isabella truly hoped to Christianize the Native Americans. She decreed that because *"Indians . . . run away from the Christians . . . I order you . . . to compel the Indians to have dealings with the Christian settlers . . . to work on their buildings, to mine and collect gold . . . and to work on their farms and crop fields."*

Christopher Columbus
Italian Explorer

On his voyages, Columbus proved himself to be a great navigator and sailor. He believed he would discover great riches and new lands while exploring the Atlantic on the way to Asia. Before his first voyage, Columbus wrote: *"Your Highnesses commanded me . . . [to] go to . . . India, and for this accorded me great rewards and ennobled [praised] me so that from that time henceforth I might style myself 'Don' and be high admiral of the Ocean Sea and . . . Governor of the islands and continent which I should discover."*

CRITICAL Thinking

1. **Explaining** Based on the quotation, what were Columbus's goals for himself and his voyage?
2. **Analyzing** Which do you think was more important to Queen Isabella: converting the Native Americans to her religion or getting them to work? Explain your answer.

Activity: Creating a Time Line

Summarizing Ask students to create a time line of Columbus's voyages. Have them use colored pencils, markers, or pictures cut from magazines to illustrate the time line, using its general themes, such as old ships, navigational instruments, and the Spanish flag. **Ask:** How many voyages did Columbus make? What country did he represent on his trips? (*Check students' time lines for correct chronological order, relative spacing, and appropriateness of illustrations. Columbus made four voyages for Spain, in 1492, 1493, 1498, and 1502.*) **BL, ELL**

W Writing Support

Expository Writing Ask students to research the people who lived on San Salvador when Columbus arrived. Tell them to learn about their houses, physical appearance, culture, and attitude toward the Europeans. Students should then present their findings in one-page papers. **OL**

European Voyages of Exploration NATIONAL GEOGRAPHIC

Map Skills Answer

Vespucci, sailing for Spain, traveled right along the coast. Students might answer Cabral, who was sailing for Portugal. The map shows that Cabral, however, sailed more throughout the Atlantic Ocean.

Map Skills Practice

Have students look at the routes of other explorers on the map and note those explorers who sailed near land and those who sailed the open sea. Discuss the benefits of sailing along a coastline. (*Explorers would acquire more knowledge about the land's geographic features and inhabitants, along with better proximity to food and fresh water.*) **OL**

Differentiated Instruction

European Voyages of Exploration NATIONAL GEOGRAPHIC

John Cabot suggested that a voyage across the Atlantic could be quickened by sailing at a more northerly latitude than Columbus's route.

Spanish
➝ Christopher Columbus (1492–1493)
➝ Amerigo Vespucci (1499–1500)
Portuguese
➝ Pedro Cabral (1500)
English
➝ John Cabot (1497–1498)
➝ Martin Frobisher (1576–1578)
French
➝ Giovanni da Verrazano (1524)
➝ Jacques Cartier (1535)
Dutch
➝ Henry Hudson (1609)

Verrazano explored the Atlantic coast from present-day Cape Fear, North Carolina, to perhaps as far north as Newfoundland.

Map Skills

Movement Which explorer traveled along the coast of Brazil? For which country did he sail?

Maps In Motion See StudentWorks™ Plus or glencoe.com.

He told the men, "I made this voyage to go to the Indies, and [I] shall continue until I find them, with God's help." To convince the crew that they had not traveled too far from home, Columbus **altered,** or changed, the distances in his ship's log.

"Tierra! Tierra!"

On October 12, 1492, at two o'clock in the morning, a lookout shouted, *"Tierra! Tierra!"*—"Land! Land!" He had spotted a small island, part of the group of islands now called the Bahamas. Columbus went ashore, claimed the island for Spain, and named it San Salvador. Although he did not know it, Columbus had reached the Americas.

W Columbus explored the area for several months, convinced he had reached the East Indies, the islands off the coast of Asia. Today the Caribbean Islands are often referred to as the West Indies. Columbus called the local people Indians. He noted that they regarded the Europeans with wonder and often touched them to find out "if they were flesh and bones like themselves."

Columbus returned to Spain in triumph. Queen Isabella and King Ferdinand received him with great honor and agreed to finance his future voyages to the lands in the west. Columbus earned the title of Admiral of the Ocean Sea.

Columbus's Later Voyages

Columbus made three more voyages from Spain, in 1493, 1498, and 1502. He explored the Caribbean islands of Hispaniola (present-day Haiti and the Dominican Republic), Cuba, and Jamaica. He also sailed along the coasts of Central America and northern South America. He claimed the new lands for Spain and established settlements. Columbus also mapped the coastline of Central America.

Later explorations made it clear that Columbus had not reached Asia at all.

Leveled Activities

BL Reading Essentials and Note-Taking Guide, p. 13

OL Reteaching Activity, URB p. 65

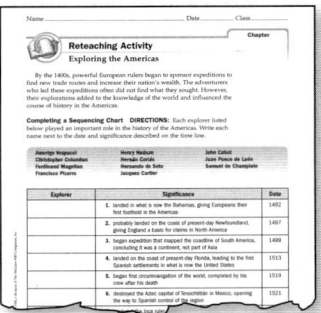

ELL Academic Vocabulary, URB p. 47

He had found a part of the globe that was unknown to Europeans, Asians, and Africans. In the following years, the Spanish explored most of the Caribbean region. In time their voyages led to the establishment of the Spanish Empire in the Americas.

Dividing the World

Both Spain and Portugal wanted to protect their claims, and they turned to Pope Alexander VI for help. In 1493 the pope drew a **line of demarcation,** an imaginary line running down the middle of the Atlantic from the North Pole to the South Pole. Spain was to control all lands to the west of the line; Portugal controlled all lands to the east of the line. Portugal, however, protested that the division favored Spain. As a result, in 1494 the two countries signed the Treaty of Tordesillas (TOHR•day•SEE•yuhs), an agreement to move the line farther west. The treaty divided the entire unexplored world between Spain and Portugal.

Exploring America

After Columbus, other voyagers explored the Americas. In 1502 **Amerigo Vespucci** sailed along South America's coast. Vespucci concluded that South America was a conti-

nent, not part of Asia. European geographers soon began calling the continent America, in honor of Amerigo Vespucci.

Another Spaniard, Vasco Núñez de Balboa (bal•BOH•uh), heard stories of the "great waters" beyond the mountains of Panama, in Central America. He hiked through steamy rain forests until he reached the opposite coast. There, in 1513, Balboa found a vast body of water, claiming it and the adjoining lands for Spain. Balboa was the first European to see the Pacific Ocean from the Americas.

Sailing Around the World

In 1520 **Ferdinand Magellan,** a Portuguese seaman sailing for Spain, reached the southernmost tip of South America. He sailed through the stormy waters of a **strait,** or narrow sea passage, into the ocean Balboa had seen. The waters were so peaceful—*pacifico* in Spanish—that Magellan named the ocean the Pacific. Although Magellan later died in the Philippine Islands, his crew continued west, arriving in Spain in 1522. They became the first known people to **circumnavigate,** or sail around, the world.

✓ **Reading Check** Describing Why did Spain finance Columbus's voyage?

C Critical Thinking

Predicting Consequences Ask: How do you predict other countries viewed the Line of Demarcation? *(Answers will vary, but students may say that other countries ignored the line or that the line would lead to conflict among countries.)* **BL**

S Skill Practice

Creating a Time Line Ask students to create a time line showing when other voyagers explored the Americas. **OL**

✓ **Reading Check** **Answer:** so he could find a trade route to Asia and spread Christianity

Assess

History ONLINE

Study Central™ provides summaries, interactive games, and online graphic organizers to help students review content.

Close

Discussing As a class, discuss why Spain and Portugal desired a sea route to Asia. **OL**

Section 2 Review

History ONLINE
Study Central™ To review this section, go to glencoe.com.

Vocabulary

1. Using complete sentences, define the following terms: saga, devote, alter, line of demarcation, strait, circumnavigate.

Main Ideas

2. **Identifying** What route did the Portuguese explorers follow to get to Asia? Which explorer arrived first?

3. **Describing** How did Spain and Portugal divide up the entire unexplored world?

Critical Thinking

4. **Analyzing** How did Henry the Navigator further exploration?

5. **Persuasive Writing** Write a paragraph explaining why Americans might celebrate Eriksson Day rather than Columbus Day.

6. **Sequencing** Use a time line like the one below to show when the following explorers carried out their journeys: Columbus, Eriksson, Magellan, Balboa.

Answer the
7. **Essential Question**
Why did Spain and Portugal want to find a sea route to Asia?

Exploring the Americas **Chapter 2** 41

Section 2 Review

Answers

1. Students should write sentences in which the terms are defined.
2. around the southern tip of Africa; Vasco da Gama
3. The pope drew an imaginary line down the middle of the Atlantic Ocean from the North Pole to the South Pole; Spain controlled lands west of the line and Portugal controlled lands to the east of it. A year later the Treaty of Tordesillas moved the line farther west.

4. He founded a "school of navigation" at Sarges, in Portugal, where he planned voyages and analyzed findings of explorers. He also brought together astronomers, geographers, and mathematicians to share knowledge with sailors and shipbuilders.
5. Students will write persuasive paragraphs in favor of honoring Leif Eriksson's exploration of Vinland in North America, which occurred before Columbus's voyages.

6. Students should list the explorers in this order: Eriksson (1000), Columbus (1492), Balboa (1513), Magellan (1520).
7. If the Portuguese and Spanish could find a sea route to Asia, they could trade directly with India and China.

Focus

Section 3

Spain in America

Bellringer
Daily Test Practice Transparency 2–3

Reading Guide
Answers to Graphic:
Top to bottom: *peninsulares*, creoles, mestizos, Native Americans, enslaved Africans

Section Spotlight Video

Have students watch the Section Spotlight Video "Spain in North America" to learn more about the conquistadors.

Essential Question
How did Spain's conquests affect the economic and social development of the Americas?

Reading Guide

Content Vocabulary
conquistador *(p. 43)*   encomienda *(p. 47)*
pueblo *(p. 46)*   plantation *(p. 47)*
mission *(p. 46)*

Academic Vocabulary
grant *(p. 43)*   found *(p. 46)*

Key People
Hernán Cortés *(p. 43)*
Montezuma *(p. 43)*
Francisco Pizarro *(p. 44)*
Atahualpa *(p. 44)*
Hernando de Soto *(p. 46)*

Reading Strategy
Taking Notes As you read, use a diagram like the one below to rank the social classes in the Spanish colonies.

Enslaved Africans

ILLINOIS STANDARDS
The American Journey

16.A.3a Describe how historians use models for organizing historical interpretation (e.g., biographies, political events, issues and conflicts).

17.A.3a Explain how people use geographic markers and boundaries to analyze and navigate the Earth (e.g., hemispheres, meridians, continents, bodies of water).

17.C Understand relationships between geographic factors and society.

18.B.3a Analyze how individuals and groups interact with and within institutions (e.g., educational, military).

American Diary

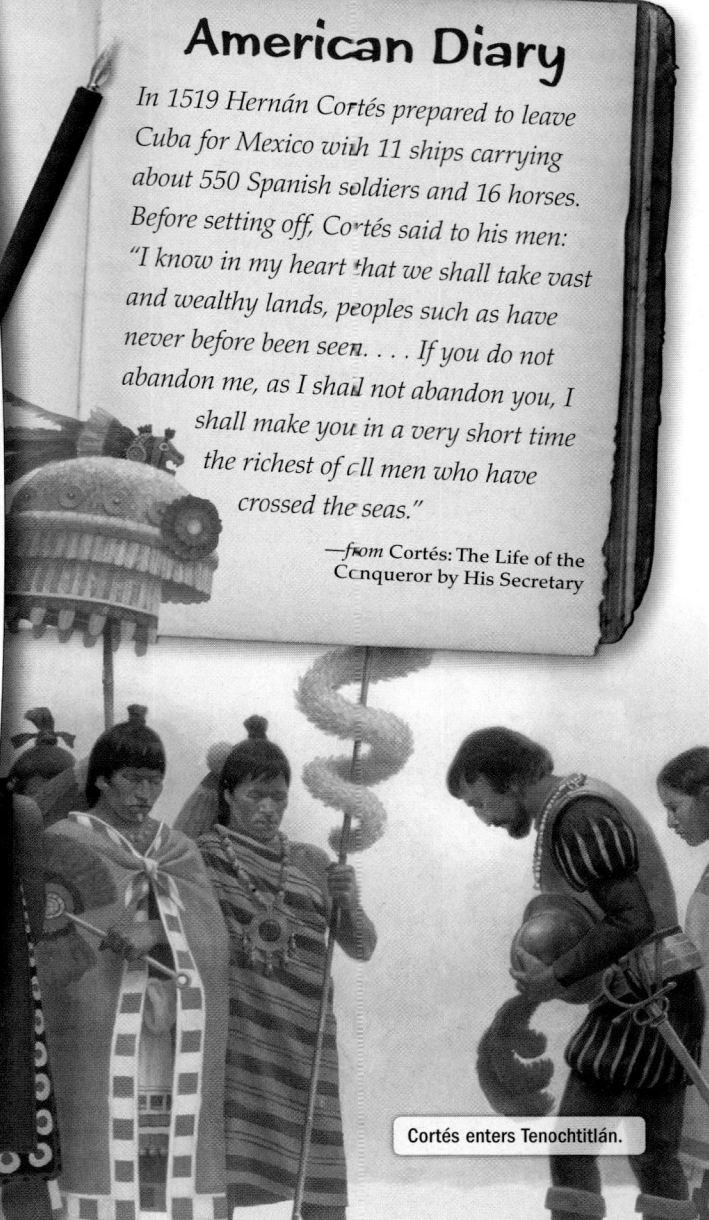

In 1519 Hernán Cortés prepared to leave Cuba for Mexico with 11 ships carrying about 550 Spanish soldiers and 16 horses. Before setting off, Cortés said to his men: "I know in my heart that we shall take vast and wealthy lands, peoples such as have never before been seen. . . . If you do not abandon me, as I shall not abandon you, I shall make you in a very short time the richest of all men who have crossed the seas."

—*from* Cortés: The Life of the Conqueror by His Secretary

Cortés enters Tenochtitlán.

Resource Manager

R Reading Strategies	**C** Critical Thinking	**D** Differentiated Instruction	**W** Writing Support	**S** Skill Practice
Teacher Edition • Questioning, p. 43 • Identifying, p. 44 • Visualizing, p. 46 **Additional Resources** • Guid. Read., URB p. 69 • Content Vocab., URB p. 45 • Acad. Vocab., URB p. 47 • Pri. Source Read., URB p. 49 • Read. Ess., p. 16	**Teacher Edition** • Predict. Conseq., p. 43 • Making General., p. 46 **Additional Resources** • Quizzes and Tests, p. 13 • Link. Past & Pres., URB p. 61	**Teacher Edition** • Verbal/Linguistic, p. 47 **Additional Resources** • Reteach, URB p. 65 • School-to-Home, URB p. 63	**Teacher Edition** • Descriptive Writing, p. 45	**Teacher Edition** • Using Geo. Skills, p. 45 **Additional Resources** • Daily Test Pract. Transp. 2-3 • Lesson Transp., 2B, 2C • Soc. Stud. Skills, URB p. 53 • Time Line Skills, URB p. 62

Explorers and Conquests

Main Idea Spanish explorers conquered Native American empires and found new lands.

History and You What would you look for as you hike along a nature trail? Read to learn what some Spanish explorers looked for as they traveled on foot through the Americas.

Stories of gold, silver, and kingdoms wealthy beyond belief greeted the early Spanish explorers in the Americas. The reports led them far and wide in search of fabulous riches.

These explorers, known as **conquistadors** (kahn•KEES•tuh•dawrs), received **grants,** or special privileges, from the Spanish rulers. These grants gave them the right to explore and establish settlements in the Americas. In exchange, they agreed to give the Spanish crown one-fifth of any gold or other treasure discovered. This arrangement allowed Spanish rulers to launch expeditions with little risk. If a conquistador failed, he lost his own fortune. If he succeeded, both he and Spain gained wealth and glory.

Cortés Conquers the Aztec

When **Hernán Cortés** landed on the east coast of present-day Mexico in 1519, he was looking for gold and glory. He came with more than 500 soldiers, some horses, and a few cannons. Cortés soon learned about the great Aztec Empire and its capital of Tenochtitlán (tay•NAWCH•teet•LAHN). **R**

The Aztec conquered many cities in Mexico to build their empire. These cities were forced to give crops, clothing, gold, and precious stones to the Aztec as tribute, or money paid for protection. Cortés formed alliances with a number of these conquered people against the Aztec. Then he marched into Tenochtitlán with his small army and his Native American allies. **C**

The Aztec emperor, **Montezuma** (MAHN•tuh•ZOO•muh)—also spelled Moctezuma—welcomed Cortés and his soldiers and provided them with food and a fine palace. However, Cortés took advantage of the hospitality and made Montezuma his prisoner. The Aztec rebelled in the spring of 1520. During the fighting, which lasted for days, Montezuma was killed.

Teach

R Reading Strategy

Questioning Have students use clues in the paragraph to predict what might happen when the Spanish and the Aztec meet. Remind students to ask themselves questions to make their predictions, such as "Why would Cortés travel with soldiers and cannons?" **BL**

C Critical Thinking

Predicting Consequences Ask: Do you think the people who paid tribute to the Aztec would feel loyalty to them? *(No, they probably felt resentment or hatred.)* **OL**

Primary Source

Critical Thinking Answer
Students may say that the Aztec stressed how fearsome Cortés's men were; Cortés stressed loyalty and how he would help make his men rich.

Primary Source / The Aztec and the Spanish

An Aztec View Hernán Cortés and his soldiers arrived on the Mexican coast in April 1519. The people of eastern Mexico felt fear and awe as they watched the soldiers. One Aztec later recalled:

"They came in battle array, as conquerors . . . their spears glinted in the sun, and their pennons [banners] fluttered like bats. They made a loud clamor as they marched, for their coats of mail and their weapons clashed and rattled. . . . They terrified everyone who saw them."

—from *The Broken Spears*

Critical Thinking

Comparing and Contrasting How do you think the Aztec's report differs from Cortés's speech?

Differentiated Instruction

Leveled Activities

BL Guided Reading,
URB p. 69

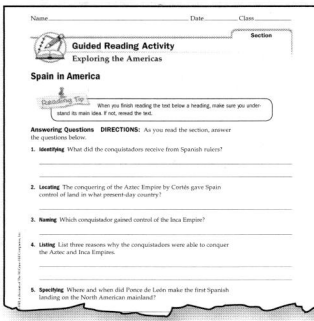

OL Time Line Skills Activity,
URB p. 62

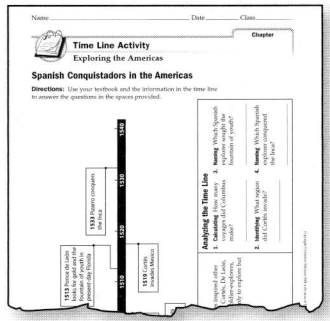

ELL Primary Source Reading
Activity, URB p. 49

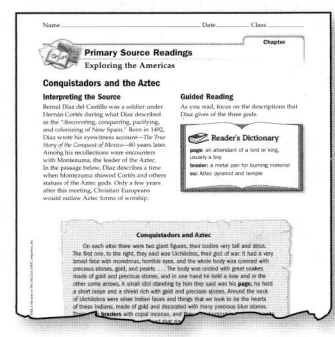

R Reading Strategy

Identifying Ask: What is the main idea of this text? *(It is a sad time because the Aztec nation has been destroyed.)* **OL**

This **READING SKILL** (Identifying the Main Idea) was introduced in this unit.

Spanish Explorers 1513–1598   NATIONAL GEOGRAPHIC

Map Skills Answer

De Soto

Graph Skills Practice

What was the value of the gold and silver sent to Spain from 1576 to 1580? *(17.5 million pesos)* **OL**

Additional Support

Eventually, the Spanish were forced to leave Tenochtitlán. Cortés, however, was determined to retake the city. He waited until more Spanish troops arrived, and then he attacked and destroyed the Aztec capital in 1521. An Aztec poem describes the scene:

> **PRIMARY SOURCE**
>
> "Without roofs are the houses,
> And red are their walls with blood.
> . . . .
> Weep, my friends,
> Know that with these disasters
> We have lost our Mexican nation."
>
> —from *Stolen Continents*

The Aztec Empire disintegrated, and Spain seized control of the region.

Pizarro Conquers the Inca

The conquistador **Francisco Pizarro** sailed down the Pacific coast of South America with about 180 Spanish soldiers. Pizarro had heard tales of the incredibly wealthy Inca Empire in what is now Peru. In 1532 Pizarro captured the Inca ruler, **Atahualpa** (AH•tah•WAHL•pah), and destroyed much of the Inca army.

The following year, the Spanish falsely accused Atahualpa of crimes and executed him. Without their leader, the Inca were not able to fight effectively. Pizarro soon gained control of most of the vast Inca Empire.

Why Spain Succeeded

The conquistadors' victories over the Aztec and Inca were quick and lasting. How could Cortés and Pizarro, with only their small armies, conquer such mighty empires?

First, the Spanish arrived with weapons—guns and cannons—and animals that the Aztec and Inca had never seen. The Spanish rode horses and had huge, ferocious dogs. To the Native Americans, the Spanish seemed almost like gods. Second, some Native Americans in the region disliked their Aztec overlords.

Spanish Explorers, 1513–1598   NATIONAL GEOGRAPHIC

Ponce de León 1513
Cabeza de Vaca 1528–1536
De Soto 1539–1542
Coronado 1540–1542
Oñate 1598–1605
Present-day boundaries

800 kilometers
800 miles
Lambert Azimuthal Equal-Area projection

By the Numbers

American Wealth Sent to Spain

Value of gold and silver in millions of pesos

1503–05	1536–40	1576–80	1616–20
1	7	17.5	23

Source: *American Treasure and the Price of Revolution in Spain*

Map Skills

Movement Which conquistador explored areas along the southern half of the Mississippi River?

Maps in MOtion See StudentWorks™ Plus or glencoe.com.

Fast Facts

The Inca Empire Beginning in the 1440s, the Inca extended their empire from what is now Peru to Ecuador, central Chile, and the edge of the Amazon basin. The empire included perhaps 12 million people.

The young men of the Inca Empire served in the army. When a new region was conquered by the impressive army, a noble was sent to govern the region; local leaders could remain if they were loyal to the Inca ruler.

The Inca created buildings and monuments that stunned early European visitors. They had a road system of some 24,800 miles (around 40,000 km) that, like other Inca public works projects, was built by subjects in mandatory labor service. The Inca, like other people in the early Americas, did not use the wheel. They carried supplies by llama. Other accomplishments of the Inca included terraced and irrigated farms, a method of keeping records using a system of knotted strings (the *quipu*), and an active theater tradition.

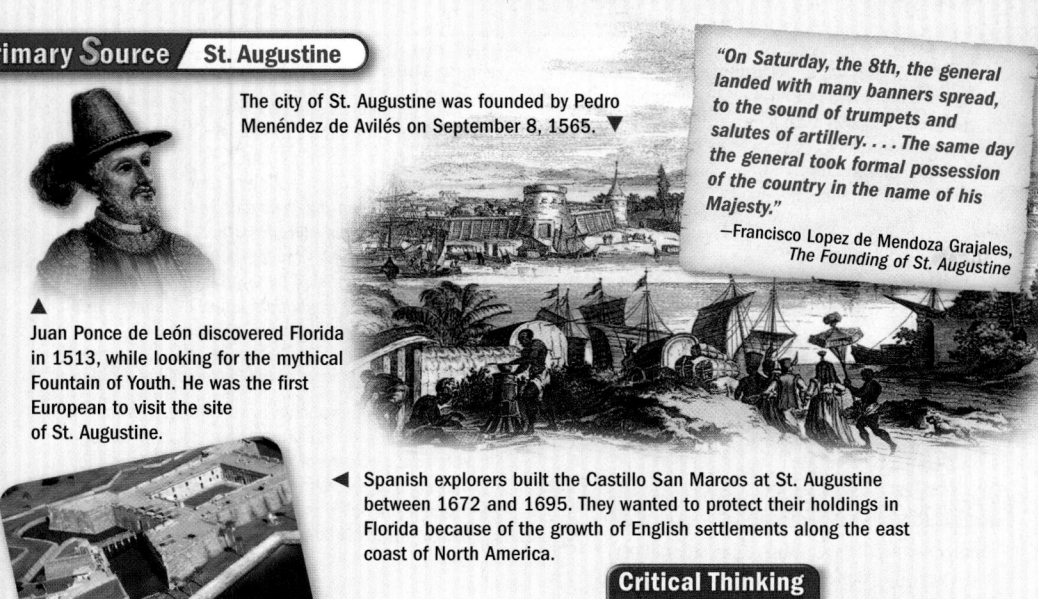

Primary Source / St. Augustine

The city of St. Augustine was founded by Pedro Menéndez de Avilés on September 8, 1565. ▼

"On Saturday, the 8th, the general landed with many banners spread, to the sound of trumpets and salutes of artillery. . . . The same day the general took formal possession of the country in the name of his Majesty."

—Francisco Lopez de Mendoza Grajales, *The Founding of St. Augustine*

▲ Juan Ponce de León discovered Florida in 1513, while looking for the mythical Fountain of Youth. He was the first European to visit the site of St. Augustine.

◀ Spanish explorers built the Castillo San Marcos at St. Augustine between 1672 and 1695. They wanted to protect their holdings in Florida because of the growth of English settlements along the east coast of North America.

Critical Thinking

Explaining Why did the Spanish fortify St. Augustine?

These peoples assisted the conquistadors in overthrowing the Aztec. Finally, disease played an extremely large role in the Spanish conquest. With no immunity to European diseases, the Aztec and the Inca quickly fell victim to epidemics of smallpox and other diseases. This situation weakened their resistance to the invaders.

Spain in North America

S Mexico and Peru were rich in silver and gold. Hoping to find similar wealth to the north, conquistadors explored the southeastern and southwestern parts of North America.

W Juan Ponce de León made the first Spanish landing on the North American mainland, arriving on the east coast of present-day Florida in 1513. According to legend, Ponce de León hoped to find not only gold but also the legendary fountain of youth, "a spring of running water of such marvelous virtue" that drinking it "makes old men young again." Ponce de León's exploration led to the first Spanish settlement in what is now the United States. In 1565, the Spanish built a fort at St. Augustine, Florida.

The Seven Cities of Cibola

Many other conquistadors searched for quick riches and several lost their lives trying. Álvar Núñez Cabeza de Vaca (cah•BAY•sah day VAH•cah) was part of a Spanish expedition to Florida in 1528.

After encountering troubles in Florida, the expedition, led by Pánfilo de Narváez, sailed south toward Mexico. However, in November 1528, three of the five boats were lost in a storm. The two boats that survived went aground on an island near what is now the state of Texas. Within a few months, only a handful of the Spaniards were still alive.

To survive among the Native Americans, de Vaca and an enslaved African named Estevanico became medicine men. Cabeza de Vaca later wrote that their method of healing was "to bless the sick, breathing on them," and to recite Latin prayers.

Exploring the Americas **Chapter 2** **45**

CHAPTER 2
Section 3

S Skill Practice

Using Geography Skills Ask: Which explorer traveled farthest west in North America according to the map on the previous page? *(Oñate)* **BL**

W Writing Support

Descriptive Writing Ask students to take the role of an explorer who is searching for the legendary fountain of youth. Have students describe the search in a letter to a family member back home in Spain. **OL**

Primary Source

Critical Thinking Answer
to protect their holdings in Florida against the English settlers

Skills Practice Have students describe Castillo San Marcos and why it would help protect St. Augustine. *(Its high, thick walls could protect people inside the fort and make it easier to defend.)*

Hands-On Chapter Project
Step 3

Creating a Historical Calendar

Step 3: Writing a Description of Each Image Each group will write interesting descriptions of the images in its calendar.

Essential Question: How did Spain's conquests affect the economic and social development of the Americas?

Directions Ask students to divide the 12 images or groups of images among the members of the group. Have students gather information about their images and write a short paragraph for each. These will be placed near that image or group of images in the calendar. Stress that the paragraphs should describe what the images show and how the person, technological development, or event was important in the early exploration and colonization of the Americas. Tell students to include information about the economy and society of the Americas where possible.

Identifying Have each group choose an image that illustrates an economic or social characteristic of the Americas. As a class, discuss how those images illustrate the effects of conquest by Spain or another colonizing nation.

(Chapter Project continued in Section 4)

45

C Critical Thinking

Making Generalizations Ask: What generalization can you make about the seven cities of gold? *(They did not exist.)* **BL**

R Reading Strategy

Visualizing Remind students that good readers visualize images in their minds as they read. Have students read the paragraph and create a mental map of a mission community. **OL**

Reading Check **Answer:** The Spanish had weapons (guns and cannons), horses, and dogs, making them seem godlike; many Native Americans helped the Spanish fight their Aztec rulers; the Spanish weakened the Native Americans by unknowingly exposing them to European diseases.

DBQ Document-Based Questions

Answer

The Spanish persecuted and murdered the Native Americans, as well as decimated their population.

Differentiated Instruction

Primary Source | Spanish Treatment of Native Peoples

Native Americans in Slavery Mistreatment of the native peoples by the Spanish led the missionary Father Bartolomé de Las Casas to come to the native peoples' defense. His account led Spanish officials to prohibit the enslavement of local peoples.

DBQ Document-Based Questions

Analyzing According to Las Casas, what effect did Spanish treatment have on the Native American population?

"[T]he Spaniards still do nothing save tear the natives to shreds, murder them and inflict upon them untold misery, suffering and distress, tormenting, harrying and persecuting them mercilessly.... When the Spanish first journeyed there, the indigenous population of the island of Hispaniola stood at some three million; today only two hundred survive."

—Bartolomé de Las Casas,
A Short Account of the Destruction of the Indies

"[O]ne of the most important things in which the Audiencias [courts] are to serve us is in taking very especial care of the good treatment of the Indians and preservation of them.... We have ordered provision to be made that from henceforward the Indians in no way be made slaves."

—from *Colonialism*

In 1533 the Spaniards set off on a long trip across the Southwest. Reaching Mexico in 1536, Cabeza de Vaca related tales about seven cities of gold.

Inspired by these stories, **Hernando de Soto** led an expedition to the west. For three years they wandered throughout the present-day southeastern United States, seizing food and supplies from Native Americans. In 1541 De Soto crossed the Mississippi River. After reaching what is today Oklahoma, de Soto died of fever.

Francisco Vásquez de Coronado also wanted to find the "Seven Cities of Cibola." Traveling through northern Mexico and present-day Arizona and New Mexico, his expedition reached a Zuni settlement in 1540. They realized at once that there was no gold. Members of the expedition traveled west to the Colorado River and east into what is now Kansas. They found nothing but "windswept plains" and strange "shaggy cows" (buffalo).

Reading Check **Analyzing** How were Spaniards able to defeat Native American empires?

Spanish Rule

Main Idea As the Spanish settled their colonies in the Americas, a strict social class structure formed.

History and You Have you ever visited or seen pictures of old Spanish missions in the American Southwest? Read to learn how the Spanish settled the Americas.

Spanish law called for three kinds of settlements in the Americas—pueblos, missions, and presidios. **Pueblos,** or towns, were established as centers of trade. **Missions** were religious communities that usually included a small town, surrounding farmland, and a church. A presidio, or fort, was usually built near a mission.

The Spanish sent Juan de Oñate (day ohn•YAH•tay) from Mexico to gain control over frontier lands to the north and to convert the inhabitants to Christianity. In 1598 Oñate **founded,** or established, the province of New Mexico and introduced cattle and horses to the Pueblo people there.

Understanding the Parts of a Map

Objective: To read and create a map

Focus: Ask students why it is important to know how to read maps.

Teach: Have students practice their map skills using the questions and activity.

Assess: Have students evaluate their skills using the self-assessment checklist.

Close: Discuss how students use maps in their daily lives.

Differentiated Instruction Strategies

BL Have students find locations on a map of their school.

AL Ask students to use an Internet mapping program to get directions from their home to school. Have them verify the accuracy of the directions.

ELL Have students list unfamiliar words in the activity and create a glossary to learn their definitions.

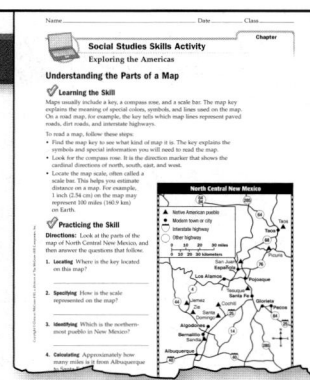

Social Studies Skills, URB p. 53

Social Classes

A class system developed in Spain's empire. At the top were people who were born in Spain, called *peninsulares*. The *peninsulares* owned the land, served in the Catholic Church, and ran the local government. Below them were the creoles, people who were born in the Americas to Spanish parents. Lower in order were the mestizos (meh•STEE•zohs), people with Spanish and Native American parents. Still lower were the Native Americans, most of whom lived in great poverty. At the bottom were enslaved Africans.

In the 1500s, the Spanish government granted conquistadors who settled in the Americas an *encomienda,* the right to demand taxes or labor from Native Americans living on the land. This system turned the Native Americans into slaves. Grueling labor took its toll. Many Native Americans died from malnutrition and disease.

A Spanish priest, Bartolomé de Las Casas, condemned the cruel treatment of the Native Americans. He pleaded for laws to protect them. Las Casas claimed that millions had died because the Spanish "made gold their ultimate aim, seeking to load themselves with riches in the shortest possible time."

Las Casas's reports influenced the Spanish government to pass the New Laws in 1542. These laws forbade making slaves of Native Americans. Although not always enforced, these laws did correct the worst abuses.

The Plantation System

Some Spanish settlers made large profits by exporting crops and raw materials to Spain. In the West Indies, the main exports were tobacco and sugarcane. To raise these crops, the Spanish developed the plantation system. A **plantation** is a large estate.

The Spanish used Native Americans to work their plantations. Las Casas suggested replacing them with enslaved Africans— a suggestion he bitterly regretted later. He thought the Africans could endure the labor better than the Native Americans. As a result, thousands of Africans from West Africa were brought to the Americas. The Africans who survived the brutal ocean voyage were sold to plantation owners. By the late 1500s, plantation slave labor was an essential part of the economy of the colonies.

Reading Check Identifying Whom did Las Casas try to protect?

History ONLINE
Study Central™ To review this section, go to glencoe.com.

D Differentiated Instruction

Verbal/Linguistic Ask: What does the word "creole" mean? *(those born in the Americas to Spanish parents)* **BL**

Reading Check **Answer:** Native Americans living on land that had been overtaken by the Spaniards

Assess

History ONLINE

Study Central™ provides summaries, interactive games, and online graphic organizers to help students review content.

Close

Identifying As a class, discuss the ways that the economy and culture of the Americas changed when Spanish explorers arrived. **OL**

Section 3 Review

Vocabulary

1. Write sentences or short paragraphs in which you define the following terms: conquistador, grant, pueblo, mission, found, *encomienda*, plantation.

Main Ideas

2. **Explaining** What were the first adventurers to explore North America looking for?

3. **Discussing** How did slavery begin in the Americas?

Critical Thinking

4. **Analyzing** Why were some Native Americans willing to form alliances with Cortés?

5. **Categorizing** Use a diagram like the one below to identify the explorers who went to each region.

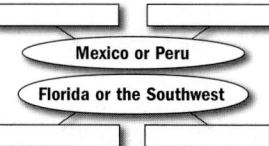

Mexico or Peru

Florida or the Southwest

6. **Expository Writing** Write a short essay describing the Spanish exploration and settlement of the Americas.

Answer the
Essential Question
7. How did Spain's conquests affect the economic and social development of the Americas?

Section 3 Review

Answers

1. Students' sentences or short paragraphs should define the terms.
2. gold and other riches, the fountain of youth
3. Las Casas suggested that Africans would be better able to endure plantation work than Native Americans. When thousands of West African slaves were brought to the Americas, slave labor became important for the colonial economy.
4. They resented the Aztec, who had conquered them and demanded tribute to support the lavish Aztec cities.

5. Mexico or Peru: Cortés, Pizarro, Coronado; Florida or the Southwest: Ponce de León, Cabeza de Vaca, de Narváez, De Soto, Coronado, Oñate
6. Students' essays should identify Spanish explorers and the regions they covered, as well as the development of Spanish settlements.

7. Answers will vary but should include the following: The Spanish destroyed the Aztec and Inca Empires; settled in pueblos, missions, and presidios; introduced Catholicism, cattle, and horses; relegated Native Americans to the lower classes; introduced slaves to support tobacco and sugarcane plantations and exports.

Focus

Section 4

Exploring North America

Bellringer
Daily Test Practice Transparency 2–4

Reading Guide
Answers to Graphic:
John Cabot; Giovanni da Verrazano; Jacques Cartier; Henry Hudson

Section Spotlight Video

Have students watch the Section Spotlight Video "Exploring North America" to learn more about the Vikings.

Essential Question ◀
Why did European nations establish colonies in North America?

Reading Guide

Content Vocabulary

mercantilism (p. 50)	Northwest Passage (p. 51)
Columbian Exchange (p. 51)	coureur de bois (p. 52)

Academic Vocabulary

globe (p. 51)   chart (p. 51)

Key People and Events
Martin Luther (p. 49)
Protestant Reformation (p. 49)
John Calvin (p. 49)
John Cabot (p. 51)
Jacques Cartier (p. 51)
Henry Hudson (p. 51)

Reading Strategy
Taking Notes As you read, use a diagram like the one below to list the explorers who tried to find the Northwest Passage.

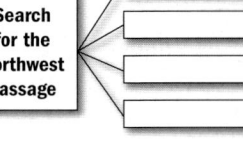

Search for the Northwest Passage

ILLINOIS STANDARDS
The American Journey

15.D Understand trade as an exchange of goods or services.

16.C.3a (US) Describe economic motivations that attracted Europeans and others to the Americas, 1500-1750.

16.D Understand, Illinois, United States and world social history.

18.B.3a Analyze how individuals and groups interact with and within institutions (e.g., educational, military).

American Diary

In 1639 a French nun named Marie of the Incarnation arrived in Quebec, New France's first colony. To convert Native Americans, she learned their languages and wrote religious books in those languages. In a letter, she wrote:
"You will perhaps laugh that at the age of fifty years I am beginning to study a new tongue [language], but one must undertake all things for the service of God and the salvation of one's neighbour."

—*from the book* Word From New France

Sister Marie and other French nuns arrive in Quebec.

Resource Manager

R Reading Strategies	C Critical Thinking	D Differentiated Instruction	W Writing Support	S Skill Practice
Teacher Edition • Taking Notes, p. 51 • Making Connect., p. 52 **Additional Resources** • Guid. Read., URB p. 70 • Content Vocab., URB p. 45 • Academic Vocab., URB p. 47 • Read. Ess., p. 19	**Teacher Edition** • Compar. & Contrast., p. 49 • Compar. & Contrast., p. 50 **Additional Resources** • Quizzes and Tests, p. 14	**Teacher Edition** • Kinesthetic, p. 51 **Additional Resources** • Reteach, URB p. 65 • School-to-Home, URB p. 63	**Teacher Edition** • Expository Writing, p. 50 **Additional Resources** • Citizen. & Dec. Mak., URB p. 3	**Teacher Edition** • Using Geo. Skills, p. 50 **Additional Resources** • Daily Test Pract. Transp. 2-4 • Geo. & Hist., URB p. 59

A Divided Church

Main Idea Protestantism became a powerful religious force in Europe during the 1600s.

History and You What motivates people to demand changes? Read to find out why Christianity changed in the 1500s.

. . . .

The desire to spread Christianity was a major reason that Europeans explored and settled North America. The earlier explorers and settlers were Roman Catholics. As overseas exploration was advancing in the 1500s, a religious upheaval in Europe was sparking religious divisions.

In 1517 **Martin Luther,** a German priest, nailed a list of complaints about the Catholic Church on a local church door. Luther declared that the Bible was the only true guide for Christians. He rejected many Church practices—even the authority of the pope—because they were not mentioned in the Bible. Luther also believed that faith rather than good deeds was the way to salvation.

Within a few years, Luther had many followers who broke away from Catholicism

to begin their own Christian churches. Luther's protests were the start of a great religious and historical movement known as the **Protestant Reformation.**

Protestantism Spreads in Europe

From Germany, Luther's ideas spread rapidly. **John Calvin,** a French religious thinker who lived in Geneva, Switzerland, also broke away from the Catholic Church. Like Luther, Calvin rejected the idea that good works alone would ensure a person's salvation and believed in the all-powerful nature of God.

Calvinists spread their faith to other people. Missionaries were sent from Geneva to all parts of Europe. Calvinism was established in France, the Netherlands, Scotland, and central and eastern Europe.

In England, King Henry VIII also left the Catholic Church, but not for strictly religious reasons. Pope Clement VII refused Henry's request to declare his first marriage invalid. In 1534 the English Parliament, working with the king, denied the authority of the pope and recognized the king as the head of the new Church of England.

Primary Source / Fur Trader Among the Native Americans

The Peacemaker Born in France, Jean Nicollet arrived in Quebec in 1618 at the age of 19. He became a fur trader and set out to learn Native American languages. For two years he lived among the Algonquins, *"always accompanying [them] on their expeditions and travels."* In about 1622 he succeeded in making peace between the Algonquins and the Iroquois. Eventually, Nicollet settled among the Nipissings, *"having his cabin apart, doing his own fishing and trading,"* but taking part in their frequent councils.

—from *The American Geologist*

▲ French fur trader Jean Nicollet and Native Americans participate in a peacemaking ceremony.

Critical Thinking

Comparing and Contrasting Do you think Nicollet's actions toward Native Americans were like or unlike the actions of other Europeans in North America? Explain.

Teach

. . . .

C Critical Thinking

Comparing and Contrasting Ask: How did King Henry VIII differ from others who left the Catholic Church? *(Others left the Catholic Church because of disagreements about Church teachings, but Henry VIII left because the pope refused to declare his marriage invalid.)* **BL**

Primary Source

Critical Thinking Answer
Nicollet's actions were different because he lived among the Native Americans and participated in their cultural practices.

Skills Practice Have students study the painting of Nicollet. **Ask:** What does the painting tell us about the relationship between Nicollet and Native Americans? *(Nicollet is shown in European dress as he appears to be participating in a Native American ritual. It can be inferred that he had close relationships with the Native Americans while retaining his European ways.)* **AL**

Hands-On Chapter Project
Step 4

Creating a Historical Calendar

Step 4: Creating the Calendar Students will use the images they collected and the descriptions they wrote in previous steps to create a calendar that represents the early exploration and colonization of the Americas.

Essential Question: Why did European nations establish colonies in North America?

Directions Show students the sample calen-

dars again for design ideas. Then have each group make its own calendar using the images they collected and the paragraphs they wrote.

Discussing Lead a class discussion about the motives behind European exploration and colonization of the Americas. Have students illustrate the motives using pages from their completed calendars.

(Chapter Project continued on the Visual Summary page)

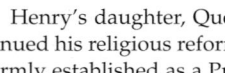

W Writing Support

Expository Writing Have students find the names and accomplishments of some famous people who lived during the reign of England's Elizabeth I. Instruct them to write a paragraph summarizing their findings. **OL**

S Skill Practice

Using Geography Skills The text describes the regions of the country settled by Spanish, French, Dutch, and English colonists. Organize students into small groups, and have them look at a road atlas. Ask students to list place names in each region that reflect the nationality of early settlers. **OL**

C Critical Thinking

Comparing and Contrasting Use a local newspaper to discuss the average price of a vacant lot in your community. Compare it to the amount the Dutch paid to buy New Amsterdam. **OL**

✔ **Reading Check**) **Answer:** Both Protestant and Catholic Europeans explored and settled in North America to spread their faith or to practice their beliefs more freely.

Additional Support

W Henry's daughter, Queen Elizabeth I, continued his religious reforms. England became firmly established as a Protestant nation.

Religious Rivalries in the Americas

The religious divisions between Catholics and Protestants in Europe also crossed the Atlantic. Spanish and French Catholics worked to spread their faith to the Native Americans. The Spanish settled in the southwestern and southeastern regions of North America, and the French settled in the northeast.

S Dutch and English Protestants established colonies in lands along the Atlantic coast between the French and the Spanish settlements. Some of the English settlements were founded by Protestants who wanted to practice their beliefs in peace.

✔ **Reading Check** **Explaining** What role did religion play in the exploration of North America?

Economic Rivalry

Main Idea European nations competed to establish colonies in the Americas.

C **History and You** Do you know if land in some parts of your neighborhood is more valuable than in other parts? Read to learn what the Dutch paid for Manhattan Island.

Religion was only one of the factors that pushed European nations across the Atlantic Ocean. The promise of great wealth was equally strong, especially as other Europeans watched Spain acquire gold and other riches from its colonies.

According to the economic theory of **mercantilism**, which was popular at the time, a nation's power is based on its wealth. Rulers tried to increase their nation's total wealth by acquiring gold and silver and by developing a continuing trade with other regions.

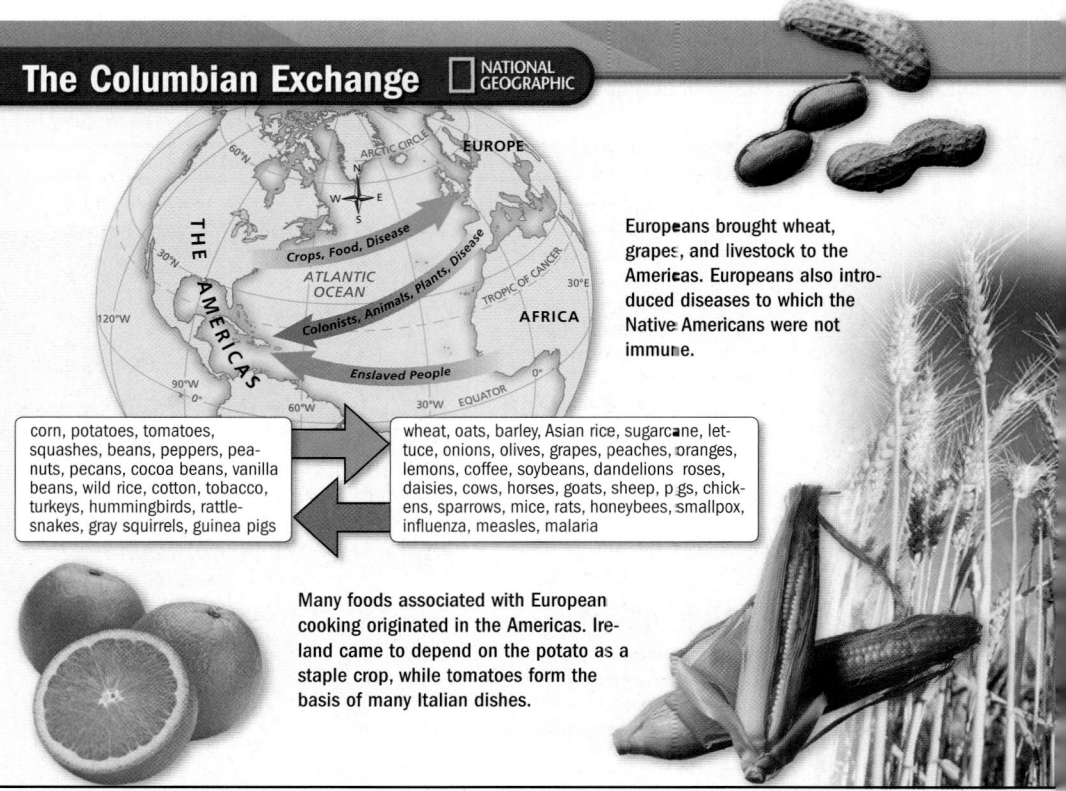

The Columbian Exchange NATIONAL GEOGRAPHIC

THE AMERICAS — ATLANTIC OCEAN — EUROPE — AFRICA

Crops, Food, Disease
Colonists, Animals, Plants, Disease
Enslaved People

Europeans brought wheat, grapes, and livestock to the Americas. Europeans also introduced diseases to which the Native Americans were not immune.

corn, potatoes, tomatoes, squashes, beans, peppers, peanuts, pecans, cocoa beans, vanilla beans, wild rice, cotton, tobacco, turkeys, hummingbirds, rattlesnakes, gray squirrels, guinea pigs

wheat, oats, barley, Asian rice, sugarcane, lettuce, onions, olives, grapes, peaches, oranges, lemons, coffee, soybeans, dandelions roses, daisies, cows, horses, goats, sheep, pigs, chickens, sparrows, mice, rats, honeybees, smallpox, influenza, measles, malaria

Many foods associated with European cooking originated in the Americas. Ireland came to depend on the potato as a staple crop, while tomatoes form the basis of many Italian dishes.

Economics Connection

Making Connections As a class, discuss the economic theory of mercantilism. Make sure students understand its underlying assumptions. **Ask: Do you think that nations today base their actions and policies on mercantilism?** This activity might be best suited to an all-class exploration and discussion. First, talk about how nations today define power, whether as wealth, military strength, cultural accomplishments, and so on. Then talk about how a nation's actions and policies reflect its idea of what power is and how it can be obtained. **OL**

Mercantilism provided great opportunities for individual merchants to make money. It also increased rivalry between nations.

Several countries in Europe competed for overseas territory that could produce wealth. They wanted to acquire colonies in the Americas that could provide valuable resources, such as gold and silver, or raw materials. The colonies also would serve as a place to sell European products.

The Columbian Exchange

The voyages of Columbus and other European explorers brought together two parts of the **globe** that previously had no contact: the continents of Europe, Asia, and Africa in one hemisphere and the Americas in the other. These contacts led to an exchange of plants, animals, and diseases that greatly altered life on both sides of the Atlantic Ocean. Scholars refer to this transfer as the **Columbian Exchange.**

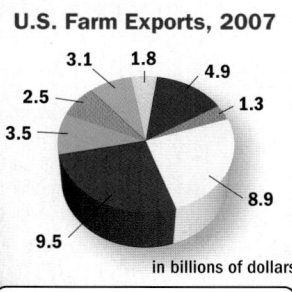

European Products in the United States

Food products introduced from Europe to the Americas are today a significant part of U.S. agriculture. The United States now exports many of these products to other countries, including Europe.

U.S. Farm Exports, 2007

3.1 1.8 4.9
2.5 1.3
3.5
8.9
9.5

in billions of dollars

- ■ Wheat   ■ Others
- ■ Rice   ■ Pork
- □ Corn   ■ Poultry and products
- ■ Soybean □ Dairy products

Source: U.S. Department of Agriculture estimates

Critical Thinking

Identifying Which of the agricultural exports in the chart above originated in the Americas? What percentage of exports did that product represent in 2007?

A Northwest Passage

The Treaty of Tordesillas had divided the Americas between Spain and Portugal. It did not allow for claims by other nations. England, France, and the Netherlands ignored the treaty. During the 1500s and early 1600s, these countries sent explorers to **chart,** or map, the coast of North America and, later, establish trade and colonies. Because the voyage to Asia—either around the southern tip of Africa or around South America—was long and difficult, they hoped to discover a **Northwest Passage** to Asia, a direct water route through the Americas.

In 1497 England sent **John Cabot,** an Italian, to look for a northern route to Asia. Cabot probably landed on the coast of present-day Newfoundland. England used Cabot's voyage as the basis for its claims to North America.

In 1524 France hired an Italian, Giovanni da Verrazano, to look for a northern sea route. Verrazano explored the coast of North America from present-day Nova Scotia down to the Carolinas.

In 1535, French explorer **Jacques Cartier** (KAR•tyay) sailed up the St. Lawrence River, hoping it would lead to the Pacific. From a mountain next to a Huron village on the river, Cartier wrote, "one sees a very great distance." He named the peak Mont-Royal, which means "royal mountain." This is the site of the city now called Montreal. Cartier heard stories about gold, but he found neither gold nor a sea route to Asia.

Hudson's Discoveries

The Netherlands, too, wanted to find a passage through the Americas. The Dutch nation hired **Henry Hudson,** an English sailor, to explore. In 1609 he discovered the river that now bears his name. In his ship, the *Half Moon,* Hudson sailed north on the Hudson River as far as the site of present-day Albany. Deciding that he had not found a passage to India, he turned back. The following year Hudson tried again, this time sent by England.

R Reading Strategy

Taking Notes Ask students to take notes as they read the rest of the section. Tell them to fold a sheet of paper in half lengthwise. At the top of the left column they should write "Country," and at the top of the right column, "Territory Explored or Settled." **OL**

D Differentiated Instruction

Kinesthetic Organize the class into small groups. Give each group a set of note cards, and have them write one product from the Columbian Exchange on each card and shuffle them. Take the class outside or to the gym. Each group will set two pieces of paper 10 feet (3 m) apart. Have them label one sheet "From Europe" and the other, "From the Americas." Groups should then compete to see which one can put the cards in the correct place the fastest. **OL**

The Columbian Exchange

NATIONAL GEOGRAPHIC

Critical Thinking Answer

corn, poultry and other products (turkeys); 8.9 percent and 3.1 percent

Differentiated Instruction

Leveled Activities

BL **School-to-Home Connection Activity, URB p. 63**

OL **Geography and History Activity, URB p. 59**

AL **Citizenship and Decision Making Skills Activity, URB p. 3**

R Reading Strategy

Making Connections Ask: Why did place names in America begin with the word "New"? *(They are named after the origin of the settlers.)* **ELL**

✓ Reading Check **Answer:** Mercantilism held that power is based on wealth, so nations tried to build their wealth. Nations believed that American colonies would provide them with resources and markets. They would become more wealthy and, thus, more powerful.

Assess

Study Central™ provides summaries, interactive games, and online graphic organizers to help students review content.

Close

Summarizing As a class, summarize the reasons European nations established colonies in North America. **OL**

On this voyage, Hudson and his crew discovered the huge bay that today bears his name. Thinking he had reached the Pacific, Hudson spent months looking for an outlet. His unhappy crew, however, rebelled. Hudson, his son, and a few sailors were set adrift in a small boat—and never seen again.

French Trading Posts

France showed little interest in building an empire in the Americas. Its rulers focused on political and religious conflicts at home. The French saw North America as an opportunity to make profits from fishing and fur trading rather than as a place to settle.

Furs were popular in Europe. Traders made large profits from beaver pelts acquired in North America from Native Americans. In 1608 a French fur-trading company sent Samuel de Champlain to found a settlement in Quebec in what is now Canada. Champlain made several trips to the region and discovered Lake Champlain. He described the beautiful scenery and abundant wildlife, as well as the Native Americans he met there.

From Quebec, the French moved into other parts of Canada, where they built trading posts to collect furs gathered by Native Americans and French trappers. The trappers were called **coureurs de bois** (ku•RUHR duh BWAH), meaning "runners of the woods."

Dutch Settlements

After Hudson's voyage, the Dutch began to explore North America. Eager for world trade, the Netherlands had a large fleet of trading ships that sailed all over the world. In 1621 the Dutch West India Company set up a colony, New Netherland, in North America. There they settled at Fort Orange (later Albany) on the Hudson River and on Burlington Island in New Jersey. They also set up Fort Nassau near what is today Philadelphia.

The center of the new colony was New Amsterdam, located on the tip of Manhattan Island, where the Hudson River enters New York Harbor. In 1626 Governor Peter Minuit paid the Manhates people 60 Dutch guilders (about $24) in goods—cloth, axes, and hoes—for the island, which is today New York City.

✓ Reading Check **Analyzing** How did mercantilism create rivalries between European nations?

Section 4 Review

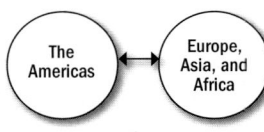

History ONLINE
Study Central™ To review this section, go to glencoe.com.

Vocabulary

1. Explain the significance of each of the following terms by using it in a sentence: mercantilism, globe, Columbian Exchange, chart, Northwest Passage, coureur de bois.

Main Ideas

2. **Explaining** What was the Protestant Reformation?

3. **Discussing** How did France's goals in North America differ from those of other European nations?

Critical Thinking

4. **Comparing and Contrasting** Discuss how Martin Luther's beliefs differed from those of Roman Catholics of his time.

5. **Diagramming** Use a diagram like the one below to identify the resources that moved between the two hemispheres in the Columbian Exchange.

The Americas ↔ Europe, Asia, and Africa

6. **Persuasive Writing** Write a speech that Henry Hudson might have given to his crew when they rebelled and threatened to kill him.

Answer the Essential Question

7. Why did European nations establish colonies in North America?

Section 4 Review

Answers

1. Sentences should relate to North American exploration.
2. the religious movement that resulted in the formation of new Christian churches by former Catholics
3. Most nations wanted colonies and empires, whereas France mainly wanted to profit from fishing and fur trading.

4. Luther believed the Bible was the only true guide and that salvation was based on faith rather than good deeds. He also rejected the authority of the pope.
5. Answers may include the following: *From the Americas:* crops, food, disease; *From Europe, Asia, and Africa:* colonists, animals, plants, disease, enslaved people.

6. Speeches may focus on Hudson's achievements as reasons not to kill him.
7. to spread their faith or to practice their beliefs freely; to become wealthy and, thus, powerful; to obtain resources; to trade or sell European products

Visual Summary

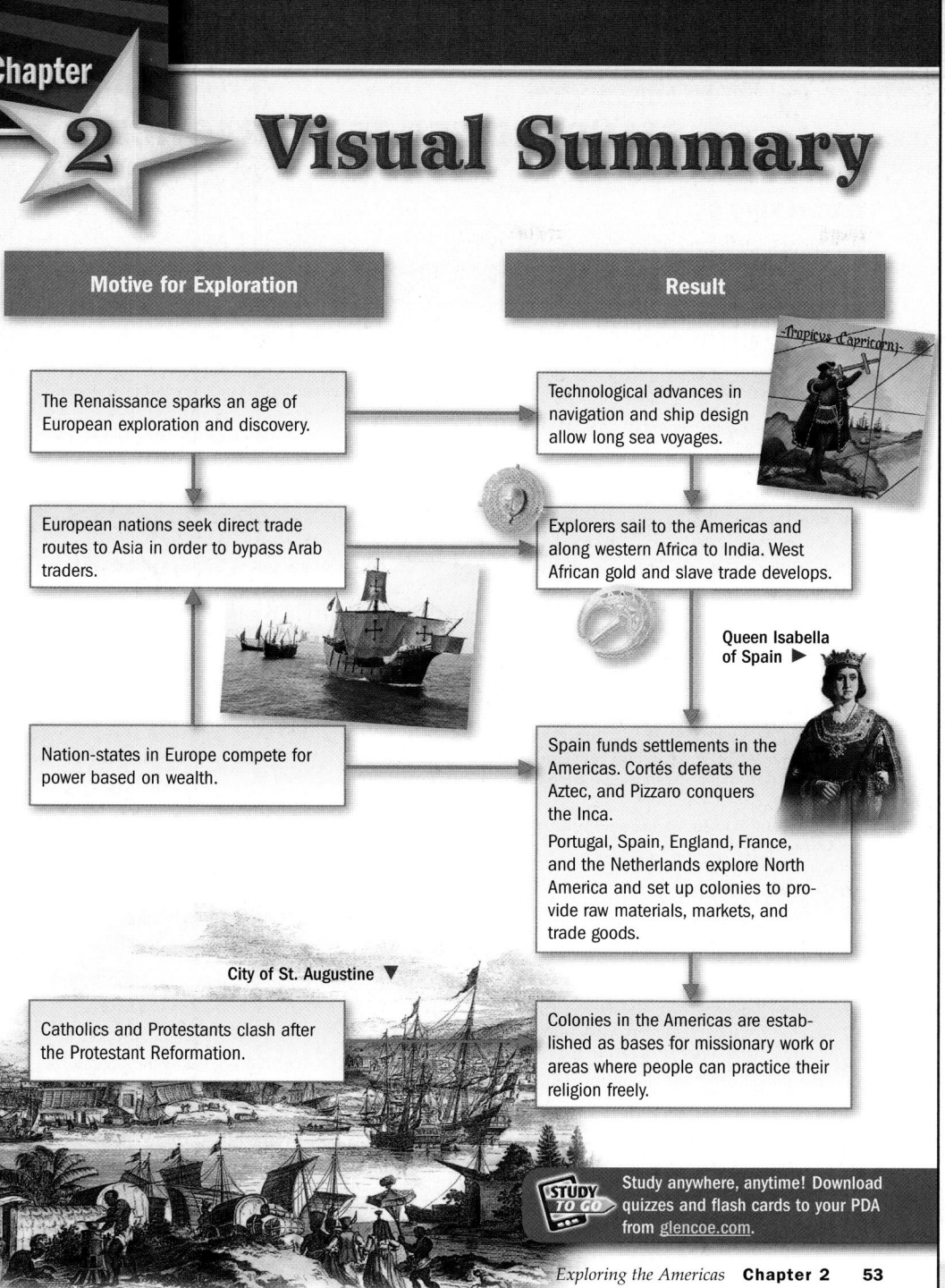

Motive for Exploration

The Renaissance sparks an age of European exploration and discovery.

European nations seek direct trade routes to Asia in order to bypass Arab traders.

Nation-states in Europe compete for power based on wealth.

Catholics and Protestants clash after the Protestant Reformation.

Result

Technological advances in navigation and ship design allow long sea voyages.

Explorers sail to the Americas and along western Africa to India. West African gold and slave trade develops.

Queen Isabella of Spain ►

Spain funds settlements in the Americas. Cortés defeats the Aztec, and Pizarro conquers the Inca.

Portugal, Spain, England, France, and the Netherlands explore North America and set up colonies to provide raw materials, markets, and trade goods.

City of St. Augustine ▼

Colonies in the Americas are established as bases for missionary work or areas where people can practice their religion freely.

STUDY TO GO Study anywhere, anytime! Download quizzes and flash cards to your PDA from glencoe.com.

Exploring the Americas **Chapter 2** **53**

Visual Summary

Summarizing Ask: Portugal led other nations in the exploration of the Americas. Who were the major Portuguese explorers of the late 1400s, and what were their accomplishments? *(Portuguese explorers de Gama and Cabral both reached Brazil in the late 1400s. Cabral claimed the land for Portugal. Vespucci explored South America, and Magellan sailed around the tip of South America. He and his crew were the first to circumnavigate the world.)* What technological advance gave Portugal an advantage over other European countries? Why? *(the three-masted caravel; it moved fast and could travel in shallow water.)* **OL**

Distinguishing Fact From Opinion Ask students to read the visual summary. **Ask:** Are these statements facts or opinions? *(facts)* How do you know? *(They can be proven.)* What words act as clues that a statement is an opinion? *(Answers will vary, but students should use phrases such as "best," "I believe," and other statements that cannot be proven true or false.)* **OL**

Hands-On Chapter Project
Step 5: Wrap-Up

Creating a Historical Calendar

Step 5: Learning From the Calendars Students will synthesize what they have learned in Steps 1 through 4.

Directions Ask students how the process of making a calendar has changed their understanding of the early exploration and colonization of the Americas. Tell each group to choose one explorer, technological development, or event from its calendar that it feels best represents the spirit of early American exploration or colonization. List each group's choice on the board.

Synthesizing In a class discussion, talk about what each item in the list illustrates about early exploration or colonization as described in the chapter. **Ask:** How did this explorer, technological development, or event affect North and South America today? The discussion might address how things might be different today if the item on the list had not existed, been discovered, or occurred.

Answers and Analyses
Reviewing the Main Ideas

1. B The text mentions none of the answers except B. Choice D is obviously incorrect because trading with Arab merchants was the only way Europeans could acquire goods from Asia. **17.C.3a**

2. C The lack of a Mediterranean port spurred Portugal to find a new route to India and China. Students might answer A, because the Portuguese sailors were indeed well trained by the school set up by Henry the Navigator. Portuguese sailors did use the compass (choice B), but it was invented in China. **16.C.3a (US)**

3. A Cortés conquered the Aztec. Choice B, Pizarro, conquered the Inca. Columbus and De Soto, choices C and D, were explorers rather than conquerors (although Columbus did claim San Salvador for Spain). **18.B**

4. B Martin Luther believed that salvation was achieved by faith rather than good deeds. Choice A is incorrect because Luther rejected Roman Catholicism. Choice D is wrong because Luther rejected the pope's authority. **18.B.3a**

Short-Answer Question

5. Columbus was describing the Native Americans he encountered, possibly in San Salvador. He assumed he was in the East Indies and may have been trying to reconcile what he saw with what he expected to see. He included details because the people were like none the Europeans had seen before. Some Europeans would have seen or known about the Canary Island inhabitants, so he compared what he saw with what might have been more familiar to Europeans. **16.A.3c**

Chapter 2 Assessment

STANDARDIZED TEST PRACTICE

TEST-TAKING **TIP**

> For multiple-choice questions, think of answers in your head before looking at the possible answers on the test. Doing so will help you recognize a correct answer immediately.

Reviewing the Main Ideas

Directions: Choose the best answer for each of the following questions.

1. Why did Europeans seek trade routes to the East that bypassed Arab merchants?
  - **A** European rulers forbade trading with non-Christians.
  - **B** Arab merchants charged high prices for their goods.
  - **C** Arab merchants offered inferior goods.
  - **D** Arabs refused to trade with Europeans.

2. The Portuguese took the lead in exploring the boundaries of the known world because
  - **A** they were the best sailors in the world.
  - **B** their invention of the compass gave them an advantage in navigation.
  - **C** lack of a Mediterranean port prevented Portugal from joining in the profitable trade between Asia and Europe.
  - **D** they wanted to convert the entire world to Christianity.

3. Who conquerored the Aztec?
  - **A** Hernán Cortés   **C** Christopher Columbus
  - **B** Francisco Pizarro   **D** Hernando de Soto

4. The German priest Martin Luther
  - **A** helped strengthen Roman Catholicism.
  - **B** rejected the idea that good works alone would ensure a person's salvation.
  - **C** taught the doctrine of predestination, the idea that God had already chosen those who would be saved.
  - **D** believed the pope's authority should take precedence over the teachings of the Bible.

Short-Answer Question

Directions: Base your answer to question 5 on the excerpt below and on your knowledge of social studies.

> *All whom I saw were young, not above thirty years of age, well made, with fine shapes and faces; their hair short . . . combed toward the forehead, except a small portion which they suffer to hang down behind, and never cut. Some paint themselves with black, which makes them appear like those of the Canaries [Canary Islands], neither black nor white; others with white, others with red. . . . Some paint the face, and some the whole body; others only the eyes, and others the nose.*
>
> —Christopher Columbus, *The Log of Christopher Columbus*

5. Who was Columbus describing, and why did he include such detail?

Review the Essential Questions

6. Essay Explain how exploration brought about great change in Europe and the Americas.

To help you write your essay, review your answers to the Essential Questions in the section reviews and the chapter Foldables Study Organizer. Your essay should include:
  - technological innovations of the 1300s and 1400s;
  - growth of trade among Europe, Africa, and Asia;
  - reasons behind European exploration and colonization of the Americas;
  - treatment of Native Americans under the Spanish; and
  - the influence of mercantilism and the impact of the Columbian Exchange.

GO ON ➤

Review the Essential Questions

6. Students should use their answers to the Essential Questions and their Foldables to describe how exploration profoundly changed Europe and the Americas. Essays should include an analysis of mercantilism and religious goals, technological innovations, trade, and the Spanish treatment of the Aztec and Inca. **16.C.3a (US)**

History ONLINE
For additional test practice, use **Self-Check Quizzes**—Chapter 2 at glencoe.com.

Chapter 2 Assessment

Document-Based Questions

Directions: Analyze the documents and answer the short-answer questions that follow.

Document 1

This excerpt from *The Saga of Eric the Red* describes the Norsemen's encounters with the native peoples, whom the Norsemen called Skrellings, in Vinland.

> *The Skrellings put down their bundles then, and loosed them, and offered their wares [for barter], and were especially anxious to exchange these for weapons; but Karlsefni forbade his men to sell their weapons, and, taking counsel with himself, he bade the women carry out milk to the Skrellings, which they no sooner saw than they wanted to buy it, and nothing else.*

Source: *The Saga of Eric the Red,* 1387

7. Based on this document, describe the relations between the Norsemen and the native Vinlanders. What did the two peoples trade and why?

Document 2

This is an excerpt from *A Short Account of the Destruction of the Indies* (1542) by Bartolome de Las Casas.

> *The pattern established at the outset has remained unchanged to this day, and the Spaniards still do nothing save tear the native to shreds, murder them and inflict upon them untold misery, suffering and distress, tormenting . . . and persecuting them mercilessly.*

Source: *A Short Account of the Destruction of the Indies*

8. Based on the document, what was the view of Las Casas toward Spanish treatment of the native peoples they encountered? Explain.

Document 3

The following excerpt is from Thomas Mun's *England's Treasure By Forraign Trade* (1664).

> The ordinary means therefore to increase our wealth and *treasure* is by Forraign Trade, wherein wee must ever observe this rule; to sell more to strangers yearly than wee consume of theirs in value.

Source: *England's Treasure By Forraign Trade,* 1664

9. Based on the document, state the central belief of mercantilism.

Document 4

The Protestant Reformation spread a number of new Christian religions across Europe.

Religions of Western Europe

Catholic
Calvinist
Church of England
Lutheran

0   400 kilometers
0   400 miles
Lambert Azimuthal
Equal-Area projection

10. Which parts of Europe were predominantly Lutheran? Calvinist? Catholic?

11. Expository Writing Using the information from the four documents and your knowledge of social studies, write an essay in which you:

- explain how and why Europeans became leaders in world trade; and

- identify at least one consequence of the Protestant Reformation on the colonization of the Americas.

8. Las Casas describes horrifying treatment of the native peoples by the Spanish. Although he does not say so explicitly in the excerpt, the language that he uses hints that he finds the actions of the Spanish appalling. **18.B.3a**

9. The document supports the belief that wealth is acquired by nations that export more than they import. **15.D.3a**

10. Lutheran: central and northeast Europe; Calvinist: central and southwest Europe and Scotland; Catholic: Ireland, Spain, Portugal, France, Italy, and Poland **17.A.3b**

11. Students' essays should reflect an understanding of the four documents and how they relate to the chapter material. Essays should describe how the pursuit of trade, mercantilism, technological innovations, and the rise of Protestantism affected European nations and their effect on the Americas. Students' essays should use transitional words that reflect cause-and-effect relationships. **16.C.3b (US)**

History ONLINE
Have students visit the Web site at glencoe.com to review Chapter 2 and take the Self-Check Quiz.

Need Extra Help?

Have students refer to the pages listed if they miss any of the questions.

Need Extra Help?											
If you missed questions...	1	2	3	4	5	6	7	8	9	10	11
Go to page...	29	35	43	49	39–40	26–52	38	44–45	50–51	49–50	26–52

Document-Based Questions

7. The Norsemen and the native Vinlanders appear to be interacting amicably, with fear on neither side. The Norsemen refuse to sell their weapons, though, implying they may not trust the Vinlanders completely. The passage does not specify the wares the Vinlanders have to trade; the Norsemen trade milk, probably because the Vinlanders have no cows, sheep, or goats—or not enough milk to fill their needs. **16.C.3a (US)**

Chapter Planning Guide

3

Key to Ability Levels
- **BL** Below level
- **OL** On level
- **AL** Above level
- **ELL** English Language Learners

Key to Teaching Resources
- 📁 Print Material
- 💿 CD-ROM
- 📀 DVD
- 🖨 Transparency

Levels (BL / OL / AL / ELL)		Resources	Chapter Opener	Section 1	Section 2	Section 3	Section 4	Chapter Assess
BL OL AL ELL	🖨	**Daily Test Practice Transparencies**		3–1	3–2	3–3	3–4	
FOCUS								
OL AL	📁	**Geography and History Activity, URB**					p. 87	
BL OL ELL	📁	**Time Line Skills Activity, URB**			p. 90			
BL OL AL ELL	📁	**Writing Skills Activity, URB**			p. 79			
BL OL AL ELL	📁	**Content Vocabulary Activity, URB**		p. 73	p. 73	p. 73	p. 73	
BL OL AL ELL	📁	**Academic Vocabulary Activity, URB**		p. 75	p. 75	p. 75	p. 75	
BL OL ELL	📁	**Social Studies Skills Activity, URB**				p. 81		
BL OL AL ELL	📁	**Differentiated Instruction Activity, URB**				p. 83		
BL OL AL ELL	📁	**Critical Thinking Skills Activity, URB**				p. 85		
BL OL AL ELL	📁	**Linking Past and Present Activity, URB**		p. 89				
OL AL	📁	**Primary Source Readings, URB**					p. 77	
BL OL AL ELL	📁	**School-to-Home Connection Activity, URB**		p. 91	p. 91	p. 91	p. 91	
BL OL ELL	📁	**Guided Reading Activity, URB***		p. 95	p. 96	p. 97	p. 98	
BL OL ELL	📁	**Reading Essentials and Note-Taking Guide***		p. 22	p. 25	p. 28	p. 31	
BL OL AL ELL	🖨	**Lesson Transparencies**			3A	3B	3C	
OL	📁	**American Biographies**					p. 5	
BL OL AL ELL	📁	**Outline Map Resource Book**	p. 9					
OL AL	🖨	**American Art and Architecture Transparencies, Strategies, and Activities**			3	6		

Note: Please refer to the *Unit Resource Book: The Americas: Worlds Meet* for this chapter's materials.

* Also available in Spanish

Levels				Resources		Chapter Opener	Section 1	Section 2	Section 3	Section 4	Chapter Assess
BL	OL	AL	ELL								
TEACH *(continued)*											
BL	OL	AL	ELL		NGS US Desk Map			✓	✓	✓	✓	
BL	OL	AL	ELL		American Literature Library		✓	✓	✓	✓	
BL	OL	AL	ELL		Writer's Guidebook		✓	✓	✓	✓	
	OL	AL			American History Primary Source Document Library CD-ROM		✓	✓	✓	✓	✓
BL	OL	AL	ELL		American Music Hits Through History	✓	✓	✓	✓	✓	
BL	OL	AL	ELL		StudentWorks™ Plus CD	✓	✓	✓	✓	✓	✓
BL	OL	AL	ELL		Section Spotlight Videos		✓	✓	✓	✓	
BL	OL	AL	ELL		Writing Process Transparencies		✓	✓	✓	✓	✓
BL	OL	AL	ELL		Presentation Plus! With MindJogger CheckPoint CD	✓	✓	✓	✓	✓	✓
ASSESS											
BL	OL	AL	ELL		Quizzes and Tests		p. 21	p. 22	p. 23	p. 24	pp. 25, 27, 29
BL	OL	AL	ELL		Authentic Assessment With Rubrics		p. 3				
BL	OL	AL	ELL		Standardized Test Practice						p. 5
BL	OL	AL	ELL		*ExamView® Assessment Suite* CD-ROM*		3–1	3–2	3–3	3–4	Ch. 3
CLOSE											
BL			ELL		Reteaching Activity, URB*		p. 93	p. 93	p. 93	p. 93	p. 93
BL	OL		ELL		Reading and Study Skills Foldables Activity	p. 54	p. 54	p. 54	p. 54	p. 54	p. 54
BL	OL	AL	ELL		*The American Journey* in Graphic Novel						p. 15
BL			ELL		Reading Strategies and Activities for the Social Studies Classroom		✓	✓	✓	✓	
BL	OL	AL	ELL		Graphic Organizer Transparencies & Strategies		✓	✓	✓	✓	

TeacherWorks Plus
All-In-One Planner and Resource Center

- Interactive Lesson Planner
- Interactive Teacher Edition
- Fully editable blackline masters
- Section Spotlight Videos Launch
- Differentiated Lesson Plans
- Printable reports of daily assignments
- Standards Tracking System

Professional Development Resources

- Strategies for Success
- Building Academic Vocabulary
- Success With English Learners DVD
- Differentiated Instruction Strategies DVD
- Teaching Literacy Strategies in Social Studies DVD
- Assessment DVD
- Standards-Based Instruction DVD

Integrating Technology

3

Using *ExamView*® Assessment Suite

QuickTest

Technology Product

Glencoe's *ExamView*® *Assessment Suite* CD-ROM includes powerful assessment tools and enables you to quickly create, adapt, and assess tests for your students.

ExamView® allows you to

- develop online testing materials that focus on the specific skills and competencies of what has been taught in the classroom;
- create several versions of these test materials that are adjusted to meet the different ability levels of your students;
- provide a variety of test formats, including Multiple Choice, True/False, Yes/No, Matching, Completion (Fill-in-the-Blank), and Numeric Response.

Steps

- Open the *ExamView*® Test Generator.
- Select **Create a new test using the QuickTest Wizard** and click **OK.**
- Name the test you are creating
- From the list, select the *Chapter Banks* you would like to use. Click **Next.**
- Indicate the number of questions you want per question type. Click **Next.**
- Enter the number of matching groups. Click **Next.**
- Verify summary of selections and click **Finish.**
- The *QuickTest Wizard* will build your test. Print the test or save it for students so that they can take the test on a computer using the Internet.

History ONLINE at glencoe.com

	Student	Teacher	Parent
Media Center			
• Student Edition Audio	●		
• Spanish Summaries	●		
• Section Spotlight Videos	●	●	
Social Studies Online Learning Center			
Classroom Tools			
• Multi-Language Glossaries	●	●	●
• Teaching Today		●	
• TIME Current Events	●	●	●
• Beyond the Textbook	●	●	
***The American Journey* Online Learning Center**			
• Study-to-Go™	●	●	●
• Study Central™	●	●	●
• Chapter Overview	●	●	
• Concepts in Motion	●	●	
• ePuzzles and Games	●	●	
• Literature Connections	●	●	
• Online Student Edition	●	●	●
• Self-Check Quizzes	●	●	●
• Student Web Activities	●	●	
• Vocabulary eFlashcards	●	●	
• Web Activity Lesson Plans	●	●	●
• Vocabulary PuzzleMaker	●	●	●

56C

READING SUPPORT FROM JAMESTOWN EDUCATION

- **Timed Readings Plus in Social Studies** helps students increase their reading rate and fluency while maintaining comprehension. The 400-word passages are similar to those found on state and national assessments.

- **Reading in the Content Area: Social Studies** concentrates on six essential reading skills that help students better comprehend what they read. The book includes 75 high-interest nonfiction passages written at increasing levels of difficulty.

- **Reading Social Studies** includes strategic reading instruction and vocabulary support in Social Studies content for ELLs and native speakers of English.

- **Content Vocabulary Workout** (Grades 6–8) accelerates reading comprehension through focused vocabulary development. Social Studies content vocabulary comes from the glossaries of Glencoe's Middle School Social Studies texts.

www.jamestowneducation.com

NATIONAL GEOGRAPHIC

Index to National Geographic Magazine:

The following article relates to this chapter:

- *"Legacy of Jamestown: America, Found and Lost,"* Charles C. Mann, May 2007.

National Geographic Society Products

To order the following, call National Geographic at 1-800-368-2728:

National Geographic Atlas of the World (Book).

Access National Geographic's new dynamic MapMachine Web site and other geography resources at:

www.nationalgeographic.com

www.nationalgeographic.com/mapmachine

Reading List Generator CD-ROM — **GLENCOE BOOKLINK 3**

Use this database to search more than 30,000 titles to create a customized reading list for your students.

- Reading lists can be organized by students' reading level, author, genre, theme, or area of interest.

- The database provides Degrees of Reading Power™ (DRP) and Lexile™ readability scores for all selections.

- A brief summary of each selection is included.

Leveled reading suggestions for this chapter:

For students at a Grade 6 reading level:
- *Tapenum's Day: A Wampanoag Indian Boy in Pilgrim Times,* by Kate Waters

For students at a Grade 7 reading level:
- *The Seekers,* by Ellis Dillon
- *Worlds Apart,* by Kathleen Karr

For students at a Grade 8 reading level:
- *The Serpent Never Sleeps,* by Scott O'Dell
- *The Double Life of Pocahontas,* by Jean Fritz

For students at a Grade 9 reading level:
- *The Witch of Blackbird Pond,* by Elizabeth George Speare
- *Caesar's Story,* by Joan Lowery Nixon

For students at a Grade 10 reading level:
- *William Penn: Founder of Democracy,* by Norma Jean Lutz
- *The Story of the Salem Witch Trials,* by Zachary Kent

The following videotape program is available from Glencoe as a supplement to the chapter:

- **Pocahontas: Her True Story** (ISBN 1-56-501555-X)

To order, call Glencoe at 1-800-334-7344. To find classroom resources to accompany this video, check the following home pages:

A&E Television: www.aetv.com

The History Channel: www.history.com

Chapter Objectives

After studying this chapter, students will be able to:

- Explain why the English settled in North America.
- Understand why the Separatists and Puritans left England and settled in North America.
- Describe how the Middle Colonies developed.
- Explain how and why the Southern Colonies grew.

Motivating Activity

Analyzing Students will learn that the colonists formed friendly relationships with Native Americans in some regions. In Pennsylvania, William Penn's beliefs helped the colonists live peacefully with their Native American neighbors. **Ask:** How do you think the colonists would benefit from making friends with the Native Americans? (*Native Americans could provide knowledge of the land and how to survive on it; could trade for supplies*) How might colonists create friendly relationships with Native Americans? (*treat them fairly and with respect; do not cheat them when trading with them; respect treaties*) **OL**

Previewing the Essential Questions

As you begin teaching each section, use these questions and activities to help students focus on the Essential Questions.

Chapter 3
Colonial America 1587–1770

William Penn meets with Native Americans in his colony of Pennsylvania.

1607 ★ English establish first permanent settlement at Jamestown

1612 ★ Tobacco planted in Virginia

1620 ★ Pilgrims land at Plymouth Rock

1630 ★ Puritans begin settling Massachusetts Bay

Americas
World

1550   1600   1650

1585 ★ Hideyoshi becomes dictator of Japan

★ **1588** England defeats Spanish Armada

★ **c. 1605** Shakespeare writes *King Lear*

★ **1609** Tea from China arrives in Europe

56   Chapter 3

Section 1

Early English Settlements Ask: Why would a country want to establish a colony in another region? (*Possible answer: to extract its resources*) Point out to students that in Section 1 they will learn about an early English settlement that survived and one that did not. **OL**

Section 2

New England Colonies Ask: What makes people leave their homeland to live in another country? (*desire for religious freedom; to escape persecution; more economic opportunities*) Tell students that Section 2 discusses the journey of the Puritans and the growth of the New England settlements. **OL**

Section 1: Early English Settlements
Essential Question Why did the English settle in North America?

Section 2: New England Colonies
Essential Question Why did the Separatists and Puritans leave England and settle in North America?

Section 3: Middle Colonies
Essential Question How did the Middle Colonies develop?

Section 4: Southern Colonies
Essential Question How and why did the Southern Colonies grow?

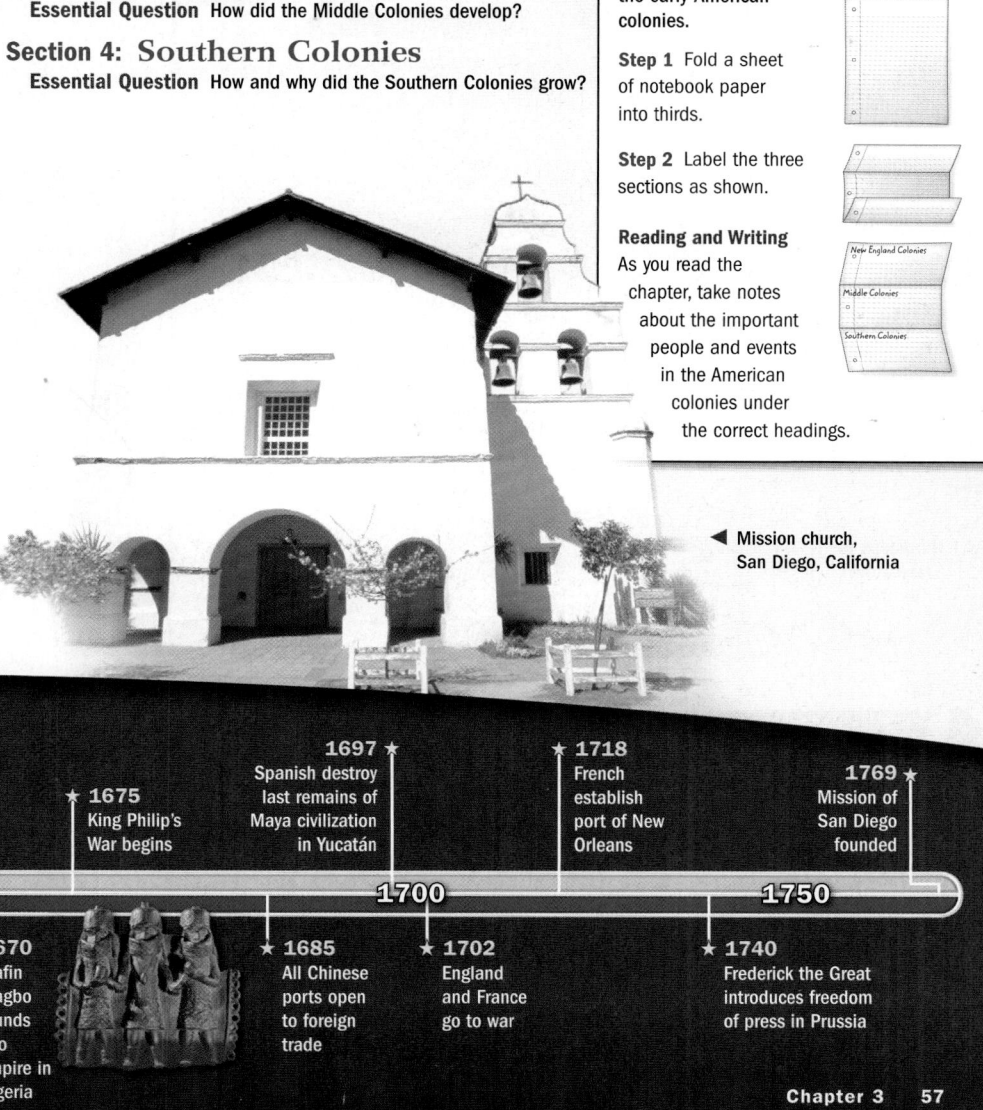

◄ Mission church, San Diego, California

FOLDABLES Study Organizer
Summarizing Information

Make this Foldable to help you summarize what you learn about the early American colonies.

Step 1 Fold a sheet of notebook paper into thirds.

Step 2 Label the three sections as shown.

Reading and Writing As you read the chapter, take notes about the important people and events in the American colonies under the correct headings.

New England Colonies
Middle Colonies
Southern Colonies

Time line

★ **1670** Alafin Ajagbo founds Oyo empire in Nigeria

★ **1675** King Philip's War begins

★ **1685** All Chinese ports open to foreign trade

★ **1697** Spanish destroy last remains of Maya civilization in Yucatán

1700

★ **1702** England and France go to war

★ **1718** French establish port of New Orleans

1750

★ **1740** Frederick the Great introduces freedom of press in Prussia

★ **1769** Mission of San Diego founded

Introducing Chapter 3

Time Line Activity

If you have not already done so, have students review the time line. **Ask:** What years are covered in this chapter? *(1550–1769)* Which European nations were active in the Americas during this time? *(England, Spain, France)* What world event on the time line suggests that conflict might erupt in the colonies? Why? *(England and France went to war in 1702. Both nations were active in North America around this time, suggesting that conflict between them might spill over to the colonies.)*

FOLDABLES Study Organizer
Dinah Zike's Foldables

Purpose This Foldable helps students identify key facts about the New England, Middle, and Southern Colonies. The completed Foldable will help them prepare for assessment.

📁 More Foldables activities for this chapter can be found in *Dinah Zike's Reading and Study Skills Foldables.*

History ONLINE

Introduce students to chapter content and key terms by having them access the **Chapter Overview** at glencoe.com.

Section 3

Middle Colonies Ask: What made England powerful in the mid to late 1600s? *(its navy)* Tell students that in Section 3 they will learn how England's navy helped the country acquire Dutch colonies and extend its influence to North America. **OL**

Section 4

Southern Colonies Ask: Why might slave labor be important to an economy that was based on agriculture? *(There would be more people to plant and harvest crops.)* Explain to students that Section 4 explores the expanding agricultural settlements in the South. **OL**

Focus

Early English Settlements

🔔 Bellringer
Daily Test Practice Transparency 3–1

Reading Guide
Answers to Graphic:
disease, hunger, conflict with Native Americans

Section Spotlight Video

To learn more about Sir Francis Drake, watch the Section Spotlight Video "Early English Settlements."

Essential Question
Why did the English settle in North America?

Reading Guide

Content Vocabulary

charter (p. 60)
joint-stock company (p. 60)
headright (p. 61)
burgesses (p. 61)

Academic Vocabulary

expand (p. 61)

Key People and Events
Sir Francis Drake (p. 59)
Sir Walter Raleigh (p. 59)
Captain John Smith (p. 61)
Pocahontas (p. 61)
House of Burgesses (p. 61)

Reading Strategy
Taking Notes As you read, use a diagram like the one below to list the hardships faced by the Jamestown settlers.

ILLINOIS STANDARDS
The American Journey

15.D Understand trade as an exchange of goods and services.

16.A Apply the skills of historical analysis and interpretation.

16.C.3a (US) Describe economic motivations that attracted Europeans and others to the Americas, 1500–1750.

17.C.3a Explain how human activity is affected by geographic factors.

American Diary

Captain John Smith, a leader of England's Jamestown colony, told an amazing tale of his capture by Native Americans. According to Smith, the Native Americans were prepared "to beat out his brains." Just then, Pocahontas, the 11-year-old daughter of Chief Powhatan, "got his head in her arms, and laid her own upon his to save him from death." The gesture moved the chief to spare Smith's life.

—*from* The Generall Historie of Virginia

Resource Manager

R Reading Strategies	**C** Critical Thinking	**D** Differentiated Instruction	**W** Writing Support	**S** Skill Practice
Teacher Edition • Reading Secondary Sources, p. 59 • Identifying, p. 60 **Additional Resources** • Guid. Read., URB p. 95 • Content Vocab., URB p. 73 • Academic Vocab., URB p. 75 • Read. Ess., p. 22	**Additional Resources** • Quizzes and Tests, p. 21 • Authentic Assess., p. 3	**Teacher Edition** • ELL, p. 59 **Additional Resources** • School-to-Home, URB p. 91 • Reteaching Act., URB p. 93	**Teacher Edition** • Narrative Writing, p. 60 **Additional Resources** • Link. Past & Pres., URB p. 89	**Teacher Edition** • Analyzing Information, p. 61 **Additional Resources** • Daily Test Pract. Transp. 3-1

England in America

Main Idea After defeating the Spanish Armada, England became more interested in establishing colonies in North America.

History and You Do you like reading mystery novels? Read to learn about the disappearance of the English colonists on Roanoke Island.

The story of Smith and Pocahontas, whether true or not, comes from the earliest period of English settlement in America. Compared to the Spanish, who were their economic rivals, the English were slow to seek colonies.

The Spanish Armada

Trading rivalry and religious differences had been pushing England and Spain toward war for years. King Philip II, the powerful ruler of Spain, wanted to put a Catholic ruler on the throne of England. He did not consider Queen Elizabeth, a Protestant, the rightful ruler of England.

Also, English adventurers, such as **Sir Francis Drake,** had attacked Spanish ships and ports. Philip thought that Elizabeth should punish Drake for his raids. Instead, she honored Drake with knighthood. Philip

sent the Spanish Armada, Spain's fleet of warships, to conquer England, but it failed completely. Although war between England and Spain continued until 1604, the defeat of the armada marked the end of Spanish control of the seas. The way was clear for England to start colonies in North America.

The Lost Colony of Roanoke

The English had made several attempts to establish a base in North America. Sir Humphrey Gilbert claimed Newfoundland for Queen Elizabeth in 1583. However, before he could find a place for a colony, Gilbert died at sea.

The following year, Queen Elizabeth gave **Sir Walter Raleigh** the right to claim land in North America. Raleigh sent an expedition to find a good place to settle. His scouts made an enthusiastic report of Roanoke Island, off the coast of present-day North Carolina.

The first settlers, 100 men, had a difficult winter on the island and returned to England. In 1587 Raleigh then sent 91 men, 17 women, and 9 children to Roanoke. John White, artist and mapmaker, led the group. Shortly after arriving on the island, White's daughter gave birth. Virginia Dare was the first English child born in North America.

Ships arrive at Jamestown, Virginia.

Time Line / Early English Settlements

Settling America Most of the early English settlements were founded by private investors who asked the English monarch for charters, or documents, that granted the right to establish colonies in America. Later, England's government placed direct controls on the American colonies.

★ **1590** Settlers at Roanoke vanish

★ **1583** Sir Humphrey Gilbert claims Newfoundland for Queen Elizabeth

★ **1607** Colonists settle at Jamestown

Critical Thinking

Theorizing Why do you think people in England invested in the founding of colonies in America?

Teach

R Reading Strategy

Reading Secondary Sources Have students read several reliable accounts of the life of Pocahontas. Have them prepare a report identifying information about her that is probably true and information that might be legend. They should include their sources and the reasons they consider those sources to be reliable. **AL**

D Differentiated Instruction

English Language Learners Ask your Hispanic students what "armada" or "armado" means in Spanish. *(armed)* **Ask:** What was the Spanish Armada? *(a fleet of armed ships)* **ELL**

Time Line

Critical Thinking Answer
to make a profit

Hands-On Chapter Project
Step 1

Reenacting Colonial Life

Step 1: Planning the Scene Students will research one colony and plan a scene of colonial life.

Essential Question: Why did the English settle in North America?

Directions Organize students into groups and assign a region to each group: New England Colonies, Middle Colonies, or Southern Colonies. Explain that they are actors who will take the roles of colonists. They will educate tourists about colonial life as they lead the tourists through a reproduction of a typical colonial town. Have the groups select one colony in their region. Ask them to gather information and visuals about life in their colony. They should learn where the colonists came from and why, how a typical town was organized, and how colonists made a living in the town. Groups should use the research to plan a town scene to portray for tourists.

Comparing As a class, compare the reasons colonists in different regions settled in North America. **OL**

(Chapter Project continued in Section 2)

W Writing Support

Narrative Writing Have students take the role of a Native American on Roanoke Island. Have them speculate about what happened to the colony and write an account from the Native Americans' point of view. **OL**

R Reading Strategy

Identifying Ask: How did the Virginia Company expect their colony to make a profit? *(from finding gold and trading in fish and furs)* **BL**

Primary Source

Critical Thinking Answer
homes taken apart, wall of tree trunks, no cross, no sign of distress

✓ Reading Check Answer: trading rivalry and religious differences

Differentiated Instruction

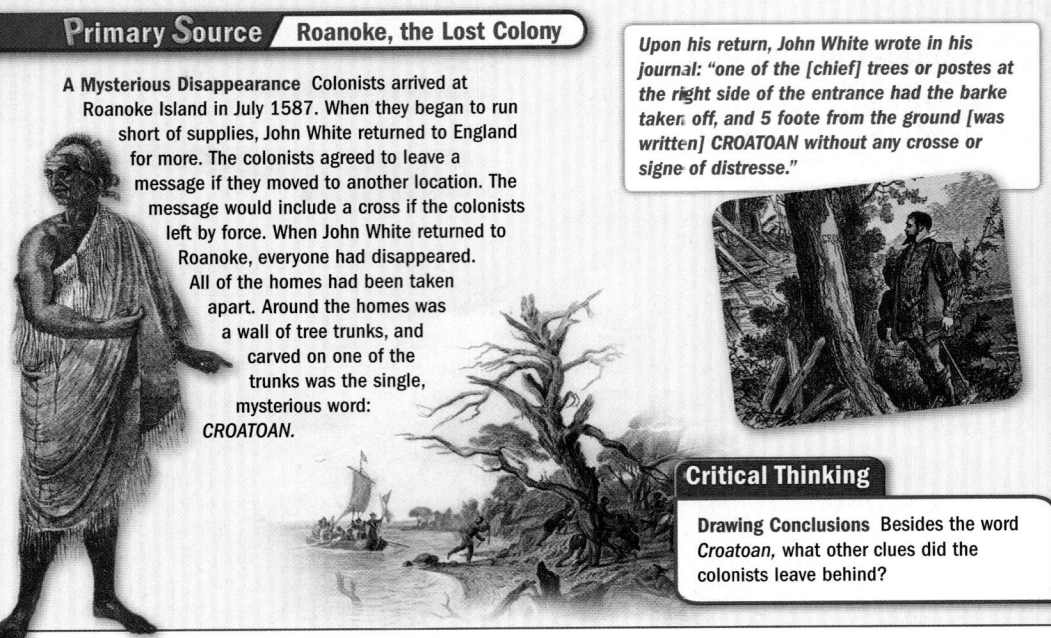

Primary Source | Roanoke, the Lost Colony

A Mysterious Disappearance Colonists arrived at Roanoke Island in July 1587. When they began to run short of supplies, John White returned to England for more. The colonists agreed to leave a message if they moved to another location. The message would include a cross if the colonists left by force. When John White returned to Roanoke, everyone had disappeared. All of the homes had been taken apart. Around the homes was a wall of tree trunks, and carved on one of the trunks was the single, mysterious word: CROATOAN.

Upon his return, John White wrote in his journal: "one of the [chief] trees or postes at the right side of the entrance had the barke taken off, and 5 foote from the ground [was written] CROATOAN without any crosse or signe of distresse."

Critical Thinking

Drawing Conclusions Besides the word *Croatoan*, what other clues did the colonists leave behind?

White explored the area and drew pictures of what he saw. In a book illustrated by White, another colonist described the Native American towns the settlers encountered:

PRIMARY SOURCE

"Their towns are small . . . a village may contain but ten or twelve houses—some . . . as many as twenty."
—from *A Brief and True Report of the New Found Land of Virginia*

Nine days after his granddaughter's birth, White returned to England for supplies. Although he had hoped to be back within a few months, the war with Spain delayed his return for nearly three years. When he returned to Roanoke, White found it deserted. Finding the word *Croatoan* carved on a gatepost, White believed the colonists had gone to Croatoan Island, about 50 miles to the south. Bad weather kept White from investigating, or examining further. The Roanoke colonists were never seen again.

✓ Reading Check Explaining Why were England and Spain at war in the late 1500s?

Jamestown Settlement

Main Idea The first permanent English settlement in North America was at Jamestown.

History and You What obstacles would you have to overcome to create a home in the wilderness? Read to learn about the hardships of the Jamestown settlers.

For a time, the failure of the Roanoke colony discouraged others from planning English colonies in North America. However, the idea emerged again in 1606. Several groups of merchants sought **charters**, documents granting the right to organize settlements in an area, from King James I.

The Virginia Company

One group of merchants, the Virginia Company of London, received a charter. The Virginia Company was a **joint-stock company.** Investors bought stock, or part ownership, in the company in return for a share of its future profits. Settlers in America were to search for gold and establish trade in fish and furs.

Popular Rule

Objective: To research voting statistics for past elections

Focus: Ask students to predict the percentage of voting-age citizens who voted in recent presidential elections.

Teach: Have students research voting statistics and complete the chart with their data.

Assess: Ask students to compare their results.

Close: Discuss why many eligible voters do not vote in presidential elections.

Differentiated Instruction Strategies

BL Discuss whether students would vote in an upcoming election if they were of voting age.

AL Have students use computer software to create a bar graph showing the data they have found.

ELL Make sure students understand how to compute the percentage of citizens who voted.

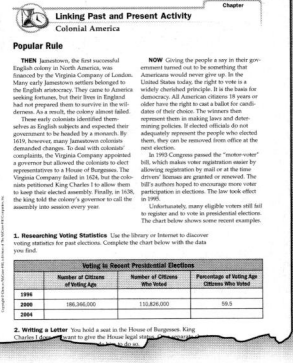

Linking Past and Present Activity, URB p. 89

In December 1606, the company sent 144 settlers in three ships to build a new colony in North America. In April 1607, the ships entered Chesapeake Bay and then sailed up a river flowing into the bay. The colonists named the river the James and their new settlement Jamestown to honor their king.

Jamestown Survives

The colonists faced hardships of disease and hunger. The colony survived its first two years because of 27-year-old **Captain John Smith,** an experienced explorer. Smith forced the settlers to work, explored the area, and sought corn from the local Native Americans led by Chief Powhatan. When John Smith returned to England, Jamestown lacked a strong leader. The winter of 1609–1610 became known as "the starving time." Fighting also broke out with the Native Americans.

The Virginia colonists finally discovered a way to make money for the investors by growing a type of tobacco using seeds from the West Indies. Soon planters all along the James River were raising tobacco.

The colony of Virginia began to prosper. Relations with the Native Americans improved after a colonist, John Rolfe, married **Pocahontas,** the daughter of Chief Powhatan. Land ownership was **expanded** when the Virginia Company gave a **headright,** or land grant, of 50 acres to settlers who paid their own way to the colony. Colonists also participated in government. The **House of Burgesses** first met in 1619. The **burgesses** were representatives of the colony's towns, and they could make local laws for the colony.

When the Virginia Company sent women to Jamestown, marriage and children became a part of life in Virginia. Another part of that life was slavery, first recognized in Virginia law in the 1660s.

By the 1620s, the Virginia Company faced financial troubles with Jamestown returning little profit. In 1624 King James canceled the company's charter and made Jamestown England's first royal colony in America.

✓ Reading Check Analyzing Why was the House of Burgesses important?

History ONLINE
Study Central™ To review this section, go to glencoe.com.

S Skill Practice

Analyzing Information Ask: How did the headright system benefit the settlers? How did it benefit the Virginia Company? *(Settlers received free land. The company expanded its colony without having to pay passage for the new settlers.)* **OL**

✓ Reading Check **Answer:** It gave colonists a say in government and in making laws.

Assess

History ONLINE

Study Central™ provides summaries, interactive games, and online graphic organizers to help students review content.

Close

Summarizing As a class, discuss the reasons the English established colonies in North America and why Jamestown survived. **OL**

Section 1 Review

Vocabulary

1. Use each of the following terms in a paragraph about the Jamestown settlement: charter, joint-stock company, expand, headright, burgesses.

Main Ideas

2. Making Connections Why was the defeat of the Spanish Armada important to England's quest for overseas colonies?

3. Explaining How did the Jamestown settlement survive the first two years?

Critical Thinking

4. Making Inferences Why do you think the king of England let a group of merchants try to establish a colony in North America?

5. Organizing Use a diagram like the one below to describe three attempts by the English to establish colonies in North America and the results.

Attempts to Colonize

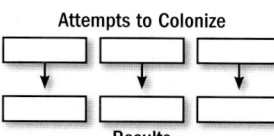

Results

6. Descriptive Writing Imagine that you are a Native American who witnessed the arrival of the Jamestown colonists. Describe your first impression of these people in a report to Chief Powhatan.

Answer the

7. Essential Question
Why did the English settle in North America?

Answers

1. Students' paragraphs should reflect knowledge of Jamestown and use the terms correctly.
2. ended Spain's control of the seas, clearing the way for England to pursue overseas colonies
3. John Smith forced the settlers to work and received food from local Native Americans.

4. Possible response: The king wanted the political power from ruling overseas colonies and economic rewards without risking his nation's resources on the venture.
5. Newfoundland: leader died at sea before finding suitable location; **Roanoke:** colonists disappeared and were never

found; **Jamestown:** survived and grew, giving England a permanent foothold in North America
6. Students should describe the new strangers from the point of view of a Native American who has never before seen Europeans.
7. The English hoped to profit from resources found in America.

GEOGRAPHY & HISTORY

Focus

C Critical Thinking

Drawing Conclusions Point out to students that the English colonists of Jamestown built their triangular fort in just 19 days. **Ask:** Why did the colonists of Jamestown build their triangular fort so quickly? *(to protect themselves from Native American attacks)* **OL**

Have students complete a graphic organizer like the one below that shows the structures the colonists built within their fort. Have students add more ovals to suggest other elements that could have been built within a fort in a new settlement. *(meeting house, lodging house, gardens, and so on)* **OL**

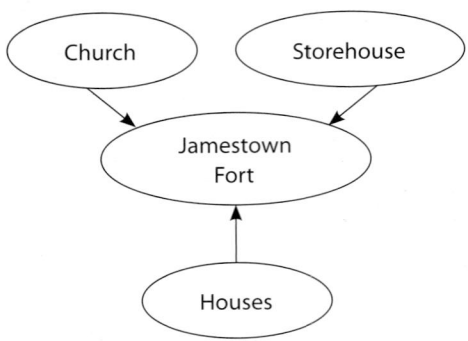

Church → Jamestown Fort ← Storehouse

Houses → Jamestown Fort

Additional Support and Answers

GEOGRAPHY & HISTORY

Jamestown

On May 14, 1607, English colonists began work on a settlement near the James River. They built a triangular fort of upright logs, about an acre in size, in just 19 days. Made of a storehouse, a church, and a number of houses, the fort was near water deep enough for ships to anchor. It also was in a secure place, where enemy ships could not fire directly into the fort. Relations with the local Native Americans were often difficult, although at times the colonists were able to trade copper and iron goods for badly needed food.

How Did Geography Affect Jamestown?

The Jamestown settlers faced the hardships of an unfamiliar climate—colder winters and warmer, humid summers. They also discovered that they had built their fort beside the dirtiest part of the James River. River water was drinkable only part of the year; in the summer, it turned salty and slimy. By autumn, disease, salt poisoning, and starvation had killed almost half the colonists.

Powhatan's territory

Native American settlement

Rappahannock R.
Potomac R.
Chesapeake Bay
Mattaponi R.
Pamunkey R.
Chickahominy R.
Toppahanock
Wighcoconoco
Powhatan
Arrohateck Chickahominy
Waenoc
Werowocomoco
Accomack
James R.
Jamestown
Nansemond
ATLANTIC OCEAN

39°N
37°N
77°W

0   40 kilometers
0   40 miles
Albers Equal-Area projection

Strategic Location Jamestown's upriver location, well inland from the Atlantic Ocean, was chosen in part because of its strategic position for defense of the river as well as to hide from Spanish ships that might be in the area.

Jamestown was built on a swampy, uninhabited site along the James River, which brought salty water from the ocean in the summer.

Activity: Technology Connection

Determining Cause and Effect Relationships between the Jamestown colonists and the local Native Americans were erratic—at times the groups traded and aided one another and at other times they fought fiercely. Have students research the marriage between John Rolfe and Pocahontas and the ensuing history of Jamestown. **Ask:** What effect did the marriage of Pocahontas and John Rolfe have on the relationship between Native Americans and English settlers? How and why did that relationship change when Chief Powhatan died? *(Because Pocahontas was the daughter of Chief Powhatan, hostilities between the two groups ceased. The lack of warfare and the success of tobacco farming allowed the colony to prosper. After Powhat-an's death, however, hostilities again arose, including massacres carried out by both sides. The conflict continued for decades, until only a few hundred Native Americans remained.)* Have students use a drawing program or a word processing program on the computer to create either a cause-and-effect diagram or a time line to illustrate their answers. **OL**

Jamestown Fort, 1607 The walls along the land sides were each 100 yards (91 meters) long. The wall along the river was 140 yards (128 meters) long.

The Scope of Suffering

Master George Percy was 27 years old when he helped establish the Jamestown Colony in 1607. He was one of the 38 aristocrats in the expedition and later served twice as the colony's governor before he returned to England.

"There were never Englishmen left in a foreign country in such misery as we were in this new-discovered Virginia."

Analyzing Geography

1. **Location** Why did the colonists choose Jamestown as their settlement site?

2. **Analyzing** In what ways was the fort's location a poor choice?

Teach

W Writing Support

Expository Writing Have students examine the diagram of the fort and write a short essay describing any elements of the fort's construction that were meant for defense. *(Examples may include the log walls with pointed tops, weapons pointed in all directions, closable gates, and the trench outside the walls.)* **OL**

C Critical Thinking

Contrasting Remind students that 38 of the Jamestown colonists were noblemen. **Ask:** How might a nobleman's opinion of Jamestown differ from that of a person from the working class? *(A nobleman might not be used to manual labor and poor conditions, so his opinion of Jamestown might be harsher than that of someone from the working class.)* **OL**

Assess/Close

D Differentiated Instruction

Interpersonal Have students take the role of Jamestown settlers and stage a debate on whether they should stay or abandon the settlement. **OL**

Answers

1. It was located in water deep enough for their ships to anchor, it was a secure location where enemy ships could not fire directly into the fort, and it was well hidden from passing ships.

2. It was built near the dirtiest part of the James River. The water was not drinkable for part of the year, which led to disease and salt poisoning. The climate of the area was unfamiliar and harsh. Native Americans were nearby.

New England Colonies

Focus

Bellringer
Daily Test Practice Transparency 3–2

Reading Guide
Answers to Graphic:
Separatist: Plymouth; **Puritan:** Massachusetts Bay, Connecticut, Rhode Island and Providence Plantations, New Hampshire

Section Spotlight Video

Watch the Section Spotlight Video "New England Colonies" to learn more about Plymouth Rock.

Resource Manager

Essential Question ◄
Why did the Separatists and Puritans leave England and settle in North America?

Reading Guide

Content Vocabulary
dissent (p. 65)
Puritan (p. 65)
Separatist (p. 65)
Pilgrim (p. 65)
Mayflower Compact (p. 66)
Fundamental Orders of Connecticut (p. 68)

Academic Vocabulary
policy (p. 68)

Key People and Events
William Bradford (p. 66)
Squanto (p. 66)
John Winthrop (p. 67)
Roger Williams (p. 68)

Reading Strategy
Taking Notes As you read, use a diagram like the one below to list the colonies that the Separatists and Puritans formed in North America.

Colonies in North America

| Separatist | Puritan |

ILLINOIS STANDARDS
The American Journey

14.F3a Analyze historical influences on the development of political ideas and practices as enumerated in the Declaration of Independence, the United States Constitution, the Bill of Rights and the Illinois Constitution.

17.C Understand relationships between geographic factors and society.

18.B.3b Explain how social institutions contribute to the development and transmission of culture.

64

American Diary

Edward Winslow, a settler in New England, was thankful that the Pilgrims had survived their first year in America. Winslow wrote to a friend in England, "We have built seven-dwelling houses. . . . We set the last spring some twenty acres of Indian corn . . . and according to the manner of the Indians, we manured our ground. . . . God be praised, we had a good increase of Indian corn."

—from Pilgrim Edward Winslow to a friend in England

The Pilgrims built their colony, Plymouth, along Cape Cod Bay in what is today Massachusetts.

R Reading Strategies	C Critical Thinking	D Differentiated Instruction	W Writing Support	S Skill Practice
Teacher Edition • Comparing and Contrasting, p. 65 • Activating Prior Knowledge, p. 67 • Identifying, p. 68 **Additional Resources** • Guid. Read., URB p. 96 • Content Vocab., URB p. 73 • Acad. Voc., URB p. 75 • Read. Ess., p. 25	**Teacher Edition** • Making Inferences, p. 65 • Drawing Conclusions, p. 66 • Drawing Conclusions, p. 67 **Additional Resources** • Quizzes and Tests, p. 22	**Teacher Edition** • ELL, p. 69 **Additional Resources** • School-to-Home, URB p. 91 • Reteaching Act., URB p. 93	**Teacher Edition** • Narrative Writing, p. 66 • Personal Writing, p. 68 **Additional Resources** • Writ. Skills, URB p. 79	**Teacher Edition** • Reading Primary Sources, p. 66 • Creating a Chart, p. 67 **Additional Resources** • Daily Test Pract. Transp. 3-2 • Lesson Transparency 3A • Time Line Skills, URB p. 90

Religious Freedom

Main Idea To practice their religion more freely, a group of Separatists established the Plymouth colony in North America.

History and You Have you and a friend ever disagreed so much on an issue that you considered ending your friendship? Read about the reason why the Pilgrims settled in Plymouth.

• •

Unlike the Jamestown settlers, the next wave of colonists arrived in search of religious freedom. England had been a Protestant country since 1534, when King Henry VIII broke away from the Roman Catholic Church and formed the Anglican Church. Not everyone in England was happy with the new church, however. Many people **dissented;** that is, they disagreed with the beliefs or practices of the Anglicans. English Catholics, for example, still considered the pope the head of the church. They were often persecuted, or treated harshly, for that reason.

Some Protestants wanted to change, or reform, the Anglican Church. Others wanted to break away from it altogether. The Protestants who wanted to reform the Anglican Church were called **Puritans.** Those who wanted to leave and set up their own churches were known as **Separatists.**

The Separatists were persecuted in England, and some fled to the Netherlands. Though they found religious freedom there, the Separatists had difficulty finding work. They also worried that their children were losing their religious values and their English way of life.

The Pilgrims' Journey

Some Separatists in the Netherlands made an arrangement with the Virginia Company. The Separatists could settle in Virginia and practice their religion freely. In return they would give the company a share of any profits they made.

The Separatists considered themselves **Pilgrims** because their journey had a religious purpose. Only 35 of the 102 passengers who boarded the *Mayflower* in September 1620 were Pilgrims. The others were called "strangers." They were common people—servants, craftspeople, and poor farmers—who hoped to find a better life in America. Because Pilgrim beliefs shaped life in the Plymouth colony, however, all the early settlers are usually called Pilgrims.

If You Were There / A Teenage Pilgrim Girl

Creating a Home As a teenage Pilgrim girl, you help your mother cook, keep house, do laundry, and raise the younger children. When the men and boys eat their meals, you stand quietly behind the table. At a church gathering, you cannot talk, and you must keep your head covered with a bonnet when in public. You are taught to read, but not to write. Your clothes are usually a full skirt, an apron, and an upper garment with long sleeves—much like your mother wears.

Critical Thinking

Making Connections How does the life of a Pilgrim teenager compare to your life today?

Activity: Interdisciplinary Connection

Art Organize students into small groups. Have the groups do research to find out how to make a colonial craft of their choice. Possibilities include decorative work such as quilling and silhouette making; toys such as tops, whirligigs, kites, and rag or corn-husk dolls; and items such as gourd rattles and bowls, corn-husk hot pads, mats, and baskets. Have the groups explain their crafts to the class and display their finished items. **OL**

Teach

• • • • • • • • • • • • • • • • • •

R Reading Strategy

Comparing and Contrasting Have students create a Venn diagram showing how Puritans and Separatists were alike and how they were different. (***Both:*** *disagreed with beliefs and practices of Anglican Church;* ***Puritans:*** *wanted to reform Church;* ***Separatists:*** *wanted to break away from Church*) **OL**

C Critical Thinking

Making Inferences Ask: Why do you think the "strangers" accepted the Pilgrims' way of life in Plymouth? (*The Separatists made the arrangements. The "strangers" probably had to agree to follow Separatist rules to be allowed to live in the colony.*) **OL**

If You Were There

Critical Thinking Answer Answers will vary but may include more equal rights for girls in today's society.

Additional Support

Teacher Tip

Art To introduce this activity, ask students to describe things they have made by hand. Have them describe the materials they used and their methods for fastening pieces together.

W Writing Support

Narrative Writing Have students take the role of a Pilgrim who has just landed on Cape Cod. Ask them to write a letter to a friend in England, expressing their feelings about their new home. **OL**

S Skill Practice

Reading Primary Sources Ask: How does the phrase "better ordering and preservation" reflect the purpose of the Mayflower Compact? *(It was created to establish an orderly society so that they could all survive.)* **ELL**

C Critical Thinking

Drawing Conclusions Ask: What can you conclude about the Pilgrims from their first few months in Plymouth? *(They were unprepared and lacked basic skills for living.)* **OL**

✔ **Reading Check** **Answer:** It was a step in the development of representative government in America.

Differentiated Instruction

The Mayflower Compact

The *Mayflower's* passengers planned to settle in the Virginia colony. The first land they sighted was Cape Cod, well north of their target. It was November, and winter was fast approaching. The colonists decided to drop anchor in Cape Cod Bay. They went ashore on a cold, bleak day in December at a place called Plymouth. **William Bradford,** their leader and historian, reported that "all things stared upon them with a weather-beaten face."

Plymouth was outside the territory of the Virginia Company and its laws. Before going ashore, the Pilgrims drew up a formal document, the **Mayflower Compact.** The compact pledged their loyalty to England. It also declared their intention of forming "a civil body politic, for our better ordering and preservation." The signers also promised to obey the laws passed "for the general good of the colony." The Mayflower Compact was a necessary step in the development of representative government in the new American colonies.

Help From the Native Americans

During their first winter in America, almost half the Pilgrims died of malnutrition, disease, and cold. In the spring, two Native Americans, **Squanto** and Samoset, befriended the colonists.

Squanto and Samoset showed the Pilgrims how to grow corn, beans, and pumpkins and where to hunt and fish. Without their help, the Pilgrims might not have survived. Squanto and Samoset also helped the Pilgrims make peace with the Wampanoag people who lived in the area. Massasoit, a Wampanoag leader, signed a treaty with the Pilgrims in March 1621. The two groups lived in harmony.

✔ **Reading Check** **Analyzing** What was the significance of the Mayflower Compact?

The *Mayflower*

The *Mayflower*
In September 1620, 102 passengers set off on the *Mayflower* on the journey across the Atlantic. The 2,750-mile trip took more than two months. In early November, the *Mayflower* reached the shores of America.

Leveled Activities

BL Reading Essentials and Note-Taking Guide, p. 25

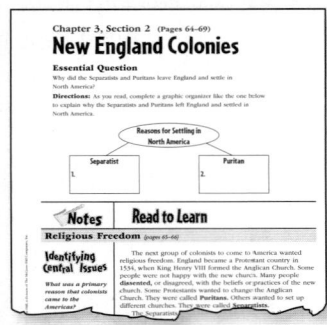

OL Writing Skills Activity, URB p. 79

ELL Content Vocabulary Activity, URB p. 73

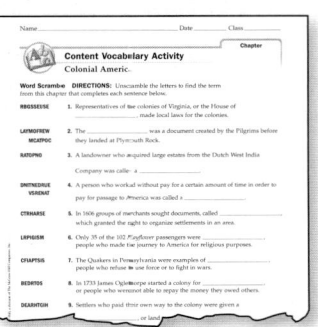

New Settlements

Main Idea To escape religious persecution in England, thousands of Puritans migrated to North America and set up new colonies.

History and You How would you react if someone set up camp in your backyard? Read about the conflict between Native Americans and the settlers in New England.

· ·

In 1625 Charles I became the king of England. Charles objected to the Puritans' calls for reform in the Anglican Church. Persecution of Puritans within the country increased again. As a result, some Puritans wanted to leave England.

In 1629 a group of Puritans formed the Massachusetts Bay Company. They received a royal charter to establish a colony north of Plymouth. This was the Puritans' chance to create a new society in America—a society based on the Bible.

The company chose **John Winthrop** to be the colony's governor. In 1630 Winthrop led about 900 men, women, and children to Massachusetts Bay. Most of them settled in a place they called Boston.

Growth and Government

During the 1630s, more than 15,000 Puritans journeyed to Massachusetts to escape religious persecution and economic hard times in England. This movement of people became known as the Great Migration.

At first John Winthrop and his assistants made the colony's laws. They were chosen by the General Court, which was made up of the colony's stockholders. In 1634 settlers demanded a larger role, or part, in the government. The General Court became an elected assembly. Adult male church members were allowed to vote for the governor and for their town's representatives to the General Court. In later years they also had to own property to vote.

Mayflower Key

1 Most of the crew slept in the tiny cabins in the **forecastle,** which also served as the ship's kitchen.

2 The *Mayflower* was a supply ship. It was not built to carry passengers. **'Tween decks** was where the passengers of the *Mayflower* slept and kept their belongings.

3 The **main hold** was the main cargo area. It held most of the ship's stores of food, supplies, and tools.

4 The **helmsman** moved a lever called the **whipstaff,** which moved the rudder and steered the ship.

5 The **great cabin** was the quarters for the commander of the ship.

Critical Thinking

Drawing Conclusions How comfortable were the passengers onboard the *Mayflower*? Explain.

The New England Colonies — NATIONAL GEOGRAPHIC

Products
- Cattle
- Fish
- Furs
- Grain
- Iron
- Lumber
- Rum
- Ships
- Whales

Area claimed by New York and New Hampshire

Massachusetts

46°N

New Hampshire

ATLANTIC OCEAN

Portsmouth

Salem

Massachusetts
Boston

42°N

Plymouth

Connecticut

Newport

New Haven

Rhode Island

0   100 kilometers
0   100 miles
Albers Equal-Area projection

72°W   68°W

C Critical Thinking

Drawing Conclusions Ask: Why do you think King Charles was willing to give the Puritans a royal charter? *(He probably wanted them to leave England.)* **OL**

R Reading Strategy

Activating Prior Knowledge Ask: What are stockholders? *(investors)* Have students reread the description of a joint-stock company in Section 1. **BL**

S Skill Practice

Creating a Chart Have students create a chart of the government of Boston before and after 1634. (*before: stockholders chose governor who made the laws; after: adult male church members elected governor and town representatives*) **OL**

The Mayflower

Critical Thinking Answer

It was probably not very comfortable. The ship was not designed to carry passengers.

Hands-On Chapter Project
Step 2

Reenacting Colonial Life

Step 2: Writing the Script Students will write a script for their characters.

Essential Question: Why did the Separatists and Puritans leave England and settle in North America?

Directions Have the groups decide who their characters will be. Each student should have a role. The roles should portray different parts of town life, such as work, family, government,

education, security, and fun. Have the groups write a speech for each character to perform for the tourists. Remind them that as actors, they will speak from their characters' points of view. Together, the speeches should create a complete picture of daily life in their town.

Determining Cause and Effect As a class, discuss how Puritan beliefs influenced the organization of New England towns. **OL**

(Chapter Project continued in Section 3)

W Writing Support

Personal Writing Have students write an essay expressing their opinions about whether a government should be based on religion. They should explain their opinions using supporting details. **AL**

R Reading Strategy

Identifying This section discusses three steps toward representative government. Have students identify and describe them. (*Mayflower Compact: agreement to form government;* *first elected assembly: gave settlers a role in government;* *Fundamental Orders of Connecticut: America's first written constitution*) **OL**

DBQ Document-Based Questions

Answers

1. Winthrop might see them as corrupt.
2. Possible response: A voyage can be a symbol of life's journey. A ship transports a variety of people who must live with each other during the voyage.

YOU DECIDE

W Should government be based on religion?

John Winthrop, a founder of the Massachusetts Bay Colony, believed that the colony should be governed on religious principles. Others, such as Roger Williams, disagreed and were banished from Massachusetts.

YES JOHN WINTHROP

It is yourselves who have called us to this office, and, being called by you, we have our authority from God. . . . If you stand for your natural corrupt liberties . . . you will not endure the least weight of authority . . . but if you will be satisfied to enjoy such civil and lawful liberties, such as Christ allows you, then will you quietly and cheerfully submit unto that authority which is set over you . . . for your good.
—from "'Little Speech' on Liberty"

ROGER WILLIAMS

I . . . only propose this case; There goes many a ship to sea, with many hundred souls in one ship, [which] is a true picture of a commonwealth. . . . It hath fallen out some times, that both Papists [Catholics] and Protestants, Jews and Turks, may be embarked in one ship; upon which supposal, I affirm . . . that none of the Papists, Protestants, Jews, or Turks, be forced to come to the ship's prayers or worship, or compelled from their own particular prayers or worship.
—from a letter to the town of Providence

DBQ Document-Based Questions

1. **Evaluating** How might Winthrop view people who held different religious views?
2. **Analyzing** Why might Williams have used the image of a ship at sea to make his case for religious freedom?

The Puritans came to America to put their religious beliefs into practice. They had little toleration for different beliefs, however. They criticized or persecuted people of other faiths. This lack of toleration led people to form new colonies in neighboring areas.

Connecticut and Rhode Island

The fertile Connecticut River valley, south of Massachusetts, was better for farming than was the stony soil around Boston. In the 1630s colonists began to settle in this area.

One such colonist, Massachusetts minister Thomas Hooker, grew dissatisfied with the way that Winthrop and other Puritan leaders ran the Massachusetts colony. In 1636 Hooker led his congregation through the wilderness to Connecticut where he founded the town of Hartford. Three years later Hartford and two other towns, Windsor and Wethersfield, formed a colony. They adopted a plan of government called the **Fundamental Orders of Connecticut.** This was the first written constitution in America. It described the organization of representative government in detail.

Good land drew colonists to Connecticut, but Rhode Island was settled by a minister named **Roger Williams** and other colonists who were forced out of Massachusetts. Williams felt that people should not be persecuted for their religious practices and that government should not force people to worship in a certain way. Williams also believed it was wrong for settlers to take land away from the Native Americans.

His ideas caused Massachusetts leaders to banish him in 1635. Williams took refuge with the Narraganset people. They later sold him land, where he founded the town of Providence. Williams received a charter in 1644 for a colony east of Connecticut called Rhode Island and Providence Plantations. With its **policy**—plan of action—of religious toleration, Rhode Island became a safe place for dissenters. It was the first place in America where people of all faiths—including Jews—could worship freely.

Differentiated Instruction

Colonial America

Objective: To create a time line of colonial leaders and governments in America

Focus: Remind students that all the colonies had to establish some type of government.

Teach: Have students read the background information and prepare their time lines.

Assess: Have students compare their time lines for similarities and differences.

Close: Discuss what characteristics made each person a leader.

Differentiated Instruction Strategies

BL Ask students to take notes from the background information before they create their time lines.

AL Have students write a report on which colonial leader they admire most and why.

ELL Have pairs of students collaborate on time lines, with one student identifying leaders and the other student listing governments.

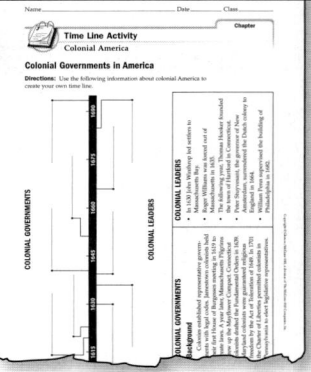

Time Line Skills Activity, URB p. 90

Others followed Williams's example, including John Wheelwright, who, in 1638, led a group of dissidents from Massachusetts to the north. They founded the town of Exeter in New Hampshire. Other Puritans settled Hampton the same year. New Hampshire became an independent colony in 1679.

Conflict With Native Americans

Native Americans traded furs for settlers' goods such as iron pots, blankets, and guns. In Virginia the colonists encountered the many tribes of the Powhatan confederacy. In New England the settlers met the Wampanoags, Narragansets, and other groups.

Conflicts arose, however. Usually settlers moved onto Native American lands without permission or payment. Throughout the colonial period, English settlers and Native Americans competed fiercely for the land.

In 1636 war broke out. Two traders were killed in Pequot territory, and Massachusetts sent troops to punish the Pequot. A Pequot attack then killed nine people in Connecticut. In May 1637, troops from Connecticut burned the main Pequot village, killing hundreds.

History ONLINE
Student Web Activity Visit glencoe.com and complete the Chapter 3 Web Activity about King Philip's War.

In 1675 New England went to war against the Wampanoag people and their allies. Metacomet, the Wampanoag chief, was known to settlers as King Philip. He wanted to stop the settlers from moving onto Native American lands. Metacomet tried to form a federation of local peoples, and many New England groups joined with him. The war began after settlers executed three Wampanoags for murder. Metacomet's forces then attacked towns across the region, killing hundreds of people.

The settlers and their Native American allies fought back. King Philip's War, as the conflict was called, ended in defeat for the Wampanoag and their allies. The war destroyed the power of the Native Americans in New England. The colonists were now free to expand their settlements.

✓ **Reading Check** **Identifying** Which colony let people of all faiths worship freely?

Section 2 Review

History ONLINE
Study Central™ To review this section, go to glencoe.com.

Vocabulary
1. Use each of these terms in a sentence that will help explain its meaning: dissent, Puritan, Separatist, Pilgrim, Mayflower Compact, Fundamental Orders of Connecticut, policy.

Main Ideas
2. **Explaining** Why did the Pilgrims settle in Cape Cod instead of Virginia?
3. **Discussing** What was the significance of King Philip's War?

Critical Thinking
4. **Comparing** What did the Mayflower Compact and the Fundamental Orders of Connecticut have in common?
5. **Determining Cause and Effect** Use a diagram like the one below to describe the ways in which interactions with Native Americans helped Plymouth colony survive.

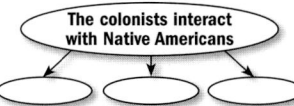
The colonists interact with Native Americans

6. **Creative Writing** Create a song that the Pilgrims might have sung as they crossed the Atlantic on the *Mayflower*. Write the lyrics from what you know about why the Pilgrims sailed to North America.

Answer the
7. **Essential Question**
Why did the Separatists and Puritans leave England and settle in North America?

Colonial America **Chapter 3** **69**

CHAPTER 3
Section 2

CHAPTER 3
Section 2

D **Differentiated Instruction**

English Language Learners In a two-column table, have students list colonial leaders on the left and their colonies on the right. *(William Bradford: Plymouth; John Winthrop: Massachusetts Bay; Thomas Hooker: Connecticut; Roger Williams: Rhode Island; John Wheelwright: New Hampshire)* **ELL**

History ONLINE
Objectives and answers to the Student Web Activity can be found at glencoe.com under the Web Activity Lesson Plan for this chapter.

✓ **Reading Check** **Answer:** Rhode Island

Assess

History ONLINE

Study Central™ provides summaries, interactive games, and online graphic organizers to help students review content.

Close

Summarizing As a class, discuss the reasons why the Separatists and Puritans left England. **OL**

Section 2 Review

Answers

1. Students should use terms correctly in sentences.
2. Winter was approaching, so they landed at the first location they sighted, which was Cape Cod.
3. The war destroyed Native American power in New England, opening the way for settlements to expand.

4. Both provided for the organization of a government.
5. The colonists learned how to grow corn, beans, and pumpkins; they learned where to hunt and fish; the treaty with the Wampanoag allowed settlers and Native Americans to live in harmony.

6. Students' songs should reflect knowledge of the values, hopes, and dreams of the Pilgrims.
7. **Separatists:** escape persecution but maintain their religious values and English way of life; **Puritans:** escape persecution and establish a new society based on their religious beliefs

69

Focus

R₁ Reading Strategy

Paraphrasing Have students find the vocabulary words within the selection. Then have them paraphrase the sentences in which each word occurs. **OL**

D Differentiated Instruction

Interpersonal Organize the class into small groups, and assign a role from the passage to each person in the group. Have the groups act out the passage in front of the class. Ask students if they learned anything more about the characters because they took on their roles. **OL**

R₂ Reading Strategy

Visualizing Have students identify words in the paragraph that may help them visualize the scene. *(Words should include heavy, untouched, dreadful, and ached.)* **OL**

Additional Reading

Review suggested books before assigning them.

Fiction: *My Lady, Pocahontas,* by Kathleen V. Kudlinski, begins in 1607 when Pocahontas is watching the activities of English colonists. The story combines fact and fiction about this courageous and intelligent woman's life.

Fiction: *The Winter People,* by Joseph Bruchac and James Bernardin, follows 14-year-old Saxso's race to rescue his mother and sisters after they are kidnapped by the British. This action-packed book is based on a real event that occurred during the French and Indian War.

Fiction: *Johnny Tremain,* by Esther Forbes, is the story of a 14-year-old silversmith's apprentice in Boston. When he injures his hand at work, he becomes involved in the Sons of Liberty at the start of the American Revolution.

For further reading, see **BookLink 3**.

America's LITERATURE

Meet the Author

Elizabeth George Speare (1908–1994) based her novel *The Witch of Blackbird Pond* on events in Wethersfield, Connecticut, her home for 20 years. Speare's research into the town's history resulted in the diverse and rich characters at the center of this tale.

Building Background

Elizabeth George Speare used her native New England as the backdrop for many novels. In *The Witch of Blackbird Pond,* Kit leaves her home in Barbados to live with her aunt and uncle in Connecticut. There she befriends a Quaker woman accused of practicing witchcraft. Many authors use plot as the basis of their stories; however, the characters drive the plot in this tale. As you read this excerpt, pay attention to how one character responds to another.

Vocabulary

R₁

fatigue tiredness

consternation fear

hysterical very emotional

consorting keeping company

slander speak ill of

D THE WITCH OF BLACKBIRD POND

Elizabeth George Speare

Kit busied herself to prepare a meal which none of them could eat. With fingers so heavy from **fatigue** and fear that she could scarcely **R₂** force them to move, she cleared the table and put away the untouched food. She wondered if ever again she would escape from the sound of that dreadful breathing. Her own lungs ached with every sighing breath that Mercy drew.

Then without warning a new fear came rushing in upon her. From without the house there was an approaching sound of stamping feet and murmuring voices, gathering volume in the roadway outside. There was a crashing knock on the outer door. The three women's eyes met in **consternation.** Matthew

Wood reached the door in one stride and flung it open.

"How dare you?" he demanded in low-voiced anger. "Know you not there is illness here?"

"Aye, we know right enough," a voice replied.

"There's illness everywhere. We need your help to put a stop to it."

"What do you want?"

"We want you to come along with us. We're going for the witch.". . .

The voices sounded **hysterical.** "We should have run her out long ago."

"Time and again she's been seen **consorting** with the devil down in that meadow!"

"Now she's put a curse on our children. God knows how many more will be dead before morning!". . .

"You'd better come with us, Matthew. Your own daughter's like to die. You can't deny it."

"I'll have naught to do with it," said Matthew firmly. "I'll hold with no witch hunt."

"You'd better hold with it!" the woman's voice shrilled suddenly. "You'd better look to the witch in your own household!"

"Ask that high and mighty niece of yours where she spends her time!" another woman shouted from the darkness. "Ask her what she knows about your Mercy's sickness!"

The weariness dropped suddenly from Matthew Wood. With his shoulders thrown back he seemed to tower in the doorway.

"Begone from my house!" he roared, his caution drowned in anger. "How dare you speak the name of a good, God-fearing girl? Any man who **slanders** one of my family has me to reckon with!"

There was a silence. "No harm meant," a man's voice said uneasily. "'Tis only woman's talk."

"If you won't come there's plenty more in the town who will," said another. "What are we wasting our time for?"

The voices receded down the pathway, rising again in the darkness beyond. Matthew bolted the door and turned back to the dumfounded women.

"Did they wake her?" he asked dully.

"No," sighed Rachel. "Even that could not disturb her, poor child."

For a moment, there was no sound but that tortured breathing. Kit had risen to her feet and stood clinging to the table's edge. Now the new fear that was stifling her broke from her lips in an anguished whisper.

"What will they do to her?"

Her aunt looked up in alarm. Matthew's black brows drew together darkly. "What concern is that of yours?"

"I know her!" she cried. "She's just a poor helpless old woman! Oh, please tell me! Will they harm her?"

"This is Connecticut," answered Matthew sternly. "They will abide by the law. They will bring her to trial, I suppose. If she can prove herself innocent she is safe enough."

Analyzing Literature

1. **Respond**
   (a) How would you describe the tone of this passage?
   (b) What words and phrases evoke this tone?

2. **Interpret and Analyze** How do Matthew's emotions change throughout the passage?

3. **Evaluate and Predict**
   (a) What can you conclude about Matthew after reading this passage?
   (b) Based on Matthew's final comment, what action do you think the townspeople will take?

Teach

C Critical Thinking

Determining Cause and Effect
Ask: What happened when a woman accused Matthew Wood's niece of being a witch? (He rose up and demanded that the group leave his house.) **OL**

D Differentiated Instruction

English Language Learners Students may have difficulty following who is speaking in the passage. Take notes on the board to show who is speaking and what he or she said. **ELL**

Assess/Close

As a class, discuss the use of point of view in creative writing. Remind your students that this passage is written from Kit's point of view. **Ask:** How would this be different if it were written from Matthew's viewpoint? (He would know the names of the people who are speaking; he might feel more anger.) From the sleeping girl's viewpoint? (She would have seen and heard nothing, so she would rely on what others told her.)

Answers

1. (a) Possible answers include fearful, suspenseful.
   (b) Possible answers include *fear, darkness beyond, anguished whisper.*

2. His emotions change from anger, defeat, bewilderment, and then to anger again.

3. (a) Possible answer: He is fair and does not judge others based on rumor.
   (b) They will persecute the old woman as a witch.

Focus

Middle Colonies

Bellringer
Daily Test Practice Transparency 3–3

Reading Guide
Answers to Graphic:
New York: New York, New Jersey;
Pennsylvania: Pennsylvania, Delaware

Section Spotlight Video

To learn more about New Amsterdam, watch the Section Spotlight Video "Middle Colonies."

Essential Question ◄
How did the Middle Colonies develop?

Reading Guide

Content Vocabulary
patroon (p. 73)
proprietary colony (p. 74)
pacifist (p. 75)

Academic Vocabulary
ethnic (p. 74)   function (p. 75)

Key People
Duke of York (p. 74)
William Penn (p. 75)
Quakers (p. 75)

Reading Strategy
Taking Notes As you read, use a diagram like the one below to show how the New York and Pennsylvania colonies split to form the four Middle Colonies under British rule.

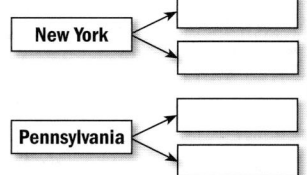

New York	

Pennsylvania	

ILLINOIS STANDARDS
The American Journey

15.D Understand trade as an exchange of goods and services.

16.B.3a (US) Describe how different groups competed for power within the colonies and how that competition led to the development of political institutions during the early national period.

16.D.3a (US) Describe characteristics of different kinds of communities in various sections of America during the colonial/frontier periods and the 19th century.

18.B Understand the roles and interactions of individuals and groups in society.

American Diary

In August 1664, strong English forces demanded the surrender of the Dutch colony of New Netherland. Peter Stuyvesant, the colony's governor, at first flatly refused to surrender. Leading citizens pleaded with Stuyvesant to avoid "the absolute ruin and destruction of about fifteen hundred innocent souls." Reluctantly Stuyvesant surrendered on September 8. The colony became New York.

—quoted in A New World

Citizens persuade Governor Peter Stuyvesant not to open fire on the British.

Resource Manager

R Reading Strategies	C Critical Thinking	D Differentiated Instruction	W Writing Support	S Skill Practice
Teacher Edition • Predicting, p. 75 **Additional Resources** • Guid. Read., URB p. 97 • Content Vocab., URB p. 73 • Academic Vocab., URB p. 75 • Read. Ess., p. 28	**Teacher Edition** • Comparing and Contrasting, p. 74 • Analyzing Information, p. 75 **Additional Resources** • Quizzes and Tests, p. 23 • Crit. Think. Skills, URB p. 85	**Additional Resources** • School-to-Home, URB p. 91 • Reteaching Act., URB p. 93 • Differ. Inst., URB p. 83	**Teacher Edition** • Expository Writing, p. 73	**Teacher Edition** • Identifying the Main Idea, p. 73 • Using Map Skills, p. 74 **Additional Resources** • Daily Test Pract. Transp. 3-3 • Lesson Transparency 3B • Soc. Stud. Skills, URB p. 81

England and the Colonies

Main Idea After seizing the Dutch colony of New Netherland, the English renamed the colony New York and formed the New Jersey colony.

History and You Have you ever won a prize and then shared it with your friends? Read how the English seized the New Netherland colony and then formed the New Jersey colony.

. . . .

In England, the Puritans who controlled Parliament struggled for power against King Charles I. In 1642 a civil war began. Led by Oliver Cromwell, a Puritan, the Parliamentary forces defeated the king. Many Puritans from New England returned to England to join in this struggle.

Charles I was beheaded in 1649 on charges of treason. A new government was established with Cromwell as Protector. After Cromwell died in 1658, Parliament restored the monarchy but with new limitations. When Charles II became king in 1660, his reign was known as the Restoration.

In 1660 England had two clusters of colonies in what is now the United States. In the north were Massachusetts, New Hampshire, Connecticut, and Rhode Island. Maryland and Virginia were in the south. Between the two groups of English colonies were lands that the Dutch controlled.

The main settlement of the New Netherland colony was New Amsterdam, located on Manhattan Island. Blessed with a good seaport, New Amsterdam became a center of shipping to and from the Americas.

The Dutch West India Company wanted **W** to increase the number of settlers in its colony. It offered large estates to anyone who could bring at least 50 settlers to work the land. The landowners who acquired these estates were called **patroons.** The patroons ruled like kings. They had their own courts and laws. Settlers owed the patroons labor and a share of their crops.

England Takes Over

New Netherland had an excellent harbor and a thriving river trade. The English wanted to acquire this valuable Dutch colony. In 1664 the English sent a fleet to **S** attack New Amsterdam. At that time Peter Stuyvesant was governor of the colony. He was unprepared for a battle and surrendered the colony to the English forces.

Primary Source / New Netherland

Colonial Dutch Crafts By the mid-1600s, New Netherland had a growing population and a prosperous economy. Immigrant artisans from the Netherlands and other parts of Europe settled in the Dutch colony. They produced outstanding furniture, silverware, and other household items, such as this finely crafted silver bowl.

Two-handed silver bowl ▶

Critical Thinking
Drawing Conclusions Why do you think New Netherland, later New York, was a valuable colony?

Teach

. . . .

W Writing Support

Expository Writing Have students research the Dutch colonization of America. Ask them to write a two-page report. The report should include at least one chart, graph, or illustration. **AL**

S Skill Practice

Identifying the Main Idea Have students note the main idea of this paragraph and supporting details in a graphic organizer. (***main idea:*** *English took over New Netherland;* ***details:*** *harbor and river trade made colony valuable; English sent fleet to attack; Dutch surrendered)* **OL**

This **READING SKILL** (Identifying the Main Idea) was introduced in this unit.

Primary Source

Critical Thinking Answer
It had a prosperous economy, skilled artisans, a good harbor, and thriving trade.

Hands-On Chapter Project
Step 3

Reenacting Colonial Life

Step 3: Designing the Set Students will construct the scenery and props for their reenactment.

Essential Question: How did the Middle Colonies develop?

Directions Instruct the groups to design a set for each character. For example, if their town has a blacksmith, they will want to create scenery depicting a blacksmith shop. They should include details from their research that will make the scene realistic. Groups should also plan the props each character will need in the performance. The groups should then gather materials and construct the sets and props.

Contrasting As a class, discuss how daily life in the Middle Colonies differed from life in New England. **OL**

(Chapter Project continued in Section 4)

S Skill Practice

Using Map Skills Refer students to the map. **Ask:** What main products helped New York prosper? *(cattle, grain, lumber, iron, rum, fish)* **BL**

C Critical Thinking

Comparing and Contrasting Ask: How did New Jersey compare to New York politically, socially, and economically? *(**politically:** unlike New York, New Jersey had elected assembly; **socially:** both had ethnic and religious diversity; **economically:** New Jersey was less prosperous due to lack of a port.)* **OL**

The Middle Colonies NATIONAL GEOGRAPHIC

Map Skills Answer

Philadelphia: on river with inlet to ocean; **New York:** on coast, good harbor; **both:** between Northern and Southern Colonies

Reading Check Answer: There were no natural harbors.

Differentiated Instruction

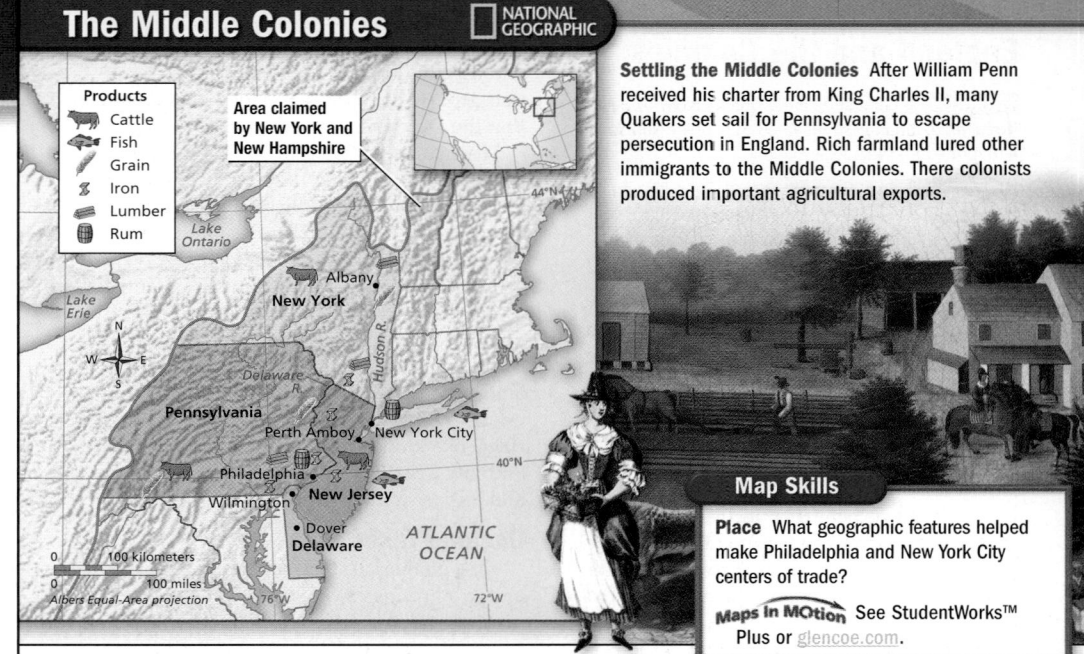

The Middle Colonies NATIONAL GEOGRAPHIC

Products
- Cattle
- Fish
- Grain
- Iron
- Lumber
- Rum

Area claimed by New York and New Hampshire

Settling the Middle Colonies After William Penn received his charter from King Charles II, many Quakers set sail for Pennsylvania to escape persecution in England. Rich farmland lured other immigrants to the Middle Colonies. There colonists produced important agricultural exports.

Map Skills

Place What geographic features helped make Philadelphia and New York City centers of trade?

Maps In MOtion See StudentWorks™ Plus or glencoe.com.

King Charles II gave the colony to his brother, the **Duke of York,** who renamed it New York. New York was a **proprietary colony,** a colony in which the owner, or proprietor, owned all the land and controlled the government. It differed from the New England colonies, where voters elected the governor and an assembly. Not until 1691 did the English government allow citizens of New York to elect their legislature.

New York continued to prosper under English control. It had a diverse population made up of Dutch, German, Swedish, and Native American people. Also among the population were Brazilian Jews, the first Jews to settle in North America.

In 1664 New York had about 8,000 inhabitants. That population also included at least 300 enslaved Africans. By 1683 the colony's population swelled to about 12,000 people. New York City, which was called New Amsterdam when it was controlled by the Dutch, was one of the fastest-growing locations in the colony.

New Jersey

The Duke of York gave the southern part of his colony, between the Hudson and Delaware Rivers, to Lord John Berkeley and Sir George Carteret. The proprietors named their colony New Jersey after the island of Jersey in the English Channel, where Carteret was born. To attract settlers, they offered large tracts of land and also promised freedom of religion, trial by jury, and a representative assembly. The assembly would make local laws and set tax rates.

Like New York, New Jersey was a place of **ethnic** and religious diversity. New Jersey had no natural harbors, so it did not develop a major port or city like New York, and New Jersey's proprietors made few profits. Both proprietors eventually sold their shares in the colony. By 1702 New Jersey had returned to the king, becoming a royal colony. However, the colonists continued to make local laws.

Reading Check Explaining Why did no major port develop in New Jersey?

Reading a Bar Graph

Objective: To learn how to create and read a bar graph

Focus: Remind students that graphs are useful for understanding and comparing data.

Teach: Have students create their bar graphs for class attendance.

Assess: Have students assess their graphs using the checklist.

Close: Discuss the advantages of using bar graphs.

Differentiated Instruction Strategies

BL Ask students to explain how bars in the graphs can be either vertical or horizontal.

AL Have students convert the bar graph data to create circle graphs.

ELL Ask students to use the terms "horizontal axis" and "vertical axis" to label the appropriate lines on their graphs.

Social Studies Skills Activity, URB p. 81

Pennsylvania

Main Idea William Penn founded the colony of Pennsylvania and designed the city of Philadelphia.

History and You If given a choice, would you take land or money for a debt someone owed you? Read to learn how William Penn acquired Pennsylvania.

· ·

In 1681, **William Penn,** a wealthy English Quaker, received land as payment for a debt that King Charles II owed to Penn's father. The king gave Penn a tract of land in America stretching inland from the Delaware River. The new colony, named Pennsylvania, was nearly as large as England.

William Penn saw Pennsylvania as a "holy experiment," a chance to put his Quaker ideals into practice. The **Quakers,** or Society of Friends, believed that everyone was equal. People could follow their own "inner light" to salvation. They did not need clergy to guide them. Quakers were also **pacifists,** or people who refuse to use force or to fight in wars. They were considered a threat in England and were persecuted.

In 1682 Penn sailed to America to supervise the building of Philadelphia, the "city of brotherly love." Penn designed the city himself and wrote Pennsylvania's first constitution. Penn believed that the land belonged to the Native Americans and that settlers should pay for it. He negotiated several treaties with local Native Americans.

Penn advertised the colony throughout Europe. By 1683 more than 3,000 English, Welsh, Irish, Dutch, and German settlers had arrived. In 1701, in the Charter of Liberties, Penn granted colonists the right to elect representatives to the legislature.

Swedes had settled southern Pennsylvania before the Dutch and then the English took over the area. The Charter of Privileges allowed these lower counties to form their own legislature. The counties then **functioned,** or operated, as a separate colony known as Delaware under Pennsylvania's governor.

✓ **Reading Check** **Inferring** What was William Penn's primary purpose for founding the colony of Pennsylvania?

Section 3 Review

History ONLINE
Study Central™ To review this section, go to glencoe.com.

Vocabulary

1. Define each of the following vocabulary terms and use each in a sentence: patroon, proprietary colony, ethnic, pacifist, function.

Main Ideas

2. **Describing** How were the colonies of New York and New Jersey governed?

3. **Summarizing** Describe three beliefs of the Quakers.

Critical Thinking

4. **Making Connections** Why do you think the Church of England might consider the Quakers a threat?

5. **Contrasting** Re-create the diagram below and describe how settlers in Pennsylvania and New England differed in the way they acquired land from Native Americans.

| Land Acquired From Native Americans |
| New England settlers | Pennsylvania settlers |

6. **Persuasive Writing** Take on the role of William Penn. Write an advertisement to persuade settlers to come to Pennsylvania. Include details about the Pennsylvania colony that people would find attractive.

Answer the
7. **Essential Question**
How did the Middle Colonies develop?

Colonial America **Chapter 3** 75

R Reading Strategy

Predicting Almost a hundred years later, Americans will fight for independence from England. **Ask:** What stand do you think the Quakers will take during the American Revolution? Why? *(They will refuse to fight because they are pacifists.)* **OL**

C Critical Thinking

Analyzing Information Ask: What policies of Pennsylvania reflected Quaker beliefs? *(The colony allowed citizens to elect representatives to the legislature, treated Native Americans fairly, and welcomed diversity.)* **OL**

✓ **Reading Check** **Answer:** Penn wanted to put his Quaker ideals into practice.

Assess
· ·

History ONLINE

Study Central™ provides summaries, interactive games, and online graphic organizers to help students review content.

Close
· ·

Summarizing As a class, discuss the founding and development of the Middle Colonies. **OL**

Section 3 Review

Answers

1. Sentences should reflect an understanding of the terms.
2. **New York:** controlled by proprietor; later elected legislature; **New Jersey:** owned by proprietor, but representative assembly made local laws and set tax rates.
3. equality of all people; people could follow own inner light to salvation; pacifism
4. The Quakers believed people did not need clergy to achieve salvation.
5. **New England:** Settlers moved onto Native American lands without permission or payment; **Pennsylvania:** Settlers paid Native Americans for the land.
6. Advertisements should include attractive details such as Quaker belief in equality and pacifism, peaceful coexistence with Native Americans, a constitution, and an elected legislature.
7. **New York:** thriving Dutch colony seized by English; major port; proprietary colony; diverse population; **New Jersey:** piece of New York given to other proprietors; land and freedoms offered to attract settlers; diverse population; lacked major port so less profitable; became royal colony; **Pennsylvania:** established under Quaker ideals; welcomed diverse immigrants; constitution; elected legislature; **Delaware:** lower part of Pennsylvania settled by Swedes; allowed to function as separate colony

Southern Colonies

Focus

Bellringer
Daily Test Practice Transparency 3–4

Reading Guide
Answers to Graphic:
criminals and prisoners of war: to gain release from prison; **enslaved Africans:** against their will as labor for farms and plantations; **indentured servants:** to pay for passage to the Americas

Section Spotlight Video

Watch the Section Spotlight Video "Southern Colonies" to learn about the Mason-Dixon Line.

Resource Manager

Essential Question ◄
How and why did the Southern Colonies grow?

Reading Guide

Content Vocabulary

indentured servant (p. 77)
constitution (p. 79)
debtor (p. 80)
tenant farmer (p. 81)
mission (p. 82)

Academic Vocabulary

estate (p. 77)

Key People and Events
Sir George Calvert, Lord Baltimore (p.77)
Nathaniel Bacon (p. 78)
James Oglethorpe (p. 80)
Louis Joliet (p. 81)
Jacques Marquette (p. 81)
René-Robert Cavelier, Sieur de La Salle (p. 81)

Reading Strategy
Taking Notes As you read, use a chart like the one below to identify the types of workers who came to the South and their reasons for coming.

Workers	Why They Came
indentured servants	

ILLINOIS STANDARDS
The American Journey

16.A Apply the skills of historical analysis and interpretation.

16.C.3a (US) Describe economic motivations that attracted Europeans and others to the Americas, 1500–1750.

16.D.3a (US) Describe characteristics of different kinds of communities in various sections of America during the colonial/frontier periods and the 19th century.

17.C.3a Explain how human activity is affected by geographic factors.

American Diary

Anthony Johnson was one of the first Africans in colonial Virginia. Arriving in 1621, Johnson worked on a tobacco plantation along the James River. He and his wife, Mary, eventually bought their way out of bondage. They acquired their own land and raised livestock. After Johnson's death, however, a Virginia court ruled that because he was an African "and by consequence an alien [foreigner]," the land rightly belonged to the British Crown.

—quoted in Africans in America

A Virginia plantation owner oversees the packing of tobacco leaves to be shipped to England.

R Reading Strategies	C Critical Thinking	D Differentiated Instruction	W Writing Support	S Skill Practice
Teacher Edition • Read. Pri. Sou., p. 79 • Identifying, p. 80 **Additional Resources** • Guid. Read., URB p. 98 • Content Vocab., URB p. 73 • Academic Vocab., URB p. 75 • Pri. Source Read., URB p. 77	**Teacher Edition** • Making Inferences, p. 77 • Identifying Central Issues, p. 79 • Speculating, p. 81 **Additional Resources** • Quizzes and Tests, p. 24	**Teacher Edition** • Naturalist, p. 79 **Additional Resources** • School-to-Home, URB p. 91 • Reteaching Act., URB p. 93	**Teacher Edition** • Narrative Writing, p. 78 • Persuasive Writing, p. 80 • Expository Writing, p. 82	**Teacher Edition** • Using Geo. Skills, p. 77 • Using Map Skills, p. 78 **Additional Resources** • Daily Test Pract. Transp. 3-4 • Lesson Transparency 3C • Geo. & Hist., URB p. 87

Maryland and Virginia

Main Idea While Maryland grew and dealt with Protestant-Catholic conflicts, Virginia settlers continued to push westward.

History and You Can you build a house wherever you want? Read about how Virginia settlers responded to restrictions placed on where they could live.

Former enslaved Africans such as Anthony Johnson rarely owned land in colonial America. White males controlled most property, especially plantations which became important to the economic growth of the Southern **[S]** Colonies. As the number of plantations grew, the need for workers increased.

Not all people came to work in the colonies of their own free will. English criminals and prisoners of war were shipped to the colonies. They could earn their release by working for a period of time—usually seven years. African rulers sold their prisoners of war to **[C]** European slave traders, who took the enslaved prisoners to the colonies. Many people also came to the colonies as **indentured servants.** To pay for their passage to America, they agreed to work without pay for a certain length of time.

Establishing Maryland

Maryland arose from the dream of **Sir George Calvert, Lord Baltimore.** Calvert wanted a safe place for his fellow Catholics who were being persecuted in England. King Charles I gave Calvert a proprietary colony north of Virginia. However, Calvert died before receiving the grant. His son, Cecilius, inherited the colony and named it Maryland. Cecilius sent two of his brothers to run the colony. They reached America in 1634.

Cecilius gave large **estates,** or pieces of land, to English aristocrats. He also granted land to other settlers. As the number of plantations grew and more workers were needed, the colony imported indentured servants and enslaved Africans.

For years the Calvert and Penn families argued over the boundary between Maryland and Pennsylvania. In the 1760s, they hired Charles Mason and Jeremiah Dixon to map the boundary and lay a line of stones bearing the Penn and Calvert crests—the Mason-Dixon line.

By the Numbers / Slavery in Colonial America

North and South Slavery was important to the economy of many of the American colonies. Most enslaved Africans lived in the Southern Colonies, where many worked on plantations, or large farms. The Northern Colonies had a smaller number of enslaved people but also profited from the international trade in Africans.

Enslaved People in the Colonies, 1650–1710

Year	North	South	Total
1650	880	720	1,600
1670	1,125	3,410	4,535
1690	3,340	13,389	16,729
1710	8,303	36,563	44,866

Enslaved People in the Colonies, 1650–1710

Source: The Gilder Lehrman Institute of American History

Critical Thinking

Speculating Why do you think more enslaved people lived in the Southern Colonies than in the Northern Colonies?

CHAPTER 3
Section 4

Teach

[S] Skill Practice

Using Geography Skills Ask: How do you think the geography of the South promoted the development of large plantations? *(Mild climate and fertile soil created favorable conditions for farming.)* **AL**

[C] Critical Thinking

Making Inferences Ask: Why might a plantation owner prefer enslaved workers over prisoners and indentured servants? *(Enslaved workers were a permanent workforce. Other workers could leave at the ends of their terms.)* **OL**

By the Numbers

Critical Thinking Answer Plantations were more common in the South than in the North. Plantations required more labor than did the small farms in the North.

Additional Support

Fast Facts

The Mason-Dixon Line Charles Mason was an astronomer. Jeremiah Dixon was a surveyor. Using the stars to calculate their path, Mason and Dixon positioned their stones along a constant latitude, marking a 233-mile (375-km) boundary between Pennsylvania and Maryland. A north-south segment marked an 83-mile (134-km) boundary between Maryland and Delaware. Each stone weighed between 300 and 600 pounds (136 to 272 kg). The stones were hauled through the wilderness by wagon and placed one mile (1.6 km) apart. The task took five years. Recent surveys reveal that Mason and Dixon missed their mark by only an inch (2.54 cm) in some places and never by more than 800 feet (244 m).

S Skill Practice

Using Map Skills Refer students to the map. **Ask:** What natural barrier formed the western border of the Southern Colonies? *(Appalachian Mountains)* **BL**

W Writing Support

Narrative Writing Have students write a report to King George about Bacon's Rebellion from William Berkeley's point of view. **OL**

✓ Reading Check **Answer:** Bacon believed that the colonial government was dominated by easterners and resented the governor's pledge to stay out of Native American territory.

The Southern Colonies
NATIONAL GEOGRAPHIC

Critical Thinking Answer

The map shows tobacco as a major product of Maryland, Virginia, and North Carolina.

Differentiated Instruction

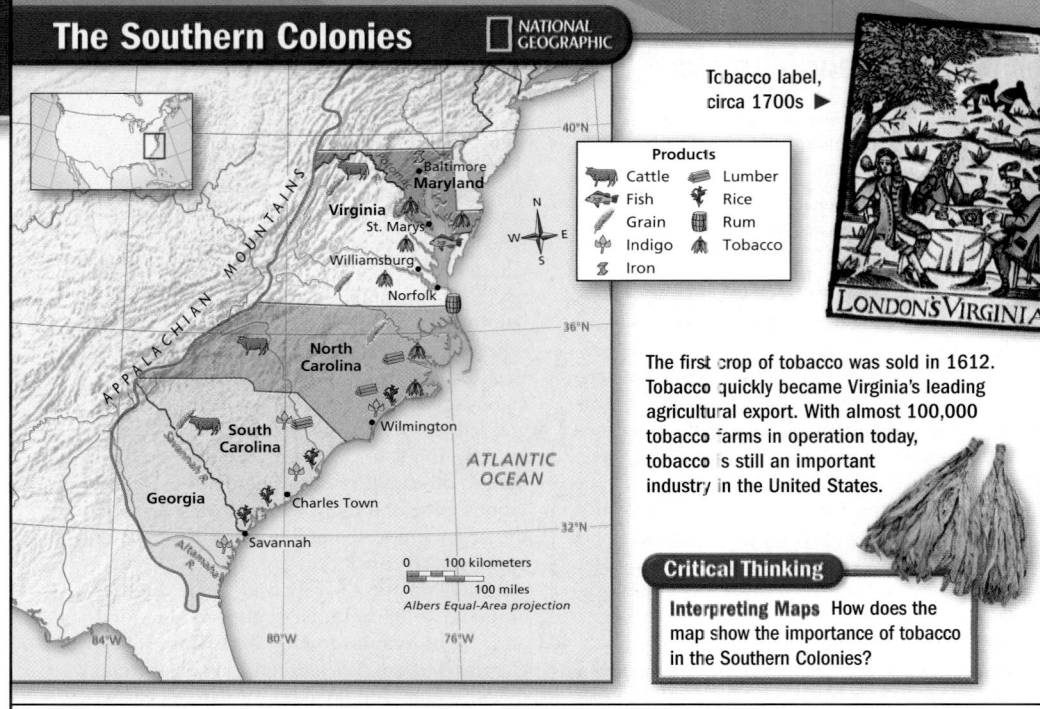

The Southern Colonies
NATIONAL GEOGRAPHIC

Products
Cattle Lumber
Fish Rice
Grain Rum
Indigo Tobacco
Iron

Tobacco label, circa 1700s ▶

LONDON'S VIRGINIA.

The first crop of tobacco was sold in 1612. Tobacco quickly became Virginia's leading agricultural export. With almost 100,000 tobacco farms in operation today, tobacco is still an important industry in the United States.

Critical Thinking

Interpreting Maps How does the map show the importance of tobacco in the Southern Colonies?

Another conflict was harder to resolve. The Calverts had welcomed Protestants as well as Catholics in Maryland. Protestant settlers outnumbered Catholics. To protect the Catholics, the Act of Toleration was passed in 1649. The act granted Protestants and Catholics the right to worship freely. However, tensions continued. In 1692 the Protestant-controlled assembly made the Anglican Church the official church in Maryland. Catholics then faced the same restrictions as they had in England.

Bacon's Rebellion in Virginia

While other colonies were being founded, Virginia continued to grow. Settlers moved west and settled Native American lands. In the 1640s, to avoid conflicts, Virginia governor William Berkeley made a pledge to Native Americans. In exchange for a large piece of land, he agreed to keep settlers from pushing farther into their territory.

Nathaniel Bacon, a young planter in western Virginia, opposed the colonial government because it was dominated, or controlled, by easterners. Many westerners also resented Berkeley's pledge to stay out of Native American territory. Some settled in the forbidden areas. They then blamed the government for not protecting them.

In 1676 Bacon led attacks on Native American villages. His army also marched to Jamestown and drove Berkeley into exile. Only Bacon's sudden death kept him from governing Virginia. England then recalled Berkeley and sent troops to restore order.

Bacon's Rebellion showed that settlers would not be limited to the coast. The colonial government formed a militia to control Native Americans and opened up more land for settlement.

✓ Reading Check **Analyzing** Why did Bacon oppose the colonial government?

Leveled Activities

BL Academic Vocabulary Activity, URB p. 75

OL School-to-Home Connection, URB p. 91

ELL Guided Reading Activity, URB p. 98

The Carolinas and Georgia

Main Idea The Carolinas and Georgia developed into major Southern Colonies.

History and You Do you believe that people who are in debt should be given a fresh start in life? Read to learn the reasons why Georgia was created.

. . . .

In 1663 King Charles II created a proprietary colony south of Virginia called Carolina—Latin for "Charles's land." The king gave the colony to eight nobles who had helped him regain his throne. The proprietors set up estates and sold or rented land to settlers brought from England.

John Locke, an English philosopher, wrote a **constitution,** or plan of government, for the colony that covered topics such as land divisions and social ranking. Concerned with principles and rights, Locke argued that

"every man has a property in his own person. . . . The labour of his body, and the work of his hands . . . are properly his."

Carolina, however, did not develop as planned. It split into northern and southern Carolina, creating two colonies.

Northern and Southern Carolina

Farmers from inland Virginia settled northern Carolina. They grew tobacco and sold timber and tar. The northern Carolina coast lacked a good harbor, so farmers used Virginia's ports to conduct their trade.

Southern Carolina, however, prospered from fertile farmland and the harbor at Charles Town (later Charleston). Settlements there spread, and trade in deerskin, lumber, and beef thrived.

Two crops came to dominate Carolina agriculture. In the 1680s planters discovered that rice grew well in the wet coastal lowlands.

Founding the Thirteen Colonies

	Colony	1st Permanent Settlement	Reasons Founded	Founders or Leaders
New England Colonies	Massachusetts Plymouth Mass. Bay Colony	1620 1630	Religious freedom Religious freedom	John Carver, William Bradford John Winthrop
	New Hampshire	c. 1620	Profit from trade and fishing	Ferdinando Gorges, John Mason
	Rhode Island	1636	Religious freedom	Roger Williams
	Connecticut	1635	Profit from fur trade, farming; religious and political freedom	Thomas Hooker
Middle Colonies	New York	1624	Expand trade	Dutch settlers
	Delaware	1638	Expand trade	Swedish settlers
	New Jersey	1638	Profit from selling land	John Berkeley, George Carteret
	Pennsylvania	1682	Profit from selling land; religious freedom	William Penn
Southern Colonies	Virginia	1607	Expand trade	John Smith
	Maryland	1634	To sell land; religious freedom	Cecil Calvert
	North Carolina	c. 1660s	Profit from trade and selling land	Group of eight aristocrats
	South Carolina	1670	Profit from trade and selling land	Group of eight aristocrats
	Georgia	1733	Religious freedom; protection against Spanish Florida; safe home for debtors	James Oglethorpe

Chart Skills

Sequencing Which colony was the first to be settled? Which was the last?

Charts In Motion See StudentWorks™ Plus or glencoe.com.

Activity: Connecting Past to Present

Technology Organize students into groups to make a bulletin board display comparing colonial and modern technology. Each group should work on a different category, such as farm tools, kitchen utensils, shop tools, logging tools, or cloth-making equipment. Students should research and then draw the equipment or collect pictures from print or online publications. Have them create informational labels for their displays. **OL**

C **Critical Thinking**

Identifying Central Issues Ask: What topics would you include in a constitution? *(Topics might include how to select leaders, make laws, handle violations of law, and protect rights.)* **AL**

R **Reading Strategy**

Reading Primary Sources To help students understand this quotation, have them restate it in their own words. *(Possible answer: People own their own bodies. Therefore, people have a right to profit from their own labor.)* **ELL**

D **Differentiated Instruction**

Naturalist Ask: What is tar? *(thick liquid made by heating coal or wood)* Have students research to find out the uses of wood tar in colonial times and report their findings to the class. *(Uses included preserving rope and wood and caulking seams of wooden sailing ships.)* **AL**

Founding the Thirteen Colonies

Chart Skills Answer

Virginia; Georgia

Additional Support

R Reading Strategy

Identifying Ask: What two crops did farmers in Carolina grow most? *(rice, indigo)* Have students go back to the map of the Southern Colonies and locate where these crops were grown in the Carolinas. *(mainly along the coast)* **BL**

W Writing Support

Persuasive Writing Ask students to take the role of James Oglethorpe. Have them write a letter to King George, asking him to grant a charter for the Georgia colony. Letters should include the reasons for founding the colony and ways the colony might benefit England. **OL**

✔**Reading Check** **Answer:** Georgia was founded to serve as a place for debtors and poor people to make a fresh start and to act as a barrier for stopping Spanish expansion.

R Growing rice required much labor, so the demand for slave labor rose. Another important crop, indigo, was developed in the 1740s by a young Englishwoman named Eliza Lucas. Indigo, a blue flowering plant, was used to dye textiles.

By the early 1700s, Carolina's settlers wanted political power. In 1719 settlers in southern Carolina seized control from its proprietors. In 1729 Carolina became two royal colonies—North Carolina and South Carolina.

Georgia

W Georgia, founded in 1733, was the last British colony set up in America. **James Oglethorpe** received a charter for a colony where debtors and poor people could make a fresh start. In Britain, **debtors**—those who were not able to repay debts—were imprisoned.

British officials also had hoped that Georgia, located north of Spanish Florida, would protect the other colonies from Britain's enemy, Spain. Oglethorpe and the first group of settlers built the forts and town of Savannah as a barrier against Spanish expansion.

Georgia did not develop as Oglethorpe planned. Few debtors settled there. Instead, hundreds of poor people came from Britain. Religious refugees from Central Europe and a small group of Jews also arrived.

Many settlers complained about Oglethorpe's rules, especially the limits on landholding and the bans on slave labor and rum. A frustrated Oglethorpe finally agreed to their demands. Disappointed with the colony's slow growth, he gave up and turned Georgia back over to the king in 1751.

By that time, the British had been in eastern North America for almost 150 years. They had lined the Atlantic coast with colonies.

✔**Reading Check** **Explaining** Why was Georgia founded?

People IN HISTORY

Anne Hutchinson

Dissenter banished from Massachusetts Bay Colony

Hutchinson held meetings in her home in Boston to discuss and give her views on recent sermons. Puritan leaders charged her with *"dishonoring"* the commonwealth. In her trial, she defended herself by arguing, *"there lyes a clear rule in Titus [book in the Christian Bible New Testament], that the elder women should instruct the younger."* She was convicted and banished in 1637.

Margaret Brent

Landowner in Maryland

Brent, one of Maryland's largest landowners and most powerful citizens, requested a vote in the Maryland Assembly on January 21, 1648. When her request was denied because she was a woman, the Assembly noted in its minutes that, *"the s[ai]d Mrs Brent protested ag[ain]st all proceedings in this . . . Assembly, unless shee may . . . have [a] vote."* Brent was so angry that she moved to Virginia, where she spent the rest of her life.

Hands-On Chapter Project
Step 4

Reenacting Colonial Life

Step 4: Creating the Costumes Students will create simple costumes for their characters.

Essential Question: How and why did the Southern Colonies grow?

Directions Have the groups plan the costumes for their characters. They should use images from their research to help them visualize the clothing typical of the time and their region. They should create simple costumes from available materials and clothes they already own.

Comparing As a class, compare the clothing from different regions. **Ask:** How did a person's dress reflect his or her role in society? **OL**

(Chapter Project continued on the Visual Summary page)

The French and Spanish in North America

Main Idea The French and the Spanish expanded their lands in North America.

History and You What might it be like to explore a large, unknown river that runs for hundreds of miles? Read to learn about the French explorers who traveled along the Mississippi River.

The British were not the only Europeans colonizing North America. Elsewhere on the continent, the Spanish and the French built settlements of their own.

The French founded Quebec in 1608. At first they had little interest in large-scale settlement in North America. They were mainly concerned with fishing and trapping animals for their fur. French trappers and missionaries went far into the interior of North America. Forts and trading posts were built to protect their profitable trade.

In 1663 New France became a royal colony. King Louis XIV limited the privileges of the fur companies. He appointed a royal governor who supported new explorations.

Down the Mississippi River

In the 1670s, two Frenchmen—a fur trader, **Louis Joliet,** and a priest, **Jacques Marquette**—explored the Mississippi River by canoe. Joliet and Marquette hoped to find gold, silver, or other precious metals. They were also looking for a water passage to the Pacific Ocean. When they realized that the Mississippi flowed south into the Gulf of Mexico rather than west into the Pacific, they turned around and headed back upriver.

A few years later, **René-Robert Cavelier, Sieur de La Salle,** followed the Mississippi River all the way to the Gulf of Mexico. La Salle claimed the region for France, calling it Louisiana in honor of King Louis XIV. In 1718 the French governor founded the port of New Orleans. Later, French explorers and missionaries traveled west to the Rocky Mountains and southwest to the Rio Grande.

Growth of New France

French settlement in North America advanced slowly. New France was made up of estates along the St. Lawrence River. Estate holders received land in return for bringing settlers. Known as **tenant farmers,** the settlers paid their lord an annual rent and worked for him for a fixed number of days each year.

The French had better relations with the Native Americans than did other Europeans. French trappers and missionaries traveled deep into Indian lands. They lived among the Native American peoples, learned their languages, and respected their ways.

Although the missionaries had come to convert Native Americans to Catholicism, they did not try to change their customs. Most importantly, the French colony grew so slowly that Native Americans were not pushed off their lands.

Colonial America **Chapter 3** 81

Eliza Lucas Pinckney

Successful plantation manager in South Carolina

Lucas managed her father's three plantations in South Carolina and experimented with many crops. She marketed the colony's first crop of indigo, used to make blue dye. Lucas was proud of her work, writing, *"I am making a large plantation of Oaks which I look upon as my own property, whether my father gives me the land or not."*

CRITICAL Thinking

1. **Synthesizing** How did these three women challenge traditional views of women's roles?
2. **Analyzing** What evidence do you see in each of the quotes that the women's activities were not entirely accepted at that time?

C Critical Thinking

Speculating Ask: How might America have developed differently if the French had established colonies earlier? *(Possible response: increased conflict between France and England for territory; the United States might now be divided into French and English sections like Canada; greater French influence on American culture)* **OL**

People IN HISTORY

Critical Thinking Answers

1. Hutchinson voiced her views, Brent owned land and requested a vote, and Lucas managed a plantation.
2. Hutchinson had to cite the Bible to justify why she could state her views. Brent was denied voting rights. Lucas was unsure if she would receive the land she managed.

Differentiated Instruction

Colonial America

Objective: To complete geography skills activities about North American colonies in 1753

Focus: Remind students that Britain, Spain, and France all had interests in colonial America.

Teach: Have students complete the map questions.

Assess: Review the correct answers for each question.

Close: Discuss any questions that were problematic.

Differentiated Instruction Strategies

BL Have students express all mileage figures in metric measurements.

AL Ask students to select one of the thirteen colonies and create an itinerary for touring colonial-era sites.

ELL Have students work in pairs to complete the activities.

Geography and History Activity, URB p. 87

Section ★ Review

W Writing Support

Expository Writing Have students research one Spanish mission in New Mexico, Arizona, Texas, or California and write a report on its history. **OL**

✔ **Reading Check** **Answer:** Spain established missions to convert Native Americans to Christianity, establish land claims in California, and use Native Americans as field laborers.

Assess

History ONLINE

Study Central™ provides summaries, interactive games, and online graphic organizers to help students review content.

Close

Discussing As a class, discuss the economic activities that helped the Southern Colonies grow. **OL**

Spanish Interests

In the early 1600s, England, France, and the Netherlands began colonizing North America. The Spanish, however, still controlled most of Mexico, the Caribbean, and Central and South America. They also expanded into the western and southern parts of the present-day United States.

Spain wanted to keep the other European powers from threatening its empire in America. To protect their claims, the Spanish sent soldiers, missionaries, and settlers north into present-day New Mexico. In 1609 or 1610, the Spanish founded Santa Fe. They also went to what is now Arizona in the late 1600s. When France claimed land around the Mississippi River, the Spanish moved into what is now Texas. Spain wanted to control the area between the French territory and Mexico. In the early 1700s, Spain built San Antonio and other military posts in Texas.

Spanish priests built a string of missions along the Pacific coast. **Missions** are religious settlements established to convert people to a faith. The missions helped the Spanish claim California. The Spanish did more than convert local Native Americans to Christianity.

Spanish missionaries and soldiers also brought them to the missions—often by force—to labor in fields and workshops.

In 1769 Junípero Serra, a Franciscan monk, founded a mission at San Diego. Over the next 15 years, Father Serra set up other missions in California along a route called *El Camino Real* (The Royal Highway). These missions later became cities, such as Los Angeles and Monterey. Serra traveled on foot to supervise the missions. Serra also supported Native Americans' rights by working to prevent Spanish soldiers from mistreating them.

European Conflicts

Rivalries between European nations carried over into the Americas. In North America, France and Britain were expanding their settlements. Both nations fought several wars in the early 1700s. When the two countries warred in Europe, fighting often erupted between their colonies in North America. In the late 1700s, wars in Europe would greatly shape events in America.

✔ **Reading Check** **Explaining** Why did Spain establish missions in California?

History ONLINE
Study Central™ To review this section, go to glencoe.com.

Section 4 Review

Vocabulary

1. Use each of these terms in a sentence that will help explain its meaning: indentured servant, estate, constitution, debtor, tenant farmer, mission.

Main Ideas

2. **Describing** How did Maryland deal with tensions between Protestant and Catholic settlers?

3. **Identifying** Who was John Locke, and what did he do for Carolina?

4. **Explaining** Why were the French slow to settle in North America?

Critical Thinking

5. **Analyzing** Why did demand for enslaved workers increase as the Southern Colonies grew?

6. **Determining Cause and Effect** Use a diagram like the one below to describe the causes and effects of Bacon's Rebellion.

[ ] → **Bacon's Rebellion** → [ ]

7. **Descriptive Writing** Suppose you are a member of La Salle's expedition. Write an entry in your journal that describes your experiences along the Mississippi River for one day. Include things that you experienced through each of your five senses: sight, sound, taste, touch, and smell.

Answer the
Essential Question

8. How and why did the Southern Colonies grow?

Answers

1. Sentences should demonstrate an understanding of the terms.
2. At first Maryland protected the right to worship freely; later, it made the Anglican Church the official church, restricting Catholics.
3. English philosopher; wrote Carolina's constitution
4. The French were more interested in fishing and trapping than in large-scale settlement.
5. The number of plantations increased as more settlers arrived, increasing the need for a cheap source of permanent labor.

6. **Causes:** westerners resented domination of Virginia government by easterners and governor's pledge to forbid settlement of Native American lands; **Effects:** more western land opened to settlement, supported by militia force
7. Journal entries should include things experienced through each of the five senses.
8. **Maryland:** established as safe place for Catholics; land granted to English aristocrats and other settlers; enslaved Africans and indentured servants imported to work

on plantations; **Virginia:** settlers pushed west into Native American lands; Bacon led rebellion to open more lands for settlement; **Carolinas:** proprietary colony; split into two royal colonies; produced tobacco, timber, tar, rice, and indigo; **Georgia:** began as place for debtors and poor people and as military barrier against Spanish expansion; colony attracted poor people and religious refugees; slow growth led proprietor to return colony to the king

Visual Summary

Visual Summary

Colonies

- Early settlements: Roanoke, Jamestown
- New England Colonies: Massachusetts, Rhode Island, Connecticut, New Hampshire
- Middle Colonies: New York, Pennsylvania, New Jersey, Delaware

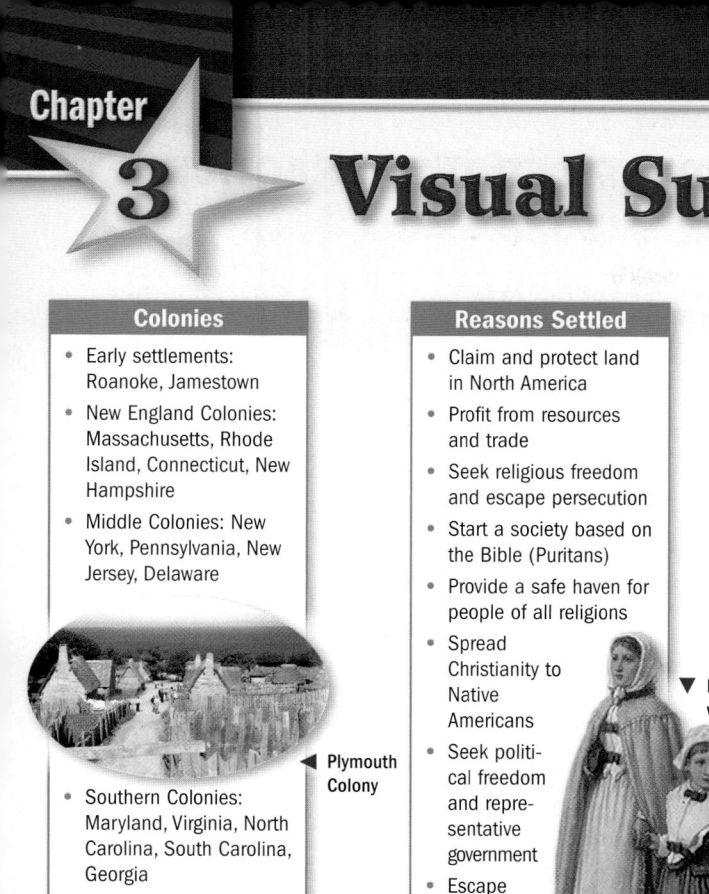

◄ Plymouth Colony

- Southern Colonies: Maryland, Virginia, North Carolina, South Carolina, Georgia
- French colonies: New France
- Spanish colonies

◄ William Penn meets with Native Americans.

Reasons Settled

- Claim and protect land in North America
- Profit from resources and trade
- Seek religious freedom and escape persecution
- Start a society based on the Bible (Puritans)
- Provide a safe haven for people of all religions
- Spread Christianity to Native Americans
- Seek political freedom and representative government
- Escape economic hard times

▼ Pilgrim women

Relations With Native Americans

- Trade and exchange of skills
- Learn Native American languages and customs (French)
- Often did not pay for land or honor treaties (British)
- Hostilities and fighting common

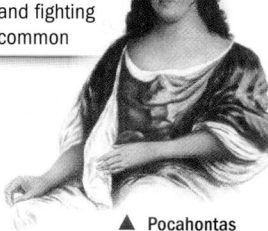

▲ Pocahontas

Types of Government

- Representative
- Proprietary
- Royal governor

Status of Slavery

- Permitted by law (originally banned in Georgia)
- Increasingly important to colonies as farms and plantations grew

STUDY TO GO Study anywhere, anytime! Download quizzes and flash cards to your PDA from glencoe.com.

Comparing Ask: What are some reasons people left their homelands to settle in America? *(to seek religious freedom, find a better life, start over, make a profit, escape persecution or famine, complete prison term, enslavement)* Why do people migrate today? *(Possible reasons: new jobs; better pay; more suitable lifestyle; some are escaping war, famine, or persecution)* How are today's reasons similar to those of the colonists? *(People are seeking a better life in some way, escaping violence or poor conditions.)* **OL**

Synthesizing Ask: What factors helped the colonies prosper and grow? *(Factors include: good leadership, help from Native Americans, discovery of crops that grew well in the area, use of available natural resources, access to good ports for trade, organized government, European investment, use of enslaved workers, resourcefulness, and hard work.)* **OL**

Hands-On Chapter Project
Step 5: Wrap-Up

Reenacting Colonial Life

Step 5: Performing the Reenactment Students will rehearse and perform their reenactment.

Directions Have the groups organize their sets and add signs directing tourists to each set. Then have the groups meet privately for a dress rehearsal. Advise them to practice their movements and use props as they speak. Invite other classes and guests to attend the reenactment. Students should remain in character as they answer any questions.

Drawing Conclusions Historical reenactments draw many visitors to historical sites each year. Some travel companies create reenactments for tourist participation, such as traveling by covered wagon to experience pioneer life. **Ask:** Why do you think people like to participate in reenactments? *(Reenactments can make history come alive. By participating, people can get a sense of what life was really like for people of that time and place.)* **OL**

Answers and Analyses
Reviewing Main Ideas

1. C Have students identify the key word in the question: *seas.* Ask them to identify the choice that has something to do with the sea. They should recognize that the Spanish Armada was a fleet of ships. **16.A.3b**

2. B Students should immediately eliminate choice D because Williams was clashing with leaders who were intolerant. Students can further narrow the choices by recognizing that the clash was most likely due to religious differences. **18.B.3a**

3. A Remind students that profit was a main reason why the English wanted colonies. Also, remind them that New Netherland became New York, which has a good harbor at New York City. **17.C.3a**

4. C Have students identify the nation that settled Mexico and the American Southwest. As a further clue, mention place names such as Los Angeles and San Francisco, and have them identify the language of these names. **18.B.3b**

Short-Answer Question

5. He rejected the European beliefs, observing that if France were as wonderful as the Europeans claimed, people would not be leaving France to settle in North America. **18.B.3a**

STANDARDIZED TEST PRACTICE

TEST-TAKING TIP

Carefully consider changing your answer to a multiple-choice test question. Unless you misread the question, your first answer choice is often correct.

Reviewing Main Ideas

Directions: Choose the best answer for each of the following questions.

1. The end of Spanish control of the seas was a result of

  A King Philip II's powerful rule of Spain.

  B the discovery of gold in Central America.

  C the defeat of the Spanish Armada by England.

  D the establishment of the Jamestown colony in Virginia.

2. Rhode Island minister Roger Williams clashed with Puritan leaders in Massachusetts because

  A he converted to Roman Catholicism.

  B he believed people should not be persecuted for their religious practices.

  C he argued that settlers should take as much land as possible from the Native Americans.

  D his views were considered too harsh and intolerant.

3. The English wanted to acquire the Dutch colony of New Netherland because

  A it had an excellent harbor and a thriving river trade.

  B they wanted to free the Dutch colonists from the control of the patroons who ruled over them like kings.

  C England and the Netherlands declared war on each other in 1649.

  D the Dutch West India Company refused to trade with England.

4. Missions were established along the Pacific coast of North America by the

  A English.   **C** Spanish.

  B French.   **D** Dutch.

Short-Answer Question

Directions: Base your answer to question 5 on the excerpt below and on your knowledge of social studies.

> Thou sayest of us [the Micmac people of eastern Canada] . . . that we are the most miserable and most unhappy of all men, living without religion, without manners, without honour, without social order, and, in a word, without any rules, like the beasts in our woods and our forests . . . [but] if France, as thou sayest, is a little terrestrial [earthly] paradise, art thou sensible to leave it?
>
> —A Micmac's statement to French priest Christian LeClerq, 1670

5. How does the Micmac respond to the European beliefs about Native Americans?

Review the Essential Questions

6. Essay Discuss the social, economic, and political differences of the New England, Middle, and Southern Colonies.

To help you write your essay, review your answers to the Essential Questions in the section reviews and the chapter Foldables Study Organizer. Your essay should include:

- the reasons behind the founding of each of the colonies;
- how New York and Pennsylvania became English colonies, and how other colonies developed from them;
- settlers' relations with Native Americans;
- types of commerce that developed in the different colonies; and
- the circumstances surrounding Bacon's Rebellion.

GO ON ➡

Review the Essential Questions

6. Essays should compare the religious and economic motivations of settlers, the degrees of religious and social tolerance, the use of enslaved workers in the colonies, especially in the South, and subsistence farming in New England versus the production of cash crops in the South. **15.D**

History ONLINE
For additional test practice, use **Self-Check Quizzes**—Chapter 3 at glencoe.com.

Chapter 3 Assessment

Document-Based Questions

Directions: Analyze the documents and answer the short-answer questions that follow.

Document 1

Indian leader Powhatan expressed these thoughts to Captain John Smith in 1608.

> What will it availe [get] you to take . . . by force [what] you may quickly have by love, or to destroy them that provide you food. What can you get by [war], when we can hide our provisions [food supplies] and fly to the woods? whereby you must famish [starve] by wronging us your friends.

Source: John Smith, *The Generall Historie of Virginia*

7. Based on this document, describe why Powhatan believed that English settlers should establish peaceful relations with his people.

Document 2

This map shows when areas of the British colonies were settled.

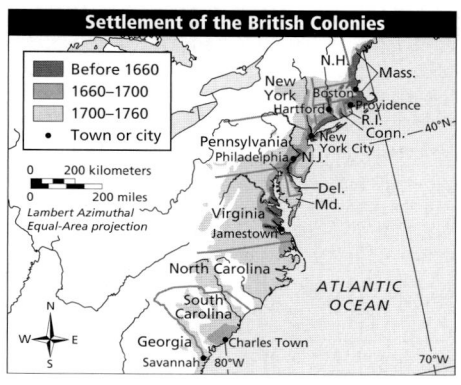

Settlement of the British Colonies

Before 1660
1660–1700
1700–1760
• Town or city

0   200 kilometers
0   200 miles
Lambert Azimuthal Equal-Area projection

ATLANTIC OCEAN

8. Based on the map, which colonies were most heavily settled before 1660?

Document 3

In this excerpt written in 1542, Cabeza de Vaca describes the people living on what is today Galveston Island, Texas.

> Their method of cure is to blow on the sick, the breath and the laying-on of hands supposedly casting out the infirmity [illness]. . . . We scoffed [laughed] at their cures and at the idea we knew how to heal. . . . An Indian told me I knew not whereof I spoke in saying their methods had no effect. Stones and other things growing about in the fields, he said, had a virtue whereby passing a pebble along the stomach could take away pain and heal; surely extraordinary men like us embodied such powers over nature.

Source: Cyclone Covey, translator, *Cabeza de Vaca's Adventures in the Unknown Interior of America*

9. Based on this document, why did the people de Vaca encountered believe that he and his men were healers?

Document 4

William Penn wrote this description of Pennsylvania to friends in England.

> The soil is good, air serene and sweet from the cedar, pine and sassafras, with wild myrtle of great fragrance. I have had better venison, bigger, more tender, as fat as in England. Turkeys of the wood I had of forty and fifty pounds weight. Fish in abundance, especially shad and rock. Oysters are monstrous for bigness. In the woods are divers [many different] fruits.

Source: M. Struthers Burt, *Philadelphia: Holy Experiment*

10. Explain how Penn's description of his colony might influence the people who read it.

11. Expository Writing Using the information from the four documents and your knowledge of social studies, write an essay in which you:
- identify major cultural differences between European settlers and Native Americans; and
- discuss the ways settlers dealt with these differences.

10. The description might persuade people to move to his colony. It describes the land as fertile and having a variety of animals and fish. **16.A.3c**

11. Students should discuss the different views about land, nature, religion, and ways of settling differences. Students should explain that some settlers treated Native Americans with respect and made treaties to gain land and settle differences. Other settlers cheated the Native Americans and took what they wanted, often resulting in violent conflict. **18.B**

History ONLINE
Have students visit the Web site at glencoe.com to review Chapter 3 and take the Self-Check Quiz.

Need Extra Help?

Have students refer to the pages listed if they miss any of the questions.

Need Extra Help?

If you missed question. . .	1	2	3	4	5	6	7	8	9	10	11
Go to page. . .	59	68	73	82	81	56–82	61	67	82	75	56–82

Document-Based Questions

7. Powhatan knew that the English settlers needed food. They would have to establish peaceful relations with the Native Americans in order to get it. **16.A.3b**

8. Massachusetts, Virginia **17.A.3b**

9. The people thought of de Vaca and his men as "extraordinary," and extraordinary men would have power over nature. **16.A.3b**

Chapter Planning Guide

4

Levels					Resources	Chapter Opener	Section 1	Section 2	Section 3	Section 4	Chapter Assess
BL	OL	AL	ELL								
FOCUS											
BL	OL	AL	ELL	📽	Daily Test Practice Transparencies		4–1	4–2	4–3	4–4	
TEACH											
	OL	AL		📁	Geography and History Activity, URB		p. 115				
BL	OL		ELL	📁	Time Line Skills Activity, URB				p. 118		
BL	OL	AL	ELL	📁	Writing Skills Activity, URB				p. 107		
	OL	AL		📁	American Literature Readings, URB			p. 9			
BL	OL	AL	ELL	📁	Content Vocabulary Activity, URB		p. 101	p. 101	p. 101	p. 101	
BL			ELL	📁	Academic Vocabulary Activity, URB		p. 103	p. 103	p. 103	p. 103	
BL			ELL	📁	Reading Skills Activity, URB			p. 7			
BL			ELL	📁	Social Studies Skills Activity, URB			p. 109			
BL	OL	AL	ELL	📁	Differentiated Instruction Activity, URB			p. 111			
BL	OL	AL	ELL	📁	Critical Thinking Skills Activity, URB		p. 113				
BL	OL	AL	ELL	📁	Linking Past and Present Activity, URB					p. 33	
	OL	AL		📁	Primary Source Readings, URB			p. 105			
BL	OL	AL	ELL	📁	School-to-Home Connection Activity, URB		p. 119	p. 119	p. 119	p. 119	
BL	OL		ELL	📁	Guided Reading Activity, URB*		p. 123	p. 124	p. 125	p. 126	
	OL	AL		📁	Economics and History Activity, URB					p. 5	
BL	OL		ELL	📁	Reading Essentials and Note-Taking Guide*		p. 34	p. 37	p. 40	p. 43	
BL	OL	AL	ELL	📽	Lesson Transparencies		4C	4B	4A		
	OL	AL		📁	Interpreting Political Cartoons, URB				p. 13		
	OL			📁	American Biographies			p. 5		p. 8	
BL	OL	AL	ELL	📁	Outline Map Resource Book	pp. 5, 9, 10, 23, 25					
	OL	AL		📽	American Art and Architecture Transparencies, Strategies, and Activities					4	

Note: Please refer to the *Unit Resource Book: The Americas: Worlds Meet* for this chapter's URB materials.

* Also available in Spanish

BL	OL	AL	ELL		Resources	Chapter Opener	Section 1	Section 2	Section 3	Section 4	Chapter Assess
					TEACH (continued)						
BL	OL	AL	ELL		NGS US Desk Map		✓	✓	✓	✓	
BL	OL	AL	ELL		American Literature Library		✓	✓	✓	✓	
BL	OL	AL	ELL		Writer's Guidebook		✓	✓	✓	✓	
	OL	AL			American History Primary Source Document Library CD-ROM		✓	✓	✓	✓	✓
BL	OL	AL	ELL		American Music: Hits Through History	✓	✓	✓	✓	✓	
BL	OL	AL	ELL		StudentWorks™ Plus CD	✓	✓	✓	✓	✓	✓
BL	OL	AL	ELL		Section Spotlight Videos		✓	✓	✓	✓	
BL	OL	AL	ELL		Writing Process Transparencies		✓	✓	✓	✓	✓
BL	OL	AL	ELL		Presentation Plus! With MindJogger CheckPoint CD	✓	✓	✓	✓	✓	✓
					ASSESS						
BL	OL	AL	ELL		Quizzes and Tests		p. 31	p. 32	p. 33	p. 34	pp. 35, 37, 39
BL	OL	AL	ELL		Authentic Assessment With Rubrics			p. 4			
BL	OL	AL	ELL		Standardized Test Practice						p. 7
BL	OL	AL	ELL		*ExamView® Assessment Suite* CD-ROM*		4–1	4–2	4–3	4–4	Ch. 4
					CLOSE						
BL			ELL		Reteaching Activity, URB*		p. 121	p. 121	p. 121	p. 121	p. 121
BL	OL		ELL		Reading and Study Skills Foldables Activity	p. 56	p. 56	p. 56	p. 56	p. 56	p. 56
BL	OL	AL	ELL		*The American Journey* in Graphic Novel			p. 23			
BL			ELL		Reading Strategies and Activities for the Social Studies Classroom		✓	✓	✓	✓	
BL	OL	AL	ELL		Graphic Organizer Transparencies & Strategies		✓	✓	✓	✓	

TeacherWorks Plus
All-In-One Planner and Resource Center

- Interactive Lesson Planner
- Interactive Teacher Edition
- Fully editable blackline masters
- Section Spotlight Videos Launch
- Differentiated Lesson Plans
- Printable reports of daily assignments
- Standards Tracking System

Professional Development Resources

- Strategies for Success
- Building Academic Vocabulary
- Success With English Learners DVD
- Differentiated Instruction Strategies DVD
- Teaching Literacy Strategies in Social Studies DVD
- Assessment DVD
- Standards-Based Instruction DVD

Using the Glencoe Media Center

Research Using Spotlight Videos

Technology Product

Glencoe's Media Center allows you and your students to browse digital media associated with your textbook. This online resource center provides access to powerful educational technology solutions such as

- downloading audio files into a MP3 player;
- viewing videos that correspond to textbook content.

Objectives

Viewing the Spotlight Video features helps students

- recall vivid details that deepen their curiosity and comprehension skills;
- reinforce their understanding of the topics presented in the textbook.

Steps

- Go to the glencoe.com Web site, and click the link for the Glencoe Media Center.
- Click the entry button to arrive at the Media Selection screen.
- Click the "Social Studies" link. Use the drop-down menu to find the appropriate textbook.
- Click the "Video" tab, then select the appropriate Spotlight Video and click the "View/Listen" button.
- Have students watch the Spotlight Video, taking notes on the topic that is presented.
- Have students write an essay about what they have learned.

History ONLINE at glencoe.com

	Student	Teacher	Parent
Media Center			
• Student Edition Audio	●		
• Spanish Summaries	●		
• Section Spotlight Videos	●	●	
Social Studies Online Learning Center			
Classroom Tools			
• Multi-Language Glossaries	●	●	●
• Teaching Today		●	
• TIME Current Events	●	●	●
• Beyond the Textbook	●	●	
***The American Journey* Online Learning Center**			
• Study-to-Go™	●	●	●
• Study Central™	●	●	●
• Chapter Overview	●	●	
• Concepts in Motion	●	●	
• ePuzzles and Games	●	●	
• Literature Connections	●	●	
• Online Student Edition	●	●	●
• Self-Check Quizzes	●	●	●
• Student Web Activities	●	●	
• Vocabulary eFlashcards	●	●	
• Web Activity Lesson Plans	●	●	●
• Vocabulary PuzzleMaker	●	●	●

READING SUPPORT FROM JAMESTOWN EDUCATION

- **Timed Readings Plus in Social Studies** helps students increase their reading rate and fluency while maintaining comprehension. The 400-word passages are similar to those found on state and national assessments.

- **Reading in the Content Area: Social Studies** concentrates on six essential reading skills that help students better comprehend what they read. The book includes 75 high-interest nonfiction passages written at increasing levels of difficulty.

- **Reading Social Studies** includes strategic reading instruction and vocabulary support in Social Studies content for ELLs and native speakers of English.

- **Content Vocabulary Workout** (Grades 6–8) accelerates reading comprehension through focused vocabulary development. Social Studies content vocabulary comes from the glossaries of Glencoe's Middle School Social Studies texts.

www.jamestowneducation.com

NATIONAL GEOGRAPHIC

Index to National Geographic Magazine:

The following articles relate to this chapter:

- *"Last Voyage of the Slave Ship* Henrietta Marie,*"* Jennifer Steinberg, August 2002.

- *"Blackbeard Lives,"* Joel K. Bourne, Jr., July 2006.

National Geographic Society Products

To order the following, call National Geographic at 1-800-368-2728:

National Geographic Atlas of the World (Book)

Access National Geographic's new dynamic MapMachine Web site and other geography resources at:

www.nationalgeographic.com

www.nationalgeographic.com/mapmachine

Reading List Generator CD-ROM — GLENCOE BOOKLINK 3

Use this database to search more than 30,000 titles to create a customized reading list for your students.

- Reading lists can be organized by students' reading level, author, genre, theme, or area of interest.

- The database provides Degrees of Reading Power™ (DRP) and Lexile™ readability scores for all selections.

- A brief summary of each selection is included.

Leveled reading suggestions for this chapter:

For students at a Grade 6 reading level:
- *The Last of the Mohicans (Adapted),* James Fenimore Cooper
- *Calico Bush,* Rachel Field

For students at a Grade 7 reading level:
- *In the Middle Colonies,* Deborah Kent
- *Soldiers of the French and Indian War,* Diane Smolinski

For students at a Grade 8 reading level:
- *The Architects,* Leonard Everett Fisher
- *The Colonies,* Rebecca Stefoff

For students at a Grade 9 reading level:
- *Colonial American Medicine,* Susan Neiburg Terkel
- *Virginia,* Karen Price Hossel

For students at a Grade 10 reading level:
- *Delaware,* Stuart A. Kallen
- *Georgia,* Christina M. Girod

The following videotape programs are available from Glencoe as supplements to the chapter:

- **Benjamin Franklin: Citizen of the World** (ISBN 1-56-501426-X)

- **George Washington: Founding Father** (ISBN 1-56-501377-8)

To order, call Glencoe at 1-800-334-7344. To find classroom resources to accompany many of these videos, check the following home pages:

A&E Television: www.aetv.com

The History Channel: www.history.com

Chapter Objectives

After studying this chapter, students will be able to:

- Explain how geography affected the economic development of the three colonial regions.
- Describe ways in which an American culture was developing during the colonial period.
- Understand why conflict arose in North America between France and Great Britain.
- Discuss how the outcome of the French and Indian War determined control of North America.

Motivating Activity

Making Generalizations Students will learn about life in the Thirteen Colonies and how the different regions (New England, Middle, and Southern Colonies) differed culturally and economically. **Ask:** In what ways might you expect life to be different in each region? *(Students may mention climate and how it affects growing seasons. The growth of cities and trade would affect the economy of each region. Culture and religion may be different based on who migrated to each region and settled there.)*

Previewing the Essential Questions

As you begin teaching each section, use these questions and activities to help students focus on the Essential Questions.

4 Growth of the Thirteen Colonies 1607–1770

Colonial scene, 1701

◀ Iroquois mask

★ c. 1570 Iroquois Confederacy forms

★ 1651 First Navigation Act regulates colonial trade

Americas

World

1550

1600

1650

Japanese samurai ▶

1603 ★ Tokugawa Shogunate emerges in Japan

★ 1610 Galileo observes planets and stars with telescope

★ 1644 Qing Dynasty is established in China

86   Chapter 4

Section 1

Life in the Colonies Ask: What effects might geography have on a region's economy? *(Climate, soil conditions, and terrain impact the type of farming. The availability of natural resources might affect trade and industry.)* Point out to students that in Section 1 they will learn how geography affected the economic development of New England, the Middle Colonies, and the Southern Colonies. **OL**

Section 2

Government, Religion, and Culture Ask: What areas of life might reflect a developing "American" culture? *(government; the importance of the family, religion, and education; freedom of the press)* Point out to students that Section 2 discusses ways in which a distinct culture was developing in the colonial period. **OL**

Section 1: Life in the Colonies
Essential Question How did geography affect the economic development of the three colonial regions?

Section 2: Government, Religion, Culture
Essential Question In what ways was an American culture developing during the colonial period?

Section 3: France and Britain Clash
Essential Question Why did conflict arise in North America between France and Great Britain?

Section 4: The French and Indian War
Essential Question How did the outcome of the French and Indian War determine who controlled North America?

Great Awakening preacher, John Wesley ▶

FOLDABLES Study Organizer

Organizing Information
Make this Foldable to help summarize what you learn about the growth of the colonies.

Step 1 Fold two sheets of paper in half and cut along the fold.

Step 2 Fold both sheets in half and then in half again.

Step 3 Cut tabs into three sheets so each sheet has its own tab. Leave the fourth sheet whole.

Step 4 Label your Foldable as shown.

| Life in the Colonies | Government, Religion, and Culture | France and Britain Clash | The French and Indian War |

Growth of the Thirteen Colonies

Reading and Writing As you read the chapter, list facts about life in the colonies and the challenges colonists faced.

Introducing Chapter 4

Time Line Activity

If you have not already done so, have students review the time line. **Ask:** What events on this time line relate to trade in the colonies? *(First Navigation Act regulates trade; Enslaved Africans brought to America; Potato becomes most popular food in Europe)* How many years passed between the formation of the Iroquois confederacy and the Proclamation of 1763? *(about 193 years)*

FOLDABLES Study Organizer **Dinah Zike's Foldables**
Purpose This Foldable helps students understand the growth of the thirteen colonies. The completed Foldable will help them prepare for assessment. **OL**

📁 More Foldable activities for this chapter can be found in *Dinah Zike's Reading and Study Skills Foldables*.

History ONLINE
Introduce students to chapter content and key terms by having them access the **Chapter Overview** at glencoe.com.

1676 Bacon's Rebellion

1700s Enslaved Africans brought to America

c. 1740 Great Awakening peaks

1754 French and Indian War begins

1763 Proclamation of 1763

1700

1750

1689 English Bill of Rights signed

English rulers William and Mary ▶

1730 Emperor Yung Cheng reduces slavery in China

1748 Montesquieu's The Spirit of Laws

1765 Potato becomes most popular food in Europe

1767 Burma invades Siam

Chapter 4 **87**

Section 3

France and Britain Clash Ask: Why did France and Britain have conflict in North America? *(Both countries were competing for wealth and empire around the world.)* Tell students that Section 3 will explore the roots of the rivalry between Britain and France in America and the beginning of the French and Indian War. **OL**

Section 4

The French and Indian War Ask: How might the outcome of a war between the French and British affect North America? *(There might be loss of life, changing alliances with Native Americans, loss or gain of territories, and change in the balance of power.)* Explain to students that in Section 4, they will learn how the outcome of the French and Indian War determined who controlled North America. **OL**

Focus

Life in the Colonies

Bellringer
Daily Test Practice Transparency 4–1

Essential Question
How did geography affect the economic development of the three colonial regions?

Reading Guide

Content Vocabulary

subsistence farming (p. 89)	Tidewater (p. 94)
triangular trade (p. 90)	backcountry (p. 94)
Middle Passage (p. 91)	overseer (p. 94)
cash crop (p. 92)	slave code (p. 95)
surplus (p. 93)	

Academic Vocabulary

rely (p. 89)   principal (p. 93)

Key People and Events
Olaudah Equiano (p. 91)

Reading Strategy
Taking Notes As you read, use a diagram like the one below to describe the triangular trade route.

Reading Guide
Answers to Graphic:
West Indies to British Colonies: sugar and molasses; **British Colonies to West Africa:** rum, iron, and tools; **Africa to the West Indies:** enslaved persons, gold, and pepper; **British Colonies to Britain:** rice, indigo, tobacco, furs; **Britain to Africa:** cloth, manufactured goods; **West Indies to Britain:** sugar, molasses, fruit

Section Spotlight Video

Have students watch the Section Spotlight Video "Life in the Colonies" to learn about the slave trade in the American colonies.

ILLINOIS STANDARDS
The American Journey

15.D Understand trade as an exchange of goods or services.

16.D.3a (US) Describe characteristics of different kinds of communities in various sections of America during the colonial/frontier periods and the 19th century.

16.E.3a (US) Describe how early settlers in Illinois and the United States adapted to, used and changed the environment prior to 1818.

17.C.3a Explain how human activity is affected by geographic factors.

American Diary

In 1760 Englishman Andrew Burnaby traveled in the American colonies, observing daily life. He could not imagine that these colonies would ever unite for they were as different from one another as "fire and water," and each colony was jealous of the other. "In short, such is the difference of character, of manners, of religion, of interest, of the different colonies, that I think, . . . were they left to themselves, there would soon be a civil war, from one end of the continent to the other."

—from Travels Through the Middle Settlements in North America

Philadelphia, Pennsylvania, was one of the major seaports in colonial America.

Resource Manager

R **Reading Strategies**	C **Critical Thinking**	D **Differentiated Instruction**	W **Writing Support**	S **Skill Practice**
Teacher Edition • Organizing, p. 93 • Making Connec., p. 94 **Additional Resources** • Guid. Read., URB p. 123 • Cont. Vocab., URB p. 101 • Ac. Vocab., URB p. 103 • Read. Ess., p. 34	**Teacher Edition** • Analyzing Info., p. 90 • Making Compar., p. 92 • Id. Cent. Issues, p. 95 **Additional Resources** • Quizzes and Tests, p. 31 • Econ. & Hist., URB p. 5 • Crit. Think. Skills, URB p. 113	**Teacher Edition** • Verbal/Linguistic, p. 89 • Auditory/Musical, p. 91 **Additional Resources** • Reteach, URB p. 121 • School-to-Home Connect. Act., URB p. 119	**Teacher Edition** • Persuasive Writing, p. 90 • Expository Writing, p. 94	**Teacher Edition** • Using Geo. Skills, p. 89 • Using Geo. Skills, p. 92 **Additional Resources** • Daily Test Pract. Transp. 4-1 • Geo. & Hist., URB p. 115 • Lesson Transparency 4C

The New England Colonies

Main Idea The economies of the New England Colonies focused on shipbuilding, fishing, and trade.

History and You Do people in your community manufacture products that are sold to other countries? Read to learn about how the economies of New England developed.

A lthough Burnaby believed the colonies would never unite, they continued to grow. The number of people living in the colonies rose from about 250,000 in 1700 to approximately 2.5 million by the mid-1770s. The population of African Americans increased at an even faster rate—from about 28,000 to more than 500,000.

Immigration was important to this growth. Between 1607 and 1775, almost a million people—an estimated 690,000 Europeans and 278,000 Africans—came to the colonies. By 1775, about 2,500 Jewish immigrants lived in the colonies. Most people lived in the cities of New York, Philadelphia, Charles Town, Savannah, and Newport, where they were allowed to worship as they pleased.

There was another reason for the growing population. Colonial women tended to marry early and have large families. In addition, America—especially New England—turned out to be a very healthy place to live.

Most people in New England lived in well-organized towns. The meetinghouse stood in the center of the town. This building was used for both church services and town meetings. The meetinghouse faced a piece of land called the *green* or *common*. Here cows grazed and the citizen army trained. Farmers lived in the town and worked in fields on its outskirts.

Farming was the main economic activity in all of the colonies. New England farms were smaller than those farther south. Long winters and thin, rocky soil made large-scale farming difficult. Farmers in New England practiced **subsistence farming.** This means that they generally produced just enough to meet their families' needs, with little left over to sell or exchange. Most Northern farmers **relied,** or depended, on their children for labor. Everyone in the family worked—spinning yarn, preserving fruit, milking cows, fencing in fields, and sowing and harvesting grain.

Commerce in New England

New England also had a large number of small businesses. Some people used the water-power from the streams on their land to run mills for grinding grain or sawing lumber.

Primary Source | Travel in Colonial America

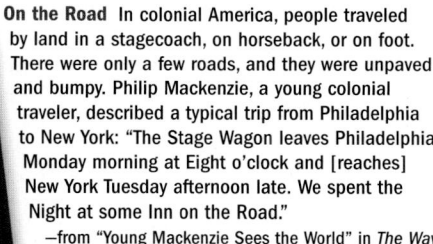

On the Road In colonial America, people traveled by land in a stagecoach, on horseback, or on foot. There were only a few roads, and they were unpaved and bumpy. Philip Mackenzie, a young colonial traveler, described a typical trip from Philadelphia to New York: "The Stage Wagon leaves Philadelphia Monday morning at Eight o'clock and [reaches] New York Tuesday afternoon late. We spent the Night at some Inn on the Road."

—from "Young Mackenzie Sees the World" in *The Way Our People Lived: An Intimate American History*

Critical Thinking

Making Connections How do you think geographic distance affected the unity of the American colonies?

Growth of the Thirteen Colonies **Chapter 4** **89**

Teach

S Skill Practice

Using Geography Skills Have students use a map of colonial America to locate major cities in the New England colonies. **Ask:** Do the locations of these cities have anything in common? *(Yes; all are located on water.)* **BL**

D Differentiated Instruction

Verbal/Linguistic Ask: Why do you think the land near a meetinghouse was called the "green" or the "common"? *(It was used for grazing, so it would have been covered by grass. Because it was located next to the meetinghouse it was used for a variety of purposes in the community.)* **OL**

Primary Source

Critical Thinking Answer Distance may have had a negative effect on the colonial unity because travel was difficult, making it hard for colonists to interact.

Additional Support

Activity: Interdisciplinary Connection

Daily Life To help students understand colonial daily life, begin by discussing work family members do today to keep a household running. They might include shopping, cooking, cleaning, buying clothes, laundry, caring for pets, and keeping things in working order. List students' responses on the board. **Ask:** How did daily chores differ in colonial America? Tell students to work in small groups. Give each group one or two activities from the list of household activities. Have students research how the activity or work was performed in a New England colony and then compare it to life today. *(For example, colonists may have spun wool or flax into thread and woven fabric for clothing themselves. People would have fixed broken things themselves rather than throwing them away or calling a repair shop.)* **OL**

W Writing Support

Persuasive Writing Discuss the economy of colonial New England. Have students create brochures to attract immigrants to the area. Brochures should depict the variety of available jobs in the region. *(Brochures should reflect the idea that work could be found in farming, grain and lumber mills, skilled crafts, shipbuilding, fishing, whaling, shipping, and rum manufacturing.)* **OL**

C Critical Thinking

Analyzing Information Ask: What role did the colonies play in the slave trade? *(Ships from New England traded rum and other goods in exchange for enslaved Africans in West Africa, who would then be shipped to the colonies for continued enslavement on plantations.)* **OL**

Primary Source

Critical Thinking Answer
Native American whale hunting tradition, abundant wood for building whaling vessels, demand for whale products

Differentiated Instruction

Primary Source — Whaling in New England

American Whaling English colonists observed Native Americans hunting whales along the coast and took up the practice themselves. In the 1600s, whalers hunted right whales for their oil and bone. When the number of right whales began to decline in the early 1700s, the whalers started using ships to hunt the more profitable sperm whales that lived in the deep water.

Abundant wood from New England's forests allowed Americans to build excellent whaling vessels. ▶

◀ Whale oil lamps

◀ Oarsmen rowed boats within range, and whalers hurled harpoons with an attached line into the whale. Once the animal exhausted itself, it was killed and towed ashore. Whale bone was used to make corsets, collars, and other products.

Critical Thinking

Determining Cause and Effect What factors led to the development of a large whaling industry in New England?

Women made cloth, garments, candles, and soap for their families. They sometimes made enough of these products to sell or trade. Large towns attracted skilled craftspeople. These people were blacksmiths, shoemakers, furniture makers, gunsmiths, metalsmiths, and printers.

Shipbuilding was an important industry in New England. The lumber for building ships came from the nearby forests. Lumber was transported down rivers to the shipyards in coastal towns.

The region also relied on fishing. New Englanders fished for many types of seafood: cod, halibut, crabs, oysters, and lobsters. Some New Englanders ventured far out to sea to hunt whales for oil and whalebone.

Colonial Trade

Northern coastal cities were the center of the shipping trade. They linked the Northern Colonies with the Southern Colonies. They also linked America to other parts of the world. New England ships sailed south along the Atlantic coast. They traded with the colonies and with islands in the West Indies. Ships also traveled across the Atlantic Ocean, carrying fish, furs, and fruit to trade for manufactured goods in both England and Europe.

These colonial merchant ships followed many different trading routes. Some went directly to England and back. Others followed routes that came to be called the **triangular trade** because the routes formed a triangle.

On one leg of the route, ships brought sugar and molasses from the West Indies to New England. In New England, the molasses would be made into rum. Next, the rum and other goods were shipped to West Africa and traded for enslaved Africans.

Slavery was widely practiced throughout West Africa. Many West African kingdoms enslaved those they defeated in war. Some of the enslaved people were then sold to Arab slave traders. Others were forced to work in gold mines or farm fields. With the arrival of the Europeans, enslaved Africans also began to be shipped to America in exchange for goods.

Leveled Activities

BL Reading Essentials, URB p. 34

OL Geography and History Activity, URB p. 115

AL Economics and History Activity, URB p. 5

ELL Content Vocabulary Activity, URB p. 101

The Middle Passage

For enslaved Africans, the voyage to America usually began with a march to a European fort on the West African coast. Tied together with ropes around their necks and hands, they were traded to Europeans, branded, and forced aboard a ship.

The cruelty continued when enslaved Africans were shipped to the West Indies. This part of the voyage was known as the **Middle Passage. Olaudah Equiano,** a young African, was forced onto a ship to America. He later described the journey:

PRIMARY SOURCE

"We were all put under deck. . . . The closeness . . . the heat . . . added to the number in the ship, which was so crowded that each had scarcely room to turn himself, almost suffocated us. . . . The shrieks . . . the groans of the dying, rendered [made] the whole a scene of horror."

—from *The Interesting Narrative and Other Writings*

D Chained together for more than a month, prisoners such as Equiano could hardly sit or stand. They were given little food or water. Africans who died or became sick were thrown overboard. Those who refused to eat were whipped.

Africans who survived the Middle Passage faced another terror when they reached American ports—the slave market. Examined and prodded by plantation owners, most Africans were sold to work as laborers. Historians estimate that about 12 million Africans were forcibly transported to the Americas between the late 1400s and mid-1800s.

With its part in the triangular trade and its shipbuilding and fishing industries, New England flourished. Its population grew, and towns and cities developed.

✓ Reading Check Explaining Where was the shipping center in America, and where did its trade extend?

D Differentiated Instruction

Auditory/Musical Tell students to imagine they survived the Middle Passage as well as a slave market in North America. Have them list sounds they might have heard since they left Africa. *(Sounds might include whips, water, wind, shrieks, groans, chains, and voices.)* **BL**

Economics & History

Critical Thinking Answer

Rum, iron, and tools were shipped from the colonies to West Africa. Rice, tobacco, indigo, and furs were shipped to Great Britain and continental Europe. The pattern was triangular because the trade involved Britain, Africa, and America.

✓ Reading Check **Answer:** Northern coastal cities were the center of the shipping trade. Trade extended to the Southern Colonies, the West Indies, England, Europe, and West Africa.

Economics & History

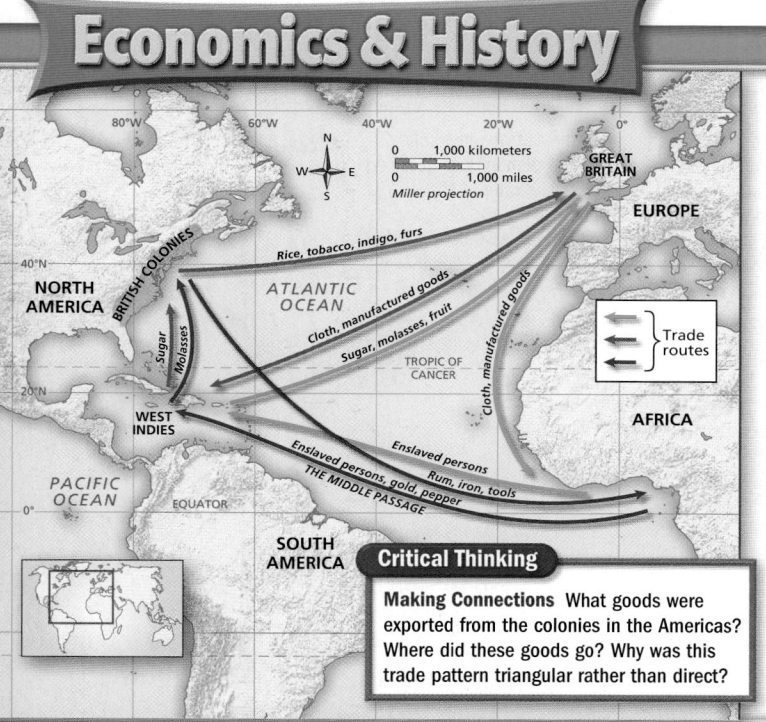

Triangular Trade During the colonial era, the desire for enslaved Africans to work plantations in the Americas led to a changed pattern of trade. Trade among Britain, Africa, and the American colonies formed a triangle. The trade in enslaved people formed one leg of the triangle—the terrible Middle Passage. Merchants sold British manufactured goods in Africa, bought enslaved Africans, and carried them to the West Indies to work on plantations. Plantation products, such as sugar, went to Europe, completing the triangle.

Critical Thinking

Making Connections What goods were exported from the colonies in the Americas? Where did these goods go? Why was this trade pattern triangular rather than direct?

Distinguishing Fact From Opinion

Objective:	To identify facts versus opinions while reading about history
Focus:	Ask students to define "fact" and "opinion"; have them give examples from daily life.
Teach:	Have students tell whether each sentence is fact or opinion, and explain why.
Assess:	Assess each answer for accuracy, and discuss why incorrect answers are wrong.
Close:	Ask students how they will use their ability to tell fact from opinion as they read.

Differentiated Instruction Strategies

BL Create three fact sentences and three opinion sentences.

AL Ask students to write a news article and an editorial about the Middle Passage.

ELL Create simple sentences that illustrate the difference between fact and opinion.

Critical Thinking Skills Activity, URB p. 113

S Skill Practice

Using Geography Skills Discuss the definition of "geography." **Ask:** *In what ways were the Middle Colonies shaped by their geographic characteristics? (Geography relates to the physical, environmental, and cultural features of an area. In the Middle Colonies, climate and soil conditions favored farming; availability of ports that allowed shipping and trade; abundant raw materials led to lumbering, mining, and manufacturing; immigrants from many countries in Europe led to cultural diversity and tolerance.)* **AL**

C Critical Thinking

Making Comparisons Ask: *How did the presence of non-English immigrants set the Middle Colonies apart from New England? (Immigrants brought many new ideas to the Middle Colonies, such as European agricultural methods; also experienced more cultural diversity, which created a tolerance for cultural differences.)* **OL**

Reading Check Answer: farm goods that are grown to be sold in colonial markets and overseas

Additional Support

The Middle Colonies

Main Idea The economies of the Middle Colonies depended on the sale of cash crops, such as wheat and corn.

History and You Have you ever visited a farm? What types of crops or animals were raised there? Read to learn about the effects farming had on the Middle Colonies.

With more fertile soil and a milder climate than New England's, the farms in the Middle Colonies produced bigger harvests. In New York and Pennsylvania, farmers grew large quantities of wheat and other **cash crops.** These crops were used by the farmers' families, but they also were sold in colonial markets and overseas.

Farmers sent cargoes of wheat and livestock to New York City and Philadelphia for shipment. These cities became busy ports. By the 1760s New York City, with 18,000 people, and Philadelphia, with 24,000 people, were the largest cities in the American colonies.

Industries of the Middle Colonies

Like the New England Colonies, the Middle Colonies also had industries. Some were home-based crafts such as carpentry and flour making. Others were larger businesses, such as lumbering, mining, and small-scale manufacturing. One iron mill in northern New Jersey employed several hundred workers. Many of these workers were from Germany. Other, smaller ironworks operated in New Jersey and Pennsylvania.

German Immigrants

Nearly 100,000 German immigrants came to America in the colonial era. Most settled in Pennsylvania. They successfully farmed the land using European agricultural methods.

The Germans, Dutch, Swedish, and other non-English immigrants gave the Middle Colonies a cultural diversity, or variety, not found in New England. This diversity created a tolerance for the many cultural differences.

Reading Check Explaining What are cash crops?

Primary Source The African Slave Trade

A Terrible Trade The transatlantic slave trade began in the 1500s when colonists needed a large labor force to work in their mines and plantations. West African slave traders sold captives acquired through wars and raids. Between 1520 and 1860, nearly 12 million Africans were enslaved. Many did not survive the march to the coastal trading sites or the voyage across the Atlantic. Between 9 and 10 million people faced a life of slavery in the Americas.

◀ Captains added platforms between decks to fit more captives onto their ships. Crowded slave compartments were covered with human waste, blood, and filth.

African slave traders set up road and river routes to move the captives to the coast. At the coastal trading sites, slaves were confined in wooden pens. ▶

92 Chapter 4 *Growth of the Thirteen Colonies*

Activity: Connecting Past and Present

Describing Many German, Dutch, and Swedish immigrants settled in the Middle Colonies. **Ask:** *How is the cultural heritage of European immigrants reflected in New York, New Jersey, Pennsylvania, and Delaware today?* Have students select a town, city, or neighborhood in one of these four states that hosts a holiday or celebration based on its German, Dutch, or Swedish heritage. Tell students to research the celebration on the Internet or at the library or by contacting the chamber of commerce in that city. They should investigate activities, food, dress, and participation. Have each student create a colorful display that includes highlights of the celebration and how the activities relate to life in Germany, Holland, or Sweden. **OL**

The Southern Colonies and Slavery

Main Idea Slavery played a role in the economic success of the Southern Colonies.

History and You Think about the types of resources that are needed to manage a large farm. Read to learn about how the economies of the Southern Colonies developed as a result of the physical features of the land and enslaved Africans.

Rich soil and a warm climate made the Southern Colonies well suited to certain kinds of farming. Southern farmers could cultivate large areas of land and produce harvests of cash crops. Most settlers in the Southern Colonies made their living from farming, and little commerce or industry developed. For the most part, London merchants rather than local merchants managed Southern trade.

Tobacco and Rice

Tobacco was the **principal,** or most important, cash crop of Maryland and Virginia.

Most tobacco was sold in Europe, where the demand for it was strong. Growing tobacco and preparing it for sale required a good deal of labor. At first, planters used indentured servants to work in the fields. When indentured servants became scarce and expensive, Southern planters began using enslaved Africans instead.

Slaveholders with large farms grew wealthy from their tobacco crop. Sometimes, however, a **surplus,** or extra amounts, of tobacco on the market caused prices to fall. As a result, the growers' profits also fell. In time, some tobacco planters switched to growing other crops, such as corn and wheat.

The main cash crop in South Carolina and Georgia was rice. In low-lying areas along the coast, planters built dams to create rice fields, called paddies. These fields were flooded when the rice was young and drained when the rice was ready to harvest. Work in the rice paddies was extremely strenuous. It involved standing knee-deep in the mud all day with no protection from the blazing sun or biting insects.

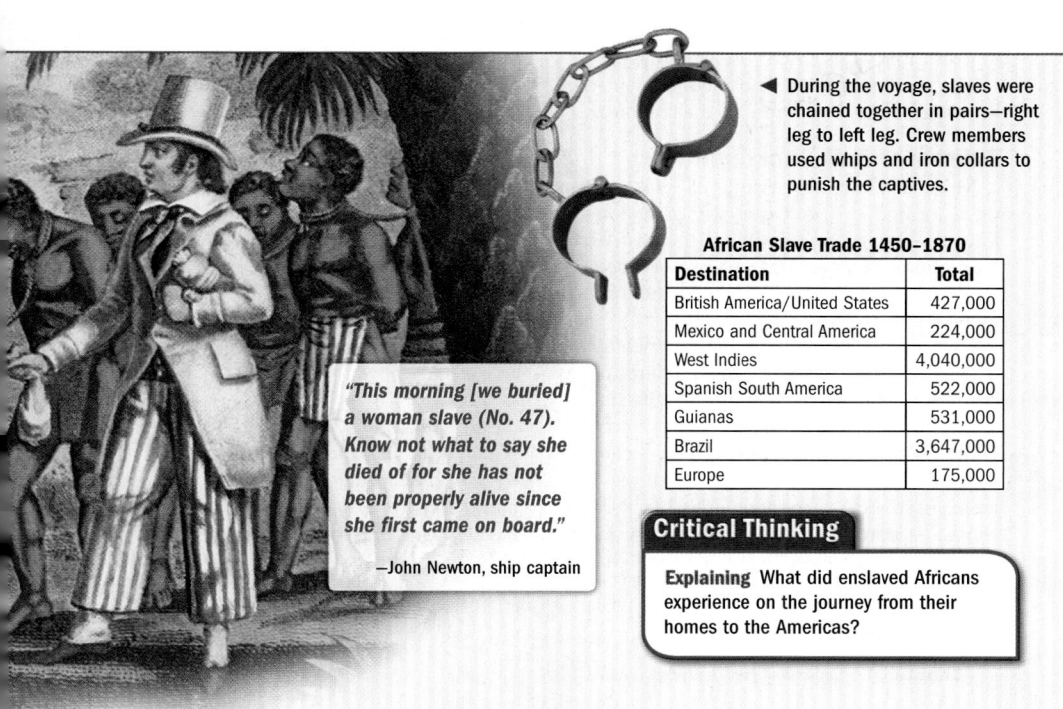

◄ During the voyage, slaves were chained together in pairs—right leg to left leg. Crew members used whips and iron collars to punish the captives.

"This morning [we buried] a woman slave (No. 47). Know not what to say she died of for she has not been properly alive since she first came on board."

—John Newton, ship captain

African Slave Trade 1450–1870

Destination	Total
British America/United States	427,000
Mexico and Central America	224,000
West Indies	4,040,000
Spanish South America	522,000
Guianas	531,000
Brazil	3,647,000
Europe	175,000

Critical Thinking

Explaining What did enslaved Africans experience on the journey from their homes to the Americas?

Activity: Technology Connection

Discussing Agriculture is still an important part of the economy in the South. In the past, the South relied on enslaved workers to provide the extensive labor needed to grow and harvest crops. **Ask:** How many people does it take to work a modern farm? What types of equipment might be used? Students will begin to answer the question by choosing a crop and learning how it is currently grown, harvested, and processed in the South. They will then research to learn how many people are employed in farming today and their characteristics (typical age, gender, country of origin, and salary and benefits). Have students create posters that compare and contrast farming methods and workers from the past compared to modern day. Hang the posters in the classroom. **Ask:** What might agriculture in the South be like in the future? **OL**

R Reading Strategy

Making Connections Ask: What was the relationship between the popularity of rice in Europe and slavery in the Southern Colonies? *(As rice became popular its price increased, making it more profitable to grow in the Southern Colonies. Because harvesting rice was labor intensive, enslaved Africans were used as a source of cheap labor.)* **OL**

W Writing Support

Expository Writing Ask students to research the characteristics of relationships between enslaved workers, plantation owners, and overseers. Then ask students to watch the movie *Gone With the Wind*. They will write a one-page essay in which they discuss the interactions between the enslaved African Americans and the plantation owners in the movie. Essays should explain whether the relationships in the movie were realistic. **AL**

Primary Source

Critical Thinking Answer
Answers might include losing enslaved Africans to illness, crop failure due to weather conditions, falling crop prices, and supervision of enslaved workers.

Hands-On Chapter Project
Step 1

Creating a Blog

Step 1: Creating a Character Students will work in groups to create a fictitious colonist in preparation for writing that individual's blog.

Essential Question: How did geography affect the economic development of the three colonial regions?

Primary Source / Plantation Life

Plantations—Large and Small Owners of small plantations—those of a few hundred acres—usually owned fewer than 50 slaves. Wealthy planters, in contrast, typically required 200 or more slaves to work their vast estates, which covered several thousand acres.

◄ Plantations often included a Big House, where the owner and his family lived, as well as slaves' cabins, stables, livestock pens, gardens, a kitchen, a sick house, and workshops for blacksmiths, weavers, and tanners.

▼ Most slaves worked in the fields from dawn to sunset. The landowner or a hired worker supervised the enslaved Africans.

"I rose at 5 o'clock this morning and . . . ate milk for breakfast. I said my prayers. Jenny and Eugene [two house slaves] were whipped. I danced my dance [physical exercises]. I read law in the morning and Italian in the afternoon. . . . I walked about the plantation."

—Virginia plantation owner, 1709

Critical Thinking

Theorizing What problems do you think a Southern plantation owner commonly faced in the 1700s?

R Because rice harvesting required so much strenuous work, rice growers relied on slave labor. Rice proved to be an even more profitable crop than tobacco. As rice became popular in Europe, its price rose steadily. By the 1750s, South Carolina and Georgia had the fastest-growing economies in the colonies.

Tidewater and Backcountry

Most of the large Southern plantations were located in the **Tidewater,** a region of flat, low-lying plains along the seacoast. Plantations, or large farms, were often located on rivers so crops could be shipped to market by boat.

W Each plantation was a self-contained community with fields stretching out around a cluster of buildings. The planter's wife supervised the main house and the household servants. A plantation included slave cabins, barns, and stables, as well as buildings that were used for carpenter and blacksmith shops, storerooms, and kitchens. A large plantation might also have its own chapel and school.

West of the Tidewater lay a region of hills and forests climbing up toward the Appalachian Mountains. This region was known as the **backcountry** and was settled in part by hardy newcomers to the colonies. The backcountry settlers grew corn and tobacco on small farms. They usually worked alone or with their families. Some of these families had one or two enslaved Africans to help them with their families.

In the Southern Colonies, the independent small farmers of the backcountry greatly outnumbered the large plantation owners. The plantation owners, however, were much wealthier and had more influence. They controlled the economic and political life of the region.

Slavery

W Most enslaved Africans lived on plantations. Some did housework, but most worked in the fields and often suffered great cruelty. The large plantation owners hired **overseers,** or bosses, to keep the enslaved Africans working hard.

In 1705, the colony of Virginia created a **slave code.** These were strict rules that

---

Directions Organize students into small groups. Explain that each group will take the role of someone living in one of the British colonies and that the group will begin a blog in which its character talks about his or her life. Ask each group to decide which colony its character lives in and the individual's age, gender, and race. Have students discuss how the person makes a living or spends a typical day, taking into account the person's location and other characteristics.

Summarizing Ask each group to describe the individual it created and explain how local geography and economic development would affect that individual's work and daily life.

(Chapter Project continued in Section 2)

governed the behavior and punishment of enslaved Africans and helped define the relationship between enslaved people and free people. Many other colonies soon followed with their own slave codes.

Some codes did not allow slaves to leave the plantation without the slaveholder's written permission. Some made it illegal to teach enslaved people to read or write. Many of the codes made it illegal for enslaved people to move about freely or assemble in large groups. The codes usually allowed slaves to be whipped for minor offenses and hanged or burned to death for serious crimes. Slaves who ran away were punished severely when caught.

African Traditions

Enslaved Africans had strong family ties. Often, however, their families were torn apart when a slaveholder sold family members to other slaveholders. Slaves turned to their African roots as a source of strength. They developed a culture that drew on the languages, customs, and traditions of their homelands in West Africa.

Some enslaved Africans learned trades such as carpentry, blacksmithing, or weaving. Skilled workers could sometimes set up shops, sharing their profits with the slaveholders. Some slaves were able to buy their freedom and joined the small population of free African Americans.

Criticism of Slavery

The majority of white Southerners were not slaveholders. Slavery, however, played an important role in the economic success of the Southern Colonies. That success came to be built on the idea that one human being could own another. Some colonists did not believe in slavery. There was less support for slavery in the Northern Colonies. For example, many Puritans refused to own enslaved people. In Pennsylvania, Quakers and Mennonites condemned slavery. Eventually the debate over slavery would erupt in a bloody war, setting the North against the South.

Reading Check Describing What was the purpose of slave codes?

History ONLINE
Study Central™ To review this section, go to glencoe.com.

Section 1 Review

Vocabulary

1. Define the following terms by using each one in a sentence: subsistence farming, rely, triangular trade, Middle Passage, cash crop, principal, surplus, Tidewater, backcountry, overseer, slave code.

Main Ideas

2. **Discussing** How did the coastal location of the New England colonies affect their prosperity?

3. **Explaining** Why were the Middle Colonies able to grow large quantities of crops?

4. **Identifying** How did cash crops affect the development of slavery?

Critical Thinking

5. **Comparing and Contrasting** Use a Venn diagram like the one below to compare and contrast characteristics of the Tidewater and the backcountry in Southern Colonies.

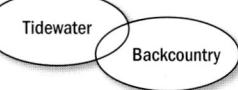

6. **Expository Writing** As a New England farmer, write a letter to relatives in Europe describing your family's daily life.

Answer the
7. **Essential Question**
How did geography affect the economic development of the three colonial regions?

Growth of the Thirteen Colonies **Chapter 4** 95

C Critical Thinking

Identifying Central Issues Tell students that the slave codes made life even more difficult for enslaved people. **Ask:** Do you think enslaved workers would try to rebel against their owners? *(Students should explain their answers.)* **AL**

Reading Check Answer: to govern the behavior and punishment of enslaved workers

Assess

History ONLINE

Study Central™ provides summaries, interactive games, and online graphic organizers to help students review content.

Close

Discussing As a class, discuss how geography impacted the economic activities of the colonies. **OL**

Answers

1. Sentences should use terms according to their definitions in the section and the Glossary.
2. It allowed an economy based on shipbuilding, fishing, and trade with the other colonies, Africa, Europe, and the West Indies.
3. They had fertile soil and a mild climate. Also, German immigrants brought improved European farming methods.
4. The cultivation of tobacco and rice was labor intensive. Indentured servants were expensive and scarce, and slaves were used as cheap labor to work in the fields.
5. Tidewater: plantations, more wealth and influence; Backcountry: small farms, more farmers; Both: tobacco, slavery
6. Student letters should use descriptive language and include details about life in New England.
7. New England: Harsh climate and rocky soil led to subsistence farming; coastal location led to shipbuilding and other industries, fishing, and trade. Middle Colonies: fertile soil and milder climate led to larger farms and cash crops; availability of natural resources led to small-scale manufacturing, lumbering, and mining; good ports allowed trade. Southern Colonies: Rich soil and warm climate led to large farms, cash crops, the development of the plantation system, and an economy based on slavery.

Focus

S Skill Practice

Using Geography Skills Have students use the world map in the Reference Atlas. Ask them to locate the African country of Guinea. Point out that Venture Smith traveled by ship from Guinea to Connecticut. Have them trace the route on the map. **Ask:** In which direction did Venture Smith's ship travel? *(northwest)* **BL**

Teach

R Reading Strategy

Paraphrasing Discuss the meaning of Franklin's quotation. Have students rewrite it in their own words. **OL**

D Differentiated Instruction

Logical/Mathematical Have students identify which city had the greatest population increase from 1710 to 1760. *(Philadelphia)* **OL**

Additional Support and Answers

What were people's lives like in the past?

These two pages will give you some clues to everyday life in the United States as you step back in time with TIME Notebook.

American Notes

FROM PRINCE TO ENSLAVEMENT TO LANDOWNER

In the 1700s, a formerly enslaved African, **VENTURE SMITH**, *wrote about his life in a book titled* A Narrative of the Life and Adventures of Venture. *Here is an excerpt of his story.*

"I was born in Dukandarra, in Guinea [in Africa], about the year 1729.... My father's name was Saungm Furro, Prince of the tribe of Dukandarra."

At 6, Venture Smith was kidnapped by an enemy tribe and later sold to the crew of a slave ship. He wrote, "I was bought on board by one Robert Mumford... for four gallons of rum, and a piece of calico, and called Venture, on account of his having purchased me with his own private venture [property]. Thus I came by my name. All the slaves that were bought for that vessel's cargo were two hundred and sixty."

NORTH WIND PICTURE ARCHIVES / ALAMY

Venture was brought to Connecticut—where he was sold several times. When he was about 35 he was able to purchase his freedom for "seventy-one pounds, two shillings." He earned this money doing odd jobs, such as "cleaning ...minks, raising potatoes and carrots, and by fishing in the night."

After years of more work—including sailing on a whaler—he was able to buy the freedom of his wife and children. In his book, Venture wrote, "My freedom is a privilege which nothing else can equal. Notwithstanding all the losses I have suffered ...by the injustice of knaves. ...I am now possessed of more than one hundred acres of land, and three habitable dwelling houses."

96

WHAT PEOPLE ARE SAYING

❝Those who would give up essential Liberty, to purchase a little temporary Safety, deserve neither Liberty nor Safety.❞
BENJAMIN FRANKLIN, *1755*

❝I wish for nothing more than to attain a small degree of knowledge in the military art.❞
GEORGE WASHINGTON,
in 1755, agreeing to fight with the British army and for King George II in the French and Indian War

❝Amazing Grace, how sweet the sound, That saved a wretch like me.❞
JOHN NEWTON,
former slave trader who realized the error of his ways during a violent storm in 1748 that nearly sank his ship. Later he wrote hymns, including "Amazing Grace," and became an abolitionist.

BOOM!

Bustling sea trade helped the populations of these port towns grow by leaps and bounds.

	1710	1730	1760
Boston	9,000	13,000	15,600
New York	5,700	8,600	18,000
Philadelphia	6,500	11,500	23,750
Charleston	3,000	4,500	8,000

BOSTON HARBOR IN 1750

MARY EVANS PICTURE LIBRARY / ALAMY

Fast Facts

What's in a Name? Venture Smith was not born with that name; instead, it was a name given to him by his owner. Enslaved people who were brought to America from Africa were often renamed by their owners. Africans were sometimes given their new names on the boats that brought them to America or by their owners once they arrived. The names were often based on popular names of the time such as Tom and Bill, biblical names such as Adam and Eve, and classical names such as Nero and Venus. Some owners named the enslaved Africans using the surnames of American leaders as first names, such as Washington, Jefferson, and Madison.

MANNERS

Oh, Behave!

George Washington, sometime before the age of 16, copied by hand a list of rules from a book called *Rules of Civility & Decent Behaviour in Company and Conversation: a Book of Etiquette.* It contains over 100 different things NOT to do in polite society. We have listed four of these tips below . . . and for fun we have added a fake. Can you spot the phony rule?

NORTH WIND PICTURE ARCHIVES / ALAMY

W

— Every action done in company ought to be with some sign of respect to those that are present.

— When in company, put not your radio on too loudly as it might congest the ears of others with noise.

— In the presence of others, sing not to yourself with a humming noise, nor drum with your fingers or feet.

— If you cough, sneeze, sigh, or yawn, do it not loud but privately; and speak not in your yawning, but put your handkerchief or hand before your face and turn aside.

— When you sit down, keep your feet firm and even, without putting one on the other or crossing them.

Answer: The second item is the fake—the radio had not been invented yet!

COLONIAL GAMES

Play Quoits

Do you feel left out of the fun when all your friends play quoits—the hot game of the 1700s? Just remember that quoits is a lot like horseshoes— only in this game you toss rings made of rope. Here is how to play one version:

JACK CAREY / ALAMY

1) Put two sets of four stakes in the ground—the sets should be 18 feet apart.

2) Standing next to one set, take turns with another player tossing two rings at the other set, while trying to loop them around the stakes.

3) Scoring:
   a. 2 points if your two rings land closer to a stake than either of your opponent's.
   b. 4 points if your ring goes around a stake—this is a "ringer."
   c. 3 points if your "ringer" lands on top of your opponent's ring.

4) Once a loop touches the ground, it's "dead." Even if it bounces up over a stake, it does not count.

5) After tossing their rings from one set, players start a new round by tossing from the other set.

6) The first player to score 21 points wins.

NUMBERS

UNITED STATES AT THE TIME

25 Percent of enslaved people who did not survive crossing the Atlantic from Africa to the Americas

D

0 Number of American political cartoons before Benjamin Franklin's first one appeared in the *Pennsylvania Gazette* in 1754; Franklin wanted the colonies to join together to defend themselves against a threat by the French and Native Americans

JOIN, or DIE.

CORBIS

3 to 10 About the number of years indentured servants had to work in the 1700s to pay back the person who paid for their passage to the Americas

2 Number of tines, or points, on that new thing called the fork, which has just appeared on a table near you; talk is there will soon be three or four tines by the end of the century

CRITICAL THINKING

Comparing and Contrasting How are George Washington's etiquette rules similar to and different from today's rules of good manners?

Hypothesizing Does sea trade today affect cities in the same way it did in the 1700s? Explain your answer.

97

Focus

Section 2

Government, Religion, Culture

Bellringer
Daily Test Practice Transparency 4–2

Reading Guide
Answers to Graphic:

Great Awakening: stronger faith, new churches

Enlightenment: increased interest in science, observation, and publishing; belief that knowledge, reason, and science will improve society

Section Spotlight Video

Have students watch the Section Spotlight Video "Government, Religion, and Culture" to learn about the principles of government outlined in the Magna Carta.

Essential Question ◄
In what ways was an American culture developing during the colonial period?

Reading Guide

Content Vocabulary
export (p. 99)

import (p. 99)

charter colony (p. 101)

proprietary colony (p. 101)

royal colony (p. 101)

Academic Vocabulary
successor (p. 99)

Key People and Events
Glorious Revolution (p. 99)

Navigation Acts (p. 100)

Great Awakening (p. 102)

Enlightenment (p. 103)

Reading Strategy
Taking Notes As you read, use a diagram like the one below to explain how the Great Awakening and the Enlightenment affected the colonists.

Great Awakening ⟹ ☐

Enlightenment ⟹ ☐

ILLINOIS STANDARDS
The American Journey

14.C.3 Compare historical issues involving rights, roles and status of individuals in relation to municipalities, states and the nation.

14.F.3a Analyze historical influences on the development of political ideas and practices as enumerated in the Declaration of Independence, the United States Constitution, the Bill of Rights and the Illinois Constitution.

18.B.3a Analyze how individuals and groups interact with and within institutions (e.g., educational, military).

American Diary

At 16 years old, Eliza Lucas Pinckney took over the family plantation when her father went to war. In 1741 she recorded: "Wrote to Mr. Murray to send down a boat load of white oak [strips], bacon and salted beef. . . . Sent up at the same time a barrel [of] salt." Eliza's major achievement, however, was finding a better way to make blue dye from the indigo plant. Used in military uniforms, the dye was in high demand. Eliza's success turned indigo into a very profitable crop.

—from the Journal of Eliza Lucas Pinckney

Drayton Hall, located near Charleston, South Carolina, was a rice plantation.

Resource Manager

R Reading Strategies	**C** Critical Thinking	**D** Differentiated Instruction	**W** Writing Support	**S** Skill Practice
Teacher Edition • Identify. Main Idea, p. 99 • Deter. Import., p. 100 **Additional Resources** • Guid. Read., URB p. 124 • Cont. Vocab., URB p. 101 • Ac. Vocab., URB p. 103 • Read. Skills, URB p. 7 • Am. Lit. Read., URB p. 9 • Pri. Source Read., URB p. 105	**Teacher Edition** • Compar. & Contrast., p. 100 • Draw. Conclus., p. 103 **Additional Resources** • Quizzes and Tests, p. 32	**Teacher Edition** • ELL, p. 99 • Verbal/Linguist., p. 102 • Naturalist, p. 103 **Additional Resources** • Reteach., URB p. 121 • School-to-Home Connect. Act., URB p. 119 • Differ. Inst., URB p. 111	**Teacher Edition** • Expository Writing, p. 100 • Expository Writing, p. 102 **Additional Resources** • Authentic Assess., p. 4	**Teacher Edition** • Using Chart Skills, p. 101 **Additional Resources** • Daily Test Pract. Transp. 4-2 • Soc. Stud. Skills, URB p. 109 • Lesson Transparency 4B

English Colonial Rule

Main Idea Although the American colonies developed some self-government, the British still set many laws, especially those concerning trade.

History and You How would you react if you were forced to buy clothes from only one store? Read to learn about the trade restrictions that England placed on its colonies.

In her writings and activities, Eliza Lucas Pinckney celebrated a new American spirit. This spirit signaled that Americans were beginning to view themselves differently from the way Great Britain viewed them.

Trouble was brewing in England—and in the colonies—during the mid-1600s. England's monarchy was restored with Charles II on the throne. Many people, however, were not satisfied with his rule. James II, Charles's **successor**—the next king—attempted to take back the powers Parliament won during the English Civil War. He also tried to tighten royal control over the colonies.

In 1688 Parliament took action. It forced out James and placed his daughter Mary and her Dutch husband, William of Orange, on the throne. This change demonstrated the power of the elected representatives over the monarch. This period came to be known as the **Glorious Revolution.**

William and Mary signed an English Bill of Rights in 1689 guaranteeing certain basic rights to all citizens. This document became an important part of the heritage of English law that the American colonists shared. Some hundred years later, it inspired the people who created the American Bill of Rights.

England viewed its North American colonies as an economic resource. The colonies provided England with raw materials such as lumber. English manufacturers used these materials to produce finished goods, which they then sold to the colonists. This process followed an economic theory called mercantilism. As you learned earlier, this theory states that as a nation's trade grows, its gold reserves increase. The nation then becomes more powerful. To make money from its trade, England had to **export,** or sell abroad, more goods than it **imported,** or bought from foreign markets.

To ensure that only England benefited from trade with the colonies, Parliament passed several laws between 1651 and 1673.

If You Were There / Plantation Life

The Planter's Family As the son or daughter of a plantation owner, you enjoy great wealth and privilege. Your father serves in the colonial government, perhaps as a member of the royal governor's council. Your mother hosts elegant parties. If you are a planter's son, you are receiving the education of a British gentleman and learning business skills to run the plantation. If you are a daughter, you study art and music and are becoming skilled in managing a plantation household. Your home is decorated with the most fashionable furnishings imported from Britain.

Critical Thinking

Drawing Conclusions Do you think Eliza Lucas Pinckney's responsibilities were typical of a woman of the 1700s? Explain.

Teach

D Differentiated Instruction

English Language Learners Ask students what smaller word is found in "successor" that may explain its meaning. *(Most will suggest "success.")* Point out that "succeed," meaning "to come after," is the more appropriate smaller word to help understand the meaning of "successor." **ELL**

R Reading Strategy

Identifying the Main Idea Ask: What is the main idea of this paragraph? *(The English Bill of Rights guaranteed basic rights to all of its citizens.)* **OL**

This **READING SKILL** (Identifying the Main Idea) was introduced in this unit.

If You Were There

Critical Thinking Answer
No, most women of the time did not manage entire plantations. Most girls her age would have been studying the arts and just beginning to learn how to manage a household.

Additional Support

Activity: Making Connections

Comparing Give each student a copy of the English Bill of Rights. **Ask:** What rights in this document do U.S. citizens possess today? *(Talk about the fact that many of the rights are ones we take for granted in the United States today. Explain that our Bill of Rights—the first ten amendments to the U.S. Constitution—was inspired by the English Bill of Rights.)* Organize students into several groups, with each group choosing one of the first 10 amendments to the U.S. Constitution. Have each group write a paragraph discussing how that amendment is reflected in the English Bill of Rights. If an amendment is similar to part of the English document, ask students to speculate on why the colonists would have copied that idea from England. If the right in an amendment seems to have originated in America, students should discuss why it was important to people at that time. **AL**

W Writing Support

Expository Writing The Navigation Act regulated trade between England and the colonies. Have students write a paragraph that explains these policies from the British point of view and then from the point of view of an American colonist. **AL**

C Critical Thinking

Comparing and Contrasting Discuss forms of representative government in your school, such as student council or another club. Ask students to write a letter to the principal in which they suggest changes to their student council or club that might allow it to better represent the students. **OL**

R Reading Strategy

Determining Importance Have students read the paragraph and identify the fact that is most significant to the U.S. system of government. *(two principles of government—limited government and representative government)* **OL**

Hands-On Chapter Project
Step 2

Creating a Blog

Step 2: Making the First Blog Entry Each group will introduce its character in a blog entry that reflects the emerging American culture.

Essential Question: In what ways was an American culture developing during the colonial period?

These **Navigation Acts** directed the trade between England and the colonies. Colonial merchants who had goods to send to England could not use foreign ships—even if those ships offered cheaper rates. The Navigation Acts also prevented the colonists from sending certain products, such as sugar or tobacco, outside the area that made up England's empire.

The colonists at first accepted the trade laws because they were guaranteed a place to sell their raw materials. Later, the colonists came to resent British restrictions. Merchants wanted to make their own manufactured goods and sell their products where they could get higher prices. Some colonists ignored these laws and began smuggling, or trading illegally, with other nations. Controls on trade would later cause even more conflict between the American colonies and England.

Reading Check **Identifying** What country strictly controlled shipping and trade with the colonies and why?

Colonial Government

Main Idea As the colonies grew, they developed some self-government.

History and You Does your school have a student council to represent students? Read to learn how colonists were represented in colonial governments.

. . . .

The English colonists brought with them ideas about government and a respect for education that had been developing in England for centuries. By the 1600s, the English people had won political liberties, such as trial by jury, that were largely unknown elsewhere. At the heart of the English system were two principles of government—limited government and representative government. These two principles greatly influenced the development of the United States.

When the colonists reached North America, they believed that government was not all-powerful. This idea was already an accepted part of the English system of government.

Primary Source | Colonial Printing and Education

An Educated Population Literacy rates were generally high in New England and the Middle Colonies. Education in the South was limited primarily to the wealthy. By the 1700s, many printed materials were available throughout the colonies. Colonists' ability to read and express ideas in print would play a major role in the later struggle for independence.

◄ The first printing press in the colonies was set up in Cambridge, Massachusetts, in 1639. By the mid-1700s, presses were found throughout the colonies.

Newspapers started appearing in colonial cities in the first half of the 1700s. ▶

Massachusetts schoolmasters used *The New England Primer* to teach generations of students how to read and write. ▶

Directions Have each group research the kind of family life, religion, and education its character might have experienced. Have the groups decide on names for the blogs that represent their characters. Then have them collaborate on writing the first entry for their blogs. In this entry, the characters will introduce themselves and describe their lives. Tell students to include images they find or create to illustrate the entry.

Analyzing Ask students to share their blogs and discuss details about their characters. How do the blogs illustrate ways in which colonial American culture was developing?

(Chapter Project continued in Section 3)

It first appeared in the Magna Carta, or the Great Charter. The Magna Carta was signed by King John on June 15, 1215.

The Magna Carta established the principle of limited government. This means that the power of the king, or government, is limited. This document also provided for protection against unjust punishment. It protected against the loss of life, liberty, and property.

As the colonies grew, their town meetings developed into small governments, responsible for making local laws. By the 1760s, there were three types of colonies in America—charter colonies, proprietary colonies, and royal colonies.

Charter Colonies

Connecticut and Rhode Island were **charter colonies.** Settlers were given a charter, or a grant of rights and privileges, to establish charter colonies. These colonists elected their own governors and the members of the legislature. Great Britain had the right to approve the governor, but the governor could not veto the acts of the legislature.

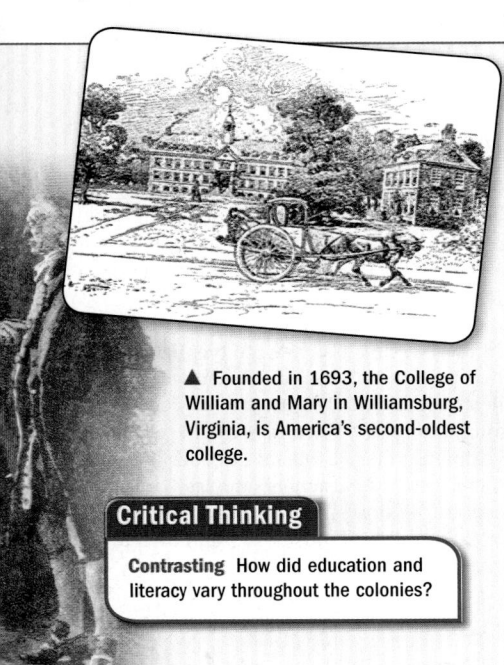

▲ Founded in 1693, the College of William and Mary in Williamsburg, Virginia, is America's second-oldest college.

Critical Thinking

Contrasting How did education and literacy vary throughout the colonies?

History ONLINE
Student Web Activity Visit glencoe.com and complete the Chapter 4 Web Activity about the Magna Carta.

Proprietary Colonies

The **proprietary colonies** of Delaware, Maryland, and Pennsylvania were ruled by proprietors. Proprietors were individuals or groups to whom Britain granted land. They were generally free to rule as they wished. Proprietors appointed the governor and members of the upper house of the legislature. The colonists elected the lower house.

Royal Colonies

By the 1760s, Georgia, Massachusetts, New Hampshire, New Jersey, New York, North Carolina, South Carolina, and Virginia were **royal colonies.** Britain directly ruled all royal colonies. In each, the king appointed a governor and council, known as the upper house, and the colonists elected an assembly called the lower house. The governor and the members of the council usually did what the British leaders told them to do. However, this often led to conflict with the colonists in the assembly. Most conflicts occurred when officials tried to enforce tax laws and trade restrictions.

Voting Rights

Colonial legislatures gave only some people a voice in government. Generally, white men who owned property had the right to vote. Most women, indentured servants, landless poor, and African Americans could not vote. In spite of these limits, the proportion of people involved in government was higher in the colonies, estimated at 80 to 90 percent, than anywhere in Europe. This strong participation in government gave Americans training that was valuable when the colonies became independent.

✔ **Reading Check** **Drawing Inferences** How did the Magna Carta influence governments in the colonies?

Growth of the Thirteen Colonies **Chapter 4** **101**

S Skill Practice

Using Chart Skills Ask students to create a bar graph that charts the kinds of colonies and the number of colonies in each category. **Ask:** Which type of colony was the most common? *(royal colony)* **OL**

Primary Source

Critical Thinking Answer
New England and the Middle Colonies had high literacy rates, while education and ability to read was limited to the wealthy in the South.

History ONLINE
Objectives and answers to the Student Web Activity can be found at glencoe.com under the Web Activity Lesson Plan for this chapter.

✔ **Reading Check** **Answer:** It established the idea that the power of the government was limited.

Differentiated Instruction

Reading a Table

Objective:	To understand how to read a table and organize information in tabular format	
Focus:	Explain the parts of a table and how tables may be understood and used.	
Teach:	Have students read the first table and complete the second table using the choices given and their knowledge of the text.	
Assess:	Have students use the Self-Assessment Checklist.	
Close:	Discuss types of information that are easier to understand when presented in a table.	

Social Studies Skills Activity, URB p. 109

Differentiated Instruction Strategies

BL As students examine the tables, have them point to each cell and explain what that cell contains.

AL Ask students to find two passages in their textbooks that could be presented in a table and then have them create the two tables.

ELL Have students write the information given in the first table in paragraph form.

D Differentiated Instruction

Verbal/Linguistic Discuss the term "revival" and its root "revive" (to become active again). Ask students to find other words in the bracketed text that relate to the idea of bringing to life. (*awakening, birth, formation*) **OL**

W Writing Support

Expository Writing Discuss the roles of husbands, wives, sons, daughters, and unmarried women in colonial society. Have students write two paragraphs in which they explain the roles of people in these categories. **OL**

People IN HISTORY

Critical Thinking Answers

1. They could pursue a variety of interests.
2. Franklin's experiments with electricity would have been dramatic, caught the public's imagination, and made science seem more real.

Differentiated Instruction

People IN HISTORY

Benjamin Franklin
American Scientist and Revolutionary Leader

Although he was born in a poor family, Ben Franklin made a fortune as a printer in Philadelphia. By the age of 42, Franklin was one of the richest men in the colonies. He chose to retire from active business and become a "gentleman." He began to pursue "philosophical studies and amusements." He was especially curious about electricity, and his experiments made him famous. He wrote in his autobiography: *"What gave my book the more sudden and general celebrity, was the success of one of its proposed experiments, . . . drawing lightning from the clouds. . . . After [the experiments] were performed before the king and court, all the curious of Paris flocked to see them."*

CRITICAL Thinking

1. **Identifying** What does Franklin's autobiography tell you about the lives of gentlemen in the colonies?
2. **Analyzing** Why do you think Franklin's experiments with electricity made him famous?

An Emerging Culture

Main Idea An American culture, influenced by religion and education, began to develop in the colonies.

History and You What items or activities do you consider part of American culture? Grilled hamburgers? Playing baseball? Read to find out how the colonists began forming a culture that was different from European cultures.

From the 1720s through the 1740s, a religious revival called the **Great Awakening** swept through the colonies. In New England and the Middle Colonies, ministers called for "a new birth," a return to the strong faith of earlier days. One popular preacher was Jonathan Edwards of Massachusetts. People thought his sermons were powerful and convincing.

The English preacher George Whitefield started religious revivals beginning in 1739. Whitefield inspired worshipers throughout the colonies. The Great Awakening led to the formation of many new churches.

Family Roles

People adapted their traditions to the new conditions of life in America. Religion, education, and the arts contributed to a new American culture. The family, however, formed the basic foundation of colonial society.

Men were the formal heads of the households and represented the family in the community. Men worked in the fields and built barns, houses, and fences. Sons could work as indentured servants for local farmers. Young men also could be apprentices, or assistants, to workers who taught them a trade.

Women ran their households and cared for children. Many worked in the fields with their husbands. Married women were under their husbands' authority and had few rights. Young unmarried women might work for wealthy families as maids or cooks. Widows might work as teachers, nurses, or seamstresses. Widows and women who never married could run businesses and own property, but they could not vote.

Leveled Activities

BL Reading Skills Activity, URB p. 7

OL Reteaching Activity, URB p. 121

AL Primary Source Reading Activity, URB p. 105

Education

Most colonists valued education. Parents often taught their children to read and write at home. In New England and Pennsylvania, in particular, people set up schools to make sure everyone could read and study the Bible. In 1647 the Massachusetts Puritans passed a public education law. Each community with 50 or more homes was required to have a school.

By 1750, New England had a high level of literacy with about 85 percent of the men and about half of the women able to read. Many learned from *The New England Primer,* which **C** combined lessons in good conduct with reading and writing.

Widows or unmarried women ran many colonial schools. Quakers and other religious groups in the Middle Colonies ran others. In towns and cities, craftspeople set up night schools for their apprentices.

The colonies' early colleges were founded to train ministers. The first was Harvard College, established in 1636 by the Puritans in Cambridge, Massachusetts. Anglicans founded William and Mary College in Virginia in 1693.

The Enlightenment

By the middle of the 1700s, many educated colonists were influenced by the **Enlightenment.** This movement began in Europe and was based upon the idea that knowledge, reason, and science could improve **D** society. In the colonies, the Enlightenment increased interest in science. People observed nature, staged experiments, and published their findings. The best-known American scientist was Benjamin Franklin.

Freedom of the Press

In 1735 John Peter Zenger of the *New York Weekly Journal* faced charges of libel. He had printed a critical report about the royal governor of New York. Andrew Hamilton argued that free speech was a basic right of English people. He defended Zenger by asking the jury to base its decision on whether Zenger's article was true, not whether it was offensive. The jury found Zenger not guilty. Today the case is regarded as an important step in the development of a free press in America.

✓ Reading Check **Analyzing** In what ways did the Great Awakening influence culture in the colonies?

History ONLINE
Study Central™ To review this section, go to glencoe.com.

Section 2 Review

Vocabulary

1. Define each of the following terms and use it in a sentence: successor, guarantee, export, import, charter colony, proprietary colony, royal colony.

Main Ideas

2. Explaining How did the Navigation Acts affect colonial trade?

3. Illustrating Discuss how people in the charter colonies participated in government.

4. Identifying What was taught from *The New England Primer?*

Critical Thinking

5. Summarizing Use a diagram like the one below to identify and describe the three types of colonies in America.

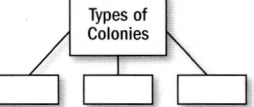

Types of Colonies

6. Persuasive Writing Write a short speech that Andrew Hamilton might have used to defend John Peter Zenger.

Answer the
7. Essential Question
In what ways was an American culture developing during the colonial period?

Growth of the Thirteen Colonies **Chapter 4** **103**

C Critical Thinking

Drawing Conclusions Ask: What information supports the idea that the colonists valued education? *(They taught reading and writing at home, established schools, had mandatory education in some areas, and founded colleges.)* **BL**

D Differentiated Instruction

Naturalist Have students research Benjamin Franklin's scientific experiments and discoveries. Each student will choose one and describe it to the class. **OL**

✓ Reading Check **Answer:** The Great Awakening was a religious revival that led to the formation of many new churches.

Assess

History ONLINE

Study Central™ provides summaries, interactive games, and online graphic organizers to help students review content.

Close

Discussing As a class, discuss the characteristics of the distinct culture that was developing in colonial America. **OL**

Section 2 Review

Answers

1. Students will define the terms and use them in sentences.
2. Merchants could no longer ship goods cheaply via non-English ships and also had to trade some products only with England.
3. The colonists elected their own governors, who then had to be approved by Great Britain, and their own legislature.
4. reading, writing, and good conduct

5. Charter: colonists elected governor and legislature; governor could not veto acts of legislature; Proprietary: was ruled by proprietors, who were granted land by Britain; proprietors appointed governor and upper house; colonists elected lower house; Royal: was ruled directly by Britain; king appointed governor and upper house; colonies elected lower house

6. Students' speeches should be persuasive and defend Zenger.
7. The colonists adopted ideas of limited government and representative government. Distinct religious and educational ideas contributed to culture; family was the basis of society; interest in science and invention grew; freedom of the press was defended.

Focus

Section 3

France and Britain Clash

Bellringer
Daily Test Practice Transparency 4–3

Reading Guide
Answers to Graphic:
Relations With the British: British wanted to seize Native American land
Relations With the French: French established a fur trade; married Native Americans and adopted their customs; shared Christianity

Section Spotlight Video

Have students watch the Section Spotlight Video "France and Britain Clash" to learn about the Iroquois Confederacy.

Resource Manager

Essential Question ◄
Why did conflict arise in North America between France and Great Britain?

Reading Guide

Content Vocabulary
Iroquois Confederacy (p. 105) militia (p. 107)

Academic Vocabulary
convert (p. 105)   design (p. 106)

Key People and Events
George Washington (p. 106)
Albany Plan of Union (p. 107)

Reading Strategy
Taking Notes As you read, use a diagram like the one below to summarize why, in general, Native Americans had better relations with the French than with the British.

Native Americans
Relations With the British	Relations With the French

ILLINOIS STANDARDS
The American Journey

16.A Apply the skills of historical analysis and interpretation.
17.C Understand relationships between geographic factors and society.
18.B.3a Analyze how individuals and groups interact with and within institutions (e.g., educational, military).

American Diary

In 1754 a small force of colonial soldiers, led by a young George Washington, fought the French in what is today western Pennsylvania. Washington later stated that the French "kept up a constant . . . fire upon us; which was returned [until] . . . the most tremendous rain . . . filled our trenches with Water, [and] Wet . . . the Ammunition . . . in a small temporary [post] . . . called Fort Necessity . . . and left us nothing but a few . . . Bayonets for defence."

—quoted in An Eyewitness History: The Colonial Era

George Washington's colonial troops surrendering to the French outside Fort Necessity

R Reading Strategies	**C** Critical Thinking	**D** Differentiated Instruction	**W** Writing Support	**S** Skill Practice
Teacher Edition • Identifying, p. 106 **Additional Resources** • Guid. Read., URB p. 125 • Cont. Vocab., URB p. 101 • Ac. Vocab., URB p. 103 • Read. Ess., p. 40	**Teacher Edition** • Determin. Cause & Effect, p. 106 **Additional Resources** • Quizzes and Tests, p. 33 • Inter. Polit. Cartoons, URB p. 13	**Teacher Edition** • Interpersonal, p. 105 **Additional Resources** • Reteach., URB p. 121 • School-to-Home Connect. Act., URB p. 119	**Teacher Edition** • Persuas. Writing, p. 107 **Additional Resources** • Writ. Skills, URB p. 107	**Teacher Edition** • Making a Time Line, p. 105 **Additional Resources** • Daily Test Pract. Transp. 4-3 • Time Line Skills, URB p. 118 • Lesson Transparency 4A

British-French Rivalry

Main Idea Rivalry between Great Britain and France led to a war for control of North America.

History and You Is it sometimes difficult to stay out of a conflict when people around you are arguing? Read to learn how Native Americans became involved in the conflict between the British and French.

⎯⎯⎯⎯⎯⎯⎯⎯⎯⎯⎯⎯⎯⎯

As a young military officer, George Washington fought with British forces against the French. Both forces wanted control of lands west of the Appalachian Mountains. During the 1700s, Britain and France were two of the strongest powers in Europe. They competed for wealth and empire in different parts of the world. This rivalry caused bitter feelings between British and French colonists in North America.

This bitterness increased when British interests turned to the Ohio River valley. The French regarded this territory as their own. They did not want British colonists sharing in their profitable fur trade.

In the 1740s hostility between the two forces grew. British fur traders built a fort at a place called Pickawillany. Acting quickly, the French attacked Pickawillany and drove the British traders out of Ohio. French troops also

S began raiding towns in Maine and New York. In response, some New Englanders captured the important French fortress at Louisbourg on Cape Breton Island, north of Nova Scotia. Much to the disgust of the New Englanders, Britain returned Louisbourg to France.

Native Americans Take Sides

The French and British both knew that assistance from Native Americans could help them win control of North America. The French had an advantage over the British because they had many Native American allies.

Unlike the British, the French were interested mainly in fur trading. They did not want to take over Native American land. Also, French trappers and fur traders often married Native American women and followed their customs. French missionaries **converted**—changed the religious beliefs of—many Native Americans to Catholicism. For these reasons, Native Americans often helped the French and raided British settlements.

The Iroquois Confederacy

The most powerful group of Native Americans in the East was the **Iroquois Confederacy,** based in the New York area.

Primary Source / Fort Necessity

A Fort for Defense Washington's Fort Necessity was built on open grassland near a stream and was surrounded by a forest. When completed, the fort contained a small log storehouse in the center of a round stockade, or a defensive line of wooden posts. Raised walls of soil, or earthworks, were built outside the stockade.

Stockade

Earthworks

Log Cabin

N

0 5 10 20   50 Feet

Critical Thinking

Making Inferences Why do you think Washington chose to build such a fort?

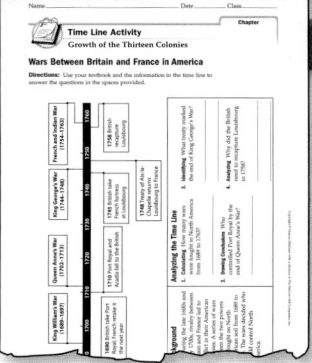

Time Line Activity
Growth of the Thirteen Colonies

Wars Between Britain and France in America

Directions: Use your textbook and the information in the time line to answer the questions in the spaces provided.

**Time Line Skills Activity,
URB p. 118**

Teach

S Skill Practice

Making a Time Line Have students create a time line of events as they read the section to help them understand the background of the French and Indian War. **OL**

D Differentiated Instruction

Interpersonal Organize students into two groups and stage a debate. One team will represent French interests in the Ohio Valley, and the other will represent British colonists there. Each team will try to convince the audience that it has the right to control the area. **AL**

Primary Source

Critical Thinking Answer The open land where the fort stood would have allowed Washington's troops to see the enemy approach, and the stockade and earthworks would have provided protection to people defending the fort. The river would have supplied drinking water.

Differentiated Instruction

Growth of the Thirteen Colonies

Objective: To practice reading a time line

Focus: Discuss the parts of the time line and what each shows.

Teach: Have students answer the questions using their textbooks and the information in the time line.

Assess: Use the Answer Key to discuss why incorrect answers are wrong.

Close: Ask students to summarize why time lines are useful in studying history.

Differentiated Instruction Strategies

BL Ask students to explain how to determine the number of years between two events on a time line.

AL Have students choose two points on the time line and add items to show more detail from that time period.

ELL Have students explain one event on the time line.

R Reading Strategy

Identifying Ask: How did the Iroquois upset the balance of power between the French and British colonists? *(The British moved into the Ohio Valley and pressured the Iroquois for trading rights.)* **OL**

C Critical Thinking

Determining Cause and Effect Ask: How do you think the British might have reacted to the French colonists? *(They may have wanted to take strong action against the French.)* **OL**

INTERPRETING
POLITICAL CARTOONS

Answers

1. NY: New York; NJ: New Jersey; P: Pennsylvania; M: Maryland; V: Virginia; NC: North Carolina; SC: South Carolina; G: Georgia

2. The colonies must unite because they are harmless apart.

✔ **Reading Check** **Answer:** The British tried to control the Ohio River valley, which the French regarded as theirs.

Hands-On Chapter Project
Step 3

Primary Sources
INTERPRETING
POLITICAL CARTOONS

America's first political cartoon, drawn by Benjamin Franklin in 1754, promoted his Albany Plan of Union. It reflects a popular superstition that a dead snake would come back to life if the pieces were placed next to each other. Each section represents a colony. The New England colonies are combined as one section.

1. **Identifying** The abbreviation *NE* stands for "New England." What colonies do the other sections represent?

2. **Interpreting** What warning does Franklin's cartoon convey about the approaching war with France?

The confederacy initially included five nations—the Mohawk, Seneca, Cayuga, Onondaga, and Oneida. Other groups of Native Americans later joined or were conquered by the Iroquois. After the Tuscarora joined in 1722, the English referred to the confederacy as the Six Nations.

The Iroquois managed to remain independent by trading with both the British and the French. By skillfully playing the British and French against each other, the Iroquois dominated the Great Lakes area.

By the mid-1700s, however, the Iroquois came under greater pressure as the British moved into the Ohio Valley. Eventually, the leaders of the confederacy gave certain trading rights to the British and reluctantly became their allies. By taking this step, the Iroquois upset the balance of power between the French and British that had been so difficult to establish.

✔ **Reading Check** **Explaining** Why did hostilities between the French and British increase during the early 1740s?

American Colonists Take Action

Main Idea The American colonists prepared to defend themselves against the French and their Native American allies.

History and You Has anyone ever tried to take something that was yours? How did you react? Read to learn how the colonists responded to the growing conflict between France and Great Britain.

. . . .

A group of Virginians had plans for settling the Ohio valley. In the fall of 1753, Governor Robert Dinwiddie of Virginia sent a surveyor named **George Washington** into the Ohio country. Washington was 21 years old. His mission was to tell the French that they were trespassing on land that Great Britain claimed. He was to demand that they leave.

Washington delivered the message, but it did no good. "The French told me," Washington said later, "that it was their absolute **design**, or plan, to take possession of the Ohio, and by God they would do it."

Creating a Blog

Step 3: Writing a Political Blog Entry Students will work in groups to create a second blog entry for their characters.

Essential Question: Why did conflict arise in North America between France and Great Britain?

Directions Have student groups prepare a second blog entry. This time their characters will discuss the rising tension between France and Britain, their views on this problem, and ways in which it affects their daily life.

Discussing Ask each group whether its character would have been affected by the British-French conflict more or less than people in other colonies. In defending their answers, they should show an understanding of the conflict and give examples that reflect the profile they created of their individual.

(Chapter Project continued in Section 4)

Washington's First Command

In the spring of 1754, Dinwiddie made Washington a lieutenant colonel. He then sent Washington back to the Ohio country with a **militia**—a group of civilians trained to fight in emergencies—of 150 men. The militia had instructions to build a fort where the Allegheny and Monongahela Rivers meet to form the Ohio River—the site of present-day Pittsburgh. Washington and his troops arrived to find the French already building Fort Duquesne (doo•KAYN) on that spot.

Washington established a small post nearby, called Fort Necessity. Although greatly outnumbered, the troops of the inexperienced Washington attacked a French force. The French quickly forced Washington's soldiers to surrender. The British soldiers were later released, and they returned to Virginia. Washington's published account of the ordeal made him famous throughout the colonies and Europe. Washington had been defeated at Fort Necessity. The colonists, however, regarded him as a hero who struck the first blow against the French.

The Albany Plan of Union

Meanwhile, representatives from several colonies met in Albany, New York, in June 1754 to discuss the threat of war. They wanted to find a way to defend themselves against the French. They also hoped to persuade the Iroquois to support the British.

The representatives adopted Benjamin Franklin's **Albany Plan of Union** for a united colonial government. Franklin's plan called for "one general government" for eleven of the American colonies. Not a single colonial assembly, however, approved the plan. No colony was willing to give up any of its power. Disappointed, Franklin wrote: "Everybody cries, a Union is necessary; but when they come to the manner and form of the union, [they] are perfectly distracted."

The Albany meeting failed to unite the colonists in fighting the French. Soon, a full-scale war—the French and Indian War—erupted.

Reading Check **Describing** Describe Washington's expeditions into French territory.

W Writing Support

Persuasive Writing Have students write a letter to the editor of a colonial newspaper. Explain that they are to defend Washington as a hero. Ask them to use their knowledge of Washington's first command to support their views. **OL**

Reading Check **Answer:** The two expeditions were failures. The first ended when the French rejected his demands. The second ended in quick defeat because Washington's troops were inexperienced and outnumbered.

Assess

History ONLINE

Study Central™ provides summaries, interactive games, and online graphic organizers to help students review content.

Close

Identifying As a class, review the causes and effects of the growing conflict between France and Great Britain and whether it could have been prevented. **OL**

Section 3 Review

History ONLINE
Study Central™ To review this section, go to glencoe.com.

Vocabulary

1. Define each of the following terms by using it in a complete sentence: convert, Iroquois Confederacy, design, militia.

Main Ideas

2. **Explaining** How did the Iroquois remain independent from both the British and the French? How did that change?

3. **Identifying** What happened as a result of Washington's defeat at Fort Necessity?

Critical Thinking

4. **Analyzing** Why did Benjamin Franklin propose the Albany Plan of Union?

5. **Determining Cause and Effect** Use a diagram like the one below to identify the causes of the increasing rivalry between the French and the British in North America.

Cause ➝ British-French Rivalry
Cause ➝

6. **Creative Writing** Write a short newspaper article describing the battle at Fort Necessity.

Answer the Essential Question

7. Why did conflict arise in North America between France and Great Britain?

Answers

1. Students' sentences should use terms according to their definitions in the section and in the Glossary.
2. The Iroquois formed a confederacy of Native American nations. They traded with both the British and French. This independence changed when the Iroquois were pressured to give some trading rights to the British and became their allies.

3. The defeat raised Washington to hero status and also was greeted with support because it was the first blow against the French.
4. Franklin wanted to unite the colonists against the French.
5. Answers may include their competition for wealth and empire in different parts of the world, competition for fur trade, and the desire for control of Ohio Valley.

6. Students' articles should include relevant details.
7. France and Britain were competing worldwide for wealth and empire. This competition intensified in North America when the two nations struggled for control of the Ohio River valley, which the French considered their territory.

Section 4

Focus

Bellringer
Daily Test Practice Transparency 4–4

Reading Guide
Answers to Graphic:
To Britain: Canada, lands east of the Mississippi River; **To Spain:** Louisiana Territory, New Orleans

Section Spotlight Video

Have students watch the Section Spotlight Video "The French and Indian War" to learn about the struggle for control of North America.

Resource Manager

Section 4

Essential Question ◄
How did the outcome of the French and Indian War determine who controlled North America?

Reading Guide

Content Vocabulary
alliance (p. 109) speculator (p. 112)

Academic Vocabulary
prospect (p. 110)

Key People and Events
General Edward Braddock (p. 109)
Seven Years' War (p. 110)
William Pitt (p. 110)
Jeffrey Amherst (p. 111)
James Wolfe (p. 111)
Treaty of Paris (p. 111)
Pontiac's War (p. 112)
Proclamation of 1763 (p. 112)

Reading Strategy
Taking Notes As you read, use a diagram like the one below to list the lands that France lost when the Treaty of Paris of 1763 was signed.

French Lands → To Britain / To Spain

ILLINOIS STANDARDS
The American Journey

17.D Understand the historical significance of geography.
17.D.3a Explain how and why spatial patterns of settlement change over time.
18.B.3a Analyze how individuals and groups interact with and within institutions (e.g. educational, military).

The French and Indian War

American Diary

Commanded by General James Wolfe, about 1,800 British troops landed "on the North Shore [of Quebec] . . . an Hour before Day Break." To get in position to attack, the soldiers had to climb a steep cliff. Scrambling up the slope, the British soldiers ran into "a little Firing" from French guards. They continued to climb until they "gained the top of the [cliff]." By the time the sun rose over Quebec, British and French soldiers were prepared to battle on the Plains of Abraham outside the city.

—*from a letter by General George Townshend*

In 1759 British troops climbed steep cliffs in order to attack the French stronghold of Quebec.

R Reading Strategies	C Critical Thinking	D Differentiated Instruction	W Writing Support	S Skill Practice
Teacher Edition • Predicting, p. 109 • Anal. Prim. Sources, p. 110	**Teacher Edition** • Drawing Con., p. 110 • Deter. Cause & Effect, p. 112	**Teacher Edition** • Gifted & Talent., p. 110	**Teacher Edition** • Exposit. Writing, p. 109 • Descrip. Writing, p. 111	**Teacher Edition** • Using Geo. Skills, p. 111
Additional Resources • Guid. Read., URB p. 126 • Cont. Vocab., URB p. 101 • Ac. Vocab., URB p. 103 • Read. Ess., p. 43	**Additional Resources** • Quizzes and Tests, p. 34	**Additional Resources** • Reteach, URB p. 121 • School-to-Home Connect. Act., URB p. 119	**Additional Resources** • Link. Past & Pres., URB p. 117	**Additional Resources** • Daily Test Pract. Transp. 4-4

The British Take Action

Main Idea William Pitt helped turn the tide of the French and Indian War to the colonists' favor.

History and You Has a friend ever given you advice that you wished you had followed? Read to learn why one British general was defeated because of his failure to accept advice.

The Battle of Quebec, fought in 1759, was a deciding moment in the conflict between Britain and France. That conflict was known as the French and Indian War. This war raged in North America through the late 1750s and early 1760s. The French and Indian War was part of a larger struggle between the British and the French. That struggle involved, or included, control of world trade and power on the seas.

In 1754 the governor of Massachusetts made an announcement to the colonial assembly. He told them that the French were on the way to "making themselves masters of this Continent."

The French were building well-armed forts throughout the Great Lakes region and the Ohio River valley. Their network of **alliances**, or unions, with Native Americans allowed the French to control large areas of land, stretching from the St. Lawrence River in Canada all the way south to New Orleans. The French and their Native American allies seemed to be winning control of the American frontier. The final showdown was about to begin.

During the early stages of the French and Indian War, the British colonists fought the French and the Native Americans with little help from Britain. In 1754, however, the government in London decided to intervene in the conflict. It was alarmed by the new forts the French were building and by Washington's defeat at Fort Necessity. In the fall of 1754, Great Britain appointed **General Edward Braddock** commander in chief of the British forces in America. Braddock's mission was to drive the French forces from the Ohio Valley region.

Braddock Marches to Duquesne

In June 1755, Braddock started out from Virginia with about 1,400 red-coated British soldiers and a smaller force of blue-coated colonial militia. George Washington served as an aide to Braddock during the campaign.

Primary Source | **Two Heroes: Wolfe and Montcalm**

Known as outstanding commanders, both the British General Wolfe and the French General Montcalm lost their lives in the Battle of Quebec. During the fighting, Wolfe was shot in the chest and was "carried off wounded to the rear of the front line." He reportedly heard cries of "they [the French] run." Told that the French lines had broken, Wolfe died peacefully, satisfied that the British had won. Montcalm also was wounded in battle. As he lay in bed, Montcalm asked how long he had to live. When told "about a dozen hours," the French general said, "So much the better. . . . I am happy I shall not live to see the surrender of Quebec."

—from *Historical Journal of the Campaigns in North America*

General James Wolfe ▼

◄ Marquis de Montcalm

Critical Thinking

Making Generalizations Why are Wolfe and Montcalm considered heroes? What qualities do you think make a person a hero?

Leveled Activities

R Reading Strategy

Analyzing Primary Sources Ask: What is Washington saying about Braddock's strategy? *(that he was too slow)* Discuss the use of exaggeration in description. *(Mole hills and streams are small and do not interfere with an army's movements. Washington used them to make a point about Braddock.)* **OL**

D Differentiated Instruction

Gifted and Talented Have groups of students research the Seven Years' War. Each group will then create a magazine that includes articles and illustrations on causes of the war, countries involved, major battles, how the war ended, and the long-term effect on Europe. **AL**

C Critical Thinking

Drawing Conclusions Ask: Which side appears to have had an advantage early in the war? *(France)* What factors contributed to its success? *(British tactics were not suited to the American frontier. The French had lived there and had the aid of their Native American allies.)* **OL**

On the march to Fort Duquesne, Washington reported that Braddock:

R

PRIMARY SOURCE
"[halted] to level every mole hill, and to erect bridges over every brook, by which means we were four days in getting twelve miles."
—from *Life of Washington*

Washington told Braddock that his army's style of marching was not well suited to fighting on the frontier. Lined up in columns and rows wearing bright-colored uniforms, the troops became easy targets. Braddock ignored Washington's advice.

Native Americans and French troops ambushed the British on July 9. The British were confused and frightened. They could not even see their attackers, who were hidden in the forest and shooting at them from behind trees. Braddock was killed. Defeated, the British lost nearly 1,000 men. Washington led the survivors back to Virginia.

Britain Declares War on France

The fighting in America helped start a new war in Europe. This war was known as the **Seven Years' War.** After arranging an alliance with Prussia, Britain declared war on France in 1756. Prussia fought France and its allies in Europe. Britain fought France in the Caribbean, India, and North America.

D

Early in the war, French troops captured several British forts, and their Native American allies began raiding frontier farms from New York to Pennsylvania. They killed settlers, burned farmhouses and crops, and drove many families back toward the coast. French forces from Canada captured British forts at Lake Ontario and at Lake George.

C

Pitt Takes Charge

Great Britain's **prospects,** or chances for success, in America improved after **William Pitt** came to power. Pitt served as secretary of state and then as prime minister of Great Britain and was a great military planner.

The French and Indian War, 1754–1763
NATIONAL GEOGRAPHIC

A War for North America During the French and Indian War, Great Britain and France each fought for control of the North American continent. Native American leaders, who had long played the European rivals against each other, were forced to choose sides.

Hands-On Chapter Project
Step 4

Creating a Blog

Step 4: Blogging About the War Students will write a final blog entry in which their characters talk about the effects of the French and Indian War on the colonies.

Essential Question: How did the outcome of the French and Indian War determine who controlled North America?

Directions For the final blog entry, tell students to have their characters discuss an aspect of the French and Indian War that the characters might have personally witnessed or read about in a newspaper. Have the characters include images and descriptive terms to illustrate their observations or reports to heighten the emotional impact of the entry.

Explaining Ask each group to describe how the war might have affected its character. Talk about ways in which the impact would vary according to the person's location, age, race, and activities.

(Chapter Project continued on the Visual Summary page)

To avoid arguments from the colonists about the cost of the war, Pitt decided that Great Britain would pay for the war supplies—no matter the cost. Pitt ran up an enormous debt. After the war the British raised the colonists' taxes to help pay this debt. Pitt had only delayed the moment when the colonists had to pay their share of the bill.

Pitt wanted more than just a clear path to the Western territories. He also intended to conquer French Canada. He sent British troops to North America under commanders **Jeffrey Amherst** and **James Wolfe**. In 1758 a British assault recaptured the fortress at Louisbourg. That same year a group of New Englanders, led by British officers, captured Fort Frontenac at Lake Ontario. Still another British force took Fort Duquesne in Pennsylvania, which was renamed Fort Pitt.

✔ Reading Check **Describing** Why was William Pitt successful at managing the war for Britain?

"[Swords] and hatchets playing on every quarter with much . . . blood but our New Hampshire forces being fresh & courageous and the Enemy tired and much discouraged with the Defeat they met with, retreated and made their escape toward a Creek. . . . The day after ye battle three Frenchmen were taken up by the Guard of Fort Lymon who upon examination declared that their Army was entirely [defeated]."

—Colonist Robert Moses,
diary entry, 1755

◄ Mohawk chief Joseph Brant was an important British ally.

Map Skills

Region Which country controlled the territory around the Great Lakes?

Maps In MOtion See StudentWorks™ Plus or glencoe.com.

The Fall of New France

Main Idea The fall of Quebec and Montreal ended the French and Indian War in North America.

History and You What factors lead to success or failure in battle? Read to learn how the British defeated the French in the French and Indian War.

The British had so many victories in 1759 that people said the church bells of London wore thin with joyous ringing. The greatest victory of the war, though, took place in the heart of New France.

The Battle of Quebec

Quebec was the capital of New France and was located on top of a cliff overlooking the St. Lawrence River. Quebec was thought to be impossible to attack. In September 1759, British general James Wolfe's scouts spotted a poorly guarded path along the back of the cliff. During the night, Wolfe's soldiers overwhelmed the French guards and scrambled up the path. The British troops then surprised and defeated the French army on a field called the Plains of Abraham.

The Treaty of Paris

The fall of Quebec and General Amherst's capture of Montreal the following year brought an end to the fighting in North America. The **Treaty of Paris** of 1763 forced France to give Canada and most of its lands east of the Mississippi River to Great Britain. Great Britain also received Florida from France's ally, Spain. Spain acquired French lands west of the Mississippi River—the Louisiana Territory—as well as the port of New Orleans.

The Treaty of Paris marked the end of France as a power in North America. The continent was now divided between Great Britain and Spain.

✔ Reading Check **Determining Cause and Effect** What happened to France's territory as a result of its defeat in the war?

Growth of the Thirteen Colonies **Chapter 4** **111**

W Writing Support

Descriptive Writing Have students create the front page of a British newspaper after the Battle of Quebec. Articles should use descriptive terms to help readers visualize the battle and what its outcome meant for the British. OL

S Skill Practice

Using Geography Skills Have students use the map on the facing page as a guide and draw a map showing French and British territory after the Treaty of Paris. OL

The French and Indian War 1754–1763
 NATIONAL GEOGRAPHIC

Map Skills Answer
France

✔ Reading Check **Answer:** Pitt was an outstanding military planner.

✔ Reading Check **Answer:** France gave Canada and most of its lands east of the Mississippi River to Britain. Spain received the French lands west of the Mississippi River (the Louisiana Territory), as well as New Orleans.

Additional Support

Activity: Connecting Past and Present

Analyzing Visuals Information about wars can be communicated through drawings, paintings, sculptures, and photographs. Students will analyze what can be learned from these images. Have students research on the Internet to find paintings, drawings, or statues depicting the Battle of Quebec. **Ask:** What information about the Battle of Quebec or its participants does the artist convey? *(Information might include number of people involved, what is occurring, reactions of participants in the battle, and reactions of bystanders.)* Next, students will gather drawings and photographs of the war in Iraq. Suggest that they look on the Internet, in newspapers and magazines, and in books. **Ask:** What information about the war in Iraq or its participants does the artist or photographer convey? Have students participate in a panel discussion about what artists and photographers choose to convey about a war and the ways in which they transmit their ideas and information. OL

C Critical Thinking

Determining Cause and Effect

Ask: What did the British do to anger the Native Americans after the French and Indian War? *(They raised prices, refused to compensate the Native Americans for using their land, and moved onto their lands.)* **BL**

 Answer: The Proclamation of 1763 prevented further westward expansion and it also denied colonists land claims, so some people lost their investments.

Assess

History ONLINE

Study Central™ provides summaries, interactive games, and online graphic organizers to help students review content.

Close

Analyzing As a class, discuss the changes in territory and political control that took place as a result of the French and Indian War. **OL**

Section 4 Review

Trouble on the Frontier

Main Idea Continued conflict between Native Americans and British settlers led to the Proclamation of 1763.

History and You How would you feel if a CD you ordered and paid for never arrived? Read to learn why some land investors were furious about the Proclamation of 1763.

The French loss dealt a blow to the Native Americans of the Ohio River valley. They had lost their French allies and trading partners. The British raised the prices of their goods and, unlike the French, refused to pay the Native Americans for the use of their land. Worst of all, more British settlers began moving west onto Native American lands.

Pontiac's War

Pontiac, chief of an Ottawa village near Detroit, regarded British settlers as a threat to his people's way of life. Just as Benjamin Franklin tried to bring the colonies together with his Albany Plan, Pontiac wanted Native American groups to unite to fight the British.

In the spring of 1763, Pontiac gathered forces and captured the British fort at Detroit and other British outposts. That summer, Native Americans killed settlers along the Pennsylvania and Virginia frontiers during **Pontiac's War.** The war finally ended in August 1765 after the British defeated Pontiac's allies. Pontiac signed a peace treaty, and the British pardoned him.

The Proclamation of 1763

To prevent more fighting, Britain called a halt to the settlers' westward expansion. The **Proclamation of 1763** set the Appalachian Mountains as the temporary western boundary for the colonies. The proclamation especially angered those who owned shares in land companies. These **speculators,** or investors, had already bought land west of the mountains. They were furious that Britain ignored their land claims. More conflicts would soon arise between Britain and the colonists.

Reading Check **Examining** Why were some colonists angered by the Proclamation of 1763?

Section 4 Review

History ONLINE
Study Central™ To review this section, go to glencoe.com.

Vocabulary

1. Using complete sentences, define the following terms: involve, alliance, prospect, speculator.

Main Ideas

2. **Identifying** Before Pitt took charge, what advantages did the French have in North America?

3. **Summarizing** What effect did the Treaty of Paris have on France?

4. **Discussing** Why did Pontiac want the Native Americans to join forces?

Critical Thinking

5. **Identifying Problems and Solutions** Use a chart like the one below to list the problems of General Braddock's army. List actions he could have taken that might have brought about France's defeat.

Problem	Solution

6. **Creative Writing** Write a conversation between two French fur trappers that describes how they might have felt about the Treaty of Paris.

Answer the
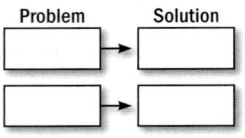
7. **Essential Question** How did the outcome of the French and Indian War determine who controlled North America?

Answers

1. Students should use terms according to their definitions in the section and in the Glossary.
2. The French had extensive forts; they also had alliances with the Native Americans and thus were able to control large areas.
3. France lost its power in North America, as it was forced to give its territory to Great Britain and Spain.
4. to fight the British threat to the Native Americans' way of life
5. Answers might include the following. Problem: inappropriate marching style for frontier; Solution: scatter troops and wear more camouflaged uniforms; Problem: not able to see their attackers in forests; Solution: avoid places where attackers could hide
6. Students should use historical detail and descriptive language.
7. In the Treaty of Paris, Britain and Spain acquired almost all of the land formerly controlled by France.

Visual Summary

Main Idea	Supporting Details
Geography affects the economic development of the American colonies.	• Regional geographic characteristics lead to: - subsistence farming and commerce in New England, - an economy based on cash crops and industry in the Middle Colonies, and - a farming economy dependent on slavery in the South.
A distinctly American culture begins to develop during the colonial period.	• Americans embrace religion, education, science and the arts, the family, and freedom of the press.
American ideas about government have their beginnings in both British law and colonial government.	• The colonists are inspired by the English Bill of Rights and by the English ideals of limited government and representative government.
Native Americans generally have better relations with French settlers than British settlers.	• The British want the support of Native Americans in fighting the French but seize Native American land without paying them for it. • The French receive more Native American help because they trade with them and do not try to take their land.
Worldwide competition between Britain and France for wealth and land leads to conflict in North America.	• Both Britain and France want control of North American resources. • Conflicts over fur trading in the Ohio River valley eventually lead to the French and Indian War.
The French and Indian War shifts the balance of power in North America.	• The Treaty of Paris divides North America between Britain and Spain. • Conflicts build between the settlers and the Native Americans, as well as between the colonists and Britain.

▲ Powder horn from the French and Indian War

◀ New England whalers

STUDY TO GO Study anywhere, anytime! Download quizzes and flash cards to your PDA from glencoe.com.

Predicting Ask: Based on your knowledge of colonial economics and politics, do you think any of the colonies would have been able to exist without the help of other colonies or England? *(Students' responses should reflect knowledge of colonial government and trade, as well as relationships with England, the other colonies, and other parts of the world.)* **OL**

Speculating Ask: How might your classroom experience be different if France had won the French and Indian War? *(Students might suggest they would be speaking French, studying more French history, seeing a different mix of ethnic groups at school, or eating different foods in the cafeteria.)* **OL**

Explaining Ask: If you had lived in the colonies, do you think you would have supported slavery? *(Students probably will automatically say no. Lead a class discussion to show that they may indeed have supported slavery, because geography, vocation, and religious beliefs affected attitudes and values.)* **OL**

Hands-On Chapter Project
Step 5: Wrap-Up

Creating a Blog

Step 5: Responding to Blogs Students will respond to the blog entries created by others in Steps 1 through 4.

Directions Have student groups trade the blogs they created in the earlier steps. In their small groups, have students write a response to one of the blog entries, keeping in the character of the colonists they created. Remind students that blog readers comment to rebut opinions, add helpful information, point out errors in information or make corrections, and to express admiration.

Synthesizing Ask: How did individual bloggers reflect the culture in which that individual lived? Lead a discussion about ways in which each blog reflects culture such as immigration, race relations, religious and educational ideas, ideas on the family, and interest in science and invention.

Answers and Analyses

Reviewing Main Ideas

1. B The text answers this question, which involves recall. Students might find a clue in the strong German cultural influence on Pennsylvania today. **17.C.3c**

2. C Great Britain did not directly rule charter colonies (choice A) but instead granted them rights and privileges and had the right to approve their governors. Heads of proprietary colonies were free to rule as they wished, so choice B also is incorrect. **14.B**

3. D The plan failed because no colony was willing to surrender any of its power. Choice B is incorrect because the lands west of the Appalachians were considered very valuable. Choice C is incorrect because there was no united colonial government. **14.C.3**

4. C Choice A is incorrect because the British did not pay the Native Americans to use their land. Choice D is wrong because the British raised, rather than lowered, prices. That leaves choices B and C. Students should have learned that the French lost their land after the French and Indian War, so they would have been less likely to trade with the Native Americans on land that was now British. **17.C.3a**

Short-Answer Question

5. The colony traded with the Native Americans and depended on them for protection—perhaps from other Native Americans or the French. **16.A.3b**

TEST-TAKING TIP

> For a short-answer or essay question, take time to review what you have written. Does it completely answer the question? Do you need to add any more information?

Reviewing Main Ideas

Directions: Choose the best answer for each of the following questions.

1. Most German immigrants settled in

  A Massachusetts.   **C** Virginia.

  B Pennsylvania.   **D** New York.

2. Great Britain *directly* ruled

  A charter colonies.

  B proprietary colonies.

  C royal colonies.

  D all of the above.

3. The Albany Plan of Union was not approved by the colonies because

  A it called for the colonies to declare their independence from Britain.

  B most colonists did not consider the lands west of the Appalachian Mountains to be valuable.

  C it diminished the strength of the united colonial government.

  D colonies were not willing to give up any of their power.

4. How did the British victory over the French affect the Native Americans of the Ohio River valley?

  A It helped them because the British, unlike the French, paid the Native Americans for the use of their land.

  B It hurt them because it resulted in a huge rush of French refugees into Native American lands.

  C It hurt them because they lost their French allies and trading partners.

  D It helped them because the British lowered the prices of their goods.

Short-Answer Question

Directions: Base your answer to question 5 on the excerpt below and on your knowledge of social studies.

> "The concerns of this country are so closely connected and interwoven with Indian affairs, and not only a great branch of our trade, but even the safety of this province, do so much depend upon our continuing in Friendship with the Indians, that I thought it highly necessary to gain all the knowledge I could of them."
>
> —South Carolina Governor James Glen, 1763

5. Why did Glen's colony have a relationship with Native Americans?

Review the Essential Questions

6. Essay Identify three events in the mid-1700s that were most responsible for changing (a) life in colonial America and (b) the influence of the British Empire in North America. Explain your choices.

To help you write your essay, review your answers to the Essential Questions in the section reviews and the chapter Foldables Study Organizer. Your essay should include:

- the economies of the three colonial regions;
- the growth of slavery in the colonies;
- the impact of the Great Awakening and the Enlightenment; and
- the causes and effects of the French and Indian War and the outcome of the conflict.

GO ON ➡

Review the Essential Questions

6. Students should use their answers to the Essential Questions and their Foldables to describe three events that changed life and the British influence in colonial America. Students should defend their choices with information on the colonial economy, slavery, the Great Awakening and Enlightenment, and the French and Indian War. **16.B.3a (US)**

History ONLINE
For additional test practice, use **Self-Check Quizzes**—Chapter 4 at glencoe.com.

Chapter 4 Assessment

Document-Based Questions

Directions: Analyze the documents and answer the short-answer questions that follow.

Document 1

This map illustrates trade and industry in the American colonies around 1750.

Colonial Trade and Industry, 1750

- Cattle and grain
- Tobacco
- Rice and indigo
- Fur and skins
- Fishing
- Lumber
- Shipbuilding
- Ironworks

ATLANTIC OCEAN

Boston, Newport, New York City, Philadelphia, Baltimore, Williamsburg, Richmond, Fayetteville, New Bern, Charles Town, Savannah

APPALACHIAN MTS.

0   200 kilometers
0   200 miles
Lambert Azimuthal Equal-Area projection

Source: *Historical Atlas of the United States*

7. Use the map to identify two differences between the economies of the New England and Middle Colonies and those of the Southern Colonies.

Document 2

"The Dutiful Child's Promises" is taken from the 1727 edition of *The New England Primer*.

> "I Will fear GOD, and honour the KING.
> I will honour my Father & Mother
> I will Obey my superiors.
> I will Submit to my Elders.
> I will Love my Friends.
> I will forgive my Enemies, and pray to God for them."

Source: *The New England Primer*

8. Identify at least two traits that reflect the culture of colonial America in the document.

Document 3

This is the introduction to the Albany Plan of Union (1754).

> "It is proposed that humble application be made for an act of Parliament of Great Britain, by virtue of which one general government may be formed in America, including all the said colonies, within and under which government each colony may retain its present constitution."

Source: Albany Plan of Union

9. Based on this document, what was the Albany Plan proposing? How would it have affected colonial constitutions?

Document 4

This is part of a 1755 British statement to the Acadians who were French settlers in Nova Scotia living in the region after Britain took control of it in 1710.

> "Your land and tenements [houses], cattle of all kinds and livestock of all sorts are forfeited [given over] to the Crown with all other effects saving your money and household goods and you are to be removed from this province."

Source: *Eyewitness to America*

10. What are the Acadians being told to do? Why would Britain have issued this statement?

11. Persuasive Writing Using the information from the four documents and your knowledge of social studies, write an essay in which you:
- compare and contrast cultural values of the colonial period with those of today; and
- explain how values from the colonial period influenced American values today.

10. The British are telling the Acadians to leave the area and give them everything except their household goods and money. The map in Section 4 shows that Acadia was disputed territory, so Britain may have been trying to exert control there in banishing French settlers. **16.A.3b**

11. Student essays should reflect an understanding of the four documents and how they relate to the chapter material. Essays might refer to values related to immigration, race relations, basic rights, religion, the role of family, education, freedom of the press, and treatment of Native Americans. Student essays should be organized in order to clearly compare colonial American values and values today. **18.A**

History ONLINE
Have students visit the Web site at glencoe.com to review Chapter 4 and take the Self-Check Quiz.

Need Extra Help?

Have students refer to the pages listed if they miss any of the questions.

Need Extra Help?

If you missed questions...	1	2	3	4	5	6	7	8	9	10	11
Go to page...	92	101	107	112	109–112	88–112	88–95	102–103	105	108–111	88–112

Document-Based Questions

7. The New England and the Middle Colonies had fishing, shipbuilding, and ironworks; the Southern Colonies had rice and indigo. **17.A.3b**

8. emphasis on religion and family, British rule **18.B.3a**

9. The plan wanted to unite all the colonies under one government. The document proposed that each colony keep its constitution. **14.F.3a**

Unit 2 Planning Guide

UNIT PACING CHART

	Unit 2	Chapter 5	Chapter 6	Chapter 7
Day 1	Unit Opener, Reading History	Chapter Opener, Section 1	Chapter Opener, Section 1	Chapter Opener, Section 1
Day 2		Section 2, America's Literature	Section 2, TIME Notebook	Section 2, You Decide
Day 3		Section 3	Section 3, Section 4	Section 3, Visual Summary
Day 4		Section 4, Visual Summary	Section 4, Geography & History, Visual Summary	Chapter Assessment
Day 5		Declaration of Independence	Chapter Assessment	Civics in Action: Constitution Handbook
Day 6		Chapter Assessment		Civics in Action: Constitution Handbook

 Teacher to Teacher

**Gayla Bailey
Russellville Junior
High School
Russellville, AR**

Writing a Children's Book Organize students into 10 groups. Assign each group one of the amendments from the Bill of Rights. Students will write and illustrate a children's book that describes the amendment. Each person in the group should be assigned a task. Tasks include planning the content to be presented, researching the amendment, organizing the layout, writing the narrative, and illustrating the narrative. Discuss as a class the type of characteristics that appeal to elementary students, such as bright colors and interesting narrative. Remind students to incorporate these ideas into their books. Provide time in class for students to complete their projects using construction paper and markers. Then have students present their books to the class. As a class, evaluate the books for their content accuracy, reading level, and designs.

Author Note

Dear American History Teacher,

The time period between the Revolutionary War and the adoption of the Constitution remains critical for understanding the rest of American history. The arguments and admonishments made by the leaders of that time continue to resonate, and our national government still operates under the Constitution they adopted.

The Declaration of Independence articulated our highest national ideals of human equality and freedom. The Constitution, however, is a less idealistic document. Its framers were trying to create a stronger national government but not one that was so strong that it tyrannized its people. The Framers achieved this by dividing the powers of government among three separate branches. James Madison explained their reasoning by noting "Ambition must be made to counteract ambition." As a result of this separation of power, presidents have struggled with Congress over the creation of domestic and foreign policies, and sometimes these policies are judged by the courts.

Despite the fact that citizens have the power to influence policy making by voting, public participation in the political process has been low. Often only half of those citizens eligible to vote cast ballots in presidential elections—and even fewer citizens vote in midterm congressional elections. Students will be eligible to vote at age 18, so they need to develop an awareness of national policies and a realization that they play a role in policy issues when they step into the polling booth.

The United States Constitution is remarkably compact—shorter and less detailed than most state constitutions. Only 27 amendments have been added to it since 1789—the first 10 almost before the ink on the original document was dry. Its brevity means that the Constitution implies as much it specifies, leaving it open to interpretation and disagreement about what its authors actually meant. Its potency, however, is no abstraction. The Constitution protects the basic rights and liberties of all American citizens. All of us must know these rights in order to preserve them for ourselves and future generations.

Donald A. Ritchie

Unit Objectives

After studying this unit, students will be able to:

- Explain how changes in British policies in North America caused dissatisfaction among colonists.
- Describe the outbreak of hostilities between Patriot and British forces.
- Discuss the preparation of and key points in the Declaration of Independence and the Constitution.

Introducing the Unit

Analyzing As students prepare to study the unit, ask them to think about who has power over them. **Ask:** How would you feel if your government made laws that affected you, but you did not have any say in the laws that were created? *(Students might note that they would oppose such a government and that they would want a system in which power was shared.)* Discuss with students that they will learn how the American colonists became angry with British policies, how escalating events led to the American Revolution, and how Americans took steps to build a new nation after the war. **OL**

Unit 2

Creating a Nation
1763–1790

Chapter 5
The Spirit of Independence
1763–1776

Chapter 6
The American Revolution
1776–1783

Chapter 7
A More Perfect Union
1777–1790

Seven-dollar bill, U.S., 1776

116

Activity: Why It Matters

Why Study the American Revolution? Tell students what they can expect to learn in the upcoming unit. **Ask:** Why would the colonists want to be independent of England? *(Students might answer that the colonists felt they were being treated unfairly and differently from persons who lived in England.)* As students read through the unit, have them write in their notebooks the reasons why Americans fought the Revolutionary War. **OL**

> "I only regret that I have but one life to lose for my country."
> —Nathan Hale

Washington Enforces the Surrender at Yorktown by Eugene Hess

117

Connect to Past Learning

Creating a Nation In the previous unit, students learned about how and why people came to North America and settled into colonies. In this unit, students will learn how the colonies united for a common cause—freedom from tyranny. Once independent, the colonies had to work at staying united while dealing with their differences. This resulted in the Constitution of the United States, which outlines our form of government.

More About the Image

Visual Literacy In 1861 Eugene Hess painted the "Surrender of Yorktown" as part of a series of 30 scenes of world history commissioned by Maximilian II, the King of Bavaria. Hess was apparently unfamiliar with the location and event because he painted a European fortress on a cliff in the background and a Native American on Washington's right. In addition, the other men around Washington are not wearing the correct uniforms. However, it is true that British General Cornwallis found himself surrounded by American and French troops in Yorktown in 1781. With no escape route and unable to receive reinforcements or supplies, Cornwallis surrendered after 11 days of fighting.

Why Making Connections Is Important

Making connections between material being learned and material that is already known is important in building one's knowledge. In honing this skill, students can begin to see the interconnectedness of seemingly dissimilar subjects and understand the importance of each to the others.

Learn It!

Ask students to name a few Constitutional amendments, and write them on the board (or simply write a few on the board before class). Ask students to consider what each amendment means historically, politically, or to them personally. (*For example, because of the Nineteenth Amendment, female citizens may vote in elections just as males may.*)

Ask students if they understood what was meant by the first amendment they saw written on the board, the first time they read it. What information did they already know that facilitated that understanding?

Use this discussion to show students how historical events have relevance to their present-day lives. **OL**

Practice It!

Students' answers will vary according to their personal knowledge. Based on the reading, students might make connections to the following facts:

1. To have value, paper money must be backed by gold and silver.
2. When you pay higher prices for the same items, you won't be able to afford as much as you did before.
3. When you pay higher prices for the same items, you won't have extra money available to buy as many other items. **OL**

Unit 2 Reading History

READING SKILL Making Connections

Learn It! When you make connections while reading, you connect the text with information you already know. This knowledge may be in math, science, geography, or any other subject area. You can also connect the text to personal experience.

Connect to Your Knowledge
What do you know about the Fourth of July?

1. The Fourth of July is the U.S. holiday celebrating the country's independence.
2. The Fourth of July is also known as Independence Day.
3. The term *freedom* also means "independence."

—from Chapter 6, p. 153

The Liberty Bell was rung every Fourth of July and for many public events until a crack appeared in about 1846. Today, the Liberty Bell is a symbol of freedom in the United States and throughout the world.

Practice It! Read the paragraph below. On another sheet of paper, write three facts from your own knowledge that connect to the text.

—from Chapter 6, p. 164

To pay for the war, the Congress and the states printed hundreds of millions of dollars' worth of paper money. The bills quickly lost their value, though. The amount of bills in circulation grew faster than the supply of gold and silver backing them. This led to **inflation,** which means that it took more and more money to buy the same amount of goods. The Congress stopped issuing the paper money because no one would use it.

Connect to Your Knowledge
What do you know about inflation and paying higher prices for the same items?

1. _____
_____
2. _____
_____
3. _____
_____

Reading Strategy Making Connections

Making Connections In learning to make connections, students can begin to understand why it is important to study history—how we can learn from events of the past and how those events have relevance to our lives today. Assign students a subsection in one of the chapters in this unit, and have them make a list of past issues or events and why they are important in their present-day lives. Have them organize the list into two simple columns: "Then" and "Now." **AL**

Academic Vocabulary Preview

Listed below are the academic vocabulary words and their definitions that you will come across as you study Unit 2. Practice It! will help you study the words and definitions.

Academic Vocabulary	Definition	**Practice It!**
Chapter 5 The Spirit of Independence		
prohibit (proh · HIH · buht) p. 123	to stop; disallow	*Identify the term from Chapter 5 that best completes the sentences.*
violate (VY · uh · LAYT) p. 124	to disturb or disregard	**1.** The British created a proclamation to _____ colonists from western settlement.
occupy (AH · kyuh · PY) p. 127	to control	
encounter (ihn · KOWN · tuhr) p. 127	an unexpected meeting	**2.** During wartime, enemy soldiers sometimes _____ homes and cities.
approach (uh · PROHCH) p. 135	to move toward	**3.** Many soldiers _____ to serve in their country's military.
volunteer (VAH · luhn · TIHR) p. 136	to willingly step forward	
debate (dih · BAYT) p. 141	a discussion of opposing opinions	
status (STA · tus) p. 142	a rank or position	
Chapter 6 The American Revolution		
transfer (TRANS · FUHR) p. 155	to move from one place to another	*Choose the word that best matches the meaning of each vocabulary term from chapter 6 listed below.*
previous (PREE · vee · uhs) p. 155	earlier; coming before	
aid (AYD) p. 161	to help	**4. transfer** **6. pursue**
issue (IH · shoo) p. 165	a point or matter of discussion	**a.** to move **a.** to continue
impact (IHM · PAKT) p. 171	an effect	**b.** to retain **b.** to retreat
sustain (suh · STAYN) p. 173	to suffer	**c.** to command **c.** to neglect
strategy (STRA · tuh · jee) p. 175	a plan of action	**5. issue** **7. strategy**
pursue (puhr · SOO) p. 177	to continue	**a.** a story **a.** a game
		b. a paper **b.** a plan
		c. a matter **c.** a work
Chapter 7 A More Perfect Union		
abandon (uh · BAN · duhn) p. 189	to give up	*Choose terms from Chapter 7 to complete the paragraph.*
clause (KLAWZ) p. 191	a condition added to a document	A legal document may have a _____ that adds a condition to the document's terms. Leaders may hold a _____ to create legal documents. At these times, leaders may vote to _____ a document if they want it changed.
convention (kuhn · VEHN · shuhn) p. 198	a formal meeting	
amend (uh · MEHND) p. 199	to alter; improve	
tradition (truh · DIH · shuhn) p. 205	cultural beliefs and practices	
reside (rih · ZYD) p. 208	to exist or live within	

Academic Vocabulary Preview

Give students some time in class to create flash cards of the unit definitions. The term should be written on one side of the card and the definition and phonetic spelling of the term on the other side.

Organize students into pairs, and ask them to quiz each other on the terms, using the flash cards. The student giving the answers should be able to say the term and give the definition. Ask students to switch places as they finish each chapter until they have made it through every chapter of the unit. **BL**

Practice It!

Answers
1. prohibit
2. occupied
3. volunteer
4. a
5. c
6. a
7. b

Completion: clause, convention, amend

 Reading Strategy   **Read to Write**

Personal Writing Making connections is often an unconscious mental process. Students will read certain information and understand it based on previous knowledge or experience but will not necessarily realize that the connections are happening. Ask students to review a subsection in the unit. Tell them to note the topic of the subsection as they read the first paragraph. Then have them write down the connections they make as they read the rest of the passage. Have volunteers read their papers aloud and describe how making connections to what they already knew helped them better understand the main idea. **OL**

Chapter Planning Guide

5

Levels (BL / OL / AL / ELL)		Resources	Chapter Opener	Section 1	Section 2	Section 3	Section 4	Chapter Assess
FOCUS								
BL OL AL ELL	🖳	**Daily Test Practice Transparencies**		5–1	5–2	5–3	5–4	
TEACH								
OL AL	📁	**Geography and History Activity, URB**			p. 31			
BL OL ELL	📁	**Time Line Skills Activity, URB**			p. 34			
BL OL AL ELL	📁	**Writing Skills Activity, URB**		p. 23				
BL OL AL ELL	📁	**Content Vocabulary Activity, URB**		p. 17	p. 17	p. 17	p. 17	
BL OL AL ELL	📁	**Academic Vocabulary Activity, URB**		p. 19	p. 19	p. 19	p. 19	
BL ELL	📁	**Reading Skills Activity, URB**					p. 7	
BL OL ELL	📁	**Social Studies Skills Activity, URB**				p. 25		
BL OL AL ELL	📁	**Differentiated Instruction Activity, URB**			p. 27			
BL OL AL ELL	📁	**Critical Thinking Skills Activity, URB**					p. 29	
BL OL AL ELL	📁	**Linking Past and Present Activity, URB**					p. 33	
OL AL	📁	**Primary Source Readings, URB**					p. 21	
BL OL AL ELL	📁	**School-to-Home Connection Activity, URB**		p. 35	p. 35	p. 35	p. 35	
BL OL ELL	📁	**Guided Reading Activity, URB***		p. 39	p. 40	p. 41	p. 42	
AL	📁	**Enrichment Activity, URB**			p. 11			
BL OL ELL	📁	**Reading Essentials and Note-Taking Guide***		p. 46	p. 49	p. 52	p. 55	
BL OL AL ELL	🖳	**Lesson Transparencies**				5A	5B, 5C	
OL	📁	**American Biographies**			p. 6	pp. 11, 12	p. 7	
BL OL AL ELL	📁	**Outline Map Resource Book**	p. 9					
OL AL	🖳	**American Art and Architecture Transparencies, Strategies, and Activities**					5, 8	

Note: Please refer to the *Unit Resource Book: Creating a Nation* for this chapter's URB materials.

* Also available in Spanish

Levels					Resources	Chapter Opener	Section 1	Section 2	Section 3	Section 4	Chapter Assess
TEACH *(continued)*											
BL	OL	AL	ELL		**NGS US Desk Map**		✓	✓	✓	✓	
BL	OL	AL	ELL		**American Literature Library**		✓	✓	✓	✓	
BL	OL	AL	ELL		**Writer's Guidebook**		✓	✓	✓	✓	
	OL	AL			**American History Primary Source Document Library CD-ROM**		✓	✓	✓	✓	✓
BL	OL	AL	ELL		**American Music Hits Through History**	✓	✓	✓	✓	✓	
BL	OL	AL	ELL		**StudentWorks™ Plus CD**	✓	✓	✓	✓	✓	✓
	OL	AL			**Section Spotlight Videos**		✓	✓	✓	✓	
BL	OL	AL	ELL		**Writing Process Transparencies**		✓	✓	✓	✓	✓
BL	OL	AL	ELL		**Presentation Plus! With MindJogger CheckPoint CD**	✓	✓	✓	✓	✓	✓
ASSESS											
BL	OL	AL	ELL		**Quizzes and Tests**		p. 41	p. 42	p. 43	p. 44	pp. 45, 47, 49
BL	OL	AL	ELL		**Authentic Assessment With Rubrics**				p. 5		
BL	OL	AL	ELL		**Standardized Test Practice**						p. 9
BL	OL	AL	ELL		*ExamView®* **Assessment Suite CD-ROM***		5–1	5–2	5–3	5–4	Ch. 5
CLOSE											
BL			ELL		**Reteaching Activity, URB***		p. 37	p. 37	p. 37	p. 37	p. 37
BL	OL		ELL		**Reading and Study Skills Foldables Activity**	p. 58	p. 58	p. 58	p. 58	p. 58	p. 58
BL	OL	AL	ELL		*The American Journey* **in Graphic Novel**				p. 31		
BL			ELL		**Reading Strategies and Activities for the Social Studies Classroom**		✓	✓	✓	✓	
BL	OL	AL	ELL		**Graphic Organizer Transparencies & Strategies**		✓	✓	✓	✓	

Plus
TeacherWorks
All-In-One Planner and Resource Center

- Interactive Lesson Planner
- Interactive Teacher Edition
- Fully editable blackline masters
- Section Spotlight Videos Launch

- Differentiated Lesson Plans
- Printable reports of daily assignments
- Standards Tracking System

Professional Development Resources

- Strategies for Success
- Building Academic Vocabulary
- Success With English Learners DVD
- Differentiated Instruction Strategies DVD
- Teaching Literacy Strategies in Social Studies DVD
- Assessment DVD
- Standards-Based Instruction DVD

5

Using the Primary Source Document Library

Searching by Chronology

Technology Product

Glencoe's *American History Primary Source Document Library* CD-ROM includes more than 200 primary source documents. The documents provide access to sources and encourage students to think critically about history. The *American History Primary Source Document Library* allows you to

- select chronological periods from Prehistory through Modern America;
- choose from selected documents within each time period to read and/or listen to;
- utilize **Teaching Strategies, Questions/Answers,** and **Blackline Masters** resources in conjunction with the primary source document to maximize student learning.

Steps

- Launch the **Primary Source Document Library CD-ROM,** choose the **Chronology** button, and select a topic.
- Select from the list of documents available. An **audio clip** icon indicates documents that include audio.
- Review the **Document Overview** and **Guided Reading Questions**.
- Click on the **User's Guide and Teaching Strategies** link. Select **To the Teacher** and **Teaching Strategies** for teaching suggestions and procedures.
- Select **Questions/Activities** and **Blackline Masters** for worksheets and organizers.

History ONLINE at glencoe.com

	Student	Teacher	Parent
Media Center			
• Student Edition Audio	●		
• Spanish Summaries	●		
• Section Spotlight Videos	●	●	
Social Studies Online Learning Center			
Classroom Tools			
• Multi-Language Glossaries	●	●	●
• Teaching Today		●	
• TIME Current Events	●	●	●
• Beyond the Textbook	●	●	
***The American Journey* Online Learning Center**			
• Study-to-Go™	●	●	●
• Study Central™	●	●	●
• Chapter Overview	●	●	
• Concepts in Motion	●	●	
• ePuzzles and Games	●	●	
• Literature Connections	●	●	
• Online Student Edition	●	●	●
• Self-Check Quizzes	●	●	●
• Student Web Activities	●	●	
• Vocabulary eFlashcards	●	●	
• Web Activity Lesson Plans	●	●	●
• Vocabulary PuzzleMaker	●	●	●

READING SUPPORT FROM

JAMESTOWN EDUCATION

- **Timed Readings Plus in Social Studies** helps students increase their reading rate and fluency while maintaining comprehension. The 400-word passages are similar to those found on state and national assessments.

- **Reading in the Content Area: Social Studies** concentrates on six essential reading skills that help students better comprehend what they read. The book includes 75 high-interest nonfiction passages written at increasing levels of difficulty.

- **Reading Social Studies** includes strategic reading instruction and vocabulary support in Social Studies content for ELLs and native speakers of English.

- **Content Vocabulary Workout** (Grades 6–8) accelerates reading comprehension through focused vocabulary development. Social Studies content vocabulary comes from the glossaries of Glencoe's Middle School Social Studies texts.

www.jamestowneducation.com

NATIONAL GEOGRAPHIC

Index to National Geographic Magazine:

The following article relates to this chapter:

- *"Boston's North Enders,"* Erla Zwingle, October 2000.

National Geographic Society Products

To order the following, call National Geographic at 1-800-368-2728:

National Geographic Atlas of the World (Book)

Access National Geographic's new dynamic MapMachine Web site and other geography resources at:

www.nationalgeographic.com

www.nationalgeographic.com/mapmachine

Reading List Generator CD-ROM

GLENCOE BOOKLINK 3

Use this database to search more than 30,000 titles to create a customized reading list for your students.

- Reading lists can be organized by students' reading level, author, genre, theme, or area of interest.
- The database provides Degrees of Reading Power™ (DRP) and Lexile™ readability scores for all selections.
- A brief summary of each selection is included.

Leveled reading suggestions for this chapter:

For students at a Grade 6 reading level:
- *The Secret of Sarah Revere,* by Ann Rinaldi

For students at a Grade 7 reading level:
- *Patsy and the Declaration,* by Elizabeth Massie

For students at a Grade 8 reading level:
- *Early Thunder,* by Jean Fritz
- *Redcoat in Boston,* by Ann Finlayson

For students at a Grade 9 reading level:
- *Guns for General Washington,* by Seymour Reit
- *Samuel Adams,* by Veda Boyd Jones

For students at a Grade 10 reading level:
- *The Battles of Lexington and Concord,* by Judith Peacock

The following videotape programs are available from Glencoe as supplements to the chapter:

- **Patrick Henry: Voice of Liberty** (ISBN 1-56-501645-9)
- **John and Abigail Adams: Love & Liberty** (ISBN 0-76-704991-8)
- **Independence Day: History of July 4th** (ISBN 0-76-700359-4)

To order, call Glencoe at 1-800-334-7344. To find classroom resources to accompany many of these videos, check the following home pages:

A&E Television: www.aetv.com

The History Channel: www.history.com

Chapter Objectives

After studying this chapter, students will be able to:

- Describe how the British government angered the American colonists after the French and Indian War.
- Explain how the colonists reacted to British policies.
- Discuss how the American colonists and the British soldiers came to open warfare at Lexington and Concord.
- Discuss why the Americans chose to declare independence from Britain.

Motivating Activity

Making Connections Students will learn how the American colonists moved toward independence from Britain. Direct students' attention to the image on this page. **Ask:** What is happening in this scene? *(A young man, presumably a colonist by his clothing, carries a gun as he says good-bye to his family. It appears that he is going off to fight.)* How can you relate this scene to family life today? *(Answers will vary, but students may stress the timelessness of young people going off to war and the resulting mixed emotions of pride, determination, sadness, and fear.)*

Previewing the Essential Questions

As you begin teaching each section, use these questions and activities to help students focus on the Essential Questions.

Chapter

5

The Spirit of Independence
1763–1776

Colonial militia members, known as minutemen, left their homes on short notice to fight the British.

British tax stamp ▶

United States

★ 1763
Treaty of Paris signed

★ 1765
Colonists protest Stamp Act

★ 1770
British troops clash with civilians in Boston Massacre

1763   1766   1769

World

★ 1764
Mozart writes first symphony at age eight

★ 1770
Industrial Revolution begins in England

120   Chapter 5

Section 1

Taxation Without Representation
Ask: Why would the British government pass laws that the American colonists considered unfair? *(Britain was more interested in protecting its interests in the colonies than in pleasing the colonists.)* Point out to students that in Section 1 they will learn why the British passed laws and prohibitions that angered the colonists. **OL**

Section 2

Building Colonial Unity Ask: How do you think the colonists will react to the British actions? *(Colonists' anger built up as the British continued to pass unpopular laws. Eventually, the colonists came to consider the British actions to be "intolerable.")* Explain to students that Section 2 discusses how the American colonists reacted to British laws that affected them. **OL**

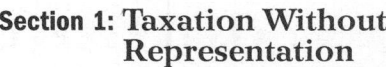

Section 1: Taxation Without Representation

Essential Question Following the French and Indian War, how did the British government anger the American colonists?

Section 2: Building Colonial Unity

Essential Question How did colonists react to British policies?

Section 3: A Call to Arms

Essential Question What brought about the clash between American colonists and British soldiers at Lexington and Concord?

Section 4: Moving Toward Independence

Essential Question Why did the American colonies choose to declare independence?

History ONLINE
Chapter Overview Visit glencoe.com and click on **Chapter 5—Chapter Overviews** to preview chapter information.

FOLDABLES
Study Organizer

Organizing Information
Make this four-tab Foldable to help you learn about the events that led to the American Revolution.

Step 1 Fold the top and bottom of a piece of paper into the middle.

Step 2 Fold the paper in half from side to side.

Step 3 Open and cut along the inside fold lines to form four tabs.

Step 4 Label the tabs as shown.

Reading and Writing
As you read the chapter, take notes about each section under the appropriate head. Use your Foldable to help you write a summary for each section.

| Taxation Without Representation | Building Colonial Unity |
| A Call to Arms | Moving Toward Independence |

Liberty Bell ▶

Statue of Minuteman, Concord, MA ▶

▲ Tea leaves from the Boston Tea Party

1773 Patriots carry out Boston Tea Party

1774 First Continental Congress meets

1775 Battles fought at Lexington and Concord

1772

1775

1772 Poland partitioned among Russia, Prussia, and Austria

1774 Louis XVI becomes king of France

◀ Chair owned by Louis XVI

Introducing Chapter 5

Time Line Activity

If you have not already done so, have students review the time line. **Ask:** What years are covered in this chapter? *(1763–1775)* Have students note the date of 1772 and the partitioning of Poland among Russia, Prussia, and Austria. **Ask:** What might American colonists have thought about this event? *(The colonists might have empathized with the Polish people who, like the Americans, were subject to the decisions of others outside their own country.)*

FOLDABLES
Study Organizer
Dinah Zike's Foldables

Purpose This Foldable helps students organize their notes about the issues and conflicts between Britain and the American colonies before independence. The completed Foldable will help them prepare for assessment.

More Foldables activities for this chapter can be found in *Dinah Zike's Reading and Study Skills Foldables.*

History ONLINE
Introduce students to chapter content and key terms by having them access the **Chapter Overview** at glencoe.com.

Section 3

A Call to Arms Ask: What can happen when people work together to achieve the same goal? *(People who join a common cause, such as the colonists' fight for independence, are more effective at achieving their goal.)* Tell students that Section 3 will explore the ways in which the colonists came together to fight the British in the first battles for American independence. **OL**

Section 4

Moving Toward Independence Ask: How do you think the members of the Second Continental Congress felt when they signed the Declaration of Independence? *(Answers may include pride that they had taken this important step, concern over what might happen next, defiance against Britain's likely reaction, and satisfaction in what the delegates had achieved together.)* **OL**

Taxation Without Representation

Focus

Bellringer
Daily Test Practice Transparency 5–1

Reading Guide
Answers to Graphic:
Policy: Sugar Act
View: Writs of assistance violated colonists' security in their homes, and new trial procedures violated their right to be considered "innocent until proven guilty."
Policy: Stamp Act
View: Parliament had no right to tax colonists directly or without their consent.
Policy: Townshend Acts
View: Only colonial representatives had the right to tax the colonists.

Section Spotlight Video

To learn more about the Stamp Act, have students watch the Section Spotlight Video "Taxation Without Representation."

Resource Manager

Essential Question
Following the French and Indian War, how did the British government anger the American colonists?

Reading Guide

Content Vocabulary

revenue (p. 123)
resolution (p. 125)
boycott (p. 125)
repeal (p. 125)

writs of assistance (p. 123)
effigy (p. 125)
nonimportation (p. 125)

Academic Vocabulary

prohibit (p. 123)   violate (p. 124)

Key People and Events
Stamp Act (p. 124)
Patrick Henry (p. 125)
Samuel Adams (p. 125)

Reading Strategy
Taking Notes As you read, identify British policies that affected the colonists. Then describe the colonists' view of each policy.

British Policy	Colonists' View

ILLINOIS STANDARDS
The American Journey

14.C.3 Compare historical issues involving rights, roles and status of individuals in relation to municipalities, states and the nation.

14.F.3a Analyze historical influences on the development of political ideas and practices as enumerated in the Declaration of Independence, the United States Constitution, the Bill of Rights and the Illinois Constitution.

15.E.3a Identify the types of taxes levied by differing levels of governments (e.g., income tax, sales tax, property tax).

American Diary

In London, Benjamin Franklin stated the American view on British taxes: "They will oppose it to the last. They do not consider it as at all necessary for you to raise money . . . by your taxes. . . . America has been greatly misrepresented . . . [as] refusing to bear any part of [the war's] expense. The Colonies . . . paid and clothed near 25,000 men during the last war, a number equal to [that of] Britain."
—in an interview before the House of Commons, 1766

R Reading Strategies	C Critical Thinking	D Differentiated Instruction	W Writing Support	S Skill Practice
Teacher Edition • Inferring, p. 123 **Additional Resources** • Guid. Read., URB p. 39 • Content Vocab., URB p. 17 • Academic Vocab., URB p. 19 • Read. Ess., p. 46	**Teacher Edition** • Identify. Central Iss., p. 124 **Additional Resources** • Quizzes and Tests, p. 41	**Teacher Edition** • Visual, p. 125 **Additional Resources** • Reteaching Act., URB p. 37 • School-to-Home, URB p. 35	**Teacher Edition** • Persuasive Writing, p. 124 **Additional Resources** • Writ. Skills, URB p. 23	**Teacher Edition** • Using Geo. Skills, p. 123 **Additional Resources** • Daily Test Pract. Transp. 5-1

Relations With Britain

Main Idea After the French and Indian War, Great Britain passed laws to protect British interests in the colonies.

History and You How do you feel when someone treats you unfairly? Read to learn how the colonists felt about British laws that affected them.

With victory in the French and Indian War, the British gained control of a vast territory in North America. However, they faced the challenge of protecting their interests in the colonies and new territory. With the Proclamation of 1763, the British government set up new provinces. The proclamation also **prohibited,** or prevented, colonists from moving west of the Appalachian Mountains.

Limiting western settlement provided several advantages for Britain. It allowed the British government to control westward movement and to avoid conflict with Native Americans. Also, keeping colonists near the East Coast ensured a market for British goods in the coastal cities, where trade flourished.

Finally, closing western settlement allowed Britain to control the fur trade in the frontier. Britain planned to station 10,000 troops in the colonies to protect these interests.

Britain needed new **revenue,** or incoming money, to pay troop expenses. Also, the French and Indian War left Britain with a huge debt. The king and Parliament believed that the colonists should pay part of the cost, so they issued new taxes on the colonies and began to enforce existing taxes more strictly.

Britain's Trade Laws

In 1763 George Grenville, prime minister of Britain, decided to act against smuggling. When the colonists smuggled goods to avoid taxes, Britain lost revenue.

Grenville knew that American juries often found smugglers innocent. He convinced Parliament to pass a law allowing smugglers to be sent to vice-admiralty courts, which were run by officers and did not have juries. In 1767 Parliament authorized **writs of assistance.** These legal documents allowed customs officers to enter any location to search for smuggled goods.

The Sugar Act

In 1764 Parliament passed the Sugar Act. This act lowered the tax on imported molasses. Grenville hoped the lower tax would convince colonists to pay the tax instead of smuggling. The act also let officers seize goods from smugglers without going to court.

During the colonial period, the British built a number of forts throughout their American colonies.

By the Numbers — Pounds and Shillings

Britain's Per-Capita War Debt, 1765

Share of the debt per person:

Britain: £ £ £ £ £ £ £ £ £ £
£ £ £ £ £ £ £ £

Colonies: S S S S S S S S S
S S S S S S S S

£ = 1 British pound   S = 1 British shilling

1 Pound (£) = 20 Shillings

Source: Don Cook. *The Long Fuse: How England Lost the American Colonies, 1760–1785.*

Britain's National Debt At the end of the French and Indian War, Great Britain's national debt soared to more than £140 million. British citizens paid far more on the debt per person than their counterparts in the colonies.

Critical Thinking

Analyzing How much more per-capita debt did residents of Britain have compared to residents of the colonies?

Declaring Independence

Step 1: Identifying Grievances Small groups of students will protest actions of the British government.

Essential Question: Following the French and Indian War, how did the British government anger the American colonists?

Directions Organize students into five groups. Each group should develop a campaign to protest the Proclamation of 1763, writs of assistance, the Sugar Act, the Stamp Act, or the Townshend Acts. Students should research the action and the colonists' reaction. Then groups should create two protests against the British action, only one of which may be written (for example, a group member could give a speech in addition to writing a pamphlet). Have students present their work to the class.

Teach

R Reading Strategy

Inferring Ask: How do you think the colonists felt about the Proclamation of 1763? Explain your answer. *(Answers may include that settlers resented the Proclamation because it prohibited them from moving west or required them to leave lands they had already claimed west of the line.)* **OL**

S Skill Practice

Using Geography Skills Have students look at the map of the Proclamation of 1763 on the next page. **Ask:** What geographic feature marked the Proclamation line? *(the Appalachian Mountains)* In what area of North America west of the Proclamation line were Native American rights not protected by the Proclamation? *(the area held by the Spanish west of the Mississippi River)* **BL**

By the Numbers

Critical Thinking Answer
16 pounds, 2 shillings

Hands-On Chapter Project
Step 1

Identifying Points of View Each group should describe how colonists felt about the British action. **Ask:** How might colonists react if their protests are ignored? *(Anger and resentment could possibly lead to a violent response.)* Tell students they will investigate this response in the next step. **OL**

(Chapter Project continued in Section 2)

W Writing Support

Persuasive Writing Have students write a letter to the editor of a colonial newspaper protesting the Sugar Act. Ask volunteers to read their letters to the class. Discuss the reasons colonists opposed the Sugar Act. **AL**

C Critical Thinking

Identifying Central Issues Ask: Why did colonists object to the Stamp Act? *(Colonists opposed Parliament levying taxes on printed materials in the colonies, which they called a direct tax. They also believed they should not be taxed without their consent.)* **BL**

The Proclamation of 1763 ☐ NATIONAL GEOGRAPHIC

Critical Thinking Answer

It prevented colonists from settling west of the Proclamation line and taking Native American lands.

✔ **Reading Check Answer:** American juries often found smugglers innocent. Vice-admiralty courts were run by officers and did not have juries.

Differentiated Instruction

The Proclamation of 1763 ☐ NATIONAL GEOGRAPHIC

"I can never look upon that Proclamation in any other light . . . than as a temporary expedient [solution] to quiet the Minds of the Indians and must fall . . . when those Indians are consenting to our Occupying the Lands."
—George Washington, 1767

Provisions of the Proclamation of 1763

- Created governments for the new North American territories won from France as a result of the French and Indian War
- Sought to prevent future conflicts with Native Americans
- Protected Native Americans by reserving the British Crown's right to enter into all land negotiations with them
- Forbade settlement of lands west of the Proclamation line
- Required settlers who had already moved west of the Proclamation line to move east of it
- Stated that the Native Americans were to govern the Proclamation territory under their own laws

Critical Thinking

Analyzing How did the Proclamation of 1763 attempt to protect Native American rights and lands?

The Sugar Act and the new laws to control smuggling angered colonists. They believed these British actions **violated,** or interfered with, their rights as English citizens. Writs of assistance violated their right to be secure in their homes. Vice-admiralty courts violated their right to a jury trial. Also, in vice-admiralty courts, defendants had to prove their innocence. This contradicted a British law stating "innocent until proved guilty."

These measures alarmed the colonists. James Otis, a lawyer in Boston, argued:

PRIMARY SOURCE

"No parts of [England's colonies] . . . can be taxed without their consent . . . every part has a right to be represented."

—from *The Rights of the British Colonies*

✔ **Reading Check Explaining** Why did George Grenville want smugglers sent to vice-admiralty courts?

New Taxes

Main Idea As the British government passed new tax laws, resistance by the colonists grew.

History and You Suppose everyone in your community refused to buy from a certain store. How would this decision affect the store? Read to learn how boycotts by the colonists affected British merchants.

In 1765 Parliament passed the **Stamp Act.** This law placed a tax on almost all printed material, including newspapers, wills, and playing cards. All printed material had to have a stamp. British officials applied the stamp after the tax was paid.

Opposition to the Stamp Act centered on two points. Parliament had interfered in colonial affairs by taxing the colonies directly. In addition, it taxed the colonists without their consent.

Presenting Evidence to Support Arguments

Objective: To learn how to present evidence to support an argument.

Focus: Ask students what strategies they use when trying to persuade others to support a cause.

Teach: Have students write compositions to persuade others to join the Sons of Liberty.

Assess: Tell students to complete the self-assessment checklist.

Close: Discuss ways in which students could improve their compositions.

Differentiated Instruction Strategies

BL Ask students to read their compositions to each other and complete their checklists.

AL Have students review editorials from local newspapers and identify examples of effective persuasive arguments.

ELL Ask students to define the terms "evidence," "persuade," "support," and "argument."

Writing Skills Activity, URB p. 23

Protesting the Stamp Act

A member of the Virginia House of Burgesses, **Patrick Henry,** persuaded the burgesses to take action against the Stamp Act. The Virginia assembly passed a **resolution**—a formal expression of opinion—declaring it had "the only and sole exclusive right and power to lay taxes" on its citizens.

In Boston **Samuel Adams** helped start an organization called the Sons of Liberty to protest the Stamp Act. People in other cities also organized the Sons of Liberty groups. Protesters burned **effigies**—rag figures—representing tax collectors and destroyed houses belonging to royal officials.

In October delegates from nine colonies met in New York at the Stamp Act Congress. They drafted a petition to the king and Parliament declaring that the colonies could not be taxed except by their own assemblies.

In colonial cities, people refused to use the stamps. They urged merchants to **boycott**—refuse to buy—British and European goods in protest. Thousands of merchants signed **nonimportation** agreements—pledges not to buy or use goods imported from Britain. As the boycott spread, British merchants lost so much business that they begged Parliament to **repeal,** or cancel, the Stamp Act. In March 1766, Parliament repealed the law. However, on the same day, it passed the Declaratory Act. This law stated that Parliament had the right to tax and make decisions for the British colonies "in all cases."

The Townshend Acts

In 1767 Parliament passed a set of laws that came to be known as the Townshend Acts. British leaders knew from the Stamp Act that the colonists would resist internal taxes—those paid inside the colonies. As a result, the new taxes would apply only to imported goods such as glass, tea, and paper, with the tax being paid at the port of entry.

By this time, *any* British taxes angered the colonists. They believed that only their own representatives had the right to tax them. The colonists organized another boycott.

Throughout the colonies, women formed groups, sometimes called the Daughters of Liberty. They urged Americans to wear homemade fabrics and produce other goods they needed rather than buy British goods.

✔ **Reading Check** **Describing** How did the Sons of Liberty attempt to influence British policy?

D Differentiated Instruction

Visual Have students create a flyer that might have been posted in colonial cities to urge residents to boycott British goods in response to the Stamp Act. Display the flyers around the classroom. **OL**

✔ **Reading Check** **Answer:** The Sons of Liberty tried to frighten tax collectors and royal officials into not collecting the taxes and enforcing the law. They burned effigies that represented tax collectors and destroyed the houses of royal officials.

Assess

History ONLINE

Study Central™ provides summaries, interactive games, and online graphic organizers to help students review content.

Close

Analyzing As a class, discuss how the events of the 1770s unified the colonists in their opposition to the British. **OL**

Section ⭐ **Review**

Section 1 Review

History ONLINE
Study Central™ To review this section, go to glencoe.com.

Vocabulary

1. Use each of these terms in a sentence that will help explain its meaning: prohibit, revenue, writs of assistance, violate, resolution, effigy, boycott, nonimportation, repeal.

Main Ideas

2. Specifying What advantages did the British gain by limiting westward settlement?

3. Explaining Why did some colonists smuggle goods?

4. Identifying Opposition to the Stamp Act centered on what two main points?

Critical Thinking

5. Contrasting How did the British and the colonists differ on the issue of taxes?

6. Determining Cause and Effect Describe the responses of the colonists to the Stamp Act and the result. Use a diagram like the one below.

Stamp Act → Responses → Result

7. Persuasive Writing Write a letter to the editor of a colonial newspaper. Your goal is to try to persuade fellow colonists to boycott British goods.

Answer the Essential Question

8. Following the French and Indian War, how did the British government anger the American colonists?

The Spirit of Independence **Chapter 5** **125**

Answers

1. Sentences should use vocabulary words according to their definitions in the section and Glossary.

2. Limiting westward settlement allowed the British government to control westward movement and to avoid conflict with Native Americans; keeping colonists near the East Coast ensured a market for British goods in coastal cities; closing western settlement allowed Britain to control the frontier's fur trade.

3. to avoid paying taxes on them

4. (1) Parliament interfered in colonial affairs by taxing the colonists directly; (2) Britain taxed the colonists without their consent.

5. Parliament believed that the colonists should be taxed to pay their part of the cost of Britain's huge debt. The colonists claimed that they should not be taxed by Parliament directly or be taxed only with their consent.

6. Stamp Act > Responses: passage of resolutions against the Act; formation of Sons of Liberty; Stamp Act Congress petition; boycotts of British goods; nonimportation

agreements > Result: repeal of Stamp Act but passage of Declaratory Act by Parliament

7. Letters should include reasons for boycotting British goods.

8. Parliament believed the colonists should pay for some of Britain's War debt. Parliament issued the Sugar Act, Stamp Act, and Townshend Acts, which increased the colonists' anger. They issued boycotts and nonimportation agreements.

Section 2

Building Colonial Unity

Focus

Bellringer
Daily Test Practice Transparency 5–2

Reading Guide
Answers to Graphic:
Any three of the following are acceptable: closed Boston Harbor; other colonies unified to support Boston; town meetings banned; colonists argued that the Intolerable Acts violated their rights; Bostonians were forced to shelter British soldiers.

Section Spotlight Video

To learn more about the Boston Tea Party, have students watch the Section Spotlight Video "Building Colonial Unity."

Essential Question
How did the colonists react to British policies?

Reading Guide

Content Vocabulary
propaganda *(p. 127)*
committee of correspondence *(p. 128)*

Academic Vocabulary
occupy *(p. 127)*   encounter *(p. 127)*

Key People and Events
Crispus Attucks *(p. 127)*
Boston Massacre *(p. 127)*
Tea Act *(p. 128)*
Boston Tea Party *(p. 129)*
George III *(p. 129)*
Coercive Acts *(p. 129)*

Reading Strategy
Taking Notes As you read, take notes on how the Intolerable Acts affected the colonists.

Intolerable Acts

ILLINOIS STANDARDS
The American Journey

16.B Understand the development of significant political events.

16.A.3c Identify the differences between historical fact and interpretation.

16.B.3b (US) Explain how and why the colonies fought for their independence and how the colonists' ideas are reflected in the Declaration of Independence and the United States Constitution.

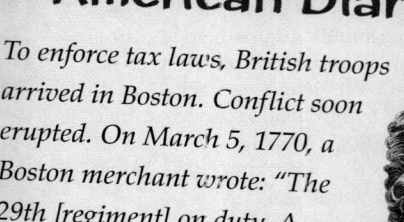

American Diary

To enforce tax laws, British troops arrived in Boston. Conflict soon erupted. On March 5, 1770, a Boston merchant wrote: "The 29th [regiment] on duty. A quarrel between the soldiers and inhabitants; . . . A party of the 29th . . . fired on the people; they killed five, wounded several others. . . . The inhabitants are greatly enraged."

—*from* The Diary of John Rowe

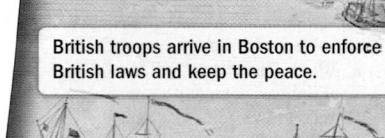

British troops arrive in Boston to enforce British laws and keep the peace.

Resource Manager

R Reading Strategies	**C** Critical Thinking	**D** Differentiated Instruction	**W** Writing Support	**S** Skill Practice
Teacher Edition • Summarizing, p. 127 **Additional Resources** • Guid. Read., URB p. 40 • Content Vocab., URB p. 17 • Academic Vocab., URB p. 19 • Read. Ess., p. 49	**Additional Resources** • Quizzes and Tests, p. 42	**Teacher Edition** • English Learners, p. 129 **Additional Resources** • Differ. Inst., URB p. 27 • Reteaching Act., URB p. 37 • School-to-Home, URB p. 35	**Teacher Edition** • Descriptive Writing, p. 127 **Additional Resources** • Enrichment Act., URB p. 11	**Teacher Edition** • Reading a Time Line, p. 128 **Additional Resources** • Daily Test Pract. Transp. 5-2 • Geo. & Hist., URB p. 31 • Time Line Skills, URB p. 34

Trouble in Boston

Main Idea A violent clash between townspeople and British soldiers in Boston intensified anti-British feeling in the colonies.

History and You When someone taunts you, how do you react? Read to learn how British soldiers responded to the jeers of Bostonians.

By 1768, protests by the colonists were making British colonial officials nervous. They sent word to Britain that the colonies were on the brink of rebellion. Parliament sent troops to Boston. As angry Bostonians jeered, the "redcoats" set up camp in the center of the city.

Many colonists felt that the British had pushed them too far. First the British had passed laws that violated colonial rights. They also had sent an army to **occupy,** or control, colonial cities.

To make matters worse, the soldiers in Boston acted rudely and sometimes even violently toward the colonists. Mostly poor men, the redcoats earned little pay. Some stole goods from local shops or scuffled with boys who taunted them in the streets. The soldiers also competed off-hours for jobs that Bostonians wanted.

The Boston Massacre

On March 5, 1770, a fight broke out between Bostonians and the soldiers. While some British officers tried to calm the crowd, one man shouted, "We did not send for you. We will not have you here. We'll get rid of you, we'll drive you away!"

The angry townspeople moved toward the customhouse, where British taxes were collected, picking up sticks, stones, and clubs. As the crowd approached, the sentry panicked and called for help. The crowd threw sticks and stones at the soldiers. "Fire, you bloodybacks, you lobsters," the crowd screamed. "You dare not fire."

After one soldier was knocked down, the nervous redcoats did fire, killing five colonists. One Bostonian cried: "Are the inhabitants to be knocked down in the streets? Are they to be murdered . . . ?" Among the dead was **Crispus Attucks,** a dockworker who was part African, part Native American. The colonists called the tragic **encounter,** or unexpected meeting, the **Boston Massacre.**

The Word Spreads

Colonial leaders used the killings as **propaganda**—information made to influence public opinion. Samuel Adams put up posters that described the "Boston Massacre."

CHAPTER 5
Section 2

Teach

R Reading Strategy

Summarizing Have students write a sentence summarizing how the actions of British soldiers in Boston contributed to colonists' anger toward Britain. **OL**

W Writing Support

Descriptive Writing Ask students to write accounts of the Boston Massacre that might appear in a London newspaper and a Boston newspaper. Have student volunteers read their accounts aloud. Discuss the differences between the points of view about the events of March 5, 1770. **AL**

Primary Source

Critical Thinking Answer
Students may note that descriptive words, such as "horrid," "wallowing in their gore," and "inhumanly murdered," are used to incite blame and anger toward the British.

Primary Source / Protesting the Boston Massacre

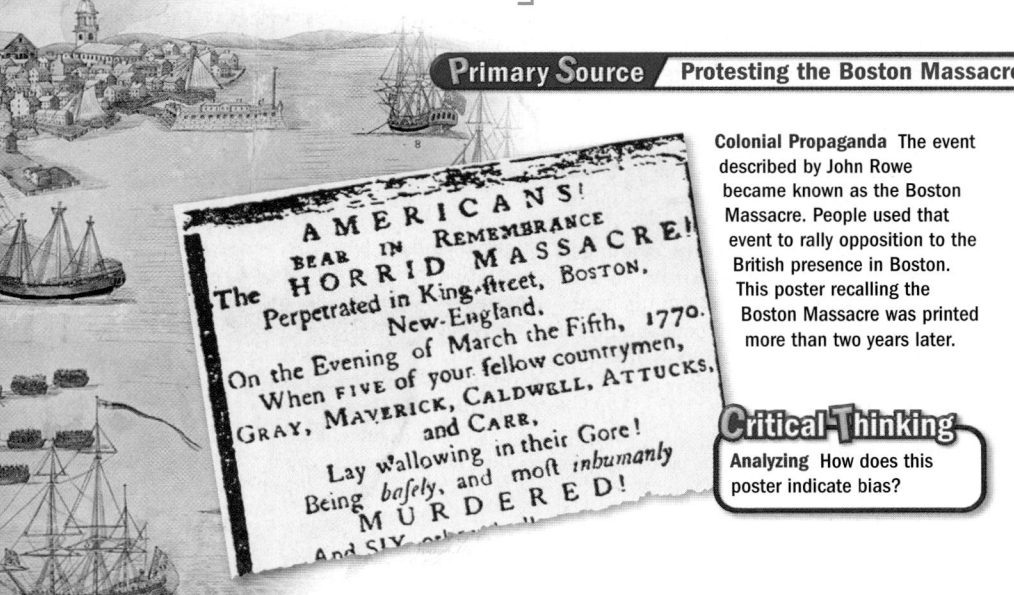

AMERICANS!
BEAR IN REMEMBRANCE
The HORRID MASSACRE!
Perpetrated in King-street, Boston,
New-England,
On the Evening of March the Fifth, 1770.
When FIVE of your fellow countrymen,
GRAY, MAVERICK, CALDWELL, ATTUCKS,
and CARR,
Lay wallowing in their Gore!
Being basely, and most inhumanly
MURDERED!
And SIX others...

Colonial Propaganda The event described by John Rowe became known as the Boston Massacre. People used that event to rally opposition to the British presence in Boston. This poster recalling the Boston Massacre was printed more than two years later.

Critical Thinking
Analyzing How does this poster indicate bias?

Hands-On Chapter Project
Step 2

Declaring Independence

Step 2: Using Propaganda to Influence Opinion Students will create propaganda that will encourage the colonies to rebel against Britain.

Essential Question: How did the colonists react to British policies?

Directions Students will create propaganda posters that will reflect an anti-British feeling. Assign each group one of the following: the Boston Massacre, the Tea Act, the Boston Tea Party, the Intolerable Acts, and the Quebec Act. Each group should create a propaganda poster about their event. First, students should decide what group or individuals might create this poster. Students should then create artwork and write slogans to turn public opinion against the British.

Distinguishing Fact From Opinion Display the finished posters in the classroom. Discuss each poster. **Ask:** What factual information does this poster include? What opinions does this poster express? **OL**

(Chapter Project continued in Section 3)

S Skill Practice

Reading a Time Line Refer students to the time line on this page. **Ask:** What events followed the passage of the Tea Act? *(Boston citizens voted to prevent tea from being unloaded; citizens staged the Boston Tea Party; Britain closed Boston's port.)* How long did it take for Britain to close Boston Harbor after the Boston Tea Party? *(3½ months)* Why do you think it took so long? *(News traveled slowly between Britain and the colonies.)* **BL**

Primary Source

Critical Thinking Answer
Students might say that the colonists wanted to disguise themselves or that the disguises distinguished themselves as more American than British.

Reading Check **Answer:** Colonists used anger over the Boston Massacre to raise support for the boycott of British goods, which led Parliament to repeal the Townshend Acts.

Differentiated Instruction

Primary Source / **The Boston Tea Party**

★ **May 1773** Parliament passes the Tea Act.

★ **November 30, 1773** Citizens of Boston vote to prevent three shiploads of tea from being unloaded.

★ **December 16, 1773** Boston Tea Party: Boston citizens disguised as Native Americans board the ships and empty the tea into Boston Harbor.

★ **March 31, 1774** George III and Parliament respond by closing Boston's port.

◄ Tea from the Boston Tea Party

"Fellow countrymen, we cannot afford to give a single inch! If we retreat now, everything we have done becomes useless!"
—Samuel Adams, December 1773

Critical Thinking

Speculating Why do you think the colonists disguised themselves as Native Americans to carry out the Boston Tea Party?

His posters showed a slaughter of innocent Americans by bloodthirsty redcoats. An engraving by Paul Revere showed British troops firing on an orderly crowd.

The Boston Massacre led many colonists to call for stronger boycotts on British goods. Aware of the opposition to its policies, Parliament repealed all the Townshend Acts taxes except the one on tea. The colonists ended their boycotts, except on tea. Trade with Britain resumed.

Some colonial leaders, however, continued to call for resistance to British rule. In 1772 Samuel Adams revived the Boston **committee of correspondence,** an organization used in earlier protests. Soon committees throughout the colonies were airing their grievances against Great Britain.

Reading Check **Explaining** How did the colonists use the Boston Massacre to their advantage?

A Crisis Over Tea

Main Idea New British laws restricting colonial rights further enraged the colonists.

History and You If you destroyed someone else's property, would you expect to be punished for your actions? Read to find out about the consequences of the Boston Tea Party.

. . . .

S In 1773 the British East India Company faced ruin. To save the company, Parliament passed the **Tea Act.** This law allowed the company a virtual monopoly, or sole control, of the trade for tea in America. The act let the company sell tea directly to shopkeepers and bypass colonial merchants who normally distributed the tea.

Colonial merchants called for a new boycott. Colonists vowed to stop the East India Company's ships from unloading.

The Spirit of Independence

Objective:	To use a time line to understand Parliament's actions and the colonists' reactions
Focus:	Point out that colonial resistance was the result of British legislation.
Teach:	Have students review the information provided and answer the questions.
Assess:	Ask pairs of students to compare their answers for similarities and differences.
Close:	Discuss what finally happened as the result of the colonists' reactions to Britain's policies.

Differentiated Instruction Strategies

BL Have students use their fingers to track the dates along the time line while they read the information.

AL Ask students to create a flow chart, showing the same sequence of events.

ELL Ask students to define the terms "policy changes" and "conflict."

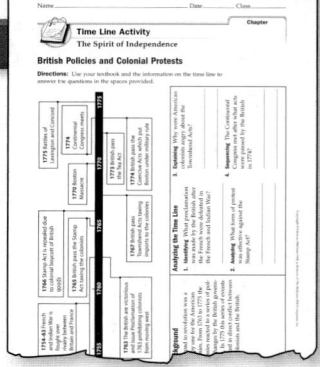

Time Line Skills Activity, URB p. 34

The Daughters of Liberty issued a pamphlet declaring that rather than part with freedom, "we'll part with our tea."

The Boston Tea Party

Despite warnings of a brewing crisis, the East India Company shipped tea to a number of colonial cities. The colonists forced the ships sent to New York and Philadelphia to turn back. Three tea ships arrived in Boston Harbor in late 1773. The royal governor refused to let the ships leave and ordered them to be unloaded. The Boston Sons of Liberty acted swiftly. On December 16, a group of men disguised as Mohawks boarded the ships at midnight. They threw 342 chests of tea overboard, an event that became known as the **Boston Tea Party.**

Word of this act of defiance spread. Colonists gathered to celebrate. Yet no one spoke of challenging British rule. Most colonists saw themselves as British citizens.

The Intolerable Acts

When news of the Boston Tea Party reached London, King **George III** realized that Britain was losing control of the colonies. He declared, "We must master them or totally leave them alone." The British government responded by passing the **Coercive Acts** in 1774. These harsh laws were intended to punish the people of Massachusetts for their resistance to British law.

The Coercive Acts closed Boston Harbor until the Massachusetts colonists paid for the ruined tea. This action prevented the arrival of food and other supplies that normally came by ship. Worse, the laws took away certain rights. For example, the laws banned most town meetings in New England.

The Coercive Acts also forced Bostonians to shelter soldiers in their own homes. Parliament planned to isolate Boston with these acts. Instead the other colonies sent food and clothing to support Boston. The colonists held that the Coercive Acts violated their rights as English citizens. These rights included no quartering of troops in private homes and no standing army in peacetime.

Parliament then passed the Quebec Act. This law set up a government for Quebec. It also gave Quebec the area west of the Appalachians and north of the Ohio River. This provision ignored colonial claims to the area. The colonists expressed their feelings in *their* name for the new laws—the Intolerable Acts.

✔ **Reading Check** **Describing** How did the British react to the Boston Tea Party?

History ONLINE
Study Central™ To review this section, go to glencoe.com.

Section 2 Review

Vocabulary

1. Write a short paragraph in which you use all of the following vocabulary terms: occupy, encounter, propaganda, committee of correspondence.

Main Ideas

2. **Describing** Describe the events leading up to and following the Boston Massacre.

3. **Explaining** How did the Tea Act give an unfair advantage to the British East India Company?

Critical Thinking

4. **Evaluating** How did Samuel Adams and Paul Revere try to sway public opinion about the Boston Massacre?

5. **Organizing** Use a diagram like the one below to identify events and policies that led to rising tensions in the 1770s.

Rising Tensions

6. **Creative Writing** Write an account of the Boston Massacre from the point of view of a British soldier involved in the event.

Answer the
Essential Question

7. How did the colonists react to British policies?

The Spirit of Independence **Chapter 5** 129

D Differentiated Instruction

English Language Learners Have students use a dictionary to find the meanings of the words "coercive" and "intolerable." Ask them to write each word in a sentence. Finally, discuss why the British called the Acts "coercive" and why the colonists called them "intolerable." **ELL**

✔ **Reading Check** **Answer:** The British reacted by passing the Coercive Acts to punish Massachusetts. The Acts closed Boston Harbor, banned town meetings, and forced colonists to quarter British troops.

Assess

History ONLINE

Study Central™ provides summaries, interactive games, and online graphic organizers to help students review content.

Close

Analyzing As a class, discuss how the events of the 1770s unified the colonists in opposition to the British. **OL**

Answers

1. Paragraphs should use vocabulary words with their correct definitions.

2. British troops were stationed in Boston, and many of them treated the colonists rudely. On March 5, 1770, a fight broke out between the soldiers and residents of Boston. Nervous soldiers fired on the crowd, killing five Bostonians. Colonial leaders used the Boston Massacre to influence public opinion and unify colonists.

3. lowered taxes for the East India Company and allowed the company to sell it at a lower price than the colonies could

4. Adams and Revere portrayed the Boston Massacre as a deliberate British slaughter of innocent colonists. This heightened colonial resistance to British laws that colonists considered unjust.

5. Any four: British occupation of Boston, the Boston Massacre, organization of committees of correspondence, the passage of the Tea Act, the Boston Tea Party, the passage of the Coercive Acts, the passage of the Quebec Act

6. Students should include information about the angry crowd, British attempts to calm the crowd, and the soldiers' nervousness.

7. Colonists objected to the occupation of Boston and used the Boston Massacre as anti-British propaganda. The Tea Act spurred protest throughout the colonies, but especially in Massachusetts, where colonists staged the Boston Tea Party. The Coercive Acts led other colonies to support Massachusetts and oppose British policies.

Focus

C Critical Thinking

Making Connections Have students reread the author biography. Ask your students how they might have reacted to the American Revolution if they were alive back then. *(They might have ignored or supported the boycott or belonged to the Committee.)* **OL**

R Reading Strategy

Activating Prior Knowledge Denenberg does not explain why the Fitch sisters should not sell British goods. **Ask:** Why didn't the Committee want the Fitch sisters to sell British goods? *(The colonies were boycotting British items to protest taxes.)* **AL**

Additional Reading

Review suggested books before assigning them.

America's LITERATURE

Meet the Author

C **Barry Denenberg** (1946–) has said that the American Revolution is often presented to young people as a distant event. In writing *The Journal of William Thomas Emerson: A Revolutionary War Patriot*, Denenberg wanted to "bring the revolution to life by showing how it affected ordinary people and how they affected it."

Vocabulary

crown king

trampled crush

cowering crouching

feeble weak

soot ash

Building Background

In *The Journal of William Thomas Emerson: A Revolutionary War Patriot*, Barry Denenberg depicts life in Boston in the months leading up to the American Revolution as told by Will, a young orphan boy. Will works for Mr. Wilson, a tavern owner and member of the Committee, a group of colonists who oppose the British. As you read this excerpt, think about the actions of the Committee toward ordinary citizens and their effect on the political climate at the time.

THE JOURNAL OF WILLIAM THOMAS EMERSON: A REVOLUTIONARY WAR PATRIOT

Barry Denenberg

The Fitch Sisters and the Committee

Mrs. Thompson is still angry about the Fitch sisters, who have a shop on Milk Street. She never raises her voice like that.

R "It's just like them to think they could bring in British goods and get away with it. You can count on the Fitch sisters to be concerned only about themselves, even in times like these. Imagine, claiming they are just trying to keep a roof

---

Nonfiction: *The American Revolutionaries: A History in Their Own Words 1750–1800,* by Milton Meltzer, tells how the people living during the American Revolution felt as their world changed. The book contains letters, diaries, and journals from soldiers, civilians, and leaders on both sides.

Historical Fiction: *My Brother Sam Is Dead,* by James Lincoln Collier, is about a family whose older son joins the Continental Army, even though the father is a Tory. As the Revolution begins, the younger son, Tim, has to make a choice between supporting his brother or his father.

Nonfiction: *Fight for Freedom: The American Revolutionary War,* by Benson Bobrick, explores the causes of the Revolution, individual battles, leaders from both sides, and the role of women during the Revolution.

For further reading, see **BOOKLINK 3**.

over their heads and food on the table. Isn't that all any of us are doing?"

The Fitch sisters say that if they didn't have British goods to sell they would find themselves poor in no time. But Mrs. Thompson says they're only making it harder on themselves by defending their actions and they should just admit their mistake. . . .

"They ought to get the same treatment as Mr. Carlisle," Mrs. Thompson said.

C Henry told me all about Mr. Carlisle. We saw him one day walking down King Street dressed in lace and ruffles. Henry said he has long been suspected of being loyal to the **crown** and one night he finally got what he deserved. Some of the men from town marched out to his house. Mr. Carlisle is very rich, Henry said, "Almost as rich as Mr. Dudley. Mr. Carlisle's house was one of the grandest in Boston."

As soon as the crowd arrived they **trampled** the lawn, hacked down the trees, and overran the gate that surrounds the house. They smashed the big front doors with axes and then poured into the house, where they tore up the floorboards, ripped the curtains from the windows and, after finding Mr. Carlisle's portrait, tore the eyes out.

They dragged his finely carved furniture outside and smashed it to bits, ran off with his carpets and drank his wine cellar dry.

They found Mr. Carlisle **cowering** upstairs, trying to hide behind his bed curtains. They pulled him out despite his **feeble** efforts to hold on to the bedpost and then took his feather bed and threw it out the window. A ladder was put up and Mr. Carlisle was lowered to those waiting below.

Once they had him outside, they stripped off his nightclothes, smeared him with hot tar and covered him with the insides of the feather bed.

When the house caught fire someone wanted to call for the firemen, but the crowd shouted him down, yelling, "LET IT BURN, LET IT BURN," and so they did. The flames, Henry said, could be seen for miles by dawn. . . .

D Most of the men pulled nightcaps over their heads or darkened their faces with chimney **soot** so they wouldn't be recognized. Some were armed with sticks and clubs and Henry said that Mr. Carlisle was lucky not to have suffered even greater injury to his person than to his pride.

Of course, Mrs. Thompson didn't say any of this to me. I overheard it when she was talking to Mr. Wilson right before he went into the regular Tuesday night meeting with the Committee.

That's why I stay put on Tuesday nights. I never go anywhere. They meet late, after the tavern closes, in the small room next to the big barroom. As soon as I hear them all coming in I just lie there quietly on my cot and listen. . . .

Analyzing Literature

1. **Respond** If asked to take sides in Mr. Carlisle's situation, which side would you take and why?

2. **Recall and Interpret**
   (a) Who tarred and feathered Mr. Carlisle? How do you know?
   (b) Why do you think the Committee acted so drastically?

3. **Evaluate**
   (a) What do you think will happen to the Fitch sisters?
   (b) Do you think the author does a good job in bringing the American Revolution to life for readers? Explain your answer.

Teach

C ### Critical Thinking

Determining Cause and Effect Remind your students that Henry never told Will that Mr. Carlisle was proven to be "loyal to the crown." People only suspected that he was. **Ask:** Could there be another reason that he was attacked? *(People might have been jealous.)* Does the reason make a difference in whether the attack was justified? *(Students may say that no attack on a man walking down the street is justified.)* **OL**

D ### Differentiated Instruction

Interpersonal The men who attacked Mr. Carlisle hid their faces and acted as a mob. As a class, discuss whether people will do things (good or ill) in a group that they might not do otherwise. Also discuss how the wearing of disguises can affect people's behaviors. **OL**

Assess/Close

Tell students to take the role of a Fitch sister. Students should write a letter to the Committee explaining why they are not following the boycott. Discuss the different reasons the Fitches had for their actions. **OL**

Answers

1. Possible answer: the citizens' side because students may believe that Mr. Carlisle should not have been loyal to the British

2. (a) The Committee; Will says he does not go out on Committee meeting nights because of what happened to Mr. Carlisle.
   (b) Students might say because he was loyal to the Crown or because he was rich.

3. (a) Possible answer: They will be persecuted like Mr. Carlisle.
   (b) Students may say that the author vividly describes people's hostility toward the Crown.

Section 3

A Call to Arms

Focus

Bellringer
Daily Test Practice Transparency 5–3

Reading Guide
Answers to Graphic:
Drafted a statement of grievances calling for a repeal of 13 laws; voted to boycott trade with Britain; endorsed resolutions calling for people to arm themselves against the British

Section Spotlight Video

To learn more about the clash between American colonists and British soldiers at Lexington and Concord, watch the Section Spotlight Video "A Call to Arms."

Resource Manager

Essential Question
What brought about the clash between American colonists and British soldiers at Lexington and Concord?

Reading Guide

Content Vocabulary
militia (p. 133)   Loyalist (p. 137)
minutemen (p. 134)   Patriot (p. 137)

Academic Vocabulary
approach (p. 135)   volunteer (p. 136)

Key People and Events
Continental Congress (p. 133)
John Adams (p. 133)
John Jay (p. 133)
Richard Henry Lee (p. 133)
George Washington (p. 133)
Paul Revere (p. 135)

Reading Strategy
Taking Notes As you read, list three key actions of the Continental Congress. Use a diagram like the one below.

ILLINOIS STANDARDS
The American Journey

16.A.3b Make inferences about historical events and eras using historical maps and other historical sources.

16.B.3b (US) Explain how and why the colonies fought for their independence and how the colonists' ideas are reflected in the Declaration of Independence and the United States Constitution.

18.B.3a Analyze how individuals and groups interact with and within institutions (e.g., educational, military).

American Diary

Many colonists were frustrated by British efforts to exert authority over the colonies. At an inn, John Adams overheard a Massachusetts farmer saying: "If Parliament can take away Mr. Hancock's wharf . . . they can take away your barn and my house." Another replied, "Well, it is high time for us to rebel. We must rebel . . . and we had better rebel now."

—quoted in the book John Adams

Messengers spread the news about the first battle between the Patriot and British forces at Lexington.

R Reading Strategies	C Critical Thinking	D Differentiated Instruction	W Writing Support	S Skill Practice
Teacher Edition • Reading Prim. Sources, p. 134 • Predicting, p. 134 • Making Connections, p. 137 **Additional Resources** • Guid. Read., URB p. 41 • Con. Vocab., URB p. 17 • Acad Vocab., URB p. 19 • Read. Ess., p. 52	**Teacher Edition** • Analyz. Prim. Sources, p. 133 **Additional Resources** • Quizzes and Tests, p. 43	**Teacher Edition** • Gifted and Talented, p. 133 • English Learners, p. 136 **Additional Resources** • Reteach. Act., URB p. 37 • School-to-Home, URB p. 35	**Teacher Edition** • Personal, p. 134 **Additional Resources** • Authentic Assess., p. 5	**Teacher Edition** • Using Geog. Skills, p. 135 **Additional Resources** • Daily Test Pract. Transp., 5-3 • Soc. Stud. Skills, URB p. 25 • Lesson Trans. 5A

The Continental Congress

Main Idea Colonial leaders met in Philadelphia to discuss their opposition to British policy.

History and You Have you ever worked with a group to accomplish a shared goal? Read to learn about the common goal that united the Continental Congress.

In September 1774, 55 delegates from all the colonies except Georgia arrived in Philadelphia. They had come to establish a political body to represent American interests and challenge British control. They called the new organization the **Continental Congress.**

Delegates to the Congress

Political leaders from across the colonies attended the Congress. Massachusetts sent fiery Samuel Adams and his cousin **John Adams,** a lawyer. New York sent **John Jay,** another lawyer. From Virginia came **Richard Henry Lee** and Patrick Henry, two outspoken defenders of colonial rights, as well as **George Washington.** Patrick Henry summed up the meaning of the gathering:

PRIMARY SOURCE

"The distinctions between Virginians, Pennsylvanians, New Yorkers, and New Englanders, are no more. I am not a Virginian, but an American."

—Patrick Henry, at the Continental Congress

Decisions of the Congress

The delegates drafted a statement of grievances calling for the repeal of 13 acts of Parliament. They believed these laws violated the "laws of nature, the principles of the English constitution, and the several charters" of the colonies. The delegates voted to boycott British trade. No British goods could be brought in or used in the colonies. No colonial goods could be sold to Britain.

The Congress also decided to endorse the Suffolk Resolves, so named because they were prepared by the people of Suffolk County, Massachusetts. These resolutions called on the people of the county to arm themselves against the British. The people responded by forming **militias**—groups of citizen soldiers.

Reading Check Explaining What was the purpose of the Continental Congress?

If You Were There / Militias in the Colonies

Citizen Soldiers Even before the American Revolution, the American colonists had a long tradition of serving in the military. If you were a member of a militia, you were an important part of the defense of your town. You trained and drilled with the other soldiers. You practiced musket and cannon drills. You were required to provide your own weapons—usually a musket—and ammunition. As the break between Great Britain and the American colonies grew, town governments also supplied their militias. The chart to the left shows arms purchased by the town of Salem, Massachusetts.

Purchases authorized by Salem Provincial Congress, October 1774	
20 tons grape- and round shot, from 3 to 24 lb. @ £15	£300
10 tons bomb shells @ £20	£200
5 tons lead balls @ £33	£165
1,000 barrels of powder @ £8	£8,000
5,000 arms and bayonets @ £2	£10,000
And 75,000 flints	£100

Critical Thinking

Speculating What advantages would local militias have against British soldiers?

Declaring Independence

Step 3: Create a Loyalist or Patriot Pamphlet Students will create a pamphlet advocating either the Loyalist or Patriot viewpoint.

Essential Question: What brought about the clash between American colonists and British soldiers at Lexington and Concord?

Directions Organize students into groups of three or four. Each group will prepare a pamphlet from either a Loyalist or a Patriot viewpoint, using research and taking notes. Next, each group should write a pamphlet to convince other colonists of their viewpoint. Make copies of all finished pamphlets for others to read. Then have each student write a short essay responding to the arguments and identifying his or her own opinion.

Teach

D Differentiated Instruction

Gifted and Talented Have students choose one political leader and research his life. Then have students write a short biography about the leader that describes his inspiration for his revolutionary ideas. **AL**

C Critical Thinking

Analyzing Primary Sources Ask: Why was it important that Patrick Henry no longer considered himself a Virginian? (*In order to be successful, the colonies had to unite rather than focus on their own interests.*) **OL**

Reading Check **Answer:** to represent the colonists' common interests and to challenge British laws and control

If You Were There

Critical Thinking Answer
Militias would know the local terrain much better than British soldiers and have a greater stake in a battle's outcome because it was their land.

Hands-On Chapter Project
Step 3

Speculating Discuss the events of 1774 and 1775. **Ask:** Do you think war could have been avoided? If so, how? (*Possible answer: By this time, events had reached a point that it was unlikely either side would have backed down.*) **OL**

(*Chapter Project continued in Section 4*)

W

W Writing Support

Personal Ask students to assume the role of a New England person serving in a militia during the winter of 1774–1775, and create a diary entry describing the preparations being made for fighting. **AL**

R₁ Reading Strategy

Reading Primary Sources Ask: What did King George mean when he announced that "blows must decide"? *(He meant that Britain and the colonists would have to settle their conflict militarily.)* **BL**

R₂ Reading Strategy

Predicting Ask: What do you think will happen when the British arrive in Concord? Why? *(Students' answers will vary but should include that the colonists and Britain will probably have an armed confrontation because the colonists have been preparing to fight.)* **OL**

Differentiated Instruction

The First Battles

Main Idea America's fight for independence began when British troops clashed with minutemen at Lexington and Concord.

History and You Why would the element of surprise be a valuable weapon during a war? Read to learn how the minutemen used the element of surprise to their advantage.

Colonists expected that if fighting against the British broke out, it would begin in New England. Militia companies in Massachusetts held frequent training sessions, made bullets, and stockpiled rifles and muskets. Some companies, known as **minutemen,** boasted they would be ready to fight on a minute's notice. In the winter of 1774–1775, a British officer stationed in Boston noted in his diary:

PRIMARY SOURCE

"The people are evidently making every preparation for resistance. They are taking every means to provide themselves with Arms."

—from *Diary of Frederick Mackenzie*

Britain Sends Troops

The British also prepared for conflict. King George announced to Parliament that the New England Colonies were "in a state of rebellion" and said that "blows must decide" who would control America. By April 1775, several thousand British soldiers were in and around Boston. with many more on the way. Their general, Thomas Gage, had instructions to take away the weapons of the Massachusetts militia and arrest the leaders.

Gage learned that the militia was storing arms and ammunition at Concord, a town about 20 miles (32 km) northwest of Boston. He ordered 700 troops under Lieutenant Colonel Francis Smith to march "to Concord, where you will seize and destroy all the artillery and ammunition you can find."

Alerting the Colonists

On the night of April 18, 1775, Dr. Joseph Warren walked the streets of Boston looking for any unusual activity by the British army. He saw a regiment form ranks in Boston Common and begin to march out of the city.

The Battles of Lexington and Concord, 1775 NATIONAL GEOGRAPHIC

- Colonial troops
- Colonial messengers
- British troops
- ★ Colonial victory
- ✶ British victory

North Bridge

Concord April 19

PRESCOTT — MINUTEMEN

SMITH

Lexington April 19

Revere captured; Dawes turns back; Dr. Samuel Prescott continues ride.

Menotomy (Arlington)

Medford

Massachusetts

Cambridge

Charlestown

Boston

Boston Harbor

Dorchester Neck

Roxbury

0   2 kilometers
0   2 miles
Albers Equal-Area projection

▲ British uniform coat

"Stand your ground. Don't fire unless fired upon, but if they mean to have a war, let it begin here."
— Captain John Parker to the Lexington Militia

Recognizing Time and Sequence

Objective: To create a time line to show the time and sequence of historical events

Focus: Remind students that historical events occur as the result of previous actions or situations.

Teach: Ask students to first read the passage and then create their own time lines.

Assess: Have students assess their time lines using the self-assessment checklist.

Close: Discuss the need for time lines to be concise.

Differentiated Instruction Strategies

BL Ask students to explain how chronological order helps us understand cause-and-effect relationships.

AL Have students create a bulletin board display in chronological order with illustrations.

ELL Have students circle words in the passage that act as clues to chronological order.

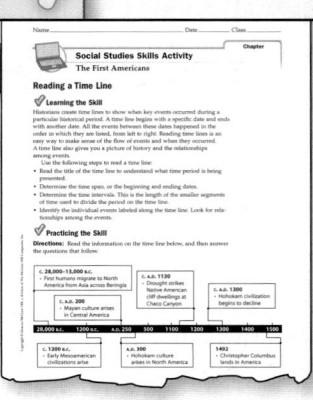

Social Studies Skills Activity, URB p. 25

Warren rushed to alert **Paul Revere** and William Dawes, members of the Sons of Liberty. Revere and Dawes rode to Lexington, a town east of Concord, to warn Samuel Adams and John Hancock that the British were coming. Revere galloped across the moonlit countryside, shouting, "The regulars are out!" to people along the way. Upon hearing the news, Adams exclaimed, "What a glorious morning this is!" Adams was ready to fight for independence.

Lexington and Concord

At dawn the redcoats **approached,** or moved closer to, Lexington. There they discovered about 70 minutemen who had been alerted by Revere and Dawes. Led by Captain John Parker, the minutemen stood on the town common with muskets in hand. A minuteman reported:

PRIMARY SOURCE

"There suddenly appeared a number of the king's troops . . . the foremost of which cried, 'Throw down your arms, ye villains, ye rebels!'"

—from *The Military Journals of Two Private Soldiers*

A shot was fired, and then both sides let loose an exchange of bullets. When the fighting ended, eight minutemen lay dead. The British troops continued their march to Concord. When they arrived, they found that most of the militia's gunpowder had already been removed. They destroyed the remaining supplies. At Concord's North Bridge, waiting minutemen turned back the British.

Messengers on horseback had spread word of the British movements. All along the road from Concord to Boston, farmers, blacksmiths, and clerks hid behind trees and stone fences. As the British marched down the road, the militia fired. By the time the redcoats reached Boston, at least 174 were wounded and 73 were dead.

Looking back, the poet Ralph Waldo Emerson wrote in "The Concord Hymn" that the Americans at Lexington and Concord had fired the "shot heard 'round the world." The battle for independence had begun.

Reading Check **Explaining** How were the colonists preparing for war with Britain?

◄ The North Bridge today

The North Bridge at Concord was the site of the first American victory in the Revolutionary War. ►

▲ On the night of April 18, British troops secretly set out from Boston to Concord. Messengers, including Paul Revere (above), were sent to spread the alarm. When the British reached Lexington, Patriot minutemen were waiting.

Critical Thinking

Analyzing What happened after British forces reached Lexington?

Maps in Motion See StudentWorks™ Plus or glencoe.com.

The Spirit of Independence **Chapter 5** 135

S Skill Practice

Using Geography Skills Have students review the map showing the battles of Lexington and Concord. **Ask:** Where did Paul Revere's ride begin? *(Boston)* Where did the British victory occur? *(Lexington)* The colonial victory? *(Concord)* **BL**

Battles of Lexington and Concord, 1775

 NATIONAL GEOGRAPHIC

Critical Thinking Answer

In Lexington, several minutemen were killed. The British traveled to Concord, where they were turned back by the colonists. During their return to Boston, the British were fired upon by the militia, and many soldiers were killed.

Reading Check **Answer:** Colonists were stockpiling muskets, rifles, ammunition, and training militias.

Additional Support

Interdisciplinary Connection

Literature Distribute copies of Henry Wadsworth Longfellow's poem "Paul Revere's Ride." Have students analyze the poem by comparing the events Longfellow describes with what actually occurred. **Ask:** How does Longfellow's poem portray events differently from what really happened? *(Revere was not the only rider; Dr. Warren, not lanterns, alerted Revere; Revere was captured at one point by the British.)* Why do you think Longfellow wrote this poem? *(Possible answer: to commemorate Revere as a hero or to stir patriotic feelings)* How do poems such as this one influence American patriotism? *(Students may note how poems like these describe people's actions to inspire others.)* **OL**

People IN HISTORY

D Differentiated Instruction

English Language Learners Have students find the definitions for "traitor" and "treason" in the dictionary. **Ask:** How do you think colonists felt about Benedict Arnold after the fall of Fort Ticonderoga? *(They probably thought of him as a hero.)* How do you think they felt about him after his treason was discovered? *(They probably did not like or trust him.)* **ELL**

People IN HISTORY

Critical Thinking Answers

1. Henry and Adams were early supporters of independence.
2. Henry meant that he was willing to take up arms and fight for the colonies' independence from Britain.

History ONLINE
Objectives and answers to the Student Web Activity can be found at glencoe.com under the Web Activity Lesson Plan for this chapter.

Differentiated Instruction

Patrick Henry
Lawyer and Revolutionary

Henry was one of the first members of the Virginia House of Burgesses to argue for independence from Britain. In a debate over whether the state should form a militia, he vowed, *"Give me liberty or give me death!"*

Samuel Adams
Patriot Leader in Boston

Adams argued that Massachusetts should be independent from Britain long before anyone else did. After the Townshend Acts were passed, he wrote that it was *"irreconcilable to . . . common sense and reason, that a British house of commons, should have a right . . . to give and grant the property of the Colonists."*

CRITICAL Thinking

1. **Synthesizing** What did Patrick Henry and Samuel Adams have in common?
2. **Analyzing** What do you think Patrick Henry meant when he said, "Give me liberty or give me death!"?

More Military Action

Main Idea As colonial militias formed and the fighting continued, American loyalties were split.

History and You Have you ever taken sides in a dispute between two friends? Read to learn how the issue of independence divided Americans.

D Shortly after Lexington and Concord, Benedict Arnold, a captain in the Connecticut militia, was authorized to raise a force of 400 men to seize Fort Ticonderoga on Lake Champlain. Ticonderoga was not only strategically located but also rich in military supplies.

Arnold learned that Ethan Allen was also mounting an expedition in Vermont to attack the fort. Arnold joined his militia with Allen's force, known as the Green Mountain Boys. Together they caught the British by surprise. Fort Ticonderoga surrendered on May 10, 1775.

Later during the war, Arnold sold military information to the British. When he conspired to surrender the key fort of West Point to the British, his treason was discovered. Arnold fled to British-controlled New York City. He was given command of British troops and led raids against the Americans in Virginia and Connecticut.

Building Forces

After Lexington and Concord, the committees of correspondence sent out calls for **volunteers,** or helpers, to join the militias. Soon the colonial militia assembled around Boston was about 20,000 strong. For several weeks, the American and British armies waited nervously to see who would make the next move.

History ONLINE
Student Web Activity Visit glencoe.com and complete the Chapter 5 Web Activity about Benedict Arnold.

Leveled Activities

BL Academic Vocabulary Activity, URB p. 19

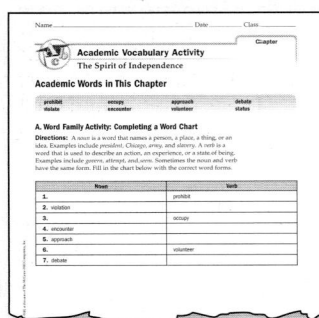

OL School-to-Home Connection Activity, URB p. 35

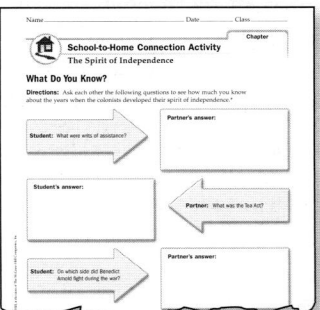

ELL Reading Essentials and Note-Taking Guide, p. 52

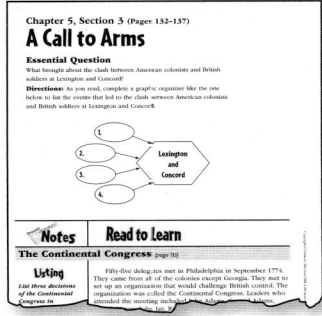

The Battle of Bunker Hill

On June 16, 1775, about 1,200 militiamen under the command of Colonel William Prescott set up fortifications at Bunker Hill and nearby Breed's Hill, across the harbor from Boston.

The British decided to drive the Americans from their strategic locations overlooking the city. The next day the redcoats assembled at the bottom of Breed's Hill. Bayonets drawn, they charged up the hill. With his forces low on ammunition, Colonel Prescott reportedly shouted the order, "Don't fire until you see the whites of their eyes." The Americans opened fire, forcing the British to retreat. The redcoats charged two more times, receiving furious fire. In the end the Americans ran out of gunpowder and had to withdraw.

The British won the Battle of Bunker Hill but suffered heavy losses—more than 1,000 dead and wounded. As one British officer wrote in his diary, "A dear bought victory, another such would have ruined us." The British had learned that defeating the Americans on the battlefield would not be quick or easy.

Choosing Sides

As American colonists heard about these battles, they faced a major decision. Should they join the rebels or remain loyal to Great Britain? Those who chose to stay with Britain, the **Loyalists,** did not consider unfair taxes and regulations good reasons for rebellion. Some Loyalists lived in relative isolation and had not been part of the wave of discontent that turned many Americans against Britain. Still others expected Britain to win the war and wanted to gain favor with the British.

The **Patriots,** on the other hand, were colonists who supported the war for independence. They believed that British rule had become unbearable. The Patriots were determined to fight the British until American independence was won.

The American Revolution was not just a war between the Americans and the British. It was also a civil war among colonists—Patriots against Loyalists.

Reading Check Analyzing What did the British learn from the Battle of Bunker Hill?

History ONLINE
Study Central™ To review this section, go to glencoe.com.

Section 3 Review

Vocabulary

1. Define each of the following terms and use them in a paragraph: militia, minutemen, approach, volunteer, Loyalist, Patriot.

Main Ideas

2. **Explaining** How did endorsement of the Suffolk Resolves by the Continental Congress push the colonies closer to war?

3. **Describing** What tactics did the colonists use against the British troops on their march back from Concord to Boston?

Critical Thinking

4. **Interpreting** Reread Patrick Henry's quote about the Continental Congress. What change was occurring in the way the colonists saw themselves?

5. **Comparing and Contrasting** Use a diagram like the one below to show the similarities and differences between Patriots and Loyalists.

Loyalists | Both | Patriots

6. **Creative Writing** Write a one-act play in which ordinary people in a small town react to the news of the Battle of Lexington. Remember that not all colonists wanted independence from Britain.

Answer the Essential Question

7. What brought about the clash between American colonists and British soldiers at Lexington and Concord?

R Reading Strategy

Making Connections Ask: If you had been an American colonist, would you have considered yourself a Loyalist or a Patriot? Why? *(Student answers will vary but may include the following: Loyalist— would not consider unfair taxes and regulations a reason for rebellion; Patriot—would think that British rule was unbearable.)* **OL**

This **READING SKILL** (Making Connections) was introduced in this unit.

Reading Check Answer: The British learned that they could not defeat the Americans quickly or without heavy losses.

Assess

History ONLINE

Study Central™ provides summaries, interactive games, and online graphic organizers to help students review content.

Close

Drawing Conclusions As a class, discuss how the actions of the Continental Congress contributed to the outbreak of the Revolutionary War. **OL**

Section 3 Review

Answers

1. Paragraphs should use vocabulary words according to their definitions in the section and Glossary.

2. By endorsing the Suffolk Resolves, the Continental Congress called on people to arm themselves against the British. This action led to the formation of militias.

3. The colonists hid behind fences and trees, firing upon the British from their hiding places.

4. Colonists were beginning to view themselves as citizens of one nation, rather than citizens of individual colonies, and entitled to freedom from British rule. They believed that if they could not be "free," they would prefer death.

5. Similarities: Both believed taxes and regulations were unfair; Differences: Loyalists did not consider taxes a reason for rebellion; often lived in isolation; expected the British to win the war. Patriots believed British rule was unbearable and that the colonies could win their independence.

6. Plays should include details about the Battle of Lexington and should include both Loyalist and Patriot points of view.

7. Americans were arming themselves and expected an armed confrontation with British troops. The British gave the Americans an excuse to confront them when British soldiers were ordered to march to Concord and seize artillery and weapons.

Section 4

Moving Toward Independence

Focus

Bellringer
Daily Test Practice Transparency 5–4

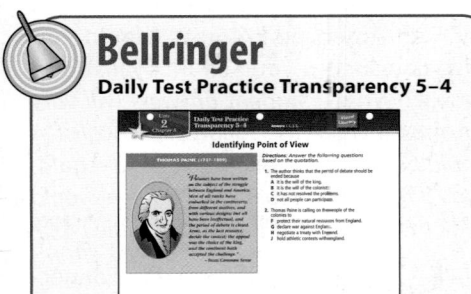

Reading Guide
Answers to Graphic:

Part 1: an introduction, or a preamble, stating that the people wanted to form a new country

Part 2: lists the rights colonists believed they should have and the right of people to abolish a government that does not protect those rights

Part 3: lists grievances against the British king and Parliament

Part 4: announcement of independence

Section Spotlight Video

To learn more about the Declaration of Independence, have students watch the Section Spotlight Video "Moving Toward Independence."

Resource Manager

Essential Question
Why did the American colonies choose to declare independence?

Reading Guide

Content Vocabulary
petition (p. 140)   preamble (p. 142)

Academic Vocabulary
debate (p. 141)   status (p. 142)

Key People and Events
Second Continental Congress (p. 139)
Continental Army (p. 139)
Olive Branch Petition (p. 140)
Thomas Paine (p. 140)
Common Sense (p. 140)
Declaration of Independence (p. 141)

Reading Strategy
Taking Notes As you read, describe the parts of the Declaration of Independence. Use a diagram like the one below.

Declaration of Independence

Part 1:
Part 2:
Part 3:
Part 4:

ILLINOIS STANDARDS
The American Journey

14.F.3a Analyze historical influences on the development of political ideas and practices as enumerated in the Declaration of Independence, the United States Constitution, the Bill of Rights and the Illinois Constitution.

16.B.3b (US) Explain how and why the colonies fought for their independence and how the colonists' ideas are reflected in the Declaration of Independence and the United States Constitution.

18.C.3a Describe ways in which a diverse U.S. population has developed and maintained common beliefs (e.g., life, liberty and the pursuit of happiness; the Constitution and the Bill of Rights).

American Diary

Colonists debated the wisdom of pursuing peace or declaring independence from Britain. Thomas Paine wrote: "I have heard it asserted by some, that as America has flourished under her former connection with Great Britain, the same connection is necessary towards her future happiness. . . . Nothing can be more [false]. . . . We may as well assert that because a child has thrived upon milk, that it is never to have meat. . . . A government of our own is our natural right."

—*from* Common Sense

The Declaration of Independence is presented to the Second Continental Congress.

Reading Strategies	**Critical Thinking**	**D** **Differentiated Instruction**	**W** **Writing Support**	**S** **Skill Practice**
Teacher Edition • Summarizing, p. 139 **Additional Resources** • Guid. Read., URB p. 42 • Content Vocab., URB p. 17 • Acad. Vocab., URB p. 19 • Read. Ess., p. 55 • Pri. Source Read., URB p. 21	**Teacher Edition** • Predicting Consequences, p. 140 **Additional Resources** • Quizzes and Tests, p. 44 • Link. Past & Pres., URB p. 33 • Read. Skills, URB p. 7	**Teacher Edition** • English Learners, p. 139 **Additional Resources** • Reteaching Act., URB p. 37 • School-to-Home, URB p. 35	**Teacher Edition** • Expository Writing, p. 141 • Descriptive Writing, p. 142	**Teacher Edition** • Visual Literacy, p. 141 **Additional Resources** • Daily Test Pract. Transp. 5-4 • Crit. Think. Skills, URB p. 29 • Lesson Transp. 5B, 5C

Colonial Leaders Emerge

Main Idea When the Second Continental Congress met for the first time, many leaders were not yet ready to call for independence.

History and You Do newspapers, books, or television news programs affect your opinion on important issues? Read to learn how a pamphlet by Thomas Paine influenced colonial opinion.

On May 10, 1775, the **Second Continental Congress** assembled for the first time. However, many delegates were not yet prepared to break away from Great Britain. It would be another year before John Adams would ask Thomas Jefferson to write the Declaration of Independence.

The delegates to the Second Continental Congress included some of the greatest political leaders in America. Among those attending were John and Samuel Adams, Patrick Henry, Richard Henry Lee, and George Washington—all delegates to the First Continental Congress held in 1774. Several distinguished new delegates came as well.

Benjamin Franklin, one of the most respected men in the colonies, had been an influential member of the Pennsylvania legislature. In 1765, during the Stamp Act crisis, he represented the colonies in London and helped secure the repeal of the act.

John Hancock of Massachusetts was a wealthy merchant. He funded many Patriot groups, including the Sons of Liberty. The delegates chose Hancock as president of the Second Continental Congress.

Thomas Jefferson, only 32, had already earned a reputation as a brilliant thinker and writer. He served in the Virginia legislature. **D**

The Second Continental Congress began to govern the colonies. It authorized the printing of money and set up a post office with Franklin in charge. It established committees to communicate with Native Americans and with other countries. Most important, the Congress created the **Continental Army** to fight against Britain in a more organized way than the colonial militias could. On John Adams's recommendation, the Congress unanimously chose George Washington to be the army's commander. **R**

Primary Source / Creating the Declaration

Adams and Jefferson By June 1776, the Second Continental Congress was ready to separate from Britain. John Adams, Benjamin Franklin, Thomas Jefferson, Robert Livingston, and Roger Sherman formed the committee to draft a statement. Adams asked Jefferson to write the document because "he was so prompt, frank, explicit, and decisive upon committees and in conversation." Jefferson was reluctant, but Adams persuaded him, saying: "Reason first—You are a Virginian, and a Virginian ought to appear at the head of this business. Reason second—I am obnoxious, suspected, and unpopular. You are very much otherwise. Reason third—you can write ten times better than I can."

—from *The Writings of Thomas Jefferson*

◄ Early draft of the Declaration of Independence

Critical Thinking

Explaining What were Adams's reasons for wanting Jefferson to draft the Declaration of Independence?

Teach

D Differentiated Instruction

English Language Learners Have students look at Adams's description of Jefferson in the Primary Source on this page. **Ask:** What adjectives did Adams use to describe Jefferson? *(prompt, frank, explicit, decisive)* What adjectives did Adams use to describe himself? *(obnoxious, suspected, unpopular)* Have students find the dictionary definition of each word. Then have them write a paragraph describing Adams's view of Jefferson's personality. **ELL**

R Reading Strategy

Summarizing Have students create a list of key actions that the Second Continental Congress took soon after it met. **BL**

Primary Source

Critical Thinking Answer
He might have wanted a Virginian to draft it because the British viewed Massachusetts as a troublemaking colony, and having a resident from a different colony draft the Declaration would show colonial unity.

Hands-On Chapter Project
Step 4

Declaring Independence

Step 4: Debating Independence Students will review their work and debate whether they should declare American independence from Britain.

Essential Question: Why did the American colonies choose to declare independence?

Directions Organize the class into three groups. One group will argue in favor of declaring independence from Britain, one group will argue against it, and one group will serve as a moderator. Have student pairs within each group do research to identify a member of the Second Continental Congress who held their point of view. After students have finished their research, the moderators should lead a discussion of whether the colonies should declare independence from Britain. Notes should be written on the board.

Summary Use the notes the student moderators have written on the board to lead a discussion summarizing the arguments in favor of and against declaring independence from Britain. **OL**

(Chapter Project continued on the Visual Summary page)

C Critical Thinking

Predicting Consequences Ask: Based on the events in 1775 and early 1776, how successful do you think Patriot forces will be in the early months of the war? *(The military engagements seem to suggest that the Patriot forces will do well in the early months of the war. However, if the British send more soldiers and change their strategies, they might have the advantage.)* **OL**

DBQ Document-Based Questions

Answers

1. The colonists should declare their independence so that the losses of those who fought and died would not have been in vain.
2. The colonies' ports would be ruined, and many colonists would be killed or become impoverished.

✓ Reading Check Answer: Colonists meant to give Great Britain a way to avoid war, but the king responded with a larger military buildup.

Additional Support

Teacher Tip

Reading Primary and Secondary Sources Remind students that primary sources are often first-hand accounts by someone who actually lived through what is being described. Secondary sources are secondhand accounts.

YOU DECIDE

Independence: Yes or No?

Many Americans were uncertain whether independence was the correct course for the colonies. After Americans and British troops had fought, however, other colonists felt strongly that independence should be their goal.

In 1776 Thomas Paine made an impassioned appeal for independence in his pamphlet *Common Sense*:

THOMAS PAINE **YES**

"Every thing that is right or natural pleads for separation. The blood of the slain, the weeping voice of nature cries, 'tis time to part.'"

Other Americans did not want to break away from Britain. Colonists who felt a strong sense of loyalty to the king were called Loyalists. They believed British law should be upheld.

Loyalist Charles Inglis argued against going to war with Britain, saying:

CHARLES INGLIS **NO**

"Ruthless war, with all its aggravated horrors, will ravage our once happy land—our seacoasts and ports will be ruined, and our ships taken. Torrents of blood will be spilt, and thousands reduced to beggary and wretchedness."

DBQ Document-Based Questions

1. **Analyzing** What is Paine's argument in favor of independence?
2. **Identifying** What did Inglis believe would result from war with Britain?

After Washington left to take charge of the forces in Boston, the delegates offered Britain one last chance to avoid war. The Congress sent a **petition,** or formal request, to George III. Called the **Olive Branch Petition,** it assured the king of the colonists' desire for peace and asked him to protect the colonists' rights. George III refused to receive the Olive Branch Petition. Instead he prepared for war, hiring more than 30,000 German troops to fight beside British troops.

The Colonies Take the Offensive

Meanwhile the Congress learned that British troops in what is now Canada were planning to invade New York. The Americans decided to strike first. Marching north from Fort Ticonderoga, a Patriot force captured Montreal. An American attack on Quebec led by Benedict Arnold failed, however.

Washington reached Boston in July 1775, a few weeks after the Battle of Bunker Hill. While he found the size of the militia growing every day, Washington realized that the members lacked discipline, organization, and leadership. He began the hard work of shaping these armed civilians into an army.

By March 1776, Washington judged the Continental Army ready to fight. He positioned the army in a semicircle around Boston and gave the order for its cannons to bombard the British forces. The redcoats, under Sir William Howe, hurriedly withdrew from the city. On March 17, Washington led his jubilant troops into Boston. The British troops sailed to Halifax, Nova Scotia.

Moving Toward Independence

In early 1776, support for the position of absolute independence was growing. In January 1776, **Thomas Paine** published a pamphlet called **Common Sense.** In bold language, Paine called for complete independence. *Common Sense* greatly influenced opinion throughout the colonies.

✓ Reading Check Explaining What was the significance of the Olive Branch Petition?

Technology Connection

Analyzing Primary Sources Ask: What is a primary source? Have students work in pairs to find two primary sources on the Internet, one written by a Patriot and one written by a Loyalist. Direct each student to summarize each document. **Ask:** What do you think is a strength of the author's argument? What do you believe is a weakness?

Student pairs should compare their summaries and evaluate the strengths and weaknesses of both documents. Finally, ask volunteers to discuss their documents with the class and identify which argument is more effective and why. **OL**

The Colonies Declare Independence

Main Idea The Declaration of Independence announced the birth of a new nation, committing Americans to a struggle for independence.

History and You How do you celebrate the Fourth of July? Read to learn how Americans celebrated at the reading of the Declaration of Independence.

At the Second Continental Congress in Philadelphia, the meeting hall was filled with spirited discussion, or **debate**: Should the colonies declare themselves an independent nation or stay under British rule? Virginia's Richard Henry Lee proposed a bold resolution:

PRIMARY SOURCE

"That these United Colonies are, and of right ought to be, free and independent States . . . and that all political connection between them and the State of Great Britain is, and ought to be, totally dissolved."

—Richard Henry Lee, resolution for independence

The Debate Over Independence

Congress debated Lee's resolution. Some delegates thought the colonies were not ready to form a separate nation. Others argued that war had already begun. Still others feared Britain's power to crush the rebellion.

As they debated, the Congress chose a committee to draft a **Declaration of Independence.** Jefferson was selected to write the declaration. Jefferson drew some ideas from English philosopher John Locke in his arguments for freedom. Locke wrote that people were born with certain natural rights to life, liberty, and property; that people formed governments to protect these rights; and that a government interfering with these rights might rightfully be overthrown. **W**

On July 2, 1776, the Congress finally voted on Lee's resolution for independence. Twelve colonies voted for it. New York did not vote but later announced its support. Congress then took up Jefferson's draft of the Declaration of Independence, which they approved with some changes on July 4, 1776. **S**

Primary Source / Independence Day

"The Second Day of July 1776, will be the most memorable [day], in the History of America. . . . It ought to be solemnized with Pomp and Parade, with Shews [shows], Games, Sports, Guns, Bells, Bonfires and Illuminations from one End of this Continent to the other from this Time forward forever more."
— John Adams, in a letter to his wife Abigail

Advertisement for railroad transportation to Fourth of July celebration, 1876 ▶

◀ A Fourth of July celebration in New York in the early 1800s

The committee assigned ▶ to draft the Declaration: Benjamin Franklin, Thomas Jefferson, and John Adams

A Day to Celebrate John Adams expected the Second Continental Congress's vote for independence on July 2, 1776, to be celebrated as a great national holiday. Instead, it was the date of the adoption of the Declaration of Independence that has come to be celebrated as Independence Day.

Critical Thinking
Analyzing How has Independence Day come to be celebrated?

The Spirit of Independence **Chapter 5** 141

W Writing Support

Expository Writing Have students write a defense of American independence using Locke's idea of natural rights and his view that the government was formed to protect those rights. Students should use their knowledge of events leading up to the Declaration of Independence to illustrate their points. **AL**

S Skill Practice

Visual Literacy Have students examine the illustration of a Fourth of July celebration in New York in the early 1800s on this page. **Ask:** What parts of the illustration show that this is a Fourth of July celebration? *(Students may mention the American flag, the gathering of people on a main boulevard, and the well-dressed New Yorkers.)* **OL**

Primary Source

Critical Thinking Answer
Students may answer that people today hang American flags to show their patriotism; parades are still held in American cities and towns.

Differentiated Instruction

Reading Skills Activity, p. 7

Creating a Nation

Objective:	To make connections when reading
Focus:	Ask students why it is important to make connections between what they read and what they already know.
Teach:	Have students read the passages and complete the activities.
Assess:	Discuss the answers to the activities.
Close:	Review how students can make connections as they read their textbooks.

Differentiated Instruction Strategies

BL Have students write a list of the three guidelines to make connections. Have them refer to it as they read their textbooks.

AL Ask students to select articles from their favorite magazines and find examples of the three connections.

ELL Ask students to define the following terms: "guideline," "connection," and "concept."

141

W Writing Support

Descriptive Writing Have students write a short newspaper article describing the scene in Worcester when the Declaration of Independence was read. Students should use descriptive language and historical detail. **OL**

✓ Reading Check Answer: The purpose of government is to protect people's natural rights to life, liberty, and property.

Assess

History ONLINE

Study Central™ provides summaries, interactive games, and online graphic organizers to help students review content.

Close

Discussing As a class, create a graphic organizer on the board that contains the following categories to identify people who supported a declaration of independence: Who? (for example, Thomas Paine); What? (wrote *Common Sense*); and Belief: (Paine stated the colonies should have complete independence from Britain.) **OL**

Section 4 Review

John Hancock was the first to sign. Hancock remarked that he wrote his name large enough for King George to read it without his glasses. Eventually 56 delegates signed the paper announcing the birth of the United States.

W Copies of the Declaration went out to the newly declared states. Washington had it read to his troops on July 9. In Worcester, Massachusetts, the reading of the Declaration of Independence was followed by "repeated [cheers], firing of musketry and cannon, bonfires, and other demonstrations of joy."

The Declaration of Independence

The Declaration has four major sections. It includes a **preamble,** or introduction, which states that people who wish to form a new country should explain their reasons for doing so. The next sections list the rights the colonists believed they should have and their complaints against Britain. The final section proclaims the existence of the new nation.

The Declaration of Independence states what Jefferson and many Americans thought were universal principles. It begins by describing traditional English rights:

PRIMARY SOURCE

"We hold these truths to be self-evident, that all men are created equal, that they are endowed by their Creator with certain unalienable Rights, that among these are Life, Liberty, and the pursuit of Happiness."
—Thomas Jefferson, *Declaration of Independence*

The Declaration states that government exists to protect these rights. If it does not, "it is the Right of the People to alter or to abolish it and to institute new Government." The Declaration goes on to list grievances against the king and Parliament. These include "cutting off our trade with all parts of the world" and "imposing taxes on us without our consent." Americans had "Petitioned for Redress" of these grievances. These petitions, however, were ignored or rejected by Britain.

The Declaration ends by announcing America's new **status,** or position. Now pledging "to each other our Lives, our Fortunes, and our sacred Honor," the Americans declared themselves a new nation.

✓ Reading Check Summarizing According to John Locke, what is the purpose of government?

Section 4 Review

History ONLINE
Study Central™ To review this section, go to glencoe.com.

Vocabulary

1. Use each of these terms in a sentence that will help explain its meaning: petition, debate, preamble, status.

Main Ideas

2. Explaining What actions did the Second Continental Congress take to begin governing the colonies?

3. Summarizing What grievances against King George III were included in the Declaration of Independence?

Critical Thinking

4. Interpreting Reread the Primary Source quote from the Declaration of Independence above. Rewrite this quote in your own words, and explain its significance.

5. Organizing Information Using a diagram like the one below, describe each leader's role in the movement toward independence.

Leader	Role
Benjamin Franklin →	
John Hancock →	
Thomas Jefferson →	
George Washington →	

6. Expository Writing Prepare a help-wanted ad to locate a person who is qualified to write the Declaration of Independence. Describe the responsibilities of the job as well as the experience and character traits needed.

Answer the Essential Question

7. Why did the American colonies choose to declare independence?

Answers

1. Sentences should use vocabulary words as they are defined in the section and Glossary.
2. The Second Continental Congress authorized the printing of money and established a post office; it set up committees to communicate with Native Americans and foreign countries; it created the Continental Army, with George Washington as its leader.
3. Grievances against King George III included cutting off the colonies' trade with other countries, taxing the colonists without their consent, and ignoring their petitions.
4. Sample answer: All men are equal and God has given them certain rights that cannot be taken away, including the right to live, to be free, and to be happy.
5. Franklin: led the movement to repeal the Stamp Act; Hancock: funded patriot groups and was the first to sign the Declaration of Independence; Jefferson: drafted the Declaration of Independence; Washington: led the Continental Army
6. The ad should include many of the characteristics of Thomas Jefferson: gifted thinker

and writer, well respected, and familiar with John Locke's ideas.
7. Students should mention several reasons, including that King George III ignored the colonists' Olive Branch Petition, in which they tried to avoid war; they learned the British were planning to invade New York; Thomas Paine published an influential pamphlet, *Common Sense*, which called for complete independence.

To help pay for the French and Indian War, Great Britain passed new laws and imposed new taxes on the American colonies.

The Boston Tea Party ▼

The colonists responded to the new laws by organizing boycotts and other protests. Tensions rose with the Boston Massacre and the Boston Tea Party.

▲ British uniform coat

The Continental Congress, a political body formed by representatives from the colonies, met for the first time and drafted a list of grievances with British policy.

Liberty Bell ▼

Fighting broke out between British troops and colonial militia at Lexington and Concord.

▲ Fighting at Concord's North Bridge

While the fighting continued, the Second Continental Congress approved the Declaration of Independence on July 4, 1776.

STUDY TO GO Study anywhere, anytime! Download quizzes and flash cards to your PDA from glencoe.com.

Visual Summary

Making Connections The colonists successfully boycotted British and European goods in order to hurt business in those foreign countries. **Ask:** Can you think of situations today in which people have used boycotts for political purposes? *(Possible answers: Boycotts have been used to protest the presence of "invaders" in foreign countries, such as China's presence in Tibet or the Soviet Union's presence in Afghanistan. Boycotts have also been used to show disapproval of the treatment of groups of people, such as migrant workers.)* **AL**

This **READING SKILL** (Making Connections) was introduced in this unit.

Narrative Writing Have students do online or library research on the life of Crispus Attucks and his death in the Boston Massacre. Ask students to write a report on what is known about Attucks. **Ask:** Why is it interesting to learn about someone like Crispus Attucks? *(Possible answer: Historical people like Crispus Attucks demonstrate that even "ordinary" people play a role in making history.)* **OL**

Hands-On Chapter Project
Step 5: Wrap-Up

Declaring Independence

Step 5: Review and Discussion Students will review their work and discuss why Americans chose to declare their independence from Britain.

Directions Have students return to their original groups. Ask the groups to make a list of the reasons Americans finally chose to declare their independence from Britain. When students have finished their group work, help the class create a time line on the board that identifies the events leading up to the Declaration of Independence.

Speculating Ask: Was there any other way that the colonists' differences with Britain could have been resolved? *(Answers will vary but may include asking other countries for diplomatic help or sending Patriot representatives to England to meet with the king to discuss solutions. Students may also say that given the Parliament's actions and the colonists' reactions, only conflict could result.)* **OL**

Answers and Analyses
Reviewing Main Ideas

1. C Students should remember that American juries often found smugglers innocent. Vice-admiralty courts, on the other hand, were run by British officers and did not have juries. Students should then choose choice C. **16.B.3b (US)**

2. A Students should remember that the Coercive Acts were passed in response to the Boston Tea Party and were meant to punish the people of Massachusetts for resisting British law. Closing Boston Harbor punished Massachusetts by preventing the arrival of food and other supplies. **16.B.3b (US)**

3. B Students should immediately eliminate choice A because Patriots were those who fought for independence. Ask students to define "loyal." They should then be able to make choice B. **18.B**

4. D Remind students of the four sections of the Declaration of Independence. Ask them to define "preamble." Knowing that a preamble is an introduction should help them make choice D. **16.B.3b (US)**

Short-Answer Question

5. As students read the excerpt, have them find the definitions in a dictionary for the words they do not know. The speaker believed that in the future, too many Americans would not know what it was like to be "free" and would therefore not support any action against Britain. **16.B.3b (US)**

STANDARDIZED TEST PRACTICE

TEST-TAKING TIP

Do not pick an answer choice just because it sounds good at first reading. Sometimes a choice is meant to sound correct but is not. Read all of the answer choices very carefully, and then select the best one.

Reviewing Main Ideas

Directions: Choose the best answer for each of the following questions.

1. American colonists objected to vice-admiralty courts because they

   A prevented them from trading with other nations besides England.

   B taxed the colonists without their consent.

   C violated their right to a jury trial.

   D violated their right to be secure in their homes.

2. The Coercive Acts

   A closed Boston Harbor until the Massachusetts colonists paid for tea ruined in the Boston Tea Party.

   B gave Quebec the area west of the Appalachians and north of the Ohio River.

   C lowered the tax on imported molasses.

   D placed a tax on almost all printed material sold in the colonies.

3. American colonists who sided with Britain during the American Revolution were called

   A Patriots.   **C** Whigs.

   B Loyalists.   **D** Libertarians.

4. The preamble to the Declaration of Independence

   A lists colonists' complaints against Britain.

   B lists the rights the colonists believed they should have.

   C proclaims the existence of the new nation.

   D states that people who wish to form a new country should explain their reasons for doing so.

Short-Answer Question

Directions: Base your answer to question 5 on the excerpt below and on your knowledge of social studies.

> We must *fight*, if we can't otherwise rid ourselves of British taxation, all revenues, and the constitution or form of government enacted for us by the British parliament. It is evil against right—utterly intolerable to every man who has any idea or feeling of right or liberty.
>
> It is *now* or never, that we must assert our liberty. . . . [Otherwise, they] who shall be born will not have any idea of a free government.
>
> —from *Principles and Acts of the Revolution*

5. Explain why the speaker believed that colonists should fight for their independence from Britain as soon as possible.

Review the Essential Questions

6. Essay Explain why American colonists had strong views about self-government.

To help you write your essay, review your answers to the Essential Questions in the section reviews and the chapter Foldables Study Organizer. Your essay should include:

- colonial reaction to the Proclamation of 1763;
- colonial arguments against various acts passed by the British government;
- the ways colonists showed their opposition to actions taken by the British government;
- the resolutions adopted at the First Continental Congress; and
- Jefferson's sources for the ideas expressed in the Declaration of Independence.

GO ON ➤

Review the Essential Questions

6. If students completed their Foldables correctly, they should be able to describe American colonists' views about self-government. Students may mention the English traditions of limited government, the practice of self-government in the colonies, and the ideas of English philosophers such as John Locke. **14.F.3a**

History ONLINE

For additional test practice, use **Self-Check Quizzes**—Chapter 5 at glencoe.com.

Chapter 5 Assessment

Document-Based Questions

Directions: Analyze the documents and answer the short-answer questions that follow.

Document 1

This is an excerpt from British writer Samuel Johnson's 1775 pamphlet, *Taxation No Tyranny.*

> He who goes voluntarily to America, cannot complain of losing what he leaves in Europe. . . . By his own choice he has left a country where he had a vote and little property, for another where he has great property, but no vote.

Source: *The Works of Samuel Johnson*

7. Based on this document, did Johnson agree with colonists' opposition to British actions that taxed them directly and without their consent? Explain.

Document 2

In this 1774 political cartoon, a group of Boston men force tea down the throat of John Malcolm, a British tax collector.

Source: The Art Archive

8. What message is the artist trying to depict? How do the Patriots seem to feel toward the tax collector?

Document 3

This is a proclamation issued by British general Sir Henry Clinton, printed in *Rivington's Royal Gazette*, July 21, 1779.

> Protection and Encouragement is hereby given to the possessors of Farms, and Gardens, to raise plentiful supplies of Grain, Provisions, Vegetables, and Forage [food for animals]. —Whatever Person or Persons shall presume to take away, or destroy any Part of the Cattle, Stock, or other Produce . . . shall, upon Proof thereof, be most severely punished.

Source: Sir Henry Clinton, *Proclamation*

9. Why would a British general want to protect American farmers and encourage them to grow food? Why would some want to destroy the food or land?

Document 4

John Adams expressed these thoughts on the authority of colonial governments in 1775.

> I agree, that "two supreme and independent authorities cannot exist in the same state," any more than two supreme beings in one universe; And, therefore, I contend, that our provincial legislatures are the only supreme authorities in our colonies.

Source: John Adams, "Novanglus"

10. Based on the document, cite one reason Adams supported American independence from Britain.

11. Expository Writing Using the information from the four documents and your knowledge of social studies, write an essay in which you:

- defend the Patriot cause; and
- identify at least one characteristic of a legitimate government.

Need Extra Help?

If you missed questions...	1	2	3	4	5	6	7	8	9	10	11
Go to page...	123–124	129	137	142	122–129	122–142	122–125	128–129	136–137	132–133	122–142

---

8. The artist is pro-Loyalist. The Patriots are depicted as savages attacking a British tax collector. **16.A**

9. The farmers were supplying the British troops with food; Patriots wanted to destroy the food and the farms to make it more difficult for the British army to get food. **16.A.3b**

10. Adams believed that only one legitimate government can exist in any particular region; in America, that government should be administered locally, not from abroad. **16.A.3b**

11. Students' essays should focus on the grievances of the Patriots, including their belief that Britain did not have the right to tax them because they had no vote in Parliament. Students should mention that the Patriots believed that a legitimate government should represent the interests of the people being governed. **14.F**

Have students visit the Web site at glencoe.com to review Chapter 5 and take the Self-Check Quiz.

Need Extra Help?

Have students refer to the pages listed if they miss any of the questions.

Document-Based Questions

7. Students should look for clue words or phrases that help them answer the question. Johnson did not agree that colonists had a right to oppose British taxes. The title of his pamphlet is *Taxation No Tyranny,* which signals his opposition to the view that "taxation without representation is tyranny." Other phrases students might cite include "goes voluntarily to America," "cannot complain," and "By his own choice." **15.E.3a**

Focus

R Reading Strategy

Paraphrasing Ask students to read the Preamble and rewrite it in their own words. **Ask:** What is the main point of the Preamble? (*It states the reasons why the colonists were severing their ties with Great Britain.*) **OL**

C Critical Thinking

Analyzing Primary Sources Tell students that statements in the Declaration of Independence proclaim some of the most important ideas on which democratic government is based. **Ask:** What statements in the Declaration of Independence are important values in a democracy? (*All people are created equal; all people possess certain basic rights, the purpose of government is to secure these rights for the people; the power and authority of governments are derived from the people.*) **OL**

Additional Support

The Declaration of Independence

In Congress, July 4, 1776. The unanimous Declaration of the thirteen United States of America,

Words spelled as originally written.

What It Means
The Preamble The Declaration of Independence has four parts. The Preamble explains why the Continental Congress drew up the Declaration.

impel: force

What It Means
Natural Rights The second part, the Declaration of Natural Rights, lists the rights of the citizens. It goes on to explain that, in a republic, people form a government to protect their rights.

endowed: provided

usurpations: unjust uses of power
despotism: unlimited power

What It Means
List of Grievances The third part of the Declaration lists the colonists' complaints against the British government. Notice that King George III is singled out for blame.

[Preamble]

R When in the Course of human events, it becomes necessary for one people to dissolve the political bands which have connected them with another, and to assume among the powers of the earth, the separate and equal station to which the Laws of Nature and of Nature's God entitle them, a decent respect to the opinions of mankind requires that they should declare the causes which **impel** them to the separation.

[Declaration of Natural Rights]

We hold these truths to be self-evident, that all men are created equal, that they are **endowed** by their Creator with certain unalienable Rights, that among these are Life, Liberty, and the pursuit of Happiness.

That to secure these rights, Governments are instituted among Men, deriving their just powers from the consent of the governed,

C That whenever any Form of Government becomes destructive of these ends, it is the Right of the People to alter or to abolish it, and to institute new Government, laying its foundation on such principles and organizing its powers in such form, as to them shall seem most likely to effect their Safety and Happiness. Prudence, indeed, will dictate that Governments long established should not be changed for light and transient causes; and accordingly all experience hath shewn, that mankind are more disposed to suffer, while evils are sufferable, than to right themselves by abolishing the forms to which they are accustomed. But when a long train of abuses and **usurpations,** pursuing invariably the same Object evinces a design to reduce them under absolute **Despotism,** it is their right, it is their duty, to throw off such Government, and to provide new Guards for their future security.

[List of Grievances]

Such has been the patient sufferance of these Colonies; and such is now the necessity which constrains them to alter their former Systems of Government. The history of the present King of Great Britain is a history of repeated injuries and usurpations, all having in direct object the establishment of an absolute Tyranny

---

Activity: Interdisciplinary Connection

Language Arts Have students discuss the reading difficulty presented by the Declaration of Independence. Tell them that Thomas Jefferson was selected to be the author because he was known to be a powerful writer. However, the document was not submitted exactly as Jefferson wrote it. Benjamin Franklin and John Adams made edits to the draft. **Ask:** If you were Jefferson's editor, how would you rewrite the Declaration of Natural Rights part of the document for modern readers? Advise students to use simple sentences to explain their ideas. Have them share their writing with the class. **AL**

over these States. To prove this, let Facts be submitted to a candid world.

He has refused his Assent to Laws, the most wholesome and necessary for the public good.

He has forbidden his Governors to pass Laws of immediate and pressing importance, unless suspended in their operation till his Assent should be obtained; and when so suspended, he has utterly neglected to attend to them.

He has refused to pass other Laws for the accommodation of large districts of people, unless those people would **relinquish** the right of Representation in the Legislature, a right **inestimable** to them and formidable to tyrants only.

He has called together legislative bodies at places unusual, uncomfortable, and distant from the depository of their public Records, for the sole purpose of fatiguing them into compliance with his measures.

He has dissolved Representative Houses repeatedly, for opposing with manly firmness his invasions on the rights of the people.

He has refused for a long time, after such dissolutions, to cause others to be elected; whereby the Legislative Powers, incapable of **Annihilation,** have returned to the People at large for their exercise; the State remaining in the mean time exposed to all the dangers of invasion from without, and **convulsions** within.

He has endeavoured to prevent the population of these States; for that purpose obstructing the Laws for **Naturalization of Foreigners;** refusing to pass others to encourage their migrations hither, and raising the conditions of new Appropriations of Lands.

He has obstructed the Administration of Justice, by refusing his Assent to Laws for establishing Judiciary powers.

He has made Judges dependent on his Will alone, for the **tenure** of their offices, and the amount and payment of their salaries.

He has erected a multitude of New Offices, and sent hither swarms of Officers to harass our people, and eat out their substance.

He has kept among us, in times of peace, Standing Armies without the Consent of our legislatures.

He has affected to render the Military independent of and superior to the Civil power.

He has combined with others to subject us to a jurisdiction foreign to our constitution, and unacknowledged by our laws; giving his Assent to their Acts of pretended Legislation:

relinquish: give up
inestimable: priceless

annihilation: destruction

convulsions: violent disturbances

Naturalization of Foreigners: process by which foreign-born persons become citizens

tenure: term

The Declaration of Independence **147**

Teach

R Reading Strategy

Evaluating Organize students into small groups, and assign each group several of the grievances. Have the groups find specific events, acts, or statements made by the king or Parliament that relate to at least one of their grievances. Then have the groups present their findings to the class. **AL**

C Critical Thinking

Making Inferences Ask: Why might holding government meetings in unusual and inconvenient places have offended the colonists? (*Students should note that the king was trying to make it so difficult for legislators to meet that they would simply give up. The colonists would feel like their views were not valued.*) **OL**

Activity: Technology Connection

Using the Declaration of Independence Today Tell students that although the Declaration of Independence was written hundreds of years ago, it is still relevant in today's society. Have pairs of students search an Internet news database, such as Google News www.news.google.com or Lexis-Nexis, using the search term "Declaration of Independence." Tell students to pick three news stories that reference the Declaration and note the context in which the document is mentioned. Have the pairs share their findings during a class discussion. **OL**

The Declaration of Independence

C Critical Thinking

Making Inferences Have students read this paragraph. **Ask:** What does it mean? *(The colonists have tried to ask for relief from these problems, but those efforts were ignored.)* What is the purpose of making this statement? *(to show that the colonists did not simply jump into a rebellion but had no choice)* **OL**

W Writing Support

Persuasive Writing Tell students to take the role of a Patriot or Loyalist newspaper editor from 1776, and write an editorial reacting to the Declaration of Independence. **OL**

Additional Support

---

quartering: lodging

render: make

abdicated: given up

perfidy: violation of trust

insurrections: rebellions

petitioned for redress: asked formally for a correction of wrongs

unwarrantable jurisdiction: unjustified authority

For **Quartering** large bodies of armed troops among us:

For protecting them, by a mock Trial, from punishment for any Murders which they should commit on the Inhabitants of these States:

For cutting off our Trade with all parts of the world:

For imposing Taxes on us without our Consent:

For depriving us in many cases, of the benefits of Trial by Jury:

For transporting us beyond Seas to be tried for pretended offences:

For abolishing the free System of English Laws in a neighbouring Province, establishing therein an Arbitrary government, and enlarging its Boundaries so as to **render** it at once an example and fit instrument for introducing the same absolute rule into these Colonies:

For taking away our Charters, abolishing our most valuable Laws, and altering fundamentally the Forms of our Governments:

For suspending our own Legislatures, and declaring themselves invested with power to legislate for us in all cases whatsoever.

He has **abdicated** Government here, by declaring us out of his Protection and waging War against us.

He has plundered our seas, ravaged our Coasts, burnt our towns, and destroyed the lives of our people.

He is at this time transporting large Armies of foreign Mercenaries to compleat the works of death, desolation and tyranny, already begun with circumstances of Cruelty & **perfidy** scarcely paralleled in the most barbarous ages, and totally unworthy the Head of a civilized nation.

He has constrained our fellow Citizens taken Captive on the high Seas to bear Arms against their Country, to become the executioners of their friends and Brethren, or to fall themselves by their Hands.

He has excited domestic **insurrections** amongst us, and has endeavoured to bring on the inhabitants of our frontiers, the merciless Indian Savages, whose known rule of warfare, is an undistinguished destruction of all ages, sexes and conditions.

C In every stage of these Oppressions We have **Petitioned for Redress** in the most humble terms: Our repeated Petitions have been answered only by repeated injury. A Prince whose character is thus marked by every act which may define a Tyrant, is unfit to be the ruler of a free People.

W Nor have We been wanting in attentions to our Brittish brethren. We have warned them from time to time of attempts by their legislature to extend an **unwarrantable jurisdiction** over us. We have reminded them of the circumstances of our emigration and settlement here. We have appealed to their native justice and magnanimity, and we have conjured them by the ties of our common kindred to disavow these usurpations, which, would inevitably interrupt our connections and correspondence.

148   *The Declaration of Independence*

Activity: Technology Connection

Tracing the Influence of the Declaration of Independence Tell students that France's Declaration of the Rights of Man and of the Citizen was as important to the French Revolution as the Declaration of Independence was to the American Revolution. The French document was written by the Marquis de Lafayette and was partly inspired by the American Declaration. In fact, Thomas Jefferson was the U. S. minister to France at the time the document was drafted. Lafayette and Jefferson were friends and often discussed Lafayette's work.

Have students read the translation of the document online at www.constitution.org/fr/fr_drm.htm. As they read, students should note differences and similarities between the ideas in the two documents. Have students share their findings with the class. As a class, make a Venn diagram that shows how the two documents are the same and different. **AL**

They too have been deaf to the voice of justice and of **consanguinity.** We must, therefore, acquiesce in the necessity, which denounces our Separation, and hold them, as we hold the rest of mankind, Enemies in War, in Peace Friends.

consanguinity: originating from the same ancestor

[Resolution of Independence by the United States]

> **What It Means**
>
> **Resolution of Independence** The final section declares that the colonies are "Free and Independent States" with the full power to make war, to form alliances, and to trade with other countries.

We, therefore, the Representatives of the united States of America, in General Congress, Assembled, appealing to the Supreme Judge of the world for the **rectitude** of our intentions, do, in the Name, and by Authority of the good People of these Colonies, solemnly publish and declare, That these United Colonies are, and of Right ought to be Free and Independent States; that they are Absolved from all Allegiance to the British Crown, and that all political connection between them and the State of Great Britain, is and ought to be totally dissolved; and that as Free and Independent States, they have full Power to levy War, conclude Peace, contract Alliances, establish Commerce, and to do all other Acts and Things which Independent States may of right do. And for the support of this Declaration, with a firm reliance on the protection of divine Providence, we mutually pledge **C** to each other our Lives, our Fortunes and our sacred Honor.

rectitude: rightness

Critical Thinking

Analyzing Primary Sources Ask: What does the closing of the document mean, in which the signers "mutually pledge to each other our Lives, our Fortunes and our sacred Honor"? *(The delegates promise their lives, their wealth, and their reputations to each other in a vow to carry out the work of independence.)* **OL**

Assess/Close

Identifying Central Issues Have students list the powers the new free and independent states planned to claim. *(to levy war, conclude peace, make alliances, establish commerce, and all other things governments do)* **OL**

> **What It Means**
>
> **Signers of the Declaration** The signers, as representatives of the American people, declared the colonies independent from Great Britain. Most members signed the document on August 2, 1776.

John Hancock
    President from
    Massachusetts

Georgia
Button Gwinnett
Lyman Hall
George Walton

North Carolina
William Hooper
Joseph Hewes
John Penn

South Carolina
Edward Rutledge
Thomas Heyward, Jr.
Thomas Lynch, Jr.
Arthur Middleton

Maryland
Samuel Chase
William Paca
Thomas Stone
Charles Carroll
    of Carrollton

Virginia
George Wythe
Richard Henry Lee
Thomas Jefferson
Benjamin Harrison
Thomas Nelson, Jr.
Francis Lightfoot Lee
Carter Braxton

Pennsylvania
Robert Morris
Benjamin Rush
Benjamin Franklin
John Morton
George Clymer
James Smith
George Taylor
James Wilson
George Ross

Delaware
Caesar Rodney
George Read
Thomas McKean

New York
William Floyd
Philip Livingston
Francis Lewis
Lewis Morris

New Jersey
Richard Stockton
John Witherspoon
Francis Hopkinson
John Hart
Abraham Clark

New Hampshire
Josiah Bartlett
William Whipple
Matthew Thornton

Massachusetts
Samuel Adams
John Adams
Robert Treat Paine
Elbridge Gerry

Rhode Island
Stephen Hopkins
William Ellery

Connecticut
Roger Sherman
Samuel Huntington
William Williams
Oliver Wolcott

The Declaration of Independence **149**

Fast Facts

Signers of the Declaration Richard Henry Lee and Francis Lightfoot Lee, from Virginia, were brothers, and John and Samuel Adams, from Massachusetts, were cousins. At age 26, Edward Rutledge, from South Carolina, was the youngest signer of the Declaration of Independence. Despite his age, Rutledge was an influential member of the Congress. However, he was initially opposed to independence for the colonies. He even worked to delay the vote for declaring independence. When a vote finally took place, the South Carolina and New Hampshire delegations voted no. After Rutledge realized that he was in the minority, he encouraged the South Carolina legislators to reconsider their vote to support independence.

Chapter Planning Guide

6

BL	OL	AL	ELL		Resources	Chapter Opener	Section 1	Section 2	Section 3	Section 4	Chapter Assess
					FOCUS						
BL	OL	AL	ELL	🖨	**Daily Test Practice Transparencies**		6–1	6–2	6–3	6–4	
					TEACH						
	OL	AL		📁	**Geography and History Activity, URB**				p. 59		
BL	OL		ELL	📁	**Time Line Skills Activity, URB**					p. 62	
BL	OL	AL	ELL	📁	**Writing Skills Activity, URB**			p. 51			
BL	OL	AL	ELL	📁	**Content Vocabulary Activity, URB**		p. 45	p. 45	p. 45	p. 45	
BL	OL	AL	ELL	📁	**Academic Vocabulary Activity, URB**		p. 47	p. 47	p. 47	p. 47	
BL	OL		ELL	📁	**Social Studies Skills Activity, URB**		p. 53				
BL	OL	AL	ELL	📁	**Differentiated Instruction Activity, URB**					p. 55	
BL	OL	AL	ELL	📁	**Critical Thinking Skills Activity, URB**		p. 57				
BL	OL	AL	ELL	📁	**Linking Past and Present Activity, URB**			p. 33			
	OL	AL		📁	**Primary Source Readings, URB**			p. 49			
BL	OL	AL	ELL	📁	**School-to-Home Connection Activity, URB**		p. 63	p. 63	p. 63	p. 63	
BL	OL		ELL	📁	**Guided Reading Activity, URB***		p. 67	p. 68	p. 69	p. 70	
BL	OL		ELL	📁	**Reading Essentials and Note-Taking Guide***		p. 58	p. 61	p. 54	p. 67	
BL	OL	AL	ELL	🖨	**Lesson Transparencies**		6A, 6C		6B		
	OL			📁	**American Biographies**				p 9		
BL	OL	AL	ELL	📁	**Outline Map Resource Book**	p. 9					
	OL	AL		🖨	**American Art and Architecture Transparencies, Strategies, and Activities**		14				

Note: Please refer to the *Unit Resource Book: Creating a Nation* for this chapter's materials.

* Also available in Spanish

Levels					Resources	Chapter Opener	Section 1	Section 2	Section 3	Section 4	Chapter Assess
BL	OL	AL	ELL								
					TEACH (continued)						
BL	OL	AL	ELL	📁	**NGS US Desk Map**		✓	✓	✓	✓	
BL	OL	AL	ELL	📁	**American Literature Library**		✓	✓	✓	✓	
BL	OL	AL	ELL	📁	**Writer's Guidebook**		✓	✓	✓	✓	
	OL	AL		💿	**American History Primary Source Document Library CD-ROM**		✓	✓	✓	✓	✓
BL	OL	AL	ELL	💿	**American Music: Hits Through History**	✓	✓	✓	✓	✓	
BL	OL	AL	ELL	💿	**StudentWorks™ Plus CD**	✓	✓	✓	✓	✓	✓
BL	OL	AL	ELL	📹	**Section Spotlight Videos**		✓	✓	✓	✓	
BL	OL	AL	ELL	🖥	**Writing Process Transparencies**		✓	✓	✓	✓	✓
BL	OL	AL	ELL	💿	**Presentation Plus! With MindJogger Checkpoint CD**	✓	✓	✓	✓	✓	✓
					ASSESS						
BL	OL	AL	ELL	📁	**Quizzes and Tests**		p. 51	p. 52	p. 53	p. 54	pp. 55, 57, 59
BL	OL	AL	ELL	📁	**Authentic Assessment With Rubrics**					p. 6	
BL	OL	AL	ELL	📁	**Standardized Test Practice**						p. 11
BL	OL	AL	ELL	💿	*ExamView® Assessment Suite* CD-ROM*		6–1	6–2	6–3	6–4	Ch. 6
					CLOSE						
BL			ELL	📁	**Reteaching Activity, URB***		p. 65	p. 65	p. 65	p. 65	p. 65
BL	OL		ELL	📁	**Reading and Study Skills Foldables Activity**	p. 60	p. 60	p. 60	p. 60	p. 60	p. 60
BL	OL	AL	ELL	📁	*The American Journey* in Graphic Novel						p. 37
BL			ELL	📁	**Reading Strategies and Activities for the Social Studies Classroom**		✓	✓	✓	✓	
BL	OL	AL	ELL	🖥	**Graphic Organizer Transparencies & Strategies**		✓	✓	✓	✓	

TeacherWorks™ Plus
All-In-One Planner and Resource Center

- Interactive Lesson Planner
- Interactive Teacher Edition
- Fully editable blackline masters
- Section Spotlight Videos Launch
- Differentiated Lesson Plans
- Printable reports of daily assignments
- Standards Tracking System

Professional Development Resources

- Strategies for Success
- Building Academic Vocabulary
- Success With English Learners DVD
- Differentiated Instruction Strategies DVD
- Teaching Literacy Strategies in Social Studies DVD
- Assessment DVD
- Standards-Based Instruction DVD

6

Using a Web Browser

Objective
- Students will find credible information online and incorporate it into projects.

Technology
- Glencoe TechCONNECT™ is an online program. (For more information or to get a free 30-day trial of Glencoe TechCONNECT™ for your classroom, visit techconnect.glencoe.com and click the **Free Trial** button.)

Focus/Teach
- Log on to TechCONNECT and click the **Find your textbook** link. You can also search for activities. After you log on, click **Activity Search.** Choose **Social Studies, Web Browsers,** and your grade level.

- Have students log on and enter the letters AC and the three-digit activity number.
- Have students read each page of the activity and follow the on-screen instructions.

Assess
- Have students complete the activity's self-assessment rubric.
- Students may also complete the activity's TechCheck, a five-question, multiple-choice quiz. Enter the letters TC and the three-digit activity number, such as TC068.

Close
- Review this activity with the class.

History ONLINE at glencoe.com

	Student	Teacher	Parent
Media Center			
• Student Edition Audio	●		
• Spanish Summaries	●		
• Section Spotlight Videos	●	●	
Social Studies Online Learning Center			
Classroom Tools			
• Multi-Language Glossaries	●	●	●
• Teaching Today		●	
• TIME Current Events	●	●	●
• Beyond the Textbook	●	●	
***The American Journey* Online Learning Center**			
• Study-to-Go™	●	●	●
• Study Central™	●	●	●
• Chapter Overview	●	●	
• Concepts in Motion	●	●	
• ePuzzles and Games	●	●	
• Literature Connections	●	●	
• Online Student Edition	●	●	●
• Self-Check Quizzes	●	●	●
• Student Web Activities	●	●	
• Vocabulary eFlashcards	●	●	
• Web Activity Lesson Plans	●	●	●
• Vocabulary PuzzleMaker	●	●	●

- **Timed Readings Plus in Social Studies** helps students increase their reading rate and fluency while maintaining comprehension. The 400-word passages are similar to those found on state and national assessments.

- **Reading in the Content Area: Social Studies** concentrates on six essential reading skills that help students better comprehend what they read. The book includes 75 high-interest nonfiction passages written at increasing levels of difficulty.

- **Reading Social Studies** includes strategic reading instruction and vocabulary support in Social Studies content for ELLs and native speakers of English.

- **Content Vocabulary Workout** (Grades 6–8) accelerates reading comprehension through focused vocabulary development. Social Studies content vocabulary comes from the glossaries of Glencoe's Middle School Social Studies texts.

www.jamestowneducation.com

NATIONAL GEOGRAPHIC
Index to National Geographic Magazine:

The following article relates to this chapter:

- **"Reconstructing a President,"** Whitney Dangerfield, February 2006.

National Geographic Society Products

To order the following, call National Geographic at 1-800-368-2728:

National Geographic Atlas of the World (Book)

Access National Geographic's dynamic MapMachine Web site and other geography resources at:

www.nationalgeographic.com
www.nationalgeographic.com/mapmachine

Reading List Generator CD-ROM / GLENCOE BOOKLINK 3

Use this database to search more than 30,000 titles to create a customized reading list for your students.

- Reading lists can be organized by students' reading level, author, genre, theme, or area of interest.
- The database provides Degrees of Reading Power™ (DRP) and Lexile™ readability scores for all selections.
- A brief summary of each selection is included.

Leveled reading suggestions for this chapter:

For students at a Grade 6 reading level:
- *Five Smooth Stones: Hope's Diary,* by Kristiana Gregory

For students at a Grade 7 reading level:
- *War Comes to Willy Freeman,* by James Collier and Christopher Collier
- *I'm Deborah Sampson,* by Patricia Clapp

For students at a Grade 8 reading level:
- *A Boy's Will,* by Erik Christian Haugaard
- *An Enemy Among Them,* by Deborah H. Deford and Harry S. Stout

For students at a Grade 9 reading level:
- *Heroines of the American Revolution: America's Founding Mothers,* by Diane Silcox-Jarrett
- *Why Not, Lafayette?* by Jean Fritz

For students at a Grade 10 reading level:
- *The Revolutionary War,* by Anne Todd

The following videotape program is available from Glencoe as a supplement to the chapter:

- **The American Revolution** (Six-Video Set) (ISBN 1-56-501436-7)

To order, call Glencoe at 1-800-334-7344. To find classroom resources to accompany this video, check the following home pages:

A&E Television: www.aetv.com

The History Channel: www.history.com

Chapter Objectives

After studying this chapter, students will be able to:

- Summarize the challenges faced by the American revolutionaries at the start of the war.
- Explain how the United States gained allies and aid during the Revolutionary War.
- Discuss how fighting in the West and South affected the course of the Revolutionary War.
- Describe how the Battle of Yorktown led to American independence.

Motivating Activity

Activating Prior Knowledge Review the circumstances that led to the writing of the Declaration of Independence in 1776. In this chapter, students will learn about the challenges the colonists faced to remove British rule. **Ask:** Will Americans have any chance of successfully becoming an independent nation? *(Although the colonists lacked strong, experienced armed forces, they would be fighting on familiar ground. Also, the colonies had already shown the ability to come together and work toward a common cause.)*

Previewing the Essential Questions

As you begin teaching each section, use these questions and activities to help students focus on the Essential Questions.

Chapter 6

The American Revolution
1776–1783

American soldiers in battle

★ **1776**
Declaration of Independence written

★ **1777**
Battle of Saratoga

★ **1778**
Act of Congress prohibits import of slaves into U.S.

Americas
1774   1776   1778

World

1774 ★
Joseph Priestley discovers oxygen

1775 ★
England hires German mercenaries for war in North America

1776 ★
Adam Smith's *Wealth of Nations* published

150   The American Revolution

Section 1

The Early Years Ask: Why might some Americans oppose war with Britain? *(People might have considered themselves British and loyal to the king; some opposed armed conflict; others may have feared Britain's military power.)* Point out to students that Section 1 discusses major challenges facing the Americans at the start of war. **OL**

Section 2

The War Continues Ask: Why might France and Spain choose to side with the Americans? *(They were Britain's rivals and would want to see Britain defeated.)* Point out to students that in Section 2, they will learn why other European nations chose to support the American cause. **OL**

Section 1: The Early Years
Essential Question What challenges did the American revolutionaries face at the start of the war?

Section 2: The War Continues
Essential Question How did the United States gain allies and aid during the Revolutionary War?

Section 3: The War Moves West and South
Essential Question How did fighting in the West and South affect the course of the Revolutionary War?

Section 4: The War Is Won
Essential Question How did the Battle of Yorktown lead to American independence?

◀ Continental infantryman

FOLDABLES
Study Organizer

Summarizing Information
Make this Foldable to help you summarize what you learn about the Revolutionary War.

Step 1 Begin with a 11" x 17" piece of paper.

Step 2 Fold the sides of the paper into the middle to make a shutter fold.

Step 3 Label the tabs as shown.

Reading and Writing
As you read the chapter, list important battles, people, and other facts under the correct tabs.

British Victories, Leaders, and Allies | Patriot Victories, Leaders, and Allies

History ONLINE
Chapter Overview Visit glencoe.com and click on **Chapter 6—Chapter Overviews** to preview chapter information.

★ **1779**
Spain declares war on Britain

★ **1780**
Britain declares war on Holland

★ **1780**
British forces capture Charles Town, South Carolina

1780

★ **1781**
British surrender at Yorktown

★ **1782**
Spain completes conquest of Florida

1782

★ **1783**
Treaty of Paris

★ **1783**
Famine in Japan

The American Revolution **151**

Time Line Activity

If you have not already done so, have students review the time line. **Ask:** How long did the American Revolution last, from the Declaration of Independence to the Treaty of Paris that ended the war? *(about 7 years)* Have students identify world events that might have influenced Britain's ability to fight in America. *(England gained soldiers by hiring Germans to fight in North America. Britain was fighting Spain and Holland during this same time, which may have stretched Britain's military resources.)*

FOLDABLES
Study Organizer
Dinah Zike's Foldables
Purpose This Foldable helps students summarize the key battles, people, and facts about the Revolutionary War. The completed Foldable will help them prepare for assessment.

📁 More Foldables activities for this chapter can be found in the *Dinah Zike's Reading and Study Skills Foldables.*

History ONLINE
Introduce students to chapter content and key terms by having them access the **Chapter Overview** at glencoe.com.

Section 3 ★

The War Moves West and South
Ask: The British navy blockaded American harbors. How would this impact the Americans' ability to fight? *(The Americans could not get supplies or reinforcements as easily.)* Tell students that Section 3 will describe the course of the war in the South and West. **OL**

Section 4 ★

The War Is Won Ask: How might an American victory in a large battle help end the war? *(High numbers of casualties might convince Britain that the cost of continued fighting was too high.)* Explain to students that in Section 4, they will learn how the Battle of Yorktown helped convince Britain to agree to a peace treaty. **OL**

151

Focus

Section 1

The Early Years

Bellringer
Daily Test Practice Transparency 6–1

Reading Guide
Answers to Graphic:

Defeats: Battle of Long Island, Battle of Brandywine, Battle of Paoli, capture of Philadelphia, Battle of Germantown, Battle of Fort Ticonderoga

Victories: Battle of Trenton, Battle of Princeton, Battle of Fort Stanwix, Battle of Saratoga

Section Spotlight Video

To learn more about events at the start of the Revolutionary War, watch the Section Spotlight Video "The Early Years."

Resource Manager

Essential Question
What challenges did the American revolutionaries face at the start of the war?

Reading Guide

Content Vocabulary
mercenary (p. 155)   recruit (p. 155)

Academic Vocabulary
transfer (p. 155)   previous (p. 155)

Key People and Events
Hessian (p. 155)
Molly Pitcher (p. 155)
General William Howe (p. 156)
Nathan Hale (p. 156)
Lemuel Hayes (p. 157)
Peter Salem (p. 157)
Benedict Arnold (p. 159)
General Horatio Gates (p. 159)

Reading Strategy
Taking Notes As you read, use a diagram like the one below to list the Patriot defeats and victories during the early years of the American Revolution.

Early Battles	
Defeats	Victories

ILLINOIS STANDARDS
The American Journey

14.C.3 Compare historical issues involving rights, roles, and status of individuals in relation to municipalities, states and the nation.

16.B.3b (US) Explain how and why the colonies fought for their independence and how the colonists' ideas are reflected in the Declaration of Independence and the United States Constitution.

18.B Understand the roles and interactions of individuals and groups in society.

18.C.3a Describe ways in which a diverse U.S. population has developed and maintained common beliefs (e.g., life, liberty and the pursuit of happiness; the Constitution and the Bill of Rights).

American Diary

On the night of July 9, 1776, General George Washington asked that the Declaration of Independence be read to his assembled troops in New York City. Later that night, a crowd of American soldiers and civilians marched to a park, where they toppled a gold-leafed statue of Britain's king George III on horseback. "In it were 4,000 Pounds of Lead," a lieutenant in the Continental Army said, ". . . to be run up into Musquet Balls [bullets] for the use of the Yankies."

— from the Journal of Lieutenant Isaac Bangs

Colonists pull down a statue of King George III in New York City.

R Reading Strategies	C Critical Thinking	D Differentiated Instruction	W Writing Support	S Skill Practice
Teacher Edition • Taking Notes, p. 153 • Making Conn., p. 155 • Using Word Parts, p. 156 • Using Con. Clues, p. 158 **Additional Resources** • Guid. Read., URB p. 67 • Cont. Vocab., URB p. 45 • Aca. Vocab., URB p. 47	**Teacher Edition** • Making Inferences, p. 153 • Analy. Information, p. 154 • Pred. Consequences, p. 156 **Additional Resources** • Crit. Think. Skills, URB p. 57 • Quizzes and Tests, p. 51	**Teacher Edition** • Visual/Spatial, p. 158 • Verbal/Linguistic, p. 159 **Additional Resources** • School-to-Home, URB p. 63 • Reteach Act., URB p. 65	**Teacher Edition** • Narr. Writing, p. 154 • Persuasive Writing, p. 157 • Personal Writing, p. 159 **Additional Resources** • Soc. Stud. Skills, URB p. 53	**Teacher Edition** • Using Geo. Skills, p. 154 • Using Geo. Skills, p. 156 **Additional Resources** • Daily Test Pract. Transp. 6-1 • Lesson Transp., 6A, 6C

The Opposing Sides

Main Idea The British and American forces each had advantages and disadvantages during the war for American independence.

History and You What qualities should a leader have? Read to learn how George Washington's leadership qualities were an advantage for the Patriots.

. . . .

As the toppling of the king's statue demonstrated, tensions between the colonies and Great Britain had reached a critical point after years of disagreement and negotiation. After the colonies declared independence from Britain in July 1776, the war for freedom was unavoidable.

Both sides expected the war for independence to be short. The British planned to crush the rebellion by force. Most of the Patriots—Americans who supported independence—believed the British would give up after losing one or two major battles. Few Patriots believed John Adams when he predicted in April 1776: "We shall have a long . . . and bloody war to go through."

At first glance the British had an overwhelming advantage in the war. They had the strongest navy in the world. They also had an experienced, well-trained army and the wealth of a worldwide empire. Great Britain also had a much larger population than the United States. More than 8 million people resided in Britain, compared with only 2.5 million in the United States. **C**

The colonists suffered serious disadvantages. They lacked a regular army and a strong navy. American soldiers also lacked experience. Weapons and ammunition were in short supply. Many Patriots belonged to militia groups—local forces. However, they were volunteer soldiers who fought for short periods of time before returning home. **R**

The Patriots faced another obstacle. Not all Americans supported the struggle for independence. Some people were neutral, taking neither side in the conflict. The Quakers, for example, would not participate in the war because they opposed all armed conflict. Still other Americans remained loyal to Britain.

The Loyalists

Those Americans who remained loyal to Britain and opposed the war for independence were called Loyalists or Tories. At least one American in five were thought to be Loyalists—perhaps as many as one in three. Some people changed sides during the war,

Primary Source / The Liberty Bell

Symbol of Freedom "Get us a good bell," wrote Isaac Norris, a Pennsylvania political leader to an aide in London in 1751. Arriving in 1752, the Liberty Bell was hung in the Pennsylvania State House (now Independence Hall). Its most famous ringing, on July 8, 1776, announced the first public reading of the Declaration of Independence. The Liberty Bell was rung every Fourth of July and for many public events until a crack appeared in about 1846. Today, the Liberty Bell is a symbol of freedom in the United States and throughout the world.

Critical Thinking
Speculating Why do you think symbols, such as statues, flags, and bells, are important to the people of a country?

Teach
. . . .

C Critical Thinking

Making Inferences How might a large population help a nation during wartime? *(more people to serve as soldiers and as workers making war supplies or sailors transporting supplies to the troops)* **OL**

R Reading Strategy

Taking Notes Have students prepare a bulleted list of the Patriots' disadvantages. *(lacked regular army and strong navy, lacked experience, short on weapons and ammunition, soldiers were volunteers, not all Americans supported war)* **BL**

Primary Source

Critical Thinking Answer
Students might mention the role of symbols in representing and reinforcing shared values or ideals.

Skills Practice Ask: How do you think Americans felt when they heard the Liberty Bell ring? *(Students might say proud or patriotic.)* **OL**

Additional Support

Activity: Debating the Issues

Identifying Points of View Have students form three groups, each representing a point of view on the war: Patriots, Loyalists, and neutral. Have each group do research to learn more about why the people felt as they did about the war. Direct students to use primary and secondary sources. Students should take notes during their research and then compile their notes into a fact sheet. Tell each group to select two or three students to take part in a debate on whether the colonists should go to war with Britain. Begin the debate by having each group summarize their view. Students' exchanges should use evidence from primary and secondary sources to support their points of view. After the debate, lead a class discussion about why Americans held different views. **Ask:** What position might you have taken if you lived during this period? **OL**

W Writing Support

Narrative Writing Have students write a letter as if they were William Franklin writing to his father about why he chose to remain loyal to Great Britain. Ask students to express the son's feelings as well as his reasons for taking that position. **OL**

C Critical Thinking

Analyzing Information Have students look up the meaning of "civil war" in the glossary. *(conflict between opposing groups of citizens of the same country)* **Ask:** In what ways was the American Revolution a civil war? *(People who lived in the colonies were divided over support of the war. One in three Americans was a Loyalist; some Americans changed sides during the war; some African Americans fought for British; even members of some families chose different sides.)* **OL**

S Skill Practice

Using Geography Skills Have students use the Reference Atlas to locate the country of Sierra Leone in Africa. **BL**

Additional Support

LINKING PAST TO PRESENT — Women in War

THEN In 1776 women could not officially join the army. Yet their contributions proved critical to the war effort. Some women spied on British soldiers while others traveled with the troops, serving as cooks, seamstresses, and nurses. A few women even disguised themselves as men in order to become soldiers.

◄ Female Continental soldier

Colonist Lydia Darrah spied on the British and passed information to the Continental Army. ►

depending on which army was closer. Loyalist support varied from region to region throughout the war. In general, it was strongest in the Carolinas and Georgia and weakest in New England.

Loyalists supported Britain for different reasons. Some people remained loyal because they were members of the Anglican Church, headed by the British king. Others depended on the British for their jobs. Some Loyalists feared the disorder that might break out from challenging the established government. Others simply could not understand what all the commotion was about and why the colonies wanted independence. No other country, one Loyalist complained, "faced a rebellion arising from such trivial causes."

W Friends and families were divided over their loyalty to Britain. For example, William Franklin, son of Patriot Benjamin Franklin, was a Loyalist who had served as a royal governor. As one Connecticut man observed:

PRIMARY SOURCE

C "Neighbor [was] . . . against neighbor, father against son and son against father, and he that would not thrust his own blade through his brother's heart was called an infamous villain."
—from *Less Than Glory*, by Norman Gelb

African Americans in the War

Some African Americans also sided with the Loyalists. At the start of the war, the British appealed to enslaved Africans to join them. Lord Dunmore, the royal governor of Virginia, announced that enslaved people who fought on the British side would be freed. Many men answered his call. Eventually some of them ended up free in Canada. **S** Others settled in the British colony of Sierra Leone in Africa.

Patriot Advantages

The Americans held some advantages. They were fighting on their own ground and fought with great determination to protect

---

Fast Facts

Lydia Darrah: Spy When British troops occupied Philadelphia, General Howe established headquarters near the home of Lydia Darrah. By eavesdropping, Darrah gathered information about British plans. She would write the information in simple code on scraps of paper and then hide the scraps inside large buttons on her clothing. She was able to easily carry them to Patriot officials. One night General Howe's assistant told Darrah that her family must go to bed early so that British officers could hold a private meeting in the back room of her home. Listening at the door, Darrah overheard British plans for a surprise attack on Washington's troops. The following day, Darrah persuaded Howe to grant her a pass through British lines so she could go to a mill to buy flour. Darrah rushed toward Washington's camp and turned over the information. When the British attacked, the Continental Army was ready for them. **Ask:** Why do you think Howe's assistant felt safe in telling Darrah about the private meeting? *(He might have believed that women did not pose a threat.)* **OL**

NOW Today, women play a critical role in the U.S. military. By the mid-1990s, Congress had opened nearly all military jobs to women, including combat roles. Today, about one in every seven soldiers on active duty is a woman, and many women hold leadership positions throughout the armed forces.

Critical Thinking

Analyzing The Revolutionary War was fought on American soil. How do you think this fact influenced the role of women in the war?

it. The British, however, had to wage war in a faraway land. They were forced to ship soldiers and supplies thousands of miles across the Atlantic.

Another advantage for the Americans was the type of soldiers fighting for the British. The British relied on **mercenaries**—hired soldiers—to fight for them. The Americans called the mercenaries **Hessians,** after the region in Germany from where most of them came. The Patriots were fighting for the freedom of their own land. They believed they had a much greater stake in winning the war than the hired soldiers did, who were fighting for money. This belief gave the Americans an edge over the Hessians in battle.

The Americans' greatest advantage was probably their leader, George Washington. Few could match him for courage, honesty, **R** and determination. The war might have taken a different turn without Washington.

Raising an Army

The Americans placed great value on liberty and personal freedom for citizens. After throwing off the rule of the British Parliament, they were unwilling to **transfer**—or move—power to their own Continental Congress. In some ways the American Revolution was really 13 separate wars, with each state pursuing its own interests. As a result, the Congress experienced difficulty enlisting soldiers and raising money to fight the war.

The militia played an essential role in the Patriots' forces. However, the Americans also needed well-trained soldiers who could fight anywhere in the colonies. The Congress established the Continental Army but depended on the states to **recruit,** or enlist, soldiers.

At first, soldiers signed up for one year of army service. General Washington appealed for longer terms. "If we ever hope for success," he said, "we must have men enlisted for the whole term of the war." Eventually the Continental Congress offered enlistments for three years or for the length of the war. Most soldiers, however, still signed up for only one year.

It was also difficult to recruit officers. The best officers in the Continental Army were veterans of **previous,** or earlier, wars or young men who were recruited from the ranks.

Women also fought with the Patriot forces. Margaret Corbin of Pennsylvania went with her husband when he joined the Continental Army. After he died in battle, she took his place. Mary Ludwig Hays McCauley also joined her husband in battle. The soldiers called her "Moll of the Pitcher," or **Molly Pitcher,** because she carried water pitchers to the soldiers. As a teenager, Deborah Sampson of Massachusetts watched her brothers and their friends go off to war. She then disguised herself as a boy and enlisted.

Reading Check **Summarizing** What disadvantages did the Patriots face?

R Reading Strategy

Making Connections Ask students to think about someone who has inspired them to do their best. That person might be a teacher, coach, relative, or some famous person. **Ask:** What traits do you admire in this person? *(Students might note traits such as honesty, enthusiasm, vision, wisdom, creativity, skill, courage, determination, and trustworthiness.)* Point out that a good leader is someone who inspires others to follow willingly. **OL**

This **READING SKILL** (Making Connections) was introduced in this unit.

Reading Check **Answer:** They did not have a strong navy or a regular army with experience, were short on weapons and ammunition, and did not have support from all Americans.

LINKING PAST TO PRESENT

Critical Thinking Answer
The closeness of the war made it possible for women to follow the troops and provide support. It also put them in contact with British soldiers, enabling them to serve as spies.

Additional Support

Activity: Connecting Past and Present

Analyzing Now, as then, the government recruits people for military service. Organize students into groups. Have them collect military recruitment advertisements and choose three ads to analyze. Their analyses should focus on what the ads are appealing to and consider whether the ads are effective. *(Students should note emotional appeals as well as offers such as money and job training.)* Have the groups display their ads as they present their analyses to the class. After the last presentation, ask the class to speculate about why people might join the military today. **Ask:** How are these reasons similar to or different from the reasons people joined the Continental Army? *(Patriotism and money will likely be common motivations.)* How might the recruitment message differ in wartime versus peacetime? *(Emotional appeals may be more effective in wartime, while offers such as job training and educational benefits may be used more in peacetime.)* **AL**

S Skill Practice

Using Geography Skills Ask: About how many miles would British troops travel as they crossed the Atlantic to New York? Have students use the Reference Atlas to estimate the length of the journey. *(more than 3,000 mi./5,000 km)*

R Reading Strategy

Using Word Parts Ask: Based on the first sentence, which army had the larger number of soldiers? *(British)* Write on the board: The British outnumbered the Patriots. **Ask:** What does "outnumbered" mean? *(having a larger number)* Have students look up the word "maneuver." *(skillful troop movement)* **Ask:** What does "outmaneuvered" mean? *(made more skillful troop movements)* **ELL**

C Critical Thinking

Predicting Consequences Ask: How might the lack of supplies affect the size of the Continental Army over the winter? *(The army might get smaller.)* Why? *(Some soldiers might die from cold or lack of food, and others might go home.)* **OL**

Differentiated Instruction

Patriot Defeats and Victories

Main Idea After suffering defeat at the Battle of Long Island, the Americans rallied and won victories at Trenton and Princeton.

History and You Do you think a single victory can help a struggling sports team with a losing record? Read to learn how American troops rallied following a crushing defeat by the British.

. . . .

Most of the early battles in the war involved few troops. At Bunker Hill, for example, about 2,200 British soldiers fought 1,200 Americans. The British had not yet won a decisive victory over the Patriots, however. They realized they would need more troops to end the war quickly.

During the summer of 1776, Britain sent 32,000 troops across the Atlantic to New York. The British commander, **General William Howe,** hoped the sheer size of his army would convince the Patriots to give up. He was soon disappointed.

Defeat on Long Island

Although Washington and the Patriots had fewer than 20,000 troops, they were determined to fight. In late August the two sides clashed in the Battle of Long Island. Outnumbered and outmaneuvered, the Continental Army suffered a serious defeat at the hands of the British forces.

One Patriot, **Nathan Hale,** proved himself a hero at Long Island. A teacher from Connecticut, Hale volunteered to spy on British troops. He disguised himself as a Dutch schoolteacher. The British discovered his true identity, however, and hanged him. According to tradition, just before his hanging Hale said, "I only regret that I have but one life to lose for my country."

Although the Americans showed bravery, they ran short of supplies for the army. In the autumn of 1776, a British officer wrote that many of the Patriot soldiers killed on Long Island had not been wearing shoes, socks, or jackets. "They are also in great want of blankets," he said, predicting that the rebels would suffer during the winter.

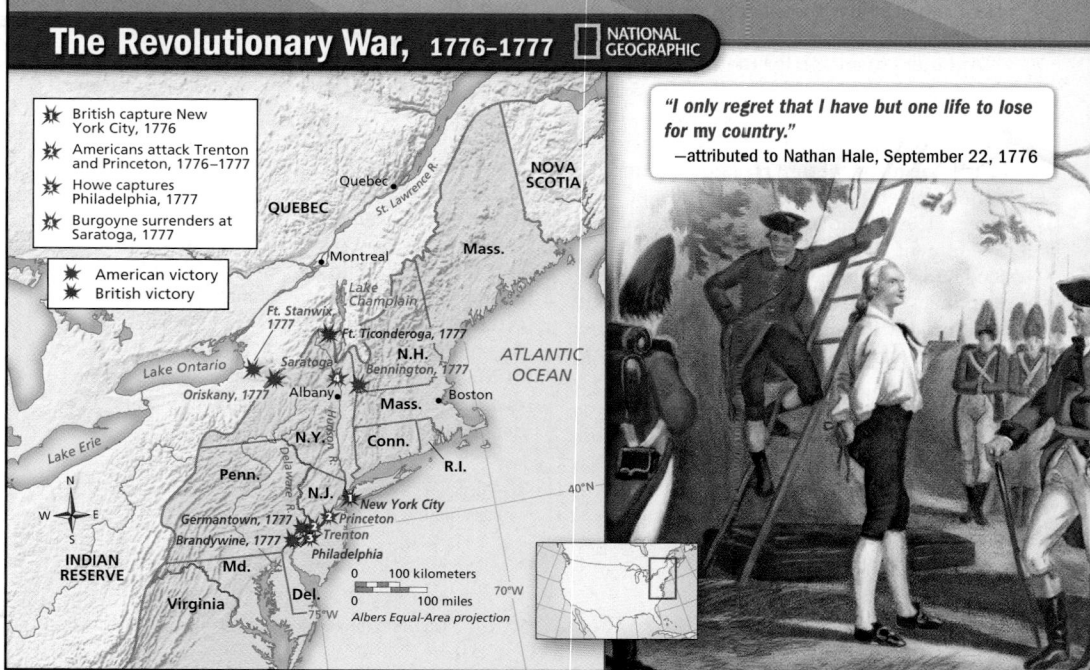

The Revolutionary War, 1776–1777
NATIONAL GEOGRAPHIC

⚔ British capture New York City, 1776
⚔ Americans attack Trenton and Princeton, 1776–1777
⚔ Howe captures Philadelphia, 1777
⚔ Burgoyne surrenders at Saratoga, 1777

★ American victory
★ British victory

QUEBEC
Quebec
St. Lawrence R.
NOVA SCOTIA
Montreal
Mass.
Lake Champlain
Ft. Stanwix 1777
Ft. Ticonderoga, 1777
Lake Ontario
Saratoga
N.H.
Bennington, 1777
ATLANTIC OCEAN
Oriskany, 1777
Albany
Mass.
Boston
Lake Erie
N.Y.
Conn.
R.I.
Penn.
N.J.
New York City
40°N
Germantown, 1777
Princeton
Brandywine, 1777
Trenton
INDIAN RESERVE
Md.
Philadelphia
Virginia
Del.
70°W
75°W
0   100 kilometers
0   100 miles
Albers Equal-Area projection

"I only regret that I have but one life to lose for my country."
—attributed to Nathan Hale, September 22, 1776

Reading a Military Map

Objective:	To learn how to read a military map
Focus:	Ask students why maps increase understanding of military campaigns.
Teach:	Have students study the map, answer the questions, and complete the activity.
Assess:	While some students read their journal entries, others find the places mentioned on the map.
Close:	Discuss how British and American soldiers might have used military maps in their campaigns.

Differentiated Instruction Strategies

BL Ask students to use the map scale to explain what it indicates about the battles shown.

AL Ask students to select another time period during the war and use geography resources to plot key battles and campaigns on a map.

ELL Have students explain what each symbol means in the map's key.

Social Studies Skills Activity
The American Revolution

Reading a Military Map

✓ Learning the Skill

A military map shows where battles occurred. Symbols show troop movements, victories, and defeats. This kind of map may also show geographic features that influence military strategy.
To read a military map, use the following steps:
• Read the title of the map.
• Decide what features the map emphasizes.
• Study the scale to determine how much area is covered.
• Look at the compass rose to determine the directions relating to the features.

✓ Practicing the Skill

Directions: Use the military map below to answer these questions.

1. **Locating** In which three states did most of the fighting in 1776–1777 take place?

2. **Identifying** What symbol is used to indicate American troop movements?

3. **Specifying** From what direction did the British troops march on Philadelphia?

4. **Identifying** Which side won victories at Trenton and Princeton?

Social Studies Skills Activity, URB p. 53

After the defeat on Long Island, Washington retreated to Manhattan. With the British in pursuit, the Continental Army retreated across New Jersey into Pennsylvania.

A Low Point

In the winter of 1776–1777, the Patriots' cause was near collapse. The size of the Continental Army had dwindled. Some soldiers completed their terms of service and went home. Other soldiers ran away.

Washington wrote his brother that if new soldiers were not recruited soon, "I think the game is pretty near up." Still, he could not believe that the fight for liberty would truly fail.

Washington pleaded with the Continental Congress for more troops. He even asked that the Congress allow free African Americans to enlist. Early in the war, however, the Southern states had persuaded the Congress not to allow African Americans in the Continental Army. Many white people in the South felt uncomfortable about giving guns to African Americans and allowing them to serve as soldiers. In those Southern states that had large enslaved populations, the whites feared revolts.

African Americans Join the Fight

As the need for soldiers grew, some states ignored the ban and enlisted African Americans. Rhode Island raised an all–African American regiment in 1778. By the war's end, every state except South Carolina enlisted African Americans to fight.

Historians estimate that as many as 5,000 African Americans joined the Patriots. Among them were **Lemuel Hayes** and **Peter Salem,** who fought at Concord. African Americans fought because they believed in the Patriot cause or they needed the money. Some were enslaved Africans who had run away from slaveholders and fought to earn their freedom.

W American Victories in New Jersey

The British settled in New York for the winter, leaving some troops in Princeton and Trenton, New Jersey. Washington saw a chance to catch the British off guard.

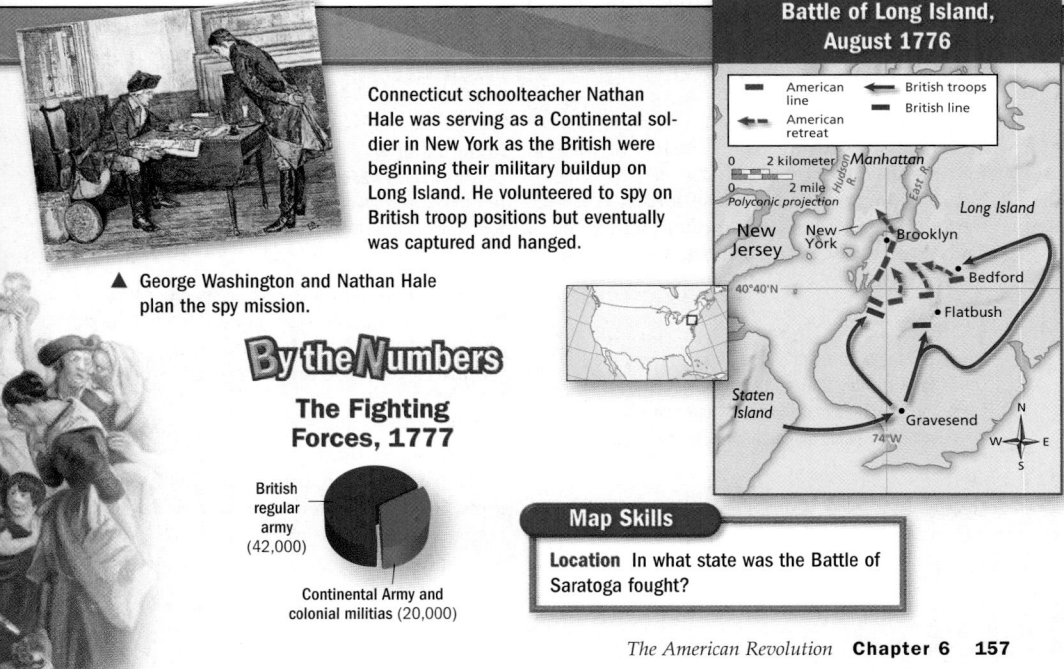

Connecticut schoolteacher Nathan Hale was serving as a Continental soldier in New York as the British were beginning their military buildup on Long Island. He volunteered to spy on British troop positions but eventually was captured and hanged.

▲ George Washington and Nathan Hale plan the spy mission.

Battle of Long Island, August 1776

American line
American retreat
British troops
British line

0   2 kilometer
0   2 mile
Polyconic projection

New Jersey   New York   Brooklyn   Long Island   Bedford   Flatbush   Staten Island   Gravesend

40°40'N   74°W

Manhattan   Hudson R.   East R.

By the Numbers

The Fighting Forces, 1777

British regular army (42,000)

Continental Army and colonial militias (20,000)

Map Skills

Location In what state was the Battle of Saratoga fought?

The American Revolution **Chapter 6** 157

W Writing Support

Persuasive Writing Have students take the role of members of the Continental Congress. They are responsible for recruiting more troops for the Continental Army, including African Americans. *(Messages should include offers that might motivate men to enlist.)* **OL**

The Revolutionary War 1776–1777

NATIONAL GEOGRAPHIC

Map Skills Answer
1. New York

Map Skills Practice
Ask: Based on what you read and the map, how many times would the Continental Army have to cross water during its retreat from the Battle of Long Island? *(At least twice: once to get to New York and again to get to New Jersey.)*

Differentiated Instruction

Leveled Activities

BL School-to-Home Connection, URB p. 63

OL Reteaching Activity, URB p. 65

AL Critical Thinking Skills Activity, URB p. 57

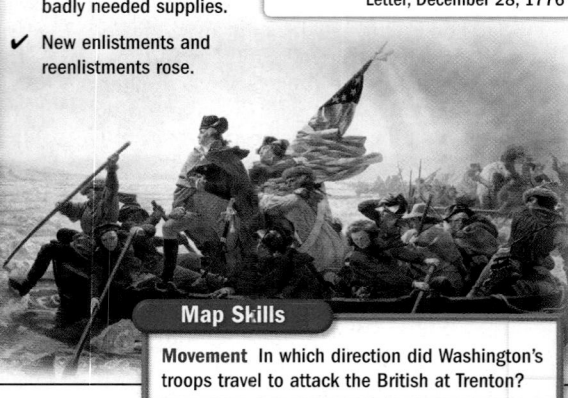
R Reading Strategy

Using Context Clues Read this quote aloud to the class. **Ask:** What is a scale? *(an instrument for measuring weight)* What do you think "turn the scale" means? *(The weight went from one side to the other—the British were winning, but the advantage shifted to the American side.)* **ELL**

D Differentiated Instruction

Visual/Spatial Have students draw a compass rose on their papers. Then ask them to draw a graphic organizer showing the parts of the British battle plan and the direction of each attack. *(Organizers should show Burgoyne's troops marching south, St. Leger's troops moving east, and Howe's group moving north, all planning to converge on Albany.)* **BL**

The Battle of Trenton ☐ NATIONAL GEOGRAPHIC

Map Skills Answer

southeast

✓ Reading Check **Answer:** The Patriots' cause was near collapse, but Washington's successful attacks around Christmas of 1776 rekindled his army's fighting spirit.

Hands-On Chapter Project
Step 1

Washington's leadership at the Battle of Trenton led to an important victory for the Patriots:

✔ Washington's troops gained confidence.

✔ The Continental Army won badly needed supplies.

✔ New enlistments and reenlistments rose.

> "Our Men pushed on with such rapidity, that they soon carried four pieces of Cannon out of Six, Surrounded the Enemy, and obliged 30 Officers and 886 privates to lay down their Arms without firing a Shot. Our loss was only two Officers and two or three privates wounded. The Enemy had between 20 and 30 killed."
> —George Washington, Letter, December 28, 1776

Map Skills

Movement In which direction did Washington's troops travel to attack the British at Trenton?

Washington was stationed in Pennsylvania across the Delaware River from the British camp in New Jersey. On Christmas night 1776, Washington and 2,400 troops crossed the icy river and surprised the enemy at Trenton the next day. The British sent reinforcements under Lord Charles Cornwallis, but Washington evaded those forces. Washington then marched to Princeton, where his army drove away the British. One British observer wrote:

> **PRIMARY SOURCE**
>
> R "A few days ago, [the Americans] had given up the cause for lost. Their late successes have turned the scale and now they are all liberty-mad again."
> —Nicholas Cresswell, quoted in *George Washington's War*

✓ Reading Check **Explaining** Why was the winter of 1776–1777 significant?

D A British Plan for Victory

Main Idea The British plan to separate New England from the Middle Colonies was foiled at the Battle of Saratoga.

History and You Do you like to play chess or other games in which you outmaneuver your opponent? Read how the Americans outmaneuvered a British army and won a stunning victory.

. . . .

The British worked out a battle plan for 1777. They would take Albany, New York, and gain control of the Hudson River. This would separate New England from the Middle Colonies.

The plan involved a three-pronged attack. General John Burgoyne would lead nearly 8,000 troops south from Canada. A second force, under Lieutenant Colonel Barry St. Leger, would move east from Lake Ontario.

Writing War Correspondence

Step 1: Understanding Point of View Students will write letters that demonstrate opposing points of view.

Essential Question: What challenges did the American revolutionaries face at the start of the war?

Directions Working in small groups, students will compile a list of challenges faced by the British and Continental armies. Posing as spies for either the British or Americans, have groups write letters to their commanders outlining the challenges their enemy faces and the prospects for victory.

Analyzing As a class, discuss ways that the challenges facing the Patriots could cause the colonies to fail in their bid for independence. **OL**

(Chapter Project continued in Section 2)

A third group, under General Howe, would move north from New York City. The three British forces would meet at Albany and destroy the Patriot troops.

The British Capture Philadelphia

Howe won battles in September 1777 at Brandywine and Paoli, near Philadelphia. Then Howe's troops captured Philadelphia, forcing the Continental Congress to flee. In early October, Washington attacked the British at nearby Germantown but had to withdraw. Howe decided to spend the winter in Philadelphia instead of going to Albany.

Patriots Slow the British

Meanwhile, problems delayed the British from taking Albany. In August, American soldiers halted St. Leger's advance at Fort Stanwix, New York. Led by **Benedict Arnold,** the Americans forced the British to retreat.

General Burgoyne's army was not making much progress toward Albany either. In July he captured Fort Ticonderoga, but trouble followed. Because he enjoyed good food and fine clothes, Burgoyne traveled with 30 **D** wagons of luxury goods. This baggage, along with the trees downed by the Americans to block the British, slowed Burgoyne's journey.

Burgoyne needed supplies. He sent 800 troops and Native Americans to capture the American supply base at Bennington, Vermont. A local militia group, the Green Mountain Boys, attacked and defeated them. Desperate for supplies, Burgoyne retreated in October to Saratoga, New York.

The Battle of Saratoga

Burgoyne faced serious trouble at Saratoga. The British forces he expected did not arrive. The Americans had stopped St. Leger's army at Fort Stanwix, and Howe's forces were still in Philadelphia. In addition, American troops under the command of **General Horatio Gates** blocked Burgoyne's path to the south. **W** Burgoyne found himself surrounded by a larger army. Burgoyne made a desperate attack on October 7. The Americans held firm.

On October 17, 1777, General Burgoyne surrendered. The British plan had failed. General Howe resigned as commander of the British troops in America. He was replaced by General Henry Clinton.

✔ **Reading Check** **Analyzing** Why was the Battle of Saratoga a turning point in the war?

History ONLINE
Study Central™ To review this section, go to glencoe.com.

Section 1 Review

Vocabulary

1. Use the terms mercenary, transfer, recruit, and previous in separate sentences that explain their meanings.

Main Ideas

2. Discussing What disadvantages did British forces face in the American Revolution?

3. Explaining Why were African Americans at first banned from serving in the Continental Army?

4. Analyzing What difficulties did General Burgoyne face at the Battle of Saratoga?

Critical Thinking

5. Analyzing Use a diagram like the one below to explain why the Loyalists supported Britain.

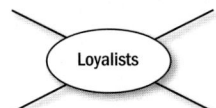

Loyalists

6. Persuasive Writing As a colonist, write a letter to the editor of your local newspaper. Point out the colonies' strengths and why you think you will win the war for independence.

Answer the
7. Essential Question
What challenges did the American revolutionaries face at the start of the war?

The American Revolution **Chapter 6** **159**

Answers

1. Sentences should use terms correctly according to their definitions in the section and the Glossary.

2. The British were fighting in a faraway land and had to ship in soldiers and supplies. They also relied on mercenaries, who fought only for money and had little stake in the outcome.

3. The Southern states persuaded Congress not to allow African Americans to enlist. Fearing revolts, many white Southerners felt uncomfortable about giving guns to African Americans so they could serve as soldiers.

4. British reinforcements did not arrive. American troops blocked his path to the south. A larger American force surrounded his army.

5. Loyalists were members of the Anglican Church; depended on the British for work; feared disorder; and thought rebellion was trivial.

6. Students' letters should use the colonies' strengths described in the section to argue persuasively that the Patriots will win the war.

7. Americans had fewer people and less wealth; they lacked a regular army and a strong navy; they lacked military experience, weapons, and ammunition; not all Americans supported the cause; and some Americans fought for the British.

The War Continues

Focus

Bellringer
Daily Test Practice Transparency 6–2

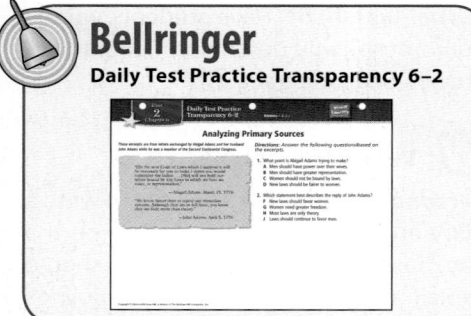

Reading Guide
Answers to Graphic:

Allies: France, Spain, and other European nations, Mexico, Cuba; **Individuals:** de Gálvez, Lafayette, Kościuszko, Pulaski, von Steuben, de Miralles; **Volunteers:** Martha Washington and others who made clothes or cared for the sick

Section Spotlight Video

Watch the Section Spotlight Video "The War Continues" to learn more about African American contributions to the war effort.

Essential Question ◄
How did the United States gain allies and aid during the Revolutionary War?

Reading Guide

Content Vocabulary
desert (p. 162)   inflation (p. 164)

Academic Vocabulary
aid (p. 161)   issue (p. 165)

Key People and Events
Bernardo de Gálvez (p. 161)
Marquis de Lafayette (p. 163)
Friedrich von Steuben (p. 163)
Juan de Miralles (p. 163)
Judith Sargeant Murray (p. 165)
Abigail Adams (p. 165)

Reading Strategy
Taking Notes As you read, use a diagram like the one below to determine what aid the Patriots received during the American Revolution.

Sources of Aid to the Patriots

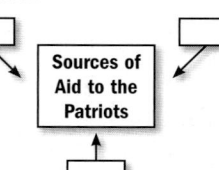

ILLINOIS STANDARDS
The American Journey

15.E Understand the impact of government policies and decisions on production and consumption in the economy.

16.A.3b Makes inferences about historical events and eras using historical maps and other historical sources.

16.B.3b (US) Explain how and why the colonies fought for their independence and how the colonists' ideas are reflected in the Declaration of Independence and the United States Constitution.

18.B.3a Analyze how individuals and groups interact with and within institutions (e.g., educational, military).

American Diary

The Continental Congress sent Jonathan Austin of Boston to France to deliver the news of the American victory at Saratoga. Benjamin Franklin was already in France trying to get that country to help the Americans fight against the British. As soon as Austin arrived, Franklin nervously inquired, "Sir, is Philadelphia taken?" Austin answered, "Yes sir. . . . But sir, I have greater news than that. General Burgoyne and his whole army are prisoners of war!"

—quoted in Liberty! The American Revolution

Benjamin Franklin arrives at the Court of the French king, Louis XVI.

Resource Manager

R **Reading Strategies**	C **Critical Thinking**	D **Differentiated Instruction**	W **Writing Support**	S **Skill Practice**
Teacher Edition • Taking Notes, p. 161 • Visualizing, p. 164 **Additional Resources** • Guid. Read., URB p. 68 • Cont. Vocab., URB p. 45 • Aca. Vocab., URB p. 47 • Pri. Source Read., URB p. 49	**Teacher Edition** • Analyzing Info., p. 163 • Ident. Cent. Issues, p. 165 • Compare and Contrast, p. 165 **Additional Resources** • Link. Past & Pres., URB p. 33 • Quizzes and Tests, p. 52	**Teacher Edition** • Auditory/Musical, p. 162 **Additional Resources** • School-to-Home, URB p. 63 • Reteaching Act., URB p. 65	**Teacher Edition** • Narrative Writing, p. 163 **Additional Resources** • Writ. Skills, URB p. 51	**Teacher Edition** • Using Geo. Skills, p. 162 **Additional Resources** • Daily Test Pract. Transp. 6-2

Gaining Allies

Main Idea Even with aid from other nations and individuals, the Patriots had difficulty financing their war for independence.

History and You Have you ever had to ask friends for help when you could not complete a task? Was the task easier to complete? Read about how the Americans sought help during their fight for independence.

Like Ben Franklin, many Americans were excited by news of the victory at Saratoga in October 1777. Even more, Saratoga marked a turning point in the war. The European nations, especially France, realized that the Americans might actually win their war against Great Britain.

Now was the time for the Americans to seek support from Great Britain's rivals. By late 1777, Benjamin Franklin had been in Paris for a year. He was trying to get the French to support the Americans' fight for independence. With his skill and charm, Franklin gained many friends for the United States. The French had given the Americans money secretly, but they had not fully committed to an alliance.

France

News of the American victory at Saratoga caused a shift in France's policy. Realizing that the Americans had a chance of defeating Britain, the French openly announced support for the United States. In February 1778, the French and the Americans worked out a trade agreement and an alliance. France declared war on Britain and sent money, equipment, and troops to **aid,** or help, the American Patriots.

Spain

Other European nations also helped the American cause. They did so mostly because they hated the British. Although Spain did not recognize American independence until after the Revolution, Spain declared war on Britain in 1779. The Spanish governor of Louisiana, **Bernardo de Gálvez** (GAHL•ves), raised an army. Gálvez's soldiers forced British troops from Baton Rouge and Natchez. Then the army captured British forts at Mobile in 1780 and Pensacola in 1781. Gálvez's campaign through hundreds of miles of wilderness diverted British troops from other fronts of the war.

Primary Source / Franklin Memorabilia

The World's First Celebrity While serving as America's first ambassador to France, Benjamin Franklin was greatly admired by the country's nobles and thinkers. After all, he was a man of great charm and many talents—philosopher, writer, printer, scientist, inventor, politician, and diplomat. Much like a singer or movie star today, Franklin became so popular in America and Europe that his likeness appeared on many items—medallions, rings, watches, and small boxes. Fashionable ladies even adopted a hairstyle that resembled the famous fur cap that Franklin wore.

Critical Thinking

Making Connections How do you think Franklin used his personality and talents to benefit the American cause? Would you consider him a celebrity? Are there any celebrities today who are like Franklin? Explain.

Writing War Correspondence

Step 2: Persuasive Writing Students will write letters that persuade the reader to support the American cause.

Essential Question: How did the United States gain allies and aid during the Revolutionary War?

Directions Have the groups consider the role of Benjamin Franklin in Paris. Using what they learned about the weaknesses faced by the Americans, have groups write letters to the French king that persuade him to openly support the Patriots. Letters should make specific requests, as well as appeal to the French view of the British.

Predicting As a class, discuss how allies and aid from other nations might affect the course of the war. **OL**

(Chapter Project continued in Section 3)

Teach

R Reading Strategy

Taking Notes As they read the section, have students create a problem/solution chart. They should list problems that the Americans faced in the left hand. In the right-hand column, they should note how each problem was addressed. *(Lists might include lack of money > aid from foreign countries, some money from states, printed money; troops outnumbered > made allies who contributed troops; difficulty delivering supplies to Valley Forge > soldiers built huts and gathered supplies from the countryside, and volunteers made clothes and cared for the sick; inflation > stopped printing money.)* **OL**

Primary Source

Critical Thinking Answer
Students might suggest that Franklin could use his charm and popularity to gain allies and aid from other nations. A celebrity is a famous person, so Franklin could be considered a celebrity. Students might name musicians who give concerts to benefit a charity or sports stars who use their fame in advertisements to persuade people to buy products.

Hands-On Chapter Project
Step 2

Dear Folks,

S Skill Practice

Using Geography Skills Have students research to learn how geography influenced Washington's decision to camp at Valley Forge. **Ask:** *What resources were available in the area to help the soldiers survive? (Answers should include the nearby rivers and streams, nearby farms, and forests for building materials.) Why was the distance from Valley Forge to Philadelphia important? (It was close enough to monitor British movements but far enough to avoid a surprise attack.)* **AL**

D Differentiated Instruction

Auditory/Musical To keep up their spirits, the soldiers at Valley Forge sang military and patriotic songs. Have groups of students write the words to a song about the Revolutionary War, set to a familiar tune. The words should include historical details, but the tone should be hopeful or optimistic. Have the groups perform their songs for the class. **OL**

Differentiated Instruction

Winter at Valley Forge

Word of the French-American alliance did not reach the United States until the spring of 1778. Meanwhile, British general Howe and his forces spent the winter in comfort in Philadelphia. Washington set up camp at Valley Forge, about 20 miles (32 km) to the west of the British. Washington and his troops endured a winter of terrible suffering. They lacked decent food, clothing, shelter, and medicine. Washington's greatest challenge at Valley Forge was keeping the Continental Army together.

Because it was difficult to get supplies delivered due to snowstorms and damaged roads, the Continental Army built huts and gathered supplies from the countryside. Several volunteers—including Washington's wife, Martha—made clothes for the troops and cared for the sick. Washington declared that no army had ever suffered "such uncommon hardships" with such "patience and fortitude."

Joseph Martin, a young private from Connecticut, spent the winter at Valley Forge.

"We had a hard duty to perform," he wrote years later, "and little or no strength to perform it with." Most of the men lacked blankets, shoes, and shirts. Martin made a pair of rough moccasins for himself out of a scrap of cowhide, which hurt his feet.

PRIMARY SOURCE

"The only alternative I had, was to endure this inconvenience or to go barefoot, as hundreds of my companions had to, till they might be tracked by their blood upon the rough frozen ground."

—Joseph Martin, in *A Narrative of a Revolutionary Soldier*

Not surprisingly, many men **deserted,** or left without permission, while the Continental Army was camped at Valley Forge. Some officers resigned. The army seemed to be falling apart.

Yet with strong determination, the Continental Army survived the winter. Conditions gradually improved and new soldiers joined the ranks in the spring. "The army grows stronger every day," one officer wrote. "There is a spirit of discipline among the troops that is better than numbers."

Primary Source / A Turning Point at Valley Forge

Winter Soldiers For the Continental Army, the winter of 1777 at Valley Forge was terrible. Soldiers suffered through a lack of food and clothing, and many became ill and died. By March, better weather had arrived along with a trickle of food and supplies. By April, Baron von Steuben was turning the troops into a fighting force.

"Naked and starving as they are, we cannot enough admire the incomparable patience and fidelity [faithfulness] of the soldiery."
—George Washington, Letter to Governor George Clinton, February 16, 1778

◀ Washington and Lafayette at Valley Forge, winter 1777

Camp bed used at Valley Forge ▼

Leveled Activities

BL **Guided Reading Activity, URB p. 68**

OL **Primary Source Reading Activity, URB p. 49**

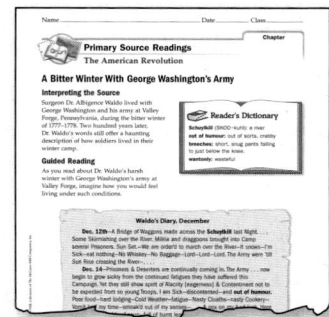

AL **Linking Past and Present Activity, URB p. 33**

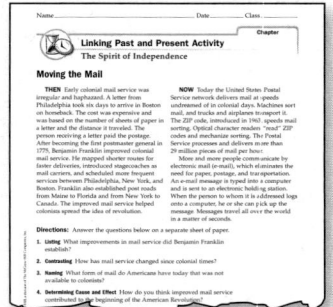

ELL **Content Vocabulary Activity, URB p. 45**

In April 1778, Washington told his troops of the Patriots' alliance with France. Everyone's spirits rose at the thought of help from overseas. The Continental Army celebrated with a religious service and a parade.

Help From Overseas

Among the leaders at Valley Forge was a French noble, the **Marquis de Lafayette** (LAH•fee•EHT). Lafayette was filled with enthusiasm for the ideas expressed in the Declaration of Independence and he rushed to join the battle for freedom. Lafayette wrote: "The future of America is closely bound up with the future of all mankind."

Upon his arrival in Philadelphia, Lafayette offered his services to General Washington. Lafayette became a trusted aide to Washington.

Other Europeans also volunteered to work for the Patriot cause. Two Poles—Thaddeus Kościuszko (kawsh•CHUSH•koh), an engineer, and Casimir Pulaski, a cavalry officer—contributed to the American efforts. Promoted to general, Pulaski died in 1779, fighting for the Continental Army.

Friedrich von Steuben (STOO•buhn), a former army officer from Prussia, also came to help Washington. Von Steuben drilled the Patriot troops at Valley Forge, teaching them military discipline. He spoke little English, so he used aides to translate drills and a training manual that he wrote. Von Steuben turned the ragged Continental Army into a more effective fighting force.

Juan de Miralles (mee•RAH•yays) arrived in Philadelphia in 1778 as a representative of Spain. At his urging, Spain, Cuba, and Mexico sent financial aid to the colonies. Miralles befriended many Patriot leaders and loaned money to the cause.

Other Europeans who had recently moved to the United States also joined the Patriot cause. In fact, almost two-thirds of soldiers in the Pennsylvania regiments were foreign-born.

Even with the help of foreign nations like France and Spain, the Patriots would find it difficult to defeat the British. The Continental Army still needed large amounts of money to continue to fight the war.

W Writing Support

Narrative Writing Have students consider Washington's personality. Then have them write a quote that reflects what they think the general might have said about one of the following topics: the progress of the war thus far; conditions at Valley Forge; alliances; or military experts who arrived recently from Europe. Select several students to read their quotes to the class. **OL**

C Critical Thinking

Analyzing Information Ask: How did alliances help the Continental Army overcome the disadvantages described in Section 1? (*Troops and experienced military leaders from other countries strengthened the Continental Army. Allies sent money, which could be used for supplies.*) **OL**

Primary Source

Critical Thinking Answer
Friedrich von Steuben helped train the troops, turning them into a fighting force. Many soldiers remained through the winter, despite the hardships.

Additional Support

Valley Forge today ▲

Baron von Steuben drills American recruits at Valley Forge, 1778. ▶

The Continental Army received important help from Europeans. Friedrich von Steuben was a Prussian officer who arrived at Valley Forge on February 23, 1778. Von Steuben began by training a "model company" of 100 chosen men. Each company commander was responsible for training the men in his company, including new recruits.

Critical Thinking
Describing What happened at Valley Forge to change the course of the war?

The American Revolution **Chapter 6** **163**

Activity: Interdisciplinary Connection

Literature The situation looked bleak for the Patriots in late 1776. Washington's army was falling apart. In the winter of 1776, Thomas Paine published *The American Crisis* to boost the Americans' spirit. The pamphlet began with the stirring words "These are the times that try men's souls." George Washington found Paine's words so moving that he ordered a reading of this pamphlet to his troops at Valley Forge. Distribute copies of the first paragraph of *The American Crisis*. Have students work in pairs to analyze it. Then ask a student to read the paragraph aloud, pausing after each sentence for interpretation from the class. At the end of the reading, discuss why this passage is so inspirational. **AL**

People IN HISTORY

Molly Pitcher

Heroine at the Battle of Monmouth Court House

Molly Pitcher may have done more than carry water to American soldiers at the Battle of Monmouth Court House in New Jersey on June 28, 1778. According to legend, when her husband collapsed from the heat, she heroically took his place in battle. On February 21, 1822, Pennsylvania recognized Molly Pitcher's service to the nation by granting her an annual pension of $40.

Abigail Adams

Wife of John Adams, delegate to the Continental Congress

Abigail Adams famously argued for women's rights in a letter to her husband, telling him, "If [particular] care and attention is not paid to the Ladies we are determined to [start] a [rebellion], and will not hold ourselves bound by any Laws in which we have no voice, or Representation."

CRITICAL Thinking

1. **Analyzing** Why do you think Molly Pitcher became a legendary heroine?
2. **Evaluating** Both Molly Pitcher and Abigail Adams challenged traditional women's roles. Why do you think their actions were accepted by society at that time?

R Reading Strategy

Visualizing To help students understand the meaning of inflation, ask them to visualize a balloon. **Ask:** What happens when you inflate a balloon? *(It gets larger.)* Explain that in times of inflation, prices are inflating—they are growing larger. **BL**

People IN HISTORY

Critical Thinking Answers

1. Students might suggest that her courage was inspiring.
2. Possible response: This was a time of crisis, and women were helping the cause in important ways.

Critical Thinking Practice

Read the quote from Abigail Adams aloud. **Ask:** To what American document does her statement seem to refer? *(Declaration of Independence)* **OL**

✔ Reading Check **Answer:** He came with enthusiasm for the cause and became a trusted aide to General Washington.

Differentiated Instruction

Money Problems

Getting money to finance the war was a major problem. The Continental Congress had no power to raise money through taxes. Although the Congress received some money from the states and from foreign countries, much more was needed to finance the war.

To pay for the war, the Congress and the states printed hundreds of millions of dollars' worth of paper money. The bills quickly lost their value, though. The amount of bills in circulation grew faster than the supply of gold and silver backing them. This led to **R** **inflation,** which means that it took more and more money to buy the same amount of goods. The Congress stopped issuing the paper money because no one would use it. However, the Americans had no other way to finance their fight for independence.

✔ Reading Check **Describing** How did Lafayette help the Patriot cause?

Life on the Home Front

Main Idea The ideals of liberty and freedom that inspired the American Revolution carried through to the issues of women's interests and slavery.

History and You Have you ever taken on more duties at home when another person was away? Read how women's roles changed during the American Revolution.

The war changed the lives of all Americans, even those who stayed at home. Thousands of men were away in military service, so many women took charge of their families. Other women ran their husbands' or their own businesses.

Changing Attitudes

The ideals of liberty and freedom inspired the American Revolution. These same ideals also caused some women to question their place and treatment in American society.

Brainstorming Ideas

Objective:	To learn how to brainstorm writing ideas
Focus:	Ask students how they get ideas when preparing a creative assignment for a class.
Teach:	Have students read about learning the skill; then have them practice and apply the skill.
Assess:	Have students assess their brainstorming strategies by using the self-assessment checklist.
Close:	Ask for class volunteers to present their strategies, and then discuss them as a class.

Differentiated Instruction Strategies

BL Provide students with a list of questions to help stimulate their brainstorming.

AL Have students research methods used by a writer, an artist, or a musician to get creative ideas.

ELL Ask students to define the term "brainstorming" in their own words.

Writing Skills Activity, URB p. 51

In an essay on education, **Judith Sargeant Murray** of Massachusetts argued that women's minds are as good as men's. Girls, therefore, should get as good an education as boys. Most girls received little schooling, so this was a radical idea.

Abigail Adams also stood up for women's interests. She wrote to her husband, John Adams, a member of Congress:

PRIMARY SOURCE

"I can not say that I think you [are] very generous to the Ladies, for whilst you are proclaiming peace and good will to Men, Emancipating all Nations, you insist upon retaining an absolute power over Wives."
—from *Adams Family Papers*

Hopes for Equality

The Revolutionary War ideals of freedom and liberty inspired some white Americans to question slavery. As early as the Stamp Act crisis, religious groups and other groups had voted to condemn slavery.

In 1778 Governor William Livingston of New Jersey asked the legislature to free all enslaved people in the state. He said slavery was "utterly inconsistent with the principles of Christianity and humanity." African

Americans made similar arguments. In New Hampshire enslaved people asked the legislature for their freedom "so that the name of *slave* may not be heard in a land gloriously contending for the sweets of freedom."

From the start of the war, African Americans fought for the American cause and hoped the Revolution would help end slavery. Vermont, New Hampshire, Massachusetts, and Pennsylvania attempted to abolish slavery in their states. The **issue,** or matter, of slavery would remain unsettled for many years, however.

Treatment of Loyalists

During the war, thousands of Loyalists fought on the side of the British. Some Loyalists spied and informed on the Patriots. Many Loyalists, however, fled the colonies.

Loyalists who remained in the United States faced difficult times. Their neighbors often shunned them. Some became victims of mob violence. Loyalists who actively helped the British could be arrested and tried as traitors. Patriots executed a few Loyalists, but such measures were unusual.

✓ **Reading Check** **Describing** How were Loyalists treated by the Patriots during the war?

C1 Critical Thinking

Identifying Central Issues Ask: Why was slavery at odds with the ideals of the American Revolution? *(White Americans were seeking freedom from Britain's tyranny but were denying freedom to enslaved African Americans.)* **BL**

C2 Critical Thinking

Comparing and Contrasting Have students research and report on the treatment of German and Japanese Americans in World War II. **AL**

 Reading Check **Answer:** Neighbors shunned them. Some suffered violence or were arrested and tried as traitors.

Assess

 History ONLINE

Study Central™ provides summaries, interactive games, and online graphic organizers to help students review content.

Close

Inferring As a class, discuss what might have resulted if the Patriots did not have strong allies. **OL**

Section 2 Review

Section 2 Review

History ONLINE
Study Central™ To review this section, go to glencoe.com.

Vocabulary

1. Write a paragraph that explains how the following terms relate to the war for independence: aid, desert, inflation, issue.

Main Ideas

2. **Explaining** Why did the Patriots find it hard to finance the war for independence?

3. **Discussing** How did the war for independence affect slavery in the United States?

Critical Thinking

4. **Determining Cause and Effect** Use a diagram like the one below to identify the effects of the Revolutionary War on women who remained at home.

Effects of the War on Women

5. **Creative Writing** Write a paragraph in which you describe what Martha Washington might have experienced when she helped the soldiers during the winter at Valley Forge.

Answer the
Essential Question
6. How did the United States gain allies and aid during the Revolutionary War?

Answers

1. Paragraphs should explain how the terms relate to the American Revolution.
2. The Continental Congress did not have the power to impose taxes, and not enough money came from the colonies and foreign countries. Inflation made the paper money they printed almost worthless.
3. Answers will vary but should touch on ideals that led to questioning slavery, attempts to end slavery in some states, and African Americans' role in the war.

4. Women at home took charge of families, ran businesses, and promoted ideas of equality.
5. Paragraphs might touch on Martha Washington's sympathy for the suffering troops and what she could do to help.
6. Britain had many European rivals, especially France. In Paris, Benjamin Franklin used his skill and charm to convince the French to send money secretly. When the Patriot victory at Saratoga showed that the Americans

might win, France, Spain, and other rivals took the opportunity to oppose Britain by supporting the Americans openly. Spain declared war on Britain. The French noble Lafayette was inspired to join the Patriots because of the ideals expressed in the Declaration of Independence. The Spanish representative de Miralles loaned money to the Patriots and convinced Spain, Cuba, and Mexico to send financial aid.

Focus

C Critical Thinking

Determining Cause and Effect
Ask: What caused Martin to feel discouraged? *(He had not eaten in four days.)* Do you think his age affected his outlook? *(Students may be surprised by Martin's young age, which might have made it harder for him to live with the situation.)* **OL**

Teach

S Skill Practice

Visual Literacy Have students study the artwork of the soldiers at Valley Forge. **Ask:** What do you think the soldiers in the picture are feeling? *(cold, exhausted, hurt)* How is this reflected in the painting? *(They are huddled by a fire; some are bandaged.)* **BL**

R Reading Strategy

Using Context Clues Discuss how the word "hang" has two different meanings here. Have students identify the meaning in each instance. *(first reference means "staying together"; second reference means "being killed")* **OL**

Additional Support and Answers

TIME NOTEBOOK

What were people's lives like in the past?

These two pages will give you some clues to everyday life in the United States as you step back in time with TIME Notebook.

American Voices

ONE TEEN'S WRITINGS FROM THE "WINTER OF DEATH"

At 15, **JOSEPH PLUMB MARTIN** *signed up with the Continental Army. At first, Martin was sure of his decision. But the fierce winter and lack of food and supplies at Valley Forge in 1778 shook his confidence. Here is what Martin wrote about during that long winter that killed over 2,000 soldiers.*

"We were absolutely literally starved. I do solemnly declare that I did not put a morsel of victuals [food] into my mouth for four days and as many nights, except a little black birch bark which I gnawed off a stick of wood, if that can be called victuals. I saw several of the men roast their old shoes and eat them, and I was afterwards informed . . . that some of the officers killed and ate a favorite little dog that belonged to one of them. If this is not 'suffering' I request to be informed what can pass under the name."

STOCK MONTAGE, INC. / GETTY IMAGES

EXHAUSTED AND HUNGRY SOLDIERS AT VALLEY FORGE, 1778

Fan-tastic

Do you like to gossip at parties but are afraid others are listening? Then this "secret language" is for you. Just grab a fan and start gabbing!

ACTION	WHAT IT MEANS
Open fan and wave it in front of your face.	"I'm jealous."
Close fan and strike it against your palm.	"I'm angry."
Open fan and wave it very slowly.	"I think you're interesting."
Close the fan and place one end against your lips.	"I don't want to talk."
Open fan and quickly wave it.	"I'm concerned."

166

VERBATIM

WHAT PEOPLE ARE SAYING

❝ I have not yet begun to fight. ❞
JOHN PAUL JONES,
America's first naval war hero, in 1779, upon hearing that his ship was sinking while battling the British warship, Serapis

❝ There, I guess King George will be able to read that. ❞
JOHN HANCOCK,
after signing the Declaration of Independence with his huge signature in 1776

❝ We must all hang together, or most assuredly we shall all hang separately. ❞
BENJAMIN FRANKLIN,
on signing the Declaration of Independence in 1776

❝ The New England governments are in a state of rebellion, blows must decide whether they are to be subject to this country or independent. ❞
KING GEORGE III OF ENGLAND,
1774

❝ . . . if particular care and attention are not paid to the ladies, we are determined to foment [cause] a rebellion and will not hold ourselves bound to obey laws in which we have no voice or representation. ❞
ABIGAIL ADAMS,
in a letter to her husband John around the time of the signing of the Declaration of Independence

---

Fast Facts

Women and Politics Many of Abigail Adams's words have lived on through the letters she wrote to her husband John while he was living abroad and she was managing their home and caring for the couple's children.

Even though Abigail encouraged her husband to pay particular attention to the ladies in drafting the Declaration of Independence, she did not push for the right of women to vote. In the late 1700s, in fact, allowing women to vote was practically unheard of. Abigail did, though, favor the abolition of slavery and a woman's right to an education. She wrote her husband that "you need not be told how much female education is neglected, nor how fashionable it has been to ridicule female learning." Abigail is thought to have played a significant role in her husband's political career.

COLONIAL GAMES
Nine Man Morris Scores a Ten!

What are all the colonial kids playing?
It is that entertaining game **Nine Man Morris**.

1. Get nine copper coins, nine silver coins, and a friend to play with you.
2. Make a drawing like the one shown on a piece of paper.
3. Give yourself the copper coins and your friend the silver ones.
4. Take turns placing your coins on the dots in the drawing.
5. Be the first to line up three of your coins in a row.
6. Capture one of the other player's coins when you get three in a row.
7. Keep playing until one player is down to two coins. The other player wins!

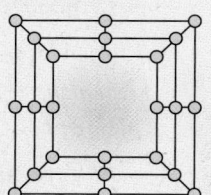

MILESTONES
EVENTS AND PEOPLE OF THE TIME

AMAZED. In 1771 world-famous composer Amadeus Mozart upon hearing the glass armonica, which was just invented by Benjamin Franklin. This musical instrument touches different spinning glasses to make music. It is similar to rubbing the rim of a glass to make a sound. Rumor has it that Mozart might someday compose music for Franklin's invention.

THE GLASS ARMONICA

PROHIBITED. Slavery, by the New England Quakers at their yearly meeting in 1770. The first colonial American group to do so, the Quakers have declared the enslavement of others to be wrong.

TRAINED. American soldiers at Valley Forge in 1778 by German aristocrat, Baron von Steuben, who speaks very little English. Hired by George Washington to get his soldiers in shape, Von Steuben ranted, screamed, and yelled at the troops—while an aide translated. But his raving paid off. He taught the soldiers to load rifles correctly and fight in formation. By the end of the long winter, the Americans were a more unified fighting force.

NUMBERS
UNITED STATES AT THE TIME

342 Number of crates—which held thousands of pounds of tea—dumped into Boston Harbor by angry Patriots who dressed as Native Americans on December 16, 1773

6 Days it takes to travel between Boston and New York in 1772 by stagecoach. Each day, travelers spend 18 hours on the bumpy roads and, each night, sleep in their clothes at inns

350 About the number of miles ridden in 6 days (a record time) by Israel Bissell, 23, in 1775, warning colonists, "To arms, to arms, the war has begun!"; the day after Paul Revere's more famous 20-mile ride

10,000 The approximate number of enslaved persons who earned their freedom by fighting against the British

40 Number of newspapers in the colonies during the American Revolution—six of which are published by women

CRITICAL THINKING

Explaining What does King George III mean when he says "blows must decide"? (See Verbatim)

Analyzing Primary Sources What was Joseph Martin's mood at Valley Forge in 1778? Do you think modern-day troops in war face similar issues? Explain your answer.

W Writing Support

Expository Writing Have students select one of the events in "Milestones." Ask them to research their subjects, thinking about the five Ws: *Who, What, When, Where,* and *Why.* Students should take notes and then write a newspaper article on the subject. They should create a headline for the article in language that might have been used during the late 1700s. Their articles should try to answer the five questions in the first few paragraphs. Have student volunteers read their articles to the class. **AL**

C Critical Thinking

Comparing and Contrasting Review the information in "Numbers" about how people traveled between Boston and New York in 1772. Have students compare and contrast traveling between the two cities today with traveling in 1772. **OL**

Assess/Close

As a class, discuss how people's lives are affected when their country is at war. Think from the perspective of not only soldiers and political leaders but also everyday citizens. Ask how people in the late 1700s who were opposed to the war might have expressed their opinions. How is it different from how people express opposing views today? **OL**

167

Answers

Explaining He means that a physical confrontation, or war, is the only way to settle the rebellion.

Analyzing Primary Sources He is discouraged, hungry, and tired. Student answers about modern-day troops should compare conditions at Valley Forge with conditions today and reflect knowledge of the difficulty of fighting in a war.

Section 3

Section 3

The War Moves West and South

Focus

Bellringer
Daily Test Practice Transparency 6–3

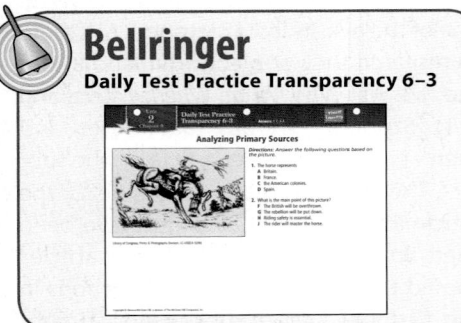

Reading Guide
Answers to Graphic:
built fleet of warships; authorized use of privateers

Section Spotlight Video

To learn more about the war in different regions of the country, watch the Section Spotlight Video "The War Moves West and South."

Essential Question
How did fighting in the West and South affect the course of the Revolutionary War?

Reading Guide

Content Vocabulary
blockade (p. 170)
privateer (p. 170)
guerrilla warfare (p. 172)

Academic Vocabulary
impact (p. 171)   sustain (p. 173)

Key People and Events
Joseph Brant (p. 169)
George Rogers Clark (p. 169)
John Paul Jones (p. 170)
Battle of Moore's Creek (p. 171)
General Charles Cornwallis (p. 171)
Francis Marion (p. 172)
Nathanael Greene (p. 173)

Reading Strategy
Taking Notes As you read, use a diagram like the one below to analyze how the Americans responded to the British naval blockade.

Response to British Naval Blockade

ILLINOIS STANDARDS
The American Journey

16.B.3b (US) Explain how and why the colonies fought for their independence and how the colonists' ideas are reflected in the Declaration of Independence and the United States Constitution.

17.C.3a Explain how human activity is affected by geographic factors.

18.B.3a Analyze how individuals and groups interact with and within institutions (e.g. educational, military)

American Diary

A brave Mohawk war chief, Joseph Brant, blended Native American and British ways. Brant, however, spoke strongly on behalf of his people. On a 1776 visit to London, he said the Mohawks have "[shown] their zeal and loyalty to the . . . King; yet they have been very badly treated by his people. . . . Indeed, it is very hard when we have let the King's subjects have so much of our lands . . . [and] they should want to cheat us."

—Joseph Brant, speech, March 14, 1776

Loyalists and their Native American allies attack an American settlement in Pennsylvania's Wyoming Valley in the summer of 1778.

Resource Manager

R Reading Strategies	**C** Critical Thinking	**D** Differentiated Instruction	**W** Writing Support	**S** Skill Practice
Teacher Edition • Skimming, p. 169 **Additional Resources** • Guid. Read., URB p. 69 • Content Vocab., URB p. 45 • Academic Vocab., URB p. 47 • Read. Ess., p. 64	**Teacher Edition** • Analy. Info., p. 170 • Ident. Cent. Issues, p. 171 • Deter. Cause & Effect, p. 173 **Additional Resources** • Quizzes and Tests, p. 53	**Teacher Edition** • ELL, p. 171 • ELL, p. 172 **Additional Resources** • School-to-Home, URB p. 63 • Reteaching Act., URB p. 65	**Teacher Edition** • Narrative Writing, p. 172	**Teacher Edition** • Using Geo. Skills, p. 170 **Additional Resources** • Daily Test Pract. Transp. 6-3 • Geo. & Hist., URB p. 59 • Lesson Transp., 6B

War in the West

Main Idea The British, along with their Native American allies, led attacks against settlers in the West.

History and You Do you have a nickname? If so, how did you get it? Read to learn the nickname of Henry Hamilton, the British commander at Detroit.

The concerns of Mohawk chief **Joseph Brant** and other Native Americans about their lands became entangled in the events of the American Revolution. As a result, several important battles involving Native Americans took place along the western frontier. Some Native Americans helped the Patriots, but more sided with the British. For them, the British seemed less of a threat than the Americans.

The British and Native Americans

West of the Appalachian Mountains, the British and their Native American allies raided American settlements. Joseph Brant led a number of brutal attacks in southwestern New York and northern Pennsylvania.

R Henry Hamilton, British commander at Detroit, was called the "hair buyer." He earned this nickname because he paid Native Americans for settlers' scalps.

Victory at Vincennes

George Rogers Clark, a lieutenant colonel in the Virginia militia, set out to end the British attacks on western settlers. In July 1778, Clark and 175 soldiers sailed west down the Ohio River. After a march of about 120 miles (193 km), the Patriots seized the British post at Kaskaskia (ka•SKAS•kee•uh) in present-day Illinois. They then captured the British town of Vincennes (vihn•SEHNZ) in present-day Indiana.

British troops under Henry Hamilton's command recaptured Vincennes that December. Clark vowed to get it back. In February 1779, Clark and his troops led a surprise attack against the British and forced Hamilton to surrender. George Rogers Clark's victory at Vincennes strengthened the American position in the West.

✓ **Reading Check** **Summarizing** Describe events in the Revolutionary War in the west.

Time Line | **Native Americans in the Revolution**

The War on the Frontier At the time of the American Revolution, about 200,000 Native Americans lived along the western frontier. Their loyalties were divided between the British and the Americans.

★ **1775** Mohawk pledge neutrality

★ **1776** Loyalist Cherokee attack North Carolina Patriots

★ **1777** Mohawk turn to the British; defeated Cherokee lose land to Americans

★ **1782** Americans force peace on the Mohawk

▲ Native American war club

Critical Thinking
Hypothesizing Why do you think many Native Americans supported the British rather than the Americans?

Activity: Collaborative Learning

Verbal/Linguistic Organize students into four groups. Assign each group one of these leaders: Joseph Brant, George Rogers Clark, Francis Marion, or Nathanael Greene. Have students do research to learn more about the person's activities during the Revolutionary War. Ask each group to write a skit about an event during the war involving that person. Each group member should have a role to play. Have the groups perform their skits for the class. **OL**

Teach

R **Reading Strategy**

Skimming Have students skim this page and write a statement summarizing the main idea in each paragraph. *(Possible statements: Most Native Americans sided with the British. British and their Native American allies raided American settlements in the West. George Rogers Clark captured British posts at Kaskaskia and Vincennes. Clark lost Vincennes but won it back, strengthening the American position in the West.)* **BL**

Time Line

Critical Thinking Answer
Answers should reflect Native American desire to keep their land and resist further American settlement.

✓ **Reading Check** **Answer:** Kaskaskia and Vincennes

Additional Support

Teacher Tip

Collaborating Students may be more engaged in the activity if they are allowed to choose their group. Write the names of the leaders on the board. Have students choose the leader who most appeals to them.

S Skill Practice

Using Geography Skills Refer students to the map on the following page. **Ask:** How did the British navy use the location of the American colonies to its advantage? *(The larger colonial cities were located mainly along the coast and depended on their ports for supplies. The strong British navy could stop the flow of supplies into the colonies by blockading these ports.)* **OL**

C Critical Thinking

Analyzing Information Ask: What are the pros and cons of employing privateers to help fight the war? *(Students might note that the lure of profit attracted much-needed fighters. However, privateers might not fight as hard for money as would people motivated by patriotism.)* **OL**

Primary Source

Critical Thinking Answer
Students might suggest that a fast ship would help Jones strike quickly and escape.

Reading Check Answer: Jones won a decisive battle against a British warship and became a naval hero to the Patriots.

Differentiated Instruction

Glory at Sea

Main Idea The American navy and American privateers had some successes against the powerful British navy.

History and You Besides George Washington, what other heroes of the American Revolution do you know? Read to learn about John Paul Jones, who became a naval hero during the Revolutionary War.

....

As fighting continued on the western frontier, other battles raged at sea. Great Britain's powerful navy kept the ships of the Patriots and of their allies from entering or leaving American harbors. This **blockade** prevented supplies and reinforcements from reaching the Continental Army.

Privateers

To break the blockade, the Second Continental Congress ordered construction of 13 American warships. Only two of these ships, however, sailed to sea. Several were quickly captured by the British. The American navy was too weak to operate effectively.

The Congress authorized approximately 2,000 ships to sail as **privateers.** These were privately owned merchant ships with weapons. Finding crews for these ships was not difficult. Privateering was a profitable trade. Privateers captured more British ships at sea than the American navy.

John Paul Jones

A daring American naval officer, **John Paul Jones,** raided British ports. Near the coast of Great Britain in September 1779, Jones's ship, *Bonhomme Richard,* met the British warship *Serapis* escorting a fleet of merchant ships. The *Bonhomme Richard* and the *Serapis* fought for hours. The British captain asked whether Jones wished to surrender. Jones is said to have answered, "I have not yet begun to fight."

In the end, the *Serapis* surrendered, but the *Bonhomme Richard* sank not long after the battle. Still, his victory made John Paul Jones a naval hero to the American Patriots.

Reading Check Describing How did privateers contribute to the American war effort?

Primary Source / John Paul Jones

The warships *Bonhomme Richard* and *Serapis*

"*I wish to have no Connection with any Ship that does not Sail fast, for I intend to go in harm's way.*"
—Captain John Paul Jones, Letter, 1778

Cannons like this one were used on the *Bonhomme Richard.* ▼

Critical Thinking
Analyzing Why did John Paul Jones want a fast ship?

The American Revolution at Sea

Objective: To learn about the role of naval power during the War of Independence

Focus: Ask students to explain why almost all the cities in the colonies were major ports.

Teach: Have students read the information and study the map.

Assess: Students should complete the four questions in the activity.

Close: Have students briefly summarize the effect of naval power for the Americans and the British.

Differentiated Instruction Strategies

BL Ask students to create a graphic organizer comparing information about the British and colonial naval powers.

AL Have students research and write a report on the role of privateers in the Continental Navy.

ELL Have students define the following terms: "port," "vessel," and "privateer."

Geography and History Activity, URB p. 59

The Revolutionary War in the West and South, 1778–1781   NATIONAL GEOGRAPHIC

200 kilometers
200 miles
Lambert Azimuthal Equal-Area projection

Ft. Detroit
Lake Erie
N.Y.
West Point
Mass.
Conn.
Wabash R.
Ft. Miami
HAMILTON
Pa.
R.I.
New York City
Cahokia July 9, 1778
Vincennes Feb. 25, 1779
Ft. Pitt
Valley Forge
N.J.
Ohio River
CLARK
Md.
Del.
Kaskaskia July 4, 1778
Va.
Yorktown
APPALACHIAN
GREENE
N.C.
CORNWALLIS
Cowpens
Kings Mtn.
CORNWALLIS
Wilmington
S.C.
MARION
Camden
Charles Town
CLINTON, 1780
DE GRASSE
Ga.
CAMPBELL, 1778
ATLANTIC OCEAN
Savannah

British capture Savannah, 1778
Patriots victorious at Kaskaskia, Cahokia, and Vincennes
Patriots victorious at Kings Mountain and Cowpens
4 Washington and Rochambeau rush toward Virginia, Aug. 1781
5 French Admiral De Grasse keeps British ships away
Cornwallis trapped; the British surrender at Yorktown, 1781

A tin lantern used by a Revolutionary War soldier

American and/or allied forces
British forces
American victory
British victory
Fort

85°W   80°W   75°W

Map Skills

Region What can you conclude about the strength of the Patriot army based on the events in the West and the South?

Maps in Motion See StudentWorks™ Plus or glencoe.com.

Struggles in the South

Main Idea Great Britain hoped that a strong campaign in the South would help the war.

History and You Has a strategy ever helped your team score a victory or helped you to do better on a test? Read to find out about American and British strategies in the South.

In the war's early years, the Americans won several battles in the South. In 1776 they crushed Loyalists at the **Battle of Moore's Creek,** near Wilmington, North Carolina. They also saved Charles Town, South Carolina, from the British. Although a small battle, its **impact,** or effect, was great.

By 1778 the British realized that bringing the American colonies back into the empire would not be easy. As a result, they changed their strategy and planned a hard-hitting offensive to finish the war.

The British concentrated their efforts in the South, where there were many Loyalists. They hoped to use British sea power and the support of the Loyalists to win decisive victories in the Southern states. Initially the strategy worked.

British Victories

In late 1778, General Henry Clinton sent 3,500 British troops from New York to take Savannah, Georgia. The British occupied the coastal city and overran most of the state.

In early 1780, Clinton himself headed south with a large army to attack the port of Charles Town, South Carolina. Charles Town surrendered in May, and the British took thousands of prisoners. It marked the worst American defeat of the war.

Clinton returned to New York, leaving **General Charles Cornwallis** in command of British forces in the South. The Continental Congress sent forces under General Horatio Gates to face Cornwallis. The two armies met at Camden, South Carolina, in August 1780. Although the British won, Cornwallis soon found that he could not control the area he had conquered. He and his troops faced a new kind of warfare.

The American Revolution **Chapter 6** **171**

C Critical Thinking

Identifying Central Issues Ask: On what strengths did the British base their battle plan in the South? *(There were many Loyalists in the South; the British had superior sea power.)* **OL**

D Differentiated Instruction

English Language Learners Students may have difficulty following the progress of the war in the South. Encourage them to use their fingers to trace the troop movements as they read about each battle. At the end of each battle description, ask students to state the winner to help them remember. **BL**

The Revolutionary War in the West and South   NATIONAL GEOGRAPHIC

Map Skills Answer
Students might suggest that the Patriot army was getting stronger. The Patriots won more key battles than did the British in these areas.

Hands-On Chapter Project
Step 3

Writing War Correspondence

Step 3: Personal Writing Students will write letters that describe civilian life near the battlefront.

Essential Question: How did fighting in the West and South affect the course of the Revolutionary War?

Directions Instruct groups to take the role of Loyalists living in the South during the war.

Have them write letters to friends in New York that describe the battles taking place, how their daily lives are affected, and whether they will remain Loyalists or switch their support to the Patriots.

Assessing As a class, discuss how the war seems to be going for the Patriots at this point. **OL**

(Chapter Project continued in Section 4)

D Differentiated Instruction

English Language Learners Ask the class what "guerrilla" means in Spanish. *(little war)* **Ask:** How was the guerrilla battle technique like a "little war"? *(Guerrilla warfare involved many small battles instead of major battles between large armies.)* **ELL**

W Writing Support

Narrative Writing Have students write a short legend, or story, glorifying the adventures of the Swamp Fox. Tell them that often a legend is based in fact, but the events in the story may be exaggerated to create a character who is larger than life. **OL**

INTERPRETING POLITICAL CARTOONS

Answers

1. The figure representing Britain is holding a cat-of-nine-tails, or whip.
2. The horse is in the process of throwing the rider, suggesting that the colonists will succeed in throwing off British rule.

Differentiated Instruction

Primary Sources
INTERPRETING
POLITICAL CARTOONS

This British cartoon was drawn in 1779, before the American Revolution ended. It shows a rider being thrown off of a horse.

1. **Analyzing** What evidence in the cartoon suggests that Britain was harsh toward the colonies?
2. **Drawing Conclusions** What outcome of the war does the cartoonist predict?

A. America B. Great Britain
C. Revolutionary War soldier

THE HORSE AMERICA THROWS HIS MASTER.

Guerrilla Warfare

The British received less help than they had expected from Loyalists in Southern states. Instead, as British troops moved through the countryside, small forces of Patriots attacked them. These bands of soldiers appeared suddenly, struck their blows, and then disappeared. This hit-and-run technique of **guerrilla warfare** caught the British off guard.

One successful guerrilla leader, **Francis Marion,** operated out of the swamps of eastern South Carolina. Known as the Swamp Fox, Marion was quick and smart. One British colonel grumbled that "the devil himself" could not catch Marion.

Help From Spain

When Bernardo de Gálvez became governor of Louisiana, Spain was neutral. That did not stop Gálvez from helping the colonists. He loaned thousands of dollars to the Americans and opened the port of New Orleans to free trade. Gálvez also had tons of supplies and ammunition shipped up the Mississippi River to American troops in the Northwest Territory. With this help, George Rogers Clark captured the key posts of Kaskaskia, Cahokia, and Vincennes.

In the summer of 1779, Spain declared war on Britain. Gálvez raised an army of Spanish soldiers along with Creoles, Native Americans, and African Americans and marched on British posts along the lower Mississippi. He captured Baton Rouge, Natchez, Mobile, and Pensacola. Gálvez's victories opened supply lines for military goods from Spain, France, Cuba, and Mexico.

According to historian Buchanan Parker Thomson, Gálvez had given:

PRIMARY SOURCE

". . . the most vital aid contributed by any one man to the struggling American colonies. In winning this triumphant victory over the last great British outpost, he had not only served his King to the limit of his strength, but had made to the United States the most important gift an ally could offer: the security of their southeastern and western frontiers."

—from *Spain: Forgotten Ally of the American Revolution*

Leveled Activities

BL Reading Essentials and Note-Taking Guide, p. 64

OL Reteaching Activity, URB p. 65

ELL Content Vocabulary Activity, URB p. 45

Patriot Victories

After their victory at Camden, South Carolina, the British moved northward through the Carolinas in September 1780. At Kings Mountain, a British officer and more than 1,000 Loyalists defended an outpost against Patriot attack. The Patriots forced the British to retreat. The victory brought new support for independence from Southerners. They wanted to see an end to the war that was destroying their homes and farms.

In October 1780, **Nathanael Greene** replaced Gates as commander of the Continental forces in the South. Rather than lead an all-out attack on Cornwallis's forces, Greene split his army in two. In January 1781 one section of the army, led by General Daniel Morgan, defeated the British at Cowpens, South Carolina. Another section joined Marion's guerrilla raids.

Greene reunited his forces in March to meet Cornwallis's army at Guilford Courthouse, in present-day Greensboro, North Carolina. Greene's army was forced to retreat, but the British **sustained,** or suffered, great losses in the process. General Cornwallis abandoned the Carolina campaign.

History ONLINE
Student Web Activity Visit glencoe.com and complete the Chapter 6 Web Activity about the Revolutionary War in the South.

British Retreat

Cornwallis realized that the British had to act quickly to win the war. More French troops were on their way to America, and the Patriots still held Virginia. Troops and supplies were still moving south. In April 1781, Cornwallis marched north to Virginia. His troops carried out raids throughout the state. They nearly captured Governor Thomas Jefferson and the Virginia legislature in June. Jefferson fled on horseback, just ahead of the advancing British troops.

General Washington sent Lafayette and General Anthony Wayne south to fight Cornwallis. Meanwhile, Cornwallis set up camp at Yorktown, which was located on the Virginia coast. There he awaited further orders from Clinton in New York. The battle for the South was entering its final phase.

Reading Check **Evaluating** What effect did the Patriot victory at Kings Mountain produce?

History ONLINE
Study Central™ To review this section, go to glencoe.com.

Section 3 Review

Vocabulary
1. Define each of the following terms, and use it in a sentence: blockade, privateer, impact, guerrilla warfare, sustain.

Main Ideas
2. **Stating** Which side did more Native Americans take in the war for independence and why?
3. **Discussing** Why did the Americans need to break the British naval blockade?

4. **Explaining** How did Spain help to undermine Great Britain's Southern strategy?

Critical Thinking
5. **Creative Writing** Write a short play based on John Paul Jones and the battle between the *Bonhomme Richard* and the *Serapis.*

6. **Determining Cause and Effect** Use a diagram like the one below to show why the British lost control in the South.

British Defeats in the South

Answer the Essential Question
7. How did fighting in the West and South affect the course of the Revolutionary War?

The American Revolution **Chapter 6** 173

C Critical Thinking
Determining Cause and Effect
Ask: How did the battles in the Carolinas affect the course of the war? *(They brought new support for independence from Southerners and cost the British great losses, convincing Cornwallis to abandon the Carolina campaign.)* **OL**

History ONLINE
Objectives and answers to the Student Web Activity can be found at glencoe.com under the Web Activity Lesson Plan for this chapter.

Reading Check **Answer:** It brought new support for independence from Southerners.

Assess
History ONLINE

Study Central™ provides summaries, interactive games, and online graphic organizers to help students review content.

Close
Summarizing As a class, discuss the key events in the South and West that helped the Americans gain an advantage in the war. **OL**

Section 3 Review

Answers

1. Definitions should use terms as they are defined in the section and the Glossary.
2. Most sided with the British, as they seemed to pose less of a threat than did the Americans.
3. Because of the blockade, the ships of the Patriots and their allies could not enter or leave American harbors, and the army could not receive supplies and reinforcements.

4. Gálvez's army captured British posts along the lower Mississippi River, opening supply lines for military aid from Spain, France, Cuba, and Mexico.
5. Students' plays should include relevant facts and details of the battle.
6. The British received less help from the Loyalists than expected; guerrilla warfare by Patriots; help for Patriots from Spain and Gálvez.

7. George Rogers Clark's victories helped strengthen the American position in the West. In the South, the American strategy of guerrilla warfare, along with aid from the Spanish, helped defeat the British campaign there.

Focus

The War Is Won

Bellringer
Daily Test Practice Transparency 6–4

Reading Guide
Answers to Graphic:
Lafayette's troops, Washington's and Rochambeau's American-French army, de Grasse's French fleet

Section Spotlight Video

Watch the Section Spotlight Video "The War Is Won" to learn more about how Americans gained their independence.

Essential Question
How did the Battle of Yorktown lead to American independence?

Reading Guide

Content Vocabulary
ratify (p. 177)   ambush (p. 178)

Academic Vocabulary
strategy (p. 175)   pursue (p. 177)

Key People and Events
Comte de Rochambeau (p. 175)
François de Grasse (p. 175)
Battle of Yorktown (p. 176)
Benjamin Franklin (p. 177)
John Adams (p. 177)
John Jay (p. 177)
Treaty of Paris (p. 177)

Reading Strategy
Taking Notes As you read, use a diagram like the one below to list the forces that met Cornwallis at Yorktown.

ILLINOIS STANDARDS
The American Journey

16.A.3c Identify the differences between historical fact and interpretation.

16.B.3b (US) Explain how and why the colonies fought for their independence and how the colonists' ideas are reflected in the Declaration of Independence and the United States Constitution.

18.B.3a Analyze how individuals and groups interact with and within institutions (e.g. educational, military)

American Diary

At the Battle of Yorktown, a Pennsylvania soldier named Ebenezer Denny saw a drummer boy on the British side beat a signal for a meeting. The cannon fire immediately stopped. From the British lines came an officer. Then an officer from the American side ran to meet him. Denny wrote in his journal, "Firing ceased totally. . . . I never heard a drum equal to it—the most delightful music to us all."

—*from* Record of Upland, and Denny's Military Journal

British forces under General Charles Cornwallis surrender at Yorktown, Virginia.

Resource Manager

R Reading Strategies	C Critical Thinking	D Differentiated Instruction	W Writing Support	S Skill Practice
Teacher Edition • Activat. Prior Knowl., p. 177 • Organizing, p. 178 **Additional Resources** • Guid. Read., URB p. 70 • Content Vocab., URB p. 45 • Academic Vocab., URB p. 47 • Read. Ess., p. 67	**Teacher Edition** • Predict. Conseq., p. 175 • Analyz. Information, p. 176 **Additional Resources** • Authentic Assess., p. 6 • Quizzes and Tests, p. 54	**Teacher Edition** • Auditory/Musical, p. 176 • Kinesthetic, p. 178 **Additional Resources** • School-to-Home, URB p. 63 • Reteaching Act., URB p. 65	**Teacher Edition** • Expository Writing, p. 177 **Additional Resources** • Differ. Inst., URB p. 55	**Additional Resources** • Daily Test Pract. Transp. 6-4 • Time Line Skills, URB p. 62

Victory at Yorktown

Main Idea Washington's complicated battle plan led to the important American victory at Yorktown.

History and You How important is planning to the successful outcome of a project? Read to learn how Washington's planning helped the Americans win an important victory.

Denny was proud to witness the steps leading to the British surrender at Yorktown. The buildup to this great event began a few months earlier. At that time, the Revolutionary War was at a critical point and both armies sought a victory. General Washington made plans to attack the British at Yorktown, Virginia, rather than in New York City. The Patriots hoped for help from the French.

In July 1780, French warships appeared off Newport, Rhode Island. The ships carried the promised French aid: soldiers commanded by **Comte de Rochambeau** (ROH•SHAM•BOH). Unfortunately, the British fleet arrived soon afterward and trapped the French ships in Newport.

In the autumn of 1780, Washington camped north of New York City. He waited for a second fleet of French ships. He also kept a close eye on the British army based in New York that General Clinton commanded. Washington planned to attack Clinton's army as soon as the second French fleet arrived. He had to wait a year to put this plan into action. The French fleet did not set sail for America until the summer of 1781.

Change in Plans

Washington followed the reports of the fighting in the South during 1780 and 1781. He knew that Cornwallis's troops were camped in Yorktown, Virginia, and that Lafayette was keeping them bottled up on the Yorktown peninsula. He also learned that Admiral **François de Grasse,** the French naval commander, was heading toward Chesapeake Bay instead of New York. Washington quickly changed his plans. He would advance on the British at Yorktown rather than at New York City.

Washington kept his new **strategy,** or plan of action, secret. He wanted Clinton to think the Patriots still planned to attack the British in New York. This, he hoped, would keep Clinton from sending aid to Cornwallis. Meanwhile, in July Rochambeau had marched his troops from Newport to join Washington.

Primary Source | Revolutionary Music

"Yankee Doodle" The song "Yankee Doodle" was played at the Yorktown surrender ceremony to annoy the British. British forces first sang "Yankee Doodle" to poke fun at what they considered the awkward ways of the Americans. The song tells the story of a poorly dressed Yankee "doodle," or simple person. The Americans, however, quickly made "Yankee Doodle" their own. They created new verses that made fun of the British and praised the Continental Army and its commander, George Washington.

Critical Thinking

Interpreting Do you think songs and other forms of music are important in fighting a war? Explain.

Teach

C Critical Thinking

Predicting Consequences Ask: What might have happened if Clinton had learned of Washington's new strategy? *(Students might suggest that Clinton would march his troops toward Yorktown. The additional troop strength might have made the battle longer and bloodier, and resulted in a British victory.)* **OL**

Primary Source

Critical Thinking Answer
Students might state that songs and music express feelings and may be helpful in encouraging or motivating people to support the cause.

Differentiated Instruction

The American Revolution

Objective: To understand a time line of important dates in the Revolutionary War

Focus: Remind students that time lines can help them understand the chronology of events.

Teach: Have students read the Background section, study the time line, and complete the questions.

Assess: Review the correct answers to the questions.

Close: Discuss any questions or answers that are challenging for students.

Differentiated Instruction Strategies

BL Have students refer to the chapter maps for more help.

AL Ask students to use the dates in the activity to create a time line of cultural or scientific achievements in Britain and America.

ELL Make sure students understand that the terms "Patriots" and "Americans" refer to the same group.

C Critical Thinking

Analyzing Information Ask: Why do you think Washington chose not to reveal his plan even to his own soldiers? *(Students might note that a secret is easier to keep if only a few people know it.)* **OL**

D Differentiated Instruction

Auditory/Musical One version of "The World Turned Upside Down" goes like this: "If buttercups buzz'd after the bee,/ If boats were on land, churches on sea,/ If ponies rode men and if grass ate the cows/ . . . Then all the world would be upside down." Read these lyrics to the class. **Ask:** Why would the world seem upside down to the British at this time? *(Students might note that the British were the world's strongest military power. It may have been difficult to believe that the Continental Army could defeat them.)* **OL**

✓ Reading Check Answer: Washington advanced because Lafayette was keeping Cornwallis bottled up at Yorktown and the French fleet was heading there instead of to New York.

Hands-On Chapter Project
Step 4

Writing War Correspondence

Step 4: Narrative Writing Students will write letters that describe the end of the war.

Essential Question: How did the Battle of Yorktown lead to American independence?

Directions Have the groups take the role of American or British soldiers and write

Washington and Rochambeau then rushed south with their armies. The secrecy was so strict that most soldiers did not know where they were going. One soldier wrote, "We do not know the object of our march, and are in perfect ignorance whether we are going against New York, or . . . Virginia."

Washington's troops marched 200 miles (322 km) in 15 days. General Clinton in New York did not detect the forces heading south toward Virginia. Three groups—Lafayette's troops, Washington's and Rochambeau's American-French army, and de Grasse's French fleet—would meet at Yorktown.

The Siege of Yorktown

Washington's plan worked perfectly. The British were thoroughly confused. By the end of September, 14,000 American and French troops had trapped Cornwallis's 8,000 British and Hessian troops at Yorktown. Meanwhile, de Grasse's fleet kept Cornwallis from escaping by sea. General Clinton and the rest of the British army waited in New York. They were unable to help Cornwallis.

Cornwallis's Defeat

On October 9, the Americans and French began a tremendous bombardment. One Hessian soldier wrote in his diary, "One saw men lying everywhere . . . whose heads, arms, and legs had been shot off."

British supplies began running low. Many soldiers were wounded or sick. On October 14, Washington's aide, Alexander Hamilton, led an attack that captured key British defenses. Cornwallis realized the hopelessness of his situation. On October 19 he surrendered his troops. The Patriots had won the **Battle of Yorktown.** They took nearly 8,000 British prisoners and captured more than 200 guns.

As the British marched between rows of French and American troops to hand over their weapons, a French band played "Yankee Doodle." A British band responded with a children's tune, "The World Turned Upside Down." Indeed it had.

✓ Reading Check Explaining Why did Washington advance on Yorktown?

Chance & Error in History

What If Washington Had Stepped Down?

Throughout the Revolutionary War, Washington succeeded in holding his army together, despite many difficulties. He had to deal with low morale among soldiers who lived on poor rations and received low pay. The Continental Congress often interfered with his military operations. During the gloomy winter at Valley Forge, some congressmen and army officers plotted to replace Washington as commander in chief.

Washington accepts the British surrender at Yorktown. ▼

Washington as president ▶

From Soldier to Leader
Washington was commissioned as a lieutenant colonel in 1754 in the French and Indian War. An excellent soldier, he was made brigadier general and was a major factor in Britain's defeat of the French.

Wilderness fighting had made Washington a trained military man. This training helped prepare him for his greatest military challenge—leading the American revolutionary forces.

"The fate of unborn millions will now depend, under God, on the courage and conduct of this army."

◀ Washington as a young soldier

letters to family at home that explain the events leading up to the Battle of Yorktown. Letters should describe the British surrender and demonstrate the point of view of the author.

Identifying Central Issues Ask: How might each army view the Battle of Yorktown and the British surrender? *(Soldiers on both sides might be relieved that the war*

was finally over; British soldiers might feel negatively about surrendering, or losing. Americans would be excited to have defeated the British army and glad to have accomplished their goal.) **OL**

(Chapter Project continued on the Visual Summary page)

Independence

Main Idea The Patriots' spirit and resolve helped them win independence.

History and You What sort of influence do you think America's fight for independence had on the rest of the world? Read to find out how American ideals affected the world.

The fighting did not end with Cornwallis's surrender at Yorktown. The British still held Savannah, Charles Town, and New York. A few more clashes took place on land and sea. The victory at Yorktown, however, convinced the British that the war was too costly to **pursue,** or continue.

The two sides sent delegates to Paris to work out a treaty. **Benjamin Franklin, John Adams,** and **John Jay** represented the United States. The American Congress **ratified,** or approved, the preliminary treaty in April 1783. The final **Treaty of Paris** was signed on September 3, 1783. By that time Britain had also made peace with France and Spain.

◄ Dr. Benjamin Rush

Dr. Benjamin Rush, one of Washington's critics, served as surgeon general in the Continental Army. In a letter to John Adams, Rush compared Washington unfavorably to the hero of Saratoga, Horatio Gates.

"I have heard several officers who have served under General Gates compare his army to a well regulated family. . . . [They] have compared General Washington's imitation of an army to an unformed mob."

Critical Thinking

Analyzing What pressures did Washington face as a leader? Why do you think he did not quit?

The Treaty of Paris was a triumph for the Americans. Great Britain recognized the United States as an independent nation. The British promised to withdraw all their troops from American territory. They also agreed to give Americans the right to fish in the waters off the coast of Canada.

The United States, in turn, agreed that British merchants could collect debts that Americans owed them. The treaty also stated that the Congress would advise the states to return to Loyalists the properties taken from them.

The Newburgh Conspiracy

Washington headquartered his strong army in Newburgh, New York, after the British surrendered. The Congress refused to fund the soldiers' pensions and failed to provide them with other pay. The soldiers' anger mounted. In disgust, some officers circulated a letter in March 1783. If their demands were not met, the letter said, the army should use force against Congress.

Washington realized that this threat of revolt was dangerous. The new nation could be destroyed. He persuaded the angry soldiers to be patient. Then Washington urged the Congress to meet their just demands. Washington's leadership ended the threat to the new nation. The Congress soon acted on the demands.

Washington Resigns

British troops left New York City in late November 1783. The war had truly ended. Washington could at last give up his command. On December 4, Washington said farewell to his troops. Three weeks later he formally resigned at a meeting of the Second Continental Congress. Washington said, "Having now finished the work assigned me I retire . . . and take my leave of all the employments of public life."

Washington returned home to Mount Vernon, Virginia, in time for Christmas. There he planned to remain and live quietly with his family.

W Writing Support

Expository Writing Have some students take the role of George Washington and write a press release announcing the end of the war. Have other students take the role of King George and write a press release to the British people announcing the end of the war. Have students read their announcements and discuss differences in point of view. **OL**

R Reading Strategy

Activating Prior Knowledge Ask: Will Washington stay retired from public life? *(No. Students should know that Washington would become the nation's first president.)* Why do you think his nation would again call him to public service? *(Students might note that Washington displayed his leadership skills and patriotism in the war, and he was widely respected.)* **OL**

Chance & Error in History

Critical Thinking Answer

Washington faced low morale of soldiers due to poor rations and low pay, interference from the Continental Congress, and attempts to replace him. He did not quit because he had courage, honesty, and determination.

Differentiated Instruction

Leveled Activities

BL Academic Vocabulary Activity, URB p. 47

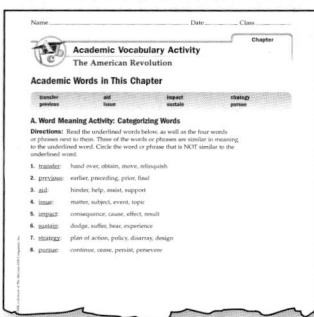

OL Authentic Assessment With Rubrics, p. 6

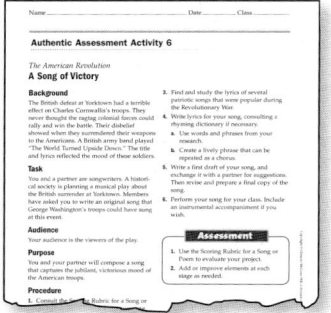

ELL Content Vocabulary Activity, URB p. 45

177

R Reading Strategy

Organizing Have students make a bulleted list of reasons the Americans won the war. Then ask them to organize their notes into a graphic organizer. **BL**

D Differentiated Instruction

Kinesthetic Have students draw a time line and label it with dates indicating the years of the American, French, and Haitian revolutions. **BL**

 Reading Check Answer: He realized that a disgruntled army could lead to a revolt, which could destroy the new nation.

Assess

History ONLINE

Study Central™ provides summaries, interactive games, and online graphic organizers to help students review content.

Close

Drawing Conclusions As a class, discuss the events leading to victory at Yorktown and the significance of this victory in achieving independence. **OL**

Section 4 Review

Why the Americans Won

How did the Americans manage to win the Revolutionary War? How did they defeat Britain, the world's greatest power?

The Americans had several advantages in the war. First, they fought on their own land while the British had to bring troops and supplies from thousands of miles away. The siege of Yorktown showed how much the British depended on the sea. When their ships were blocked, the British troops had no support. Also, the Americans knew the local terrain and where to lay an **ambush**—a surprise attack. The British, in contrast, had much difficulty controlling the American countryside once they occupied the cities.

Second, help from other nations contributed to the American victory. The French supplied soldiers, ships, and loans. The Spanish gave aid when they attacked the British in the Mississippi Valley and along the Gulf of Mexico.

Perhaps most important, the American Revolution was a people's movement. Its outcome depended not on any one battle or event but on the determination and spirit of all Patriots. As Washington remarked about the patriotic crowds, "Here is an army they [the British] will never conquer."

Influence of the American Revolution

In 1776 the American colonists began a revolution. They made clear the principles of freedom and the rights outlined in the Declaration of Independence. These ideas bounded back across the Atlantic to influence the French Revolution. French rebels in 1789 fought in defense of "Liberty, Equality, and Fraternity." The French upheld these principles: "Men are born and remain free and equal in rights."

In 1791 the ideals of the American and French Revolutions traveled across the Caribbean and the Atlantic to the French colony of Saint Domingue. Inspired by talk of freedom, enslaved Africans took up arms. Led by Toussaint-Louverture, they shook off French rule. In 1804 Saint Domingue—present-day Haiti—became the second nation in the Americas to achieve independence from colonial rule. "We have asserted our rights," declared the revolutionaries. "We swear never to yield them to any power on earth."

Reading Check **Explaining** Why did Washington take action to end the Newburgh Conspiracy?

History ONLINE

Study Central™ To review this section, go to glencoe.com.

Section 4 Review

Vocabulary

1. Using complete sentences, define the following terms: strategy, pursue, ratify, ambush.

Main Ideas

2. **Summarizing** What role did the French play in the Patriot victory at Yorktown?

3. **Explaining** Why were the Americans successful in their fight for independence?

Critical Thinking

4. **Categorizing** Use a diagram like the one below to show what the United States and Great Britain agreed to in the Treaty of Paris.

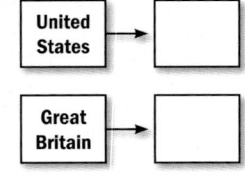

5. **Expository Writing** Write a paragraph comparing Washington's original plans to attack the British with his new secret strategy.

Answer the Essential Question

6. How did the Battle of Yorktown lead to American independence?

Answers

1. Sentences should use terms as they are defined in the section and Glossary.
2. Rochambeau joined his forces with Washington's on the march to Yorktown. Lafayette's troops already had the British bottled up at Yorktown. De Grasse's fleet kept Cornwallis from escaping by sea.
3. Americans fought on their own land, able to supply troops and stage ambushes from familiar terrain; other nations helped the Americans; the Patriots' spirit and determination helped them win.
4. **United States:** granted British merchants right to collect debts owed them by Americans, would advise states to return Loyalist property; **Great Britain:** recognized the United States as an independent nation, promised to withdraw all troops from American territory, granted Americans right to fish in Canadian coastal waters
5. Students' paragraphs should note that Washington had planned to attack New York but changed the target to Yorktown when he realized he would have French help there.
6. The British losses at Yorktown convinced Britain that the war was too costly to pursue.

Visual Summary

The American Revolution

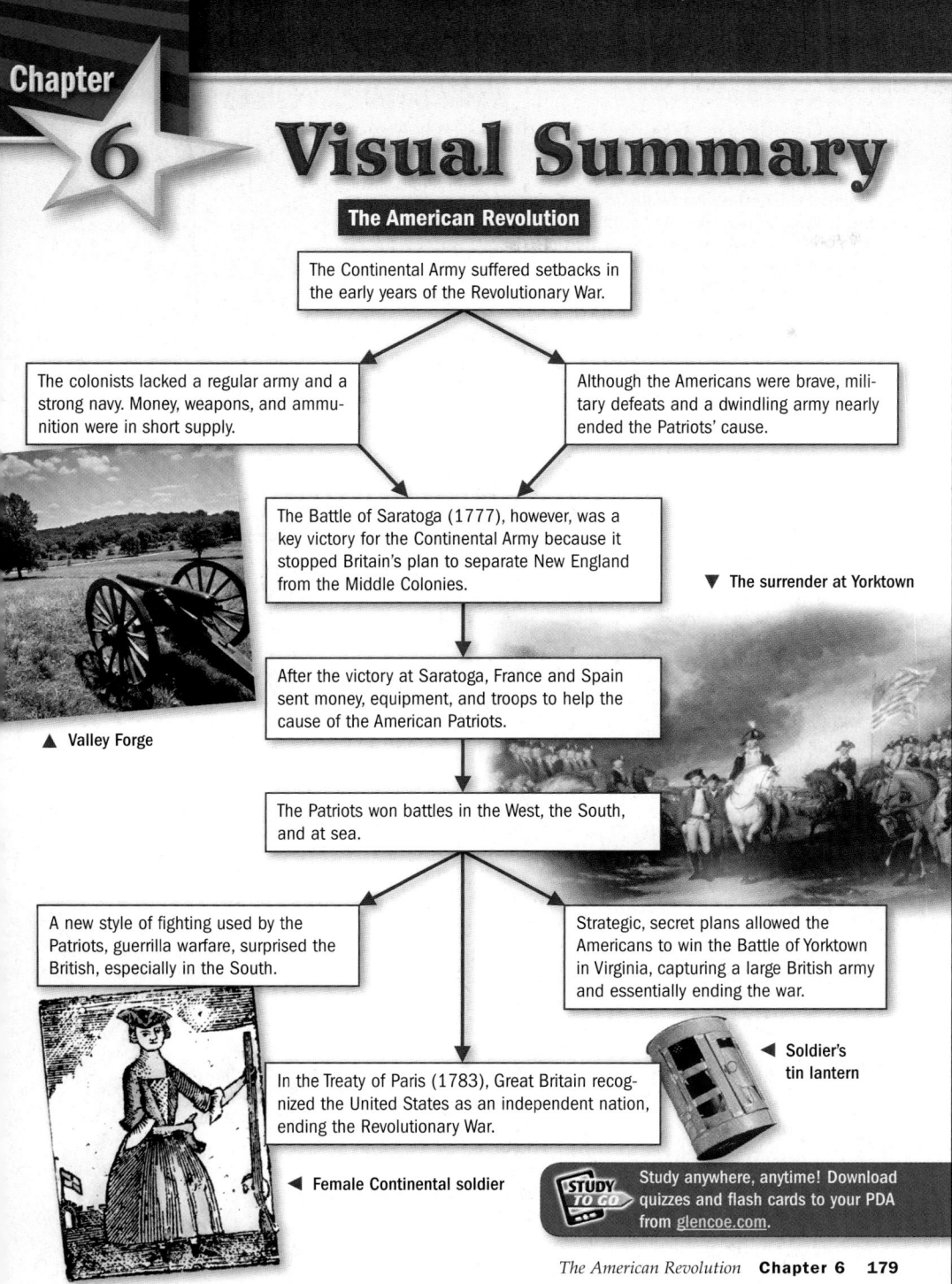

The Continental Army suffered setbacks in the early years of the Revolutionary War.

The colonists lacked a regular army and a strong navy. Money, weapons, and ammunition were in short supply.

Although the Americans were brave, military defeats and a dwindling army nearly ended the Patriots' cause.

The Battle of Saratoga (1777), however, was a key victory for the Continental Army because it stopped Britain's plan to separate New England from the Middle Colonies.

▼ The surrender at Yorktown

After the victory at Saratoga, France and Spain sent money, equipment, and troops to help the cause of the American Patriots.

The Patriots won battles in the West, the South, and at sea.

A new style of fighting used by the Patriots, guerrilla warfare, surprised the British, especially in the South.

Strategic, secret plans allowed the Americans to win the Battle of Yorktown in Virginia, capturing a large British army and essentially ending the war.

◀ Soldier's tin lantern

In the Treaty of Paris (1783), Great Britain recognized the United States as an independent nation, ending the Revolutionary War.

▲ Valley Forge

◀ Female Continental soldier

STUDY TO GO Study anywhere, anytime! Download quizzes and flash cards to your PDA from glencoe.com.

The American Revolution **Chapter 6 179**

Visual Summary

Activating Prior Knowledge Ask students to recall the disadvantages facing the Patriots at the start of the war. *(no regular army or navy, little experience, few supplies, not much money, and popular support was divided)* **Ask:** How did the Patriots overcome these disadvantages? *(Other nations provided troops, naval support, experienced leaders, and money. Popular support grew with Patriot victories. Patriots also used strengths—home turf, guerrilla tactics, and determination.)* **OL**

Drawing Conclusions The American Revolution influenced the people of France and Saint Domingue to overthrow their governments. **Ask:** Why do you think the American Revolution inspired these actions? *(Ideals of liberty and equality would appeal to the people who felt oppressed by their government.)* Do you think that successful revolutions are always a good thing? Explain. *(Students might note these drawbacks: revolutionary leaders may be more interested in power than in improving the lives of the people; revolutions can result in bloodbaths and disorder, as the French Revolution did.)* **OL**

Hands-On Chapter Project
Step 5: Wrap-Up

Writing War Correspondence

Step 5: Collecting the Letters Students will compile the letters into a book that portrays the experiences of individual people during the American Revolution.

Directions As a class, gather copies of all the letters written during the project.

Assemble the letters into chapters by topic, and write a table of contents. Have each group select a chapter and write an introduction, explaining what the reader can expect to learn about the American Revolution through the letters in that chapter. Create a cover for the book, and make copies for the class.

Comparing and Contrasting Ask: How does point of view affect perceptions and opinions about war? *(How people view events depends on their values, ideas, and circumstances.)* **OL**

Focus

C Critical Thinking

Analyzing Information Discuss with students the different geographic factors that led to the surrender at Yorktown. **Ask:** Why were British troops unsuccessful in defending Yorktown and Gloucester Point? *(The location of the city allowed attacks by sea and land; British troops were outnumbered by American and French troops; after Chesapeake Bay was seized, the British were unable to get supplies and reinforcements.)* **OL**

Have students complete a graphic organizer that illustrates the main events that affected Yorktown in 1871. **BL**

Time	Event
Spring	British troops move into Tidewater region to protect Chesapeake Bay harbor.
August	American and French troops move toward Yorktown from the north.
September	French navy seizes Chesapeake Bay.
October	Cornwallis surrenders.

Additional Support and Answers

GEOGRAPHY & HISTORY

Battle of Yorktown

British general Charles Cornwallis moved into the Tidewater region of Virginia in the spring of 1781. He was ordered to provide a protected harbor for the British fleet in the lower Chesapeake Bay. He selected a spot near the city of Yorktown, Virginia, whose deep-water harbor on the York River seemed perfect. Cornwallis spent most of the summer fortifying Yorktown and Gloucester Point across the York River.

How Did Geography Affect the Battle of Yorktown?

C Although Yorktown seemed a good choice, the city's location would make it impossible to defend. In September the French navy seized Chesapeake Bay. With the bay in French hands, Cornwallis was unable to get supplies or reinforcements coming by sea. By the end of September, nearly 18,000 American and French soldiers had gathered on the outskirts of Yorktown, while about 8,000 British soldiers occupied the town and Gloucester Point. Cornwallis was surrounded, his back to the York River. He soon surrendered and the Revolutionary War was all but over.

Cornwallis leads British forces north to Virginia in the spring of 1781.

American and French troops move toward Yorktown from the north in August 1781.

In September the French navy under Admiral de Grasse drives British ships away from Chesapeake Bay.

← American and allied forces
← British forces
✶ American victory

March to Victory Washington, de Grasse, and Rochambeau led their forces to Yorktown.

George Washington—American general and commander of the Continental Army. Forces under Washington. Lafayette also moved toward Yorktown from the north.

François de Grasse—French admiral whose 28 ships took control of Chesapeake Bay; 3,000 soldiers aboard those ships landed at Yorktown

Rochambeau—French general whose troops joined Washington's Continental Army in its march toward Yorktown

180 Unit 2 *Creating a Nation*

Fast Facts

When Washington changed his plan of attack, he wanted British General Henry Clinton to think that he was still planning to attack New York so that Clinton would not send help to Yorktown. To accomplish this goal, Washington used several clever tactics. He built large army camps with huge brick ovens visible from New York to give Clinton the impression that his troops were staying in the area. He also wrote false papers about attacking Clinton and purposely allowed the papers to be discovered by the British. Last, he did not take all of his troops to Yorktown; instead he left a small group at camp to be seen by Clinton.

The Yorktown Campaign

Realizing he was both outmanned and outgunned, Cornwallis sent for help. Before the reinforcements arrived, Cornwallis was forced to surrender his army on October 19. **R** **S**

0   1 kilometer
0   1 mile
Polyconic projection

The mortar barrel was elevated on a flat, wooden bed to launch bombs behind enemy lines.

York River

Gloucester

Swamp

Cornwallis 8,000

Yorktown

Rochambeau 9,000

French lines

American lines

Mill Pond

Field of British Surrender

General Lincoln

Lafayette's Headquarters

General Steuben

General Lafayette 8,000

Washington's Headquarters

The *Ville de Paris* was the flagship of Admiral de Grasse during his operations **C** in Virginia waters in the autumn of 1781. Reported to be the largest warship of its time, the *Ville de Paris* boasted 110 guns on 3 gun decks.

Map Key
- ■ British troops
- ⌐⌐ British defensive lines
- ← American and French attacks October 6–15
- ▬ American troops
- ▬ French troops
- ⛵ French fleet
- ⚔ French and American artillery

◀ On October 14–15, Americans and French stormed the small British forts (called redoubts) to the south of Yorktown.

Analyzing Geography

1. **Movement** From which direction did de Grasse's ships travel to Yorktown?
2. **Place** Why did Cornwallis choose Yorktown as the British base of operations? Why did this decision leave his forces vulnerable?

Creating a Nation **Unit 2** **181**

Teach

R Reading Strategy

Academic Vocabulary Make sure students understand the terminology used in the captions. Ask the meanings of "outmanned" *(more manpower or forces)* and "outgunned" *(more firepower or weapons).* **ELL**

S Skill Practice

Using Geography Skills The map shows that French and American troops surrounded Yorktown. Ask students to use the map key, compass rose, and scale to determine the locations of troops. **Ask:** On which side of Yorktown were most French troops located? American troops? The French fleet? *(west & southwest; south & southeast; north)* How far away were the British troops in Gloucester from the British troops in Yorktown? *(less than 1 mile [1.609 km])* **OL**

Assess/Close

C Critical Thinking

Making Connections Describe the operations of de Grasse's fleet during the campaign. Why was the French fleet vital to the American victory at Yorktown? **OL**

Answers

1. northwest
2. for its location on a deep water harbor; when the French navy seized Chesapeake Bay, his escape route was eliminated

181

Answers and Analyses
Reviewing Main Ideas

1. B Remind students that this attack occurred early in the war and was successful, eliminating choices A and C. The attack also occurred during the winter of 1776–1777, a low point for the Patriots. **17.C.3a**

2. A Remind students that the government lacked the ability to tax. **15.E**

3. C A good way for students to approach questions involving terms is to first eliminate those that they know do not fit the given definition. This will narrow the choices and increase their chances to identify the correct answer if they have to guess. **17.C.3a**

4. A Students should recognize that the Treaty of Paris ended the American Revolution, and the main outcome of the war was independence. **16.B.3b (US)**

Short-Answer Question
5. Their families at home were being neglected because they did not have enough supplies. **18.B.3a**

TEST-TAKING TIP

When answering a test question that uses a map, study the map key and make sure you understand the information presented on the map.

Reviewing Main Ideas

Directions: Choose the best answer for each of the following questions.

1. Washington's surprise attack across the Delaware River on Christmas night
   A was the last battle of the Revolutionary War.
   B boosted the morale of the Patriots.
   C was followed by calls for his resignation.
   D was successful but caused a great number of American casualties.

2. Americans had problems getting enough money to finance the war because
   A the Continental Congress did not have the power to raise money through taxes.
   B the states were against the war.
   C no foreign countries would help the Patriots pay for the war.
   D the British closed all colonial banks at the start of the war.

3. In the Southern states, small forces of Patriots attacked the British in a hit-and-run technique known as
   A privateering.   **C** guerrilla warfare.
   B quartering.   **D** blockading.

4. Which of the following was one of the terms of the Treaty of Paris?
   A Great Britain recognized the United States as an independent nation.
   B British merchants agreed not to collect debts that Americans owed them.
   C Great Britain and the United States agreed to form a naval alliance.
   D Loyalists would be punished for their actions.

Short-Answer Question

Directions: Base your answer to question 5 on the excerpt below and on your knowledge of social studies.

> Yesterday upwards of fifty Officers in Gen. Greene's Division resigned their Commissions—Six or Seven of our Regiment are doing the like to-day. All this is occasion'd by Officers Families being so much neglected at home on account of Provisions [supplies].
>
> —Dr. Albigence Waldo
> December 28, 1777

5. According to Waldo, why were so many officers in the Continental Army resigning their commissions?

Review the Essential Questions

6. Essay Describe the events and circumstances that led to America's victory in the Revolutionary War.

To help you write your essay, review your answers to the Essential Questions in the section reviews and the chapter Foldables Study Organizer. Your essay should include:

- American and British strengths and weaknesses.
- the role of American allies in the war effort;
- results of important battles;
- economic issues and changes;
- events and tactics used during battles in the Southern states; and
- events that lead to the end of the war.

GO ON ➤

Review the Essential Questions

6. Students' responses should include key factors in America's victory, such as alliances and aid from other countries, advantages of fighting on familiar ground, Patriot determination, the success of Washington's surprise attack across the Delaware River, de Gálvez's help in opening supply lines along the Mississippi River, and Washington's secret plan and French support at the Battle of Yorktown. **16.B.3b (US)**

History ONLINE
For additional test practice, use **Self-Check Quizzes**—Chapter 6 at glencoe.com.

Chapter 6 Assessment

Document-Based Questions

Directions: Analyze the documents and answer the short-answer questions that follow.

Document 1

This is an excerpt from a document known as the Connecticut Slaves Petition for Freedom dated May 11, 1779.

> And we not only groan under our own burden, but with concern, & Horror, look forward, & contemplate, the miserable Condition of our Children, who are training up, and kept in Preparation, for a like State of Bondage, and Servitude. [We ask] your Honours serious Consideration, whether it is consistent with the present Claims, of the united States, to hold so many Thousands . . . in perpetual Slavery.

Source: Connecticut Slaves Petition for Freedom (1779)

7. What basic argument against slavery did the writers base their petition on?

Document 2

This is an excerpt from a letter from George Washington to John Hancock dated September 24, 1776.

> When Men are irritated, and the Passions inflamed, they fly hastely and chearfully to Arms; but after the first emotions are over, to expect, among such People, as compose the bulk of an Army, that they are influenced by any other principles than those of Interest, is to look for what never did, and I fear never will happen; the Congress will deceive themselves therefore if they expect it.

Source: *From Revolution to Reconstruction*

8. Based on the document, did Washington believe people could successfully be persuaded to join the Continental Army simply by appealing to their feelings of patriotism? Explain.

Document 3

In this document, Andrew Sherburne describes his experiences on a privateer ship during the Revolutionary War.

> I was not yet fourteen years of age. . . . The boys were employed in waiting on the officers, but in time of action a boy was quartered [assigned] to each gun to carry cartridges.

Source: "Andrew Sherburne's Experiences on a Privateer During the Revolutionary War (1828)"

9. How old was Sherburne and what were his duties aboard ship?

Document 4

The following map shows areas of Patriot and Loyalist strength during the Revolutionary Era.

Patriot and Loyalist Strongholds

Loyalists
Patriots
Neutral

0 400 kilometers
0 400 miles
Albers Equal-Area projection

10. According to the map, where was Loyalist sentiment the strongest?

11. Expository Writing Using the information from the four documents and your knowledge of social studies, write an essay in which you:
- explain how the war demonstrated the democratic ideals of the Patriots; and
- describe some ways those ideals were *not* upheld.

9. He was 13. Between battles, his job was to serve the officers. During a battle, he was expected to carry ammunition to a particular gun. **16.A.3b**

10. in the Carolinas and New York **17.A.3b**

11. These ideals were demonstrated by the patriotism and self-sacrifice of the many Americans who fought for independence. However, hardships at Valley Forge and elsewhere led to desertion. The Newburgh Conspiracy demonstrated unfair treatment of soldiers by Congress. The democratic ideals also faltered in the failure to end slavery across the nation, the failure to grant equal rights to women, and the abuse of Loyalists. **16.A.3b**

History ONLINE
Have students visit the Web site at glencoe.com to review Chapter 6 and take the Self-Check Quiz.

Need Extra Help?

Have students refer to the pages listed if they miss any of the questions.

Need Extra Help?

If You Missed Questions...	1	2	3	4	5	6	7	8	9	10	11
Go to Page...	158	163–164	172	177	155–157	153–176	154–157	155	170	153–154	164–165

The American Revolution **Chapter 6 183**

Document-Based Questions

7. The argument against slavery was that the United States's fight for independence was inconsistent with the keeping of enslaved people. **16.A.3c**

8. Washington seems to be saying that although strong feelings might first cause some people to take up arms, self-interest is ultimately a stronger motivation. **18.B.3a**

Chapter Planning Guide

BL	OL	AL	ELL		Resources	Chapter Opener	Section 1	Section 2	Section 3	Chapter Assess
					FOCUS					
BL	OL	AL	ELL	🖨	Daily Test Practice Transparencies		7–1	7–2	7–3	
					TEACH					
	OL	AL		📁	Geography and History Activity, URB		p. 87			
BL	OL		ELL	📁	Time Line Skills Activity, URB			p. 90		
BL	OL	AL	ELL	📁	Writing Skills Activity, URB		p. 79	p. 79		
	OL	AL		📁	American Literature Readings, URB			p. 9		
BL	OL	AL	ELL	📁	Content Vocabulary Activity, URB		p. 73	p. 73	p. 73	
BL			ELL	📁	Academic Vocabulary Activity, URB		p. 75	p. 75	p. 75	
	OL	AL		📁	Citizenship and Decision-Making Activity, URB				p. 3	
BL			ELL	📁	Social Studies Skills Activity, URB			p. 81		
BL	OL	AL	ELL	📁	Differentiated Instruction Activity, URB			p. 83		
BL	OL	AL	ELL	📁	Critical Thinking Skills Activity, URB				p. 85	
BL	OL	AL	ELL	📁	Linking Past and Present Activity, URB		p. 89			
	OL	AL		📁	Primary Source Readings, URB		p. 77			
BL	OL	AL	ELL	📁	School-to-Home Connection Activity, URB		p. 91	p. 91	p. 91	
BL	OL		ELL	📁	Guided Reading Activity, URB*		p. 95	p. 96	p. 97	
	OL	AL		📁	Economics and History Activity, URB		p. 5			
BL	OL		ELL	📁	Reading Essentials and Note-Taking Guide*		p. 70	p. 73	p. 76	
BL	OL	AL	ELL	🖨	Lesson Transparencies			7B	7A, 7C	
	OL	AL		📁	Interpreting Political Cartoons, URB				p. 3	
	OL			📁	American Biographies			p. 12		
BL	OL	AL	ELL	📁	Outline Map Resource Book	p. 9				

Note: Please refer to the *Unit Resource Book: Creating a Nation* for this chapter's URB materials.

* Also available in Spanish

Levels					Resources	Chapter Opener	Section 1	Section 2	Section 3	Chapter Assess
BL	OL	AL	ELL		**TEACH** (continued)					
BL	OL	AL	ELL	📁	**NGS US Desk Map**		✓	✓	✓	
BL	OL	AL	ELL	📁	**American Literature Library**		✓	✓	✓	
BL	OL	AL	ELL	📁	**Writer's Guidebook**		✓	✓	✓	
	OL	AL		💿	**American History Primary Source Document Library CD-ROM**		✓	✓	✓	✓
BL	OL	AL	ELL	💿	**American Music: Hits Through History**	✓	✓	✓	✓	
BL	OL	AL	ELL	💿	**StudentWorks™ Plus CD**	✓	✓	✓	✓	✓
BL	OL	AL	ELL	🔒	**Section Spotlight Videos**		✓	✓	✓	
BL	OL	AL	ELL	🖨	**Writing Process Transparencies**		✓	✓	✓	✓
BL	OL	AL	ELL	💿	**Presentation Plus! With MindJogger CheckPoint CD**	✓	✓	✓	✓	✓
BL	OL	AL	ELL		**ASSESS**					
BL	OL	AL	ELL	📁	**Quizzes and Tests**		p. 61	p. 62	p. 63	pp. 65, 67, 69
BL	OL	AL	ELL	📁	**Authentic Assessment With Rubrics**			p. 7		
BL	OL	AL	ELL	📁	**Standardized Test Practice**					p. 13
BL	OL	AL	ELL	💿	*ExamView® Assessment Suite* **CD-ROM***		7–1	7–2	7–3	Ch. 7
BL	OL	AL	ELL		**CLOSE**					
BL			ELL	📁	**Reteaching Activity, URB***		p. 93	p. 93	p. 93	p. 93
BL	OL		ELL	📁	**Reading and Study Skills Foldables Activity**	p. 62	p. 62	p. 62	p. 62	p. 62
BL	OL	AL	ELL	📁	*The American Journey* **in Graphic Novel**					p. 37
BL			ELL	📁	**Reading Strategies and Activities for the Social Studies Classroom**		✓	✓	✓	
BL	OL	AL	ELL	🖨	**Graphic Organizer Transparencies & Strategies**		✓	✓	✓	

TeacherWorks Plus
All-In-One Planner and Resource Center

- Interactive Lesson Planner
- Interactive Teacher Edition
- Fully editable blackline masters
- Section Spotlight Videos Launch
- Differentiated Lesson Plans
- Printable reports of daily assignments
- Standards Tracking System

Professional Development Resources

- Strategies for Success
- Building Academic Vocabulary
- Success With English Learners DVD
- Differentiated Instruction Strategies DVD
- Teaching Literacy Strategies in Social Studies DVD
- Assessment DVD
- Standards-Based Instruction DVD

Integrating Technology

Student Web Activities

Using the Glencoe Web Site

Technology Product

The Glencoe Web site provides Web activities to students that reinforce and enrich chapter content. The Student Web Activities

- introduce topics relevant to chapter content, along with links to Web sites that provide information about the topic;
- prompt students to complete tasks specific to the activity.

Objectives

The Student Web Activities help students

- learn online research and study skills;
- practice reading and comprehension skills.

Steps

- Locate the Web page for the textbook on the Glencoe Web site glencoe.com.
- Click on **Student Center** under the textbook title.
- In the Student Center, select a unit from the Unit Resources menu and a chapter from the Chapter Activities menu using the drop-down arrows.
- Click on the **Student Web Activities** link.
- Have students complete the activity on the page and answer the questions.
- Provide students with an e-mail address to submit their answers for grading.

History ONLINE at glencoe.com

	Student	Teacher	Parent
Media Center			
• Student Edition Audio	●		
• Spanish Summaries	●		
• Section Spotlight Videos	●	●	
Social Studies Online Learning Center			
Classroom Tools			
• Multi-Language Glossaries	●	●	●
• Teaching Today		●	
• TIME Current Events	●	●	●
• Beyond the Textbook	●	●	
The American Journey **Online Learning Center**			
• Study-to-Go™	●	●	●
• Study Central™	●	●	●
• Chapter Overview	●	●	
• Concepts in Motion	●	●	
• ePuzzles and Games	●	●	
• Literature Connections	●	●	
• Online Student Edition	●	●	●
• Self-Check Quizzes	●	●	●
• Student Web Activities	●	●	
• Vocabulary eFlashcards	●	●	
• Web Activity Lesson Plans	●	●	●
• Vocabulary PuzzleMaker	●	●	●

- **Timed Readings Plus in Social Studies** helps students increase their reading rate and fluency while maintaining comprehension. The 400-word passages are similar to those found on state and national assessments.

- **Reading in the Content Area: Social Studies** concentrates on six essential reading skills that help students better comprehend what they read. The book includes 75 high-interest nonfiction passages written at increasing levels of difficulty.

- **Reading Social Studies** includes strategic reading instruction and vocabulary support in Social Studies content for ELLs and native speakers of English.

- **Content Vocabulary Workout** (Grades 6–8) accelerates reading comprehension through focused vocabulary development. Social Studies content vocabulary comes from the glossaries of Glencoe's Middle School Social Studies texts.

www.jamestowneducation.com

NATIONAL GEOGRAPHIC

Index to National Geographic Magazine:

The following articles relate to this chapter:

- *"Endangered Revolution,"* Andrew Meier, March 2006.

- *"True Colors: Divided Loyalties in Puerto Rico,"* Andrew Cockburn, March 2003.

National Geographic Society Products

To order the following, call National Geographic at 1-800-368-2728:

National Geographic Atlas of the World (Book)

Access National Geographic's dynamic MapMachine Web site and other geography resources at:

www.nationalgeographic.com

www.nationalgeographic.com/mapmachine

Reading List Generator CD-ROM — GLENCOE BookLink 3

Use this database to search more than 30,000 titles to create a customized reading list for your students.

- Reading lists can be organized by students' reading level, author, genre, theme, or area of interest.
- The database provides Degrees of Reading Power™ (DRP) and Lexile™ readability scores for all selections.
- A brief summary of each selection is included.

Leveled reading suggestions for this chapter:

For students at a Grade 6 reading level:
- *A More Perfect Union: The Story of Our Constitution,* by Betsy Maestro

For students at a Grade 7 reading level:
- *The Articles of Confederation,* by Karen Price Hossell
- *The Young United States: 1783 to 1830,* by Edwin Tunis

For students at a Grade 8 reading level:
- *Our Congress,* by Michael Weber
- *Our Constitution,* by Hal Marcovitz

For students at a Grade 9 reading level:
- *God and Government: The Separation of Church and State,* by Ann E. Weiss

For students at a Grade 10 reading level:
- *To Establish Justice: Citizenship and the Constitution,* by Patricia McKissack & Arlene Zarembka

The following videotape program is available from Glencoe as a supplement to the chapter:

- **Patrick Henry: Voice of Liberty** (ISBN 1-56-501645-9)

To order, call Glencoe at 1-800-334-7344. To find classroom resources to accompany this video, check the following home pages:

A&E Television: www.aetv.com

The History Channel: www.history.com

Chapter Objectives

After studying this chapter, students will be able to:

- Assess the effectiveness of the government under the Articles of Confederation.
- Explain why the Constitution is a document of compromises.
- Discuss the ideas and features found in the United States Constitution.

Motivating Activity

Identifying Central Issues The colonists successfully took a stand against the tyranny of kings by fighting for their freedom in the American Revolution. However, they were then faced with the challenge of creating a system of government that allowed for strong leadership as well as representative democracy. **Ask:** How would you expect the Constitution to make the United States "a more perfect union"? Have students write a list of concerns and issues they think the colonists might have hoped the Constitution would address.

Previewing the Essential Questions

As you begin teaching each section, use these questions and activities to help students focus on the Essential Questions.

Chapter

⭐ **7**

A More Perfect Union 1777–1790

Delegates to the Constitutional Convention, 1787

1781 ⭐
Robert Morris serves as superintendent of finance for the U.S.

1777 ⭐
Articles of Confederation written

⭐ **1783**
Treaty of Paris

U.S. Events
World Events

1776 — 1779 — 1782

1778 ⭐
France goes to war against Britain

1780 ⭐
League of Armed Neutrality is formed

1782 ⭐
Rama I starts new dynasty in Siam

Palace, Bangkok, Thailand (Siam) ▶

184   Chapter 7

Section ⭐ 1

The Articles of Confederation Ask: Was the new U.S. government effective under the Articles of Confederation? Why or why not? *(It was ineffective because the national government did not have enough political and economic power.)* Point out to students that in Section 1 they will learn about the strengths and weaknesses of the Articles of Confederation. **OL**

Section ⭐ 2

Convention and Compromise Ask: Why is the Constitution considered a document of compromises? *(The delegates had to compromise on issues such as distribution of powers, representation, and slavery.)* Point out to students that Section 2 discusses compromises made by the delegates. **OL**

Section 1: The Articles of Confederation

Essential Question How effective was government under the Articles of Confederation?

Section 2: Convention and Compromise

Essential Question Why is the Constitution a document of compromises?

Section 3: A New Plan of Government

Essential Question What ideas and features are found in the United States Constitution?

History ONLINE
Chapter Overview Visit glencoe.com and click on **Chapter 7—Chapter Overviews** to preview chapter information.

FOLDABLES **Study Organizer**

Organizing Information
Make this Foldable to help you organize what you learn about the differences between the Articles of Confederation and the Constitution.

Step 1 Fold an 11" x 17" piece of paper lengthwise to create three equal sections.

Step 2 Then fold it into four equal columns.

Step 3 Label your Foldable as shown.

Reading and Writing As you read, describe each document by identifying its purpose and features, and evaluate how effective it was for governing.

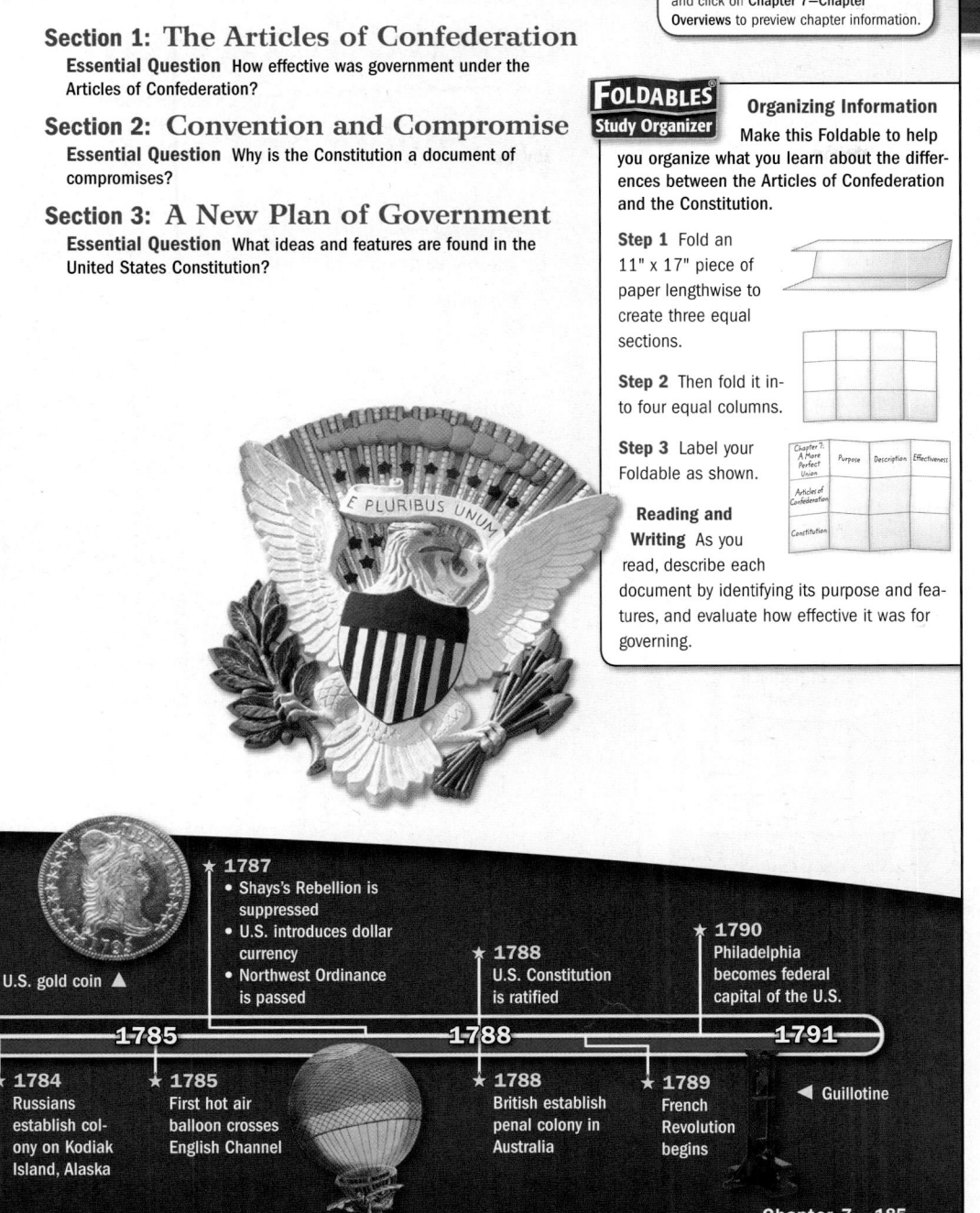

E PLURIBUS UNUM

1787
• Shays's Rebellion is suppressed
• U.S. introduces dollar currency
• Northwest Ordinance is passed

1788
U.S. Constitution is ratified

1790
Philadelphia becomes federal capital of the U.S.

U.S. gold coin ▲

1785
1788
1791

1784
Russians establish colony on Kodiak Island, Alaska

1785
First hot air balloon crosses English Channel

1788
British establish penal colony in Australia

1789
French Revolution begins

◄ Guillotine

Chapter 7 **185**

Time Line Activity

If you have not already done so, have students review the time line. **Ask:** What years are covered in this time line? *(1776–1791)* Have students identify two world events that might have been influenced by the Revolutionary War. *(Students may suggest France's war with Britain and the start of the French Revolution.)* Ask students to offer reasons for their choices. *(The French sided with the colonists against Britain. The colonists' successful rebellion encouraged others to rebel against Britain.)*

FOLDABLES **Study Organizer** **Dinah Zike's Foldables**

Purpose This Foldable helps students identify the differences between the Articles of Confederation and the Constitution. The completed Foldable will help them prepare for assessment. **OL**

📁 More Foldables activities for this chapter can be found in *Dinah Zike's Reading and Study Skills Foldables.*

History ONLINE
Introduce students to chapter content and key terms by having them access the **Chapter Overview** at glencoe.com.

Section 3

A New Plan of Government Ask: What principles of government are established in the United States Constitution? *(government run by the people; division of power between local, state, and national governments; system of checks and balances prevents any one branch of government from having* too much power; Bill of Rights added after the Constitution was ratified.) Tell students that Section 3 will explore the impact of scholars and philosophers on the document. They will learn about some specific objections and how they were resolved. **OL**

Focus

The Articles of Confederation

Bellringer
Daily Test Practice Transparency 7–1

Reading Guide
Answers to Graphic:
conduct foreign affairs, maintain armed forces, borrow money, issue currency

Section Spotlight Video

Have students watch the Section Spotlight Video "The Articles of Confederation" to learn more about how America unites under its first plan of government.

Resource Manager

Essential Question ◄
How effective was government under the Articles of Confederation?

Reading Guide

Content Vocabulary

constitution (p. 187)	petition (p. 190)
bicameral (p. 187)	ordinance (p. 190)
republic (p. 188)	depreciate (p. 191)

Academic Vocabulary

abandon (p. 189)	clause (p. 191)

Key People and Events
Articles of Confederation (p. 188)
John Adams (p. 193)

Reading Strategy
Taking Notes As you read, use a diagram like the one below to identify the powers of the national government under the Articles of Confederation.

Powers of National Government

ILLINOIS STANDARDS
The American Journey

14.A Understand and explain the basic principles of the United States government.

16.B.3a (US) Describe how different groups competed for power within the colonies and how that competition led to the development of political institutions during the early national period.

17.C.3c Analyze how human processes influence settlement patterns including migration and population growth.

17.D.3a Explain how and why spatial patterns of settlement change over time.

American Diary

As British forces approached Philadelphia on September 19, 1777, John Adams and members of the Second Continental Congress fled to York, Pennsylvania. Adams wrote to his wife: "War has no Charms for me. If I live much longer in Banishment I shall scarcely know my own Children. Tell my little ones, that if they will be very good, Pappa will come home."

—from Letters of Delegates to Congress

Congress Hall in Philadelphia (building in the left front) was the meeting place of the U.S. Congress from 1790 to 1800.

R Reading Strategies	C Critical Thinking	D Differentiated Instruction	W Writing Support	S Skill Practice
Teacher Edition • Identifying, p. 187 • Organizing, p. 190 • Act. Prior Know., p. 192	**Teacher Edition** • Under. Cause & Effect, p. 188 • Predict. Conseq., p. 188 • Making Infer., p. 191 • Draw. Conclus., p. 192 • Making Infer., p. 193	**Teacher Edition** • Intrapersonal, p. 188 • ELL, p. 190	**Teacher Edition** • Persuasive Writ., p. 189 • Narrative Writ., p. 192	**Teacher Edition** • Visual Literacy, p. 190 • Using Geo. Skills, p. 191
Additional Resources • Guid. Read., URB p. 95 • Cont. Vocab., URB p. 73 • Academic Vocab., URB p. 75 • Read. Ess., p. 70 • Pri. Source Read., URB p. 77	**Additional Resources** • Quizzes and Tests, p. 61 • Econ. & Hist., URB p. 5 • Link. Past & Pres., URB p. 89	**Additional Resources** • School-to-Home, URB p. 91 • Reteaching Act., URB p. 93	**Additional Resources** • Writ. Skills, URB p. 79	**Additional Resources** • Daily Test Pract. Transp. 7–1 • Geo. & Hist., URB p. 87

From Independent States to a Republic

Main Idea The Articles of Confederation created a weak central government and strong state governments.

History and You How hard is it to get a group of friends to agree on what type of movie to watch or game to play? Read about what was necessary for the new Congress to pass a law.

. . . .

It was important for the Second Continental Congress to create a plan for government that would satisfy the needs of all 13 states. The states were united against the British, but would they be able to work together and still maintain their independence? How would each state's government be organized? After rejecting British rule, the states' first task was to establish their own political institutions.

State Constitutions

In May 1776, the Continental Congress asked the states to organize their governments. Each state moved quickly to adopt a state **constitution,** or plan of government. By the end of 1776, eight states had drafted constitutions. New York and Georgia followed in 1777 and Massachusetts in 1780. Connecticut and Rhode Island kept their colonial charters as state constitutions.

Their experience with British rule made Americans cautious about placing too much power in the hands of a single ruler. For that reason, the states adopted constitutions that limited the power of the governor. Pennsylvania even replaced the office of governor with an elected council of 12 members.

Limiting Power

States also divided government functions between the governor (or Pennsylvania's council) and the legislature. Most states established two-house, or **bicameral,** legislatures to divide the power even further.

The writers of the constitutions not only wanted to prevent abuses of power in the states, but they also wanted to keep power in the hands of the people. State legislators were popularly elected, and elections were frequent. In most states, only white males who were at least 21 years old could vote. These citizens also had to own a certain amount of property or pay a certain amount of taxes. Some states allowed free African American males to vote.

When and Where — Capitals of the United States

Capital Cities of the United States

City	Length of Time as U.S. Capital
Philadelphia, Pennsylvania	May 10, 1775 to December 12, 1776
Baltimore, Maryland	December 20, 1776 to February 27, 1777
Philadelphia, Pennsylvania	March 4, 1777 to September 18, 1777
Lancaster, Pennsylvania	September 27, 1777 (one day)
York, Pennsylvania	September 30, 1777 to June 27, 1778
Philadelphia, Pennsylvania	July 2, 1778 to June 21, 1781
Princeton, New Jersey	June 30, 1783 to November 4, 1783
Annapolis, Maryland	November 26, 1783 to August 19, 1784
Trenton, New Jersey	November 1, 1784 to December 24, 1784
New York City, New York	January 11, 1785 to August 12, 1790
Philadelphia, Pennsylvania	December 6, 1790 to May 14, 1800
Washington, D.C.	November 17, 1800 to present

Nine different cities have served as capitals, or seats of government, of the United States.

Critical Thinking

Making Inferences Why do you think the United States had numerous capital cities between 1775 and 1800? Do you think it is important for a country to have a permanent location for its seat of government? Explain.

Teach

. . . .

R **Reading Strategy**

Identifying Ask: Why did the state constitutions limit the power of the governor? (*The colonists rejected placing too much power in the hands of a single ruler because of their experiences under British rule.*) **OL**

When and Where

Critical Thinking Answer Answers should mention the effects of war and the need to move the capital from areas of combat; a permanent capital city reflects stability and permanence of a government.

Skills Practice Ask: What inventions have made it easier for politicians to live far from our nation's capital today? (*Answers may include airplanes, trains, cars, cell phones, computers, and e-mail.*) **OL**

Differentiated Instruction

Leveled Activities

BL **Content Vocabulary Activity, URB p. 73**

OL **Reading Essentials and Note-Taking Guide, p. 70**

AL **Primary Source Reading Activity, URB p. 77**

Section 1

C₁ Critical Thinking

Understanding Cause and Effect Have students create a cause-and-effect diagram for each of the two sentences. *(Cause: State constitutions restricted powers of governors; Effect: Legislatures became most powerful branch of government. Cause: State legislatures struggled to make taxes fair; Effect: Disagreements arose.)* **OL**

D Differentiated Instruction

Intrapersonal Discuss the role of authority figures in society. **Ask:** When is it helpful to have someone in authority over you? *(for protection, leadership)* What challenges might require states to work together under a single authority? *(fighting a war or dealing with other nations)* **AL**

C₂ Critical Thinking

Predicting Consequences Ask: What might be the result of the Congress not having the power to impose taxes? *(Students should see that the government would not have any money, making it weak and ineffective.)* **OL**

Additional Support

Teacher Tip

Make sure students search your state's official Web site. The Web address should end in .gov. **OL**

Primary Source | **The Articles of Confederation**

Richard Henry Lee of Virginia moved on June 7, 1776, that

"a plan of confederation be prepared and transmitted to the respective colonies, for their consideration and approbation [approval]."

Writing the Articles Even though he opposed independence, John Dickinson was asked to chair the committee to draft the Articles of Confederation because of his knowledge of government institutions.

★ **1781** March 1 Articles of Confederation ratified

★ **1783** March 10 Troops demand back pay from Congress, threaten to mutiny

★ **1786** September 14 Annapolis Convention to reform regulation of commerce

★ **1787** May 17 Constitutional Convention convenes in Philadelphia

★ **1783** November 2 Continental Army officially disbanded

★ **1785** July 6 Congress approves a currency system based on the dollar

★ **1787** February 21 Congress calls convention to amend Articles of Confederation

C₁ State constitutions generally restricted the powers of the governors, which made the legislatures the most powerful branch of government. The state legislatures struggled to make taxes more fair, but disagreements arose. New challenges emerged as dependent colonies became self-governing states.

Forming a Republic

D Americans agreed that their country should be a **republic,** a government in which citizens rule through elected representatives. They could not agree, however, on the organization and powers of their new republic. At first, most Americans favored a weak central government. They assumed the states would be like small, independent countries—similar to the way the colonies had been organized. The states would act independently on most issues, working together through a central government only to wage war and handle relations with other nations.

Planning a New Government

In 1776 the Second Continental Congress appointed a committee to draw up a plan for a new government. After much debate, the Congress adopted the **Articles of Confederation** in November 1777. The Articles, America's first constitution, provided for a new central government under which the states kept most of their power. For the states, the Articles of Confederation were "a firm league of friendship" in which each state retained "its sovereignty, freedom and independence." Under the Articles of Confederation, Congress had the authority to conduct foreign affairs, maintain armed forces, borrow money, and issue currency.

C₂ Congress, however, did not have the power to regulate trade, force citizens to join the army, or impose taxes. If Congress needed to raise money or troops, it had to ask the state legislatures—but they were not required to contribute.

188 **Chapter 7** *A More Perfect Union*

Activity: Technology Connection

Making Connections Ask: When was our state constitution written? *(Some students might know, but most will not.)* Have students use the Internet to find the official government Web site for your state. Next, have students locate the date your state constitution was first ratified. Next, have students list other information about the history of your state that they can find at the Web site. Have students summarize what they learned in an encyclopedia entry. **OL**

Weaknesses of the Articles of Confederation

- Congress had no authority to raise money by collecting taxes
- Congress had no control over foreign trade
- Congress could not force states to carry out its laws
- All 13 states had to agree to any amendments, making it nearly impossible to correct problems

A Common Currency The national currency had little value. States issued their own money, and values varied from state to state.

According to George Washington, the Articles of Confederation were *"little more than the shadow without the substance."*

Regulating Trade Under the Articles of Confederation, the federal government did not have the authority to regulate commerce. In 1784 Congress wanted to take control of commerce for 15 years. The states, however, refused because they were afraid that Congress would then have too much power.

Critical Thinking

Predicting What economic problems might develop if a country uses different types of currency?

In addition, the government lacked a chief executive. The Confederation government carried on much of its business, such as selling western lands, through congressional committees.

The Articles of Confederation were not wholly supported by the states. Under the new plan, each state had one vote, regardless of its population, and all states had to approve the Articles and any amendments. States with large populations, however, believed they should have more votes. The states were also divided by whether or not they claimed land in the West. Maryland refused to approve the Articles until New York, Virginia, and other states **abandoned**, or gave up, land claims west of the Appalachian Mountains. Finally the states settled their differences. With Maryland's ratification, all 13 states approved the Articles. On March 1, 1781, the Confederation formally became the government of the United States of America.

The Confederation Government

The years between 1781 and 1789 were a critical period for the young American republic. The Articles of Confederation did not provide a government strong enough to handle the problems facing the United States. The Congress had limited authority. It could not pass a law unless 9 states voted in favor of it. Any attempt to change the Articles required the consent of all 13 states. This made it difficult for the Congress to pass laws when there was any opposition. Despite its weaknesses, the Confederation made some important achievements. Under the Confederation government, Americans won their independence from Britain and expanded the country's foreign trade. The Confederation also aided with settling and governing the nation's western territories.

W

✔ **Reading Check** **Specifying** How many votes did each state have in the new Congress?

A More Perfect Union **Chapter 7** 189

CHAPTER 7

Section 1

W Writing Support

Persuasive Writing Assume the role of a small business owner in 1785. Write a letter to your state's representative in Congress expressing one specific concern you have about the Articles of Confederation. Offer a possible solution. **OL**

Primary Source

Critical Thinking Answer
States might not honor each other's currency; exchange rates might restrict trade.

Critical Thinking Practice
Ask: Why were the states unwilling to allow Congress to control commerce? *(Students should recall the colonists' struggle against the taxes imposed by Parliament during the Revolutionary War.)* **OL**

✔ **Reading Check** **Answer:** one vote, regardless of population

Hands-On Chapter Project
Step 1

Creating a Constitution

Step 1: Finding a Problem Groups will read the Articles of Confederation to find areas where improvement is needed.

Essential Question: How effective was government under the Articles of Confederation?

Directions Organize the class into groups and assign each group one of the original 13 states. Tell groups they will be creating a new constitution based on problems they find in the Articles of Confederation. Have groups read the Articles of Confederation and discuss its strengths and weaknesses. Students must research facts about their assigned states during the late 1780s, including sources of income, state governor and his ideals, and debt incurred during the Revolutionary War.

Analyzing Based on their research, have each group create a two- to three-sentence declaration that states why they believe the Articles are in need of revision.

(Chapter Project continued in Section 2)

R Reading Strategy

Organizing Ask: What actions did Congress take to extend its authority over the frontier and allow for new states to form? Have students write the steps in order, as a numbered list. *(1. States gave up their claims to lands; 2. Central government took control over these lands; 3. Congress divided territory into districts; 4. District population reached the size of the smallest state; 5. District could petition for statehood.)* **BL**

S Skill Practice

Visual Literacy Ask: Which is larger, a section or a township? *(township)* Have students draw an imaginary territory and divide it as Congress did. Ask them to label each different-sized part. *(Drawings should illustrate acres, an imaginary territory, sections, townships.)* **OL**

D Differentiated Instruction

English Language Learners Ask: What is a land speculator? *(Students may infer from the context that these are people who buy land when it is cheap and sell it later for a profit.)* **OL**

Differentiated Instruction

New Land Policies

Main Idea As people moved west, the country needed a process for new states joining the Union.

History and You Do you have to meet certain requirements to join some clubs or organizations? Read to learn the requirements for territories to become states.

. . . .

At the beginning of the Revolutionary War, only a few thousand settlers lived west of the Appalachian Mountains. By the 1790s, the number was approaching 120,000. These western settlers hoped to organize their lands as states and join the Union. The Articles of Confederation, however, did not contain a provision for adding new states. Congress realized that it had to extend its national authority over the frontier. During the 1780s, all of the states except Georgia gave up their claims to lands west of the Appalachians. The central government took control of these lands. In 1784 Congress divided the western territory into self-governing districts. When the number of people in a district reached the population of the smallest existing state, that district could **petition,** or apply to, Congress for statehood.

The Ordinance of 1785

In 1785 the Confederation Congress passed an **ordinance,** or law, that established a procedure for surveying and selling the western lands north of the Ohio River. The new law divided this massive territory into townships 6 miles long (9.7 km) and 6 miles wide (9.7 km). These townships were to be further divided into 36 sections of 640 acres (259 ha) each that would be sold at public auction for at least a dollar an acre. Land speculators viewed the law as an opportunity to accumulate large tracts of land cheaply. Concerned about lawless people moving into western lands, Richard Henry Lee, the president of the Congress, urged that "the rights of property be clearly defined" by the government. The Congress drafted another ordinance to protect the interests of hardworking settlers.

The Northwest Territory
NATIONAL GEOGRAPHIC

Lake Superior

SPANISH LOUISIANA

Mississippi River

Wisconsin

Lake Michigan

Lake Huron

Lake Ontario

Michigan

Lake Erie

Illinois   Indiana   Ohio   40°N

Ohio River

N W E S

90°W   80°W

Northwest Territory
Present-day state boundaries

0   200 kilometers
0   200 miles
Lambert Azimuthal Equal-Area projection

New Land The British gave up their claim to the Northwest Territory in the Treaty of Paris. After acquiring the land, Congress had to convince individual states to give up any claims they had on it. Then Congress had to negotiate treaties with Native Americans who were living in the Northwest Territory.

Township: American Building Block

Western lands north of the Ohio River were divided into townships 6 miles to a side. Each township contained 36 square miles, or "sections."

Township baseline 6 miles

Range line 6 miles

36	30	24	18	12	6
35	29	23	17	11	5
34	28	22	16	10	4
33	27	21	15	9	3
32	26	20	14	8	2
31	25	19	13	7	1

Reserved for schools
Reserved for federal government

Section 19
Half Section 320 acres
1 mile
Quarter Section 160 acres

Differentiated Instruction

The Ordinances of 1785 and 1787

Objective: To learn about the new land policies

Focus: Ask students how they think the lands to the west of the Appalachian Mountains could be organized.

Teach: Read the first article and have small groups develop a plan to divide the land and create new states.

Assess: Assess each plan for its fairness.

Close: Discuss the solutions provided by the Ordinances of 1785 and 1787.

Differentiated Instruction Strategies

BL Ask students to identify which states did not have land claims.

AL Have students create a list of reasons a state with large holdings should cede its territory.

ELL Ask students to create two land claim maps representing different years.

Geography and History Activity, URB p. 87

The Northwest Ordinance

The Northwest Ordinance, passed in 1787, created a single Northwest Territory out of the lands north of the Ohio River and east of the Mississippi River. The lands were to be divided into three to five smaller territories. When the population of a territory reached 60,000, the people could petition for statehood. Each new state would have the same rights and privileges as the original 13 states. The Northwest Ordinance included a bill of rights for the settlers, guaranteeing freedom of religion and trial by jury. It also stated, "There shall be neither slavery nor involuntary servitude in said territory." This **clause,** or condition added to a document, marked the first attempt to stop the spread of slavery in the United States. The Ordinance of 1785 and the Northwest Ordinance opened the way for settlement of the Northwest Territory in a stable and orderly manner.

Reading Check **Explaining** What rule did the Northwest Ordinance have about slavery?

Trouble on Two Fronts

Main Idea Financial problems and disputes with Britain and Spain revealed serious weaknesses of the Confederation government.

History and You Imagine paying ten times the normal price for a gallon of milk or a loaf of bread. Read about the economic problems of the late 1700s.

. . . .

The Confederation government did not have enough power to deal with the country's financial problems and issues with other nations.

Financial Problems

By 1781, the money printed during the Revolutionary War **depreciated,** or fell in value, so far that it was almost worthless. Unable to collect taxes, the Continental Congress and the states printed their own paper money. No gold or silver backed up these bills, so they had no real value.

S Skill Practice

Using Geography Skills Have students look at a map of the Northwest Territory. **Ask:** Which areas of the territory were likely to be settled first? Why? *(areas just north of the Ohio River; because they are easily accessible from the Ohio River and from Pennsylvania and Kentucky, which were already settled areas)* **OL**

C Critical Thinking

Making Inferences Ask: Why was it important for Congress to let new states enter the Union with the same rights and privileges as the original states? *(It encouraged people to settle in new areas and petition to join the Union.)* **OL**

The Northwest Territory
NATIONAL GEOGRAPHIC

Critical Thinking Answer

They could petition for statehood, had the same rights and privileges as citizens of the original 13 states, and were guaranteed freedom of religion and trial by jury.

Reading Check **Answer:** It banned slavery in the Northwest Territory.

Paying Debts The government needed money to pay off the debt from the Revolutionary War. Much of the new territory's land was sold at auction to raise money to pay off that debt. The government did not have enough money to pay the Revolutionary War veterans' salaries. Instead, it gave veterans land in the Northwest Territory. ▼

▲ **New Settlements** Land speculators also bought large tracts of land in the Northwest Territory to sell to settlers for a profit. A group of land speculators built Campus Martius when they arrived in the Northwest Territory. Campus Martius served as a fort until the town of Marietta, in present-day Ohio, was established.

Critical Thinking

Analyzing How did settlers benefit from the Northwest Ordinance of 1787?

A More Perfect Union **Chapter 7** **191**

Fast Facts

Prime Real Estate The land west of the Appalachians was a valuable asset for the national government. The Ohio Company, an organization of Revolutionary War veterans, approached Congress in 1787 about buying large amounts of land. Congress was motivated to quickly write and pass the Northwest Ordinance, partly because it wanted to resolve the land issue permanently but also because they were des-

perate for money. At the rate of $1 per acre, the sale of present-day Illinois could have brought more than $36 million to the government.

The Northwest Ordinance was a major accomplishment when it was passed. Later, it would serve as the model for managing new territories as the United States expanded westward throughout the nineteenth and twentieth century.

During the summer of 1787, as Congress was writing the Northwest Ordinance, leaders were also meeting to establish a new plan of government. Many of the ideas included in the Northwest Ordinance were written into the newly drafted Constitution later that same year. The money from the sale of lands in new territories would bring revenue into the new federal treasury for years to come.

Economics & History

Money is anything that is widely accepted as payment. Throughout the history of the American colonies and the United States, a number of different items served as currency.

▲ Native American wampum, or clam-shell beads, served as money during the 1600s.

In colonial Virginia, tobacco leaves were accepted as paper money. ▶

Greenbacks, named for their color, were used during the Civil War. ▼

In the U.S. today, people pay with Federal Reserve notes. ▼

▲ Continentals were printed to pay for the Revolutionary War.

Purposes of Money

1. **Medium of exchange** People accept money as payment for goods and services.
2. **Standard of value** Money is a way to measure how much something is worth—its price.
3. **Store of value** Money can be saved and used in the future.

Critical Thinking

Making Inferences Why do you think paper money was created?

W Writing Support

Narrative Writing Have students write a story about how a typical family dealt with the soaring price of food and other goods. Stories should include dialogue as well as historical details. **OL**

C Critical Thinking

Drawing Conclusions Ask: Would individual states be affected by a collapse of the country's finances? *(Answers should discuss the payments owed to soldiers who fought in the Revolution, as well as other debts held by the government.)* **AL**

R Reading Strategy

Activating Prior Knowledge Ask: What made the Articles of Confederation so weak that it was impossible to pass a tax law? *(Every state had to agree to any amendments.)* **OL**

Economics & History

Critical Thinking Answer
Students may say that paper money is easier to carry than coins and takes up less space.

Additional Support

W As more Continental dollars, or "Continentals," flowed into circulation, people realized that Congress could not redeem these bills for gold or silver. The public lost confidence in the money, and the value of the bills plummeted. Between 1779 and 1781, the number of Continental dollars required to buy one Spanish silver dollar rose from 40 to 146. "Not worth a Continental" became a common saying. At the same time, the price of food and other goods soared. In Boston and some other areas, high prices led to food riots.

The war for independence left the Continental Congress with a large debt. Congress had borrowed money from American citizens and foreign governments during the war. It still owed the Revolutionary soldiers their pay for their military service. Lacking the power to tax, the Confederation could not pay its debts. The Continental Congress requested funds from the states, but they were not required to contribute. The amount that was collected from the states amounted to only a small portion of the total money needed to pay off the debt.

Robert Morris's Import Tax

C In 1781, faced with a total collapse of the country's finances, Congress created a department of finance led by Philadelphia merchant Robert Morris. While serving in Congress, Morris had proposed a 5 percent tax on imported goods to help pay the national debt. The plan required that the Articles of Confederation be charged to give Congress the power to levy the tax. Although 12 states approved the plan, Rhode Island's opposition **R** killed it. A second effort in 1783 also failed to win unanimous approval by the states, and the financial crisis continued to worsen.

Activity: Collaborative Learning

Designing Currency Tell students they will be designing new currency to be used in the United States in the late 1700s. **Ask:** What does paper currency represent? *(its value in gold or silver)* **Ask:** What sorts of things are typically printed on currency? *(famous people or landmarks, value, serial number, name of the nation, and so on)* Organize students into small groups.

Have each group sketch a preliminary design for its currency. Next, distribute art supplies, scissors, rulers, and unlined paper. Have the groups create a final copy of their currency. Have students share their work with the class by explaining the symbols they chose.
Numismatics Tell students that many people enjoy collecting unusual or old money. **Ask:** Is anyone here a numismatist? Explain that a numismatist collects coins or currency. Because paper currency is fragile, most numismatists collect coins. Have students visit www.moneyfactory.gov at the U.S. Bureau of Engraving and Printing to learn more about paper money. **OL**

Problems With Britain

The weaknesses of the new American government became more evident as the United States encountered problems with other countries. In the Treaty of Paris of 1783, Britain promised to withdraw from the lands east of the Mississippi River. British troops, however, continued to occupy several strategic forts in the Great Lakes region.

British trade policy caused other problems. American merchants complained that the British were keeping Americans out of the West Indies and other profitable British markets. In 1785 Congress sent **John Adams** to London to discuss these difficulties. The British, however, were not willing to talk. They pointed to the failure of the United States to honor *its* promises made in the Treaty of Paris. The British claimed that Americans had agreed to pay Loyalists for the property taken from them during the Revolutionary War. The Congress had, in fact, recommended that the states pay the Loyalists. However, the states refused, and Congress could not require them to pay.

Problems With Spain

If American relations with Great Britain were poor, affairs with Spain were worse. Spain, which controlled Florida as well as lands west of the Mississippi River, was anxious to stop American expansion into its territory. As a result, Spain closed the lower Mississippi River to American shipping in 1784. Western settlers no longer had access to the Mississippi River, which they used for trade.

In 1786 American diplomats reached an agreement with Spain. Representatives from the Southern states, however, blocked the agreement because it did not include the right to use the Mississippi River. The weakness of the Confederation and its inability to deal with problems worried many leaders, including George Washington. Americans began to agree that the country needed a stronger government.

✓ Reading Check Analyzing Why did Spain close the lower Mississippi River to American shipping in 1784?

History ONLINE
Study Central™ To review this section, go to glencoe.com.

Section 1 Review

Vocabulary

1. Define each of the following terms in a sentence: constitution, bicameral, republic, abandon, petition, ordinance, clause, depreciate.

Main Ideas

2. Explaining Why did most states limit the power of their governors and divide the legislature into two bodies?

3. Specifying According to the Northwest Ordinance, when might the people of a territory petition for statehood?

4. Explaining Why did the Continental Congress have difficulty raising money?

Critical Thinking

5. Predicting How do you think the Northwest Ordinance would affect Native Americans?

6. Analyzing Use a graphic organizer like the one below to summarize the strengths and weaknesses of the Confederation government.

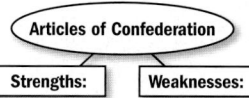

Articles of Confederation

Strengths: Weaknesses:

7. Persuasive Writing You are a delegate to the Second Continental Congress. Congress is debating whether to allow the central government to impose taxes. Take a stand on this issue, and write a short essay defending your position. Give specific reasons for your opinion.

Answer the
8. Essential Question
How effective was government under the Articles of Confederation?

CHAPTER 7
Section 1

C Critical Thinking

Making Inferences Ask: What do you think might happen because of Spain's refusal to allow U.S. traders to use the Mississippi River? *(Students may suggest that the United States may use diplomacy or threaten military action.)* **OL**

✓ Reading Check **Answer:** to stop American expansion into its territory

Assess

History ONLINE

Study Central™ provides summaries, interactive games, and online graphic organizers to help students review content.

Close

Discussing As a class, discuss the accomplishments and failures of the government under the Articles of Confederation. **Ask:** What issues could be resolved by creating a stronger government? **OL**

Section ⭐ Review

193

Answers

1. Students should use vocabulary words as they are defined in the section and the Glossary.
2. Experience with British rule made them cautious about giving too much power to single rulers or political bodies.
3. when the territory's population reached 60,000
4. It lacked the power to tax or require the states to contribute money to the government.

5. Students should recognize that Native Americans would be forced to give up lands and move or fight to stay.
6. **Strengths:** could conduct foreign affairs, maintain armed forces, borrow money, issue currency; **Weaknesses:** Congress could not pass a law unless all states voted in favor of it; consent of all states was required to change the Articles; Congress could not regulate trade, force soldiers to join the army, or impose taxes.

7. Essays should give specific reasons the central government should or should not be allowed to impose taxes.
8. Students may argue that it was ineffective because the Congress lacked important economic and diplomatic powers.

Convention and Compromise

Focus

Bellringer
Daily Test Practice Transparency 7–2

Reading Guide
Answers to Graphic:
Randolph: introduced the Virginia Plan; **Madison:** author of the Virginia Plan, known as the "Father of the Constitution"; **Sherman:** proposed Great Compromise calling for a two-house legislature; **Morris:** as author of much of the Constitution, he accepted its basic principles

Section Spotlight Video

Have students watch the Section Spotlight Video "Convention and Compromise" to learn more about the Constitution as a document of compromise.

Resource Manager

Essential Question
Why is the Constitution a document of compromises?

Reading Guide

Content Vocabulary

depression (p. 195)   proportional (p. 199)
manumission (p. 197)   compromise (p. 200)

Academic Vocabulary

convention (p. 198)   amend (p. 199)

Key People and Events

Shays's Rebellion (p. 196)
James Madison (p. 197)
Alexander Hamilton (p. 197)
Virginia Plan (p. 199)
New Jersey Plan (p. 199)
Great Compromise (p. 200)
Three-Fifths Compromise (p. 201)

Reading Strategy

Taking Notes As you read, use a graphic organizer like the one below to take notes about each individual's plan for creating a new government.

Leader	Role
Edmund Randolph	
James Madison	
Roger Sherman	
Gouverneur Morris	

ILLINOIS STANDARDS
The American Journey

14.F Understand the development of United States political ideas and traditions.

16.B.3a (US) Describe how different groups competed for power within the colonies and how that competition led to the development of political institutions during the early national period.

16.B.3b (US) Explain how and why the colonies fought for their independence and how the colonists' ideas are reflected in the Declaration of Independence and the United States Constitution.

16.C.3b (US) Explain relationships among the American economy and slavery, immigration, industrialization, labor and urbanization, 1700-present.

American Diary

By 1786 many Americans were blaming the inadequate Confederation for the nation's foreign policy problems as well as its economic troubles. Edmund Randolph of Virginia, one of 55 delegates called to Philadelphia for the specific purpose of revising the Articles of Confederation, delivered the opening speech saying, "It is absolutely necessary in this difficult crisis to prevent America's downfall."

—from Our Nation's Great Heritage

Independence Hall, Philadelphia

R Reading Strategies	**C** Critical Thinking	**D** Differentiated Instruction	**W** Writing Support	**S** Skill Practice
Teacher Edition • Act. Prior Know., p. 198 • Deter. Import., p. 198 • Categorizing, p. 199 **Additional Resources** • Guid. Read., URB p. 96 • Content Vocab., URB p. 73 • Academic Vocab., URB p. 75 • Read. Ess., p. 73 • Am. Lit. Read., URB p. 9	**Teacher Edition** • Predict. Conseq., p. 196 • Analyzing, p. 199 • Identify. Central Iss., p. 200 • Contrasting, p. 201 **Additional Resources** • Quizzes and Tests, p. 62 • Differ. Inst., URB p. 83	**Teacher Edition** • Visual/Spatial, p. 195 • Logic./Math., p. 198 **Additional Resources** • School-to-Home, URB p. 91 • Reteaching Act., URB p. 93	**Teacher Edition** • Persuasive Writ., p. 196 • Narrative Writ., p. 197 • Personal Writ., p. 200 **Additional Resources** • Authentic Assess., p. 7 • Writing Skills, URB p. 79	**Additional Resources** • Daily Test Pract. Transp. 7–2 • Soc. Stud. Skills, URB p. 81 • Time Line Skills, URB p. 90 • Lesson Transp. 7B

A Call for Change

Main Idea The government under the Articles of Confederation faced many problems.

History and You You make a plan, but the plan is not working—what do you do? Read to learn about the issues that challenged the government.

Many Americans called for the Articles of Confederation to be changed. They believed that the Confederation government was too weak to deal with the nation's problems. Those problems, however, were very difficult to solve. After the Revolutionary War, the United States experienced a **depression,** a period when economic activity slows and unemployment increases. Southern plantations were damaged during the war, and rice exports dropped sharply. Trade also decreased when the British closed the profitable West Indies market to American merchants. The little money that the government did have went to pay foreign debts, resulting in a serious currency shortage.

Shays's Rebellion

American farmers suffered because they could not sell their goods. They had trouble paying the money requested by the states to meet Revolutionary War debts. As a result state officials seized farmers' lands to pay their debts and threw many farmers in jail. Grumblings of protest soon grew into revolt. Resentment grew especially strong in Massachusetts. Farmers viewed the new government as just another form of tyranny. They wanted the government to issue paper money and make new policies to relieve debtors. In a petition to state officials, a number of farmers proclaimed:

PRIMARY SOURCE

"Surely your honours are not strangers to the distresses [problems] of the people but . . . know that many of our good inhabitants are now confined in [jail] for debt and taxes."

—"Petition from the Town of Greenwich, Massachusetts"

In 1786 angry farmers lashed out. Led by Daniel Shays, a former Continental Army captain, they forced courts in western Massachusetts to close so judges could not take away farmers' lands.

In January 1787, Shays led more than 1,000 farmers toward the federal arsenal in Springfield, Massachusetts, in search of guns and ammunition. The state militia ordered the advancing farmers to halt and then fired over their heads, but the farmers did not stop.

By the Numbers | Framers of the Constitution

Lawyers 31
Merchants 8
Politicians 4
Others 12

Occupations of the Framers Edmund Randolph was a lawyer and a graduate of William and Mary College. Although he did not sign the United States Constitution, he had much in common with his fellow delegates at the Federal Convention of 1787. Of the 55 men designing and debating the Constitution, nearly half were college educated and almost two-thirds practiced law.

· Judges
· Physicians
· Planters
· Philosopher
· Professor
· Surveyor

Source: *Fifty-Five Fathers: The Story of the Constitutional Convention*

Critical Thinking

Evaluating Do you think it is important for government leaders to have a college education? Why or why not?

Teach

D Differentiated Instruction

Visual/Spatial Have students review the information about Shays's Rebellion and design a poster to support or oppose the rebels. Encourage appealing graphics and accurate details and information. **OL**

By the Numbers

Critical Thinking Answer Students may state that the issues leaders face require a firm base of knowledge and an understanding of history and law; a college education could provide that.

Skills Practice Ask: How does a circle graph represent the number of merchants better than just the numeral itself? *(The graph shows the proportion of merchants best.)* **AL**

Differentiated Instruction

American Literature Reading, URB p. 9

Domestic Tranquility

Objective: To recognize two points of view regarding Shays's Rebellion

Focus: Ask students if there can be two valid sides to an issue.

Teach: Have students compare the two servants and their politics as they read the excerpt.

Assess: Students should understand the issues of social position and Shays's Rebellion.

Close: Have students summarize both sides of the Shays's Rebellion issue.

Differentiated Instruction Strategies

BL Ask students to create a two-column chart listing facts about Jonathan and Jessamy.

AL Have students write continued dialogue between the servants.

ELL Tell students to use a dictionary to restate the last statement by Jonathan.

W Writing Support

Persuasive Writing Have students read the statements of Washington and Jefferson about Shays's Rebellion and write a letter to the editor of your local newspaper supporting or opposing the rebellion. **OL**

C Critical Thinking

Predicting Consequences Ask: What did many Southerners fear would happen if slavery was abolished? *(They would lose a valuable source of labor.)* **OL**

History ONLINE

Objectives and answers to the Student Web Activity can be found at glencoe.com under the Web Activity Lesson Plan for this chapter.

Primary Source

Critical Thinking Answer Students may agree with Jefferson that preserving the rights of citizens to protest is good for protecting liberties. Students who agree with Adams will view rebellion as dangerous for a republic. Adams's views do not support that right.

Additional Support

Primary Source / Shays's Rebellion

Farmers Rebel in Massachusetts In 1787 Daniel Shays and rebellious farmers clashed with the state militia at the federal arsenal at Springfield.

◀ The federal arsenal at Springfield was used to store weapons and ammunition.

Shays and his followers attack the arsenal. ▶

"*What country can preserve its liberties if their rulers are not warned from time to time that their people preserve the spirit of resistance?*"
—Thomas Jefferson, in a letter to William S. Smith, November 13, 1787

"*Rebellion [against a king] may be pardoned, or lightly punished, but the man who dares to rebel against the laws of a republic ought to suffer death.*"
—Samuel Adams

Critical Thinking

Evaluating In your opinion, is Jefferson or Adams correct in his thinking? Justify your answer.

The militia fired again, killing four farmers. Shays and his followers scattered, and the uprising was over. **Shays's Rebellion** frightened many Americans. They worried that the government could not control unrest and prevent violence. On hearing of the rebellion, George Washington wondered whether "mankind, when left to themselves, are unfit for their own government." Thomas Jefferson, minister to France at the time, had a different view. "A little rebellion, now and then," he wrote, "is a good thing."

C The Issue of Slavery

The Revolutionary War brought attention to the contradiction between the American battle for liberty and the practice of slavery. Between 1776 and 1786, 11 states—all except South Carolina and Georgia—outlawed or heavily taxed the importation of enslaved people.

Although slavery was not a major source of labor in the North, it existed and was legal in all the Northern states. Many individuals and groups began to work to end the institution of slavery in America. In 1774 Quakers in Pennsylvania organized the first American antislavery society. Six years later Pennsylvania passed a law that provided for the gradual freeing of enslaved people. Between 1783 and 1804, Connecticut, Rhode Island, New York, and New Jersey passed laws that gradually ended slavery.

Still, free African Americans faced discrimination. They were barred from many public places, and few states gave free African Americans the right to vote. The children of most free blacks had to attend separate schools. Free African Americans established their own institutions—churches, schools, and mutual-aid societies—to seek social and economic opportunities.

The states south of Pennsylvania clung to the institution of slavery. The plantation system was built on slavery, and many Southerners feared that their economy could not survive without it.

History ONLINE

Student Web Activity Visit glencoe.com and complete the Chapter 7 Web Activity about Shays's Rebellion.

Activity: Interdisciplinary Connection

Geography Invite a local geography professor or city planner to speak to the class about how maps are made, their purposes, and professions relating to cartography. **Ask:** Why is an accurate map important? *(Answers may include settling boundary disputes, determining state/city/county lines, calculating property taxes, giving directions to travelers, etc.)* After the presentation, tell students they will be making maps. Provide an outline map of the nation in the late 1700s to each student. Have them refer to the above text to find issues relating to slavery in the 1700s and 1800s in America and depict them on their maps. Urge students to locate other events in other resources. Have students title their maps and design map keys with color codes or symbols. Encourage students to be accurate and neat as cartographers must be. **OL**

Nonetheless, an increasing number of slaveholders began freeing the enslaved people that they held after the war. Virginia passed a law that encouraged **manumission,** the freeing of individual enslaved persons, and the state's population of free African Americans grew.

The abolition of slavery in the North divided the new country on the critical issue of whether people should be allowed to keep other human beings in bondage. This division came at the time when many American leaders decided that the Articles of Confederation needed to be strengthened. In the summer of 1787, when state representatives assembled to plan a new government, they compromised on this issue. It would take a civil war to settle the slavery question.

✓ **Reading Check** Explaining How did the North and South differ on slavery?

The Constitutional Convention 🗹

Main Idea National leaders reshape the government.

History and You When your family or group of friends faces a problem, does everyone agree to a solution right away? Read about how certain political views changed the United States government.

. . . .

The American Revolution led to a union of 13 states, but it had not yet created a nation. Some leaders were satisfied with a system of independent state governments that resembled the old colonial governments. Others supported a strong national government. They demanded a reform of the Articles of Confederation. Two Americans who were active in the movement for change were **James Madison,** a Virginia planter, and **Alexander Hamilton,** a New York lawyer.

🗹 Writing Support

Narrative Writing Have students write a story for young children about a servant who accompanied a delegate to the Constitutional Convention. Have them conduct research to learn more key facts to use as they write, describing the servant's excitement and surroundings. **OL**

People IN HISTORY

Critical Thinking Answers

1. His fame and respectability made the Convention's work more likely to be accepted; he presided over the Convention; after it was over, he worked for ratification.
2. He argued that changes could be made later, as needed.

✓ **Reading Check** Answer: The economy of the North was not dependent on slave labor, while plantation farming in the South was built on slavery as cheap labor.

People IN HISTORY

George Washington

Presiding Officer of the Constitutional Convention

George Washington did not want to attend the Constitutional Convention, but he did because he worried that the nation would not survive under the weak Articles of Confederation. The delegates unanimously chose him as the presiding officer, or leader, of the Convention. Washington said very little during the debates but became one of the Constitution's strongest supporters. He argued that later generations could make any changes necessary: *"I think the people . . . can, as they will have the aid of experience on their side, decide . . . on the . . . amendments [which] shall be found necessary, . . . I do not conceive that we are more inspired—have more [wisdom]—or possess more virtue than those who will come after us."*

CRITICAL Thinking

1. **Evaluating** How did Washington contribute to the success of the Constitutional Convention?
2. **Analyzing** Why did Washington support the Constitution's ratification?

Hands-On Chapter Project
Step 2

Creating a Constitution

Step 2: Writing and Compromising Groups continue their work to create a constitution.

Essential Question: Why is the Constitution a document of compromises?

Directions Have each group list three or four weaknesses of the Articles of Confederation that they discussed in Step 1. Then have each group select a delegate to send to a constitutional convention. The delegates will meet as a group, using the list of weaknesses to write a constitution. They should make sure they protect the rights of their group (or state). Have them write their constitution on poster paper and sign it.

Identifying Points of View Discuss the different concerns of each state. Ask groups how they will represent their states' needs when others may not agree.

(Chapter Project continued in Section 3)

197

D Differentiated Instruction

Logical/Mathematical Have students calculate the percentage of the country's white male population that had college degrees in 1787. *(less than 1%)* **Ask:** What percentage of the delegates had college degrees? *(47%)* Have students research to learn which colleges the delegates attended, and create a table summarizing what they found. **AL**

R₁ Reading Strategy

Activating Prior Knowledge Ask: What do you know about George Washington that would have made his opinion carry so much weight among Americans at the time? *(He led the battle for independence and was a respected leader.)* **OL**

R₂ Reading Strategy

Determining Importance Ask: Who was called the "Father of the Constitution"? and what made his contribution so valuable? *(Madison; because he was the author of the basic plan of government that the Convention adopted)* **BL**

Additional Support

In September 1786, Hamilton proposed calling a **convention,** or meeting, in Philadelphia to discuss trade issues. He also suggested that this convention consider what possible changes were needed to make "the Constitution of the Federal Government adequate to the exigencies [needs] of the Union."

At first, George Washington was not enthusiastic about the movement to revise the Articles of Confederation. When Washington heard about Shays's Rebellion, however, he changed his mind. After Washington agreed to attend the Philadelphia convention, the meeting took on greater significance. The Philadelphia meeting began in May 1787 and continued through one of the hottest summers on record. The 55 delegates included planters, merchants, lawyers, physicians, generals, governors, and a college president. Three of the delegates were under 30 years of age, and one, Benjamin Franklin, was over 80. Many were well educated. At a time when only one white man in 1,000 went to college, 26 of the delegates had college degrees. Other groups, such as Native Americans, African

Americans, and women, were not considered part of the political process, so they were not represented at the convention.

The presence of George Washington and Benjamin Franklin ensured that many people would trust the Convention's work. Two Philadelphians also played key roles. James Wilson often read Franklin's speeches and did important work on the details of the Constitution. Gouverneur Morris, a powerful speaker and writer, wrote the final draft of the Constitution. James Madison was a keen supporter of a strong national government. Madison's careful notes documented the Convention's work. Madison is often called the "Father of the Constitution" because he was the author of the basic plan of government that the Convention adopted.

Organization

The delegates chose George Washington to preside over the meetings. The delegates also decided that each state would have one vote on all questions. A simple majority vote of those states present would make decisions.

Primary Source | **Signing of the Constitution**

"The Constitution is not an instrument for the government to restrain the people, it is an instrument for the people to restrain the government."
—Patrick Henry

Of the original 55 Convention delegates, only 39 signed the Constitution on September 17, 1787.

Activity: Connecting Past and Present

Conventions Then and Now Ask: What is a convention? *(an assembly of persons meeting for a common purpose)* **Ask:** Have you or someone in your family attended a convention? What kind? *(Responses will vary.)* Tell students that whatever the purpose of the convention may be, many preparations must be made. Work together as a class to create a "To Do List" of things the delegates to the Constitutional Convention must have had to accomplish, from answering the invitation to reporting the results at home. Then tell students that today, the major political parties hold conventions every four years to nominate candidates for president and vice president. Event planners plan and carry out the detailed preparations that go on behind the scenes. **Ask:** Why are these conventions held? *(to create a set of ideas they agree on, called a "party platform," and to elect a candidate to represent the party in the national election)* **Ask:** How are the Constitutional Convention and today's political conventions alike? *(They both serve the purpose of improving our nation.)* **OL**

No meetings could be held unless delegates from at least 7 of the 13 states were present. Sessions were not open to the public, which allowed the delegates to talk freely. **C**

The Virginia Plan

The Convention opened with a surprise from the Virginia delegation. Edmund Randolph proposed the creation of a strong national government. He introduced the **Virginia Plan,** which was largely the work of James Madison. The plan called for a two-house legislature, a chief executive chosen by the legislature, and a court system. The members of the lower house of the legislature **R** would be elected by the people. The members of the upper house would be chosen by the lower house. In both houses the number of representatives would be **proportional,** or corresponding in size, to the population of each state. This would give Virginia many more delegates than Delaware, the state with the smallest population.

Delegates from Delaware, New Jersey, and other small states immediately objected. They preferred the Confederation system in which all states were represented equally. Delegates who were unhappy with the Virginia Plan rallied around William Paterson of New Jersey. On June 15, he presented an alternative plan. This plan revised the Articles of Confederation, which was all the Convention was empowered to do.

The New Jersey Plan

Paterson's **New Jersey Plan** kept the Confederation's one-house legislature, with one vote for each state. Congress, however, could set taxes and regulate trade—powers it did not have under the Articles of Confederation. Congress would elect a weak executive branch consisting of more than one person. Paterson argued that the Convention should not deprive the smaller states of the equality they had under the Articles. Thus, his plan was designed simply to **amend,** or improve, the Articles.

✓ **Reading Check** **Making Connections** How did Shays's Rebellion influence the Constitutional Convention?

CHAPTER 7

Section 2

C Critical Thinking

Analyzing Ask: Do you agree with the delegates' decision to keep their discussions secret? *(Some will argue that secrecy led to a successful document; others may say it was unnecessary and undemocratic.)* **OL**

R Reading Strategy

Categorizing Ask: What do the Virginia and New Jersey plans have in common? *(an executive who is elected by the legislature)* **OL**

Primary Source

Critical Thinking Answer
It is an instrument for the people to restrain the government.

Visual Literacy Ask: What important delegate activities are shown? *(taking notes, participating orally, listening, and so on)*

✓ **Reading Check** **Answer:** It convinced many Americans of the need to change the plan of government.

1. Washington, George, Va.
2. Franklin, Benjamin, Pa.
3. Madison, James, Va.
4. Hamilton, Alexander, N.Y.
5. Morris, Gouverneur, Pa.
6. Morris, Robert, Pa.
7. Wilson, James, Pa.
8. Pinckney, Charles C., S.C.
9. Pinckney, Charles, S.C.
10. Rutledge, John, S.C.
11. Butler, Pierce, S.C.
12. Sherman, Roger, Conn.
13. Johnson, William Samuel, Conn.
14. McHenry, James, Md.
15. Read, George, Del.
16. Bassett, Richard, Del.
17. Spaight, Richard Dobbs, N.C.
18. Blount, William, N.C.
19. Williamson, Hugh, N.C.
20. Jenifer, Daniel, Md.
21. King, Rufus, Mass.
22. Gorham, Nathaniel, Mass.
23. Dayton, Jonathan, N.J.
24. Carroll, Daniel, Md.
25. Few, William, Ga.
26. Baldwin, Abraham, Ga.
27. Langdon, John, N.H.
28. Gilman, Nicholas, N.H.
29. Livingston, William, N.J.
30. Paterson, William, N.J.
31. Mifflin, Thomas, Pa.
32. Clymer, George, Pa.
33. FitzSimons, Thomas, Pa.
34. Ingersoll, Jared, Pa.
35. Bedford, Gunning, Jr., Del.
36. Brearley, David, N.J.
37. Dickinson, John, Del.
38. Blair, John, Va.
39. Broom, Jacob, Del.
40. Jackson, William (Secretary)

◄ Washington led the delegates in the signing of the Constitution.

Critical Thinking

Interpreting How does the Constitution limit the power of the government?

A More Perfect Union **Chapter 7** **199**

Activity: Technology Connection

Getting to Know the Delegates Ask: What is a biography? *(the story of someone's life)* Tell students they will be learning about the individual delegates who participated in the Constitutional Convention. Locate a list of the delegates. Have each student choose a different delegate and conduct research to learn about the life of his or her chosen delegate. Encourage them to begin with the material in the National Archive, but ask them to also locate at least two other sources of information about their delegates. Students should also find letters from the delegates and a portrait if possible.

Presenting Finally, have students write a two-page biography, emphasizing information that relates to the delegates' ideals and political views. Allow time for each biographer to share his or her work with the class. **AL**

C Critical Thinking

Identifying Central Issues Ask: Which issue was especially difficult to resolve? Why? *(representation; states had very different populations and wanted to be fairly represented.)* **OL**

W Writing Support

Personal Writing Ask: What issue was solved by the Great Compromise? *(representation)* What was the solution? Explain. *(A two-house legislature; representation in the House of Representatives was based on the state's population, while each state would be represented by two people in the Senate.)* **OL**

Virginia and New Jersey Plans

Critical Thinking Answer

The Virginia Plan; membership in the legislative branch is proportional to the state's population. As large states, they would have more representatives than smaller states and therefore have more power.

Differentiated Instruction

Virginia and New Jersey Plans

Both Plans

- Were federal systems with three branches—legislative, executive, and judicial
- Gave the federal government more powers than it had under the Articles of Confederation

Virginia Plan

Legislative Branch
- Powerful legislature
- Two houses, with membership proportional to state's population
- Lower house elected by the people
- Upper house elected by lower house

Executive Branch
- Chosen by legislature
- Limited power
- Could veto legislation, subject to override

Judicial Branch
- Would serve for life
- Could veto legislation, subject to override

▲ Edmund Randolph proposed the Virginia Plan.

New Jersey Plan

Legislative Branch
- One house with equal representation from all states
- Legislature could collect taxes from states

Executive Branch
- Chosen by Congress
- Would serve a single term
- Subject to recall on request of state governors

Judicial Branch
- Appointed by executive branch
- Would serve for life

▲ William Paterson proposed the New Jersey Plan.

Critical Thinking

Making Inferences Which form of government would be favored by states with large populations? Why?

Compromise Wins Out

Main Idea A new Constitution is adopted.

History and You To resolve differences of opinion in a group, do you discuss options until you reach an agreement? Read how delegates reached a compromise on important issues.

The delegates had to decide whether to simply revise the Articles of Confederation or write a constitution for a new national government. On June 19, the states voted to work toward a national government based on the Virginia Plan, but they still had to resolve the thorny issue of representation that divided the large and small states.

The Great Compromise

The Convention appointed a committee to resolve their disagreements. Roger Sherman of Connecticut suggested what came to be known as the **Great Compromise.** A compromise is an agreement between two or more sides in which each side gives up some of what it wants. Sherman proposed a two-house legislature. In the lower house—the House of Representatives—the number of seats for each state would vary based on the state's population. In the upper house—the Senate—each state would have two members.

The Three-Fifths Compromise

The delegates also compromised on how to count enslaved people. Southern states wanted to include enslaved people in their population counts to gain delegates in the House of Representatives. Northern states objected because enslaved people were legally considered property. Some Northern delegates argued that enslaved people, as property, should be counted for the purpose of taxation but not representation. Neither side, however, considered giving enslaved people the right to vote.

Leveled Activities

BL **Guided Reading Activity, URB p. 96**

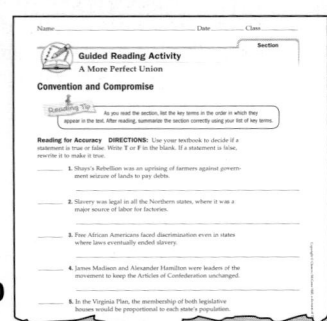

OL **Authentic Assessment With Rubrics, p. 7**

AL **Writing Skills Activity, URB p. 79**

The committee's solution, known as the **Three-Fifths Compromise,** was to count each enslaved person as three-fifths of a free person for both taxation and representation. In other words, every five enslaved persons would equal three free persons. The delegates voted to approve the Three-Fifths Compromise.

Slave Trade

Northern states banned slave trade within their borders and wanted to prohibit it nationwide. Southern states considered slavery and the slave trade essential to their economies. To keep the Southern states in the nation, Northerners agreed that the Congress could not interfere with the slave trade until 1808.

Bill of Rights

George Mason of Virginia proposed a bill of rights to be included in the Constitution. Some delegates worried that without a bill of rights the new national government might abuse its power. However, most delegates believed that the Constitution, with its carefully defined list of government powers, provided adequate protection of individual rights. Mason's proposal was defeated.

Approving the Constitution

The committees finished their work in late summer. On September 17, 1787, the delegates assembled in Philadelphia to sign the document. Three delegates refused to sign— Elbridge Gerry of Massachusetts, and Edmund Randolph and George Mason of Virginia. Gerry and Mason would not sign without a bill of rights. The approved draft of the Constitution was then sent to the states for consideration. The approval process for the Articles of Confederation required a unanimous vote of all the states. The new Constitution, however, required 9 of the 13 states to be approved. After that, the new government would come into existence.

✔ Reading Check **Analyzing** Who refused to sign the Constitution? Why?

Section 2 Review

History ONLINE
Study Central™ To review this section, go to glencoe.com.

Vocabulary

1. Define each of the following terms, and use it in a sentence: depression, manumission, convention, proportional, amend, compromise.

Main Ideas

2. **Specifying** What did the farmers in Shays's Rebellion want?

3. **Explaining** Why did New Jersey's delegates object to the Virginia Plan?

4. **Identifying** What key issues had to be resolved to create a Constitution that most states would accept?

Critical Thinking

5. **Contrasting** Use a chart like the one below to describe the differences between the Virginia and New Jersey Plans concerning the legislature, representation, and the executive branch.

	Virginia Plan	New Jersey Plan
Legislature		
Representation		
Executive Branch		

6. **Analyzing** Why do you think representation was such a thorny issue?

7. **Expository Writing** You have been asked to write a short announcement to inform your community about the Great Compromise. Summarize the key points of the agreement. Include any other details you think are important.

Answer the
8. **Essential Question**
Why is the Constitution a document of compromises?

A More Perfect Union **Chapter 7** 201

C Critical Thinking

Contrasting Ask: How did the approval process for adopting the Constitution differ from the process under the Articles of Federation? *(Unanimous approval was required for the Articles of Confederation, but under the new Constitution only 9 of 13 states were needed to adopt the new Constitution.)* **BL**

✔ Reading Check **Answer:** Elbridge Gerry, Edmund Randolph, and George Mason; Gerry and Mason would not sign the Constitution without a bill of rights.

Assess

History ONLINE

Study Central™ provides summaries, interactive games, and online graphic organizers to help students review content.

Close

Summarizing As a class, discuss the compromises that the nation's leaders resolved in order to write the new Constitution. **OL**

Section 2 Review

Answers

1. Definitions should follow vocabulary terms as they are defined in the section and the Glossary.
2. for the government to issue paper money and make new policies to relieve debtors
3. Because representation was proportional, small states like New Jersey would have fewer votes in Congress than would large states.
4. how members of Congress would be elected, representation in the legislature, count enslaved people for representation

5. **Virginia:** two houses, proportional representation, one chief executive; **New Jersey:** one house, one vote per state, executive could be recalled by state governors.
6. Students should recognize that states with more representatives in Congress would have more voting power. Small states did not want large states to dominate the government.
7. Announcements should identify the two houses in the legislature and explain how seats in each house are to be allotted to the

states. Students might discuss Roger Sherman's role.
8. Student answers should describe how delegates had to compromise on issues such as power distribution, representation, and slavery.

Focus

George Mason ▶

Independence Hall in 2007, Philadelphia, Pennsylvania

202

YOU DECIDE

Should the Constitution Be Ratified: Yes or No?

Building Background

After the delegates in Philadelphia wrote the U.S. Constitution, it had to be approved by the American people. Delegates in each state met at special conventions to decide whether to accept or reject the Constitution. The Constitution would only become the new plan of government of the United States if nine of the 13 states ratified, or approved, it.

C People who opposed the Constitution were called Antifederalists. Antifederalists feared a strong national government. They were afraid that a strong central government would take away the rights of citizens. Federalists, however, supported the Constitution. They believed that the Constitution would give the national government power to manage the problems facing the United States. At the same time, the Federalists argued, the Constitution would protect the rights of the individual.

NO

PATRICK HENRY

I look upon that paper [the Constitution] as the most fatal plan that could possibly be conceived[1] to enslave a free people.

R GEORGE MASON

There is no declaration of rights, and the laws of the general government being paramount[2] to the laws and constitutions of the several States, the declarations of rights in the separate States are no security.

---

[1] **conceived** formed
[2] **paramount** of higher authority

Fast Facts

Unifying the Nation The ratification of the Constitution in 1787 transformed American political life. By providing the federal government with a robust executive branch and with the authority to raise armies and regulate trade, the Constitution made it possible for the United States to grow into a powerful nation. Ratification profoundly changed American culture as well. Under the Articles of Confederation, citizens tended to put their own state before the Union in their loyalties. The new government, with the president as its most visible symbol, influenced its subjects to identify themselves as Americans.

YES

JAMES WILSON

I am satisfied that any thing nearer to perfection could not have been accomplished. If there are errors, it should be remembered, that the seeds of reformation³ are sown in the work itself, and the concurrence⁴ of two thirds of the congress may at any time introduce alterations and amendments. . . . I am bold to assert, that it is the BEST FORM OF GOVERNMENT WHICH HAS EVER BEEN OFFERED TO THE WORLD.

ALEXANDER HAMILTON

There is an idea . . . that a vigorous Executive is inconsistent with the genius of republican government. . . .

[However,] a feeble Executive implies a feeble execution⁵ of the government. A feeble execution is but another phrase for a bad execution; and a government ill executed, whatever it may be in theory, must be, in practice, a bad government.

▼ James Wilson

The Assembly Room where the U.S. Constitution was signed

203

---

³ **reformation** change
⁴ **concurrence** agreement
⁵ **execution** plan

DBQ Document-Based Questions

1. **Identifying** According to Wilson, how can the Constitution be changed?

2. **Drawing Conclusions** Why do you think Henry believed that the Constitution would "enslave a free people"?

3. **Analyzing** One of George Mason's objections to the Constitution was that it had no bill of rights. Do you think he objected to it for other reasons? Explain your answer.

4. **Evaluating** Which person do you think argued the most persuasively? Why? Write a paragraph that explains your opinion.

Teach

W Writing Support

Expository Writing   Ask: What does Hamilton mean by a "feeble executive"? *(a weak president)* How would the proposed Constitution improve the execution of government? *(A more powerful executive could guide the new government and nation.)* Have students write two to three paragraphs describing their beliefs about strong leadership in government or in another, more familiar organization. **OL**

Assess/Close

Discuss how the concerns of the Antifederalists were addressed after the Constitution was ratified—most importantly by the Bill of Rights.

Answers

1. The Constitution can be amended if two-thirds of Congress approves of the change.

2. Henry was afraid that the Constitution would create a strong central government that would take away the rights and freedoms of Americans.

3. He mentioned that the laws of the central government would take precedence over those of the states; he may have objected to the Constitution because of the federal government's power.

4. Students' paragraphs might describe how word choice influences a reader's opinion.

Section 3

A New Plan of Government

Focus

Bellringer
Daily Test Practice Transparency 7–3

Reading Guide
Answers to Graphic:

Executive: over Congress—can veto laws; over Court—appoints justices. **Legislative:** over president—can override veto; over Court—Senate approves appointments to Court. **Judicial:** over Congress—can rule on constitutionality of laws; over president—can rule on constitutionality of presidential acts.

Section Spotlight Video

To learn more about the challenge to ratify the Constitution, have students watch the Section Spotlight Video "A New Plan of Government."

Essential Question ◀
What ideas and features are found in the United States Constitution?

Reading Guide

Content Vocabulary

federalism (p. 206)	judicial branch (p. 208)
legislative branch (p. 207)	checks and balances (p. 208)
executive branch (p. 207)	amendment (p. 210)
Electoral College (p. 207)	

Academic Vocabulary

tradition (p. 205)   reside (p. 208)

Key People
John Locke (p. 206)
Baron de Montesquieu (p. 206)

Reading Strategy
Taking Notes As you read, use a chart like the one below to identify ways in which each branch of the federal government can check, or limit, the power of the other branches.

Branch	Example
Executive	
Legislative	
Judicial	

ILLINOIS STANDARDS
The American Journey

14.F.3a Analyze historical influences on the development of political ideas and practices as enumerated in the Declaration of Independence, the United States Constitution, the Bill of Rights and the Illinois Constitution.

14.F.3b Describe how United States political ideas and traditions were instituted in the Constitution and the Bill of Rights.

16.B.3b (US) Explain how and why the colonies fought for their independence and how the colonists' ideas are reflected in the Declaration of Independence and the United States Constitution.

American Diary

As Benjamin Franklin was leaving the last session of the Constitutional Congress, a woman asked, "Well Doctor, what have we got: a republic or a monarchy?" Franklin answered, "A republic, if you can keep it." He meant that in order to maintain a republic—a system of government in which the people elect representatives to exercise power for them—citizens must take an active role.

—quoted in the "Papers of Dr. James McHenry, 1787"

The U.S. Constitution on display at the National Archives, Washington, D.C.

Resource Manager

R Reading Strategies	C Critical Thinking	D Differentiated Instruction	W Writing Support	S Skill Practice
Teacher Edition • Listing, p. 206 • Predicting, p. 209 **Additional Resources** • Guid. Read., URB p. 97 • Content Vocab., URB p. 73 • Academic Vocab., URB p. 75 • Read. Ess., p. 76	**Teacher Edition** • Making Gen., p. 205 • Anal. Pri. Sources, p. 210 **Additional Resources** • Quizzes and Tests, p. 69 • Citizen. & Dec. Mak. Skills, URB p. 3 • Inter. Polit. Cartoons, URB p. 13 • Crit. Think. Skills, URB p. 85	**Teacher Edition** • Gifted & Tal., p. 206 • Verbal/Ling., p. 207 • Visual/Spatial, p. 209 **Additional Resources** • School-to-Home, URB p. 91 • Reteaching Act., URB p. 93	**Teacher Edition** • Personal Writ., p. 206 • Expository Writ., p. 208 • Persuasive Writ., p. 210	**Teacher Edition** • Creat. a Visual, p. 208 **Additional Resources** • Daily Test Pract. Transp. 7-3 • Lesson Transp. 7A, 7C

Roots of the Constitution

Main Idea As the Framers wrote the Constitution, they borrowed ideas from other political systems and philosophers of the Enlightenment.

History and You Has a person influenced you to do better in school or participate in an activity that helps others? Read to learn about the ideas and thinkers who helped shape the Constitution.

·······

After four long and difficult months, Franklin and the other delegates had produced a new constitution. The document provided the framework for a strong central government for the United States. Although a uniquely American document, the Constitution has roots in many other civilizations. The delegates studied and discussed the history of political thought at length—starting with ancient Greece—so that their new government could avoid the mistakes of the past. Many ideas found in the Constitution came from the study of European political institutions and political writers. British ideas and institutions influenced the delegates.

The Framers who shaped the document were familiar with the parliamentary system of Britain, and many had participated in the colonial assemblies or their state assemblies. They valued the individual rights guaranteed by the British judicial system. Although the Americans broke away from Britain, they respected many British **traditions,** or cultural beliefs and practices.

European Influences

The English Magna Carta (1215) placed limits on the power of the monarch. England's lawmaking body, Parliament, emerged, or became known, as a force that the monarch had to depend on to pay for wars and to finance the royal government. Like Parliament, the colonial assemblies controlled their colonies' funds. For that reason the assemblies had some control over colonial governors. The English Bill of Rights of 1689 provided another model for Americans. Many Americans felt that the Constitution also needed a bill of rights. The Framers of the Constitution believed in the ideas about the nature of people and government promoted by European writers of the Enlightenment. **C** The Enlightenment was a movement of the 1700s that promoted knowledge, reason, and science as a means of improving society.

By the Numbers **The Delegates Talk**

Speeches—Long and Short Except for two short breaks, the delegates met six days a week from May to September 1787. Although they met for only five to six hours each day, the heat, the debating, and the sitting often made it feel longer. During the Convention, many delegates gave speeches to share their ideas and knowledge about government. Some delegates gave more speeches than others.

Delegate	Number of Speeches
Gouverneur Morris	173
James Wilson	168
James Madison	161
George Washington	1

Gouverneur Morris ▶

Critical Thinking

Making Generalizations Do you think talking a lot convinces people to listen to you more? Explain.

Teach

·········

C **Critical Thinking**

Making Generalizations Ask: What sorts of government projects might politicians, who were influenced by the Enlightenment, propose? *(Students may suggest founding a national university, funding scientists and inventors, public education, and other projects that could improve society.)* **AL**

By the Numbers

Critical Thinking Answer People may listen more if a speaker is well respected, but listeners might ignore someone who talks a lot but has little of value to say.

Skills Practice Ask: What information is needed to calculate the percentage of speeches given by Morris? *(the total number of speeches by all delegates)* **OL**

Differentiated Instruction

Leveled Activities

BL **School-to-Home Connection Activity, URB p. 91**

OL **Reteaching Activity, URB p. 93**

ELL **Academic Vocabulary Activity, URB p. 75**

W Writing Support

Personal Writing Ask: What rights do you value the most? *Have students write their answers in personal essays that describes which rights they have and why they value them.* **OL**

D Differentiated Instruction

Gifted and Talented Ask: What is federalism? *(sharing power between the federal and state governments)* Have students give examples of federalism from current events. *(Examples could include education, environmental protection, road construction, and so on.)* **AL**

R Reading Strategy

Listing Have students help you write a list of the broad powers of the federal government gained under the Constitution. *(tax citizens, regulate trade, control the currency, raise an army, declare war, and pass laws)* **BL**

James Madison and other architects of the Constitution were familiar with the work of **John Locke** and **Baron de Montesquieu** (mahn·tuhs·KYOO), two philosophers of the Enlightenment.

Locke, an English philosopher, believed that all people have natural rights. These natural rights include the rights to life, liberty, and property. In his *Two Treatises of Civil Government* (1690), he wrote that government is based on an agreement, or contract, between the people and the ruler. Many Americans interpreted natural rights to mean the rights of Englishmen defined in the Magna Carta and the English Bill of Rights. The Framers viewed the Constitution as a contract between the American people and their government. The contract protected the people's natural rights by limiting the government's power. In *The Spirit of Laws* (1748), the French writer Montesquieu declared that the powers of government should be separated and balanced against each other. This separation would prevent any single person or group from gaining too much power. The powers of government should also be clearly defined and limited to prevent abuse. Following the ideas of Montesquieu, the Framers of the Constitution carefully specified and divided the powers of government.

The Federal System

The Constitution created a federal system of government that divided powers between the national, or federal, government and the states. In the Articles of Confederation, the states held most powers. Under the Constitution, the states gave up some powers to the federal government and kept others. **Federalism,** or sharing power between the federal and state governments, is one of the distinctive features of the United States government. Under the Constitution, the federal government gained broad powers to tax, regulate trade, control the currency, raise an army, and declare war. It could also pass laws that were "necessary and proper" for carrying out its responsibilities. This power allowed Congress to make laws as needed to deal with new situations.

LINKING PAST TO PRESENT — The United States Flag

THEN On June 14, 1777, Congress resolved that "the flag of the United States be thirteen stripes, alternate red and white; that the union be thirteen stars, white in a blue field representing a new constellation." Congress, however, did not specify how to arrange the stars. As a result, some flags had stars arranged in a circle, whereas other flags had the stars aligned.

◄ American flag, 1795–1818, had 15 stars and 15 stripes. In 1818 Congress set the number of stripes at 13.

◄ A legend claims that Betsy Ross made the first American flag, but no historical evidence supports this claim.

Hands-On Chapter Project
Step 3

Creating a Constitution

Step 3: Approving the Constitution Groups continue to work toward creating a constitution.

Essential Question: What ideas and features are found in the United States Constitution?

Directions Delegates will return to their original groups with a copy of the constitution. Each group will decide if the constitution should be approved. If approved without amendments, the group should outline an argument stating the reasons no changes are necessary. If groups want to add amendments, they will outline an amendment that they believe needs to be added. Students should use persuasive arguments to create support for amendments.

Comparing Discuss the amendments in the U.S. Constitution and compare them to what the groups are doing. **Ask:** Why are amendments an important feature of constitutions?

(Chapter Project continued in the Visual Summary)

The Constitution, however, left important powers in the hands of the states. The states had the power to regulate trade within their borders. They also could establish local governments and schools and set marriage and divorce laws.

The Constitution also allows for power to be shared between the federal and state governments. Both federal and state governments have the power to tax and administer criminal justice.

The Supreme Law of the Land

The Constitution and the laws that Congress passed were to be "the supreme law of the land." No state could make laws or take actions that went against the Constitution. Any dispute between the federal government and the states was to be settled by the federal courts on the basis of the Constitution. Under the new federal system, the Constitution became the final and supreme authority.

Reading Check Describing What is the principle of federalism?

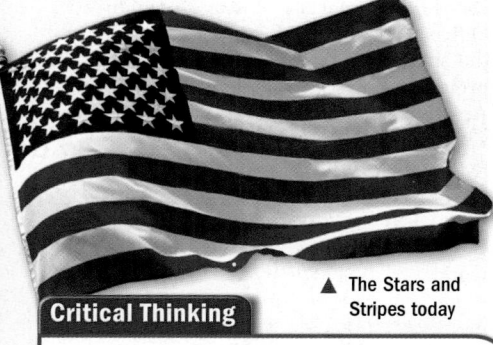

NOW A star was added as each new state entered the Union. On July 4, 1960, the number of stars reached the present total of 50. The 50th star represents Hawaii.

▲ The Stars and Stripes today

Critical Thinking

1. **Making Inferences** Why do you think Congress decided to set the number of stripes at 13?

2. **Applying** What are other symbols of our nation?

The New Government

Main Idea The Constitution divides and limits power among three branches of government.

History and You Do you think government leaders should be limited to what they can or cannot do? Read about the division of powers and responsibilities of government.

Montesquieu's idea of a division of powers led the Framers to divide the federal government into three branches—legislative, executive, and judicial. The first three articles, or parts, of the Constitution describe each branch's powers and responsibilities.

Branches of Government

Article I of the Constitution establishes Congress as the **legislative branch,** or law-making branch, of the government. Congress is composed of the House of Representatives and the Senate. As a result of the Great Compromise between large and small states, each state's representation in the House is proportional to its population. Representation in the Senate is equal—two senators for each state. The powers of Congress include collecting taxes, coining money, and regulating trade. Congress also can declare war and "raise and support armies." Finally, it makes all laws needed to fulfill its functions as stated in the Constitution. Memories of King George III's rule made some delegates reluctant to establish a powerful executive, or ruler. Others believed that the Articles of Confederation failed, in part, because it lacked an executive branch. They argued that a strong executive would limit the power of Congress.

Article II of the Constitution established the **executive branch,** headed by the president, to carry out the nation's laws and policies. The president serves as commander in chief of the armed forces and conducts relations with foreign countries. The president and a vice president are elected by a special group called the **Electoral College,** made of presidential electors.

A More Perfect Union **Chapter 7 207**

D # Differentiated Instruction

Verbal/Linguistic Explain to students that the root of the word "legislative," "leg-," comes from the Latin root "lex-," which means "law." **Ask:** What other words can you name that share this Latin root? *(legal, legislator, legitimate)* **OL**

LINKING PAST TO PRESENT

Critical Thinking Answers

1. Thirteen symbolized the number of original colonies in America.

2. Students may suggest bald eagle, Uncle Sam, Statue of Liberty, and so on.

Critical Thinking Practice

Analyzing Ask: If the United States admits another state to the Union, what will happen to the flag? *(Another star will be added.)*

Reading Check **Answer:** Powers are divided and shared between states and the national government.

Differentiated Instruction

Activity: Interdisciplinary Connection

Graphic Arts Invite a graphic arts teacher to discuss the impact of colors and graphic images on the designs of flags. Ask the speaker to discuss how manufacturing techniques might impact flag designs, as they are printed on apparel fabrics, ceramics, and other surfaces.

Remind students that the new United States Constitution solved one major concern shared by all the states: that the government would be too strong. **Ask:** How did they do this? *(by sharing power with the states)* Tell students that they will be designing a new flag for the

United States. Have them refer to the text's description of the balance of power as they sketch a design for a new U.S. flag reflecting this theme. Provide art supplies and unlined paper for students to use as they create a final copy. Display finished flags in class. **OL**

W Writing Support

Expository Writing Ask: Is the Electoral College an effective way to elect the president? Have students write essays supporting their opinions. **OL**

S Skill Practice

Creating a Visual Have students draw the three branches of government arranged in a triangle. Have them add the checks and balances between the branches. Ask students to add symbols, images, or arrows to make their content more clear. **OL**

INTERPRETING POLITICAL CARTOONS

Answers

1. the ratification vote by each state convention
2. Nine states must ratify the Constitution for it to become law.

✓ Reading Check **Answer:** to describe the powers and responsibilities of each branch of the federal government

Additional Support

Primary Sources
INTERPRETING POLITICAL CARTOONS

This cartoon was published in 1788, as the state conventions were voting to ratify the new Constitution.

1. **Interpreting** What do the pillars represent?
2. **Synthesizing** What is the significance of the ninth pillar?

The Ninth PILLAR erected !
" The Ratification of the Conventions of nine States, fhall be fufficient for the eftablifhment of this Conftitution, between the States fo ratifying the fame." *Art.* vii.
INCIPIENT MAGNI PROCEDERE MENSES.

"Incipent magni procedere menses" means "And the months enter on their mighty march."

Each state's voters select electors to cast their votes for the president and vice president. Every state has the same number of electors as it has senators and representatives in Congress. The president and vice president serve a four-year term.

Article III deals with the **judicial branch,** or court system. The nation's judicial power **resides,** or exists, in "one supreme Court" and any other lower federal courts that Congress might establish. The Supreme Court and the federal courts hear cases involving the Constitution, laws passed by Congress, and disputes between states.

System of Checks and Balances

The Framers built in a system of **checks and balances.** Each branch has ways to check, or limit, the power of the others so that no single branch can dominate the government. Both the House and the Senate must pass a bill for it to become law. The president can check Congress by vetoing, or rejecting, the bill. Congress can check the president by overriding, or voting down, the veto. To override a veto, two-thirds of the members of both houses must vote for the bill.

The system of checks and balances also applies to the Supreme Court. The president appoints Supreme Court justices, and the Senate must approve the appointments. Over time, the Court has become a check on Congress and the president by ruling on the constitutionality of laws and presidential acts. This system has kept a balance of power among the branches and has limited abuses.

National Citizens

The Constitution created citizens who choose their officials—directly or indirectly. Officials answer to the people rather than to the states. The new government pledged to protect the personal freedoms of its citizens. Americans showed the world that it was possible for a people to change its form of government through discussion and choice—rather than through chaos, force, or war. The world watched the new nation to see if its experiment in self-government really would work.

✓ Reading Check **Explaining** What is the purpose of the first three articles of the Constitution?

Activity: Connecting Past and Present

Activating Prior Knowledge Ask: What are constituents? *(people that members of Congress represent)* How do you think the delegates informed their constituents about the new U.S. Constitution? *(newspaper articles, letters, town hall meetings, handbills)* Have students write a list of main points to be included in a detailed handbill that could be distributed to

inform Americans about their new Constitution.

Ask: How do senators and representatives report on their work to their constituents today? *(letters, newsletters, Web sites, e-mail)* Tell students that today's legislators are not writing a new constitution but sometimes will propose amendments. Tell students that much of legislators'

time is spent working in committees drafting new laws, approving the budget, and making sure that the interests of their home states are well-represented in Washington.

Have students visit the Web site for your state senator or representative and find examples of that person's efforts to keep their constituents up to date. **OL**

Debate and Adoption

Main Idea After a much heated debate, the states ratified the Constitution.

History and You How do some people influence a group's decisions more than others? Read how influential leaders helped ratify the Constitution.

The delegates produced the Constitution, but before it could go into effect, nine states had to ratify, or approve, it. A great debate then took place throughout the country. In newspapers, at meetings, and in ordinary conversations, Americans discussed the arguments for and against the new Constitution.

Federalists and Antifederalists

Supporters of the new Constitution were called Federalists. Federalists enjoyed the support of two of the most respected men in America—George Washington and Benjamin Franklin. Gifted political thinkers James Madison, Alexander Hamilton, and John Jay also backed the Constitution. Madison, Hamilton, and Jay wrote a series of essays explaining and defending the Constitution. These essays appeared in newspapers around the country. Called the Federalist Papers, they were later published as a book and sent to delegates at state conventions. Jefferson called the essays "the best commentary on the principles of government which was ever written."

People who opposed the Constitution were called Antifederalists. Antifederalists responded to the Federalists by writing their own essays, now known as the Antifederalist Papers. Their main argument was that the strong national government created by the Constitution would take away the liberties Americans had fought for in the war against Great Britain. The government would ignore the will of the states and the people and favor the wealthy few over the common people.

Antifederalists favored local government that was controlled more closely by the people. A central government, they feared, would be made of a small group of individuals.

R Reading Strategy

Predicting Instruct students to read the title and subheads and look at the photos. Then remind them that the overall topic of the feature is the Constitution. **Ask:** What do you think you will learn about from reading the text on this page? (how the Constitution was debated and eventually adopted) **BL**

D Differentiated Instruction

Visual/Spatial Have students make two columns on lined paper and label them "Federalists" and "Antifederalists." As they read this article, have them record facts about each in the appropriate column. **OL**

Primary Source

Critical Thinking Answer
Students may suggest that they did not want to be identified or that a pen name would draw more attention to their ideas.

Primary Source — James Madison and the Federalist Papers

Debating the Constitution During the national debate over ratification of the Constitution, newspapers published articles for and against it. The most famous of these articles appeared as a series of essays published under the pen name "Publius" in New York newspapers. "Publius" was actually three men—John Jay, Alexander Hamilton, and James Madison. Their essays explained the benefits of the new Constitution and became known as the Federalist Papers.

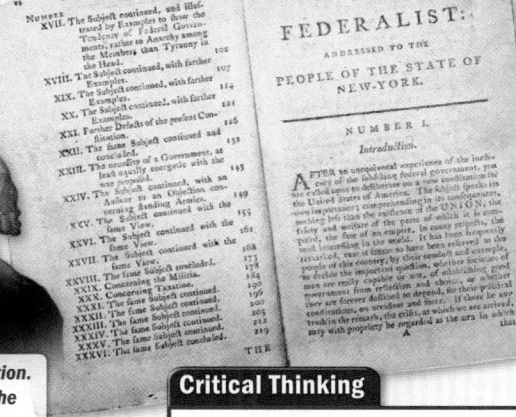

After taking a leading role in shaping the Constitution, James Madison argued for its ratification. ▶

"I believe I never have yet mentioned to you that publication. It was undertaken last fall by Jay, Hamilton, and myself. The proposal came from the two former. The execution was thrown, by the sickness of Jay, mostly on the two others."
—James Madison, in a letter to Thomas Jefferson, 1788

Critical Thinking

Speculating Why do you think that Jay, Hamilton, and Madison signed their essays with a single pen name?

A More Perfect Union **Chapter 7** **209**

Interpreting Political Cartoons, URB p. 13

Debate Over Ratification

Objective: To understand the views of Federalists and Antifederalists

Focus: Have students refer to the chapter opener time line to place this event in time.

Teach: Tell students Connecticut was divided on ratification, as were other states.

Assess: Students should answer the questions on the activity and complete what they missed during discussion.

Close: Have students summarize the main idea.

Differentiated Instruction Strategies

BL Have students refer to Shays's Rebellion in their text to explain the issue pulling Connecticut apart.

AL Tell students to add an additional speech bubble for each person pictured.

ELL Have students write the names of prominent Americans on the appropriate side of the wagon in the cartoon.

C Critical Thinking

Analyzing Primary Sources **Ask:** Which does Warren think is more important, government or individual liberty? *(individual liberty)* What did she want the Constitution to include? *(a bill of rights)* **OL**

W Writing Support

Persuasive Writing Write a letter to Patrick Henry trying to persuade him to ratify the Constitution even though it does not yet have a bill of rights. **OL**

✔ **Reading Check** **Answer:** They were the two largest states.

Assess

History ONLINE

Study Central™ provides summaries, interactive games, and online graphic organizers to help students review content.

Close

Synthesizing As a class, discuss the ideas that influenced the Framers, the form of the new government, and the process of ratification. **OL**

Section 3 Review

They agreed with Patrick Henry, who warned that the Constitution was "incompatible with [contrary to] the genius of republicanism."

Protecting Rights

Perhaps the strongest criticism of the Constitution was that it lacked a bill of rights to protect individual freedoms. Several state conventions announced that they would not ratify it without the addition of a bill of rights. Mercy Otis Warren expressed the problem:

PRIMARY SOURCE

C "We have struggled for liberty & made costly sacrifices . . . and there are still many among us who [value liberty] too much to relinquish . . . the rights of man for the Dignity of Government."

—from a letter to Catherine Graham

The Federalists feared disorder without a strong central government. Antifederalists worried about the oppression that might result if power was concentrated in a central government.

Adopting the Constitution

On December 7, 1787, Delaware became the first state to approve the Constitution. By June 21, 1788, the ninth state—New Hampshire—ratified it. In theory, that meant the new government could go into effect. However, without the support of the two largest states—New York and Virginia—the future of the new government was bleak.

In Virginia, Patrick Henry charged that the Constitution did not sufficiently limit the power of the central government. Still, Virginia ratified the Constitution after being assured that it would include a bill of rights amendment. An **amendment** is something W added to a document. The Bill of Rights would be added in 1791. In July 1788, New York finally ratified the Constitution, followed by North Carolina in November 1789 and Rhode Island in May 1790. The nation celebrated its new government.

✔ **Reading Check** **Explaining** Why was it important that New York and Virginia ratify the Constitution?

Section 3 Review

History ONLINE
Study Central™ To review this section, go to glencoe.com.

Vocabulary

1. **Use** each of these terms in a sentence that will help explain its meaning: tradition, federalism, legislative branch, executive branch, Electoral College, judicial branch, reside, checks and balances, amendment.

Main Ideas

2. **Identifying** What features of the Constitution developed from the ideas of Baron de Montesquieu?

3. **Explaining** Why does the Constitution divide power among branches of government?

4. **Specifying** Why did Virginia eventually ratify the Constitution?

Critical Thinking

5. **Interpreting** If a state law conflicts with a federal law, which law will prevail? How do you know?

6. **Identifying Central Issues** Use a diagram like the one below to summarize the Antifederalist arguments against the Constitution.

Antifederalist Arguments

7. **Persuasive Writing** Take the role of James Madison. Write an essay for the Federalist Papers, urging ratification of the Constitution. Use details that you know about the Constitution to support your argument.

Answer the
8. **Essential Question**
What ideas and features are found in the United States Constitution?

Answers

1. Sentences should use terms according to their definitions in the section and the Glossary.
2. the federal system of divided power, clearly specified powers
3. to keep any one branch from gaining too much power
4. It was promised that a bill of rights would be added.
5. The federal law will prevail because the Constitution states that the Constitution

and laws passed by Congress are "the supreme law of the land."
6. It took away individual liberties, ignored the will of the states and the people, favored the wealthy; government would be dominated by a small group of educated individuals.
7. Essays should include the need for a strong central government and safeguards such as checks and balances, shared powers, and a bill of rights.

8. **Ideas:** Enlightenment ideas about natural rights limiting government power, separation of power; **Features:** the Constitution shares power between a central government and state governments; establishes branches that make laws, carry out laws, and interpret laws; is the supreme law of the land; protects individual rights

Visual Summary

Visual Summary

The first constitution of the United States was the Articles of Confederation. The United States Constitution, ratified in 1788, replaced the Articles of Confederation and has served as the plan for government ever since.

Articles of Confederation	United States Constitution
Established a weak central government and strong state governments	Created a federal system that divided powers between the national government and state governments
"a firm league of friendship" in which each state retained its "sovereignty, freedom and independence"	"the supreme law of the land"
Congress could: • conduct foreign affairs • maintain armed forces • borrow money • issue currency	Congress can: • issue taxes • regulate trade • control currency • raise an army • declare war • pass laws that are "necessary and proper" to carry out its responsibilities
Congress could not: • regulate trade • force citizens to join the army • impose taxes	States can: • regulate trade within their borders • establish local government schools • set marriage and divorce laws
No chief executive; rule by congressional committees	Three branches of government: • legislative (makes the laws) • executive (carries out the laws) • judicial (interprets the laws) Includes a system of checks and balances so that no branch becomes more powerful than another
One state, one vote	Congress includes: • House of Representatives—number of representatives for each state based on the state's population • Senate—two senators per state
An agreement was needed by 9 of the 13 states to approve a law.	Both the House of Representatives and the Senate must approve a bill for it to become law. The president may approve or veto the bill.

◀ Independence Hall, Philadelphia, Pennsylvania

STUDY TO GO Study anywhere, anytime! Download quizzes and flash cards to your PDA from glencoe.com.

A More Perfect Union **Chapter 7** 211

Visual Summary

Making Connections Ask: How well did the Articles of Confederation work? *(Students should recall that Congress did not have the power to regulate trade, force citizens to join the army, or impose taxes.)* Discuss the importance of each of these with the class. Which of these powers does Congress have today? *(all three)* **OL**

Listing Tell students that the U.S. Constitution is a vital document in ensuring the freedom of Americans today. **Ask:** What aspects of the process of developing this document helped make it so unique? Organize students into small groups. Have all groups review the chapter and write a list of each person, event, influence, or idea that contributed to the success of the Constitutional Convention. As a class, make a master list and discuss the entries. **OL**

Hands-On Chapter Project
Step 4: Wrap-Up

Creating a Constitution

Step 4: Presenting Amendments and Ratifying the Constitution Groups finalize their work toward creating a constitution.

Directions Have each group present its proposal to the class. After each presentation, have each group cast a secret ballot as to whether the constitution should be ratified. Count the votes. Approval must be gained by three-fourths of the groups. Have delegates announce which amendments were added to the constitution. Finally, have the class present its constitution on poster board, complete with amendments. Have all delegates sign the document and display it in class.

Analyzing Discuss the role of compromise in the success of each amendment. **Ask:** Which is more important, the needs of your state or national unity? Discuss as a class.

Answers and Analyses

Reviewing Main Ideas

1. D Congress did have the power to conduct foreign affairs, maintain an army, and borrow money. Students should recall the correct wording, "force citizens to join the army," Choice D. **14.F**

2. C Choices A and D should be eliminated because there was no income tax and the Northwest Ordinance has nothing to do with Shays's Rebellion. Answer B is incorrect because farmers hoped the federal government would use paper money to relieve debtors, but it did not ignite the rebellion. **18.B.3a**

3. A Choices C and D are wrong because neither of these were mentioned as influences on the Framers. Montesquieu was concerned about the separation and balance of powers, eliminating choice B. Natural rights should be associated with John Locke. **14.F.3a (US)**

4. C Remind students that the Antifederalists feared government oppression, eliminating choice A. Religion and sales tax, choices B and D, were not mentioned. Students should recall that the Federalists wanted a strong central government to protect them from disorder. **16.B.3a (US)**

Short-Answer Question

5. As students read the excerpt, have them reword phrases to increase understanding. They should then see that Washington addressed the criticism that the Constitution was not a perfect document, that it limited state sovereignty and did not fully satisfy anyone. Washington argues that had one state dominated the document, negative consequences might have resulted for other states. **18.C.3a**

STANDARDIZED TEST PRACTICE

TEST-TAKING TIP

Think carefully before you change your answer to a multiple-choice test question. Unless you misread the question, your first answer choice is often correct.

Reviewing Main Ideas

Directions: Choose the best answer for each of the following questions.

1. Under the Articles of Confederation, Congress did not have the authority to

  A conduct foreign affairs.

  B maintain armed forces.

  C borrow money.

  D force citizens to join the army.

2. Shays's Rebellion erupted when

  A merchants and creditors in New England forced state governments to abolish income taxes.

  B the state government of Delaware issued more paper currency.

  C Massachusetts officials seized farmers' lands to pay their debts and threw many farmers in jail.

  D the Northwest Ordinance set aside funds from land sales for public schools.

3. The Framers of the Constitution wanted to protect people's natural rights. This idea was reflected in the work of

  A English philosopher John Locke.

  B French writer Baron de Montesquieu.

  C King George III.

  D Italian philosopher Niccolò Machiavelli.

4. In the debate over the ratification of the Constitution, the Federalists most feared

  A government oppression.

  B the establishment of a state religion.

  C disorder without a strong central government.

  D a national sales tax.

Short-Answer Question

Directions: Base your answer to question 5 on the excerpt below and on your knowledge of social studies.

That [the Constitution] will meet the full and entire approbation [approval] of every state is not perhaps to be expected; but each will doubtless consider, that had her interest been alone consulted, the consequences might have been particularly disagreeable or injurious to others . . . that [the Constitution] may promote the lasting welfare of that country so dear to us all, and secure her freedom and happiness, is our most ardent [eager] wish.

—George Washington, 1787

5. Which criticism of the Constitution does Washington address? How does he respond to this criticism?

Review the Essential Questions

6. Essay Discuss why the Constitution has survived for more than 200 years.

To help you write your essay, review your answers to the Essential Questions in the section reviews and the chapter Foldables Study Organizer. Your essay should include:

- an analysis of the flaws of the Articles of Confederation;
- the compromises reflected in the final version of the Constitution;
- Federalist and Antifederalist views of the Constitution;
- the responsibilities and limits of the three branches of federal government; and
- an outline of the basic rights identified in the Constitution.

GO ON ➡

Review the Essential Questions

6. Students should consult their completed Foldables to find reasons the Constitution has survived so long. Responses should mention adaptability to the changing views and needs of succeeding generations of Americans; its simplicity and relative lack of specificity, which allows for flexibility; and the checks and balances that prevent power from being centered in any one branch of government. **14.B.3**

History ONLINE
For additional test practice, use **Self-Check Quizzes**—Chapter 7 at glencoe.com.

Chapter 7 Assessment

Document-Based Questions

Directions: Analyze the documents and answer the short-answer questions that follow.

Document 1

This is Article 6 of the Northwest Ordinance (1787).

> There shall be neither slavery nor involuntary servitude in the said territory. . . . Provided, always, That any person escaping into the same, from whom labor or service is lawfully claimed in any one of the original States, such fugitive may be lawfully reclaimed and conveyed [transferred] to the person claiming his or her labor or service as aforesaid.

Source: The Northwest Ordinance

7. Based on the document, what was the legal status of an enslaved person who escaped into the Northwest Territory?

Document 2

The following is from records of the Constitutional Convention discussion (1787) about the slave trade.

> Mr. [Roger] Sherman [of Conn.] was for leaving the clause as it stands. He disapproved of the slave trade; yet, as the states were now possessed of the right to import slaves, as the public good did not require it to be taken from them, and as it was expedient [advantageous] to have as few objections as possible to the proposed scheme [plan] of government, he thought it best to leave the matter as we find it. He observed that the abolition of slavery seemed to be going on in the United States, and that the good sense of the several states would probably by degrees complete it.

Source: Records from a pro-slavery document

8. According to the document, identify two reasons Sherman had for not prohibiting the slave trade.

Document 3

This map of Massachusetts shows where support was located for the Federalists and Anti-Federalists when the state ratified the Constitution.

Massachusetts Votes on the Constitution

- Areas that voted mostly for ratification
- Areas that voted mostly against ratification

ATLANTIC OCEAN

0   40 kilometers
0   40 miles
Lambert Conformal Conic projection

9. Based on the map, where were most of the Federalist supporters located?

Document 4

This is an excerpt from "On the Equality of the Sexes" by Judith Sargent Stevens Murray (1790).

> Our souls are by nature equal to yours; the same breath of God animates, enlivens, and invigorates us.

Source: "On the Equality of the Sexes"

10. Using the document, identify the reason Murray believed women are equal to men.

11. Persuasive Writing Using the information from the documents and your knowledge of social studies to write an essay in which you:

- defend the Constitution as a great model of democracy; or

- express criticism of the Constitution based on differences between its ideals and the status of enslaved African Americans and women in the 1700s.

9. Federalist sentiment, which supported ratification, was strongest along the coast of Massachusetts. **17.A.3b**

10. Murray believes that women were made equal with men by nature and by God who created them. **16.A.3b**

11. Students' essays should support a single opinion and provide logical arguments to support it with specific references to the Constitution. **14.F.3b**

History ONLINE
Have students visit the Web site at glencoe.com to review Chapter 7 and take the Self-Check Quiz.

Need Extra Help?

Have students refer to the pages listed if they miss any of the questions.

Need Extra Help?

If you missed questions. . .	1	2	3	4	5	6	7	8	9	10	11
Go to page. . .	189	195–196	206	210	209–210	186–210	191	201	209–210	198	194–210

Document-Based Questions

7. Students should read the question first and look for the answer as they read. Fugitives who lawfully owe servitude in one of the original states may be reclaimed and returned. **16.A.3b**

8. Two of the following should be mentioned: The "public good" did not require the abolition of the slave trade; Sherman wanted to smooth over the issue to get the Constitution accepted; he believed that over time, slavery would be abolished anyway. **16.A.3b**

Focus

R Reading Strategy

Activating Prior Knowledge Remind students that the Constitution is a plan, or an outline, for government. **Ask:** What documents from English history provided the foundation for the colonists' ideas about government? (*Magna Carta, English Bill of Rights*) What other documents had been created by colonists to plan for their government? (*Mayflower Compact, Declaration of Independence, early state constitutions, Articles of Confederation*) **OL**

Reading Guide
Answers to Graphic:
Popular Sovereignty; Republicanism; Limited Government; Separation of Powers; Checks and Balances; Individual Rights

Additional Support

Civics in Action

Essential Question ◄
Why is citizen participation essential to the preservation of the U.S. political system?

Reading Guide

Content Vocabulary

Preamble (p. 215)	reserved powers (p. 216)
popular sovereignty (p. 215)	concurrent powers (p. 216)
republicanism (p. 215)	amend (p. 218)
federalism (p. 216)	implied powers (p. 219)
enumerated powers (p. 216)	

Academic Vocabulary

involve (p. 221)   diminish (p. 223)

Reading Strategy
Taking Notes As you read, use a diagram like the one below to identify the seven major principles on which the Constitution is based.

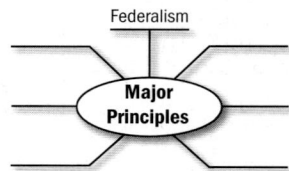

Federalism

Major Principles

214

Constitution Handbook

R *For more than 200 years, the Constitution has provided the framework for the United States government and has helped preserve the basic rights of American citizens. It is the highest authority in the nation and the basic law of the United States. It is also a symbol of our nation, representing our system of government and our basic ideals, such as liberty and freedom.*

Fast Facts

Other National Constitutions Constitutions vary from country to country. For example, Article 23 of Japan's constitution guarantees academic freedom. The constitution of Bangladesh avows that "the state religion of the Republic is Islam, but other religions may be practiced in peace and harmony in the Republic." The constitution of the Central African Republic states that "no one will be submitted to torture or to inhuman, cruel, degrading, or humiliating brutalities or treatment."

Not many governments have had the stability that the United States Constitution has provided. France, for example, has had a dozen constitutions.

The Constitution

Main Idea The Constitution sets forth the basic principles of government.

History and You What principles do you live by? Read to learn how the basic principles of the Constitution assure the rights of the people.

. . . .

The **Preamble,** or introduction, to the Constitution reflects the basic idea of American government—the right of the people to govern themselves. It also lists six goals for the United States government:

PRIMARY SOURCE

"to form a more perfect Union, establish Justice, insure domestic Tranquility [peace], provide for the common defence, promote the general Welfare, and secure the Blessings of Liberty to ourselves and our Posterity [descendents]."

—United States Constitution

Major Principles

The principles outlined in the Constitution were the Framers' solution to the problems of a representative government. The Constitution rests on seven major principles: (1) popular sovereignty, (2) republicanism, (3) limited government, (4) federalism, (5) separation of powers, (6) checks and balances, and (7) individual rights.

Popular Sovereignty The Declaration of Independence states that governments derive their powers from "the consent of the governed." The opening words of the Constitution, "We the People," reinforce this idea of **popular sovereignty**—or "authority of the people."

Republicanism Under **republicanism,** voters hold sovereign power. The people elect representatives and give them the responsibility to make laws and conduct government. For most Americans today, the terms *republic* and *representative democracy* mean the same thing: a system of limited government in which the people are the ultimate source of governmental power.

Limited Government The Framers saw both benefits and risks in creating a powerful national government. They agreed that the nation needed strong central authority but feared misuse of power. They wanted to prevent the government from using its power to give one group special advantages or to deprive another group of its rights. By creating a limited government, they made certain the government would have only those powers granted by the people.

Article I of the Constitution states the powers that the government has and the powers that it does not have. Other limits on government appear in the Bill of Rights, which guarantees certain rights and liberties to the people.

Limited government can be described as the "rule of law." No person or group of people is above the law. Government officials must obey the law.

Teach
. . . .

D **Differentiated Instruction**

English Language Learners Committing the Preamble of the Constitution to memory provides a useful language model for students' spoken language development. To aid in this memory task, ask students to write the words *who, why,* and *what* in their notebooks. Have students write the various phrases of the Preamble under the words to which they are most closely related. **ELL**

R **Reading Strategy**

Reading Primary Sources Have students paraphrase the six goals for the United States government stated in the Preamble to the Constitution. **OL**

C **Critical Thinking**

Making Inferences Ask: *Why did the Framers of the Constitution fear misuse of power by the national government?* (*They remembered their experience under British rule when they felt that the British government was abusing its power over them and limiting the rights of the colonists.*) **AL**

Activity: Collaborative Learning

Limited Government Divide the class into nine small groups. Assign each group one of the sections of Article I of the Constitution, excluding Section 1. **Ask:** How does your section limit the power of government? Ask each group to read their section, paraphrase it, and answer this question. Begin discussion by paraphrasing Section 1 for the class. Then have each group present their findings, in turn, to the rest of the class. Finish by discussing the meaning of limited government with the class as a whole. **OL**

R Reading Strategy

Reading Charts Ask: Which powers in the chart on this page are enumerated powers? *(those under national government)* Which are reserved powers? *(those under state governments)* Which are concurrent powers? *(those under national and state governments)* **BL**

C Critical Thinking

Predicting Consequences Ask students to consider how the U.S. government would be different if responsibility were not divided among three branches. **Ask:** What would be the advantages if one group conducted all legislative, executive, and judicial functions of government? *(Possible answer: The government would be more efficient, and all representatives could be directly elected by the people.)* What would be the disadvantages? *(Possible answer: There would be a greater danger of corruption, because separate branches could not serve as checks on the power of other branches.)* **AL**

Federal and State Powers

Chart Skills Answer
Both state and federal governments raise taxes to pay for expenses unique to their governments.

Additional Support

Federalism When the states banded together under the Constitution, they gave up some independence. States could no longer print their own money or tax items imported from other states. Nevertheless, each state governed itself much as it had in the past.

This system, in which the power to govern is shared between the national government and the states, is called the federal system, or **federalism.** Our federal system allows the people of each state to deal with their needs in their own way. At the same time, it lets the states act together to deal with matters that affect all Americans.

R The Constitution defines three types of government powers. **Enumerated powers** belong only to the federal government. These include the power to coin money, regulate interstate and foreign trade, maintain the armed forces, and create federal courts (Article I, Section 8).

The second kind of powers are those retained by the states, known as **reserved powers.** They include such rights as the power to establish schools, pass marriage and divorce laws, and regulate trade within a state. Although reserved powers are not listed specifically in the Constitution, the Tenth Amendment says that all powers not specifically granted to the federal government "are reserved to the States."

The third set of powers defined by the Constitution are **concurrent powers**—powers shared by the state and federal governments. Among these powers are the right to raise taxes, borrow money, provide for public welfare, and administer criminal justice.

When conflicts arise between state law and federal law, the Constitution declares that the Constitution is "the supreme Law of the Land." Conflicts between state law and federal law must be settled in a federal court.

C **Separation of Powers** To prevent any single group or institution in government from gaining too much authority, the Framers divided the federal government into three branches: legislative, executive, and judicial. Each branch has its own functions and powers. The legislative branch, Congress, makes the laws. The executive branch, headed by the president, carries out the laws. The judicial branch, consisting of the Supreme Court and other federal courts, interprets and applies the laws.

Checks and Balances As an additional safeguard, the Framers established a system of checks and balances in which each branch of government can check, or limit, the power of the other branches. This system helps maintain a balance in the power of the three branches. For example, Congress can pass a

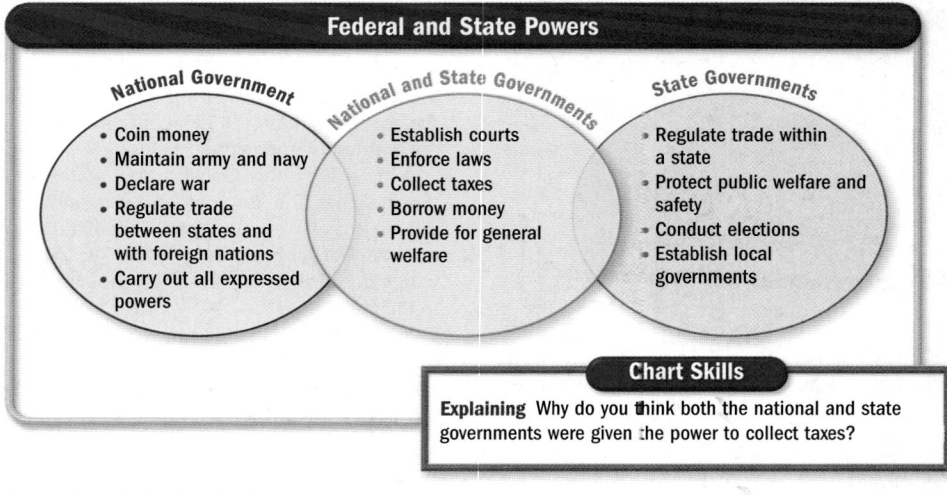

Federal and State Powers

National Government
- Coin money
- Maintain army and navy
- Declare war
- Regulate trade between states and with foreign nations
- Carry out all expressed powers

National and State Governments
- Establish courts
- Enforce laws
- Collect taxes
- Borrow money
- Provide for general welfare

State Governments
- Regulate trade within a state
- Protect public welfare and safety
- Conduct elections
- Establish local governments

Chart Skills

Explaining Why do you think both the national and state governments were given the power to collect taxes?

Activity: Connecting With Your Community

Local Government Ask: What kind of government does our local community have? Have small groups of students research the local government, beginning by looking up the definitions of "county" and "municipality" in the dictionary. **Ask:** Does our state have counties? *(yes, except in Louisiana, where counties are called parishes, and in Alaska,* *where counties are called boroughs)* Do we have a municipal government? If so, what kind? *(Answers will vary, but examples include city, town, and village governments.)* When students have answered these questions, have them research the specific form their local government takes and then create a poster displaying this information. **OL**

A System of Checks and Balances

Can impeach president;
Can override veto;
Can reject appointments;
Can refuse to approve treaties

Can impeach judges;
Can reject appointment
of judges

Can veto
legislation

Can declare
acts of legislature
unconstitutional

LEGISLATIVE BRANCH

Can appoint judges

EXECUTIVE BRANCH

Can declare presidential
actions unconstitutional

JUDICIAL BRANCH

Critical Thinking

1. **Describing** How can the judicial branch check the power of the executive branch?
2. **Describing** How can the executive branch check the power of the judicial branch?

law. Then the president can reject the law by vetoing it. However, Congress can override, or reverse, the president's veto if two-thirds of the members of both houses vote again to approve the law.

Over the years, the Supreme Court has acquired the power to determine the meaning of the Constitution and to declare that a law or a government policy goes against the Constitution. In doing so, the Court provides a check on the powers of Congress and the president. Judicial decisions—those made by the courts—can be overruled by amending the Constitution. The president and the Senate provide a check on the judicial branch through their power to appoint and approve federal judges. Congress can also change a law so that it no longer conflicts with the Constitution, or it can amend the Constitution. The Fourteenth Amendment, passed by Congress in 1866, overturned the Supreme Court's rul-

ing in the *Dred Scott* decision, which had ruled that enslaved African Americans were not citizens.

Individual Rights The Bill of Rights became part of the U.S. Constitution in 1791. These first 10 consitutional amendments protect basic liberties and rights that you may have taken for granted—including freedom of speech, freedom of the press, freedom of assembly, freedom of religion, and the right to a trial by jury.

The 17 amendments that follow the Bill of Rights expand the rights of Americans and adjust certain provisions of the Constitution. Included among them are amendments that abolish slavery, define citizenship, guarantee the right to vote to all citizens aged 18 years and older, authorize an income tax, establish the direct election of senators, and set a two-term limit on the presidency.

Constitution Handbook **217**

Constitution Handbook ★

W Writing Support

Personal Writing Have students research the freedom of religion guaranteed in the Bill of Rights. Ask students to analyze how freedom of religion affects Americans in a one-page report. Students may cite examples of how freedom of religion affects their lives at school and at home. **OL**

D Differentiated Instruction

Gifted and Talented Have each student choose one of the 17 amendments that follow the Bill of Rights. Direct them to appropriate reference sources to learn about the history of the amendment, the story of its passage and ratification, and its effects on American life. Then have students write a one- or two-page report summarizing what they have learned. **AL**

A System of Checks and Balances

Critical Thinking Answers
1. by declaring presidential actions unconstitutional
2. by appointing judges

Activity: Making Connections

The Bill of Rights Have each student create a poster showing the 10 constitutional amendments that make up the Bill of Rights. **Ask:** How do the rights outlined in the Constitution affect your lives today? *(Answers will vary but might include that students can worship as they choose and debate government actions openly.)* Have students include examples on their posters of how each of the 10 amendments affects the daily lives of Americans. Encourage students to add interest to their work by including visual materials on their posters as well. Display the posters in the classroom. **OL**

Constitution Handbook

218

S Skill Practice

Using Geography Skills Have each student choose one of the 17 amendments that follow the Bill of Rights and research the history of the amendment they have chosen. Then students should trace a map of the United States as it existed at the time the amendment was ratified, and color code which states ratified the amendment and which states did not. Finally, have students summarize what they learned from the exercise in a few paragraphs. **OL**

C Critical Thinking

Analyzing Information Ask: Why is Article I, Section 8 of the Constitution known as the "elastic clause"? *(because Congress has interpreted the clause directing Congress to "make all Laws which shall be necessary and proper" to mean that it has some powers not directly stated in the Constitution—therefore, its powers can expand as needed)* **ELL**

Primary Source

Critical Thinking Answer
because many people first came to the United States in search of religious freedom

Additional Support

Primary Source / **First Amendment Rights: Freedom of Religion**

Many people have come to the United States in search of religious freedom. The principle of religious freedom became rooted in early America as people of different religions learned to live and work together.

In 1777 Thomas Jefferson wrote a resolution on religious freedom that was adopted by the Virginia State legislature in 1786. ▶

The Virginia Statute for Religious Freedom
"No man shall be compelled to frequent or support any religious worship, place, or ministry whatsoever, nor shall be enforced, restrained, molested, or [burdened] in his body or goods, nor shall otherwise suffer on account of his religious opinions or belief; but that all men shall be free to profess, and by argument to maintain, their opinion in matters of religion, and that the same shall in no [way] diminish enlarge, or affect their civil capacities."

—from Thomas Jefferson, "The Virginia Statute for Religious Freedom"

Freedom of religion became one of the principles upon which the United States was founded. In 1791 the First Amendment to the Constitution barred the federal government from establishing a religion or from adopting any law limiting religious freedom.

Critical Thinking

Explaining Why do you think Americans regard religious freedom as an important principle?

A Living Constitution

Two years after the Constitutional Convention, Benjamin Franklin wrote, "Our Constitution is in actual operation; everything appears to promise that it will last; but in this world nothing is certain but death and taxes."

Despite Franklin's uncertainty about the Constitution's future, it is still very much alive today. The Constitution has survived because the Framers wrote a document that the nation could alter and adapt to meet changing needs. The result is a flexible document that can be interpreted in different ways in keeping with the conditions of a particular time. The Constitution's flexibility allows the government to deal with matters the Framers never anticipated—such as regulating nuclear power plants or developing a space program. In addition, the Constitution contains a provision for **amending**—changing or adding to—the document.

Amending the Constitution The Framers intentionally made the amendment process difficult to discourage minor or frequent changes. Although thousands of amendments—changes to the Constitution—have been proposed since 1788, only 27 of them have actually become part of the Constitution.

An amendment can be proposed in two ways: by the vote of two-thirds of both houses of Congress or by two-thirds of the state legislatures asking for a special convention on the amendment. The second method has never been used. Ratification of an amendment requires approval by three-fourths of the states. States ratify amendments by the approval of state legislatures or by special state conventions.

Only the Twenty-first Amendment—which repealed the Eighteenth Amendment, banning the sale of alcoholic beverages—was ratified by state conventions. Voters in each state chose the delegates to the special conventions.

Interpreting the Constitution The Constitution includes two provisions that give Congress the power to act as needed to meet changing conditions. The first of these provisions is what is known as the "elastic clause" (Article I, Section 8). It directs Congress to "make all Laws which shall be necessary and proper" for executing all the powers of government. Congress has interpreted this clause to mean that it has certain

---

Fast Facts

James Madison Madison was known as "the Father of the Constitution." He developed the Virginia Plan, which was put forward by Edmund Randolph at the Constitutional Convention. The Virginia Plan became the basis of the new government by establishing the principle of a strong national government kept in check by balancing power among three branches of government. Madison believed that the Constitution would have to be altered as new situations arose but that this had to depend on the majority. He wrote: "If the will of the majority cannot be trusted where there are diversified and conflicting interests, it can be trusted nowhere." Madison put his beliefs into practice as a member of the first House of Representatives when he sponsored the first 10 amendments to the Constitution, which became the Bill of Rights. **OL**

implied powers, powers not specifically defined in the Constitution. Over the years, Congress has drawn on its implied powers to pass laws to deal with the needs of society.

The second provision used to expand congressional authority, the "commerce clause" (Article I, Section 8), gives Congress the power to "regulate Commerce with foreign Nations, and among the several States." Congress has used this clause to expand its powers into a number of areas, such as regulation of the airline industry, radio and television, and nuclear energy.

The process of amending the Constitution and applying its principles in new areas helps keep our government functioning well. In 1974 Barbara Jordan, an African American member of Congress and a constitutional scholar, spoke about her faith in the constitutional process:

PRIMARY SOURCE

"Through the process of amendment, interpretation, and court decision I have finally been included in 'We, the people.' . . . My faith in the Constitution is whole; it is complete; it is total.
—from her speech before the House, July 25, 1974

✔ **Reading Check** Explaining What are reserved powers?

The Federal Government

Main Idea The U.S. federal government has three branches: the legislative branch, the executive branch, and the judicial branch.

History and You Have you ever written to a representative, senator, president, or chief justice? Read to learn about the duties of officials in the different branches of the federal government.

The Constitution explains how our federal, or national, government is set up and how it works. The federal government is divided among the three branches: legislative, executive, and judicial.

The Legislative Branch

Congress, the legislative branch, makes laws, imposes taxes, and declares war. It has two parts—the House of Representatives and the Senate. The House of Representatives has 435 voting members and 5 nonvoting delegates from the District of Columbia, Puerto Rico, Guam, American Samoa, and the Virgin Islands. The number of representatives from each state is determined by the state's population. Representatives, who must be at least 25 years old, serve two-year terms.

Women in Congress

◄ **Jeanette Rankin** First woman in U.S. Congress (1917)

Firsts Patsy Mink of Hawaii, elected in 1964, became the first Asian American woman and the first woman of color in the U.S. Congress. In 1968 Shirley Chisholm of Brooklyn, New York, was the first African American woman elected to Congress. The first Latino woman elected to Congress was Ileana Ros-Lehtinen of Florida. She was elected in 1988.

Nancy Pelosi First woman Speaker of the U.S. House (2007) ►

Critical Thinking

Making Generalizations Does democracy require participation in government by all groups? Explain.

Activity: Geography Connection

Using Geography Skills Have students trace a current map of the United States from the atlas in the textbook. Then have them find the current number of representatives from each state and write it in the map. Have students color code their maps to show states with similar numbers of representatives and create a key. (For example, states with 50+ representatives might be green, states with 25–35 representatives might be blue, and so on.) **Ask:** Which state has the most power in the House of Representatives? Why? (California, because it has far more representatives than any other state) Which states have fewer representatives than senators? (Alaska, Delaware, Montana, North Dakota, South Dakota, Vermont, Wyoming) **OL**

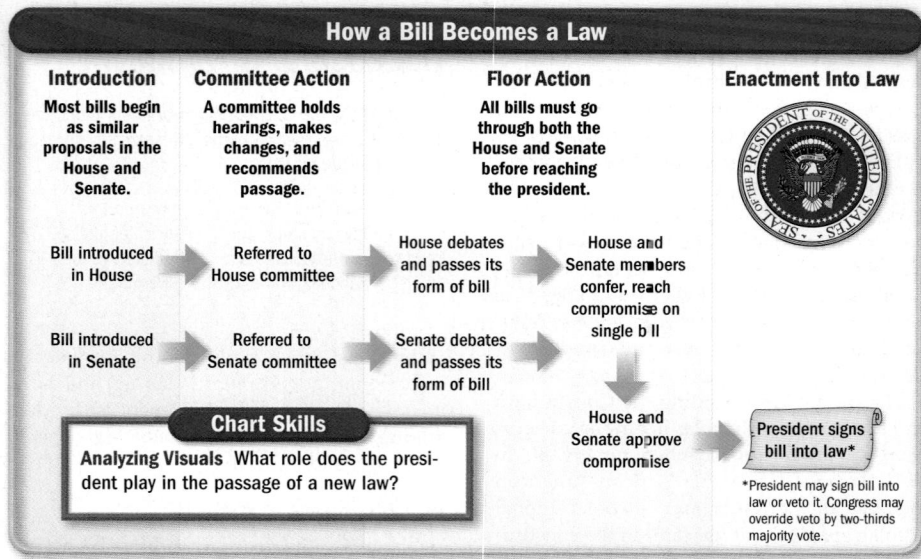

How a Bill Becomes a Law

Introduction Most bills begin as similar proposals in the House and Senate.

Committee Action A committee holds hearings, makes changes, and recommends passage.

Floor Action All bills must go through both the House and Senate before reaching the president.

Enactment Into Law

Bill introduced in House → Referred to House committee → House debates and passes its form of bill → House and Senate members confer, reach compromise on single bill

Bill introduced in Senate → Referred to Senate committee → Senate debates and passes its form of bill

House and Senate approve compromise → President signs bill into law*

*President may sign bill into law or veto it. Congress may override veto by two-thirds majority vote.

Chart Skills
Analyzing Visuals What role does the president play in the passage of a new law?

The Senate has 100 senators, 2 from each state. Senators, who must be at least 30 years old, serve six-year terms. One-third of Senate seats come up for election every 2 years.

The Role of Congress Congress makes the nation's laws and controls government spending. All tax and spending bills begin in the House of Representatives and are approved in both the House and the Senate before the president signs them into law.

Congress also keeps a check on the actions of the executive branch. The House can impeach, or bring charges against, any federal official suspected of wrongdoing. Officials found guilty may be removed from office. The Senate also holds certain special powers. It can ratify treaties and approve presidential appointments of federal officials.

R The Executive Branch

The executive branch carries out the laws passed by Congress. It includes the president, the vice president, and various offices, departments, and agencies.

The President The president carries out the nation's laws with the help of many executive offices, departments, and agencies. As head of the executive branch, the president has the following roles, each with specific powers and duties:

- **Chief Diplomat:** directs foreign policy, appoints ambassadors, and negotiates treaties with other nations.

- **Commander in Chief:** uses the military in crises at home and abroad with congressional approval or declaration of war.

- **Head of State:** representative of all Americans; receives foreign dignitaries; bestows honors on Americans.

- **Legislative Leader:** proposes laws to Congress; sets goals for legislation and working to see that they are passed. In the annual State of the Union address, the president presents goals for legislation. The vice president also serves in the Legislative branch as the President of the Senate.

Cabinet and Vice President The secretaries, or heads, of departments form the cabinet, a group that helps the president set government policy. Members of the cabinet advise the president on issues related to their departments. The Constitution gives the vice president no duties aside from presiding over the Senate. It is the president who determines what the vice president will do, such as working with Congress or making trips abroad.

The Judicial Branch

The Constitution calls for a Supreme Court and the creation of lower courts as Congress wishes. In 1789 Congress passed a Judiciary Act, which added a series of district courts to the federal court system. Appeals, or circuit courts, were added in 1891 to ease the workload of the Supreme Court.

Lower Federal Courts The duties of the lower federal courts are the following:

- **District Courts:** handle civil and criminal cases that come under federal authority; 91 district courts, with at least 1 in every state.

- **Appeals Courts:** review disctrict court decisions; overturn a verdict of the district court or order a retrial; 14 appeals courts in the United States.

The Supreme Court The Supreme Court stands at the top of the American legal system. It is one of the coequal branches of the national government, along with Congress and the president. The Supreme Court is comprised of nine justices: the chief justice of the United States and eight associate justices. Congress has the power to set this number and the power to change it.

The Constitution does not describe the duties of the justices, which have developed from laws and customs in response to national needs. The main duty of the justices is to hear and rule on cases. This duty **involves** them in three tasks: deciding which cases to hear from among thousands of appeals each year; deciding the case itself; and explaining the decision, called the Court's opinion.

The role of the judicial branch has grown as the powers implied in the Constitution have been put into practice. In the 1803 case *Marbury* v. *Madison,* Chief Justice John Marshall expanded Supreme Court powers by striking down an act of Congress. In that decision, the Court defined its right to determine whether a law violates the Constitution. Although not mentioned in the Constitution, this principle, known as judicial review, has become a major power of the judicial branch.

Reading Check **Describing** What is Congress's role in government spending?

D Differentiated Instruction

Visual/Spatial Have students create a graphic representation of the federal court system in the United States. This could be done by the class on the bulletin board or electronically by using presentation software. Tell students to caption their graphics appropriately. **OL**

C Critical Thinking

Making Generalizations Ask: *Judicial review is related to which major principle of the Constitution? (checks and balances, because it serves as a check on the power of the legislative branch)* **OL**

The Supreme Court

Critical Thinking Answer
Possible answer: to avoid a tie vote

Reading Check **Answer:** All tax and spending bills must begin in the House of Representatives and be approved by the House and the Senate.

The Supreme Court

◄ Seated left to right: Anthony Kennedy, John Paul Stevens, Chief Justice John G. Roberts, Jr., Antonin Scalia, David Souter. Standing left to right: Stephen Breyer, Clarence Thomas, Ruth Bader Ginsburg, Samuel Alito, Jr.

Critical Thinking

Describing Why do you think the number of justices is set an an uneven number?

Constitution Handbook **221**

Fast Facts

Sandra Day O'Connor In 1981 Sandra Day O'Connor became the first female Supreme Court justice. O'Connor commented: "Society as a whole benefits immeasurably from a climate in which all persons, regardless of race or gender, may have the opportunity to earn respect, responsibility, advancement, and remuneration based on ability." Ruth Bader Ginsburg, appointed by President Bill Clinton, joined O'Connor as the second female Supreme Court justice in 1993. O'Connor retired from the Court in 2006.

Rights, Duties, and Responsibilities

Rights	Duties	Responsibilities
Security protection by government **Equality** equal treatment under the law **Liberty** rights guaranteed under the Constitution	• Obey the law • Pay taxes • Defend the nation • Serve in court • Attend school	• Be informed and vote • Participate in your community and government • Respect the rights and property of others • Respect different opinions and ways of life

Chart Skills
Contrasting How do duties differ from responsibilities?

Rights and Citizen Participation

Main Idea U.S. citizenship brings with it certain rights and responsibilities.

History and You Are you a good citizen? What are the rights and responsibilities of citizenship? Read to learn why American citizens have a responsibility to their community, the environment, and the law.

All American citizens have certain basic rights, but they also have specific responsibilities. Living in a democracy means that every citizen is partly responsible for how society is governed and for the actions the government takes on each citizen's behalf.

The Rights of American Citizens

The rights of Americans fall into three broad categories: the right to be protected from unfair government actions, to have equal treatment under the law, and to enjoy basic freedoms.

Due Process The Fifth Amendment states that no person shall "be deprived of life, liberty, or property, without due process of law." Due process of law means that the government must follow procedures established by law and guaranteed by the Constitution, treating all people according to these principles.

Equal Protection All Americans, regardless of race, religion, or political beliefs, have the right to be treated the same under the law.

The Fourteenth Amendment requires every state to grant its citizens "equal protection of the laws."

Basic Freedoms The basic freedoms involve the liberties outlined in the First Amendment—freedom of speech, freedom of religion, freedom of the press, freedom of assembly, and the right to petition. In a democratic society, power exists in the hands of the people. Therefore, its citizens must be able to exchange ideas freely.

Limits on Rights Our rights are not unlimited. The government can establish laws or rules to protect the health, safety, security, and moral standards of a community. Moreover, rights may be limited to prevent one person's rights from interfering with the rights of others. The restrictions of rights, however, must be reasonable and must apply to everyone equally.

Citizen Participation

A citizen is a person who owes loyalty to and is entitled to the protection of a state or nation. How do you become an American citizen? Generally, citizenship is granted to anyone born within the borders of the United States. Citizenship is also granted to anyone born outside of the United States if one parent is a U.S. citizen. A person of foreign birth can become a citizen through the process of naturalization. Before being admitted citizenship, applicants must be willing to give up any foreign allegiance and must promise to

Activity: Why It Matters

Depicting Citizenship Ask groups of students to create collages that depict Americans exercising the rights, duties, and responsibilities of citizenship. Each group should create a theme as a basis for selecting illustrations. Tasks could include gathering used magazines and newspapers to clip pictures, working on layout, providing necessary lettering, and selecting and attaching pictures. Have group representatives explain their finished collages. **Ask:** What are your duties and responsibilities as student citizens? (*Answers will vary but may include attending school, obeying the law, respecting the rights and property of others, and respecting different opinions and ways of life.*) **OL**

obey the Constitution and the laws of the United States.

As citizens of the United States, we are expected to carry out certain duties and responsibilities. Duties are things we are required to do by law. Responsibilities are things we should do. Fulfilling both our duties and our responsibilities helps ensure that we have a good government and that we continue to enjoy our rights.

Duties One of the duties of all Americans is to obey the law. Laws help keep order; protect the health, safety, and property of citizens; and make it possible for people to live together peacefully. If you believe a law needs to be changed, you can work through your elected representatives to improve it.

Americans also have a duty to pay taxes. The government uses tax money for purposes, such as defending the nation, providing health insurance for senior citizens, and building roads and bridges.

Another duty of citizens is to defend the nation. All males aged 18 and older must register with the government in case they are needed for military service.

The Constitution guarantees all Americans the right to a trial by a jury of their peers (equals). For this reason, citizens are often called to serve on juries after they become eligible at the age of 18. Having jurors on hand is necessary to guarantee the right to a fair and speedy trial.

Responsibilities Responsibilities are not as clear-cut as duties. Because responsibilities are voluntary, people are not arrested or punished if they do not fulfill these obligations. The quality of our lives **diminishes** if responsibilities are neglected.

Perhaps your most important responsibility as a citizen will be to vote when you reach the age of 18. Voting allows you to participate in government and guide its direction. When you vote for people in government, you will be exercising your right of self-government. If you disapprove of the job your representatives are doing, you can express your views to them or help elect other people in the next election.

Reading Check **Summarizing** What is the difference between a duty and a responsibility?

Constitution Handbook Review

Vocabulary
1. Use each of these terms in a sentence: Preamble, popular sovereignty, republicanism, federalism, enumerated powers, reserved powers, concurrent powers, amend, implied powers, involve, diminish.

Main Ideas
2. **Making Connections** How are popular sovereignty and voting connected?
3. **Explaining** Are the rights of American citizens unlimited? Explain.

Critical Thinking
4. **Evaluating** What is the importance of federalism in the Constitution?
5. **Comparing** Re-create the chart below, and describe how each branch of government has power over another branch.

Branch	Power
Legislative	
Executive	
Judicial	

6. **Expository Writing** Write a short essay summarizing the major principles found in the Preamble.

Answer the
7. **Essential Question**
Why is citizen participation essential to the preservation of the U.S. political system?

Constitution Handbook **223**

Constitution Handbook

D **Differentiated Instruction**

Kinesthetic Have students research the candidates in an upcoming local, state, or national election. Have each student create a flyer encouraging people to fulfill their obligation to vote in the upcoming election. The flyers may be partisan or nonpartisan. **OL**

Reading Check **Answer:** Duties are required by law; responsibilities are voluntary.

Assess

History ONLINE

Study Central™ provides summaries, interactive games, and online graphic organizers to help students review content.

Close

Listing As a class, create a list on the board of the duties of American citizens and a list of the responsibilities of American citizens. **OL**

Constitution Handbook Review

Answers
1. Student work should reflect correct use of terms.
2. Popular sovereignty is the idea that the government reflects the wishes of the people. Voting is the way people express their wishes.
3. No; the government can establish laws to protect the health, safety, security, and moral standards of a community, and may restrict one person's rights from interfering with another person's.
4. Federalism is the system of shared power between the national government and the states. The Constitution defines three kinds of powers—enumerated powers, which belong only to the federal government; reserved powers, which are retained by the states; and concurrent powers, which are shared by state and federal governments.
5. **Legislative:** over executive—impeach president, override veto, reject appointments, reject treaties; over judicial—impeach judges, reject nomination of judges; **Executive:** over judicial—appoints judges; over legislative—veto legislation; **Judicial:** over executive and legislative branches—declare actions/laws unconstitutional
6. Essays should summarize popular sovereignty, republicanism, limited government, federalism, separate of powers, checks and balances, and individual rights.
7. The U.S. political system is a democracy and every person living in a democracy is partly responsible for how society is governed and for the actions the government takes on each citizen's behalf.

Focus

Setting a Purpose The Constitution is reproduced in its original language, some of which can be difficult due to complex sentence structure. The explanatory notes should help students grasp the purpose of major sections. Many of its difficult words are defined in marginal notes on the page where they appear. Suggest that students substitute the definitions for the original words to help them understand the point of the document. **OL**

**Additional
Support**

The Constitution
of the United States

The Constitution of the United States is truly a remarkable document. It was one of the first written constitutions in modern history. The entire text of the Constitution and its amendments follows. For easier study, those passages that have been set aside or changed by the adoption of amendments are printed in blue. Also included are explanatory notes that will help clarify the meaning of important ideas presented in the Constitution.

Fast Facts

Constitutional Style The final draft of the Constitution was prepared by a group of five delegates called the Committee of Style. Chaired by William Samuel Johnson of Connecticut, the committee included Alexander Hamilton of New York, Rufus King of Massachusetts, James Madison of Virginia, and Gouverneur Morris of Pennsylvania. The committee worked for five days, completing its task on September 12. Morris did most of the work of styling the document.

Preamble

We the People of the United States, in Order to form a more perfect Union, establish Justice, insure domestic Tranquility, provide for the common defence, promote the general Welfare, and secure the Blessings of Liberty to ourselves and our Posterity, do ordain and establish this **Constitution** for the United States of America.

Article I

Section 1

All legislative Powers herein granted shall be vested in a Congress of the United States, which shall consist of a Senate and House of Representatives.

Section 2

[1.] The House of Representatives shall be composed of Members chosen every second Year by the People of the several States, and the Electors in each State shall have the Qualifications requisite for Electors of the most numerous Branch of the State Legislature.

[2.] No Person shall be a Representative who shall not have attained the Age of twenty five Years, and been seven Years a Citizen of the United States, and who shall not, when elected, be an Inhabitant of that State in which he shall be chosen.

[3.] Representatives and direct Taxes shall be apportioned among the several States which may be included within this Union, according to their respective Numbers, which shall be determined by adding to the whole Number of free Persons, including those bound to Service for a Term of Years, and excluding Indians not taxed, three fifths of all other Persons. The actual **Enumeration** shall be made within three Years after the first Meeting of the Congress of the United States, and within every subsequent Term of ten Years, in such Manner as they shall by Law direct. The Number of Representatives shall not exceed one for every thirty Thousand, but each State shall have at Least one Representative; and until such enumeration shall be made, the State of New Hampshire shall be entitled to chuse three, Massachusetts eight, Rhode-Island and Providence Plantations one, Connecticut five, New-York six, New Jersey four, Pennsylvania eight, Delaware one, Maryland six, Virginia ten, North Carolina five, South Carolina five, and Georgia three.

[4.] When vacancies happen in the Representation from any State, the Executive Authority thereof shall issue Writs of Election to fill such Vacancies.

[5.] The House of Representatives shall chuse their Speaker and other Officers; and shall have the sole Power of **Impeachment.**

The **Preamble** introduces the Constitution and sets forth the general purposes for which the government was established. The Preamble also declares that the power of the government comes from the people.

The printed text of the document shows the spelling and punctuation of the parchment original.

What It Means

Article I. The Legislative Branch The Constitution contains seven divisions called articles. Each article covers a general topic. For example, Articles I, II, and III create the three branches of the national government—the legislative, executive, and judicial branches. Most of the articles are divided into sections.

What It Means

Representation The number of representatives from each state is based on the size of the state's population. Each state is entitled to at least one representative. *What are the qualifications for members of the House of Representatives?*

Vocabulary

preamble: introduction

constitution: principles and laws of a nation

enumeration: a census or population count

impeachment: the bringing of charges against an official

Teach

C Critical Thinking

Making Inferences Ask: What is the significance of discussing the legislative branch first? *(Answers may include the idea that the lawmaking power is the most important or that the lawmaking power logically comes first because Congress must pass laws before the president can execute them or before judges can interpret them.)* **AL**

D Differentiated Instruction

Visual/Spatial Have students research to identify the number of representatives in each state in 1992 and 2002. They should determine which states gained and which ones lost representatives. Have them create two maps comparing the two years and highlighting the differences. **OL**

What It Means

Answer
A member of the House must be at least 25 years old, be a United States citizen for at least seven years, and be an inhabitant of the state from which he or she was elected.

Activity: Technology Connection

Making Connections Have students use Internet sources to find out how many representatives each state currently has. Then have them organize the information into a chart or map. Students may chart their information by listing the states with the most representatives first, create a chart that shows representatives by political parties, or use a map to illustrate their results. Encourage students to be creative in how they display the information. **OL**

The Constitution of the United States

S Skill Practice

Analyzing Ask: How many votes does each state get in the Senate? *(two)* How many votes did each state have under the Articles of Confederation? *(one)* **BL**

C Critical Thinking

Comparing and Contrasting Ask: How much of the Senate is elected every two years? *(one-third)* How many seats in the House of Representatives are subject to an election every two years? *(all)* Which house might be more responsive to voters' wishes? Why? *(the House; because members who want to be reelected must face voters more often)* **OL**

R Reading Strategy

Monitoring Comprehension Ask: What happens if the Senate ties when holding a vote? *(The vice president has the right to cast the deciding vote.)* **OL**

What It Means

Answer
the Senate

Additional Support

What It Means

Electing Senators Originally, senators were chosen by the state legislators of their own states. The Seventeenth Amendment changed this so that senators are now elected by the people. There are 100 senators, 2 from each state. The vice president serves as president of the Senate.

▲ John Adams, the first vice president

What It Means

Impeachment One of Congress's powers is the power to impeach—to accuse government officials of wrongdoing, put them on trial, and if necessary remove them from office. *Which body has the power to decide the official's guilt or innocence?*

Vocabulary

president pro tempore: the presiding officer of Senate who serves when the vice president is absent

indictment: the charging of a person with an offense

quorum: the minimum number of members that must be present to conduct sessions

adjourn: to suspend a session

emolument: salary

bill: the draft of a proposed law

revenue: income raised by government

Section 3

[1.] The Senate of the United States shall be composed of two Senators from each State, chosen by the Legislature thereof, for six Years; and each Senator shall have one Vote.

[2.] Immediately after they shall be assembled in Consequence of the first Election, they shall be divided as equally as may be into three Classes. The Seats of the Senators of the first Class shall be vacated at the Expiration of the second Year, of the second Class at the Expiration of the fourth Year, and of the third Class at the Expiration of the sixth Year, so that one third may be chosen every second Year; and if Vacancies happen by Resignation, or otherwise, during the Recess of the Legislature of any State, the Executive thereof may make temporary Appointments until the next Meeting of the Legislature, which shall then fill such Vacancies.

[3.] No Person shall be a Senator who shall not have attained to the Age of thirty Years, and been nine Years a Citizen of the United States, and who shall not, when elected, be an Inhabitant of that State for which he shall be chosen.

[4.] The Vice President of the United States shall be President of the Senate, but shall have no Vote, unless they be equally divided.

[5.] The Senate shall chuse their other Officers, and also a **President pro tempore,** in the Absence of the Vice President, or when he shall exercise the Office of the President of the United States.

[6.] The Senate shall have the sole Power to try all Impeachments. When sitting for that Purpose, they shall be on Oath or Affirmation. When the President of the United States is tried, the Chief Justice shall preside: And no Person shall be convicted without the Concurrence of two thirds of the Members present.

[7.] Judgment in Cases of Impeachment shall not extend further than to removal from Office, and disqualification to hold and enjoy any Office of honor, Trust or Profit under the United States: but the Party convicted shall nevertheless be liable and subject to **Indictment,** Trial, Judgment and Punishment, according to Law.

Section 4

[1.] The Times, Places and Manner of holding Elections for Senators and Representatives, shall be prescribed in each State by the Legislature thereof; but the Congress may at any time by Law make or alter such Regulations, except as to the Places of chusing Senators.

[2.] The Congress shall assemble at least once in every Year, and such Meeting shall be on the first Monday in December, unless they shall by Law appoint a different Day.

Activity: Interdisciplinary Connection

History Begin a discussion of the impeachment clause. Tell students that only two sitting presidents have been impeached: Andrew Johnson and William Clinton. The House started impeachment proceedings on President Richard Nixon, but he resigned before the vote took place.

Have students work in groups to research both impeachments. Although neither President Johnson nor President Clinton was convicted by the Senate, the impeachment is part of their historical record. Have students discuss how this affects each president's place in history. **OL**

Section 5

[1.] Each House shall be the Judge of the Elections, Returns and Qualifications of its own Members, and a Majority of each shall constitute a **Quorum** to do Business; but a smaller Number may **adjourn** from day to day, and may be authorized to compel the Attendance of absent Members, in such Manner, and under such Penalties as each House may provide.

[2.] Each House may determine the Rules of its Proceedings, punish its Members for disorderly Behaviour, and, with the Concurrence of two thirds, expel a Member.

[3.] Each House shall keep a Journal of its Proceedings, and from time to time publish the same, excepting such Parts as may in their Judgment require Secrecy; and the Yeas and Nays of the Members of either House on any question shall, at the Desire of one fifth of those Present, be entered on the Journal.

[4.] Neither House, during the Session of Congress, shall, without the Consent of the other, adjourn for more than three days, nor to any other Place than that in which the two Houses shall be sitting.

Section 6

[1.] The Senators and Representatives shall receive a Compensation for their Services, to be ascertained by Law, and paid out of the Treasury of the United States. They shall in all Cases, except Treason, Felony and Breach of the Peace, be privileged from Arrest during their Attendance at the Session of their respective Houses, and in going to and returning from the same; and for any Speech or Debate in either House, they shall not be questioned in any other Place.

[2.] No Senator or Representative shall, during the Time for which he was elected, be appointed to any civil Office under the Authority of the United States, which shall have been created, or the **Emoluments** whereof shall have been encreased during such time; and no Person holding any Office under the United States, shall be a Member of either House during his Continuance in Office.

Section 7

[1.] All **Bills** for raising **Revenue** shall originate in the House of Representatives; but the Senate may propose or concur with Amendments as on other Bills,

[2.] Every Bill which shall have passed the House of Representatives and the Senate, shall, before it become a Law, be presented to the President of the United States: If he approve he shall sign it, but if not he shall return it, with his Objections to that House in which it shall have originated, who shall enter the Objections at large on their Journal, and proceed to reconsider it. If after such Reconsideration two thirds

▲ Congresswoman Nydia Velázquez represents New York's 12th District.

What It Means

Congressional Salaries To strengthen the federal government, the Founders set congressional salaries to be paid by the United States Treasury rather than by members' respective states. Originally, members were paid $6 per day. In 2006 all members of Congress received a base salary of $165,200.

What It Means

Where Tax Laws Begin All tax laws must originate in the House of Representatives. This ensures that the branch of Congress that is elected by the people every two years has the major role in determining taxes.

What It Means

How Bills Become Laws A bill may become a law only by passing both houses of Congress and by being signed by the president. The president can check Congress by rejecting—vetoing—its legislation. *How can Congress override the president's veto?*

The Constitution of the United States

R **Reading Strategy**

Understanding Vocabulary Direct students' attention to the bottom of the previous page for a definition of "quorum." **Ask:** How many members of the 100-person Senate are needed for a quorum? *(51)* **OL**

C **Critical Thinking**

Drawing Conclusions Ask: Why is Congress required to make its proceedings public? *(to let people know what members said on particular issues)* Why is Congress allowed to keep some discussions secret? *(Answers may include the need to maintain security.)* **OL**

S **Skill Practice**

Analyzing Ask: What is meant by the "Yeas and Nays"? *(the yes and no votes that members of Congress register on a bill)* **AL**

What It Means

Answer
A bill can become a law, despite not being signed by the president, if two-thirds of the House of Representatives and two-thirds of the Senate approve it a second time.

Activity: Collaborative Learning

Describing In this activity, students will use the Internet and other sources to find out what representatives and senators do on a daily basis. Form small groups and instruct students to begin their research with a list of questions, such as: Do new senators and representatives get training? What do they do? What kind of work constitutes a typical day?

How long does it take to learn all the rules?

Next, students will conduct their research. Encourage students to write to their state representatives or senators to get a personal answer to their questions. Have students document the results of their research in a poster. **OL**

The Constitution of the United States

What It Means

Powers of Congress Expressed powers are those powers directly stated in the Constitution. Most of the expressed powers of Congress are listed in Article I, Section 8. These powers are also called enumerated powers because they are numbered 1–18. *Which clause gives Congress the power to declare war?*

▲ Civil War money

Vocabulary

resolution: legislature's formal expression of opinion

impost: tax

naturalization: procedure by which a citizen of a foreign nation becomes a citizen of the United States

tribunal: a court

letter of marque: authority given to a citizen to outfit an armed ship and use it to attack enemy ships in time of war

reprisal: taking by force property or territory belonging to another country or to its citizens

of that House shall agree to pass the Bill, it shall be sent, together with the Objections, to the other House, by which it shall likewise be reconsidered, and if approved by two thirds of that House, it shall become a Law. But in all such Cases the Votes of both Houses shall be determined by yeas and Nays, and the Names of the Persons voting for and against the Bill shall be entered on the Journal of each House respectively. If any Bill shall not be returned by the President within ten Days (Sundays excepted) after it shall have been presented to him, the Same shall be a Law, in like Manner as if he had signed it, unless the Congress by their Adjournment prevent its Return, in which Case it shall not be a Law.

[3.] Every Order, **Resolution,** or Vote to which the Concurrence of the Senate and House of Representatives may be necessary (except on a question of Adjournment) shall be presented to the President of the United States; and before the Same shall take Effect, shall be approved by him, or being disapproved by him, shall be repassed by two thirds of the Senate and House of Representatives, according to the Rules and Limitations prescribed in the Case of a Bill.

Section 8

[1.] The Congress shall have the Power To lay and collect Taxes, Duties, **Imposts** and Excises, to pay the Debts and provide for the common Defence and general Welfare of the United States; but all Duties, Imposts and Excises shall be uniform throughout the United States;

[2.] To borrow Money on the credit of the United States;

[3.] To regulate Commerce with foreign Nations, and among the several States, and with the Indian Tribes;

[4.] To establish an uniform Rule of **Naturalization,** and uniform Laws on the subject of Bankruptcies throughout the United States;

[5.] To coin Money, regulate the Value thereof, and of foreign Coin, and fix the Standard of Weights and Measures;

[6.] To provide for the Punishment of counterfeiting the Securities and current Coin of the United States;

[7.] To establish Post Offices and post Roads;

[8.] To promote the Progress of Science and useful Arts, by securing for limited Times to Authors and Inventors the exclusive Right to their respective Writings and Discoveries;

[9.] To constitute **Tribunals** inferior to the supreme Court;

[10.] To define and punish Piracies and Felonies committed on the high Seas, and Offences against the Law of Nations;

[11.] To declare War, grant **Letters of Marque** and **Reprisal,** and make Rules concerning Captures on Land and Water;

[12.] To raise and support Armies, but no Appropriation of Money to that Use shall be for a longer Term than two Years;

[13.] To provide and maintain a Navy;

[14.] To make Rules for the Government and Regulation of the land and naval Forces;

[15.] To provide for calling forth the Militia to execute the Laws of the Union, suppress **Insurrections** and repel Invasions;

[16.] To provide for organizing, arming, and disciplining, the Militia, and for governing such Part of them as may be employed in the Service of the United States, reserving to the States respectively, the Appointment of the Officers, and the Authority of training the Militia according to the discipline prescribed by Congress;

[17.] To exercise exclusive Legislation in all Cases whatsoever, over such District (not exceeding ten Miles square) as may, by Cession of particular States, and the Acceptance of Congress, become the Seat of Government of the United States, and to exercise like Authority over all Places purchased by the Consent of the Legislature of the State in which the Same shall be, for the Erection of Forts, Magazines, Arsenals, dock-Yards, and other needful Buildings;—And

[18.] To make all Laws which shall be necessary and proper for carrying into Execution the foregoing Powers, and all other Powers vested by this Constitution in the Government of the United States, or in any Department or Officer thereof.

Section 9

[1]. The Migration or Importation of such Persons as any of the States now existing shall think proper to admit, shall not be prohibited by the Congress prior to the Year one thousand eight hundred and eight, but a Tax or **duty** may be imposed on such Importation, not exceeding ten dollars for each Person.

[2.] The Privilege of the Writ of Habeas Corpus shall not be suspended, unless when in Cases of Rebellion or Invasion the public Safety may require it.

[3.] No Bill of Attainder or ex post facto Law shall be passed.

[4.] No Capitation, or other direct, Tax shall be laid, unless in Proportion to the Census or enumeration herein before directed to be taken.

[5.] No Tax or Duty shall be laid on Articles exported from any State.

[6.] No Preference shall be given by any Regulation of Commerce or Revenue to the Ports of one State over those of another; nor shall Vessels bound to, or from, one State, be obliged to enter, clear, or pay Duties in another.

[7.] No Money shall be drawn from the Treasury, but in Consequence of **Appropriations** made by Law; and a regular Statement and Account of the Receipts and Expenditures of all public Money shall be published from time to time.

[8.] No Title of Nobility shall be granted by the United States: And no Person holding any Office of Profit or Trust under them, shall, without the Consent of the Congress, accept of any present, Emolument, Office, or Title, of any kind whatever, from any King, Prince, or foreign State.

What It Means

Elastic Clause The final enumerated power is often called the "elastic clause." This clause gives Congress the right to make all laws "necessary and proper" to carry out the powers expressed in the other clauses of **Article I.** It is called the elastic clause because it lets Congress "stretch" its powers to meet situations the Founders could never have anticipated.

What does the phrase **"necessary and proper"** in the elastic clause mean? Almost from the beginning, this phrase was a subject of dispute. The issue was whether a strict or a broad interpretation of the Constitution should be applied. The dispute was first addressed in 1819, in the case of *McCulloch v. Maryland*, when the Supreme Court ruled in favor of a broad interpretation.

What It Means

Habeas Corpus A writ of habeas corpus issued by a judge requires a law official to bring a prisoner to court and show cause for holding the prisoner. A bill of attainder is a bill that punished a person without a jury trial. An "ex post facto" law is one that makes an act a crime after the act has been committed. *What does the Constitution say about bills of attainder?*

Vocabulary

insurrection: rebellion

duty: tax

appropriations: funds set aside for a specific use

C Critical Thinking

Analyzing Information Ask: Is the term "elastic clause" appropriate for Section 8, Clause 18? Why or why not? *(Students may say that it is appropriate because Congress can stretch the clause to cover many actions.)* **OL**

S Skill Practice

Analyzing Explain that this clause prevented Congress from passing any law banning the importation of Africans as slaves before 1808. This language was a compromise between delegates who wanted to ban the importation of slaves and those who wished to continue the practice. **Ask:** Which part of the country was represented by pro-slavery delegates? *(the South)* **OL**

R Reading Strategy

Reading Primary Sources Ask: What limits does this clause (Section 9, Clause 7) place on the federal government? *(prevents it from spending any money unless authorized by Congress)* **OL**

What It Means

Answer
Congress cannot pass such bills.

Fast Facts

Seat of the Government The Founders wanted to completely remove the nation's capital from the control of any state. The notion stemmed from a June 1783 incident in Philadelphia in which a group of 80 soldiers threatened and verbally abused members of Congress. No local or state authorities offered aid; however, Congressional members eventually were allowed to leave Independence Hall. Congress is the local and national legislature for Washington, D.C.

Habeas Corpus President Abraham Lincoln suspended the Writ of Habeas Corpus during the Civil War on the grounds that the Constitution allowed suspension in cases of rebellion. The Supreme Court ruled in *Ex parte Merryman* that Lincoln's move violated the Constitution because only Congress had the power to suspend habeas corpus.

The Constitution of the United States

R₁ Reading Strategy

Taking Notes Have students create a two-column chart in which they list the powers denied the states in one column and the clause in which that power is granted to Congress in the other. **OL**

R₂ Reading Strategy

Organizing Information Have students read Article II to find the powers of the president. Suggest that they classify those powers under the headings "Executive," "Legislative," "Diplomatic," "Military," and "Judicial." **OL**

R₃ Reading Strategy

Monitoring Comprehension Ask: Who are the only two members of the executive branch specified in the Constitution? *(the president and vice president)* **BL**

What It Means

Limitations on the States Section 10 lists limits on the states. These restrictions were designed, in part, to prevent an overlapping in functions and authority with the federal government. **R₁**

What It Means

Article II. The Executive Branch Article II creates an executive branch to carry out laws passed by Congress. Article II lists the powers and duties of the presidency, describes qualifications for office and procedures for electing the president, and provides for a vice president.

▲ United States coins

Section 10

[1.] No State shall enter into any Treaty, Alliance, or Confederation; grant Letters of Marque and Reprisal; coin Money; emit Bills of Credit; make any Thing but gold and silver Coin a Tender in Payment of Debts; pass any Bill of Attainder, ex post facto Law, or Law impairing the Obligation of Contracts, or grant any Title of Nobility.

[2.] No State shall, without the Consent of the Congress, lay any Imposts or Duties on Imports or Exports, except what may be absolutely necessary for executing it's inspection Laws: and the net Produce of all Duties and Imposts, laid by any State on Imports or Exports, shall be for the Use of the Treasury of the United States; and all such Laws shall be subject to the Revision and Controul of the Congress.

[3.] No State shall, without the Consent of Congress, lay any Duty of Tonnage, keep Troops, or Ships of War in time of Peace, enter into any Agreement or Compact with another State, or with a foreign Power, or engage in War, unless actually invaded, or in such imminent Danger as will not admit of delay.

Article II   R₂

Section 1

[1.] The executive Power shall be vested in a President of the United States of America. He shall hold his Office during the Term of four Years, and, together with the Vice President, chosen for the same Term, be elected, as follows: R₃

[2.] Each State shall appoint, in such Manner as the Legislature thereof may direct, a Number of Electors, equal to the whole Number of Senators and Representatives to which the State may be entitled in the Congress: but no Senator or Representative, or Person holding an Office of Trust or Profit under the United States, shall be appointed an Elector.

[3.] The Electors shall meet in their respective States, and vote by Ballot for two Persons, of whom one at least shall not be an Inhabitant of the same State with themselves. And they shall make a List of all the Persons voted for, and of the Number of Votes for each; which List they shall sign and certify, and transmit sealed to the Seat of the Government of the United States, directed to the President of the Senate. The President of the Senate shall, in the Presence of the Senate and House of Representatives, open all the Certificates, and the Votes shall then be counted. The Person having the greatest Number of Votes shall be the President, if such Number be a Majority of the whole Number of Electors appointed; and if there be more than one who have such Majority, and have an equal Number of Votes, then the House of Representatives shall immediately chuse by Ballot one of them for President; and if no person have a Majority,

Activity: Interdisciplinary Connection

Language Arts The Constitution outlines the basic qualifications of the president of the United States and how elections should be run. It does not, however, provide a list of traits the president should have.

Have students write a newspaper ad in which they describe the perfect president.

Advertisements should include personality traits, work experience, and principles that they think a person should possess to run as president. Ask students if any past or current presidents measure up to the standards they have created. **OL** then from the five highest on the List the said House shall in like Manner chuse the President. But in chusing the President, the Votes shall be taken by States, the Representation from each State having one Vote; A quorum for this Purpose shall consist of a Member or Members from two thirds of the States, and a Majority of all the States shall be necessary to a Choice. In every Case, after the Choice of the President, the Person having the greatest Number of Votes of the Electors shall be the Vice President. But if there should remain two or more who have equal Votes, the Senate shall chuse from them by Ballot the Vice President.

[4.] The Congress may determine the Time of chusing the Electors, and the Day on which they shall give their Votes; which Day shall be the same throughout the United States.

[5.] No Person except a natural born Citizen, or a Citizen of the United States, at the time of the Adoption of this Constitution, shall be eligible to the Office of President; neither shall any Person be eligible to that Office who shall not have attained to the Age of thirty five Years, and been fourteen Years a Resident within the United States.

[6.] In Case of the Removal of the President from Office, or of his Death, Resignation, or Inability to discharge the Powers and Duties of the said Office, the Same shall devolve on the Vice President, and the Congress may by Law provide for the Case of Removal, Death, Resignation or Inability, both of the President and Vice President, declaring what Officer shall then act as President, and such Officer shall act accordingly, until the Disability be removed, or a President shall be elected.

[7.] The President shall, at stated Times, receive for his Services, a Compensation, which shall neither be increased nor diminished during the Period for which he shall have been elected, and he shall not receive within that Period any other Emolument from the United States, or any of them.

[8.] Before he enter on the Execution of his Office, he shall take the following Oath or Affirmation:—"I do solemnly swear (or affirm) that I will faithfully execute the Office of President of the United States, and will to the best of my Ability, preserve, protect and defend the Constitution of the United States."

Section 2

[1.] The President shall be Commander in Chief of the Army and Navy of the United States, and of the Militia of the several States, when called into the actual Service of the United States; he may require the Opinion, in writing, of the principal Officer in each of the executive Departments, upon any Subject relating to the Duties of their respective Offices, and he shall have Power to grant Reprieves and Pardons for Offences against the United States, except in Cases of Impeachment.

What It Means

Previous Elections The Twelfth Amendment, added in 1804, changed the method of electing the president stated in Article II, Section 3. The Twelfth Amendment requires that the electors cast separate ballots for president and vice president.

What It Means

Qualifications The president must be a citizen of the United States by birth, at least 35 years of age, and a resident of the United States for 14 years.

What It Means

Vacancies If the president dies, resigns, is removed from office by impeachment, or is unable to carry out the duties of the office, the vice president becomes president. The Twenty-fifth Amendment sets procedures for presidential succession.

What It Means

Salary Originally, the president's salary was $25,000 per year. The president's current salary is $400,000 plus a $50,000 nontaxable expense account per year. The president also receives living accommodations in two residences—the White House and Camp David.

What It Means

The Cabinet Mention of "the principal officer in each of the executive departments" is the only suggestion of the president's cabinet to be found in the Constitution. The cabinet is an advisory body, and its power depends on the president. Section 2, Clause 1, also makes the president—a civilian—the head of the armed services. This established the principle of civilian control of the military.

W₁ Writing Support

Persuasive Writing Have students write an essay in which they argue whether or not, in modern times, a person who is 35 years old is adequately prepared for the complex demands of serving as president of the United States. If they believe the age is not old enough, tell them to specify the minimum age they would set. **OL**

W₂ Writing Support

Expository Writing Have students research and prepare an oral presentation on the vice presidents who later became president. Have them explain why they were chosen as vice presidents, how they became presidents, and whether or not they were elected. **OL**

S Skill Practice

Analyzing Primary Sources Ask: What pledge does the president make when taking the oath of office? *(to preserve, protect, and defend the Constitution)* What does that pledge mean? *(Answers may include that the president's actions should uphold the Constitution and not undermine it.)* **OL**

The Constitution of the United States **231**

Activity: Interdisciplinary Connection

History The Constitution did not originally limit the number of terms the president could serve. It was George Washington who set the precedent, serving two terms, or eight years. All presidents followed this unspoken rule except for President Franklin D. Roosevelt. He served four terms in office.

Have students work in groups to discuss why some people were opposed to this and why the Twenty-second Amendment was written. Then have groups debate the pros and cons of the Twenty-second Amendment. **OL**

The Constitution of the United States

C Critical Thinking

Defending Ask: As long as judges are on good behavior they can serve. This is interpreted as serving for life. Do you think Supreme Court justices should serve such long terms? How does this affect our laws? *(Answers will vary. Appointment of Supreme Court justices does not occur frequently. Thus, many of their decisions cannot be reversed. Students may consider this advantageous or detrimental.)* **OL**

R Reading Strategy

Questioning Ask: What does the Constitution mean by saying that judges "hold their Offices during good Behaviour"? If students are unable to answer, explain that this means federal judges hold office for life unless they retire, resign, or are impeached and removed from office. **OL**

Additional Support

What It Means

Presidential Powers An executive order is a command issued by a president to exercise a power which he or she has been given by the U.S. Constitution or by a federal statute. In times of emergency, presidents sometimes have used the executive order to override the Constitution of the United States and the Congress. During the Civil War, President Lincoln suspended many fundamental rights guaranteed in the Constitution and the Bill of Rights. He closed down newspapers that opposed his policies and imprisoned some who disagreed with him. Lincoln said that these actions were justified to preserve the Union.

What It Means

Article III. The Judicial Branch The term "judicial" refers to courts. The Constitution set up only the Supreme Court but provided for the establishment of other federal courts. The judiciary of the United States has two different systems of courts. One system consists of the federal courts, whose powers derive from the Constitution and federal laws. The other includes the courts of each of the 50 states, whose powers derive from state constitutions and laws.

What It Means

Statute Law Federal courts deal mostly with "statute law," or laws passed by Congress, treaties, and cases involving the Constitution itself.

[2.] He shall have Power, by and with the Advice and Consent of the Senate, to make Treaties, provided two thirds of the Senators present concur; and he shall nominate, and by and with the Advice and Consent of the Senate, shall appoint Ambassadors, other public Ministers and Consuls, Judges of the supreme Court, and all other Officers of the United States, whose Appointments are not herein otherwise provided for, and which shall be established by Law: but the Congress may by Law vest the Appointment of such inferior Officers, as they think proper, in the President alone, in the Courts of Law, or in the Heads of Departments.

[3.] The President shall have Power to fill up all Vacancies that may happen during the Recess of the Senate, by granting Commissions which shall expire at the End of their next Session.

Section 3

He shall from time to time give to the Congress Information of the State of the Union, and recommend to their Consideration such Measures as he shall judge necessary and expedient; he may, on extraordinary Occasions, convene both Houses, or either of them, and in Case of Disagreement between them, with Respect to the Time of Adjournment, he may adjourn them to such Time as he shall think proper; he shall receive Ambassadors and other public Ministers; he shall take Care that the Laws be faithfully executed, and shall Commission all the Officers of the United States.

Section 4

The President, Vice President and all civil Officers of the United States, shall be removed from Office on Impeachment for, and Conviction of, Treason, Bribery, or other high Crimes and Misdemeanors.

Article III

Section 1

The judicial Power of the United States shall be vested in one supreme Court, and in such inferior Courts as the Congress may from time to time ordain and establish. The Judges, both of the supreme and inferior Courts, shall hold their Offices during good Behaviour, and shall, at stated Times, receive for their Services a Compensation, which shall not be diminished during their Continuance in Office.

Section 2

[1.] The judicial Power shall extend to all Cases, in Law and Equity, arising under this Constitution, the Laws of the United States, and Treaties made, or which shall be made, under their Authority;—to all Cases affecting Ambassadors, other public Ministers and Consuls;—to all Cases of admiralty and maritime Jurisdiction;—to Controversies to which the United States shall be a Party;—to Controversies

---

Fast Facts

State of the Union It is the president's responsibility to inform Congress of the status of the country as well as recommend actions that Congress should consider taking in the next year. Article II, Section 3 of the United States Constitution does not specify how often State of the Union messages should be delivered, but George Washington set the precedent beginning in 1790 with delivering an address every year he was in office.

Although the first twelve messages were delivered orally, Thomas Jefferson began the practice of submitting a written State of the Union Address in 1801. It was not until 1913 that President Wilson reintroduced the practice of addressing Congress in person.

The State of the Union Address with the fewest number of words was Washington's in 1789. It contained 1,089 words. The longest was President Carter's address in 1981 with 33,667 words.

between two or more States;—between a State and Citizens of another State;—between Citizens of different States;—between Citizens of the same State claiming Lands under Grants of different States, and between a State, or the Citizens thereof, and foreign States, Citizens or Subjects.

R₁

[2.] In all Cases affecting Ambassadors, other public Ministers and Consuls, and those in which a State shall be Party, the supreme Court shall have **original Jurisdiction.** In all the other Cases before mentioned, the supreme Court shall have **appellate Jurisdiction,** both as to Law and Fact, with such Exceptions, and under such Regulations as the Congress shall make.

[3.] The Trial of all Crimes, except in Cases of Impeachment, shall be by Jury; and such Trial shall be held in the State where the said Crimes shall have been committed; but when not committed within any State, the Trial shall be at such Place or Places as the Congress may by Law have directed.

Section 3

R₂

[1.] **Treason** against the United States, shall consist only in levying War against them, or in adhering to their Enemies, giving them Aid and Comfort. No Person shall be convicted of Treason unless on the Testimony of two Witnesses to the same overt Act, or on Confession in open Court.

[2.] The Congress shall have Power to declare the Punishment of Treason, but no Attainder of Treason shall work Corruption of Blood, or Forfeiture except during the Life of the Person attainted.

Article IV

Section 1

Full Faith and Credit shall be given in each State to the public Acts, Records, and judicial Proceedings of every other State. And the Congress may by general Laws prescribe the Manner in which such Acts, Records and Proceedings shall be proved, and the Effect thereof.

Section 2

[1.] The Citizens of each State shall be entitled to all Privileges and Immunities of Citizens in the several States.

[2.] A Person charged in any State with Treason, Felony, or other Crime, who shall flee from Justice, and be found in another State, shall on Demand of the executive Authority of the State from which he fled, be delivered up, to be removed to the State having Jurisdiction of the Crime.

[3.] No Person held to Service of Labour in one State, under the Laws thereof, escaping into another, shall, in Consequence of any Law or Regulation therein, be discharged from such Service or Labour, but shall be delivered up on Claim of the Party to whom such Service or Labour may be due.

What It Means

The Supreme Court A court with "original jurisdiction" has the authority to be the first court to hear a case. The Supreme Court has "appellate jurisdiction" and mostly hears cases appealed from lower courts.

What It Means

Article IV. Relations Among the States Article IV explains the relationship of the states to one another and to the national government. This article requires each state to give citizens of other states the same rights as its own citizens, addresses admitting new states, and guarantees that the national government will protect the states.

Vocabulary

original jurisdiction: authority to be the first court to hear a case

appellate jurisdiction: authority to hear cases that have been appealed from lower courts

treason: violation of the allegiance owed by a person to his or her own country, for example, by aiding an enemy

The Constitution of the United States **233**

R₁ ## Reading Strategy

Analyzing Text Structure Ask: Which branch of the government is described in more detail in the Constitution, the legislative or the judicial? *(legislative)* Explain that as a result, Congess had to pass laws, starting with the Judiciary Act of 1789, to set up the federal courts. **OL**

R₂ ## Reading Strategy

Summarizing Ask: What kinds of cases are heard in federal courts? *(disputes involving officials of the federal government; cases about ships; cases involving the government; cases that involve two state governments, a citizen of one state and the government of another state, or citizens of different states; cases involving land grants by different states; cases between a citizen or state and a foreign person or government)* **AL**

Activity: Interdisciplinary Connection

History Until the late 1900s, all Supreme Court justices were white males. Lead a discussion on how this may have influenced Supreme Court decisions. Point out that the first African American justice was Thurgood Marshall, and the first woman was Sandra Day O'Connor.

Next, have students research the names of other minorities who have served in Congress. Charts should include dates and states.

Ask students to speculate when they think a minority will serve as president of the United States. **OL**

The Constitution of the United States

R Reading Strategy

Activating Prior Knowledge Ask: How many states were needed to approve an amendment to the Articles of Confederation? *(all of them)* How many are needed to amend the Constitution? *(two-thirds of the states in Congress or in the state legislatures for proposing amendments; three-fourths for approving one)* **OL**

C Critical Thinking

Drawing Conclusions A political scientist once named the supremacy clause as "the most important single provision of the Constitution." **Ask:** Do you agree or disagree? Why? Discuss students' answers as a class. **OL**

Additional Support

What It Means

Republic Government can be classified in many different ways. The ancient Greek philosopher Aristotle classified government based on the question: Who governs? According to Aristotle, all governments belong to one of three major groups: (1) autocracy—rule by one person; (2) oligarchy—rule by a few persons; or (3) democracy—rule by many persons. A republic is a form of democracy in which the people elect representatives to make the laws and conduct government.

What It Means

Article VI. National Supremacy
Article VI contains the "supremacy clause." This clause establishes that the Constitution, laws passed by Congress, and treaties of the United States "shall be the supreme Law of the Land." The "supremacy clause" recognized the Constitution and federal laws as supreme when in conflict with those of the states.

Vocabulary

amendment: a change to the Constitution

ratification: the process by which an amendment is approved

234 *The Constitution of the United States*

Section 3

[1.] New States may be admitted by the Congress into this Union; but no new State shall be formed or erected within the Jurisdiction of any other State; nor any State be formed by the Junction of two or more States, or Parts of States, without the Consent of the Legislatures of the States concerned as well as of the Congress.

[2.] The Congress shall have Power to dispose of and make all needful Rules and Regulations respecting the Territory or other Property belonging to the United States; and nothing in this Constitution shall be so construed as to Prejudice any Claims of the United States, or of any particular State.

Section 4

The United States shall guarantee to every State in this Union a Republican Form of Government, and shall protect each of them against Invasion; and on Application of the Legislature, or of the Executive (when the Legislature cannot be convened), against domestic Violence.

Article V

The Congress, whenever two thirds of both Houses shall deem it necessary, shall propose **Amendments** to this Constitution, or, on the Application of the Legislatures of two thirds of the several States, shall call a Convention for proposing Amendments, which, in either Case, shall be valid to all Intents and Purposes, as Part of this Constitution, when ratified by the Legislatures of three fourths of the several States, or by Conventions in three fourths thereof, as the one or the other Mode of **Ratification** may be proposed by the Congress; Provided that no Amendment which may be made prior to the Year One thousand eight hundred and eight shall in any Manner affect the first and fourth Clauses in the Ninth Section of the first Article; and that no State, without its Consent, shall be deprived of its equal Suffrage in the Senate.

Article VI

[1.] All Debts contracted and Engagements entered into, before the Adoption of this Constitution, shall be as valid against the United States under this Constitution, as under the Confederation.

[2.] This Constitution, and the Laws of the United States which shall be made in Pursuance thereof; and all Treaties made, or which shall be made, under the Authority of the United States, shall be the supreme Law of the Land; and the Judges in every State shall be bound thereby, any Thing in the Constitution or Laws of any State to the Contrary notwithstanding.

[3.] The Senators and Representatives before mentioned, and the Members of the several State Legislatures, and all executive

---

Activity: Collaborative Learning

Geography Ask students to draw a current map of the United States and fill in the states' names and the dates in which they became states. In addition, have students locate, copy, or re-create maps of the 13 colonies, the Western Land Claims of 1754, the Louisiana Purchase Territory, the Florida purchase, the Texas annexation, and the Oregon Territory. Have them discuss the importance of these acquisitions. Then, have students work in groups to create a States Quiz Game. Have groups challenge each other. **AL**

and judicial Officers, both of the United States and of the several States, shall be bound by Oath or Affirmation, to support this Constitution; but no religious Test shall ever be required as a Qualification to any Office or public Trust under the United States.

Article VII

The Ratification of the Conventions of nine States, shall be sufficient for the Establishment of this Constitution between the States so ratifying the Same.

Done in Convention by the Unanimous Consent of the States present the Seventeenth Day of September in the Year of our Lord one thousand seven hundred and Eighty seven and of the Independence of the United States of America the Twelfth. In witness whereof We have hereunto subscribed our Names,

What It Means

Article VII. Ratification Article VII addresses ratification and declares that the Constitution would take effect after it was ratified by nine states.

Signers W4

George Washington,
President and Deputy
from Virginia

New Hampshire
John Langdon
Nicholas Gilman

Massachusetts
Nathaniel Gorham
Rufus King

Connecticut
William Samuel Johnson
Roger Sherman

New York
Alexander Hamilton

New Jersey
William Livingston
David Brearley
William Paterson
Jonathan Dayton

Pennsylvania
Benjamin Franklin
Thomas Mifflin
Robert Morris
George Clymer
Thomas FitzSimons
Jared Ingersoll
James Wilson
Gouverneur Morris

Delaware
George Read
Gunning Bedford, Jr.
John Dickinson
Richard Bassett
Jacob Broom

Maryland
James McHenry
Daniel of
    St. Thomas Jenifer
Daniel Carroll

Virginia
John Blair
James Madison, Jr.

North Carolina
William Blount
Richard Dobbs Spaight
Hugh Williamson

South Carolina
John Rutledge
Charles Cotesworth
    Pinckney
Charles Pinckney
Pierce Butler

Georgia
William Few
Abraham Baldwin

Attest:
William Jackson, Secretary

W2

W1 Writing Support

Persuasive Writing Explain that three members of the Convention did not sign the Constitution because they objected to the lack of a Bill of Rights. Have students write an essay explaining why they would or would not have signed the document. **OL**

W2 Writing Support

Research Reports Writing Have each student write a brief biography of one of the signers of the Constitution and present their findings orally. **OL**

Activity: Interdisciplinary Connection

Art The first seven articles of the Constitution provide our country with a framework for our national government. Have students create a collage that illustrates the main ideas set forth in Articles I–VII of the Constitution. Students can clip pictures from magazines or make drawings to represent the articles. Ask students to explain their work to the class. **OL**

The Constitution of the United States

The Amendments This part of the Constitution consists of amendments. The Constitution has been amended 27 times throughout the nation's history.

What It Means

The Bill of Rights The first 10 amendments are known as the Bill of Rights (1791). These amendments limit the powers of government. The First Amendment protects the civil liberties of individuals in the United States. The amendment freedoms are not absolute, however. They are limited by the rights of other individuals. *What freedoms does the First Amendment protect?*

Vocabulary

quarter: to provide living accommodations

warrant: a document that gives police particular rights or powers

probable cause: a reasonable basis to believe a person is linked to a crime

Amendment I

Congress shall make no law respecting an establishment of religion, or prohibiting the free exercise thereof; or abridging the freedom of speech, or of the press; or the right of the people peaceably to assemble, and to petition the Government for a redress of grievances.

Amendment II

A well regulated Militia, being necessary to the security of a free State, the right of the people to keep and bear Arms, shall not be infringed.

Amendment III

No Soldier shall, in time of peace be **quartered** in any house, without the consent of the Owner, nor in time of war, but in a manner to be prescribed by law.

Amendment IV

The right of the people to be secure in their persons, houses, papers, and effects, against unreasonable searches and seizures, shall not be violated, and no **Warrants** shall issue, but upon **probable cause,** supported by Oath or affirmation, and particularly describing the place to be searched, and the persons or things to be seized.

Amendment V

No person shall be held to answer for a capital, or otherwise infamous crime, unless on a presentment or indictment of a Grand Jury, except in cases arising in the land or naval forces, or in the Militia, when in actual service in time of War or public danger; nor shall any person be subject for the same offence to be twice put in jeopardy of life or limb; nor shall be compelled in any criminal case to be a witness against himself, nor be deprived of life, liberty, or property, without due process of law; nor shall private property be taken for public use, without just compensation.

Amendment VI

In all criminal prosecutions, the accused shall enjoy the right to a speedy and public trial, by an impartial jury of the State and district wherein the crime shall have been committed, which district shall have been previously ascertained by law, and to be informed of the nature and cause of the accusation; to be confronted with the witnesses against him; to have compulsory process for obtaining

Fast Facts

The Bill of Rights Critics of the Constitution believed that it did not go far enough in protecting individual rights and liberties. To answer these objections, supporters of the Constitution promised to introduce a series of amendments listing the rights of individuals. On June 8, 1789, James Madison kept his promise by proposing 12 amendments to the Constitution, 10 of which were adopted and are now known as the Bill of Rights. One amendment not adopted concerned pay raises for members of Congress. It eventually became the Twenty-seventh Amendment to the Constitution.

witnesses in his favor, and to have the Assistance of Counsel for his defence.

Amendment VII

In Suits at **common law,** where the value in controversy shall exceed twenty dollars, the right of trial by jury shall be preserved, and no fact tried by a jury, shall be otherwise re-examined in any Court of the United States, than according to the rules of common law.

Amendment VIII

Excessive **bail** shall not be required, nor excessive fines imposed, nor cruel and unusual punishments inflicted.

Amendment IX

The enumeration in the Constitution, of certain rights, shall not be construed to deny or disparage others retained by the people.

Amendment X

The powers not delegated to the United States by the Constitution, nor prohibited by it to the States, are reserved to the States respectively, or to the people.

Amendment XI

The Judicial power of the United States shall not be construed to extend to any suit in law or equity, commenced or prosecuted against one of the United States by Citizens of another State, or by Citizens or Subjects of any Foreign State.

Amendment XII

The electors shall meet in their respective states and vote by ballot for President and Vice-President, one of whom, at least, shall not be an inhabitant of the same state with themselves; they shall name in their ballots the person voted for as President, and in distinct ballots the person voted for as Vice-President, and they shall make distinct lists of all persons voted for as President, and of all persons voted for as Vice-President, and of the number of votes for each, which lists they shall sign and certify, and transmit sealed to the seat of the government of the United States, directed to the President of the Senate;—The President of the Senate shall, in the presence of the Senate and House of Representatives, open all the certificates and the votes shall then be counted;—The person

What It Means

Powers Reserved to the People This amendment prevents government from claiming that the only rights people have are those listed in the Bill of Rights.

What It Means

Powers Reserved to the States The final amendment of the Bill of Rights protects the states and the people from an all-powerful federal government. It establishes that powers not given to the national government—or denied to the states—by the Constitution belong to the states or to the people.

What It Means

Suits Against States The Eleventh Amendment (1795) limits the jurisdiction of the federal courts. The Supreme Court had ruled that a federal court could try a lawsuit brought by citizens of South Carolina against the state of Georgia. This case, *Chisholm* v. *Georgia*, decided in 1793, raised a storm of protest, leading to passage of the Eleventh Amendment.

Vocabulary

common law: law established by previous court decisions

bail: money that an accused person provides to the court as a guarantee that he or she will be present for a trial

The Constitution of the United States **237**

W **Writing Support**

Persuasive Writing Some defense lawyers say that the large amount of media coverage of some trials threatens the accused person's Sixth Amendment rights. Have students write an essay explaining why they agree or disagree. **OL**

R **Reading Strategy**

Monitoring On the board write the four phrases in the Sixth Amendment beginning with "to be informed of the nature and cause of the accusation" to the end of the amendment. Then read each of the following rewordings and ask which phrase it applies to:

- A person accused of a crime has the right to a lawyer. *(to have the assistance of counsel for his defence)*
- A person must be able to hear the words of anyone who testifies against him in a court. *(to be confronted with the witnesses against him)*
- A person must be told what crime he or she is accused of. *(to be informed of the nature and cause of the accusation)*
- The court can order people to appear as witnesses for an accused person. *(to have compulsory process for obtaining Witnesses)* **OL**

Activity: Collaborative Learning

Identifying Central Issues Ask students to form small groups. Have groups create a set of four to five scenarios or situations that illustrate the freedoms or rights in the first 10 amendments. (You may want to assign particular amendments to each group.) Each group will read or reenact the scenario, and the class will decide to which amendment the situation applies. **OL**

S Skill Practice

Analyzing Point out that the Electoral College has been criticized as being obsolete, and various ideas have been suggested for changing it or abolishing it altogether. Have students debate the question: Should the Electoral College be abolished and the president elected by popular vote? Point out that those in favor must address the concern of small states that they would have no voice in such a system. **OL**

R Reading Strategy

Activating Prior Knowledge Ask: What two principles of the Constitution are stated in Section 1 of the Fourteenth Amendment? *(due process of law; equal protection of the law)* **OL**

Additional Support

What It Means

Election of President and Vice President The Twelfth Amendment (1804) corrects a problem that had arisen in the method of electing the president and vice president. This amendment provides for the Electoral College to use separate ballots in voting for president and vice president. *If no candidate receives a majority of the electoral votes, who elects the president?* **S**

What It Means

Abolition of Slavery Amendments Thirteen (1865), Fourteen (1868), and Fifteen (1870) often are called the Civil War amendments because they grew out of that great conflict. The Thirteenth Amendment outlaws slavery.

What It Means

Rights of Citizens The Fourteenth Amendment (1868) originally was intended to protect the legal rights of the freed slaves. Today it protects the rights of citizenship in general by prohibiting a state from depriving any person of life, liberty, or property without "due process of law." In addition, it states that all citizens have the right to equal protection of the law in all states.

Vocabulary

majority: more than half
devolve: to pass on
abridge: to reduce

having the greatest number of votes for President, shall be the President, if such number be a majority of the whole number of Electors appointed; and if no person have such majority, then from the persons having the highest numbers not exceeding three on the list of those voted for as President, the House of Representatives shall choose immediately, by ballot, the President. But in choosing the President, the votes shall be taken by states, the representation from each state having one vote; a quorum for this purpose shall consist of a member or members from two-thirds of the states, and a **majority** of all the states shall be necessary to a choice. And if the House of Representatives shall not choose a President whenever the right of choice shall **devolve** upon them, before the fourth day of March next following, then the Vice-President shall act as President, as in the case of the death or other constitutional disability of the President. The person having the greatest number of votes as Vice-President, shall be the Vice-President, if such number be a majority of the whole number of Electors appointed, and if no person have a majority, then from the two highest numbers on the list, the Senate shall choose the Vice-President; a quorum for the purpose shall consist of two-thirds of the whole number of Senators, and a majority of the whole number shall be necessary to a choice. But no person constitutionally ineligible to the office of President shall be eligible to that of Vice-President of the United States.

Amendment XIII

Section 1

Neither slavery nor involuntary servitude, except as a punishment for crime whereof the party shall have been duly convicted, shall exist within the United States, or any place subject to their jurisdiction.

Section 2

Congress shall have power to enforce this article by appropriate legislation.

Amendment XIV

Section 1

All persons born or naturalized in the United States, and subject to the jurisdiction thereof, are citizens of the United States and of the State wherein they reside. No State shall make or enforce any law which shall **abridge** the privileges or immunities of citizens of the United States; nor shall any State deprive any person of life, liberty, or **R**

Fast Facts

Too Close to Call? The 1888 presidential election was extremely close. The Democratic candidate, President Grover Cleveland, won the popular election by 95,713 votes, but he lost the Electoral College vote by 65 votes. As a result, Benjamin Harrison was elected as the 23rd president of the United States.

Today, a president must have the majority of electoral votes, 270, to be elected. In situations where no candidate has the majority of electoral votes, the House of Representatives decides the outcome. This has happened only twice. The House voted for Thomas Jefferson in 1801 and John Quincy Adams in 1825.

property, without due process of law; nor deny to any person within its jurisdiction the equal protection of the laws.

Section 2

Representatives shall be apportioned among the several States according to their respective numbers, counting the whole number of persons in each State, excluding Indians not taxed. But when the right to vote at any election for the choice of electors for President and Vice-President of the United States, Representatives in Congress, the Executive and Judicial officers of a State, or the members of the Legislature thereof, is denied to any of the male inhabitants of such State, being twenty-one years of age, and citizens of the United States, or in any way abridged, except for participation in rebellion, or other crime, the basis of representation therein shall be reduced in the proportion which the number of such male citizens shall bear to the whole number of male citizens twenty-one years of age in such State.

Section 3

No person shall be a Senator or Representative in Congress, or elector of President and Vice-President, or hold any office, civil or military, under the United States, or under any State, who, having previously taken an oath, as a member of Congress, or as an officer of the United States, or as a member of any State legislature, or as an executive or judicial officer of any State, to support the Constitution of the United States, shall have engaged in **insurrection** or rebellion against the same, or given aid or comfort to the enemies thereof. But Congress may by a vote of two-thirds of each House, remove such disability.

Section 4

The validity of the public debt of the United States, authorized by law, including debts incurred for payment of pensions and bounties for service in suppressing insurrection or rebellion, shall not be questioned. But neither the United States nor any State shall assume or pay any debt or obligation incurred in aid of insurrection or rebellion against the United States, or any claim for the loss or **emancipation** of any slave; but all such debts, obligations and claims shall be held illegal and void.

Section 5

The Congress shall have power to enforce, by appropriate legislation, the provisions of this article.

What It Means

Representation in Congress This section reduced the number of members a state had in the House of Representatives if it denied its citizens the right to vote. Later civil rights laws and the Twenty-fourth Amendment guaranteed the vote to African Americans.

What It Means

Penalty for Engaging in Insurrection The leaders of the Confederacy were barred from state or federal offices unless Congress agreed to remove this ban. By the end of Reconstruction all but a few Confederate leaders were allowed to return to public life.

What It Means

Public Debt The public debt acquired by the federal government during the Civil War was valid and could not be questioned by the South. However, the debts of the Confederacy were declared to be illegal. *Could former slaveholders collect payment for the loss of their slaves?*

Vocabulary

R

insurrection: rebellion against the government

emancipation: freedom from slavery

The Constitution of the United States **239**

R Reading Strategy

Understanding Vocabulary Students may have difficulty with many words in the Constitution. Have students identify difficult words and write them in their notebooks. Then students should use a dictionary to find and write their definitions next to the words. Advise students to refer to their lists as they reread the text. **OL**

What It Means

Answer
No, they could not.

Activity: Technology Connection

Drawing Conclusions Have students use the Internet, including government sources, to find out how the Supreme Court interpreted Amendment XIV over the years, beginning with the Gitlow case in 1925 (*Gitlow* v. *New York*). Have students research the following cases: *Near* v. *Minnesota*, *DeJonge* v. *Oregon*, *Wolf* v. *Colorado*, *Pointer* v. *Texas*, and *Benton* v. *Maryland*. Students will present their findings in a chart. **Ask:** Should all the protections and rights covered by the Bill of Rights apply to state governments as well as the national government? Do you think the Framers of the Constitution wanted the states to grant all of the rights stated in the Bill of Rights? **AL**

The Constitution of the United States

C Critical Thinking

Comparing and Contrasting Ask: Did the Seventeenth Amendment make the Senate more or less democratic? Why? *(more; because all the voters in a state can choose senators)* **OL**

D Differentiated Instruction

Verbal/Linguistic Have students rephrase the Seventeenth Amendment, Section 3, in their own words. *(Senators elected under the old system will continue to serve their terms.)* **AL**

> ### What It Means
> **Answer**
> six years

Additional Support

> ### What It Means
> **Right to Vote** The Fifteenth Amendment (1870) prohibits the government from denying a person's right to vote on the basis of race. Despite the law, many states denied African Americans the right to vote by such means as poll taxes, literacy tests, and white primaries. During the 1950s and 1960s, Congress passed successively stronger laws to end racial discrimination in voting rights.

> ### What It Means
> **Direct Election of Senators** The Seventeenth Amendment (1913) states that the people, instead of state legislatures, elect United States senators. *How many years are in a Senate term?*

Vocabulary
apportionment: the distribution of seats in the House based on population

Amendment XV

Section 1
The right of citizens of the United States to vote shall not be denied or abridged by the United States or by any State on account of race, color, or previous condition of servitude.

Section 2
The Congress shall have power to enforce this article by appropriate legislation.

Amendment XVI
The Congress shall have power to lay and collect taxes on incomes, from whatever source derived, without **apportionment** among the several States, and without regard to any census or enumeration.

Amendment XVII

Section 1
The Senate of the United States shall be composed of two Senators from each State, elected by the people thereof, for six years; and each Senator shall have one vote. The electors in each State shall have the qualifications requisite for electors of the most numerous branch of the State legislatures. **C**

Section 2
When vacancies happen in the representation of any State in the Senate, the executive authority of such State shall issue writs of election to fill such vacancies: *Provided,* That the legislature of any State may empower the executive thereof to make temporary appointments until the people fill the vacancies by election as the legislature may direct.

Section 3
This amendment shall not be so construed as to affect the election or term of any Senator chosen before it becomes valid as part of the Constitution. **D**

Amendment XVIII

Section 1
After one year from ratification of this article, the manufacture, sale, or transportation of intoxicating liquors within, the importation thereof into, or the exportation

---

Activity: Economics Connection

Making Decisions Explain to students that as population increases, so do government spending and taxes. Have students create a line graph. One line will show how the average income of Americans has increased since 1915. A second line will indicate tax increases. Ask students to show their charts to family members or friends and note personal reactions. Have students share responses with the class. **Ask:** Do you agree that income tax is necessary? Should everyone pay the same rate or should it be a progressive tax (rates rise with income), as it is now? **AL**

thereof from the United States and all territory subject to the jurisdiction thereof for beverage purposes is hereby prohibited.

Section 2

The Congress and the several States shall have concurrent power to enforce this article by appropriate legislation.

Section 3

This article shall be inoperative unless it shall have been ratified as an amendment to the Constitution by the legislatures of the several States, as provided in the Constitution, within seven years from the date of the submission hereof to the States by the Congress.

Amendment XIX

Section 1

The right of citizens of the United States to vote shall not be denied or abridged by the United States or by any State on account of sex.

Section 2

Congress shall have power by appropriate legislation to enforce the provisions of this article.

Amendment XX

Section 1

The terms of the President and Vice President shall end at noon on the 20th day of January, and the terms of the Senators and Representatives at noon on the 3d day of January, of the years in which such terms would have ended if this article had not been ratified; and the terms of their successors shall then begin.

Section 2

The Congress shall assemble at least once in every year, and such meeting shall begin at noon on the 3d day of January, unless they shall by law appoint a different day.

Section 3

If, at the time fixed for the beginning of the term of the President, the **President elect** shall have died, the Vice President elect shall become President. If a President shall not have been chosen before the time fixed for the beginning of his term, or if the President elect shall have failed to qualify, then the Vice President elect shall act as President until a President shall have qualified; and the Congress may by law

What It Means

Woman Suffrage The Nineteenth Amendment (1920) guaranteed women the right to vote. By then women had already won the vote in many state elections, but the amendment made their right to vote in all state and national elections constitutional.

What It Means

"Lame Duck" The Twentieth Amendment (1933) set new dates for Congress to begin its term and for the inauguration of the president and vice president. Under the original Constitution, elected officials who retired or who had been defeated remained in office for several months. For the outgoing president, this period ran from November until March. Such outgoing officials, referred to as "lame ducks," could accomplish little. *What date was fixed as Inauguration Day?*

Vocabulary

president elect: the individual who is elected president but has not yet begun serving his or her term

---

S Skill Practice

Sequencing Point out that several states gave women the right to vote before the federal government did. Have students conduct research and create a time line showing when women gained suffrage in different states. **OL**

D₁ Differentiated Instruction

English Language Learners Students learning the English language are probably not familiar with the expression "lame duck." Explain that it refers to people who have announced they will retire or who have lost reelection but whose original term of office still has time left. They are called "lame ducks" because—like ducks who are injured and cannot fly—they are not able to do much. **ELL**

D₂ Differentiated Instruction

Below Grade Level Direct students' attention to the bottom of the page, where "president elect" is defined. **Ask:** What does "vice president elect" mean? *(a vice president who has been elected but has not yet begun serving his or her term)* **BL**

What It Means

Answer
January 20

Activity: Interdisciplinary Connection

Art and History Have groups find current or historical political cartoons that address lame duck sessions or presidents. Have each group make a scrapbook of cartoons and share the final product with the class. Students should discuss the meanings of the cartoons. Encourage students to create their own political cartoons to add to their books. **OL**

C Critical Thinking

Predicting Consequences This is the first amendment that was ratified that put a time limit on ratification. **Ask:** *Do you expect later amendments to include this language? Why or why not? (Students are likely to answer yes because once the idea was introduced, people would probably want to repeat it.)* OL

R Reading Strategy

Using Context Clues Have students read the note explaining the Twenty-first Amendment. **Ask:** *What does "repeal" mean? (to cancel an earlier law)* OL

Additional Support

provide for the case wherein neither a President elect nor a Vice President elect shall have qualified, declaring who shall then act as President, or the manner in which one who is to act shall be selected, and such person shall act accordingly until a President or Vice President shall have qualified.

Section 4

The Congress may by law provide for the case of the death of any of the persons from whom the House of Representatives may choose a President whenever the right of choice shall have devolved upon them, and for the case of the death of any of the persons from whom the Senate may choose a Vice President whenever the right of choice shall have devolved upon them.

Section 5

Sections 1 and 2 shall take effect on the 15th day of October following the ratification of this article.

Section 6

C This article shall be inoperative unless it shall have been ratified as an amendment to the Constitution by the legislatures of three-fourths of the several States within seven years from the date of its submission.

Amendment XXI

Section 1

The eighteenth article of amendment to the Constitution of the United States is hereby repealed.

Section 2

The transportation or importation into any State, Territory, or Possession of the United States for delivery or use therein of intoxicating liquors, in violation of the laws thereof, is hereby prohibited.

Section 3

This article shall be inoperative unless it shall have been ratified as an amendment to the Constitution by conventions in the several States, as provided in the Constitution, within seven years from the date of the submission hereof to the States by the Congress.

Amendment XXII

Section 1

No person shall be elected to the office of the President more than twice, and no person who has held the office of

What It Means

Repeal of Prohibition Amendment The Twenty-first Amendment (1933) repeals the Eighteenth Amendment. It is the only amendment ever passed to overturn an earlier amendment. It is also the only amendment ratified by special state conventions instead of state legislatures. **R**

What It Means

Limit on Presidential Terms The Twenty-second Amendment (1951) limits presidents to a maximum of two elected terms. It was passed largely as a reaction to Franklin D. Roosevelt's election to four terms between 1933 and 1945.

Activity: Collaborative Learning

Monitoring Organize the class into small groups. Have groups review all of the amendments and create a 20-item True/False Quiz. Have students prepare the tests with an answer key for your approval. Then have groups exchange quizzes. Decide as a class what the reward will be for achieving the highest score. OL

President, or acted as President, for more than two years of a term to which some other person was elected President shall be elected to the office of the President more than once. But this Article shall not apply to any person holding the office of President when this Article was proposed by the Congress, and shall not prevent any person who may be holding the office of President, or acting as President, during the term within which this Article becomes operative from holding the office of President or acting as President during the remainder of such term.

Section 2

This article shall be inoperative unless it shall have been ratified as an amendment to the Constitution by the legislatures of three-fourths of the several States within seven years from the date of its submission to the States by the Congress.

Amendment XXIII

Section 1

The **District** constituting the seat of Government of the United States shall appoint in such manner as the Congress may direct:

A number of electors of President and Vice President equal to the whole number of Senators and Representatives in Congress to which the District would be entitled if it were a State, but in no event more than the least populous State; they shall be in addition to those appointed by the States, but they shall be considered, for the purposes of the election of President and Vice President, to be electors appointed by a State; and they shall meet in the District and perform such duties as provided by the twelfth article of amendment.

Section 2

The Congress shall have power to enforce this article by appropriate legislation.

Amendment XXIV

Section 1

The right of citizens of the United States to vote in any primary or other election for President or Vice President, for electors for President or Vice President, or for Senator or Representative in Congress, shall not be denied or abridged by the United States or any State by reason of failure to pay any poll tax or other tax.

What It Means

Presidential Electors for the District of Columbia The Twenty-third Amendment (1961) allows citizens living in Washington, D.C., to vote for president and vice president, a right previously denied residents of the nation's capital. The District of Columbia now has three presidential electors, the number to which it would be entitled if it were a state.

What It Means

Abolition of Poll Tax The Twenty-fourth Amendment (1964) prohibits poll taxes in federal elections. Prior to the passage of this amendment, some states had used such taxes to keep low-income African Americans from voting. In 1966 the Supreme Court banned poll taxes in state elections as well.

Vocabulary

District: the site of the nation's capital, occupying an area between Maryland and Virginia

R Reading Strategy

Monitoring Make sure that students understand the differences in the limits. **Ask:** How many times can someone be elected as president? *(two)* How many times can someone be elected as president if he or she first is a vice president who succeeds to the presidency and serves two or more years? *(one)* **OL**

W Writing Support

Persuasive Writing Have students write a persuasive essay in which they argue that the two-term limit on presidents is a good or bad idea. Remind them to write a coherent statement of their thesis and have a well-supported conclusion. **OL**

C Critical Thinking

Analyzing Information Point out that although the people of the District of Columbia have presidential electors, they do not have members with full voting rights in the House or Senate. Have students discuss the issue of whether or not this situation is fair for the people of the District. **OL**

Activity: Interdisciplinary Connection

Language Arts Imagine you are a resident of Washington, D.C. You have only recently been allowed to vote in presidential elections (1963). Yet, presently, you do not have representation in Congress. No one represents the District of Columbia in the House or in the Senate. Write a letter to the Supreme Court or to the president, urging them to support you in your fight to win representation in Congress. **OL**

The Constitution of the United States

C Critical Thinking

Making Inferences Ask: Why does Section 4 of the Twenty-fifth Amendment provide a way for someone other than the president to declare that the president cannot serve? *(in case the president is too ill to be able to make the declaration)* **OL**

What It Means

Answer

the president pro tempore of the Senate (the vice president) and the Speaker of the House

Additional Support

What It Means

Presidential Disability and Succession The Twenty-fifth Amendment (1967) established a process for the vice president to take over leadership of the nation when a president is disabled. It also set procedures for filling a vacancy in the office of vice president.

This amendment was used in 1973, when Vice President Spiro Agnew resigned from office after being charged with accepting bribes. President Richard Nixon then appointed Gerald R. Ford as vice president in accordance with the provisions of the 25th Amendment. A year later, President Nixon resigned during the Watergate scandal and Ford became president. President Ford then had to fill the vice presidency, which he had left vacant upon assuming the presidency. He named Nelson A. Rockefeller as vice president. Thus, individuals who had not been elected held both the presidency and the vice presidency. *Whom does the president inform if he or she cannot carry out the duties of the office?*

▲ **President Gerald Ford**

Vocabulary

vacancy: an office or position that is unfilled or unoccupied

---

Section 2

The Congress shall have power to enforce this article by appropriate legislation.

Amendment XXV

Section 1

In case of the removal of the President from office or of his death or resignation, the Vice President shall become President.

Section 2

Whenever there is a **vacancy** in the office of the Vice President, the President shall nominate a Vice President who shall take the office upon confirmation by a majority vote of both Houses of Congress.

Section 3

Whenever the President transmits to the President pro tempore of the Senate and the Speaker of the House of Representatives his written declaration that he is unable to discharge the powers and duties of his office, and until he transmits to them a written declaration to the contrary, such powers and duties shall be discharged by the Vice President as Acting President.

Section 4

Whenever the Vice President and a majority of either the principal officers of the executive departments or of such other body as Congress may by law provide, transmit to the President pro tempore of the Senate and the Speaker of the House of Representatives their written declaration that the President is unable to discharge the powers and duties of his office, the Vice President shall immediately assume the power and duties of the office of Acting President.

Thereafter, when the President transmits to the President pro tempore of the Senate and the Speaker of the House of Representatives his written declaration that no inability exists, he shall resume the powers and duties of his office unless the Vice President and a majority of either the principal officers of the executive department or of such other body as Congress may by law provide, transmit within four days to the President pro tempore of the Senate and the Speaker of the House of Representatives their written declaration that the President is unable to discharge the powers and duties of his office. Thereupon Congress shall decide the issue, assembling within forty-eight hours for that purpose if not in session. If the Congress, within twenty-one days after receipt of the latter written

---

Activity: U.S./World Connections

Assessing On a few occasions, the president of the United States has died, been assassinated, or been disabled. Have students research the times in which the vice president of the United States has had to assume power. **Ask:** How did the people of the United States react? How did the world react? Have students write a one-page report answering the questions. **AL**

declaration, or, if Congress is not in session, within twenty-one days after Congress is required to assemble, determines by two-thirds vote of both Houses that the President is unable to discharge the powers and duties of his office, the Vice President shall continue to discharge the same as Acting President; otherwise, the President shall resume the power and duties of his office.

Amendment XXVI

Section 1

The right of citizens of the United States, who are eighteen years of age or older, to vote shall not be denied or abridged by the United States or by any State on account of age.

Section 2

The Congress shall have power to enforce this article by appropriate legislation.

Amendment XXVII

No law, varying the compensation for the services of Senators and Representatives, shall take effect, until an election of representatives shall have intervened.

What It Means

Eighteen-Year-Old Vote The Twenty-sixth Amendment (1971) guarantees the right to vote to all citizens 18 years of age and older.

What It Means

Restraint on Congressional Salaries The Twenty-seventh Amendment (1992) makes congressional pay raises effective during the term following their passage. James Madison offered the amendment in 1789, but it was never adopted. In 1982 Gregory Watson, then a student at the University of Texas, discovered the forgotten amendment while doing research for a school paper. Watson made the amendment's passage his crusade.

▼ Joint meeting of Congress

W Writing Support

Research Report Writing Have students look up the history of the Twenty-sixth Amendment. Tell them to find out what major issue facing the nation led to its approval. **OL**

C Critical Thinking

Analyzing Information Point out that the turnout in elections among people ages 18 to 21 tends to be low. **Ask:** If so few young people vote in elections, should they lose the right to vote? Have students debate the issue. **OL**

Activity: Collaborative Learning

Making Decisions Have students work with a partner. Students will review the amendments and discuss their meanings. Have students create a T-chart. One column will include a list of amendments they think should be repealed. Students should state the reasons they think the amendments should be repealed. The second column will include a list of rights they think should be added as amendments with the reasons. Finally, have students write a statement that explains why people still challenge the Constitution in present times. Share evaluations with the class. **OL**

UNIT 3 PACING CHART

	Unit 3	Chapter 8	Chapter 9	Chapter 10
Day 1	Unit Opener, Reading History	Chapter Opener, Section 1	Chapter Opener, Section 1	Chapter Opener, Section 1
Day 2		Section 1, Geography & History	Section 2, Section 3	Section 1, America's Literature
Day 3		Section 2, Section 3	Section 4, Visual Summary	Section 2, TIME Notebook
Day 4		Section 3, Visual Summary	Chapter Assessment	Section 3, Visual Summary
Day 5		Chapter Assessment		Chapter Assessment

 Teacher to Teacher

**Gabe Heselton
New Albany
Middle School
New Albany, OH**

Creating a Territorial Expansion Skit Students will work in cooperative groups to research and learn about the territories acquired by the United States during the 1800s. Organize students into cooperative groups of four or five students each, and assign each group one of the territorial acquisitions (Louisiana Purchase, Spanish Cession, Texas Annexation, Oregon Country, Mexican Cession, Gadsden Purchase). Have each group research and find information about how their territory was acquired. Next, have each group write a skit to tell the story about how their land was acquired by the United States. Students should assign each member in their group a role, including that of a narrator. Provide time for students to practice their skits. Then have each group perform their skit in front of the class. Students may use props and/or costumes for their performances.

Author Note

Dear American History Teacher,

The United States Constitution created a nation. It did this by establishing a federal government with authority over the whole country. Citizens from all of the states would vote either directly or indirectly for all of the offices under the Constitution.

The Constitution made it possible for new institutions, values, and ways of thinking to flourish. From 1789 to 1828, America became more democratic. This happened not just because the vote was extended to a majority of white men, but because in the election of 1800, the Federalists and the Republicans explicitly disagreed about such things as freedom of association and popular participation in politics. When Jeffersonians won, they supported one of the most important developments in our history: extending citizenship to all males, whether they were property owners or not. Later, women, freed slaves, and immigrants won the right to vote. The Twenty-Sixth Amendment, which lowered the voting age to 18, was part of this long democratic struggle.

The American economy changed dramatically in this period as well. Once free of Great Britain and united by a constitution that created a national market, men and women could invest their labor and money in a range of activities. Many young people left home to teach school, and from there they discovered a larger world of enterprise. Boys from the North went South as peddlers. Manufacturing firms were built near sources of water power, enabling Americans to make products that they had formerly purchased from England. Slowly, rural America began changing into industrial America, just as today industrial America is giving way to a services-based economy.

A series of popular religious revivals, called the Great Awakening, kindled a fierce religious spirit at this time. The Constitution removed the possibility of having one national, established church, so numerous different denominations sprung up, nurturing the spiritual longings of many people.

Foreign visitors were astonished at the vitality of the Americans, who were creating their own nation and identity. When we look back, we are amazed, too.

Joyce Appleby

Joyce Appleby

Unit Objectives

After studying this unit, students will be able to:

- Explain the challenges that were faced during the first presidential administrations.
- Identify and discuss the importance of various aspects of the Jefferson era.
- Discuss the Industrial Revolution and its effects, explain how sectionalism developed, and summarize the Monroe Doctrine.

Introducing the Unit

Analyzing As students prepare to study the unit, ask them to think about how a nation grows. **Ask:** How do you think a country develops? *(Students might note that a country can grow in terms of government organization or policies, expansion of land areas, or through trade and economics.)* Discuss with students that they will learn how the young United States overcame challenges in developing a new government, fighting another war, expanding its territory, and developing industries and agriculture. **OL**

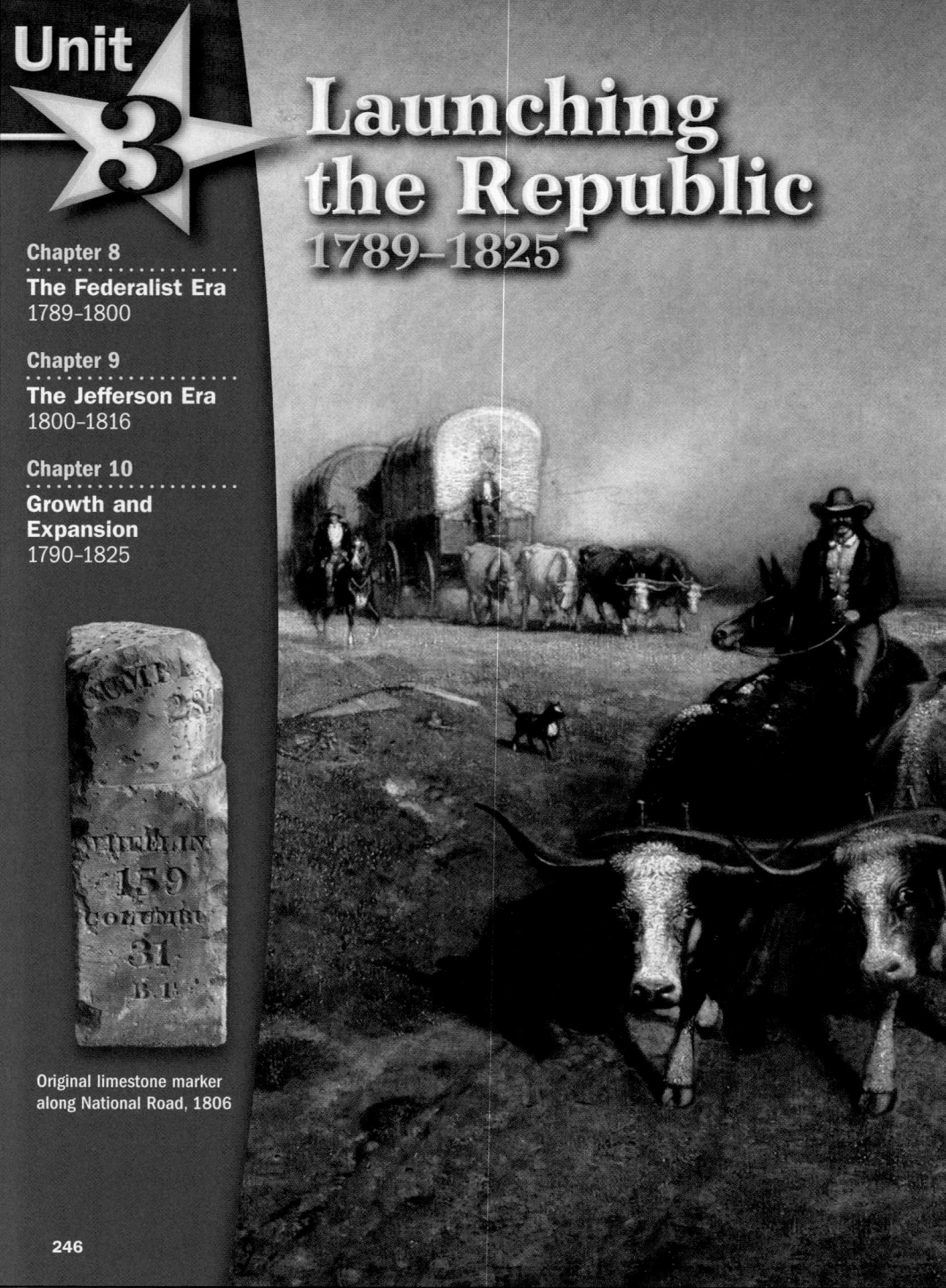

Unit 3

Chapter 8
The Federalist Era
1789–1800

Chapter 9
The Jefferson Era
1800–1816

Chapter 10
Growth and Expansion
1790–1825

Launching the Republic
1789–1825

Original limestone marker along National Road, 1806

246

Activity: Why It Matters

Why Study Launching the Republic? Tell students what they can expect to learn in the upcoming unit. **Ask:** How are government leaders chosen in the United States? *(Students should answer that open elections are held, and people can vote for the person they think is the best candidate.)* How do you think the structure of our government was created? Did it just evolve over time, or was it created through laws? *(Students may answer that our government's structure was probably created through decisions and laws that were put into effect as the result of the people's needs.)* As students study the unit, have them describe in their notebooks the ways in which the U.S. government came into being. **OL**

"Peace, commerce, and honest friend-ship with all nations, entangling alliances with none . . ."

—Thomas Jefferson

Ships of the Plains by Samuel Colman

247

Connect to Past Learning

Launching the Republic In the previous unit, students learned about the causes of the American Revolution and the major battles and strategies, as well as the imme-diate steps taken after the war to build a new nation. In this unit, students will study the challenges the new American govern-ment faced and how foreign affairs influ-enced the policies of the United States.

More About the Image

Visual Literacy This painting, by Samuel Colman, currently hangs in the Union League Club in New York City, where Col-man was a member. Colman was an Ameri-can painter who studied throughout Europe but who remains popular for his paintings of the early West. He was one of the found-ers and the first president of the American Water Color Society. The covered wagon train symbolizes frontier expansion of "civi-lized" societies into the wilderness regions inhabited by people who were considered "backward and savage." The people of the frontier illustrate the rugged individualism that is part of our national identity. Discuss with students why the painting is called "Ships of the Plains."

Why **Summarizing Information** Is **Important**

Summarizing information using the five *W* questions helps students pull smaller, more easily digestible amounts of information from large, complicated pieces of text. Being able to summarize helps students to extract important points from their reading, therefore helping with retention of the most relevant information.

Learn It!

Use the summary process in reverse: Organize students into groups of three or four, and ask them to create a short story about a person (man, woman, or child) who lived in colonial times.

Tell students to begin by assigning a scribe who will write the five *W* questions on a piece of paper and who will then record the group's decisions about *who* this person was, *when* and *where* the person lived, *what* he or she did, and *why*. From there, ask students to add some more descriptive details about this person and his or her life.

At the end of the allotted time period, ask a member of each group to tell the group's story. **OL**

Practice It!

Students should list the following as answers to the five *W* questions:

Who? Eli Whitney

What? Invented the cotton gin

When? 1793

Where? Massachusetts

Why? To quickly remove seeds from cotton fiber **OL**

Summarizing Information

Learn It!

When you summarize information, you recount key points from the text. As you read to summarize, stop occasionally to answer the 5W questions in your own words: *Who? What? Where? When? Why?*

Who? Thomas Pinckney

What? Negotiated Pinckney's Treaty

Where? Spain

When? 1795

Why? To settle differences between the U.S. and Spain

—from Chapter 8, p. 263

Spanish leaders feared that the United States and Great Britain would work together against them in North America. Thomas Pinckney was sent to Spain to settle the differences between the United States and Spain. In 1795 **Pinckney's Treaty** gave the Americans free navigation of the Mississippi River and the right to trade at New Orleans.

Practice It!

Read the paragraphs and answer the 5W questions on another sheet of paper.

—from Chapter 10, p. 306

In 1793 **Eli Whitney** of Massachusetts invented the cotton gin. The **cotton gin** was a simple machine that quickly and efficiently removed the seeds from the cotton fiber.

Whitney also started using **interchangeable parts.** These were identical machine parts that could be put together quickly to make a complete product. These parts also made machine repair easier. Interchangeable parts allowed for the production of different kinds of goods on a large scale. This reduced the price of the goods.

Who? _____

What? _____

Where? _____

When? _____

Why? _____

Reading Strategy — Read to Write

Summarizing Information Asking the five *W* questions can help students identify the most important pieces of a reading, which, in turn, will help with their overall comprehension of the class material. Assign students a subsection in one of the chapters in this unit and have them ask, and then answer, the five *W* questions for each paragraph. Then have students use the answers to create a summary for this subsection. **BL**

Academic Vocabulary Preview

Listed below are the academic vocabulary words and their definitions that you will come across as you study Unit 3. Practice It! will help you study the words and definitions.

Academic Vocabulary	Definition	Practice It!
Chapter 8 The Federalist Era		
uniform (YOO · nuh · FAWRM) *p. 255*	identical; unchanging	**Identify** *the term from Chapter 8 that best completes the sentences.*
accumulate (uh · KYOO · muh · LAYT) *p. 256*	to collect; to gather together	**1.** Many citizens prefer a _____ system of law that is identical in each state.
challenge (CHA · luhnj) *p. 261*	to try to get or obtain	
maintain (mayn · TAYN) *p. 261*	to keep; to uphold	**2.** Avoiding foreign conflicts was a _____ to the new American government.
resolve (rih · ZAHLV) *p. 269*	to bring to an end	**3.** Governments often send delegates to help _____ disputes with other countries.
principle (PRIHN · suh · puhl) *p. 270*	a basic or fundamental reason, truth, or law	
Chapter 9 The Jefferson Era		
similar (SIH · muh · luhr) *p. 278*	having common qualities	**Identify** *the term from Chapter 9 that best matches the underlined term.*
conflict (KAHN · FLIHKT) *p. 279*	a disagreement	**4.** Thomas Jefferson surrounded himself with those with <u>nearly the same</u> views..
purchase (PUHR · chuhs) *p. 284*	something bought and paid for	
authority (uh · THAHR · uh · tee) *p. 284*	power to decide; power over others	**5.** The president of the United States has the <u>power</u> to make certain decisions.
react (ree · AKT) *p. 289*	to respond	**6.** The size of the United States doubled with the <u>gain</u> of the Louisiana Territory.
restriction (rih · STRIHK · shuhn) *p. 291*	a limit	
underestimate (UHN · duhr · EHS · tuh · MAYT) *p. 295*	to misjudge	
goal (GOHL) *p. 297*	an aim; a purpose	
Chapter 10 Growth and Expansion		
contribute (kuhn · TRIH · byuht) *p. 305*	to help to cause an event or situation	**Choose** *the word that best matches the meaning of each vocabulary term listed below.*
element (EH · luh · muhnt) *p. 307*	one part of a larger whole	**7. contribute** **9. element**
reveal (rih · VEEL) *p. 313*	to show something that was hidden	**a.** help **a.** routine
region (REE · juhn) *p. 314*	a geographic area with similar features	**b.** convince **b.** part
intense (ihn · TEHNS) *p. 322*	exhibiting strong feeling	**c.** create **c.** whole
internal (ihn · TUHR · nuhl) *p. 322*	within a location such as a nation or state	**8. reveal** **10. region**
		a. show **a.** map
		b. hide **b.** globe
		c. order **c.** area

Academic Vocabulary Preview

Ask students to choose three vocabulary words from each chapter of the unit and write a sentence for each that relates to the chapter discussion. Encourage students to work from memory rather than flipping back through the chapter for the context.

After the allotted time is up, read each term and definition aloud. Invite students to volunteer to read their sentences when a term they used is called. **ELL**

Practice It!

Answers

1. uniform
2. challenge
3. resolve
4. similar
5. authority
6. purchase
7. a
8. a
9. b
10. c

Reading Strategy — Read to Write

Summarizing Explain to students that summarizing is a large part of everyday life. When they e-mail a sick friend to tell him what he missed in class or they relate a funny story about their weekend to a classmate, they are summarizing. Usually they are, even unconsciously, answering most or all of the five *W* questions in the process. Ask students to write a page describing a TV sitcom they recently watched, either on network primetime or a cable network such as Nickelodeon. Remind them to use the five *W* questions but to try to catch important details while still being concise. **BL**

249

Chapter Planning Guide

8

Levels BL	OL	AL	ELL		Resources	Chapter Opener	Section 1	Section 2	Section 3	Chapter Assess
					FOCUS					
BL	OL	AL	ELL	🖨	Daily Test Practice Transparencies		8–1	8–2	8–3	
					TEACH					
	OL	AL		📁	Geography and History Activity, URB			p. 31		
BL	OL		ELL	📁	Time Line Skills Activity, URB			p. 34		
BL	OL	AL	ELL	📁	Writing Skills Activity, URB				p. 23	
BL	OL	AL	ELL	📁	Content Vocabulary Activity, URB		p. 17	p. 17	p. 17	
BL	OL	AL	ELL	📁	Academic Vocabulary Activity, URB		p. 19	p. 19	p. 19	
	OL	AL		📁	Citizenship and Decision-Making Activity, URB		p. 3			
BL			ELL	📁	Social Studies Skills Activity, URB				p. 25	
BL	OL	AL	ELL	📁	Differentiated Instruction Activity, URB			p. 27		
BL	OL	AL	ELL	📁	Critical Thinking Skills Activity, URB			p. 29		
BL	OL	AL	ELL	📁	Linking Past and Present Activity, URB		p. 33			
	OL	AL		📁	Primary Source Readings, URB		p. 21			
BL	OL	AL	ELL	📁	School-to-Home Connection Activity, URB		p. 35	p. 35	p. 35	
BL	OL		ELL	📁	Guided Reading Activity, URB*		p. 39	p. 40	p. 41	
BL	OL		ELL	📁	Reading Essentials and Note-Taking Guide*		p. 79	p. 82	p. 85	
BL	OL	AL	ELL	🖨	Lesson Transparencies		8A	8B	8C	
	OL			📁	American Biographies		p. 10			
BL	OL	AL	ELL	📁	Outline Map Resource Book	p. 7				

Note: Please refer to the *Unit Resource Book: Launching the Republic* for this chapter's URB materials.

* Also available in Spanish

Levels					Resources	Chapter Opener	Section 1	Section 2	Section 3	Chapter Assess
BL	OL	AL	ELL							
TEACH *(continued)*										
BL	OL	AL	ELL		NGS US Desk Map		✓	✓	✓	
BL	OL	AL	ELL		American Literature Library		✓	✓	✓	
BL	OL	AL	ELL		Writer's Guidebook		✓	✓	✓	
	OL	AL			American History Primary Source Document Library CD-ROM		✓	✓	✓	✓
BL	OL	AL	ELL		American Music: Hits Through History	✓	✓	✓	✓	
BL	OL	AL	ELL		StudentWorks™ Plus CD	✓	✓	✓	✓	✓
	OL	AL			Section Spotlight Videos		✓	✓	✓	
BL	OL	AL	ELL		Writing Process Transparencies		✓	✓	✓	✓
BL	OL	AL	ELL		Presentation Plus! With MindJogger Checkpoint CD	✓	✓	✓	✓	✓
ASSESS										
BL	OL	AL	ELL		Quizzes and Tests		p. 71	p. 72	p. 73	pp. 75, 77, 79
BL	OL	AL	ELL		Authentic Assessment With Rubrics		p. 8			
BL	OL	AL	ELL		Standardized Test Practice					p. 15
BL	OL	AL	ELL		*ExamView® Assessment Suite* CD-ROM*		8–1	8–2	8–3	Ch. 8
CLOSE										
BL			ELL		Reteaching Activity, URB*		p. 37	p. 37	p. 37	p. 37
BL	OL		ELL		Reading and Study Skills Foldables Activity	p. 64	p. 64	p. 64	p. 64	p. 64
BL	OL	AL	ELL		*The American Journey* in Graphic Novel					p. 51
BL			ELL		Reading Strategies and Activities for the Social Studies Classroom		✓	✓	✓	
BL	OL	AL	ELL		Graphic Organizer Transparencies & Strategies		✓	✓	✓	

TeacherWorks *Plus*
All-In-One Planner and Resource Center

- Interactive Lesson Planner
- Interactive Teacher Edition
- Fully editable blackline masters
- Section Spotlight Videos Launch

- Differentiated Lesson Plans
- Printable reports of daily assignments
- Standards Tracking System

Professional Development Resources

- Strategies for Success
- Building Academic Vocabulary
- Success With English Learners DVD
- Differentiated Instruction Strategies DVD
- Teaching Literacy Strategies in Social Studies DVD
- Assessment DVD
- Standards-Based Instruction DVD

Using Study Central™

Build Vocabulary

Technology Product

The **Build Vocabulary** tab on the Study Central™ Web site allows you to reinforce the content vocabulary and academic vocabulary in each section of a chapter. Build Vocabulary

- provides a definition, an example of its correct usage, and a textbook page reference for each glossary term;
- allows students to test their understanding of the content vocabulary in each section through Flying Answers, an interactive vocabulary activity.

Objectives

Build Vocabulary helps students

- build vocabulary skills;
- reinforce their understanding of the content and academic vocabulary in each section.

Steps

- Locate the Web page for your textbook on the Glencoe Web site glencoe.com.
- Click on **Study Central™** under *Textbook Resources*.
- On the Study Central™ Web site (a new window will have opened), select a chapter and section using the drop-down arrows and click **Enter.**
- Click on the **Main Ideas** tab and then on the **Build Vocabulary** tab.
- Under the **Content Vocabulary** tab and the **Academic Vocabulary** tab, click on each term and discuss its definition, proper usage, and location in the textbook.
- On the **Key Vocabulary** tab, click on **Flying Answers** to engage students in the interactive game.

History ONLINE at glencoe.com

	Student	Teacher	Parent
Media Center			
• Student Edition Audio	●		
• Spanish Summaries	●		
• Section Spotlight Videos	●	●	
Social Studies Online Learning Center			
Classroom Tools			
• Multi-Language Glossaries	●	●	●
• Teaching Today		●	
• TIME Current Events	●	●	●
• Beyond the Textbook	●	●	
The American Journey **Online Learning Center**			
• Study-to-Go™	●	●	●
• Study Central™	●	●	●
• Chapter Overview	●	●	
• Concepts in Motion	●	●	
• ePuzzles and Games	●	●	
• Literature Connections	●	●	
• Online Student Edition	●	●	●
• Self-Check Quizzes	●	●	●
• Student Web Activities	●	●	
• Vocabulary eFlashcards	●	●	
• Web Activity Lesson Plans	●	●	●
• Vocabulary PuzzleMaker	●	●	●

- **Timed Readings Plus in Social Studies** helps students increase their reading rate and fluency while maintaining comprehension. The 400-word passages are similar to those found on state and national assessments.

- **Reading in the Content Area: Social Studies** concentrates on six essential reading skills that help students better comprehend what they read. The book includes 75 high-interest nonfiction passages written at increasing levels of difficulty.

- **Reading Social Studies** includes strategic reading instruction and vocabulary support in Social Studies content for ELLs and native speakers of English.

- **Content Vocabulary Workout** (Grades 6–8) accelerates reading comprehension through focused vocabulary development. Social Studies content vocabulary comes from the glossaries of Glencoe's Middle School Social Studies texts.

www.jamestowneducation.com

Index to National Geographic Magazine:

The following article relates to this chapter:

- *"Zip USA: Washington,"* Angus Phillips, July 2002.

National Geographic Society Products

To order the following, call National Geographic at 1-800-368-2728:

National Geographic Atlas of the World (Book)

Access National Geographic's new dynamic MapMachine Web site and other geography resources at:

www.nationalgeographic.com

www.nationalgeographic.com/mapmachine

Use this database to search more than 30,000 titles to create a customized reading list for your students.

- Reading lists can be organized by students' reading level, author, genre, theme, or area of interest.

- The database provides Degrees of Reading Power™ (DRP) and Lexile™ readability scores for all selections.

- A brief summary of each selection is included.

Leveled reading suggestions for this chapter:

For students at a Grade 6 reading level:
- *Benjamin Franklin: American Statesman, Scientist, and Writer,* by Bruce Durost Fish and Becky Fish

For students at a Grade 7 reading level:
- *Who Is Carrie?,* by James Collier and Christopher Collier

For students at a Grade 8 reading level:
- *George Washington,* by Genevieve Foster

For students at a Grade 9 reading level:
- *18th Century Clothing,* by Bobbie Kalman

For students at a Grade 10 reading level:
- *George Washington and the Founding of a Nation,* by Albert Marrin

The following videotape program is available from Glencoe as a supplement to the chapter:

- **Presidential Memorials: The Great American Monuments** (ISBN 1-56-501641-6)

To order, call Glencoe at 1-800-334-7344. To find classroom resources to accompany the video, check the following home pages:

A&E Television: www.aetv.com

The History Channel: www.history.com

Chapter Objectives

After studying this chapter, students will be able to:

- Identify the precedents that George Washington established as the first president of the United States.
- Discuss challenges the United States faced during Washington's administration.
- Explain how the Federalist and Republican Parties formed and identify issues about which they disagreed.

Motivating Activity

Comparing and Contrasting Students will learn that the country's Founders did not always agree about the roles of government. They had different opinions about how strong the federal government should be and what rights states and citizens should have. **Ask:** *Do you think disagreements among a nation's leaders have a positive or negative impact on the country? (Some students might say that disagreements have a positive effect because many solutions can be discussed and the best one chosen. Others might say that disagreements weaken a country because little gets done when leaders argue too much.) Can you think of an issue about which the country's leaders disagree today? (Students might mention wars, taxes, and health care.)* **OL**

Previewing the Essential Questions

As you begin teaching each section, use these questions and activities to help students focus on the Essential Questions.

Chapter 8

The Federalist Era 1789–1800

Election scene, Detroit, early 1800s

PRESIDENTS
U.S. Events
World Events

GEORGE WASHINGTON

★ **1789**
- Washington becomes first president
- Judiciary Act passes

★ **1789**
- Lavoisier's table of 33 elements published
- The French Revolution begins

1790

★ **1791**
Bill of Rights added to Constitution

1792

★ **1792**
France declares war on Austria

250   Chapter 8

Section ★ 1

The First President Ask: *How might the first leader of a new nation shape future leaders' roles? (by starting traditions, setting limits on powers, and showing how duties will be performed)* Tell students that in Section 1 they will learn how George Washington set some standards for later presidents. **OL**

Section ★ 2

Early Challenges Ask: *What kinds of challenges might a new country face? (learning to deal with other nations, setting rules for the new government, and protecting citizens)* Explain to students that Section 2 discusses challenges the United States faced during Washington's administration. **OL**

Section 1: The First President

Essential Question What were the precedents that Washington established as the first president of the United States?

Section 2: Early Challenges

Essential Question What challenges did the United States face during Washington's administration?

Section 3: The First Political Parties

Essential Question How did the Federalist and Republican Parties form, and on what issues did they disagree?

History ONLINE
Chapter Overview Visit glencoe.com and click on **Chapter 8—Chapter Overviews** to preview chapter information.

FOLDABLES **Study Organizer**

Organizing Information
Make this Foldable to organize what you learn about early political parties.

Step 1 Fold a piece of 11" x 17" paper in half.

Step 2 Fold up the bottom edge two inches. Staple the outer edges of the flap to create pockets.

Step 3 Label each side as shown. Use the pockets to hold index cards or quarter sheets of paper.

Reading and Writing
As you read the chapter, list leaders and key ideas for the Federalist and Republican Parties.

Time Line Activity

If you have not already done so, have students review the time line. **Ask:** What years are covered in this chapter? *(1789–1800)* Which two presidents served in office during this time period? *(George Washington and John Adams)* When was the Bill of Rights added to the Constitution? *(1791)* Have students refer to the "World" section of the time line to identify important events in the rest of the world during the years covered. *(Answers may include the French Revolution, development of the smallpox vaccine, and discovery of the Rosetta stone.)*

FOLDABLES **Study Organizer** **Dinah Zike's Foldables**

Purpose This Foldable helps students visually organize information about the first political parties. The completed Foldable will help them prepare for assessment.

More Foldable activities for this chapter can be found in *Dinah Zike's Reading and Study Skills Foldables.*

History ONLINE
Introduce students to chapter content and key terms by having them access the **Chapter Overview** at glencoe.com.

John Jay ▶

★ **1794** Whiskey Rebellion

★ **1795** Nation's first chief justice, John Jay, retires from court

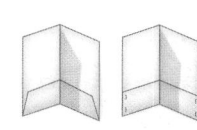
JOHN ADAMS

★ **1798**
• Alien and Sedition Acts pass
• XYZ affair

★ **1800** Congress meets in Capitol for first time

1794 ———— **1796** ———— **1798**

★ **1793** The Louvre opens as public museum in Paris

★ **1794** Slavery abolished in all French colonies

★ **1796** Jenner develops smallpox vaccine

★ **1799** Rosetta stone is discovered

Chapter 8 251

Section 3

The First Political Parties Ask: Why do you think political parties exist? *(Political parties allow people to share ideas and values for the purpose of trying to influence government policies in their favor.)* Tell students that Section 3 will explore how the first political parties—the Federalists and the Republicans—formed and on which issues they disagreed. **OL**

Focus

Bellringer
Daily Test Practice Transparency 8–1

Reading Guide
Answers to Graphic:
Department of State: Thomas Jefferson; **Department of the Treasury:** Alexander Hamilton; **Department of War:** Henry Knox

Section Spotlight Video

To learn more about Washington's presidency, have students watch the Section Spotlight Video "The First President."

Resource Manager

Section 1

Essential Question
What were the precedents that Washington established as the first president of the United States?

Reading Guide

Content Vocabulary

precedent *(p. 253)*   bond *(p. 256)*
cabinet   unconstitutional
 (p. 253)   *(p. 257)*
national debt *(p. 255)* tariff *(p. 257)*

Academic Vocabulary

uniform *(p. 255)*   accumulate *(p. 256)*

Key People and Events
Thomas Jefferson *(p. 253)*
Alexander Hamilton *(p. 253)*
John Jay *(p. 255)*
Bill of Rights *(p. 255)*

Reading Strategy
Taking Notes As you read, use a diagram like the one below to organize the departments and their secretaries under Washington's authority.

Executive Branch of Government Under Washington

ILLINOIS STANDARDS
The American Journey

14.A Understand and explain basic principles of the United States government.

14.F.3b Describe how United States political ideas and traditions were instituted in the Constitution and the Bill of Rights.

15.E.3a Identify the types of taxes levied by differing levels of governments (e.g., income tax, sales tax, property tax).

16.B.3c (US) Describe the way the Constitution has changed over time as a result of amendments and Supreme Court decisions.

The First President

American Diary

George Washington faced many challenges and had to make choices when he became the nation's first president. He understood that the destiny of the new nation was in the hands of the people. At his first inauguration, Washington said: "The preservation of the sacred fire of liberty and the destiny of the republican model of government are justly . . . staked on the experiment entrusted to the hands of the American people."

—*from Washington's First Inaugural Address*

 R	Reading Strategies	 C	Critical Thinking	 D	Differentiated Instruction	 W	Writing Support	 S	Skill Practice
	Teacher Edition • Prior Know., p. 253 • Summarizing, p. 257 **Additional Resources** • Guid. Read., URB p. 39 • Content Vocab., URB p. 17 • Acad. Vocab., URB p. 19 • Read. Ess., p. 79 • Pri. Source, URB p. 21		**Teacher Edition** • Drawing Concl., p. 253 • Ident. Central Issues, p. 254 • Analyz. Info., p. 255 **Additional Resources** • Quizzes and Tests, p. 71 • Link. Past, URB p. 33 • Authentic Assess., p. 8		**Teacher Edition** • ELL, p. 254 **Additional Resources** • School-to-Home, URB p. 35 • Reteaching Act., URB p. 37		**Teacher Edition** • Persuasive Writing, p. 255 • Personal Writing, p. 256 **Additional Resources** • Citizen. & Dec. Mak. Skills, URB p. 3		**Additional Resources** • Daily Test Pract. Transp. 8-1 • Lesson Transp. 8A

President Washington

Main Idea President Washington and the new Congress had to make many decisions about the structure of the new government.

History and You If you were founding our nation's government, what do you think would be most important? Read about the choices that Washington and the new Congress had to make.

On April 30, 1789, George Washington took the oath of office as the first president of the United States under the federal Constitution. (Several presidents served under the Articles of Confederation.) John Adams became vice president.

Washington knew that the **precedents,** or traditions, he established would shape the future of the United States. "No slip will pass unnoticed," he said. With Congress, Washington would create departments within the executive branch, set up the court system, and add the Bill of Rights to the Constitution.

The First Congress

During the summer of 1789, Congress set up three departments and two offices in the executive branch of government. Washington chose prominent political figures to head them. The State Department, led by **Thomas Jefferson,** handled relations with other nations. The Department of the Treasury, led by **Alexander Hamilton,** handled financial matters. Henry Knox provided for the nation's defense as the secretary of the Department of War. To handle the government's legal affairs, Washington chose Edmund Randolph as attorney general. The office of postmaster general also was established.

The three department heads and the attorney general became known as the **cabinet.** However, Congress debated how much power the president should have over the cabinet. Senators were evenly divided in voting on the issue.

Vice President John Adams broke the tie. He voted to allow the president the authority to dismiss cabinet officers without Senate approval. This decision strengthened the president's position and it established his authority over the executive branch.

Judiciary Act of 1789

The first Congress also had to decide how to set up the nation's judicial system.

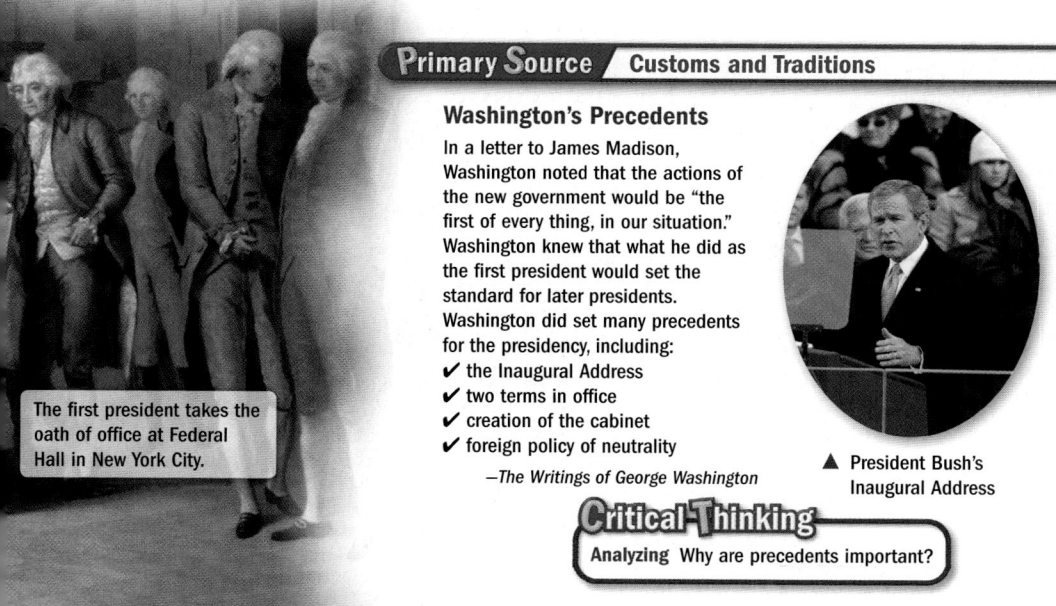

The first president takes the oath of office at Federal Hall in New York City.

Primary Source | Customs and Traditions

Washington's Precedents

In a letter to James Madison, Washington noted that the actions of the new government would be "the first of every thing, in our situation." Washington knew that what he did as the first president would set the standard for later presidents. Washington did set many precedents for the presidency, including:

✔ the Inaugural Address
✔ two terms in office
✔ creation of the cabinet
✔ foreign policy of neutrality

—*The Writings of George Washington*

▲ President Bush's Inaugural Address

Critical Thinking

Analyzing Why are precedents important?

Creating a Three-Panel Display

Step 1: Creating a Pictorial Display Groups of students will prepare a three-panel display of images about the United States during early administrations.

Essential Question: What were the precedents that Washington established as the first president of the United States?

Directions Organize students into groups. Tell them that they will be creating three-panel visual displays about the United States during Washington's and Adams's administrations. They should begin by collecting or creating pictures, maps, diagrams, time lines, facts, and so on about Washington's precedents. Together, group members should prepare the images for display and include informative captions.

Teach

R Reading Strategy

Activating Prior Knowledge Have students write down anything they know about George Washington as president. **Ask:** Based on what you already know about George Washington, what do you think you might learn about him in this section? *(Answers may refer to his leadership in the early stages of the government as well as what effect he had on the office of the presidency.)* **OL**

C Critical Thinking

Drawing Conclusions Ask: Which of Washington's precedents do you think are most important to modern presidents and why? *(Answers might include the creation of the cabinet, which helps the president do his or her job, and two terms in office, which keeps the president's power in check.)* **AL**

Primary Source

Critical Thinking Answer
Precedents start traditions and shape the way people do things in the future.

Hands-On Chapter Project
Step 1

Have the groups work on the first panel, which should be about how Washington shaped the office of the presidency, in class.

Determining Cause and Effect As a class, discuss how George Washington's decisions and actions helped shape the office of the presidency for future American leaders. **Ask:** Did Washington start beneficial traditions? **OL**

(Chapter Project continued in Section 2)

Teach

C Critical Thinking

Identifying Central Issues Have students write down which amendment they think was most important to the people of the United States in 1791. Then ask them to write down which amendment they think is most important to the people of the United States today. **Ask:** *Are the two amendments you wrote down the same or different? Explain your choice(s). (Answers will vary. Help students distinguish between early issues that are still important today and those that were of greater concern to people of the early United States.)* **AL**

D Differentiated Instruction

English Language Learners Ask students to choose one amendment and rewrite it in their own words. **Ask:** *Which part of the amendment was the most difficult for you to express? (Answers will vary. Discuss with students that difficulties with unfamiliar vocabulary may be different from difficulties with unfamiliar concepts.)* **ELL**

Answers

Bill of Rights

Ratified December 15, 1791, the first 10 amendments to the U.S. Constitution state specific guarantees of individual freedoms. These rights and protections help Americans define the meaning of liberty. Examples are given below.

▲ The Bill of Rights

> **I** Congress shall make no law respecting an establishment of religion, or prohibiting the free exercise thereof; or **abridging** the freedom of speech, or of the press; or the right of the people peaceably to assemble, and to petition the Government for a **redress** of grievances.
>
> **IV** The right of the people to be secure in their persons, houses, papers, and effects, against unreasonable searches and seizures, shall not be violated, and no **Warrants** shall issue, but upon probable cause, supported by Oath or affirmation, and particularly describing the place to be searched, and the persons or things to be seized.
>
> **VI** In all criminal prosecutions, the accused shall enjoy the right to a speedy and public trial, by an impartial jury of the State and district wherein the crime shall have been committed, which district shall have been previously ascertained by law, and to be informed of the nature and cause of the accusation; to be confronted with the witnesses against him; to have compulsory process for obtaining witnesses in his favor, and to have the Assistance of Counsel for his defence.
>
> **X** The powers not delegated to the United States by the Constitution, nor prohibited by it to the States, are reserved to the States respectively, or to the people.

I: The First Amendment combines the five separate freedoms of religion, speech, press, assembly, and petition, or formally requesting changes of the government.

IV: The Fourth Amendment protects Americans against "unreasonable searches and seizures." No soldier, government agent, or police officer can search your home or take your property without probable, or a valid, cause.

VI: In the United States of America, the government cannot imprison people without announcing a charge, keep them imprisoned without a trial, hold a trial in secret, or stop them from seeing a lawyer.

X: This amendment is meant to prevent the federal government from abusing its power by going beyond what the Constitution allows.

VOCABULARY
abridging (uh·BRIHJ·ing): reducing
redress (rih·DREHS): fair adjustment
warrants (WAWR·uhnts): documents granting authorization

Critical Thinking

1. **Differentiating** How is freedom of speech different from freedom of the press?
2. **Making Connections** Following the terrorist attacks of September 11, 2001, many have called for increased police powers. Do you think the rights listed in the Fourth and Sixth Amendments should apply to Americans suspected of terrorism?
3. **Evaluating** Why do you think the Tenth Amendment is important?

Answers

1. Freedom of speech concerns the right of individuals to express themselves, especially their disagreement with or disapproval of government policies. Freedom of the press overlaps freedom of speech but also includes the right to publish news and information free from government interference.
2. Students' answers will vary, but they may note that many believe that the extraordinary threat of terrorism makes such measures necessary. Others may say that sacrificing liberty for security is not necessary.
3. Students may say that reserving certain powers to the states or to the people prevents the federal government from becoming too powerful.

Disagreements arose between those favoring a **uniform,** or standard, national legal system and those favoring state courts. The two groups reached a compromise in the Judiciary Act of 1789 with which Congress established a federal court system with 13 district courts and three circuit courts to serve the nation. State laws remained, but the federal courts had the power to reverse state decisions.

The Supreme Court would be the final authority on many issues. President Washington nominated **John Jay** to lead the Supreme Court as chief justice. The Senate approved Jay's nomination. With the Judiciary Act, Congress took the first steps toward creating a strong and independent national judiciary.

The Bill of Rights

Americans had long feared strong central governments. They fought a revolution to get rid of one and did not want to replace it with another. Many people insisted that the Constitution needed to include guarantees of civil liberties. Some states supported the Constitution on the condition that a bill of rights be added in the near future to guarantee personal liberties.

To fulfill promises to these states, James Madison introduced a set of amendments during the first session of Congress. Congress passed 12 amendments, and the states ratified 10 of them. In December 1791, these 10 amendments, the **Bill of Rights,** were added to the Constitution.

The Bill of Rights limits the powers of government. Its purpose is to protect the rights of individual liberty, such as freedom of speech, and the rights of persons accused of crimes, including trial by jury. With the Tenth Amendment, Madison hoped to use the states as an important line of defense against a too-powerful national government. 📖 *(See the Appendix for the Bill of Rights.)*

✓ **Reading Check** **Identifying** What did the Judiciary Act do?

The New Country's Economy

Main Idea The new country's economy developed under the guidance of Alexander Hamilton.

C **History and You** Have you ever borrowed money from a family member or one of your friends? By doing so, you acquired a debt and had to figure out how to pay it back. Hamilton faced a similar challenge with the nation's debt.

．．．．．．．．．．．．．．．．．．．．．．．．．．．．．．．．．．

President Washington rarely proposed laws and almost always approved the bills that Congress passed. The first president concentrated mainly on foreign affairs and military matters. Washington left the government's economic policies to his dynamic secretary of the treasury, Alexander Hamilton. When Washington appointed him to the position, Hamilton was only 34 years old. Yet he had bold plans and definite policies to deal with the country's finances.

The new nation faced serious financial problems. The **national debt**—the amount of money owed by the nation's government—was growing. Hamilton tried to find a way to improve the government's financial reputation and strengthen the nation at the same time.

Hamilton's Plan **W**

Days after he took office, Hamilton was asked by the House of Representatives to prepare a plan for the "adequate support of public credit." This meant that the United States needed a way to borrow money for its government, its industrial development, and its commercial activity. How good the government's credit would be in the future depended on how well it could pay back the money it currently owed.

In 1790 Hamilton made his proposal. He said the new government should pay off the millions of dollars in debts owed by the Confederation government to other countries and to individual American citizens. The states fought for the nation's independence, Hamilton argued, so the national government should pay for the cost of their help.

C Critical Thinking

Analyzing Information Ask students to think about what it might be like if there were no federal court system and each state ran its courts differently. **Ask:** Why is having a uniform national legal system a good idea? *(It ensures that citizens in each state have equal rights and protection under the law.)* **AL**

W Writing Support

Persuasive Writing Have students write a short persuasive speech that supports or rejects Alexander Hamilton's argument that the new government should pay off the debts the Confederation government owed to other countries and to American citizens. If time permits, have volunteers deliver their speeches to the class. **OL**

✓ **Reading Check** **Answer:** It established a federal court system with 13 district courts and three circuit courts.

Differentiated Instruction

Leveled Activities

BL Guided Reading Activity, URB p. 39

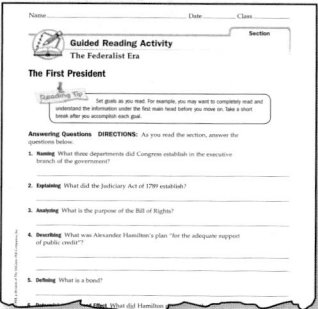

OL Primary Source Reading Activity, URB p. 21

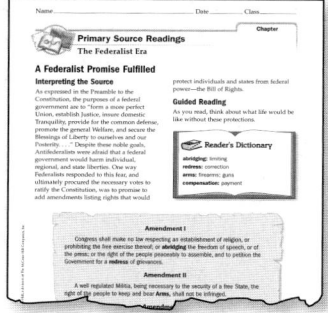

AL Citizenship and Decision Making, URB p. 3

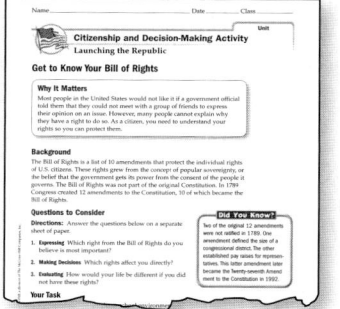

ELL Content Vocabulary Activity, URB p. 17

255

W Writing Support

Personal Writing Have students take on the role of Alexander Hamilton and write a diary entry discussing his compromise plan with Southern leaders. Students should address the reasons Hamilton and the leaders wanted to work together and what each side hoped to gain. **OL**

Economics & History

Critical Thinking Answers

1. The American hat would sell better because the British hat would cost more with the tariff added to its price.

2. Tariffs might anger the British because they would decrease the sale of British goods in the United States.

Economics & History

Protective Tariffs *In the late 1700s, American industries lacked the experience to make goods efficiently. As a result, their production costs were higher than those of their foreign competitors. A protective tariff would raise the price of imported products, helping American companies compete.*

Hat made in Britain   Hat made in U.S.

$7 $6

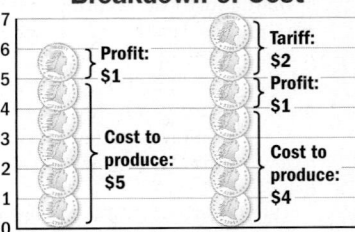

Breakdown of Cost

	U.S.	Britain
	Profit: $1	Tariff: $2
		Profit: $1
	Cost to produce: $5	Cost to produce: $4

▲ A British-made hat would cost $5 in Britain. The same hat made in America is $6. With a $2 tariff, Americans pay $7 for the imported British hat but only $6 for the American-made hat.

Critical Thinking

1. **Drawing Conclusions** Which hat would sell more with the tariff? Why?

2. **Speculating** How might the issue of tariffs impact U.S. relations with Britain?

Hamilton also believed that federal payment of state debts would give the states a strong interest in the success of the national government.

Opposition to the Plan

Congress agreed to pay money owed to other nations. However, Hamilton's plan to pay off the debt to American citizens unleashed a storm of protest. When borrowing money during the American Revolution, the government issued **bonds.** These are paper notes promising to repay the money in a certain length of time. While waiting for the payment, many of the original bond owners—shopkeepers, farmers, and soldiers—sold the bonds for less than their value. They were purchased by speculators, people who risk money in order to make a larger profit. Hamilton proposed that these bonds be paid off at their original value.

Opponents believed that Hamilton's plan would make speculators rich. They said his plan was "established at the expense of national justice, gratitude, and humanity." The original bond owners also felt betrayed by the government. They lost money on their bonds while new bond owners profited.

Even stronger opposition came from the Southern states, which **accumulated,** or collected, much less debt than the Northern states. Southern states complained that they would have to pay more than their share under Hamilton's plan.

W Compromise Results in a Capital

To win support for his plan, Hamilton worked out a compromise with Southern leaders. If they voted for his plan to pay off the state debts, he would, in return, support locating the new nation's capital in the South.

Differentiated Instruction

The City of Washington, D.C.

Objective:	To understand the history of Washington, D.C.
Focus:	Review with students the compromise that led to the location of the capital in the South.
Teach:	Have students read the background material and answer the five questions.
Assess:	Ask for volunteers to read their answers to the class.
Close:	Ask students who have visited the city to discuss their impressions of what they saw there.

Differentiated Instruction Strategies

BL Provide a city map of Washington, D.C., and ask students to locate landmarks that are familiar to them, such as the White House.

AL Have students write an essay on whether they think Washington, D.C., is a better location for the national capital than New York City would be.

ELL Ask students what other national capitals they are familiar with.

Linking Past and Present Activity, URB p. 33

A special district would be laid out between Virginia and Maryland along the banks of the Potomac River. This district became Washington, D.C. While workers prepared the new city, the nation's capital was moved from New York to Philadelphia.

The Fight Over the Bank

To help build a strong national economy, Hamilton also asked Congress to create a national bank—the Bank of the United States. Both private investors and the national government would own the Bank's stock, or shares of ownership.

In 1792 only eight other banks existed in the nation, all of them established by the states. Madison and Jefferson opposed a national bank, believing it would benefit the wealthy. They also charged that the Bank was **unconstitutional**—or inconsistent with the Constitution. Hamilton agreed that the Constitution did not specifically say a bank could be created. However, he argued, Congress still had the power to do so. Washington agreed, and a national bank was created.

Tariffs and Taxes

Hamilton believed that agricultural America would benefit from more manufacturing. He proposed a **tariff**—a tax on imports—to protect new American industries from foreign competition. The South, having little industry, opposed such tariffs. Hamilton, however, won support in Congress for low tariffs, which raised money rather than protected industry.

Hamilton's plan also called for national taxes to help the government pay off the national debt. At Hamilton's request, Congress approved a variety of taxes, including one on whiskey distilled in the United States.

Hamilton also planned to give the national government new financial powers. Opponents, such as Jefferson and Madison, however, feared a strong national government run by the wealthy. Their vision of America was very different.

Reading Check Summarizing Summarize Hamilton's plan for building the nation's economy.

R Reading Strategy

Summarizing Have students summarize who supported and who opposed a national bank, and why. *(Hamilton and Washington supported it because they hoped it would help build a strong national economy. Jefferson and Madison opposed it because they thought it was unconstitutional and would benefit the wealthy.)* **BL**

Reading Check Answer: Hamilton's economic plan would pay back debts, create a national bank, impose protective tariffs on foreign goods, and begin collecting national taxes.

Assess
History ONLINE

Study Central™ provides summaries, interactive games, and online graphic organizers to help students review content.

Close

Discussing As a class, list and discuss the issues that were addressed during Washington's time in office. Cover presidential traditions, the Bill of Rights, the national judiciary, and the economy. **OL**

Section 1 Review

Section 1 Review

History ONLINE
Study Central™ To review this section, go to glencoe.com.

Vocabulary

1. Use each term in a sentence to help explain its meaning: precedent, cabinet, uniform, national debt, bond, accumulate, unconstitutional, tariff.

Main Ideas

2. Discussing How did the first Congress support President Washington in establishing the executive branch?

3. Summarizing Why did Madison and Jefferson disagree with Hamilton's proposal for a national bank? What was the outcome?

Critical Thinking

4. Diagramming Use a diagram like the one below to show the court system established by the Judiciary Act of 1789. List the two levels and explain their powers.

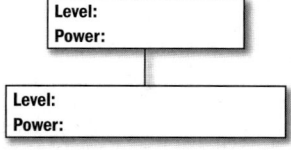

| Level: |
| Power: |

| Level: |
| Power: |

5. Contrasting Discuss the arguments of those in favor of and against Hamilton's plan to improve the economy.

6. Expository Writing Do you think the first Congress was right in giving the president the authority to dismiss cabinet members without the approval of the Senate? Write a paragraph explaining your point of view.

Answer the
7. Essential Question
What were the precedents that Washington established as the first president of the United States?

The Federalist Era **Chapter 8** **257**

Answers

1. Sentences should use vocabulary words according to their definitions in the section and Glossary.
2. Congress passed laws at Washington's request creating three departments and two offices in the executive branch.
3. Madison and Jefferson thought a national bank was unconstitutional and would benefit the wealthy. The bank was created despite their objections.

4. **Level:** Federal; **Power:** could reverse state decisions, had final judicial authority. **Level:** State; **Power:** handled most cases and interpreted state laws.
5. Answers will vary but should include summaries of both points of view.
6. Answers should include students' opinions about why the president should or should not have the authority to dismiss cabinet members without Senate approval. Some might believe it is right because the

president should be able to dismiss members of the executive branch. Others might believe it is wrong because it allows the president to possibly misuse his or her authority to dismiss people for any reason he or she chooses.
7. Washington started the traditions of the Inaugural Address, two terms in office, the creation of the cabinet, and a foreign policy of neutrality.

Focus

R Reading Strategy

Activating Prior Knowledge Ask: What other cities had served as the capital of the United States? *(Philadelphia, New York)* Discuss with students the compromise that brought the capital to Washington, D.C. Then discuss the considerations that should be taken into account when choosing a national capital. *(central location, on major transportation routes, water routes)* **Ask:** What advantages did Washington, D.C., hold over earlier capitals? Disadvantages? *(Students may suggest that Washington, D.C., was more centrally located, but transportation routes were not as good.)* **OL**

After reading the page and reviewing the map, ask students to complete a graphic organizer that shows some of the transportation plans and issues related to the new capital city. **BL**

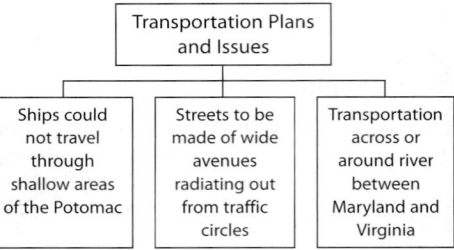

Transportation Plans and Issues

- Ships could not travel through shallow areas of the Potomac
- Streets to be made of wide avenues radiating out from traffic circles
- Transportation across or around river between Maryland and Virginia

Additional Support and Answers

Choosing the Location of Washington, D.C.

Before 1790 the United States had no permanent capital city. Early Congresses met in various cities. A political compromise established the nation's capital along the Potomac River.

How Did Geography Affect the Early Development of Washington, D.C.?

R The city's site was selected by George Washington. He may have chosen it for its natural scenery or his belief that the Potomac would become a great navigable waterway. Unfortunately, debris and silt were deposited in the shallow tidal areas around the developing city. Ships could not travel the length of the river. The stagnant water created unhealthy conditions and a rotten smell.

◄ Mathematician and inventor Benjamin Banneker was hired in 1791 to help survey the land for the new national capital. In addition to his other talents, Banneker was also a farmer and a publisher of a well-known yearly almanac.

Benjamin Banneker

Black Heritage USA 15c

◄ French architect Pierre L'Enfant designed the plan for the city of Washington, D.C., in 1791.

POTOMAC RIVER

VIRGINIA

▲ **Map of Washington, D.C., 1791** L'Enfant's basic plan included wide avenues and major streets radiating out from traffic circles. Modern Washington, D.C., still retains many of the elements of L'Enfant's plan.

◄ **The City's Location** Straddling the Potomac River, Washington, D.C., was laid out on land handed over to the federal government from both Maryland and Virginia. The Virginia land was given back to Virginia in 1846. Thus, all of the city's current area was originally part of Maryland.

258 Unit 3 *Launching the Republic*

Activity: Collaborative Learning

Making Connections Divide the class into small groups and have them research residential life in Washington, D.C., today. Encourage them to use the Internet, personal interviews, books, magazines, and other resources for their research. **Ask:** What are the advantages and disadvantages of living in Washington, D.C.? *(Students should investigate such issues as population diversity, housing availability, variety of restaurants and entertainment, transportation systems, cost of living, public schools, crime rate, and unemployment rate.)* Then divide the class into two groups and have them debate the advantages and disadvantages of living in Washington, D.C. Ask one group to support the idea and the other group to argue against it. **OL**

◄ Washington, D.C., is famous for its cherry blossoms. This scene shows blossoms along the Tidal Basin.

The Tidal Basin To help reduce the amount of stagnant water near the Potomac, an inlet called the Tidal Basin was created in the 1880s. The basin provides a means for draining the Washington Channel and flushing the channel with relatively clean water with each change of tide. **R**

1 **Washington Monument** **C₁**
2 **Jefferson Memorial**
3 **Franklin Delano Roosevelt Memorial**
4 **White House**

Washington, D.C., in 1801 The city was slowly rising from a marshy site on the Potomac River. The nation's capital had only two noteworthy buildings—the president's mansion (later called the White House) and the still-unfinished Capitol. Between them stretched about two miles of muddy streets. ► **C₂**

- MAIN · FLOOR · PLAN ·
—— PRESENT ——
· EXECUTIVE · MANSION ·
James Hoban, Original Architect, 1792

Analyzing Geography

1. **Human-Environment Interaction** One of the reasons that the site was chosen as the capital was that it was in the center of the country. What are the advantages of such a location?

2. **Location** How do you think the location of Washington, D.C., affected its early growth? Explain.

Launching the Republic **Unit 3** **259**

GEOGRAPHY & HISTORY

Teach

R Reading Strategy

Summarizing Ask: What is the purpose of the Tidal Basin? How does it work? *(The purpose of the Tidal Basin is to help reduce the amount of stagnant water near the Potomac. It helps to drain the Washington Channel and to flush the canal with cleaner water with each change of the tide.)* **OL**

C₁ Critical Thinking

Making Inferences Every state in the nation donated a memorial stone to be set on the interior walls of the Washington Monument. **Ask:** Why do you think the builders of the monument asked states to donate stones? *(to create a truly national monument representing all the states)* **OL**

Assess/Close

C₂ Critical Thinking

Comparing Ask: How is modern-day Washington, D.C., similar to the original plan for the city? *(While the city has grown tremendously, it is built around several of the original buildings.)* **AL**

Answers

1. more people can easily travel to it; representatives from all states have access to government centers

2. Its central location probably spurred growth in and around the city. Since it is the nation's capital, physical, economic, and political development brought new jobs and people to the area.

259

Focus

Early Challenges

Bellringer
Daily Test Practice Transparency 8–2

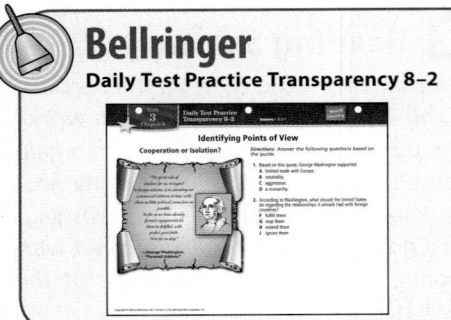

Reading Guide
Answers to Graphic:
Treaty of Greenville: Native Americans agreed to surrender most of the land in what is now Ohio; **Jay's Treaty:** The British agreed to withdraw from American soil, but the treaty failed to address impressment or British interference in American trade; **Pinckney's Treaty:** Spain agreed to let Americans freely use the Mississippi River and trade in New Orleans.

Section Spotlight Video

To learn more about the violent uprising of Pennsylvania farmers during Washington's administration, watch the Section Spotlight Video "Early Challenges."

Resource Manager

Essential Question ◄
What challenges did the United States face during Washington's administration?

Reading Guide

Content Vocabulary

neutrality (p. 262)   impressment (p. 263)

Academic Vocabulary

challenge (p. 261)   maintain (p. 261)

Key People and Events

Whiskey Rebellion (p. 261)
Battle of Fallen Timbers (p. 262)
Treaty of Greenville (p. 262)
Edmond Genêt (p. 263)
Jay's Treaty (p. 263)
Pinckney's Treaty (p. 263)

Reading Strategy

Taking Notes As you read, use a diagram like the one below to summarize how the treaties described in this section affected the United States.

Treaty	Effect
Treaty of Greenville	
Jay's Treaty	
Pinckney's Treaty	

ILLINOIS STANDARDS
The American Journey

14.E.3 Compare the basic principles of the United States and its international interests (e.g., territory, environment, trade, use of technology).

15.E Understand the impact of government policies and decisions on production and consumption in the economy.

17.D Understand the historical significance of geography.

American Diary

In 1791 Congress passed a tax on the manufacture and sale of whiskey. Opposition to the tax was strong in western Pennsylvania. Farmers refused to pay and attacked tax collectors. The federal government took action against the Whiskey Rebellion. Alexander Hamilton believed that using force to stop the rebellion would: "do us a great deal of good and add to the solidity of every thing in this country."

—from American Politics in the Early Republic

President Washington reviews the troops before their march west to shut down the Whiskey Rebellion.

R Reading Strategies	C Critical Thinking	D Differentiated Instruction	W Writing Support	S Skill Practice
Teacher Edition • Sequencing, p. 261 **Additional Resources** • Guid. Read., URB p. 40 • Content Vocab., URB p. 17 • Academic Vocab., URB p. 19 • Read. Ess., p. 82	**Teacher Edition** • Drawing Conclusions, p. 261 **Additional Resources** • Quizzes and Tests, p. 72 • Crit. Think. Skills, URB p. 29	**Teacher Edition** • Visual/Spatial, p. 263 **Additional Resources** • School-to-Home, URB p. 35 • Reteaching Act., URB p. 37 • Differ. Inst., URB p. 27	**Teacher Edition** • Personal Writing, p. 262	**Teacher Edition** • Using Vocab. Skills, p. 263 **Additional Resources** • Daily Test Pract. Transp. 8-2 • Time Line Skills, URB p. 34 • Geo. & Hist., URB p. 31 • Lesson Transp. 8B

The Whiskey Rebellion and the West

Main Idea The new government was faced with challenges in Pennsylvania and on the frontier.

History and You Have you ever opposed a government action? Read to learn how the new government handled rebellious citizens.

• •

The Whiskey Rebellion was only one **challenge,** or demanding situation, faced by the new government. Native Americans, aided by the British and Spanish, were resisting the American settlers' expansion westward. Britain and France were pressuring the United States to become more involved in their conflicts. President Washington stood firm by not involving the United States in foreign conflicts.

The Whiskey Rebellion

Washington was concerned about the growing resistance of western Pennsylvania farmers to the tax on whiskey. Their protest turned violent in July 1794. An armed mob attacked tax collectors and burned down buildings. This armed protest, called the **Whiskey Rebellion,** alarmed government leaders. Washington and his advisers decided to crush the challenge. This action sent messages that the government would use force when necessary to **maintain,** or keep, the social order.

Struggle Over the West

The new government also faced difficult problems in the West. Washington worried about European ambitions in the Northwest Territory. He signed treaties with the Native Americans, hoping to lessen the influence of the British and Spanish on them. American settlers ignored the treaties and moved onto lands promised to the Native Americans. Fighting broke out between the two groups.

Washington sent an army under General Arthur St. Clair to restore order in the Northwest Territory. In November 1791, St. Clair's forces were defeated by Little Turtle, chief of the Miami people. More than 600 American soldiers died in the battle by the Wabash River.

Many Americans believed an alliance with France would help them defeat the British, Spanish, and Native Americans in the West.

Primary Source / The Whiskey Rebellion

Thomas Jefferson accused Hamilton of orchestrating the rebellion: "an insurrection [rebellion] was announced & proclaimed & armed against, but could never be found."

▲ Rebels tar and feather a tax collector during the Whiskey Rebellion.

Critical Thinking
Explaining How did Alexander Hamilton want to respond to the rebellion?

Geography and History Activity, URB p. 31

CHAPTER 8
Section 2

Teach
• • • • • • • • • • • • • • • • • • •

C Critical Thinking

Drawing Conclusions Ask: Why did Washington believe it was important to demonstrate that the government would use force to maintain the social order? *(to prevent future rebellions; to establish the authority of the new government; and to preserve the new nation's unity)* **OL**

R Reading Strategy

Sequencing Ask: What was the order of events that led to the defeat of General St. Clair's forces? *(Washington signed a treaty with Native Americans; settlers ignored the treaty and moved onto lands promised to the Native Americans; Native Americans fought back; Washington sent an army under St. Clair to restore order; Chief Little Turtle's forces defeated the American soldiers.)* **BL**

Primary Source

Critical Thinking Answer
Hamilton wanted to use force to crush the rebellion.

Differentiated Instruction

Treaties and Forts of the Northwest Territory

Objective:	To study the treaties and forts of the Northwest Territory during the Federalist Era
Focus:	Ask students why treaties and forts would have been necessary in the Northwest Territory.
Teach:	Have students read the background information and answer the five questions.
Assess:	Discuss any answers that seem confusing to the students.
Close:	Ask students to predict what will happen to relations with Native Americans in the future.

Differentiated Instruction Strategies

BL Have students recall their earlier studies about relations between Native Americans and colonists before the Revolutionary War.

AL Ask students to research the Wyandot and Delaware nations and report their findings to the class.

ELL Have students review a map of the present-day area and point to the locations described in the activity.

W Writing Support

Personal Writing Ask students if they think neutrality was a good policy for Washington. Have students write their thoughts on neutrality as a national policy on wars between other countries. Tell them to consider questions such as these while writing: Is it always best to try to remain neutral? What should a leader do if neutrality becomes impossible? Should neutrality still be the default foreign policy of the United States? **OL**

Native American Campaigns [NATIONAL GEOGRAPHIC]

Map Skills Answer
Ohio
Reading a Map Ask: About how far did General St. Clair travel? (about 75 miles [120 km]) About how far did General Wayne travel? What battle did he and his troops fight against Native Americans? (about 175 miles [282 km]; the Battle of Fallen Timbers)

Reading Check **Answer:** to help defeat the British, Spanish, and Native Americans in the West

Hands-On Chapter Project
Step 2

Creating a Three-Panel Display

Step 2: Continuing to Create a Pictorial Display Groups of students will prepare a three-panel display of images about the United States during the Washington and Adams administrations.

Essential Question: What challenges did the United States face during Washington's administration?

Native American Campaigns [NATIONAL GEOGRAPHIC]

General Anthony Wayne wrote to the Secretary of War after the Battle of Fallen Timbers, saying, "[The Indians] abandoned themselves to flight . . . leaving our victorious army in full and quiet possession of the field of battle."

Native Americans who signed the Treaty of Greenville believed they had retained control of their lands. ▶

◀ Little Turtle was a spokesperson for the Native Americans at the peace talks.

Map Skills

Place In what present-day state was most of the land ceded by the Native Americans in the Treaty of Greenville?

Maps In Motion See StudentWorks™ Plus or glencoe.com.

Map legend:
- ← Route of General Arthur St. Clair
- ← Route of General Anthony Wayne
- ✳ Battle
- ■ Fort
- Land ceded by Native Americans

The possibility of French involvement prompted Britain to take action in the West. In 1794 the British government urged Native Americans to destroy American settlements west of the Appalachians. The British also began building a new fort in Ohio.

The Native Americans demanded that all settlers north of the Ohio River leave the territory. Washington sent another army under Anthony Wayne, a former Revolutionary War general, to challenge their demands. In August 1794 his army defeated more than 1,000 Native Americans led by the Shawnee chief Blue Jacket at the **Battle of Fallen Timbers** (near present-day Toledo, Ohio). The Battle of Fallen Timbers crushed the Native Americans' hopes of keeping their land. In the **Treaty of Greenville** (1795), they agreed to surrender most of the land in what is now Ohio.

Reading Check **Analyzing** Why did some Americans want to form an alliance with France?

Problems With Europe

Main Idea President Washington wanted the nation to remain neutral in foreign conflicts.

History and You Have you ever been in the middle of a disagreement between two friends? Read why Washington looked for middle ground in a war between Britain and France.

Most Americans cheered the French Revolution of 1789 because of its similarity to America's own revolution. By 1793, however, the French Revolution turned bloody. Public opinion was now divided.

When Britain and France went to war in 1793, some Americans sympathized with France and others supported Britain. Washington hoped that the United States could maintain its **neutrality**—not taking sides in the conflict between France and Britain. As time passed, however, remaining neutral became more difficult.

Directions Have groups continue conducting research to collect or create pictures, maps, diagrams, time lines, facts, and other items about the challenges the United States faced during Washington's terms in office. Together, group members should prepare the images for display and include informative captions. Have the groups work on the second panel, which should be about early challenges the nation faced. Explain

that they will finish their displays in the next section.

Making Generalizations As a class, discuss how Washington handled some of the crises that occurred during his presidency. **Ask:** Did Washington address these challenges effectively? **OL**

(Chapter Project continued in Section 3)

Washington Proclaims Neutrality

The French tried to involve the United States in their conflict with Britain. They sent diplomat **Edmond Genêt** (zhuh•NAY) to recruit American volunteers to attack British ships. In response, President Washington issued a Proclamation of Neutrality, which prohibited American citizens from fighting in the war. It also barred French and British warships from American ports. The British captured American ships that traded with the French and forced the American crews into the British navy. This practice of **impressment** angered the Americans.

Washington sent John Jay, chief justice of the Supreme Court, to negotiate a peaceful solution with Britain. Few Americans approved of **Jay's Treaty.** In it, the British agreed to withdraw from American soil. However, the treaty did not deal with the issue of impressment or British interference with American trade. Washington found fault with the treaty but realized it would end the crisis. The Senate narrowly approved it after a fierce debate.

D Treaty With Spain

Spanish leaders feared that the United States and Great Britain would work together against them in North America. Thomas Pinckney was sent to Spain to settle the differences between the United States and Spain. In 1795 **Pinckney's Treaty** gave the Americans free navigation of the Mississippi River and the right to trade at New Orleans.

Washington's Farewell

Washington decided not to seek a third term. In his Farewell Address, he attacked political parties and involvement in foreign affairs. He also urged his fellow citizens to:

PRIMARY SOURCE

"Observe good faith and justice toward all nations. . . . . . . It is our true policy to steer clear of permanent alliances." **S**

—from *The Annals of America*

These parting words influenced the nation's foreign policy for more than 100 years.

✔ **Reading Check** **Explaining** What was the significance of Jay's Treaty?

History ONLINE
Study Central™ To review this section, go to glencoe.com.

Section 2 Review

Vocabulary

1. Write headlines for newspaper stories about the U.S. role in the Britain-France conflict. Use and show understanding of the terms: challenge, maintain, neutrality, impressment.

Main Ideas

2. **Identifying** What did Washington's actions in crushing the Whiskey Rebellion signify to the country?

3. **Discussing** How did the British challenge U.S. neutrality in the war between France and Britain?

Critical Thinking

4. **Comparing and Contrasting** Compare and contrast U.S. attitudes and actions toward the Native Americans and U.S. actions in foreign affairs.

5. **Determining Cause and Effect** Use a diagram like the one below to show the causes and the effect of the Battle of Fallen Timbers.

Causes	Cause/Effect: Battle of Fallen Timbers	Effect

6. **Persuasive Writing** Imagine that you disagree with Washington's policy of neutrality in the war between France and Britain. Write a letter to the president to persuade him to side with France.

Answer the Essential Question

7. What challenges did the United States face during Washington's administration?

The Federalist Era **Chapter 8** 263

D Differentiated Instruction

Visual/Spatial Have students draw a political cartoon to illustrate Washington's Proclamation of Neutrality. **OL**

S Skill Practice

Using Vocabulary Skills Ask students to explain what Washington meant when he gave this advice to the nation. **ELL**

✔ **Reading Check** **Answer:** The British agreed to withdraw from American soil. Because the treaty did not address trade issues or impressment, few Americans approved of it.

Assess

History ONLINE

Study Central™ provides summaries, interactive games, and online graphic organizers to help students review content.

Close

Summarizing As a class, discuss the challenges Washington faced during his presidency and evaluate how he handled them. **OL**

Section 2 Review

Answers

1. Headlines should reflect an understanding of the terms.
2. that the government would use force if necessary to maintain order
3. by capturing American ships that traded with the French and by forcing Americans into the British navy
4. Washington preferred to stay neutral in foreign conflicts, but he sent armies to deal with Native American conflicts.
5. **Causes:** British urged Native Americans to destroy American settlements; Native Americans demanded that American settlers leave territory; Washington sent army; **Effect:** crushed Native Americans' hopes of keeping their land; Treaty of Greenville gave most of present-day Ohio to the U.S.
6. Students' letters should attempt to persuade the president to side with France in its conflict with Britain. Students should present two or more logical arguments to support their position.
7. the Whiskey Rebellion; conflicts with Native Americans, British, and Spanish in the West; trying to maintain neutrality in conflict between Britain and France

The First Political Parties

Focus

CHAPTER 8
Section 3

Bellringer
Daily Test Practice Transparency 8–3

Reading Guide
Answers to Graphic:
Federalists: wanted strong, stable central government, supported banking and shipping interests; **Republicans:** wanted to limit government's power, supported individual liberties; supported French, appealed to farmers and urban workers

Section Spotlight Video

To learn more about the first political parties, watch the Section Spotlight Video "The First Political Parties."

Resource Manager

Essential Question ◄
How did the Federalist and Republican Parties form, and on what issues did they disagree?

Reading Guide

Content Vocabulary
partisan (p. 265)   sedition (p. 270)
implied powers   nullify
  (p. 266)   (p. 270)
caucus (p. 268)   states' rights (p. 270)
alien (p. 269)

Academic Vocabulary
resolve (p. 269)   principle (p. 270)

Key People and Events
XYZ affair (p. 269)
Alien and Sedition Acts (p. 270)
Virginia and Kentucky Resolutions (p. 270)

Reading Strategy
Taking Notes As you read, create a diagram like the one below. Identify the differences between the Federalists and the Republicans on the role of the federal government.

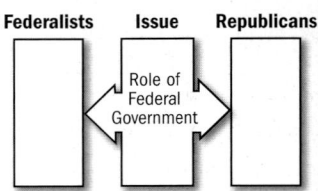

Federalists   Issue   Republicans

Role of Federal Government

ILLINOIS STANDARDS
The American Journey

14.A Understand and explain basic principles of the United States government.

14.A.3 Describe how responsibilities are shared and limited by the United States and Illinois Constitutions and significant court decisions.

14.C Understand election processes and the responsibilities of citizens.

16.B.3a (US) Describe how different groups competed for power within the colonies and how that competition led to the development of political institutions during the early national period.

American Diary

Although many Americans hailed George Washington as a great leader, the president did not escape criticism. One critic was Ben Franklin's grandson, Benjamin Franklin Bache, a writer and publisher. Washington, Bache wrote, was "but a man, and certainly not a great man." Bache even criticized Washington's military leadership during the American Revolution, describing him as "ignorant of war both in theory and useful practice."

—*from* Remarks Occasioned by the Late Conduct of Mr. Washington

George and Martha Washington

R Reading Strategies	**C** Critical Thinking	**D** Differentiated Instruction	**W** Writing Support	**S** Skill Practice
Teacher Edition • Pri. Sources, p. 267 • Using Context Clues, p. 270 **Additional Resources** • Guid. Read., URB p. 41 • Content Vocab., URB p. 17 • Acad. Vocab., URB p. 19 • Read. Ess., p. 85	**Teacher Edition** • Ident. Central Issues, p. 265 • Making Inferences, p. 266 **Additional Resources** • Quizzes and Tests, p. 73	**Teacher Edition** • Visual/Spatial, p. 268 **Additional Resources** • School-to-Home, URB p. 35 • Reteaching Act., URB p. 37	**Teacher Edition** • Narrative Writing, p. 269 **Additional Resources** • Writ. Skills, URB p. 23	**Teacher Edition** • Visual Literacy, p. 269 **Additional Resources** • Daily Test Pract. Transp. 8-3 • Soc. Stud. Skills, URB p. 25 • Lesson Transp. 8C

Opposing Views

Main Idea By 1796, Americans began to take opposing sides on issues. Two political parties emerged from the debates.

History and You When you disagree with someone, do you voice your opinion? Read to learn what happened when conflict occurred between the supporters of Hamilton and Jefferson.

President Washington's character and military record were admired by most Americans. However, harsh attacks on his policies and on his personality appeared from time to time in newspapers. One paper even called Washington "the scourge and the misfortune of his country."

Most attacks on Washington came from supporters of Thomas Jefferson. They were trying to discredit the policies of Washington and Hamilton by attacking the president. By 1796 Americans were beginning to divide into opposing groups and to form political parties.

At that time many Americans considered political parties harmful. Parties—or "factions,"

as they were called—were to be avoided as much as a strong central government. The nation's Founders did not even mention political parties when they wrote the Constitution.

Washington disapproved of political parties and warned that they would divide the nation. To others it seemed natural that people would disagree about issues. They also knew that people who hold similar views tend to band together.

In Washington's cabinet, Alexander Hamilton and Thomas Jefferson often took opposing sides on issues. They disagreed on economic policy and foreign relations. Nor could they agree on the power of the federal government or on interpretations of the Constitution. Even Washington was **partisan**—favoring one side of an issue. Although he believed he stood above politics, Washington usually supported Hamilton's positions.

Political Parties Emerge

In Congress and in the nation at large, similar differences existed. By the mid-1790s two distinct political parties formed.

Primary Source / **Political Cartoons**

Jefferson Criticized Newspapers that supported Washington and Hamilton ridiculed Thomas Jefferson in print and in cartoons. In this cartoon, Jefferson is throwing the U.S. Constitution into a fire.

Critical Thinking

Making Inferences Cartoonists often use a symbol to stand for a larger idea. What does the eagle represent? What is the eagle trying to do?

Teach

C Critical Thinking

Identifying Central Issues Ask: Why do you think some people were opposed to the formation of political parties? *(Possible answers: because parties might divide the nation, and concentrate power in the hands of a few)* Do you agree with George Washington that political parties are harmful? *(Some students might agree because they believe political parties are divisive today. Others might disagree, saying that political parties give people a way to gather with others who share their views in order to influence the government.)* **OL**

Primary Source

Critical Thinking Answer
The eagle represents the federal government. It is trying to stop Jefferson from burning the Constitution and/or harming the nation.

Hands-On Chapter Project
Step 3

Creating a Three-Panel Display

Step 3: Continuing to Create a Pictorial Display Groups of students will prepare a three-panel display of images about the United States during its early years.

Essential Question: How did the Federalist and Republican Parties form, and on what issues did they disagree?

Directions Have groups continue conducting research to collect or create pictures,

maps, diagrams, time lines, facts, and other items about the formation of the first political parties. Together, group members should prepare the images for display and include informative captions.

Compare and Contrast As a class, discuss how the Federalists and the Republicans differed and why. **Ask:** If you were alive at the time, which party would you join, if either, and why? **OL**

(Chapter Project continued in the Visual Summary)

C Critical Thinking

Making Inferences Ask: What might be the danger in Hamilton's idea of implied powers? *(The government could claim any power that the Constitution does not expressly forbid, making it more powerful than it should be.)* **AL**

DBQ Document-Based Questions

Answers

1. He worried that groups would seek revenge on each other, would become despotic and eventually look for security from one all-powerful individual.

2. He meant that, in the end, they were all Americans who wanted the nation to be successful and that it was acceptable for people to disagree about how to get there.

Differentiated Instruction

YOU DECIDE

Will Political Parties Harm the Nation?

In his Farewell Address, George Washington warned the nation that the development of political parties would lead to trouble. Thomas Jefferson believed that while the new parties had different opinions, they still had much in common.

YES GEORGE WASHINGTON

"The alternate domination of one faction [group] over another, sharpened by the spirit of revenge . . . is itself a frightful despotism [tyranny]. But this leads at length to a more formal and permanent despotism. The disorders and miseries which result gradually incline the minds of men to seek security . . . in the absolute power of an individual."

THOMAS JEFFERSON **NO**

"Every difference of opinion is not a difference of principle. . . . We are all Republicans, we are all Federalists. . . . Let us, then, with courage and confidence pursue our own Federal and Republican principles, our attachment to union and representative government."

DBQ Document-Based Questions

1. **Analyzing** Why did George Washington fear the emergence of political parties?

2. **Interpreting** What did Thomas Jefferson mean when he said, "We are all Republicans: We are all Federalists"?

The name *Federalist* was first used to describe someone who supported ratification of the Constitution. By the 1790s, the word meant the people who supported the policies of the Washington administration.

Generally, Federalists stood for a strong federal government. They admired Britain because of its stability and distrusted France because of the violent changes following the French Revolution. Federalist policies favored banking and shipping interests. Federalists received the strongest support in the Northeast, especially New England, and from wealthy plantation owners in the South.

Efforts to turn public opinion against Federalist policies began seriously in late 1791 when Philip Freneau (Freh•NOH) began publishing the *National Gazette*. Jefferson, then secretary of state, helped the newspaper get started. Later he and Madison organized people who disagreed with Hamilton. They called their party the Republicans, or the Democratic-Republicans.

The Republicans wanted to limit the government's power. They feared that a strong federal government would endanger people's liberties. They supported the French and condemned what they regarded as the Washington administration's pro-British policies. Republican policies appealed to small farmers and urban workers, especially in the Middle Atlantic states and the South.

Views of the Constitution

One difference between Federalists and Republicans was the basis of government power. In Hamilton's view, the federal government had **implied powers.** These were powers that were not expressly forbidden in the Constitution.

C Hamilton used the idea of implied powers to justify a national bank. He argued that the Constitution gave Congress the power to issue money and to regulate trade. A national bank would clearly help the government perform these responsibilities. Therefore, he reasoned, creating a bank was within the constitutional power of Congress.

Organizing and Displaying Information

Objective:	To learn how to organize information
Focus:	Remind students that the Federalists and the Republicans had different views about government.
Teach:	Ask students to apply the skill.
Assess:	Have students use the self-assessment checklist.
Close:	Ask students whether they identify more closely with Hamilton's or Jefferson's views.

Differentiated Instruction Strategies

BL Review with students how charts could be organized.

AL Have students analyze written documents or political cartoons on the early political parties and present what they find using a chart or graph.

ELL Ask students to explain the difference between a *chart* and a *graph*.

Writing Skills Activity, URB p. 23

Jefferson and Madison disagreed with Hamilton. They believed in a strict interpretation of the Constitution. They accepted the idea of implied powers but in a much more limited sense than Hamilton did. Jefferson and Madison believed that implied powers are those powers that are "absolutely necessary" to carry out the expressed powers.

The People's Role

The differences between Federalists and Republicans, however, went deeper than disagreements about the Constitution. The parties also disagreed about the role of ordinary citizens in government.

Federalists supported representative government, in which elected officials ruled in the people's name. Too much democracy, Federalists claimed, was dangerous to liberty. Therefore, they did not believe that it was wise to let the public become too involved in politics.

Hamilton said:

PRIMARY SOURCE

"The people are turbulent and changing; they seldom judge or determine right."
—from a speech at the Constitutional Convention

Public office, Federalists thought, should be held by honest and educated men of property who would protect the rights of all the nation's people. Ordinary people were too likely to be swayed by agitators.

In contrast, the Republicans feared a strong central government controlled by only a few people. They believed that democracy and liberty would be safe only if ordinary people participated fully in government. As Jefferson said in a letter:

PRIMARY SOURCE

"I am not among those who fear the people. They, and not the rich, are our dependence [what we depend on] for continued freedom."
—from The Papers of Thomas Jefferson

R Reading Strategy

Reading Primary Sources Ask students to copy the two primary source quotes from this page on two separate pieces of paper. Have them paraphrase each quote, putting it into their own words. Invite a few students to read their paraphrased statements aloud. As a class, choose the ones that best capture the speakers' intended meanings. **OL**

People IN HISTORY

Critical Thinking Answers

1. Hamilton thought the government could claim implied powers that were not directly stated in the Constitution. Jefferson thought any powers that were not given directly to the federal government in the Constitution should be left to the states.

2. Answers will differ, but students should support their opinions with logical reasons and examples.

People IN HISTORY

Alexander Hamilton

Leader of the Federalist Party

Hamilton believed that the federal government could act as needed to govern the country well, even if those powers were not stated in the Constitution. He used this argument to defend the creation of a national bank. Specifically, he concluded that:

"It is the manifest [obvious] design and scope of the Constitution to vest in Congress all the powers requisite [needed] to the effectual administration of the finances of the United States."

Thomas Jefferson

Leader of the Republican Party

Jefferson believed all powers not clearly given to the federal government in the Constitution should be left to the states. He fought against the broad federal powers used by the Washington administration, arguing: "[B]y a compact . . . [the states] constituted a General Government for special purposes,—delegated to that government certain definite powers, reserving, each State to itself, the . . . right to their own self-government."

CRITICAL Thinking

1. **Contrasting** How did Jefferson and Hamilton differ in their views on the constitutional powers of the federal government?
2. **Defending** With which view do you agree more? Why?

The Federalist Era **Chapter 8** **267**

Leveled Activities

D

Differentiated Instruction

Visual/Spatial Have students create a presidential campaign poster for Adams or Jefferson. Their posters should include a picture as well as a slogan or persuasive statement that tries to convince voters to support the candidate. **BL**

INTERPRETING
POLITICAL CARTOONS

Answers

1. The sack appears to be for money. The French are trying to get the Americans to give France a loan to help them in their conflict with Britain.

2. The British character is probably amused because he knows the French will not get money from the United States.

✓ Reading Check **Answer:** The person who won the most electoral votes became president, and the person with the second-highest number of electoral votes became vice president.

Additional Support

Teacher Tip

Making a Chart Suggest that students assign roles to members of their groups. One person might research the Electoral College, while another might be responsible for writing a summary of the group's findings.

Primary Sources

INTERPRETING
POLITICAL CARTOONS

In this British cartoon, Great Britain, on the hilltop, is greatly amused by French-American relations, while other European leaders look on.

1. **Analyzing** What appears to be in the French sack? What are the French trying to get the United States to do?

2. **Making Connections** Why is the character representing Great Britain greatly amused by the situation?

A. United States
B. French leaders
C. European leaders
D. Great Britain

PROPERTY PROTECTED à la Françoise.

Washington tried to get his two advisers to work out their differences. Knowing that Jefferson was dissatisfied, Washington wrote to Jefferson:

PRIMARY SOURCE

"I . . . ardently wish that some line could be marked out by which both of you could walk."
—from *George Washington: Letters and Addresses*

Nevertheless, Jefferson resigned as secretary of state and soon after Hamilton resigned as secretary of the treasury. The rival groups and their points of view moved further apart.

D ### The Election of 1796

In the presidential election of 1796, candidates sought office for the first time as members of rival political parties. To prepare for the election, the Federalists and the Republicans held meetings called **caucuses.** At the caucuses, members of Congress and other leaders chose their parties' candidates for office.

The Federalists nominated Vice President John Adams for president and Charles Pinckney for vice president. The Republicans put forth former secretary of state Jefferson for president and Aaron Burr for vice president. Adams and Jefferson, once good friends, became bitter rivals. The Federalists expected to easily carry the New England region. The Republicans' strength lay in the Southern states. Most of that region's votes went to Thomas Jefferson.

In the end, Adams received 71 electoral votes, winning the election. Jefferson finished second with 68 votes. Under the provisions of the Constitution at that time, the person with the second-highest number of electoral votes became vice president. Jefferson, therefore, became the new vice president. The administration that took office on March 4, 1797, had a Federalist president and a Republican vice president.

✓ Reading Check **Explaining** How did members of opposing parties become president and vice president in the election of 1796?

Activity: Connecting Past and Present

Making Connections The Electoral College still exists. Have students work in small groups to conduct research about how modern elections work. They should find out about the Electoral College and the relationship between the popular vote and the electoral vote. Have each group orally present its findings to the class. Discuss differences between the election of 1796 and elections today. **Ask:** Why might it be a problem for the vice president to be a member of a different political party than the president? *(conflicts between the two top officials; the possibility of a vice president whose beliefs differ from the majority of voters becoming president)* **OL**

President John Adams

Main Idea During his administration, President John Adams faced a dispute with France and the issue of states' rights at home.

History and You Do you think you should be free to say or write anything you want about the government? Read to find out why the Federalists passed laws restricting freedom of speech.

John Adams spent most of his life in public service. One of Massachusetts's most active patriots, he later became ambassador to France and to Great Britain and served two terms as vice president under Washington.

The XYZ Affair

When Adams became president, he inherited the dispute with France. The French regarded the 1794 Jay's Treaty as an American **S** attempt to help the British in their war with France. To punish the United States, the French seized American ships that carried cargo to Britain.

History ONLINE
Student Web Activity Visit glencoe.com and complete the Chapter 8 Web Activity about John Adams.

In the fall of 1797, Adams sent a delegation to Paris to try to **resolve**—bring to an end—the dispute. French foreign minister Charles de Talleyrand, however, refused to meet with the Americans. Instead, Talleyrand sent three agents who demanded a bribe and a loan for France from the Americans. "Not a sixpence," the Americans replied and sent a report of the incident to the United States. Adams was furious. He referred to the three French agents as X, Y, and Z. Adams urged Congress to prepare for war. The incident became known as the **XYZ affair.** **W**

Alien and Sedition Acts

As public anger rose against France, Americans became more suspicious of **aliens**—immigrants living in the country who were not citizens. Many Europeans who came to the United States in the 1790s supported the ideals of the French Revolution.

S Skill Practice

Visual Literacy Have students create a cause-and-effect chain showing the events that led up to the XYZ affair and its results *(**Causes:** French resentment of Jay's Treaty, French demands for bribe and loan, American refusal to pay; **Effects:** Adams urges Congress to prepare for war, public anger rises against France, growing suspicion of immigrants who were not citizens)* **OL**

W Writing Support

Narrative Writing Have students take on the role of a member of the American delegation in Paris in 1797. Have them write a one-page report to President Adams, explaining what happened with Talleyrand and the three French agents. **BL**

History ONLINE
Objectives and answers to the Student Web Activity can be found at glencoe.com under the Web Activity Lesson Plan for this chapter.

The Alien and Sedition Acts

Naturalization Act
Required that aliens be residents for 14 years instead of 5 years before they became eligible for U.S. citizenship

Alien Acts
Allowed the president to imprison aliens and to send those he considered dangerous out of the country

Sedition Act
Made it a crime to speak, write, or publish "false, scandalous, and malicious" criticisms of the government

Why they were passed
The Federalist-controlled Congress wanted to:
• strengthen the federal government.
• silence Republican opposition.

Results
• Discouraged immigration and led some foreigners already in the country to leave
• Convicted 10 Republican newspaper editors who had criticized the Federalists in government

Reaction
• Opposition to Federalist party grows
• Led to movement to allow states to overturn federal laws

Activity: Interdisciplinary Connection

Art Have students work in five groups to find five different examples of artwork in which John Adams is the subject. Art selections might include painted portraits, political cartoons, sculptures, campaign art, and so on. Invite an art teacher to visit your class to discuss the media and styles chosen by the artists and to make suggestions about how to analyze art. Then ask the groups to discuss their selected artwork and try to determine how each artist felt about his or her subject. Have a student from each group present its selection to the class and explain the group's analysis of it. Encourage them to point out specific details or stylistic choices in the artwork that led them to their conclusions. Invite class discussion about the artist's intentions or attitude. **OL**

R Reading Strategy

Using Context Clues Ask: What is a principle? *(a basic idea or code of conduct)* What does the principle of states' rights hold? *(that the powers of the federal government should be limited to those clearly stated in the Constitution and that the states should have all other powers not forbidden by the Constitution)* **OL**

Reading Check Answer: Peace with France split the Federalists and hurt Adams's chance for reelection.

Assess

History ONLINE

Study Central™ provides summaries, interactive games, and online graphic organizers to help students review content.

Close

Determining Cause and Effect As a class, discuss how the formation of political parties affected politics in the United States. **OL**

Section 3 Review

Some Americans questioned whether these aliens would remain loyal if the United States went to war with France.

Federalists responded with strict laws to protect the nation's security. In 1798 they passed a group of measures known as the **Alien and Sedition Acts. Sedition** refers to activities aimed at weakening the established government. The Alien Act allowed the president to imprison aliens, or send those considered dangerous out of the country.

Domestic and Foreign Affairs

In response to the Alien and Sedition Acts, Republicans looked to the states to preserve people's liberties by standing up to what they regarded as Federalist tyranny. Madison and Jefferson drafted documents of protest that the Virginia and Kentucky legislatures passed.

The **Virginia and Kentucky Resolutions** of 1798 and 1799 claimed that the Alien and Sedition Acts violated the Constitution. Therefore, they could not be put into action. The Kentucky Resolutions further suggested that states might **nullify**—legally overturn—federal laws considered unconstitutional.

The resolutions supported the **principle,** or basic idea, of **states' rights.** This principle stated that the powers of the federal government should be limited to those clearly assigned to it by the Constitution. The states should have all other powers not expressly forbidden to them. The issue of states' rights would remain an important issue.

To help themselves politically, the Federalists urged Adams to declare war on France. Adams, however, refused to rush to war. Instead, he appointed a new commission to seek peace with France.

In 1800 the French agreed to a treaty and stopped their attacks on American ships. The agreement with France was in the best interest of the United States. However, it hurt Adams's chance for reelection. Rather than applauding the agreement, Hamilton and his supporters now opposed their own president. The Federalists were split. Republican prospects for capturing the presidency were now greatly improved. The road was clear for Thomas Jefferson in the election of 1800.

Reading Check Summarizing How did peace with France affect the Federalists?

Section 3 Review

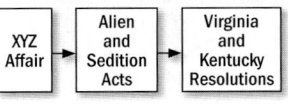

History ONLINE
Study Central™ To review this section, go to glencoe.com.

Vocabulary

1. Write sentences to demonstrate your understanding of the following words. You may combine two or more words in a sentence: partisan, implied powers, caucus, resolve, alien, sedition, nullify, principle, states' rights.

Main Ideas

2. **Discussing** How did the Federalists and the Republicans view the role of ordinary people in government?

3. **Explaining** Why did some Americans feel threatened by the passage of the Alien and Sedition Acts?

Critical Thinking

4. **Comparing** How did Jefferson's views about the Constitution's implied powers differ from the views of Alexander Hamilton?

5. **Expository Writing** Write a paragraph explaining, in your own words, how Adams tried to avoid war with France.

6. **Making Connections** Use a diagram like the one below to summarize each event and explain how it influenced the next one.

XYZ Affair → Alien and Sedition Acts → Virginia and Kentucky Resolutions

Answer the
7. **Essential Question**
How did the Federalist and Republican Parties form, and on what issues did they disagree?

Answers

1. Sentences should demonstrate understanding of the terms.
2. **Federalists:** ordinary people had poor judgment, easily swayed, should have elected officials rule in their name; **Republicans:** ordinary people should participate fully in government to keep the government in check.
3. People could be arrested for writing or speaking against the government; they felt their free speech was being threatened and that the federal government was

becoming tyrannical.
4. Jefferson believed that the federal government could claim powers only directly assigned to it by the Constitution. All other powers fell to the states. Hamilton believed that the federal government should be able to claim powers that were implied by the Constitution.
5. Students' paragraphs should include accurate details about how Adams worked to reach peace with France.
6. XYZ affair: French agents tried to bribe

the United States. Americans became suspicious of aliens. The Federalist-controlled government passed the Alien and Sedition Acts. States' rights supporters passed the Virginia and Kentucky Resolutions to protect individuals' and states' rights.
7. Groups began to disagree about how much power the federal government should have. **Federalists:** strong federal government, limit ordinary people's roles in government **Republicans:** limit federal government, protect individuals' and states' rights

Visual Summary

Precedents Set by Washington Administration

| Separation of powers | Strong and independent national court system | Limits on government's powers (Bill of Rights) | Use of force to maintain social order | Neutrality in foreign affairs |

◀ Little Turtle

Challenges Faced by Washington and Adams Administrations

| Management of the national debt | Debate over national taxes and protective tariffs | Conflicts with Europeans and Native Americans in the West | Role of ordinary people in government | Pressure to end neutrality in British-French wars | States' rights versus the power of the federal government |

Viewpoints Held by New Political Parties

	Federalists	Republicans
Economic Policy	Protective tariffs; emphasis on manufacturing	Free trade; emphasis on agriculture
Foreign Relations	Support for Britain	Support for France
Role of the Federal Government	Strong federal government	Strong state governments
Interpretation of the Constitution	Loose interpretation; federal government has implied powers	Strict interpretation; federal government limits powers to those needed to carry out the Constitution
Role of People in Government	Rule by wealthy class	Rule by ordinary people

STUDY TO GO Study anywhere, anytime! Download quizzes and flash cards to your PDA from glencoe.com.

The Federalist Era **Chapter 8** 271

Visual Summary

Technology Connection Have students visit the Internet Web site for Mount Vernon, George Washington's Virginia home. Students should read the "Meet George Washington" section, and browse through the pictures and other articles on the site. Ask them to write a one-page paper about their research, describing how what they learned from the Mount Vernon Web site contributes to their understanding of Washington's role as the first president of the United States. **OL**

Making Connections Review with students what the Federalists and the Republicans stood for in the 1790s. Then have students research the platforms of today's U.S. political parties. **Ask:** What similarities and differences do you see between political parties in the 1790s and today? *(Answers will vary but should show an understanding of disagreements over the role of people in government.)* Have students create lists of these similarities and differences and post them around the classroom. **AL**

Hands-On Chapter Project
Step 4: Wrap-Up

Creating a Three-Panel Display

Step 4: Presenting the Display Students will prepare and give a presentation to the class.

Directions Have the groups complete their displays by adding titles, captions, and additional facts and images as necessary to fill the space on the boards. Allow students to set up their displays in the classroom, library, hallway, or other area that is large enough to exhibit the completed displays. Invite other classes and guests to view the displays. Have students be available to answer questions.

Comparing and Contrasting Point out that, although they cover the same topics, all the displays are different. Call students' attention to some of the unique choices of images, graphics, or facts students included on their displays. **Ask:** What do these choices show about how different people view the same events and people in history? *(Possible answers: It shows what people think is important or noteworthy; It shows how history is open to individual interpretation; It shows how people's past experiences and knowledge can shape their views of historical events and figures.)* **OL**

Answers and Analyses

Reviewing Main Ideas

1. B Students should immediately eliminate choice C because the word "judiciary" refers to courts and judges. Remind them that the disagreement that led to this act was about how to organize the federal court system. **14.B**

2. A Students should eliminate choices C and D because there was nothing in the chapter about municipal bonds or interest charges. If they recall the controversy about implied versus stated Constitutional powers, they should then be able to select choice A. **16.B.3a (US)**

3. D Tell students that the location is the key to answering this question. If they remember that it was farmers in Pennsylvania who most strongly opposed the whiskey tax, they will know that D is the correct answer. **15.E.3a**

4. B Remind students that Madison and Jefferson supported these resolutions. Because these two were Republicans who supported states' rights, the answer cannot be A or D. Tell students that Republicans generally favored a strict interpretation of the Constitution. They should then be able to choose B as the correct answer. **16.B.3a (US)**

Short-Answer Question

5. Possible response: Madison believes that the authority of government should be based on liberty and the will of free people. **18.C.3a**

STANDARDIZED TEST PRACTICE

TEST-TAKING TIP

As you read the first part of a multiple-choice question, try to anticipate the answer before you look at the choices. If your answer is one of the choices, it is probably correct.

Reviewing Main Ideas

Directions: Choose the best answer for each of the following questions.

1. With the Judiciary Act of 1789, Congress
 A placed state courts under federal courts.
 B established a federal court system with 13 district courts and three circuit courts to serve the nation.
 C blocked state laws in favor of federal laws.
 D named judges for all federal and state courts.

2. What was one reason Madison and Jefferson opposed the idea of a national bank?
 A They believed it was unconstitutional for Congress to create a bank.
 B They wanted each state to have its own bank.
 C They feared that banking activities would threaten the purchase of municipal bonds.
 D They considered it unethical to charge interest.

3. The Whiskey Rebellion was
 A an armed uprising by farmers in Ohio.
 B a violent slave rebellion in Virginia.
 C a skirmish between U.S. soldiers and Native Americans living in the Ohio Valley.
 D a protest by Pennsylvania farmers over a federal excise tax on whiskey.

4. The Virginia and Kentucky Resolutions
 A were drafted by Federalists opposing Republican uses of federal power.
 B claimed that the Alien and Sedition Acts violated the Constitution.
 C distributed land to settlers in Virginia and Kentucky.
 D rejected the principle of states' rights.

Short-Answer Question

Directions: Base your answer to question 5 on the excerpt below and on your knowledge of social studies.

> In Europe, charters of liberty have been granted by power. America has set the example and France has followed it on charters of power granted by liberty. . . . the only earthly source of authority ought to be the vigilance [watchfulness] with which they are guarded by every citizen in private life, and the circumspection [care] with which they are executed by every citizen in the public trust.
>
> —James Madison, "Constitution," 1792

5. According to Madison, on what should the authority of government be based?

Review the Essential Questions

6. Essay George Washington never belonged to a political party, and in his Farewell Address, he warned against the establishment of them. Do you think, though, that Washington was more a Federalist or a Republican? Explain.

To help you write your essay, review your answers to the Essential Questions in the section reviews and the chapter Foldables Study Organizer. Your essay should include:

- Alexander Hamilton's economic policies;
- Washington's response to the Whiskey Rebellion;
- U.S. policies toward the British and French during the Washington administration;
- criticism of Washington; and
- Washington's Farewell Address.

GO ON

Review the Essential Questions

6. If students completed their Foldables correctly, they should be able to reach the conclusion that Washington was more of a Federalist than a Republican. Students' answers might focus on his tendency to agree with Hamilton (a Federalist) and side against Jefferson and Madison (Republicans) on the role of the federal government, the economy, dealing with internal conflicts, and foreign policy. **14.E.3**

History ONLINE
For additional test practice, use **Self-Check Quizzes**—Chapter 8 at glencoe.com.

Chapter 8 Assessment

Document-Based Questions

Directions: Analyze the documents and answer the short-answer questions that follow.

Document 1

The following passage is taken from the Treaty of Greenville, 1795.

> The Indian tribes who have a right to those lands, are quietly to enjoy them, hunting, planting, and dwelling thereon, so long as they please, without any [interference] from the United States; but when those tribes, or any of them, shall . . . sell their lands, or any part of them, they are to be sold only to the United States; and until such sale, the United States will protect all the said Indian tribes in the quiet enjoyment of their lands against all citizens of the United States. . . . And the said Indian tribes again acknowledge themselves to be under the protection of the said United States, and no other power whatever.

Source: The Treaty of Greenville

7. What does the United States government promise Native Americans in this document? What do Native Americans promise to do?

Document 2

In the following passage, Washington describes his feelings about political parties.

> I . . . warn you in the most solemn manner against the baneful [harmful] effects of the spirit of party generally.
>
> This spirit, unfortunately, is inseparable from our nature. . . . It exists under different shapes in all governments . . . but, in those of the popular form, it is seen in its greatest rankness, and is truly their worst enemy.

Source: George Washington's Farewell Address

8. According to Washington, why do political parties exist?

Document 3

This 1798 cartoon depicts a fight between two House members—Republican Matthew Lyon (center) and Federalist Roger Griswold (right)—over the Sedition Act.

Source: CORBIS

9. How are others reacting to the fight?

Document 4

Tenth Amendment to the U.S. Constitution:

> The powers not delegated to the United States by the Constitution, nor prohibited by it to the States, are reserved to the States respectively, or to the people.

Source: The Bill of Rights

10. Which political party—Federalists or Republicans—do you think supported this amendment more? Explain.

11. Persuasive Writing Using the information from the four documents and your knowledge of social studies, write an essay in which you:

- compare and contrast Federalist and Republican visions of America; and

- explain which of those visions is most closely related to the ideals on which the United States was founded.

9. Other House members appear to be encouraging the fighting. This probably reflects the disagreement between the Federalists and the Republicans over the Alien and Sedition Acts. **16.A.3c**

10. Most students will probably say that the Tenth Amendment appealed more to Republicans because it gives to the states any powers not granted to the federal government or expressly denied to the states. This supports states' rights, a key idea in the Republican philosophy. **16.B.3a (US)**

11. Essays should identify key ideas of the Federalist and Republican philosophy and highlight issues on which they agree and disagree. Students should then take a position on whether Federalism or Republicanism more closely matches the ideals on which the United States was founded. They should support their arguments with facts and examples as much as possible. **18.C.3b**

History ONLINE
Have students visit the Web site at glencoe.com to review Chapter 8 and take the Self-Check Quiz.

Need Extra Help?

Have students refer to the pages listed if they miss any of the questions.

Need Extra Help?

If you missed questions. . .	1	2	3	4	5	6	7	8	9	10	11
Go to page. . .	253–255	266–267	261	270	266–267	260–268	261–262	264–268	269–270	264–268	252–270

The Federalist Era **Chapter 8** **273**

Document-Based Questions

7. The United States promises to allow Native Americans to use their lands and to protect the Native Americans from U.S. citizens. Native Americans in turn agree to sell the land only to the United States and not accept protection from any other power. **18.B.3a**

8. Washington says it is human nature to want to form parties. **16.A.3b**

Chapter Planning Guide

9

BL	OL	AL	ELL		Resources	Chapter Opener	Section 1	Section 2	Section 3	Section 4	Chapter Assess
					FOCUS						
BL	OL	AL	ELL	🖋	**Daily Test Practice Transparencies**		9–1	9–2	9–3	9–4	
					TEACH						
	OL	AL		📁	**Geography and History Activity, URB**			p. 59			
BL	OL		ELL	📁	**Time Line Skills Activity, URB**			p. 62			
BL	OL	AL	ELL	📁	**Writing Skills Activity, URB**					p. 51	
	OL	AL		📁	**American Literature Readings, URB**				p. 9		
BL	OL	AL	ELL	📁	**Content Vocabulary Activity, URB**		p. 45	p. 45	p. 45	p. 45	
BL			ELL	📁	**Academic Vocabulary Activity, URB**		p. 47	p. 47	p. 47	p. 47	
BL			ELL	📁	**Social Studies Skills Activity, URB**					p. 53	
BL	OL	AL	ELL	📁	**Differentiated Instruction Activity, URB**			p. 55			
BL	OL	AL	ELL	📁	**Critical Thinking Skills Activity, URB**			p. 57			
BL	OL	AL	ELL	📁	**Linking Past and Present Activity, URB**				p. 61		
	OL	AL		📁	**Primary Source Readings, URB**		p. 49				
BL	OL	AL	ELL	📁	**School-to-Home Connection Activity, URB**		p. 63	p. 63	p. 63	p. 63	
BL	OL		ELL	📁	**Guided Reading Activity, URB***		p. 67	p. 68	p. 69	p. 70	
	OL	AL		📁	**Economics and History Activity, URB**		p. 5				
BL	OL		ELL	📁	**Reading Essentials and Note-Taking Guide***		p. 88	p. 91	p. 94	p. 97	
BL	OL	AL	ELL	🖋	**Lesson Transparencies**		9A	9B		9C	
	OL	AL		📁	**Interpreting Political Cartoons, URB**				p. 13		
		AL		📁	**Supreme Court Case Studies**		pp. 1, 3, 7				
	OL			📁	**American Biographies**			p. 14			
BL	OL	AL	ELL	📁	**Outline Map Resource Book**	p. 23					
	OL	AL		🖋	**American Art and Architecture Transparencies, Strategies, and Activities**		9				

Note: Please refer to the *Unit Resource Book: Launching the Republic* for this chapter's URB materials.

* Also available in Spanish

Levels					Resources	Chapter Opener	Section 1	Section 2	Section 3	Section 4	Chapter Assess
BL	OL	AL	ELL								
TEACH *(continued)*											
BL	OL	AL	ELL		NGS US Desk Map		✓	✓	✓	✓	
BL	OL	AL	ELL		American Literature Library		✓	✓	✓	✓	
BL	OL	AL	ELL		Writer's Guidebook		✓	✓	✓	✓	
	OL	AL			American History Primary Source Document Library CD-ROM		✓	✓	✓	✓	✓
BL	OL	AL	ELL		American Music: Hits Through History	✓	✓	✓	✓	✓	
BL	OL	AL	ELL		StudentWorks™ Plus CD	✓	✓	✓	✓	✓	✓
BL	OL	AL	ELL		Section Spotlight Videos		✓	✓	✓	✓	
BL	OL	AL	ELL		Writing Process Transparencies		✓	✓	✓	✓	✓
BL	OL	AL	ELL		Presentation Plus! With MindJogger CheckPoint CD	✓	✓	✓	✓	✓	✓
ASSESS											
BL	OL	AL	ELL		Quizzes and Tests		p. 81	p. 82	p. 83	p. 84	pp. 85, 87, 89
BL	OL	AL	ELL		Authentic Assessment With Rubrics				p. 9		
BL	OL	AL	ELL		Standardized Test Practice						p. 17
BL	OL	AL	ELL		*ExamView®* Assessment Suite CD-ROM*		9–1	9–2	9–3	9–4	Ch. 9
CLOSE											
BL			ELL		Reteaching Activity, URB*		p. 65	p. 65	p. 65	p. 65	p. 65
BL	OL		ELL		Reading and Study Skills Foldables Activity	p. 66	p. 66	p. 66	p. 66	p. 66	p. 66
BL	OL	AL	ELL		*The American Journey* in Graphic Novel						p. 45
BL			ELL		Reading Strategies and Activities for the Social Studies Classroom		✓	✓	✓	✓	
BL	OL	AL	ELL		Graphic Organizer Transparencies & Strategies		✓	✓	✓	✓	

TeacherWorks *Plus*
All-In-One Planner and Resource Center

- Interactive Lesson Planner
- Interactive Teacher Edition
- Fully editable blackline masters
- Section Spotlight Videos Launch

- Differentiated Lesson Plans
- Printable reports of daily assignments
- Standards Tracking System

Professional Development Resources

- Strategies for Success
- Building Academic Vocabulary
- Success With English Learners DVD
- Differentiated Instruction Strategies DVD
- Teaching Literacy Strategies in Social Studies DVD
- Assessment DVD
- Standards-Based Instruction DVD

Using StudentWorks™ Plus

Logging Daily Assignments

Technology Product

Glencoe's *StudentWorks™ Plus* CD contains the complete Student Edition and all student workbooks. *StudentWorks™ Plus* also includes a Daily Assignment and Activity Log that allows students to

- record and track progress on their daily assignments;
- log results achieved, including their grades;
- sort assignments alphabetically or by category;
- view and print the assignment and grade log.

Objectives

StudentWorks™ Plus will help your students

- take responsibility for their individual tasks;
- improve independent study skills.

Steps

Provide students with the following information:

- Launch *StudentWorks™ Plus*.
- Select the **Daily Assignment and Grade Log** button.
- Create a new file or open an existing one. The log is organized as a table, with a row of information for each assignment.
- Add information for each assignment.
- Edit rows as assignment information is provided or changed. Add a new row for each new assignment.

History ONLINE at glencoe.com

	Student	Teacher	Parent
Media Center			
• Student Edition Audio	●		
• Spanish Summaries	●		
• Section Spotlight Videos	●	●	
Social Studies Online Learning Center			
Classroom Tools			
• Multi-Language Glossaries	●	●	●
• Teaching Today		●	
• TIME Current Events	●	●	●
• Beyond the Textbook	●	●	
***The American Journey* Online Learning Center**			
• Study-to-Go™	●	●	●
• Study Central™	●	●	●
• Chapter Overview	●	●	
• Concepts in Motion	●	●	
• ePuzzles and Games	●	●	
• Literature Connections	●	●	
• Online Student Edition	●	●	●
• Self-Check Quizzes	●	●	●
• Student Web Activities	●	●	
• Vocabulary eFlashcards	●	●	
• Web Activity Lesson Plans	●	●	●
• Vocabulary PuzzleMaker	●	●	●

READING SUPPORT FROM JAMESTOWN EDUCATION

- **Timed Readings Plus in Social Studies** helps students increase their reading rate and fluency while maintaining comprehension. The 400-word passages are similar to those found on state and national assessments.

- **Reading in the Content Area: Social Studies** concentrates on six essential reading skills that help students better comprehend what they read. The book includes 75 high-interest nonfiction passages written at increasing levels of difficulty.

- **Reading Social Studies** includes strategic reading instruction and vocabulary support in Social Studies content for ELLs and native speakers of English.

- **Content Vocabulary Workout** (Grades 6–8) accelerates reading comprehension through focused vocabulary development. Social Studies content vocabulary comes from the glossaries of Glencoe's Middle School Social Studies texts.

www.jamestowneducation.com

NATIONAL GEOGRAPHIC

Index to National Geographic Magazine:

The following articles relate to this chapter:

- **"Searching for Sacagawea,"** Margaret Talbot, February 2003.

- **"Lewis and Clark's Lost Missouri,"** Cathy Riggs Salter, April 2002.

National Geographic Society Products

To order the following, call National Geographic at 1-800-368-2728:

National Geographic Atlas of the World (Book)

Access National Geographic's dynamic MapMachine Web site and other geography resources at:

www.nationalgeographic.com

www.nationalgeographic.com/mapmachine

Reading List Generator CD-ROM — GLENCOE BOOKLINK 3

Use this database to search more than 30,000 titles to create a customized reading list for your students.

- Reading lists can be organized by students' reading level, author, genre, theme, or area of interest.
- The database provides Degrees of Reading Power™ (DRP) and Lexile™ readability scores for all selections.
- A brief summary of each selection is included.

Leveled reading suggestions for this chapter:

For students at a Grade 6 reading level:
- **These Lands Are Ours: Tecumseh's Fight for the Old Northwest,** by Kate Connell

For students at a Grade 7 reading level:
- **Battles of the War of 1812,** by Diane & Henry Smolinski

For students at a Grade 8 reading level:
- **The War of 1812: "We Have Met the Enemy and They Are Ours,"** by Karen Clemens Warrick
- **Thomas Jefferson: Third President of the United States,** by Rebecca Stefoff

For students at a Grade 9 reading level:
- **The War of 1812,** by Don Nardo
- **Who Were the Founding Fathers?,** by Steven H. Jaffe

For students at a Grade 10 reading level:
- **American Wars and Heroes,** by Maurice Matloff

The following videotape programs are available from Glencoe as supplements to the chapter:

- **Lewis and Clark** (ISBN 1-56-501592-4)
- **Tecumseh: The Dream of Confederacy** (ISBN 0-76-701247-X)

To order, call Glencoe at 1-800-334-7344. To find classroom resources to accompany many of these videos, check the following home pages:

A&E Television: www.aetv.com

The History Channel: www.history.com

Chapter Objectives

After studying this chapter, students will be able to:

- Discuss the ways in which Thomas Jefferson and the Republicans limited the powers of the government.
- Explain how the Louisiana Purchase affected the nation's economy and politics.
- Identify the challenges to the nation's stability during the late 1700s and early 1800s.
- Describe how the United States benefited from its victory in the War of 1812.

Motivating Activity

The United States waged war on Great Britain in 1812, only 31 years after the Revolutionary War ended. **Ask:** Why were Americans anxious to go to war with Britain again? *(Americans had developed a nationalistic fervor and wanted to end British practices such as capturing and destroying ships, impressing sailors, and making alliances with Native Americans.)* **OL**

Previewing the Essential Questions

As you begin teaching each section, use these questions and activities to help students focus on the Essential Questions.

Chapter 9 The Jefferson Era 1800–1816

Monticello, located in Charlottesville, Virginia, was the home of Thomas Jefferson.

PRESIDENTS

THOMAS JEFFERSON 1801–1809

JAMES MADISON 1809–1817

U.S. Events

★ 1801 Robert Fulton builds first submarine

1803 Supreme Court establishes judicial review

1804 Lewis and Clark begin expedition ★

★ 1804 Alexander Hamilton duels with Aaron Burr

World Events

1800

1805

Drawing of Fulton's submarine ▶

★ 1803 War begins again between France and Britain

1804 ★ Napoleon proclaims himself emperor of France

1806 ★ Holy Roman Empire officially ends

★ 1808 Extensive excavations begin at Pompeii

274 Chapter 9

Section 1

The Republicans Take Power Ask: What kind of transition occurs today when a new president is of a different political party than the previous president? *(The transfer of power is peaceful and regulated by law.)* Tell students that in Section 1 they will learn about the transition from a Federalist to a Republican government after the 1800 election and the changes enacted by Thomas Jefferson. **OL**

Section 2

The Louisiana Purchase Ask: What benefits would a country gain by doubling in size? *(Answers might include more resources, land for settlement, and new transportation routes.)* Point out to students that Section 2 discusses the Louisiana Purchase and how it affected the economy and politics of the United States. **OL**

Section 1: The Republicans Take Power

Essential Question In what ways did Thomas Jefferson and the Republicans limit the powers of the government?

Section 2: The Louisiana Purchase

Essential Question How did the Louisiana Purchase affect the nation's economy and politics?

Section 3: A Time of Conflict

Essential Question What were the challenges to the nation's stability during the late 1700s and early 1800s?

Section 4: The War of 1812

Essential Question How did the United States benefit from its victory in the War of 1812?

FOLDABLES Study Organizer

Organizing Information
Make this four-tab Foldable to help you learn about the events of the Jefferson era.

Step 1 Fold the sides of a piece of paper into the middle to make a shutter fold.

Step 2 Cut each tab at the midpoint to form four tabs.

Step 3 Label the tabs as shown.

Reading and Writing
As you read the chapter, take notes about each section under the appropriate head. Use your Foldable to help you write a summary for each section.

◀ The U.S. Capitol after it was burned by the British in 1814.

Time Line Activity

Have students review the time line. **Ask:** Which nations experienced conflicts between 1800 and 1816? *(the United States, France, Britain, Ecuador, Spain, Russia, Venezuela)*

FOLDABLES Study Organizer **Dinah Zike's Foldables**

Purpose This Foldable helps students understand events of the Jefferson era. The completed Foldable will help them prepare for assessment.

📁 More Foldables activities for this chapter can be found in the *Dinah Zike's Reading and Study Skills Foldables.*

History ONLINE

Introduce students to chapter content and key terms by having them access the **Chapter Overview** at glencoe.com.

◀ Tecumseh

★ **1811** Tecumseh joins British forces after the Battle of Tippecanoe

★ **1812** U.S. declares war on Britain

1814 ★ British forces burn Washington, D.C.

★ **1815** Battle of New Orleans

1810 — **1812** — **1816**

★ **1809** Ecuador wins independence from Spain

1812 ★ Napoleon invades Russia

1813 ★ Simón Bolívar becomes dictator of Venezuela

★ **1814** Congress of Vienna meets

★ **1815** Napoleon defeated at Waterloo

Chapter 9   275

Section 3

A Time of Conflict Ask: What challenges might have come up as Americans continued to move westward onto lands already settled by Native Americans? *(Students might answer that conflict could arise over land rights and resources, and cultural clashes also might arise.)* Tell students that Section 3 will explore the challenges America faced as it grew. **OL**

Section 4

The War of 1812 Ask: Where was the War of 1812 fought? *(The War of 1812 was fought in many parts of the United States, including the Great Lakes, the Southeast, and the South.)* Explain to students that in Section 4, they will learn about the War of 1812 and how its outcome affected the United States. **OL**

Section 1

The Republicans Take Power

Focus

Section 1

Bellringer
Daily Test Practice Transparency 9–1

Reading Guide
Answers to Graphic:
Republicans decreased the size of government and the military, reduced military spending, and repealed federal internal taxes.

Section Spotlight Video

Have students watch the Section Spotlight Video "The Republicans Take Power" to learn about the changes that occurred in the Jefferson presidency.

Resource Manager

Essential Question ◀
In what ways did Thomas Jefferson and the Republicans limit the powers of the government?

Reading Guide

Content Vocabulary
laissez-faire (p. 278)   judicial review (p. 279)
customs duties (p. 278)

Academic Vocabulary
similar (p. 278)   conflict (p. 279)

Key People and Events
Thomas Jefferson (p. 277)
Aaron Burr (p. 277)
Judiciary Act of 1801 (p. 279)
Marbury v. Madison (p. 279)

Reading Strategy
Taking Notes As you read, use a diagram like the one below to identify how the Republicans reduced the role of government.

```
        Reducing the
      Role of Government
       /    |    \
     ( )   ( )   ( )
```

ILLINOIS STANDARDS
The American Journey

14.B Understand the structures and functions of the political systems of Illinois, the United States and other nations.

14.A.3 Describe how responsibilities are shared and limited by the United States and Illinois Constitutions and significant court decisions.

16.A Apply the skills of historical analysis and interpretation.

16.B.3c (US) Describe the way the Constitution has changed over time as a result of amendments and Supreme Court decisions.

American Diary

For eight years, Thomas Jefferson opposed the Federalists and eventually won the presidency as a member of a new political party—the Democratic-Republicans. In his Inaugural Address, Jefferson tried to reach out to Federalists and bridge the gap that developed between the two parties. "We are all Republicans, we are all Federalists. . . . Let us, then, with courage and confidence pursue our own Federal and Republican principles, our attachment to union and representative government."

—from Jefferson's first Inaugural Address, 1801

The Capitol, Washington, D.C., 1800

R Reading Strategies	**C** Critical Thinking	**D** Differentiated Instruction	**W** Writing Support	**S** Skill Practice
Teacher Edition • Deter. Importance, p. 279	**Teacher Edition** • Analyz. Information, p. 278	**Teacher Edition** • Visual/Spatial, p. 277	**Teacher Edition** • Persuasive Writing, p. 278	**Teacher Edition** • Using Geo. Skills, p. 277
Additional Resources • Guid. Read., URB p. 67 • Content Vocab., URB p. 45 • Academic Vocab., URB p. 47 • Read. Ess., p. 88 • Pri. Source Read., URB p. 49	**Additional Resources** • Quizzes and Tests, p. 81 • Econ. and Hist., URB p. 5	**Additional Resources** • School-to-Home, URB p. 63 • Reteaching Act., URB p. 65		**Additional Resources** • Daily Test Pract. Transp. 9-1 • Lesson Transp. 9A

The Election of 1800

Main Idea The election of 1800 showed that power could be peacefully transferred even when the political parties were in disagreement.

History and You Think about today's political campaigns. Are they based on emotional appeals or serious discussion of the issues? Read to find out how the presidential election campaign of 1800 was conducted.

. . . .

The Federalist and Republican Parties fought a bitter election campaign in 1800. Federalists supported President Adams for a second term and Charles Pinckney for vice president. Republicans nominated **Thomas Jefferson** for president and **Aaron Burr** as his running mate.

The election campaign of 1800 differed greatly from campaigns of today. Neither Adams nor Jefferson traveled around the country to gather support. This would have been considered inappropriate. Instead, the candidates and their supporters began a letter-writing campaign. They sent hundreds of letters to leading citizens and newspapers to make their views public. Federalists

accused Jefferson, who believed in freedom of religion, of being "godless." Republicans warned that the Federalists favored the wealthy and would bring back monarchy.

Election Deadlock

Jefferson and Burr each received 73 electoral votes. Because of the tie vote, the House of Representatives had to decide the election. At this time, the electors voted for each candidate individually. The candidate with the majority of votes became president. The candidate with the next-largest number of votes became vice president.

In the House, Federalists saw a chance to prevent the election of Jefferson. They supported Burr. For 35 ballots, the election remained tied. Finally, at Alexander Hamilton's urging, one Federalist decided not to vote for Burr. Jefferson became president, and Burr became vice president.

To prevent another tie between a presidential and vice-presidential candidate, Congress passed the Twelfth Amendment to the Constitution in 1803. Electors now had to vote for the president and vice president on separate ballots.

By the Numbers / **Election Results, 1800**

Boundary disputed by Britain and the U.S.

N W E S

0 400 kilometers
0 400 miles
Albers Equal-Area projection

VT 4 — NH 6
NY 12 — MA 16
— RI 4
Terr. NW of Ohio R. — PA 8 — NJ 7 — CT 9
Indiana Terr. — KY 4 — VA 21 — DE 3
— MD 3
TN 3 — NC 8 4
Terr. South of Ohio R. — SC 8
GA 4
Miss. Terr.

Presidential Candidate
☐ Jefferson (Democratic-Republican)
■ Adams (Federalist)
3 Electoral votes

Critical Thinking

Speculating Do you think a person's political views will always match those of his or her political party?

Creating a Children's Story

Step 1: Choosing a Topic to Explore In-Depth Students will select a topic from the Jefferson era and locate research sources in preparation for creating a children's story that explores the topic in-depth.

Essential Question: In what ways did Thomas Jefferson and the Republicans limit the powers of the government?

Directions Tell students to form small groups. Ask each group to choose a topic from the chapter that it finds interesting and locate three sources on the topic to learn more about it. Possible topics include the life of Thomas Jefferson, the "midnight judges," Conestoga wagon travel, the Louisiana Purchase, the Lewis and Clark expedition, the Barbary Wars, and the War of 1812.

Problem Solving As a class, discuss how the topic of Jeffersonian limits on the powers of government could be simplified and presented as a children's story. Students should think about how they can use these ideas to simplify the presentations of their own topics in their stories. **OL**

(Chapter Project continued in Section 2)

Teach
. . . .

S Skill Practice

Using Geography Skills Have students look at the map on this page. **Ask:** Which color appears on the map but not on the key? *(Green)* What does it represent? *(It is used to show territories, which would not have voted in the election.)* **BL**

D Differentiated Instruction

Visual/Spatial Have students make a Venn diagram on a piece of paper showing the similarities and differences between presidential election campaigning in 1800 and today. *(**1800 only:** no travel, intensive letter writing. **Area of similarity:** criticizing of other candidates. **Today:** extensive travel; TV, radio, and print ads.)* **OL**

By the Numbers

Critical Thinking Answer Students might answer that a person's political views probably match those of his or her political party more than they match the views of other parties but that most people's views probably differ from the party's views to some degree.

Hands-On Chapter Project
Step 1

C Critical Thinking

Analyzing Information Ask: Why did Thomas Jefferson oppose a large federal government? *(Jefferson believed that state governments were more able to reflect the will of the people and thus protect freedom and liberty.)* **OL**

W Writing Support

Persuasive Writing Ask: Did Thomas Jefferson really believe that people should do as they choose? Have students write a persuasive essay in which they defend their answer to this question. **AL**

Primary Source

Critical Thinking Answer
Students might state that successful inventors need to be curious, persistent, and open to new ideas.

✓ **Reading Check Answer:** The Twelfth Amendment requires Americans to vote for the offices of president and vice president separately.

Differentiated Instruction

Primary Source / Inventor and Architect

Invention and Design Thomas Jefferson was a passionate inventor and architect. He invented a plow that was easy to use on hills, a machine to make macaroni, and a device to encode secret messages. Jefferson also designed his Monticello home and the Rotunda on the campus of the University of Virginia.

"One new idea leads to another, that to a third, and so on through a course of time until some one, with whom no one of these ideas was original, combines all together, and produces what is justly called a new invention."
—*The Writings of Thomas Jefferson*

▲ Jefferson employed other people's inventions at his Monticello home. He used a copying machine, known as a "polygraph," invented by John Isaac Hawkins. This machine used two pens to copy words at the same time, allowing the writer to create automatic duplicates of documents.

◄ Thomas Jefferson and Charles-Louis Clerisseau were the architects for Virginia's State Capitol in Richmond. Jefferson's design was inspired by first-century Roman architecture.

Critical Thinking

Drawing Conclusions What characteristics do you think a person should have in order to be a successful inventor?

Jefferson's Inauguration

Jefferson, dressed in everyday clothes, walked from his boardinghouse to the Senate to be sworn in as president. President Adams chose not to attend the ceremony.

C In his Inaugural Address, Jefferson tried to bridge the gap between the political parties. Then he outlined some of his goals. They included "a wise and frugal government" and "the support of state governments in all their rights." Jefferson believed a large federal government threatened liberty. The states, he believed, could better protect freedom.

W Jefferson believed in reducing the power and size of the government. These ideas were **similar** to the French philosophy known as **laissez-faire** (LEH•SAY FEHR). This phrase means "let people do as they choose."

✓ **Reading Check Describing** What does the Twelfth Amendment require?

Jefferson's Presidency

Main Idea Thomas Jefferson wanted to reduce the power of the federal government.

History and You How do you think government should balance individual liberty with national interests? Read about Jefferson's views.
• •

Thomas Jefferson had strong ideas about how to make the United States a great nation. He surrounded himself with those who shared his views.

Cutting Costs

Jefferson and Albert Gallatin, secretary of the treasury, reduced the national debt. They scaled down military expenses. All federal internal taxes, including the whiskey tax, were repealed. Government funds would come only from **customs duties**—taxes on imported goods—and from the money raised

Leveled Activities

BL Academic Vocabulary Activity, URB p. 47

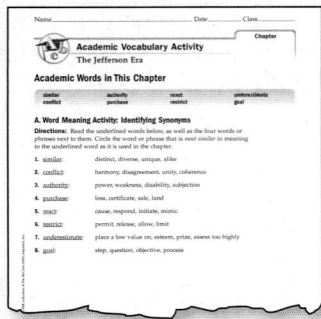

OL Reading Essentials and Note-Taking Guide, p. 88

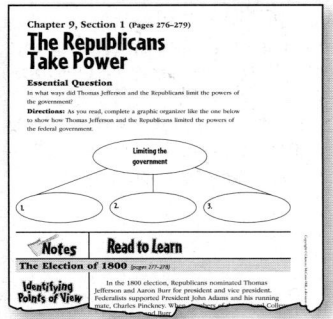

AL Economics and History Activity, URB p. 5

from the sale of western lands. Jefferson also limited the number of federal government workers to a few hundred people.

Judiciary Act of 1801

Before Jefferson took office, the Federalists passed the **Judiciary Act of 1801.** This act set up regional courts for the United States with 16 judges and other judicial officials.

In his last days as president, John Adams made hundreds of appointments to these judicial positions with the approval of the Federalist-controlled Congress. Adams also asked John Marshall, secretary of state, to serve as chief justice. Thus, Adams shut Jefferson out of the appointment process and ensured Federalist control of the courts.

Adams and Marshall worked around the clock to process these judicial appointments. The appointments could not take effect, however, until the papers, also known as commissions, for these last-minute "midnight judges" were received. When Jefferson became president, a few of the commissions had not yet been delivered. He told his Secretary of State James Madison not to deliver them. One commission was to go to William Marbury.

Marbury v. Madison

To force the delivery of his commission, Marbury took his case directly to the Supreme Court. He claimed this court had jurisdiction. John Marshall wrote an opinion turning down Marbury's claim. He noted that the Constitution did not give the Court jurisdiction to decide Marbury's case.

In ***Marbury v. Madison,*** three principles of **judicial review** were established: (1) the Constitution is the supreme law; (2) the Constitution must be followed when there is a **conflict,** or disagreement, between it and any other law; and (3) the judicial branch must uphold the Constitution and nullify, or cancel, unconstitutional laws.

Marshall broadened federal power at the expense of the states. In *McCulloch v. Maryland* (1819), the Court held that Congress is allowed to do more than the Constitution expressly authorizes it to do. In *Gibbons v. Ogden* (1824), the Court held that federal law takes precedence over state law in interstate transportation.

Reading Check **Summarizing** Summarize the three principles of judicial review.

History ONLINE
Study Central™ To review this section, go to glencoe.com.

Section 1 Review

Vocabulary

1. Use the following terms in sentences that show you understand their meanings: similar, laissez-faire, customs duties, judicial review, conflict.

Main Ideas

2. Discussing How did President Jefferson's Inaugural Address reflect his beliefs about government?

3. Explaining Explain how the Federalists benefited from the Judiciary Act of 1801.

Critical Thinking

4. Identifying Central Issues Use a diagram like the one below to show how the powers of the Supreme Court and federal law were extended.

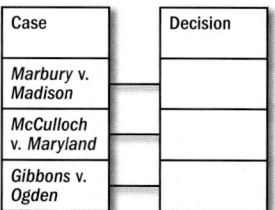

Case		Decision
Marbury v. Madison		
McCulloch v. Maryland		
Gibbons v. Ogden		

5. Persuasive Writing You are a supporter of Thomas Jefferson in the 1800 election. Write a letter to voters that will appear in all the newspapers in your state.

Answer the
6. Essential Question
In what ways did Thomas Jefferson and the Republicans limit the powers of the government?

The Jefferson Era **Chapter 9** **279**

CHAPTER 9
Section 1

R Reading Strategy

Determining Importance After reading the text on *Marbury v. Madison,* have students work in pairs to write a sentence telling the main idea of the subsection. Remind them to use their own words. **OL**

Reading Check **Answer:** The Constitution is the supreme law and must be followed when it conflicts with another law. Any unconstitutional law must be nullified.

Assess

History ONLINE

Study Central™ provides summaries, interactive games, and online graphic organizers to help students review content.

Close

Discussing Have small groups discuss the changes that Thomas Jefferson brought to government when he became president. **OL**

Section ★ Review

Answers

1. Students will write sentences correctly using the terms.

2. First, Jefferson wore his everyday clothes to show he was not above the people he served. Then, in his Inaugural Address, he outlined his goals of a thrifty government and the support of states to better protect their freedoms than a large federal body.

3. The act set up regional courts in which judicial positions were filled with Federalists.

Thus, Republicans were shut out of the judicial appointment process giving Federalists control of the courts.

4. *Marbury v. Madison:* Judicial review principles confirm the ultimate authority of the Supreme Court. *McCulloch v. Maryland:* Congress can do more than what is expressly authorized in the Constitution. *Gibbons v. Ogden:* Federal law takes precedence over state law in interstate transportation.

5. Students will write persuasive letters that should include why Jefferson's beliefs will make him a better leader.

6. They reduced military spending and size, repealed all federal internal taxes, and kept government small.

Focus

Reading Guide
Answers to Graphic:

Lewis and Clark: from St. Louis westward to the Pacific Ocean

Zebulon Pike: upper Mississippi valley to Colorado, northern Rio Grande to southern Texas

Section Spotlight Video

Have students watch the Section Spotlight Video "The Louisiana Purchase" to learn about Lewis and Clark's exploration of the land later acquired in the Louisiana Purchase.

Resource Manager

Section 2

Essential Question ◄
How did the Louisiana Purchase affect the nation's economy and politics?

Reading Guide

Content Vocabulary
Conestoga wagon *(p. 281)*
secede *(p. 285)*

Academic Vocabulary
purchase *(p. 283)*   authority *(p.283)*

Key People and Events
Napoleon Bonaparte *(p. 282)*
Meriwether Lewis *(p. 284)*
William Clark *(p. 284)*
Sacagawea *(p. 284)*
Zebulon Pike *(p. 285)*

Reading Strategy
Taking Notes As you read, use a diagram like the one below to describe the areas that Lewis and Clark and Zebulon Pike explored.

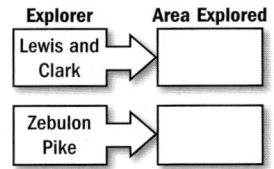

Explorer	Area Explored
Lewis and Clark →	
Zebulon Pike →	

ILLINOIS STANDARDS
The American Journey

17.C Understand relationships between geographic factors and society.
17.D.3a Explain how and why spatial patterns of settlement change over time.
17.D.3b Explain how interactions of geographic factors have shaped present conditions.

The Louisiana Purchase

American Diary

In this journal entry from May 5, 1805, Meriwether Lewis describes America's bounty along the trail: "Buffalo Elk and goats or Antelopes feeding in every direction; we kill whatever we wish, the buffalo furnish us with fine veal and fat beef, we also have venison and beaver tails when we wish them; the flesh of the Elk and goat are less esteemed, and certainly are inferior. We have not been able to take any fish for some time past. The country is as yesterday beautiful! in the extreme."

—*from the journals of Lewis and Clark*

Lewis and Clark explore the lands west of the Mississippi River.

R Reading Strategies	**C** Critical Thinking	**D** Differentiated Instruction	**W** Writing Support	**S** Skill Practice
Teacher Edition • Summarizing, p. 281 • Questioning, p. 285 **Additional Resources** • Guid. Read., URB p. 68 • Content Vocab., URB p. 45 • Academic Vocab., URB p. 47 • Read. Ess., p. 91	**Teacher Edition** • Predicting Consequences, p. 282 **Additional Resources** • Quizzes and Tests, p. 82 • Crit. Think. Skills, URB p. 57	**Teacher Edition** • English Language Learners, p. 281 • Verbal/Linguistic, p. 284 **Additional Resources** • School-to-Home, URB p. 63 • Reteaching Act., URB p. 65 • Differ. Inst., URB p. 55	**Teacher Edition** • Persuasive Writing, p. 283 • Expository Writing, p. 284	**Teacher Edition** • Using Geo. Skills, p. 282 • Using Geo. Skills, p. 283 **Additional Resources** • Daily Test Pract. Transp. 9-2 • Time Line Skills, URB p. 62 • Geo. & Hist., URB p. 59 • Lesson Transp. 9B

Western Territory

Main Idea As Americans moved west in the early 1800s, Spain and France made a secret agreement about land that affected American trade.

History and You If you have ever moved to a new city or state, what challenges did you face? How did you learn where grocery stores or your school were located? Read to learn about challenges that the pioneers experienced as they moved west.

During the early 1800s, Americans moved west in search of land and adventure. Pioneers traveled over the mountains into Kentucky and Tennessee. Many also set out for the less settled areas of the Northwest Territory. Most of these pioneers were farmers. They made a long and exhausting journey over the Appalachian Mountains. Pioneers heading to the western lands had to trudge along crude, muddy roads or cut their way through dense forests.

Settlers loaded their household goods into **Conestoga wagons,** sturdy vehicles topped with white canvas. These westward-bound **D** pioneers traveled with their two most valued possessions: rifles and axes. Rifles were **R** carried for protection and for hunting animals for food. Axes helped the settlers cut through the dense forests so that their wagons could travel through them.

In 1800 the territory of the United States extended only as far west as the Mississippi River. The area to the west of the river was known as the Louisiana Territory. This region belonged to Spain. It was an enormous area of land, anchored to the south by the city of New Orleans and extending west to the Rocky Mountains. Its northern boundaries remained undefined.

Many of the pioneers established farms along rivers that fed into the upper Mississippi River. They used the river system to ship their crops to markets. The goods they sent downriver were unloaded in New Orleans. The goods were then loaded onto other ships and sent to markets on the East Coast. If the farmers did not have access to the Mississippi River, then there was no way to ship their goods.

Even though the Spanish controlled the region, they allowed the Americans to sail on the lower Mississippi and trade in New Orleans. For the western farmers, this agreement was vital to their economic survival.

Primary Source / The Journals

Exploring the West From 1804 to 1806, Meriwether Lewis and William Clark explored and mapped more than 7,000 miles (11,265 km) from St. Louis to the Pacific Ocean and back. During the journey, they met with many Native Americans and accumulated valuable information about the western frontier.

In addition to their travel supplies, the expedition also took along items that were used to trade or give as gifts to the Native Americans. These items included:

- 12 dozen pocket mirrors
- 144 small pairs of scissors
- 8 brass kettles
- 33 pounds (15 kg) of tiny beads of assorted colors

Critical Thinking

Speculating What challenges do you think the expedition might have faced?

Teach

R Reading Strategy

Summarizing Have students write a summary of the text that describes the area west of the Mississippi River in the early 1800s. To prevent students from repeating the text word for word, tell them their summaries can be no longer than four sentences. **OL**

This **READING SKILL** (Summarizing Information) was introduced in this unit.

D Differentiated Instruction

English Language Learners Have students draw a picture of a group of Conestoga wagons at the edge of a forest. Instruct them to include a caption explaining how early settlers moved through dense trees. **ELL**

Primary Source

Critical Thinking Answer
Answers might include severe weather, relations with Native Americans, illness, food shortages, and dangerous river conditions.

Differentiated Instruction

Early Pioneer Medicine

Objective: To learn about early pioneer medicine

Focus: Ask students what medical practices were used when pioneers began to move west.

Teach: Have students study the table and answer the questions.

Assess: Use the Answer Key, and discuss the answers where needed.

Close: Discuss whether similar remedies are used today.

Differentiated Instruction Strategies

BL Ask students to name plants used in promoting health today.

AL Ask students to conduct research to create a table of herbal medicine today.

ELL Have students make a list of herbal remedies used in their country of origin. Instruct them to use English names when possible.

Differentiated Instruction Activity, URB p. 55

C Critical Thinking

Predicting Consequences Ask: How might America be different if Napoleon had taken over Santo Domingo in the early 1800s? *(Answers should address the fact that France would have had a naval base to help control an American empire, so part of the United States today might be French.)* **OL**

S Skill Practice

Using Geography Skills Have students locate Haiti on a map of the Western Hemisphere. **Ask:** What island nations are near Haiti? *(Answers might include Cuba, Dominican Republic, and Puerto Rico.)* **BL**

Primary Source

Critical Thinking Answer
Answers might include food, equipment and materials for repairs, clothes for warmth, and medicine.

Reading Check **Answer:** Jefferson worried that farmers might not be allowed to send their goods down the Mississippi River to New Orleans, thereby cutting off trade with East Coast markets.

Hands-On Chapter Project
Step 2

Creating a Children's Story

Step 2: Researching the Topic Students will research the topics of their stories using the sources they located in Step 1.

Essential Question: How did the Louisiana Purchase affect the nation's economy and politics?

Primary Source / The Conestoga Wagon

Wagons to Go West Conestoga wagons were first built in the Conestoga Creek region of Lancaster, Pennsylvania. During the mid-1700s, these sturdy wagons transported settlers over the Appalachian Mountains. As people pushed even farther westward, Conestoga wagons could be seen rolling across the plains toward Oregon and California.

1 Six to eight draft horses or a dozen oxen pull the wagon. The driver rides or walks beside the animals.

2 The boat-shaped wagon's high front and back keep goods from falling out on steep mountain trails.

3 A **toolbox** attached to the side of the wagon holds spare parts for needed repairs.

4 A white canvas cloth stretches over the hoops, or **wagon bows.** This cover protects passengers and cargo from heat, rain, and snow.

5 Broad **wheels** help keep the heavy wagon from being mired in the mud.

The average Conestoga wagon was 21 feet (6 m) long and 11 feet (3 m) high. It could carry up to 12,000 pounds (5,443 kg) of cargo.

Critical Thinking

Listing List three things a family traveling by wagon will have to plan for.

The French Threat

In 1802, however, the Spanish suddenly changed their policy. They refused to allow American goods to move into or past New Orleans. President Jefferson confirmed that Spain and France had secretly agreed to transfer the Louisiana Territory to France.

Jefferson was alarmed. This agreement between Spain and France posed a serious diplomatic and economic threat to the United States. France's leader, **Napoleon Bonaparte,** had plans to create empires in Europe and the Americas. Jefferson believed French control would put American trade on the Mississippi River at risk. Jefferson authorized Robert Livingston, the new minister to France, to offer as much as $10 million for New Orleans and West Florida in order to gain control of the territory. Jefferson believed that France had gained Florida as well as Louisiana in its secret agreement with Spain.

Revolt in Santo Domingo

Napoleon saw Santo Domingo as an important Caribbean naval base from which he could control an American empire. Events in Santo Domingo, however, ended Napoleon's dream of a Western empire.

The ideas of the French Revolution inspired enslaved Africans and other laborers in Santo Domingo to revolt against the island's plantation owners. Toussaint-Louverture (TOO•SA LOO•vuhr•TYUR) led the rebels. After fierce fighting, the rebels won and declared the colony an independent republic. Toussaint-Louverture established a new government.

In 1802 Napoleon sent troops to regain control of Santo Domingo, but they were not successful. By 1804, the French were driven out of Santo Domingo. The country regained its original name of Haiti.

Reading Check **Explaining** Why did French control of the Louisiana Territory worry Jefferson?

Directions Have students take notes as they research their topics. Then ask them to review their notes and create an outline for a story. Tell them to think about the story's audience and how they might present the information in a clear, fun, and educational way.

Analyzing As a class, discuss how the Louisiana Purchase might be used as the subject of a story. Talk about what details might be interesting to children and the ways in which they might be presented. **OL**

(Chapter Project continued in Section 3)

The Nation Expands

Main Idea The Louisiana Purchase opened a vast area to exploration and settlement.

History and You Imagine you are preparing to lead an expedition to explore new lands. Who would you travel with? What would you like to research? Read about the exploration of the Louisiana Territory.

. . . .

Without Santo Domingo, Napoleon had little use for Louisiana. Napoleon, however, needed money to finance his plans for war against Britain. The French believed that it was time to sell the Louisiana Territory.

French foreign minister Charles de Talleyrand informed the American diplomats that the entire Louisiana Territory was for sale. Robert Livingston and James Monroe, who was Jefferson's new special representative, were taken completely by surprise. They were not authorized to accept such an offer. The deal, however, was too good to pass up. After a few days of negotiation, the parties agreed on a price of $15 million.

The new territory would provide cheap and abundant land for farmers for future generations and give the United States control of the Mississippi River. Jefferson worried, though, about whether the **purchase** was legal. The Constitution said nothing about acquiring new territory. By what **authority**, or power, could he justify the purchase? Livingston wrote from Paris. He urged Jefferson to accept the deal before Napoleon changed his mind. Jefferson decided the government's treaty-making powers allowed the purchase of the new territory. The Senate approved it in October 1803. The size of the United States doubled.

Lewis and Clark

Little was known about the newly acquired land west of the Mississippi. Even before the deal was complete, Jefferson had been making plans to learn more about the western territory. He persuaded Congress to sponsor an expedition to gather information about the new land. Jefferson was particularly interested in the expedition as a scientific venture.

W Writing Support

Persuasive Writing Have students write a persuasive speech that Thomas Jefferson might have delivered to Congress asking it to fund an exploration of lands gained in the Louisiana Purchase. Remind them to use information they learned about Jefferson earlier in the chapter, including his passion for knowledge and invention. **AL**

S Skill Practice

Using Geography Skills Have students study the map of westward expansion on this page. **Ask:** What generalization can you make about how the explorers chose their routes? *(The explorers tended to travel along rivers.)* As a class, discuss why these explorers would have preferred river travel over other modes of transportation. **OL**

Louisiana Purchase & Westward Expansion NATIONAL GEOGRAPHIC

Critical Thinking Answer

Lewis and Clark were given the task of finding and mapping the "Northwest Passage" to Asia.

Additional Support

Louisiana Purchase and Westward Expansion NATIONAL GEOGRAPHIC

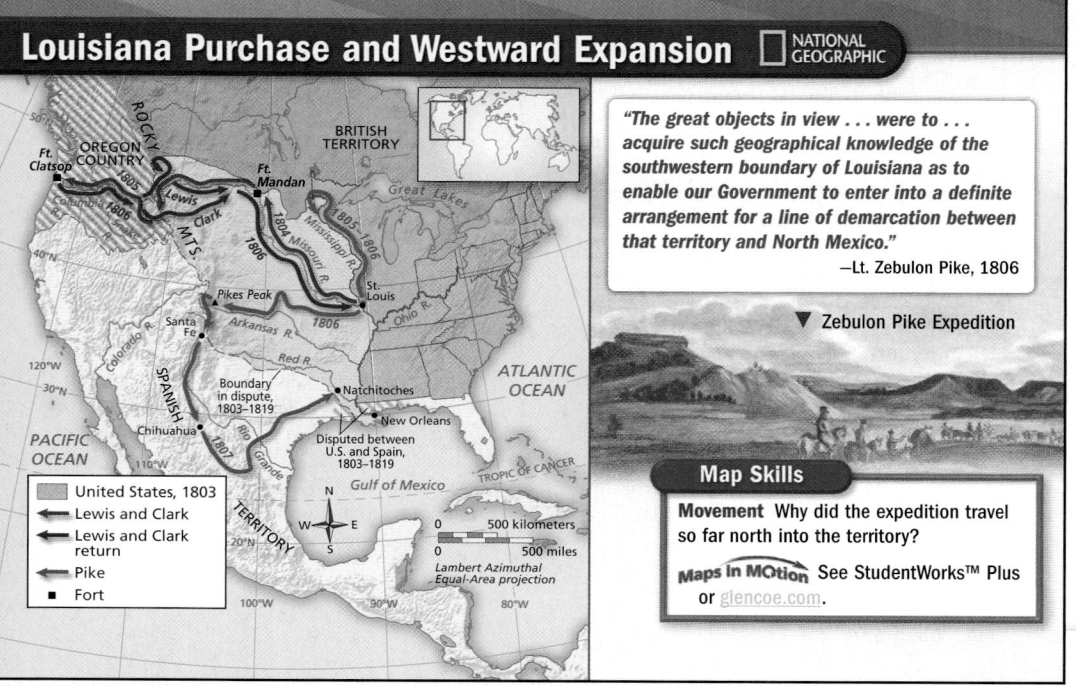

"The great objects in view . . . were to . . . acquire such geographical knowledge of the southwestern boundary of Louisiana as to enable our Government to enter into a definite arrangement for a line of demarcation between that territory and North Mexico."
—Lt. Zebulon Pike, 1806

▼ Zebulon Pike Expedition

United States, 1803
← Lewis and Clark
← Lewis and Clark return
← Pike
■ Fort

Map Skills

Movement Why did the expedition travel so far north into the territory?

 Maps in MOtion See StudentWorks™ Plus or glencoe.com.

Collaborative Learning

Speculating Have students form small groups and research the Lewis and Clark expedition. Tell them to choose a particularly difficult experience for the explorers and write a newspaper account of the event. The students should include details about how the explorers handled the situation and report the story as if they were accompanying the group. **Ask:** What advantages would you have if you explored the same route today? *(Students might answer that they would be able to use cell phones to call for help, they would encounter more people along the way, they would have good maps for navigation, and they would be able to take along more effective medicines.)* **OL**

Teacher Tip

Evaluating The most accurate source for information on the Lewis and Clark expedition is the journals written by the participants. If students choose to use Internet sources, remind them to ask these questions: Who created the information? Is the source reliable? What is the purpose of the Web site?

People IN HISTORY

William Clark's journal ▼

Sacagawea
Shoshone Interpreter

Sacagawea, the daughter of a Shoshone chief, was kidnapped by the Hidatsa Indians when she was a young girl. Later, she was sold to a French Canadian fur trader who married her.

The couple brought along their infant son when they were hired as interpreters by Meriwether Lewis and William Clark for their expedition to the Pacific Ocean.

Sacagawea made herself invaluable. She negotiated the purchases of horses, found edible wild plants, and made moccasins and clothing. Clark wrote that her presence alone calmed fears among Native Americans:

"The sight of This Indian woman . . . confirmed those people of our friendly intentions, as no woman ever accompanies a war party of Indians in this quarter [region]."
—from the journals of Lewis and Clark

CRITICAL Thinking

Theorizing What challenges might the expedition have faced without Sacagawea?

Writing Support

W **Expository Writing** Ask students to read first-hand accounts written by Lewis and Clark. Then have them imagine they spent a week with the expedition party. Have students write a magazine article describing the experience and including headlines and illustrations of what they might have seen. **AL**

D Differentiated Instruction

Verbal/Linguistic Have students write a poem or journal entry describing how Lewis and Clark might have felt as they embarked on their expedition. Remind them to think about what the explorers knew of the area they were to visit, the dangers they expected to encounter, and their backgrounds. **OL**

People IN HISTORY

Critical Thinking Answers

Answers might include language barriers, hunger, relations with Native Americans, and the ability to stay warm and dry.

Differentiated Instruction

W The expedition would document findings about the territory's plants and animals and recommend sites for future forts.

The expedition was also responsible for finding and mapping the fabled "Northwest Passage." In order to trade with Asia, Europeans had to sail around Africa. The route was time-consuming and costly, so European explorers searched, unsuccessfully, for a more direct route. Once the Americas were colonized, Americans and Europeans continued to sail around Africa or around the tip of South America in order to reach Asia. It became more important than ever to find a water route across North America.

To head the expedition, Jefferson chose **Meriwether Lewis,** his 28-year-old private secretary. During the Whiskey Rebellion, Lewis joined the militia and had been in the army since that time. The expedition's coleader was **William Clark.** Clark was 32 years old and a friend of Lewis's.

Both Lewis and Clark were well-informed amateur scientists. They both had conducted business with Native Americans. Together they assembled a crew of expert river men, gunsmiths, carpenters, scouts, and a cook. Two men of mixed Native American and French heritage served as interpreters. An African American named York was also a member of the group.

D The expedition left St. Louis in the spring of 1804 and worked its way up the Missouri River. Lewis and Clark kept a journal and made notes on what they saw and did.

Along their journey, the members of the expedition encountered many Native American groups. One young Shoshone woman named **Sacagawea** (sA•kuh•juh•WEE•uh) joined their group as a guide. After 18 months and nearly 4,000 miles (6,437 km), Lewis and Clark reached the Pacific Ocean. They spent the winter there, and then both explorers headed back east along separate routes.

Leveled Activities

BL Guided Reading Activity, URB p. 68

OL Time Line Skills Activity, URB p. 62

AL Geography and History Activity, URB p. 59

The expedition returned in September 1806. Lewis and Clark collected valuable information about people, plants, animals, and the geography of the West. Perhaps most important, their journey inspired people to move westward.

Pike's Expedition

Jefferson sent others to explore the wilderness in addition to Lewis and Clark. Lieutenant **Zebulon Pike** led two expeditions between 1805 and 1807. He traveled through the upper Mississippi River valley and into present-day Colorado. In Colorado he found a snowcapped mountain he called Grand Peak, known today as Pikes Peak. Americans learned about the Great Plains and Rocky Mountains from his travels. Pike also mapped part of the Rio Grande and traveled across northern Mexico and what is now southern Texas.

Federalists Plan to Secede

Many Federalists opposed the Louisiana Purchase. They feared that states created from the territory would be Republican and the Federalists would lose power. A group of Federalists in Massachusetts plotted to **secede,** or withdraw, from the Union. New England would become the "Northern Confederacy."

The plotters wanted their plan to be successful. They realized that the Northern Confederacy would have to include New York. The Massachusetts Federalists needed a powerful friend in that state who would support their plan. They turned to Aaron Burr. The Republicans cast aside Burr when he refused to withdraw from the 1800 election. The Federalists gave Burr their support when he ran for governor of New York in 1804.

Burr and Hamilton

Alexander Hamilton had never trusted Aaron Burr. Now Hamilton was concerned about rumors of secession. He heard that Burr had secretly agreed to lead New York out of the Union. Hamilton accused Burr of plotting treason. When Burr lost the election for governor, he blamed Hamilton and challenged him to a duel. In July 1804, the two men—armed with pistols—met in Weehawken, New Jersey. Hamilton hated dueling and pledged not to shoot at his rival. Burr, however, aimed to hit Hamilton and shot him. Hamilton was seriously wounded and died the next day. Burr fled to avoid arrest.

Reading Check Summarizing Why did France sell the Louisiana Territory to the United States?

History ONLINE
Study Central™ To review this section, go to glencoe.com.

Section 2 Review

Vocabulary

1. Define each of the following terms: Conestoga wagon, purchase, authority, secede.

Main Ideas

2. **Specifying** How did the secret agreement between Spain and France affect American settlers?

3. **Summarizing** Discuss the reaction of the Federalists to the Louisiana Purchase.

Critical Thinking

4. **Organizing** Create a graphic organizer like the one below that lists the benefits of acquiring the Louisiana Territory.

Benefits

5. **Creative Writing** You are the cook on the Lewis and Clark expedition. Write a one-paragraph diary entry that describes the crew and how you feel about the trip so far.

Answer the
6. **Essential Question**
How did the Louisiana Purchase affect the nation's economy and politics?

R Reading Strategy

Questioning Have students turn the subhead into a question, such as "Why did the Federalists consider secession?" Then have pairs of students take turns reading the subsection aloud to find the answer. **OL**

Reading Check **Answer:** Napoleon had no need for the land after the Santo Domingo revolt ended his plans for an American empire. He also needed money to finance his war with England.

Assess
....

History ONLINE

Study Central™ provides summaries, interactive games, and online graphic organizers to help students review content.

Close
....

Summarizing Ask students to summarize in a few sentences how the Louisiana Purchase changed the United States. **OL**

Section 2 Review

Answers

1. Students will correctly define the terms.
2. Spain no longer controlled the Louisiana Territory and refused to let Americans use the port of New Orleans. This action threatened U.S. trade on the Mississippi and thus the livelihood of Western farmers who relied on river travel to get their goods to market in the East.

3. The Federalists opposed the Louisiana Purchase because they suspected that new states would be Republican and jeopardize the balance of power. Some Federalists planned to secede.
4. land for settlement, access to the Mississippi and the port of New Orleans, access to a possible Northwest Passage

5. Students will write descriptive paragraphs.
6. It secured the Mississippi trade route; provided cheap, abundant land for farming; inspired westward expansion; and raised fears of increased support for the Republicans which, in turn, caused some Federalists to call for secession.

Focus

Section 3

A Time of Conflict

Bellringer
Daily Test Practice Transparency 9–3

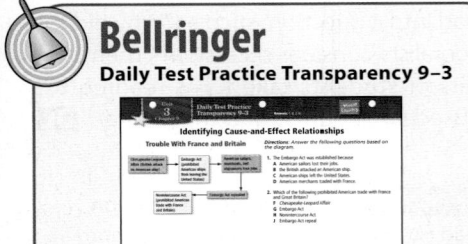

Reading Guide
Answers to Graphic:
Demand for Tribute: war with Tripoli;
Attacks on the *Chesapeake*: Embargo
Act and Nonintercourse Act; **Tecumseh's
Confederation:** Battle of Tippecanoe

Section Spotlight Video

Have students watch the Section Spotlight Video "A Time of Conflict" to learn about problems with Native Americans on the frontier.

Resource Manager

Essential Question ◄
What were the challenges to the nation's stability during the late 1700s and early 1800s?

Reading Guide

Content Vocabulary
tribute (p. 287)   embargo (p. 290)
neutral rights (p. 289)   nationalism (p. 293)
impressment (p. 289)

Academic Vocabulary
react (p. 289)   restriction (p. 291)

Key People and Events
Embargo Act (p. 290)
Nonintercourse Act (p. 290)
Tecumseh (p. 291)
Battle of Tippecanoe (p. 293)
Henry Clay (p. 293)
John Calhoun (p. 293)

Reading Strategy
Taking Notes As you read, create a chart like the one below, and describe the actions the United States took in each of the situations.

	Action Taken
Demand for Tribute	
Attacks on the *Chesapeake*	
Tecumseh's Confederation	

ILLINOIS STANDARDS
The American Journey

14.E Understand United States foreign policy as it relates to other nations and international issues.

14.E.3 Compare the basic principles of the United States and its international interests (e.g., territory, environment, trade, use of technology).

15.D.3a Explain the effects of increasing and declining imports and exports to an individual and to the nation's economy as a whole.

17.D Understand the historical significance of geography.

American Diary

"We are now about to embark upon an expedition, which may terminate in our sudden deaths, our perpetual [eternal] slavery, or our immortal glory. The event is left for futurity [the future] to determine. The first quality of a good seaman, is, personal courage,—the second, obedience to orders,—the third, fortitude [strength] under sufferings; to these may be added, an ardent [passionate] love of country. I am confident you possess them all."

—Lt. Stephen Decatur to the crew of the USS **Essex**

Stephen Decatur and U.S. sailors attack a gunboat in Tripoli's harbor.

R Reading Strategies	**C** Critical Thinking	**D** Differentiated Instruction	**W** Writing Support	**S** Skill Practice
Teacher Edition • Previewing, p. 287 • Determining Importance, p. 291 **Additional Resources** • Guid. Read., URB p. 69 • Content Vocab., URB p. 45 • Academic Vocab., URB p. 47 • Read. Ess., p. 94 • Am. Lit. Read., URB p. 9	**Teacher Edition** • Det. Cause and Effect, p. 289 • Analyz. Pri. Sources, p. 292 **Additional Resources** • Quizzes and Tests, p. 83 • Inter. Polit. Cartoons, URB p. 13 • Link. Past and Pres., URB p. 61	**Teacher Edition** • Interpersonal, p. 288 **Additional Resources** • School-to-Home, URB p. 63 • Reteaching Act., URB p. 65	**Teacher Edition** • Persuasive Writing, p. 289 • Descriptive Writing, p. 291 **Additional Resources** • Authentic Assess., p. 9	**Teacher Edition** • Using Geo. Skills, p. 287 • Reading a Time Line, p. 293 **Additional Resources** • Daily Test Pract. Transp. 9-3

Americans on Foreign Seas

Main Idea Pirates made travel by sea dangerous and brought the United States into conflict with Tripoli.

History and You Think about the dangers at sea that sailors face. Read to learn about the challenges of those Americans who traded on the open seas in the early 1800s.

Sea travel was dangerous in the early 1800s. Sailors fought deadly storms and were threatened by pirates. Many Americans, however, depended on trade with foreign nations and were forced to rely on traveling by ship.

In 1785 the *Empress of China* returned to New York from China with a highly prized cargo of tea and silk. The goods sold for a fabulous profit. Soon, ships from New York, Philadelphia, and New England sailed regularly to China and India, transporting furs and other goods. American merchant ships began sailing to South America, Africa, and lands along the Mediterranean Sea.

War between France and Britain in the mid-1790s gave an additional boost to American shipping. To avoid being captured or destroyed by the enemy, many French and British merchant ships remained at home. American shippers profited from the situation and increased their trade. By 1800, the United States had almost 1,000 merchant ships trading around the world.

Barbary Pirates

Sailing on foreign seas could be dangerous because of piracy. For example, pirates from the Barbary Coast states of North Africa—Morocco, Algiers, Tripoli, and Tunis—terrorized European ships that were sailing on the Mediterranean Sea. Pirates demanded **tribute,** or protection money, from their country's governments to let their ships pass safely. European countries routinely paid tribute so that their ships would be undisturbed. They believed that it was less expensive to pay the Barbary Coast pirates than it was to go to war with them.

War With Tripoli

The United States, too, had to pay tribute to the Barbary Coast states. The ruler of Tripoli, however, did not think it was enough. In 1801 he asked the United States for more money. When President Jefferson refused, Tripoli declared war on the United States.

Primary Source / **USS Constitution**

Still Serving In 1794 President George Washington authorized the construction of six warships, including the *Constitution,* to protect American merchant ships. Today, the USS *Constitution* is the oldest active ship serving in the United States Navy.

The USS *Constitution* in Boston Harbor ▶

Critical Thinking
Speculating Why do you think the newly created United States needed a navy?

Teach

R Reading Strategy

Previewing Set a timer for two minutes, and have students preview the subsection. Remind them to skim the main idea, headings, and images. After they finish, have them close their books and complete this sentence on a piece of paper: In this subsection, I will learn about _____. **OL**

S Skill Practice

Using Geography Skills Have students look at a current map of North Africa and try to locate the Barbary Coast states (Morocco, Algiers, Tripoli, and Tunis). **Ask:** Which of these nations exist today? (*Students will note that only Morocco still exists and that Algiers is the capital of Algeria, Tripoli is the capital of Libya, and Tunis is the capital of Tunisia.*) **ELL**

Primary Source

Critical Thinking Answer
Answers might include the need to protect American trade and to defend the nation.

Differentiated Instruction

Leveled Activities

BL **Reteaching Activity, URB p. 65**

OL **Content Vocabulary Activity, URB p. 45**

AL **Linking Past and Present Activity, URB p. 61**

D Differentiated Instruction

Interpersonal Have students organize into small groups and read aloud the text description of the war with Tripoli. Instruct each group to list the important events in the war. Have each group member draw a separate event on a sheet of paper. Tape together papers in chronological order to form a cartoon strip. **BL**

Primary Source

Critical Thinking Answer
Students might answer that Europeans viewed the U.S. actions as courageous. Because the wars did not completely end the need for tribute payments, though, they might also have been seen as ineffective.

Reading Check **Answer:** The United States refused to pay any more tribute.

Hands-On Chapter Project
Step 3

Creating a Children's Story

Step 3: Writing the Text Students will use their research notes and outlines to write a children's story about a topic that is relevant to the time period of Jefferson.

Essential Question: What were the challenges to the nation's stability during the late 1700s and early 1800s?

Jefferson sent ships to blockade Tripoli. The Americans, though, could not defeat the pirates, and the conflict continued.

Pirates seized the United States warship *Philadelphia* in 1804. They towed the ship into Tripoli Harbor and threw the crew into jail. Stephen Decatur, a 25-year-old U.S. Navy captain, took action. He slipped into the heavily guarded harbor with a small raiding party. Decatur burned the captured ship to prevent the pirates from using it. A British admiral praised the deed as the "most bold and daring act of the age."

The war ended in June 1805. Tripoli agreed to stop demanding tribute, but the United States had to pay $60,000 for the prisoners to be released. It would not be until 1815, however, that American tribute payments ended completely.

Reading Check **Explaining** Why did Tripoli declare war on the United States?

Primary Source / The Barbary Wars

An Ongoing War The first Barbary War took place from 1801 to 1805. In 1805 Tripoli agreed to stop demanding tribute from the United States. Pirate raids, however, continued on American ships. After the War of 1812, Stephen Decatur and the United States Navy used military force to stop the raids and end tribute payments permanently.

The USS *Enterprise* defeated and captured the pirate vessel *Tripoli* in 1801. Seventy-five percent of the *Tripoli*'s crew was killed in the fighting, while there were no casualties on the *Enterprise.* ▼

Stephen Decatur and his crew attack one of Tripoli's gunboats. Decatur became a national hero as a result of his actions in the Barbary Wars. ▼

Commodore Edward Preble took command of the U.S. Mediterranean fleet in 1803. His leadership helped defeat Tripoli and end the war. ▶

Critical Thinking
Predicting How do you think European countries viewed the U.S. actions after the wars?

Freedom of the Seas

Main Idea A war between Great Britain and France threatened the security of the United States, as well as American shipping and trade.

History and You What problems might develop when a country refuses to trade with other countries? What do you think happens to that country's industries and its standard of living? Read to find out what happened when Thomas Jefferson tried to stop trade to avoid getting drawn into a war.

Thomas Jefferson was reelected in 1804, and his second term began with the nation at peace. Across the Atlantic Ocean, however, Great Britain and France were fighting a war that threatened to interfere with American trade. The United States ended the war with Tripoli in 1805. Now the United States was caught in the middle of a war between Great Britain and France.

Directions Discuss ways to target the book to the intended audience, such as simplifying the language, keeping the book short, and using descriptions, action words, and attractive illustrations. Then have each group use its notes and outline to write a children's story with those guidelines in mind. Instruct students to make notes where illustrations would help convey ideas or add more detail and interest.

Discussing Discuss how the inclusion of conflict and resolution helps create a powerful storyline. Ask students to share challenges to the nation that add interest to their stories. **OL**

(Chapter Project continued in Section 4)

Economics & History

A nation's balance of trade is the difference between the value of a nation's exports and its imports. A nation has a **trade surplus** when it exports more than it imports. For example, if the United States exported $100 in cotton and imported $50 in tea, it would be experiencing a trade surplus, or positive balance of trade.

▼ New Orleans, 1841

Graph Skills

Applying In 1810 did the United States have a positive or negative balance of trade? Explain.

Graphs In Motion See StudentWorks™ Plus or glencoe.com.

Imports and Exports, 1800–1820

Millions of $

(Noncourse Act, Embargo Act, Panic of 1819, War of 1812 labeled)

Year: 1800, 1805, 1810, 1815, 1820

1 Exports: goods sold
2 Imports: goods purchased
3 Balance of trade: difference between the value of a nation's exports and its imports

Source: *Historical Statistics of the United States*

C Critical Thinking

Determining Cause and Effect To help students understand the events leading up to the Embargo Act and the Nonintercourse Act, have them make a list of British actions toward U.S. shipping interests. **OL**

W Writing Support

Persuasive Writing Have students write a letter to the editor of an American newspaper after the attack on the *Chesapeake*. Tell them to argue either for going to war with Britain or for peaceful settlement. **OL**

Economics & History

Graphic Skills Answer
The United States had a negative balance of trade, because it imported more than it exported.

Neutral Rights Violated

When Britain and France went to war in 1803, America had a prosperous trade with both countries. As long as the United States remained neutral, shippers could continue doing business. A nation not involved in a conflict had **neutral rights.** That is, it had the right to sail the seas and not take sides.

For two years, American shipping prospered. By 1805, however, Britain and France lost patience with American "neutrality." Britain blockaded the French coast and threatened to search all ships trading with France. France later announced that it would search and seize ships caught trading with Britain.

American Sailors Kidnapped

The British were in desperate need of sailors for their naval war. Many of their own sailors had deserted due to the terrible living conditions in the British Royal Navy. British naval ships began stopping American ships to search for suspected British deserters. The

British then forced these deserters to return to the British navy. This practice of forcing people to serve in the navy was **impressment.** While some of those taken were deserters from the British navy, the British also impressed thousands of native-born and naturalized American citizens.

Attack on the *Chesapeake*

Often the British waited for American ships outside an American harbor where they boarded and searched them. This occurred in June 1807 off the coast of Virginia. The *Leopard,* a British warship, stopped the American vessel *Chesapeake.* The *Leopard's* captain demanded to search the American ship for British deserters, but the *Chesapeake's* captain refused. The British opened fire, crippling the *Chesapeake* and killing three crew members.

News of the attack spread. Americans **reacted** with an anti-British fury not seen since the Revolutionary War. Secretary of State James Madison responded to the news.

Additional Support

The Jefferson Era **Chapter 9** **289**

Fast Facts

Impressment Until the early 1800s, the British Royal Navy dealt with the short supply of recruits during times of war by capturing sailors and forcing them to serve. When the British began to search American ships for Royal Navy deserters and captured

American sailors along with them, the new nation took note. In fact, this practice was one of the causes of the War of 1812.

Impressment was legalized in Britain in the 1500s. Although its practice had restrictions such as age and citizenship status,

these rules were often overlooked. Impressment ended in Britain after the Napoleonic Wars (1803–1815). Since then the British Navy has relied on compulsory enrollment, also known as *conscription* or *the draft,* to meet its needs. **OL**

INTERPRETING POLITICAL CARTOONS

Answers

1. They are robbing Thomas Jefferson.

2. Students might reply that the cartoon does not support Jefferson's embargo policy; its point is that attacks on American interests are continuing despite the policy.

Reading Check **Answer:** Britain simply turned to other countries for its goods, yet American commerce with other nations was wiped out.

History ONLINE

Objectives and answers to the Student Web Activity can be found at glencoe.com under the Web Activity Lesson Plan for this chapter.

Differentiated Instruction

Primary Sources
INTERPRETING
POLITICAL CARTOONS

Jefferson's embargo policy had a disastrous effect on American trade, and it did not stop the British and French from seizing American ships.

1. **Interpreting** What are King George and Napoleon Bonaparte doing?

2. **Drawing Conclusions** Do you think this cartoon supports Jefferson's embargo policy? Why or why not?

A. King George of England

B. Thomas Jefferson

C. Napoleon Bonaparte of France

He called the attack an outrage. Many Americans demanded war against Britain. President Jefferson, though, sought a course of action other than war.

A Disastrous Trade Ban

Because Britain violated America's neutral rights, Jefferson banned some trade with Britain. The attack on the *Chesapeake* triggered even stronger measures.

In December 1807, Congress passed the **Embargo Act.** An **embargo** prohibits trade with another country. In addition to Britain, the act banned imports from and exports to *all* foreign countries. Jefferson wanted to prevent Americans from using other countries to trade with France and Britain indirectly. Jefferson and Madison wanted to avoid war, but they also wanted to hurt Britain by banning the trade of agricultural products.

The embargo of 1807 was a disaster. It wiped out all American commerce with other nations and was ineffective against Britain. The British simply turned to Latin America for agricultural goods. Congress then enacted

the weaker **Nonintercourse Act.** This act prohibited trade only with Britain and France and their colonies, but it too was unpopular and unsuccessful.

Jefferson Leaves Office

Jefferson followed Washington's precedent by making it clear that he would not be a candidate for a third term. The Republicans chose James Madison as their candidate for president. The Federalists nominated Charles Pinckney and hoped that anger over the embargo would help them win. Pinckney carried most of New England, but the Federalist ticket gained little support from the other regions. Madison won the presidency with 122 electoral votes to Pinckney's 47 votes.

Reading Check **Summarizing** Why was the Embargo Act ineffective?

History ONLINE

Student Web Activity Visit glencoe.com and complete the Web Activity about American trade issues in the early 1800s.

The Embargo Act of 1807

Objective: To learn about the Embargo Act while analyzing a political cartoon

Focus: Ask students to explain the Embargo Act restrictions in their own words.

Teach: Have students answer the questions.

Assess: Assess each answer, and discuss incorrect answers.

Close: As a class, discuss how the cartoon reflects the artist's political beliefs.

Differentiated Instruction Strategies

BL Have students write a paragraph that describes the cartoon's action.

AL Have students draw a cartoon showing Americans' reaction to the Nonintercourse Act.

ELL Have students write the word "Ograbme" backwards to reveal its meaning.

Interpreting Political Cartoons Activity, URB p. 13

War Fever

Main Idea Trade issues with Britain and France and tensions between Native Americans and settlers challenged James Madison.

History and You Why do you think tension between different groups occurs? Read about the conflicts among the various groups during the early 1800s.

James Madison took office as president under unfavorable conditions. At home and abroad, the nation was involved in the embargo crisis. Meanwhile, Britain continued to halt American ships. Cries for war with Britain grew louder.

Closer to War

In 1810 Congress passed a law permitting direct trade with either France or Britain, depending on which country first lifted its trade **restrictions,** or limits, against America. Napoleon seized the opportunity and promised to end France's trade restrictions.

The French, however, continued to seize American ships, selling them and pocketing the proceeds. Americans were deeply divided. The nation was on the verge of war, but it was hard to decide whether the enemy was Britain or France. Madison believed that Britain was the bigger threat to the United States.

Frontier Conflicts

Madison also received news about problems in the West. Ohio became a state in 1803. White settlers wanted more land in the Ohio Valley. Native Americans already gave up many millions of acres. However, the settlers continued to move onto lands that were guaranteed to Native Americans by the treaty.

Tensions increased as some Native Americans renewed their contacts with British agents and fur traders in Canada.

Other Native Americans pursued a new strategy. **Tecumseh** (tuh•KUHM•suh), a powerful Shawnee chief, built a confederacy among Native American nations in the Northwest.

R
W

R Reading Strategy

Determining Importance Have students skim the text to identify sources of conflict for the United States when James Madison became president. *(embargo crisis; relations with Britain, France, and Native Americans)* **OL**

W Writing Support

Descriptive Writing Have students learn more about Tecumseh and write a report about the Shawnee chief. The report should be illustrated in a way that adds descriptive detail to the facts in the text. **AL**

Territorial Expansion 1800–1820 [NATIONAL GEOGRAPHIC]

Critical Thinking Answer

In 1800 the French territory covered about a third of the landmass, but by 1820 the French had no territory.

Territorial Expansion, 1800–1820 [NATIONAL GEOGRAPHIC]

Map Skills

Place Describe the changes in French territory between 1800 and 1820.

Additional Support

Activity: Debating the Issues

Defending Beginning in 1805, both Britain and France violated American neutrality on the seas. The trade ban established in retaliation by the United States in 1807 devastated the American economy. The drums of war were getting louder and louder. **Ask:** Do you think the United States should have chosen to go to war with Britain or France? Organize students into four groups and have them research the events leading up to the War of 1812. Stage a debate between two of the groups, with one side promoting war with Britain and the other side promoting war with France. Have the remaining two groups conduct a similar debate after the first one is completed. Remind students to consider all the factors discussed in the chapter, including economic conditions, impressment, seizure of U.S. ships, frontier conflicts, and pressure from the War Hawks. **AL**

C Critical Thinking

Analyzing Primary Sources
Ask: According to Tecumseh, how would the United States have to change in order to avoid war with the Native Americans? *(He said peace could not be maintained as long as the United States incited war by killing Native Americans, taking their land, playing favorites, and keeping them from uniting.)* **OL**

Primary Source

Critical Thinking Answer
Students might answer that Tecumseh was able to organize Native Americans into a more powerful confederation. Also, he opposed the idea of ownership of land, which Americans held dear.

Additional Support

Primary Source / Tecumseh

Tecumseh organized a confederation of 14 Native American nations to oppose white settlement on lands in the Northwest. He recognized that individual Native American groups had little power to negotiate with the United States government.

"The only way to stop this evil [white settlement of Indians' land], is for all the red men to unite in claiming a common and equal right in the land as it was at first, and should be now—for it never was divided, but belongs to all. . . . Sell a country! Why not sell the air, the clouds, and the great sea, as well as the earth?"
—Tecumseh in a letter to President Harrison, 1810

Tecumseh's brother Tenskwatawa, known as the Prophet, founded Prophetstown in Indiana. This village served as the spiritual, social, and political capital of the confederation of Native American nations.

▼ The Prophet

Tecumseh's ceremonial pipe ►

When Tecumseh died at the Battle of the Thames, hopes for a lasting Native American confederacy ended.

Critical Thinking

Making Inferences Why do you think American leaders feared Tecumseh?

Tecumseh believed that a strong alliance—with the backing of the British in Canada—could halt white movement into Native American lands. A commanding speaker, Tecumseh had great political skills. He believed the U.S. government's treaties with separate Native American nations were worthless. "The Great Spirit gave this great island to his red children," he said. No one nation had the right to give it away.

Tecumseh had a powerful ally in his brother, Tenskwatawa, known as the Prophet. The Prophet urged Native Americans to return to their ancestors' customs. His message attracted a large following. The Prophet founded Prophetstown in northern Indiana, located near where the Tippecanoe and Wabash Rivers meet.

A Meeting With Harrison

William Henry Harrison, governor of the Indiana Territory, became alarmed by the growing power of the two Shawnee brothers.

He feared they would form an alliance with the British. Harrison warned Tecumseh in a letter that the United States had more warriors than all the Indian nations combined. Tecumseh replied to Harrison in person.

PRIMARY SOURCE

"Brother . . . Since the peace was made, you have killed some Shawnees, Delawares and Winnebagoes. . . . You have taken land from us and I do not see how we can remain at peace if you continue to do so. You try to force red people to do some injury. It is you that are pushing them on to some mischief. You endeavor [try] to make distinctions. You try to prevent the Indians from doing as they wish—to unite and let them consider their lands common property of the whole."
—from Tecumseh, an Indian Moses

The Battle of Tippecanoe

When Tecumseh went south to expand the confederacy, Harrison attacked Prophetstown on the Tippecanoe River. After more than two hours, the Prophet's forces fled in defeat.

Activity: Connecting Past and Present

Comparing and Contrasting Tecumseh believed that only through unity could Native Americans have a chance at defending their rights against the United States. **Ask:** What problems and conflicts cause today's Native Americans to join together to find a solution? Have students organize into small groups and learn about Native American alliances and the causes they represent. Instruct each group to choose one Native American alliance that is active today and create an informational poster about it. Remind them to clearly present the problem, the nature of the group, and the proposed solution or activity. **OL**

The **Battle of Tippecanoe** was declared a glorious victory for the Americans. Harrison's victory, however, resulted in something the American people hoped to prevent. Tecumseh joined forces with the British, whom, settlers believed, had supplied his confederacy with guns.

War Hawks

In the meantime, President Madison faced demands for a more aggressive policy toward Britain. The most pressure came from a group of young Republicans known as the War Hawks. They wanted war with Britain. The leading War Hawks were Kentucky's **Henry Clay** and South Carolina's **John Calhoun.**

The War Hawks were mainly from the West and South. They supported increases in military spending and were driven by hunger for land. War Hawks from the West wanted the fertile forests of southern Canada, whereas Southerners desired Spanish Florida. The War Hawks also wanted to expand the nation's power. Their **nationalism**—or loyalty to their country—appealed to a renewed American patriotism.

Not everyone, however, wanted war. The Federalists in the Northeast remained strongly opposed to it.

Declaring War

By the spring of 1812, Madison knew that war with Britain was inevitable. In a message to Congress on June 1, he cited:

PRIMARY SOURCE

"Such is the spectacle of injuries and indignities which have been heaped on our country."
—from Madison's "War Message"

Madison asked for a declaration of war.

Meanwhile, the British had decided to end their policy of search and seizure of American ships. Unfortunately, it took much time for this news to travel across the Atlantic, and leaders in Washington, D.C., did not know about Britain's change in policy. Word of the policy change arrived too late. Once set in motion, the war machine could not be stopped.

✔ Reading Check **Summarizing** What factors led to the war with Britain?

S Skill Practice

Reading a Time Line Direct students to the time line at the beginning of the chapter. **Ask:** What events were occurring in the world around the time of the Battle of Tippecanoe? *(Within two years of that battle were Ecuador's independence from Spain and Napoleon's invasion of Russia.)* **BL**

✔ Reading Check **Answer:** The British continued to search and seize United States ships and formed alliances with Native Americans. Also, the War Hawks increased their pressure for war with Britain.

Assess

History ONLINE

Study Central™ provides summaries, interactive games, and online graphic organizers to help students review content.

Close

Describing Have students describe to partners the challenges to U.S. stability during the late 1700s and early 1800s. **OL**

Section 3 Review

Section 3 Review

History ONLINE
Study Central™ To review this section, go to glencoe.com.

Vocabulary

1. Define each of the following terms in a sentence: tribute, neutral rights, impressment, react, embargo, restriction, nationalism.

Main Ideas

2. **Discussing** How widespread was American trade by 1800? Include information about the types of goods that were traded.

3. **Explaining** Explain why U.S. security was threatened as a result of the war between Britain and France.

4. **Summarizing** How did conflict on the American frontier increase tensions between the United States and Britain?

Critical Thinking

5. **Drawing Conclusions** Use a diagram like the one below to identify how people from each region felt about going to war with Britain.

War With Britain
South
Northeast
West

6. **Expository Writing** Take the role of William Henry Harrison. Write a letter to the president explaining why you plan to attack Prophetstown.

Answer the
7. **Essential Question**
What were the challenges to the nation's stability during the late 1700s and early 1800s?

The Jefferson Era **Chapter 9** **293**

Answers

1. Students will write sentences correctly defining the terms.
2. Trade extended to South America, Africa, the Mediterranean, India, and China. Trade goods included furs, tea, and silk.
3. Both France and Britain seized and searched United States ships. The British stopped United States ships and impressed Americans into naval service.
4. As American settlers continued to move onto lands that had been given by treaties

to Native Americans, the Native Americans made more contacts with the British and formed a confederacy headed by Tecumseh. He supported an alliance with the British to fight for territory.
5. **South:** War Hawks wanted war to get land and power; **North:** Federalists opposed war; **West:** War Hawks wanted war to acquire southern Canadian forests and power.
6. Students should write letters that show an understanding of Harrison's motives.

7. Answers should include some of the following: (1) threats to trade, including Barbary pirates, seizure of U.S. ships by Britain and France, and U.S. trade bans; (2) tension in the West between settlers and Native Americans; and (3) British–Native American alliances.

Focus

Section 4

The War of 1812

Bellringer
Daily Test Practice Transparency 9–4

Reading Guide
Answers to Graphic:

Lake Erie: Americans won control of the lake and access to Canada.

Washington, D.C.: British seized the city and burned parts of it.

New Orleans: Americans won a decisive victory, and Andrew Jackson became a hero.

Section Spotlight Video

Have students watch the Section Spotlight Video "The War of 1812" to learn the story of this conflict.

Essential Question

How did the United States benefit from its victory in the War of 1812?

Reading Guide

Content Vocabulary

frigate (p. 296)   privateer (p. 296)

Academic Vocabulary

underestimate (p. 295)

goal (p. 297)

Key People and Events

Andrew Jackson (p. 296)
Battle of Horseshoe Bend (p. 296)
Francis Scott Key (p. 297)
Treaty of Ghent (p. 298)
Battle of New Orleans (p. 298)

Reading Strategy

Taking Notes As you read, re-create the diagram below and describe each battle's outcome.

Battle   Outcome

Lake Erie ⟶ ☐

Washington, D.C. ⟶ ☐

New Orleans ⟶ ☐

ILLINOIS STANDARDS
The American Journey

14.E Understand United States foreign policy as it relates to other nations and international issues.

14.E.3 Compare the basic principles of the United States and its international interests (e.g., territory, environment, trade, use of technology).

16.A.3c Identify the differences between historical fact and interpretation.

18.A.3 Explain how language, literature, the arts, architecture and traditions contribute to the development and transmission of culture.

American Diary

"When the detachment [small military unit], sent out to destroy Mr. Madison's house, entered his dining parlor, they found a dinner table spread. . . . You will readily imagine, that these preparations were beheld, by a party of hungry soldiers, with no indifferent eye. . . . They sat down to it, therefore, not indeed in the most orderly manner . . . and having satisfied their appetites . . . they finished by setting fire to the house which had so liberally entertained them."

—quoted from George Robert Gleig, a British soldier, in 1814

In August 1814, British troops burn Washington, D.C.

Resource Manager

R **Reading Strategies**	C **Critical Thinking**	D **Differentiated Instruction**	W **Writing Support**	S **Skill Practice**
Teacher Edition • Identifying, p. 295 • Outlining, p. 296	**Teacher Edition** • Analyzing Information, p. 298	**Teacher Edition** • Auditory/Musical, p. 297	**Teacher Edition** • Expository Writing, p. 297	**Teacher Edition** • Using Geo. Skills, p. 295
Additional Resources • Guid. Read., URB p. 70 • Content Vocab., URB p. 45 • Academic Vocab., URB p. 47 • Read. Ess., p. 97	**Additional Resources** • Quizzes and Tests, p. 84	**Additional Resources** • School-to-Home, URB p. 63 • Reteaching Act., URB p. 65	**Additional Resources** • Writing Skills, URB p. 51	**Additional Resources** • Daily Test Pract. Transp. 9-4 • Soc. Stud. Skills, URB p. 53 • Lesson Transp. 9C

War Begins

Main Idea The United States was unprepared for war with Great Britain.

History and You Have you ever been unprepared for a quiz or a test? Read to learn how the United States was unprepared for the War of 1812.

....

The War Hawks were confident that they would achieve a quick victory over the British. The Americans, however, were overall unprepared for war.

The regular army had fewer than 7,000 troops, and the states had between 50,000 and 100,000 poorly trained militia. Military commanders who were veterans of the American Revolution were too old for warfare. Support for the conflict was not unanimous, and some states opposed "Mr. Madison's War." In addition, the Americans **underestimated,** or misjudged, the strength of the British and their Native American allies.

The war began in July 1812. General William Hull led the American army from Detroit into Canada. Tecumseh and his warriors met **[S]** Hull, who feared a massacre by the Native Americans. Hull surrendered Detroit to the British. General William Henry Harrison also made an unsuccessful attempt to invade Canada. Harrison decided that the Americans could make no headway into Canada as long as the British controlled Lake Erie.

Naval Battles

Oliver Hazard Perry, who commanded the Lake Erie naval forces, was ordered to seize the lake from the British. On September 10, 1813, Perry's ships defeated the British naval force. After the battle, Perry sent General Harrison the message "We have met the enemy and they are ours."

Lake Erie was now under American control. The British and their Native American allies tried to pull back from the Detroit area, but Harrison cut them off. In the Battle of the Thames on October 5, Tecumseh was killed.

The Americans also attacked the town of York (present-day Toronto), burning the parliament buildings. Even though Canada remained unconquered, the Americans had **[R]** won some victories by the end of 1813.

Primary Source | Escape from Washington

Dolley Madison wrote her sister the day before British forces burned Washington, D.C.

"At this late hour, a wagon has been procured; I have had it filled with the . . . most valuable portable articles belonging to the house [White House].

I insist on waiting until the large picture of General Washington is secured. . . . And now, dear sister, I must leave this house. . . . When I shall again write to you, or where I shall be to-morrow, I cannot tell!!"

—Dolley Madison in a letter to her sister, 1814

Critical Thinking

Making Inferences Why do you think the British burned the White House?

▲ Dolley Madison, wife of President James Madison

Teach

....

[S] Skill Practice

Using Geography Skills Have students study the map on the next page and note the distances between the battle sites in the War of 1812. Instruct them to write a paragraph in which they discuss problems that the Americans might have faced because of the extreme distances. *(Answers might include slow communication, difficulty getting supplies to the troops, and coordination.)* **OL**

[R] Reading Strategy

Identifying Ask: *What victories did the United States win in 1812 and 1813?* *(United States forces defeated the British on Lake Erie and defeated British and Native Americans at the Battle of the Thames. They killed Tecumseh and captured or destroyed numerous British ships.)* **BL**

Primary Source

Critical Thinking Answer
The White House was a powerful symbol of America, so burning it would symbolically destroy an important part of the nation.

Hands-On Chapter Project
Step 4

Creating a Children's Story

Step 4: Illustrating the Text Students will illustrate their children's stories.

Essential Question: How did the United States benefit from its victory in the War of 1812?

Directions Have each group use colored pencils, crayons, paints, or computer graphics to illustrate their children's stories. Remind students to make the illustrations interesting by including action and historically accurate details.

Identifying Ask students what drawings they might include in a story about the War of 1812. Discuss the use of color, point of view, detail, and simplification. **OL**

(Chapter Project continued on the Visual Summary page)

THE WAR OF 1812

...a story for children

The War of 1812

The War of 1812

NATIONAL GEOGRAPHIC

Additional Support

The U.S. Navy had three of the fastest **frigates,** or warships, afloat. When the *Constitution* destroyed two British vessels within four months, Americans rejoiced. **Privateers,** armed private ships, also captured numerous British vessels, boosting American morale.

Setbacks for Native Americans

Before the Battle of the Thames, Tecumseh talked with the Creeks in the Mississippi Territory about a confederation. However, hopes for a confederation died with Tecumseh.

In March 1814, **Andrew Jackson** attacked the Creeks. Jackson's forces slaughtered more than 550 Creek people. Known as the **Battle of Horseshoe Bend,** the defeat forced the Creeks to give up most of their lands.

✓ **Reading Check** **Evaluating** Do you think the United States was prepared to wage war? Explain.

R The British Offensive

Main Idea Americans were instilled with a sense of national pride after the Battle of New Orleans.

History and You When have you heard "The Star-Spangled Banner"? Read how the War of 1812 inspired the creation of the national anthem.

British fortunes improved in the spring of 1814. After winning the war against Napoleon, Britain was able to send more forces to America.

Attack on Washington, D.C.

The British sailed into Chesapeake Bay in August 1814. Their destination was Washington, D.C. On the outskirts of the capital, British troops quickly overpowered the American militia. They then marched into the city.

The War of 1812

NATIONAL GEOGRAPHIC

New Boundaries During the War of 1812, approximately 286,000 Americans fought the British and an estimated 2,200 died. Although the Treaty of Ghent ended the war in 1815, it was not until 1818 that the United States and Britain agreed on a boundary line between the United States and Canada.

The British navy blockades the coast, 1812

Perry defeats the British on Lake Erie, 1813

Harrison defeats British and Native American forces at the Battle of Thames, 1813

The British burn Washington, D.C. Americans recapture the city and defeat the British at Ft. McHenry, 1814

Americans win the Battle of Lake Champlain, 1814

Jackson defeats the British at New Orleans, 1815

▲ United States military hat from 1813

□ Fort
← American forces
← British forces
✹ American victory
✶ British victory
⚓ British naval blockade

Map Skills

1. **Movement** How did the British navy support the British land troops?
2. **Location** Who won the Battle of New Orleans?

Maps In Motion See StudentWorks™ Plus or glencoe.com.

Activity: Technology Connection

Describing Lead a class discussion on the use of embedded reporters in the war in Iraq and Afghanistan. Have students locate examples of news stories and blogs by embedded reporters. Talk about the differences between what a writer would say in an official news story compared to a personal blog. *(Blog entries would likely contain personal opinions and speculation, whereas official news stories would report facts and describe events as objectively as possible.)* **Ask:** What would an embedded reporter have blogged about during the War of 1812? Instruct students to choose one of the battles in the War of 1812 and conduct research to learn more about that event. Then tell them to create blog entries for an embedded reporter. Have them share their blogs and comment on one another's entries. **OL**

The Battle of New Orleans

A Final Battle As a large British fleet approached New Orleans, the Americans prepared for battle. On January 8, 1815, the British attacked New Orleans. Andrew Jackson's force of about 7,000 troops hid behind cotton bales and concentrated their fire on the advancing British. Andrew Jackson's troops won the battle within half an hour.

There were 289 British killed during the battle compared to 71 Americans. The victory made Andrew Jackson a national hero. ▼

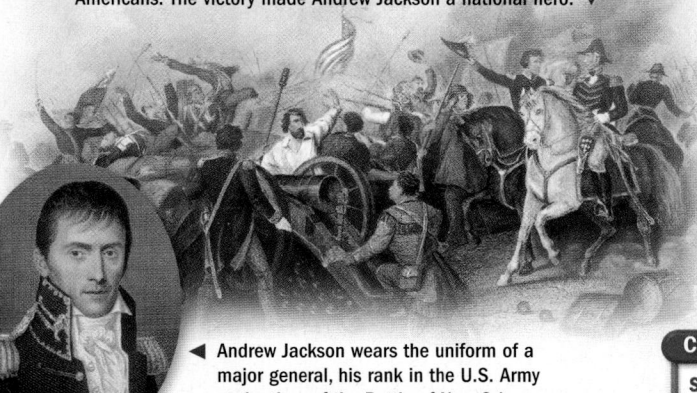

Jean Lafitte was a ▲ famous smuggler along the Gulf Coast. Hoping to gain a pardon for his illegal activities, he provided the Americans with information about British activities in the area.

◄ Andrew Jackson wears the uniform of a major general, his rank in the U.S. Army at the time of the Battle of New Orleans.

Critical Thinking

Speculating Why do you think people support presidential candidates who have had successful military careers?

"They proceeded, without a moment's delay, to burn and destroy everything in the most distant degree connected with the government," reported a British officer.

The Capitol and the president's mansion were among the buildings burned. Fortunately, a thunderstorm put out the fires before they could do more damage. August 24, 1814, was a low point for Americans.

Baltimore Holds Firm

To everyone's surprise, the British did not try to hold Washington, D.C. They left the city and sailed north to Baltimore. In mid-September, the people of Baltimore were ready for the attack and held firm against the British. A determined defense and fierce artillery fire from Fort McHenry in the harbor kept the British from entering the city.

Francis Scott Key, an attorney, watched the bombs burst over Fort McHenry during the night of September 13–14. That morning he saw the American flag still flying over the fort. Deeply moved, Key wrote a poem that became known as "The Star-Spangled Banner." Congress designated "The Star-Spangled Banner" as the national anthem in 1931.

Defeat at Plattsburgh

Meanwhile, General Sir George Prevost led more than 10,000 British troops into New York from Canada. His **goal** was to capture Plattsburgh, a key city on the shore of Lake Champlain. The invasion was stopped when an American naval force on the lake defeated the British fleet in September 1814. Fearing the Americans would surround them, the British retreated into Canada.

After the Battle of Lake Champlain, the British decided the war in North America was too costly and unnecessary. They had defeated Napoleon in Europe. To keep fighting the United States would result in little gain and was not worth the effort.

The Jefferson Era **Chapter 9** 297

W Writing Support

Expository Writing Have students work with partners to find out more about the British attack on Washington, D.C., in the War of 1812. Encourage them to use primary sources where possible. Then have each pair write a newspaper article to inform Americans about the attack. **AL**

D Differentiated Instruction

Auditory/Musical Have students write down as many of the lyrics of "The Star-Spangled Banner" as they can remember. Organize the class into small groups, and have group members work together to figure out all the words. Instruct each student to create a glossary of words that are unfamiliar. **ELL**

The Battle of New Orleans

Critical Thinking Answer

Students might answer that individuals who have had successful military careers probably possess leadership skills.

Additional Support

Activity: Interdisciplinary Connection

Music "The Star-Spangled Banner," the United States national anthem, originally was written as a poem. Music was added later. **Ask:** Why do musicians often turn to poetry when they seek lyrics for their tunes? *(Students might respond that poetry has rhythm and rhyme, which are well suited to music. Also, musicians might not be able to write well, and poets are not necessarily gifted in music.)* Distribute copies of the lyrics of "The Star-Spangled Banner" to the class. Have them organize into groups of five, distributing class members who enjoy singing and playing musical instruments evenly among the groups. Instruct the students to write a new tune for the national anthem, which they can memorize or transcribe in any way they choose. Ask students to rehearse their pieces for a concert, incorporating voice, standard or original musical instruments, or even dance. Then have the groups perform their music for the class. **OL**

Section 4

C Critical Thinking

Analyzing Information Review the meaning of the word "adjective" with the class. **Ask:** What adjectives would you use to describe the soldiers in the Battle of New Orleans? *(Answers might include "outnumbered," "resourceful," and "creative.")* **BL**

✓ Reading Check **Answer:** The Federalist Party lost strength, American patriotism and national identity grew, and the United States gained status in the world.

Assess

History ONLINE

Study Central™ provides summaries, interactive games, and online graphic organizers to help students review content.

Close

Summarizing Have students write a paragraph summarizing an important battle or battlefront in the War of 1812. **OL**

Section 4 Review

The War Ends

American and British representatives signed a peace agreement in December 1814 in Ghent, Belgium. The **Treaty of Ghent** did not change any existing borders. Nothing was mentioned about the impressment of sailors. Even neutral rights became a dead issue because of Napoleon's defeat.

Before word of the treaty reached the United States, one final—and ferocious—battle occurred at New Orleans. British army troops moved toward New Orleans in December 1814. Andrew Jackson and his troops were waiting for them.

C The British troops advanced on January 8, 1815. The redcoats were no match for Jackson's soldiers. Jackson's soldiers hid behind thick cotton bales. The bales absorbed the British bullets, while the British advancing in the open provided easy targets for American troops. In a short but gruesome battle, hundreds of British soldiers were killed. At the **Battle of New Orleans,** Americans achieved a decisive victory. Andrew Jackson became a hero, and his fame helped him win the presidency in 1828.

American Nationalism

New England Federalists opposed "Mr. Madison's War" from the start. These unhappy Federalists gathered in December 1814 at the Hartford Convention in Connecticut. A few favored secession, but most wanted to remain with the Union. To protect their interests, they made a list of proposed amendments to the Constitution.

In the triumph following the war, the Federalists' grievances seemed unpatriotic. The party lost the public's respect and was weakened. The War Hawks took over the leadership of the Republican Party and carried on the Federalist philosophy of a strong national government. They favored trade, western expansion, the energetic development of the economy, and a strong army and navy.

After the War of 1812, Americans felt a new sense of patriotism and a strong national identity. The young nation also gained new respect from other nations in the world.

✓ Reading Check **Identifying Cause and Effect** What were the effects of the War of 1812?

Section 4 Review

History ONLINE
Study Central™ To review this section, go to glencoe.com.

Vocabulary

1. Define each of the following terms in a sentence: underestimate, frigate, privateer, goal.

Main Ideas

2. Specifying Why was the Battle of the Thames important for the United States in the War of 1812?

3. Determining Cause and Effect How did the outcome of the war affect the Federalist Party?

Critical Thinking

4. Summarizing Use a diagram like the one below to describe how the War Hawks influenced the Republican Party after the War of 1812.

Ideas Favored by War Hawks

5. Making Connections In what way did the writing of "The Star-Spangled Banner" represent the American spirit at the end of the War of 1812?

6. Expository Writing Take the role of an American who has witnessed the burning of Washington, D.C. Write a letter to your family out West describing your feelings about the British actions.

Answer the Essential Question

7. How did the United States benefit from its victory in the War of 1812?

Answers

1. Students will write sentences correctly defining the terms.

2. Tecumseh was killed, which ended the possibility of a Native American confederation to oppose the United States.

3. The nationalistic fervor after the war made the Federalists' positions seem unpatriotic, and they were weakened.

4. Answers might include a strong national government, trade, western expansion, economic development, and a strong military.

5. The poem/song reflects Francis Scott Key's patriotism and mirrors the strong pride and identity of the new nation as it gained worldwide respect after the war.

6. Students will use information from the text to describe the burning of the city and how they feel witnessing it.

7. Answers will vary but should touch on an end to the threat of a Native American confederation, as well as growth of national pride, national identity, and respect abroad.

Visual Summary

Jefferson's Influence on Government

- The federal government's size and power are reduced.
- The Constitution is the supreme law.
- The power of the Supreme Court and federal law are strengthened.

▲ Thomas Jefferson

War of 1812

- War with Britain is fueled by nationalism and a desire for land.
- Tecumseh's death weakens both Native Americans and the British defense.
- The Federalists lose support after the U.S. victory.
- The United States gains worldwide respect.
- Patriotism grows.

▲ Tecumseh

▲ Conestoga wagon

Louisiana Purchase

- The U.S. purchases the Louisiana Territory from France for $15 million.
- The newly-acquired land doubles the size of the United States.
- The Mississippi River trade route is secured.
- Westward exploration and settlement increase.
- Some Federalists want to secede.

War with Tripoli ▶

Challenges to U.S. Stability

- Spain and France control Mississippi River trade and the Northwest Territory.
- Napoleon plans to build an American empire.
- War breaks out with Tripoli.
- France and Britain violate U.S. neutrality.
- A trade embargo creates political and economic problems.
- Frontier conflicts with the British and Native Americans continue.

STUDY TO GO Study anywhere, anytime! Download quizzes and flash cards to your PDA from glencoe.com.

The Jefferson Era **Chapter 9** 299

Visual Summary

Predicting Ask: What problems might the United States encounter if Congress passed a second embargo act today? *(Students should be encouraged to consider the importance of imports and exports to the United States economy. The discussion might cover the sources of our food supply, electronics, clothing, and energy resources and what we might do if we suddenly had to rely on just our own resources.)* **OL**

Explaining Ask: If you had been a United States citizen in 1807, would you have supported war against Britain after the attack on the *Chesapeake? (Students may be divided in their opinions. Lead a class discussion to clarify the pros and cons of that war. Individuals in favor of the war might argue that winning a war would avenge the Chesapeake attack, end impressment and British violations of American neutrality at sea, satisfy nationalistic feelings, and provide more land. Reasons to oppose the war might include opposition to military spending and violence and a desire for a peaceful solution to the differences.)* **OL**

Hands-On Chapter Project
Step 5: Wrap-Up

Creating a Children's Story

Step 5: Learning From the Children's Stories Students will read their stories to a group of younger children and evaluate their work using audience feedback.

Directions Instruct students to read their stories to a group of younger children. Have them encourage audience members to ask questions and say what they like or do not like about the story.

Evaluating Ask: What techniques are important in presenting historical events to children? Students should consider which techniques best conveyed their ideas and held the attention of the audience. Each group might then revise its story and illustrations accordingly. **OL**

Answers and Analyses
Reviewing Main Ideas

1. A Judicial review essentially states that the Constitution is the highest law. Thus, choices B and C are wrong because they claim that state law or any other law can overrule the Constitution. Choice D is incorrect because judicial review holds that it is the judicial branch, not the legislative branch, that is responsible for upholding the Constitution. **16.B.3c (US)**

2. C When his troops were unable to control Santo Domingo, Napoleon lost his hopes of a naval base to control an American empire. He then had no reason to hold on to the Louisiana Territory. **14.E**

3. C To increase their naval force, the British stopped American ships and practiced impressment, forcing United States sailors to serve in the British navy. **18.B.3a**

4. A Tecumseh was a British ally, so his death was a setback to the British. Choice C is incorrect because the British burning of Washington, D.C., was a victory for them. Choice D, the Hartford Convention, did not concern the British but involved Federalist proposals to amend the Constitution. **16.A**

Short-Answer Question

5. The first proposal showed dissatisfaction with the Embargo Act and the Nonintercourse Act. The second proposal showed the Federalists' dissatisfaction with the War of 1812; it appears that they believed the war did not reflect the wishes of a representative number of Americans. **16.A.3b**

STANDARDIZED TEST PRACTICE

TEST-TAKING TIP

Try to answer the question before you look at the answer choices. Then see if your answer is listed in the choices.

Reviewing Main Ideas

Directions: Choose the best answer for each of the following questions.

1. Which of the following statements is a principle of judicial review?

  A The Constitution is the supreme law of the land.

  B State law takes precedence over federal law.

  C The Constitution should not be followed when it conflicts with any other law.

  D The legislative branch is responsible for upholding the Constitution.

2. Which factor influenced Napoleon's decision to sell the Louisiana Territory to the United States?

  A the movement of American settlers west

  B France's plans to wage war against Russia

  C the loss of the naval base at Santo Domingo

  D Spain's refusal to allow American goods to move into or past New Orleans

3. Because the British desperately needed sailors for their naval war with France, they

  A recruited thousands of Barbary pirates.

  B increased their sailors' pay.

  C forced American citizens to serve in the navy.

  D begged the U.S. to fight against France.

4. Which of the following was a setback for the British in the War of 1812?

  A the death of Tecumseh

  B the British victory over Napoleon

  C the burning of Washington, D.C.

  D the Hartford Convention

Short-Answer Question

Directions: Base your answer to question 5 on the excerpt below and on your knowledge of social studies.

> Third.—Congress shall not have power to lay any embargo on the ships or vessels of the citizens of the United States, in the ports or harbors thereof, for more than sixty days.
>
> Fifth.—Congress shall not make or declare war, or authorize acts of hostility against any foreign nation, without the concurrence of two-thirds of both Houses, except such acts of hostility be in defense of the territories of the United States when actually invaded.
>
> —Amendments to the Constitution Proposed by the Hartford Convention, 1814

5. Explain how these proposals reflected Federalist dissatisfaction with the policies of Jefferson and Madison.

Review the Essential Questions

6. Essay Were the Republicans or the Federalists in a stronger political position following the War of 1812? Explain.

To help you write your essay, review your answers to the Essential Questions in the section reviews and the chapter Foldables Study Organizer. Your essay should include:

- Jefferson's Inaugural Address;
- westward expansion and the Louisiana Purchase;
- the buildup to the War of 1812; and
- the Hartford Convention and the postwar rise of American nationalism.

GO ON

Review the Essential Questions

6. Students should use their answers to the Essential Questions and their Foldables to explain whether the Republicans or Federalists held a stronger political position after the War of 1812. Students should support their arguments with information about Jefferson's Inaugural Address, territorial expansion, events leading to the War of 1812, the Hartford Convention, and nationalism. **17.C.3a**

History ONLINE
For additional test practice, use **Self-Check Quizzes**—Chapter 9 at glencoe.com.

Chapter 9 Assessment

Document-Based Questions

Directions: Analyze the documents and answer the short-answer questions that follow.

Document 1

This passage describes a visit from a German baron to Jefferson's White House.

> As [the baron] sat by the table, among the newspapers that were scattered about, he perceived one that was always filled with the most virulent [hateful] abuse of Mr. Jefferson, calumnies [lies] the most offensive, personal as well as political. "Why are these libels [lies] allowed?" asked the Baron taking up the paper, 'Why is not this libelous journal suppressed, or its Editor at least, fined and imprisoned?'
>
> Mr. Jefferson smiled, saying, "Put that paper in your pocket Baron, and should you hear the reality of our liberty, the freedom of our press, questioned, show this paper, and tell where you found it."

Source: Margaret Bayard Smith, *Forty Years of Washington Society,* 1906

7. Why did Jefferson not stop the libels printed about him?

Document 2

Lewis and Clark presented these medals to Native Americans on their expedition.

8. Why do you think these medals were given to Native Americans?

Document 3

In October 1811, William Henry Harrison recorded his observations about Tecumseh after meeting with him at Vincennes, the capital of the Indiana Territory.

> If it is his [Tecumseh's] object to begin with the surprise of this place, it is impossible that a more favorable situation could have been chosen, than the one he occupies: it is just so far off as to be removed from immediate observation, and yet so near as to enable him to strike us, when the water is high, in twenty-four hours.

Source: David Colbert, *Eyewitness to America*

9. Based on the document, what strategic advantage did Tecumseh's forces have over Harrison's?

Document 4

In this passage, an unknown eyewitness describes an incident during the Battle of New Orleans.

> As the British Officer came in, Paleface [one of the American soldiers] demanded his sword. He hesitated about giving it to him, probably thinking it was derogatory to his dignity, to surrender to a private all over begrimed with dust and powder and that some Officer should show him the courtesy to receive it.

Source: Robert Vincent Remini, *The Battle of New Orleans*

10. Based on the document, why did the British officer not want to surrender his sword to Paleface?

11. Persuasive Writing Using the information from the four documents and your knowledge of social studies, write an essay in which you:

- agree with the belief of many historians that the election of 1800 was a "revolution"; or
- disagree with the viewpoint.

9. Tecumseh's forces had an isolated position that allowed them to observe without being noticed and that enabled them to launch a surprise attack. **16.A.3c**

10. The British officer believed it would be undignified to surrender his sword to a mere private—especially a dirty one. **16.A.3c**

11. Students' essays should explain why the election of 1800 was or was not revolutionary. The essays should explain the term "revolution," support or refute the statement using facts, and reflect an understanding of the four documents and how they relate to the chapter material. **16.A**

History ONLINE
Have students visit the Web site at glencoe.com to review Chapter 9 and take the Self-Check Quiz.

Need Extra Help?

Have students refer to the pages listed if they miss any of the questions.

Need Extra Help?

If you missed questions...	1	2	3	4	5	6	7	8	9	10	11
Go to page...	279	283	289	297	298	276–298	276–279	283–285	291–293	298	276–298

Document-Based Questions

7. Jefferson believed that freedom of the press was an important liberty. **16.A.3b**

8. Possible answer: The "peace and friendship" motto would have indicated that Lewis and Clark had positive motives. Also, the medals, with their rendering of the president, might have impressed the Native Americans. **16.A.3b**

Chapter Planning Guide

10

Levels BL	OL	AL	ELL		Resources	Chapter Opener	Section 1	Section 2	Section 3	Chapter Assess
					FOCUS					
BL	OL	AL	ELL	🖶	Daily Test Practice Transparencies		10–1	10–2	10–3	
					TEACH					
	OL	AL		📁	Geography and History Activity, URB			p. 87		
BL	OL		ELL	📁	Time Line Skills Activity, URB		p. 90			
BL	OL	AL	ELL	📁	Writing Skills Activity, URB		p. 79			
BL	OL	AL	ELL	📁	Content Vocabulary Activity, URB		p. 73	p. 73	p. 73	
BL			ELL	📁	Academic Vocabulary Activity, URB		p. 75	p. 75	p. 75	
BL			ELL	📁	Reading Skills Activity, URB			p. 7		
BL			ELL	📁	Social Studies Skills Activity, URB				p. 81	
BL	OL	AL	ELL	📁	Differentiated Instruction Activity, URB				p. 83	
BL	OL	AL	ELL	📁	Critical Thinking Skills Activity, URB				p. 85	
BL	OL	AL	ELL	📁	Linking Past and Present Activity, URB		p. 89			
	OL	AL		📁	Primary Source Readings, URB			p. 77		
BL	OL	AL	ELL	📁	School-to-Home Connection Activity, URB		p. 91	p. 91	p. 91	
BL	OL		ELL	📁	Guided Reading Activity, URB*		p. 95	p. 96	p. 97	
		AL		📁	Enrichment Activity, URB			p. 11		
BL	OL		ELL	📁	Reading Essentials and Note-Taking Guide*		p. 100	p. 103	p. 106	
BL	OL	AL	ELL	🖶	Lesson Transparencies		10A, 10B	10C		
		AL		📁	Supreme Court Case Studies				pp. 3, 7	
	OL			📁	American Biographies		pp. 13, 16	p. 15	p. 20	
BL	OL	AL	ELL	📁	Outline Map Resource Book	pp. 6, 7, 11				
	OL	AL		🖶	American Art and Architecture Transparencies, Strategies, and Activities			p. 21		

Note: Please refer to the *Unit Resource Book: Launching the Republic* for this chapter's URB materials.

* Also available in Spanish

Levels					Resources	Chapter Opener	Section 1	Section 2	Section 3	Chapter Assess
BL	OL	AL	ELL							
TEACH *(continued)*										
BL	OL	AL	ELL	📁	NGS US Desk Map		✓	✓	✓	
BL	OL	AL	ELL	📁	American Literature Library		✓	✓	✓	
BL	OL	AL	ELL	📁	Writer's Guidebook		✓	✓	✓	
	OL	AL		💿	American History Primary Source Document Library CD-ROM		✓	✓	✓	✓
BL	OL	AL	ELL	💿	American Music: Hits Through History	✓	✓	✓	✓	
BL	OL	AL	ELL	💿	StudentWorks™ Plus CD	✓	✓	✓	✓	✓
BL	OL	AL	ELL	🔒	Section Spotlight Videos		✓	✓	✓	
BL	OL	AL	ELL	🖎	Writing Process Transparencies		✓	✓	✓	✓
BL	OL	AL	ELL	💿	Presentation Plus! With MindJogger CheckPoint CD	✓	✓	✓	✓	✓
ASSESS										
BL	OL	AL	ELL	📁	Quizzes and Tests		p. 91	p. 92	p. 93	pp. 95, 97, 99
BL	OL	AL	ELL	📁	Authentic Assessment With Rubrics				p. 10	
BL	OL	AL	ELL	📁	Standardized Test Practice					p. 19
BL	OL	AL	ELL	💿	*ExamView® Assessment Suite* CD-ROM*		10–1	10–2	10–3	Ch. 10
CLOSE										
BL			ELL	📁	Reteaching Activity, URB*		p. 93	p. 93	p. 93	p. 93
BL	OL		ELL	📁	Reading and Study Skills Foldables Activity	p. 68	p. 68	p. 68	p. 68	p. 68
BL	OL	AL	ELL	📁	*The American Journey* in Graphic Novel		p. 51			
BL			ELL	📁	Reading Strategies and Activities for the Social Studies Classroom		✓	✓	✓	
BL	OL	AL	ELL	🖎	Graphic Organizer Transparencies & Strategies		✓	✓	✓	

TeacherWorks Plus
All-In-One Planner and Resource Center

- Interactive Lesson Planner
- Interactive Teacher Edition
- Fully editable blackline masters
- Section Spotlight Videos Launch
- Differentiated Lesson Plans
- Printable reports of daily assignments
- Standards Tracking System

Professional Development Resources

- Strategies for Success
- Building Academic Vocabulary
- Success With English Learners DVD
- Differentiated Instruction Strategies DVD
- Teaching Literacy Strategies in Social Studies DVD
- Assessment DVD
- Standards-Based Instruction DVD

Using CyberScout

Research Using *Famous Person*

Technology Product

CyberScout is a convenient and dynamic search engine that provides several easy ways to locate information outside the McGraw-Hill Learning Network. CyberScout searches only Web sites that have been reviewed by teachers, so the information students find is always appropriate and accurate.

Objectives

Encourage students to research global and historical issues using CyberScout.

- Enable students to exercise research and study skills.
- Give students the opportunity to practice writing skills.

Steps

- Choose CyberScout from the References menu on the navigation bar to access the home page.
- Enter a name in the Famous Person field and click the Go button.
- The CyberScout page displays a set of results.
- Scroll down by continuing to click result links until coming to a Web site of interest. Click that link.
- Students navigate through the chosen Web site to gain information on their topic and take notes.
- Have students write a summary report of what they have learned.

History ONLINE at glencoe.com

	Student	Teacher	Parent
Media Center			
• Student Edition Audio	●		
• Spanish Summaries	●		
• Section Spotlight Videos	●	●	
Social Studies Online Learning Center			
Classroom Tools			
• Multi-Language Glossaries	●	●	●
• Teaching Today		●	
• TIME Current Events	●	●	●
• Beyond the Textbook	●	●	
***The American Journey* Online Learning Center**			
• Study-to-Go™	●	●	●
• Study Central™	●	●	●
• Chapter Overview	●	●	
• Concepts in Motion	●	●	
• ePuzzles and Games	●	●	
• Literature Connections	●	●	
• Online Student Edition	●	●	●
• Self-Check Quizzes	●	●	●
• Student Web Activities	●	●	
• Vocabulary eFlashcards	●	●	
• Web Activity Lesson Plans	●	●	●
• Vocabulary PuzzleMaker	●	●	●

READING SUPPORT FROM JAMESTOWN EDUCATION

- **Timed Readings Plus in Social Studies** helps students increase their reading rate and fluency while maintaining comprehension. The 400-word passages are similar to those found on state and national assessments.

- **Reading in the Content Area: Social Studies** concentrates on six essential reading skills that help students better comprehend what they read. The book includes 75 high-interest nonfiction passages written at increasing levels of difficulty.

- **Reading Social Studies** includes strategic reading instruction and vocabulary support in Social Studies content for ELLs and native speakers of English.

- **Content Vocabulary Workout** (Grades 6–8) accelerates reading comprehension through focused vocabulary development. Social Studies content vocabulary comes from the glossaries of Glencoe's Middle School Social Studies texts.

www.jamestowneducation.com

NATIONAL GEOGRAPHIC

Index to National Geographic Magazine:

The following articles relate to this chapter:

- *"China's Instant Cities,"* Peter Hessler, June 2007.

- *"Down the Drain?"* John G. Mitchell, September 2002.

National Geographic Society Products

To order the following, call National Geographic at 1-800-368-2728:

National Geographic Atlas of the World (Book)

Access National Geographic's new dynamic MapMachine Web site and other geography resources at:

www.nationalgeographic.com

www.nationalgeographic.com/mapmachine

Reading List Generator CD-ROM — GLENCOE BOOKLINK 3

Use this database to search more than 30,000 titles to create a customized reading list for your students.

- Reading lists can be organized by students' reading level, author, genre, theme, or area of interest.

- The database provides Degrees of Reading Power™ (DRP) and Lexile™ readability scores for all selections.

- A brief summary of each selection is included.

Leveled reading suggestions for this chapter:

For students at a Grade 6 reading level:
- *Erie Canal: Canoeing America's Great Waterway,* by Peter Lourie

For students at a Grade 7 reading level:
- *Robert Fulton,* by Elaine Landau
- *Westward Expansion: Exploration and Settlement,* by Frank De Varona

For students at a Grade 8 reading level:
- *Beyond the Mississippi: Early Westward Expansion of the United States,* by Angela M. Herb
- *Mill,* by David Macaulay

For students at a Grade 9 reading level:
- *Inventors,* by Martin W. Sandler
- *Industrial Revolution,* by John D. Clare

For students at a Grade 10 reading level:
- *The American Frontier,* by Roger Barr

The following videotape programs are available from Glencoe as supplements to the chapter:

- **Textiles: Birth of an American Industry** (ISBN 1-76-700624-0)

- **The Erie Canal** (ISBN 0-76-703154-7)

To order, call Glencoe at 1-800-334-7344. To find classroom resources to accompany many of these videos, check the following home pages:

A&E Television: www.aetv.com

The History Channel: www.history.com

Chapter Objectives

After studying this chapter, students will be able to:

- Discuss the effects of the Industrial Revolution on the U.S. economy.
- Explain how land and water transportation affected westward expansion.
- Explain how nation-building issues were resolved in the 1800s.

Motivating Activity

Identifying Central Issues As the frontier expanded west, settlers needed easier ways to transport goods. Have students look at the painting. **Ask:** What advantages did the Erie Canal offer merchants? *(an easy, dependable way to move their goods long distances)* **Ask:** What disadvantages might transport by canal include? *(Canal routes might be limited; transferring cargo to wagons or other forms of transportation might be difficult.)* Tell students that the Erie Canal can still be accessed today. People enjoy hiking, biking, or cross-country skiing along the paths trod by mules 200 years ago.

Chapter 10

Growth and Expansion
1790–1825

The Erie Canal provided a new transportation route for merchants and travelers.

PRESIDENTS

GEORGE WASHINGTON

JOHN ADAMS

THOMAS JEFFERSON

U.S. Events

★ 1790 Washington, D.C., founded

★ 1793 Eli Whitney invents cotton gin

★ 1807 Robert Fulton designs first practical steamboat

1790

1800

World Events

★ 1792 Russia invades Poland

◄ Russian general's uniform

★ 1804 Haiti claims independence from France

302 Chapter 10

Previewing the Essential Questions

Answering the Essential Question will help students understand important concepts in the section.

Section 1

Economic Growth Ask: How did the Industrial Revolution affect the U.S. economy? *(In many places, the Industrial Revolution led to a change from an agricultural economy to an industrial one. New machinery allowed the mass production of goods.)* Point out to students that in Section 1 they will learn about the enormous changes in the United States brought about by the Industrial Revolution. **OL**

Section 2

Westward Bound Ask: What advantages did better roads and water travel bring? *(Better roads and advances in water transport—such as canals and steamboats—allowed easier travel and cheaper shipping. These advances also encouraged the growth of towns and united the country.)* Point out to students that Section 2 discusses the role of transportation in westward expansion. **OL**

Section 1: Economic Growth

Essential Question What effects did the Industrial Revolution have on the U.S. economy?

Section 2: Westward Bound

Essential Question How did land and water transportation affect westward expansion?

Section 3: Unity and Sectionalism

Essential Question How were nation-building issues resolved in the early 1800s?

FOLDABLES Study Organizer

Organizing Information
Make this Foldable to help organize what you learn about how transportation methods changed in the early 1800s.

Step 1 Place two sheets of paper on top of one another about one inch apart.

Step 2 Fold the papers to form four equal tabs.

Step 3 Staple the sheets, and label each tab as shown.

Transportation: Growth and Expansion
Roads
Rivers
Canals

Reading and Writing As you read the chapter, list the inventors, inventions, and routes that changed transportation in the United States in the early 1800s.

This flag from Fort McHenry inspired Key to write "The Star-Spangled Banner." ▶

1814 ★
Francis Scott Key writes poem that becomes national anthem
JAMES MADISON

JAMES MONROE

1820
Missouri Compromise passed

JOHN Q. ADAMS

★ **1825**
Erie Canal completed

1810 **1820** **1830**

1813 ★
Jane Austen writes *Pride and Prejudice*

★ **1815**
Napoleon defeated at Battle of Waterloo

★ **1822**
Franz Liszt debuts as pianist in Vienna at age 11

★ **1823**
Mexico becomes a republic

Chapter 10   303

Introducing Chapter 10

Time Line Activity

If you have not already done so, have students review the time line. **Ask:** What years does this chapter cover? *(1790–1830)* Have students identify two events related to the arts. *(Francis Scott Key's poem, Jane Austen's* Pride and Prejudice, *or Franz Liszt's debut)*

FOLDABLES Study Organizer **Dinah Zike's Foldables**

Purpose This Foldable helps students identify the inventors, inventions, and routes that changed transportation in the United States in the early 1800s. The completed Foldable will help them prepare for assessment.

📁 More Foldables activities for this chapter can be found in *Dinah Zike's Reading and Study Skills Foldables.*

History ONLINE
Introduce students to chapter content and key terms by having them access the **Chapter Overview** at glencoe.com.

Section 3 ★

Unity and Sectionalism Ask: What sort of issues might have arisen as the United States developed and grew as a country? *(Problems between the states and different sections of the country might have arisen as new laws and the powers of the federal and state governments were tested. Disputes with* neighboring countries and the European powers could also have erupted.) Tell students that in Section 3, they will learn how Americans solved problems without the use of military force. They will explore the ways nation-building issues were solved through negotiation, treaties, and doctrines. **OL**

303

Economic Growth

Focus

Bellringer
Daily Test Practice Transparency 10–1

Reading Guide
Answers to Graphic:
competition, profit, private property, economic freedom

Section Spotlight Video

Have students watch the Section Spotlight Video "Economic Growth" to learn more about the cotton industry.

Resource Manager

Essential Question ◄
What effects did the Industrial Revolution have on the U.S. economy?

Reading Guide

Content Vocabulary

cotton gin (p. 306)   capitalism (p. 307)
interchangeable   capital
  parts (p. 306)   (p. 307)
patent (p. 306)   free enterprise (p. 307)
factory system (p. 306)

Academic Vocabulary

contribute (p. 305)   element (p. 307)

Key People and Events
Industrial Revolution (p. 305)
Eli Whitney (p. 306)

Reading Strategy
Taking Notes As you read, use a diagram like the one below to identify the major elements of the free enterprise system.

Free Enterprise System

ILLINOIS STANDARDS
The American Journey

15.D.3a Explain the effects of increasing and declining imports and exports to an individual and to the nation's economy as a whole.

15.E Understand the impact of government policies and decisions on production and consumption in the economy.

16.C.3b (US) Explain relationships among the American economy and slavery, immigration, industrialization, labor and urbanization, 1700-present.

17.C.3a Explain how human activity is affected by geographic factors.

American Diary

Lucy Larcom started working in the textile mills of Lowell, Massachusetts, at 11 years of age. She later recalled her life in the factory. "I had learned to do a spinner's work, and I obtained permission to tend some frames that stood directly in front of the river-windows with only them and the wall behind me, extending half the length of the mill,—and one young woman beside me. . . . I was, when with strangers, rather a reserved girl; so I kept myself occupied with the river, my work, and my thoughts."

—*from* A New England Girlhood

Winslow Homer painted young women heading to work in the mills.

R **Reading Strategies**	C **Critical Thinking**	D **Differentiated Instruction**	W **Writing Support**	S **Skill Practice**
Teacher Edition • Scanning, p. 305 • Summarizing, p. 306 • Mak. Connections, p. 308	**Teacher Edition** • Mak. General., p. 305 • Draw. Conclusions, p. 306	**Teacher Edition** • Below Grade Level, p. 306 • Gift. & Talent., p. 307 • Logical/Math., p. 308	**Teacher Edition** • Expository Writ., p. 306 • Personal Writ., p. 309	**Teacher Edition** • Using Graph Skills, p. 309
Additional Resources • Guid. Read., URB p. 95 • Content Vocab., URB p. 73 • Academic Vocab., URB p. 75 • Read. Ess., p. 100	**Additional Resources** • Quizzes and Tests, p. 91 • Link. Past & Pres., URB p. 89	**Additional Resources** • School-to-Home, URB p. 91 • Reteaching Act., URB p. 93	**Additional Resources** • Writing Activity, URB p. 79	**Additional Resources** • Daily Test Pract. Transp. 10-1 • Lesson Transparency 10A, B • Time Line Skills, URB p. 90

The Growth of Industry

Main Idea New technology changed the way things were made.

History and You Do you know someone who works in a factory? What is his or her job like? Read to learn how new technology spurred the Industrial Revolution in New England.

Lucy Larcom was one of the many young women who worked in the new industries that developed in the Northeast during the early 1800s. Since colonial times, most people lived and worked on farms. Thus, workers were in short supply for jobs outside of the home. To make up for this lack of workers, Americans developed tools that made their jobs easier and more efficient.

People working in their homes or in workshops made cloth and most other goods. Using hand tools, they made furniture, farm equipment, household items, and clothing.

In the mid-1700s, however, the way goods were made began to change. These changes appeared first in Great Britain. British inventors created machinery to perform some of the work involved in cloth making, such as spinning. Because these machines ran on waterpower, British cloth makers built textile mills along rivers and installed the new machines in these mills. People left their homes and farms to work in the mills and earn wages. This historic development is so important that it is known as the **Industrial Revolution.**

Industrial Revolution in New England

The Industrial Revolution took root in the United States around 1800. The changes appeared first in New England. The region's geography **contributed,** or added, to the development of the Industrial Revolution.

First, farming was difficult with New England's poor soil. Many people willingly gave up farming to find work elsewhere. Second, New England had rivers and streams to provide the waterpower needed to run the machines in the new factories. Third, New England was close to other resources, including coal and iron deposits in Pennsylvania. Fourth, the area had many ports. Raw materials like cotton, as well as finished goods like cloth, were shipped through these ports.

If You Were There / Lowell Mill Girls

On the Job You work long hours—from sunrise to sunset. The work is boring, and you usually perform one task over and over again. You make about $3 per week, and half of your pay is used to rent a room and to buy food. You live in a company-owned boardinghouse. You are required to be in bed by ten o'clock and to attend church on Sunday. You can read, write letters, and attend lectures, but you are not allowed to drink alcohol or play cards.

◀ Lowell Girls, 1840s

Critical Thinking

Making Connections What would you like or dislike about working at the mill? How do you think your job at Lowell would compare with the kinds of jobs young people have today?

Teach

R Reading Strategy

Scanning Tell students that certain words within a question can be the key to answering it. Have them identify one such word in the following question *(tools)*, then scan to find the answer. **Ask:** What inspired Americans to develop tools? *(lack of workers)* **BL**

C Critical Thinking

Making Generalizations Ask students to write a generalization about the physical characteristics of places they would expect large American cities to develop. *(Answers might include proximity to rivers and streams, natural resources, or ports.)* **OL**

If You Were There

Critical Thinking Answer
Students may mention long hours, low pay, and poor working conditions. Independence from home might be a positive aspect. Students might note the variety of jobs available today and the greater legal protections, pay, and benefits.

Differentiated Instruction

Writing "Business" Documents

Objective: To learn about business writing

Focus: Show students want ads from the local newspaper.

Teach: Read the directions and have students write the ad, following the checklist and including appropriate duties and skills.

Assess: Assess the ads.

Close: Discuss the best-written ads.

Writing Skills Activity, URB p. 79

Differentiated Instruction Strategies

BL Ask students to circle the skills and underline the responsibilities in the job posting.

AL Have students create a list of qualifications for three different jobs of the early 1800s.

ELL Ask students to rewrite the job posting, removing the unnecessary sentence.

D Differentiated Instruction

Below Grade Level Ask: What are four advantages of interchangeable parts? *(They could be put together quickly to make a complete product, made machine repair easier, allowed for production of goods on a large scale, and reduced the price of goods.)* **BL**

W Writing Support

Expository Writing Ask students to think of an invention of their own design that they would like to see patented. Have them describe their invention in one or two paragraphs. A third paragraph should explain why the invention is needed. They can include sketches. **OL**

R Reading Strategy

Summarizing Ask students to read the passage and summarize the information into one paragraph. **OL**

C Critical Thinking

Drawing Conclusions Ask: What was a major economic advantage of the factory system? *(Students should recognize that bringing all the stages of production together would save money on transportation of materials and products.)* **OL**

Differentiated Instruction

New Technology

The invention of new machines and technology led to the Industrial Revolution. For example, the spinning jenny, the water frame—which spun thread—and the power loom—which wove the thread into cloth—allowed many steps in making cloth to be done by machine. These machines saved both time and money.

In 1793 **Eli Whitney** of Massachusetts invented the **cotton gin.** The cotton gin was a simple machine that quickly and efficiently removed the seeds from the cotton fiber.

Whitney also started using **interchangeable parts.** These were identical machine parts that could be put together quickly to make a complete product. These parts also made machine repair easier. Interchangeable parts allowed for the production of different kinds of goods on a large scale. This reduced the price of the goods.

Patents and Factories

In 1790 Congress passed a patent law to protect the rights of inventors. A **patent** gives an inventor the sole legal right to the invention and its profits for a certain period of time.

Although the British tried to keep their new industrial technology a secret, a few British workers brought their knowledge to the United States. One such worker was Samuel Slater. He memorized the design of the machines used in the British factory in which he worked.

Once in the United States, Slater took over the management of a cotton mill in Pawtucket, Rhode Island. There he duplicated the British machines that made cotton thread. Women working in their homes then wove the thread into cloth. Slater's mill marked an important step in the Industrial Revolution in the United States.

Francis Cabot Lowell improved on Slater's process in 1814. In Lowell's textile plant in Massachusetts, all the stages of cloth making were performed under one roof. Lowell began the **factory system,** where all manufacturing steps are brought together in one place to increase efficiency.

Primary Source / Technology and Industry

Growth of Industry New England was the perfect location for the Industrial Revolution to begin in the United States because its rushing rivers provided power to run the machinery. The industrial growth that began in New England spread to other areas of the country. By 1870, the nation's industrial cities were growing.

Slater Mill in Pawtucket, Rhode Island Because Britain prohibited the export of textile machinery, Slater had to design his factory and build the machines from memory. It was an immediate success. ▼

"If thou canst do this thing, I invite thee to come to Rhode Island, and have the credit of introducing cotton-manufacture into America."
—Moses Brown, in a letter to Samuel Slater in 1789

Growth of Industrial Cities

Leveled Activities

BL Content Vocabulary Activity, URB p. 73

OL Time Line Skills Activity, URB p. 90

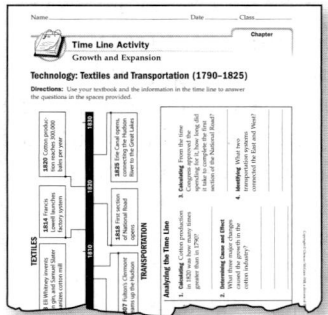

AL Linking Past and Present Activity, URB p. 89

Free Enterprise

Industrial growth requires an economic system that allows competition to flourish with little government interference. **Capitalism** is the economic system of the United States. Under capitalism, individuals put their **capital,** or money, into a business, hoping that the business will be successful and make a profit.

Free enterprise is another term used to describe the American economy. In a free enterprise economy, people are free to buy, sell, and produce whatever they want. They can also work wherever they wish. The major **elements,** or parts, of free enterprise are competition, profit, private property, and economic freedom. Business owners have the freedom to produce the products that they think will sell the best and be the most profitable. In a free enterprise economy, buyers also compete to find the best products at the lowest prices.

D

✔ **Reading Check** **Describing** How did New England's physical geography support the growth of industries?

Agriculture Expands

Main Idea Agriculture expanded and remained the leading occupation of most Americans in the 1800s.

History and You Do any of your relatives own and work on a farm? Read to learn how agriculture expanded in the 1800s.

....

Although many New Englanders went to work in factories during the first half of the 1800s, agriculture remained the country's leading economic activity. Most Americans still lived and worked on farms.

In the Northeast, farms were small and worked by families. Farmers in the Northeast usually marketed their produce locally. In the South, cotton production rose dramatically. The demand for cotton grew steadily with the development of the textile industries of New England and Europe.

History ONLINE

Student Web Activity Visit glencoe.com and complete the Chapter 10 Web Activity about the Industrial Revolution.

D Differentiated Instruction

Gifted and Talented Have students research a company and describe the company and its product in terms of capitalism and free enterprise. **AL**

Primary Source

Critical Thinking Answer
Students may suggest that better technology led people to build more factories. However, such factories were so successful that they surely inspired people to design better technology.

History ONLINE

Objectives and answers to the Student Web Activity can be found at glencoe.com under the Web Activity Lesson Plan for this chapter.

✔ **Reading Check** **Answer:** Farming was difficult so there were more available workers; rivers and streams provided waterpower for machines; resources were located nearby; ports were available to ship goods.

Textile Mill The Lowell factory system was designed to bring work and workers together. A typical Lowell textile mill in 1830 housed 4,500 spindles, 120 power looms, and more than 200 employees under one roof.

◄ A water frame was used to spin thread.

1 The first steps in textile production were to clean the raw cotton and turn loose cotton into crude yarn.

2 The spinning process transforms the yarn into thread.

3 At the weaving stage, power looms interlace the threads into coarse cloth or fabric.

4 Fabric is measured and batched for dyeing. Vegetable dyes were the earliest known dyes.

Critical Thinking

Determining Cause and Effect Did the increase of factories lead to better technology, or did better technology lead to more factories? Explain.

Growth and Expansion **Chapter 10 307**

Additional Support

Teacher Tip

Researching Students will probably enjoy discovering the manufacturing techniques for their favorite items, and you may need to limit their viewing time. One helpful Web site for this project is http://manufacturing.stanford.edu/. **OL**

Activity: Technology Connection

Touring a Factory Ask: What was produced in factories in the early 1800s? *(cloth, tools, farm implements, and so on)* Have pairs of students locate online factory tours and select a factory that interests them. As they follow their online tours, ask students to pay careful attention to the machinery and the skills that would be required to design the machines. **Ask:** Why are patents important? *(Students should understand that patents ensure that an inventor earns payment for his or her ideas, which helps the inventor continue to invent.)* Have students write a paragraph presenting their views on the following statement: "Inventors should be subsidized by the federal government for the benefit of the nation." **OL**

R Reading Strategy

R Reading Strategy

Making Connections Ask: What might have been some of the effects of increased cotton production in the Southern states? *(Students may suggest more and larger plantations, higher profits for plantation owners, increased need for slave labor.)* **AL**

D Differentiated Instruction

Logical/Mathematical Ask: How many times greater was cotton production in 1820 than in 1790? *(300,000/3,000 = 100 times)* How long did it take for cotton production to increase that much? *(1820 − 1790 = 30 years)* **OL**

Population of the United States, 1820
NATIONAL GEOGRAPHIC

Map Skills Answers
1. New York, Pennsylvania, and Virginia
2. Louisiana

Hands-On Chapter Project
Step 1

Making a Book

Step 1: Organizing the Book Bring samples of nonfiction books to class to familiarize students with the cover, table of contents, chapters, glossary, index, photographs, and diagrams.

Population of the United States, 1820 **NATIONAL GEOGRAPHIC**

The tremendous growth in population helped spur the growth of industry.

Urban and Rural Population, 1820

Rural 92.8%

Urban 7.2%

By the Numbers

Population Growth, 1800–1840

Population (in millions): 0, 5, 10, 15, 20

Year: 1800, 1810, 1820, 1830, 1840

Source: *Historical Statistics of the United States.*

▼ Philadelphia, 1799

Map Skills

1. **Place** Which states had a population of more than 1 million in 1820?
2. **Regions** Which state had a larger population, Louisiana or Mississippi?

Maps In MOtion See StudentWorks™ Plus or glencoe.com.

R Southern plantation owners used enslaved workers from Africa to plant, tend, and pick the cotton. The recently invented cotton gin encouraged the planters to raise even larger amounts of the crop. The new machine made it possible to clean cotton faster and more cheaply than could be done by hand. Between 1790 and 1820, cotton production soared from 3,000 bales produced per year to more than 300,000 bales produced per year in the South.

D Agriculture also expanded in the West. Southern farmers seeking new land moved west to plant cotton. Western farmers in the region north of the Ohio River concentrated on raising pork and cash crops such as corn and wheat.

✓ **Reading Check** **Contrasting** How was agriculture different in the Northeast than in the South?

Economic Independence

Main Idea The growth of factories and trade led to the development of corporations and cities.

History and You If you had your choice, would you prefer living in the city or in the country? Why? Read to learn about the growth of cities in the 1800s.

Small investors, such as shopkeepers, merchants, and farmers, financed most new businesses. These people invested their money in hopes of earning profits if the new businesses succeeded. Low taxes, minimum government regulations, and competition encouraged people to invest in new industries.

Corporations Develop

Large businesses called corporations began to develop rapidly in the 1830s when legal obstacles to their formation were removed.

Essential Question: What effects did the Industrial Revolution have on the U.S. economy?

Directions Tell students that they will be creating a book on the Industrial Revolution. Organize students into groups of four and have each group choose a topic for its chapter about the Industrial Revolution. As a class, discuss the best way to organize the book, such as chronologically or by type of industry. Assign a chapter number to each group.

Cause and Effect Ask the class to discuss the causes of the Industrial Revolution in Britain. **OL**

(Chapter Project continued in Section 2)

The rise of these new corporations made it easier to sell stock—shares of ownership in a company—to finance improvement and development.

Cities Come of Age

The growth of factories and trade led to the growth of towns and cities. Many cities developed along rivers because factories could take advantage of the water power and ship goods to markets more easily. Older cities such as New York, Boston, and Baltimore also grew as centers of commerce and trade.

Along New York City's South Street, shipping piers extended for 3 miles (4.8 km). The value of merchandise shipped from these piers rose from $84 million in 1825 to $146 million in 1836. An English traveler wrote of the busy New York City waterfront: **S**

PRIMARY SOURCE

"Every thought, word, look, and action of the multitude seemed to be absorbed by commerce."

—quoted in *The Growing Years*, by Margaret L. Coit

Moving westward, towns such as Pittsburgh, Cincinnati, and Louisville profited from their locations on major rivers. As farmers in the West shipped more of their products by water, these towns grew rapidly.

Cities and towns looked quite different from modern urban areas. Buildings were made of wood or brick. Streets and sidewalks were unpaved, and barnyard animals often roamed freely. There were no sewers to carry away waste and dirty water, so the danger of diseases such as cholera and yellow fever was very real. In 1793, for example, a yellow fever epidemic in Philadelphia killed thousands.

Fire posed another threat to cities. Sparks from a fireplace or chimney could easily ignite a wooden building and spread to others. Few towns or cities had organized fire companies, thus fires could be disastrous. **W**

Cities and towns offered many opportunities, such as a variety of jobs to choose from and steady wages. As cities grew, libraries, museums, and shops were built, providing people with places to enjoy during their leisure time. For many, the jobs and attractions of city life outweighed any of the dangers.

✔ **Reading Check** Analyzing Why were rivers important for the growth of cities?

History ONLINE
Study Central™ To review this section, go to glencoe.com.

Section 1 Review

Vocabulary

1. Define each term in a sentence: contribute, cotton gin, interchangeable parts, patent, factory system, capitalism, capital, free enterprise, element.

Main Ideas

2. **Summarizing** How did inventions like the cotton gin and interchangeable parts revolutionize the textile industry?

3. **Explaining** Why were Southern plantations able to increase their cotton production between 1790 and 1821?

4. **Specifying** What conditions encouraged people to invest in the new businesses?

Critical Thinking

5. **Determining Cause and Effect** Use a diagram like the one below to identify why the Industrial Revolution first began in New England.

Characteristics of New England

Industrial Revolution

6. **Personal Writing** It is 1830, and you have just moved to New York City. Write a letter to your friends back on the farm describing what your new life is like.

Answer the Essential Question

7. What effects did the Industrial Revolution have on the U.S. economy?

Growth and Expansion **Chapter 10** 309

Answers

Focus

W Writing Support

Expository Writing Have students reread the author biography and point out that a newspaper article prompted Anderson to write *Fever 1793*. Ask students to bring in a newspaper. Have them identify an article about a topic or an idea they would like to explore further. Have them research their topic on the Internet and write three paragraphs about it. **AL**

R₁ Reading Strategy

Analyzing Text Structure Have students read this phrase aloud. **Ask:** Why did the author say "my feet moved" instead of "I walked"? *(Mattie is wandering, not deciding where to go. Students might say she is on "automatic pilot.")* **OL**

R₂ Reading Strategy

Visualizing Read the paragraph aloud to the class, and ask them to visualize the scene. **Ask:** What words bring the scene to life? *(shoes tapping across the cobblestones, [the homes] were all deserted, darkened with my sweat)* **OL**

Additional Reading

Meet the Author

W Laurie Halse Anderson (1961–) began researching *Fever 1793* after reading a newspaper article about an epidemic that killed 10 percent of the population of Federalist-era Philadelphia. During her studies, she examined the politics, food, religion, and medicine of the period. This information helped her create realistic details in the life of Mattie, the main character in the story.

Building Background

In *Fever 1793*, Laurie Halse Anderson tells the story of Mattie, a young girl living through the horrors of a yellow fever outbreak in Philadelphia. At the time, Philadelphia was the young country's largest city and capital. During the epidemic, the American government, along with many residents, fled the city. Throughout the novel, Anderson weaves historical facts with the fictional story. In the following scene, Mattie wanders the city alone after the death of her grandfather. While reading, pay attention to the actions that depict Mattie's personal strength and maturity.

Vocabulary

acquainted familiar

shift dress

tethered tied

exorbitant very high

thrive gain in health

quill feather shaft

pestilence contagious disease

Second Street in Philadelphia, 1790s ▶

FEVER 1793

Laurie Halse Anderson

R₁ My feet moved, taking me up one street and down the next. I didn't see another person for blocks, not even a grave digger or a physician. **R₂** The sound of my shoes tapping across the cobblestones echoed down the street like a latecomer sneaking into church. I walked past the homes of people **acquainted** with my family. They were all deserted. My **shift** darkened with sweat. Surely I wasn't the only person left in Philadelphia?

* * *

When I came upon the open windows of the *Federal Gazette* office, it was a shock. A horse was **tethered** by the door. I stumbled through the door, eager for a friendly face.

310

Review suggested books before assigning them.

Biography: *Thomas Jefferson: Man on a Mountain,* by Natalie S. Bober, shows readers that Jefferson was a man with personal flaws and strengths and experienced great joys and sorrows. This book uses writings by Jefferson and the people who knew him, along with other historical documents, to describe the man.

Fiction: *Bold Journey: West With Lewis and Clark,* by Charles H. Bohner, follows Lewis and Clark's exploration team into the unknown. Based on real-life events, the explorers race rapids, scale mountains, and make wild discoveries on their journey across the West.

Fiction: *The Gold-Lined Box,* by Marjory Hall, is based on a true story that took place during the War of 1812. Sixteen-year-old Matilda O'Neill's father is captured by the British, and she must try to rescue him from a British warship that is guarded by soldiers.

For further reading, see **BOOKLINK 3**.

"Can I help you?"

"It's me, Mr. Brown. William Cook's granddaughter."

The printer looked up from his desk. The dark circles under his eyes and lines of worry across his brow made him look as if he had aged years in the course of a month.

"What do you need, Matilda? I've no time for social calls today."

I hesitated. What could Mr. Brown do? I couldn't work a press; he couldn't bring Grandfather back from the grave.

"Please, Sir," I said. "I would like to place an advertisement in your newspaper. I'm searching for my mother. She's gone."

Mr. Brown pulled a stained kerchief out of his trouser pocket and rubbed it over his face and neck.

"Matilda, there is nothing I'd rather do than run an advertisement for your mother. But look about you." He spread his arms to take in the shop. "There is hardly any paper to be had for a hundred miles. The *Gazette* is the last paper being printed in the city, and I have to print on half-sheets. Five other newspapers have closed down. I wish I could flee myself."

He paused and looked out the window. I thought he had forgotten me.

"But I must stay. This paper is the only method of communication left in the city. I must print physicians' notices, orders from the mayor . . ."

"Mr. Brown? Sir?"

He took a deep breath and looked up.

"In the beginning of August, this was the largest city in the United States. Forty thousand people lived here. Near as I can **R**

tell," he pointed to the jumble of notes and letters on the desk before him, "more than half the city has fled, twenty thousand people."

"How many dead, Sir?"

"More than three thousand, enough to fill house after house, street after street."

---

*I'm searching for my mother.
She's gone.*

"I went to the market, but found no food," I said.

"Few farmers dare come into town. They charge **exorbitant** prices for their wares, and get whatever they ask," he said bitterly. "Those who don't die of the fever are beginning to starve. You've seen the rats?"

I nodded.

"The rats **thrive**. I should write that." He dipped a **quill** into the ink pot and scribbled a note. "The only creatures to benefit from this **pestilence** are the rats. Go home, Matilda, take my regards to your grandfather, but tell him he must lock all the doors and pray for frost." **C**

I started to tell him what had happened, but a man burst through the door waving a letter and shouting. Mr. Brown shooed me from his shop with a wave of his hand. No matter. Telling him wouldn't bring Grandfather back, and it was clear he couldn't help me.

Analyzing Literature

1. **Respond and Connect**
   (a) How might Mattie feel at the beginning of the passage as she walks the streets alone?
   (b) How does Mattie feel as she encounters Mr. Brown?

2. **Recall and Interpret**
   (a) What is Mr. Brown's occupation?
   (b) Why is a newspaper important during this plague?

3. **Evaluate** What actions show Mattie's maturity during this crisis?

Section 2

Focus

Bellringer
Daily Test Practice Transparency 10–2

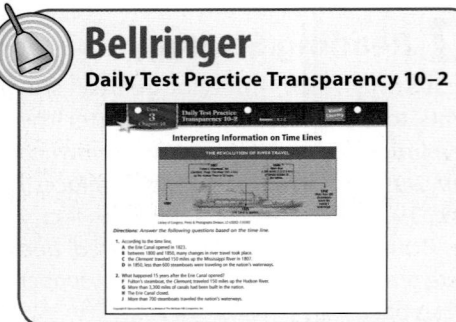

Reading Guide
Answers to Graphic:
1807: Steamboat *Clermont* operates successfully; **1811:** Construction of the National Road begins; **1818:** First section of the National Road opens; **1825:** Erie Canal opens

Section Spotlight Video

Have students watch the Section Spotlight Video "Westward Bound" to learn more about the Erie Canal.

Resource Manager

Section 2

Essential Question ◄
How did land and water transportation affect westward expansion?

Reading Guide

Content Vocabulary
census (p. 313)   canal (p. 315)
turnpike (p. 313)   lock (p. 316)

Academic Vocabulary
reveal (p. 313)   region (p. 314)

Key People
Robert Fulton (p. 314)
De Witt Clinton (p. 315)

Reading Strategy
Taking Notes As you read, use a time line like the one below to identify major developments in transportation during the early 1800s.

1800   1810   1820   1830

ILLINOIS STANDARDS
The American Journey

15.D.3c Explain how workers can affect their productivity through training and by using tools, machinery and technology.
16.D.3b (US) Describe characteristics of different kinds of families in America during the colonial/frontier periods and the 19th century.
17.C.3c Analyze how human processes influence settlement patterns including migration and population growth.
17.D.3a Explain how and why spatial patterns of settlement change over time.

Westward Bound

American Diary

In the early 1800s, pioneers wrote many letters that praised the qualities of the territory west of the Appalachians. One immigrant wrote about the land in Illinois: "[It has] the most fertile soil in the U[nited] States. . . . [In] general, the farmer has nothing to do, but fence in his fields: plough his ground and plant his crop. He may then expect, from an acre, from 50 to 100 bushels [of] corn; and from 10 to 50 of wheat; the quality of both which articles is superior to that of any I ever saw."

—quoted in Westward Expansion: An Eyewitness History

Fort Dearborn, at the site of Chicago, Illinois, 1820

R **Reading Strategies**	C **Critical Thinking**	D **Differentiated Instruction**	W **Writing Support**	S **Skill Practice**
Teacher Edition • Deter. Impor., p. 313 • Making Connec., p. 314 **Additional Resources** • Con. Vocab., URB p. 73 • Acad. Vocab., URB p. 75 • Read. Ess., p. 103 • Read. Skills, URB p. 7 • Pri. Source Read., URB p. 77	**Teacher Edition** • Identify Central Iss., p. 313 • Deter. Cause & Effect, p. 316 **Additional Resources** • Quizzes and Tests, p. 92 • Enrichment Act., URB p. 11	**Teacher Edition** • Interpersonal, p. 315 **Additional Resources** • School-to-Home, URB p. 91 • Reteaching Act., URB p. 93	**Teacher Edition** • Persuasive Writ., p. 314 • Personal Writ., p. 317	**Teacher Edition** • Using Map Skills, p. 316 **Additional Resources** • Daily Test Pract. Transp. 10-2 • Lesson Transp. 10C • Geo. & Hist., URB p. 87

Moving West

Main Idea Transportation routes such as roads improved as settlers moved west, and steamboats greatly improved the transport of goods along rivers.

History and You Have you ever taken a trip to another state? How did you get there? Read to learn about the new network of roads that connected the country.

. . . .

Settlers poured into Illinois and other frontier areas west of the Appalachian Mountains during the 1800s. The typical frontier family moved from place to place as the line of settlement continued to push westward.

The first **census**—the official count of a population—of the United States in 1790 **revealed** a population of nearly 4 million. Most Americans at that time lived east of the Appalachian Mountains and within a few hundred miles of the Atlantic coast.

Within a few decades this pattern changed. The number of settlers heading west increased dramatically. In 1811 a Pennsylvania resident reported seeing 236 wagons filled with people and their possessions traveling on the road to Pittsburgh. A man in Newburgh, New York, counted 60 wagons rolling by in a single day. By 1820, just 30 years after the first census, the population of the United States had more than doubled to about 10 million people. Nearly 2 million of these people lived west of the Appalachians.

Traveling west was not easy. The 363-mile (584 km) trip from New York City to Buffalo could take as long as three weeks. A pioneer family moving west faced hardships and dangers along the way.

Roads and Turnpikes

The nation needed good inland roads for travel and for the shipment of goods. Private companies built many **turnpikes,** or toll roads. The fees travelers paid to use those roads helped finance their construction. Many of the roads had a base of crushed stone. The land was often muddy in some areas. To aid travel, companies built "corduroy roads." These roads consisted of logs laid side by side, like the ridges of corduroy cloth.

Ohio became a state in 1803. The new state asked the federal government to build a road to connect it with the East. In 1806 Congress approved funds for a national road to the West and five years later agreed on the route.

By the Numbers / Western Settlement

A Road to the West

New States Between 1800 and 1830, westward expansion increased the population in three new states—Ohio, Indiana, and Illinois.

Population in Ohio, Indiana, and Illinois

Year	Ohio	Indiana	Illinois
1800	42,159	2,632	2,458
1810	230,760	24,520	12,282
1820	581,434	147,178	55,211
1830	937,903	343,031	157,445

Source: *Historical Statistics of the United States.*

Critical Thinking

Synthesizing How do you think a region's physical geography influenced where people settled?

Teach

. . . .

C Critical Thinking

Identifying Central Issues Ask: What pattern changed between 1790 and 1820? *(Americans went from almost all living east of the Appalachians to one-fifth of them living to the west of them.)* **AL**

R Reading Strategy

Determining Importance Ask: What advantages did turnpikes provide for westward expansion? *(They provided inland roads for travel and the shipment of goods.)* **OL**

By the Numbers

Critical Thinking Answer
Students might describe how the availability of fertile land or the nearness to waterways might have influenced where people settled.

Skill Practice Ask: Which state had the greatest increase in population from 1800 to 1830? *(Ohio)* Why did Illinois's population take longer to increase than the other two states? *(It's farthest west.)* **OL**

Differentiated Instruction

Leveled Activities

W Writing Support

Persuasive Writing Ask: Who should pay for the construction of new roads? *(Responses may include: those who will use them, or all citizens in the area, or the federal government.)* Have each student select a location within the United States in 1805. Have them write a letter from a resident of that area to a legislator, either supporting or opposing the building of the National Road. **OL**

R Reading Strategy

Making Connections Ask: Do you know anyone who has invented something in order to solve a problem? *(Answers will vary.)* What problem was Robert Fulton trying to solve? *(Earlier steamboats were not powerful enough to travel on large rivers or other bodies of water.)* Why do you think one invention leads to another? *(Responses may include that each succeeding invention will do the job better or more efficiently or that inventors are attracted to profits from improving successful inventions.)* **OL**

Additional Support

Construction of the road began in 1811 at the Potomac River in Cumberland, Maryland. However, work on the road stopped during the War of 1812. The first section, from Maryland to Wheeling, Virginia (now West Virginia), did not open until 1818. The route closely followed that of a military road built by George Washington in 1754. In later years, the national road reached Ohio and continued on to Vandalia, Illinois. Congress viewed the National Road as a military necessity, but it did not take on any other road-building projects.

River Travel

River travel had definite advantages over travel by wagon and horse. It was far more comfortable than traveling by roads, which were at that time often nothing more than wide, rough paths. Also, boats or river barges could carry far larger loads of farm products or other goods than a wagon.

River travel had two problems, however. The first was a result of the geography of the eastern part of the United States. Most major rivers in the **region** flowed in a north-south direction, not east to west, the direction in which most people and goods were headed. Second, traveling upstream by barge against the current was extremely difficult and slow.

Steam engines were already being used in the 1780s and 1790s to power boats in quiet waters. Inventor James Rumsey equipped a small boat on the Potomac River with a steam engine. John Fitch, another inventor, built a steamboat that navigated the Delaware River. Neither boat, however, had enough power to withstand the strong currents and winds found in and along large rivers or open bodies of water.

In 1802 Robert Livingston, a political and business leader, hired **Robert Fulton** to develop a steamboat with a powerful engine. Livingston wanted the steamboat to carry cargo and passengers up the Hudson River from New York City to Albany.

In 1807 Fulton had his steamboat, the *Clermont*, ready for a trial on the Hudson. A newly designed engine powered the boat. The *Clermont* made the 150-mile (241 km) trip

LINKING PAST TO PRESENT   Roads: Tying the Nation Together

THEN For a large part of the early 1800s, the National Road was the nation's busiest land route to the West. It stimulated trade, as well as settlement on the western frontier.

Major Roads Before the Civil War

In an 1879 interview, a man recalled the heyday of the National Road: "The wagons were so numerous that the leaders of one team [of horses] had their noses in the trough [feed box] at the end of the next wagon ahead."
—"The Old National Pike," *Harper's New Monthly Magazine,* November 1879

The National Road was the nation's first federally funded highway. When completed in 1837, the gravel road covered almost 800 miles (1,287 km), connecting Cumberland, Maryland, to Vandalia, Illinois.

Some roads in the East were rough corduroy roads. ▶

Activity: Economics Connection

Home-Based to Factory Workers Ask: What personal expenses might have increased when people went from working at home to working in factories? *(Students may suggest costs for transportation or boarding, food, clothing.)* What would be some advantages of factory work? *(social* interaction, possibly higher pay, materials would be provided by the employer, and so on)

Modern Home-Based Workers Ask: What jobs are done at home today? Have students offer job ideas and list them on the board. How have jobs for home-based workers changed? *(Many home-based jobs* today involve telecommuting, or working via computer.)* What are some economic advantages of today's home-based work? *(Students may mention savings in transportation costs, flexible work hours, ability to care for family, and so on.)* **OL**

from New York City to Albany in the unheard-of time of 32 hours. Using only sails, the trip would have taken four days.

About 140 feet (43 m) long and 14 feet (4 m) wide, the *Clermont* offered great comforts to its passengers. They could sit or stroll about on deck. At night they could relax in the sleeping compartments below deck. The engine was noisy, but its power provided a fairly smooth ride.

Steamboats ushered in a new age in river travel. They greatly improved the transport of goods and passengers along major inland rivers. Shipping goods became cheaper and faster. Regular steamboat service began along the Mississippi River, between New Orleans and Natchez, Mississippi, in 1812. Steamboats also contributed to the growth of other river cities like Cincinnati and St. Louis. By 1850, some 700 steamboats were carrying cargo and passengers within the United States.

Reading Check Identifying What advantages did river travel offer?

Canals

Main Idea Business and government officials developed a plan to build a canal to link the eastern and western parts of the country.

History and You Have you ever worked long and hard to build something? Read to learn about the accomplishment of thousands of laborers who constructed the Erie Canal.

. . . .

Steamboats were a great improvement in transportation, but their routes depended on the existing river system. Because most major rivers in the eastern United States flowed north to south, steamboats could not effectively tie together the eastern and western parts of the country.

Business and government officials led by **De Witt Clinton** in New York developed a plan to link New York City with the Great Lakes region. They would build a **canal**—an artificial waterway—across New York state. The canal would connect Albany on the Hudson River with Buffalo on Lake Erie.

D Differentiated Instruction

Interpersonal Organize students into groups. Have each group research the effect of the Erie Canal on the development of a city along its route and prepare a visual display to show the changes. **OL**

LINKING PAST TO PRESENT

Critical Thinking Answers

1. It provided a faster and easier east-west route for moving people and goods.

2. Students may suggest that highways allow visits to distant places; access to fresh produce and foods from other regions; reduced air quality.

Reading Check **Answer:** Travel by river was much faster than travel by wagon and horse. It was also cheaper, more comfortable, and allowed the transport of larger loads.

Major U.S. Highways Today

— Eisenhower Interstate Highway System

NOW The development of automobiles brought about new demand for national highways. Construction on Route 40 began in the 1920s. It followed the National Road for much of its route and covered 3,220 miles (5,182 km). In the 1970s, Interstate 70 was built. It runs parallel to sections of Route 40 and is today a major east-west highway.

Critical Thinking

1. **Determining Cause and Effect** How did the National Road help westward expansion?

2. **Making Connections** How does the National Highway System affect your life?

Hands-On Chapter Project
Step 2

Making a Book

Step 2: Gathering Information Have groups research their topics.

Essential Question: How did land and water transportation affect westward expansion?

Directions Have each group research its chapter using the Internet or the library. Have them create outlines for their chapter and choose artwork, diagrams, graphs, charts, or photographs.

Analyzing Information As a class, discuss how transportation affected the Industrial Revolution. **Ask:** *What kinds of jobs did new transportation create? (steamboat operators, ditchdiggers for canals, road builders, etc.)* **OL**

(Chapter Project continued in Section 3)

C Critical Thinking

Determining Cause and Effect
Ask: What cause-and-effect relationship can you state about the explosion in canal building? *(The success of the Erie Canal [cause] led to the explosion in canal building, [effect].)* **OL**

S Skill Practice

Using Map Skills Have students compare the map on this page to the map titled "Major Roads Before the Civil War" earlier in this section. **Ask:** Where were most canals built in relation to the National Road? *(to its north)* **OL**

Canals 1820–1860 · NATIONAL GEOGRAPHIC

Map Skills Answer
Lake Michigan and the Illinois River

Map Skills Practice
Ask: What were most canals named after? *(the bodies of water and cities they connected or by the names of the states they crossed)*

✓ Reading Check Answer: to link the eastern and western regions of the country

Differentiated Instruction

Canals, 1820–1860 · NATIONAL GEOGRAPHIC

"But when we consider that this canal will open a way into the great rivers that fall into the Mississippi . . . and that it will communicate with . . . the most productive regions of America; there can be no question respecting the blessings that it will produce [and] the riches that it will create."
—De Witt Clinton in a letter, November 1823

Canal Mileage, 1850
- OH, 792 miles
- IN, 214 miles
- IL, 100 miles
- Other states, 800 miles
- NY and PA, 1,757 miles

The Canal Boom The success of the Erie Canal sparked a wave of canal-building across the United States. Engineers who had worked on the Erie Canal spread out across the country to assist in numerous canal projects.

▲ To celebrate the opening of the Erie Canal, Governor Clinton pours water from Lake Erie into the Atlantic Ocean.

Map Skills
Location What bodies of water were connected by the Illinois and Michigan Canal?

Building the Erie Canal

Thousands of laborers, many of them Irish immigrants, worked on the construction of the 363-mile (584 km) Erie Canal. Along the canal they built a series of **locks**—separate compartments in which water levels were raised or lowered. Locks provided a way to raise and lower boats at places canal levels changed.

Construction of the canal proved dangerous for workers. Diggers were buried when canal beds collapsed and others died in blasting accidents. The swamps in which they toiled led to disease among the workers.

After more than two years of construction, the Erie Canal opened on October 26, 1825. Clinton boarded a barge in Buffalo and traveled on the canal to Albany. From there he sailed down the Hudson River to New York City. As crowds cheered, the officials poured water from Lake Erie into the Atlantic Ocean.

Improving Canal Travel

In its early years, the Erie Canal did not allow steamboats. Their powerful engines could damage the canal's earthen embankments. Instead, teams of mules or horses hauled the boats and barges. A two-horse team pulled a 100-ton (91 t) barge about 24 miles (39 km) in one day. This was fast compared with travel by wagon. In the 1840s, the canal banks were reinforced to accommodate steam tugboats that could pull the barges.

The success of the Erie Canal led to an explosion in canal building. By 1850, the United States had more than 3,600 miles (5,794 km) of canals. Canals lowered the cost of shipping goods and brought prosperity to the towns along their routes. Perhaps most important, they linked regions of a growing country.

✓ Reading Check **Finding the Main Idea** Why were canals built?

Summarizing Information

Objective: To learn techniques for summarizing
Focus: Ask students why writing is grouped into paragraphs.
Teach: Have students identify an important detail in each paragraph and write it in the box.
Assess: Students should complete the summary and the second skill activity.
Close: Review details and summaries.

Differentiated Instruction Strategies

BL Ask students to identify and underline each detail in a selected passage.

AL Have students find a challenging passage in this section, list details, and summarize.

ELL Tell students to highlight difficult words and look them up as they read the first passage.

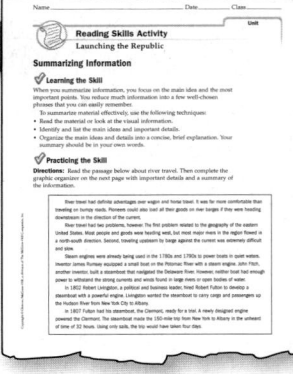

Reading Skills Activity, URB p. 7

Western Settlement

Main Idea Americans continued to move westward, settling near rivers so they could ship their goods to markets.

History and You Think about what your life might be like if you could not watch TV or use the computer. Read to learn about the lives of Western families in the early 1800s.

· ·

Americans moved westward in waves. The first wave began before the 1790s and led to the admission of four new states between 1791 and 1803—Vermont, Kentucky, Tennessee, and Ohio. A second wave of westward growth began between 1816 and 1821. Five new western states were created—Indiana, Illinois, Mississippi, Alabama, and Missouri.

The new states reflected the dramatic growth of the region west of the Appalachians. In 1800 only 387,000 white settlers lived west of the Appalachian Mountains. By 1820, that number had grown to more than 2.4 million people. Ohio, for example, had only 45,000 settlers in 1800. By 1820, it had 581,000 settlers.

Pioneer families tended to settle in communities along the great rivers, such as the Ohio and the Mississippi. They settled by rivers so they could ship their crops and other goods to markets. The canals, which crisscrossed the land in the 1820s and 1830s, allowed people to live farther away from the rivers.

People also often preferred to settle with others from their home communities. Indiana, for example, was settled mainly by people from Kentucky and Tennessee. Michigan's pioneers came mostly from the New England area.

Western families often gathered together for social events. Men took part in sports such as wrestling. Women met for quilting and sewing parties. Both men and women participated in cornhuskings. These were gatherings where farm families shared the work of stripping the outer layers from corn.

Life in the West did not include the conveniences of Eastern town life. However, the pioneers had not traveled to the West to live a pampered life. They wanted to make a new life for themselves and their families. America's population continued to spread westward in the years ahead.

Reading Check **Describing** What was life like for families on the western frontier?

W Writing Support

Personal Writing Have students take the role of someone who has just settled along the Ohio or Mississippi River. Write a letter to a relative in New England, describing new friends and activities. **OL**

Reading Check **Answer:** They settled with others from their home communities along rivers, gathered for social events and to share work, and lived without modern conveniences.

Assess

· ·

History ONLINE

Study Central™ provides summaries, interactive games, and online graphic organizers to help students review content.

Close
· ·

Summarizing As a class, discuss the effects of improvements in land and water transportation on westward expansion. **OL**

Section 2 Review

History ONLINE
Study Central™ To review this section, go to glencoe.com.

Vocabulary
1. Define the following terms by using each one in a sentence: census, reveal, turnpike, region, canal, lock.

Main Ideas
2. Discussing How were the improvements in westward travel financed in the early 1800s?

3. Identifying What were the benefits of canal travel?

4. Listing What determined where people would settle as they moved westward?

Critical Thinking
5. Analyzing Use a chart like the one below to describe why each item was important to the nation's growth.

	Significance
National Road	
Clermont	
Erie Canal	

6. Persuasive Writing Would you have preferred Eastern city life or life in a western settlement in 1820? Write a paragraph to persuade people to join you in one of the two places.

Answer the
7. Essential Question
How did land and water transportation affect westward expansion?

Growth and Expansion **Chapter 10** **317**

Answers

1. Students will write sentences using the vocabulary in an appropriate context.

2. Private companies built turnpikes, which charged travelers fees to pay for the construction. The federal government built the National Road.

3. faster transportation, lower shipping costs, prosperity to towns along their routes, unification of the growing country

4. proximity to waterways; proximity to others from their home communities

5. National Road: connected east and west, better travel and cheaper shipping; *Clermont:* first steamboat powerful enough to travel upriver, faster and more comfortable travel, cheaper cargo shipping on major rivers; **Erie Canal:** united the country and allowed cheaper shipping, led to the building of more canals

6. Students' paragraphs should focus on the benefits of living in the region of their choice.

7. Better roads allowed easier travel and cheaper shipping. Steamboats brought cheaper and faster shipping and spurred the growth of river cities. The Erie Canal and other canals made shipping cheaper, encouraged the growth of towns, and united the country.

Focus

C₁ Critical Thinking

Making Inferences Have students read "American Voices." Read aloud the first sentence of the italicized paragraph under "American Voices." **Ask:** If Robert Fulton did not invent the steamboat, what do you think his role was in the history of the steamboat? *(He designed a steamboat using existing technology; he was the first to advance steamboat use for passengers.)* **AL**

Teach

W Writing Support

Descriptive Writing Have students write a paragraph about Robert Fulton's first steamboat ride from the point of view of one of the passengers on board. Ask for student volunteers to read their paragraphs aloud. **OL**

C₂ Critical Thinking

Drawing Conclusions Read aloud the quote in "Verbatim" from the first political cartoon. **Ask:** Why do you think the term "Uncle Sam" was created? *(The character's initials are "U.S." and the term gave the government a name and a face.)* **OL**

Additional Support and Answers

TIME Notebook

What were people's lives like in the past?
These two pages will give you some clues to everyday life in the United States as you step back in time with TIME Notebook.

BETTMANN / CORBIS

American Voices

FULL STEAM AHEAD!

ROBERT FULTON *might not have invented the steamboat, but he does believe in its potential to turn waterways into business routes and transform America's economic future. In 1807 he's ready for his trial run of the first commercial passenger steamboat. The boat is 150 feet (46 m) long and only 13 feet (4 m) wide and will travel from New York City to Albany—and back again. People are terrified the engines that power the ship's two paddle wheels will explode, so he has a tough time getting passengers onboard. In this letter, Fulton describes what happens just as the ship leaves the dock in New York City.*

NORTH WIND PICTURE ARCHIVES / ALAMY

ROBERT FULTON

"The moment arrived in which the word was to be given for the boat to move. My friends were in groups on the deck. There was anxiety mixed with fear among them. They were silent, sad, and weary. I read in their looks nothing but disaster, and almost repented of my efforts. The signal was given and the boat moved on a short distance and then stopped and became immovable. To the silence of the preceding moment, now succeeded murmurs of discontent, and agitations, and whispers and shrugs. I could hear distinctly repeated, 'I told you it was so; it is a foolish scheme: I wish we were well out of it.' . . . I went below and examined the machinery, and discovered that the cause was a slight maladjustment . . . The boat was again put in motion."

318

Sea Talk

The **U.S.S. CONSTITUTION,** *the world's largest warship with its 54 cannons, was instrumental in helping the United States win the War of 1812. Want to join its crew of 450? If so, you'll have to learn some sea terms. Here's a seafaring glossary.*

1. **KEEL OVER:** Putting a ship in for repair

2. **TACK:** The course or direction boats take into the wind

3. **LET THE CAT OUT OF THE BAG:** Sailors who do wrong are disciplined with a cat-o'-nine-tails whip that's kept in a red sack

4. **SHIPSHAPE:** Good condition

BETTMANN / CORBIS

Fast Facts

A Man of Many Talents Robert Fulton was an inventor, an engineer, and even an artist. Born in 1765 to Irish immigrants, Fulton began his career as an artist by painting portraits on ivory lockets at a jewelry shop. When he realized that he would not make it as a painter, though, he turned his attention to canal engineering. But his canal ideas, like his art, were not successful.

He then traveled to Paris, where he proposed the idea of the "Nautilus," a submarine that France could use in its war against Britain, creeping under British warships to plant explosives. The French government, however, rejected the idea as a dishonorable way to fight.

Fulton's first steamboat, with partner Robert L. Livingston, was not successful either; the engine broke the hull. In 1807 the steamboat journey from New York City to Albany and back made Fulton famous, and he helped build other steamboats for commercial use.

Fulton did not die a rich man; however, he spent much of his wealth defending his steamboat patents, investing in paintings, and providing financial aid to family members and young artists.

First Things First

Someone's got to be first—see if you can match up each name with the correct description.

1. Thomas Hopkins Gallaudet
2. Thomas Jefferson
3. James Madison
4. James Madison Randolph
5. Frederick Graff

a. First president to wear pants instead of knee breeches.
b. First child born in the White House (1806)—his grandfather was Thomas Jefferson.
c. Founder of first school for advanced education of hearing-impaired students.
d. First president to shake hands instead of bowing when meeting people.
e. Engineer for Philadelphia Water Works who installed the country's first fire hydrant in 1801.

Answers: 1. c; 2. d; 3. a; 4. b; 5. e

ILLUSTRATION WORKS / GETTY IMAGES

MILESTONES

EVENTS AND PEOPLE OF THE TIME

BORROWED. The music from the English song "To Anacreon in Heaven" by Francis Scott Key for **D** his new poem "The Star-Spangled Banner," which he wrote in 1814.

STARVED. Many Vermont farmers and their families as snow falls all summer in 1816—a year some call "eighteen hundred and froze-to-death." Some think the bizarre weather is caused by last year's volcanic eruption in the Dutch East Indies that sent dust and ash far up into the air where it blocked out the sun.

DUG. First shovel of dirt as work on the proposed 363-mile-long Erie Canal begins in 1817. Many are labeling it "The Big Ditch."

BITTEN. United States officials, by insects in 1800 as the country's government moves from Philadelphia to Washington, D.C.—a place many complain is a bug-infested swamp.

NORTH WIND PICTURE ARCHIVES / ALAMY

RESCUED. Treasures, such as the original Declaration of Independence and a famous portrait of George Washington, by First Lady Dolley Madison after the British set fire to the White House in 1814.

NUMBERS

UNITED STATES AT THE TIME

$15 million Price the United States pays for the Louisiana Purchase in 1803

16 Number of states in the Union in 1800—that number will grow to 23 by 1820

17 Age of Sacagawea when she started guiding Lewis and Clark on their famous expedition

BETTMANN / CORBIS

18 Months it takes Lewis and Clark to reach the Pacific in 1805

19th Date in August 1812 that the U.S.S. *Constitution* earns its nickname "Old Ironsides" after defeating the British warship, *Guerriere* **R**

CRITICAL THINKING

Describing What was the atmosphere like on board Fulton's steamboat on its first voyage?

Theorizing Was Tecumseh, the chief of the Shawnees, justified in his response to President Madison's message? Explain your answer.

319

Answers

Describing Students' answers should reflect the uncomfortable, fearful atmosphere during the initial stage of the voyage, followed by the agitated state felt when the engine stopped, and finally feelings of relief and happiness when the steamboat completed the voyage safely and successfully.

Theorizing Student answers should show sensitivity to the plight of the Native Americans and justifications for not moving to new lands.

Section 3

Unity and Sectionalism

Focus

Bellringer
Daily Test Practice Transparency 10–3

Reading Guide
Answers to Graphic:
protective tariffs, internal improvements, national bank

Section Spotlight Video

Have students watch the Section Spotlight Video "Unity and Sectionalism" to learn more about the Monroe Doctrine.

Resource Manager

Essential Question
How were nation-building issues resolved in the early 1800s?

Reading Guide

Content Vocabulary
sectionalism (p. 322)
state sovereignty (p. 322)
American System (p. 323)

Academic Vocabulary
intense (p. 322)   internal (p. 322)

Key People and Events
Missouri Compromise (p. 323)
McCulloch v. Maryland (p. 324)
Gibbons v. Ogden (p. 324)
Adams-Onís Treaty (p. 326)
Monroe Doctrine (p. 326)

Reading Strategy
Taking Notes As you read, create a diagram like the one below to list the three parts of Henry Clay's American System.

American System

ILLINOIS STANDARDS
The American Journey

14.A.3 Describe how responsibilities are shared and limited by the United States and Illinois Constitutions and significant court decisions.

14.D Understand the roles and influences of individuals and interest groups in the political systems of Illinois, the United States, and other nations.

14.E.3 Compare the basic principles of the United States and its international interests (e.g., territory, environment, trade, use of technology).

16.B.3c (US) Describe the way the Constitution has changed over time as a result of amendments and Supreme Court decisions.

American Diary

"If we look to the history of other nations, ancient or modern, we find no example of a growth so rapid—so gigantic; of a people so prosperous and happy. In [thinking about] what we still have to perform, the heart of every citizen must expand with joy when he reflects how near our Government has approached to perfection."

—from James Monroe's Inaugural Address, March 1817

Philadelphia residents celebrate the Fourth of July in 1819.

R Reading Strategies	**C** Critical Thinking	**D** Differentiated Instruction	**W** Writing Support	**S** Skill Practice
Teacher Edition • Summarizing, p. 322 • Predicting, p. 325 • Questioning, p. 326 **Additional Resources** • Guid. Read., URB p. 97 • Content Vocab., URB p. 73 • Academic Vocab., URB p. 75 • Read. Ess., p. 106	**Teacher Edition** • Draw Conclusions, p. 324 • Making Infer., p. 325 • Making General., p. 326 **Additional Resources** • Quizzes and Tests, p. 93 • Authentic Assess., p. 10 • Crit. Think. Skills, URB p. 85	**Teacher Edition** • ELL, p. 321 • Below Grade Level, p. 322 • Gifted & Talented, p. 323 **Additional Resources** • School-to-Home, URB p. 91 • Reteaching Act., URB p. 93 • Differ. Inst., URB p. 83	**Teacher Edition** • Descriptive Writ., p. 321 • Expository Writ., p. 322	**Teacher Edition** • Using Geo. Skills, p. 324 **Additional Resources** • Daily Test Pract. Transp. 10-3 • Soc. Stud. Skills, URB p. 81

The Era of Good Feelings

Main Idea After the War of 1812, a new spirit of nationalism spread throughout the United States.

History and You Do you believe your favorite sports team is better than any other team? Read on to find out about the national pride many Americans felt for their country.

The absence of major political divisions after the War of 1812 helped forge a sense of national unity. In the 1816 presidential election, James Monroe, the Republican candidate, faced almost no opposition. The Federalists, weakened by doubts of their loyalty during the War of 1812, barely existed as a national party. Monroe won the election by an overwhelming margin.

Although the Federalist Party had almost disappeared, many of its programs had gained popularity. Support grew for tariffs to protect industries and a national bank.

Political differences among citizens, however, seemed to fade. A Boston newspaper called these years the Era of Good Feelings. President James Monroe symbolized these good feelings. Monroe had been involved in national politics since the American Revolution. He wore breeches, or short pants, and

powdered wigs—styles no longer in fashion at that time. With his sense of dignity, Monroe represented a united America, free of political strife.

Early in his term, Monroe toured the nation. No president since George Washington had done so. Monroe even paid for the trip using his own expenses and tried to travel without an official escort. Local officials everywhere greeted the president and celebrated his visit.

Monroe arrived in Boston, the former Federalist stronghold, in the summer of 1817. About 40,000 well-wishers cheered him. John Adams, the second president, invited Monroe to his home. Abigail Adams praised the new president's "unassuming manner."

Monroe did not think the demonstrations were meant for him personally. He wrote James Madison that they revealed a "desire in the body of the people to show their attachment to the union."

Two years later Monroe continued his tour throughout the country. He traveled as far south as Savannah and as far west as Detroit. In 1820 President Monroe won reelection, receiving all but one electoral vote.

✓ Reading Check Summarizing Why did James Monroe appeal to people?

Primary Source / Celebrating Independence

Fourth of July Independence Day was first observed on July 8, 1776. On that day in Philadelphia, the Declaration of Independence was read in public for the first time. The next year, Philadelphia honored the nation's independence on July 4—the day the Declaration of Independence was adopted by the Continental Congress. People celebrated the occasion with bonfires, parades, and fireworks. In 1826 Thomas Jefferson wrote: "Let the annual return of this day forever refresh our recollections of [our] rights, and an undiminished devotion to them."

Critical Thinking

Making Connections How do people express patriotism for the United States today?

Teach

W Writing Support

Descriptive Writing Instruct students to take the role of a reporter for a local Boston newspaper. Have them write an article about Monroe's visit to Boston in the summer of 1817. Include descriptions of Monroe and the crowd. **OL**

D Differentiated Instruction

English Language Learners Have students restate the quotation in the selection using their own words. **Ask:** Why didn't Monroe think the crowd's greetings were for him personally? (He felt that they were expressing their loyalty to the nation they loved.) **OL**

Primary Source

Critical Thinking Answer
flying flags, patriotic music, parades, fireworks

✓ Reading Check Answer: Monroe was viewed as an experienced, dignified politician who toured the nation in a simple manner.

Additional Support

Activity: Why It Matters

Making Connections Invite a representative from the U.S. military, a scoutmaster, or a member of the American Legion or Veterans of Foreign Wars to discuss American flag etiquette. Ask the speaker to discuss the disposal techniques for tattered flags and the appropriate use of the flag as a decorative device on clothing and other

items. Allow question-and-answer time at the end. **Ask:** Why do we treat the flag so carefully? (as a sign of respect for our nation) Have students write a five-question quiz about flag etiquette, writing the answers on the back of the page. Have students exchange papers and take the quiz. Next, have each student write one of their

questions neatly on a small piece of paper. Glue only the top edge of each piece of paper to a large folded paper to create a thank-you card for your guest. Have students write the answers and sign their names beneath the questions they wrote. **OL**

W Writing Support

Expository Writing Have students write an essay comparing and contrasting Calhoun, Webster, and Clay. In particular, have them address the issues of states' rights and tariffs. **OL**

R Reading Strategy

Summarizing Have students sum up the first paragraph in a single sentence. *(Sample summary sentence: Most Americans felt more loyalty to their regions than to the nation.)* **OL**

This **READING SKILL** (Summarizing Information) was introduced in this unit.

D Differentiated Instruction

Below Grade Level Have students summarize John C. Calhoun's beliefs before the 1820s. *(support for internal improvements, development of industries, and a national bank)* Next, have them suggest statements that he might have made to Congress. **Ask:** How did Calhoun's views change in the 1820s? *(He supported each state's right to sovereignty and opposed national programs.)* Have students suggest some new statements for Calhoun. **BL**

Differentiated Instruction

W Sectionalism and the American System

Main Idea Regional differences brought an end to the Era of Good Feelings.

History and You Why do people support certain political leaders? Read about three influential spokespeople in Congress during the early 1800s.

R Regional differences soon brought an end to the Era of Good Feelings. Most Americans felt a strong allegiance to the region where they lived. They thought of themselves as Westerners or Southerners or Northerners. This **sectionalism,** or loyalty to their region, grew more **intense** over national policies.

Most white Southerners, for example, supported slavery. They argued that states were given the right in the Constitution to govern themselves. Southerners believed the federal government and people in the North were interfering with a state's right to maintain the institution of slavery.

The different regions also disagreed strongly on the need for tariffs, a national bank, and **internal** improvements. Internal improvements were federal, state, and privately funded projects, such as canals and roads, to develop the nation's transportation system. Three regional spokespersons emerged in Congress.

John C. Calhoun

John C. Calhoun, a planter from South Carolina, had called for war with Great Britain in 1812. He remained a nationalist for some time after the war. Calhoun supported internal improvements, the development of industries, and a national bank. He believed D that these programs would benefit the South.

In the 1820s, however, Calhoun's views began to change. He emerged as a chief supporter of **state sovereignty,** the idea that states have autonomous power, or the right to govern themselves. Calhoun became a strong opponent of national programs.

People IN HISTORY

John C. Calhoun

Politician from South Carolina

Calhoun was a fierce supporter of states' rights. He believed that if the federal government passed a law where it overstepped its authority over states, then people had the right to refuse to obey it. *"Let it never be forgotten that, where the majority rules without restriction, the minority is the subject."*

Daniel Webster

Politician from New England

Webster argued against the right of states to declare laws invalid. He stated, *"I say, the right of a state to annul [declare invalid] a law of Congress, cannot be maintained, but on the ground of the unalienable right of man to resist [the cruel use of power]; that is to say, upon the ground of revolution."*

Leveled Activities

BL Guided Reading Activity, URB p. 97

OL Reteaching Activity, URB p. 93

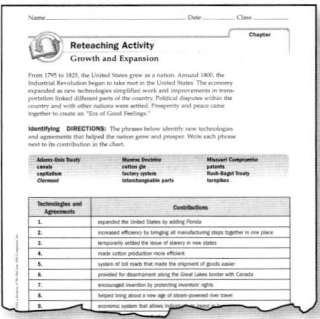

ELL Academic Vocabulary Activity, URB p. 75

Calhoun and other Southerners opposed high tariffs. Calhoun argued that tariffs raised the prices of manufactured goods that they could not make for themselves and that high tariffs protected inefficient manufacturers.

Daniel Webster

Daniel Webster was first elected to Congress in 1812 to represent his home state of New Hampshire. He later represented Massachusetts in both the House and the Senate. Webster at first supported free trade and the shipping interests of New England. In time Webster came to favor the Tariff of 1816, which protected American industries from foreign competition. He also supported other policies that he thought would strengthen the nation and help the North.

Webster gained fame as one of the greatest public speakers of his day. As a U.S. senator, he spoke eloquently in defense of the nation as a whole against sectional interests. In one of his most memorable speeches, Webster declared, "Liberty and Union, now and forever, one and inseparable!"

Henry Clay

Henry Clay of Kentucky was another leading War Hawk. He became speaker of the House of Representatives in 1811 and a leader who represented the interests of the Western states. He also served as a member of the delegation that negotiated the Treaty of Ghent, ending the War of 1812. Above all, Henry Clay became known as the national leader who tried to resolve sectional disputes.

The Missouri Compromise

Sectional tension reached new heights in 1820. The issue was whether to allow slavery in states when they joined the Union. The South wanted Missouri admitted as a slave state, whereas Northerners wanted it to be free of slavery. The issue was further complicated when Maine, still a part of Massachusetts, also applied for statehood.

Eventually Henry Clay helped work out a compromise that preserved the balance between North and South. The **Missouri Compromise,** reached in March 1820, provided for the admission of Missouri as a slave state and Maine as a free state. Slavery was banned in the rest of the Louisiana Territory north of the 36°30'N parallel.

Henry Clay believed his policies would benefit all sections of the nation. In an 1824 speech, he called his program the "American System." The **American System** included three parts: (1) a protective tariff, (2) a program of internal improvements, and (3) a national bank. Not everyone saw Clay's program in such positive terms. Many Southerners did not see the benefits of the tariff or internal improvements.

In the end, little of Clay's American System went into effect. Congress eventually adopted some internal improvements, but they were not on the scale Clay hoped for. Congress created a Second National Bank in 1816, but it remained controversial.

Henry Clay

Politician from Kentucky

Clay's ability to resolve arguments earned him the nickname "The Great Compromiser." He was a strong nationalist. In a speech on the Senate floor, he said: *"If the . . . sad event of the dissolution [breaking up] of this Union is to happen, that I shall not survive to behold the sad and heart-rending [distressing] spectacle."*

CRITICAL Thinking

1. **Comprehending** According to Webster, when might a state declare the federal government's laws invalid?
2. **Contrasting** Describe the differences in the three men's views about the power of government.
3. **Analyzing** How does Clay's statement reflect nationalist views?

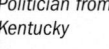

Differentiated Instruction

Gifted and Talented Ask: Do you think high tariffs protect inefficient manufacturers? Why or why not? *(Answers will vary, but students may argue that high tariffs discourage competition from foreign goods that may be superior to domestic goods.)* **AL**

People IN HISTORY

Critical Thinking Answers

1. when there is a cruel use of federal power
2. Calhoun believed that the power of the federal government should be limited. Webster felt federal power superceded state power. Clay felt national unity was deeply important.
3. It reflects regret at the idea of a national breakup.

Hands-On Chapter Project
Step 3

Making a Book

Step 3: Writing and Organizing Have groups complete their chapters.

Essential Question: How were nation-building issues resolved in the early 1800s?

Directions Have each group write its chapter and insert artwork, charts, or graphs where appropriate. Each chapter should have a distinct title. Have groups exchange chapters and give each other feedback on the material. Groups should revise as necessary.

Identifying Central Issues Discuss how regional differences affected industry in the North and the South. *(Southerners wanted to keep slavery and opposed tariffs and national programs. Northerners favored tariffs and other federal programs.)* **OL**

(Chapter Project continued in the Visual Summary)

C Critical Thinking

Drawing Conclusions Ask: What single issue do both court cases and the Missouri Compromise have in common? *(All have to do with establishing an acceptable amount of federal power while still allowing an acceptable level of states' rights.)* **AL**

S Skill Practice

Using Geography Skills Have students examine a road map of the United States. **Ask:** What would happen if states could interfere with interstate commerce? *(Travel would be disrupted; businesses would be affected.)* Do you agree with the Supreme Court's ruling? *(Answers will vary.)* **OL**

The Missouri Compromise
NATIONAL GEOGRAPHIC

Map Skills Answer
closed by the Missouri Compromise

✓Reading Check **Answer:** The Supreme Court strengthened the power of the federal government over the power of the states. Chief Justice John Marshall argued that the Constitution gives specific powers to the federal government, which take precedence over state government powers.

Additional Support

The Missouri Compromise
NATIONAL GEOGRAPHIC

A Compromise on Slavery Missouri's application for statehood sparked a national debate over the issue of slavery. Northern Congressional leaders sought to restrict the entry of Missouri as a slave state. Southern leaders retaliated by blocking Maine's application for statehood. The Missouri Compromise allowed for Missouri to be admitted as a slave state and Maine as a free state.

> "All know that permitting the slaves of the South to spread in the West . . . will dilute [weaken] the evil everywhere . . . getting finally rid of it."
> —Thomas Jefferson in a letter, December 1820

Map legend:
- Free state/territory
- Closed to slavery by the Missouri Compromise
- Slave state/territory
- Territory opened to slavery by the Missouri Compromise

> "Freedom and slavery are the parties which stand this day before the senate, and upon its decision the empire of the one or the other will be established in the new state which we are about to admit into the Union."
> —Senator Rufus King, February 1820

Map Skills

Location Was the Unorganized Territory open or closed to slavery?

Maps in MOtion See StudentWorks™ Plus or glencoe.com.

McCulloch v. Maryland

The Supreme Court also became involved in sectional and states' rights issues at this time. Its decisions strengthened the power of the national government. The state of Maryland imposed a tax on the Baltimore branch of the Second National Bank of the United States, a federal institution. The Bank refused to pay the state tax. The case, **McCulloch v. Maryland,** reached the Court in 1819.

Speaking for the Court, Chief Justice John Marshall ruled that Maryland had no right to tax the Bank. Marshall argued that the Constitution gave certain powers to the federal government, such as collecting taxes, borrowing money, and regulating commerce. Marshall claimed that the national bank helped the federal government carry out these powers.

Next, Marshall stated that the government could use any method that was necessary to carry out its powers, as long as it was not forbidden by the Constitution. Finally, Marshall claimed that a state government could not interfere with a federal agency that was using its constitutional powers in that state. The tax was interfering with the bank and its constitutional powers and was, thus, unconstitutional.

Gibbons v. Ogden

Another Supreme Court case, **Gibbons v. Ogden,** established that states could not enact legislation that would interfere with congressional power over interstate commerce. People who supported states' rights believed that the Court's decisions in these cases increased federal power at the expense of state power. Nationalists welcomed the rulings' support for federal power.

✓Reading Check **Explaining** Describe how the Supreme Court's decisions affected the power of the federal government.

Activity: Interdisciplinary Connection

Dramatic Arts Organize students into groups of five or six. Have the groups read more about *McCulloch* v. *Maryland* online or at the library. Have them make a list of possible roles—both historical and fictional, if necessary—for a reenactment of this high court drama. Next, have them write the script, including details, so that someone who has not read about the case would be able to understand it when they act out their play. Have each group present its play to the class. Audience members should take notes on the facts emphasized in each play.

Using Summarizing Skills When all the plays have been presented, have each student write a short paragraph summarizing the main points made by Chief Justice Marshall in his ruling. **OL**

Foreign Affairs

Main Idea The United States defined its role in the Americas with the Monroe Doctrine.

History and You Have you ever had to take a stand on an issue with a friend? Read about American foreign policies in the early 1800s.

• •

The War of 1812 heightened Americans' pride in their country. Americans also realized that the United States had to establish a new relationship with the "Old World." **C**

Relations With Britain

In the 1817 Rush-Bagot Treaty, the United States and Britain agreed to limit the number of naval vessels on the Great Lakes and remove weapons located along the border of the United States and British Canada.

The Convention of 1818 set the boundary of the Louisiana Territory between the United States and Canada at the 49th parallel. The convention also created a secure and demilitarized border. In other words, each country agreed to maintain its border without armed forces. Through Secretary of State John Quincy Adams's efforts, Americans also gained the right to settle in the Oregon Country.

Relations With Spain

Spain owned East Florida and also claimed West Florida. The United States argued that West Florida was part of the Louisiana Purchase. In 1810 and 1812, Americans simply added parts of West Florida to Louisiana and Mississippi. Spain objected but took no action.

General Andrew Jackson was ordered to stop Seminole raids on America from Florida. In April 1818, Jackson invaded Spanish East Florida and seized two Spanish forts. Secretary of State Adams had not authorized Jackson's actions, but he did nothing about them. **R**

C Critical Thinking

Making Inferences Ask: Why was it in the best interests of the United States to have good relations with European powers? *(Students should mention the chance of economic growth from trade with Europe, avoiding war, and a chance to negotiate ownership of territories.)* **OL**

R Reading Strategy

Predicting Ask: What problem might result from General Jackson's actions? *(Students might predict that trouble with Spain could develop.)* **OL**

Latin America and the Monroe Doctrine

Critical Thinking Answer

Students may suggest that nationalists, encouraged by the revolutions, began to fight for their own independence.

Latin America and the Monroe Doctrine

Seeking Freedom in Latin America By the early 1800s, Spain had a large colonial empire that extended from North America to South America. People in the Spanish colonies wanted their own political and economic freedom. They were inspired by the successful revolutions for independence in the United States and France and began their own liberation movements.

In 1823 President Monroe and his advisers developed the Monroe Doctrine to prevent further European colonization in the Western Hemisphere. ▼

◀ Simón Bolívar and other Venezuelans declared independence from Spain on July 5, 1811, before driving them from the colony. Bolívar also helped Colombia, Panama, Bolivia, and Ecuador win their freedom.

◀ As a general in the Argentinian army, José de San Martín helped drive the Spanish from Buenos Aires before helping Chile and Peru achieve independence.

Critical Thinking

Identifying Cause and Effect How did the American and French Revolutions influence the independence movements in South America?

Differentiated Instruction

Creating a Web Diagram

**Social Studies Skills,
URB p. 81**

Objective:	To use web diagramming as a tool for comprehension
Focus:	Tell students that a web diagram can help them organize and understand content.
Teach:	Have students refer to the text to find ideas to complete their diagrams.
Assess:	Have students use the Self-Assessment Checklist as they work.
Close:	Have students make corrections while you review the correct answers.

Differentiated Instruction Strategies

BL Let students work in pairs to complete the first two webs.

AL Tell students to investigate how a web diagram relates to the parts of a chapter. Then have them create a large web diagram of this chapter to display.

ELL Have students do only the web diagrams in Practicing the Skill.

Section 3

C Critical Thinking

Making Generalizations Ask: What generalizations can you make about how the United States settled border disputes? Have students share and support their generalizations. *(Students may suggest that the U.S. often settled disputes through negotiation.)* **OL**

R Reading Strategy

Questioning Have students write two questions about the Monroe Doctrine. Then have them exchange questions with partners and answer them. **OL**

✓ **Reading Check** **Answer:** to reduce European involvement in the Americas

Assess

History ONLINE

Study Central™ provides summaries, interactive games, and online graphic organizers to help students review content.

Close

Summarizing Discuss with the class the nation-building issues of the 1800s and how each was resolved. **OL**

Section 3 Review

Jackson's raid demonstrated American military strength. Secretary of State Adams believed that the Spanish did not want war and wanted to settle the dipute. His assumption was correct.

C Adams-Onís Treaty and Mexico

With the **Adams-Onís Treaty** in 1819, the United States gained East Florida, and Spain also abandoned all claims to West Florida. In return the United States gave up its claims to Spanish Texas and agreed to border boundaries. As a result, the United States gained a territory in the Pacific Northwest.

Meanwhile Spain was losing power in its vast empire, especially in Mexico. In the fall of 1810 a priest, Miguel Hidalgo (ee•DAHL•goh), led a rebellion in Mexico. Hidalgo called for racial equality and the redistribution of land. The Spanish defeated the revolutionary forces and executed Hidalgo. In 1821 Mexico finally gained its independence.

Bolívar and San Martín

Simón Bolívar, also known as "the Liberator," led the independence movement that won freedom for the present-day countries of Venezuela, Colombia, Panama, Bolivia, and Ecuador. José de San Martín successfully achieved independence for Chile and Peru. By 1824, Spain lost control of most of South America.

The Monroe Doctrine

In 1822 the Quadruple Alliance—France, Austria, Russia, and Prussia—discussed a plan to help Spain regain its American holdings. The possibility of increased European involvement in North America led President Monroe to take action.

R The president issued a statement, later known as the **Monroe Doctrine,** on December 2, 1823. The United States would not interfere with any existing European colonies in the Americas. However, North and South America "are henceforth not to be considered as subjects for future colonization by any European powers." The Monroe Doctrine became an important element in American foreign policy.

✓ **Reading Check** **Making Inferences** Why was the Monroe Doctrine issued?

Section 3 Review

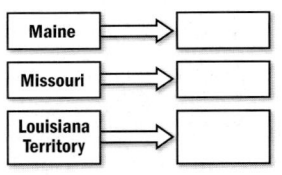

History ONLINE
Study Central™ To review this section, go to glencoe.com.

Vocabulary

1. Define the following terms using complete sentences: sectionalism, intense, internal, state sovereignty, American System.

Main Ideas

2. **Describing** Describe the overall feeling in the U.S. after the War of 1812.

3. **Listing** What issues divided the country at the end of the Era of Good Feelings?

4. **Explaining** Why was the Monroe Doctrine issued?

Critical Thinking

5. **Organizing** Use a diagram like the one below to show the effects of the Missouri Compromise.

Maine	→	
Missouri	→	
Louisiana Territory	→	

6. **Persuasive Writing** If you had been a congressperson at the time, do you think you would have supported the ideas of John C. Calhoun or Henry Clay? Write a paragraph explaining who you would support and why.

7. **Answer the Essential Question** How were nation-building issues resolved in the early 1800s?

Answers

1. Students will write sentences defining the vocabulary terms.
2. A lack of significant political divisions led to a strong sense of national unity.
3. slavery, states' rights, need for tariffs, a national bank, internal improvements
4. to prevent Spain or other European powers from colonizing any more land in the Americas

5. Maine: admitted as a free state; Missouri: admitted as a slave state; Louisiana Territory: slavery banned in the rest of the territory
6. Students' paragraphs should describe their views of states' rights along with the view of the congressman with whom they sided.
7. Answers may include: sectional differences brought about the Missouri Compromise; the Supreme Court issued decisions that

strengthened the power of the federal government over state governments; territorial issues were resolved in agreements with Britain and Spain, while the Monroe Doctrine stopped further land disputes with European countries.

Visual Summary

Growth and Expansion

The Economy Grows

- The Industrial Revolution and the factory system energize the U.S. economy.
- Free enterprise encourages economic growth.
- Agriculture expands in the South and West.
- Corporations emerge, and people invest in new industries.
- Towns and cities develop as a result of increased trade.

Westward Expansion Occurs

- Turnpikes are constructed to make it easier to travel and trade.
- Steamboats improve the transportation of goods and passengers along rivers.
- Canals are built to link the eastern and western parts of the U.S.
- America's population continues to move west.

▲ Corduroy road

Sectional Differences Emerge

- People living in different regions disagree about national policies.
- The issue of slavery continues to divide Southerners and Northerners.
- The Missouri Compromise attempts to resolve the issue of slavery in states being admitted in the Union.
- The Supreme Court supports federal power over states' rights.

▲ Slater Mill, Pawtucket, Rhode Island

The U.S. Defines Its Role With Europe

- Policy agreements are made peacefully with Britain.
- The U.S. acquires West and East Florida from Spain.
- Spain loses most of its colonies in South America as a result of independence movements.
- The U.S. issues the Monroe Doctrine to prevent the establishment of new European colonies in the Western Hemisphere.

▲ Water frame

Study anywhere, anytime! Download quizzes and flash cards to your PDA from glencoe.com.

◀ Discussing the Monroe Doctrine

Growth and Expansion **Chapter 10** 327

Visual Summary

Summarizing Ask: What helped the United States grow both economically and physically? Encourage students to explain the conditions related to the growth of the country in a class discussion. Have all students take notes during the discussion. *(Responses should include the shift to the factory system, the growth of industry, capitalism and free enterprise, and improvements in transportation.)* **OL**

Organizing Ask: During this nation-building period, what documents and decisions allowed peace to prevail when disputes arose, and what issues did they resolve? As students offer ideas, list them for all to see. *(Missouri Compromise—sectional differences between the Northern and Southern states; the Supreme Court decisions in the matters of McCulloch v. Maryland and Gibbons v. Ogden—strengthened the power of the federal government over state governments; Monroe Doctrine—prevented further land disputes with European nations)* **OL**

Hands-On Chapter Project
Step 4: Wrap-Up

Making a Book

Step 4: Putting It All Together Students will design a cover and assemble their book.

Directions Have the class decide on a title for the book as well as a cover design. Assign a couple of students to create the cover and the table of contents. Assemble the books and distribute a copy to everyone in the class.

Analyzing Remind the class the book is attempting to cover the Industrial Revolution. **Ask:** What are some outstanding contributions, and why? Invite class members to offer positive comments about each other's work. **OL**

INDUSTRIAL REVOLUTION

Answers and Analyses
Reviewing Main Ideas

1. B Choice A is incorrect, as cotton was not grown in the Northeast. C is incorrect since the cotton gin greatly increased the demand for cotton. Because cotton was in demand, enslaved workers would not have been freed, so D is wrong. Students should recall that the cotton gin helped speed processing, which led Southern farmers to plant more acreage; choice B is correct. **15.D.3c**

2. A Choices B, C, and D are not related to the physical gathering of factory processes for efficient manufacturing. The answer is A, the factory system. **16.C.3b (US)**

3. D Choice B will attract students, but the key idea is that the families were *settling,* not traveling. Since settling on a river did not offer any protection from Native Americans, A is incorrect. Many settlements had other sources of fresh water, so C is wrong. Being able to ship crops to market was an important consideration, making D the correct choice. **16.D.3a (US)**

4. B Remind students that tariffs protected Northeastern factory owners, eliminating choice A. Westerners and freedmen living in the North, C and D, did not protest tariffs. Students should recall that the Southern planters spoke out against tariffs since they sought lower prices on manufactured goods. B is the correct answer. **15.D.3a**

Short-Answer Question

5. European nations are reassured that the United States would not interfere their regional colonies, in which they had a legitimate interest. However, the United States did not want European nations to become involved in countries that had maintained independence. **14.E.3**

STANDARDIZED TEST PRACTICE

TEST-TAKING TIP

Eliminate answers that you know for certain are incorrect. Then choose the most likely answer from those remaining.

Reviewing Main Ideas

Directions: Choose the best answer for each of the following questions.

1. The invention of the cotton gin

  A encouraged farmers in the Northeast to begin planting cotton.

  B led to a dramatic increase in Southern cotton production.

  C had no impact on the demand for cotton.

  D encouraged many plantation owners to free their enslaved workers.

2. The system in which all manufacturing steps are brought together in one place to increase efficiency is called the

  A factory system.

  B patent system.

  C capital system.

  D corporation system.

3. Pioneer families tended to settle in communities along major rivers

  A to gain greater protection from Native Americans.

  B to make it easier for them to travel east.

  C because they provided fresh drinking water.

  D so that they could more easily ship their crops to market.

4. In the mid-1800s, by whom were tariffs *least* likely to be supported?

  A Northeastern factory owners

  B Southern planters

  C Westerners living on the frontier

  D free African Americans living in the North

Short-Answer Question

Directions: Base your answer to question 5 on the following excerpt and on your knowledge of social studies.

> With the existing colonies . . . of any European power we have not interfered and shall not interfere. But with the [Latin American] governments who have declared their independence and maintained it . . . we could not view any [involvement] for the purpose of oppressing them . . . by any European power in any other light than as the [showing] of an unfriendly disposition toward the United States.
>
> —James Monroe, Speech to Congress, December 1823

5. In this excerpt, what distinction does Monroe make between European involvement in their American colonies and in independent Latin American nations?

Review the Essential Questions

6. Essay Describe the forces that tended to unify Americans in the early 1800s. What were some important points of dispute?

To help you write your essay, review your answers to the Essential Questions in the section reviews and the chapter Foldables Study Organizer. Your essay should include:

- the Industrial Revolution and the growth of American cities;
- the Western settlement of the United States;
- transportation systems in early and mid-1800s in America;
- sectional conflicts and the American System; and
- America's relations with foreign nations.

GO ON ➡

Review the Essential Questions

6. Students should consult their completed Foldables to find the unifying forces, such as expansionism/nationalism, optimism, a belief in progress, and self-improvement. Points of dispute may include slavery, tariffs, internal improvements, and states' rights. **17.C.3c**

History ONLINE
For additional test practice, use **Self-Check Quizzes**—Chapter 10 at glencoe.com.

Chapter 10 Assessment

Document-Based Questions

Directions: Analyze the documents and answer the short-answer questions that follow.

Document 1

In this passage, Harriet Hanson Robinson recounts the 1836 strike of the mill girls of Lowell, Massachusetts.

> Cutting down their wages was not [the workers'] only grievance, nor the only cause of the strike. Hitherto the corporations had paid twenty-five cents a week toward the board of each operative, and now it was their purpose to have the girls pay the sum; and this, in addition to the cut in the wages, would make a difference of at least a dollar a week.

Source: *Loom and Spindle,* 1898

7. Based on the excerpt, why did the Lowell mill girls go on strike in 1836?

Document 2

In this excerpt, the English writer Frances Trollope records a conversation with a man in Cincinnati, Ohio.

> "You [Americans] spend a good deal of time in reading the newspapers."
>
> "And I'd like you to tell me how we can spend it better. How should freemen spend their time, but looking after their government, and watching that them fellers as we gives offices to, does their duty, and gives themselves no airs?"
>
> "But I sometimes think, sir, that your fences might be in more thorough repair, and your roads in better order, if less time was spent in politics."

Source: *Domestic Manners of the Americans,* 1832

8. According to the man, why do Americans spend so much time reading newspapers? What is the writer's opinion about this?

Document 3

This is a portion of the Missouri Compromise.

> Section 8. *And be it further enacted,* that in all that territory ceded by France to the United States, under the name of Louisiana, . . . slavery and involuntary servitude . . . shall be, and is hereby, forever prohibited.

Source: Missouri Compromise

9. What historical issue is addressed in the document?

Document 4

This map shows the sequence of the acquisition of Florida.

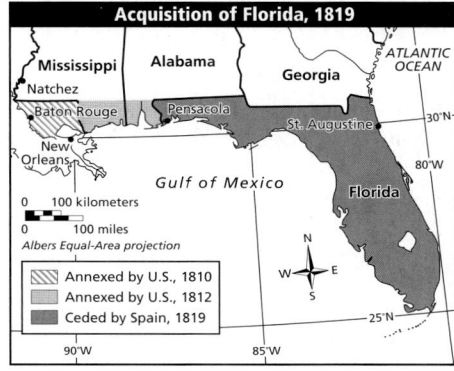

Acquisition of Florida, 1819

ATLANTIC OCEAN
Mississippi
Alabama
Georgia
Natchez
Pensacola
Baton Rouge
St. Augustine
New Orleans
Gulf of Mexico
Florida
30°N
80°W
25°N
90°W
85°W

0   100 kilometers
0   100 miles
Albers Equal-Area projection

N W E S

⧄ Annexed by U.S., 1810
▨ Annexed by U.S., 1812
■ Ceded by Spain, 1819

10. Based on the map, in which direction did the U.S. acquire the various parts of Florida?

11. Expository Writing Using the information from the four documents and your knowledge of social studies, write an essay in which you:

- describe how Americans generally felt about themselves and their place in the world in the early 1800s; and

- explain why they felt this way and which Americans might have thought differently.

9. This portion of the Missouri Compromise addresses the issue of slavery and where it was to be allowed in the Louisiana Territory. **16.A.3b**

10. from west to east **17.A.3b**

11. Students' essays should note that many Americans felt proud of their individual freedoms and their economic, technological, and territorial accomplishments. However many groups such as women, African Americans, factory workers, and immigrants, may not have felt they shared equally in freedoms and prosperity. **16.A.3b**

History ONLINE
Have students visit the Web site at glencoe.com to review Chapter 10 and take the Self-Check Quiz.

Need Extra Help?

Have students refer to the pages listed if they miss any of the questions.

Need Extra Help?

If you missed questions...	1	2	3	4	5	6	7	8	9	10	11
Go to page...	306	306	317	322–323	326	302–326	304–307	313	323–324	325–326	302–326

Document-Based Questions

7. The Lowell mill girls were being asked to take a cut in wages and spend more on board, lowering their overall pay considerably. **15.A.3b**

8. The American says it is important for citizens to stay well-informed so they are capable of looking after their government. The English woman seems to believe that the focus on politics interferes with the completion of other, important, tasks. **16.A.3c**

Unit 4 Planning Guide

UNIT PACING CHART

	Unit 4	Chapter 11	Chapter 12	Chapter 13	Chapter 14
Day 1	Unit Opener, Reading History	Chapter Opener, Section 1	Chapter Opener, Section 1	Chapter Opener, Section 1	Chapter Opener, Section 1
Day 2		Section 2	You Decide, Section 2	Section 2	Section 1, TIME Notebook
Day 3		Section 3, Visual Summary	Section 3	Section 3, America's Literature	Section 2, Geography & History
Day 4		Chapter Assessment	Section 4, Visual Summary	Section 4, Visual Summary	Section 3, Visual Summary
Day 5			Chapter Assessment	Chapter Assessment	Chapter Assessment

 Teacher to Teacher

**Donald Cygan
Sagewood
Middle School
Parker, CO**

Debating the Missouri Compromise Before students learn about the final results of the Missouri Compromise, hold a debate among Henry Clay, Daniel Webster, and John C. Calhoun to understand the issues. Organize students into three groups. One group represents the Southern states in Congress and elects a student to be John C. Calhoun. Another group represents the Northern states and elects someone to be Daniel Webster. The third group represents the new Western states and territories and chooses a student to be Henry Clay. Each group should use the maps and other information in their textbooks to learn about the issue that developed in 1819 when the Missouri Territory applied for admission into the Union as a slave state. It was feared that if Missouri was admitted as a slave state, it would upset the balance of power and state representation in Congress. Students in each group will research how the admission would affect their region and write their suggestions for resolving the issue. Each region should present its suggestions through those students who are acting as Clay, Webster, and Calhoun. These representatives will present their plan and recommendations to the whole class. Students can then vote on which argument they support. At the end of the lesson, students should read about the results of the real Missouri Compromise and discuss whether they think it was a fair resolution.

Author Note

Dear American History Teacher,

The four decades preceding the Civil War were a time of rapid economic growth, political conflict, and territorial expansion for our young nation. It was also an era of tremendous reform zeal by men and women who dedicated themselves to improving people's lives.

This time of conflict and change occurred during the Jackson Era. "Old Hickory," as Andrew Jackson was commonly known, was a hero of the War of 1812. He lost a contentious election for president in 1824 to John Quincy Adams. Jackson's victory over Adams in 1828 brought sweet revenge, and Jackson was thrust into office as a man of the people. Jackson was a strong-willed man who openly shared his beliefs about issues, including his support for the removal of Native Americans from their land.

The United States economy grew rapidly between 1820 and 1861, and slavery expanded. The nation gained territory through purchase, treaty, and wars. Indeed, many Americans believed that it was the God-given mission of the United States to expand from coast to coast. This belief in "manifest destiny" explained why the United States expanded its western borders to the Oregon coast and then in the American Southwest. The territory in the Southwest was acquired from Mexico and vastly expanded the size of the United States. It also reignited the divisive question of whether slavery should exist in the territories.

The reform movement was particularly strong between 1830 and 1860, as people reexamined their feelings about slavery, the mentally challenged, alcohol usage, and education. The abolitionist movement clearly overshadowed each of these reform movements. Men and women—including William Lloyd Garrison, Frederick Douglass, Harriet Beecher Stowe, and Dorothea Dix—dedicated their lives to helping others. The desire to improve the plight of those in need via the democratic process is a common theme throughout American history.

Albert S. Broussard

Albert S. Broussard

Introducing Unit

Unit 4

Unit Objectives

After studying this unit, students will be able to:

- Describe key political and social events of the Jackson Era.
- Explain the concept of Manifest Destiny.
- Compare and contrast the economy and people of the North with those of the South.
- Discuss the social history of the early and mid-1800s.

Introducing the Unit

Visualizing As students prepare to study the unit, ask them to think about what it would be like to be a pioneer moving into a new or unknown area. **Ask:** How would you feel if you were a pioneer in the United States in the early 1800s? *(Students might say excited, interested, or eager; or they might say frightened, anxious, or lonely for civilization.)* Discuss with students that they will learn how pioneers settled new areas of the country and how the different regions of the United States took on their own special characteristics. **OL**

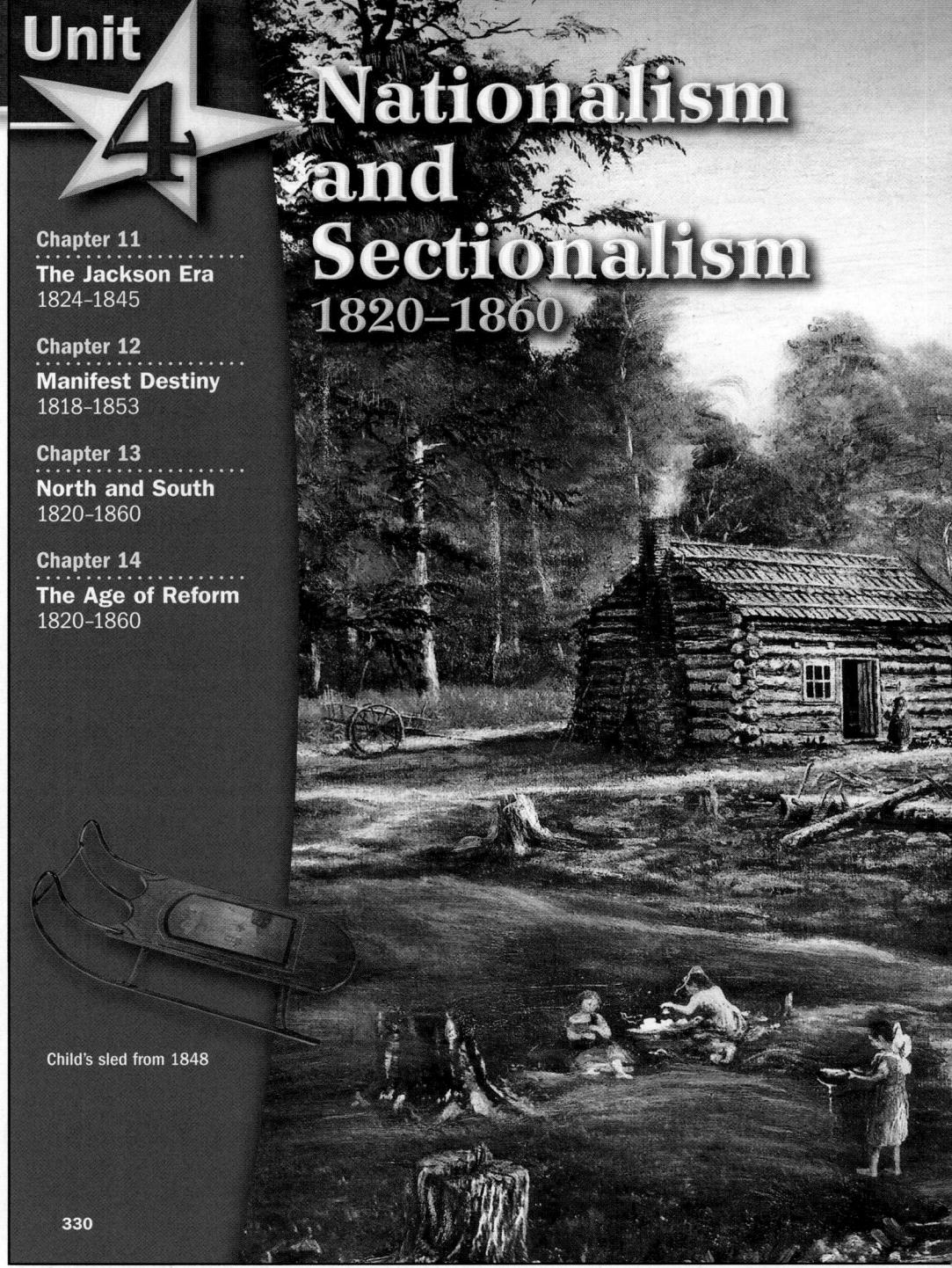

Unit 4 Nationalism and Sectionalism 1820–1860

Child's sled from 1848

330

Activity: Why It Matters

Why Study Manifest Destiny? Tell students what they can expect to learn in the upcoming unit. **Ask:** How do California and Texas affect the present-day political and economic power of the United States? *(Students should answer that these are two heavily populated states that can* influence presidential elections, and they have large economies because of the number of people working in the state.) As they study the unit, have students write in their notebooks what the United States would be like if California or Texas were part of another country. **OL**

"We are the nation of human progress, and who will, what can, set limits to our onward march?"

—John L. O'Sullivan

Log cabin and farm site in Ohio, 1831

331

Connect to Past Learning

Nationalism and Sectionalism In the previous unit, students learned about the challenges the new American government faced, Washington's administration, the War of 1812, and the industrial and westward growth of the country. In this unit, they will learn about Andrew Jackson's impact on the country, more westward expansion, and the sectional differences between Northern and Southern states, as well as religious, educational, and cultural reform movements.

More About the Image

Visual Literacy This image is a lithograph of a painting of James Garfield's birthplace in Orange (Cuyahoga County), Ohio. Log cabins are the symbol of pioneer life. Pioneers built log cabins using their ingenuity and materials that were readily available: trees, mud, and straw. Once the trees were felled and notched, the pioneers stacked them and put mud and straw in the cracks. Over time, log cabins began to signify self-sufficiency, practicality, independence, and the ability to overcome adversity. This painting shows the tree stumps that remained after the trees were cut down, which also helped clear the land for other uses.

Unit 4 Reading History

Why Making Inferences Is Important

Being able to infer is an important learning skill. Understanding that sometimes it is important to make inferences, and having the tools for doing so, will help students as they move into higher grade levels and increasingly more difficult subject matter, where every important fact is not always spelled out.

Learn It!

In our everyday lives, inferences can be made in many different ways, not only by using our prior background information, but also by paying attention to certain body language and situational clues.

Have students give examples of statements whose more literal meaning can be inferred by one of these other kinds of clues. For example, from the statement, "We are going to Grandma's for brunch on Sunday," one can infer approximately what time the action will occur without it being expressly stated. Or, one may infer the meaning of the statement "You're in big trouble!" in different ways, depending on if it is said with a smile and a shake of the head or with a frown and a stern voice. **BL**

Practice It!

Students should work through the inference process as follows:

Text Clue: People lived on farms or plantations that were far apart.

Text Clue: Families decided for themselves how to educate their children.

Background Knowledge: Answers will vary. **OL**

READING SKILL **Making Inferences**

Learn It!

To comprehend some texts, you will need to make inferences. When you infer, you use clues from the text along with your own knowledge to figure out the author's meaning.

Question: Why do you think the Cherokees' journey west is called the Trail of Tears?

Inference Process

> **Text Clue:**
> Cherokee leaders were reluctant to relocate their people.

> **Text Clue:**
> Many Cherokee died on the journey.

> **Background Knowledge:**
> It is difficult to lose your home and experience the loss of family and friends.

—from Chapter 11, p. 346
Filled with sadness and anger, their leaders gave in, and the long march to the West began. . . . Around 2,000 Cherokee died in camps waiting for the move to begin. About another 2,000 died along the way from starvation, disease, and exposure to brutal weather.

Practice It!

Read the paragraph, and follow the inference process on another sheet of paper.

—from Chapter 13, p. 412
The South was behind other sections of the country in **literacy,** the number of people able to read and write. One reason . . . was the South's geography. The South had few people per square mile. Many families could not send their children great distances to attend school. In addition, many Southerners believed that education was a private matter, not a state function.

Question: How did the South's agricultural economy affect its children's education?

Inference Process

> **Text Clue:**
> _____

> **Text Clue:**
> _____

> **Background Knowledge:**
> _____

332 **Unit 4** *Nationalism and Sectionalism*

Reading Strategy **Inferring**

Making Inferences Being able to make inferences is essential to students' academic success, especially as their classes increase in difficulty. Create a list of questions to correspond with a subsection of one of the chapters in this unit. Ask students to answer the questions using the inference process, writing down one or two text clues along with a piece of their own background knowledge, in order to come to a final conclusion. **ELL**

Academic Vocabulary Preview

Listed below are the academic vocabulary words and their definitions that you will come across as you study Unit 4. The activities in the Practice It! column will help you study the words and definitions.

Academic Vocabulary	Definition	Practice It!
Chapter 11 The Jackson Era		
select (suh · LEHKT) p. 337	to choose	**Choose** *terms from Chapter 11 to complete the paragraph.* The president of the United States is an elected member of the **1.** _____ government. In an election, if no presidential candidate receives a majority of electoral votes, members of the House of Representatives **2.** _____ the president. The House is an **3.** _____ of the U.S. legislative government.
participate (pahr · TIH · suh · PAYT) p. 340	to take part in	
federal (FEH · duh · ruhl) p. 343	the central governing authority	
survive (suhr · VYV) p. 347	to continue to live	
institution (IHN · stuh · TOO · shuhn) p. 349	an organization	
symbol (SIHM · buhl) p. 352	an object representing something else	
Chapter 12 Manifest Destiny		
access (AK · sehs) p. 359	the ability to get to	**Identify** *the term from Chapter 12 that best completes the sentence.* **4.** In the early 1800s, many Americans wanted _____ to the Pacific Ocean. **5.** Spain encouraged families to _____ a colony in Texas. **6.** Before earning statehood, California wrote a _____ that banned slavery.
establish (ihs · TA · blihsh) p. 367	to set up	
resource (REE · SOHRS) p. 374	an available source of wealth	
commence (kuh · MENTS) p. 375	to begin	
constitution (KAHNT · stuh · TOO · shuhn) p. 380	a list of fundamental laws to support a government	
incorporate (ihn · KAWR · puh · RAYT) p. 382	to include; to bring into	
Chapter 13 North and South		
innovation (IH · nuh · VAY · shuhn) p. 389	a new idea or method	**Identify** *the term from Chapter 13 that best matches the underlined word or phrase.* **7.** Canals and railways <u>changed</u> trade in the United States in the early 1800s. **8.** Many <u>towns</u> in the North did not allow enslaved people to attend school. **9.** Today, slavery is not <u>allowed by law</u> in the United States.
transform (trants · FAWRM) p. 391	to change	
community (kuh · MYOO · nuh · tee) p. 396	a group of people living in a particular place	
license (LY · suhnts) p. 397	to grant official authority	
consequence (KAHNT · suh · kwehnts) p. 402	a result	
legal (LEE · guhl) p. 409	permitted by law	
Chapter 14 The Age of Reform		
lecture (LEHK · chuhr) p. 419	a speech intended as a warning	**Choose** *the word that best matches the meaning of each vocabulary term listed below.* **10. lecture** a. praise b. essay c. speech **11. capable** a. able b. loud c. unable
route (ROOT) p. 430	a line of travel	
capable (KAY · puh · buhl) p. 437	having the necessary abilities	
ministry (MIH · nuh · stree) p. 438	religious services	

Nationalism and Sectionalism **Unit 4 333**

Academic Vocabulary Preview

Write the words *Synonyms* and *Antonyms* as column heads on the board. To the left, as the first row, write the first vocabulary word on the list.

Ask students what is meant by the words *synonym* and *antonym*. Then ask them to quickly call out as many of each as they can for the vocabulary word on the board. Continue the exercise with each vocabulary word, or a smaller selection of them, depending on your time limitations. **OL**

Practice It!

Answers
1. federal
2. select
3. institution
4. access
5. establish
6. constitution
7. transformed
8. communities
9. legal
10. c
11. a

Reading Strategy — Read to Write

Narrative Writing Narratives are stories of lives or events, and they may, in the process of the telling, impart a lesson. Have students write a story about a time when they or someone they know missed or misunderstood an important inference. Why did it happen? What was the result? When was the mistake realized? How was it corrected? Begin by telling your own story and emphasizing the importance of paying attention to clues in every aspect of our lives. **AL**

Chapter Planning Guide

11

Levels					Resources	Chapter Opener	Section 1	Section 2	Section 3	Chapter Assess
BL	OL	AL	ELL		**FOCUS**					
BL	OL	AL	ELL	🖨	Daily Test Practice Transparencies		11–1	11–2	11–3	
					TEACH					
	OL	AL		📁	Geography and History Activity, URB		p. 31			
BL	OL		ELL	📁	Time Line Skills Activity, URB		p. 34			
BL	OL	AL	ELL	📁	Writing Skills Activity, URB		p. 23			
	OL	AL		📁	American Literature Readings, URB			p. 9		
BL	OL	AL	ELL	📁	Content Vocabulary Activity, URB		p. 17	p. 17	p. 17	
BL			ELL	📁	Academic Vocabulary Activity, URB		p. 19	p. 19	p. 19	
	OL	AL		📁	Citizenship and Decision-Making Skills Activity, URB			p. 3		
BL			ELL	📁	Social Studies Skills Activity, URB				p. 25	
BL	OL	AL	ELL	📁	Differentiated Instruction Activity, URB			p. 27		
BL	OL	AL	ELL	📁	Critical Thinking Skills Activity, URB			p. 29		
BL	OL	AL	ELL	📁	Linking Past and Present Activity, URB				p. 33	
	OL	AL		📁	Primary Source Readings, URB			p. 21		
BL	OL	AL	ELL	📁	School-to-Home Connection Activity, URB		p. 35	p. 35	p. 35	
BL	OL		ELL	📁	Guided Reading Activity, URB*		p. 39	p. 40	p. 41	
	OL	AL		📁	Economics and History Activity, URB				p. 5	
BL	OL		ELL	📁	Reading Essentials and Note-Taking Guide*		p. 109	p. 112	p. 115	
BL	OL	AL	ELL	🖨	Lesson Transparencies		11B, 11C	11A		
		AL		📁	Supreme Court Case Studies			p. 9	p. 3	
	OL			📁	American Biographies			p. 19		
BL	OL	AL	ELL	📁	Outline Map Resource Book	pp. 5, 7, 23				

Note: Please refer to the *Unit Resource Book: Nationalism and Sectionalism* for this chapter's URB materials.

* Also available in Spanish

Levels					Resources	Chapter Opener	Section 1	Section 2	Section 3	Chapter Assess
BL	OL	AL	ELL							
					TEACH *(continued)*					
BL	OL	AL	ELL	📁	NGS US Desk Map		✓	✓	✓	
BL	OL	AL	ELL	📁	American Literature Library		✓	✓	✓	
BL	OL	AL	ELL	📁	Writer's Guidebook		✓	✓	✓	
	OL	AL		💿	American History Primary Source Document Library CD-ROM		✓	✓	✓	✓
BL	OL	AL	ELL	💿	American Music: Hits Through History	✓	✓	✓	✓	
BL	OL	AL	ELL	💿	StudentWorks™ Plus CD	✓	✓	✓	✓	✓
BL	OL	AL	ELL	🔒	Section Spotlight Videos		✓	✓	✓	
BL	OL	AL	ELL	🖥	Writing Process Transparencies		✓	✓	✓	✓
BL	OL	AL	ELL	💿	Presentation Plus! With MindJogger CheckPoint CD	✓	✓	✓	✓	✓
					ASSESS					
BL	OL	AL	ELL	📁	Quizzes and Tests		p. 101	p. 102	p. 103	pp. 105, 107, 109
BL	OL	AL	ELL	📁	Authentic Assessment With Rubrics			p. 11		
BL	OL	AL	ELL	📁	Standardized Test Practice					p. 21
BL	OL	AL	ELL	💿	*ExamView® Assessment Suite* CD-ROM*		11–1	11–2	11–3	Ch. 11
					CLOSE					
BL			ELL	📁	Reteaching Activity, URB*		p. 37	p. 37	p. 37	p. 37
BL	OL		ELL	📁	Reading and Study Skills Foldables Activity	p. 70	p. 70	p. 70	p. 70	p. 70
BL	OL	AL	ELL	📁	*The American Journey* in Graphic Novel			p. 67		
BL			ELL	📁	Reading Strategies and Activities for the Social Studies Classroom		✓	✓	✓	
BL	OL	AL	ELL	🖥	Graphic Organizer Transparencies & Strategies		✓	✓	✓	

TeacherWorks *Plus*
All-In-One Planner and Resource Center

- Interactive Lesson Planner
- Interactive Teacher Edition
- Fully editable blackline masters
- Section Spotlight Videos Launch

- Differentiated Lesson Plans
- Printable reports of daily assignments
- Standards Tracking System

Professional Development Resources

- Strategies for Success
- Building Academic Vocabulary
- Success With English Learners DVD
- Differentiated Instruction Strategies DVD
- Teaching Literacy Strategies in Social Studies DVD
- Assessment DVD
- Standards-Based Instruction DVD

11

Using TechCONNECT™

Using E-mail Responsibly

Technology Product

Glencoe's TechCONNECT™ is an e-mail applications program. (For more information or to get a free 30-day trial of Glencoe TechCONNECT™ for your classroom, visit techconnect.glencoe.com **and click the Free Trial button.**) Using TechCONNECT™ will allow students to

- see online activities related to e-mail;
- complete a self-assessment rubric;
- complete a TechCheck quiz.

Objective

- Students will learn the basics of responsible e-mailing.

Steps

- Log on to TechCONNECT™ and click the **Find your textbook** link.
- After you log on, click **Activity Search.**
- Choose **E-Mail** and your grade level.
- Have students log on and enter the letters AC and the three-digit activity number.
- Have students read each page and follow the on-screen instructions.
- Have students complete the activity's self-assessment rubric.
- Students must also complete the TechCheck, a five-question, multiple-choice quiz, by entering the letters TC and the three-digit activity number.

History ONLINE at glencoe.com

	Student	Teacher	Parent
Media Center			
• Student Edition Audio	●		
• Spanish Summaries	●		
• Section Spotlight Videos	●	●	
Social Studies Online Learning Center			
Classroom Tools			
• Multi-Language Glossaries	●	●	●
• Teaching Today		●	
• TIME Current Events	●	●	●
• Beyond the Textbook	●	●	
***The American Journey* Online Learning Center**			
• Study-to-Go™	●	●	●
• Study Central™	●	●	●
• Chapter Overview	●	●	
• Concepts in Motion	●	●	
• ePuzzles and Games	●	●	
• Literature Connections	●	●	
• Online Student Edition	●	●	●
• Self-Check Quizzes	●	●	●
• Student Web Activities	●	●	
• Vocabulary eFlashcards	●	●	
• Web Activity Lesson Plans	●	●	●
• Vocabulary PuzzleMaker	●	●	●

READING SUPPORT FROM JAMESTOWN EDUCATION

- **Timed Readings Plus in Social Studies** helps students increase their reading rate and fluency while maintaining comprehension. The 400-word passages are similar to those found on state and national assessments.

- **Reading in the Content Area: Social Studies** concentrates on six essential reading skills that help students better comprehend what they read. The book includes 75 high-interest nonfiction passages written at increasing levels of difficulty.

- **Reading Social Studies** includes strategic reading instruction and vocabulary support in Social Studies content for ELLs and native speakers of English.

- **Content Vocabulary Workout** (Grades 6–8) accelerates reading comprehension through focused vocabulary development. Social Studies content vocabulary comes from the glossaries of Glencoe's Middle School Social Studies texts.

www.jamestowneducation.com

NATIONAL GEOGRAPHIC

Index to National Geographic Magazine:

The following articles relate to this chapter:

- *"Seasons of Smoke,"* Adam Goodheart, August 2006.

- *"Indian Renaissance,"* Joseph Bruchac, September 2004.

National Geographic Society Products

To order the following, call National Geographic at 1-800-368-2728:

National Geographic Atlas of the World (Book)

Access National Geographic's new dynamic MapMachine Web site and other geography resources at:

www.nationalgeographic.com

www.nationalgeographic.com/mapmachine

Reading List Generator CD-ROM — GLENCOE BOOKLINK 3

Use this database to search more than 30,000 titles to create a customized reading list for your students.

- Reading lists can be organized by students' reading level, author, genre, theme, or area of interest.

- The database provides Degrees of Reading Power™ (DRP) and Lexile™ readability scores for all selections.

- A brief summary of each selection is included.

Leveled reading suggestions for this chapter:

For students at a Grade 6 reading level:
- *Andrew Jackson: Young Patriot,* George Stanley

For students at a Grade 7 reading level:
- *The Cherokee: An Independent Nation,* Anne M. Todd

For students at a Grade 8 reading level:
- *Andrew Jackson: 7th President of the United States,* Rebecca Stefoff

For students at a Grade 9 reading level:
- *America's Third-Party Presidential Candidates,* Nathan Aaseng
- *What Shall We Do With the Land?* Laurence Pringle

For students at a Grade 10 reading level:
- *O'odham Poet Strives to Preserve Languages,* Pila Martinez

The following videotape programs are available from Glencoe as supplements to the chapter:

- **Andrew Jackson: A Man for the People** (ISBN 1-56-501647-5)

- **John and Abigail Adams: Love & Liberty** (ISBN 0-76-704991-8)

To order, call Glencoe at 1-800-334-7344. To find classroom resources to accompany many of these videos, check the following home pages:

A&E Television: www.aetv.com

The History Channel: www.history.com

Chapter Objectives

After studying this chapter, students will be able to:

- Explain how political beliefs and events shaped Andrew Jackson's presidency.
- Understand how Andrew Jackson's presidency affected Native Americans.
- Describe how economic issues affect the president and presidential elections.

Motivating Activity

Making Inferences The Jackson era was a time of conflict with Native Americans. The government created the Indian Territory in the West and forced many Native Americans to move there. **Ask:** What are the Native Americans doing in this painting? *(traveling west on the Trail of Tears)* **Ask:** What evidence can you see that supports the inference that the Indians are undergoing hardship? *(Students may mention bad weather, cold weather clothing, people carrying their heavy belongings, or small children and young animals walking far.)* **OL**

Previewing the Essential Questions

As you begin teaching each section, use these questions and activities to help students focus on the Essential Questions.

Chapter 11
The Jackson Era 1824–1845

In the 1830s, many Native Americans were forced to move west along what became known as the Trail of Tears.

PRESIDENTS

JAMES MONROE 1817–1825

JOHN Q. ADAMS 1825–1829

ANDREW JACKSON 1829–1837

U.S. Events

★ 1823 Monroe Doctrine issued

1830 ★ Indian Removal Act

★ 1833 Force Bill passes

World Events

1820

1825

1830

★ 1822 Brazil gains independence from Portugal

1826 ★ French scientist Niépce produces first photograph

★ 1829 Louis Braille publishes reading system for the blind

334 Chapter 11

Section 1

Jacksonian Democracy Have students describe the types of advertisements, speeches, and interviews they see on TV during the days before an election. Discuss how the candidates promote their messages. Point out to students that in Section 1 they will learn how events and beliefs shaped Jackson's presidency. **OL**

Section 2

Conflicts Over Land Ask: How have Native Americans been treated by settlers based on what we have learned so far? *(Although some settlers have treated Native Americans fairly, many have taken their lands.)* Point out to students that Section 2 will focus on the events and issues surrounding the removal of Native Americans to the Oklahoma Territory. **OL**

Section 1: Jacksonian Democracy

Essential Question How did political beliefs and events shape Andrew Jackson's presidency?

Section 2: Conflicts Over Land

Essential Question How did Andrew Jackson's presidency affect Native Americans?

Section 3: Jackson and the Bank

Essential Question How do economic issues affect the president and presidential elections?

History ONLINE
Chapter Overview Visit glencoe.com and click on **Chapter 11—Chapter Overviews** to preview chapter information.

FOLDABLES Study Organizer

Organizing Information Make this Foldable to organize what you learn about the Jackson era.

Step 1 Fold a sheet of paper into fourths from top to bottom.

Step 2 Fold the paper into thirds along the long axis. You have formed a table with three columns and four rows.

Step 3 Label the left column with the chapter number and the titles of the sections. Label column two "Problems." Label column three "Solutions."

Chapter 11	Problems	Solutions
Jackson Democracy		
Conflicts Over Land		
Jackson and the Bank		

Reading and Writing As you read, use your Foldable to write down the problems that arose during the Jackson era and attempts to solve these problems.

Abraham Lincoln, "The Rail Splitter" ▶

★ **1834** Abraham Lincoln elected to Illinois legislature

★ **1836** "Nature" by Ralph Waldo Emerson published in Boston

MARTIN VAN BUREN 1837–1841

★ **1838** Cherokee forced to move west

WILLIAM HENRY HARRISON 1841

JOHN TYLER 1841–1845

1835 — 1840 — 1845

Queen Victoria's Imperial State Crown ▶

★ **1837** Victoria becomes Queen of Great Britain

★ **1839** Scottish blacksmith, Kirkpatrick Macmillan, produces first bicycle

Chapter 11 335

Introducing Chapter 11

Time Line Activity

Have students look at the time line and identify two events that might reflect a cause-and-effect relationship. *(Students should identify the 1830 Indian Removal Act and the Cherokee being forced to move west in 1838.)* Tell students that in this chapter, they will learn how white settlement impacted the Native Americans.

FOLDABLES Study Organizer **Dinah Zike's Foldables**

Purpose This Foldable helps students identify the problems that challenged the Jackson presidency and the actions he took to resolve them. The completed Foldable will help students prepare for assessment.

▱ More Foldables activities for this chapter can be found in *Dinah Zike's Reading and Study Skills Foldables.*

History ONLINE
Introduce students to chapter content and key terms by having them access the **Chapter Overview** at glencoe.com.

Section 3

Jackson and the Bank Ask: What type of influence does the president have over the economy? *(Students may think that the president controls the economy. In reality, however, the president has little control over the American economy. Economic issues, though, affect presidencies and elections.)* Tell students that Section 3 will explore the impact of economic issues on the presidents and on their elections. **OL**

Section 1

Section 1

Jacksonian Democracy

Focus

Bellringer
Daily Test Practice Transparency 11–1

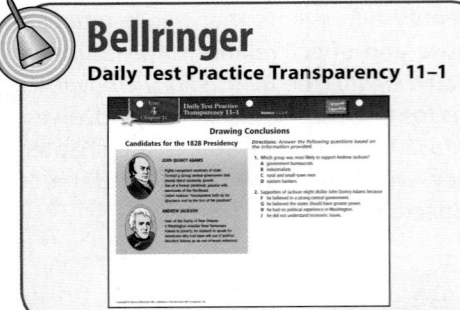

Reading Guide
Answers to Graphic:
Democratic-Republicans: Jackson; favored states' rights and mistrusted strong central government; **National Republicans:** John Quincy Adams; wanted a strong central government that supported federal measures that would shape the U.S. economy

Section Spotlight Video

Have students watch the Section Spotlight Video "Jacksonian Democracy" to learn more about Andrew Jackson.

Resource Manager

Essential Question
How did political beliefs and events shape Andrew Jackson's presidency?

Reading Guide

Content Vocabulary
majority (p. 337)
plurality (p. 337)
spoils system (p. 340)
caucus (p. 340)
nominating convention (p. 340)
tariff (p. 341)
nullify (p. 341)
secede (p. 341)

Academic Vocabulary
select (p. 337)
participate (p. 340)

Key People and Events
Andrew Jackson (p. 337)
John Quincy Adams (p. 337)
Nullification Act (p. 341)

Reading Strategy
Taking Notes As you read about the parties competing in the election of 1828, use a diagram like the one below to organize the information.

Party → Candidate → Views

ILLINOIS STANDARDS
The American Journey

14.C Understand the election process and responsibilities of citizens.

15.D.3a Explain the effects of increasing and declining imports and exports to an individual and to the nation's economy as a whole.

18.B.3a Analyze how individuals and groups interact with and within institutions (e.g., educational, military).

American Diary

As a supporter of the "common man," Andrew Jackson lost the 1824 presidential election to John Quincy Adams. Because no candidate won an electoral vote majority, the election went to the House of Representatives, which elected Adams. Jackson's supporters, "the humble members of society—the farmers, mechanics and laborers," believed Jackson was cheated out of the presidency by a "corrupt bargain."

—from The White House Historical Association

Andrew Jackson's inauguration in 1828

R Reading Strategies	C Critical Thinking	D Differentiated Instruction	W Writing Support	S Skill Practice
Teacher Edition • Identifying, p. 337 • Seq. Information, p. 338 • Making Connections, p. 339 **Additional Resources** • Guid. Read., URB p. 39 • Content Vocab., URB p. 17 • Academic Vocab., URB p. 19 • Read. Ess., p. 109	**Teacher Edition** • Evaluating, p. 337 • Pred. Consequences, p. 340 **Additional Resources** • Quizzes and Tests, p. 101	**Teacher Edition** • ELL, p. 338 **Additional Resources** • Reteach, URB p. 37 • School-to-Home, URB p. 35	**Teacher Edition** • Personal Writing, p. 338 • Expository Writing, p. 340 **Additional Resources** • Writ. Skills, URB p. 23	**Teacher Edition** • Using Geo. Skills, p. 341 **Additional Resources** • Daily Test Pract. Transp. 11-1 • Lesson Transp. 11B, 11C • Time Line Skills, URB p. 34 • Geo. & Hist., URB p. 31

Elections of 1824 and 1828

Main Idea John Quincy Adams and Andrew Jackson introduced new ways of campaigning in the presidential elections of 1824 and 1828.

History and You Think of the ways that presidential candidates campaign today. What methods do they use? Read to find out about the new ways of campaigning that John Quincy Adams and Andrew Jackson brought about.

From 1816 to 1824, the United States had only one political party, the Jeffersonian Republicans, or the Republican Party. In 1824, when James Monroe declined to run for a third term as president, four candidates from the party competed for the presidency. The views of the four candidates differed on the role of the federal government. Their views also differed because they represented different regions of the country.

The party nominated William H. Crawford, a former congressman from Georgia. The other three candidates were favorite sons—meaning they were backed by their home states rather than the national party. **Andrew Jackson** and Henry Clay came from the West. Clay, of Kentucky, was Speaker of the House of Representatives. Jackson, of Tennessee, was not a Washington politician, but he was a hero of the War of 1812. Raised in poverty, he claimed to speak for the Americans who had been left out of politics. **John Quincy Adams,** of Massachusetts, son of former president John Adams, was popular with merchants of the Northeast.

Striking a Bargain

In the election, Jackson received the largest number of popular votes. However, no candidate received a **majority,** or more than half, of the electoral votes. Jackson won a **plurality,** or the largest single share. According to the Twelfth Amendment of the Constitution, when no candidate receives a majority of electoral votes, the House of Representatives **selects,** or chooses, the president.

While the House was preparing to vote on the next president, Henry Clay met with John Quincy Adams. Clay agreed to use his influence as Speaker of the House to defeat Jackson. In return, Clay may have hoped to gain the position of secretary of state.

With Clay's help, Adams was elected president in the House. Adams quickly named Clay as secretary of state, traditionally the stepping-stone to the presidency. Jackson's followers accused the two men of making a "corrupt bargain" and stealing the election.

By the Numbers / Presidential Elections

Election of 1824

Candidate*	Electoral Votes	House Votes
John Q. Adams	84	13
Andrew Jackson	99	7
William H. Crawford	41	4
Henry Clay	37	-

Election of 1828

Candidate*	Electoral Votes
Andrew Jackson Democratic Republican	178
John Q. Adams National Republican	83

*All candidates represented the Democratic Republican Party.

Critical Thinking

Analyzing What major differences can you see between the results of the two elections?

Teach

R Reading Strategy

Identifying Ask: In what two primary ways did the views of each of the main candidates differ? *(They differed on the role of the federal government; their views represented different regions of the country.)* **BL**

C Critical Thinking

Evaluating Ask: Do you think the agreement between Clay and Adams was fair? *(Students may say yes, the agreement was an effective way to achieve a majority and represent more people from the West and the East, or no, they should have let the House of Representatives select the winners without any deal agreements.)* **OL**

By the Numbers

Critical Thinking Answer Answers may include that in 1824, Jackson won by a slim margin in the Electoral College, but Adams won in the House. Jackson won the 1828 election much more solidly.

Additional Support

Activity: Interdisciplinary Connection

Mathematics Invite a math teacher from your school or the local junior college to discuss the difference between a majority and a plurality. *(A majority is when more than 50% of the voters vote for one person. A plurality is when there are more than two candidates in an election and the number of votes cast for one is greater than the number cast for any other candidate but not more than half the total votes cast.)* Ask your guest to show students how to convert numbers of electoral votes in the 1824 election to a percentage of the whole. (261 electoral votes = 100%) Have students sketch ideas for a poster that illustrates this difference as it applies to the 1824 presidential election. Ask students to use mathematical representations, such as bar and circle graphs, to make their posters visually appealing. When the sketches are ready, distribute poster paper and art materials such as colored pencils or markers. Provide mathematical tools such as rulers, protractors, and compasses. Display students' posters as they are completed. **OL**

Hands-On Chapter Project
Step 1

Creating a Political Cartoon About the Jackson Era

Step 1: Learning About Political Cartoons Students will learn how political cartoons expressed political opinions in the Jackson Era.

Essential Question: How did political beliefs and events shape Andrew Jackson's presidency?

The Adams Presidency

D Adams and Clay denied any wrongdoing, and no evidence of a deal ever emerged. Still, the charge of a "corrupt bargain" cast a long shadow over Adams's presidency. A hard-working and intelligent man, Adams was determined to leave his mark on the presidency.

In his first message to Congress, Adams announced an ambitious program of legislation. In addition to improving roads and waterways, Adams urged that the government spend money to build a national university, set up astronomical observatories, and support scientific research.

R Adams's proposals, however, horrified his opponents who desired a more limited role for the federal government. It would be wrong, they believed, to spend the taxpayers' money on such projects.

In the end, Congress granted the president funds for improving rivers, harbors, and roads, but this was far less than Adams wanted. The rejection of many of Adams's proposals set the stage for the president's defeat in his 1828 reelection attempt.

The Election of 1828

By 1828, the Republican Party had divided into two separate parties: the Democratic-Republicans, who supported Jackson, and the National Republicans, who supported Adams. Jackson's Democratic-Republicans, or Democrats, favored states' rights and mistrusted strong central government. Many Democrats were people from the frontier, immigrants, or workers in the big cities.

The National Republicans wanted a strong central government. They supported federal measures, such as road building and the Bank of the United States, that would shape the nation's economy. Many National Republicans were merchants or farmers.

W During the campaign both parties resorted to mudslinging, or attempts to ruin their opponents' reputations with insults. The Democratic-Republicans accused Adams of betraying the people. They put out a handbill

Primary Source / The Campaign of 1828

Jackson Attacked The presidential campaign of 1828 was one of the dirtiest in American history. Supporters of President John Quincy Adams attacked Andrew Jackson in print. The so-called "coffin handbills" (below) criticized Jackson's execution of six soldiers for desertion during the War of 1812. The handbills backfired, either because they exaggerated too much or because most Americans approved of what Jackson did. In addition, Jackson's opponents accused his wife, Rachel Donelson Jackson, of bigamy. When Rachel died before the inauguration, Jackson blamed those who slandered her.

Rachel Donelson Jackson ▲

"Gentle reader, it is for you to say, whether this man, who carries a sword cane, and is willing to run it through the body of any one who may presume to stand in his way, is a fit person to be our President."

—from the "Coffin Handbill"

Directions Review the political cartoon in the feature "The Campaign of 1828." Cartoons that were critical of Jackson appeared in newspapers and handbills and were seen by many people. Tell students that they will be creating their own political cartoon about an issue or event during the Jackson Era.

Selecting Have students skim the chapter to find other political cartoons that were created during this time. **Ask:** What are two characteristics of political cartoons? *(exaggeration and symbolism)* Tell students they will select an issue or event and create a new political cartoon about it. Allow time for students to select an issue or event from the chapter. **OL**

(Chapter Project continued in Section 2)

calling the election a contest "between an honest patriotism, on the one side, and an unholy, selfish ambition, on the other." The National Republicans fought back. They created a vicious campaign song to play up embarrassing incidents in Jackson's life. One involved Jackson's order in the War of 1812 to execute soldiers who deserted.

Mudslinging was not the only new tactic introduced in the 1828 campaign. Election slogans, rallies, buttons, and events such as barbecues also were used to stir up enthusiasm. All of these new features became a permanent part of American political life.

In the election of 1828, Jackson received most of the votes cast in the frontier states. He also received many votes in the South, where his support for states' rights was popular. John C. Calhoun of South Carolina, who had been Adams's vice president, switched parties to run with Jackson. Calhoun also supported states' rights. Jackson won the election in an overwhelming victory, or landslide.

Reading Check Identifying What campaign practices of the 1828 election still are used today?

Philadelphia editor John Binns published several "coffin handbills" attacking Andrew Jackson. This cartoon shows Binns **A** struggling to carry a burden consisting of coffins for Secretary of State Henry Clay **B** and President John Quincy Adams **C**. Adams is clinging to the presidential chair that he was soon to lose.

Critical Thinking

Interpreting What is the cartoonist trying to say about the coffin handbills?

Jackson as President

Main Idea Andrew Jackson made the American political system more democratic.

History and You What are the requirements for today's citizens to be eligible to vote? Read on to learn how President Jackson expanded voting rights to include a larger number of people.

. . . .

Andrew Jackson was everything most Americans admired—a patriot, a self-made man, and a war hero. Thousands of farmers and laborers arrived in Washington to hear Jackson's Inaugural Address. Later, a crowd attended the White House reception. They filled the elegant rooms, trampling carpets with muddy shoes and spilling food on chairs. They were there to shake the hand of the president who seemed just like them.

"Old Hickory"

Like many of his supporters, Andrew Jackson was born in a log cabin. During the War of 1812, he defeated the Creek Nation in the Battle of Horseshoe Bend and the British at the Battle of New Orleans. His troops called him "Old Hickory" because he was as tough as a hickory stick.

Small farmers, craftspeople, and others who felt left out of the expanding American economy loved Jackson. They felt that his rise from a log cabin to the White House demonstrated the American success story.

New Voters

President Andrew Jackson promised "equal protection and equal benefits" for all Americans—at least for all white American men. During his first term, a spirit of equality spread throughout American politics.

In the nation's early years, only men who owned property or paid taxes had suffrage, or the right to vote. By the 1820s, many states had loosened the property requirements. Democracy expanded as people who had not been allowed to vote became new voters.

The Jackson Era **Chapter 11** 339

R **Reading Strategy**

Making Connections Ask: How do candidates use technology today to reach voters? *(Sample answers might include participating in Internet debates and maintaining blogs.)* **OL**

Reading Check **Answer:** mudslinging, election slogans, rallies, buttons, and events such as barbecues or dinners

Primary Source

Critical Thinking Answer

The coffin handbills were a burden to Binns put on him by Adams and Clay.

Differentiated Instruction

Leveled Activities

Writing Support

W **Expository Writing** Have students write an 1828 newspaper article explaining to citizens how the change in their state's constitution will broaden democracy. **OL**

Critical Thinking

C **Predicting Consequences Ask:** What are some possible effects of the spoils system? *(Students may suggest citizens will be angry because of lost jobs and fear far-reaching changes because of the increased power in the presidency.)* **AL**

Primary Source

Critical Thinking Answer

For: A state could nullify any federal law if it was against state interests. **Against:** Jackson issued a proclamation declaring that nullification was unconstitutional and that threatening to secede was an act of treason.

✓ **Reading Check** **Answer:** a system in which major candidates are chosen by members of Congress

Differentiated Instruction

Primary Source / The Nullification Crisis

In 1832 South Carolina called a state convention to declare the tariffs of 1828 and 1832 null and void. In addition, the state threatened to secede, or withdraw, from the Union if the federal government attempted to use force to collect those tariffs within its borders.

"It is hereby declared . . . that the . . . laws for the imposing of duties . . . on the importation of foreign commodities. . . are null, void, and no law, nor binding upon this State. . . .

Any act authorizing the employment of a military or naval force against the State of South Carolina, . . . [is] inconsistent with the . . . continuance of South Carolina in the Union."

—from the South Carolina Ordinance of Nullification

Vice President John C. Calhoun argued that any state had the authority to call a formal convention to declare null and void any federal law it considered unconstitutional. Tensions between Calhoun and President Jackson increased when Jackson sided with those opposing nullification.

The Nullification Proclamation declared that nullification was unconstitutional. It also stated that threatening to secede was an act of treason.

"I consider, then, the power to annul a law of the United States, assumed by one State, incompatible with the existence of the Union, . . . and destructive of the great object for which it was formed."

—President Andrew Jackson's proclamation from the nullification

President Andrew Jackson privately threatened to march an army into South Carolina to hang Calhoun. Instead, he issued a proclamation against nullification. Congress passed a bill to lower tariffs—along with a bill to enforce it.

Critical Thinking

Comparing and Contrasting How did each side in the nullification crisis defend its position?

For the first time, white male sharecroppers, factory workers, and others **participated,** or took part, in the political process. Women, however, could not vote, and African Americans and Native Americans had few rights of any kind.

W Also, by 1828, 22 of the 24 states had changed their constitutions to allow the people, rather than the state legislatures, to choose presidential electors. This change further broadened democracy.

The Spoils System

C Democrats wanted to open up government jobs to people from all walks of life. They argued that ordinary citizens could handle any government job. Many Democrats were disturbed that the federal government had become a bureaucracy, a system in which nonelected officials carry out laws.

President Jackson fired many federal workers and replaced them with his supporters. The fired employees protested.

They charged that Jackson was acting like a tyrant. Jackson responded that new federal employees would be good for democracy.

One Jackson supporter said: "To the victors belong the spoils." In other words, because the Jacksonians won the election, they had the right to the spoils, or the benefits of victory. The practice of replacing government employees with the winner's supporters is called the **spoils system.**

Electoral Changes

Jackson's supporters abandoned the unpopular **caucus** system, in which major candidates were chosen by members of Congress. The caucuses were replaced by **nominating conventions** in which delegates from the states chose the party's presidential candidate. This system allowed many people to participate in the selection of candidates.

✓ **Reading Check** **Describing** What is a caucus system?

Growth of Democracy (1815–1840)

Objective:	To learn how American life changed during the Jackson Era
Focus:	Ask students to calculate the number of years represented.
Teach:	Have students discuss the major changes in elections made during this time.
Assess:	Students should summarize the main idea.
Close:	Have students write about how the Jacksonian Era affected the nation.

Differentiated Instruction Strategies

BL Have students illustrate the cause-and-effect relationship in question 3.

AL Ask students to predict how President Jackson might feel about the voting age requirement today.

ELL Have students explain the 1815 entry in a paragraph.

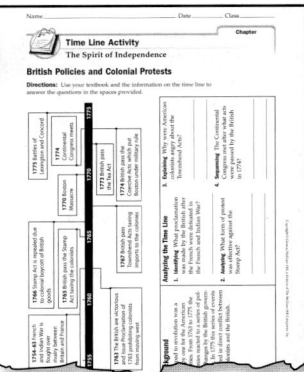

Time Line Skills Activity, URB p. 34

The Tariff Debate

Main Idea A fight over tariffs ignited a crisis on the question of states' rights versus the rights of the federal government.

History and You Can you ignore a school rule? Read how South Carolina rejected a federal law.

· ·

A tariff is a fee paid on imported goods. The high tariff on European manufactured goods pleased Northeastern factory owners. Tariffs made European goods more expensive, prompting American consumers to buy American-made goods. Southerners hated the tariff, because tariffs meant higher prices.

John C. Calhoun of South Carolina argued that a state had the right to **nullify,** or cancel, a federal law if it was considered to be against state interests. Because the states created the federal government, he argued, the states are the final authority. Daniel Webster disagreed, claiming that nullification would destroy the Union.

Nobody knew Jackson's views. At a dinner, however, Jackson spoke directly to Calhoun: "Our federal union . . . must be preserved!" Answering the challenge, Calhoun said, "The Union—next to our liberty, most dear." He meant that the Union must take second place to a state's liberty to overrule the Constitution if its interests were threatened.

In 1832 Congress enacted a lower tariff, but it did not cool the protest. South Carolina passed the **Nullification Act,** declaring it would not pay the "illegal" tariffs of 1828 and 1832. The state threatened to **secede,** or break away, from the Union if the U.S. federal government interfered.

To ease the crisis, Jackson backed a bill that would gradually lower the tariff. Jackson, however, had Congress pass the Force Bill, allowing him to use the military to enforce acts of Congress. South Carolina accepted the new tariff but nullified the Force Bill.

S

✓**Reading Check** **Explaining** How would Northeastern factory owners react to a high tariff?

History ONLINE
Study Central™ To review this section, go to glencoe.com.

Section 1 Review

Vocabulary
1. Define each of the following words by using it in a sentence: majority, plurality, select, participate, spoils system, caucus, nominating convention, tariff, nullify, secede.

Main Ideas
2. **Specifying** What key issue split the Republican Party in the 1828 presidential election?
3. **Explaining** Why did Andrew Jackson fire many government employees?
4. **Summarizing** Why was the issue of states' rights versus federal authority serious?

Critical Thinking
5. **Making Inferences** Why do you think Speaker of the House Henry Clay was willing to make the "corrupt bargain"?
6. **Organizing** Use a diagram like the one below to describe the changes that took place in the political system under Andrew Jackson.

Changes

7. **Creative Writing** Write three questions you would ask President Andrew Jackson if you interviewed him. Then write answers to the questions as you think Jackson might have responded.

Answer the
8. **Essential Question**
How did political beliefs and events shape Andrew Jackson's presidency?

The Jackson Era **Chapter 11** 341

S Skill Practice

Using Geography Skills Ask: Why might South Carolina want to purchase manufactured goods from Europe? *(They were cheaper.)* Have students locate South Carolina on a map. **Ask:** What geographic feature might have allowed South Carolina to secede and still easily purchase manufactured goods? *(Charleston is a major shipping port on the coast, and European goods could have been received there.)* **OL**

✓**Reading Check** **Answer:** The high tariff on European manufactured goods pleased Northeastern factory owners because Americans would consume more of their products.

Assess
· ·

Study Central™ provides summaries, interactive games, and online graphic organizers to help students review content.

Close
· ·

Summarizing Review with students the changes brought about by the 1828 election. **OL**

Section 1 Review

Answers

1. Students should use vocabulary words in sentences that include their correct definitions.
2. states' rights versus a strong central government
3. Jackson felt that new federal employees would be good for democracy and that, as the victor, his party had a right to the spoils.
4. States' rights were important to the South, and Jackson's vice president, John Calhoun,

supported that view, gaining support for Jackson.
5. Clay did it to defeat Jackson and because he would be made secretary of state, the stepping-stone to the presidency.
6. more democratic process for nominating political candidates; expansion of suffrage; introduction of spoils system
7. Questions and answers should show an understanding of the democratic process.

8. Students' essays should reflect an understanding of how Jackson's beliefs in limiting the strength of the federal government, in states' rights, in the broadening of democracy, and in the spoils system shaped his presidency. They should also mention how nullification challenged his ideals.

Section 2

Focus

Bellringer
Daily Test Practice Transparency 11-2

Reading Guide
Answers to Graphic:
Cherokee: unsuccessfully negotiated treaties with Georgia and the federal government; **Sauk/Fox:** returned and planted crops on their lands but were slaughtered; **Seminole:** some successfully resisted removal by fighting U.S. troops

Section Spotlight Video

Have students watch the Section Spotlight Video "Conflicts Over Land" to learn more about the Trail of Tears.

Resource Manager

Section 2

Essential Question
How did Andrew Jackson's presidency affect Native Americans?

Reading Guide

Content Vocabulary
relocate (p. 343)
guerrilla tactics (p. 347)

Academic Vocabulary
federal (p. 343)
survive (p. 347)

Key People and Events
Indian Removal Act (p. 343)
Indian Territory (p. 344)
General Winfield Scott (p. 345)
Trail of Tears (p. 346)
Black Hawk (p. 346)
Osceola (p. 347)

Reading Strategy
Taking Notes As you read, use a diagram like the one below to describe how each group of Native Americans resisted removal and the result.

Cherokee   Sauk/Fox   Seminole

ILLINOIS STANDARDS
The American Journey

16.D.3a Describe characteristics of different kinds of communities in various sections of America during the colonial/frontier periods and the 19th century.

17.C.3c Analyze how human processes influence settlement patterns including migration and population growth.

17.D.3a Explain how and why spatial patterns of settlement change over time.

18.B.3a Analyze how individuals and groups interact with and within institutions (e.g., educational, military).

342

Conflicts Over Land

American Diary

As they moved west in 1838 during a forced removal from their lands, the Cherokee were said to be on a "Trail of Tears." A legend developed that a Cherokee rose appeared along the road wherever a Cherokee tear landed. Poet Rick Brown described the event:

"As wagons, weighted, marked their way, from New Echota to where they close; where each tear fell, as some will tell, will be seen a Cherokee rose."

—quoted from "A Cherokee Rose"

The Seminole people of Florida fought against being forced to abandon their homes and way of life.

R Reading Strategies	C Critical Thinking	D Differentiated Instruction	W Writing Support	S Skill Practice
Teacher Edition • Visualizing, p. 346 **Additional Resources** • Guid. Read., URB p. 40 • Content Vocab., URB p. 17 • Acad. Voc., URB p. 19 • Read. Ess., p. 112 • Am. Lit. Read., URB p. 9 • Pri. Source Read., URB p. 21	**Teacher Edition** • Predict. Conseq., p. 343 • Draw. Infer., p. 343 • Identify Central Issues, p. 347 **Additional Resources** • Quizzes and Tests, p. 102 • Citizen. & Dec. Mak., URB p. 3 • Crit. Think. Skills, URB p. 29	**Teacher Edition** • Gift. & Talent., p. 344 **Additional Resources** • Reteach, URB p. 37 • School-to-Home, URB p. 35 • Differ. Inst., URB p. 27	**Teacher Edition** • Persuasive Writing, p. 345	**Teacher Edition** • Reading a Map, p. 344 **Additional Resources** • Daily Test Pract. Transp. 11-2 • Lesson Transp. 11A

Moving Native Americans

Main Idea Thousands of Native Americans were forced to abandon their lands to white settlers and move West.

History and You How long have you lived in your community? How would you feel if you were forced to leave your home? Read how Native Americans reacted to their forced move.

While the nation had expanded westward by the 1830s, many Native Americans still lived in the eastern part of the country. The "Five Civilized Tribes"—the Cherokee, Creek, Seminole, Chickasaw, and Choctaw—lived in Georgia, Alabama, Mississippi, and Florida. These tribes had established farming societies with successful economies.

Because the area west of the Mississippi was dry and seemed unsuitable for farming, few white Americans lived there. Many settlers wanted the **federal**—or national—government to **relocate** Native Americans living in the Southeast to this area. They wanted to force the Native Americans to leave their land and move west.

President Andrew Jackson, a man of the frontier himself, supported the settlers' demand for Native American land. Jackson had fought the Creek and Seminole peoples in Georgia and Florida. In his Inaugural Address, he stated that he intended to move all Native Americans to the Great Plains.

Many Americans believed that the Great Plains was a wasteland that would never be settled. They thought that if they moved Native Americans to that region, the nation's conflict with them would be over.

Indian Removal Act

In 1830 President Jackson pushed the **Indian Removal Act** through Congress. The act allowed the federal government to pay Native Americans to move west.

Jackson then sent officials to make treaties with the Native Americans in the Southeast.

By the Numbers / Forced Migration

The Five Civilized Tribes east of the Mississippi were forced to migrate to Oklahoma under provision of Congress. Thousands died along the way.

Forced Migration, 1830–1840

Choctaw
Creek
Chickasaw
Cherokee
Seminole

0   5,000   10,000   15,000   20,000
Number of people

Critical Thinking

Analyzing What would be the advantage to white settlers if Congress forced Native Americans off their Eastern lands?

Teach

C₁ Critical Thinking

Predicting Consequences Ask: What characteristic describes the "Five Civilized Tribes"? *(established farming societies with successful economies)* Why might these tribes be upset when forced to relocate? *(because they would not have wanted to leave their good land for less suitable land)* **OL**

C₂ Critical Thinking

Drawing Inferences Ask: What personal experience influenced Jackson's view of Native Americans? *(He had fought the Creek and the Seminole people in Georgia and Florida.)* **AL**

By the Numbers

Critical Thinking Answer White settlers would have more fertile land to settle, and there would be less conflict with Native Americans.

Differentiated Instruction

Citizenship and Decision Making Skills Activity, URB p. 3

Connecting With Native Americans

Objective: To learn about the cultures of Native Americans

Focus: Discuss how cultures express their values in songs and poems.

Teach: Have students research the customs and traditions of a Native American group.

Assess: Have students explain what they learned about Native American cultures.

Close: Compare and contrast the themes found in Native American poems with those of today's poems.

Differentiated Instruction Strategies

BL Have students describe a family custom or tradition.

AL Have students research and write an essay about their own cultural heritage.

ELL Have students paraphrase the second paragraph of the Background section.

CHAPTER 11
Section 2

S Skill Practice

Reading a Map Have students study the map at the top of the page. **Ask:** Which group of Native Americans traveled the farthest? *(Seminole)* Which groups moved from Alabama? *(Cherokee and Creek)* **OL**

D Differentiated Instruction

Gifted and Talented Ask: What does the Cherokee speaker mean by "land of our fathers"? *(the land on which their ancestors lived)* Have students find the complete text of the Cherokee appeal. Ask them to find at least two arguments the Cherokee give for not leaving their land and report on them to the class. **OL**

History ONLINE
Objectives and answers to the Student Web Activity can be found at glencoe.com under the Web Activity Lesson Plan for this chapter.

Additional Support

Teacher Tip

Background Information Students may not know what a census is and how it works. Explain to students that the federal government collects data on the population of the United States every 10 years. For more information, refer students to the Web site www.census.gov.

344

Removal of Native Americans, 1820–1840   NATIONAL GEOGRAPHIC

Chief Black Hawk led Native Americans back to Illinois in 1832, but they were driven away.

The Cherokee took their refusal to move to the Supreme Court and won. Federal troops forced them to leave anyway.

Chief Osceola led the Seminole in rebellion.

▲ This seal appeared on all official documents from 1871 until Oklahoma became a state.

Ceded by Native Americans
Ceded to Native Americans
Common removal route
Cherokee removal route
Chickasaw removal route
Choctaw removal route
Creek removal route
Seminole removal route
□ Fort
Borders as of 1840

Dade Massacre 1835
Seminole area, 1740–1822
Seminole area, 1822–1842
Seminole reservation, 1823–1832
□ Fort ✷ Battle

Most Native American leaders felt forced to accept payment for their lands. In 1834 Congress created the **Indian Territory.** This was an area in present-day Oklahoma that was set aside for the relocation of Native Americans from the Southeast.

The Cherokee Nation

The Cherokee, however, refused to give up their land. In treaties of the 1790s, the federal government recognized the Cherokee in Georgia as a separate nation. Georgia, however, refused to recognize Cherokee laws. As pressure to leave mounted, the Cherokee appealed to the people of the United States:

History ONLINE
Student Web Activity Visit glencoe.com and complete the Web Activity about the struggles of Native Americans.

PRIMARY SOURCE

"We are aware, that some persons suppose it will be for our advantage to remove beyond the Mississippi. . . . Our people universally think otherwise. . . . We wish to remain on the land of our fathers."
—Cherokee appeal, 1830

When the government's position did not change, the Cherokee sued the state of Georgia. Eventually the Cherokee took their case to the Supreme Court. In *Worcester* v. *Georgia* (1832), Chief Justice John Marshall ruled that Georgia had no right to interfere with the Cherokee. Only the federal government had power in Cherokee matters.

President Jackson supported Georgia's efforts to remove the Cherokee. He declared that he would ignore the Supreme Court, saying, "John Marshall has made his decision, now let him enforce it."

344 **Chapter 11** *The Jackson Era*

Fast Facts

Oklahoma "Oklahoma" is from the Choctaw words for people, "okla" and red, "humma." Though Oklahoma today has more Native Americans than any other state, Native Americans make up only 8.1% of the state's population. Native American Oklahomans include descendants of the 67 tribes that lived in Jackson's Indian Territory.

◀ A Cherokee village in the Southeast

"My troops already occupy many positions in the country that you are to abandon, and thousands and thousands are approaching from every quarter, to render [make] resistance and escape alike hopeless. All those troops, regular and militia, are your friends. . . . Obey them when they tell you that you can remain no longer in this country."

—General Winfield Scott's address to the Cherokee Nation, 1838

▼ John Ross was elected chief of the Cherokee Nation in 1828 and held that post until his death in 1866. In the late 1830s, he led the fight against removal.

"A [false] Delegation, . . . proceeded to Washington City with this pretended treaty, and by false and fraudulent representations [replaced] . . . the legal and accredited Delegation of the Cherokee people, and obtained for this instrument, . . . the recognition of the United States Government. And now it is presented to us as a treaty, ratified by the Senate, and approved by the President."

—letter to the Senate and House of Representatives, 1836

◀ Wilma Mankiller, first female chief of the Cherokee, at a monument to John Ross on the Cherokee Reservation in Oklahoma, 2000

Critical Thinking

Making Inferences Do you think that General Scott wanted a peaceful solution to the government's disagreement with the Cherokee Nation? Why or why not?

Maps In MOtion See StudentWorks™ Plus or glencoe.com.

The Trail of Tears

By 1835, the Cherokee were divided and feeling hopeless. That year, the federal government persuaded a small number—about 500—of Cherokee to sign The Treaty of New Echota, giving up their people's land. The treaty gave Jackson the legal document he needed to remove Native Americans. Approval of the treaty by the U.S. Senate sealed the fate of the Cherokee. Among the few who spoke out against approving the treaty were Daniel Webster and Henry Clay, but the treaty passed by a single vote.

Most of the 17,000 Cherokee, however, refused to honor the treaty. Cherokee Chief John Ross wrote a letter to the United States government. The letter explained that the Cherokee who had signed the treaty did not represent the Cherokee people. The letter asked the government not to enforce the treaty. This plea, however, did not soften the resolve of President Jackson or the white settlers.

The Cherokee resisted the government's offer of western lands until 1838 when Jackson's successor, Martin Van Buren, began their removal. General John Wool resigned his command in protest. This delayed the action, but only temporarily. His replacement, **General Winfield Scott**, arrived at New Echota, the Cherokee capital, in May 1738. With 7,000 federal troops, General Scott 🅦 and the U.S. Army began the invasion of the Cherokee Nation.

Scott threatened to use force if the Cherokee did not leave. He told them he had positioned troops all around the country so that resistance and escape were hopeless. The Cherokee knew that fighting would lead to their destruction.

🅦 Writing Support

Persuasive Writing Have students compose in today's language a persuasive speech for General Scott to present to the Native Americans. Encourage students to reflect Scott's attitudes and add additional thoughts he might have expressed to encourage cooperation. **OL**

Removal of Native Americans 1820–1840

Critical Thinking Answer General Scott wanted the Native Americans to peacefully abandon thoughts of resistance and escape and to see the soldiers as their friends.

Analyzing Primary Sources Ask: What main point did Chief John Ross support in his letter to Congress? *(He told them that the delegation to Washington and the treaty were fraudulent.)* **OL**

Hands-On Chapter Project
Step 2

Creating a Political Cartoon About the Jackson Era

Step 2: Exploring an Issue or Event Students will explore the issue or event they selected in Step 1.

Essential Question: How did Andrew Jackson's presidency affect Native Americans?

Directions Ask: Why might it be difficult to create a cartoon about the Indian Removal Act today? *(Exaggerated drawings of Native Americans would be insulting.)* Advise students that using symbols can solve this type of problem. Tell students that though Jackson believed in expanding democracy to represent the common man, this respect for people did not extend to Native Americans. Tell students that know-

ing this background information can help create a more effective political cartoon. Have them explore the subject they selected in Step 1 to use this background information in their cartoons. **OL**

Gathering Background Allow class time for students to conduct research. Tell them that their cartoons should show an understanding of the event or issue in the Jackson era and express a clear opinion about it.

345

R Reading Strategy

Visualizing Suggest that students visualize the scene as you read the account aloud to them. **Ask:** Why is it called the Trail of Tears? *(It was a forced removal and many people died along the way.)* **OL**

People IN HISTORY

Critical Thinking Answers

1. Both leaders wanted to empower their people. Black Hawk wanted to retain tribal lands; Sequoyah developed a written language.

2. Sequoyah's actions had a better result because the Cherokee developed a written language. Black Hawk's people were killed and lost their land.

Reading Check **Answer:** to provide more good land for settlement and end conflicts between white settlers and Native Americans

Differentiated Instruction

People IN HISTORY

Black Hawk

Leader of a group of Sauk and Fox Native Americans

Black Hawk led 1,000 people, including old men, women, and children, back into Illinois in order to plant crops in their old tribal lands. He did not plan on an armed confrontation but believed that they still owned the land. *"We had never sold our country. We never received any annuities [payments] from our American father! And we are determined to hold on to our village!"*

Sequoyah

Developed the written alphabet for the Cherokee language

Sequoyah believed that Europeans had power because of their written language. He spent 12 years developing 86 symbols to represent all the syllables of the Cherokee language. A Cherokee poet, Alexander Lawrence Posey, wrote about the importance of Sequoyah's achievement: *"Thy name shall descend to every age. . . . The people's language cannot perish—nay."*

CRITICAL Thinking

1. **Analyzing** What did each Native American leader hope to accomplish?

2. **Evaluating** Which leader's actions had a better result? Why?

Filled with sadness and anger, the Cherokee leaders gave in, and the long march to the West began. One traveler from Main witnessed seeing hundreds of Cherokee marching by:

PRIMARY SOURCE

"[The] aged . . . nearly ready to drop into the grave, were traveling with heavy burdens attached to the back—on the frozen ground . . . with no covering for the feet."

—from *The Trail of Tears*

Around 2,000 Cherokee died in camps waiting for the move to begin. About another 2,000 died along the way from starvation, disease, and exposure to brutal weather. Their forced journey west became known to the Cherokee people as the Trail Where They Cried. Historians call it the **Trail of Tears.**

Reading Check **Explaining** What was the purpose of the Indian Removal Act?

Native American Resistance

Main Idea Some groups of Native Americans attempted to resist relocation. Most were taken from their lands by force.

History and You Think about how you might react if you were forced to do something that you thought was wrong. Would you attempt to resist? Read how some Native Americans responded to relocation.

In 1832 the Sauk chieftain, **Black Hawk,** led a group of Sauk and Fox people back to Illinois, their homeland. They wanted to recapture this area, which had been given up in a treaty. The Illinois state militia and federal troops responded with force, gathering nearly 4,500 soldiers. They chased the Fox and Sauk to the Mississippi River and slaughtered most of them as they tried to flee westward into present-day Iowa.

Leveled Activities

BL **Differentiated Instruction Activity, URB p. 27**

OL **Primary Source Reading Activity, URB p. 21**

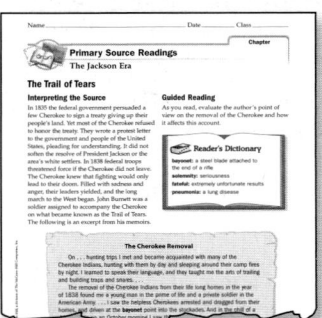

AL **American Literature Reading, URB p. 9**

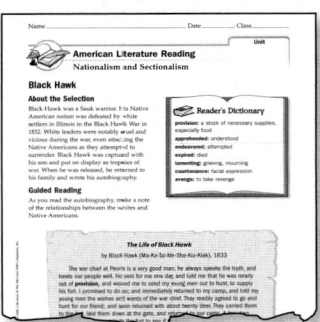

The Seminole people of Florida were the only Native Americans who successfully resisted their removal. Although they were pressured in the early 1830s to sign treaties giving up their land, the Seminole chief, **Osceola,** and some of his people refused to leave Florida. The Seminole decided to go to war against the United States instead.

In 1835 the Seminole joined forces with a group of African Americans who had run away to escape slavery. Together they attacked white settlements along the Florida coast. They used **guerrilla tactics,** making surprise attacks and then retreating back into the forests and swamps. In December 1835, the Seminole ambushed soldiers under the command of Major Francis Dade. Only a few of the 110 soldiers **survived,** or lived through, the attack. The Dade Massacre prompted a call for more troops to fight the Seminole.

By 1842, more than 1,500 Americans had died in the Seminole wars. The government gave up and allowed some Seminole to stay in Florida. Many, however, had died fighting. Many more were caught and forced to move west.

After 1842, only a few scattered groups of Native Americans lived east of the Mississippi. Most had been moved west. Native Americans had given up more than 100 million acres (40 million ha) of Eastern land to the federal government. In return, they received about $68 million and 32 million acres (13 million ha) in lands west of the Mississippi River. There they lived, organized by tribes, on reservations. Eventually, white settlements would extend into these areas as well.

The Five Civilized Tribes were relocated in the eastern half of present-day Oklahoma on lands claimed by several Plains groups, including the Osage, Comanche, and Kiowa. U.S. Army leaders got agreements from the Plains groups to let the Five Civilized Tribes live in peace. Settled in their new homes, the Five Civilized Tribes developed governments and built farms and schools. They also created a police force, the Lighthorsemen, to maintain safety in the area.

✔ Reading Check **Analyzing** What was the significance of the Dade Massacre?

C Critical Thinking

Identifying Central Issues Ask: What would you have done to resolve the conflict between the Seminole and the United States in Florida? *(Answers may include negotiate a treaty, offer to share territory, and so on.)* **OL**

✔ Reading Check **Answer:** The Dade Massacre showed that Native Americans could be tough opponents, so more troops were called to fight them. Eventually, some Seminole were allowed to stay in Florida.

Assess
. . . .

Study Central™ provides summaries, interactive games, and online graphic organizers to help students review content.

Close
. . . .

Identifying Cause and Effect As a class, discuss the actions taken by the federal government to remove Native Americans from lands in the East and how the Native Americans responded. **OL**

Section 2 Review

Section 2 Review

History ONLINE
Study Central™ To review this section, go to glencoe.com.

Vocabulary

1. Define each of the following terms and use the terms in a paragraph about conflicts over land: federal, relocate, guerrilla tactics, survive.

Main Ideas

2. Explaining Why did white settlers want the government to move Native Americans from the Southeast to the Great Plains?

3. Describing What were some of the features of the new Native American communities in the West?

Critical Thinking

4. Sequencing Identify the events that resulted in the eventual removal of the Cherokee from their land. Use a diagram like the one below.

5. Contrasting Faced with removal from their lands, how did the response of the Seminole differ from that of the Cherokee?

6. Persuasive Writing Write a letter to Andrew Jackson discussing whether the Native Americans should be allowed to stay on their homelands.

Answer the
7. Essential Question
How did Andrew Jackson's presidency affect Native Americans?

The Jackson Era **Chapter 11** **347**

Answers

1. The vocabulary words should be used in a paragraph that reflects their accurate definitions.

2. White settlers wanted more fertile land to settle and to end conflicts with Native Americans.

3. New Native American communities in the West developed governments and built farms and schools.

4. Most Cherokee refuse to sign treaty→ Chief John Ross writes letter to Congress requesting government not enforce treaty→Gen. Scott's forces invade Cherokee Nation

5. The Seminole successfully waged a guerrilla war while the Cherokee unsuccessfully negotiated treaties.

6. Letters, in appropriate format, should give specific reasons that support students' opinions.

7. Answers should include Jackson's belief that the federal government should deal with Native American matters; his intention to move all Native Americans to the Great Plains; the Indian Removal Act he pushed through Congress; his support for Georgia's efforts to remove the Cherokee; and the Treaty of Echota, which gave him the legal power to remove Native Americans.

Focus

Bellringer
Daily Test Practice Transparency 11–3

Reading Guide
Answers to Graphic:
Jackson vetoes bill→Orders withdrawal of government deposits from Bank→Refuses to sign new Bank charter→Bank of United States closes

Section Spotlight Video

Have students watch the Section Spotlight Video "Jackson and the Bank."

Resource Manager

Essential Question
How do economic issues affect the president and presidential elections?

Reading Guide

Content Vocabulary

veto (p. 349)   laissez-faire (p. 351)
depression (p. 350)

Academic Vocabulary

institution (p. 349)   symbol (p. 352)

Key People and Events

Henry Clay (p. 349)
Daniel Webster (p. 349)
Martin Van Buren (p. 349)
William Henry Harrison (p. 351)
John Tyler (p. 351)
James Polk (p. 352)

Reading Strategy

Taking Notes As you read, use a diagram like the one below to identify the actions by Andrew Jackson that put the Bank of the United States out of business.

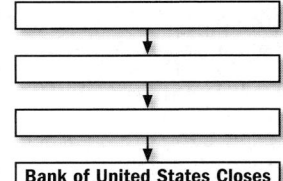

↓
↓
↓
Bank of United States Closes

ILLINOIS STANDARDS
The American Journey

14.C Understand the election process and responsibilities of citizens.

15.E Understand the impact of government policies and decisions on production and consumption in the economy.

18.B.3a Analyze how individuals and groups interact with and within institutions (e.g., educational, military).

Jackson and the Bank

American Diary

President Jackson rested at the Hermitage, his home outside of Nashville, Tennessee, when he wanted to escape his critics in Washington. Many accused him of considering himself a "king," especially when he wanted to dissolve the national bank. To explain his actions Jackson declared the president must protect, "the liberties and rights of the people and the integrity of the Constitution against the Senate, or the House of Representatives, or both together."

—*from* The American Presidency

Andrew Jackson's home, the Hermitage

R **Reading Strategies**	**C Critical Thinking**	**D Differentiated Instruction**	**W Writing Support**	**S Skill Practice**
Teacher Edition • Paraphrasing, p. 350 • Using Context Clues, p. 351 **Additional Resources** • Guid. Read., URB p. 41 • Content Vocab., URB p. 17 • Academic Vocab., URB p. 19 • Read. Ess., p. 115	**Teacher Edition** • Drawing Con., p. 349 **Additional Resources** • Quizzes and Tests, p. 103 • Econ. & Hist., URB p. 5 • Link. Past & Present, URB p. 33	**Teacher Edition** • Below Grade Level, p. 349 **Additional Resources** • Reteach, URB p. 37 • School-to-Home, URB p. 35	**Teacher Edition** • Descriptive Writing, p. 352 **Additional Resources** • Authentic Assess., p. 11	**Teacher Edition** • Creating a Time Line, p. 350 **Additional Resources** • Daily Test Pract. Transp. 11-3 • Soc. Stud. Skills, URB p. 25

War Against the Bank

Main Idea President Jackson forced the National Bank to close, and economic problems split the Democratic Party.

History and You Do you have a bank account? What would happen to your money if an economic crisis occurred? Read to find out about the economic problems of the 1830s.

For years, Jackson attacked the Bank of the United States as being an organization of wealthy Easterners that ordinary citizens could not control. The Bank of the United States was a powerful **institution,** or organization. It held the federal government's money and controlled much of the country's money supply. However, many western settlers, who borrowed money to run their farms, were unhappy with the Bank's strict lending policies. Although the Bank was chartered by Congress, it was run by private bankers rather than elected officials.

The Bank's president, Nicholas Biddle, represented everything Jackson disliked. Jackson prided himself on being a self-made man who started with nothing. Biddle, however, came from a wealthy Philadelphia family and had a good education, social status, and experience in financial matters.

The Bank as an Election Issue

In 1832 Jackson's opponents gave him the chance to take action against the Bank. Senators **Henry Clay** and **Daniel Webster,** friends of Biddle, planned to use the Bank to defeat Jackson in the 1832 presidential election. They persuaded Biddle to apply early for a new charter—a government permit to operate the Bank—even though the Bank's current charter did not expire until 1836.

Clay and Webster believed the Bank had popular support. They thought that an attempt by Jackson to veto the charter would lead to his defeat and allow Henry Clay to be elected president.

When the bill to renew the Bank's charter came to Jackson to sign, he was sick in bed. Jackson told his friend **Martin Van Buren,** "The bank . . . is trying to kill me. But I will kill it!" Jackson **vetoed,** or rejected, the bill. Jackson felt the Bank was unconstitutional despite the Supreme Court's decision to the contrary in *McCulloch* v. *Maryland* (1819). Jack-

Primary Source "King Andrew the First"

BORN TO COMMAND.

KING ANDREW THE FIRST.

◄ This political cartoon of Andrew Jackson shows him being a tyrant who was trampling on the rights of all Americans.

Critical Thinking

Interpreting What tells you the cartoonist is depicting Jackson as a dictatorial leader? What is Jackson seen walking on?

Teach

C Critical Thinking

Drawing Conclusions Ask: Why did Jackson disapprove of the Bank of the United States? *(He believed that it was a powerful organization of wealthy Easterners. It controlled the country's money supply, and it was run by private bankers rather than elected officials. Jackson also believed it was unconstitutional.)* **OL**

D Differentiated Instruction

Below Grade Level Tell students that two senators tried to use the Bank against Jackson. **Ask:** Which sentence shows that the senators thought most people wanted the Bank? *(Clay and Webster believed the Bank had popular support.)* Discuss the meaning of "popular support" with students. **BL**

Primary Source

Critical Thinking Answer

Jackson is dressed as a king. He is walking on the Constitution.

Differentiated Instruction

Leveled Activities

349

R Reading Strategy

Paraphrasing Have students paraphrase the quotation. *(Sample answer: When laws favor the rich and powerful, common people, who do not have these advantages, have the right to ask the government for help.)* **BL**

S Skill Practice

Creating a Time Line Have students create a time line showing the major events of the Bank, starting with the election of 1832 and ending with the creation of the federal treasury. **OL**

INTERPRETING
POLITICAL CARTOONS

Answers

1. They are supporters of the Bank. They are running from Jackson, the Bank's chief opponent, and toward the crumbling Bank. They appear scared of Jackson.

2. Average citizens support Jackson's action against the Bank.

Primary Sources
INTERPRETING
POLITICAL CARTOONS

President Andrew Jackson struck a fatal blow to the Bank of the United States when he ordered the withdrawal of all federal deposits from the Bank.

1. **Making Inferences** Are the members of Congress supporters or opponents of the Bank? How do you know?

2. **Interpreting** What meaning does the cartoonist convey with his portrayal of Major Jack Downing?

A. Bank of the United States B. members of Congress C. President Andrew Jackson D. Major Jack Downing, mythical character representing the average citizen

son angrily stated his beliefs about the Bank to Congress:

> **PRIMARY SOURCE**
>
> "When the laws . . . make the rich richer and the potent more powerful, the humble members of society . . . who [lack] . . . the means of securing like favors to themselves, have a right to complain of the injustice of their government."
>
> —Andrew Jackson, on vetoing the Bank's charter

S The Election of 1832

The Bank did play a large part in the election of 1832. The strategy for gaining support for Clay as president, however, backfired. Most people supported Jackson's veto, and Jackson was reelected. Jackson decided on a plan to "kill" the Bank ahead of the 1836 schedule. He ordered the withdrawal of all government deposits from the Bank and placed the funds in smaller state banks. In 1836 he refused to sign a new charter for the Bank, and it closed.

The Panic of 1837

When Jackson decided not to run for a third term in 1836, the Democrats chose Martin Van Buren, Jackson's friend and vice president. Van Buren faced opposition from the Whigs, a new party that included former National Republicans and other anti-Jackson forces. The Whigs nominated three different candidates, each of whom had a following in a different part of the nation. Jackson's popularity and his personal support helped Van Buren win easily.

Soon after the election, the country entered a severe economic **depression,** a period in which business and employment fall to a very low level. The depression began with the Panic of 1837. Land values dropped, investments declined, and banks failed. Thousands of businesses closed. Many people lost their jobs. In the South, cotton prices fell to record lows. Farmers plunged into debt and lost their land. In the cities, many people could not afford food or rent.

350 **Chapter 11** *The Jackson Era*

Differentiated Instruction

The National Bank

Objective: To learn about the National Bank and the Federal Reserve System

Focus: Have students tell what happened after the Panic of 1837.

Teach: Discuss the role of the Federal Reserve.

Assess: Have students summarize the main idea.

Close: Tell students to write a generalization about economic changes that took place in 1913.

Differentiated Instruction Strategies

BL Have students draw circle graphs for each entry on the first chart.

AL Ask students to create a chart with the categories "Before," "Then," and "Now" to identify the economic changes.

ELL Have students write the dated facts on cards and arrange them to create a time line.

Economics and History Activity, URB p. 5

President Van Buren believed in the principle of **laissez-faire**—that government should interfere as little as possible in the nation's economy. Van Buren persuaded Congress to establish an independent federal treasury in 1840. The government would no longer deposit its money in private banks as it had been doing during Jackson's presidency. Instead, the government would store its money in the federal treasury. The private banks had used government funds to back their banknotes. The new treasury system would keep banks from using government funds in this way and help prevent further bank crises.

Van Buren and his supporters hailed the new law as a "second declaration of independence." Members of Van Buren's own Democratic Party, however, along with the Whigs, criticized the act. The split in the Democratic Party gave the Whigs a chance to win the presidency in 1840.

Reading Check Explaining What was the purpose of the new treasury system?

The Whigs Take Power

R **Main Idea** After Harrison's death, Tyler took the presidency in a direction that went against the Whigs' goals, and the Whigs lost power.

History and You Do you think political ads portray candidates as they really are? Read to find out how the Whigs came to power.

. . . .

The Democrats had been in control of the presidency for 12 years. With the country still in the depths of depression, though, the Whigs thought they had a chance to win the election in 1840.

The Log Cabin Campaign

The Whigs nominated **William Henry Harrison,** a hero of the War of 1812, to run against President Van Buren. **John Tyler,** a planter from Virginia, was Harrison's running mate. Because Harrison had gained national fame by defeating Tecumseh's followers in the Battle of Tippecanoe, the Whigs' campaign slogan was "Tippecanoe and Tyler Too."

R **Reading Strategy**

Using Context Clues Ask: Why is "hands off" a good restatement of *laissez-faire*? (The term refers to a government policy of not interfering with the economy, or keeping its "hands" off it.) **BL**

Primary Source

Critical Thinking Answer

It was intended as an insult to Harrison but instead depicted him as a man of the people, which helped him win the election.

Skills Practice Ask: What did supporters want people to remember when they heard "Tippecanoe and Tyler, Too"? (Harrison's famous victory at Tippecanoe and of his running mate Tyler, a planter from Virginia) **OL**

Primary Source | Harrison's Log Cabin Campaign

A Baltimore journalist made fun of William Henry Harrison, writing, "Give him a barrel of hard cider, and . . . he will sit the remainder of his days in his log cabin by the side of the fire and study moral philosophy!" The Whigs turned the insult to their advantage by creating the log cabin campaign, which depicted Harrison as a man of the people.

Stunts and Songs Harrison supporters from Kentucky rolled a large paper ball from Kentucky to Baltimore in support of their candidate (below). This event inspired a campaign jingle. ▶

What has caused this great commotion, motion
Our country through?
It is the ball rolling on
For Tippecanoe and Tyler too
And with them we'll beat the little
Van, Van, Van
Van is a used-up man!

Campaign Practices The Whigs used the symbol of the log cabin to present Harrison as a simple farmer. The party raised money to support their candidate by selling memorabilia, such as this china pitcher (above left).

Critical Thinking

Summarizing How did the log cabin insult backfire?

Hands-On Chapter Project
Step 3

Creating a Political Cartoon About the Jackson Era

Step 3: Drawing a Political Cartoon Students will draw the political cartoon they selected in Step 1.

Essential Question: How do economic issues affect the president and presidential elections?

Directions Review the cartoon on the previous page with the class. Ask students to predict how their political cartoons could have affected people's opinions of the issues or events.

Drawing Encourage students to incorporate exaggeration and symbols as they develop their cartoons. Provide a supply of sketching paper for students to use. Advise students that they will display their work in Step 4.

(Chapter Project continued on the Visual Summary page)

W Writing Support

Descriptive Writing Have students write a journalist's report of Harrison's inauguration. Encourage them to include descriptions of those who might have attended, how they were dressed, and Harrison's appearance. **OL**

✔ **Reading Check** **Answer:** The Whigs lost power because they could not agree on their party's goals and voted according to sectional ties.

Assess

History ONLINE

Study Central™ provides summaries, interactive games, and online graphic organizers to help students review content.

Close

Discussing As a class, describe how economic issues impacted the 1840 presidential election. **OL**

Section 3 Review

To win the election, Harrison had to gain the support of the laborers and farmers who had voted for Jackson. The Whigs adopted a log cabin as their **symbol,** or an object that represents something else. Political cartoons in newspapers showed Harrison, a wealthy man from Virginia, in front of a log cabin. The Whigs wanted to show that their candidate was a "man of the people."

W The Whigs also ridiculed Van Buren as "King Martin," a wealthy snob who had spent the people's money on fancy furniture for the White House. The log cabin campaign seemed to work, and Harrison went on to defeat Van Buren by a wide margin. William Henry Harrison became the first Whig president.

Inauguration day, 1841, was bitterly cold. Harrison, however, insisted on delivering his speech without a hat or coat. He died of pneumonia 32 days later. Harrison served the shortest term of any American president. John Tyler of Virginia became the first vice president to gain the presidency because the elected president died in office.

Tyler's Presidency

Although Tyler had been elected vice president as a Whig, he had once been a Democrat. Whig party leaders had placed Tyler on the ticket with Harrison mainly to attract Southern voters. As president, Tyler vetoed several bills sponsored by Whigs in Congress, including a bill to recharter the Bank of the United States. His lack of party loyalty outraged many Whigs. Most of Tyler's cabinet resigned. Whig leaders in Congress expelled Tyler from the party.

It seemed that the Whigs could not agree on their party's goals. Increasingly, Whigs voted according to sectional ties—North, South, and West—not party ties. This division may explain why the Whig candidate, Henry Clay, lost the election of 1844 to Democratic candidate **James Polk.** After only four years, the Whigs were out of power again.

✔ **Reading Check** **Describing** How did the Whigs lose power in the election of 1844?

Section 3 Review

History ONLINE
Study Central™ To review this section, go to glencoe.com.

Vocabulary

1. Define each of the following terms and use each word in a sentence: institution, veto, depression, laissez-faire, symbol.

Main Ideas

2. Explaining Why did President Van Buren do little to solve the nation's economic problems?

3. Describing How did the log cabin campaign help Harrison win the election?

Critical Thinking

4. Interpreting Reread Andrew Jackson's quote about the

National Bank. Based on his words, why did Jackson want to close the Bank of the United States?

5. Diagramming Use a diagram like the one below to describe Henry Clay's strategy to win the 1832 election. Explain the actual result.

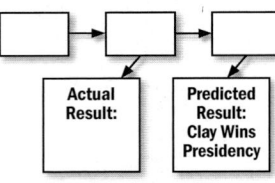

| Actual Result: | Predicted Result: Clay Wins Presidency |

6. Creative Writing Write a "catchy" campaign slogan for either Andrew Jackson or Henry Clay that would help the candidate win the 1832 presidential election.

Answer the Essential Question

7. How do economic issues affect the president and presidential elections?

Answers

1. Sentences should use vocabulary terms correctly according to their definitions in the section and Glossary.

2. Van Buren believed in laissez-faire, the idea that the government should not interfere in the nation's economy.

3. It helped Harrison defeat Van Buren by building up his image as a "man of the people."

4. Jackson felt the Bank favored the rich and powerful but did not serve the needs of the common man, and it was unconstitutional.

5. Biddle renews Bank's charter early→Jackson vetoes bill→*Actual Result:* Jackson reelected; *Predicted Result:* People object to veto→Clay wins presidency; students should emphasize that the plan backfired because most people supported Jackson's veto.

6. Slogans will vary but should accurately reflect section content.

7. Student responses should reflect economic issues such as the closing of the Bank, the Panic of 1837, and the economic depression that followed.

Visual Summary

Main Idea	Supporting Details
The Election of 1828 transformed American political campaigns.	• Mudslinging, election slogans, rallies, buttons, and campaign events were first practiced in 1828.
President Andrew Jackson made changes to the American political system.	• Jackson established the spoils system (replacing government employees with supporters of the winning candidate). • His supporters created nominating conventions to select presidential candidates.
President Jackson supported the demands of western settlers for Native American land.	• In 1830 Jackson pushed the Indian Removal Act through Congress. This law forced Native Americans to move west.
Some Native American groups resisted relocation.	• The Cherokee Nation sued to keep its land. However, after a few Cherokee signed a treaty in 1835, thousands were forced to move west on the "Trail of Tears." • The Seminole resisted removal by using guerrilla tactics to attack white settlements on the Florida coast.
President Jackson opposed the Bank of the United States.	• Jackson believed the national bank was undemocratic and unconstitutional. He vetoed a bill extending the bank's charter, eventually forcing it to close.

STUDY TO GO Study anywhere, anytime! Download quizzes and flash cards to your PDA from glencoe.com.

The Jackson Era **Chapter 11** 353

Visual Summary

Making Connections Ask: How did the media of the 1800s influence the way people viewed political candidates? *(Students' responses should reflect an awareness of techniques used in the presidential campaigns of the mid-1800s.)* **Ask:** What influence does today's media have on people's perceptions about candidates? *(Students should mention that today's media allows people to judge candidates themselves and allows candidates to defend their reputations against slander; the media, however, can expose traits that people may consider unacceptable in a leader.)* **OL**

Making Inferences Ask: What can you infer about Andrew Jackson's feelings about Native Americans based on his actions and statements presented in this chapter? Organize students into small groups. Have all groups review the chapter while members take notes to help them each form an inference. Students should write a sentence that states their inferences. When students are ready, discuss the inferences that students made. **OL**

Hands-On Chapter Project
Step 4: Wrap-Up

Creating a Political Cartoon About the Jackson Era

Step 4: Learning From the Cartoons Students will synthesize what they have learned in steps 1 through 3.

Directions Write all three Essential Questions on the board. Discuss the students' political cartoons. Review their symbols to be sure that all students understand their meanings.

Wrapping Up Ask: How did the political cartoons answer each of the Essential Questions? Invite students to explain why a classmate's political cartoon expresses an issue or event particularly well. **OL**

Answers and Analyses

Reviewing Main Ideas

1. C Remind students that Jackson's party favored states' rights and mistrusted a strong central government. Choice A may confuse them because it refers to a strong central government, but in reading the answer more closely, students should select choice C. **14.F.3a**

2. A Chief Justice Marshall ruled that Georgia had no right to interfere with the Cherokee. He supported the federal government's power in Cherokee matters. The correct answer is A. **18.B.3a**

3. D Students should immediately eliminate choices A and C because those who ran the Bank were not elected officials, and the Bank did not have relationships with foreign nations. Students should also eliminate choice B because the Bank did not make loans to all citizens but favored the wealthy Easterners who controlled it. Students should then choose choice D. **15.E**

4. D Remind students that Harrison's election was helped by the Log Cabin Campaign. The "corrupt bargain" was between Clay and Adams, eliminating choice A. The Democrats were actually divided over Van Buren's new law, not the man himself, so choice B is incorrect. Answer C can be eliminated as it was Democrats who led the nation through the Panic of 1837. Students should then be able to make choice D. **14.C**

Short-Answer Question

5. Students should indicate that Smith's attitude toward the crowd was tolerant, as she realized that Jackson represented not only the wealthy, but all people. Further details should reflect an understanding of Jackson's ideals. **16.A.3b**

STANDARDIZED TEST PRACTICE

TEST-TAKING TIP

Read an extended-response question carefully. Are you being asked to explain something or to demonstrate what you know about a subject? Be sure to understand what you are being asked.

Reviewing Main Ideas

Directions: Choose the best answers for each of the following questions.

1. In the 1828 presidential election, Andrew Jackson's Democratic-Republican Party

  A wanted a strong central government.

  B supported setting up a national bank.

  C favored states' rights.

  D was dominated by merchants and farmers.

2. In *Worcester* v. *Georgia* (1832), Chief Justice John Marshall ruled that

  A Georgia had no right to interfere with the Cherokee.

  B the "spoils system" was unconstitutional.

  C the federal government had no authority over Native Americans.

  D states had to support a national bank.

3. Jackson attacked the Bank of the United States because

  A it was being run by corrupt elected officials.

  B it provided loans to all citizens.

  C it financed foreign business deals that put Americans out of work.

  D it was controlled by wealthy Easterners.

4. One reason the Whigs won the presidential election of 1840 was that

  A they made a "corrupt bargain" with Henry Clay to steal the presidency.

  B the Democrats split over Van Buren.

  C they ended the Panic of 1837.

  D they gained support from laborers and farmers rather than the wealthy elite.

Short-Answer Question

Directions: Base your answer to question 5 on the excerpt below and on your knowledge of social studies.

> Carriages, wagons and carts all pursuing him [Jackson] to the President's house. . . . Ladies fainted, men were seen with bloody noses and such a scene of confusion took place as is impossible to describe. . . . This concourse [event] had not been anticipated and therefore not provided against. Ladies and gentlemen, only had been expected at this Levee [reception], not the people en masse [as a whole]. But it was the People's day, and the People's President and the People would rule.
>
> —a letter by Margaret Bayard Smith describing Jackson's inauguration in 1829

5. What is Smith's attitude toward Jackson and his enthusiastic supporters? Explain.

Review the Essential Questions

6. Essay Andrew Jackson is often considered by historians to be one of the 10 greatest presidents in American history. Write an essay in which you agree or disagree with this position.

To help you write your essay, review your answers to the Essential Questions in the section reviews and the chapter Foldables Study Organizer. Your essay should include:

- Jackson's campaign and the election of 1828;
- Jacksonian policies regarding suffrage, the spoils system, tariffs, and states' rights;
- the removal of Native Americans; and
- Jackson's war against the Bank.

GO ON →

Review the Essential Questions

6. Students' essays should include information about Jackson's policies and decisions. Students may argue that Jackson is considered a great president because he was decisive and had strong opinions about democracy. **14.D.3**

History ONLINE
For additional test practice, use **Self-Check Quizzes**—Chapter 11 at glencoe.com.

Chapter 11 Assessment

Document-Based Questions

Directions: Analyze the documents and answer the short-answer questions that follow.

Document 1

In the 1840 election campaign, the Whigs marched in parades, carrying miniature log cabins on poles.

7. Based on the photo, explain why Harrison's supporters made the log cabin their symbol.

8. What political symbols do political parties use today?

Document 2

Massachusetts Senator Daniel Webster made these comments in 1830 regarding the nullification crisis.

> If anything be found in the national constitution . . . which ought not to be in it, the people know how to get rid of it. If any construction . . . [is] unacceptable to them so as to become practically a part of the constitution, they will amend it.

Source: Daniel Webster, *The Writings and Speeches of Daniel Webster*

9. Based on the excerpt, what did Webster think was a better solution than nullification if the people disapproved of a law?

Document 3

This is a selection from William Coodey's account of the Cherokee removal to Indian Territory.

> I almost fancied a voice of divine indignation for the wrongs of my poor and unhappy countrymen, driven by brutal power from all they loved and cherished in the land of their fathers, to gratify the cravings of [greed].

Source: David Colbert, *Eyewitness to America*

10. Based on the document, does Coodey approve of the removal of the Cherokee?

11. What reasons does Coodey give for their removal?

Document 4

Frederick Marryat recorded these views about life in New York City during the Panic of 1837.

> Go to the theaters and places of public amusement, and, instead of change, you receive an IOU from the treasury.—It is the same every where. . . . The barbers give you tickets, good for so many shaves; and were there beggars in the streets, I presume they would give you tickets in change, good for so much philanthropy.

Source: Captain Frederick Marryat, *Diary in America*

12. Based on the excerpt, describe one effect the Panic of 1837 had on the economy.

13. **Expository Writing** Using the information from the four documents and your knowledge of social studies, write an essay in which you:
   - discuss the economics and social climate of the United States during the Jackson era; and
   - describe the Jackson presidency and any changes it brought to American politics.

Need Extra Help?												
If you missed questions. . .	1	2	3	4	5	6	7	8	9	10	11	12	13
Go to page. . .	338	344	349	351	336-340	336-350	351-352	336-350	341	350-351	343-347	350-351	336-350

Document-Based Questions

7. Student explanations should include details from the photo that explain the role of the Log Cabin Campaign, and how it helped Harrison gain the support of laborers and farmers who had voted for Jackson. **16.A.3a**

8. Students may list the elephant and the donkey, which represent the Republican and Democratic Parties. **14.D.3**

9. Tell students that by carefully paraphrasing this passage, it will be easier to understand. Webster believed that the United States Constitution already included a way to change federal law: the amendment process. He believed that nullification was not necessary. **16.B.3c (US)**

10. Coodey does not support their removal. **16.A.3b**

11. Explain to students that "divine indignation" in this excerpt means that Coodey believes God would not approve of the removal of the Cherokee. Students should mention that he calls the Cherokee "my poor and unhappy countrymen, " showing that he sympathizes with them. He also says that the reason this is being done is to satisfy greed. **18.B.3a**

12. Responses should describe the use of paper IOUs from the treasury instead of change from a cash payment. The Panic of 1937 caused banks to fail, which resulted in decreasing the exchange of actual money. **15.E**

13. Students should use the four documents and their knowledge from this chapter to write essays. Student essays should discuss the economics and social climate of the United States during the Jackson Era, a description of the Jackson presidency, and the changes it brought to American politics. **16.A.3a**

History ONLINE
Have students visit the Web site at glencoe.com to review Chapter 11 and take the Self-Check Quiz.

Need Extra Help?

Have students refer to the pages listed if they miss any of the questions.

Key to Ability Levels

BL Below level   AL Above level
OL On level   ELL English Language Learners

Key to Teaching Resources

Print Material   DVD
CD-ROM   Transparency

BL	OL	AL	ELL		Resources	Chapter Opener	Section 1	Section 2	Section 3	Section 4	Chapter Assess
					FOCUS						
BL	OL	AL	ELL	🖨	**Daily Test Practice Transparencies**		12–1	12–2	12–3	12–4	
					TEACH						
	OL	AL		📁	**Geography and History Activity, URB**			p. 59			
BL	OL		ELL	📁	**Time Line Skills Activity, URB**			p. 62			
BL	OL	AL	ELL	📁	**Writing Skills Activity, URB**		p. 51				
BL	OL	AL	ELL	📁	**Content Vocabulary Activity, URB**		p. 45	p. 45	p. 45	p. 45	
BL			ELL	📁	**Academic Vocabulary Activity, URB**		p. 47	p. 47	p. 47	p. 47	
BL			ELL	📁	**Reading Skills Activity, URB**					p. 7	
BL			ELL	📁	**Social Studies Skills Activity, URB**				p. 53		
BL	OL	AL	ELL	📁	**Differentiated Instruction Activity, URB**					p. 55	
BL	OL	AL	ELL	📁	**Critical Thinking Skills Activity, URB**		p. 57				
BL	OL	AL	ELL	📁	**Linking Past and Present Activity, URB**		p. 61				
	OL	AL		📁	**Primary Source Readings, URB**					p. 49	
BL	OL	AL	ELL	📁	**School-to-Home Connection Activity, URB**		p. 63	p. 63	p. 63	p. 63	
BL	OL		ELL	📁	**Guided Reading Activity, URB***		p. 67	p. 68	p. 69	p. 70	
BL	OL		ELL	📁	**Reading Essentials and Note-Taking Guide***		p. 118	p. 121	p. 124	p. 127	
BL	OL	AL	ELL	🖨	**Lesson Transparencies**		12A	12B		12C	
	OL			📁	**American Biographies**					p. 24	
BL	OL	AL	ELL	📁	**Outline Map Resource Book**	pp. 23, 31					

Note: Please refer to the *Unit Resource Book: Nationalism and Sectionalism* for this chapter's URB materials.

* Also available in Spanish

Levels					Resources	Chapter Opener	Section 1	Section 2	Section 3	Section 4	Chapter Assess
BL	OL	AL	ELL								
TEACH *(continued)*											
BL	OL	AL	ELL	📁	**NGS US Desk Map**		✓	✓	✓	✓	
BL	OL	AL	ELL	📁	**American Literature Library**		✓	✓	✓	✓	
BL	OL	AL	ELL	📁	**Writer's Guidebook**		✓	✓	✓	✓	
	OL	AL		💿	**American History Primary Source Document Library CD-ROM**		✓	✓	✓	✓	✓
BL	OL	AL	ELL	💿	**American Music: Hits Through History**	✓	✓	✓	✓	✓	
BL	OL	AL	ELL	💿	**StudentWorks™ Plus CD**	✓	✓	✓	✓	✓	✓
BL	OL	AL	ELL	📹	**Section Spotlight Videos**		✓	✓	✓	✓	
BL	OL	AL	ELL	🖨	**Writing Process Transparencies**		✓	✓	✓	✓	✓
BL	OL	AL	ELL	💿	**Presentation Plus! With MindJogger CheckPoint CD**	✓	✓	✓	✓	✓	✓
ASSESS											
BL	OL	AL	ELL	📁	**Quizzes and Tests**		p. 111	p. 112	p. 113	p. 114	pp. 115, 117, 119
BL	OL	AL	ELL	📁	**Authentic Assessment With Rubrics**		p. 12				
BL	OL	AL	ELL	📁	**Standardized Test Practice**						p. 23
BL	OL	AL	ELL	💿	*ExamView® Assessment Suite CD-ROM*		12–1	12–2	12–3	12–4	Ch. 12
CLOSE											
BL			ELL	📁	**Reteaching Activity, URB***		p. 65	p. 65	p. 65	p. 65	p. 65
BL	OL		ELL	📁	**Reading and Study Skills Foldables Activity**	p. 72	p. 72	p. 72	p. 72	p. 72	p. 72
BL	OL	AL	ELL	📁	*The American Journey* in Graphic Novel					p. 69	
BL			ELL	📁	**Reading Strategies and Activities for the Social Studies Classroom**		✓	✓	✓	✓	
BL	OL	AL	ELL	🖨	**Graphic Organizer Transparencies & Strategies**		✓	✓	✓	✓	

TeacherWorks *Plus*
All-In-One Planner and Resource Center

- Interactive Lesson Planner
- Interactive Teacher Edition
- Fully editable blackline masters
- Section Spotlight Videos Launch
- Differentiated Lesson Plans
- Printable reports of daily assignments
- Standards Tracking System

Professional Development Resources

- Strategies for Success
- Building Academic Vocabulary
- Success With English Learners DVD
- Differentiated Instruction Strategies DVD
- Teaching Literacy Strategies in Social Studies DVD
- Assessment DVD
- Standards-Based Instruction DVD

Using the Primary Source Document Library Database

Searching by Keyword, Author, or Title

Technology Product

Glencoe's *American History Primary Source Document Library* CD-ROM has more than 200 primary source documents.

Objectives

The *American History Primary Source Document Library* allows you to

- perform a search based on key words, author, or titles of documents;
- read or listen to documents;
- utilize **Teaching Strategies, Questions/Answers,** and **Blackline Masters** resources in conjunction with the primary source document to maximize student learning.

Steps

- After launching the **Primary Source Document Library CD-ROM,** choose the **Search** button.
- Click on the Search icon and enter key words related to a subject, author, or title.
- Make a selection from the list of documents in the "Results" window.
- Review the **Document Overview** and **Guided Reading Questions** located at the top of each document.
- Click on the **User's Guide** and **Teaching Strategies** link. Select **To the Teacher** and **Teaching Strategies** for teaching suggestions using the primary source documents.
- Select **Questions/Activities** and **Blackline Masters** for worksheets and organizers.

History ONLINE at glencoe.com

	Student	Teacher	Parent
Media Center			
• Student Edition Audio	●		
• Spanish Summaries	●		
• Section Spotlight Videos	●	●	
Social Studies Online Learning Center			
Classroom Tools			
• Multi-Language Glossaries	●	●	●
• Teaching Today		●	
• TIME Current Events	●	●	●
• Beyond the Textbook	●	●	
The American Journey **Online Learning Center**			
• Study-to-Go™	●	●	●
• Study Central™	●	●	●
• Chapter Overview	●	●	
• Concepts in Motion	●	●	
• ePuzzles and Games	●	●	
• Literature Connections	●	●	
• Online Student Edition	●	●	●
• Self-Check Quizzes	●	●	●
• Student Web Activities	●	●	
• Vocabulary eFlashcards	●	●	
• Web Activity Lesson Plans	●	●	●
• Vocabulary PuzzleMaker	●	●	●

Additional Resources

READING SUPPORT FROM JAMESTOWN EDUCATION

- **Timed Readings Plus in Social Studies** helps students increase their reading rate and fluency while maintaining comprehension. The 400-word passages are similar to those found on state and national assessments.

- **Reading in the Content Area: Social Studies** concentrates on six essential reading skills that help students better comprehend what they read. The book includes 75 high-interest nonfiction passages written at increasing levels of difficulty.

- **Reading Social Studies** includes strategic reading instruction and vocabulary support in Social Studies content for ELLs and native speakers of English.

- **Content Vocabulary Workout** (Grades 6–8) accelerates reading comprehension through focused vocabulary development. Social Studies content vocabulary comes from the glossaries of Glencoe's Middle School Social Studies texts.

www.jamestowneducation.com

NATIONAL GEOGRAPHIC

Index to National Geographic Magazine:

The following articles relate to this chapter:

- **"Once Upon a Time in Laredo,"** Mimi Swartz, November 2006.
- **"The Way West,"** John G. Mitchell, September 2000.

National Geographic Society Products

To order the following, call National Geographic at 1-800-368-2728:

National Geographic Atlas of the World (Book)

Access National Geographic's new dynamic MapMachine Web site and other geography resources at:

www.nationalgeographic.com

www.nationalgeographic.com/mapmachine

Reading List Generator CD-ROM — GLENCOE BOOKLINK 3

Use this database to search more than 30,000 titles to create a customized reading list for your students.

- Reading lists can be organized by students' reading level, author, genre, theme, or area of interest.
- The database provides Degrees of Reading Power™ (DRP) and Lexile™ readability scores for all selections.
- A brief summary of each selection is included.

Leveled reading suggestions for this chapter:

For students at a Grade 6 reading level:
- *Lost in Death Valley: The True Story of Four Families in California's Gold Rush,* Connie Goldsmith

For students at a Grade 7 reading level:
- *Hurry Freedom: African Americans in Gold Rush California,* Jerry Stanley
- *The Mexican War: "Mr. Polk's War,"* Charles W. Carey

For students at a Grade 8 reading level:
- *Westward Expansion,* Michael V. Uschan
- *Explorers, Missionaries, and Trappers: Trailblazers of the West,* Kieran Doherty

For students at a Grade 9 reading level:
- *The California Gold Rush,* Tom Ito

For students at a Grade 10 reading level:
- *Secretaries of State: Making Foreign Policy,* Jason Richie

The following videotape programs are available from Glencoe as supplements to the chapter:

- **The Battle of the Alamo** (ISBN 1-56-501357-3)
- **California and the Dream Seekers** (ISBN 0-76-700555-4)

To order, call Glencoe at 1-800-334-7344. To find classroom resources to accompany many of these videos, check the following home pages:

A&E Television: www.aetv.com

The History Channel: www.history.com

Chapter Objectives

After studying this chapter, students will be able to:

- Discuss how the belief in Manifest Destiny influenced western settlement.
- Explain why Texas fought for independence from Mexico.
- Describe how Mexican lands in the West became part of the United States.
- Summarize the effects of the Gold Rush on California history.

Motivating Activity

Predicting Explain to students that chapter-opening visuals often depict an overall theme of a chapter. Tell students to study the image on this page and identify objects they see. *(cattle, covered wagon, mountainous terrain)* **Ask:** Where have you seen a covered wagon? *(Answers may include on television shows depicting pioneers and westward expansion, at museums, and in books.)* Who appear to be traveling in the wagons? *(families)* What clues indicate the U.S. region in the photo? *(The terrain in the background is mountainous, with a steep decline to flatlands, indicative of western regions of the United States.)* Based on this image, what information might you expect to find in this chapter? *(Answers may include information about western settlement.)* **OL**

Previewing the Essential Questions

As you begin teaching each section, use these questions and activities to help students focus on the Essential Questions.

Chapter ★ 12 Manifest Destiny 1818–1853

Traveling along the Oregon Trail

PRESIDENTS
- JAMES MADISON 1809–1817
- JAMES MONROE 1817–1825
- JOHN Q. ADAMS 1825–1829
- ANDREW JACKSON 1829–1837

U.S. Events
World Events

★ **1809** Elizabeth Ann Seton founds Sisters of Charity

1810

★ **1821** Mexico declares independence from Spain

1824 Russia surrenders land south of Alaska

★ **1824** U.S. House elects John Q. Adams president

1820

★ **1826** First Burmese War ends

1830

★ **1830** France occupies Algeria

356   Chapter 12

Section ★ 1

The Oregon Country Ask: What motivates people to move to a new country, state, or city? *(Answers may include work opportunities, better quality of life, and access to resources such as natural resources, education, and medical care.)* Point out to students that in Section 1 they will learn how the beliefs of Americans influenced their movement to western regions. **OL**

Section ★ 2

Independence for Texas Ask: What conditions might justify a fight for independence? *(Answers may include tyranny, corruption, and abuse by a country's government.)* Explain to students that Section 2 describes the events that led to Texas's independence from Mexico. **OL**

Section 1: The Oregon Country
Essential Question How did the belief in Manifest Destiny influence western settlement?

Section 2: Independence for Texas
Essential Question Why did Texans fight for their independence from Mexico?

Section 3: War With Mexico
Essential Question How did Mexican lands in the West become part of the United States?

Section 4: California and Utah
Essential Question What factors affected the settlement of California and Utah in the West?

History ONLINE
Chapter Overview Visit glencoe.com and click on **Chapter 12—Chapter Overviews** to preview chapter information.

FOLDABLES
Study Organizer

Organizing Information Make this Foldable to help organize what you learn about the expansion of the United States.

Step 1 Fold four sheets of paper in half from top to bottom. Cut each paper in half along the folds.

Step 2 Fold each piece of paper in half from top to bottom again.

Step 3 On each folded paper, make a cut 1 inch from the side on the top flap.

Step 4 Place the folded papers one on top of the other, and staple the sections together.

Manifest Destiny

Reading and Writing As you read, note dates and events about new territories in Oregon, Texas, New Mexico, California, and Utah.

Introducing Chapter 12

Time Line Activity

Have students review the time line. Ask them to read the events in the U.S. time line. **Ask:** What land exchanges took place during the 1800s? *(Russia surrendered land south of Alaska, and the United States annexed Texas.)* Have students refer to the "World" section of the time line to identify land exchanges that took place globally. *(Mexico declared independence from Spain, and Great Britain gained Hong Kong.)*

FOLDABLES
Study Organizer **Dinah Zike's Foldables**

Purpose This Foldable helps students organize visual information about the expansion of the United States. The completed Foldable will help them prepare for assessment.

More Foldables activities for this chapter can be found in *Dinah Zike's Reading and Study Skills Foldables.*

History ONLINE
Introduce students to chapter content and key terms by having them access the **Chapter Overview** at glencoe.com.

Numerous Engravings....12½ cts.
Mexican Treacheries and Cruelties.
INCIDENTS AND SUFFERINGS
IN THE
MEXICAN WAR;
WITH
Accounts of Hardships endured; Treacheries of the Mexicans; Battles Fought, and Success of American Arms;
The "Heroine of Fort Brown."
Also, an Account of Valiant Soldiers Fallen,
AND THE PARTICULARS OF THE
Death and Funeral Services in honor of
Capt. George Lincoln, of **Worcester.**
BY A VOLUNTEER RETURNED FROM THE WAR.
BOSTON AND NEW YORK:
1847.

MARTIN VAN BUREN 1837–1841

1839 Mutiny occurs on slave ship *Amistad*

WILLIAM HENRY HARRISON 1841

JOHN TYLER 1841–1845

★ **1845** U.S. annexes Texas

★ **1846** Congress declares war on Mexico

JAMES POLK 1845–1849

ZACHARY TAYLOR 1849–1850

1840

1850

★ **1839** Opium War begins between Britain and China

◄ A man pulls Chinese women in a rickshaw

★ **1842** Treaty of Nanking gives Hong Kong to Great Britain

★ **1846** Neptune discovered

Section 3

War With Mexico Refer students to a current U.S. map. **Ask:** What states might have been disputed territory in a war with Mexico? *(Answers may include Arizona, New Mexico, and Texas.)* Tell students that Section 3 will describe the conflict between the United States and Mexico as the United States acquired more territory. **OL**

Section 4

California and Utah Ask: How might the discovery of natural resources affect a country's population? *(Answers may include that large numbers of people might move to areas close to the natural resources and that the financial gain from the natural resources could lure others to specific areas.)* Tell students that Section 4 explains the history of California after the discovery of gold. **OL**

Focus

Bellringer

Daily Test Practice Transparency 12–1

Reading Guide

Answers to Graphic:

1819: United States and Spain negotiate the Adams-Onís Treaty; **1825:** United States and Britain extend joint occupation of Oregon; **1836:** First U.S. settlers arrive in Oregon; **1846:** United States and Britain compromise on Oregon border

Section Spotlight Video

Have students watch the Section Spotlight Video "The Oregon Country" to learn more about western settlement.

Essential Question

How did the belief in Manifest Destiny influence western settlement?

Reading Guide

Content Vocabulary

joint occupation (p. 359)

mountain man (p. 360)

rendezvous (p. 360)

emigrant (p. 362)

prairie schooner (p. 362)

Manifest Destiny (p. 363)

Academic Vocabulary

plus (p. 359)   access (p. 359)

Key People and Events

Adams-Onís Treaty (p. 359)

Oregon Trail (p. 362)

Henry Clay (p. 363)

Reading Strategy

Taking Notes As you read, list key events in a time line like the one below.

1819   1825   1836   1846

ILLINOIS STANDARDS
The American Journey

15.D Understand trade as an exchange of goods or services.

16.A.3b Make inferences about historical events and eras using historical maps and other historical sources.

17.C.3a Explain how human activity is affected by geographic factors.

17.D.3a Explain how and why spatial patterns of settlement change over time.

American Diary

Families left everything familiar behind when they made the often uncomfortable and dangerous trip to the Western frontier. Martha Gay was a 13-year-old who, in 1851, left Springfield, Missouri, in a covered wagon. She later wrote about the experience of leaving loved ones and friends behind: "Farewell sermons were preached and prayers offered for our safety. . . . All places of business and the schools were closed . . . and everybody came to say goodbye to us."

—from One Woman's West

A mountain man gives advice to pioneers.

Resource Manager

R Reading Strategies	**C** Critical Thinking	**D** Differentiated Instruction	**W** Writing Support	**S** Skill Practice
Teacher Edition • Reading Maps, p. 359 • Outlining, p. 360 • Questioning, p. 361 • Deter. Import., p. 363 **Additional Resources** • Guid. Read., URB p. 67 • Content Vocab., URB p. 45 • Acad. Vocab., URB p. 47	**Teacher Edition** • Analyz. Infor., p. 360 • Deter. Cause and Effect, p. 361 • Making Inferences, p. 362 **Additional Resources** • Quizzes and Tests, p. 111 • Crit. Think., URB p. 57	**Teacher Edition** • ELL, p. 359 **Additional Resources** • School-to-Home, URB p. 63 • Reteaching Act., URB p. 65	**Teacher Edition** • Narrative Writing, p. 362 **Additional Resources** • Writ. Skills, URB p. 51	**Teacher Edition** • Using Geo. Skills, p. 359 • Using Geo. Skills, p. 362 **Additional Resources** • Daily Test Pract. Transp. 12-1 • Lesson Transp. 12A

Rivalry in the Northwest

Main Idea Several nations claimed the Oregon Country, but many Americans wanted the land for its access to the Pacific Ocean.

History and You If you were deep in the wilderness and starving, what might you do to survive? Read to learn how pioneers survived as they traveled west.

The Oregon Country was the huge area located between the Pacific Ocean and the Rocky Mountains north of California. It included all of what is now Oregon, Washington, and Idaho **plus** parts of Montana and Wyoming. The region also contained about half of what is now the Canadian province of British Columbia.

In the early 1800s, four nations claimed the vast, rugged land known as the Oregon Country. The United States based its claim on Robert Gray's discovery of the Columbia River in 1792 and on the Lewis and Clark expedition. Great Britain based its claim on British explorations of the Columbia River. Spain, which had also explored the Pacific coast in the late 1700s, controlled California to the south. Russia had settlements that extended south from Alaska into Oregon.

Adams-Onís Treaty

Many Americans wanted control of Oregon in order to **access,** or get to, the Pacific Ocean. In 1819 Secretary of State John Quincy Adams negotiated the **Adams-Onís Treaty** with Spain. The Spanish agreed to set the limits of their territory at what is now California's northern border and to give up all claims to Oregon. In 1824 Russia also gave up its claim to the land south of Alaska.

In 1818 Adams worked out an agreement with Britain for **joint occupation** of the area. This meant that people from both the United States and Great Britain could settle there. When Adams became president in 1825, he proposed that the two nations divide Oregon along the 49°N line of latitude. Britain refused, insisting on a larger share. Unable to resolve their dispute, the two countries agreed to extend the joint occupation. In the following years, thousands of Americans streamed into the Oregon Country.

If You Were There / "Hard Tack Snack"

Ingredients:
3 cups flour
3 teaspoons salt
1 cup water

Directions:
Mix all ingredients stirring until the dough is too stiff to stir anymore. Knead the dough, adding flour so mixture is very dry. Roll out dough to 1/4 inch thick sheet. With a fork, poke holes all over the dough. Bake for 30 minutes in a very hot oven or over a fire until hard. Break into pieces and store in a bag or box.

▲ As you traveled west, you might have snacked on hard tack.

Critical Thinking
Describing What types of food might be good to take on a long trip in a covered wagon?

Teach

S Skill Practice

Using Geography Skills Have students use a U.S. map to locate the area included in the Oregon Country. **Ask:** In what region of the United States was the Oregon Country located? *(the Northwest region)* **OL**

D Differentiated Instruction

English Language Learners Help students understand the term "joint occupation" by defining "joint" (together) and "occupy" (to hold or take up). **ELL**

R Reading Strategy

Reading Maps Provide students with maps of North America that include lines of latitude and longitude. Have students locate the dividing line Adams proposed. Ask students to locate alternative divisions that might have been more appealing to Britain. **OL**

If You Were There

Critical Thinking Answer
Answers may include dry foods such as bread, crackers, and dried meat.

Differentiated Instruction

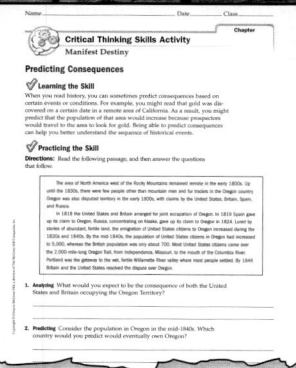

Predicting Consequences

Objective: To use personal knowledge to make predictions

Focus: Ask students to define "educated guess."

Teach: Write a scenario on the board. Have students make educated guesses about what will happen next.

Assess: Have students read text headings and make educated guesses about the text.

Close: Explain that educated guesses in reading are predictions.

Differentiated Instruction Strategies

BL Help students see underlying patterns to determine consequences.

AL Define "butterfly effect" for students and have them analyze causes that lead to the butterfly effect.

ELL Define "educated guess" for students, and help them see that a prediction does not have a right or wrong answer.

Mountain Men, 1825–1840   NATIONAL GEOGRAPHIC

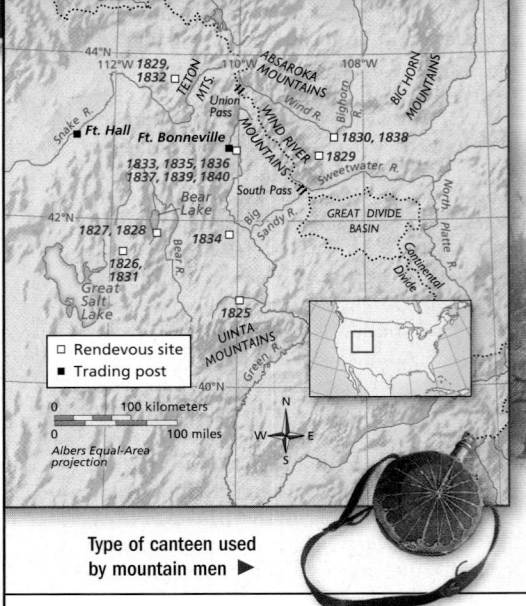

Type of canteen used by mountain men ▶

Life in the Mountains The lives of mountain men were difficult and unpredictable. Mountain men often faced the threat of starvation, dehydration, extreme heat, frigid cold, and deadly attacks by animals and hostile Native Americans.

> *"I defy the annals of chivalry to furnish the record of a life more wild and perilous than that of a Rocky Mountain trapper."*
> —Francis Parkman,
> *The Oregon Trail*

Map Skills

Location What rendezvous site was used most often?

Maps In Motion See StudentWorks™ Plus or glencoe.com.

R Mountain Men

The first Americans to reach the Oregon Country were not farmers but fur traders. They came to trap beaver, whose skins were in great demand in the eastern United States and in Europe. The British established several trading posts in the region, as did merchant John Jacob Astor of New York. In 1808 Astor organized the American Fur Company. It became the most powerful fur company in America. Astor traded on the East Coast, the Pacific Northwest, and China.

At first the merchants traded for furs that the Native Americans supplied. Gradually American adventurers joined the trade. These people, who spent most of their time in the Rocky Mountains, came to be known as **mountain men.** These tough, independent men made their living by trapping beaver. Many had Native American wives and adopted Native American ways. They lived in buffalo-skin lodges and dressed in fringed buckskin pants, moccasins, and beads.

Some mountain men worked for fur-trading companies; others worked for themselves. Throughout the spring and early summer, they hiked across the mountains, setting traps and then collecting the beaver pelts. As they did their work, the mountain men explored the mountains, valleys, and trails of the West. Jim Beckwourth, an African American from Virginia, explored Wyoming's Green River. Robert Stuart and Jedediah Smith found the South Pass, a broad break through the Rockies. South Pass later became the main route that settlers took to Oregon.

In late summer, mountain men gathered for a **rendezvous** (RAHN•dih•voo), or meeting. The annual rendezvous was the most important event of the year for mountain men. They met with the trading companies to exchange **C** their "hairy banknotes"—beaver skins—for traps, guns, coffee, and other goods. They met old friends and exchanged news. They relaxed by competing in races and swapping stories about their most exciting adventures.

Mountain men had to be resourceful. They needed courage and intelligence in order to survive in the wilderness. For example, trapper Joe Meek told how, when faced with starvation, he once held his hands "in an anthill until they were covered with ants, then greedily licked them off." The mountain men took pride in joking about the dangers they faced.

Over time, the mountain men could no longer make a living by trapping because most of the beaver were killed. Some moved to Oregon and settled on farms. With their knowledge of the western lands though, several mountain men, such as Jim Bridger and Kit Carson, found work as guides. They led the parties of settlers now streaming west. Beginning in the 1830s, the mountain men carved out several east-to-west passages that played a vital role in western settlement. The most popular route was the Oregon Trail. Others included the California Trail and the Santa Fe Trail.

C

✓ **Reading Check** **Explain** Why did trading posts develop in the Oregon Country?

Oregon and Manifest Destiny

Main Idea Many people believed that God had given the entire continent to Americans and wanted them to settle western land.

History and You When you prepare to take a trip, what types of items do you pack? Read how pioneers made a 2,000-mile journey, carrying only what they would need in a covered wagon.

. . . .

In the 1830s, Americans began traveling to the Oregon Country to settle. Economic troubles in the East and reports of Oregon's fertile land made the West look attractive.

R

The Whitman Mission

Among the first settlers of the Oregon Country were missionaries who wanted to bring Christianity to the Native Americans. Dr. Marcus Whitman and his wife, Narcissa, went to Oregon in 1836 and built a mission among the Cayuse people near the present site of Walla Walla, Washington.

Primary Source **The Whitman Mission**

A Settlement in the Oregon Country In 1836 Dr. Marcus Whitman and his new bride, Narcissa, arrived at Waiilatpu, on the Walla Walla River in present-day Washington. The Whitmans built a mission to provide medical care and convert the Cayuse to Christianity. Narcissa's journals provide a vivid account of their experiences. Her initial optimism turned to frustration as the Cayuse resisted their efforts.

"They [the Cayuse] are an exceedingly proud . . . people, and keep us constantly . . . [practicing] patience and forbearance. . . . Notwithstanding all this, there are many redeeming qualities in them, else we should have been discouraged long ago. We are more and more encouraged the longer we stay among them."
—Narcissa Whitman, in a letter to her mother

▼ The Whitman Mission became a primary stopping point for settlers traveling along the Oregon Trail. In 1847 a measles epidemic broke out, killing many Cayuse children.

Critical Thinking

Drawing Conclusions Why would people traveling to the Oregon Country stop at the Whitman mission?

Activity: Economics Connection

Hypothesizing Explain to students that fur traders engaged in bartering, a form of payment that has been in existence since prehistoric times. Before the existence of currency, people exchanged cattle, agricultural goods, and even shells. Ask students to think of examples of bartering today. *(Answers may include trading music CDs or babysitting for a neighbor in exchange for a concert ticket.)* Have students think of benefits and drawbacks of bartering and share their thoughts with the class. As a class, compare and contrast bartering with currency payment. Then instruct the class to write a brief essay hypothesizing how the U.S. and world economies might operate if everyone used a barter system instead of a currency system. Tell them to consider agricultural, industrial, and cultural effects of bartering. **AL**

C **Critical Thinking**

Determining Cause and Effect Ask: What were the effects of overhunting the beaver? *(Most of the beaver were killed, so mountain men could no longer make a living by hunting them. Instead, they became farmers or guides.)* **OL**

R **Reading Strategy**

Questioning Read the paragraph aloud. Tell students to think of three questions they would like answered as they read this section. If students have difficulty, provide them with keywords to use in forming questions. Have students note their answers as they find them in the text. After reading, ask students to share their questions and answers and any questions that remain unanswered. **BL**

Primary Source

Critical Thinking Answer
There were few places to stop along the route, and the mission provided medical care and a place to take a much-needed rest.

✓ **Reading Check** **Answer:** to conduct business with fur traders in the West

Additional Support

Teacher Tip

Defining Before the activity, define the terms "bartering" and "currency."

W Writing Support

Narrative Writing Instruct students to write a letter from a settler to a family member on the East Coast. In the letter, explain the measles epidemic, the reaction of the Cayuse, and the aftermath of the killings. **OL**

C Critical Thinking

Making Inferences Ask: What was "Oregon fever"? *(the desire to settle in the Oregon Country and the resulting mass migration to that region)* **OL**

S Skill Practice

Using Geography Skills Instruct students to refer to the map on this page. **Ask:** Near which city did settlers enter Mexico's territory? *(Salt Lake City)* Which mountains did settlers have to cross while on the trail? *(Rocky Mountains)* **OL**

Oregon Country, 1846 — NATIONAL GEOGRAPHIC

Map Skills Answer

the Great Salt Lake

Differentiated Instruction

New settlers unknowingly brought measles to the mission. An epidemic killed many children of the Cayuse. Blaming the Whitmans for the sickness, the Cayuse attacked the mission in November 1847 and killed the Whitmans and 11 others. Despite this, the flood of settlers into Oregon continued.

The Oregon Trail

In the early 1840s, "Oregon fever" swept through the Mississippi Valley. The depression caused by the Panic of 1837 hit the region hard. People formed societies to gather information about Oregon and to plan and make the long trip. The "great migration" had begun. Tens of thousands of people made the trip. These pioneers were called **emigrants** because they left the United States to go to Oregon.

Before the difficult 2,000-mile (3,219-km) journey, these pioneers stuffed their canvas-covered wagons, called **prairie schooners,** with supplies. From a distance these wagons looked like schooners, or ships, at sea. Gathering in Independence in Missouri, they followed the **Oregon Trail** across the Great Plains, along the Platte River, and through the South Pass of the Rocky Mountains. After they crossed the mountains, they traveled north and west along the Snake and Columbia Rivers into the Oregon Country.

Oregon Country, 1846 — NATIONAL GEOGRAPHIC

Settling the Northwest After the War of 1812, the United States and Britain agreed that settlers from both countries could live in the Oregon Country. Most of the British who lived in the region were trappers, while most of the Americans were farmers. The British Hudson's Bay Company maintained order.

Native Americans relied on the Columbia River for transportation, as well as a source of food. The river was also valuable to white settlers. ▼

"The buffalo will dwindle away, and the large wandering communities [of Native Americans] who depend on them . . . must be broken and scattered. . . . Within a few years the traveler may pass in tolerable security through their country. . . . Its danger and its charm will have disappeared."
—Francis Parkman, *The Oregon Trail*

◄ Most emigrants packed their wagons so full that they had to make the long trip on foot.

Map Skills

Location What geographic feature lies at about 41° N and 115° W?

Maps in Motion See StudentWorks™ Plus or glencoe.com.

Leveled Activities

BL Writing Skills Activity, URB p. 51

OL Authentic Assessment With Rubrics, p. 12

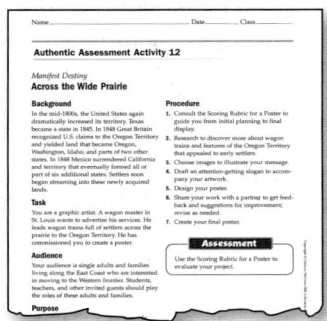

AL Linking Past and Present Activity, URB p. 61

Manifest Destiny

Since colonial times many Americans had believed their nation had a special role to fulfill. For years people thought the nation's mission should be to serve as a model of freedom and democracy. In the 1800s that vision changed. Many believed that the mission of the United States was to spread freedom by occupying the entire continent. In 1819 John Quincy Adams expressed what many Americans were thinking when he said expansion to the Pacific was as inevitable "as that the Mississippi should flow to the sea."

In the 1840s, New York newspaper editor John O'Sullivan expressed the idea of a national mission in more specific words. O'Sullivan declared it was America's "**Manifest Destiny** to overspread and to possess the whole of the continent which Providence has given us." O'Sullivan meant that the United States was clearly destined—set apart for a special purpose—by God to extend its boundaries all the way to the Pacific Ocean.

"Fifty-Four Forty or Fight"

Many Americans wanted the United States to own all of Oregon. In the 1844 presidential election, James K. Polk, the Democratic nominee, supported this demand. Democrats used the slogan "Fifty-Four Forty or Fight," referring to the line of latitude they believed should be the nation's northern border in Oregon.

Polk's Whig opponent, **Henry Clay,** did not take a strong position on the Oregon issue. Polk won the election because Whig support was not united behind Clay.

A firm believer in Manifest Destiny, Polk was focused on making Oregon part of the United States. Britain, however, would not accept a border at "Fifty-Four Forty." This would mean giving up its land claim entirely. In 1846 the two countries finally compromised. They set the border between American and British parts of Oregon at latitude 49°N.

 **Reading Check** **Defining** What is Manifest Destiny?

R Reading Strategy

Determining Importance Have students scan the text in this subsection to identify important facts about the U.S.–British border in the Oregon Country. **Ask:** How did Manifest Destiny affect the 1844 presidential election? *(Many Americans wanted the United States to own all of Oregon, and James K. Polk agreed. He beat his opponent, Henry Clay, who did not take a strong position on the issue.)* **OL**

Reading Check **Answer:** the American belief that the U.S. was meant to extend its boundaries to the Pacific Ocean

Assess

History ONLINE

Study Central™ provides summaries, interactive games, and online graphic organizers to help students review content.

Close

Summarizing As a class, summarize what life was like for mountain men. **OL**

Section 1 Review

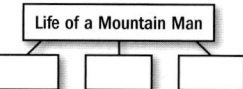 **History ONLINE**
Study Central™ To review this section, go to glencoe.com.

Vocabulary

1. Use each of these terms in a sentence that will help explain its meaning: plus, access, joint occupation, mountain man, rendezvous, emigrant, prairie schooner, Manifest Destiny.

Main Ideas

2. Specifying Which nations claimed the Oregon Country? How did John Quincy Adams help resolve the claims?

3. Explaining What was James K. Polk's campaign slogan in the 1844 election? What did the slogan mean?

Critical Thinking

4. Analyzing During the 1840s, many more Americans than British settled in the Oregon Country. How do you think this influenced negotiations over the territory?

5. Summarizing Create a diagram like the one below to list details about what life was like for a mountain man. Add more boxes to your diagram if necessary.

> Life of a Mountain Man
> [ ] [ ] [ ]

6. Creative Writing Take the role of a pioneer about to travel to the Oregon Country. A friend asks why you are leaving. Write your answer in the voice of your character. Include details about who you are, your reasons for going, and your feelings about the journey ahead.

Answer the
7. Essential Question
How did the belief in Manifest Destiny influence western settlement?

Manifest Destiny **Chapter 12** 363

Section 1 Review

Answers

1. Sentences should reflect a correct understanding of the terms.

2. United States, Great Britain, Spain, Russia; Adams negotiated treaties with Spain and Russia to give up their claims and with Britain for joint occupation.

3. "Fifty-four Forty or Fight"; it referred to a line of latitude that Democrats believed should be the nation's northern border in Oregon.

4. It strengthened American claims while making the British more willing to compromise.

As a result, the British agreed to 49°N, the line they rejected in 1825.

5. Answers may include: mountain men had to be tough and independent; many had Native American wives and adopted Native American ways; worked for fur-trading companies or for themselves; gathered in late summer for a rendezvous; they had to be resourceful, courageous, and intelligent.

6. Stories should be written in first person from the character's viewpoint. Students

should express details that are realistic for the situation.

7. The idea that Americans had a right to this land helped them feel justified in taking it away from others who were already living on the land or held claim to it.

Focus

S Skill Practice

Using Geography Skills Display a map of the United States. Ask students to identify the main obstacles to westward expansion at various points in history: first the Appalachian Mountains and potentially hostile Native Americans and lands later owned by Spain and Mexico. **Ask:** How did the United States overcome these various obstacles in pursuit of the country's Manifest Destiny? (*Students should recognize that advances in transportation, treaties, and wars all helped the United States claim and settle lands to the west.*) **OL**

R Reading Strategy

Summarizing After students read Gallatin's speech, ask them to summarize his ideas in their own words. Students should write one sentence summarizing each of the three paragraphs. Help students use context clues to decipher challenging vocabulary. **OL**

Additional Support and Answers

Spanish mission in the Southwest

YOU DECIDE

Was Manifest Destiny Justified?

Building Background

In 1845 a magazine editor named John L. O'Sullivan declared that it was the "manifest destiny" of Americans to expand westward to the Pacific Ocean. Many Americans believed in this concept of Manifest Destiny—the idea that God had given **S** the continent to Americans and wanted them to settle western land. Manifest Destiny did have its opponents, however. Longtime public servant Albert Gallatin expressed his opposition to Manifest Destiny and to war with Mexico in an 1847 pamphlet *Peace with Mexico.*

NO

ALBERT GALLATIN

It is said, that the people of the United States have a hereditary superiority of race over the Mexicans, which gives them the right to subjugate[1] and keep in bondage the inferior nation. . . .

Is it compatible with the principle of Democracy, which rejects every hereditary claim of individuals, to admit a hereditary superiority of races? . . . Can you for a moment suppose, that a very doubtful descent from men, who lived one thousand years ago, has transmitted to you a superior- **R** *ity over your fellow-men? . . . At this time, the claim is but a pretext for covering and justifying unjust usurpation[2] and unbounded ambition. . . .*

Among ourselves, the most ignorant, the most inferior, either in physical or mental faculties,[3] is recognized as having equal rights, and he has an equal vote with any one, however superior to him in all those respects. This is founded on the immutable[4] principle that no one man is born with the right of governing another man.

---

[1] **subjugate** conquer
[2] **usurpation** seizure

[3] **faculties** abilities
[4] **immutable** unchanging

Activity: Connecting Past and Present

Theorizing The idea that the United States has a moral duty to project its influence beyond its borders has been a continuing theme in American history. Every president since World War II has stressed the nation's global responsibilities as leader of the "Free World." Today, artifacts of American culture—from blue jeans to hamburgers to rock music videos—are popular in virtually every corner of the world, especially with young people. Draw on students' familiarity with pop culture in a discussion linking Manifest Destiny to the recent spread of American culture through what is called "globalization." **Ask:** Is the globalization of American media and pop culture a new form of Manifest Destiny? (*Students may note that while globalization involves a vigorous and deliberate campaign to increase America's economic influence around the world, it does not involve the acquisition of actual territory.*)

YES

JOHN L. O'SULLIVAN

Texas is now ours. Already, before these words are written, her convention has undoubtedly ratified the acceptance, by her congress, of our proffered[5] invitation into the Union. . . . Her star and her stripe may already be said to have taken their place in the glorious blazon[6] of our common nationality. . . .

The next session of Congress will see the representatives of the new young state in their places in both our halls of national legislation, side by side with those of the old Thirteen. . . .

Other nations have undertaken to intrude themselves into [the question of Texas. They have come] between us and the proper parties to the case, in a spirit of hostile interference against us, for the avowed[7] object of thwarting[8] our policy and hampering our power, limiting our greatness and checking the fulfillment of our manifest destiny to overspread the continent allotted by Providence for the free development of our yearly multiplying millions.

Texas celebrates entering the Union.

[5] **proffered** offered
[6] **blazon** showy display

[7] **avowed** declared openly
[8] **thwarting** stopping

DBQ Document-Based Questions

1. **Summarizing** According to O'Sullivan, what was Manifest Destiny?
2. **Making Inferences** Why do you think O'Sullivan mentions Texas's future representation in Congress?
3. **Analyzing** What does Albert Gallatin think is the real motivation underlying the idea of Manifest Destiny?
4. **Evaluating** Imagine you could interview Gallatin and O'Sullivan. Write a list of three questions you could ask each man about his views on Manifest Destiny.

Teach

R Reading Strategy

Paraphrasing Read the last paragraph of O'Sullivan's excerpt aloud to the class. Discuss the meaning of the words *avowed* and *thwarting*. **Ask:** What does "Providence" mean? *(God)* What does "yearly multiplying millions" mean? *(expanding population)* Then, ask students to paraphrase the last paragraph in their own words. Have some students read their paragraphs aloud. **AL**

Assess/Close

Lead a closing discussion on whether the concept of Manifest Destiny survives in American culture today.

365

Answers

1. Manifest Destiny was the God-given right of the United States to expand westward to the Pacific Ocean and become a great nation.
2. to emphasize that the annexation of Texas spreads democracy
3. the seizure of territory not rightfully part of the United States
4. Answers will vary. Accept all reasonable answers.

Independence for Texas

Focus

Bellringer
Daily Test Practice Transparency 12–2

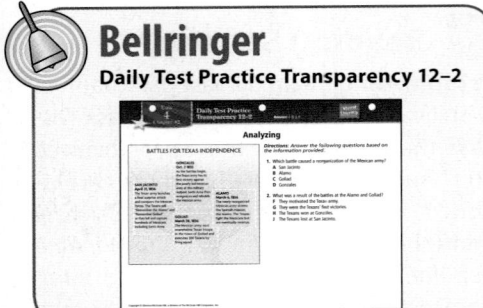

Reading Guide
Answers to Graphic:
October 1835: battle between Texas and Mexico in Gonzales; **December 1835:** Texans freed San Antonio from Mexican forces; **February 1836:** Battle of the Alamo; **March 1836:** Texas declares independence from Mexico; **April 1836:** Texans attack Mexican troops at San Jacinto; **May 1836:** Santa Anna signs treaty with Texas; **September 1836:** Texas elects Sam Houston president and asks for U.S. annexation

Section Spotlight Video

Have students watch the Section Spotlight Video "Independence for Texas" to learn more about the war for Texas independence.

Resource Manager

Essential Question ◄
Why did Texans fight for their independence from Mexico?

Reading Guide

Content Vocabulary
Tejano (p. 367) decree (p. 368)
empresario (p. 367) annex (p. 371)

Academic Vocabulary
establish (p. 367) remove (p. 368)

Key People and Events
Stephen F. Austin (p. 367)
Antonio López de Santa Anna (p. 368)
Alamo (p. 369)
Sam Houston (p. 370)

Reading Strategy
Taking Notes Use a time line like the one below to list key events in Texas history.

1835   1836

| Oct. | | Mar. | May |

| | Dec. | Feb. | Apr. | Sept. |

ILLINOIS STANDARDS
The American Journey

16.A.3c Identify the differences between historical fact and interpretation.

16.D.3b Describe characteristics of different kinds of families in America during the colonial/frontier periods and the 19th century.

17.D.3a Explain how and why spatial patterns of settlement change over time.

18.B.3a Analyze how individuals and groups interact with and within institutions (e.g., educational, military).

American Diary

Thomas Jefferson Pilgrim was an immigrant who heard about opportunities in Texas. In New Orleans, he bought a ticket to Texas and a new life. "We were now on the Gulf. . . . Soon all on board were seasick except the crew and me and many wished that they had never started. . . . [After landing at Matagorda Bay] the others went eastward to the Brazos, I on foot and alone, made my way north to San Felipe, about 60 miles distant."

—from the diary of Thomas J. Pilgrim

Settlers lived on estates in southeast Texas.

R Reading Strategies	**C** Critical Thinking	**D** Differentiated Instruction	**W** Writing Support	**S** Skill Practice
Teacher Edition • Taking Notes, p. 367 • Using Word Parts, p. 368 • Sequencing, p. 369 • Making Conn., p. 370 **Additional Resources** • Guid. Read., URB p. 68 • Content Vocab., URB p. 45 • Acad. Vocab., URB p. 47	**Teacher Edition** • Det. Cause and Effect, p. 367 • Making Inferences, p. 368 **Additional Resources** • Quizzes and Tests, p. 112	**Teacher Edition** • Gifted and Talented, p. 369 • Interpersonal, p. 371 **Additional Resources** • School-to-Home, URB p. 63 • Reteaching Act., URB p. 65	**Teacher Edition** • Expository Writing, p. 368	**Teacher Edition** • Using Geo. Skills, p. 370 **Additional Resources** • Daily Test Pract. Transp. 12-2 • Time Line Skills, URB p. 62 • Geo. & Hist., URB p. 59 • Lesson Transp. 12B

A Clash of Cultures

Main Idea People from the United States and Mexico settled Texas.

History and You If someone from a different culture offered you a large amount of land on the condition that you adopt his or her language and customs, would you take it? Read to find out how settlers in Texas reacted to a similar situation.

Conflict over Texas began in 1803, when the United States bought the Louisiana Territory from France. Americans claimed that the land in present-day Texas was part of the purchase. Spain protested. In the Adams-Onís Treaty, the United States agreed to drop its claim to the region.

Land Grants

At the time, few people lived in Texas. Most residents—about 3,000—were **Tejanos** (teh•HAH•nohs), or Mexicans who claimed Texas as their home. Native Americans, such as the Comanches, Apaches, and Kiowas, also lived in the area. Because the Spanish wanted to promote the growth of Texas, they offered vast tracts of land to people who agreed to

bring families to settle there. The people who obtained these grants and recruited the settlers were called **empresarios.**

American Moses Austin received the first land grant in 1821. He died, however, before he could **establish,** or set up, his colony. Mexico won its independence from Spain in 1821. Austin's son, **Stephen F. Austin,** received permission from the new Mexican government to organize the colony. Austin recruited 300 American families to settle in Texas. Austin's success made him a leader among the American settlers.

From 1823 to 1825, Mexico passed laws offering new settlers land at extremely low prices. In return the colonists agreed to learn Spanish, become Mexican citizens, convert to Catholicism—the religion of Mexico—and obey Mexican law. Mexican leaders hoped to attract settlers from all over, but most settlers came from the United States.

Growing Tension

By 1830 Americans in Texas far outnumbered Mexicans. Further, these American colonists had not adopted Mexican ways. In the meantime, the United States had twice offered to buy Texas from Mexico.

Primary Source | Migration to Texas

Texas's Appeal By 1830 there were 4,000 members of Austin's colonies and approximately 16,000 Americans in Texas—four times the Mexican population. Inexpensive land drew many to Texas. The efforts of Mary Austin Holley, a cousin and close friend of Stephen F. Austin, also helped. Holley's books and letters provided information for settlers. Her descriptions of Texas as a land of "surpassing beauty . . . a *splendid* country—an enchanting spot" attracted many settlers.

Cost of Land in 1825	
Land in the U.S.	$1.25 per acre
Land in Texas	4¢ per acre

Critical Thinking
Predicting How do you think settlers made a living in Texas?

**Geography and History
Activity, URB p. 59**

Teach

R Reading Strategy

Taking Notes To help students understand the events leading to Texas's independence, instruct them to take notes on this chapter. Students' notes should include phrases and key words to help them understand the time period at a glance. **OL**

C Critical Thinking

Determining Cause and Effect Ask: What led to tension between Americans and Mexicans in Texas? *(The Americans outnumbered the Mexicans, and the Americans did not adopt Mexican ways.)* **OL**

Primary Source

Critical Thinking Answer
Students should focus on land-related work such as farming or cattle ranching.

Calculating Ask: How much would you pay if you purchased 100 acres of land in Texas? *($4.00)* **OL**

Differentiated Instruction

Manifest Destiny

Objective: To explain the influence of Spanish culture on the cattle industry

Focus: Write the word "cowboy" on the board. Ask students who the first cowboys were.

Teach: Have students read the article, then research the history of vaqueros.

Assess: Have students write five trivia questions using the information they gathered.

Close: Ask students to explain the connection of vaqueros to modern-day ranch hands.

Differentiated Instruction Strategies

BL Highlight information about vaqueros in the activity.

AL Instruct students to brainstorm and research other industries that were affected by Spanish culture.

ELL Help students see the meanings in compound words and phrases such as "cowboy," "longhorn," and "ranch hand."

W Writing Support

Expository Writing Have students do research to learn more about Stephen F. Austin and General Santa Anna, including characteristics of the men. Ask students to write an essay comparing and contrasting the two leaders. **AL**

C Critical Thinking

Making Inferences Ask: Based on information in this paragraph, would Santa Anna support a democracy? Why or why not? *(Santa Anna made himself dictator and threw out the Mexican constitution. These actions do not describe a democracy.)* **OL**

R Reading Strategy

Using Word Parts Ask: What is the root word in "unavoidable"? *(avoid)* List some avoidable events. *(being late for class and watching too much television)* **Ask:** What does the prefix "un-" mean? *(not)* Help students see that "unavoidable" means "not avoidable." **BL**

✔Reading Check Answer: They obtained land grants and recruited settlers.

Differentiated Instruction

The Mexican government viewed the growing American influence in Texas with alarm. In 1830 the Mexican government issued a **decree,** or official order, that stopped all immigration from the United States. At the same time, the decree encouraged the immigration of Mexican and European families with generous land grants. Trade between Texas and the United States was discouraged by placing a tax on goods that were imported from the United States.

These new policies angered the Texans. The prosperity of many citizens depended on trade with the United States. Many had friends and relatives who wanted to come to Texas. In addition, those colonists who held slaves were uneasy about the Mexican government's plans to end slavery.

Attempt at Reconciliation

Some of the American settlers called for independence. Others hoped to stay within Mexico but on better terms. In 1833 General **Antonio López de Santa Anna** became president of Mexico. Stephen F. Austin traveled to Mexico City with the Texans' demands to **remove,** or take away, the ban on American settlers and to make Texas a separate state of Mexico.

Santa Anna agreed to the first request but refused the second. Austin sent a letter back to Texas, suggesting that plans for independence get underway. The Mexican government intercepted the letter and arrested Austin.

While Austin was in jail, Santa Anna named himself dictator and overthrew Mexico's constitution of 1824. Without a constitution to protect their rights, Texans felt betrayed. Santa Anna placed Texas under greater central control. This loss of local power dismayed many people. Even Austin, finally released from prison, now saw that dealing with Santa Anna was impossible. He concluded that war was unavoidable.

✔Reading Check Explaining What role did empresarios play in colonization?

Chance & Error in History

What If the Defenders Had Abandoned the Alamo?

William Travis and almost 200 other defenders—mostly volunteers—were determined to hold the Alamo for a cause in which they believed. In February 1836, Travis wrote several unsuccessful letters, asking the people of Texas and the United States for help.

General Antonio López de Santa Anna, Mexico's president, hoped the fall of the Alamo would convince other Texans that it was useless to resist his armies. Instead, the heroism of those in the Alamo inspired Texans to carry on the struggle. "Remember the Alamo!" became the battle cry of the Texas army.

Travis's Appeal for Aid at the Alamo, February 24, 1836
To the People of Texas & all Americans in the world—
Fellow citizens & compatriots—I am besieged, by a thousand or more of the Mexicans under Santa Anna—I have sustained a continual Bombardment & cannonade for 24 hours & have not lost a man. . . . I shall never surrender or retreat. Then, I call on you in the name of Liberty, of patriotism & everything dear to the American character, to come to our aid, with all dispatch. . . . If this call is neglected, I am determined to sustain myself as long as possible & die like a soldier who never forgets what is due to his own honor & that of his country—

Victory or Death
William Barret Travis
Lt. Col. comdt.

368 **Chapter 12** *Manifest Destiny*

Leveled Activities

BL School-to-Home Connection Activity, URB p. 63

OL Reteaching Activity, URB p. 65

ELL Academic Vocabulary Activity, URB p. 47

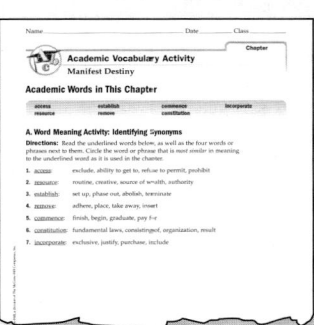

The Struggle for Independence

Main Idea Texans fought for their independence from Mexico.

History and You Did you know that Texas was once a nation? Read why Texas remained independent before it became a state.

. . . .

During 1835 unrest among Texans sometimes erupted in open conflict. Santa Anna sent an army into Texas to punish the rebels. In October some Mexican troops tried to seize a cannon held by Texans at the town of Gonzales. The Texans taunted the Mexicans. They put a white flag on the cannon, bearing the words "Come and Take It." After a brief battle, the Texans drove back the Mexican troops. Texans consider this to be the first fight of the Texan Revolution.

The Texans called for volunteers. Many answered, including African Americans and Tejanos. In December 1835, the Texans freed San Antonio from a larger Mexican force.

Santa Anna's Letter Explaining the Attack
"[Travis's] responses were insulting, which made it imperative to assault the fort before it could be reinforced by Samuel Houston. . . . The obstinacy [stubbornness] of Travis and his soldiers was the cause of the death of the whole of them, for not one would surrender."

Critical Thinking

1. **Identifying Cause and Effect** What effect did the defeat of the Alamo have on the Texas independence movement?

2. **Speculating** What do you think might have happened to the independence movement had the defenders of the Alamo abandoned the fort?

Despite these victories, problems arose. Various groups argued over who would lead and what actions to take. In early 1836, when Texas should have been preparing to face Santa Anna, plans had stalled.

The Battle of the Alamo

Santa Anna marched north, furious at the loss of San Antonio. When his army reached San Antonio in late February 1836, it found a small Texan force barricaded inside a nearby mission called the **Alamo.**

Although the Texans had cannons, they lacked gunpowder. The Texans were at a further disadvantage because they had only about 180 soldiers to take on Santa Anna's army of several thousand. The Texans had brave leaders, however, including Davy Crockett and a tough Texan named Jim Bowie. The commander, William B. Travis, who was only 26 years old, was determined to hold his position at the Alamo. Travis managed to send messages through Mexican lines. Several messages appealed to the people of Texas and the United States for aid.

For 12 long days, through several attacks, the defenders of the Alamo kept Santa Anna's army at bay with rifle fire. On March 6, 1836, Mexican cannon fire smashed the Alamo's walls.

The Mexicans were too numerous to hold back. They entered the fortress, killing all the defenders, including Travis, Crockett, and Bowie. Only a few women and children and some servants survived to tell of the battle.

The defenders had killed hundreds of Mexican soldiers. But more important, they had bought Texans some much-needed time.

Texas Declares Its Independence

During the siege at the Alamo, Texan leaders were meeting at Washington-on-the-Brazos, where they were writing a new constitution. There, on March 2, 1836—four days before the fall of the Alamo—American settlers and Tejanos declared independence from Mexico. They then established the Republic of Texas.

Manifest Destiny **Chapter 12** 369

R Reading Strategy

Sequencing Information Read the Main Idea aloud. Have students draw a line on a sheet of paper. Instruct students to write key events and their dates on the line, in order of occurrence, as they read. Then as a class, discuss students' time lines. **BL**

D Differentiated Instruction

Gifted and Talented Tell students to do research to learn more about the Battle of the Alamo. Have students revise the Texans' military strategy to change the outcome of the event. Instruct students to consider weaponry, timing, and logical reactions from Mexican troops in their plans. **AL**

Chance & Error in History

Critical Thinking Answers
Answers may include:
1. The defeat angered the Texans, motivating them to continue fighting.
2. They would not have gained time that they needed to prepare for Mexican troops and create the Republic of Texas.

Additional Support

Activity: Collaborative Learning

Auditory/Musical Tell students that they will reenact the Battle of the Alamo and include music in their performance. As a class, have students use the textbook as well as library and online resources to write a script for their reenactment. Instruct students to include major characters such as Davy Crockett, Jim Bowie, and William B. Travis. Remind them to include adequate dialogue and sound effects as well as appropriate action. When finished, have the students research appropriate music such as songs from the musical play *Liberty! The Siege of the Alamo.* After rehearsing their reenactment, invite another class to view the performance. **OL**

R Reading Strategy

Making Connections Ask: How is the Declaration of Independence of Texas similar to the U.S. Declaration of Independence? *(Both call for freedom, independence, and a sovereign government, and both declare their independence from a ruling country, Britain in the U.S. Declaration and Mexico in the Texas declaration.)* `OL`

S Skill Practice

Using Geography Skills Have students locate Goliad on the map and trace the route of Mexican forces. **Ask:** In what general direction did the Mexican troops travel to San Antonio? *(northeast)* `BL`

Texas War for Independence, 1835–1836 NATIONAL GEOGRAPHIC

Map Skills Answer

Battle of San Jacinto

Skills Practice

Predicting Consequences Ask: What might have happened if Texas had formed an alliance with Britain? *(Answers may indicate that Texas might not have joined the United States.)* `OL`

Hands-On Chapter Project
Step 2

Creating an Illustrated Encyclopedia

Step 2: Creating a "Republic of Texas" Entry Groups of students will create an encyclopedia entry for "Republic of Texas."

Essential Question: Why did Texans fight for their independence from Mexico?

Directions Assign each group a topic related to the Republic of Texas, such as the

---

Texas War for Independence, 1835–1836 NATIONAL GEOGRAPHIC

Map legend:
- → Mexican forces
- ✷ Mexican victory
- ■ Texan forces
- ✷ Texan victory
- Austin's colony
- Disputed territory

UNITED STATES
Unorganized Terr.
Arkansas
REPUBLIC OF TEXAS
Louisiana
Boundary claimed by Mexico
Washington-on-the-Brazos 1836
Alamo, March 6, 1836
San Jacinto April 21, 1836
HOUSTON
San Antonio Bexar, Dec. 10, 1835
Gonzales, Oct. 2, 1835
Brazoria
Boundary claimed by Texas
Goliad, March 20, 1836
Refugio, March 14, 1836
San Patricio Feb. 27, 1836
Gulf of Mexico
SANTA ANNA 1836
URREA 1836
Nueces R.
Rio Grande
MEXICO
0 200 kilometers
0 200 miles
Albers Equal-Area projection
28°N
26°N
96°W   94°W

"In my judgment it would be far better for this Country that Texas should remain an independent State if this were possible."
—Senator James Buchanan

From Independence to Statehood Texas remained independent for several years. At first the United States refused to annex Texas. To pressure the United States, Texas threatened to form an alliance with Great Britain. The United States did not want the British near its southern border, and in 1845 Texas was admitted to the Union as a slave state.

The Republic of Texas had a three-branch government. Its first Congress met in 1837 at this house in present-day Houston. ▼

▲ Texas banknote, 1838

Map Skills

Location What battle was fought northeast of Brazoria?

Maps In MOtion See StudentWorks™ Plus or glencoe.com.

The Texas Declaration stated that the government of Santa Anna had violated the Mexican Constitution. It noted that the Texans' protests against these violations were met with force. The declaration proclaimed the following:

R PRIMARY SOURCE

"The people of Texas, in solemn convention assembled, appealing to a candid world for the necessities of our condition, do hereby resolve and declare, that our political connection with the Mexican nation has forever ended, and that the people of Texas do now constitute a free, Sovereign, and independent republic."
—The Declaration of Independence of Texas

With Mexican troops in Texas, it was not possible to hold an election to ratify the constitution and vote for leaders. Texas leaders set up a temporary government.

The government named **Sam Houston** as commander in chief of the Texas forces. Houston wanted to prevent the Mexicans from overrunning other forts. He ordered the troops at Goliad to abandon their position. As **S** they retreated, however, they came face to face with Mexican troops. After a fierce fight, several hundred Texans surrendered. On Santa Anna's orders, the Texans were executed. This action outraged Texans, who called it the "Goliad Massacre."

370 Chapter 12 *Manifest Destiny*

Battle of the Alamo, the Battle of San Jacinto, Stephen F. Austin, and Sam Houston. Instruct students to research their topics, using the textbook and library and online sources. Students should collect facts and study related photos, maps, and illustrations. Groups should then discuss their research and decide which facts and images to include in their entries. Group members should prepare the text and illustrations for

their entries and include informational captions. Explain that they will add more entries to the encyclopedia in the next two sections.

Sequencing As a class, sequence the events leading up to Texas independence and statehood and verify that the information is correct in the encyclopedia entry. `OL`

(Chapter Project continued in Section 3)

The Battle of San Jacinto

Houston gathered an army of about 900 at San Jacinto (SAN huh•SIHN•toh), near the site of present-day Houston. Santa Anna was camped nearby with an army of more than 1,300. On April 21, the Texans launched a surprise attack, shouting, "Remember the Alamo! Remember Goliad!" They killed more than 600 soldiers and captured about 700 more—including Santa Anna. On May 14, 1836, Santa Anna signed a treaty that recognized the independence of Texas.

The Lone Star Republic

In September 1836, Texans elected Sam Houston as their president. Mirabeau Lamar, who had fought at the Battle of San Jacinto, served as vice president. Houston sent a delegation to Washington, D.C., asking the United States to **annex,** or take control of, Texas.

Andrew Jackson, however, refused their request. An addition of another slave state would upset the balance of slave and free states in Congress. For the moment, Texas would remain an independent country.

The Road to Statehood

After winning independence, Texas still had difficulties with Mexico, and it faced a mounting debt. Many Texans wanted to join the United States. Southerners favored Texas annexation, but Northerners opposed admitting another slave state to the Union. President Martin Van Buren did not want to inflame the slavery issue or risk war with Mexico. He put off the question of annexing Texas. John Tyler, who became president in 1841, supported Texas annexation. The Senate, however, was still divided over the slavery issue and failed to ratify the annexation treaty.

The situation changed with the 1844 presidential campaign. Manifest Destiny was a popular idea at the time. The South wanted Texas. The North favored gaining all of Oregon. Candidate James K. Polk supported both actions. After Polk won, Congress passed a resolution to annex Texas. In 1845 Texas joined the Union.

Reading Check **Identifying** What was the role of Sam Houston in Texas history?

D Differentiated Instruction

Interpersonal Have students form groups of three. Assign each student in a group the role of President Van Buren, President Tyler, or President Polk. As president, have each student discuss his stance on Texas annexation, using information from the text as support for the opinion. **OL**

Reading Check **Answer:** Sam Houston was Texas's first commander in chief. He led Texas troops to victory at the Battle of San Jacinto and later became president of Texas.

Assess

History ONLINE

Study Central™ provides summaries, interactive games, and online graphic organizers to help students review content.

Close

Listing As a class, list the key events from this section. **OL**

Section 2 Review

Section 2 Review

History ONLINE
Study Central™ To review this section, go to glencoe.com.

Vocabulary

1. Write a short paragraph in which you use all of the following vocabulary terms: Tejano, empresario, establish, decree, remove, annex.

Main Ideas

2. **Explaining** How did Stephen Austin try to resolve tensions with the Mexican government?

3. **Specifying** Why was the Battle of San Jacinto important?

Critical Thinking

4. **Contrasting** In a diagram like the one below, describe the Mexican government's expectations for the settlement of Texas. Describe how the actual settlement differed from these expectations and the result.

Expectation: → Actual: → Result:

5. **Synthesizing** How did the Texan defeats at the Alamo and Goliad affect Texans?

6. **Persuasive Writing** Take the role of Stephen Austin. Write what you would say to President Santa Anna to persuade him to agree to Texans' demand for independence.

Answer the Essential Question

7. Why did Texans fight for their independence from Mexico?

Manifest Destiny **Chapter 12** **371**

Answers

1. Paragraphs should reflect a correct understanding of the terms.
2. He traveled to Mexico City to ask the government to remove the ban on American settlers and to make Texas a separate state.
3. Texans captured Santa Anna, forcing him to sign a treaty recognizing Texas independence.

4. **Expectations:** Settlers would come from all over, including other parts of Mexico, and would adopt Mexican ways. **Actual:** Most settlers came from the United States and did not adopt Mexican ways. **Result:** tension and finally war
5. It bought Texans needed time to organize a government and form an army.

6. Students should promote Texans' demands in a persuasive, nonconfrontational tone.
7. Americans in Texas were upset about the actions of the Mexican government, including limitations placed on immigration from the United States; taxation on U.S. imports, which discouraged trade and hurt Texans' livelihoods; and plans to end slavery.

Focus

Section 3

War With Mexico

Bellringer

Daily Test Practice Transparency 12–3

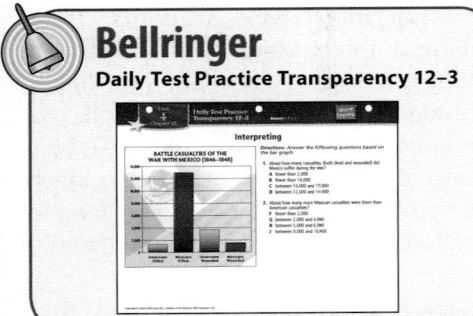

Reading Guide

Answers to Graphic:

William Becknell: First American trader to reach Santa Fe

John C. Frémont: Mapmaker who wrote about California's mild climate and vast natural resources; formed the Bear Flag Republic

Winfield Scott: Army general who captured Veracruz, Mexico

Section Spotlight Video

Have students watch the Section Spotlight Video "War With Mexico" to learn more about President James K. Polk's plans to acquire New Mexico and California.

Resource Manager

Reading Guide

Content Vocabulary

rancho (p. 374)

Californios (p. 376)

ranchero (p. 374)

cede (p. 377)

Academic Vocabulary

resource (p. 374)

commence (p. 375)

Key People and Events

Santa Fe Trail (p. 373)

John C. Frémont (p. 374)

Winfield Scott (p. 377)

Treaty of Guadalupe Hidalgo (p. 377)

Mexican Cession (p. 377)

Gadsden Purchase (p. 377)

Reading Strategy

Taking Notes As you read, describe the achievements of each individual in the chart below.

	Achievements
William Becknell	
John C. Frémont	
Winfield Scott	

ILLINOIS STANDARDS
The American Journey

14.E Understand United States foreign policy as it relates to other nations and international issues.

17.C.3a Explain how human activity is affected by geographic factors.

17.C.3c Analyze how human processes influence settlement patterns including migration and population growth.

17.D.3a Explain how and why spatial patterns of settlement change over time.

American Diary

Spanish conquistadors brought the first cattle and horses to North America. As Mexicans settled in present-day California, many became cowhands. They herded cattle on California's large ranches. These Mexican cowhands were called vaqueros *and were the first cowboys of the American West. People of other nationalities soon populated the region, but Spanish culture still influences California's people today.*

Mexican cowboys roping cattle

R Reading Strategies	C Critical Thinking	D Differentiated Instruction	W Writing Support	S Skill Practice
Teacher Edition • Activ. Prior Knowledge, p. 374 • Monitoring, p. 376 • Academic Vocab., p. 377 **Additional Resources** • Guid. Read., URB p. 69 • Content Vocab., URB p. 45	**Teacher Edition** • Analyz. Information, p. 373 • Drawing Conclusions, p. 374 • Analyz. Information, p. 376 **Additional Resources** • Quizzes and Tests, p. 113	**Teacher Edition** • Kinesthetic, p. 373 **Additional Resources** • School-to-Home, URB p. 63 • Reteaching Act., URB p. 65	**Teacher Edition** • Persuasive Writing, p. 375	**Teacher Edition** • Using Geo. Skills, p. 377 **Additional Resources** • Daily Test Pract. Transp. 12-3 • Soc. Stud. Skills, URB p. 53

The New Mexico Territory

Main Idea The Santa Fe Trail was a busy trade route from Missouri to the large Mexican province of New Mexico.

History and You Can you imagine finding your way from Missouri to New Mexico without roads? Read how a trader established the Santa Fe Trail.

In the early 1800s, New Mexico was the vast region between the Texas and California territories. It included all of present-day New Mexico, Arizona, Nevada, and Utah and parts of Colorado and Wyoming. Native Americans had lived in the area for thousands of years. Spanish conquistadors began exploring there in the late 1500s and made it part of Spain's colony of Mexico. In 1610 the Spanish founded the settlement of Santa Fe. Missionaries followed soon after.

When Mexico won its independence in 1821, it inherited New Mexico from Spain. The Spanish had tried to keep Americans away from Santa Fe, fearing that Americans would want to take over the area. The Mexican government, however, welcomed American traders. It hoped that the trade would boost the economy of the province.

William Becknell, the first American trader to reach Santa Fe, arrived in 1821 with a supply of goods. Becknell's route came to be known as the **Santa Fe Trail.** The trail started near Independence, Missouri, and crossed the prairies to the Arkansas River. It followed the river west toward the Rocky Mountains before turning south into New Mexico. The trail was mostly flat, and Becknell used wagons to transport his goods.

Other traders followed Becknell, and the Santa Fe Trail became a busy trade route. As trade with New Mexico increased, Americans began settling in the area. Many saw New Mexico as part of the Manifest Destiny of the United States.

Reading Check Describing Where did the Santa Fe Trail begin and end?

By the Numbers | Los Angeles in 1850

Types of Employment A census of Los Angeles County, California, was taken in 1850. Many people in Los Angeles were farmers, miners, merchants, watchmakers, blacksmiths, and physicians.

Los Angeles Population, 1850
- Males 61%
- Females 39%

Los Angeles Ages, 1850
- People 40 and older 13%
- People 39 and younger 87%

Source: 1850 Federal Census Los Angeles County, California

Critical Thinking
Analyzing Describe the characteristics of Los Angeles' population.

Creating an Illustrated Encyclopedia

Step 3: Creating "New Mexico" and "California" Entries Groups of students will create encyclopedia entries for "New Mexico" and "California."

Essential Question: How did Mexican lands in the West become part of the United States?

Directions Assign each group a topic related to New Mexico and California, such as the Santa Fe Trail and war with Mexico. Instruct students to research their topics. They should collect facts and study related photos, maps, and illustrations. Groups should then decide which facts and images to include in their entries. Group members should prepare the text and illustrations and include captions. Explain that they will add more entries in the next section.

Identifying Central Issues As a class, discuss the role of Manifest Destiny in the war with Mexico. **OL**

(Chapter Project continued in Section 4)

Teach

C Critical Thinking

Analyzing Information Ask: How did the Mexican government view the American traders? *(The Mexican government viewed the traders favorably because the government believed the traders would boost the economy of the province.)* **OL**

D Differentiated Instruction

Kinesthetic Ask students to create a mural or relief map depicting the Santa Fe Trail. **OL**

By the Numbers

Critical Thinking Answer
The population of Los Angeles was mainly young and male.

Making Inferences Ask: Why did so few older adults live in Los Angeles in 1850? *(probably because the difficult journey to California prevented older people from traveling)* **OL**

Reading Check **Answer:** The trail began in Independence, Missouri, and ended in Santa Fe, New Mexico.

Hands-On Chapter Project
Step 3

R Reading Strategy

Activating Prior Knowledge Ask students to cite Spanish words and examples of Spanish culture. Explain that the text on this page tells how the Spanish influenced California's culture. **BL**

C Critical Thinking

Drawing Conclusions Ask: How would U.S. merchants benefit by the addition of California to the United States? *(They could use California port cities for trade and gain access to California's natural resources.)* **OL**

The Santa Fe Trail NATIONAL GEOGRAPHIC

Map Skills Answer
Ft. Zarah, Ft. Larned

✔ **Reading Check** **Answer:** to convert Native Americans to Christianity

History ONLINE
Objectives and answers to the Student Web Activity can be found at glencoe.com under the Web Activity Lesson Plan for this chapter.

Differentiated Instruction

The Santa Fe Trail NATIONAL GEOGRAPHIC

Westward Trade When Mexico gained its independence from Spain in 1821, trade also opened up in New Mexico. That year, William Becknell set out from Missouri to trade with the Native Americans and traveled on to Santa Fe. By 1860, $3.5 million in goods were transported along the trail.

▲ The 900-mile-long Santa Fe Trail served as the main highway between Missouri and New Mexico. Unlike the Oregon Trail, it was used mainly by traders and the military.

"I travelled from the Spanish village of Taos, to Fort Osage, on the Missouri, in thirty-four days. . . . By the route which I travelled on my return, I avoided the so much dreaded sand hills, where adventurers have frequently been forced to drink the blood of their mules, to allay their thirst."
—from the journal of William Becknell

▲ Freight wagons on the Santa Fe Trail

Military forts were built along the Santa Fe Trail to protect travelers. These are the ruins of Fort Union in New Mexico.

Map Skills
Movement Which forts would you pass if you traveled from Independence to Fort Dodge?

Maps in MOtion See StudentWorks™ Plus or glencoe.com.

California's Spanish Culture

Main Idea California was settled by Mexicans.

R **History and You** Did you know that *Los Angeles* means "the angels" in Spanish? Read to learn about California's Spanish heritage.

Spanish explorers and missionaries from Mexico settled California in the 1700s. Captain Gaspar de Portolá and Father Junípero Serra built a chain of missions that eventually extended from San Diego to Sonoma.

The missions were used to convert Native Americans to Christianity. Native Americans also farmed the land and worked at weaving and other crafts. American mountain man Jedediah Smith described the missions as "large farming and grazing establishments."

After Mexico gained its independence from Spain in 1821, California became a state in the new Mexican nation. Mexican settlers bought available mission lands and set up huge estates called **ranchos**. Native Americans worked the land in return for food and shelter. **Rancheros**—ranch owners—treated Native Americans almost like slaves.

In the 1840s, more Americans reached California. **John C. Frémont,** an army officer, wrote of the region's mild climate and vast natural **resources.** Americans began to talk about adding California to the Union. They argued that the nation would then be safely bordered by the Pacific Ocean rather than by a foreign country. Shippers also hoped to build ports on the Pacific coast for trade with East Asia.

C

✔ **Reading Check** **Examining** What was the purpose of the California missions?

History ONLINE
Student Web Activity Visit glencoe.com and complete the Chapter 12 Web Activity about California missions.

Leveled Activities

BL **Guided Reading Activity, URB p. 69**

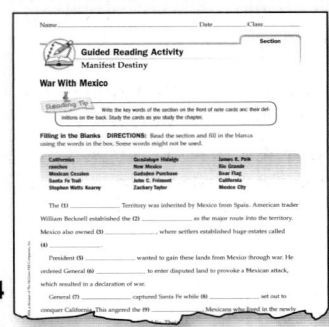

OL **Reading Essentials and Note-Take Guide, p. 124**

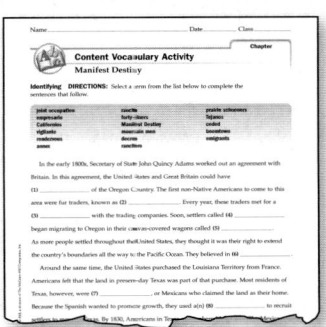

ELL **Content Vocabulary Activity, URB p. 45**

War With Mexico

Main Idea War broke out between the United States and Mexico.

History and You Think about how important California is to the United States. Read to find out how the United States acquired this land from Mexico.

• •

President Polk saw New Mexico and California as belonging to the United States. After Mexico refused to sell the lands, Polk plotted to gain them through war. Polk, however, wanted to provoke Mexico to strike first so that he could justify a war.

Relations between the two countries were strained. Mexico still claimed Texas as its own. The two nations also disagreed about the Texas-Mexico border. The United States insisted that the Rio Grande formed the border. Mexico claimed that the border lay along the Nueces (nu•AY•suhs) River, 150 miles (241 km) farther north.

Conflict Begins

Polk sent John Slidell to Mexico to propose a deal. Slidell was authorized to offer $30 million for California and New Mexico in return for Mexico's acceptance of the Rio Grande as the Texas boundary. In addition the United States would take over payment of Mexico's debts to American citizens. The Mexican government refused to discuss the offer and announced its intention to reclaim Texas for Mexico.

Polk ordered General Zachary Taylor to march his soldiers across the disputed borderland. On April 24, 1846, Mexican soldiers attacked Taylor's force. Taylor sent the report the president wanted to hear: "Hostilities may now be considered as **commenced** [begun]."

On May 11, the president told Congress that Mexico had "invaded our territory and shed American blood upon the American soil." Congress passed a declaration of war against Mexico.

W Writing Support

Persuasive Writing Instruct students to write a letter from President Polk to the Mexican government, persuading Mexico to accept the U.S. proposal for California. Tell students to use convincing language to help persuade the Mexican government. **OL**

People IN HISTORY

Critical Thinking Answers

1. The Mexican government could not provide a settled and stable government, which was reflected in their treatment of California settlers.
2. He supported the revolt because it would establish a settled and stable government for the settlers and their property.

People IN HISTORY

John C. Frémont

Western Explorer and Supporter of the Bear Flag Revolt

John C. Frémont was a mapmaker who led several western expeditions. He set out on his third expedition in 1845 when the United States was on the verge of a war with Mexico over the annexation of Texas. In June 1846, during the Bear Flag Revolt, he supported a small group of Americans who declared the area independent. They named it the Bear Flag Republic. Frémont later wrote that he saw their actions as *"movements with the view of establishing a settled and stable government, which may give security to their persons and property."*

CRITICAL Thinking

1. **Theorizing** Based on Frémont's quotation, how do you think the Mexican government treated California settlers?
2. **Speculating** Why do you think Frémont supported the revolt?

Differentiated Instruction

Social Studies Skills Activity, URB p. 53

Reading a Time Line

Objective:	To identify dates in time-line intervals
Focus:	Draw a number line on the board showing multiples of 10. Ask students how many years are between each number. *(nine)*
Teach:	Show students how to find dates located between marked numbers on a time line.
Assess:	Have students demonstrate how to find a specific year on a time line.
Close:	Discuss the different intervals possible on a time line.

Differentiated Instruction Strategies

BL Provide students with a specific, written process for interpreting time lines.

AL Have students create questions using the time line.

ELL Define the term "interval" for students, and have them identify an interval on a time line.

C Critical Thinking

Analyzing Information Ask: *Why was the order of the parts important to the success of Polk's plan? (If the United States did not secure the border first, then Mexican troops could defend New Mexico and California, preventing the United States from capturing those territories.)* **OL**

R Reading Strategy

Monitoring The events in these passages occur at the same time. Struggling readers may become confused by the overlapping dates. Remind students to stop and reread—and paraphrase and take notes, if needed—to understand the text. **BL**

War With Mexico
1846–1848 NATIONAL GEOGRAPHIC

Map Skills Answer

the number of American victories, which is shown by the blue "starbursts"

Additional Support

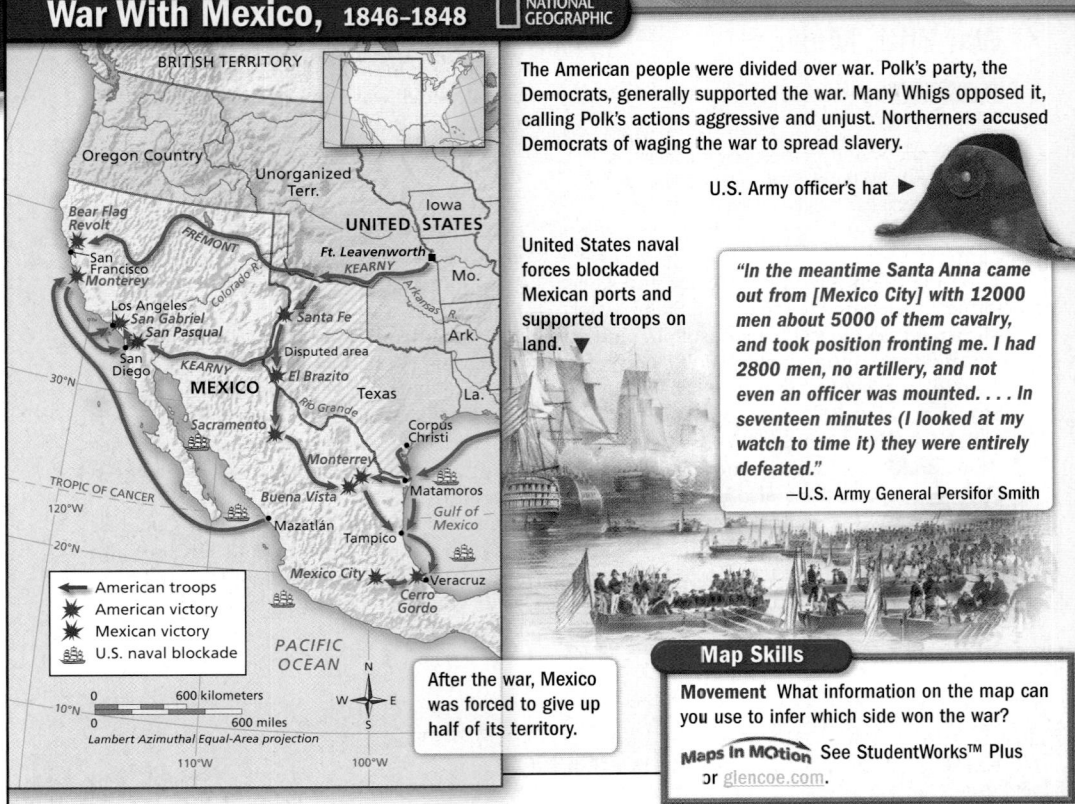

War With Mexico, 1846–1848 NATIONAL GEOGRAPHIC

The American people were divided over war. Polk's party, the Democrats, generally supported the war. Many Whigs opposed it, calling Polk's actions aggressive and unjust. Northerners accused Democrats of waging the war to spread slavery.

U.S. Army officer's hat ▶

United States naval forces blockaded Mexican ports and supported troops on land. ▼

"In the meantime Santa Anna came out from [Mexico City] with 12000 men about 5000 of them cavalry, and took position fronting me. I had 2800 men, no artillery, and not even an officer was mounted. . . . In seventeen minutes (I looked at my watch to time it) they were entirely defeated."

—U.S. Army General Persifor Smith

American troops
★ **American victory**
✦ **Mexican victory**
⚓ **U.S. naval blockade**

After the war, Mexico was forced to give up half of its territory.

Map Skills

Movement What information on the map can you use to infer which side won the war?

Maps In MOtion See StudentWorks™ Plus or glencoe.com.

Polk's War Plan

C Polk's war plan had three parts. First, American troops would drive Mexican forces out of the disputed border region in Texas and secure the border. Second, the United States would seize New Mexico and California. Finally, American forces would take Mexico City, the capital of Mexico.

Zachary Taylor accomplished the first goal. By early 1847, his army had captured the towns of Matamoros, Monterrey, and Buena Vista. The Texas border was secure.

R While Taylor made progress in northern Mexico, American forces also advanced farther west. General Stephen Watts Kearny led about 1,500 troops along the Santa Fe Trail from Fort Leavenworth to New Mexico. The

Mexican governor fled, allowing the Americans to capture New Mexico's capital, Santa Fe, on August 18, 1846, without firing a shot. Kearny then led his army across the deserts toward California.

The Bear Flag Republic

In June 1846, a small group of Americans seized the town of Sonoma north of San Francisco and proclaimed the independent Republic of California. They called the new country the Bear Flag Republic.

John C. Frémont and mountain man Kit Carson also met in Sonoma. Frémont declared that he would conquer California. Many **Californios,** the Mexicans who lived in California, were outraged by his declaration.

Fast Facts

The Bear Flag On June 9, 1846, a group of Americans captured the town of Sonoma in an effort to protect American settlers in the area. Less than a week later, the Mexican General Vallejo was captured, and the area was declared an independent republic. The Americans then designed a flag to represent their new country. The flag contained a star and a grizzly bear and the words "California Republic." Because of the flag design, the Americans who claimed independence became known as the Bears, and their country was called the Bear Flag Republic. The flag brought the new republic much ridicule because the bear resembled a hog. The original bear flag survived until 1906, when it was destroyed in the San Francisco earthquake and subsequent fire. **OL**

They might have supported a revolt for local control, but they opposed what looked like an attempt to seize land.

In July 1846, a United States Navy force under Commodore John Sloat captured the ports of Monterey and San Francisco. Sloat declared California annexed to the United States. Sloat's fleet sailed for San Diego, carrying Frémont and Carson. The Americans captured San Diego and moved north to Los Angeles.

After Sloat's ships left, many Californios in San Diego rose up against the Americans who had taken over the city. General Kearny and his troops put down the revolt. By January 1847, California was fully controlled by the United States.

The Capture of Mexico City

President Polk gave the task of capturing Mexico City to General **Winfield Scott.** In March 1847, Scott's army landed near the Mexican port of Veracruz. The army captured Veracruz after a three-week siege and then fought its way some 300 miles to Mexico City. By mid-September 1847, the Americans had taken Mexico City. The Mexican government surrendered. It would also be forced to surrender half of its territory.

The United States Expands

The **Treaty of Guadalupe Hidalgo** (GWAH•duhl•OOP hih•DAL•goh) was signed in February 1848. Mexico gave up Texas and agreed to the Rio Grande as the border between Texas and Mexico. In what was called the **Mexican Cession,** Mexico **ceded,** or gave, California and New Mexico to the United States for the price of $15 million.

In 1853 the United States paid Mexico $10 million for the **Gadsden Purchase,** a strip of land along the southern edge of present-day Arizona and New Mexico. With the Gadsden Purchase, the U.S. mainland reached its present size.

✓ **Reading Check** Evaluating Was President Polk's war plan successful? Explain.

S Skill Practice

Using Geography Skills Have students use a map to trace Sloat's route. **OL**

R Reading Strategy

Academic Vocabulary Ask: What does "ceded" mean? *(gave)* Who gave California to the United States? Remind students that they can replace the vocabulary word with the easier definition (gave) to help them understand the meaning of the text. **BL**

✓ **Reading Check Answer:** Yes, by 1847, California was under the control of the United States.

Assess
. . . .

History ONLINE

Study Central™ provides summaries, interactive games, and online graphic organizers to help students review content.

Close
. . . .

Stating As a class, tell why the United States wanted control of California. **OL**

Section 3 Review

History ONLINE
Study Central™ To review this section, go to glencoe.com.

Vocabulary

1. Define each of the following terms in a sentence: rancho, ranchero, resource, commence, Californios, cede.

Main Ideas

2. Specifying What was the original purpose of the Santa Fe Trail?

3. Explaining Why did Americans want to acquire California?

4. Identifying What issues existed between the United States and Mexico before they went to war?

Critical Thinking

5. Analyzing Describe how trade promoted United States territorial growth.

6. Organizing Use a diagram like the one below to describe each part of Polk's war plan and the goal he was trying to achieve.

Polk's War Plan

Goal

7. Creative Writing Write the words to a short national anthem for the Bear Flag Republic. Include details designed to evoke pride among the citizens of the country.

Answer the
8. Essential Question
How did Mexican lands in the West become part of the United States?

Answers

1. Sentences should demonstrate a correct understanding of the terms.
2. to serve as a trade route
3. to build Pacific ports for trade with China and Japan; to be safely bordered by the sea instead of by a foreign power; belief in Manifest Destiny
4. dispute over location of Texas-Mexico border; annexation of Texas, which Mexico still claimed

5. Trade interests led American traders to Santa Fe, creating the Santa Fe Trail; the Santa Fe Trail gave other traders a westward route to follow; and an interest in port cities was one factor in the acquisition of California.
6. Plan: drive Mexican forces out of border region in Texas and secure border, seize New Mexico and California, take Mexico City; **Goal:** gain California and New Mexico for the United States

7. Lyrics should reflect a positive image of the Bear Flag Republic.
8. most were gained in treaty following war, final piece gained through Gadsden Purchase

Section 4

California and Utah

Focus

Bellringer
Daily Test Practice Transparency 12–4

Reading Guide
Answers to Graphic:

Forty-niners: People who arrived in California in 1849; **Role:** stayed in California after the Gold Rush and helped settle the state

Mormons: members of the Church of Jesus Christ of Latter-day Saints; **Role:** built a new settlement in Utah

Brigham Young: Mormon leader; **Role:** led the Mormons to Utah

Section Spotlight Video

Have students watch the Section Spotlight Video "New Settlers in California and Utah" to learn more about the Mormons.

Resource Manager

Essential Question
What factors affected the settlement of California and Utah in the West?

Reading Guide

Content Vocabulary
forty-niner (p. 379)   vigilante (p. 380)
boomtown (p. 379)

Academic Vocabulary
constitution (p. 380)   incorporate (p. 382)

Key People and Events
Levi Strauss (p. 380)
Mormon (p. 381)
Joseph Smith (p. 381)
Brigham Young (p. 382)

Reading Strategy
Taking Notes As you read, take notes in a diagram like the one below. Describe what a person or group did and what their roles were in the settlement of California and Utah.

ILLINOIS STANDARDS
The American Journey

17.C.3a Explain how human activity is affected by geographic factors.

17.C.3c Analyze how human processes influence settlement patterns including migration and population growth.

18.B Understand the roles and interactions of individuals and groups in society.

18.C.3a Describe ways in which a diverse U.S. population has developed and maintained common beliefs (e.g., life, liberty and the pursuit of happiness; the Consitution and the Bill of Rights).

American Diary

From early 1848—when John Sutter discovered gold in California—until late 1849, the population of California increased from 15,000 to more than 100,000. Wild-eyed prospectors came from all over the world. "Farmers left their fields untilled and went off. . . . Workmen quit their jobs without notice. . . . In every town . . . one might buy gold-seekers' manuals, guides and maps."

—*from* The Way Our People Lived

Gold mining in California

R Reading Strategies	C Critical Thinking	D Differentiated Instruction	W Writing Support	S Skill Practice
Teacher Edition • Visualizing, p. 379 • Sequencing Information, p. 381 **Additional Resources** • Guid. Read., URB p. 70 • Content Vocab., URB p. 45 • Read. Ess., p. 127 • Read. Skills, URB p. 7	**Teacher Edition** • Evaluating, p. 379 • Comparing and Contrasting, p. 380 **Additional Resources** • Quizzes and Tests, p. 114 • Differ. Inst., URB p. 55	**Teacher Edition** • Intrapersonal, p. 382 **Additional Resources** • School-to-Home, URB p. 63 • Reteaching Act., URB p. 65	**Teacher Edition** • Descriptive Writing, p. 380	**Teacher Edition** • Visual Literacy, p. 381 **Additional Resources** • Daily Test Pract. Transp. 12-4 • Lesson Transp. 12C

California Gold Rush

Main Idea The discovery of gold led to rapid growth and eventual statehood for California.

History and You Do you think searching for treasure would be an exciting life? Read what life was like during the California Gold Rush.

When gold was discovered in California in 1848, people from all over the world traveled to the region in search of riches. Those who arrived in 1849 were called **forty-niners.** As one official reported, "the farmers have thrown aside their plows, the lawyers their briefs, the doctors their pills, the priests their prayer books, and all are now digging gold." Many people arrived by sea. Others traveled on the Oregon Trail or the Santa Fe Trail.

Americans made up about 80 percent of the forty-niners. Others came from Mexico, South America, Europe, and Australia. About 300 men arrived from China, the first large group of Asian immigrants to settle in America. Although some eventually returned to China, others remained and established California's Chinese American community.

The Californios

The Treaty of Guadalupe Hidalgo ended the war with Mexico and made Californios citizens of the United States. The treaty also guaranteed them the rights to their lands. The Land Law of 1851, however, established a group of reviewers who examined the Californios' land rights. When a new settler claimed a Californio's land, the two parties would go to court, and the Californio had to prove that he or she owned the land. Some Californios were able to prove their claims. Many, however, lost their land.

Life in California

As people rushed to a new area to look for gold, they built new communities, called **boomtowns,** almost overnight. At one site on the Yuba River where only two houses stood in September 1849, a miner arrived the next year to find a town of 1,000 people "with a large number of hotels, stores, groceries, bakeries, and . . . gambling houses."

Cities also flourished during the Gold Rush. As ships arrived daily with gold seekers, San Francisco grew from a tiny village to a city of about 20,000 people.

Teach

C **Critical Thinking**

Evaluating Ask: Why was the Land Law of 1851 created? *(Many people hoped to discover gold on property already settled by Californios. The Land Law helped resolve ownership disputes between new settlers and Californios.)* **OL**

R **Reading Strategy**

Visualizing Tell students that visualizing, or creating pictures in one's mind, can help them understand what they read. Ask students to visualize a boomtown as they read this paragraph. Then have them sketch a picture using the description in the paragraph. **BL**

By the Numbers

Critical Thinking Answer
There were few stores in mining towns, so miners had to pay the prices the store owners set, even if the prices were high.

Calculating Ask: What was the least amount of money a miner made for three days of labor? *($6 × 3 = $18)* What was the most a miner made in three days? *($10 × 3 = $30)*

Differentiated Instruction

By the Numbers / Gold Rush Prices

Costs Miners might mine $10 worth of gold one day but $2,000 the next day. Even though their income was unpredictable, miners still had to buy supplies. What did goods cost in San Francisco in 1849?

Gold Rush Era California

Item	Cost
Flour	$18 per pound
Coffee	$16 per pound
Butter	$1 per pound
Rice	$10 per pound
Wood	$20 per cord
Sleeping Room	$12 per week
Labor (earned money)	$6–10 per day

Critical Thinking

Analyzing San Francisco's prices were 20 times higher than those in the rest of the country. Why would miners pay high prices?

Leveled Activities

BL **Lesson Transparency 12C**

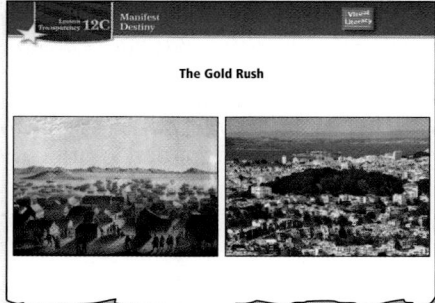

OL **Differentiated Instruction Activity, URB p. 55**

AL **Primary Source Readings Activity, URB p. 49**

379

C Critical Thinking

Comparing and Contrasting Ask: How were the goals of miners and merchants similar? *(Both wanted to profit from the Gold Rush.)* How did their results differ? *(Merchants became wealthy, but miners rarely did.)* **OL**

W Writing Support

Descriptive Writing Tell students they are members of a mining camp sending postcards to loved ones. Have students write descriptions of the mining camp on index cards and draw pictures of the camp on the fronts of the postcards. **OL**

INTERPRETING
POLITICAL CARTOONS

Answers

1. They acted eager and excited.
2. Favorable, because the image is one of celebration, however the cartoonist seems to poke fun at how insistent travelers are to get to California.

Reading Check **Answer:** to search for gold

Hands-On Chapter Project
Step 4

WESTERN EXPANSION ENCYCLOPEDIA

Primary Sources
INTERPRETING
POLITICAL CARTOONS

People from all over the world traveled to California in search of gold.

1. **Interpreting** Describe how people in the cartoon acted as they left for California.

2. **Drawing Conclusions** Do you think the cartoonist views the California Gold Rush as favorable? Why or why not?

Most forty-niners had no experience in mining. Whenever they heard that gold had been discovered at a particular site, they rushed to it and attacked the hillsides with pickaxes and shovels. They spent hours bent over streambeds, "washing" or "panning" the water for gold dust and nuggets.

The California Gold Rush more than doubled the world's supply of gold. For all their hard work, however, very few forty-niners achieved lasting wealth. Most found little or no gold. Many of those who did lost their riches through gambling or wild spending.

Boomtown merchants, however, made huge profits. They could charge whatever they liked for food and other essential items because there were no other nearby stores that sold these products. For example, an immigrant named **Levi Strauss** sold the miners sturdy pants made of denim. His "Levi's" made him rich.

Gold Rush Society

Mining camps contained men of all backgrounds, but few women. Lonely and suffering hardships, many men spent their free hours drinking, gambling, and fighting. Mining towns had no police or prisons. As a result, citizens formed committees of groups known as **vigilantes** (vih•juh•LAN•teez) to protect themselves. Vigilantes took the law into their own hands and acted as police, judge, jury, and sometimes executioner.

Economic and Political Progress

The Gold Rush had lasting effects on California. Agriculture, shipping, and trade grew to meet the demand for food and other goods. Many people who had arrived looking for gold stayed to farm or run a business.

Rapid growth brought the need for better government. In 1850, Californians applied for statehood and wrote a **constitution**—a list of laws to support the government. The constitution's ban on slavery, however, caused a crisis in Congress. Southern states opposed California's admission. California did not enter the Union until a compromise was reached later that year.

Reading Check **Explaining** Why did the forty-niners travel to California?

Creating an Illustrated Encyclopedia

Step 4: Creating "Gold Rush" and "Utah" Entries Groups of students will create encyclopedia entries for "Gold Rush" and "Utah."

Essential Question: What factors affected the settlement of California and Utah in the West?

Directions Assign each group a topic related to the Gold Rush and Utah, such as boomtowns and Mormon settlers. Instruct students to research their topics. Students should collect facts and study related photos, maps, and illustrations. Groups should then decide which facts and images to include in their entries. Group members should prepare the text and illustrations and include captions.

Speculating As a class, discuss how history might have been different if gold had not been discovered in California. **OL**

(Chapter Project continued on the Visual Summary page)

A Religious Refuge in Utah

Main Idea The Mormons settled in Utah.

History and You Think about how you would plan to build a city in a desert. Learn how the Mormons created a thriving city in the harsh terrain of a desert.

A visitor to the Utah Territory in the 1850s wrote admiringly: "The whole of this small nation occupy themselves as usefully as the working bees of a hive." This account described the **Mormons,** or members of the Church of Jesus Christ of Latter-day Saints. Mormons settled in Utah to fulfill their vision of the godly life.

The First Mormons

The Church of Jesus Christ of Latter-day Saints was among a number of religious movements that sprang up during the religious awakenings of the 1830s and 1840s. The founder of the Mormon Church was **Joseph Smith,** a New Englander living in western New York. Smith claimed that he had received visions that led him to build a new Christian church. He began preaching Mormon ideas in 1830.

Smith published *The Book of Mormon* that year, announcing that it was a translation of words written on golden plates that he had received from an angel. The text told of the coming of God and the need to build a kingdom on Earth to receive him.

Smith hoped to use his visions to build an ideal society. He believed that property should be held in common. He also supported polygamy, the idea that a man could have more than one wife. This angered a large number of people. Mormons eventually gave up this practice.

Smith formed a community in New York, but unsympathetic neighbors disapproved of the Mormons' religion and forced them to leave. The Mormons eventually settled in Illinois. In 1839 they bought the town of Commerce, Illinois, and renamed it Nauvoo. Nauvoo became a prosperous community.

Primary Source / The Mormons

West to Utah Strong anti-Mormon feelings in the United States convinced Brigham Young to lead Mormons west. Young hoped to settle in a place where his people could live and worship freely.

Mormons gave people carts to help them carry their possessions on the journey west. By 1860, about 40,000 Mormons had settled in the Utah Territory. ▼

"In our Mountain home we feel not the withering sources of influence of political or even fashionable [tyranny]. . . . I have found the satisfaction of having been [very] successful, and peace again smiles upon all our settlements, and that too without a resort to arms."
—Brigham Young

▲ Mormons minted coins and issued paper money in the 1840s and 1850s.

The Mormon Temple, Salt Lake City, Utah ▼

Critical Thinking

Analyzing Why did Young feel satisfied after the Mormons' journey west?

Reading Skills Activity, URB p. 7

R Reading Strategy

Sequencing Information As students read the text, have them complete a time line of events depicting the founding and settlement of the Mormons. **OL**

S Skill Practice

Visual Literacy Have students read the quotation and refer to the feature on this page. **Ask:** What evidence in the painting reflects the speaker's opinion? *(Some people in the picture are busy working.)* Ask students to look at the image of the Mormon Temple. **Ask:** Based on the painting and photo, would you predict the Mormons were successful in settling Utah? What makes you think so? *(yes, because their temple is grand and elaborate, which is a sign of success)* **OL**

Primary Source

Critical Thinking Answer
He believed the Mormons had found a peaceful area away from tyranny and persecution.

Differentiated Instruction

Making Inferences

Objective: To identify hidden meanings in text in order to draw inferences

Focus: Ask students what it means to "read between the lines."

Teach: Demonstrate how to find hidden meanings in short statements or paragraphs.

Assess: Have students find the hidden meaning in a sample passage, quotation, or poem.

Close: Discuss the importance of critical reading versus "word calling."

Differentiated Instruction Strategies

BL Provide students with real-life scenarios that contain hidden meaning.

AL Have students create inference questions from the text.

ELL Help students understand the language of inference questions to help them identify when to use their own experience to find hidden meaning.

Section 4

D Differentiated Instruction

Intrapersonal Ask: What does independence mean to you? *(Answers may include freedom to make one's own choices and live on one's own.)* How did the Mormons exhibit independence? *(Students may note that they created their own community, practiced their religion freely, and became self-sufficient.)* **OL**

✓ **Reading Check Answer:** Joseph Smith

Assess

History ONLINE

Study Central™ provides summaries, interactive games, and online graphic organizers to help students review content.

Close

Naming Ask students to name the territory settled by the Mormons. **OL**

Section 4 Review

Persecution of the Mormons, however, continued. In 1844 a mob of local residents killed Joseph Smith. After Smith's death, **Brigham Young** took over as head of the Mormons. Young decided that the Mormons should move again to escape persecution and find religious freedom. This time, the Mormons would move west to the Great Salt Lake in present-day Utah. Although part of Mexico at the time, no Mexicans had settled in the region because of its harsh terrain.

A Haven in the Desert

The Mormon migration began in 1846. About 12,000 Mormons made the trek. It was the largest single migration in American history. The Mormons forged their way along a path that became known as the Mormon Trail. Like the Oregon Trail, the Mormon Trail served as a valuable route into the western United States.

In 1847 the Mormons finally reached the Great Salt Lake. It was there that Young declared that the Mormons would build a new settlement. The land was dry and wild. Nevertheless, the Mormons staked a claim on the land they called Deseret. Soon they had set up farming communities.

D At first life was difficult for the settlers. The Mormons, however, made Deseret flourish because of their hard work and determination to succeed. They planned their towns, such as Salt Lake City, carefully and built irrigation canals to water their farms. Property was taxed, and the use of water, timber, and other natural resources was regulated. Mormons also founded industries so they could be self-sufficient. Mormon merchants sold supplies to the forty-niners who passed through Utah on their way to California.

In 1848 the United States acquired the Salt Lake area as part of the settlement with the war with Mexico. In 1850 Congress established the Utah Territory. President Millard Fillmore made Brigham Young the governor of the Utah Territory.

By 1860 there were numerous Mormon communities throughout the Utah region. Utah was not easily **incorporated**, or included, into the United States. The Mormons often had conflicts with federal officials. In 1857 and 1858, war almost broke out between the Mormons and the United States Army. Utah did not become a state until 1896.

✓ **Reading Check Identifying** Who founded the Church of Jesus Christ of Latter-day Saints?

Section 4 Review

History ONLINE
Study Central™ To review this section, go to glencoe.com.

Vocabulary
1. Define each of the following terms and use them in a paragraph about the California Gold Rush: forty-niner, boomtown, vigilante, constitution, incorporate.

Main Ideas
2. **Explaining** Why was California's entry into the Union delayed?
3. **Explaining** Why did the Mormons leave New York?

Critical Thinking
4. **Making Connections** How did the Gold Rush affect California's population?
5. **Organizing** In a diagram like the one below, list the reasons Deseret was able to flourish.

Success of Deseret

6. **Creative Writing** You are living in a California boomtown in the mid-1800s. Write a journal entry that describes what your daily life is like.

Answer the
7. **Essential Question**
What factors affected the settlement of California and Utah in the West?

Answers

1. Paragraphs should reflect a correct understanding of the terms.
2. Its constitution banned slavery, so Southern states objected that admitting it would upset the balance of free and slave states.
3. They were seeking safe haven, as disapproving neighbors forced them to move on.
4. It made California more diverse, as people arrived from all over the world. Those from China established California's Chinese American community.
5. Mormons' hard work and determination to succeed; careful planning of towns; built irrigation canals to water their farms; property was taxed; use of natural resources was regulated; Mormons founded industries so they could be self-sufficient.
6. Journal entries should reflect facts about boomtowns from the text.
7. caused rapid growth in population and in economic activity to serve the growing population; growth led to need for more effective government, resulting in the writing of a state constitution and statehood in 1850

Visual Summary

Oregon Territory

- The area includes present-day Oregon, Washington, and Idaho and parts of Montana, Wyoming, and British Columbia.
- The United States, Great Britain, Spain, and Russia claim the Oregon Territory.
- Mountain men create east-west passages that are vital for trade and settlement.
- Manifest Destiny is the belief that God has given Americans the right to extend the country's western boundaries.
- In 1846 Britain and the U.S. set the border at latitude 49° N.

Texas

- Americans receive land grants from Mexico and settle in Texas.
- Texas colonists agree to learn Spanish, become Mexican citizens, convert to Catholicism, and obey Mexican law in exchange for land at low prices.
- Texans wins their independence from Mexico in 1836.
- Texas joins the Union in 1845.

New Mexico

- The territory includes all of present-day New Mexico, Arizona, Nevada, and Utah and parts of Colorado and Wyoming.
- The first American trader arrives in New Mexico in 1821.
- The Santa Fe Trail trade route begins near Independence, Missouri, and ends in New Mexico.

Utah Territory

- The Mormons, founded by Joseph Smith, seek to escape religious persecution.
- In 1846 Brigham Young leads the Mormons west; they settle near the Great Salt Lake.
- The Mormons establish successful farming communities.
- Utah becomes a state in 1896.

California

- Spanish explorers and Mexican missionaries settle the region.
- In June 1846, American settlers proclaim California's independence from Mexico.
- After the war with Mexico, the United States buys California and New Mexico for $15 million.
- The Gold Rush fuels settlement and economic growth.
- California becomes a state in 1850.

 Study anywhere, anytime! Download quizzes and flash cards to your PDA from glencoe.com.

Visual Summary

Understanding Question-Answer Relationships Have students work in pairs to write questions based on the Visual Summary. Have each pair write eight questions on index cards, one per card. Then have the pair write the answers, using eight more cards. For example, an answer might be "Brigham Young" and the question might be "Who led the Mormons to Utah?" Ask students to exchange answers with another pair of students, identify the matching questions, and discuss the answers and questions. **OL**

Specifying Organize students into small groups. Instruct them to take turns reading a bulleted item from the Visual Summary. After a student reads the item, the other students should name the state or territory that corresponds to the event. Tell students to try to name the state or territory without using their books. **OL**

Identifying the Main Idea Instruct students to use the headings in the Visual Summary to construct main-idea statements that fit the chapter content. When finished, have students compare their sentences. **OL**

Hands-On Chapter Project
Step 5: Wrap-Up

Creating an Illustrated Encyclopedia

Step 5: Publishing the Encyclopedia Students will publish their encyclopedia.

Directions Have the groups complete the encyclopedia by creating a front and back cover and title page and then binding the book. Have students make color copies of their encyclopedia for use in other classrooms or in the school library. Students can also create an online version by scanning the hard-copy encyclopedia and placing the file on a class or library computer.

Determining Cause and Effect Ask: What were the benefits and drawbacks of Manifest Destiny? *(Benefits might be access to natural resources and the establishment of valuable port cities on the Pacific; drawbacks might include strained U.S.–Mexican and U.S.–British relations.)* Do you think Manifest Destiny is a viable philosophy today? *(Answers may include no, because the United States must maintain good foreign relations, and taking more territory would create conflicts with other countries.)* **OL**

Answers and Analyses
Reviewing Main Ideas

1. B Remind students that the United States negotiated with Spain, not Britain or Russia, for the Oregon Country. Under the treaty, the United States did not gain possession of the territory. Britain and the United States jointly occupied the territory. **14.E**

2. C Students can eliminate answer choice A because Spain attracted empressarios to Texas; Spain did not jail them. Answer choice B is incorrect because Mexico taxed U.S. imports to prevent more Americans from settling Texas. Answer choice D is incorrect because Americans had freedom of religion in the United States and did not have to settle Texas to practice their religion. **17.C.3c**

3. C Students should recall that economics was one motivating factor for statehood, and West Coast ports would allow for increased trade. **17.C.3a**

4. A The settlement's name, Deseret, may be a clue to the type of environment of the settlement: the desert. Irrigation was needed for farming in the desert. **16.E.3b (US)**

Short-Answer Question

5. Senator Corwin states that Southerners should not fight Mexico for land only to be told slavery would not be allowed there. **16.A.3b**

STANDARDIZED TEST PRACTICE

TEST-TAKING TIP

Skim through a test before you start to answer the questions. This strategy will help you decide how to pace yourself.

Reviewing Main Ideas

Directions: Choose the best answer for each of the following questions.

1. In the Adams-Onís Treaty of 1819,

  A the United States and Britain agreed to jointly occupy Oregon.

  B Spain gave up claims to Oregon.

  C the United States gained sole possession of the Oregon Territory.

  D Russia gave up claims to the Oregon Territory.

2. How did Mexico attract settlers to Texas?

  A It jailed the *empresarios* for keeping most of the land in Texas for themselves.

  B It removed all taxes on American-made goods.

  C It offered land to people who agreed to settle it.

  D It agreed to allow freedom of religion.

3. Why did many Americans in the 1840s want to make California a state?

  A to convert Native Americans to Christianity

  B to abolish the Spanish missions

  C to build ports on the Pacific coast

  D to sell Native Americans into slavery

4. Mormons used irrigation to water crops at

  A Deseret.

  B New York City.

  C San Francisco.

  D boomtowns in California.

Short-Answer Question

Directions: Base your answer to question 5 on the following excerpt and on your knowledge of social studies.

> I allude to the question of Slavery. Opposition to its further extension . . . is a deeply-rooted determination with men of all parties in what we call the non-slave-holding States. . . . How is it in the South? Can it be expected that they should expend in common, their blood and their treasure, in the acquisition of immense territory, and then willingly forgo the right to carry thither their slaves, and inhabit the conquered country if they please to do so? Sir, I know the feelings and opinions of the South too well to calculate on this.
>
> —Senator Thomas Corwin, from a speech in opposition to the impending Mexican-American War

5. Based on the excerpt, explain why Corwin opposed war with Mexico.

Review the Essential Questions

6. Essay Explain how westward expansion affected California, Texas, and Utah.

To help you write your essay, review your answers to the Essential Questions in the section reviews and the chapter Foldables Study Organizer. Your essay should include:

- Manifest Destiny;
- the settlement of Texas;
- life in California before and after the discovery of gold;
- reasons for and consequences of the Mexican-American War; and
- the Mormon migration.

GO ON

Review the Essential Questions

6. If students completed their Foldables correctly, they should be able to explain how westward expansion affected California, Texas, and Utah. They should mention the Gold Rush in California, the war with Mexico in Texas, and the Mormon settlement in Utah. **17.C.3a**

History ONLINE
For additional test practice, use **Self-Check Quizzes**—Chapter 12 at glencoe.com.

Chapter 12 Assessment

Document-Based Questions

Directions: Analyze the documents and answer the short-answer questions that follow.

Document 1

This excerpt from *The Prairie and Overland Traveler* offers advice for organizing groups of immigrants to head west.

> After a particular route has been selected to make the journey across the plains . . . their first business should be to organize themselves into a company and elect a commander. The company should be of sufficient [size] to herd and guard animals, and for protection against [Native Americans].
>
> From 50 to 70 men, properly armed and equipped, will be enough for these purposes.

Source: R. B. Marcy, *The Prairie and Overland Traveler*

7. State the reasons why immigrants were advised to travel west in a relatively large group.

Document 2

This excerpt describes a Texas settlement in 1828.

> The Americans from the North, at least the great part of those I have seen, eat only salted meat, bread made by themselves out of corn meal, coffee, and homemade cheese. To these the greater part . . . add strong liquor, for they are in general, in my opinion, lazy people of vicious character. Some of them cultivate their small farms by planting corn; but this task they usually entrust to their . . . slaves, whom they treat with considerable harshness.

Source: José María Sánchez, "A Trip to Texas in 1828"

8. Who planted the corn on farms run by Americans?

9. Based on the excerpt, how would you characterize the attitudes of the Tejanos toward American settlers?

Document 3

Mary Ballou ran a boardinghouse in a mining town; this is an excerpt from a letter to her son.

> I would not advise any Lady to come out here and suffer the toil and fatigue that I have suffered for the sake of a little gold. . . . [An] associate . . . said if she had as good a home as I had got she would not stay twenty five minutes in California. . . . I have been to church to hear a methodist sermon. . . . I was the only Lady that was present and about forty gentleman.

Source: Mary B. Ballou, *"I Hear the Hogs in My Kitchen": A Woman's View of the Gold Rush*

10. What challenges did women face in mining towns during the Gold Rush?

Document 4

This print depicts the murder of Joseph Smith.

Source: Library of Congress

11. What was Smith doing before he was killed?

12. Expository Writing Using the information from the four documents and your knowledge of social studies, write an essay in which you:

- explain how Manifest Destiny was justified;
- explain why Americans settled in new territories; and
- explain how American expansion affected Native Americans and other nations.

If you missed questions...	1	2	3	4	5	6	7	8	9	10	11	12
Go to page...	359	367	374	382	375	358-382	362	367-368	367-368	379-380	381-382	358-382

Need Extra Help?

---

9. Have students consider negative and positive comments as they read the document. The author is critical of Americans' food, their drinking habits, and their work ethic and treatment of slaves. The words "vicious character" are particularly negative. **16.A.3b**

10. Point out to students that the question is asking about challenges for women, so they should look for hardships in the document. The author mentions hard work, fatigue, and the lack of other women in California. **16.A**

11. Smith was seated at a table, reading a book. **16.A.3c**

12. Essays should explain how the idea of Manifest Destiny led many Americans to justify the taking over of other lands. Students should also explain the factors that led to westward expansion, such as increased trade, the Gold Rush, and religious freedom. Students' essays should also address the poor treatment of Native Americans and the war with Mexico. **17.C.3c**

History ONLINE
Have students visit the Web site at glencoe.com to review Chapter 12 and take the Self-Check Quiz.

Need Extra Help?
Have students refer to the pages listed if they miss any of the questions.

Document-Based Questions

7. Refer students to the last sentence in the paragraph, which discusses the "company" size. The text cites the reasons as herding and guarding animals and protecting each other against Native Americans. **16.A.3b**

8. Some Americans planted the corn, but usually their slaves were responsible for this task. **18.B.3a**

Chapter Planning Guide

13

Levels BL	OL	AL	ELL		Resources	Chapter Opener	Section 1	Section 2	Section 3	Section 4	Chapter Assess
					FOCUS						
BL	OL	AL	ELL	🖨	Daily Test Practice Transparencies		13–1	13–2	13–3	13–4	
					TEACH						
	OL	AL		📁	Geography and History Activity, URB			p. 87			
BL	OL		ELL	📁	Time Line Skills Activity, URB		p. 90				
BL	OL	AL	ELL	📁	Writing Skills Activity, URB					p. 79	
BL	OL	AL	ELL	📁	Content Vocabulary Activity, URB		p. 73	p. 73	p 73	p. 73	
BL	OL	AL	ELL	📁	Academic Vocabulary Activity, URB		p. 75	p. 75	p 75	p. 75	
BL	OL		ELL	📁	Social Studies Skills Activity, URB			p. 81			
BL	OL	AL	ELL	📁	Differentiated Instruction Activity, URB					p. 83	
BL	OL	AL	ELL	📁	Critical Thinking Skills Activity, URB					p. 85	
BL	OL	AL	ELL	📁	Linking Past and Present Activity, URB		p. 89				
	OL	AL		📁	Primary Source Readings, URB			p. 77			
BL	OL	AL	ELL	📁	School-to-Home Connection Activity, URB		p. 91	p. 91	p. 91	p. 91	
BL	OL		ELL	📁	Guided Reading Activity, URB*		p. 95	p. 96	p. 97	p. 98	
BL	OL		ELL	📁	Reading Essentials and Note-Taking Guide*		p. 130	p. 133	p. 136	p. 139	
BL	OL	AL	ELL	🖨	Lesson Transparencies		13A		13B	13C	
	OL			📁	American Biographies		p. 15		p. 13		
BL	OL	AL	ELL	📁	Outline Map Resource Book	pp. 11, 15, 17, 18					

Note: Please refer to the *Unit Resource Book: Nationalism and Sectionalism* for this chapter's URB materials.

* Also available in Spanish

Levels					Resources	Chapter Opener	Section 1	Section 2	Section 3	Section 4	Chapter Assess
BL	OL	AL	ELL								
TEACH *(continued)*											
BL	OL	AL	ELL		NGS US Desk Map		✓	✓	✓	✓	
BL	OL	AL	ELL		American Literature Library		✓	✓	✓	✓	
BL	OL	AL	ELL		Writer's Guidebook		✓	✓	✓	✓	
	OL	AL			American History Primary Source Document Library CD-ROM		✓	✓	✓	✓	✓
BL	OL	AL	ELL		American Music Hits Through History	✓	✓	✓	✓	✓	
BL	OL	AL	ELL		StudentWorks™ Plus CD	✓	✓	✓	✓	✓	✓
	OL	AL			Section Spotlight Videos		✓	✓	✓	✓	
BL	OL	AL	ELL		Writing Process Transparencies		✓	✓	✓	✓	✓
BL	OL	AL	ELL		Presentation Plus! With MindJogger CheckPoint CD	✓	✓	✓	✓	✓	✓
ASSESS											
BL	OL	AL	ELL		Quizzes and Tests		p. 121	p. 122	p. 123	p. 124	pp. 125, 127, 129
BL	OL	AL	ELL		Authentic Assessment With Rubrics		p. 13	p. 13	p. 13	p. 13	
BL	OL	AL	ELL		Standardized Test Practice						p. 25
BL	OL	AL	ELL		*ExamView® Assessment Suite* CD-ROM*		13–1	13–2	13–3	13–4	Ch. 13
CLOSE											
BL			ELL		Reteaching Activity, URB*		p. 93	p. 93	p. 93	p. 93	p. 93
BL	OL		ELL		Reading and Study Skills Foldables Activity	p. 74	p. 74	p. 74	p. 74	p. 74	p. 74
BL	OL	AL	ELL		*The American Journey* in Graphic Novel				p. 77		
BL			ELL		Reading Strategies and Activities for the Social Studies Classroom		✓	✓	✓	✓	
BL	OL	AL	ELL		Graphic Organizer Transparencies & Strategies		✓	✓	✓	✓	

TeacherWorks *Plus*
All-In-One Planner and Resource Center

- Interactive Lesson Planner
- Interactive Teacher Edition
- Fully editable blackline masters
- Section Spotlight Videos Launch

- Differentiated Lesson Plans
- Printable reports of daily assignments
- Standards Tracking System

Professional Development Resources

- Strategies for Success
- Building Academic Vocabulary
- Success With English Learners DVD
- Differentiated Instruction Strategies DVD
- Teaching Literacy Strategies in Social Studies DVD
- Assessment DVD
- Standards-Based Instruction DVD

Using Study Central™

Main Ideas

Technology Product

The Study Central™ Web site lists the main ideas for each section of a chapter. The main ideas

- serve as a starting point for class discussions;
- reinforce section content as students pose and answer questions based on the main ideas;
- provide practice and review of test-taking skills.

Objectives

The main ideas help students

- build comprehension and study skills;
- practice developing and answering questions.

Steps

- Locate the Web page for the textbook being studied on the Glencoe Web site glencoe.com.
- Click on **Study Central™** under *Textbook Resources.*
- Select a chapter and section using the drop-down arrows and click **Enter.**
- Click on the **Main Ideas** tab and then on a Main Idea to engage in a discussion on that topic.
- Have students write and review questions based on the statement, using examples as needed.
- Click on Steps 2 and 3 to discuss the skills involved in answering the questions.
- Discuss the questions again with students to evaluate their answers.

History ONLINE at glencoe.com

	Student	Teacher	Parent
Media Center			
• Student Edition Audio	●		
• Spanish Summaries	●		
• Section Spotlight Videos	●	●	
Social Studies Online Learning Center			
Classroom Tools			
• Multi-Language Glossaries	●	●	●
• Teaching Today		●	
• TIME Current Events	●	●	●
• Beyond the Textbook	●	●	
***The American Journey* Online Learning Center**			
• Study-to-Go™	●	●	●
• Study Central™	●	●	●
• Chapter Overview	●	●	
• Concepts in Motion	●	●	
• ePuzzles and Games	●	●	
• Literature Connections	●	●	
• Online Student Edition	●	●	●
• Self-Check Quizzes	●	●	●
• Student Web Activities	●	●	
• Vocabulary eFlashcards	●	●	
• Web Activity Lesson Plans	●	●	●
• Vocabulary PuzzleMaker	●	●	●

READING SUPPORT FROM
JAMESTOWN EDUCATION

- **Timed Readings Plus in Social Studies** helps students increase their reading rate and fluency while maintaining comprehension. The 400-word passages are similar to those found on state and national assessments.

- **Reading in the Content Area: Social Studies** concentrates on six essential reading skills that help students better comprehend what they read. The book includes 75 high-interest nonfiction passages written at increasing levels of difficulty.

- **Reading Social Studies** includes strategic reading instruction and vocabulary support in Social Studies content for ELLs and native speakers of English.

- **Content Vocabulary Workout** (Grades 6–8) accelerates reading comprehension through focused vocabulary development. Social Studies content vocabulary comes from the glossaries of Glencoe's Middle School Social Studies texts.

www.jamestowneducation.com

NATIONAL GEOGRAPHIC
Index to National Geographic Magazine:

The following articles relate to this chapter:

- **"21st-Century Slaves,"** Andrew Cockburn, September 2003.

- **"Last Voyage of the Slave Ship** Henrietta Marie,"** Jennifer Steinberg, August 2002.

National Geographic Society Products

To order the following, call National Geographic at 1-800-368-2728:

National Geographic Atlas of the World (Book)

Access National Geographic's new dynamic MapMachine Web site and other geography resources at:

www.nationalgeographic.com

www.nationalgeographic.com/mapmachine

Reading List Generator CD-ROM
GLENCOE BOOKLINK 3

Use this database to search more than 30,000 titles to create a customized reading list for your students.

- Reading lists can be organized by students' reading level, author, genre, theme, or area of interest.
- The database provides Degrees of Reading Power™ (DRP) and Lexile™ readability scores for all selections.
- A brief summary of each selection is included.

Leveled reading suggestions for this chapter:

For students at a Grade 6 reading level:
- ***So Far From Home: The Diary of Mary Driscoll, an Irish Mill Girl,*** by Barry Denenberg

For students at a Grade 7 reading level:
- ***Trouble Don't Last,*** by Shelley Pearsall
- ***Streets of Gold,*** by Karen Branson

For students at a Grade 8 reading level:
- ***Narrative of the Life of Frederick Douglass,*** by Frederick Douglass
- ***The Slave Dancer,*** by Paula Fox

For students at a Grade 9 reading level:
- ***Amistad: A Long Road to Freedom,*** by Walter Dean Myers
- ***Slave Narratives: The Journey to Freedom,*** by Elaine Landau

For students at a Grade 10 reading level:
- ***Eli Whitney: Cotton Gin Genius,*** by Kaye Patchett

The following videotape programs are available from Glencoe as supplements to the chapter:

- **Frederick Douglass** (ISBN 0-76-700120-6)
- **Textiles: Birth of an American Industry** (0-76-700624-0)

To order, call Glencoe at 1-800-334-7344. To find classroom resources to accompany many of these videos, check the following home pages:

A&E Television: www.aetv.com

The History Channel: www.history.com

Introducing Chapter 13

Chapter Objectives

After studying this chapter, students will be able to:

- Describe the innovations in industry, travel, and communications that changed the lives of Americans in the 1800s.
- Discuss the impact of immigration on cities, industry, and culture in the North.
- Explain how the South's industry and economy differed from the North's industry and economy.
- Describe how unique elements of culture developed among enslaved African Americans in the South.

Motivating Activity

Expressing Students will learn that cities grew rapidly in the mid-1800s, especially in the North. Jobs in factories drew people from the countryside and from other nations, transforming towns into cities. **Ask:** Would you prefer to live in a large city or a small town? Why? *(Students might like the excitement of city life and the variety of entertainment and employment options available there. Students who prefer small towns might point to overcrowding, crime, fast pace, or impersonal lifestyle in cities as drawbacks.)* Point out that many of the advantages and disadvantages of city life today were true of cities in the mid-1800s as well.

Previewing the Essential Questions

As you begin teaching each section, use these questions and activities to help students focus on the Essential Questions.

Chapter 13 ▸ North and South 1820–1860

New York City in 1857

PRESIDENTS
- JAMES MONROE 1817–1825
- JOHN Q. ADAMS 1825–1829
- ANDREW JACKSON 1829–1837
- MARTIN VAN BUREN 1837–1841

U.S. Events 1820 — 1830

- ★ 1824 U.S. and Russia settle Northwest coast land claims
- ★ 1826 *The Last of the Mohicans* published
- ★ 1834 McCormick reaper is patented

World Events
- ★ 1820 Antarctica discovered
- ★ 1825 World's first public railroad opens in England
- ★ 1832 Greece recognized as independent state

Section 1

The North's Economy **Ask:** How might the development of an east-west railroad network influence life in the Midwest? *(More efficient transportation of goods and people could speed settlement and industrialization of the Midwest.)* Point out that Section 1 describes innovations that transformed American life. **OL**

Section 2

The North's People **Ask:** Why might the arrival of many immigrants change American culture? *(They brought diverse languages, customs, religions, and traditions with them.)* Point out that Section 2 discusses the impact of large numbers of immigrants on American society. **OL**

Section 1: The North's Economy
Essential Question What innovations in industry, travel, and communications changed the lives of Americans in the 1800s?

Section 2: The North's People
Essential Question How did immigration have an impact on cities, industry, and culture in the North?

Section 3: Southern Cotton Kingdom
Essential Question How did the South's industry and economy differ from the industry and economy of the North?

Section 4: The South's People
Essential Question How did unique elements of culture develop among enslaved African Americans in the South?

History ONLINE
Chapter Overview Visit glencoe.com and click on **Chapter 13—Chapter Overviews** to preview chapter information.

FOLDABLES Study Organizer

Organizing Information
Make this Foldable to help summarize what you learn about similarities and differences between the North and the South.

Step 1 Mark the center of a sheet of notebook paper.

Step 2 Fold the sheet of notebook paper into thirds.

Step 3 Sketch a map of the United States on the front and label your Foldable as shown.

North (1820–1860)

South (1820–1860)

Reading and Writing After you finish taking notes in your Foldable, list the causes and effects of the differences that led to conflict between these regions.

◄ California gold miner

WILLIAM HENRY HARRISON 1841

JOHN TYLER 1841–1845

★ **1845** James Marshall discovers gold in California

JAMES POLK 1845–1849

ZACHARY TAYLOR 1849–1850

MILLARD FILLMORE 1850–1853

FRANKLIN PIERCE 1853–1857

JAMES BUCHANAN 1857–1861

1840   **1850**   **1860**

★ **1845** Great Irish Famine begins

★ **1848** Johannes Rebmann is first European to see Kilamanjaro

Kilimanjaro in Tanzania ►

★ **1857** Sepoy Rebellion begins in India

★ **1859** Darwin's *On the Origin of Species* is published

Chapter 13   387

Time Line Activity

If you have not already done so, have students review the time line. **Ask:** What years are covered in this chapter? Who was president when McCormick patented his reaper? *(1820–1860; Andrew Jackson)* What world event might influence immigration to the United States? Why? *(Irish famine; people of Ireland might immigrate to escape the famine.)*

FOLDABLES Study Organizer   **Dinah Zike's Foldables**

Purpose This Foldable helps students summarize the similarities and differences between the North and the South. The completed Foldable will help them prepare for assessment. **OL**

📁   More Foldables activities for this chapter can be found in the *Dinah Zike's Reading and Study Skills Foldables.*

History ONLINE
Introduce students to chapter content and key terms by having them access the **Chapter Overview** at glencoe.com.

Section 3

Southern Cotton Kingdom Ask: How might high demand for cotton influence the way the South's economy developed? *(Southern farmers grew more cotton, increasing the South's dependence on the crop.)* Tell students that Section 3 will explore differences in the economies of the North and the South. **OL**

Section 4

The South's People Ask: How did enslaved people cope with their situation? *(They developed their own culture that blended African and American traditions and Christianity.)* Explain to students that in Section 4 they will learn what life was like for the people of the South. **OL**

The North's Economy

Focus

Bellringer
Daily Test Practice Transparency 13–1

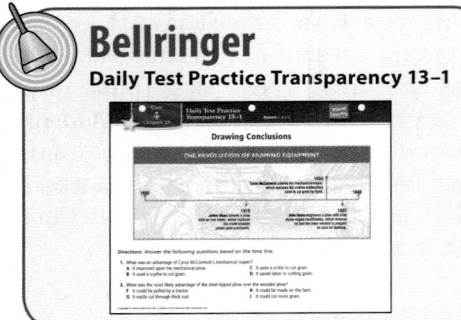

Reading Guide
Answers to Graphic:
Phase 1: manufacturers made products by dividing tasks among workers; **Phase 2:** manufacturers built factories to bring specialized workers together; **Phase 3:** workers used machinery to perform some of their work

Section Spotlight Video

To learn more about industrialization in the Northern states, watch the Section Spotlight Video "The North's Economy."

Resource Manager

Essential Question
What innovations in industry, travel, and communications changed the lives of Americans in the 1800s?

Reading Guide

Content Vocabulary
clipper ship (p. 390)
telegraph (p. 391)
Morse code (p. 392)

Academic Vocabulary
innovation (p. 389)   transform (p. 391)

Key People
Elias Howe (p. 389)
Robert Fulton (p. 390)
Peter Cooper (p. 390)
Samuel Morse (p. 391)
John Deere (p. 393)
Cyrus McCormick (p. 393)

Reading Strategy
Taking Notes As you read, use the diagram below to describe the three phases of the development of industrialization in the North.

Development of Industrialization

Phase 1
↓
Phase 2
↓
Phase 3

ILLINOIS STANDARDS
The American Journey

15.A Understand how different economic systems operate in the exchange, production, distribution and consumption of goods and services.

15.D.3c Explain how workers can affect their productivity through training and by using tools, machinery and technology.

16.C.3b (US) Explain relationships among the American economy and slavery, immigration, industrialization, labor and urbanization, 1700-present.

16.E.3b (US) Describe how the largely rural population of the United States adapted, used and changed the environment after 1818.

American Diary

Railroad travel in the mid-1840s was uncomfortable. English novelist Charles Dickens described what it was like to travel on a train. "There is a great deal of jolting, a great deal of noise, a great deal of wall, not much window, a locomotive engine, a shriek, and a bell. The cars are like shabby omnibusses, but larger; holding thirty, forty, fifty people. . . . In the center of the carriage there is usually a stove, fed with charcoal . . . which is for the most part red-hot. It is insufferably close."

—from American Notes for General Circulation

The number of railroad routes increased dramatically from 1840 to 1860.

R Reading Strategies	C Critical Thinking	D Differentiated Instruction	W Writing Support	S Skill Practice
Teacher Edition	**Teacher Edition**	**Teacher Edition**	**Teacher Edition**	**Teacher Edition**
• Making Connections, p. 389	• Contrasting, p. 389	• Kinesthetic, p. 392	• Narrative Writing, p. 390	• Using Art Skills, p. 390
• Reading Primary Sources, p. 391	• Making Inferences, p. 390	**Additional Resources**		• Using Geo. Skills, p. 393
Additional Resources	• Drawing Conclusions, p. 392	• School-to-Home, URB p. 91		**Additional Resources**
• Guid. Read., URB p. 95	**Additional Resources**	• Reteaching Act., URB p. 93		• Daily Test Pract. Transp. 13-1
• Content Vocab., URB p. 73	• Quizzes and Tests, p. 121			• Lesson Transp. 13A
	• Authentic Assess., p. 13			• Time Line Skills, URB p. 90

Technology and Industry

Main Idea Industry, travel, and communications greatly expanded during the 1800s.

History and You How often do you use e-mail or text messaging during any one day? Read to learn about the invention of the telegraph, which greatly improved communications in the 1800s.

Early trains differed from and offered few of the comforts of modern-day trains. They were noisy and often dirty. As Charles Dickens noted, they also provided a jolty ride. Locomotives were part of the wave of industrialization during the 1800s. **Innovations**—new ideas or methods—in industry and technology began changing the way Americans worked, traveled, and communicated.

Industrialization

The industrialization of the North developed in three phases. In the first phase, manufacturers made products by dividing the tasks involved among the workers. For example, one worker would spin thread all day, and another would weave cloth. This was faster than having one person spin and then weave. During the second phase, manufacturers built factories to bring specialized workers together. Products could be made more quickly than before.

In the third phase, factory workers used machinery to perform some of their work. Many of the new machines ran on water-power or steam power. For example, power-driven looms took over the task of weaving. The worker's job changed from weaving to tending the machine. This change produced more fabric in less time.

Mass production of cotton textiles began in New England in the early 1800s. **Elias Howe** invented the sewing machine in 1846. Using this machine and machine-made fabrics, workers produced clothing on a large scale. Other types of industries developed during the same period. By 1860, the Northeast's factories produced at least two-thirds of the country's manufactured goods.

Improved Transportation

Transportation improvements contributed to the success of America's new industries. Between 1800 and 1850, construction crews built thousands of miles of roads and canals.

Primary Source — Railroad Expansion, 1860

Major Railroads, 1860

Total Length of Railroad Tracks	
1840	3,000 miles (4,828 km)
1850	9,000 miles (14,484 km)
1860	30,000 miles (48,280 km)

— Railroads

0   200 kilometers
0   200 miles
Albers Equal-Area projection

Making Tracks Trains were important not only for transporting people across the country, but they also allowed goods to be shipped greater distances than ever before. Beginning in the early 1800s, industrialization and technology began to change the way Americans worked, traveled, and communicated.

Critical Thinking
Making Inferences What region might have an advantage for transporting goods and people more easily?

Teach

R Reading Strategy

Making Connections Ask students to name a recent innovation. *(Students might name the latest electronic device.)* Point out that an innovation can be a device, but it can also be a new idea or a new way of doing something. **BL**

C Critical Thinking

Contrasting Ask: Before industrialization, how was a shirt produced? *(One craftsperson made the entire shirt.)* How did the worker's role in making shirts change in the first phase of industrialization? *(Tasks were divided up, with each worker performing only part of the job.)* What was the worker's role by the final phase of industrialization? *(tending machines)* **OL**

Primary Source

Critical Thinking Answer
The North would have an advantage, because it had more railroad tracks.

Differentiated Instruction

Leveled Activities

W Writing Support

Narrative Writing Have students take the role of a passenger on an early steamboat. Have them write a letter to a friend, describing the experience. **OL**

C Critical Thinking

Making Inferences "Tom Thumb" was the stage name of Charles Stratton, a midget performer in P. T. Barnum's circus in the mid-1800s. **Ask:** What can you infer about Peter Cooper's locomotive, based on its name? *(It was small and unusual.)* **OL**

This ▶READING SKILL◀ (Making Inferences) was introduced in this unit.

S Skill Practice

Using Art Skills In 1860 the last railroad tracks were laid between New York City and Jamestown, New York. The people of Jamestown held a great celebration. Have students create posters announcing the coming of the steam locomotive. Posters should highlight the advantages of the railroad for the town. **BL**

Hands-On Chapter Project
Step 1

Creating a Slide Show

Step 1: Learning About Innovations Students will research important innovations of the 1800s.

Essential Question: What innovations in industry, travel, and communications changed the lives of Americans in the 1800s?

Directions Organize students into groups. Each group should choose one of these

390

Primary Source / Steamboats and Clipper Ships

Powered by Steam In 1807 Robert Fulton launched his first steamboat, the *Clermont*, on the Hudson River. The first upriver voyage on the Mississippi, from New Orleans to Pittsburgh, was made in 1815. Within a few years, a large fleet of steamboats traveled on the Mississippi and its tributaries. Steamboats revolutionized transportation and played a large part in the settling of the Midwest.

"From every point on the river whence the boat, announced by the smoke of its chimney, could be seen, we saw the inhabitants collect; they waved their handkerchiefs and hurrahed for Fulton."
—from an eyewitness account of the first voyage of the *Clermont*

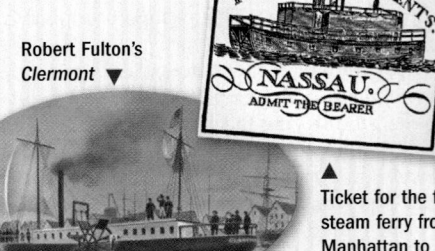

Robert Fulton's *Clermont* ▼

▲ Ticket for the first steam ferry from Manhattan to Brooklyn in 1814

▲ Steamboats congregated in great numbers at Cincinnati, a major river port, in the 1800s. Today, Cincinnati celebrates that heritage with a yearly festival (above far right).

Canals opened new shipping routes by connecting many lakes and rivers. Upstream travel against the current was extremely difficult though. That changed in 1807, when inventor **Robert Fulton** demonstrated a reliable steamboat. Steamboats could carry goods and passengers more cheaply and quickly along inland waterways than flatboats or sail-powered vessels.

In the 1840s, builders began to widen and deepen canals to accommodate steamboats. By 1860 about 3,000 steamboats traveled the country's major rivers and canals, as well as the Great Lakes, spurring the growth of cities such as Cincinnati, Buffalo, and Chicago.

Sailing ships also were improved in the 1840s. The **clipper ships**—with sleek hulls and tall sails—were the pride of the open seas. They could sail 300 miles (483 km) per day, as fast as most steamships at that time. The ships got their name because they "clipped" time from long journeys. Before the clippers, the voyage from New York to Great Britain took about 21 to 28 days. A clipper ship could usually make that trip in half the time.

Locomotives

The development of railroads in the United States began with short stretches of tracks to connect mines with nearby rivers. Horses, rather than locomotives, pulled the early trains. The first steam-powered passenger locomotive, the *Rocket*, began operating in Britain in 1829.

Peter Cooper designed and built the first American steam locomotive in 1830. Called the *Tom Thumb*, it got off to a bad start. In a race against a horse-drawn train in Baltimore, the *Tom Thumb*'s engine failed. Engineers soon improved the engine, and within 10 years steam locomotives were pulling trains in the United States.

A Railway Network

In 1840 the United States had almost 3,000 miles (4,828 km) of railroad track. By 1860, it had almost 31,000 miles (49,890 km), mostly in the North and Midwest areas. One railway linked the cities of New York City and Buffalo. Another connected the Pennsylvania cities of Philadelphia and Pittsburgh.

---

innovations: sewing machine, steamship, clipper ship, steam locomotive, telegraph, reaper, thresher, or cotton gin. Explain to students that they are inventors. They have an idea for a great innovation, but they need money from investors to develop it. Each group will prepare a presentation with electronic slides in order to convince investors to support their project. Groups should do research to collect images and facts about their innovations. They should take

notes about how the innovations work and their effects on the economy and on daily life.

Determining Cause and Effect Discuss the inventions as a class. **Ask:** Which ones directly impact workers? *(sewing machine, reaper, thresher, cotton gin)* **OL**

(Chapter Project continued in Section 2)

Wind in the Sails Clipper ships were designed to carry small, but highly profitable, cargoes over long distances at high speeds. In 1851 one of those ships, the *Flying Cloud*, made the passage from New York to San Francisco in 89 days—a record never beaten by another sailing ship. The age of the clipper ship ended in the late 1800s due to decreased shipping costs on steamships. After that, only ships that could carry large cargoes could make a profit.

◄ A poster announces a clipper ship sailing from New York to San Francisco.

The *Flying Cloud* under full sail ►

"Steamers were improving, but they could not stand up with the clippers in honest competition. . . . The editor of Harper's Magazine . . . predicted 'if our steam-men do not look to their oars [there will be] a return to the old and wholesome service of wind and sail.'"

—from *Clipper Ship Men*

Critical Thinking

Speculating Why do you think that ocean-going sailing ships were still being designed after the invention of the steamboat?

Yet another linked Baltimore and Wheeling, Virginia (now West Virginia). Railway builders connected these eastern lines to lines being built farther west in Ohio, Indiana, and Illinois. By 1860, a network of railroad track united the Midwest and the East.

Moving Goods and People

Along with canals, the railways **transformed,** or changed, trade in the nation's interior. The changes began with the opening of the Erie Canal in 1825 and the first railroads of the 1830s. Before this time, agricultural goods were carried down the Mississippi River to New Orleans. From there they were shipped to the East Coast or to other countries.

The development of the east-west canal and the rail network allowed grain, livestock, and dairy products to move directly from the Midwest to the East. Goods could now be moved faster and more cheaply. As a result, manufacturers in the East could offer them at lower prices.

The railroads also played an important role in the settlement and industrialization of the Midwest. Fast, affordable train travel brought people into Ohio, Indiana, and Illinois. The populations of these states grew. As more people moved into the area, new towns and industries developed.

Faster Communication

The growth of industry and the new pace of travel created a need for faster methods of communication over the vast distances. The **telegraph**—an apparatus that used electric signals to transmit messages—filled that need.

Samuel Morse, an American inventor, was seeking support for a system of telegraph lines. On May 24, 1844, Morse got the chance to demonstrate that he could send messages instantly along wires. As a crowd in the U.S. capital watched, Morse tapped in the words "What hath God wrought!" A few moments later, the telegraph operator in Baltimore sent the same message back in reply. The telegraph worked! Soon telegraph messages were flashing back and forth between Washington, D.C., and Baltimore.

North and South **Chapter 13** 391

Activity: Interdisciplinary Activity

Science The first successful transatlantic cable was laid in 1858. Financed by Cyrus Field, a wealthy New York paper manufacturer, it stretched from Newfoundland to Ireland. The telegraph, however, would not have been possible without the discovery of electricity. Have students research early experiments with electricity. **Ask:** How did electricity help with the development of the telegraph? *(Sending an electric current over wire activated an electromagnet, which moved a marker to produce written codes on a paper strip.)* Have students report their findings in essays. **AL**

People IN HISTORY

Differentiated Instruction

D

Kinesthetic Distribute a copy of the Morse code alphabet. Write this code on the board, and ask students to translate it: . . . - - - . . . *(SOS, which means "help")* Have students write a word in Morse code and then work in pairs to tap out a word for their partners to translate. **OL**

Critical Thinking

C

Drawing Conclusions Ask: How might advances in transportation and farm technology affect consumers? *(Foods would arrive fresher and in greater quantity and variety.)* **AL**

People IN HISTORY

Critical Thinking Answers

1. Both were inventors.
2. **telegraph:** cheering crowd; **plow:** high sales

Reading Check Answer: They created a more direct way to get from the East Coast to the Midwest, vastly improving trade in the nation's interior. People and goods could be moved more quickly.

Differentiated Instruction

John Deere
Inventor of the Steel-Tipped Plow

Because the heavy Midwestern soil stuck to cast-iron plows, farmers had to stop every few feet to clean the plow blades. Blacksmith John Deere set out to create a polished steel plow that would clean itself. The plows became a successful new business. Within 10 years he was selling 1,000 plows per year. Deere constantly improved his design. He was quoted as saying, *"I will never put my name on a product that does not have in it the best that is in me."*

Samuel Morse
Inventor of the Telegraph

Samuel Morse had trouble convincing Congress to build a telegraph line. When he finally did, however, Americans were thrilled with the telegraph's speed. In a letter to his brother, Sidney, Morse described the scene that day: *"The enthusiasm of the crowd . . . was excited to the highest pitch. . . . They gave the Telegraph three cheers, and I was called to make my appearance at the window where three cheers were given to me by some hundreds present."*

CRITICAL Thinking

1. **Analyzing** What did Samuel Morse and John Deere have in common?
2. **Identifying** What showed the popularity of the telegraph? Of the steel-tipped plow?

D Morse transmitted his message in **Morse code.** This code, which Morse developed and which bears his name, is a series of dots and dashes representing the letters of the alphabet. A skilled Morse code operator could rapidly tap out words in the dot-and-dash alphabet.

Americans adopted the telegraph eagerly. A British visitor marveled at the speed with which Americans formed telegraph companies and erected telegraph lines. Americans, he wrote, were driven to "annihilate [wipe out] distance" in their vast country. To speed the transmission of news using the telegraph, the Associated Press was formed in 1848. By 1852, there were about 23,000 miles (37,015 km) of telegraph lines in the United States.

Reading Check **Explaining** How did canals and railways transform trade in the interior of the United States?

Agriculture

Main Idea Revolutionary inventions in the 1830s changed farming methods, and agriculture became more profitable.

History and You Have you or your family ever bought produce from a farmers market? Read to learn how agriculture boomed during the 1800s.

C The railroads gave farmers access to new markets far from their homes in which to sell their products. At the same time, advances in agricultural technology allowed farmers to greatly increase the size of the harvests they produced.

In the early 1800s, few farmers had ventured into the treeless Great Plains west of Missouri, Iowa, and Minnesota. Even areas of mixed forest and prairie west of Ohio and Kentucky seemed too difficult for farming.

From Hand Tools to Tractors

Objective: To understand how the development of farm machines in the 1830s changed agriculture

Focus: Ask students why horse-drawn farm machines would be preferable to manual labor.

Teach: Have students explain how agriculture progressed from manual labor to horse-drawn machinery to internal combustion-powered processes.

Assess: Students should complete the five questions.

Close: Discuss how agricultural techniques might evolve in the future.

Differentiated Instruction Strategies

BL Have students refer to the diagram to explain how the McCormick reaper worked.

AL Have students research and report on present-day agricultural methods in American "family" farming.

ELL Ask students to explain why the American Midwest is called the "Breadbasket of the World."

Linking Past and Present Activity, URB p. 89

Settlers worried that their wooden plows could not break the prairie's matted sod. Further, they worried that the soil would not be fertile enough to support fields of crops.

Revolution in Agriculture

Three revolutionary inventions of the 1830s changed farming methods and encouraged settlers to cultivate larger areas of the Midwest. One invention was the steel-tipped plow that **John Deere** invented in 1837. Far sturdier than the wooden plow, Deere's plow easily cut through the hard-packed prairie sod. Equally important were the mechanical reaper, which sped up the harvesting of wheat, and the thresher, which quickly separated the grain from the stalk.

McCormick's Reaper

Born on a Virginia farm, **Cyrus McCormick** became interested in machines that would ease the burden of farmwork. McCormick designed and constructed the mechanical reaper. He made a fortune manufacturing and selling it.

For hundreds of years, farmers harvested grain with handheld sickles, or cutting tools. McCormick's reaper could harvest grain much faster than a person using a sickle.

History ONLINE
Student Web Activity Visit glencoe.com and complete the Chapter 13 Web Activity about agriculture in the mid-1800s.

Because farmers could harvest wheat so quickly, they began planting more of it. Growing wheat became profitable. McCormick's reaper ensured that raising wheat would remain the main economic activity on the Midwestern prairies.

New machines and the accessibility to railroads allowed farmers to devote more acres to cash crops—crops raised strictly for sale. Midwestern farmers began growing wheat as a cash crop and shipping it east by train and canal barge. Farmers in the Northeast and Middle Atlantic states increased their production of fruits and vegetables.

Despite improvements in agriculture, the North turned away from farming and toward industry. It was difficult to make a living farming the rocky soil of New England. Industry, however, flourished in the area. The number of people working in factories continued to rise. **S**

Reading Check **Identifying** What innovation sped up the harvesting of wheat?

History ONLINE
Objectives and answers to the Student Web Activity can be found at glencoe.com under the Web Activity Lesson Plan for this chapter.

S Skill Practice

Using Geography Skills Ask: What geographic conditions made agriculture difficult? *(The rocky soil and colder climate were not favorable for farming.)* **BL**

Reading Check **Answer:** the mechanical reaper

Assess

History ONLINE

Study Central™ provides summaries, interactive games, and online graphic organizers to help students review content.

Close

Summarizing Review the innovations discussed in the section. Assess the impact of each on the lives of Americans. **OL**

Section 1 Review

History ONLINE
Study Central™ To review this section, go to glencoe.com.

Vocabulary

1. Write a paragraph in which you explain why each of these terms appears in a chapter about American life in the first half of the nineteenth century: innovation, clipper ship, transform, telegraph, Morse code.

Main Ideas

2. Summarizing How were messages sent via telegraph? Why was this invention important?

3. Identifying List innovations in farming methods in the 1830s.

Critical Thinking

4. Making Connections Use a diagram like the one below to show factors that encouraged the settlement of the Midwest.

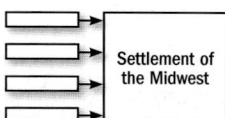
Settlement of the Midwest

5. Expository Writing Write a paragraph discussing why industrial growth and the new pace of travel created a desire for faster communication.

Answer the
6. **Essential Question**
What innovations in industry, travel, and communications changed the lives of Americans in the 1800s?

North and South **Chapter 13** 393

Section 1 Review

Answers

1. Paragraphs should use the terms as they are defined in the section and in the Glossary.

2. The telegraph used electric signals as dots and dashes to send messages instantly along wires. It provided a faster method of communicating over vast distances.

3. steel-tipped plow, mechanical reaper, thresher

4. steamboats; railroads; canals; farming technology (steel plow, mechanical reaper, thresher)

5. Paragraphs might include the need for a faster way to communicate orders as manufacturing increased. People may have wanted to communicate more quickly with friends and family as they settled in distant locations.

6. Industry: division of labor, factories that used steam- and water-powered machines, mass production; **Travel:** locomotives, steamboats, clipper ships, roads, canals, railroad networks; **Communications:** telegraph

Focus

Bellringer
Daily Test Practice Transparency 13–2

Reading Guide
Answers to Graphic:
growth of industry; immigration

Section Spotlight Video

To learn more about how the potato famine in Ireland affected immigration to America, watch the Section Spotlight Video "The North's People."

Section 2

Essential Question ◄
How did immigration have an impact on cities, industry, and culture in the North?

Reading Guide

Content Vocabulary

trade union (p. 396) discrimination (p. 396)
strike (p. 396) famine (p. 398)
prejudice (p. 396) nativist (p. 399)

Academic Vocabulary

community (p. 396) license (p. 397)

Key People and Events

Henry Boyd (p. 396)
Samuel Cornish (p. 396)
John B. Russwurm (p. 396)
Macon B. Allen (p. 397)
Sarah G. Bagley (p. 397)
Know-Nothing Party (p. 399)

Reading Strategy

Taking Notes As you read, use a diagram like the one below to list two reasons for the growth of cities.

```
        Growth of Cities
         /        \
       (  )      (  )
```

ILLINOIS STANDARDS
The American Journey

16.C.3b (US) Explain relationships among the American economy and slavery, immigration, industrialization, labor and urbanization, 1700-present.

16.E.3c (US) Describe the impact of urbanization and suburbanization, 1850-present, on the environment.

17.D Understand the historical significance of geography.

18.C.3b Explain how diverse groups have contributed to U.S. social systems over time.

394

The North's People

American Diary

"Over there [Germany], alas, common sense and free speech lie in shackles. . . . I invite you to come over here, should you want to obtain a clear notion of genuine public life, freedom of people and sense of being a nation. . . . I have never regretted that I came here, and never! never! again shall I bow my head under the yoke of despotism and folly."

—August Blümner, a German immigrant quoted in News from the Land of Freedom

Immigrants arriving in New York Harbor

Resource Manager

R Reading Strategies	**C** Critical Thinking	**D** Differentiated Instruction	**W** Writing Support	**S** Skill Practice
Teacher Edition • Making Conn., p. 395 • Academic Vocab., p. 396 • Identifying, p. 399 **Additional Resources** • Guid. Read., URB p. 96 • Cont. Vocab., URB p. 73 • Academic Vocab., URB p. 75	**Teacher Edition** • Analyzing Information, p. 395 • Finding the Main Idea, p. 397 **Additional Resources** • Quizzes and Tests, p. 122 • Authentic Assess., p. 13	**Teacher Edition** • Interpersonal, p. 399 **Additional Resources** • School-to-Home, URB p. 91 • Reteaching Act., URB p. 93	**Teacher Edition** • Expository Writing, p. 396 • Persuasive Writing, p. 397	**Teacher Edition** • Using Chart Skills, p. 398 **Additional Resources** • Daily Test Pract. Transp. 13-2 • Soc. Stud. Skills, URB p. 81 • Geo. & Hist., URB p. 87

Northern Factories

Main Idea Many workers in the mid-1800s saw the need for reforms in working conditions.

History and You Do you babysit or mow lawns to earn money? Is the pay fair? Read to learn why workers in the mid-1800s wanted to earn more pay and improve their working conditions.

For many immigrants like August Blümner, America meant freedom and liberty. Immigrants often settled in cities and found work in the many mills and factories there. Working conditions were harsh, however, and reforms were needed.

Between 1820 and 1860, America's manufacturing increasingly shifted to mills and factories. As numerous machines took over more production tasks, these tasks were brought under one roof—creating the factory system. In addition to textiles and clothing, factories produced items such as shoes, watches, guns, sewing machines, and agricultural machinery.

Working Conditions

As the factory system developed, working conditions worsened. Employees worked long hours, averaging 11.4 hours per day by 1840. Factory work involved many dangerous conditions, and longer workdays caused on-the-job accidents.

For example, long leather belts connected the machines to the factory's water-powered driveshaft. These belts had no protective shields. Workers, especially children, often suffered injuries from the rapidly spinning belts. Many workers lost their fingers or broke their bones.

Employees often labored under unpleasant conditions. Factories were miserably hot and stifling in the summer. The machines gave off heat, and air-conditioning had not yet been invented. Most factories had no heating in the winter, and workers were cold.

Factory owners were often more concerned about profits than about employees' comfort and safety. No laws existed to regulate working conditions or to protect workers.

By the Numbers / Immigration in the Mid-1800s

Sources of Immigration Newcomers came to America from many different countries in the mid-1800s, but the overwhelming majority came from Ireland and Germany.

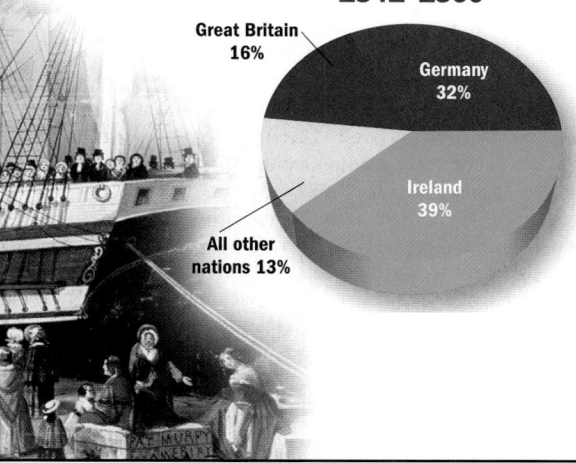

Sources of U.S. Immigration, 1841–1860

Great Britain 16%
Germany 32%
Ireland 39%
All other nations 13%

Immigration, 1820–1860

Annual immigration (in thousands)

400
300
200
100
0

1820 1830 1840 1850 1860
Year

Critical Thinking

Predicting Why might people leave their homeland for another country?

R Reading Strategy

Academic Vocabulary Ask: What is the difference between prejudice and discrimination? *(Prejudice is an unfair opinion that is not based on facts. Discrimination is unfair treatment of a group.)* **ELL**

W Writing Support

Expository Writing Have students do research and write a short biography of one of these African American businesspersons. Biographies should include the person's major accomplishments. **OL**

Primary Source / The Lowell Textile Mills

Lowell Girls In Lowell, Massachusetts, the textile mills were staffed mainly by young female workers known as "Lowell girls." They toiled long hours in a hot, dangerous working environment for low wages. While they sought better working conditions, the girls had opportunities to attend social gatherings and educational programs.

> "Pleasures there are, even in factory life; and we have many. . . . Where can you find a more pleasant place for contemplation?"
> —Sarah G. Bagley, "Pleasures of Factory Life"

▶ Power loom of the type used at the Lowell factories

◀ Cover of the *Lowell Offering*, a magazine published by the women at the Lowell mills

Critical Thinking
Analyzing Refer to the quotation and the pictures, and describe what it was like to work in the Lowell mills.

Workers' Attempts to Organize

By the 1830s, workers began organizing to improve working conditions. Fearing the growth of the factory system, skilled workers formed **trade unions**—organizations of workers with the same trade, or skill. Steadily worsening working conditions also led unskilled workers to organize.

In the mid-1830s, skilled workers in New York City staged a series of **strikes.** They refused to work in order to put pressure on employers. Workers wanted to receive higher wages and to limit their workday to 10 hours. Groups of skilled workers formed the General Trades Union of New York.

In the early 1800s, going on strike was illegal. Striking workers could be punished for breaking the law, or they could be fired from their jobs. In 1842 a Massachusetts court ruled that workers did have the right to strike. It would be many years, however, before workers received other legal rights.

African American Workers

Slavery largely disappeared from the North by the 1830s. However, racial **prejudice**—an unfair opinion not based on facts—and **discrimination**—unfair treatment of a group—remained. For example, New York no longer required white men to own property in order to vote. However, few African Americans were allowed to vote. Rhode Island and Pennsylvania passed laws to keep free African Americans from voting.

Most **communities** would not allow free African Americans to attend public schools. Many communities barred them from public facilities as well. Often African Americans were forced into segregated, or separate, schools and hospitals.

A few African Americans rose in the business world. **Henry Boyd** owned a furniture manufacturing company in Cincinnati, Ohio. In 1827 **Samuel Cornish** and **John B. Russwurm** founded *Freedom's Journal*, the

---

Differentiated Instruction

Changing the Landscape for Industry

Objective: To understand how Lowell, Massachusetts, developed into a planned industrial city

Focus: Ask students why they think the Industrial Revolution developed in New England.

Teach: Have students read the background information and study the map.

Assess: Students should complete the five questions.

Close: Review how geography and human modifications made Lowell an industrial city.

Differentiated Instruction Strategies

BL Have students explain why it was important for industries to locate near rivers and streams.

AL Ask students to research and present information on whether Lowell is still a textile center today.

ELL Have students create a graphic organizer showing how natural features and human modifications helped industrialization in Lowell.

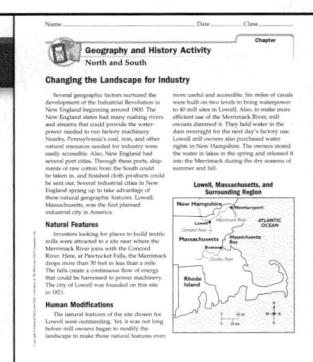

Geography and History Activity, URB p. 87

first African American newspaper, in New York City. In 1845 **Macon B. Allen** became the first African American **licensed,** or given official authority, to practice law in the United States. Most African Americans, however, were extremely poor.

Women Workers

Employers also discriminated against women, paying them less than male workers. Men excluded women from unions and wanted them kept out of the workplace.

Some female workers tried to organize in the 1830s and 1840s. **Sarah G. Bagley,** a weaver from Massachusetts, founded the Lowell Female Labor Reform Organization. Her group petitioned for a 10-hour workday in 1845. Because most of the petitioners were women, the legislature did not consider the petition. Women like Sarah Bagley, however, paved the way for later movements to correct the injustices against female workers.

W

✔ **Reading Check** Describing How did conditions for workers change as the factory system developed?

The Rise of Cities

| Main Idea | European immigrants often faced hardships and discrimination when they settled in Northern cities.

History and You Do you have Irish or German ancestors or know someone who does? Read to learn why many Irish and Germans came to the United States.

. . . .

The growth of factories and immigration—the movement of people into a country—went hand in hand with the growth of Northern cities. Both natural-born citizens and immigrants flocked to the cities, where most of the factories were located. American manufacturers welcomed immigrants, many of whom were willing to work for low pay.

C

Increase in Urban Population

Between 1820 and 1840, some Midwestern towns that had been small villages located along rivers developed into major cities.

W **Writing Support**

Persuasive Writing Have students write a letter from Sarah Bagley to the Massachusetts legislature, asking for a 10-hour workday. The letter should include reasons supporting the request. **OL**

C **Critical Thinking**

Finding the Main Idea Ask: Why did factory managers hire immigrants? *(Many immigrants were willing to work for low pay.)* **BL**

Primary Source

Critical Thinking Answer
Most immigrants were Catholic, while nativists were mainly Protestant. Nativists may have feared that their children would be influenced toward Catholic beliefs by immigrant children at school.

✔ **Reading Check** **Answer:** Conditions worsened. Workers labored long hours under uncomfortable and often dangerous conditions.

Primary Source / Nativism

Anti-immigrant Sentiment Nativists feared the impact new immigrants would have on American culture. Many of the new immigrants were Catholic, while nativists were mainly Protestant. Nativists from the American Party (also called the Know-Nothing Party) tried to block immigration and limit the political rights of immigrants.

◀ American Party emblem, 1854

"Americans must rule America; *and to this end* native-*born citizens should be selected for all State, Federal and municipal offices of government employment, in preference to all others.*"
—the American Party platform, from the American National Convention, 1856

By the Numbers

Immigrants as a Percentage of the Population

1820

99.5%

less than 1%

1860

87%

13%

■ American Citizens
■ Immigrants (not naturalized)

Source: Historical Census Browser, University of Virginia

◀ Protestants and Catholics battle in the streets of Philadelphia in 1844 over the issue of Catholicism in the schools.

Critical Thinking

Making Connections How was the issue of Catholicism in schools related to nativism?

Differentiated Instruction

Leveled Activities

BL **Guided Reading Activity, URB p. 96**

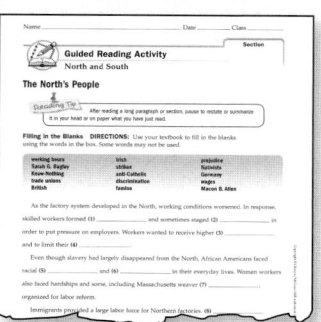

OL **Social Studies Skills Activity, URB p. 81**

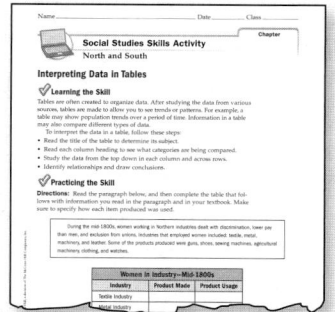

ELL **Content Vocabulary Activity, URB p. 73**

S Skill Practice

Using Chart Skills Draw outlines of these cause-and-effect charts on the board and have students fill in the reasons for Irish and German immigration. **BL**

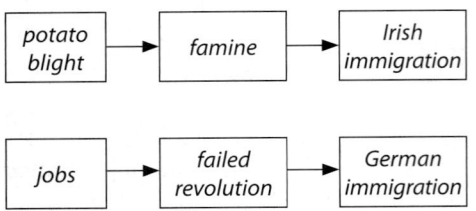

potato blight → famine → Irish immigration

jobs → failed revolution → German immigration

INTERPRETING
POLITICAL CARTOONS

Critical Thinking Answer

1. The British don't want immigrants to go; John Bull is trying to hold back an immigrant, and the lion looks sad.

2. better wages; the statement on the sign

Hands-On Chapter Project
Step 2

Creating a Slide Show

Step 2: Writing an Oral Presentation Students will write a presentation about their innovation.

Essential Question: How did immigration have an impact on cities, industry, and culture in the North?

Directions Instruct each group to use its research to write a presentation about its

---

Primary Sources
INTERPRETING
POLITICAL CARTOONS

Many Irish immigrants journeyed to the United States in the mid-1800s. Castle Garden, the building in the upper left, was the processing facility for immigrants at that time.

1. **Interpreting** According to this cartoon, how do the British feel about the migration? How do you know?

2. **Analyzing** What reason does the cartoon suggest for why the immigrants are leaving? How do you know?

   A. Uncle Sam (United States)
   B. Irish immigrants
   C. John Bull (Britain)
   D. British lion

St. Louis, Pittsburgh, Cincinnati, and Louisville profited from their waterfront locations. They became growing centers of trade that linked the farmers of the Midwest with the cities of the Northeast. After 1830, the Great Lakes became a center for shipping, and new urban centers such as Buffalo, Detroit, Milwaukee, and Chicago arose.

The larger cities became even larger. The population of New York City, the nation's largest city, passed 800,000. Philadelphia had more than 500,000 people in 1860.

Immigration

Immigration to the United States increased dramatically between 1840 and 1860. The largest group of immigrants to the United States at that time were from Ireland. Between 1846 and 1860, more than 1.5 million Irish immigrants arrived in the country. They came to the United States because of a potato blight that destroyed most of the Irish potato crops in the 1840s. A **famine,** an extreme shortage of food, struck Ireland. More than a million people died.

Mostly farmers, the Irish immigrants were too poor to buy land. For this reason many settled in the Northeast and took low-paying factory jobs in the cities. Many of the Irish men also worked on the railroads. Accounting for nearly half of the immigrants, Irish women became servants and factory workers in the Northern cities.

The second-largest group of immigrants in the United States between 1820 and 1860 came from Germany. Some sought work and opportunity. Others came because the German democratic revolution had failed. Many arrived with enough money to buy farms or open their own business. They prospered and founded their own communities and self-help organizations. Some German immigrants settled in New York and Pennsylvania, but many moved to the Midwest and the western territories.

The Impact of Immigration

The European immigrants who came to the United States between the years of 1820 and 1860 changed the character of the country.

---

innovation. Remind students that their goal is to persuade potential investors to provide money for their project. The presentation should describe their innovation in an interesting way and motivate people to invest in their product. It should also explain the benefits of the innovation to both businesses and individuals. Explain that in the next two steps, the groups will create electronic slides to use when they give their oral presentations.

Determining Cause and Effect Ask: How did innovations contribute to the growth of factories in the North? Factories were able to grow because of new methods of dividing tasks, bringing together specialized workers, and the creation of new machines. **OL**

(Chapter Project continued in Section 3)

These people brought their languages, customs, religions, and traditions with them. Some of their ways of life filtered into American culture.

Before the early 1800s, the country had relatively few Catholics. Most of them lived around Baltimore, New Orleans, and St. Augustine. Most Irish immigrants and about one-half of the German immigrants were Roman Catholics. Many Catholic immigrants settled in cities of the Northeast. The Church provided spiritual guidance and served as a center of community life for the newcomers.

The German immigrants brought their language as well as their religion. When they settled, they founded their own publications and established musical societies.

Immigrants Face Prejudice

In the 1830s and 1840s, anti-immigrant feelings rose. Some Americans feared that immigrants were changing the character of the United States too much.

People opposed to immigration were known as **nativists**. They believed that immigration threatened the future of "native"—American-born—citizens. Some nativists accused immigrants of taking jobs from "real"

Americans and were angry that immigrants would work for lower wages. Others accused immigrants of bringing crime and disease to American cities. Immigrants who lived in city slums were likely targets of this prejudice.

The Know-Nothing Party

Nativists formed secret anti-Catholic societies. In the 1850s, they formed a new political party: the American Party. Because members of nativist groups often answered questions about their organization with the statement "I know nothing," their party came to be known as the **Know-Nothing Party.**

The Know-Nothings called for stricter citizenship laws. They wanted to extend the immigrants' waiting period for citizenship from 5 to 21 years and to ban foreign-born citizens from holding office.

In the mid-1850s, the Know-Nothing movement split into a Northern branch and a Southern branch over the question of slavery. At this time the slavery issue was also dividing the Northern and Southern states of the nation.

✓ **Reading Check** Identifying Which two nations did most immigrants come from in the mid-1800s?

History ONLINE
Study Central™ To review this section, go to glencoe.com.

Section 2 Review

Vocabulary
1. Use each of these terms in a sentence that will help explain its meaning: trade union, strike, prejudice, discrimination, community, license, famine, nativist.

Main Ideas
2. **Listing** List some of the early attempts at work reforms in the North.

3. **Discussing** Why did some Americans object to immigration?

Critical Thinking
4. **Classifying** Create a diagram like the one below to identify the two major groups of immigrants to the United States in the first half of the 1800s and show where they settled.

Group		Area Settled
	→	
	→	

5. **Creative Writing** Imagine that you are an African American child living in the North in the mid-1800s. Write a poem in which you describe how you feel about your treatment.

Answer the
6. **Essential Question**
How did immigration have an impact on cities, industry, and culture in the North?

Answers

1. Students' sentences should use terms as they are defined in the section and Glossary.
2. formation of trade unions, organization of unskilled workers, strikes, formation of Lowell Female Labor Reform Organization and its petition for a 10-hour workday
3. Some Americans feared that immigrants were changing the character of the United States too much; they accused immigrants

of taking "their" jobs; they were upset that immigrants worked for lower wages; and they accused immigrants of bringing crime and disease.
4. **Irish:** Northeastern cities; **Germans:** New York, Pennsylvania, Midwest, western territories

5. Students' poems should show the effects of prejudice and discrimination.
6. The cheap labor provided by immigrants spurred factory and city growth. Their languages, customs, religions (especially Roman Catholicism), and ways of life spread into U.S. culture.

D Differentiated Instruction

Interpersonal Have students identify elements of American culture that came from their immigrant ancestors. *(Students might mention place names, music, dress, and food.)* **ELL**

R Reading Strategy

Identifying Remind students that nativists believed that immigration threatened the future of "native" citizens. **Ask:** What was inconsistent about the nativists' viewpoint? *(Nativists ignored the fact that their ancestors were immigrants.)* **AL**

✓ **Reading Check** **Answer:** Ireland and Germany

Assess
· ·

Study Central™ provides summaries, interactive games, and online graphic organizers to help students review content.

Close
· ·

Summarizing Use a graphic organizer to summarize the effects of immigration on the North's cities, industry, and culture. **OL**

Section 2 Review

Southern Cotton Kingdom

Focus

Bellringer
Daily Test Practice Transparency 13–3

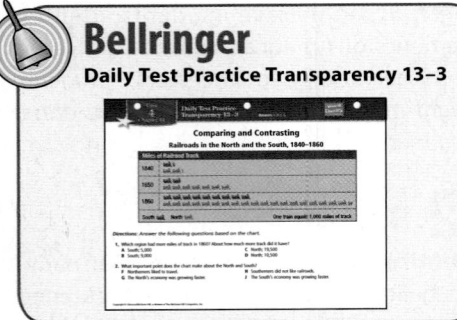

Reading Guide
Answers to Graphic:
Boom in Cotton Production: (1) boom in cotton sales, (2) ready source of labor—enslaved African Americans; **Slow Industrial Growth:** (1) boom in cotton sales (agriculture was more profitable), (2) lack of interest in industry

Section Spotlight Video

Watch the Section Spotlight Video "Southern Cotton Kingdom" to learn more about Eli Whitney and the invention of the cotton gin.

Resource Manager

Essential Question
How did the South's industry and economy differ from the industry and economy of the North?

Reading Guide

Content Vocabulary
cotton gin (p. 401)   capital (p. 403)

Academic Vocabulary
consequence (p. 402) process (p. 402)

Key People and Events
Eli Whitney (p. 401)
William Gregg (p. 403)
Joseph Reid Anderson (p. 403)

Reading Strategy
Taking Notes As you read, use a diagram like the one below to show reasons cotton production grew but industrial growth was slower in the South.

Boom in Cotton Production

Slow Industrial Growth

ILLINOIS STANDARDS
The American Journey

15.D Understand trade as an exchange of goods or services.

15.D.3c Explain how workers can affect their productivity through training and by using tools, machinery and technology.

16.C.3b (US) Explain relationships among the American economy and slavery, immigration, industrialization, labor and urbanization, 1700-present.

17.C.3a Explain how human activity is affected by geographic factors.

American Diary

"I have just returned from Philadelphia. My business there was to lodge a Model of my machine and receive a Patent for it. I accomplished everything agreeable to my wishes. I had the satisfaction to hear it declared by a number of the first men in America that my machine is the most perfect & the most valuable invention that has ever appeared in this Country. I have received my Patent."

—Eli Whitney, letter to his father, March 30, 1794

Cotton gin being used on Southern plantation

R Reading Strategies	C Critical Thinking	D Differentiated Instruction	W Writing Support	S Skill Practice
Teacher Edition • Predicting, p. 403	**Teacher Edition** • Making Connections, p. 401	**Teacher Edition** • Visual/Spatial, p. 401	**Teacher Edition** • Persuasive Writing, p. 403	**Teacher Edition** • Using Economics Skills, p. 402
Additional Resources • Guid. Read., URB p. 97 • Content Vocab., URB p. 73 • Academic Vocab., URB p. 75 • Read. Ess., p. 136	**Additional Resources** • Quizzes and Tests, p. 123 • Authentic Assess., p.13	**Additional Resources** • School-to-Home, URB p. 91 • Reteaching Act., URB p. 93		**Additional Resources** • Daily Test Pract. Transp. 13-3 • Lesson Transp. 13B

Rise of the Cotton Kingdom

Main Idea The economy in the South, unlike that in the North, remained largely agricultural.

History and You What fabric is your favorite T-shirt or pair of sweats made of? Read to learn how cotton was a major economic asset to the Deep South.

. . . .

Eli Whitney transformed cotton production with his new invention, the cotton gin. To the cotton planters of the South, Whitney's cotton gin was indeed the "most perfect and the most valuable invention."

Changes in the South

In 1790 the South seemed to be an underdeveloped agricultural region. Most Southerners lived along the Atlantic coast in Maryland, Virginia, and North Carolina. This area was known as the Upper South.

By 1850 the South had changed. Its population had spread inland to the Deep South—which included Georgia, South Carolina, Alabama, Mississippi, Louisiana, and Texas.

The economy of the South was thriving. That economy depended, however, on slavery. Having all but disappeared from the North, slavery was growing stronger than ever in the South.

Cotton Rules the Deep South

In colonial times, rice, indigo, and tobacco made up the South's main crops. After the American Revolution, demand for these crops decreased. European mills now wanted Southern cotton. However, cotton took time and labor to produce. After harvest, workers had to carefully separate the plant's sticky seeds from the cotton fibers.

Cotton production was revolutionized when **Eli Whitney** invented the cotton gin in 1793. The **cotton gin** was a machine that could remove seeds from cotton fibers, dramatically increasing the amount of cotton that could be processed. A worker could clean 50 times more cotton each day with the machine than by hand. Furthermore, the gin was small enough for one person to carry from place to place.

By the Numbers — Cotton Production, 1820–1860

The South's Agricultural Economy Agriculture was very profitable in the South. By 1860, cotton production made up 57.5 percent of U.S. exports.

1820

Missouri · Kentucky · Virginia · North Carolina · Tennessee · South Carolina · Arkansas Territory · Miss. · Georgia · Texas (Spain) · Louisiana · Alabama · Fla.
ATLANTIC OCEAN
Gulf of Mexico
0 200 kilometers
0 200 miles
Albers Equal-Area projection
■ Major cotton-producing areas, 1820

1860

Missouri · Kentucky · Virginia · North Carolina · Tennessee · South Carolina · Arkansas · Miss. · Georgia · Texas · Louisiana · Alabama · Fla.
ATLANTIC OCEAN
Gulf of Mexico
0 200 kilometers
0 200 miles
Albers Equal-Area projection
■ Major cotton-producing areas, 1860

Critical Thinking

Predicting How might an agricultural economy increase the need for workers?

Teach

. . . .

D Differentiated Instruction

Visual/Spatial Have students trace the Upper South with their fingers on both maps. Then have them trace the Deep South. **Ask:** In which region did cotton farming expand most? *(Deep South)* **BL**

C Critical Thinking

Making Connections Ask: Why did slavery largely disappear from the North? *(The North's small farms did not need enslaved workers.)* **OL**

Primary Source

Critical Thinking Answer
Farming required a lot of labor. As profits rose, farmers wanted to grow more, increasing the need for workers.

Analyzing Information Ask: How would planters benefit from the invention of the cotton gin? *(The cotton gin allowed planters to grow and process more cotton and earn higher profits.)* **OL**

Differentiated Instruction

Leveled Activities

401

S Skill Practice

Using Economics Skills Refer students to the feature. **Ask:** If an enslaved worker cost $1 a day to maintain, how much would 1 pound of cotton cost to produce without the cotton gin? *($1)* with the cotton gin? *($1/50 pounds = 2 cents)* **AL**

Economics & History

Critical Thinking Answers

1. more efficient work methods; improvement in the workers' education or skills, improved equipment
2. The price would go down, because the cost for producing and transporting the shirt to market would go down.

✓ Reading Check **Answer:** It increased demand for enslaved workers and made cotton production more profitable for Southern planters.

Hands-On Chapter Project
Step 3

Cotton Gin

402

Economics & History

Productivity is the amount of goods and services a worker can produce in a given period of time, such as an hour or a day.

▲ Elias Howe's sewing machine enabled workers to make large amounts of clothing in a day.

Productivity in services increased too. The steamboat could move cotton goods to market faster. ▶

Advances in technology increased productivity in the 1800s. Before the invention of the cotton gin, a worker could produce 1 pound of cotton a day by hand. With the cotton gin, a worker could produce 50 pounds of cotton a day. This increase in productivity meant (a) farmers could grow more cotton to sell; and (b) the use of slave labor increased. By the mid-1800s, cotton made up more than one-half of U.S. exports.

Cotton Production as a Percentage of U.S. Exports

1800	1820
	7.1%	32%

1840	1860
51.6%	57.5%

Source: *Historical Statistics of the United States*

Critical Thinking

1. **Making Inferences** In addition to technology, what other factors might increase productivity?
2. **Determining Cause and Effect** How do you think increases in productivity affected the price consumers paid for a cotton shirt? Why?

Whitney's invention had important **consequences,** or results. Because the cotton gin **processed,** or prepared, cotton fibers so quickly, farmers wanted to grow more cotton to increase their profits. Thus, they needed more laborers. Many Southern planters relied on slave labor to plant and pick their cotton.

By 1860 the economies of the Deep South and the Upper South had developed in different ways. Both parts of the South were agricultural. The Upper South produced tobacco, hemp, wheat, and vegetables. The Deep South was committed to cotton and, in some areas, to rice and sugarcane.

The value of enslaved people increased because of their key role in producing cotton and sugar. The Upper South became a center for the sale and transport of enslaved people throughout the region.

✓ Reading Check **Describing** What effect did the cotton gin have on the South's economy?

Industry in the South

Main Idea Industry developed slowly in the South for a variety of reasons.

History and You To get to school, do you take the bus, ride in a car, or walk? Read to learn how the people of the South traveled.

. . . .

The economy of the South became increasingly different from that of the North. The mostly rural South contributed only a small percentage of the nation's manufacturing value by 1860. The entire South had a lower value of manufactured goods than the state of Pennsylvania.

Barriers to Industry

There were many reasons why industry developed so slowly in the South. One reason was the boom in cotton sales. Agriculture, especially cotton, was extremely profitable.

Creating a Slide Show

Step 3: Making a Diagram Students will draw diagrams of their innovations and make an electronic slide of them.

Essential Question: How did the South's industry and economy differ from the industry and economy of the North?

Directions As inventors, students should realize that potential investors want to understand how the innovation works before committing money to it. Have the groups use their research

to draw diagrams showing the main parts of their innovations, using color to make the diagrams attractive. Have them scan their diagrams and make electronic slides. They should then use their software to create labels that identify and explain the main parts of the diagrams.

Making Inferences Ask: How did the cotton gin affect the economies of the North as well as the South? *(In the South, the cotton gin increased the production of cotton that was used in Northern factories to make cloth.)* **OL**

(Chapter Project continued in Section 4)

Another stumbling block in the South was the lack of **capital**—money to invest in businesses. Planters would have had to sell enslaved people or land to raise the money to build factories. In addition, the market for manufactured goods in the South was small. The large population of enslaved people had no money to buy merchandise. This limited local market discouraged industries from developing. Yet another reason is that some Southerners simply did not want industry. One Texas politician, Louis Wigfall, summed up that Southern point of view:

PRIMARY SOURCE

"We want no manufactures: we desire no trading, no mechanical or manufacturing classes. As long as we have our rice, our sugar, our tobacco and our cotton, we can command wealth to purchase all we want."
—quoted in *Louis T. Wigfall, Southern Fire-eater*

Southern Factories

Some Southern leaders wanted to develop industry in the region. They argued that the South depended too much on the North for manufactured goods. These leaders also argued that factories would help the less prosperous economy of the Upper South.

Two Southerners shared this view. **William Gregg,** a South Carolina merchant, opened his own textile factory. In Virginia, **Joseph Reid Anderson** took over the Tredegar Iron Works and made it one of the nation's leading iron producers. During the Civil War, Tredegar provided artillery and other iron products for the Southern forces. These industries, however, were the exception rather than the rule in the South.

Southern Transportation

Natural waterways were used to transport goods in the South. Most towns were located on coasts or along rivers. Few canals existed, and roads were poor.

The South had fewer railroads than the North. Southern rail lines were short, local, and not interlinked. Thus Southern cities grew more slowly than Northern cities where railways were major routes of commerce and settlement. By 1860 only about one-third of the nation's rail lines lay within the South. This rail shortage would seriously hinder the South during the Civil War.

Reading Check Explaining What is capital? Why is it important for economic growth?

History ONLINE
Study Central™ To review this section, go to glencoe.com.

Section 3 Review

Vocabulary

1. Use cotton gin, consequence, process, and capital in complete sentences to define the terms.

Main Ideas

2. **Discussing** Discuss the similarities and differences between the economies of the Upper South and the Deep South around 1860.

3. **Explaining** Why did some Southerners feel that industrial growth would benefit the region?

Critical Thinking

4. **Identifying** Re-create the diagram below to show the barriers to Southern transportation.

5. **Persuasive Writing** Look again at the words of the Texas politician who said, "We want no manufactures." Add a second paragraph to his quotation that explains, in words you imagine could be his, why he opposes industry for the South.

6. **Answer the Essential Question**
How did the South's industry and economy differ from the industry and economy of the North?

North and South **Chapter 13** 403

CHAPTER 13
Section 3

W Writing Support

Persuasive Writing Have students write an editorial arguing for the development of industry in the South. **OL**

R Reading Strategy

Predicting Ask: How might a rail shortage hinder the South during the Civil War? *(The shortage would make it harder for the South to move troops and supplies.)* **OL**

Reading Check **Answer:** Capital is money to invest in businesses. Without ready money to invest, people cannot establish or maintain businesses.

Assess

History ONLINE

Study Central™ provides summaries, interactive games, and online graphic organizers to help students review content.

Close

Discussing As a class, discuss the economic differences between the North and South and reasons for these differences. **OL**

Section 3 Review

Answers

1. Sentences should use terms according to their definitions in the section and Glossary.
2. The economies of both regions depended on agriculture rather than industry and relied on enslaved workers. The agricultural products differed (**Upper South:** tobacco, hemp, wheat, and vegetables; **Deep South:** cotton, rice, sugarcane).
3. They thought industrial growth would lessen the dependence of the South on the North for manufactured goods and could help the economy of the Upper South.
4. lack of canals; poor roads; short, local rail lines
5. Students might give reasons such as favorable growing conditions in the South, strong demand for the South's agricultural products, and confidence that the South's agricultural economy will continue to prosper. The tone should reflect the strength of the politician's convictions.
6. The South's economy was based on agriculture; the North's economy was based on industry. The South's economy depended on slavery, while slavery had almost disappeared in the North.

Focus

C Critical Thinking

Recognizing Bias Have students read the author's biography. **Ask:** How do you think the enslaved girl's picture made the author feel when he looked at it? *(Possible answers include angry, sympathetic, or protective.)* How do you think it affected how he wrote about these characters, and whom he sympathized with? *(It probably caused him to feel sympathy toward the enslaved characters.)* **AL**

D Differentiated Instruction

English Language Learners Remind students of what they have read about slavery in the United States. Ask them to explain why the auction is called the "weeping time." *(When enslaved people were auctioned, or sold, families were broken apart and often did not see each other again.)* **OL**

R Reading Strategy

Using Context Clues Ask: Why are names capitalized in some sections and not others? *(Names are not capitalized when a character is thinking. They are capitalized when a character speaks.)* **BL**

Additional Reading

Review suggested books before assigning them.

America's LITERATURE

Meet the Author

C **Julius Lester** (1939–) took inspiration for *Day of Tears* from several sources, one being a photograph of an enslaved girl, about nine years old, holding a white baby. This girl served as Emma, the main character of the novel, and Lester kept her photograph on his desk while he wrote the book.

Building Background

D In *Day of Tears*, Julius Lester uses dialogue to tell the story of the largest auction of enslaved people in U.S. history, which took place in Savannah, Georgia, in 1859. More than 400 enslaved people were put up for sale. The readers hear the words and thoughts of more than 20 characters, including the enslaved and their slaveholders, as they describe the horrors of the auction. This was known as the "weeping time." As you read this excerpt from *Day of Tears*, consider how Lester's use of dialogue affects the overall theme of humanity.

Slave Market by Eyre Crowe ▶

Vocabulary

strident high-pitched

verge edge

coach carriage

DAY OF TEARS

Julius Lester

Characters

Emma 12-year-old enslaved girl
Will Emma's father
Mattie Emma's mother
Pierce Butler slaveholder
Sarah Master Butler's daughter
Frances Master Butler's daughter

emma

The lady in the long blue dress and slave-seller were looking in this direction. Ain't nothing over here for them to see. Now the slave-**R** seller say something to Master [Butler] and then Master and the lady start talking. Master shakes his head. She talks some more. Master don't shake his head this time.

404

Autobiography: *Narrative of the Life of Frederick Douglass, An American Slave,* by Frederick Douglass, describes slavery in the words of someone who lived through it. Douglass links his quest to learn to read with his journey to become a free man because slaveholders maintained power by keeping slaves ignorant.

Nonfiction: *The Forbidden Schoolhouse: The True and Dramatic Story of Prudence Crandall and Her Students,* by Suzanne Jurmain, describes the reaction of a Northern town in 1831 when an African American teen wants to attend school. The issue sharply divides the town's people.

Fiction: *A Gathering of Days: A New England Girl's Journal,* by Joan W. Blos, uses journal entries to tell the story of a 14-year-old girl living in New Hampshire in the 1830s.

For further reading, see

She talk some more. This time Master nods slowly. The woman holds out her hand and Master shakes it. The woman turn around and look over here again. Miss Frances is looking over this way, too. Master look like he found something very interesting on the floor to stare at. Master say something to Frances and she starts in this direction.

I see Papa. He's staring at Master and looks angry about something.

FRANCES: *(Calls out loudly as she comes near.)* Sarah! Papa wants you!

SARAH: *(Starts toward her sister, still holding Emma's hand.)* Come on, Emma. It's time to go home.

FRANCES: *(Close enough to Sarah and Emma that she doesn't have to raise her voice.)* Emma can't come.

SARAH: Why not?

FRANCES: Because. . . .

EMMA: *(Beginning to understand what she just witnessed.)* Frances? Did Master Butler sell me to that lady? Is that what they was shaking hands about?

FRANCES: *(Refuses to look at Emma.)* Come on, Sarah! Now! *(Her voice is* **strident** *and she is on the* **verge** *of tears.)* Please, Sarah! Papa wants you to come with me!

SARAH: Emma? Papa wouldn't sell you. I know he wouldn't do that.

EMMA: *(Puts her arms around Sarah and holds her tightly, blinking her eyes rapidly to hold back her own tears.)* You go on with your sister. Your papa wants you. You go on now.

SARAH: But, what about you? I want you to come.

EMMA: You go on. Everything will be all right. *(Takes her arms from* around Sarah, looks at Frances and opens her arms. Frances runs to Emma's embrace, tears trickling down her face. The two hug tightly. After a moment, Emma releases her.)* You go on now. You don't want to keep your papa waiting.

* * *

mattie

I knew something terrible had happened the minute I heard that girl [Sarah] screaming. From way down the road I could hear her, and the closer they got, the louder her screaming was. I ran outside and the **coach** had hardly stopped before she was out the door and running to me.

"Papa sold Emma! Papa sold Emma!" she sobbed. . . .

> *I knew something terrible had happened the minute I heard that girl screaming.*

[Will] got down from the coach and come over to where I was outside the door to the kitchen and he hugged me real hard and kept saying over and over, "I'm sorry, Mattie. I'm sorry," like it was his fault. Sarah was there in between us like she wanted as much of the hugging as she could get, and Will picked her up. She put one arm around my neck and one around Will's and the three of us had ourselves a good cry.

Analyzing Literature

1. **Respond** What surprised you most about Master Butler's sale of Emma?

2. **Recall and Interpret** What actions show Master Butler is unhappy about selling Emma?

3. **Evaluate**
   (a) How does the dialogue structure affect point of view in the story?
   (b) In your opinion, which character seems most sympathetic toward the slaves—Sarah, Frances, or Master Butler? Why?

405

Teach

R Reading Strategy

Predicting Ask students if they were surprised that Emma was sold. **Ask:** When did you first suspect that she might be sold? *(Possible answers include: when the woman in the blue dress looked over at Emma; when the woman and the slave seller spoke to Emma's master and when he stared at the floor; when Will (Papa) looked angry; and when Frances would not tell Emma what was happening.)* **OL**

Assess/Close

As a class, discuss the use of point of view in creative writing. **Ask:** How many points of view are used in this scene? *(Four: Emma's, Will's, Mattie's, and third person (he, she, they) that allows readers to see the whole scene)* Why do you think Lester describes what people are thinking? *(Possible answers: to emphasize that everyone there was a human being with feelings and to give readers a more complete view of the scene)*

Answers

1. Possible answer: Sarah's and Frances's reactions to the sale.

2. At first he refuses the sale; after selling Emma, he cannot look at her.

3. (a) Possible answer: Readers know what each character is thinking as the story takes place.
   (b) Possible answer: Sarah, because she cries with Will and Mattie over the sale of Emma

Focus

Bellringer
Daily Test Practice Transparency 13–4

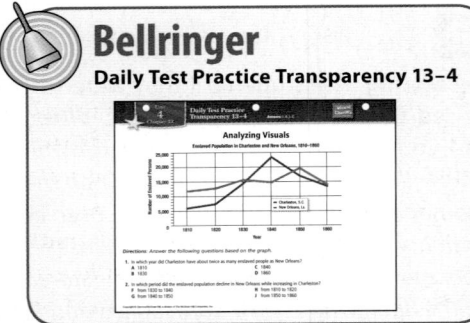

Reading Guide
Answers to Graphic:
(1) domestic work—cleaning house, laundry, sewing, cooking, serving meals; **(2)** pasture work—tending to livestock; **(3)** field work—planting, tending, and harvesting crops; **(4)** trade work—blacksmithing, carpentry, shoemaking, weaving

Section Spotlight Video

To learn more about the Underground Railroad, watch the Section Spotlight Video "The South's People."

Resource Manager

Section 4

Essential Question
How did unique elements of culture develop among enslaved African Americans in the South?

Reading Guide

Content Vocabulary

yeoman (p. 407)	spiritual (p. 409)
tenant farmer (p. 407)	slave codes (p. 410)
overseer (p. 408)	literacy (p. 412)

Academic Vocabulary

legal (p. 409)	brief (p. 410)

Key People and Events
Nat Turner (p. 410)
Harriet Tubman (p. 411)
Frederick Douglass (p. 411)
Underground Railroad (p. 411)

Reading Strategy
Taking Notes As you read, use a diagram like the one below to describe the work that was done on Southern plantations.

ILLINOIS STANDARDS
The American Journey

16.D.3a (US) Describe characteristics of different kinds of communities in various sections of America during the colonial/frontier periods and the 19th century.

16.D.3b (US) Describe characteristics of different kinds of families in America during the colonial/frontier periods and the 19th century.

18.A.3 Explain how language, literature, the arts, architecture and traditions contribute to the development and transmission of culture.

18.C.3b Explain how diverse groups have contributed to U.S. social systems over time.

The South's People

American Diary

"We lodged in log huts, and on the bare ground. . . . In a single room were huddled, like cattle, ten or a dozen persons, men, women, and children. . . . Our beds were collections of straw and old rags, thrown down in the corners and boxed in with boards; a single blanket the only covering. . . . The wind whistled and the rain and snow blew in through the cracks, and the damp earth soaked in the moisture till the floor was miry [muddy] as a pigsty [enclosed area where pigs live]."

—*from* Father Henson's Story of His Own Life

Former slave quarters on a plantation in South Carolina

R Reading Strategies	**C** Critical Thinking	**D** Differentiated Instruction	**W** Writing Support	**S** Skill Practice
Teacher Edition • Making Connections, p. 407 • Act. Prior Know., p. 410 • Identifying, p. 411 • Inferring, p. 412 **Additional Resources** • Guid. Read., URB p. 98 • Content Vocab., URB p. 73	**Teacher Edition** • Identifying Central Issues, p. 408 • Making Inferences, p. 408 • Analyzing Information, p. 409 **Additional Resources** • Quizzes and Tests, p. 124	**Teacher Edition** • Visual/Spatial, p. 407 • ELL, p. 410 **Additional Resources** • School-to-Home, URB p. 91 • Reteaching Act., URB p. 93 • Differ. Inst., URB p. 83	**Teacher Edition** • Desc. Writing, p. 409 • Personal Writing, p. 410 • Narr. Writing, p. 411 **Additional Resources** • Writ. Skills, URB p. 79	**Teacher Edition** • Classifying, p. 408 **Additional Resources** • Daily Test Pract. Transp. 13-4 • Lesson Transp. 13C

Farms and Plantations

Main Idea The South had far more small farms than large plantations.

History and You Would you like to own your own business one day? Read to learn about what it took to keep a plantation operating.

The Southern economy was based on agriculture. Enslaved workers like Josiah Henson were used to farm the land. The South before 1860 is usually portrayed as a land of stately plantations that wealthy white slaveholders owned. In reality most white Southerners were either small farmers without enslaved people or planters with a handful of enslaved workers. Most white Southerners fit into four categories: yeomen, tenant farmers, the rural poor, or plantation owners.

Small Farmers and the Rural Poor

Yeomen—farmers who did not have enslaved workers—made up the largest group of whites in the South. Most yeomen owned land, ranging from 50 to 200 acres (20 to 81 ha). They grew crops for their own use and to sell, trading produce with local merchants. Yeomen lived mostly in the Upper South and in the hilly areas of the Deep South.

Not all Southern whites owned land. Some rented land or worked as **tenant farmers** on landlords' estates. The majority of Southern whites lived in simple homes—cottages or log cabins. Others—the rural poor—lived in crude cabins in wooded areas. Looked down on by other whites, the rural poor were stubbornly independent. They were proud of being self-sufficient and avoided jobs that were normally done by enslaved people.

Plantations

A large plantation might cover several thousand acres. Plantation owners usually lived in comfortable but not luxurious farmhouses. They measured their wealth partly by the number of enslaved people they controlled. Only about 4 percent of plantation owners held 20 or more enslaved workers in 1860. Most slaveholders held fewer than 10 enslaved workers. A few free African Americans also held enslaved workers. Some free African Americans purchased members of their own families to free them.

By the Numbers | Southern Population, 1860

A Slaveholding Society In 1860 about 400,000 households in the South held enslaved workers. Nearly 4 million African Americans remained in slavery.

African Americans — 32%
Whites — 17%
2%
49%

African Americans
- Enslaved
- Free

Whites
- Slaveholders
- Not slaveholders

*Total population = 12 million

Source: Geospatial and Statistical Data Center

The Legree Plantation, Capers Island, South Carolina ▶

Critical Thinking
Identifying What percentage of the total Southern population did African Americans make up?

Teach

D Differentiated Instruction

Visual/Spatial Use a Venn diagram on the board to compare yeomen and tenant farmers. Have the class identify the facts to put in the diagram. *(yeomen: largest group of whites in South, owned small amounts of land; tenant farmers: rented land to work; both: white, poor, held no enslaved workers)* **BL**

R Reading Strategy

Making Connections Ask: When you think of a plantation house, what image comes to mind first? *(Students might suggest an elegant mansion.)* How was reality different from this image? *(The house was comfortable but not luxurious.)* **OL**

By the Numbers

Critical Thinking Answer 34%

Differentiated Instruction

Critical Thinking Skills Activity, URB p. 85

Drawing Conclusions

Objective:	To learn how to draw conclusions when reading
Focus:	Tell students that this activity will teach them how to better understand what they read.
Teach:	Have students read Clayton Holbert's story and answer the questions.
Assess:	Ask student volunteers to explain how they reached their answers to the questions.
Close:	Discuss how people draw conclusions in other forms of daily life, such as in conversations.

Differentiated Instruction Strategies

BL Have students use colored pencils to circle the excerpt material that supplies the answers to the questions.

AL Ask students to write a summary of Clayton Holbert's life.

ELL Make sure students understand the phrase "drawing conclusions." Ask them to explain it in their own words.

C1 Critical Thinking

Identifying Central Issues Ask: Why did planters use agents? *(They wanted to wait to sell their cotton until the price rose.)* Under this system, how did planters pay their expenses? *(with credit from their agents)* **OL**

C2 Critical Thinking

Making Inferences Ask: Why do you think some planters allowed their wives to keep the financial records? *(The planters were away much of the time, and the women were capable of doing the task.)* **OL**

S Skill Practice

Classifying Ask: What were four kinds of jobs done by enslaved workers? *(housework, skilled crafts, pasture work, field work)* **BL**

✓ **Reading Check** **Answer:** yeomen

Hands-On Chapter Project
Step 4

Teacher Tip

Making Slides Tell students that bullet points need not be complete sentences. Each point should contain just a few key words, so the audience can focus more on listening than on reading the slides.

LINKING PAST TO PRESENT — Roots of American Music

THEN Enslaved people drew on the rhythms of their African homeland to create uniquely American musical forms. One form was the *work song* or *field holler.* A worker led a rhythmic call-and-response song, which sometimes included shouts and moans. The beat set the tempo for their work.

Conversion of enslaved African Americans to Christianity gave rise to *spirituals,* or religious folk songs. Often spirituals combined a longing for freedom with religious themes, as in "Swing Low, Sweet Chariot."

"Swing Low, Sweet Chariot"
Swing low, sweet chariot
Coming for to carry me home.
I looked over Jordan and what did I see
Coming for to carry me home
A band of angels coming after me
Coming for to carry me home

"While on their way [to work], they [the slaves] would make the dense old woods . . . [echo] with their wild songs, revealing at once the highest joy and the deepest sadness."
—Frederick Douglass, *Narrative of the Life of Frederick Douglass*

The main economic goal for large plantation owners was to earn profits. Such plantations had fixed costs. These are regular operating expenses that remain much the same year after year—housing and feeding workers, for example.

Cotton prices, however, varied from season to season, depending on the market. To receive the best prices, planters sold their cotton to agents in large cities, such as New Orleans and Charleston. The cotton exchanges, or trade centers, were of vital importance to the cotton economy. The agents extended credit—a form of loan—to the planters and held the cotton for several months until the price rose. Then the agents sold the cotton. Only at that time were the planters paid for their cotton. This system kept the planters in debt.

Plantation Wives

Wives of plantation owners took charge of their households. They supervised the buildings and the fruit and vegetable gardens. They watched over the enslaved domestic workers and sometimes tended to them when they became ill. In addition, they might keep the plantation's financial records. Their life was often difficult and lonely. Planters were often absent to deal with cotton agents. Their wives spent long periods alone.

Work on the Plantation

Large plantations needed many different kinds of workers. Some enslaved people did domestic work. They cleaned the house, cooked, did laundry and sewing, and served meals. Others were trained as blacksmiths, carpenters, shoemakers, or weavers. Still others worked in the pastures, tending the livestock. Most enslaved African Americans, however, were field hands. They worked from sunrise to sunset to plant, tend, and harvest crops. An **overseer,** or plantation manager, supervised them.

✓ **Reading Check** **Identifying** What group made up the largest number of whites in the South?

408 **Chapter 13** *North and South*

Creating a Slide Show

Step 4: Preparing the Slides Students will create electronic slides of key points.

Essential Question: How did unique elements of culture develop among enslaved African Americans in the South?

Directions Have the groups summarize the main ideas from their written presentations by creating bulleted lists. Then have them create electronic slides of their lists, adding headings. Students should use visuals on their slides to illustrate their points. Remind students to keep the information on each slide brief. Oral presentations will include more detail.

Analyzing As a class, discuss whether enslaved African Americans would benefit from any of the innovations selected by students. **OL**

(Chapter Project continued on the Visual Summary Page)

NOW Out of the rhythmic patterns and themes of work songs and spirituals arose a new musical form—the blues. The blues influenced later styles, including jazz, rock and roll, and rap.

"[Jazz] is the highest [interpretation] of individual emotion in the history of Western music."
—Wynton Marsalis

◄ Jazz musician Wynton Marsalis

Critical Thinking

1. **Interpreting** What is the religious theme in "Swing Low, Sweet Chariot"? How might this song also be about slavery?

2. **Making Inferences** Why do you think enslaved African Americans sang?

Life Under Slavery

Main Idea Despite their hardships, enslaved African Americans found methods to help them cope with their lack of freedom.

History and You Can you imagine moving to a foreign land that has different customs? Read to learn how enslaved African Americans coped with their situation.

....

Enslaved African Americans suffered hardships and misery. They worked hard, earned no money, and had little hope of freedom. One of their worst fears was being sold to another planter and separated from their loved ones. In the face of these brutal conditions, they had to cope with their situation. Enslaved African Americans maintained their family life as best they could and developed a culture all their own, blending African and American elements. They resisted slavery through a variety of clever methods and looked ahead to the day when they would be set free.

Family Life

Enslaved people had few comforts beyond the bare necessities. Uncertainty and danger were constant threats in their lives. American laws in the early 1800s did not protect enslaved families. A slaveholder's death could lead to the breakup of an enslaved family. A husband or wife could be sold and moved away. Although not recognized by law, marriages between enslaved people occurred. Their marriage vows included the phrase "until death or separation do us part." Couples recognized and lived with the possibility that one of them could be sold.

Enslaved people needed some measure of stability in their lives. They established a network of relatives and friends who made up their extended family. If a father or mother were sold, an aunt, an uncle, or a close friend could raise the children left behind. Large, close-knit, extended families became a vital feature of African American culture.

African American Culture

In 1808 Congress outlawed the slave trade. Slavery remained **legal,** or permitted by law, but no new enslaved people could enter the United States. By 1860, almost all the enslaved people in the South had been born there.

These native-born African Americans held on to their African customs. They continued to perform African music and dance. They passed traditional African folk stories on to their children. Some wrapped colored cloth around their heads in the African style. Although many enslaved African Americans accepted Christianity, they often followed the religious beliefs and practices of their African ancestors as well.

African American Christianity

For many enslaved African Americans, Christianity became a religion of hope and resistance. They prayed intensely for the day when they would be free from bondage.

The passionate beliefs of the enslaved Southerners found expression in the **spiritual,** an African American religious folk song.

North and South **Chapter 13** 409

W Writing Support

Descriptive Writing Have students take the role of an enslaved African American who has been sold. Ask them to write a diary entry, expressing their feelings at being separated from family and friends. **OL**

C Critical Thinking

Analyzing Information Ask: Why did the enslaved population continue to grow even after the slave trade was outlawed? *(Children born to enslaved people in the United States added to the enslaved population.)* **OL**

LINKING PAST TO PRESENT

Critical Thinking Answers

1. going to heaven; might also reflect a longing to escape bondage

2. Possible response: to express their feelings; singing might have helped ease the pain of slavery.

Additional Support

Fast Facts

African American Tales Enslaved African Americans enjoyed telling tales of the trickster, Brer Rabbit. The character of Brer Rabbit had its roots in East African stories of Kalulu the Rabbit, whose wit got him into trouble but also provided a way out. In America, Brer Rabbit took on characteristics of some Native American folktales. Obtain a copy of "Brer Rabbit Meets a Tar Baby" and read it aloud to the class. Discuss how Brer Rabbit overcame his stronger rival, Brer Fox. Point out that Brer Rabbit often outsmarted more powerful animals. **Ask:** Why do you think the tales of Brer Rabbit might appeal to enslaved people? *(The tales came from African tradition. Also, Brer Rabbit overcame more powerful foes, as enslaved people hoped to do.)*

Differentiated Instruction

English Language Learners Ask: What emotions might a "lament" express? *(sorrow, regret, sadness, grief)* **ELL**

Reading Strategy

Activating Prior Knowledge Have students look back at the feature on population earlier in this section. **Ask:** Why was a slave rebellion a threat to white Southerners? *(There were nearly 4 million enslaved people—32% of the Southern population. A widespread revolt could be hard to stop.* **AL**

Writing Support

Personal Writing Assign each student one of the following roles: planter, yeoman, enslaved person, and free African American. Have students write their reaction to the Nat Turner uprising from the viewpoint of their assigned persons. **OL**

Primary Source

Critical Thinking Answer
Emotional misery, fear, physical suffering, anger, or hopelessness might increase.

Additional Support

The spiritual below, for example, refers to the biblical story of Daniel, who was saved from the lions' den:

PRIMARY SOURCE

"Didn't my Lord deliver Daniel
Deliver Daniel, deliver Daniel
Didn't my Lord deliver Daniel
An' why not-a every man."
—from "Didn't My Lord Deliver Daniel"

Spirituals enabled enslaved people to communicate secretly among themselves. Many spirituals combined elements related to the enslaved people's Christian faith with laments about earthly suffering.

Slave Codes

Between 1830 and 1860, life under slavery became even more difficult. The **slave codes**—the laws in the Southern states that controlled enslaved people—became more severe. Slave codes had existed since the 1700s. One purpose of the codes was to prevent the event that white Southerners dreaded most—the slave rebellion. For this reason slave codes prohibited enslaved people from assembling in large groups. The codes also required enslaved people to have written passes before leaving the slaveholder's property.

Slave codes made it a crime to teach enslaved people to read or write. White Southerners feared that an educated enslaved person might start a revolt. An enslaved person who could not read and write, whites believed, was less likely to rebel.

Resistance to Slavery

Some enslaved African Americans did rebel openly against their owners. One was **Nat Turner.** He was a popular religious leader among enslaved people. Turner had taught himself to read and write. In 1831 he led a group of followers on a **brief,** or short, violent rampage in Southhampton County, Virginia. Before being captured, Turner and his followers killed at least 55 whites. Nat Turner was hanged, but his rebellion frightened white Southerners. Turner's rebellion led to more severe slave codes.

Primary Source / Slave Codes

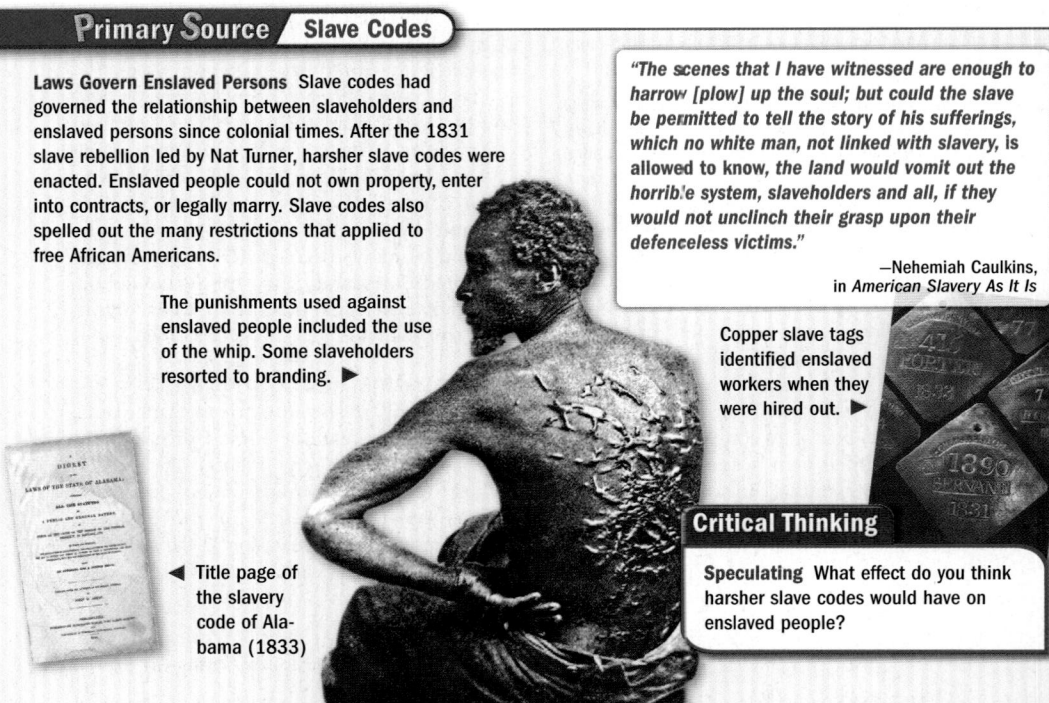

Laws Govern Enslaved Persons Slave codes had governed the relationship between slaveholders and enslaved persons since colonial times. After the 1831 slave rebellion led by Nat Turner, harsher slave codes were enacted. Enslaved people could not own property, enter into contracts, or legally marry. Slave codes also spelled out the many restrictions that applied to free African Americans.

The punishments used against enslaved people included the use of the whip. Some slaveholders resorted to branding. ▶

"The scenes that I have witnessed are enough to harrow [plow] up the soul; but could the slave be permitted to tell the story of his sufferings, which no white man, not linked with slavery, is allowed to know, the land would vomit out the horrible system, slaveholders and all, if they would not unclinch their grasp upon their defenceless victims."
—Nehemiah Caulkins, in *American Slavery As It Is*

Copper slave tags identified enslaved workers when they were hired out. ▶

◀ Title page of the slavery code of Alabama (1833)

Critical Thinking

Speculating What effect do you think harsher slave codes would have on enslaved people?

Activity: Interdisciplinary Connection

Music Many spirituals from African American tradition are still performed today. Organize students into groups. Have each group choose a spiritual to perform for the class. Possible choices include "Go Down, Moses," "Great Day," "Nobody Knows the Trouble I've Seen," "My Lord, What a Morning," "Roll, Jordan, Roll," and "Joshua Fit the Battle of Jericho." Have students find a recording and lyrics for their spiritual and practice singing it. Encourage them to respond to the music, as appropriate. Have the groups do research to prepare a short introduction to the music, including historical background and possible meanings. Each group should read their introduction before performing its spiritual. **OL**

The Nat Turner Rebellion

Violent Uprising In 1831 Nat Turner saw an eclipse of the sun and took it to be a sign from God commanding him to kill his enemies. He and six of his men killed his slaveholder's family and then went from farm to farm, killing all the whites they encountered. Turner and his followers were caught and executed, but slaveholders lived in fear of another violent uprising.

While in jail, Turner was interviewed by Thomas Gray, who recorded his confession. ▶

Nat Turner and his followers meet in the woods to plan their uprising. ▼

"*And about this time I had a vision, and I saw white spirits and black spirits engaged in battle, and the sun was darkened; the thunder rolled in the heavens, and blood flowed in streams; and I heard a voice saying, '. . . let it come, rough or smooth, you must surely bear it.'*"
—*The Confessions of Nat Turner*

"The course has been by no means a direct one. [Northern traders] began first by making [the slaves] religious . . . telling the blacks . . . the black man was as good as the white; that all men were born free and equal; that they can not serve two masters."
—Governor John Floyd of Virginia, in a letter responding to the rebellion, 1831

Critical Thinking

1. **Interpreting** To what "two masters" was Governor John Floyd referring?
2. **Determining Cause and Effect** According to Floyd and Nat Turner, what were the causes of the rebellion?

Armed revolts were rare, however. African Americans in the South knew that they would only lose. For the most part, enslaved people resisted slavery by working slowly or by pretending to be ill. Occasionally resistance was more active. Some enslaved workers would set fire to a plantation building or break tools. Resistance helped enslaved African Americans tolerate their lack of freedom. Even if they were not free, they could strike back at the slaveholders. Resistance also helped set boundaries that slaveholders would respect.

Escaping Slavery

Some enslaved African Americans tried to run away to the North. A few succeeded. **Harriet Tubman** and **Frederick Douglass** were two African American leaders who were born into slavery. They both gained their freedom when they fled to the North.

Getting to the North was difficult for most enslaved people. Most who succeeded escaped from the states of the Upper South.

The **Underground Railroad** offered aid to enslaved people who had escaped. It was a network of "safe houses" owned by free blacks and whites who opposed slavery.

Some enslaved people sought to find relatives on plantations or to escape punishment. Rarely did they plan to flee to the North. Moses Grandy, who did escape, spoke about the problems runaways faced:

PRIMARY SOURCE

"They hide themselves during the day in the woods and swamps; at night they travel. . . . In these dangerous journeys they are guided by the north-star, for they only know that the land of freedom is in the north."
—from *Life of a Slave*

Most runaways were caught and returned to their owners. Discipline was severe. The most common punishment was whipping.

✓ **Reading Check** Explaining How did the African American spiritual develop?

North and South **Chapter 13** 411

R **Reading Strategy**

Identifying Ask: What are some ways that enslaved people resisted slavery? *(working slowly, pretending to be ill, setting fire to a plantation building, breaking tools)* **BL**

W **Writing Support**

Narrative Writing Have students do research to learn more about the experience of people escaping slavery on the Underground Railroad. Ask them to take the role of an escaping person and write a series of diary entries, describing the journey to freedom. **AL**

The Nat Turner Rebellion

Critical Thinking Answers

1. slaveholder and God
2. **Floyd:** introducing enslaved people to religion; **Turner:** a command from God

✓ **Reading Check** **Answer:** It developed as a way to communicate secretly and combine prayer with laments about suffering.

Differentiated Instruction

Leveled Activities

BL **Differentiated Instruction Activity, URB p. 83**

OL **Lesson Transparency 13C**

AL **Writing Skills Activity, URB p. 79**

R Reading Strategy

Inferring Ask: Since free African Americans lived in Southern cities, why couldn't they have become an effective political force? *(The rights of free African Americans were not secure. They were denied an equal share in political life.)* **AL**

✓ **Reading Check** **Answer:** They were located at the crossroads of the railways.

Assess

History ONLINE

Study Central™ provides summaries, interactive games, and online graphic organizers to help students review content.

Close

Summarizing Have students identify unique elements of culture among enslaved African Americans and discuss how each element developed. **OL**

Section 4 Review

City Life and Education

Main Idea By the mid-1800s, the South had several large cities, and education had begun to expand throughout the region.

History and You How far do you travel to get to your school? Read to learn why some Southern families may not have been able to send their children to school.

• •

The South was primarily agricultural. It had several large cities by the mid-1800s, however, including Baltimore and New Orleans. The ten largest cities in the South were either seaports or river ports.

Life in Southern Cities

Cities located at the crossroads of the railways also began to grow. Among them were Chattanooga, Montgomery, and Atlanta. Whites, enslaved workers, and many free African Americans lived in cities.

R In the cities, free African Americans had the opportunity to form their own communities. They practiced trades and founded churches and institutions. Free African Amer-

icans' lives were not secure. Their rights were limited. Most states would not allow them to move from state to state. Free African Americans were denied an equal share in economic and political life.

Education

During this era, no statewide public school systems existed. People who could afford to do so sent their children to private schools. Some of the larger cities established public schools. By the mid-1800s, however, education was growing. North Carolina and Kentucky set up and ran public schools.

The South was behind other sections of the country in **literacy,** the number of people able to read and write. One reason for this situation was the South's geography. The South had few people per square mile. Many families could not send their children great distances to attend school. In addition, many Southerners believed that education was a private matter, not a state function.

✓ **Reading Check** **Identifying** Why did Southern cities such as Atlanta and Montgomery grow?

Section 4 Review

History ONLINE
Study Central™ To review this section, go to glencoe.com.

Vocabulary

1. Using complete sentences, define the following terms: yeoman, tenant farmer, overseer, legal, spiritual, slave code, brief, literacy.

Main Ideas

2. **Describing** Other than plantation owners, what kinds of farmers existed in the South?

3. **Discussing** How did the family structure of enslaved African Americans help them survive life under slavery?

4. **Explaining** Why did education in the South lag behind other areas of the United States?

Critical Thinking

5. **Organizing** Use a diagram like the one below to keep track of key people, events, and practices in resistance to slavery.

Resistance to Slavery

6. **Persuasive Writing** Write a dialogue between an enslaved husband and wife. One wants to try to escape to the North, and the other argues against doing so.

Answer the Essential Question

7. How did unique elements of culture develop among enslaved African Americans in the South?

Answers

1. Sentences should use terms according to their definitions in the section and the Glossary.
2. Yeomen owned land and grew crops for their own use and for profit. Tenant farmers rented land or worked on landlords' estates.
3. Families were broken up as people were sold, but extended families of relatives and friends provided stability.
4. Because the South had few people per square mile, schools were too far away for many families to send their children. Also,

many Southerners felt that education was a private matter, not a state function.
5. Nat Turner (led armed rebellion), active resistance (setting fires, breaking tools), passive resistance (faking illness, working slowly), Underground Railroad (assisted enslaved people who escaped), Harriet Tubman (an enslaved African American who escaped and became a leader), Frederick Douglass (an enslaved African American who escaped and became a leader)

6. Students' dialogues should reflect the hopes and risks of trying to escape.
7. Answers will vary but might include: The possibility of family separation led to large, close-knit extended families. Christianity and African religious beliefs were practiced simultaneously and blended. Christianity stressed hope for freedom and resistance to bondage, and out of it came the spiritual, which evolved as a secret communication method.

Visual Summary

Comparing North and South

The North and the South developed differently during the first half of the 1800s. The North built an industrial economy, while the South pursued an agricultural economy based on slavery. Those economies influenced the labor force and the development of transportation in the regions.

Plantation workers using a cotton gin ▶

	North	South
Economy	• Industrial • New technology fuels growth of industry • Industry develops rapidly Power loom ▶	• Agricultural • Revolutionary cotton gin makes cotton crop highly profitable • Industry develops slowly
People	• Immigrants, including many from Ireland, work factory jobs • Slavery has mostly disappeared by 1830s, but racial prejudice and discrimination remain ◀ Mill workers	• The South had more small farms than large plantations • Most small farmers work land themselves • Slavery on large cotton plantations grows due to increased demand for labor • By 1860 about 4 million African Americans lived under slavery
Transportation	• Roads, canals, and railroads are built for transportation and shipping	• Natural waterways for shipping; fewer railroads are built than in the North

◀ Steamboats in Cincinnati

STUDY TO GO Study anywhere, anytime! Download quizzes and flash cards to your PDA from glencoe.com.

Visual Summary

Making Inferences Point out that although the economies of the North and South were very different, they were interconnected. **Ask:** In what ways did the economies of the North and South depend on one another? *(The South depended on the North for manufactured goods. The North relied on the South for raw materials, such as cotton for its textile mills. By 1860, cotton made up nearly 60% of U.S. exports. [Point to the circle graph in Section 3.] Many of these exports were carried overseas by Northern merchant ships.)* **AL**

Hands-On Chapter Project
Step 5: Wrap-Up

Creating a Slide Show

Step 5: Presenting the Slide Show Each group will give its oral presentation.

Directions Have the groups give their presentations to the class. Each group member should have a speaking role. Tell the audience that they are playing the role of investors who are trying to decide which innovation to support. The investors should ask questions for the presenting group to answer. After all groups have presented, have the class vote on the presentation that most convinced them to invest in the innovation. Students may not vote for their own presentation. As a class, discuss why the winning presentation was convincing.

Analyzing Ask: Why is investment important for innovation? *(Developing an idea into a practical device requires money. Money from investors can enable development to continue.)* Why do investors choose to invest in a new idea? *(They hope to make a profit.)* **OL**

413

Answers and Analyses
Reviewing Main Ideas

1. B Advise students to look for clues to the sequence of events. Choice B describes specialization, so it must occur before specialized workers are brought together in factories (choice D). This sequence also eliminates choices A and C, which involve factories. **16.C.3b (US)**

2. C Remind students that this party began as a secret anti-Catholic society. This information eliminates choice D and suggests choice C as the likely answer. **18.B**

3. B Remind students that under capitalism, people conduct business to make a profit. When a business is especially profitable, as cotton production was in the South, a large portion of the people in that area will to go into that business. **16.C.3b (US)**

4. A Remind students that only a small portion of white Southerners held slaves, eliminating choice D. **16.D.3a (US)**

Short-Answer Question

5. Industrialization, brought on by innovations such as specialization and power-driven machinery, led to an increase of factory jobs. Mass production increased jobs in transportation and trade as well as jobs in mining raw materials. Although innovations also spurred agricultural growth, jobs created by industrialization far outnumbered those in agriculture. **16.C.3b (US)**

TEST-TAKING **TIP**

> Make sure the number of answer spaces on the answer sheet matches the number of questions on the test you are taking.

Reviewing Main Ideas

Directions: Choose the best answer for each of the following questions.

1. What happened in the first phase of industrialization in the North?

   A Factory workers used machinery to perform some of their work.

   B Manufacturers made products by dividing the tasks involved among the workers.

   C Waterpower and steam power were used to produce more products in less time.

   D Manufacturers built factories to bring specialized workers together.

2. The American Party was sometimes called the Know-Nothing Party because

   A its opponents believed party members knew nothing about the important issues.

   B party members did not support education.

   C party members responded to questions about the group by saying, "I know nothing."

   D party members were mainly Catholics who knew nothing about Protestantism.

3. What was the main reason that the Southern economy remained largely agricultural?

   A Southerners lacked the capital to start industries.

   B Cotton sales were very profitable.

   C Southerners refused to work in factories.

   D Costs to ship goods to markets were too high.

4. The largest group of whites in the South were

   A yeomen.   **C** the rural poor.

   B tenant farmers.   **D** plantation owners.

Short-Answer Question

Directions: Base your answer to question 5 on the following table and on your knowledge of social studies.

Occupational Distribution of American Workers

	1820	1860
Agriculture	79%	53%
Mining	0.4%	1.6%
Construction	—	4.7%
Manufacturing	3%	14%
Trade	—	8%
Transport	1.6%	6.4%
Service	4.1%	6.4%

5. Explain how the technological innovations of the early 1800s affected the change in the percentage of Americans working in agriculture and manufacturing.

Review the Essential Questions

6. Essay How did industrialization and immigration affect different parts of the United States in the first half of the 1800s?

To help you write your essay, review your answers to the Essential Questions in the section reviews and the chapter Foldables Study Organizer. Your essay should include:

- innovations in technology, communications, and transportation in the 1800s;
- the development of factories and cities in various parts of the United States;
- influences of immigration and patterns of settlement;
- reasons for and effects of the growing importance of cotton in the Southern economy; and
- the spread of slavery in the South.

GO ON ➡

Review the Essential Questions

6. Students' Foldables should help with their answers. Industrialization especially affected the Northeast, where factory cities and seaports grew rapidly—in part because of immigrants, who provided cheap labor. The population of the Midwest grew as agricultural innovations made wheat farming profitable and transportation innovations opened new markets for farm products. The growth of Northern factories increased the demand for Southern cotton. Inventions such as the cotton gin allowed more cotton to be produced, leading to the spread of slavery throughout the Deep South. **17.C.3c**

History ONLINE
For additional test practice, use **Self-Check Quizzes**—Chapter 13 at glencoe.com.

Chapter 13 Assessment

Document-Based Questions

Directions: Analyze the documents and answer the short-answer questions that follow.

Document 1

A Southern newspaper publisher wrote the following in 1856.

> Every Roman Catholic in the known world is under the absolute control of the Catholic Priesthood. . . . And it is . . . this power of the Priesthood to control the Catholic community, and cause a vast multitude of ignorant foreigners to vote as a unit . . .

Source: William G. Brownlow, *Americanism Contrasted*

7. Based on the document, what did the writer believe about Catholic immigrants to the U.S.?

Document 2

This map shows the 15 most populous American cities in 1840.

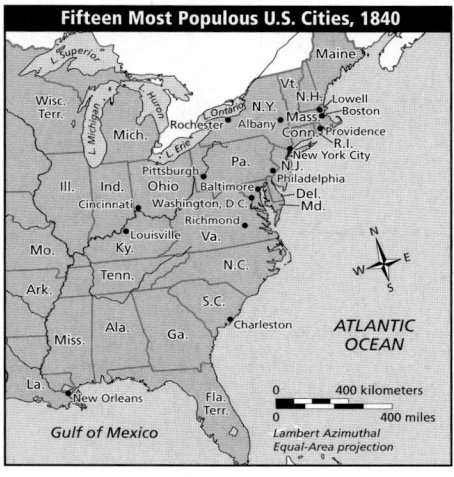

Fifteen Most Populous U.S. Cities, 1840

ATLANTIC OCEAN

Gulf of Mexico

0 400 kilometers
0 400 miles
Lambert Azimuthal Equal-Area projection

8. Use the map and your knowledge of geography and economics to explain the distribution of major U.S. cities in the mid-1800s.

Document 3

The following is an excerpt from a work contract from around 1830.

> We . . . agree to work for such wages per week, and prices by the job, as the Company may see fit to pay. . . . We also agree not to be engaged in any [labor union], whereby the work may be [delayed], or the company's interest in any work [harmed].

Source: Cocheco Manufacturing Company

9. Based on the excerpt, what can you conclude about the relationship between employees and employers in factories in the early 1800s?

Document 4

In this passage, Jacob Stroyer describes the aftermath of a beating he received as an enslaved boy.

> I went to mother with my complaint and she came out to the man who had whipped me. . . . Then he took a whip and started for her. . . . I ran back and forth between mother and him until he stopped beating her. [Afterward], he took me back to the stable yard and gave me a severe flogging.

Source: Jacob Stroyer, *My Life in the South*

10. According to the document, how did Jacob's mother react to his beating? What was the final outcome?

11. Expository Writing Using the information from the four documents and your knowledge of social studies, write an essay in which you:

- take the role of an immigrant to America in 1840 and decide whether to settle in the North or the South; and

- describe the conditions in both sections of the country that led to your decision.

9. Employers held the most power. Workers accepted whatever the company wanted to pay. Labor unions were active, and employers were concerned about them. **16.A.3b**

10. She tried to confront the man who was beating her son. Jacob got another serious whipping. **18.B.3a**

11. Students' essays should compare conditions in the North and South and use this comparison to support their decision about where to settle. **17.C.3c**

History ONLINE

Have students visit the Web site at glencoe.com to review Chapter 13 and take the Self-Check Quiz.

Need Extra Help?

Have students refer to the pages listed if they miss any of the questions.

Need Extra Help?

If You Missed Questions...	1	2	3	4	5	6	7	8	9	10	11
Go to Page...	389	399	401–403	407	389–393	386–412	399	397–399	395–397	409–411	386–412

Document-Based Questions

7. The writer believed that the immigrants were ignorant and controlled by priests, who would tell them how to vote. **16.A.3b**

8. Cities grew more rapidly in the North as workers flocked to factory jobs. Because Southern rail lines were short, local, and did not connect all parts of the region, Southern cities grew more slowly than those in the North and Midwest, where railways provided major routes of commerce and settlement. **17.A.3b**

Chapter Planning Guide

14

BL	OL	AL	ELL		Resources	Chapter Opener	Section 1	Section 2	Section 3	Chapter Assess
					FOCUS					
BL	OL	AL	ELL	🖨	Daily Test Practice Transparencies		14–1	14–2	14–3	
					TEACH					
	OL	AL		📁	Geography and History Activity, URB		p. 115			
BL	OL		ELL	📁	Time Line Skills Activity, URB				p. 118	
BL	OL	AL	ELL	📁	Writing Skills Activity, URB				p.107	
BL	OL	AL	ELL	📁	Content Vocabulary Activity, URB		p. 101	p. 101	p. 101	
BL	OL	AL	ELL	📁	Academic Vocabulary Activity, URB		p. 103	p. 103	p. 103	
BL	OL		ELL	📁	Social Studies Skills Activity, URB		p. 109			
BL	OL	AL	ELL	📁	Differentiated Instruction Activity, URB				p. 111	
BL	OL	AL	ELL	📁	Critical Thinking Skills Activity, URB				p. 113	
BL	OL	AL	ELL	📁	Linking Past and Present Activity, URB		p. 117			
	OL	AL		📁	Primary Source Readings, URB				p. 105	
BL	OL	AL	ELL	📁	School-to-Home Connection Activity, URB		p. 119	p. 119	p. 119	
BL	OL		ELL	📁	Guided Reading Activity, URB*		p. 123	p. 124	p. 125	
		AL		📁	Enrichment Activity, URB			p. 11		
BL	OL		ELL	📁	Reading Essentials and Note-Taking Guide*		p. 142	p. 145	p. 148	
BL	OL	AL	ELL	🖨	Lesson Transparencies		14A	14C	14B	
	OL	AL		📁	Interpreting Political Cartoons, URB			p. 13		
		AL		📁	Supreme Court Case Studies			p. 9		
	OL			📁	American Biographies		pp. 17, 18, 25	pp. 21, 22	pp. 23,26	
	OL	AL		🖨	American Art and Architecture Transparencies, Strategies, and Activities		12			

Note: Please refer to the *Unit Resource Book: Nationalism and Sectionalism* for this chapter's materials.

* Also available in Spanish

Levels					Resources	Chapter Opener	Section 1	Section 2	Section 3	Chapter Assess
BL	OL	AL	ELL							
TEACH *(continued)*										
BL	OL	AL	ELL	📁	NGS US Desk Map		✓	✓	✓	
BL	OL	AL	ELL	📁	American Literature Library		✓	✓	✓	
BL	OL	AL	ELL	📁	Writer's Guidebook		✓	✓	✓	
	OL	AL		💿	American History Primary Source Document Library CD-ROM		✓	✓	✓	✓
BL	OL	AL	ELL	💿	American Music: Hits Through History	✓	✓	✓	✓	
BL	OL	AL	ELL	💿	StudentWorks™ Plus CD	✓	✓	✓	✓	✓
	OL	AL		🖥	Section Spotlight Videos		✓	✓	✓	
BL	OL	AL	ELL	🖏	Writing Process Transparencies		✓	✓	✓	✓
BL	OL	AL	EL	🖥	Presentation Plus! With MindJogger CheckPoint CD	✓	✓	✓	✓	✓
ASSESS										
BL	OL	AL	ELL	📁	Quizzes and Tests		p. 131	p. 132	p. 133	pp. 135, 137, 139
BL	OL	AL	ELL	📁	Authentic Assessment With Rubrics		p. 14			
BL	OL	AL	ELL	📁	Standardized Test Practice					p. 27
BL	OL	AL	ELL	💿	*ExamView® Assessment Suite* CD-ROM*		14–1	14–2	14–3	Ch. 14
CLOSE										
BL			ELL	📁	Reteaching Activity, URB*		p. 121	p. 121	p. 121	p. 121
BL	OL		ELL	📁	Reading and Study Skills Foldables Activity	p. 76	p. 76	p. 76	p. 76	p. 76
BL			ELL	📁	Reading Strategies and Activities for the Social Studies Classroom		✓	✓	✓	
BL	OL	AL	ELL	🖏	Graphic Organizer Transparencies & Strategies		✓	✓	✓	

TeacherWorks *Plus*
All-In-One Planner and Resource Center

- Interactive Lesson Planner
- Interactive Teacher Edition
- Fully editable blackline masters
- Section Spotlight Videos Launch

- Differentiated Lesson Plans
- Printable reports of daily assignments
- Standards Tracking System

Professional Development Resources

- Strategies for Success
- Building Academic Vocabulary
- Success With English Learners DVD
- Differentiated Instruction Strategies DVD
- Teaching Literacy Strategies in Social Studies DVD
- Assessment DVD
- Standards-Based Instruction DVD

Using PuzzleMaker™ 3.1

Online Word Search Puzzles

Technology Product

Glencoe's Vocabulary PuzzleMaker™ 3.1 lets you create your own puzzles based on the glossary. The PuzzleMaker allows you to

- create word search puzzles;
- create online or paper word search puzzles.

Objectives

After students complete the word search puzzles, they will be able to

- recall vocabulary terms based on the clues provided;
- reinforce their understanding of the vocabulary.

Steps

- Download, install, and run PuzzleMaker™ 3.1 from glencoe.com. Click on **Create a New Puzzle**.
- Select the *Puzzle Database* for the vocabulary.
- The *PuzzleMaker Wizard* will help you select a puzzle type and grid type.
- Make selections from the list. Indicate whether you want the words selected randomly or manually.
- Select the language and words you wish to use for the puzzle. Click **Finish**.
- Save your word search puzzle with PuzzlePlayer™ 3.1, or print copies for your students to complete.
- Use PuzzlePlayer™ 3.1 to review students' puzzles.

History ONLINE at glencoe.com

	Student	Teacher	Parent
Media Center			
• Student Edition Audio	●		
• Spanish Summaries	●		
• Section Spotlight Videos	●	●	
Social Studies Online Learning Center			
Classroom Tools			
• Multi-Language Glossaries	●	●	●
• Teaching Today		●	
• TIME Current Events	●	●	●
• Beyond the Textbook	●	●	
The American Journey **Online Learning Center**			
• Study-to-Go™	●	●	●
• Study Central™	●	●	●
• Chapter Overview	●	●	
• Concepts in Motion	●	●	
• ePuzzles and Games	●	●	
• Literature Connections	●	●	
• Online Student Edition	●	●	●
• Self-Check Quizzes	●	●	●
• Student Web Activities	●	●	
• Vocabulary eFlashcards	●	●	
• Web Activity Lesson Plans	●	●	●
• Vocabulary PuzzleMaker	●	●	●

Additional Resources

- **Timed Readings Plus in Social Studies** helps students increase their reading rate and fluency while maintaining comprehension. The 400-word passages are similar to those found on state and national assessments.

- **Reading in the Content Area: Social Studies** concentrates on six essential reading skills that help students better comprehend what they read. The book includes 75 high-interest nonfiction passages written at increasing levels of difficulty.

- **Reading Social Studies** includes strategic reading instruction and vocabulary support in Social Studies content for ELLs and native speakers of English.

- **Content Vocabulary Workout** (Grades 6–8) accelerates reading comprehension through focused vocabulary development. Social Studies content vocabulary comes from the glossaries of Glencoe's Middle School Social Studies texts.

www.jamestowneducation.com

Index to National Geographic Magazine:

The following articles relate to this chapter:

- *"Views of Africa,"* David Quammen, September 2005.
- *"Zip USA: 02557,"* Perry Garfinkel, June 2003.

National Geographic Society Products
To order the following, call National Geographic at 1-800-368-2728:

National Geographic Atlas of the World (Book)

Access National Geographic's new dynamic MapMachine Web site and other geography resources at:

www.nationalgeographic.com
www.nationalgeographic.com/mapmachine

Use this database to search more than 30,000 titles to create a customized reading list for your students.

- Reading lists can be organized by students' reading level, author, genre, theme, or area of interest.
- The database provides Degrees of Reading Power™ (DRP) and Lexile™ readability scores for all selections.
- A brief summary of each selection is included.

Leveled reading suggestions for this chapter:

For students at a Grade 6 reading level:
- *Who Comes With Cannons?* by Patricia Beatty
- *Send One Angel Down,* by Virginia Frances Schwartz

For students at a Grade 7 reading level:
- *True North,* by Kathryn Lasky
- *Sojourner Truth: Voice for Freedom,* by Kathleen Kudlinski

For students at a Grade 8 reading level:
- *Elizabeth Blackwell: The First Woman Doctor,* by Francene Sabin
- *By Secret Railway,* by Enid LaMonte Meadowcroft

For students at a Grade 9 reading level:
- *Harriet Tubman,* by Ann Petry
- *Many Thousand Gone: African-Americans From Slavery to Freedom,* by Virginia Hamilton

For students at a Grade 10 reading level:
- *Uncle Tom's Cabin,* by Harriet Beecher Stowe

The following videotape programs are available from Glencoe as supplements to the chapter:

- **Susan B. Anthony: Rebel for the Cause** (ISBN 1-56-501646-7)
- **Frederick Douglass** (ISBN 0-76-700120-6)

To order, call Glencoe at 1-800-334-7344. To find classroom resources to accompany many of these videos, check the following home pages:

A&E Television: www.aetv.com

The History Channel: www.history.com

Chapter Objectives

After studying this chapter, students will be able to:

- Describe how religion influenced the social reforms in the United States during the early and mid-1800s.
- Explain how abolitionists influenced the antislavery movement.
- Explain the effects of the women's rights movement of the middle to late 1800s.

Motivating Activity

Making Inferences Students will learn that certain people were not allowed to attend school in the 1800s. **Ask:** Based on this picture, what group of children was typically denied the right to attend school? *(African Americans)* Point out that girls were often excluded as well, because parents thought girls did not need an education for their roles as wives and mothers. **Ask:** If you could not go to school, how might your future be different? *(Answers may include limited job opportunities, lower pay, and lower standard of living.)* **OL**

Previewing the Essential Questions

As you begin teaching each section, use these questions and activities to help students focus on the Essential Questions.

Chapter 14
The Age of Reform 1820–1860

During the 1800s, most American students attended one-room schools.

PRESIDENTS

JAMES MONROE 1817–1825

JOHN Q. ADAMS 1825–1829

ANDREW JACKSON 1829–1837

MARTIN VAN BUREN 1837–1841

U.S. Events

★ **1821** Sequoya develops Cherokee alphabet

★ **1827** New York bans slavery

★ **1830** *Book of Mormon* published

World Events

1820

1830

★ **1821** Mexico becomes independent nation

★ **1837** Victoria becomes queen of England

416   Chapter 14

Section 1

Social Reform Ask: How do religious congregations serve society today? *(Possible answer: run soup kitchens, free stores, schools, and clinics; minister to the sick)* Point out to students that in Section 1 they will learn how religious and other reformers tried to improve society in the 1800s. **OL**

Section 2

The Abolitionists Ask: What could opponents of slavery do to try to end the practice? *(write or speak against it; help enslaved people escape or shelter them)* Point out to students that Section 2 discusses the efforts of antislavery activists who took great risks to try to end slavery. **OL**

Section 1: Social Reform

Essential Question How did religion influence the social reforms in the United States during the early and mid-1800s?

Section 2: The Abolitionists

Essential Question How did abolitionists influence the antislavery movement?

Section 3: The Women's Movement

Essential Question What were the effects of the women's rights movement of the middle to late 1800s?

◀ Elizabeth Cady Stanton at the Seneca Falls Convention ▶

History ONLINE
Chapter Overview Visit glencoe.com and click on **Chapter 14—Chapter Overviews** to preview chapter information.

FOLDABLES Study Organizer

Organizing Information Make this Foldable to organize what you learn about the reform movements of the 1800s.

Step 1 Fold a sheet of paper in half lengthwise.

Step 2 Fold the paper into three equal sections.

Step 3 Cut the folds on the top flap.

Step 4 Label the tabs as shown.

| Reform and Society | Reform and Slavery | Reform and Women |

Reading and Writing As you read the chapter, take notes in your Foldable about how reformers addressed problems in society and issues facing enslaved people and women.

Time Line Activity

If you have not already done so, have students review the time line. **Ask:** What years are covered in this chapter? Who was president when New York banned slavery? *(1820–1860; John Q. Adams)* What nations gained independence during this period? *(Mexico, Liberia)*

FOLDABLES Study Organizer **Dinah Zike's Foldables**

Purpose This Foldable helps students organize what they learn about the reform movements of the 1800s. The completed Foldable will help them prepare for assessment.

More Foldables activities for this chapter can be found in *Dinah Zike's Reading and Study Skills Foldables.*

History ONLINE
Introduce students to chapter content and key terms by having them access the **Chapter Overview** at glencoe.com.

WILLIAM HENRY HARRISON 1841

JOHN TYLER 1841–1845

JAMES POLK 1845–1849

★ **1848** Seneca Falls Convention held

ZACHARY TAYLOR 1849–1850

MILLARD FILLMORE 1850–1853

FRANKLIN PIERCE 1853–1857

JAMES BUCHANAN 1857–1861

1840   **1850**   **1860**

★ **1843** Maori revolt against British in New Zealand

★ **1847** Liberia claims independence

★ **1850** Taiping Rebellion begins in China

★ **1853** Crimean War begins

★ **1859** Belgian inventor Lenoir builds first practical internal-combustion engine

Chapter 14   417

Section 3

The Women's Movement Ask: What rights and opportunities do women have today that they did not have in the early 1800s? *(rights to vote, own property after marriage, seek divorce and custody of children; equality in jobs, pay, and education)* Tell students that Section 3 will explore the impact of the women's movement in the 1800s. **OL**

417

Section 1

Section 1

Social Reform

CHAPTER 14
Section 1

Focus

Bellringer
Daily Test Practice Transparency 14–1

Reading Guide
Answers to Graphic:
Gallaudet: developed a method to educate people who were hearing impaired, opened the Hartford School for the Deaf;
Dix: educated the public about poor conditions for prisoners and the mentally ill

Section Spotlight Video

To learn more about reform movements of the 1800s, watch the Section Spotlight Video "Social Reform."

Resource Manager

Essential Question ◄
How did religion influence the social reforms in the United States during the early and mid-1800s?

Reading Guide

Content Vocabulary
revival (p. 419)
utopia (p. 419)
temperance (p. 419)
normal school (p. 420)
transcendentalist (p. 421)
civil disobedience (p. 421)

Academic Vocabulary
lecture (p. 419)   author (p. 421)

Key People and Events
Second Great Awakening (p. 419)
temperance movement (p. 419)

Reading Strategy
Taking Notes As you read, use a diagram like the one below to identify the reformers' contributions.

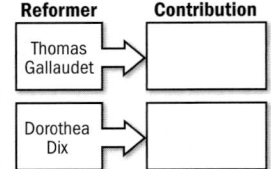

Reformer	Contribution
Thomas Gallaudet →	
Dorothea Dix →	

ILLINOIS STANDARDS
The American Journey

14.F.3b Describe how United States political ideas and traditions were instituted in the Constitution and the Bill of Rights.

16.D.3a (US) Describe characteristics of different kinds of communities in various sections of America during the colonial/frontier periods and the 19th century.

18.A.3 Explain how language, literature, the arts, architecture and traditions contribute to the development and transmission of culture.

18.B.3b Explain how social institutions contribute to the development and transmission of culture.

American Diary

"The noise was like the roar of Niagara [Falls]. The vast sea of human beings seemed to be agitated as if by a storm. . . . Some of the people were singing, others praying, some crying for mercy. . . . While witnessing these scenes, a peculiarly-strange sensation, such as I had never felt before, came over me. My heart beat tumultuously [violently], my knees trembled, my lip quivered, and I felt as though I must fall to the ground."

—*from Autobiography of Rev. James B. Finley*

Religious revivals could attract thousands of people for days of prayers and songs.

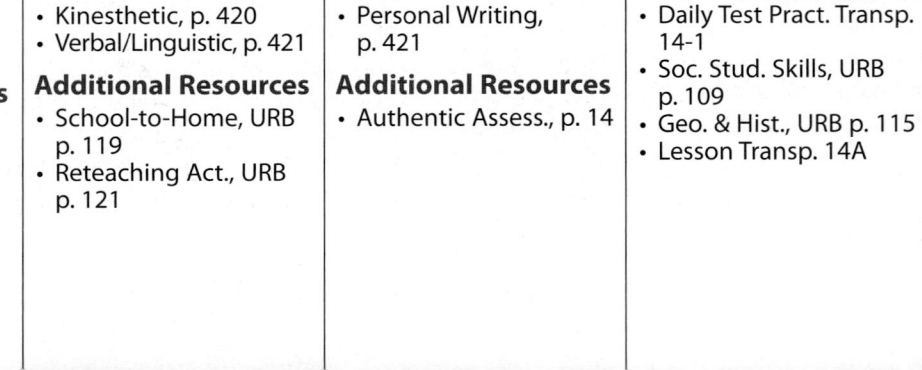

R Reading Strategies	**C** Critical Thinking	**D** Differentiated Instruction	**W** Writing Support	**S** Skill Practice
Teacher Edition • Using Parts of Words, p. 419 **Additional Resources** • Guid. Read., URB p. 123 • Content Vocab., URB p. 101 • Academic Vocab., URB p. 103 • Read. Ess., p. 142	**Teacher Edition** • Analyzing Primary Sources, p. 419 **Additional Resources** • Quizzes and Tests, p. 131 • Link. Past & Pres., URB p. 117	**Teacher Edition** • Kinesthetic, p. 420 • Verbal/Linguistic, p. 421 **Additional Resources** • School-to-Home, URB p. 119 • Reteaching Act., URB p. 121	**Teacher Edition** • Personal Writing, p. 421 **Additional Resources** • Authentic Assess., p. 14	**Additional Resources** • Daily Test Pract. Transp. 14-1 • Soc. Stud. Skills, URB p. 109 • Geo. & Hist., URB p. 115 • Lesson Transp. 14A

Religion and Reform

Main Idea The Second Great Awakening influenced social and educational reforms.

History and You Do you volunteer to help people, such as the elderly, with their daily chores? You are probably familiar with individuals or organizations who help people in need. Read about how reformers felt a responsibility to help others.

Religious camp meetings, called **revivals,** were quite common in the early 1800s. People would travel great distances to hear preachers speak and to pray, sing, weep, and shout. This was the time when a wave of religious fervor—known as the **Second Great Awakening**—stirred the nation. The first Great Awakening had spread through the colonies in the mid-1700s.

There was a new spirit of reform throughout America in the early 1800s. This spirit brought changes to American religion, education, and literature. Some reformers sought to improve society by forming **utopias.** These communities were based on a vision of the perfect society. However, most were founded on impractical ideas and only a few groups, like the Mormons, were able to establish stable, lasting communities.

The Religious Influence

Attending revivals often made men and women eager to reform both their own lives and the world. Some people became involved in missionary work and social reform movements. Among those movements was the push to ban alcohol.

Lyman Beecher, a Connecticut minister, crusaded against the use of alcohol. He wanted to protect society from "rum-selling, tippling folk, infidels [nonbelievers], and ruffscruff." Beecher and other reformers called for **temperance,** drinking little or no alcohol. They used **lectures,** pamphlets, and revival-style rallies to warn people of the dangers of liquor.

The **temperance movement** led to some victories when Maine and other states passed laws banning the manufacture and sale of alcoholic beverages. Most of these laws, however, were later repealed, or canceled.

Primary Source / **Responsibility for Others**

Helping Others Reformer Dorothea Dix encouraged others to help the less fortunate. She said, "Become the [protectors] of your race, the just guardians of the solemn rights you hold in trust. Raise up the fallen, [aid] the desolate, restore the outcast, defend the helpless, and for your eternal and great reward receive the [blessing]."

—from *Memorial to the Massachusetts Legislature*

Dorothea Dix ▶

Critical Thinking

Comparing Do you know any people today who share beliefs similar to Second Great Awakening reformers? What are their beliefs?

Teach

C Critical Thinking

Analyzing Primary Sources Have students read the quote from Dix in the feature. **Ask:** What religious influence do you see in her words? *(The reward for helping the less fortunate is eternal blessing—that is, a place in heaven.)* **OL**

R Reading Strategy

Using Parts of Words Read this sentence aloud: "She had to temper her excitement at the good news." **Ask:** What does "temper" mean? *(tone down)* How did temperance reformers want to change the way people drank alcohol? *(They wanted them to tone it down.)* **ELL**

Primary Source

Critical Thinking Answer
Students might identify celebrities who speak out or perform concerts to benefit the poor.

Hands-On Chapter Project
Step 1

Influencing Public Policy

Step 1: Researching an Issue Students will do research to learn more about a reform issue.

Essential Question: How did religion influence the social reforms in the United States during the early and mid-1800s?

Directions Organize students into groups. Assign each group one of the following reform issues: temperance, education, prisons, abolition, women's rights. Tell students they are taking on the roles of reform activists. Their state representative has asked them to present their views at a hearing of the state legislature. Each group will prepare a pamphlet and a presentation. Have students gather facts, supporting details, images, and quotes from reformers to use in their pamphlets. The goal is to influence state legislators to pass a reform law.

Determining Cause and Effect Ask: How might the revival of religious spirit motivate people to try to reform society? *(In seeking to reform their own lives according to religious teaching, people might naturally think about improving the society in which they live.)* **OL**

(Chapter Project continued in Section 2)

D Differentiated Instruction

Kinesthetic Print out and project the Braille alphabet from National Braille Press, www.nbp.org. Explain that raised dots in different positions form letters. Pass around a Braille book. Have students close their eyes, feel the dots, and then look at the alphabet sheet to find the letters. **OL**

INTERPRETING POLITICAL CARTOONS

Answers

1. The man drinks progressively more and degrades physically and morally until he dies.

2. the man's wife and child; suggests that the man has obligations to his family that drinking is causing him to neglect

✓ **Reading Check** **Answer:** Howe developed a system of raised letters that people with sight impairments could read with their fingers.

Differentiated Instruction

Primary Sources
INTERPRETING
POLITICAL CARTOONS

This cartoon, by Nathaniel Currier, is titled "The Drunkard's Progress." It was created in 1846, during the temperance movement.

1. **Summarizing** How would you describe the "progress" from step 1 through step 9?
2. **Making Inferences** Who do the people under the arch represent? Why are they shown in the cartoon?

Reforming Education

Reformers also wanted to improve education. In the mid-1850s, most schools were poorly funded, and many teachers lacked training. Some people opposed compulsory, or required, education.

In addition, restrictions were placed on who could attend school. Girls were often excluded because parents thought education was wasted on future wives and mothers. Many African Americans were also denied the right to attend school.

Massachusetts lawyer Horace Mann was a leader of educational reform. Partly because of his efforts, in 1839 Massachusetts founded the nation's first state-supported **normal school** where high-school graduates were trained to become teachers. Other states soon adopted Mann's reforms.

Many new colleges and universities were created during the age of reform. Most admitted only men, but gradually, higher education became available to groups that had been denied the opportunity. Oberlin College of Ohio, for example, founded in 1833, admitted both women and African Americans.

People With Special Needs

Some reformers focused on the problem of teaching people with disabilities. Thomas Gallaudet (GA•luh•DEHT) developed a method to educate people who were hearing impaired. He opened the Hartford School for the Deaf in Connecticut in 1817. At about the same time, Samuel Gridley Howe advanced the cause of people who were visually impaired. He developed books with large raised letters that people with sight impairments could "read" with their fingers. Howe headed the Perkins Institute, a school for the blind, in Boston.

Schoolteacher Dorothea Dix began visiting prisons in 1841. She found some prisoners chained to the walls with little or no clothing, often in unheated cells. Dix also learned that some of the inmates were guilty of no crime. They were people who were mentally ill. Dix made it her life's work to educate the public about the poor conditions for prisoners and the mentally ill.

✓ **Reading Check** **Identifying** How did Samuel Howe help the visually impaired?

Creating a Web Organizer

Objective:	To learn how to organize information into a web diagram
Focus:	Ask students why it is important to identify the central ideas in their reading.
Teach:	Have students review the web diagram, answer the questions, and then create their own web diagrams.
Assess:	Ask students to complete the checklist.
Close:	Have volunteers share their diagrams.

Differentiated Instruction Strategies

BL Before students begin their own web diagrams, discuss with them possible life events they could select.

AL Have students create their web diagrams using presentation software.

ELL Ask students to explain, in their own words, the term "central idea."

Social Studies Skills Activity, URB p. 109

Cultural Trends

Main Idea A distinct type of American literature emerged in the 1820s.

History and You Have you read works by Thoreau, Emerson, or Dickinson? Read to learn how these writers changed American literature.

The changes in American society also influenced art and literature. Beginning in the 1820s, American artists developed their own style and explored American themes.

The American spirit of reform influenced the **transcendentalists.** These thinkers and writers stressed the relationship between humans and nature and the importance of the individual conscience. Margaret Fuller, Ralph Waldo Emerson, and Henry David Thoreau were leading transcendentalists.

Through her writings, Fuller supported women's rights. In his works, Emerson urged people to listen to the inner voice of conscience and to overcome prejudice. Thoreau practiced **civil disobedience** by refusing to obey laws he considered unjust. In 1846 Thoreau went to jail rather than pay a tax to support the Mexican War.

Numerous poets also created great works during this period. Henry Wadsworth Longfellow wrote narrative, or story, poems such as the *Song of Hiawatha*. Poet Walt Whitman captured the new American spirit and confidence in his *Leaves of Grass*. Emily Dickinson wrote simple, deeply personal poems. In a poem called "Hope," written in 1861, she compares hope to a bird:

PRIMARY SOURCE

"'Hope' is the thing with feathers—
That perches in the soul—
And sings the tune without the words—
And never stops—at all—"
—from *Emily Dickinson: Selected Poems*

During this time, women were the **authors** of the most popular fiction. Harriet Beecher Stowe wrote the most successful best-seller of the mid-1800s, *Uncle Tom's Cabin*. Stowe's novel explores the injustice of slavery, an issue that took on new urgency during the age of reform.

Reading Check Identifying Cause and Effect How did the spirit of reform influence American authors?

W Writing Support

Personal Writing Have students write a four-line poem on one of the themes of the transcendentalists. **OL**

D Differentiated Instruction

Verbal/Linguistic Ask: Why do you think Dickinson compared hope to a bird? *(Hope creates the same uplifting feeling that a singing bird does.)* **AL**

Reading Check **Answer:** It inspired themes of the relationship between humans and nature, the importance of individual conscience, and the injustice of slavery.

Assess

History ONLINE

Study Central™ provides summaries, interactive games, and online graphic organizers to help students review content.

Close

Making Connections Discuss the relationship between religious revival and the spirit of reform during this period. **OL**

Section 1 Review

History ONLINE
Study Central™ To review this section, go to glencoe.com.

Vocabulary

1. Use the following key terms to write a paragraph about social reform: revival, utopia, temperance, lecture, normal school, transcendentalist, civil disobedience, author.

Main Ideas

2. **Identifying** What problems spurred reform in the area of education?

3. **Explaining** What themes did the transcendentalists focus on in their writings?

Critical Thinking

4. **Synthesizing** In what ways did the writers of the mid-1800s demonstrate the American spirit of the times?

5. **Analyzing** What reforms resulted from the Second Great Awakening? Use a diagram like the one below to organize your answer.

Second Great Awakening

6. **Persuasive Writing** Create a brochure about the newly established Oberlin College to send to potential students. Explain why the college differs from others, and describe the advantages of this college experience.

Answer the
7. **Essential Question**
How did religion influence the social reforms in the United States during the early and mid-1800s?

The Age of Reform **Chapter 14** 421

Section 1 Review

Answers

1. Students should use the terms correctly in a paragraph about social reform.
2. Problems included poorly trained teachers, poorly funded schools, opposition to compulsory education, few educational opportunities for females or African Americans, and the problem of teaching people with disabilities.
3. The themes included the relationship between humans and nature and the importance of the individual conscience.
4. Students might mention that the writers

showed the spirit of reform; authors wrote about the importance of the individual in relation to nature, standing up for what one believes, equality through overcoming prejudice, women's rights, and the injustice of slavery.
5. utopian communities, temperance laws, new colleges including the first normal school, techniques for teaching people with disabilities, better conditions for prisoners and the mentally ill
6. Students' brochures will differ but should

mention that men, women, and African Americans are all welcome as members of the student body.
7. The revival of religious spirit inspired people to reform their own lives and improve the ills of society. Reformers of this period wanted laws restricting alcohol; better teacher training and school funding; more colleges; more universal access to education for women, African Americans, and people with special needs; and better conditions for prisoners and the mentally ill.

Focus

C Critical Thinking

Making Inferences Ask students: Why do you think Audubon became successful during this time? *(Students should note that his writings and drawings were based on personal observations. Also, during this time, more people were settling the West and were interested in learning about the new environments.)* **OL**

Teach

R Reading Strategy

Paraphrasing Have students read the quotation by President Tyler. Discuss his use of metaphors in the sentences. Ask students to rewrite the quotation without using metaphors. **OL**

Additional Support and Answers

What were people's lives like in the past?

These two pages will give you some clues to everyday life in the United States as you step back in time with TIME Notebook.

PHOTO RESEARCHERS

Profile

"My best friends solemnly regard me as a madman." That's what the artist **JOHN JAMES AUDUBON** *writes about himself in his journal.* And he does seem to be a bit peculiar. After all, he put a band around a bird's foot so he could tell if it returned from the South in the spring. No one's ever done that before. Audubon is growing more famous thanks to his drawings. His love of the wild and his skill as an artist have awakened a new sense of appreciation for animal life in the United States. Here is what he wrote while on a trip to New Orleans in 1821.

C

"I took a walk with my gun this afternoon to see . . . millions of Golden Plovers [medium-sized shorebirds] coming from the northeast and going nearly south—the destruction . . . was really astonishing—the Sportsmen here are more numerous and at the same time more expert at shooting on the wing than anywhere in the United States. . . . 400 Gunners were out. Supposing that each man killed 40 dozen that day, 192,000 plovers must have been destroyed."

PLUVIALIS DOMINICA, AMERICAN GOLDEN PLOVER, DRAWN BY AUDUBON

THE NATURAL HISTORY MUSEUM / ALAMY

R

" What hath God wrought? "
SAMUEL MORSE,
in the first official message sent over his telegraph in 1844

" O, Susanna,
Now don't you cry for me,
For I come from Alabama
With my banjo on my knee. "
STEPHEN FOSTER,
author of this campfire tune in 1848

" . . . Some very good houses, broad streets, and marble-fronted shops . . . though it is never likely to vie, in point of elegance or beauty, with Cincinnati. "
CHARLES DICKENS,
British author, on his visit to St. Louis in 1842

" The tide of emigration seems as usual to be flowing to the west. . . . Counties which three or four years ago were but a trackless wilderness, contain now five, six, and seven hundred voters. "
INDIANAPOLIS JOURNAL, *1829*

" In 1840 I was called from my farm to undertake the administration of public affairs and I foresaw that I was called to a bed of thorns. I now leave that bed which has afforded me little rest . . . "
U.S. PRESIDENT JOHN TYLER,
on why he won't run for reelection in 1844

SPORTS

Baseball for Beginners

Want to take up the new game of baseball? Keep your eye on the ball—because the rules keep changing!

REGULATION. LEAGUE BALL

1845
• bases are set 90 feet (27 m) apart in a diamond shape
• only nine men play on each side
• pitches are thrown underhand
• a ball caught on the first bounce is an "out"
1846
• at first base, a fielder can tag the bag before the runner reaches it and so make an out
1847
• players may no longer throw the ball at a runner to put him out

---

Fast Facts

John James Audubon The National Audubon Society is an organization whose mission is to conserve and restore natural ecosystems, focusing on birds, other wildlife, and their habitats. The organization has a national network of nature centers and advocates sustaining important bird populations.

Although John James Audubon had no role in the creation of the organization, he is the organization's namesake and inspiration. Audubon was a businessman who created drawings of birds as a hobby. When Audubon experienced financial difficulties, he set off on a quest to capture the images of America's birds. He sailed along the Mississippi River with a gun, drawing materials, and an assistant. His collection of drawings was a huge success and featured life-sized portraits of birds and a description of wilderness life.

Even today, Audubon's drawings have set the standard against which other ornithological drawings are judged. The name "Audubon" remains synonymous with bird conservation.

NORTH WIND PICTURE ARCHIVES / ALAMY

Going for the Gold?

You probably know the 1849 rush of gold seekers to California has given us new phrases like pay dirt, pan out, *and* strike it rich. *But are you aware that the demands of all those people have reduced supplies and sent prices skyrocketing? See if you can match the item below with the price you'd pay for it in California—thanks to the Gold Rush.*

1.	Barrel of flour	a.	$36
2.	Dozen eggs	b.	$800
3.	A shovel	c.	$100
4.	Barrel of sugar	d.	$400

Pretty steep when you remember that most workers are only making about $2 a day!

Answers: 1. b; 2. a; 3. c; 4. d

NUMBERS

UNITED STATES AT THE TIME

0 Amount of national debt in 1835 and 1836. During the Jackson administration, the United States entirely paid off its national debt

30 Number of minutes a person has to sit to have a photo taken to get the correct exposure in 1839

D. HURST / ALAMY

300 Number of families who traveled with Stephen Austin as the first American colonists to the Mexican state of Texas in 1821 and 1822

3,000 Number of pioneers who took the Overland trails west in 1845; many people headed for the Willamette Valley in Oregon, while others followed the newly improved California Trail over the Sierra Nevada to California **S**

MILESTONES

EVENTS AND PEOPLE OF THE TIME

INVENTED. The first sewing machine in the United States by Walter Hunt in 1834. Too bad Hunt didn't bother to patent his invention—Elias Howe patented his own sewing machine a few years later and grew extremely rich. Hunt *did* patent the first fountain pen and the first repeating rifle. He also invented the safety pin after four hours of twisting wire. It's a billion-dollar idea—so why did he sell the patent rights for only $100?

MARCHED. 17,000 Cherokee forced by federal troops from their Georgia homeland to reservations in the West from 1838 to 1839. About 4,000 Native Americans died on the 116-day-long march, now known as the "Trail of Tears." **W**

EMIGRATED. In 1845, to England, Frederick Douglass, former slave, author, and abolitionist leader, to escape danger in reaction to his autobiography, *Narrative of the Life of Frederick Douglass.*

BETTMANN / CORBIS

ELIAS HOWE'S SEWING MACHINE

CRITICAL THINKING

Theorizing Why do you think pioneers sang or played tunes around campfires? Are those reasons similar to why people play or sing music today? Explain your answer.

Hypothesizing Why do you think prices of everyday items skyrocketed during the Gold Rush?

423

W **Writing Support**

Descriptive Writing Ask students to research the events surrounding the Native American march known as the "Trail of Tears." Have them write a one-page essay that describes the march. **AL**

S **Skill Practice**

Using Geography Skills Have students use maps to locate the Willamette Valley in Oregon and the Sierra Nevada in California. Ask students to use the map scale to estimate the distances between their hometown and these locations. **BL**

Assess/Close

Discuss with the class how American pioneers moved west between 1820 and 1850 to settle new lands. **Ask:** What type of person might have wanted to head west to settle these new territories? What was life like for the pioneers? What types of problems did they encounter? What do you think the settlers were ultimately looking for? **OL**

Answers

Theorizing Students' answers should reflect that singing tunes around campfires gave pioneers the opportunity to talk about their experiences and to pass the time; it also was a form of entertainment. Today, people play or sing music for entertainment as well, and some people use music as a way to express their emotions.

Hypothesizing Students' answers should include knowledge of supply and demand. Because the amount of goods was too low to accommodate all of the people who wanted them, prices increased.

Focus

Bellringer
Daily Test Practice Transparency 14–2

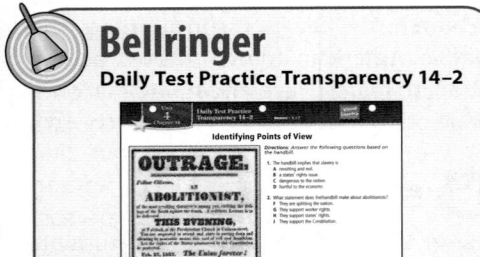

Reading Guide
Answers to Graphic:

William Lloyd Garrison: editor of *The Liberator,* started two antislavery societies; **Sarah and Angelina Grimké:** lectured and wrote against slavery, freed enslaved persons held by their family; **David Walker:** published an argument against slavery; **Frederick Douglass:** influential speaker, editor of *North Star*; **Sojourner Truth:** traveled throughout the North speaking of her experiences in slavery; **Harriet Tubman:** conductor on Underground Railroad; **Elijah Lovejoy:** editor of anti-slavery newspaper

Section Spotlight Video

Watch the Section Spotlight Video "The Abolitionists" to learn more about Frederick Douglass.

Resource Manager

Essential Question ◄
How did abolitionists influence the antislavery movement?

Reading Guide

Content Vocabulary
abolitionist (p. 425)
Underground Railroad (p. 430)

Academic Vocabulary
route (p. 430)   medical (p. 431)

Key People and Events
American Colonization Society (p. 425)
William Lloyd Garrison (p. 426)
Sarah Grimké (p. 427)
Angelina Grimké (p. 427)
David Walker (p. 428)
Frederick Douglass (p. 428)
Sojourner Truth (p. 429)
Elijah Lovejoy (p. 431)

Reading Strategy
Taking Notes As you read, use a diagram like the one below to identify five abolitionists. Below each name, write a brief description of his or her role in the movement.

ILLINOIS STANDARDS
The American Journey

18.B.3a Analyze how individuals and groups interact with and within institutions (e.g., educational, military).
18.C.3a Describe ways in which a diverse U.S. population has developed and maintained common beliefs (e.g., life, liberty and the pursuit of happiness; the Constitution and the Bill of Rights).
18.C.3b Explain how diverse groups have contributed to U.S. social systems over time.

The Abolitionists

American Diary

Sojourner Truth was an enslaved woman who gained her freedom in 1827. Although she lacked a formal education, her eloquent and deeply religious antislavery speeches attracted huge crowds. Truth believed that just as African Americans deserved equal rights, so too did women. Sojourner Truth's most famous speech, "Ain't I a Woman?", was given in Akron, Ohio, in 1851. Truth asked, "I have plowed and reaped and husked and chopped and mowed, and can any man do more than that?"

—quoted in Sojourner Truth As Orator

Enslaved children work outside their living quarters in Savannah, Georgia.

R **Reading Strategies**	C **Critical Thinking**	D **Differentiated Instruction**	W **Writing Support**	S **Skill Practice**
Teacher Edition	**Teacher Edition**	**Teacher Edition**	**Teacher Edition**	**Teacher Edition**
• Using Parts of Words, p. 425	• Evaluating, p. 426	• Auditory/Musical, p. 427	• Expository Writing, p. 426	• Using Analytical Skills, p. 429
• Identifying, p. 427	• Analyz. Information, p. 429	• Verbal/Linguistic, p. 428	• Persuasive Writing, p. 428	• Using Questioning Skills, p. 431
• Reading Primary Sources, p. 428	• Making Inferences, p. 429	• Visual/Spatial, p. 430		
• Organizing, p. 430				**Additional Resources**
	Additional Resources	**Additional Resources**		• Daily Test Pract. Transp. 14-2
Additional Resources	• Quizzes and Tests, p. 132	• School-to-Home, URB p. 119		• Lesson Transp. 14C
• Guid. Read., URB p. 124	• Enrichment Act., URB p. 11	• Reteaching Act., URB p. 121		
• Content Vocab., URB p. 101				

Early Efforts to End Slavery

Main Idea During the early 1800s, some Americans began to call for an end to slavery.

History and You What issues divide our nation today? Read to learn how the issue of slavery continued to divide the nation in the early 1800s.

. . . .

The spirit of reform that swept the United States in the early 1800s was not limited to improving education and expanding the arts. It also included the efforts of **abolitionists** like Sojourner Truth. Abolitionists were among the growing band of reformers who worked to abolish, or end, slavery.

Even before the American Revolution, some Americans had tried to limit or end slavery. At the Constitutional Convention in 1787, the delegates did not agree on this difficult issue. Instead, they reached a compromise by agreeing to let each state decide whether to allow slavery. By the early 1800s, slavery had ended in the Northern states. It continued, however, to be a part of the economy in Southern states.

The reform movement of the early and mid-1800s gave new life to the antislavery movement. Many Americans came to believe that slavery was wrong. Yet not all Northerners shared this view. The conflict over slavery continued to build.

Many who led the antislavery movement came from the Quaker faith. One Quaker, Benjamin Lundy, founded a newspaper in 1821 to spread the abolitionist message. He wrote:

PRIMARY SOURCE

"I heard the wail of the captive, I felt his pang of distress, and the iron entered my soul."

—quoted in "The Underground Railroad in Ohio"

American Colonization Society

The first large-scale antislavery effort was not aimed at abolishing slavery. Its aim was to resettle African Americans in Africa or the Caribbean. The **American Colonization Society,** formed in 1816 by a group of white Virginians, freed enslaved workers by buying them from slaveholders and sending them abroad to start new lives.

Teach

. . . .

R Reading Strategy

Using Parts of Words Have students give synonyms for the verb "abolish." *(to end, stop, eliminate, prohibit)* Point out that "abolition" is the noun form. Adding "ist" makes the word refer to a person. **Ask:** What is an "abolitionist"? *(a person who wants to end something—in this case, slavery)* **ELL**

Time Line

Critical Thinking Answer
Students might note that slavery was a deeply ingrained part of the economy. Major change takes much adjustment and often comes with the upheaval of long-standing customs.

Skills Practice
Ask: How did the compromise reached at the Constitutional Convention of 1787 affect slavery and the abolition movement? *(The compromise allowed each state to decide whether to allow slavery. Therefore, the Southern states retained the practice.)* **OL**

Time Line / The Abolition Movement

Early Opposition Early antislavery societies called for a gradual end to slavery. In the 1830s, however, more groups were inspired by the American reform movement and argued that enslaved people should be freed immediately.

★ **1787** States given authority to decide whether to allow slavery

★ **1831** William Lloyd Garrison begins publishing *The Liberator*

★ **1833** American Anti-Slavery Society founded

★ **1816** American Colonization Society founded

★ **1832** New England Anti-Slavery Society founded

★ **1840s** Sojourner Truth's speeches draw huge crowds

Critical Thinking
Making Inferences Why do you think some people supported a gradual end to slavery?

Differentiated Instruction

Leveled Activities

BL Reteaching Activity, URB p. 121

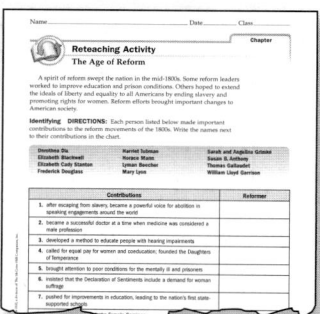

OL School-to-Home Connection Activity, URB p. 119

ELL Content Vocabulary Activity, URB p. 101

W Writing Support

Expository Writing Have students do research to learn about Liberia today. Ask them to write a summary of challenges facing Liberia and signs of progress. **AL**

C Critical Thinking

Evaluating Ask: For an enslaved person, what were some advantages and disadvantages of going to Liberia? (**Advantages:** *freedom, chance for self-rule;* **Disadvantages:** *unknown land*) **OL**

Primary Source

Critical Thinking Answer
Students might suggest that many whites in the United States likely disapproved of the resettlement activities.

Reading Check **Answer:** The Society bought enslaved workers, freed them, and sent them abroad to begin new lives.

Differentiated Instruction

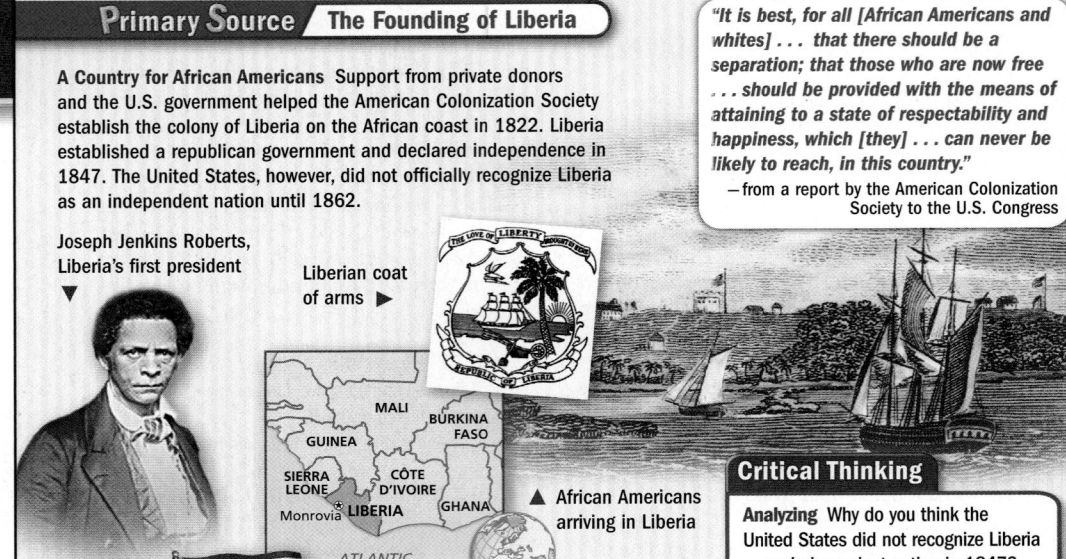

Primary Source / **The Founding of Liberia**

A Country for African Americans Support from private donors and the U.S. government helped the American Colonization Society establish the colony of Liberia on the African coast in 1822. Liberia established a republican government and declared independence in 1847. The United States, however, did not officially recognize Liberia as an independent nation until 1862.

Joseph Jenkins Roberts, Liberia's first president ▼

Liberian coat of arms ▶

▲ African Americans arriving in Liberia

Liberian flag ▶

"It is best, for all [African Americans and whites] . . . that there should be a separation; that those who are now free . . . should be provided with the means of attaining to a state of respectability and happiness, which [they] . . . can never be likely to reach, in this country."
—from a report by the American Colonization Society to the U.S. Congress

Critical Thinking

Analyzing Why do you think the United States did not recognize Liberia as an independent nation in 1847?

The society raised money from private donors, Congress, and a few state legislatures to send several groups of African Americans out of the country. Some traveled to the west coast of Africa, where the society acquired land for a colony. The first African American settlers arrived in this colony, called Liberia—Latin for "place of freedom"—in 1822. Some 12,000 to 20,000 African Americans settled in the new country between 1822 and 1865.

The American Colonization Society did not stop the growth of slavery. The number of enslaved people continued to increase. The society could resettle only a small number of African Americans. Furthermore, most African Americans did not want to go to Africa. Many were from families that had lived in America for generations. They simply wanted to be free in American society. Some African Americans feared that the society might actually strengthen slavery.

Reading Check **Explaining** How did the American Colonization Society fight slavery?

The Movement Changes

Main Idea Beginning in the 1830s, slavery became the most pressing issue for reformers.

History and You Is there a leader or a person whom you admire? Does he or she stand up for others? Read to learn how abolitionists worked to end slavery.

Reformers realized that the gradual approach to ending slavery had failed. Moreover, the numbers of enslaved persons had sharply increased because the cotton boom in the Deep South made planters increasingly dependent on slave labor. Beginning in about 1830, the American antislavery movement took on new life. Slavery became the most pressing social issue for reformers.

William Lloyd Garrison

Massachusetts abolitionist **William Lloyd Garrison** had a great influence on the antislavery movement. In 1831, he started the antislavery newspaper, *The Liberator*.

Disputes Over Slavery

Objective: To interpret a political cartoon about the issue of slavery and abolitionism

Focus: Review with students how visual cues in a political cartoon can help them interpret its meaning.

Teach: Have students study the cartoon and answer the questions.

Assess: Review students' answers to the questions.

Close: Discuss why the cartoon is more sympathetic to the abolitionists than to the South.

Differentiated Instruction Strategies

BL Discuss with students how this cartoon uses irony to express its viewpoint.

AL Have students draw a cartoon on "Northern Ideas of Liberty" from the Southern point of view.

ELL Students may need extra discussion and explanation in order to understand the cartoon's caption.

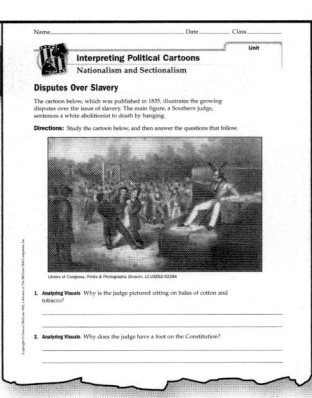

Interpreting Political Cartoons, URB p. 13

Garrison was one of the first white abolitionists to call for the immediate freeing of enslaved people. He denounced the slow, gradual approach of other reformers. In the first issue of his paper, he wrote, "I *will be* as harsh as truth, and as uncompromising as justice. . . . I will not retreat a single inch—AND I WILL BE HEARD."

Garrison *was* heard. He attracted enough followers to start the New England Anti-Slavery Society in 1832 and the American Anti-Slavery Society the next year. The abolitionist movement grew rapidly. By 1838, the antislavery societies Garrison started had more than 1,000 chapters, or local branches.

The Grimké Sisters

Among the first women who spoke out publicly against slavery were **Sarah** and **Angelina Grimké.** The sisters were born in South Carolina to a wealthy slaveholding family. The women moved to Philadelphia in 1832. While living in the North, the Grimké sisters lectured and wrote against slavery. At one antislavery meeting, Angelina Grimké exclaimed:

PRIMARY SOURCE

"As a Southerner I feel that it is my duty to stand up . . . against slavery. I have seen it—I have seen it."
—from a speech at Pennsylvania Hall

The Grimkés persuaded their mother to give them their share of the family inheritance. Instead of money or land, the sisters asked for several of the enslaved workers, whom they immediately freed.

The Grimkés and Angelina's husband, abolitionist Theodore Weld, wrote *American Slavery As It Is* in 1839. This book collected firsthand accounts of life under slavery. It was one of the most powerful abolitionist publications of its time.

History ONLINE
Student Web Activity Visit glencoe.com and complete the Chapter 14 Web Activity about African American abolitionists.

People IN HISTORY

Harriet Beecher Stowe
Author of Uncle Tom's Cabin

Stowe wrote many books and stories about social reform. *Uncle Tom's Cabin,* published in 1852, was her most famous work. The novel shows slavery as a cruel and brutal system. Stowe later said that while she was writing it, "My heart was bursting with the anguish excited by the cruelty and injustice our nation was showing to the slave." *Uncle Tom's Cabin* had a major impact on public feelings about slavery. Even President Abraham Lincoln is claimed to have said that Harriet Beecher Stowe wrote the book that started the American Civil War.

CRITICAL Thinking

1. **Analyzing** Why did Stowe write *Uncle Tom's Cabin?*
2. **Evaluating** Why do you think Stowe might be accused of starting a civil war?

The Age of Reform **Chapter 14** 427

R **Reading Strategy**

Identifying Ask: What evidence suggests that the abolitionist movement grew between 1832 and 1838? *(The antislavery societies founded in 1832 had more than 1,000 chapters by 1838.)* BL

D **Differentiated Instruction**

Auditory/Musical Have students work in small groups to write an abolitionist song. They should use a tune they already know and adapt the lyrics to fit the message. Have students perform their songs. BL

People IN HISTORY

Critical Thinking Answers

1. Stowe wanted to expose the cruelty and injustice of slavery.
2. The book was popular. It made Northerners realize how unjust slavery was and encouraged them to fight it.

History ONLINE
Objectives and answers to the Student Web Activity can be found at glencoe.com under the Web Activity Lesson Plan for this chapter.

Additional Support

Interdisciplinary Connection

Literature During the Depression, the federal government sent unemployed writers to interview people and write their life stories as part of the Federal Writer's Project of the Works Progress Administration. The collection includes more than 2,300 first-person accounts from African Americans who experienced slavery. The Slave Narrative Collection is available at the Library of Congress site, http://memory.loc.gov/ammem/snhtml. Print segments of several narratives and distribute one segment to each student. Have students read the narrative and write a summary of what they learned about life under slavery. Have some students read their narratives aloud for class discussion. OL

W Writing Support

Persuasive Writing Have students take the role of Samuel Cornish and write an antislavery editorial for *Freedom's Journal*. **OL**

R Reading Strategy

Reading Primary Sources Ask: What reason did Walker give to support his belief that America rightly belonged to African Americans? *(The nation was built on African American labor.)* **OL**

D Differentiated Instruction

Verbal/Linguistic Have students write and act out a short play in which Frederick Douglass explains why he escaped from slavery and worked with abolitionists to fight slavery. **OL**

Hands-On Chapter Project
Step 2

Teacher Tip

Abridging Advise students in the use of ellipses to shorten a quote. Explain that they can omit words that are not necessary for understanding, but they must not change the meaning.

Primary Source **Views About Slavery**

Different Views In the 1820s, antislavery sentiment strengthened in the North. Abolitionists formed the American Anti-Slavery Society in 1833. The Society attacked slavery in its literature and speeches. In response, Southerners developed a theory to defend slavery.

"As slaveholders and their apologists are . . . flooding the world with testimony that their slaves are kindly treated; that they are well fed, well clothed, well housed, well lodged, moderately worked, and bountifully provided with all things needful for their comfort. . . . We will prove that the slaves in the United States are treated with barbarous inhumanity."

▲ **Theodore Weld**   —from *American Slavery As It Is*

▲ In an announcement for a meeting of the Massachusetts Anti-Slavery Society, a poem by John Greenleaf Whittier was included:
"On, woman! from thy happy hearth
Extend thy gentle hand to save
The poor and perishing of earth—
The chained and stricken slave!
Oh, plead for all the suffering of thy kind—
For the crushed body and the darkened mind."

African American Abolitionists

African Americans also played a major role in the abolitionist movement. The abolition of slavery was an especially important goal to the free African Americans of the North.

Most African Americans in the North lived in poverty in cities. They were excluded from most jobs. White mobs often attacked them. These African Americans, however, were proud of their freedom, and many wanted to help those who were still enslaved.

African Americans helped organize and direct the American Anti-Slavery Society. They subscribed in large numbers to *The Liberator*. In 1827 Samuel Cornish and John Russwurm started the country's first African American newspaper, *Freedom's Journal*.

Born a free man in North Carolina, writer **David Walker** of Boston published his argument against slavery. He challenged African Americans to rebel and overthrow slavery. He wrote, "America is more our country than it is the whites'—we have enriched it with our blood and tears."

In 1830 free African American leaders held their first convention in Philadelphia. Delegates met "to devise ways and means for the bettering of our condition." They discussed starting an African American college and encouraging free African Americans to emigrate to Canada.

Frederick Douglass

Frederick Douglass, the most widely known African American abolitionist, was born enslaved in Maryland. After teaching himself to read and write, he escaped from slavery in Maryland in 1838. He settled first in Massachusetts and then moved to New York.

As a runaway, Douglass could have been captured and returned to slavery. Still, he joined the Massachusetts Anti-Slavery Society. He traveled widely to address abolitionist meetings. Douglass was a powerful speaker who often moved listeners to tears with his message. At an Independence Day gathering, he told the audience:

428   Chapter 14 *The Age of Reform*

Influencing Public Policy

Step 2: Planning the Pamphlet Students will plan the content and layout of their pamphlets.

Essential Question: How did abolitionists influence the antislavery movement?

Directions Have the groups decide what to include in the pamphlet. Remind them that their goal is to influence lawmakers to pass a reform law. The content of their pamphlets should focus on getting this law passed. They should select a quote that supports their argument and abridge it to keep it short. Have them sketch the pamphlet's layout on a separate piece of paper. Provide promotional pamphlets as examples.

Analyzing Read aloud the quote in the feature on this page. Discuss the role of abolitionists in educating the public about the true nature of slavery. **OL**

(Chapter Project continued in Section 3)

◄ Selling enslaved people at auction

▲ Defenders of slavery described plantations as ideal settings where enslaved persons were well treated.

▲ Poster announcing the raffle of a horse and an enslaved female

"In all social systems there must be a class to do the menial duties, to perform the drudgery of life. That is, a class requiring but a low order of intellect and but little skill. . . . Such a class you must have, or you would not have that other class which leads progress, civilization, and refinement. . . . Fortunately for the South, she found a race adapted to that purpose. "
—Senator James Henry Hammond in a speech to Congress, 1858

Critical Thinking

Analyzing Primary Sources What pro-slavery arguments are discussed in the quotations from Weld and Hammond?

S **Skill Practice**

Using Analytical Skills Ask: What did the Fourth of July mean to white Americans? *(freedom, independence)* How did African Americans feel about the Fourth of July celebration? Why? *(It was a sham, because whites were celebrating freedom while holding people in bondage.)* **OL**

C₁ **Critical Thinking**

Analyzing Information Ask: Why might many whites consider Douglass's message radical? *(He advocated full equality with whites.)* **OL**

C₂ **Critical Thinking**

Making Inferences Ask: What "truths" might Sojourner Truth express to her listeners? *(truths about slavery—that it was a barbaric institution)* **OL**

This **READING SKILL** (Making Inferences) was introduced in this unit.

Primary Source

Critical Thinking Answer
The pro-slavery arguments are that enslaved people were well treated and that African Americans were an inferior race suited only for life's menial tasks.

Additional Support

PRIMARY SOURCE

"What, to the American slave, is your 4th of July? I answer; a day that reveals to him, more than all other days in the year, the gross injustice and cruelty to which he is the constant victim. To him, your celebration is a sham . . . your national greatness, swelling vanity; your sounds of rejoicing are empty and heartless; . . . your shouts of liberty and equality, hollow mockery." **S**
—from *Frederick Douglass: Selected Speeches and Writings*

Douglass was editor of the antislavery newspaper *North Star* and won admiration as a powerful and influential speaker and writer. He even traveled abroad. Douglass spoke to huge antislavery audiences in London and the West Indies.

Douglass returned to the United States because he believed abolitionists must fight slavery at its source. He insisted that African Americans receive not just their freedom but full equality with whites as well. In 1847 friends helped Douglass buy his freedom from the slaveholder from whom he had fled in Maryland. **C₁**

Sojourner Truth

"I was born a slave in Ulster County, New York," Isabella Baumfree began when she told her story to audiences. Called "Belle," she lived in the cellar of a slaveholder's house. She escaped in 1826 and gained official freedom in 1827 when New York banned slavery. Quaker friends then helped her find her son who had been sold as a slave. She eventually settled in New York City with her two youngest children. In 1843 Belle chose a new name:

PRIMARY SOURCE

"The Lord [named] me Sojourner . . . Truth, because I was to declare the truth to the people."
—from *Sojourner Truth: Slave, Prophet, Legend*

Sojourner Truth worked with a number of other abolitionists, including William Lloyd Garrison and Frederick Douglass, to bring about the end of slavery. She traveled throughout the North and spoke about her experiences as an enslaved person. Sojourner Truth was also an active supporter of the women's rights movement. **C₂**

The Age of Reform **Chapter 14** **429**

Activity: Collaborative Learning

Understanding Perspective Organize students into small groups. Each group will represent one person who was involved in the Underground Railroad: the runaway enslaved person, the person hired to track down the runaway, and the Underground Railroad station conductor.

After conducting research at the library or on the Internet, have each group write a one-page diary entry from the perspective of their person. "Runaways" should address why they are running and their hopes and plans for the future. "Slave trackers" should include their reasons for hunting down the runaways. "Underground Railroad conductors" must explain why they are willing to risk their lives and livelihoods to help slaves get to freedom.

All groups should include information on how they felt, and what they saw, said, or did in their diary entries. One person from each group should read aloud their completed diary entry to the class. Together discuss each perspective. **AL**

D Differentiated Instruction

Visual/Spatial Show a film about Harriet Tubman or the Underground Railroad. Have students discuss their reactions to it and what they learned. **OL**

R Reading Strategy

Organizing Have students make a graphic organizer to summarize three main reasons for Northern opposition to abolition. *(threat to social order—African Americans would not blend in, might start a war, might take jobs belonging to whites)* **OL**

Primary Source

Critical Thinking Answer
The literature was destroyed to stop the spread of abolitionist ideas.

Reading Check **Answer:** places such as barns, basements, and attics where passengers stayed during the daytime

---

Additional Support

Primary Source / Reactions Against Abolitionism

Anti-Abolitionists Opposition to abolitionism was almost as strong in the North as it was in the South. Southerners viewed abolitionism as an attack on their way of life. Many Northerners feared the effect abolition might have upon them. In both areas, anti-abolitionists violently responded to literature that supported abolitionism.

In 1837 in Alton, Illinois, a mob killed abolitionist newspaper editor Elijah Lovejoy, destroyed his press (right), and burned his house (below).

▲ Southerners burn antislavery documents in Charleston, South Carolina, in 1830.

"And men, like the abolitionist . . . [who goes] about meddling with other Peoples' affairs . . . [should] pay attention to his own affairs, & let his neighbor alone. . . . If these matters are going to be [agitated it will] . . . lead to the separation of the Union."
—from a letter by E. W. Taylor (a New Yorker who moved to South Carolina)

Critical Thinking

Analyzing Why did anti-abolitionists destroy pro-abolition literature?

The Underground Railroad

Some abolitionists risked prison—even death—by helping African Americans escape from slavery. The network of escape **routes**—lines of travel—from the South to the North was called the **Underground Railroad.**

Passengers on this "railroad" traveled through the night, often on foot, and went north. The North Star was their guide. During the day passengers rested at "stations"—barns, basements, and attics—until the next night's journey. The railroad's "conductors" were whites and African Americans who helped guide the runaways to freedom in the Northern states or Canada. Harriet Tubman became the most famous conductor on the Underground Railroad.

The Underground Railroad helped only a tiny fraction of the enslaved population. Still, the Railroad gave hope to people who suffered in slavery. It also gave abolitionists a way to help some enslaved people.

Reading Check **Explaining** What were "stations" on the Underground Railroad?

Clashes Over Abolitionism

Main Idea Many Southerners and Northerners opposed abolition.

History and You Can you think of a time when you feared change, even if it was for the better? Read to learn why many people opposed abolition.

The antislavery movement triggered a strong reaction against abolitionism. Many Southerners opposed the idea of ending slavery. They held that abolitionism threatened the South's way of life, which depended on enslaved labor.

Not all Northerners were abolitionists. The abolitionists in the North made up only a small fraction of the population. Many Northerners saw the antislavery movement as a threat to the nation's social order. They believed that once freed, the African Americans could never blend into American society. Other Northerners feared that the abolitionists could begin a war between the North and South.

Fast Facts

Harriet Tubman Harriet Tubman carried a pistol when helping enslaved people escape. This was necessary not only to defend her group from pursuers but also to force tired or panicked runaways to move on. She knew that dead runaways could not inform on her. Using her experiences as a conductor on the Underground Railroad, Tubman became a valuable scout and spy for the Union Army during the Civil War. After the war, she lived in Auburn, New York, where she established a home for elderly African Americans.

Many Northerners also had economic fears. They did not want to lose their jobs to the emancipated workers who might travel to the North and work for cheaper wages.

Opposition to abolitionism sometimes erupted into violence against the abolitionists themselves. Philadelphia's antislavery headquarters was burned, which set off a bloody race riot. A Boston mob attacked and threatened to hang abolitionist William Lloyd Garrison. Authorities saved his life by putting him in jail.

Elijah Lovejoy in Illinois was not so lucky. Angry whites invaded his antislavery newspaper offices and wrecked his presses three times. Each time Lovejoy installed new presses and resumed publication. The fourth time the mob set fire to the building. When Lovejoy came out of the blazing building, he was shot and killed.

The South Reacts

Southerners fought abolitionism with arguments in defense of slavery. They claimed that slavery was essential to the Southern economy and had allowed Southern whites to reach a high level of culture.

Southerners also argued that they treated enslaved people well. They claimed that Northern workers were worse off than enslaved workers because they worked in factories for long hours at low wages. These jobs were repetitious and often dangerous. Also, Northern workers had to pay for their own goods and services from their small earnings, whereas the system of slavery provided food, clothing, and **medical** care to its workers.

Other defenses of slavery were based on racism. Many whites believed that African Americans were better off under white care than on their own.

The conflict between pro-slavery and antislavery groups continued to mount. At the same time, a new women's rights movement was growing.

✔ **Reading Check** **Explaining** How did many Southerners defend the instituion of slavery?

History ONLINE
Study Central™ To review this section, go to glencoe.com.

Section 2 Review

Vocabulary

1. Write complete sentences that define the following terms: abolitionist, route, Underground Railroad, medical.

Main Ideas

2. Specifying What effect did the American Colonization Society have on slavery? How did enslaved African Americans view that group and its efforts?

3. Discussing Discuss the role of African Americans in the abolitionist movement.

4. Comparing and Contrasting How did Northerners and Southerners view abolitionism differently?

Critical Thinking

5. Outlining Use a format like the one below to make an outline of this section. Write each main heading on a line with a Roman numeral, and then list important facts below it. The number of key facts may vary from this sample.

    I. First main heading
       A. Key fact #1
       B. Key fact #2
    II. Second main heading
       A. Key fact #1
       B. Key fact #2
    III. Third main heading
       A. Key fact #1
       B. Key fact #2

6. Creative Writing Write a conversation that might have taken place between a Southern plantation owner and a Massachusetts abolitionist about the abolition of slavery. Have each character explain his or her point of view.

Answer the
7. Essential Question
How did abolitionists influence the antislavery movement?

The Age of Reform **Chapter 14** **431**

S Skill Practice

Using Questioning Skills **Ask:** Why did white Northerners fear employers would hire African Americans instead of white workers? *(African Americans would likely work for lower wages.)* **BL**

✔ **Reading Check** **Answer:** Southerners claimed slavery was essential to the Southern economy. They argued that enslaved people were treated well and that African Americans would not survive as well on their own.

Assess

History ONLINE

Study Central™ provides summaries, interactive games, and online graphic organizers to help students review content.

Close

Summarizing Have students identify different methods that abolitionists used to try to end slavery. Note these methods on the board. **OL**

Section 2 Review

Answers

1. Students will write sentences that correctly define the vocabulary terms.

2. The society did not stop the growth of slavery; in fact, the number of enslaved people increased. Resettlement in Africa was not embraced by most African Americans, whose families had lived in America for generations. Some also feared the society might strengthen slavery.

3. The role of African Americans included: organizing and directing the American Anti-Slavery Society, running antislavery newspapers, writing and speaking against slavery, and serving as conductors on the Underground Railroad.

4. Many Southerners believed that abolition threatened their way of life, which depended on enslaved labor. Many Northerners opposed abolition as well, fearing that ending slavery would upset the social order, tear the nation apart, and take jobs away from whites.

5. Students will outline Section 2.

6. Conversations should reflect opposing points of view and may include some of the following points: for abolition—it is morally wrong to enslave people; against abolition—slavery is vital to the economy.

7. Abolitionists published antislavery newspapers, organized antislavery societies, bought enslaved workers to free them and send them abroad, lectured and wrote books to promote their views, and helped enslaved African Americans escape to the North via the Underground Railroad.

GEOGRAPHY & HISTORY

Focus

R Reading Strategy

Summarizing Make sure students understand that the Underground Railroad was not a true railway. **Ask:** What was the Underground Railroad? *(a system of secret routes for helping slaves escape to free states or Canada)* **ELL**

Members of the Underground Railroad used railroad terminology as code names for people and places. To check understanding, ask students to complete a graphic organizer that gives the literal meanings of the four terms used below. **BL**

Term	Meaning
Underground Railroad	system of secret routes to help slaves escape to free states
conductor	person who guided the slaves
passenger	escaped slave
station	safe house

Additional Support and Answers

GEOGRAPHY & HISTORY

NATIONAL GEOGRAPHIC

R The Underground Railroad

The Underground Railroad was a loosely organized system of secret routes for helping enslaved people escape to Canada or to areas of safety in free states. However, the popular notion of lantern-wielding "conductors" guiding families of enslaved people through forests in the South is largely inaccurate. In fact, few Southerners were willing to assist an enslaved person escape. For the most part, fugitives were on their own until they reached border states. There they could find assistance from loosely-connected groups of abolitionists. This network was the true Underground Railroad.

How Did Geography Affect the Underground Railroad?

Few abolitionists escorted runaways from the Deep South into free territory. Most runaways—typically single young men—probably lived in the upper South, close to free territories. Antislavery Northerners—mostly free African Americans—in border towns such as Ripley, Ohio, and Wilmington, Delaware, hid escapees from police and professional slave catchers and helped them move farther north.

▲ *The Underground Railroad*, Charles T. Webber, 1893
The painting portrays a group of enslaved African Americans arriving at a safe house "station" on the Underground Railroad. Three abolitionists, Levi Coffin and his wife, Catharine, as well as Hannah Haddock, are also pictured. The scene most likely takes place at the Coffin farm in Cincinnati, Ohio.

This "hidey hole" built in a safe house in Fountain City, Indiana, was used to conceal fugitives from the police and professional slave catchers. The beds could be moved in front of the hole to conceal it. ▼

◄ This poster refers to Anthony Burns, a runaway enslaved man. Burns's arrest and trial under the Fugitive Slave Act of 1850 sparked protests by abolitionists in Boston and other Northern cities.

A MAN KIDNAPPED!
A PUBLIC MEETING AT
FANEUIL HALL!
WILL BE HELD
THIS FRIDAY EVEN'G,
May 26th, at 7 o'clock,
To secure justice for A MAN CLAIMED AS A SLAVE by a
VIRGINIA KIDNAPPER!

432 Unit 4 *Nationalism and Sectionalism*

Activity: Interdisciplinary Connection

Art Some historians believe that the patterns sewn into quilts may have served as a code to aid escaping enslaved persons. Sympathizers on the Underground Railroad would sew coded messages into the quilts, then hang the pieces outside—as if they were hanging laundry—to help guide the escapees. Some of the patterns used were a wrench, a wagon wheel, tumbling blocks, a bear's paw, a star, and a cabin. Have students research to find the meaning of these pictures and ask them to try to find more pictures and meanings. *(wrench: prepare tools needed for escape; wagon wheel: prepare for long journey; tumbling blocks: safe to travel; bear's paw: go through mountains; star: follow the North Star; a cabin: a safe house)* After students have completed their research, have them use squares of construction paper to create their own miniature coded quilt. **OL**

Escape Routes Escapees used two main corridors to flee into the North. Enslaved people from inland Southern states generally made their way toward Ohio, Illinois, Indiana, and Michigan. Runaways from Southern states along the Atlantic coast tended to follow the coastline into Pennsylvania, New Jersey, and New York. Many of these runaways eventually headed into Canada. ▼ **S**

Routes to Freedom

CANADA

Great Lakes

Unorganized Terr.

Nebraska Territory

Minn.

Wis.

Mich.

Iowa
Des Moines

Percival

Kansas Territory

Mo.
Chester
Cairo

N. Mex. Terr.

Indian Territory

Ark.
Little Rock

Miss.
Jackson

Texas

La.

New Orleans

MEXICO

Gulf of Mexico

Milwaukee

Chicago

Ind.

Quincy
Springfield
Ill.

Toledo

Ohio

Indianapolis

Cincinnati

Evansville

Jeffersonville

Nashville

Tenn.

Atlanta

Montgomery

Ala.

London
Windsor

Cleveland

Columbus

Ironton

Ohio R.

Ky.

S.C.

Ga.

Savannah

Tallahassee

Fla.

Oswego
Rochester
Buffalo

Albany

Pa.

Cumberland
Marietta
Richmond
Va.
Norfolk

New Bern

Charleston

Mississippi R.

Missouri R.

Arkansas R.

N.H.
Vt.
Maine

N.Y.

Portland
Boston
Mass.
Providence
R.I.
Conn.
New York City
N.J.
Philadelphia
Del.
Md.

ATLANTIC OCEAN

N.C.

40°N

80°W
90°W
70°W
30°N

Slaveholding regions
Non-slaveholding regions
→ **Underground Railroad route**
— **1860 boundary**

0   400 kilometers
0   400 miles
Albers Equal-Area projection

Ellen Craft (1826–1891) was the daughter of an African American enslaved woman and her slaveholder. Passing as white, Ellen escaped from slavery in Georgia in 1848 by dressing as a Southern male slaveholder (pictured below left). Her darker-skinned husband, **William Craft** (pictured right), accompanied her by pretending to be her valet. **W**

Analyzing Geography

1. **Place** From which state do you think more African Americans successfully escaped slavery to freedom: Kentucky or Alabama? Explain your answer.

2. **Regions** On the map, locate the cities of Toledo, Cleveland, and Buffalo. Why do you think these cities became important points along the Underground Railroad?

Nationalism and Sectionalism **Unit 4** 433

GEOGRAPHY & HISTORY

Teach

S Skill Practice

Using Map Skills Remind students that there were various Underground Railroad routes that many slaves used. **Ask:** What route might an escaped slave take to get from Charleston, South Carolina, to Canada? *(travel from Charleston to Philadelphia by sea; then travel to Buffalo through Rochester; then cross the border to Canada)* Why did some slaves travel to Canada instead of stopping when they reached a free Northern state? *(They would have less chance of being captured if they went all the way to Canada.)* **OL**

Assess/Close

W Writing Support

Creative Writing Have students write a short, fictional account of the escape of Ellen and William Craft. They may wish to do outside research to include realistic details about their journey. **OL**

Answers

1. Since Kentucky bordered free states to the North, more slaves probably escaped from here. To escape from Alabama would have been more difficult because slaves would have a longer journey through other Southern states.

2. These cities are close to Canada, and Canada was a final destination for many slaves.

Focus

Section 3

The Women's Movement

Bellringer
Daily Test Practice Transparency 14-3

Reading Guide
Answers to Graphic:
Mott: organized Philadelphia Female Anti-Slavery Society; helped organize first women's rights convention. **Stanton:** helped organize first women's rights convention; insisted that woman suffrage be included in the Declaration of Sentiments and Resolutions issued by the convention; co-led the women's movement with Anthony. **Anthony:** called for equal pay, college training for girls, coeducation, and suffrage; co-led the women's movement with Stanton.

Section Spotlight Video

To learn more about the Seneca Falls convention, watch the Section Spotlight Video "The Women's Movement."

Resource Manager

Essential Question
What were the effects of the women's rights movement of the middle to late 1800s?

Reading Guide

Content Vocabulary
suffrage (p. 435)   coeducation (p. 437)

Academic Vocabulary
capable (p. 437)   ministry (p. 438)

Key People and Events
Lucretia Mott (p. 435)
Elizabeth Cady Stanton (p. 435)
Susan B. Anthony (p. 437)
Catherine Beecher (p. 437)
Emma Hart Willard (p. 437)
Mary Lyon (p. 438)
Elizabeth Blackwell (p. 438)

Reading Strategy
Taking Notes As you read, use a diagram like the one below to identify the contributions these individuals made to women's rights.

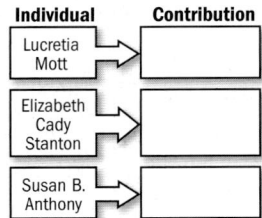

Individual	Contribution
Lucretia Mott	
Elizabeth Cady Stanton	
Susan B. Anthony	

ILLINOIS STANDARDS
The American Journey

18.B.3a Analyze how individuals and groups interact with and within institutions (e.g., educational, military).

18.C.3a Describe ways in which a diverse U.S. population has developed and maintained common beliefs (e.g., life, liberty and the pursuit of happiness; the Constitution and the Bill of Rights).

18.C.3b Explain how diverse groups have contributed to U.S. social systems over time.

American Diary

When Lucy Stone attended college, she faced many challenges. Her daughter, Alice Stone Blackwell, recalled, "At the low wages then paid to women, it took Lucy nine years to save up money enough to enter college." Stone attended Oberlin College in Ohio, which was the first college in the United States to admit women. Stone graduated from Oberlin in 1847 and became a strong supporter of women's rights.

—*from* Lucy Stone: Pioneer of Woman's Rights

Mount Holyoke Female Seminary in South Hadley, Massachusetts, was the first women's college in the United States.

R Reading Strategies	**C** Critical Thinking	**D** Differentiated Instruction	**W** Writing Support	**S** Skill Practice
Teacher Edition • Outlining, p. 436 • Inferring, p. 438 **Additional Resources** • Guid. Read., URB p. 125 • Content Vocab., URB p. 101 • Academic Vocab., URB p. 103 • Read. Ess., p. 148 • Pri. Source Read., URB p. 105	**Teacher Edition** • Making Generalizations, p. 435 • Making Inferences, p. 437 **Additional Resources** • Quizzes and Tests, p. 133 • Crit. Think. Skills, URB p. 113	**Teacher Edition** • Visual/Spatial, p. 435 **Additional Resources** • School-to-Home, URB p. 119 • Reteaching Act., URB p. 121 • Differ. Inst., URB p. 111	**Teacher Edition** • Narrative Writing, p. 435 • Persuasive Writing, p. 436 **Additional Resources** • Writ. Skills, URB p. 107	**Teacher Edition** • Creating a Time Line, p. 437 • Using Contrasting Skills, p. 438 **Additional Resources** • Daily Test Pract. Transp. 14-3 • Lesson Transp. 14B • Time Line Skills, URB p. 118

Women and Reform

Main Idea Women organized to win equal rights.

History and You Can you imagine a time when women were not allowed to vote and had limited access to education and jobs? Read to learn how women worked to change their status in America.

Many women abolitionists also worked for women's rights. Like many of the women reformers, **Lucretia Mott** was a Quaker. Quaker women enjoyed a certain amount of equality in their own communities. Mott helped fugitive enslaved workers and organized the Philadelphia Female Anti-Slavery Society. At the world antislavery convention in London, she met **Elizabeth Cady Stanton.** There, they joined forces to work for women's rights.

The Seneca Falls Convention

In July 1848, Stanton, Mott, and other women organized the first women's rights convention in Seneca Falls, New York. About 200 women and 40 men attended.

The convention issued a Declaration of Sentiments and Resolutions. The declaration called for an end to laws that discriminated against women. It also demanded that women be allowed to enter the all-male world of trades, professions, and businesses. The most controversial issue at the Seneca Falls Convention, however, was about **suffrage,** or the right to vote.

Elizabeth Stanton insisted that the declaration include a demand for woman suffrage. The delegates, however, thought the idea of women voting was too radical. Lucretia Mott told her friend, "Lizzie, thee will make us ridiculous." Standing with Stanton, the abolitionist Frederick Douglass argued powerfully for women's right to vote. After a heated debate, the convention voted to include the demand for woman suffrage in the United States.

Growth of the Women's Movement

The Seneca Falls Convention paved the way for the growth of the women's rights movement. During the 1800s women held several national conventions, including the first national women's rights convention, in Worcester, Massachusetts. A number of reformers, both male and female, joined the growing movement.

Time Line / Women's Rights

Struggling for Equality Women who fought to end slavery also began to argue for their own rights and an equal place in society.

★ **1833** Oberlin College admits women and African Americans

★ **1844** Female textile workers in Massachusetts form labor association

★ **1837** Mary Lyon establishes Mount Holyoke Female Seminary

★ **1848** First women's rights convention held in Seneca Falls, New York

◄ Mary Lyon

Critical Thinking
Speculating Why do you think the Declaration of Independence is often referred to by people struggling to gain rights?

CHAPTER 14
Section 3

Teach

W Writing Support

Narrative Writing Working in pairs, students should write a dialogue between Elizabeth Cady Stanton and Lucretia Mott, debating whether to include suffrage in the declaration. **OL**

D Differentiated Instruction

Visual/Spatial Have students sketch a political cartoon about woman suffrage from the viewpoint of an opponent. **ELL**

C Critical Thinking

Making Generalizations Ask: How could a convention help a movement get started? *(Possible response: A convention brings together people with common goals so they can share ideas on how to achieve them and brings public attention to the issues.)* **OL**

Time Line

Critical Thinking Answer
Rights were the focus of the Declaration of Independence, and Americans had to fight to get those rights.

Hands-On Chapter Project
Step 3

Influencing Public Policy

Step 3: Preparing the Pamphlet Students will complete their pamphlets and plan their presentations for the hearing.

Essential Question: What were the effects of the women's rights movement of the middle to late 1800s?

Directions Have students complete their pamphlets using illustration software or on heavy paper. They should include key points with supporting details, images, and a quote. They should add headings and captions. Their pamphlets should include a description of the reform bill and a call for legislators to pass it into law. Have the groups plan their presentations.

Making Inferences Ask: How did society view women before the women's movement? *(Possible answer: as weak, not sufficiently well informed to vote intelligently, incapable of handling the same responsibilities as men)* **OL**

(Chapter Project continued on the Visual Summary page)

Answers

W Writing Support

Persuasive Writing Ask students to write a letter to the editor of a newspaper in July 1848. The letter should argue in support of or against the Seneca Falls Declaration. **Ask:** What statement in the declaration most influenced your position? *(Students may indicate that a phrase such as "all men and women are created equal" won their support. Or they may have found the statement that "the history of mankind is a history of repeated injuries . . . on the part of man toward woman" to be too strong an assertion, thereby turning them against the declaration.)* **OL**

R Reading Strategy

Outlining To help students visualize the progress made by women following the Seneca Falls Convention, have them outline the text of Section 3, using the heads "Suffrage," "Education," "Marriage Laws," and "Professional Employment." **Ask:** How did the gains made by women address the declaration's claim of "disfranchisement"? *(The term means "deprivation of rights, especially the right to vote." Therefore, women's gains in voting rights, educational and professional opportunities, and marriage and property laws directly addressed issues in the declaration.)* **BL**

Primary Source

The Seneca Falls Declaration

The first women's rights convention adopted resolutions proclaiming women's equality and calling for women's right to vote, to speak publicly, and to run for office. Before the meeting, the women published a "Declaration of Sentiments" in the local newspaper to state their goals.

▲ Elizabeth Cady Stanton

W When, in the course of human events, it becomes necessary for one portion of the family of man to assume among the people of the earth a position different from that which they have **hitherto** occupied, but one to which the laws of nature and of nature's God entitle them, a decent respect to the opinions of mankind requires that they should declare the causes that impel them to such a course.

We hold these truths to be self-evident: that all men and women are created equal; that they are **endowed** by their Creator with certain **inalienable** rights; that among these are life, liberty, and the pursuit of happiness. . . .

The history of mankind is a history of repeated injuries and **usurpations** on the part of man toward woman, having in direct object the establishment of an absolute tyranny over her. To prove this, let facts be submitted to a candid world. . . .

R Now, in view of this entire **disfranchisement** of one-half the people of this country, their social and religious **degradation**—in view of the unjust laws above mentioned, and because women do feel themselves aggrieved, oppressed, and fraudulently deprived of their most sacred rights, we insist that they have immediate admission to all the rights and privileges which belong to them as citizens of the United States.

> This document reflects the ideas in the Declaration of Independence. Like the patriots of 1776, women are announcing the need for revolutionary change.

> Here two important words—*and women*—are added to Thomas Jefferson's famous phrase.

> During this time, husbands were legal masters of their wives.

> A list of specific grievances follows this paragraph.

> In addition to the right to vote, most educational and employment opportunities at this time were unavailable to women.

> In 1920—more than 70 years after Seneca Falls—American women finally gained the right to vote.

VOCABULARY
hitherto (HIH·thuhr·TOO): before
endowed (ihn·DAU·ehd): provided
inalienable (ih·NAYL·yuh·nuh·buhl): impossible to surrender
usurpations (YOO·suhr·PAY·shuhnz): wrongful seizures of power
disfranchisement (DIH·suhn·FRAN·CHYZ·muhnt): deprivation of rights, especially the right to vote
degradation (DEH·gruh·DAY·shuhn): lowering in status

436   Chapter 14   *The Age of Reform*

Critical Thinking

1. **Drawing Conclusions** Why did the authors of this document use the Declaration of Independence as a model?
2. **Speculating** How do you think the authors would have responded to critics who ridiculed them as being too bold?
3. **Making Inferences** How did this document, along with the women's convention, help women acquire more rights?

Answers

1. The authors draw parallels between the movement for American independence and the movement for women's rights to emphasize the message that a dramatic change is needed.

2. The authors would probably argue that what people considered to be women's "proper behavior" needed to change.
3. The Seneca Falls Convention brought a great deal of attention to the idea of

women's rights, leading many women to speak out and work for change.

People IN HISTORY

Maria Mitchell
First professional woman astronomer

Mitchell was educated by her father and became fascinated with astronomy. She discovered the orbit of a new comet in 1847, and her accomplishments became widely known. Mitchell accepted a position at Vassar College when it opened in 1865. She wrote, *"It seems to me that the needle is the chain of woman. . . . Emancipate her from the 'stitch, stitch, stitch,' . . . and she would have time for studies which would engross as the needle never can."*

Mary Lyon
Founder of Mount Holyoke

After working as a teacher for 20 years, Lyon began raising funds for Mount Holyoke Female Seminary in 1834. She became the school's first principal when it opened in 1837. Lyon wrote that women should be educated in order to *"promote human happiness. To advance everything excellent. . . . Promote the best interests of this life & that which is to come. . . . The great secret of the whole in some respects is female education."*

CRITICAL Thinking

1. **Analyzing** What beliefs did Maria Mitchell and Mary Lyon share?
2. **Identifying** What did Mitchell mean by the phrase "the needle is the chain of woman"?

Susan B. Anthony was the daughter of a Quaker abolitionist in New York. Anthony worked for women's rights and temperance. She called for equal pay for women, college training for girls, and **coeducation**—the teaching of males and females together. Anthony organized the country's first women's temperance association, the Daughters of Temperance.

Anthony met Elizabeth Cady Stanton at a temperance meeting in 1851. They became lifelong friends and partners in the struggle for women's rights and suffrage. For the rest of the century, Anthony and Stanton led the women's movement. They worked with other women to win the right to vote. Beginning with Wyoming in 1890, several states granted women suffrage. It would not be until 1920, however, that women would gain the right to vote throughout the United States.

[S]

Reading Check **Explaining** What is suffrage?

Progress by Women

Main Idea Women made progress in achieving equality in education, marriage laws, and professional employment.

History and You Are there some laws that you consider unfair or unjust? Read to learn how some women worked to change laws and social customs that they thought were unjust.

Pioneers in women's education began to call for more opportunity. Early champions such as **Catherine Beecher** and **Emma Hart Willard** believed that women should be educated for their traditional roles in life. They also thought that women could be **capable,** or skillful, teachers. The Milwaukee College for Women created courses based on Beecher's ideas "to train women to be healthful, intelligent, and successful wives, mothers, and housekeepers." **[C]**

The Age of Reform **Chapter 14** **437**

CHAPTER 14
Section 3

S Skill Practice

Creating a Time Line Have students conduct research to create a time line of key events in the struggle for woman suffrage. The time line should begin with the Seneca Falls Convention and end with victory in 1920. Encourage gifted students to use an electronic time-line template. **AL**

C Critical Thinking

Making Inferences Ask: Why might society be willing to accept the ideas of the early champions of women's education? *(They advocated education but only to prepare women for their traditional roles.)* **OL**

People IN HISTORY

Critical Thinking Answers

1. They believed that women should be educated.
2. The needle represents society's definition of a woman's role as homemaker. If women were freed from the limits of that role, they could pursue an education.

Reading Check **Answer:** Suffrage is the right to vote.

Differentiated Instruction

Leveled Activities

BL **Differentiated Instruction Activity, URB p. 111**

OL **Time Line Skills Activity, URB p. 118**

AL **Writing Skills Activity, URB p. 107**

ELL **Academic Vocabulary Activity, URB p. 103**

437

S Skill Practice

Using Contrasting Skills Ask: How was the Troy Female Seminary different from the Milwaukee College for Women? *(Troy offered courses in traditionally "male" subjects.)* **OL**

R Reading Strategy

Inferring Ask: Before the mid-1800s, who became the guardian of the children after a divorce? *(the man)* **BL**

✔ **Reading Check** **Answer:** Gains included the establishment of colleges for women and the study of subjects considered traditionally "male," such as science and mathematics.

Assess

History ONLINE

Study Central™ provides summaries, interactive games, and online graphic organizers to help students review content.

Close

Discussing Have students identify gains made by the early women's movement. Discuss each one. **OL**

Section 3 Review

Education

Some young women began to make their own opportunities. They broke the barriers to female education and helped other women do the same.

After her marriage, Emma Willard educated herself in subjects considered suitable only for males, such as science and mathematics. In 1821 Willard set up the Troy Female Seminary in upstate New York. Willard's seminary taught mathematics, history, geography, and physics, as well as the usual homemaking subjects.

Mary Lyon established Mount Holyoke Female Seminary in Massachusetts in 1837. She modeled its curriculum on that of nearby Amherst College.

Marriage and Family Laws

During the mid to late 1800s, women made some gains in marriage and property laws. New York, Pennsylvania, Indiana, Wisconsin, Mississippi, and the new state of California recognized the right of women to own property after their marriage.

Some states passed laws permitting divorced women to share the guardianship of their children with their husbands. Indiana was the first of several states that allowed women to seek divorce if their husbands were chronic abusers of alcohol.

Breaking Barriers

In the 1800s, women had few career choices. They could become elementary teachers, but school boards often paid lower salaries to women than to men. Employment in professions that were dominated by men, such as medicine and the **ministry**, or Christian service, was even more difficult. Some strong-minded women, however, succeeded.

For example, **Elizabeth Blackwell's** medical school application was turned down repeatedly. Finally accepted by Geneva College in New York, Blackwell graduated first in her class and achieved fame as a doctor.

Despite the accomplishments of notable women, and their gains in education, state laws, and employment opportunities, women remained limited by social customs and expectations. Women had just begun the long struggle to achieve their goal of equality.

✔ **Reading Check** **Identifying** What gains were made by women in the field of education?

Section 3 Review

History ONLINE
Study Central™ To review this section, go to glencoe.com.

Vocabulary

1. Write a short paragraph about the women's movement of the middle to late 1800s that uses the following terms correctly: suffrage, coeducation, capable, ministry.

Main Ideas

2. Listing What opportunities were reserved for males in the middle to late 1800s?

3. Explaining Describe the rights within marriage that women gained in the 1800s.

Critical Thinking

4. Making Connections Many reformers in the 1800s focused on abolition and woman suffrage. Use a diagram like the one below to help you consider ways in which the two movements were similar.

| Suffrage movement | Abolitionist movement |

Similarities

5. Expository Writing What arguments might have been used by women who supported suffrage? You are a female pioneer traveling west. Write a paragraph explaining why women should have the right to vote.

Answer the Essential Question

6. What were the effects of the women's rights movement of the middle to late 1800s?

Answers

1. Students' paragraphs should demonstrate understanding of the terms and the women's movement.

2. Opportunities included entrance into the trades, professions, and the business world; voting; fair pay; college; and quality education.

3. In some states, married women could own property, share child guardianship,

and divorce if their husbands abused alcohol.

4. Answers might include a concern for equal rights; desire for freedom; spreading of ideas through rallies, lectures, and writings; and people involved in both movements, such as Mott and Stanton.

5. Students' paragraphs should support their argument for suffrage.

6. Women gained the right to vote in several states, greater access to education, expanded rights within marriage in some states, and greater public awareness of issues affecting women.

Chapter 14

Visual Summary

What were some social and educational reforms of the early 1800s?

- Temperance movement
- Expansion of higher education
- Education targeting the blind and deaf
- Improving prison conditions
- Transcendentalism in literature

Methodist camp meeting ▶

Abolitionist and reformer Frederick Douglass ▼

How did abolitionists fight slavery?

- Founded African colony for formerly enslaved people
- Published antislavery newspapers and books
- Established antislavery societies
- Spoke publicly against slavery
- Created Underground Railroad to help enslaved people escape to freedom

◀ Meeting notice, Massachusetts Anti-Slavery Society

How did Southerners defend slavery?

- Claimed slavery was essential to Southern economy
- Argued that enslaved workers were treated well
- Argued that system of slavery provided for needs of workers

What were the goals of the women's movement?

- Access to all-male professions
- Woman suffrage (the right to vote)
- Equal pay for women
- Higher education for women
- Right to own property

Elizabeth Cady Stanton and Susan B. Anthony, leaders in the woman suffrage movement ▶

STUDY TO GO Study anywhere, anytime! Download quizzes and flash cards to your PDA from glencoe.com.

The Age of Reform **Chapter 14** 439

Visual Summary

Making Connections Point out that being part of a reform movement wasn't easy. Women's rights activists were taunted and scorned. Abolitionists were attacked and even killed. Many of these activists believed passionately in their cause. Ask students to think about problems and injustices in today's world. **Ask:** Is there a cause that you feel deeply about? On the board, list the causes students mention. Have students select a cause and discuss the actions they would take to promote it. **OL**

Analyzing Information Have students review the reasons people opposed abolition. Point out that other movements faced similar opposition. **Ask:** Who might oppose temperance for economic reasons? *(bar owners, alcohol producers)* Who might oppose for social reasons? *(people who liked to drink or for whom drinking alcohol was traditional)* Why might many men oppose women's rights? *(Men would have to share social, economic, and political power with women.)* Select a few current causes from the previous activity. Have the class identify who in society might be opposed and why. **AL**

Hands-On Chapter Project
Step 4: Wrap-Up

Influencing Public Policy

Step 4: Giving the Presentation Students will make their presentations to the legislators.

Directions Have the groups distribute copies of their pamphlets or display them on an overhead projector during their presentations. The class will play the role of the state legislators at the hearing and ask questions of the presenters. After all groups have presented, discuss the effectiveness of each group in supporting the group's views and persuading legislators to pass the reform law.

Analyzing Ask: How do advocacy groups benefit society today? *(They bring problems to light, educate the public, propose possible solutions, and influence public policy toward positive change.)* Do you think the changes proposed by advocacy groups are always good for society? *(No. There are different sides to every issue—some proposals have more merit than others. Some groups may seek change that benefits their members more than society.)* **OL**

Answers and Analyses
Reviewing Main Ideas

1. B Students can narrow the possible choices by recalling that transcendentalists reflected the reform spirit of their time. **18.A.3**

2. A Students can eliminate choice B by recognizing that most abolitionists were in the North, where slavery was mostly gone. They can eliminate choice C by recalling that many Northerners opposed abolition because they feared African Americans would take their jobs. **18.B.3a**

3. C Remind students that the Seneca Falls Convention was about women's rights, eliminating choices A and B. Have them think about which issue of the early women's movement was most controversial. **18.C.3b**

Short-Answer Question

4. The passage mimics the words of the Declaration of Independence. The temperance society might have used this style to gain attention and to associate their cause with the widely respected principles stated in the Declaration. **16.A.3b**

STANDARDIZED TEST PRACTICE

TEST-TAKING TIP

Eliminate answers that do not make sense. For example, if an answer refers to a subject that does not relate to the question, you know it cannot be correct.

Reviewing Main Ideas

Directions: Choose the best answer for each of the following questions.

1. A major subject of transcendentalist literature was

  A realism.

  B the relationship between humans and nature and the importance of the individual conscience.

  C anti-abolitionism.

  D the relationship between humans and technology and the importance of industrialism.

2. Which of the following arguments did pro-slavery Southerners use against abolitionists?

  A They claimed that slave labor was essential to the South, allowing Southern whites to reach a high level of culture.

  B They argued that many abolitionists were also secretly slaveholders.

  C They argued that abolitionists only wanted to free enslaved workers so that they could work in Northern factories.

  D They stated that abolitionists wanted to steal Southerners' farms.

3. What happened at the Seneca Falls Convention in 1848?

  A Delegates called for an end to child labor.

  B Delegates passed a resolution in favor of voting rights for all African Americans.

  C Delegates demanded that women be given the right to vote.

  D Delegates petitioned the states to add an Equal Rights Amendment to the Constitution.

Short-Answer Question

Directions: Base your answer to question 4 on the excerpt below and on your knowledge of social studies.

> We hold these truths to be self-evident; that all men are created temperate [without the need to drink alcohol]; that they are endowed by their Creator with certain natural and innocent desires; that among these are the appetite for cold water and the pursuit of happiness!
>
> —*Manifesto of the Washington Total Abstinence Societies*

4. Which important American document does this passage imitate? Why do you think the writers chose this style?

Review the Essential Questions

5. Essay Describe the roots, goals, and achievements of the social reform, education reform, and women's rights movements, and explain their similarities and differences.

To help you write your essay, review your answers to the Essential Questions in the section reviews and the chapter Foldables Study Organizer. Your essay should include:

- religious and cultural trends of the mid-1800s;
- the temperance movement and reforms in education;
- the abolitionist movement; and
- the women's rights movement.

GO ON

Review the Essential Questions

5. If students completed their Foldables correctly, they should be able to discuss different reform movements. Students' essays should note the religious roots of reform efforts and the goals to improve society. Temperance laws were passed in some states but were later repealed. Abolitionists built public awareness and helped many enslaved people escape, but they failed to end slavery. The early women's movement made some gains in marriage and property laws and won the right to vote in several states, but not nationally. Education reformers helped improve teacher training, establish colleges, and open more opportunities for women, African Americans, and people with special needs to gain an education. **18.A.3**

History ONLINE
For additional test practice, use **Self-Check Quizzes**—Chapter 14 at glencoe.com.

Chapter 14 Assessment

Document-Based Questions

Directions: Analyze the documents and answer the short-answer questions that follow.

Document 1

This excerpt is from an 1848 report that Horace Mann wrote to the Massachusetts Board of Education.

> According to the European theory, men are divided into classes,—some to toil and earn, others to seize and enjoy. According to the Massachusetts theory, all are to have an equal chance for earning, and equal security in the enjoyment of what they earn. . . . Education, then, beyond all other devices of human origin, is the great equalizer of the conditions of men.

Source: Horace Mann, "Report No. 12 of the Massachusetts School Board"

6. What did Mann consider the difference to be between European and Massachusetts theories of society?

Document 2

The following is taken from Ralph Waldo Emerson's essay "Self-Reliance."

> And so the reliance on Property, including the reliance on governments which protect it, is the want of self-reliance. Men have looked away from themselves and at things so long, that they have come to esteem . . . the religious, learned, and civil institutions as guards of property. . . . They measure their esteem of each other, by what each has, not by what each is.

Source: Ralph Waldo Emerson, *Essays: First Series*

7. Based on the document, what does Emerson see as one of the basic problems within American society?

Document 3

The following is one of a series of cards issued in 1863 by H. T. Helmbold, a drug and chemical company, to promote its products.

THE PARTING "Buy us too."

8. Based on the image, do you believe Helmbold issued the cards to rally support for or against the abolition of slavery? Explain.

Document 4

The following is an excerpt from an 1853 essay that appeared in *Harper's New Monthly Magazine*.

> There is danger that laws giving the right of separate property, and of course the management of separate property, to the wife, may in time vitally affect that oneness which is so essential to the marriage idea.

Source: Henry Raymond, "Woman's Rights"

9. Why does the writer suggest that women should not receive marriage property rights?

10. Creative Writing Using the information from the four documents and your knowledge of social studies, write an essay in which you:

- assume the role of a mid-1800s reformer and explain your goals for American society; and
- describe the challenges you face and how you will address them.

---

8. The cards were issued to win support for abolition. This card shows a heartbreaking scene of an African American family being separated because one member was sold. **16.A.3b**

9. Marriage was supposed to join two people into a single unit. Separate property rights promoted separateness, not oneness. **18.C.3b**

10. Essays should be written in first person from the viewpoint of a reformer in one of the movements of the mid-1800s. Students should clearly state the movement's goals, the challenges facing the movement, and realistic ways to overcome those challenges. **18.B**

History ONLINE
Have students visit the Web site at glencoe.com to review Chapter 14 and take the Self-Check Quiz.

Need Extra Help?

Have students refer to the pages listed if they miss any of the questions.

Need Extra Help?

If you missed questions. . .	1	2	3	4	5	6	7	8	9	10
Go to page. . .	421	431	435	419	418–438	420	421	424–431	438	418–438

Document-Based Questions

6. European society was divided between classes that did the work and classes that enjoyed the fruits of that labor. The Massachusetts theory held that everyone was equal, with an equal chance to work and to benefit from their own labor. **18.C**

7. Emerson believed that people had come to value property too much and rely too much on public institutions to protect their property. He wanted people to become more self-reliant and to base respect for each other on character, not possessions. **16.A.3b**

UNIT PACING CHART

	Unit 5	Chapter 15	Chapter 16	Chapter 17
Day 1	Unit Opener, Reading History	Chapter Opener, Section 1	Chapter Opener, Section 1	Chapter Opener, Section 1
Day 2		Section 2, Section 3	Section 2, America's Literature	Section 2
Day 3		Section 3, Section 4	Section 3, Section 4	Section 3, TIME Notebook
Day 4		Section 4, You Decide, Visual Summary	Section 5, Visual Summary	Section 4, Geography & History, Visual Summary
Day 5		Chapter Assessment	Chapter Assessment	Chapter Assessment

 Teacher to Teacher

Erin Farley
New Albany
Middle School
New Albany, OH

Create a Civil War Board Game Students will create a board game using information about the Civil War. The students can work in pairs or groups of three to create their game. The game needs to be based on trivia, not chance. The game will allow students to explore, in detail, the battles, key people, issues, and culture of the American Civil War Era. Have the students submit their game plans and directions to you, along with a description of the strategy that is needed in order to win. (The North does not always have to win.) Once approved, the students can begin their research and construction. The game needs to have a board, the necessary pieces (dice, trivia cards, and so on), and a box in which to store the game. The game should have a name and a unique, colorful design. Then, when the games are due, allow students to play them. The students can play each other's games while providing feedback about how well the game worked.

Author Note

Dear American History Teacher,

The American Revolution gave birth to the United States but left the infant republic with two potentially fatal diseases. The first was the inherent vulnerability of all republics to divisive factions that could lead to either civil war or totalitarianism. The founding generation was painfully aware of the fate of most republics throughout history. Would the United States succumb to this same fate? Could it survive as one nation, indivisible, with a republican form of government based on male suffrage? Or would it collapse into warring factions, division, and anarchy, or succumb to a strong-armed dictator? The question remained unresolved through the first four score and seven years of our history as a nation.

The second potentially fatal disease was slavery. The United States was founded on a contradiction. Its founding document declared all men created equal, with a natural right of liberty. Yet every one of the 13 states in 1776 was a slave state. Proudly calling itself the "land of liberty," the United States by 1850 was the largest slaveholding country in the world. This issue remained unresolved until it finally tore the country apart in 1861.

The outcome of the Civil War cured these diseases and ensured the republic a long life as a unified nation. No state has seriously threatened to secede from the United States since 1865. What Abraham Lincoln called "the monstrous injustice of slavery" came to an end. The central issue of the Reconstruction years after the Civil War was whether that liberty for all would also become justice for all. The Fourteenth Amendment to the Constitution, ratified in 1868, enshrined equal citizenship for freed slaves. It would not be until the twentieth century, however, that full citizenship would be extended to another group of Americans: women.

James M. McPherson

Unit Objectives

After studying this unit, students will be able to:

- Explain how differences between the North and the South led to the Civil War.
- Detail the major campaigns of the war.
- Describe Reconstruction policies and their effects on the former Confederacy.

Introducing the Unit

Analyzing Visuals As students prepare to study the unit, have them look at the photo on the Unit Opener. Ask students to think about how weapon technology might influence the outcome of a war. **Ask:** How do you think the use of cannons might affect warfare? *(Students might note that cannons could have a disastrous effect on infantry.)* Tell students that as they study the unit on the Civil War, they will learn how new technology changed the way wars were fought. New technology was used in addition to traditional strategies, such as bayonet charges, which drastically increased the number of casualties and deaths. Also point out to students that they will learn why war broke out and how the goals changed during the war. **OL**

Unit 5
Civil War and Reconstruction
1820–1896

Chapter 15
Toward Civil War
1820–1861

Chapter 16
The Civil War
1861–1865

Chapter 17
Reconstruction and the New South
1865–1896

FIRED FROM FORT MOULTRIE INTO CHARLESTON, S.C. 1861

Spent cannon round from the attack on Fort Sumter, April 1861

442

Activity: Why It Matters

Why Study the Civil War and Reconstruction? Ask: What is a civil war? *(Students should answer that it is a war that takes place within a region or country between groups.)* What might be some reasons why people fight civil wars? *(Students might discuss how some groups fight to create a new government based on their views.)* Tell students what they can expect to learn in the upcoming unit. As students read through the unit, have them write in their notebooks the reasons Americans fought a civil war in the 1860s. **OL**

> *"It is well that war is so terrible; we would grow too fond of it."*
> —Robert E. Lee

Union soldiers with a cannon, June 1862

443

Connect to Past Learning

Civil War and Reconstruction In the previous unit, students learned about the development of distinct ways of life in the nation's regions and the further expansion of the United States. In this unit, they will learn how those regional differences led to increasing hostility between the North and the South over slavery in the territories and how that conflict led to the Civil War, the end of slavery, and attempts at Reconstruction in the South.

More About the Image

Visual Literacy The Federal forces began the war with more than 4,000 pieces of artillery. The Union had the distinct advantage of having several foundries that were able to shift over to wartime production, as well as an abundant supply of raw materials. This allowed the government to produce a formidable artillery arm and augment it with a few imports and captured Southern weapons. This was an advantage the South was never able to match. As the Federal blockade of Southern ports intensified, the Confederacy had to rely more on the fortunes of battle to capture Union artillery and ammunition. By the end of the war, the South still had only a few armories and foundries compared to the larger number in the North.

Unit 5 Reading History

Why Identifying Cause and Effect Is Important

Being able to identify the causes (the reasons that something occurs) and the effects (the results and consequences) is an important critical thinking skill. Students use cause-and-effect relationships every day, whether or not they are aware of it. Cause-and-effect relationships are also used to organize many kinds of writing.

Learn It!

Create a cause-and-effect graphic organizer on the board. Write "Joey received a low grade on his math exam" in the middle. Include spaces for several causes and several effects.

Ask students to volunteer possible causes for Joey's poor performance. *(For example: He didn't study, he suffered from test anxiety, or he couldn't sleep the night before.)* Then ask them to list several possible effects of his failure. *(His basketball coach benched him, his parents grounded him, or he had to study extra hard for the rest of the semester.)*

Use the exercise to point out that an event can have many causes and many effects. **OL**

Practice It!

Multiple effects are given in the paragraph. Students should list the following:

Cause: Reconstruction

Effect: Public schools were created for both races.

Effect: About 50 percent of white children and 40 percent of African American children in the South were enrolled in public schools. **OL**

READING SKILL ## Identifying Cause and Effect

Learn It! A *cause* is an action or event that makes something happen. What happens as a result is the *effect*.

Cause
The slavery issue splits the Democratic Party.

Effect
Northern Democrats nominate Stephen Douglas.

Effect
Southern Democrats nominate John C. Breckinridge.

—from Chapter 15, p. 463

The issue of slavery split the Democratic Party. The northern Democrats nominated Stephen Douglas. They supported popular sovereignty. Southern Democrats vowed to uphold slavery. Their candidate was John C. Breckinridge.

Practice It! Read the paragraph and write down the cause and effect(s) on another sheet of paper.

—from Chapter 17, p. 531

In the 1870s, Reconstruction governments created public schools for both races. Within a few years, about 50 percent of white children and 40 percent of African American children in the South were enrolled.

Cause
_____

Effect
_____

Effect
_____

Reading Strategy | Questioning

Identifying Cause and Effect Asking questions can help students identify cause-and-effect relationships. Students need to ask themselves questions as they read, such as "Why did this happen?" and "What happened as a result?" Assign students a subsection in one of the chapters in this unit and have them ask, and then answer, questions to determine cause-and-effect relationships. Use the questions and answers to create a cause-and-effect graphic organizer for this subsection. **BL**

Academic Vocabulary Preview

In addition to content vocabulary, you will also find academic vocabulary in this unit. Knowing academic vocabulary will help you understand content that is taught in all of your classes, not just social studies. Learning these words will also help you perform well on tests. Below are the academic vocabulary terms that appear in Unit 5.

Academic Vocabulary	Definition	Practice It!
Chapter 15 Toward Civil War		
temporary (TEHM · puh · REHR · ee) *p. 449*	brief	**Identify** *the term from Chapter 15 that best completes the sentences.*
regulate (REH · gyuh · LAYT) *p. 450*	to control	**1.** The Underground Railroad was a secret _____ of people opposed to slavery.
network (NEHT · WUHRK) *p. 453*	an interconnected system	
inevitable (ih · NEH · vuh · tuh · buhl) *p. 455*	unavoidable	**2.** When Southern states seceded from the Union, it signaled the _____ coming of the Civil War.
rigid (RIH · juhd) *p. 458*	firm and inflexible	
topic (TAH · pihk) *p. 460*	a subject of discussion	**3.** The _____ of slavery was one that divided families as well as the nation.
reject (rih · JEHKT) *p. 464*	to refuse to accept	
justify (JUHS · tuh · FY) *p. 464*	to find reason(s) to support	
Chapter 16 The Civil War		
contrast (kuhn · TRAST) *p. 476*	completely opposite	**Identify** *the term from Chapter 16 that best matches the underlined term or terms.*
challenge (CHA · luhnj) *p. 479*	a demanding situation	
abandon (uh · BAN · duhn) *p. 481*	to leave behind	**4.** Many women collected food, clothing, and medicine to give out to the troops.
impact (ihm · PAKT) *p. 487*	to effect or influence	
distribute (dih · STRIH · byuht) *p. 493*	to divide and give out	**5.** A person could avoid the draft by hiring a replacement to serve in his place.
substitute (SUHB · stuh · TOOT) *p. 496*	a replacement	
nevertheless (NEH · vuhr · thuh · LEHS) *p. 501*	however	**6.** Under attack, Union soldiers decided to leave the fort.
encounter (ihn · KAUN · tuhr) *p. 502*	to come upon; meet	
series (SIHR · eez) *p. 507*	sequence	
interpret (ihn · TUHR · pruht) *p. 509*	to explain the meaning of something	
Chapter 17 Reconstruction and the New South		
radical (RA · dih · kuhl) *p. 520*	extreme	**Choose** *the synonym that best matches the meaning of each vocabulary word listed below.*
adjust (uh · JUHST) *p. 520*	to adapt	
convince (kuhn · VIHNS) *p. 523*	to persuade (someone) that something is true	**7. radical** **9. suspend** **a.** method **a.** believe **b.** drastic **b.** eliminate **c.** envy **c.** delay
suspend (suh · SPEHND) *p. 526*	to temporarily prevent	
credit (KREH · diht) *p. 530*	extra time to pay for purchased goods	**8. convince** **10. outcome** **a.** bother **a.** conclusion **b.** believe **b.** expense **c.** persuade **c.** anew
academy (uh · KA · duh · mee) *p. 531*	a school that provides special training	
outcome (AUT · KUHM) *p. 536*	a result	
commission (kuh · MIH · shuhn) *p. 536*	a special group	

Civil War and Reconstruction **Unit 5** **445**

Academic Vocabulary Preview

Randomly divide the class into two even teams, and then instruct each team to line up on opposite sides of the classroom.

Give the first person on Team One a vocabulary word, and ask the student to provide the definition (or give them the definition and ask for the word, or mix it up throughout the game as you see fit). If the student is correct, award the team a point, and move to Team Two. If the student is incorrect, give Team Two the chance to answer correctly and steal the point. Move down the line of students on each team, giving each student a new term. Award the winning team a special privilege. **OL**

Practice It!

Answers

1. network
2. inevitable
3. topic
4. distribute
5. substitute
6. abandon
7. b
8. c
9. c
10. a

Reading Strategy   Read to Write

Writing Essays Cause-and-effect essays may be written in chronological order or may be organized by the relative importance of the causes and effects. All essays should begin with a paragraph introducing the event being explored. Each additional paragraph should explore one cause or one effect. Have students choose an event in this unit that demonstrates a cause-and-effect relationship. Before writing the essay, tell students to brainstorm the possible causes and effects of the event. They may want to create a cause-and-effect graphic organizer to help them construct their essays. **OL**

Chapter Planning Guide

15

Key to Ability Levels
- **BL** Below level
- **OL** On level
- **AL** Above level
- **ELL** English Language Learners

Key to Teaching Resources
- Print Material
- CD-ROM
- DVD
- Transparency

BL	OL	AL	ELL		Resources	Chapter Opener	Section 1	Section 2	Section 3	Section 4	Chapter Assess
FOCUS											
BL	OL	AL	ELL	🖨	Daily Test Practice Transparencies		15–1	15–2	15–3	15–4	
TEACH											
	OL	AL		📁	Geography and History Activity, URB		p. 31				
BL	OL		ELL	📁	Time Line Skills Activity, URB				p. 34		
BL	OL	AL	ELL	📁	Writing Skills Activity, URB					p. 23	
BL	OL	AL	ELL	📁	Content Vocabulary Activity, URB		p. 17	p. 17	p. 17	p. 17	
BL	OL	AL	ELL	📁	Academic Vocabulary Activity, URB		p. 19	p. 19	p. 19	p. 19	
BL	OL		ELL	📁	Social Studies Skills Activity, URB			p. 25			
BL	OL	AL	ELL	📁	Differentiated Instruction Activity, URB				p. 27		
BL	OL	AL	ELL	📁	Critical Thinking Skills Activity, URB			p. 29			
BL	OL	AL	ELL	📁	Linking Past and Present Activity, URB		p. 33				
	OL	AL		📁	Primary Source Readings, URB				p. 21		
BL	OL	AL	ELL	📁	School-to-Home Connection Activity, URB		p. 35	p. 35	p. 35	p. 35	
BL	OL		ELL	📁	Guided Reading Activity, URB*		p. 39	p. 40	p. 41	p. 42	
BL	OL		ELL	📁	Reading Essentials and Note-Taking Guide*		p. 151	p. 154	p. 157	p. 160	
BL	OL	AL	ELL	🖨	Lesson Transparencies		15A, 15B	15A, 15B	15B	15C	
		AL		📁	Supreme Court Case Studies				p. 11		
BL	OL	AL	ELL	📁	Outline Map Resource Book	pp. 5, 6					

Note: Please refer to the *Unit Resource Book: Civil War and Reconstruction* for this chapter's URB materials.

* Also available in Spanish

446A

Levels					Resources	Chapter Opener	Section 1	Section 2	Section 3	Section 4	Chapter Assess
BL	OL	AL	ELL								
TEACH *(continued)*											
BL	OL	AL	ELL	📁	**NGS US Desk Map**		✓	✓	✓	✓	
BL	OL	AL	ELL	📁	**American Literature Library**		✓	✓	✓	✓	
BL	OL	AL	ELL	📁	**Writer's Guidebook**		✓	✓	✓	✓	
	OL	AL		💿	**American History Primary Source Document Library CD-ROM**		✓	✓	✓	✓	✓
BL	OL	AL	ELL	💿	**American Music: Hits Through History**	✓	✓	✓	✓	✓	
BL	OL	AL	ELL	💿	**StudentWorks™ Plus CD**	✓	✓	✓	✓	✓	✓
BL	OL	AL	ELL	🔒	**Section Spotlight Videos**		✓	✓	✓	✓	
BL	OL	AL	ELL	🖨	**Writing Process Transparencies**		✓	✓	✓	✓	✓
BL	OL	AL	ELL	💿	**Presentation Plus! With MindJogger CheckPoint CD**	✓	✓	✓	✓	✓	✓
ASSESS											
BL	OL	AL	ELL	📁	**Quizzes and Tests**		p. 141	p. 142	p. 143	p. 144	pp. 145, 147, 149
BL	OL	AL	ELL	📁	**Authentic Assessment With Rubrics**					p. 15	
BL	OL	AL	ELL	📁	**Standardized Test Practice**						p. 29
BL	OL	AL	ELL	💿	*ExamView® Assessment Suite CD-ROM**		15–1	15–2	15–3	15–4	Ch. 15
CLOSE											
BL			ELL	📁	**Reteaching Activity, URB***		p. 37	p. 37	p. 37	p. 37	p. 37
BL	OL		ELL	📁	**Reading and Study Skills Foldables Activity**	p. 78	p. 78	p. 78	p. 78	p. 78	p. 78
BL	OL	AL	ELL	📁	*The American Journey* **in Graphic Novel**						p. 77
BL			ELL	📁	**Reading Strategies and Activities for the Social Studies Classroom**		✓	✓	✓	✓	
BL	OL	AL	ELL	🖨	**Graphic Organizer Transparencies & Strategies**		✓	✓	✓	✓	

TeacherWorks Plus
All-In-One Planner and Resource Center

- Interactive Lesson Planner
- Interactive Teacher Edition
- Fully editable blackline masters
- Section Spotlight Videos Launch

- Differentiated Lesson Plans
- Printable reports of daily assignments
- Standards Tracking System

Professional Development Resources

- Strategies for Success
- Building Academic Vocabulary
- Success With English Learners DVD
- Differentiated Instruction Strategies DVD
- Teaching Literacy Strategies in Social Studies DVD
- Assessment DVD
- Standards-Based Instruction DVD

Using CyberScout

Researching Using *Keyword*

Technology Product

CyberScout is a convenient and dynamic search engine that provides several easy ways to locate information outside the McGraw-Hill Learning Network. CyberScout searches only Web sites that have been reviewed by teachers, so the information students find is always appropriate and accurate.

Objectives

After students learn using CyberScout, they will be able to

- research topics and issues in economics using CyberScout;
- exercise research and study skills;
- practice writing skills.

Steps

- From the McGraw-Hill Learning Network home page (www.mhln.com), click on **For Students**.
- Choose **CyberScout** below **Homework Help**.
- Enter a keyword or phrase in the **Keyword** field and click on the **Go** button.
- Click on the link to a Web site of interest.
- Students will be redirected to the Web site in a new window.
- Students navigate through the chosen Web site to acquire information about their topics and take notes.

History ONLINE at glencoe.com

	Student	Teacher	Parent
Media Center			
• Student Edition Audio	●		
• Spanish Summaries	●		
• Section Spotlight Videos	●	●	
Social Studies Online Learning Center			
Classroom Tools			
• Multi-Language Glossaries	●	●	●
• Teaching Today		●	
• TIME Current Events	●	●	●
• Beyond the Textbook	●	●	
***The American Journey* Online Learning Center**			
• Study-to-Go™	●	●	●
• Study Central™	●	●	●
• Chapter Overview	●	●	
• Concepts in Motion	●	●	
• ePuzzles and Games	●	●	
• Literature Connections	●	●	
• Online Student Edition	●	●	●
• Self-Check Quizzes	●	●	●
• Student Web Activities	●	●	
• Vocabulary eFlashcards	●	●	
• Web Activity Lesson Plans	●	●	●
• Vocabulary PuzzleMaker	●	●	●

- **Timed Readings Plus in Social Studies** helps students increase their reading rate and fluency while maintaining comprehension. The 400-word passages are similar to those found on state and national assessments.

- **Reading in the Content Area: Social Studies** concentrates on six essential reading skills that help students better comprehend what they read. The book includes 75 high-interest nonfiction passages written at increasing levels of difficulty.

- **Reading Social Studies** includes strategic reading instruction and vocabulary support in Social Studies content for ELLs and native speakers of English.

- **Content Vocabulary Workout** (Grades 6–8) accelerates reading comprehension through focused vocabulary development. Social Studies content vocabulary comes from the glossaries of Glencoe's Middle School Social Studies texts.

www.jamestowneducation.com

Index to National Geographic Magazine:

The following articles relate to this chapter:

- *"The Kurds In Control,"* Frank Viviano, January 2006.

- *"The Future Is Calling,"* Thomas B. Allen, December 2001.

National Geographic Society Products

To order the following, call National Geographic at 1-800-368-2728:

National Geographic Atlas of the World *(Book)*

Access National Geographic's dynamic MapMachine Web site and other geography resources at:

www.nationalgeographic.com

www.nationalgeographic.com/mapmachine

Use this database to search more than 30,000 titles to create a customized reading list for your students.

- Reading lists can be organized by students' reading level, author, genre, theme, or area of interest.
- The database provides Degrees of Reading Power™ (DRP) and Lexile™ readability scores for all selections.
- A brief summary of each selection is included.

Leveled reading suggestions for this chapter:

For students at a Grade 6 reading level:
- *Mine Eyes Have Seen,* by Ann Rinaldi
- *Lightning Time,* by Douglas Rees

For students at a Grade 7 reading level:
- *Underground Man,* by Milton Meltzer
- *Jayhawker,* by Patricia Beatty

For students at a Grade 8 reading level:
- *Abraham Lincoln,* by George Sullivan
- *A Yankee Girl at Fort Sumter,* by Alice Turner Curtis

For students at a Grade 9 reading level:
- *Before the Creeks Ran Red,* by Carolyn Reeder
- *Dred and Harriet Scott: A Family's Struggle for Freedom,* by Gwenyth Swain

For students at a Grade 10 reading level:
- *The Abraham Lincoln You Never Knew,* by James Lincoln Collier
- *A Free Black Girl Before the Civil War: The Diary of Charlotte Forten, 1854,* by Christy Steele & Kerry Graves

The following videotape programs are available from Glencoe as supplements to the chapter:

- **Abraham Lincoln: Preserving the Union** (ISBN 0-76-700034-X)

- **Images of the Civil War** (ISBN 1-56-501171-6)

To order, call Glencoe at 1-800-334-7344. To find classroom resources to accompany many of these videos, check the following home pages:

A&E Television: www.aetv.com

The History Channel: www.history.com

Chapter Objectives

After studying this chapter, students will be able to:

- Evaluate the effectiveness of compromises that Congress made to address slavery and sectionalism.
- Explain how popular sovereignty led to violence in Kansas.
- Discuss the significance of the *Dred Scott* decision.
- Explain the theory of states' rights and discuss its role in the outbreak of the Civil War.

Motivating Activity

Making Connections Students will learn about the issues that divided the North and South and how failure to resolve those issues led to the Civil War. Direct students' attention to the image on this page. **Ask:** What is happening in this scene? *(Confederate forces are attacking a federal fort.)* How would you feel if one part of the country broke away from and attacked another part of the country today? *(Answers will vary, but students may talk about feelings of anger, sadness, worry, fear, and disbelief.)* **OL**

Chapter 15 Toward Civil War 1840–1861

Confederate forces bombarded Fort Sumter on April 12, 1861. The attack on the fort, located in Charleston Harbor, South Carolina, marked the beginning of the Civil War.

PRESIDENTS

WILLIAM HENRY HARRISON 1841

JOHN TYLER 1841–1845

JAMES POLK 1845–1849

★ 1846 Congress establishes the Smithsonian Institution

ZACHARY TAYLOR 1849–1850

MILLARD FILLMORE 1850–1853

U.S. Events

World Events

1840 — 1845 — 1850

1843 ★ Charles Dickens: *A Christmas Carol* published

1845 ★ Many Irish emigrate to escape famine

1848 ★ Marx publishes *The Communist Manifesto*

446 Chapter 15

Previewing the Essential Questions

As you begin teaching each section, use these questions and activities to help students focus on the Essential Questions.

Section 1

Slavery and the West Ask: What do you know about ways of life in the North and the South? *(Students may answer that the North was industrialized while the South was agricultural, and that the South depended on a slave labor force while the North did not.)* Point out to students that in Section 1 they will learn how the expansion of slavery into the territories became a divisive issue that led to the Civil War. **OL**

Section 2

A Nation Dividing Ask: If people who opposed slavery were required by law to help catch runaways, how do you think they would react? *(They might be angry and refuse to obey the law.)* Tell students that Section 2 discusses Northern and Southern reactions to the Fugitive Slave Act, as well as the reasons behind the violence in "Bleeding Kansas." **OL**

Section 1: Slavery and the West
Essential Question Did the compromises that Congress made effectively address slavery and sectionalism?

Section 2: A Nation Dividing
Essential Question How did popular sovereignty lead to violence in Kansas?

Section 3: Challenges to Slavery
Essential Question What was the significance of the *Dred Scott* decision?

Section 4: Secession and War
Essential Question What role did the theory of states' rights play in the outbreak of the Civil War?

History ONLINE
Chapter Overview Visit glencoe.com and click on **Chapter 15—Chapter Overviews** to preview chapter information.

FOLDABLES
Study Organizer

Organizing Information
Make this Foldable to help organize what you learn about events leading up to the Civil War.

Step 1 Fold an 11" x 17" sheet of paper accordion style.

Step 2 Fold the bottom edge up three inches. Glue the edges to make pockets.

Step 3 Label the panels with the section titles as shown. Use the pockets to hold notes taken on index cards.

| Slavery & the West | A Nation Dividing | Challenges to Slavery | Secession & War |

Reading and Writing As you read the chapter, take notes on key issues and key events in the years leading up to war.

◀ Edwin Drake drills the first oil well near Titusville, Pennsylvania.

1857 ★
U.S. Supreme
Court makes
Dred Scott
decision

FRANKLIN PIERCE 1853–1857

1854 ★
Kansas-
Nebraska
Act passes

JAMES BUCHANAN 1857–1861

1859
The Drake
Well
becomes
first U.S.
oil well

1861 ★
Civil War
begins

ABRAHAM LINCOLN 1861–1865

1855   **1860**

1855 ★
Florence Nightingale
improves health care
during Crimean War

1856 ★
Henry Bessemer
introduces process
for making steel
inexpensively

1861 ★
Alexander II
frees serfs
in Russia

Chapter 15   447

Introducing Chapter 15

Time Line Activity

Have students review the time line. **Ask:** What years are covered in this chapter? *(1840–1861)* Tell students that the Kansas-Nebraska Act and the *Dred Scott* decision were crucial events leading up to the Civil War. **Ask:** What happened in 1861 that might have influenced President Lincoln? *(the freeing of serfs in Russia)*

FOLDABLES
Study Organizer
Dinah Zike's Foldables

Purpose This Foldable helps students organize information about the divisions between North and South and the conflicts over slavery that led to the Civil War. The completed Foldable will help them prepare for assessment. **OL**

▱ More Foldables activities for this chapter can be found in *Dinah Zike's Reading and Study Skills Foldables.*

History ONLINE
Introduce students to chapter content and key terms by having them access the **Chapter Overview** at glencoe.com.

Section 3

Challenges to Slavery Ask: What could people do if the established political parties fail to address issues that are important to many voters? *(Third parties might form.)* Tell students that Section 3 will explain how antislavery advocates formed the Republican Party, which would become a major force in American politics, in 1854. **OL**

Section 4

Secession and War Ask: How do you think Southerners reacted to Abraham Lincoln's election to the presidency in 1860? *(Answers may include: worried that he would abolish slavery and not respect their rights; secession; Civil War.)* Tell students that they will learn in Section 4 about the formation of the Confederacy and the attack in 1861 that began the Civil War.

447

Slavery and the West

CHAPTER 15
Section 1

Focus

Bellringer
Daily Test Practice Transparency 15–1

Reading Guide
Answers to Graphic:
Missouri Compromise: admit Missouri (slave state) and Maine (free state) at the same time, ban slavery from the rest of Louisiana Purchase north of 36°30' N latitude; **Compromise of 1850:** admit California (free state), no limits on slavery in New Mexico, end slave trade in Washington, D.C.

Section Spotlight Video

Have students watch the Section Spotlight Video "Slavery and the West" to learn more about the Missouri Compromise.

Resource Manager

Essential Question
Did the compromises that Congress made effectively address slavery and sectionalism?

Reading Guide

Content Vocabulary
sectionalism (p. 449)   secede (p. 451)
fugitive (p. 451)   abstain (p. 451)

Academic Vocabulary
temporary (p. 449)   regulate (p. 450)

Key People and Events
Missouri Compromise (p. 449)
Stephen A. Douglas (p. 451)
Compromise of 1850 (p. 451)

Reading Strategy
Taking Notes As you read, use a diagram like the one below to describe how two compromises addressed the issue of slavery in new states.

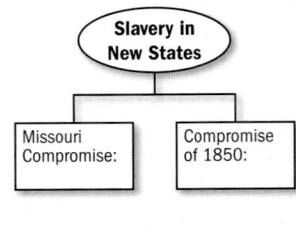

Slavery in New States

Missouri Compromise:

Compromise of 1850:

ILLINOIS STANDARDS
The American Journey

14.C.3 Compare historical issues involving rights, roles and status of individuals in relation to municipalities, states and the nation.

16.D Understand Illinois, United States and world social history.

17.C.3a Explain how human activity is affected by geographic factors.

18.B.3a Analyze how individuals and groups interact with and within institutions (e.g., educational, military).

American Diary

When Missouri applied for statehood in 1819, controversy arose in Congress. Slavery was legal in Missouri, and Missouri's admission would change the balance between free states and slave states. The Missouri debate became so bitter that Thomas Jefferson wrote: "This momentous question, like a fire bell in the night, awakened and filled me with terror. I considered it at once as the knell [funeral bell] of the Union."

—letter to John Holmes

A riverboat traveling on the Mississippi River at St. Louis

R Reading Strategies	C Critical Thinking	D Differentiated Instruction	W Writing Support	S Skill Practice
Teacher Edition • Reading Maps, p. 449 • Questioning, p. 450	**Teacher Edition** • Analyzing Information, p. 450	**Teacher Edition** • Verbal/Linguistic, p. 451	**Teacher Edition** • Expository Writing, p. 450	**Teacher Edition** • Using Geo. Skills, p. 449
Additional Resources • Guid. Read., URB p. 39 • Content Vocab., URB p. 17 • Academic Vocab., URB p. 19 • Read. Ess., p. 151	**Additional Resources** • Quizzes and Tests, p. 141 • Link. Past and Pres., URB p. 33	**Additional Resources** • School-to-Home, URB p. 35 • Reteaching Act., URB p. 37		**Additional Resources** • Daily Test Pract. Transp. 15-1 • Lesson Transparencies 15A and 15B • Geo. and Hist., URB p. 31

The Missouri Compromise

Main Idea The Missouri Compromise temporarily resolved the issue of whether new states would be slave states or free states.

History and You Do you feel loyalty to your school during a contest with another school? Read how differences between the North and the South created feelings of loyalty to a region.

Many settlers brought enslaved African Americans into Missouri with them. When Missouri applied for statehood, its constitution allowed slavery. The request sparked an angry debate in Congress. In 1819, 11 states permitted slavery and 11 did not. The Senate—with two members from each state—was, therefore, evenly balanced between slave and free states. The admission of a new state would upset that balance.

In addition, the North and the South, with their different economic systems, were competing for new lands in the western territories. At the same time, a growing number of Northerners wanted to restrict or ban slavery. Southerners, even those who disliked slavery,

opposed these antislavery efforts. They resented the interference by outsiders in Southerners' affairs. These differences between the North and the South grew into **sectionalism**—an exaggerated loyalty to a particular region of the country.

The Senate suggested a way to resolve the crisis—allow Missouri to join as a slave state and admit Maine at the same time as a free state. Maine, formerly part of Massachusetts, had also applied for statehood. The Senate wanted to settle the issue of slavery in the territories for good. It proposed banning slavery in the rest of the Louisiana Purchase north of 36°30′ N latitude.

Speaker of the House Henry Clay carefully guided the bill through the House of Representatives, which passed it by a close vote in 1820. Maine joined the union that year. In 1821 Missouri became the twenty-fourth state. The **Missouri Compromise** preserved the balance between slave and free states in the Senate. It also brought about a **temporary,** or brief, lull in the debate over slavery.

Reading Check **Explaining** Why was the admission of a new state controversial in 1819?

By the Numbers | The Missouri Compromise

The Vote The map shows how the House of Representatives voted on provisions in a law restricting slavery.

- For extending slavery
- Against extending slavery
- Tie vote

ATLANTIC OCEAN

Gulf of Mexico

0 200 kilometers
0 200 miles
Albers Equal-Area projection

Critical Thinking

Comparing Which region united in favor of extending slavery? Which region opposed extending slavery?

Teach

S Skill Practice

Using Geography Skills Have students look at the map of the United States in the atlas in the textbook and compare it with the map of slave and free states on this page. Ask them to explain why Missouri might become a battleground between pro- and antislavery activists. **OL**

R Reading Strategy

Reading Maps Ask: How does the map on this page provide an example of sectionalism? *(Sectionalism is an exaggerated loyalty to a particular region of the country. The map shows that states voted on a law restricting slavery strictly by region.)* **OL**

By the Numbers

Critical Thinking Answer The South united in favor; the North opposed it.

Reading Check Answer: It would upset the balance of power between slave and free states.

Hands-On Chapter Project
Step 1

Investigating Sectionalism

Step 1: Debating the Compromise of 1850 Small groups of students will debate the Compromise of 1850 in a Senate hearing.

Essential Question: Did the compromises that Congress made effectively address slavery and sectionalism?

Directions Organize students into five groups. Each group will represent one of the following: a free-soiler, Daniel Webster,

John C. Calhoun, a wealthy Southern plantation owner, and Stephen A. Douglas. Each group will research its assigned individual's point of view on the Compromise of 1850. One person will take the role of the group's assigned individual and present his views in a Senate hearing (to the class) on the proposed provisions of the compromise. Senators Webster, Calhoun, and Douglas will question the free-soiler and the Southern plantation owner about their views on

slavery and its expansion. Then each senator will give a brief two- or three-minute speech summing up his views.

Predicting Ask students to consider the different points of view expressed in the debate. **Ask:** What problems might occur in the nation in the near future? Tell students they will learn more about the failures of compromise in the next section. **OL**

(Chapter Project continued in Section 2)

New Territories and the Free-Soil Party

NATIONAL GEOGRAPHIC

New Territories and the Free-Soil Party

NATIONAL GEOGRAPHIC

W Writing Support

Expository Writing Assign a one- or two-page essay in which students explain why bitter regional divisions over slavery flared up once again in the 1840s. **OL**

C Critical Thinking

Analyzing Information Ask: Why did Southerners object to the Wilmot Proviso? *(because it would ban slavery in any lands acquired from Mexico, upsetting the balance of power between slave and free states)* **OL**

R Reading Strategy

Questioning Ask: Was John C. Calhoun antislavery or pro-slavery? How do you know? *(pro-slavery, because he suggested that Congress did not have the authority to regulate or ban slavery)* **BL**

Critical Thinking Answer

the debate over slavery in the territories gained from Mexico

Differentiated Instruction

A New Party Forms The acquisition of New Mexico and California brought the slavery issue into the open. Many Southern senators argued that Congress had no constitutional power to forbid slavery in the new territories. In 1848, a new party—the Free-Soil Party—formed. Free-Soilers supported the Wilmot Proviso, which banned the spread of slavery into the new territories gained from Mexico.

The Van Buren-Adams Free-Soil ticket received nearly 300,000 votes in 1848. Later the Republican Party would adopt many principles from the Free-Soil Party.

> "Gen. [Zachary] Taylor and Gen. [Lewis] Cass are proslavery candidates. Mr. Van Buren and Mr. Adams are antislavery candidates. The former are the shameless tools of the slave-power. The latter bravely resist it."
> —Gerrit Smith, New York abolitionist, August 1848

Critical Thinking

Finding the Main Idea What led to the formation of the Free-Soil Party?

A New Compromise

Main Idea The Compromise of 1850 addressed several issues, including slavery in the territories.

History and You Do you engage in some give and take in order to settle an argument? Read how Congress settled its differences in 1850.

. . . .

The debate over slavery in new territories erupted again in the 1840s. The annexation of Texas, where slavery already existed, became the main issue in the presidential election of 1844. Democrat James Polk won the election and pressed forward on acquiring Texas. Texas became a state in 1845. At the same time, support grew in the South for taking New Mexico and California from Mexico. Government actions led to war with Mexico.

Conflicting Views

Soon after the Mexican War began, Representative David Wilmot of Pennsylvania introduced a proposal. Called the Wilmot Proviso, it would ban slavery in any lands that might be acquired from Mexico.

Southerners protested. They believed that any antislavery policy about the territories endangered slavery everywhere. They wanted California and New Mexico to remain open to slavery. Senator John C. Calhoun of South Carolina countered with another proposal. It stated that neither Congress nor any territorial government had the authority to ban slavery from a territory or **regulate,** or control, it.

Neither proposal passed, but both caused bitter debate. By the 1848 presidential election, the United States had gained California and New Mexico from Mexico but took no action on slavery in those areas.

The Free-Soil Party

In 1848 the Whigs selected Zachary Taylor, a Southerner and a hero of the Mexican War, as their candidate. The Democrats chose Senator Lewis Cass of Michigan. Both candidates ignored the slavery issue.

North and South: Taking Sides on Slavery

Objective: To analyze the balance between Northern and Southern states over slavery

Focus: Ask students why the loyalty of Northerners and Southerners to their regions created problems.

Teach: Have students read the material and answer the questions.

Assess: Review any answers that are problematic.

Close: Ask students if compromise is effective in deciding political issues.

Differentiated Instruction Strategies

BL Have students use a drawing of an old-fashioned balance scale to illustrate the issues in this debate.

AL Have students discuss why compromise on this issue ultimately failed.

ELL Ask students to explain in their own words what "compromise" and "concession" mean.

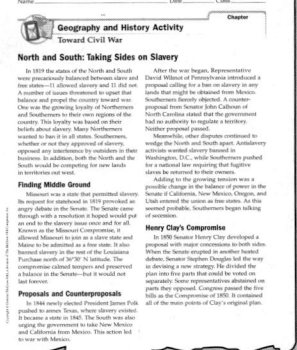

Geography and History Activity, URB p. 31

This failure to take a stand angered voters. Many opponents of slavery left their parties and formed the Free-Soil Party. Adopting the slogan "Free Soil, Free Speech, Free Labor, and Free Men," they chose former president Martin Van Buren as their candidate. Taylor won, but the Free-Soil Party gained several seats in Congress.

The Compromise of 1850

With the backing of President Taylor, California applied to become a free state in 1849. Meanwhile, antislavery forces wanted to ban slavery in Washington, D.C. Southerners, however, wanted a strong national law that required states to return **fugitive,** or runaway, enslaved people. The key issue, however, remained the balance of power in the Senate. If California entered as a free state, the slave-holding states would be outvoted in the Senate. Southerners talked about **seceding** from, or leaving, the Union.

In 1850 Senator Henry Clay tried to find a compromise. He proposed that California enter as a free state, while the rest of the new territories would have no limits on slavery. In addition, the slave trade, but not slavery itself, would be banned in Washington, D.C. Finally, Clay pushed for a stronger fugitive slave law.

A heated debate began in Congress. Senator Calhoun opposed Clay's plan. He felt that the Union could be saved only by protecting slavery. Senator Daniel Webster supported the plan. He reasoned that slavery had little chance in the new territories because the land was not suited to plantations.

When President Taylor—an opponent of Clay's plan—died unexpectedly, Vice President Millard Fillmore succeeded him and favored a compromise. To end the crisis, Illinois Senator **Stephen A. Douglas** divided Clay's plan into parts that could be voted on separately. Fillmore had several Whigs **abstain,** or not vote, on the parts they opposed. Congress finally passed five bills in 1850. Taken together, these laws became known as the **Compromise of 1850.**

✔ **Reading Check** **Explaining** Who formed the Free-Soil Party and why?

Section 1 Review

History ONLINE
Study Central™ To review this section, go to glencoe.com.

Vocabulary

1. Use each of the following terms in a sentence that clearly expresses its meaning: sectionalism, temporary, regulate, fugitive, secede, abstain.

Main Ideas

2. Describing How did the Missouri Compromise preserve the balance of power in the U.S. Senate?

3. Explaining How did Stephen Douglas help win approval of the Compromise of 1850?

Critical Thinking

4. Analyzing What was the Wilmot Proviso? Why was this amendment to a bill so controversial?

5. Comparing Describe what the North and South each gained from the Compromise of 1850. Use a diagram like the one below.

Compromise of 1850

North Gains: South Gains:

6. Creative Writing Write a dialogue in the form of a conversation in which John Calhoun and Daniel Webster express their views on the Compromise of 1850.

Answer the
7. Essential Question
Did the compromises that Congress made effectively address slavery and sectionalism?

Toward Civil War **Chapter 15** **451**

CHAPTER 15
Section 1

D **Differentiated Instruction**

Verbal/Linguistic Have students write more campaign slogans dealing with the formation and purpose of the Free-Soil Party and the election of 1848. **OL**

✔ **Reading Check** **Answer:** antislavery Democrats and Whigs because their parties refused to take a stand on slavery in the territories

Assess

History ONLINE

Study Central™ provides summaries, interactive games, and online graphic organizers to help students review content.

Close

Analyzing Discuss how the Missouri Compromise and the Compromise of 1850 settled the issue of slavery for a time. **OL**

Section ★ Review

Answers

1. Sentences should use vocabulary words according to their definitions in the section and Glossary.

2. by admitting two states at the same time, Missouri as a slave state and Maine as a free state

3. He divided Clay's plan into parts that members of Congress could vote on separately.

4. It was a proposal to ban slavery in any lands acquired from Mexico. Southerners had hoped to keep the California and New Mexico territories open to slavery.

5. North: California admitted as free state, slave trade banned in Washington, D.C.; **South:** no limits on slavery in New Mexico, slavery allowed in Washington, D.C., stronger fugitive slave law

6. The dialogue should address the disagreements between Calhoun and Webster over the Compromise of 1850, including why Calhoun opposed the plan and why Webster supported it.

7. Student answers will vary but should note that the compromises primarily dealt with immediate issues of admittance of new states and maintaining a balance in Congress. The compromises did not address slavery at a national level.

451

Focus

A Nation Dividing

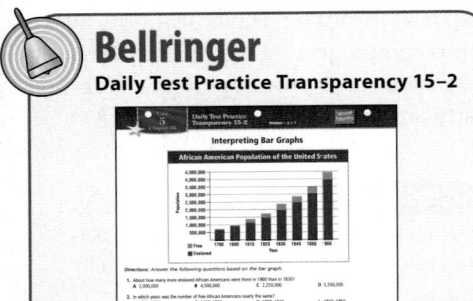

Bellringer
Daily Test Practice Transparency 15–2

Reading Guide
Answers to Graphic:

Antislavery: opposed; law repealed Missouri Compromise, which had established this territory as free **Pro-slavery:** supported; expected slavery supporters from Missouri to settle the territory and vote to keep slavery legal there

Section Spotlight Video

Have students watch the Section Spotlight Video "A Nation Dividing" to learn more about John Brown.

Resource Manager

Essential Question
How did popular sovereignty lead to violence in Kansas?

Reading Guide

Content Vocabulary
popular sovereignty (p. 454)　　civil war (p. 455)
border ruffians (p. 455)

Academic Vocabulary
network (p. 453)　　inevitable (p. 455)

Key People and Events
Fugitive Slave Act (p. 453)
Kansas-Nebraska Act (p. 454)
John Brown (p. 455)

Reading Strategy
Taking Notes Use a diagram like the one below to note reactions to the Kansas-Nebraska Act. Also, summarize the reasons for these reactions.

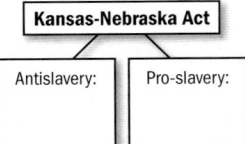

Kansas-Nebraska Act

Antislavery:　　Pro-slavery:

ILLINOIS STANDARDS
The American Journey

14.C.3 Compare historical issues involving rights, roles and status of individuals in relation to municipalities, states and the nation.

16.A Apply the skills of historical analysis and interpretation.

18.B.3a Analyze how individuals and groups interact with and within institutions (e.g., educational, military).

American Diary

On May 24, 1854, the people of Boston erupted in outrage. Federal officers had seized Anthony Burns, a runaway enslaved African American who lived in Boston, to return him to slavery. Abolitionists tried to rescue Burns from the federal courthouse, and city leaders attempted to buy his freedom. All efforts failed. Federal troops escorted Burns to a ship that would carry him back to Virginia and into slavery. In a gesture of bitter protest, Bostonians draped buildings in black and hung the American flag upside down.

The Underground Railroad by James Michael Newell

R Reading Strategies	C Critical Thinking	D Differentiated Instruction	W Writing Support	S Skill Practice
Teacher Edition • Predicting, p. 454 **Additional Resources** • Guid. Read., URB p. 40 • Content Vocab., URB p. 17 • Academic Vocab., URB p. 19 • Read. Ess., p. 154	**Additional Resources** • Quizzes and Tests, p. 142 • Crit. Think. Skills, URB p. 29	**Teacher Edition** • Interpersonal, p. 455 **Additional Resources** • School-to-Home, URB p. 35 • Reteaching Act., URB p. 37	**Teacher Edition** • Persuasive Writing, p. 453	**Teacher Edition** • Using Geo. Skills, p. 454 **Additional Resources** • Daily Test Pract. Transp. 15-2 • Lesson Transparencies 15A and 15B • Soc. Stud. Skills, URB p. 25

The Fugitive Slave Act

Main Idea The Fugitive Slave Act required all citizens to help catch runaways, yet many Northerners refused to cooperate.

History and You Have you ever tried to protect someone from a bully? Read how Northerners tried to thwart the efforts of slave hunters.

A̲s part of the Compromise of 1850, Senator Henry Clay of Kentucky convinced Congress to pass the **Fugitive Slave Act** as an attempt to pacify slaveholders. The Fugitive Slave Act of 1850 required all citizens to help catch runaways. Anyone who aided a fugitive could be fined or imprisoned. People in the South believed the law would force Northerners to recognize the rights of Southerners. Instead, enforcement of the law convinced more people in the North of the evils of slavery.

After the passage of the Fugitive Slave Act, slaveholders stepped up their efforts to catch runaway enslaved people. They even tried to capture runaways who had lived in freedom in the North for years. Sometimes they seized African Americans who were not trying to escape and forced them into slavery.

History ONLINE
Student Web Activity Visit glencoe.com and complete the Chapter 15 Web Activity about the Underground Railroad.

In spite of the penalties, some Northerners refused to cooperate with the law. They justified their opposition on moral grounds. In his 1849 essay "Civil Disobedience," Henry David Thoreau wrote that if the law "requires you to be the agent [cause] of injustice to another, then I say, break the law."

The Underground Railroad, a **network**, or interconnected system, of free African Americans and whites, helped runaways make their way to freedom. Antislavery groups tried to rescue African Americans who were being pursued or to free those who were captured. In Boston, members of one such group followed federal agents shouting, "Slave hunters—there go the slave hunters." People contributed funds to buy the freedom of African Americans. Northern juries refused to convict those accused of violating the Fugitive Slave Act.

✔ **Reading Check** **Explaining** What was the purpose of the Underground Railroad?

Primary Source / Reward Poster

A poster advertises a substantial reward for a runaway enslaved man.

$150 REWARD

RANAWAY from the subscriber, on the night of the 2d instant, a negro man, who calls himself Henry May, about 22 years old, 5 feet 6 or 8 inches high, ordinary color, rather chunky built, bushy head, and has it divided mostly on one side, and keeps it very nicely combed; has been raised in the house, and is a first rate dining-room servant, and was in a tavern in Louisville for 18 months. I expect he is now in Louisville trying to make his escape to a free state, (in all probability to Cincinnati, Ohio.) Perhaps he may try to get employment on a steamboat. He is a good cook, and in any capacity as a house servant. Had on when he left, a dark ... dark striped cassinett pantaloons, new—he had other ... and if taken in Louisville, 100 dollars if taken out ... State, and 150 dollars if taken out ... ... BURKE.

Critical Thinking

Making Inferences Under the Fugitive Slave Act of 1850, any citizen might be required to help capture a runaway slave. Why do you think some people condemned this law?

Teach

W **Writing Support**

Persuasive Writing Have students write a speech that might have been given by an abolitionist to protest the Fugitive Slave Act. **AL**

✔ **Reading Check** **Answer:** to help runaway enslaved African Americans make their way to freedom

Primary Source

Critical Thinking Answer
Answers may include that they opposed slavery and that they worried free African Americans would be captured and enslaved.

History ONLINE
Objectives and answers to the Student Web Activity can be found at glencoe.com under the Web Activity Lesson Plan for this chapter.

Hands-On Chapter Project
Step 2

Investigating Sectionalism

Step 2: Traveling the Underground Railroad Students will use maps of the Underground Railroad and primary source accounts to trace the experience of an enslaved person's escape to freedom.

Essential Question: How did popular sovereignty lead to violence in Kansas?

Directions Direct student groups to appropriate online materials to collect information about routes and stations on the Underground Railroad as well as accounts of slaves' escapes to freedom. Then have students create a large poster that includes a map showing the possible route and each stop of one person's escape from slavery. They should also incorporate an account of the trip into their poster, using primary sources and their own imaginations. When students have finished, have them present their work to the rest of the class.

Comparing and Contrasting Ask: Passage of which laws led to renewed antislavery activism in the North? *(passage of the Fugitive Slave Act and passage of the Kansas-Nebraska Act in 1854)* How did protests against these laws differ? *(The Underground Railroad network was peaceful; protests in Kansas involved violent confrontations.)* **OL**

(Chapter Project continued in Section 3)

453

Slavery and Sectionalism
NATIONAL GEOGRAPHIC

The Compromise of 1850

Kansas-Nebraska Act, 1854

Free states | Territory open to slaveholding
Slave states | Territory closed to slaveholding
Indian Territory

◀ Stephen Douglas sponsored the controversial Kansas-Nebraska Act.

Map Skills

Regions What territories were non-slaveholding in 1854?

Maps in Motion See StudentWorks™ Plus or glencoe.com.

The Kansas-Nebraska Act

Main Idea The Kansas-Nebraska Act resulted from another dispute over slavery in Congress.

History and You Do you recall how the Missouri Compromise limited slavery in the territories? Read how this agreement fell apart in the 1850s.

. . . .

Franklin Pierce, a New Hampshire Democrat, became president in 1853. Pierce intended to enforce the Fugitive Slave Act.

In 1854 Stephen A. Douglas, the Illinois senator who forged the Compromise of 1850, introduced a bill in Congress. He proposed organizing the region west of Missouri and Iowa as the territories of Kansas and Nebraska. Douglas hoped his plan to expand the nation would be acceptable to both the North and the South.

Because of their location, Kansas and Nebraska seemed likely to become free states. Both lay north of 36°30′N latitude, the line set in the Missouri Compromise as the limit of slavery. Douglas knew Southerners would object to admitting Kansas and Nebraska as

free states because it would give free states more votes in the Senate. As a result, Douglas proposed abandoning the Missouri Compromise and letting the settlers in each territory vote on whether to allow slavery. He called this **popular sovereignty**—allowing the people to decide.

Passage of the Act

Many Northerners protested. Douglas's plan to repeal the Missouri Compromise would allow slavery into areas that had been free for more than 30 years. Southerners in Congress, however, supported the bill. They expected Kansas to be settled mostly by slaveholders from Missouri who would vote to keep slavery legal. With some support from Northern Democrats and the backing of President Pierce, Congress passed the **Kansas-Nebraska Act** in 1854.

Conflict in Kansas

Right after the law passed, pro-slavery and antislavery groups rushed into Kansas. When elections took place, a pro-slavery legislature was elected.

454 Chapter 15 *Toward Civil War*

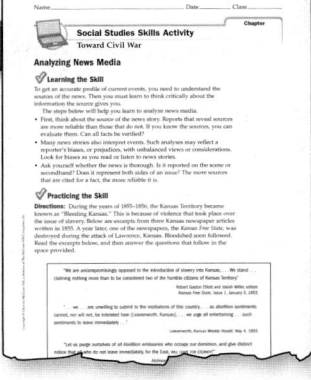

Although only about 1,500 voters lived in Kansas at the time, more than 6,000 people cast ballots. Thousands of pro-slavery supporters from Missouri crossed the border just to vote in the election. These Missourians traveled in armed groups and became known as **border ruffians.**

Soon, the new Kansas legislature passed laws supporting slavery. One law even restricted political office to pro-slavery candidates.

The antislavery people refused to accept these laws. Instead they armed themselves, held their own elections, and adopted a constitution that banned slavery. By January 1856, rival governments existed in Kansas—one for and one against slavery.

"Bleeding Kansas"

With both sides arming themselves, an outbreak of violence became **inevitable,** or unavoidable. In May 1856, 800 slavery supporters attacked the town of Lawrence, a stronghold of antislavery settlers. The attackers burned the Free State Hotel and destroyed two newspaper offices and many homes. Soon after, antislavery forces retaliated.

John Brown, a fervent abolitionist, believed God chose him to end slavery. The attack on Lawrence enraged Brown. He vowed to "strike terror in the hearts of the pro-slavery people." One night Brown led a group along Pottawatomie Creek, where they seized and killed five supporters of slavery. **D**

Armed bands soon roamed the territory. Newspapers referred to "Bleeding Kansas" and "the Civil War in Kansas." A **civil war** is a conflict between citizens of the same country. In October 1856 the territorial governor sent federal troops to stop the bloodshed.

Violence also broke out in Congress. Senator Charles Sumner of Massachusetts lashed out against pro-slavery forces in Kansas. He also criticized pro-slavery senators, such as Andrew P. Butler of South Carolina. Two days later, Butler's cousin, Representative Preston Brooks, walked into the Senate chamber and hit Sumner with a cane. Sumner fell to the floor, unconscious and bleeding. This incident and the Kansas feud revealed the rising hostility between North and South.

Reading Check **Explaining** What events led to "Bleeding Kansas"?

Section 2 Review

History ONLINE
Study Central™ To review this section, go to glencoe.com.

Vocabulary

1. Use each of these terms in a sentence that will help explain its meaning: network, popular sovereignty, border ruffians, inevitable, civil war.

Main Ideas

2. **Listing** What were some ways that Northerners defied the Fugitive Slave Act?

3. **Explaining** How would the issue of slavery in Kansas and Nebraska be decided under the Kansas-Nebraska Act?

Critical Thinking

4. **Contrasting** How did Southerners expect Northerners to react to the Fugitive Slave Act? How did Northerners actually react?

5. **Sequencing** Use a diagram like the one below to list the steps leading to bloodshed in Kansas.

6. **Persuasive Writing** Decide whether you would have been for or against the Kansas-Nebraska Act and the concept of popular sovereignty. Then write a newspaper editorial arguing your position.

Answer the
Essential Question

7. How did popular sovereignty lead to violence in Kansas?

Toward Civil War **Chapter 15** 455

CHAPTER 15
Section 2

D **Differentiated Instruction**

Interpersonal Organize students into pairs. Have one student write a pro-slavery editorial about the attack on Lawrence. Have the other student write an anti-slavery editorial on the same event. Have students exchange papers and discuss the differences. **OL**

Reading Check **Answer:** Pro-slavery and antislavery supporters rushed to Kansas, where a pro-slavery legislature was elected. Antislavery people set up a rival government, and both sides armed themselves.

Assess

History ONLINE

Study Central™ provides summaries, interactive games, and online graphic organizers to help students review content.

Close

Sequencing As a class, create an annotated time line showing the events discussed in this section beginning with the Fugitive Slave Act of 1850. **OL**

Section 2 Review

Answers

1. Sentences should use vocabulary words with their correct definitions.
2. ran the Underground Railroad; tried to rescue pursued or captured African Americans; gave funds to buy freedom; refused to convict law breakers
3. by popular sovereignty—the settlers would decide by voting

4. **Expected:** Northerners would recognize Southerners' rights; **Actual:** with anger, more convinced of evils of slavery, refused to cooperate
5. Kansas-Nebraska Act passed; supporters and opponents of slavery rushed to Kansas; voters from Missouri helped elect pro-slavery legislature in Kansas; legislature

passed pro-slavery laws; antislavery people set up rival government; both sides armed
6. Editorials should reflect an understanding of the concept of popular sovereignty and the effects it might have on the nation.
7. Outsiders corrupted the election, and fighting broke out over the results.

455

Challenges to Slavery

Focus

Bellringer
Daily Test Practice Transparency 15–3

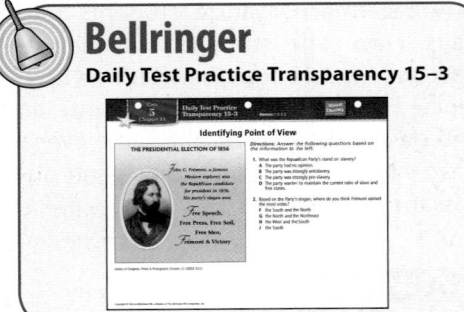

Reading Guide
Answers to Graphic:
Republican: John C. Frémont, free territories; **Democrat:** James Buchanan, popular sovereignty; **American Party:** Millard Fillmore, anti-immigrant; **Election Result:** Buchanan elected

Section Spotlight Video

Have students watch the Section Spotlight Video "Challenges to Slavery" to learn more about the *Dred Scott* decision.

Resource Manager

Essential Question
What was the significance of the *Dred Scott* decision?

Reading Guide

Content Vocabulary
arsenal (p. 461)   martyr (p. 461)

Academic Vocabulary
rigid (p. 458)   topic (p. 460)

Key People and Events
Republican Party (p. 457)
John C. Frémont (p. 457)
James Buchanan (p. 457)
Dred Scott (p. 458)
Abraham Lincoln (p. 460)

Reading Strategy
Taking Notes As you read, use a diagram like the one below to note each party's candidate and platform in the 1856 presidential election. Also record the election result.

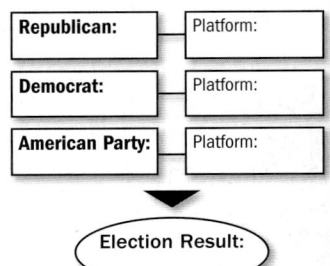

Republican:	Platform:
Democrat:	Platform:
American Party:	Platform:

Election Result:

ILLINOIS STANDARDS
The American Journey

14.C Understand election processes and responsibilities of citizens.

16.B.3c (US) Describe the way the Constitution has changed over time as a result of amendments and Supreme Court decisions.

18.B.3a Analyze how individuals and groups interact with and within institutions (e.g., educational, military).

17.D Understand the historical significance of geography.

American Diary

A few years after the attacks in Kansas, John Brown led a raid in Harpers Ferry, Virginia. Many people considered Brown and his followers to be ruthless murderers. The Fredericksburg Herald declared that, "shooting is a mercy they should be denied." Others viewed Brown as a freedom fighter. When Brown was executed in 1859, writer Henry David Thoreau wrote, "He is not Old Brown any longer, [but] an angel of light."

—quoted in "John Brown at Harpers Ferry" and from Thoreau's "A Plea for Capt. John Brown"

John Brown leaving Charleston jail on his way to his execution

Reading Strategies	**Critical Thinking**	**Differentiated Instruction**	**Writing Support**	**Skill Practice**
Teacher Edition • Identifying, p. 458 • Paraphrasing, p. 461 **Additional Resources** • Guid. Read., URB p. 41 • Content Vocab., URB p. 17 • Academic Vocab., URB p. 19 • Read. Ess., p. 157 • Pri. Source Read., URB p. 21	**Teacher Edition** • Det. Cause and Effect, p. 457 **Additional Resources** • Quizzes and Tests, p. 143	**Teacher Edition** • English Language Learners, p. 460 • Below Grade Level, p. 461 **Additional Resources** • School-to-Home, URB p. 35 • Reteaching Act., URB p. 37	**Teacher Edition** • Personal Writing, p. 459 • Narrative Writing, p. 460 **Additional Resources** • Differ. Inst., URB p. 27	**Teacher Edition** • Visual Literacy, p. 457 • Using Geo. Skills, p. 458 **Additional Resources** • Daily Test Pract. Transp. 15-3 • Lesson Transparency 15B • Time Line Skills, URB p. 34

A New Political Party

Main Idea Opponents of slavery from different political parties came together to form the new Republican Party.

History and You Which of today's political issues is most important to your family? Read to learn how the parties stood on key issues of the 1854 and 1856 elections.

• •

Even before Brown's raid, other events drove the North and South further apart. After the Kansas-Nebraska Act, the Democratic Party began to divide along sectional lines, with Northern Democrats leaving the party. Differing views over the slavery issue destroyed the Whig Party.

The Election of 1854

In 1854 additional antislavery Whigs and Democrats joined forces with Free-Soilers to form the **Republican Party.** The Republicans challenged the pro-slavery Whigs and Democrats, choosing candidates to run in the state and congressional elections of 1854. Their main message was that the government should ban slavery from new territories. The

Republican Party quickly showed its strength in the North. In the election, the Republicans won control of the House of Representatives and of several state governments. In the South, the Republican Party had almost no support.

Almost three-fourths of the Democratic candidates from free states lost in 1854. The Democrats were increasingly becoming a Southern party.

The Election of 1856

Democrats and Republicans met again in the presidential election of 1856. The Whig Party, disintegrating over the slavery issue, did not offer a candidate of its own.

The Republicans chose **John C. Frémont** of California as their candidate for president. Frémont gained fame as an explorer in the West. The party platform called for free territories, and its campaign slogan became "Free soil, Free speech, and Frémont."

The Democratic Party nominated **James Buchanan** of Pennsylvania, an experienced diplomat and former member of Congress. Buchanan wanted to appease the South in order to save the Union. As a result, the party endorsed the idea of popular sovereignty.

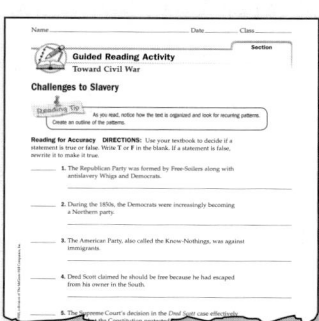

Primary Source | Hero or Villain?

Views of John Brown Some Northerners regarded John Brown as a hero. In a letter to Brown, a free African American in Indiana wrote: "I thank you that you have been brave enough to reach out your hands to the crushed and blighted of my race." A Southern newspaper, however, wrote: "The miserable old traitor and murderer belongs to the gallows, and the gallows will have its own."

Critical Thinking

Evaluating In what ways might a Northerner and a Southerner view John Brown's actions differently?

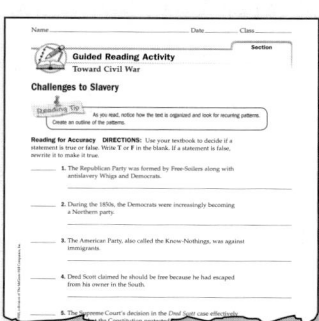

Teach

• •

S Skill Practice

Visual Literacy Ask: Which of the images on this page likely appeared in a Southern publication? Which in a Northern publication? (South: the cartoon of Brown looking like a madman; North: the image of Brown kissing an African American child) **OL**

C Critical Thinking

Determining Cause and Effect Ask: Why was the Republican Party formed? (to bring together those who opposed slavery's spread to the territories) **OL**

This **READING SKILL** (Determining Cause and Effect) was introduced in this unit.

Primary Source

Critical Thinking Answer
A Northerner might have thought Brown's actions were heroic, but a Southerner would view him as a criminal.

Differentiated Instruction

Leveled Activities

S Skill Practice

Using Geography Skills Refer students to the map on this page. **Ask:** In which part of the country did people seem more committed to sectional interests above all else? How do you know? *(in the South, because some Northern states voted for the Democratic candidate, but no Southern state voted for the Republican one)* **OL**

R Reading Strategy

Identifying Ask: Who was Dred Scott? *(an enslaved African American who was moved by his master into territories where slavery was outlawed and who later sued for his freedom)* **BL**

The Election of 1856 NATIONAL GEOGRAPHIC

Map Skills Answer

the Northeast; Pennsylvania and New Jersey

Map Skills Practice

Place In which state were voters most concerned about immigration and Catholicism? *(Maryland)* **OL**

Reading Check **Answer:** the Democratic Party

Hands-On Chapter Project
Step 3

Investigating Sectionalism

Step 3: Create a Political Protest Students will work in groups to create items meant to be used to protest the *Dred Scott* decision.

Essential Question: What was the significance of the *Dred Scott* decision?

The Election of 1856 NATIONAL GEOGRAPHIC

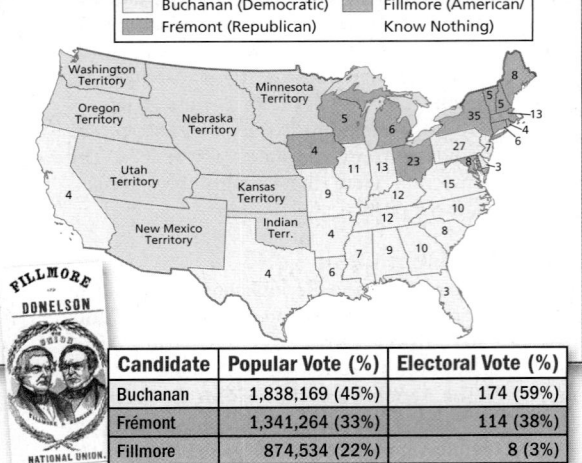

Candidate	Popular Vote (%)	Electoral Vote (%)
Buchanan	1,838,169 (45%)	174 (59%)
Frémont	1,341,264 (33%)	114 (38%)
Fillmore	874,534 (22%)	8 (3%)

Legend: Buchanan (Democratic), Frémont (Republican), Fillmore (American/Know Nothing)

▲ Third-party candidate Fillmore appealed to voters concerned about immigration and Catholicism.

Democrats stressed that Buchanan was the candidate of conciliation and stability and believed that a Frémont victory would lead to civil war. ▶

Northern States for Buchanan The presidential election of 1856 was decided in the swing states of Pennsylvania, Illinois, and Indiana. Democratic candidate James Buchanan won all three. Only 1,200 of Republican John Frémont's 1.34 million popular votes came from slaveholding states.

The Republican ticket of John C. Frémont and William L. Dayton opposed slavery's expansion into the territories. ▶

Map Skills

Regions In which region was Frémont most successful? Which states in that area did he not win?

Maps In Motion See StudentWorks™ Plus or glencoe.com.

The American Party, or Know Nothings, grew quickly between 1853 and 1856 by attacking immigrants. The Know Nothings nominated former president Millard Fillmore. Most of the Northern delegates, however, walked out of the convention when the party refused to call for the repeal of the Kansas-Nebraska Act.

S The presidential vote divided along **rigid**—firm and inflexible—sectional lines. Buchanan won the election. He took all Southern states except Maryland and received 174 electoral votes compared to 114 for Frémont and 8 for Fillmore. Frémont did not receive a single electoral vote south of the Mason-Dixon line, but he carried 11 of the 16 free states.

Reading Check **Identifying** Which political party was emerging as the party of the South in the 1854 and 1856 elections?

The *Dred Scott* Case

Main Idea The Supreme Court's decision in the *Dred Scott* case dealt a severe blow to antislavery forces and further divided the country.

History and You How would you feel if the Supreme Court decided that you were "property"? Read to find out how the decision in the *Dred Scott* case shocked the nation.

Dred Scott was an enslaved African American bought by an army doctor in Missouri, a slave state. In the 1830s, the doctor moved his household to Illinois, a free state, and then to **R** the Wisconsin Territory, where slavery was banned by the Northwest Ordinance of 1787. Later the family returned to Missouri, where the doctor died. In 1846, with the help of antislavery lawyers, Scott sued for his freedom.

Directions Have students work together to create an antislavery campaign meant to protest the *Dred Scott* decision. Each group should produce at least three items that might be used by an antislavery group. For example, a group might write a speech to be given by an abolitionist to church groups, create a flyer to be handed out on street corners, and lay out a newspaper advertisement. Encourage students to use their imaginations. When students have finished, display the materials in the classroom.

Analyzing Information Discuss the *Dred Scott* decision. **Ask:** Why would the Court's reasoning outrage antislavery activists? *(because it meant that slavery could not be outlawed anywhere)* **OL**

(Chapter Project continued in Section 4)

Scott claimed he should be free because he once lived in areas of the North where slavery was prohibited.

Eleven years later, as anger grew over the slavery issue, the case reached the Supreme Court. The case attracted enormous attention across the country. While the immediate issue was Dred Scott's status, the Court also had the opportunity to rule on the question of slavery in the territories.

The Court's Decision

The Court's decision electrified the nation. Chief Justice Roger B. Taney (TAW•nee) said that Dred Scott was still an enslaved person. As such, Scott was not a citizen and had no right to bring a lawsuit. Taney continued on, addressing broader issues.

Taney wrote that Scott's residence on free soil did not make him free. An enslaved person was property, and the Fifth Amendment prohibits Congress from taking away property without "due process of law."

Finally, Taney wrote that Congress had no power to prohibit slavery in any territory. The Missouri Compromise—which banned slavery north of 36°30'N latitude—was unconstitutional. For that matter, so was popular sovereignty. Not even the voters in a territory could prohibit slavery because that would amount to taking away a person's property. In effect, the decision meant that the Constitution protected slavery.

Reaction to the Decision

Rather than settling the issue, the decision divided the country even more. The Court upheld what many in the South had always maintained: Nothing could legally stop the spread of slavery. The Republicans' main issue—limiting the spread of slavery—was ruled unconstitutional.

Republicans and other antislavery groups were outraged. They called the *Dred Scott* decision "a wicked and false judgment" and "the greatest crime" ever committed in the nation's courts.

W

✓ **Reading Check** **Applying** Based on the *Dred Scott* decision, could voters ban slavery? Explain.

W Writing Support

Personal Writing Have students write a one- or two-page personal response paper to the Court's findings in the *Dred Scott* decision. Ask them to include their thoughts about the case's effect on the nation and on the slaveholding controversy. **OL**

✓ **Reading Check** **Answer:** no, because that would amount to taking someone's property, which was unconstitutional

Primary Source

Critical Thinking Answer
The decision would have increased sectional tensions in the country, because it upset the balance of power between the North and South in favor of the South and slavery.

Primary Source | The *Dred Scott* Decision

A Controversial Ruling In his ruling in the *Dred Scott* case, Chief Justice Roger B. Taney declared the Missouri Compromise unconstitutional because it deprived slaveholders of their property without due process or compensation. Southerners praised the decision, which opened all U.S. territory to slavery.

Supreme Court Chief Justice Roger B. Taney ▶

◀ Newspaper announcing the *Dred Scott* decision

▲ The Old Courthouse in St. Louis where the *Dred Scott* case was heard

"They [African Americans] had for more than a century before been regarded as beings of an inferior order and altogether unfit to associate with the white race . . . and so far inferior that they had no rights which the white man was bound to respect. . . . No one . . . should induce the Court to give to the words of the Constitution a more liberal construction in their favor than they were intended to bear when the instrument was framed and adopted."
—Roger Taney, *Scott* v. *Sandford* decision, March 1857

Critical Thinking
Assessing How do you think the *Dred Scott* decision affected sectional tensions in the country?

Differentiated Instruction

Debate and Division

Objective:	To use information from the time line to answer the related questions
Focus:	Review with students why the 1850s were a critical decade for the slavery issue.
Teach:	Have students review the time line and answer the questions.
Assess:	Ask for volunteers to read their answers to the class.
Close:	Discuss answers that were problematic.

Time Line Skills Activity,
URB p. 34

Time Line Activity
Toward Civil War

Debate and Division (1850–1859)

Differentiated Instruction Strategies

BL Remind students that they can use their textbooks for this activity.

AL Have students debate which time-line event had the most important effect on the slavery issue.

ELL Have students select a time-line event and explain, in their own words, what happened.

Primary Source / The Raid on Harpers Ferry

A Raid to Fight Slavery John Brown gained notoriety fighting against pro-slavery forces in Kansas in the mid-1850s. Financed by wealthy abolitionists, Brown led a raid in 1859 to capture the federal arsenal at Harpers Ferry, Virginia. Brown hoped to use the weapons at the arsenal to spark an uprising by enslaved people in Virginia.

John Brown and his men barricaded themselves in this brick engine house to fight off attacks from federal troops. ▼

"Now if . . . I should forfeit my life for the furtherance of the ends of justice and MINGLE MY BLOOD . . . with the blood of millions in this slave country whose rights are disregarded by wicked, cruel, and unjust enactments—I submit; so LET IT BE DONE."
—John Brown's statement to the Virginia Court

▲ Federal troops commanded by Colonel Robert E. Lee crushed Brown's raid. More than half of Brown's force, including two of his sons, died in the fighting. Brown and his surviving men were captured and Brown was later hanged.

Critical Thinking

Drawing Conclusions Was the raid on Harpers Ferry a success for abolitionists? Why or why not?

Lincoln and Douglas

Main Idea The Lincoln-Douglas debates placed the little-known Lincoln into the national spotlight.

History and You Do you like to root for the underdog? Read how Abraham Lincoln skillfully debated against the powerful Stephen Douglas.

In the congressional election of 1858, the Senate race in Illinois was the center of national attention. The contest pitted the current senator, Democrat Stephen A. Douglas, against Republican challenger **Abraham Lincoln.** People considered Douglas a likely candidate for president in 1860. Lincoln was nearly an unknown.

Douglas, a successful lawyer, joined the Democratic Party and won election to the House in 1842 and to the Senate in 1846. Short, stocky, and powerful, Douglas was called "the Little Giant." He disliked slavery but thought that the controversy over it would interfere with the nation's growth. He believed the issue could be resolved through popular sovereignty.

Born in the poor backcountry of Kentucky, Abraham Lincoln moved to Indiana as a child, and later to Illinois. Like Douglas, Lincoln was intelligent, ambitious, and a successful lawyer. He had little formal education—but excellent political skills. He had served in the Illinois legislature and in the U.S. House of Representatives. Lincoln saw slavery as morally wrong but admitted there was no easy way to end slavery where it existed. He was certain, though, that slavery should not be allowed to spread.

The Lincoln-Douglas Debates

Not as well-known as Douglas, Lincoln challenged the senator to a series of debates. Douglas reluctantly agreed. The two met seven times in August, September, and October of 1858 in cities and villages throughout Illinois. Thousands came to these debates. The main **topic,** or subject of discussion, was slavery.

Activity: Collaborative Learning

The Lincoln-Douglas Debates Have students form groups of three. Direct each group to appropriate online sources for transcripts of the Lincoln-Douglas debates. Each group should then choose one debate to read and analyze. **Ask:** What are the values of each candidate? How are the candidates' values similar and different? Have students discuss the content of their debate using these questions as a starting point. Then have students work together to outline and write a short essay comparing and contrasting the values, views, and policy recommendations of Lincoln and Douglas. Students should identify the strengths and weaknesses in each candidate's argument. **AL**

During the debate at Freeport, Lincoln pressed Douglas about his views on popular sovereignty. Could the people of a territory legally exclude slavery before becoming a state? Douglas replied that the people could exclude slavery by refusing to pass laws protecting slaveholders' rights. Douglas's response, which satisfied antislavery followers but lost him support in the South, became known as the Freeport Doctrine.

Douglas claimed that Lincoln wanted African Americans to be fully equal to whites. Lincoln denied this. Still, Lincoln said, "in the right to eat the bread . . . which his own hand earns, [an African American] is my equal and the equal of [Senator] Douglas, and the equal of every living man." The real issue, Lincoln said, is "between the men who think slavery a wrong and those who do not think it wrong. The Republican Party think it wrong."

Following the debates, Douglas won a narrow victory in the election. Lincoln lost the election but did not come away empty-handed. He gained a national reputation as a man of clear thinking who could argue with force and persuasion.

The Raid on Harpers Ferry

After the 1858 election, Southerners felt threatened by Republicans. In late 1859, an act of violence added to their fears. On October 16 the abolitionist John Brown led a group on a raid on Harpers Ferry, Virginia. His target was an **arsenal,** a storage site for weapons. Brown hoped to arm enslaved African Americans and start a revolt against slaveholders. Abolitionists had paid for the raid.

Brown's raid was defeated by local citizens and federal troops. Convicted of treason and murder, Brown was sentenced to hang. His execution shook the North. Some antislavery Northerners denounced Brown's use of violence. Others saw Brown as a **martyr**—a person who dies for a great cause.

John Brown's death rallied abolitionists. When Southerners learned of Brown's abolitionist ties, their fears of a great Northern conspiracy against them seemed to be confirmed. The nation was on the brink of disaster.

✓ **Reading Check** Identifying Why did John Brown raid the arsenal at Harpers Ferry?

Section 3 Review

History ONLINE
Study Central™ To review this section, go to glencoe.com.

Vocabulary

1. Define each of the following terms, and use each in a sentence: rigid, topic, arsenal, martyr.

Main Ideas

2. **Specifying** What issue led to the formation of the Republican Party, and what stand did the new party take on that issue?

3. **Explaining** What reasons did Taney give for Dred Scott's status as an enslaved person?

4. **Identifying** How did the Lincoln-Douglas debates benefit Lincoln?

Critical Thinking

5. **Identifying Points of View** Use a diagram like the one below to compare the views of Lincoln and Douglas on the issue of slavery.

6. **Making Inferences** Why do you think the raid on Harpers Ferry by a mere 18 men seemed so threatening to Southerners?

7. **Persuasive Writing** Write a rebuttal, or response, to Roger B. Taney on the *Dred Scott* decision. Address the points he made in his remarks on the Court's decision.

Answer the Essential Question

8. What was the significance of the *Dred Scott* decision?

Toward Civil War **Chapter 15** 461

CHAPTER 15
Section 3

D Differentiated Instruction

Below Grade Level Have students use each of the following words in a sentence that correctly expresses its meaning: "abolitionist," "arsenal," and "martyr." **BL**

R Reading Strategy

Paraphrasing Have students read John Brown's words in the Primary Source feature on the previous page and paraphrase the statement in one sentence. **ELL**

✓ Reading Check **Answer:** to take arms to give to enslaved African Americans and start a rebellion against slaveholders

Assess

. . . .

History ONLINE

Study Central™ provides summaries, interactive games, and online graphic organizers to help students review content.

Close

. . . .

Determining Importance As a class, discuss the significance of the *Dred Scott* decision. **OL**

Section 3 Review

Answers

1. Sentences should use vocabulary words according to their definitions.
2. Slavery in the territories; the Republicans opposed it.
3. Scott was not a citizen and had no right to bring a lawsuit; an enslaved person is property, and property may not be taken away without due process of law.
4. By skillfully debating the more prominent Douglas, Lincoln gained a national reputation.

5. **Douglas:** disliked slavery, issue could be resolved through popular sovereignty, people could exclude slavery by refusing to protect slaveholders' rights; **Lincoln:** believed slavery was morally wrong, no easy way to eliminate it where it already existed but should not be allowed to spread, African Americans have equal right to enjoy benefits of their work
6. Possible response: It was backed by abolitionists, making it seem like part of a

larger conspiracy against the South. Also, the prospect of guns in the hands of thousands of enslaved persons probably terrified Southern whites.
7. Rebuttals should address the assertion that enslaved people are property and therefore have no rights.
8. It meant that the Constitution protected slavery—neither Congress nor voters could ban slavery and earlier compromises were meaningless.

Focus

Bellringer
Daily Test Practice Transparency 15-4

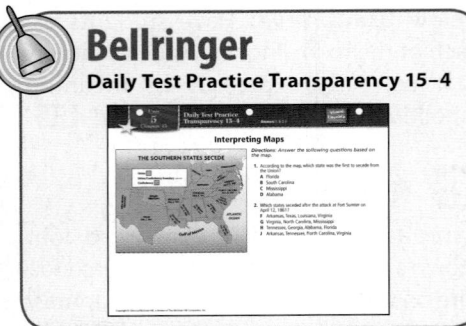

Reading Guide
Answers to Graphic:
Nov. 1860: Lincoln elected president; **Dec. 1860:** S.C. secedes; **Feb. 1861:** Confederacy formed; **March 1861:** Lincoln's Inaugural Address; **April 1861:** attack on Fort Sumter begins Civil War

Section Spotlight Video

Have students watch the Section Spotlight Video "Secession and War" to learn more about the Confederacy.

Resource Manager

Essential Question

What role did the theory of states' rights play in the outbreak of the Civil War?

Reading Guide

Content Vocabulary
secession (p. 463)   states' rights (p. 464)

Academic Vocabulary
reject (p. 464)   justify (p. 464)

Key People and Events
John Crittenden (p. 463)
Confederate States of America (p. 464)
Jefferson Davis (p. 464)
Fort Sumter (p. 466)

Reading Strategy
Taking Notes As you read, list the major events on a time line like the one below.

| Nov. 1860 | Feb. 1861 | April 1861 |

| Dec. 1860 | March 1861 |

ILLINOIS STANDARDS
The American Journey

16.A Apply the skills of historical analysis and interpretation.
16.A.3c Identify the differences between historical fact and interpretation.
17.C Understand relationships between geographic factors and society.
17.D Understand the historical significance of geography.

462

Secession and War

American Diary

The events at Harpers Ferry inflamed slaveholders. In 1859 the Charleston Mercury declared "The day of compromise is passed. . . . There is no peace for the South in the Union." Republicans argued that the South leaving the Union was a tactic to frighten voters from casting their ballots for Abraham Lincoln. To many Southerners, however, Lincoln's election would signal that their position in the Union was hopeless.

—from the Charleston Mercury

The Wigwam in Chicago was the site of the 1860 Republican Convention.

R Reading Strategies	**C** Critical Thinking	**D** Differentiated Instruction	**W** Writing Support	**S** Skill Practice
Teacher Edition • Identifying, p. 463 • Summarizing, p. 464 **Additional Resources** • Guid. Read., URB p. 42 • Content Vocab., URB p. 17 • Academic Vocab., URB p. 19 • Read. Ess., p. 160	**Teacher Edition** • Analyz. Information, p. 466 **Additional Resources** • Quizzes and Tests, p. 144 • Authentic Assess., p. 15	**Teacher Edition** • Visual/Spatial, p. 464 • Logical/Mathematical, p. 465 **Additional Resources** • School-to-Home, URB p. 35 • Reteaching Act., URB p. 37	**Teacher Edition** • Persuasive Writing, p. 463 **Additional Resources** • Writ. Skills, URB p. 23	**Teacher Edition** • Visual Literacy, p. 464 • Using Geo. Skills, p. 465 **Additional Resources** • Daily Test Pract. Transp. 15-4 • Lesson Transparency 15C

Secession

Main Idea Fearing that President Lincoln would not protect Southern rights, first South Carolina and then other states voted to leave the Union.

History and You Have you ever been so angry that you needed to leave a room? Read to learn about the South's decision to secede.

Would the Union break up? That was the burning question as the presidential election of November 1860 approached.

The Election of 1860

The issue of slavery split the Democratic Party. The northern Democrats nominated Stephen Douglas. They supported popular sovereignty. Southern Democrats vowed to uphold slavery. Their candidate was John C. Breckinridge. Moderates from the North and the South who formed the Constitutional Union Party chose John Bell. This party took no position on slavery.

The Republicans nominated Abraham Lincoln. Their platform was that slavery should be left undisturbed where it existed, but that it should be excluded from the territories. **[W]**

Many Southerners feared, however, that a Republican victory would encourage slave revolts.

With the Democrats divided, Lincoln won a clear majority of the electoral votes. The vote was along purely sectional lines. Lincoln's name did not even appear on the ballot in most Southern states, but he won every Northern state. In effect, the more populous North outvoted the South.

Attempt at Compromise

The Republicans promised not to disturb slavery where it already existed. Many Southerners, though, did not trust the Republican Party to protect their rights. On December 20, 1860, South Carolina voted to secede from the Union. **[R]**

As other Southern states debated the question of **secession,** or withdrawal from the Union, leaders in Congress worked frantically to fashion a compromise. Senator **John Crittenden** of Kentucky proposed a series of amendments to the Constitution. Central to his plan was a provision to protect slavery south of 36°30′N latitude—the line set by the Missouri Compromise—in all territories "now held or hereafter acquired."

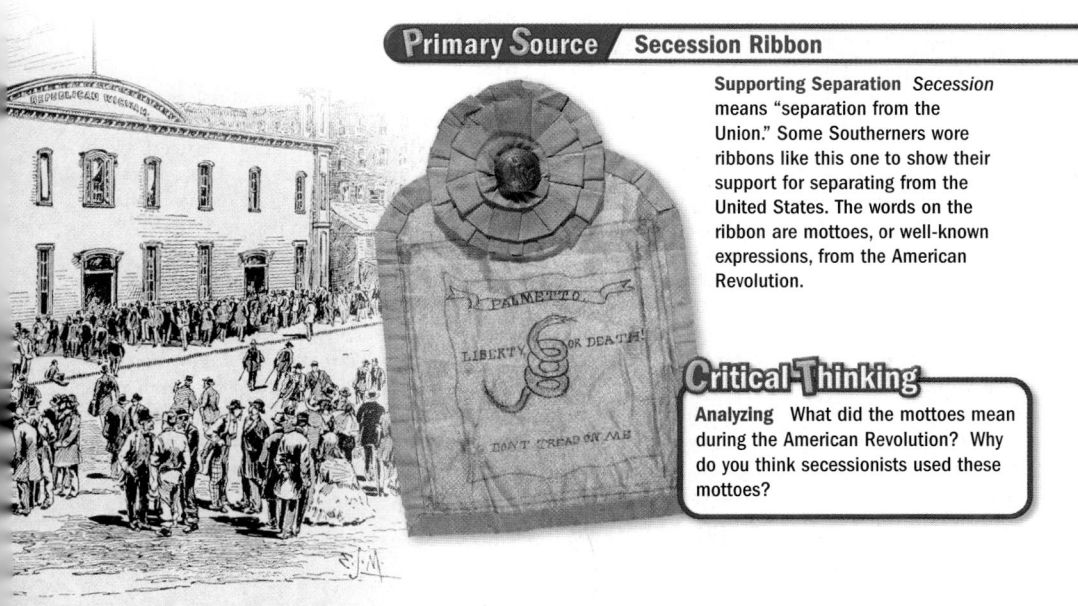

Primary Source | **Secession Ribbon**

Supporting Separation *Secession* means "separation from the Union." Some Southerners wore ribbons like this one to show their support for separating from the United States. The words on the ribbon are mottoes, or well-known expressions, from the American Revolution.

PALMETTO

LIBERTY OR DEATH

DON'T TREAD ON ME

Critical Thinking

Analyzing What did the mottoes mean during the American Revolution? Why do you think secessionists used these mottoes?

463

S Skill Practice

Visual Literacy Have students read the first paragraph and then look at the cartoon on this page. **Ask:** What does the cartoonist believe the effects of Southern secession will be on the Union? Explain your answer. *(The Union is shown as a strong tree; cutting off a branch will have little effect on it.)* **OL**

R Reading Strategy

Summarizing Have students summarize in one or two sentences the reasoning Southern states used to justify secession. **ELL**

D Differentiated Instruction

Visual/Spatial Have each student create a political cartoon that expresses his or her view on the secession crisis. **OL**

INTERPRETING POLITICAL CARTOONS

Answers

1. states that are seceding
2. angry, spiteful
3. Secession will hurt the states that secede far more than it will hurt the Union.

Differentiated Instruction

Primary Sources
INTERPRETING POLITICAL CARTOONS

This cartoon was created in 1861, just before the outbreak of the Civil War. Secession was breaking up the United States.

1. **Interpreting** What do the men in the cartoon represent?
2. **Analyzing** Look at each person's expression. How would you describe their expressions?
3. **Identifying Points of View** What does the cartoonist think will result from the men's action?

SECESSIONISTS LEAVING THE UNION

Republicans **rejected,** or refused to accept, this provision. They had just won an election on the principle that slavery would not be extended in any territories. "Now we are told . . ." Lincoln wrote, "the government shall be broken up unless we surrender to those we have beaten." Leaders in the South also rejected the plan. "We spit upon every plan to compromise," exclaimed one Southern leader. "No human power can save the Union," wrote another.

The Confederacy

By February 1861, Texas, Louisiana, Mississippi, Alabama, Florida, and Georgia joined South Carolina and also seceded. On February 4, delegates from these states and South Carolina met to form a new nation. Calling themselves the **Confederate States of America,** they chose **Jefferson Davis** as their president.

Southerners **justified,** or found reasons to support, secession with the theory of **states' rights.** The states, they argued, had voluntarily chosen to enter the Union. They defined the Constitution as a contract among the independent states. They believed the national government violated that contract by refusing to enforce the Fugitive Slave Act and by denying the Southern states equal rights in the territories. As a result, they argued, the states had a right to leave the Union.

Reactions to Secession

Many Southerners welcomed secession, ringing church bells and celebrating in the streets. Other Southerners, however, were alarmed. Virginian Robert E. Lee expressed concern about the future. "I only see that a fearful calamity is upon us," he wrote.

In the North, some abolitionists preferred to allow the Southern states to leave. If the Union could be kept together only by compromising on slavery, they declared, then let the Union be destroyed. Most Northerners, however, believed that the Union must be preserved. For Lincoln the issue was "whether in a free government the minority have the right to break up the government whenever they choose."

464 **Chapter 15** *Toward Civil War*

Identifying Facts and Opinions

Objective: To learn how to differentiate between facts and opinions

Focus: Ask students how they identify facts and opinions in their daily lives.

Teach: Have students read the background information, practice the skill, and then apply the skill.

Assess: Ask students to use the self-assessment checklist.

Close: Discuss why it is important to consider arguments that may oppose your position.

Differentiated Instruction Strategies

BL To practice, have students underline words that indicate the statement is an opinion rather than a fact.

AL Have students stage a verbal debate on their topics.

ELL Ask students to define "position," "support," and "downplay," and write a sentence using each word.

Writing Skills Activity, URB p. 23

Lincoln Takes Office

Lincoln had won the election, but he was not yet president. James Buchanan's term ran until March 4, 1861. In December 1860, Buchanan sent a message to Congress saying that the Southern states had no right to secede from the Union. Then he added that he had no power to stop them from doing so.

As Lincoln prepared for his inauguration on March 4, 1861, people throughout the United States wondered what he would say and do. They wondered, too, what would happen in Virginia, North Carolina, Kentucky, Tennessee, Missouri, and Arkansas. These slave states chose to remain in the Union, but the decision was not final. If the United States used force against the Confederate States of America, the remaining slave states also might secede.

In his Inaugural Address, Lincoln spoke to the seceding states directly, mixing tough-ness with words of peace. He said that secession would not be permitted, that "the Union of these States is perpetual [forever]." He vowed to hold federal property in the South, including a number of forts and military installations, and to enforce the laws of the United States. At the same time, Lincoln pleaded with the South:

PRIMARY SOURCE

"In your hands, my dissatisfied fellow countrymen, and not in mine, are the momentous issues of *civil war*. The Government will not assail you. You can have no conflict without being yourselves the aggressors. . . . We are not *enemies*, but *friends*. We must not be enemies. Though passion may have strained, it must not break our bonds of affection."

—Abraham Lincoln, on reconciliation

Reading Check **Explaining** What was John Crittenden's proposal to save the Union?

Seceding States, 1860–1861   NATIONAL GEOGRAPHIC

West Virginia separated from Virginia in 1861 and was admitted to the Union in 1863.

Jefferson Davis ▶

On February 4, 1861, delegates met in Alabama to form a new nation.

South Carolina was the first state to secede from the Union.

0   600 kilometers
0   600 miles
Lambert Azimuthal Equal-Area projection

Union territories
Union free state
Union slave state
Slave state seceding before siege of Ft. Sumter, April 1861
Slave state seceding after siege of Ft. Sumter, April 1861
Boundary between Union & Confederacy

Map Skills
1. **Regions** Which states seceded before the attack on Fort Sumter?
2. **Regions** Which states did not secede until after the attack on Fort Sumter?

Maps In Motion See StudentWorks™ Plus or glencoe.com.

CHAPTER 15
Section 4

D Differentiated Instruction

Logical/Mathematical Ask: How much time passed between Lincoln's inauguration and the formation of the Confederacy? *(about $3\frac{1}{2}$ months)* How did the Union deal with the crisis during that time? *(Buchanan said he could do nothing about it.)* **OL**

S Skill Practice

Using Geography Skills Have students examine the map on this page. **Ask:** In relation to the rest of the Confederate states, where were the states that waited to secede until after the attack on Fort Sumter? *(farther north)* Why do you think these states waited to secede? *(Possible answer: Those states' economies might be less dependent on slave labor and therefore less invested in protecting slavery.)* **OL**

Seceding States, 1860–1861   NATIONAL GEOGRAPHIC

Map Skills Answers
1. Texas, Louisiana, Mississippi, Alabama, Georgia, Florida, South Carolina
2. Virginia, North Carolina, Tennessee, Arkansas

Hands-On Chapter Project
Step 4

Investigating Sectionalism

Step 4: Writing Newspaper Articles Students will work together to write two articles reporting on Lincoln's inauguration.

Essential Question: What role did the theory of states' rights play in the outbreak of the Civil War?

Directions Have students form their original groups. They will write two newspaper articles reporting on the inauguration of President Lincoln—one for an Atlanta newspaper and one for a Boston newspaper. Students will list the topics they want to cover (for example, Lincoln's political experience, Lincoln's election, or the secession crisis) and the facts they need. Finally, students will write two articles that follow the original outline, one reflecting Northerners' biases and one reflecting Southerners' biases.

Distinguishing Fact From Opinion Ask: What is the difference between a fact and an opinion? *(A fact is verifiable; an opinion is a personal view that cannot be verified.)* Lead a class discussion about the facts and opinions students used in their articles. List facts on the board. Ask for examples of biased opinions that groups used in their articles. **OL**

(Chapter Project continued on the Visual Summary page)

C Critical Thinking

Analyzing Information Ask: Why do you think Virginia, North Carolina, Tennessee, and Arkansas voted to secede when they did? *(Possible answer: Residents of those states had hoped to avoid a war. Once shots were fired, however, they felt they had to choose sides and felt more allegiance to the South.)* **AL**

✔ **Reading Check** **Answer:** Lincoln did not want to begin the Civil War; he wanted to leave the decision to start fighting up to the Confederates.

Assess

History ONLINE

Study Central™ provides summaries, interactive games, and online graphic organizers to help students review content.

Close

Evaluating As a class, discuss the reasons the Confederacy seceded from the Union. **OL**

Section 4 Review

Fort Sumter

Main Idea The Civil War began when Confederate forces attacked Fort Sumter in South Carolina.

History and You Have you ever argued with a family member over an item that you each felt you owned? Read to learn about events at Fort Sumter.

Confederate forces had already seized some U.S. forts within their states. Although Lincoln did not want to start a war by trying to take the forts back, allowing the Confederates to keep them would amount to admitting their right to secede.

The day after taking office, Lincoln received a message from the commander of **Fort Sumter**, a U.S. fort on an island guarding Charleston Harbor. The message warned that the fort was low on supplies and the Confederates demanded its surrender.

Lincoln responded by sending a message to Governor Francis Pickens of South Carolina. He informed Pickens that he was sending an unarmed expedition with supplies to Fort Sumter. Lincoln promised that Union forces would not "throw in men, arms, or ammunition" unless they were fired upon. The president thus left the decision to start shooting up to the Confederates.

Jefferson Davis made a fateful choice. He ordered his forces to attack Fort Sumter before the Union supplies could arrive. Confederate guns opened fire early on April 12, 1861. Union captain Abner Doubleday witnessed the attack from inside the fort:

PRIMARY SOURCE

"Showers of balls . . . and shells . . . poured into the fort in one incessant stream, causing great flakes of masonry to fall in all directions."

—quoted in *Fort Sumter*

High seas kept Union relief ships from reaching the fort. Fort Sumter surrendered on April 14. Thousands of shots were fired during the siege, but there was no loss of life.

President Lincoln issued a call for troops, and volunteers quickly signed up. Meanwhile, Virginia, North Carolina, Tennessee, and Arkansas voted to join the Confederacy. The Civil War had begun.

✔ **Reading Check** **Explaining** Why did Lincoln decide not to send armed troops to Fort Sumter?

Section 4 Review

History ONLINE
Study Central™ To review this section, go to glencoe.com.

Vocabulary

1. Use each of the following vocabulary terms in a sentence that will help explain its meaning: secession, reject, justify, states' rights.

Main Ideas

2. **Specifying** What action did South Carolina take after Lincoln won the election of 1860? Why?

3. **Explaining** What was the significance of the attack on Fort Sumter?

Critical Thinking

4. **Drawing Conclusions** How would you describe President Lincoln's priorities as he took office in March 1861?

5. **Sequencing** In a diagram like the one below, trace the events leading to the surrender of Fort Sumter.

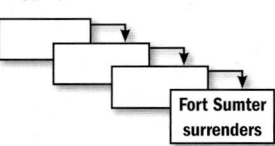

Fort Sumter surrenders

6. Descriptive Writing
Imagine that you are a Confederate journalist. Write a brief announcement about the attack on Fort Sumter for your newspaper. Then write another brief announcement of the event—this time from a Union journalist's point of view.

Answer the
7. **Essential Question**
What role did the theory of states' rights play in the outbreak of the Civil War?

Answers

1. Sentences should use vocabulary words according to their definitions in the section and Glossary.

2. South Carolina seceded; many Southerners did not trust a Republican administration to protect their rights.

3. turned the North-South dispute into a shooting war and brought several more Southern states into the Confederacy.

4. He was determined to preserve the Union by opposing secession but hoped to prevent war.

5. Fort Sumter's commander sends message about low supplies and demand for surrender, Lincoln informs South Carolina governor that unarmed supply expedition is on the way, Davis orders troops to attack fort before supplies arrive

6. Announcements should show different points of view.

7. The theory held that the Constitution was a contract among independent states, which the states had agreed to voluntarily. When the federal government violated the rights of the states, as Southerners believed it had, the contract was void. Southerners used this theory to justify secession.

Visual Summary

Visual Summary

Making Connections Many stops on the Underground Railroad have become museums or have been otherwise documented by local historical societies. Help the class research the location of the nearest stop on the Underground Railroad. Then have students write letters requesting more information from the museums and historical societies. Have them continue to research other historical information about the stop. After the class has collected a variety of brochures, reproductions of images, and letters, have them create a large bulletin board in the classroom displaying the information. **OL**

Auditory/Musical Have students work in pairs to write a poem or song about the attack on Fort Sumter from the point of view of someone who witnessed the event. Make sure students have identified whose point of view they are taking as they write. Then have pairs perform their compositions for the rest of the class. **OL**

1848–1854

1848 The Free-Soil Party forms to oppose slavery in territories.

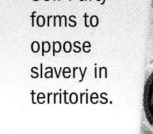

Van Buren-Adams poster, 1848 ▶

1850
- The Compromise of 1850 temporarily eases debate on slavery in Congress.
- The Fugitive Slave Act stirs up antislavery feelings in North.

1854
- The Kansas-Nebraska Act declares popular sovereignty in territories.
- Missouri voters help elect proslavery legislature in Kansas.
- The Republican Party forms as antislavery party.

1855–1859

1856

Jan. Kansas antislavery forces set up a rival government.

May Slavery supporters unleash violence in Kansas.

Oct. Federal troops are sent to end violence in "Bleeding Kansas."

1857 The *Dred Scott* decision rules that slavery is protected by the Constitution.

1858 Lincoln-Douglas debates focus on slavery and give Lincoln national recognition.

1859

Oct. John Brown raids Harpers Ferry arsenal uniting abolitionists.

1860–1861

1860

Nov. Lincoln is elected president.

Dec. South Carolina secedes; other Southern states follow.

1861

Feb. Southern states form Confederate States of America.

March Lincoln speaks of preserving the Union and preventing war in his Inaugural Address.

April The Confederate attack on Fort Sumter begins the Civil War.

◀ Fighting at Harpers Ferry

▲ Confederate attack on Fort Sumter

 Study anywhere, anytime! Download quizzes and flash cards to your PDA from glencoe.com.

Toward Civil War **Chapter 15** **467**

Investigating Sectionalism

Step 5: Review and Discussion Students will review their work and discuss the sectional differences that led to the outbreak of the Civil War.

Directions Have students return to their original five groups. Ask groups to list the disagreements between the North and South that led to the Civil War. Then have them list the attempts to resolve differences between the two regions.

When students have finished their group work, lead a class discussion. Create a list of disagreements on the board as well as a list of compromises and other agreements between the two sides that were attempts to avert civil war.

Speculating Ask: Could differences between the North and South have been resolved without war? *(Answers will vary but could include gradual abolition of slavery with federal compensation for slaveholders or provisions of the Crittenden plan.)* **OL**

Hands-On Chapter Project
Step 5: Wrap-Up

Disagreements | Compromises/Agreements
1. slavery in new territories | 1. Missouri Compromise
2. Fugitive Slave Act | 2. Compromise of 1850
3. Kansas-Nebraska Act
4. "Bleeding Kansas"
5. Dred Scott Case
6. Raid on Harper's Ferry
7. Secession

Focus

R Reading Strategy

Previewing Before reading the two excerpts, have students predict what they think the two presidents' main arguments will be. Then have them compare their predictions to the excerpts. **BL**

W Writing Support

Persuasive Writing Discuss as a class how Lincoln tried to persuade both sides to resolve their differences. *(Students should observe that Lincoln appealed to their shared history and the common interest to do what is morally right.)* **Ask:** Were Lincoln's arguments strong enough to keep the South from seceding? Why or why not? Students should write a short essay that presents their opinions about whether secession should have been an option for the Southern states. **OL**

Additional Support and Answers

YOU DECIDE

Abraham Lincoln's first inauguration, March 4, 1861

468

Did the South Have the Right to Secede?

Building Background

When Abraham Lincoln was inaugurated to his first term as president, on March 4, 1861, the unfinished Capitol dome seemed to reflect the uncertain future of the United States. Seven Southern states had already voted to secede from the Union and form the Confederate States of America.

The Confederate president, Jefferson Davis, had been inaugurated earlier, on February 18. Each man's inauguration address presented a different view on the basic question of whether a state had the right to secede from the Union.

NO

ABRAHAM LINCOLN

One section of our country believes slavery is right and ought to be extended, while the other believes it is wrong and ought not to be extended. This is the only substantial dispute. . . .

The [President] derives all his authority from the people, and they have referred none upon him to fix terms for the separation of the States. The people themselves can do this if also they choose, but the Executive as such has nothing to do with it. His duty is to administer[1] the present Government as it came to his hands and to transmit it unimpaired[2] by him to his successor. . . .

We are not enemies, but friends. We must not be enemies. Though passion may have strained it must not break our bonds of affection. The mystic chords of memory, stretching from every battlefield and patriot grave to every living heart and hearthstone all over this broad land, will yet swell the chorus of the Union, when again touched, as surely they will be, by the better angels of our nature.

[1] **administer** manage
[2] **unimpaired** unharmed

Fast Facts

The Confederate Constitution Delegates from the seven states that had seceded met in Montgomery, Alabama, on February 4, 1861, to draft a constitution for their newly formed nation. The next month, the delegates adopted the Confederate Constitution, which had many similarities to the U.S. Constitution. Among the key differences: It permitted slavery in states and territories; it banned protective tariffs; and it granted the president only one six-year term, along with a line-item veto.

YES

JEFFERSON DAVIS

An agricultural people, whose chief interest is the export of a commodity required in every manufacturing country, our true policy is peace, and the freest trade which our necessities will permit.... There can be but little rivalry between ours and any manufacturing or navigating community, such as the Northeastern States of the American Union. It must follow, therefore, that a mutual interest would invite good will and kind offices. If, however, passion or the lust of dominion[3] should cloud the judgment or inflame the ambition of those States, we must prepare to meet the emergency and to maintain, by the final arbitrament[4] of the sword, the position which we have assumed among the nations of the earth. We have entered upon the career of independence, and it must be inflexibly pursued.... As a necessity, not a choice, we have resorted to the remedy of separation; and henceforth our energies must be directed to the conduct of our own affairs, and the perpetuity[5] of the Confederacy which we have formed.

---

[3] **dominion** territory
[4] **arbitrament** power to decide
[5] **perpetuity** lasting life

DBQ Document-Based Questions

1. **Identifying** What are Abraham Lincoln's and Jefferson Davis's basic arguments against or in favor of secession?

2. **Making Inferences** What issue seems most important to Lincoln? To Davis?

3. **Analyzing** Did either president refer to the economies of the different regions? If so, how were they described?

4. **Evaluating** In your opinion, which of the two addresses makes the more powerful appeal to emotions? Explain your answer in a short essay.

Jefferson Davis's inauguration in Montgomery, Alabama, February 18, 1861

469

Teach

C Critical Thinking

Analyzing Primary Sources Ask: Why do you think Davis makes a distinction between the agricultural economy of the South and the manufacturing economy of the North? *(perhaps to suggest that the economic interests of the South and the North are different enough to warrant secession and the formation of a different country)* **OL**

Assess/Close

As a class, discuss the power of descriptive language to persuade readers. List the metaphors each author uses and the feelings they try to evoke with their words.

Answers

1. Lincoln believes that as chief executive, he must preserve the government as it existed when he took office. He does not believe that the people gave him the authority to allow secession. Davis believes that the agricultural interests of the South's economy should be pre-served, which by inference requires slavery. Secession was a necessity to maintain their way of life.

2. Lincoln wants to preserve the Union as is; Davis wants to preserve the agricultural economy of the South.

3. Davis makes an economic argument for secession. He describes the relationship between the agricultural South and the industrial North.

4. Students' essays should use evidence from either quote to explain their views.

Answers and Analyses
Reviewing Main Ideas

1. B Students should remember the controversy surrounding whether slavery would be permitted in any territory acquired from Mexico as a result of the war with Mexico. The Compromise of 1850 proposed that California would be a free state, but slavery would not be limited in other territories acquired from Mexico. The Wilmot Proviso, on the other hand, would have banned slavery in all territories acquired from Mexico. Therefore, choice B is correct. **18.C.3a**

2. D Students should remember that the Fugitive Slave Act required all citizens to help catch runaways and made it a criminal offense to help fugitives. This resulted in much resentment among people in the North, leading students to select choice D. **18.B.3a**

3. B Students should immediately eliminate choice A, because the decision stated that slaves could not bring lawsuits, and C, because *Dred Scott* did not have to do with the slave trade. The decision stated that Congress could not take away property without "due process of law," and therefore, Congress had no power to prohibit slavery anywhere. Students should then be able to select choice B. **14.C.3**

4. C Remind students that the Republicans, while pledging to keep slavery from spreading, promised not to disturb slavery where it already existed in the hopes of keeping the Union together. This should lead them to select choice C. **16.B**

Short-Answer Question

5. Possible answer: Northerners would be outraged and think the attack was an example of the violence of the Southern system. Southerners might feel either ashamed of the attack or that the attack was justified because of Sumner's criticism of pro-slavery senators. **16.A.3b**

TEST-TAKING TIP

Read all the choices before selecting your answer. You may overlook the correct answer if you are hasty!

Reviewing Main Ideas

Directions: Choose the best answer for each of the following questions.

1. Which of the following was a proposal to ban slavery in any lands acquired from Mexico?

  A Compromise of 1850

  B Wilmot Proviso

  C Missouri Compromise

  D Freeport Doctrine

2. What resulted from the Fugitive Slave Act?

  A Passage of the law quieted widespread violence in Kansas and Nebraska.

  B Most Northerners believed Southern slaveholders' rights should be upheld.

  C Abolitionists were jailed in the North.

  D The law angered the North, convincing many of the evils of slavery.

3. The Supreme Court's decision in the *Dred Scott* case stated that

  A enslaved persons could bring lawsuits.

  B Congress had no power to prohibit slavery in any territory.

  C the slave trade should be abolished.

  D the Missouri Compromise was constitutional.

4. Which was included in the Republican Party platform of the election of 1860?

  A The question of slavery should be decided by popular sovereignty.

  B In a free society, the minority has the right to break up the government.

  C Slavery should be left where it existed but be excluded from the territories.

  D Slavery should be protected in all territories south of 36°30'N latitude.

Short-Answer Question

Directions: Base your answer to question 5 on the political cartoon below and on your knowledge of social studies.

SOUTHERN CHIVALRY — ARGUMENT versus CLUB'S.

Source: Bettmann/CORBIS

5. This cartoon shows the attack on Massachusetts Senator Charles Sumner in the Senate chamber. What emotions might the event in this cartoon have stirred up in the North and in the South?

Review the Essential Questions

6. Essay Describe the various attempts to find a compromise between the demands of the North and the South.

To help you write your essay, review your answers to the Essential Questions in the section reviews and the chapter Foldables Study Organizer. Your essay should include:

- the compromises Congress made regarding sectionalism and slavery; and
- reactions by antislavery and pro-slavery forces.

GO ON ➡

Review the Essential Questions

6. Students should describe the arguments used by Northerners and Southerners to justify their positions on slavery. They may mention legal arguments such as the Missouri Compromise, the Compromise of 1850, and the *Dred Scott* decision, as well as emotional arguments revolving around violence in Kansas or the actions of John Brown. **16.B**

History ONLINE
For additional test practice, use **Self-Check Quizzes**—Chapter 15 at glencoe.com.

Chapter 15 Assessment

Document-Based Questions

Directions: Analyze the documents and answer the short-answer questions that follow.

Document 1

In this passage, Erastus D. Ladd describes voters from Missouri crossing the border to vote in an 1855 election in Kansas.

> They claimed to have a legal right to vote in the Territory [Kansas], and that they were residents by virtue of their being then in the Territory. They said they were free to confess that they came from Missouri; that they lived in Missouri, and voted as Missourians.

Source: Albert Bushnell Hart, *Source-Book of American History*

7. Were the actions of these voters legal? How did the voters from Missouri justify voting in Kansas?

Document 2

This is an excerpt from a speech by Georgia congressperson Robert Toombs in 1849.

> I do not . . . hesitate to avow [admit] before this House and the country, and in the presence of the living God, that if by your legislation you seek to drive us from the territories of California and New Mexico, purchased by the common blood and treasure of the whole people, and to abolish slavery in this District, thereby attempting to fix a national degradation [shame] upon half the States of this Confederacy, I am for disunion.

Source: Representative Robert Toombs of Georgia, 1849

8. Based on the excerpt, do you think Toombs favored or opposed the legalization of slavery in California and New Mexico? On what did Toombs base his views?

Document 3

In this passage from 1851, Richard Henry Dana, Jr., speaks of the Fugitive Slave Act of 1850.

> If the law were constitutional, which I firmly believe it is not, it would be the duty of a citizen not to resist it by force, unless he was prepared for revolution and civil war; but we rejoice in the escape of a victim of an unjust law as we would in the escape of an ill-treated captive deer or bird.

Source: Charles Francis Adams, *Richard Henry Dana*

9. Suppose Dana was a member of a jury during a trial of someone accused of breaking the Fugitive Slave Act. Based on the passage, do you think he would find the accused guilty or not guilty? Why?

Document 4

This is a campaign ribbon from the 1856 presidential election.

Source: David J. & Janice L. Frent Collection/CORBIS

10. Does this ribbon support or oppose John C. Frémont for president? Explain.

11. Expository Writing Using the information from the four documents and your knowledge of social studies, write an essay in which you:

* identify ways Northerners and Southerners appealed to emotion *and* to legal arguments to justify their positions; and

* explain which type of argument you find most persuasive, and why.

9. He likely would have found the accused not guilty of breaking the Fugitive Slave Law because he believed the law was unjust and unconstitutional. **16.A.3b**

10. It opposes Frémont. The ribbon depicts a runaway enslaved man with an image of a skull and crossbones, suggesting that the election of Frémont—who called for free territories—would result in a dangerous increase in fugitive enslaved people. **16.A**

11. Students' answers may discuss aspects such as the emotionalism of individuals like John Brown, the Supreme Court's decision in the *Dred Scott* case, or theories of states' rights. Essays should use examples to explain which argument students found most persuasive. **18.B**

History ONLINE
Have students visit the Web site at glencoe.com to review Chapter 15 and take the Self-Check Quiz.

Need Extra Help?

Have students refer to the pages listed if they miss any of the questions.

Need Extra Help?

If you missed questions. . .	1	2	3	4	5	6	7	8	9	10	11
Go to page. . .	450	453	458–459	463	455	448–466	454–455	451	453	457–458	448–466

Toward Civil War **Chapter 15** 471

Document-Based Questions

7. Thousands of pro-slavery supporters from Missouri routinely crossed the border into Kansas to vote for pro-slavery candidates in Kansas's elections. Though this was illegal, these voters claimed they could legally vote in Kansas because they were "residing" in Kansas at the time they voted. **18.B.3a**

8. He favored slavery in California and New Mexico, arguing that all Americans—including slaveholding Southerners—had fought in the war with Mexico to acquire these territories. **16.A.3b**

Chapter Planning Guide

16

Levels BL	OL	AL	ELL		Resources	Chapter Opener	Section 1	Section 2	Section 3	Section 4	Section 5	Chapter Assess
FOCUS												
BL	OL	AL	ELL	🖋	Daily Test Practice Transparencies		16–1	16–2	16–3	16–4	16–5	
					TEACH							
	OL	AL		📁	Geography and History Activity, URB						p. 59	
BL	OL		ELL	📁	Time Line Skills Activity, URB		p. 62	p. 62	p. 62	p. 62	p. 62	
BL	OL	AL	ELL	📁	Writing Skills Activity, URB					p. 51		
	OL	AL		📁	American Literature Readings, URB					p. 9		
BL	OL	AL	ELL	📁	Content Vocabulary Activity, URB		p. 45	p. 45	p. 45	p. 45	p. 45	
BL	OL	AL	ELL	📁	Academic Vocabulary Activity, URB		p. 47	p. 47	p. 47	p. 47	p. 47	
BL	OL		ELL	📁	Social Studies Skills Activity, URB		p. 53					
BL	OL	AL	ELL	📁	Differentiated Instruction Activity, URB			p. 55				
BL	OL	AL	ELL	📁	Critical Thinking Skills Activity, URB					p. 57		
BL	OL	AL	ELL	📁	Linking Past and Present Activity, URB					p. 61		
	OL	AL		📁	Primary Source Readings, URB				p. 49			
BL	OL	AL	ELL	📁	School-to-Home Connection Activity, URB		p. 63	p. 63	p. 63	p. 63	p. 63	
BL	OL		ELL	📁	Guided Reading Activity, URB*		p. 67	p. 68	p. 69	p. 70	p. 71	
		AL		📁	Enrichment Activity, URB						p. 11	
BL	OL		ELL	📁	Reading Essentials and Note-Taking Guide*		p. 163	p. 166	p. 169	p. 172	p. 175	
BL	OL	AL	ELL	🖋	Lesson Transparencies		16A	16B		16C		
	OL	AL		📁	Interpreting Political Cartoons, URB			p. 13				
	OL			📁	American Biographies			p. 27				
BL	OL	AL	ELL	📁	Outline Map Resource Book	pp. 14, 15						

Note: Please refer to the *Unit Resource Book: Civil War and Reconstruction* for this chapter's URB materials.

472A

* Also available in Spanish

Levels BL	OL	AL	ELL		Resources	Chapter Opener	Section 1	Section 2	Section 3	Section 4	Section 5	Chapter Assess
					TEACH (continued)							
BL	OL	AL	ELL		NGS US Desk Map		✓	✓	✓	✓	✓	
BL	OL	AL	ELL		American Literature Library		✓	✓	✓	✓	✓	
BL	OL	AL	ELL		Writer's Guidebook		✓	✓	✓	✓	✓	
	OL	AL			American History Primary Source Document Library CD-ROM		✓	✓	✓	✓	✓	✓
BL	OL	AL	ELL		American Music: Hits Through History	✓	✓	✓	✓	✓	✓	
BL	OL	AL	ELL		StudentWorks™ Plus CD	✓	✓	✓	✓	✓	✓	✓
BL	OL	AL	ELL		Section Spotlight Videos		✓	✓	✓	✓	✓	
BL	OL	AL	ELL		Writing Process Transparencies		✓	✓	✓	✓	✓	✓
BL	OL	AL	ELL		Presentation Plus! With MindJogger CheckPoint CD	✓	✓	✓	✓	✓	✓	✓
					ASSESS							
BL	OL	AL	ELL		Quizzes and Tests		p. 151	p. 152	p. 153	p. 154	p. 155	pp. 157, 159, 161
BL	OL	AL	ELL		Authentic Assessment With Rubrics		p. 16	p. 16	p. 16	p. 16	p. 16	p. 16
BL	OL	AL	ELL		Standardized Test Practice							p. 31
BL	OL	AL	ELL		ExamView® Assessment Suite CD-ROM*		16–1	16–2	16–3	16–4	16–5	Ch. 16
					CLOSE							
BL			ELL		Reteaching Activity, URB*		p. 65	p. 65	p. 65	p. 65	p. 65	p. 65
BL	OL		ELL		Reading and Study Skills Foldables Activity	p. 80	p. 80	p. 80	p. 80	p. 80	p. 80	p. 80
BL	OL	AL	ELL		The American Journey in Graphic Novel							p. 85
BL			ELL		Reading Strategies and Activities for the Social Studies Classroom		✓	✓	✓	✓	✓	
BL	OL	AL	ELL		Graphic Organizer Transparencies & Strategies		✓	✓	✓	✓	✓	

TeacherWorks Plus
All-In-One Planner and Resource Center

- Interactive Lesson Planner
- Interactive Teacher Edition
- Fully editable blackline masters
- Section Spotlight Videos Launch

- Differentiated Lesson Plans
- Printable reports of daily assignments
- Standards Tracking System

Professional Development Resources

- Strategies for Success
- Building Academic Vocabulary
- Success With English Learners DVD
- Differentiated Instruction Strategies DVD
- Teaching Literacy Strategies in Social Studies DVD
- Assessment DVD
- Standards-Based Instruction DVD

16

Using PuzzleMaker™ 3.1

Online Jumble Puzzles

Technology Product

Glencoe's Vocabulary PuzzleMaker™ 3.1 lets you create your own puzzles based on the glossary. The PuzzleMaker allows you to

- create jumble puzzles based on content vocabulary and academic vocabulary;
- create online or paper jumble puzzles.

Objectives

After students complete the jumble puzzles, they will be able to

- recall and identify scrambled terms with the help of clues;
- reinforce their understanding of the vocabulary.

Steps

- Download, install, and run PuzzleMaker™ 3.1. Click on **Create a New Puzzle**.
- Select the appropriate database for the vocabulary.
- Select a puzzle type and grid type.
- Select one or more chapters from the list. Indicate whether you want the words selected randomly or manually.
- Select the language and words. Click **Finish**.
- Save your jumble puzzle or print copies for your students to complete.
- Use PuzzlePlayer™ 3.1 to review students' puzzles.

History ONLINE at glencoe.com

	Student	Teacher	Parent
Media Center			
• Student Edition Audio	●		
• Spanish Summaries	●		
• Section Spotlight Videos	●	●	
Social Studies Online Learning Center			
Classroom Tools			
• Multi-Language Glossaries	●	●	●
• Teaching Today		●	
• TIME Current Events	●	●	●
• Beyond the Textbook	●	●	
***The American Journey* Online Learning Center**			
• Study-to-Go™	●	●	●
• Study Central™	●	●	●
• Chapter Overview	●	●	
• Concepts in Motion	●	●	
• ePuzzles and Games	●	●	
• Literature Connections	●	●	
• Online Student Edition	●	●	●
• Self-Check Quizzes	●	●	●
• Student Web Activities	●	●	
• Vocabulary eFlashcards	●	●	
• Web Activity Lesson Plans	●	●	●
• Vocabulary PuzzleMaker	●	●	●

READING SUPPORT FROM JAMESTOWN EDUCATION

- **Timed Readings Plus in Social Studies** helps students increase their reading rate and fluency while maintaining comprehension. The 400-word passages are similar to those found on state and national assessments.

- **Reading in the Content Area: Social Studies** concentrates on six essential reading skills that help students better comprehend what they read. The book includes 75 high-interest nonfiction passages written at increasing levels of difficulty.

- **Reading Social Studies** includes strategic reading instruction and vocabulary support in Social Studies content for ELLs and native speakers of English.

- **Content Vocabulary Workout** (Grades 6–8) accelerates reading comprehension through focused vocabulary development. Social Studies content vocabulary comes from the glossaries of Glencoe's Middle School Social Studies texts.

www.jamestowneducation.com

NATIONAL GEOGRAPHIC

Index to National Geographic Magazine:

The following articles relate to this chapter:

- **"Iron vs. Oak: The Day the Wooden Navy Died,"** Joel K. Bourne, Jr., March 2006.

- **"The H. L. Hunley: Secret Weapon of the Confederacy,"** Glen Oeland, July 2002.

National Geographic Society Products

To order the following, call National Geographic at 1-800-368-2728:

National Geographic Atlas of the World (Book)

Access National Geographic's dynamic MapMachine Web site and other geography resources at:

www.nationalgeographic.com
www.nationalgeographic.com/mapmachine

Reading List Generator CD-ROM

GLENCOE BOOKLINK 3

Use this database to search more than 30,000 titles to create a customized reading list for your students.

- Reading lists can be organized by students' reading level, author, genre, theme, or area of interest.
- The database provides Degrees of Reading Power™ (DRP) and Lexile™ readability scores for all selections.
- A brief summary of each selection is included.

Leveled reading suggestions for this chapter:

For students at a Grade 6 reading level:
- **Civil War on Sunday,** by Mary Pope Osborne
- **Numbering All the Bones,** by Ann Rinaldi

For students at a Grade 7 reading level:
- **Joseph's Choice: 1861,** by Bonnie Pryor
- **The River Between Us,** by Richard Peck

For students at a Grade 8 reading level:
- **Private Captain: A Story of Gettysburg,** by Marty Crisp
- **The Story of Clara Barton,** by Rachel A. Koestler-Grack

For students at a Grade 9 reading level:
- **The Battle of Gettysburg: Turning Point of the Civil War,** by Gina DeAngelis
- **Growing Up in the Civil War: 1861 to 1865,** by Duane Damon

For students at a Grade 10 reading level:
- **Across Five Aprils,** by Irene Hunt
- **Little Women,** by Louisa May Alcott

The following videotape programs are available from Glencoe as supplements to the chapter:

- **Abraham Lincoln: Preserving the Union** (ISBN 0-76-700034-X)
- **Robert E. Lee** (ISBN 1-56-501973-3)
- **American Civil War** (ISBN 0-76-700102-8)

To order, call Glencoe at 1-800-334-7344. To find classroom resources to accompany many of these videos, check the following home pages:

A&E Television: www.aetv.com

The History Channel: www.history.com

Chapter Objectives

After studying this chapter, students will be able to:

- Identify the strengths and weaknesses of the North and the South.
- Explain why neither the North nor the South had a distinct advantage in the early stages of the war.
- Discuss the social, political, and economic changes that occurred as a result of the war.
- Understand how the battles of Vicksburg and Gettysburg changed the course of the war.
- Describe the events that led to the end of the Civil War.

Motivating Activity

Speculating Give students the following information. At the beginning of the Civil War, 21 million people lived in the North and 9 million in the South. Of those living in the South, 4 million were enslaved. **Ask:** How do you think these factors would affect the odds of the South winning the war? *(Students may note that the North was able to raise larger forces and that Southern armies would be at a disadvantage.)* Do you think other factors are as important? *(Students may suggest resources, strategy, and leadership.)* **OL**

Chapter 16

The Civil War
1861–1865

Civil War: First at Vicksburg, 1863 by H. Charles McBarron, Jr.

PRESIDENTS

ABRAHAM LINCOLN

U.S. Events

World Events

1861 ★ Conflict at Fort Sumter, South Carolina, begins Civil War

1861 ★ Robert E. Lee named commander of Confederate armies

1861

1862

★ **1861**
- Russia emancipates serfs
- First ironclad warship completed in England

★ **1862**
International Red Cross established; American Red Cross organized 10 years later

Previewing the Essential Questions

As you begin teaching each section, use these questions and activities to help students focus on the Essential Questions.

Section 1

The Two Sides Ask: What is the relationship between economic resources and military strength? *(Economic resources make it easier for a country or region to build up its military.)* Point out to students that in Section 1 they will learn about the strengths and weaknesses of the North and the South at the beginning of the Civil War. **OL**

Section 2

Early Stages of the War Ask: What might be necessary for either the North or the South to gain an advantage during the early years of the war? *(a large army, strong leadership, and several early military victories)* Point out to students that Section 2 discusses Northern and Southern leadership, strategies, and mistakes made during the war. **OL**

Section 1: The Two Sides

Essential Question What were the strengths and weaknesses of the North and the South?

Section 2: Early Stages of the War

Essential Question Why did neither the Union nor the Confederacy gain a strong advantage during the early years of the war?

Section 3: Life During the War

Essential Question What social, political, and economic changes resulted from the war?

Section 4: The Strain of War

Essential Question How did the events at Gettysburg and Vicksburg change the course of the war?

Section 5: The War's Final Stages

Essential Question What events led to the end of the war?

History ONLINE
Chapter Overview Visit glencoe.com and click on **Chapter 16—Chapter Overviews** to preview chapter information.

FOLDABLES Study Organizer

Organizing Information
Make this Foldable to help organize what you learn about the Civil War.

Step 1 Fold a sheet of paper in half from side to side.

> Fold it so the left edge lies about ½ inch from the right edge.

Step 2 Turn the paper and fold it into thirds.

> This will make three tabs.

Step 3 Unfold and cut the top layer only along both folds.

Step 4 Label your Foldable as shown.

Before the War	During the War	After the War

The Civil War

Reading and Writing As you read the chapter, list events that occurred before, during, and after the Civil War under the appropriate tabs of your Foldable.

1863
- Emancipation Proclamation issued
- Grant named commander of Union armies

1864 Sherman's March to the Sea begins

ANDREW JOHNSON

1865 Civil War ends

1863   1864   1865

1863 London subway opens

1864 First Geneva Convention establishes rules for treatment of prisoners of war

1865 French writer Jules Verne publishes a novel about a trip to the moon

Chapter 16   473

Introducing Chapter 16

Time Line Activity

If you have not already done so, have students review the time line. **Ask:** What years are covered in this chapter? *(1861–1865)* Who were the presidents during this period? *(Abraham Lincoln and Andrew Johnson)* Have students identify a world event that might have influenced people living in the United States during the Civil War. *(Students may describe how the emancipation of Russian serfs might have strengthened the abolitionist movement. The development of the first ironclad warship in England might have had an impact on warfare technology used by the North and the South.)*

FOLDABLES Study Organizer **Dinah Zike's Foldables**

Purpose This Foldable helps students identify the major events of the Civil War. The completed Foldable will help them prepare for assessment.

More Foldables activities for this chapter can be found in the *Dinah Zike's Reading and Study Skills Foldables.*

History ONLINE
Introduce students to chapter content and key terms by having them access the **Chapter Overview** at glencoe.com.

Section 3

Life During the War Ask: What changes do you think people in the Northern states experienced during the Civil War? The Southern states? *(Possible answer: The roles of women at home might change because men are away at war.)* Tell students that Section 3 will explore the impact of the war on women and the economy. Students will also consider opposition to the war and the decision to suspend *habeus corpus.* **OL**

Section 4

The Strain of War Ask: Why might a few key military victories change the course of the war? *(Winning a battle could give an army control of a key geographic location or transportation route. Important leaders and many men could be killed or wounded.)* Explain to students that in Section 4, they will learn more about decisive victories for the Union forces, which greatly affected the war's outcome. **OL**

Section 5

The War's Final Stages Ask: How might the final days of the war impact the process of rebuilding? *(Areas that saw many battles would need to be rebuilt.)* Point out to students that the South experienced a great deal of destruction during the war. They will learn more about the extreme measures taken by the North to end the war, as well as the early days of peace. **OL**

The Two Sides

Focus

Bellringer
Daily Test Practice Transparency 16-1

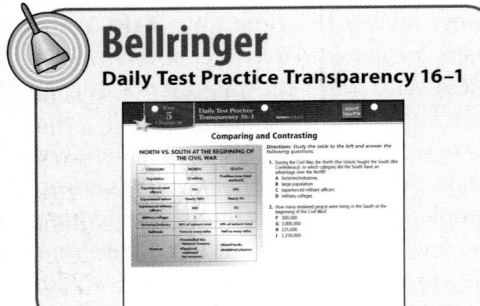

Reading Guide
Answers to Graphic:
North: *Strengths*—large population; more railroads, farms, exports, manufactured goods; *Weaknesses*—war would be fought on unfamiliar territory; **South:** *Strengths*—excellent military leaders, strong fighting spirit; knowledge of the territory; *Weaknesses*—smaller population; fewer resources and industry

Section Spotlight Video

To learn more about who fought in the Civil War, have students watch the Section Spotlight Video "The Two Sides."

Resource Manager

Essential Question
What were the strengths and weaknesses of the North and the South?

Reading Guide

Content Vocabulary
border state (p. 475)   export (p. 477)
blockade (p. 477)

Academic Vocabulary
contrast (p. 476)   challenge (p. 479)

Key People and Events
Abraham Lincoln (p. 475)
Anaconda Plan (p. 477)

Reading Strategy
Taking Notes As you read, take notes on the differences and similarities between the two sides.

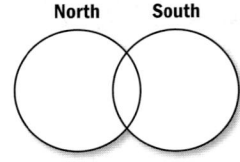

North   South

ILLINOIS STANDARDS
The American Journey

15.E Understand the impact of government policies and decisions on production and consumption in the economy.

17.C.3a Explain how human activity is affected by geographic factors.

18.B.3a Analyze how individuals and groups interact with and within institutions (e.g., educational, military).

474

American Diary

At the Battle of Malvern Hill in 1862, a Union sergeant named Driscoll shot a young Confederate soldier. Hurrying forward, Driscoll turned the soldier's face up to see if the young man was dead. But when he looked at the dying soldier's face, he received a terrible shock. Looking up, the boy murmured, "Father," and then closed his eyes forever. The soldier was his son, who had gone south before the war.

R Reading Strategies	C Critical Thinking	D Differentiated Instruction	W Writing Support	S Skill Practice
Teacher Edition • Making Inferences, p. 476 • Drawing Conclusions, p. 479 **Additional Resources** • Guid. Read., URB p. 67 • Content Vocab., URB p. 45 • Academic Vocab., URB p. 47 • Read. Ess., p. 163	**Teacher Edition** • Identify. Central Issues, p. 478 **Additional Resources** • Quizzes and Tests, p. 151	**Teacher Edition** • Verbal/Linguistic, p. 476 **Additional Resources** • Reteaching Act., URB p. 65 • School-to-Home, URB p. 63	**Teacher Edition** • Persuasive Writing, p. 475 • Narrative Writing, p. 478 **Additional Resources** • Authentic Assess., p. 16	**Teacher Edition** • Using Geo. Skills, p. 477 **Additional Resources** • Daily Test Pract. Transp. 16-1 • Soc. Stud. Skills, URB p. 53 • Lesson Transp. 16A • Time Line Skills, URB p. 62

Goals and Strategies

Main Idea The North and the South had many different strengths, strategies, and purposes in the Civil War.

History and You Is it better for an army to have plenty of soldiers or a powerful will to fight? Why? Read to learn how these characteristics affected the Civil War.

Like the Driscolls, many families were divided by the war. Neither side imagined, however, that the war would cost such a terrible price in human life. During the four years of fighting, hundreds of thousands of Americans had lost their lives. Many thousands more were wounded in battle.

The Border States

For most states, choosing sides in the Civil War was easy. The **border states** of Delaware, Maryland, Kentucky, and Missouri, however, were bitterly divided. Slavery was legal in all four states, though none had many enslaved people. All four had ties to the North and the South.

These states were vital to the Union because of their strategic locations. Missouri could control parts of the Mississippi River and major routes to the West. Kentucky controlled the Ohio River. Delaware was close to Philadelphia.

Maryland, perhaps the most important of the border states, was close to Richmond, the Confederate capital. Most significantly, Washington, D.C., lay within the state. If Maryland seceded, the North's government would be surrounded.

President **Abraham Lincoln** worked tirelessly to keep the four border states in the Union. In the end, he was successful.

Still, many border state residents supported the Confederacy. The president had his hands full trying to restrain these opponents of the war. In September 1861, Lincoln wrote:

PRIMARY SOURCE

"I think to lose Kentucky is nearly the same as to lose the whole game. . . . We would as well consent to separation at once, including the surrender of this capitol."

—from *Abraham Lincoln: His Speeches and Writings*

By the Numbers / The Fighting Forces

More than 400,000 Union and Confederate soldiers were wounded in battle during the Civil War.

Organization of the Armies The smaller Confederate army and the larger Union army were organized in roughly the same way.

1861–1865

Union soldiers 2,100,000

Confederate soldiers 900,000

50 Soldiers	= 1 Platoon
2 Platoons	= 1 Company
10 Companies	= 1 Regiment
4–6 Regiments	= 1 Brigade
4–5 Brigades	= 1 Division
3 Divisions	= 1 Corps

Critical Thinking

Concluding Why do you think the armed forces were divided into units?

Teach

W Writing Support

Persuasive Writing Discuss the efforts of President Lincoln to keep the border states from seceding. Then have each student choose one border state. Ask students to write a letter from President Lincoln to the governor or legislature of that state, persuading them to remain with the Union. **OL**

By the Numbers

Critical Thinking Answer Armed forces were divided into units to better organize the movements and activities of large numbers of soldiers and personnel.

Skills Practice Ask: How many more soldiers did the Union have, compared to the Confederacy? *(1,200,000 more soldiers)* About how many companies would be in a brigade? *(40 to 60 companies)* How many soldiers would be in a regiment? *(1,000 soldiers)* **OL**

Differentiated Instruction

Leveled Activities

BL **Reteaching Activity, URB p. 65**

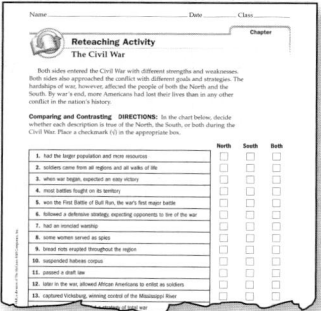

OL **School-to-Home Connection Activity, URB p. 63**

ELL **Content Vocabulary Activity, URB p. 45**

Resources in the North and South

Resources in the North and South

D Differentiated Instruction

Verbal/Linguistic Have students choose a role as a member of Jefferson Davis's cabinet. Then have them write a speech that outlines the priorities for the new Confederate government. Students can give their speeches to the class. Discuss the challenges the South faced in trying to establish itself as a separate nation. **AL**

R Reading Strategy

Making Inferences Ask: *Was freeing enslaved African Americans a goal of President Lincoln in the early years of the war? (No; he wanted to save the Union and would have upheld slavery if it had meant saving the Union.)* **OL**

Resources in the North and South

Graph Skills Answer
manufactured goods and railroad mileage

Graph Skills Practice
Ask: *How might exports have benefited the South's economy? (Goods sold overseas would bring money into the Confederate economy.)* **OL**

Additional Support

Graph Skills

Comparing In what areas did the North have the greatest advantage over the South?

Graphs In MOtion See StudentWorks™ Plus or glencoe.com.

Source: U.S. Census Bureau, *Historical Statistics of the United States*

Comparing North and South

When the war began, both sides had advantages and disadvantages. How they would use those strengths and weaknesses would determine the war's outcome.

The North had a larger population and better resources than the South. The South had other advantages, such as excellent military leaders and a strong fighting spirit. Also, because most of the war was fought in the South, the Confederacy knew the land and had the will to defend it.

War Aims

The North and the South had different aims in fighting the Civil War. The South's goal was to establish itself as an independent nation. To do this, the South did not have to invade the North or destroy the Union army. The Confederacy needed only to fight hard enough and long enough to convince Northerners that the war was not worth its cost.

In **contrast,** the Northern goal was to restore the Union. That meant invading the South and forcing the breakaway states to give up their quest for sovereignty. Although slavery helped drive a wedge between Northerners and Southerners, President Lincoln's original aim was not to defeat slavery. He wrote in 1862:

PRIMARY SOURCE

"If I could save the Union without freeing *any* slave I would do it."
—from *Abraham Lincoln: His Speeches and Writings*

Confederate Strategies

The South expected support from Britain and France, whose supply of Southern cotton was being disrupted by the war. Southerners reasoned that these nations might pressure the North to end the war.

The South's basic strategy, however, was to conduct a defensive war. This meant that the South would hold on to as much territory as possible. Southerners felt that if they showed determination to be independent, Northerners would tire of the war. The only exception to this defensive strategy was a plan to attack Washington, D.C.

476 Chapter 16 *The Civil War*

Activity: Collaborative Learning

Speculating In his Inaugural Address, Abraham Lincoln said, "We are not enemies, but friends. We must not be enemies." However, Jefferson Davis announced in his own Inaugural Address: "We have entered upon the career of independence, and it must be inflexibly pursued." **Ask:** *What might have happened if President Lincoln were unwilling to use military force to preserve the Union? (The Confederacy would have set up a separate nation with its own government and laws. Slavery might have continued to be legal in the Confederacy, and the economy of both countries would be affected.)* Organize the class into small groups. Have groups research to find other countries that have experienced civil wars. **Ask:** *What was the role of diplomacy before the Civil War? Do you think the war could have been avoided? Why?* Then, ask students what the presidents of the Union and Confederacy could have done, if anything, to resolve their disagreements diplomatically. **OL**

Union Strategies

The North's war plan came from General Winfield Scott, hero of the war with Mexico. Knowing that the North would have to subdue the South completely, he proposed three main strategies for winning the war.

First, the Union should **blockade,** or close, Southern ports. This strategy would prevent supplies from reaching the Confederacy. It also would keep the South from **exporting** its cotton crop—or selling it to other countries.

Second, the North intended to gain control of the entire Mississippi River, which would split the Confederacy in two and cut Southern supply lines. Scott's plan was called the **Anaconda Plan,** after the snake that squeezes its prey to death.

Third, the North planned to capture Richmond, Virginia, the Confederate capital.

✓ **Reading Check** **Explaining** Why was it to the South's advantage to fight a defensive war?

Americans Against Americans

Main Idea Soldiers in the Civil War came from every region, and each side expected an early victory.

History and You What motivates men and women to join the armed forces today? Read to find out about the backgrounds of the Civil War soldiers.

The Civil War was more than a war between the states. It pitted brother against brother and neighbor against neighbor. Kentucky senator John Crittenden had two sons who became generals. One fought for the Confederacy, the other for the Union. Even President Lincoln's wife, Mary Todd Lincoln, had relatives in the Confederate army.

Many left their homes and families to enlist in the Union or Confederate armies. Soldiers on both sides had many reasons for signing up. Some were motivated by patriotism and loyalty to their causes.

Economics & History

Enlisted men in both the Union and Confederate armies were paid monthly. Compare the pay rates to those in later wars.

Army Salaries (monthly)

Rank	Civil War	World War II 1942	Vietnam War 1965	Iraq War 2007
Private	*$13	$50	$85	$1,203 – 1,543.20
Corporal	$14	$66	$210	$1,699.50
Sergeant	$17	$78	$261	$1,854 – 2,339.10
Sergeant Major	$21	$138	$486	$4,110

*Until 1864, African Americans in the Civil War were paid only $7.00 per month.

Source: *Bureau of Economic Analysis*; Princeton Review; www.militaryfactory.com

$7.20	Overcoat	$1.14	Pair of Shoes
$6.71	Dress Coat	$1.35	Hat
$2.95	Blanket	$0.88	Undershirt
$2.63	Blouse	$0.55	Underwear
$3.03	Trousers	$0.26	Socks

Soldiers had to replace any of the clothing they lost out of their own pay.

Union soldier's cap ▲

$100 BOUNTY
$13 PAY PER MONTH
$6 STATE PAY for MARRIED MEN
$4 STATE PAY for SINGLE MEN
$3.50 PER MONTH FOR CLOTHES
& RATIONS FOUND.

...N GUARDS!
...ON, Colonel William Bryan...
...Beverly. A few more
...YOUNG MEN WANTED
...FILL THIS COMPANY.
...AND PROCEED TO CAMP AT ONCE
...TING STATION.
...AN'S, SECOND ST
...Market and Plum Sts.
..., N JERSEY.
APT. R. GRAHAM CLARKE.

To get more men to enlist, Union recruiters put up posters offering a sign-up bonus or bounty.

Critical Thinking

Calculating What was a private's weekly salary in the Civil War?

S Skill Practice

Using Geography Skills Give students a historical map of the United States and have them illustrate the Anaconda Plan. **Ask:** Which Southern ports would require blockades? *(Norfolk, Savannah, Charleston, Mobile, New Orleans)* What geographic features would affect the movement of armies? *(Appalachian Mountains, rivers)* **OL**

Economics & History

Critical Thinking Answer
About $3.25

Skills Practice Have students select two wars from the chart and research to find the cost of food, clothes, and homes during those wars. Have students calculate monthly expenses. **Ask:** Do you think soldiers were paid enough to support themselves? Their families? *(Answers should include information from the chart and their research.)* **AL**

✓ **Reading Check** **Answer:** they wanted to hold on to as much territory as possible; believed Northerners would tire of the war

Differentiated Instruction

Time Line Activity
The Civil War

President Lincoln's Decisions (1860–1865)

Time Line Skills Activity, URB p. 62

President Lincoln's Decisions

Objective: To complete a time line of Abraham Lincoln's decisions from 1860 to 1865

Focus: Ask students to recount what they already know about President Lincoln.

Teach: Have students read the background information and then fill in their time lines.

Assess: Ask for volunteers to fill in a time line on the board with their entries.

Close: Discuss with students which events on the time line they consider most important.

Differentiated Instruction Strategies

BL Have students work in pairs to complete their time lines.

AL Ask students to select one of the events on their time lines, research the topic, and report back to the class with additional information.

ELL Have students use their fingers to trace the progression of the completed time lines while reading the information they have entered.

On Average The typical soldier was 5'8", 143 pounds, nearly 26 years of age, and unmarried. He grew up on a farm and practiced the Protestant religion.

Private Edwin Francis Jennison, 2nd Louisiana Cavalry

Private George A. Stryker, New York Regiment

Critical Thinking

Explaining Why do you think many new soldiers had their picture taken in uniform?

W Writing Support

Narrative Writing Have students write a letter as if they were William Stone writing to his sister about why he was eager to join the army. They should use descriptive language and historical detail. **OL**

C Critical Thinking

Identifying Central Issues Ask: What advantages might soldiers who grew up on farms have over those who grew up in the city? *(They might be more accustomed to living and working outdoors, be strong from physical work, and have experience with firearms.)* **BL**

Primary Source

Critical Thinking Answer
They might have been proud to be soldiers.
Skills Practice Ask: What do the soldiers have in common? *(They are both in uniform and carrying their weapons, they are white Americans, and they appear serious.)* **BL**

Others thought they would be called cowards if they did not serve. Still others yearned for excitement. The sister of William Stone of Louisiana wrote that her brother was:

PRIMARY SOURCE

W "wild to be off to Virginia [to join the Confederate army]. He so fears that the fighting will be over before he can get there."
—from *Brokenburn: The Journal of Kate Stone*

The quest for excitement was especially strong among younger soldiers. Many recruits on both sides were hardly adults. Tens of thousands of soldiers were under 18, and some were younger than 14. To get into the army, many teenagers ran away from home or lied about their ages.

Although teenage boys were accepted into military service, one group of men was not permitted to fight during the early days of the war. Unwilling to provide enslaved people with weapons, the Confederacy barred African Americans from the army. The Union also refused to let freed people enlist. Northern leaders worried that white troops would

not accept African American soldiers. Later in the war, though, this policy was changed.

False Hopes

When the war began, each side expected an easy victory. Northerners could not imagine the Confederates holding out for long against the Union's greater resources. They boasted that the war would end in a quick and glorious triumph for the Union.

Confederates found it impossible to believe that the North could ever subdue the fighting spirit of the South. Both sides were wrong. In the end, the war lasted far longer than most Americans could have guessed.

Who Were the Soldiers?

Soldiers came from every region and all walks of life. Most, though, came from farms. Almost half of the North's troops and more than 60 percent of the South's had owned or worked on farms. Lincoln's early terms of enlistment asked governors to supply soldiers for 90 days. When the conflict did not end quickly, soldiers' terms became longer.

478 Chapter 16 *The Civil War*

Hands-On Chapter Project
Step 1

Publishing a Newspaper

Step 1: Setting Up a Newspaper Small groups of students will organize a staff for a new city newspaper for a Union or Confederate city during the Civil War.

Essential Question: What were the strengths and weaknesses of the North and the South?

Directions Organize students into five groups and explain that they will be creat-

ing newspapers about the events of the Civil War from the perspective of journalists living in either a Union or a Confederate city. Have students select a city and create a name for their paper. Tell students to gather historical information and visuals about their city from 1860 to 1865. Students can look for information about city leaders and industries, as well as stories about people who may have lived there during the Civil War. Provide samples of current newspapers

to show students how information is presented. Students should also find out how residents felt about the outbreak of the war. Then have students summarize what they have learned in a short essay.

Analyzing Ask each group to describe how Americans felt about the Civil War in 1860. Tell students they will publish their first "newspaper" in the next step. **OL**

(Chapter Project continued in Section 2)

By the summer of 1861, the Confederate army had about 112,000 soldiers, who were sometimes called Rebels. The Union had about 187,000 soldiers, or Yankees, as they were also known. By the end of the war, about 900,000 men fought for the Confederacy and about 2.1 million men for the Union. The Union army included just under 200,000 African Americans and about 10,000 Latino soldiers.

The Life of a Soldier

In both the North and the South, civilians and soldiers suffered terrible hardships and faced new **challenges.** In letters to their families and friends at home, soldiers described what they saw and how they felt. Many wrote about their boredom, discomfort, sickness, fear, and horror.

Most of the time the soldiers lived in camps. Camp life had its pleasant moments of songs, stories, letters from home, and baseball games. Often, however, a soldier's life was dull—a seemingly unchanging routine of drills, bad food, marches, and rain.

During lulls between battles, Confederate and Union soldiers sometimes forgot they were enemies. A private described his wartime experiences:

PRIMARY SOURCE

"A part of Co K and some of the enemy came together and stacked arms and talked for a long time. Our men cooked coffee and treated them and [afterward] . . . each one took up his position again and they began to fire at each other again, but not as hard as before."
—from *The Life of Billy Yank*

The Reality of War

In spite of fleeting moments of calm, the reality of war was never far away. Both sides suffered terrible losses. The new rifles used during the Civil War fired with greater accuracy than the muskets of earlier wars.

Medical facilities were overwhelmed by the thousands of casualties. After the Battle of Shiloh, the wounded lay in the rain for more than 24 hours waiting for treatment. A Union soldier recalled, "Many had died there, and others were in the last agonies as we passed. Their groans and cries were heart-rending."

Faced with such horrors, many men deserted. About one of every 11 Union soldiers and one of every 8 Confederates ran away because of fear, hunger, or sickness.

Reading Check Explaining Why did both sides think the war would end quickly?

History ONLINE
Study Central™ To review this section, go to glencoe.com.

Section 1 Review

Vocabulary

1. Write a short paragraph in which you use all the following vocabulary terms: border state, contrast, blockade, export, challenge.

Main Ideas

2. **Explaining** Why were the border states important to both the North and South?

3. **Evaluating** What was the purpose of the Anaconda Plan?

Critical Thinking

4. **Predicting** What do you think would be the South's greatest advantage in the war?

5. **Comparing** Create a diagram to compare Northern and Southern aims and strategies.

	North	South
Aims		
Strategies		

6. **Descriptive Writing** You are a Southerner or Northerner in 1861. Write a journal entry that explains your reasons for joining the Confederate or Union army.

Answer the
7. **Essential Question**
What were the strengths and weaknesses of the North and the South?

R Reading Strategy

Drawing Conclusions Ask: Based on this description, how close must the armies have been in relation to each other? *(close enough to talk, trade, and share coffee)* **OL**

Reading Check Answer: Northerners didn't believe the Confederates could hold out for long against the Union's greater resources; Southerners did not believe the North could subdue the fighting spirit of the South.

Assess

History ONLINE

Study Central™ provides summaries, interactive games, and online graphic organizers to help students review content.

Close

Discussing As a class, discuss the challenges faced by the North and the South at the beginning of the Civil War. **OL**

Section ★ Review

Answers

1. Paragraphs should use vocabulary words with their correct definitions.
2. These were strategic locations because they were near major cities, as well as trade and transportation routes.
3. to split the Confederacy in two and cut Southern supply lines
4. Students may say they were fighting on familiar territory or had a strong determination to win their independence.

5. **North:** *Aims*—bring South back into Union; *Strategies*—blockade, control Mississippi, capture Richmond; **South:** *Aims*—independence and slavery; *Strategies*—fight until North gives up, gain foreign support
6. Journal entries will vary but should include personal and historical details.
7. **North:** *Strengths*—larger population; more railroads, farms, exports, manufactured goods; *Weaknesses*—war would be fought

on unfamiliar territory; **South:** *Strengths*—excellent military leaders, strong fighting spirit, knowledge of the territory; *Weaknesses*—smaller population; fewer resources and industry

Early Stages of the War

Focus

Bellringer
Daily Test Practice Transparency 16–2

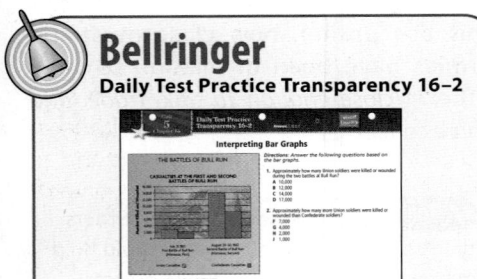

Reading Guide
Answers to Graphic:

Answers may include **1861:** First Battle of Bull Run, Confederate victory; **1862:** Battle of the ironclads, indecisive; Shiloh, Union victory; **1863:** Vicksburg, Union victory, won control of the Mississippi; Gettysburg, Union victory

Section Spotlight Video

Watch the Section Spotlight Video "Early Stages of the War" to learn more about the battle between the *Monitor* and the *Merrimac.*

Resource Manager

Essential Question ◄
Why did neither the Union nor the Confederacy gain a strong advantage during the early years of the war?

Reading Guide

Content Vocabulary
tributary (p. 482)   casualty (p. 483)
ironclad (p. 483)

Academic Vocabulary
abandon (p. 481)   impact (p. 487)

Key People and Events
Stonewall Jackson (p. 481)
Ulysses S. Grant (p. 482)
Battle of Shiloh (p. 483)
Robert E. Lee (p. 485)
Battle of Antietam (p. 486)
Frederick Douglass (p. 487)
Emancipation Proclamation (p. 487)

Reading Strategy
Taking Notes As you read, place the early Civil War battles described in the text on a time line and take notes on what happened during each one.

ILLINOIS STANDARDS
The American Journey

14.C.3 Compare historical issues involving rights, roles and status of individuals in relation to municipalities, states and the nation.

17.A Locate, describe and explain places, regions, and features on Earth.

18.C.3a Describe ways in which a diverse U.S. population has developed and maintained common beliefs (e.g., life, liberty and the pursuit of happiness; the Constitution and the Bill of Rights).

American Diary

Captain Van Brunt, of the U.S. Navy, described the historic first battle between metal-plated ships in 1862: "[The Monitor] laid herself right alongside of the Merrimack, *and the contrast was that of a pigmy to a giant. Gun after gun was fired by the* Monitor, *which was returned with whole broadsides from the rebels with no more effect, apparently, than so many pebblestones thrown by a child."*

—*quoted in* Official Records of the Union and Confederate Navies in the War of the Rebellion, *1898*

R Reading Strategies	C Critical Thinking	D Differentiated Instruction	W Writing Support	S Skill Practice
Teacher Edition • Outlining, p. 481 • Visualizing, p. 481 • Det. Cause and Effect, p. 482 • Act. Prior Know., p. 483 • Making Infer., p. 486 **Additional Resources** • Guid. Read., URB p. 68 • Cont. Voc., URB p. 45 • Acad. Vocab., URB p. 47 • Read. Ess., p. 166	**Teacher Edition** • Making Gen., p. 483 • Analyzing Info., p. 484 • Analyzing Info., p. 486 **Additional Resources** • Quizzes and Tests, p. 152 • Inter. Polit. Cartoons, URB p. 13	**Teacher Edition** • ELL, p. 482 • Below Grade Level, p. 482 • Gifted and Talented, p. 485 **Additional Resources** • Reteaching Act., URB p. 65 • School-to-Home, URB p. 63 • Differ. Inst., URB p. 55	**Teacher Edition** • Persuasive Writing, p. 487 **Additional Resources** • Authentic Assess., p. 16	**Teacher Edition** • Using Geo. Skills, p. 484 **Additional Resources** • Daily Test Pract. Transp. 16-2 • Lesson Transp. 16B • Time Line Skills, URB p. 62

War on Land and Sea

Main Idea The Confederates decisively won the First Battle of Bull Run.

History and You Would you eat a picnic lunch while a battle was raging all around you? Read to learn what happened in 1861 when many people did exactly that.

The Civil War was fought on sea as well as on land. While the Union and Confederacy mobilized their armies, the Union navy began operations against the South. In April 1861, President Lincoln proclaimed a blockade of all Confederate ports.

Southerners hoped to break the Union blockade with a secret weapon—the *Merrimack,* an **abandoned** Union warship. The Confederates rebuilt and covered the wooden ship in iron. The armored vessel, renamed the *Virginia,* could withstand Union cannon fire.

First Battle of Bull Run

Pressure mounted in the summer of 1861, leading to the first major battle of the Civil War. On July 21, about 30,000 inexperienced

R1 Union troops commanded by General Irvin McDowell attacked a smaller, equally inexperienced Confederate force led by General P. G. T. Beauregard. The fighting took place in northern Virginia, about 5 miles (8 km) from the town of Manassas Junction near a small river called Bull Run. Hundreds of Washington, D.C., residents went to the battle site to picnic and watch.

The Yankees drove the Confederates back at first. Then the Rebels rallied, inspired by reinforcements under General Thomas Jackson. Jackson was seen holding out heroically, "like a stone wall," and became known thereafter as **"Stonewall" Jackson.** The Confederates unleashed a savage counterattack that forced Union lines to break. The Union retreat turned into a mad stampede when retreating Union troops collided with the civilians, fleeing in panic back to Washington, D.C. R2

The outcome shocked Northerners. They began to understand that the war could be a long, difficult, and costly struggle. President Lincoln appointed a new general, George B. McClellan, to head and organize the Union army of the East—called the Army of the Potomac—and to train the troops.

Primary Source / Naval Warfare

The Ironclads The *Monitor* was small for a warship—about 172 feet (52 m) long—and constructed almost entirely of iron. A revolving armored tower called a turret housed the guns.

The Union's *Monitor* (below) battled the ironclad *Merrimack* (left), called the *Virginia* by the Confederates, on March 9, 1862.

iron turret rotates on a pivot

11-inch (28-cm) cannon housed inside rotating turret

layered armor plating

Critical Thinking

Making Inferences What advantages would an iron warship have over a wooden ship? Explain.

Teach

R1 Reading Strategy

Outlining Have students make an outline of this section by using the subheads. Then have them complete the outline as they read by adding key details beneath each subhead. **BL**

R2 Reading Strategy

Visualizing Ask: What does the author want the reader to picture with the phrase "mad stampede"? *(a herd of cattle or other animals running as fast as they can)* What would it be like to witness this event? *(Answers will vary.)* What words would you choose to help readers visualize the battle? *(Answers may include confusing, frightening, or dangerous.)* **OL**

Primary Source

Critical Thinking Answer
An iron warship is protected from gunfire and is less likely to catch fire and burn.

Skills Practice Ask: How might this technology benefit the North's war strategy? *(Ports could be blockaded by these iron ships that could deflect gunfire.)* **OL**

Differentiated Instruction

Leveled Activities

BL School-to-Home Connection Activity, URB p. 63

OL Reading Essentials and Note-Taking Guide, p. 166

ELL Academic Vocabulary Activity, URB p. 47

R Reading Strategy

Determining Cause and Effect
Ask: What effect do you think the number of casualties might have on morale in the North? *(Students may suggest that morale or support for the war in the North might decrease as the number of casualties increased.)* **OL**

D₁ Differentiated Instruction

English Language Learners Remind students that some words can be understood by looking at the word parts. Write "discouraged" on the board. **Ask:** What does the root word "courage" mean? *("Courage" means "brave.")* Explain that adding "dis" would make it mean the opposite. **Ask:** What might "discouraged" mean? *(having no courage, or being afraid)* Have students look up "discouraged" in the dictionary to check their answers. **ELL**

D₂ Differentiated Instruction

Below Grade Level Ask students to explain the term "unconditional" and why it became Grant's nickname. **BL**

Hands-On Chapter Project
Step 2

The loss at Bull Run discouraged Union supporters. Although dismayed by the results, President Lincoln was also determined. Within days he issued a call for more volunteers for the army. He signed two bills requesting a total of 1 million soldiers to serve for three years. Victories in the West raised Northern spirits and also increased enlistment.

The War in the West

In the West, the major Union goal was to control the Mississippi River and its **tributaries,** the smaller rivers that flow into a larger river. With control of the river, Union ships on the Mississippi could prevent the states of Louisiana, Arkansas, and Texas from supplying the rest of the Confederacy. Control would also let Union gunboats and troops move into the heart of the South.

The battle for the rivers began in February 1862 when Union forces captured Fort Henry on the Tennessee River. The assault was led by naval commander Andrew Foote and army general **Ulysses S. Grant.** Soon afterward, Grant and Foote moved against Fort Donelson on the Cumberland River. The Confederates in Fort Donelson realized that they had no chance of winning the battle, so they asked Grant what terms, or incentives, he would give them to give up the fort. Grant said:

PRIMARY SOURCE
"No terms except an unconditional and immediate surrender can be accepted."
—General Grant to General Buckner, February 1862

"Unconditional Surrender" Grant became the North's new hero.

War of the Ironclads

As conflict was raging on the rivers of the West, ships of the Union and Confederate navies were fighting in the Atlantic Ocean.

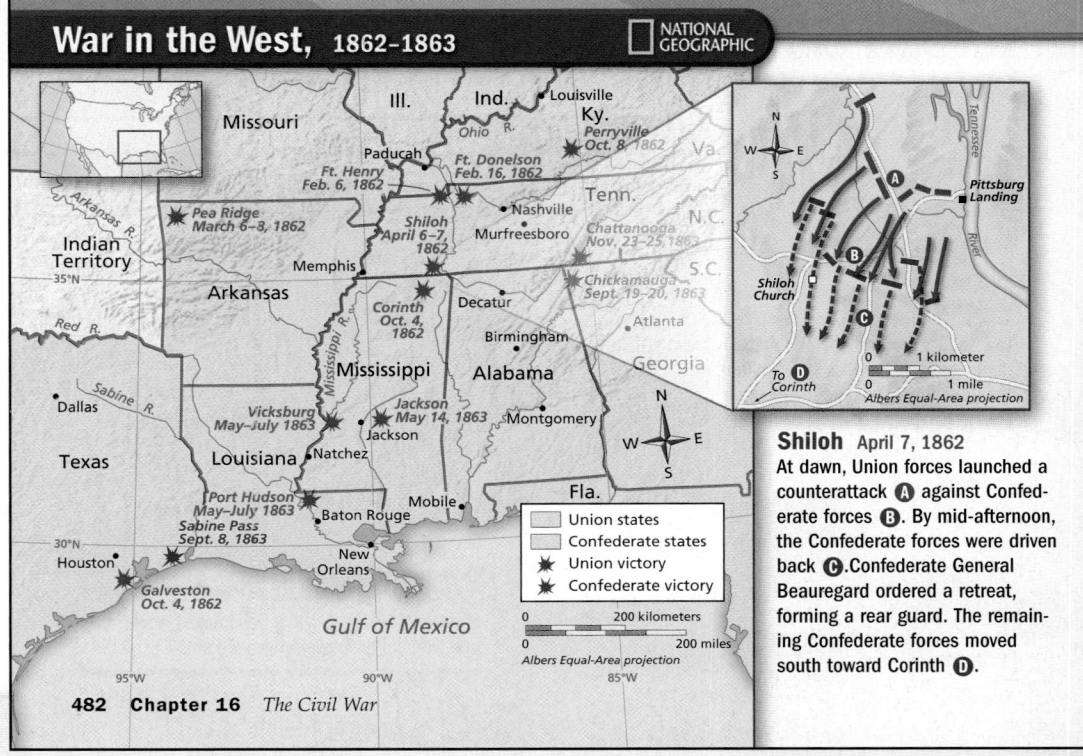

War in the West, 1862–1863
NATIONAL GEOGRAPHIC

Union states
Confederate states
★ Union victory
★ Confederate victory

Shiloh April 7, 1862
At dawn, Union forces launched a counterattack **A** against Confederate forces **B**. By mid-afternoon, the Confederate forces were driven back **C**. Confederate General Beauregard ordered a retreat, forming a rear guard. The remaining Confederate forces moved south toward Corinth **D**.

482   Chapter 16   *The Civil War*

Publishing a Newspaper

Step 2: Writing as a Journalist Students will write articles discussing the early stages of the Civil War.

Essential Question: Why did neither the Union nor the Confederacy gain a strong advantage during the early years of the war?

Directions Students should write articles about news events during the Civil War, which include historical detail and accurate dates.

Groups should assemble their work into one document. Using word processing software, they may design their document like a newspaper. Have students print enough for the class.

Comparing and Contrasting Discuss how each newspaper reports events differently. **Ask:** How do journalists from Union and Confederate cities differ in their reporting? What do they have in common?

(Chapter Project continued in Section 3)

On March 8, 1862, the *Merrimack,* renamed the *Virginia,* attacked a group of Union ships off the coast of Virginia. The North's wooden warships could not damage the Confederate ship—shells simply bounced off its iron sides. Some Northern leaders feared the South would use the **ironclad** warship to destroy the Union navy, steam up the Potomac River, and bombard Washington, D.C.

The North, though, had an ironclad ship of its own, the *Monitor,* and this ship rushed toward Virginia. On March 9, the two ironclads met in battle. Neither ship could sink the other. Although the battle was indecisive, it was also historic because it was the first ever between metal-covered ships.

The Battle of Shiloh

Meanwhile, in the West, General Grant and about 40,000 troops headed south along the Tennessee River toward Corinth, Mississippi, an important railroad junction. In early April 1862, the Union army camped at Pittsburg Landing, 20 miles (32 km) from Corinth. Nearby was a church named Shiloh. Additional Union forces came from Nashville to join Grant.

Confederate leaders decided to strike first, before the reinforcements arrived. Early in the morning of April 6, Confederate forces led by Albert Sidney Johnston and P. G. T. Beauregard launched a surprise attack on the Union troops. The **Battle of Shiloh** lasted two days, with some of the most bitter, bloody fighting of the war. Even though Shiloh was a narrow victory for the Union forces, the losses were enormous. Together the two armies suffered more than 23,000 **casualties**—people killed or wounded.

After Shiloh, Union forces gained control of Corinth on May 30. Memphis, Tennessee, fell to Union armies on June 6. The North seemed well on its way to controlling the Mississippi River.

C Critical Thinking

Making Generalizations Have students read the account of the Battle of Shiloh. **Ask:** What generalizations can you make about the battle strategy? (*Students might suggest that striking first is a good tactic because it can surprise the enemy; reinforcements can change a battle's outcome.*) **AL**

R Reading Strategy

Activating Prior Knowledge Ask: What is a casualty? (*a person who is either killed or wounded*) During the Battle of Shiloh, most casualties did not die. **ELL**

War in the West
1862–1863

Critical Thinking Answer

The statements of both men sound as though they believed they could win the Battle of Shiloh after the first day. Most military leaders would make similar statements because they want to encourage their troops to keep fighting, even when the battle situation seems challenging.

Additional Support

The Battle of Shiloh

More than 23,000 troops were killed or wounded in the Battle of Shiloh. This was the highest number of casualties of any Civil War battle to date. The Union victory was an important step toward the goal of controlling the Mississippi River.

Day One

A surprise attack by the Confederate army gave it an early advantage. Union general William T. Sherman remarked to General Grant, *"Well, Grant, we've had the devil's own day of it, haven't we?"*

"Yes," Grant replied, *"Lick 'em tomorrow, though."*

◀ William T. Sherman

Day Two

With Union reinforcements, the battle changed direction, resulting in a Union victory. Confederate general P. G. T. Beauregard lamented, *"I thought I had General Grant just where I wanted him and could finish him up in the morning."*

P. G. T. Beauregard ▶

Critical Thinking

Analyzing Did either Beauregard or Sherman accept the fact that his side might lose the Battle of Shiloh? Do you think their statements reflect what most military leaders would say in this situation? Explain.

Activity: Interdisciplinary Connection

Geography Many Civil War battles have two names. The Union often named battles after the nearest body of water. The Confederacy usually named battles after the nearest settlement. The Battle of Bull Run (a river) in the North was known as the Battle of Manassas (a settlement) in the South. Have students survey the chapter and list the major battles of the Civil War. Then, have them research to identify names given to each battle by both the Union and the Confederate armies.

Organize students into groups. Give each group a relief map of the United States from this period that includes settlement names. Half the class should find the Union-named battles on the map, and the other half can find the Confederate-named battles. Make a comparison list of all the battles the students find. Have students identify geographic features near major battlefields. Then, transfer the battle locations to a large map at the front of the classroom. **Ask:** What patterns do you see? (*Many battles took place in the South.*) How might landforms have affected the outcomes of battles? (*Mountains and foothills would limit movement of armies; waterways could be used to transport goods and troops.*) **OL**

S Skill Practice

Using Geography Skills Have students look at the maps in this section. **Ask:** About how far was Vicksburg from New Orleans? *(about 200 miles)* What other ports could the Confederacy use to ship goods after New Orleans fell? *(Galveston, Mobile, Norfolk)* **OL**

C Critical Thinking

Analyzing Information Direct students' attention to the map on this page. **Ask:** How much time elapsed between each of the battles shown on the map? *(about 3 months; about 2 months; about 3 weeks; about 3 months; about 5 months; about 2 months)* How many Confederate victories are shown on the map? *(four)* How many Union victories are shown? *(two)* **OL**

✔ **Reading Check** **Answer:** Similar—both battles took place early in the war; the victors in both battles had to rally to win. Different—Confederacy won First Battle of Bull Run, Union won Battle of Shiloh; Bull Run was one day, Shiloh was fought over two days. Casualties at Shiloh were much higher.

Additional Support

War in the East, 1862–1863 ☐ NATIONAL GEOGRAPHIC

Battle Dates

Monitor & Virginia
Mar. 9, 1862
Seven Days
June 25–July 1, 1862
Bull Run
(2nd Battle)
Aug. 29–30, 1862
Antietam
Sept. 17, 1862
Fredericksburg
Dec. 13, 1862
Chancellorsville
May 1–4, 1863
Gettysburg
July 1–3, 1863

← Union advance
◄◄◄ Union retreat
← Confederate advance
◄◄◄ Confederate retreat
✦ Union victory
✦ Confederate victory
✦ Inconclusive battle

New Orleans Falls

A few weeks after Shiloh, the North won another important victory. On April 25, 1862, Union naval forces under David Farragut captured New Orleans, Louisiana, the largest city in the South. Farragut, who was of Spanish descent, grew up in the South but remained loyal to the Union. His capture of New Orleans, near the mouth of the Mississippi River, meant that the Confederacy could no longer use the river to carry its goods to sea. Together with Grant's victories to the north, the capture of New Orleans gave the Union control of most of the Mississippi River. Only the city of Vicksburg, Mississippi, blocked Union control of the river and the success of the Union's western strategy.

✔ **Reading Check** **Comparing and Contrasting** How was the Battle of Shiloh like the First Battle of Bull Run? How were the two battles different?

C War in the East

Main Idea The South won several important victories in the East during 1862, but the Union responded with a vital triumph of its own.

History and You What is the most valuable thing you have lost? Read to learn what happened when a Confederate officer lost some important papers.

W hile Union and Confederate forces were struggling for control of Tennessee and the Mississippi River, another major campaign was being waged in the East to capture Richmond, Virginia. Richmond, the capital of the Confederacy, was close to the northern Confederate border and vulnerable to attack. Yet it was a matter of pride to defend it at all costs. Repelling one Union advance after another, Confederate armies prevented the fall of Richmond until the end of the war.

Activity: Technology Connection

Creating a Time Line Ask students to use appropriate software to create a time line from the following information about a day in the life of a Civil War soldier (who was not engaged in battle): 5:00 A.M.—Reveille played; 5:15 A.M.—Roll call and special orders; 5:30 A.M.–8:00 A.M.—Breakfast, tend horses, infirmary calls, cleanup duty, and necessary chores; 8:00 A.M.–2:00 P.M.—Out of six hours; two hours of sentry duty; 8:00 A.M.–12:00 P.M.—Drill if not on sentry duty; 12:00 P.M.—Lunch followed by more drill; 4:30 P.M.—Polish weapons and care for uniforms; 5:45 P.M.—Retreat ceremony with roll call, inspection, and dress parade; 7:30 P.M.—Supper; 8:30 P.M.—Assembly and last roll call; 9:00 P.M.—Taps sounded and lights out. **Ask:** What do you think it might have been like to be a soldier in the Confederate or Union army? *(Check students' time lines for correct chronological order. Students may describe the routine drills as boring.)* **OL**

By the Numbers

The Battle of Antietam was the bloodiest one-day battle in the war and in American history. Several battles in the East were costly in terms of total casualties (killed, wounded, missing, and captured).

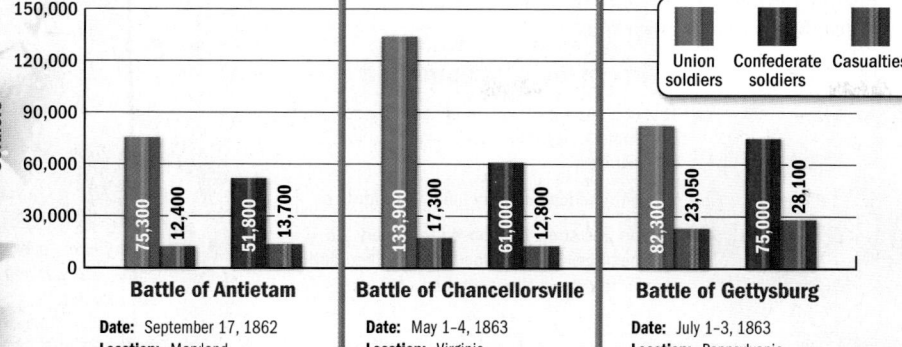

Legend: Union soldiers | Confederate soldiers | Casualties

Battle of Antietam (75,300 / 12,400 / 51,800 / 13,700)
Date: September 17, 1862
Location: Maryland
Commanders:
  Union: George B. McClellan
  Confederate: Robert E. Lee
Result: Indecisive (Strategic Union Victory)

Battle of Chancellorsville (133,900 / 17,300 / 61,000 / 12,800)
Date: May 1–4, 1863
Location: Virginia
Commanders:
  Union: Joseph Hooker
  Confederate: Robert E. Lee
Result: Victory for Confederacy

Battle of Gettysburg (82,300 / 23,050 / 75,000 / 28,100)
Date: July 1–3, 1863
Location: Pennsylvania
Commanders:
  Union: George G. Meade
  Confederate: Robert E. Lee
Result: Victory for Union

Source: U.S. Army Center of Military History

Graph Skills

Calculating About how many soldiers fought at Chancellorsville?

Graphs in MOtion See StudentWorks™ Plus or glencoe.com.

Victories for the Confederacy

Southern victories in the East were largely the result of the leadership of General **Robert E. Lee** and Stonewall Jackson. Through knowledge of the terrain, speed of movement, and the ability to inspire their troops, Confederate forces managed to defeat Union forces sometimes twice as large as their own.

In 1862 Confederate forces turned back General George B. McClellan at the Seven Days' Battle, General John Pope at the Second Battle of Bull Run, and General Ambrose Burnside at Fredericksburg. In May 1863, at Chancellorsville, Virginia, Lee's army defeated a Union army twice its size. "My God, my God," Lincoln said when he learned of the defeat, "What will the country say!"

Victories in the East did not include victories outside the Confederacy. Lee's two attempts to invade the North failed. In September 1862,

Lee's army was turned back at the Battle of Antietam. Less than a year later, Confederate forces would face the same fate at Gettysburg. You will read about the Battle of Gettysburg in Section 4.

Invasion of the North

Washington, D.C., presented a tempting target for the Confederates, but the city was too well guarded for Lee to consider an attack. On the urging of Confederate president Jefferson Davis, Lee moved his troops instead into western Maryland—Union territory. His goal now was to sweep into Pennsylvania and carry the war into the Northern states. Lee knew that McClellan was pursuing him with a sizable force, so he concentrated on moving forward. Lee's forces crossed into Maryland and began an invasion of the North.

The Civil War **Chapter 16** 485

Differentiated Instruction

Gifted and Talented Have students research the lives of one Union and one Confederate general. Have students write short biographies of each general, comparing their military service and personal experiences. **AL**

War in the East 1862–1863

NATIONAL GEOGRAPHIC

Graph Skills Answer

194,900 fought at Chancellorsville.

Graph Skills Practice

Using Mathematics Skills Ask: How many more Union soldiers than Confederate soldiers were at each battle? *(Antietam: 23,500 more; Chancellorsville: 72,900 more)* Is there a relationship between the number of soldiers who fought in a battle and the army that won? *(Students may say that there is not always a relationship because the Confederacy won the Battle of Chancellorsville with a much smaller army.)* **OL**

Differentiated Instruction

"The Battle Cry of Freedom"

Objective: To analyze a Civil War–era song

Focus: Ask students how the modern-day songs they listen to make them feel.

Teach: Have students read the lyrics of the song and then answer the questions.

Assess: Discuss the answers provided by the students.

Close: Discuss with students how music can stir emotions and act as a morale booster.

Differentiated Instruction Strategies

BL Have students orally describe what they envision when they read the song's lyrics.

AL Ask students to design a cover page for the sheet music of the song, using appropriate words and images.

ELL Ask students to identify similar songs from their native cultures.

Differentiated Instruction
Activity, URB p. 55

485

C Critical Thinking

Analyzing Information Ask: What might have happened if Lee's orders had not been found? *(McClellan would not have known Lee's plans and that his army was split.)* **OL**

R Reading Strategy

Making Inferences Ask: Why would Lincoln be reluctant to move against slavery because of the border states? *(Many people in border states held slaves, and he did not want to alienate them and risk their secession.)* **OL**

Primary Source

Critical Thinking Answer
Abolitionists wanted to use the war to end slavery; Lincoln knew that England and France would be less willing to help the South because those countries were opposed to slavery.

Reading Check Answer: At the end of a one-day battle, the Union won a costly victory, and Lee retreated to Virginia.

Additional Support

Primary Source / Emancipation Proclamation

Lincoln declared in the Emancipation Proclamation that:

"all persons held as slaves within any state . . . in rebellion against the United States, shall be then, thenceforward and forever free."

Results of the Proclamation

✔ It sent a clear message to enslaved people and the Confederacy that slavery would no longer be tolerated.

✔ African American military units were formed.

✔ Europe was strongly opposed to slavery. No European government would defend the South in its war to protect the institution of slavery.

"The white man's happiness cannot be purchased by the black man's misery."
—Frederick Douglass, 1849

"If my name ever goes into history, it will be for this act."
—Abraham Lincoln, 1863

Critical Thinking

Explaining What political reasons did Lincoln have for issuing the Emancipation Proclamation?

The Battle of Antietam

Once in Maryland, Lee split his army in four parts and instructed them to move in different directions. He hoped to confuse McClellan about the size and destination of his army. A Confederate officer, however, lost his copy of Lee's orders describing this plan. The paper was found by two Union soldiers, who brought it to McClellan.

McClellan did not attack immediately. Lee reassembled his troops, and on September 17, 1862, the two sides met in the **Battle of Antietam** near Sharpsburg, Maryland.

About 6,000 soldiers were killed. About 17,000 more were badly wounded. It was the deadliest single day of fighting during the war. Antietam was an important victory for the Union. Because of the great losses, Lee chose to retreat to Virginia after the fighting. At least for the time being, his strategy of invading the North had failed. The Union could breathe a little more easily.

Reading Check Summarizing What was the outcome of the Battle of Antietam?

The Emancipation Proclamation

Main Idea Lincoln's Emancipation Proclamation had an enormous effect in America and abroad.

History and You How do you make difficult decisions? Read to learn about the debate over the war's purpose and how Lincoln eventually settled on a course of action.

. . . .

At first, Abraham Lincoln cast the Civil War as a battle for the Union rather than as a fight against slavery. As the conflict progressed, however, Lincoln changed the way he thought about slavery and its role in the war.

The Debate

Lincoln hated slavery, yet he was reluctant to make the Civil War a battle to end it. He feared that many Union supporters would strongly oppose such a decision. At the beginning of the war, Lincoln hesitated to move against slavery because of the border states.

Activity: Collaborative Learning

Determining Importance Give students a copy of the Emancipation Proclamation. Working in pairs, students should read the proclamation carefully and then choose the part they think is the most important and rewrite it in their own words. **Ask:** Which sections would be most important for enslaved people living in the Confederacy? *(the section that gives them their freedom)* What section would impact the military? *(the section that permits former enslaved people to enlist in the armed services of the United States)* How do you think news of the proclamation was received by slaveholders in Confederate states? *(They may have disregarded it because they believed they were not subject to President Lincoln's authority; they may have been more motivated to fight in the Civil War to protect slavery in their areas.)* By enslaved persons? *(They may have celebrated the proclamation; some may have left their owners, while others may have waited to see what would happen with the war.)* Have students research to find primary-source accounts of reactions to the Emancipation Proclamation. **AL**

Even many Northerners who disapproved of slavery were not eager to risk their lives to end it. Other Americans held a different opinion, however.

From the start of the war, abolitionists, including orator **Frederick Douglass** and newspaper editor Horace Greeley, urged Lincoln to make the war a fight to end slavery. These Northerners made several arguments to support their position. First, they argued, slavery was a moral wrong that needed to be abolished. Second, they pointed out that slavery was the root of the divisions between North and South. Therefore, the nation could never be fully restored if slavery continued.

Finally, Douglass and others brought up the issue of foreign policy. Britain and France each sympathized with the South for economic reasons. Southern leaders were trying to persuade Britain and France to recognize the Confederacy's independence.

Public opinion in England and France was strongly antislavery. By casting the war as a fight for freedom, Douglass pointed out, Lincoln would make Britain and France less willing to support the South. That, in turn, would help the Union cause.

Lincoln Decides

Lincoln knew that the Constitution did not give him the power to end slavery. The Constitution did, however, give him the power to take property from an enemy in wartime—and, by law, enslaved people were property. On September 22, 1862, soon after the North's victory at Antietam, Lincoln announced that he would issue the **Emancipation Proclamation**—a decree freeing all enslaved people in rebel territory on January 1, 1863.

Effects of the Proclamation

The Emancipation Proclamation did not actually free a single enslaved person. The proclamation applied only to enslaved people in areas held by the Confederacy. There Lincoln had no power to enforce the new policy.

The proclamation had an important **impact** in America, however. By issuing the Emancipation Proclamation, the government declared slavery to be wrong. If the Union won the war, slavery would be banned forever.

✓ **Reading Check** Summarizing Why did abolitionists believe that Lincoln should make the end of slavery a goal of the war?

W Writing Support

Persuasive Writing Have students write a letter to President Lincoln that persuades him to issue the Emancipation Proclamation. Students should explain their views and include historical information. **OL**

✓ **Reading Check** **Answer:** Abolitionists believed that slavery was morally wrong, it was the source of disagreement between the North and the South, and it should be abolished to prevent Britain or France from siding with the Confederacy.

Assess

History ONLINE

Study Central™ provides summaries, interactive games, and online graphic organizers to help students review content.

Close

Summarizing As a class, discuss the reasons neither the Union nor the Confederacy gained a strong advantage during the early years of the war. **OL**

Section 2 Review

History ONLINE
Study Central™ To review this section, go to glencoe.com.

Vocabulary

1. Use each of these terms in a sentence that will help explain its meaning: abandon, tributary, ironclad, casualty, impact.

Main Ideas

2. Analyzing What factors helped the Confederates win the First Battle of Bull Run?

3. Summarizing What was the final outcome of the Battle of Shiloh?

4. Explaining What did the Emancipation Proclamation state?

Critical Thinking

5. Analyzing Why was controlling the Mississippi River vital to the North and the South? Explain your answer in a diagram like the one shown here.

Control of the Mississippi

6. Evaluating Which of Frederick Douglass's arguments for making the abolition of slavery an aim of the war do you find most convincing? Why?

7. Expository Writing You read about General Lee's lost battle orders. Write a short paragraph explaining the role of chance and error in this discovery, as well as General McClellan's use of the information.

Answer the
8. Essential Question
Why did neither the Union nor the Confederacy gain a strong advantage during the early years of the war?

Answers

1. Definitions for the vocabulary words are found in the section and in the Glossary.
2. Confederates were aided by the leadership of "Stonewall" Jackson, as well as reinforcements that he brought.
3. The Union won a narrow victory; both sides had heavy casualties; and the Union army took control of Corinth, Mississippi, which was an important railroad junction.
4. All slaves in rebel territory were free.

5. **North:** could block western Confederate states from supplying the rest of the Confederacy; could also move gunboats and troops into the heart of the South. **South:** could use it to move troops and supplies; vital to South's economy to allow farmers to ship goods to markets
6. Answers will vary but should include references to specific quotes by Douglass.

7. Answers should explain the role of chance and error, as well as how McClellan did not immediately take action based on the discovered orders.
8. Student answers should discuss decisions made by leaders as well as key battles won by the Union and the Confederacy.

Focus

C₁ Critical Thinking

Making Inferences Have students read the author biography. Remind students that the author had never seen a wartime battle but described it in enough detail that veterans found it realistic. **Ask:** How might the author have learned about the battles of the Civil War? *(He may have learned about them in school or in books, or he may have interviewed people who were there.)* **OL**

R Reading Strategy

Paraphrasing Have students find the vocabulary words within the selection. Then have them paraphrase the sentences in which each word occurs. **OL**

C₂ Critical Thinking

Making Inferences Ask: What is the soldier doing? *(He is in a battle and may be getting his weapons ready to fire.)* Why do you think the author describes the soldier's task this way? *(He has done it so many times that he can work fast and think about other things.)* **OL**

Additional Reading

Review suggested books before assigning them.

America's LITERATURE

Meet the Author

C₁ **Stephen Crane** (1871–1900) had never seen a battlefield when he wrote *The Red Badge of Courage*, which he based on accounts of the Confederate victory at Chancellorsville. Even so, he described the experience of war so realistically that even combat veterans admired his work.

Building Background

The American novelist Stephen Crane, who created the most famous depiction of Civil War combat in his 1895 novel *The Red Badge of Courage*, did not describe warfare in traditional, heroic terms. Instead, he tried to present an objective, almost scientific examination of the effect of battle on individuals. As you read this excerpt from *The Red Badge of Courage*, be aware of how Crane creates an effect of realism.

Vocabulary

careering speeding

exasperation extreme irritation

R **impotency** powerlessness

imprecations curses

pummeling beating

exultant very joyful

THE RED BADGE OF COURAGE

Stephen Crane

He was at a task. He was like a carpenter who has made many boxes, making still another box, only there was furious haste in his movements. He, in his thought, was **careering** off in other places, even as the carpenter who as he works whistles and thinks of his friend or his enemy, his home or a saloon. And these jolted dreams were never perfect to him afterward, but remained a mass of blurred shapes.

Presently he began to feel the effects of the war atmosphere—a blistering sweat, a sensation that his eyeballs were about to crack like hot stones. A burning roar filled his ears.

488

Fiction: *Who Comes With Cannons?* by Patricia Beatty, begins when orphan Truth Hopkins moves to the South to live with relatives. When the Civil War begins, her cousins are forced to join the Confederate army. One of them is captured, and Truth is the only one who can rescue him.

Fiction: *The Deep Cut,* by Susan Rosson Spain, is based partly on true Civil War events. People thought that the quiet, teenaged Lonzo was "slow," but he is the only one who can foil a murder plot.

Nonfiction: *The President Is Shot!* by Harold Holzer, describes the assassination of President Abraham Lincoln, with careful attention given to the events and background leading up to the assassination.

For further reading, see BOOKLINK 3.

Following this came a red rage. He developed the acute **exasperation** of a pestered animal, a well-meaning cow worried by dogs. He had a mad feeling against his rifle, which could only be used against one life at a time. He wished to rush forward and strangle with his fingers. He craved a power that would enable him to make a world-sweeping gesture and brush all back. His **impotency** appeared to him, and made his rage into that of a driven beast.

A burning roar filled his ears.

Buried in the smoke of many rifles his anger was directed not so much against the men whom he knew were rushing toward him as against the swirling battle phantoms which were choking him, stuffing their smoke robes down his parched throat. He fought frantically for respite for his senses, for air, as a babe being smothered attacks the deadly blankets.

There was a blare of heated rage mingled with a certain expression of intentness on all faces. Many of the men were making low-toned noises with their mouths, and these subdued cheers, snarls, **imprecations,** prayers, made a wild, barbaric song that went as an undercurrent of sound, strange and chantlike with the resounding chords of the war march. The man at the youth's elbow was babbling. In it there was something soft and tender like the monologue of a babe. . . .

The lieutenant of the youth's company had encountered a soldier who had fled screaming at the first volley of his comrades. Behind the lines these two were acting a little isolated scene. The man was blubbering and staring with sheeplike eyes at the lieutenant, who had seized him by the collar and was **pummeling** him. He drove him back into the ranks with many blows. The soldier went mechanically, dully, with his animal-like eyes upon the officer. Perhaps there was to him a divinity expressed in the voice of the other—stern, hard, with no reflection of fear in it. He tried to reload his gun, but his shaking hands prevented. The lieutenant was obliged to assist him.

The men dropped here and there like bundles. The captain of the youth's company had been killed in an early part of the action. His body lay stretched out in the position of a tired man resting, but upon his face there was an astonished and sorrowful look, as if he thought some friend had done him an ill turn. . . .

At last an **exultant** yell went along the quivering line. The firing dwindled from an uproar to a last vindictive popping. As the smoke slowly eddied away, the youth saw that the charge had been repulsed. The enemy were scattered into reluctant groups. He saw a man climb to the top of the fence, straddle the rail, and fire a parting shot. The waves had receded, leaving bits of dark *débris* upon the ground.

Analyzing Literature

1. **Respond** What surprised you most about Stephen Crane's description of combat?

2. **Recall and Interpret**
   (a) What is the "dark *débris*" left on the battlefield?
   (b) What is the effect of using this phrase?

3. **Evaluate and Connect**
   (a) In your opinion, which details in this passage contribute most powerfully to the effect of realism Crane was striving to create?
   (b) What conclusions can you draw from Crane's depiction of battle?

489

Teach

D Differentiated Instruction

Visual/Spatial Have students draw, paint, or create storyboards to illustrate the scene described by Crane. **OL**

W Writing Support

Descriptive Writing Tell students to take the role of a reporter. Have them write an interview with someone who was present at the battle of Chancellorsville. They should include the questions they would ask and the answers a soldier might have given. **OL**

Assess/Close

Ask: How would the impact of this account be different if it were written as a military report? *(It would include more facts and figures and less colorful language.)* As a newspaper article? *(It would include dates, times, and names of people involved, and it might be shorter.)* Do you think the account would still appeal to readers? *(Answers will vary, but students might mention that Crane's account is more interesting because it includes story-telling details.)*

Answers

1. Students might say they were surprised by the intensity of the battle or the way the soldier was preparing his weapon without having to think about it.

2. (a) The term "dark debris" refers to wounded or dead soldiers.
   (b) This term suggests that the value of human life is diminished during battles or wars.

3. (a) Students may say descriptions about wounded or dying soldiers create a sense of realism.
   (b) Battles were chaotic, violent, and intense.

Life During the War

Focus

Bellringer
Daily Test Practice Transparency 16–3

Reading Guide
Answers to Graphic:
worked in hospitals; took over jobs that were held by men; saved money to buy necessities for their families

Section Spotlight Video

Have students watch the Section Spotlight Video "A Call for Freedom" to learn more about the changes that resulted from the war.

Essential Question
What social, political, and economic changes resulted from the war?

Reading Guide

Content Vocabulary
habeas corpus (p. 495)
draft (p. 496)
bounty (p. 496)
greenback (p. 497)
inflation (p. 497)

Academic Vocabulary
distribute (p. 493)   substitute (p. 496)

Key People and Events
Mary Edwards Walker (p. 492)
Dorothea Dix (p. 492)
Clara Barton (p. 492)
Sally Tompkins (p. 492)
bread riots (p. 494)

Reading Strategy
Taking Notes As you read the section, complete a diagram like the one below by describing three ways that women in the North and the South contributed to the war effort.

Contributions

ILLINOIS STANDARDS
The American Journey

14.C.3 Compare historical issues involving rights, roles and status of individuals in relation to municipalities, states and the nation.

16.A.3c Identify the differences between historical fact and interpretation.

18.B.3a Analyze how individuals and groups interact with and within institutions (e.g., educational, military).

American Diary

Drummer boy Delavan Miller, who served in a New York Regiment, recalls: "The day after a battle is always a sad one in a regiment. Men search for missing comrades and some are found cold in death who were full of life the day before. No jests are spoken. The terribleness of war has been forcibly impressed on all participants."

—*from* Drum Taps in Dixie

Men with the 36th Pennsylvania Infantry Regiment drill at their winter quarters near Langley, Virginia.

Resource Manager

R Reading Strategies	C Critical Thinking	D Differentiated Instruction	W Writing Support	S Skill Practice
Teacher Edition • Summarizing, p. 491 • Organizing, p. 492 • Skimming, p. 493 • Monitoring, p. 495 **Additional Resources** • Guid. Read., URB p. 69 • Content Vocab., URB p. 45 • Academic Vocab., URB p. 47 • Read. Ess., p. 169	**Teacher Edition** • Analyz. Pri. Sources, p. 491 • Predicting, p. 492 • Drawing Conclusions, p. 494 • Deter. Cause and Effect, p. 497 **Additional Resources** • Quizzes and Tests, p. 153	**Teacher Edition** • Interpersonal, p. 492 • Logical/Math., p. 494 • Visual/Spatial, p. 496 **Additional Resources** • Reteaching Act., URB p. 65 • School-to-Home, URB p. 63	**Teacher Edition** • Persuasive Writing, p. 496 **Additional Resources** • Authentic Assess., p. 16	**Teacher Edition** • Creating a Time Line, p. 493 • Using Analysis Skills, p. 496 **Additional Resources** • Daily Test Pract. Transp. 16-3 • Time Line Skills, URB p. 62

A Different Way of Life

Main Idea The Civil War affected civilians as well as soldiers.

History and You How does war change the everyday life of citizens? Read on to find out how Americans tried to adjust to wartime conditions.

Thirteen-year-old Delavan Miller served as a drummer for a New York regiment. He recalls that:

PRIMARY SOURCE

"The great majority of the men really felt that the war would be ended before we had a chance to take a hand in. I may say that the drummer boys, full of young red blood, were as eager for [battle] as the older men, but most of us had got enough of war before we reached Appomattox."

—from _Drum Taps in Dixie_

Life at Home

When the Civil War began, Miller, like many other teenagers, left everything that was familiar to him to serve in the military. This meant leaving family, friends, and school.

Almost everyone who stayed home was touched in some way by the war. Only about one-half of the 12 million school-age children attended school. Many of those who did not worked to help support their families. Schools closed during the war in some areas, especially those near the scenes of battles and skirmishes. Many schools and churches served as hospitals for the wounded.

Shortages in the South

Although the war affected everyone, life in the South changed most dramatically. Both armies spent most of their time on Southern soil, and the South therefore suffered the greatest destruction. Southerners who lived in the paths of marching armies lost crops and homes. Thousands became refugees, and even those who lived outside the war zones suffered. As one observer noted, the South depended on the outside world "for everything from a hairpin to a toothpick, and from a cradle to a coffin." As the war dragged on, shortages of food, supplies, and even household items became commonplace.

✓ **Reading Check** **Explaining** What problems did the Southern people face during the war?

If You Were There / Drummer Boys in the Civil War

Duties and Tasks At 13, you join the army and train as a drummer. Your day begins at 5 A.M. Your drums call the soldiers to meals, roll call, drills, bed, and lights out. You also do chores for officers and surgeons. Your meals, when you can eat, are usually plain biscuits called hardtack and barely cooked bacon.

◄ "Drummer" Jackson served with an African American regiment.

Critical Thinking

Making Inferences What is your daily routine like? How do you think you would have handled the life of a drummer?

"Men of Color, to Arms!"

Objective: To analyze an editorial by Frederick Douglass, urging African Americans to fight against the South

Focus: Review with students what role Douglass played in America in the 1800s.

Teach: Have students read the editorial and answer the questions.

Assess: Discuss students' answers to the questions.

Close: Ask students to predict whether Douglass's hopes for African Americans will come true.

Teach

C Critical Thinking

Analyzing Primary Sources Ask: Why do you think the author compared the eagerness of the drummer boys to the older men? _(He may have wanted to communicate that they were brave even though they were young.)_ **OL**

R Reading Strategy

Summarizing Ask: How does this sentence reflect what the South's economy was like? _(The South did not manufacture many goods, so it needed to import them.)_ **ELL**

✓ **Reading Check** **Answer:** The war was fought mostly on Southern soil; people lost crops and homes; the long war resulted in shortages of many products.

If You Were There

Critical Thinking Answer Students should describe their daily routines and whether they would have liked a drummer boy's life.

Differentiated Instruction

Differentiated Instruction Strategies

BL Have students underline specific sections of the editorial that provide answers to the questions.

AL Ask students to assume the role of enslaved men and discuss whether they would have followed Douglass's call to arms.

ELL Direct students' attention to the Reader's Dictionary for definitions of words they may not know.

R Reading Strategy

Organizing Have students list the women named in this section, the roles they filled during the Civil War, and which side they served on. **BL**

C Critical Thinking

Predicting Direct students' attention to the feature entitled "Women in the War." **Ask:** What might it be like for Francis Clailin to hide her identity as a woman while serving as a soldier? *(She may have been glad to be with her husband, or afraid of the danger of war, or anxious about being discovered.)* **OL**

D Differentiated Instruction

Interpersonal Ask: Which woman would you like to meet? Why? *(Students' answers will vary but should include specific reasons for their choices.)* Have students research to learn more about the woman they chose. Ask them to write a short biography about that woman. **OL**

**Hands-On
Chapter Project
Step 3**

R New Roles for Women

Main Idea Many Northern and Southern women took on new responsibilities during the war.

History and You Think of ways that your family would be affected by a war in your backyard. Read to learn the many ways families were affected by the Civil War.

. . . .

Against the advice of family and friends, Kate Cumming, a young woman from Mobile, Alabama, left home to begin a career as a nurse with the Confederate Army of the Mississippi. Cumming was one of the many women whose lives changed greatly because of the Civil War.

In both the North and the South, women kept the farms and factories going. They ran offices, taught school, and kept government records. Women suffered the stress of having husbands away at war and the pain of losing family members. They scrimped and saved to make do without many things they were used to, and they prayed to keep their families together.

Treating the Sick and Wounded

In the Civil War, for the first time, thousands of women served as nurses. At first many doctors did not want women nurses, saying that women were too delicate for the grisly work required on the battlefields. Men thought of nursing as work for males and believed it was improper for women to tend the bodies of unknown men.

Strong-minded women disregarded these objections. **Mary Edwards Walker** became the first woman army surgeon and later received the Congressional Medal of Honor. **Dorothea Dix** convinced officials to let women work as nurses and recruited large numbers of women to serve. Another Northerner, **Clara Barton,** became famous for her work with wounded soldiers. In the South, **Sally Tompkins** established a hospital for soldiers in Richmond, Virginia.

Kate Cumming, who nursed the wounded in Corinth after the Battle of Shiloh, wrote, "Nothing that I had ever heard or read had given me the faintest idea of the horrors witnessed here."

Primary Source / Women in the War

New Roles Women filled many roles during the Civil War. Many offered their services as nurses. A few were spies, and as many as 400 disguised themselves as men to serve as Union or Confederate soldiers. They cut their hair, donned men's clothing, and changed their names to fight alongside men in battle. Many were following brothers or husbands to war, but some wanted to fight because they believed in the cause.

"Francis Clailin" ▶

Nurse in field hospital ▼

Frances Louisa Clayton changed her name to Francis Clailin and enlisted as a Union soldier to be with her husband. Like the woman described below, Clayton's identity was revealed in a hospital.

"Maybe she would have remained undiscovered for a long time if she hadn't fainted. She was given a warm bath which gave the secret away."

Frances Clayton ▶

Publishing a Newspaper

Step 3: Writing Letters to the Editor Students will write editorial letters to their city newspapers.

Essential Question: What social, political, and economic changes resulted from the war?

Directions Each student in the group should write a letter to the editor that expresses his or her views about the role of women in the war, political disagreement over President Lincoln's policies, or economic difficulties people faced. Students' work should reflect the perspective of residents in their chosen city and include historical detail as well as persuasive language.

Recognizing Bias Discuss the points of view represented by the editorials. How does writing an editorial differ from reporting on an actual event? **OL**

(Chapter Project continued in Section 4)

Spies

Some women were spies. Rose O'Neal Greenhow entertained Union leaders in Washington, D.C. She gathered information about Union plans that she passed to the South. Greenhow eventually was caught, convicted of treason, and exiled. Belle Boyd, of Front Royal, Virginia, informed Confederate generals of Union army movements in the Shenandoah Valley.

Some women disguised themselves as men and became soldiers. Loretta Janeta Velázquez fought for the South at the First Battle of Bull Run and at the Battle of Shiloh. Later she became a Confederate spy.

Harriet Tubman, an important "conductor" on the Underground Railroad, also served as a spy and scout for the Union. In 1863 Tubman led a mission that freed hundreds of enslaved people and disrupted southern supply lines.

Reading Check Making Inferences How do you think women felt about how the war changed their lives?

Elizabeth Van Lew lived in Richmond and secretly sent information about Confederate activities to President Lincoln.

"For my loyalty to my country I have two beautiful names— here I am called 'Traitor,' farther North a 'Spy.'"

Elizabeth Van Lew ▲

Critical Thinking

Analyzing Did the Civil War change the traditional roles of women? How?

Prison Camps and Field Hospitals

Main Idea When Americans went to war, most were not prepared for the horrors of battle.

History and You What goes through the mind of a doctor or nurse in the middle of battle? Read to learn about battlefield medicine.

A fter the terror on the battlefield, many men suffered the agony of their wounds. Still others faced the humiliation and suffering of being taken prisoner.

In the Hands of the Enemy

Throughout the war, each side treated its enemy soldiers with a mixture of sympathy and hostility. At first, the two sides exchanged prisoners. However, when each realized that the men simply returned to fight again, they set up prison camps. Prisoners were generally allowed to keep their blanket and a cup or canteen when they were captured. These few provisions were all they had during their imprisonment. Food shortages also added to the suffering. Volunteers **distributed,** or gave out, bread and soup among the wounded, but in the prisons there was little or nothing to eat.

Andersonville prison, in Georgia, was opened in early 1864. It was built to hold 10,000 prisoners, but by August, 33,000 were crammed into it. The men slept in shallow holes dug in the ground and daily received a teaspoon of salt, three tablespoons of beans, and eight ounces of cornmeal. They drank and cooked with water from a stream that also served as a sewer. Almost 13,000 Union prisoners died there, mostly from disease.

The Union prison in Elmira, New York, was no better. Captured soldiers from the sunny South suffered through the winter months without blankets and warm clothes. The hospital was in a flooded basement, and a pond within the compound served as both toilet and garbage dump. Almost one quarter of all prisoners at Elmira died.

The Civil War **Chapter 16** 493

R **Reading Strategy**

Skimming Have students skim the paragraph. **Ask:** What is the main idea of this paragraph? *(It discusses how each side handled prisoners of war.)* **BL**

S **Skill Practice**

Creating a Time Line Explain that one of the principles of the Geneva Conventions establishes international law for the fair treatment of prisoners of war. Have students research the Geneva Conventions and later challenges to those principles. Ask students to present their findings in a time line that includes major milestones for the law. **AL**

Reading Check **Answer:** Some women suffered because of the war's impact on their lives; others may have been glad to help the cause by serving in hospitals or having new responsibilities.

Primary Source

Critical Thinking Answer
The war gave many women new opportunities for work. Other women had more responsibilities at work or at home because many men were fighting in the war.

Additional Support

Activity: Connecting Past and Present

Discussion Have students form three groups to gather information about women's roles during wartime. Assign one group the Civil War, another World War II, and the third the most recent war in Iraq. Direct students to use both primary and secondary sources. Students should take notes during their research and then compile their notes in a fact sheet. Tell each group to select two or three students to take part in a panel discussion of women's roles during wartime. Begin the discussion by having each group summarize what they learned and share quotes from women who lived during the wars. Begin the discussion with the following question. **Ask:** How do women's roles during wartime reflect the needs of their society at that time? *(In earlier wars, women were able to take on new roles in order to fill in for men who were not* available. Today women do whatever needs to be done in the war or at home.) How were the roles of women in each war similar, as well as unique? *(In each war, women had to fill roles vacated by men who became soldiers. During World War II, women were permitted to serve in the military in support roles; many women have served in Iraq, and some have been in combat positions.)* **AL**

C Critical Thinking

Drawing Conclusions Ask: What risks did surgeons face? *(Hospitals on battlefields were dangerous because of flying bullets and cannonballs.)* **OL**

D Differentiated Instruction

Logical/Mathematical Have students research the number of casualties from the Civil War. They should find data on the total number of wounded on both sides, soldiers who became ill or were wounded in battle, and the numbers of soldiers who died as a result of injuries or illness. Have students create bar graphs that represent their data. **OL**

✓ Reading Check Answer: Similar—bad/little food, poor sanitation; Different—Prisoners in the Northern camp had no blankets or warm clothes during winter.

Teacher Tip

Evaluating Students may need help evaluating Internet sources. Tell them to use these questions: Who created the information? What is its purpose? Is the information from a reliable source?

Field Hospitals

C Surgeons traveled with the troops and set up hospitals near battlefields. There, with bullets and cannonballs flying past their heads, they bandaged wounds and amputated limbs. A nurse recalls:

PRIMARY SOURCE

"We have to walk, and when we give the men anything kneel, in blood and water; but we think nothing of it."
—*from Kate: The Journal of a Confederate Nurse*

D The war produced many casualties, and doctors struggled to tend to the wounded. Disease was a constant threat, and some regiments lost half their men to illness before ever going into battle. Crowded together in army camps and drinking from unsanitary water supplies, many soldiers became sick. Smallpox, when it erupted, could be deadly, as could a number of other diseases, including dysentery, typhoid, and pneumonia.

✓ Reading Check Comparing and Contrasting How were the prison camps at Andersonville and Elmira alike, and how were they different?

Political and Economic Change

Main Idea The Civil War led to political change and strained the economies of the North and the South.

History and You Can you think of a time when you disagreed or opposed something? Did you take action? Read to learn why and how people opposed the Civil War, and how Presidents Lincoln and Davis responded.

· ·

Throughout the Civil War, numerous smaller "civil wars" raged in the North and the South.

In the South

Many Southerners opposed the war in the first place. After two years, the war had taken huge amounts of food, materials, and money, and shortages were widespread.

Bread riots erupted throughout the South as hungry people took to the streets. In Richmond, a mob, mostly made of women and

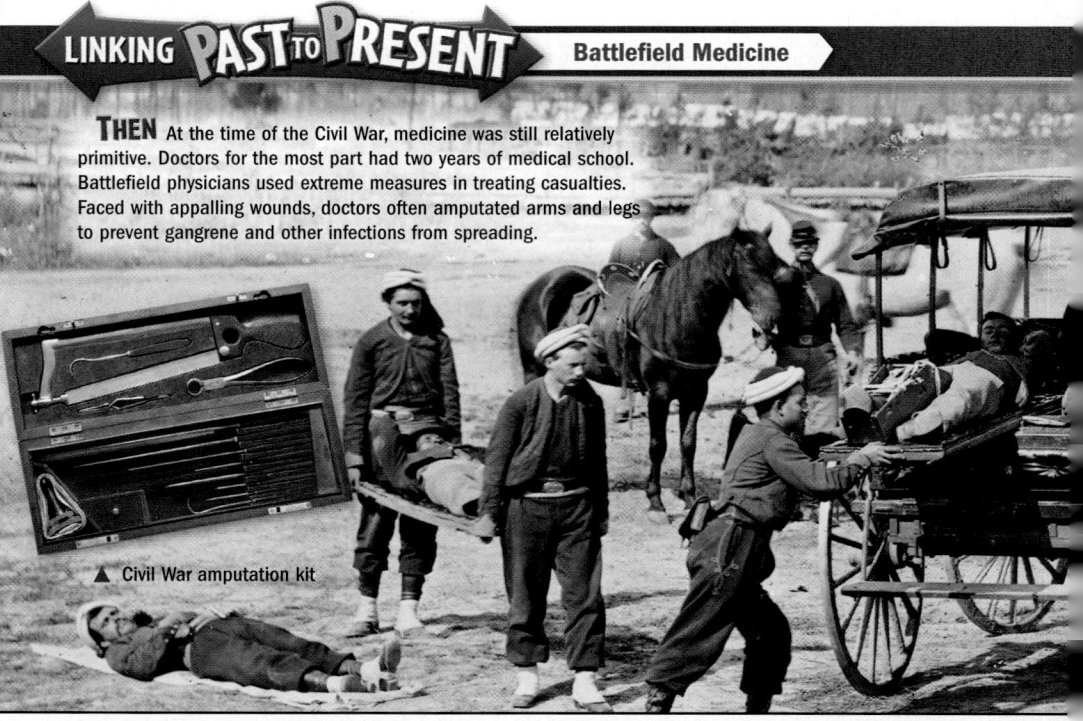

LINKING PAST TO PRESENT — Battlefield Medicine

THEN At the time of the Civil War, medicine was still relatively primitive. Doctors for the most part had two years of medical school. Battlefield physicians used extreme measures in treating casualties. Faced with appalling wounds, doctors often amputated arms and legs to prevent gangrene and other infections from spreading.

▲ Civil War amputation kit

Activity: Technology Connection

Making Connections Ask: What innovations in medicine may have come about during the Civil War? *(new surgical procedures, medicines, women serving as nurses)* Have students work in groups to learn more about battlefield medicine during the Civil War and how doctors and nurses improved treatment and care based upon what they learned on the battlefield as well as through other research. Ask students to identify differences and similarities between the medical practices and technology used during the Civil War and modern-day medical technology on the battlefield. Finally, ask students to summarize their information in a one-page essay. **OL**

children, gathered peacefully to protest but soon started smashing shop windows and stealing food.

In the North

The Union, too, had its war opponents. The Democratic Party, which always opposed Lincoln, was split down the middle. The War Democrats were sharply critical of how the Republican administration was running the war. The Peace Democrats, in contrast, argued for an immediate end to fighting. They called for reuniting the states through negotiation. Mostly from the Midwestern states of Ohio, Illinois, and Indiana, the Peace Democrats were viewed by some as traitors. This earned them the nickname Copperheads, after the poisonous snake. However, by 1863, they proudly embraced this label and wore copper pennies as badges because the coins had "Lady Liberty" on them.

As in the South, some Northerners who opposed the war discouraged enlistment. Occasionally they went further, helping Confederate prisoners of war escape. Some historians claim that the activities of the Peace Democrats encouraged the South and that the war dragged on because the South believed that the North would abandon the struggle.

Jail Without Trial

As a way of dealing with war opponents in the North, President Lincoln suspended **habeas corpus.** This legal proceeding is a protection against unlawful imprisonment. A prisoner uses it to ask for a court hearing to determine if he or she is being held lawfully. The Constitution provides that habeas corpus can be suspended only "when in cases of rebellion or invasion, the public safety may require it."

As a result of Lincoln's action, thousands of Northerners were jailed without trials. When people—even supporters of the war—spoke out against the suspension, they were labeled treasonous Copperheads. Lincoln's critics were right to be concerned. Although many who were in jail actively helped the enemy, others were simply political leaders who had stated their opinions.

R Reading Strategy

Monitoring Tell students that *habeas corpus* is a Latin phrase meaning "you should have the body." It comes from the opening words of a court order that required law-enforcement officials to produce the person they had arrested. Have students use the U.S. Constitution in their textbooks to find the reference to *habeas corpus.* **Ask:** What kind of situation could require the president to suspend *habeas corpus? (a war or rebellion on U.S. soil; a terrorist attack or invasion)* **OL**

LINKING PAST TO PRESENT

Critical Thinking Answers

1. In the Civil War, the wounded were transported by stretcher and wheeled cart. In modern warfare, they use stretchers and helicopter ambulances known as Medevacs.

2. They must have medical training, remain calm in stressful situations, make decisions quickly, and be courageous.

Differentiated Instruction

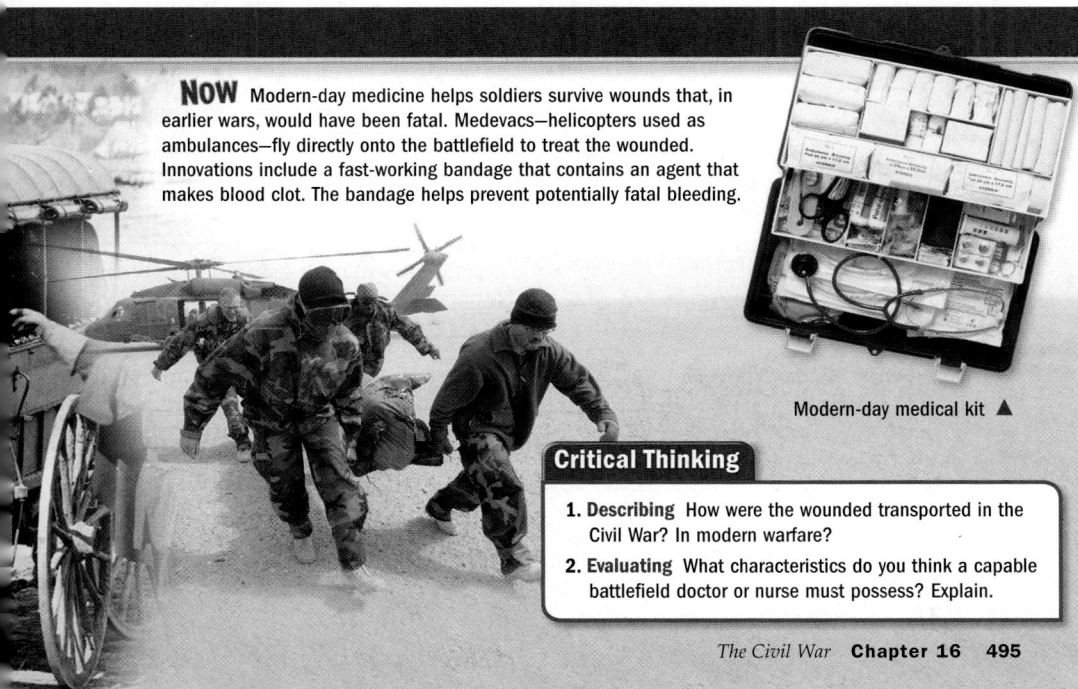

NOW Modern-day medicine helps soldiers survive wounds that, in earlier wars, would have been fatal. Medevacs—helicopters used as ambulances—fly directly onto the battlefield to treat the wounded. Innovations include a fast-working bandage that contains an agent that makes blood clot. The bandage helps prevent potentially fatal bleeding.

Modern-day medical kit ▲

Critical Thinking

1. **Describing** How were the wounded transported in the Civil War? In modern warfare?

2. **Evaluating** What characteristics do you think a capable battlefield doctor or nurse must possess? Explain.

The Civil War **Chapter 16** **495**

Leveled Activities

BL Guided Reading Activity, URB p. 69

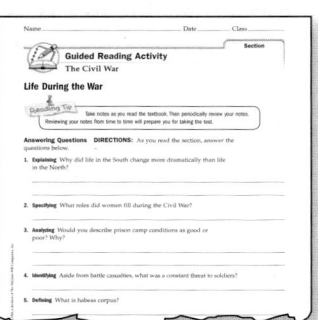

OL Time Line Skills Activity, URB p. 62

ELL Content Vocabulary Activity, URB p. 45

Primary Sources
INTERPRETING
POLITICAL CARTOONS

A Northern newspaper ran this cartoon in 1863. It shows Lady Liberty warding off an attack of the Peace Democrats, or Copperheads.

1. **Identify** Who does the woman represent?
2. **Points of View** What is the cartoonist expressing about the Peace Democrats? How can you tell?

A. Lady Liberty   B. Copperheads

THE COPPERHEAD PARTY—IN FAVOR OF A VIGOROUS PROSECUTION OF PEACE!

In the South, President Jefferson Davis also suspended the right of habeas corpus. He, too, believed he needed to deal harshly with opponents of the war. However, by suspending habeas corpus, Davis upset many loyal supporters. In early 1864, North Carolina's Governor Vance wrote him:

PRIMARY SOURCE

"I hear with deep regret that a bill is certainly expected to pass . . . suspending the writ of habeas corpus, throughout the Confederacy, and that certain arrests will immediately be made."
—letter to Confederate President Jefferson Davis

Draft Laws

After the initial excitement of the war had disappeared, both the North and the South had trouble recruiting troops. In 1862 the Confederate Congress passed a **draft** law requiring able-bodied white men between 18 and 35 to serve for three years. Later the range was extended to cover men between 17 and 50. There were several exceptions. If he could afford it, a man could hire a **substitute**, or replacement, to serve for him. Later, if a man had 20 or more enslaved people, he did not have to serve.

The North, at first, offered a **bounty**, or a sum of money paid to encourage volunteers. Then, in March 1863, it too passed a draft law. All men from age 20 to 45 had to register. As in the South, a man could avoid the draft, either by hiring a substitute or by paying $300. Such exceptions met with great protest. In both the North and the South, people complained it was "a rich man's war and a poor man's fight."

Antidraft sentiment led to riots in several Northern cities. The worst disturbance was the New York City draft riots in July 1863. Members of the working class, many of them Irish immigrants, attacked government and military buildings. Then mobs turned their attacks against African Americans. Many white workers had opposed the Emancipation Proclamation, fearing that freed blacks would take their jobs. After four days of terror, more than 100 people were dead. Federal troops had to be rushed in to stop the riots.

496 Chapter 16 *The Civil War*

Activity: Collaborative Learning

Economic Effects

The war strained the economies of the North and the South. However, the North, with its greater resources, was better able to cope with the immense costs of the war.

The two governments had three ways of paying for the war:

1. They borrowed money by selling war bonds that promised high interest.
2. They imposed new taxes, including income taxes.
3. They printed money. Northern money was called **greenbacks** because of its color.

The North Prospers

Northern industry profited from the war effort. It produced guns, ammunition, shoes, and uniforms. Farmers prospered as they sold their crops to provide a steady supply of food for the troops. However, prices rose faster than wages because goods were in high demand. This **inflation,** or general increase in prices, caused a great hardship for working people. Still, the Northern economy boomed during the war years.

Economic Troubles in the South

The war's economic strain was felt more sharply in the South, where warfare destroyed farmland and railroad lines. Also, the blockade prevented the shipping of trade goods. Vital materials could not reach the Confederacy. Salt was so desperately needed that women scraped the floors of smokehouses to recover it. Food shortages led to riots in Atlanta, Richmond, and other cities.

Inflation, too, was much worse in the South. As early as 1862, citizens begged Confederate leaders for help. In North Carolina, citizens wrote desperate letters to the governor:

PRIMARY SOURCE

"If it is Constitutional, and if your position . . . gives you the power to do so, in the name of . . . suffering humanity, of the cries of widows and orphans, *do* put down the Speculation and extortion in this . . . State."
—R. L. Abernethy to Governor Zebulon Vance, 1862

✓ **Reading Check** Determining Cause and Effect Describe at least three causes of discontent among people in the North and the South.

History ONLINE
Study Central™ To review this section, go to glencoe.com.

C Critical Thinking

Determining Cause and Effect
Ask: How did the South's economy of the prewar period help cause severe shortages during the war? *(The South's dependence on cotton for export before the war meant that it had little industry to produce what it needed during the war.)* **OL**

This **READING SKILL** (Identifying Cause and Effect) was introduced in this unit.

✓ **Reading Check Answer:** *South*—war was expensive, shortages, high inflation, difficulty recruiting troops; *North*—trouble recruiting troops, inflation, Peace Democrats' opposition to the war

Assess

History ONLINE

Study Central™ provides summaries, interactive games, and online graphic organizers to help students review content.

Close

Summarizing As a class, discuss the reasons for the social, political, and economic changes that took place during the Civil War. **OL**

Section 3 Review

Vocabulary

1. Use each of these terms in a complete sentence that will help explain its meaning: distribute, habeas corpus, draft, substitute, bounty, greenback, inflation.

Main Ideas

2. **Describing** What role did Sally Tompkins play in the war effort? Which women played a similar role in the North?

3. **Summarizing** Who were the Copperheads? What was their position on fighting the war?

4. **Explaining** Why did the Union and the Confederacy institute drafts?

Critical Thinking

5. **Describing** Explain three ways that the governments raised money for the war effort.

```
      Raising Funds
      /    |    \
     ( )  ( )  ( )
```

6. **Persuasive Writing** President Lincoln suspended writs of habeas corpus to prevent interference with the draft. Do you think suspending civil liberties is justified in some situations? Write a short essay explaining your position and defend it.

Answer the
7. **Essential Question**
What social, political, and economic changes resulted from the war?

Answers

1. Sentences should use vocabulary words according to their definitions in the section and Glossary.
2. She established a hospital for soldiers in Richmond, Virginia; Mary Edwards Walker, Dorothea Dix, and Clara Barton all worked in the medical field.
3. Also known as the Peace Democrats, the Copperheads were Northerners who were opposed to the war.

4. Draft laws were passed in order to recruit troops.
5. They sold war bonds; they raised taxes; they printed more money.
6. Answers will vary but should include specific reasons for opinions.
7. **Social:** Women's roles changed during the war as they had more opportunity and responsibility. **Political:** There were many political disagreements in the North and

South over the war and the economy. **Economic:** The war was expensive for the North and South, and both sides had to try to raise money to pay for the war, as well as establish new policies for keeping the economy going.

Section 3 Review

Focus

Section 4

The Strain of War

Bellringer
Daily Test Practice Transparency 16–4

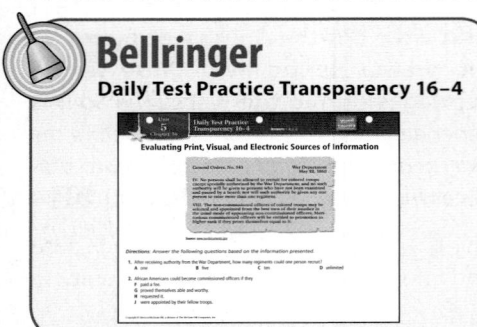

Reading Guide
Answers to Graphic:
Fredericksburg: entrenchments used by Lee, Confederate victory, Burnside resigned; **Chancellorsville:** clever strategy led to Confederate victory, Stonewall Jackson died after being injured in battle; **Gettysburg:** three-day battle with heavy losses on both sides, Pickett's Charge failed, Union victory; **Siege of Vicksburg:** Grant led successful 47-day campaign to take this important city on Mississippi River, few civilian casualties

Section Spotlight Video

To learn more about battlefield medicine during the Civil War, have students watch the Section Spotlight Video "Life During the Civil War."

Resource Manager

Essential Question
How did the events at Gettysburg and Vicksburg change the course of the war?

Reading Guide

Content Vocabulary
entrench *(p. 499)*   siege *(p. 505)*

Academic Vocabulary
nevertheless *(p. 501)*   encounter *(p. 502)*

Key People and Events
54th Massachusetts *(p. 501)*
Pickett's Charge *(p. 503)*
Gettysburg Address *(p. 505)*

Reading Strategy
Taking Notes As you read, use a chart like the one shown below to write at least one important fact about each of these battles.

Battle	Importance
Fredericksburg	
Chancellorsville	
Gettysburg	
Siege of Vicksburg	

ILLINOIS STANDARDS
The American Journey

16.A.3b Make inferences about historical events and eras using historical maps and other historical sources.

17.C.3a Explain how human activity is affected by geographic factors.

18.B.3a Analyze how individuals and groups interact with and within institutions (e.g., educational, military).

American Diary

The battle at Chancellorsville raged well into the moonlit night. In the confusion, Confederate soldiers shot their own general, hero Stonewall Jackson. An officer recalls the confusion: "To hear shell whizzing and bursting over you, . . . and not know from whence death comes to you, is trying beyond all things."

—*from* The History of a Brigade of South Carolinians

Stonewall Jackson

	R Reading Strategies	**C** Critical Thinking	**D** Differentiated Instruction	**W** Writing Support	**S** Skill Practice
Teacher Edition	• Paraphrasing, p. 499 • Skimming, p. 500 • Using Context Clues, p. 502 • Analyz. Pri. Sources, p. 503	• Ident. Cen. Iss., p. 502 • Analyz. Info., p. 503 • Ident. Cent. Iss., p. 504 • Draw. Concl., p. 504 • Analyz. Pri. Sources, p. 505	• Visual/Spatial, p. 500 • Mathematical, p. 502	• Expository Writing, p. 501 • Personal Writing, p. 503	• Using Geo. Skills, p. 499
Additional Resources	• Guid. Read., URB p. 70 • Cont. Voc., URB p. 45 • Acad. Voc., URB p. 47 • Read. Ess., p. 172	• Quizzes and Tests, p. 154 • Crit. Think. Skills, URB p. 57	• Reteaching Act., URB p. 65 • School-to-Home, URB p. 63	• Authentic Assess., p. 16 • Writ. Skills, URB p. 51 • Link. Past & Pres., URB p. 61	• Daily Test Pract. Transp. 16-4 • Lesson Transp. 16C • Time Line Skills, URB p. 62

Southern Victories

Main Idea In the winter of 1862 and the spring of 1863, the South seemed to be winning the Civil War.

History and You How do leadership qualities make a difference to what happens in life? Read to learn the qualities of some Civil War battle commanders that led to victories and to defeat.

· ·

Southern victories in the East were largely the result of the military leadership of generals Robert E. Lee and Stonewall Jackson. Through knowledge of the terrain and the ability to inspire troops, these two managed to defeat larger Union forces. Jackson's death at Chancellorsville not only removed one of the South's great strategists, it affected the morale of its army and its citizens. As Jackson lay dying, Lee said, "He has lost his left arm; I have lost my right."

Battle of Fredericksburg

After Antietam, Robert E. Lee moved his army out of Maryland into Virginia. This encouraged Union leaders to attack. The new Union commander, General Ambrose Burnside, boldly marched his troops toward the Confederate capital at Richmond.

Lee chose to intercept the Union troops near the town of Fredericksburg. He moved his forces to hills south of the town and ordered them to dig trenches so they could fire down on the enemy from a protected position. On December 13, 1862, the Union army attacked. Lee's **entrenched** forces drove the Union troops back soundly. Devastated by his failure, General Burnside resigned and was replaced by General Joseph Hooker.

Battle of Chancellorsville

In May 1863, Lee again used strategy brilliantly. He divided his forces in Virginia in response to General Hooker's having done the same thing—even though Hooker had twice as many men. Some Confederate troops stayed to defend Fredericksburg, and some confronted the main Union force at Chancellorsville. A third group made a daring maneuver that caught the Union army by surprise. Under the leadership of Stonewall Jackson, Confederate troops marched around the side of Hooker's position.

Stonewall Jackson mortally wounded at the battle of Chancellorsville in Virginia

Primary Source | West Point and the Civil War

Thomas Jackson is, "quite a smart youth in every respect for his age and opportunity." This description comes from Jackson's letter of recommendation to the U.S. Military Academy at West Point, New York. Jackson and 21 other graduates of the class of 1846 served as Union and Confederate generals during the Civil War.

Soldiers who trained together now faced each other in battle. Confederate general A.P. Hill led forces against Union general George McClellan, "as if Mac were the most hated of his enemies, rather than the dear roommate of his West Point years."

—from *The Class of 1846: From West Point to Appomattox*

A.P. Hill

George McClellan

Critical Thinking

Speculating What do you think is the main reason some leaders decided to fight for the Confederacy? For the Union?

CHAPTER 16
Section 4

Teach
· · · · · · · · · · · · · · ·

R Reading Strategy

Paraphrasing Have students rewrite this paragraph in their own words. **Ask:** What do you expect to read about in this section? *(Confederate victories due to effective leadership; battle of Chancellorsville; death of Stonewall Jackson)* **OL**

S Skill Practice

Using Geography Skills Have students turn to a map of the United States in the Reference Atlas in this book. **Ask:** How far was the capital of the Confederacy from the capital of the Union? *(Richmond, the capital of the Confederacy, is about 150 miles [241 km] from Washington, D.C.)* **BL**

Primary Source

Critical Thinking Answer
Soldiers who chose to fight for the Confederacy were usually from Southern states, wanted to uphold the principle of states' rights, or supported slavery. Soldiers fighting for the Union were usually from Northern states, wanted to preserve the Union, or opposed slavery.

Differentiated Instruction

Leveled Activities

BL Reteaching Activity, URB p. 65

OL Critical Thinking Skills Activity, URB p. 57

AL Writing Skills Activity, URB p. 51

ELL Content Vocabulary Activity, URB p. 45

D Differentiated Instruction

Visual/Spatial Have students diagram this battle on a map, using different colors or symbols for the Union and Confederate armies. Students' maps should indicate the directions armies moved and the generals who led each army. **OL**

R Reading Strategy

Skimming Ask: *How many different Union generals are mentioned here?* (four) *How might the soldiers have been affected by these frequent changes in leadership?* (It may have been difficult to have new generals and new strategies, or perhaps soldiers were encouraged by the active leadership of President Lincoln's attempts to win the war.) **OL**

✔ Reading Check Answer: He organized his troops to surround Union armies; he dug entrenchments to fire on Union soldiers from positions of strength.

D
Then, suddenly, Jackson's army turned and attacked the Union forces in the rear. At the same time, Lee struck from the front. Sandwiched between the two Confederate forces, Hooker eventually withdrew his men. One of the Confederate companies fired on Stonewall Jackson's company by mistake, wounding the general in the left arm. Jackson's arm had to be amputated, and he died a week later.

Weak Union Generals

R
In less than a year, three different generals led the Union forces. Lincoln was frustrated by their conduct of the war. Major General George McClellan commanded the Union forces at the Battle of Antietam in March 1862. He prepared well but was reluctant to engage the enemy. Said Lincoln, "If McClellan doesn't want to use the army, I'd like to borrow it for awhile."

The last straw came when, after victory at Antietam, McClellan failed to obey Lincoln's order to follow the retreating Confederate troops and "destroy the rebel army."

Lincoln pushed his next commander, General Ambrose Burnside, to take aggressive action. Burnside quickly lost the president's favor after a crushing loss at Fredericksburg.

Next, Lincoln appointed Major General Joseph Hooker, who had often been critical of other generals. Hooker's attitude matched the president's.

PRIMARY SOURCE

"May God have mercy on General Lee, for I will have none."

—General Joseph Hooker to his staff, April 1863

Words, however, were not enough to defeat Lee, who crushed Hooker's forces at Chancellorsville. Within two months, Hooker resigned.

Lincoln's next commander needed to prove himself quickly. Major General George Meade assumed command three days before one of the most important battles of the war.

✔ Reading Check Synthesizing What strategies did General Lee use to defeat Union armies that were much larger than his?

Primary Source / African American Soldiers

Union Recruits Of the more than 2 million soldiers who served in the Union army and navy, nearly 200,000 were African American. As news of the Emancipation Proclamation spread, many African Americans from the North and the South enlisted. More than half were formerly enslaved.

▼ Union soldiers

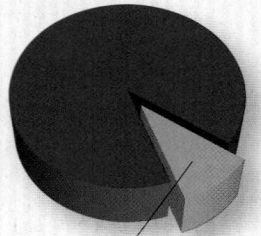

Union Army

Union Navy

Nearly 10% of the soldiers in the Union army were African American.

About 18% of sailors in the Union navy were African American.

Hands-On Chapter Project
Step 4

Publishing a Newspaper

Step 4: Visual Literacy Students will research photos from the Civil War.

Essential Question: How did the events at Gettysburg and Vicksburg change the course of the war?

Directions Students should find and collect a variety of images that depict everyday life or an event that took place during the Civil War. Have them write captions for their images. Then groups should present their work as a poster. Display their work in the classroom, and discuss what they have learned.

Analyzing Discuss how information can be communicated through a photo, compared to an article. **Ask:** *How do captions help the reader understand images?* (by giving important details) *How might photojournalists influence people's opinions about the war?* (Students may say that photos might influence people's views about an event.) **OL**

(Chapter Project continued in Section 5)

African Americans in the War

Main Idea African Americans showed courage and skill as soldiers in the Union army.

History and You What does it mean to act bravely? Read to learn about the 54th Massachusetts regiment and the battle for Fort Wagner.

．．．．．．．．．．．．．．．．．．．．．．．．．．．．．．．

At first, both the North and the South barred African Americans from serving in their armies. As time passed, the North relaxed its rules.

In the South

African Americans made up more than 30 percent of the Southern population, but Confederate leaders never seriously considered allowing them to enlist. Confederate leaders feared that African American soldiers, once armed, would attack their fellow troops or even begin a general revolt. The Confederates felt that the advantage of having more soldiers in their army did not justify this risk.

▲ Recruitment poster

History ONLINE
Student Web Activity Visit glencoe.com and complete the Chapter 16 Web Activity about African Americans in the war.

In the North

President Lincoln at first resisted appeals to enlist African Americans in the Union army. He feared that such a policy would be resented in the border states. By 1862, though, it was evident that the North needed more soldiers, and many Union African Americans were eager to fight. As a result, Congress decided to allow the formation of all-African American regiments.

These new soldiers were in a tough position. Many white regiments from the North doubted their fighting ability. Others resented their presence. Many Southern troops hated the African American soldiers and often focused their fiercest gunfire on African American Northern regiments.

Still, African Americans joined. By the end of the war, they comprised about 10 percent of the Union army. Some were freed people from the North; others were runaway enslaved African Americans from the South. These men fought hard and effectively, too. As one white Union officer wrote about an all-African American Kansas regiment:

PRIMARY SOURCE

"They make better soldiers in every respect than any troops I have ever had under my command."
—Union general James G. Blunt

The 54th Massachusetts

The best-known African American regiment was the **54th Massachusetts.** In 1863 this regiment took part in an assault on Fort Wagner in South Carolina. The 54th served in the front lines of this battle. Confederate gunfire battered the men, causing nearly 300 casualties in this regiment alone. **Nevertheless,** the soldiers bravely fought on. Though the Union could not capture the fort, the 54th became famous for the courage and sacrifice of its members.

✓ Reading Check Comparing and Contrasting How were Union and Confederate policies regarding African American soldiers alike and different?

Critical Thinking

Speculating Do you think using enslaved African Americans as soldiers would have helped the Confederacy win the war? Why or why not?

W Writing Support

Expository Writing Have students write an article for a Northern newspaper that describes President Lincoln's decision to enlist African American soldiers. Be sure to include information on how African Americans might have reacted to the news. **AL**

✓ Reading Check Answer: Both refused to enlist African American soldiers during the early years of the war. The North changed course in 1862 and accepted African Americans into all-black regiments.

Primary Source

Critical Thinking Answer
Answers will vary but should mention that not many African Americans would want to help a government that preserved slavery, and the Confederacy had other challenges such as a weak economy and not enough industry that would make it difficult to win the war.

History ONLINE
Objectives and answers to the Student Web Activity can be found at glencoe.com under the Web Activity Lesson Plan for this chapter.

Additional Support

Activity: Collaborative Learning

Debating the Issues Have students form two groups to gather information on the life of African Americans in the Union states. Direct students to use both primary and secondary sources. Students should take notes during their research and then compile their notes into a fact sheet. Tell each group to select two or three students to take part in a debate on whether the North should have permitted African American soldiers from the beginning of the war. First have each group summarize its views. Students' exchanges should use evidence from primary and secondary sources to support their points of view. After the debate, have each student write a short essay responding to the arguments and identifying his or her opinion. **OL**

C Critical Thinking

Identifying Central Issues Ask: Why did Lee decide to take the war into the North? *(He hoped that a victory there would encourage the British and French to aid the Confederacy.)* **BL**

R Reading Strategy

Using Context Clues Ask students to explain, in their own words, the phrase "the two sides encountered one another." *(The Union and Confederate soldiers came across each other.)* **ELL**

D Differentiated Instruction

Mathematical Ask: How many total casualties were sustained during the Battle of Gettysburg? *(48,000)* **BL**

DBQ Document-Based Questions

Answers

1. Students may say that the possibility of getting support from Europe made it worth the risk.
2. Failure would allow the North to gain a significant advantage.

Differentiated Instruction

YOU DECIDE

Should Lee Have Invaded the North?

The war was fought in Southern territory for the most part. Lee's first invasion was turned back at Antietam. In 1863 he tried again.

The Alternatives

Play it safe	Be bold
Should the South continue its defensive strategy?	Should Lee launch a second invasion of the North?

Considering the Consequences

If the invasion fails
- The Confederacy makes no further attempt to invade the North.
- The tide of war turns in favor of the North.

If the invasion succeeds
- The Confederacy likely gains support from Europe.
- Union antiwar feeling grows.

The Decision

Could Lee's forces conquer the army of the Potomac on its own soil? Confident after the brilliant victory at Chancellorsville, Lee decided to invade the North.

The Results

- Lee's army in northern Virginia is defeated.
- The Confederacy makes no further attempt to invade the North.
- The tide of war turns in favor of the North.

DBQ Document-Based Questions

1. **Analyzing** In your opinion, did Lee have valid reasons for invading the North?
2. **Explaining** What do you think was the best reason for not invading the North?

The Tide of War Turns

Main Idea The Battle of Gettysburg marked a turn in the war as the Union forces defeated the Confederates.

History and You Have you ever made a decision that seemed right at the time but turned out to be disastrous? Read to learn what happened when General Lee decided to invade the North.

In spring of 1863, the South had the upper hand, but that was soon to change. The Confederate victory at Chancellorsville ruined Union plans for attacking Richmond. Robert E. Lee, emboldened by his victories, decided to take the war into the North. A win there might impress France and Britain.

The South's strategy recalled that of the colonies in the Revolutionary War—though far outnumbered, they were aided by France and had won. Now, France and Britain missed the goods—especially cotton—they were accustomed to buying from Southern planters. If the Confederates appeared to be winning, those nations might help.

The Battle of Gettysburg

In July 1863, a small town in southern Pennsylvania became the site of one of the most decisive battles in the Civil War. Gettysburg was not a capital, a strategic port, or the location of an important fort. That such serious fighting took place there was almost an accident.

The Confederates entered the town for much-needed supplies. General Lee hoped to avoid fighting troops in an unfamiliar area. However, the two sides **encountered** one another. When Lee's armies crawled out of Gettysburg four grueling days later, it was after sustaining 25,000 casualties. The Union—the victor—suffered the loss of 23,000.

The battle started at 5:30 A.M. on July 1. Outnumbered, Union troops retreated to a section of high ground called Cemetery Ridge. Reinforcements for both sides arrived, and on the second day of fighting, Southern generals

Battlefield Medicine

Objective: To learn about sanitation and medical issues during the Civil War and today

Focus: Ask students to describe the relationship between sanitation and good health.

Teach: Have students create a pamphlet about a sanitation or medical issue.

Assess: Students should assess each pamphlet for its information.

Close: Discuss what sanitary and medical issues challenge Americans today.

Differentiated Instruction Strategies

BL **Provide magazines for students to help them identify issues.**

AL **Have students discuss how sanitation and medical solutions are financed.**

ELL **Tell students to create a graphic organizer to illustrate the information.**

Linking Past and Present Activity, URB p. 61

tried to dislodge Union forces from hills named Round Top and Little Round Top. However, after furious fighting, Union forces under the command of General George Meade held their positions.

That night, Meade made the decision not to retreat. The next day, Lee also made an important decision. He ordered an attack designed to "create a panic and virtually destroy the [Union] army."

The Confederates started by firing nearly 140 cannons at the Union lines. Then, under the leadership of General George Pickett, thousands of Confederate troops attacked the Union's center position at Cemetery Ridge. Putting themselves directly in the way of musket and artillery fire, they advanced across open land.

At first, it seemed that **Pickett's Charge** might work—the Confederates broke the first line of Union defense. In the end, however, three-quarters of those who started the attack

lay dead or wounded on the ground. Lee later wrote:

PRIMARY SOURCE

"The army did all it could. I fear I required of it impossibilities."

—from *Memoirs of Robert E. Lee*

Gettysburg put an end to one goal of Confederate foreign policy: gaining help from Britain and France. The South hoped to receive from the British two ironclads that would be used to sweep Union shipping from the Atlantic. However, in October 1863, the British government decided not to release the ships.

The Vicksburg Siege

On July 4, the day that Lee retreated from Gettysburg, the Confederacy suffered another major military blow. The important river city of Vicksburg, Mississippi, fell under the control of Union troops led by Ulysses S. Grant.

C Critical Thinking

Analyzing Information Under General Pickett, thousands of Confederate troops advanced on Cemetery Ridge, putting themselves directly in the way of enemy fire. **Ask:** Do you think that the Confederate soldiers were deliberately sacrificed in this attack? *(Student answers will vary but should show evidence of thoughtful consideration of the facts.)* **OL**

W Writing Support

Personal Writing Have students write a letter from a Union or Confederate soldier after the Battle of Gettysburg, explaining its outcome. **OL**

R Reading Strategy

Analyzing Primary Sources Ask: How might Lee's statement have affected the soldiers' morale? *(They may have been encouraged by his honesty and motivated to keep fighting.)* **OL**

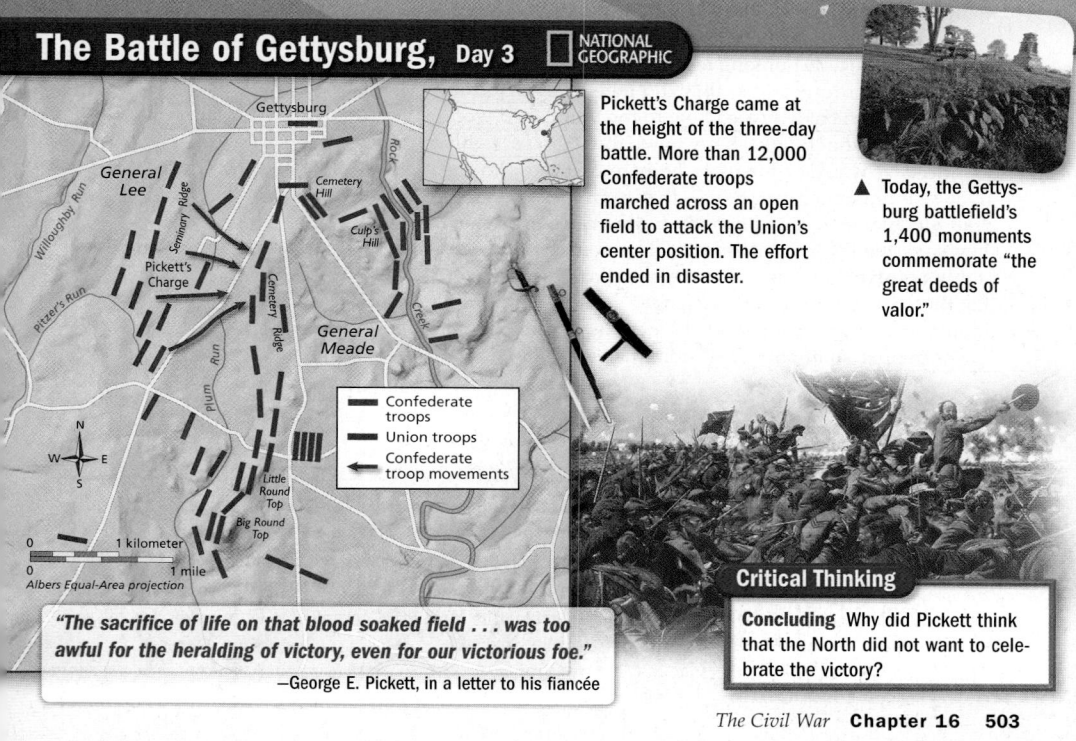

The Battle of Gettysburg, Day 3 — NATIONAL GEOGRAPHIC

Gettysburg

General Lee

Cemetery Hill

Culp's Hill

Pickett's Charge

Cemetery Ridge

General Meade

Little Round Top

Big Round Top

Willoughby Run

Seminary Ridge

Pitzer's Run

Plum Run

Rock Creek

0   1 kilometer
0   1 mile
Albers Equal-Area projection

- Confederate troops
- Union troops
- Confederate troop movements

N / W / E / S

Pickett's Charge came at the height of the three-day battle. More than 12,000 Confederate troops marched across an open field to attack the Union's center position. The effort ended in disaster.

▲ Today, the Gettysburg battlefield's 1,400 monuments commemorate "the great deeds of valor."

"The sacrifice of life on that blood soaked field . . . was too awful for the heralding of victory, even for our victorious foe."
—George E. Pickett, in a letter to his fiancée

Critical Thinking

Concluding Why did Pickett think that the North did not want to celebrate the victory?

The Civil War   **Chapter 16**   503

The Battle of Gettysburg, Day 3 — NATIONAL GEOGRAPHIC

Critical Thinking Answer

Pickett knew that even though the North had won, the terrible loss of life overshadowed any cause for celebration.

Additional Support

Fast Facts

Reaction to the Gettysburg Address President Abraham Lincoln delivered the Gettysburg Address on November 19, 1863, during the dedication of the Gettysburg National Cemetery. The dedication was in honor of the more than 7,000 Union and Confederate soldiers who died in the Battle of Gettysburg earlier that year. Lincoln's brief speech is recognized as one of the finest speeches in the English language. It is

also one of the most moving speeches in the nation's history.

On the day following the Gettysburg dedication, many of the nation's newspapers printed the speech. The *Chicago Tribune* noted that: "The dedicatory remarks by President Lincoln will live among the annals of men." Other newspapers did not think it was a worthy address by a president. The *Harrisburg* (Pennsylvania) *Patriot* criti-

cized the speech, noting, "We pass over the silly remarks of the President; for the credit of the Nation we are willing that the veil of oblivion shall be dropped over them and that they shall no more be repeated or thought of." **Ask:** Why do you think some people criticized the speech? *(They may have opposed the war and believed that too many lives were lost.)*

Teach

C₁ Critical Thinking

Identifying Central Issues Have students read the first sentence. **Ask:** What was Lincoln's argument for going to war in 1861? *(to preserve the Union)* How did this goal change in 1862? *(Lincoln announced his plans to free all enslaved people in the South with the Emancipation Proclamation.)* What phrase in the Gettysburg Address hints at this change of goals? *(... dedicated to the proposition that all men are created equal)* **AL**

C₂ Critical Thinking

Drawing Conclusions Ask: Where else in the Gettysburg Address does Lincoln refer to this new war goal? *(... shall have a new birth of freedom...)* **OL**

Primary Source

The Gettysburg Address

On November 19, 1863, President Abraham Lincoln gave a short speech at the dedication of a national cemetery on the battlefield of Gettysburg. His simple yet eloquent words expressed his hopes for a nation divided by civil war.

▲ Monument at Gettysburg

> **C₁** Four **score** and seven years ago our fathers brought forth on this continent a new nation, conceived in liberty, and dedicated to the **proposition** that all men are created equal.
>
> Now we are engaged in a great civil war, testing whether that nation, or any nation so conceived and so dedicated, can long **endure**. We are met on a great battlefield of that war. We have come to dedicate a portion of that field as a final resting place for those who here gave their lives that that nation might live. It is altogether fitting and proper that we should do this.
>
> But, in a larger sense, we can not dedicate—we can not **consecrate**—we can not **hallow**—this ground. The brave men, living and dead, who struggled here, have consecrated it far above our poor power to add or detract. The world will little note nor long remember what we say here, but it can never forget what they did here. It is for us, the living, rather, to be dedicated here to the unfinished work which they who fought here have thus far so nobly advanced. It is rather for us to be here dedicated to the great task remaining before us—that from these honored dead we take increased devotion to that cause for which they gave the last full measure of devotion; that we here highly **resolve** that these dead shall not have died in vain; **C₂** that this nation, under God, shall have a new birth of freedom; and that government of the people, by the people, for the people, shall not perish from the earth.

Lincoln is referring to the nation declaring its independence in 1776—87 years before.

Union soldiers were fighting to keep the nation (North and South) together.

The soldiers who died made the supreme sacrifice. Lincoln believes it is up to those who are still living to carry on their unfinished work.

The U.S. government was created to serve the people. People are the source of the government's power.

VOCABULARY

score: twenty

proposition (PRAH·puh·zi·shun): an idea or a belief

endure: to continue or last

consecrate (KAHN·suh·KRAT): to dedicate to a sacred purpose

hallow (ha·LOH): to respect greatly

resolve: to make a firm decision

Critical Thinking

1. **Making Inferences** How is the Civil War going to "test" whether or not the United States can endure?

2. **Interpreting** Why do you think Lincoln thought it was so important to honor those who fought and died at Gettysburg?

3. **Finding the Main Idea** According to Lincoln, why was the war being fought?

504 **Chapter 16** *The Civil War*

Answers

Answers

1. It will test whether a nation that was born from democratic ideals and freedoms can survive.

2. The soldiers gave their lives to save the Union.

3. The war was being fought to preserve the Union and to provide freedom to all the people of that Union.

Grant first launched his attack in April, surrounding the 30,000 Confederate troops holding Vicksburg. In May, Grant began a **siege** against the town, blockading it to prevent food and supplies from entering. Union gunships on the river supported Grant's 77,000 troops by firing thousands of mortar shells into the city.

During the 47-day siege, both sides suffered heavy casualties. More than 9,000 Confederate and 10,000 Union troops died, many of disease or starvation. Remarkably, fewer than 20 civilians were killed in the siege.

The bad news did not end there for the South, though. A few days later, it lost Port Hudson in Louisiana, its last stronghold on the vital Mississippi River. The Union strategy to split the South in two had succeeded. Arkansas, Louisiana, and Texas were now cut off. In a single month, July 1863, the Civil War reached a major turning point.

Lincoln's Gettysburg Address

On November 19, 1863, Soldiers' National Cemetery was dedicated at Gettysburg. At the ceremony, former governor of Massachusetts Edward Everett delivered a two-hour speech. After him, President Abraham Lincoln spoke for about two minutes. In 272 words, Lincoln was able to honor the soldiers and the cause for which they had fought and died, as well as state his vision for the country.

PRIMARY SOURCE

"These dead shall not have died in vain. . . . Government of the people, by the people, for the people shall not perish from the earth."

—from the Gettysburg Address

Reactions to Lincoln's **Gettysburg Address** in the press were mixed. Everett, along with the *New York Times, Chicago Tribune,* and *Springfield* (Mass.) *Republican,* thought the speech was a success. The *Republican* wrote, "His little speech is a perfect gem; deep in feeling, compact in thought and expression, and tasteful . . . in every word and comma."

✔ **Reading Check** **Explaining** How do the events of this section demonstrate that the "tide" of war turned?

Section 4 Review

History ONLINE
Study Central™ To review this section, go to glencoe.com.

Vocabulary

1. Define each of these terms in a sentence that will help explain its meaning: entrench, nevertheless, encounter, siege.

Main Ideas

2. Explaining Why was the battle of Chancellorsville important?

3. Contrasting How were African American soldiers treated differently than white soldiers?

4. Explaining In the Gettysburg Address, what did Lincoln say was the duty of "the living" to accomplish?

Critical Thinking

5. Making Inferences Why do you think many leaders called for African Americans to be allowed to fight in the Civil War?

6. Organizing Using a graphic organizer similar to the one below, list the results of the Battle of Gettysburg.

Battle of Gettysburg
high casualties

7. Expository Writing Refer to Lincoln's Gettysburg Address in this section. Write an essay discussing Lincoln's ideas on freedom and the importance of saving the Union.

Answer the
8. Essential Question
How did the events at Gettysburg and Vicksburg change the course of the war?

C Critical Thinking

Analyzing Primary Sources Have students read the full Gettysburg Address located in their textbooks. **Ask:** What are the main themes of the Gettysburg Address? *(The battle to preserve the Union and the cause of liberty was worth it, even though the cost was high.)* **OL**

✔ **Reading Check** **Answer:** Although the South won key victories at Fredericksburg and Chancellorsville, major Union victories at Gettysburg and Vicksburg set the stage for future victory.

Assess

History ONLINE

Study Central™ provides summaries, interactive games, and online graphic organizers to help students review content.

Close

Activating Prior Knowledge Ask: Which battle allowed the Union armies to accomplish one of their war goals outlined in the Anaconda Plan? *(Victory at Vicksburg allowed the Union to divide the South and control the Mississippi River.)* **OL**

Section 4 Review

Answers

1. Sentences should use vocabulary words according to their definitions in the section and Glossary.

2. It was a strategic victory for the Confederacy, but it cost them a key general when Stonewall Jackson died from injuries.

3. White soldiers doubted the African Americans' ability to fight, and Southern soldiers fought them fiercely.

4. The living had the duty to carry on the unfinished work of the soldiers who died.

5. It would allow the Union Army to add many soldiers; African Americans wanted to end slavery and would be motivated to fight.

6. heavy losses on both sides; invasion of the Union failed; site of Lincoln's famous address

7. Students' essays should reflect Lincoln's emphasis on freedom and liberty in the United States and the importance of preserving those values.

8. Defeat at Gettysburg ended the Confederate hopes for invading the North. Victory at Vicksburg allowed the Union to divide the Southern states and control the Mississippi River.

Section 5

The War's Final Stages

Focus

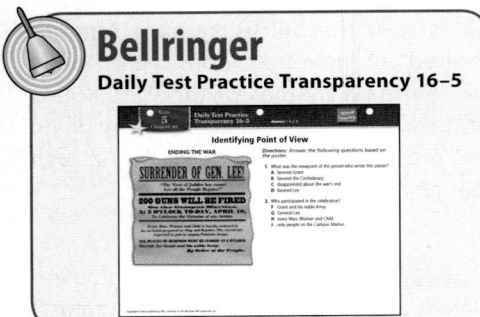

Bellringer
Daily Test Practice Transparency 16–5

Reading Guide
Answers to Graphic:
Students' answers should include: Union blockade of Confederate ports; Wilderness campaign; Mississippi River blockade; Sherman's March to the Sea; fall of Richmond; surrender at Appomattox.

Section Spotlight Video

Have students watch the Section Spotlight Video "The Way to Victory" to learn more about the events that led to the end of the Civil War.

Resource Manager

Essential Question
What events led to the end of the war?

Reading Guide

Content Vocabulary
total war *(p. 507)*   resistance *(p. 509)*

Academic Vocabulary
series *(p. 507)*   interpret *(p. 509)*

Key People and Events
David Farragut *(p. 509)*
March to the Sea *(p. 510)*
Appomattox Court House *(p. 512)*

Reading Strategy
Taking Notes As you read, take notes on the significance of battles late in the war.

Battle	Importance

ILLINOIS STANDARDS
The American Journey

16.B.3c (US) Describe the way the Constitution has changed over time as a result of amendments and Supreme Court decisions.
17.C.3a Explain how human activity is affected by geographic factors.
18.C.3a Describe ways in which a diverse U.S. population has developed and maintained common beliefs (e.g., life, liberty and the pursuit of happiness; the Constitution and the Bill of Rights).

American Diary

After Union forces took control of Atlanta on September 2, 1864, General William Sherman ordered the city burned and the citizens to leave. When the mayor of Atlanta pleaded with Sherman to change his mind, Sherman refused. He responded: "War is cruelty, and you cannot refine it. . . . You might as well appeal against the thunderstorm as against these terrible hardships of war."

—from Memoirs of General William T. Sherman

Atlanta and many other Southern cities, including Richmond as shown here, suffered large-scale destruction as the war continued.

R Reading Strategies	**C** Critical Thinking	**D** Differentiated Instruction	**W** Writing Support	**S** Skill Practice
Teacher Edition • Visualizing, p. 508 • Summarizing, p. 510 • Reading Circle Graphs, p. 511 **Additional Resources** • Guid. Read., URB p. 71 • Content Vocab., URB p. 45 • Academic Vocab., URB p. 47 • Read. Ess., p. 175	**Teacher Edition** • Pred. Consequences, p. 507 • Compare/Contrast, p. 508 • Analyz. Pri. Sources, p. 511 **Additional Resources** • Quizzes and Tests, p. 155 • Enrichment Act., URB p. 11	**Teacher Edition** • Gifted/Talented, p. 508 • Mathematical, p. 510 • ELL, p. 511 **Additional Resources** • Reteaching Act., URB p. 65 • School-to-Home, URB p. 63	**Teacher Edition** • Narrative Writing, p. 509 • Personal Writing, p. 512 **Additional Resources** • Authentic Assess., p. 16	**Teacher Edition** • Using Geo. Skills, p. 510 **Additional Resources** • Daily Test Pract. Transp. 16-5 • Time Line Skills, URB p. 62 • Geo. & Hist., URB p. 59

Total War Strikes the South

Main Idea After a long, bloody summer, Union forces captured major Southern strongholds, and as a result, Lincoln won reelection.

History and You Have you ever had a goal that was difficult to reach? Did you have a strategy to reach your goal? Read to learn how Grant and the Union forces executed their plan.

General William Sherman's destruction of Atlanta and other areas of the South was part of a deliberate strategy to bring the horrors of war—terror, starvation, violence, and homelessness—to the Southern people. This systematic destruction of an entire land—not just its army—is called **total war.**

Union Strategy

By 1864, Union forces surrounded the South. Union ships blocked the Confederate coast, strangling its export economy and cutting off supplies. The Union controlled the Mississippi River, and the western Confederate states were cut off. A bold plan of attack was needed. General Grant would be the one to draw up such a plan.

Grant in Charge

Ulysses S. Grant was only an average student and a failure as a farmer and businessperson. At soldiering, however, he was brilliant. He chalked up victories at Shiloh and Vicksburg and at another important battle in Chattanooga, Tennessee. In March 1864, President Lincoln put General Grant in charge of all the Union armies.

Grant then devised his plan. He would deliver killing blows from all sides. His armies would move on to Richmond, the Confederate capital. At the same time, William Tecumseh Sherman would lead his troops in attacks across the Deep South.

Grant soon put his strategy into effect. In May and June of 1864, Grant's army of 115,000 men smashed into Lee's 64,000 troops in a **series** of three battles near Richmond, Virginia—the battles of the Wilderness, Spotsylvania Courthouse, and Cold Harbor. Each time Confederate lines held, but each time Grant quickly resumed the attack.

"Whatever happens, there will be no turning back," Grant promised Lincoln. He was determined to march southward, attacking Lee's forces relentlessly until the Confederacy surrendered.

By the Numbers | Costs of the War

The South in Ruins By the end of the war, many Southern roads, railroads, farms, and industrial plants were in ruins.

Millions of Dollars

	Physical Destruction	Government Expenditures
Union	$2,302,000	$1,032,000
Confederacy	$0	$1,487,000

Legend: Union, Confederacy

Critical Thinking
Interpreting Were most battles fought on Union or Confederate soil? How can you tell?

Source: EH.Net Encyclopedia

Teach

C Critical Thinking

Predicting Consequences Remind students that the Anaconda Plan was an early Union strategy to win the war by blockading Southern ports, dividing the South by controlling the Mississippi River, and capturing Richmond. **Ask:** How did the success of the Anaconda Plan set the stage for the Union to win battles in the last year of the war? *(Because the Union controlled ports and the Mississippi River, its armies could focus on capturing Richmond, the Confederate capital.)* **OL**

By the Numbers

Critical Thinking Answer Most battles were fought on Confederate soil. The Confederacy experienced much more physical destruction than the Union did.

Skills Practice Ask: According to the chart, what was the cost of the war to the South? *($3,334,000)* Which economy do you think would be better able to recover after the war? *(the North, because there was less physical destruction, and strong industry was already in place)* **OL**

Differentiated Instruction

Leveled Activities

507

D Differentiated Instruction

Gifted/Talented Have groups of students write a short play about the Wilderness campaign. As a class, stage a performance of the best one or two plays. **AL**

R Reading Strategy

Visualizing Ask: Based on this description, what challenges might the commanders of each army have faced? *(difficulty communicating, knowing the location of their troops and enemy troops, finding and helping wounded soldiers, motivating soldiers to keep fighting)* **OL**

C Critical Thinking

Comparing and Contrasting Have students compare Grant's actions following the battles at Wilderness, Spotsylvania, and Cold Harbor with McClellan's actions after Antietam. Contrast President Lincoln's reactions to both generals' decision making. *(Grant resumed the attack, while McClellan refused to follow Lee's army into Virginia. Lincoln approved of Grant's aggressiveness, while he eventually fired McClellan for his inaction.)* **OL**

Hands-On Chapter Project
Step 5

The Wilderness Campaign

In the northeast corner of the Confederacy, about halfway between Washington, D.C., and Richmond, Virginia, lay an area of dense woods called the Wilderness. Here, on May 5, 1864, the six bloodiest weeks of the war began. For two days, the forces of Grant and Lee struggled among a tangle of trees through which they could scarcely see. Said a Union private, "It was a blind and bloody hunt to the death."

Lee had only about 60,000 men to Grant's more than 100,000. Both sides suffered huge casualties. Grant, who lost 17,000 men, cried in his tent at the end of the second day. Meanwhile, brushfires raged through the forest, burning alive 200 wounded men. On the morning of the third day, with no clear winner, Grant moved his forces south toward Richmond.

The next battles were fought at nearby Spotsylvania Courthouse and at Cold Harbor. On June 2, the night before this third battle began, a Union general observed that men were "writing their names and home addresses on slips of paper and pinning them to the backs of their coats" to help people identify their bodies. The war seemed hopeless. Grant, however, was determined. He explained to the White House:

PRIMARY SOURCE

"I propose to fight it out on this line, if it takes all summer."

—Dispatch to Washington, May 11, 1864

Grant's critics in the North called him a "butcher" because of the huge loss of life among his own troops—50,000 in 30 days. Lincoln, however, said, "I can't spare this man. He fights."

People IN HISTORY

Robert E. Lee
General, commander in chief of the Confederate armies

Lee, a brilliant scholar and a daring soldier, was willing to take risks. However, when his orders caused enormous loss of lives, he was filled with sadness. When he finally surrendered, he told his troops he had *"unceasing admiration of your constancy and devotion to your country."*

Abraham Lincoln
Sixteenth president of the United States

Lincoln would not give up. He lost seven elections on the way to winning the presidency. His perseverance helped him stand against all opposition to the war. He believed, *"A house divided against itself cannot stand."* He would see the war through until the country was reunited.

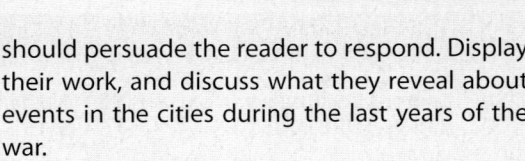

Publishing a Newspaper

Step 5: Persuasive Writing Students will write advertisements for their newspapers.

Essential Question: What events led to the end of the war?

Directions Students should write and illustrate an advertisement for a product or a classified ad in which they are trying to sell something. Students' ideas should reflect the events in their city during the last year of the war. Their writing should persuade the reader to respond. Display their work, and discuss what they reveal about events in the cities during the last years of the war.

Evaluating What was life like during the last year of the Civil War? How do you think the advertisements might differ from what would be found in newspapers during times of peace? **OL**

(Chapter Project continued on the Visual Summary page)

The Petersburg Siege

Continuing his movement south, Grant went on to Petersburg, a railroad center that was vital to the Confederate movement of troops and supplies. If Grant could take Petersburg, then Richmond would be cut off from the rest of the Confederacy. Grant laid siege. The Confederates defended the city, but they could not win. Trains brought food and reinforcements to the Union troops. The Confederates could get neither. For nine long months, however, they held out.

Sherman in Georgia

Meanwhile, William Tecumseh Sherman took off for Georgia. In early July, his troops circled Atlanta. There they faced the brilliant Confederate general, John Hood, whose forces put up major **resistance.** Sherman laid siege. Finally, on September 1, Hood abandoned the

city. The mood in the South was desperate. Mary Chesnut, a Georgian who kept a diary throughout the war, wrote, "There is no hope, but we will try to have no fear."

Farragut at Mobile Bay

The highest-ranking officer in the Union navy was **David Farragut,** the son of a Latino military man. Young David Farragut joined the navy when he was only 12 years old. Now, in August 1864, he was leading a fleet of 18 ships through a narrow channel into Mobile Bay in Alabama. The Confederates had two forts on either side of the channel, and they had mined the waters with torpedoes. Guns were firing from both forts. What was Farragut to do? He gave his famous order, "Damn the torpedoes, full speed ahead!"

Farragut, who was suffering from dizziness, had himself tied to the ship's rigging so he could stay in the battle. His invasion was a success, and the last Southern port east of the Mississippi was blocked.

The Election of 1864

Through most of 1864, opposition to the war in the North grew stronger. A presidential election was coming up in November, and it looked unlikely that Lincoln would win reelection. His loss could mean an end to the war and recognition of the Confederate government as an independent country. Southerners clung to this hope.

After Atlanta fell and Mobile Bay was blocked, Northerners began to believe again that they could win. Lincoln won a second term handsomely—with 55 percent of the popular vote, 212 to 21 electoral votes.

Lincoln **interpreted,** or explained, his reelection as a clear sign from the voters to end slavery permanently by amending the Constitution. On January 31, 1865, Congress passed the Thirteenth Amendment, which banned slavery in the United States.

Reading Check Summarizing What was the Union strategy in 1864, and what were the results?

Ulysses S. Grant

General of the United States Army and eighteenth president of the United States

Grant was a fearless soldier and an expert horseman at a time when soldiers rode horses in battle. Grant's strategy seemed ruthless at times, but he said, *"I have never advocated [war] except as a means of peace."*

CRITICAL Thinking

1. **Synthesizing** What characteristics do you think these three men shared?
2. **Describing** Select a quote from one of the men described. What does the quote reveal about that person?

The Civil War **Chapter 16** 509

CHAPTER 16
Section 5

W Writing Support

Narrative Writing Have students write a short story about a soldier in the Union navy at the Battle of Mobile Bay. Students should use descriptive language and historical detail. **OL**

Reading Check Answer: Grant wanted to move armies to take Richmond; Sherman would begin a "total war" campaign to crush the South. The Union had key victories, but the war continued.

People IN HISTORY

Critical Thinking Answers

1. Students may say determination and courage.
2. Students' selections should use the quotes they choose to explain their responses.

Skills Practice
Lee said of Grant: "I doubt his superior can be found in all of history." **Ask:** What things might have influenced Lee to say this about his enemy? *(his determination, strategic skill, and leadership qualities)*

Additional Support

Fast Facts

Election of 1864 During most of 1864, it seemed unlikely that Lincoln would be reelected. Across the Union, widespread disagreement over the suspension of civil liberties, the military draft, emancipation, and the high cost of the war turned voters against the Republican president.

The Democratic Party tried to take advantage of doubts about Lincoln and fatigue with the war. During their convention in

Chicago during August 1864, the party agreed to a platform that included a willingness to end the war without abolishing slavery. They nominated former Union general George McClellan as their candidate.

The Republican Party changed its name to the National Union Party and held its convention in Baltimore on June 7–8, 1864. Their platform stated the commitment to continue the war, adopt a Constitutional amend-

ment for abolition, encourage immigration, and construct a transcontinental railroad.

The party's hopes were dim until a series of Union victories, including the fall of Atlanta, turned the tide of public opinion. Victory for the Union now seemed possible. Lincoln won a landslide victory with 55 percent of the popular vote and a powerful margin in the Electoral College, 212 to 21.

Skill Practice

Using Geography Skills Have students perform research to learn the population at the time for each city that Sherman marched through. Discuss the impact of Sherman's March to the Sea on cities and the people living there. **OL**

Reading Strategy

Summarizing Ask: How did Sherman's March to the Sea fulfill the Union's "total war" strategy? *(He wanted to break the will of the South and make it impossible for them to continue to fight. His soldiers burned cities and farmlands, took food, destroyed railroad lines and fields, and killed livestock.)* **OL**

Differentiated Instruction

Mathematical Have students use maps to determine how much distance General Sherman covered during his March to the Sea. **AL**

Differentiated Instruction

The Final Battles, 1864–1865 — NATIONAL GEOGRAPHIC

Battle Dates

The Wilderness
May 5–6, 1864

Cold Harbor
June 3, 1864

Petersburg siege
June 5, 1864–April 3, 1865

Kennesaw Mountain
June 27, 1864

Atlanta
July 20–Sept. 2, 1864

Franklin
Nov. 30, 1864

Nashville
Dec. 15–16, 1864

Wilmington
Feb. 12–22, 1865

Bentonville
March 19–21, 1865

Appomattox Court House
April 9, 1865

Map Skills

1. **Location** Where did Sherman's March to the Sea begin and end?
2. **Analyzing Information** Which battle was considered "indecisive"? Why?

Maps in MOtion See StudentWorks™ Plus or glencoe.com.

The War's End

Main Idea After four years of fighting against unfavorable odds, the South finally surrendered.

History and You How would you treat an enemy who said, "I give up"?

. . . .

From the beginning of the war, the Union army wanted to capture the Confederate capital. When Grant finally drove Lee's army out of Petersburg, Virginia, Jefferson Davis knew that Richmond was doomed.

Sherman's March to the Sea

The last months of the war saw the Union determined to break the will of the South. Sherman and his men became destroyers.

Before Sherman's army left Atlanta in November, it burned much of this beautiful city. From Atlanta, Sherman's troops burned cities and farmlands as they marched across Georgia to the Atlantic coast. This trail of destruction is known as Sherman's **March to the Sea.**

Sherman continued his path of destruction through the Carolinas to join Grant's forces near Richmond. Union troops took what food they needed, tore up railroad lines and fields, and killed livestock in an effort to destroy anything that was useful to the South.

White Southerners deplored Sherman's march, but thousands of African Americans left their plantations to follow the protection of his army. For them, this was a march to freedom.

510   Chapter 16 *The Civil War*

Waging War Between the States

Objective:	To identify locations of importance in the Civil War
Focus:	Remind students of the roles played by Grant, Sherman, and Lee in the final years of the war.
Teach:	Have students read the background material and answer the questions.
Assess:	Ask for volunteers to discuss their answers with the class.
Close:	Review any questions and answers that were problematic for students.

Differentiated Instruction Strategies

BL Have students use a dictionary to define words they do not know.

AL Have students select a particular battle and prepare a report on what the surrounding area is like today.

ELL With the instructor's permission, have students watch a video documentary about some aspect of the Civil War.

Geography and History Activity, URB p. 59

The Union Advances

1861

ATLANTIC OCEAN

Gulf of Mexico

Early Stages Confederate troops won most of the battles in the first year of the Civil War.

1863

ATLANTIC OCEAN

Gulf of Mexico

Union Gains Union control of the Mississippi River cut off Texas and Arkansas, the South's leading food producers, from the Confederacy.

1865

ATLANTIC OCEAN

Gulf of Mexico

Final Stages By 1865, the Union controlled large parts of the Confederacy.

By the Numbers

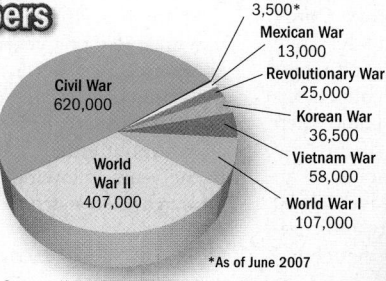

Lives Lost More lives were lost in the Civil War than in any other major American conflict. Deadly weapons, poor medical practices, infection, and disease all contributed.

Civil War 620,000

World War II 407,000

Iraqi War 3,500*

Mexican War 13,000

Revolutionary War 25,000

Korean War 36,500

Vietnam War 58,000

World War I 107,000

*As of June 2007

Sources: *United States Civil War Center, For the Common Defense*

Unknown Soldiers A gravestone in Gettysburg Cemetery commemorates the loss of 425 Civil War soldiers who were never identified.

UNKNOWN. 425 BODIES

The Fall of Richmond

Meanwhile, Grant continued the siege of Petersburg. Lee and his troops defended the town, but sickness, casualties, and desertion weakened them. Finally, on April 2, 1865, the Confederate lines broke and Lee withdrew.

Word of Lee's retreat came to the Confederate president. As the Union army marched toward Richmond, Davis and his cabinet gathered documents, gave orders that bridges and weapons useful to the enemy be set on fire, and fled the city. An observer wrote:

PRIMARY SOURCE

"The trains came and went, wagons, vehicles, and horsemen rumbled and dashed to and fro. . . . As night came on . . . rioting and robbing took place."
—from *Battles and Leaders of the Civil War*

The armory, with its stores of ammunition, exploded. Boom after boom rang through the city, and fires raged out of control.

Two days later, President Lincoln and his son Tad arrived to tour the fallen capital. Said Lincoln, "Thank God I have lived to see this. It seems to me that I have been dreaming a horrid nightmare for four years, and now the nightmare is over."

Joyful African Americans followed Lincoln everywhere, singing, laughing, and reaching out to touch him. When one man knelt down to thank him, Lincoln replied, "Don't kneel to me. You must kneel to God only, and thank Him for your freedom."

At the Confederate president's house, Lincoln sat in a chair in Davis's office and "looked far off with a dreamy expression."

The Civil War **Chapter 16 511**

R Reading Strategy

Reading Circle Graphs Refer students to the By the Numbers feature. **Ask:** Other than the Civil War, which war had the highest number of deaths? *(World War II)* Which war had the fewest? *(the Iraq War)* **BL**

C Critical Thinking

Analyzing Primary Sources Ask: What does the author mean when he states, "As night came on… rioting and robbing took place"? *(After Davis and his cabinet retreated, there was a breakdown in law and order. People stole goods and rioted in the city.)* **OL**

D Differentiated Instruction

English Language Learners Have students use a dictionary to find the meanings of the word "raged." Then have them rewrite this sentence in their own words. **ELL**

Additional Support

Activity: Technology Connection

Making Connections The Framers of the U.S. Constitution gave the president authority to conduct wars on behalf of the United States.

Have students use the circle graph in the By the Numbers feature to list major wars in which the United States has been involved. Have students list the men who were president during each war. Ask students to select one president and war to compare and contrast with President Lincoln and the Civil War. Students should use Internet research to focus on how the president conducted the war, dealt with public and political opinions on the war, confronted the painful reality of casualties, and celebrated the end of the war.

Finally, have students use presentation software to display their results. **AL**

W Writing Support

Personal Writing Have students take the role of a Union or Confederate soldier who has just heard about the surrender at Appomattox. Have them write a letter to a family member, explaining the soldier's feelings about the war's end. **OL**

 Reading Check **Answer:** Sherman's March to the Sea and the fall of Richmond

Assess

History ONLINE

Study Central™ provides summaries, interactive games, and online graphic organizers to help students review content.

Close

Analyzing As a class, discuss the effects of the war on the North and the South. How did they differ? **OL**

Section ★ Review

At Libby Prison, where the Union held Confederate prisoners of war, Lincoln was asked what to do with the prisoners and replied, "If I were in your place, I'd let 'em up easy, let 'em up easy."

Surrender at Appomattox

The formal end of the war came a few days later, on April 9, 1865. Two days earlier, Grant asked Lee to surrender, writing, "The result of last week must convince you of the hopelessness of further resistance."

Yet Lee believed he must fight on. However, when the Union captured the train carrying food to his troops and Lee was completely surrounded, he knew it was over.

In the little town of **Appomattox Court House,** Virginia, Grant met with Lee. They shook hands and talked a little. Then Grant offered his terms. Lee's soldiers could keep their small firearms, the officers could keep their horses, and no one would disturb the soldiers as they made their way home. In an act of generosity, Grant also gave 25,000 rations to feed Lee's troops. Dignity and compassion were the order of the day that ended America's deadliest war.

The Toll of War

More lives were lost in the Civil War than in any other conflict in American history. More than 600,000 soldiers died. The war cost billions of dollars. In the South, cities and farmlands were destroyed, and it would take years and a massive national effort to rebuild.

The war had other consequences as well. The North's victory saved the Union. The federal government was strengthened and was now clearly more powerful than the states. Finally, the war freed millions of African Americans. The end of slavery, however, did not solve the problems that the newly freed African Americans were to face.

Following the war, many questions remained. No one yet knew how to bring the Southern states back into the Union, nor what the status of African Americans would be in Southern society. Americans from the North and the South tried to answer these questions in the years following the Civil War—an era known as Reconstruction.

Reading Check **Evaluating** What events led to Lee's surrender?

History ONLINE
Study Central™ To review this section, go to glencoe.com.

Section 5 Review

Vocabulary
1. Define each of the following terms, and use them in a paragraph about the last year of the Civil War: total war, series resistance, interpret.

Main Ideas
2. **Explaining** How did events on the battlefield affect Lincoln's reelection?
3. **Describing** Why did Sherman burn and destroy the South's land?

4. **Explaining** What were Grant's terms of surrender at Appomattox Court House?

Critical Thinking
5. **Analyzing** Complete a graphic organizer similar to the one below to explain the effects of the Civil War on the nation.

6. **Descriptive Writing** Take on the role of a reporter living in Georgia during Sherman's March to the Sea. Write a brief article describing the Union's actions and their effects on the people living there.

Answer the
7. **Essential Question**
What events led to the end of the war?

Answers

1. Paragraphs should use vocabulary words according to their definitions.
2. Lincoln's chances for reelection were slim while the North was losing major battles during most of 1864.
3. The Union was determined to break the will of the South. "Total war" was a deliberate strategy by the North to end the conflict.

4. Lee's soldiers could keep their small firearms, officers could keep their horses, Confederate soldiers returning home would be left alone, and Grant gave Lee 25,000 rations to feed his troops.
5. Answers could include: saved the Union; strengthened federal government; 600,000 soldiers died; cities and farmland in the South destroyed; billions spent on war.

6. Students' articles should describe the effects of Sherman's march on the residents of Georgia.
7. Students' responses should include descriptions of the Wilderness campaign, the blockade of Mobile Bay, Sherman's March to the Sea, total war, and the fall of Richmond.

Visual Summary

1861	1862	1863	1864
Feb. Southern states form the Confederacy	**Mar.** The *Monitor* and the *Virginia* fight the first battle between ironclad ships	**Jan.** Lincoln issues Emancipation Proclamation	**Mar.** General Ulysses Grant assumes command of all Union armies
Apr. Union surrenders Fort Sumter	*Virginia*	**July** Lee's invasion of the North turned back at Gettysburg	**Nov.** Lincoln reelected to second term
June Four border states stay in the Union	**Apr.** Farragut's naval forces capture New Orleans	**July** Fall of Vicksburg results in Union control of the Mississippi River	
July First major battle fought at Bull Run in Virginia	**Sept.** Antietam is the first major battle on Northern soil		

UNKNOWN SOLDIER
CIVIL WAR

FOR PRESIDENT
A. LINCOLN
1864

1865
Feb. Sherman's forces march through the Carolinas
Apr. 2 Lee evacuates Richmond; Union forces capture capital
Apr. 9 Surrender at Appomattox Court House
Apr. 14 Lincoln is assassinated

▲ A Union soldier with his family in a Washington, D.C., camp in 1862

STUDY TO GO Study anywhere, anytime! Download quizzes and flash cards to your PDA from glencoe.com.

The Civil War **Chapter 16** 513

Visual Summary

Identifying Points of View Ask: Based on the events leading up to the end of the war, how do you think soldiers on each side felt about Lee's surrender at Appomattox? *(Soldiers on both sides may have been relieved that the long war was over; Confederate soldiers may have been frustrated at surrendering or fearful of how they would be treated.)* How might enslaved African Americans have felt? *(relief at being free; perhaps confused about what to do; hostility toward former slave owners)* **OL**

Predicting Ask: Do you think former Confederate states should have been automatically readmitted to the Union? *(Students' responses should reflect the challenges each side faced in planning for postwar recovery.)* Ask students to predict how the Union might accept the return of the Confederate states. Who might oversee the process, and what would need to be in place before a state could rejoin the Union? **OL**

Hands-On Chapter Project
Step 6: Wrap-Up

Publishing a Newspaper

Step 6: Printing the Newspaper Students will compile their work into a newspaper.

Directions Have student groups review their work. As a team, students should select articles, editorials, images, and advertisements to compile into a newspaper. Using word processing or design software, students should create page layouts, write headlines, and assemble their selected content. Newspapers should reflect the experience of the residents and journalists of the students' chosen city and include historical detail. Have students print their newspapers and distribute them to the rest of the class.

Analyzing Discuss the role of journalism in American culture. **Ask:** How do newspapers reflect historical events? *(by reporting on events as they happen)* How might events be shaped by journalists? *(Through the stories and images they choose to print and the editorials they write, journalists can create public awareness about certain issues.)* How are newspapers important to the historian? *(They provide perspectives about issues and events that journalists and their readers were interested in.)* **OL**

513

STANDARDIZED TEST PRACTICE

Answers and Analyses

Reviewing Main Ideas

1. B Have students identify the key word in the question: *advantage.* Then ask students to think about synonyms for the word. They should use these synonyms to help them answer the question. **17.C.3a**

2. C Remind students to think about where the Mississippi and Tennessee Rivers are located. Students should then be able to select choice C. **17.C.3a**

3. A Students should remember that Northern armies traveled south, so it was the Confederacy that fought a defensive war. Also, bounties were not paid to increase the number of recruits. The correct answer is A. **15.E**

4. B Students should recall that McClellan, Burnside, and Hooker lost several important battles, while Grant was a brilliant soldier who led the North to victory. Students should then choose choice B. **16.A**

Short-Answer Question

5. As students read the excerpt, have them find the definitions in a dictionary for the words they do not know. Lincoln argues that people are morally obligated to take care of each other. He also believes that by taking care of those who were hurt by the war, peace will replace any anger and resentment people might have. **16.A.3b**

TEST-TAKING TIP

> Answer the questions you know first and go back to those for which you need more time.

Reviewing Main Ideas

Directions: Choose the best answer for each of the following questions.

1. What was one advantage the Southern states had during the Civil War?

  A They received military support from Britain and France.

  B Many battles occurred on lands with which Southerners were more familiar.

  C The largest weapons factories were located in the South.

  D Most people in the country agreed with the position of the Southern states.

2. By gaining control of the Mississippi and Tennessee Rivers, what was the Union able to do?

  A capture Fort Sumter

  B force the Confederacy to surrender

  C split the Confederacy

  D defeat the Confederate forces at Gettysburg

3. During the war, the economy of the South

  A was severly strained from the blockade instituted by the North and the destruction of Southern land and property.

  B remained unchanged because most of the battles took place on Northern soil.

  C was strengthened due to inflation.

  D was strengthened because bounties were paid to army recruits.

4. Which Union general proved to be most effective?

  A General McClellan   **C** General Burnside

  B General Grant   **D** General Hooker

Short-Answer Question

Directions: Base your answer to question 5 on the excerpt below and on your knowledge of social studies.

> With malice toward none, with charity for all, with firmness in the right as God gives us to see the right, let us strive on to finish the work we are in, to bind up the nation's wounds, to care for him who shall have borne the battle and for his widow and his orphan—to do all which may achieve and cherish a just and lasting peace among ourselves and with all nations.
>
> —from Abraham Lincoln's second Inaugural Address

5. In his address, Lincoln did not focus on the Union victory in the Civil War. State *two* reasons why this is so.

Review the Essential Questions

6. Essay How did the Civil War affect the North and the South?

To help you write your essay, review your answers to the Essential Questions in the section reviews and the chapter Foldables Study Organizer. Your essay should include:

- the strengths and weaknesses of the two sides;
- the results of early battles;
- social, political, and economic changes;
- how Vicksburg and Gettysburg changed the course of the war; and
- the end of the Civil War.

GO ON ▶

Review the Essential Questions

6. If students completed their Foldables correctly, they should be able to describe how the Civil War affected the North and the South. The North, which was heavily industrialized before the war, was able to use its resources to win the war. The South, which had an economy based on agriculture and slavery with little industry before the war, was completely devastated as a result of advancing Northern armies. After the war, the South's plantation system was destroyed and slavery ended. **17.C.3a**

History ONLINE
For additional test practice, use **Self-Check Quizzes**—Chapter 16 at glencoe.com.

Chapter 16 Assessment

Document-Based Questions

Directions: Analyze the documents and answer the short-answer questions that follow.

Document 1

In July 1861 Confederate diplomat John Slidell describes one advantage the South holds.

> We shall have the enormous advantage of fighting on our own territory and for our very existence.

Source: James M. McPherson, *Ordeal By Fire*

7. Why would fighting on familiar territory be an advantage?

Document 2

A Union cavalry man taken prisoner describes the conditions of the Andersonville prison.

> July 6. Boiling hot, camp reeking with filth, and no sanitary privileges; men dying off over 140 per day . . . .Disease is here and mowing down good and true men. . . .Bread today and it is so coarse as to do more hurt than good to a majority of the prisoners.

Source: *Eyewitness to America*

8. What was life like for prisoners during the Civil War?

Document 3

The diaries of Mary Chesnut of South Carolina describe life in the South during the Civil War.

> Since we left Chester nothing but solitude, nothing but tall blackened chimneys, to show that any man has trod here before. This is Sherman's track.

Source: Mary Boykin Chesnut, *A Diary From Dixie*

9. What does this excerpt reveal about Sherman's strategy in fighting the South?

Document 4

This political cartoon appeared in an August 1862 edition of *Punch*, a British magazine.

LINCOLN'S TWO DIFFICULTIES.

Source: Corbis

10. Based on this cartoon, identify *two* challenges the Union faced in fighting the war.

Document 5

Frederick Douglass led the movement to allow African American men to enlist.

> Once let the black man get upon his person the brass letters U.S. . . . and a musket on his shoulder and bullets in his pocket, and there is no power on earth which can deny that he has earned the right to citizenship [in the United States].

Source: James M. McPherson, *Battle Cry of Freedom*

11. Based on this document, identify *one* reason Douglass wanted African American men to fight in the war.

12. Expository Writing Using the information from the five documents and your knowledge of social studies, write an essay in which you:

- discuss the main goals for the Union and the Confederacy in fighting the Civil War; and

- discuss the effects of the war on soldiers and civilians.

9. The description of the burning of Atlanta reveals Sherman's use of destructive total war to bring the South to its knees. **16.A.3b**

10. The cartoon shows Lincoln learning that he does not have enough money or soldiers to fight the Civil War. Lincoln had to find ways to raise revenue and add soldiers to the military. **16.A**

11. Douglass argues that if African Americans defended the Union, they earned the right to be made citizens. **18.C.3b**

12. Students' essays should focus on the differences between the North and the South and how each side chose to fight the war. Topics that should be covered in essays include: slavery, popular sovereignty, Northern and Southern industry and agriculture, the Emancipation Proclamation, and the military and political strategies that led to the Union victory. Students' essays should use transitional words and phrases that reflect cause-and-effect relationships. **18.C.3a**

History ONLINE
Have students visit the Web site at glencoe.com to review Chapter 16 and take the Self-Check Quiz.

Need Extra Help?

If you missed questions. . .	1	2	3	4	5	6	7	8	9	10	11	12
Go to page. . .	476	482–483	494–497	500	506–512	472–512	475–476	493	506–510	498–505	501	472–512

Need Extra Help?

Have students refer to the pages listed if they miss any of the questions.

Document-Based Questions

7. The soldier sees the war as a noble cause in support of "American civilization," for which he is willing to give his life. **16.A.3b**

8. Both sides treated enemy soldiers with a mixture of sympathy and hostility. Prison camps were set up, but few provisions were available and food shortages added to the suffering. As a result, disease was a constant threat. **18.B.3a**

Chapter Planning Guide

17

Levels				Resources	Chapter Opener	Section 1	Section 2	Section 3	Section 4	Chapter Assess
BL	OL	AL	ELL							
FOCUS										
BL	OL	AL	ELL	Daily Test Practice Transparencies		17–1	17–2	17–3	17–4	
TEACH										
	OL	AL		Geography and History Activity, URB		p. 89				
BL	OL		ELL	Time Line Skills Activity, URB			p. 92			
BL	OL	AL	ELL	Writing Skills Activity, URB		p. 81				
BL	OL	AL	ELL	Content Vocabulary Activity, URB		p. 75	p. 75	p. 75	p. 75	
BL	OL	AL	ELL	Academic Vocabulary Activity, URB		p. 77	p. 77	p. 77	p. 77	
BL			ELL	Reading Skills Activity, URB			p. 7			
	OL	AL		Citizenship and Decision-Making Skills Activity, URB			p. 3			
BL	OL		ELL	Social Studies Skills Activity, URB		p. 83				
BL	OL	AL	ELL	Differentiated Instruction Activity, URB		p. 85				
BL	OL	AL	ELL	Critical Thinking Skills Activity, URB			p. 87			
BL	OL	AL	ELL	Linking Past and Present Activity, URB					p. 91	
	OL	AL		Primary Source Readings, URB					p. 79	
BL	OL	AL	ELL	School-to-Home Connection Activity, URB		p. 93	p. 93	p. 93	p. 93	
BL	OL		ELL	Guided Reading Activity, URB*		p. 97	p. 98	p. 99	p. 100	
	OL	AL		Economics and History Activity, URB				p. 5		
BL	OL		ELL	Reading Essentials and Note-Taking Guide*		p. 178	p. 181	p. 184	p. 187	
BL	OL	AL	ELL	Lesson Transparencies		17A, 17B			17C	
	OL			American Biographies		p. 28		p. 29		
BL	OL	AL	ELL	Outline Map Resource Book	p. 6					

Note: Please refer to the *Unit Resource Book: Civil War and Reconstruction* for this chapter's URB materials.

* Also available in Spanish

Levels					Resources	Chapter Opener	Section 1	Section 2	Section 3	Section 4	Chapter Assess
TEACH *(continued)*											
BL	OL	AL	ELL		**NGS US Desk Map**		✓	✓	✓	✓	
BL	OL	AL	ELL		**American Literature Library**		✓	✓	✓	✓	
BL	OL	AL	ELL		**Writer's Guidebook**		✓	✓	✓	✓	
	OL	AL			**American History Primary Source Document Library CD-ROM**		✓	✓	✓	✓	✓
BL	OL	AL	ELL		**American Music: Hits Through History**	✓	✓	✓	✓	✓	
BL	OL	AL	ELL		**StudentWorks™ Plus CD**	✓	✓	✓	✓	✓	✓
BL	OL	AL	ELL		**Section Spotlight Videos**		✓	✓	✓	✓	
BL	OL	AL	ELL		**Writing Process Transparencies**		✓	✓	✓	✓	✓
BL	OL	AL	ELL		**Presentation Plus! With MindJogger CheckPoint CD**	✓	✓	✓	✓	✓	✓
ASSESS											
BL	OL	AL	ELL		**Quizzes and Tests**		p. 163	p. 164	p. 165	p. 166	pp. 167, 169, 171
BL	OL	AL	ELL		**Authentic Assessment With Rubrics**		p. 17				
BL	OL	AL	ELL		**Standardized Test Practice**						p. 33
BL	OL	AL	ELL		***ExamView® Assessment Suite* CD-ROM***		17–1	17–2	17–3	17–4	Ch. 17
CLOSE											
BL			ELL		**Reteaching Activity, URB***		p. 95	p. 95	p. 95	p. 95	p. 95
BL	OL		ELL		**Reading and Study Skills Foldables Activity**	p. 82	p. 82	p. 82	p. 82	p. 82	p. 82
BL	OL	AL	ELL		***The American Journey* in Graphic Novel**						p. 93
BL			ELL		**Reading Strategies and Activities for the Social Studies Classroom**		✓	✓	✓	✓	
BL	OL	AL	ELL		**Graphic Organizer Transparencies & Strategies**		✓	✓	✓	✓	

TeacherWorks Plus
All-In-One Planner and Resource Center

- Interactive Lesson Planner
- Interactive Teacher Edition
- Fully editable blackline masters
- Section Spotlight Videos Launch
- Differentiated Lesson Plans
- Printable reports of daily assignments
- Standards Tracking System

Professional Development Resources

- Strategies for Success
- Building Academic Vocabulary
- Success With English Learners DVD
- Differentiated Instruction Strategies DVD
- Teaching Literacy Strategies in Social Studies DVD
- Assessment DVD
- Standards-Based Instruction DVD

Integrating Technology

17

Using Study Central™

Online Quiz

Technology Product

Students can check their comprehension of section content with quizzes on the Study Central™ Web site. Each quiz

- consists of five multiple-choice questions;
- is scrambled so students can take quizzes multiple times;
- provides immediate feedback to students.

Objectives

The quizzes on Study Central™ help students

- assess their comprehension of chapter content;
- build study skills;
- identify areas for additional study and reinforcement.

Steps

- Locate the textbook's Web page at glencoe.com.
- Click on **Study Central™** under *Textbook Resources*.
- Select a chapter and section using the drop-down arrows and click **Enter**.
- Click on the **Quiz** tab.
- Have students answer the questions.
- Identify and reteach the concepts the students had problems with as they engaged in the quiz.

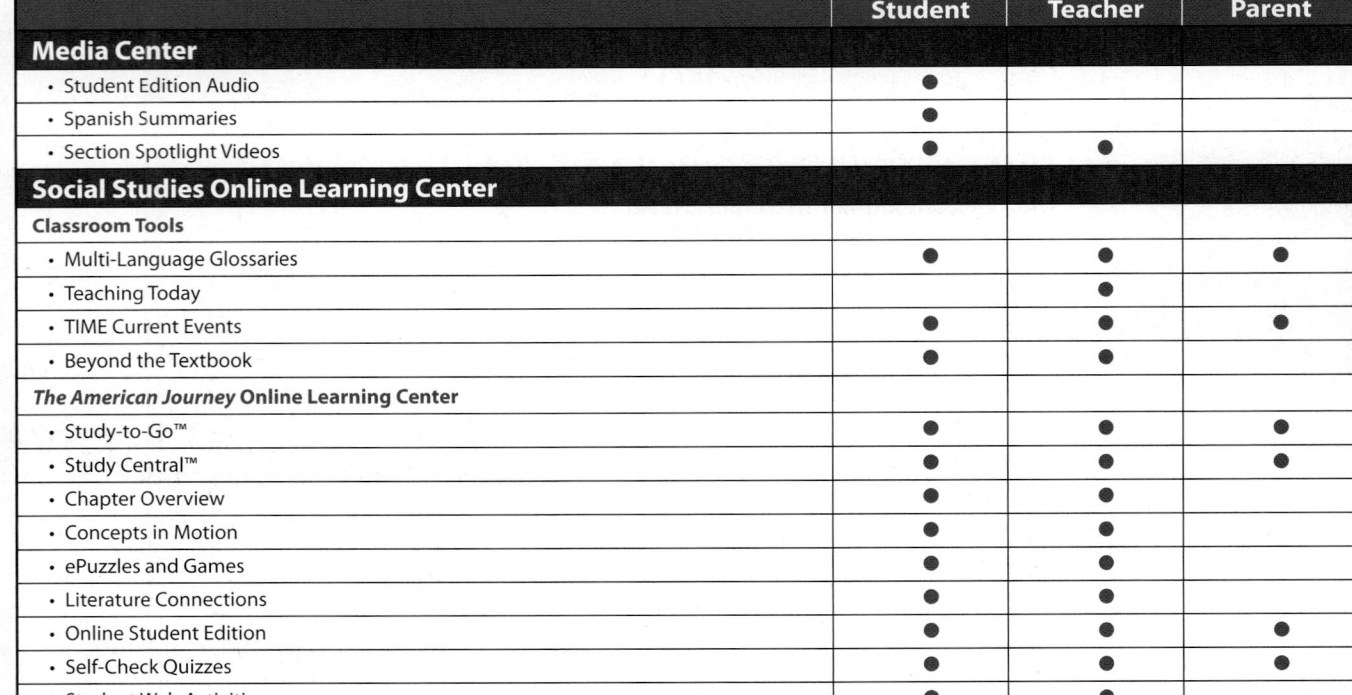

History ONLINE at glencoe.com

	Student	Teacher	Parent
Media Center			
• Student Edition Audio	●		
• Spanish Summaries	●		
• Section Spotlight Videos	●	●	
Social Studies Online Learning Center			
Classroom Tools			
• Multi-Language Glossaries	●	●	●
• Teaching Today		●	
• TIME Current Events	●	●	●
• Beyond the Textbook	●	●	
***The American Journey* Online Learning Center**			
• Study-to-Go™	●	●	●
• Study Central™	●	●	●
• Chapter Overview	●	●	
• Concepts in Motion	●	●	
• ePuzzles and Games	●	●	
• Literature Connections	●	●	
• Online Student Edition	●	●	●
• Self-Check Quizzes	●	●	●
• Student Web Activities	●	●	
• Vocabulary eFlashcards	●	●	
• Web Activity Lesson Plans	●	●	●
• Vocabulary PuzzleMaker	●	●	●

READING SUPPORT FROM JAMESTOWN EDUCATION

- **Timed Readings Plus in Social Studies** helps students increase their reading rate and fluency while maintaining comprehension. The 400-word passages are similar to those found on state and national assessments.

- **Reading in the Content Area: Social Studies** concentrates on six essential reading skills that help students better comprehend what they read. The book includes 75 high-interest nonfiction passages written at increasing levels of difficulty.

- **Reading Social Studies** includes strategic reading instruction and vocabulary support in Social Studies content for ELLs and native speakers of English.

- **Content Vocabulary Workout** (Grades 6–8) accelerates reading comprehension through focused vocabulary development. Social Studies content vocabulary comes from the glossaries of Glencoe's Middle School Social Studies texts.

www.jamestowneducation.com

NATIONAL GEOGRAPHIC
Index to National Geographic Magazine:

The following articles relate to this chapter:

- *"Arlington Cemetery,"* Rick Atkinson, June 2007.
- *"Lost Gold: Bounty From a Civil War Ship,"* Priit J. Vesilind, September 2004.

National Geographic Society Products

To order the following, call National Geographic at 1-800-368-2728:

National Geographic Atlas of the World (Book)

Access National Geographic's dynamic MapMachine Web site and other geography resources at:

www.nationalgeographic.com

www.nationalgeographic.com/mapmachine

Reading List Generator CD-ROM — GLENCOE BOOKLINK 3

Use this database to search more than 30,000 titles to create a customized reading list for your students.

- Reading lists can be organized by students' reading level, author, genre, theme, or area of interest.
- The database provides Degrees of Reading Power™ (DRP) and Lexile™ readability scores for all selections.
- A brief summary of each selection is included.

Leveled reading suggestions for this chapter:

For students at a Grade 6 reading level:
- *An Acquaintance With Darkness,* by Ann Rinaldi
- *Be Ever Hopeful, Hannalee,* by Patricia Beatty

For students at a Grade 7 reading level:
- *Fires of Jubilee,* by Alison Hart
- *The Red Rose Box,* by Brenda Woods

For students at a Grade 8 reading level:
- *Bigger,* by Patricia Calvert
- *Tancy,* by Belinda Hurmence

For students at a Grade 9 reading level:
- *Unconditional Surrender: U.S. Grant and the Civil War,* by Albert Marrin
- *Cane River,* by Lalita Tademy

For students at a Grade 10 reading level:
- *Ulysses S. Grant: 18th President of the United States,* by Lucille Falkof
- *Buffalo Soldiers,* by Catherine Reef

The following videotape programs are available from Glencoe as supplements to the chapter:

- **John Wilkes Booth** (ISBN 1-56-501715-3)
- **Fragile Freedom: African American Historic Sites** (ISBN 0-76-704670-6)

To order, call Glencoe at 1-800-334-7344. To find classroom resources to accompany many of these videos, check the following home pages:

A&E Television: www.aetv.com

The History Channel: www.history.com

Chapter Objectives

After studying this chapter, students will be able to:

- Contrast the different plans to unify the nation after the Civil War.
- Discuss the results of Radical Reconstruction.
- Describe how government in the Southern states changed during Reconstruction.
- Explain how the South changed politically, economically, and socially when Reconstruction ended.

Motivating Activity

Making Inferences Students will learn that enslaved African Americans were freed from slavery at the end of the Civil War. For African Americans, both in the former Confederacy as well as across the country, the struggle to achieve full equality was just beginning. **Ask:** Why do you think all the children in this picture are African American? *(African American children were not allowed to attend the same schools as white children in most Southern states.)* Do you think African Americans in the South received an education equal to that of whites during this period? Why or why not? *(No. African American schools probably received fewer resources than white schools because of the continuing hostility of many Southern whites toward African Americans.)* **OL**

Previewing the Essential Questions

As you begin teaching each section, use these questions and activities to help students focus on the Essential Questions.

Chapter 17

Reconstruction and the New South 1865–1896

A teacher and her students in front of the Freedmen's School in North Carolina

PRESIDENTS

ABRAHAM LINCOLN 1861–1865

ANDREW JOHNSON 1865–1869

ULYSSES S. GRANT 1869–1877

U.S. Events

1867
- Alaska purchased
- First Reconstruction Act passed

1870 Fifteenth Amendment ratified

1877 Reconstruction ends

1860   1870

World Events

★ **1866** First transatlantic cable connects North America to Europe

★ **1868** Meiji era begins in Japan

★ **1871** Bismarck unifies Germany

★ **1874** First major exhibit of impressionist art in Paris

516   Chapter 17

Section 1

Reconstruction Plans Ask: After the Civil War ended, do you think the Confederates should have been punished? Why or why not? *(Some students might see secession as a punishable crime. Others might note that a pardon would help unify the nation.)* Point out that Section 1 describes different views on how to bring the former Confederate states back into the Union. **OL**

Section 2

Radicals in Control Ask: How do you think white Southerners treated newly freed African Americans? *(Many whites tried to control and exploit them.)* Point out to students that in Section 2, they will learn about laws that denied rights to African Americans as well as ways the federal government tried to protect them. **OL**

Section 1: Reconstruction Plans
Essential Question How did plans to unify the nation differ after the Civil War?

Section 2: Radicals in Control
Essential Question What were the results of Radical Reconstruction?

Section 3: The South During Reconstruction
Essential Question In what ways did government in the Southern states change during Reconstruction?

Section 4: Change in the South
Essential Question How did the South change politically, economically, and socially when Reconstruction ended?

History ONLINE
Chapter Overview Visit glencoe.com and click on **Chapter 17—Chapter Overviews** to preview chapter information.

FOLDABLES®
Study Organizer

Organizing Information
Make this Foldable to help you summarize what you learn about Reconstruction and the New South.

Step 1 Fold an 11" x 17" piece of paper lengthwise to create a shutterfold.

Step 2 Fold a 3-inch tab along the bottom, and glue or staple the seams to create four pockets.

Step 3 Label the Foldable as shown.

| Sect 1: Reconstruction Plans Essential Question: | Sect 2: Radicals in Control Essential Question: | Sect 3: The South During Reconstruction Essential Question: | Sect 4: Change in the South Essential Question: |

Reading and Writing As you read the chapter, take notes on notecards about key events and issues covered in each section. Use your Foldable to store the cards, and then answer the Essential Questions for each section.

Jane Addams, founder of Hull House ▶

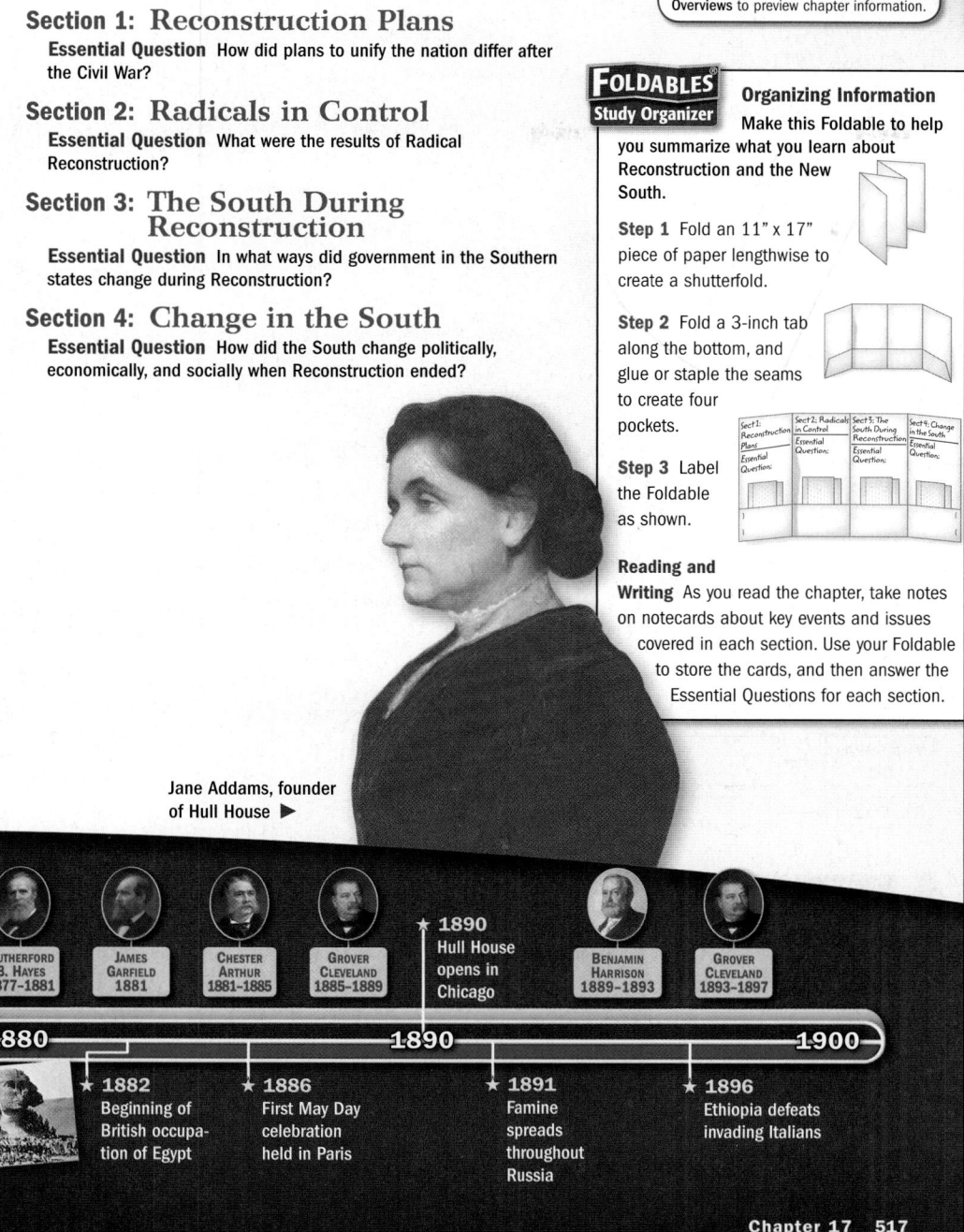

| RUTHERFORD B. HAYES 1877–1881 | JAMES GARFIELD 1881 | CHESTER ARTHUR 1881–1885 | GROVER CLEVELAND 1885–1889 | ★ 1890 Hull House opens in Chicago | BENJAMIN HARRISON 1889–1893 | GROVER CLEVELAND 1893–1897 |

1880 · **1890** · **1900**

★ **1882** Beginning of British occupation of Egypt

★ **1886** First May Day celebration held in Paris

★ **1891** Famine spreads throughout Russia

★ **1896** Ethiopia defeats invading Italians

Chapter 17   517

Introducing Chapter 17

Time Line Activity

If you have not already done so, have students review the time line. **Ask:** What years are covered in this chapter? Which president ended Reconstruction during his first year in office? *(1865–1896; Rutherford B. Hayes)* Have students identify three world events that occurred during the Reconstruction period in the United States. *(Meiji era begins in Japan, Bismarck unifies Germany, first major exhibit of impressionist art in Paris)* **OL**

FOLDABLES
Study Organizer

Dinah Zike's Foldables
Purpose This Foldable helps students summarize what they learn about Reconstruction and the New South. The completed Foldable will help them prepare for assessment. **OL**

📁 More Foldables activities for this chapter can be found in the *Dinah Zike's Reading and Study Skills Foldables.*

History ONLINE
Introduce students to chapter content and key terms by having them access the **Chapter Overview** at glencoe.com.

Section 3

The South During Reconstruction
Ask: How might governments in the South be affected by African Americans gaining the right to vote? *(More African Americans might be elected to public office.)* Tell students that in Section 3, they will learn about the role of the Republican party in Southern politics, as well as the tensions that arose over Reconstruction policies and the rights of African Americans. **OL**

Section 4

Change in the South Ask: Do you think you would be willing to vote if you had to pay a fee or a tax before you could cast your ballot? *(Students' answers may vary.)* Explain that Section 4 explores political, economic, and social changes in the South when Reconstruction ended, including restrictions placed on African Americans. **OL**

517

Focus

Reconstruction Plans

Bellringer
Daily Test Practice Transparency 17–1

Reading Guide
Answers to Graphic:

Ten Percent Plan: 10% swear loyalty to the Union, ban slavery, amnesty to all except Confederate leaders; **Wade-Davis Plan:** majority swear loyalty to the Union, ban slavery, Confederates cannot vote for delegates or hold office; **Restoration:** most Southerners who swear loyalty are pardoned and can vote for delegates, high-ranking Confederates appeal to president, denounce secession, ban slavery, ratify Thirteenth Amendment

Section Spotlight Video

To learn more about how the assassination of President Lincoln affected plans for reconstruction in the South after the war, watch the Section Spotlight Video "Reconstruction Plans."

Resource Manager

Essential Question
How did plans to unify the nation differ after the Civil War?

Reading Guide

Content Vocabulary
Reconstruction (p. 519)   amnesty (p. 519)

Academic Vocabulary
radical (p. 520)   adjust (p. 520)

Key People and Events
Ten Percent Plan (p. 519)
Radical Republicans (p. 520)
Thaddeus Stevens (p. 520)
Wade-Davis Bill (p. 520)
Freedmen's Bureau (p. 520)
John Wilkes Booth (p. 521)
Andrew Johnson (p. 521)

Reading Strategy
Taking Notes As you read, use a diagram like the one below to describe each Reconstruction plan.

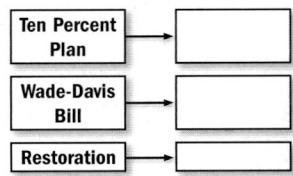

Ten Percent Plan	→	
Wade-Davis Bill	→	
Restoration	→	

ILLINOIS STANDARDS
The American Journey

14.F3a Analyze historical influences on the development of political ideas and practices enumerated in the Declaration of Independence, the United States Constitution, the Bill of Rights and the Illinois Constitution.

16.B.3c (US) Describe the way the Constitution has changed over time as a result of amendments and Supreme Court decisions.

16.A Apply the skills of historical analysis and interpretation.

American Diary

Major Henry Rathbone tried to seize John Wilkes Booth after Booth shot President Lincoln at Ford's Theater. As Booth leaped over the railing of the presidential box onto the stage, Rathbone cried, "Stop that man." Rathbone later stated: "I then turned to the President. . . . I saw that he was unconscious, and, supposing him mortally wounded, rushed to the door for the purpose of calling medical aid."

—from The Assassination of President Lincoln and the Trial of the Conspirators

The funeral train that carried Lincoln's body traveled more than 1,700 miles (2,736 km) and stopped in 10 major cities before arriving in Springfield, Illinois.

R Reading Strategies	C Critical Thinking	D Differentiated Instruction	W Writing Support	S Skill Practice
Teacher Edition • Using Word Parts, p. 519 **Additional Resources** • Guid. Read., URB p. 97 • Content Vocab., URB p. 75 • Academic Vocab., URB p. 77 • Read. Ess., p. 178	**Teacher Edition** • Making Inferences, p. 519 **Additional Resources** • Quizzes and Tests, p. 163 • Authentic Assess., p. 17	**Teacher Edition** • Interpersonal, p. 521 **Additional Resources** • School-to-Home, URB p. 93 • Reteaching Act., URB p. 95 • Differ. Inst., URB p. 85	**Teacher Edition** • Expository Writing, p. 520 • Narrative Writing, p. 521 **Additional Resources** • Writ. Skills, URB p. 81	**Teacher Edition** • Using Analysis Skills, p. 520 **Additional Resources** • Daily Test Pract. Transp. 17-1 • Lesson Transparency 17B • Soc. Stud. Skills, URB p. 83 • Geo. & Hist., URB p. 89

Reconstruction Debate

Main Idea Government leaders disagreed about how Southern states could rejoin the Union.

History and You Have you ever had an argument with a friend? How did you resolve your differences? Read to learn how the North and South tried to work out their problems after the Civil War.

. . . .

Major Henry Rathbone and the rest of the nation were deeply shocked by Abraham Lincoln's assassination. Four years of civil war, followed by the president's death, shook the nation. The Union was saved, but Americans still faced the difficult challenges of reuniting and rebuilding their country.

Southern states, because they had left the Union in 1861, needed to be readmitted. The economy and society of the devastated South also needed to be rebuilt. Americans disagreed bitterly, however, about how to accomplish these tasks. This period of rebuilding is called **Reconstruction**. This term also refers to the various plans for readmitting Southern states to the Union.

Lincoln's Plan

Before his assassination, President Lincoln offered the first plan for accepting the Southern states back into the Union. In December 1863, during the Civil War, the president announced what came to be known as the **Ten Percent Plan.** When 10 percent of the voters of a state took an oath of loyalty to the Union, the state could form a new government and adopt a new constitution that banned slavery.

Lincoln wanted to encourage Southerners who supported the Union to take charge of the state governments. He believed that punishing the South would serve no useful purpose and would only delay healing the torn nation. Lincoln offered **amnesty**—a pardon— to all white Southerners who were willing to swear loyalty to the Union, except Confederate leaders. In 1864 three states under Union occupation—Louisiana, Arkansas, and Tennessee—set up governments under the plan. These states then became caught in controversy when Congress refused to seat the states' representatives.

Teach

R Reading Strategy

Using Word Parts Ask: What is the root verb in "Reconstruction"? (*construct*) What does it mean? (*to construct; to build*) What does the prefix "re" mean? (*again*) **ELL**

C Critical Thinking

Making Inferences Ask: Why did Lincoln offer amnesty to white Southerners who would swear loyalty to the Union? (*He believed that punishing the South had no useful purpose.*) **BL**

If You Were There

Critical Thinking Answers
Residents of Springfield, Illinois, a Union state, would mourn the loss of their hometown hero, who had saved the Union. Some Southerners may have been sad at his death; others may have viewed him as an enemy and would not be sorry he was killed.

If You Were There / Viewing Lincoln's Funeral Train

Springfield, Illinois At 9 P.M. on Wednesday, May 3, you stand with a large crowd at Springfield's railroad station. The funeral train carrying President Lincoln's body arrives from Chicago. A horse-drawn carriage takes the president's coffin to the state capitol. Once the coffin is placed on an elaborate platform, thousands of people walk past it, paying their last respects.

ABRAHAM LINCOLN'S
FUNERAL MARCH,
Dedicated to the
PEOPLE OF THE UNITED STATES

Route of Lincoln's Funeral Train

CANADA

New York
Buffalo   Albany
Chicago   Cleveland   New York City
Ohio   Columbus   Penn.   ATLANTIC
Harrisburg   Philadelphia   OCEAN
Indianapolis   Baltimore
Springfield   Washington, Md.
Ill.   Ind.   D.C.

0   200 kilometers
0   200 miles
Albers Equal-Area projection

Critical Thinking

Identifying Central Issues As a resident of Springfield, how might you feel about Lincoln's death? If you were a Southerner, would you feel the same way? Explain.

Differentiated Instruction

Writing Letters

Objective: To learn how to write and format a letter correctly

Focus: Ask students why it is important to be able to write a professional letter of inquiry.

Teach: Have students read the information, practice the skill, and apply the skill.

Assess: Students should use the self-assessment checklist.

Close: Ask volunteers to read their letters and explain how they followed the steps in writing a letter of inquiry.

Writing Skills Activity, URB p. 81

Differentiated Instruction Strategies

BL Ask students to explain why a letter of inquiry should not contain unnecessary material.

AL Have students write a hypothetical letter of inquiry to a college or a business of interest to them, asking for information.

ELL Ask students to define the terms "return address," "inside address," "salutation," and "complimentary close."

519

Section 1

S Skill Practice

Using Analysis Skills Ask: In what way was Thaddeus Stevens's view "radical"? *(He wanted to completely change the South.)* **OL**

W Writing Support

Expository Writing Have students write an essay that describes the challenges faced by formerly enslaved people in their transition to living as free individuals. Students should include examples from primary sources and other historical documents. **AL**

Primary Source

Critical Thinking Answer
Formerly enslaved people would benefit from learning to read and write and from learning practical skills that would allow them to find jobs.

Reading Check **Answer:** Lincoln did not want to punish the South, wanted states to rejoin the Union, and take charge of their governments. Radical Republicans wanted to change the institutions of the South and viewed Lincoln's plan as too forgiving.

Hands-On Chapter Project
Step 1

Creating a Web Site

Step 1: Researching Students will do research to learn more about the lives of freedmen after the Civil War.

Essential Question: How did plans to unify the nation differ after the Civil War?

Directions Tell the class that they are members of a historical society. For Black

---

Primary Source / Freed people's Schools

Course of Study African Americans who were enrolled in freedmen's schools learned practical skills such as sewing as well as academic subjects. A popular textbook was Lydia Maria Child's *Freedmen's Book*, a collection of essays and poems used to teach and inspire freed African Americans.

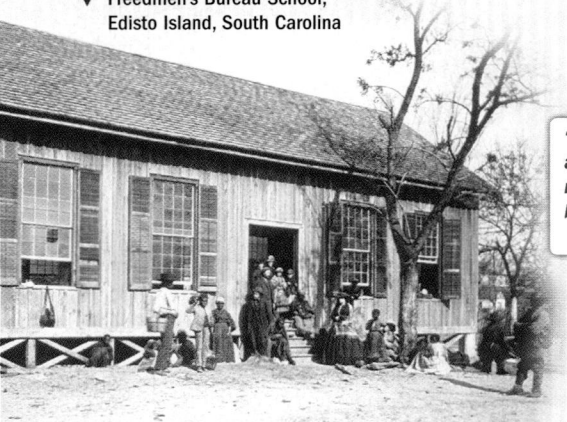

▼ Freedmen's Bureau School, Edisto Island, South Carolina

"Yesterday . . . my sister and I formally opened school. . . . We had more than one thousand (1,000) children, and seventy-five adults; and found time, after disciplining them, to hear the readers, to instruct the writers, and to teach the multitude from the blackboard."
—Lucy Chase, April 1865

"We have glorious schools in full blast—And I am so satisfied with the work here that nothing in the world could make me wish to be in another place, or doing anything else."
—Sarah Chase, February 1866

Critical Thinking

Analyzing Why do you think practical skills and academic subjects were taught at freed people's schools?

The Radicals' Plan

Some Republicans considered Lincoln's plan too forgiving. They favored a more **radical**, or extreme, approach and were called **Radical Republicans.** Radical Republican **Thaddeus Stevens** declared that Southern institutions "must be broken up and relaid, or all our blood and treasure have been spent in vain." Congress was controlled by the Radical Republicans and voted to deny seats to representatives from any state that was readmitted under Lincoln's plan.

In July 1864, Congress passed the **Wade-Davis Bill.** To rejoin the Union, a state had to meet several requirements. First, a majority of the state's white males had to swear loyalty to the Union. Second, only white males who swore they had not fought against the Union could vote for delegates to a state constitutional convention. Finally, any new state constitution had to ban slavery. The bill would also bar former Confederates from holding public office.

Lincoln refused to sign the bill, but he wanted new state governments to form quickly so that order could be restored in the South as soon as possible. Lincoln realized that he would have to compromise with the Radical Republicans.

The Freedmen's Bureau

In March 1865, Lincoln and Congress set up the **Freedmen's Bureau.** The bureau helped African Americans **adjust,** or adapt, to freedom. It provided food, clothing, and medical services. It helped freed people acquire land or find work for fair wages.

The bureau also set up schools, staffed mostly by teachers from the North. It gave aid to new African American institutions of higher learning, such as Atlanta University, Howard University, and Fisk University.

Reading Check **Contrasting** What were the differences between Lincoln's views and the Radical Republicans' views concerning Reconstruction?

520   Chapter 17 *Reconstruction and the New South*

History Month, they will prepare Web pages about the lives of African Americans during Reconstruction. Organize students into groups of two or three. Each group will create one Web page. Assign each group one of these topics: Freedmen's Bureau, education, black codes, Fourteenth Amendment, African Americans in government, violence against African Americans, sharecropping, voting restrictions, or segregation. Have

them do research to gather related information and images.

Analyzing Information As a class, discuss the reasons Lincoln and Congress set up the Freedmen's Bureau. *(African Americans emerged from slavery without paying jobs or education. They needed help starting new lives as citizens.)* **OL**

(Chapter Project continued in Section 2)

Johnson's Plan

Main Idea After Lincoln was assassinated, Andrew Johnson became president and announced his plan of "Restoration."

History and You How do you think Abraham Lincoln's death might affect plans to unify the nation? Read about President Johnson's Reconstruction plan.

Shortly after the Freedmen's Bureau was founded, a tragic event took place that shocked the nation. On April 14, 1865, President Lincoln attended a play at Ford's Theater in Washington, D.C. **John Wilkes Booth,** an actor and Confederate sympathizer, entered the private box and shot Lincoln in the head. Lincoln died several hours later.

News of the president's assassination swept across the nation. African Americans mourned the man who helped them win their freedom. Northern whites grieved for the leader who had saved the Union.

When Lincoln died, Vice President **Andrew Johnson** became president. Johnson was born in the South but supported the Union during the war. Johnson soon revealed his plan for Reconstruction. Called "Restoration," his plan would grant amnesty to most Southerners once they swore loyalty to the Union. High-ranking Confederates could be pardoned only by appealing to the president. This provision revealed Johnson's desire to humiliate the leaders who he believed had tricked the South's people into seceding.

Johnson also allowed only loyal, pardoned whites to vote for delegates to the state constitutional conventions. Stating that "white men alone must manage the South," Johnson opposed equal rights for African Americans.

Before a state could reenter the Union, it had to denounce secession and ban slavery. States also had to ratify the Thirteenth Amendment to the Constitution, passed by Congress in January 1865. This amendment abolished slavery throughout the United States. By the end of 1865, all former Confederate states, except Texas, had new governments and were ready to rejoin the Union.

✔ **Reading Check** **Specifying** What did the Thirteenth Amendment accomplish?

History ONLINE
Study Central™ To review this section, go to glencoe.com.

W **Writing Support**

Narrative Writing Have students write a diary entry for April 15, 1865, that describes their reaction to hearing the news of President Lincoln's assassination. **AL**

D **Differentiated Instruction**

Interpersonal Have students work in pairs to write and perform a skit showing an interaction between President Johnson and a high-ranking Confederate who is appealing for amnesty. **OL**

✔ **Reading Check** **Answer:** It abolished slavery throughout the United States.

Assess

History ONLINE

Study Central™ provides summaries, interactive games, and online graphic organizers to help students review content.

Close

Contrasting Have students use their completed Reading Strategy graphic organizer on the first page of this section to identify the differences among the Reconstruction plans. **OL**

Section ★ Review

Section 1 Review

Vocabulary

1. Write a short paragraph in which you use all of the following vocabulary terms:
Reconstruction, amnesty, radical, adjust.

Main Ideas

2. Explaining Why did Lincoln disagree with the harsh Reconstruction plan of the Radical Republicans?

3. Specifying Under Johnson's Restoration plan, how could high-ranking or wealthy Confederates gain a pardon?

Critical Thinking

4. Contrasting Using a diagram like the one below, compare the Reconstruction plans of Lincoln and the Radical Republicans.

Reconstruction Plans

Lincoln	Radical Republicans

5. Drawing Conclusions Do you think President Johnson's Southern heritage influenced his Reconstruction plan? Explain your answer.

6. Persuasive Writing Write a one-paragraph response to the Radical Republicans' plan for Reconstruction from Abraham Lincoln's point of view. Explain why you think the South should be treated less harshly.

Answer the
Essential Question

7. How did plans to unify the nation differ after the Civil War?

Answers

1. Paragraphs should reflect a correct understanding of the terms.

2. Lincoln believed punishment served no useful purpose and would only delay healing.

3. only by appealing to Johnson

4. Lincoln (Ten Percent Plan): 10% of voters must swear loyalty to the Union, amnesty to all except Confederate leaders; **Radical Republicans (Wade-Davis):** majority of white males must swear loyalty to the Union, former Confederates could not vote for convention delegates or hold office.

5. Johnson's plan granted amnesty to most Southerners but treated Confederate leaders harshly, reflecting a feeling of kinship with the South's people but anger toward the leaders who he believed had tricked them. Also, Johnson's plan denied voting rights to African Americans, reflecting Southern racism.

6. Responses should focus on Lincoln's desire to bring the nation together, avoid punishment, and promote healing.

7. Lincoln wanted to avoid punishing to promote healing, so he offered amnesty to all white Southerners except Confederate leaders. Radical Republicans favored harsher measures that would break up and rebuild the South's institutions and ban former Confederates from holding office. Johnson wanted to pardon most Southerners but humiliate Confederate leaders.

Focus

Section 2

Bellringer
Daily Test Practice Transparency 17–2

Reading Guide
Answers to Graphic:
What: formal charge of wrongdoing;
Who: President Andrew Johnson;
Outcome: The Senate failed to achieve the two-thirds majority required for conviction, so Johnson completed his term in office.

Section Spotlight Video

Watch the Section Spotlight Video "Radicals in Control" to learn more about rebuilding and reconstruction.

Essential Question ◄
What were the results of Radical Reconstruction?

Reading Guide

Content Vocabulary
black codes (p. 523)   impeach (p. 527)
override (p. 524)

Academic Vocabulary
convince (p. 523)   suspend (p. 526)

Key People and Events
Civil Rights Act of 1866 (p. 523)
First Reconstruction Act (p. 525)
Second Reconstruction Act (p. 526)
Tenure of Office Act (p. 526)
Edwin Stanton (p. 526)
Ulysses S. Grant (p. 527)

Reading Strategy
Taking Notes As you read, use a diagram like the one below to answer the questions about impeachment.

Impeachment
- What Is It?
- Who Was Impeached?
- Outcome of Trial?

ILLINOIS STANDARDS
The American Journey

14.C.3 Compare historical issues involving rights, roles and status of individuals in relation to municipalities, states and the nation.

16.B.3c (US) Describe the way the Constitution has changed over time as a result of amendments and Supreme Court decisions.

18.C.3b Explain how diverse groups have contributed to U.S. social systems over time.

Radicals in Control

American Diary

For three days in May 1866, white mobs in Memphis, Tennessee, burned African American churches, schools, and homes. An army officer investigating the causes of the riot later reported: "Three [African American] churches were burned, also . . . about fifty (50) private dwellings, owned, occupied or inhabited by freedmen as homes, and . . . in many instances containing the hard earnings of months of labor."

—from "Reports of Outrages, Riots and Murders, Jan. 15, 1866–Aug. 12, 1868" by Colonel Charles F. Johnson

Memphis rioters set fire to an African American schoolhouse built by the Freedmen's Bureau.

Resource Manager

R Reading Strategies	C Critical Thinking	D Differentiated Instruction	W Writing Support	S Skill Practice
Teacher Edition	**Teacher Edition**	**Teacher Edition**	**Teacher Edition**	**Teacher Edition**
• Find. Main Ideas, p. 523	• Predict. Con., p. 523	• ELL, p. 527	• Personal Writing, p. 526	• Using Note-Taking Skills, p. 524
• Monitoring, p. 525	• Ident. Cause & Effect, p. 524	**Additional Resources**	• Persuasive Writing, p. 527	• Using Map Skills, p. 525
Additional Resources	• Drawing Conclusions, p. 526	• School-to-Home, URB p. 93		**Additional Resources**
• Guid. Read., URB p. 98		• Reteaching Act., URB p. 95		• Daily Test Pract. Transp. 17-2
• Content Vocab., URB p. 75	**Additional Resources**			• Citizen. & Dec. Mak. Skills, URB p. 3
• Acad. Vocab., URB p. 77	• Quizzes and Tests, p. 164			• Time Line Skills, URB p. 92
• Read. Skills, URB p. 7	• Crit. Think. Skills, URB p. 87			• Lesson Transp. 17A

African Americans' Rights

Main Idea When Northerners realized that African Americans in the South were still being mistreated, they worked to find a way to help them.

History and You Think about the rights American citizens have. Read to find out how Congress made sure that formerly enslaved African Americans became citizens.

Many Northerners saw the Memphis riot as an attempt by whites to terrorize African Americans and keep them from enjoying and practicing their new freedoms. The Memphis incident and similar riots in other Southern cities helped **convince,** or persuade, Radical Republicans that President Johnson's Reconstruction plan was not strong enough.

During the fall of 1865, Southern states created new governments based on Johnson's plan. They also elected new representatives to Congress. When the Southern representatives arrived in Washington, D.C., however, Congress refused to seat them. Many Republicans refused to readmit the Southern states on such easy terms.

Black Codes

By early 1866, Southern states had passed **black codes,** or laws to control freed men and women. The black codes trampled the rights of African Americans. They allowed plantation owners to exploit African American workers and allowed officials to arrest and fine jobless African Americans. The codes also banned African Americans from owning or renting farms. To freed men and women and many Northerners, the black codes resembled slavery.

In early 1866, Congress passed a bill giving the Freedmen's Bureau new powers. The agency could now set up special courts to try individuals charged with violating the rights of African Americans. African Americans could also serve on juries in these courts.

Congress then passed the **Civil Rights Act of 1866.** This act granted full citizenship to African Americans and gave the federal government the power to intervene in state affairs to protect their rights. The law overturned the black codes. It also contradicted the 1857 *Dred Scott* decision of the Supreme Court, which had ruled that African Americans were not citizens.

Primary Source / Freed People's Schools

Freedom to Learn Throughout the South, African Americans of all ages attended freed men and women's schools to learn basic reading, writing, and mathematical skills. As one freed person declared, education was "the next best thing to liberty." Many white Southerners, however, opposed schooling for African Americans. During the Memphis riots, white mobs burned down freed people's schools and attacked teachers and students. Despite the violence, African Americans continued to enroll in the schools.

—from *Forever Free: The Story of Emancipation and Reconstruction*

▲ Freed people's school, Richmond, Virginia, 1866

Critical Thinking

Hypothesizing Why do you think freed African Americans were eager to receive an education?

Teach

R Reading Strategy

Finding Main Ideas Ask: Why did Congress refuse to seat the new Southern representatives? *(Republicans felt that Johnson's terms for readmitting states were too easy.)* **BL**

C Critical Thinking

Predicting Consequences Ask: What did the Civil Rights Act of 1866 accomplish? *(gave full citizenship to African Americans; gave the federal government the power to intervene in local affairs to protect their rights)* How might some Southerners view the Act? *(resist the federal government's involvement in local issues, unwilling to rejoin the Union, hope that the Supreme Court could overturn it based on its 1857* Dred Scott *ruling)* **AL**

Primary Source

Critical Thinking Answer
Education was denied them when they were enslaved, and they viewed education as a pathway to success.

Additional Support

Activity: Collaborative Learning

Political Science Have students use library and Internet resources to research the harsh restrictions placed on African Americans by the black codes and the action by Congress to protect African Americans with the Civil Rights Act of 1866. Then ask students to work in pairs to create political cartoons that express their reaction to these laws. Encourage students to share their completed cartoons with the class and have others interpret their meanings. **Ask:** How might a former abolitionist view the black codes? *(that the codes were intended to keep African Americans in a position similar to slavery)* Ask students to find present-day political cartoons that address racial discrimination. Have students share these cartoons with the class. **OL**

C Critical Thinking

Identifying Cause and Effect Ask: How did the ability of Congress to override Johnson's vetoes affect Reconstruction plans? *(The ability to override put the Radical Republicans in control of Reconstruction. Johnson could not stop them.)* **OL**

This **READING SKILL** (Identifying Cause and Effect) was introduced in this unit.

S Skill Practice

Using Note-Taking Skills Have students create a graphic organizer showing the three main provisions of the Fourteenth Amendment. *(granted citizenship to everyone born or naturalized in the United States; forbade states to take away a citizen's rights without due process of law; provided all citizens equal protection of the laws)* **BL**

Primary Source

Critical Thinking Answer
It has been applied in many situations to protect equal rights for all citizens.

Hands-On Chapter Project
Step 2

Teacher Tip

Point out that a good Web page is visually pleasing and easy to read. Avoid long passages. Break up the material into chunks with headings and illustrations.

Primary Source / The Fourteenth Amendment

Protection of Rights The Fourteenth Amendment gave African American males their citizenship and tried to prevent the Southern states from taking away their rights. Since its ratification in 1868, the Supreme Court has written several landmark decisions related to the Fourteenth Amendment.

> "All persons born or naturalized in the United States, and subject to the jurisdiction thereof, are citizens of the United States and of the State wherein they reside. No State shall make or enforce any law which shall abridge the privileges or immunities of citizens of the United States; nor shall any State deprive any person of life, liberty, or property, without due process of law; nor deny to any person within its jurisdiction the equal protection of the laws."
> —Fourteenth Amendment, Section I

The Supreme Court limited the Fourteenth Amendment in a series of rulings in the late 1800s. These rulings led to segregation and voter restrictions in the South.

In 1954 the Supreme Court ruled in *Brown* v. *Board of Education, Topeka, Kansas* that the equal protection clause forbade segregation. The Court ordered the desegregation of the nation's public schools. ▶

During the 2000 presidential election, the Supreme Court ruled in *Bush* v. *Gore* that the Florida recount violated the equal protection clause. The Court argued that since vote counters used different standards to count the votes, the recount did not treat all voters equally.

Responding to an ▶ appeal by Clarence Gideon, the Supreme Court in 1963 ruled in *Gideon* v. *Wainwright* that all defendants were entitled to legal counsel in cases involving possible jail time, including those who were too poor to hire a lawyer.

Critical Thinking

Assessing How has the Fourteenth Amendment influenced the rights of individual Americans?

President Johnson vetoed both bills. He argued that the federal government was overstepping its authority. He also argued that the Freemen's Bureau bill and the Civil Rights Act were unconstitutional because they were approved by a Congress that did not include representatives from all of the states. By raising this issue, Johnson indirectly threatened to veto any law passed by this Congress.

C Republicans in Congress had enough votes to **override,** or defeat, both vetoes, and the bills became law. The chances of the president and Congress working together faded. The Radical Republicans abandoned the idea of compromise and drafted a new Reconstruction plan—one created by Congress.

S The Fourteenth Amendment

Fearing that the Civil Rights Act might be overturned in court, Congress passed a new amendment to the Constitution in 1866. The Fourteenth Amendment was enacted in 1868. It granted full citizenship to all people born in the United States. Because most African Americans in the United States had been born in the country, they became full citizens.

The amendment also stated that no state could take away a citizen's life, liberty, or property "without due process of law." In addition to this, every citizen was entitled to "equal protection of the laws." If a state prevented any adult male citizen from voting, then it could lose some of its representation in Congress.

Creating a Web Site

Step 2: Planning a Web Page Groups will plan their page layout and write the copy.

Essential Question: What were the results of Radical Reconstruction?

Directions Have students examine their favorite Web pages for ideas about designing a page. Instruct groups to use information and images from their research to plan their page. They should plan the layout and write the copy. Remind students that their purpose as a historical society is to create interest as well as to inform.

Identifying Central Issues As a class, discuss how the First and Second Reconstruction Acts benefited African Americans. **OL**

(Chapter Project continued in Section 3)

The amendment also barred former Confederate leaders from holding national or state office unless pardoned by Congress. The Fourteenth Amendment also excluded Native Americans from citizenship.

Congress declared that Southern states had to ratify the amendment to rejoin the Union. Of the 11 Southern states, only Tennessee ratified it. The refusal of the other Southern states to ratify delayed the amendment's adoption until 1868.

Republican Victory

In the congressional elections of 1866, President Johnson campaigned vigorously against the Radical Republicans. Many Northerners objected to the nasty tone of Johnson's campaign and feared clashes between whites and African Americans. The Republicans won a solid victory, giving Congress the signal to take Reconstruction into its own hands.

Reading Check **Explaining** Why did Johnson consider the civil rights bill unconstitutional?

Radical Reconstruction

Main Idea Radical Republicans were able to put their version of Reconstruction into action.

History and You If you were a member of Congress at this time, what changes would you like to see in a Reconstruction plan? Read to find out how the Radical Republicans shaped Reconstruction.

· ·

President Johnson could do little to stop Republicans because they could easily override his vetoes in Congress. Thus began a period known as Radical Reconstruction.

Reconstruction Acts of 1867

The **First Reconstruction Act** passed in 1867 called for the creation of new governments in the 10 Southern states that had not ratified the Fourteenth Amendment. Tennessee, which ratified, kept its government and rejoined the Union.

History ONLINE
Student Web Activity Visit glencoe.com and complete the Chapter 17 Web Activity about Reconstruction.

R Reading Strategy

Monitoring Ask: How could the refusal of Southern states to ratify the Fourteenth Amendment delay its adoption? *(A constitutional amendment requires approval of three fourths of the states to take effect.)* **OL**

S Skill Practice

Using Map Skills Ask: Based on the map, what states did Philip Sheridan govern during Reconstruction? *(Texas and Louisiana)* **BL**

Military Reconstruction Districts, 1867
NATIONAL GEOGRAPHIC

Map Skills Answer

Tennessee

Reading Check **Answer:** The bill was approved by a Congress that did not include representatives from all the states.

History ONLINE
Objectives and answers to the Student Web Activity can be found at glencoe.com under the Web Activity Lesson Plan for this chapter.

Differentiated Instruction

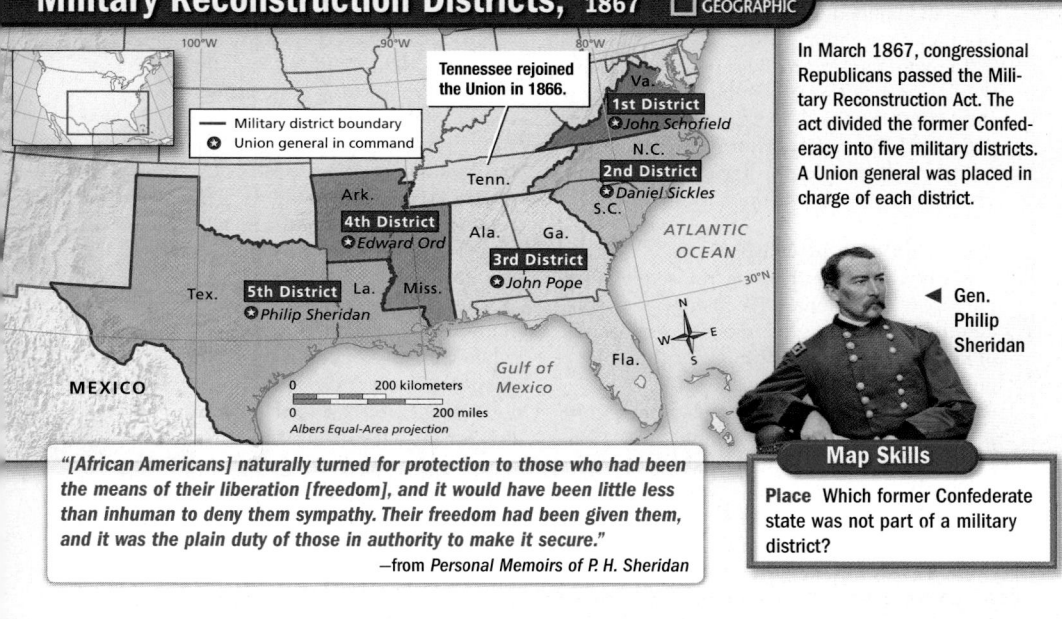

Military Reconstruction Districts, 1867
NATIONAL GEOGRAPHIC

Tennessee rejoined the Union in 1866.

— Military district boundary
⊕ Union general in command

1st District
⊕ John Schofield

2nd District
⊕ Daniel Sickles

3rd District
⊕ John Pope

4th District
⊕ Edward Ord

5th District
⊕ Philip Sheridan

Va.
N.C.
S.C.
Tenn.
Ark.
Ala.
Ga.
Miss.
La.
Tex.
Fla.
ATLANTIC OCEAN
Gulf of Mexico
MEXICO
100°W 90°W 80°W
30°N

0   200 kilometers
0   200 miles
Albers Equal-Area projection

In March 1867, congressional Republicans passed the Military Reconstruction Act. The act divided the former Confederacy into five military districts. A Union general was placed in charge of each district.

◀ Gen. Philip Sheridan

"[African Americans] naturally turned for protection to those who had been the means of their liberation [freedom], and it would have been little less than inhuman to deny them sympathy. Their freedom had been given them, and it was the plain duty of those in authority to make it secure."
—from *Personal Memoirs of P. H. Sheridan*

Map Skills

Place Which former Confederate state was not part of a military district?

Leveled Activities

BL **Reading Skills Activity,** URB p. 7

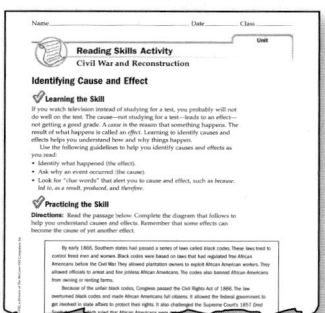

Reading Skills Activity
Civil War and Reconstruction

Identifying Cause and Effect

OL **Critical Thinking Skills Activity,** URB p. 87

Critical Thinking Skills Activity
Reconstruction and the New South

Making Generalizations

AL **Citizenship and Decision-Making Skills Activity,** URB p. 3

Citizenship and Decision-Making Activity
Civil War and Reconstruction

Voting: A Right and a Responsibility

ELL **Reteaching Activity,** URB p. 95

Reteaching Activity
Reconstruction and the New South

C Critical Thinking

Drawing Conclusions Ask: How did the Second Reconstruction Act influence Southern elections? *(It guaranteed African American men the right to vote, who helped Republicans gain control of Southern state governments.)* **OL**

W Writing Support

Personal Writing Have students take the role of an African American who has just voted for the first time. Have them write a letter to a friend in the North, expressing their feelings about the experience. **OL**

Chance & Error in History

Critical Thinking Answers

1. Lincoln was popular, compassionate, and a unifier. Johnson was unpopular and had a distasteful personality.
2. Possible response: Lincoln would have been willing to compromise during Reconstruction.

Differentiated Instruction

Chance & Error in History

What If Lincoln Had Survived?

Abraham Lincoln wanted the South to be treated compassionately when the war ended. The Radicals expected that the new president, Andrew Johnson, would adopt a firm policy toward the South.

◀ Lincoln's funeral procession, Columbus, Ohio

◀ President Johnson and the Radicals had little in common, and Johnson had little popular support. Many people thought Johnson was self-righteous, hot-tempered, stubborn, and crude.

Second Inaugural Address, March 1865

"With malice toward none, with charity for all, with firmness in the right as God gives us to see the right, let us strive on to finish the work we are in, to bind up the nation's wounds, to care for him who shall have borne the battle and for his widow and his orphan."

—Abraham Lincoln

Critical Thinking

1. **Contrasting** Describe the leadership qualities of Abraham Lincoln and Andrew Johnson.
2. **Speculating** How do you think Reconstruction might have been different if Lincoln had not been assassinated? Explain.

The act divided the 10 Southern states into 5 military districts, each run by a military commander until new governments were formed. The act also guaranteed African American men the right to vote in state elections and banned former Confederate leaders from holding political office.

To rejoin the Union, the states had to ratify the Fourteenth Amendment and submit new state constitutions to Congress for approval. A **Second Reconstruction Act** required the military commanders to register voters and prepare for state constitutional conventions.

Readmission of States

Many white Southerners refused to take part in the elections for constitutional conventions and state governments. Thousands of newly registered African American voters, however, voted.

In the elections, Republicans gained control of Southern state governments. By 1868, seven Southern states—Alabama, Arkansas, Florida, Georgia, Louisiana, North Carolina,

and South Carolina—had established new governments and met the requirements for readmission. By 1870, Mississippi, Virginia, and Texas were restored to the Union.

Impeaching the President

Strongly opposed to Radical Reconstruction, President Johnson had the power as commander in chief of the army to direct the actions of the military governors. For this reason, Congress passed a series of laws to limit the president's power, such as the **Tenure of Office Act.** It prohibited the president from removing government officials, including members of his own cabinet, without the Senate's approval.

The conflict between Johnson and the Radicals grew more intense. In August 1867—when Congress was not in session—Johnson **suspended** (removed from office temporarily) Secretary of War **Edwin Stanton** without the Senate's approval. When the Senate met again and refused to approve the suspension, Johnson removed Stanton from office.

The Rise and Fall of Civil Rights (1865–1896)

Objective: To use time-line information to answer questions about civil rights in the 1800s

Focus: Direct students' attention to the three amendments on the time line.

Teach: Have students review the time line and answer the questions.

Assess: Discuss the answers to any questions that are difficult for students.

Close: Ask students to explain why this activity refers to the "rise and fall of civil rights."

Differentiated Instruction Strategies

BL Have students work in pairs to answer the questions.

AL Ask students to write a one-act play from the point of view of a freed African American in the years just following the Civil War.

ELL Remind students that they can use their textbooks when answering the questions.

Time Line Skills Activity, URB p. 92

This action was a deliberate violation of the Tenure of Office Act. Johnson also appointed people who the Radical Republicans opposed to command some of the Southern military districts.

Outraged by Johnson's actions, the House of Representatives voted to **impeach** the president, or formally charge him, with wrongdoing. In 1868 the case went to the Senate for a trial that lasted almost three months. Johnson's defenders claimed that the president was exercising his right to challenge laws he considered unconstitutional. They argued that Congress impeached the president because of politics, without accusing him of a crime. Johnson's critics disputed that Congress held supreme power to make the laws and that Johnson's use of the veto improperly interfered with this function.

The senators failed to achieve the two-thirds majority required for conviction. Some moderate Republicans supported the president, arguing that Johnson should not be removed from office because of political differences. As a result, Johnson stayed in office until the end of his term in March 1869.

The Fifteenth Amendment

By the presidential election of 1868, most Southern states had rejoined the Union, and many Americans hoped that Reconstruction was over. Abandoning Johnson, the Republicans nominated **Ulysses S. Grant,** the Civil War hero. The Democrats chose Horatio Seymour. Grant received most of the African American votes in the South and won the presidency. The 1868 election showed that voters supported the Republican approach to Reconstruction.

In 1869 Congress passed the Fifteenth Amendment. It prohibited the state and federal governments from denying the right to vote to any male citizen because of "race, color, or previous condition of servitude."

African American men won the right to vote when the amendment was ratified and became law in 1870. Republicans thought the power of the vote would enable African Americans to protect themselves. That belief, however, was too optimistic.

✓ **Reading Check** Explaining How did Republicans organize the South during Reconstruction?

History ONLINE
Study Central™ To review this section, go to glencoe.com.

Section 2 Review

Vocabulary

1. Define each of the following terms and use it in a sentence: convince, black codes, override, suspend, impeach.

Main Ideas

2. **Specifying** What requirement was necessary for African Americans to become citizens under the Fourteenth Amendment?

3. **Explaining** Why was President Johnson unable to stop Radical Republicans from putting their Reconstruction plan into action?

Critical Thinking

4. **Comparing** How were black codes similar to slavery?

5. **Determining Cause and Effect** Describe the impact of the Fourteenth and Fifteenth Amendments on African Americans. Use a diagram like the one below.

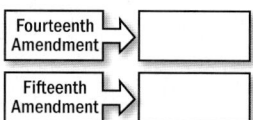

| Fourteenth Amendment | → | |
| Fifteenth Amendment | → | |

6. **Persuasive Writing** Assume the role of Andrew Johnson. Write a short speech to give at your trial, explaining why the senators should not convict you of wrongdoing.

Answer the
Essential Question

7. What were the results of Radical Reconstruction?

Reconstruction and the New South **Chapter 17** **527**

W Writing Support

Persuasive Writing Have students take the role of a citizen in 1868 and write a letter to their senator, urging him to vote either for or against convicting Johnson. **OL**

D Differentiated Instruction

English Language Learners Have students explain in their own words the phrase "because of race, color, or previous condition of servitude." **ELL**

✓ **Reading Check** **Answer:** into five military districts, each run by a military commander

Assess
. . . .
History ONLINE

Study Central™ provides summaries, interactive games, and online graphic organizers to help students review content.

Close
. . . .
Discussing As a class, discuss the effects of Radical Reconstruction on the South. **OL**

Section 2 Review

Answers

1. Students should define terms accurately, and their sentences should reflect an understanding of the definitions.
2. They had to be born in the United States.
3. Radical Republicans had enough votes in Congress to override Johnson's vetoes.
4. Like slavery, black codes were designed to control African Americans. The codes allowed exploitation of African Americans and trampled their rights.
5. **Fourteenth Amendment:** most African Americans gained full citizenship, and the

principles of equal protection and due process were intended to protect their rights; **Fifteenth Amendment:** African American men gained the right to vote
6. Speeches might note that the presidential veto is a power granted by the Constitution, Johnson was not charged with a crime, and limiting his ability to remove members of his own cabinet is unreasonable.
7. African Americans gained full citizenship with the rights due all citizens, although protecting these rights proved difficult.

African American men gained the right to vote. African American voters, combined with the refusal of many white Southerners to vote, put Republicans in control of Southern state governments. By 1870 all of the Southern states had met the requirements under Radical Reconstruction and were restored to the Union.

Focus

Section 3

The South During Reconstruction

Bellringer
Daily Test Practice Transparency 17–3

Reading Guide
Answers to Graphic:
new public school systems for both races; academies offering advanced education to African Americans

Section Spotlight Video

To learn more about African Americans in government in the South during Reconstruction, watch the Section Spotlight Video "The South During Reconstruction."

Essential Question
In what ways did government in the Southern states change during Reconstruction?

Reading Guide

Content Vocabulary
scalawag (p. 529)   integrate (p. 531)
carpetbagger (p. 530)   sharecropping (p. 531)
corruption (p. 530)

Academic Vocabulary
credit (p. 530)   academy (p. 531)

Key People and Events
Hiram Revels (p. 529)
Blanche K. Bruce (p. 529)

Reading Strategy
Taking Notes As you read, use a diagram like the one below to describe improvements in the South in the field of education.

Improvements in Education

ILLINOIS STANDARDS
The American Journey

17.C.3c Analyze how human processes influence settlement patterns including migration and population growth.

18.B.3a Analyze how individuals and groups interact with and within institutions (e.g., educational, military).

18.B.3b Explain how social institutions contribute to the development and transmission of culture.

American Diary

John Roy Lynch, once enslaved, ran a business in Mississippi. In the 1869 election—the first in which African Americans could vote—Lynch was elected to the Mississippi state legislature. Lynch later recalled that "the campaign was aggressive . . . the election resulted in a sweeping Republican victory. That party not only elected the state ticket . . . but also had a large majority in . . . the state legislature."

—from Reminiscences of an Active Life: The Autobiography of John Roy Lynch

Newly freed African Americans from rural areas moved to Southern cities, such as Richmond, where they sought jobs, voted for the first time, and joined local branches of the Republican Party.

Resource Manager

R Reading Strategies	C Critical Thinking	D Differentiated Instruction	W Writing Support	S Skill Practice
Teacher Edition • Academic Vocabulary, p. 530 **Additional Resources** • Guid. Read., URB p. 99 • Content Vocab., URB p. 75 • Academic Vocab., URB p. 77 • Read. Ess., p. 184	**Teacher Edition** • Contrasting, p. 529 • Drawing Conclusions, p. 531 **Additional Resources** • Quizzes and Tests, p. 165	**Additional Resources** • School-to-Home, URB p. 93 • Reteaching Act., URB p. 95	**Teacher Edition** • Expository Writing, p. 529 **Additional Resources** • Econ & Hist., URB p. 5	**Teacher Edition** • Using Cause-and-Effect Skills, p. 529 **Additional Resources** • Daily Test Pract. Transp. 17-3

Reconstruction Politics

Main Idea As African Americans began to take part in civic life in the South, they faced resistance, including violence, from whites.

History and You Do some people today use mean names to refer to someone they don't like? Read to learn what former Confederates called Republican supporters in the South.

∙∙∙∙∙∙∙∙∙∙∙∙∙∙∙∙∙∙∙∙∙∙∙∙∙∙∙∙∙∙∙∙∙∙

During Reconstruction, Republicans dominated Southern politics. Support for the Republican Party came from African Americans, white Southerners who supported Republican policies, and white settlers from the North. These groups were in charge of the state governments.

African Americans in Government

African Americans played an important role in Reconstruction politics, both as voters and as elected officials. In some states they contributed heavily to Republican victories. African Americans did not control any state government, although they briefly held a majority in the lower house of the South Carolina legislature. In other Southern states, they held important positions, but never in proportion to their numbers.

At the national level, 16 African Americans served in the House of Representatives and 2 in the Senate between 1869 and 1880. **Hiram Revels,** one of the African American senators, was an ordained minister who had recruited African Americans for the Union army. He also started a school for freed African Americans in Missouri and served as chaplain of an African American regiment in Mississippi. Revels remained in Mississippi after the war and was elected to the U.S. Senate in 1870.

Blanche K. Bruce, the other African American senator, also came from Mississippi. A former escaped slave, Bruce taught in a school for African Americans in Missouri when the war began. In 1869 he went to Mississippi, entered politics, and was elected to the U.S. Senate in 1874.

Scalawags and Carpetbaggers

Some Southern whites—such as pro-Union business leaders and non-slaveholding farmers—backed the Republicans. Former Confederates called them **scalawags,** a term meaning "scoundrel" or "worthless rascal."

Primary Source / The African American Church

Creating a Community After the Civil War, many African Americans formed their own churches free of white control. In addition to providing a place of worship, churches supported schools, social events, and political meetings. Elias Campbell Morris was a popular African American preacher and a leader of the Republican Party in Arkansas. He encouraged African Americans to participate in politics, saying that improvements in society "will depend in a large measure upon what we prove able to do for ourselves."

—from *This Far by Faith: Stories from the African American Religious Experience*

◀ In many African American homes, the social, political, and economic life of the family centered around religion.

Critical Thinking

Analyzing Information Why do you think churches played such an important political and social role in the African American community?

Teach

∙∙∙∙∙∙∙∙∙∙∙∙∙∙∙∙∙∙∙∙∙∙∙∙

S Skill Practice

Using Cause-and-Effect Skills Ask: How did African American voters affect Southern politics? *(helped elect Republicans and African Americans)* **OL**

W Writing Support

Expository Writing Have students research and then write a short profile of one of these African American members of Congress during Reconstruction: Richard Cain, Henry Cheatham, Jeremiah Haralson, John Hyman, John Langston, Jefferson Long, or John Lynch. **OL**

C Critical Thinking

Contrasting Ask: How were scalawags different from former Confederates? *(Scalawags supported Republicans.)* **BL**

Primary Source

Critical Thinking Answer
Possible response: African American churches were not under white control, so churches could serve as centers for social and political gatherings for the African American community.

Differentiated Instruction

Economics and History Activity, URB p. 5

Reconstruction and the Economy of the South

Objective:	To analyze information about Southern economic problems after the Civil War
Focus:	Ask students why they think the South faced severe economic problems.
Teach:	Have students read the information, study the chart, and answer the questions.
Assess:	Discuss why sharecropping replaced slavery in the South.
Close:	Ask students if they think that sharecropping was an improvement over slavery for African Americans.

Differentiated Instruction Strategies

BL Have students create a list of advantages and disadvantages of the sharecropping system for landowners and tenants.

AL Have students research and report on what happened to the sharecropping system in the South.

ELL Ask students to explain the difference between landowners and tenants.

People IN HISTORY

Blanche K. Bruce
African American senator from Mississippi

In Mississippi, the election of 1876 was controversial. Many people thought that African Americans were pressured to vote for white Democrats. Bruce stated: *"The conduct of the late election in Mississippi . . . put in question and jeopardy the sacred rights of the citizen."*

Hiram Revels
First African American senator

Revels wanted to find common ground between African Americans and white Southerners. He felt that in most places in Mississippi, *"white people . . . accept as a fact that all men are born free and equal, and . . . are ready to guarantee to my people every right and privilege guaranteed to an American citizen."*

CRITICAL Thinking

1. **Analyzing** How do Revels and Bruce differ in their views of Mississippi politics?
2. **Evaluating** Which view of Mississippi politics do you think is more accurate? Explain your answer.

R Reading Strategy

Academic Vocabulary Point out that "supremacy" is the noun form of the word "supreme." **Ask:** What did white supremacy groups want? *(for whites to hold the greatest power)* **ELL**

People IN HISTORY

Critical Thinking Answers

1. Revels believed that white people were ready to recognize African Americans as citizens, while Bruce saw corruption during the 1876 election as a sign that rights were in jeopardy.
2. Most students will likely support Bruce's view, pointing to the strong resistance of whites to Reconstruction.

✓ **Reading Check** Answers: *Scalawags:* Southern whites who backed Republicans; *Carpetbaggers:* Northern whites who moved to the South after the war and supported Republicans. Many Southerners viewed Republican state governments as corrupt and resented Republican supporters.

Hands-On Chapter Project
Step 3

Many Northern whites who moved to the South after the war also supported the Republicans. Critics called these Northerners **carpetbaggers** because they arrived with all their belongings in cheap suitcases made of carpet fabric. Although some carpetbaggers were dishonest, most were not. Many were reformers who wanted to help the South.

Many Southerners accused Reconstruction governments of **corruption**—or dishonest or illegal actions. Although some officials made money illegally, probably less corruption occurred in the South than in the North.

Resistance to Reconstruction

Most Southern whites opposed efforts to expand African Americans' rights. Life soon became difficult for African Americans. Most white landowners refused to rent land to freed people. Store owners refused them **credit**—extra time to pay for goods—and employers would not hire them.

Secret societies, such as the Ku Klux Klan, used fear and violence to deny rights to freed men and women. Wearing white sheets and hoods, Klan members killed thousands of African Americans and their white friends. They beat and wounded many more and burned African American homes, schools, and churches. Many Southerners, especially planters and Democrats, backed the Klan. These people, who had the most to gain from the return of white supremacy, saw violence as a defense against Republican rule.

In 1870 and 1871, Congress passed several laws to try to stop the growing violence of the Klan. These laws met with limited success. Most white Southerners refused to testify against those who attacked African Americans and their white supporters.

✓ **Reading Check** Explaining Who were the scalawags and carpetbaggers? Why did many Southerners resent them?

Creating a Web Site

Step 3: Creating a Web Page Students will create storyboards or Web pages.

Essential Question: In what ways did government in the Southern states change during Reconstruction?

Directions Have each group create a colorful storyboard on large poster material for the group's page. If students have access to computers, they should use software to create actual Web-style pages. Each page should include the written content, illustrations, and an overall heading. Have the groups include links that would be appropriate for their page, including a link to a home page, which they will create in the next step.

Analyzing As a class, discuss likely challenges facing the first African Americans elected to office. **OL**

(Chapter Project continued in Section 4)

Education and Farming

Main Idea Education improved for both races in the South, but the sharecropping system limited economic opportunities for African Americans.

History and You If you could not attend school, how would the course of your life change? Read about advances in education in the South.

During Reconstruction, African Americans created their own schools. The Freedmen's Bureau also helped spread education. Northern women and African Americans came south to teach in schools. In the 1870s, Reconstruction governments created public schools for both races. Within a few years, about 50 percent of white children and 40 percent of African American children in the South were enrolled. Northern missionary societies set up **academies**—schools for special training. These academies grew into a network of African American colleges and universities, including Fisk University in Tennessee and Morehouse College in Georgia.

Generally, African American and white students attended different schools. Only a very few states required that schools be **integrated**—include both whites and African Americans—but the laws were not enforced.

Along with education, most freed people wanted land. Some African Americans purchased land with the help of the Freedmen's Bank, but most failed to get their own land. The most common form of farmwork for freed people was **sharecropping**. In this system, a landowner rented a plot of land to a sharecropper, or farmer, along with a crude shack, some seeds and tools, and perhaps a mule. In return, sharecroppers shared a percentage of their crops with the landowners.

After paying the landowners, sharecroppers often had little left to sell. Sometimes there was barely enough to feed their families. For many, sharecropping was little better than slavery.

Reading Check **Describing** What was the relationship between sharecroppers and landowners?

History ONLINE
Study Central™ To review this section, go to glencoe.com.

C Critical Thinking

Drawing Conclusions Ask: *Why did most African Americans fail to get their own land? (They emerged from slavery poor, and sharecropping and black codes kept them poor. Also, white landowners resisted selling to them.)* **OL**

Reading Check **Answer:** Landowners rented land to sharecroppers in exchange for a percentage of the crop.

Assess

History ONLINE

Study Central™ provides summaries, interactive games, and online graphic organizers to help students review content.

Close

Contrasting Have students contrast Southern state governments before the Civil War to Southern state governments during Reconstruction. **OL**

Section 3 Review

Vocabulary

1. Use each of these terms in a sentence that will help explain its meaning: scalawag, carpetbagger, corruption, credit, academy, integrate, sharecropping.

Main Ideas

2. **Specifying** What kinds of resistance did African Americans face as they tried to exercise their rights as citizens in the South?

3. **Describing** How did Reconstruction governments reform education in the South?

Critical Thinking

4. **Organizing** Use a diagram like the one below to identify the three main groups that made up the Southern Republican Party.

Southern Republican Party

5. **Analyzing** How did the sharecropping system work to keep African Americans from improving their lives?

6. **Expository Writing** Imagine that you are a journalist in 1869. You are preparing to interview an African American senator from Mississippi, a carpetbagger, and a white Southern planter. Write three questions you would ask each about Reconstruction. Suggest how each person would respond.

Answer the
7. **Essential Question**
In what ways did government in the Southern states change during Reconstruction?

Reconstruction and the New South **Chapter 17** 531

Section 3 Review

Answers

1. Sentences should reflect a correct understanding of the terms.
2. White landowners refused to rent them land. Store owners refused them credit. Employers would not hire them. Violent groups killed or injured them and burned their buildings. Few Southern whites would testify against these attackers.
3. They created public school systems for both races.

4. African Americans, some white Southerners, whites from the North
5. After paying the landowner, sharecroppers had little crop left over to sell. As a result, they could not save to buy their own land or start their own businesses. Few could move out of poverty.
6. Questions and responses should show understanding of the different goals of the groups represented by the interviewees.

7. Before the Civil War, only whites could vote or hold office in the South. During Reconstruction, African American men gained these rights. African American voters mostly supported Republicans, helping Radical Republicans take control of Southern state governments. Also, several African Americans were elected to office.

Focus

S Skill Practice

Visual Literacy Have students study the drawing that shows the completion of the transcontinental railroad. **Ask:** Who are the people in this drawing? *(owners of the railroad, government officials, workers)* Ask students to write a caption for the drawing. **OL**

Teach

C Critical Thinking

Comparing and Contrasting Have students research to learn how long it would take to travel by land from New York City to San Francisco in 1869 and in 2008. **Ask:** How has travel changed since the completion of the first transcontinental railroad? *(Today, people can travel by car or bus on interstate highways, by plane, or by train.)* **AL**

R Reading Strategy

Paraphrasing Have students read the "Verbatim" quotations. Discuss how they reflect changes in American culture during the last part of the nineteenth century. Have students select a quotation and rewrite it in their own words. **OL**

Additional Support and Answers

TIME NOTEBOOK

What were people's lives like in the past?

These two pages will give you some clues to everyday life in the United States as you step back in time with TIME Notebook.

PHOTO RESEARCHERS

New Railway Crosses the Country

GETTING THERE

By now, you have probably heard that the tracks of the Union Pacific and Central Pacific railways met up in Utah on May 10, 1869—completing the first transcontinental railroad in the United States. A pioneer named **ALEXANDER TOPONCE** *wrote about the events that day:*

"When they came to drive the last spike, Governor Stanford, president of the Central Pacific, took the sledge, and the first time he struck he missed the spike and hit the rail.

"What a howl went up! Irish, Chinese, Mexicans, and everybody yelled with delight. 'He missed it. Yee.' The engineers blew the whistles and rang their bells. Then Stanford tried it again and tapped the spike and the telegraph operators had fixed their instruments so that the tap was reported in all the offices east and west, and set bells to tapping in hundreds of towns and cities. . . . Then Vice President T. C. Durant of the Union Pacific took up the sledge and he missed the spike the first time. Then everybody slapped everybody else again and yelled, 'He missed it too, yow!'

"It was a great occasion, everyone carried off souvenirs and there are enough splinters of the last tie in museums to make a good bonfire."

Fast Facts

Fighting Fires The Great Chicago Fire destroyed about 18,000 buildings and left about 100,000 of the city's 300,000 residents homeless. More than 200 firefighters worked for 30 hours to quench the flames.

Many other cities experienced the devastation caused by fires. Boston experienced a major fire in November 1872. Beginning in a dry goods store, the fire spread quickly to the nearby wooden roofs of surrounding buildings. Nearly 1,700 firefighters from Boston and the surrounding area battled the inferno. Weak water pressure was just one of the challenges they faced. Eventually, they used explosives to destroy buildings and create a firebreak. The controversial plan worked. Almost 800 buildings were devastated by the fire. The cost of the fire was about $75 million—the equivalent of about $1 billion today. The Boston fire chief lost his job after the fire, but he became an advocate for nationwide fire codes for buildings.

TIME NOTEBOOK

VIRGINIA STATS
State of the Union

Richmond had been the capital of the Confederacy—and Virginia paid the price after the Civil War. One of the states most ravaged by battles, Virginia's farm values sank from fifth in the country to tenth. The state tried to get new business by lowering taxes. That led to more factories, but they produced less than in the past.

CORBIS

	1860	1870
Number of Farms	86,468	73,849
Value of Farm Land	$371.8 million	$213 million
Number of Factories	5,385	5,933
Value of Manufactured Products	$50.7 million	$38.4 million

MILESTONES
EVENTS AND PEOPLE OF THE TIME

DRAWN. An elephant to represent jittery Republican voters by Thomas Nast before the presidential election in 1874. Looks like his symbol for Republicans might stick—after all, Nast is the artist who drew a mule to represent Democrats.

STRETCHED. Baseball fans in 1882 in what is becoming known as the "seventh inning stretch." The athletic director of New York's Manhattan College baseball team felt sorry for fidgety students in the crowd and told them to stand up and stretch during a game. Word has it that New York Giants fans will copy the practice.

DRIVEN OUT. African American members of the Georgia legislature in 1868, after white members claimed that African Americans might vote but not hold office.

THE REPUBLICAN VOTE

BETTMANN / CORBIS

NUMBERS
UNITED STATES AT THE TIME

2 cents About the price per acre the United States paid for Alaska in 1867—the total price is $7.2 million **D**

600,000 Approximate number of African Americans in the South who had enrolled in school by 1877

$125 Price of a typewriter, invented by Christopher Sholes in 1868

120,000,000,000 Number of locusts in a swarm that reached a mile high, 100 miles wide (161 km), and up to 300 miles long (483 km), wiping out crops in the West in 1874 **W**

MARY EVANS PICTURE LIBRARY / ALAMY

10,000 Number of people who went to the first Kentucky Derby horse race in 1875

CRITICAL THINKING

Speculating Based on Susan B. Anthony's reaction to her voting fine, what personal and philosophical qualities do you think she had?

Assessing How might the values of Virginia's farm and manufacturing economies have affected the lives of its citizens after the Civil War? Use the table to help explain your answer.

533

Change in the South

Focus

Bellringer
Daily Test Practice Transparency 17–4

Reading Guide
Answers to Graphic:

Industry: Build a strong industrial economy based on the region's abundant coal, iron, tobacco, cotton, and lumber.

Agriculture: Create small, profitable farms raising a variety of crops rather than large plantations devoted to cotton.

Section Spotlight Video

Watch the Section Spotlight Video "Change in the South" to learn more about the rise of the "New South."

Resource Manager

Essential Question ◄

How did the South change politically, economically, and socially when Reconstruction ended?

Reading Guide

Content Vocabulary

cash crop (p. 539)	grandfather clause (p. 539)
poll tax (p. 539)	segregation (p. 540)
literacy test (p. 539)	lynching (p. 540)

Academic Vocabulary

outcome (p. 536)	commission (p. 536)

Key People and Events
Amnesty Act (p. 535)
Rutherford B. Hayes (p. 536)
Compromise of 1877 (p. 536)
Jim Crow laws (p. 540)
Plessy v. Ferguson (p. 540)

Reading Strategy
Taking Notes As you read, use a diagram like the one below to summarize the goals for industry and for agriculture that leaders hoped to achieve in the "New South."

```
        The New South
        /           \
   Goal for       Goal for
   Industry:      Agriculture:
```

ILLINOIS STANDARDS
The American Journey

14.C.3 Compare historical issues involving rights, roles and status of individuals in relation to municipalities, states and the nation.

15.E.3b Explain how laws and government policies (e.g., property rights, contract enforcement, standard weights/measurements) establish rules that help a market economy function effectively.

18.B.3a Analyze how individuals and groups interact with and within institutions (e.g., educational, military).

American Diary

In 1875 Mississippi's governor, Adelbert Ames, appealed for federal troops to end racial violence in his state. The attorney general responded: "The whole public are tired out with these . . . outbreaks in the South. . . . Preserve the peace by the forces in your own state." His sharp tone revealed the desire of the Grant administration to end the federal government's involvement with Reconstruction.

—quoted in The Great Betrayal

Intent on securing white rule in Louisiana, a group called the "White League" takes over the statehouse in 1874.

R Reading Strategies	C Critical Thinking	D Differentiated Instruction	W Writing Support	S Skill Practice
Teacher Edition • Acad. Vocab., p. 535 • Act. Prior Know., p. 536 **Additional Resources** • Guid. Read., URB p. 100 • Content Vocab., URB p. 75 • Acad. Vocab., URB p. 77 • Pri. Source Read., URB p. 79	**Teacher Edition** • Ident. Cent. Iss., p. 535 • Making Infer., p. 536 • Pred. Conseq., p. 538 • Det. Cause & Effect, p. 538 **Additional Resources** • Quizzes and Tests, p. 166 • Link Past & Pres., URB p. 91	**Teacher Edition** • Gifted and Talented, p. 536 • Visual/Spatial, p. 540 **Additional Resources** • School-to-Home, URB p. 93 • Reteaching Act., URB p. 95	**Teacher Edition** • Persuasive Writing, p. 538 • Expository Writing, p. 540	**Teacher Edition** • Using Note-Taking Skills, p. 537 • Using Map Skills, p. 537 • Using Econ. Skills, p. 539 **Additional Resources** • Daily Test Pract. Transp. 17-4 • Lesson Transparency 17C

The End of Reconstruction

Main Idea Democrats steadily regained control of Southern governments as support for Radical Reconstruction policies decreased.

History and You Would you lose respect for a famous sports star if you learned he or she was cheating? Read how scandals weakened public support for the Radical Republicans.

During the Grant administration, Northerners began losing interest in Reconstruction. Many believed it was time for the South to solve its own problems.

Reconstruction declined for other reasons as well. The old Radical leaders began to disappear from politics. Thaddeus Stevens died in 1868. Others retired or lost elections.

Opponents of Reconstruction also exploited racial prejudice in the North. They argued that only Southerners really knew how to deal with African Americans and that the fate of the freed people should be left to the South. Southerners protested what they called "bayonet rule"—the use of federal troops to support Reconstruction governments. Grant tried to avoid any clashes with the South.

Republican Revolt

In the early 1870s, reports of corruption in Grant's administration and in Reconstruction governments spread. Some Republicans split with the party over the issue of corruption. Another group broke with the party over Reconstruction, proposing peaceful reconciliation—coming together again—with Southern whites. Calling themselves Liberal Republicans, these two groups nominated Horace Greeley, a newspaper editor, to run against Grant in 1872. Despite the split among Republicans, Grant was reelected.

Democrats Regain Power

In 1872 Liberal Republicans helped pass the **Amnesty Act,** which pardoned most former Confederates. Nearly all white Southerners could vote and hold office again. The amnesty changed the political balance in the South by restoring full rights to people who supported the Democratic Party.

In Southern states where a majority of voters were white, Democrats soon regained control of state governments. In states where African Americans held a majority, the Ku Klux Klan helped the Democrats take power by terrorizing Republican voters.

By the Numbers / Politics in Mississippi

Mississippi House of Representatives

1870

82 Republicans

25 Democrats

1875

97 Democrats

20 Republicans

End of Reconstruction After the Civil War, Republican state governments in Mississippi and other Southern states set up schools, built hospitals, and ended racial discrimination laws. By 1880, these reforms that began under Reconstruction came to an end as the more conservative Democrats returned to power throughout the South.

Mississippi State Budgets	
1870	$1,061,250
1871	$1,729,046
1876	$518,709
1877	$697,019
1880	$803,191

Source: *Cyclopaedia of Political Science*, 1899.

Critical Thinking

Interpreting Why do you think state government spending in Mississippi declined around 1876? How do you think the state's African American population was affected by this and other changes?

Primary Source Reading Activity, URB p. 79

Teach

R Reading Strategy

Academic Vocabulary Ask: What is a bayonet? *(a blade attached to the end of a rifle)* What does "bayonet rule" mean? *(that the government rules through the threat of force)* **ELL**

C Critical Thinking

Identifying Central Issues Ask: How did the Amnesty Act help Democrats regain control of state governments? *(It restored voting rights to most former Confederates, who supported the Democratic Party.)* **OL**

By the Numbers

Critical Thinking Answers Possible response: The shift in power from reform-minded Republicans to conservative Democrats led to lower government spending for reforms, such as schools and social services. These changes reversed the gains made by African Americans under Reconstruction.

Differentiated Instruction

Letter to a Former Slaveholder

Objective: To read an excerpt and interpret the source

Focus: Ask students why many African Americans started new lives away from their former plantations.

Teach: Have students read the excerpt and answer the questions.

Assess: Ask students what they think of Jourdan Anderson's letter and whether they agree with it.

Close: Discuss why Jourdan asked his former master for back wages.

Differentiated Instruction Strategies

BL Have students discuss what Jourdan should do about Colonel Anderson's offer.

AL Have students role-play a conversation between Jourdan and his former master.

ELL Tell students to refer to the Reader's Dictionary for definitions of unfamiliar words.

Section 4

The Republicans had other problems as well. In 1873 a series of political scandals came to light. Investigations uncovered top government officials making unfair business deals, scheming to withhold public tax money, and accepting bribes. One scandal involved the vice president and another the secretary of war. These scandals further damaged the Grant administration and the Republicans.

In addition to political scandals, Grant and the nation endured a severe economic depression. The crisis began in 1873 when a series of bad railroad investments forced the powerful banking firm of Jay Cooke and Company to declare bankruptcy. A wave of fear known as the Panic of 1873 quickly spread through the nation's financial community. The panic forced small banks to close and the stock market to plummet. Thousands of businesses shut down, and tens of thousands of Americans were thrown out of work. Blame for the hard times fell on the Republicans.

In the congressional elections of 1874, Democrats gained seats in the Senate and won control of the House. For the first time since the Civil War, the Democratic Party controlled a part of the federal government. This situation further weakened Congress's commitment to Reconstruction and protecting the rights of African Americans.

The Election of 1876

President Grant considered running for a third term in 1876. Most Republican leaders preferred a new candidate—one who could win back the Liberal Republicans and unite the party. The Republicans nominated **Rutherford B. Hayes**, governor of Ohio. A champion of political reform, Hayes had a reputation for honesty, and he held moderate views on Reconstruction. The Democrats nominated New York governor Samuel Tilden. Tilden gained fame for fighting political corruption in New York City.

After the election, Tilden appeared to be the winner, receiving almost 250,000 more votes than Hayes. However, disputed returns from four states—representing 20 electoral

Struggle of Reconstruction

Extending Liberties Laws and amendments were passed during Reconstruction to extend civil liberties to African Americans.

Civil Rights Amendments and Laws

Civil Rights Act of 1866
Granted citizenship and equal rights to all persons born in the United States (except Native Americans)
Fourteenth Amendment (1870)
Granted citizenship and equal protection of the laws to all persons born in the United States (except Native Americans)
Fifteenth Amendment (1870)
Protected the voting rights of African Americans
Civil Rights Act of 1875
Outlawed racial segregation in public services Ensured the right of African Americans to serve as jurors

votes—kept the **outcome**, or results, in doubt. Tilden had 184 electoral votes, only 1 short of what he needed to win. Yet if Hayes received all 20 of the disputed votes, he would have the 185 electoral votes required for victory.

To review the election results, Congress created a special **commission**, or group, of 15 persons made up equally of members of the House of Representatives, the Senate, and the Supreme Court. The commission had 7 Republicans, 7 Democrats, and 1 independent. But the independent resigned, and a Republican took his place. The commission voted 8 to 7 to award all 20 electoral votes, and the election, to Hayes. The vote followed party lines.

Compromise of 1877

Democrats in Congress threatened to fight the commission's decision. Republican and Southern Democratic leaders reportedly met in secret to work out an agreement. On March 2, 1877, Congress declared Hayes the winner.

The agreement—called the **Compromise of 1877**—included some favors to the South.

Fast Facts

Disputed Election of 1876

Rutherford B. Hayes ▶

Disputed Election of 1876 NATIONAL GEOGRAPHIC

One of Oregon's three electoral votes was in doubt.

Disputed electoral vote

People living in territories could not vote in national elections.

Northern troops still occupied three states.

Washington Territory 3
Montana Territory
Dakota Territory 5
Idaho Territory
Wyoming Territory
3
Oregon 3
Utah Terr. 3
6
Arizona Territory
New Mexico Territory
Unorg. Terr.
10
11
5
15
12
21 15 22
11
29
35
5 5 13
4
6
9
3
8
5 11
10
7
8 10 11
6
12
8
8
4

Candidate	Electoral Vote	Popular Vote	Political Party
Hayes	185	4,036,572	Republican
Tilden	184	4,284,020	Democrat

Critical Thinking

Comparing Which laws are most similar to each other?

The new government would give more aid to the South. Republicans agreed to withdraw all remaining troops from Southern states. Without soldiers to support them, the remaining Republican governments in South Carolina and Louisiana quickly collapsed. The Democrats, in turn, promised to maintain African American rights.

A New Policy

In his Inaugural Address, Hayes declared that what the South needed most was the restoration of "wise, honest, and peaceful local self-government." During a goodwill trip to the South, Hayes announced his intention of letting Southerners handle racial issues. Hayes's message was clear. The federal government would no longer attempt to reshape Southern society. Reconstruction had come to an end.

✔ **Reading Check** Summarizing How did the Compromise of 1877 affect Reconstruction?

Change in the South

Main Idea After Reconstruction, the South experienced a political shift and industrial growth.

History and You Do you recall that lack of industry put the South at a disadvantage during the Civil War? Read to learn how Southerners vowed to create a strong industrial "New South."

. . . .

Many Southern whites hated Republicans for their role in the Civil War and in Reconstruction. When Reconstruction ended, power in the South shifted to the Democrats.

Democrats in Control

In some regions, the ruling Democrats were the large landowners and other groups that held power before the Civil War. In many areas, however, new leaders took charge. Among their ranks were merchants, bankers, and other business leaders who supported economic development.

Reconstruction and the New South **Chapter 17** 537

Activity: Interdisciplinary Connection

Civics Remind students that a presidential candidate can win the popular vote yet lose the presidency. Explain that when Americans vote in a presidential election, they are not voting directly for a candidate. Instead, they are voting for that candidate's electors. The votes cast by the electors officially elect the president. Have students do research to create a chart listing the key arguments for and against the Electoral College system. Tell students to come to class prepared to debate the issue with their classmates. **AL**

C₁ Critical Thinking

Predicting Consequences Ask: How would you expect the conservative tax policies of the Democrats to affect African Americans? *(Funding for social services benefiting African Americans, including education, would likely be cut.)* **OL**

W Writing Support

Persuasive Writing Have students take the role of Henry Grady and write an editorial for the *Atlanta Constitution*, urging Southerners to build a "New South." **OL**

C₂ Critical Thinking

Determining Cause and Effect Ask: Why do you think the major industries to develop in the South were manufacturers of textiles, steel, and tobacco products? *(The South produced an abundance of cotton, iron ore, and tobacco, which these industries needed to make their products. The South also had a cheap, reliable workforce and an expanding railroad system.)* **OL**

Change in Politics

These Democrats called themselves "Redeemers" because they had "redeemed," or saved, the South from Republican rule. The Redeemers adopted conservative policies, such as lower taxes and reduced government spending. They drastically cut, or even eliminated, many social services started during Reconstruction, including public education. Their one-party rule and conservative policies dominated Southern politics well into the 1900s.

Rise of the "New South"

By the 1880s, forward-looking Southerners were convinced that their region must develop a strong industrial economy. They argued that the South lost the Civil War because its industry did not match the North's. Henry Grady, editor of the *Atlanta Constitution*, headed a group that urged Southerners to "out-Yankee the Yankees" and build a "New South." This "New South" would have industries based on the region's abundant coal, iron, tobacco, cotton, and lumber. Southerners would create this new economy by embracing a spirit of hard work and regional pride.

Industry in the South made dramatic gains in the 1880s. Textile mills sprang up across the South. The American Tobacco Company, developed largely by James Duke of North Carolina, eventually controlled almost all tobacco manufacturing in the nation. By 1890, Southern mills produced nearly 20 percent of the nation's iron and steel. Much of the industry was in Alabama near deposits of iron ore.

Southern industry grew as a result of a cheap and reliable workforce. Most factory workers put in long hours for low wages. A railroad-building boom also aided industrial development. By 1870, the Southern railroad system, which had been destroyed during the war, was largely rebuilt. The miles of rail track more than doubled between 1880 and 1890. Still, the South did not develop an industrial economy as strong as the North's. Agriculture remained the South's main economic activity.

Differentiated Instruction

Primary Source / Sharecropping

Denied Land During the Civil War, formerly enslaved African Americans hoped to acquire abandoned or confiscated Confederate lands. The government under President Johnson, however, returned Southern plantations to their former slaveholders.

Southern laws forced sharecroppers to work the land until they paid off their debts. A system emerged in the South that closely resembled slavery. ▼

Formerly enslaved African Americans often ended up working as sharecroppers on land that belonged to their former owners. ▼

Typical sharecropper contract ▶

To secure payment of said rent and supply bill, the said Dawson [the sharecropper] grants unto said Solid South [the landowner] a special privilege and right of pledge on all the products raised on said land, and on all his stock, farming implements, and personal property, and hereby waives in favor of said Solid South the benefit of any and all homestead laws and exemption laws now in force, or which may be in force, in Louisiana, and agrees that all his property shall be seized and sold to pay said rent and supply bill in default of payment thereof as herein agreed. Any violation of this contract shall render the lease void.

Leveled Activities

BL School-to-Home Connection Activity, URB p. 93

OL Linking Past and Present Activity, URB p. 91

ELL Guided Reading Activity, URB p. 100

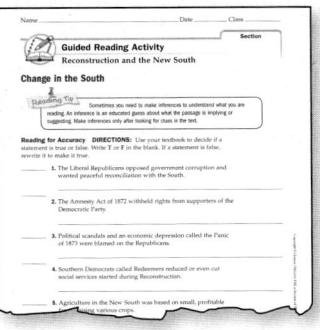

Rural Economy

Supporters of the New South hoped to change Southern agriculture as well as industry. Their goal was small, profitable farms raising a variety of crops rather than large plantations devoted to cotton. A different economy emerged, however. Some plantations were broken up, but many large landowners held on to their land. When estates were divided, much of the land went to sharecropping and tenant farming, neither of which was profitable.

Debt also caused problems. Poor farmers used credit to buy supplies. Merchants who sold on credit charged high prices, and farmers' debts rose. To repay debts, farmers grew **cash crops**—crops that could be sold for money. As in the past, the main cash crop was cotton. Too much cotton forced prices down, however. Farmers then had to grow even more cotton to try to recover their losses. Sharecropping and reliance on one cash crop kept Southern agriculture from advancing.

Reading Check Describing Why did industry in the South grow during this period?

Agricultural Production in the South, 1850–1890

Increased production lowered cotton prices and left much of the rural South in poverty after the Civil War.

Source: *Historical Statistics of the South*

Critical Thinking

Comparing and Contrasting How was the South after the Civil War similar to and different from the South before the Civil War?

Graphs In Motion See StudentWorks™ Plus or glencoe.com.

A Divided Society

Main Idea As Reconstruction ended, true freedom for African Americans became a distant dream.

History and You How would you feel if you had to pass a test on a subject you never studied in order to graduate? Read to learn about a test African Americans in the South had to pass in order to vote.

As Reconstruction ended, African Americans' dreams for justice faded. In the last 20 years of the 1800s, racism became firmly set in the culture. Individuals took steps to keep African Americans separated from whites and to deny them basic rights.

Voting Restrictions

The Fifteenth Amendment prohibited any state from denying an individual the right to vote because of race. Southern leaders, however, found ways to get around the amendment and prevent African Americans from voting.

Many Southern states required a **poll tax,** a fee people had to pay to vote. Because many African Americans could not afford the tax, they could not vote. The tax also kept many poor whites from voting.

Another approach was to make prospective voters take a **literacy test** in which they had to read and explain difficult parts of state constitutions or the federal Constitution. Because most African Americans had little education, literacy tests prevented many from voting.

Literacy tests could also keep some whites from voting. For this reason some states passed **grandfather clauses.** These laws allowed people who did not pass the literacy test to vote if their fathers or grandfathers voted before Reconstruction. Because African Americans could not vote until 1867, they were excluded. By the end of the 1800s, such laws and the constant threat of violence caused African American voting to decline drastically.

Reconstruction and the New South **Chapter 17** 539

S Skill Practice

Using Economics Skills Ask: How did dependence on one cash crop—cotton—harm the South? *(Producing too much cotton drove prices and profits down.)* How would producing a variety of crops have helped Southern farmers? *(They would have been less likely to overproduce a crop, keeping prices up. If the price of one crop did fall, farmers could recover their losses with profits from other crops.)* **OL**

Primary Source

Critical Thinking Answer
Similarities: Whites owned the land and poor African Americans worked the land. **Differences:** African Americans were sharecroppers instead of slaves; cotton was more profitable before the war.

Reading Check Answer: leaders favored industrial development; South had abundant resources and a cheap and reliable workforce; boom in railroad building

Hands-On Chapter Project
Step 4

Creating a Web Site

Step 4: Creating a Home Page Students will create a home page for their Web site.

Essential Question: How did the South change politically, economically, and socially when Reconstruction ended?

Directions Have the class brainstorm a name for their historical society. Have students look at home pages on the Web as examples and discuss the kinds of information they want for their home page. Then have volunteers work together to create a home page, either as a storyboard or an electronic page. The home page should introduce the site's purpose and include links to all the groups' pages, forming a Web site.

Determining Cause and Effect As a class, discuss how the end of Reconstruction affected African Americans politically, economically, and socially. **OL**

(Chapter Project continued on the Visual Summary page)

D Differentiated Instruction

Visual/Spatial Have students collect images of segregation in the South from different time periods. Have groups work together to create a collage of images with captions. `OL`

W Writing Support

Expository Writing Have students write a paragraph that explains the meaning of this statement by W.E.B. Du Bois. `OL`

✔ **Reading Check** **Answer:** with Jim Crow laws

Assess

History ONLINE

Study Central™ provides summaries, interactive games, and online graphic organizers to help students review content.

Close

Summarizing Create columns on the board labeled "political," "economic," and "social," and have students identify changes that occurred in the South in each category. `OL`

Section 4 Review

Jim Crow Laws

By the 1890s, **segregation,** or the separation of the races, had become a common feature of the South. Southern states passed so-called **Jim Crow laws** that required African Americans and whites to be separated in almost every public place.

In 1896 the Supreme Court upheld segregation laws in ***Plessy v. Ferguson.*** The case involved a Louisiana law requiring separate sections on trains for African Americans. The Court ruled that segregation was legal as long as African Americans had access to public places equal to those of whites.

One problem, however, was that the facilities were separate but in no way equal. Southern states spent much more money on schools and other facilities for whites than on those for African Americans. This "separate but equal" doctrine gave legal support to Southern segregation for more than 50 years. White violence against African Americans also rose. One form of violence was **lynching,** in which an angry mob killed a person by hanging. African Americans were lynched because they were suspected of crimes—or because they did not behave as whites thought they should behave.

Reconstruction's Impact

Reconstruction was both a success and a failure. It helped the South rebuild its economy. Yet much of the South remained agricultural and poor. African Americans gained greater equality, created their own institutions, and shared in government with whites. Their advances, however, did not last. In the words of African American writer and civil rights leader W.E.B. Du Bois, "The slave went free; stood a brief moment in the sun; then moved back again toward slavery."

✔ **Reading Check** **Describing** How was segregation applied?

History ONLINE
Study Central™ To review this section, go to glencoe.com.

Section 4 Review

Vocabulary

1. Use each of these terms in a sentence that will help explain its meaning: outcome, commission, cash crop, poll tax, literacy test, grandfather clause, segregation, lynching.

Main Ideas

2. **Explaining** How did the Amnesty Act help Democrats regain control of Southern state governments?

3. **Describing** How did forward-thinking Southerners want to change the South's economy?

4. **Explaining** Why did African American voting in the South decline drastically by the late 1800s?

Critical Thinking

5. **Determining Cause and Effect** Use a diagram like the one below to describe the two issues that split the Republican Party for the 1872 election. Then name the group these dissatisfied Republicans came together to form.

Issues That Divided Republicans

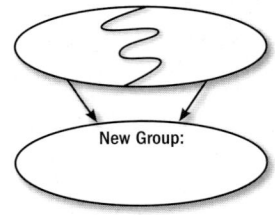

New Group:

6. **Analyzing** Did agriculture in the New South achieve the shift envisioned by its supporters? Why or why not?

7. **Descriptive Writing** You are an African American in 1899. When you took a seat on a train, the white conductor told you to move to a separate section. Write a letter to W.E.B. Du Bois, describing the incident and your feelings about it.

Answer the Essential Question

8. How did the South change politically, economically, and socially when Reconstruction ended?

Answers

1. Sentences should reflect a correct understanding of the terms.
2. It restored full voting rights to most former Confederates—white Southerners who supported the Democratic Party.
3. They wanted to create a stronger industrial economy and agriculture that was based on small farms and a variety of crops instead of large plantations devoted to cotton.
4. because of poll taxes, literacy tests, and the constant threat of violence

5. **Issues:** corruption, Reconstruction policy—favored peaceful reconciliation with Southern whites; **New group:** Liberal Republicans
6. No. Many large landowners held on to their land. When estates were divided, much of the land went to sharecropping and tenant farming, neither of which was profitable. Poor farmers relied on a single cash crop—mainly cotton—to repay debts.
7. Letters might describe feelings of humilia-

tion or outrage and perhaps the less comfortable conditions of the African American section of the train.
8. **Politically:** power shifted to Democrats, who instituted conservative policies; **Economically:** developed more industries, agriculture included sharecropping and tenant farming as well as large plantations; **Socially:** laws created segregation and limited African American voting rights, white violence against African Americans increased

Reconstruction Plans

- The South is rebuilt and readmitted to the Union during Reconstruction.
- Lincoln's Ten Percent Plan is designed to heal the Union quickly.
- The Radical Republicans' Wade-Davis Bill has strict requirements for states to be readmitted.
- The Freedmen's Bureau helps African Americans adjust to freedom.
- Abraham Lincoln is assassinated in April 1865.
- President Johnson's "Restoration" plan calls for states to ratify the amendment to abolish slavery.

◄ Freedmen's school

Lincoln's funeral ▼

Radical Reconstruction

- Radical Republicans believe Johnson's plan is too easy on the South.
- Southern states pass black codes to control freed African Americans, but Congress passes the Civil Rights Act of 1866 to protect their freedoms.
- The Fourteenth Amendment gives African Americans citizenship and equal protection of the laws.
- Radical Republicans win Congress and enact their own Reconstruction plans.
- Congress impeaches Johnson but fails to convict him.
- The Fifteenth Amendment gives African American men the right to vote.

Andrew Johnson ▲

Reconstruction in the South

- African Americans vote and take part in Southern politics.
- Some whites resist the expansion of African Americans' rights and form the Ku Klux Klan.
- Sharecropping limits economic opportunities for African Americans.

Reconstruction Ends

- Republicans lose power as a result of political corruption and economic crisis.
- Democrats regain control of Southern state governments.
- Southern Democrats encourage economic growth but limit the rights of African Americans.

 STUDY TO GO Study anywhere, anytime! Download quizzes and flash cards to your PDA from glencoe.com.

Reconstruction and the New South **Chapter 17** **541**

Visual Summary

Analyzing Ask: What factors led to Radical Reconstruction? *(Lincoln's death, riots against African Americans in the South, Northern reaction to black codes, Republicans could override Johnson's vetoes, solid Republican victory in 1866 congressional elections)* What factors helped end Reconstruction? *(loss of interest in the North, radical leaders died or lost elections, racial prejudice, corruption and scandals in government, Amnesty Act, Ku Klux Klan terrorized Republican voters, Republicans blamed for economic depression, Democrats won control of House in 1874, Compromise of 1877, removal of troops from South)* **OL**

Evaluating Ask: In what ways was Reconstruction a success? *(It helped rebuild the South's economy; laws and amendments offered the promise of equality for African Americans; African Americans created own institutions and shared in government.)* In what ways was Reconstruction a failure? *(Much of the South remained agricultural and poor; restrictive laws and threats of violence prevented African Americans from enjoying truly equal rights.)* **OL**

Hands-On Chapter Project
Step 5: Wrap-Up

Creating a Web Site

Step 5: Assembling the Web Site Students will combine their pages into a Web site display.

Directions Have the groups prepare a display of their Web site. They can create a bulletin board display with storyboards or printouts of each page linked with string or yarn to the home page. If the class has access to computer projection, have students display their pages electronically. Discuss how the collection of Web pages provides a good overview of the effects of Reconstruction and its aftermath on African Americans.

Analyzing Discuss the changes that took place in the South after the Civil War.

Ask: In what ways did people experience Reconstruction differently? *(Answers should* reflect an understanding of the challenges faced by African Americans, as well as political issues, and the struggle to rebuild the South.)* How does the Internet allow historians to educate and inform people about the past? *(Web sites allow historians to gather a variety of information from several sources and points of view. Images and maps can also be presented, as well as links to other Web sites of interest.)* **OL**

Focus

C Critical Thinking

Analyzing Primary Sources Have students read and analyze Henry Grady's quote about taking revenge on the South. **Ask:** How do the leaders calling for a "New South" feel about the North? What emotions are expressed in the quote? *(The South's leaders understood that they were still competing with the North economically. This competitiveness, and lingering resentment over the Civil War, are apparent in the quote.)* **OL**

Have students complete a graphic organizer like the one shown here that identifies the industries that developed in the "New South." **BL**

Textiles — Timber — Tobacco — New industries — Iron — Coal — Cotton

Additional Support and Answers

Southern Industry After the Civil War

Before the Civil War, the backbone of the Southern economy was agriculture. After Reconstruction, industry in the South made dramatic gains.

How Did Geography Affect Southern Industry?

Many Southern industries after the Civil War centered around regional agricultural products such as tobacco and cotton. In the 1880s textile mills sprang up throughout the South. Additionally, Southern forests provided lumber for new homes, factories, railroad ties, and above all, furniture.

Other Southern industries centered on the region's rich reserves of coal and iron. By 1900, the South led the world in coal production; this same period saw a large growth in iron and steel mills.

Map legend:
- Coal
- Cotton
- Iron
- Lumber
- Textiles
- Tobacco

▲ While the economy of the Old South focused on cotton and tobacco production, distinct industrial regions began to develop after the Civil War.

Manufacturing in the Southern States, 1860–1900*

State	1860	1880	1900
Alabama	1,459	2,070	5,602
Arkansas	518	1,202	4,794
Florida	185	426	2,056
Georgia	1,890	3,593	7,504
Louisiana	1,744	1,553	4,350
Mississippi	976	1,479	4,772
North Carolina	3,689	3,802	7,226
South Carolina	1,230	2,078	3,762
Tennessee	2,572	4,326	8,016
Texas	983	2,996	12,289
TOTAL	**15,246**	**23,525**	**60,371**

*Number of Manufacturing Establishments

Thomas Nast's illustration for an 1882 cover of *Harper's Weekly* compares the Old South's "King Cotton" of 1861 to the New South's "Queen of Industry." ▶

What they were saying . . .

Atlanta *Constitution* editor Henry Grady was one of the leaders calling for a "New South," a South that is industrialized and part of a modern national economy.

"We are going to take a noble revenge . . . by invading every inch of your territory [the North] with iron, as you invaded ours twenty-nine years ago."

C

Activity: Connecting the Past and Present

Determining Cause and Effect Tobacco has played a major role in the South's economy. Along with cotton, it supported the agricultural economy of the South. As industry grew after the Civil War, tobacco processing became a major industry in the South. Ask students to research changes in the tobacco industry since the post–Civil War years. **Ask:** What role does tobacco play in the economy of the South today? What factors have changed the importance of the crop? *(The South continues to plant tobacco and it remains an important crop in many areas. However, there are many factors that are influencing tobacco production and processing. Students may point out that many of these factors—such as awareness of health risks, lawsuits against tobacco companies, limits on advertising, rising prices of tobacco products, and heavy taxation—have reduced the number of tobacco users over the years.)* Hold a class discussion on how the decrease in tobacco use may affect the South's economy and what alternatives Southern tobacco producers might consider. *(With less demand, prices may drop. It may cause a loss of jobs in the industry. States may consider planting alternative crops.)* **OL**

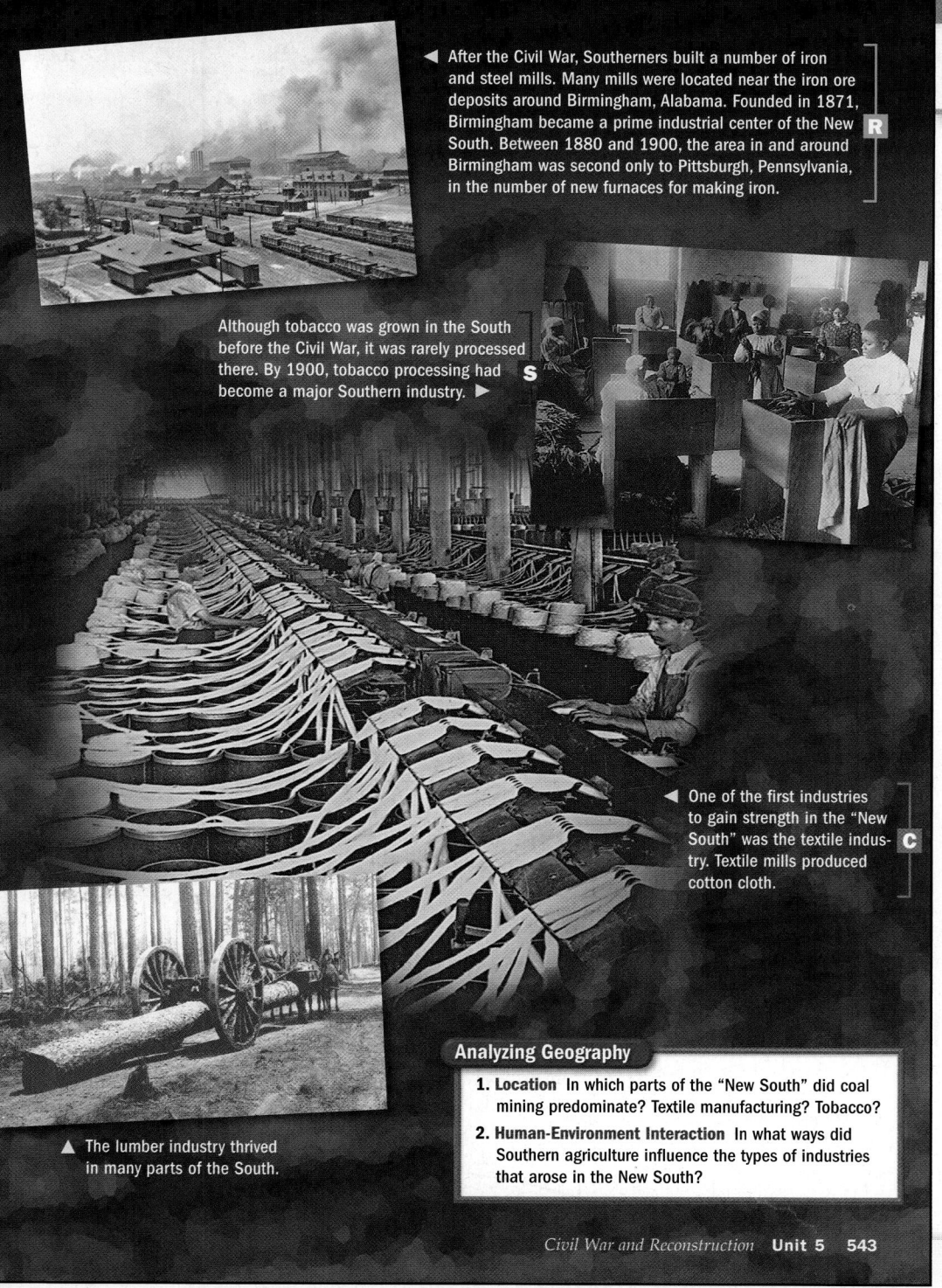

After the Civil War, Southerners built a number of iron and steel mills. Many mills were located near the iron ore deposits around Birmingham, Alabama. Founded in 1871, Birmingham became a prime industrial center of the New South. Between 1880 and 1900, the area in and around Birmingham was second only to Pittsburgh, Pennsylvania, in the number of new furnaces for making iron. **R**

Although tobacco was grown in the South before the Civil War, it was rarely processed there. By 1900, tobacco processing had become a major Southern industry. ▶ **S**

One of the first industries to gain strength in the "New South" was the textile industry. Textile mills produced cotton cloth. **C**

▲ The lumber industry thrived in many parts of the South.

Analyzing Geography

1. **Location** In which parts of the "New South" did coal mining predominate? Textile manufacturing? Tobacco?

2. **Human-Environment Interaction** In what ways did Southern agriculture influence the types of industries that arose in the New South?

Civil War and Reconstruction **Unit 5 543**

Teach

R Reading Strategy

Inferring Ask: Why did Birmingham succeed as an industrial center? *(The area had rich reserves of iron, so it was a logical place to build steel mills.)* **OL**

S Skill Practice

Visual Literacy Have students examine the photograph of the workers processing tobacco. Ask them to explain how the available workforce affected the growth of industry in the South. *(The cheap workforce, often made up of women, children, and African Americans, allowed higher profits and growth of industry.)* **OL**

Assess/Close

C Critical Thinking

Determining Cause and Effect Why was the textile industry the first to recover after the Civil War? *(Textile mills produced cotton cloth. The main resource for this industry—cotton—was abundant and was the South's main crop.)* **OL**

Answers

1. **coal mining:** Virginia, Tennessee, and Alabama; **textile manufacturing:** Virginia, North Carolina, South Carolina, Tennessee, Georgia, Alabama, and Mississippi; **tobacco:** Virginia, North Carolina, Tennessee, and Arkansas

2. Southerners began to develop industries to process the tobacco and cotton that they grew.

Answers and Analyses
Reviewing Main Ideas

1. B Remind students that the Wade-Davis bill was the Radical Republican plan, so it would be harsh toward former Confederates. **14.C.3**

2. B Students should immediately eliminate choices A and C by recalling that Johnson and Congress strongly disagreed over Reconstruction plans. **16.A**

3. A Students should immediately eliminate choices B and D because freed people and many sharecroppers were African American. They can eliminate carpetbaggers by recalling that these people were Northerners. **18.B.3a**

4. C Students can choose the correct answer by recalling that support for Reconstruction was decreasing during the Grant administration. **18.B.3a**

Short-Answer Question

5. He thought most African Americans would earn their living as farmers in the South. He thought the future for African Americans looked bright, expecting them to advance themselves and to contribute greatly to American society. **16.A.3b**

TEST-TAKING TIP

Be sure to pay attention to specific words in a question. Words can act as clues to help you identify the correct answer.

Reviewing Main Ideas

Directions: Choose the best answer for each of the following questions.

1. Which of the following was a provision of the 1864 Wade-Davis bill?

  A African American males in a state had to swear loyalty to the Union.

  B Ex-Confederates could not hold public office.

  C Confederate states could be readmitted to the Union even if they kept slavery.

  D Half of all delegates to a constitutional convention had to be formerly enslaved people.

2. What was Andrew Johnson's reaction to the Civil Rights Act of 1866?

  A He supported the law even though he believed it did not protect African Americans.

  B He said it was unconstitutional because it was passed by a Congress that did not include representatives from all the states.

  C He persuaded Congress to pass the bill.

  D He vetoed it because it gave states too much power.

3. Southern whites who supported the Republicans were called

  A scalawags.   **C** carpetbaggers.

  B sharecroppers. **D** freed men and women.

4. During the Grant administration,

  A Radical Republicans became more powerful.

  B corruption charges weakened Democrats.

  C many Northerners began to think the South should solve its own problems.

  D most white Southerners supported Republicans.

Short-Answer Question

Directions: Base your answer to question 5 on the excerpt below and on your knowledge of social studies.

> I have confidence . . . in the endurance, capacity, and destiny of my people [African Americans]. We will . . . seek our places, sometimes in the field of letters, arts, sciences, and the professions. More frequently mechanical pursuits will attract and elicit our efforts; more still of my people will find employment . . . as the cultivators of the soil. The bulk of this people—by surroundings, habits, adaptation, and choice—will continue to find their homes in the South. . . . Whatever our ultimate position in the . . . Republic . . . we will not forget our instincts for freedom nor our love of country.
>
> —Senator Blanche K. Bruce, from a speech in 1876

5. According to the document, how did Bruce expect most African Americans to earn a living? How did he view their futures?

Review the Essential Questions

6. Essay What do you think was Reconstruction's greatest success? What was its greatest failure? Explain your answers.

To help you write your essay, review your answers to the Essential Questions in the section reviews and the chapter Foldables Study Organizer. Your essay should include:

- the various plans for Reconstruction;
- the actions of the Radical Republicans and their conflicts with Johnson;
- the changes in the South and white Southern responses; and
- reasons why Reconstruction ended.

GO ON ➡

Review the Essential Questions

6. If students completed their Foldables correctly, they should be able to summarize the successes and failures of Reconstruction. Successes might include rebuilding the South's economy, laws and amendments promoting greater equality for African Americans, and expanded education for both races. Failures might include the failure of the South to develop a diverse agricultural and industrial economy, persistent poverty in the South, short-lived impact of laws protecting African American rights, persistent racism, and restrictive laws and violence toward African Americans. **16.A**

History ONLINE
For additional test practice, use **Self-Check Quizzes**—Chapter 17 at glencoe.com.

Chapter 17 Assessment

Document-Based Questions

Directions: Analyze the documents and answer the short-answer questions that follow.

Document 1

New England journalist Sidney Andrews recorded these remarks in 1865 from a man in Charleston, South Carolina.

> You Northern people are making a great mistake in your treatment of the South. We are thoroughly whipped; we give up slavery forever; and now we want you to quit [criticizing] us. Let us back into the Union, and then come down here and help us build up the country.

Source: Sidney Andrews, *The South Since the War*

7. Based on the excerpt, do you think the person Andrews spoke to would most likely support Lincoln's Ten Percent Plan or the Wade-Davis Bill? Explain.

Document 2

President Andrew Johnson made these remarks in his veto of the First Reconstruction Act of 1867.

> The power . . . given to the commanding officer . . . of each district is that of an absolute monarch. His mere will is to take the place of all law. . . .
> It reduces the whole population of the ten States . . . to the most abject and degrading slavery.

Source: Andrew Johnson, "From Revolution to Reconstruction"

8. According to the document, why did Johnson veto the First Reconstruction Act?

Document 3

The illustration at the top right is from the December 28, 1868, *Harper's Weekly* magazine. It shows two members of the Ku Klux Klan.

Source: Corbis

9. Why did Klan members wear disguises?

Document 4

The following are examples of Jim Crow laws passed throughout the South.

> No person or corporation shall require any white female nurse to nurse in wards or rooms in hospitals, either public or private, in which negro men are placed. *Alabama*
>
> The schools for white children and the schools for negro children shall be conducted separately. *Florida*
>
> Books shall not be interchangeable between the white and colored schools, but shall continue to be used by the race first using them. *North Carolina*

Source: Martin Luther King, Jr., National Historic Site

10. How were African American freedoms limited?

11. **Expository Writing** Using the information from the four documents and your knowledge of social studies, write an essay in which you:

- describe the political issues related to Reconstruction, including the effect of Lincoln's death on the process; and
- describe how Reconstruction affected the various groups in the South.

Need Extra Help?

If you missed questions. . .	1	2	3	4	5	6	7	8	9	10	11
Go to page. . .	520	524	529	535	530	518–540	519–520	525	530	539–540	518–540

Reconstruction and the New South **Chapter 17** 545

9. Klan members probably wanted to hide their identities, because Reconstruction governments were cracking down on the Klan at this time. Also, the disguises could frighten and intimidate their victims. **16.A**

10. These laws limited African Americans' access to equal education and services, such as health care. The laws also enforced separation of the races. **14.C.3**

11. **Political issues:** Lincoln favored amnesty and healing. His death opened the way for more radical leaders to make Reconstruction policy. The Radicals divided the South into military districts and required states to ratify the Fourteenth Amendment to rejoin the Union. The Amnesty Act and Compromise of 1877 brought Reconstruction to an end. **Effects on African Americans:** laws and amendments protecting their rights, expanded education, participation in government, and white backlash, including violence and restrictive local laws. **Effects on Southern whites:** had to share power and forge a new way of life without slavery. **14.C.3**

History ONLINE
Have students visit the Web site at glencoe.com to review Chapter 17 and take the Self-Check Quiz.

Need Extra Help?

Have students refer to the pages listed if they miss any of the questions.

Document-Based Questions

7. Ten Percent Plan. Lincoln wanted to encourage Southerners who supported the Union to take charge of state governments. He believed that punishing the South would serve no purpose and would only delay healing the nation. **16.A.3b**

8. The act divided 10 Southern states into five military districts and placed each under the authority of a military commander until new governments were formed. Johnson believed that the act gave too much power to the commanding officer of each district. **16.A.3b**

UNIT PACING CHART				
	Unit 6	Chapter 18	Chapter 19	Chapter 20
Day 1	Unit Opener, Reading History	Chapter Opener, Section 1, America's Literature	Chapter Opener, Section 1	Chapter Opener, Section 1, TIME Notebook
Day 2		Section 2	Section 2	Section 2
Day 3		Section 3, Geography & History	Section 3, You Decide	Section 3, Visual Summary
Day 4		Section 4, Visual Summary	Section 4, Visual Summary	Chapter Assessment
Day 5		Chapter Assessment	Chapter Assessment	

 Teacher to Teacher

Cheryl Tentschert
Margaret Buerkle
Middle School
Mehlville R-IX
School District
St. Louis, MO

Race Toward the West! To help students understand the opening of the West, mark three areas in your gymnasium or outside your school: the East, the Plains (across the middle), and the West. Organize your class into miners, settlers, soldiers, and Native Americans. In the Plains, place markers or cones to represent choice pieces of farmland; in the West, place markers or cones to represent mining areas. Have a select set of students be Native Americans living in the West. After giving this group directions to protect their land, and the miners and settlers the goal of reaching the mining areas and farmland, respectively, play a game of tag. Settlers should cross the Plains to reach the "farmland" without being tagged, while the miners cross into the West to reach the mining areas. Take a head count of the miners and settlers who reached their goal; then tell everyone to go back to their places. At this time, place the soldiers on the Plains and in the West. Play a second round of tag with the miners and settlers again trying to reach their desired areas. Again, take a head count of those who made it safely. As a class, discuss the challenges each group faced in order to achieve its goal. Tell students that this activity introduces why these different groups came into conflict with each other as people moved west.

Author Note

Dear American History Teacher,

Americans were restless at the end of the Civil War and sought to expand the country's physical territory. They were also in search of gold and silver and eager to settle new lands in the West or on the Great Plains. The passage of the Homestead Act in 1862 set many of these developments in motion. Americans, as eager to own land and build homes as their predecessors, flocked by the thousands to the western states and territories.

Their desires often conflicted, however, with the presence of the Plains Indians. The Plains Indians were a rich variety of Native American peoples, who had lived on the Great Plains for thousands of years and depended on the buffalo for survival. Neither American citizens nor the federal government showed much respect or patience for the Native Americans. The goal of many of the federal policies was to relocate them onto reservations. The Dawes Act represented a departure from this policy and was designed to make farmers and ranchers out of Native Americans.

The late nineteenth century also represented a great forward surge in American business. Many fortunes were made in the railroad, oil, and steel industries. Students will be intrigued to learn how men such as John D. Rockefeller and Andrew Carnegie made great fortunes but also felt obligated to share their wealth with others.

America has always been a nation of immigrants, but the number and the type of immigrant who came to the United States differed dramatically after 1880. The "new" immigrant, who hailed from eastern and southern Europe, significantly outnumbered the "old" immigrant, who had originated from western Europe. Most immigrants settled in cities.

Indeed, cities served as magnets for people because they offered jobs and a respite from the monotony of rural life. As more Americans crowded into cities, their physical space was transformed. Streetcars, skyscrapers, and unimaginable feats of architecture, such as the Brooklyn Bridge and the Woolworth Building, graced the urban landscape. Cities, however, also included tenement housing and slums. Pollution increased, and diseases spread quickly. America had seldom undergone such rapid transformations in such a short time period.

Albert S. Broussard

Albert S. Broussard

Unit Objectives

After studying this unit, students will be able to:

- Discuss the development of the West.
- Explain the role of railroad barons, inventions, and labor in America in the late 1800s and early 1900s.
- Describe the social history of the late 1800s and early 1900s.

Introducing the Unit

Speculating As students prepare to study the unit, ask them to think about the effects of changes in transportation on the development of the United States. **Ask:** How do you think the expansion of the railroad affected the United States? *(Students might note that expansion made it easier and faster to move people and products, and that towns and cities would probably develop near railroad lines.)* Discuss with students that they will learn how the railroad influenced the development of the West and eventually succeeded in binding regions of the nation together. This, along with the advances of the Industrial Age, created an urban society in the United States. **OL**

Unit 6

Reshaping the Nation 1858–1914

The gramophone was an early player of musical recordings.

546

Activity: Why It Matters

Why Study Immigration and Its Effects on the Nation? Tell students what they can expect to learn in the upcoming unit. Explain that the late 1800s and early 1900s were a time of significant immigration of people into the United States. **Ask:** What changes might a person need to make when coming to the United States from a different country? *(Students might answer that immigrants would have to learn about U.S. customs and laws. They would experience different foods, and they would have to learn the English language and new ways of life.)* As they study the unit, have students write in their notebooks the reasons people wanted to come to this country and what effects the immigrants had on the nation and its society. **OL**

> "Once I moved about like the wind. Now I surrender to you and that is all."
>
> —Geronimo

Grand Opening of the Brooklyn Bridge, May 24, 1883

547

Connect to Past Learning

Reshaping the Nation In the previous unit, students learned about the social, economic, and political differences between the North and South and the effects of the resulting Civil War. In this unit, students will study changes that took place in the 1800s and early 1900s in the United States including the development of the Western frontier, the growth of industry and immigration, and the birth of an urban society.

More About the Image

Visual Literacy On May 24, 1883, New York City and Brooklyn celebrated the grand opening of the Brooklyn Bridge, which at the time, was the world's longest steel suspension bridge at more than 5,900 feet (1,798 m). The bridge officially opened at 2:00 P.M. and was dedicated by President Chester Arthur and Governor Grover Cleveland. More than 150,000 people paid one cent to cross the bridge on the first day. The festivities closed with an hour-long display of fireworks. On May 24, 1983, the bridge's 100th anniversary was celebrated with parades, a procession of tall ships, and fireworks. President Ronald Reagan traveled across the bridge along the same route that President Chester Arthur took in 1883.

Why Comparing and Contrasting Is Important

Comparing (looking for similarities among people, things, or ideas) and contrasting (looking for differences) helps students understand relationships. Being able to compare and contrast can help students make inferences and draw conclusions.

Learn It!

Draw a Venn diagram on the board. In it write "Youth in 1800s," "Similarities," and "Youth in 2000s."

Ask students to compare and contrast their generation with the youth of the past. Remind students that in a Venn diagram, unique characteristics are written under the appropriate category heading. Students might compare and contrast categories such as music, fashion, or entertainment. **OL**

Practice It!

Students should include the following within their Venn diagrams:

Streetcars: Pulled by horses

Similarities: Ran on tracks

Cable-cars: Powered by motors **OL**

Unit 6 Reading History

READING SKILL Comparing and Contrasting

Learn It! When you *compare* people, things, or ideas, you look for similarities among them. When you *contrast,* you look for differences.

Central Pacific
Hired Chinese laborers

Similarities
Both companies were working to build the transcontinental railroad. Workers labored for low wages in harsh conditions.

Union Pacific
Hired Irish and African American workers

—from Chapter 18, p. 556

Two companies accepted the challenge to build the [transcontinental] railroad. . . .The Central Pacific hired about 10,000 Chinese laborers to work on its tracks. The first Chinese were hired in 1865 at about $28 per month. The Union Pacific relied on Irish and African American workers. All workers toiled for low wages in harsh conditions.

Practice It! Read the paragraph. Then on another sheet of paper, draw a Venn diagram and compare and contrast forms of public transportation in the late 1800s.

—from Chapter 20, p. 625

As cities grew, people needed new means of transportation. Streetcars, which horses pulled on tracks, provided public transportation at the time. In 1873 San Francisco began construction of cable-car lines. A large underground cable powered by a motor at one end of the rail line moved passengers along.

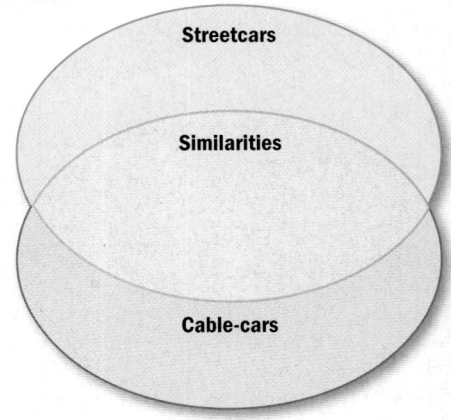

Streetcars

Similarities

Cable-cars

Reading Strategy **Organizing Information**

Comparing and Contrasting Explain to students that another way to see similarities and differences easily is to organize them in a comparison frame. A comparison frame is a chart with a column for each of the subjects that are being compared and a row for each of the areas of comparison. For example, if you are comparing an orange and a carrot, "Orange" and "Carrot" would be the column headings, and "Color" and "Shape" could be two of the row labels. Important facts about each of the areas of comparison should be listed in the boxes under each of the column headings. Have students create a comparison frame to compare and contrast two presidents in this unit. **ELL**

Academic Vocabulary Preview

Listed below are the academic vocabulary words and their definitions that you will come across as you study Unit 6. The activities in the Practice It! column will help you study the words and definitions.

Academic Vocabulary	Definition	Practice It!
Chapter 18 Opening the West		
sum (SUHM) *p. 553*	amount; total	**Identify** *the term from Chapter 18 that best completes each sentence.*
extract (ehk · STRAKT) *p. 553*	to remove, usually by force	**1.** Mining companies use machinery to _____ ore from the land.
locate (LOH · kayt) *p. 561*	to establish; settle	**2.** At one time, the United States had a gold-based _____ , instead of metal coins and paper notes.
factor (FAK · tuhr) *p. 563*	contributing circumstance	
ensure (ihn · SHUR) *p. 567*	make certain	**3.** Some prospectors made large _____(s) of money during the California Gold Rush.
widespread (WYD · SPREHD) *p. 569*	far-reaching	
create (kree · AYT) *p. 575*	to form; to make	
currency (KUHR · uhnt · see) *p. 577*	metal coins and paper notes used as money	
Chapter 19 The Industrial Age		
labor (LAY · buhr) *p. 585*	to work	**Identify** *the term from Chapter 19 that best matches the underlined word or phrase.*
individual (IHN · duh · VIHJ · wuhl) *p. 585*	person	
transmit (trants · MIHT) *p. 589*	send from one place to another	**4.** The telegraph was used to <u>send</u> messages in Morse code.
mechanism (MEH · kuh · NIH · zuhm) *p. 592*	mechanical device	**5.** In the early 1900s, labor unions helped create safer <u>working conditions</u> in urban factories.
partner (PAHRT · nuhr) *p. 597*	associate who agrees to operate a business with another	**6.** African American inventors developed much-needed <u>mechanical devices</u> for consumers and industry.
trend (TREHND) *p. 599*	general direction or movement	
identify (eye · DEHN · tuh · FY) *p. 604*	recognize	
environment (ihn · VY · ruhn · muhnt) *p. 605*	the conditions of a location	
Chapter 20 An Urban Society		
attitude (A · tuh · TOOD) *p. 617*	way of thinking and acting	**Choose** *the word that best matches the meaning of each vocabulary term listed below.*
affect (uh · FEHKT) *p. 617*	to have an impact on	

major (MAY · juhr) *p. 621*	greater in size, extent, or importance	**7. major** **9. minor**
		   a. greater **a.** equal
		   b. lower **b.** lesser
		   c. wiser **c.** greater

minor (MY · nuhr) *p. 623*	lesser in size, extent, or importance	

philosophy (fuh · LAH · suh · fee) *p. 627*	a set of ideas and beliefs	**8. philosophy** **10. isolate**
		   a. education **a.** gather
		   b. beliefs **b.** control
		   c. government **c.** separate

isolate (EYE · suh · LAYT) *p. 628*	cut off; separate	

Reshaping the Nation **Unit 6** **549**

Academic Vocabulary Preview

Distribute a bingo sheet to each student in the class. As you call out the letters/numbers, also say one of the vocabulary definitions. Students who have that square on their cards should write the correct vocabulary term in or beside the square.

When a student gets bingo, check his or her sheet to ensure that the correct vocabulary terms are written. If the answers are correct, award that student a special privilege. If several terms are still left, continue the game until one or two more winners are awarded. **OL**

Practice It!

Answers
1. extract
2. currency
3. sums
4. transmit
5. environments
6. mechanisms
7. a
8. b
9. b
10. c

Reading Strategy   Read to Write

Organizing an Essay In a compare and contrast essay, students can use two paragraphs to explain the similarities and differences between two items. Have students choose two groups who traveled west to compare and contrast. They will compare and contrast each group's reasons for moving to the frontier. For their first paragraph, tell students to explain how the groups are similar. In the next paragraph, have them identify their differences. Be sure that students use words such as "like" or "both" when discussing the groups' similarities and "in contrast" or "unlike" when addressing their differences. **BL**

Chapter Planning Guide

18

Levels					Resources	Chapter Opener	Section 1	Section 2	Section 3	Section 4	Chapter Assess
BL	OL	AL	ELL								
					FOCUS						
BL	OL	AL	ELL	🖨	Daily Test Practice Transparencies		18–1	18–2	18–3	18–4	
					TEACH						
	OL	AL		📁	Geography and History Activity, URB			p. 31			
BL	OL		ELL	📁	Time Line Skills Activity, URB					p. 34	
BL	OL	AL	ELL	📁	Writing Skills Activity, URB		p. 23				
BL	OL	AL	ELL	📁	Content Vocabulary Activity, URB		p. 17	p. 17	p. 17	p. 17	
BL	OL	AL	ELL	📁	Academic Vocabulary Activity, URB		p. 19	p. 19	p. 19	p. 19	
BL			ELL	📁	Reading Skills Activity, URB		p. 7				
	OL	AL		📁	Citizenship and Decision-Making Skills Activity, URB				p. 3		
BL	OL		ELL	📁	Social Studies Skills Activity, URB				p. 25		
BL	OL	AL	ELL	📁	Differentiated Instruction Activity, URB			p. 27			
BL	OL	AL	ELL	📁	Critical Thinking Skills Activity, URB				p. 29		
BL	OL	AL	ELL	📁	Linking Past and Present Activity, URB			p. 33			
	OL	AL		📁	Primary Source Readings, URB				p. 21		
BL	OL	AL	ELL	📁	School-to-Home Connection Activity, URB		p. 35	p. 35	p. 35	p. 35	
BL	OL		ELL	📁	Guided Reading Activity, URB*		p. 39	p. 40	p. 41	p. 42	
	OL	AL		📁	Economics and History Activity, URB		p. 5				
BL	OL		ELL	📁	Reading Essentials and Note-Taking Guide*		p. 190	p. 193	p. 196	p. 199	
BL	OL	AL	ELL	🖨	Lesson Transparencies		18A	18B, 18C	18C		
	OL	AL		📁	Interpreting Political Cartoons, URB				p. 13		
	OL			📁	American Biographies				pp. 30, 31		
BL	OL	AL	ELL	📁	Outline Map Resource Book	pp. 12, 13					
	OL	AL		🖨	American Art and Architecture Transparencies, Strategies, and Activities		16		17		

Note: Please refer to the *Unit Resource Book: Reshaping the Nation* for this chapter's URB materials.

*Also available in Spanish

Levels					Resources	Chapter Opener	Section 1	Section 2	Section 3	Section 4	Chapter Assess
BL	OL	AL	ELL								
TEACH *(continued)*											
BL	OL	AL	ELL	📁	**NGS US Desk Map**		✓	✓	✓	✓	
BL	OL	AL	ELL	📁	**American Literature Library**		✓	✓	✓	✓	
BL	OL	AL	ELL	📁	**Writer's Guidebook**		✓	✓	✓	✓	
	OL	AL		💿	**American History Primary Source Document Library CD-ROM**		✓	✓	✓	✓	✓
BL	OL	AL	ELL	💿	**American Music: Hits Through History**	✓	✓	✓	✓	✓	
BL	OL	AL	ELL	💿	**StudentWorks™ Plus CD**	✓	✓	✓	✓	✓	✓
BL	OL	AL	ELL	🔒	**Section Spotlight Videos**		✓	✓	✓	✓	
BL	OL	AL	ELL	🖐	**Writing Process Transparencies**		✓	✓	✓	✓	✓
BL	OL	AL	ELL	💿	**Presentation Plus! With MindJogger CheckPoint CD**	✓	✓	✓	✓	✓	✓
ASSESS											
BL	OL	AL	ELL	📁	**Quizzes and Tests**		p. 173	p. 174	p. 175	p. 176	pp. 177, 179, 181
BL	OL	AL	ELL	📁	**Authentic Assessment With Rubrics**			p. 18			
BL	OL	AL	ELL	📁	**Standardized Test Practice**						p. 35
BL	OL	AL	ELL	💿	*ExamView® Assessment Suite* CD-ROM*		18–1	18–2	18–3	18–4	Ch. 18
CLOSE											
BL			ELL	📁	**Reteaching Activity, URB***		p. 37	p. 37	p. 37	p. 37	p. 37
BL	OL		ELL	📁	**Reading and Study Skills Foldables Activity**	p. 84	p. 84	p. 84	p. 84	p. 84	p. 84
BL	OL	AL	ELL	📁	*The American Journey* in Graphic Novel						p. 99
BL			ELL	📁	**Reading Strategies and Activities for the Social Studies Classroom**		✓	✓	✓	✓	
BL	OL	AL	ELL	🖐	**Graphic Organizer Transparencies & Strategies**		✓	✓	✓	✓	

TeacherWorks *Plus*
All-In-One Planner and Resource Center

- Interactive Lesson Planner
- Interactive Teacher Edition
- Fully editable blackline masters
- Section Spotlight Videos Launch

- Differentiated Lesson Plans
- Printable reports of daily assignments
- Standards Tracking System

Professional Development Resources

- Strategies for Success
- Building Academic Vocabulary
- Success With English Learners DVD
- Differentiated Instruction Strategies DVD
- Teaching Literacy Strategies in Social Studies DVD
- Assessment DVD
- Standards-Based Instruction DVD

Using TechCONNECT™

Using Word Processing

Objective
Students will create word processing documents.

Technology
- Glencoe TechCONNECT™ is an online program. (For more information or to get a free 30-day trial of Glencoe TechCONNECT™ for your classroom, visit techconnect.glencoe.com and click the **Free Trial** button.)

Focus/Teach
- Log on to TechCONNECT™ and click the **Find your textbook** link. After you log on, click **Activity Search**. Choose **Social Studies, Word Processing**, and your grade level.

- Have students log on and enter the letters AC and the three-digit activity number.
- Have students follow the on-screen instructions.

Assess
- Have students complete the self-assessment rubric.
- Students may also complete the activity's TechCheck, a five-question, multiple-choice quiz.

Close
- Review this activity with the class.
- Have students who are in need of remediation repeat the activity.

History ONLINE at glencoe.com

	Student	Teacher	Parent
Media Center			
• Student Edition Audio	●		
• Spanish Summaries	●		
• Section Spotlight Videos	●	●	
Social Studies Online Learning Center			
Classroom Tools			
• Multi-Language Glossaries	●	●	●
• Teaching Today		●	
• TIME Current Events	●	●	●
• Beyond the Textbook	●	●	
***The American Journey* Online Learning Center**			
• Study-to-Go™	●	●	●
• Study Central™	●	●	●
• Chapter Overview	●	●	
• Concepts in Motion	●	●	
• ePuzzles and Games	●	●	
• Literature Connections	●	●	
• Online Student Edition	●	●	●
• Self-Check Quizzes	●	●	●
• Student Web Activities	●	●	
• Vocabulary eFlashcards	●	●	
• Web Activity Lesson Plans	●	●	●
• Vocabulary PuzzleMaker	●	●	●

READING SUPPORT FROM JAMESTOWN EDUCATION

- **Timed Readings Plus in Social Studies** helps students increase their reading rate and fluency while maintaining comprehension. The 400-word passages are similar to those found on state and national assessments.

- **Reading in the Content Area: Social Studies** concentrates on six essential reading skills that help students better comprehend what they read. The book includes 75 high-interest nonfiction passages written at increasing levels of difficulty.

- **Reading Social Studies** includes strategic reading instruction and vocabulary support in Social Studies content for ELLs and native speakers of English.

- **Content Vocabulary Workout** (Grades 6–8) accelerates reading comprehension through focused vocabulary development. Social Studies content vocabulary comes from the glossaries of Glencoe's Middle School Social Studies texts.

www.jamestowneducation.com

NATIONAL GEOGRAPHIC
Index to National Geographic Magazine:

The following articles relate to this chapter:

- **"Change of Heartland: The Great Plains,"** John G. Mitchell, May 2004.

- **"The Big Open,"** John G. Mitchell, August 2001.

National Geographic Society Products

To order the following, call National Geographic at 1-800-368-2728:

National Geographic Atlas of the World *(Book)*

Access National Geographic's dynamic MapMachine Web site and other geography resources at:

www.nationalgeographic.com

www.nationalgeographic.com/mapmachine

Reading List Generator CD-ROM — GLENCOE BOOKLINK 3

Use this database to search more than 30,000 titles to create a customized reading list for your students.

- Reading lists can be organized by students' reading level, author, genre, theme, or area of interest.
- The database provides Degrees of Reading Power™ (DRP) and Lexile™ readability scores for all selections.
- A brief summary of each selection is included.

Leveled reading suggestions for this chapter:

For students at a Grade 6 reading level:
- *On the Banks of Plum Creek,* by Laura Ingalls Wilder
- *Away to the Goldfields!* by Pat Derby

For students at a Grade 7 reading level:
- *Sing Down the Moon,* by Scott O'Dell
- *Soldier Boy,* by Brian Burks

For students at a Grade 8 reading level:
- *Sitting Bull and the Battle of the Little Bighorn,* by Sheila Black
- *Snow Mountain Passage,* by James D. Houston

For students at a Grade 9 reading level:
- *Born to Be a Cowgirl: A Spirited Ride Through the Old West,* by Candace Savage
- *Laura Ingalls Wilder: A Biography,* by William Anderson

For students at a Grade 10 reading level:
- *Voices From the West: Life Along the Trail,* by Katharine Emsden
- *Wounded Knee: An Indian History of the American West,* by Dee Brown

The following videotape programs are available from Glencoe as supplements to the chapter:

- **The Best of the Real West** (ISBN 1-56-501352-2)
- **Sitting Bull: Chief of the Lakota Nation** (ISBN 1-56-501684-X)

To order, call Glencoe at 1-800-334-7344. To find classroom resources to accompany many of these videos, check the following home pages:

A&E Television: www.aetv.com

The History Channel: www.history.com

Chapter Objectives

After studying this chapter, students will be able to:

- Discuss the causes and effects of mining booms in the West.
- Explain how cattle ranchers and farmers adapted to life in the West.
- Trace the effects of westward expansion on Native Americans.
- Explain why economic reform movements developed in the late 1800s.

Motivating Activity

Questioning Students will learn about the Western frontier in this chapter. Ask students if they have ever seen a "Western." **Ask:** What is a typical plot of a "Western"? *(Cowboys often fight Native Americans, outlaws, or corrupt officials.)* Do you think Westerns realistically portray life on the frontier? *(Answers will vary, but students may recognize that while Westerns contain some realistic aspects, other aspects are greatly exaggerated.)* Why do you think Westerns portray life in the West as they do? *(for entertainment purposes)* **OL**

Chapter 18
Opening the West 1858–1896

Railroad companies hired buffalo hunters to provide their workers with fresh meat.

▲ Ruins after Chicago Fire

PRESIDENTS

| JAMES BUCHANAN 1857–1861 | ABRAHAM LINCOLN 1861–1865 | ANDREW JOHNSON 1865–1869 | ULYSSES S. GRANT 1869–1877 | | RUTHERFORD B. HAYES 1877–1881 | JAMES GARFIELD 1881 |

★ 1871 Great Chicago Fire destroys most of city

U.S. Events
World Events

1860 — 1870 — 1880

★ 1861 Italians establish a united kingdom

★ 1869 Suez Canal opens

1871 ★ Stanley and Livingstone meet in Africa

★ 1878 Russo-Turkish War ends

550 Chapter 18

Previewing the Essential Questions

As you begin teaching each section, use these questions and activities to help students focus on the Essential Questions.

Section 1

The Mining Booms Ask: What do you think happened when gold and silver were discovered in the mountains of the West? *(Many people rushed there, hoping to get rich.)* Point out to students that in Section 1 they will learn about the results of the mining booms, including boomtowns and expansion of the nation's railroads. **OL**

Section 2

Ranchers and Farmers Ask: Besides mining, how did people make a living on the Western frontier? *(farming and ranching)* Tell students that Section 2 discusses the lifestyles of cowhands, the effects of railroads, and new methods of farming that developed in the Great Plains. **OL**

Section 1: The Mining Booms
Essential Question What were the causes and effects of mining booms in the West?

Section 2: Ranchers and Farmers
Essential Question How did cattle ranchers and farmers adapt to life in the West?

Section 3: Native American Struggles
Essential Question How did westward expansion affect Native Americans?

Section 4: Farmers in Protest
Essential Question Why did economic reform movements develop in the late 1800s?

Apache leader Geronimo ▶

FOLDABLES®
Study Organizer

Organizing Information Make this Foldable to help organize what you learn about the opening of the West in the late 1800s.

Step 1 Fold an 11" x 17" piece of paper lengthwise to create 4 equal sections.

Step 2 Label your Foldable as shown.

The Mining Booms | Ranchers & Farmers | Native American Struggles | Farmers in Protest

Reading and Writing As you read the chapter, use the Foldable to take notes on each section. Be sure to write down important people, dates, and events.

History ONLINE
Chapter Overview Visit glencoe.com and click on **Chapter 18—Chapter Overviews** to preview chapter information.

Time line

★ **1882** Congress limits immigration with Chinese Exclusion Act

CHESTER ARTHUR 1881–1885

★ **1886**
• Geronimo surrenders to U.S. military
• U.S. accepts Statue of Liberty from France

GROVER CLEVELAND 1885–1889

★ **1892**
• Populist Party forms
• Sierra Club organizes in San Francisco

BENJAMIN HARRISON 1889–1893

GROVER CLEVELAND 1893–1897

1890   **1900**

★ **1882** Triple Alliance forms among Germany, Austria, Italy

★ **1885** European powers divide Africa

★ **1891** Construction of Trans-Siberian railroad begins

★ **1896** First modern Olympics held in Athens

Chapter 18   551

Introducing Chapter 18

Time Line Activity

If you have not already done so, have students review the time line. **Ask:** What years are covered in this chapter? *(1860–1900)* Do the U.S. Events on the time line deal with urban or rural concerns, or both? Explain. *(Both. Time line mentions Chicago fire and Statue of Liberty in New York. It also mentions the surrender of Geronimo and creation of the Sierra Club in the West.)*

FOLDABLES
Study Organizer
Dinah Zike's Foldables

Purpose This Foldable helps students organize information about the opening of the West in the late 1800s. The completed Foldable will help them prepare for assessment.

📁 More Foldables activities for this chapter can be found in *Dinah Zike's Reading and Study Skills Foldables.*

History ONLINE
Introduce students to chapter content and key terms by having them access the **Chapter Overview** at glencoe.com.

Section 3

Native American Struggles Ask: How would you respond if the government took your home and the land it was built on and forced you to live in a less desirable location? *(Students may respond that they would be angry or fight to get their land back.)* Tell students that Section 3 will explore the ways in which Native Americans resisted white settlement in the West. **OL**

Section 4

Farmers in Protest Ask: What might farmers do if their crops fail or if prices for their crops fall drastically? *(quit farming and sell their farms; go into debt)* Tell students that they will learn in Section 4 why and how farmers in the late 1800s protested the economic hardships they suffered. **OL**

551

Focus

Section 1

The Mining Booms

Bellringer
Daily Test Practice Transparency 18–1

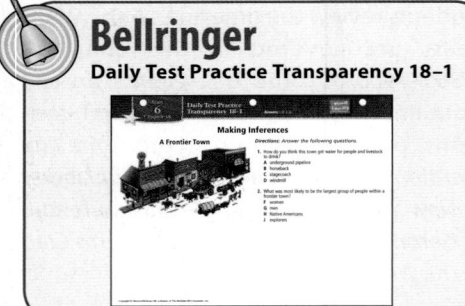

Essential Question
What were the causes and effects of mining booms in the West?

Reading Guide

Content Vocabulary
vigilante (p. 553)
subsidy (p. 555)
transcontinental (p. 555)
time zone (p. 557)

Academic Vocabulary
sum (p. 553)   extract (p. 553)

Key People and Events
Comstock Lode (p. 553)
Leland Stanford (p. 556)

Reading Strategy
Taking Notes As you read, identify the effects of the mining booms.

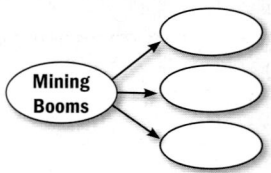

Reading Guide
Answers to Graphic:

Towns sprang up overnight; Western areas became populated and eventually became states; railroads connected East and West; a new wave of settlers went west.

Section Spotlight Video

Have students watch the Section Spotlight Video "The Mining Booms" to learn more about Chinese laborers and the transcontinental railroad.

ILLINOIS STANDARDS
The American Journey

15.B.3a Describe the "market clearing price" of a good or service.

16.D.3a (US) Describe characteristics of different kinds of communities in various sections of America during the colonial/frontier periods and the 19th century.

17.C.3a Explain how human activity is affected by geographic factors.

American Diary

In 1859 a Kansas newspaper article tried to inspire people to travel to Pikes Peak in Colorado where gold had been discovered: "Hurra for Pike's Peak! Hurra for Pike's Peak! / There's gold in the Mount'n, there's gold in the vale, / There's plenty for all who are willing to seek / Believe me; believe me—'tis no idle tale. / Come, hurra for Pike's Peak!" Stories about the discoveries of gold and silver lured thousands of fortune seekers west."

—from "A Call to the Mines"

People traveled west to Colorado in search of gold and silver.

Resource Manager

R Reading Strategies	**C** Critical Thinking	**D** Differentiated Instruction	**W** Writing Support	**S** Skill Practice
Teacher Edition • Reading Graphs, p. 554 **Additional Resources** • Guid. Read., URB p. 39 • Content Vocab., URB p. 17 • Academic Vocab., URB p. 19 • Read. Ess., p. 190 • Read. Skills, URB p. 7	**Teacher Edition** • Deter. Cause & Effect, p. 553 • Drawing Conclusions, p. 555 • Analyz. Pri. Sources, p. 556 **Additional Resources** • Quizzes and Tests, p. 173	**Teacher Edition** • Visual/Spatial, p. 553 • Logical/Mathematical, p. 555 **Additional Resources** • School-to-Home, URB p. 35 • Reteaching Act., URB p. 37	**Teacher Edition** • Persuasive Writing, p. 555 • Expository Writing, p. 556 **Additional Resources** • Writ. Skills, URB p. 23	**Teacher Edition** • Using Geo. Skills, p. 554 • Using Context Skills, p. 557 **Additional Resources** • Daily Test Pract. Transp. 18-1 • Lesson Transp. 18A • Econ. & Hist., URB p. 5

Gold, Silver, and Boomtowns

Main Idea Miners found gold in the West, leading to the creation of new states.

History and You What opportunities today might tempt your family to move to a new state? Read to learn how the discovery of gold encouraged people to move West.

By the mid-1850s, the California Gold Rush had ended. Disappointed miners, still hoping to strike it rich, began prospecting in other parts of the West.

In 1858 gold was found at Pikes Peak in the Colorado Rockies. Newspapers claimed that miners were making $20 a day panning for gold—a large **sum,** or amount of money, at a time when servants earned less than a dollar a day. By the spring of 1859, about 50,000 prospectors had flocked to the goldfields of Colorado.

Prospectors skimmed gold dust from streams or scratched gold particles from the land. Most of the gold, however, was deep in underground lodes, which are rich streaks of ore running between rock layers. Mining this ore and then **extracting,** or removing, the gold particles required machinery, workers, and

an organized business. Companies stood a better chance of getting rich from mining for gold than did individuals.

Boom and Bust

In 1859 several prospectors found one of the world's richest deposits of silver-bearing ore near Nevada's Carson River. The discovery was called the **Comstock Lode** after Henry Comstock, who owned a share of the claim. Thousands of mines opened near the site, but only a few were profitable.

Gold strikes created boomtowns—towns that developed almost overnight around mining sites. The Comstock boomtown was Virginia City, Nevada. Boomtowns were lively, and often lawless, places. Money came quickly—and was often lost just as quickly through spending and gambling. Violence was also part of life in boomtowns, where many people carried guns and a lot of cash. Few boomtowns had police or prisons, so ordinary people known as **vigilantes** sometimes acted to punish criminals.

Men mostly lived in boomtowns, but some women opened businesses or worked as laundresses, cooks, or entertainers. Women often founded schools and churches.

By the Numbers / Life of a Mining Boomtown

A Boomtown's Population Virginia City, Nevada, became one of the largest cities in the West after gold was discovered in the region. Once all of the gold was extracted from the ground, however, Virginia City's population declined.

Population of Virginia City, Nevada

(Population axis: 0 to 30,000; Year axis: 1860, 1870*, 1880, 1890, 1900, 1910, 1920)

*Estimate according to various Nevada historical sources

Source: Nevada State Library and Archives, 2007.

Critical Thinking
Summarizing Describe the changes in population in Virginia City, Nevada, from 1860 to 1920.

CHAPTER 18
Section 1

Teach

C Critical Thinking

Determining Cause and Effect
Ask: Why did individuals rarely get rich from prospecting gold in the Colorado Rockies? *(because most gold was in underground lodes and required machinery and workers to be extracted)* **OL**

D Differentiated Instruction

Visual/Spatial Have students create Venn diagrams comparing and contrasting the lives and activities of men and women in boomtowns. **OL**

By the Numbers

Critical Thinking Answer The population rose sharply between 1860 and 1870 to a high of 30,000 people. It then started a steep decline. By 1900, the town had few residents.

Skills Practice Ask: What do you think happened between 1870 and 1880? *(Most of the precious metals were extracted from the ground.)* **OL**

Differentiated Instruction

Leveled Activities

BL Reading Skills Activity, URB p. 7

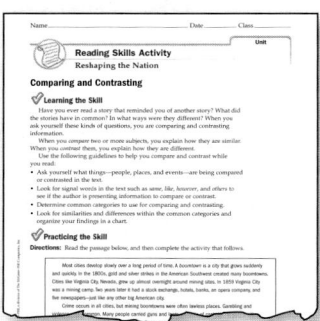

OL Economics and History Activity, URB p. 5

ELL Academic Vocabulary Activity, URB p. 19

R Reading Strategy

Reading Graphs Have students look at the graph tracing the population of Virginia City, Nevada, on the previous page. **Ask:** In what year did the population of Virginia City peak? *(1870)* Was Virginia City a ghost town in 1920? Explain. *(No; the population had not totally disappeared.)* **OL**

S Skill Practice

Using Geography Skills Group students into pairs and refer them to the map on this page. Have them take turns, one student naming a town while the other student names what precious metal was nearby. **BL**

Mining and the West, 1848–1890 NATIONAL GEOGRAPHIC

Map Skills Answer
Black Hills—gold; Tombstone—silver

✔ **Reading Check** **Answer:** because when the ore was gone, people left the towns

Differentiated Instruction

Mining and the West, 1848–1890 NATIONAL GEOGRAPHIC

Gold, Silver, and Growth The expansion of mining led to growth in population and the addition of new states.

In the mining boomtowns, real estate, rent, and prices soared. Here, miners exchange gold dust for bank notes. ▶

"[Denver's] prosperity, of course, depends on the activity of mining operations in the mountains. There is at present a stagnation [economic slowdown]. . . . Wages are so high that many companies have been forced to suspend [temporarily stop] business."
—Bayard Taylor, from the *New York Tribune*, 1866

Map Skills
Location Which mineral was found in the Black Hills? In the area around Tombstone?
Maps in MOtion See StudentWorks™ Plus or glencoe.com.

R Despite the promise of prosperity, many mining "booms" were followed by "busts." When the ore was gone, people left, and the boomtowns became ghost towns.

The United States Expands West

S As the gold and silver disappeared, the mining of other metals, including copper, lead, and zinc, increased. As these mining areas developed and became more populated, they eventually became states. Colorado joined the United States in 1876. North Dakota, South Dakota, Washington, and Montana became states in 1889. Wyoming and Idaho were admitted to the Union in 1890.

✔ **Reading Check** **Explaining** Why did many boomtowns turn into ghost towns?

Railroads Connect East and West

Main Idea Railroads transported gold and silver to market and brought supplies to the miners.

History and You What type of transportation would you take if you had to travel from the East Coast to the West Coast? Read to learn how people and goods were transported in the mid-1800s.

The western mines operated far from the industrial centers of the East and Midwest. For this reason, transportation played a vital role in the survival of mining communities. Gold and silver had little value unless they could reach factories, ports, and markets.

554 **Chapter 18** *Opening the West*

Engaging Readers' Interest: Writing a Strong Lead

Objective:	To learn how to write a strong lead
Focus:	Ask students what draws their interest when they first read a story or an article.
Teach:	Ask students to read the background material, answer the questions, and then apply the skill.
Assess:	Have students use the self-assessment checklist.
Close:	Review with students why their leads were or were not effective.

Differentiated Instruction Strategies

BL Ask students to explain what type of lead most often catches their interest.

AL Have students find examples of several different styles of writing, then identify the leads in the writing and comment on their effectiveness.

ELL Ask students to explain in their own words what a *lead* is.

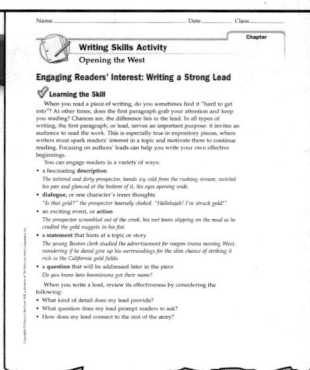

Writing Skills Activity, URB p. 23

At the same time, people living in the boom-towns needed shipments of food and other supplies.

Wagons and stagecoaches could not move people and goods fast enough to meet these demands, but railroads did. The nation's railroad network expanded rapidly between 1865 and 1890. During that time, the length of track in the United States soared from about 35,000 miles (56,327 km) to more than 150,000 miles (241,402 km).

Government and the Railroads

Railroad construction was often supported by large government **subsidies**—financial aid and land grants from the government. Railroad executives made the argument that their companies should receive free public land on which to lay track because a rail network connecting East and West would bring important benefits to the entire nation.

The national government and states agreed. In all, the federal government granted more than 130 million acres (52,609,180 ha) of land to the railroad companies. Much of the land was purchased or obtained by treaties from Native Americans. The government grants included the land for the tracks plus strips of land along the railway, 20 to 80 miles (32 to 129 km) wide. Railroad companies sold those strips of land to raise additional money.

States and local communities also helped the railroads. Towns offered cash subsidies to make sure that the railroads were constructed near their communities. For example, Los Angeles gave the Southern Pacific Railroad money and paid for a passenger terminal to ensure that the railroad would be built near the town.

Spanning the Continent

The search for a route for a **transcontinental** rail line—one that would span the continent and connect the Atlantic and Pacific coasts—began in the 1850s. Southerners wanted the route to run through the South, and Northerners wanted it to pass through the North. During the Civil War, the Union government chose a northerly route. The government offered land grants to railroad companies willing to build the transcontinental line.

The challenge was enormous—laying track for more than 1,700 miles (2,736 km) across hot plains and through rugged mountains.

D Differentiated Instruction

Logical/Mathematical Ask: The number of miles of railroad track increased by about what percentage between 1865 and 1890? *(by more than 400%)* What was the average length of track laid per year during that period? *(4,600 miles [7,401 km])* **OL**

W Writing Support

Persuasive Writing Ask: Do you think that government support of private railroad building was justified? Write an editorial in support of your position. **AL**

C Critical Thinking

Drawing Conclusions Ask: How did the Civil War affect transportation in the nation? *(During the war, the Union government decided on a northerly route for the transcontinental railroad.)* **OL**

The Steam Locomotive

Critical Thinking Answer

Possible answer: They were faster, more reliable, and did not depend on animals for power.

The Steam Locomotive

The railroads that were so important to the growth of the West were dependent upon the technology of the steam locomotive.

1 The **firebox** burns coal, wood, or sometimes oil.

2 Water in the **boiler**, heated by gases from the firebox, creates steam.

3 The **smoke box** draws hot gases from the firebox and keeps an even fire burning.

4 In the **steam header tank**, the heated steam expands and creates great pressure.

5 Hot steam is piped to the **pistons**. The pistons power the **drive rods**, which in turn push the **drive wheels**.

Critical Thinking

Making Inferences What advantages did steam locomotives have over other forms of transportation available in the mid-1800s?

Hands-On Chapter Project
Step 1

Creating an Atlas

Step 1: Mapping Boomtowns and Railroads Small groups of students will create maps showing the locations of boomtowns and railroads in the West.

Essential Question: What were the causes and effects of mining booms in the West?

Directions Organize students into several small groups. Provide each group with two outline maps of the United States, or have groups trace maps using the atlas in this textbook. Students should mark state and territory boundaries, using the "Mining and the West, 1848–1890" map in this section as a guide. On one map, have students mark boomtowns and locations of precious metals. Each group should research to find at least three other boomtowns to include on this map. On the second map, have students mark the route of the transcontinental railroad. Direct students to research to find the routes of other railroads built before 1890. Students should mark the route of each railroad, its name, and the date it was opened.

Drawing Conclusions Have students compare their two maps. **Ask:** Is there any relationship between railroad routes and the locations of boomtowns? Tell students they will investigate the geography of the West further in the next step. **OL**

(Chapter Project continued in Section 2)

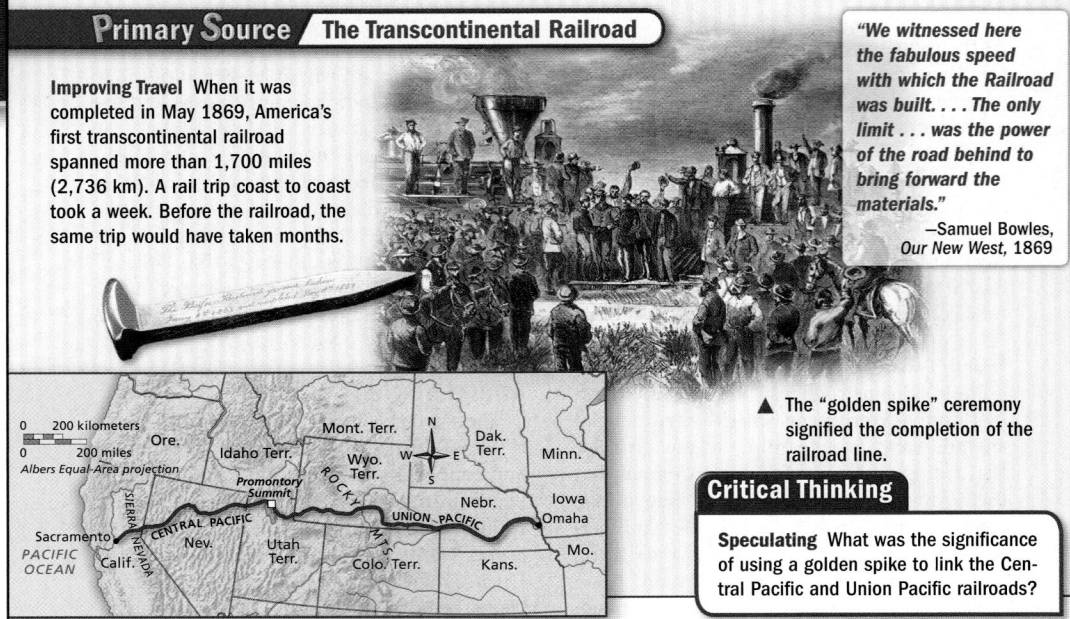

Primary Source — The Transcontinental Railroad

Improving Travel When it was completed in May 1869, America's first transcontinental railroad spanned more than 1,700 miles (2,736 km). A rail trip coast to coast took a week. Before the railroad, the same trip would have taken months.

"We witnessed here the fabulous speed with which the Railroad was built. . . . The only limit . . . was the power of the road behind to bring forward the materials."
—Samuel Bowles, *Our New West,* 1869

▲ The "golden spike" ceremony signified the completion of the railroad line.

Critical Thinking

Speculating What was the significance of using a golden spike to link the Central Pacific and Union Pacific railroads?

Two companies accepted the challenge to build the railroad. The Union Pacific Company began laying track westward from Omaha, Nebraska, while the Central Pacific Company worked eastward from the city of Sacramento, California.

The two companies competed furiously. Each wanted to cover a greater distance than the other in order to receive more of the government subsidies.

The Central Pacific hired about 10,000 Chinese laborers to work on its tracks. The first Chinese were hired in 1865 at about $28 per month. The Union Pacific relied on Irish and African American workers. All workers toiled for low wages in harsh conditions. In the choking heat of summer and the icy winds of winter, the workers cleared forests, blasted tunnels through mountains, and laid hundreds of miles of track across the vast center of the country. In the end, the Central Pacific workers, who covered a much harsher terrain, laid 742 miles (1,194 km) of track. The Union Pacific workers laid 1,038 miles (1,670 km) of track.

The Transcontinental Railway

On May 10, 1869, construction was completed. A Chinese crew was chosen to lay the final 10 miles (16 km) of track, which was completed in only 12 hours. The two sets of track met at Promontory Summit in Utah Territory. **Leland Stanford,** governor of California, drove a final golden spike into a tie to join the two railroads. Almost as the event occurred, telegraph lines flashed the news across the country: "The last rail is laid. . . . [T]he last spike driven. . . . The Pacific Railroad is completed."

Effects of the Railroads

By 1883, two more transcontinental lines and dozens of shorter lines connected cities in the West with the rest of the nation. The economic consequences were enormous. The railroads brought thousands of workers west. Trains carried metals and produce east and manufactured goods west. As more tracks were laid, more steel was needed, and the demand boosted the nation's steel industry.

Fast Facts

The Transcontinental Railroad When the transcontinental railway opened in 1869, it was not directly connected to the railroads of the East. Initially, train cars were ferried across the Missouri River. In 1872 a bridge opened that connected the railroads on each side of the river.

Although the transcontinental railway opened to much fanfare, traffic was light. Only one eastbound and one westbound train ran per week, which was more than adequate to meet the demand. Almost another 10 years would pass before demand was heavy enough to justify additional trains.

Coal producers, railroad car manufacturers, and construction companies also benefited from the expansion.

Numerous towns sprang up along the rail lines that carried the settlers' agricultural goods to market. Some of these towns eventually grew into large cities such as Denver, Colorado. Railroads also brought the next wave of settlers to the West—ranchers and farmers.

Railroads even changed how people measured time. Before the 1880s, each community kept its own time based on the sun's position at noon. Clocks in Boston, for example, were 11 minutes ahead of clocks in New York City. Having local time zones interfered with train scheduling, however, and at times even threatened passenger safety. When two trains were traveling on the same track, collisions could result from scheduling errors caused by differences in timekeeping.

To make rail service across the country safer and more reliable, the American Railway Association—an organization that included the nation's railroad companies—divided the country into four **time zones** in 1883. All of the communities located within a time zone would share the same time. Each zone was exactly one hour later than the zone to its west. Congress made the time zones official in 1918.

Meanwhile, new locomotive technology and the invention of air brakes enabled railroads to pull longer and heavier trains on their lines. When combined with large, well-organized railroad systems, operations became so efficient that the average cost per mile for a ton of freight dropped from two cents in 1860 to three-quarters of a cent in 1900.

The nationwide rail network also helped unite Americans in different regions. The *Omaha Daily Republican* newspaper in Nebraska observed in 1883 that railroads had "made the people of the country homogenous [alike], breaking the peculiarities and provincialisms [local ways] which marked separate and unmingling regions." This was a bit of an exaggeration, but it recognized that railroads were changing American society.

✓ Reading Check Determining Cause and Effect How did railroads affect the American economy in the middle to late 1800s?

Section 1 Review

History ONLINE
Study Central™ To review this section, go to glencoe.com.

Vocabulary

1. Use each of these terms in a sentence that will help explain its meaning: sum, extract, vigilante, subsidy, transcontinental, time zone.

Main Ideas

2. **Describing** What was life like in the boomtowns?

3. **Explaining** Why did the government provide subsidies to railroad companies?

Critical Thinking

4. **Evaluating** What are some problems that might be caused by allowing vigilantes to punish people for crimes? Record your ideas in a diagram like this one.

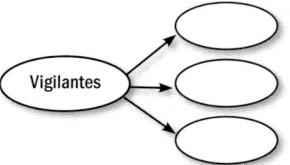

5. **Making Inferences** Why do you think the government chose a northern route for the transcontinental railroad?

6. **Descriptive Writing** From the point of view of a miner in a boomtown, write a letter to your family in Boston describing your new life and your reasons for moving west.

Answer the
7. **Essential Question** What were the causes and effects of mining booms in the West?

Opening the West **Chapter 18** 557

S Skill Practice
Using Context Skills Ask students to explain what time zones are and how and why they were created by the American Railway Association. Have students study a map that shows time zones in the U.S. (or across the globe) today. **ELL**

✓ Reading Check Answer: The railroads brought workers west. They also brought raw materials east and manufactured goods west. Industries involved in railroad building boomed, and towns sprang up along the rail lines, some eventually growing into large cities.

Assess
....
History ONLINE

Study Central™ provides summaries, interactive games, and online graphic organizers to help students review content.

Close
....
Analyzing As a class, discuss how mining and railroad building opened up the West. **OL**

Section ★ Review

Answers

1. Sentences should correctly use vocabulary words according to their definitions in the section and Glossary.
2. Life in boomtowns was lively and often lawless and violent. With no police or prisons, vigilantes punished criminals. Also, there were more men than women in the towns.
3. Building a transcontinental railroad was expensive, and the railroad companies argued that the government should help

pay for it because a railroad would bring benefits to the entire nation.
4. Answers will vary but may include the following: may not follow the law; might use inhumane punishment; might mistakenly punish innocent people.
5. The decision was made during the Civil War, when the South had seceded from the Union and the North hoped to gain the benefits created by the railroad.

6. Letters should include key details about boomtowns.
7. The discovery of various metals in the West led to the mining booms. Effects of the booms included creation of new states, construction of the transcontinental railroad, a new wave of settlers, and benefits to industry.

Focus

D Differentiated Instruction

English Language Learners Remind students that this selection is from a book entitled *Roughing It.* **Ask:** *Why do you think that Twain called his book that?* (because the journey out West was difficult) **ELL**

R Reading Strategy

Previewing Have students read the vocabulary words and their definitions. Ask them what types of images they think of when they read the words. Discuss what they think the story will be about based on the vocabulary. **OL**

W Writing Support

Descriptive Writing Tell students to read the first two paragraphs of the selection. Have students describe in their own words what Carson City looked like. Then have your students write about a trip they have taken. Students should describe the place using adjectives. **OL**

Additional Reading

Review suggested books before assigning them.

Meet the Author

Mark Twain (1835–1910) was born Samuel Longhorne Clemens in Missouri. He took his pen name from a phrase used by pilots on Mississippi riverboats. A legendary American writer, lecturer, and humorist, Twain published newspaper and magazine articles as well as novels and short stories. *Roughing It,* Twain's second major work, contains the imagery and humor that serve as hallmarks of Twain's writing.

Building Background

D *Roughing It* is the personal account of Mark Twain's travels to the Nevada Territory in 1861, when few Americans had first-hand knowledge about the West. The following excerpt is Twain's description of his arrival in Carson City. As you read the passage, think about Twain's choice of words and note the images that his words bring to mind.

Vocabulary

barren bare

alkali salt mixture

burthen burden

R serenity calmness

impertinent bothersome

intermeddling interfering

rebuke scold

rivulets streams

Miner, Nevada Territory, 1867 ▶

ROUGHING IT

Mark Twain

WE were approaching the end of our long journey. It was the morning of the twentieth day. At noon **W** we would reach Carson City, the capital of Nevada Territory. . . .

Visibly our new home was a desert, walled in by **barren,** snow-clad mountains. There was not a tree in sight. There was no vegetation but the endless sage-brush and greasewood. All nature was gray with it. We were plowing through great deeps of powdery **alkali** dust that rose in thick clouds and floated across the plain like smoke from a burning house. . . . Every twenty steps we passed the skeleton of some dead beast of **burthen,** with its dust-coated skin stretched tightly

558

Biography: *Geronimo: Wolf of the Warpath,* by Ralph Moody, explores the story of the most famous Apache. Geronimo was so skilled that he eluded the U.S. Army for 25 years.

Biography: *Full Steam Ahead: The Race to Build a Transcontinental Railroad,* by Rhoda Blumberg, reads like a tall tale about the real "great race" to build the first cross-country railroad. Photographs and maps help tell the story.

Fiction: *Rockbuster,* by Gloria Skurzynski and Michael Benny, follows 16-year-old Tommy Quinlan into the coal mines to support his mother and himself. After a man is unjustly convicted of murder, Tom must decide whether to do nothing or fight for justice.

For further reading, see **BOOKLINK 3**.

over its empty ribs. Frequently a solemn raven sat upon the skull or the hips and contemplated the passing coach with meditative **serenity**. . . .

We arrived, disembarked, and the stage went on. [Carson City] was a "wooden" town; its population two thousand souls. The main street consisted of four or five blocks of little white frame stores which were too high to sit down on, but not too high for various other purposes; in fact, hardly high enough. They were packed close together, side by side, as if room were scarce in that mighty plain. . . . **[C₁]**

We were introduced to several citizens, at the stage-office and on the way up to the Governor's from the hotel—among others, to a Mr. Harris, who was on horseback; he began to say something, but interrupted himself with the remark: **[C₂]**

"I'll have to get you to excuse me a minute; yonder is the witness that swore I helped to rob the California coach—a piece of **impertinent intermeddling**, sir, for I am not even acquainted with the man."

Then he rode over and began to **rebuke** the stranger with a six-shooter, and the stranger began to explain with another. When the pistols were emptied, the stranger resumed his work . . . and Mr. Harris rode by with a polite nod, homeward bound, with a bullet through one of his lungs, and several in his hips; and from them issued little **rivulets** of blood that coursed down the horse's sides. . . . This was all we saw that day, for it was two o'clock, now, and according to custom the

daily "Washoe Zephyr" set in; a soaring dust-drift about the size of the United States set up edgewise came with it, and the capital of Nevada Territory disappeared from view.

Every twenty steps we passed the skeleton of some dead beast of burthen, with its dust-coated skin stretched tightly over its empty ribs.

Still, there were sights to be seen which were not wholly uninteresting to new comers; for the vast dust cloud was thickly freckled with things strange to the upper air—things living and dead . . . appearing and disappearing among the rolling billows of dust—hats, chickens and parasols sailing in the remote heavens; blankets, tin signs, sage-brush and shingles a shade lower; door-mats and buffalo robes lower still; shovels and coal scuttles on the next grade; glass doors, cats and little children on the next; disrupted lumber yards, light buggies and wheelbarrows on the next; and down only thirty or forty feet above ground was a scurrying storm of emigrating roofs and vacant lots.

It was something to see that much. I could have seen more, if I could have kept the dust out of my eyes.

Analyzing Literature

1. **Respond** After reading the passage, how would you describe Carson City?

2. **Recall and Interpret** What occurred between Mr. Harris and the stranger? Why?

3. **Evaluate**
   (a) In Twain's description of the dust cloud, how did he create the image of movement?
   (b) In your opinion, is the description of the dust cloud meant to inform, entertain readers, or both? Explain your thinking.

559

Teach

C₁ Critical Thinking

Drawing Conclusions Remind students that Twain did not see trees in Carson City. Ask them where they think the wood came from. *(Possible answer: It was delivered by the railroad.)* **Ask:** Why were the buildings so small and close together? *(Possible answer: They were small because of the lack of wood and close together to share walls.)* **AL**

C₂ Critical Thinking

Analyzing Information Ask: Does Mr. Harris ever say that the witness lied? *(No, we don't know if Mr. Harris robbed the coach.)* Ask your students if they think he was guilty and explain why. *(Students may say that shooting at the witness inclines them to believe in Mr. Harris's guilt.)* **OL**

Assess/Close

As a class, discuss how exaggerations and understatements can make things funny. Ask students to find examples of exaggeration *("a soaring dust-drift about the size of the United States")* and understatement *("rebuke the stranger with a six-shooter")*, and discuss what Twain might have actually seen.

Answers

1. Possible answer: a dusty, rough town

2. A gunfight; Mr. Harris believed the stranger meddled in his business and accused him of robbery.

3. (a) He describes how it soared and hid the capital.
   (b) Students might say that it is to entertain, because the description of specific items in the cloud is humorous.

Focus

Ranchers and Farmers

Bellringer
Daily Test Practice Transparency 18–2

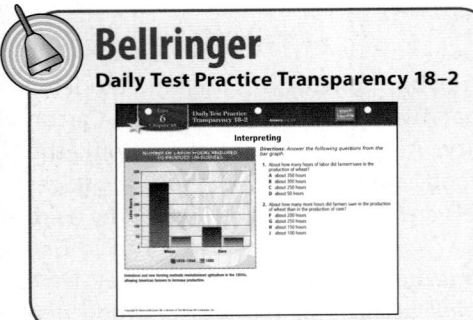

Reading Guide
Answers to Graphic:

Answers may include profit from cattle; railroads provided easy and cheap travel; Homestead Act; better farming methods; immigrants and African Americans sought freedom and independence.

Section Spotlight Video

Have students watch the Section Spotlight Video "Ranchers and Farmers" to learn more about the Oklahoma Land Rush.

Essential Question
How did cattle ranchers and farmers adapt to life in the West?

Reading Guide

Content Vocabulary

Long Drive *(p. 561)*   sodbuster *(p. 565)*
vaquero *(p. 562)*   dry farming *(p. 565)*
homestead *(p. 563)*

Academic Vocabulary

locate *(p. 561)*   factor *(p. 563)*

Key People and Events
Homestead Act *(p. 563)*

Reading Strategy
Taking Notes As you read, use a cause-and-effect diagram like the one below to identify reasons people settled on the Great Plains.

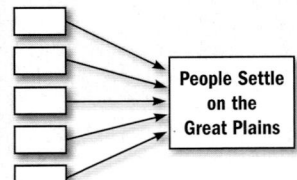

People Settle on the Great Plains

ILLINOIS STANDARDS
The American Journey

16.D.3b (US) Describe characteristics of different kinds of families in America during the colonial/frontier periods and the 19th century.

16.E.3b (US) Describe how the largely rural population of the United States adapted, used and changed the environment after 1818.

17.D.3a Explain how and why spatial patterns of settlement change over time.

American Diary

Texas cowhand E. C. Abbott recalled the early days of riding the trail: "Here [were] all these cheap long-horned steers overrunning Texas; here was the rest of the country crying for beef—and no railroads to get them out. So they trailed them out, across hundreds of miles of wild country that was thick with Indians. . . . In 1867 the town of Abilene was founded at the end of the Kansas Pacific railroad and that was when the trail really started."

—*from* We Pointed Them North

In his painting *Jerked Down*, western painter Charles Russell depicted cowhands lassoing cattle on the open range.

Resource Manager

R Reading Strategies	**C** Critical Thinking	**D** Differentiated Instruction	**W** Writing Support	**S** Skill Practice
Teacher Edition • Questioning, p. 561 • Taking Notes, p. 562 • Summarizing, p. 564 **Additional Resources** • Guid. Read., URB p. 40 • Content Vocab., URB p. 17 • Academic Vocab., URB p. 19 • Read. Ess., p. 193	**Teacher Edition** • Analyz. Pri. Sources, p. 563 • Comparing & Contrasting, p. 565 **Additional Resources** • Quizzes and Tests, p. 174 • Link. Past & Pres., URB p. 33 • Authentic Assess., p.18	**Teacher Edition** • Below Grade Level, p. 563 • Visual/Spatial, p. 564 **Additional Resources** • School-to-Home, URB p. 35 • Reteaching Act., URB p. 37 • Differ. Inst., URB p. 27	**Teacher Edition** • Descriptive Writing, p. 562 • Narrative Writing, p. 565 **Additional Resources** • Geo. & Hist., URB p. 31	**Teacher Edition** • Using Geo. Skills, p. 561 • Visual Literacy, p. 562 **Additional Resources** • Daily Test Pract. Transp. 18-2 • Lesson Transp. 18B, 18C

Cattle on the Plains

Main Idea Ranchers herded their cattle to railroad towns and shipped them to new markets in the North and East.

History and You Have you ever wondered whether the beef in your grocery store was raised in your state or another state? Read to learn how ranchers got their cattle to market.

When the Spanish settled Mexico and Texas, they brought a tough breed of cattle with them. Called longhorns because of their prominent horns, these cattle gradually spread across Texas.

Even though very large cattle ranches were found throughout the state, much of Texas was open range—which means it was not fenced or divided into lots. Cattle roamed free on the open range. Ranchers added to their own herds by rounding up wild cattle. The ranchers burned a brand, or symbol, into the animals' hides to show who owned the cattle.

Railroads and Cow Towns

Although Texas ranchers had plenty of cattle, the markets for beef were in the North and the East. By 1865, the Missouri Pacific Railroad reached Kansas City, Missouri, and the value of Texas cattle suddenly increased. Texas cattle could now be herded to Missouri and loaded onto trains for shipment to northern and eastern cities, where new markets for beef were expanding. Some Texans drove their combined herds—sometimes 260,000 head of cattle—north to Sedalia, Missouri, the nearest rail point. Longhorns that were worth $3 each quickly rose in value to $40.

The Long Drive

This increase in the longhorns' value set off what became known as the **Long Drive**—the herding of cattle 1,000 miles (1,609 km) or more to meet the railroads. Cattle drives left Texas in the spring, when there was enough grass along the way to feed the cattle. They traveled to cow towns—towns **located**, or established, near railroads. Some of the largest Long Drives led from central Texas to Abilene, Kansas, on the Chisholm Trail. From the late 1860s to the mid-1880s, more than 5 million cattle moved north on cattle drives.

✓ **Reading Check** Determining Cause and Effect
How did railroads increase the value of Texas cattle?

If You Were There / African American Cowboys

A New Life Following the Civil War, a large number of formerly enslaved persons moved to the West to work in the cattle industry. Many became cowhands, working the cattle trails that headed north from Texas. African American cowhands faced some of the same prejudices found in the South and the East. They could not stay in the same hotels or eat in the same restaurants as whites. Despite these differences, however, African American cowhands often received the same pay as white cowhands.

Critical Thinking

Inferring How do you think life was different for formerly enslaved persons who went west to work as cowhands?

Teach

R Reading Strategy

Questioning Ask: What do you think were the costs of cattle ranching in Texas? *(Answers may include hiring cowboys to round up wild cattle and drive them to market; branding; possibly buying additional cattle.)* **OL**

S Skill Practice

Using Geography Skills Direct students to the map on the following page. **Ask:** Through what present-day states did the Chisholm Trail pass? *(Texas, Oklahoma, Kansas)* What trail would Texas cowboys use to get cattle to the railroad station in Denver? *(the Goodnight-Loving Trail)* **OL**

If You Were There

Critical Thinking Answer Answers may indicate that formerly enslaved persons could now travel freely and were paid for their work.

✓ **Reading Check** **Answer:** Railroads made it easier to ship cattle to markets in the North and East. As a result, the value of the cattle increased.

Hands-On Chapter Project
Step 2

Creating an Atlas

Step 2: Mapping Cattle Trails Small groups of students will map cattle trails in the West.

Essential Question: How did cattle ranchers and farmers adapt to life in the West?

Directions Have students join their small groups. First, have them add the railroads shown on the "Cowhands and Cattle Drives" map (on the following page) to the map of railroads they created in Step 1. Next, have students make a new map of cattle trails. On another outline or traced map, have students mark states and territories as in Step 1. They should then mark the cattle trails shown in the "Cowhands and Cattle Drives" map. Have students research to find additional cattle trails to add to their maps.

Predicting Ask: How would you expect the locations of cattle trails to change over time? *(Trails would change as railroad lines extended or as new and better routes to railroad cities were established.)* **OL**

(Chapter Project continued in Section 3)

S Skill Practice

Visual Literacy Direct students to examine the images of cowhands in this section. Have them list several adjectives to describe the cowhands depicted in the images. **Ask:** Do the cowhands shown fit the stereotypes of the Wild West? Explain. *(Students may note that some images seem very standard, while the images of the African American cowhands may be less well known.)* **OL**

W Writing Support

Descriptive Writing Have students write a song, poem, or short children's story about the life of a cowhand. **OL**

R Reading Strategy

Taking Notes Have students note three facts about the origins of cowhand culture in the American West. **OL**

Reading Check Answer: Cowhands faced violent storms, cattle rustlers, and stampedes on the trail.

Additional Support

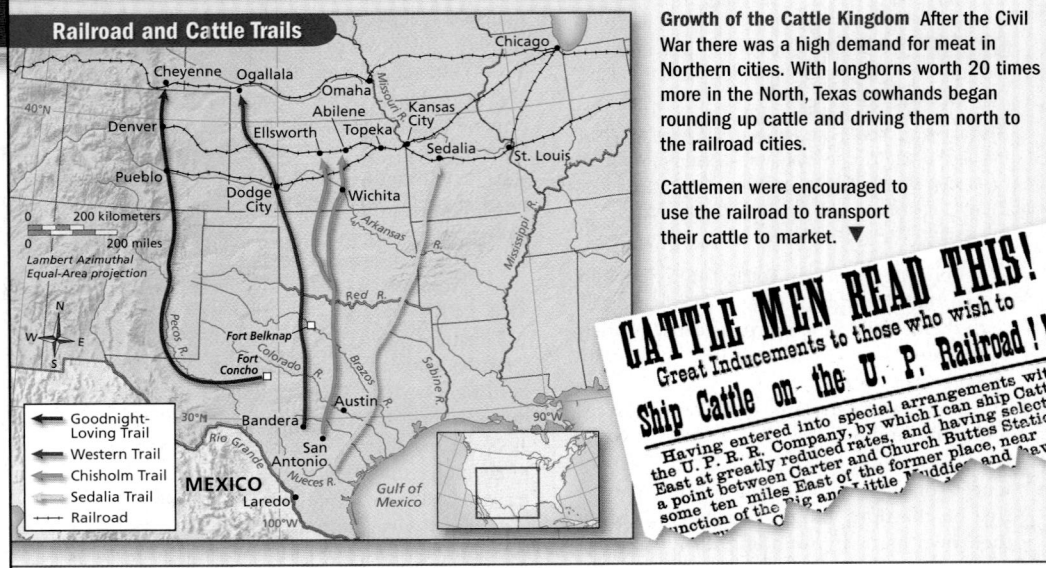

Primary Source / Cowhands and Cattle Drives

Railroad and Cattle Trails

Goodnight-Loving Trail
Western Trail
Chisholm Trail
Sedalia Trail
Railroad

Growth of the Cattle Kingdom After the Civil War there was a high demand for meat in Northern cities. With longhorns worth 20 times more in the North, Texas cowhands began rounding up cattle and driving them north to the railroad cities.

Cattlemen were encouraged to use the railroad to transport their cattle to market. ▼

CATTLE MEN READ THIS!
Great Inducements to those who wish to
Ship Cattle on the U. P. Railroad !!

Life on the Great Plains

Main Idea Cowhands and ranchers lived difficult lives on the Plains.

History and You Think about Old West movies you have seen. Read to find out what life was really like on the Plains.

The cattle drives and the cowhands who worked on them captured the imagination of the nation. Cattle driving was hard work. Cowhands rode in the saddle up to 15 hours every day, in driving rain, dust storms, and blazing sun. Life on the trail was lonely, too. Cowhands saw few outsiders. Cowhands also faced many dangers: violent storms, "rustlers" who tried to steal cattle, and stampedes, when thousands of cattle ran in panic. During a stampede, cowhands had to race on horseback and bring the cattle under control.

Cowhands included veterans of the Civil War and African Americans who moved west in search of a better life. Some cowhands were Hispanics. In fact, cattle herding traditions began in the Spanish Southwest when Hispanic ranch hands, known as **vaqueros,** developed the riding, roping, and branding skills used by cowhands. Much of the language of the rancher today comes from Spanish words used by vaqueros for centuries. Even the word *ranch* comes from the Spanish word *rancho.*

The Cattle Kingdom Ends

Ranching eventually began to replace the cattle drives, because ranchers were able to produce hardier, plumper cattle. The ranchers became rich when cattle prices boomed. Then, as a result of too many cattle for sale on the beef market, cattle prices fell, bringing an end to the "Cattle Kingdom." The cattle industry survived but was changed forever. Another type of economic activity would rise in the Plains—farming.

Reading Check **Describing** Why were the trails dangerous for cowhands?

Interdisciplinary Connection

Music Distribute copies of the lyrics to "Home on the Range." Have students highlight words and phrases that paint a picture of what cowhands experienced on the Plains. **Ask:** Which words and phrases are descriptive? *("the skies are not cloudy all day"; "the light of glittering stars"; and so on)*

Ask students to create a collage of images that corresponds to the words of the song.

Then have students look up the definition of *romanticize.* As a class, discuss the ways in which "Home on the Range" presents a romantic picture of cowhand life. **OL**

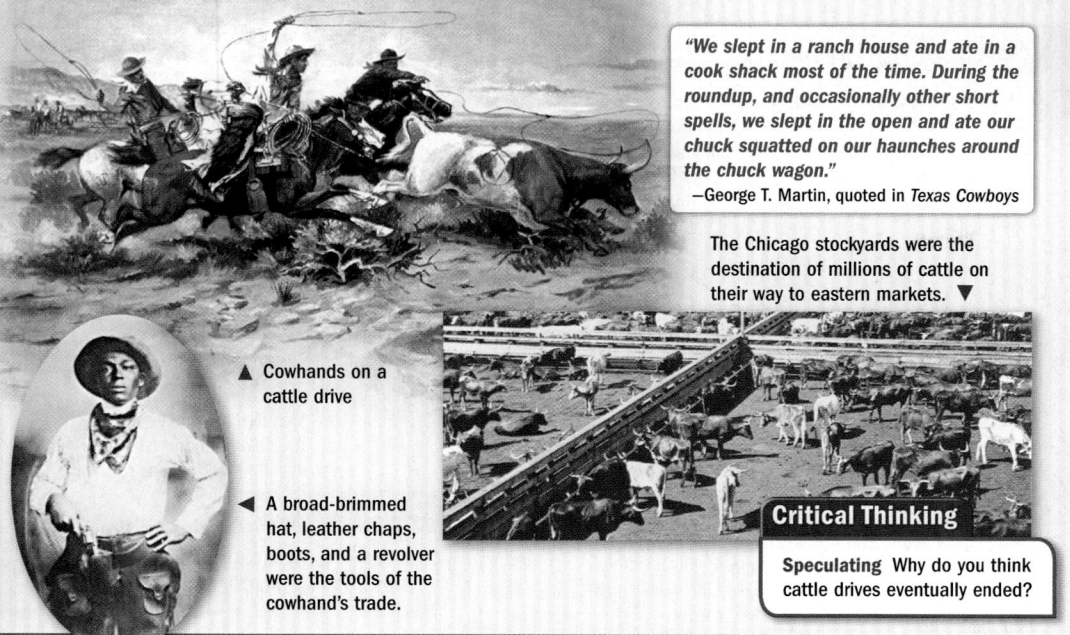

"We slept in a ranch house and ate in a cook shack most of the time. During the roundup, and occasionally other short spells, we slept in the open and ate our chuck squatted on our haunches around the chuck wagon."
—George T. Martin, quoted in *Texas Cowboys*

The Chicago stockyards were the destination of millions of cattle on their way to eastern markets. ▼

▲ Cowhands on a cattle drive

◄ A broad-brimmed hat, leather chaps, boots, and a revolver were the tools of the cowhand's trade.

Critical Thinking

Speculating Why do you think cattle drives eventually ended?

Farmers Settle the Plains

Main Idea Free land and new farming methods brought many settlers to the Great Plains.

History and You Have you ever experienced a drought or flood? Read on to learn about the challenges farmers faced on the Great Plains.

• •

The early pioneers who reached the Great Plains did not believe they could farm the dry, treeless area. In the late 1860s, however, farmers began settling there. Much of the Plains soon changed from "wilderness" to farmland. In 1872 a Nebraska farmer wrote, "One year ago this was a vast, houseless, uninhabited prairie. . . . Today I can see more than thirty dwellings from my door."

Several **factors,** or contributing circumstances, brought settlers to the Plains. Railroads made the journey west easier and cheaper. New laws offered free land. Finally, above-average rainfall in the late 1870s made the land better suited to farming.

The Homestead Act

In 1862 the government encouraged settlement on the Plains by passing the **Homestead Act.** This law gave up to 160 free acres (65 ha) of land to a settler who paid a $10 filing fee and lived on the land for five years. Later government acts increased the size of the tracts available. The federal land policy brought farmers to the Plains to homestead— earn ownership of land by settling on it.

Homesteading attracted thousands of new settlers to the Plains. With their property rights secured, settlers were more willing to move west. Some of these settlers were immigrants who had begun the process of becoming American citizens and were eligible to file for land. Other homesteaders were women. Although married women could not claim land, single women and widows had the same rights as men—and they used the Homestead Act to acquire property. In Colorado and Wyoming, for example, 12 percent of all those who filed claims were women.

Opening the West **Chapter 18** 563

C Critical Thinking

Analyzing Primary Sources Ask: What caused the change noted by the Nebraska farmer? *(Railroads made the journey west easier; free land was offered; above-average rainfall helped farmers.)* **OL**

D Differentiated Instruction

Below Grade Level Have students list "Who?" "What?" "When?" "Where?" and "Why?" in their notebooks and then answer the following questions about the Homestead Act: Who could take advantage of the act? What were the requirements of the act? When was the act passed? Where did the act apply? Why was the act passed? **BL**

Primary Source

Critical Thinking Answer
Possible answer: Railroads extended farther and farther into the Southwest, making trailing unnecessary.

Skills Practice
Ask: What were a cowhand's tools used for? *(A hat offered protection from the sun, leather chaps and boots protected legs and feet, and a revolver could drive away rustlers.)* **OL**

Differentiated Instruction

Leveled Activities

563

Primary Source

Critical Thinking Answer

The government was pressured to open up Indian Territory to white settlement; the government purchased two million acres from Native Americans; on April 22, 1889, thousands raced to claim land; people drove stakes, erected tents, and built wooden shanties, then registered their claims at a land office.

Skills Practice

Ask: Why was there such a rush to claim land in Oklahoma? *(Much of the rest of the West's lands had already been settled.)* **OL**

Primary Source / The Oklahoma Land Rush

Open for Settlement During the 1880s, pressure increased to open Indian Territory in Oklahoma to white settlement. Early in 1889, the government yielded and purchased nearly 2 million acres of land from Native Americans. The Oklahoma Land Rush officially began at noon on April 22, 1889.

◄ Oklahoma City on the first day of the land rush.

◄ On horseback, in wagons, in buggies, and on foot, thousands raced forward to claim land.

▲ Men line up outside a land office. The chaotic land rush led to many disputed land claims.

"The race was not over when you reached the particular lot. . . . The contest still was who should drive their stakes first, who would erect their little tents soonest, and then, who would quickest build a little wooden shanty."
—Hamilton S. Wicks, "The Opening of Oklahoma," 1889

Critical Thinking

Sequencing What steps were involved in claiming land during the Oklahoma Land Rush?

New Groups of Settlers

Homesteaders settled on the Plains to own land and be independent. Advertising paid for by railroads, steamship companies, land speculators, and western states and territories also lured people to the Plains. Railroad companies sold the strips of land alongside the rail lines to raise cash. Steamship travel companies advertised the Plains in Scandinavia where many people were searching for economic opportunities. Scandinavian influence remains strong in Minnesota and the Dakotas today.

Thousands of African Americans also migrated from the Southern states to Kansas in the late 1870s. They called themselves "Exodusters," from the biblical book of Exodus, which describes the Jews' escape from slavery in Egypt.

The end of Reconstruction in 1877 had meant the end of federal protection for African Americans. Fearing for their safety in former slave regions, freed people sought land farther west. By 1881, more than 40,000 African Americans had migrated to Kansas.

Challenges of Farming the Frontier

The climate of the Plains presented farmers with their greatest challenge. During some years excessive rainfall caused flooding. The region, however, also experienced drought. In times of drought, brushfires swept rapidly through a region, destroying crops, livestock, and homes. Summer might bring plagues of grasshoppers.

Winters presented even greater dangers. Winds howled across the open Plains, and deep snow could bury animals and trap families in their homes. Farm families had to plan ahead and store food for the winter.

Meeting the challenges of farming on the Great Plains was a family affair. Men labored hard in the fields. Women often did the same work, but they also cared for the children, sewed clothing, made candles, and cooked and preserved food. When the men were away, women bore all responsibility for keeping the farm running. When children grew old enough, they helped work on the farm. Farmwork often kept children from attending school.

564 **Chapter 18** *Opening the West*

New Farming Methods

The Plains could not be farmed by the methods of the 1860s. Most of the region had little rainfall and few streams for irrigation. Plains farmers, known as **sodbusters,** needed new methods and tools.

One approach, called **dry farming,** was to plant seeds deep in moist ground. However, wooden plows could not penetrate the tough layer of sod. By the late 1870s, farmers could use the new lightweight steel plow that was better for digging into sod.

The sodbusters had other tools to help them—windmills to pump water from deep in the ground and a new fencing called barbed wire. Farmers did not have wood to build fences, so they substituted these wire fences to protect their land.

Dry farming, however, did not produce large yields, and the 160-acre (65 ha) grants were too small. Most farmers needed at least 300 acres (121 ha) and advanced machinery, to make a profit. Many farmers went into debt. Others lost ownership of their farms and then had to pay rent for the land.

The Oklahoma Land Rush

The last region of the Plains to be settled was the Oklahoma Territory, which Congress designated as "Indian Territory" in the 1830s. In 1889, after years of pressure from land dealers and settlers, the government opened Oklahoma to homesteaders.

On the morning of April 22, 1889—the official opening day—more than 10,000 people lined up on the edge of this land. At the sound of a bugle, the homesteaders charged across the border to stake their claims. The eager boomers, as the homesteaders were called, discovered that some settlers had already slipped into Oklahoma. These "sooners" already claimed most of the best land. Within a few years, all of Oklahoma was opened to settlement.

Not long after the land rush, the 1890 census revealed that the frontier was no more. Settlement had greatly changed the Plains, especially for Native Americans.

Reading Check **Identifying** What new farming methods were used on the Great Plains?

C Critical Thinking

Comparing and Contrasting Have students carry out research and then create a Venn diagram to compare and contrast farming and farming methods in the East and in the Plains. **AL**

This **READING SKILL** (Comparing and Contrasting) was introduced in this unit.

W Writing Support

Narrative Writing Have students write a letter from a "boomer" to a relative back East, relating the events of the Oklahoma land rush. **OL**

Reading Check **Answer:** dry farming, steel plows, windmills, barbed wire

Assess

History ONLINE

Study Central™ provides summaries, interactive games, and online graphic organizers to help students review content.

Close

Comparing and Contrasting As a class, compare and contrast the lives of cattle ranchers and farmers on the Plains. **OL**

Section 2 Review

History ONLINE
Study Central™ To review this section, go to glencoe.com.

Vocabulary

1. Use each of these terms in a sentence that will help explain its meaning: Long Drive, locate, vaquero, factor, homestead, sodbuster, dry farming.

Main Ideas

2. **Explaining** Why did the Long Drive develop?

3. **Analyzing** Why do you think cowhands captured the imaginations of many Americans?

4. **Predicting** How do you think the Oklahoma Land Rush affected Native Americans?

Critical Thinking

5. **Analyzing** Create a diagram that shows how new farming methods solved some of the problems of farming on the Plains.

Problem		Solution
☐	→	☐
☐	→	☐
☐	→	☐
☐	→	☐

6. **Explaining** Why did many African Americans move west?

7. **Persuasive Writing** Design a brochure that might have been printed by a steamship company in Scandinavia. Include a few sentences explaining why Scandinavians should move to the American plains.

Answer the
Essential Question

8. How did cattle ranchers and farmers adapt to life in the West?

Answers

1. Sentences should clearly explain the meanings of vocabulary words.
2. The price of cattle went up, so cattle ranchers began herding their cattle toward railroad towns where they could be sent to market.
3. Cowhand life was difficult and dangerous, but it probably seemed like a great adventure.
4. Possible answer: Students might point out that the Native Americans were forced from their land.

5. **Problem:** little rainfall, **Solution:** dry farming; **Problem:** tough layer of sod to dig, **Solution:** steel plow; **Problem:** getting water from ground, **Solution:** windmills; **Problem:** lack of wood for fences, **Solution:** barbed wire
6. After Reconstruction, many freed African Americans moved west because they feared for their safety in the South because they were no longer protected by the federal government.

7. Students' brochures might include information about large amounts of available cheap land.
8. **Cattle ranchers:** learned riding, branding, and roping techniques; developed the Long Drive to get cattle to market; faced dangers such as stampedes, weather, and rustlers. **Farmers:** invented new farming techniques such as dry farming, and new technology, including barbed wire and lightweight steel plows.

Focus

Bellringer

Daily Test Practice Transparency 18–3

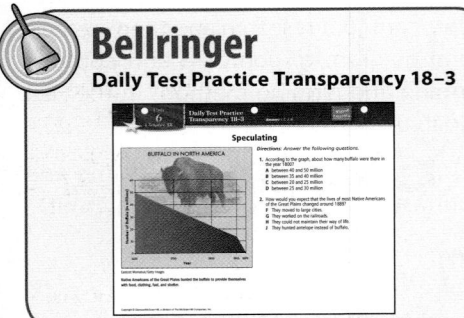

Reading Guide
Answers to Graphic:

moved Native Americans to large reservations; attacked Native American groups that resisted resettlement; Dawes Act broke up reservations and gave Native Americans plots of land

Section Spotlight Video

Have students watch the Section Spotlight Video "Native American Struggles" to learn more about Native Americans of the Plains.

Resource Manager

Section 3

Essential Question
How did westward expansion affect Native Americans?

Reading Guide

Content Vocabulary

nomadic (p. 567)   reservation (p. 568)

Academic Vocabulary

ensure (p. 567)   widespread (p. 569)

Key People and Events
Crazy Horse (p. 569)
Sitting Bull (p. 570)
Geronimo (p. 571)
Dawes Act (p. 571)
Wounded Knee (p. 571)

Reading Strategy
Taking Notes As you read, record the actions of the U.S. government toward Native Americans.

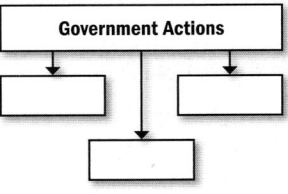

Government Actions

ILLINOIS STANDARDS
The American Journey

16.D.3a (US) Describe characteristics of different kinds of communities in various sections of America during the colonial/frontier periods and the 19th century.

17.C.3c Analyze how human processes influence settlement patterns including migration and population growth.

17.D.3a Explain how and why spatial patterns of settlement change over time.

Native American Struggles

American Diary

In 1867 government officials traveled to Fort Laramie, Wyoming, to sign a peace treaty with Red Cloud and other Sioux chiefs. After the U.S. troops were withdrawn, at Red Cloud's request, the treaty was signed. One Crow leader, Bear Tooth, however, sharply criticized the actions of white people. "If I went into your country to kill your animals, what would you say? Would I not be wrong, and would you not make war on me?"

—*from* The Mammoth Book of Native Americans

Signers of the Treaty of Fort Laramie, May 1868

Reading Strategies	C Critical Thinking	D Differentiated Instruction	W Writing Support	S Skill Practice
Teacher Edition • Reading Graphs, p. 568 • Summarizing, p. 569 **Additional Resources** • Guid. Read., URB p. 41 • Content Vocab., URB p. 17 • Academic Vocab., URB p. 19 • Read. Ess., p. 196 • Pri. Source Read., URB p. 21	**Teacher Edition** • Making Inferences, p. 567 • Analyzing Information, p. 571 **Additional Resources** • Quizzes and Tests, p. 175 • Inter. Polit. Cartoons, URB p. 13 • Crit. Think. Skills, URB p. 29	**Teacher Edition** • English Language Learners, p. 568 • Interpersonal, p. 570 **Additional Resources** • School-to-Home, URB p. 35 • Reteaching Act., URB p. 37	**Teacher Edition** • Descriptive Writing, p. 567 • Narrative Writing, p. 570	**Teacher Edition** • Visual Literacy, p. 568 • Reading a Time Line, pp. 569, 570 **Additional Resources** • Daily Test Pract. Transp. 18-3 • Lesson Transp. 18C • Citizen. & Dec. Mak. Skills, URB p. 3 • Soc. Stud. Skills, URB p. 25

Following the Buffalo

Main Idea Native Americans of the Great Plains depended on buffalo to survive, but railroads threatened this lifestyle.

History and You What is one thing in your life that you could not live without? Read to learn what Native Americans were forced to give up.

⸻

The government officials who met with Red Cloud wanted to **ensure,** or make certain of, the safety of whites moving into Native American territory. In the mid-1850s, miners, ranchers, and farmers began to settle on the Plains. Conflict between Native Americans and whites grew as Native Americans tried to preserve their civilizations. Red Cloud mourned, "The white children [settlers] have surrounded me and left me nothing but an island."

The Great Plains had been home to many Native American nations for centuries. Some, like the Omaha and the Osage nations, lived in communities as farmers and hunters. Most of the Plains Indians, however, including the Sioux, the Comanche, and the Blackfeet, lived a **nomadic** life. They traveled vast distances following their main source of food—great herds of buffalo.

Despite their differences, the people of the Plains were similar in many ways. Their nations, sometimes numbering several thousand people, were divided into bands consisting of up to 500 people each. A governing council headed each band, but most members participated in decisions.

The women raised the children, cooked, and prepared hides. The men hunted, traded, and performed military tasks. Most Native Americans of the Plains believed in the spiritual power of the natural world.

For most of their history, the Plains Native Americans had millions of buffalo to supply their needs. After the Civil War, however, American hunters hired by the railroads began slaughtering the animals to feed the crews building the railroads. The railroad companies also wanted to prevent the giant herds of buffalo from blocking the trains. Starting in 1872, hunters targeted buffalo to sell the hides back East.

✓ **Reading Check** Comparing and Contrasting How were the lifestyles of different Plains people similar? How were they different?

⸻

If You Were There / Life on the Plains

Skills of a Warrior Young Native Americans on the Plains learned the skills they would need in battle. Boys ran races, wrestled, rode horses, and learned how to shoot arrows. As they grew older, they learned about battle strategies, including the tactic of sending young men to fight hand-to-hand with the enemy while other warriors surrounded and attacked the opponents. Courage during battle was highly valued by the Native Americans of the Plains. Before a battle, for example, the Lakota would often yell, "It is a good day to die!"

Critical Thinking

Making Connections What types of skills are you learning that will help you as an adult?

⸻

Teach

W Writing Support

Descriptive Writing Have students research and write a one- or two-page descriptive essay about the lifestyles and beliefs of one Plains Indian group. **AL**

C Critical Thinking

Making Inferences Ask: How might the killing of buffalo by whites affect the lifestyles of Plains Indians? *(Nomadic groups might have to travel further for hunting buffalo or have to begin farming instead of relying on buffalo for food.)* **OL**

✓ **Reading Check Answer:** Some groups were nomadic, while others lived in farming communities. All nations were divided into bands, which had governing councils. Women and men had gender-specific roles, and most believed in the spiritual power of the natural world.

If You Were There

Critical Thinking Answer Students might suggest that the basic skills they are learning in schools now, such as math and English, will help them in future careers.

Differentiated Instruction

⸻

Critical Thinking Skills Activity
Opening the West

Predicting Consequences

✓ **Learning the Skill**

When you look at historical maps, you can sometimes predict consequences based on certain facts or conditions. For example, you might look at a map that shows the first transcontinental railroad route. You might predict that many cities and towns would someday grow along this route.

✓ **Practicing the Skill**

Directions: Use the maps below to answer the questions that follow.

Range of Buffalo in North America (1500) — **Map A**
North American Grassland Before European Settlement — **Map B**

Critical Thinking Skills Activity, URB p. 29

⸻

Predicting Consequences

Objective:	To learn how to predict consequences
Focus:	Ask students why buffalo were important to Native Americans on the Plains.
Teach:	Have students read the information, answer the questions, and apply the skill.
Assess:	Discuss the process by which the killing of the buffalo and the elimination of the grasslands affected Native Americans.
Close:	Have students predict what might happen to the buffalo and the grasslands in the future.

Differentiated Instruction Strategies

BL Have students draw a cause-and-effect graphic organizer that sums up the information in this activity.

AL Ask students to create a multimedia presentation on the protected buffalo reserves in the U.S.

ELL Have students explain, in their own words, the meaning of the phrase "predicting consequences."

R Reading Strategy

Reading Graphs Have students look at the "Native American Population" graph. **Ask:** By how many thousands did the Native American population decline between 1850 and 1900? *(about 200,000)* About what percentage decline was that? *(about 50%)* **OL**

D Differentiated Instruction

English Language Learners Ask students to write phrases from the text that describe life on a reservation. Have them look up any words they are unfamiliar with. Then have them summarize reservation life in a few sentences. **ELL**

S Skill Practice

Visual Literacy Have students review the map in the Primary Source feature. Ask them to list the dates and locations of the conflicts between Native Americans and whites. **BL**

Hands-On Chapter Project
Step 3

Creating an Atlas

Step 3: Mapping Reservations and Battles Students will create maps showing Native American reservations and battles in the Plains.

Essential Question: How did westward expansion affect Native Americans?

R Conflict

Main Idea Conflict between Native Americans and whites grew as Native Americans were forced onto reservations.

History and You Think about how you might feel if the government told you where to live. Read to learn how this affected Native Americans.

· ·

When white people began to settle the Plains, conflict developed with Native American groups. In 1867 the federal government appointed the Indian Peace Commission to develop a policy toward Native Americans. The commission recommended moving the Native Americans to a few large **reservations**—tracts of land set aside for them. The army was given authority to deal with any groups that would not move. Moving Native Americans to reservations was not a new policy, but the government increased its efforts in that direction.

Reservation Life

One large reservation was in Oklahoma, the "Indian Territory" that Congress created in the 1830s for Native Americans who were relocated from the Southeast. A second large reservation was created for the Sioux in the Dakota Territory. The federal Bureau of Indian Affairs would manage the reservations.

D Government agents often used trickery to persuade Native American nations to move to the reservations. Many reservations were located on poor land. In addition, the government often failed to deliver promised food and supplies, and the goods that were delivered were of poor quality.

A great many Native Americans accepted the reservation policy at first, and they agreed to move to the lands that had been set aside for them. However, some Native Americans refused to move, while others who tried reservation life eventually abandoned it. The **S** stage was set for conflict.

Primary Source / Conflicts With Native Americans

Cultures Under Pressure Westward migration of white settlers in the mid-1800s caused conflicts with Native Americans on the Great Plains. White settlers fought with many groups, including the Sioux, Cheyenne, Apache, and Navajo. After the Civil War, the U.S. government implemented a reservation policy. Some Native Americans agreed to move to reservations; others resisted.

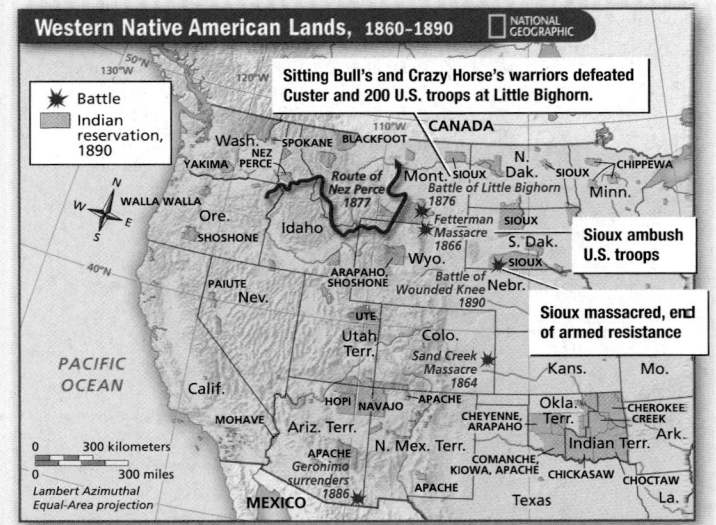

Western Native American Lands, 1860–1890

Sitting Bull's and Crazy Horse's warriors defeated Custer and 200 U.S. troops at Little Bighorn.

Sioux ambush U.S. troops

Sioux massacred, end of armed resistance

By the Numbers

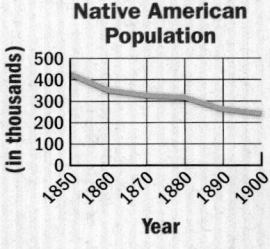

Native American Population

"You might as well expect all rivers to run backward as that any man who was born a free man should be contented when penned up and denied liberty to go where he pleases."
—Chief Joseph of the Nez Perce, on a visit to Washington, D.C., 1879

Directions Have students form their small groups. Provide, or have each group trace, two outline maps of the United States. Groups should then add and label states and territories as in Step 1. On one map, have them mark the reservations shown on the map on this page. On the other map, have them mark the locations of battles shown on the map. Have students research to find additional battles between Native Americans

and whites to add to their maps. Students should keep notes about the causes and results of these additional battles.

Speculating Ask: Is there any relationship between the locations of reservations and battles in the West? *(Some battles were fought near reservations, perhaps because there were large numbers of Native Americans in the area.)* **OL**

(Chapter Project continued in Section 4)

Conflict Begins

During the 1860s, many armed clashes between Native Americans and whites took place. Minnesota Territory was the site of one especially bloody confrontation. Resentful of the settlers, Sioux warriors led by Red Cloud burned and looted white settlers' homes in the summer of 1862. Hundreds died before troops put down the uprising.

The Sioux, along with Cheyenne and Arapaho, staged a series of attacks from 1865 to 1867. The bloodiest occurred on December 21, 1866. Army troops were stationed at a fort on the Bozeman Trail, which was used by prospectors to reach gold mines in Montana. A Sioux military leader, **Crazy Horse,** acting as a decoy, lured the troops into a deadly trap, where hundreds of warriors wiped out the entire detachment. This incident was known as the Fetterman Massacre.

Colorado was another site of conflict between Native Americans and whites. A growing number of miners flocked to Colorado in search of gold and silver. Bands

S of Cheyenne and Arapaho began raiding wagon trains and stealing cattle and horses from ranches. By the summer of 1864, white people traveling to Denver or the mining camps were no longer safe. Many ranches were burned, and about 200 settlers were killed. The territorial governor of Colorado ordered the Native Americans to surrender at Fort Lyon, where he said they would be given food and protection.

Although several hundred Native Americans surrendered at the fort, many did not. In November 1864, Chief Black Kettle traveled **R** with several hundred Cheyenne to negotiate a peace agreement. They camped at Sand Creek. On their way to the fort, Colonel John Chivington led the Colorado Volunteers on an attack against the unsuspecting Cheyenne. Fourteen volunteers and hundreds of Cheyenne died. Retaliation by the Cheyenne was swift, provoking **widespread,** or far-reaching, uprisings before some of the Cheyenne and Arapaho leaders agreed to stop the fighting in October 1865.

"When I look back now from this high hill of my old age, I can still see the butchered women and children [at Wounded Knee]. . . . And I can see that something else died there in the bloody mud. . . . A people's dream died there."
—Black Elk, *Black Elk Speaks* (1932)

Sioux "ghost shirt" worn at ▶ Wounded Knee

▲ The massacre of 200 Native American men, women, and children at Wounded Knee marked the end of the Indian Wars.

◀ Chief Gall, a Sioux leader at the Battle of Little Bighorn

▲ Custer's defeat at Little Bighorn shocked the nation and prompted the U.S. government to send large armies west.

DBQ **Document-Based Questions**

Comparing and Contrasting What similarities are there in the quotations from Chief Joseph and Black Elk? How do the quotations differ?

Opening the West **Chapter 18** 569

Additional Support

Connecting Past and Present

Reservations Today Tell students that Native American reservations still exist today. They are managed by Native American tribes under the Bureau of Indian Affairs. **Ask:** What do you think conditions are like on reservations today? *(Students may answer that conditions on many reservations are difficult because they have few natural resources. They may also mention casinos.)* Direct pairs of students to research conditions on reservations today. Have each pair select one reservation during its research and take notes on its history and current conditions. Have each pair present to the class a 3- to 5-minute report on what they find. When all pairs have finished, discuss as a class how the nineteenth-century policy of containing Native Americans on reservations still affects Native American people today. **OL**

People IN HISTORY

Skill Practice

Reading a Time Line Have students add events on this spread to the time line created earlier in this section. **OL**

Writing Support

Narrative Writing Have students research and write a brief biographical sketch of either Sitting Bull, Crazy Horse, or Geronimo. **OL**

Differentiated Instruction

Interpersonal Have students work in pairs to choose a battle mentioned in this spread and then research its details, including its causes, effects, and important leaders. Student pairs should then create a poster incorporating visuals, captions, time lines, and other materials explaining the battle. **OL**

People IN HISTORY

Critical Thinking Answers

1. because his people already owned the land wanted by the whites
2. Both men greatly distrusted whites.

Differentiated Instruction

Sitting Bull
Sioux Chief

Sitting Bull distrusted the U.S. government and resisted its attempts to control the Sioux. One journalist reported that Sitting Bull said, *"I never taught my people to trust Americans. I have told them the truth—that the Americans are great liars. I never dealt with the Americans. Why should I? The land belonged to my people."*

Geronimo
Leader of the Apache

Geronimo once said that he might have lived peacefully with white settlers if their promises to his people had been kept. Instead, he wrote, *"We were reckless of our lives, because we felt that every man's hand was against us. If we returned to the reservation we would be put in prison and killed; f we stayed in Mexico they would continue to send soldiers to fight us."*

CRITICAL Thinking

1. **Interpreting** Why did Sitting Bull choose not to negotiate with the U.S. government?
2. **Analyzing** What did Sitting Bull and Geronimo have in common?

Little Bighorn

An 1868 treaty was supposed to bring peace, but tensions remained and erupted in more fighting. This time the conflict arose over the Black Hills of the Dakotas. The government had promised that "No white person or persons shall be permitted" to settle on the Black Hills. However, the hills were rumored to contain gold, and white prospectors swarmed into the area.

The Sioux protested against the trespassers. Instead of protecting the Sioux's rights, the government tried to buy the hills. **Sitting Bull,** an important leader of the Lakota Sioux, refused. "I do not want to sell any land. Not even this much," he said, holding a pinch of dust.

Sitting Bull gathered the combined Sioux and Cheyenne warriors along the Little Bighorn River in present-day Montana. There they were joined by Crazy Horse, another Sioux chief, and his forces. With only about 250 soldiers, Lieutenant Colonel George Custer of the U.S. Army faced thousands of Sioux and Cheyenne warriors. In less than 30 minutes, Custer and all of his men lost their lives at Little Bighorn.

News of the army's defeat shocked the nation. Yet the army soon crushed the uprising, sending most of the Native Americans to reservations. Sitting Bull and his followers fled north to Canada. By 1881, exhausted and starving, the Lakota and Cheyenne agreed to live on a reservation.

Leveled Activities

BL Social Studies Skills Activity, URB p. 25

OL Interpreting Political Cartoons, URB p. 13

AL Citizenship and Decision-Making Skills Activity, URB p. 3

ELL Reteaching Activity, URB p. 37

The Apache Wars

Trouble also broke out in the Southwest. In the 1870s, the Chiracahua Apache were moved to a reservation in Arizona. The Apache leader, **Geronimo,** then fled to Mexico. During the 1880s, he led raids in Arizona. Thousands of troops pursued Geronimo and his warriors. In 1886 Geronimo finally gave up—the last Native American to surrender.

A Changing Culture

Many factors changed Native American life—the movement of whites onto their lands, the slaughter of the buffalo, U.S. army attacks, and the reservation policy. Change also came from reformers who wanted to absorb Native Americans into white culture.

In 1887 Congress passed the **Dawes Act.** It aimed to remove what whites regarded as two weaknesses of Native American life: the lack of private property and the nomadic tradition. The act called for the breakup of reservations and an end to identification with a tribal group. Each Native American would receive a plot of reservation land. Reformers hoped that the native peoples would become farmers and, in time, American citizens. Some Native Americans succeeded as farmers or ranchers, but many had little training or enthusiasm for either pursuit. Like homesteaders, they often found their land too small to be profitable, and so they sold it.

Wounded Knee

A ceremony called the Ghost Dance became popular with many western Native Americans. The ceremony celebrated a hoped-for day when the settlers would disappear and the buffalo would return. As the Ghost Dance spread, white officials became alarmed and banned the ritual. Believing that Sitting Bull led the movement, police tried to arrest him. During a scuffle, they shot and killed him.

After Sitting Bull's death, several hundred Lakota Sioux gathered at a creek called **Wounded Knee** in southwestern South Dakota. In December 1890, the army went there to collect Sioux weapons. When a shot rang out, the army responded with fire. More than 200 Sioux and 25 soldiers were killed. Wounded Knee marked the end of armed conflict beween the U.S. government and Native Americans.

✓ **Reading Check** Evaluating How effective was the Dawes Act?

Section 3 Review

Vocabulary

1. Define each of the following terms: ensure, nomadic, reservation, widespread.

Main Ideas

2. **Specifying** Why did American railroad workers hunt buffalo?

3. **Evaluating** Was the Dawes Act an improvement on previous government policy toward Native Americans? Why or why not?

Critical Thinking

4. **Predicting** What do you think happened to Native Americans after Wounded Knee?

5. **Contrasting** List the similarities and differences between nomadic life and reservation life. Use a Venn diagram like the one below.

Nomadic Life — Both — Reservation Life

6. **Creative Writing** Write a poem describing the Ghost Dance and its importance to Native Americans.

Answer the
7. **Essential Question**
How did westward expansion affect Native Americans?

History ONLINE
Study Central™ To review this section, go to glencoe.com.

C **Critical Thinking**

Analyzing Information Ask: Why did white officials ban the Ghost Dance? *(White officials became alarmed as the Ghost Dance spread, fearing it could lead to an uprising.)* **OL**

✓ **Reading Check Answer:** The Dawes Act was not effective because most Native Americans did not succeed at farming or ranching.

Assess

History ONLINE

Study Central™ provides summaries, interactive games, and online graphic organizers to help students review content.

Close

Discussing As a class, discuss conflicts between Native Americans and white settlers and the consequences for Native Americans. **OL**

Section 3 Review

Answers

1. Sentences should use vocabulary words according to their definitions in the section and Glossary.

2. to prevent buffalo herds from blocking the tracks; to feed railroad workers; to sell hides in the East

3. Possible answer: No, the Dawes Act was not an improvement. Even though the new act did not force Native Americans to live on reservations, it forced them to give up their way of life.

4. Possible answer: Native Americans were most likely forced to follow policies set by the government.

5. **Nomadic life:** moved with food source; relied on buffalo for food and supplies; **Both:** Native Americans maintained cultural traditions; **Reservation life:** stayed in one place; farmed; relied on government for food and supplies

6. Students' poems should include information about the purposes behind the Ghost Dance.

7. Railroad building harmed the buffalo herds, a major food source; westward expansion led to continual conflict between whites and Native Americans, with the Native Americans often losing; the government forced Native Americans to live on reservations and abandon cultural traditions.

Focus

Making Inferences Ask: Why did the Great Plains Native Americans travel so much instead of settling in one area? *(They followed game, including buffalo herds—their main source of food. They did not farm the Plains like the white settlers would.)* **OL**

R **Reading Strategy**

Explaining Ask: Why did homesteaders build soddies and houses dug out of the side of hills? *(They did not have wood to build traditional buildings.)* **BL**

Ask students to complete a graphic organizer like the one below that compares and contrasts tepees and sod houses. **OL**

Tepees
* Used by Native Americans
* Quick setup
* Made with animal skin
* Transportable

(center overlap)
* Fire can be made inside
* Roof can leak

Sod Houses
* Used by homesteaders
* Took long time to build
* Made with sod from ground
* Permanent

Additional Support and Answers

NATIONAL GEOGRAPHIC

GEOGRAPHY & HISTORY

Skin Houses, Sod Houses: Plains Indians and Homesteaders

As many as 100,000 Native Americans lived on the Great Plains in the middle of the 1800s. Many groups, such as the Crow and Sioux, were nomadic hunters who trekked across the plains following game: deer, elk, antelope, and most importantly buffalo. Over time Native Americans had learned to live in the harsh landscape. By contrast white settlers who entered the region in the mid-1800s were accustomed to entirely different surroundings.

How Did Geography Affect Housing on the Great Plains?

Great Plains Native Americans lived in portable shelters that they could carry from place to place. These shelters, called tepees, were made from buffalo skins. Most homesteaders, however, were farmers who wanted more permanent homes. The Great Plains had few trees, so little wood was available for building. Some settlers built shelters called dugouts by tunneling directly into the sides of hills. Others constructed freestanding sod houses—or *soddies*—made of bricks cut from the ground.

The Great Plains Covering most of the central United States is a vast area called the Great Plains. In the early 1800s, the area's relative lack of water and wood made it seem unfit for settlement and farming. The region was labeled the "Great American Desert" on many maps of the day. This inhospitable environment made the Great Plains the last refuge of independent Native Americans.

Native American Lands

Native American Lands
- 1860
- 1890
- Great Plains (Great American Desert)

400 kilometers
400 miles
Lambert Azimuthal Equal-Area projection

▲ Handbill promoting Plains settlement

◄ "Boomers" race into the Oklahoma Territory to claim land, April 1889

Activity: Technology Connection

Analyzing Native Americans of the Great Plains used the buffalo for food, clothing, weapons, tools, utensils, and shelter. When white settlers came to the Great Plains, the buffalo started to disappear. Have students use the Internet and find several sites that answer questions about the uses of buffalo by Native Americans and whites. **Ask:** Why did the Plains peoples kill buffalo? *(For survival—they used every part of the buffalo and wasted none of it.)* Encourage students to research specific uses of the buffalo parts, such as the use of hooves to make glue; horns to make cups and spoons; skins to make tepee covers, clothing, and moccasins; and hair to make headdresses and ropes. Why did the white settlers kill buffalo? *(They killed buffalo for food, but only used the meat. The rest was usually wasted. They also killed buffalo when the animals interfered with railroad expansion and for sport.)* After students research the answers to these questions, ask them to organize the information into a report or multimedia presentation. **OL**

Skin Houses A tepee had a cover made of tanned buffalo skins fastened together and stretched over a cone-like framework of poles. Typically 3 or 4 poles were tied together near the top and raised upright. Up to 12 additional poles were leaned against these, again tied at the top. The cover was then positioned around the frame and tied to an anchor inside the tepee. The bottom was tied down or held down with stones. A door flap was pinned into place. Two women could typically raise a tepee in less than an hour.

Where the sides of the tepee cover met, pins acted as a wooden seam. The door flap was also attached with a pin.

Plains Indians built other structures besides tepees, such as earth lodges, sweat lodges, storage pits, and platforms for drying food.

A completed tepee was about 15 feet in diameter. Objects inside the tepee were used in specific ways: ceremonial items at the back, beds and pillows along the sides.

About 36 tons of sod were needed to make a house.

Only grass that had strong roots could be used so that the soil held together.

The direction of the bricks was reversed every few layers to make the wall strong.

Sod Houses Homesteaders built *soddies* by plowing ground into strips 12 inches wide and 4 inches thick; these strips were then cut into about 3-foot lengths. The builder laid two bricks side by side lengthwise to construct a wall, placing every third layer crosswise to bind the walls. Sod was laid with the grass side down. Wooden door and window frames were set in place with wooden pegs as the walls reached proper height. Roofs were thin wooden planks nailed to rafters and topped with a layer of sod.

A sod house needed to be at least 8 x 10 feet to meet the requirements of the Homestead Act of 1862. The sun-hardened sod created a solid structure. The house's thick walls provided good insulation.

Analyzing Geography

1. **Human-Environment Interaction** Do you think living in a *soddie* was comfortable? What kinds of problems do you think homesteaders typically had with their *soddies*? Explain your answer.
2. **Human-Environment Interaction** What materials did Native Americans use to build their tepees?

Reshaping the Nation **Unit 6** 573

Teach

D **Differentiated Instruction**

Logical/Mathematical Remind students of the formulas used to calculate area. The area of a circle is pi x radius^2. (pi = 3.14) The area of a rectangle is length x width. **Ask:** Which has more floor space—a typical 15-foot tepee or an 8 x 10-foot sod house? *(A 15-foot tepee. It has an area of about 177 square feet (3.14 x 7.5^2). The area of the sod house is 80 square feet.)* **OL**

Assess/Close

R **Reading Strategy**

Making Connections Ask: How did the type of housing that Native Americans and homesteaders built represent their ways of life? *(Native Americans built transportable tepees because of their nomadic ways. Homesteaders preferred to stay in one area, so they built permanent sod houses and dugouts.)* **OL**

Answers

1. Students may recognize that since the sod houses were well insulated, they were probably warm in the winter and cool in the summer; however, they might also be damp, dark, and infested with insects.
2. tanned buffalo skins, poles, and wooden pins

Section 4

Farmers in Protest

Focus

Bellringer
Daily Test Practice Transparency 18–4

Reading Guide
Answers to Graphic:
National Grange: *Successes*—provided education, fellowship, support; *Failures*—cooperatives failed.
Farmers' Alliance: *Successes*—sponsored education and cooperative buying; *Failures*—separate alliances did not unite.
Populist Party: *Successes*—many Populist reforms passed; *Failures*—did not get a Populist president elected.

Section Spotlight Video

Have students watch the Section Spotlight Video "Farmers in Protest" to learn more about the creation of the Populist Party.

Resource Manager

Essential Question ◄
Why did economic reform movements develop in the late 1800s?

Reading Guide

Content Vocabulary
National Grange *(p. 575)*
cooperative *(p. 575)*
populism *(p. 577)*

Academic Vocabulary
create *(p. 575)*　　currency *(p. 577)*

Key People and Events
William Jennings Bryan *(p. 578)*
William McKinley *(p. 578)*

Reading Strategy
Taking Notes As you read, use a chart like the one below to identify the successes and failures of the National Grange, Farmers' Alliances, and the Populist Party.

	Successes	Failures
National Grange		
Farmers' Alliances		
Populist Party		

ILLINOIS STANDARDS
The American Journey

15.A Understand how different economic systems operate in the exchange, production, distribution, and consumption of goods and services.
18.B.3a Analyze how individuals and groups interact with and within institutions (e.g., educational, military).
18.C.3a Describe ways in which a diverse U.S. population has developed and maintained common beliefs (e.g., life, liberty and the pursuit of happiness; the Constitution and the Bill of Rights).

American Diary

In the late 1800s, farmers experienced great economic hardships, suffering from falling prices and rising costs. They expressed their frustration in the following popular song called "The Farmer Is the Man":
"The farmer is the man,
Lives on credit till the fall—
With the interest rates so high
It's a wonder he don't die,
For the mortgage man's the one
who gets it all."

—*from* Songs of Work and Protest

Farmworkers on a combine harvester and thresher, 1903

R Reading Strategies	**C** Critical Thinking	**D** Differentiated Instruction	**W** Writing Support	**S** Skill Practice
Teacher Edition • Reading Graphs, p. 575 • Identifying, p. 575 **Additional Resources** • Guid. Read., URB p. 42 • Content Vocab., URB p. 17 • Academic Vocab., URB p. 19 • Read. Ess., p. 199	**Teacher Edition** • Drawing Conclusions, p. 576 • Comparing and Contrasting, p. 576 **Additional Resources** • Quizzes and Tests, p. 176	**Teacher Edition** • English Language Learners, p. 575 • Verbal/Linguistic, p. 577 **Additional Resources** • School-to-Home, URB p. 35 • Reteaching Act., URB p. 37	**Teacher Edition** • Persuasive Writing, p. 577 • Expository Writing, p. 578	**Teacher Edition** • Using Geo. Skills, p. 578 **Additional Resources** • Daily Test Pract. Transp. 18-4 • Time Line Skills, URB p. 34

The Farmers Organize

Main Idea The National Grange and the Farmers' Alliances tried to help farmers.

History and You Are you a member of any groups or organizations? Read to find out why farmers united in groups.

. . . .

After the Civil War, farming expanded in the West and South. The supply of crops grew faster than the demand for them, however, and prices fell steadily. In 1866 a bushel of wheat sold for $1.45. By the mid-1880s, the price dropped to 80 cents, and by the mid-1890s, it dropped to 49 cents. At the same time, farmers' expenses—for transporting their goods to market, for seed, and for equipment and other manufactured goods—remained high.

Farmers blamed their troubles on three groups in particular. They resented the railroad companies, which charged farmers more to ship crops than they charged manufacturers to ship goods. They were angry at Eastern manufacturers, who charged high prices for their products. They also resented

bankers, who charged high interest rates to farmers when they borrowed money for seed, equipment, and other necessary items. Senator William A. Peffer of Kansas summarized farmers' problems when he noted that the railroad companies "took possession of the land" and the bankers "took possession of the farmer."

The National Grange

Farmers began to organize in an effort to solve their problems. Within a short time, they had **created,** or formed, a mass political movement.

The first farmers' organization was a network of local organizations that eventually was called the **National Grange.** The Grange offered farmers education, fellowship, and support. For inexperienced farmers, the Grange provided a library with books on planting and livestock raising. For lonely farm families, it also organized social gatherings.

Above all, the Grange tried to encourage economic self-sufficiency for farmers. It set up "cash-only" **cooperatives,** stores where farmers bought products from each other.

By the Numbers / Farmers Face Hard Times

A Drop in Crop Prices As farming grew, so did the amount of crops grown, such as wheat. The price of wheat dropped because there was too much wheat available to sell.

Wheat Production

Millions of Bushels

500
400
300
200

1870   1880   1890

Year

Wheat Prices

$ per Bushel

1.50
1.20
0.90
0.60

1870   1880   1890

Year

Source: U.S. Census Bureau, Historical Statistics of the United States.

Critical Thinking

Predicting What might happen to the price of a product if there were not enough of it available to sell?

Teach

. . . .

R₁ Reading Strategy

Reading Graphs Have students look at the graphs on this page. **Ask:** In what year were both wheat production and wheat prices relatively high? *(1880)* **OL**

R₂ Reading Strategy

Identifying Ask: At which three groups were farmers angry? *(railroad companies, Eastern manufacturers, and bankers)* **BL**

D Differentiated Instruction

English Language Learners Have students define the word *cooperate.* **Ask:** How does knowing the definition of *cooperate* help you define *cooperative?* *(Cooperatives must have been founded for the members' mutual benefit.)* Ask students what sort of activities may have occurred in the cooperatives. **ELL**

By the Numbers

Critical Thinking Answer The price of the product would probably increase.

Hands-On Chapter Project
Step 4

Creating an Atlas

Step 4: Mapping the Election of 1896 Students will create maps showing the results of the presidential election of 1896.

Essential Question: Why did economic reform movements develop in the late 1800s?

Directions Provide students outline maps of the U.S. Have them again draw and label states and territories as in Step 1. Ask them to reproduce the Election of 1896 map in this section. Have them

research Populists elected to governorships or national office and note this on their maps.

Identifying Central Issues Ask: Why did the northeast, midwest, and west coast regions favor McKinley? *(He was a pro-business candidate who advocated a high tariff to protect domestic industry.)* Why did the South favor Bryan? *(He was the free-silver candidate; farmers thought more currency would help them pay debts; the South had a primarily agricultural economy.)* **OL**

(Chapter Project continued on the Visual Summary page)

ATLAS

Section 4

C₁ Critical Thinking

Drawing Conclusions Ask: What was good about the "cash-only" policy of cooperatives? *(It kept farmers from buying items on credit and going into debt.)* What was bad about "cash-only"? *(Cooperatives could not survive because farmers did not have cash.)* **OL**

C₂ Critical Thinking

Comparing and Contrasting Ask: How were the Grange and the Farmers' Alliances alike? How were they different? *(Both sponsored education and cooperative buying and selling; the alliances, however, lobbied for a government plan that would provide indebted farmers with some federal protection.)* **OL**

The Election of 1896

Map Skills Answer
McKinley carried most of the industrial states; Bryan captured most of the agricultural states.

✔ **Reading Check Answer:** Farmers organized to solve their conflicts with railroads, manufacturers, and bankers.

Differentiated Instruction

The Election of 1896 [NATIONAL GEOGRAPHIC]

McKinley (R)
Bryan (D)

Campaigns in Contrast In 1896 the Democratic presidential nominee was William Jennings Bryan, who ran on a free-silver platform. The Republicans nominated William McKinley, a pro-business candidate who favored the gold standard and a high tariff.

◄ Democrat William Jennings Bryan campaigned that free silver would help farmers and the working class.

▲ Republican William McKinley said that the gold standard would ensure prosperity for all.

Map Skills

Regions In the 1896 election, which candidate carried most of the industrial states? Which candidate carried most of the agricultural states?

Cooperatives charged lower prices than regular stores while also providing an outlet for farmers' crops. The cash-only policy prevented farmers from buying items on credit, which often led to debt.

In the 1870s, the Grange tried to cut farmers' costs by getting state legislatures to limit railroad shipping rates. Many Midwestern states passed such laws. By 1878, however, the railroads put so much pressure on state legislatures that these states repealed the rate regulations.

The Grange's cooperatives also failed. Farmers were always short of cash and had to borrow money until their next crop was sold. The cash-only cooperatives could not survive if borrowing was necessary. By the late 1870s, the Grange had declined.

The Farmers' Alliances

The Farmers' Alliances were a network of organizations that sprang up in the West and the South in the 1880s. The alliances grew rapidly. By 1890, the Southern Alliance had more than 3 million members, and the Colored Farmers' National Alliance, a separate organization of African American farmers, had 1 million members.

Like the Grange, the Farmers' Alliances sponsored education and cooperative buying and selling. The alliances also proposed a plan in which the federal government would store farmers' crops in warehouses and lend money to the farmers. When the crops were sold, the farmers would pay back the loans. It was hoped that such a plan would reduce the power that railroads, banks, and merchants had over farmers. The plan would also offer farmers some federal protection.

The alliances could have been a powerful force. Regional differences and personality clashes, however, kept the alliances apart.

✔ **Reading Check Determining Cause and Effect** Why did farmers create organizations such as the Grange and the Farmers' Alliances?

Farmers' Protest Movement (1862–1896)

Objective: To complete a time line on the farmers' protest movement in the 1800s

Focus: Ask students to recount some of the reasons farmers began to create a mass political movement.

Teach: Have students read the background information and then complete the time line.

Assess: Review the correct answers and discuss any that are problematic.

Close: Discuss whether the farmers' protest movement ultimately was a failure.

Differentiated Instruction Strategies

BL Tell students that the National Grange still exists today. Have interested students find out more about the organization.

AL Ask students to write a protest song or poem that could have been used by the farmers' movement.

ELL Have students define the term *populism* and explain what it symbolized in the name *Populist Party*.

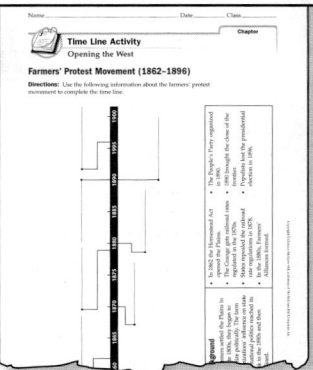

Time Line Skills Activity, URB p. 34

A Party of the People

Main Idea The Populist Party supported the views of farmers and the common people.

History and You What political parties exist in the United States today? Read to learn about the People's, or Populist, Party that was created in 1890.

In the 1890 election, the Farmers' Alliances became active in political campaigns. Their candidates won 6 governorships, 3 seats in the U.S. Senate, and 50 seats in the House of Representatives.

As a result of their successes, Alliance leaders worked to turn the movement into a national political party. In February 1890, Alliance members had formed the People's Party of the U.S.A., also known as the Populist Party. The goals of this new party were rooted in **populism,** or appeal to the common people.

The Populist Party

The Populist Party claimed that the government, not private companies, should own the railroads and telegraph lines. The Populists also wanted to replace the country's gold-based **currency,** or money, system with a flexible currency system that was based on free silver, or the unlimited production of silver coins. They believed that putting more silver coins into the economy would give farmers more money to pay their debts.

The Populist Party also supported several political and labor reforms. They promoted political reforms such as limiting the president and vice president to a single term, electing senators directly, and introducing the use of secret ballots. They also called for shorter hours for workers and the creation of a national income tax that would tax higher earnings more heavily.

In 1892 the Populists nominated James B. Weaver of Iowa as its presidential candidate. Although Weaver did not win, support for the Populist Party strengthened.

History ONLINE
Student Web Activity Visit glencoe.com and complete the **Chapter 18** Web Activity about farming in the late 1800s.

Primary Sources
ANALYZING POLITICAL CARTOONS

In 1896 William Jennings Bryan campaigned for the unlimited production of silver coins to help poor farmers. Opponents viewed free silver as repudiation, or a refusal to pay their debts.

1. **Identifying Points of View** Does the cartoon support or oppose free silver? How do you know?

2. **Interpreting** According to the cartoon, what is happening to the free-silver movement?

Supporters of the free-silver movement:
A. Senator Ben Tillman of South Carolina B. William Jennings Bryan C. Governor John P. Altgeld of Illinois

---

W Writing Support

Persuasive Writing Ask students to write a letter to the editor explaining and arguing in favor of the economic proposals of the Populist Party. **OL**

D Differentiated Instruction

Verbal/Linguistic Have students write and deliver a short campaign speech for James B. Weaver's presidential bid. **AL**

INTERPRETING POLITICAL CARTOONS

Answers

1. The cartoon opposes free silver. The free-silver supporters appear comical.

2. The free-silver movement is running out of control and headed for a crash.

History ONLINE
Objectives and answers to the Student Web Activity can be found at glencoe.com under the Web Activity Lesson Plan for this chapter.

Differentiated Instruction

Leveled Activities

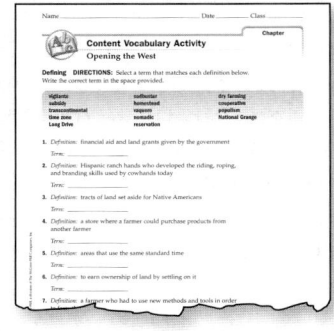
577

W Writing Support

Expository Writing Have students write a one-page essay describing support for and opposition to the Populist Party. **OL**

S Skill Practice

Using Geography Skills Refer students to the Election of 1896 map. **Ask:** Residents of what parts of the United States did not vote? *(the territories)* **BL**

✓ Reading Check **Answer:** The Populists focused on issues that concerned the common people.

Assess

History ONLINE

Study Central™ provides summaries, interactive games, and online graphic organizers to help students review content.

Close

Listing As a class, list problems that led to the development of economic reform movements in the late 1800s. **OL**

Section 4 Review

The Populists did well in the state and local elections of 1894 and had hopes for building even more support in the presidential election of 1896. Despite having energetic candidates, however, the Populists lacked money and organization.

Free Silver

In addition to these problems, hostility between the North and the South following the Civil War caused divisions within the Populist Party. Also, many white Southerners could not bring themselves to join forces with Populists who were African American.

Another problem for populism was that in the 1890s, Democrat-controlled Southern state legislatures placed limits on the rights of African Americans to vote. Many freedmen—who might have supported the Populists—were unable to vote.

Farmers were joined by debtors in supporting free silver. Debtors hoped that free silver would mean their loans could be repaid more cheaply. Silver-mining companies in the West also supported the cause. If the government coined large quantities of silver, the mining companies would have a place to sell their metal.

S The Election of 1896

In 1896 the Democrats chose a candidate for president who supported free silver and other Populist goals. He was 36-year-old **William Jennings Bryan,** known as the Great Commoner because of his appeal to average Americans. Bryan passionately believed in farmers' causes. The Populists endorsed Bryan as their candidate. His opponent was Republican **William McKinley** of Ohio, who opposed free silver.

Bryan was a fiery speaker and proved to be an outstanding campaigner. He traveled across the nation giving dynamic speeches, attacking bankers and other money interests. Yet by the time of the election, the economic depression that had slowed business in the early 1890s was nearly over. Bryan's message no longer seemed urgent. McKinley won the election in a landslide.

Despite the loss, Populist ideas made an impact. In the 1900s, the United States abandoned the gold standard and adopted an eight-hour workday, an income tax, the secret ballot, and the direct election of senators.

✓ Reading Check **Evaluating** Why did people support the Populist Party?

History ONLINE
Study Central™ To review this section, go to glencoe.com.

Section 4 Review

Vocabulary

1. Define each of the following terms, and use each of them in a sentence: create, National Grange, cooperative, populism, currency.

Main Ideas

2. Explaining How did cooperatives help farmers? Why did the cooperatives fail?

3. Analyzing Why did the Populists believe free silver would help farmers and debtors?

Critical Thinking

4. Evaluating Was the Populist Party successful? Explain your answer.

5. Identifying Points of View Use a chart to describe what each person's opinion might be about the Populist Party.

	Opinion
Factory Worker	
Wealthy Factory Owner	
Southern African American Farmer	

6. Persuasive Writing Write a speech that William Jennings Bryan might have given during the election of 1896.

Answer the Essential Question

7. Why did economic reform movements develop in the late 1800s?

Answers

1. Sentences should use vocabulary words according to their definitions in the section and Glossary.

2. Cooperatives provided a market for farmers' goods and products at lower costs. They did not work because farmers often had to buy on credit, and the cooperatives were a cash-only system.

3. The Populists believed that having more silver coins in circulation would give farmers more money to pay their debts.

4. Possible answers: Yes, many Populist reforms were adopted in the 1900s. No, the Populists did not succeed in placing their candidates in high office.

5. Possible answers: **Factory worker:** supports party because it calls for an eight-hour workday. **Wealthy factory owner:** opposes party because it supports limited work hours and the income tax. **Southern African American farmer:** supports party because it calls for economic reforms to help farmers.

6. Students' speeches should include information about free silver and political reforms.

7. Students should address issues farmers faced, such as the high costs charged by railroads and manufacturers and the debt constantly facing farmers.

Visual Summary

Miners

- Pikes Peak in Colorado and the Comstock Lode in Nevada bring many miners west.
- Boomtowns spring up near mining sites and are abandoned when mining ended.
- Population growth leads to statehood for Colorado, North Dakota, South Dakota, Washington, Montana, Wyoming, and Idaho.

Ranchers

- Railroads open up profitable new markets for beef in the North and East.
- Cowhands herd cattle from Texas on long drives.
- Ranching spreads from Texas to the northern Plains.
- The "Cattle Kingdom" ends when a surplus of cattle causes prices to fall.

Farmers

- The Homestead Act attracts thousands of settlers with the promise of free land on the Great Plains.
- New technology helps pioneers overcome the harsh realities of farming on the Plains.
- Organizations such as the Grange and Farmers' Alliances help farmers financially and politically.

Native Americans

- Plains Indians are forced off their lands with the promise of receiving new land.
- White settlers move into land promised to Native Americans.
- The slaughter of the buffalo removes a major part of the Native American way of life.
- The Dawes Act aims to break up reservations and end tribal identification among Native Americans.

Study anywhere, anytime! Download quizzes and flash cards to your PDA from glencoe.com.

Opening the West **Chapter 18** 579

Visual Summary

Analyzing Information Some historians have argued that the existence of the Western frontier shaped American culture and that the farther people moved to the West, the more "American" they became. **Ask:** What characteristics of people in the West do you think these authors viewed as distinctly "American"? *(Possible answers: individualistic, adventurous, militaristic, strong, tended toward vigilantism, democratic, and so on.)* **AL**

Applying Organize the class into small groups. Have them discuss the following question in their groups. **Ask:** Had you been a voter in 1896, would you have voted for Bryan or McKinley? Explain your answer. *(Students should evaluate the political platforms of Bryan and McKinley and discuss the groups that supported their choices of candidates.)* **OL**

Creating an Atlas

Step 5: Assembling the Atlas Students will compile their maps into an atlas.

Directions Have student groups review their work. Each map should have a title and a legend. Students could include other materials from the chapter in their atlases as well, such as short introductory paragraphs for their maps. Finally, each group should write an introduction for its atlas, describing what it includes and what it can be used to show.

Analyzing Ask: How does viewing the maps as a group contribute to your understanding of the West in the late 1800s? *(Answers will vary.)* **OL**

Hands-On Chapter Project
Step 5: Wrap-Up

Teacher Tip

Displaying If you have access to a color photocopier, photocopy student maps onto transparencies. Students can then lay one map over another to compare and contrast the information on them.

Answers and Analyses

Reviewing Main Ideas

1. D Students should remember that the Comstock Lode was one of the world's richest deposits of silver-bearing ore. This should lead students to select choice D. Other western mines contained the ores listed in choices A, B and C. **17.C.3a**

2. B Students should remember that Hispanic ranch hands were called "vaqueros," making choice A incorrect. Choices C and D are wrong as settlers in Oklahoma were called "boomers," and citizens who punished criminals were called "vigilantes." The only choice left is B. **16.E.3b (US)**

3. B Students can eliminate choice D, because the Ghost Dance emerged later. Geronimo did not surrender until 1886, eliminating choice C. The Cheyenne were massacred while on their way to negotiate a peace settlement, which should lead students to choose B. **18.B.3a**

4. B Students should immediately eliminate returning to the gold standard and extending the term of the president—choices A and C—both of which the Populists opposed. Choice D can be eliminated since the Fifteenth Amendment is unrelated to the Populists. Students should remember that Populists were angry at railroads for high shipping rates, leading them to choice B. **16.A**

Short-Answer Question

5. Based on visions received from the ghosts of his ancestors, Kicking Bear believed Native Americans would regain their lands from whites with help from the spirit world. **16.A.3b**

STANDARDIZED TEST PRACTICE

TEST-TAKING TIP

Answer the questions you know first and go back to those for which you need more time.

Reviewing Main Ideas

Directions: Choose the best answer for each of the following questions.

1. Discovered in 1859, Nevada's Comstock Lode contained
   A scattered deposits of gold and iron ore.
   B large concentrations of coal.
   C the biggest seam of copper ever found.
   D a rich lode of silver-bearing ore.

2. Who were the "Exodusters"?
   A Hispanic ranch hands in the Southwest
   B African Americans who migrated into Kansas
   C settlers who staked claims in Oklahoma
   D ordinary citizens who punished criminals

3. Which of the following events occurred in 1868 along the Little Bighorn River in present-day Montana?
   A Several hundred Cheyenne negotiated a peace deal with the U.S. government.
   B Sioux and Cheyenne warriors defeated a U.S. army unit led by Lt. Col. George Custer.
   C Apache leader Geronimo was the last Native American to surrender formally to the U.S.
   D Thousands of Lakota Sioux gathered for a Ghost Dance ritual.

4. One of the goals of the Populist Party was
   A returning to the gold currency standard.
   B government ownership of railroads.
   C extending the term of the president.
   D passage of the Fifteenth Amendment.

Short-Answer Question

Directions: Base your answer to question 5 on the excerpt below and on your knowledge of social studies.

> My brothers, I bring to you the promise of a day in which there will be no white man to lay his hand on the bridle of the Indian's horse; when the red men of the prairie will rule the world and not be turned from the hunting-grounds by any man. I bring you word from your fathers the ghosts, that they are now marching to join you, led by the Messiah who came once to live on earth with the white men, but was cast out and killed by them. I have seen the wonders of the spirit-land, and have talked with the ghosts.
>
> —from Kicking Bear's speech to a council of Sioux, 1890

5. According to the document, what changes did Kicking Bear expect to occur in the relationship between Native Americans and whites? Why did he think this?

Review the Essential Questions

6. **Essay** Discuss the contributions of different ethnic groups to the history of the American West in the middle to late 1800s.

To help you write your essay, review your answers to the Essential Questions in the section reviews and the chapter Foldables Study Organizer. Your essay should include:

- western mining booms;
- westward expansion;
- ranchers and homesteaders;
- settlers' relations with Native Americans; and
- Populist Party activities.

GO ON

Review the Essential Questions

6. Using their Foldables, students should discuss factors such as: Chinese, Irish, and African American railroad workers; Hispanic and African American ranch hands; African American homesteaders (Exodusters); Native American struggles; and African American political activity in the Populist Party. **17.C.3c**

History ONLINE
For additional test practice, use **Self-Check Quizzes**—Chapter 18 at glencoe.com.

Chapter 18 Assessment

Document-Based Questions

Directions: Analyze the documents and answer the short-answer questions that follow.

Document 1

This is an excerpt from Grenville M. Dodge's 1869 report on the transcontinental railway.

> Telegraphic wires were so connected that each blow of the descending [sledgehammer] could be reported instantly to all parts of the United States. . . . And with the last blow of the sledge a cannon was fired at Fort Point [in San Francisco].

Source: David Colbert, *Eyewitness to America*

7. Based on the excerpt, was the completion of the railroad considered an important national event? How do you know?

Document 2

J. Ross Browne recorded these impressions of Virginia City, Nevada, in 1865.

> The business part of the town has been built up with astonishing rapidity. In the spring of 1860 there was nothing of it save a few frame shanties and canvas tents, and one or two rough stone cabins. It now presents some of the distinguishing features of a metropolitan city.

Source: *The Mammoth Book of Eyewitness America*

8. According to Browne, how had Virginia City changed?

9. What might be distinguishing features of a metropolitan city in 1865?

Document 3

This 1891 cartoon is about the Populist Party.

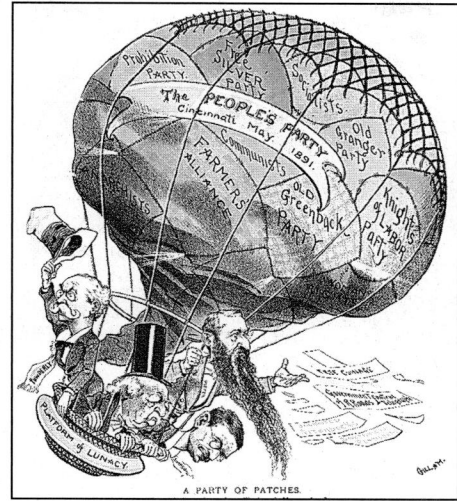

A PARTY OF PATCHES.

10. The title of the cartoon is "A Party of Patches." What does this say about the organization of the party?

11. Expository Writing Using the information from the three documents and your knowledge of social studies, write an essay in which you:

- explain why railroads are the key to understanding the development of the American West; and

- discuss at least one problem or conflict directly related to the spread of railroads in the West.

9. Students may answer that it would have a thriving business district, including permanent and impressive buildings, roads, perhaps transportation hubs, and so on. **16.E.3c(US)**

10. Possible answer: The cartoon title and the drawing of the balloon indicate that the Populist Party is made up of different groups that may or may not work together well. The tipping of the balloon indicates that there are problems with how the pieces fit together. **16.A.3b**

11. Students may cite a number of reasons, such as: Railroads brought thousands of workers and settlers to the west; they carried metals and produce to the East and manufactured goods to the west; ranching became more profitable and widespread as railroads opened new markets in the North and the East; towns sprang up along the rail lines that carried the settlers' agricultural goods to market; creation of time zones. Problems cited could include railroads' effects on Native American culture or farmers' resentment of railroad shipping costs and ownership of land, leading to changes in American politics. **16.C.3b(US)**

History ONLINE
Have students visit the Web site at glencoe.com to review Chapter 18 and take the Self-Check Quiz.

Need Extra Help?

If you missed questions. . .	1	2	3	4	5	6	7	8	9	10	11
Go to page. . .	553	564	570	577	568–571	552–578	554–557	557	557	577–578	552–578

Need Extra Help?

Have students refer to the pages listed if they miss any of the questions.

Document-Based Questions

7. Yes, it was considered an important national event because the telegraph was used to transmit each hammer blow to the nation, and a cannon was fired at the last blow in faraway San Francisco. **15.E**

8. According to Browne, just five years earlier the town consisted of only a few shanties and tents; by 1865, it had grown rapidly, and came to resemble in part a large metropolitan city. **16.D.3a (US)**

Chapter Planning Guide

19

Levels BL	OL	AL	ELL		Resources	Chapter Opener	Section 1	Section 2	Section 3	Section 4	Chapter Assess
FOCUS											
BL	OL	AL	ELL	📇	**Daily Test Practice Transparencies**		19–1	19–2	19–3	19–4	
TEACH											
	OL	AL		📁	**Geography and History Activity, URB**				p. 59		
BL	OL		ELL	📁	**Time Line Skills Activity, URB**					p. 62	
BL	OL	AL	ELL	📁	**Writing Skills Activity, URB**		p. 51				
BL	OL	AL	ELL	📁	**Content Vocabulary Activity, URB**		p. 45	p. 45	p. 45	p. 45	
BL	OL	AL	ELL	📁	**Academic Vocabulary Activity, URB**		p. 47	p. 47	p. 47	p. 47	
BL	OL		ELL	📁	**Social Studies Skills Activity, URB**			p. 53			
BL	OL	AL	ELL	📁	**Differentiated Instruction Activity, URB**					p. 55	
BL	OL	AL	ELL	📁	**Critical Thinking Skills Activity, URB**					p. 57	
BL	OL	AL	ELL	📁	**Linking Past and Present Activity, URB**			p. 61			
	OL	AL		📁	**Primary Source Readings, URB**				p. 49		
BL	OL	AL	ELL	📁	**School-to-Home Connection Activity, URB**		p. 63	p. 63	p. 63	p. 63	
BL	OL		ELL	📁	**Guided Reading Activity, URB***		p. 67	p. 68	p. 69	p. 70	
BL	OL		ELL	📁	**Reading Essentials and Note-Taking Guide***		p. 202	p. 205	p. 208	p. 211	
BL	OL	AL	ELL	📇	**Lesson Transparencies**			19A, 19B	19C		
		AL		📁	**Supreme Court Case Studies**		p. 21		p. 29	p. 25	
	OL			📁	**American Biographies**				p. 32	pp. 33, 34	
BL	OL	AL	ELL	📁	**Outline Map Resource Book**	p. 6					
	OL	AL		📇	**American Art and Architecture Transparencies, Strategies, and Activities**				18, 19		

Note: Please refer to the *Unit Resource Book: Reshaping the Nation* for this chapter's URB materials.

* Also available in Spanish

Levels				Resources	Chapter Opener	Section 1	Section 2	Section 3	Section 4	Chapter Assess
BL	OL	AL	ELL	**TEACH** *(continued)*						
BL	OL	AL	ELL	NGS US Desk Map		✓	✓	✓	✓	
BL	OL	AL	ELL	American Literature Library		✓	✓	✓	✓	
BL	OL	AL	ELL	Writer's Guidebook		✓	✓	✓	✓	
	OL	AL		American History Primary Source Document Library CD-ROM		✓	✓	✓	✓	✓
BL	OL	AL	ELL	American Music: Hits Through History	✓	✓	✓	✓	✓	
BL	OL	AL	ELL	StudentWorks™ Plus CD	✓	✓	✓	✓	✓	✓
BL	OL	AL	ELL	Section Spotlight Videos		✓	✓	✓	✓	
BL	OL	AL	ELL	Writing Process Transparencies		✓	✓	✓	✓	✓
BL	OL	AL	ELL	Presentation Plus! With MindJogger CheckPoint CD	✓	✓	✓	✓	✓	✓
BL	OL	AL	ELL	**ASSESS**						
BL	OL	AL	ELL	Quizzes and Tests		p. 183	p. 184	p. 185	p. 186	pp. 187, 189, 191
BL	OL	AL	ELL	Authentic Assessment With Rubrics					p. 19	
BL	OL	AL	ELL	Standardized Test Practice						p. 37
BL	OL	AL	ELL	*ExamView® Assessment Suite* CD-ROM*		19–1	19–2	19–3	19–4	Ch. 19
BL	OL	AL	ELL	**CLOSE**						
BL			ELL	Reteaching Activity, URB*		p. 65	p. 65	p. 65	p. 65	p. 65
BL	OL		ELL	Reading and Study Skills Foldables Activity	p. 86	p. 86	p. 86	p. 86	p. 86	p. 86
BL	OL	AL	ELL	*The American Journey* in Graphic Novel						p. 107
BL			ELL	Reading Strategies and Activities for the Social Studies Classroom		✓	✓	✓	✓	
BL	OL	AL	ELL	Graphic Organizer Transparencies & Strategies		✓	✓	✓	✓	

TeacherWorks *Plus*
All-In-One Planner and Resource Center

- Interactive Lesson Planner
- Interactive Teacher Edition
- Fully editable blackline masters
- Section Spotlight Videos Launch
- Differentiated Lesson Plans
- Printable reports of daily assignments
- Standards Tracking System

Professional Development Resources

- Strategies for Success
- Building Academic Vocabulary
- Success With English Learners DVD
- Differentiated Instruction Strategies DVD
- Teaching Literacy Strategies in Social Studies DVD
- Assessment DVD
- Standards-Based Instruction DVD

Integrating Technology

19

Using a Whiteboard

Physical Geography of the United States

Objective

Students will locate major physical features of the U.S.

Technology Product

- Interactive whiteboard
- *The American Journey TeacherWorks™ Outline Map Resource Book*, page 6

Focus/Teach

- Project the map of the U.S. found in the Outline Map Resource Book on page 6. Explain to students that they are going to draw the major physical features of the U.S.
- The class can be organized into teams of four, or students can participate individually.

- List the major mountains, rivers, deserts, lakes, oceans, and so on.
- Have each team create a label for its physical feature, using a colored pen and map symbol. Teams may use the atlas in the text for help. Have team members draw the symbols and colors in the key.

Assess

- Have students review the map projection.

Close

- Project the completed outline map.
- Review this activity with the class.

History ONLINE at glencoe.com

	Student	Teacher	Parent
Media Center			
• Student Edition Audio	●		
• Spanish Summaries	●		
• Section Spotlight Videos	●	●	
Social Studies Online Learning Center			
Classroom Tools			
• Multi-Language Glossaries	●	●	●
• Teaching Today		●	
• TIME Current Events	●	●	●
• Beyond the Textbook	●	●	
***The American Journey* Online Learning Center**			
• Study-to-Go™	●	●	●
• Study Central™	●	●	●
• Chapter Overview	●	●	
• Concepts in Motion	●	●	
• ePuzzles and Games	●	●	
• Literature Connections	●	●	
• Online Student Edition	●	●	●
• Self-Check Quizzes	●	●	●
• Student Web Activities	●	●	
• Vocabulary eFlashcards	●	●	
• Web Activity Lesson Plans	●	●	●
• Vocabulary PuzzleMaker	●	●	●

Timed Readings Plus in Social Studies helps students increase their reading rate and fluency while maintaining comprehension. The 400-word passages are similar to those found on state and national assessments.

Reading in the Content Area: Social Studies concentrates on six essential reading skills that help students better comprehend what they read. The book includes 75 high-interest nonfiction passages written at increasing levels of difficulty.

Reading Social Studies includes strategic reading instruction and vocabulary support in Social Studies content for ELLs and native speakers of English.

Content Vocabulary Workout (Grades 6–8) accelerates reading comprehension through focused vocabulary development. Social Studies content vocabulary comes from the glossaries of Glencoe's Middle School Social Studies texts.

www.jamestowneducation.com

Index to National Geographic Magazine:

The following articles relate to this chapter:

- *"Biofuels: Green Dreams,"* Joel K. Bourne, Jr., October 2007.
- *"Silicon Valley: Inside the Dream Incubator,"* Cathy Newman, December 2001.

National Geographic Society Products

To order the following, call National Geographic at 1-800-368-2728:

National Geographic Atlas of the World *(Book)*

Access National Geographic's dynamic MapMachine Web site and other geography resources at:

www.nationalgeographic.com

www.nationalgeographic.com/mapmachine

Use this database to search more than 30,000 titles to create a customized reading list for your students.

- Reading lists can be organized by students' reading level, author, genre, theme, or area of interest.
- The database provides Degrees of Reading Power™ (DRP) and Lexile™ readability scores for all selections.
- A brief summary of each selection is included.

Leveled reading suggestions for this chapter:

For students at a Grade 6 reading level:
- *The Gold Cadillac,* by Mildred D. Taylor

For students at a Grade 7 reading level:
- *Henry Ford: A Photo-Illustrated Biography,* by Erika L. Shores

For students at a Grade 8 reading level:
- *CLICK! A Story About George Eastman,* by Barbara Mitchell

For students at a Grade 9 reading level:
- *Queen of Inventions: How the Sewing Machine Changed the World,* by Laurie Carlson

For students at a Grade 10 reading level:
- *Thomas A. Edison: The World's Greatest Inventor,* by Anna Sproule

The following videotape programs are available from Glencoe as supplements to the chapter:

- **Andrew Carnegie and the Age of Steel** (ISBN 0-76-700620-8)
- **Henry Ford: Tin Lizzy Tycoon** (ISBN 1-56-501380-8)

To order, call Glencoe at 1-800-334-7344. To find classroom resources to accompany many of these videos, check the following home pages:

A&E Television: www.aetv.com

The History Channel: www.history.com

Chapter Objectives

After studying this chapter, students will be able to:

- Understand how railroad expansion affected the U.S. economy.
- Discuss how inventions revolutionized society in the late 1800s.
- Describe how Americans built fortunes in the oil and steel industries.
- Explain why workers formed labor unions in the middle to late 1800s.

Motivating Activity

Making Inferences Students will learn that the growth of industry in the late 1800s created many new jobs in factories. **Ask:** What do the workers in this image have in common? *(All are women working at machines.)* Point out that by 1900, more than 1 million women had joined the industrial workforce. **Ask:** Why might factory managers hire women? *(Students may say that managers could pay women less than men.)* Point out that factory workers often did the same simple task for 10 or 12 hours per day, six days per week. **OL**

Previewing the Essential Questions

As you begin teaching each section, use these questions and activities to help students focus on the Essential Questions.

Chapter 19

The Industrial Age 1865–1914

Working at a factory in Dayton, Ohio, 1902

PRESIDENTS

A. JOHNSON 1865–1869	
U. S. GRANT 1869–1877	
R. B. HAYES 1877–1881	
J. GARFIELD 1881	

1869 ★ First transcontinental railroad completed

★ **1870** Rockefeller organizes Standard Oil Company

1876 ★ Bell patents the telephone

★ **1879** Edison invents electric light

U.S. Events
World Events

1860 — 1870 — 1880

1867 ★ Diamonds discovered in Cape Colony, a province in South Africa

★ **1880** Unions win the right to strike in Great Britain

582 Chapter 19

Section 1

Railroads Lead the Way Ask: How might the development of a nationwide network of railroads help businesses? *(They could get raw materials to factories faster and from farther away, they could open markets in more distant places, and they could transport finished goods to more markets.)* Explain that Section 1 explores how railroads helped the economy grow. **OL**

Section 2

Inventions Ask: How would your life be different if the telephone had not been invented? *(Students might say that they could not keep up with their friends as closely. Remind them that the Internet would not exist without telephone technology.)* Explain that in Section 2, students will learn about inventions of the late 1800s that transformed society. **OL**

Section 1: Railroads Lead the Way

Essential Question How did railroad expansion affect the United States economy?

Section 2: Inventions

Essential Question How did the inventions of the late 1800s revolutionize society?

Section 3: An Age of Big Business

Essential Question How did Americans build fortunes in the oil and steel industries?

Section 4: Industrial Workers

Essential Question Why did workers form labor unions in the middle to late 1800s?

History ONLINE
Chapter Overview Visit glencoe.com and click on Chapter 19—Chapter Overviews to preview chapter information.

FOLDABLES Study Organizer

Organizing Information

Make this Foldable to help organize what you learn about the growth of industry in the late 1800s.

Step 1 Fold four sheets of paper in half from top to bottom.

Step 2 On each folded paper, make a cut 1 inch from the side on the top flap.

Step 3 Place the folded papers one on top of the other, and staple the sections together. Label the pages with headings appropriate for the sections.

Railroad Industry

Main ideas, dates, events, diagrams, etc.

Reading and Writing As you read, note dates, events, and visuals from the chapter to help you summarize its main ideas.

Model T touring car, 1908 ▶

★ **1890** Sherman Antitrust Act passes

1892 Iron- and steel-workers strike in the U.S.

C. ARTHUR 1881–1885

G. CLEVELAND 1885–1889

B. HARRISON 1889–1893

G. CLEVELAND 1893–1897

W. MCKINLEY 1897–1901

T. ROOSEVELT 1901–1909

★ **1903** First powered flight by Wright brothers

1908 Ford introduces Model T

1890   **1900**

1893 ★ Karl Benz builds four-wheel car

1895 ★ Marconi sends first radio signals

1895 Lumière brothers introduce motion pictures

◀ French inventor Louis Lumière

Chapter 19   583

Introducing Chapter 19

Time Line Activity

If you have not already done so, have students review the time line. **Ask:** What years are covered in this chapter? *(1860–1908)* What innovations did Americans introduce in this period? *(telephone, electric light, motorized airplane, Model T)* **Ask:** Which inventions shown here made later inventions possible? *(electric light—motion pictures; four-wheel car—Model T)*

FOLDABLES Study Organizer Dinah Zike's Foldables

Purpose This Foldable helps students organize information about the growth of industry in the 1800s. The completed Foldable will help them prepare for assessment. **OL**

📁 More Foldables activities for this chapter can be found in the *Dinah Zike's Reading and Study Skills Foldables.*

History ONLINE

Introduce students to chapter content and key terms by having them access the **Chapter Overview** at glencoe.com.

Section 3

An Age of Big Business Ask: How might people organize businesses to make the most profit? *(keep wages low, charge high prices, keep production costs low, control different phases of production)* Point out that Section 3 explains how individuals gained control of the oil and steel industries, enabling them to build great fortunes. **OL**

Section 4

Industrial Workers Ask: What do you think conditions were like for workers in factories in the 1800s? *(long hours, unsafe and unhealthy conditions, accidents were common)* Explain that in Section 4, students will learn how workers formed labor unions to try to gain better working conditions. **OL**

583

Section 1

Railroads Lead the Way

Focus

Bellringer
Daily Test Practice Transparency 19–1

Reading Guide
Answers to Graphic:

spurred growth of iron, steel, timber, and coal industries; provided thousands of jobs; helped industry and population expand into the West

Section Spotlight Video

To learn more about the development of railroads, watch the Section Spotlight Video "Railroads Lead the Way."

Essential Question ◀
How did railroad expansion affect the United States economy?

Reading Guide

Content Vocabulary
consolidation (p. 585)
rebate (p. 587)
railroad baron (p. 585)
pool (p. 587)
standard gauge (p. 586)

Academic Vocabulary
labor (p. 585)   individual (p. 585)

Key People and Events
George Westinghouse (p. 587)
Eli H. Janney (p. 587)
Gustavus Swift (p. 587)
George M. Pullman (p. 587)

Reading Strategy
Taking Notes As you read, use a diagram like the one below to record the effects of railroad expansion in the United States.

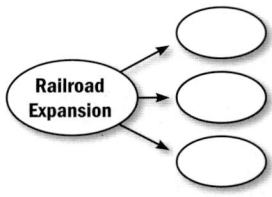

Railroad Expansion

ILLINOIS STANDARDS
The American Journey

15.B.3b Explain the effects of choice and competition on individuals and the economy as a whole.

15.C.3 Identify and explain the effects of various incentives to produce a good or service.

18.B.3a Analyze how individuals and groups interact with and within institutions (e.g., educational, military).

American Diary

In 1869 writer Samuel Bowles described his journey west: "Marked, indeed, was the contrast between the stage [stagecoach] ride . . . and the Railroad ride . . . across the Plains. The then long-drawn, tedious [boring] endurance of six days and nights, running the gauntlet of hostile Indians, was now accomplished in a single twenty-four hours, safe in a swiftly-moving train, and in a car that was an elegant drawing-room by day and a luxurious bedroom at night."

—from **Our New West**

Resource Manager

R Reading Strategies	C Critical Thinking	D Differentiated Instruction	W Writing Support	S Skill Practice
Teacher Edition • Inferring, p. 585 **Additional Resources** • Guid. Read., URB p. 67 • Content Vocab., URB p. 45 • Academic Vocab., URB p. 47 • Read. Ess., p. 202	**Teacher Edition** • Ident. Central Issues, p. 586 **Additional Resources** • Quizzes and Tests, p. 183	**Teacher Edition** • Logical/Mathematical, p. 585 **Additional Resources** • School-to-Home, URB p. 63 • Reteaching Act., URB p. 65	**Teacher Edition** • Persuasive Writing, p. 586 **Additional Resources** • Writ. Skills, URB p. 51	**Teacher Edition** • Using Research Skills, p. 587 **Additional Resources** • Daily Test Pract. Transp. 19-1 • Lesson Transp. 19A

Railroad Expansion

Main Idea The railroad system expanded rapidly in the late 1800s, building large fortunes for some wealthy businesspeople.

History and You In what industries do people make large amounts of money today? Read to learn about the profits generated by railroad expansion.

During the Civil War, trains carried troops and supplies to the front. After the war, the railroad system grew rapidly and drove economic growth in the United States. In 1860 the United States had about 30,000 miles (48,280 km) of railroad track. By 1900, the nation had nearly 193,000 miles (310,603 km) of track. Work songs such as "John Henry" and "I've Been Working on the Railroad" were popular among those who **labored,** or worked, to build these miles of track.

Railroad expansion was accompanied by **consolidation**—the practice of combining separate companies—in the industry. Large railroad companies bought smaller companies or drove them out of business. Consolidation made the large companies more efficient. These companies established standard prices and made industrial processes more uniform.

Railroad Barons

After consolidation, a few powerful **individuals,** or persons, known as **railroad barons** controlled the nation's rail traffic. New Yorker Cornelius Vanderbilt, one of the first railroad barons, made a fortune by consolidating several companies. His railroad empire stretched from New York City to the Great Lakes. Another railroad baron, James J. Hill, built the Great Northern line between Minnesota and Washington State. Other barons, including Collis P. Huntington and Leland Stanford, founded the Central Pacific, which connected California and Utah. The railroad barons were aggressive and competitive. They lived in an age when there were few laws that regulated business.

✔ **Reading Check** **Analyzing** What are the advantages and disadvantages of consolidation?

By the Numbers / Railroad Tracks

Connecting the Country Railroads expanded rapidly in the years following the Civil War. By the late 1800s, all major U.S. cities from the West Coast to the East Coast were connected by rail.

U.S. Railroad Track Miles

Year	Miles of track
1860	30,635
1870	52,922
1880	92,147
1890	163,597
1900	193,346

Source: Association of American Railroads; *Historical Statistics of the United States: Colonial Times to 1970*

Critical Thinking

Calculating Which decade saw the largest increase in track miles?

The Union Pacific Railroad depot at La Grande, Oregon, c. 1870

Teach

D Differentiated Instruction

Logical/Mathematical Ask: Between 1860 and 1900, the miles of railroad track grew by about what percentage? *(193,000/30,000 = 6.43 = 643%)* **AL**

R Reading Strategy

Inferring Point out that in medieval Europe, barons were nobles who owned large estates with many serfs. **Ask:** Why were men like Hill and Vanderbilt called railroad barons? *(They were wealthy, powerful men who controlled huge companies with many workers.)* **OL**

By the Numbers

Critical Thinking Answer
1880 to 1890

✔ **Reading Check** **Answer:** *Advantage:* Large companies become more efficient. *Disadvantage:* Smaller companies may be forced out of business.

Differentiated Instruction

Narrowing a Research Topic

Writing Skills Activity
The Industrial Age

Narrowing a Research Topic

Objective: To learn how to narrow a research topic

Focus: Ask students why it would be important to know how to narrow a research topic.

Teach: Have students read the material, answer the questions, and apply the skill.

Assess: Students should complete the self-assessment checklist.

Close: Ask students to read their research topics aloud. Have the class determine if each topic is narrow enough to write a report on it.

Writing Skills Activity,
URB p. 51

Differentiated Instruction Strategies

BL Have students use different-colored pencils to fill in the groups of web circles as they narrow their topics.

AL Ask students to research and write their reports on the topics they selected.

ELL Before students work on their topics, have them define the following terms: "research topic," "web circle," and "scope."

The Growth of Railroads
NATIONAL GEOGRAPHIC

W Writing Support

Persuasive Writing Have students take the role of a railroad baron and write a newspaper advertisement to attract people to work for the railroad. **OL**

C Critical Thinking

Identifying Central Issues Ask: Before the consolidation of railroad companies, why did cargo have to be moved from one train to another during shipment? *(Trains from different railroads could not use the same track because the widths of the tracks differed.)* **BL**

The Growth of Railroads
NATIONAL GEOGRAPHIC

Map Skills Answers
Eastern and Central regions; these regions had the most people and the most industry.

Hands-On Chapter Project
Step 1

Conducting a Seminar

Step 1: Researching Students will research key innovations and developments of the late 1800s and early 1900s.

Essential Question: How did railroad expansion affect the U. S. economy?

Directions Organize the class into four groups. Assign each group one of these

---

The Growth of Railroads NATIONAL GEOGRAPHIC

Time Zones Before railroads, each community established its own time. In order to create sensible schedules, the railroad companies divided the country into four time zones. Each zone was one hour apart from the zone on either side of it.

Railroads in 1890

	Pacific Time Zone
	Mountain Time Zone
	Central Time Zone
	Eastern Time Zone
——	Railroads built by 1870
——	Railroads built by 1890

*Time zones and borders shown as of 1890

This advertisement shows the "Hotel" car introduced by George Pullman in 1867. It had both sleeping and dining facilities and greatly improved the experience of rail travel.

Map Skills

Regions Which time zone regions had the greatest lengths of railroad tracks? Why was that so?

Maps In Motion See StudentWorks™ Plus or glencoe.com.

W Railroads Stimulate the Economy

Main Idea Railroads brought major changes to American industry and American life in general.

History and You Think about how the expansion of one industry leads to the growth of others. Read to learn how railroads influenced other industries.

· ·

Railroads carried raw materials such as iron ore, coal, and timber to factories. They also carried manufactured goods from factories to markets and transported produce from farming areas to the cities.

At first the demand for iron tracks and locomotives helped the iron mining and processing industries grow. Around 1880, railroad companies began using tracks of steel—a strong metal made by adding carbon and other elements to refined iron. The use of steel in railroad tracks stimulated America's steel industry. Railroads also had an effect on the lumber industry, which supplied wood for railway ties, and the coal industry, which provided fuel. In addition, railroad companies provided work for thousands of people.

Improving the Railroads

C Increased use made it necessary for railroads to expand and unify their systems. While railroads were being built across the country, different lines used rails of different gauges, or widths. As a result, trains of one line could not use another line's tracks. The gaps in service made travel extremely slow.

As the railroad companies consolidated, companies adopted a **standard gauge** of 4 feet, 8.5 inches (1 m, 41.6 cm) as the width of the railroad track. A standard gauge allowed faster shipment of goods at a reduced cost. It was no longer necessary to load and unload goods from one train to another.

586 Chapter 19 *The Industrial Age*

---

topics: (1) railroad barons and innovators of railroad technology; (2) inventors; (3) entrepreneurs and industrial leaders, and (4) labor union leaders. Explain that each group will create an educational seminar with these people as panelists. The seminar will take place in the early 1900s. The goal is to educate the audience about important changes occurring at this time and the effects on business and society. Have the groups research their assigned people and innovations and gather images.

Discussing Have the railroad group share their notes on the effects of railroad expansion. As a class, discuss how railroads changed daily life. **OL**

(Chapter Project continued in Section 2)

Railroad Technology

Railway transportation also improved with the introduction of new technology. Four developments were particularly important. Inventor **George Westinghouse** devised air brakes that improved the system for stopping trains, making train travel safer. Janney car couplers, named after inventor **Eli H. Janney,** made it easier for railroad workers to link cars. Refrigerated cars, developed by **Gustavus Swift,** enabled the railroads to ship meat and other perishable goods over long distances. Finally, **George M. Pullman** developed the Pullman sleeping car—a luxury railway car with seats that converted into beds for overnight journeys.

Competing for Customers

Railroad companies competed fiercely with one another to keep old customers and to win new ones. Large railroads offered secret discounts called **rebates** to their biggest customers. Smaller railroads that could not match these rebates were often forced out of business. Giving discounts to big customers, however, raised freight rates for farmers and other customers who shipped small amounts of goods.

The railroad barons also made secret agreements among themselves, known as **pools.** They divided business among their companies and set rates. With no other competition in its region, a railroad could charge higher rates and earn greater profits. There were some laws to regulate the railroads, but they did little to stop the barons.

Railroads Change America

The growing railroad network helped American industry expand into the West. For example, the manufacturing center for agricultural equipment moved from central New York State to Illinois and Wisconsin. Trains also redistributed the American population. They transported homesteaders into the Great Plains and the West and people from rural areas to the cities.

Reading Check **Describing** What were some of the new technologies that improved railroad travel?

History ONLINE
Study Central™ To review this section, go to glencoe.com.

Section 1 Review

Vocabulary

1. Use each of these terms in a sentence that will help explain its meaning: labor, consolidation, individual, railroad baron, standard gauge, rebate, pool.

Main Ideas

2. **Explaining** How did railroad barons build their fortunes?

3. **Evaluating** Do you think Congress should have allowed railroad barons to make agreements about business and rates? Explain your answer.

Critical Thinking

4. **Classifying** What are some industries that benefited from the expansion of the railroad system?

Railroad Industry

5. **Making Inferences** Do you think owners of small farms supported the rebates given by railroad companies?

6. **Expository Writing** Write a paragraph explaining how the adoption of standard-gauge track affected the railroads.

Answer the
7. **Essential Question**
How did railroad expansion affect the United States economy?

S Skill Practice

Using Research Skills Have students look into the history of trains from the early days of railroading to the present, focusing on locomotives and power sources. Have them present their findings as images with captions. **AL**

Reading Check **Answer:** air brakes, Janney car couplers, refrigerated cars, Pullman sleeping cars

Assess

History ONLINE

Study Central™ provides summaries, interactive games, and online graphic organizers to help students review content.

Close

Predicting On the board, make a list of the potential effects of railroad expansion on the U.S. economy in the late 1800s. **OL**

Section 1 Review

The Industrial Age **Chapter 19** **587**

Answers

1. Students' sentences should demonstrate an understanding of the terms.
2. By consolidating small companies into large companies; individuals gained control of the nation's rail traffic.
3. Answers will vary but should discuss rebates, pools, and whether Congress should regulate business.

4. iron, steel, lumber, coal
5. no, because the rebates were given only to large customers, and freight rates increased for small farmers
6. Paragraphs should mention that standard-gauge track allowed faster shipment of goods, or travel for people, at lower cost,

because it meant one train could make the entire trip.
7. Railroad expansion allowed a few powerful individuals to build great fortunes; it benefited lumber, coal, iron, and steel industries; it moved industries to the West; and it opened the entire United States to economic growth.

Section 2

Section 2

Inventions

Focus

Bellringer
Daily Test Practice Transparency 19–2

Reading Guide
Answers to Graphic:

telegraph: sped up everyday communications for businesses and individuals, linked Europe and United States by transatlantic cable; **telephone:** first businesses and then homes could communicate with one another by voice; **electric lightbulb:** became the main way of illuminating the night, led to further developments in the use and distribution of electrical power

Section Spotlight Video

Watch the Section Spotlight Video "Inventions" to learn more about innovations that spurred economic growth during industrialization.

Resource Manager

Essential Question
How did the inventions of the late 1800s revolutionize society?

Reading Guide

Content Vocabulary

Model T (p. 593)   mass production (p. 593)

assembly line (p. 593)

Academic Vocabulary

transmit (p. 589)   mechanism (p. 592)

Key People and Events

Cyrus Field (p. 589)
Alexander Graham Bell (p. 590)
George Eastman (p. 590)
John Thurman (p. 590)
Lewis Howard Latimer (p. 592)
Granville Woods (p. 592)
Elijah McCoy (p. 592)
Jan E. Matzeliger (p. 592)
Henry Ford (p. 592)

Reading Strategy

Taking Notes As you read, use a chart like the one below to identify the effects of major inventions.

	Effects
Telegraph	
Telephone	
Electric lightbulb	

ILLINOIS STANDARDS
The American Journey

15.A.3a Explain how market prices signal producers about what, how and how much to produce.

15.D.3c Explain how workers can affect their productivity through training and by using tools, machinery and technology.

16.C.3b (US) Explain relationships among the American economy and slavery, immigration, labor and urbanization, 1700-present.

American Diary

The Cleveland Plain Dealer described the lighting of a park in 1879:

"Thousands of people gathered . . . and as the light shot around and through the Park a shout was raised. . . . Soon afterward a section of artillery on the lake shore began firing a salute in honor of the occasion.

The Telegraph Supply Company's establishment . . . was thrown open to as many people as could be accommodated . . . [to] inspect the machinery which sends light over the wire."

—from Men and Volts

Electricity lights up Luna Park on Coney Island in New York, 1890.

R **Reading Strategies**	C **Critical Thinking**	D **Differentiated Instruction**	W **Writing Support**	S **Skill Practice**
Teacher Edition • Previewing, p. 589 • Making Connections, p. 593 **Additional Resources** • Guid. Read., URB p. 68 • Content Vocab., URB p. 45 • Academic Vocab., URB p. 47 • Read. Ess., p. 205	**Teacher Edition** • Making Inferences, p. 591 • Analyzing Information, p. 593 **Additional Resources** • Quizzes and Tests, p. 184	**Teacher Edition** • Auditory/Musical, p. 589 • Gifted and Talented, p. 590 • Verbal/Linguistic, p. 591 **Additional Resources** • School-to-Home, URB p. 63 • Reteaching Act., URB p. 65	**Teacher Edition** • Expository Writing, p. 590 • Descriptive Writing, p. 590	**Teacher Edition** • Creating a Time Line, p. 592 **Additional Resources** • Daily Test Pract. Transp. 19-2 • Link. Past & Pres., URB p. 61 • Soc. Stud. Skills, URB p. 53 • Lesson Transp. 19B

Communications

Main Idea New inventions revolutionized communications, making faraway places seem closer.

History and You Do you talk on a cell phone or e-mail people in other states or countries? Read to learn how long-distance communication changed in the late 1800s.

By 1910, Americans in cities drove cars through streets lit with electric lights. They went to department stores where they bought everything from kitchen sinks to shoes. Americans also could do their shopping by mail—or pick up the telephone and order groceries from the local store. The automobile, the electric light, and the telephone were invented after 1870. Within a generation, they became part of everyday life for millions of people. These new inventions helped people communicate more quickly over long distances. Improvements in communication helped unify the country and promoted economic growth.

The Telegraph

Samuel Morse had introduced the telegraph in 1844. By 1860 the United States had thousands of miles of telegraph lines, managed mostly by the Western Union Telegraph Company. At telegraph offices, trained operators **transmitted**, or sent, messages in Morse code.

Telegrams offered almost instant communication and served many purposes. Shopkeepers relied on telegrams to order goods, and reporters used them to transmit stories to their newspapers. Americans also used telegrams to send personal messages.

The telegraph soon linked the United States and Europe. In the 1860s, news from Europe was relayed to the United States by ship and took several weeks. **Cyrus Field** wanted to speed up the process. In 1866, after several unsuccessful attempts, Field managed to lay a telegraph cable across the Atlantic Ocean. The new transatlantic telegraph transmitted messages in a matter of seconds, bringing the United States and Europe closer together.

Primary Source / Lewis Latimer

Improving Technology Lewis Latimer was a draftsman and an inventor who received numerous patents for his inventions. In 1876 he was hired to draft the patent drawings for Alexander Graham Bell's telephone. Later, he improved on Edison's version of the lightbulb, creating one that lasted much longer. Latimer directed the installation of electric streetlights in New York City, Philadelphia, Montreal, and London.

Critical Thinking
Making Connections What types of technology today make your life easier?

Conducting a Seminar

Step 2: Writing Questions and Answers Students will begin writing the seminar topics.

Essential Question: How did the inventions of the late 1800s revolutionize society?

Directions Ask students to discuss or research the subject of seminars to see how the format works. Choose a moderator for the class. Group members will be panelists who answer questions posed by the moderator. Each panelist should play the role of a person living in the late 1800s. Have groups write questions and answers for the other groups. Some questions should focus on the effects of new developments on business and society. Point out that some developments, such as monopolies and labor strikes, were controversial. In these cases, some questions should require panelists to justify their views.

Discussing Have the inventors group describe some effects of inventions on nineteenth-century life for class discussion. **OL**

(Chapter Project continued in Section 3)

Teach

R **Reading Strategy**

Previewing Ask: Based on this introductory paragraph, which innovations will you learn about in this section? *(automobile, electric lights, department stores, mail-order shopping, telephone)* **BL**

D **Differentiated Instruction**

Auditory/Musical Go to the Web site www.learnmorsecode.com and play the slow sample of Morse code for the class. As students listen, they should write the code they hear: a dash for a long sound and a dot for a short sound. Then display the Morse code alphabet on the overhead projector and help students translate the sounds they recorded into letters. **ELL**

Primary Source

Critical Thinking Answer
Possible responses: cell phones, Internet, computers

Hands-On Chapter Project
Step 2

Differentiated Instruction

D **Differentiated Instruction**

Gifted and Talented Have interested students work together to research how voices can be transmitted through electrical wires. Have them prepare one or more diagrams to explain the process to the class. **AL**

W₁ **Writing Support**

Expository Writing Have students take the role of one of the inventors discussed in "The Genius of Invention." Ask them to write an announcement of their invention, explaining its benefits for business, for society, or both. **OL**

W₂ **Writing Support**

Descriptive Writing Have students choose an object that they use often. Looking at the object as a new invention, students should write a description of it. They should not name the object but should explain what it does, how it works, and what it looks like. Then have students exchange descriptions and try to guess each other's inventions. **BL**

Reading Check **Answer:** The telegraph carries messages in Morse code. The telephone carries voice communications.

Primary Source | The Wright Brothers

Taking Flight Inventors experimented with engine-powered aircraft in the 1800s, but attempts were not successful until 1903. Orville and Wilbur Wright made the world's first flight in an engine-powered glider at Kill Devil Hill, near Kitty Hawk, North Carolina.

◄ Orville and his brother Wilbur operated a bicycle shop in Dayton, Ohio, in the 1890s. Both expert mechanics, they became interested in the concept of human flight.

▲ On December 17, 1903, the Wright brothers fitted their glider with a gasoline engine. They made four flights at Kitty Hawk, the longest covering 852 feet (260 m) and lasting 59 seconds.

◄ The Wright brothers designed and tested gliders. From these experiments, they learned how to control an aircraft.

The Telephone Rings In

Alexander Graham Bell invented a device that revolutionized communications even more. Born and educated in Scotland, Bell moved to the United States, where he studied methods for teaching hearing-impaired people to speak. He also experimented with sending voices through electrical wires.

By 1876 Bell developed a device that transmitted speech—the telephone. While preparing to test the device, he accidentally spilled battery acid on his clothes. Panicked, Bell called out to his assistant in another room: "Mr. Watson, come here. I want you!" Watson heard Bell's voice coming through the telephone. The invention was a success.

Bell formed the Bell Telephone Company in 1877. By the 1890s, he had sold hundreds of thousands of phones. Businesses were the first customers to use telephones. Before long, though, telephones were common in homes.

Reading Check **Comparing** Describe the difference between a telegraph and a telephone.

W₁ The Genius of Invention

Main Idea Revolutionary new inventions changed business and everyday life in the 1800s.

History and You Have you ever had an idea for an invention that would make life easier? Read about **W₂** inventions that improved people's lives.

The late 1800s saw a burst of inventiveness in the United States. Between 1860 and 1890, the United States government granted more than 400,000 patents for new inventions.

Many of the inventions were designed to help businesses operate more efficiently. Among these were Christopher Sholes's typewriter (1868) and William Burroughs's adding machine (1888).

Other inventions affected everyday life. In 1888 **George Eastman** invented a small box camera—the Kodak—that made it easier and less costly to take photographs. **John Thurman** developed a vacuum cleaner in 1899 that simplified housework.

Air Travel

Objective: To create a time line on events in aviation history

Focus: Ask students if they have ever flown and, if so, whether they recall what the plane was like.

Teach: Have students research the aviation events and complete their time lines.

Assess: Draw the time line on the board and have the class decide on the correct answers.

Close: Discuss with students why the airplane has had such a significant impact on human history.

Differentiated Instruction Strategies

BL Ask students to research images of some of the airplanes mentioned in the activity.

AL Have students select a foreign city they would like to visit and use the Internet to create a travel itinerary to fly there.

ELL Tell students to use available resources to create a list of major airlines in various countries.

Linking Past and Present Activity, URB p. 61

In 1908 Wilbur created a sensation in France by controlling his aircraft in different types of wind. He also set new distance and altitude records. ▶

"The airplane became the promise of the future, and pilots were the popular heroes. . . . Even the routine flights of today retain a touch of magic, reminiscent of the Wright brothers' real intent, which was not speed, money, or military might but simply to break the bonds of Earth and see the world in a new way."

—Astronaut Edwin "Buzz" Aldrin, May 1998

◀ As shown by this aerial bomb test in 1911, the Wrights' invention soon attracted the attention of the U.S. military as well as militaries around the world.

Critical Thinking

Analyzing Primary Sources According to Buzz Aldrin, what was the Wright brothers' greatest accomplishment?

The Wizard of Menlo Park

Thomas Edison was called "dull" by his teachers. Because of his poor hearing, he had trouble in school and often did not attend. His mother finally removed him from school and taught him at home. Edison loved anything related to science, and his mother allowed him to set up a chemistry lab in the family's basement.

When he was 12, Edison got a job working for the railroad, where he set up a new lab in an empty freight car. One day, Edison saved the life of a child who had fallen onto the tracks of an oncoming train. The child's father took an interest in Edison and taught him to use the telegraph. Edison's first invention was a gadget that sent automatic telegraph signals—which he invented so he could sleep on the job.

While still in his 20s, Edison decided to go into the "invention business." In 1876 he set up a workshop in Menlo Park, New Jersey. Out of this famous laboratory came the phonograph, the motion picture projector, the telephone transmitter, and the storage battery. Edison's most important invention by far, though, was the electric lightbulb.

Edison developed the first workable lightbulb in 1879. He then designed power plants that could produce electric power and distribute it to lightbulbs. For Christmas in 1880, Edison used 40 bulbs to light up Menlo Park. Visitors flocked to see the "light of the future." Then, in 1882, Edison built the first central electric power plant in New York City—illuminating 85 buildings!

Inventor George Westinghouse took Thomas Edison's work with electricity even further. In 1885 Westinghouse developed and built transformers that could send electric power more cheaply over longer distances. As a result of Westinghouse's work, factories, trolleys, streetlights, and lamps throughout the United States could be powered by electricity. Westinghouse also created a method for transporting natural gas and invented many safety devices.

The Industrial Age **Chapter 19** **591**

Activity: Technology Connection

Comparing and Contrasting Have students make a list of all the electrical equipment in their homes, such as the refrigerator, TV, computer, and radio. Then have students research to discover when each item was invented and present the information in a time line. Students can interview adults they know at home or at school to find out what life was like before each new innovation became popular. **Ask:** What does the time line tell you about the explosion in the number of inventions in the recent past? (Students might be surprised at the electrical items they consider necessities that were not available in previous generations.) **Ask:** What inventions may change your life or the lives of your children? Discuss as a class. **OL**

S Skill Practice

Creating a Time Line Direct students to the Primary Source feature. Have them choose the automobile or another invention featured on this page. Ask them to research and create a time line of key events related to this invention from its introduction to today. **AL**

Primary Source

Critical Thinking Answer
Student responses should demonstrate an understanding of the effect of the invention they cite.

Skills Practice
Ask: How did these inventions create new jobs for Americans? *(Possible answers: The typewriter led to the hiring of typists and secretaries; the telephone led to the hiring of operators, installers, and maintenance people; the camera led to jobs for photographers and developers; and so on.)* **OL**

✓ Reading Check **Answer:** Students may mention the lightbulb, because it led to further innovations in the distribution of electric power and is part of everyday life for people around the world.

Differentiated Instruction

Primary Source   An Age of Invention

Lightbulbs and Vacuum Cleaners The late 1800s could be called the age of invention. The inventions helped change the everyday lives of Americans.

▼ Alexander Graham Bell's first phone

In 1888 George Eastman marketed the Kodak camera. After taking 100 pictures, a user could send it back to the company. The developed photos and a reloaded camera were returned to the customer by mail. ▲

★ **1876** Telephone
★ **1879** Lightbulb
★ **1888** Kodak camera

★ **1868** Typewriter
★ **1877** Phonograph
★ **1888** Adding machine
★ **1899** Motorized vacuum cleaner

▼ Alexander Graham Bell patented the telephone in 1876. There were two million in use by 1900.

◄ Thomas Edison's invention of the phonograph in 1877 attracted worldwide attention.

DBQ Document-Based Questions
Evaluating Which invention do you think affected people's lives the most? Why?

African American Inventors

A number of African Americans contributed to the era of invention. Engineer **Lewis Howard Latimer** developed an improved wire for the lightbulb and joined Thomas Edison's company. **Granville Woods,** an electrical and mechanical engineer from Ohio, patented dozens of inventions. Among them were an electric incubator and railroad improvements such as an electromagnetic brake and an automatic circuit breaker. **Elijah McCoy** invented a **mechanism,** or mechanical device, for oiling machinery.

Jan E. Matzeliger, another African American inventor, developed a shoe-making machine that performed many steps previously done by hand. His device, which revolutionized the shoe industry, was used in in the United States and overseas.

✓ Reading Check **Evaluating** Which of Edison's inventions do you think is the most valuable to our world today? Explain your reasoning.

S A Changing Society

Main Idea Henry Ford's automobile and assembly line changed industry and society forever.

History and You How might your life be different if the automobile had never been invented? Read to learn about the invention of the automobile.

I n the 1900s, improvements ushered in a new era of transportation. After much experimentation, the automobile became a practical machine for traveling from place to place.

Henry Ford's Automobiles

Henry Ford had a vision. He wanted to build an inexpensive car that would last a lifetime. While working as an engineer in Detroit, Michigan, in the 1890s, Ford experimented with an automobile engine that was powered by gasoline. In 1903 he established his own auto-making company in Detroit and began designing cars.

Leveled Activities

In 1906 Ford had an idea for a new type of car. He told Charles Sorenson, later Ford's general superintendent, "We're going to get a car now that we can make in great volume and get the prices way down." For the next year, Ford and Sorenson worked on the **Model T,** building the car and testing it on rough roads. In 1908 Ford introduced the Model T to the public. Sorenson described the sturdy black vehicle as "a car which anyone could afford to buy, which anyone could drive anywhere, and which almost anyone could keep in repair." These qualities made the Model T immensely popular. During the next 18 years, Ford's company sold 15 million Model Ts.

Henry Ford also pioneered a new, less expensive way to manufacture cars—the **assembly line.** On the assembly line, each worker performed an assigned production task again and again. The assembly line revolutionized other industries as well. It enabled manufacturers to produce large quantities of goods more quickly. This **mass production** of goods decreased manufacturing costs, so products could be sold more cheaply.

Selling Goods

Merchants looked for more efficient ways to sell their goods. One method was through the mail. Before 1863 people picked up their mail at post offices. After 1863 mail was delivered directly to people's homes.

Merchants could now send goods cross country nearly as easily as across town. Some firms developed mail order businesses—receiving and shipping orders by mail. Companies such as Montgomery Ward and Sears Roebuck published catalogs that offered a wide range of goods from shoes to farm equipment.

Chain stores—stores with identical branches in many places—grew rapidly. F. W. Woolworth's chain of "five-and-ten-cent stores" specialized in the sale of everyday household and personal items at bargain prices. By 1911, more than 1,000 Woolworths were in operation. The Woolworth Building, erected in New York City in 1913, stood 792 feet (241 m) tall—the tallest building in the world at that time.

✓ Reading Check Identifying What was Henry Ford's vision?

History ONLINE
Study Central™ To review this section, go to glencoe.com.

C Critical Thinking

Analyzing Information Ask: Why would mail-order businesses appeal to rural residents? *(Rural areas had few stores. Catalogs made a wide variety of products available to rural residents.)* **AL**

R Reading Strategy

Making Connections Ask: Why do you think chains can often sell at bargain prices? *(Chains can order merchandise in large quantities, so manufacturers give them discounts.)* **OL**

✓ Reading Check Answer: build a car that was affordable, easy to drive and repair

Assess

History ONLINE

Study Central™ provides summaries, interactive games, and online graphic organizers to help students review content.

Close

Summarizing On the board, list the inventions discussed in this section as students identify them. For each invention, have students identify at least one effect on society. **OL**

Section 2 Review

Section 2 Review

Vocabulary

1. Use each of these terms in a sentence that will help explain its meaning: transmit, mechanism, Model T, assembly line, mass production.

Main Ideas

2. Assessing What was the significance of the transatlantic telegraph cable?

3. Explaining How did George Westinghouse build upon Thomas Edison's inventions?

4. Analyzing What effect did the assembly line have on the manufacturing industry?

Critical Thinking

5. Evaluating In your opinion, what were the five most important inventions of this time? List them in order in a chart, and provide your reasons.

Top 5 Inventions	Reasons

6. Concluding How did companies change the way goods were sold to the public in the late 1800s?

7. Expository Writing Some people believe that the Internet has been the most revolutionary invention in communications since the telegraph. Write a paragraph in which you compare the two inventions and explain whether you support this view. *Venn*

Answer the
8. Essential Question
How did the inventions of the late 1800s revolutionize society?

Answers

1. Students' sentences should demonstrate an understanding of the terms.

2. Previously, messages from the United States to Europe had to travel by ship and took several weeks. With transatlantic telegrams, messages traveled in a matter of seconds.

3. Westinghouse developed transformers that could send electric power cheaply over long distances.

4. Large quantities of goods could be produced more quickly and for less money so products could then be sold more cheaply.

5. Answers will vary but should be supported with examples and analysis.

6. Some companies began to sell goods through the mail, and chain stores sold goods at low prices.

7. Students will write paragraphs comparing the telegraph and the Internet. They should state whether or not they believe the Internet was the most revolutionary invention in communications since the telegraph and support their views.

8. Inventions helped unify the country and promoted economic growth.

Section ⭐ 3

Focus

An Age of Big Business

Bellringer

Daily Test Practice Transparency 19–3

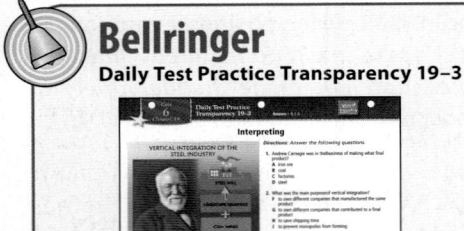

Reading Guide
Answers to Graphic:

Oil: *Leader:* John D. Rockefeller; *Reason for Growth:* oil valuable for producing heat and smoke-free light and for lubricating machinery; *Method Used:* horizontal integration; **Steel:** *Leader:* Andrew Carnegie; *Reason for Growth:* steel was the ideal material for railroad tracks, bridges, and many other products; Bessemer process and open-hearth process made steel affordable; *Method Used:* vertical integration

Section Spotlight Video

To learn more about the growth of monopolies and trusts during industrialization, watch the Section Spotlight Video "An Age of Big Business."

Resource Manager

Essential Question ◀
How did Americans build fortunes in the oil and steel industries?

Reading Guide

Content Vocabulary

corporation (p. 596)   trust (p. 597)
stock (p. 596)   monopoly (p. 597)
shareholders (p. 596)   merger (p. 599)
dividend (p. 596)

Academic Vocabulary

partner (p. 597)   trend (p. 599)

Key People and Events
John D. Rockefeller (p. 597)
Andrew Carnegie (p. 598)
Sherman Antitrust Act (p. 599)

Reading Strategy
Taking Notes As you read, create a diagram like the one below to organize information about the oil and steel industries.

ILLINOIS STANDARDS
The American Journey

15.A.3c Describe the relationship between consumer purchases and businesses paying for productive resources.

16.C.3c (US) Describe how economic developments and government policies after 1865 affected the country's economic institutions including corporations, banks and organized labor.

17.C.3b Explain how patterns of resources are used throughout the world.

American Diary

A man once told author Ida M. Tarbell that, "The only time I ever saw John Rockefeller enthusiastic was when a report came in from the creek that his buyer had secured a cargo of oil at a figure much below the market price. He bounded from his chair with a shout of joy, danced up and down, hugged me, threw up his hat, acted so like a madman that I have never forgotten it."

—from The History of the Standard Oil Company

Oil wells in Los Angeles, California, area during the late 1800s

---

R Reading Strategies	**C** Critical Thinking	**D** Differentiated Instruction	**W** Writing Support	**S** Skill Practice
Teacher Edition • Making Connections, p. 596 • Identifying, p. 598 **Additional Resources** • Guid. Read., URB p. 69 • Content Vocab., URB p. 45 • Aca. Vocab., URB p. 47 • Read. Ess., p. 208 • Pri. Source Read., URB p. 49	**Teacher Edition** • Making Inferences, p. 596 • Det. Cause and Effect, p. 597 **Additional Resources** • Quizzes and Tests, p. 185	**Teacher Edition** • Visual/Spatial, p. 595 • Verbal/Linguistic, p. 599 **Additional Resources** • School-to-Home, URB p. 63 • Reteaching Act., URB p. 65	**Teacher Edition** • Personal Writing, p. 597 • Narrative Writing, p. 598	**Teacher Edition** • Using Categorizing Skills, p. 595 • Using Geo. Skills, p. 598 **Additional Resources** • Daily Test Pract. Transp. 19-3 • Geo. and Hist., URB p. 59

Foundations for Growth

Main Idea New technology and abundant natural resources led to economic growth.

History and You If you wanted to start your own small business, what resources would you need? Read about the resources that were available for the oil and steel industries.

In western Pennsylvania, a sticky black substance—petroleum—seeped from the ground. For a while, promoters sold the oil as medicine. Then, in the 1850s, researchers found they could burn petroleum to produce heat and smoke-free light. It could also be used to lubricate machinery. Suddenly, oil became valuable.

Edwin L. Drake believed that he could find petroleum by digging a well. Many people thought Drake was wrong. At that time, few people knew that pools of oil did indeed exist underground. They did not imagine that oil wells could lead to great fortune.

In 1859 Drake drilled a well in Titusville, Pennsylvania, and struck oil. This led to the creation of a multimillion-dollar petroleum industry.

Factors of Production

During the late 1800s, new technology, transportation, and business methods allowed the country to tap its rich supply of natural resources and increase production.

The change from an agricultural economy to an industrial one was possible because the United States had the resources needed for a growing economy. Among these resources were what economists call the factors of production: land, labor, and capital.

The first factor of production, land, refers not just to the land itself but all natural resources. The United States held a variety of natural resources that were useful for industrial production.

The second factor of production is labor. Large numbers of workers were needed to turn raw materials into goods. This need was met by rapid population growth. Between 1860 and 1900, the population of the country more than doubled.

The third factor of production is capital, which are the manufactured goods used to make other goods and services. The machines, buildings, and tools used to assemble automobiles, for example, are capital goods.

Primary Source / Big Business

Monopolies Big corporations were often portrayed as "monopoly monsters" that were too powerful to be controlled.

The United States is swallowed by the Giant of Monopoly, ca. 1890. ▶

Critical Thinking

Evaluating Why might laws be passed to control monopolies?

Conducting a Seminar

Step 3: Preparing the Material Students will prepare note cards and an introduction to the seminar.

Essential Question: How did Americans build fortunes from oil and steel?

Directions Have the groups select the questions they want to use. The moderator should then write each question on a separate note card. Have panelists prepare their responses on note cards. Ask the groups to write an introduction for their topic. Tell them to come up with a name for their seminar, such as "Technology Today." Presentations should run about 10 minutes.

Questioning Have the class brainstorm questions for men such as Carnegie or Rockefeller. Have the corporate group consider using some of these questions in their seminar. **OL**

(Chapter Project continued in Section 4)

Teach

D Differentiated Instruction

Visual/Spatial Have interested students do research to identify some of the many products made from petroleum today. Have them work together to gather images of petroleum products and create a labeled collage. **OL**

S Skill Practice

Using Categorizing Skills On the board, write the three factors of production: land, labor, capital. Then have students identify the correct category for each of these resources: hammer *(capital)*, farmer *(labor)*, trees *(land)*, bank building *(capital)*, accountant *(labor)*, iron ore *(land)*, investment money *(capital)*. **OL**

Primary Source

Critical Thinking Answer
Monopolies eliminated competition. Without competition, corporations could take advantage of consumers by controlling prices or supplies.

Hands-On Chapter Project
Step 3

Teacher Tip

When making note cards for a speech, students should list only key talking points. Rather than write out or memorize their speeches, they should talk naturally, using the key points as prompts.

C Critical Thinking

Making Inferences Ask: Why would an entrepreneur want to form a corporation rather than own the business alone? *(The company might need more capital than the entrepreneur has to invest.)* **AL**

R Reading Strategy

Making Connections Ask: Could you become a partial owner of a corporation? How? *(yes, by buying some of the corporation's stock)* **OL**

Primary Source

Critical Thinking Answer
1. capital
2. Possible response: willingness to take risks and to work hard, talent, ability to organize tasks and manage people, vision to recognize opportunity and create new products

✓ **Reading Check** **Answer:** Capital is needed to buy raw materials and equipment, pay workers, and cover shipping and advertising costs.

Additional Support

The term *capital* also means "money for investment." One source of money is the sale of stock by corporations. Another is corporate savings, or businesses investing some of their earnings in better equipment.

Raising Capital

With the economy growing after the Civil War, many railroads and other businesses looked for ways to expand. To do so, they had to raise capital. They needed capital to buy raw materials and equipment, to pay workers, and to cover shipping and advertising costs.

One way a company could raise capital was by becoming a **corporation.** A corporation is a company that sells shares, or **stock,** of its business to the public. People who invest in the corporation by buying stock are its **shareholders,** or partial owners.

During periods of strong economic growth, shareholders earn **dividends**—cash payments from the corporation's profits—on the stock they own. If the company fails, however, the shareholders lose their investment. In the late 1800s, hundreds of thousands of people bought and sold stocks in special markets known as stock exchanges.

The growth of corporations helped fuel America's industrial expansion in the years following the Civil War. Railroads were the first businesses to form corporations, followed by manufacturing firms and other businesses. Banks also played a major role in this period of economic growth. They made profits by lending money to new businesses.

✓ **Reading Check** **Explaining** Why is capital important for economic growth?

Primary Source | Factors of Production

"I am a woman who came from the cotton fields of the South. I was promoted from there to the wash-tub. Then I was promoted to the cook kitchen, and from there I promoted myself into the business of manufacturing hair goods and preparations. . . . I have built my own factory on my own ground."
—Madam C. J. Walker, quoted in *On Her Own Ground*

Land Natural resources

Labor Human skills and effort

Capital Buildings, tools, equipment

▲ Madam C. J. Walker, American entrepreneur

Entrepreneurs People bring together the factors of production to create products and services. They accept the risk of running a business to earn a profit.

Products and Services

Critical Thinking

1. **Categorizing** You use a calculator to complete your math homework. Which factor of production is your calculator?
2. **Theorizing** What qualities should a person have to become a successful entrepreneur?

Activity: Economics Connection

Reading Graphs Use the New York Stock Exchange site www.nyse.com to introduce students to the concept of stock trading. Enter any stock symbol to bring up company data as an example. Select "month" for the graph of stock prices. Project this Web page in class, if possible, or distribute a printout.

Use the graph to explain that stock prices go up and down constantly. Select a day, and have students identify the share price on that day. **Ask:** How much would you have paid for 100 shares that day? Then select a different day, and have students identify the price on that day. **Ask:** How much would you have received if you sold your 100 shares on that day? Then subtract the amounts on the board to show the amount gained or lost in this stock transaction. Use this demonstration to start a discussion of the risks and rewards of investing in corporations. **OL**

Primary Sources
INTERPRETING
POLITICAL CARTOONS

This 1800s cartoon represents John D. Rockefeller's near-total control of the oil industry.

1. **Identifying** What type of character does Rockefeller represent in this cartoon?

2. **Analyzing** Why is Rockefeller shown holding the world in his hand?

A. John D. Rockefeller
B. oil lamp
C. world

The Oil Business

Main Idea John D. Rockefeller's Standard Oil Company controlled the booming oil industry.

History and You Recall how the railroad barons became powerful. Read how similar events occurred in the oil industry.

. . . .

The oil industry grew rapidly in the late 1800s. As word of Edwin Drake's success spread, prospectors and investors hurried to western Pennsylvania. "Oil rush" towns with names such as Oil City and Petroleum Center sprang up overnight. The oil boom expanded as prospectors struck oil in Ohio and West Virginia.

Great fortunes were made from oil. Born in Richford, New York, in 1839, **John D. Rockefeller** was the most famous figure of the oil industry. When Rockefeller was 26 years old, he and four **partners**, or associates who agree to operate a business together, built an oil refinery—a plant to process oil—in Cleveland, Ohio.

In 1870 Rockefeller organized the Standard Oil Company of Ohio and set out to dominate the oil industry. One method he used was horizontal integration—combining competing companies into one corporation. Standard Oil grew powerful and wealthy.

The Standard Oil Trust

Rockefeller lowered his prices to drive his competitors out of business, pressured customers not to deal with rival companies, and persuaded the railroads to give him special rates. In 1882 he formed a **trust,** a group of companies managed by the same board of directors. Rockefeller did this by acquiring stock in many different oil companies. The shareholders of these companies traded their stock for Standard Oil stock, which paid higher dividends. As a result, Standard Oil became part owner of the other companies. Rockefeller had created a **monopoly**—total control of an industry by a single producer.

✓ **Reading Check** **Describing** How did Standard Oil become a monopoly?

The Industrial Age **Chapter 19** **597**

W Writing Support

Personal Writing Have students write an essay either applauding or condemning Rockefeller's business methods. Students should include reasons they believe as they do. **OL**

C Critical Thinking

Determining Cause and Effect
Ask: How would a monopoly affect the price of oil? Why? *(The price may rise because producers could charge whatever they want. If people want oil, they have to pay whatever price the single producer sets.)* **AL**

INTERPRETING
POLITICAL CARTOONS

Critical Thinking Answers

1. a king

2. It suggests that by controlling oil, he controls the world.

✓ **Reading Check** **Answer:** Standard Oil lowered prices to drive competitors out of business, pressured customers not to deal with other companies, got special rates from railroads, and formed trusts.

Differentiated Instruction

Leveled Activities

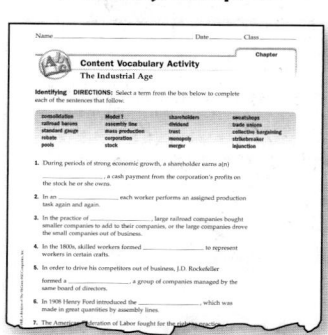

R Reading Strategy

Identifying Ask: What two new processes helped turn steel making into a profitable industry? *(the Bessemer process and the open-hearth process)* **BL**

S Skill Practice

Using Geography Skills Ask: Why did large steel mills locate in Pittsburgh, Pennsylvania? *(Sources of the iron ore needed for steel production were located near Pittsburgh.)* **BL**

W Writing Support

Narrative Writing Have students research the life of Andrew Carnegie and create a list of the major events in his life. **OL**

Economics & History

Diagram Skills Answer
Horizontal integration is achieved by purchasing competing companies in the same industry. Vertical integration is achieved by purchasing companies at all levels of production.

Differentiated Instruction

Economics & History

During the late 1800s, vertical and horizontal integration helped businesses grow into monopolies.

Vertical Integration
Purchase of companies at all levels of production

Ace Meat Industries

Delivery wagons
Meat packing plants
Cooled warehouse
Refrigerated railroad cars
Slaughterhouse
Cattle

Horizontal Integration
Purchase of competing companies in same industry

U.S. Oil Company

Independent Oil Refineries

Diagram Skills
Contrasting What is the difference between vertical integration and horizontal integration?

The Steel Business

Main Idea New processes for making steel created an important industry.

History and You Have you heard of Carnegie Hall in New York City? Read to learn about the influential man for whom this cultural landmark is named.

Steel also became a huge business in the late 1800s. A strong and long-lasting form of iron treated with carbon, steel was the ideal material for railroad tracks, bridges, and many other products.

Steel Industry Growth

Two new methods of making steel—the Bessemer process, developed by English inventor Henry Bessemer, and the open-hearth process—changed the industry. With these new methods, mills could produce steel at affordable prices and in large quantities. In the 1870s, large steel mills were built near sources of iron ore in western Pennsylvania and eastern Ohio. Pittsburgh, Pennsylvania, became the steel capital of the United States. Cleveland, Chicago, Detroit, and Birmingham, Alabama, also became important hubs for steel production.

W Andrew Carnegie

The leading figure in the early years of the American steel industry was **Andrew Carnegie,** the son of a Scottish immigrant. Starting as a messenger and telegraph operator, Carnegie worked his way up to become manager of the Pennsylvania Railroad. In 1865 he invested in the growing iron industry. Carnegie soon realized that there was an enormous market for steel. After learning about the Bessemer process, he built a steel plant near Pittsburgh.

The Benefits and Obligations of Wealth

Objective: To analyze an excerpt written by Andrew Carnegie about the obligation of the wealthy

Focus: Ask students how they would spend their wealth if they became rich.

Teach: Have students read the excerpt and answer the questions.

Assess: Discuss whether students think that Carnegie's viewpoint was shared by other industrial millionaires of the time.

Close: Ask students if they agree with Carnegie.

598

Differentiated Instruction Strategies

BL Ask students to underline the main idea of each paragraph in the excerpt.

AL Have students find an interview or article where a public figure today discusses his or her views on wealth.

ELL Remind students to check the Reader's Dictionary for definitions of words they do not know.

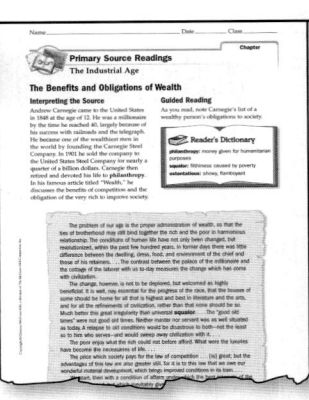

Primary Source Reading Activity, URB p. 49

By 1890 Andrew Carnegie dominated the steel industry. His company became powerful through vertical integration—acquiring companies that provided the equipment and services he needed. Carnegie bought iron and coal mines, warehouses, ore ships, and railroads to gain control of all parts of the business of making and selling steel. By 1900 the Carnegie Steel Company was producing one-third of the nation's steel.

Philanthropists

Andrew Carnegie, John D. Rockefeller, and other industrial millionaires of the era grew interested in philanthropy—the use of money to benefit the community. They used their huge fortunes to found schools, universities, and other civic institutions.

Carnegie donated $350 million to various organizations. He built Carnegie Hall—one of the world's most famous concert halls—in New York City and created more than 2,000 libraries worldwide. Rockefeller used his fortune to establish the University of Chicago in 1890 and New York's Rockefeller Institute for Medical Research.

Corporations Grow Larger

In 1889 New Jersey encouraged the **trend,** or general movement, toward business monopolies by allowing holding companies to obtain charters. A holding company would buy the stock of other companies instead of purchasing the companies outright. Rockefeller formed Standard Oil of New Jersey so that the corporation could expand its holdings. Other states also passed laws that made corporate **mergers**—the combining of companies—easier.

Many Americans admired the efficiencies of large businesses, but others argued that a lack of competition hurt consumers. Without competition, corporations had no reason to improve—or keep prices low.

In 1890 Congress passed the **Sherman Antitrust Act,** which prohibited trusts and monopolies. In its early years, however, the Sherman Antitrust Act did little to curb the power of big business.

✓ **Reading Check** Making Inferences What is one advantage of vertical integration?

History ONLINE
Study Central™ To review this section, go to glencoe.com.

Section 3 Review

Vocabulary

1. Use each of these terms in a sentence that will help explain its meaning: corporation, stock, shareholder, dividend, partner, trust, monopoly, trend, merger.

Main Ideas

2. **Describing** What is the relationship between a corporation and its shareholders?

3. **Explaining** What methods did Rockefeller use to build his oil empire?

4. **Defending** Did the Sherman Antitrust Act support competition? Explain.

Critical Thinking

5. **Speculating** Why do you think the industrial millionaires became philanthropists?

6. **Comparing and Contrasting** Create a diagram to list the similarities and differences between Carnegie and Rockefeller.

Carnegie — Rockefeller

7. **Persuasive Writing** As a member of Congress, write a speech supporting the Sherman Antitrust Act.

Answer the
8. **Essential Question**
How did Americans build fortunes in the oil and steel industries?

The Industrial Age **Chapter 19 599**

Answers

1. Students' sentences should reflect an understanding of the terms.
2. The shareholders are partial owners of the corporation.
3. Rockefeller used horizontal integration, lowered prices to drive competitors out of business, and formed a trust by acquiring stock in other companies.
4. Yes. It prohibited trusts and monopolies.

5. Possible response: They might have wanted to give back to the community, create a positive image of themselves, or create a lasting legacy.
6. **Carnegie:** steel industry, vertical integration; **Rockefeller:** oil industry, horizontal integration; **Both:** built monopolies, gained large fortunes, were philanthropists

7. Students' speeches might suggest that without competition, companies have little incentive to improve or to keep prices fair for consumers.
8. formed corporations; used methods of vertical integration and horizontal integration; formed trusts and monopolies

Focus

D Differentiated Instruction

Intrapersonal Ask students to name some of the wealthiest Americans of the past and present, from John D. Rockefeller to Bill Gates to Oprah Winfrey. Have them write a journal entry that describes their attitudes about or stereotypes they hold concerning the very wealthy. **OL**

C Critical Thinking

Making Generalizations Ask: What is the role of the wealthy, according to Carnegie? *(to elevate the race and spend money for the benefit of the community)* Is there anything in his statement that may cause the "poorer brethren" to resent Carnegie? *(the idea that the wealthy are wiser and better able to take care of the poor than they are themselves)* **OL**

Additional Support and Answers

Carnegie Steel Company plant in Homestead, Pennsylvania

600

YOU DECIDE

Were Wealthy Industrialists "Robber Barons"?

Building Background

After the Civil War, businesses, especially those in oil, steel, and railroads, formed a few dominating corporations. Some people viewed the industrial millionaires, such as Andrew Carnegie, as ingenious businesspeople who also gave back to the communities through charity.

Other people, mostly laborers, referred to the leaders of the corporations as robber barons, those who robbed the poor to build their fortunes. In May 1886, after Chicago police fired into a crowd of striking workers, killing several, labor leaders criticized business owners and urged workers to continue their protests.

NO

ANDREW CARNEGIE

The surplus wealth of the few will become, in the best sense, the property of the many. . . . This wealth, passing through the hands of the few, can be made a much more potent[1] force for the elevation of our race than if it had been distributed in small sums to the people themselves. Even the poorest can be made to see this, and to agree that great sums gathered by some of their fellow-citizens and spent for public purposes, from which the masses reap the principal benefit, are more valuable to them than if scattered among them through the course of many years in trifling amounts.

This, then, is held to be the duty of the man of Wealth: . . . to consider all surplus revenues which come to him simply as trust funds, which he is called upon to administer, . . . [in order] to produce the most beneficial result for the community—the man of wealth thus [becomes] the sole agent and trustee for his poorer brethren, bringing to their service his superior wisdom [and] experience . . . doing for them better than they would or could do for themselves.

---

[1] **potent** powerful

Activity: Economics Connection

Simulating The Haymarket Square Riot of 1886 took place amid a massive laborers' campaign to limit the workday to eight hours in the factories of Chicago. Employers had tried to replace striking workers with strikebreakers, who were protected by police, and the confrontation led to several days of violence. Six years later, Andrew Carnegie sent in militias to end a strike at his steel plant in Homestead, Pennsylvania. Prepare students to role-play a labor union meeting in which workers will debate whether or not to go on strike. **Ask:** What might the union accomplish by walking off the job? What are the risks? What will you do if the bosses bring in nonunion "scabs" (strikebreakers)? How will you and your families survive during the strike? What will happen if the union chooses not to strike? *(Encourage students to take the perspective of immigrants and other poor laborers, thinking through the options and weighing the pros and cons of any actions.)*

YES

AD FOR LABOR MEETING

Your masters sent out their bloodhounds—the police—; they killed six of your brothers at McCormicks this afternoon. They killed the poor wretches, because they, like you, had the courage to disobey the supreme will of your bosses. They killed them, because they dared ask for the shortening of the hours of toil. They killed them to show you, "Free American Citizens," that you must be satisfied and contented with whatever your bosses . . . allow you, or you will get killed!

You have for years endured the most abject[2] humiliations . . . you have worked yourself to death; you have endured the pangs of want and hunger; . . . in short: You have been miserable and obedient slaves all these years: Why? To satisfy the insatiable[3] greed, to fill the coffers[4] of your lazy thieving master? When you ask them now to lessen your burden, he sends his bloodhounds out to shoot you, kill you!

If you are men . . . then you will . . . destroy the hideous monster that seeks to destroy you. To arms we call you, to arms!

R

---

[2] **abject** miserable
[3] **insatiable** unquenchable
[4] **coffers** money boxes

DBQ Document-Based Questions

1. **Summarizing** According to Andrew Carnegie, what responsibility does a man of wealth have to society?

2. **Making Inferences** Why did Carnegie think that giving his wealth to worthy causes would do more to improve the lives of working people than would paying them higher wages?

3. **Explaining** Why did the author of the advertisement for the meeting in Chicago urge working people to rise up and fight?

4. **Evaluating** Why do you think the phrase "robber barons" developed during this period? Explain your answer.

Newspaper engraving of Chicago's Haymarket Riot, May 4, 1886

601

Focus

Section 4

Bellringer
Daily Test Practice Transparency 19–4

Reading Guide
Answers to Graphic:

Haymarket Riot: *Reason:* protest killings of striking workers the previous day; *Outcome:* many Americans began associating unions with terrorism and disorder; **Homestead Strike:** *Reason:* company cut wages; *Outcome:* plant reopened with nonunion workers; steelworkers union dwindled; **Pullman Strike:** *Reason:* company cut wages; *Outcome:* federal troops broke up strike; union movement weakened

Section Spotlight Video

Watch the Section Spotlight Video "Industrial Workers" to learn more about working conditions in the industrial age.

Resource Manager

Essential Question
Why did workers form labor unions in the middle to late 1800s?

Reading Guide

Content Vocabulary
sweatshop (p. 603)   strikebreaker (p. 606)
trade union (p. 604)   injunction (p. 606)
collective bargaining (p. 605)

Academic Vocabulary
identify (p. 604)   environment (p. 605)

Key People and Events
Knights of Labor (p. 604)
Terence V. Powderly (p. 604)
American Federation of Labor (p. 604)
Samuel Gompers (p. 605)
Eugene V. Debs (p. 606)

Reading Strategy
Taking Notes As you read, use a chart like the one below to record the reasons the events occurred and what happened as a result.

	Reason	Outcome
Haymarket Riot		
Homestead Strike		
Pullman Strike		

ILLINOIS STANDARDS
The American Journey

15.A.3b Explain the relationship between productivity and wages.

15.A.3d Describe the causes of unemployment (e.g., seasonal fluctuation in demand, changing jobs, changing skill requirements, national spending).

18.B.3a Analyze how individuals and groups interact with and within institutions (e.g., educational, military).

Industrial Workers

American Diary

The life of an industrial worker during the early 1900s was exhausting. Many factory laborers worked twelve-hour shifts, often without a break. William McQuade worked in one of Carnegie's steel mills. "We stop only the time it takes to oil the engine. While they are oiling they eat, at least some of the boys, some of them; a great many of them in the mill do not carry anything to eat at all, because they haven't got time to eat."

—*from "The Steel Business: The Lot of a Steelworker"*

Reading Strategies	C Critical Thinking	D Differentiated Instruction	W Writing Support	S Skill Practice
Additional Resources • Guid. Read., URB p. 70 • Content Vocab., URB p. 45 • Academic Vocab., URB p. 47 • Read. Ess., p. 211	**Teacher Edition** • Comp. and Contrast., p. 604 • Det. Cause and Effect, p. 605 **Additional Resources** • Quizzes and Tests, p. 186 • Crit. Think. Skills, URB p. 57 • Authentic Assess., p. 19	**Teacher Edition** • Visual/Spatial, p. 606 **Additional Resources** • School-to-Home, URB p. 63 • Reteaching Act., URB p. 65	**Teacher Edition** • Narrative Writing, p. 603 • Expository Writing, p. 605 **Additional Resources** • Differ. Inst., URB p. 55	**Teacher Edition** • Using Math Skills, p. 603 **Additional Resources** • Daily Test Pract. Transp. 19-4 • Time Line Skills, URB p. 62 • Lesson Transp. 19C

Working Conditions

Main Idea Factory workers toiled under terrible conditions.

History and You When you are working on a project, do you take breaks? Why are breaks necessary? Read to learn what life was like for factory workers.

T he industrial growth of the late 1800s created new jobs. Yet factory workers paid a price for economic progress. As mass production increased, factories became larger and less personal.

Industrial laborers worked for 10 or 12 hours a day, six days a week. They could be fired at any time for any reason. Many lost their jobs during business downturns or were replaced by immigrants who were willing to work for lower pay.

People worked in unsafe and unhealthy factory conditions, and accidents were common in factories and mines. Steelworkers suf-

fered burns. Coal miners died in cave-ins and from the effects of gas and coal dust. Garment workers toiled in crowded and dangerous urban factories called **sweatshops.**

Women and Children

By 1900 more than one million women had joined the industrial workforce. Because there were no laws that regulated workers' salaries, women, in general, earned about half of what men did for the same work.

Hundreds of thousands of children under 16 years of age also worked in factories. Many states passed child-labor laws that said children working in factories had to be at least 12 years old and should not work more than 10 hours a day. Employers, however, widely ignored child-labor laws.

Reading Check Calculating How many hours a week did industrial laborers typically work?

History ONLINE
Student Web Activity Visit glencoe.com and complete the Chapter 19 Web Activity about industrial workers.

By the Numbers / Cost of Living

Working for a Living For industrial workers in the early 1900s, life was difficult. Most family members, including children, worked for long hours and low pay. Employers often hired and paid on a weekly or daily basis. A worker did not get paid if he or she was unable to work because of illness or if an employer closed the factory because business was slow.

Average Hourly Wages*
Bricklayers: 50¢
Plasterers: 50¢
Newspaper compositors: 36¢
Machine woodworkers: 25¢
Construction workers: 17¢
Metalworkers: 16¢

(*in Chicago, 1903)

Average Expenses*
Rent: $4–10 per month
Butter: 22¢ per pound
Milk: 6¢ per quart
Bread: 5¢ per loaf
Rib roast: 13¢ per pound
Postage: 2¢ per ounce

(*in Chicago, 1903)

Critical Thinking
Speculating What do you think is the biggest expense today for workers?

Workers repair train wheels in 1904.

Teach

S Skill Practice

Using Math Skills Refer students to the chart on this page. **Ask:** Working 10 hours per day and 6 days per week, how much would a metal factory worker earn in a month? *($38.40)* **OL**

W Writing Support

Narrative Writing Have students research to learn more about the lives of child laborers. Have them take the role of a young factory worker and write six daily journal entries, describing a typical week in his or her life. **OL**

By the Numbers

Critical Thinking Answer
Students might suggest housing.

History ONLINE
Objectives and answers to the Student Web Activity can be found at glencoe.com under the Web Activity Lesson Plan for this chapter.

Reading Check **Answer:** 60–72 hours per week

Differentiated Instruction

Leveled Activities

BL Guided Reading Activity, URB p. 70

OL Authentic Assessment With Rubrics, p. 19

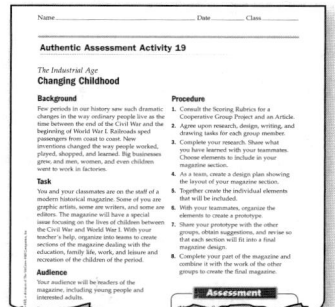

ELL Differentiated Instruction Activity, URB p. 55

C Critical Thinking

Comparing and Contrasting Ask: How were trade unions of the early 1800s similar to and different from unions of the later 1800s? *(Both brought workers together to demand better pay and working conditions. Early unions were made of skilled workers in the same trade and were too small to be effective. Later unions included all types of workers and were larger, so they had more power.)* **OL**

This **READING SKILL** (Comparing and Contrasting) was introduced in this unit.

The Labor Movement
1877–1914
NATIONAL GEOGRAPHIC

Critical Thinking Answer

Silver Mine Unrest, Anthracite Coal Strike, Ludlow Massacre

Critical Thinking Practice

Have students select one of the strikes listed, research the events, and prepare a report that details who, what, when, where, and why. **OL**

Hands-On Chapter Project
Step 4

Conducting a Seminar

Step 4: Preparing Visuals Students will prepare visuals for their seminar.

Essential Question: Why did workers form labor unions in the middle to late 1800s?

Directions Instruct the groups to choose images from their research to support the points the panelists will make. Images might include a diagram showing how an invention works, a chart showing the growth of labor unions, or a picture of people constructing railroad tracks. Ask them to prepare their visuals as large posters. Each group should plan how to blend the visuals into their presentations. Have them prepare cards showing the name and occupation of each panelist. They should construct the cards to stand up on a table in front of the panelists. Give the groups time to rehearse their seminar.

Summarizing For class discussion, ask the union group to summarize the conditions that gave rise to labor unions. **OL**

(Chapter Project continued on the Visual Summary page)

Growth of Labor Unions

Main Idea Workers organized unions in order to acquire better wages, benefits, and working conditions.

History and You Have you ever been a part of a group that was working for a common goal? Did the group achieve its goal? Why or why not? Read to learn about labor unions and their goals.

Dissatisfied workers organized into groups—labor unions—to demand better pay and working conditions from their employers. Earlier in the 1800s, skilled workers had formed unions to represent workers in certain crafts or trades, such as carpentry. These **trade unions** had little influence because each represented only one trade and were too small to be effective. By the mid-1800s, as working conditions worsened, labor leaders looked to expand their unions.

In 1869 garment cutters in Philadelphia founded a trade union known as the Noble and Holy Order of the **Knights of Labor.** Employers fired workers who joined labor organizations, so the Knights met secretly and used special handshakes to **identify,** or recognize, one another.

Under the leadership of **Terence V. Powderly,** the Knights of Labor became a national labor organization in the 1880s. Unlike most unions, the Knights recruited people who were traditionally kept out of trade unions, including women, African Americans, immigrants, and unskilled laborers.

The Knights of Labor grew to more than 700,000 members by 1886. A wave of strikes, however, turned public opinion against the union, and it lost power in the 1890s.

In 1881 a group of national trade unions formed the **American Federation of Labor** (AFL). The AFL represented skilled workers in various crafts.

The Labor Movement, 1877–1914
NATIONAL GEOGRAPHIC

0 400 kilometers
0 400 miles
Albers Equal-Area projection

❶ **1877 Great Railway Strike**
Workers protest pay cuts

❷ **1886 Haymarket Affair**
Labor rally ends in violence

❸ **1892 New Orleans**
Workers from 42 unions demand shorter hours and better pay

❹ **1892 Homestead Strike**
Steelworkers protest wage cut

❺ **1892 Silver Mine Unrest**
State jails hundreds of striking workers

❻ **1894 Pullman Strike**
Federal troops end riots

❼ **1902 Anthracite Coal Strike**
Miners strike to win union recognition

❽ **1914 Ludlow Massacre**
State militia burns striking miners' tent colony

Unions Struggle After the Civil War, labor leaders sought to organize large national unions. In the late 1800s, however, government opposition, internal divisions, and public disapproval limited the movement's progress.

◀ Unions gained strength in the late 1800s and worked more actively for workers' rights.

▼ Labor unrest during the Pullman Strike, 1894

Critical Thinking

Identifying Which strikes involved miners?

People IN HISTORY

Samuel Gompers
Leader of the American Federation of Labor

Samuel Gompers did not think that unions should always support the same political party. Rather, Gompers argued that unions should support any political party that worked for the unions' goals. He also believed the best way to achieve labor's goals was through collective bargaining. Gompers stressed that *"the*

individual workman is as weak against the combination of wealth as would be a straw in a cyclone." Workers could only *"stand on an equal footing with the employers"* when they were organized into labor unions.

Mary Harris Jones
Labor organizer

Mary Harris Jones, also known as "Mother Jones," traveled across the country organizing workers for the United Mine Workers union. She also supported strikes and tried to sway public opinion in favor of unions. Denounced in the United States Senate, Jones believed that *"there are no limits to which powers of privilege will not go to keep the workers in slavery."*

CRITICAL Thinking

1. **Identifying** According to Gompers, how could labor unions help workers?
2. **Synthesizing** How did Gompers and Jones view employers?

The AFL was led by **Samuel Gompers,** the tough and practical-minded president of the Cigar Makers' Union. The organization pressed for higher wages, shorter hours, better working conditions, and the right to **collective bargaining**—when unions represent workers in labor discussions with management.

Although violent strikes turned public feeling against workers and unions in the late 1880s, the AFL survived and grew. By 1904, the AFL claimed more than 1.6 million members.

Women and the Unions

Many unions would not admit women workers, so some women formed their own unions. Mary Harris Jones, also known as Mother Jones, spent 50 years fighting for workers' rights.

In 1911 a fire broke out at the Triangle Shirtwaist Company factory, a sweatshop in New York City. The workers, mostly young immigrant women, could not escape because the company locked the doors to prevent employees from leaving early. Nearly 150 workers died. The disaster led the International Ladies' Garment Workers Union (ILGWU) to push for a safer working **environment.**

The Unions Act

Economic depressions in the 1870s and the 1890s forced companies to lower wages and, in some cases, fire workers. Unions responded with large strikes that sometimes sparked violence.

After a financial panic in 1873, an economic depression hit the nation. To cut costs, companies forced their workers to take pay cuts.

The Industrial Age **Chapter 19 605**

W Writing Support

Expository Writing The district attorney of West Virginia, Reese Blizzard, called Mother Jones "the most dangerous woman in America." Have students write an essay about why some people of the time might have agreed with this statement and others would not. **OL**

C Critical Thinking

Determining Cause and Effect Ask: How did economic conditions lead to strikes? *(Companies cut wages and fired workers to cut costs during depressions, and workers responded by striking.)* **OL**

People IN HISTORY

Critical Thinking Answers

1. put workers on equal footing with employers in collective bargaining
2. willing to use their power against workers

Differentiated Instruction

Identifying the Main Idea

Objective:	To learn how to identify the main idea
Focus:	Ask for volunteers to explain who Samuel Gompers was and whom he represented.
Teach:	Have students read the excerpt, answer the questions, and apply the skill.
Assess:	Review with students why is it important to be able to identify the main idea.
Close:	Ask students if they consider Gompers's speech to be effective and to defend their point of view.

Critical Thinking Skills Activity, URB p. 57

Differentiated Instruction Strategies

BL Have students alternate reading each sentence in the excerpt aloud.

AL Ask students to use their own drawings or to locate images with which they can create a collage illustrating Gompers's speech.

ELL Have students explain, in their own words, the following terms: "main idea" and "topic sentence."

D Differentiated Instruction

Visual/Spatial Have students take the role of a striking worker in one of the strikes described here. Have them create a sign to carry as they march. The sign should contain a slogan or demand and a supporting picture. **ELL**

Reading Check **Answer:** Strikes disrupted daily life and sometimes resulted in violence.

Assess

History ONLINE

Study Central™ provides summaries, interactive games, and online graphic organizers to help students review content.

Close

Evaluating As a class, discuss the reasons for the rise of labor unions in the late 1800s. **OL**

Section 4 Review

In July 1877, angry strikers burned rail yards, ripped up track, and destroyed railroad property. The companies hired **strikebreakers** to replace the striking workers, and federal troops restored order.

Antilabor feeling grew stronger after a bloody clash between police and strikers in Chicago's Haymarket Square in May 1886. Striking workers from the McCormick Harvester Company gathered to protest the killings of four strikers the previous day. When police ordered the crowd to break up, an unidentified person threw a bomb that killed a police officer. Several more were killed in a riot that followed. Following the Haymarket Riot, many Americans associated the labor movement with terrorism and disorder.

In 1892 workers went on strike at Andrew Carnegie's steel plant in Homestead, Pennsylvania. In the attempt to weaken the steelworkers' union, plant managers had cut workers' wages. When the union called a strike, Homestead managers hired nonunion workers and brought in 300 armed guards to protect them. A fierce battle left at least 10 people dead.

Pennsylvania's governor sent the state's militia to Homestead to restore order. The plant reopened with nonunion workers, protected by the troops. After the failure of the Homestead Strike, the number of members in the steelworkers' union dwindled.

The employees of George Pullman's railway-car plant near Chicago went on strike in May 1894, when the company cut their wages. Pullman responded by closing the plant. One month later, workers in the American Railway Union supported the strikers by refusing to handle Pullman cars. As a result, rail traffic was paralyzed.

Pullman and the railroad owners fought back with the help of the government. They persuaded U.S. Attorney General Richard Olney to obtain an **injunction,** or court order, to stop the union from "obstructing the railways and holding up the mails." Yet the union and its leader, **Eugene V. Debs,** still refused to end the strike. Debs was sent to jail.

President Grover Cleveland sent federal troops to Chicago, and soon the strike was over. The failure of the Pullman Strike dealt another blow to the union movement. Despite these setbacks, however, workers continued to organize to campaign for better wages and working conditions.

Reading Check **Explaining** Why were there growing antilabor feelings during the late 1800s?

History ONLINE
Study Central™ To review this section, go to glencoe.com.

Section 4 Review

Vocabulary

1. Use each of these terms in a sentence that will help explain its meaning: sweatshop, trade union, identify, collective bargaining, environment, strikebreaker, injunction.

Main Ideas

2. **Describing** How were women and children treated as members of the industrial workforce?

3. **Making Inferences** Why did employers fire workers who joined labor organizations?

Critical Thinking

4. **Comparing** Compare the Pullman Strike and the Homestead Strike. Create a Venn diagram like the one below to identify their similarities.

Pullman Strike — Homestead Strike

5. **Evaluating** Were the early labor unions successful? Explain.

6. **Persuasive Writing** As a member of Congress, write a speech supporting federal child-labor laws.

7. **Essential Question** Why did workers form labor unions in the middle to late 1800s?

Answers

1. Students' sentences should demonstrate an understanding of the terms.
2. Women were paid about half of what men earned for the same work; employers widely ignored child-labor laws requiring that child workers be 12 years old and not work more than 10 hours per day.
3. Unions gave workers more power to push for better wages and working conditions, which would cut into a corporation's profits.
4. **Pullman Strike:** railway workers; **Homestead Strike:** steel workers; **Both:** factory cut wages; workers went on strike, strikes failed
5. no, because they were generally small trade unions and had little influence
6. Students' speeches should give reasons children needed protection from businesses.
7. Laborers were working long hours in unsafe and unhealthy factory conditions. Wealthy, powerful employers could fire workers for any reason or cut their pay. Individually, workers had little power. However, by working together as a union, they could put pressure on employers to improve conditions.

Visual Summary

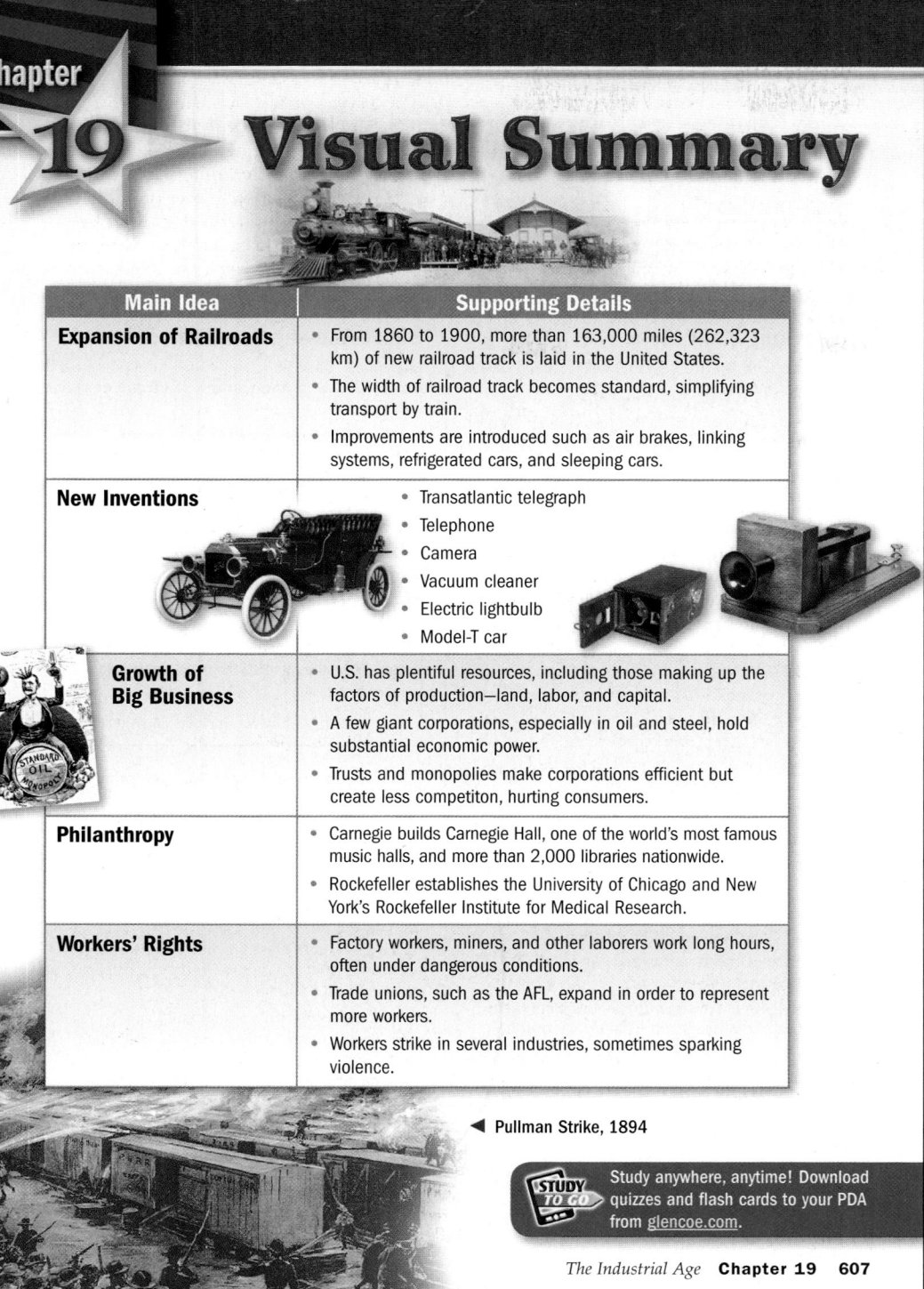

Main Idea	Supporting Details
Expansion of Railroads	• From 1860 to 1900, more than 163,000 miles (262,323 km) of new railroad track is laid in the United States. • The width of railroad track becomes standard, simplifying transport by train. • Improvements are introduced such as air brakes, linking systems, refrigerated cars, and sleeping cars.
New Inventions	• Transatlantic telegraph • Telephone • Camera • Vacuum cleaner • Electric lightbulb • Model-T car
Growth of Big Business	• U.S. has plentiful resources, including those making up the factors of production—land, labor, and capital. • A few giant corporations, especially in oil and steel, hold substantial economic power. • Trusts and monopolies make corporations efficient but create less competiton, hurting consumers.
Philanthropy	• Carnegie builds Carnegie Hall, one of the world's most famous music halls, and more than 2,000 libraries nationwide. • Rockefeller establishes the University of Chicago and New York's Rockefeller Institute for Medical Research.
Workers' Rights	• Factory workers, miners, and other laborers work long hours, often under dangerous conditions. • Trade unions, such as the AFL, expand in order to represent more workers. • Workers strike in several industries, sometimes sparking violence.

◀ Pullman Strike, 1894

STUDY TO GO Study anywhere, anytime! Download quizzes and flash cards to your PDA from glencoe.com.

The Industrial Age **Chapter 19** **607**

Visual Summary

Visual Summary

Synthesizing Ask: In what ways was daily life improving for most Americans during this time? *(Inventions were making life easier and more enjoyable. For the first time, many Americans had electric lights and telephones. They enjoyed phonographs and cameras, and vacuum cleaners eased housework. The booming economy created many jobs. Mass production provided new products at affordable prices; and railroads, chain stores, and mail-order businesses made these products available across the country.)* **OL**

Analyzing Points of View Ask: Why might many Americans at this time admire people such as Vanderbilt, Rockefeller, and Carnegie? *(They helped create an economic boom, built great wealth, and gave back to the community through philanthropy.)* Why might some people of the time view these leaders as villains? *(They used ruthless tactics to run competitors out of business, and they took advantage of workers.)* **OL**

Hands-On Chapter Project
Step 5: Wrap-Up

Conducting a Seminar

Step 5: Presenting the Seminar Students will conduct their seminar.

Directions Provide a table and chairs and perhaps a lectern. Have the groups present their seminars. The moderator should begin by introducing the seminar's topic and the panelists and then lead the question-and-answer session. The rest of the class will act as the audience. After each group's seminar, have the moderator ask for questions from the audience. The panelists should respond to questions in character.

Analyzing Ask: How did innovations in technology and manufacturing affect the economy and working conditions? How did they affect society? **OL**

Answers and Analyses
Reviewing Main Ideas

1. C Remind students that a discount reduces the price of something. Choices A and B are wrong because they add to the cost of something, so they can be eliminated. Pools were used by railroad companies to divide business and set rates, not to offer discounts. **15.C.3**

2. D Have students try to recall who invented each item so that they can eliminate the choices they know are incorrect. Students should recall that Thomas Edison invented the lightbulb and the phonograph, and the typewriter was invented by Christopher Sholes, eliminating choices A and B. **15.C.3**

3. D Students can immediately eliminate choice B because dividends are not a factor of production. Remind students that "land" refers both to land and all available natural resources and "labor" is the term for workers, so they can eliminate choices A and C as well. **15.D.3c**

4. B It may help students to recall that Andrew Carnegie's steel plant was located in Homestead, Penn. Choice A relates to the Pullman Strike, and choice C deals with the strike in Haymarket Square in Chicago. Choice D describes the Triangle Shirtwaist Company factory fire. **18.B.3a**

Short-Answer Question

5. Workers have been accused of being selfish for wanting more pay and better hours, yet the desire for more money is common to people at all income levels. **16.A.3b**

TEST-TAKING TIP

Answer the questions you know first. Then go back to answer those for which you need more time.

Reviewing Main Ideas

Directions: Choose the best answer for each of the following questions.

1. Large railroads of the 1800s offered their biggest customers secret discounts called

  A tariffs.

  B tolls.

  C rebates.

  D pools.

2. Which of the following was invented by George Eastman?

  A lightbulb

  B typewriter

  C phonograph

  D Kodak camera

3. Which factor of production refers to buildings, machinery, and tools?

  A land

  B dividends

  C labor

  D capital

4. The 1892 Homestead Strike erupted after

  A railway workers paralyzed rail traffic in protest over job cuts.

  B managers at Andrew Carnegie's steel plant cut workers' wages to weaken the union.

  C workers from the McCormick Harvester Company demanded a 40-hour workweek.

  D a fire killed workers at a garment factory, leading to calls for safer working conditions.

Short-Answer Question

Directions: Base your answer to question 5 on the excerpt below and on your knowledge of social studies.

> We want eight hours [work day] and nothing less. We have been accused of being selfish, and it has been said that we will want more; that last year we got an advance of ten cents and now we want more. We do want more. You will find that a man generally wants more. . . . You ask a workingman, who is getting two dollars a day, and he will say that he wants ten cents more. . . . The man who receives five thousand dollars a year wants six thousand dollars a year, and the man who owns eight or nine hundred thousand dollars will want a hundred thousand dollars more to make it a million.
>
> —Samuel Gompers, labor union leader

5. Restate the main idea of this excerpt in your own words.

Review the Essential Questions

6. Essay Explain why the late 1800s and early 1900s became known as the Age of Big Business.

To help you write your essay, review your answers to the Essential Questions in the section reviews and the chapter Foldables Study Organizer. Your essay should include:

- the effect of railroad expansion;
- the abundance of inventions in the late 1800s and their impact;
- factors of production and the business practices of industrial leaders; and
- government responses to labor unions.

GO ON ➡

Review the Essential Questions

6. If students completed their Foldables correctly, they should be able to discuss several factors in the growth of business, including the expansion of railroads; inventions such as the electric light and telephone; the discovery of oil and the technology to extract and refine it; the availability of productive resources; the development of the assembly line, leading to mass production; the formation of corporations, enabling companies to raise large amounts of capital for expansion; and public and government hostility toward labor unions. **15.D.3c**

History ONLINE
For additional test practice, use **Self-Check Quizzes**—Chapter 19 at glencoe.com.

Chapter 19 Assessment

Document-Based Questions

Directions: Analyze the documents and answer the short-answer questions that follow.

Document 1

The following words are from the workers' song "Drill, Ye Tarriers, Drill." "Tarrier" was the name given to Irish drillers who dug tunnels for the railroads.

> The new foreman is Dan McCann, / I'll tell you sure he's a blame mean man, / Last week a premature blast went off, / And a mile in the air went big Jim Goff.
>
> [Chorus:] Then drill, ye tarriers, drill, / Drill, ye tarriers, drill, / Oh it's work all day without sugar in your tay / When ye work beyant [beyond] on the railway, / And drill, ye tarriers, drill.
>
> When pay day next it came around, / Poor Jim's pay a dollar short he found, / "What for?" says he, then came this reply, / "You were docked for the time you were up in the sky."

Source: Norm Cohen, *Long Steel Rail: The Railroad in American Folksong*

7. How does the song reflect the challenges that railroad workers faced?

Document 2

Tall skyscrapers were built in the late 1800s. In 1879 Benjamin Oppenheimer submitted the drawing to the right with his patent application.

8. What do you think is the purpose of Oppenheimer's invention?

Source: A. E. Brown and H. A. Jeffcott, Jr., *World's Wackiest Inventions*

Document 3

John D. Rockefeller stated the following:

> God gave me my money. . . . Having been endowed with the gift I possess, I believe it is my duty to make money and still more money and to use the money I make for the good of my fellow man according to the dictates of my conscience.

Source: Suzy Platt, *Respectfully Quoted*

9. How did Rockefeller explain his own wealth? How do you think he might explain why some people are not wealthy?

Document 4

The following article, "Christianity and Wealth," is by Congregationalist minister Washington Gladden.

> During the past fourteen years the wealth of this nation has increased much faster than the population, but the people who work for wages are little if any better off than they were fourteen years ago. . . .
>
> But this is not saying that . . . the state [should] . . . take the property of the rich and distribute it among the poor. . . . There are, however, one or two things that [are] . . . the immediate duty of the state. Certain outrageous monopolies exist that the state is bound to crush. . . . Another gigantic public evil that the state must exterminate is that of gambling in stocks and produce.

Source: Washington Gladden, *Century Illustrated*

10. What problems does Gladden describe in the excerpt? What solution does he propose?

11. Expository Writing Using the information from the four documents and your knowledge of social studies, write an essay in which you:

- explain why this time period might be referred to as the beginning of modern America; and
- name at least one way American society today resembles the Industrial Age and one way it is different.

Need Extra Help?											
If you missed questions. . .	1	2	3	4	5	6	7	8	9	10	11
Go to page. . .	587	590	595	606	605	584–606	603	590	597	603	584–606

The Industrial Age **Chapter 19** 609

9. He believes God gave him the ability to make money. He might explain economic inequality by attributing it to God's will. **16.A.3c**

10. Gladden says that America's growing wealth is unfairly divided among workers and owners and that workers are not being given their fair share of the wealth they are producing. He suggests outlawing certain monopolies and stock/commodity speculation. **16.A.3b**

11. Students might point to modernizing changes such as the many inventions of this time; the formation of corporations and resulting business growth; the expansion of railroads that brought people and industry to the West; mass production methods resulting in a wide variety of affordable products; and the development of chain stores and mail-order selling. Large industries are still part of American life today, and people are still creating valuable innovations. Conditions for workers have improved since the industrial age. **18.A**

History ONLINE
Have students visit the Web site at glencoe.com to review Chapter 19 and take the Self-Check Quiz.

Need Extra Help?

Have students refer to the pages listed if they miss any of the questions.

Document-Based Questions

7. The work was difficult and dangerous; in the song, one of the workers (Jim Goff) was blown into the sky by an explosion. The song also suggests that workers were not treated well. If they missed work due to an on-the-job injury, for example, they simply were not paid. (Jim Goff was "docked" for the time he was in the sky.) **18.A.3**

8. In the event of an emergency, the parachutelike invention was supposed to allow the user to safely jump out of the window of a tall building and land without injury on the ground. **16.A**

Chapter Planning Guide

20

Levels					Resources	Chapter Opener	Section 1	Section 2	Section 3	Chapter Assess
BL	OL	AL	ELL							
FOCUS										
BL	OL	AL	ELL	🖌	Daily Test Practice Transparencies		20–1	20–2	20–3	
TEACH										
	OL	AL		📁	Geography and History Activity, URB				p. 87	
BL	OL		ELL	📁	Time Line Skills Activity, URB			p. 90		
BL	OL	AL	ELL	📁	Writing Skills Activity, URB		p. 79			
	OL	AL		📁	American Literature Readings, URB		p. 9			
BL	OL	AL	ELL	📁	Content Vocabulary Activity, URB		p. 73	p. 73	p. 73	
BL			ELL	📁	Academic Vocabulary Activity, URB		p. 75	p. 75	p. 75	
BL			ELL	📁	Reading Skills Activity, URB			p. 7		
BL			ELL	📁	Social Studies Skills Activity, URB				p. 81	
BL	OL	AL	ELL	📁	Differentiated Instruction Activity, URB			p. 83		
BL	OL	AL	ELL	📁	Critical Thinking Skills Activity, URB		p. 85			
BL	OL	AL	ELL	📁	Linking Past and Present Activity, URB				p. 89	
	OL	AL		📁	Primary Source Readings, URB			p. 77		
BL	OL	AL	ELL	📁	School-to-Home Connection Activity, URB		p. 91	p. 91	p. 91	
BL	OL		ELL	📁	Guided Reading Activity, URB*		p. 95	p. 96	p. 97	
		AL		📁	Enrichment Activity, URB		p. 11			
BL	OL		ELL	📁	Reading Essentials and Note-Taking Guide*		p. 214	p. 217	p. 220	
BL	OL	AL	ELL	🖌	Lesson Transparencies		20A	20B	20C	
	OL			📁	American Biographies				p. 40	
	OL	AL		🖌	American Art and Architecture Transparencies, Strategies, and Activities				22	

Note: Please refer to the *Unit Resource Book: Reshaping the Nation* for this chapter's URB materials.

* Also available in Spanish

Levels				Resources	Chapter Opener	Section 1	Section 2	Section 3	Chapter Assess
BL	OL	AL	ELL						
				TEACH (continued)					
BL	OL	AL	ELL	📁 **NGS US Desk Map**		✓	✓	✓	
BL	OL	AL	ELL	📁 **American Literature Library**		✓	✓	✓	
BL	OL	AL	ELL	📁 **Writer's Guidebook**		✓	✓	✓	
	OL	AL		💿 **American History Primary Source Document Library CD-ROM**		✓	✓	✓	✓
BL	OL	AL	ELL	💿 **American Music: Hits Through History**	✓	✓	✓	✓	
BL	OL	AL	ELL	💿 **StudentWorks™ Plus CD**	✓	✓	✓	✓	✓
BL	OL	AL	ELL	🔒 **Section Spotlight Videos**		✓	✓	✓	
BL	OL	AL	ELL	🖨 **Writing Process Transparencies**		✓	✓	✓	✓
BL	OL	AL	ELL	💿 **Presentation Plus! With MindJogger Checkpoint CD**	✓	✓	✓	✓	✓
				ASSESS					
BL	OL	AL	ELL	📁 **Quizzes and Tests**		p. 193	p. 194	p. 195	pp. 197, 199, 201
BL	OL	AL	ELL	📁 **Authentic Assessment With Rubrics**		p. 20			
BL	OL	AL	ELL	📁 **Standardized Test Practice**					p. 39
BL	OL	AL	ELL	💿 *ExamView® Assessment Suite CD-ROM**		20–1	20–2	20–3	Ch. 20
				CLOSE					
BL			ELL	📁 **Reteaching Activity, URB***		p. 93	p. 93	p. 93	p. 93
BL	OL		ELL	📁 **Reading and Study Skills Foldables Activity**	p. 88	p. 88	p. 88	p. 88	p. 88
BL	OL	AL	ELL	📁 *The American Journey* **in Graphic Novel**					p. 111
BL			ELL	📁 **Reading Strategies and Activities for the Social Studies Classroom**		✓	✓	✓	
BL	OL	AL	ELL	🖨 **Graphic Organizer Transparencies & Strategies**		✓	✓	✓	

Teacher Works *Plus*
All-In-One Planner and Resource Center

- Interactive Lesson Planner
- Interactive Teacher Edition
- Fully editable blackline masters
- Section Spotlight Videos Launch

- Differentiated Lesson Plans
- Printable reports of daily assignments
- Standards Tracking System

Professional Development Resources

- Strategies for Success
- Building Academic Vocabulary
- Success With English Learners DVD
- Differentiated Instruction Strategies DVD
- Teaching Literacy Strategies in Social Studies DVD
- Assessment DVD
- Standards-Based Instruction DVD

Integrating Technology

20

Using StudentWorks™ Plus

Read and Listen

Technology Product

Glencoe's *StudentWorks™ Plus* CD contains the complete Student Edition, text in audio, all student workbooks, and links to online activities and resources.

- Students can read chapters if they have software that allows them to view PDF files.
- The complete textbook is available with audio via the *StudentWorks™ Plus* CD.
- Students can read and listen simultaneously with page-by-page audio.

Objectives

Using *StudentWorks™ Plus* will help your students

- practice their reading skills,

- improve their comprehension.

Steps

Provide students with the following information:

- Launch *StudentWorks™ Plus*.
- Select **Student Edition with Audio** from the launch screen.
- Use the bookmarks along the left side to navigate to the desired chapter or use the **Page Navigator** link in the bookmarks to link to the exact page number in the Student Edition.
- Click on the audio icon located on each page in the upper left corner to launch the audio.
- Read along with the audio.

History ONLINE at glencoe.com

	Student	Teacher	Parent
Media Center			
• Student Edition Audio	●		
• Spanish Summaries	●		
• Section Spotlight Videos	●	●	
Social Studies Online Learning Center			
Classroom Tools			
• Multi-Language Glossaries	●	●	●
• Teaching Today		●	
• TIME Current Events	●	●	●
• Beyond the Textbook	●	●	
***The American Journey* Online Learning Center**			
• Study-to-Go™	●	●	●
• Study Central™	●	●	●
• Chapter Overview	●	●	
• Concepts in Motion	●	●	
• ePuzzles and Games	●	●	
• Literature Connections	●	●	
• Online Student Edition	●	●	●
• Self-Check Quizzes	●	●	●
• Student Web Activities	●	●	
• Vocabulary eFlashcards	●	●	
• Web Activity Lesson Plans	●	●	●
• Vocabulary PuzzleMaker	●	●	●

READING SUPPORT FROM JAMESTOWN EDUCATION

- **Timed Readings Plus in Social Studies** helps students increase their reading rate and fluency while maintaining comprehension. The 400-word passages are similar to those found on state and national assessments.

- **Reading in the Content Area: Social Studies** concentrates on six essential reading skills that help students better comprehend what they read. The book includes 75 high-interest nonfiction passages written at increasing levels of difficulty.

- **Reading Social Studies** includes strategic reading instruction and vocabulary support in Social Studies content for ELLs and native speakers of English.

- **Content Vocabulary Workout** (Grades 6–8) accelerates reading comprehension through focused vocabulary development. Social Studies content vocabulary comes from the glossaries of Glencoe's Middle School Social Studies texts.

www.jamestowneducation.com

NATIONAL GEOGRAPHIC

Index to National Geographic Magazine:

The following articles relate to this chapter:

- *"Hip Hop Planet,"* James McBride, April 2007.
- *"Our Wall,"* Charles Bowden, May 2007.

National Geographic Society Products

To order the following, call National Geographic at 1-800-368-2728:

National Geographic Atlas of the World *(Book)*

Access National Geographic's dynamic MapMachine Web site and other geography resources at:

www.nationalgeographic.com

www.nationalgeographic.com/mapmachine

Reading List Generator CD-ROM — GLENCOE BOOKLINK 3

Use this database to search more than 30,000 titles to create a customized reading list for your students.

- Reading lists can be organized by students' reading level, author, genre, theme, or area of interest.
- The database provides Degrees of Reading Power™ (DRP) and Lexile™ readability scores for all selections.
- A brief summary of each selection is included.

Leveled reading suggestions for this chapter:

For students at a Grade 6 reading level:
- *Shutting Out the Sky: Life in the Tenements of New York: 1880–1924,* Deborah Hopkinson
- *The Colors of Freedom: Immigrant Stories,* Janet Bode

For students at a Grade 7 reading level:
- *Immigrant Kids,* Russell Freedman
- *Newcomers to America,* Judith E. Greenberg

For students at a Grade 8 reading level:
- *A Century of Immigration: 1820–1924,* Christopher Collier & James Lincoln Collier
- *Bound for America: The Story of the European Immigrants,* Milton Meltzer

For students at a Grade 9 reading level:
- *Life on Ellis Island,* Renee C. Rebman
- *A Nation of Strangers,* Vance Packard

For students at a Grade 10 reading level:
- *What's American About America?* Ishmael Reed
- *Mexican Immigration,* LeeAnne Gelletly

The following videotape programs are available from Glencoe as supplements to the chapter:

- **Ellis Island DVD** (ISBN 0-76-704451-7)
- **The Statue of Liberty** (ISBN 1-56-501468-5)

To order, call Glencoe at 1-800-334-7344. To find classroom resources to accompany many of these videos, check the following home pages:

A&E Television: www.aetv.com

The History Channel: www.history.com

Chapter Objectives

After studying this chapter, students will be able to:

- Identify characteristics of the new wave of immigrants that arrived after 1865.
- Relate how cities changed during the late 1800s.
- Discuss ways American culture changed in the late 1800s.

Motivating Activity

Analyzing Discuss with students how transportation and city life are related. **Ask:** How might the introduction of the railroad and motorized vehicles have changed American city life? *(The railroad and motorized vehicles allowed more people to travel to cities for work and probably made transportation more affordable.)* **Ask:** How do motorized vehicles affect our lives today? *(Possible answers: people use cars to travel into cities for work, allowing for the growth of suburbs. Environmental issues have become a concern in part because of motorized vehicles.)* **OL**

Previewing the Essential Questions

As you begin teaching each section, use these questions and activities to help students focus on the Essential Questions.

Chapter 20

An Urban Society 1865–1914

The Brooklyn Bridge with a view of the surrounding area, 1898

PRESIDENTS

| ANDREW JOHNSON 1865–1869 | ULYSSES S. GRANT 1869–1877 | RUTHERFORD B. HAYES 1877–1881 | JAMES GARFIELD 1881 | CHESTER ARTHUR 1881–1885 | GROVER CLEVELAND 1885–1889 | BENJAMIN HARRISON 1889–1893 |

U.S. Events
World Events

1865 — 1875 — 1885

★ 1866
Transatlantic telegraph line successfully completed

1882 ★
Robert Louis Stevenson's *Treasure Island* published

1889 ★
Eiffel Tower erected

Section 1

The New Immigrants Ask: How might immigration affect family life, language, and other cultural aspects of American life? *(Immigrants might introduce their language and traditions to Americans. American family life might change to adapt to others' cultures.)* Tell students that in Section 1 they will learn about the new wave of immigrants to America. **OL**

Section 2

Moving to the City Ask: What problems might a city face when many people arrive in a short time? *(Answers may include a housing shortage and a scarcity of jobs and resources.)* Explain to students that Section 2 discusses the changes that occurred in cities in the late 1800s as a new influx of immigrants arrived to live and work in America. **OL**

Section 1: The New Immigrants
Essential Question What were some characteristics of the new wave of immigrants that arrived after 1865?

Section 2: Moving to the City
Essential Question How did cities change during the late 1800s?

Section 3: A Changing Culture
Essential Question In what ways did American culture change in the late 1800s?

History ONLINE
Chapter Overview Visit glencoe.com and click on **Chapter 20—Chapter Overviews** to preview chapter information.

Organizing Information

Make this Foldable to help organize what you learn about changes to the culture of the United States.

Step 1 Place two sheets of paper on top of one another about one inch apart.

Step 2 Fold the papers to form four equal tabs.

Step 3 Staple the sheets, and label each tab as shown.

Reading and Writing As you read the chapter, write down key events and ideas that relate to the Essential Questions.

An Urban Society 1865–1914
Section 1: The New Immigrants Essential Question:
Section 2: Moving to the City Essential Question:
Section 3: A Changing Culture Essential Question:

◀ Ford factory, Detroit, Michigan

★ 1892 Ellis Island admits immigrants

GROVER CLEVELAND 1893–1897
WILLIAM McKINLEY 1897–1901
THEODORE ROOSEVELT 1901–1909

1906 ★ San Francisco rocked by earthquake

WILLIAM HOWARD TAFT 1909–1913

★ 1913 Ford develops first moving assembly line

1895 **1905** **1915**

1895 ★ First complete performance of *Swan Lake*

1900 ★ First trial flight of Zeppelin

★ 1907 Cubism arises in art

Chapter 20 611

Introducing Chapter 20

Time Line Activity

If you have not already done so, have students review the time line. **Ask:** What years are covered in this chapter? *(1865–1915)* What were some of the technological achievements that occurred in the world during this time? *(Eiffel Tower erected, transatlantic telegraph line completed, first flight of Zeppelin, first assembly line developed)* Which of these accomplishments took place in the United States? *(the development of the assembly line)*

FOLDABLES Study Organizer **Dinah Zike's Foldables**
Purpose This Foldable helps students identify key events and ideas that influenced the culture of the United States. The completed Foldable will help them prepare for assessment. **OL**

📁 More Foldable activities for this chapter can be found in *Dinah Zike's Reading and Study Skills Foldables.*

History ONLINE
Introduce students to chapter content and key terms by having them access the **Chapter Overview** at glencoe.com.

Section ★ 3

A Changing Culture Ask: How might the industrialization of cities affect recreation in America? *(Answers may include that industrial workers might have more leisure time for sports, cultural, and arts events.)* Tell students that Section 3 will describe how leisure activities changed in the late 1800s, as a new American culture evolved. **OL**

Focus

The New Immigrants

Bellringer
Daily Test Practice Transparency 20–1

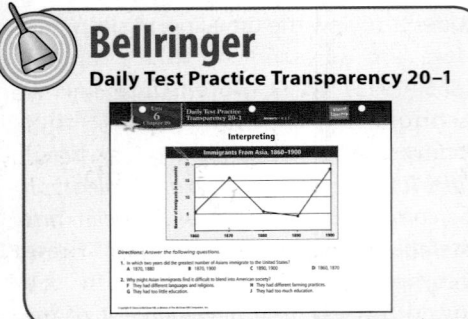

Reading Guide

Answers to Graphic:

1882: Chinese Exclusion Act—prohibited Chinese workers from entering the United States; **1892 and 1902:** extensions of the Chinese Exclusion Act—prohibited Chinese workers from entering the United States; **1907:** agreement with Japan—limited the number of Japanese immigrants; **1917:** Immigration Act of 1917—required immigrants to be able to read and write in any language

Section Spotlight Video

Have students watch the Section Spotlight Video "The New Immigrants" to learn more about the wave of immigration in the late 1800s.

Resource Manager

Essential Question
What were some characteristics of the new wave of immigrants that arrived after 1865?

Reading Guide

Content Vocabulary

emigrate (p. 613)   sweatshop (p. 615)

ethnic group (p. 614)   assimilate (p. 616)

steerage (p. 614)

Academic Vocabulary

attitude (p. 617)   affect (p. 617)

Key People and Events

Emma Lazarus (p. 614)

Chinese Exclusion Act (p. 617)

Immigration Act of 1917 (p. 617)

Reading Strategy

Taking Notes As you read, place the immigration laws on a time line like the one below, and take notes on the purpose of each law.

1882   1892   1902   1907   1917

ILLINOIS STANDARDS
The American Journey

16.C.3b (US) Explain relationships among the American economy and slavery, immigration, industrialization, labor, and urbanization, 1700–present.

17.C.3c Analyze how human processes influence settlement patterns including migration and population growth.

18.C.3b Explain how diverse groups have contributed to U.S. social systems over time.

American Diary

At the end of a long ocean voyage, immigrants waited for entry into the United States. "The steerage passengers have before them more rigid examinations . . . so in spite of . . . the glad greetings shouted to and fro, they sink again into awe-struck and confused silence. When the last . . . passenger has disappeared from the dock, the immigrants with their baggage are loaded into barges and taken to Ellis Island for their final examination."

—*from* On the Trail of the Immigrant *by Edward A. Steiner*

Newly arrived immigrants at Ellis Island

R Reading Strategies	C Critical Thinking	D Differentiated Instruction	W Writing Support	S Skill Practice
Teacher Edition • Previewing, p. 613 • Predicting, p. 615 **Additional Resources** • Guid. Read., URB p. 95 • Content Vocab., URB p. 73 • Academic Vocab., URB p. 75 • Read. Ess., p. 214 • Am. Lit. Read., URB p. 9	**Teacher Edition** • Compar. & Contrast, p. 614 • Making Infer., p. 615 • Drawing Con., p. 616 **Additional Resources** • Quizzes and Tests, p. 193 • Enrichment Act., URB p. 11 • Crit. Think. Skills, URB p. 85	**Teacher Edition** • ELL, p. 613 • Interpersonal, p. 617 **Additional Resources** • School-to-Home, URB p. 91 • Reteaching Act., URB p. 93	**Teacher Edition** • Persuasive Writ., p. 617 **Additional Resources** • Writ. Skills, URB p. 79 • Authentic Assess., p. 20	**Teacher Edition** • Visual Lit., p. 614 **Additional Resources** • Daily Test Pract. Transp. 20-1 • Lesson Transp. 20A

A Flood of Immigrants

Main Idea New immigrants began to arrive in the late 1800s, seeking opportunities in the United States.

History and You Have you seen pictures of or visited the Statue of Liberty? Read to learn the statue's significance to millions of immigrants.

Before 1865, most immigrants to the United States—except for enslaved Africans—came from northern and western Europe. After the Civil War, immigrants from other countries began making the journey to the United States.

New Immigration

In the mid-1880s, the pattern of immigration started to change. Large groups of "new" immigrants arrived from eastern and southern Europe. Greeks, Russians, Hungarians, Italians, Turks, and Poles were among the newcomers. At the same time, the number of "old" immigrants from northern and western Europe started to decrease. By 1907, 80 percent of immigrants came from southern and eastern Europe.

Many of these newcomers were Catholics or Jews. Few spoke English. Because of this, they did not blend into American society as easily as the "old" immigrants had. Often, they clustered together in neighborhoods made up of people of the same nationality.

After 1900, immigration from Mexico also increased. In addition, many people came to the United States from China and Japan. They, too, brought unfamiliar languages and religious beliefs and had difficulty blending into American society.

Leaving Troubles Behind

Why did so many people leave their homelands for the United States in the late 1800s and early 1900s? They were "pushed" away by difficult conditions at home. At the same time, many were "pulled" to the United States by new opportunities.

Many people **emigrated,** or left their homelands, because of economic troubles. In Italy and Hungary, overcrowding and poverty made jobs scarce. Farmers in Croatia and Serbia could not own enough land to support their families. Sweden suffered major crop failures. New machines such as looms put many craft workers out of work.

Primary Source | **Responding to New Immigrants**

Differing Opinions People had different opinions about immigration. Although some believed the United States should welcome immigrants with open arms, others saw the flood of people entering the country as a problem. These views were reflected in political cartoons of the day.

◀ This magazine cover demonstrates one reaction to making Ellis Island a new processing station for immigrants. The cartoon on the cover shows the Statue of Liberty frowning as immigrants are dumped at her feet.

Critical Thinking

Comparing and Contrasting What symbols does the artist use to represent the United States? What message is the artist trying to convey about new immigrants?

Name _____ Date _____ Class _____

Enrichment Activity
Launching the Republic

Unit

The United States Census

Representation and direct Taxes shall be apportioned among the several States which may be included within this Union according to their respective Numbers. . . . The actual Enumeration shall be made within three Years after the first Meeting of the Congress of the United States, and within every subsequent Term of ten Years, in such Manner as they shall by Law direct.
—Article I, Section 2 of the Constitution of the United States

With this statement, the Founding Fathers created the U.S. census. The first census count, conducted in 1790, consisted of a door-to-door survey by U.S. marshals and their assistants. Their goal was to determine the number of free white males and females, the number of free persons, and the number of enslaved people, in each household. The information was written on paper that the marshals furnished themselves, and the results were posted in public areas for all to inspect. The census information was used to ensure that every state had fair representation in the U.S. House of Representatives based on population.

Since that time, the U.S. Census Bureau has conducted more than 20 census counts. In later censuses, members of households were asked more questions, such as occupation, place of birth, and school enrollment. Census data is now used for many purposes, including redistricting, federal aid distribution, and environmental impact analysis.

Maps and the Census

In the late 1800s, the U.S. Census Bureau began using maps to present population, economic, and other data by geographic area. Since then, the Census Bureau's mapmaking has progressed from simple outline maps to electronic databases and computerized map output. The areas mapped not only include large geographic areas but also areas as small as city blocks.

Using maps, government workers and decision makers in private industry can more easily visualize census data. By comparing maps from different years, trends in population growth and migration can be seen. For example, the map on the next page, which is based on data from the 1790 census, shows that the population of the newly formed United States was concentrated along the East Coast. It also shows that Virginia had the largest population at that time.

Teach

R Reading Strategy

Previewing Have students preview the section content by reading the main idea, the section headings, and the key terms. **Ask:** Based on your preview, what do you think this section will be about? *(Answers may include immigrants' reasons for moving to the United States and the challenges they faced when they arrived.)* **BL**

D Differentiated Instruction

English Language Learners Ask students to read the sentence silently. **Ask:** What is the definition of *emigrate*? *(to leave one's homeland)* Ask students to compare the word *emigrate* to *immigrate*. Explain that *emigrate* means "to leave" and *immigrate* means "to enter." **OL**

Primary Source

Critical Thinking Answer The Statue of Liberty and Washington, D.C.; the immigrants are Europe's unwanted citizens.

Differentiated Instruction

U.S. Immigration in the Late 1800s

Objective:	To create and present a graph using historical data
Focus:	Ask students what they know about the Statue of Liberty and Ellis Island.
Teach:	Have students research and create their graphs.
Assess:	Have students use the Self-Assessment Checklist.
Close:	Ask students what their findings might mean for the country's immediate future.

Differentiated Instruction Strategies

BL Discuss appropriate sources for the information in the graph.

AL Have students present the information in other types of graphs such as circle or bar graphs.

ELL Discuss the elements of a graph, including the legend.

C Critical Thinking

Comparing and Contrasting Ask: Why did immigrants want to live in America? *(They saw the United States as a place to work, buy land, and find new opportunities.)* **Ask:** Compare reasons for immigration to the U.S. today with those in the late 1800s. Are immigrants' reasons for coming to America the same or different? *(Students may say they are the same because most immigrants come to the United States to live a better life.)* **OL**

S Skill Practice

Visual Literacy Have students look at the photos of the Statue of Liberty and read the captions. **Ask:** Which symbols on the statue relate the message of freedom? *(the torch and the broken chain)* **OL**

Hands-On Chapter Project
Step 1

Presenting an American Cultural Fair

Step 1: Conducting Research Groups of students will research one of the immigrant groups to arrive in the United States in the late 1800s.

Essential Question: What were some characteristics of the new wave of immigrants that arrived after 1865?

Seeking Fairness

Persecution also drove people from their homelands. Some countries passed laws or set policies against certain **ethnic groups**—minorities that spoke different languages or followed different customs from those of most people in a country. Members of these ethnic groups often emigrated to escape discrimination or unfair laws. Many Jews fled persecution in Russia in the 1880s and came to the United States.

Seeking Opportunity

Immigrants saw the United States as a place of jobs, plentiful land, and opportunities for a better life. Although some immigrants returned to their homelands after a few years, most came to America to stay.

Immigrants often had a difficult journey to America. Many had to first travel to a seaport to board a ship. Often they traveled for hundreds of miles and through foreign countries to get to port cities.

Then came the long ocean voyage to the United States—12 days across the Atlantic or several weeks across the Pacific. Immigrants usually could afford only the cheapest tickets and traveled in **steerage**—cramped quarters on the lower decks of the ships.

Entering America

Most immigrants landed at New York City. After 1836, the magnificent sight of the Statue of Liberty greeted immigrants as they sailed into New York Harbor. The statue, a gift from the people of France, seemed to promise hope for a better life in the new country. On its base, the stirring words of **Emma Lazarus,** an American poet, welcomed the many immigrants arriving in the country from Europe: "Give me your tired, your poor, Your huddled masses yearning to breathe free, The wretched refuse of your teeming shore. Send these, the homeless, tempest-tossed to me, I lift my lamp beside the golden door!"

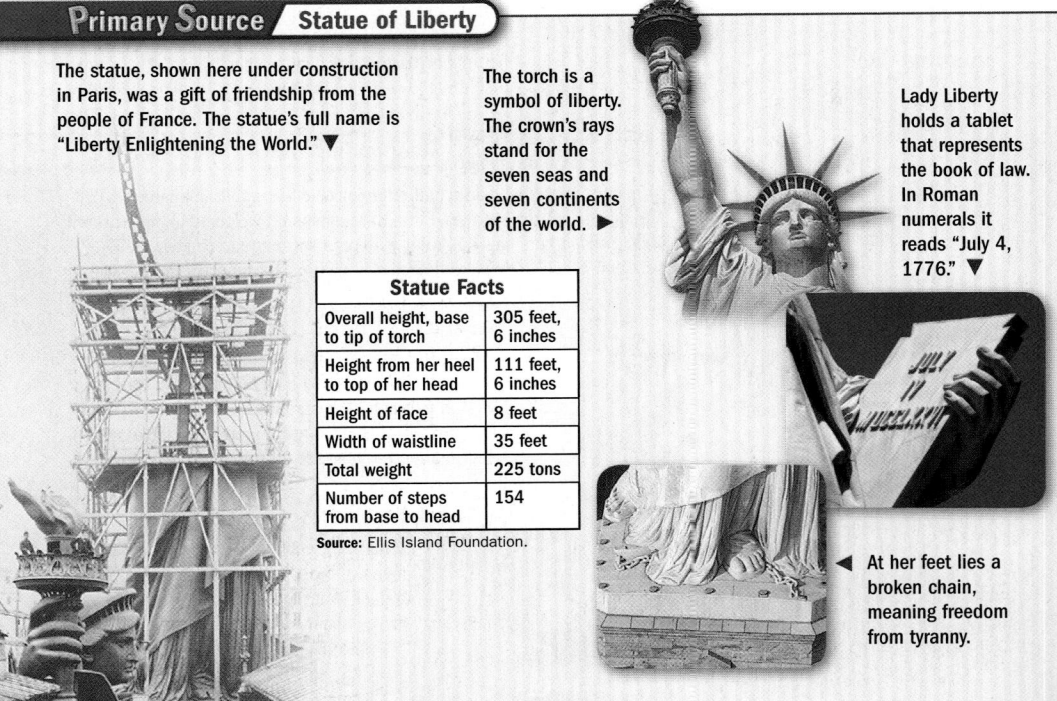

Primary Source / Statue of Liberty

The statue, shown here under construction in Paris, was a gift of friendship from the people of France. The statue's full name is "Liberty Enlightening the World." ▼

The torch is a symbol of liberty. The crown's rays stand for the seven seas and seven continents of the world. ▶

Lady Liberty holds a tablet that represents the book of law. In Roman numerals it reads "July 4, 1776." ▼

Statue Facts	
Overall height, base to tip of torch	305 feet, 6 inches
Height from her heel to top of her head	111 feet, 6 inches
Height of face	8 feet
Width of waistline	35 feet
Total weight	225 tons
Number of steps from base to head	154

Source: Ellis Island Foundation.

◀ At her feet lies a broken chain, meaning freedom from tyranny.

Directions Organize students into small groups, and assign each group one of the immigrant groups mentioned in the chapter. Explain that each group will create a booth for an American cultural fair. Have students read this section and the next and take notes on the languages and religions of the groups and their patterns of settlement in American cities. Then have students research their group in greater detail using the library and online sources. Tell students to discuss what they want to include in their booth as they conduct research.

Summarizing After students have conducted their research, meet with each group. Ask students to summarize their findings.

(Chapter Project continued in Section 2)

Before the new arrivals could actually pass through the "golden door" to America, however, they had to register at government reception centers. In the East, immigrants were processed at Castle Garden, a former fort on Manhattan Island. After 1892, they went through Ellis Island in New York Harbor. Most Asian immigrants arrived in the United States on the West Coast in California and went through the processing center on Angel Island in San Francisco Bay.

Examiners at the centers recorded the immigrants' names—sometimes shortening or simplifying a name they found too difficult to write. The examiners asked the immigrants where they came from, their occupation, and whether they had relatives in the United States. New immigrants also were given health examinations. Immigrants with contagious illnesses could be refused permission to enter the United States.

Reading Check Explaining Why was the voyage to America often difficult?

"We will not forget that Liberty has here made her home."
—President Grover Cleveland, Statue of Liberty dedication ceremony

◄ The unveiling, New York Harbor, October 28, 1886

Critical Thinking

1. **Making Connections** How does the date on the tablet relate to the broken chain?
2. **Finding Main Ideas** What American values are represented in the statue's symbols?

The Immigrant Experience

C

Main Idea Immigrants adjusted to life in America, finding work, forming communities, and adapting to a new culture. R

History and You Are you familiar with parts of cities that are known as Little Italy or Chinatown? Read to learn how these neighborhoods might have formed.

After passing through the reception centers, most immigrants gained entry to the United States. Where would they go? How would they live? Some had relatives or friends to stay with and to help them find jobs. Others knew no one and would have to strike out on their own.

Finding Work

An immigrant's greatest challenge was finding work. Sometimes organizations in his or her homeland recruited workers for jobs in the United States. These organizations supplied American employers with unskilled workers who worked unloading cargo or digging ditches.

Some of America's fastest-growing industries hired immigrant workers. In the steel mills of Pittsburgh, for example, most of the laborers in the early 1900s were immigrant men. They might work 12 hours per day, seven days per week.

Many immigrants, including women and children, worked in **sweatshops** in the garment industry. These were dark, crowded shops where workers made clothing. The work was repetitious and hazardous, the pay low, and the hours long.

Pauline Newman, who later became an official in the International Ladies' Garment Workers Union, worked in a New York sweatshop as a child. She recalled: "We started work at 7:30 [in the morning] and during the busy season we worked until nine o' clock in the evening. They didn't pay any overtime and didn't give you anything for supper money. At times they would give you . . . a little apple pie . . . for your supper."

An Urban Society **Chapter 20** 615

C Critical Thinking

Making Inferences Ask: Why do you think the U.S. port was referred to as the "golden door"? *(because the United States stood for wealth and opportunity)* **OL**

R Reading Strategy

Predicting Read the Main Idea aloud. Have students make predictions about new immigrants' experiences in the United States. **BL**

Reading Check **Answer:** Immigrants often had to travel hundreds of miles to board a ship and then sail 12 days across the Atlantic or weeks across the Pacific. On board, immigrants travelled in steerage, the cheapest, most cramped quarters.

Primary Source

Critical Thinking Answers

1. The date is the date of U.S. independence, when the United States broke free (broke the chain) of British rule.
2. torch: liberty; chain: freedom; book: law

Differentiated Instruction

Leveled Activities

BL **Reteaching Activity, URB p. 93**

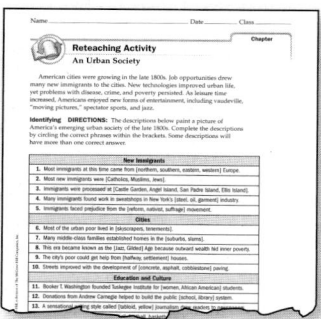

OL **Writing Skills Activity, URB p. 79**

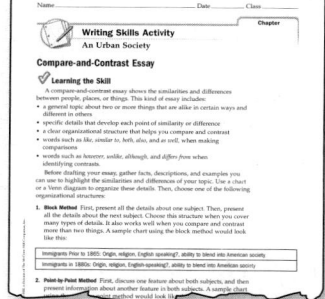

AL **Critical Thinking Skills Activity, URB p. 85**

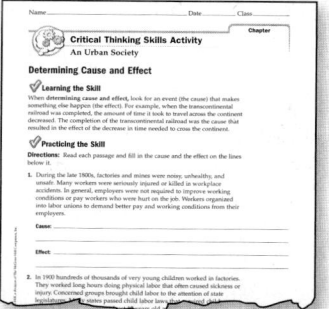

ELL **Content Vocabulary Activity, URB p. 73**

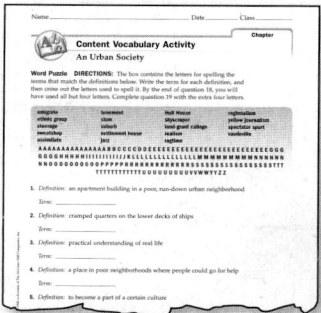

C Critical Thinking

Drawing Conclusions Ask: How might separate ethnic communities contribute to racial strife in cities? *(Such segregation might lead to distrust and prejudice among groups.)* **Ask:** Is the challenge of separate communities the same today? Why? *(Students may answer yes, since prejudice remains a problem today.)* **AL**

INTERPRETING
POLITICAL CARTOONS

Answers

1. They are trying to prevent new immigrants from entering the United States.

2. They would see the shadows of their forefathers. The cartoonist is saying that successful Americans should not forget that they or their ancestors were once immigrants, too.

Reading Check **Answer:** They wanted to feel at home in a new land.

Additional Support

Primary Sources
INTERPRETING
POLITICAL CARTOONS

This cartoon comments on successful Americans who wanted to limit immigration.

1. **Interpreting** How are the successful Americans treating the new immigrant?

2. **Analyzing** If the Americans looked backward, as the title suggests, what would they see? What is the cartoonist saying?

A. New, poor immigrant   B. Successful Americans
C. Immigrant forefathers of the Americans

LOOKING BACKWARD THEY WOULD CLOSE TO THE NEWCOMER THE BRIDGE THAT CARRIED THEM AND THEIR FATHERS OVER.

Adjusting to America

In their new homes, immigrants tried to preserve their own cultures. At the same time, most wanted to **assimilate,** or become part of the American culture. These two desires sometimes came into conflict.

Many immigrant parents, for example, continued to speak their native languages. Their children spoke English at school and with friends, but they spoke their native language at home. The grandchildren of many immigrants spoke only English.

Furthermore, in the United States, women generally had more freedom than women in European and Asian countries. New lifestyles conflicted with traditional ways and sometimes caused family friction.

Building Communities

Most of the new immigrants were from rural areas. Because they lacked the money to buy farmland in America, however, they often settled in industrial cities. With little or no education, they usually worked as unskilled laborers.

People of the same ethnic group tended to form separate communities. As a result, neighborhoods of Jewish, Italian, Polish, Chinese, and other groups quickly developed in New York, Chicago, San Francisco, and other large cities.

Immigrants sought to re-create some of the life they had left behind. The communities they established revolved around a number of traditional institutions. Most important were the houses of worship—the churches and the synagogues—where worship was conducted and holidays were celebrated as they were in their homelands. Priests and rabbis often acted as community leaders.

The immigrants published newspapers in their native languages, opened stores and theaters, and organized social clubs. Ethnic communities helped the immigrants preserve their cultural heritage.

Reading Check **Analyzing** Why would immigrants re-create traditional institutions in their new land?

Activity: Interdisciplinary Connection

Literature Many historical novels have been written depicting life as an immigrant at the turn of the century. Have students read excerpts from *The Boxer* (Kathleen Karr) or *A Tree Grows in Brooklyn* (Betty Smith). Instruct students to note the historical references in the text and the language and dialect of the characters. **Ask:** What hardships discussed in the text are evident in the stories? *(Answers will vary depending on the excerpt discussed.)* How do the authors convey character traits through the character's voice? *(The authors use language and dialect in dialogue to give readers a sense of ethnicity.)* As an extension, have students read excerpts from both novels and use a Venn diagram to compare the lives of each main character. **OL**

The Nativist Movement

Main Idea Some people opposed immigration, while others appreciated the positive contributions made by immigrants.

History and You Did any of your relatives immigrate to the United States from another country? If so, when? Read to find out how immigrants were regarded by American society.

. . . .

Assimilation also was slowed by the **attitudes**—ways of thinking and acting—of many native-born Americans, who resented the new wave of immigrants. They feared that the new immigrants would take away their jobs or drive down everyone's wages by accepting lower pay. These Americans also argued that the new immigrants—with their foreign languages, unfamiliar religions, and distinctive customs—would not fit into American society.

People found it easy to blame immigrants for increasing crime, unemployment, and other problems. The nativist movement, which had opposed immigration since the 1830s, gained strength during the late 1800s. Calls for restrictions on immigration mounted.

Lawmakers responded quickly to the tide of anti-immigrant feeling. In 1882 Congress passed the **Chinese Exclusion Act,** which prohibited Chinese workers from entering the United States for 10 years. Congress extended this law in 1892 and again in 1902. Similarly, in 1907 the federal government and Japan came to a "gentleman's agreement" that aimed to limit the number of Japanese immigrants.

Other legislation **affected,** or had an impact on, immigrants from all nations. In 1897 Congress passed a bill that required immigrants to be able to read and write in some language. Although the president vetoed the bill, Congress later passed the **Immigration Act of 1917,** which included a similar literacy requirement.

On the other hand, some Americans supported immigration. These people recognized that immigrants supplied the country's growing industries with workers. Immigrants also enriched the United States with the culture of their homelands.

✓**Reading Check** **Explaining** Why did some Americans blame immigrants for the nation's problems?

History ONLINE
Study Central™ To review this section, go to glencoe.com.

D Differentiated Instruction

Interpersonal Have small groups discuss the attitude of nativists. **Ask:** Has there been a similar situation in your own life with a new student or neighbor? **OL**

W Writing Support

Persuasive Writing Have students write a letter to lawmakers persuading them to refrain from passing the Chinese Exclusion Act. **OL**

✓**Reading Check** **Answer:** Americans thought immigrants would take away jobs, drive down wages, and not assimilate into American culture.

Assess

History ONLINE

Study Central™ provides summaries, interactive games, and online graphic organizers to help students review content.

Close

Discussing As a class, discuss the family life of U.S. immigrants in the late 1800s. **OL**

Section ★ Review

Section 1 Review

Vocabulary

1. Use each of these terms in a sentence that will help explain its meaning: emigrate, ethnic group, steerage, sweatshop, assimilate, attitude, affect.

Main Ideas

2. **Contrasting** How did immigration change after 1865?

3. **Describing** What were the working conditions in sweatshops?

4. **Evaluating** What is your opinion of the nativist movement?

Critical Thinking

5. **Determining Cause and Effect** What was the effect of each of the following immigration laws?

Chinese Exclusion Act	
"Gentleman's Agreement"	
Immigration Act of 1917	

6. **Speculating** What was an immigrant's greatest challenge upon arriving in the United States?

7. **Expository Writing** Write a paragraph explaining what happened at government reception centers for immigrants.

Answer the
8. **Essential Question**
What were some characteristics of the new wave of immigrants that arrived after 1865?

An Urban Society **Chapter 20** 617

Answers

1. Sentences should use vocabulary words according to their definitions in the section and Glossary.
2. New groups of immigrants came from southern and eastern Europe, as well as from Mexico, China, and Japan.
3. Sweatshops were dark and crowded, work was repetitive and hazardous, and the pay was low.
4. Answers will vary but may include nativists unfairly feared the new immigrants, and they did not appreciate the many contributions immigrants made to American life.
5. **Chinese Exclusion Act:** prohibited Chinese workers from entering the United States; **"Gentleman's Agreement":** limited the number of Japanese immigrants; **Immigration Act of 1917:** required that immigrants be literate
6. Students may suggest that an immigrant's greatest challenge was finding work or a place to live.
7. Student paragraphs should include details about recording names; the questions asked of immigrants; and health examinations.
8. Many were from southern and eastern Europe; some did not speak English; some were Catholics or Jews; they did not blend into society as easily as previous groups of immigrants had; some formed separate communities.

Focus

C Critical Thinking

Comparing and Contrasting Have students study the photo of the automobile race. Ask them to contrast the features of the automobile shown in the photo with modern-day automobiles. **Ask:** What are some of the features on this automobile that have been updated, and why do you think the changes were made? *(We now have steering wheels to make turning easier; wheels are smaller and made of rubber for speed and better wear and tear; many cars are enclosed or covered, and they are made of metal to be safer; we now have seat belts for safety.)* **OL**

Teach

W Writing Support

Descriptive Writing Ask students to think about what it might have been like to be with Thomas Edison viewing the first lightbulb. Ask them to write a descriptive paragraph about the experience. **OL**

Additional Support and Answers

TIME NOTEBOOK

What were people's lives like in the past?

These two pages will give you some clues to everyday life in the United States as you step back in time with TIME Notebook.

AMERICA'S FIRST AUTO RACE
Built for Speed

BETTMANN / CORBIS

In 1893 two brothers, **CHARLES** and **FRANK DURYEA**, built the first American automobile in Springfield, Massachusetts. It could travel up to 7.5 miles per hour (mph). In 1895 the two bicycle mechanics held the first automobile race. The course was 54 miles (87 km), going from Chicago to Evanston, Illinois, and back again. Six cars started the race that snowy morning—the Duryea's second automobile, two electric cars and three gas-powered Benzes from Germany. Here is how Frank Duryea describes the race:

The machine made good going of the soft unpacked snow in Jackson Park.... While still in the lead, the left front wheel struck a bad rut at such an angle that the steering arm was broken off.... We, fortunately, located a blacksmith shop where we forged down, threaded, and replaced the arm.... The Macy Benz passed us and held the lead as far as Evanston, where we regained it. Having made the turn at Evanston, elated at being in the lead again, we started on the home trip.

"... One of the two cylinders ceased firing.... This repair was completed in fifty-five minutes and we got going, feeling that the Macy Benz must surely be ahead of us, but learned later that the Macy did not get that far. After a stop for gasoline ... we continued on to the finish.... The motor had at all times shown ample power, and at no time were we compelled to get out and push."

Averaging 7.3 mph, Frank Duryea's car was the first to finish the race in just over 10 hours. He won the $2,000 prize.

CORBIS

The Eighth Wonder of the World

Fourteen years after construction began, the **BROOKLYN BRIDGE** —the largest suspension bridge in the world—opens in 1883. Schools and shops in Brooklyn are closed so everyone can celebrate.

With a span half again as long as that of any previous bridge, it hangs from steel cables. Its designer and builder, John Roebling, was killed on the job. His son, Washington, continued directing the work until he was injured. Then Washington's wife, Emily, completed the job, making her possibly the first woman field engineer.

618

VERBATIM
WHAT PEOPLE ARE SAYING

❝Assassination can be no more guarded against than death by lightning; and it is best not to worry about either.❞
PRESIDENT JAMES GARFIELD,
Second United States president to be assassinated; he died from a gunshot wound in 1881

❝The greatest bane [curse] of modern civilization.❞
DR. JOHN HARVEY KELLOGG,
describing modern cooking in 1894. He had just invented a new "toasted corn flake" for the breakfast table

❝I pledge allegiance to the flag of the United States of America ...❞
YOUTH'S COMPANION,
the first magazine to publish the Pledge of Allegiance in 1892

❝We sat and looked as the lamp continued to burn, and the longer it burned, the more fascinated we were. None of us could go to bed. There was no sleep for any of us for 40 hours.❞
THOMAS EDISON,
on inventing the lightbulb, which he patented in 1883

❝I asked a man in prison once how he happened to be there and he said he had stolen a pair of shoes. I told him if he had stolen a railroad, he would be a United States senator.❞
"MOTHER" MARY JONES,
labor activist

Fast Facts

Questions of Authority After just four months in office, President James Garfield was shot in the back at a railroad station in Washington, D.C. He was shot by Charles J. Guiteau, who was disappointed at not being appointed to a political office. Guiteau surrendered to the police, stating, "I am a Stalwart [a conservative division of the Republican Party]. Arthur is now president of the United States."

The president would survive for 80 days after the shooting, but he was unable to perform his duties. Although the vice president was empowered to assume the presidential duties, it was not clear whether Vice President Chester A. Arthur should serve as acting president or permanently replace the ailing Garfield. There was uncertainty in the Constitution about this situation, and the question could not be presented before Congress for debate because Congress was not in session.

The president's cabinet decided that the president would have to be consulted to make a decision, but Garfield's doctors did not think he was capable of such a task. Before the issue was resolved, however, Garfield died.

The Well-Dressed Cowhand

These are prices from the Montgomery Ward catalogs of the 1880s.

Stetson hat $10.00
Cotton shirt (no collar) $1.25
Chaps and pants $8.00
Leather boots $20.00
Spurs $0.70
Colt pistol $12.20
Holster, cartridge belt $2.00
Saddle $40.00
Horse (usually
provided by ranch) $35.00
Lariat (lasso) $7.75

BETTMANN / CORBIS

MILESTONES

EVENTS AND PEOPLE OF THE TIME

OFFERED. A "company of fifty lady sharpshooters" to President William McKinley in 1898 at the start of the Spanish-American War, by the famous sharpshooter and performer, Annie Oakley. She promised each would bring along her own rifle and ammunition—McKinley has yet to respond to the offer.

CALLED. Government officials by President Rutherford B. Hayes, who took office in 1877; he was the first president to use the new telephone in the White House.

DRAWN. The first comic strip, *The Yellow Kid,* by R. F. Outcault in 1896—it has provided the name for dishonest reporting: "yellow journalism."

DEDICATED. The new Statue of Liberty in New York Harbor by President Cleveland in 1886.

SHOWN. First moving picture in 1896; featured are two girls dancing with umbrellas and two men boxing.

OPENED. Hull House in Chicago by Jane Addams in 1889—providing meals, health care, and education for the poor, including many immigrants.

HULTON-DEUTSCH COLLECTION / CORBIS

ANNIE OAKLEY

NUMBERS

UNITED STATES AT THE TIME

5 The number of transcontinental railroads crisscrossing the country in 1900

10 The number of years Chinese people must wait after applying to immigrate to the United States, according to the Chinese Immigration Act passed by Congress in 1882

21 The age of Frances Folsom when she married President Cleveland in 1886, making her the youngest First Lady

27,000,000
The number of visitors to the Chicago Exposition—sometimes called the first world's fair—in 1893, where visitors rode G.W. Ferris's new 250-foot-high invention, the Ferris wheel

VISUAL ARTS LIBRARY (LONDON) / ALAMY

200 Approximate number of Sioux Indians, mostly women and children, killed at Wounded Knee, South Dakota, when they were attacked by the American 7th Cavalry

CRITICAL THINKING

Describing Name the inventions and structures mentioned in this Notebook. How did each change the lives of Americans?

Analyzing Primary Sources Based on Duryea's diary of the race, why was it considered a daring and unusual adventure to race, or even drive, a car in 1893?

619

Section 2

Moving to the City

Focus

Bellringer
Daily Test Practice Transparency 20–2

Reading Guide
Answers to Graphic:

Growth of cities: Tenements became slums, which housed poor immigrants; the middle class grew; the wealthy built mansions in cities.

Section Spotlight Video

Have students watch the Section Spotlight Video "Moving to the City" to learn more about the Gilded Age.

Resource Manager

Essential Question
How did cities change during the late 1800s?

Reading Guide

Content Vocabulary
tenement (p. 622)	settlement house (p. 623)
slum (p. 622)	Hull House (p. 623)
suburb (p. 622)	skyscraper (p. 624)

Academic Vocabulary
major (p. 621) minor (p. 623)

Key People and Events
Gilded Age (p. 622)
Jane Addams (p. 623)
Louis Sullivan (p. 624)
Frederick Law Olmsted (p. 625)

Reading Strategy
Taking Notes As you read, describe three effects of the growth of cities.

ILLINOIS STANDARDS
The American Journey

16.E.3c (US) Describe the impact of urbanization and suburbanization, 1850–present, on the environment.

17.C.3c Analyze how human processes influence settlement patterns including migration and population growth.

18.B.3b Explain how social institutions contribute to the development and transmission of culture.

American Diary

Americans across the United States were leaving farms and towns and moving to cities. Henry Fletcher wrote, "Undeniably the city has superior attractions as a place of residence for the well-to-do; even the poorest classes, who live in filthy tenements and are completely shut out from the enjoyments of nature, seem to find in the noises, the crowds, the excitements, even in the sleepless anxieties of the daily struggle for life, a charm they are powerless to resist."

—from "The Drift of Population to Cities: Remedies"

Chicago, Illinois, grew from 109,000 residents in 1860 to nearly 1.7 million in 1900.

R Reading Strategies	**C** Critical Thinking	**D** Differentiated Instruction	**W** Writing Support	**S** Skill Practice
Teacher Edition • Questioning, p. 623 • Identifying, p. 624 **Additional Resources** • Guid. Read., URB p. 96 • Content Vocab., URB p. 73 • Academic Vocab., URB p. 75 • Read. Ess., p. 217 • Pri. Source Read., URB p. 77	**Teacher Edition** • Identify. Central Iss., p. 621 • Deter. Cause & Effect, p. 624 **Additional Resources** • Quizzes and Tests, p. 194	**Teacher Edition** • Logic./Math., p. 621 • Visual/Spatial, p. 624 • Naturalist, p. 625 **Additional Resources** • School-to-Home, URB p. 91 • Reteaching Act., URB p. 93 • Differ. Inst., URB p. 83	**Teacher Edition** • Narrative Writ., p. 622 • Personal Writ., p. 623	**Teacher Edition** • Using Geo. Skills, p. 625 **Additional Resources** • Daily Test Pract. Transp. 20-2 • Time Line Skills, URB p. 90 • Lesson Transp. 20B

Growth of Cities

Main Idea Immigrants and others flooded to American cities, where extremes of poverty and wealth existed.

History and You What is the largest city in your state? Read to learn how many American cities grew rapidly during the late 1800s.

American cities grew rapidly after the Civil War. In 1870 one American in four lived in cities with 2,500 or more people. By 1910, nearly half of the American population were city dwellers. The United States was changing from a rural to an urban nation.

Immigrants played an enormous part in the growth of cities. In **major,** or larger, urban centers such as New York, Detroit, and Chicago, immigrants and their children made up 80 percent or more of the population in 1890. Native-born Americans also contributed to the urban growth, moving in huge numbers from farming areas to cities, looking for jobs.

The industrialization of America had changed work on farms. New farm machinery made it possible to produce crops using fewer farmworkers. In addition, women in rural areas no longer had to make clothing and household goods. These items, made by machine, could now be bought in stores or from catalogs. Freed from such chores, many women left farms to look for jobs in the cities.

African Americans also migrated to cities in large numbers. After the Civil War, many African Americans began moving to Southern cities in search of jobs. Beginning in 1914, a large number of African Americans moved to Northern cities, where they hoped to find less discrimination.

Transportation and Resources

America's expanding railroad network fed the growth of cities. Railroads helped people move, and they also transported the raw materials for industry. Trains carried cattle to Chicago and Kansas City, making these cities large meatpacking centers.

Some cities flourished because of nearby resources. Pittsburgh developed rapidly as a center for iron and steel manufacturing because both iron ore and coal—to fuel the industry's huge furnaces—were found in the area. Seaports such as New York and San Francisco developed as American trade with the rest of the world increased.

By the Numbers | Urban and Rural Population Growth

Urban and Rural Population Growth, 1860–1900

Population (in millions) — Urban / Rural — 1860 1870 1880 1890 1900

Source: *Historical Statistics of the United States.*

Critical Thinking

Analyzing Which year saw the least difference between urban and rural populations?

Activity: Connecting Past to Present

Comparing and Contrasting As a class, discuss the role of resources on the geography of cities. **Ask:** How do waterways, trade, transportation routes, and natural resources affect where cities are located? (*Cities tend to grow near valuable natural resources and along transportation routes, which affects trade.*) Tell students they will conduct research to find out what factors affected the location of a city, either their own or a large city nearby. Instruct students to use online state and city Web sites to identify the resources that drive the city's industry. Have students use online maps to identify important transportation routes and how they affect trade. When finished, discuss students' findings in class. **OL**

Teach

D Differentiated Instruction

Logical/Mathematical Ask: What percentage of Americans lived in cities in 1870? (*25 percent*) How much did this percentage increase by 1910? (*25 percent*) **OL**

C Critical Thinking

Identifying Central Issues Ask: How did industry improve the lives of farmers? (*Farmers could produce crops with fewer workers. Women no longer had to make clothing and household goods; they could find work in cities.*) **OL**

By the Numbers

Critical Thinking Answer
1900

Skills Practice Ask: How would you expect the urban and rural populations to compare in 100 years? (*The urban population will probably exceed the rural population.*)

Additional Support

Teacher Tip

Questioning Suggest that students think of questions related to their chosen city before they begin researching to help direct them in their search.

W Writing Support

Narrative Writing Have students conduct research to learn more about the conditions of tenement houses in New York City and Chicago at the time. Then have them write a children's picture book in which the main character is a child who lives in a tenement slum. Remind students to include a beginning, middle, and end to their story and a main conflict or problem. Students should create or recommend artwork to accompany their writing. **OL**

Primary Source

Critical Thinking Answer
Students may suggest that immigrants chose to live with others from their country and that tenement housing was affordable for poor immigrants.

Reading Check Answer: Tenement living was difficult because the tenements were run-down and crowded with families.

Hands-On Chapter Project
Step 2

Presenting an American Cultural Fair

Step 2: Conducting Interviews Groups of students will interview immigrants or descendants of immigrants to learn information about the culture of their homeland.

Primary Source | **Life in the Tenements**

Crowded Conditions Immigrant families usually lived in tenements in Irish, German, Jewish, or other ethnic neighborhoods. A typical tenement apartment consisted of three rooms, most without windows. Such an apartment might house a family of seven or more.

"To-day three-fourths of its [New York's] people live in the tenements, and the . . . drift of the population to the cities is sending ever-increasing multitudes to crowd them. The fifteen thousand tenant houses that were the despair of the sanitarian [public health specialist] in the past generation have swelled into thirty-seven thousand, and more than twelve hundred thousand persons call them home."
—Jacob Riis, *How the Other Half Lives*, 1890

◀ A crowded tenement building in New York City

▲ Many immigrant families did piecework in their tenement apartments, making clothing for the garment industry.

◀ Jacob Riis, a newspaper reporter and reformer, documented the living conditions in New York tenements.

Critical Thinking

Speculating Why do you think that so many immigrants ended up living in tenements in ethnic neighborhoods?

Tenement Living

In the biggest, most crowded cities, the poorest residents—including most immigrants—lived in **tenements.** Originally a tenement was simply a building in which several families rented rooms. By the late 1800s, however, a tenement had come to mean an apartment building in the **slums**—poor, run-down urban neighborhoods.

Several people lived in each room. Usually several families had to share a cold-water tap and a toilet. A government inspector wrote of the "filthy and rotten tenements" of the Chicago slums in 1896, where children filled "every nook, eating and sleeping in every windowsill, pouring in and out of every door."

The Middle Class

The cities also had a growing middle class, which included the families of doctors, lawyers, and ministers, as well as managers, salaried office clerks, and others. The middle class enjoyed a comfortable life. Many families moved to the **suburbs,** residential areas that sprang up outside city centers. There they lived in houses with hot water, indoor toilets, and—by 1900—electricity. Middle-class families might have servants and the leisure time to enjoy music, art, and literature.

The Very Rich

At the top of the economic and social ladder were the very rich. They built enormous mansions in the cities and huge estates in the country. In these mansions, the rich lived lives of extreme luxury. Because of their extravagant wealth—and the terrible poverty that lay beneath it—this time period became known as the **Gilded Age.** The word *gilded* refers to something covered with a thin layer of gold.

Reading Check Describing Why was tenement living difficult?

Essential Question: How did cities change during the late 1800s?

Directions Have groups interview immigrants or descendants of immigrants from their chosen country. Instruct students to brainstorm questions before the interview. Tell students to include questions about specific traditions, such as family roles and celebrations and religious practices. When finished, students should conduct additional research to find out more about the traditions and their origins.

Comparing and Contrasting As a class, discuss the similarities and differences of the immigrants' traditions as compared to common "American" traditions.

(Chapter Project continued in Section 3)

Cities in Crisis

Main Idea Growing cities suffered from health and sanitation problems, poverty, fire, and crime.

History and You How do cities handle health and sanitation today? Read to learn about the problems of city life in the 1800s.

The rapid growth of cities produced serious problems. Garbage and horse manure accumulated in city streets, and the sewers could not handle the flow of human waste. Fires were another ever-present threat.

Health problems were widespread in the cities, because the filth was a breeding ground for quickly spreading diseases. In one Chicago neighborhood in 1900, babies often died of whooping cough, diphtheria, or measles before reaching their first birthday. One section of New York City was called the "lung block" because so many of its residents were suffering from tuberculosis. In an effort to control the spread of disease, New York City began to screen schoolchildren for contagious diseases, provide visiting nurses to mothers with young children, and establish public health clinics.

Yet disease was not the only threat to city life. Poverty in the cities led to crime as well. Orphaned and homeless children sometimes resorted to committing **minor,** or less serious, crimes in order to survive. Gangs roamed the poor neighborhoods.

The problems of the cities did not go unnoticed. Many dedicated people worked to improve urban life and help the poor. Some of this help came from religious groups that ran orphanages, prisons, hospitals, and recreation centers. The poor also received assistance from establishments called **settlement houses.** One of the most famous settlement houses was Chicago's **Hull House,** founded by **Jane Addams** in 1889.

✓ **Reading Check** **Explaining** Why did disease spread so rapidly in large cities?

Primary Source — Settlement Houses

An Approach to Social Reform During the late 1800s, reformers such as Jane Addams established settlement houses in poor neighborhoods. The women who ran settlement houses provided everything from medical care, recreation programs, and English classes to hot lunches for factory workers.

Hull House, begun in Chicago by Jane Addams and Ellen Gates Starr in 1889, was surrounded by tenements and factories. ▶

"The Settlement, then, is an experimental effort to aid in the solution of the social and industrial problems which are engendered by the modern conditions of life in a great city. . . . It is an attempt to relieve, at the same time, the over-accumulation at one end of society and the destitution at the other."
—Jane Addams, *Philanthropy and Social Progress*

▼ The crowded areas of Chicago near Hull House had poor sanitation, and most residents lived in poverty.

Children at Hull House ▼

Critical Thinking

Making Connections What kinds of organizations offer help to people today?

R **Reading Strategy**

Questioning Read the first sentence aloud. Have students create a question using the sentence. For example, students might ask, "What serious problems were produced by the rapid growth of cities?" Tell students to look for the answer to the question as they read. **BL**

W **Writing Support**

Personal Writing Have students take the role of someone from this time period and write a paragraph about what they would do to help improve urban life, either for the city in general or for the poor. **OL**

✓ **Reading Check** **Answer:** Neighborhoods were filthy and crowded, which allowed diseases to spread quickly.

Primary Source

Critical Thinking Answer
Answers may include schools, churches, other charitable organizations, and government agencies.

Differentiated Instruction

Leveled Activities

C Critical Thinking

Determining Cause and Effect Ask: How did limited space in cities affect architects' work? *(They began building skyscrapers.)* **BL**

R Reading Strategy

Identifying Write the following dates on the board: 1852, 1884, 1913. Have students identify the accomplishment associated with each date. **Ask:** Which accomplishment made the other two possible? *(the elevator)* **OL**

D Differentiated Instruction

Visual/Spatial Have students design an urban landscape that allows for skyscrapers as well as elements of nature. If possible, students can create three-dimensional models to represent their cities. **OL**

Primary Source

Critical Thinking Answer
because the bridge was both long and high; the development of woven steel cable wire

Differentiated Instruction

Primary Source — The Brooklyn Bridge

The Great Bridge To accommodate the growing population of New York City, the Brooklyn Bridge was built over the East River to connect Manhattan and Brooklyn. Its long, high span was designed to allow for the passage of ships beneath. The bridge took 14 years to build. When completed in 1883, it was the longest suspension bridge in the world.

Workers finish a cable on the Brooklyn Bridge during construction. ▶

◀ The Brooklyn Bridge was the first suspension bridge to use woven steel cable wire, a technology developed by John Roebling, chief engineer. Four suspension cables support the bridge, and each cable contains 5,434 wires.

"The contemplated work [the bridge] . . . will not only be the greatest bridge in existence, but it will be the greatest engineering work of this continent, and of the age. . . . [It will be] a great work of art, and . . . a successful specimen of advanced bridge engineering."
—John A. Roebling, quoted in *The Great Bridge*

◀ The Brooklyn Bridge, view from the Brooklyn side toward Manhattan, 1883

Critical Thinking

Explaining Why was it important for the Brooklyn Bridge to be a suspension bridge? What innovation made this possible?

The Changing City

Main Idea New technology in transportation and architecture reshaped cities.

History and You What is the tallest building you have ever visited? Read to learn how skyscrapers forever changed American cities.

Urban growth led to new developments. In the late 1800s, the look and feel of American cities changed with the introduction of skyscrapers, new kinds of public transportation, new bridges, and public parks.

Building Up—Not Out

C Because of the limited space in cities, imaginative architects began building upward rather than outward. In the 1860s, architects started to use iron frames to strengthen the building walls. Iron supports—together with the safety elevator that Elisha Otis invented in 1852—made taller buildings possible.

R In 1884 William LeBaron Jenney constructed a 10-story office building in Chicago. Supported by an iron-and-steel frame, it was the world's first **skyscraper**. **Louis Sullivan** was one of the first to design skyscrapers. Soon architects were designing higher structures. New York's Woolworth Building, completed in 1913, soared an incredible 55 stories—792 feet (241 m) high. People called the building the Cathedral of Commerce.

New Designs

D Some people looked to reshape the urban landscape. A group known as the "City Beautiful" movement believed city dwellers should be able to enjoy the beauties of nature.

Achievements of America's Cities (1852–1904)

Objective: To practice reading a time line

Focus: Ask students how entries can be displayed on a time line.

Teach: Explain how to locate events on a time line and calculate time between events.

Assess: Draw the time line on the board and have students place the events.

Close: Discuss how time lines can help students in their study of history.

Differentiated Instruction Strategies

BL Use basic math to calculate the number of years between points or a time line.

AL Ask students how generalizations can be made using a time line.

ELL Discuss the use of the terms "on" and "about" when placing events in time.

Time Line Skills Activity, URB p. 90

Frederick Law Olmsted, a leader in this movement, designed New York's Central Park as well as several parks in Boston.

Olmsted designed the fairgrounds for the World's Fair held in Chicago in 1892 and 1893. The fair revealed that American architecture was dynamic and original. The best architects thoroughly understood European styles and adapted them for modern use.

New Forms of Transportation

As cities grew, people needed new means of transportation. Streetcars, which horses pulled on tracks, provided public transportation at the time. In 1873 San Francisco began construction of cable-car lines. A large underground cable powered by a motor at one end of the rail line moved passengers along. In 1888 Richmond, Virginia, pioneered the use of the trolley car, a motorized train that was powered by electricity supplied through overhead cables. By 1900, the trolley was everywhere. In 1897 Boston opened the nation's first subway, or underground railway. In 1904 New York City opened the first section of what was to become the largest subway system in the world.

Building Bridges

Bridge construction also improved urban transportation. Many American cities were divided or bounded by rivers. Architects and engineers designed huge steel bridges to link sections of cities that were divided by rivers. The 520-foot (158-m) Eads Bridge across the Mississippi River in St. Louis opened in 1874. Nine years later, New York's majestic Brooklyn Bridge, with a main span of 1,600 feet (488 m) long, connected Manhattan and Brooklyn. Both bridges remain in use today.

New forms of transportation not only helped people travel within the cities, they also helped the cities grow. Middle-class suburbs developed along train or trolley lines stretching away from city centers. People who moved out of city centers could easily travel downtown to work, shop, or seek entertainment.

The increase in immigration and the growth of the cities went hand in hand with other changes in American life. Education, culture, and recreation were changing too.

✓ **Reading Check** **Summarizing** What were the new forms of urban transportation?

History ONLINE
Study Central™ To review this section, go to glencoe.com.

Section 2 Review

Vocabulary

1. Use each of these terms in a sentence that will help explain its meaning: major, tenement, slum, suburb, minor, settlement house, Hull House, skyscraper.

Main Ideas

2. Contrasting During the Gilded Age, how was life different for the poor, the middle class, and the very rich?

3. Listing What problems did cities face in the 1800s?

4. Describing How did American architecture change during this period?

Critical Thinking

5. Problem Solving How did Americans respond to the following problems in cities?

Disease	
Poverty	
Lack of Space	

6. Determining Cause and Effect What effect did the new forms of transportation have on city life?

7. Descriptive Writing As a settlement house worker in the 1800s, write a diary entry explaining the problems you see in cities.

Answer the
8. Essential Question
How did cities change during the late 1800s?

An Urban Society **Chapter 20** **625**

D Differentiated Instruction

Naturalist Have students research the work of Frederick Law Olmsted and his Central Park project. Tell them to identify the natural elements that Olmsted felt were important to include in the park. **OL**

S Skill Practice

Using Geographic Skills Have students use an online map of New York City to locate the Brooklyn Bridge. Encourage them to locate other bridges that connect Manhattan to other mainland areas. **OL**

✓ **Reading Check** **Answer:** streetcar, cable car, trolley car, subway

Assess

History ONLINE

Study Central™ provides summaries, interactive games, and online graphic organizers to help students review content.

Close

Summarizing As a class, summarize architectural changes that took place in the late 1880s. **OL**

Section 2 Review

Answers

1. Sentences should reflect an understanding of the terms.
2. Poor—lived in tenements in unhealthy and crowded conditions; middle class—lived in suburbs, may have had servants, had leisure time; very wealthy—lived in huge mansions; held extravagant parties
3. disease, poor sanitation, poverty, crime, fire
4. Skyscrapers were built; prominent American architects adapted European architecture for modern use.

5. New York screened schoolchildren for disease, provided nurses, established public health clinics; settlement houses provided assistance to the poor; architects built skyscrapers.
6. helped people travel within the cities; contributed to the growth of suburbs
7. Students will write diary entries that relate to urban problems in areas such as health, housing, education, and employment.

8. Cities grew, causing serious problems involving health and safety; architecture and the city landscape changed; public transportation improved; society became divided into the very poor, the middle class, and the very rich.

Section 3

A Changing Culture

Section 3

Focus

Bellringer
Daily Test Practice Transparency 20–3

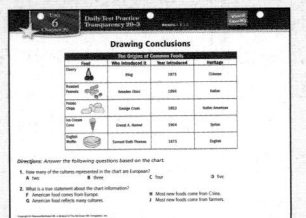

Reading Guide
Answers to Graphic:

Booker T. Washington: founded Tuskegee Institute

Edith Wharton: wrote about the upper class; won the Pulitzer Prize

Paul Laurence Dunbar: first African American poet to receive national acclaim

Section Spotlight Video

Have students watch the Section Spotlight Video "A Changing Culture" to learn more about Thomas Eakins.

Resource Manager

Essential Question ◄
In what ways did American culture change during the late 1800s?

Reading Guide

Content Vocabulary
land-grant college (p. 628)
realism (p. 629)
regionalism (p. 629)
yellow journalism (p. 630)
spectator sport (p. 631)
vaudeville (p. 631)
jazz (p. 632)
ragtime (p. 632)

Academic Vocabulary
philosophy (p. 627)   isolate (p. 628)

Key People
George Washington Carver (p. 628)
Mark Twain (p. 629)
Joseph Pulitzer (p. 630)
William Randolph Hearst (p. 630)

Reading Strategy
Taking Notes As you read, describe the achievements of the persons listed.

Individual	Achievement
Booker T. Washington	
Edith Wharton	
Paul Laurence Dunbar	

ILLINOIS STANDARDS
The American Journey

18.A.3 Explain how language, literature, the arts, architecture, and traditions contribute to the development and transmission of culture.

18.B.3a Analyze how individuals and groups interact with and within institutions (e.g., educational, military).

18.B.3b Explain how social institutions contribute to the development and transmission of culture.

American Diary

New ideas about education were changing how people viewed physical education for girls. Gertrude Dudley wrote: "This matter of playing games is one to be determined, not by comparison of the sexes, but by an educational principle. If women can be trained well enough to make athletics beneficial . . . to themselves, then it is good for them to play; if athletics develop . . . qualities valuable to them as individuals . . . then also is it well for them to play."

—from *Athletic Games in the Education of Women*
by Gertrude Dudley

A team of young Cherokee athletes, c. 1910

R Reading Strategies	C Critical Thinking	D Differentiated Instruction	W Writing Support	S Skill Practice
Teacher Edition • Outlining, p. 627 • Ident. the Main Idea, p. 629 • Mak. Connect., p. 631 **Additional Resources** • Guid. Read., URB p. 97 • Content Vocab., URB p. 73 • Academic Vocab., URB p. 75 • Read. Ess., p. 220	**Teacher Edition** • Analyzing Info., p. 628 • Comparing, p. 630 **Additional Resources** • Quizzes and Tests, p. 195 • Link. Past & Pres., URB p. 89	**Teacher Edition** • Naturalist, p. 628 • Verbal/Ling., p. 629 • Aud./Music., p. 632 **Additional Resources** • School-to-Home, URB p. 91 • Reteaching Act., URB p. 93	**Teacher Edition** • Personal Writ., p. 627 • Narrative Writ., p. 630	**Teacher Edition** • Visual Lit., p. 631 **Additional Resources** • Daily Test Pract. Transp. 20-3 • Soc. Stud. Skills, URB p. 81 • Geo. & Hist., URB p. 87 • Lesson Transp. 20C

Expanding Education

Main Idea Educational opportunities were extended to many more Americans, as the system of public schools and colleges expanded.

History and You How would American life be different if people attended only four years of school? Read to learn how more Americans began attending school during this period.

Most Americans in 1865 had attended school for an average of only four years. Government and business leaders as well as reformers believed that for the nation to progress, the people needed more schooling. Toward the end of the 1800s, the "treasure" of education became more widely available to Americans.

By 1914, most states required children to have at least some schooling. More than 80 percent of all children between the ages of 5 and 17 were enrolled in elementary and secondary schools.

Public Schools

The expansion of public education was particularly notable in high schools. The number of public high schools increased from 100 in 1860 to 6,000 in 1900 and increased

to 12,000 in 1914. Despite this huge increase, however, many teenagers did not attend high school. Boys often went to work instead of attending school. The majority of high school students were girls.

The benefits of a public school education, however, were not shared equally by everyone. In the South, many African Americans received little or no education. In many parts of the country, African American children had no choice but to attend segregated elementary and secondary schools.

Progressive Education

Around 1900, a new **philosophy**—ideas and beliefs—of education emerged in the United States. Supporters of this "progressive education" wanted to shape the characters of the students and teach them good citizenship as well as facts. They also believed children should learn through the use of hands-on activities. These ideas had the greatest effect in elementary schools.

John Dewey, the leading spokesperson for progressive education, criticized schools for stressing too much memorization of facts. Instead, Dewey argued, schools should relate learning to the interests, problems, and concerns of students.

Primary Source | **First Day of School**

A Day to Remember Public education was important to newcomers to America. Mary Antin came to the United States in 1894 and described her first day of school this way: "That day I must always remember, even if I live to be so old that I cannot tell my name. To most people their first day at school is a memorable occasion. In my case the importance of the day was a hundred times magnified, on account of the years I had waited, the road I had come, and the conscious ambitions I entertained."

Critical Thinking
Speculating Why do you think going to school in America was such a memorable experience for an immigrant like Mary Antin?

Teach

W Writing Support

Personal Writing Have students write a journal response explaining their feeling about the "treasure" of education and why they think the U.S. government mandates schooling for children from elementary through high school. **OL**

R Reading Strategy

Outlining To help students comprehend the ideas behind progressive education, instruct them to create a T-chart titled "Progressive Education" with the column headings "Dos" and "Don'ts." As students read the text under the subheading, have them classify the information as something progressives would want schools to do or not do. **OL**

Primary Source

Critical Thinking Answer
Answers may include because immigrants did not have access to schools in their homeland and recognized the value of education.

Hands-On Chapter Project
Step 3

Presenting an American Cultural Fair

Step 3: Preparing the Booths Groups of students will prepare booths that display the language and cultural and religious aspects of American immigrant groups.

Essential Question: In what ways did American culture change in the late 1800s?

Directions Have groups use the research they completed in Steps 1 and 2 to plan their booths.

Have them design a decorative banner that reflects their immigrant group's cultural traditions, along with a brief summary of the group's history, religion, and politics. Encourage students to include examples of music, art, and food.

Displaying Have students assemble and present their booths to the class. Then invite students from other classes to attend the fair.

(Chapter Project continued on the Visual Summary page)

C Critical Thinking

Analyzing Information Ask: What does the increase in college enrollment of women in the late 1800s tell you about the roles of women at that time? *(Women were beginning to pursue careers and interests outside the home.)* **AL**

D Differentiated Instruction

Naturalist Instruct students to research how the peanut is processed to create materials like plastics and paper. **OL**

✔ **Reading Check** **Answer:** They were new women's colleges.

Primary Source

Critical Thinking Answer
Answers may include that students gained self-esteem and received an education that would help them find professional jobs with higher salaries.

Differentiated Instruction

Higher Education

Colleges and universities changed and expanded. The 1862 Morrill Act gave states federal land that could be sold to raise money for education. States used these funds to start schools called **land-grant colleges.**

In 1865 few American colleges admitted women. The new land-grant schools admitted women students, as did new women's colleges—Vassar, Smith, Wellesley, and Bryn Mawr. By 1910, almost 40 percent of all American college students were women.

Some new colleges, such as Hampton Institute in Virginia and Howard University in Washington, D.C., provided higher education for African Americans. Prominent Howard graduates of today include Supreme Court Justice Thurgood Marshall and author Toni Morrison. One Hampton Institute student, Booker T. Washington, became an educator. In 1881 he founded the Tuskegee Institute in Alabama to train teachers and provide practical education for African Americans. Then, in 1896, scientist **George Washington Carver** joined the Tuskegee faculty. His research transformed agriculture in the South. From the peanut, Carver developed hundreds of products, including plastics and paper.

Schools for Native Americans

Reservation schools and boarding schools also opened to train Native Americans for jobs. Although these schools provided Native Americans with training for jobs in industry, they also **isolated,** or cut off, Native Americans from their tribal traditions. Boarding schools were sometimes located hundreds of miles away from a student's family.

✔ **Reading Check** **Comparing** What did Bryn Mawr, Vassar and Smith have in common?

Primary Source | The Tuskegee Institute

Washington Founds a School In 1881 Booker T. Washington founded Tuskegee Institute, a school for the education of African American men and women. Tuskegee combined academics with vocational training and an emphasis on self-reliance. The school began in a one-room building with 30 students. By the time of Washington's death in 1915, the school had grown to 100 buildings, 200 faculty, and 1,500 students.

These students erecting a school building show Tuskegee's early emphasis on self-reliance and education in the trades. ▲

Tuskegee combined academics with vocational training. ▶

"If one thing more than another has taught me to have confidence in the masses of my own people it has been their willingness (and even eagerness) to learn and their disposition to help themselves."
—Booker T. Washington, *My Larger Education,* 1911

Critical Thinking
Predicting What effect do you think the Tuskegee Institute had on the lives of African Americans who went to school there?

Leveled Activities

BL School-to-Home Connection Activity, URB p. 91

OL Academic Vocabulary Activity, URB p. 75

AL Geography and History Activity, URB p. 87

People IN HISTORY

Paul Laurence Dunbar

Poet, playwright, and songwriter

Dunbar was the first African American poet to gain national attention. He was forced to make a living by writing for white audiences who preferred his black dialect poetry. For example, in *"Song of Summer,"* he portrayed the South as an idyllic and peaceful place: *"Sky all white wif streaks o' blue,/Sunshine softly gleamin',/D'ain't no wuk hit 's right to do,/Nothin' 's right but dreamin'."* In other writings, Dunbar was an advocate for civil rights and higher education for African Americans.

Edith Wharton

Pulitzer Prize–winning author

Edith Wharton was born into a rich family. However, she came to dislike the manners and lifestyle of the upper-class Americans she often wrote about. *"Such dreariness, such whining sallow [pale] women, such utter absence of the amenities [pleasantries], such crass [foul] food, crass manners, crass landscape!!"* . . . *"What a horror it is for a whole nation to be developing without the sense of beauty."*

CRITICAL Thinking

1. **Describing** Describe the attitudes of Wharton and Dunbar toward the people they wrote about.
2. **Evaluating** How do you think writing for a white audience affected Dunbar's poetry?

A Nation of Readers

Main Idea Educated Americans found new reading material in public libraries, a growing literary culture, and thriving newspapers.

History and You Do you ever borrow books from your public library? Read to learn which prominent industrialist gave support to libraries.

As opportunities for education grew, more Americans became interested in reading. New books, magazines, and newspapers were published, and more libraries opened. In 1881 Andrew Carnegie, the steel industrialist, pledged to build a public library in any city that would pay its operating costs. With gifts from Carnegie and others, and the efforts of state and local governments, every state in the Union established free public libraries.

Changes in Literature

Many writers of the era explored new themes and subjects. Their approach to literature was called **realism** because they sought to describe the lives of people. Related to realism was **regionalism,** writing that focused on a particular region of the country.

Mark Twain was a realist and a regionalist. Many of his books, including *Adventures of Huckleberry Finn* and *The Adventures of Tom Sawyer,* are set along the Mississippi River, where Twain grew up.

Stephen Crane wrote about city slums in *Maggie* and about the Civil War in *The Red Badge of Courage.* In books such as *The Call of the Wild* and *The Sea Wolf,* Jack London portrayed the lives of miners and hunters in the far Northwest. Edith Wharton described upper-class Easterners in *The House of Mirth* and *The Age of Innocence.*

An Urban Society **Chapter 20 629**

R **Reading Strategy**

Identifying the Main Idea Read the paragraph aloud and have students identify the main idea and supporting details. *(Main idea: As opportunities for education grew, more Americans became interested in reading; new books, magazines, and newspapers were published, and more public libraries were built.)* **BL**

D **Differentiated Instruction**

Verbal/Linguistic Twain is known for his humor and wit. Ask students to discuss Twain's message in the following quotation: "Always do right. This will gratify some people and astonish the rest." **OL**

People IN HISTORY

Critical Thinking Answers

1. While Dunbar was an advocate for the African Americans he wrote about, Wharton disliked upper-class Americans.
2. He may have written in a way not to offend or upset whites.

Additional Support

Fast Facts

Philanthropy and Public Libraries Andrew Carnegie learned the value of free public libraries as a young man, when he was forbidden membership to a private library. This event, along with his belief that education was the key to a successful life, led him to help fund free public libraries throughout the country in the late 1800s. One of these libraries, the Carnegie Library of Pittsburgh, was established in 1895 when Carnegie contributed $1 million to build a main library and five branches. In 1899, the library established the first children's library department in the country, and a few years later the library began offering services for the blind. In providing free access to information, the Carnegie libraries help fulfill Andrew Carnegie's mission to provide for the education of the American public. **OL**

History ONLINE
Student Web Activity Visit glencoe.com and complete the Chapter 20 Web Activity about the literature of realism.

Paul Laurence Dunbar, the son of former enslaved Africans, wrote books that used the dialects and folktales of Southern African Americans. Dunbar was one of the first African American writers to gain fame around the world.

Inexpensive paperback books appeared for the first time in the late 1800s. Horatio Alger wrote a series of young-adult books with titles such as *Work and Win* and *Luck and Pluck*. Based on themes of hard work and honesty, Alger's books sold millions of copies.

Spreading the News

Technological advances in printing, paper-making, and communications made it possible to publish a daily paper for a large number of readers. The growing cities provided readers for the newspapers.

In 1883 **Joseph Pulitzer** purchased the New York *World* and created a new kind of newspaper. The paper grabbed the reader's attention with illustrations, cartoons, and sensational stories with huge headlines—such as "ANOTHER MURDERER TO HANG." Under Pulitzer's management, the *World* had more than 1 million readers every day.

Other newspapers soon imitated Pulitzer's style. The New York *Morning Journal,* purchased by **William Randolph Hearst** in 1895, became even more successful than the *World* by exaggerating dramatic or gruesome aspects of stories. This sensational writing style became known as **yellow journalism.**

Ethnic and minority newspapers thrived as well. By 1900, six daily Jewish-language newspapers were operating in New York City. African Americans started more than 1,000 newspapers between 1865 and 1900.

More magazines took advantage of printing improvements and mass-circulation techniques to reach a national market. Between 1865 and 1900, the number of magazines in the United States rose from about 700 to 5,000. Some magazines of that era—the *Atlantic Monthly, Harper's Magazine,* and *Ladies' Home Journal*—are still published today.

✔ **Reading Check** **Discussing** How did yellow journalism attract readers?

LINKING PAST TO PRESENT — American Football

THEN Football began in 1869 as a soccer-style game between college teams. In the 1870s, the game became more like English rugby, with players carrying the ball and tackling. The game was brutal. Players did not even wear helmets at first. A new rule in 1894 banned projecting nails from shoes.

◀ Knute Rockne in 1913 was an all-American end for Notre Dame. Later, he coached Notre Dame to six national championships.

▲ College football scrimmage, c. 1905

Writing Support

Narrative Writing Have students locate and read works by Horatio Alger. Then have them write a short young adult story with the same style and theme as Alger's stories but using modern teen characters. **OL**

Critical Thinking

Comparing Instruct students to use online and library sources to read examples of yellow journalism from the *Morning Journal.* Then have students compare those examples with popular newspapers today, including tabloids. Ask them to identify which newspaper comes closest to the style of yellow journalism. **OL**

✔ **Reading Check** **Answer:** with illustrations, cartoons, and sensational stories under huge headlines

History ONLINE
Objectives and answers to the Student Web Activity can be found at glencoe.com under the Web Activity Lesson Plan for this chapter.

Differentiated Instruction

Researching on the Internet

Objective: To identify ways to successfully research on the Internet

Focus: Ask students what keywords they might use to research early spectator sports.

Teach: Have students research their event and complete their outline.

Assess: Have students use the Self-Assessment Checklist.

Close: Discuss how to evaluate online sources.

Differentiated Instruction Strategies

BL Have students work in groups to research their event.

AL Have students support the reliability of their sources.

ELL Help students develop keywords to use in their search.

Social Studies Skills Activity, URB p. 81

Leisure and the Arts

Main Idea American culture moved away from European influence and became distinctively American.

History and You What are your favorite movies? Read to learn which famous inventor introduced the first "moving pictures."

. . . .

During this era, Americans enjoyed increasing amounts of leisure time. Unlike round-the-clock farmwork, professional and industrial jobs gave people hours and even days of free time. To fill their leisure time, Americans developed new forms of recreation, including sports, art, and music.

A Changing World of Sports

A favorite leisure-time activity for many people was watching and following sports. Baseball became the most popular **spectator sport** in America. By the early 1900s, the National and American Leagues were founded—each made up of teams from major cities. Their games drew large crowds of enthusiastic fans, and in 1903 the first World Series was held.

NOW Football has evolved into an exciting style of play. Rule changes and better protective gear have made the game safer. Each week millions watch high school, college, and pro teams in action.

Critical Thinking

Comparing What do you think is the biggest difference in football between the two eras?

Another popular spectator sport was football, which developed from the English game of rugby. The first college football game was played between Rutgers and Princeton in 1869. By the 1890s, college football games were drawing huge crowds. **[S]**

Basketball, invented by Dr. James Naismith of Springfield, Massachusetts, also became popular. Naismith developed the game in the 1890s as an indoor winter sport for the students in his YMCA physical education classes. Considered the only major sport that is completely American in origin, basketball soon spread to other countries.

Americans not only watched but also participated in sports. The wealthy played tennis and golf, usually in exclusive private clubs. Bicycling grew in popularity after the "safety" bicycle was developed. Older bicycles had a large wheel in front and a small one in back, but the new ones had two air-filled rubber tires of the same size.

These improvements helped bicycle riding take the country by storm. One romantic song celebrated the bicycle: "It won't be a stylish marriage, I can't afford a carriage, But you'll look sweet upon the seat of a bicycle built for two."

Vaudeville and Movies

Not only did Americans watch sports, they also became eager fans of shows and movies. Large cities had many theaters. Plays performed ranged from serious dramas by Shakespeare to **vaudeville** shows, which were variety shows with dancing, singing, comedy, and magic acts.

Many people could afford the price of a ticket, and in the early 1900s, vaudeville offered the most popular shows in town. The circus was another popular attraction that brought large crowds. In 1910 the United States had about 80 traveling circuses that moved from town to town. **[R]**

Prominent inventor Thomas Edison introduced "moving pictures" in the 1880s. The "movies" soon became enormously popular in the United States.

An Urban Society **Chapter 20** 631

Skill Practice

Visual Literacy Ask students to study the football uniform in the Linking Past to Present feature. **Ask:** How have uniforms changed? *(Helmets have face guards, players wear more pads.)* Why do you think these changes were made? *(to improve safety)* **OL**

Reading Strategy

Making Connections Ask students if they have ever been to a play, circus, or movie. Have them describe what they saw. **Ask:** How has popular entertainment changed since the late 1800s? *(Students may recognize that the movie industry has grown tremendously in that period.)* **BL**

LINKING PAST TO PRESENT

Critical Thinking Answer

Answers will vary, but students may suggest the football itself, the uniforms, padding, or equipment.

S Skill Practice

R Reading Strategy

Additional Support

Activity: Collaborative Learning

Expressing Vaudeville made its debut in the late 1800s, providing much-needed entertainment for thousands of people. Vaudeville acts included comedians, dancers, musicians, acrobats, animal trainers, and other specialized talents, such as plate-spinners. **Ask:** Which type of act would you find most entertaining? Instruct students to research vaudeville acts online. Then have students work together to create a vaudeville show. Students may work in small groups to create a musical or dance act, or they may create an individual act displaying a particular talent. Provide rehearsal time, and invite other classes to attend the show. **OL**

D Differentiated Learning

Auditory/Musical Play samples of the types of music described in the text. Have students write in their journals the types of sounds they hear and their reactions to each type of music. Then discuss the influence of the various cultures that are evident in the music. **OL**

 Reading Check Answer: work songs, gospel music, spirituals, and African rhythms

Assess

History ONLINE

Study Central™ provides summaries, interactive games, and online graphic organizers to help students review content.

Close

Determining Cause and Effect As a class, discuss changes to the American culture and landscape in the late 1800s and early 1900s. **OL**

Section 3 Review

Theaters called nickelodeons got their name because they charged five cents to see short films. The nickelodeons marked the beginning of today's film industry.

American Artists and Musicians

For most of the 1800s, the work of American artists and musicians reflected a European influence. After the Civil War, Americans began to develop a distinctively American style.

Some American painters pursued realist themes in their works. Thomas Eakins of Philadelphia painted the human anatomy and surgical operations as well as rowers and other athletes. One of Eakins's students, Henry Tanner, depicted warm family scenes of Americans in the South. Frederic Remington portrayed the American West, focusing on subjects such as cowhands and Native Americans. Winslow Homer painted Southern farmers, Adirondack campers, and stormy sea scenes. James Whistler's *Arrangement in Grey and Black,* commonly known as "Whistler's Mother," is one of the best-known American paintings. Mary Cassatt was influential in the Impressionist school of painting that arose during the late 1800s. Impressionists tried to capture the play of light, color, and patterns as they made immediate impressions on the senses.

Distinctively American kinds of music were also becoming popular. Bandleader John Philip Sousa composed many rousing marches, including "The Stars and Stripes Forever."

African American musicians in New Orleans in the late 1800s developed another entirely new kind of music—jazz. **Jazz** combined elements of work songs, gospel music, spirituals, and African rhythms. One of jazz's major characteristics was syncopation, a shifting of the usual musical accent. Related to jazz was **ragtime** music. One of the best ragtime composers was Scott Joplin. He wrote "Maple Leaf Rag" and many other well-known works.

The symphony orchestras of New York, Boston, and Philadelphia, all founded before 1900, were among the world's finest orchestras. Great singers and conductors from all over the world came to perform at New York's Metropolitan Opera House.

 Reading Check Describing What elements make up jazz music?

Section 3 Review

Vocabulary

1. Use each of these terms in a sentence that will help explain its meaning: philosophy, land-grant college, isolate, realism, regionalism, yellow journalism, spectator sport, vaudeville, jazz, ragtime.

Main Ideas

2. Explaining What was the goal of progressive education?

3. Contrasting How did realism and regionalism differ?

4. Describing What forms of entertainment were popular during this era?

Critical Thinking

5. Making Connections Identify the causes that sparked an increase in the number of publications in the late 1800s.

Causes

6. Making Inferences In what ways did schools have a negative effect on Native Americans?

7. Creative Writing Write a local newspaper article in the style of yellow journalism.

8. Answer the Essential Question
In what ways did American culture change in the late 1800s?

Answers

1. Sentences should demonstrate understanding of the terms.

2. to shape the character of students and teach them good citizenship as well as facts

3. Realism describes the lives of people; regionalism focuses on a particular region of the country.

4. spectator and participatory sports, theater, movies, art, and music

5. Publications increased because more people were educated and interested in reading, technology made printing for large audiences possible, and more libraries opened.

6. separated Native American children from their families and their culture

7. Student articles should use a sensational writing style and include a large, bold headline.

8. Education expanded; newspapers, magazines, and books gained wide readership; new leisure activities, such as sports and shows, became popular; literature, music, and art developed a distinctively American style.

Visual Summary

Immigration

- New groups of immigrants arrive in the U.S. from eastern and southern Europe.
- Reasons for immigration include: economic troubles, persecution in the native country, and better opportunities in the United States.
- New industries, such as steel and garment manufacturing, offer low-paying jobs for immigrant workers.
- Ethnic groups establish separate communities to re-create former lifestyles.
- Nativists fear immigration and call for restrictions.

City Life

- Industry and immigration lead to the growth of cities.
- In the poorest parts of crowded cities, people live in tenements and slums.
- Overcrowding leads to sanitation problems, disease, and crime.
- "The Gilded Age" refers to American riches overshadowing the poverty in many areas.

Technology and Culture

- Architects address the lack of space in cities by building skyscrapers.
- Streetcars, trolleys, subways, and bridges all improve transportation in cities.
- The American educational system expands and offers new opportunities.
- Public libraries and new forms of literature and journalism add to culture in the cities.

Leisure Activities

- Middle-class Americans have newfound leisure time for sports, arts, and music.
- Sports, including baseball, football, and basketball, grow in popularity.
- Vaudeville shows, traveling circuses, and the first movies offer other new forms of entertainment.
- Distinctively American forms of music, including jazz and ragtime, become popular.

STUDY TO GO Study anywhere, anytime! Download quizzes and flash cards to your PDA from glencoe.com.

Visual Summary

Identifying the Main Idea Instruct students to use the headings in the Visual Summary to write main-idea sentences related to the chapter content. Model the process by changing "City Life" to "A wave of immigration changed city life in the late 1800s." **OL**

Evaluating Ask: What were some benefits of immigration in the late 1800s? *(Immigration provided workers for America's growing industry; introduced new cultural traditions to the U.S.)* What were some drawbacks of immigration? *(Cities became crowded and tenement slums formed; immigrants were willing to work for low wages, which created a class of working poor; overcrowding resulted in the spread of disease, sanitation problems, and an increase in crime.)* **OL**

Hands-On Chapter Project
Step 4: Wrap-Up

Presenting an American Cultural Fair

Step 4: Learning From the Booths Students will synthesize what they have learned in Steps 1–3.

Directions Write the Essential Questions on the board. Use students' booths as a springboard for discussion of the questions. Have students name the languages, religions, and traditions of each country and list them on the board. Ask which traditions, languages, and religions can be found in the culture of the United States today. Discuss why these religions, languages, and cultural traditions remain while others have faded away. Then have students respond to the following question in their journals: What is "American" culture?

Identifying Points of View Ask: Based on what you learned in your research, what additional challenges not discussed in the book might your particular immigrant group face when coming to the United States? *(Answers might include difficulties in school and work because of language differences and difficulties adapting to American culture.)* **Ask:** What message would you like to give to new immigrants? *(Answers may include the value of education in gaining employment and the importance of participating in American democracy.)* **OL**

633

Answers and Analyses
Reviewing Main Ideas

1. C Choice A is incorrect since most of the new immigrants came from southern and eastern Europe. Choices B and D are wrong as the new immigrants experienced difficulty blending into American society, and most took unskilled jobs. C is the correct choice. **17.C.3c**

2. B Students should recognize that slums and tenements were the homes of the poorer classes, so choices C and D are wrong. Choice A refers to farmers, so it is incorrect. B is the correct choice. **17.C.3c**

3. D Students might recall from their reading that Frederick Law Olmsted was responsible for the design of Central Park in New York City, as well as parks in Boston. From this, students can infer that he was part of the "City Beautiful" movement. **18.C.3b**

4. A Choice B is wrong, since progressive education objected to rote memorization. While choices C and D are related to this period, they are not a part of progressive education. Choice A is correct. **18.B.3a**

Short-Answer Question

5. According to the table, Hungarians were more likely to return to Europe (22 percent). In answering the second question, students should look for the greatest number in the second column, which is Italians (320 men). **17.A.3b**

TEST-TAKING TIP

Consider carefully before changing your answer to a multiple-answer test question. Unless you misread the question, your first answer choice is often correct.

Reviewing Main Ideas

Directions: Choose the best answer for each of the following questions.

1. Most of the immigrants who arrived in the United States in the late 1800s

  A came from Latin America.

  B immediately blended into American society.

  C were from rural areas.

  D sought highly skilled technical jobs.

2. By the 1900s, where were middle-class Americans increasingly likely to live?

  A in rural areas

  B in the suburbs

  C in slums

  D in tenements

3. What was Frederick Law Olmsted's major contribution to American cities?

  A His safety elevator made taller buildings possible.

  B He founded settlement houses to help the urban poor.

  C He invented the electric trolley car, making city travel easier.

  D He led the "City Beautiful" movement, which promoted urban parks.

4. Supporters of "progressive education" emphasized which of the following?

  A character education

  B rote memorization of facts

  C the opening of libraries

  D land-grant schools for women

Short-Answer Question

Directions: Base your answer to question 5 on the table below and on your knowledge of social studies.

Family Characteristics of Major Immigrant Groups, 1909–1914

Group	Percentage Returning to Europe	Males per 100 Females	Percentage Under Age 14
Czechs	5	133	19
English	6	136	16
Finnish	7	181	8
Germans	7	132	18
Greeks	16	170	4
Hungarians	22	141	16
Italians	17	320	12
Poles	13	188	10
Slovaks	19	162	12

Source: "Immigrant America," Digital History

5. According to the table, which group was the most likely to return to Europe? Which group had the most uneven ratio between the sexes?

Review the Essential Questions

6. Essay Explain how immigration contributed to (a) the rise of the modern city; (b) the expansion of education; and (c) the development of a distinctly American culture by the early 1900s.

To help you write your essay, review your answers to the Essential Questions in the section reviews and the chapter Foldables Study Organizer. Your essay should include:

- characteristics and challenges of immigrants;
- changes and living conditions of cities;
- expansion of education and reading; and
- leisure activities and the arts.

GO ON ➡

Review the Essential Questions

6. Students' essays should address the difficult assimilation process for immigrants, the overcrowded and unhealthy conditions of city living, the educational changes taking place, and the increase in leisure time, especially for the middle class. **16.E.3c (US)**

History ONLINE
For additional test practice, use **Self-Check Quizzes**—Chapter 20 at glencoe.com.

Chapter **20** Assessment

Document-Based Questions

Directions: Analyze the documents and answer the short-answer questions that follow.

Document 1

> The immigrant of the former time came almost exclusively from western and northern Europe. . . . Immigrants from southern Italy, Hungary, Austria, and Russia . . . made up hardly more than one per cent of our immigration. To-day the proportion has risen to something like forty per cent. . . . These people . . . are beaten men from beaten races; representing the worst failures in the struggle for existence. . . . They have none of the ideas and [abilities] which fit men to take up readily and easily the problem of self-care and self-government.

Source: F. A. Walker, "Restriction of Immigration," 1907

7. Identify *two* reasons Walker opposed immigration from southern and eastern Europe.

Document 2

U.S. President Theodore Roosevelt stated the following.

> There is no room in this country for hyphenated Americanism. . . .
> . . . The one absolutely certain way of bringing the nation to ruin . . . would be to permit it to become a tangle of squabbling nationalities.

Source: address to Knights of Columbus, 1915

8. What did Roosevelt mean by "hyphenated Americanism"?

9. Based on the quote, did he favor or oppose the acceptance of immigrants into the American society? Explain your answer.

Document 3

This photo of three homeless boys sleeping in an alley appeared in Jacob Riis's *How the Other Half Lives: Studies Among the Tenements of New York,* 1890.

Source: Bettmann/CORBIS

10. Who was the "other half" referred to in the title of Riis's book? What did Riis hope to accomplish by publishing pictures such as this?

Document 4

In this passage, African American composer W. C. Handy—the "Father of the Blues"—explains what the blues are all about.

> My purpose was to capture in fixed form the highly distinctive music of my race. Everything I have written has its roots deep in the folk life of the South.

Source: "The Birth of the Blues," 1911

11. Based on the passage, what was the inspiration for Handy's music?

12. Expository Writing Using the information from the four documents and your knowledge of social studies, write an essay in which you:

- identify ways that American society by the early 1900s had become a true "melting pot" of assimilated cultures; and

- point out ways in which Americans remained separated in the early 1900s.

9. Roosevelt favored acceptance of immigrants; he wanted them to assimilate into American society and become simply "American." **16.A.3b**

10. The author is referring to poor immigrants. Publishing a photo of such horrid conditions for children, the author hoped to gain sympathy and aid for the poor. **18.A.3**

11. Handy states he found inspiration in his race and in his roots in the South. **18.A.3**

12. Essays should identify the ethnicities of immigrants and their attempts at assimilation, such as children attending school and learning to speak English and families working with others in industry. These acts led to a merging of cultures, known as the "melting pot." Essays should also point out the separation of cultures in cities, such as the formation of ethnic communities with separate newspapers, businesses, and social clubs, as well as the role of prejudice in isolating immigrants. **18.C.3b**

History ONLINE
Have students visit the Web site at glencoe.com to review Chapter 20 and take the Self-Check Quiz.

Need Extra Help?

If you missed questions. . .	1	2	3	4	5	6	7	8	9	10	11	12
Go to page. . .	613	622	625	627	614	612–632	617	617	619	622–623	621	612–632

Need Extra Help?

Have students refer to the pages listed if they miss any of the questions.

Document-Based Questions

7. He argued that these men were failures in their own countries and lacked the abilities to care for themselves and participate effectively in government. **16.A.3b**

8. Roosevelt was referring to the perception of immigrants as from their old countries, rather than as simply Americans. **16.A.3b**

UNIT PACING CHART

	Unit 7	Chapter 21	Chapter 22	Chapter 23
Day 1	Unit Opener, Reading History	Chapter Opener, Section 1, America's Literature	Chapter Opener, Section 1	Chapter Opener, Section 1
Day 2		Section 2	Section 2, Section 3	Geography & History, Section 2
Day 3		Section 3	Section 3, Section 4	Section 3, Section 4
Day 4		Section 4, Visual Summary	Section 4, You Decide, Visual Summary	Section 5, TIME Notebook, Visual Summary
Day 5		Chapter Assessment	Chapter Assessment	Chapter Assessment

Teacher to Teacher

Lisa Ray
Chapin
Middle School
Chapin, SC

Understanding Themes in History The study of history can be organized into four major themes: civil rights, change, conflict/resolution, and migration. Explain to students that the theme of civil rights addresses the ongoing struggle for equality among people. Change refers to new ways people learn to work or perform daily activities. The theme of conflict/resolution addresses the ways in which wars and conflicts change how people live. Migration explains the reasons people move. As students read the unit, they will organize the information according to the appropriate theme and then create a poster that reflects the themes. Have students write each theme at the top of a page in their notebooks. As they read the chapters, have them take notes under the appropriate theme. Then, have students work in groups of four to discuss their notes to be sure that they are concise and inclusive. Each person in the group will be responsible for illustrating a theme, whether through photos or drawings, on the poster. Students should display their posters and explain how their images reflect each theme.

Author Note

Dear American History Teacher,

At the beginning of the nineteenth century, the United States was an insignificant nation on the periphery of the European world. Its population of 6 million people was about the same as Ireland's. Its economy was overwhelmingly agricultural, and its international trade involved mainly the exchange of raw materials for manufactured goods produced in Europe. By the end of the century, however, all of that had changed radically, and it changed even more by the eve of World War I. In the 1880s, the United States surpassed Britain in manufacturing output. By 1913, American mills, factories, and shops produced as much as those of Britain, Germany, and France combined. The American population of 76 million was larger than that of any other Western country. Although still focused inward politically and economically, the United States, by virtue of its size and productivity, could scarcely escape becoming a player on the world stage.

This growth and development did not occur without significant social costs. Clashes were common in the years after the Civil War between the following groups: management and labor; farmers and bankers; immigrants and native-born; African Americans and whites in the South; and Native Americans and Euro-Americans in the West. The violent nature of some of these conflicts threatened to tear apart the country's social fabric. Major economic depressions in the 1870s and 1890s were characterized by suffering and violence. The growth of cities and factories spewed toxic fumes into the atmosphere. Industrial accidents maimed thousands. Mining and deforestation ravaged the West.

These problems generated a variety of reform movements that, collectively, were known as the Progressive Movement. The reformers of these movements sought to ease the social and economic problems that developed as a result of America's rapid industrialization. They also sought to promote a better quality of life for all Americans, especially workers, farmers, immigrants, women, and children. Thanks to their efforts, the social welfare of the American people had begun to catch up with the nation's industrial might by the time America entered World War I in 1917.

James M. McPherson

James M. McPherson

Unit Objectives

After studying this unit, students will be able to:

- Discuss the need for and attempts at governmental and social reform during the late 1800s and early 1900s.
- Explain how and why the United States expanded its influence in the Pacific and in Latin America.
- Describe the causes, course, and outcome of World War I.

Introducing the Unit

Making Connections As students prepare to study the unit, ask them to recall the isolationist policy that George Washington endorsed. Then ask them to think about current U.S. foreign policy. **Ask:** Do you consider present-day U.S. foreign policy to be "isolationist"? Why or why not? (Students will probably note that today the United States is active in the affairs of other countries.) Discuss with students that they will learn about why the United States became involved in world affairs in the late 1800s. **OL**

Unit 7
Reform and Empire
1865–1920

Chapter 21
The Progressive Era
1877–1920

Chapter 22
Rise to World Power
1865–1917

Chapter 23
World War I
1914–1919

Program cover for women's right to vote demonstration, Washington, D.C., 1913

636

Activity: Why It Matters

Why Study the Progressive Movement? Tell students what they can expect to learn in the upcoming unit. Mention that the Progressive Era was a time of significant change in many aspects of American life. **Ask:** What are some current reform issues? (Students might answer that healthcare and immigration are issues that are being debated today.) As they study the unit, have them write in their notebooks how a current reform issue affects their lives and whether there are any parallels to those of the Progressive Era. **OL**

*"Give me your tired,
your poor,
your huddled masses
yearning to
breathe free . . ."*
—Emma Lazarus

Members of the famous 369th Colored Infantry return from World War I.

Connect to Past Learning

Reform and Empire In the previous unit, students learned about the development of the Western frontier, the growth of industry, immigration, and the development of cities. In this unit, they will learn about progressive reforms that brought many changes to American life, how the United States expanded and took a more active role in international affairs, and what the causes and effects were of World War I.

More About the Image

Visual Literacy This photograph shows members of the 369th Infantry, also known as the "Harlem Hellfighters," in Hoboken, New Jersey. During World War I, 380,000 African Americans served in the army, of which 42,000 saw combat. The 369th Infantry spent 191 days in combat, longer than any other American unit in the war. Some of the men in the 369th received France's Croix de Guerre medal for gallantry in action. Because of their valor, the unit became famous in Europe and in America. Before leaving for Europe, the unit was not allowed to march in a farewell parade in New York City but upon their return in February 1919, they were honored with a victory parade on Fifth Avenue.

Reading History

Why **Paraphrasing** Is Important

Paraphrasing requires a complete understanding of the text. In order to create a paraphrased version that is accurate and makes sense, students must first process the information and then change it into words they use. Paraphrasing aids with comprehension.

Learn It!

Before class begins, write several famous historical quotes or pieces from historical writings on the board. (For example: "Taxation without representation is tyranny," "We hold these truths to be self-evident, that all men are created equal, that they are endowed by their Creator with certain unalienable Rights…" "Speak softly and carry a big stick," or "The buck stops here.")

Ask students to volunteer possible paraphrases for each quote, and write them under the quote. Confirm that this is how others in the class understand the quote, and if not, discuss what their understanding is. **AL**

Practice It!

Answers will vary, but a possible response is:

We still need: the freedom to work, go to school, and live our lives as we see fit.

By making sure each of us has all these freedoms, together we: can become a stronger world community through understanding and acceptance. **OL**

READING SKILL **Paraphrasing**

Learn It! When you paraphrase, you use your own words to retell the information. You can improve your understanding of difficult passages by rewording, or paraphrasing, them.

Paraphrased Version
As the army asks for your solid and steady support, think about the courage and strength of our ancestors. Your support will help ensure that America's democratic values will not be destroyed.

—from Chapter 23, p. 722
General John J. Pershing
"Invoking the spirit of our forefathers, the army asks for your unflinching support, to the end that the high ideals for which America stands may endure upon the earth."

Practice It! Read the quote below. On another sheet of paper, paraphrase the passage by completing the sentences with your own words.

—from Chapter 21, p. 662
W.E.B. Du Bois
"Freedom . . . we still seek,—the freedom of life and limb, the freedom to work and think, the freedom to love and aspire. Work, culture, liberty,—all these we need, not singly but together, . . . all striving toward that vaster ideal . . . the ideal of human brotherhood, gained through the unifying ideal of Race."

Paraphrased Version
We still need _____
_____.
By making sure each of us has all these freedoms, together we _____
_____.

Reading Strategy **Identifying**

Paraphrasing Paraphrasing can be helpful to students in understanding concepts, but students should also understand that paraphrasing is a major part of teaching history. Historical writings—official documents, letters, and so on—can be difficult for today's laypeople to decipher, so historians use paraphrasing to make the information understandable to the general public. Ask students to review a chapter or subsection of a chapter in this unit and identify information that the author may have paraphrased from historical documents or quotations. **AL**

Academic Vocabulary Preview

Listed below are the academic vocabulary words and their definitions that you will come across as you study Unit 7. Practice It! will help you study the words and definitions.

Academic Vocabulary	Definition	Practice It!
Chapter 21 The Progressive Era		
behalf (bih · HAF) *p. 646*	in the interest of	**Identify** *the term from Chapter 21 that best completes each sentence.*
accurate (A · kyuh · ruht) *p. 647*	correct	
professional (pruh · FEHSH · nuhl) *p. 651*	a person in an occupation requiring special knowledge or education	**1.** U.S. laws make sure that food and drug labels are _____ .
intelligence (ihn · TEH · luh · juhnts) *p. 651*	the ability to understand and use knowledge	**2.** One goal of progressive reforms is to eliminate _____ against women and minorities.
inspect (ihn · SPEHKT) *p. 658*	to carefully examine	**3.** In the early 1900s, most _____ jobs for women were in teaching.
primary (PRY · MEHR · ee) *p. 660*	an election in which a political party chooses its candidate	
deny (dih · NY) *p. 664*	to not allow access to	
bias (BY · uhs) *p. 665*	an unbalanced view or consideration	
Chapter 22 Rise to World Power		
communicate (kuh · MYOO · nuh · KAYT) *p. 676*	to transmit information so it is received or understood	**Choose** *the word that best matches the meaning of each vocabulary term listed below.*
vision (VIH · zhuhn) *p. 676*	an imagined plan	
consult (kuhn · SUHLT) *p. 681*	to seek opinions or information from	**4. annual** **6. vision**
exploit (ihk · SPLOYT) *p. 682*	to make use of	a. always a. plan
trigger (TRIH · guhr) *p. 686*	to start	b. yearly b. work
eventual (ih · VEHNT · shuh · wuhl) *p. 689*	occurring later	c. often c. process
eliminate (ih · LIH · muh · NAYT) *p. 691*	to end	**5. trigger** **7. eliminate**
annual (AN · yuh · wuhl) *p. 691*	yearly	a. stop a. include
		b. tease b. end
		c. start c. explain
Chapter 23 World War I		
dimension (duh · MEHN · shuhn) *p. 709*	magnitude or extent	**Choose** *terms from Chapter 23 to complete the paragraph.*
equip (ih · KWIHP) *p. 709*	to provide with	During World War I, the plane added a new **8.** _____ to combat. Fighter planes were **9.** _____ with machine guns and flown by daring pilots. Airplanes, as well as other sophisticated weapons, helped the Allies **10.** _____ victory.
stress (STREHS) *p. 713*	to call particular attention to	
revolution (REH · vuh · LOO · shuhn) *p. 716*	a war to overthrow a government	
proceed (proh · SEED) *p. 720*	to continue on	
consent (kuhn · SEHNT) *p. 723*	to agree to	
consume (kuhn · SOOM) *p. 726*	to use	
perceive (puhr · SEEV) *p. 727*	to recognize; understand	
final (FY · nuhl) *p. 730*	last	
achieve (uh · CHEEV) *p. 730*	to accomplish; to gain by effort	

Reform and Empire **Unit 7** **639**

Academic Vocabulary Preview

Play "What Term Am I?" (or a clever name of your choice). Tape one piece of paper with a unit term written on it onto each student's back. Make sure the student does not see what it is. (If you have more students than terms, use some terms from previous units.)

Once each student has a term, allow the students to move around the classroom and gather information from their classmates regarding what term they are. Classmates can provide definitions or text clues only (no rhyming words or saying, "It starts with…"). Once students have correctly guessed their terms, they may remove their paper but continue to help their classmates until every term has been identified. **OL**

Practice It!

Answers
1. accurate
2. bias
3. professional
4. b
5. c
6. a
7. b
8. dimension
9. equipped
10. achieve

Reading Strategy Read to Write

Paraphrasing Paraphrasing is a useful tool for students who may be struggling with reading comprehension. Encourage students to take time with difficult passages and to try to "translate" information into language they understand. Provide students with a historical document that may be difficult for them, such as a part of the Declaration of Independence or the Gettysburg Address, and ask them to rewrite it in their own words. It does not need to be a formal essay; rather it should be written in a way that helps them understand the meaning. **BL**

Key to Ability Levels

BL Below level		**AL** Above level	
OL On level		**ELL** English Language Learners	

Key to Teaching Resources

📁 Print Material   💿 DVD
🔘 CD-ROM   🖨 Transparency

Levels BL	OL	AL	ELL		Resources	Chapter Opener	Section 1	Section 2	Section 3	Section 4	Chapter Assess
FOCUS											
BL	OL	AL	ELL	🖨	Daily Test Practice Transparencies		21–1	21–2	2–3	21–4	
TEACH											
	OL	AL		📁	Geography and History Activity, URB					p. 31	
BL	OL		ELL	📁	Time Line Skills Activity, URB				p. 34		
BL	OL	AL	ELL	📁	Writing Skills Activity, URB			p. 23			
	OL	AL		📁	American Literature Readings, URB				p. 9		
BL	OL	AL	ELL	📁	Content Vocabulary Activity, URB		p. 17	p. 17	p. 17	p. 17	
BL			ELL	📁	Academic Vocabulary Activity, URB		p. 19	p. 19	p. 19	p. 19	
	OL	AL		📁	Citizenship and Decision-Making Activity, URB				p. 3		
BL			ELL	📁	Social Studies Skills Activity, URB					p. 25	
BL	OL	AL	ELL	📁	Differentiated Instruction Activity, URB		p. 27				
BL	OL	AL	ELL	📁	Critical Thinking Skills Activity, URB				p. 29		
BL	OL	AL	ELL	📁	Linking Past and Present Activity, URB				p. 33		
	OL	AL		📁	Primary Source Readings, URB			p. 21			
BL	OL	AL	ELL	📁	School-to-Home Connection Activity, URB		p. 35	p. 35	p. 35	p. 35	
BL	OL		ELL	📁	Guided Reading Activity, URB*		p. 39	p. 40	p. 41	p. 42	
	OL	AL		📁	Economics and History Activity, URB		p. 5				
BL	OL		ELL	📁	Reading Essentials and Note-Taking Guide*		p. 223	p. 226	p. 229	p. 232	
BL	OL	AL	ELL	🖨	Lesson Transparencies			21B	21A	21C	
	OL	AL		📁	Interpreting Political Cartoons, URB			p. 13			
		AL		📁	Supreme Court Case Studies		pp. 23, 25	p. 33			
	OL			📁	American Biographies		p. 36	pp. 35, 38, 40		pp. 37, 39, 43	
	OL	AL		🖨	American Art and Architecture Transparencies, Strategies, and Activities			19			

Note: Please refer to the *Unit Resource Book: Reform and Empire* for this chapter's URB materials.

* Also available in Spanish

Levels BL	OL	AL	ELL		Resources	Chapter Opener	Section 1	Section 2	Section 3	Section 4	Chapter Assess
					TEACH *(continued)*						
BL	OL	AL	ELL		**NGS US Desk Map**		✓	✓	✓	✓	
BL	OL	AL	ELL		**American Literature Library**		✓	✓	✓	✓	
BL	OL	AL	ELL		**Writer's Guidebook**		✓	✓	✓	✓	
	OL	AL			**American History Primary Source Document Library CD-ROM**		✓	✓	✓	✓	✓
BL	OL	AL	ELL		**American Music: Hits Through History**	✓	✓	✓	✓	✓	
BL	OL	AL	ELL		**StudentWorks™ Plus CD**	✓	✓	✓	✓	✓	✓
BL	OL	AL	ELL		**Section Spotlight Videos**		✓	✓	✓	✓	
BL	OL	AL	ELL		**Writing Process Transparencies**		✓	✓	✓	✓	✓
BL	OL	AL	ELL		**Presentation Plus! With MindJogger CheckPoint CD**	✓	✓	✓	✓	✓	✓
					ASSESS						
BL	OL	AL	ELL		**Quizzes and Tests**		p. 203	p. 204	p. 205	p. 206	pp. 207, 209, 211
BL	OL	AL	ELL		**Authentic Assessment With Rubrics**			p. 21			
BL	OL	AL	ELL		**Standardized Test Practice**						p. 41
BL	OL	AL	ELL		*ExamView® Assessment Suite* **CD-ROM***		21–1	21–2	21–3	21–4	Ch. 21
					CLOSE						
BL			ELL		**Reteaching Activity, URB***		p. 37	p. 37	p. 37	p. 37	p. 37
BL	OL		ELL		**Reading and Study Skills Foldables Activity**	p. 90	p. 90	p. 90	p. 90	p. 90	p. 90
BL	OL	AL	ELL		*The American Journey* **in Graphic Novel**			p. 119			
BL			ELL		**Reading Strategies and Activities for the Social Studies Classroom**		✓	✓	✓	✓	
BL	OL	AL	ELL		**Graphic Organizer Transparencies & Strategies**		✓	✓	✓	✓	

TeacherWorks *Plus*
All-In-One Planner and Resource Center

- Interactive Lesson Planner
- Interactive Teacher Edition
- Fully editable blackline masters
- Section Spotlight Videos Launch

- Differentiated Lesson Plans
- Printable reports of daily assignments
- Standards Tracking System

Professional Development Resources

- Strategies for Success
- Building Academic Vocabulary
- Success With English Learners DVD
- Differentiated Instruction Strategies DVD
- Teaching Literacy Strategies in Social Studies DVD
- Assessment DVD
- Standards-Based Instruction DVD

21

Using Study Central™

Section Previews

Technology Product

The Study Central™ Web site offers an in-depth, section-based preview that summarizes the content of the section of a chapter. The preview

- summarizes and reinforces the content in the section for the student;
- highlights key points for the student that will be used in other tabs of the Study Central™ Web site;
- provides discussion points for the teacher to bring up in class.

Objectives

The preview help students

- prepare for better understanding of section content;

- practice reading and comprehension skills.

Steps

- Locate the Web page for your textbook at glencoe.com.
- Click on **Study Central™** under *Textbook Resources*.
- On the Study Central™ Web site (a new page will have opened), select a chapter and section using the drop-down arrows and then click **Enter**.
- The page should open to the Section Preview tab; otherwise, click on the **Section Preview** tab.
- Read the content in the Section Preview with the class.
- Lead a class discussion about what your students learned from the Section Preview.

History ONLINE at glencoe.com

	Student	Teacher	Parent
Media Center			
• Student Edition Audio	●		
• Spanish Summaries	●		
• Section Spotlight Videos	●	●	
Social Studies Online Learning Center			
Classroom Tools			
• Multi-Language Glossaries	●	●	●
• Teaching Today		●	
• TIME Current Events	●	●	●
• Beyond the Textbook	●	●	
***The American Journey* Online Learning Center**			
• Study-to-Go™	●	●	●
• Study Central™	●	●	●
• Chapter Overview	●	●	
• Concepts in Motion	●	●	
• ePuzzles and Games	●	●	
• Literature Connections	●	●	
• Online Student Edition	●	●	●
• Self-Check Quizzes	●	●	●
• Student Web Activities	●	●	
• Vocabulary eFlashcards	●	●	
• Web Activity Lesson Plans	●	●	●
• Vocabulary PuzzleMaker	●	●	●

READING SUPPORT FROM
JAMESTOWN EDUCATION

- **Timed Readings Plus in Social Studies** helps students increase their reading rate and fluency while maintaining comprehension. The 400-word passages are similar to those found on state and national assessments.

- **Reading in the Content Area: Social Studies** concentrates on six essential reading skills that help students better comprehend what they read. The book includes 75 high-interest nonfiction passages written at increasing levels of difficulty.

- **Reading Social Studies** includes strategic reading instruction and vocabulary support in Social Studies content for ELLs and native speakers of English.

- **Content Vocabulary Workout** (Grades 6–8) accelerates reading comprehension through focused vocabulary development. Social Studies content vocabulary comes from the glossaries of Glencoe's Middle School Social Studies texts.

www.jamestowneducation.com

NATIONAL GEOGRAPHIC
Index to National Geographic Magazine:

The following articles relate to this chapter:

- **"Yellowstone and the Tetons,"** Alexander Fuller, November 2003.

- **"Our National Parks in Peril,"** John G. Mitchell, October 2006.

National Geographic Society Products

To order the following, call National Geographic at 1-800-368-2728:

National Geographic Atlas of the World (Book)

Access National Geographic's dynamic MapMachine Web site and other geography resources at:

www.nationalgeographic.com

www.nationalgeographic.com/mapmachine

Reading List Generator CD-ROM

GLENCOE BOOKLINK 3

Use this database to search more than 30,000 titles to create a customized reading list for your students.

- Reading lists can be organized by students' reading level, author, genre, theme, or area of interest.
- The database provides Degrees of Reading Power™ (DRP) and Lexile™ readability scores for all selections.
- A brief summary of each selection is included.

Leveled reading suggestions for this chapter:

For students at a Grade 6 reading level:
- *The Jungle,* Upton Sinclair

For students at a Grade 7 reading level:
- *Fight On!: Mary Church Terrell's Battle for Integration,* Dennis Brindell Fradin & Judith Bloom Fradin
- *We Shall Not Be Moved: The Women's Factory Strike of 1909,* Joan Dash

For students at a Grade 8 reading level:
- *Failure Is Impossible!: The History of American Women's Rights,* Martha E. Kendall
- *Prejudice,* Tish Davidson

For students at a Grade 9 reading level:
- *Elizabeth Cady Stanton: The Right Is Ours,* Harriet Sigerman

For students at a Grade 10 reading level:
- *Cleaning Nature Naturally,* Kathlyn Gay

The following videotape programs are available from Glencoe as supplements to the chapter:

- **Teddy Roosevelt: An American Lion DVD Set** (ISBN 0-76-705176-9)

- **Ku Klux Klan: A Secret History** (ISBN 0-76-700878-2)

To order, call Glencoe at 1-800-334-7344. To find classroom resources to accompany many of these videos, check the following home pages:

A&E Television: www.aetv.com

The History Channel: www.history.com

Chapter Objectives

After studying this chapter, students will be able to:

- Explain how the progressives fought corruption in business and government.
- Illustrate ways in which reforms affected the lives of women and other groups in the late 1800s.
- Discuss why Theodore Roosevelt and William Howard Taft were known as progressive presidents.
- Describe how minority groups reacted to discrimination.

Motivating Activity

Women fought hard to obtain the right to vote. Full woman suffrage was achieved with the ratification of the Nineteenth Amendment in 1920. **Ask:** Did gaining the right to vote put women on an equal standing with men in other areas of politics? *(Students probably will say no. Reasons might include the unequal representation of women in national government.)*

Previewing the Essential Questions

As you begin teaching each section, use these questions and activities to help students focus on the Essential Questions.

Chapter 21
The Progressive Era 1877–1920

Woman suffrage parade, New York City, 1915

Ferris wheel at Columbian Exposition ▶

RUTHERFORD B. HAYES 1877–1881	JAMES GARFIELD 1881	CHESTER ARTHUR 1881–1885	GROVER CLEVELAND 1885–1889	BENJAMIN HARRISON 1889–1893	GROVER CLEVELAND 1893–1897

PRESIDENTS
U.S. Events
World Events

1880

1890

1893 ★ World's Columbian Exhibition held in Chicago

★ 1879 British win Zulu War

1889 ★ Brazil becomes a republic

★ 1890 First general election in Japan

★ 1893 New Zealand grants woman suffrage

Japanese Parliament ▶

Section 1

The Progressive Movement Ask: What kinds of corruption can occur in business and government? *(Answers might include dishonesty, bribes, patronage, and so on.)* Point out to students that in Section 1 they will learn how progressives fought corruption in business and in government. **OL**

Section 2

Women and Progressives Ask: In what ways does our school work to improve the lives of students or other people in the community? *(Answers might include lunch programs, educating students for better jobs, and clubs that work to help others in the community.)* Point out to students that Section 2 discusses ways in which reforms affected the lives of women and other groups in the late 1800s. **OL**

Section 1: The Progressive Movement

Essential Question How did the progressives fight corruption in business and in government?

Section 2: Women and Progressives

Essential Question How did reforms affect the lives of women and other groups in the late 1800s?

Section 3: Progressive Presidents

Essential Question Why were Theodore Roosevelt and William Howard Taft known as progressive presidents?

Section 4: Excluded From Reform

Essential Question How did minority groups react to discrimination?

History ONLINE
Chapter Overview Visit glencoe.com and click on **Chapter 21—Chapter Overviews** to preview chapter information.

FOLDABLES **Study Organizer**

Organizing Information

Make this Foldable to help you organize information about the Progressive Era.

Step 1 Fold an 11" x 17" sheet of paper lengthwise to create five equal sections.

Step 2 Then fold it to form five columns.

Step 3 Label your Foldable as shown.

Chapter 21: The Progressive Era	The Progressive Movement	Women and Progressives	Progressive Presidents	Excluded From Reform
Essential Question				
Key Events and Dates				
1877–1910 Attitudes				
Current Attitudes				

Reading and Writing As you read the chapter, take notes about the people, places, and events related to the Progressive Era in the correct place on the chart.

Time Line Activity

If you have not already done so, have students review the time line. **Ask:** Was the United States the first country to grant women the right to vote? *(No. New Zealand granted woman suffrage in 1893, and other countries not on the time line may have done so earlier.)*

FOLDABLES **Study Organizer** **Dinah Zike's Foldables**

Purpose This Foldable helps students organize information about the Progressive Era. The completed Foldable will help them prepare for assessment. **OL**

More Foldable activities for this chapter can be found in *Dinah Zike's Reading and Study Skills Foldables.*

History ONLINE
Introduce students to chapter content and key terms by having them access the **Chapter Overview** at glencoe.com.

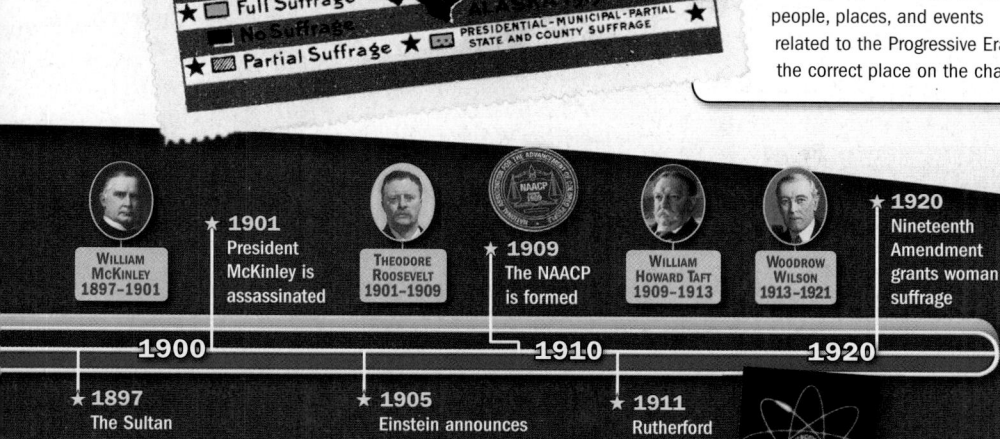

★ **VOTES FOR WOMEN** ★
THE MAP PROVES IT A SUCCESS

☐ Full Suffrage
■ No Suffrage
▨ Partial Suffrage
PRESIDENTIAL - MUNICIPAL - PARTIAL STATE AND COUNTY SUFFRAGE

WILLIAM McKINLEY 1897–1901

★ **1901** President McKinley is assassinated

THEODORE ROOSEVELT 1901–1909

★ **1909** The NAACP is formed

WILLIAM HOWARD TAFT 1909–1913

WOODROW WILSON 1913–1921

★ **1920** Nineteenth Amendment grants woman suffrage

1900   **1910**   **1920**

★ **1897** The Sultan of Zanzibar abolishes slavery

★ **1905** Einstein announces theory of relativity

★ **1911** Rutherford discovers structure of atom

Chapter 21 641

Section 3

Progressive Presidents Ask: Why might Theodore Roosevelt deserve to be depicted on Mount Rushmore? *(Answers might refer to his achievements as president, and particularly his role in conservation.)* Tell students that Section 3 will describe the presidencies of Theodore Roosevelt and William Howard Taft. **OL**

Section 4

Excluded From Reform Ask: What kinds of discrimination do minority groups face today? *(Answers might include access to quality education and housing, as well as fair legal treatment.)* Explain to students that in Section 4, they will learn how minority groups worked for civil rights reform in the Progressive Era. **OL**

Section 1

Section 1

The Progressive Movement

Focus

Bellringer
Daily Test Practice Transparency 21–1

Reading Guide
Answers to Graphic:

Before: State legislatures (often controlled by party bosses and big business) chose senators.

After: Voters chose senators in direct elections.

Section Spotlight Video

Have students watch the Section Spotlight Video "The Progressive Movement" to learn about how Ida Tarbell reformed the oil industry.

Essential Question
How did the progressives fight corruption in business and in government?

Reading Guide

Content Vocabulary
oligopoly (p. 645)   referendum (p. 647)
muckraker (p. 647)   recall (p. 647)
initiative (p. 647)

Academic Vocabulary
behalf (p. 646)   accurate (p. 647)

Key People and Events
Pendleton Act (p. 644)
Sherman Antitrust Act (p. 645)
Interstate Commerce Act (p. 645)
Eugene V. Debs (p. 646)
Ida Tarbell (p. 647)
Upton Sinclair (p. 647)

Reading Strategy
Taking Notes As you read, use a diagram like the one below to show how the Seventeenth Amendment reformed the political process.

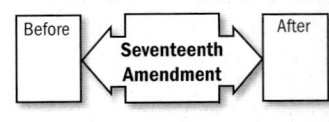

| Before | Seventeenth Amendment | After |

ILLINOIS STANDARDS
The American Journey

15.E Understand the impact of government policies and decisions on production and consumption in the economy.

16.B.3c (US) Describe the way the Constitution has changed over time as a result of amendments and Supreme Court decisions.

16.C.3c (US) Describe how economic developments and government policies after 1865 affected the country's economic institutions including corporations, banks and organized labor.

American Diary

Boss Tweed was a dishonest but powerful political official in New York City in the late 1800s. During this time, bribery, fixed elections, and kickbacks were common practices in city government. Journalists and reformers, however, exposed these activities and tried to change the political system. Political cartoonist from the time, Thomas Nast, said: "I made up my mind not long ago to put some of those fellows behind bars, and I am going to put them there."

—quoted in The Great Bridge by David McCullough

The former New York County Courthouse, also known as Tweed Courthouse

Resource Manager

R Reading Strategies	**C** Critical Thinking	**D** Differentiated Instruction	**W** Writing Support	**S** Skill Practice
Teacher Edition • Taking Notes, p. 646 • Monitoring, p. 646 **Additional Resources** • Guid. Read., URB p. 39 • Content Vocab., URB p. 17 • Academic Vocab., URB p. 19 • Read. Ess., p. 223	**Teacher Edition** • Predict. Conseq., p. 644 **Additional Resources** • Quizzes and Tests, p. 203 • Econ. & Hist., URB p. 5	**Teacher Edition** • Kinesthetic, p. 645 • Gifted & Talent., p. 646 **Additional Resources** • School-to-Home, URB p. 35 • Reteaching Act., URB p. 37 • Differ. Inst., URB p. 27	**Teacher Edition** • Expository Writ., p. 643 • Expository Writ., p. 647	**Teacher Edition** • Visual Lit., p. 643 **Additional Resources** • Daily Test Pract. Transp. 21-1

Fighting Corruption

Main Idea Americans took action against corruption in business and government.

History and You How would you feel if the team members who paid the coach the most money got to be the starting players on your school's basketball team? Read to find out how reformers worked to fight corruption in city governments.

Many Americans called for reform in the late 1800s. The reformers, called progressives, had many different goals. Progressives focused on urban problems, government, and business. They claimed that government and big business were taking advantage of the American people rather than serving them.

Fighting the Political Machines

Political machines were powerful organizations linked to political parties. These machines controlled local government in many cities. In each ward, or political district within a city, a machine representative controlled jobs and services. This person was the political boss. A political boss was often a citizen's closest link to local government. Although they helped people, many bosses were dishonest.

Corrupt politicians found different ways to make money. They accepted bribes from tenement landlords to overlook violations of city housing codes. They took campaign contributions from contractors who hoped to do business with the city. They also took kickbacks, or illegal payments. For example, a contractor would pad, or add to, the amount of the bill for city work. The contractor then paid, or "kicked back," a percentage of that amount to the bosses.

Some politicians profited illegally from city business. One corrupt city boss was William M. Tweed. Known as Boss Tweed, he headed New York City's Democratic political machine in the 1860s and 1870s. Boss Tweed led a network of city officials called the Tweed ring.

By the Numbers / Stealing From the People

Courthouse Corruption As the New York County Courthouse was built in the late 1800s, dishonest construction workers and city officials stole money from the city's treasury by submitting bills for fraudulent work. An investigation by the *New York Times* found that more than $12 million was billed for questionable work on the courthouse. Evidence about corrupt practices prompted a public outcry against Boss Tweed and his political machine. Some of the huge charges recorded by the city are listed in the chart below.

Payment for Work Completed on New Courthouse

To	For	Amount
Andrew Garvey	Plastering, Repairs	$2,870,464
Keyser & Co.	Plumbing	$1,200,000
Ingersoll	Chairs	$170,727.60
Ingersoll	Cabinets, Furniture	$2,817,469.19
George Miller	Carpentry	$360,751.61

▲ Cartoon showing Boss Tweed

Critical Thinking

Inferring How does the right of a free press contribute to a democracy?

CHAPTER 21
Section 1

Teach

W Writing Support

Expository Writing Have students imagine they have discovered that their local mayor or village manager has been accepting bribes. Instruct them to write a letter to the local newspaper in which they expose the corruption and suggest a solution. **OL**

S Skill Practice

Visual Literacy Tell students that the caricature of Boss Tweed on this page was drawn by Thomas Nast. **Ask:** Why does Nast show such a contrast in size between the police officer and Boss Tweed? (*He wanted to show that the power of the police was dwarfed by the power Boss Tweed had through his corrupt political machine.*) **OL**

By the Numbers

Critical Thinking Answer A press that is able to convey ideas freely can expose government abuses and help ensure that the government represents the people without abusing its power.

Additional Support

Activity: Connecting Past and Present

Political Corruption Progressive reformers fought political corruption manifested as machine politics, bribes and kickbacks, the spoils system, and patronage. **Ask:** Is political corruption an issue in our local or state government? Tell students to work in small groups and try to find examples of historic or current government corruption. Remind students that the corrupt activities may be documented or be undergoing investigation. Instruct each group to make a chart that lists the type of corruption, the source of the corruption, and effects on citizens' lives. Remind them to clarify whether the charges have been proven. **OL**

C Critical Thinking

Predicting Consequences Ask: Why do you think the spoils system would lead to inefficient government? *(Students might respond that when government employees are hired because of their political support rather than their expertise, they are not necessarily the people best qualified to do the job or to carry out the tasks most efficiently.)* **OL**

Primary Source

Critical Thinking Answer
Other cities might note that the commission plan oversaw the successful rebuilding of Galveston after the mayor–city council system failed to do so. The text infers that the commission plan is more efficient.

Reading Check **Answer:** Under the Pendleton Act, people had to show their skills in exams administered by the Civil Service Commission. Under the spoils system, jobs were awarded to political supporters.

Hands-On
Chapter Project
Step 1

Creating a Reform Campaign

Step 1: Choosing a Progressive Cause Students will select one of the targets of progressive reform to study and promote.

Essential Question: How did the progressives fight corruption in business and in government?

Primary Source / Good Government in Galveston, Texas

A New Type of City Government After a hurricane in September 1900 devastated Galveston, Texas, killing some 8,000 of the city's people and destroying about half the city's homes, the task of rebuilding the city overwhelmed the mayor and city council. Galveston's citizens persuaded the Texas state legislature to approve a new charter that placed the city government in the hands of five commissioners. The new commission successfully rebuilt the city. Soon, many other cities adopted the new form of government.

▲ Galveston following the hurricane of 1900

◄ A new seawall is built in Galveston following the hurricane.

Critical Thinking

Analyzing Why would other cities adopt the commission plan of government?

The Tweed ring controlled the city's police, the courts, and even some newspapers. They collected millions of dollars in illegal payments from companies doing business with the city. Political cartoonist Thomas Nast exposed the Tweed ring's operations in his cartoons for *Harper's Weekly*. Tweed was convicted and sentenced to prison.

Reformers wanted to break the power of political bosses. They founded organizations such as the National Municipal League in Philadelphia. They worked to make city governments more honest and efficient. Galveston, Texas, for example, changed to a government run by five commissioners. By 1917, commissioners governed nearly 400 cities.

Fighting the Spoils System

Since the presidency of Andrew Jackson, the spoils system had been common practice. Under this system, political supporters were rewarded with jobs and favors. When a new president came to power, job seekers flooded the nation's capital. Also called patronage, the spoils system could be found at all levels of government and led to abuses. Many people who received government jobs were not qualified, and some were dishonest.

Presidents Rutherford B. Hayes (1877–1881) and James Garfield (1881) tried to change the spoils system. Hayes tried to reform the civil service, the body of government workers who are not elected. Neither major political party backed his efforts. Before Garfield could launch his reforms, he was assassinated by an unsuccessful office seeker.

When Vice President Chester A. Arthur succeeded Garfield as president, he tried to end the spoils system. In 1883 Congress passed the **Pendleton Act,** which established the Civil Service Commission to give examinations for federal jobs. Job seekers had to demonstrate their skills in these tests. By 1900, the commission controlled the hiring of many federal workers.

Reading Check **Contrasting** How was the hiring of government employees under the Pendleton Act different from how people were hired in the spoils system?

Directions Tell students to form small groups. Ask each group to select one of the progressive reforms discussed in the chapter and locate sources so they can learn more about that reform and its targets. Examples of reform targets include government corruption; control of the economy and government by trusts; social problems such as unsafe food, poverty, and child labor; lack of women suffrage; drunkenness; need for conservation; discrimination; and racial violence.

Identifying As a class, discuss what kinds of government corruption existed in the Progressive Era and how reformers tried to fight it.

(Chapter Project continued in Section 2)

Controlling Business

Main Idea The government passed acts to regulate businesses and transportation.

History and You Do you think the government should have a role in managing big businesses? Read to learn how the government became more involved in regulating businesses.

Many Americans believed that trusts, or groups of companies, had too much control over the economy and the government. This concern led to new laws regulating big business. In 1890 Congress passed the **Sherman Antitrust Act,** the first federal law to control trusts and monopolies.

During the 1890s, however, the government rarely used the Sherman Act to curb business. Instead, it applied the act against labor unions. The government claimed that labor strikes hurt trade. It was not until the early 1900s that the Sherman Act was used to win cases against trusts.

Reining in the Railroads

The railroads formed an **oligopoly,** a few large companies that controlled prices for an entire industry. Reformers called for rules on railroad rates. In 1887 Congress passed the **Interstate Commerce Act,** requiring railroads to charge and publish "reasonable and just" rates. The act set up the Interstate Commerce Commission (ICC) to oversee the railroad and, later, trucking industries.

Lowering Tariffs

Reformers wanted to lower tariffs. They believed that higher tariffs increased the price of goods. In 1890 the Republicans raised tariffs sharply to protect U.S. businesses from foreign competition. Voters opposing high tariffs sent many Democrats to Congress. Grover Cleveland, who became president in 1893, also favored lower tariffs.

✓ **Reading Check** **Explaining** How did the government gain control over powerful businesses?

D **Differentiated Instruction**

Kinesthetic The game of Monopoly® was not created until 1934, but monopolies were a part of American business in the 1800s. Have students organize into groups of four and play a game of Monopoly®. Have them write a paragraph that explains why the game is called Monopoly®. *(The more railroads or properties a player owns, the more money they make.)* **BL**

✓ **Reading Check** **Answer:** passed the Sherman Antitrust Act, the Interstate Commerce Act, and also lowered tariffs

---

Primary Sources
INTERPRETING POLITICAL CARTOONS

1. **Analyzing** Why do you think the cartoonist chose to depict the trust as an animal with many heads?

2. **Interpreting** Does the beast look trustworthy to you? Why or why not?

A. Andrew Carnegie
B. Uncle Sam
C. Carnegie's steel trust

A quote by Andrew Carnegie inspired the cartoon below:
"The public may regard trusts or combinations with serene confidence."
—from the *New York Times*, October 9, 1888

A TRUSTWORTHY BEAST

INTERPRETING POLITICAL CARTOONS

Answers

1. The heads of the beast represent the different companies that make up a trust.

2. Students may say that the beast does not look trustworthy. The heads are horned and angry, with forked tongues.

Differentiated Instruction

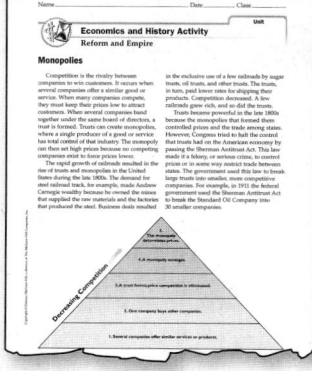

Economics and History Activity, URB p. 5

Monopolies

Objective: To learn the history of monopolies

Focus: Have students define *competition, trust,* and *monopoly* in their own words.

Teach: Have students answer the questions.

Assess: Assess each answer according to the Answer Key, and discuss incorrect answers.

Close: Ask students to identify monopolies that affect the U.S. economy today.

Differentiated Instruction Strategies

BL Have students create three questions about the text and supply the answers.

AL Ask students to research monopolistic activities by airlines and summarize their findings.

ELL Have students identify a monopoly in their countries of origin and discuss how it affects daily life or society.

R₁ Reading Strategy

Taking Notes Ask students to keep a list of attempts at progressive reform as they read this subsection. After they have analyzed their lists, have them explain what a "progressive" is in their own words. **OL**

D Differentiated Instruction

Gifted and Talented Invite interested students to conduct research into the policies of Bernie Sanders, the first socialist elected to the U.S. Senate. Have them summarize their findings and present them to the class. **AL**

R₂ Reading Strategy

Monitoring Ask: How did the muckrakers contribute to the Progressive movement? *(Muckrakers used reporting and writing to raise awareness about corruption and social problems.)* **OL**

Primary Source

Critical Thinking Answer
Students might answer that the people these reformers tried to help were powerless, unable to help themselves, or being exploited for profit.

Differentiated Instruction

Primary Source / Muckrakers

Exposing Corruption Between 1900 and 1910, muckrakers wrote articles for several popular magazines that exposed the social hardships caused by corrupt big business. Public outrage caused by the stories inspired some politicians to take the lead in passing some social reforms.

Samuel Hopkins Adams's articles in *Collier's* exposed patent medicines—sold as cure-alls—as frauds and led to the 1906 Pure Food and Drug Act. He wrote that without patent medicines, **"the nation would be richer not only in lives and money, but in drunkards and drug fiends saved."**

In order to be committed to an asylum for poor women, reporter Nellie Bly pretended to be insane. She later wrote about her experiences in *Ten Days in a Mad-House*. Her account shocked readers and led to improvements in the care of the insane. **"So I have at least the satisfaction of knowing that the poor unfortunates will be the better cared for because of my work."**

Lewis Hine's work for the National Child Labor Committee took him across the country to photograph children at work. His photographs of dirty coal miners, anemic mill workers, and tired oyster shuckers made the plight of working children real to Americans. *"My child labor photos have . . . set the authorities to work to see 'if such things can be possible,'"* he wrote.

"They try to get around them by crying 'fake,' but therein lies the value of data & a witness."

Critical Thinking

Analyzing What did the groups of people that Bly, Hine, and Adams tried to help have in common?

R₁ The New Reformers

Main Idea Writers exposed corruption in business and government, and voters gained more power in choosing candidates.

History and You What sorts of problems do your local TV investigative reporters try to resolve? Read how reporters brought about reforms in business and government.

In the early 1900s, reformers in America had new ideas for ending injustice and solving social problems. These ideas included socialism and progressivism.

Socialists believed the government should own and operate resources and major industries on **behalf**, or in the interest, of all the people. **Eugene V. Debs** helped found the American Socialist Party in 1898. With Debs as its leader, the party gained some support in the early 1900s. Debs ran for president five times, but he never received more than 6 percent of the popular vote.

At the same time, progressives brought new energy to the reform movement. Like the socialists, many progressives were alarmed by the fact that only a few people held most of America's wealth and power. Unlike the socialists, they wanted government to regulate industry rather than own it. They also wanted government to be more efficient and less influenced by powerful businesses. Society, progressives believed, had a duty to protect and help all its members. Many of their reforms were aimed at helping people who did not have wealth or power.

Muckrakers Expose Problems

Journalists aided the reformers. Investigative reporters wrote newspaper and magazine stories that alerted people about problems.

Leveled Activities

BL **School-to-Home Connection Activity, URB p. 35**

OL **Academic Vocabulary Activity, URB p. 19**

AL **Differentiated Instruction Activity, URB p. 27**

Called **muckrakers,** these reporters "raked"—or exposed—the "muck"—dirt and corruption—underlying society.

One of the most effective muckrakers was Lincoln Steffens. Working for *McClure's Magazine,* Steffens exposed corrupt machine politics in New York and other cities. **Ida Tarbell,** also with *McClure's,* described the oil trust's unfair practices. Her articles increased public pressure for more government control over big business.

In his novel *The Jungle* (1906), **Upton Sinclair** described the horrors of the Chicago meatpacking industry. His vivid descriptions shocked people in America. In response, Congress passed the Meat Inspection Act and the Pure Food and Drug Act in 1906. Now food and medicine had to be **accurately** labeled, and harmful food could not be sold.

Progressives also backed many reforms designed to increase the people's direct control of government. Robert La Follette reformed Wisconsin's electoral system. He introduced the "Wisconsin idea," a direct primary election in which party candidates were chosen by voters instead of by party bosses and state conventions.

The Oregon System

Oregon also made important reforms. With the **initiative,** voters could place an issue on the ballot in a state election. Voters could accept or reject measures that the state legislature enacted with the **referendum.** The **recall** allowed voters to remove incompetent elected officials. These reforms, called the Oregon System, were adopted by other states.

The Seventeenth Amendment

Progressives also changed the way U.S. senators were elected. The Constitution gave state legislatures the responsibility of choosing senators. Party bosses and business interests, however, often controlled the process. Progressives wanted to give people the opportunity to vote for their senators directly. Support for this idea grew. In 1912 Congress passed the Seventeenth Amendment to the Constitution. This amendment set forth the direct election of senators. Ratified in 1913, the amendment gave the people a voice in choosing their representatives.

✔ **Reading Check** **Summarizing** How did progressive reformers reinforce democratic ideas?

Section 1 Review

History ONLINE
Study Central™ To review this section, go to glencoe.com.

Vocabulary

1. Define each of the following terms in a sentence: oligopoly, behalf, muckraker, accurate, initiative, referendum, recall.

Main Ideas

2. Listing Identify some ways in which political machines were corrupt in the late 1800s.

3. Discussing Why did reformers want regulation of the railroads, and what was the government's response?

4. Identifying How did muckrakers bring about reform?

Critical Thinking

5. Determining Cause and Effect Use a diagram like the one below to show which problem reformers were trying to resolve with each legislation.

	Sherman Antitrust Act
	Pendleton Act
	Interstate Commerce Act

6. Persuasive Writing You are a muckraker. Choose something you think is unfair in your school or community and write a two- or three-paragraph article about it. Try to move your readers to improve the situation.

Answer the
7. Essential Question
How did the progressives fight corruption in business and in government?

The Progressive Era **Chapter 21** **647**

Answers

1. Students should use vocabulary words as they are defined in the section and Glossary.

2. Many political bosses were dishonest; politicians accepted bribes to overlook code violations, gave contracts in return for campaign contributions, and accepted kickbacks; corrupt officials controlled police, the courts, and some newspapers.

3. Railroads controlled their own rates. The government responded with the Interstate Commerce Act and the Interstate Commerce Commission.

4. The muckrakers publicized problems and thus increased public pressure for reform.

5. Sherman Antitrust Act: excessive control of economy and government by trusts and monopolies; **Pendleton Act:** spoils system; **Interstate Commerce Act:** railroad oligopoly

6. Students should write persuasive articles.

7. They enacted civil service reform to end the spoils system. They also exposed corruption in government, business, and industry through muckraking journalism, and they backed reforms that increased direct control of government by the people.

Focus

C Critical Thinking

Drawing Conclusions Have students reread the "Building Background" paragraph. Remind them that even though Grace's mother, father, and older sister work at the mill, Grace must work to help support the family. **Ask:** Do you think the mill pays its workers very much? *(no, because one or two people cannot make enough money to feed and house a family)* **OL**

R₁ Reading Strategy

Using Context Clues Ask students to read the selection and not look at the definitions. **Ask:** What is a bobbin? *(a toy)* What are mumblety-peg and roll the bobbin? *(games)* What words in the selection helped you figure that out? *("dolly" and "I played")* **OL**

R₂ Reading Strategy

Predicting Have students reread the section about skating. **Ask:** Does this sound like fun? *(yes)* What does it remind you of? *(skating, sledding)* Does it sound like a safe working environment? *(no)* What might happen when you combine slippery floors and big machines? *(accidents)* **BL**

Additional Reading

Review suggested books before assigning them.

Meet the Author

Elizabeth Winthrop (1948–) was inspired to write *Counting on Grace* after seeing a photograph of a 12-year-old girl named Addie at work in a textile mill in Vermont. The photograph, taken by child labor photographer Lewis Hine in 1910, has been reprinted hundreds of times and has even appeared on a U.S. postage stamp.

Vocabulary

bobbin a small round device or which thread or yarn is wound

mumblety-peg game in which players throw or flip a jackknife in various ways so that the knife sticks in the ground

dawdles wastes time

Building Background

In *Counting on Grace*, the main character is a 12-year-old girl who leaves school to work at the thread mill in a Vermont town in 1910. Grace had been in the mill "lots of times" before to play and bring lunch to her family. Now she works to help support her family. Her mother, Mamère, her father, and her sister, Delia, also work in the mill. French Johnny, a French-Canadian second hand in the mill, is in charge of the spinning rooms where Grace and her family work. As you read Grace's description, think about the difficulties that the workers had to endure.

This photograph of mill worker Addie Card inspired Elizabeth Winthrop to write the novel *Counting on Grace.* ▶

COUNTING ON GRACE

Elizabeth Winthrop

I've been in the mill lots of times. Summers ever since I was nine, I've been cooking the hot meal for Mamère and Papa and Delia and taking in the dinner pails in the middle of the day. Delia let me push her **bobbin** dolly. I played **mumblety-peg** or roll the bobbin with Dougie and Bridget and Felix when he was a summer sweeper boy in the spinning room. And grease skating. That's the best. Thomas invented that game. Too bad he can't play it no more with his twisted foot.

With all the oil dripping off the machines, bare feet slide around easy. The boys draw a line at the end of one alley, between the frames where French Johnny can't see us, and we run and set our legs into a

648

Biography: *Escape!: The Story of the Great Houdini,* by Sid Fleischman, tells the story of the poor boy who became the world's most famous magician and escape artist.

Biography: *Jane Addams: Champion of Democracy,* by Dennis Brindell Fradin, describes Jane Addams as a woman whose bravery and creativity helped change Chicago, as well as the nation.

Fiction: *Here Lies the Librarian,* by Richard Peck, stars orphans PeeWee and Jake in 1914 Indiana. This novel features the "newfangled motorcar" racing, four librarians who know cars, and the bad Kirby Brothers.

For further reading, see **BOOKLINK 3**.

long slide. I'm skinny for my age and I've got big feet, but I can go the farthest 'cause I know how to keep myself low to the floor. Sometimes you slip and fall. That's a chance you take.

But now I'm here to work, not play.

The air in the mill is stuffy and linty and sweaty at the same time 'cause all day long water sprays down on the frames from little hoses in the ceiling. Wet keeps the threads from breaking. The windows are shut tight even in the summer. You don't breathe too deep for fear of what you might be sucking down your throat.

People complain about the noise, but it's not so bad in the spinning room. The belts up above our heads slap and the big roll drives turn and the bobbins spin like a thousand bees buzzing. You get used to it so you almost miss it when you step outside. The world seems too quiet all of a sudden.

The weaving room is the worst. In there you get a pounding sound every time a beam slaps into place. And there are a hundred beams slapping at once and the whole floor shakes and jumps. Most of the people who work in weaving go deaf early on. That's why I say Delia should stay in the spinning room even if she won't make as much money.

You're not supposed to work in the mill until you're fourteen, but visiting is fine. French Johnny likes us kids going in and out all the time. He says, that way we get used to the work.

The only people you worry about are the state inspectors. When French Johnny blows the whistle, all the kids in the mill, even the ones just visiting, know to run as fast as we can so he can hide us in the elevator that carries the cotton between the floors. The inspector always stops in at the front office and **dawdles** around there for a while so us kids have time to hide. Seems to me he don't really want to find us. We skitter across the room like those big cockroaches that come up through the floorboards in the summertime. Our mothers make a wall out of themselves to hide us.

You don't breathe too deep for fear of what you might be sucking down your throat.

It gets hot in that old elevator and the inspector can take hours to look through the mill, top to bottom. A couple of kids fainted last August and French Johnny had to throw cold water on them when he slid open the metal doors.

I didn't feel so good myself, but I didn't say a word.

"You look kind of green," Pierre Gagnon said to me when we filed out.

"Green Grace, green Grace," Felix shouted, and everybody called me that for a while. When nobody was looking, I smacked Felix hard on the top of his head. By the time he turned around I was gone. I've got fast feet, fast hands, and fast fingers.

Now I'm really going to need them.

Analyzing Literature

1. **Respond** Describe the relationship between Grace and the other young workers.

2. **Recall and Interpret** Stories sometimes contain a symbol—an object that stands for something else, often an idea. What do you think the elevator in this story might symbolize?

3. **Evaluate** What conclusions can you draw from the reading about Grace's character? In your opinion, would she be a good friend? Is Grace a conscientious worker? Explain.

Teach

C Critical Thinking

Identifying Central Issues With students, read the three-paragraph description of the inside of the mill. **Ask:** Does this sound like a place that you want to work? *(no)* Why are the windows always closed? *(so workers cannot leave at will or steal fabric)* What other problems do you recognize? *(Answers may include noise, stuff in air that affects breathing.)* **AL**

D Differentiated Instruction

Intrapersonal Point out that Grace doesn't think that her sister should become a weaver, even though the weavers make more money. **Ask:** Do you agree with her? Why or why not? *(Answers will vary, based on students' perspectives.)* **OL**

Assess/Close

Remind students to make connections between what they are reading and what they have read before. As a class, discuss earlier readings on mill conditions and child labor. Note that Graces thinks that the state inspectors don't want to find kids in the mill. **Ask:** Why do you think the state inspectors might not want to find problems at the mill?

Answers

1. She has fun with them but doesn't have a special friend.

2. Possible answers include the mill (it is closed, airtight, hot) and the "invisibility" of mill workers (the children become invisible inside the elevator, and the problems of mill workers were invisible to society).

3. Grace is conscientious and hardworking (she has been cooking and bringing her family lunch since age 9), loves fun (the games), is smart (her comments about the mill and the inspector), and sticks up for herself when teased ("green Grace" incident).

Focus

Women and Progressives

Bellringer
Daily Test Practice Transparency 21–2

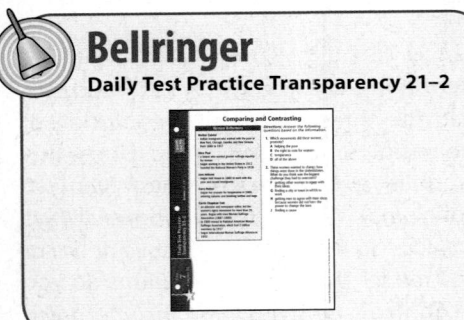

Reading Guide
Answers to Graphic:
Eighteenth: Prohibited making, transporting, or selling alcohol; **Nineteenth:** Gave women the right to vote

Section Spotlight Video

Have students watch the Section Spotlight Video "Women and Progressives" to learn about women's struggle to attain the right to vote.

Essential Question
How did reforms affect the lives of women and other groups in the late 1800s?

Reading Guide

Content Vocabulary
suffragist *(p. 652)*   prohibition *(p. 655)*

Academic Vocabulary
professional *(p. 651)*
intelligence *(p. 651)*

Key People and Events
Jane Addams *(p. 651)*
Mother Cabrini *(p. 651)*
Mary Church Terrell *(p. 652)*
Frances Willard *(p. 655)*

Reading Strategy
Taking Notes As you read, use a diagram like the one below to describe the two constitutional amendments.

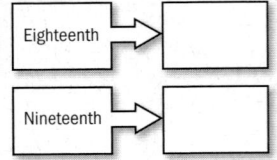

Amendment	Description
Eighteenth →	
Nineteenth →	

ILLINOIS STANDARDS
The American Journey

16.B.3c (US) Describe the way the Constitution has changed over time as a result of amendments and Supreme Court decisions.

18.B.3a Analyze how individuals and groups interact with and within institutions (e.g., educational, military).

18.C.3b Explain how diverse groups have contributed to U.S. social systems over time.

American Diary

Progressive women formed clubs and organizations to socialize and to make a difference in people's lives. Women's leader, Mary Eastman, said: "We must learn sympathy, learn unity, learn the great lesson of organization. . . . This club and other clubs reach out into the new life for women. It is certainly a new life. These clubs have made a new world, and we have got to adapt ourselves to it and to educate the world around us."

—*quoted in* History of the Woman's Club Movement in America

By the end of the 1800s, middle-class women had more free time to organize clubs and to socialize.

Resource Manager

R Reading Strategies	**C** Critical Thinking	**D** Differentiated Instruction	**W** Writing Support	**S** Skill Practice
Teacher Edition • Using Con. Clues, p. 651 • Summarizing, p. 654	**Teacher Edition** • Making General., p. 651 • Analyz. Info., p. 652	**Teacher Edition** • Auditory Music., p. 653 • Intrapersonal, p. 654	**Teacher Edition** • Persuasive Writ., p. 653 • Personal Writ., p. 655	**Teacher Edition** • Using Chart Skills, p. 652 • Using Geo. Skills, p. 653
Additional Resources • Guid. Read., URB p. 40 • Content Vocab., URB p. 17 • Academic Vocab., URB p. 19 • Read. Ess., p. 226 • Pri. Source Read., URB p. 21	**Additional Resources** • Quizzes and Tests, p. 204 • Inter. Polit. Cartoons, URB p. 13	**Additional Resources** • School-to-Home, URB p. 35 • Reteaching Act., URB p. 37	**Additional Resources** • Writ. Skills, URB p. 23 • Authentic Assess., p. 21	**Additional Resources** • Daily Test Pract. Transp. 21-2 • Lesson Transp. 21B

Women's Roles Change

Main Idea Roles began to change for middle-class women in the late 1800s.

History and You Do you believe women today have unlimited career choices? Read to learn how women's career choices began to expand in the late 1800s.

Many leaders of urban reform were women of the middle class. The lives of middle-class women changed during the late 1800s. As people moved from farms to cities, fewer children were needed to help a family survive. As a result, families became smaller. More children spent the day at school, and men worked away from home. Women also gained more free time as technology made housework easier. Because of these factors, women's lives became less centered around maintaining a home.

With more free time, more middle-class women began to pursue higher education. About 40 percent of all college students in 1910 were women.

Educated women were starting professional careers. Most **professional** women, those in occupations requiring special knowledge or education, were teachers, but others worked in nursing, medicine, and other fields. Between 1890 and 1910, the number of women in the workforce increased from 4 million to nearly 7.5 million.

The "New Woman"

These changes created the "new woman." This term was a popular way to refer to educated, modern women who pursued interests outside their homes. For example, **Jane Addams** set up Hull House, a settlement house, in Chicago. She became a pioneer in the emerging field of social work. Working with disadvantaged people gave Addams an outlet for her energy and **intelligence.**

Women became writers, public speakers, fund-raisers, and social or political reformers. Many young women followed the example of talented public figures such as Jane Addams. Others were inspired by the life of **Mother Cabrini,** an Italian nun who came to the United States to work with the poor.

Primary Source / **Demonstrating for the Right to Vote**

A Parade for Suffrage Women who fought for the right to vote were known as suffragists. Beatrice Forbes-Robertson Hale described a suffrage parade: "A little time ago I found myself in a great American city, where a Woman Suffrage Parade was to be held for the first time. . . . Some large stores had hung out the yellow suffrage flag, and yellow daffodils were being worn by many in the crowd. . . . Presently came the beat of a drum, then the fifes . . . they were here! Line upon line of white-clad figures with yellow badges, short-skirted, booted, and hatted in simple white. . . . Eyes front, earnest faces, marching feet, down the sunshine of the street they came."

—from *What Women Want*

Critical Thinking

Analyzing What types of issues are important to women today?

Teach

C Critical Thinking

Making Generalizations Ask: Why did the number of working women increase around the turn of the century? (*Some women had more free time and pursued college degrees and professional careers.*) **OL**

R Reading Strategy

Using Context Cues Ask: Using clues from the paragraph, define "settlement house." (*Students can guess that a settlement house was a place disadvantaged people or those who needed help with integration into society received aid.*) Lead a class discussion about similar community services available today. (*Answers might include YMCAs, community centers, churches, and senior citizen centers.*) **OL**

Primary Source

Critical Thinking Answer
Answers might include family leave, ability to serve at all levels of government, and equal pay for equal work.

Additional Support

Activity: Why It Matters

Comparing Jane Addams was an early proponent of social welfare. The debate about what services should be provided to the nation's poor and underserved continues today. **Ask:** Why should private organizations and the government help individuals in need? Lead a class discussion that begins with students listing categories of people who might benefit from social welfare programs. (*Examples include people living in poverty, people with disabilities, and victims of natural disasters such as floods and fires, and elderly individuals.*) Then talk about world events that help illustrate what life might be like in a country without a social safety net. Discussion topics might include AIDS orphans and victims of earthquakes or famine. Next, have students participate in a panel discussion about how American life would be different if services were not available to help individuals in need. **OL**

C Critical Thinking

Analyzing Information Ask: How did the motto "Lifting As We Climb" describe the goals of the National Association of Colored Women? *(Not only did the members gain rights and privileges [climb], they also helped [lifted] others along the way.)* **OL**

S Skill Practice

Using Chart Skills Have students conduct research to learn the percentage of eligible women and eligible men who voted in the most recent presidential election. Ask them to create a bar graph to present their findings visually. **AL**

Primary Source

Critical Thinking Answer
The words "justice," "equal chance," and "free kindergartens" show social issues that were important to Terrell.

✔ **Reading Check** **Answer:** Characteristics might include educated, modern, having interests outside the home, and being interested in social welfare.

Differentiated Instruction

A Leader of Women Mary Church Terrell was well educated and was eventually appointed to the District of Columbia Board of Education, the first African American to hold such a position in the United States. Terrell also became active in the women's club movement.

"With courage, born of success achieved in the past . . . we look forward to a future large with promise and hope. Seeking no favors because of our color, nor patronage because of our needs, we knock at the bar of justice, asking an equal chance."

In Washington, D.C., Terrell worked to establish kindergarten classes for African American children as well as a nursery for the children of working mothers. ▼

"Free kindergartens in every city and hamlet of this broad land we must have, if the children are to receive from us what it is our duty to give."

▲ Terrell helped found the National Association of Colored Women in 1896. Members focused on education and community work as well as racial issues.

Critical Thinking

Evaluating How do the quotes from Mary Church Terrell show what social issues were important to her?

Women's Clubs

Women found another way to use their talents and energy in women's clubs. The number of women's clubs increased rapidly. At first the clubs focused on cultural activities, such as music and painting. Many clubs, however, became more concerned about social problems.

Some clubs refused to admit African Americans. In response, African American women set up their own network of clubs. Clubs such as the Phyllis Wheatley Club of New Orleans set up classes, recreational activities, and social services. In 1896 women from these clubs formed the National Association of Colored Women. Its founder and first president, **Mary Church Terrell,** was an active leader for women's rights. The association founded homes for orphans, established hospitals, and worked for woman suffrage. It fulfilled its motto "Lifting As We Climb."

✔ **Reading Check** **Identifying** Describe the characteristics of the "new woman" of the late 1800s.

The Fight for Suffrage

S ▶ **Main Idea** Women in the United States gained the right to vote in 1920.

History and You Think about how your life might be different if only men were allowed to vote. Read to learn about some suffragists who fought for women's right to vote.

Ratified after the Civil War in 1870, the Fifteenth Amendment gave voting rights to freed men but did not extend them to women. Women were excluded. Some leading abolitionists became **suffragists.** These men and women fought for woman suffrage, or women's right to vote.

Like other reformers, the suffragists formed organizations to promote their cause. Two woman suffrage associations merged in 1890 to form the National American Woman Suffrage Association.

Anna Howard Shaw, a minister and doctor, and Carrie Chapman Catt, an educator and newspaper editor, led the new group.

652 Chapter 21 *The Progressive Era*

Interpreting the Source

Objective:	To learn to interpret a primary source
Focus:	Explain how primary sources can add to what students learn in textbooks.
Teach:	Have students read Addams's description and answer the questions.
Assess:	Use the Answer Key, and discuss incorrect answers.
Close:	Discuss what Addams learned about child labor through observation.

Differentiated Instruction Strategies

BL Ask students to identify unfamiliar words in the passage and find their definitions.

AL Ask students to summarize the primary source as if they were writing an entry on child labor for an encyclopedia.

ELL Have students write sentences using the words in the Reader's Dictionary.

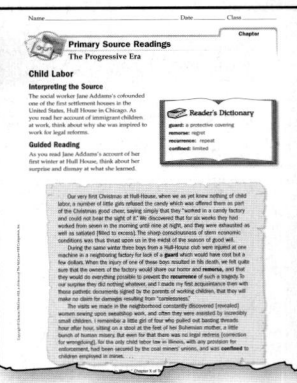

Primary Source Reading Activity, URB p. 21

By 1917, the National American Woman Suffrage Association had more than 2 million members. In a speech to the association in 1902, Catt said:

PRIMARY SOURCE

"The whole aim of the [women's] movement has been to destroy the idea that obedience is necessary to women . . . and to train men to such comprehension of equity [fairness] they would not exact [demand] it."
—quoted in The American Reader

Opposition to Woman Suffrage

Groups protested the idea of giving women the vote. Some women, as well as men, supported these groups. They claimed that woman suffrage would upset society's "natural" balance and lead to divorce and neglect of children. As the progressive movement gained momentum, however, many middle-class women concluded that they needed the vote to promote the reforms they favored. Many working-class women also wanted the vote to pass labor laws protecting women. The suffrage movement also gained strength when respected people such as Jane Addams spoke out in support of the vote for women.

As the movement grew, women began lobbying lawmakers, organizing marches, and delivering speeches on street corners. On March 3, 1913, the day before President Woodrow Wilson's inauguration, suffragists marched on Washington, D.C. **W**

The suffragists won their early victories in the West. First as a territory and then as a state, Wyoming led the nation in giving women the vote. Between 1910 and 1913, five other states adopted woman suffrage. By 1919, women could vote in at least some elections in most of the 48 states. **S**

Continuing the Fight

Meanwhile, suffragists continued their struggle to win the vote everywhere. Alice Paul, a Quaker social worker, founded the National Woman's Party in 1916. She sought greater economic and legal equality, as well as suffrage, for women.

In 1917 Alice Paul met with President Woodrow Wilson but failed to win his support for woman suffrage. In response, Paul led women protesters in front of the White House. They were arrested for blocking the sidewalk. **D**

W ## Writing Support

Persuasive Writing Have students write a speech that a suffragist might have given in a public park in your town in 1919. Remind them that both men and women were suffragists and that the speech would have varied somewhat depending on geographic location. **OL**

S ## Skill Practice

Using Geography Skills As a class, discuss what the map at the bottom of the page shows about nationwide trends in woman suffrage. (*It shows that voting rights for women were geographically distributed, with the West the most progressive and the East the least.*) **BL**

D ## Differentiated Instruction

Auditory/Musical Ask students to write a song or chant that Paul's women protest group might have sung at the White House in 1917. Tell them to include their goals and persuasive reasons they are important. **OL**

Voting Rights for Women, 1919

Map Skills Answer
Answers will vary by state.

Voting Rights for Women, 1919   NATIONAL GEOGRAPHIC

Equal suffrage, date effective
Partial suffrage
No statewide suffrage

CANADA

Wash. 1910
Ore. 1912
Idaho 1896
Mont. 1914
N. Dak.
Minn.
Wyo. 1869
S. Dak. 1918
Wis.
Mich. 1918
N.Y. 1917
Vt. Maine
N.H. Mass. R.I.
Nev. 1914
Utah 1870
Colo. 1893
Nebr.
Iowa
Ill. Ind. Ohio
Pa.
Conn. N.J.
Calif. 1911
Kans. 1912
Mo.
Ky.
W. Va. Va.
Del. Md.
Ariz. 1912
N. Mex.
Okla. 1918
Ark.
Tenn.
N.C.
S.C.
ATLANTIC OCEAN
Tex.
Miss. Ala. Ga.
La.
Fla.

PACIFIC OCEAN

130°W
120°W
90°W
80°W
70°W
40°N
30°N

0   400 kilometers
0   400 miles
Albers Equal-Area projection

MEXICO
Gulf of Mexico

Map Skills

Place What was the status of woman suffrage in your state by 1919?

Maps In MOtion See StudentWorks™ Plus or glencoe.com.

Leveled Activities

BL **Content Vocabulary Activity, URB p. 17**

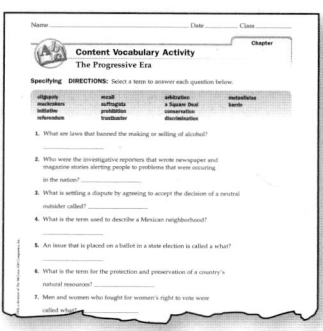

OL **Interpreting Political Cartoons, URB p. 13**

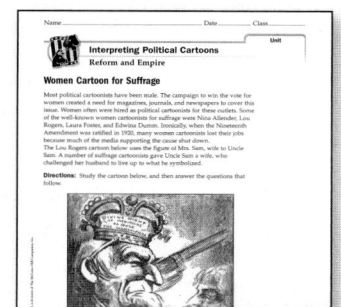

AL **Writing Skills Activity, URB p. 23**

Primary Source / The Woman's Christian Temperance Union

Reading Strategy

Summarizing Have students work in pairs to summarize the text in the subsection "Women and Social Reform." Tell students to include the terms "temperance," "law," "reform," "progressive," and "Prohibition." **OL**

D Differentiated Instruction

Intrapersonal Have students organize into small groups and discuss how people they know or have read about are working to improve the lives of others. Then instruct them to write a paragraph that summarizes various ways individuals can get together and make social change possible. **BL**

Primary Source

Critical Thinking Answer
Students should support their opinions and include examples.

Reading Check **Answer:** Opponents felt women's suffrage was unnatural and would lead to divorce and child neglect.

Hands-On Chapter Project
Step 2

Creating a Reform Campaign

Step 2: Learning More About the Need for Reform Students will continue to research the reform they chose and analyze why it was needed.

Primary Source / The Woman's Christian Temperance Union

Campaigning Against Alcohol The Woman's Christian Temperance Union (WCTU), founded in 1874, became the largest and most powerful women's organization in the country. To promote temperance, the WCTU used education on the dangers of alcohol.

Frances Willard, president of the WCTU, believed in the motto "Do Everything." She thought all social problems were connected and activists should embrace many social reforms. ▶

◀ The WCTU was founded after the successful Women's Crusade of the winter of 1873–1874. During the Crusade, women demonstrated outside saloons, praying and singing hymns.

The WCTU joined with the Anti-Saloon League to push through the Eighteenth Amendment in 1919. The amendment outlawed making and selling alcohol. ▼

Critical Thinking

Drawing Conclusions Do you agree with Frances Willard that all social problems are connected? Explain.

After their arrest, the women started a much-publicized hunger strike. Alva Belmont, one of the protesters, proudly said that all the women did was stand there "quietly, peacefully, lawfully, and gloriously."

Women Vote Nationally

By 1917, the national tide was turning in favor of woman suffrage. New York and, a year later, South Dakota and Oklahoma, granted equal suffrage. As more states granted women the right to vote, Congress debated the issue.

In 1918 the House of Representatives passed a woman suffrage amendment. The next year, the Senate also passed the amendment. After three-fourths of the states had ratified it, the Nineteenth Amendment went into effect in 1920. The amendment came in time for women to vote in that year's presidential election. For the first time, American women could take part in the election of their leaders on a national level.

Reading Check **Explaining** Why were some groups against giving women the right to vote?

Do activity "B"

R Women and Social Reform

Main Idea Women were active in many social reform efforts to improve the lives of others.

History and You Do you know anyone who has worked hard for a cause? Read to learn how women worked for reforms to help improve life for themselves and others.

During the Progressive Era, women became involved in many reform movements in addition to woman suffrage.

Working for a Better Life

Many middle-class women worked to improve the lives of others. They helped working-class people, immigrants, and society as a whole. The women supported and staffed libraries, schools, and settlement houses. They also raised money for various charities.

Some women worked for other causes. They sponsored laws to regulate the labor of both women and children and to require the regular inspection of workplaces by the government.

Essential Question: How did reforms affect the lives of women and other groups in the late 1800s?

Directions Instruct student groups to keep notes as they read about how progressives worked for their reform. Ask them to assess the following: What would your life have been like without this reform? What specific changes were needed to improve your life and the lives of others?

Analyzing Ask students how their lives would change if this reform were successfully enacted.

(Chapter Project continued in Section 3)

Their pressure on Congress helped create the Children's Bureau in the Labor Department. Women also worked for reforms in the food and medicine industries. They pressured state legislatures to provide pensions for widows and for abandoned mothers with children.

Working women also were active in the reform movement. In 1903 the Women's Trade Union League (WTUL) was formed. The WTUL urged working women to form labor unions. It also supported laws to protect the rights of women factory workers. WTUL members raised money to help striking workers pay bail for women who were arrested for striking.

The Temperance Crusade

The crusade against alcohol was led by the Woman's Christian Temperance Union (WCTU), founded in 1874, and the Anti-Saloon League, set up 20 years later. They called for temperance, urging individuals to stop drinking. They also supported **prohibition**—laws that would ban making or selling alcohol.

In 1879 **Frances Willard** became head of the WCTU. Willard educated the public about the dangers of alcohol abuse. The WCTU's goal was prohibition, but it also supported other causes, including prison reform, woman suffrage, improved working conditions, and world peace. Through state WCTU chapters, women combined their role as guardians of the home with social activism.

Carry Nation was a colorful crusader for temperance in the early 1900s. During her protests, she would enter saloons and destroy the bottles and kegs of alcohol there with an ax.

Progressive reformers also wanted to ban alcohol for social reasons. Other Americans opposed alcohol for moral reasons. In response, Congress in 1917 passed a constitutional amendment declaring it illegal to make, transport, or sell alcohol in the United States. The Eighteenth Amendment, known as the Prohibition Law, was ratified in 1919.

Reading Check **Describing** What was the goal of the temperance movement?

Section 2 Review

History ONLINE
Study Central™ To review this section, go to glencoe.com.

Vocabulary

1. Use complete sentences to define the following terms: professional, intelligence, suffragist, prohibition.

Main Ideas

2. **Summarizing** In what ways did middle-class women's roles change near the end of the 1800s?

3. **Explaining** Why was 1920 a good year for the passage of the Nineteenth Amendment?

4. **Identifying** In what ways did reformers try to improve the lives of working women?

Critical Thinking

5. **Drawing Conclusions** Why was gaining the right to vote important to women?

6. **Creative Writing** Write a dialogue between a man and a woman before 1920 in which they discuss whether women should be allowed to vote for the president.

7. **Sequencing** Complete a time line like the one below to show important steps in woman suffrage.

1890   1896   1916 1920

Answer the
8. **Essential Question**
How did reforms affect the lives of women and other groups in the late 1800s?

The Progressive Era **Chapter 21** **655**

W Writing Support

Personal Writing Have students choose a progressive reform described in the text that they feel is similar to a problem today. Ask them to write a short essay. The first paragraph should summarize the social problem; the second paragraph, possible solutions; and the third paragraph, ways in which students could help solve the problem. **OL**

Reading Check **Answer:** The goal of the temperance movement was prohibition and laws that banned the making and selling of alcohol.

Assess

History ONLINE

Study Central™ provides summaries, interactive games, and online graphic organizers to help students review content.

Close

Categorizing Have students identify one social reform and paraphrase the information given about it in the text. **OL**

Section 2 Review

Answers

1. Students should use vocabulary words as they are defined in the section and Glossary.
2. Women's lives moved to the public arena. More women achieved higher education, entered professional careers, and joined the urban reform movement.
3. 1920 was a presidential election year. The amendment allowed women to vote, so their first vote was in a national election.
4. Reformers sponsored laws to improve working conditions and protect the rights

of women factory workers. Reformers also helped striking workers.
5. more control over their lives, a voice in government, equality, protection under the law, and a greater ability to promote reforms
6. Students will write a dialogue.
7. **1890:** Formation of National American Woman Suffrage Association; **1896:** Formation of National Association of Colored Women; **1916:** Foundation by Alice Paul

of National Woman's Party; **1920:** Nineteenth Amendment
8. Women became more educated and entered more job fields. Reforms led to settlement houses, hospitals, and charities to help the poor. Reformers pushed for equality and rights for African Americans. Thus, reforms helped immigrants, children, African Americans, and the poor, as well as women.

Section 3

Progressive Presidents

Focus

Reading Guide

Answers to Graphic:
Roosevelt: balanced business interests and conservation; wanted lower tariffs
Taft: favored business over conservation; did not lower tariffs **Similarities:** favored business regulation, antitrust activities

Section Spotlight Video

Have students watch the Section Spotlight Video "Progressive Presidents" to learn about early efforts to preserve the American wilderness.

Essential Question
Why were Theodore Roosevelt and William Howard Taft known as progressive presidents?

Reading Guide

Content Vocabulary

trustbuster (p. 657)   Square Deal (p. 658)
arbitration (p. 658)   conservation (p. 659)

Academic Vocabulary

inspect (p. 658)   primary (p. 660)

Key People and Events
Federal Reserve Act (p. 661)
Clayton Antitrust Act (p. 661)

Reading Strategy
Taking Notes As you read, use a diagram like the one below to identify how the beliefs of Theodore Roosevelt were similar to but different from William Howard Taft's.

Roosevelt   Taft

ILLINOIS STANDARDS
The American Journey

15.E.3a Identify the types of taxes levied by differing levels of governments (e.g., income tax, sales tax, property tax).

16.C.3c (US) Describe how economic developments and government policies after 1865 affected the country's economic institutions including corporations, banks and organized labor.

16.E.3c Describe the impact of urbanization and suburbanization, 1850-present, on the environment.

American Diary

Progressive reformers wanted to protect America's wilderness and environment. President Theodore Roosevelt was an enthusiastic supporter of their cause. Describing his travels in California in 1903, he wrote: "The first night was clear and we lay down in the darkening aisles of the great sequoia grove. The majestic trunks, beautiful in symmetry [proportion], rose round us like the pillars of a mightier cathedral than ever was conceived."

—*quoted in* Roosevelt the Explorer

Theodore Roosevelt riding at a western ranch

Resource Manager

R Reading Strategies	C Critical Thinking	D Differentiated Instruction	W Writing Support	S Skill Practice
Teacher Edition • Questioning, p. 657 • Taking Notes, p. 660 • Identifying, p. 661 **Additional Resources** • Guid. Read., URB p. 41 • Content Vocab., URB p. 17 • Academic Vocab., URB p. 19 • Read. Ess., p. 229 • Am. Lit. Read., URB p. 9	**Teacher Edition** • Compar. & Contrast., p. 658 • Analyzing Info., p. 660 **Additional Resources** • Quiz. & Tests, p. 205 • Citizen. & Dec. Mak. Skills, URB p. 3 • Crit. Think., URB p. 29 • Link. Past & Pres., URB p. 33	**Teacher Edition** • ELL, p. 658 • Naturalist, p. 659 **Additional Resources** • School-to-Home, URB p. 35 • Reteaching Act., URB p. 37	**Teacher Edition** • Narrative Writ., p. 658 • Persuasive Writ., p. 661	**Teacher Edition** • Using Chart Skills, p. 657 **Additional Resources** • Daily Test Pract. Transp. 21-3 • Time Line Skills, URB p. 34 • Lesson Transp. 21A

Theodore Roosevelt

Main Idea Theodore Roosevelt believed that businesses must be regulated.

History and You Are there powerful businesses in your community? Read to learn how big business was regulated when Theodore Roosevelt was president.

Theodore Roosevelt won the Republican vice presidential nomination in 1900. Mark Hanna, the Republican leader, called Roosevelt "that cowboy" and warned that only one life would stand between Roosevelt and the White House. When the Republicans won, Hanna told President McKinley, "Now it is up to you to live." Less than one year later, McKinley was assassinated. Suddenly 42-year-old Theodore Roosevelt became president. He was the youngest president in the nation's history. When Roosevelt moved into the White House in 1901, he brought progressive ideas with him.

The "Trustbuster"

President McKinley favored big business. President Roosevelt, in contrast, supported the regulation of business and other progressive reforms. During his term, Roosevelt tackled certain trusts that violated the Sherman Antitrust Act.

His first target was the Northern Securities Company. This railroad monopoly fought the accusations of illegal activity all the way to the Supreme Court. In 1904 the Supreme Court decided that Northern Securities had illegally limited trade. The Court ordered that the trust be taken apart.

During the rest of Roosevelt's term, he obtained indictments, or legal charges, against trusts in the beef, oil, and tobacco industries. Although called a **trustbuster**, Roosevelt did not want to break up all trusts. He thought trusts should be regulated, not destroyed. He grouped trusts into "good" and "bad" ones. Good trusts, he believed, were concerned with public welfare, but bad trusts were not.

Labor Crisis

In 1902 Roosevelt faced a major labor crisis. More than 100,000 Pennsylvania coal miners, members of the United Mine Workers, went on strike. They demanded better pay, an eight-hour workday, and recognition of the union's right to represent its members in discussions with mine owners.

By the Numbers | **Protecting America's Wilds**

Theodore Roosevelt is said to have remarked that "birds in the trees and on the beaches were much more beautiful than on women's hats."
—from *Theodore Roosevelt: The Naturalist*

Setting Aside American Lands While he was president, Roosevelt used his authority to create a number of parks, preserves, and monuments to protect birds, wildlife, and millions of acres of American land.

Lands Protected Under Theodore Roosevelt	
4	Federal Game Preserves
5	National Parks
18	National Monuments
51	Federal Bird Preserves
150	National Forests

Critical Thinking

Speculating What might happen if the federal government did not protect natural resources and wildlife?

Teach

R Reading Strategy

Questioning Have students write one question based on each heading within this subsection. **OL**

S Skill Practice

Using Chart Skills Explain that President Roosevelt pursued conservation of the American wilderness. Have students use the chart at the bottom of the page to create a bar graph showing what kinds of land Roosevelt protected. Then ask them to make up two questions about their chart and provide the answers. **OL**

By the Numbers

Critical Thinking Answer
Students might respond that business interests and free enterprise might destroy the nation's natural resources and wildlife habitat because development would be more profitable in the short run.

Differentiated Instruction

Learning About Labor Unions

American Literature Reading, URB p. 9

Objective:	To interpret a fictional account of a union member
Focus:	Discuss the conditions of mine workers in the late 1800s.
Teach:	Have students read the passage and answer the questions.
Assess:	Assess the answers using the Answer Key, and discuss incorrect answers.
Close:	Ask students what they learned about union members from the reading.

Differentiated Instruction Strategies

BL Have students indicate the speaker for each line of dialogue in the passage.

AL Have students write a dialogue that might have occurred between BB and Owen the day *before* the convention met.

ELL Have students create a glossary of unfamiliar terms in the passage.

Differentiated Instruction

W Writing Support

Narrative Writing Have students imagine they are at the White House meeting between the coal miners and the mine owners. Instruct them to write a one-act play that shows the interactions among the president, miners, and owners. **OL**

D Differentiated Instruction

English Language Learners Ask: Why did President Roosevelt use the term "square" to describe his policies? (*The dictionary defines "square" not only as a shape but also as meaning "just" or "fair." President Roosevelt called his platform the Square Deal to emphasize that he would treat everyone fairly and equally.*) **ELL**

C Critical Thinking

Comparing and Contrasting Ask: Is the economic system in America today closer to Jefferson's laissez-faire approach or to Roosevelt's Square Deal? Have students write a paragraph in which they defend the answer to this question. (*Students will probably assert that we are closer to Roosevelt's policies because the government regulates many aspects of business.*) **AL**

The mine owners refused to negotiate with the workers. The coal strike dragged on for months. As winter approached, coal supplies dwindled. Public feeling began to turn against the owners. As public pressure mounted, Roosevelt invited representatives of the owners and miners to a meeting at the White House. He was angry when the owners refused to negotiate. Roosevelt threatened to send federal troops to work in the mines and produce the coal. The owners finally agreed to **arbitration**—settling the dispute by agreeing to accept the decision of a neutral outsider. Mine workers won a pay increase and a reduction in hours, but they did not gain recognition for their union.

Roosevelt's action marked a departure from normal patterns of labor relations at the time. Earlier presidents used troops against strikers. In contrast, Roosevelt used the government's power to force the company owners to negotiate. In other labor actions, however, Roosevelt supported employers in disputes with workers.

Square Deal

Roosevelt ran for president in 1904. He promised the people a **Square Deal**—fair and equal treatment for all. He easily won the election with more than 57 percent of the popular vote.

Roosevelt's Square Deal called for the government regulation of business. This attitude toward business differed from the presidency of Thomas Jefferson. That approach was called laissez-faire (LEH•say FEHR). This French term generally means "let people do as they choose." In economics, it refers to an economic policy in which there is little government involvement in the affairs of businesses.

Roosevelt introduced a new era of government regulation. He supported the Meat Inspection Act and the Pure Food and Drug Act. These acts gave the Department of Agriculture and the Food and Drug Administration the power to visit businesses and **inspect**, or carefully examine, the products that were produced there.

LINKING PAST TO PRESENT — Conserving Wild Places

THEN By the mid-1800s, Americans began to view wild places as more than obstacles to overcome or resources to use. The nation began setting aside areas of natural beauty for future generations. President Theodore Roosevelt greatly expanded the system of national parks and forests.

The conservation movement began partly as a response to uncontrolled logging. Roosevelt understood, though, that the nation also needed to use its resources: "Conservation means development as much as it does protection." ▼

"There are no words that can tell the hidden spirit of the wilderness, that can reveal its mystery . . . and its charm."
—Theodore Roosevelt

◄ Visitors enjoying Yosemite National Park, 1920

Leveled Activities

BL Reading Essentials and Note-Taking Guide, p. 229

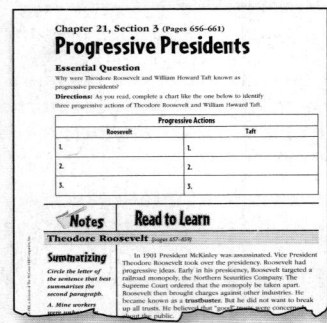

OL Linking Past and Present Activity, URB p. 33

AL Citizenship and Decision-Making Skills Activity, URB p. 3

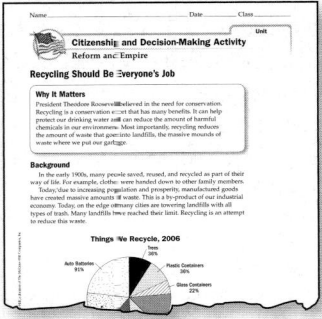

Conserving the Wilderness

Roosevelt had a lifelong enthusiasm for the great outdoors and the wilderness. He strongly believed in the need for **conservation,** the protection and preservation of the country's natural resources.

As president, Roosevelt took steps to conserve the country's forests, mineral deposits, and water resources. In 1905 he proposed the U.S. Forest Service. He pressured Congress to set aside millions of acres of national forests to create the nation's first wildlife sanctuaries. Roosevelt also formed the National Conservation Commission, which produced the first survey of the country's natural resources.

Roosevelt has been called America's first environmental president. He made conservation an important public issue. Roosevelt, however, also saw the need for economic growth and development. He tried to balance business interests with conservation.

Reading Check **Describing** What was Roosevelt's approach to labor relations?

William Howard Taft

Main Idea Conflict between Roosevelt and Taft led to Woodrow Wilson's election as president.

History and You Has a friend ever disappointed you by an action he or she has taken? Read to learn about the conflict between Theodore Roosevelt and William Howard Taft.

. . . .

No president had ever served more than two terms. In keeping with that tradition, Roosevelt decided not to run for reelection in 1908. Instead he chose William Howard Taft to run for president. Taft easily defeated Democrat William Jennings Bryan.

Taft lacked Roosevelt's flair. Still, he carried out—and went beyond—many of Roosevelt's policies. The Taft administration won more antitrust cases in four years than Roosevelt won in seven. Taft also favored safety standards for mines and railroads.

Taft supported the Sixteenth Amendment. It allowed Congress to tax citizens' incomes to collect money for the federal government.

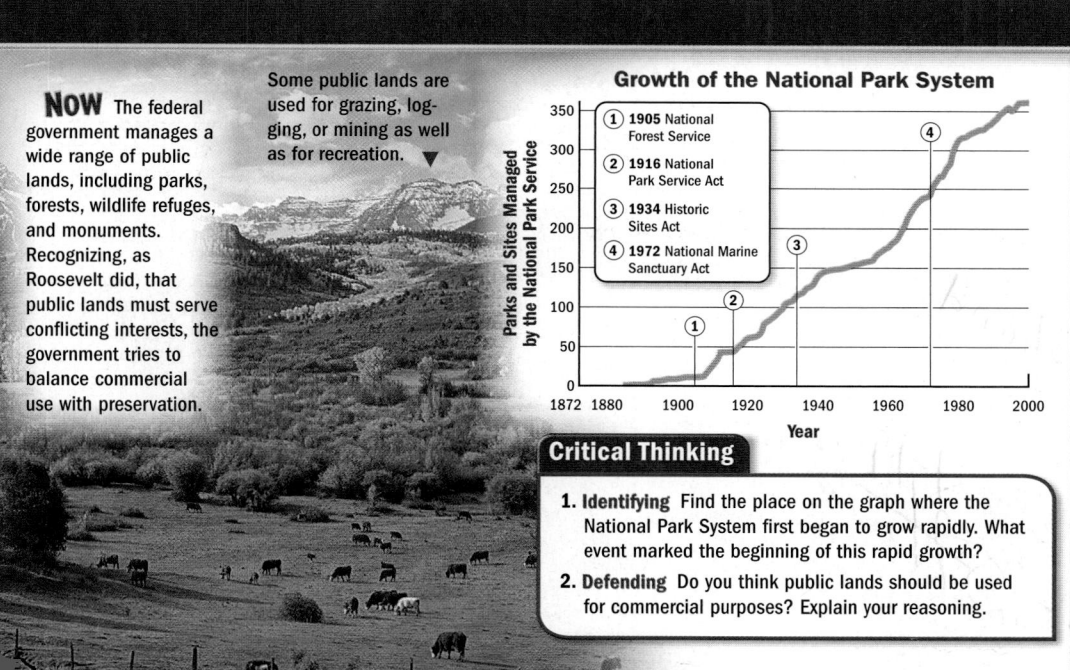

NOW The federal government manages a wide range of public lands, including parks, forests, wildlife refuges, and monuments. Recognizing, as Roosevelt did, that public lands must serve conflicting interests, the government tries to balance commercial use with preservation.

Some public lands are used for grazing, logging, or mining as well as for recreation. ▼

Growth of the National Park System

① **1905** National Forest Service
② **1916** National Park Service Act
③ **1934** Historic Sites Act
④ **1972** National Marine Sanctuary Act

Parks and Sites Managed by the National Park Service (y-axis: 0, 50, 100, 150, 200, 250, 300, 350)

Year (x-axis: 1872 1880, 1900, 1920, 1940, 1960, 1980, 2000)

Critical Thinking

1. **Identifying** Find the place on the graph where the National Park System first began to grow rapidly. What event marked the beginning of this rapid growth?

2. **Defending** Do you think public lands should be used for commercial purposes? Explain your reasoning.

Activity: Fast Facts

A President and the Teddy Bear
Ask: How does the story of the teddy bear reflect Theodore Roosevelt's love of nature? President Theodore "Teddy" Roosevelt was a student of nature and a proponent of wilderness conservation. Therefore, it should have been no surprise when the president refused to shoot for sport a bear that had been injured by the hunting dogs and tied up to make the hunt easier. Clifford Berryman, a political cartoonist, publicized this story in a cartoon showing Roosevelt halting a hunt with an outstretched arm while a guide holds a bear on a leash. Berryman then began to include cute bear cubs in his cartoons about the president.

Stuffed bears were not common at that time, but a Brooklyn shopkeeper had an idea. He took stuffed bears sewn by his wife and named them "Teddy" in honor of the president. The toys sold well, and their popularity has continued to this day. **BL**

R Reading Strategy

Taking Notes Ask pairs of students to create a two-column chart labeled "Roosevelt" and "Taft." Tell students that they will use the chart to take notes as they read the subsection. Remind them to write important words or phrases rather than complete sentences directly from the text. **OL**

C Critical Thinking

Analyzing Information Ask: Which candidate would you have voted for in the 1912 presidential election? Have students write paragraphs to support their answers. **OL**

Economics & History

Critical Thinking Answer
$20; $40

Skills Practice Ask: How many years ago did U.S. workers begin to pay income taxes? To arrive at their answers, students will subtract 1862 from the current year. **OL**

2011 - 149 yrs.

Progressives believed income taxes to be fairer and hoped the taxes would allow the government to lower tariffs and relieve the hardship of the poor. The Sixteenth Amendment, added to the Constitution in 1913, did not state how income would be taxed. Congress passed further laws so that higher incomes were taxed at a higher rate than lower incomes.

Taft made progressive reforms. Yet he disappointed many progressives such as Theodore Roosevelt. The two important areas where progressives believed Taft was weak were tariffs and conservation. Taft failed to fight for a lower tariff, and he altered a number of conservation policies so that they favored businesses.

Roosevelt Challenges Taft

By 1912, Roosevelt had become disappointed in Taft. Claiming that Taft "completely twisted around" his own policies, Roosevelt decided to challenge Taft for the Republican presidential nomination.

The showdown between Roosevelt and Taft came at the Republican national convention in Chicago in June. Roosevelt had won every **primary**—an election in which a political party chooses its candidates—and had many supporters. Taft, however, had the backing of party leaders. Taft also had the support of business interests that controlled the party machinery. Taft was nominated on the first ballot.

Roosevelt charged the Republican Party leaders with stealing the nomination from him. He led his supporters out of the convention hall. They formed a new party, the Progressive Party. In August the Progressives held their own convention in Chicago and nominated Roosevelt for president.

A reporter asked Roosevelt about his health. The candidate thumped himself on the chest and declared, 'I feel as strong as a bull moose!' From then on, the Progressive Party was known as the Bull Moose Party.

Economics & History

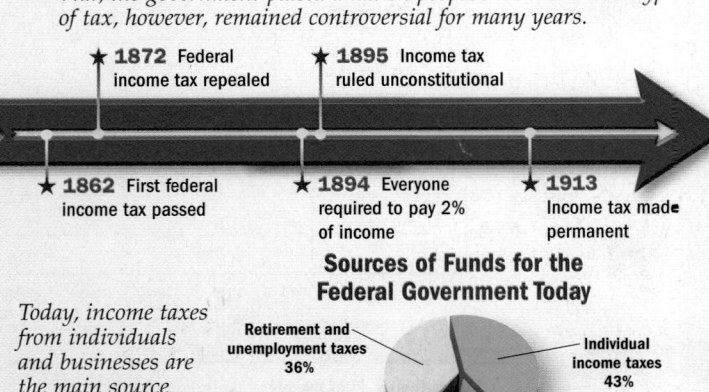

Before the Civil War, the federal government received most of its funds from tariffs, or taxes on imported goods. During the Civil War, the government placed a tax on people's incomes. This type of tax, however, remained controversial for many years.

★ **1872** Federal income tax repealed

★ **1895** Income tax ruled unconstitutional

★ **1862** First federal income tax passed

★ **1894** Everyone required to pay 2% of income

★ **1913** Income tax made permanent

Federal Income Taxes

1864	Earnings	Tax Rate
	$600–$5,000	5%
	over $10,000	10%

1894	Earnings	Tax Rate
	all	2%

Income taxes today are progressive—rates are based on ability to pay. People who earn more pay a larger percentage of their income in taxes than do people who earn less.

Sources of Funds for the Federal Government Today

Today, income taxes from individuals and businesses are the main source of funds for the federal government.

- Retirement and unemployment taxes 36%
- Borrowing 1%
- Other taxes 7%
- Individual income taxes 43%
- Business income taxes 13%

Source: Internal Revenue Service

Critical Thinking

Calculating Suppose you earned $1,000 in 1894. How much income tax would you pay? Your friend earned $2,000. How much tax would he or she pay?

Hands-On Chapter Project
Step 3

CONSERVE OUR FORESTS

Creating a Reform Campaign

Step 3: Planning a Peaceful Demonstration Students will plan a peaceful demonstration to publicize their reform ideas and motivate others to join the cause.

Essential Question: Why were Theodore Roosevelt and William Howard Taft known as progressive presidents?

Directions Have each group plan a peaceful demonstration to let others know about its progressive cause. Tell each group to make posters that the demonstrators can hold and create chants to let others know about their proposed reforms. Stress the need to make clear, concise points when delivering their message.

Theorizing Have each group discuss how Presidents Roosevelt and Taft might have reacted to these reform proposals.

(Chapter Project continued in Section 4)

The Election of 1912

The split in the Republican Party hurt both Taft and Roosevelt. While Republicans and the Progressive Party battled at the polls, Democrat Woodrow Wilson, a progressive reformer and former governor of New Jersey, gathered enough support to win the election. Wilson received only 42 percent of the popular vote. Roosevelt received 27 percent, and Taft got 23 percent. Wilson, though, won the presidency by the largest electoral majority up to that time. He swept 435 of the 531 electoral votes.

Wilson in the White House

Woodrow Wilson had criticized big government, as well as big business, during his campaign. He called his program the "New Freedom."

In 1913 Wilson achieved a long-held progressive goal—tariff reform. He persuaded the Democrat-controlled Congress to adopt a **W** lower tariff on imports. Wilson believed that foreign competition would force American manufacturers to improve their products and lower their prices. The government income that was lost by lowering tariffs would be replaced by the new income tax.

That same year Congress passed the **Federal Reserve Act** to regulate banking. The act created 12 regional banks supervised by a central board in Washington, D.C. Banks that operated nationally were required to join the Federal Reserve System and follow the rules established by the Reserve's board.

Wilson also worked to strengthen government control over business. In 1914 Congress established the Federal Trade Commission (FTC). The FTC was to investigate corporations for unfair trade practices. Wilson also supported the **Clayton Antitrust Act** of 1914. This act, like the Sherman Antitrust Act, was one of the government's chief weapons used against trusts. The government also tried to regulate child labor. The Keating-Owen Act of 1916 banned goods produced by child labor from being sold in interstate commerce. This legislation, however, was struck down as unconstitutional two years later.

By the end of Wilson's first term, progressive support was declining. Americans turned to world affairs—especially the war that began in Europe in 1914.

R

✓ **Reading Check** **Analyzing** How did Roosevelt's run for the presidency affect the election of 1912?

History ONLINE
Study Central™ To review this section, go to glencoe.com.

Section 3 Review

Vocabulary

1. Define the following terms in sentences: trustbuster, arbitration, Square Deal, inspect, conservation, primary.

Main Ideas

2. Identifying Cause and Effect How did President Roosevelt's Square Deal affect American businesses?

3. Discussing On what issues did Roosevelt and Taft disagree by 1912?

Critical Thinking

4. Predicting How do you think Roosevelt might have felt about President Wilson's policies?

5. Organizing Use a diagram like the one below to show the legislation that President Roosevelt supported to further regulation and conservation.

Roosevelt's Square Deal

6. Expository Writing Write a paragraph summarizing the progressive reforms made during Woodrow Wilson's presidency.

Answer the
7. Essential Question
Why were Theodore Roosevelt and William Howard Taft known as progressive presidents?

The Progressive Era **Chapter 21** 661

W **Writing Support**

Persuasive Writing Have students write a speech in which the newly elected president Wilson explains to Americans his goals for the country. **OL**

R **Reading Strategy**

Identifying Ask: What is another name for "the war that began in Europe in 1914"? *(World War I)* **BL**

✓ **Reading Check** **Answer:** By running for president, Roosevelt split the Republican vote. Wilson was thus able to win the election.

Assess

History ONLINE

Study Central™ provides summaries, interactive games, and online graphic organizers to help students review content.

Close

Identifying As a class, discuss the progressive reforms initiated by Presidents Roosevelt and Taft. **OL**

Section 3 Review

Answers

1. Students should write sentences in which they define the vocabulary terms.

2. Roosevelt increased government regulation of businesses in an effort to provide fair and equal treatment for all.

3. lowering tariffs and favoring business versus conservation interests

4. Answers will vary but should mention that both men were progressive reformers and favored government regulation of business, lower tariffs, and trust busting.

5. Meat Inspection Act, Pure Food and Drug Act, U.S. Forest Service, Formation of National Conservation Commission

6. Students should base their summaries on information from the readings.

7. Both men were reformers. For example, Roosevelt supported conservation, reining in trusts, and other government regulation of business. Taft oversaw antitrust activity and promoted safer working conditions.

Focus

Excluded From Reform

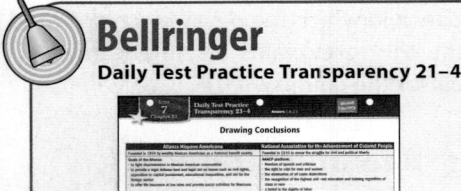

Bellringer
Daily Test Practice Transparency 21–4

Guide to Reading

Answers to Graphic:

Booker T. Washington: Equality and civil rights would come from education, job skills, and economic power.

W.E.B. Du Bois: Equality and civil rights depend on the right to vote.

Section Spotlight Video

Have students watch the Section Spotlight Video "Excluded From Reform" to learn about violence against African Americans.

Essential Question
How did minority groups react to discrimination?

Reading Guide

Content Vocabulary
discrimination (p. 663)
mutualista (p. 668)
barrio (p. 668)

Academic Vocabulary
deny (p. 664)   bias (p. 665)

Key People and Events
Ku Klux Klan (p. 664)
Booker T. Washington (p. 666)
W.E.B. Du Bois (p. 666)

Reading Strategy
Taking Notes As you read, use a diagram like the one below to show how Booker T. Washington and W.E.B. Du Bois differed in their beliefs for achieving equality.

	Beliefs
Booker T. Washington	
W.E.B. Du Bois	

ILLINOIS STANDARDS
The American Journey

14.D.3 Describe roles and influences of individuals, groups and media in shaping current Illinois and United States public policy (e.g., general public opinion, special interest groups, formal parties, media).

18.C.3a Describe ways in which a diverse U.S. population has developed and maintained common beliefs (e.g., life, liberty and the pursuit of happiness; the Constitution and the Bill of Rights).

18.C.3b Explain how diverse groups have contributed to U.S. social systems over time.

American Diary

Many people, such as African Americans, did not enjoy the benefits of progressive reforms. W.E.B. Du Bois spoke forcefully for equality for African Americans: "Freedom . . . we still seek,—the freedom of life and limb, the freedom to work and think, the freedom to love and aspire. Work, culture, liberty,— all these we need, not singly but together, . . . all striving toward that vaster ideal . . . the ideal of human brotherhood, gained through the unifying ideal of Race."

—from The Souls of Black Folk

Students at the Hampton Institute, Hampton, Virginia, 1899

662

Resource Manager

R Reading Strategies	**C** Critical Thinking	**D** Differentiated Instruction	**W** Writing Support	**S** Skill Practice
Teacher Edition • Previewing, p. 663 • Identifying, p. 665 • Identifying, p. 666 **Additional Resources** • Guid. Read., URB p. 42 • Content Vocab., URB p. 17 • Academic Vocab., URB p. 19 • Read. Ess., p. 232	**Teacher Edition** • Deter. Cause & Effect, p. 664 • Compar. & Contrast., p. 666 • Making Infer., p. 667 **Additional Resources** • Quizzes and Tests, p. 206	**Teacher Edition** • Special Ed., p. 663 • Gifted & Talent., p. 664 **Additional Resources** • School-to-Home, URB p. 35 • Reteaching Act., URB p. 37	**Teacher Edition** • Personal Writ., p. 664 • Persuasive Writ., p. 666 • Expository Writ., p. 668	**Teacher Edition** • Using Chart Skills, p. 665 • Read. a Time Line, p. 667 **Additional Resources** • Daily Test Pract. Transp. 21-4 • Soc. Stud., URB p. 25 • Geo. & Hist., URB p. 31 • Lesson Transp. 21C

Prejudice and Discrimination R

Main Idea Many members of ethnic and religious minority groups in the United States faced discrimination and even violence.

History and You How would you feel if, after moving to a new land and hoping to start a new life, you were told that you could go only to certain schools or hold certain low-paying jobs? Read to learn about the challenges that some immigrants faced.

During the 1800s, the majority of Americans were white Protestants who were born in the United States. Many believed that the United States should remain a white Protestant nation. Nonwhite, non-Protestant, and non-native residents often faced **discrimination.** People who face discrimination receive unequal treatment because of their race, religion, ethnic background, or place of birth. The government rarely addressed discrimination in the late 1880s.

Anti-Catholicism

Some Americans faced discrimination because of their religion. America's largely Protestant population feared that Catholic immigrants threatened the "American" way of life. Anti-Catholic Iowans formed the American Protective Association (APA) in 1887. Its members vowed not to hire or to vote for Catholics.

By the mid-1890s, the APA claimed to have 2 million members across the nation. Among other activities, the APA spread false rumors that Catholics were making plans to take over the country.

Anti-Semitism

Many Jewish immigrants came to the United States to escape discrimination in their homelands but found the same anti-Semitic, or anti-Jewish, attitudes in America. Landlords, employers, and even schools discriminated against Jews.

Eastern European Jews faced even more discrimination because they were Jewish and from eastern Europe. Many Americans regarded eastern Europeans as more "foreign" than western Europeans because their languages, customs, and traditions were so different than those of earlier immigrants.

Primary Source | **Pursuing Reforms**

Denouncing Discrimination In 1909 the National Negro Committee, a group of whites and African Americans, drafted a statement of opposition to discrimination. The Committee declared:

We denounce the ever-growing oppression of our 10,000,000 colored fellow citizens as the greatest menace that threatens the country. . . . We regard with grave concern the attempt . . . to deny black men the right to work and to enforce this demand by violence and bloodshed.

We demand of Congress and the Executive:

(1.) That the Constitution be strictly enforced and the civil rights guaranteed under the Fourteenth Amendment be secured impartially to all.

(2.) That there be equal educational opportunities for all and in all the States, and that public school expenditure be the same for the Negro and white child.

(3.) That in accordance with the Fifteenth Amendment the right of the Negro to the ballot on the same terms as other citizens be recognized in every part of the country.

Critical Thinking

Speculating How might whites and African Americans working together help end discrimination?

Creating a Reform Campaign

Step 4: Advertising the Peaceful Demonstration Students will create brochures or posters to let others know about their upcoming peaceful demonstration.

Essential Question: How did minority groups react to discrimination?

Directions Have each group create a poster or brochure to advertise its cause and the upcoming demonstration. Tell them to discuss what their audience would need to know, including the place, time, problem, reform targets, and proposed reform.

Discussing Ask the groups with causes that involve discrimination to discuss what methods they might have used to fight for equality.

(Chapter Project continued on the Visual Summary page)

Primary Source / Discrimination and Prejudice

New Immigrants In the late 1800s, the character of immigration changed. Most "new" immigrants who entered the United States after 1880 were from southern and eastern Europe rather than from England, Ireland, and Germany. The new immigrants changed the ethnic makeup of the nation.

▲ Prejudice against Catholic immigrants is presented in this cartoon, which shows a bishop forcing children to attend a Catholic school, rather than a public school.

◄ Some Americans urged the government to turn back the new wave of immigrants, fearing that the newcomers were criminals or of lower moral character.

Anti-Asian Policies

W Discrimination also was based on race. In California and other Western states, Asians faced prejudice and resentment. White Americans claimed that Chinese immigrants, who worked for lower wages, took jobs away from them. Congress passed the Chinese Exclusion Act in 1882 to prevent Chinese immigrants from coming to the United States.

C America's westward expansion created opportunities for thousands of Japanese immigrants. Many came to the United States to work on railroads or farms. Like the Chinese before them, Japanese immigrants met with prejudice. California would not allow them to become citizens and made it illegal for them to buy land. Other Western states passed similar laws.

President Theodore Roosevelt yielded to a rising tide of anti-Japanese feeling. He authorized the Gentlemen's Agreement with Japan in 1907. This accord restricted Japanese immigration to the United States, but it did not bring an end to anti-Japanese feeling.

Discrimination Against African Americans

African Americans faced discrimination in the North and the South. Although officially free, African Americans were continually **denied,** or refused, the basic rights held by white citizens.

Four-fifths of the nation's African Americans lived in the South. Most worked as rural sharecroppers or in low-paying jobs in the cities. African Americans were separated from white society. They had their own neighborhoods, schools, parks, restaurants, theaters, and even cemeteries. In 1896 the Supreme Court legalized segregation in the case of *Plessy* v. *Ferguson*. This case recognized "separate but equal" facilities for blacks and whites.

D The **Ku Klux Klan,** which terrorized African Americans during Reconstruction, was reborn in Georgia in 1915. The new Klan wanted to restore white, Protestant America. The Klan lashed out against minorities, including Catholics, Jews, and immigrants, as well as African Americans.

664 **Chapter 21** *The Progressive Era*

Activity: Collaborative Learning

Making Connections Ask: How would you feel if you were treated differently than your classmates because of an irrelevant difference, and how might you react? Have students form small groups. Each group will write a play in which they will depict what it feels like to be the victim of discriminatory policies. Tell students that the basic premise of their play will be a classroom in which the teacher has asked students wearing blue to sit on one side and students not wearing blue to sit on the other side. The teacher then treats each side differently based on the color of their clothing. Instruct students to include in the play topics such as how the treatment differs, how the students react to the treatment, and what they do to try to end the discrimination. **OL**

Rebirth of the Ku Klux Klan The Ku Klux Klan (KKK) underwent a resurgence in the early 1900s following the release of D.W. Griffith's 1915 movie *The Birth of a Nation*, which presented a romantic vision of the KKK. Following a brief growth spurt, in which membership climbed into the millions, the Klan began to decline in 1924 after a series of scandals involving the group's leadership. Membership shrank and politicians who supported the Klan were voted out of office. The Klan declared bankruptcy and disbanded again in 1944.

KKK Membership	
Year	Members
1915	5,000
1920	100,000
1924	4,000,000
1930	30,000

Ku Klux Klan march in Washington, D.C. ▲

Critical Thinking

Analyzing Why were the late 1800s a time of fear and prejudice in the United States?

Calling for "100 percent Americanism," the number of Klan supporters continued to **S** grow and even spread beyond the South. Many Klan members were from Northern as well as Southern cities and towns.

Racial Violence

Many people lost their jobs during the economic depressions of 1893 and 1907. Frustrated and desperate, they sometimes unleashed their anger against African Americans and other minorities. More than 2,600 African Americans were lynched between 1886 and 1916, mostly in the South. Lynching also was used to terrorize Chinese immigrants in the West.

Progressivism and Prejudice

In the late 1800s and the early 1900s, many Americans held **biased**, or unbalanced, views. They believed that white, male, native-born Americans had the right to make decisions for all of society.

Most of the progressive reformers came from the middle and upper classes. They saw themselves as moral leaders who worked to improve the lives of less fortunate people in their communities and throughout the nation. The reforms they supported, though, often discriminated against one group as they tried to help another group.

Trade unions often did not allow African Americans, women, or immigrants to join. The unions argued that skilled laborers could obtain better working conditions if they did not demand improved conditions for all workers.

Sometimes progressive reforms were really efforts to control a particular group. The temperance movement, for example, was partly an attempt to control the behavior of Irish **R** Catholic immigrants. Civil service reforms required job applicants to be educated. This change reduced the political influence that immigrants, who were largely uneducated, began to achieve in some cities. In spite of their mixed results, though, progressive reforms did improve conditions for many Americans.

prejudiced

Reading Check **Identifying** Which Supreme Court decision legalized segregation?

The Progressive Era **Chapter 21** **665**

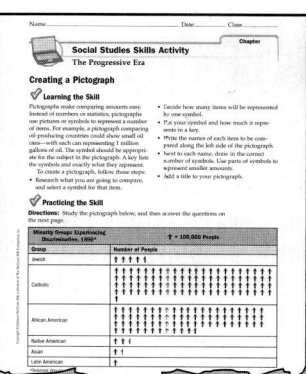

Social Studies Skills Activity, p. 25

665

R Reading Strategy

Identifying Ask: What did the Tuskegee Institute teach? *(farming and industrial skills)* **BL**

W Writing Support

Persuasive Writing Discuss the differing views of Washington and Du Bois on how African Americans could best achieve equality. Ask students to determine which plan was more workable and write a paragraph supporting their choice. **OL**

People IN HISTORY

Critical Thinking Answers

1. He believed that African Americans must gain economic power before they could attain social equality or civil rights.

2. W.E.B. Du Bois. Du Bois advocated protest. Also, Washington felt that education was primary and that equality would follow, so he might have believed that segregated schools were better than no schools.

Additional Support

Struggle for Equal Opportunity

Main Idea Minority groups in the United States sought to end discrimination and obtain equal rights.

History and You Have you ever been part of a group that worked for a common cause? Read to find out how some groups fought discrimination.

Minorities were often banned from joining progressive organizations because of prejudice. They had to battle for justice and opportunity on their own. African Americans, Native Americans, and Mexican Americans took steps to form organizations that would work to improve their lives.

+ Jewish Americans

Struggle for Equality

W **R**
African Americans rose to the challenge of achieving equality. Born enslaved, **Booker T. Washington** taught himself to read. In 1881 he founded the Tuskegee Institute. The school taught African Americans farming and industrial skills.

Washington believed African Americans needed more economic power. With such power, they would be better able to demand social equality and civil rights. Washington founded the National Negro Business League. The League wanted to promote business development among African Americans.

In his autobiography, *Up from Slavery,* Washington advised African Americans to patiently work for equality. He argued that African Americans needed education and skills. These would help African Americans become more valuable members of their community and lead to equality.

W.E.B. Du Bois also worked for civil rights. He was the first African American to receive a doctorate degree from Harvard University. As an educator, Du Bois took a different approach than did Booker T. Washington. Du Bois rejected Booker T. Washington's emphasis on job skills and argued that the right to vote was the way to end racial inequality, stop lynching, and gain better schools. "The power of the ballot we need in

People IN HISTORY

Booker T. Washington
African American educator and leader

Washington urged African Americans to work hard for economic security before looking for ways to end discrimination and segregation. In one speech, he said that the opportunity to

"earn a dollar in a factory" was worth much more than the opportunity to "spend a dollar in an opera house."

W.E.B. Du Bois
Sociologist and advocate of civil rights for African Americans

Du Bois believed that African Americans should protest their unequal treatment in American society. An African American, he wrote,

"simply wishes to . . . be both a Negro and an American, without being cursed and spit upon by his fellows, without having the doors of Opportunity closed roughly in his face."

CRITICAL Thinking

1. **Making Inferences** What did Washington mean when he said the opportunity to earn a dollar was worth more than the opportunity to spend one in an opera house?

2. **Synthesizing** Which leader would be more likely to protest having separate schools for African Americans and whites? Explain your answer.

666 **Chapter 21** *The Progressive Era*

Activity: Debating the Issues

Evaluating African American reformers in the Progressive Era disagreed on the best way to end racial discrimination and achieve equality. Booker T. Washington believed that social equality and civil rights would come after economic gains were achieved. W.E.B. Du Bois, in contrast, believed that protesting and attaining the right to vote were keys to civil rights. **Ask:** Would the strategies of Washington and Du Bois help solve today's racial issues? As a class, discuss what kinds of racial inequalities exist today. Have students brainstorm to develop two different strategies to tackle those problems. Then divide into two groups and stage a debate between the two strategies. After the debate, discuss which strategy is more workable in America today. **OL**

sheer self-defense," he said, "else what shall save us from a second slavery?" Du Bois helped start the Niagara Movement in 1905. This movement demanded equal economic and educational opportunity for African Americans and insisted on an end to legalized segregation and discrimination.

Although it never gained great support, the Niagara Movement led to the creation of the National Association for the Advancement of Colored People in 1910. This organization was greatly influential in the fight for African American civil rights throughout the twentieth century.

Some African Americans thought that they would be better off in separate societies. These societies could be located either in the United States or in Africa. To achieve this goal, groups were founded to establish African American towns. A back-to-Africa movement began, but its ideas were not popular. The goals of these movements gained few supporters among African Americans.

African American Women Take Action

African American women also formed groups to end discrimination. The National Association of Colored Women fought lynchings and other forms of racial violence. Ida B. Wells was editor of an African American newspaper in Memphis, Tennessee. She was forced to leave town after publishing the names of people involved in a lynching. Wells started a national crusade against the terrible practice of lynching.

In 1895 Wells published a book, *A Red Record*. She showed that lynching was used mainly against African Americans who became prosperous or who had competed with white businesses. "Can you remain silent and inactive when such things are done in your own community and country?" she asked. Although Congress rejected an antilynching bill, the number of lynchings declined significantly due in great part to the efforts of Wells and other activists.

Carlos Velasco

Founder of the Alianza Hispano-Americo

Velasco, born in Mexico in 1837, was forced to flee across the border to Arizona several times because of his political beliefs. In the 1890s, he began publishing *El Fronterizo*, a daily newspaper that fought discrimination and mistreatment of Mexicans in the United States. In 1894 he founded the Alianza Hispano-Americo and served as its first president.

Zitkala-Sa (Red Bird), also known as Gertrude Bonnin

Native American activist

Zitkala-Sa served as the secretary of the Society of American Indians. She wanted to preserve Native American culture, and she came to believe that Indian schools run by whites threatened that culture. Of those schools, she wrote, *"few [whites] . . . have paused to question whether real life or long-lasting death lies beneath [them]."*

CRITICAL Thinking

1. **Analyzing** What did Zitkala-Sa mean by "long-lasting death"?
2. **Evaluating** What was each activist fighting for?

W Writing Support

Expository Writing Have students research to learn more about George Washington Carver. Instruct them to write paragraphs that summarize either his early life and education or his research. **OL**

History ONLINE

Objectives and answers to the Student Web Activity can be found at glencoe.com under the Web Activity Lesson Plan for this chapter.

✔ **Reading Check** **Answer:** achieve equal educational and economic opportunity for African Americans; end legalized segregation and discrimination

Assess

History ONLINE

Study Central™ provides summaries, interactive games, and online graphic organizers to help students review content.

Close

Discussing As a class, choose a minority group. Discuss how that group reacted to discrimination in the Progressive Era and problems that group faces today. **OL**

Section 4 Review

History ONLINE
Student Web Activity Visit glencoe.com and complete the Chapter 21 Web Activity about the Progressive Era.

African American Successes

African Americans achieved success in many professions. George Washington Carver, a chemist at Tuskegee Institute, helped improve the South's economy through his research on plant products. Maggie Lena founded the St. Luke Penny Savings Bank in Richmond. She served as America's first woman bank president.

Native Americans Seek Justice

The federal government's efforts to blend Native Americans into white society threatened their traditional cultures. In 1911 Native American leaders formed the Society of American Indians to improve living conditions for Native Americans and to teach white America about native cultures.

One of the society's founders was Dr. Carlos Montezuma. An Apache, Montezuma revealed government abuse of Native American rights. Montezuma believed that Native Americans should leave the reservations and make their own way in white society.

Mexican Americans Work Together

In the early 1900s, the Mexican American population quickly grew. Many crossed the border to escape conflict and economic woes in Mexico. Like other groups, Mexican Americans faced discrimination and violence.

Mexican Americans often relied on their own efforts. Their *mutualistas*—self-defense groups—provided insurance and legal help. One of the first *mutualistas* was the *Alianza Hispano-Americo* (Hispanic American Alliance). Another, the *Orden Hijos de America* (Order of Sons of America), promoted Mexican American rights. In labor camps and Mexican neighborhoods called **barrios,** *mutualistas* handled issues such as overcrowding and poor public services.

Widespread prejudice kept Mexican Americans from many reform groups. Yet Mexican Americans had dynamic leaders who formed organizations to fight for justice.

✔ **Reading Check** **Identifying** What was the purpose of the Niagara Movement?

Section 4 Review

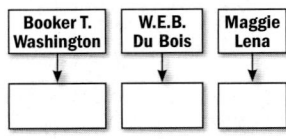
History ONLINE
Study Central™ To review this section, go to glencoe.com.

Vocabulary
1. Define the following terms in complete sentences: discrimination, deny, bias, *mutualista*, barrio.

Main Ideas
2. **Discussing** Why did many Americans and recent immigrants face discrimination in the Progressive Era?
3. **Summarizing** How did Mexican Americans organize to fight discrimination and violence?

Critical Thinking
4. **Making Connections** If you lived in the early 1900s, which organization would you join to help fight discrimination? Why?
5. **Organizing** Use a diagram like the one below to show the organizations founded by African Americans in the later 1800s.

Booker T. Washington	W.E.B. Du Bois	Maggie Lena

6. **Expository Writing** Read the quotation again in this section from Ida B. Wells's book *A Red Record*. Write a paragraph that answers Wells's question.

Answer the Essential Question
7. How did minority groups react to discrimination?

Answers

1. Students should write sentences using the vocabulary terms.
2. People faced discrimination because of religion, race, country of origin, or ethnicity. Many people feared that immigrants would take their jobs and other opportunities. To compound the problem, the government rarely addressed discrimination.
3. They formed *mutualistas* and other organizations to raise money for aid, work for equality, and combat overcrowding and deficient public services.
4. Students should explain their answers.
5. Booker T. Washington: Tuskegee Institute and National Negro Business League; W.E.B. Du Bois: Niagara Movement; Maggie Lena: St. Luke Penny Savings Bank
6. Students' paragraphs should reflect an understanding of the question she asks and its implications.
7. They formed organizations to fight discrimination and violence, seek economic equality, improve living standards, and achieve education. They educated others by publishing their ideas and cultural information in books and newspapers.

Visual Summary

Business and Politics

Target	Reform
Corrupt politics at all levels of government	• City commissioners • Civil Service Commission
More participation in government	• Seventeenth Amendment • Election reform
Trusts and big business	• Sherman Antitrust Act • Theodore Roosevelt's "Square Deal" • Federal Trade Commission • Clayton Antitrust Act
Railroad oligopoly	• Interstate Commerce Act/Commission
Conservation interests	• U.S. Forest Service • National Conservation Commission
High tariffs	• Sixteenth Amendment • "New Freedom" tariff reform
Banking regulation	• Federal Reserve Act

▲ Yosemite National Park

Prohibition agents dump alcohol ▶

◀ Educator Booker T. Washington

Gender and Race

Target	Reform
Equal voting rights for women	• Woman suffrage movement • State-by-state voting rights • National Woman's Party • Nineteenth Amendment
Prejudice and discrimination	• Tuskegee Institute • National Negro Business League • Niagara Movement • National Association for the Advancement of Colored People • Society of American Indians • Mexican American *mutualistas*

Society

Target	Reform
Social problems related to alcohol	• Women's Christian Temperance Union • Anti-Saloon League • Eighteenth Amendment
Unsafe food and medicine	• Meat Inspection Act • Pure Food and Drug Act
Difficult working conditions	• Children's Bureau of Labor Department • Women's Trade Union League • Mine/railroad safety standards • Keating-Owen Act

STUDY TO GO Study anywhere, anytime! Download quizzes and flash cards to your PDA from glencoe.com.

Visual Summary

Speculating Ask: Why didn't the government do much to address the problems of racial discrimination in the United States during the Progressive Era? *(Answers will vary but might mention that the targets of discrimination were not represented in the government at the time.)* **OL**

Comparing and Contrasting Ask: How do minority groups today work to end discrimination? *(Answers should refer to representation by members of minority groups in government today. Other actions include writing books and editorials, hosting television programs, and participating in organizations such as the NAACP.)* **OL**

Hands-On Chapter Project
Step 5: Wrap-Up

Creating a Reform Campaign

Step 5: Staging and Assessing the Peaceful Demonstration Students will stage peaceful demonstrations to promote their agendas.

Directions Have student groups take over a part of the classroom and stage their demonstrations. As they do so, the audience members should take notes on their feelings upon watching.

Evaluating Ask: Which demonstration was the most effective? Students should consider which group explained its cause and its proposed solutions most clearly and made audience members want to join the group to help promote the reform. As a class, discuss methods the most successful rallies used to educate and motivate the audience.

Answers and Analyses

Reviewing Main Ideas

1. C The text answers this question, which involves recall. Students might answer choice D, because the railroad oligopoly resembles a trust. However, it was the Sherman Antitrust Act that was passed to control trusts in general.
15.E.3b

2. B This question is answered by recall. Carry Nation was a temperance crusader.
18.C.3a

3. A President Roosevelt broke up many trusts during his first term, but he differentiated between trusts that concerned public welfare (good trusts) and those that did not (bad trusts). Choice C, Taft, also broke up many trusts but did not characterize them as good or bad. **16.A**

4. A Du Bois believed that African Americans could gain racial equality only after they could vote. It was Washington who believed that gaining employable skills would help end discrimination (choice B). Choice C is incorrect because Du Bois did not advocate violence. Choice D is wrong because *mutualistas* aided Mexican Americans, not African Americans. **18.C.3a**

Short-Answer Question

5. Justice Brewer believes that working too much has detrimental effects on women and their ability to raise healthy children and thus goes against the best interests of society. Proponents of equal rights might have argued that women are not automatically weaker or less able to work just because of their gender. Feminists might have argued that men also could raise vigorous children.
18.B.3a

STANDARDIZED TEST PRACTICE

TEST-TAKING TIP

Answer the questions you know first and go back to those for which you need more time.

Reviewing Main Ideas

Directions: Choose the best answer for each of the following questions.

1. The Interstate Commerce Act was an attempt to control
  A the spoils system.
  B excessive union activity.
  C railroad oligopoly.
  D the excessive influence of trusts.

2. For which cause was Carry Nation best known as a crusader?
  A labor rights
  B temperance
  C woman suffrage
  D immigration reform

3. Grouping trusts into "good" and "bad" ones was a characteristic of
  A Theodore Roosevelt's first term in office.
  B William Jennings Bryan's 1908 presidential campaign.
  C William Howard Taft's administration.
  D Woodrow Wilson's first term in office.

4. How did W.E.B. Du Bois differ from Booker T. Washington regarding racial discrimination?
  A Du Bois strongly promoted political involvement by African Americans.
  B Du Bois put the responsibility on the individual to gain employable skills.
  C Du Bois called for minorities to use violence against the Ku Klux Klan.
  D Du Bois encouraged *mutualistas* to help African Americans solve problems.

Short-Answer Question

Directions: Base your answer to question 5 on the excerpt below and on your knowledge of social studies.

That woman's physical structure and the performance of maternal [motherly] functions place her at a disadvantage in the struggle for subsistence is obvious. This is especially true when the burdens of motherhood are upon her. Even when they are not, . . . continuance for a long time on her feet at work, repeating this from day to day, tends to injurious effects upon the body, and as healthy mothers are essential to vigorous offspring, the physical well-being of woman becomes an object of public interest.

—Supreme Court Justice David J. Brewer,
Muller v. Oregon, 1908

5. In this opinion, Justice Brewer upholds a law limiting women's workday to 10 hours. What reasons does Justice Brewer give for not striking down the law? Why might some equal-rights feminists have opposed Brewer's decision?

Review the Essential Questions

6. Essay Compare and contrast the role of government with the role of private citizens in the progressive movement.

To help you write your essay, review your answers to the Essential Questions in the section reviews and the chapter Foldables Study Organizer. Your essay should include:

- differences and similarities among progressives, socialists, and muckrakers;
- the role of women in reform;
- the policies and actions of Roosevelt, Taft, and Wilson; and
- attempts of minorities to effect change.

GO ON

Review the Essential Questions

6. Students should use their answers to the Essential Questions and their Foldables to compare and contrast the role of government and private citizens in the progressive movement. Students should include in their discussion the roles of socialists, muckrakers, women, the presidents, and minorities, among others. **18.B.3a**

History ONLINE
For additional test practice, use Self-Check Quizzes—Chapter 21 at glencoe.com.

Chapter 21 Assessment

Document-Based Questions

Directions: Analyze the documents and answer the short-answer questions that follow.

Document 1

In 1916, Theodore Roosevelt stated the following about conservation.

> It is entirely in our power as a nation to preserve large tracts [areas] of wilderness, which are valueless for agricultural purposes and unfit for settlement . . . so that it shall continue to exist for the benefit of all lovers of nature. . . . But this end can only be achieved by wise laws. . . . Lack of such legislation and administration will result in harm to all of us, but most of all in harm to the nature lover who does not possess vast wealth. Already there have sprung up here and there through the country . . . large private preserves.

Source: Theodore Roosevelt, *Outdoor Pastimes of an American Hunter*

7. According to Roosevelt, why should wilderness areas be preserved?

Document 2

George Washington Plunkitt was a powerful state senator in New York. This is what he had to say about the political machine system.

> Have you ever thought what would become of the country if the bosses were put out of business, and their places were taken by a lot of cart-tail orators and college graduates? It would mean chaos. It would be just like takin' a lot of dry-goods clerks and settin' them to run express trains on the New York Central Railroad.

Source: William L. Riordon, *Plunkitt of Tammany Hall*

8. Based on the document, do you think Plunkitt favored or opposed reforms to the political machine system? Explain.

Document 3

This map shows the spread of woman suffrage in the United States from 1890 to 1920.

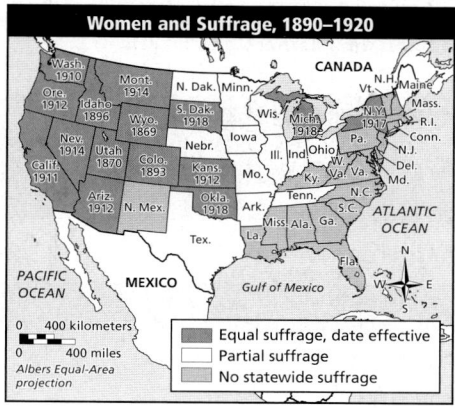

Women and Suffrage, 1890–1920

Equal suffrage, date effective
Partial suffrage
No statewide suffrage

9. Based on the map, which area was most resistant to woman suffrage?

Document 4

This is an excerpt from *The Jungle*, a novel about the meatpacking industry.

> There would be meat that had tumbled out on the floor, in the dirt and sawdust, where the workers had tramped and spit. . . . There would be meat stored in great piles in rooms; . . . and thousands of rats would race about on it.

Source: Upton Sinclair, *The Jungle*

10. Why do you think *The Jungle* was written?

11. Creative Writing Using the information from the four documents and your knowledge of social studies, write an essay in which you:

- take on the role of a reformer for a cause of your choice; and
- describe the challenges you face and the tactics you will use to succeed.

9. The area including the southern and eastern states was most resistant to the suffrage movement. **17.A.3b**

10. Students might respond that Upton Sinclair had researched the meatpacking industry and wanted people to know the appalling conditions so they would be motivated to enact reforms. **18.A.3**

11. Student essays should clearly describe the reformer's cause, the challenges faced by the reformer, and the strategies that individual might have adopted to achieve his or her goals. The organization of the essays should be logical and help clarify the points. **18.C.3b**

History ONLINE
Have students visit the Web site at glencoe.com to review Chapter 21 and take the Self-Check Quiz.

Need Extra Help?

Have students refer to the pages listed if they miss any of the questions.

Need Extra Help?

If you missed questions . . .	1	2	3	4	5	6	7	8	9	10	11
Go to page . . .	645	655	657	666–667	651–654	642–668	659	643–644	652–654	647	642–668

Document-Based Questions

7. Lack of wilderness preservation areas would harm everyone and make nature inaccessible to all but individuals who were wealthy enough to be able to purchase it. **16.A.3b**

8. Plunkitt seemed to support the political machine system. He believed that the political bosses and their workers made the political system work and that the alternative would be amateurs who would not be able to handle the job. **16.A.3b**

671

Chapter Planning Guide

22

Levels BL	OL	AL	ELL		Resources	Chapter Opener	Section 1	Section 2	Section 3	Section 4	Chapter Assess
					FOCUS						
BL	OL	AL	ELL	🖼	Daily Test Practice Transparencies		22–1	22–2	22–3	22–4	
					TEACH						
	OL	AL		📁	Geography and History Activity, URB			p. 59			
BL	OL		ELL	📁	Time Line Skills Activity, URB			p. 62			
BL	OL	AL	ELL	📁	Writing Skills Activity, URB			p. 51			
BL	OL	AL	ELL	📁	Content Vocabulary Activity, URB		p. 45	p. 45	p. 45	p. 45	
BL	OL	AL	ELL	📁	Academic Vocabulary Activity, URB		p. 47	p. 47	p. 47	p. 47	
BL	OL		ELL	📁	Social Studies Skills Activity, URB					p. 53	
BL	OL	AL	ELL	📁	Differentiated Instruction Activity, URB				p. 55		
BL	OL	AL	ELL	📁	Critical Thinking Skills Activity, URB					p. 57	
BL	OL	AL	ELL	📁	Linking Past and Present Activity, URB		p. 61				
	OL	AL		📁	Primary Source Readings, URB		p. 49				
BL	OL	AL	ELL	📁	School-to-Home Connection Activity, URB		p. 63	p. 63	p. 63	p. 63	
BL	OL		ELL	📁	Guided Reading Activity, URB*		p. 67	p. 68	p. 69	p. 70	
		AL		📁	Enrichment Activity, URB				p. 11		
BL	OL		ELL	📁	Reading Essentials and Note-Taking Guide*		p. 235	p. 238	p. 241	p. 244	
BL	OL	AL	ELL	🖼	Lesson Transparencies		22A	22B	22B	22C	
BL	OL	AL	ELL	📁	Outline Map Resource Book	pp. 8, 28, 30, 32, 50					

Note: Please refer to the *Unit Resource Book: Reform and Empire* for this chapter's URB materials.

* Also available in Spanish

672A

	Levels				Resources	Chapter Opener	Section 1	Section 2	Section 3	Section 4	Chapter Assess
BL	OL	AL	ELL								

TEACH (continued)

Levels					Resources	Chapter Opener	Section 1	Section 2	Section 3	Section 4	Chapter Assess
BL	OL	AL	ELL		NGS US Desk Map		✓	✓	✓	✓	
BL	OL	AL	ELL		American Literature Library		✓	✓	✓	✓	
BL	OL	AL	ELL		Writer's Guidebook		✓	✓	✓	✓	
	OL	AL			American History Primary Source Document Library CD-ROM		✓	✓	✓	✓	✓
BL	OL	AL	ELL		American Music: Hits Through History	✓	✓	✓	✓	✓	
BL	OL	AL	ELL		StudentWorks™ Plus CD	✓	✓	✓	✓	✓	✓
BL	OL	AL	ELL		Section Spotlight Videos		✓	✓	✓	✓	
BL	OL	AL	ELL		Writing Process Transparencies		✓	✓	✓	✓	✓
BL	OL	AL	ELL		Presentation Plus! With MindJogger CheckPoint CD	✓	✓	✓	✓	✓	✓

ASSESS

Levels					Resources	Chapter Opener	Section 1	Section 2	Section 3	Section 4	Chapter Assess
BL	OL	AL	ELL		Quizzes and Tests		p. 213	p. 214	p. 215	p. 216	pp. 217, 219, 221
BL	OL	AL	ELL		Authentic Assessment With Rubrics				p. 22		
BL	OL	AL	ELL		Standardized Test Practice						p. 43
BL	OL	AL	ELL		ExamView® Assessment Suite CD-ROM*		22–1	22–2	22–3	22–4	Ch. 22

CLOSE

Levels					Resources	Chapter Opener	Section 1	Section 2	Section 3	Section 4	Chapter Assess
BL			ELL		Reteaching Activity, URB*		p. 65	p. 65	p. 65	p. 65	p. 65
BL	OL		ELL		Reading and Study Skills Foldables Activity	p. 92	p. 92	p. 92	p. 92	p. 92	p. 92
BL	OL	AL	ELL		The American Journey in Graphic Novel						p. 127
BL			ELL		Reading Strategies and Activities for the Social Studies Classroom		✓	✓	✓	✓	
BL	OL	AL	ELL		Graphic Organizer Transparencies & Strategies		✓	✓	✓	✓	

TeacherWorks Plus
All-In-One Planner and Resource Center

- Interactive Lesson Planner
- Interactive Teacher Edition
- Fully editable blackline masters
- Section Spotlight Videos Launch
- Differentiated Lesson Plans
- Printable reports of daily assignments
- Standards Tracking System

Professional Development Resources

- Strategies for Success
- Building Academic Vocabulary
- Success With English Learners DVD
- Differentiated Instruction Strategies DVD
- Teaching Literacy Strategies in Social Studies DVD
- Assessment DVD
- Standards-Based Instruction DVD

Using the Glencoe Web Site

Chapter Overviews

Technology Product

The Glencoe Web site offers in-depth overviews that summarize the content of each chapter. The overviews consist of brief chapter summaries and separate overviews for each section. The chapter overviews

- summarize and reinforce chapter content;
- provide discussion points to use in class.

Objectives

The overviews help students

- prepare for better understanding of chapter content;
- practice reading and comprehension skills.

Steps

Provide students with the following steps to complete the activities:

- Locate the Web page for your textbook at the Glencoe Web site glencoe.com.
- Click on **Student Center** under the textbook title.
- Once you are in the Student Center, select a unit from the Unit Resources menu and a chapter from the Chapter Activities menu using the drop-down arrows.
- Click on the **Chapter Overviews** link.

Have students read the chapter overview in preparation for a reading assignment or activity.

History ONLINE at glencoe.com

	Student	Teacher	Parent
Media Center			
• Student Edition Audio	●		
• Spanish Summaries	●		
• Section Spotlight Videos	●	●	
Social Studies Online Learning Center			
Classroom Tools			
• Multi-Language Glossaries	●	●	●
• Teaching Today		●	
• TIME Current Events	●	●	●
• Beyond the Textbook	●	●	
The American Journey **Online Learning Center**			
• Study-to-Go™	●	●	●
• Study Central™	●	●	●
• Chapter Overview	●	●	
• Concepts in Motion	●	●	
• ePuzzles and Games	●	●	
• Literature Connections	●	●	
• Online Student Edition	●	●	●
• Self-Check Quizzes	●	●	●
• Student Web Activities	●	●	
• Vocabulary eFlashcards	●	●	
• Web Activity Lesson Plans	●	●	●
• Vocabulary PuzzleMaker	●	●	●

READING SUPPORT FROM JAMESTOWN EDUCATION

- **Timed Readings Plus in Social Studies** helps students increase their reading rate and fluency while maintaining comprehension. The 400-word passages are similar to those found on state and national assessments.

- **Reading in the Content Area: Social Studies** concentrates on six essential reading skills that help students better comprehend what they read. The book includes 75 high-interest nonfiction passages written at increasing levels of difficulty.

- **Reading Social Studies** includes strategic reading instruction and vocabulary support in Social Studies content for ELLs and native speakers of English.

- **Content Vocabulary Workout** (Grades 6–8) accelerates reading comprehension through focused vocabulary development. Social Studies content vocabulary comes from the glossaries of Glencoe's Middle School Social Studies texts.

www.jamestowneducation.com

NATIONAL GEOGRAPHIC

Index to National Geographic Magazine:

The following articles relate to this chapter:

- *"Alaska's Giant of Ice and Stone,"* John G. Mitchell, March 2003.

- *"Hawai'i,"* Paul Theroux, December 2002.

National Geographic Society Products

To order the following, call National Geographic at 1-800-368-2728:

National Geographic Atlas of the World (Book)

Access National Geographic's dynamic MapMachine Web site and other geography resources at:

www.nationalgeographic.com

www.nationalgeographic.com/mapmachine

Reading List Generator CD-ROM

GLENCOE BOOKLINK 3

Use this database to search more than 30,000 titles to create a customized reading list for your students.

- Reading lists can be organized by students' reading level, author, genre, theme, or area of interest.

- The database provides Degrees of Reading Power™ (DRP) and Lexile™ readability scores for all selections.

- A brief summary of each selection is included.

Leveled reading suggestions for this chapter:

For students at a Grade 6 reading level:
- *World Myths and Legends II: The Caribbean,* by Joseph Curran

For students at a Grade 7 reading level:
- *A Visit to Cuba,* by Alta Schreier

For students at a Grade 8 reading level:
- *Hawaii: Facts and Symbols,* by Emily McAuliffe

For students at a Grade 9 reading level:
- *The People of the Philippines,* by Dolly Brittan

For students at a Grade 10 reading level:
- *The Panama Canal,* by Patricia Maloney Markun

The following videotape programs are available from Glencoe as supplements to the chapter:

- **Teddy Roosevelt: An American Lion DVD Set** (ISBN 0-76-705176-9)

- **Pancho Villa: Outlaw Hero** (ISBN 0-76-700315-2)

To order, call Glencoe at 1-800-334-7344. To find classroom resources to accompany many of these videos, check the following home pages:

A&E Television: www.aetv.com

The History Channel: www.history.com

Chapter Objectives

After studying this chapter, students will be able to:

- Discuss why the United States extended its influence to other regions in the late 1800s.
- Explain why the United States expanded its role in the Pacific.
- Analyze how the Spanish-American War helped the United States become a world power.
- Relate how the beliefs of the U.S. presidents shaped Latin American foreign policies.

Motivating Activity

Comparing and Contrasting Students will learn that the United States was once aggressively imperialistic. In other words, most Americans wanted to add large amounts of new land to the nation's territory and expand U.S. influence in the world. **Ask:** Do you think the United States is still imperialistic? Explain. *(Some students might say that the United States is still imperialistic because, although it is no longer aggressively adding territory, it is still expanding its influence in the world; others might say that the United States is not imperialistic because it no longer claims countries it defeats as its territory.)* **OL**

Previewing the Essential Questions

As you begin teaching each section, use these questions and activities to help students focus on the Essential Questions.

Chapter ⭐ 22 Rise to World Power 1865–1917

When American Commodore Matthew Perry arrived in Tokyo in 1853–54, he presented the Japanese with a miniature steam locomotive.

PRESIDENTS

ANDREW JOHNSON 1865–1869

★ 1867 Russia purchases Alaska

ULYSSES S. GRANT 1869–1877

RUTHERFORD B. HAYES 1877–1881

JAMES GARFIELD 1881

CHESTER ARTHUR 1881–1885

GROVER CLEVELAND 1885–1889

U.S. Events
World Events

1865 — 1875 — 1885

★ 1867 Japan ends shogun rule

★ 1871 Italian law gives pope possession of Vatican

★ 1875 British take control of Suez Canal

★ 1883 Vietnam becomes French protectorate

St. Peter's Basilica in Vatican City ►

672 Chapter 22

Section ⭐ 1

Expanding Horizons Ask: Why might some Americans have favored imperialism during the late 1800s? *(to make the country more powerful, to find new natural resources, and to expand trade)* Tell students that in Section 1 they will learn about the expansion of American influence in the world during the late 1800s. **OL**

Section ⭐ 2

Imperialism in the Pacific Ask: Why do you think the Pacific islands are valuable to the United States? *(natural resources, trade, ports near Asia, and tourism)* Explain to students that Section 2 discusses reasons the United States increased its role in the Pacific and in Asia. **OL**

Section 1: Expanding Horizons
Essential Question Why did the United States extend its influence to other regions in the late 1800s?

Section 2: Imperialism in the Pacific
Essential Question Why did the United States expand its role in the Pacific?

Section 3: Spanish-American War
Essential Question How did the Spanish-American War help the United States become a world power?

Section 4: Latin American Policies
Essential Question How did the beliefs of the U.S. presidents shape Latin American foreign policies?

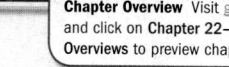
History ONLINE
Chapter Overview Visit glencoe.com and click on **Chapter 22—Chapter Overviews** to preview chapter information.

FOLDABLES Study Organizer
Organizing Information Make this four-tab Foldable to help you learn about how the United States expanded its influence around the world.

Step 1 Fold the sides of three pieces of paper into the middle to make a shutter fold.

Step 2 Cut each flap at the midpoint to form tabs.

Step 3 Label the tabs as shown.

Reading and Writing As you read the chapter, take notes about the role the United States played in each region. Use your Foldable to help you prepare for assessment.

| Alaska and Hawaii | Asia |
| Latin America | Africa |

Time Line Activity

If you have not already done so, have students review the time line. **Ask:** What years are covered in this chapter? *(1865–1916)* What major U.S. events are listed? *(Russia purchases Alaska, Spanish-American War erupts, and the National Park Service is established)* Which two events happened in 1867? *(Russia purchased Alaska, and Japan ended shogun rule)* Have students refer to the "World" section of the time line to identify important events in the rest of the world during the years covered. *(Examples: Shogun rule ends in Japan, the British take control of the Suez Canal, Vietnam becomes a French protectorate, and the Qing dynasty is overthrown in China)* **OL**

FOLDABLES Study Organizer — Dinah Zike's Foldables
Purpose This Foldable helps students visually organize information about how the United States expanded its influence around the world during the late 1800s and early 1900s. The completed Foldable will help them prepare for assessment. **OL**

More Foldables activities for this chapter can be found in *Dinah Zike's Reading and Study Skills Foldables.*

History ONLINE
Introduce students to chapter content and key terms by having them access the **Chapter Overview** at glencoe.com.

| BENJAMIN HARRISON 1889–1893 | GROVER CLEVELAND 1893–1897 | **1898** Spanish-American War erupts | WILLIAM McKINLEY 1897–1901 | THEODORE ROOSEVELT 1901–1909 | WILLIAM HOWARD TAFT 1909–1913 | WOODROW WILSON 1913–1921 | **1916** National Park Service established |

1895   **1905**   **1915**

★ **1895** José Martí leads revolt in Cuba

★ **1900** Boxer uprising in China

★ **1907** Shackleton organizes expedition to Antarctica

★ **1911** Qing dynasty overthrown in China

Chapter 22   673

Section 3

Spanish-American War Ask: How might the outcome of a war transform a country into a world power? *(by showing that the country can stand up to older, stronger nations; by showing that it has the determination to fight hard and make sacrifices; and by showing that its military is strong)* Tell students that Section 3 will cover the Spanish-American War and how it made the United States into a world power. **OL**

Section 4

Latin American Policies Ask: What are some ways that one country can affect events in other countries? *(diplomacy, military action, trade, communications, alliances, technology, and education)* Tell students that Section 4 will explore how U.S. presidents' foreign policies affected events in Latin America during the late 1800s and early 1900s. **OL**

Expanding Horizons

Focus

Section 1

Bellringer
Daily Test Practice Transparency 22–1

Reading Guide
Answers to Graphic:

Possible answers: by moving west and south within the North American continent; by opening ports overseas; by purchasing Alaska; by starting the Pan-American Union; by expanding U.S. naval power; by speeding up global communication and trade

Section Spotlight Video

To learn more about U.S. imperialism during the late 1800s, have students watch the Section Spotlight Video "Expanding Horizons."

Resource Manager

Essential Question ◄

Why did the United States extend its influence to other regions in the late 1800s?

Reading Guide

Content Vocabulary

isolationism (p. 675)   imperialism (p. 676)
expansionism (p. 675)

Academic Vocabulary

communication (p. 676) vision (p. 676)

Key People and Events

Matthew Perry (p. 675)
William H. Seward (p. 676)
Pan-American Union (p. 677)

Reading Strategy

Taking Notes As you read, use a diagram like the one below to describe how the United States was able to expand its influence during the age of imperialism.

ILLINOIS STANDARDS
The American Journey

14.E.3 Compare the basic principles of the United States and its international interests (e.g., territory, environment, trade, use of technology).

16.B.3d (US) Describe ways in which the United States developed as a world political power.

17.C.3b Explain how patterns of resources are used throughout the world.

American Diary

In 1899 Albert J. Beveridge was elected to the U.S. Senate as a Republican from Indiana. A brilliant speaker, Beveridge praised the new strength of the U.S. Navy and called on the country to expand its influence overseas. In a speech in 1900, Beveridge declared: "The Philippines are ours forever. . . . And just beyond the Philippines are China's [vast] markets. We will not retreat from either. . . . The Pacific is our ocean."

—from "In Support of an American Empire"

By the late 1890s, the United States had created a fleet of modern warships.

R **Reading Strategies**	C **Critical Thinking**	D **Differentiated Instruction**	W **Writing Support**	S **Skill Practice**
Teacher Edition • Summarizing, p. 676 **Additional Resources** • Guid. Read., URB p. 67 • Content Vocab., URB p. 45 • Academic Vocab., URB p. 47 • Read. Ess., p. 235 • Pri. Source Read., URB p. 49	**Teacher Edition** • Ident. Cent. Issues, p. 675 **Additional Resources** • Quizzes and Tests, p. 213 • Link. Past & Pres., URB p. 61	**Additional Resources** • School-to-Home, URB p. 63 • Reteaching Act., URB p. 65	**Teacher Edition** • Persuasive Writing, p. 677	**Teacher Edition** • Using Map Skills, p. 676 **Additional Resources** • Daily Test Pract. Transp. 22-1 • Lesson Transp. 22A

American Foreign Policy

Main Idea The influence of the United States began to extend to other world regions.

History and You How many products do you own that are made in Japan? Read to learn about the beginning of U.S. trade with Japan.

∙∙

Senator Albert Beveridge was not alone in his opinions. Many Americans yearned for an empire abroad. This idea greatly differed from earlier attitudes.

In his Farewell Address, George Washington warned Americans to "steer clear of permanent alliances with any portion of the foreign world." This principle guided American foreign policy for about 100 years. Some people, however, interpreted Washington's words differently. They said he supported a policy of **isolationism,** or noninvolvement, in world affairs. Others said Washington supported trade with other countries and not complete isolation from the rest of the world.

Americans expanded their territory by moving west and south. This **expansionism** was a driving force in American history. Most of the land between the Atlantic Coast and the Pacific Coast was settled. The American "frontier" had ended.

Americans then looked beyond the nation's borders to frontiers overseas. American merchants already traded with China, but they also wanted to trade with Japan, which had long been isolated from the West.

In 1853 Commodore **Matthew Perry** traveled to Japan. He steamed into Tokyo Bay with four warships and asked the Japanese to open their ports to U.S. ships. He told them he would return in several months for their answer. When Perry returned in 1854, the Japanese signed the Treaty of Kanagawa. They opened two ports to American ships. Perry's mission marked the start of greater U.S. involvement in Asia.

✔ **Reading Check** **Making Inferences** What effect do you think Perry's warships had on Japan's decision to trade with the United States?

Primary Source | Modern Battleships

A New Navy Moving away from wooden ships powered solely by the wind, the U.S. Navy built steel-hulled ships with steam-powered engines that included sails. One of the U.S. Navy's first armored battleships was the USS *Maine.*

❶ **Torpedo tubes** are devices to launch torpedoes.
❷ **Steam boilers** power the engines.
❸ **Munitions** were stored in the **magazine.**
❹ **Cowls** provided fresh air below deck.

Critical Thinking
Interpreting What do you think Senator Beveridge meant when he said "The Pacific is our ocean"?

Teach

C Critical Thinking

Identifying Central Issues Some people thought George Washington supported a policy of isolationism. Others thought he meant to trade with other countries and not have complete isolation from the rest of the world. **Ask:** What do you think Washington meant? *(Students might say that Washington's actual words were to avoid permanent alliances, which trade agreements are. This supports the idea that Washington was encouraging isolationism. Others might point out that Washington encouraged trade during his administration but that he wanted to remain politically neutral. This supports the second point of view.)* **AL**

Primary Source

Critical Thinking Answer
The navy was strong enough to dominate the Pacific, and Beveridge wanted to take advantage of it.

✔ **Reading Check** **Answer:** The Japanese likely felt intimidated by the warships in Tokyo Bay and might have felt that they had to accept the trade relationship.

Differentiated Instruction

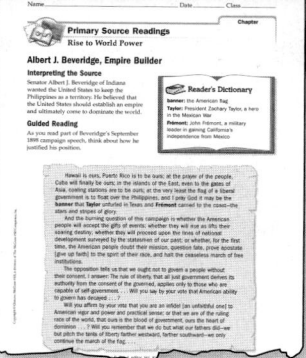

Primary Source Reading Activity, URB p. 49

Albert J. Beveridge, Empire Builder

Objective:	To analyze Albert J. Beveridge's statements about American foreign policy
Focus:	Review with students how expansionism became important to Americans in the nineteenth century.
Teach:	Have students read the excerpt and answer the questions.
Assess:	Discuss any questions that are problematic.
Close:	Ask students whether they agree with Beveridge's point of view.

Differentiated Instruction Strategies

BL Have students refer to a map or globe while they read the excerpt.

AL Have one group of students create a poster that favors expansionism while a second group prepares a poster that does not.

ELL Remind students to check the Reader's Dictionary for definitions of words they do not know.

Primary Source — The Alaska Purchase

Expanding Northward In 1867 Secretary of State William Seward negotiated a treaty to buy Alaska from Russia for $7.2 million. Congress approved his Alaska treaty because it eliminated the Russian presence from North America. Though Seward acquired the vast territory for only two cents per acre, many Americans ridiculed the purchase. Critics at the time called Alaska "a large lump of ice" and "Seward's Folly."

> "I can see no good reason for adopting at this time the treaty with Russia for the purchase of 'Alaska,' a country which . . . we know but little about, and judging from its location, doubtful if any of it will . . . induce persons to settle there under a homestead law; and as to minerals, we have little or no reliable information."
>
> —George Miller,
> speech in the House of Representatives, July 14, 1868

◄ Seward and the president's Cabinet discussing the Alaska purchase

A gold miner in Alaska ►

District of Alaska — NATIONAL GEOGRAPHIC

Map shows: RUSSIA, Bering Strait, Arctic Ocean, Beaufort Sea, Alaska, Nome, Yukon River, CANADA, Mt. McKinley, Skagway, Gulf of Alaska, Juneau, Pacific Ocean. 0–400 kilometers, 0–400 miles. Lambert Azimuthal Equal-Area projection.

Critical Thinking

Identifying Points of View Why did some Americans oppose the purchase of Alaska?

An Age of Imperialism

Main Idea The United States expanded its territory when it bought Alaska and extended its influence in Latin America.

History and You Think about what you have seen on TV and read about Alaska. Read to learn about how Alaska became a territory of the United States.

Other Western nations, in addition to the United States, also began to expand their trade and influence in Asia and other parts of the world. The late 1800s and the early 1900s were called an age of **imperialism.** During this time, powerful European nations created large empires by gaining economic and political control over weaker nations.

The search for materials and markets drove imperialism. The industrial nations of Europe needed raw materials and new markets for the goods they manufactured. This led to competition among European powers for influence in Asia and Africa.

Toward an Empire

After the Civil War, some Americans wanted the nation to build an empire. By annexing new lands, they argued, the United States would join the ranks of the world's great powers. Their country could take its rightful place at the center of power.

Secretary of State **William H. Seward,** appointed by Abraham Lincoln, supported this view. Seward pictured an American empire dominating the Caribbean, Central America, and the Pacific. This vast empire would be connected by a canal across Central America linking the Atlantic and Pacific Oceans, a transcontinental railroad system, and the telegraph, which would provide rapid **communication.**

The Purchase of Alaska

In 1867 Seward moved closer to making his **vision,** or imagined plan, a reality when he bought Alaska from Russia for $7.2 million. It was a great bargain for a territory twice the size of Texas.

Essential Question: Why did the U.S. extend its influence to other regions in the late 1800s?

Directions Organize students into small groups and distribute a large outline map of the world to each group. Have students research to locate the borders of the U.S. and its areas of influence in 1865. Tell them to color-code their world maps. One color should show the official territory of the U.S. One or more other colors should show areas of the world with which the U.S. had influence, such as trade agreements, treaties of peace or alliance, and so on.

Drawing Conclusions Discuss reasons the U.S. chose to begin expanding its influence in the world during the late 1800s. **Ask:** Why did the U.S. choose imperialism at the end of the 1800s? *(The U.S. joined European nations in the search for materials and markets.)* **OL**

(Chapter Project continued in Section 2)

Many people ridiculed Seward's actions. They mocked the purchase as "Seward's Ice Box" and a "polar bear garden." Alaska was viewed as an icy, barren place. However, after gold was discovered there in the 1890s, Seward's "folly" seemed more like a wise purchase. In 1912 Alaska became a territory of the United States.

A Sense of Mission

Some Americans had another reason for favoring imperialism. They believed they could "lift up" the world's "uncivilized" people by sharing Christianity and Western civilization. Josiah Strong, a Congregational minister, proposed an "imperialism of righteousness." He thought Americans should bring their religion and culture to Africa, Asia, and Latin America.

American Interest in Latin America

The United States had a flourishing trade with Latin America. Taking advantage of the Monroe Doctrine, American merchants wanted to further extend U.S. economic influence in the region. In 1884 James G. Blaine, then the Republican nominee for president, declared that the United States should "improve and expand its trade with the nations of America."

As secretary of state in 1889, Blaine invited Latin American leaders to attend a Pan-American Conference in Washington, D.C. Blaine hoped to develop closer ties among the Latin American nations. The conference led to the **Pan-American Union,** which promoted cooperation among member nations.

Building Sea Power

As the United States expanded its influence overseas, Captain Alfred Thayer Mahan, president of the Naval War College, wanted to improve the navy. "Sea power," Mahan said, "is essential to the greatness of every splendid people." The United States would be able to use its colonies as bases to refuel its ships.

During the 1880s, the U.S. Navy shifted from sails to steam power and from wooden to steel hulls. By the early 1900s, the United States had the naval power needed to support its expanded role in foreign affairs.

✓ **Reading Check** Explaining What factors led to imperialism?

Section 1 Review

History ONLINE
Study Central™ To review this section, go to glencoe.com.

Vocabulary

1. Define each of the following terms in a sentence: isolationism, expansionism, imperialism, communication, vision.

Main Ideas

2. Discussing Why did the U.S. begin to expand overseas?

3. Summarizing Summarize why many Americans favored imperialism in the late 1800s and early 1900s.

Critical Thinking

4. Predicting Do you think George Washington would support the Pan-American Union? Why or why not?

5. Determining Cause and Effect Use a diagram like the one below to discuss the causes and effects of the Treaty of Kanagawa.

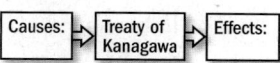
Causes: → Treaty of Kanagawa → Effects:

6. Persuasive Writing You are William H. Seward, and you have just read a newspaper article criticizing your purchase of Alaska. Write a letter to the paper defending your purchase.

Answer the
7. Essential Question
Why did the United States extend its influence to other regions in the late 1800s?

Rise to World Power **Chapter 22 677**

W Writing Support

Persuasive Writing Ask students to imagine they are the U.S. secretary of state during the late 1800s. Have them write a report listing why the United States should adopt a policy of imperialism. *(Students should list reasons such as expanding trade, finding new resources, and spreading Christianity and democracy.)* **OL**

✓ **Reading Check** **Answer:** the desire to expand U.S. trade and power, a desire to spread Christianity and democracy, and a stronger navy

Assess

History ONLINE

Study Central™ provides summaries, interactive games, and online graphic organizers to help students review content.

Close

Discussing List and discuss why the United States began expanding its influence during the late 1800s. Then talk about the methods used and the effectiveness of each. **OL**

Section ★ Review

Answers

1. Sentences should use vocabulary words according to their definitions in the section and Glossary.

2. to increase trade, to compete for resources and markets, to show its naval power to other countries, and to spread Christianity and democracy

3. They wanted to compete with European powers, which were building empires. They wanted to become a world power and accumulate wealth.

4. Answers will vary. Some students will say that Washington would not support the Pan-American Union because it was a permanent foreign alliance. Others might say that Washington supported international trade and would have approved of the union but might have wanted to maintain political neutrality despite the trade agreement.

5. Causes: The United States wanted to trade with Japan; Perry brought U.S. warships to Tokyo Bay to persuade Japan to trade.

Effects: Japan opened two ports to American ships; U.S. involvement in Asia increased.

6. Letters should include reasons such as getting Russia out of the Western Hemisphere, the possibility of unknown resources in Alaska, the low price, and the size of the land.

7. Answers might include competing with European powers, wanting to become a world power, gaining wealth, making new alliances, and spreading Christianity and democracy.

Section 2

Imperialism in the Pacific

Focus

Bellringer
Daily Test Practice Transparency 22–2

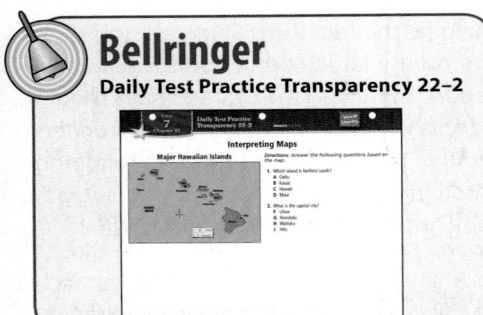

Reading Guide
Answers to Graphic:

Treaty of Portsmouth: peace agreement between Japan and Russia, but Japan continued expansionist activities

1906 San Francisco Board of Education Policy: ordered Asian students to attend separate schools; Roosevelt changed the policy and Japan promised to restrict emigration, but the Japanese people resented the situation and relations grew worse

Section Spotlight Video

To learn more about trade with China, the Open Door policy, and the Chinese reaction to foreigners in their country, watch the Section Spotlight Video "Imperialism in the Pacific."

Resource Manager

Essential Question ◄
Why did the United States expand its role in the Pacific?

Reading Guide

Content Vocabulary
provisional government *(p. 680)*
spheres of influence *(p. 682)*

Academic Vocabulary
consult *(p. 681)*   exploit *(p. 682)*

Key People and Events
Liliuokalani *(p. 680)*
John Hay *(p. 682)*
Open Door policy *(p. 682)*
Russo-Japanese War *(p. 683)*
Treaty of Portsmouth *(p. 683)*

Reading Strategy
Taking Notes As you read, use a diagram like the one below to explain why these events strained relations between Japan and the United States.

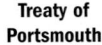

| Treaty of Portsmouth | → | |

| 1906 San Francisco Board of Education Policy | → | |

ILLINOIS STANDARDS
The American Journey

14.E Understand United States foreign policy as it relates to other nations and international issues.

16.B.3d (US) Describe ways in which the United States developed as a world political power.

17.C.3a Explain how human activity is affected by geographic factors.

American Diary

On a trip to England in 1887, Hawaii's Princess Liliuokalani heard about a "revolutionary movement, [begun] by those of . . . American birth" in her Pacific island homeland. The royal party set out by ship for Honolulu, Hawaii's capital. Later, the princess wrote: "As our vessel was entering the harbor . . . we knew, although no word was spoken, the changes which had . . . been forced upon the king. We were received by the members of the new [council] of the king . . . all men of foreign birth."

—from Hawaii's Story

United States Marines arrive in Hawaii to support the overthrow of the Hawaiian monarchy in 1893.

R Reading Strategies	**C** Critical Thinking	**D** Differentiated Instruction	**W** Writing Support	**S** Skill Practice
Teacher Edition • Skimming, p. 679 • Inferring, p. 682 **Additional Resources** • Guid. Read., URB p. 68 • Content Vocab., URB p. 45 • Academic Vocab., URB p. 47 • Read. Ess., p. 238	**Teacher Edition** • Det. Cause & Effect, p. 680 • Making Inferences, p. 681 **Additional Resources** • Quizzes and Tests, p. 214	**Teacher Edition** • Gifted and Tal., p. 681 • ELL, p. 683 **Additional Resources** • School-to-Home, URB p. 63 • Reteaching Act., URB p. 65	**Teacher Edition** • Narrative Writing, p. 682 **Additional Resources** • Writ. Skills, URB p. 51	**Teacher Edition** • Using Geo. Skills, p. 679 **Additional Resources** • Daily Test Pract. Transp. 22-2 • Lesson Transp. 22B • Time Line Skills, URB p. 62 • Geo. & Hist., URB p. 59

Hawaii

Main Idea The United States strengthened its foothold in the Pacific by annexing Hawaii and part of Samoa.

History and You Has anyone ever taken something that belonged to you without your approval? Read to learn why the Hawaiians resisted American influence in their country.

Princess Liliuokalani (lih•LEE•uh•woh•kuh•LAH•nee) realized that time was running out for her people. American planters and businesspeople were tightening their control of Hawaii and threatening the much-loved monarchy.

Since the mid-1800s, many Americans had wanted to build an American trading empire in the Pacific. In 1867 Secretary of State William H. Seward acquired the Pacific islands of Midway. These islands were more than 3,000 miles (4,800 km) west of California. They would serve as an important stopping place for American ships en route to China. American merchants and the U.S. Navy, however,

R needed more than two islands to establish a firm foothold in the vast stretches of the Pacific.

The Hawaiian Islands

The Hawaiian Islands, a chain of eight large and about 100 smaller islands, lay about 2,000 miles (3,200 km) west of California. The Hawaiian people in the 1800s lived in independent communities, each with its own chieftain. The people depended on the lush environment for farming and fishing. American trading ships and whalers often stopped at the islands for supplies and water.

In the 1790s, Americans and Hawaiians began to trade with each other. About that same time, King Kamehameha I began to unify the islands. Because they had good ports, the villages of Honolulu and Lahaina (luh•HY•nuh) grew in importance. Trade continued to flourish.

American and European ships also brought infectious diseases to the islands. These diseases devastated the island population just as they had once devastated the Native Americans.

Primary Source | The Republic of Hawaii

Taking Control of the Islands On January 17, 1893, a group of American businesspeople overthrew Hawaii's monarchy. A temporary government was then set up that would "exist until terms of union with the United States . . . have been . . . agreed upon." Sanford B. Dole, an elderly judge, became its leader. U.S. president Grover Cleveland opposed the takeover. Dole, however, refused to hand power back to the Hawaiian queen, saying, "We do not recognize the right of the President of the United States to interfere in our domestic affairs." On July 4, 1894, Hawaii officially became an independent republic, with Dole as president.

—from *History of Later Years of the Hawaiian Monarchy and the Revolution of 1893*

▲ Sanford B. Dole

Critical Thinking
Explaining Why do you think Hawaii is important to the United States today?

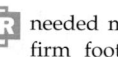
Activity: Economics Connection

Making Connections Tell students that economic factors were the driving force behind the United States's interest and involvement in Hawaii. Have students make a chart that shows what economic factors brought Americans to Hawaii, how involvement in Hawaii affected the United States and Hawaiian economies, and how Hawaii affects the United States economy today. **Ask:** Economically speaking, was Hawaii a good addition to the United States? *(Possible answer: Yes, because it provided a place for American ships to stop and get supplies; it offered abundant natural resources; and it is an attractive tourist destination.)* **OL**

People IN HISTORY

C Critical Thinking

Determining Cause and Effect Have students create a cause-and-effect chart showing what caused the American take-over of Hawaii and its effects. (*Causes: Missionaries, merchants, and whalers began to settle in the islands; American planters brought sugarcane and made huge profits; American businesspeople took over most Hawaiian land; Congress imposed tariffs on Hawaiian sugar.* **Effects:** *Americans took over Hawaii so that it would be an American territory and tariffs wouldn't apply; the Hawaiian queen tried to take back power; Americans overthrew the queen.*) **AL**

People IN HISTORY

Critical Thinking Answers

1. She started the Oni pa'a movement, and she asked the United States for help.
2. She probably meant that actions to take over Hawaii had been against Hawaiian law and that she had not been given a chance to argue her case for her legal claim to be the head of Hawaii's government.

Differentiated Instruction

Liliuokalani
Queen of Hawaii

After she was removed from power in 1893, Queen Liliuokalani continued her fight to take back the throne. She headed the Oni pa'a ("Stand Firm") movement, whose motto was "Hawaii for the Hawaiians." She appealed to the U.S. government to "do justice in this matter and to restore to me this property." In this 1898 letter to the U.S. House of Representatives, she wrote, *"I, Liliuokalani of Hawaii . . . do hereby earnestly and respectfully protest against the assertion [declaration] of ownership by the United States of America of the so-called Hawaiian Crown Islands. . . . I especially protest against such . . . taking of property without due process of law."*

CRITICAL Thinking

1. **Explaining** How did Liliuokalani fight the overthrow of the Hawaiian government?
2. **Evaluating** What did Liliuokalani mean when she wrote that she especially protested the taking of Hawaii without "due process of law"?

Missionaries and Sugar Growers

In 1820 Christian missionaries from the United States arrived in Hawaii. They established schools, created a written Hawaiian alphabet, and translated the Bible into Hawaiian. Many American merchants in the whaling trade also came to settle in the Hawaiian Islands.

An American firm introduced sugarcane in Hawaii in the 1830s. The missionaries and traders began buying land and establishing sugar plantations. The United States agreed not to impose tariffs on Hawaiian sugar. The sugar industry grew quickly, and American planters reaped huge profits. Gradually the Americans took control of most of the land and businesses. They also served as advisers to the Hawaiian ruling family. The United States recognized Hawaiian independence in 1842, but American influence remained strong.

Then, in the early 1890s, Congress began imposing tariffs on Hawaiian sugar. As a result, sugar exports to the United States dropped sharply. Facing ruin, the sugar planters plotted a way to avoid the new tariff. They argued that because the United States already had a naval base at Pearl Harbor, Hawaii could be made a territory of the United States.

American Planters' Revolt

The Hawaiians, meanwhile, had begun to resist the growing influence of the Americans. In 1891 the new ruler, Queen **Liliuokalani,** came to the throne. Wanting Hawaiians to regain economic control of their islands, she took away the powers of the American sugar planters. In response, the white planters overthrew Liliuokalani and set up their own **provisional government,** or temporary government, in 1893. The queen yielded:

PRIMARY SOURCE

"Now, to avoid any collision of armed forces, and perhaps the loss of life, I . . . yield my authority."
—Queen Liliuokalani

680 **Chapter 22** *Rise to World Power*

Writing Summaries

Objective:	To learn how to summarize information
Focus:	Discuss with students what steps to take in writing a summary.
Teach:	Have students read the information, answer the questions, and then apply the skill.
Assess:	Have students use the self-assessment checklist.
Close:	Ask for volunteers to read their summaries aloud.

Differentiated Instruction Strategies

BL Have students create flash cards containing the steps to writing a successful summary.

AL Ask students to summarize the information about one foreign country in this section of the textbook.

ELL Have students locate an excerpt relating to the history of their native country and summarize it.

Writing Skills Activity, URB p. 51

Annexation

The success of the planters' revolt was due in part to the support of John Stevens. Stevens was the chief American diplomat in Hawaii. He arranged for marines from the warship *Boston* to assist in the revolt. Stevens immediately recognized the new government. A delegation was sent to Washington to seek a treaty that would annex, or add, Hawaii to the United States. President Benjamin Harrison signed the treaty and sent it to the Senate for approval.

The Senate, however, did not ratify the treaty before President Harrison left office. The new president, Grover Cleveland, opposed annexation and withdrew the treaty from the Senate when he found out that Hawaiians did not support the revolt. Cleveland called American interference in the Hawaiian revolution "disgraceful."

Most Hawaiians opposed annexation, but a small, powerful group of sugar growers, traders, and missionaries, along with their allies and leaders in the United States, supported it. After William McKinley became president, Congress approved the annexation of Hawaii, and in 1900 it became a territory of the United States.

The Islands of Samoa

About 3,000 miles (4,800 km) south of Hawaii lay the Samoa Islands. Samoa allowed the Americans to build a naval station at Pago Pago. Samoa also granted special trading rights to the United States. Because Great Britain and Germany secured trading rights in the islands, tensions grew as the three powers competed for power in Samoa.

In 1899 the United States, Great Britain, and Germany met in Berlin. Without **consulting**—seeking an opinion from—the Samoans, the United States and Germany split Samoa, and the United States quickly annexed its portion. Great Britain withdrew from the area in return for rights to other Pacific islands.

Reading Check **Explaining** Why did the planters want Hawaii as a U.S. territory?

United States Overseas Possessions, 1900 NATIONAL GEOGRAPHIC

Map Skills

Place When were the Hawaiian Islands acquired?

D Differentiated Instruction

Gifted and Talented Pair students and have them take opposing sides in a brief debate about whether or not it would be right to annex Hawaii against many Hawaiians' wishes. Then discuss the outcome of students' debates as a class. **AL**

C Critical Thinking

Making Inferences Ask: If you were a Samoan person in 1899, how would you feel about being annexed by the United States or Germany without being consulted? *(Students might say that they would feel resentful; others might say that they would be happy about being protected by a larger, wealthier country.)* **OL**

United States Overseas Possessions, 1900 NATIONAL GEOGRAPHIC

Map Skills Answer

1898

Reading Check **Answer:** The planters were making huge profits from sugarcane grown in Hawaii, and their crops would not be subject to U.S. tariffs if Hawaii became a U.S. territory.

Hands-On Chapter Project
Step 2

Creating a Chronological Series of Maps

Step 2: Creating the Second Map Students will prepare the second map, which will show the U.S. and the world as it was in about 1870.

Essential Question: Why did the United States expand its role in the Pacific?

Directions Distribute a large outline map of the world to each group of students. Have them research to locate the borders of the U.S. and its areas of influence in 1870. Tell them to color-code their world maps. One color should show the official territory of the U.S. One or more other colors should show areas of the world with which the U.S. had influence, such as trade agreements, treaties of peace or alliance, and so on. Students will make the next map in Section 3.

Analyzing Information List Pacific islands acquired by the U.S. by 1870. **Ask:** What were the goals of the U.S. in the Pacific? In your opinion, were these goals accomplished by 1870? **OL**

(Chapter Project continued in Section 3)

R Reading Strategy

Inferring Have students read the information about China and the Open Door policy. **Ask:** What evidence in this subsection implies that the Chinese people were worried about losing their independence? *(Foreign powers had carved China into spheres of influence, the Boxers revolted against "foreign devils", and the second Open Door policy maintained China's independence and respected its borders.)* **OL**

W Writing Support

Narrative Writing Have students write a brief newspaper article about the Boxer Rebellion and the second Open Door proposal that resulted from it. **OL**

Primary Source

Critical Thinking Answer
Possible answer: to keep China safe, peaceful, and independent so that the United States and other countries could trade freely in China

✔ **Reading Check Answer:** to protect and expand U.S. trading interests in China

Differentiated Instruction

Primary Source — The United States in Asia

Extending Influence At the turn of the century, the United States used diplomatic and military tactics to protect its economic interests in Asia. Maintaining access to the vast Chinese market was a major American foreign policy goal.

▼ American troops fighting in Peking during the Boxer Rebellion.

"The policy of the Government of the United States is to seek a solution which may bring about permanent safety and peace to China, preserve Chinese territorial and administrative entity [existence], protect all rights to friendly powers by treaty and international law, and safeguard for the world . . . trade with all parts of the Chinese Empire."
—John Hay

America's "Great White ▶ Fleet" helped convince Japan to reaffirm the Open Door policy in China and to maintain the status quo in the Pacific.

Critical Thinking

Making Inferences Based on the quote from John Hay, what were the United States's intentions in China?

R China and the Open Door

Main Idea The Open Door policy protected and expanded U.S. trading interests in China.

History and You Do you remember reading about a trade agreement with Japan in the 1850s? Read to learn about trade between the U.S. and China.

Pacific island territories were stepping-stones to a larger prize—China. Weakened by war, China also lacked industry. It could not resist the efforts of foreign powers that wanted to **exploit,** or make use of, its vast resources and markets.

Rivalries in China

By the late 1890s, Japan and European powers had carved out **spheres of influence** in China. These were sections of the country where each of the foreign nations enjoyed special rights and powers. Japan, Germany, Great Britain, France, and Russia all had spheres of influence in China.

An Open Door to China

Some U.S. government and business leaders worried about being left out of the profitable China trade. To protect and expand American trading interests, Secretary of State **John Hay** proposed an **Open Door policy.** It gave each foreign nation in China rights to trade freely in the other nations' spheres of influence. The other powers hesitated to accept the policy.

The Boxer Rebellion

In 1899 a secret Chinese society, the Boxers, revolted against the "foreign devils" in China, and many foreigners died. The next year, foreign troops defeated the Boxers.

The Boxer Rebellion led to a second Open Door proposal. This version stressed the importance of maintaining China's independence and respecting its borders. Alarmed by the revolt, the other foreign powers accepted Hay's policy.

✔ **Reading Check Analyzing** Explain the purpose of the Open Door policy.

Leveled Activities

BL Academic Vocabulary Activity, URB p. 47

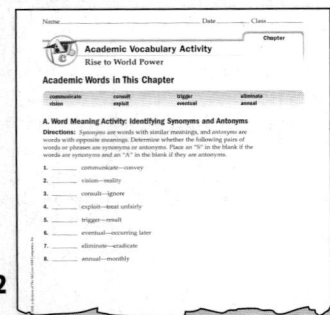

OL Geography and History Activity, URB p. 59

ELL Content Vocabulary Activity, URB p. 45

Japan

Main Idea The relations between Japan and the United States were strained in the early 1900s.

History and You Have you ever tried to help two friends agree on an issue? Read to learn how the United States helped settle the Russo-Japanese War.

Eager to expand its power in Asia, Japan began to ignore the Open Door policy. Japan's actions led to war with Russia and conflict with the United States.

In the early 1900s, Japan and Russia clashed over Manchuria, a Chinese province rich in natural resources. On February 8, 1904, Japan attacked the Russian fleet in Manchuria, starting the **Russo-Japanese War.** By the spring of 1905, both Japan's and Russia's resources were nearly exhausted. Both countries were eager to make peace.

Treaty of Portsmouth

President Theodore Roosevelt met with the Russian and Japanese leaders in Portsmouth, New Hampshire, to help settle the conflict. In September 1905, Japan and Russia signed the **Treaty of Portsmouth.** This recognized Japan's control of Korea in return for Japan's pledge to halt expansion. Roosevelt hoped the treaty would preserve a balance of power in Asia, but it failed. Japan became the strongest naval power in the Pacific and challenged the United States in the region.

Strained Relations

Many people in Japan immigrated to the United States during the Russo-Japanese War and settled in California. In 1906 the San Francisco Board of Education ordered all Asian students to attend separate schools. The Japanese government protested. President Roosevelt forced the school board to change its policies. In return, Japan promised to restrict emigration. The Japanese, however, resented the agreement, and relations between Japan and the United States worsened. Some Americans called for war.

President Roosevelt had no plan for war. He sent 16 gleaming white battleships on a cruise around the world. The "Great White Fleet" greatly impressed the Japanese. By 1909, the United States and Japan resolved many of their differences.

Reading Check **Describing** What role did the U.S. play in the end of the Russo-Japanese War?

D Differentiated Instruction

English Language Learners Have students draw a comic-strip-style row of three to five captioned pictures showing the sequence of events that led to strained relations between the United States and Japan. *(Possible pictures: Russo-Japanese War, Treaty of Portsmouth, Japan's strengthening navy, Japanese immigration to the United States, San Francisco Board of Education's segregation policy, American calls for war, and the Great White Fleet)* **ELL**

Reading Check **Answer:** President Roosevelt met with Russian and Japanese leaders to help settle the conflict with the Treaty of Portsmouth.

Assess

History ONLINE

Study Central™ provides summaries, interactive games, and online graphic organizers to help students review content.

Close

Identifying Central Issues As a class, list reasons the United States worked to expand its influence in the Pacific during the late 1800s. **OL**

Section 2 Review

Section 2 Review

History ONLINE
Study Central™ To review this section, go to glencoe.com.

Vocabulary

1. Define each of the following terms in a sentence: provisional government, consult, exploit, spheres of influence.

Main Ideas

2. **Explaining** How did planters and missionaries become powerful in Hawaii?

3. **Identifying Cause and Effect** Explain the effect of the Boxer Rebellion on foreign powers in China.

4. **Making Inferences** Why did Japan want control of Manchuria?

Critical Thinking

5. **Organizing** Draw a diagram like the one below. In each oval, describe the relationship between the United States and the location listed.

Hawaii · Samoa · Relationship With the U.S. · China · Japan

6. **Persuasive Writing** Write a speech that Theodore Roosevelt might have delivered to the San Francisco Board of Education to convince it to reverse its decision of sending Asian students to different schools.

Answer the
7. **Essential Question**
Why did the United States expand its role in the Pacific?

Answers

1. Sentences should reflect a correct understanding of the terms.
2. by gradually taking over most of the land and businesses and by advising the Hawaiian royal family
3. The Boxer Rebellion scared many foreign powers enough that they accepted the second Open Door proposal.
4. Manchuria was rich in natural resources, and Japan wanted exclusive trading rights there.
5. **Hawaii:** American planters overthrew the royal family, and the U.S. annexed it.

Samoa: allowed a U.S. naval base and gave special trading privileges to the United States; United States annexed part of Samoa without asking. **China:** United States wanted open trade with China; proposed Open Door policy to respect Chinese independence and borders. **Japan:** strained relationship because Japan did not honor Open Door policy and became aggressive in the Pacific; Japanese immigrants to U.S. caused tension.

6. Speeches should offer two logical arguments about why the schools should not separate Japanese students from other students. For example, it opposes the idea of equality, which Americans value.

7. Possible answers: to gain wealth through trade; to obtain natural resources; to keep other nations from getting too powerful or shutting the United States out of Pacific and Asian markets; to place American military bases in the Pacific; and to have stopovers for merchant, military, and whaling ships

Section 3

Spanish-American War

Focus

Bellringer
Daily Test Practice Transparency 22–3

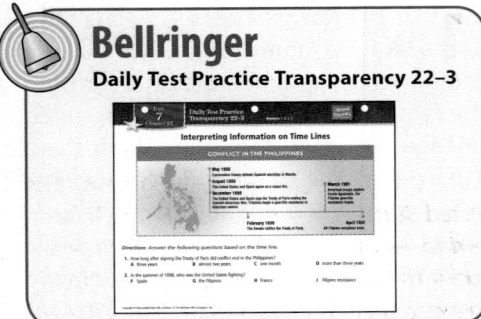

Reading Guide
Answers to Graphic:
Cuba, Guam, Puerto Rico, and the Philippines

Section Spotlight Video

To learn more about the Rough Riders U.S. Cavalry volunteers during the Spanish-American War, watch the Section Spotlight Video "Spanish-American War."

Essential Question
How did the Spanish-American War help the United States become a world power?

Reading Guide

Content Vocabulary
yellow journalism (p. 686)   protectorate (p. 688)
armistice (p. 687)   territory (p. 688)

Academic Vocabulary
trigger (p. 686)   eventual (p. 689)

Key People and Events
Rough Riders (p. 687)
Battle of San Juan Hill (p. 687)
Platt Amendment (p. 688)

Reading Strategy
Taking Notes As you read, use a diagram like the one below to identify the lands that the United States acquired after the Spanish-American War.

Land Acquired

ILLINOIS STANDARDS
The American Journey

14.E.3 Compare the basic principles of the United States and its international interests (e.g., territory, environment, trade, use of technology).

16.A.3c Identify the differences between historical fact and interpretation.

18.B.3a Analyze how individuals and groups interact with and within institutions (e.g., educational, military).

American Diary

Soldiers of the Ninth and Tenth Cavalry made the charge up San Juan Hill. In the face of enemy fire, Colonel Theodore Roosevelt on horseback encouraged his Rough Riders forward. He later recalled: "Some forty yards from the top [of the hill] I . . . jumped off [the horse]. . . . As I ran up to the hill, [my orderly] stopped to shoot, and two Spaniards fell. . . . Almost immediately afterward the hill was covered by the troops, both Rough Riders and the [African American] troopers of the Ninth [Cavalry]."

—*from* The Rough Riders

American artist Frederic Remington painted the Rough Riders' charge up San Juan Hill.

Resource Manager

R Reading Strategies	**C** Critical Thinking	**D** Differentiated Instruction	**W** Writing Support	**S** Skill Practice
Teacher Edition • Making Connections, p. 686 • Det. Importance, p. 686 • Using Word Parts, p. 688 **Additional Resources** • Guid. Read., URB p. 69 • Content Vocab., URB p. 45 • Read. Ess., p. 241	**Teacher Edition** • Det. Cause and Effect, p. 685 • Making Inferences, p. 688 • Analyz. Information, p. 689 **Additional Resources** • Quizzes and Tests, p. 215	**Teacher Edition** • Verbal/Linguistic, p. 687 **Additional Resources** • School-to-Home, URB p. 63 • Reteaching Act., URB p. 65 • Differ. Inst., URB p. 55	**Additional Resources** • Enrichment Act., URB p. 11	**Teacher Edition** • Using Geo. Skills, p. 685 **Additional Resources** • Daily Test Pract. Transp. 22-3 • Lesson Transp. 22B

"A Splendid Little War"

Main Idea Events in Cuba led to war between the United States and Spain in 1898.

History and You Why do countries go to war? Read to learn why the United States declared war on Spain.

The charge of the Rough Riders took place in Cuba, a Caribbean island about 90 miles (145 km) from American shores. The Cubans had lived under Spanish rule for centuries. They rebelled several times in the late 1800s. Each time, however, the Spanish overpowered them and shattered their dreams of independence.

José Martí was one hero of the Cuban independence movement. He fled to the United States to gather money, arms, and troops. In 1895 Martí returned to Cuba to lead his people in a new revolt.

Martí's revolution led to huge losses in human life and property. The rebels burned sugarcane fields and destroyed buildings in hopes of forcing the Spanish to leave. In response, Spanish troops herded Cuban people into camps to separate them from the rebels and to destroy their morale. Thousands of Cubans died of starvation and disease in the conflict.

War Fever

The Cuban people's struggle caused great concern in the United States. Businesspeople worried about the loss of their investments and trade in Cuba. Government leaders were concerned about a rebellion taking place so close to the United States. Many Americans were horrified by the violence against Cuban citizens, and they called for the U.S. government to do something about it.

President Grover Cleveland opposed any American involvement in Cuba. In March 1897, William McKinley became president. He, too, hoped for a peaceful settlement.

The American press reported the tragedy in Cuba in graphic detail. Coverage fueled the debate over America's role in the crisis. Newspapers, including Joseph Pulitzer's *World* and William Randolph Hearst's *Journal*, tried to outdo one another. They printed shocking reports about the revolution.

Hearst, it is said, told an artist who was illustrating a news story on Cuba, "You furnish the pictures, and I'll furnish the war."

Primary Source | **Sheet Music**

THE CHARGE OF THE ROUGH RIDERS

GRAND GALOP MILITAIRE BY EDUARD HOLST.

HOWLEY, HAVILAND & Co.

Rallying Support During the 1890s, popular music was sold primarily as sheet music. Friends and families gathered around pianos in homes and sang to the latest music. The Spanish-American War was a popular theme in much of this sheet music. Many songwriters wrote patriotic marches and stirring songs to rally American support for the war. War heroes were celebrated in musical numbers, such as "The Charge of the Rough Riders." Patriotic music not only provided entertainment, it also shaped people's attitudes about the war.

Critical Thinking

Making Connections Do you think popular music shapes people's attitudes about major events today? Explain.

Teach

S Skill Practice

Using Geography Skills Ask: How did Cuba's location affect Americans' feelings about the rebellion that was taking place there? *(Because it is so close to the United States—just 90 miles [145 km] from Florida—Americans were especially nervous about the violence there affecting Americans and American interests.)* **OL**

C Critical Thinking

Determining Cause and Effect Ask: What caused rising "war fever" among Americans? *(sympathy for Cuban rebels based on detailed reports in the American press)* **OL**

Primary Source

Critical Thinking Answer Some students might say that popular music does shape people's attitudes, such as antiwar or pro-American songs. Others might say that there are relatively few such songs, so they do not necessarily have a strong impact on public opinion.

Hands-On Chapter Project
Step 3

Creating a Chronological Series of Maps

Step 3: Creating the Third Map Student groups will prepare the third map, which will show the U.S. and the world as it was in about 1900.

Essential Question: How did the Spanish-American War help the United States become a world power?

Directions Distribute another large outline map of the world to each group of students. Have them research to locate the borders of the U.S. and its areas of influence in 1900. Tell them to color-code maps to show the official territory of the U.S. and areas of the world with which the U.S. had influence.

Determining Cause and Effect Ask: What was the effect of the Spanish-American War on the United States' reputation in the world? *(Because the U.S. could stand up to Spain, it became clear that the U.S. had become a world power.)* **OL**

(Chapter Project continued in Section 4)

The United States and the World, 1900

R₁ Reading Strategy

Making Connections Ask: Do you think the modern media tries to influence people's opinions about current events? Why or why not? (*Some students might give examples of media bias and say it does try to influence public opinion; others might say they believe most of the media tries to be fair.*) **AL**

R₂ Reading Strategy

Determining Importance After students read the subsection entitled "Remember the *Maine*," ask them to reread it and decide what was the most important factor that made the United States decide to declare war on Spain. (*Most will probably say it was the explosion of the* Maine. *A case could also be made that it was Americans' eagerness for war due to press coverage of Cuba or that it was Spain's refusal to meet American demands.*) **BL**

The Spanish-American War ⬜ NATIONAL GEOGRAPHIC

Map Skills Answers
1. Cuba
2. Cuba and Puerto Rico

Differentiated Instruction

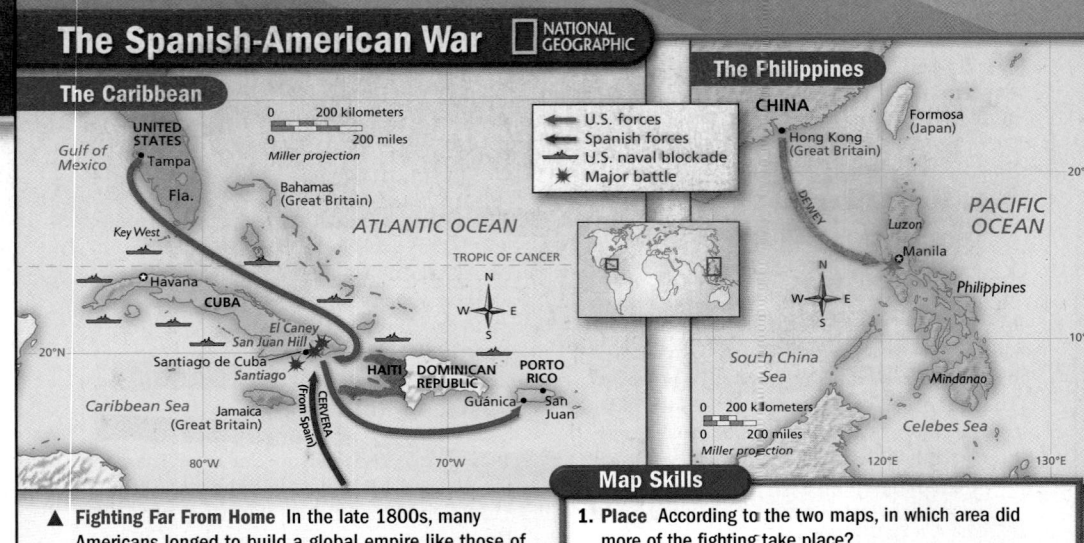

The Spanish-American War ⬜ NATIONAL GEOGRAPHIC

The Caribbean

The Philippines

Legend: ← U.S. forces, ← Spanish forces, ⚓ U.S. naval blockade, ★ Major battle

▲ **Fighting Far From Home** In the late 1800s, many Americans longed to build a global empire like those of the imperial European powers. Victories in the Spanish-American War led to American acquisitions in the Caribbean and the Pacific.

Map Skills

1. **Place** According to the two maps, in which area did more of the fighting take place?
2. **Location** On what two Caribbean islands did U.S. forces land?

Maps In Motion See StudentWorks™ Plus or glencoe.com.

R₁

This type of sensational, biased, and often false reporting is called **yellow journalism.** It played a major role in the formation of pro-war opinion in the United States.

R₂ "Remember the *Maine*"

The pressure on President McKinley to take action seemed to grow by the hour. Rioting broke out in the Cuban capital of Havana in January 1898. McKinley responded by sending the battleship *Maine* to Havana to protect American citizens and property.

The ship remained quietly at anchor in Havana Harbor for three weeks. Then, on the night of February 15, 1898, a huge explosion shattered the *Maine*, killing 260 officers and crew members. American newspapers immediately blamed the Spanish. Spain denied responsibility for the explosion. Much later, evidence indicated that the explosion may have been accidental. At the time, however, Americans wanted war with Spain. The slogan "Remember the *Maine*" became a rallying cry for revenge.

After the *Maine* incident, President McKinley sent the Spanish a strong note. He demanded a truce and an end to brutality against the Cubans. The Spanish agreed to some American demands, but not enough to satisfy McKinley or Congress. On April 19 Congress recognized Cuban independence and it also demanded the withdrawal of Spanish forces from the island. McKinley was authorized to use the army and navy to enforce American aims. On April 25, 1898, Congress declared war on Spain.

War in the Philippines

Events in Cuba **triggered,** or started, the Spanish-American War. The war's first military actions, however, occurred thousands of miles away in the Spanish colony of the Philippines. These islands served as a base for part of the Spanish fleet.

In late February 1898, Assistant Secretary of the Navy Theodore Roosevelt had wired Commodore George Dewey to prepare for possible military action in the Philippines.

Leveled Activities

BL Reteaching Activity, URB p. 65

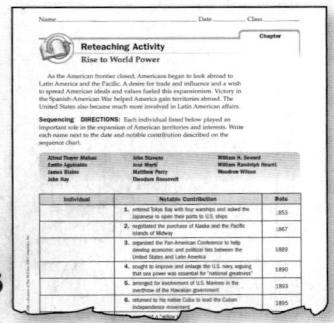

OL School-to-Home Conn. Activity, URB p. 63

AL Enrichment Activity, URB p. 11

ELL Guided Reading Activity, URB p. 69

Articles and cartoons in American "yellow" newspapers highlighted Spanish atrocities in Cuba. Many Americans wanted to rescue Cuba from the "villainous" Spanish. ▶

▼ The U.S. battleship *Maine* blew up in Havana Harbor on February 15, 1898. The cause of the explosion was a mystery—the Spanish had little motive to destroy a U.S. ship, but Cuban rebels had much to gain by increasing hostilities between the United States and Spain.

In the early morning hours of May 1, Dewey launched a surprise attack on the Spanish fleet in Manila Bay. Dewey destroyed most of the Spanish ships.

American troops arrived in July, and Filipino rebels, led by Emilio Aguinaldo (AH•gee•NAHL•doh), helped the Americans capture the city of Manila. Using American weapons, the rebels then took the main island of Luzon and declared independence. They expected American support, but the United States debated what to do with the islands.

Fighting in Cuba

Meanwhile in the Caribbean, a Spanish fleet entered the harbor of Santiago in Cuba on May 19. American ships soon blockaded the coast, trapping the Spanish in the harbor.

About 17,000 American troops—nearly a quarter of them African American—then came ashore while forces under Cuban general Calixto García drove off the Spanish soldiers. As the Cuban and American forces advanced, heavy fighting followed.

History ONLINE
Student Web Activity Visit glencoe.com and complete the Chapter 22 Web Activity about the Rough Riders.

The Rough Riders

Theodore Roosevelt resigned his position as assistant secretary of the navy to join the fighting in Cuba. He led the First Regiment of U.S. Cavalry Volunteers. The regiment was an assorted group of former cowhands and college students, popularly known as the **Rough Riders.** On July 1, the Rough Riders, with African American soldiers of the Ninth and Tenth Cavalries, joined the **Battle of San Juan Hill.** "I waved my hat and we went up the hill with a rush," Roosevelt wrote later.

The Americans captured San Juan Hill after intense fighting. Two days later the Spanish fleet attempted to break out of the Santiago harbor. In a battle that lasted about four hours, the Spanish fleet was destroyed, ending Spanish resistance in Cuba.

The United States then turned to the Spanish colony of Puerto Rico. American troops landed on Puerto Rico in late July and quickly took control of the island. On August 12, the Spanish signed an **armistice,** or peace agreement, and the war ended.

Losses in the War

Secretary of State John Hay called the Spanish-American War "a splendid little war." The war lasted fewer than four months. About 400 Americans were killed in battle or died from wounds received in the fighting.

Yet the war had other aspects that were not at all "splendid." More than 2,000 Americans died of yellow fever, malaria, and other diseases found in the tropical climate. The African Americans who served during this war faced the additional burden of discrimination. They were placed in segregated units, but they fought alongside the Cuban rebel army, in which African American and white troops fought as equals.

Reading Check Identifying Who were the Rough Riders?

D Differentiated Instruction

Verbal/Linguistic Have students write short poems about one aspect of the Spanish-American War and share them with the class. They might write about fighting, the Rough Riders, or the war's outcome. They can write from an American point of view or from the point of view of an islander. **AL**

History ONLINE
Objectives and answers to the Student Web Activity can be found at glencoe.com under the Web Activity Lesson Plan for this chapter.

Reading Check **Answer:** The Rough Riders were a cavalry regiment made of former cowhands and college students, led by Theodore Roosevelt. They became war heroes because of their boldness and bravery.

Additional Support

Activity: Interdisciplinary Connection

Art Have students work in five groups to find five different examples of artwork in which the Spanish-American War is the subject. Art selections might include paintings, political cartoons, sculptures, or newspaper illustrations. Invite an art teacher to visit your class to discuss the media and styles chosen and to help students analyze the art. Then ask the groups to discuss their selected artwork and try to determine how each artist felt about the war. Have each group write a brief analysis of their artwork, explaining from the artist's point of view the message he or she hoped to convey about the war or its outcome. Encourage them to point out specific details or stylistic choices in the art that led them to their conclusions. If time permits, invite groups to present their art and analyses to the class. **OL**

R Reading Strategy

Using Word Parts Ask: What is the root word of "acquisitions"? *(acquire)* What does it mean? *(to take possession of something)* What are some other words based on this root word? *(acquirable, acquisitive, and acquiring)* **ELL**

C Critical Thinking

Making Inferences Have students list the conditions the United States put on Cuba's independence. *(The Cuban constitution would have to state that Cuba would not make treaties with other nations, would give the United States control of a naval base at Guantanamo Bay, and would allow the United States to intervene in Cuban affairs if Cuban independence were threatened.)* **OL**

INTERPRETING
POLITICAL CARTOONS

Answers

1. islands to take over

2. Imperialist; Uncle Sam views the territories as his to take.

Differentiated Instruction

Primary Sources
INTERPRETING
POLITICAL CARTOONS

Uncle Sam's menu includes "Cuba Steak," "Porto Rico Pig," "the Philippine Floating Islands," and "the Sandwich Islands."

1. **Interpreting** What does Uncle Sam's menu represent?

2. **Analyzing** Does the cartoon depict President McKinley as an imperialist or as an anti-imperialist? How do you know?

A. Uncle Sam (United States)
B. President William McKinley C. Menu

"Well, I Hardly Know Which to Take First"

R Acquisitions

Main Idea The American empire became a reality after the Spanish-American War.

History and You Think about what it means to be independent. Read to learn how Cuba was ruled after the Spanish-American War.

• •

The United States and Spain signed the Treaty of Paris on December 10, 1898, ending the war. The treaty dissolved most of the Spanish Empire.

Cuba became an American **protectorate**. A protectorate is technically an independent country, but it is under the control of another country. Puerto Rico and Guam became **territories** of the United States. A territory is an area that is completely controlled by another country. Spain also surrendered the Philippines to the United States in exchange for $20 million. The American empire became a reality despite criticism that it was contrary to the democratic values on which the country was based.

Cuban Protectorate

Americans debated what to do about Cuba. Finally, in 1901 the United States granted Cubans full independence, but only if their new constitution included clauses giving the United States certain rights. Known as the **Platt Amendment,** these conditions prohibited Cuba from making treaties with other nations. They gave the United States control of a naval base at Guantanamo Bay. The United States also could intervene in Cuban affairs if the country's independence was threatened.

New Government for Puerto Rico

After the war, Puerto Rico remained under direct military rule. In 1900 the United States set up a new Puerto Rican government under the Foraker Act. The American government controlled the new administration. In 1917 the Jones Act made Puerto Rico a territory of the United States. American citizenship was granted to all Puerto Ricans. Many Puerto Ricans, however, still wanted independence.

The American Anti-Imperialist League

Objective: To analyze information about the American Anti-Imperialist League

Focus: Ask students why some Americans felt it necessary to form an anti-imperialist league.

Teach: Have students read the information and answer the questions.

Assess: Discuss with students why the league's standpoint was not popular.

Close: Ask students why they agree or disagree with the league's viewpoint.

Differentiated Instruction Strategies

BL Ask students to list the words in the excerpt they do not know and then write definitions obtained from the dictionary.

AL Ask students to obtain more information about the league and then prepare a time line of its activities.

ELL Have students underline words and phrases in the excerpt that describe or reinforce the league's principles.

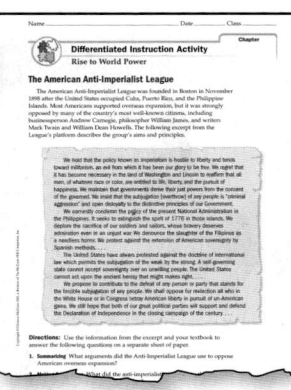

Differentiated Instruction Activity, URB p. 55

Acquiring the Philippines

The United States had gained possession of the Philippines in the treaty that ended the Spanish-American War. Acquisition of the Philippines, however, aroused fierce debate among American citizens.

During the 1890s, the anti-imperialists—people who opposed American foreign expansion—fought approval of the treaty. Some argued that American rule of the Philippines went against the democratic principles on which the United States was founded. Others opposed the large standing army that would be necessary to control the Philippines. Still others feared competition from Filipino laborers. Many Americans—including Andrew Carnegie, Carl Schurz, and Mark Twain—joined the anti-imperialist campaign.

The imperialists, however, led by Senators Henry Cabot Lodge and Albert Beveridge, eventually won out. They emphasized what they believed to be the benefits of taking the islands. Some argued that the Philippines would provide the United States with another Pacific naval base, a stopover on the way to China, and a large market for American goods. Others felt that the Americans had a duty to help "less civilized" peoples. As a result, the Senate ratified the Treaty of Paris on February 6, 1899.

Rebellion in the Philippines

The United States quickly learned that controlling its new empire would not be easy. In February 1899, Emilio Aguinaldo's forces began a fight for independence. This conflict became a gigantic undertaking for the United States. More than 4,000 Americans died. Filipinos suffered far greater casualties—at least 200,000 soldiers and civilians died.

When Aguinaldo was captured in March 1901, many Filipino military officers and soldiers surrendered. Others refused to give up even after Aguinaldo urged them to stop fighting.

In the summer of 1901, the United States transferred authority from a military to a civilian government headed by William Howard Taft. Taft set out to prepare the islands for **eventual,** or later, self-rule. The Philippines gained independence in 1946.

✔ Reading Check **Contrasting** What is the difference between a protectorate and a territory?

C Critical Thinking

Analyzing Information Ask: Who do you think was right about the acquisition of the Philippines—the imperialists or the anti-imperialists? Why? *(imperialists—because the Philippines provided a market for American goods and a stopping place in the Pacific; anti-imperialists—taking the Philippines against its will went against American democratic ideals)* **OL**

✔ Reading Check **Answer:** A protectorate is an independent country but under the control of another country. A territory is completely controlled by another country.

Assess

History ONLINE

Study Central™ provides summaries, interactive games, and online graphic organizers to help students review content.

Close

Determining Cause and Effect Discuss the outcome of the Spanish-American War and how it made the United States into a world power. **OL**

Section 3 Review

History ONLINE
Study Central™ To review this section, go to glencoe.com.

Vocabulary

1. Define each of the following terms in a sentence: yellow journalism, trigger, armistice, protectorate, territory, eventual.

Main Ideas

2. Explaining How did newspapers contribute to America's declaration of war against Spain in 1898?

3. Discussing Why did some Americans oppose empire building by the United States?

Critical Thinking

4. Summarizing Use a time line like the one below to summarize the events in the Philippines after the end of Spanish rule in 1898.

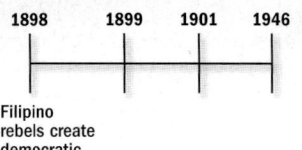

1898 1899 1901 1946

Filipino rebels create democratic republic

5. Creative Writing Write an account of the Battle of San Juan Hill from the point of view of an African American soldier of the Ninth Cavalry.

Answer the
6. Essential Question
How did the Spanish-American War help the United States become a world power?

Answers

1. Sentences should demonstrate correct understanding of the terms.
2. By printing detailed, upsetting, and sometimes false accounts of the Cuban rebellion and Spanish mistreatment of the rebels, the press convinced many Americans that the United States needed to do something to help the Cubans throw off Spanish rule.
3. They believed it went against the democratic ideals on which the United States was founded.

4. **1899:** Treaty of Paris signed and Filipinos begin fighting for independence; **1901:** United States transfers authority from a military to a civilian government under Taft; **1946:** the Philippines gain independence
5. Students' accounts might mention seeing the Rough Riders advance up the hill, fighting alongside Cuban rebels, dealing with discrimination and segregation in the American army, or enjoying equality when fighting alongside Cuban fighters.

6. Possible answers: It showed the world that the United States could now easily defeat one of the world's stronger navies, which meant that it could hold its own against any world power. Also, by acquiring several new important territories, the United States became an empire and joined other world powers in the fight to acquire territories in the Pacific and the Caribbean and trading rights in Asia.

Section 4

Latin American Policies

Focus

Bellringer
Daily Test Practice Transparency 22–4

Reading Guide
Answers to Graphic:

Roosevelt Corollary: should intervene in Latin America whenever those nations seemed unstable; **Dollar Diplomacy:** should intervene in other countries only if they threatened American business interests; **Moral Diplomacy:** should intervene to teach Latin Americans to "elect good men"

Section Spotlight Video

To learn more about the U.S. presidents' influence on foreign policy and the Panama Canal, watch the Section Spotlight Video "Latin American Policies."

Resource Manager

Essential Question ◄
How did the beliefs of U.S. presidents shape Latin American foreign policies?

Reading Guide

Content Vocabulary
isthmus *(p. 691)*
anarchy *(p. 693)*
dollar diplomacy *(p. 694)*

Academic Vocabulary
eliminate *(p. 691)*   annual *(p. 691)*

Key People and Events
Roosevelt Corollary *(p. 694)*
Francisco "Pancho" Villa *(p. 696)*
John J. Pershing *(p. 696)*

Reading Strategy
Taking Notes As you read, use a diagram like the one below to compare the principles on which each American foreign policy was based.

Policy	Principle
Roosevelt Corollary	
Dollar Diplomacy	
Moral Diplomacy	

ILLINOIS STANDARDS
The American Journey

14.E.3 Compare the basic principles of the United States and its international interests (e.g., territory, environment, trade, use of technology).

15.E Understand the impact of government policies and decisions on production and consumption in the economy.

16.B.3d (US) Describe ways in which the United States developed as a world political power.

American Diary

On August 15, 1914, the Ancon, a cargo ship, made the first official trip through the Panama Canal. One traveler onboard the Ancon noted: "So quietly did [the ship] pursue [its] way that . . . a strange observer coming suddenly upon the scene would have thought that the canal had always been in operation, and that the Ancon was only doing what thousands of other vessels must have done before [it]."

—quoted in **The Path Between the Seas**

Since the *Ancon*'s voyage, more than 800,000 ships have passed through the Gaillard (Culebra) Cut, the narrowest channel of the Panama Canal.

R Reading Strategies	**C** Critical Thinking	**D** Differentiated Instruction	**W** Writing Support	**S** Skill Practice
Teacher Edition • Making Connections, p. 693 • Using Context Clues, p. 694 **Additional Resources** • Guid. Read., URB p. 70 • Content Vocab., URB p. 45 • Read. Ess., p. 244	**Teacher Edition** • Drawing Conclusions, p. 692 • Inferring, p. 695 • Ident. Central Issues, p. 696 **Additional Resources** • Quizzes and Tests, p. 216 • Crit. Think. Skills, URB p. 57	**Teacher Edition** • Logical/Mathematical, p. 693 **Additional Resources** • School-to-Home, URB p. 63 • Reteaching Act., URB p. 65	**Teacher Edition** • Persuasive Writing, p. 692 **Additional Resources** • Authentic Assess., p. 22	**Teacher Edition** • Using Geo. Skills, p. 691 • Visual Literacy, p. 692 **Additional Resources** • Daily Test Pract. Transp. 22-4 • Lesson Transp. 22B, 22C • Soc. Stud. Skills, URB p. 53

Panama

Main Idea The United States negotiated with Panama to build the Panama Canal.

History and You Have you negotiated for better pay for lawn mowing or babysitting services? Read to learn how the United States negotiated in order to build the Panama Canal.

The opening of the Panama Canal in 1914 was the fulfillment of a long-held dream. For hundreds of years, Americans and Europeans had wanted to build a canal across Central America to connect the Atlantic and Pacific Oceans. They wanted that connection to **eliminate** the long and dangerous sea voyage around South America. Now that the United States controlled territory in both oceans, it was even more important to have a canal that would allow easier access to American overseas territories.

Panama was an **isthmus**—a narrow strip of land connecting two larger bodies of land—about 50 miles (80 km) wide. Wedged between the Caribbean Sea and the Pacific Ocean, Panama seemed like the perfect site for the canal.

In 1879 a French company acquired a lease from Colombia to build a canal across Colombia's northern province of Panama. French efforts to build a canal failed, however, because of lack of funds and terrible losses from disease among the workers.

The United States had long considered two possible canal sites, one through Nicaragua and one through Panama. The French company eased this choice by offering to sell its rights and property in Panama to the United States.

In 1901 the United States bought the lease from the French for $40 million. Secretary of State John Hay negotiated a treaty with Colombia in 1903 that granted the United States a 99-year lease on a strip of land across Panama. That lease cost the United States a payment of $10 million with an **annual** rent of $250,000.

Revolution in Panama

The Colombian Senate, however, rejected the U.S. offer to lease the strip of land. President Roosevelt then looked for other ways to get land for the canal. He wrote that he would "be delighted if Panama were an independent state."

If You Were There / Working on the Panama Canal

Digging the "Big Ditch" With tropical diseases under control, you and thousands of workers begin digging. In grassy and swampy coastal areas, you struggle against the extreme heat, but your equipment works well. It is difficult work when you reach the rugged inland mountains, though. Heavy rains create mud and landslides. You also have to blast away solid rock with dynamite. After the blasts, giant steam shovels scoop up the rocks and dump them into nearby railroad cars. President Theodore Roosevelt is excited about the project, and he arrives at the site in 1906. He is photographed sitting at the controls of a steam shovel. With such presidential backing, how can you not succeed? In 1913 digging ends at last, and one of the greatest engineering projects of your time is almost complete.

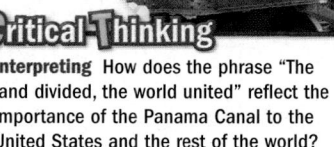

Critical Thinking

Interpreting How does the phrase "The land divided, the world united" reflect the importance of the Panama Canal to the United States and the rest of the world?

CHAPTER 22
Section 4

Teach

S Skill Practice

Using Geography Skills Show students a map of Central America. Point out Nicaragua and Panama, the two canal sites considered by the United States. **Ask:** Which site do you think is better and why? *(Possible answer: probably Panama, because it is the narrowest point; however, Nicaragua had the advantage of Lago de Nicaragua and/or major rivers)* **What geographical features might make a site a better or worse choice for the canal?** *(**Better:** flat land, bodies of water that can be made part of the canal system; **Worse:** mountainous and rocky land, no bodies of water, a wider part of the isthmus)* **OL**

If You Were There

Critical Thinking Answer
Possible answer: Cutting across the Panamanian isthmus produced a faster path from one side of the world to the other. This changed global trade, transportation, and communication forever.

Hands-On Chapter Project
Step 4

Creating a Chronological Series of Maps

Step 4: Creating the Fourth Map Student groups will prepare the fourth map, which will show the U.S. and world as it was in about 1915.

Essential Question: How did the beliefs of U.S. presidents shape Latin American foreign policies?

Directions Have students meet in their groups. Distribute another large outline map of the world to each group. Have students conduct research to locate the borders of the U.S. and its areas of influence by 1915. Tell them to color-code their world maps using one color to show the official territory of the U.S. Other colors should show areas of the world with which the U.S. had influence, such as trade

agreements, treaties of peace or alliance, and so on.

Drawing Conclusions Ask: How did the U.S. presidents' foreign policies during the early 1900s change the map? *(Possible answer: U.S. influence spread strongly in Latin America, and the Panama Canal Zone was added to its territories.)* **OL**

(Chapter Project continued on the Visual Summary page)

C Critical Thinking

Drawing Conclusions Ask: Why did the United States support Panama's revolution? *(because an independent Panama would lease the land for the canal to the United States, but Colombia would not)* **BL**

W Writing Support

Persuasive Writing Ask students to write a few paragraphs in which they support or oppose Roosevelt's actions in Panama. Encourage students to justify their points of view with two or more logical arguments supported by facts and details from the text. **AL**

S Skill Practice

Visual Literacy Direct students' attention to the map on this page. **Ask:** How many sets of locks are there in the Panama Canal, and what are they called? *(three: Gatún, Pedro Miguel, and Miraflores Locks)* What is the purpose of the locks? *(to raise and lower ships as they move through the canal)* **OL**

Differentiated Instruction

The Panamanians had staged a number of revolts against Colombia in the past, but those uprisings had never met with success. This time, however, the Panamanians had reason to believe that the Americans would support them in a revolt against Colombia.

On November 2, 1903, the American warship *Nashville* steamed into the port of Colón on the Caribbean coast of Panama. Encouraged by this show of support, the Panamanians revolted the next day and declared their independence. Colombia sent forces to stop the revolt, but the United States intervened and turned them back.

The Panama Canal

On November 6, the United States recognized Panama's independence. Less than two weeks later, Hay signed a treaty with the new nation of Panama. It gave the United States a 10-mile (16-km) strip of land across the country for the same amount offered earlier to Colombia. The United States now had land to build a canal.

Roosevelt's actions did not meet with praise from everyone, however. Many Latin Americans, some Congress members, and other Americans were angered. The president, however, took great pride in his accomplishment. He later said: "I took the canal zone and let Congress debate, and while the debate goes on, the canal does also."

The United States could now start work on the canal—not an easy undertaking. Disease struck the workers. An English writer described Panama as "a damp, tropical jungle, intensely hot, swarming with mosquitoes." Those mosquitoes carried two deadly diseases—yellow fever and malaria.

The Grand Opening

The Panama Canal opened on August 15, 1914. A cargo ship named the *Ancon* made the first voyage through the new waterway.

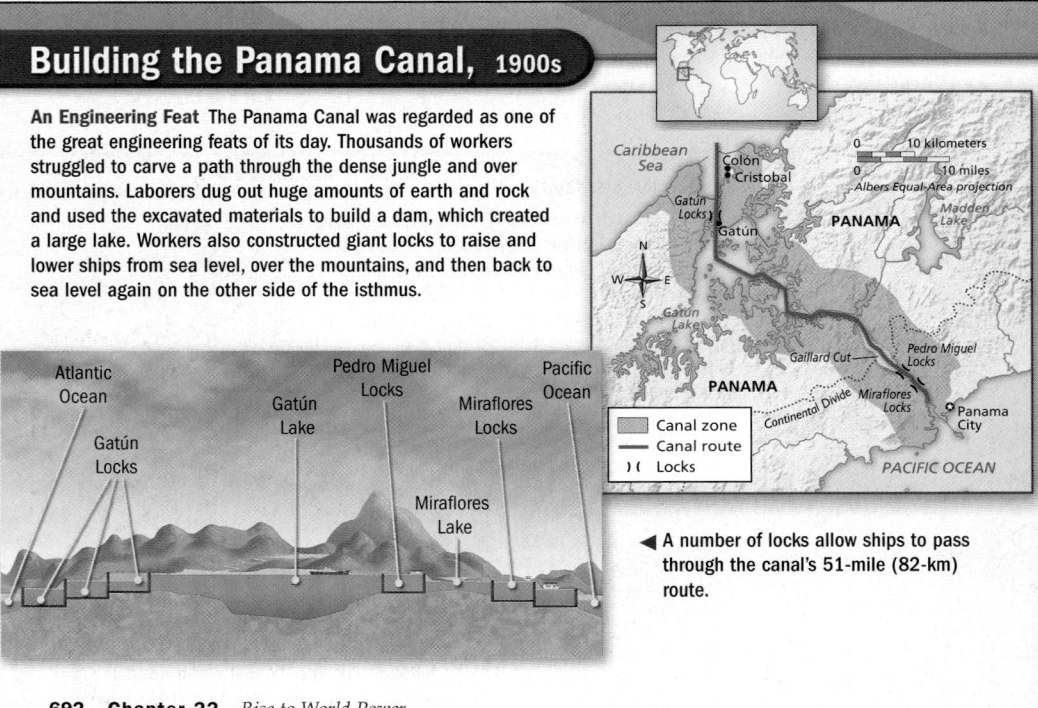

Building the Panama Canal, 1900s

An Engineering Feat The Panama Canal was regarded as one of the great engineering feats of its day. Thousands of workers struggled to carve a path through the dense jungle and over mountains. Laborers dug out huge amounts of earth and rock and used the excavated materials to build a dam, which created a large lake. Workers also constructed giant locks to raise and lower ships from sea level, over the mountains, and then back to sea level again on the other side of the isthmus.

◄ A number of locks allow ships to pass through the canal's 51-mile (82-km) route.

Leveled Activities

BL Social Studies Skills Activity, URB p. 53

OL Authentic Assessment With Rubrics, p. 22

ELL Reading Essentials and Note-Taking Guide, p. 244

From the start, the canal was a great success. Before the canal opened, ships sailing from New York to San Francisco traveled 12,600 miles (20,277 km) around the treacherous tip of South America. Afterwards, the trip was only 4,900 miles (7,886 km). It could be completed in less than half the time, significantly reducing shipping costs.

The Panama Canal also helped extend American naval power. The U.S. naval fleet could now move freely between the Atlantic and Pacific Oceans. The canal was a valuable property that the United States intended to protect. Thus, it guaranteed that there would be a strong American presence in Latin America. Yet many Latin Americans remained bitter over how the canal land had been acquired. This resentment soured relations between the United States and Latin America for years.

✓ **Reading Check** Identifying What problem faced workers on the canal?

Policing the Western Hemisphere

D **Main Idea** Using its economic and military power, the United States policed the Western Hemisphere.

History and You Have you ever heard the proverb "Speak softly and carry a big stick"? What does that mean? Read to learn about American foreign policies in Latin America.

. . . .

President Roosevelt often quoted an African proverb, "Speak softly and carry a big stick." He believed the United States should respond **R** to foreign crises not with threats but with military action. Roosevelt became known for his "big stick" approach to foreign affairs.

Roosevelt also believed that America must exercise "an international police power." He felt that this was necessary to preserve order and to prevent the world from falling into **anarchy**—disorder and lawlessness.

More than 6,000 men used shovels, explosives, and a system of railways to create the Gaillard (Culebra) Cut. Below, a sailing ship is towed through the finished passageway.

◄ Colonel William Gorgas

Eliminating Disease Colonel William Gorgas, an army doctor who helped eliminate yellow fever in Cuba, went to Panama to improve health conditions. Gorgas instructed workers to drain swamps, spray insecticides, spread oil on stagnant pools of water, and cut grassy marshes in order to destroy mosquito breeding places. Workers who did become ill were isolated in "pens" to stop the spread of the disease. By 1906, these measures eliminated yellow fever and greatly reduced the number of malaria cases. Without controlling disease, the United States could not have built the canal.

Critical Thinking

Making Inferences What do the efforts devoted to the construction of the Panama Canal reveal about how U.S. leaders felt about the project?

Rise to World Power **Chapter 22** 693

D **Differentiated Instruction**

Logical/Mathematical Ask: How much shorter was the route from New York to San Francisco through the Panama Canal than the route around South America? *(7,700 miles [12,391 km] shorter)* **OL**

R **Reading Strategy**

Making Connections Ask: Do you think Roosevelt would approve of the foreign policy of the United States today? *(Some may say that Roosevelt would approve of U.S. military actions that are intended to keep order, spread democracy, and protect U.S. interests. Others might say that Roosevelt would not approve because the U.S. does not intervene in every situation where lawlessness is a problem.)* **OL**

Building the Panama Canal, 1900s

Critical Thinking Answer

U.S. leaders were intent on building the canal and would not allow any obstacle to stop them.

✓ **Reading Check Answer:** mosquito-borne diseases (malaria and yellow fever)

Critical Thinking Skills Activity, URB p. 57

Drawing Conclusions

Objective: To learn how to draw conclusions in order to understand a political cartoon

Focus: Ask students to list some of the foreign countries in which the U.S. had influence in 1909.

Teach: Have students study the cartoon, answer the questions, and apply the skill.

Assess: Ask students if the conclusions they drew from the cartoon are accurate.

Close: Ask students if they agree with the U.S. acting as a world "police officer" in the early 1900s.

Differentiated Instruction Strategies

BL Have students verbally explain the meaning of the cartoon before they answer the questions.

AL Have students draw a cartoon about the U.S. in 1909 from the rest of the world's viewpoint.

ELL Ask students to explain who Uncle Sam is.

693

Primary Sources
INTERPRETING
POLITICAL CARTOONS

When European powers threatened to send warships to the Dominican Republic to collect debts owed them, the United States applied the Roosevelt Corollary to stop them.

1. **Analyzing** How is the Dominican Republic portrayed? What does this suggest about American opinion of Latin Americans?

2. **Interpreting** According to the cartoon, how did the Monroe Doctrine prevent European intervention in Latin America?

A. President Theodore Roosevelt
B. European powers
C. Republic of Santo Domingo (Dominican Republic)

HANDS OFF!

Roosevelt Corollary

Theodore Roosevelt was worried about instability in the Caribbean region. He feared that European powers would try to intervene there. In 1904 Roosevelt asserted America's right to act as a "policeman" in Latin America and to intervene "however reluctantly . . . in cases of wrongdoing."

This policy, known as the **Roosevelt Corollary,** was an addition to the Monroe Doctrine. The United States used the Monroe Doctrine only to prevent European intervention in Latin America. Under the Roosevelt Corollary, the United States now claimed the right to intervene in the affairs of Latin American nations whenever those nations seemed unstable.

The United States first applied the Roosevelt Corollary in 1905 when it took control of the Dominican Republic's finances following a revolution that had toppled the country's government. Then in 1906, the United States used the policy again when troops were sent to Cuba to stop a revolution there.

Dollar Diplomacy

Theodore Roosevelt thought of American power mostly in military terms. His successor, William Howard Taft, had a different view. Taft hoped to change American foreign policy by "substituting dollars for bullets." That is, he was willing to intervene in other nations' affairs if they threatened American business interests.

Taft's policy was known as **dollar diplomacy.** This policy had some positive and some negative effects. First, American investments in Latin America grew. Roads, railroads, and harbors built with American investments helped increase trade and profits. Second, the United States played a stronger role overseas. When U.S. business interests in Latin America were threatened, military intervention often followed. Of course, such action led to increased anti-U.S. feelings throughout Latin America.

☑ **Reading Check Contrasting** How were Taft's views about power different from Roosevelt's?

Relations With Mexico

Main Idea During the early 1900s, the United States and Mexico almost went to war with each other.

History and You Think about a country today that is experiencing a long civil war. Then read about the United States's involvement in the Mexican revolution.

· ·

In the early 1900s, Mexico was a poor country. A tiny group of rich landholders controlled the nation. Investors in the United States invested millions of dollars in Mexican oil wells and other businesses.

Then, in 1910, events in Mexico began to threaten American investments. This period also revealed the weaknesses of dollar diplomacy and forced the United States to use military intervention to protect its interests in the area.

In 1911 a popular Mexican reformer named Francisco Madero (muh•DEHR•oh) led a successful revolution. His goal was to overthrow Mexico's brutal dictator, Porfirio Díaz (DEE•ahs). Foreign businesses and some Mexican politicians and landowners prospered under the rule of Díaz. The lives of most Mexicans, however, had grown worse.

Just two years after taking power, Madero was overthrown and killed by General Victoriano Huerta (WEHR•tuh). Like Díaz, Huerta favored the wealthy and foreign interests. President Woodrow Wilson, who had just taken office, refused to recognize Huerta's "government of butchers."

Primary Source | Relations With Mexico

American Troops in Mexico In 1916 Mexican rebel Pancho Villa, angered by American support for a political rival, began attacking Americans. He killed 16 American miners in Mexico, then crossed the U.S. border and burned the town of Columbus, New Mexico, killing even more Americans. American president Woodrow Wilson sent 6,000 soldiers under the leadership of General John Pershing into Mexico to capture Villa. Though Mexican president Carranza also wanted to capture Villa, he opposed the presence of U.S. forces in Mexican territory.

Pursuing Pancho Villa

▲ American soldiers used motorcycles, trucks, and horses in their unsuccessful search for Villa.

"Villa is entirely familiar with every foot of Chihuahua, and the Mexican people, through friendship or fear, have always kept him advised of our every movement. He carries little food, lives off the country, rides his mounts hard and replaces them with fresh stock taken wherever found. Thus he has had the advantage since the end of the first twenty-four hours after the Columbus raid occurred."

—from a report by General John Pershing, April 1916

◄ Bold and ruthless, Villa commanded a strong rebel force in northern Mexico. ▶

Critical Thinking

Drawing Conclusions Why do you think U.S. forces failed to capture Pancho Villa?

Activity: Debating the Issues

Understanding Points of View Pair students and have them role-play U.S. President Wilson and Mexican President Carranza having a debate about American troops going into Mexico to try to capture Pancho Villa. During their discussions, they should explain their points of view and reasons for believing as they do. For example, Wilson might express a strong desire to find Villa and bring him to justice for killing Americans, explaining that he thinks his well-armed troops could do it quickly and easily without causing trouble in Mexico. Carranza might agree about capturing Villa but protest against foreign troops in his country because he considers it an invasion. He might offer instead to have Mexican troops capture Villa. Invite pairs to conduct their discussions in front of the class. **OL**

Section 4

C Critical Thinking

Identifying Central Issues Ask: Do you approve or disapprove of Wilson's "moral diplomacy" foreign policy? Why? *(Some might approve because it was intended to improve life for Latin Americans and spread democracy. Others might disapprove because it imposed American values on others against their will, and it assumed that Americans always know best.)* **OL**

Reading Check **Answer:** It was Wilson's idea that the United States had a duty to teach Latin Americans "to elect good men," which he was willing to use military force to do.

Assess

History ONLINE

Study Central™ provides summaries, interactive games, and online graphic organizers to help students review content.

Close

Determining Cause and Effect Discuss Roosevelt's, Taft's, and Wilson's foreign policies. Have students summarize each president's philosophy and give an example of how he applied it while in office. **OL**

Section 4 Review

Wilson's "Moral Diplomacy"

In foreign affairs, Woodrow Wilson hoped to avoid further imperialism by the United States. He sought to promote democracy in other nations as a means of ensuring stability and preventing war and revolution. According to Wilson, the United States had a duty "to teach the South American republics to elect good men." Like Roosevelt and Taft, Wilson recognized the importance of military power and economic interests. Wilson however, wished to base his foreign policy on moral principles.

C Wilson's "moral diplomacy" faced a serious challenge in Mexico. After Huerta took power, a civil war broke out in Mexico. Wilson hoped that the Huerta government, without American support, would fall. That did not happen. Wilson then authorized arms sales to Huerta's rival, Venustiano Carranza (kuh•RAN•zuh).

Problems came to a head in April 1914. When Huerta's troops arrested some American sailors, Wilson ordered U.S. troops to seize the port of Veracruz. This show of force strengthened Carranza's position. Huerta was forced to flee in August. Carranza took power, and American troops withdrew.

Francisco "Pancho" Villa

Huerta's departure did not end the civil war. Rebel leader **Francisco "Pancho" Villa** rose up against Carranza. In January 1916, Villa held and shot 16 Americans because of U.S. support for the Carranza government. Villa hoped to damage Mexican-American relations, but the United States did not act against Mexico. Then Villa and his rebels crossed into New Mexico, burning the town of Columbus and killing 18 Americans.

Villa's actions angered the United States. Troops led by General **John J. Pershing** crossed the border into Mexico and pursued Villa for almost a year. Many Mexicans protected Villa from capture. After America's attention turned to the war raging in Europe in 1917, Pershing's troops left Mexico. American actions had brought the countries close to war and led to great resentment in Mexico. As in the Caribbean, America's experience in Mexico showed other nations that the United States would willingly use its power when its interests or its honor was threatened.

Reading Check **Defining** What was "moral diplomacy"?

History ONLINE
Study Central™ To review this section, go to glencoe.com.

Section 4 Review

Vocabulary

1. Define the following terms, using each one in a sentence: eliminate, isthmus, annual, anarchy, dollar diplomacy.

Main Ideas

2. **Identifying** How did the United States benefit from the construction of the Panama Canal? What were the drawbacks?

3. **Explaining** Why did President Roosevelt believe the United States should assert its military power in Latin America?

4. **Discussing** What event prevented an outbreak of war between the United States and Mexico in 1917? What did the United States prove by its actions in Mexico?

Critical Thinking

5. **Evaluating** Use a diagram like the one below to identify the positive and negative effects of Taft's dollar diplomacy in Latin America.

| Positive Effects | Dollar Diplomacy | Negative effects |

6. **Creative Writing** You are a follower of Francisco "Pancho" Villa. Write a paragraph explaining why you support him.

Answer the
7. **Essential Question**
How did the beliefs of U.S. presidents shape Latin American foreign policies?

Answers

1. Sentences should demonstrate correct understanding of the terms.
2. **Benefits:** a faster path between U.S. coasts, lower shipping costs, revenues from ships using the canal, and a presence in Central America; **Drawbacks:** Latin Americans were angry at how the U.S. obtained the land, many workers died during construction
3. to protect American business interests, to influence events and keep order in the Western Hemisphere, and to show U.S. power

4. the war in Europe; it would use its power when its interests or its honor were threatened.
5. **Positive effects:** temporarily lessened U.S. military intervention in Latin America, encouraged U.S. business investments in Latin America; **Negative effects:** failed to prevent violence, failed to adequately protect U.S. business interests
6. Paragraphs should include several reasons students support Villa.

7. Possible answers: Roosevelt's belief in using military force made the Panama Canal a reality, which benefited the entire world. His policy caused anger in Latin America that lasted for decades. Taft's "dollar diplomacy" increased American business in Latin America but also failed to stop instability there. Wilson's "moral diplomacy" helped bring U.S.-approved leaders to power in Mexico, but it also offended many.

Visual Summary

Main Idea	Supporting Details
American influence around the world expands in the late 1800s.	• After the closing of the frontier, the U.S. looks overseas to expand its territory. • Matthew Perry's expedition in 1854 opens Japan to U.S. trade. • The U.S. competes with European nations for overseas markets and resources. • Americans seek to spread Christianity and Western culture. • The United States purchases Alaska from Russia and seeks to develop friendly relations with Latin America. • U.S. Navy is strengthened to support overseas territories.
America seeks an empire in the Pacific.	• American sugar planters overthrow Hawaii's Queen Liliuokalani; Hawaii becomes a U.S. territory. • Germany and the United States divide the Samoa Islands. • The Open Door Policy protects and expands American trade in China. • Japan threatens U.S. power in the Pacific.
The Spanish-American War helps the United States become a world power.	• War erupts over concerns about Spanish rule in Cuba; explosion of the USS *Maine*. • U.S. defeats Spain; acquires Puerto Rico, Guam, and the Philippines.
U.S. involvement in Latin America increases in the early 1900s. **America's "Great White Fleet"** ▶	• U.S. seeks to build a canal across Central America to ease travel between the oceans. • U.S. supports Panama's revolt against Colombia to gain canal site. • The construction of the Panama Canal guarantees a strong American influence in the region.
The U.S. uses its military and economic power to maintain its interests in Latin America.	• The Roosevelt Corollary supports the use of American military force to prevent instability in Latin America. • Taft's "dollar diplomacy" calls for American intervention to protect U.S. business and economic interests. • Wilson's "moral diplomacy" supports the spread of democracy in Latin America.

▲ Queen Liliuokalani

◀ American troops in Mexico

STUDY TO GO Study anywhere, anytime! Download quizzes and flash cards to your PDA from glencoe.com.

Visual Summary

Determining Importance Ask: What do you think is the most important supporting detail for each main idea? Why? (*Students should justify their selections with logical reasons. For example, a student might say that the closing of the American frontier is the most important detail of the United States' spread of influence in the world. The justification might be that if the frontier had not been settled yet, the United States would not have looked to expand beyond its borders.*) **OL**

Personal Writing Have students write a poem or the lyrics for a song about the Age of Imperialism in the United States. Tell them they can write approvingly or disapprovingly about the nation's rise to world power. Their poems or lyrics should reference some historical facts and details from the chapter. **OL**

Hands-On Chapter Project
Step 5: Wrap-Up

Creating a Chronological Series of Maps

Step 5: Presenting the Map Series Students will display their maps and give a brief presentation to the class.

Directions Have groups arrange their maps in order on a wall, poster board, or some other display area. They should add titles, dates, legends, and other necessary information to make clear the order of the maps. Invite groups to show their maps to the class, pointing out how American territory and influence in the world grew between the late 1800s and early 1900s.

Comparing and Contrasting Point out that although the changes on the maps seem small, they represent the time period when the United States became a serious world power, setting the stage for its superpower status today. **Ask:** How might the world be different today if the United States had not been imperialistic during the late 1800s and early 1900s? (*Possible answers: There might be less freedom in the world without the U.S. to protect weaker allies; U.S. might be a poor country with still-developing industries; more Pacific islands would belong to European powers; or China might have been colonized by other powers or been consumed by decades of war.*) **OL**

Focus

R Reading Strategy

Previewing Have students read the title of this feature. **Ask:** Based on their knowledge of the Panama Canal, how would they answer this question? *(Students may justify the canal based on the fact that it has been in operation since it was built.)* After they finish reading both pages, ask students if their position has changed and discuss their views. **OL**

C Critical Thinking

Analyzing Lead a discussion on the main claims made by Roosevelt in his excerpt. Write these points on the board under the heading "Roosevelt's argument." Then, **ask:** Do you accept the logic of this argument? If so, why? Would you seek to challenge it? If so, how? *(Students may suggest that Roosevelt exaggerated the case for Panamanian independence to get the canal built or that the canal was important enough to warrant Roosevelt's actions.)* **AL**

Additional Support and Answers

698

YOU DECIDE

R Did the United States Have the Right to Build the Panama Canal?

Building Background

Theodore Roosevelt wanted the United States to be one of the world's great powers. He believed that the citizens of weaker countries were incapable of governing themselves. His beliefs guided him to help Panama secede from Colombia, enabling the United States to build a canal in the area.

Rubén Darío, an influential poet and journalist from Nicaragua, became increasingly concerned about the possibility of U.S. colonization of Latin America. In 1904 Darío wrote a poem entitled "To Roosevelt."

YES

THEODORE ROOSEVELT

I did not lift my finger to incite the revolutionists.... I simply ceased to stamp out the different revolutionary fuses that were already burning.... We gave to the people of Panama self-government, and freed them from subjection to alien oppressors.... When we did act and recognize Panama, Colombia at once acknowledged her own guilt by promptly offering to do what we had demanded, and what she had protested it was not in her power to do. But the offer came too late.... It would have necessitated our abandoning the people of Panama, our friends, and turning them over to

C *their and our foes.... If, as representing the American people, I had not acted precisely as I did, I would have been an unfaithful or incompetent representative; and inaction at that crisis would have meant not only indefinite delay in building the canal, but also practical admission on our part that we were not fit to play the part on the Isthmus which we had arrogated[1] to ourselves....*

I deeply regretted, and now deeply regret, the fact that the Colombian Government [forced] me to take the action I took; but I had no alternative, consistent with the full performance of my duty to my own people, and to the nations of mankind.

[1] **arrogated** claimed

Fast Facts

Defying Authority American leaders recognized that a canal across Panama would provide a tremendous boost for the American economy, because cargo ships on the Atlantic seaboard could reach the West Coast without sailing around the tip of South America. By the year 1900, advances in engineering had made this feat possible.

At the urging of the multimillionaire J.P. Morgan and other financiers, the U.S. government bought property on the Panamanian isthmus. But the government of Colombia, which controlled Panama at the time, refused to allow the Americans to build a canal. One of Morgan's business partners, William Nelson Cromwell, persuaded two managers of the Panama Railroad Company to defy the Colombian authorities and declare Panama's independence in November 1903. President Theodore Roosevelt's administration recognized the new nation immediately, and canal construction began the following year. The Panama Canal opened for traffic in 1914.

RUBÉN DARÍO

You think that life is fire,
that progress is eruption,
that wherever you shoot
you hit the future.

. . . .

But our America, that has had poets
since the ancient times of Netzahualcoyotl,[2]

has lived on light, on fire, on perfume, on love,
America of the great Montezuma, of the Inca,
the fragrant America of Christopher Columbus,
Catholic America, Spanish America,
the America in which noble Cuahtemoc[3] said:
"I'm not in a bed of roses"; that America
that trembles in hurricanes and lives on love,
it lives, you men of Saxon[4] eyes and barbarous soul.
And it dreams. And it loves, and it vibrates, and it is the
daughter of the Sun.
Be careful. Viva Spanish America!
There are a thousand cubs loosed from the Spanish lion.
Roosevelt, one would have to be, through God himself,
the-fearful Rifleman and strong Hunter,
to manage to grab us in your iron claws.

Building the Panama Canal

699

---

[2] **Netzahualcoyotl** ruler in 1400s Mexico
[3] **Cuahtemoc** last emperor of the Aztecs
[4] **Saxon** a person of English birth or descent

DBQ Document-Based Questions

1. **Interpreting** What did Roosevelt believe was his duty?

2. **Making Inferences** What do you think was more important to Roosevelt: Panamanian independence or the Panama Canal? Why?

3. **Analyzing** According to Darío, what are the differences between the United States and Latin America?

4. **Evaluating** In your opinion, which man made a stronger argument for his position? Explain your answer.

Teach

D Differentiated Instruction

Verbal/Linguistic Before you provide a dramatic reading of the poem, instruct students to listen to the emotional tone in the poem, and notice how they respond to the poem's imagery. Ask them to pick out one or two specific images or phrases to analyze. **Ask:** What is Dario saying? How do the images convey both ideas and feelings? **OL**

Assess/Close

Direct students to look at the two excerpts side by side. **Ask:** How does each author try to make his own viewpoint seem morally correct? *(Roosevelt asserts that America acts upon virtues such as justice, patience, and freedom; Dario associates "the naive America" with love, poetry, and ancient heritage, while accusing the United States of aggression and abuse of power.)* Ensuing discussions could try to draw connections between these opposing value systems and relations between the United States and Latin America.

Answers

1. Roosevelt implies that his duty was to intervene in Panama to help the nation achieve independence. This action would permit the Panama Canal to be built, under American control.

2. Students who say the canal was more important may support the point by noting that Roosevelt expresses regret but also defends his action as necessary to get the Panama Canal built.

3. Dario depicts the United States as powerful, warlike, and arrogant. In contrast, his poem emphasizes Latin America's rich cultural history, its connection to ancient times, and its ability to survive.

4. Answers will vary but should use specific references to the primary sources to support their arguments.

Answers and Analyses
Reviewing Main Ideas

1. D If students remember that Perry had something to do with Japan, that narrows their choices to C and D. Remind them that President Roosevelt himself stepped in to end the Russo-Japanese War, and students will be able to select choice D.
16.B.3d (US)

2. A A rebellion is a revolt or an uprising. This means students can eliminate B and D because they do not have anything to do with a rebellion. Remind students that the Boxer Rebellion resulted in a second Open Door proposal, and they should be able to select choice A. **16.A**

3. C Hawaii was not involved in the Spanish-American War, so students can eliminate choices A and D. Spain was never a protectorate of the United States, so the answer cannot be B. Students should be able to use a process of elimination to select choice C. **17.C.3a**

4. B If students remember that the Roosevelt Corollary had something to do with Latin America, they can eliminate A and C. Tell students that it pertained to what Roosevelt thought the United States itself should do, and they should be able to select choice B. **14.E**

Short-Answer Question

5. Possible response: because he believed it was the duty of Americans to spread democracy and Christianity
16.A.3b

TEST-TAKING TIP

Do not wait until the last minute to prepare for a test. Make sure you ask questions in class after you have studied, but before you take the test.

Reviewing Main Ideas

Directions: Choose the best answer for each of the following questions.

1. Commodore Matthew Perry is most associated with
   A the purchase of Alaska.
   B improving and expanding U.S. trade.
   C ending the Russo-Japanese War.
   D the opening of Japanese ports to U.S. ships.

2. What was the Boxer Rebellion?
   A a Chinese uprising against foreigners
   B a brief skirmish between the United States and Germany over the division of Samoa
   C a revolt of sugar planters in Hawaii
   D a clash between Japan and Russia

3. Which of the following became U.S. territories or protectorates following America's victory in the Spanish-American War?
   A Cuba, Puerto Rico, and Hawaii
   B Spain and Cuba
   C Cuba, Puerto Rico, and Guam
   D the Philippines and Hawaii

4. The Roosevelt Corollary stated that
   A all European nations had the right to trade freely in China.
   B the U.S. had the right to get involved in Latin America to preserve order.
   C the United States was destined to expand from the Atlantic to the Pacific Ocean.
   D no European nation should intervene in Latin American affairs.

Short-Answer Question

Directions: Base your answer to question 5 on the excerpt below and on your knowledge of social studies.

> The two great needs of mankind, that all men may be lifted up into the light of the highest Christian civilization, are, first, a pure, spiritual Christianity, and, second, civil liberty. . . . It follows, then, that the Anglo-Saxon, as the great representative of these two ideas, . . . is . . . to be, in a peculiar sense, his brother's keeper.
>
> —Josiah Strong, on imperialism and the Spanish-American War, 1885

5. Based on the document, explain why Josiah Strong supported American imperialism.

Review the Essential Questions

6. **Essay** Which do you believe was the *most important* factor in American imperialism from 1865 to 1914: economic gain, military-strategic interest, or ideology? Explain and defend your answer.

To help you write your essay, review your answers to the Essential Questions in the section reviews and the chapter Foldables Study Organizer. Your essay should include:
- the actions and ideas of James G. Blaine and Alfred Thayer Mahan;
- the annexation of Hawaii, division of Samoa, and Open Door policy;
- events before, during, and after the Spanish-American War;
- the Panama Canal; and
- the foreign policies of Roosevelt, Taft, and Wilson.

GO ON

Review the Essential Questions

6. Students might defend any of the three options. Those who choose economic gain might point out that almost all foreign policy of the time was targeted at securing paths to Asia for the purposes of trade or for protecting American business interests in Latin America. Those who choose military-strategic interest might point out that the United States set up military bases in most of the areas it gained territory or influence, clearly indicating that this was a priority. Those who choose ideology should point out that the United States tried to spread democracy and Christianity everywhere it went as well. **14.E.3**

History ONLINE

For additional test practice, use **Self-Check Quizzes**—Chapter 22 at glencoe.com.

Chapter 22 Assessment

Document-Based Questions

Directions: Analyze the documents and answer the short-answer questions that follow.

Document 1

This is an excerpt from Alfred Thayer Mahan's 1890 book, *The Influence of Sea Power Upon History.*

> The government should . . . build up for the nation a navy which, if not capable of reaching distant countries, shall at least be able to keep clear the chief approaches to its own. . . . It is essential to the welfare of the whole country that the conditions of trade and commerce should remain, as far as possible, unaffected by an external war.

Source: Alfred Thayer Mahan, *The Influence of Sea Power Upon History*

7. Based on the excerpt, identify one reason why Mahan wanted the United States to strengthen its sea presence.

Document 2

The following is taken from a June 1897 letter from Hawaiian queen Liliuokalani to President McKinley concerning the proposed U.S. annexation of Hawaii.

> My people, about forty thousand in number, have in no way been consulted by those, . . . who claim the right to destroy the independence of Hawaii.
>
> [The] treaty ignores, not only the civic rights of my people, but, further, the hereditary property of their chiefs.
>
> [The] treaty ignores, . . . all treaties made by . . . sovereigns with other and friendly powers, and it is thereby in violation of international law.

Source: Queen Liliuokalani, *Hawaii's Story*

8. Use the document to explain Queen Liliuokalani's arguments against annexation.

Document 3

This cartoon shows Roosevelt "taking" Panama.

Source: Bettmann/CORBIS

9. What is this cartoon's message? Explain.

Document 4

Woodrow Wilson made these remarks in a speech in Mobile, Alabama, on October 27, 1913.

> It is a very [dangerous] thing to determine . . . foreign policy . . . in the terms of material interest. . . . Human rights, national integrity, and opportunity as against material interests—that, . . . is the issue which we now have to face. I want to . . . say that the United States will never again seek . . . territory by conquest.

Source: John Woolley and Gerhard Peters, *The American Presidency Project*

10. How do Wilson's remarks reflect his rejection of "dollar diplomacy"?

11. Persuasive Writing Using the information from the four documents and your knowledge of social studies, write an essay in which you:

- state the principles you think should govern American foreign policy; and

- explain when the United States is justified in interfering in a foreign nation.

9. It is critical of Roosevelt for his arrogance in supporting/inciting rebellion in Panama in order to get the land for the canal. **16.A.3b**

10. His comments make clear that he thinks it is wrong to conquer other lands for the purpose of economic gain, such as forcing trade or taking natural resources. He would, therefore, be opposed to a form of diplomacy that authorizes U.S. intervention simply because U.S. business interests are threatened. **14.E**

11. Essays should identify students' ideas of the ideal foreign policy. They should justify their opinions with three or more logical arguments, with facts and details from the text or from their understanding of social studies and current events. **14.E.3**

History ONLINE

Have students visit the Web site at glencoe.com to review Chapter 22 and take the Self-Check Quiz.

Need Extra Help?

Have students refer to the pages listed if they miss any of the questions.

Need Extra Help?

If you missed questions. . .	1	2	3	4	5	6	7	8	9	10	11
Go to page. . .	675	682	688	694	676–677	674–698	677	678–681	691–693	694–696	674–698

Document-Based Questions

7. Possible answer: to defend its own coastlines and keep them clear for trade **16.A.3b**

8. She points out that Hawaiians have not been asked if they want to be annexed, that the treaty takes away Hawaiians' property and rights, and that it is in violation of international law. **16.A**

Key to Ability Levels	
BL Below level	**AL** Above level
OL On level	**ELL** English Language Learners

Key to Teaching Resources	
Print Material	DVD
CD-ROM	Transparency

BL	OL	AL	ELL		Resources	Chapter Opener	Section 1	Section 2	Section 3	Section 4	Section 5	Chapter Assess
FOCUS												
BL	OL	AL	ELL	📠	Daily Test Practice Transparencies		23–1	23–2	23–3	23–4	23–5	
TEACH												
	OL	AL		📁	Geography and History Activity, URB						p. 87	
BL	OL		ELL	📁	Time Line Skills Activity, URB		p. 90					
BL	OL	AL	ELL	📁	Writing Skills Activity, URB			p. 79				
BL	OL	AL	ELL	📁	Content Vocabulary Activity, URB		p. 73	p. 73	p. 73	p. 73	p. 73	
BL	OL	AL	ELL	📁	Academic Vocabulary Activity, URB		p. 75	p. 75	p. 75	p. 75	p. 75	
BL			ELL	📁	Reading Skills Activity, URB			p. 7				
BL	OL		ELL	📁	Social Studies Skills Activity, URB					p. 81		
BL	OL	AL	ELL	📁	Differentiated Instruction Activity, URB				p. 83			
BL	OL	AL	ELL	📁	Critical Thinking Skills Activity, URB		p. 85					
BL	OL	AL	ELL	📁	Linking Past and Present Activity, URB						p. 89	
	OL	AL		📁	Primary Source Readings, URB						p. 77	
BL	OL	AL	ELL	📁	School-to-Home Connection Activity, URB		p. 91	p. 91	p. 91	p. 91	p. 91	
BL	OL		ELL	📁	Guided Reading Activity, URB*		p. 95	p. 96	p. 97	p. 98	p. 99	
BL	OL		ELL	📁	Reading Essentials and Note-Taking Guide*		p. 247	p. 250	p. 253	p. 256	p. 259	
BL	OL	AL	ELL	📠	Lesson Transparencies		23A, 23B	23A	23C			
	OL	AL		📁	Interpreting Political Cartoons, URB						p. 13	
		AL		📁	Supreme Court Case Studies					p. 37		
	OL			📁	American Biographies				p. 47			
BL	OL	AL	ELL	📁	Outline Map Resource Book	p. 39						
	OL	AL		📠	American Art and Architecture Transparencies, Strategies, and Activities			25				

Note: Please refer to the *Unit Resource Book: Reform and Empire* for this chapter's URB materials.

* Also available in Spanish

BL	OL	AL	ELL		Resources	Chapter Opener	Section 1	Section 2	Section 3	Section 4	Section 5	Chapter Assess
					TEACH (continued)							
BL	OL	AL	ELL		NGS US Desk Map		✓	✓	✓	✓	✓	
BL	OL	AL	ELL		American Literature Library		✓	✓	✓	✓	✓	
BL	OL	AL	ELL		Writer's Guidebook		✓	✓	✓	✓	✓	
	OL	AL			American History Primary Source Document Library CD-ROM		✓	✓	✓	✓	✓	✓
BL	OL	AL	ELL		American Music: Hits Through History	✓	✓	✓	✓	✓	✓	
BL	OL	AL	ELL		StudentWorks™ Plus CD	✓	✓	✓	✓	✓	✓	✓
	OL	AL			Section Spotlight Videos		✓	✓	✓	✓	✓	
BL	OL	AL	ELL		Writing Process Transparencies		✓	✓	✓	✓	✓	✓
BL	OL	AL	ELL		Presentation Plus! With MindJogger CheckPoint CD	✓	✓	✓	✓	✓	✓	✓
					ASSESS							
BL	OL	AL	ELL		Quizzes and Tests		p. 223	p. 224	p. 225	p. 226	p. 227	pp. 229, 231, 233
BL	OL	AL	ELL		Authentic Assessment With Rubrics							p. 23
BL	OL	AL	ELL		Standardized Test Practice							p. 45
BL	OL	AL	ELL		*ExamView® Assessment Suite* CD-ROM*		23–1	23–2	23–3	23–4	23–5	Ch. 23
					CLOSE							
BL			ELL		Reteaching Activity, URB*		p. 93	p. 93	p. 93	p. 93	p. 93	p. 93
BL	OL		ELL		Reading and Study Skills Foldables Activity	p. 94	p. 94	p. 94	p. 94	p. 94	p. 94	p. 94
BL	OL	AL	ELL		*The American Journey* in Graphic Novel					p. 135		
BL			ELL		Reading Strategies and Activities for the Social Studies Classroom		✓	✓	✓	✓	✓	
BL	OL	AL	ELL		Graphic Organizer Transparencies & Strategies		✓	✓	✓	✓	✓	

Teacher Works Plus
All-In-One Planner and Resource Center

- Interactive Lesson Planner
- Interactive Teacher Edition
- Fully editable blackline masters
- Section Spotlight Videos Launch
- Differentiated Lesson Plans
- Printable reports of daily assignments
- Standards Tracking System

Professional Development Resources

- Strategies for Success
- Building Academic Vocabulary
- Success With English Learners DVD
- Differentiated Instruction Strategies DVD
- Teaching Literacy Strategies in Social Studies DVD
- Assessment DVD
- Standards-Based Instruction DVD

Using Study Central™

Take Notes

Technology Product

The Study Central™ Web site offers a section-based review.

Objectives:

Take Notes supplies graphic organizers that students can fill out as they study.

- It helps students build note-taking skills.
- It teaches students to think differently.

Steps:

- Locate the Web page for your textbook at glencoe.com.
- Under Textbook Resources, click on **Study Central™**.
- Click on the **Study Central™** link at the bottom of the page to access the Study Central™ Web site.
- Select a chapter and section and then click **Enter**.
- Click on the **Take Notes** tab.
- Discuss the type of graphic organizer being used.
- Discuss the topic in the second panel and how the students will use the graphic organizer.
- Click on **Open Organizer** and have the students complete the graphic organizer.
- Help students complete the graphic organizer.

History ONLINE at glencoe.com

	Student	Teacher	Parent
Media Center			
• Student Edition Audio	●		
• Spanish Summaries	●		
• Section Spotlight Videos	●	●	
Social Studies Online Learning Center			
Classroom Tools			
• Multi-Language Glossaries	●	●	●
• Teaching Today		●	
• TIME Current Events	●	●	●
• Beyond the Textbook	●	●	
***The American Journey* Online Learning Center**			
• Study-to-Go™	●	●	●
• Study Central™	●	●	●
• Chapter Overview	●	●	
• Concepts in Motion	●	●	
• ePuzzles and Games	●	●	
• Literature Connections	●	●	
• Online Student Edition	●	●	●
• Self-Check Quizzes	●	●	●
• Student Web Activities	●	●	
• Vocabulary eFlashcards	●	●	
• Web Activity Lesson Plans	●	●	●
• Vocabulary PuzzleMaker	●	●	●

READING SUPPORT FROM JAMESTOWN EDUCATION

- **Timed Readings Plus in Social Studies** helps students increase their reading rate and fluency while maintaining comprehension. The 400-word passages are similar to those found on state and national assessments.

- **Reading in the Content Area: Social Studies** concentrates on six essential reading skills that help students better comprehend what they read. The book includes 75 high-interest nonfiction passages written at increasing levels of difficulty.

- **Reading Social Studies** includes strategic reading instruction and vocabulary support in Social Studies content for ELLs and native speakers of English.

- **Content Vocabulary Workout** (Grades 6–8) accelerates reading comprehension through focused vocabulary development. Social Studies content vocabulary comes from the glossaries of Glencoe's Middle School Social Studies texts.

www.jamestowneducation.com

NATIONAL GEOGRAPHIC

Index to National Geographic Magazine:

The following articles relate to this chapter:

- *"War Letters,"* Andrew Carroll, November 2005.

- *"Flight of Vimy: Early Aviation History"*.

National Geographic Society Products

To order the following, call National Geographic at 1-800-368-2728:

National Geographic Atlas of the World *(Book)*

Access National Geographic's dynamic MapMachine Web site and other geography resources at:

www.nationalgeographic.com

www.nationalgeographic.com/mapmachine

Reading List Generator CD-ROM — GLENCOE BookLink 3

Use this database to search more than 30,000 titles to create a customized reading list for your students.

- Reading lists can be organized by students' reading level, author, genre, theme, or area of interest.

- The database provides Degrees of Reading Power™ (DRP) and Lexile™ readability scores for all selections.

- A brief summary of each selection is included.

Leveled reading suggestions for this chapter:

For students at a Grade 6 reading level:
- *Fighter Planes,* Jay Schleifer

For students at a Grade 7 reading level:
- *World War I,* Virginia Schomp
- *Hell Fighters: African American Soldiers in World War I,* Michael L. Cooper

For students at a Grade 8 reading level:
- *World War I: Life in the Trenches,* Stephen Currie
- *Woodrow Wilson: Visionary for Peace,* James T. Rogers

For students at a Grade 9 reading level:
- *Germany,* William R. Horne
- *World War I,* Sean Connolly

For students at a Grade 10 reading level:
- *The Generation of 1914,* Robert Wohl

The following videotape programs are available from Glencoe as supplements to the chapter:

- **Woodrow Wilson: Reluctant Warrior** (ISBN 0-76-700101-X)

- **The Red Baron: Master of the Air** (ISBN 1-56-501582-7)

To order, call Glencoe at 1-800-334-7344. To find classroom resources to accompany many of these videos, check the following home pages:

A&E Television: www.aetv.com

The History Channel: www.history.com

Chapter Objectives

After studying this chapter, students will be able to:

- Explain how militarism contributed to the outbreak of World War I.
- State the reasons why the United States entered World War I.
- Describe how the United States helped the Allies win World War I.
- Summarize how the United States mobilized its resources to fight the war.
- Discuss why Wilson's peace plan failed.

Motivating Activity

Evaluating Write the following two statements on the board: "A country should not become involved in conflicts between other nations" and "A country has an obligation to become involved in conflicts between other countries." Have students raise their hands to show which statement reflects their position on isolationism. Ask volunteers to cite reasons for their opinions. Tell students that the United States debated these two opinions while European countries were fighting in World War I. In this chapter, students will read about the U.S. decision to give up isolationism and enter the war. **OL**

Previewing the Essential Questions

As you begin teaching each section, use these questions and activities to help students focus on the Essential Questions.

Chapter ★ 23 ★ World War I 1914–1919

U.S. soldiers on the battlefront

EVEN A DOG ENLISTS WHY NOT YOU?

PRESIDENTS
WOODROW WILSON 1913–1921

U.S. Events

★ **1914** Millions of immigrants from southern and eastern Europe enter U.S.

★ **1915** Germany torpedoes the *Lusitania*

1917 ★
- Zimmermann telegram angers United States
- United States enters World War I
- Selective Service Act passed

1914 — — 1916 —

World Events

1914 ★ Franz Ferdinand assassinated

★ **1914** World War I begins

★ **1915** International Congress of Women held at The Hague

Lenin addresses a crowd, 1917 ▶

1917 ★ Lenin leads Bolshevik Revolution

702 Chapter 23

Section ★ 1

War in Europe Ask: How might people respond when they feel threatened by others? *(Students may say that people become defensive and are ready to fight back.)* Point out to students that in Section 1 they will learn how the threat of attack and invasion caused tensions to escalate in the years before World War I. **OL**

Section ★ 2

America's Road to War Ask: What conditions might justify U.S. entry into another country's war? *(Answers may include tyranny, genocide, or direct threats to the United States.)* Explain to students that Section 2 explains the reasons why the United States abandoned its policy of isolationism and entered World War I. **OL**

Section 1: War in Europe

Essential Question How did militarism contribute to the outbreak of World War I?

Section 2: America's Road to War

Essential Question Why did the United States enter World War I?

Section 3: Americans Join the Allies

Essential Question How did the United States help the Allies win the war?

Section 4: The War at Home

Essential Question How did the United States mobilize its resources to fight the war?

Section 5: Searching for Peace

Essential Question Why did Wilson's peace plan fail?

History ONLINE
Chapter Overview Visit glencoe.com and click on **Chapter 23—Chapter Overviews** to preview chapter information.

FOLDABLES Study Organizer

Organizing Information

Make this Foldable to help organize what you learn about World War I.

Step 1 Place two sheets of paper on top of one another about one inch apart.

Step 2 Fold the papers to form four equal tabs.

Step 3 Staple the sheets and label each tab as shown.

> World War I
> 1914–1919
> War in Europe
> America in the War
> Searching for Peace

Reading and Writing As you read the chapter, list the key events of World War I in Europe and in the United States.

◄ President Woodrow Wilson on tour to promote the League of Nations

1918 ★
National War Labor Board established

1919 ★
President Woodrow Wilson wins Nobel Peace Prize

1920 ★
Senate rejects League of Nations

1918 — **1920**

1918 ★
World War I ends

1918 ★
Flu epidemic kills more than 20 million people

1919 ★
Treaty of Versailles signed

1920 ★
The Hague chosen as seat of International Court of Justice

1920 ★
League of Nations headquarters moves to Geneva

Chapter 23   703

Time Line Activity

If you have not already done so, have students review the time line. **Ask:** Who was president of the United States during the war years? *(Woodrow Wilson)* What events show countries' efforts toward international peace? *(the signing of the Treaty of Versailles and the creation of the League of Nations)*

FOLDABLES Study Organizer Dinah Zike's Foldables

Purpose This Foldable helps students organize information about key events of World War I in Europe and the United States. The completed Foldable will help them prepare for assessment. **OL**

📂 More Foldables activities for this chapter can be found in *Dinah Zike's Reading and Study Skills Foldables.*

History ONLINE

Introduce students to chapter content and key terms by having them access the **Chapter Overview** at glencoe.com.

Section 3 ★

Americans Join the Allies Ask: How can a country help an ally fight a war? *(Answers may include sending troops and supplies.)* Tell students that Section 3 describes how the United States helped its allies win the war. **OL**

Section 4 ★

The War at Home Ask: How does the attitude of a nation's people help their soldiers fight a war? *(Answers may note that support from citizens increases soldiers' strength to fight.)* Tell students that Section 4 describes how U.S. citizens took action at home during World War I. **OL**

Section 5 ★

Searching for Peace Ask: What challenges do you think countries face when discussing a peace plan? *(Answers may include disagreement over national boundaries and refusal to disarm.)* Tell students that Section 5 discusses the aftermath of World War I. **OL**

Section 1

War in Europe

Focus

Bellringer
Daily Test Practice Transparency 23–1

Reading Guide
Answers to Graphic:

improved weapons, larger shells that could travel longer distances, poison gas, armored tanks, fighter planes

Section Spotlight Video

Have students watch the Section Spotlight Video "War in Europe" to learn more about the outbreak of World War I.

Resource Manager

Essential Question
How did militarism contribute to the outbreak of World War I?

Reading Guide

Content Vocabulary

nationalism (p. 705)

ethnic group (p. 705)

militarism (p. 706)

alliance system (p. 706)

balance of power (p. 706)

U-boat (p. 709)

Academic Vocabulary

dimension (p. 709) equip (p. 709)

Key People and Events

Archduke Franz Ferdinand (p. 705)

Battle of Verdun (p. 708)

Reading Strategy

Taking Notes As you read, use a diagram like the one below to list the new technologies used in World War I.

New Technologies in World War I

ILLINOIS STANDARDS
The American Journey

16.A.3a Describe how historians use models for organizing historical interpretation (e.g., biographies, political events, issues and conflicts).

17.C.3a Explain how human activity is affected by geographic factors.

18.B.3a Analyze how individuals and groups interact with and within institutions (e.g., educational, military).

American Diary

In the spring of 1914, President Woodrow Wilson sent his chief adviser, Colonel E. M. House, to evaluate the political situation in Europe. Relations were hostile between Europe's nations and were growing worse. His attempt at maintaining peace, however, failed. Colonel House reported:

"The situation is extraordinary. It is militarism run stark mad. . . . There is too much hatred, too many jealousies."

—*from* The Intimate Papers of Colonel House

German men march through the streets of Berlin in response to the call to mobilize.

R Reading Strategies	**C** Critical Thinking	**D** Differentiated Instruction	**W** Writing Support	**S** Skill Practice
Teacher Edition • Outlining, p. 705 • Sequencing Info., p. 707 **Additional Resources** • Guid. Read., URB p. 95 • Content Vocab., URB p. 73 • Academic Vocab., URB p. 75	**Teacher Edition** • Analyz. Info., p. 705 • Det. Cause and Effect, p. 706 • Making Infer., p. 707 • Drawing Conclusions, p. 709 **Additional Resources** • Quizzes and Tests, p. 223 • Crit. Think. Skills, URB p. 85	**Teacher Edition** • Verbal/Linguistic, p. 706 **Additional Resources** • School-to-Home, URB p. 91 • Reteaching Act., URB p. 93	**Teacher Edition** • Expository Writing, p. 708	**Teacher Edition** • Using Geo. Skills, p. 706 **Additional Resources** • Daily Test Pract. Transp. 23-1 • Time Line Skills, URB p. 90 • Lesson Transparencies 23A, 23B

Troubles in Europe

Main Idea Several factors led to the outbreak of World War I.

History and You Why might one country defend another country that was attacked? Read about why most European nations went to war in 1914.

On the morning of June 28, 1914, the people of Sarajevo, Bosnia, crowded the city streets to see **Archduke Franz Ferdinand,** who was the next in line to the throne of the Austro-Hungarian Empire. The archduke and his wife were on a state visit to Bosnia, an Austrian province. Suddenly shots rang out. The royal couple were shot and died soon after.

The assassination destroyed the delicate balance of European stability. Within weeks Europe was at war. The tensions that led to World War I, however, went back many years. The conflicts grew as European nations pursued dreams of new empires, built up their armies, and formed alliances.

Nationalism

Nationalism, a feeling of intense loyalty to one's country or group, caused much of the tension in Europe. Nationalism encouraged new nations, such as Italy and Germany, to unify and establish their power in the world. Italy became a kingdom in the 1860s, and the German states united in the 1870s. Their actions threatened the power of older nations such as Great Britain and France.

Nationalism also inspired certain groups of people to break away from existing nations. Some of these **ethnic groups**—people who share a common language and traditions—demanded independent nations of their own.

Imperial Expansion

Tension in Europe increased as nations expanded their empires. Nations competed for colonies in Africa, Asia, and other parts of the world. These colonies not only provided new markets and raw materials, they also boosted a nation's status.

Primary Source | **Forming Alliances**

Taking Sides European nations made alliances with one another for mutual self-defense. Alliances were sometimes broken or dissolved and new ones created. This 1915 propaganda poster ridicules Italy for changing sides. Italy allied with Germany and Austria-Hungary at first, then formed an alliance with France, Russia, and Great Britain.

BISMARKS AUSSPRUCH:
GOTT HAT DEN MENSCHEN NACH SEINEN EBENBILDE ER-SCHAFFEN, DEN ITALIENER ABER NACH JENEM DES JUDAS

Critical Thinking

Making Inferences Should a country form military alliances with other nations? Explain.

CHAPTER 23
Section 1

Teach

R Reading Strategy

Outlining As they read, have students create an outline using the headings from the text. After students complete their outlines, discuss how the outline provides details about the main idea. **BL**

C Critical Thinking

Analyzing Information Ask: What are some benefits of nationalism? *(Nationalism can inspire pride in and loyalty to one's country.)* What are some drawbacks of nationalism? *(The desire to break apart nations based on ethnic groups can cause conflict and war. Extreme nationalism can result in disrespect of other nations and lead to conflict.)* **AL**

Primary Source

Critical Thinking Answer
Answers may include yes, because they need the protection of other countries.

Making Inferences Ask: Which country might have created this propaganda poster? *(one of Italy's first allies, such as Germany or Austria-Hungary)* **OL**

**Hands-On
Chapter Project
Step 1**

Creating a War Documentary

Step 1: Researching the Causes of War Groups of students research the causes of World War I.

Essential Question: How did militarism contribute to the outbreak of World War I?

Directions Tell students that they will create a documentary about World War I. If possible, show students an example of a war documentary. To begin the project, teach several students how to operate a video camera and video editing software. Have the camera operators accompany small groups as they research the causes of World War I in Europe. Tell student researchers to gather information they can use to narrate the documentary as well as photos, maps, and illustrations to use as visuals. Have the camera operators record the visual information and upload it onto the computer.

Determining Cause and Effect As a class, discuss how militarism contributed to the outbreak of the war. **OL**

(Chapter Project continued in Section 2)

Croatia, Slovenia, Romania, Bulgaria, Albania, Serbia, Bosnia, Macedonia (8 countries)

C Critical Thinking

Determining Cause and Effect Help students identify the key word in this sentence that indicates a cause-effect relationship. *("result")* Draw a graphic organizer on the board showing the cause and effect in this sentence. **BL**

D Differentiated Instruction

Verbal/Linguistic Define "simile" for students. *(a figure of speech comparing two like things and indicated by the words "like" or "as")* Read the sentence aloud, and have students identify the simile. **Ask:** What is the author trying to convey? *(The tensions between European countries were like fuel for an explosion that could be set off with a small spark.)* **OL**

S Skill Practice

Using Geography Skills Have students use a world map to locate the Balkan Peninsula. **OL**

✓ Reading Check **Answer:** to keep peace by creating a balance of power

Additional Support

Great Britain and France already had large overseas empires, but both nations wanted to expand them even more. Germany, Italy, and Russia wanted to increase their colonial holdings as well. Expansion by one European nation often brought it into conflict with another country.

Military Buildup

As European nations competed for colonies, they strengthened their armies and navies to protect their interests. If one nation increased its military strength, its rivals felt threatened and built up their military. In this atmosphere of **militarism,** Germany, France, and Russia developed huge armies in the early 1900s.

Great Britain had the world's largest and strongest navy. Germany began to challenge Britain's naval power in the early 1900s. A bitter rivalry grew between the two nations. The rivalry led to an arms race that threatened the peace of Europe.

Formation of Alliances

As a result of military buildups, an **alliance system** developed. When a country joined an alliance, it agreed to defend other alliance countries if they were attacked. By 1914, two major alliances were established. Germany, Austria-Hungary, and Italy formed the Triple Alliance. Great Britain, France, and Russia formed the Triple Entente. An entente is an understanding among nations.

The purpose of alliances was to keep peace by creating a **balance of power.** This system prevents any one country from dominating the others. However, the alliance system posed a great danger because an attack on one nation could easily trigger a war involving many countries.

Europe was like a keg of gunpowder. One American diplomat noted that it would take "only a spark to set the whole thing off." That spark was ignited in the Balkans.

✓ Reading Check **Describing** What was the purpose of the alliance system?

Crisis in the Balkans

Main Idea War spread throughout Europe as a result of the alliance system.

History and You When your friends argue, is it difficult for you not to take sides? Read to learn how World War I began in Europe.

The Balkan Peninsula was a hotbed of nationalist and ethnic rivalries in the early 1900s. Several nations argued over territory. Slavic nationalists hoped to unite all Slavic peoples in the region. One conflict was especially bitter. The Slavic people in Austria-Hungary wanted independence, and Serbia supported them.

An Assassination Leads to War

Gavrilo Princip, Franz Ferdinand's assassin, belonged to a Serbian nationalist group. Princip and other terrorists plotted the mur-

Europe Goes to War

Time of Crisis Despite more than 40 years of general peace, tensions among European nations were building in 1914. Militarism was on the rise. Rival countries had formed alliances. Because of the way the alliances were set up, an attack on one nation by another was all that was needed to trigger a war.

◄ The assassination of Archduke Franz Ferdinand on June 28, 1914, provided the incident that ignited Europe into war.

Fast Facts

The Black Hand The main objective of the Black Hand was to end Austro-Hungarian rule and unite all of the South Slavs into one nation known as Greater Serbia. By 1914, there were about 2,500 members.

The leaders wanted to assassinate Archduke Franz Ferdinand because he was opposed to the creation of Greater Serbia. Hearing of the archduke's plan to visit

Sarajevo in June 1914, the Black Hand sent three of its members to assassinate him.

Early in the royal procession, one of the would-be assassins threw a bomb at Franz Ferdinand's car. The bomb bounced off the back of the car and exploded underneath the next car, injuring the riders. The procession resumed, and the archduke rode to the Town Hall, where he gave a short speech.

Afterwards, the archduke and his wife made their way to the hospital to visit the wounded members of their party. It was on this leg of their trip that they were shot at point blank range by Gavrilo Princip. The archduke and his wife were rushed to the palace, where they bled to death. **OL** der of Ferdinand to bring down the Austro-Hungarian Empire and unite the Slavs.

Austria-Hungary moved to crush Serbia. With Germany's support, it gave Serbia a list of harsh demands, which Serbia refused. Austria-Hungary declared war on Serbia on July 28, 1914.

Europe's alliance system caused the war to spread quickly. Russia, which was Serbia's protector, prepared for war. Germany then came to the side of its ally Austria-Hungary. Germany declared war on Russia on August 1, 1914, and then declared war on France, Russia's ally, on August 3.

A day later, Germany invaded Belgium, violating a treaty that guaranteed Belgium's neutrality. Great Britain, honoring a pledge to protect Belgium, declared war on Germany.

Reading Check Identifying Cause and Effect How did nationalism contribute to the outbreak of World War I?

A World War Begins

Main Idea World War I was a long, deadly war as a result of new technologies and battle strategies.

History and You Think about the technology you use as you go about your everyday routines. Read to learn how new technology affected armies during World War I.

The "Great War" had begun. On one side were the Allied Powers, or the Allies. They included Great Britain, France, and Russia. On the other side, Germany, Austria-Hungary, and the Ottoman (Turkish) Empire made up the Central Powers.

Japan, a rival of Germany in Asia, joined the Allies in late August 1914. Italy refused to honor its alliance with Germany and Austria-Hungary. Instead, it joined the Allies in 1915 after being promised territory in Austria after the war.

R **Reading Strategy**

Sequencing Information Write the following events on the board:

a. Germany declared war on Russia.

b. Great Britain declared war on Germany.

c. Austria-Hungary declared war on Serbia.

d. Germany declared war on France.

e. Germany invaded Belgium

Have students place these events in order to help them understand the events that led to war. (c, a, d, e, b) **OL**

C **Critical Thinking**

Making Inferences Ask: Why was World War I called the "Great War"? (because it involved many countries) **OL**

Europe Goes to War NATIONAL GEOGRAPHIC

Map Skills Answer

Germany, Austria-Hungary, and the Ottoman Empire

Reading Check **Answer:** Princip, a Serb nationalist, wanted South Slavs to be independent. He shot Archduke Franz Ferdinand in order to end Austro-Hungarian rule in the region.

Differentiated Instruction

Europe Goes to War — NATIONAL GEOGRAPHIC

THE HEIR TO AUSTRIAN THRONE ASSASSINATED.

① June 28 Franz Ferdinand assassinated

② June 28 Austria-Hungary declares war on Serbia

③ July 30 Russia mobilizes armed forces

④ Aug. 1 Germany declares war on Russia

⑤ Aug. 3 Germany declares war on France

⑥ Aug. 4 Germany invades Belgium

⑦ Aug. 4 Britain declares war on Germany

⑧ Aug. 6 Austria-Hungary declares war on Russia

⑨ Aug. 12 France and Britain declare war on Austria-Hungary

Map legend:
- Allies
- Central Powers
- Neutral nations

0 200 kilometers
0 200 miles
Lambert Azimuthal Equal-Area projection

Map Skills

Regions What nations made up the Central Powers in 1914?

World War I **Chapter 23** **707**

Leveled Activities

BL **Guided Reading Activity, URB p. 95**

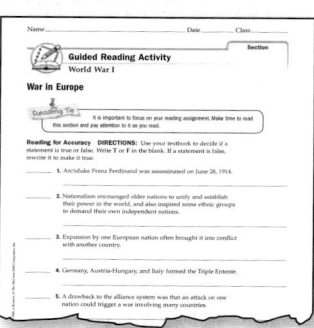

OL **Time Line Skills Activity, URB p. 90**

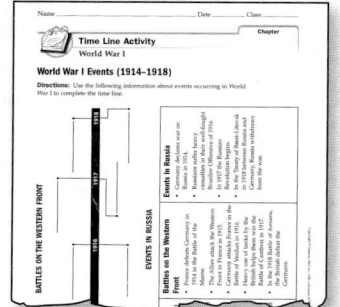

ELL **Reading Essentials and Note-Taking Guide, p. 247**

Chapter 23, Section 1 (Pages 704–709)
War in Europe

W Writing Support

Expository Writing Tell students to conduct research to gather additional information on trench warfare during World War I. Have students write a report explaining the benefits and drawbacks of trench warfare and its overall effectiveness. **OL**

Primary Source

Critical Thinking Answer
Casualties increased dramatically. Machine guns could quickly fire many bullets, and poison gas could be used against enemy soldiers. Airplanes observed and bombed enemy positions, while tanks attacked across battle lines.

Critical Thinking Practice
Ask: Which weapons might be effective against soldiers in trenches? *(bombs from aircraft, poison gas, tanks)* **OL**

Differentiated Instruction

Primary Source | Deadly Technology

Changing Nature of Warfare Warring nations employed several weaponry innovations during World War I. Machine guns, modern artillery, poison gas, tanks, aircraft, and submarines produced horrific casualty rates.

◄ Both sides used aircraft for observation, ground support, and bombing missions.

Armies on both sides used poison gas. Soldiers without gas masks faced death or damage to the lungs. ▼

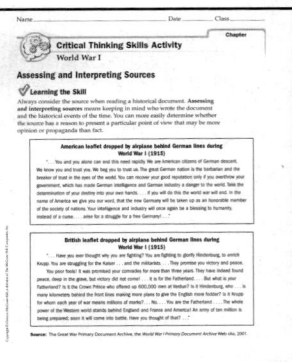

▲ The British introduced the tank in 1916.

◄ German soldiers fire a machine gun.

Critical Thinking
Explaining How did new technology affect the deadliness of combat?

Fighting on the Western Front
Germany launched its offensive through Belgium because it hoped to defeat France and then move troops east against Russia. The plan almost succeeded. The Belgians, however, held out for nearly three weeks against the powerful German army. This delay gave the French and British time to prepare their armies for war.

After defeating the Belgians, the Germans marched into France. They advanced to within 15 miles (24 km) of Paris. The British and French met the Germans at the Marne River just a few miles east of the city. The Battle of the Marne, fought between September 5 and 12, 1914, stopped the German advance and boosted French morale. The battle also made it clear that neither side was capable of winning the war quickly or easily.

The fighting in western Europe reached a stalemate, where neither side made any military advances. For the next three years, the opposing armies faced each other across a complex network of deep trenches. Trenches along the front lines provided protection from flying bullets and artillery shells. Trenches behind the lines served as first-aid stations, headquarters, and storage areas.

To break the standstill, both sides launched major offensives in 1916. The German offensive, the **Battle of Verdun** in northeastern France, began in February. It continued until December. At first the Germans made small gains, but these gains were lost after the French counterattacked. Verdun was one of the longest and bloodiest battles of the war. When it was over, more than 750,000 French and German soldiers had lost their lives.

While the Battle of Verdun raged, the Allies launched their own offensive in July. This was known as the Battle of the Somme. Again the number of casualties was high. The Allies gained only 7 miles (11.2 km) in the offensive.

Technology of War
New deadly weapons caused large numbers of injuries and deaths. Improved cannons and other artillery fired larger shells at great distances. Better rifles enabled soldiers to hit targets with greater accuracy.

Assessing and Interpreting Sources

Objective:	To learn how to consider the source when reading a historical document
Focus:	Ask students if they believe everything they read.
Teach:	Have students read the information, answer the questions, and apply the skill.
Assess:	Ask students what they would have thought of the leaflets had they been German soldiers.
Close:	Discuss whether it is ever possible to find out "the truth" during a time of war.

Differentiated Instruction Strategies

BL Ask students to work in pairs to read the excerpts to each other and then answer the questions.

AL Have students compose a leaflet from the Germans to drop behind American lines.

ELL Have students define the term "propaganda" in their own words.

Critical Thinking Skills Activity, URB p. 85

The Germans first used poison gas against Allied troops in April 1915. The gas could kill or seriously injure anyone who breathed it. A British officer said:

PRIMARY SOURCE

"They fought with their terror, running blindly in the gas cloud, and dropping . . . in agony."
—quoted in *Avoiding Armageddon*

The Allies began to use poison gas as well. Soldiers started to carry gas masks.

The armored tank, first used in World War I in January 1916, could cross battle lines and fire on the enemy at close range. By crushing barbed wire, tanks also provided an easier route for advancing troops. After seeing the effectiveness of the Allies' tanks, the Germans produced them, too.

The most dramatic new weapon—the airplane—added a new **dimension**, or magnitude, to fighting in World War I. Both sides used airplanes to watch the movements of enemy troops and bomb targets. Daring pilots waged duels in the skies called "dogfights."

The first fighter planes were **equipped,** or outfitted, only with machine guns fastened to the top wing. The most famous pilots included Germany's Baron von Richthofen—the "Red Baron"—and Eddie Rickenbacker, an American who served in the French air force. The Germans used the zeppelin, or blimp, to bomb Allied cities.

On the Seas

With their land armies deadlocked in western Europe, both sides turned to the sea. Great Britain blockaded all ports under German control, eventually causing severe shortages. Many Germans went without food and other supplies.

Germany had an effective naval weapon of its own: the submarine. Known as **U-boats**—from the German word *Unterseeboot*—submarines sunk ships carrying supplies to Britain. U-boat attacks on ships at sea eventually brought the United States into the war.

✓ **Reading Check** **Explaining** What did both sides realize after the Battle of the Marne?

Section 1 Review

History ONLINE
Study Central™ To review this section, go to glencoe.com.

Vocabulary

1. Define the following terms in a sentence: nationalism, ethnic group, militarism, alliance system, balance of power, dimension, equip, U-boat.

Main Ideas

2. **Stating** Why did nations form alliances with other nations?

3. **Discussing** Discuss the role of the Slavic nationalist movement in Austria-Hungary in the early 1900s.

4. **Explaining** How did the Central Powers and the Allies try to break the deadlock caused by trench warfare?

Critical Thinking

5. **Organizing** Use a diagram like the one below to identify the Allies and the Central Powers.

6. **Expository Writing** Write a paragraph to explain why the airplane became an important weapon during World War I.

Answer the
7. **Essential Question**
How did militarism contribute to the outbreak of World War I?

C Critical Thinking

Drawing Conclusions Ask: Based on the quotation, what conclusions can you draw about the effectiveness of poison gas? *(Poison gas was effective because it caused agony and terror for soldiers who breathed it.)* **OL**

✓ **Reading Check** **Answer:** that neither side was capable of winning the war easily nor quickly

Assess

History ONLINE

Study Central™ provides summaries, interactive games, and online graphic organizers to help students review content.

Close

Describing Ask students to describe the types of weapons used during World War I. **OL**

Section ★ Review

Answers

1. Sentences should reflect a correct understanding of the terms.
2. to create a balance of power and keep peace
3. The Slavic people in Austria-Hungary wanted independence. Serbia and the Serbian nationalist movement supported them. When terrorists in the movement assassinated the heir to the Austro-Hungarian Empire, Austria-Hungary declared war on Serbia to crush the nationalists.
4. Both went on the offensive—Germany with the Battle of Verdun, and France and Britain with the Battle of the Somme.
5. **Allies:** Great Britain, France, Russia, Japan, Italy; **Central Powers:** Germany, Austria-Hungary, Ottoman Empire
6. Students' paragraphs should include information about watching troop movements and bombing cities.
7. Students should note that militarism created the need for the alliance system and that as armies were built up, nations looked for new types of technology to create superior armies.

Focus

S Skill Practice

Using Geography Skills Have students use the map key and labels to determine the direction traveled by different armies. **Ask:** Who gained ground as a result of the Battle of the Marne? The Battle of the Somme? How can you tell? *(Allied forces gained ground in both cases. You can tell by locating the rivers, looking for the symbol for the major battles, and then seeing that the blue arrow that represents the Allies continues past the battle location.)* **OL**

Have students use a geographic organizer like the one below and information from the map to show the general flow of events on the Western Front. **OL**

```
┌─────────────────────────────┐
│ Line of trench warfare      │
│ 1915–1917                   │
└─────────────────────────────┘
              ↓
┌─────────────────────────────┐
│ German offensives push      │
│ line back into France       │
└─────────────────────────────┘
              ↓
┌─────────────────────────────┐
│ Allied offensives force     │
│ Germans to retreat, push    │
│ line back into Belgium      │
└─────────────────────────────┘
              ↓
┌─────────────────────────────┐
│ Armistice,                  │
│ Nov. 11, 1918               │
└─────────────────────────────┘
```

Additional Support and Answers

World War I and Trench Warfare

The Germans were determined to hold onto the parts of France and Belgium that they still occupied after the Battle of the Marne. They dug trenches for protection from the advancing French and British troops. The Allies could not break through the German trenches and began digging their own. For the next three years, neither side advanced more than a few miles along the line of trenches that became known as the Western Front.

How Did Geography Affect Trench Warfare?

The nature of trench warfare resulted in the development of its own unique form of geography. In the forward zone, traditional methods of transportation such as roads and rail were replaced by a network of trenches and light tramways. Occupying the high ground was critically important. Savage battles were fought just to gain possession of a small hill. Many farmhouses and groves of trees were fought over simply because they were the largest identifiable features of the landscape.

The Western Front

Line of trench warfare, 1915–1917

Farthest advance of Central Powers, 1918

Allied offensive

Major battle involving U.S. forces

German offensive

Armistice Line, Nov. 11, 1918

▲ On the Western Front where Allied and German armies faced each other, the troops dug a network of trenches that **S** stretched from the English Channel through parts of France and Germany.

◄ American artist Mal Thompson served in France as a lieutenant with the U.S. Army. After the war, he published a volume of his sketches of war life entitled *In France with the American Expeditionary Forces.*

710   Unit 7   *Reform and Empire*

War Poetry British soldier and poet Wilfred Owen became famous for his realistic verses about life in the trenches. He was killed just one week before the end of the war. This is an excerpt from his poem "Dulce et Decorum Est." The title is taken from a Latin phrase: *Dulce et decorum est pro patria mori* ("How sweet and lovely it is to die for your country").

Gas! Gas! Quick, boys!—An ecstasy of fumbling,
Fitting the clumsy helmets just in time;
But someone still was yelling out and stumbling
And flound'ring like a man in fire or lime . . .
Dim, through the misty panes and thick green light,
As under a green sea, I saw him drowning.

Activity: Interdisciplinary Connection

Health Not all of the injuries and deaths during World War I were related to battle. Conditions in the trenches led to many diseases and disorders as well. For instance, trench foot and trench fever were common. Lice and rats plagued the soldiers, and even frogs caused problems. Though it was not recognized at the time, a psychological disorder called shell shock (now known as post-traumatic stress disorder) was also common. Ask students to research one of these diseases or disorders in detail and present an oral report to the class on their topic. If possible, invite a medical professional to your class to discuss health issues related to troops in combat. **OL**

Aircraft were used to assess enemy troops before an attack.

Long range artillery 4–5 miles (6–8 km) behind the front line fired on advancing enemy troops.

Rows of barbed wire slowed down advancing troops.

Concrete block house for a machine gun

Reserve trench

Support trench

Front-line trench

A deep dugout could protect from artillery shells but could trap soldiers underground.

Front-line dug-outs provided some protection but could be hit by an artillery shell from above.

No Man's Land was the area between the trenches of opposing sides. Churned mud and hardened ruts made it difficult for troops to cross.

American nurses in France make their way through a trench carrying gas masks. Poison gas attacks could cause vomiting, blindness, and suffocation. Gas masks were a necessary part of equipment for soldiers and nurses. ▶

Today the trenches at Vimy Ridge in northern France are preserved in a memorial park. ▼

▲ Soldiers set up living quarters in dugouts and caves that were joined to the trenches. This picture from 1915 shows makeshift beds lined up against the walls of a dugout. In many cases, soldiers tried to make dugouts as much like home as possible.

Analyzing Geography

1. **Location** Use the text and map to determine in which countries the Western Front of World War I was located.

2. **Human-Environment Interaction** Why was it a tactical advantage for troops in World War I to occupy the high ground?

Reform and Empire **Unit 7** **711**

Teach

R Reading Strategy

Activating Prior Knowledge Ask: List three new weapons used during World War I. How were they used? How did their effects differ from those of prior wars? *(Aircraft: used to assess enemy troops and to battle in the sky; improved cannons with larger shells: used to fire from longer distances; poison gas: released on and breathed in by enemies; better rifles: allowed greater accuracy; and armored tanks: crushed barbed wire to advance across enemy lines and fired at close range. New weapons resulted in more deaths and injuries than in previous wars.)* **OL**

Assess/Close

W Writing Support

Narrative Writing Have each student write a story about life as a soldier in the trenches and dugouts during World War I. **OL**

Answers

1. France, Germany, and a small part of Belgium

2. They could see and fire upon the approaching enemy, and attacking uphill was more difficult.

Focus

Section 2

America's Road to War

Bellringer

Daily Test Practice Transparency 23–2

Reading Guide

Answers to Graphic:

1915: Germany would sink any vessels that entered or left British ports.

1917: Germany would sink on sight all merchant vessels, armed or unarmed.

Section Spotlight Video

Have students watch the Section Spotlight Video "America's Road to War" to learn why the United States entered World War I.

Essential Question

Why did the United States enter World War I?

Reading Guide

Content Vocabulary

propaganda *(p. 713)*   autocracy *(p. 716)*

Academic Vocabulary

stress *(p. 713)*   revolution *(p. 716)*

Key People and Events

Lusitania *(p. 714)*

Selective Service Act *(p. 717)*

Reading Strategy

Taking Notes As you read, use a diagram like the one below to compare how Germany's policy on submarine warfare changed between 1915 and 1917.

Policy in 1915   **Policy in 1917**

ILLINOIS STANDARDS
The American Journey

14.E.3 Compare the basic principles of the United States and its international interests (e.g., territory, environment, trade, use of technology).

16.B.3d (US) Describe ways in which the United States developed as a world political power.

18.B.3a Analyze how individuals and groups interact with and within institutions (e.g., educational, military).

American Diary

In 1914 many Americans believed that the war in Europe was a European conflict in which the United States should not be involved. Mississippi Congressperson Percy E. Quin strongly opposed building an army just to be ready because "When our country really needs soldiers to defend it, millions of patriots will rush to arms and rally to the flag." That time was drawing near.

—*from America's Great War: World War I and the American Experience*

U.S. members of the Women's Peace Party arrive in Europe to call for negotiations to end the war.

Resource Manager

R Reading Strategies	**C** Critical Thinking	**D** Differentiated Instruction	**W** Writing Support	**S** Skill Practice
Teacher Edition	**Teacher Edition**	**Teacher Edition**	**Teacher Edition**	**Teacher Edition**
• Monitoring, p. 714 • Reading Pri. Sources, p. 716	• Dist. Fact from Opinion, p. 713 • Det. Cause and Effect, p. 714 • Analyz. Information, p. 715 • Comparing and Contrasting, p. 717	• Gifted and Talented, p. 715 • Interpersonal, p. 716	• Descriptive Writing, p. 714	• Reading a Time Line, p. 717
Additional Resources		**Additional Resources**		**Additional Resources**
• Guid. Read., URB p. 96 • Content Vocab., URB p. 73 • Academic Vocab., URB p. 75 • Read. Skills Activity, URB p. 7	**Additional Resources** • Quizzes and Tests, p. 224	• School-to-Home, URB p. 91 • Reteaching, URB p. 93		• Daily Test Pract. Transp. 23-2 • Lesson Transparency 23C

American Neutrality

Main Idea The United States tried to remain neutral in the war in Europe.

History and You Do you think the newspaper in your city or town reports on national events accurately? Read how propaganda influenced people's ideas about the war in Europe.

President Wilson had to make some difficult decisions. He declared that the United States would be neutral in the war in Europe. Most Americans did not think that the war concerned them. Many shared the view expressed in an editorial in a New York newspaper.

PRIMARY SOURCE

"There is nothing reasonable in such a war . . . and it would be [foolish] for this country to sacrifice itself to . . . a clash of ancient hatreds which is urging the Old World to destruction."

—from the *New York Sun*

Despite pleas for neutrality, Americans soon began to take sides. More than one-third of the nation's 92 million people were either foreign-born or the children of immigrants. Many naturally favored their countries of origin. Some of the 8 million Americans of German or Austrian descent and the 4.5 million Irish Americans—who hated the British because they ruled Ireland—favored the Central Powers.

Even more Americans, however, including President Wilson, favored the Allies. Ties of language, customs, and traditions linked the United States to Great Britain. President Wilson told the British ambassador: "Everything I love most in the world is at stake." A German victory "would be fatal to our form of government and American ideals."

Using Propaganda

To gain support, both sides in the war used **propaganda.** This term describes information used to influence opinion. Allied propaganda **stressed,** or called attention to, the German invasion of neutral Belgium and included horror stories of German atrocities. It called the Germans "Huns" and barbarians.

Teach

C Critical Thinking

Distinguishing Fact from Opinion Call on volunteers to find words that demonstrate bias in the quotation. (*"nothing reasonable," "foolish," "sacrifice," "clash," "ancient hatreds," "destruction"*) As a class, discuss how the words support a neutral position in the war. **OL**

By the Numbers

Critical Thinking Answer
The Allied Powers had more troops.

Calculating Ask: Which country had the largest army? (*Germany*) About how many more troops did Germany have than its ally? (*1,500,000*) **BL**

By the Numbers — Land Forces

Size of Armies, August 1914

Central Powers   Allied Powers

*Although not yet involved in the war, American troops totaled about 119,250 enlisted men.

Source: *Encyclopaedia Britannica;* U.S. Census Bureau

German soldier, 1916 ▶

Critical Thinking
Analyzing How did the armies of the Central and Allied powers compare in size?

Differentiated Instruction

Leveled Activities

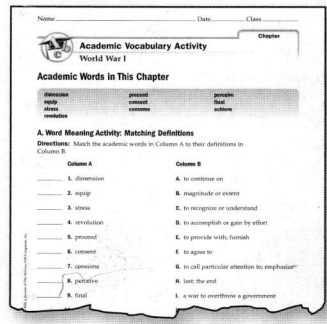
713

Reading Strategy

Monitoring Remind students to ask questions as they read the passage, such as "Why was trade with Germany difficult?" and "How did the United States feel about the British blockade of German ports?" **BL**

Critical Thinking

Determining Cause and Effect Ask: How did the war in Europe affect the U.S. economy? *(The United States enjoyed an economic boom. Trade increased dramatically, as did loans by U.S. banks to Allied nations.)* **OL**

Writing Support

Descriptive Writing Have students do research to learn more about submarines. Then have them write a paragraph describing submarines, including their weapons and the effects of submarine attacks. **OL**

War at Sea: The Submarine

Critical Thinking Answer
1. diving rudders
2. Americans were killed when German submarines attacked British and American ships.

Hands-On Chapter Project
Step 2

Creating a War Documentary

Step 2: Interviewing Historical Experts Groups of students will interview historians about World War I.

Essential Question: Why did the United States enter World War I?

Directions Explain to students that they will be including recorded comments from historical experts in their documentary.

War at Sea: The Submarine

The United States began building its own submarine fleet during the war. The fastest American submarines reached a top surface speed of 14 knots (a little more than 16 miles per hour).

Captured German submarine on display in Hoboken, New Jersey, 1919 ▶

❶ The **conning tower** is the attack center.

❷ The **diving rudders** guide the submarine to different depths.

❸ The **rudder** steers the vessel.

❹ About 12 **torpedoes** could be carried at a time.

Periscope

Deck gun

Engine room   Control room   Crew's quarters

Critical Thinking

1. **Naming** What part of the craft guided the submarine up and down?
2. **Summarizing** How did submarine warfare lead to U.S. entry into the war?

The propaganda from the Central Powers was equally horrible, but because of sympathy for the British, Allied propaganda was more effective in influencing Americans.

America's Early Involvement

Trade between the United States and the Allies helped build support for the Allied cause. As a neutral nation, America sought to trade with both sides. However, Britain's blockade of Germany made this difficult.

Stopping and searching American ships headed for German ports, the British navy often seized the ships' goods. The United States protested that its ships should be able to pass without interference. The British responded with the defense that they were fighting for their survival. "If the American shipper grumbles," wrote a London newspaper, "our reply is that this war is not being conducted for his pleasure or profit." The U.S. government could do nothing about the blockade. Barred from trading with Germany, it continued trading with Britain.

Indeed, American trade with the Allies soared. In addition, Great Britain and France borrowed billions of dollars from American banks to help pay for their war efforts. All this business caused an economic boom in the United States. It also upset the Germans, who watched the United States—supposedly a neutral nation—helping the Allies.

Submarine Warfare

To stop American aid to Britain, Germany stated in February 1915 that it would sink any vessels that entered or left British ports. President Wilson warned that the United States would hold Germany responsible for any American lives lost in submarine attacks. The Germans ignored Wilson's threat. On May 7, 1915, a German U-boat torpedoed the British passenger liner *Lusitania* near the coast of Ireland. The captain reported:

714 **Chapter 23** *World War I*

Have students identify people who might serve as experts on World War I, such as a history teacher, college history professors, history writers, and politicians. In small groups, have students brainstorm appropriate questions to ask interviewees. Remind students to ask open-ended questions to avoid "yes" and "no" answers. Then have students set up and interview the experts. Be sure students ask permission to record the interviews. After the interviews, discuss with students how they can incorporate the experts' comments as voiceovers in their documentary.

Analyzing As a class, discuss common themes and ideas related by the various experts. **OL**

(Chapter Project continued in Section 3)

PRIMARY SOURCE

"I saw a torpedo speeding toward us, and immediately I tried to change our course, but was unable to [maneuver] out of the way. There was a terrible impact as the torpedo struck the starboard side of the vessel, and a second torpedo followed almost immediately."

—from W. T. Turner, captain of the *Lusitania*

More than 1,000 people died, including 128 American citizens, when the *Lusitania* sank. Americans were outraged, and President Wilson denounced the attack. Later it was learned that the ship carried war materials.

Within a few months, several Americans were injured when a German U-boat attacked the unarmed French passenger ship *Sussex*. Germany feared that the Americans might enter the war. To pardon itself, Germany offered money to people who were injured on the *Sussex* and promised to warn neutral ships and passenger vessels before attacking. The *Sussex* Pledge seemed to resolve the issue.

✓ **Reading Check** Describing What is the purpose of propaganda?

The End of Neutrality

Main Idea Relations with Germany worsened, and the United States entered World War I.

History and You Why did the United States enter into a war with Iraq in 2003? Read to learn why the United States finally entered World War I.

. . . .

The crisis over submarine warfare led Congress, in the summer of 1916, to pass legislation to strengthen the military. Congress doubled the size of the army and provided funding for the construction of new navy warships. President Wilson still hoped, however, to stay out of the war.

Antiwar sentiment remained very strong. Some Americans saw the nation's military buildup as a step toward entering the war. The phrase "He [Wilson] Kept Us Out of War" became the Democrats' campaign slogan in 1916. Wilson, however, only narrowly defeated the Republican candidate, Charles Evans Hughes.

People IN HISTORY

Jeannette Rankin

First Female Member of the U.S. Congress

Rankin voted against the declaration of war on Germany just a few days after taking office in 1917. During the vote, she said, *"I want to stand by my country—but I cannot vote for war."* Her pacifism probably cost her the Republican Senate nomination in 1918. She was reelected to Congress in 1940 on an antiwar platform. She was the only member of Congress to vote against the declaration of war on Japan after the bombing of Pearl Harbor in December 1941. The vote met with wide disapproval, and Rankin did not seek reelection the following year.

CRITICAL Thinking

1. **Analyzing** Why do you think Rankin made the statement "I want to stand by my country" at the time she voted against a declaration of war on Germany?

2. **Synthesizing** Did voters agree or disagree with Rankin's position on war? How do you know?

C **Critical Thinking**

Analyzing Information Ask: What signs indicated that Congress was preparing for war? *(They doubled the size of the army and provided funds to build new warships.)* **OL**

D **Differentiated Instruction**

Gifted and Talented Have students study the effects of war on political elections. Using online or library resources, have students find and share examples of presidential elections in which war influenced the outcome. **AL**

People IN HISTORY

Critical Thinking Answers

1. She might have wanted to be clear that she supported the U.S. even though she did not agree with the decision to go to war.

2. Students may note that Rankin lost a chance to be nominated to the Senate, suggesting that voters disagreed with her vote.

✓ **Reading Check** **Answer:** to gain citizens' support

Additional Support

Activity: Technology Connection

Analyzing Primary Sources Have students work in small groups to research original newspaper articles about the attack on the *Lusitania*. Instruct students to find a variety of articles, such as news reports, editorials, and articles with firsthand accounts, along with photos or illustrations related to the topic. After their research, have students analyze the articles for evidence of public opinion, nationalism, and bias. Students should also try to find inconsistencies between articles. As a class, have students compare their sources to determine commonalities in reports. As a class, discuss the role of journalism in recording events as they happen, as well as representing the way people view those events. **AL**

Chance & Error in History

What If the British Had Not Intercepted the Zimmermann Note?

In January 1917, German foreign minister Arthur Zimmermann proposed that Mexico help Germany if the United States entered the war. A British official intercepted Zimmermann's telegram.

The Telegram

"We shall endeavor . . . to keep the United States of America neutral. In the event of this not succeeding, we make Mexico a proposal of alliance on the following basis: make war together, make peace together, generous financial support and an understanding on our part that Mexico is to reconquer the lost territory in Texas, New Mexico, and Arizona."

Reaction to Telegram

The Zimmermann telegram angered Americans and helped build popular sentiment for the war. Then, in mid-March, four American merchant ships were sunk without warning. On April 2, 1917, President Wilson asked Congress to declare war on Germany.

Critical Thinking

Analyzing If there were no Zimmermann note, do you think the United States would have: (a) entered the war when it did in April; (b) entered the war at a later time; or (c) not been drawn into the war at all? Explain.

D ## Differentiated Instruction

Interpersonal Have students brainstorm a list of pro and con statements that President Wilson and his cabinet may have made as they considered the move from neutrality to war. Have students use their list to debate U.S. entry into the war. **OL**

R ## Reading Strategy

Reading Primary Sources Ask: Who does "we" refer to in the first line of the quotation? *(Germany)* Explain to students that it is important to identify who is speaking in order to correctly interpret quotations. **BL**

Chance & Error in History

Critical Thinking Answers

Answers may include no, the United States would not have entered the war when it did because it would not have felt a threat so close to home.

Differentiated Instruction

On the Brink of War

In January 1917, Germany announced that it would sink on sight all merchant vessels, armed or unarmed, sailing to Allied ports. The Germans knew they risked bringing Americans into the war. However, the Germans believed they could defeat the Allies before the United States became too involved. An angry President Wilson broke off diplomatic relations with Germany.

Then a few weeks later, British agents intercepted a secret telegram sent by the German foreign minister, Arthur Zimmermann. It offered an alliance with Mexico against the United States if war broke out. Newspapers published the Zimmermann telegram, and Americans reacted angrily to the German offer. The telegram set off a new wave of anti-German feeling.

Revolution in Russia

Dramatic events continued to push the United States into the war. First, in March 1917 a **revolution**—a war to overthrow the government—took place in Russia. The Rus-

sian people overthrew the monarchy and established a temporary government that promised free elections. The new Russian government also vowed to continue the fight to defeat Germany.

This change from an **autocracy,** in which one person with unlimited powers rules, to a more democratic government, raised Allies' hopes. Wilson could now argue that the Allies were fighting a war for democracy.

Other critical events took place at sea. In March 1917, within a few days' time, the Germans attacked and sank four American merchant ships. Thirty-six lives were lost.

D President Wilson continued to struggle with his conscience. His cabinet, on the other hand, strongly favored war. One government official later explained:

PRIMARY SOURCE

R "If we had stayed out of the war and Germany had won there would no longer have been a balance of power in Europe or a British fleet to support the Monroe Doctrine and protect America."

—from "The Duties of the Citizen," 1917

Paraphrasing

Objective:	To learn how to paraphrase
Focus:	Ask students how they would feel if someone copied their work and presented it as his or her own.
Teach:	Have students read the information, answer the questions, and apply the skill.
Assess:	Discuss why changing only a few words and phrases is not considered paraphrasing.
Close:	Review the steps students should take when paraphrasing.

Differentiated Instruction Strategies

BL Ask students to restate their paraphrased material verbally before they write it down.

AL Have students research famous cases of plagiarism and their outcomes.

ELL Have students define the terms "plagiarizing" and "paraphrasing" in their own words.

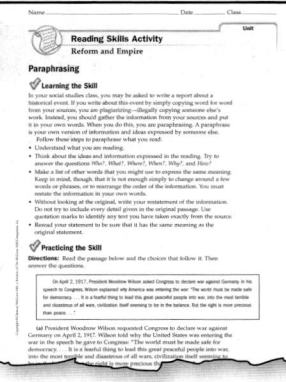

Reading Skills Activity, URB p. 7

America Enters the War

President Wilson decided that the United States could no longer remain neutral. On the cold, rainy evening of April 2, 1917, he asked Congress for a declaration of war against Germany:

PRIMARY SOURCE

"The world must be made safe for democracy. . . . . . . It is a fearful thing to lead this great, peaceful people into war, into the most terrible and disastrous of all wars. . . . But the right is more precious than peace."

—from *Democracy Today: An American Interpretation*

Congress did not agree at once to a war resolution. In the end, however, most members agreed that the nation must defend its rights if it wished to remain a great world power. As a result, Congress passed a declaration of war, and Wilson signed it on April 6. Fifty-six members of the House and Senate voted against war. One of those 56 was Jeannette Rankin of Montana—the first woman to serve as a representative in Congress.

The United States had to raise an army quickly. On May 18, Congress passed the **Selective Service Act,** setting up a military draft. Men aged 21 to 30 registered by the millions. By war's end, some 24 million men had registered. Of them, about 3 million were called to serve. Another 2 million joined voluntarily. In addition, for the first time, women enlisted in the armed forces. They served in noncombat roles, such as radio operators, clerks, and nurses.

More than 300,000 African Americans joined the armed forces, but they faced discrimination and racism. Most held low-level jobs at military bases. Among the 140,000 African American soldiers sent to Europe, 40,000 fought in combat. Many served with honor, including a regiment that received medals for bravery from France. One of its members, Henry Johnson, was the first American to receive the French Croix de Guerre [Cross of War], a medal for bravery.

✓ **Reading Check** **Describing** What was the purpose of the Selective Service Act?

S Skill Practice

Reading a Time Line Assign students to work in small groups to create time lines that list all of the events which led the United States to declare war. Have students use the time line in the opening pages of this chapter as an example. **OL**

C Critical Thinking

Comparing and Contrasting Ask: How did the roles of women differ from those of men? *(Women were not allowed to fight in combat, whereas many men were assigned combat roles.)* **OL**

✓ **Reading Check** **Answer:** to raise an army quickly

Assess

Study Central™ provides summaries, interactive games, and online graphic organizers to help students review content.

Close

Evaluating As a class, discuss the options President Wilson might have weighed as he considered whether or not to enter the war. **OL**

Section 2 Review

Section 2 Review

Study Central™ To review this section, go to glencoe.com.

Vocabulary

1. Define each of the following terms in a sentence: propaganda, stress, revolution, autocracy.

Main Ideas

2. **Summarizing** Why did many Americans favor the Allies?

3. **Explaining** Why did the revolution in Russia push the United States toward entering the war?

Critical Thinking

4. **Analyzing** How is propaganda used as a "weapon" in war?

5. **Determining Cause and Effect** Use a diagram like the one below to show the consequences of Germany's attacks on various ships.

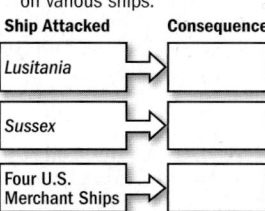

Ship Attacked		Consequence
Lusitania	→	
Sussex	→	
Four U.S. Merchant Ships	→	

6. **Persuasive Writing** Write a letter to President Wilson to persuade him to keep the United States out of the war.

Answer the
7. **Essential Question**
Why did the United States enter World War I?

World War I **Chapter 23** **717**

Answers

1. Sentences should reflect a correct understanding of the terms.
2. Many people had come from Allied countries, felt cultural ties to Great Britain, and were influenced by Allied propaganda. Also, the United States traded exclusively with Britain because of the British blockade of Germany. German submarine attacks on the *Lusitania* and the *Sussex* enraged Americans.
3. The government in Russia was democratic and was believed to be planning to join the

Allies. Wilson, in looking for justification for entering the war, now could say that it was a war for democracy.
4. Propaganda rouses support from citizens and sways public opinion about war.
5. *Lusitania:* Wilson denounces the attack. *Sussex:* Germany, afraid that the United States might enter the war, pledges to warn neutral ships and passenger ships before attacking. **Four U.S. Merchant Ships:** Congress declares war.

6. Students may argue that the war is a European affair and that the U.S. military is unprepared for war.
7. Answers should include cultural ties to Allies, Germany's new policy of sinking all merchant vessels sailing to Allied ports, the Zimmermann telegram, the Russian Revolution, and continued sinking of U.S. ships by Germany.

Section 3

Americans Join the Allies

Focus

Bellringer
Daily Test Practice Transparency 23-3

Reading Guide
Answers to Graphic:
helped the British destroy German submarines; escorted groups of merchant ships across the Atlantic

Section Spotlight Video

Have students watch the Section Spotlight Video "Americans Join the Allies" to learn about trench warfare.

Resource Manager

Essential Question
How did the United States help the Allies win the war?

Reading Guide

Content Vocabulary

convoy (p. 719)   kaiser (p. 723)

armistice (p. 723)

Academic Vocabulary

proceed (p. 720)   consent (p. 723)

Key People and Events

Bolsheviks (p. 719)

Vladimir Lenin (p. 719)

Treaty of Brest-Litovsk (p. 720)

John J. Pershing (p. 720)

Reading Strategy

Taking Notes As you read, use a diagram like the one below to describe how the U.S. Navy helped get much-needed supplies to Great Britain.

```
    ○        ○
     ↖      ↗
   ╭─────────────╮
   │  Supplies to │
   │ Great Britain│
   ╰─────────────╯
```

ILLINOIS STANDARDS
The American Journey

14.E.3 Compare the basic principles of the United States and its international interests (e.g., territory, environment, trade, use of technology).

16.B.3d (US) Describe ways in which the United States developed as a world political power.

17.D Understand the historical significance of geography.

American Diary

"Late one afternoon our captain . . . formed the company and, with great solemnity [seriousness], announced: 'This company is going to France. We are going right away. Is there a man here who does not want to go?' No one replied. He commanded: 'Dismissed.' I have often wondered if that company did not have a pack of silent liars."

—*quoted in* Doughboy War:The American Expeditionary Force in World War I

A French couple greets U.S. soldiers.

R Reading Strategies	**C** Critical Thinking	**D** Differentiated Instruction	**W** Writing Support	**S** Skill Practice
Teacher Edition • Skimming, p. 719 • Identifying, p. 721 • Making Connections, p. 723 **Additional Resources** • Guid. Read., URB p. 97 • Content Vocab., URB p. 73 • Academic Vocab., URB p. 75 • Read. Ess., p. 253	**Teacher Edition** • Predict. Conseq., p. 719 • Analyz. Information, p. 720 • Analyzing, p. 723 **Additional Resources** • Quizzes and Tests, p. 225	**Teacher Edition** • ELL, p. 721 **Additional Resources** • School-to-Home, URB p. 91 • Reteaching Act., URB p. 93 • Differ. Inst., URB p. 83	**Teacher Edition** • Expository Writing, p. 722 **Additional Resources** • Writ. Skills, URB p. 79	**Teacher Edition** • Using Geo. Skills, p. 720 **Additional Resources** • Daily Test Pract. Transp. 23-3 • Lesson Transparency 23C

Supplying the Allies

Main Idea Russia withdrew from the war, but the American troops helped turn the tide in favor of the Allies.

History and You Can you complete a task more quickly by working alone or by working with a team? Read to learn how the American soldiers fought with the Allies in the war.

In 1917 the Allies desperately needed the help of American soldiers. Years of trench warfare had exhausted the Allied armies. Some French troops refused to continue fighting after a failed offensive in 1917. The British started to run out of war supplies and food, so their people were starving. Furthermore, German submarines were taking a deadly toll on Allied shipping. They sank one of every four ships that left British ports.

American entry into the war made an immediate difference. To ensure that needed supplies reached Great Britain, the U.S. Navy helped the British destroy German submarines. Then **convoys,** or teams, of navy destroyers escorted groups of merchant ships across the Atlantic.

R If German submarines wanted to attack a merchant ship, they had to get past the American ships protecting it. The convoy system worked well. In one year it reduced Allied shipping losses from 900,000 to 300,000 tons per month. With the convoy system, not one American soldier bound for Europe was lost to submarine attack.

Russian Withdrawal **C**

The Allies also needed more troops because of a second revolution in Russia. In March 1917, Czar Nicholas II, leader of the Russian Empire, gave up his throne in the first revolution. Political leadership was handed to a temporary government that supported the war. This government, however, was unable to solve major problems, such as food shortages, that plagued the nation.

In November 1917, riots broke out over the government's handling of the war and over the scarcity of food and fuel. The **Bolsheviks,** a group of Communists, overthrew the democratic Russian government and established a Communist government. Led by **Vladimir Lenin,** the Bolsheviks wanted to pull out of the war so they could concentrate their efforts on setting up a new Communist state.

Primary Source / **Soldiers' IDs**

Dog Tags Before World War I, the U.S. military often had a difficult time identifying dead soldiers after a battle. By 1917, each American soldier was required to wear an identification badge around the neck. Soldiers nicknamed them "dog tags."

LT. P. HENRY N. FLYNT
USA

Critical Thinking

Making Inferences Why do you think identifying fallen soldiers was an important issue for soldiers and their families?

Teach

R Reading Strategy

Skimming Remind students that skimming means "to quickly read over a passage to get a general idea of the text." Instruct students to skim the headings, illustrations, and boldface words in this section. **BL**

C Critical Thinking

Predicting Consequences Ask: What do you think would happen to the Allied countries when Russia pulled out of the war? *(The Allied countries would have more difficulty fighting the Central Powers because Allied forces would have fewer troops.)* **OL**

Primary Source

Critical Thinking Answer
The dog tags ensure that injured soldiers do not get lost on the battlefield. If soldiers should die in battle, their bodies can be found and returned to their families.

Hands-On Chapter Project
Step 3

Creating a War Documentary

Step 3: Researching the Causes of War Groups of students will research Americans' reaction to and their support for the war.

Essential Question: How did the United States help the Allies win the war?

Directions Students will work in small groups to research Americans' feelings about entering the war and their support for the troops fighting in Europe. Instruct students to find information related to U.S. public opinion regarding the politics of war, as well as the cultural and social effects of entering the war. As students gather facts

for their documentary script, remind them to select background music from the time period.

Explaining Have students explain how the United States supported the Allies in the war. **OL**

(Chapter Project continued in Section 4)

History ONLINE

S Skill Practice

Using Geography Skills Refer students to the map on this page to trace the movement from the Eastern Front to the Western Front. **Ask:** Between 1914 and 1918, where did most battles take place? *(along the Western Front)* How many major battles took place in France? *(five)* **OL**

C Critical Thinking

Analyzing Information Ask: What words and phrases in the quotation show that Paris welcomed General Pershing? *("shook with cheers" "terrific roar" "took Pershing by storm")* What do you think the French people were hoping? *(that Pershing and his troops would help them defeat Germany)* **OL**

History ONLINE
Objectives and answers to the Student Web Activity can be found at glencoe.com under the Web Activity Lesson Plan for this chapter.

Additional Support

Lenin took Russia out of the war, and in March 1918, he signed the **Treaty of Brest-Litovsk** with Germany. As a result of this treaty, Russia lost substantial territory to the Germans. Russia's withdrawal from the war allowed the Germans to move thousands of troops from the Eastern Front, or line of battle, to the Western Front in France.

New German Offensive

In March 1918, the Germans launched a massive attack along the Western Front. German military leaders hoped to drive a wedge in the Allied lines. They wanted to capture the city of Amiens before **proceeding** to Paris. Between March and June 1918, the Germans hammered at Allied lines. They pushed the Allies back to within 40 miles (64 km) of

History ONLINE
Student Web Activity Visit glencoe.com and complete the Chapter 23 Web Activity about World War I.

Paris. After years of stalemate along the Western Front—the area along the French-German border—it looked as if Germany might win the war.

American Troops Arrive in France

In May 1917, General **John J. Pershing** was named supreme commander of the American Expeditionary Force (AEF), the American army in Europe. American correspondent Floyd Gibbons described the welcome for the first American troops to arrive in France:

PRIMARY SOURCE

"The sooty girders of the Gare du Nord [railroad station] shook with cheers when the special train pulled in. . . .

. . . A minute later, there was a terrific roar from beyond the walls of the station. The crowds outside had heard the cheering within. . . . Paris took Pershing by storm."

—from *"And They Thought We Wouldn't Fight"*

Europe During World War I, 1914–1918

NATIONAL GEOGRAPHIC

Allies
Central Powers
Neutral nations
Eastern Front
Western Front

Major Battles

Tannenberg, Aug. 1914
1st Marne, Sept. 1914
Gallipoli, Apr. 1915–Jan. 1916
Verdun, Feb.–Dec. 1916
Somme, July–Nov. 1916
Château-Thierry and Belleau Wood, June 1918
2nd Marne, July 1918
St. Mihiel, Sept. 1918
Meuse-Argonne, Sept.–Nov. 1918

Activity: Interdiciplinary Connection

Health Ask students to imagine the daily life of a soldier in the trenches. **Ask:** What do you think living conditions were like in the trenches? *(Answers may include cold in winter, wet during rainy periods, and dirty.)* Have students research the effects of trench warfare on the health of soldiers. Students should use online and print resources to locate information about the common health problems soldiers faced, the causes of the problems, and the treatment soldiers received. As a class, discuss the students' findings. Present them with the conditions soldiers face during wartimes today. Ask students to predict the types of health problems that today's soldiers might face. **OL**

The AEF was ready for battle in Europe by the spring of 1918. The French and British wanted to use the American soldiers to build up their own troops. However, General Pershing refused. He preferred to keep the AEF a separate force.

Doughboys in Battle

American soldiers, or "doughboys," saw their first serious fighting in early June 1918. They were nicknamed "doughboys" because of their brass uniform buttons that resembled boiled dough dumplings, a popular food. In June, the AEF helped turn back a German offensive at Château-Thierry on the Marne River east of Paris. The American troops then advanced to nearby Belleau Wood. For 24 hours a day for the next three weeks, American forces fought their way through the forest against a solid wall of German machine-gun fire.

The Americans and the French fought back German attacks on Allied forces along the Marne and the Somme Rivers and stopped the German offensive. General Pershing wrote that the battles had "turned the tide of war."

The Battle of the Argonne Forest

The Allies now began an offensive of their own. In mid-September, about 500,000 American soldiers fought and defeated the Germans at Saint Mihiel, east of Verdun. Later that month, more than 1 million American troops joined the Allies in the Battle of the Argonne Forest. It became the most massive attack in American history.

The Battle of the Argonne Forest raged for nearly seven weeks. Soldiers struggled over the rugged, heavily forested ground. Rain, mud, barbed wire, and fire from German machine guns hindered the Allies' advance. Many lives were lost.

African Americans in World War I

World War I gave African Americans the opportunity to show their loyalty and patriotism. In 1917 the War Department created two divisions of primarily African American combat units. Discrimination remained, however. Units were forced to train separately. Four regiments fought alongside the French, where they were treated as equals and fought valiantly.

"These Negroes are American citizens. Naturally I cannot and will not discriminate against these soldiers."

—General John Pershing's response to British protest of using African American troops

The 369th regiment fought on the front lines for 191 days, five days longer than any other U.S. regiment. The entire unit received the French Croix de Guerre medal for bravery. ▶

Critical Thinking

Making Inferences Why do you think some African American soldiers wanted to stay in Europe after the war?

World War I **Chapter 23** 721

R Reading Strategy

Identifying Ask: Who were the doughboys? *(American soldiers)* **ELL**

D Differentiated Instruction

English Language Learners Help students understand the adjective + noun structure used in English, especially students whose native language places adjectives behind or otherwise away from the nouns they are modifying. Instruct students to match adjectives with their modified nouns when they read. For example, "rugged, heavily forested ground" means "rugged ground" and "heavily forested ground." **ELL**

Europe During World War I, 1914–1918 NATIONAL GEOGRAPHIC

Critical Thinking Answer

Answers may include because they felt less discrimination from Europeans than from Americans.

Differentiated Instruction

Writing Skills Activity,
URB p. 79

Choosing a Form of Writing

Objective: To learn how to choose a writing mode

Focus: Explain why it is necessary to consider different writing modes.

Teach: Have students read the information, answer the questions, and apply the skill.

Assess: Have students use the self-assessment checklist.

Close: Discuss any challenges that students have when using the different writing modes.

Differentiated Instruction Strategies

BL Remind students that there are several different writing modes that can work for a specific purpose.

AL Have students discuss the advantages of the different writing modes.

ELL Ask students to create a graphic organizer that lists the different purposes and writing modes, and use this when applying the skill.

People IN HISTORY

W Writing Support

Expository Writing Tell students to conduct research on either Alvin York or Eddie Rickenbacker. Have students use their research to write official commendations for the honored soldier explaining the action that earned the soldier the Medal of Honor and describing the soldier's character. **AL**

People IN HISTORY

Critical Thinking Answers

1. to inspire support from the American people
2. He uses words such as "spirit of our forefathers" to appeal to Americans' loyalty and patriotism.

✓ **Reading Check** **Answer:** The Allies pushed back the Germans and broke through enemy lines, effectively invading Germany.

General John J. Pershing

Commander of the American Expeditionary Force during World War I

Pershing was a skillful military leader. He insisted that the American Expeditionary Force remain independent from the French and British armies. In a message he recorded for the American people during the battle of Picardy and Flanders in April 1918, he said, *"Three thousand miles from home, an American army is fighting for you. Everything you hold worthwhile is at stake. . . . Invoking the spirit of our forefathers, the army asks your unflinching support, to the end that the high ideals for which America stands may endure upon the earth."*

CRITICAL Thinking

1. **Analyzing** What was the purpose of Pershing's message?
2. **Evaluating** How does Pershing appeal to his listeners' emotions?

The Battle of the Argonne Forest ended in early November. The Allies had pushed back the Germans and broken through the enemy lines. The Germans now were faced with an invasion of their own country.

W Although the war led to many acts of bravery, the actions of two Americans captured the nation's imagination. During the fighting at Argonne Forest, Corporal Alvin York killed several German soldiers, captured machine guns, and took 132 prisoners. Captain Eddie Rickenbacker was a member of the 94th Aero Squadron. He fought in 134 air battles and shot down 26 aircraft. Both York and Rickenbacker were awarded the Medal of Honor for their actions.

✓ **Reading Check** **Summarizing** Why was the Battle of the Argonne Forest important?

The End of the War

Main Idea By late 1918, Germany was losing the war and appealed for an armistice to end the fighting.

History and You Think about the reasons a nation decides to stop fighting a war. Read to learn why Germany asked for peace.

While fighting raged along the Western Front, Germany's allies faced certain defeat. In late 1918, the Ottoman Empire was on the brink of collapse, and a revolution engulfed Austria-Hungary. Street protests in Vienna, Budapest, and other cities led to the end of the centuries-old empire. In October 1918, the ethnic territories within the empire began to break away. Poland, Hungary, and Czechoslovakia, for example, declared independence.

Differentiated Instruction

Leveled Activities

BL School-to-Home Connection Activity, URB p. 91

OL Reteaching Activity, URB p. 93

ELL Differentiated Instruction Activity, URB p. 83

By early in November, the governments of Austria-Hungary and the Ottoman Empire had surrendered to the Allied Powers.

Request for an Armistice

Meanwhile, military leaders in Germany realized they had little chance of winning the war. American troops and supplies had fortified and added new determination to the Allied war effort. In addition, the Germans on the home front were suffering greatly from severe shortages of food and other needed supplies.

On October 4, 1918, the German government appealed to President Wilson for an **armistice.** An armistice is an agreement to end the fighting. Wilson **consented,** or agreed, but only under certain conditions. Germany must accept his plan for peace and promise not to renew hostilities. All German troops must leave Belgium and France. Finally, Wilson would deal only with civilian leaders, not with the military.

While German leaders considered Wilson's demands, political unrest erupted in Germany. On November 3, sailors in Kiel, the main base of the German fleet, revolted. Within days,

groups of workers and soldiers seized power in other German towns. As the revolution spread, the German **kaiser,** or emperor, decided to step down. On November 9, Germany was declared a republic. The new leaders of Germany agreed to Wilson's terms for an armistice.

Peace Begins

The armistice began on November 11, 1918—the 11th hour on the 11th day of the 11th month. Germany agreed to withdraw all land forces west of the Rhine River, withdraw its fleet to the Baltic Sea, and surrender huge amounts of equipment. The fighting stopped, and the Great War ended. President Wilson said:

PRIMARY SOURCE

"Everything for which America fought has been accomplished. It will now be our fortunate duty to assist by example, by sober friendly counsel and by material aid in the establishment of a just democracy throughout the world."
—from "Proclamation of the Armistice with Germany"

✓ **Reading Check** Describing What conditions did Germany accept to end the fighting?

History ONLINE
Study Central™ To review this section, go to glencoe.com.

Section 3 Review

Vocabulary

1. Define the following terms in a sentence: convoy, proceed, armistice, consent, kaiser.

Main Ideas

2. Explaining Why did the war intensify on the Western Front after the second Russian revolution?

3. Determining Cause and Effect What factor led to Germany's acceptance of a peace agreement?

Critical Thinking

4. Predicting If the war had continued on the Eastern Front, do you think the Allies still could have won? Why or why not?

5. Determining Cause and Effect Draw a diagram like the one below to list three reasons the Allies needed the help of U.S. forces.

U.S. Help

6. Creative Writing Think about what it was like for a soldier serving on the front line in WWI. Write a letter home describing battle conditions.

Answer the
7. Essential Question
How did the United States help the Allies win the war?

World War I **Chapter 23 723**

C Critical Thinking

Analyzing Ask: Why did the Germans appeal for an armistice? *(They had little chance of victory.)* **OL**

R Reading Strategy

Making Connections Ask: What holiday does the U.S. celebrate on November 11? *(Veterans Day)* Tell students that Veterans Day, originally called Armistice Day, was first proclaimed by President Wilson in 1919. **OL**

✓ **Reading Check** **Answer:** to withdraw all land forces west of the Rhine River and its fleet from the Baltic Sea, and surrender huge amounts of equipment

Assess
. . . .
History ONLINE

Study Central™ provides summaries, interactive games, and online graphic organizers to help students review content.

Close
. . . .
Summarizing As a class, summarize the ways the Americans helped the Allies. **OL**

Section 3 Review

Answers

1. Sentences should reflect a correct understanding of the terms.

2. Lenin took Russia out of the war, which allowed the Germans to move troops from the Eastern Front to the Western Front.

3. The German people revolted, the kaiser stepped down, and the new leaders of Germany agreed to Wilson's terms for an armistice.

4. Students' answers will probably recognize that the fresh American troops, coupled with America's industrial might, would have posed a significant threat to Germany's ability to win the war, particularly when the German home front was in upheaval.

5. (1) Years of trench warfare had exhausted Allied armies, and some French troops refused to continue fighting after a failed offensive in 1917. (2) The British were starving without supplies and food. (3) German submarines were crippling Allied shipping.

6. Students' letters should describe the terrible conditions in the trenches and on the battlefields.

7. The U.S. Navy helped the British destroy German submarines, and Allied convoys escorted merchant ships. The American forces provided more troops to the Allies. American soldiers helped win significant battles and stopped the German offensive.

Focus

Section 4

Bellringer
Daily Test Practice Transparency 23–4

Reading Guide
Answers to Graphic:

Espionage Act: set stiff penalties for espionage

Sabotage Act: made it a crime to say, print, or write any criticism about the government

Sedition Act: made it a crime to say, print, or write any criticism about the government

Section Spotlight Video

Have students watch the Section Spotlight Video "The War at Home" to learn about the role of women in World War I.

Resource Manager

Essential Question ◄
How did the United States mobilize its resources to fight the war?

Reading Guide

Content Vocabulary
mobilization (p. 725)   pacifist (p. 727)
ration (p. 726)   dissent (p. 727)
socialist (p. 727)

Academic Vocabulary
consume (p. 726)   perceive (p. 727)

Key People and Events
Great Migration (p. 725)
Espionage Act (p. 727)
Sabotage Act (p. 727)
Sedition Act (p. 727)

Reading Strategy
Taking Notes As you read, use a chart like the one below to describe how these three acts controlled public opinion.

	Description
Espionage Act	
Sabotage Act	
Sedition Act	

ILLINOIS STANDARDS
The American Journey

14.C.3 Compare historical issues involving rights, roles and status of individuals in relation to municipalities, states and the nation.

16.C.3c (US) Describe how economic developments and government policies after 1865 affected the country's economic institutions including corporations, banks and organized labor.

17.C.3c Analyze how human processes influence settlement patterns including migration and population growth.

The War at Home

American Diary

As American men left their homes for war, American women grabbed tools and went to work. Ella May Stumpe, in her early twenties, described her contribution: "When the harvest time came, there weren't enough young men left to work the fields. So an old bachelor organized a bunch of us, about a dozen young women, and came with a wagon and took us out to the fields to shuck grain. He told us we were helping the war effort."

—quoted in Centenarians: The Story of the 20th Century by the Americans Who Lived It

Workers prepare missiles in a factory.

R Reading Strategies	**C** Critical Thinking	**D** Differentiated Instruction	**W** Writing Support	**S** Skill Practice
Teacher Edition • Setting a Purpose, p. 725	**Teacher Edition** • Det. Cause and Effect, p. 725	**Teacher Edition** • Gifted and Talented, p. 727	**Teacher Edition** • Persuasive Writing, p. 726	**Teacher Edition** • Visual Literacy, p. 726
Additional Resources • Guid. Read., URB p. 98 • Content Vocab., URB p. 73 • Academic Vocab., URB p. 75 • Read. Ess., p. 256	**Additional Resources** • Quizzes and Tests, p. 226	**Additional Resources** • School-to-Home, URB p. 91 • Reteaching, URB p. 93		**Additional Resources** • Daily Test Pract. Transp. 23-4 • Soc. Stud. Skills, URB p. 81

Mobilizing the Nation

Main Idea The United States prepared to fight the war.

History and You If you have a summer job, do you manage the work for someone who is on vacation? Read to learn how the United States had to adjust its workforce during World War I.

. . . .

After the United States declared war on Germany in 1917, Americans began focusing their energies on getting ready to fight the war. **Mobilization,** or the gathering of resources and the preparation for war, affected almost every part of American life.

To ensure production of vital war materials, the government created the National War Labor Board in April 1918. The board pressured businesses to grant some of the most important demands of workers. As a result, workers won an eight-hour working day. They also received overtime pay, equal pay for women, and the right to form unions. In return, workers agreed not to go on strike.

R Workers During the War

To pay for the war, the United States government sold war bonds and increased taxes. Then industries had to expand in order to produce war materials. During this time, however, there was a labor shortage. Millions of men left their jobs to serve in the armed forces. Also, immigration slowed during the war. Fewer immigrants were arriving to take on the jobs.

The labor shortage provided new job opportunities for women. Many women joined the workforce for the first time by taking on jobs previously held by men.

The prospect of finding good jobs also brought hundreds of thousands of African Americans to Northern cities from the rural South. From 1914 to 1920, between 300,000 and 500,000 African Americans left their homes in the rural South to settle in Northern cities and find jobs. This huge population movement was known as the **Great Migration.** In addition, thousands of Mexicans migrated to the United States in search of jobs.

Primary Source / Saving Resources

Make-Do Recipes
The Food Administration enlisted 20 million housewives to promote awareness of the need to follow the rules for conserving food. Eggs, butter, milk, and wheat flour were to be used sparingly so that enough food was available to feed the soldiers. In 1918 the Royal Baking Company even published a book of recipes that identified ingredients that could be substituted for those that were needed for the troops.

Barley or Oat Flour Biscuits

2 cups barley or oat flour	1 tablespoon sugar
4 teaspoons Royal Baking Powder	1 tablespoon shortening
1/2 teaspoon salt	2/3 cup milk

Sift dry ingredients together. Rub in shortening and add enough milk to make a soft dough. Roll out on board to about one-half inch thick and cut with biscuit cutter. Bake in very hot oven 15 to 20 minutes.

Critical Thinking

Analyzing If you lived in the United States during World War I, how could you have contributed to the war effort?

Social Studies Skills Activity, URB p. 81

Teach

. . . .

R Reading Strategy

Setting a Purpose Write the following statements on the board:

1. The U.S. government sold war bonds to pay for the war.

2. African Americans opened factories in the South to produce needed supplies.

3. Pacifists supported the war.

Tell students to read the chapter to find out whether these statements are true or false. *(true, false, false)* **OL**

C Critical Thinking

Determining Cause and Effect
Ask: What was the effect of the labor shortage on women? *(New job opportunities were open to women.)* **OL**

Primary Source

Critical Thinking Answer
Answers may include conserving food items and taking odd jobs to help provide family income.

Differentiated Instruction

Analyzing Information Using Graphs

Objective:	To learn how to analyze information using graphs
Focus:	Review with students the different types of graphs with which they are familiar.
Teach:	Have students read the information, answer the questions, and apply the skill.
Assess:	Have students use the self-assessment checklist.
Close:	Ask students to compare their charts, and then have the class list the most common activities on the board.

Differentiated Instruction Strategies

BL Ask students to add up the percentages in the graphs and explain why the total should be 100%.

AL Have students prepare their circle graphs using software.

ELL Ask students to explain why a circle graph is also called a "pie chart."

Primary Source / Propaganda Posters

Building Support The Committee on Public Information launched a massive campaign to build support for the war. Posters were an important part of this campaign.

▲ James Montgomery Flagg's depiction of Uncle Sam for the U.S. Army is the most famous American wartime poster.

With millions of men serving in the military, women were needed to take their places in the labor force. ▼

The government sold war bonds to help pay for the cost of the war. ▶

◀ The Food Administration urged people to observe "Wheatless Mondays," "Meatless Tuesdays," and "Porkless Thursdays," and to add to their own store of food by planting "victory gardens." Slogans such as "Serve Just Enough" and "Use All Leftovers" reminded Americans to conserve food.

Critical Thinking

Synthesizing What common message is found in all four posters?

Producing Supplies

The United States had to produce food not only for its own needs but also for the Allies. President Wilson appointed Herbert Hoover to head a new Food Administration. This agency's campaign encouraged American farmers to produce more and persuaded the public to eat less.

The Food Administration also put price controls on many agricultural products to encourage voluntary **rationing,** or the limitation of use. As a result of such efforts, Americans **consumed,** or used, less food, expanded food production, and increased food exports.

Another government agency, the War Industries Board, supervised the nation's industrial production. The board's responsibilities included overseeing the changeover of factories to produce war-related goods and setting prices for key consumer products. Finally, the Fuel Administration managed the nation's coal and oil. To save energy, the agency introduced daylight savings time and called for "Heatless Mondays."

Mobilizing Support

The federal government also needed to mobilize public support for the war. Antiwar sentiment remained strong even after the United States entered the war. The president appointed journalist George Creel to head the Committee on Public Information. The purpose of the committee was to promote the war as a battle for democracy and freedom.

The Committee on Public Information launched a massive propaganda campaign. The Committee distributed millions of pro-war pamphlets, posters, articles, and books, and it provided newspapers with government accounts of the war and advertisements. The committee hired speakers, writers, artists, and actors to build support for the war.

✔ **Reading Check** **Explaining** Why did the United States face a labor shortage during the early days of World War I?

Creating a War Documentary

Step 4: Compiling a Documentary Groups of students will compile and edit a documentary about World War I.

Essential Question: How did the United States mobilize its resources to fight the war?

Directions Students will now compile and edit their documentary. Divide the students into three groups. Have each group take a portion of the research material and choose the images and text that best convey the events of World War I. As a class, select a narrator for the documentary. Have one group of students write the script for the narrator. Have another group use video-editing software to edit the images, text, music, and voiceovers into a complete film. Instruct another group to create a movie poster advertising their film.

Analyzing As a class, discuss the overall theme of the documentary. **OL**

(Chapter Project continued in Section 5)

Public Opinion and the War

Main Idea During World War I, the American government approved legislation to control public opinion.

History and You Have you ever spoken out against a government action? Read to learn how the government tried to stop people from speaking out against the war.

World War I helped the American economy. Yet the war had harmful effects on American society. To create a sense of national unity, the government tried to silence opposition. Some Americans became intolerant of those who were different.

Controlling Public Opinion

Even after America entered the war, opposition to it remained strong. Some German Americans and Irish Americans sympathized with the Central Powers. Many **socialists**—people who believe industries should be publicly owned—opposed the war. They thought it would only help rich business owners and hurt working people. **Pacifists**—people who are opposed to the use of violence—were also against the war.

During the war, the Committee on Public Information began trying to silence **dissent.** Dissent is disagreement or opposition. It portrayed people who were against the war as unpatriotic. The **Espionage Act** of 1917 gave the government a new weapon to combat dissent to the war. The law provided stiff penalties for espionage, or spying. People who aided the enemy or interfered with army recruiting also could be penalized.

Congress passed even harsher measures in 1918—the **Sabotage Act** and the **Sedition Act.** These laws made it a crime to say, print, or write any criticism **perceived,** or recognized, as negative about the government. Such acts were considered sabotage—secret action to damage the war effort. Thousands of people were convicted under the laws.

Some people spoke out against these laws and the intolerance they produced. Most Americans, however, believed that in wartime no measure could be "too drastic" toward traitors and disloyal Americans.

✔ Reading Check Making Inferences Why do you think Congress passed laws to penalize people who criticized the government?

Section 4 Review

History ONLINE
Study Central™ To review this section, go to glencoe.com.

Vocabulary

1. Define the following terms in a sentence: mobilization, ration, consumed, socialist, pacifist, dissent, perceive.

Main Ideas

2. Identifying How did World War I benefit workers?

3. Explaining For what reasons did some people oppose the U.S. involvement in World War I?

Critical Thinking

4. Organizing Draw a diagram like the one below that explains why each organization was created.

Government Body	Purpose
National War Labor Board	
Food Administration	
War Industries Board	
Committee on Public Information	

5. Persuasive Writing Make a poster to encourage the people in your town to eat less so more food can be given to the Allied troops.

Answer the
6. Essential Question
How did the United States mobilize its resources to fight the war?

World War I **Chapter 23** **727**

D Differentiated Learning

Gifted and Talented Instruct students to research primary and secondary sources about the laws that were passed to silence dissent. Have students write an essay stating their position either for or against these acts. Tell students they must provide support for their opinions. Have the students share their essays with the class. Discuss more recent legislation such as the Patriot Act, and how it compares with the legislation passed during World War I. **AL**

✔ Reading Check **Answer:** to create a sense of national unity

Assess

History ONLINE

Study Central™ provides summaries, interactive games, and online graphic organizers to help students review content.

Close

Explaining Have students explain the changes to the workforce during World War I. **OL**

Section 4 Review

Answers

1. Sentences should reflect a correct understanding of the terms.
2. To ensure production, the National War Labor Board pressured businesses to hire women and give them equal pay with men. All workers got an eight-hour workday, overtime pay, and the right to unionize in return for not striking.
3. Some German Americans and Irish Americans sympathized with the Central Powers. Socialists believed the war would hurt the workers and help business owners. Pacifists opposed all forms of violence.
4. **National War Labor Board:** ensure U.S. production of war materials; **Food Administration:** ensure food production for Americans and the Allies through voluntary rationing, increased food production, decreased consumption, and increased export of food; **War Industries Board:** supervise U.S. industrial production, set prices for some consumer products; **Committee on Public Information:** promote the war as a battle for democracy and freedom
5. Students' posters should reflect themes about patriotic sacrifice.
6. Students should address how the United States mobilized its economic resources, including materials production and workers, along with promoting the war through a propaganda campaign.

Searching for Peace

Focus

Bellringer
Daily Test Practice Transparency 23–5

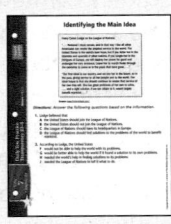

Reading Guide
Answers to Graphic:

accept full responsibility for the war; pay billions of dollars in reparations to the Allies; disarm completely; give up overseas colonies and some territory in Europe

Section Spotlight Video

Have students watch the Section Spotlight Video "Searching for Peace" to learn more about Woodrow Wilson.

Resource Manager

Essential Question
Why did Wilson's Peace Plan fail?

Reading Guide

Content Vocabulary
national self-determination (p. 729)
reparation (p. 730)

Academic Vocabulary
final (p. 730)   achieve (p. 730)

Key People and Events
Fourteen Points (p. 729)
League of Nations (p. 730)
Treaty of Versailles (p. 731)
Henry Cabot Lodge (p. 732)

Reading Strategy
Taking Notes As you read, use a diagram like the one below to list the conditions that Germany agreed to under the Treaty of Versailles.

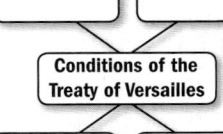

Conditions of the Treaty of Versailles

ILLINOIS STANDARDS
The American Journey

14.E.3 Compare the basic principles of the United States and its international interests (e.g., territory, environment, trade, use of technology).

16.A Apply the skills of historical analysis and interpretation.

16.B.3d (US) Describe ways in which the United States developed as a world political power.

728

American Diary

"We want Wilson," the war-weary crowd roared. "Long live Dr. Wilson!" British students with American flags smiled, tossing flowers in the president's path. Everywhere in Europe the Wilsons visited—Paris, Rome, Milan—the reception was jubilant. Boosted by the cheers of the European crowds, Wilson walked into the Paris Peace Conference at the Palace of Versailles with confidence. He was sure that his plan for a just and lasting peace would win swift approval in Europe and the United States.

President Woodrow Wilson leads the procession after the signing of the Treaty of Versailles.

R Reading Strategies	**C** Critical Thinking	**D** Differentiated Instruction	**W** Writing Support	**S** Skill Practice
Teacher Edition • Using Word Parts, p. 729 • Organizing, p. 732 **Additional Resources** • Guid. Read., URB p. 99 • Content Vocab., URB p. 73 • Academic Vocab., URB p. 75 • Pri. Source Read., URB p. 77	**Teacher Edition** • Analyz. Info., p. 729 • Analyz. Info., p. 731 **Additional Resources** • Quizzes and Tests, p. 227 • Link. Past and Pres., URB p. 89 • Inter. Polit. Cartoons, URB p. 13	**Teacher Edition** • Interpersonal, p. 730 **Additional Resources** • School-to-Home, URB p. 91 • Reteaching Act., URB p. 93	**Teacher Edition** • Personal Writing, p. 730	**Teacher Edition** • Visual Literacy, p. 731 **Additional Resources** • Daily Test Pract. Transp. 23-5 • Geo. and Hist., URB p. 87

Making a Peace

Main Idea World War I ended, but the Allies opposed Wilson's plan for peace.

History and You Think about the destruction caused by war. Read to learn why the Allies wanted to punish Germany.

World leaders from 27 nations gathered in Paris, France, in January 1919. They met for the peace conference following World War I. When President Woodrow Wilson arrived in the city, huge crowds cheered him. With great hope, Europeans looked to Wilson to help build a better postwar world, but enormous problems lay ahead.

Europe was in ruins. Its landscape, farms, and towns were destroyed. The human losses were huge. France, Russia, Germany, and Austria-Hungary each lost between 1 million and 2 million people in the fighting. Millions more were wounded. More than 50,000 Americans were killed in battle, while another 60,000 soldiers died from disease. Estimates put the number of soldiers killed worldwide at nearly 9 million. Millions of civilians also lost their lives.

Europe faced social and political turmoil. Millions of people were homeless and hungry, and civil war raged in Russia. Poles, Czechs, and other peoples struggled to form their own nations. The search for peace and stability was difficult.

Wilson's Fourteen Points

Woodrow Wilson had a vision of a just and lasting peace. He outlined his peace plan in the **Fourteen Points.** Several of the proposals dealt with adjusting boundaries in Europe and creating new nations. These points reflected Wilson's belief in **"national self-determination"**—the right of the people to decide how they should be governed.

Wilson also proposed a number of principles for conducting international relations. They included calls for free trade and freedom of the seas.

By the Numbers — The Human Cost of War

Total Mobilized Forces
- Allies 42 million
- Central Powers 23 million

Military Deaths
- Allies 5.1 million
- Central Powers 3.4 million

Critical Thinking
Calculating What percent of the Allies' mobilized forces were killed in the war? The Central Powers?

Teach

C Critical Thinking

Analyzing Information Write the main idea on the board. Have students work together to locate evidence in the text that supports this statement. *(Europeans believed that some of Wilson's points did not provide clear solutions and wanted to punish the defeated nations. Wilson was forced to compromise.)* **OL**

R Reading Strategy

Using Word Parts Ask: What is the first word in "self-determination"? *("self")* What is the root word in "determination"? *(determine)* Ask students to define "determination." *(the act of making a choice)* Tell students to put the two meanings together to find the meaning of "self-determination." Have students brainstorm other words that begin with the word "self." **ELL**

Primary Source

Critical Thinking Answer
Allies: 12%;
Central Powers: 15%

Hands-On Chapter Project
Step 5

Creating a War Documentary

Step 5: Preparing for a Movie Premiere
Students will prepare to show their documentary to an audience.

Essential Question: Why did Wilson's peace plan fail?

Directions Students will organize a movie premiere event to show their documentary to an audience. Divide the students into small groups. Assign one group the task of writing an introduction for the documentary, which will explain the making of the film to the audience and introduce each of the students who worked on the project. Assign another group to address the audience after the film, raising questions about the future ramifications of the Treaty of Versailles. Assign other groups of students to create invitations to the premiere, to create advertising materials, and to create a schedule for the event.

Speculating Have students speculate how their audience might feel before and after they view the film. **OL**

(Chapter Project continued on the Visual Summary page)

W Writing Support

Personal Writing Have students read the passage. Then have them write a journal entry expressing their thoughts and ideas about the role of the League of Nations. **OL**

D Differentiated Instruction

Interpersonal Divide students into four groups, and assign each group one of the Big Four leaders. Have each group brainstorm a list of questions for their assigned leader. When students complete their lists, have them compare and discuss questions. **OL**

Europe After World War I
NATIONAL GEOGRAPHIC

Map Skills Answer

Poland and Czechoslovakia

Differentiated Instruction

Europe After World War I
NATIONAL GEOGRAPHIC

The Postwar World

- Treaties changed the boundaries of Europe.
- Allied nations weakened the Central Powers by dividing their land.
- Germany's land area was greatly reduced.
- New nations emerged in Eastern Europe, including Poland, Czechoslovakia, and Yugoslavia.
- Economic depression aided the rise of dictatorships in Europe and Japan.

Map Skills

Regions Which new nations bordered Germany?

Maps In MOtion See StudentWorks™ Plus or glencoe.com.

In addition, Wilson supported an end to secret treaties or agreements among nations. He also called for limits on arms and peaceful settlement of disputes over colonies.

League of Nations   1920–1946

Wilson's **final**, or last, point was the creation of a **League of Nations.** The League's member nations would help preserve peace and prevent future wars. They would respect and protect one another's independence.

At first, many Europeans welcomed Wilson's ideas, but problems developed when nations put their own interests first. Also, some of Wilson's points did not provide clear solutions to difficult questions, such as how to **achieve**, or accomplish, self-determination in regions where different ethnic groups lived closely together.

The Allies Disagree

The Allies did not invite either Germany or Russia to the peace talks. The major participants were called the Big Four. In this group was President Wilson; Prime Minister David Lloyd George of Great Britain; France's premier, Georges Clemenceau; and Italian prime minister Vittorio Orlando.

The European leaders showed little enthusiasm for the Fourteen Points. Wilson opposed punishing the defeated nations. In contrast, the Europeans sought revenge.

Clemenceau wanted to make sure that Germany could never invade France again. He believed that Germany should be broken up into smaller countries. Both he and Lloyd George demanded that Germany make large **reparations,** or payments, for the damage Germans caused in the war. Wilson struggled to uphold the principles of his Fourteen Points at the Paris meeting, yet he was forced to compromise or give in to the demands of the other Allies.

At the same time, the Allies had to decide how to deal with the new Bolshevik government of Russia. Fearing the spread of communism, France, Britain, and the United States supported anti-Bolshevik forces fighting in a civil war for control of Russia. All three countries sent troops to Russia.

730   Chapter 23 *World War I*

Leveled Activities

BL **Academic Vocabulary Activity, URB p. 75**

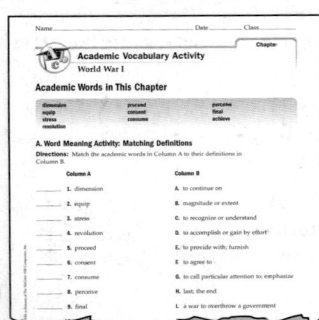

OL **Primary Source Reading Activity, URB p. 77**

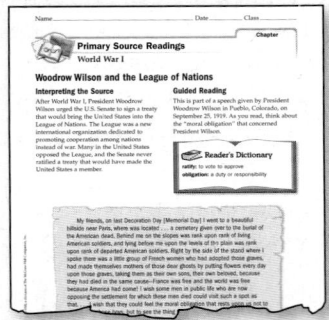

AL **Linking Past and Present Activity, URB p. 89**

ELL **Content Vocabulary Activity, URB p. 73**

The Treaty of Versailles

On June 28, 1919, the Allies and Germany signed the **Treaty of Versailles.** The treaty dealt harshly with the Germans but because they were defeated, they had no choice but to sign. Under the treaty's terms, Germany had to accept full responsibility for the conflict. It had to pay billions of dollars in reparations to the Allies. Also, Germany had to disarm completely and give up its overseas colonies and some territory in Europe.

The treaty carved up the Austro-Hungarian and Russian Empires as well. New nations were created and old nations restored. The new nations fulfilled Wilson's vision of national self-determination. Border disputes, however, would lead to future conflicts.

Wilson succeeded in having the League of Nations included in the treaty. He believed that the League would correct any mistakes in the rest of the treaty.

✓ Reading Check Identifying Cause and Effect Why didn't Great Britain, France, and Italy support Wilson's Fourteen Points?

C Opposition at Home

Main Idea The U.S. Senate rejected the Treaty of Versailles and the League of Nations.

History and You Think about how Americans might have felt after World War I. Read to learn how the U.S. Senate reacted to the treaty and the League of Nations.

• •

Wilson presented the Treaty of Versailles to the U.S. Senate for ratification in July 1919. "Dare we reject it and break the heart of the world?" he asked. In spite of Wilson's plea, a difficult struggle lay ahead.

Many Americans had doubts about the treaty. Some thought it dealt too harshly with Germany, while others worried that the League of Nations marked a permanent American commitment to international affairs. **S**

In 1919 the Republicans controlled the Senate, which had to ratify the treaty. Some Republican senators saw the ratification issue as a chance to embarrass President Wilson.

Primary Sources

INTERPRETING POLITICAL CARTOONS

Under the Covenant (constitution) of the League of Nations, members pledged to defend any member nation attacked by any other nation. Many Americans, however, believed the Covenant violated national sovereignty. It would allow other nations to commit American troops to foreign conflicts.

NOT ROOM FOR BOTH

1. **Interpreting** What is the League Covenant trying to do in the cartoon?
2. **Identifying Point of View** Does the cartoon express a view for or against joining the League of Nations? How do you know?

World War I **Chapter 23** **731**

C Critical Thinking

Analyzing Information Have students create a list of benefits and drawbacks of U.S. ratification of the Treaty of Versailles. Discuss students' lists and opinions. **AL**

S Skill Practice

Visual Literacy Ask: Based on this cartoon, do you think the U.S. public will agree with Wilson? Why or why not? *(No, because the cartoon reflects the public's idea that the League is not needed.)* **OL**

INTERPRETING POLITICAL CARTOONS

Answers

1. force its way onto the "throne"
2. against joining the League, because the caption says "Not room for both."

✓ Reading Check **Answer:** They wanted to punish the defeated nations.

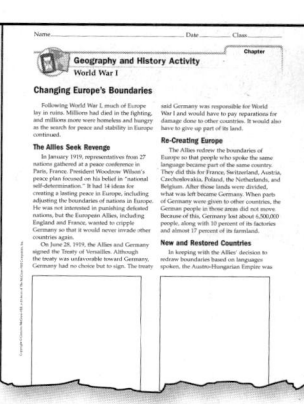

Geography and History Activity, URB p. 87

Changing Europe's Boundaries

Objective: To understand how Europe's boundaries changed after World War I

Focus: Review with students what motives the Allies had when they redrew Europe's boundaries.

Teach: Have students read the information, study the maps, and answer the questions.

Assess: Discuss any answers that are problematic for students.

Close: Have students predict possible future outcomes of the redrawing of Europe's boundaries.

Differentiated Instruction Strategies

BL Have students discuss what it would be like to be a German who was "given" to another country after the war.

AL Have students debate whether changing Europe's boundaries after the war was justified.

ELL Ask students to discuss issues of national individuality, border changes, and language identity.

731

Section 5 Review

R Reading Strategy

Organizing Ask students to create a T-chart, labeling one column "Lodge" and the other column "Wilson." Have students list what they know about the positions Lodge and Wilson took on the Treaty of Versailles. **BL**

✓ **Reading Check** **Answer:** The Republican-controlled Senate rejected the treaty in order to weaken the Democrats and because many Americans did not approve of the League of Nations and felt the treaty punished Germany too severely.

Assess

History ONLINE

Study Central™ provides summaries, interactive games, and online graphic organizers to help students review content.

Close

Identifying Points of View Have students identify the points of view of the Allies and the United States regarding the Treaty of Versailles and the League of Nations. **OL**

Section 5 Review

Some Republicans viewed it as an opportunity to weaken the Democratic Party before the upcoming elections of 1920. Other senators had sincere concerns about the treaty, particularly the League of Nations. A few senators opposed signing any treaty.

R Lodge vs. Wilson

The most powerful opponent of the treaty was **Henry Cabot Lodge** of Massachusetts. Lodge was head of the Senate Foreign Relations Committee and a longtime foe of President Wilson. Lodge said that membership in the League would mean that:

> *PRIMARY SOURCE*
>
> "American troops and American ships may be ordered to any part of the world by nations other than the United States, and that is a proposition to which I, for one, can never assent."
>
> —from *Vital Forces in Current Events*, 1920

Lodge delayed a vote on the treaty so that opponents could present their cases. He then proposed a number of reservations that would limit America's obligations under the treaty.

Wilson went on a national tour in September to rally support for the treaty and League of Nations. When he returned to Washington, he suffered a stroke. During the president's illness, his wife, Edith Wilson, shielded him from pressures and took a major role in deciding which issues to raise with him.

The Treaty Is Rejected

In the months after Wilson's stroke, opposition to the treaty grew. In March 1920, the Senate voted on the treaty with Lodge's changes. Opposed by most Republicans and deserted by former supporters, the Treaty of Versailles was rejected in the Senate.

Wilson hoped the 1920 election would be a "great and solemn referendum" on the League. He even considered running for a third term. In the end, however, Wilson did not run. In 1921 the United States signed a separate peace treaty with each of the Central Powers. The United States never joined the League of Nations.

✓ **Reading Check** **Explaining** Why did the Senate reject the Treaty of Versailles?

Section 5 Review

Vocabulary

1. Define the following terms in a sentence: *national self-determination, final, achieve, reparation.*

Main Ideas

2. **Explaining** Why did Woodrow Wilson think a lasting peace could be achieved in Europe?

3. **Identifying Cause and Effect** What effect did Wilson's illness have on the ratification of the Treaty of Versailles?

Critical Thinking

4. **Analyzing** Use a diagram like the one below to identify the challenges that the United States and Europe faced after the war.

Challenges Facing U.S. and Europe

5. **Expository Writing** If you were in Paris for the peace talks, do you think you would support Wilson's plan? Why or why not? Write a paragraph that explains your point of view.

Answer the Essential Question

6. Why did Wilson's Peace Plan fail?

Answers

1. Sentences should reflect a correct understanding of the terms.

2. Wilson believed that lasting peace could be achieved by allowing people the right of national self-determination, establishing principles for conducting free trade and international relations, ending secret treaties, and settling disputes peacefully.

3. Wilson's illness interrupted his campaign to gain public support for the treaty. As his illness continued, he was unable to effectively lobby members of Congress for their support.

4. Answers may include ruined European infrastructure, injured veterans, homelessness, hunger, civil war, struggles for independence, creation of lasting peace, ethnic conflicts, debate over the role of the United States in foreign conflicts, spread of communism, and treatment of Germany.

5. Students' paragraphs should include their opinions with details and examples to support them.

6. Some Americans thought the treaty was unfairly harsh to Germany, many objected to the League of Nations, and some senators used opposition to it as a way to weaken the Democrats before the next election.

Visual Summary

Visual Summary

Visual Summary

1914	
June	Archduke Franz Ferdinand assassinated
July	Austria-Hungary declares war on Serbia
Aug.	Germany declares war on Russia and France, and invades Belgium; World War I begins

1915	
May	German U-boat torpedoes the British *Lusitania*, killing 128 Americans

1916	
Feb.	The Germans launch a major offensive at the Battle of Verdun
July	Allies begin their offensive at the Battle of the Somme
Nov.	Woodrow Wilson wins presidential reelection

1917	
Jan.	Germany requests an alliance with Mexico if the U.S. entered the war
March	Germany attacks and sinks four American ships
April	U.S. Congress declares war against Germany
May	Selective Service Act sets up a military draft
Dec.	Russia's new Communist government pulls out of the war

I WANT YOU FOR U.S. ARMY
NEAREST RECRUITING STATION

1918	
March	Treaty of Brest-Litovsk shifts German troops to the Western Front
Sept.–Nov.	Battle of the Argonne Forest turns war in favor of Allies
Nov.	Germany becomes a republic; armistice begins

1919	
Jan.	World leaders meet at Paris peace conference
June	Germany and the Allies sign the Treaty of Versailles

1920	
March	U.S. Senate rejects the Treaty of Versailles and League of Nations

STUDY TO GO › Study anywhere, anytime! Download quizzes and flash cards to your PDA from glencoe.com.

Visual Summary

Speculating Have students review the events of World War I. Ask them to speculate about the future of Europe. **Ask:** How do you think Germany might cope with the demands in the Treaty of Versailles? *(Answers may indicate that Germans might be resentful of the conditions imposed on them by the treaty.)* How do you think the United States might respond to international conflicts after the war? *(Answers may indicate that Americans might become involved in international conflicts only when they pose a serious threat to the United States.)* **OL**

Visual/Spatial Have students study the illustrations in the Visual Summary. Explain that the illustrations were chosen to help readers recall the main ideas in the chapter. Have the students read the text on the page. Then have them create a mural depicting at least one event from each year. Tell students they should label the events with the year in which each took place and must keep the events in the correct order. Have students display their work in the classroom. **OL**

Hands-On Chapter Project
Step 6: Wrap-Up

Creating a War Documentary

Step 6: Presenting the Documentary Students will synthesize what they have learned in Steps 1–5.

Directions On the day of the "premiere," have the students prepare the viewing room for the audience. As the audience arrives,

have students welcome them and introduce the film. After the viewing, have the students invite audience questions and comments. Students should use the information they learned about World War I and film making to answer the questions.

Evaluating Ask: Based on the audience response, what feelings did the film create

for them? *(Answers might include sadness over the loss of life and pride in the United States and Allied troops.)* What message would you like to give to future generations about war? *(Answers may indicate the value of peaceful negotiations and respect for other countries' values, customs, and governments.)* **OL**

733

TIME NOTEBOOK

Focus

C Critical Thinking

Analyzing Primary Sources Have students read Frank Cobb's account of his conversation with President Wilson. **Ask:** Based upon his tone, how do you think Cobb felt about President Wilson and his decision to go to war? *(Cobb indicates respect for the president and understanding of the difficult situation the president was in.)* **OL**

Teach

R Reading Strategy

Paraphrasing Read aloud the public service message in "Verbatim." Ask students to explain the meaning of the sentence in their own words. **ELL**

W Writing Support

Personal Writing Have students read the quote in "Verbatim" by Emma Lazarus. **Ask:** What does this statement mean? *(America welcomed immigrants.)* Ask students to write an essay on whether they feel immigrants are welcomed in the United States today. **AL**

Additional Support and Answers

What were people's lives like in the past?

These two pages will give you some clues to everyday life in the United States as you step back in time with TIME Notebook.

BETTMANN / CORBIS

FRANK COBB

American Voices

MEETING WITH A TROUBLED PRESIDENT

Just one day before President Wilson appeared before Congress in 1917 to ask for a declaration of war against Germany, he was struggling with whether or not it was the right thing to do. He sent for his friend, **FRANK COBB**, *editor of the* New York World *newspaper. Here is how Cobb remembers that late-night meeting at the White House:*

"[Wilson] was waiting for me sitting in his study. . . . I'd never seen him so worn down. He said he was probably going before Congress the next day to ask a declaration of war, and he'd never been so uncertain about anything in his life as about that decision. For nights, he said, he'd been lying awake going over the whole situation—over the provocation [outrage] given by Germany, over the probable feeling in the United States, over the consequences to the settlement to the world at large if we entered the [war].

"He said he couldn't see any alternative. . . . 'I think I know what war means,' he said, and he added that if there were any possibility of avoiding war he wanted to try it. 'What else can I do?' he asked. 'Is there anything else I can do?'

"I told him his hand had been forced by Germany, that so far as I could see we couldn't keep out."

AMERICAN SCENE
Average Life Spans in 1900

Average life expectancy: **47.3 YEARS**	
Male life expectancy: **46.3 YEARS**	
Female life expectancy: **48.3 YEARS**	
White life expectancy: **47.6 YEARS**	
Nonwhite life expectancy: **33.0 YEARS**	

0 years   10   20   30   40   50

VSTOCK / ALAMY

VERBATIM

WHAT PEOPLE ARE SAYING

❝ The . . . crowds rarely raised a cheer. . . . It was enough to walk . . . with 10,000 strangers, and to realize in that moment of good news not one of them was really a stranger. ❞

AN OBSERVER OF THE ARMISTICE DAY PARADE, *celebrating the end of World War I in New York City, 1918*

❝ I can predict with absolute certainty that within another generation there will be another world war if the nations of the world do not concert [agree on] the method by which to prevent it. ❞

WOODROW WILSON, *1919*

❝ Obey the laws, and wear the gauze; protect your jaws from septic paws. ❞

A PUBLIC SERVICE MESSAGE, *reminding people to wear masks to protect themselves from catching or spreading influenza and pneumonia, which in October 1918 killed about 194,000 people*

❝ Mountains! Look at them! ❞

EDWARD CORSI, *10-year-old Italian immigrant on spotting the high-rise buildings in New York City for the first time in 1907*

❝ Give me your tired, your poor, your huddled masses yearning to breathe free. ❞

WORDS BY EMMA LAZARUS, *engraved on the Statue of Liberty in 1903*

Fast Facts

A Pandemic of Epic Proportions The influenza epidemic of 1918 claimed more lives than World War I. Although the war cost an estimated 16 million lives, the influenza epidemic killed an estimated 20 to 50 million people worldwide. One-fifth of the world's population was attacked by this virus, which killed more people than any other illness in recorded history.

The first wave of influenza, which occurred in late spring of 1918, was relatively mild. Few deaths were reported, and victims recovered within several days. But when the disease struck again in the fall, it was much more severe. At first, scientists, doctors, and health officials were unable to identify the disease. Sometimes people died just hours after their first flu symptoms

appeared. Other patients developed pneumonia quickly, and their lungs filled with fluid that suffocated them.

People ages 20 to 40, who were usually unaffected by these types of diseases, were hard hit by the flu. It is estimated that 550,000 people in the United States died of influenza, which was transmitted from person to person through airborne respiratory secretions.

The Slang Game R

Want to express yourself more clearly? Then test your knowledge of the latest slang of the early 1900s! Match the word or phrase with the correct description.

1. Big bug
2. Bully for you
3. Dude
4. Greased lightning
5. Full of grit
6. Into a pucker
7. Schoolmarm
8. Waking snakes

a. Well-dressed person
b. Causing a ruckus
c. Very important person
d. Female teacher
e. Upset
f. Brave
g. Quick speed
h. Good job!

Answers: 1. c; 2. h; 3. a; 4. g; 5. f; 6. e; 7. d; 8. b

MILESTONES

EVENTS AND PEOPLE OF THE TIME

BETTMANN / CORBIS

GRADUATED. Helen Keller from Radcliffe College in 1904. Deaf and blind from a childhood illness, Keller has been assisted by her lifelong friend and teacher, Anne Sullivan. Keller was introduced to Sullivan by none other than Alexander Graham Bell, inventor of the telephone and teacher of the hearing impaired.

NAMED. The "hot dog," after a drawing in 1906 showed a dachshund—a small, long dog—inside a frankfurter bun.

SUNG. The "Star-Spangled Banner" for the first time before a baseball game in 1918. The owner of the Boston Red Sox wanted to honor the many wounded veterans of World War I who were in the stands to watch the Sox take on the Chicago Cubs.

STRUCK. Oil in Spindletop, Texas, in 1901, triggering what many believe will be an oil boom in the American Southwest. Oil companies are springing up quickly as this new fuel is used to heat homes and run trains.

ESTABLISHED. Mother's Day, by President Woodrow Wilson in 1914—after all, it is only fair since Father's Day was created in 1910.

It Is the Law

Two laws were passed in 1902 to deal with the automobile.

1. Tennessee demands that all drivers give the public a week's notice before they start any trip.
2. Vermont states that an adult waving a red flag has to walk in front of any moving automobile.

NUMBERS

UNITED STATES AT THE TIME

12 cents
Price of a dozen eggs in 1910

$12 Price of a sewing machine in 1900

$12 Lowest price for a steamship ticket from Italy to America in 1905 — S

$12 Average weekly salary (seven-day weeks/12-hour days) for arriving immigrants in 1907

12 seconds
Air time of Wright brothers' first flight in 1903

BETTMANN / CORBIS

1.2 million Approximate number of immigrants who entered the United States in 1907 — D

395,000 Approximate number of immigrants in 1908 who gave up on the American dream and returned to their homelands

CRITICAL THINKING

Creative Writing Write a story about how you would feel arriving in a strange land and starting a new life as an immigrant.

Contrasting Use the graph to determine who had the longest and shortest life expectancies in 1900. What do you think accounts for the differences in life expectancies?

735

R Reading Strategy

Making Connections Have students review "The Slang Game." Ask them to identify currently used words or phrases that match each of the descriptions shown in the column on the right. **BL**

S Skill Practice

Using Math Skills Have students use the Internet or go to the library to research the average weekly salary in the United States today. Ask them to calculate the percentage increases in weekly salaries over the last century. **OL**

D Differentiated Instruction

Interpersonal Have students interview someone who immigrated to the United States. **Ask:** What kinds of experiences has he or she had? **OL**

Assess/Close

As a class, discuss how the number of immigrants increased in the late 1800s and early 1900s. Ask students why they think so many people wanted to leave their homelands and settle in the United States. Discuss the challenges that they faced. **OL**

Answers and Analyses
Reviewing Main Ideas

1. B Students can immediately eliminate answer choices C and D because these ideas were not discussed in the chapter. Remind students that nationalism relates to patriotism and a feeling of pride in and loyalty to one's country. **18.B**

2. C The Zimmermann telegram was the communication Germany sent to Mexico. Germany's action was secretive, so their offer would not be proposed in a public treaty; therefore, answer choice A can be eliminated. The Selective Service Act was a U.S. law, and the Triple Entente was an alliance established before Germany's proposal to Mexico. **14.E**

3. C Remind students that Russia's withdrawal meant that Germany did not have to fight against Russia on the Eastern Front. Therefore, Germany could move its forces to the Western Front. **16.A**

Short-Answer Question

4. Senator Lodge believed that the "power to send American soldiers and sailors" to war should not be "taken from the American people." According to Lodge, the American people are given this power through sovereignty. **16.A.3b**

STANDARDIZED TEST PRACTICE

TEST-TAKING TIP

When reviewing for a test, pay special attention to bold type, questions, and summary paragraphs in your text.

Reviewing Main Ideas

Directions: Choose the best answer for each of the following questions.

1. Nationalism caused much of the tension in Europe that led to World War I. *Nationalism* can best be defined as

　A the practice of one nation extending its control over another nation.

　B a feeling of intense loyalty to one's country or group.

　C a political system based on military strength.

　D a structure of defense agreements among nations.

2. In 1917 Germany offered Mexico an alliance against the United States in the

　A Treaty of Brest-Litovsk.

　B Selective Service Act.

　C Zimmermann telegram.

　D Triple Entente.

3. Russia's withdrawal from World War I in December 1917

　A convinced German military leaders that they had little chance of winning the war.

　B allowed the Germans to move hundreds of thousands of troops from the Eastern to the Western Front.

　C eliminated the Allies' need for help from American soldiers.

　D caused thousands of French and British soldiers to refuse to continue fighting.

Short-Answer Question

Directions Base your answer to question 4 on the excerpt below and on your knowledge of social studies.

In what I have already said about other nations putting us into war I have covered one point of sovereignty [supreme power] which ought never to be yielded—the power to send American soldiers and sailors everywhere, which ought never to be taken from the American people.

—Senator Henry Cabot Lodge, "The League of Nations Must Be Revised," 1919

4. According to the document, why did Senator Lodge oppose U.S. participation in the League of Nations?

Review the Essential Questions

5. Essay When World War I began, many Americans felt torn and personally involved. Why? How did Americans' attitudes toward the war change as the conflict progressed?

To help you write your essay, review your answers to the Essential Questions in the section reviews and the chapter Foldables Study Organizer. Your essay should include:

- the causes and start of World War I;
- American neutrality and the eventual entry of the United States into war;
- the impact of the American military on the war effort;
- mobilization of the war effort at home and the control of public opinion; and
- Wilson's Fourteen Points, the League of Nations, and the Treaty of Versailles.

GO ON ▶

Review the Essential Questions

5. If students completed their Foldables correctly, they should be able to explain why many Americans felt torn and personally involved at the beginning of the war. Students should include the events mentioned to describe how Americans' attitudes changed as the war progressed. **14.E**

History ONLINE
For additional test practice, use **Self-Check Quizzes**—Chapter 23 at glencoe.com.

Chapter 23 Assessment

Document-Based Questions

Directions: Analyze the documents and answer the short-answer questions that follow.

Document 1

Theodore Roosevelt wrote the following about the American war effort in 1917.

> The German-language papers carry on a consistent campaign in favor of Germany against England. They should be put out of existence for the period of this war. . . . Every disloyal native-born American should be disfranchised [deprived of rights] and interned [confined]. It is time to strike our enemies at home heavily and quickly.

Source: *The Foes of Our Own Household*

6. How did Roosevelt think disloyal Americans should be treated during the war? Why?

Document 2

This American poster from 1917 was directed toward recent immigrants to the U.S.

Remember Your First Thrill of AMERICAN LIBERTY

YOUR DUTY-*Buy* United States Government *Bonds* 2ⁿᵈ Liberty Loan of 1917

Source: The Granger Collection, New York

7. Why does this poster encourage recent immigrants to remember their "first thrill of American liberty"? Name two goals the poster hoped to achieve.

Document 3

The following table shows the number of military deaths by country in World War I.

Country	Number of Deaths
Austria-Hungary	1,200,000
France	1,375,800
Germany	1,773,700
Great Britain	908,371
Italy	650,000
Russia	1,700,000
U.S.	126,000

Source: Susan Everett, *History of World War I*

8. Which two countries had the most deaths? Why were U.S. deaths comparatively low?

Document 4

Sir Harold Nicolson, a British delegate, described the signing of the Treaty of Versailles.

> Through the door at the end appear two huissiers [court officers] with silver chains. . . . After them come four officers of France, Great Britain, America and Italy. And then, isolated and pitiable, come the two German delegates. . . . They keep their eyes fixed away from those two thousand staring eyes [ceremony attendees], fixed upon the ceiling. They are deathly pale. They do not appear as representatives of a brutal militarism.

Source: Harold Nicolson, *Peacemaking 1919*

9. What is the tone of this passage? How does Nicolson seem to feel about events? Explain.

10. Expository Writing Using the information from the four documents and your knowledge of social studies, write an essay in which you:

- discuss the war's most important impact on American society; and
- compare this to its most important impact on Allied and Central Powers.

Need Extra Help?

If you missed questions. . .	1	2	3	4	5	6	7	8	9	10
Go to page. . .	705	716	720	732	704–732	727	725	728	731	704–732

World War I **Chapter 23** **737**

8. Students should see that the countries are organized alphabetically in the first column and not by the number of deaths. Therefore, students will need to search for the highest numbers in the second column to find the answer to the first question. *(Germany and Russia)* From their reading, students should recall that the United States entered the war late, so it did not suffer as many casualties. **16.A**

9. Students should identify specific words that relate an ominous tone in the quotation. *(isolated, pitiable, deathly pale)* Students might conclude that Nicolson does feel the Allies are justified in their treatment of Germany. **16.A.3b**

10. Essays should identify the effects of the war on American society, such as workforce and family changes. Essays should compare these effects to the effects on the Central Powers, such as loss of territory and its great loss of life. **14.E**

History ONLINE
Have students visit the Web site at glencoe.com to review Chapter 23 and take the Self-Check Quiz.

Need Extra Help?
Have students refer to the pages listed if they miss any of the questions.

Document-Based Questions

6. Refer students to the bracketed text that defines Roosevelt's original words. Roosevelt thought disloyal Americans should be deprived of rights and confined because he considered them enemies at home. This idea is evident in his words: "It is time to strike our enemies at home heavily and quickly." **16.A.3b**

7. Ask students to identify the statue in the poster and the ideas the statue symbolizes. Students should understand that the poster attempted to remind immigrants about the benefits of living in America. Tell students to read the words on the poster to identify the poster's second goal: to encourage immigrants to buy war bonds. **16.A.3b**

UNIT PACING CHART

	Unit 8	Chapter 24	Chapter 25	Chapter 26
Day 1	Unit Opener, Reading History	Chapter Opener, Section 1, Geography & History	Chapter Opener, Section 1	Chapter Opener, Section 1
Day 2		Section 2, Section 3	Section 2, You Decide	Section 2, Section 3
Day 3		Section 4	Section 3, TIME Notebook	Section 4
Day 4		America's Literature, Visual Summary	Section 4, Visual Summary	Section 5, Visual Summary
Day 5		Chapter Assessment	Chapter Assessment	Chapter Assessment

 Teacher to Teacher

Trissa McCabe
Reno Valley
Middle School
Hutchinson, KS

Comparing Prices Students will compare prices before, during, and after the Great Depression. Have students use the Internet to research prices for six household items (soap, eggs, clothes, refrigerator, car, and so on). Students should find how much each item cost in 1922, 1932, and 1942. Students will then create a line graph for each year to show how the price changed for each item. In order to do this, you should discuss how to calculate the percent of increase (the difference in prices divided by the original price). Students should then make a list of how many of the items they could buy for $1,000 before 1922. They should create a similar list for 1932 and 1942 using the same number of items. Ask students to compare how the three lists are different and summarize their observations in a paragraph.

Author Note

Dear American History Teacher,

This unit includes three very different periods of American history: a period of tremendous prosperity and optimism; a period of unprecedented economic difficulty and great turbulence; and a period in which the United States joined the greatest and most terrible war in human history. Students will have no difficulty understanding the differences among these three eras. You will want, however, to encourage them to see the connections among these time periods as well.

The so-called "New Era" of the 1920s created some of the preconditions of the Great Depression. During this era, there was experimentation with economic and political ideas that would shape the important programs of the New Deal of the 1930s.

The crises of the 1930s were not just economic ones but also included events that would lead to World War II. The United States would find itself fighting a war on two fronts. The war would help the country come out of its economic depression and become a leading world power.

Alan Brinkley

Alan Brinkley

Unit Objectives

After studying this unit, students will be able to:

- Evaluate the effects of the 1920s on American culture.
- Discuss the causes and outcomes of the Great Depression.
- Relate the causes of World War II, and summarize the role of the United States in the war.

Introducing the Unit

Predicting As students prepare to study the unit, ask them to think about how difficult it can be to find a good job. **Ask:** What might happen in the United States today if there were widespread unemployment and business failures? *(Students might note that life would become hard for most citizens. People might have trouble finding an affordable place to live or making enough money to buy food. The country's economy would also suffer if people didn't have money to purchase what they needed.)* Tell students that they will learn about what happened when many people lost their jobs during the Great Depression. **OL**

Unit ★8

Chapter 24
....
The Jazz Age
1920–1929

Chapter 25
....
The Depression and the New Deal
1929–1939

Chapter 26
....
America and World War II
1939–1945

King Kong film poster, 1933

738

Change and Conflict
1920–1945

Activity: Why It Matters

Why Study the Depression and the New Deal? Tell students what they can expect to learn in the upcoming unit. **Ask:** What do you know about the Depression? *(Students might know that the Depression was a time when many people were out of work and the country's economy collapsed.)* What do you think the phrase "New Deal" means?

(Students may say that it could refer to a different plan or arrangement from what came before.) As they study the unit, have students list in their notebooks the events that brought about the Depression and how the New Deal attempted to solve the economic crisis. **OL**

"The only thing we have to fear is fear itself."

—Franklin D. Roosevelt

Drought refugees with stalled truck on New Mexico highway, 1937

739

Connect to Past Learning

Change and Conflict In the previous unit, students learned about progressive reforms and imperialism in the late 1800s and early 1900s, as well as the role of the United States in World War I. In this unit, they will study how the events of the three decades after World War I affected Americans: the flourishing culture of the 1920s, the focus on domestic issues during the Great Depression, and the sacrifices people made and the unity they demonstrated during World War II.

More About the Image

Visual Literacy Dorothea Lange was a portrait photographer in San Francisco before documenting the Dust Bowl and Great Depression. With little business after the stock market crash, Lange made it her goal to show the world, through her photographs, the plight of the rural poor. She captured images depicting the social upheaval and economic vulnerability of farm families moving west through the Dust Bowl and the migrant workers who toiled in California. Lange was the most widely published government photographer of the 1930s.

Unit 8 Reading History

Reading History

Why **Questioning** Is Important

Questioning helps students clarify what they have read. As students ask questions of instructors or of themselves, they improve their comprehension.

Learn It!

Show students how questioning helps them specify more exactly what they mean.

Ask a student, "What's your favorite food?" As the student answers, ask another question ("Do you like it the way it's prepared in a restaurant, or do you prefer homemade?"). After each answer, ask another question, until you move from, for example, "pizza" to "thin-crust pepperoni from Antonio's down the street, especially on Sundays when my whole family sits down together to eat and talk." **BL**

Practice It!

Students should include the following answers:

Question: How were jobs created for the unemployed?

Answer: Congress created the Works Progress Administration to put the unemployed to work building airports, public facilities, bridges, and roads. **OL**

READING SKILL — Questioning

Learn It! One way to understand what you are reading is to interact with the text by asking questions.

> Practice asking questions by turning headings into questions. For instance, the heading "Government Action" can be turned into the question "What actions did the government take to deal with the Great Depression?"

—from Chapter 25, p. 777
Government Action
Eventually Hoover recognized that the federal government had to take steps to combat the Depression. In 1931 he authorized additional federal spending on public works—projects such as highways, parks, and libraries—to create new jobs.

> As you read, you should be able to find the answer in the next paragraph or section.

Practice It! Read the paragraph. Turn the heading into a question and write your answer on another sheet of paper.

—from Chapter 25, p. 796
Creating Jobs
Millions of people—20 percent of the workforce—were still unemployed in 1935. In April Congress created the Works Progress Administration (WPA) to give people jobs and help the country. Led by Harry Hopkins, the WPA kept about 2 million people employed between 1935 and 1941. WPA workers built or repaired airports, public buildings, bridges, and roads.

Question
_____

Answer
_____
_____

740   Unit 8   *Change and Conflict*

Reading Strategy — Question-Answer Relationships

Questioning As students will see from the Learn It! exercise, answers very often produce more questions; and the more questions that arise from each answer, the more information that is gathered from the process. Direct students to a chapter or subsection of a chapter in this unit, and show them how the material is arranged to answer more specific questions. The main head can be written to ask a central question. The subheads can be written to ask more specific questions related to the central question. In the body of the text, more answers are uncovered until an entire story has emerged. **ELL**

Academic Vocabulary Preview

Listed below are the academic vocabulary words and their definitions that you will come across as you study Unit 8. Practice It! will help you study the words and definitions.

Academic Vocabulary	Definition	Practice It!
Chapter 24 The Jazz Age		
normal (NAWR · muhl) *p. 745*	typical; average	**Identify** *the term from Chapter 24 that best completes the sentence.*
dynamic (dy · NA · mihk) *p. 747*	active and energetic	
detect (dih · TEHKT) *p. 752*	to uncover or discover the true character of	**1.** Mass production _____ led to increased productivity and lower prices.
intervene (IHN · tuhr · VEEN) *p. 753*	to involve oneself in the affairs of another	**2.** Businesses hired _____ to help them develop new products.
expert (EHK · spuhrt) *p. 755*	a person with advanced knowledge	**3.** Most people did not want the United States to _____ in the affairs of other countries.
technique (tehk · NEEK) *p. 755*	a skillful method	
device (dih · VYS) *p. 759*	an instrument or piece of equipment	
enormous (ih · NAWR · muhs) *p. 760*	huge	
Chapter 25 The Depression and The New Deal		
decline (dih · KLYN) *p. 774*	to descend; drop	**Identify** *the word from Chapter 25 that best matches the underlined term.*
collapse (kuh · LAPS) *p. 775*	to break down	**4.** When prices <u>fall</u>, many investors sell their stock.
promote (pruh · MOHT) *p. 782*	to help advance	
generate (JEH · nuh · RAYT) *p. 782*	to create	**5.** President Roosevelt's fireside chats were designed to <u>build</u> people's confidence.
migrate (MY · GRAYT) *p. 788*	to relocate; move	
advocate (AD · vuh · KAYT) *p. 790*	to support	**6.** Many Dust Bowl families had to leave their homes and <u>move</u> to California in search of work.
scheme (SKEEM) *p. 795*	a plan	
welfare (WEHL · FEHR) *p. 797*	standard care; well-being	
Chapter 26 America and World War II		
obtain (uhb · TAYN) *p. 806*	to gain	**Choose** *the word that best matches the meaning of each vocabulary term listed below.*
unify (YOO · nuh · FY) *p. 807*	to join together	
target (TAHR · guht) *p. 809*	an object of attack	**7. obtain** **9. tense**
fund (FUHND) *p. 813*	a reserve or source of money	a. select a. anxious
shift (SHIHFT) *p. 815*	to move	b. acquire b. loose
overseas (OH · vuhr · SEEZ) *p. 816*	across the ocean	c. remove c. colorful
concentrate (KAHN · suhn · TRAYT) *p. 821*	to focus	**8. shift** **10. conflict**
tense (TEHNS) *p. 823*	anxious; nervous	a. delay a. theory
secure (sih · KYUR) *p. 830*	to gain control	b. create b. fight
conflict (KAHN · FLIHKT) *p. 832*	a war; prolonged struggle	c. change c. plan

Change and Conflict **Unit 8** **741**

Academic Vocabulary Preview

Before students begin the Practice It! activities, take a moment to play the ultimate answer-question game, Jeopardy!

Break the unit terms (and terms from other units, if needed) into a few categories, and write the categories on the board. Chose a student to begin, let the student choose a category, and read the "answer." If the student cannot give the question in the allotted amount of time, open it up to the class—the first hand up wins. Continue to work through the remaining terms this way. **OL**

Practice It!

Answers
1. techniques
2. experts
3. intervene
4. decline
5. promote
6. migrate
7. b
8. c
9. a
10. b

Reading Strategy   Read to Write

Expository Writing Expository writing is all about answering questions. By now, students should realize that questions often are not simple, and one seemingly straightforward question could lead to a surplus of answers with additional questions. Have students write an expository paper explaining a sport or hobby that they enjoy. Suggest that students begin by asking questions of themselves and watching how the answers naturally lead to another question. Encourage them to use a main head and subheads in their paper, as in the text, to present and answer increasingly specific questions about the process they are explaining. **OL**

Chapter Planning Guide

24

Levels (BL)	(OL)	(AL)	(ELL)		Resources	Chapter Opener	Section 1	Section 2	Section 3	Section 4	Chapter Assess
					FOCUS						
BL	OL	AL	ELL	📇	Daily Test Practice Transparencies		24–1	24–2	24–3	24–4	
					TEACH						
	OL	AL		📁	Geography and History Activity, URB		p. 31				
BL	OL		ELL	📁	Time Line Skills Activity, URB					p. 34	
BL	OL	AL	ELL	📁	Writing Skills Activity, URB					p. 23	
	OL	AL		📁	American Literature Readings, URB				p. 9		
BL	OL	AL	ELL	📁	Content Vocabulary Activity, URB		p. 17	p. 17	p. 17	p. 17	
BL	OL	AL	ELL	📁	Academic Vocabulary Activity, URB		p. 19	p. 19	p. 19	p. 19	
BL			ELL	📁	Social Studies Skills Activity, URB		p. 25		p. 25		
BL	OL	AL	ELL	📁	Differentiated Instruction Activity, URB			p. 27			
BL	OL	AL	ELL	📁	Critical Thinking Skills Activity, URB				p. 29		
BL	OL	AL	ELL	📁	Linking Past and Present Activity, URB					p. 33	
	OL	AL		📁	Primary Source Readings, URB		p. 21				
BL	OL	AL	ELL	📁	School-to-Home Connection Activity, URB		p. 35	p. 35	p. 35	p. 35	
BL	OL		ELL	📁	Guided Reading Activity, URB*		p. 39	p. 40	p. 41	p. 42	
BL	OL		ELL	📁	Reading Essentials and Note-Taking Guide*		p. 262	p. 265	p. 268	p. 271	
BL	OL	AL	ELL	📇	Lesson Transparencies		24B	24C		24A	
	OL			📁	American Biographies				pp. 49, 50, 51, 53, 56		
	OL	AL		📇	American Art and Architecture Transparencies, Strategies, and Activities					27, 28	

Note: Please refer to the *Unit Resource Book: Change and Conflict* for this chapter's URB materials.

* Also available in Spanish

Levels BL	OL	AL	ELL		Resources	Chapter Opener	Section 1	Section 2	Section 3	Section 4	Chapter Assess
					TEACH (continued)						
BL	OL	AL	ELL	📁	**NGS US Desk Map**		✓	✓	✓	✓	
BL	OL	AL	ELL	📁	**American Literature Library**		✓	✓	✓	✓	
BL	OL	AL	ELL	📁	**Writer's Guidebook**		✓	✓	✓	✓	
	OL	AL		💿	**American History Primary Source Document Library CD-ROM**		✓	✓	✓	✓	✓
BL	OL	AL	ELL	💿	**American Music: Hits Through History**	✓	✓	✓	✓	✓	
BL	OL	AL	ELL	💿	**StudentWorks™ Plus CD**	✓	✓	✓	✓	✓	✓
BL	OL	AL	ELL	🔒	**Section Spotlight Videos**		✓	✓	✓	✓	
BL	OL	AL	ELL	🖨	**Writing Process Transparencies**		✓	✓	✓	✓	✓
BL	OL	AL	ELL	💿	**Presentation Plus! With MindJogger CheckPoint CD**	✓	✓	✓	✓	✓	✓
					ASSESS						
BL	OL	AL	ELL	📁	**Quizzes and Tests**		p. 235	p. 236	p. 237	p. 238	pp. 239, 241, 243
BL	OL	AL	ELL	📁	**Authentic Assessment With Rubrics**					p. 24	
BL	OL	AL	ELL	📁	**Standardized Test Practice**						p. 47
BL	OL	AL	ELL	💿	*ExamView® Assessment Suite* **CD-ROM***		24–1	24–2	24–3	24–4	Ch. 24
					CLOSE						
BL			ELL	📁	**Reteaching Activity, URB***		p. 37	p. 37	p. 37	p. 37	p. 37
BL	OL		ELL	📁	**Reading and Study Skills Foldables Activity**	p. 96	p. 96	p. 96	p. 96	p. 96	p. 96
BL	OL	AL	ELL	📁	*The American Journey* **in Graphic Novel**						p. 139
BL			ELL	📁	**Reading Strategies and Activities for the Social Studies Classroom**		✓	✓	✓	✓	
BL	OL	AL	ELL	🖨	**Graphic Organizer Transparencies & Strategies**		✓	✓	✓	✓	

TeacherWorks *Plus*
All-In-One Planner and Resource Center

- Interactive Lesson Planner
- Interactive Teacher Edition
- Fully editable blackline masters
- Section Spotlight Videos Launch

- Differentiated Lesson Plans
- Printable reports of daily assignments
- Standards Tracking System

Professional Development Resources

- Strategies for Success
- Building Academic Vocabulary
- Success With English Learners DVD
- Differentiated Instruction Strategies DVD
- Teaching Literacy Strategies in Social Studies DVD
- Assessment DVD
- Standards-Based Instruction DVD

Integrating Technology

Using TechCONNECT™

Using Graphics Effectively

Technology Product

Glencoe's TechCONNECT™ is an online graphics program. (For more information or to get a free 30-day trial of Glencoe TechCONNECT™ for your classroom, **visit** techconnect.glencoe.com **and click the Free Trial button.**) This program allows you to

- choose, resize, and place graphics in a project;
- search for activities correlated to this textbook;
- complete a self-assessment activity or TechCheck quiz.

Objective

The CD-ROM will help students

- understand historical perspective.

Steps

- Log on to TechCONNECT and click the "find your textbook" link.
- After you log on, click **Activity Search, Choose Social Studies, Graphics,** and your grade level.
- Enter the letters AC and the three-digit activity number.
- Read each page and follow the on-screen instructions.
- Complete the activity's self-assessment rubric.
- Students may also complete the TechCheck, a five-question, multiple-choice quiz by entering the letters TC and the three-digit activity number.

History ONLINE at glencoe.com

	Student	Teacher	Parent
Media Center			
• Student Edition Audio	●		
• Spanish Summaries	●		
• Section Spotlight Videos	●	●	
Social Studies Online Learning Center			
Classroom Tools			
• Multi-Language Glossaries	●	●	●
• Teaching Today		●	
• TIME Current Events	●	●	●
• Beyond the Textbook	●	●	
The American Journey **Online Learning Center**			
• Study-to-Go™	●	●	●
• Study Central™	●	●	●
• Chapter Overview	●	●	
• Concepts in Motion	●	●	
• ePuzzles and Games	●	●	
• Literature Connections	●	●	
• Online Student Edition	●	●	●
• Self-Check Quizzes	●	●	●
• Student Web Activities	●	●	
• Vocabulary eFlashcards	●	●	
• Web Activity Lesson Plans	●	●	●
• Vocabulary PuzzleMaker	●	●	●

READING SUPPORT FROM JAMESTOWN EDUCATION

- **Timed Readings Plus in Social Studies** helps students increase their reading rate and fluency while maintaining comprehension. The 400-word passages are similar to those found on state and national assessments.

- **Reading in the Content Area: Social Studies** concentrates on six essential reading skills that help students better comprehend what they read. The book includes 75 high-interest nonfiction passages written at increasing levels of difficulty.

- **Reading Social Studies** includes strategic reading instruction and vocabulary support in Social Studies content for ELLs and native speakers of English.

- **Content Vocabulary Workout** (Grades 6–8) accelerates reading comprehension through focused vocabulary development. Social Studies content vocabulary comes from the glossaries of Glencoe's Middle School Social Studies texts.

www.jamestowneducation.com

NATIONAL GEOGRAPHIC

Index to National Geographic Magazine:

The following articles relate to this chapter:

- *"Changing America,"* Joel L. Swerdlow, September 2001.

- *"Wings of Change: From the Wright Flyer to the B-2 Bomber,"* Michael Klesius, December 2003.

National Geographic Society Products

To order the following, call National Geographic at 1-800-368-2728:

National Geographic Atlas of the World (Book)

Access National Geographic's dynamic MapMachine Web site and other geography resources at:

www.nationalgeographic.com
www.nationalgeographic.com/mapmachine

Reading List Generator CD-ROM

GLENCOE BOOKLINK 3

Use this database to search more than 30,000 titles to create a customized reading list for your students.

- Reading lists can be organized by students' reading level, author, genre, theme, or area of interest.

- The database provides Degrees of Reading Power™ (DRP) and Lexile™ readability scores for all selections.

- A brief summary of each selection is included.

Leveled reading suggestions for this chapter:

For students at a Grade 6 reading level:
- *Black Boy,* by Richard Wright

For students at a Grade 7 reading level:
- *Ellis Island: Gateway to the New World,* by Leonard Everett Fisher
- *Forward Into Light: The Struggle for Woman's Suffrage,* by Madeleine Meyers

For students at a Grade 8 reading level:
- *The Day the Women Got the Vote,* by George Sullivan
- *A Fashionable History of Dresses and Skirts,* by Helen Reynolds

For students at a Grade 9 reading level:
- *Legendary Labor Leaders,* by Thomas Streissguth

For students at a Grade 10 reading level:
- *Pride and Promise: The Harlem Renaissance,* by Kathryn Cryan-Hicks

The following videotape program is available from Glencoe as a supplement to the chapter:

- **Lucky: The Story of Charles Lindbergh** (ISBN 1-56-501501-0)

To order, call Glencoe at 1-800-334-7344. To find classroom resources to accompany this video, check the following home pages:

A&E Television: www.aetv.com

The History Channel: www.history.com

Chapter Objectives

After studying this chapter, students will be able to:

- Understand how prejudice and labor strife affected the nation after World War I.
- Discuss how the election of Harding and Coolidge reflected America's changing mood.
- Explain how new technology and forms of transportation changed American life.
- Describe how social change affected the arts, the role of women, and minorities.

Motivating Activity

Identifying Central Issues The end of World War I ushered in a time of transition in domestic affairs for the United States. New businesses and jobs would create wealth and opportunity for some, while other people would be left behind. Rapid changes in technology and communications would take place, and new tensions over political issues and social values would arise. **Ask:** What effect do you think change has on people? Have students make a list of changes that occurred throughout the world during their lifetimes. As they read the chapter, discuss connections between what they have experienced and the transformations that occurred in the 1920s.

Previewing the Essential Questions

Answering the section-based Essential Question will help students understand important concepts in the section.

Chapter 24 — The Jazz Age 1920–1929

After World War I, many Americans enjoyed a time of prosperity and confidence.

PRESIDENTS

U.S. Events

World Events

★ **1920**
- Prohibition begins
- Nineteenth Amendment grants woman suffrage

WARREN G. HARDING

★ **1922**
Teapot Dome Scandal

1918

1921

★ **1918**
Flu pandemic kills millions worldwide

★ **1921**
- Ireland becomes an independent country
- Albert Einstein wins Nobel Prize for Physics

Gauze masks were worn to protect against the flu. ▶

742   Chapter 24

Section 1

Time of Turmoil Ask: Was American society able to return to the way it was before World War I? Why or why not? *(No. There was racial strife and fear of radicalism.)* Point out to students that in Section 1 they will learn about the roots of prejudice and labor and racial unrest after the war. **OL**

Section 2

Desire for Normalcy Ask: What values did Harding and Coolidge represent? *(Answers might include support of business, smaller government, and isolationism.)* Point out to students that Section 2 discusses how Harding and Coolidge embodied the nation's desire for "normalcy." **OL**

Section 1: Time of Turmoil
Essential Question How did prejudice and labor strife affect the nation following World War I?

Section 2: Desire for Normalcy
Essential Question In what ways did the election of Harding and Coolidge reflect America's changing mood?

Section 3: A Booming Economy
Essential Question How did new technology and forms of transportation change American life?

Section 4: The Roaring Twenties
Essential Question How did social change affect the arts, the role of women, and minorities?

Babe Ruth of the New York Yankees ►

FOLDABLES Study Organizer
Organizing Information
Make this four-pocket Foldable to help organize what you learn about the 1920s.

Step 1 On an 11" x 17" sheet of paper, make a fold as shown.

Step 2 Fold the sheet into four equal parts. Staple or glue the ends of the paper to make four pockets.

Step 3 Label the pockets of your Foldable as shown.

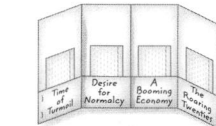

Reading and Writing As you read the chapter, list key people and events on index cards. Place the cards in the appropriate pocket. Use your cards to help you study for quizzes and tests.

Introducing Chapter 24

Time Line Activity

If you have not already done so, have students review the time line. **Ask:** *What years are covered in this time line? What achievements were made by women during this period?* (1918–1930; obtained woman suffrage, were represented by governors in two states) Have students discuss how the Kellogg-Briand Pact might have reflected the American mood during this decade. (The pact called for outlawing war. Americans and their presidents favored peace and isolationism.)

FOLDABLES Study Organizer — Dinah Zike's Foldables
Purpose This Foldable helps students organize information about the 1920s. The completed Foldable will help them prepare for assessment. **OL**

☞ More Foldables activities for this chapter can be found in the *Dinah Zike's Reading and Study Skills Foldables.*

History ONLINE
Introduce students to chapter content and key terms by having them access the **Chapter Overview** at glencoe.com.

CALVIN COOLIDGE

★ **1924**
• Wyoming and Texas elect female governors
• Model T sells for less than $300

◄ Nellie Tayloe Ross, governor of Wyoming

★ **1927**
• Lindbergh flies across Atlantic
• Babe Ruth hits 60 home runs

1924 — **1927** — **1930**

★ **1924**
First Winter Olympics staged in Chamonix, France

★ **1928**
Kellogg-Briand Pact aims to outlaw war

Chapter 24   743

Section 3
A Booming Economy Ask: What advances in technology and transportation affected American life? (Technology: electricity for factories, electric appliances at home, mass-production techniques; Transportation: automobiles) Tell students that Section 3 explores the impact of innovations in technology and transportation after World War I. **OL**

Section 4
The Roaring Twenties Ask: How do you think the invention of radio and movies changed America's culture? (Students might say that fashion, music, and language changed.) Explain to students that in Section 4, they will learn more about the social changes that occurred in the 1920s. **OL**

Section 1

Time of Turmoil

Focus

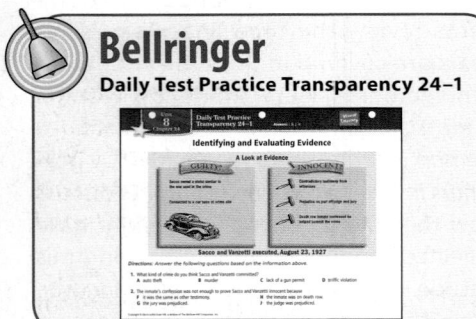

Reading Guide
Answers to Graphic:
raids, arrests, deportations

Section Spotlight Video

Watch the Section Spotlight Video "Time of Turmoil" to learn about the dramatic events surrounding the trial of Sacco and Vanzetti.

Essential Question ◄
How did prejudice and labor strife affect the nation following World War I?

Reading Guide

Content Vocabulary

capitalism (p. 745)   deport (p. 745)

anarchist (p. 745)

Academic Vocabulary

normal (p. 745)   dynamic (p. 747)

Key People and Events

Red Scare (p. 745)

Calvin Coolidge (p. 747)

Marcus Garvey (p. 747)

Reading Strategy

Taking Notes On a diagram like the one below, list the ways the U.S. government dealt with people they thought were a threat to the government.

Government Action	

ILLINOIS STANDARDS
The American Journey

14.C.3 Compare historical issues involving rights, roles and status of individuals in relation to municipalities, states and the nation.

14.D.3 Describe roles and influences of individuals, groups and media in shaping current Illinois and United States public policy (e.g., general public opinion, special interest groups, formal parties, media).

16.C.3c (US) Describe how economic developments and government policies after 1865 affected the country's economic institutions including corporations, banks and organized labor.

American Diary

A wave of strikes after World War I fueled fears that Communists were conspiring to start a revolution in the United States. Attorney General A. Mitchell Palmer viewed them as a threat to the American values of religion, private property, and democracy. Declaring that "the blaze of revolution [is] eating its way into the homes of the American workman," Palmer was ready to take action.

—*from* New World Coming

Resource Manager

R Reading Strategies	**C** Critical Thinking	**D** Differentiated Instruction	**W** Writing Support	**S** Skill Practice
Teacher Edition • Questioning, p. 745	**Teacher Edition** • Diagramming, p. 747	**Teacher Edition** • Interpersonal, p. 746	**Teacher Edition** • Expository Writing, p. 747	**Teacher Edition** • Making a Time Line, p. 745
Additional Resources • Guid. Read., URB p. 39 • Content Vocab., URB p. 17 • Academic Vocab., URB p. 19 • Pri. Source Read., URB p. 21 • Read. Ess., p. 262	**Additional Resources** • Quizzes and Tests, p. 235	**Additional Resources** • School-to-Home, URB p. 35 • Reteaching Act., URB p. 37		**Additional Resources** • Daily Test Pract. Transp. 24-1 • Lesson Transp. 24B • Soc. Stud. Skills, URB p. 25 • Geo. and Hist., URB p. 31

Fear of Radicalism

Main Idea Events after World War I made some Americans intolerant of immigrants and foreign ideas.

History and You How do you feel about ideas and practices that are different from your own? Read to find out how Americans responded to people who had new ideas about social change.

As the 1920s began, Americans were coping with the uncertainties that followed World War I. Tired of war and world responsibilities, Americans wanted to return to a **normal,** or typical, way of life. As a result, they grew more suspicious of foreigners and those holding views that were different from their own.

Some Americans were especially disturbed by the Russian Revolution. In 1917 the Bolsheviks set up a Communist state in Russia. They urged workers around the world to overthrow **capitalism**—an economic system based on private property and free enterprise. Many Americans feared that "bolshevism" threatened American society.

Fanning those fears were the actions of **anarchists**—people who believe there should be no government. A series of anarchist bombings in 1919 in New York City, Seattle, and other cities frightened Americans.

The Red Scare

This wave of fear led to the **Red Scare,** a period when the government went after "Reds"—as Communists were known—and others with radical views. In late 1919 and early 1920, Attorney General A. Mitchell Palmer and his deputy, J. Edgar Hoover, ordered the arrest of more than 10,000 people suspected of being Communists and anarchists." Palmer and Hoover also staged raids on the headquarters of "suspicious" groups. They did not find the large stockpiles of weapons and dynamite they claimed they were seeking.

The government **deported**—expelled from the United States—a few hundred of the aliens it arrested but quickly released many others for lack of evidence.

Primary Source | The Alien Act

Rights v. Security The Alien Act, passed by Congress in October 1918, stated that "any alien who, at any time after entering the United States, is found to have been at the time of entry, or to have become thereafter, a member of any anarchist organization" could be deported. Journalist and critic H. L. Mencken spoke out about the erosion of rights. "Government, today, is growing too strong to be safe. There are no longer any citizens in the world; there are only subjects."

Critical Thinking

Defending Do you think the federal government should have the power to curtail individual rights during times of war or during times of great crisis? Why or why not?

Creating a Political Advertisement

Step 1: Analyzing the Political Climate Students will analyze social and political issues in the United States after World War I.

Essential Question: How did prejudice and labor strife affect the nation following World War I?

Directions Organize students into groups of five or six. Explain that one person in each group will be running in a presidential election in the 1920s and that each group will create a political advertisement for its candidate. Have each group choose a candidate and begin to define its candidate's opinions. Groups should address how their candidates feel about labor issues and prejudice.

Teach

R Reading Strategy

Questioning Have students restate the Main Idea as a question. **Ask:** What do you expect to learn? (to learn about events after World War I that made some Americans less tolerant of immigrants and foreign ideas) **OL**

This **READING SKILL** (Questioning) was introduced in this unit.

S Skill Practice

Making a Time Line Have students make a time line of events leading up to the Red Scare. **Ask:** How did the government respond to these events? (It ordered raids, arrests, and deportations of suspected communists and radicals.) Organize the class into two teams to debate the government's actions. **OL**

Primary Source

Critical Thinking Answer
Answers should reflect the challenge for leaders to balance the interests of public safety with those of individual rights.

Hands-On Chapter Project
Step 1

Identifying Central Issues Discuss how political leaders can influence people's views. Then talk about how candidates might resolve labor unrest and issues about discrimination and prejudice.

(Chapter Project continued in Section 2)

People IN HISTORY

People IN HISTORY

D Differentiated Instruction

Interpersonal Have students research how people in their communities reacted to labor unrest and racial tension during the 1920s. Discuss as a class. Ask students to think about how they might have reacted. **AL**

Critical Thinking Answer

The Great Migration was a movement that encouraged Southern African Americans to move to Northern cities for jobs and to escape discrimination. Competition for jobs increased as many African Americans moved north. Many whites resented African Americans because of that increased competition.

✓ Reading Check **Answer:** the arrest of suspected Communists and anarchists; raids on their headquarters; deportation of aliens; public support for the execution of Sacco and Vanzetti

Differentiated Instruction

A. Philip Randolph

Labor leader and civil rights activist

A. Philip Randolph worked tirelessly for more than a decade to win union recognition for the Brotherhood of Sleeping Car Porters. He said, *"Freedom is never given; it is won. And the Negro people must win their freedom. . . . This involves struggle, continuous struggle."* Years later, when President Kennedy's Civil Rights Bill stalled in Congress, Randolph helped organize the March on Washington. More than 250,000 people rallied near the Lincoln Memorial on August 28, 1963, to show their support for civil rights.

Robert Sengstacke Abbott

Newspaper publisher

By the beginning of World War I, the *Chicago Defender*, founded by Robert Sengstacke Abbott, was the nation's most influential African American weekly newspaper. The paper led the Great Migration, a movement that encouraged African Americans in the South to move to Northern cities to escape segregation and to fill a labor shortage in factories. His paper wrote, *"To die from the bite of frost is far more glorious than at the hands of a mob."*

CRITICAL Thinking

Explaining What was the Great Migration? What effect did it have on Northern cities?

Sacco and Vanzetti

An event that for many came to symbolize fear of immigrants and radical ideas was the trial of Nicola Sacco and Bartolomeo Vanzetti. These two Italian immigrants and anarchists were accused of killing two men during a robbery in Massachusetts. The two men were tried and convicted in July 1921 and were sentenced to death.

Many Americans demanded that the death sentence be carried out. In 1927 a special Massachusetts commission upheld the verdict. Sacco and Vanzetti—proclaiming their innocence—were executed.

✓ Reading Check **Synthesizing** What events of the 1920s might be cited as evidence of prejudice against immigrants?

Labor and Racial Strife

Main Idea The 1920s brought increased labor unrest and racial tensions, often marked by violence.

History and You Do you think people of very different backgrounds can live together peacefully? Read to see how this issue affected Americans during the 1920s.

After World War I, industrial workers launched strikes to get wage increases that would keep up with rapidly rising prices. Many Americans believed that Bolsheviks and radicals were causing this labor unrest. At the same time, racial tensions increased. In the North, many whites resented African American competition for factory jobs.

Leveled Activities

BL Reteaching Activity, URB p. 37

OL Primary Source Reading, URB p. 21

ELL Geography and History Activity, URB p. 31

Strikes Sweep Country

In September 1919, about 350,000 steelworkers went on strike, demanding an increase in wages and an eight-hour workday. The steel companies accused the strikers of being "Red agitators." This charge cost the strikers public support and forced them to end the strike—but not before 18 strikers died in a riot in Gary, Indiana.

That same month, Boston police officers went on strike for the right to form a union. This strike by public employees angered many Americans, and they applauded when Massachusetts governor **Calvin Coolidge** called out the National Guard. When the strike collapsed, the entire police force was fired.

Many workers did not join labor unions, linking them with radicalism. Distrust of unions, as well as pressure from employers and government, led to a sharp drop in union membership in the 1920s.

Despite the unions' decline, a **dynamic,** or energetic, African American, A. Philip Randolph, started the Brotherhood of Sleeping Car Porters. This union of railroad workers began to grow in the 1930s, when the government began to encourage unions.

Racial Unrest

In 1919 rising racial tensions led to violence. In the South, more than 70 African Americans were lynched. In Chicago a violent riot broke out after a group of whites stoned an African American youth who was swimming in Lake Michigan. The youth drowned and the incident set off rioting. For two weeks African American and white gangs roamed city streets, attacking each other and burning buildings. The riot left 15 whites and 23 African Americans dead and more than 500 people injured.

Many African Americans turned to **Marcus Garvey** for answers. Marcus Garvey was born to a poor family in Jamaica. A powerful leader with a magnetic personality, Garvey opposed integration. Instead he supported a "back-to-Africa" movement, urging African Americans to establish their own country in Africa. Garvey founded the Universal Negro Improvement Association (UNIA) in 1914 to promote African American pride. It also helped African Americans start businesses. Garvey gained a large following.

✔ **Reading Check** **Explaining** Did Marcus Garvey support or oppose integration? Explain.

C Critical Thinking

Diagramming Have students create a cause-and-effect diagram that illustrates different reactions to labor disputes during this period. **OL**

W Writing Support

Expository Writing Lead a class discussion about racial unrest in America. **Ask:** Does racism exist in the United States today? Have students write an essay that explains their answer. **OL**

✔ **Reading Check** **Answer:** Garvey opposed integration and wanted African Americans to establish a country in Africa.

Assess

History ONLINE

Study Central™ provides summaries, interactive games, and online graphic organizers to help students review content.

Close

Discussing Ask students to identify one event discussed in the section and explain how business or the government could have responded differently. **OL**

Section 1 Review

History ONLINE
Study Central™ To review this section, go to glencoe.com.

Vocabulary

1. Use each of these words in a sentence that explains its meaning: normal, capitalism, anarchist, deport, dynamic.

Main Ideas

2. **Explaining** What was the outcome of the Boston police strike of 1919?

3. **Describing** What was the UNIA? What was its purpose?

Critical Thinking

4. **Analyzing** Why did Americans fear anarchists? What did Americans expect to happen?

5. **Determining Cause and Effect** Create a diagram like the one below to identify reasons why union membership dropped in the 1920s.

6. **Expository Writing** Write a news summary of the arrest and trial of Sacco and Vanzetti.

Answer the
7. **Essential Question**
How did prejudice and labor strife affect the nation following World War I?

The Jazz Age **Chapter 24** **747**

Answers

1. Sentences should use vocabulary words as they are defined in the section and Glossary.
2. The National Guard was called in, the strike collapsed, and the entire police force was fired.
3. Universal Negro Improvement Association; to promote pride in the African American community and help African Americans start businesses

4. Students may say Americans feared anarchists because many were Bolsheviks. People feared they would destroy the basic U.S. principles of capitalism, democracy, religious freedom, and private property.
5. Many Americans equated labor unions with radicalism; workers distrusted unions; employers and the government pressured workers not to join unions.
6. News summaries will vary but should

include historical details and describe the public's reaction.
7. Prejudice against foreigners led to deportations of aliens and stifling of dissenting views. Prejudice against African Americans led to unequal treatment and violence. Labor unrest inspired distrust of radicals, strong responses from business and government to end strikes, and decreasing union membership.

Focus

C Critical Thinking

Making Inferences Ask students how the Great Migration changed the makeup of the nation. **Ask:** How do you think white factory workers felt about the African American migration to the North? *(Many were probably bitter because they thought African Americans were taking away jobs from them and lowering wages.)* **OL**

Complete a graphic organizer like the one below that shows the reasons that factory owners in the Northern states tried to recruit African American workers. **OL**

```
( Labor        )
( shortages    ) ────┐
                     ├──→ ( Recruitment )
                     │    ( of African  )
                     │    ( Americans   )
( Limits on    ) ────┘
( immigration  )
```

Additional Support and Answers

The Great Migration

Before World War I, most African Americans lived in the rural South. Most were farmers or sharecroppers; almost all were poor. Racial barriers kept them from moving into better-paying jobs. Legal racial segregation and frequent harassment were facts of life.

How Did Geography Affect the Great Migration?

Employment opportunities in Northern cities spurred migration. Labor shortages and limits on immigration after World War I prompted Northern factory owners to actively recruit African American workers. By 1920, almost 500,000 African Americans had moved to industrial cities such as Chicago, Detroit, New York, and Philadelphia. Many hoped to escape the racial injustice and economic hardship they faced in the South. This massive population movement, which became known as the Great Migration, radically changed the racial makeup of the entire nation.

Map legend: Southern states · ← Primary migration routes · 0 400 kilometers · 0 400 miles · Albers Equal-Area projection

Map labels: Chicago, Detroit, Cleveland, Pittsburgh, New York City, Philadelphia, Indianapolis, Cincinnati, Ky., Va., N.C., Ark., Tenn., S.C., Miss., Ala., Ga., Tex., La., Fla., ATLANTIC OCEAN, Gulf of Mexico · 40°N, 70°W, 30°N, 80°W, 90°W

◄ Many African American soldiers returning to the United States after World War I settled in the North, seeking better lives for themselves and their families.

The Harlem Renaissance

Painter Jacob Lawrence (1917–2000) moved from the South to Harlem in New York City. He was a member of the movement called the Harlem Renaissance, in which African American writers and artists began creating works grounded in their own experiences and culture. His work included the series of paintings called "The Migration of the Negro" (1940–1941). This panel from the series shows African Americans buying train tickets to Northern cities. ▶

Activity: Collaborative Learning

Analyzing Information Have students work in groups of three to research and gain an understanding of the most recent U.S. census data available (www.census.gov). Ask them to look for data that show the states that have the highest and lowest percentages of African Americans today. Encourage them to use the U.S. Census Bureau website or print materials. **Ask:** What ten states have the largest population of African Americans today? What ten states have the smallest population of African Americans today? Do you think this has changed much since the early 1900s? Next, assign a different state to each group. Ask them to find the total population of their assigned state and the percentages of each race that make up the population. They should create a pie chart to display their findings and then share their chart with the class. Discuss changing ethnic populations today as a class. **OL**

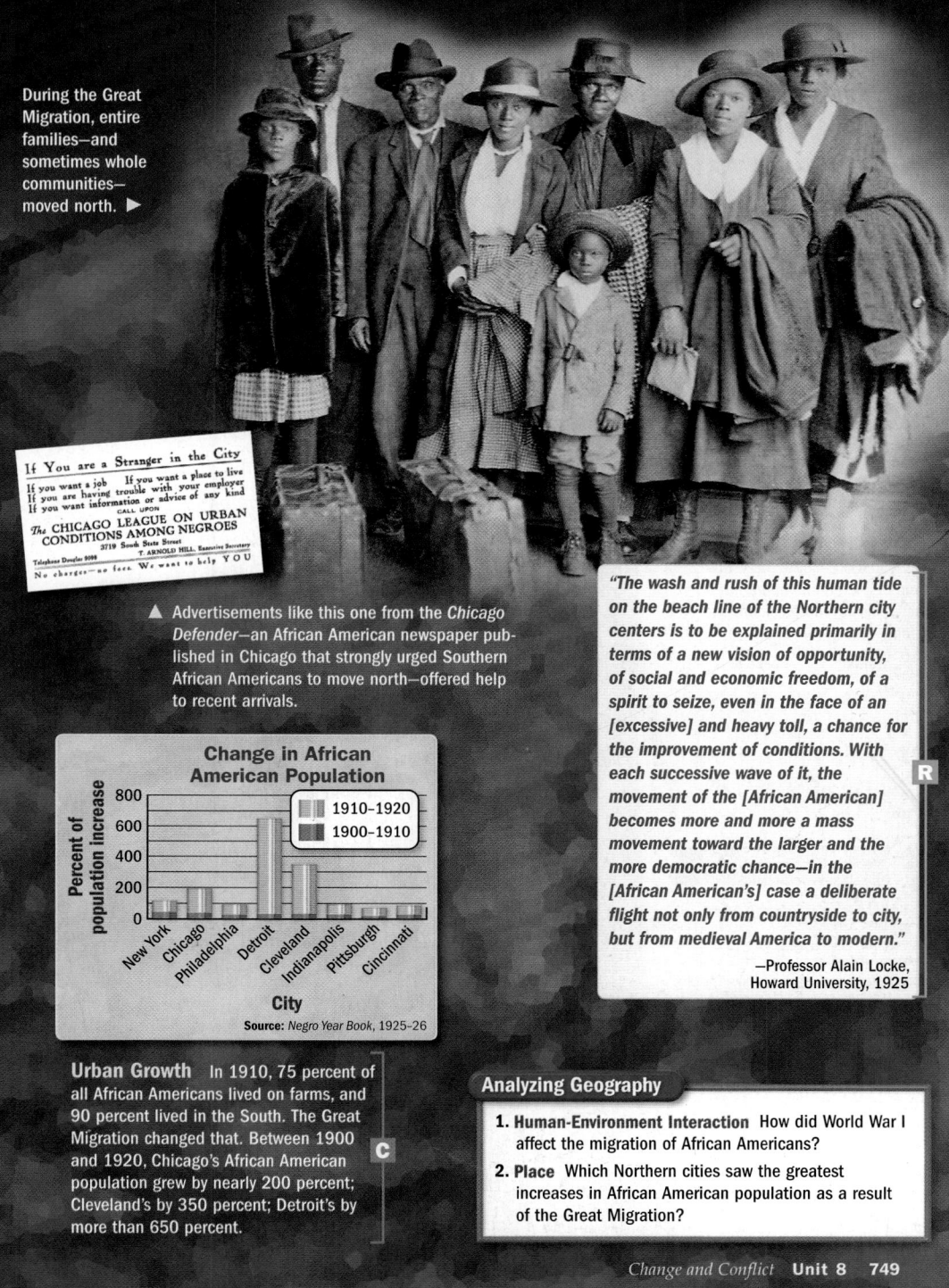

During the Great Migration, entire families—and sometimes whole communities—moved north. ▶

If You are a Stranger in the City

If you want a job   If you want a place to live
If you are having trouble with your employer
If you want information or advice of any kind
                    CALL UPON

The CHICAGO LEAGUE ON URBAN
CONDITIONS AMONG NEGROES
3719 South State Street
Telephone Douglas 9090   T. ARNOLD HILL, Executive Secretary

No charges—no fees. We want to help YOU

▲ Advertisements like this one from the *Chicago Defender*—an African American newspaper published in Chicago that strongly urged Southern African Americans to move north—offered help to recent arrivals.

Change in African American Population

Percent of population increase

- 1910–1920
- 1900–1910

City: New York, Chicago, Philadelphia, Detroit, Cleveland, Indianapolis, Pittsburgh, Cincinnati

Source: *Negro Year Book,* 1925–26

Urban Growth In 1910, 75 percent of all African Americans lived on farms, and 90 percent lived in the South. The Great Migration changed that. Between 1900 and 1920, Chicago's African American population grew by nearly 200 percent; Cleveland's by 350 percent; Detroit's by more than 650 percent.

"The wash and rush of this human tide on the beach line of the Northern city centers is to be explained primarily in terms of a new vision of opportunity, of social and economic freedom, of a spirit to seize, even in the face of an [excessive] and heavy toll, a chance for the improvement of conditions. With each successive wave of it, the movement of the [African American] becomes more and more a mass movement toward the larger and the more democratic chance—in the [African American's] case a deliberate flight not only from countryside to city, but from medieval America to modern."

—Professor Alain Locke,
Howard University, 1925

Analyzing Geography

1. **Human-Environment Interaction** How did World War I affect the migration of African Americans?

2. **Place** Which Northern cities saw the greatest increases in African American population as a result of the Great Migration?

Change and Conflict Unit 8 **749**

Focus

Section 2

Desire for Normalcy

Bellringer
Daily Test Practice Transparency 24-2

Reading Guide

Answers to Graphic:

Harding: corruption and scandals; **Coolidge:** honesty, income tax cuts for wealthy and corporations, higher tariffs, less regulation of child labor and wages, support for U.S. business in Latin America through negotiation; **Both:** *laissez-faire* attitude toward government, supported isolationism, promoted peace

Section Spotlight Video

Watch the Section Spotlight Video "Desire for Normalcy" to investigate the famous Teapot Dome scandal that occurred during President Harding's administration.

Essential Question
In what ways did the election of Harding and Coolidge reflect America's changing mood?

Reading Guide

Content Vocabulary
lease (p. 751)   isolationism (p. 753)

Academic Vocabulary
detect (p. 752)   intervene (p. 753)

Key People and Events
Warren G. Harding (p. 751)
Teapot Dome (p. 751)

Reading Strategy
Taking Notes Re-create the Venn diagram below, and compare the characteristics of the presidencies of Harding and Coolidge.

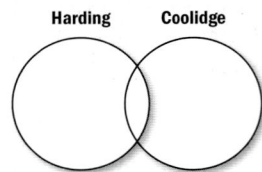

Harding   Coolidge

ILLINOIS STANDARDS
The American Journey

14.C. Understand the election processes and responsibilities of citizens.

14.E. Understand United States foreign policy as it relates to other nations and international issues.

15.E.3b Explain how laws and government policies (e.g., property rights, contract enforcement, standard weights/measurements) establish rules that help a market economy function effectively.

American Diary

In the summer of 1920, the Republicans gathered in Chicago to nominate a candidate for president. They had no outstanding leaders to head the party ticket. Senator Warren G. Harding of Ohio attracted attention with his friendly personality and fine voice. Harding had earned a reputation as a loyal Republican. Ohio political boss Harry Daugherty promoted Harding as a candidate for the nomination. "He looks like a president," Daugherty explained.

Harding's easygoing nature won the goodwill of the voters.

Resource Manager

R Reading Strategies	C Critical Thinking	D Differentiated Instruction	W Writing Support	S Skill Practice
Additional Resources • Guid. Read., URB p. 40 • Content Vocab., URB p. 17 • Academic Vocab., URB p. 19 • Read. Ess., p. 265	**Teacher Edition** • Predict. Conseq., p. 751 **Additional Resources** • Quizzes and Tests, p. 236	**Teacher Edition** • ELL, p. 753 **Additional Resources** • Differ. Inst., URB p. 27 • Reteaching Act., URB p. 37 • School-to-Home, URB p. 35	**Teacher Edition** • Descriptive Writing, p. 752	**Teacher Edition** • Using Geo. Skills, p. 753 **Additional Resources** • Daily Test Pract. Transp. 24-2 • Lesson Transp. 24C

Harding and Coolidge

Main Idea The Harding and Coolidge administrations favored business and wanted a smaller government.

History and You Have you ever enjoyed a restful moment after working or playing hard? Read to find out about two presidents who tried to turn America from fast-paced change to quieter ways.

In his campaign, **Warren G. Harding** promised a return to "normalcy." What Harding meant by "normalcy" was not really explicit, but the word sounded reassuring to Americans who wanted an end to foreign involvement and domestic turmoil.

Harding and his running mate, Massachusetts governor Calvin Coolidge, won a landslide victory in November 1920—the first presidential election in which women could vote. The Republican team easily defeated the Democratic candidate, Governor James Cox of Ohio, and his young running mate, Franklin Delano Roosevelt of New York. Harding named several talented people to his cabinet—Charles Evans Hughes, a former Supreme Court justice, as secretary of state; Andrew Mellon, a Pittsburgh banker and financier, to head the Treasury Department; and Herbert Hoover, a skilled organizer, as secretary of commerce.

Scandals

President Harding also gave government jobs to many of his political supporters—the so-called Ohio Gang. Many of these appointees were unqualified; some turned out to be corrupt. The biggest scandal of the administration involved Albert Fall, the secretary of the interior. In 1922 Fall secretly **leased,** or rented, government oil reserves in Elk Hills, California, and Teapot Dome, Wyoming, to the owners of two oil companies. In exchange, Fall received more than $400,000. Fall was convicted of bribery and became the first cabinet official ever to go to prison. **Teapot Dome** became a symbol of the corruption in the Harding administration.

Harding himself was not directly involved in any scandals, but as the rumors spread, he became troubled. In the summer of 1923, before the full story of the scandals came out, Harding took a trip west to escape the political troubles of Washington. During the trip, he became ill, suffered a heart attack, and died.

Primary Source | **Campaign Items**

Showing Support Political buttons and posters have long been used in campaigns to show support for a candidate.

WARREN G. HARDING & CALVIN COOLIDGE
PRESIDENT & VICE PRESIDENT

PEACE WITH HONOR
OUR CHOICE
COX FOR PRESIDENT
ROOSEVELT FOR VICE PRESIDENT

Critical Thinking

Analyzing How do these campaign items portray the candidates? Which one do you think is more effective? Explain.

Teach

C Critical Thinking

Predicting Consequences Ask: How might Harding's administration have been different if he had appointed people because of their skills instead of their political connections? *(The president may have had government employees who performed their duties with integrity instead of self-interest.)* **AL**

Primary Source

Critical Thinking Answer
Both items show the candidates in similar poses with patriotic symbols. Students may say the Cox-Roosevelt item is more effective because it makes a political statement.

Skills Practice Ask: What slogan or phrase might Harding and Coolidge have chosen for their buttons? *(Answers should include phrases such as "Return to Normalcy.")* **OL**

Hands-On Chapter Project
Step 2

Creating a Political Advertisement

Step 2: Creating a Political Platform Students will analyze what Americans wanted from their government by reading about the Harding and Coolidge presidential election campaigns and positions.

Essential Question: In what ways did the elections of Harding and Coolidge as presidents reflect America's changing mood?

Directions Have students assemble in their small groups and review the social and political ideas in the United States after World War I. Ask each group to create a campaign slogan and a platform for its candidate. Slogans and platforms should explain the candidate's ideas as well as appeal to potential voters.

Summarizing As a class, share the slogans and platforms. Discuss whether they would appeal to Americans in the 1920s.

(Chapter Project continued in Section 3)

W Writing Support

Descriptive Writing Ask students to take the role of a reporter at the end of the 1924 elections. Have them write a news story about the victory party for either Nellie Tayloe Ross or Miriam Ferguson. **AL**

History ONLINE
Objectives and answers to the Student Web Activity can be found at glencoe.com under the Web Activity Lesson Plan for this chapter.

INTERPRETING POLITICAL CARTOONS

Answers

1. business prosperity during the Coolidge administration
2. They say, "What a friend we have in Coolidge!" because he does not support the control or regulation of business.

Reading Check **Answer:** Americans were weary after problems at home and abroad during World War I and probably associated the term "normalcy" with comfort.

Differentiated Instruction

Primary Sources
INTERPRETING
POLITICAL CARTOONS

This cartoon was drawn by Daniel R. Fitzpatrick, who worked as the editorial cartoonist for the *St. Louis Post-Dispatch* in 1924. It shows business leaders gathered around a cash register singing about their friend, President Calvin Coolidge.

1. **Identifying** What does the cash register represent?
2. **Analyzing** What are the business leaders saying about President Coolidge? Why?

"Silent Cal" Takes Over

Vice President Calvin Coolidge was visiting his father in Vermont when he heard the news of Harding's death. Coolidge's father, a justice of the peace, administered the presidential oath of office. As president, Calvin Coolidge was in many ways the opposite of Harding. Harding loved to talk and meet people; in contrast, Coolidge said very little and earned the nickname "Silent Cal." In addition, Coolidge had a reputation for honesty. After becoming president, he allowed the investigations into the Harding scandals to proceed without interference. He replaced corrupt members of the Ohio Gang with honest officials.

Coolidge, like Harding, took a hands-off, or laissez-faire, approach to government. He once said, "If the federal government should go out of existence, the common run of the people would not **detect** the difference for a considerable length of time."

History ONLINE
Student Web Activity Visit glencoe.com and complete the Chapter 24 Web Activity about the Jazz Age.

A Friend to Business

The Coolidge administration and the Republican-controlled Congress held that support of business would aid prosperity. The government cut spending and lowered income tax rates on wealthy Americans and corporations. It also raised tariffs to protect business and overturned laws regulating child labor and women's wages.

A New Term

Coolidge seemed to be what the country wanted. At the 1924 Republican national convention, Coolidge was nominated without opposition. The Democrats named John W. Davis of West Virginia as their candidate. Wisconsin senator Robert La Follette was the choice of a third party, the Progressives. Coolidge swept the 1924 presidential race with 54 percent of the popular vote. For the first time in America's history, women won governors' races—Nellie Tayloe Ross in Wyoming and Miriam Ferguson in Texas.

W

Reading Check **Describing** Why was Harding's emphasis on "normalcy" an effective campaign strategy?

Leveled Activities

BL **Guided Reading Activity, URB p. 40**

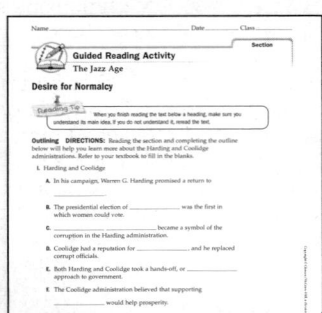

OL **Reading Essentials, p. 265**

AL **Differentiated Instruction Activity, URB p. 27**

ELL **Academic Vocabulary, URB p. 19**

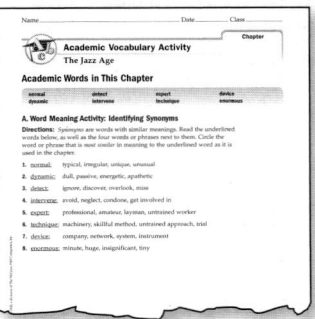

Foreign Policy

Main Idea Harding and Coolidge aimed to limit the role of the United States in foreign affairs.

History and You Have you ever wanted to stay out of an argument between two other people? Read on to see how the United States tried to avoid involvement in international disputes.

Harding and Coolidge both favored a limited role for the nation in world affairs. They desired world peace but did not want the nation to enter the League of Nations or join foreign alliances. Harding had promised the American people that he would not lead them into the League "by the side door, back door, or cellar door." Many Americans supported this policy of **isolationism.**

Promoting Peace

The Harding administration made serious efforts to promote peace. After the war the United States, Britain, and Japan began a naval arms race. In 1921 Secretary of State Hughes invited Japan and Britain to Washington, D.C., to discuss the problem. In February 1922, the three nations, along with France and Italy, signed the Five-Power Treaty to limit the size of the nations' navies. The treaty marked the first time in modern history that world powers agreed to disarm.

In August 1928 the United States joined 14 other nations in signing the Kellogg-Briand Pact, which called for outlawing war. Within a few years, 48 other nations signed the pact, but it lacked any means of enforcing peace.

A More Friendly Neighbor

The United States **intervened,** or got involved, in Latin America several times in the early 1900s to support American business interests. By 1920 American troops were stationed in the Dominican Republic and Nicaragua, and relations with Mexico were tense.

After the Dominican Republic and Nicaragua held elections in the mid-1920s, the United States withdrew its troops from those countries. American investors asked President Coolidge to send troops into Mexico when its government threatened to take over foreign-owned oil and mining companies. Coolidge chose to negotiate instead, and the United States reached a peaceful settlement with Mexico.

Reading Check **Explaining** Why would the Kellogg-Briand Pact prove to be ineffective?

History ONLINE **Study Central™** To review this section, go to glencoe.com.

Section 2 Review

Vocabulary

1. Use each of these terms in a complete sentence that will help explain its meaning: lease, detect, isolationism, intervene.

Main Ideas

2. **Analyzing** Why did President Harding give important government jobs to people who were unqualified for their positions? What happened as a result?

3. **Summarizing** What did the Harding and Coolidge administrations do to promote world peace?

Critical Thinking

4. **Explaining** How does an increase in tariffs help the business community?

5. **Comparing** Create a table and list reasons for and against American isolationism.

Isolationism	
For	Against

6. **Persuasive Writing** Neither Harding nor Coolidge wanted the United States to join the League of Nations. Do you agree with their position? Write a paragraph that explains your point of view.

7. **Answer the Essential Question**
In what ways did the election of Harding and Coolidge reflect America's changing mood?

The Jazz Age **Chapter 24** **753**

D **Differentiated Instruction**

English Language Learners Ask: What does "by the side door, back door, or cellar door" mean? *(All are ways to enter a place other than the front door. Harding meant that he would not mislead Americans by joining the League.)* **ELL**

S **Skill Practice**

Using Geography Skills Have students locate a map of Latin America in the Reference Atlas. **Ask:** Which nation is the nearest to the U. S.? *(Mexico)* **BL**

Reading Check **Answer:** The pact did not include a way to enforce peace.

Assess

History ONLINE

Study Central™ provides summaries, interactive games, and online graphic organizers to help students review content.

Close

Summarizing As a class, summarize the mood of the United States in the early 1920s and how it led to the elections of Harding and Coolidge. **OL**

Section 2 Review

Answers

1. Sentences should use vocabulary words in sentences that clarify their meanings as provided in the section and Glossary.
2. Harding was rewarding them for their political support. Some were corrupt, scandals emerged, and the Harding administration was viewed as corrupt.
3. Harding's administration hosted discussions about the arms race and limited naval size by signing the Five-Power Treaty. The Coolidge administration supported the Kellogg-Briand Pact to outlaw war. Coolidge

also preferred negotiation over military action in settling Latin American business disputes.
4. Tariffs make foreign goods more expensive, which encourages Americans to buy products made by U.S. businesses.
5. **For:** Answers may include keeping the country out of war and avoiding the problems of other nations. **Against:** Answers may include not having allies to help in case of war or other problems, as well as lack of cooperation among foreign

countries to resolve issues.
6. Paragraphs should explain Harding's and Coolidge's positions on the League and a detailed defense or criticism of those positions.
7. Americans were disturbed by foreign conflict and racial and labor problems at home, so the promise of continued peace and a return to normalcy appealed to them. Harding and Coolidge favored business over labor and promised this support would lead to prosperity.

A Booming Economy

Focus

Bellringer
Daily Test Practice Transparency 24–3

Reading Guide
Answers to Graphic:
Business Practice/Goal: hiring efficiency experts/lower costs and increased productivity; mass-production techniques/increased productivity and lower production costs; welfare capitalism/worker loyalty to company and less union participation; advertising/increased buying; installment buying plans/increased buying

Section Spotlight Video

Watch the Section Spotlight Video "A Booming Economy" to learn more about the assembly line.

Resource Manager

Essential Question
How did technology and new forms of transportation change American life?

Reading Guide

Content Vocabulary
recession (p. 755)
productivity (p. 755)
gross national product (p. 755)
installment buying (p. 756)

Academic Vocabulary
expert (p. 755)
technique (p. 755)

Key People and Events
Henry Ford (p. 756)

Reading Strategy
Taking Notes Re-create the chart below and record new American business management changes and what they were intended to achieve.

Business Practice	Goal

 ILLINOIS STANDARDS
The American Journey

15.A.3b Explain the relationship between productivity and wages.

15.D.3c Explain how workers can affect their productivity through training and by using tools, machinery and technology.

16.C.3b (US) Explain relationships among the American economy and slavery, immigration, industrialization, labor and urbanization, 1700-present.

American Diary

After a brief decline, the American economy began to grow steadily; this lasted most of the 1920s. Higher wages and shorter workdays kept the economy booming. In a speech in 1925, President Calvin Coolidge said, "The chief business of the American people is business. . . . The accumulation of wealth means the multiplication of schools, the increase of knowledge, . . . the expansion of liberties."

—from Address to the American Society of Newspaper Editors

R Reading Strategies	C Critical Thinking	D Differentiated Instruction	W Writing Support	S Skill Practice
Teacher Edition • Activating Prior Know., p. 757	**Teacher Edition** • Predicting Consequences, p. 757	**Teacher Edition** • Intrapersonal, p. 755	**Teacher Edition** • Descriptive Writing, p. 756	**Teacher Edition** • Analyzing Statistics, p. 755
Additional Resources • Guid. Read., URB p. 41 • Content Vocab., URB p. 17 • Academic Vocab., URB p. 19 • Read. Ess., p. 268	**Additional Resources** • Quizzes and Tests, p. 237 • Crit. Think. Skills, URB p. 29	**Additional Resources** • School-to-Home, URB p. 35 • Reteaching Act., URB p. 37		**Additional Resources** • Daily Test Pract. Transp. 24-3 • Soc. Stud. Skills, URB p. 25

Growth in the 1920s

Main Idea The United States experienced amazing economic growth during the 1920s.

History and You As you get ready for school, think about all the ways that you use electricity. Read to find out how electricity improved the lives of people living in the 1920s.

A **recession,** or economic downturn, lingered after World War I. The economy then began a steady growth that lasted most of the decade. In 1922 the nation's **gross national product** (GNP)—the total value of all goods and services produced—was $70 billion. By 1929 it rose to $100 billion.

Technology spurred, or stimulated, rapid industrial growth, and electricity powered American industry. Before World War I, only 30 percent of the nation's factories were run by electricity. By 1929, this figure had risen to 70 percent. Electricity was cheaper than steam power. By cutting the costs of production, businesses could lower prices and increase profits.

Management and Workers

New ways of managing businesses helped the economy grow. Many employers used scientific management—hiring **experts,** or people with advanced knowledge, to adopt more efficient work methods. These methods lowered costs and increased **productivity**—the amount of work each worker could do.

Many businesses adopted mass-production techniques, or skillfull methods, using the assembly line, which was first introduced in Henry Ford's automobile factories. Assembly lines increased productivity and cut production costs.

Businesses also tried to build better relations with workers. They set up safety programs that lowered the risk of death or injury on the job. Some provided health and accident insurance. Others encouraged workers to buy stock in the company. These steps—known as welfare capitalism—aimed to link workers more closely to the company they worked for. Businesses also adopted these steps to keep workers from joining independent unions.

By the Numbers / The 1920s Economy

Industry (Percentage Increase, 1922–28)		Workers (Percentage Increase, 1922–28)	
Industrial production	70%	Workers' incomes	11%
Gross national product	40%	Average workweek	-4%
Corporate profits	62%		

Source: Jules Tygiel, "The 1920s Economy: A Statistical Portrait"

Invented in the 1920s

- Push-button elevators
- Electric razors
- Spiral-bound notebooks
- Pop-up toasters
- Car radios
- Adhesive tape
- Self-winding wristwatch
- Band-Aid™

Critical Thinking

Identifying Cause and Effect How did standardized mass production change the American economy?

Teach

D Differentiated Instruction

Intrapersonal As a class, discuss mass-production and assembly line techniques. **Ask:** What are some local examples of businesses that use these methods? *(Answers could include factories, school cafeterias, and pizzerias.)* **BL**

S Skill Practice

Analyzing Statistics Ask students to identify a company that has been in business since the early twentieth century. Students should research to compare statistics from the past with current data, such as number of employees, net profits and expenses, and cost of providing benefits. Have students summarize what they found in a chart and draw conclusions about the past and present profitability of the company. **AL**

By the Numbers

Critical Thinking Answer
Industrial production, GNP, corporate profits, and incomes rose. Lower costs led to lower prices.

Hands-On Chapter Project
Step 3

Creating a Political Advertisement

Step 3: Evaluating Media Students will decide on the best medium to present their candidates' positions.

Essential Question: How did technology and new forms of transportation change American life?

Directions As a class, discuss how developments in technology and transportation affected communication in the 1920s. In their groups, have students research newspaper, magazine, radio, and motion picture advertising in the 1920s. Then ask each group to create a communications plan that will best convey its candidate's message.

Identifying Central Issues As a class, discuss the innovations in technology and transportation in the 1920s and ways in which these changes might have affected the spread of ideas and political messages.

(Chapter Project continued in Section 4)

W Writing Support

Descriptive Writing Ask students to take the role of a farmer who has just arrived in the U.S. Write a one-page letter to relatives back home describing seeing an automobile for the first time. Explain its impact on life in the United States. **OL**

Economics & History

Graph Skills Answer

The assembly line was fast and efficient, allowing Ford to produce and sell more cars.

Skills Practice Have students look at the graph showing Model T prices over time. **Ask:** What might explain the dramatic change from 1911 to 1915? (*The Model T was inexpensive to make, so as sales increased, Ford could reduce its price.*) **AL**

✓Reading Check **Answer:** New techniques allowed businesses to cut costs and lower prices.

Differentiated Instruction

Economics & History

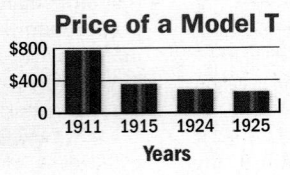

The Ford assembly line sped production and led to lower prices. Tires Ⓐ are put on the wheels; gas tanks Ⓑ slide onto the conveyor belt; and the engine Ⓒ, the radiator Ⓓ, and the auto body Ⓔ are lowered onto the moving chassis.

Price of a Model T

U.S. Auto Industry in 1914

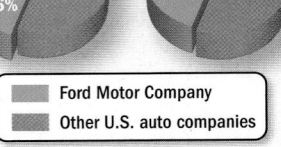

Workers: 84% / 16%
Cars produced: 48% / 52%

■ Ford Motor Company
■ Other U.S. auto companies

Source: *Encyclopaedia Britannica.*

Graph Skills

Speculating Why was the Ford Motor Company able to produce and sell more cars than its competitors?

Graphs In MOtion See StudentWorks™ Plus or glencoe.com.

The Consumer Economy

By the 1920s, more than 60 percent of American households had electricity. Companies produced and consumers acquired electric appliances—refrigerators, stoves, vacuum cleaners, and radios. Using electric appliances meant less time on household chores.

Businesses spent more money on advertising to persuade people to buy a particular product. Newspapers and magazines were filled with ads, and with the spread of radio, a new advertising form—the commercial announcement—was born.

Spurred by ads to buy more, consumers found a new way to make those purchases—**installment buying.** Consumers could now buy products by promising to pay small, regular amounts over a period of time.

✓Reading Check **Explaining** Why did the price of some consumer goods decrease?

The Automobile Age

Main Idea The automobile industry stimulated the economy and transformed the ways Americans traveled and lived.

History and You Can you think of a recent invention that has greatly changed the way in which you live? Read on to find out how the automobile changed America during the 1920s.

During the 1920s, the car became an important part of American life. The nation's economy, too, revolved around the automobile. Almost 4 million Americans **W** worked for auto companies or in related jobs. Detroit, Michigan, became the automobile manufacturing center of the world. **Henry Ford** was a pioneer in making affordable, dependable autos with his Model T, which was built using assembly-line methods.

Leveled Activities

BL **School-to-Home Connection Activity, URB p. 35**

OL **Social Studies Skills, URB p. 25**

AL **Critical Thinking Skills, URB p. 29**

The car was sturdy, reliable, and inexpensive. In 1914 Ford announced that he would pay his workers the high wage of $5 per day. Workers were happy, and Ford had more customers as he steadily dropped the price of his Model T. By the mid-1920s, other car makers, such as General Motors, cut into Ford's sales by offering autos with various improvements. Out of this competition came the practice of introducing new car models each year.

Effect on Other Industries

Americans' love of driving called for new roads and highways. Highways, in turn, needed gas stations and rest stops. Businesses along major roads profited from many people now traveling around the country by car.

The car boom affected industries that made products used in cars. For example, the steel, rubber, and glass industries grew.

Travel for pleasure became a regular part of daily life. People could now go wherever they wished. Cars also contributed to the spread of suburbs. Because people could now drive to work, they could live in a suburb and still hold a job in the city.

Those Left Behind

Despite this prosperity, many Americans did not share in the boom of the 1920s. Farmers especially had difficulties. During the war, the government had bought wheat, corn, and other products, and farmers prospered from higher prices. After the war, farmers had to compete with European agriculture again. Food prices fell, and farm income dropped. Unable to pay their debts, many farmers lost their farms.

Farmers were not alone in suffering. Railroad workers and coal miners had a difficult time as trucks took business from railroads and electricity replaced coal as a power source. Americans also were buying less cotton and more clothes made of synthetic fibers. As cotton prices plunged, many textile factories had to shut down. Workers' wages rose slightly, but the cost of living rose more. By 1929 nearly three-fourths of families had incomes below $2,500, the accepted level needed for a comfortable life.

✓ **Reading Check** **Explaining** How did the automobile change life in the United States?

R Reading Strategy

Activating Prior Knowledge Ask: What war is being referenced here? *(World War I)* **BL**

C Critical Thinking

Predicting Consequences Ask: Who might not have shared in the prosperity of the 1920s? *(storekeepers in farm or coal-mining towns, manufacturers of railroad car accessories)* **OL**

✓ **Reading Check** **Answer:** The U.S. economy became tied to auto manufacturing; jobs were created, travel boomed, related industries grew, suburbs spread, and competition emerged between the trucking and the railroad industries.

Assess

History ONLINE

Study Central™ provides summaries, interactive games, and online graphic organizers to help students review content.

Close

Listing Have the class list the ways new technology and transportation changed American life in the 1920s.

Section 3 Review

Section 3 Review

History ONLINE
Study Central™ To review this section, go to glencoe.com.

Vocabulary

1. Explain the meaning of the following terms by using each one in a sentence: recession, gross national product, expert, productivity, technique, installment buying.

Main Ideas

2. **Explaining** How did the availability of electricity change the habits of American consumers in the 1920s?

3. **Evaluating** Who benefited from the increased popularity of the automobile?

Critical Thinking

4. **Analyzing** Discuss the pros and cons of installment buying for the American consumer.

5. **Determining Cause and Effect** Create a chart like the one below. Record the major cause behind the invention of the automobile and add any additional causes and effects that occurred.

Cause	Effects	Effects

6. **Persuasive Writing** It is 1920 and you work for a company that manufactures and sells the latest home appliance—the refrigerator. Write a radio commercial explaining what a refrigerator does and the advantages of owning one.

Answer the **Essential Question**

7. How did new technology and forms of transportation change American life?

The Jazz Age **Chapter 24** 757

Answers

1. Students should use vocabulary words in sentences that explain their meanings.
2. allowed for lower prices; made chores easier and gave people more leisure time
3. workers in the auto, steel, rubber, glass, and travel industries; consumers; businesses along roads; suburban workers
4. Pros might include consumers' ability to buy items immediately instead of saving for them ahead of time. Cons might include increasing debt and overspending.

5. **Cause:** assembly line **Effects:** affordable car production, economy based on the automobile, decline of railroads; **Cause:** increased mobility of individuals **Effects:** growth of travel industry, new roads, suburbs; **Cause:** need for car products **Effects:** growth of steel, rubber, glass industries
6. Radio commercials should explain refrigerators to an audience that might not know what they are and the benefits of using the new appliance.

7. Technology led to industrial growth, lower costs, lower prices, and increased profits for business. It also created a consumer economy, more leisure time, and an improved standard of living. The travel industry grew, and suburbs developed. The railroad and coal industries suffered.

Focus

Bellringer
Daily Test Practice Transparency 24–4

Reading Guide
Answers to Graphic:
the American experience, questioning of American ideals, prejudice faced by African Americans, everyday life

Section Spotlight Video

Watch the Section Spotlight Video "The Roaring Twenties" to learn more about the life and work of Harlem Renaissance author Zora Neale Hurston.

Essential Question
How did social change affect the arts, the role of women, and minorities?

Reading Guide

Content Vocabulary

flapper (p. 759)   nativism (p. 762)
mass media (p. 759)   quota system (p. 762)
expatriate (p. 761)   evolution (p. 763)
Prohibition (p. 761)

Academic Vocabulary

device (p. 759)   enormous (p. 760)

Key People and Events
Harlem Renaissance (p. 760)
Eighteenth Amendment (p. 761)
Twenty-first Amendment (p. 762)

Reading Strategy
Taking Notes On a diagram like the one below, list the major themes that appeared in the art, writing, and music of the 1920s.

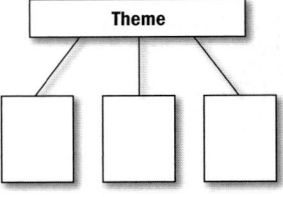

Theme

ILLINOIS STANDARDS
The American Journey

14.D.3 Describe roles and influences of individuals, groups and media in shaping current Illinois and United States public policy (e.g., general public opinion, special interest groups, formal parties, media).

18.A.3 Explain how language, literature, the arts, architecture and traditions contribute to the development and transmission of culture.

18.B.3a Analyze how individuals and groups interact with and within institutions (e.g., educational, military).

The Roaring Twenties

American Diary

On the morning of May 20, 1927, a young pilot named Charles Lindbergh made the final preparations for takeoff. Shortly before 8:00 A.M., Lindbergh climbed into his aircraft and took off for Paris. The news of his departure "flashed along the wires," the American people were united in "the exaltation of a common emotion." All minds and hearts were focused on the brave pilot who was crossing the vast Atlantic Ocean.

Resource Manager

R Reading Strategies	C Critical Thinking	D Differentiated Instruction	W Writing Support	S Skill Practice
Teacher Edition • Predicting, p. 760 • Previewing, p. 761 • Organizing, p. 764 **Additional Resources** • Guid. Read., URB p. 42 • Content Vocab., URB p. 17 • Academic Vocab., URB p. 19 • Read. Ess., p. 271	**Teacher Edition** • Making Inferences, p. 759 • Determin. Cause & Effect, p. 762 • Compar. & Contrast., p. 762 **Additional Resources** • Quizzes and Tests, p. 238 • Authentic Assess., p. 24	**Teacher Edition** • Auditory/Musical, p. 760 • ELL, p. 761 • Mathematical, p. 762 **Additional Resources** • Reteaching Act., URB p. 37 • School-to-Home, URB p. 35	**Teacher Edition** • Creative Writing, p. 759 • Narrative Writing, p. 763 **Additional Resources** • Writ. Skills, URB p. 23 • Link. Past & Pres., URB p. 33	**Teacher Edition** • Recog. Historical Perspectives, p. 760 • Using Geo. Skills, p. 763 **Additional Resources** • Daily Test Pract. Transp. 24-4 • Lesson Transp. 24A • Time Line Skills, URB p. 34

Social and Cultural Change

Main Idea During the 1920s, social changes affected the role of women and led to new forms of entertainment and culture.

History and You Have you known anyone who has moved from the United States to reside in another country? Read to find out why many American writers and artists of the 1920s settled in Europe.

In May 1927 aviator Charles Lindbergh became the first person to fly alone across the Atlantic Ocean. Americans went wild and hailed Lindbergh as a hero. The national embrace of Lindbergh showed what one historian called a "delighted concern over things that were exciting but didn't matter profoundly."

Changes for Women

The 1920s brought changes for women. One important change was the ratification of the Nineteenth Amendment in 1920. The amendment guaranteed women in all states the right to vote. Women also ran for election to political offices.

The number of women working outside the home grew steadily. Most working women became teachers or office workers, but some college-educated women began professional careers. Still, most married women remained within the home, working as mothers and homemakers.

The symbol of the new "liberated" woman of the 1920s was the **flapper**—a carefree young woman with short "bobbed" hair, heavy makeup, and short skirts. Many people saw the behavior of flappers as a sign of changing morals and new freedoms.

Movies and Radio

Cultural changes spread quickly because of the growth of **mass media**—forms of communication, such as newspapers and radio, that reach millions of people. Laborsaving **devices**, or equipment, and fewer working hours gave Americans more leisure time to enjoy newspapers, magazines, phonograph records, the radio, and the movies.

In the 1920s the motion picture industry in Hollywood, California, became a major business. For millions of Americans, the movies offered entertainment and escape. The first movies were black and white and silent, with the actors' dialog printed on the screen. In 1927 Hollywood introduced movies with sound. The first "talkie," *The Jazz Singer*, created a sensation.

Primary Source / Bessie Coleman

A Flying Pioneer Bessie Coleman was the first female African American to receive a pilot's license and the first to become a stunt pilot. She championed the cause of equal rights, refusing to perform at shows that did not admit African Americans. Coleman's achievements inspired the founding of Chicago's Coffey School of Aeronautics. Its graduates helped train the U.S. military's first African American pilots, the Tuskegee airmen, who served with distinction in World War II. A Chicago, Illinois, city council resolution stated that "Bessie Coleman continues to inspire . . . young persons with her sense of adventure, her positive attitude and her determination to succeed."

Critical Thinking

Interpreting Why was Charles Lindbergh a symbol of modern America?

Teach

W Writing Support

Creative Writing Have students research flappers to learn more about their characteristics and lifestyles. Students should then write a journal entry describing an encounter with a flapper. **OL**

C Critical Thinking

Making Inferences Ask: How might electricity have influenced the growth of mass media? *(The use of electricity allowed the development of labor-saving inventions and gave Americans more leisure time to enjoy the media. Electricity also helped in the production of movies, magazines, and the like.)* **BL**

Primary Source

Critical Thinking Answer Like Bessie Coleman, Lindbergh symbolized bravery, a spirit of adventure, a can-do attitude, and determination—all traits that Americans valued in the 1920s.

Differentiated Instruction

Leveled Activities

OL Time Line Skills, URB p. 34

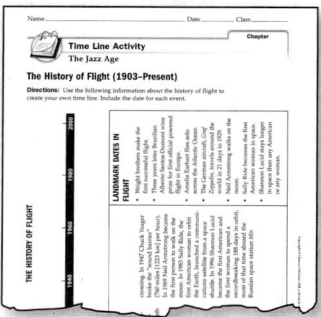

AL Linking Past and Present, URB p. 33

ELL Content Vocabulary, URB p. 17

R **Reading Strategy**

Predicting As a class, identify additional ways radio might have influenced society. *(spread of new types of music such as jazz, rapid communication with millions of people, increased sense of shared culture)* **AL**

D **Differentiated Instruction**

Auditory/Musical Play a song by Louis Armstrong for the class. As a class, discuss African American contributions to music that led to new forms of music, such as spirituals, jazz, blues, rock, and hip-hop. **OL**

S **Skill Practice**

Recognizing Historical Perspectives Ask each member of the class to bring in a poem by Langston Hughes. Read the poems aloud, and discuss how each poem's wording, themes, and overall mood reflect the society in which Hughes lived. **AL**

Hands-On Chapter Project
Step 4

Creating a Political Advertisement

Step 4: Creating the Advertisement Students create political advertisements for their presidential candidates.

Essential Question: How did social change affect the arts, the role of women, and minorities?

Directions Organize students into their small groups, and have them read the section. Have them create a captivating political ad that uses the slogan and clarifies the candidates' positions. Movie or radio ads might be prerecorded or scripted to be acted out in the next step. Newspaper and magazine ads may be displayed on poster board.

Analyzing Ask each group to describe how social change affected its candidate's ideas and the presentation of those ideas in the advertisement.

The radio brought entertainment into people's homes in the 1920s. Radio networks broadcast popular programs that included news, concerts, sporting events, and comedies. Businesses soon realized that the radio offered an **enormous,** or huge, audience for messages about their products, so they began to help finance radio programs. Radio stations sold spot advertisements, or commercials, to companies.

Sports and Fads

Radio added to the popularity of sports, such as baseball, football, and boxing, by allowing listeners to experience sporting events as they happened. Americans flocked to sporting events, and sports stars became heroes.

In the 1920s Americans took up new activities with enthusiasm, turning them into fads. Board games and crossword puzzles were all the rage. Contests such as flagpole sitting and dance marathons—often lasting three or four days—made headlines.

Jazz and the Harlem Renaissance

During the 1920s people danced to the beat of a new kind of music called jazz. Jazz captured the spirit of the era so well that the 1920s is often referred to as the Jazz Age. Rooted in African American music, jazz uses dynamic rhythms and improvisation—new rhythms and melodies created during a performance. Among the best-known African American jazz musicians were trumpeter Louis Armstrong, pianist and composer Duke Ellington, and singer Bessie Smith.

The rhythm and themes of jazz inspired a blossoming of culture in Harlem, an African American section of New York City. During this movement, called the **Harlem Renaissance,** writers such as Langston Hughes, James Weldon Johnson, and Zora Neale Hurston presented the African American experience in novels, poems, and short stories. In his autobiography, Langston Hughes described his arrival in Harlem:

Primary Source / **Women of the Harlem Renaissance**

Literature and the Arts African American women contributed greatly to the Harlem Renaissance with a wide range of talent. They opened the doors of opportunity for others who came later.

Jessie Redmon Fauset ▶

Zora Neale Hurston ▼

Zora Neale Hurston wrote about rural African American life. Her stories were among the first to feature African American women as the main characters. In her classic novel, *Their Eyes Were Watching God,* Hurston describes the force of a hurricane:

"The wind came back with triple fury, and put out the light for the last time. . . . They seemed to be staring at the dark, but their eyes were watching God."

Jessie Redmon Fauset was a mentor to the younger writers of the Harlem Renaissance, as well as a novelist herself. While others wrote about poverty, Fauset's characters were modeled after her own friends: educated, middle-class African Americans facing racial prejudice.

"The complex of color . . . every colored man feels it sooner or later. It gets in the way of his dreams, of his education, of his marriage, of the rearing of his children."

—from *There Is Confusion*

Vote for Harding
For a Return to Normalcy!

(Chapter Project continued on the Visual Summary page)

"I can never put on paper the thrill of that underground ride to Harlem. . . . I went up the steps and out into the bright September sunlight. Harlem! I stood there, dropped my bags, took a deep breath and felt happy again."

—from *The Big Sea*

A Lost Generation of Writers

While the Harlem Renaissance thrived, other writers questioned American ideals. Some influential writers were **expatriates**—people who choose to live in another country. Writer Gertrude Stein called these rootless Americans "the lost generation."

Other writers remained at home and wrote about life in America. Novelist Sinclair Lewis presented a critical view of American culture. In *Winesburg, Ohio,* Sherwood Anderson explored small-town life in the Midwest.

✓ **Reading Check Comparing** What fads were popular in the 1920s? What are two comparable fads today?

Augusta Christine Savage was the seventh of 14 children. Because her family could not afford to buy toys, she molded small animals into playthings from the red-clay soil at her Florida home. Savage studied sculpture in France and eventually taught art in Harlem to young people.

Gamin by Augusta Christine Savage ▶

Critical Thinking

Analyzing Why do you think these women chose to write about the African American lifestyle and culture?

A Clash of Cultures

Main Idea During the 1920s, American society was divided by a clash between traditional and modern values.

History and You Think of an issue that is important to you. What would you be willing to do to stand up for that issue? Read to learn how various groups in the 1920s clashed over issues they considered important.

• •

During the 1920s cities and industries grew. Many Americans, however, did not identify with this new, urban society. They believed that the America they knew and valued—a nation based on family, church, and tradition—was under attack. Disagreement arose between those who defended traditional beliefs and those who welcomed the new.

Prohibition

One issue that divided Americans was the use of alcoholic beverages. The temperance movement, the campaign against alcohol use, was rooted in religious objections to drinking alcohol and in the belief that society would benefit if alcohol were unavailable.

The movement reached its goal in 1919 with the ratification of the **Eighteenth Amendment** to the Constitution. This amendment established **Prohibition**—a total ban on the manufacture, sale, and transportation of liquor throughout the United States. In the rural South and Midwest, where the temperance movement was strong, Prohibition generally succeeded. In the cities, however, Prohibition had little support. The nation divided into two camps: the "drys"—those who supported Prohibition—and the "wets"—those who opposed it.

A continuing demand for alcohol led to widespread lawbreaking. Illegal bars and clubs, known as speakeasies, sprang up in cities. With only about 1,500 agents, the federal government could do little to enforce Prohibition. By the early 1920s, many states in the East stopped trying to enforce the laws.

The Jazz Age **Chapter 24** **761**

Activity: Interdisciplinary Connection

Literature Sherwood Anderson drew on his experience to write about American life. Have students read "The Egg" from *The Triumph of the Egg,* a collection of Anderson's short stories. (The story is available online.) Read aloud the following passage from the end of the second paragraph: "They became ambitious. The American passion for getting up in the world took possession of them."

Ask: Does Anderson feel that the pursuit of this value leads to a happy and balanced life? (*No, Anderson is critical of this and does not feel it leads to contentment or a happy life.*) Lead a class discussion about what the narrator's parents did to try to achieve success and how those actions affected their lives. **OL**

C1 Critical Thinking

Determining Cause and Effect Ask: Why did Prohibition fail to achieve its goals? *(It lacked unanimous public support and government enforcement, inspired illegal manufacture and drinking of alcohol, and encouraged organized crime.)* **OL**

D Differentiated Instruction

Mathematical Ask: How long was Prohibition in effect? *(about 14 years)* **OL**

C2 Critical Thinking

Comparing and Contrasting Lead a class discussion about nativism in U.S. society today. Students can supply news articles as examples. *(Examples might include controversy over undocumented workers, prejudice against ethnic or religious groups, and so on.)* **OL**

Education in the 1920s

Going to School Society was changing rapidly. Nowhere was change more evident than in education. Larger numbers of young people were in school than ever before. By 1930 a majority of children of high school age were in school.

1910	1920	1930
18%	35%	55%

Enrollment in grades 9–12 as a percentage of 14–17 year olds.

Source: U.S. Census Bureau, *Statistical Abstract of the United States*

Prohibition contributed to the rise of organized crime. Powerful gangsters, such as Chicago's Al Capone, made millions of dollars from bootlegging—producing and selling illegal alcohol. They used their profits to influence businesses, labor unions, and governments.

Over time many Americans realized that the "noble experiment," as Prohibition was called, had failed. Prohibition was repealed in 1933 with the **Twenty-first Amendment.** It is the only amendment ever passed to overturn an earlier amendment.

Nativism

Many native-born Americans feared the rapid changes in society. Their concerns led to an upsurge of **nativism**—the belief that native-born Americans are superior to foreigners. With this renewed nativism came a revival of the Ku Klux Klan.

The first Klan was founded in the 1860s in the South to deprive African Americans from exercising their rights. The second Klan, set up in 1915, still preyed on African Americans, but it also targeted Catholics, Jews, immigrants, and other groups it believed to represent "un-American" values. To get their way, Klan members used scare tactics, whipped or lynched people, and burned property. In the 1920s the Klan spread from the South to other areas of the country.

Nativism also arose because some Americans believed that foreigners would take away their jobs. This anti-immigrant prejudice was directed mainly at southern and eastern Europeans and Asians.

In 1921 Congress responded to these Nativist fears by passing the Emergency Quota Act. This law established a **quota system,** an arrangement that placed a limit on the number of immigrants from each country.

762 Chapter 24 *The Jazz Age*

Activity: Connecting Past and Present

Discussion Students may be hearing about the Ku Klux Klan for the first time. They may not be aware that the Klan is active today in some parts of the country. Organize students into small groups. Each group will work together to research one of the following topics about the Klan today: locations of the Klan, types of activities carried out by Klan members, groups targeted, reaction of local residents, and legal reactions. Tell each group to organize its findings and choose a member to present the information to the class. **OL**

Trends in Public Education:
- High school attendance more than doubles during the 1920s.
- Minimum legal dropout age is raised.
- By 1930 every state has mandatory attendance laws.

Crowded Classrooms During the 1920s, many small schools were combined. Some consolidated schools grew to be very large. By 1930 the country had 29 high schools with more than 5,000 students. One school, DeWitt Clinton in New York City, had more than 10,000 students. A 1923 issue of *TIME* magazine described the crowded conditions:

"On the grand average, about one child in ten must join the overflow classes in basement or improvised classrooms."

Critical Thinking

Explaining What was one effect of the great increase in student enrollment?

Graphs In MOtion See StudentWorks™ Plus or glencoe.com.

The act limited the number of immigrants to the United States in any one year to 3 percent of the total number of people in any national group that had been living in America in 1910. This policy favored immigration from northern and western Europe. In 1910 people from those regions were more numerous than those from other parts of Europe.

Congress revised the law in 1924. The National Origins Act reduced the annual country quota from 3 percent to 2 percent and based it on the census of 1890. The law also excluded Japanese immigrants completely. An earlier law passed in 1890 already excluded the Chinese.

Quotas did not apply to countries in the Western Hemisphere. As a result, immigration from Canada and Mexico increased. By 1930 more than 1 million Mexicans had come to live in the United States.

The Scopes Trial

Another cultural clash in the 1920s involved the role of religion in society. This conflict gained national attention in 1925 in one of the most famous trials of the era.

In 1925 the state of Tennessee passed a law making it illegal to teach **evolution**—the scientific theory that humans evolved over vast periods of time. The law was supported by Christian fundamentalists, who accepted the biblical story of creation. The fundamentalists saw evolution as a challenge to their values and their religious beliefs.

A young high school teacher named John Scopes deliberately broke the law against teaching evolution so that a trial could test its legality. Scopes acted with the support of the American Civil Liberties Union (ACLU). During the sweltering summer of 1925, the nation followed day-to-day developments in the Scopes trial with great interest. More than 100 journalists from around the country descended on Dayton, Tennessee, to report on the trial.

Two famous lawyers took opposing sides in the trial. William Jennings Bryan, Democratic candidate for president in 1896, 1900, and 1908 and a strong opponent of evolution, led the prosecution. Clarence Darrow, who had defended many radicals and labor union members, spoke for Scopes.

Although Scopes was convicted of breaking the law and fined $100, the fundamentalists lost the larger battle. Darrow's defense made it appear that Bryan wanted to impose his religious beliefs on the entire nation. The Tennessee Supreme Court overturned Scopes's conviction.

The Scopes case may have dealt a blow to fundamentalism, but the movement continued to thrive. Rural people, especially in the South and Midwest, remained faithful to their religious beliefs. When large numbers of farmers migrated to cities during the 1920s, they brought fundamentalism with them.

Reading Check **Analyzing** How did new laws limit immigration?

W **Writing Support**

Narrative Writing Ask students to take the role of a witness at the Scopes trial. Ask each student to prepare a one-paragraph statement in which he or she supports or criticizes Mr. Scopes's teaching of evolution. **OL**

S **Skill Practice**

Using Geography Skills Ask students to draw a rough outline of the United States on a piece of paper. Have them shade the areas of the country in which fundamentalist beliefs predominated in the 1920s. *(Students should shade in the South and Midwest.)* **BL**

Education in the 1920s

Critical Thinking Answer

Answers might include overcrowded classrooms, huge schools, and lack of school supplies.

Reading Check **Answer:** created a quota system that linked the number of immigrants permitted from a particular country to a percentage of those already in the United States based on the 1890 census; excluded Japanese immigrants

Differentiated Instruction

Authentic Assessment Activity, p. 24

Our Society of Many Cultures

Objective: To learn about the multicultural contributions to U.S. society

Focus: Have students discuss diversity in America today.

Teach: Have students find or create graphic examples of achievements by various ethnic groups, and create a bulletin board display.

Assess: Assess the display for thoroughness, objectivity, and presentation.

Close: Ask students whether our society encourages or discourages diversity.

Differentiated Instruction Strategies

BL Have students survey their classmates to find out what countries their ancestors came from and then graphically display the results.

AL Ask students to research and write an assessment of diversity issues facing two countries.

ELL Ask students to list cultural contributions of immigrants from their native country.

R Reading Strategy

Organizing Have students fold a sheet of lined paper in half lengthwise and write "Hoover" and "Smith" at the top of each column and then summarize the qualities of each candidate. **Ask:** What qualities characterized each candidate? *(Hoover: respected, known for wise use of funds, promoted government-business cooperation, symbol of middle class, favored Prohibition, Quaker; Smith: opposed Prohibition, champion of poor and working class, Roman Catholic)* **OL**

Reading Check **Answer:** Hoover's landslide victory was due to Republican prosperity and prejudice against his Roman Catholic opponent.

Assess

Study Central™ provides summaries, interactive games, and online graphic organizers to help students review content.

Close

Discussing As a class, discuss how social changes during the 1920s affected the arts, the role of women, and minorities. **OL**

Section 4 Review

The Election of 1928

Main Idea Prosperity, prohibition, and religion were the major themes of the 1928 election.

History and You If you were choosing a president of the United States, what qualifications would you look for in a candidate? Read on to find out about the candidates who ran for president in 1928.

In 1927 President Coolidge shocked people by announcing that he would not run for a second full term. Herbert Hoover declared his candidacy for the Republican nomination.

During World War I, Hoover won respect as the head of a committee providing food relief for Europe. He showed such a gift in this role that "to Hooverize" came to mean "to economize, to save and share." Later, Hoover served Presidents Harding and Coolidge as secretary of commerce.

Hoover worked tirelessly to promote cooperation between government and business. A symbol of the forward-looking middle class, he easily won the Republican nomination. Because he favored a ban on sales of alcohol, Hoover was considered the "dry" candidate.

The Democrats chose a far different kind of frontrunner—Alfred E. Smith, governor of New York. The son of immigrants and a man of the city, Smith opposed Prohibition and championed the poor and the working class. As the first Roman Catholic nominee for president, Smith was the target of anti-Catholic feeling. Many Protestants feared that the Catholic Church financed the Democrats and would rule the United States if Smith got into the White House. These attacks embarrassed Hoover, a Protestant Quaker, and he tried to stop them, but the charges seriously damaged Smith's candidacy.

Smith's bigger problem, however, was the prosperity of the 1920s, for which the Republicans took credit. Hoover won the election by a landslide due to the Republican prosperity and the religious prejudice against Smith. The contest reflected many of the tensions in American society—rural versus urban life, nativism versus foreign influences, "wets" versus "drys," Protestants versus Catholics, and traditional values versus modern values.

Reading Check **Identifying** Why was Hoover elected president by a landslide in 1928?

Study Central™ To review this section, go to glencoe.com.

Section 4 Review

Vocabulary

1. Write a sentence to explain each term: flapper, mass media, device, enormous, expatriate, Prohibition, nativism, quota system, evolution.

Main Ideas

2. **Summarizing** What forms of art and entertainment became popular during the 1920s?

3. **Describing** What did reformers hope to accomplish with Prohibition in the 1920s?

4. **Explaining** How did the politics of the election of 1928 reflect the social changes of the 1920s?

Critical Thinking

5. **Identifying** On a diagram like the one below, identify some direct results of nativism in America in the 1920s.

Nativism	

6. **Persuasive Writing** You are running for governor of your state in 1928. Write a campaign speech on the issues that will persuade your audience to vote for you.

Answer the Essential Question

7. How did social change affect the arts, the role of women, and minorities?

Answers

1. Sentences should define each of the vocabulary words.
2. newspapers, radio, magazines, phonographs, movies, jazz, sports events, board games, crossword puzzles, contests
3. Reformers hoped to benefit society by outlawing alcohol consumption, which they felt was harmful to individuals and society.
4. Issues in the election reflected social tensions such as rural versus urban life, nativism versus foreign influences, Prohibition, Protestants versus Catholics, and traditional versus modern values.
5. revival of Ku Klux Klan, Emergency Quota Act, National Origins Act
6. Campaign speeches should reflect an understanding of the issues in the 1928 election.
7. In the arts, more leisure time encouraged the growth of entertainment industries and the development of mass media. Increased participation of African Americans influenced the development of jazz and inspired the Harlem Renaissance. The clash of traditional and modern values spurred expatriate writers and criticism of American culture. Women gained the right to vote and new freedoms, so more worked outside the home and in the professions. Minorities experienced continued racial prejudice.

Visual Summary

Economic Change

Business Innovation
- Mass production reduces prices
- New technology leads to new industries
- New consumer goods fuel a manufacturing boom

Government's Role
- Little interference with business
- Cut government spending and debt
- High tariffs

Consumer Society
- Demand for product grows
- Installment buying boosts consumer spending
- Mass advertising

Effect: Prosperity for Some
The growth of new, urban industries fueled an economic boom during the 1920s. For the most part, farmers and minorities did not share in the prosperity.

Charles Lindbergh

The 1920s was the age of the automobile.

Cultural and Social Change

Time of Turmoil
- Fear of communism grows
- Labor strikes occur
- Racial tension grows

The Jazz Age
- Women gain the right to vote
- The Harlem Renaissance reflects a new spirit of pride and protest
- Art, literature, and popular culture reflect the modern age

Points of Conflict
- The Eighteenth Amendment establishes Prohibition
- The Twenty-first Amendment repeals Prohibition
- Nativism helps revive the Ku Klux Klan
- Congress passes quota laws to limit immigration
- Many fear the nation is losing its traditional values

Effect: A Clash of Values
Major social and cultural achievements took place during the 1920s. For many Americans, however, these changes meant a loss of important traditional values.

Police confiscate literature

STUDY TO GO Study anywhere, anytime! Download quizzes and flash cards to your PDA from glencoe.com.

The Jazz Age **Chapter 24** **765**

Visual Summary

Making Connections Ask: How were the fears of communism, racial tension, and labor strikes related? *(People who feared the influence of communism believed that labor unrest was spurred by the Bolsheviks. Membership in labor unions declined, in part because of this perceived radicalism, and strikes became less common. In the North, increased job competition from newly arrived African Americans caused both tension between races and further labor unrest.)* **OL**

Discussing After World War I, many people feared that America was losing its traditional values. **Ask:** What American institutions and values were endangered in the 1920s? Which institutions and values do some people feel may be breaking down today? Organize students into small groups. Half of the groups should examine the chapter to answer the first question, and the other groups should conduct research to suggest answers to the second question. Discuss the groups' answers. **OL**

Hands-On Chapter Project
Step 5: Wrap-Up

Creating a Political Advertisement

Step 5: Presenting the Political Advertisements and Voting on the Candidates

Directions Have each group present its candidate, platform, slogan, and political advertisement to the class. The ads may be prerecorded or be presented live. Students should display magazine and newspaper ads. Have the students vote on the candidate they think would be best for the country. Have each person write the selected candidate on a slip of paper. Collect the "ballots," and tally the vote. Announce the winner to the class.

Analyzing Lead a class discussion in which the students talk about the strengths and weaknesses of each campaign. **Ask:** What issues do you think were most important? Do you think the candidate won because of his or her platform or because of the quality of the advertisement? This might lead into a discussion about the quality of political advertisements today.

Focus

R Reading Strategy

Making Connections Remind your students that Hughes lived during a period of great social change. Have them refer to the textbook and discuss what events might have influenced Hughes's determination to write about his African American experience. *(Students may discuss the Harlem Renaissance when writers tried to present the African American experience or the repression of African Americans during slavery.)* **OL**

C Critical Thinking

Analyzing Primary Sources Ask: What did Hughes mean when he said: "express our individual dark-skinned selves without fear or shame"? *(Many people did not know anything about the heritage of African Americans, but by telling their stories, they were able to reach others through their experiences.)* **OL**

Additional Reading

Review suggested books before assigning them.

America's LITERATURE

Meet the Author

R Langston Hughes (1902–1967) lived during a time of great racial turmoil in the United States. His grandmother raised him in Lawrence, Kansas, until he was a young teen. When she died, he lived with his grandmother's friends and then eventually with his mother in Ohio. Throughout his childhood, he turned to books to ease his loneliness.

Building Background

C Hughes wrote poetry as a teenager, publishing "The Negro Speaks of Rivers" when he was 17 years old. That poem, along with "Mother to Son," exemplifies the pride Hughes had in his African American heritage. Hughes declared, "We younger Negro artists who create now intend to express our individual dark-skinned selves without fear or shame." As you read his poems, pay attention to how he uses words and symbols to relate the experiences of African Americans.

Vocabulary

dawns days

bosom chest

dusky dark

▲ "Jacobia Hotel" by William H. Johnson typifies the art of the Harlem Renaissance.

Fiction: *Tulsa Burning,* by Anna Myers, tells the story of Nobel Chase and his mother in Wekiwa, Oklahoma, in 1921. It is a year of change for Nobel as racial unrest grows in the dust bowl, and he and his mother must give up their farm.

Fiction: *Code Talker: A Novel About the Navajo Marines of World War II,* by Joseph Bruchac, follows Navajo Ned Begay to an American boarding school and then to the U.S. Marines where he becomes one of the World War II "code talkers."

Nonfiction: *Flying Higher: The Women Airforce Service Pilots of World War II,* by Wanda Langley, uncovers the history of the Women Airforce Service Pilots (WASPs). They tested new planes, transported materials, and faced danger and prejudice.

For further reading, see **BOOKLINK 3**.

THE NEGRO SPEAKS OF RIVERS

Langston Hughes

I've known rivers:
I've known rivers ancient as the world and older than the
    flow of human blood in human veins.

My soul has grown deep like the rivers.

I bathed in the Euphrates when **dawns** were young.
I built my hut near the Congo and it lulled me to sleep.
I looked upon the Nile and raised the pyramids above it.
I heard the singing of the Mississippi when Abe Lincoln
    went down to New Orleans, and I've seen its muddy
    bosom turn all golden in the sunset.

S

I've known rivers:
Ancient, **dusky** rivers.

My soul has grown deep like the rivers.

MOTHER TO SON

Langston Hughes

Well, son, I'll tell you:
Life for me ain't been no crystal stair.
It's had tacks in it,
And splinters,
And boards torn up,
And places with no carpet on the floor—
Bare.
But all the time
I'se been a-climbin' on,
And reachin' landin's,
And turnin' corners,
And sometimes goin' in the dark
Where there ain't been no light.
So boy, don't you turn back.
Don't you set down on the steps
'Cause you finds it's kinder hard.
Don't you fall now—
For I'se still goin', honey,
I'se still climbin',
And life for me ain't been no crystal stair.

Analyzing Literature

1. **Respond**
   (a) What is your impression about the lives of African Americans based on these poems?
   (b) What words and phrases in the poems give you that impression?

2. **Recall and Analyze**
   (a) What rivers does Hughes discuss in "The Negro Speaks of Rivers"?
   (b) How does Hughes use the rivers as a symbol for the African American experience?

3. **Evaluate** In what ways are the poems similar? How are they different?

Teach

S Skill Practice

Using Geography Skills Using a globe or world map, have students locate the rivers Hughes mentions in "The Negro Speaks of Rivers." Ask them what geographic locations would describe their—and their ancestors'—experiences. **AL**

Assess/Close

Have students read "The Negro Speaks of Rivers" aloud. Discuss the cadence, or rhythm, of the poem. Point out how the words flow like a river. Now have them read "Mother to Son" aloud. Note that the words and rhythm do not flow as smoothly. Ask them if the mother has quit because life has been hard. **Ask: Does she expect her son to quit when things become difficult?**

Answers

1. (a) Possible answer: Their lives were difficult.
   (b) Possible answers: "Life for me ain't been no crystal stair," "tacks," and "Bare"

2. (a) Euphrates, Congo, Nile, Mississippi
   (b) Hughes uses the rivers as benchmarks in African American history and also compares the speaker's soul to the rivers to show that African Americans have become stronger because of their experiences.

3. Possible answers: Each poem addresses the theme of a people's hardships. The voice varies; "The Negro Speaks of Rivers" uses a more academic voice, and "Mother to Son" uses a more conversational voice.

Answers and Analyses
Reviewing Main Ideas

1. D The government pressured workers not to join unions, which they linked with radicalism. Students should eliminate choices A and C because rising prices and unchanged wages would have encouraged their union participation. **16.C.3c (US)**

2. C Coolidge and Congress supported business. Students should eliminate choice A because the Ohio Gang is associated with President Harding. Coolidge overturned laws regulating child labor and women's wages, so students should also eliminate choices B and D. **16.C.3c (US)**

3. D Students might be tempted to answer C, because Ford's introduction of the assembly line was important. However, it was price decreases that encouraged sales. Ford kept his workers happy by increasing wages rather than establishing labor unions, so choice B can be eliminated by reading the text. **15.A.3a**

4. A Jazz is the only one of the choices that came out of the African American culture of the 1920s. **18.C.3b**

Short-Answer Question

5. Before students read the excerpt, have them find dictionary definitions for *assimilation, assimilated,* and *socket.* They should then understand that the writer is prejudiced against immigrants from central and southeastern Europe. The writer criticizes them for their refusal to conform to American life and their low standard of living. In terms of chapter concepts, the writer displays nativism. **18.B.3a**

TEST-TAKING **TIP**

> If you are stuck on a question, temporarily skip it. Return to the question once you have answered those you are sure about. Come back to the question, and if you are still unsure, take a guess.

Reviewing Main Ideas

Directions: Choose the best answer for each of the following questions.

1. What contributed to the sharp drop in labor union membership in the 1920s?

  A rising prices

  B racial tensions

  C unchanged wages

  D government pressure

2. Who prospered under Coolidge and his Republican-controlled Congress?

  A the Ohio Gang

  B female workers

  C business interests

  D American children

3. Ford increased the sales of his automobiles by

  A building new highways.

  B establishing labor unions in his factories.

  C introducing the assembly line.

  D steadily dropping the price of the Model T.

4. A form of 1920s entertainment that was rooted in African American culture is

  A jazz.

  B movies.

  C football.

  D speakeasies.

Short-Answer Question

Directions: Base your answer to question 5 on the excerpt below and on your knowledge of social studies.

> An ostrich could assimilate a croquet ball or a cobble-stone with about the same ease that America assimilated her newcomers from Central and South-eastern Europe. Most of them seem to have been inoculated [vaccinated] against assimilation before leaving home. Their standard of living in their home countries was as low as any standard of living could possibly be. If it had been any lower, it would have ceased to be a standard, and would have become a hole or socket.
>
> —from *Why Europe Leaves Home*

5. What ideas about immigration are expressed in the above statement?

Review the Essential Questions

6. Essay How did changes after World War I affect American life?

To help you write your essay, review your answers to the Essential Questions in the section review and the chapter Foldables Study Organizer. Your essay should include:

- examples illustrating fear of immigrants and persecution of unions;
- evidence of American support for business and the policy of isolationism;
- factors that led to economic growth;
- changes in the arts; and
- new roles for women and minorities.

GO ON ➡️

Review the Essential Questions

6. Students should use their answers to the Essential Questions and their Foldables to describe how changes after World War I affected American life. Essays should describe nativism, labor strife, government support for business, the popularity of isolationism, changes in technology and transportation modes, the arts, and the roles of women and minorities. **18.A.3**

History ONLINE
For additional test practice, use **Self-Check Quizzes**—Chapter 24 at glencoe.com.

Chapter 24 Assessment

Document-Based Questions

Directions: Analyze the documents and answer the short-answer questions that follow.

Document 1

This excerpt, from a 1920 memoir by Evalyn McLean, talks about the kinds of friendships Warren G. Harding developed during his presidency.

> Unhappily, for many persons [Harding] had become something other than a friend; he was to all of these no less a thing than Opportunity.

Source: Henry Steele Commager, *Witness to America*

7. Based on this document, cite one reason that Harding's administration ended in scandal.

Document 2

First Lady Grace Coolidge describes her role.

> We New England women cling to the old way and being the President's wife isn't going to make me think less about the domestic duties I've always loved.

Source: Carl Sferrazza Anthony, *First Ladies: The Saga of Presidents' Wives and Their Power, 1789–1961*

8. Based on the document, did Grace Coolidge view herself as a liberated woman of the 1920s?

Document 3

This excerpt from *A Farewell to Arms* describes the Italian front during World War I.

> At the start of the winter came the permanent rain and with the rain came the cholera. But it was checked and in the end only seven thousand died of it in the army.

Source: Ernest Hemingway

9. How would you describe the mood of the speaker in Hemingway's story?

Document 4

This political cartoon shows President Coolidge making music while big business dances.

Source: Picture Research Consultants

10. Based on this cartoon, explain the relationship between government and business during the 1920s.

11. Persuasive Writing Using the information from the five documents and your knowledge of social studies, write an essay in which you:
- summarize the needs and goals of most Americans after World War I; and
- convince readers that Harding, Coolidge, and Hoover represented/did not represent most Americans.

8. The excerpt makes it clear that Grace Coolidge did not see herself as liberated. Hints are her description of herself clinging to old ways and loving domestic duties—activities against which some women of her time rebelled. **18.B.3a**

9. Students might answer that the speaker seems resigned, detached, weary, and sarcastic ("*only* seven thousand died"). **16.A.3b**

10. The cartoon shows Big Business (as an unusually large flapper) and government (as a well-dressed musician) dancing. In other words, the two are friends and depend on each other for a good time. **16.C.3b (US)**

11. Students' essays might describe the needs and goals of the majority of Americans in the 1920s as a desire for normalcy, comfort, and peace. In explaining how the three presidents did or did not represent those needs and goals, students might include the idea that government and many Americans were willing to curtail the rights and opportunities of workers and immigrants to ensure order and prosperity. Arguments also address the presidents' relationships with business, the role of isolationism, and the lack of government aid to individuals who suffered due to the economic boom. **18.B**

History ONLINE
Have students visit the Web site at glencoe.com to review Chapter 24 and take the Self-Check Quiz.

Need Extra Help?

If you missed questions. . .	1	2	3	4	5	6	7	8	9	10	11
Go to page. . .	747	752	756–757	760	762–763	754–764	751	752	761	752	745–753

Document-Based Questions

7. In the passage "he was to all of these no less a thing than Opportunity," ask students what "all of these" refers to. If they understand that the phrase refers to the people Harding considered friends, they will grasp that the author is saying that people supported Harding only to further their own goals. When Harding appointed people to government positions on the basis of friendship rather than merit or character, it was more likely that people would take advantage of him. **16.A.3b**

Need Extra Help?

Have students refer to the pages listed if they miss any of the questions.

Chapter Planning Guide

25

Levels					Resources	Chapter Opener	Section 1	Section 2	Section 3	Section 4	Chapter Assess
BL	OL	AL	ELL								
FOCUS											
BL	OL	AL	ELL	📇	**Daily Test Practice Transparencies**		25–1	25–2	25–3	25–4	
TEACH											
	OL	AL		📁	**Geography and History Activity, URB**			p. 59			
BL	OL		ELL	📁	**Time Line Skills Activity, URB**					p. 62	
BL	OL	AL	ELL	📁	**Writing Skills Activity, URB**			p. 51			
BL	OL	AL	ELL	📁	**Content Vocabulary Activity, URB**		p. 45	p. 45	p. 45	p. 45	
BL			ELL	📁	**Academic Vocabulary Activity, URB**		p. 47	p. 47	p. 47	p. 47	
BL			ELL	📁	**Social Studies Skills Activity, URB**		p. 53				
BL	OL	AL	ELL	📁	**Differentiated Instruction Activity, URB**					p. 55	
BL	OL	AL	ELL	📁	**Critical Thinking Skills Activity, URB**			p. 57			
BL	OL	AL	ELL	📁	**Linking Past and Present Activity, URB**					p. 61	
	OL	AL		📁	**Primary Source Readings, URB**				p. 49		
BL	OL	AL	ELL	📁	**School-to-Home Connection Activity, URB**		p. 63	p. 63	p. 63	p. 63	
BL	OL		ELL	📁	**Guided Reading Activity, URB***		p. 67	p. 68	p. 69	p. 70	
	OL	AL		📁	**Economics and History Activity, URB**		p. 5				
BL	OL		ELL	📁	**Reading Essentials and Note-Taking Guide***		p. 274	p. 277	p. 280	p. 283	
BL	OL	AL	ELL	📇	**Lesson Transparencies**		25A	25B		25C	
	OL	AL		📁	**Interpreting Political Cartoons, URB**			p. 13			
		AL		📁	**Supreme Court Case Studies**				pp. 45, 51	p. 53	
	OL			📁	**American Biographies**				p. 57		
BL	OL	AL	ELL	📁	**Outline Map Resource Book**	pp. 6, 24, 40					
	OL	AL		📇	**American Art and Architecture Transparencies, Strategies, and Activities**				30, 32		

Note: Please refer to the *Unit Resource Book: Change and Conflict* for this chapter's URB materials.

* Also available in Spanish

Levels					Resources	Chapter Opener	Section 1	Section 2	Section 3	Section 4	Chapter Assess
BL	OL	AL	ELL								
	TEACH *(continued)*
BL	OL	AL	ELL	📁	NGS US Desk Map		✓	✓	✓	✓	
BL	OL	AL	ELL	📁	American Literature Library		✓	✓	✓	✓	
BL	OL	AL	ELL	📁	Writer's Guidebook		✓	✓	✓	✓	
	OL	AL		💿	American History Primary Source Document Library CD-ROM		✓	✓	✓	✓	✓
BL	OL	AL	ELL	💿	American Music: Hits Through History	✓	✓	✓	✓	✓	
BL	OL	AL	ELL	💿	StudentWorks™ Plus CD	✓	✓	✓	✓	✓	✓
BL	OL	AL	ELL	🔒	Section Spotlight Videos		✓	✓	✓	✓	
BL	OL	AL	ELL	🖨	Writing Process Transparencies		✓	✓	✓	✓	✓
BL	OL	AL	ELL	💿	Presentation Plus! With MindJogger CheckPoint CD	✓	✓	✓	✓	✓	✓
	ASSESS
BL	OL	AL	ELL	📁	Quizzes and Tests		p. 245	p. 246	p. 247	p. 248	p. 249, 251, 253
BL	OL	AL	ELL	📁	Authentic Assessment With Rubrics				p. 25		
BL	OL	AL	ELL	📁	Standardized Test Practice						p. 49
BL	OL	AL	ELL	💿	*ExamView®* Assessment Suite CD-ROM*		25–1	25–2	25–3	25–4	Ch. 25
	CLOSE
BL			ELL	📁	Reteaching Activity, URB*		p. 65	p. 65	p. 65	p. 65	p. 65
BL	OL		ELL	📁	Reading and Study Skills Foldables Activity	p. 98	p. 98	p. 98	p. 98	p. 98	p. 98
BL	OL	AL	ELL	📁	*The American Journey* in Graphic Novel						p. 147
BL			ELL	📁	Reading Strategies and Activities for the Social Studies Classroom		✓	✓	✓	✓	
BL	OL	AL	ELL	🖨	Graphic Organizer Transparencies & Strategies		✓	✓	✓	✓	

Teacher Works *Plus*
All-In-One Planner and Resource Center

- Interactive Lesson Planner
- Interactive Teacher Edition
- Fully editable blackline masters
- Section Spotlight Videos Launch

- Differentiated Lesson Plans
- Printable reports of daily assignments
- Standards Tracking System

Professional Development Resources

- Strategies for Success
- Building Academic Vocabulary
- Success With English Learners DVD
- Differentiated Instruction Strategies DVD
- Teaching Literacy Strategies in Social Studies DVD
- Assessment DVD
- Standards-Based Instruction DVD

Using TechCONNECT™

Teaching Internet Search Skills

Technology Product

Glencoe TechCONNECT™ is an engaging, activities-based online program that enhances comprehension of core subjects while teaching technology skills. For more information or to get a free 30-day trial of Glencoe TechCONNECT™ for your classroom, visit techconnect.glencoe.com and click the **Free Trial** button.

Objective

- Students will find credible information online and incorporate it into projects.

Steps

- To see activities correlated to this textbook, log on to TechCONNECT™ and click the **Find Your Textbook** link.

- You can also search for activities. After you log on, click **Activity Search**. Choose **Social Studies, Web Browsers,** and **your grade level**.
- Students can also log on and enter the letters AC and the three-digit activity number.
- Have students read each page of the activity and follow the on-screen instructions.
- Have students complete the activity's self-assessment rubric or complete the activity's TechCheck, a five-question, multiple-choice quiz.
- Review this activity with the class.

History ONLINE at glencoe.com

	Student	Teacher	Parent
Media Center			
• Student Edition Audio	●		
• Spanish Summaries	●		
• Section Spotlight Videos	●	●	
Social Studies Online Learning Center			
Classroom Tools			
• Multi-Language Glossaries	●	●	●
• Teaching Today		●	
• TIME Current Events	●	●	●
• Beyond the Textbook	●	●	
***The American Journey* Online Learning Center**			
• Study-to-Go™	●	●	●
• Study Central™	●	●	●
• Chapter Overview	●	●	
• Concepts in Motion	●	●	
• ePuzzles and Games	●	●	
• Literature Connections	●	●	
• Online Student Edition	●	●	●
• Self-Check Quizzes	●	●	●
• Student Web Activities	●	●	
• Vocabulary eFlashcards	●	●	
• Web Activity Lesson Plans	●	●	●
• Vocabulary PuzzleMaker	●	●	●

- **Timed Readings Plus in Social Studies** helps students increase their reading rate and fluency while maintaining comprehension. The 400-word passages are similar to those found on state and national assessments.

- **Reading in the Content Area: Social Studies** concentrates on six essential reading skills that help students better comprehend what they read. The book includes 75 high-interest nonfiction passages written at increasing levels of difficulty.

- **Reading Social Studies** includes strategic reading instruction and vocabulary support in Social Studies content for ELLs and native speakers of English.

- **Content Vocabulary Workout** (Grades 6–8) accelerates reading comprehension through focused vocabulary development. Social Studies content vocabulary comes from the glossaries of Glencoe's Middle School Social Studies texts.

www.jamestowneducation.com

Index to National Geographic Magazine:

The following article relates to this chapter:

- *"Great Plains,"* John G. Mitchell, May 2004.

National Geographic Society Products

To order the following, call National Geographic at 1-800-368-2728:

National Geographic Atlas of the World (Book)

Access National Geographic's dynamic MapMachine Web site and other geography resources at:

www.nationalgeographic.com

www.nationalgeographic.com/mapmachine

Use this database to search more than 30,000 titles to create a customized reading list for your students.

- Reading lists can be organized by students' reading level, author, genre, theme, or area of interest.
- The database provides Degrees of Reading Power™ (DRP) and Lexile™ readability scores for all selections.
- A brief summary of each selection is included.

Leveled reading suggestions for this chapter:

For students at a Grade 6 reading level:
- *Franklin D. Roosevelt,* Michael Burgan

For students at a Grade 7 reading level:
- *Driven From the Land: The Story of the Dust Bowl,* Milton Meltzer
- *The Dust Bowl and the Depression in American History,* Debra McArthur

For students at a Grade 8 reading level:
- *The Great Depression,* Nathaniel Harris
- *The Great Depression and the New Deal: America's Economic Collapse and Recovery,* Anne E. Schraff

For students at a Grade 9 reading level:
- *The New Freedom to the New Deal: 1913–1939,* William Loren Katz

For students at a Grade 10 reading level:
- *Voices of Protest: Huey Long, Father Coughlin, and the Great Depression,* Alan Brinkley

The following videotape programs are available from Glencoe as supplements to the chapter:

- **Norman Rockwell** (ISBN 1-56-501427-8)
- **Tennessee Valley Authority** (ISBN 0-76-700031-5)

To order, call Glencoe at 1-800-334-7344. To find classroom resources to accompany many of these videos, check the following home pages:

A&E Television: www.aetv.com

The History Channel: www.history.com

Chapter Objectives

After studying this chapter, students will be able to:

- Identify the factors that brought about the Great Depression.
- Understand how Franklin Roosevelt's leadership brought about change in the U.S. economy.
- Explain how the Great Depression affected the economic and social conditions of Americans, especially minorities.
- Discuss why some people supported Roosevelt's New Deal and why others opposed it.

Motivating Activity

Making Connections Students will learn how the Great Depression affected the economy of the United States as well as the lives of all Americans during the 1930s. Banks collapsed, people lost jobs, and many Americans sunk into poverty. The government developed many programs to address the challenges the country faced. **Ask:** What are some ways the government helps people today? *(with food stamps, unemployment, Social Security, welfare, and so on.)* As you read the chapter, discuss the different programs that Roosevelt established as part of the New Deal and how they helped Americans during the Depression.

Previewing the Essential Questions

As you begin teaching each section, use these questions and activities to help students focus on the Essential Questions.

Chapter 25
The Depression and the New Deal 1929–1939

Pickers bring baskets of produce to be weighed.

PRESIDENTS
U.S. Events
World Events

HERBERT HOOVER

FRANKLIN D. ROOSEVELT

1928   **1931**   **1934**

★ **1929** Stock market crashes

★ **1932** Bonus Marchers forced out of Washington, D.C.

★ **1930** World population reaches 2 billion

★ **1933** Hitler comes to power in Germany

Section 1

The Great Depression Ask: What factors brought about the Great Depression? *(During the 1920s, farm income shrank, industries declined, unemployment grew, large gap developed between very rich and everyone else, credit crisis led to loan defaults, stock market crashed in 1929.)* Point out to students that in Section 1 they will learn about the factors that led to the Great Depression. **OL**

Section 2

Roosevelt's New Deal Ask: How did Franklin Roosevelt's leadership bring about change in the U.S. economy? *(FDR immediately addressed the bank crisis, got Congress to pass relief legislation within the first hundred days in office, and used fireside chats to gain public confidence.)* Point out to students that Section 2 will focus on the sweeping changes made by Roosevelt to save the economy. **OL**

Section 1: The Great Depression

Essential Question What were the factors that brought about the Great Depression?

Section 2: Roosevelt's New Deal

Essential Question How did Franklin Roosevelt's leadership bring about change in the U.S. economy?

Section 3: Life During the Depression

Essential Question How did the Great Depression affect the economic and social traditions of Americans, especially minorities?

Section 4: Effects of the New Deal

Essential Question Why did some people support Roosevelt's New Deal and some oppose it?

History ONLINE
Chapter Overview Visit glencoe.com and click on **Chapter 25—Chapter Overviews** to preview chapter information.

FOLDABLES Study Organizer

Organizing Information Make this Foldable and use it to help you study the chapter vocabulary.

Step 1 Use quarter sheets of binder paper. Fold the sheets in half.

Step 2 Cut a tab along the left side of each sheet.

Step 3 Staple the multiple sections together on the left side. Record the term on the front of each tab.

Step 4 Record the definitions and examples under each tab.

Relief

Reading and Writing Use this Foldable as a self-checking vocabulary study aid by reading the word on the front of the tab, mentally defining the word, and then looking under the tab to check your response.

aid for the needy

Time Line Activity

If you have not already done so, have students review the time line. **Ask:** How many years does this chapter cover? *(12)* Have students identify an event that might have unified Americans by making them feel pride in their country. *(Students may mention that Jesse Owens won Olympic gold medals.)* What major world event came at the end of this period? *(World War II began in 1939.)*

FOLDABLES Study Organizer **Dinah Zike's Foldables**

Purpose This Foldable will help students identify the major events and programs of the Great Depression. The completed Foldable will help them prepare for assessment.

☞ More Foldables activities for this chapter can be found in the *Dinah Zike's Reading and Study Skills Foldables.*

History ONLINE

Introduce students to chapter content and key terms by having them access the **Chapter Overview** at glencoe.com.

★ **1935** Social Security Act passes

★ **1937** Court-packing bill defeated

★ **1938** Fair Labor Standards Act passes

1937

1940

★ **1936** American Jesse Owens wins four gold medals at Berlin Olympic Games

★ **1939** World War II begins

Chapter 25 **771**

Section 3

Life During the Depression Ask: How did the Great Depression affect the economic and social conditions of Americans? *(Many Americans lost their jobs, land, and other property; more women entered the workforce; people moved away from home in search of work.)* Tell students that Section 3 will explore the impact of the Depression on the American people. **OL**

Section 4

Effects of the New Deal Ask: Why did some people support Roosevelt's New Deal? *(Needy Americans, jobless workers, and labor unions supported the New Deal because they believed it helped them.)* Explain to students that in Section 4, they will learn more about those who supported and opposed the New Deal. **OL**

Focus

Bellringer
Daily Test Practice Transparency 25–1

Reading Guide
Answers to Graphic:

Late September 1929: investors began selling off their stocks; stock prices fell; margin investors were forced to sell, causing prices to decline steadily; **October 21–23:** stock prices plunged as millions of shares were sold daily; **Oct. 24:** "Black Thursday," almost 13 million shares were sold; **Oct. 25–28:** four days of calm; **Oct. 29:** more than 16 million shares were sold and stock prices plummeted; the New York Stock Exchange closed for several days

Section Spotlight Video

Have students watch the Section Spotlight Video "The Great Depression" to learn more about the Bonus Army riots.

Resource Manager

Section 1

Essential Question ◄
What were the factors that brought about the Great Depression?

Reading Guide

Content Vocabulary

stock exchange (p. 773) relief (p. 776)

default (p. 775) public works (p. 777)

Academic Vocabulary

decline (p. 774) collapse (p. 775)

Key People and Events
"Black Thursday" (p. 774)
Great Depression (p. 774)
Hooverville (p. 776)
Bonus Army (p. 777)

Reading Strategy

Taking Notes Re-create a time line like the one below to record the events that happened in September and October of 1929 that led to the stock market crash.

ILLINOIS STANDARDS
The American Journey

15.A.3d Describe the causes of unemployment (e.g., seasonal fluctuation in demand, changing jobs, changing skill requirements, national spending).

15.D.3a Explain the effects of increasing and declining imports and exports to an individual and to the nation's economy as a whole.

16.C.3c (US) Describe how economic developments and government policies after 1865 affected the country's economic institutions including corporations, banks and organized labor.

The Great Depression

American Diary

The crash of the American stock market in 1929 sent shock waves through the country. Almost overnight, the country suffered financial disaster. Many people lost their savings, homes, and jobs. In 1932 humorist Will Rogers remarked: "We'll hold the distinction of being the only Nation in the history of the world that ever went to the poor house in an automobile."

—from the Will Rogers Memorial Archives

$100. WILL BUY THIS CAR. MUST HAVE CASH. LOST ALL ON THE STOCK MARKET

For many, the stock market crash of 1929 meant bankruptcy.

R Reading Strategies	C Critical Thinking	D Differentiated Instruction	W Writing Support	S Skill Practice
Teacher Edition • Read. Pri. Sources, p. 774 • Using Context Clues, p. 775 **Additional Resources** • Guid. Read., URB p. 67 • Cont. Vocab., URB p. 45 • Ac. Vocab., URB p. 47 • Read. Ess., p. 274	**Teacher Edition** • Determin. Cause & Effect, p. 775 **Additional Resources** • Econ. & Hist., URB p. 5 • Quizzes and Tests, p. 245	**Teacher Edition** • English Learners, p. 774 • Logical/Math., p. 774 **Additional Resources** • School-to-Home, URB p. 63 • Reteaching Act., URB p. 65	**Teacher Edition** • Expository Writing, p. 773 • Narrative Writing, p. 777	**Teacher Edition** • Visual Literacy, p. 776 **Additional Resources** • Daily Test Pract. Transp. 25-1 • Soc. Stud. Skills, URB p. 53 • Lesson Transp. 25A

The Stock Market

Main Idea The stock market crash of 1929 signaled an end to the prosperity of the 1920s.

History and You You have probably heard statements on the news about the ups and downs of the stock market. Read to find out how a stock market collapse in 1929 ushered in the worst economic crisis in United States history.

In the booming economy of the 1920s, confident business and government leaders said the nation had entered a new era of prosperity for all. The chair of General Motors advised people to invest money in the stock market every month—and many followed his advice. "Grocers, motormen, plumbers, seamstresses, and . . . waiters were in the market," reported writer Frederick Lewis Allen. The "market had become a national mania." Everyone, it seemed, was trying to get rich quickly.

Suddenly, in October 1929, everything changed. Almost overnight the value of stocks plunged. Millionaires lost fortunes, and thousands of less wealthy investors lost their savings. The stock market had crashed. The nation was about to enter its worst domestic crisis since the Civil War.

The Boom

A **stock exchange** is an organized system for buying and selling shares, or blocks of investments, in corporations. In the late 1920s, the value of stocks on the New York Stock Exchange climbed to dizzying heights. This long period of rising stock prices convinced many to invest heavily in stock. By 1929, 3 to 4 million Americans, or roughly 10 percent of all households, owned stocks.

Because many investors lacked the money to continue purchasing stock, they bought on margin. This means they paid only a fraction of the stock price and borrowed the rest from their brokers. Brokers, in turn, borrowed their money from banks. As long as the value of stocks continued to rise, the buyer could sell later, pay back what was borrowed, and make a profit. If that value fell, though, investors and brokers would not have enough cash to pay off the loans.

The Crash

Fearing that the boom market would end, some investors began selling their stocks in late September. These sales made stock prices fall. Brokers began to demand repayment of loans, forcing investors who had bought on margin to sell their stock.

By the Numbers | Looking for Jobs

No Work Following the stock market crash, many Americans wanted to work but could not find jobs.

- Total available to work
- Total employed

Number of workers* (in thousands) — Years: 1929, 1930, 1931, 1932, 1933

*14 years and older   **Source:** Statistical Abstract of the United States

Critical Thinking

Analyzing What do the employment figures show about the financial health of America at this time?

Teach

W Writing Support

Expository Writing Discuss the events and fears brought about by the stock market crash of 1929. Explain one factor that accelerated the stock market crash of 1929 and one factor that made the economic effects felt by a wide sector of the American population. **OL**

By the Numbers

Critical Thinking Answer
The sharp decline in employment would limit cash flow in the U.S. economy; increased competition for jobs might recur because the number of people available to work increased during this period.

Skills Practice
Ask: Between 1929 and 1932, about how many jobs were lost? *(9 million)* How many people were available to work in 1929? *(49 million)* In 1933? *(52 million)* How many people were available but unemployed in 1933? *(13 million)* **OL**

Differentiated Instruction

Leveled Activities

BL Guided Reading, URB p. 67

OL Social Studies Skills, URB p. 53

ELL Content Vocabulary, URB p. 45

Prices **declined**, or dropped, steadily until October 21, but most experts thought there was no need to worry. Then, for three straight days, stock prices plunged as investors sold millions of shares each day. Panicked traders sold almost 13 million shares on October 24, a day that became known as **"Black Thursday."** Following a few days of calm, the crisis worsened. On Tuesday, October 29, more than 16 million shares changed hands and stock prices plummeted. Journalist Jonathan Norton Leonard described the scene:

PRIMARY SOURCE

"The selling pressure was . . . coming from everywhere. The wires to other cities were jammed with frantic orders to sell. So were the cables, radio, and telephones to Europe and the rest of the world."
—from *Ordinary Americans*

The New York Stock Exchange closed for a few days to prevent more panic selling.

✔**Reading Check** **Explaining** What is buying stock "on margin"?

The Great Depression

Main Idea The Great Depression, a worldwide economic slump, brought hardship to many Americans during the 1930s.

History and You If you were penniless and homeless, how would you try to survive? Read to find out how many Americans coped with the challenges of living through the Great Depression.

During the next two years, the nation slid into a severe economic crisis called the **Great Depression.** Total economic output dropped from $104 billion in 1929 to $58 billion in 1932. While the stock market crash shook confidence in the economy, it did not cause the Depression. Other factors, working together, sent the economy into a tailspin.

An Unbalanced Economy

The problems that led to the Great Depression began to surface in the early 1920s. Farm income shrank throughout the decade. Industries also declined.

Primary Source | **Surviving the Depression**

Hard Times During the Depression, the feelings of helplessness grew as the number of jobs dwindled and debts mounted. For many, surviving became a daily struggle.

Some people had little or no money to buy groceries. Some stores offered credit. In small farm towns, customers sometimes traded goods for groceries.

◄ Clerk and customer in small grocery store

Oklahoma shanty, 1939 ▼

A North Carolina woman hoped that a job for her husband meant better times lay ahead. *"After he gets his first pay check, we can get along. But we haven't had anything in the house to eat for a week now but two messes of flour and a peck of meal. The children has nothin' for breakfast but a biscuit or a slice of corn bread. They come home after school begging for food. But I can't give them but two meals a day."*
—from *American Life Histories*

774 **Chapter 25** *The Depression and the New Deal*

Factories began having trouble selling everything they produced. In the months before the stock market crash, the automobile and construction industries especially suffered from lagging orders. This overproduction of goods forced factory owners to slow production. Then they cut wages and laid off workers. Jobless or with reduced income, many Americans had to cut back on purchases, further reducing sales.

Another factor that fueled the Depression was the growing gap in wealth between rich people and most Americans. The prosperity of the 1920s did not help all Americans equally. In 1929 less than 1 percent of the population owned nearly one-third of the country's wealth. At the same time, about 75 percent of American families lived in poverty or on the very edge of it.

Credit Crisis

Borrowed money fueled much of the economy in the 1920s. Farmers bought land, equipment, and supplies on credit. Consumers used credit to buy cars. Investors borrowed to buy stocks. Many small banks suffered when farmers **defaulted,** or failed to meet loan payments. Large banks, which had bought stocks as an investment, suffered huge losses in the crash. These losses forced thousands of banks across the nation to close between 1930 and 1933. At that time, the government did not insure bank deposits; therefore, when banks **collapsed,** or broke down, millions of depositors lost their money.

International Depression

Other countries also had crises. One problem was the lack of loans. During the 1920s, U.S. banks made loans to stock speculators instead of lending money to foreign countries. Without these loans from U.S. banks, foreign companies purchased fewer products from American manufacturers.

Matters grew worse after Congress passed the Hawley-Smoot Tariff in 1930. A tariff is a tax on imported goods. Because goods purchased from other countries now cost more, Americans bought fewer of them. Foreign countries responded by raising their own tariffs on American products. As a result, foreign countries purchased fewer American goods.

Joblessness and Poverty

As the Depression tightened its grip on the United States, millions lost their jobs. In 1932, 25 percent of American workers were out of work. The unemployment rate remained near 20 percent throughout the decade. Workers who managed to keep their jobs worked only part-time or for reduced wages.

The newly unemployed felt devastated. New Yorker Sidney Lens, who lost his job, wrote about developing "a feeling of worthlessness—and loneliness; I began to think of myself as a freak and misfit." Some tried to earn a few cents by shining shoes or selling apples on street corners.

Long lines of hungry people snaked through the streets of the nation's cities. They waited for hours to receive a slice of bread, a cup of coffee, or a bowl of soup from soup kitchens run by local governments or charities.

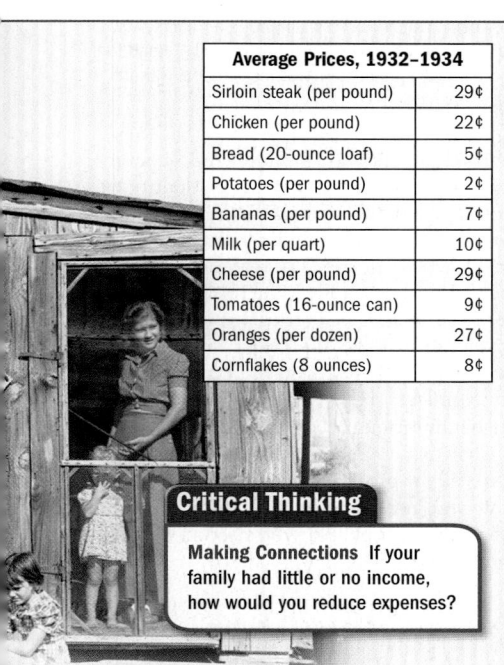

Average Prices, 1932–1934	
Sirloin steak (per pound)	29¢
Chicken (per pound)	22¢
Bread (20-ounce loaf)	5¢
Potatoes (per pound)	2¢
Bananas (per pound)	7¢
Milk (per quart)	10¢
Cheese (per pound)	29¢
Tomatoes (16-ounce can)	9¢
Oranges (per dozen)	27¢
Cornflakes (8 ounces)	8¢

Critical Thinking

Making Connections If your family had little or no income, how would you reduce expenses?

The Depression and the New Deal **Chapter 25 775**

C Critical Thinking

Determining Cause and Effect
Ask: What factor caused factory owners to slow production? *(overproduction of goods)* **OL**

R Reading Strategy

Using Context Clues Tell students that words often help identify cause-and-effect relationships. Have them focus on the international Depression on this page. **Ask:** Which words and phrases alert you to a cause-and-effect relationship? *(grew worse after, Because, responded by, As a result)* **OL**

Primary Source

Critical Thinking Answer
Students may suggest walking or bicycling instead of driving, growing vegetables at home, wearing used clothing, and so on.

Reading Charts Ask: Which item(s) is most expensive? *(steak and cheese)* Least expensive? *(potatoes)*

Additional Support

Activity: Collaborative Learning

Understanding Cause and Effect Ask: What is a vicious cycle? *(when one event causes something to get worse, which then worsens the original situation)* Tell students that they will be creating an arrangement of causes and effects that works in a vicious cycle. Organize the students into groups of three or four. Have the students research a topic from this section that contributed to America's unbalanced economy. Ask groups to list each event on a separate index card. Have groups arrange the events in such a way that they work logically in a cycle. Have groups glue the cycle events on a large sheet of paper, adding arrows to show the cycle process. For example, overproduction of goods could be where a cycle begins and ends. *(Overproduction of goods caused factory owners to slow production, cut wages, and lay off workers. Lower wages and joblessness caused many Americans to buy less, further reducing sales, which caused factory owners to further slow production, and so on.)* **OL**

S Skill Practice

Visual Literacy Ask: What can you learn about life in Shantytowns from the sentence and photographs on this page? *(Students may comment on how the houses were made of old boxes, rocks, and other found items; the people cooked outside; some might have lived outside.)* **OL**

Primary Source

Document-Based Question Answer
Students may comment that Hoovervilles were filled with people who were industrious (hardworking) and who were trying to be self-supporting.

Reading Check Answer: Tariffs raised the price of imported goods so Americans bought fewer of them. Foreign countries responded by adding tariffs to American goods, which caused them to buy fewer American goods.

Hands-On Chapter Project
Step 1

Creating a Board Game

Step 1: Planning the Game Small groups of students will design board games that explore the Great Depression.

Essential Question: What factors brought about the Great Depression?

Directions Organize students into small groups. Tell students they will create board games that will include the factors that con-

tributed to the Depression and how it affected the lives of Americans. Tell them they will design a game that requires players to move around a board and encounter positive and negative events by chance. Later, they will prepare question cards and game pieces. Have students gather historical information about banks, industries, agriculture, as well as about people who have lived during the Depression.

Primary Source / Hooverville, USA

Growing Poverty The poverty of the 1930s was most visible in the number of shantytowns that popped up across the United States. The homeless clustered together shacks made from any materials they could find, including cardboard, wood, tar paper, and tin.

A Seattle man uses bricks to hold down a tar paper roof. ▼

A family evicted from its home ▼

Jesse Jackson, an out-of-work lumberjack, talks about the tasks the people performed in a Seattle Hooverville:

"Hooverville is a colony of industrious men, the most of whom are busy trying to hold their heads up and be self-supporting and respectable. A lot of work is required in order to stay here, consequently, the lazy man does not tarry [stay] long in this place."

—from "The Story of Hooverville, In Seattle"

DBQ Document-Based Questions

Analyzing Does anything about Jesse Jackson's description surprise you? Explain.

Peggy Terry, a young girl in Oklahoma City, told how each day after school her mother sent her to the soup kitchen:

PRIMARY SOURCE

"If you happened to be one of the first ones in line, you didn't get anything but water that was on top. So we'd ask the guy that was ladling out soup into the buckets—everybody had to bring their own bucket to get the soup—he'd dip the greasy, watery stuff off the top. So we'd ask him to please dip down to get some meat and potatoes from the bottom of the kettle. But he wouldn't do it."

—from *Hard Times*, by Studs Terkel

S Families or individuals who had lost their homes built shelters out of old boxes and other debris, sometimes grouped together in pitiful "shantytowns." Some referred bitterly to the shantytowns as **Hoovervilles** because of President Hoover's failure to act. Across the country Americans wondered why the president did nothing to end the suffering.

Reading Check Describing What effect did tariffs have on imports and exports?

776 Chapter 25 *The Depression and the New Deal*

Hoover and the Crisis

Main Idea Herbert Hoover gradually involved the federal government in the economic crisis.

History and You If you ran the government, how would you fix problems in your community? Read to find out how President Hoover tried to deal with the Great Depression.

President Hoover thought the economic crisis was temporary and that prosperity was "just around the corner." He also believed that the "depression cannot be cured by legislative action or executive pronouncement." Instead, Hoover called on business leaders not to cut wages or production of goods and on charities to do their best for the needy. Voluntary action by private citizens and local governments, Hoover thought, would pull the nation through tough times.

Charities, churches, and volunteers worked heroically to provide **relief**—aid for the needy. State and local governments did as well. But the number of people who needed help was simply overwhelming.

Designing Allow time in class for students to plan their board games. Have students summarize the concepts they plan to include in a sketch. Tell them that game directions should include a way to determine a winner.

(Chapter Project continued in Section 2)

Government Action

Eventually Hoover recognized that the federal government had to take steps to combat the Depression. In 1931 he authorized additional federal spending on **public works**—projects such as highways, parks, and libraries—to create new jobs. State and local governments ran out of money, however, and the combined spending by all three levels of government declined.

In January 1932, Hoover asked Congress to create the Reconstruction Finance Corporation (RFC). The RFC lent money to businesses. It also provided funds for state and local programs. However, the RFC's directors were reluctant to make risky loans, and much of its budget remained unspent.

The Bonus Army

By 1932 Americans were growing increasingly discontented and began to take action. A march on Washington by World War I veterans turned many Americans, who were already blaming Hoover for the Depression, firmly against the president.

In 1924 Congress had agreed to give each veteran of World War I a bonus, to be distributed in 1945. Jobless veterans wanted the bonuses right away. In the summer of 1932, they formed the **Bonus Army** and marched to Washington, D.C., to demand their money. Once in Washington, the marchers camped in Hoovervilles. More veterans joined them.

When Congress voted against paying the bonus, many veterans left. About 2,000, however, vowed to remain. When the police tried to disband the veterans' camp, conflict broke out and two people were killed.

Hoover responded by calling in the army. Veterans and their families fled in terror as the troops burned their camp. Many Americans were horrified that the government had attacked its own citizens, particularly war veterans. Hoover seemed out of touch with ordinary people. Many people thought the time had come for a change in government.

✔ Reading Check **Explaining** What did the Bonus Army demand?

Section 1 Review

Vocabulary

1. Write a sentence for each of the following terms that explains its meaning: stock exchange, decline, default, collapse, relief, public works.

Main Ideas

2. **Summarizing** How did buying stocks on margin contribute to the stock market crash?

3. **Describing** What impact did the Great Depression have on employment?

4. **Explaining** How did President Hoover respond to the economic crisis?

Critical Thinking

5. **Sequencing** Re-create a flow chart like the one below to show the chain of Depression events caused by Congress agreeing to pay World War I veterans a bonus.

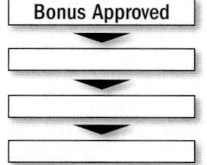

Bonus Approved

6. **Narrative Writing** You are a journalist. Write an article for your small-town newspaper that explains the stock market crash and the failure of the local bank in your community.

Answer the
Essential Question

7. What were the factors that brought about the Great Depression?

History ONLINE
Study Central™ To review this section, go to glencoe.com.

The Depression and the New Deal **Chapter 25** **777**

W Writing Support

Narrative Writing Have students write a newspaper account of the Bonus Army and its march on Washington. Articles should describe either the day two people were killed or the day troops burned the veterans' camp. **OL**

✔ Reading Check **Answer:** World War I veterans were promised a bonus to be paid in 1945. Jobless veterans wanted their bonuses right away.

Assess

History ONLINE

Study Central™ provides summaries, interactive games, and online graphic organizers to help students review content.

Close

Summarizing As a class, create a time line that illustrates factors that brought about the Great Depression and the early response by the government and U.S. citizens. **OL**

Section 1 Review

Answers

1. Students should use vocabulary words as they are defined in the section and Glossary.
2. As stock sales made prices fall, brokers demanded loan repayments from investors who had bought on margin, which forced them to sell their stock, setting off further decline.
3. Farm income and industrial production declined, causing a decline in employment, in hours worked, and in wages paid.
4. Hoover felt the government should not intervene and instead asked businesses not to cut wages or production and called on charities to provide relief. In 1931, he authorized federal spending on public works. In 1932, he had Congress create the Reconstruction Finance Corporation.
5. Bonus Army marched on Washington, D.C., to demand early payment; Congress voted against paying the bonus; police tried to disband the camp and killed two people; members of the Bonus Army burned the camp.
6. Newspaper articles should include personal and historical details.
7. Unbalanced U.S. economy, buying on margin, panic selling, overproduction, credit crisis, loan defaults, stock market crash, bank collapse

Focus

🔔 Bellringer
Daily Test Practice Transparency 25–2

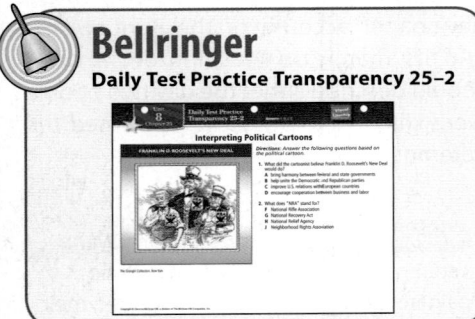

Reading Guide
Answers to Graphic:
banks, stock market, industry, agriculture, public works, relief for the poor, and conservation of resources

Section Spotlight Video

Have students watch the Section Spotlight Video "Roosevelt's New Deal" to learn more about the Hundred Days and the first New Deal.

Essential Question ◄
How did Franklin Roosevelt's leadership bring about change in the U.S. economy?

Reading Guide

Content Vocabulary
work relief (p. 781)

Academic Vocabulary
promote (p. 782)   generate (p. 782)

Key People and Events
Franklin D. Roosevelt (p. 779)
Eleanor Roosevelt (p. 779)
Hundred Days (p. 781)
New Deal (p. 781)
Tennessee Valley Authority (p. 782)

Reading Strategy
Taking Notes As you read, complete a diagram like the one below to note what areas of American life and business were affected by Roosevelt's New Deal.

Banks

New Deal

🔷 ILLINOIS STANDARDS
The American Journey

15.A.3a Explain how market prices signal producers about what, how and how much to produce.

15.A.3b Explain the relationship between productivity and wages.

15.C.3 Identify and explain the effects of various incentives to produce a good or service

15.E.3b Explain how laws and government policies (e.g., property rights, contract enforcement, standard weights/measurements) establish rules that help a market economy function effectively.

Roosevelt's New Deal

American Diary

Americans huddled around their radios on March 12, 1933, to hear newly elected president, Franklin D. Roosevelt, in his first fireside chat: "Let us unite in banishing fear. We have provided the machinery to restore our financial system, and it is up to you to support and make it work. It is your problem my friends, your problem no less than it is mine. Together we cannot fail."
In the fireside chats, Roosevelt calmly but confidently explained in simple terms the nation's problems.

Families in the 1930s gathered around the radio to hear their favorite programs.

Resource Manager

R Reading Strategies	**C** Critical Thinking	**D** Differentiated Instruction	**W** Writing Support	**S** Skill Practice
Teacher Edition • Read Prim. Sources, p. 780 • Identifying, p. 782 **Additional Resources** • Guid. Read., URB p. 68 • Cont. Vocab., URB p. 45 • Ac. Vocab., URB p. 47 • Read. Ess., p. 277	**Teacher Edition** • Mak. Infer., p. 779 • Anal. Prim. Sources, p. 781 • Drawing Con., p. 783 **Additional Resources** • Quizzes and Tests, p. 246 • Inter. Polit. Cartoons, URB p. 13 • Crit. Think. Skills, URB p. 57	**Teacher Edition** • ELL, p. 780 • Auditory/Musical, p. 781 **Additional Resources** • School-to-Home, URB p. 63 • Reteaching Act., URB p. 65	**Teacher Edition** • Persuasive Writing, p. 782 **Additional Resources** • Writ. Skills, URB p. 51	**Additional Resources** • Daily Test Pract. Transp. 25-2 • Geo. & Hist., URB p. 59 • Lesson Transp. 25B

Franklin D. Roosevelt

Main Idea Franklin D. Roosevelt promised a "new deal" to get America out of the Great Depression.

History and You If you were out of work, would you vote for someone who promised to make your life better? Read to find out about the pledge that Roosevelt made to Americans in 1932.

• •

With the nation's economy crumbling, the Democrats believed they had a good chance of winning the presidency. Meeting in Chicago in June 1932, the Democrats chose Governor **Franklin D. Roosevelt** of New York as their candidate. At the convention, Roosevelt —or FDR as he was called—told the Democrats and the nation, "I pledge you, I pledge myself, to a new deal for the American people."

The Republicans also met in Chicago and nominated President Hoover for reelection. With the country's economy worsening in 1932, Hoover's chances for being reelected seemed extremely slim. Delegates knew the Depression had turned many voters against Hoover.

Early Years of Promise

Franklin D. Roosevelt, a distant cousin of former president Theodore Roosevelt, came from a wealthy New York family. Ambitious and charming, FDR decided on a career in politics. In 1905 he married Theodore Roosevelt's niece, **Eleanor Roosevelt,** and she became a tireless partner in his public and political life.

FDR's political career began in 1910 with his election to the New York State senate. There, he was known as a forward-thinking leader who could persuade people to support his views. In 1913 Roosevelt became assistant secretary of the navy, and in 1920 the Democrats chose him as their candidate for vice president. The Democrats lost the election to Warren G. Harding, but Franklin Roosevelt's political future seemed bright.

Then in 1921 polio struck Roosevelt, paralyzing both his legs. Although there was no cure, FDR's will remained strong and he refused to give in. "Once I spent two years lying in bed trying to move my big toe," he said later. "After that, anything else seems easy."

If You Were There / America Tunes In

The Radio In the 1930s, you and your family and friends gathered around the radio for entertainment. In 1931, 2 out of every 5 families had a radio in their living rooms. By 1938, the number climbed to 4 out of 5 families. You could listen to musical shows, dramas, and comedies.

Bi-Acoustic Radio

It's "HIS MASTER'S VOICE" of the air!

RCA Victor Bi-Acoustic Radio

Radios in the United States, 1930

Percentage of families owning radios
- 50 and over
- 40–49
- 30–39
- 20–29
- 10–19
- Less than 10

PACIFIC OCEAN

ATLANTIC OCEAN

Source: U.S. Census Bureau

Critical Thinking

Interpreting How did the percentage of people who owned a radio differ in the North and in the South? What do you think was the reason for this difference?

Activity: Connecting Past and Present

Creating a Technology Time Line Tell students that the radio was an exciting new technology in the 1930s. **Ask:** What are some other technologies that entertain or communicate? (television, computers, DVDs, and so on) Have students use the Internet to search for the dates each new communication or entertainment technology was invented. Have students plot the inventions on a time line. Encourage students to include inventors' names, illustrations, or other pertinent data to enrich their work. Have students document their research with a complete list of the URL sources of their information. **OL**

Teach

• • • • • • • • • • • • • • • • • • •

C Critical Thinking

Making Inferences Ask: Considering that Hoover's inaction caused him to lose public support, what qualities might Roosevelt have needed as a candidate? *(Answers may include strong leadership, charisma, and willingness to take decisive action.)* **AL**

If You Were There

Critical Thinking Answer
Far more Northerners had radios than did Southerners. Students may suggest that the North was more industrialized and prosperous.

Skills Practice Ask: How might the radio help Roosevelt promote his ideas? *(People who had radios could hear him share his New Deal ideas.)* **OL**

Additional Support

Teacher Tip

Creating a Time Line Remind students to allow enough room for the span of years their time lines will cover. Also, make sure students leave space to add additional details for each entry.

Differentiated Instruction

R Reading Strategy

Reading Primary Sources Ask: Who was the "forgotten man"? *(people "at the bottom of the economic pyramid"; Roosevelt is referring to the many people who were poor and struggling.)* Who was Roosevelt criticizing in these quotes? *(Hoover)* **OL**

D Differentiated Instruction

English Language Learners Ask: Why did Roosevelt need to reassure Americans in the speech he gave at his inauguration? *(The economy had worsened and people were desperately afraid.)* In the second quote, which two words showed that putting people to work was important to him? *(greatest, primary)* **ELL**

✔ **Reading Check Answer:** They were a group of progressive lawyers, economists, and social workers who advised FDR as he guided the nation out of the Great Depression.

Return to Politics

After a few years, FDR decided to return to politics. He never publicly mentioned his paralyzed legs, and he asked journalists not to photograph his leg braces or wheelchair. Elected governor of New York in 1928 and reelected in 1930, Roosevelt earned a national reputation as a reformer. He drew on the advice of a group of progressive lawyers, economists, and social workers—known as the Brain Trust—to develop relief programs for the state. When he decided to run for president, he counted on the Brain Trust to help him guide the nation out of the Great Depression.

R During the 1932 campaign, Roosevelt declared that "the country needs and . . . demands bold, persistent experimentation." He also spoke of trying to help "the forgotten man at the bottom of the economic pyramid."

✔ **Reading Check Identifying** What was the Brain Trust? Why did Franklin Roosevelt rely on it?

FDR Takes Charge

Main Idea Roosevelt quickly launched programs to improve the American economy.

History and You Have you ever had to do something difficult? Who helped you gain the confidence to do it? Read to learn how Roosevelt reached out to Americans during the 1930s.

Drawn to Roosevelt's confidence, voters elected him in a landslide. Democrats also won important victories in Congress. People clearly wanted a change.

Restoring Confidence

D In the months before Roosevelt took office, the economy worsened. People became desperately afraid. At his inauguration on March 4, 1933, Roosevelt told the nation that "the only thing we have to fear is fear itself." He reassured people and pointed out that the "greatest primary task is to put people to work." He also promised immediate action to help the nation's failed banks.

Primary Source / New Deal Programs

Relief and New Jobs In about 100 days, President Roosevelt and Congress gave hope to the nation with a number of programs designed to pull Americans out of the Depression and set the country on a path to prosperity.

New Deal Program	Initials	Purpose
Civilian Conservation Corps	CCC	Provided jobs for young men to plant trees and build bridges
Tennessee Valley Authority	TVA	Built dams to provide cheap electric power to seven Southern states; set up schools and health centers
Federal Emergency Relief Administration	FERA	Gave relief to unemployed and needy
Agricultural Adjustment Administration	AAA	Paid farmers not to grow certain crops
National Recovery Administration	NRA	Helped set standards for production, prices, and wages
Public Works Administration	PWA	Built ports, schools, and aircraft carriers
Federal Deposit Insurance Corporation	FDIC	Insured savings accounts in banks approved by the government

New Deal Poster Artists created posters to publicize New Deal programs and slogans. ▶

The CCC Beginning in March 1933, the CCC offered men ages 18 to 25 the opportunity to work. ▶

Leveled Activities

Differentiated Instruction

BL Reading Essentials, p. 277

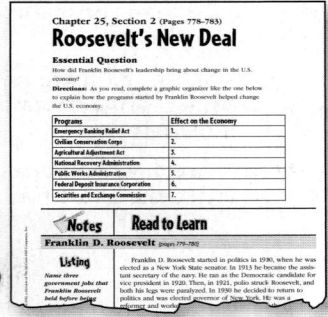

OL Interpreting Political Cartoons, URB p. 13

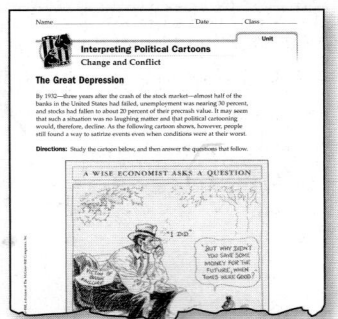

AL Critical Thinking Skills Activity, URB p. 57

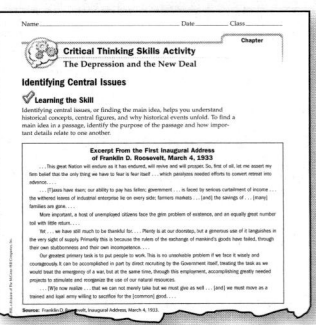

Roosevelt ordered all banks closed for four days. Congress passed the Emergency Banking Relief Act to help banks reorganize and open again. After a week in office, FDR assured Americans in a radio broadcast "that it is safer to keep your money in a . . . bank than under the mattress."

The president's radio talk was the first of many fireside chats—so called because he sat next to a fireplace in the White House as he spoke. These fireside chats helped FDR gain the public's confidence.

The Hundred Days

During a period that came to be called the **Hundred Days,** Roosevelt's proposals for new economic programs were quickly approved by Congress. It was an amazingly productive time. Optimism swept through the capital. Journalist Thomas Stokes recalled, "The gloom . . . of the closing months of the Hoover administration had vanished."

D

✔**Reading Check** **Evaluating** Why did Roosevelt broadcast his fireside chats?

Tennessee Valley Authority

Area supplied with power from the TVA
✦ Dam
■ Steam power plant

0 100 kilometers
0 100 miles
Albers Equal-Area projection

Map Skills

Place Why was the state of Tennessee a prime area to build the Tennessee Valley Authority Project?

Maps in MOtion See StudentWorks™ Plus or glencoe.com.

The New Deal Takes Shape

Main Idea Roosevelt's New Deal affected many areas of American life, including banking, the stock market, industry, agriculture, and welfare.

History and You Has a recent government action had an impact on your life? Read to learn how the New Deal changed the lives of many Americans during the 1930s.

· ·

The new laws that Congress passed during the Hundred Days—and in the months and years that followed—came to be called the **New Deal.** New Deal laws and regulations affected banking, the stock market, industry, agriculture, public works, relief for the poor, and conservation of resources. These laws changed the face of America dramatically.

Frances Perkins, Roosevelt's secretary of labor, later recalled those early, exciting days of the New Deal:

PRIMARY SOURCE

"In March 1933, the New Deal was not a plan. . . . It was a happy phrase [FDR] had coined during the campaign. . . . It made people feel better, and in that terrible period of depression they needed to feel better."

—from *The Roosevelt I Knew*

C

Jobs and Relief

Roosevelt gave high priority to creating jobs. He planned to help the unemployed with **work relief** programs, giving needy people government jobs. During his first month in office, FDR asked Congress to create the Civilian Conservation Corps (CCC). Over the next 10 years, the CCC employed about 3 million young people to work on projects that benefited the public, including planting trees to reforest areas, building levees for flood control, and improving national parks.

The president made aid to the poor and suffering another priority. Roosevelt established the Federal Emergency Relief Administration (FERA) to give money to the states for use in helping people in need.

The Depression and the New Deal **Chapter 25** 781

Writing Skills Activity
The Depression and the New Deal

Types of Sentences

✔ **Learning the Skill**

Good writers add variety to their writing by using different types of sentences and sentence structures.

Practicing the Skill

Directions: Read the paragraphs below. Then complete the activity that follows.

Writing Skills Activity, URB p. 51

W Writing Support

Persuasive Writing Ask: How did some people feel about the AAA's method of raising prices? *(It shocked people to throw away food when millions of people went hungry.)* Have students write a newspaper editorial persuading the reader to support the AAA's actions. **OL**

R Reading Strategy

Identifying Have students identify major objections people had to the TVA project. *(Funds for the TVA should support programs nationwide instead of just in Tennessee, and power companies said the program was unfair and communistic.)* **OL**

INTERPRETING POLITICAL CARTOONS

Answers

1. The letters represent New Deal programs.

2. Americans felt happy because New Deal programs were working.

Hands-On Chapter Project
Step 2

Primary Sources
INTERPRETING POLITICAL CARTOONS

This cartoon is a takeoff on the children's nursery rhyme "Ring Around the Rosie." It shows President Roosevelt standing in the middle of a group of children playing the game and singing as they dance around him.

1. **Identifying** What do the letters on the children's clothes represent?

2. **Analyzing Visuals** Why did the cartoonist draw everyone in the picture, including Roosevelt, smiling and laughing?

Roosevelt appointed Harry Hopkins, a New York social worker, to lead the FERA. Hopkins became one of FDR's closest advisers and also became involved in several other New Deal programs.

Roosevelt did not forget agriculture. On May 12, Congress passed the Agricultural Adjustment Act (AAA). The act had two goals: to raise farm prices quickly and to control production so that farm prices would stay up over the long term.

In the AAA's first year, though, the supply of food outstripped demand. The AAA could raise prices only by paying farmers to destroy crops, milk, and livestock. To many, it seemed shocking to throw away food when millions of people went hungry. However, the New Dealers claimed the action was necessary to bring up prices.

To control production and farm prices, the AAA paid farmers to leave some of their land uncultivated. If market prices of key farm products such as wheat and cotton fell below a certain level, the AAA would pay farmers subsidies—grants of money—to make up the difference. In the first three years of the New Deal, farmers' incomes rose by about 50 percent. However, the Supreme Court ruled that the AAA was unconstitutional in *United States v. Butler* (1936) for invading the reserved powers of the states.

Rebuilding a Region

One of the boldest programs launched during the Hundred Days was the **Tennessee Valley Authority** (TVA). The TVA aimed to control flooding, **promote,** or help advance, conservation and development, and bring electricity to rural areas along the Tennessee River. By building new dams and improving others, the TVA ended the region's disastrous floods. And with hydroelectric power **generating,** or creating, affordable electricity, thousands of farms and homes in some Southern states were wired for electricity for the first time.

Some critics charged that funds for the TVA should be used to support programs nationwide. Power companies also attacked the program as unfair and communistic. When the spring rains came in 1937, however, the system worked—the dams prevented the Tennessee River from flooding. In the end, most observers agreed that the TVA was an example of successful social and economic planning.

Creating a Board Game

Step 2: Creating the Board Students will create the board for the game they planned in Step 1.

Essential Question: How did Franklin Roosevelt's leadership bring about change in the U.S. economy?

Directions Provide groups with art supplies and some poster board. Have them create the game board they designed in Step 1. Encourage students to incorporate information about FDR's leadership.

Creating Allow time in class for groups to create their board surfaces. Tell them that their games should require understanding of the factors that contributed to the Great Depression and the New Deal programs that Roosevelt established. Game directions should include a way to determine a winner.

(Chapter Project continued in Section 3)

Helping Business and Labor

On the last day of the Hundred Days, Congress passed the National Industrial Recovery Act (NIRA), which Roosevelt called "the most important and far-reaching legislation" ever passed in the United States. The goal of the NIRA was to boost the economy by helping business regulate itself.

The NIRA created the National Recovery Administration (NRA), which encouraged businesses to set a minimum wage and abolish child labor. The NRA also tried to set up codes governing pricing and other practices for every industry. To promote the agency, its blue eagle symbol and slogan—"We Do Our Part"—soon appeared everywhere.

Another program that the NIRA launched was the Public Works Administration (PWA). Its goal was to stimulate the economy through the building of huge public works projects. The PWA employed many people to work on the construction of roads, shipyards, hospitals, and schools. Many PWA projects—such as New York City's Lincoln Tunnel and Kentucky's Fort Knox—still stand. The PWA spent its funds slowly, though, and the impact on unemployment was not immediate.

To avoid future banking crises, Roosevelt called for reform of the nation's financial system. Congress established the Federal Deposit Insurance Corporation (FDIC) to insure bank deposits. The government guaranteed that money placed in a bank insured by the FDIC would not be lost if the bank failed.

Congress also passed a law regulating the sale of stocks and bonds and created the Securities and Exchange Commission (SEC). This law gave the SEC the power to punish dishonest stockbrokers and speculators.

Assessing the Early New Deal

The New Deal did not cure the nation's ills. The Depression dragged on, and hardships did not cease. Farmers continued to lose their land. Unemployment remained at high levels. Many people still struggled to survive and to make ends meet.

Yet the darkest days had passed. The panic of 1932 and 1933 had receded, and the flurry of activity from the nation's capital had restored some measure of confidence.

Reading Check **Describing** What was the goal of the Public Works Administration?

Section 2 Review

History ONLINE
Study Central™ To review this section, go to glencoe.com.

Vocabulary

1. Write a short paragraph using each of the following vocabulary terms: work relief, promote, generate.

Main Ideas

2. **Describing** How did Roosevelt's political experiences prepare him to face the challenges of being president?

3. **Summarizing** What steps did Roosevelt take to restore confidence in banks and in the stock exchange?

4. **Analyzing** Explain how work relief programs benefited the economy.

Critical Thinking

5. **Comparing** Re-create the diagram below to compare the arguments for and against the TVA dam-building project.

TVA Project

For	Against

6. **Descriptive Writing** Write a proposal from the mayor of your city to President Roosevelt that outlines a Public Works Administration project you would like him to authorize. Include specific information about the work as well as how it would benefit your community.

Answer the
Essential Question

7. How did Franklin Roosevelt's leadership bring about change in the U.S. economy?

The Depression and the New Deal **Chapter 25** **783**

C Critical Thinking

Drawing Conclusions Tell students that two New Deal programs still exist today: the FDIC and the SEC. **Ask:** Why do you think these agencies are still around today? *(Banks still benefit from having deposits insured by the government. The stock market still needs to be protected from dishonest stockbrokers and speculators.)* **OL**

Reading Check **Answer:** Its goal was to stimulate the economy through huge public projects that required large numbers of workers.

Assess

History ONLINE

Study Central™ provides summaries, interactive games, and online graphic organizers to help students review content.

Close

Summarizing As a class, discuss how the New Deal was possible because of FDR's qualities as a leader. **Ask:** What issues does our country face today that require strong leadership from the president? **OL**

Section 2 Review

Answers

1. The vocabulary words should be used in a paragraph, according to their definitions in the section and the Glossary.
2. FDR's persuasive skill, his terms as a senator and governor, and his leadership in forming the Brain Trust helped him guide the nation.
3. FDR ordered banks closed while Congress passed the Emergency Banking Relief Act, which allowed banks to reorganize and open again. He also guided Congress to pass laws and regulations that affected banking and the stock market. FDR's fireside chats helped him gain the public's confidence.
4. Work relief programs allowed people to earn money, which they spent to support their families. Their spending put money back into the economy.
5. **For the TVA:** control flooding, promote conservation and development, bring affordable electricity to rural areas; **Against the TVA:** funds should be used nationwide, unfair to power companies, communistic plan
6. Answers should refer to a specific program carried out by the PWA and include specifics about the work and how it would benefit the community.
7. Answers should include FDR's use of fireside chats to reassure the American public and his persuasive skills, strong will, and confidence, which he used to persuade Congress to pass relief legislation within his first hundred days in office.

Focus

R Reading Strategy

Predicting Discuss how Americans blamed Herbert Hoover, and his "hands-off approach to the economy," for the suffering caused by the Great Depression. Also discuss how Hoover opposed the policies of the man who replaced him as president, Franklin D. Roosevelt. **Ask:** How do you think Hoover will criticize the New Deal? *(Students may speculate that Hoover will say Roosevelt is taking away states' rights or that his programs cost too much money.)* **OL**

C Critical Thinking

Analyzing Information Ask: What is Rabbi Cohen most impressed with? *(the people who want to work)* What is his main argument for why the Works Progress Administration must continue? *(It is meeting a social need that the business sector cannot meet.)* **OL**

Additional Support and Answers

Worker on a WPA project

784

YOU DECIDE

Was the New Deal an Abuse of Government Power?

Building Background

Roosevelt's New Deal program tried to regulate the American economy to ease the Great Depression. The New Deal differed from the traditional hands-off approach to the economy in American politics.

R Herbert Hoover had refused to interfere in the economy. Hungry and jobless Americans blamed the Hoover administration for their suffering. As a result, Roosevelt easily beat Hoover in the 1932 presidential election. Hoover publicly opposed Roosevelt's New Deal. The New Deal was widely supported by Americans, however, because government agencies such as the Works Progress Administration (WPA) reduced the hardships of unemployed workers.

NO

RABBI SIMON COHEN

For about two years now I have been the supervisor of a project . . . under the Works Progress Administration. . . . I wish that those who are opposing such a program could meet these people. I could furnish instance after instance of old people who have worked hard all their lives, only to face desperate need in their old age; of middle-aged workers cast adrift not through their own incapability, but of those who employed them; of young people who have just completed their education and find that the working world has no place for them. I have found some shirkers[1] and cheaters, but they are a very small minority; and the thing that has impressed me is the eagerness with which the unemployed seek for work, even the most difficult, in order that they may do their part in the community.

It goes then without question that I heartily applaud the work that the government has done in this direction and that I feel that it must continue as long as the necessity exists. . . . There is a social need which private business cannot or will not meet, it must be met by the American people as a whole, as a worth-while investment in its own citizens.

—letter to President Roosevelt, October 27, 1935

[1] **shirker** person who avoids his or her responsibility

Interdisciplinary Connection

Art Among the most lasting achievements of the Works Progress Administration was the Federal Arts Project, the largest public art program in the nation's history. The program funded out-of-work artists to produce thousands of posters, murals, paintings, and other works of art. Many WPA murals are still displayed on the walls of public schools, post offices, and municipal government buildings. Direct students to the online exhibit "By the People, For the People: Posters from the WPA" (memory.loc.gov/ammem/wpaposters/wpahome.html). Students should browse the exhibit and choose and study five specific posters in detail, noting their content and artistic features. Then ask students to write several paragraphs defining the characteristics of "public art," referring to the posters they examined. What makes "public art" different from traditional art exhibited in museums or from the artwork students produce in art classes?

YES

HERBERT HOOVER

You cannot extend the mastery of government over the daily life of a people without somewhere making it master of people's souls and thoughts. . . . Every step in that direction poisons the very roots of liberalism. It poisons political equality, free speech, free press, and equality of opportunity. It is the road not to more liberty but to less liberty. True liberalism is found not in striving to spread bureaucracy,[2] but in striving to set bounds to it. True liberalism seeks all legitimate freedom first in the confident belief that without such freedom the pursuit of other blessings is in vain. . . .

Through four years of experience this New Deal attack upon free institutions has emerged as the transcendent[3] issue in America. . . .

Surely the NRA and the AAA alone, should prove what the New Deal philosophy of government means. . . .

But their illegal invasions of the Constitution are but the minor artillery with which this New Deal philosophy of government is being forced upon us. They are now . . . taking vast sums of the people's money and then manipulating its spending to build up personal power.

—speech given October 30, 1936

[2] **bureaucracy** system of government marked by many rules and regulations
[3] **transcendent** most important

DBQ Document-Based Questions

1. **Summarizing** According to Hoover, what is the danger of the New Deal?

2. **Analyzing** Why does Cohen think the Works Progress Administration should continue?

3. **Inferring** How do you think Hoover feels about the Works Progress Administration?

4. **Evaluating** With which position do you agree more? Explain your answer.

Homeless shelters in Seattle, Washington

785

Teach

C Critical Thinking

Identifying Central Issues Read the excerpt from President Hoover and discuss the vocabulary terms. **Ask:** What seems to be Hoover's main concern about the New Deal? *(its expansion of government activities into daily life, which he calls "the transcendent issue in America")* After discussing Hoover's main point, challenge students to identify a central issue that is not mentioned in the excerpt. *(the Depression itself or the suffering and poverty it has caused)* **Ask:** What is the significance of this omission? **OL**

Assess/Close

Stress to the class that the philosophical dispute highlighted in these readings is still prominent in American politics. Liberals and conservatives still disagree on the amount of social services that should be provided by the federal government. Discuss why this controversy still exists, and have students write a journal entry describing their own perspectives on this critical issue.

Answers

1. Herbert Hoover believed that the extension of government into people's daily lives threatened individual liberty.

2. Rabbi Cohen's experience with the Works Progress Administration showed him that the program brought meaningful work to people facing poverty and need during the Great Depression. He believed that private businesses by themselves would not do enough to help people in need.

3. Hoover seems to perceive government programs like the WPA as a violation of the Constitution and a wrongful use of taxpayers' money.

4. Students' answers should take into consideration the conditions during the Depression.

Section 3

Life During the Depression

Focus

Bellringer
Daily Test Practice Transparency 25–3

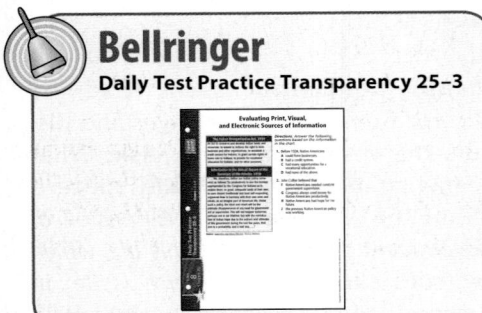

Reading Guide
Answers to Graphic:

Women—drawn into the workforce, worked harder at home; **African Americans**—lost jobs to white workers, led many to migrate north, NAACP formed, Black Cabinet formed; **Native Americans**—Indian New Deal restored culture and heritage, CCC built new schools, Indian Reorganization Act restored tribal government and enlarged reservations; **Latinos**—lost jobs, faced deportation, turned away by schools and hospitals

Section Spotlight Video

Have students watch the Section Spotlight Video "Life During the Depression" to learn more about how Americans coped with the Dust Bowl.

Resource Manager

Essential Question
How did the Great Depression affect the economic and social traditions of Americans, especially minorities?

Reading Guide

Content Vocabulary
migrant worker (p. 788)   fascist (p. 790)

Academic Vocabulary
migrate (p. 788)   advocate (p. 790)

Key People and Events
Frances Perkins (p. 787)
Dust Bowl (p. 787)
Ralph Bunche (p. 789)
Mary McLeod Bethune (p. 789)
Indian Reorganization Act (p. 789)
Spanish Civil War (p. 790)

Reading Strategy
Taking Notes Re-create a diagram like the one below to record information about the various groups that were affected during the Depression.

Group	How Affected
Women	

ILLINOIS STANDARDS
The American Journey

16.E.3b (US) Describe how the largely rural population of the United States adapted, used and changed the environment after 1818.

17.C.3a Explain how human activity is affected by geographic factors.

17.C.3c Analyze how human processes influence settlement patterns including migration and population growth.

American Diary

Dear Mrs. Roosevelt
I am writing to you for some of your old soiled dresses if you have any . . . . I am in the seventh grade in school but I have to stay out of school because I have no books or clothes to ware [wear] . . . . If you have any soiled clothes that you don't want to ware I would be very glad to get them.
Yours Truly

—*from* Dear Mrs. Roosevelt

Organized hunger marches, such as this one in Columbus, Ohio, were common during the years of the Great Depression.

R Reading Strategies	**C** Critical Thinking	**D** Differentiated Instruction	**W** Writing Support	**S** Skill Practice
Teacher Edition • Sequencing Info., p. 788 • Categorizing, p. 791 **Additional Resources** • Guid. Read., URB p. 69 • Cont. Vocab., URB p. 45 • Ac. Vocab., URB p. 47 • Read. Ess., p. 280 • Pri. Source Read., URB p. 49	**Teacher Edition** • Compar. & Contrast., p. 787 • Analyzing Info., p. 790 **Additional Resources** • Quizzes and Tests, p. 247	**Teacher Edition** • Below Grade Level, p. 787 • Naturalist, p. 788 **Additional Resources** • School-to-Home, URB p. 63 • Reteaching Act., URB p. 65	**Teacher Edition** • Personal Writing, p. 788 • Descriptive Writing, p. 789 **Additional Resources** • Authentic Assess., p. 25	**Teacher Edition** • Using Geo. Skills, p. 789 **Additional Resources** • Daily Test Pract. Transp. 25-3

Hard Times in America

Main Idea The Depression was a difficult time because many Americans faced unemployment and the loss of land and other property.

History and You Would you be willing to stay in an area that was damaged by a disaster? Read to find out what happened to people living on the Great Plains and what they did to find a better life.

The letter in the American Diary is one of thousands of letters sent to first lady Eleanor Roosevelt. Many Americans—both young and old—sought relief from the pain brought about by the Depression.

Women Go to Work

Desperation drove a large number of women into the workforce, despite the fact that many people thought that women should not hold jobs as long as men were unemployed. Many families survived on a woman's income—even though American women earned less than men.

Women also worked harder at home to make ends meet. Instead of buying clothes or groceries, they sewed their own clothing, baked their own bread, and canned their own vegetables. Some women started home businesses such as laundries or boardinghouses.

The New Deal era also opened doors for women in public life. President Roosevelt appointed the first woman ever to serve in the cabinet, **Frances Perkins.** He also named more than 100 other women to federal posts. One—Ellen Sullivan Woodward—started a program to provide jobs for women.

Eleanor Roosevelt often acted as her husband's "eyes and ears." She made fact-finding trips for the president because polio had limited his mobility. Mrs. Roosevelt campaigned vigorously for women and families in need.

The Dust Bowl

During the 1930s, while people were struggling to make ends meet, the southern Great Plains suffered an environmental disaster. Hardest hit were western Kansas and Oklahoma, northern Texas, and eastern Colorado and New Mexico—the region dubbed the **Dust Bowl.**

Primary Source / Songs of Sorrow

"Brother Can You Spare a Dime?"

They used to tell me I was building a dream
And so I followed the mob
When there was earth to plow or guns to bear
I was always there, right on the job.

They used to tell me I was building a dream
With peace and glory ahead
Why should I be standing in line
Just waiting for bread?

Once I built a railroad, I made it run
Made it race against time
Once I built a railroad, now it's done
Brother can you spare a dime?

Music of the Depression Many songs described Americans' feelings during the Great Depression. One of the more famous ballads describes the loss of hope by people who were unemployed.

Critical Thinking
Drawing Conclusions What do you think is meant by "building a dream" in the song?

CHAPTER 25
Section 3

Teach

C Critical Thinking

Comparing and Contrasting Ask: How did the daily lives of women change during the Depression? *(The Depression drove many women to work outside the home for wages. They also worked harder at home and some started their own businesses.)* **OL**

D Differentiated Instruction

Below Grade Level Tell students that the wives of previous U.S. presidents used to focus on entertaining important visitors and running the household. **Ask:** How was Eleanor Roosevelt different? *(She acted as her husband's "eyes and ears," going on fact-finding trips for him because of his polio. She also campaigned for women and families in need.)* **BL**

Primary Source

Critical Thinking Answer
Students may refer to the American dream of peace and prosperity as the reward for hard work. **OL**

Additional Support

Interdisciplinary Connection

Health Ask: What illness caused problems for FDR? *(polio)* Tell the class that FDR was honest about having polio, but during his presidency, he did not reveal how disabled he had become. At that time, disabled people were considered incapable of getting much done. **Ask:** How might having full knowledge of his disability have affected Americans' attitudes about FDR's leadership? *(People might not have trusted FDR's ability to help them out of the Great Depression.)* Have students work in small groups to research the history of polio, Roosevelt's involvement in promoting its treatment, and the development of a successful vaccine to prevent it. Finally, have each group prepare a visual display to share the information they have gathered. **OL**

R Reading Strategy

Sequencing Information Have students list in order the factors that contributed to the Dust Bowl. *(New technology allowed millions of acres to be cleared; severe drought of 1931 killed crops and dried soil; many strong winds blew away soil.)* **BL**

D Differentiated Instruction

Naturalist Ask: Why were the plains soils so easily damaged by wheat farming? *(There were no more grasses to hold the soil in place.)* Have students discuss how the plains would have looked before and after the Dust Bowl. Ask students to create a mural to illustrate the changes that took place. **OL**

W Writing Support

Personal Writing Have students take the role of a migrant worker migrating from Oklahoma to California. Ask them to write several diary entries describing their travels and search for work in California. **OL**

Reading Check Answer: The blowing dust reduced visibility to near zero.

Using new technology such as tractors and disc plows, farmers cleared millions of acres of sod for wheat farming. They did not realize that the roots of the grass held the soil in place. When a severe drought struck in 1931, the wheat crops died and the soil dried out. Strong prairie winds blew the soil away.

Each storm stripped away more soil. The drought—and the storms—continued for years. People called the storms "black blizzards" because the blowing dust reduced visibility to near zero. In some areas, sand drifts formed as high as 6 feet (1.8 m), burying roads and vehicles.

Thousands of Dust Bowl farmers went bankrupt and had to give up their farms. About 400,000 farmers **migrated,** or moved, to California and became **migrant workers,** moving from place to place to harvest fruits and vegetables. So many came from Oklahoma that people called them "Okies."

Reading Check Explaining Why were dust storms called "black blizzards"?

The Plight of Minorities

Main Idea The Great Depression placed the hardest burden on minority groups. It also led to the growth of radical political movements.

History and You What might it be like to be poor but also to face prejudice? Read to find out about the challenges and gains of African Americans, Native Americans, and Hispanic Americans during the 1930s.

The Depression fell especially hard on the minority groups who were already on the lower rungs of the American economic ladder. These groups included African Americans, Native Americans, and Hispanic Americans.

African Americans

In the South more than half of the African American population had no jobs. African Americans who lived and worked in Southern cities found their jobs taken by white people who had lost theirs. The collapse of farm prices crushed African American farmers.

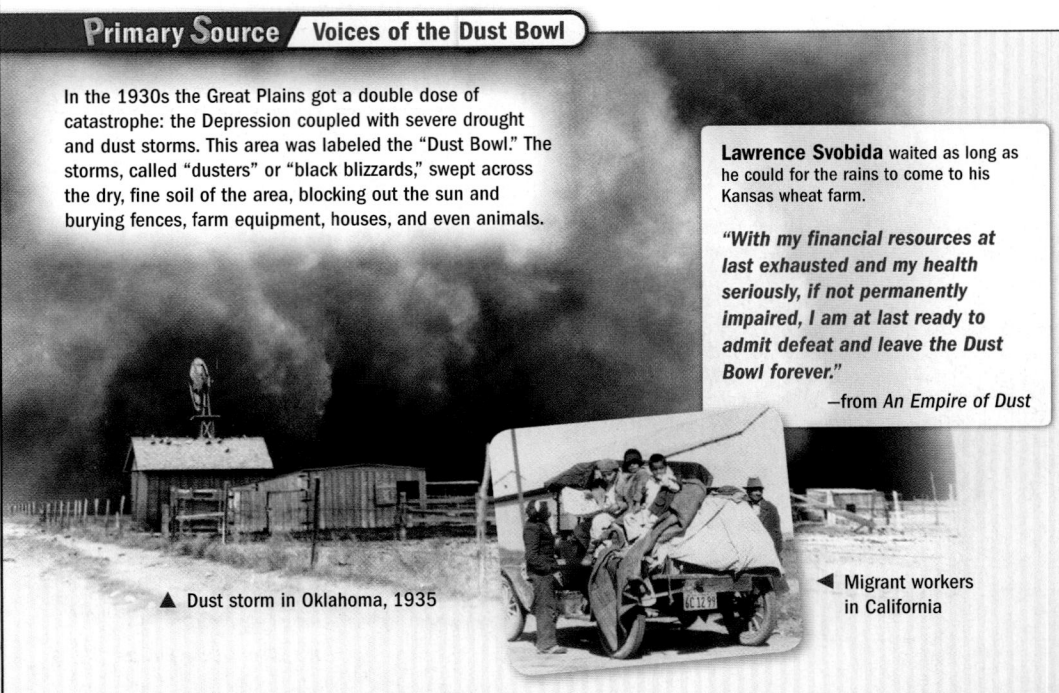

Primary Source | **Voices of the Dust Bowl**

In the 1930s the Great Plains got a double dose of catastrophe: the Depression coupled with severe drought and dust storms. This area was labeled the "Dust Bowl." The storms, called "dusters" or "black blizzards," swept across the dry, fine soil of the area, blocking out the sun and burying fences, farm equipment, houses, and even animals.

Lawrence Svobida waited as long as he could for the rains to come to his Kansas wheat farm.

"With my financial resources at last exhausted and my health seriously, if not permanently impaired, I am at last ready to admit defeat and leave the Dust Bowl forever."

—from *An Empire of Dust*

▲ Dust storm in Oklahoma, 1935

◄ Migrant workers in California

Differentiated Instruction

Leveled Activities

BL School-to-Home Connection Activity, URB p. 63

OL Reteaching Activity, URB p. 65

AL Primary Source Reading Activity, URB p. 49

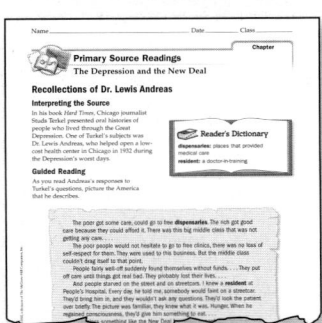

ELL Content Vocabulary Activity, URB p. 45

Seeking more opportunity, about 400,000 African American men, women, and children migrated to Northern cities during the 1930s. These migrants did not fare much better in the North, however. The jobless rate for African Americans remained high.

However, African Americans did make some social and political gains during the Depression. The National Association for the Advancement of Colored People (NAACP) worked to lessen discrimination in the labor movement. As a result, more than 500,000 African Americans were able to join labor unions. African Americans also won a greater voice in government. President Roosevelt appointed a number of African Americans to federal posts. He had a group of advisers, known as the Black Cabinet, that included Robert Weaver, a college professor, and **Ralph Bunche,** who later played an important role in the civil rights movement. **Mary McLeod Bethune,** who founded Bethune-Cookman College in Florida, also served as an adviser to the president.

African Americans continued to fight against prejudice. In 1939 opera singer Marian Anderson was denied permission to sing in Constitution Hall because she was African American. Mrs. Roosevelt helped arrange for Anderson to give a historic concert at the Lincoln Memorial.

Native Americans

The 1930s did provide some benefits to Native Americans. The head of the Bureau of Indian Affairs, John Collier, introduced a set of reforms known as the Indian New Deal. These changes would help restore Native American culture and heritage.

Collier halted the sale of reservation land, got jobs for 77,000 Native Americans in the Civilian Conservation Corps, and obtained Public Works Administration funds to build new reservation schools. Most importantly, he pushed Congress to pass the **Indian Reorganization Act** of 1934. This law restored traditional tribal government and provided money for land purchases to enlarge some reservations.

Latinos

By 1930, about 2 million people of Latino, or Hispanic, descent lived in the United States, mostly in California and the Southwest. Many had emigrated from Mexico. Some worked as farmers on small pieces of land. Others were laborers in industries or migrant workers, traveling from place to place harvesting crops.

As the Great Depression deepened, resentment against Mexican Americans grew, and many lost their jobs. Politicians and labor unions demanded that Mexican Americans be forced to leave the United States.

The government encouraged Mexican immigrants to return to Mexico. Authorities gave them one-way train tickets to Mexico or simply rounded them up and shipped them south across the border. More than 500,000 Mexican Americans left the United States during the early years of the Depression, often involuntarily.

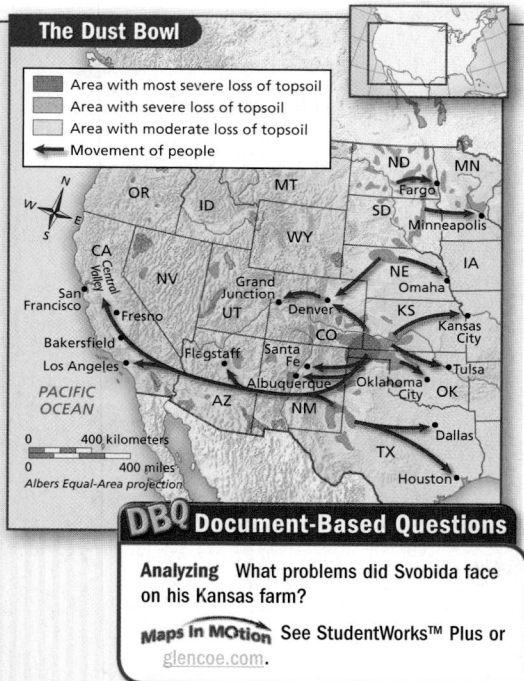

The Dust Bowl

- Area with most severe loss of topsoil
- Area with severe loss of topsoil
- Area with moderate loss of topsoil
- ← Movement of people

DBQ Document-Based Questions

Analyzing What problems did Svobida face on his Kansas farm?

Maps in MOtion See StudentWorks™ Plus or glencoe.com.

The Depression and the New Deal **Chapter 25 789**

S Skill Practice

Using Geography Skills Have students look at a map of North America in the Reference Atlas at the front of the book. **Ask:** Why did most Latinos emigrate to California and the Southwest? (*These areas are closer to Mexico.*) **AL**

W Writing Support

Descriptive Writing Radio was the source of news and entertainment in the 1930s. Write a radio script of an interview by a news reporter with a Latino parent in the 1930s. Include details that describe the impact of the Depression on a typical Latino family. **OL**

Primary Source

Document-Based Question
Svobida faced poverty and illness.

Map Practice Ask: From which area of the country did most people migrate? (*the area that Colorado, Kansas, and Oklahoma meet*) **OL**

Differentiated Instruction

Authentic Assessment, p. 25

Living Through the Great Depression

Objective:	To appreciate the daily lives of average Americans during the Depression
Focus:	Have students develop a list of topics and people they could present in the documentary.
Teach:	Have students research realistic details to include in their TV specials.
Assess:	Have students summarize the series.
Close:	Tell students to make a generalization about people's lives during the Depression.

Differentiated Instruction Strategies

BL Have students use a dictionary to define words they do not know.

AL Ask students to explore online digital archives that preserve the history of ordinary Americans during the Depression.

ELL Have students paraphrase each storyboard statement in each student's documentary.

C Critical Thinking

Analyzing Information Ask: Why did Communism attract some Americans? *(It promised to end economic and social injustice.)* Why were Communists considered radical? *(They advocated extreme and immediate change.)* **OL**

Primary Source

Document-Based Questions Answer: Teens left home to find work or adventure; the economic hardship of the Great Depression might have forced families to split up to survive. **OL**

✓ **Reading Check Answer:** It restored traditional tribal government and provided money for land purchases to enlarge some reservations.

History ONLINE

Objectives and answers to the Student Web Activity can be found at glencoe.com under the Web Activity Lesson Plan for this chapter.

Hands-On Chapter Project
Step 3

Creating a Board Game

Step 3: Writing Chance Cards Students will create the board game they planned in Step 1.

Essential Question: How did the Great Depression affect the economic and social traditions of Americans, especially minorities?

Primary Source | **Teenage Hoboes**

Riding the Rails During the Depression, at least 250,000 teenagers left home to ride the rails. They crisscrossed the country by hopping freight trains. Many went west to California or south to warmer states in search of jobs, a better life, or just plain adventure. The life of a hobo was often lonely and dangerous. In 1932 alone, nearly 6,000 hoboes were killed or injured when they attempted to jump on or off a train.

Symbol	Meaning
⊔	You can camp here
⊖	Leave quickly
⊗	Good place for food and money
‡ ‡‡	Danger, police
�羽	This water is dangerous to drink

▲ Hoboes developed their own symbols to communicate with other hoboes on the road.

"To be a hobo, you had to know how to get on a train while it is moving. Some hoboes got killed by trying to get on trains that were moving too fast."
—from Luther S. Head, National Heritage Museum

◄ Riding on trains was dangerous but free.

DBQ Document-Based Questions

Speculating How do you think the actions of these teenage hoboes reflected the effects of the Great Depression on American teenagers and families?

Those Mexican Americans who remained in the United States faced continued discrimination. They were kept from getting relief or were offered benefits far below those given to whites. Many hospitals and schools also turned away Mexican Americans. To resist job discrimination, some migrant workers tried to form labor unions, but local food producers and officials cracked down on these organizations.

Radical Political Movements

Hard times helped radical political groups gain ground in the United States during the 1930s. Radical groups **advocate,** or support, extreme and immediate change. Socialists and Communists viewed the Depression not as a temporary economic problem but as the death of a failed system. They proposed sweeping changes.

History ONLINE

Student Web Activity Visit glencoe.com and complete the Chapter 25 Web Activity about The Great Depression and the New Deal.

Communism attracted some Americans with promises to end economic and racial injustice. Although both socialism and communism had significant influence, neither became a political force in the United States.

Another political development was the rise of **fascists** in Germany and Italy. Fascism is a political philosophy that holds the individual second to the nation and advocates government by dictatorship. Although fascism never attracted many Americans, it drew enough attention to make it dangerous. During the Depression, fascists blamed Jews, Communists, and liberals for the country's troubles.

In 1936 the **Spanish Civil War** began. Germany and Italy supported fascists who were trying to take over the Spanish government. Although the United States remained neutral, more than 3,000 Americans went to Spain to fight the fascists.

✓ **Reading Check Explaining** What was the purpose of the Indian Reorganization Act?

Directions Provide index cards for each group. Each group should stripe one edge of their cards with a color you assign to them to help each group identify its cards. Tell students to use the index cards to write out questions and answers about people, events, and concepts related to the Great Depression. Encourage them to include information about changes in economic and social conditions during the Great Depression, as well as challenges faced by minorities during this period. Advise students that they will add to the cards they produce as they read Section 4.

Writing Allow sufficient class time for groups to write their cards. Suggest that the cards be reviewed by each group for accuracy and clarity.

(Chapter Project continued in Section 4)

Entertainment and the Arts

Main Idea The 1930s was a golden age of entertainment, literature, music, and art.

History and You What do you do for entertainment? Read to learn about the ways people sought fun or inspiration during the hard times of the Depression.

The Depression produced two separate trends in entertainment and the arts. One was escapism—light or romantic entertainment that helped people forget about their problems. The other was social criticism—portraits of the injustice and suffering of Depression America.

Radio and the Movies

Radio became enormously popular during the 1930s. "Soap operas" were daytime dramas sponsored by laundry detergents. Adventure programs such as *Dick Tracy* and *Superman* had millions of listeners, as did variety shows featuring comedians George Burns and Gracie Allen and Jack Benny.

Every week about 85 million people went to movie theaters, usually to escape their cares and worries. Walt Disney produced the successful animated film *Snow White and the*

R *Seven Dwarfs* in 1937. Two years later, audiences flocked to see *The Wizard of Oz*, a colorful musical that lifted viewers' spirits.

Some movies did explore serious topics. For example, *The Grapes of Wrath* (1940) was a screen version of John Steinbeck's powerful novel about farm families fleeing the Dust Bowl. The 1939 film of Margaret Mitchell's novel *Gone With the Wind*, set in the Civil War era, also portrayed people coping with hard times.

Images of the Times

Many writers and painters portrayed the grim realities of Depression life. Richard Wright's novel *Native Son* told the story of an African American man growing up in Chicago. Writer James Agee and photographer Walker Evans depicted poor Southern farm families in *Let Us Now Praise Famous Men*.

Photographer Margaret Bourke-White also recorded the plight of American farmers, and Dorothea Lange took gripping photographs of migrant workers. Painters such as Grant Wood and Thomas Hart Benton showed ordinary people facing the hardships of Depression life.

Reading Check **Analyzing** How is social criticism expressed in artwork?

R Reading Strategy

Categorizing Have students title a two-column chart and label the columns "Escapism" and "Social Criticism." Have them list the types of entertainment or art mentioned here in each column. *(Escapism—radio soap operas, adventure programs, variety shows, movies; social criticism—movies, novels, photographs, paintings)* **OL**

Reading Check **Answer:** Photographers recorded the plight of farmers and migrant workers. Painters showed ordinary people facing hardships.

Assess

Study Central™ provides summaries, interactive games, and online graphic organizers to help students review content.

Close

Discussing As a class, discuss the ways the Great Depression affected the economic and social traditions of Americans, especially minorities. **Ask:** Which group faced the greatest challenge? Which groups benefited from the changes that took place? **OL**

Section 3 Review

History ONLINE
Study Central™ To review this section, go to glencoe.com.

Vocabulary

1. Write a paragraph in which you use all of the following vocabulary terms: migrate, migrant worker, advocate, fascist.

Main Ideas

2. **Analyzing** What was the Dust Bowl? How did advanced farming technology contribute to it?

3. **Identifying** What was the Black Cabinet, and why was it important?

4. **Making Inferences** Why was radio so popular?

Critical Thinking

5. **Analyzing** In a diagram like the one below, note some examples of social criticism found in 1930s art, movies, and writing.

Social Criticism — Art, Movies, Writing

6. **Creative Writing** Imagine you are an African American man who moved to a Northern city in 1935 to find work. Write a letter to a Southern relative about your experiences.

Answer the
Essential Question

7. How did the Great Depression affect the economic and social traditions of Americans, especially minorities?

The Depression and the New Deal **Chapter 25** **791**

Answers

1. Paragraphs should use vocabulary terms according to their definitions in the section and Glossary.
2. A time of severe drought and dust storms. Farmers used machines to farm vast areas; then drought killed the crops and winds blew the away soil.
3. The Black Cabinet was a group of advisers to President Roosevelt. It was important because it allowed greater voice in government for African Americans, a group that traditionally suffered great prejudice.

4. Radio was popular in the 1930s because it helped people forget about their problems with daytime dramas, adventure programs, and variety shows.
5. **Art**—photography by Walker Evans, Margaret Bourke-White, Dorothea Lange; paintings by Grant Wood, Thomas Hart Benton; **Movies**—*The Grapes of Wrath, Gone With the Wind*; **Writing**—same as movies, plus Wright's *Native Son* and Agee's *Let Us Now Praise Famous Men*

6. Letters should include details such as the extreme poverty of the times, method of travel, and the way minorities were treated.
7. The Depression made Americans face unemployment and poverty, loss of homes and possessions, and the breakup of families. Women were drawn into the workforce, prejudice against minorities increased, radical political movements grew, and a new age of entertainment and the arts began.

Focus

R Reading Strategy

Reading Primary Sources Have a student volunteer read Dorothea Lange's description of her meeting with the mother. Discuss how Lange needed the photograph to tell the story of the mother and her children. **Ask:** In what way had Dorothea Lange "recorded the essence" of her assignment? *(Lange captured the plight of migrant farmers with one photograph.)* **AL**

Teach

D Differentiated Instruction

Visual/Spatial Ask students to research the Dust Bowl. Have them locate an image, whether online or in a book, of the black blizzards described in "Verbatim." Have them print or photocopy the image and share it with the class. **OL**

S Skill Practice

Visual Literacy Have students study the photo of Mount Rushmore and think about the working conditions of these laborers. Ask students to write a caption for the photo. **OL**

Additional Support and Answers

TIME NOTEBOOK

What were people's lives like in the past?

These two pages will give you some clues to everyday life in the United States as you step back in time with TIME Notebook.

Images of Our Nation

PICTURE OF THE PAST

In 1936 photographer **DOROTHEA LANGE** *took a picture called* Migrant Mother, Nipomo, California, *in a camp filled with seasonal agricultural workers. Shooting photos for the Farm Security Administration, Lange was trying to show how government programs might be improving the lives of people in the rural United States. However, Lange found something different from what she expected as she started to snap her photos.*

The woman in the photo was a pea-picker and the mother of seven children —all on the verge of starvation. Lange's photo ran in a San Francisco newspaper, capturing the desperation of the times perfectly. Thanks to the picture, the government immediately sent 20,000 pounds of food to the camp. Here's what Lange had to say about taking the picture:

DOROTHEA LANGE/THE LIBRARY OF CONGRESS

"I approached the hungry mother. She told me her age—that she was 32. She said that they had been living on frozen vegetables from the surrounding fields, and birds that the children killed. There she sat in that lean-to tent with her children huddled around her, and seemed to know that my pictures might help her, and so she helped me.... The pea crop ...had frozen and there was no work for anybody. I did not approach the tents ...of other stranded pea-pickers.... I knew I had recorded the essence of my assignment."

HEADLINE FROM THE TIME

Lindbergh Baby Search Still On

Nearly two months have passed since famed flyer Charles Lindbergh and his wife Anne's baby boy was kidnapped in March 1932. A ladder leading up to the baby's window, muddy footprints, and a ransom note demanding $50,000 are the three clues that have been studied by more than 5,000 FBI agents. About 100,000 police and volunteers have combed the country, searching for the baby.

VERBATIM

WHAT PEOPLE ARE SAYING

❝ These storms were like rolling black smoke. We had to keep the lights on all day. We went to school with headlights on and with dust masks on. I saw a woman who thought the world was coming to an end. ❞

A BOY IN TEXAS,
during the devastating dust storms of 1936—with its churning storms called black blizzards that had winds up to 90 miles per hour

❝ While I still have got breath in my lungs, I will tell you what a dandy car you make. I [have driven] Fords exclusively when I could get away with one. ❞

CLYDE BARROW,
(half the team of bank robbers Bonnie and Clyde) in a 1934 letter to Henry Ford

❝ American history shall march along that skyline. ❞

GUTZON BORGLUM,
in 1924, standing near the Black Hills of South Dakota, where work on his Mount Rushmore sculptures would begin three years later

UNDERWOOD & UNDERWOOD / CORBIS

Fast Facts

Carving History Mount Rushmore features the faces of four U.S. presidents: George Washington, Thomas Jefferson, Theodore Roosevelt, and Abraham Lincoln. The idea for the sculptures came from state historian Doane Robinson, who thought carvings would attract more people to the Black Hills of South Dakota.

The sculptor, Gutzon Borglum, first created a plaster model. Work began on Mount Rushmore in 1927. George Washington was the first face to be carved. Thomas Jefferson was started next, but after two years of work on him, the granite was found to be badly cracked. Jefferson's face was blasted off the mountain and started again.

As each of the presidents was completed, his face was dedicated in a public ceremony. In 1939, a full 12 years after the work on Mount Rushmore began, the final sculpture—of Theodore Roosevelt—was dedicated in a ceremony that included fireworks.

Borglum continued to work on Mount Rushmore for two more years, making finishing touches, until his death in 1941.

CHATTER OF THE DECADE

Can You Talk the Talk?

Sure, the Roaring Twenties are full of flappers and good times, but you cannot dance the Charleston forever. Sooner or later you are going to have to talk—will you know what to say? See if you can match the 1920s slang with the correct meaning.

LORDPRICE COLLECTION / ALAMY

1. sinker	a. dancer
2. speakeasy	b. doughnut
3. flyboy	c. place with illegal liquor
4. swanky	d. dollar
5. hoofer	e. pilot
6. clam	f. elegant

Answers: 1. b; 2. c; 3. e; 4. f; 5. a; 6. d

NUMBERS

UNITED STATES AT THE TIME

Number One

Gone With the Wind wins the Pulitzer Prize for 1937. Millions of readers set aside their worries as they experienced the epic drama, defeat, and triumphs of Margaret Mitchell's cast of characters

Two

Two is a charm for President Franklin Roosevelt, sworn in for the second time on January 20, 1937. FDR turned down a ride in a closed limousine—even though it was raining. He pointed toward the thousands of wet people who lined the streets of Washington, D.C., hoping to catch a glimpse of him, and said, "I'll ride in the open limo. If they can take it, I can!"

Four

Four gold medals. Adolf Hitler, Germany's fascist leader, invited the world to Berlin for the 1936 Olympic Games. Hitler hoped to prove the supposed "inferiority" of non-Aryan races. No one told that to U.S. superstar Jesse Owens, an African American athlete who won four gold medals in track and field events

25¢

25¢ First federal minimum wage, signed into law as part of the Fair Labor Standards Act (FLSA) in 1938

MILESTONES

EVENTS AND PEOPLE OF THE TIME

BETTMANN / CORBIS

FLOWN. The first helicopter in 1936, piloted by Russian-born Igor Sikorsky in Connecticut.

DIED. Harry Houdini in 1926. The world's most famous escape artist died after a trick went terribly wrong. The son of a poor Hungarian family who emigrated to the United States, he had a flair for the dramatic—escaping from tough spots, including a locked canister filled with water while in a straitjacket and hung upside down from a 50-foot-high (15 m) building.

SPACED OUT. In 1934 Wiley Post, wearing a pressurized suit, flew his plane to a height of nearly 9.5 miles (15.3 km), setting a new altitude record.

TUNED IN. 60,000 families who owned radios in 1922—that number jumps to 13,750,000 families in 1930.

CHILLED. Foods as they are cooled by the introduction of the first electric refrigerators in 1923. The new machines have quickly replaced the icebox, which uses huge blocks of ice to keep food cold.

CRITICAL THINKING

Analyzing Visuals Why did Lange's photo raise awareness of migrant workers' problems? What does the photo "say" to you?

Hypothesizing Why do you think Jesse Owens's victories at the Berlin Olympic Games thrilled Americans? What message did Owens's medals send to Hitler's Germany?

Answers

Analyzing Visuals By showing the plight of the woman and her children, Lange's photo made people aware of the suffering of migrant workers.

Hypothesizing By winning four gold medals, Owens disproved Hitler's theory of the inferiority of non-Aryan races.

Section 4

Focus

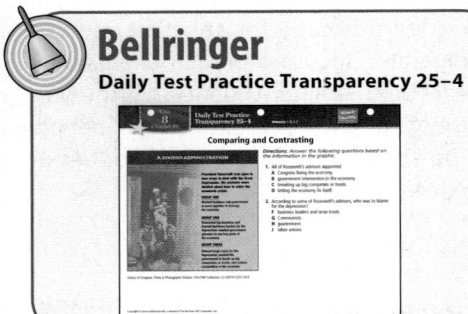
Reading Guide
Answers to Graphic:

Charles Coughlin—wanted heavy taxes on the wealthy and for the government to take over the nation's banks

Francis Townsend—wanted a monthly pension for older, retired people

Huey Long—called for taxing the rich heavily and using that money to give every American a home and $2,500 a year

Section Spotlight Video

Have students watch the Section Spotlight Video "Effects of the New Deal" to learn more about the Social Security Act.

Resource Manager

Section 4

Essential Question ◄
Why did some people support Roosevelt's New Deal and some oppose it?

Reading Guide

Content Vocabulary

pension   unemployment
(p. 795)   insurance (p. 797)

Academic Vocabulary

scheme (p. 795)   welfare (p. 797)

Key People and Events
Second New Deal (p. 796)
Social Security Act (p. 797)
John L. Lewis (p. 797)
Fair Labor Standards Act (p. 797)

Reading Strategy
Taking Notes On a chart like the one below, record the major complaint or suggestion of each of the reformers who criticized Roosevelt's New Deal.

Reformer	Complaint/ suggestion
Charles Coughlin	
Francis Townsend	
Huey Long	

ILLINOIS STANDARDS
The American Journey

14.A.3 Describe how responsibilities are shared and limited by the United States and Illinois Constitutions and significant court decisions.

16.C.3b (US) Explain relationships among the American economy and slavery, immigration, industrialization, labor and urbanization, 1700-present.

Effects of the New Deal

American Diary

Under Roosevelt's New Deal program, millions of Americans found jobs and a new sense of hope when the government created the Works Progress Administration (WPA). "Every time a man is taken from the demoralizing ranks of the jobless, every time a woman is removed from the humiliation of a breadline, and given work to do, a home somewhere becomes more secure."

—from "The Lasting Values of the WPA," a speech by Ellen Woodward

---

R Reading Strategies	C Critical Thinking	D Differentiated Instruction	W Writing Support	S Skill Practice
Teacher Edition • Identifying, p. 795 • Skimming, p. 796 **Additional Resources** • Guid. Read., URB p. 70 • Cont. Vocab., URB p. 45 • Ac. Vocab., URB p. 47 • Read. Ess., p. 283	**Teacher Edition** • Predicting Con., p. 796 • Evaluating, p. 798 **Additional Resources** • Quizzes and Tests, p. 248	**Teacher Edition** • Logical/Mathematical, p. 796 **Additional Resources** • School-to-Home, URB p. 63 • Reteaching Act., URB p. 65 • Differ. Inst., URB p. 55	**Teacher Edition** • Persuasive Writing, p. 797	**Additional Resources** • Daily Test Pract. Trans. 25-4 • Time Line Skills, URB p. 62 • Lesson Transp. 25C

Critics of the New Deal

Main Idea During the mid-1930s, Roosevelt's New Deal programs faced growing opposition.

History and You When someone proposes or makes changes, why do other people often object or criticize? Think about this as you read about the people who opposed Roosevelt's New Deal.

In the early days of his presidency, FDR counted on big business to support his efforts to revive the economy. In general, however, the business world opposed the New Deal.

Business leaders accused Roosevelt of spending too much money. They viewed the government's expansion of power as a threat to individual liberty. These conservatives wanted the government to leave business alone and play a less active role in the economy.

Demanding More Reform

At the same time, Roosevelt drew fire from those who believed that the president had not gone far enough. Three men gained wide popularity with **schemes,** or plans, to help the average American.

Father Charles Coughlin, a Detroit priest, reached millions of listeners through his weekly radio program. Once a Roosevelt supporter, Coughlin called for heavy taxes on the wealthy and for the government to take over the nation's banks. Coughlin used his radio show to attack bankers, Jews, Communists, and labor unions, as well as the New Deal. In time Coughlin lost support because of his extreme views.

Francis Townsend, a California doctor, called for a monthly **pension,** or payment, for older, retired people. Townsend's plan received little support from Congress. It did, however, force many Americans to think about the needs of the elderly poor.

Of greatest concern to Roosevelt, however, was Senator Huey Long of Louisiana. As governor of Louisiana, Long won wide support with public works projects.

His "Share Our Wealth Plan" called for taxing the rich heavily, then using that money to give every American a home and $2,500 a year. Long's plans appealed to many Americans. Polls indicated that in 1936 he might receive as many as 4 million votes on a third-party ticket. But in 1935 he was assassinated by a political opponent.

Reading Check Identifying What group was Townsend's pension plan designed to help?

VPA workers repair sidewalks, July 1936.

By the Numbers / WPA Projects

The projects completed by WPA workers were lasting and varied.

Total	Projects
651,087	Miles of highways, roads built
124,031	Bridges repaired
125,110	Public buildings erected
8,192	Public parks created
853	Airports built or improved
2,565	Murals painted
17,744	Sculptures created

Source: *The Depression and New Deal*

US 99

Critical Thinking

Explaining Why do you think WPA projects were considered beneficial to the entire nation?

Teach

R Reading Strategy

Identifying Have students read the paragraph and identify the main idea. *(Business leaders wanted the government to play a less active role in the economy.)* **Ask:** In which sentence can you find the main idea? *(last sentence)* **OL**

By the Numbers

Critical Thinking Answer Most were large-scale projects intended to benefit the public. Also, they created many jobs, which helped both individuals and the U.S. economy as a whole.

Skills Practice Ask: How many bridges were repaired? *(124,031)*

Reading Check Answer: older, retired people

Additional Support

Activity: Technology Connection

Making Connections Tell students that work relief projects both employed people and improved the nation in a wide variety of ways that can still be seen and enjoyed all over the United States. For instance, the work of the Civilian Conservation Corps (CCC) was established during the first Hundred Days of FDR's presidency. Have students identify CCC projects in their home state or in places they have visited by going to www.cccalumni.org/states/index.html. Have them select a state and view the charts listing projects accomplished by the CCC. Next, have them identify a project they have seen or would like to see and conduct research, using the name and location information from the chart. Ask students to write a one-page description of the project, its location, and how it continues to benefit people today. Provide class time for students to share their discoveries. **AL**

C Critical Thinking

Predicting Consequences Ask: Do you think wealthy people and owners of corporations voted for or against Roosevelt in the next election? *(Students will most likely predict that these people did not vote for Roosevelt.)* **OL**

D Differentiated Instruction

Logical/Mathematical Ask: If each student in this class were a working adult and 20% were unemployed, how many people would be jobless? *(number of students in class multiplied by .20 = answer)* **OL**

R Reading Strategy

Skimming Remind students that sometimes when they are trying to find the answer to a question, skimming for a term can help them find the answer. Have students listen to the question and skim the page for the answer. **Ask:** What was the purpose of the WPA? *(to give people jobs and help the country)* **BL**

Hands-On Chapter Project
Step 4

Creating a Board Game

Step 4: Creating Game Pieces Students will continue to create the board game they planned in Step 1.

Essential Question: Why did some people support Roosevelt's New Deal and some oppose it?

The Second New Deal

> **Main Idea** Roosevelt's Second New Deal introduced new programs to help jobless workers, the elderly, and labor unions.
>
> **History and You** Do your grandparents receive a monthly social security check from the federal government? Read to find out about the origins of social security under the Second New Deal.

By the mid-1930s the economy had improved slightly, but the Depression was far from over. FDR took bolder steps.

To bring in more government funds, Roosevelt pushed Congress to pass the Revenue Act of 1935. The act raised taxes on wealthy people and corporations. Critics accused him of "soaking the rich" to pay for his programs, but many Americans cheered.

In 1935 President Roosevelt launched a new set of programs and reforms, often called the **Second New Deal.** The laws passed at this time changed American life even more than the Hundred Days had done.

Creating Jobs

Millions of people—20 percent of the workforce—were still unemployed in 1935. In April Congress created the Works Progress Administration (WPA) to give people jobs and help the country. Led by Harry Hopkins, the WPA kept about 2 million people employed between 1935 and 1941. WPA workers built or repaired airports, public buildings, bridges, and roads.

The WPA also found work for unemployed writers, artists, and musicians. WPA painters decorated the new public buildings with murals. WPA produced *Life in America,* 150 volumes that recorded folktales and songs, African American narratives, and Native American traditions.

Help for Those in Need

Before the Second New Deal, America was the only advanced industrial nation without a national government program to help the needy. In August 1935, Congress passed the Social Security Act.

LINKING PAST TO PRESENT — Women in Government

THEN As the nation's first woman cabinet member, Secretary of Labor **Frances Perkins** (large image, below) worked for safe working conditions. Since 1917, when **Jeannette Rankin** (top right) of Montana became the first woman to serve in Congress, more than 240 women have served in the U.S. Congress. In 1953 **Oveta Culp Hobby** (taking oath of office) became the second woman to serve in a presidential cabinet. In 1977 **Patricia Roberts Harris** (bottom right) became the first African American woman to serve in the cabinet. She is also the first woman to hold two different cabinet posts.

796

Directions Display several sample game pieces from which students can get ideas. Provide materials such as heavy poster board, colored markers, scissors, and glue for each group to use. Game pieces should be distinctive, relate to the time period, stand up on their own, and easily fit into the spaces on their game boards. When the game pieces are prepared, have students add to their stack of question cards using the concepts covered in Section 4.

Reviewing As groups finish working, have them play their own games. As each group plays, ask members to make any improvements needed before others play their game.

(Chapter Project continued on the Visual Summary page)

The **Social Security Act** created a tax on workers and employers. That money provided monthly pensions for retired people. Another tax, on employers alone, funded **unemployment insurance** payments to people who lost their jobs. In addition, Social Security helped people with disabilities, the elderly poor, and children of parents who could not support them.

With the Social Security Act, the federal government took responsibility for the **welfare** of all citizens. The act launched the American welfare system.

The Labor Movement

Labor unions grew stronger as workers battled the Depression. In 1937 workers at the General Motors plant in Flint, Michigan, used a new technique—the sit-down strike. Strikers continuously occupied the plant and refused to work until management agreed to negotiate with them about their demands. After 44 days, the Flint strikers won the right to organize their union.

Most unions in the American Federation of Labor (AFL) represented only skilled workers. **John L. Lewis** of the United Mine Workers helped form a new union, the Congress of Industrial Organizations (CIO). The CIO set out to organize unions that included all workers, skilled and unskilled, in a particular industry. By 1938, the CIO had 4 million members, including large numbers of women and African Americans.

Unions found support in the New Deal. The 1935 National Labor Relations Act—also called the Wagner Act after its sponsor, Senator Robert Wagner of New York—guaranteed workers the right to form unions to bargain collectively with employers. In 1938 Congress passed the **Fair Labor Standards Act** (FLSA), which banned child labor and set a minimum wage of 40 cents per hour. The FLSA and the Wagner Act form the basis of American labor rights today.

Reading Check **Comparing** How did the CIO differ from the AFL?

W **Writing Support**

Persuasive Writing Have students create a radio address for President Roosevelt that builds enthusiasm for the Social Security Act. Students should explain the need for such legislation and include historical details. **OL**

LINKING PAST TO PRESENT

Critical Thinking Answer

Students who agree may reason that as more women enter politics, more will have a chance at important roles. Students may say that it depends on how people vote or whether leaders are willing to appoint women.

Critical Thinking Practice

Specifying Ask: What two characteristics set Condoleezza Rice apart from past secretaries of state? (*She is African American and female.*)

Reading Check **Answer:** The AFL represented only skilled workers. The CIO represented skilled as well as unskilled workers.

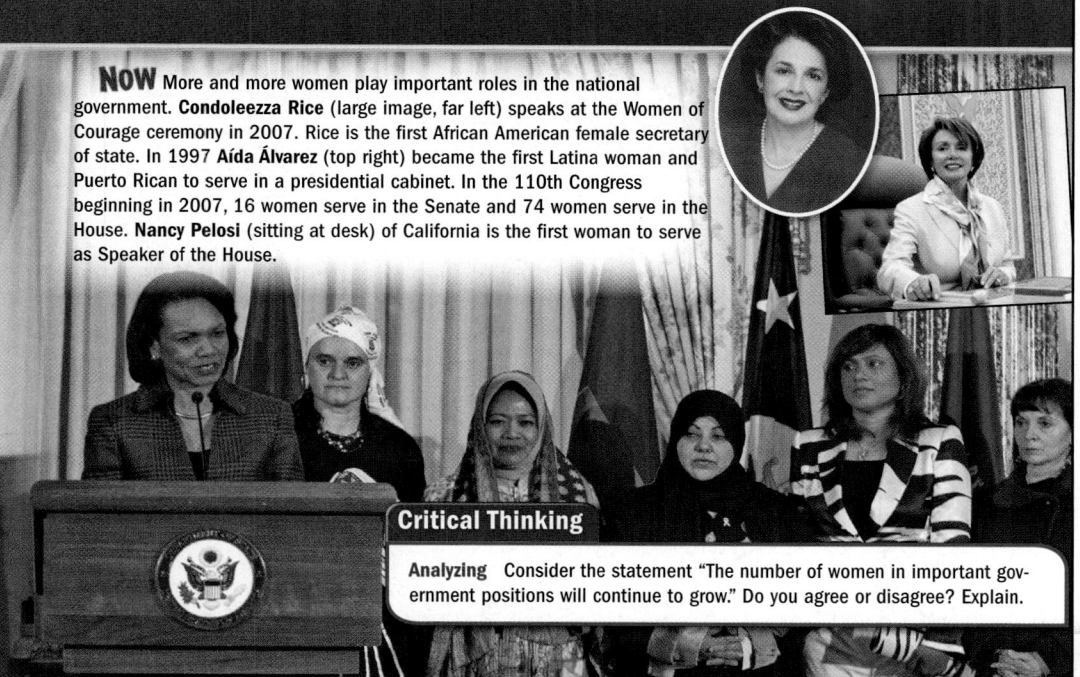

NOW More and more women play important roles in the national government. **Condoleezza Rice** (large image, far left) speaks at the Women of Courage ceremony in 2007. Rice is the first African American female secretary of state. In 1997 **Aída Álvarez** (top right) became the first Latina woman and Puerto Rican to serve in a presidential cabinet. In the 110th Congress beginning in 2007, 16 women serve in the Senate and 74 women serve in the House. **Nancy Pelosi** (sitting at desk) of California is the first woman to serve as Speaker of the House.

Critical Thinking

Analyzing Consider the statement "The number of women in important government positions will continue to grow." Do you agree or disagree? Explain.

Differentiated Instruction

Time Line Activity
The Depression and the New Deal

American Labor Movement (1869–1964)

Directions: Use the following information to make a time line about labor legislation and the rise of labor unions. Include the date for each event.

Time Line Skills Activity, URB p. 62

American Labor Movement (1869–1964)

Objective: To learn about labor legislation and the rise of labor unions

Focus: Have students describe industrial working conditions that were addressed by labor legislation.

Teach: Have students read the excerpt and identify each item of labor legislation enacted.

Assess: Ask students to summarize the main idea.

Close: Discuss the progress of labor legislation and unions between 1869 and 1964.

Differentiated Instruction Strategies

BL Have students fill in the Rise of Labor Unions facts, using only the top part of the diagram.

AL Ask students to research articles written about labor issues within the past decade.

ELL Have students use a dictionary to define words they do not know.

C Critical Thinking

Evaluating Ask: Do you think it was wise of FDR to cut spending on programs in 1937? *(Students may say it was unwise because the economy quickly went into a recession.)* **AL**

✓ Reading Check **Answer:** Filling the new positions with people who would support the New Deal plans would ruin the system of checks and balances.

Assess

History ONLINE

Study Central™ provides summaries, interactive games, and online graphic organizers to help students review content.

Close

Identifying Points of View Ask students to identify the groups who opposed the New Deal and why. Next, ask students who supported it and what their reasons were for doing so. **OL**

Section 4 Review

The Supreme Court

Main Idea Roosevelt's Second New Deal was challenged by the Supreme Court.

History and You Think about a time when someone questioned what you said or did. How did you answer that person? Read to learn how Roosevelt responded to critics of the New Deal.

Those opposed to the New Deal challenged many of its laws in the courts. Beginning in 1935, the Supreme Court began to declare New Deal legislation unconstitutional. The presidential campaign of 1936 focused on a single issue: Did the American people support FDR and the New Deal? On Election Day, FDR won 61 percent of the popular vote.

Roosevelt's "Court-Packing" Plan

After the election, FDR acted to keep the Supreme Court from undoing the New Deal. He asked Congress to increase the number of Court justices from 9 to 15. FDR planned to fill the six new positions with justices who would uphold the New Deal.

The proposal aroused bitter opposition. Critics accused the president of trying to "pack" the Court and ruin the system of checks and balances. The issue died when the Court ruled in favor of the Wagner Act and the Social Security Act. The New Deal was no longer in serious danger from the Court. The unpopularity of the court-packing plan, however, cost Roosevelt much support.

The End of the New Deal

FDR also ran into trouble with the economy. During 1937, an economic recovery seemed to be in full swing, so FDR cut spending on programs. An economic downturn, known to some as the Roosevelt Recession, took hold and lasted into 1938. Roosevelt helped reverse it with spending on public works. Still, it was clear that the economy had not fully recovered, despite wide-ranging New Deal programs. As the 1930s came to an end, however, dangerous events in Asia and Europe caused Americans to turn their attention from domestic to foreign affairs.

✓ Reading Check **Explaining** Why was FDR's Supreme Court plan criticized?

Section 4 Review

History ONLINE
Study Central™ To review this section, go to glencoe.com.

Vocabulary

1. Use each of these terms in a complete sentence that will explain its meaning: scheme, pension, unemployment insurance, welfare.

Main Ideas

2. **Discussing** Why did many business leaders criticize Roosevelt?

3. **Stating** What was the intended dual purpose of the WPA?

4. **Analyzing** What did the 1936 election say about the public's opinion of the president's policies?

Critical Thinking

5. **Identifying** On a diagram like the one below, list the major labor legislative acts passed by Congress during the Second New Deal.

```
Labor
Legislation  >—————
```

6. **Explaining** What was the Social Security Act of 1935 and why was it a significant act for Congress to pass?

7. **Persuasive Writing** Imagine you were the unemployed head of your family in 1935. Would you have supported President Roosevelt's plan to add six more justices to the Supreme Court? Write a short essay explaining and supporting your view.

Answer the
8. **Essential Question**
Why did some people support Roosevelt's New Deal and some oppose it?

Answers

1. Sentences should use vocabulary words according to their meanings.
2. They criticized FDR for spending too much money, raising taxes on the wealthy and on businesses, and because the government's expansion of power threatened individual liberty.
3. The WPA was formed to give people jobs and to help the country.
4. FDR won the election with 61% of the popular vote, which showed that the majority

of the public supported his policies.
5. Labor Legislation—the Social Security Act, the National Labor Relations (Wagner) Act, the Fair Labor Standards Act
6. It taxed workers and employers to provide pensions, fund unemployment insurance, and help the disabled, the elderly poor, and children who were not supported by their parents. It was significant because America was the only advanced industrial nation without a program to help the needy.

7. Students' essays should include one viewpoint and several supporting statements.
8. Supporters—labor unions, the needy and the jobless; because they needed help or were concerned about those who did; Opposition—business leaders felt FDR was spending too much money and that the government's expansion of power threatened individual liberty.

Stock Market Helps Trigger Depression

- Investors buy stocks on margin
- Sharp drop in market prices leaves investors in debt
- International market falters
- Stock market crashes; financial panic

Causes of the Great Depression

- Uneven distribution of income leads to low demand for goods
- Overuse of credit to make purchases
- Supply exceeds demand in industry; leads to large inventories of unsold goods
- Farmers suffer from too much production, low prices, and large debts

Effects

- Businesses lay off workers, close plants
- Millions lose jobs
- Poverty is widespread
- Businesses and banks close
- New Deal legislation enacted
- Despite periods of economic upturn, the Depression remains

STUDY TO GO Study anywhere, anytime! Download quizzes and flash cards to your PDA from glencoe.com.

The Depression and the New Deal **Chapter 25** 799

Identifying Points of View Ask: President Hoover took a hands-off approach to the economic crisis. He asked businesses not to cut wages and for charities to help out. How well did Hoover's plan work? *(Charities, volunteers, and churches tried to provide relief, as did state governments, but too many people needed help. Eventually Hoover authorized federal public works projects, but state and local governments ran out of money. He also asked Congress to create the Reconstruction Finance Corporation, but the RFC was reluctant to make risky loans, and much of the money went unspent.)* How did voters respond to Hoover in the next election? *(They elected Roosevelt instead.)* **OL**

Drawing Conclusions Ask: Do you think President Roosevelt went too far to help people during the Depression? *(Answers will vary, but students may discuss how New Deal programs helped many Americans. On the other hand, businesses accused Roosevelt of spending too much money, and many believed the government should play a less active role. Others believed Roosevelt had not done enough, such as Father Charles Coughlin, who called for heavy taxes on the wealthy. When the Supreme Court threatened to declare the New Deal legislation unconstitutional, Roosevelt tried to "pack" the Supreme Court, which angered many people.)* **OL**

Hands-On Chapter Project
Step 5: Wrap-Up

Creating a Board Game

Step 5: Learning From the Games Students will synthesize what they have learned in steps 1 through 4.

Directions Write the four Essential Questions on the board. Discuss the factors that brought about the Great Depression, the changes in economic and social conditions Americans faced, and the people, programs, and legislation that contributed to recovery. Allow time for groups to play each other's board games. Tell the class members they are to select the best game, based on how well it answered the four Essential Questions from the chapter.

Wrapping Up Ask: How did playing each game answer each of the Essential Questions? Invite students to nominate a game and explain to the class why they made that particular selection.

Answers and Analysis
Reviewing Main Ideas

1. B Remind students that in 1932, 25 percent of Americans were out of work. Because this is more than 20 percent, they should be able to make choice B. **15.A.3d**

2. D The NRA was a New Deal program that helped set standards for production, prices, and wages. The correct answer is D. **15.E.3b**

3. D Students should immediately eliminate choice C because Dust Bowl families traveled within the nation to seek employment. Students also should quickly eliminate choices A and B because Native Americans and African Americans were not immigrants. Students should then choose D. **15.E.3b**

4. C Remind students that the conservatives were business leaders who would not have wanted to pay for social programs or have a tax increase, which eliminates answers A, B, and D. Students should then be able to make choice C. **18.B.3a**

Short-Answer Question

5. The excerpt should bring to mind that WPA programs employed people. Students should also mention specific types of WPA projects, such as the building of bridges and highways, the creation of public parks, and so on. **16.A.3b**

TEST-TAKING TIP

When you take a test, do not answer the questions right away. Look over the test first. How many questions are there? How many different sections? Are some questions worth more points than others? Pace yourself accordingly.

Reviewing Main Ideas

Directions: Choose the best answer for each of the following questions.

1. What hardship did more than 20 percent of Americans face during the Great Depression?
  A inflation
  B unemployment
  C scarcity of goods
  D high stock prices

2. The National Recovery Administration helped the economy by
  A providing jobs.
  B insuring bank deposits.
  C distributing food and cash.
  D encouraging businesses to set a minimum wage.

3. Whom did the government encourage to leave the country during the Great Depression?
  A Native Americans
  B African Americans
  C Dust Bowl families
  D Mexican Americans

4. Conservative critics wanted the Roosevelt administration to
  A give every American a house.
  B impose heavy taxes on the wealthy.
  C play a less active role in the economy.
  D pay older workers to quit their jobs.

Short-Answer Question

Directions: Base your answer to question 5 on the excerpt below and on your knowledge of social studies.

> Now a lot of people remember [the WPA] as boon-doggles and raking leaves. . . . But I can take you to our town and show you things, like a river front that I used to hike through once that was a swamp and is now a beautiful park place built by WPA.
>
> —Ronald Reagan, as quoted in *The New Deal*

5. What were some lasting effects of the New Deal?

Review the Essential Questions

6. Essay Did the New Deal correct the factors that caused the Great Depression? Explain.

To help you write your essay, review your answers to the Essential Questions in the section reviews and the chapter Foldables Study Organizer. Your essay should include:

- factors that caused the Great Depression;
- New Deal programs that addressed these factors;
- changes brought about by New Deal programs; and
- evaluation of the views of supporters and opponents of the New Deal.

GO ON

Review the Essential Questions

6. If students completed their Foldables correctly, they should be able to include each of the factors that caused the Depression, the New Deal Programs designed to address them, the changes these programs brought about, and the supporters and opponents of the New Deal in their essays. **15.E.3b**

History ONLINE
For additional test practice, use **Self-Check Quizzes**—Chapter 25 at glencoe.com.

Chapter 25 Assessment

Document-Based Questions

Directions: Analyze the documents and answer the questions that follow.

Document 1

Reverend Reinhold Niebuhr recorded his thoughts about Ford's new model car in 1927.

> The car cost [laid-off] Ford workers at least fifty million in lost wages during the past year. . . . We are now asked to believe that the whole idea of waiting a year after the old car [Model T] stopped selling before bringing out a new one was a great advertising scheme.

Source: Robert Sklar, *The Plastic Age (1917–1930)*

7. What phrases in the excerpt foreshadow the coming of the Great Depression?

Document 2

"Bread Line," a poem by Florence Converse, was first published in 1932.

> What if we should be destroyed
> By our patient unemployed?

Source: David A. Shannon, *The Great Depression*

8. How does the poet think that the unemployed might react to continued hard times?

Document 3

Langston Hughes recorded these observations while in Spain during the Spanish Civil War.

> I've met wide-awake Negroes [African Americans] from various parts of the world—New York, our Middle West . . . all of them here because they know that if Fascism creeps across Spain, across Europe, and then across the world, there will be no more place for intelligent young Negroes at all.

Source: Langston Hughes, "Negroes in Spain"

9. Why did African Americans volunteer in Spain?

Document 4

This cartoon by Cliff Berryman was published in 1938.

Source: Granger Collection

10. Based on the cartoon, explain the economic downturn of the late 1930s and Roosevelt's reaction.

11. Descriptive Writing Using the information from the four documents and your knowledge of social studies, write an essay in which you:

- illustrate, with examples, hardships suffered just before and during the Great Depression; and

- describe the feelings these hardships brought out in wealthy, middle-class, and poor Americans.

Need Extra Help?											
If you missed questions. . .	1	2	3	4	5	6	7	8	9	10	11
Go to page. . .	775	783	789	795	794–798	775	790	790	790	796	786–791

---

9. Explain that "wide-awake" in this excerpt means "intelligent and knowledgeable" about world events. Students should write that "intelligent young Negroes" were fighting for the preservation of their democratic rights, such as free speech, which is not allowed under fascism. **18.C.3b**

10. During 1937, the economy was recovering well, so FDR cut spending programs, which led to an economic downturn. The cartoon shows FDR performing his economic magic a second time around by returning to spending on public works to reverse the downturn. **16.A.3c**

11. Students should use the four documents and their knowledge from this chapter to write essays. Topics must include the hardships suffered just before and during the Great Depression and the feelings these hardships brought out in wealthy, middle-class, and poor Americans. Student essays should include descriptive words as they discuss both topics. **18.B.3a**

History ONLINE
Have students visit the Web site at glencoe.com to review Chapter 25 and take the Self-Check Quiz.

Need Extra Help?

Have students refer to the pages listed if they miss any of the questions.

Document-Based Questions

7. Students should look for clue words or phrases that help them answer the question. In this passage, "laid-off Ford workers," "lost wages," and "stopped selling" foreshadow the lowered wages, the lost jobs, and the overproduction problems that contributed to the Great Depression. **16.A.3b**

8. Tell students that *The Atlantic Monthly* was a magazine favored by wealthy conservatives in the 1930s. Ask students to picture unemployed people waiting in line for food. The poet thinks that the unemployed might lose their patience with the failing economy and attack and destroy the wealthy. **16.A.3b**

Chapter Planning Guide

26

Key to Ability Levels
- **BL** Below level
- **OL** On level
- **AL** Above level
- **ELL** English Language Learners

Key to Teaching Resources
- 📁 Print Material
- 💿 CD-ROM
- 📀 DVD
- 🖨 Transparency

BL	OL	AL	ELL		Resources	Chapter Opener	Section 1	Section 2	Section 3	Section 4	Section 5	Chapter Assess
					FOCUS							
BL	OL	AL	ELL	🖨	**Daily Test Practice Transparencies**		26–1	26–2	26–3	26–4	26–5	
					TEACH							
	OL	AL		📁	**Geography and History Activity, URB**		p. 87					
BL	OL		ELL	📁	**Time Line Skills Activity, URB**					p. 90		
BL	OL	AL	ELL	📁	**Writing Skills Activity, URB**		p. 79					
BL	OL	AL	ELL	📁	**Content Vocabulary Activity, URB**		p. 73	p. 73	p. 73	p. 73	p. 73	
BL	OL	AL	ELL	📁	**Academic Vocabulary Activity, URB**		p. 75	p. 75	p. 75	p. 75	p. 75	
BL			ELL	📁	**Reading Skills Activity, URB**						p. 7	
	OL	AL		📁	**Citizenship and Decision-Making Activity, URB**				p. 3			
BL	OL		ELL	📁	**Social Studies Skills Activity, URB**				p. 81			
BL	OL	AL	ELL	📁	**Differentiated Instruction Activity, URB**						p. 83	
BL	OL	AL	ELL	📁	**Critical Thinking Skills Activity, URB**				p. 85			
BL	OL	AL	ELL	📁	**Linking Past and Present Activity, URB**			p. 89				
	OL	AL		📁	**Primary Source Readings, URB**			p. 77				
BL	OL	AL	ELL	📁	**School-to-Home Connection Activity, URB**		p. 91	p. 91	p. 91	p. 91	p. 91	
BL	OL		ELL	📁	**Guided Reading Activity, URB***		p. 95	p. 96	p. 97	p. 98	p. 99	
		AL		📁	**Enrichment Activity, URB**			p. 11				
BL	OL		ELL	📁	**Reading Essentials and Note-Taking Guide***		p. 286	p. 289	p. 292	p. 295	p. 298	
BL	OL	AL	ELL	🖨	**Lesson Transparencies**		26A	26B	26C			
		AL		📁	**Supreme Court Case Studies**						p. 63	
BL	OL	AL	ELL	📁	**Outline Map Resource Book**	p. 40						

Note: Please refer to the *Unit Resource Book: Change and Conflict* for this chapter's URB materials.

* Also available in Spanish

| Levels | | | | | Resources | Chapter Opener | Section 1 | Section 2 | Section 3 | Section 4 | Section 5 | Chapter Assess |
BL	OL	AL	ELL									
TEACH *(continued)*												
BL	OL	AL	ELL		NGS US Desk Map		✓	✓	✓	✓	✓	
BL	OL	AL	ELL		American Literature Library		✓	✓	✓	✓	✓	
BL	OL	AL	ELL		Writer's Guidebook		✓	✓	✓	✓	✓	
	OL	AL			American History Primary Source Document Library CD-ROM		✓	✓	✓	✓	✓	✓
BL	OL	AL	ELL		American Music: Hits Through History	✓	✓	✓	✓	✓	✓	
BL	OL	AL	ELL		StudentWorks™ Plus CD	✓	✓	✓	✓	✓	✓	✓
	OL	AL			Section Spotlight Videos		✓	✓	✓	✓	✓	
BL	OL	AL	ELL		Writing Process Transparencies		✓	✓	✓	✓	✓	✓
BL	OL	AL	ELL		Presentation Plus! With MindJogger CheckPoint CD	✓	✓	✓	✓	✓	✓	✓
ASSESS												
BL	OL	AL	ELL		Quizzes and Tests		p. 255	p. 256	p. 257	p. 258	p. 259	pp. 261, 263, 265
BL	OL	AL	ELL		Authentic Assessment With Rubrics		p. 26					
BL	OL	AL	ELL		Standardized Test Practice							p. 51
BL	OL	AL	ELL		*ExamView®* Assessment Suite CD-ROM*		26–1	26–2	26–3	26–4	26–5	Ch. 26
CLOSE												
BL			ELL		Reteaching Activity, URB*		p. 93	p. 93	p. 93	p. 93	p. 93	p. 93
BL	OL		ELL		Reading and Study Skills Foldables Activity	p. 100	p. 100	p. 100	p. 100	p. 100	p. 100	p. 100
BL	OL	AL	ELL		*The American Journey* in Graphic Novel							p. 155
BL			ELL		Reading Strategies and Activities for the Social Studies Classroom		✓	✓	✓	✓	✓	
BL	OL	AL	ELL		Graphic Organizer Transparencies & Strategies		✓	✓	✓	✓	✓	

TeacherWorks *Plus*
All-In-One Planner and Resource Center

- Interactive Lesson Planner
- Interactive Teacher Edition
- Fully editable blackline masters
- Section Spotlight Videos Launch

- Differentiated Lesson Plans
- Printable reports of daily assignments
- Standards Tracking System

Professional Development Resources

- Strategies for Success
- Building Academic Vocabulary
- Success With English Learners DVD
- Differentiated Instruction Strategies DVD
- Teaching Literacy Strategies in Social Studies DVD
- Assessment DVD
- Standards-Based Instruction DVD

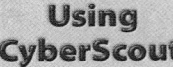

Using CyberScout

Researching Using *Subject Area*

Technology Product

CyberScout is a convenient and dynamic search engine that provides several easy ways to locate information outside the McGraw-Hill Learning Network. CyberScout searches only Web sites that have been reviewed by teachers, so the information students find is always appropriate and accurate.

Objectives

After students learn to use CyberScout, they will be able to

- research topics in history using CyberScout;
- research and study skills;
- practice writing skills.

Steps

- From the McGraw-Hill Learning Network home page (www.mhln.com), click on **For Student**.
- Choose **CyberScout** below **Homework Help**.
- Click a subject area link to narrow the search.
- The CyberScout page displays a set of results.
- Drill down by continuing to click result links until you find a Web site of interest.
- Click on the link to reach the Web site.
- The site will open in a new window.
- Students navigate through the chosen Web site to acquire information about their topics and take notes.
- Have students write a report that summarizes what they have learned.

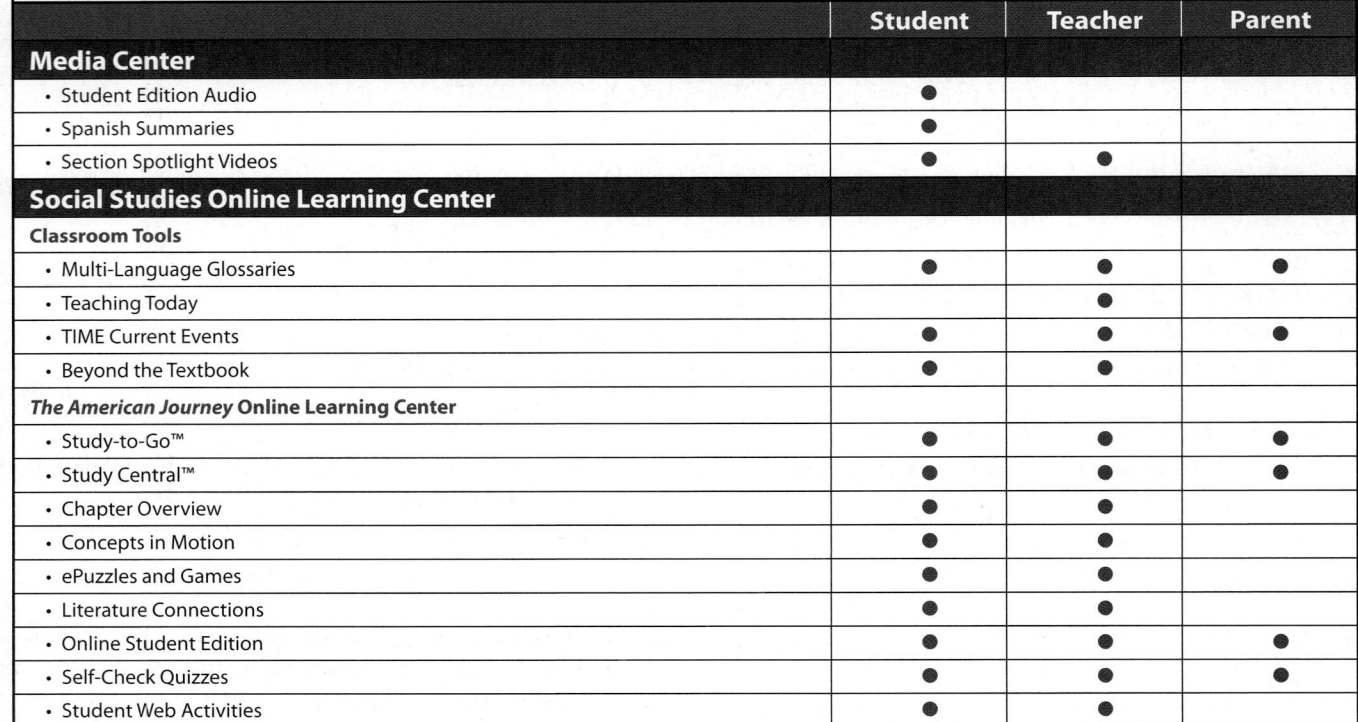

History ONLINE at glencoe.com

	Student	Teacher	Parent
Media Center			
• Student Edition Audio	●		
• Spanish Summaries	●		
• Section Spotlight Videos	●	●	
Social Studies Online Learning Center			
Classroom Tools			
• Multi-Language Glossaries	●	●	●
• Teaching Today		●	
• TIME Current Events	●	●	●
• Beyond the Textbook	●	●	
***The American Journey* Online Learning Center**			
• Study-to-Go™	●	●	●
• Study Central™	●	●	●
• Chapter Overview	●	●	
• Concepts in Motion	●	●	
• ePuzzles and Games	●	●	
• Literature Connections	●	●	
• Online Student Edition	●	●	●
• Self-Check Quizzes	●	●	●
• Student Web Activities	●	●	
• Vocabulary eFlashcards	●	●	
• Web Activity Lesson Plans	●	●	●
• Vocabulary PuzzleMaker	●	●	●

Reading Support From JAMESTOWN EDUCATION

- **Timed Readings Plus in Social Studies** helps students increase their reading rate and fluency while maintaining comprehension. The 400-word passages are similar to those found on state and national assessments.

- **Reading in the Content Area: Social Studies** concentrates on six essential reading skills that help students better comprehend what they read. The book includes 75 high-interest nonfiction passages written at increasing levels of difficulty.

- **Reading Social Studies** includes strategic reading instruction and vocabulary support in Social Studies content for ELLs and native speakers of English.

- **Content Vocabulary Workout** (Grades 6–8) accelerates reading comprehension through focused vocabulary development. Social Studies content vocabulary comes from the glossaries of Glencoe's Middle School Social Studies texts.

www.jamestowneducation.com

NATIONAL GEOGRAPHIC

Index to National Geographic Magazine:

The following articles relate to this chapter:

- **"Living With the Bomb,"** Richard Rhodes, August 2005.

- **"Embedded Memories,"** Alan Mairson, June 2004.

National Geographic Society Products

To order the following, call National Geographic at 1-800-368-2728:

National Geographic Atlas of the World (Book)

Access National Geographic's dynamic MapMachine Web site and other geography resources at:

www.nationalgeographic.com

www.nationalgeographic.com/mapmachine

Reading List Generator CD-ROM — GLENCOE BOOKLINK 3

Use this database to search more than 30,000 titles to create a customized reading list for your students.

- Reading lists can be organized by students' reading level, author, genre, theme, or area of interest.
- The database provides Degrees of Reading Power™ (DRP) and Lexile™ readability scores for all selections.
- A brief summary of each selection is included.

Leveled reading suggestions for this chapter:

For students at a Grade 6 reading level:
- **Under the Blood-Red Sun,** by Graham Salisbury
- **Don't You Know There's a War On?** by Avi

For students at a Grade 7 reading level:
- **Good Night, Mr. Tom,** by Michelle Magorian
- **Under a War-Torn Sky,** by L. M. Elliott

For students at a Grade 8 reading level:
- **Summer of My German Soldier,** by Bette Greene
- **Hiroshima,** by Laurence Yep

For students at a Grade 9 reading level:
- **Children of the Blitz: Memories of Wartime Childhood,** by Robert Westall
- **Anne Frank: The Diary of a Young Girl,** by Anne Frank

For students at a Grade 10 reading level:
- **The Homefront: America During World War II,** by Mark J. Harris
- **We Are Witnesses,** by Jacob Boas

The following videotape programs are available from Glencoe as supplements to the chapter:

- **The War in Europe** (ISBN 1-56-501993-8)
- **The War in the Pacific** (ISBN 1-56-501994-6)

To order, call Glencoe at 1-800-334-7344. To find classroom resources to accompany many of these videos, check the following home pages:

A&E Television: www.aetv.com

The History Channel: www.history.com

Chapter Objectives

After studying this chapter, students will be able to:

- Describe how dictators acquired and expanded power in Europe in the 1930s.
- Discuss how peaceful nations confronted foreign aggressors in World War II.
- List the ways that American men, women, and minorities supported the war effort at home.
- Describe the strategies the Allies pursued in Europe and Africa to defeat the Axis Powers in World War II.
- Discuss the events that led up to the turning point in the war in the Pacific.

Motivating Activity

Activating Prior Knowledge Tell students that they probably know more about World War II than they realize. **Ask:** Who fought in World War II? *(Emphasize that the United States joined the war after Britain and France.)* What else do you know about World War II? *(Students will probably mention facts about Pearl Harbor, the Holocaust, and D-Day.)* Refer to the D-Day photograph on this page. **Ask:** What other WWII photographs have you seen?

Previewing the Essential Questions

As you begin teaching each section, use these questions and activities to help students focus on the Essential Questions.

Chapter 26
America and World War II
1939-1945

American troops land in France, D-Day, June 6, 1944

PRESIDENTS

U.S. Events

World Events

FRANKLIN DELANO ROOSEVELT

1937

1939

★ **1937**
Neutrality Act limits trade with warring nations

★ **1940**
Selective Training and Service Act passes

★ **1937**
Mexico president Lázaro Cárdenas continues land, railroad reform

★ **1939**
• Germany invades Austria and Czechoslovakia
• Hitler seizes Poland

802   Chapter 26

Section 1

The Road to War Ask: How did many Germans and other Europeans respond to the Treaty of Versailles and the Great Depression? *(Many resented the treaty and were suffering during the depression.)* Point out to students that in Section 1 they will learn how dictators took advantage of people's suffering and resentment to gain power in the 1930s. **OL**

Section 2

War Begins Ask: How do you think the United States responded to German aggression in Europe? *(Students may state that the United States would support Britain and France or even go to war against Germany to combat aggression.)* Explain to students that Section 2 discusses why the United States joined with other countries to fight German and Japanese aggression. **OL**

Section 1: The Road to War

Essential Question How did dictators acquire and expand power in Europe in the 1930s?

Section 2: War Begins

Essential Question How did peaceful nations confront foreign aggressors in World War II?

Section 3: On the Home Front

Essential Question In what ways did American men, women, and minorities support the war effort at home?

Section 4: War in Europe and Africa

Essential Question What strategies did the Allies pursue in Europe and Africa to defeat the Axis powers in World War II?

Section 5: War in the Pacific

Essential Question What was the turning point in the war in the Pacific, and what led up to it?

History ONLINE
Chapter Overview Visit glencoe.com and click on **Chapter 26—Chapter Overviews** to preview chapter information.

FOLDABLES
Study Organizer

Summarizing Information
Make the following Foldable to help you summarize information about the effects of the war on women and minorities.

Step 1 Collect three sheets of paper and place them on top of each other about an inch apart.

Step 2 Fold up the bottom edges of the paper to form six tabs. This makes all tabs the same size.

Step 3 When all the tabs are the same size, crease the paper to hold the tabs in place, and staple the sheets together. Label each tab as shown.

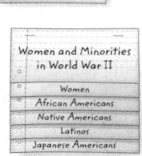

Reading and Writing As you read the chapter, write details about how the war affected women and minorities.

About 2,000 women were accepted into the Women's Air Force Service Pilots. ▶

"I've found the job where I fit best!"

FIND YOUR WAR JOB
in Industry – Agriculture – Business

★ **1941**
• Lend-Lease Act passes
• U.S. declares war

★ **1942**
• Allies capture North Africa
• U.S. increases war effort on home front

★ **1944**
Supreme Court upholds internment of Japanese American civilians

★ **1945**
U.S. drops atomic bombs on Hiroshima and Nagasaki, Japan

1941 — **1943** — **1945**

★ **1940**
• German troops occupy Paris
• Hitler orders bombing of Britain

★ **1941**
• Germany attacks Soviet Union
• Japan bombs Pearl Harbor, Hawaii

★ **1944**
D-Day, Allies invade France

◀ American cemetery, Normandy, France

Chapter 26   803

Introducing Chapter 26

Time Line Activity

If you have not already done so, have students review the time line. **Ask:** What years are covered in this chapter? *(1937–1945)* During which of these years was the United States at war? (*The United States was at war from 1941 to 1945.*) Have students refer to the "World" section of the time line to identify Germany's actions during this period. (***1939:*** *Germany invades Austria and Czechoslovakia and seizes Poland;* ***1940:*** *Germany occupies Paris and bombs Britain;* ***1941:*** *Germany attacks the Soviet Union.*)

FOLDABLES
Study Organizer
Dinah Zike's Foldables

Purpose This Foldable helps students understand cause-and-effect relationships as they list facts and details that describe how the war affected women and minorities. **OL**

📂 More Foldables activities for this chapter can be found in the *Dinah Zike's Reading and Study Skills Foldables.*

History ONLINE

Introduce students to chapter content and key terms by having them access the **Chapter Overview** at glencoe.com.

Section 3

On the Home Front Ask: How can citizens at home contribute to a nation's war effort? *(Citizens might work in defense factories, watch for suspicious activities, or send care packages to troops.)* Tell students that Section 3 will explore the ways American citizens supported the war effort during World War II. **OL**

Section 4

War in Europe and Africa Ask: What do you know about D-Day? Tell students that before the Allies invaded mainland Europe on D-Day, they first drove the Germans out of North Africa. Tell them they will learn about the Allies' military strategy to defeat Hitler in Section 4. **OL**

Section 5

War in the Pacific Ask: What effects would have to be considered before using the atomic bomb? *(Thousands of Japanese civilians would be killed, wounded, or sickened by the bomb, but many American lives would be lost if there was an invasion of Japan.)* Section 5 will discuss the decision to drop the atomic bomb on Hiroshima and Nagasaki. **OL**

803

Focus

Bellringer
Daily Test Practice Transparency 26–1

Reading Guide
Answers to Graphic:
Nazi Party: *Dictator:* Adolf Hitler; *Country:* Germany **Fascist Party:** *Dictator:* Benito Mussolini; *Country:* Italy **Communist Party:** *Dictator:* Joseph Stalin; *Country:* Soviet Union

Section Spotlight Video

To learn more about the beginnings of World War II, watch the Section Spotlight Video "Road to War."

Resource Manager

Essential Question ◄
How did dictators acquire and expand power in Europe in the 1930s?

Reading Guide

Content Vocabulary
dictator *(p. 805)*   totalitarian *(p. 806)*
fascism *(p. 805)*   appeasement *(p. 807)*
anti-Semitism *(p. 806)*

Academic Vocabulary
obtain *(p. 806)*   unify *(p. 807)*

Key People and Events
Benito Mussolini *(p. 805)*
Joseph Stalin *(p. 806)*
Munich Conference *(p. 807)*

Reading Strategy
Taking Notes Use a chart like the one below to list the dictator and country where each political party originated in the 1930s.

	Nazi Party	Fascist Party	Communist Party
Dictator			
Country			

 ILLINOIS STANDARDS
The American Journey

14.D Understand the roles and influences of individuals and interest groups in the political systems of Illinois, the United States and other nations.

14.E.3 Compare the basic principles of the United States and its international interests (e.g., territory, environment, trade, use of technology).

18.B.3a Analyze how individuals and groups interact with and within institutions (e.g., educational, military).

The Road to War

American Diary

Many people underestimated Adolf Hitler's influence, but not American journalist William Shirer. He described a rally for Hitler at Nuremberg in September 1934: "Like a Roman emperor Hitler rode into this mediæval town. . . . When Hitler finally appeared on the balcony for a moment, . . . [people] looked up at him as if he were a Messiah, their faces transformed into something positively inhuman." The passion of the Nazis shocked Shirer, and soon it would shock the world.

—*from* Berlin Diary

Nazi rally in Nuremberg, Germany

R Reading Strategies	**C** Critical Thinking	**D** Differentiated Instruction	**W** Writing Support	**S** Skill Practice
Teacher Edition • Making Inferences, p. 807 **Additional Resources** • Guid. Read., URB p. 95 • Content Vocab., URB p. 73 • Academic Vocab., URB p. 75 • Read. Ess., p. 286	**Teacher Edition** • Analyzing Primary Sources, p. 805 • Analyzing Information, p. 806 **Additional Resources** • Quizzes and Tests, p. 255 • Authentic Assess., p. 26	**Teacher Edition** • Auditory, p. 806 **Additional Resources** • School-to-Home, URB p. 91 • Reteaching Act., URB p. 93	**Additional Resources** • Writ. Skills, URB p. 79	**Teacher Edition** • Reading a Time Line, p. 805 **Additional Resources** • Daily Test Pract. Transp. 26-1 • Geo. & Hist., URB p. 87 • Lesson Transp. 26A

The Rise of Dictators

Main Idea Bitterness over the outcome of World War I and serious economic problems led to the rise of dictators in several countries.

History and You Is it ever okay for people to steal something if they need it? Read to learn how dictators in Europe and Asia used that argument to justify invading other countries.

In the 1920s, Adolf Hitler stated in his book *Mein Kampf* (My Struggle): "He who wants to live must fight, and he who does not want to fight in this world, where eternal struggle is the law of life, has no right to exist." When Hitler became Germany's leader, he put his strong words into action.

Hitler was among other ruthless leaders to rise to power in the 1920s and 1930s by taking advantage of people's anger and suffering. Some Europeans resented the Treaty of Versailles, which ended World War I. When a worldwide economic depression hit in the 1930s, frustration and fear added to this anger. Hitler and other leaders promised a better life and a glorious future. Once they won power, these men became **dictators**—leaders who control their nations by force.

Italy

Benito Mussolini won power by appealing to Italians who resented that Italy had won little in the Versailles treaty. Mussolini made **fascism**—extreme nationalism—popular. By 1922, his Fascist Party was able to force Italy's king to name Mussolini the head of government. Mussolini soon banned all political parties except his Fascist Party.

Known as *Il Duce* (the leader), Mussolini quickly ended democratic rule in Italy. Civil liberties and the free press ceased to exist. Mussolini also built up the military and vowed to regain the glory of ancient Rome.

In 1935 Mussolini took over the African nation of Ethiopia. The League of Nations banned the trade of certain goods with Italy, but it lacked the power to enforce the ban. Italy left the League and continued its expansion, seizing its neighbor Albania in 1939.

Germany

The Great Depression hit Germany extremely hard. Businesses failed, and millions of people lost their jobs. Hitler won German support by appealing to fears about the economy and bitterness over the Versailles treaty.

Teach

C Critical Thinking

Analyzing Primary Sources Discuss the meaning of "pacifism" and "pacifist" with students. **Ask:** How do you think Hitler felt about pacifists? *(Hitler might argue that pacifists "have no right to exist" because pacifists do not believe in the use of violence.)* **AL**

S Skill Practice

Reading a Time Line Direct students to examine the time line on this page. **Ask:** When did Hitler become head of the Nazi Party? *(1921)* What economic disaster preceded the Nazis' rise to power in the 1930s? *(the beginning of the Great Depression)* **OL**

Time Line

Critical Thinking Answer
A possible answer is that the hardships and despair of World War I and the Great Depression made Germans more likely to support a party that promised a better life and a glorious future.

Time Line | Rise of Nazism

Path to Power By 1933 the Nazis—once a small, obscure group—had become Germany's most powerful political party.

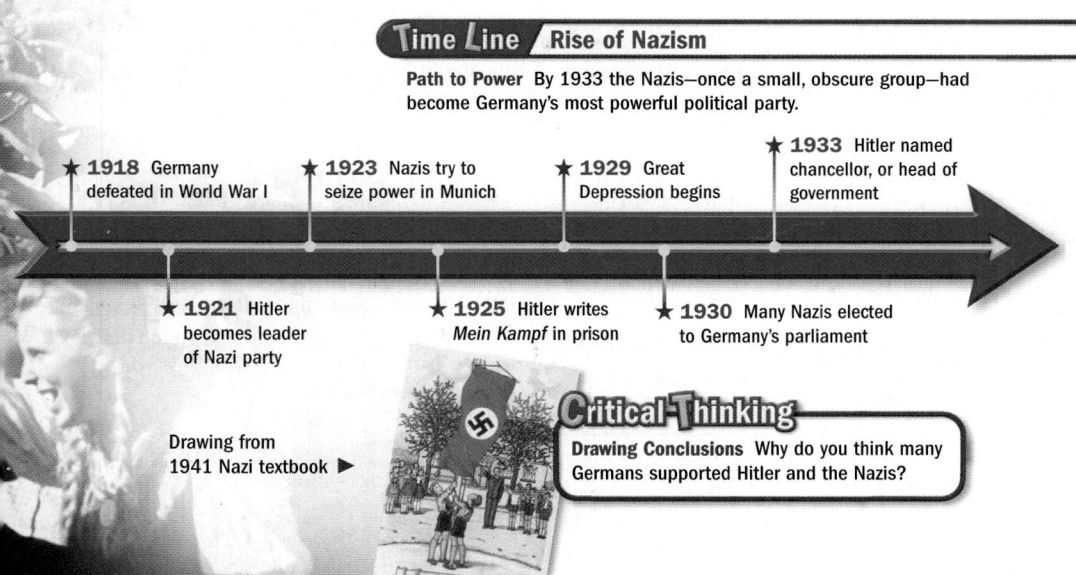

★ **1918** Germany defeated in World War I

★ **1923** Nazis try to seize power in Munich

★ **1929** Great Depression begins

★ **1933** Hitler named chancellor, or head of government

★ **1921** Hitler becomes leader of Nazi party

★ **1925** Hitler writes *Mein Kampf* in prison

★ **1930** Many Nazis elected to Germany's parliament

Drawing from 1941 Nazi textbook ▶

Critical Thinking
Drawing Conclusions Why do you think many Germans supported Hitler and the Nazis?

Differentiated Instruction

Hitler and Mussolini March Across Europe

Geography and History Activity, URB p. 87

Objective: To use a map to show German and Italian aggression in Europe from 1935 to 1939

Focus: Ask students to identify the German and Italian dictators in the 1930s.

Teach: Students should use their textbooks to complete the map activity.

Assess: Have students display their completed maps and review their answers.

Close: Ask students what might result from Germany's and Italy's actions during the 1930s.

Differentiated Instruction Strategies

BL Have students explain the information in the map's key before completing the activity.

AL Have students read a memoir of someone who lived through German or Italian aggression in the 1930s.

ELL Have students explain the terms: "aggression" and "appeasement."

D Differentiated Instruction

Auditory Have students work in pairs to create questions testing vocabulary words found in the section. **OL**

C Critical Thinking

Analyzing Information Ask: How did the United States respond to the increasing tensions in Europe? *(by passing the Neutrality Acts between 1935 and 1937 to keep the nation out of war)* **OL**

INTERPRETING
POLITICAL CARTOONS

Answers

1. Hitler is making them look more like himself. They look surprised and concerned.

2. The cartoonist implies that Hitler was the most powerful dictator of the three shown, and his policies influenced those of other dictators.

✓ **Reading Check** **Answer:** to return their countries to former glory by expanding their boundaries

Hands-On Chapter Project
Step 1

Recognizing Propaganda

Step 1: Defining Propaganda Students will define "propaganda" and investigate its use by the Nazis.

Essential Question: How did dictators acquire and expand power in Europe in the 1930s?

Directions Organize students into five groups. Have each group look up "propaganda" in the dictionary. **Ask:** What is

---

1. **Analyzing Visuals** Why is Hitler cutting the hair of Inönü and Stalin? How are they reacting?
2. **Identifying Points of View** What commentary do you think the cartoonist is making about Hitler?

A. Russia's Stalin B. Germany's Hitler
C. Turkey's Inönü

Economic problems brought dictators to power in many countries. This June 1941 cartoon comments on Hitler's strong influence.

Hitler was leader of the National Socialist Party, or the Nazi Party. Hitler and the Nazis believed the German people were superior to other groups of people. Hitler blamed the Jews, including Germans who were Jewish, for Germany's problems. His **anti-Semitism**—hatred of the Jews—would lead to unspeakable horrors.

After gaining power in 1933, Hitler ended democracy and set up **totalitarian** rule. In a **totalitarian** state, leaders crush all opposition and try to totally control all areas of society.

Hitler claimed that Germany had a right to expand. Germany's neighbors watched uneasily as he defied the Versailles treaty and rebuilt Germany's military. To win support, Hitler formed an alliance with Italy in 1936.

Growing Tension

During the Depression the Japanese suffered from lack of jobs and food shortages. Military leaders believed that Japan needed more land and resources. In September 1931, Japan's army invaded mineral-rich Manchuria, China's northeastern region.

The League of Nations condemned the Japanese invasion but did nothing about it. Japan then set up a government in Manchuria. In 1937 Japan invaded China. Three years later, Japan joined Germany and Italy in the "Axis" alliance.

In the late 1920s, **Joseph Stalin** rose to power as the Communist leader of the Soviet Union. Stalin used force to **obtain,** or gain, obedience from his people. He executed his rivals and sent millions of people suspected of disloyalty to labor camps.

American Neutrality

Most Americans wanted to avoid foreign troubles. To keep the nation out of wars, Congress passed the Neutrality Acts between 1935 and 1937. The Neutrality Acts banned weapons sales and loans to nations that were at war. Many countries had not paid back their World War I loans and Congress wanted to prevent more debts.

✓ **Reading Check** **Comparing** What plans did Mussolini and Hitler share?

---

propaganda? *(ideas, facts, or allegations spread deliberately to further one's cause or to damage an opposing cause)* How could propaganda be used by European dictators? *(to convince people to support their rule)* Have each group use the Internet to find a piece of visual propaganda produced by the Nazi Party. Each group should prepare a short presentation describing the piece. Students must analyze why the selection could be considered propaganda

and describe the message that it was promoting.

Assessing Ask: How did Hitler use propaganda to acquire power in the 1930s? *(He used propaganda to convey that the Nazis would usher in a better life and a glorious future for Germany.)* Tell students they will learn more about the outbreak of war in the next step. **OL**

(Chapter Project continued in Section 2)

Germany On the March

Main Idea Other European countries stood by as Germany expanded its territory.

History and You Is it better to stand up to bullies or give them what they want? Read to learn how Europe's leaders dealt with Adolf Hitler's demands.

⋯⋯⋯⋯⋯⋯⋯⋯⋯⋯⋯⋯⋯⋯⋯⋯⋯

Hitler moved forward with his plans for expansion. In March 1936, he ordered German troops into the Rhineland. The Versailles treaty had made the Rhineland, German lands west of the Rhine River, a neutral area.

Next, Hitler insisted that German-speaking Austria should be **unified** with Germany. In March 1938, he sent troops into Austria.

Hitler then turned to the Sudetenland, an area of Czechoslovakia where many German-speaking people lived. Falsely claiming that these people were being mistreated, Hitler declared Germany's right to take the territory.

Czechoslovakia was ready to fight to keep the Sudetenland. Britain and France, fearing a major war, sought a peaceful solution. In September 1938, European leaders met in Munich, Germany.

Britain and France thought that they could avoid war by accepting Germany's demands—a policy known as **appeasement**. At the **Munich Conference,** British and French leaders agreed to give the Sudetenland to Germany. Czechoslovakia was told to give up the Sudetenland or fight Germany on its own. Hitler pledged not to further expand Germany's territory. British prime minister, Neville Chamberlain, returned home to cheers, declaring that the agreement had preserved "peace for our time."

Hopes for peace were soon dashed. In March 1939, Hitler's army took the rest of western Czechoslovakia and set up a pro-Nazi state in the eastern part.

Meanwhile, Hitler prepared to invade Poland. He worried, however, that such an attack would anger Stalin because Poland bordered the Soviet Union. Though bitter enemies, Hitler and Stalin signed the Soviet-German Non-Aggression Pact in August 1939. Hitler was now free to attack Poland without fear of Soviet intervention.

✓ **Reading Check** **Explaining** Why was Germany able to invade Poland?

R Reading Strategy

Making Inferences Ask: How do you think the British and French governments viewed the Soviet-German Non-Aggression Pact? *(The British and French governments must have been alarmed, because the Soviet Union would no longer be a potential ally in the fight against Germany.)* **OL**

✓ **Reading Check** **Answer:** because Hitler and Stalin signed the Soviet-German Non-Aggression Pact, which eliminated the threat of Soviet intervention

Assess

⋯⋯⋯⋯⋯⋯⋯⋯⋯⋯⋯⋯⋯⋯⋯

History ONLINE

Study Central™ provides summaries, interactive games, and online graphic organizers to help students review content.

Close

⋯⋯⋯⋯⋯⋯⋯⋯⋯⋯⋯⋯⋯⋯⋯

Summarizing Have students describe how Hitler was able to acquire power in Germany. **OL**

Section 1 Review

History ONLINE
Study Central™ To review this section, go to glencoe.com.

Vocabulary

1. Use each term in a sentence: dictator, fascism, anti-Semitism, totalitarian, obtain, unify, appeasement.

Main Ideas

2. Explaining What were some of the problems that led to the rise of dictators in Germany, Italy, and Japan?

3. Theorizing How did the policy of appeasement work in Hitler's favor?

Critical Thinking

4. Interpreting Why do you think fascism became popular in Europe in the years following World War I?

5. Sequencing Create a time line like the one below to track Hitler's actions in each of the months and years noted.

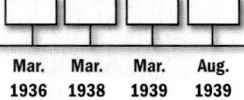

| Mar. | Mar. | Mar. | Aug. |
| 1936 | 1938 | 1939 | 1939 |

6. Persuasive Writing Write an editorial that defends or criticizes the policy of American neutrality in the 1930s. Make sure to include reasons that support your position.

Answer the
7. Essential Question
How did dictators acquire and expand power in Europe in the 1930s?

America and World War II **Chapter 26** **807**

Section 1 Review

Answers

1. Sentences should include vocabulary words with their correct definitions.

2. Some Europeans resented the Treaty of Versailles, and when the Great Depression began, people felt frustrated, angry, and afraid.

3. Appeasement allowed Hitler to build up his military and take control of Austria and the Sudetenland without interference from Britain and France.

4. People were suffering, and the extreme nationalistic feelings of fascism gave people

hope that their countries would again become great and powerful.

5. March 1936: German troops move into the Rhineland; **March 1938:** German troops march into Austria; **March 1939:** Hitler's army takes control of western Czechoslovakia and sets up a pro-Nazi state in eastern Czechoslovakia; **August 1939:** Hitler and Stalin sign the Soviet-German Non-Aggression Pact.

6. Students should include information about the Neutrality Acts as well as information

about the buildup to war in Europe during that period to support their positions.

7. Dictators took advantage of people's anger and suffering, promising a better life and a glorious future under their rule. Once in power, dictators ended democracy and set up totalitarian states in which all opposition was crushed and all areas of society were controlled by the government.

Focus

Section 2

Bellringer
Daily Test Practice Transparency 26–2

Reading Guide
Answers to Graphic:
Allied Powers: Great Britain, France, China, the Soviet Union, the United States;
Axis Powers: Germany, Italy, Japan

Section Spotlight Video

Watch the Section Spotlight Video "War Begins" to learn more about the war in Europe.

Resource Manager

Essential Question ◄
How did peaceful nations confront foreign aggressors in World War II?

Reading Guide

Content Vocabulary
blitzkrieg (p. 809)   disarmament (p. 812)

Academic Vocabulary
target (p. 809)   fund (p. 813)

Key People and Events
Allied Powers (p. 810)
Axis Powers (p. 810)
Winston Churchill (p. 810)
Atlantic Charter (p. 812)
Pearl Harbor (p. 813)

Reading Strategy
Taking Notes Use a diagram like the one below to record which countries belonged to the Allied Powers and which belonged to the Axis Powers in World War II.

ILLINOIS STANDARDS
The American Journey

16.A Apply the skills of historical analysis and interpretation.

14.E.3 Compare the basic principles of the United States and its international interests (e.g., territory, environment, trade, use of technology).

17.D Understand the historical significance of geography.

18.B Understand the roles and interactions of individuals and groups in society.

War Begins

American Diary

On the morning of September 1, 1939, President Roosevelt received an urgent phone call from Europe. The voice on the other end was that of William Bullitt, U.S. ambassador to France. Bullitt told the President, "Several German divisions are deep in Poland, and fighting is heavy. . . . There were reports of bombers over the city." Roosevelt responded, "Well, Bill, it's come at last. God help us all."

—*from* American White Paper

Military aircraft being made in American factory, 1941

R **Reading Strategies**	**C** **Critical Thinking**	**D** **Differentiated Instruction**	**W** **Writing Support**	**S** **Skill Practice**
Teacher Edition • Summarizing, p. 811 **Additional Resources** • Guid. Read., URB p. 96 • Content Vocab., URB p. 73 • Academic Vocab., URB p. 75 • Read. Ess., p. 289 • Pri. Source Read., URB p. 77	**Teacher Edition** • Analyz. Pri. Sources, p. 809 • Predict. Conseq., p. 811 • Analyz. Inform., p. 812 **Additional Resources** • Quizzes and Tests, p. 256 • Enrichment Act., URB p. 11 • Link. Past & Pres., URB p. 89	**Teacher Edition** • Verbal/Linguistic, p. 810 **Additional Resources** • School-to-Home, URB p. 91 • Reteaching Act., URB p. 93	**Teacher Edition** • Expository Writing, p. 810	**Teacher Edition** • Using Geo. Skills, p. 809 • Using Geo. Skills, p. 810 • Reading Charts, p. 813 **Additional Resources** • Daily Test Pract. Transp. 26-2 • Outline Map Resource Book, p. 40

War in Europe

Main Idea World War II began in September 1939, when Germany invaded Poland, and Great Britain and France declared war on Germany.

History and You Have you ever had to do something difficult? What helped you? Read to learn how the British endured defeats and German bombing.

In a speech in 1937, President Franklin Roosevelt expressed the feeling of many Americans toward the growing "epidemic of world lawlessness. . . . We are determined to keep out of war, yet we cannot insure ourselves against the disastrous effects of war and the dangers of involvement."

On September 1, 1939, Hitler sent his armies into Poland. Two days later, Great Britain and France declared war on Germany. World War II had begun.

The German attack on Poland was swift and fierce. German planes bombed and machine-gunned **targets**, or objects for attack. German tanks blasted holes in Polish defenses, and thousands of soldiers poured into Poland. The Germans called the offensive a **blitzkrieg**, or "lightning war." Then Soviet troops moved into and occupied eastern Poland, acting on the Soviet agreement with Germany to divide Poland.

Great Britain and France could do little to help Poland because its defeat came so quickly. In late September 1939, the conquered country was split in half by Hitler and Stalin. Stalin also forced the Baltic republics of Latvia, Lithuania, and Estonia to accept Soviet military bases. When he tried to do the same with Finland, war broke out between the two nations. The Finns held out heroically until March 1940, when the Soviets forced them to surrender.

The War Expands

All through the winter of 1939–1940, the western front was quiet. British and French forces settled in at the Maginot Line, a string of steel-and-concrete bunkers along the German border from Belgium to Switzerland. Hitler and his generals decided to attack other nations before invading France.

By the Numbers — America Prepares for War

Military Increases After Hitler's invasion of Poland, the United States began to expand its armed forces and defense plants.

U.S. Military Personnel on Active Duty	
1939	334,473
1940	458,365
1941	1,801,101
1942	3,858,791
1943	9,044,745
1944	11,541,719
1945	12,123,455

Source: Bureau of the Census, *Historical Statistics of the United States.*

U.S. Military Aircraft Production

Number of Aircraft (units): 100,000 / 80,000 / 60,000 / 40,000 / 20,000 / 0

Year: 1939, 1940, 1941, 1942, 1943, 1944, 1945

Source: John Ellis, *World War II: A Statistical Survey*

Critical Thinking

Making Inferences Why do you think increases in the armed forces and military production rose greatly after 1941?

Linking Past and Present Activity, URB p. 89

Teach

C Critical Thinking

Analyzing Primary Sources Ask: What do you think Roosevelt's goal was in this 1937 speech? *(to prepare Americans for the possibility that the country might enter the war)* **OL**

S Skill Practice

Using Geography Skills Provide students with the map of Europe on page 40 from Glencoe's *Outline Map Resource Book.* Direct students to color countries occupied by Germany in blue and by the Soviets in yellow. **OL**

By the Numbers

Critical Thinking Answer
The Japanese attacked Pearl Harbor in December 1941, and the United States entered the war.

Differentiated Instruction

Blood Banks

Blood Banks

Objective: To learn about the use of blood banks during World War II and today

Focus: Ask students why it would be necessary to store blood during wartime.

Teach: Have students complete the matching exercise at the end of the activity.

Assess: Students should check their answers and discuss any discrepancies.

Close: Discuss why it is important to maintain blood supplies in the United States today.

Differentiated Instruction Strategies

BL Ask students to find out what the different blood types are.

AL Have students research the life of Dr. Charles Drew and share their information with the class.

ELL Have students explain, in their own words, the phrase "blood bank."

S Skill Practice

Using Geography Skills As students read this page, have them update the color-coded maps they created earlier in the section, showing areas of German occupation. **Ask:** What natural barrier kept the Germans from easily moving into Britain? *(the English Channel)* **OL**

W Writing Support

Expository Writing Have students write a paragraph that predicts the effects the Battle of Britain might have had on Londoners' daily lives. **OL**

D Differentiated Instruction

Verbal/Linguistic Ask: In Churchill's speech, why does he keep repeating the phrase "we shall"? *(Churchill uses repetition to emphasize the resolve of the British people. The words inspire a sense of national unity.)* **OL**

Additional Support

In April, Hitler attacked Denmark and Norway to the north, and the following month he turned west to invade the Netherlands and Belgium. The Netherlands and Belgium immediately asked for help from Great Britain and France—the **Allied Powers,** or the Allies. After bombing raids in the Netherlands, the Dutch surrendered. The Belgians fought courageously, but they too were overwhelmed.

With the collapse of Belgium, Allied troops retreated to the port of Dunkirk in the northwest corner of France on the English Channel. They were now trapped between the advancing Germans and the French coast. In a daring move, more than 800 British ships—warships, ferries, and fishing boats—joined an operation to rescue the troops. Crossing the channel again and again, the boats evacuated more than 300,000 French and British troops to safety.

In June the Germans crossed the Somme River and continued their sweep into France. Italy joined the war on the side of Germany and attacked France from the southeast. Germany and Italy—and later Japan—formed the **Axis Powers.** On June 14, 1940, German troops marched victoriously into Paris. The French surrendered a week later.

The Battle of Britain

All that kept Hitler from taking western Europe was Great Britain. In August 1940, the Germans bombed British air bases, shipyards, and industries. German planes also bombed cities, destroying entire areas of London and killing many civilians.

Hitler's goal was to break British morale before invading Britain. The British people endured, however, in part because of the inspiration of Prime Minister **Winston Churchill.** When Hitler called for Britain to surrender, Churchill responded defiantly:

PRIMARY SOURCE

"We shall defend our island, whatever the cost may be, we shall fight on the beaches, we shall fight on the landing grounds, we shall fight in the fields and in the streets, we shall fight in the hills; we shall never surrender."

—from a speech to the British House of Commons

Primary Source / The Battle of Britain

Bombing Britain In mid-August 1940, Hitler ordered the German air force to concentrate on bombing London. Hitler's goal was to terrorize the British people into surrendering. Despite the bombing of London and other major cities, the British people stood firm against the threat of a Nazi invasion.

"Gas masks have suddenly become part of everyday civilian equipment and everybody is carrying the square cardboard cartons that look as though they might contain a pound of grapes for a sick friend. . . . Although the summer holiday is still on, village schools have reopened as centers where the evacuated hordes from London can be rested, sorted out, . . . refreshed with tea and biscuits, and distributed to their new homes."

—English writer, Mollie Panter-Downes

"It was a night when London was ringed and stabbed with fire. They came just after dark. . . . About every two minutes a new wave of planes would be over. The motors seemed to grind rather than roar, and to have an angry pulsation, like a bee buzzing in blind fury."

—journalist Ernie Pyle

Technology Connection

Analyzing Primary Sources Have students work in small groups to search the Internet for three news reports of the Battle of Britain that were published or broadcast in the United States. Students should write a paragraph summarizing each report. Have each group choose a report and present it to the class. **Ask:** How do you think Americans responded to these news reports? *(Possible answer: Because of accounts of the courage of the British, Americans would feel sympathy for them and possibly hostility toward the Germans.)* How might these reports affect the nation's involvement in the war? *(Possible answer: The reports would make Americans more supportive of helping the Allies and possibly entering the war.)* **OL**

Although the Battle of Britain continued until October, the Germans never gained control of the skies over Britain. The British Royal Air Force mounted a heroic defense and inflicted heavy losses on the German air force. Finally, Hitler ended the air attacks.

Germany Turns East

Unable to defeat the British, Hitler decided that Germany needed the resources of the Soviet Union. He also believed that the Soviets' vast land area could provide "living space" for Germans.

In June 1941, German forces attacked the Soviet Union, destroying planes and tanks and capturing half a million Soviet soldiers. As the Germans advanced, Stalin ordered a scorched-earth policy. The Soviets burned their own cities, destroyed crops, and blew up dams that produced electric power. These actions made it harder for the Germans to supply their troops and to keep advancing.

Reading Check Examining Why did Hitler end plans to invade Britain?

DBQ Document-Based Questions

Analyzing What do the two documents and the photographs reveal about the British people's reaction to the German air strikes?

America and the War

Main Idea Wanting to defend democracy, the United States gradually became involved in the European conflict on the side of the Allies.

History and You Have you ever tried to stay out of a quarrel, only to find yourself being drawn into it? Read to learn how the United States responded to the war in Europe.

. . . .

The United States watched the war in Europe with concern. Most Americans leaned toward the Allies, but they did not want war. Isolationists set up the America First Committee to further the idea that the United States should stay out of Europe's problems.

Although he vowed to remain neutral, Roosevelt prepared for war. In 1938, at his request, Congress strengthened the navy. In 1939 the president also had Congress pass a new Neutrality Act. It let warring nations buy U.S. goods as long as they paid cash and carried the goods in their own ships. In 1940 Roosevelt signed the Selective Training and Service Act, the first peacetime draft in United States history. The law applied to U.S. men between the ages of 21 and 35.

The 1940 Election

With the world in crisis, President Roosevelt chose to run for a third term, ending the tradition of serving two terms set by George Washington. Roosevelt promised Americans, "Your boys are not going to be sent into any foreign wars." The Republican candidate Wendell L. Willkie generally agreed with Roosevelt's New Deal and foreign policy, but Americans preferred to keep a president they knew. Roosevelt won an easy victory.

U.S. Involvement Grows

With the election won, Roosevelt supported the Allies openly. At Roosevelt's urging, Congress passed the Lend-Lease Act in March 1941. This law allowed the United States to sell, lend, or lease weapons to any country "vital to the defense of the United States."

C Critical Thinking

Predicting Consequences Ask students to explain why the German attack on the Soviet Union may have helped the Allies. *(The attack on the Soviet Union diverted German troops and equipment from Western Europe. In addition, the German attack would likely force the Soviet Union to join the Allies.)* **AL**

R Reading Strategy

Summarizing Have students write a paragraph summarizing the United States's growing involvement in the war. **BL**

Reading Check **Answer:** The British Royal Air Force defended the skies over Britain and inflicted heavy losses on the German air force.

DBQ Document-Based Questions

Answer

Although the terrible German air strikes were designed to break British morale, the British were able to maintain calm, continue their daily routines, and ultimately endure the attacks.

Hands-On Chapter Project
Step 2

Recognizing Propaganda

Step 2: Creating a Peace Organization
Students will create an organization that is opposed to America's deepening involvement in the war.

Essential Question: How did peaceful nations confront foreign aggressors in World War II?

Directions As a class, discuss the actions of the U.S. government that brought the nation closer to war. Brainstorm reasons some Americans would oppose these actions. Then have students break into their groups to create a peace organization. Each group should write a charter and a statement of purpose. They should then create a publicity announcement for their group.

Each group should have a name and a slogan that describes its purpose.

Distinguishing Fact from Opinion Have each group present its publicity announcement to the class. **Ask:** What statements of fact does the announcement include? What opinions? Are these announcements propaganda? Why or why not? **OL**

(Chapter Project continued in Section 3)

C Critical Thinking

Analyzing Information Have students find the definition of "neutral" in the dictionary. As a group, list the characteristics of neutral nations on the blackboard. **Ask:** Do you think Germany considered the United States a neutral nation? Why or why not? (*probably not, because Roosevelt openly helped the Allied nations by protecting British ships, providing them with weapons, and drawing up the Atlantic Charter*) **AL**

Primary Source

Critical Thinking Answer
Students' answers will vary. A possible answer is that Roosevelt was increasingly supporting the Allies; therefore, even if a planned attack had been stopped, the United States would still probably have entered the war.

✔**Reading Check** **Answer:** Isolationists argued that lend-lease, by providing the Allies with weapons, increased the United States's role in the war.

Differentiated Instruction

Primary Source | Shock at Pearl Harbor

A Surprise Attack The Japanese succeeded in their surprise attack on Pearl Harbor. Sailor Charles Christensen describes the terrible scene on the USS *Arizona*:

"The oil was on fire, and they were trying to swim out of it. They'd come up and try to get their breath. The whites of their eyes were red. Their skin was coming off."
—from *Remember Pearl Harbor*

Rescue boats move in on burning battleships. ▶

U.S. Losses at Pearl Harbor

Human Casualties	Killed	Wounded
Navy	1,998	710
Marine Corps	109	69
Army	233	364
Civilian	48	35

Ships		Aircraft	
Sunk or beached	12	Destroyed	164
Damaged	9	Damaged	159

Critical Thinking
Speculating If the Japanese attack on Pearl Harbor had not occurred, do you think the United States would have entered the war? Why or why not?

Isolationists opposed the law, arguing that it would bring America closer to war. Britain, short of cash, was the first to use lend-lease.

In mid-1941, Roosevelt also had the navy protect British ships when they were close to the United States. When the Germans fired on American destroyers, Roosevelt ordered American ships to "shoot-on-sight" German and Italian ships found in certain areas.

The Atlantic Charter

In August 1941, President Roosevelt and British prime minister Churchill met and drew up the **Atlantic Charter.** While Roosevelt made no military promises, he joined Churchill in setting goals for the world after "the final destruction of the Nazi tyranny." The two nations pledged that the people would be free to choose their own form of government and live free of "fear and want." They urged **disarmament**—giving up military weapons—and the creation of a "permanent system of general security."

✔**Reading Check** **Explaining** Why did isolationists oppose the Lend-Lease Act?

The Japanese Threat

Main Idea The United States entered World War II as a result of Japan's attack on the Pearl Harbor military base in 1941.

History and You Do you remember how the terrorist attacks on September 11, 2001, led to a war? The same thing happened in 1941 when an attack on American soil drew the United States into World War II.

While Hitler and Mussolini waged war in Europe, the Japanese made military conquests in the Far East. After seizing much of China in the 1930s, the Japanese continued their expansion. After France's fall in 1940, they seized French-ruled Indochina in Southeast Asia. Japan also planned to take the Dutch East Indies, British Malaya, and the American territory of the Philippines, primarily to acquire badly needed rubber and oil.

The United States Responds

The United States responded to Japan's moves by applying economic pressure.

Leveled Activities

BL **Content Vocabulary Activity, URB p. 73**

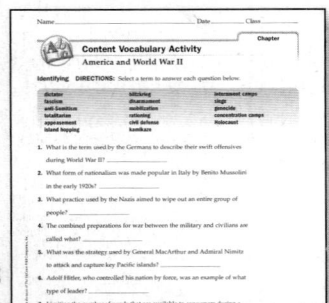

OL **Primary Source Reading Activity, URB p. 77**

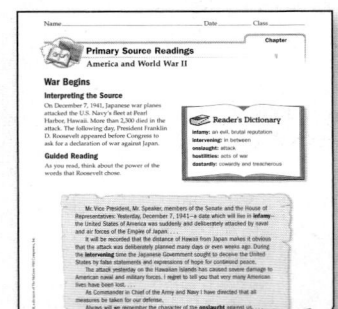

AL **Enrichment Activity, URB p. 11**

ELL **Reading Essentials and Note-Taking Guide, p. 289**

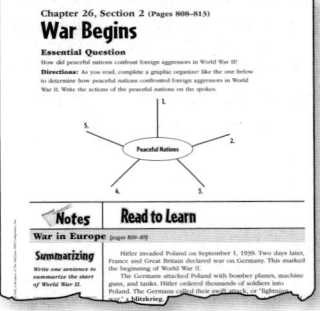

Roosevelt froze all Japanese **funds,** or reserves of money, in U.S. banks. He also stopped the sale of oil, gasoline, and other resources that Japan lacked. The action angered the Japanese.

In October 1941, the Japanese prime minister, Fumimaro Konoye, resigned. Konoye wanted to hold talks with the United States because he believed Japan could not defeat America in a war. The new leader, General Hideki Tōjō, did not share Konoye's views. Still, on November 20, talks began in Washington. Meanwhile, Tōjō's government began planning an attack on the United States.

Attack on Pearl Harbor

At 7:55 A.M. on Sunday, December 7, 1941, Japanese warplanes attacked the American military base at **Pearl Harbor,** Hawaii. Ships there were anchored in a neat row, and airplanes were grouped together on the airfield—easy targets for an air attack.

The attack destroyed many battleships, cruisers, and airplanes. More than 2,300 soldiers, sailors, and civilians were killed. Fortunately, at the time of the attack, the navy's three aircraft carriers were at sea.

The Americans at Pearl Harbor were taken completely by surprise. According to Lieutenant Commander Charles Coe:

PRIMARY SOURCE

"The capsizing of the *Oklahoma* was to me a sight beyond all belief. It was in fact the most awful thing I had ever seen. To watch this big battleship capsize and to see only her bottom sticking up out of the water like the back of a turtle and to realize that U.S. officers and men were still in there—well, I just couldn't believe it. It made me realize . . . that war had come to Hawaii."
—from *December 7, 1941*

The attack on Pearl Harbor united the country. The next day, Roosevelt asked Congress to declare war, calling December 7 "a date which will live in infamy."

On December 11, Germany and Italy—Japan's allies—declared war on the United States. Congress then declared war on them. The United States joined the Allied nations—including Great Britain, France, China, and the Soviet Union—against the Axis Powers—Germany, Italy, and Japan.

Reading Check Explaining Why did Japan attack Pearl Harbor?

Section 2 Review

History ONLINE
Study Central™ To review this section, go to glencoe.com.

Vocabulary

1. Use each of these terms in a complete sentence that will help explain its meaning: target, blitzkrieg, disarmament, fund.

Main Ideas

2. **Analyzing** What was the blitzkrieg, and why was it so effective during the war?
3. **Identifying** What was the outcome of the presidential election in 1940?

4. **Analyzing** Explain why the attack on Pearl Harbor was successful.

Critical Thinking

5. **Listing** Re-create a diagram like the one below to list the main goals of the Atlantic Charter.

6. **Creative Writing** You are a teen living in London in September 1940. Write a journal entry explaining what it is like living in a city that is daily bombarded.

7. **Answer the Essential Question**
How did peaceful nations confront foreign aggressors in World War II?

America and World War II **Chapter 26 813**

S Skill Practice

Reading Charts Tell students to examine the charts on the previous page. **Ask:** What branch of the military suffered the most casualties in the attack on Pearl Harbor? *(the navy)* Were more people killed or wounded in the attacks? *(More people were killed.)* **BL**

Reading Check **Answer:** Japan attacked because the United States was applying economic pressure on its government and the Japanese military believed Japan could defeat the United States in a war.

Assess

History ONLINE

Study Central™ provides summaries, interactive games, and online graphic organizers to help students review content.

Close

Classifying As a class, list the ways that the United States responded to German aggression. Then identify how the United States responded to Japanese aggression. **OL**

Section 2 Review

Answers

1. Sentences should use vocabulary words with their correct definitions.
2. The blitzkrieg was a method of swift and fierce warfare used by the Germans. It was effective because it gave opponents little time to prepare their defenses.
3. Roosevelt was reelected.
4. The attack was a complete surprise, and the ships and airplanes at the military base were grouped together, making easy targets for an air attack.
5. **Goals:** disarmament, creation of a permanent system to keep peace, and freedom of all people to choose their own forms of government
6. Students should include information about the Battle of Britain and the inspiring leadership of Winston Churchill.
7. While France fell to Germany, Britain mounted a courageous defense and won the Battle of Britain. When the Soviets were attacked by Germany, they burned their own cities and destroyed their own crops to make it difficult for German troops to get supplies. The United States supported the Allies openly after 1940 and declared war on Japan and Germany after Pearl Harbor was attacked.

Section 3

On the Home Front

Focus

Bellringer
Daily Test Practice Transparency 26-3

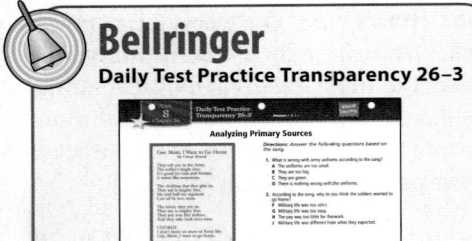

Reading Guide
Answers to Graphic:
Large numbers of women served in the military; African Americans were given combat assignments; African Americans moved to the North and West to work in industries; Native Americans became "code talkers"; many Mexicans moved to the United States to work.

Section Spotlight Video

To learn more about the Selective Service, watch the Section Spotlight Video "On the Home Front."

Resource Manager

Essential Question
In what ways did American men, women, and minorities support the war effort at home?

Reading Guide

Content Vocabulary
mobilization (p. 815) civil defense (p. 817)
ration   internment
(p. 817)   camp (p. 819)

Academic Vocabulary
shift (p. 815)   overseas (p. 816)

Key People and Events
WACs (p. 815)
WAVES (p. 815)
Tuskegee Airmen (p. 817)
bracero (p. 819)
Nisei (p. 819)

Reading Strategy
Taking Notes Re-create the diagram below, and describe the new roles adopted by American men and women during World War II.

ILLINOIS STANDARDS
The American Journey

15.B Understand that scarcity necessitates choices by consumers.

15.E.3a Identify the types of taxes levied by differing levels of governments (e.g., income tax, sales tax, property tax).

18.B.3a Analyze how individuals and groups interact with and within institutions (e.g., educational, military).

18.C.3b Explain how diverse groups have contributed to U.S. social systems over time.

American Diary

Sybil Lewis, a riveter for Lockheed Aircraft in Los Angeles, gave this description of her wartime job: "The women worked in pairs. I was the riveter and this big, strong, white girl from a cotton farm in Arkansas worked as the bucker. The riveter used a gun to shoot rivets through the metal and fasten it together. The bucker used a bucking bar on the other side of the metal to smooth out the rivets. Bucking was harder than shooting rivets; it required more muscle. Riveting required more skill."

—from "Rosie the Riveter"

During the war years, women worked at jobs traditionally held by men.

R Reading Strategies	**C** Critical Thinking	**D** Differentiated Instruction	**W** Writing Support	**S** Skill Practice
Teacher Edition • Taking Notes, p. 816 • Summarizing, p. 816 **Additional Resources** • Guid. Read., URB p. 97 • Content Vocab., URB p. 73 • Academic Vocab., URB p. 75 • Read. Ess., p. 292	**Teacher Edition** • Draw. Conclu., p. 816 • Pred. Conseq., p. 817 **Additional Resources** • Quizzes and Tests, p. 257 • Citizen. & Dec. Mak. Skills, URB p. 3 • Crit. Think. Skills, URB p. 85	**Teacher Edition** • ELL, p. 817 **Additional Resources** • School-to-Home, URB p. 91 • Reteaching Act., URB p. 93	**Teacher Edition** • Personal Writing, p. 815 • Persuasive Writing, p. 819	**Teacher Edition** • Visual Literacy, p. 815 • Using Geo. Skills, p. 818 **Additional Resources** • Daily Test Pract. Transp. 26-3 • Soc. Stud. Skills, URB p. 81 • Lesson Transp. 26C

America Prepares

Main Idea The United States had to refocus its economy to provide supplies for the war effort.

History and You Have you heard the expression "strength in numbers"? Read to find out how Americans joined together to fight World War II.

. . . .

The Japanese attack on Pearl Harbor united the American people as nothing else could. With astonishing speed, the nation's economy and its people prepared to fight the war.

Building an Army

Even before Pearl Harbor, the United States had begun raising an army under the Selective Service Acts of 1940 and 1941. More than 15 million Americans joined the armed forces during the war, both as volunteers and as draftees.

New draftees were given physical exams and injections against smallpox and typhoid. The draftees were then issued uniforms, boots, and equipment. The clothing bore the label "G.I." meaning "Government Issue." As a result, American soldiers came to be known as "GIs."

Recruits were sent to basic training for eight weeks. They learned how to handle weapons, load backpacks, read maps, pitch tents, and dig trenches.

For the first time, large numbers of women served in the military. About 250,000 women served in the **WACs** (Women's Army Corps), the **WAVES** (Women Appointed for Volunteer Emergency Service in the Navy), and women's units in the marines, Coast Guard, and army air corps. These women did not fight in combat—most performed clerical tasks or worked as nurses—but they played important roles in the war effort.

Creating a War Economy

Equipping the troops required changes in the nation's economy. To speed up **mobilization**—military and civilian preparations for war—the government created new agencies. The War Production Board supervised the conversion of industries to war production. Under its guidance, automakers **shifted**, or moved away, from building cars to produce trucks, jeeps, and tanks. The Office of Price Administration established limits on consumer prices and rents to prevent inflation.

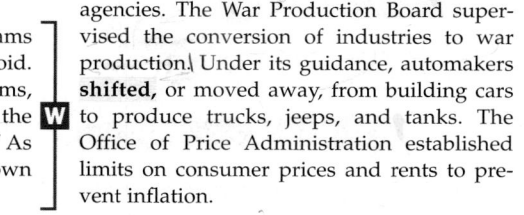

W **Writing Support**

Personal Writing Ask students to write a letter from a new draftee to his parents back home. They should use information from the text and include interesting details. **OL**

S **Skill Practice**

Visual Literacy Have students look at the poster on this page. **Ask:** What was the goal of this poster? *(to recruit women to work in defense industries)* How did the government link women's work with patriotism? *(by saying that women's work would help win the war)* How might women's attitudes toward work outside the home have changed as a result of the war? *(Women may have come to view work outside the home as a legitimate alternative to being a stay-at-home wife and mother.)* **OL**

Primary Source | Women on the Home Front Poster

The more WOMEN at work the sooner we WIN!

WOMEN ARE NEEDED ALSO AS:

FARM WORKERS, WAITRESSES, HOUSEKEEPERS, LAUNDRESSES, TYPISTS, BUS DRIVERS, ELEVATOR OPERATORS, TEACHERS, SALESPEOPLE, TAXI DRIVERS, MESSENGERS, CONDUCTORS —and in hundreds of other war jobs!

SEE YOUR LOCAL U.S. EMPLOYMENT SERVICE

Aiding the War Effort As the war progressed, women found their roles changing. Women enlisted for noncombat duties in various branches of the military. Women also found work on the home front in the construction industry or on assembly lines turning out tanks and airplanes. Eventually 2.5 million women went to work in shipyards, aircraft factories, and other manufacturing plants. Although most women left the factories after the war, their success permanently changed American attitudes about women in the workplace.

Critical Thinking

Making Connections What adjectives would you use to describe the woman in the poster? What do you think the poster says about the role of women in World War II? Explain.

Primary Source

Critical Thinking Answer
Possible adjectives: capable, patriotic, strong. Possible answer: The poster indicates that women played a crucial part in winning World War II because of their work in the nation's factories.

Differentiated Instruction

Leveled Activities

BL **Academic Vocabulary Activity, URB p. 75**

OL **Reteaching Activity, URB p. 93**

ELL **Content Vocabulary Activity, URB p. 73**

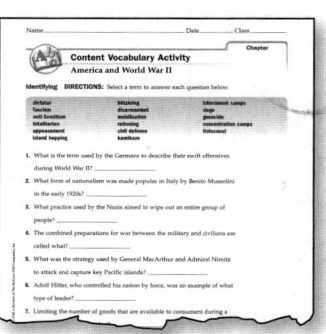

R₁ Reading Strategy

Taking Notes Have students list the new government offices and agencies discussed in this section and summarize the function of each. **BL**

R₂ Reading Strategy

Summarizing Have students write a sentence summarizing the costs of the war and how the government funded it. **OL**

C Critical Thinking

Drawing Conclusions Refer students to the information about Mexican farmworkers in the visual on this page. **Ask: Why do you think the federal government created the Bracero program?** *(Because so many men were away at war, not enough people were left to work on farms and railroads. Mexicans filled that labor need.)* **OL**

✔ **Reading Check** **Answer:** to prevent inflation by limiting consumer prices and rents

Hands-On
Chapter Project
Step 3

WOMEN!
Be a Patriot – Get a Defense Job!

Office of War Information

R₁ The National War Labor Board helped resolve labor disputes that might slow down war production. By the summer of 1942, almost all major industries and some 200,000 companies had converted to war production.

Financing the War

From 1941 to the end of the war, the U.S. spent more than $320 billion on the war effort—10 times the amount spent in World War I. Much of this money was raised through **R₂** taxes. The Revenue Act of 1942 raised corporate taxes and required most Americans to pay income taxes. Congress approved a system for withholding taxes from workers' paychecks—a practice still in effect today.

The government also borrowed money to finance the war. As in World War I, the government sold war bonds. Movie stars and other celebrities urged people to buy bonds to support the war.

✔ **Reading Check** **Explaining** What was the purpose of the Office of Price Administration?

Wartime America

Main Idea During World War II, Americans faced hardships but united to help the war effort.

History and You What would it be like to live in a country that is fighting a world war? Read to find out how American lives were shaped by World War II.

C Those who remained at home had to provide food and shelter for all those in uniform. Civilians also provided training, equipment, transportation, and medical care.

Making Sacrifices

With the war effort came many sacrifices. For many American families, the war meant separation from loved ones serving **overseas.** Those at home lived in dread of receiving a telegram announcing that a family member had been killed, wounded, or captured.

With industries geared to producing goods to fight the war, Americans faced shortages of many consumer goods.

The War and Social Change

Mexican Farmworkers ▶ In 1942 the federal government arranged for Mexican farmworkers to help with the harvest in the Southwest. The laborers were part of the Bracero Program. *Bracero* is a Spanish word meaning "worker." More than 200,000 Mexicans came to help harvest fruit and vegetables and to build and maintain railroads.

◀ Women Take New Roles The need for defense workers changed traditional patterns of American society. As millions of men joined the armed services, more women than ever before entered the labor force.

Recognizing Propaganda

Step 3: Create a Propaganda Poster Students will create a poster encouraging Americans at home to get involved in the war effort.

Essential Question: In what ways did American men, women, and minorities support the war effort at home?

Directions Student groups should choose one of these issues: convincing women to work in defense industries or convincing Americans to buy war bonds. Groups should create a propaganda poster for their issues with artwork and text, along with the name of the government office that would have issued it.

Synthesizing Ask: Why was it important for the U.S. government to get all Americans involved in the war effort? *(The government needed workers, revenue, and cooperation with rationing in order to fight the war.)* **OL**

(Chapter Project continued in Section 4)

Many things needed for the war were **rationed**—consumers could buy only limited numbers or amounts of them. Americans used government-issued books of ration coupons to buy certain items, such as gasoline, tires, sugar, and meat.

Helping the War Effort

People found other ways to help the war effort. Many planted "victory gardens" to grow vegetables, which were in short supply. Children collected scrap metal for industry.

Many people joined in **civil defense**—protective measures taken in case of attack. For example, volunteer spotters scanned the skies for possible enemy aircraft. Coastal cities enforced blackouts at night so that lights could not serve as beacons for enemy pilots.

The Office of War Information promoted patriotism to keep Americans united behind the war effort.

Reading Check Explaining Why were many consumer goods in short supply?

Opportunities for African Americans The need for workers increased the shift of African Americans from farming to manufacturing jobs. Many African Americans left the South and moved to cities in the Northeast, the Midwest, and California to work in war industries. ▼

Critical Thinking

Analyzing What effect did World War II have on migration? Explain.

Women and Minorities

Main Idea World War II brought new opportunities to women and minorities, but inequalities remained.

History and You Do you know anyone who has been discriminated against because of his or her gender or race? Read about the discrimination—and the opportunities—for women and minorities during the war.

. . . .

The war had a tremendous impact on the lives of women and minorities. It created opportunities for new jobs and new roles in society.

As millions of men joined the armed forces, more women than ever before entered the labor force. In factories women worked in jobs previously held by men. An advertising campaign featuring a character called Rosie the Riveter encouraged women to take factory jobs. For many women, this was their first opportunity to work outside the home.

Although women had new job opportunities, they usually earned less than men. Moreover, when the war ended and the troops returned home, most women would lose their jobs. Still, the war changed public opinion about women's right to work.

African Americans

About one million African Americans served in the armed forces during the war. At first, most were given low-level assignments and kept in segregated units. Gradually, military leaders assigned African Americans to integrated units. In 1942 the army began training whites and African Americans together in officer candidate school. Eventually, African Americans were allowed to take combat assignments.

The 332nd Fighter Group, known as the **Tuskegee Airmen,** shot down more than 200 enemy planes. Benjamin Davis, Jr., who trained at the Tuskegee flying school, became the first African American general in the United States Air Force. His father, Benjamin Davis, Sr., was the first African American general in the army.

America and World War II **Chapter 26** **817**

D **Differentiated Instruction**

English Language Learners Ask students to look up "civil" and "defense" in the dictionary. **Ask:** How do these definitions help you understand the meaning of "civil defense"? ("Civil" means "pertaining to citizens"; "defense" means "protection." "Civil defense" refers to ordinary citizens taking measures to defend their communities.) **ELL**

C **Critical Thinking**

Predicting Consequences Ask: How might the participation of African Americans in the military have influenced American society? (White Americans might have been more open to respecting African Americans.) **AL**

Reading Check **Answer:** Industries produced goods to fight the war rather than consumer products.

The War and Social Change

Critical Thinking Answer

Migration increased. Mexicans traveled to the United States to help harvest crops and build railroads. African Americans left the South to work in war industries.

Additional Support

Activity: Connecting Past and Present

Supporting the Military In a discussion with students, create a list on the board of the ways people at home supported the war effort during World War II. **Ask:** Do people today engage in activities that help military missions overseas? What are some ways people might do so? (Possible answers: by sending care packages to soldiers stationed overseas; giving blood or holding blood drives; donating frequent-flyer miles so soldiers can visit home) Have students research to see how people and organized groups in their community are supporting military missions overseas. Students may choose to get involved in the effort. **OL**

S Skill Practice

Using Geography Skills Have each student use the Reference Atlas at the beginning of the textbook to identify three large cities in different regions of the United States. Help students use the Census Bureau Web site to research their cities' populations between 1900 and 1970. Have students chart each city's population in a line graph. Lead a class discussion about any population shifts students identified that may have resulted from World War II migration. **AL**

Serving With Honor

Critical Thinking Answer

Some people may have viewed African Americans and Japanese Americans with less prejudice as a result of their service.

History ONLINE

Objectives and answers to the Student Web Activity can be found at glencoe.com under the Web Activity Lesson plan for this Chapter.

Differentiated Instruction

Serving With Honor

Tuskegee Airmen Although the nation's armed forces were segregated, minority groups served with courage. In early 1941, the air force created its first African American unit, the 99th Pursuit Squadron. The pilots trained in Tuskegee, Alabama and became known as the Tuskegee Airmen.

▲ Tuskegee Airmen in Italy

The Nisei Soldiers As the war progressed, second-generation Japanese Americans served in the 100th Infantry Battalion and the 442nd Regimental Combat team (right, fighting in Italy). Together, these units became the most decorated in the history of the U.S. military.

Critical Thinking

Speculating How do you think the efforts of the Tuskegee Airmen and Japanese American soldiers affected racial attitudes in America?

In civilian life, African Americans sought change. In the summer of 1941, labor leader A. Philip Randolph demanded that the government ban discrimination against African Americans in defense industries. He planned a large demonstration in Washington in support of his demands. President Roosevelt persuaded Randolph to call off the march by establishing the Fair Employment Practices Commission to combat discrimination in industries that held government contracts. The president announced that "there shall be no discrimination in the employment of workers in defense industries or government because of race, creed, color, or national origin."

The war accelerated the population shift that began during World War I. Large numbers of African Americans moved from the rural South to industrialized cities in the North and the West in search of work. In some cities, racial tensions erupted in violence. The riots inspired the African American poet Langston Hughes to write: "Yet you say we're fightin' for democracy. Then why don't democracy [i]nclude me?"

Native Americans

Thousands of Native Americans left reservations to work in defense industries and serve in the armed forces. Ira Hayes became a hero in the battle for Iwo Jima in the Pacific. A special group of Navajo formed the "code talkers." Many of the American radio communications about troop movements and battle plans were intercepted by the Japanese. The "code talkers" used a special code based on the Navajo language to send messages—a code that the Japanese never broke.

Latinos

More than 250,000 Latinos, also called Hispanic Americans, served in the armed forces. The Medal of Honor, the nation's highest military medal, was awarded to 12 Mexican Americans.

History ONLINE

Student Web Activity Visit glencoe.com and complete the Chapter 26 Web Activity about the Tuskegee Airmen.

Honoring Veterans

Objective:	To understand why it is important to honor veterans
Focus:	Ask students if any of their relatives are veterans.
Teach:	Have students read the background information and answer the questions.
Assess:	Have students discuss their answers as a group.
Close:	Students should choose one of the activities to honor veterans and complete it.

Differentiated Instruction Strategies

BL Ask students to locate a veterans' memorial in their area and report on it to the class.

AL Select students to act as group leaders in designing activities to honor local veterans.

ELL Have students present to the class information about how veterans are honored in other countries.

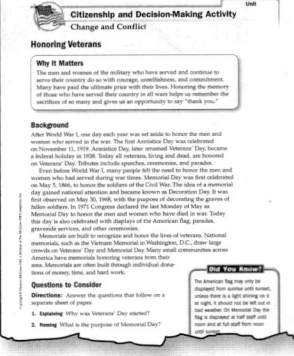

Citizen. and Dec.-Making Skills Act., URB p. 3

Mercedes Cubría of Cuba became the first Latina woman officer in the Women's Army Corps. Horacio Rivero of Puerto Rico became the first Latino four-star admiral since David Farragut to serve in the United States Navy.

Prompted by the wartime need for labor, United States labor agents recruited thousands of farm and railroad workers from Mexico. This program, called the *bracero* program, stimulated emigration from Mexico.

Like African Americans, Mexican Americans suffered from discrimination, and their presence created tensions in some cities. In 1943, for example, a four-day riot started in Los Angeles when white sailors attacked Mexican American teens.

Japanese Americans

After the Japanese bombed Pearl Harbor, Japanese Americans were feared and hated by many other Americans. About two-thirds of Japanese Americans were **Nisei**—American citizens who were born in the United States. But this fact made little difference to people who questioned their loyalty.

Military and political leaders also worried about the loyalty of Japanese Americans if Japanese forces invaded the United States. President Roosevelt directed the army to relocate more than 100,000 Japanese Americans who were living on the West Coast to detention centers. Located mostly in desert areas, these **internment camps** were crowded and uncomfortable. Conditions were harsh.

With only days to prepare for the move, most Japanese Americans left valuable possessions behind. Many abandoned their homes and businesses or sold them at a loss. Most had to stay in internment camps for the next three years. Detainee Peter Ota remembered how his father suffered. "After all those years, having worked his whole life to build a dream—having it all taken away. . . . He died a broken man."

In 1944 in *Korematsu v. United States,* the Supreme Court upheld the order providing for the relocation of Japanese Americans. In 1988 Americans acknowledged the injustice of relocation. The United States Congress issued a formal apology and agreed to give each survivor $20,000 as a token of the nation's regret.

✔ **Reading Check** **Explaining** What was the purpose of the *bracero* program?

W Writing Support

Persuasive Writing Have students state whether they think the Japanese internment was justified. Then have each student write a short essay that refutes his or her opinion. Students should use their textbooks to support their arguments. **OL**

✔ **Reading Check** **Answer:** to bring Mexican workers to the United States to help with labor shortages

Assess

History ONLINE

Study Central™ provides summaries, interactive games, and online graphic organizers to help students review content.

Close

Identifying As a class, discuss how Americans, including women and minority groups, supported the war effort at home. **OL**

Section 3 Review

Section 3 Review

History ONLINE
Study Central™ To review this section, go to glencoe.com.

Vocabulary

1. Explain the significance of each of the following terms: mobilization, shift, overseas, ration, civil defense, internment camp.

Main Ideas

2. Discussing What kinds of sacrifices did American civilians make during wartime?

3. Explaining What legal action was taken against many Japanese Americans?

Critical Thinking

4. Comparing Make a chart like the one below to record major challenges faced by each of these minority groups during the war.

Japanese Americans	
African Americans	
Native Americans	
Latinos	

5. Persuasive Writing Decide how you feel about the detention of Japanese Americans during the war. Then write a persuasive paragraph to convince a reader to agree with your point of view about this issue.

Answer the Essential Question

6. In what ways did American men, women, and minorities support the war effort at home?

America and World War II **Chapter 26** **819**

Answers

1. Explanations of terms should be accurate.

2. Some Americans were separated from loved ones, and all Americans faced rationing and shortages of consumer goods.

3. They were relocated to internment camps.

4. **Women:** entered the workforce and the military in large numbers; **African Americans:** kept segregated in the military and discriminated against in defense industries; **Native Americans:** left reservations to work in defense industries; some became "code talkers"; **Latinos:** many emigrated from Mexico and suffered discrimination.

5. Paragraphs should include details about the reasons for Japanese internment as well as the opinions about the issue.

6. Men, women, and minorities supported the war effort by working in defense industries, suffering through rationing, planting victory gardens, and joining civil defense.

Section 4

War in Europe and Africa

Focus

Bellringer
Daily Test Practice Transparency 26–4

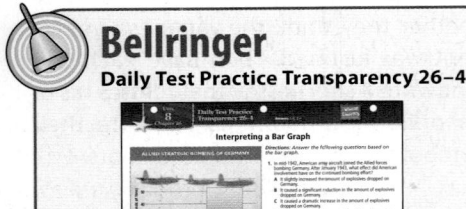

Reading Guide
Answers to Graphic:
Bottom: Allies decided to invade North Africa; **Middle:** British defeated the Germans at the Battle of El Alamein; Germans were unable to capture the Suez Canal; **Top:** Forces under Dwight D. Eisenhower joined British forces and drove the Germans out of North Africa.

Section Spotlight Video

Watch the Section Spotlight Video "War in Europe and Africa" to learn more about D-Day.

Resource Manager

Essential Question
What strategies did the Allies pursue in Europe and Africa to defeat the Axis Powers in World War II?

Reading Guide

Content Vocabulary

siege *(p. 822)*   Holocaust *(p. 825)*
genocide *(p. 825)*   concentration camp *(p. 825)*

Academic Vocabulary

concentrate *(p. 821)*   tense *(p. 823)*

Key People and Events
Dwight D. Eisenhower *(p. 821)*
George Patton *(p. 822)*
Operation Overlord *(p. 823)*
D-Day *(p. 823)*
V-E Day *(p. 824)*
Harry S. Truman *(p. 824)*

Reading Strategy
Taking Notes Fill in a pyramid like the one below with events that led to the Allied victory in North Africa.

Allied Victory

ILLINOIS STANDARDS
The American Journey

14.E.3 Compare the basic principles of the United States and its international interests (e.g., territory, environment, trade, use of technology).

16.A.3c Identify the differences between historical fact and interpretation.

17.D Understand the historical significance of geography.

18.C.3a Describe ways in which the diverse U.S. population has developed and maintained common beliefs.

American Diary

Ernie Pyle, a war correspondent, described the life of the World War II American soldier: "In the magazine the war seemed romantic and exciting, full of heroics and vitality. . . . I saw instead: men . . . suffering and wishing they were somewhere else, . . . all of them desperately hungry for somebody to talk to besides themselves, . . . cold and fairly dirty, just toiling from day to day in a world full of insecurity, discomfort, homesickness, and a dulled sense of danger."

—*from* Here Is Your War

Soldiers in a foxhole during the Allied invasion of Normandy, France, July 1944

R Reading Strategies	**C** Critical Thinking	**D** Differentiated Instruction	**W** Writing Support	**S** Skill Practice
Teacher Edition • Summarizing, p. 822 • Questioning, p. 822 • Identifying, p. 825 • Read. Pri. Sources, p. 826	**Teacher Edition** • Predicting Consequences, p. 821 • Det. Cause & Effect, p. 823 • Analyz. Information, p. 826	**Teacher Edition** • Below Grade Level, p. 823 • Auditory, p. 824 • Visual, p. 827	**Teacher Edition** • Narrative Writing, p. 824 • Personal Writing, p. 825	**Teacher Edition** • Using Geo. Skills, p. 821 • Using Geo. Skills, p. 824
Additional Resources • Guid. Read., URB p. 98 • Cont. Vocab., URB p. 73 • Acad. Vocab., URB p. 75	**Additional Resources** • Quizzes and Tests, p. 258	**Additional Resources** • School-to-Home, URB p. 91 • Reteaching Act., URB p. 93		**Additional Resources** • Daily Test Pract. Transp. 26-4 • Time Line Skills, URB p. 90

North African Campaign

Main Idea Allied armies fought a successful campaign against Axis forces in North Africa.

History and You What challenges do soldiers face when they go to battle in unfamiliar territory? Read to find out about American and other Allied forces involved in desert warfare during World War II.

O n January 1, 1942—three weeks after Pearl Harbor—the United States joined Britain, the Soviet Union, and 23 other Allied nations in vowing to defeat the Axis Powers. Although the Japanese were conquering vast areas in the Pacific, the Allied leaders decided to **concentrate,** or focus, first on defeating Hitler before dealing with Japan. The situation in Europe was desperate. German forces occupied almost all of Europe and much of North Africa. If the Germans defeated the Soviets, Germany might prove unstoppable.

Setting a Strategy

Stalin wanted the western Allies to launch a major attack on continental Europe across the English Channel. Churchill, however, argued that the United States and Britain

were not yet ready to fight strong German forces in Europe. Instead he wanted to attack the edges of Germany's empire.

Roosevelt agreed, and the Allies made plans to invade North Africa. The invasion would give untested American troops combat experience. Also, once the Americans were in North Africa, they would be able to help British forces in Egypt.

The Struggle for North Africa

The Axis forces in North Africa were led by German general Erwin Rommel, known as the "Desert Fox" because of his success in desert warfare. In November 1942, the British defeated Rommel at the battle of El Alamein. The victory prevented the Germans from capturing the Suez Canal, linking the Mediterranean and Red Seas. Rommel's forces, however, remained a serious threat.

Later that year, British and American forces under American general **Dwight D. Eisenhower** landed in Morocco and Algeria. Moving swiftly eastward, they joined British forces advancing west from Egypt to close in on Rommel. The Allies drove the Germans out of North Africa in May 1943.

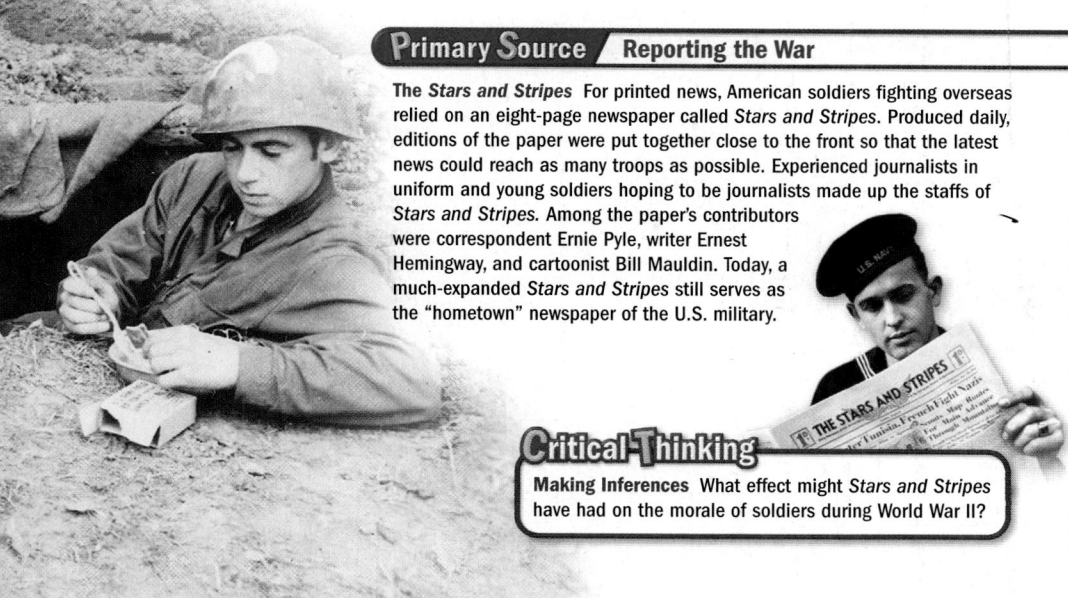

Primary Source / **Reporting the War**

The *Stars and Stripes* For printed news, American soldiers fighting overseas relied on an eight-page newspaper called *Stars and Stripes*. Produced daily, editions of the paper were put together close to the front so that the latest news could reach as many troops as possible. Experienced journalists in uniform and young soldiers hoping to be journalists made up the staffs of *Stars and Stripes*. Among the paper's contributors were correspondent Ernie Pyle, writer Ernest Hemingway, and cartoonist Bill Mauldin. Today, a much-expanded *Stars and Stripes* still serves as the "hometown" newspaper of the U.S. military.

Critical Thinking
Making Inferences What effect might *Stars and Stripes* have had on the morale of soldiers during World War II?

Teach

C Critical Thinking

Predicting Consequences Ask: What effect do you think Allied strategy had on Soviet relations with the West? Explain. *(Relations with the West might have become strained because Stalin would perceive the Allies as not willing to help the Soviets in their desperate situation.)* **AL**

S Skill Practice

Using Geography Skills Have students look at the map of World War II in Europe and North Africa on the following page. **Ask:** Why was it important for the Allies to defeat the Axis forces in North Africa? *(so that the Axis forces would not have complete control of shipping routes through the Mediterranean Sea)* **AL**

Primary Source

Critical Thinking Answer
It would help boost the morale of soldiers by giving them a sense of connection with other soldiers.

Differentiated Instruction

Leveled Activities

BL School-to-Home Connection Activity, URB p. 91

OL Academic Vocabulary Activity, URB p. 75

ELL Guided Reading Activity, URB p. 98

The Invasion of Italy

R₁ Allied troops then moved into southern Europe. They took the island of Sicily in the summer of 1943 and landed on Italy's mainland in September. Eisenhower directed the invasion. Another American general, **George Patton,** and British general Bernard Montgomery actually led the troops.

As the Allies advanced, the Italians overthrew dictator Benito Mussolini and surrendered. German forces in Italy fought on but failed to stop the Allied move into central Italy. In June 1944, the Allies finally took Rome, Italy's capital.

Meanwhile, the Allies launched an air war on Germany. Day and night, bombs battered German factories and cities and killed thousands. Yet the attacks failed to crack Germany's determination to win the war.

✔ **Reading Check** **Explaining** Why did the Allies invade North Africa first instead of Europe?

The Tide Turns in Europe

Main Idea From 1944 to 1945, the Allies fought a two-front war in Europe to defeat the Nazis.

History and You What is one memory you have that you will never forget? For many Americans who lived through World War II, June 6, 1944, stands out in their memory. Read to find out why.

During the time of the North African campaign, the Soviets and the Germans were locked in ferocious combat on Soviet territory. For months the Soviet Union bore the main brunt of Germany's European war effort.

R₂ ### The Eastern Front

After invading the Soviet Union in June 1941, German troops advanced into the country's interior. They began a **siege,** or military blockade, of the city of Leningrad that lasted nearly 900 days. As food ran out, thousands

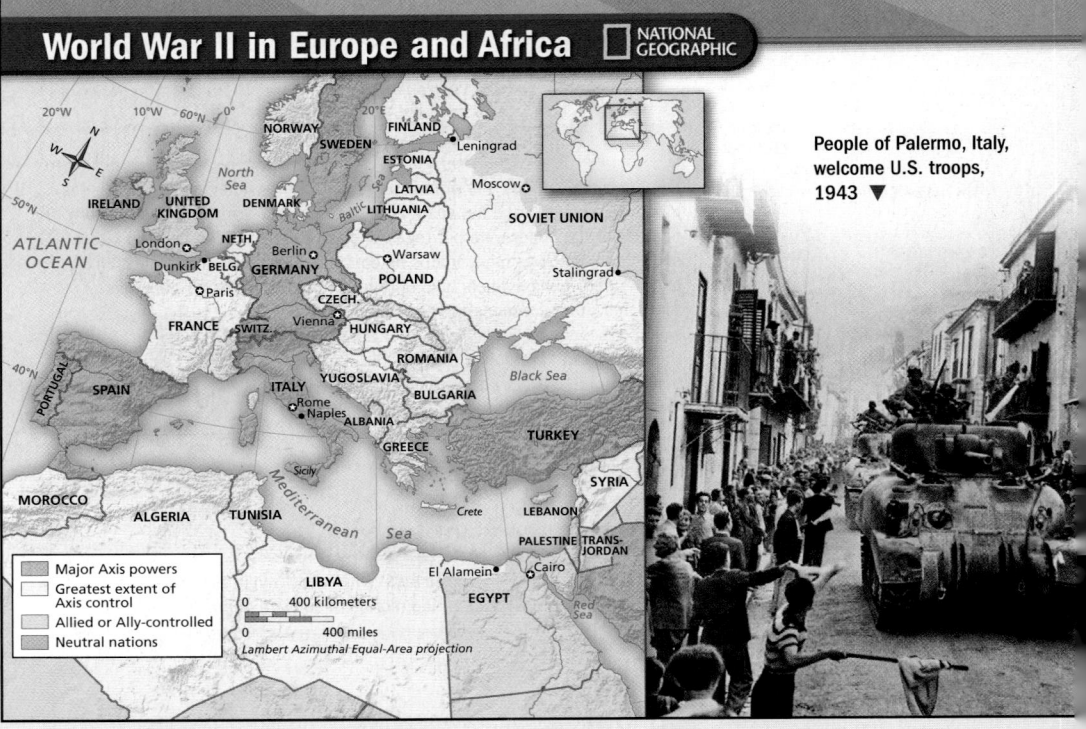

World War II in Europe and Africa 🌐 NATIONAL GEOGRAPHIC

People of Palermo, Italy, welcome U.S. troops, 1943 ▼

Major Axis powers
Greatest extent of Axis control
Allied or Ally-controlled
Neutral nations

0   400 kilometers
0   400 miles
Lambert Azimuthal Equal-Area projection

of people died. Still the Germans could not take the city, and in early 1944 the siege was broken.

German forces also attacked other Soviet cities. In 1941 the Germans tried to take Moscow, the Soviet capital. Heavy losses and wintry weather slowed them, but the Germans reached Moscow by December. When all seemed lost, the Soviets counterattacked and forced a German retreat.

In the spring of 1942, the Germans tried to take Stalingrad, a major industrial city. No sooner had the Germans won Stalingrad than Soviet forces surrounded the city, cutting off the German supply lines. Cold and starving, the Germans at Stalingrad finally surrendered in February 1943.

After Stalingrad, the Soviets drove the Germans back hundreds of miles. The Germans struck back the following summer, but their defeat at Stalingrad marked a major turning point in the war.

Invasion of France

As the Soviets pushed toward Germany from the east, Allied forces under General Eisenhower were getting ready for **Operation Overlord,** the invasion of occupied Europe. Eisenhower later wrote of the **tense,** or anxious, days of preparation: "All southern England was one vast military camp, crowded with soldiers awaiting final word to go."

On June 6, 1944, or **D-Day**—the day of the invasion—ships carried troops and equipment across the English Channel to the French province of Normandy. At the same time, paratroopers were dropped inland, east and west of the coastal beaches.

As dawn broke, the warships in the Allied fleet let loose with a tremendous barrage of fire. Thousands of shells rained down on the beaches, code-named "Utah," "Omaha," "Gold," "Sword," and "Juno." After wading ashore the troops faced land mines and fierce fire from the Germans.

C Critical Thinking

Determining Cause and Effect Ask: What was the German strategy in the Soviet Union? *(to take major cities)* Was their strategy successful? Explain. *(The Germans were not successful because the Soviet people were determined not to surrender.)* **OL**

D Differentiated Instruction

Below Grade Level Ask: What was Operation Overlord? *(the Allied invasion of Europe)* What was the significance of D-Day? *(It was the day that troops and equipment landed on the shores of France in Normandy.)* **BL**

World War II in Europe and Africa

Critical Thinking Answer

Although women did not serve in combat positions, they—like men—faced extreme danger on the battlefront.

Additional Support

Audie Murphy (1924–1971)
He wanted to join the Marines, but at 5 feet 5 inches tall, he was too short. The Navy also turned him down. Reluctantly, Audie Murphy, the orphaned son of Texas sharecroppers, enlisted in the Army. By the end of the war, Murphy was the most decorated combat soldier of World War II. When victory was declared in Europe in May 1945, Murphy had still not reached his 21st birthday. Today, through the Audie Murphy Club, the Army honors noncommissioned officers who best represent Audie Murphy's motto:

"You lead from the front."

Ruby Bradley (1907–2002)
About 440 American women serving in the military were killed during World War II. Eighty-eight were taken as prisoners of war. Colonel Ruby Bradley (left) is the nation's most decorated military woman. During World War II, she was a prisoner of war for 37 months. The experience of living in a Japanese prison camp taught her a lesson she could not have learned any other way:

"The many privileges, normally enjoyed every day, become very cherished when they no longer exist: Freedom to speak without censorship, freedom to communicate in writing without censorship . . ."

Critical Thinking

Comparing Compare the lives of American men and women on the battlefront.

Maps in MOtion See StudentWorks™ Plus or glencoe.com.

America and World War II **Chapter 26** 823

Fast Facts

Operation Fortitude Because the British broke the German intelligence code early in the war, they were able to find the German agents operating in England. Many of these spies became double agents for Britain. These double agents convinced the Germans that the Allies were going to launch an attack on Normandy as a diversion before they launched a main assault on the Pas de Calais, a region further east on the French coast. Hollywood stagehands built a dummy oil dock, landing craft, planes, tanks, and trucks at Dover, England, to convince the Germans that a force was gathering there. A few hundred men simulated an entire army with constant radio transmissions. In the days after D-Day, the Germans sent no reinforcements to Normandy because they believed that the Allies were about to launch a second, larger attack on the Pas de Calais.

Many Allied troops were hit as they stormed across the beaches to establish a foothold on high ground. By the end of the day, nearly 35,000 American troops had landed at Omaha, and another 23,000 had landed at Utah. More than 75,000 British and Canadian troops were on shore as well. The invasion succeeded.

Within a few weeks, the Allies landed a million troops in France. From Normandy the Allies pushed across France. On August 25, French and American soldiers marched through joyful crowds and liberated Paris.

Victory in Europe

Germany fought for survival as Soviet forces pushed from the east and American and British forces from the west. The advance across France was so rapid that many believed the war would soon end. In December of that year, however, the Germans counterattacked along a 50-mile front in Belgium. As their troops advanced, they pushed back the Allied lines, creating a bulge. The attack later became known as the Battle of the Bulge. After weeks of fighting, the Americans won the battle and headed into Germany.

By late 1944, the Soviets had driven the Germans from Russia to Poland. By February 1945, Soviet troops were just outside Berlin. Realizing the situation was hopeless, Hitler committed suicide in Berlin on April 30. Germany signed an unconditional surrender on May 7, ending the war in Europe. The Allies declared May 8 **V-E Day** for "Victory in Europe."

President Roosevelt did not share in the celebration. On vacation in Warm Springs, Georgia, Roosevelt died suddenly on April 12, 1945. Americans were greatly saddened by the death of the man who had led them for 12 difficult years. Vice President **Harry S. Truman** became president.

Reading Check **Explaining** Why was the Battle of the Bulge an important Allied victory?

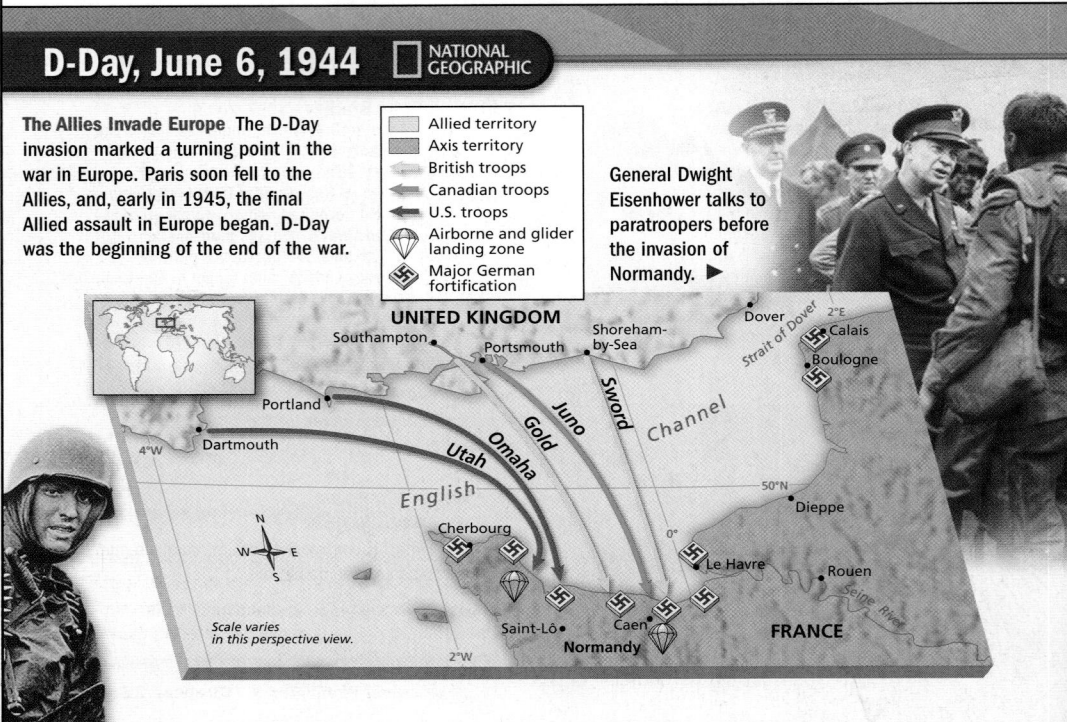

D-Day, June 6, 1944 ☐ NATIONAL GEOGRAPHIC

The Allies Invade Europe The D-Day invasion marked a turning point in the war in Europe. Paris soon fell to the Allies, and, early in 1945, the final Allied assault in Europe began. D-Day was the beginning of the end of the war.

- ☐ Allied territory
- ☐ Axis territory
- British troops
- Canadian troops
- U.S. troops
- Airborne and glider landing zone
- Major German fortification

General Dwight Eisenhower talks to paratroopers before the invasion of Normandy. ►

UNITED KINGDOM
Southampton • Portsmouth • Shoreham-by-Sea • Dover 2°E • Calais • Boulogne
Portland • Strait of Dover
Dartmouth • 4°W • Channel
English • Utah • Omaha • Gold • Juno • Sword • 50°N • Dieppe
Cherbourg • 0° • Le Havre • Rouen
Saint-Lô • Caen • Seine River
Normandy • FRANCE
Scale varies in this perspective view. • 2°W

The Holocaust

Main Idea The Nazis increased their persecution of the Jews and set up death camps in an effort to kill all of Europe's Jewish population.

History and You Today many people use the word *Nazi* to mean "someone very evil." The main reason is the Holocaust. Read on to learn about this dark chapter in human history.

. . . .

As the Allies freed German-held areas, they discovered numerous instances of Nazi cruelty. During World War II, the Nazis developed what they called "the final solution." Their "solution" was **genocide**—wiping out an entire group of people. About 6 million Jews were killed in what is known as the **Holocaust.** Millions of others—Slavs, Roma (Gypsies), communists, homosexuals, and people with handicaps—were also killed, though Jews were the only group singled out for total extermination.

Persecution of Germany's Jews

Ever since Hitler gained power in 1933, the Nazis had persecuted the Jews of Germany. They first quickly deprived Jews of many rights that all Germans had long taken for granted. In September 1935, the Nuremberg laws removed citizenship from Jewish Germans and banned marriage between Jews and other Germans. Other laws kept Jews from voting, holding public office, and employing non-Jewish Germans. Later, Jews were banned from owning businesses and practicing law and medicine. With no source of income, life became difficult for Jews in Germany.

By the end of the decade, Nazi actions against the Jews became more violent. On the night of November 9, 1938, the Nazis burned Jewish places of worship, destroyed Jewish shops, and killed many Jews. About 30,000 Jewish men were sent to **concentration camps,** large prison camps used to hold people for political reasons.

Numbers	
Allied Forces	**Casualties**
· 15,000 troops (11 divisions)	By the end of the day, 2,500 Allied soldiers were killed.
· 1,500 tanks	
· 5,300 ships and landing craft	
· 12,000 airplanes	D-Day planners had forecast 10,000 dead.
· 20,000 airborne troops	

"I could not swim when we jumped off the [landing craft]. I was tied to my platoon sergeant with a nylon rope. . . . I was too scared to even know my name."
—Dale L. Shrop, 1st Engineer Combat Battalion

Critical Thinking

Speculating What might have happened if the German forces had pushed the Allied forces back when they tried to establish a beachhead at Normandy? How might such an outcome have affected the war?

America and World War II **Chapter 26** 825

R Reading Strategy

Identifying Ask: What German laws limited the civil rights of Jews? *(the Nuremberg laws)* What rights were Jews denied? *(German citizenship, the right to marry non-Jewish Germans, the right to vote or hold public office, the right to own businesses or practice law and medicine)* **BL**

W Writing Support

Personal Writing Ask: Why do you think the Holocaust happened? *(Answers will vary.)* Allow students to do additional research on this question. They should then use their notes to write an essay outlining their points of view. **AL**

D-Day, June 6, 1944 | NATIONAL GEOGRAPHIC

Critical Thinking Answer

German forces might have retained control of Europe and could have won the war.

Differentiated Instruction

The Holocaust (1933–1945)

Objective:	To create a time line about the Holocaust
Focus:	Ask students what "Holocaust" means.
Teach:	Have students read the background information and then create their time lines.
Assess:	Have students discuss the entries they made on their time lines.
Close:	As a class, talk about the consequences of the Holocaust.

Differentiated Instruction Strategies

BL Have students list dates from the background information before creating time lines.

AL Have students research and prepare a report about the exhibits at the United States Holocaust Memorial Museum in Washington, D.C.

ELL Ask students whether their native languages have a word for "Holocaust."

C Critical Thinking

Analyzing Information Ask: Why do you think the Germans made Jews wear a yellow star on their clothing? *(to identify them and prevent them from passing as non-Jews)* **OL**

R Reading Strategy

Reading Primary Sources Ask: What was the long ditch meant to be? *(a mass grave)* Why did Josef run into the forest? *(because if he didn't, he probably would have been killed)* **BL**

Additional Support

Primary Source / Young People in the Holocaust

The Final Solution Before and during World War II, many Jewish young people in Europe suffered terrible persecution and eventual death at the hands of the Nazis.

Auschwitz, 1940 At death camps like Auschwitz (right), Jews were the Nazis' main victims. Alexander Ehrmann, a 17-year-old from Czechoslovakia, experienced a nightmarish scene when he reached one of the death camps:

"The doors flung open and we saw strange uniformed men. . . . Sentries and dogs were there, and they yelled at us . . . as they beat us out of the wagon."
—from *Children With A Star*

Hungary, 1944 Thirteen-year-old Èva Heyman described her fears as the Nazis forced her family to leave their home in Hungary:

"We are allowed to take along . . . the clothes on our bodies, and the shoes on our feet. . . . All the while I thought I was just having a bad dream. . . . I have never been so afraid."
—from *We Are Witnesses*

Critical Thinking

Analyzing What was life like for Jewish young people during the years of the Holocaust?

This event became known as *Kristallnacht,* or the "night of the shattered glass," because of the Jewish shop windows that were broken by Nazi mobs.

The Persecution Spreads

During World War II, the Nazis mistreated the Jews in the lands they conquered. They forced Jews to wear a yellow, six-pointed star on their clothing. The mass killing of Jews began when the German army invaded the Soviet Union in 1941. Special Nazi forces carried out these murders. They rounded up thousands of Jews, shooting them and throwing them into mass graves. Josef Perl, who survived a massacre of Czech Jews, wrote of the act:

PRIMARY SOURCE

"We marched into a forest where a huge long ditch was already dug. . . . I could hear . . . a machine gun going . . . . All of a sudden, . . . I saw my mother and four sisters lined up and before I had a chance to say,

'Mother!' they were already dead. Somehow time stands still. . . . But what woke me was the sight of my five nieces and nephews being marched, and the murderers had the audacity to ask them to hold hands. . . . I would have been almost the next one but all of a sudden the bombers came over, we were ordered to lay face downwards, but everyone started running . . . and I . . . ran deep into the forest.
—from *Remembering: Voices of the Holocaust*

Nazi troops crammed thousands more into railroad cars like cattle, depositing them in concentration camps, such as Buchenwald in Germany. Guards took the prisoners' belongings, shaved their heads, and tattooed camp numbers on their arms. Prisoners often had only a crust of bread or watery soup to eat. Thousands became sick and died.

The Final Solution

In January 1942, the Nazis agreed on what they called the "final solution" to destroy the Jews. They built death camps, such as those at Auschwitz and Treblinka in Poland.

Activity: Debating the Issues

Discussing Have students form two groups to gather information about what the United States government knew about the Holocaust by 1942. Tell students to use both primary and secondary sources. Students should take notes during their research and then compile their notes into a fact sheet. Tell each group to select two or three students to take part in a debate on whether the United States should have directed more effort toward combating the Holocaust earlier in the war. Begin the debate by having each group summarize its findings. After the debate, have each student write a short essay responding to the arguments and identifying their own opinions. **OL**

At these camps, many people died in poison gas chambers. Others died of starvation. Still others were victims of cruel experiments carried out by Nazi doctors. Of the estimated 1.6 million people who died at Auschwitz, about 1.3 million were Jews.

Upon arrival at a death camp, healthy prisoners were chosen for slave labor. The elderly, disabled, sick, and mothers and children were sent to the gas chambers, after which their bodies were burned in giant furnaces.

Although information about the unfolding Holocaust had reached western leaders well before 1945, Allied forces moving through Germany and Poland after V-E Day saw the unspeakable horrors of the camps firsthand. British soldier Peter Coombs described the condition of the survivors in a camp:

PRIMARY SOURCE

"One has to take a tour round and see their faces, their slow staggering gait and feeble movements. The state of their minds is plainly written on their faces, as starvation had reduced their bodies to skeletons."

—from The Holocaust

People around the world were stunned by this terrible result of Nazi tyranny. Allied governments, however, had evidence of the death camps as early as 1942. Historians today debate why and how an event as horrifying as the Holocaust could have occurred. They also discuss why so relatively little was done to stop it.

In Remembrance

The United States Holocaust Memorial Museum is located near the National Mall in Washington, D.C. This memorial provides a national mark of respect for all victims of Nazi persecution.

In 2004 the National World War II Memorial opened on a site on the National Mall. The Memorial is dedicated to the 16 million who served in the military during World War II, the more than 400,000 who died, and the men and women who supported the war effort on the home front. **D**

✔ **Reading Check** **Identifying** What groups did the Nazi government victimize?

Section 4 Review

History ONLINE
Study Central™ To review this section, go to glencoe.com.

Vocabulary

1. Write a sentence for each of the following terms that explains its meaning: concentrate, siege, tense, genocide, Holocaust, concentration camp.

Main Ideas

2. Explaining When the United States joined the Allies, why did the Allies concentrate first on defeating Hitler?

3. Identifying What was the significance of Operation Overlord?

4. Describing What was the Nazis' "final solution"?

Critical Thinking

5. Determining Cause and Effect Create a cause-and-effect chart like the one below to describe the two fronts fought in Europe to defeat the Nazis.

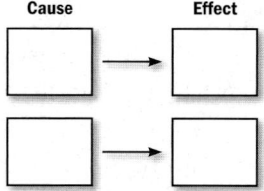

Cause		Effect

6. Persuasive Writing Take the role of an American relative of a Polish Jew. Write a letter to the editor of your local newspaper explaining what you know about the Nazi persecution of the Jews and urging the United States to take action.

Answer the Essential Question

7. What strategies did the Allies pursue in Europe and Africa to defeat the Axis Powers in World War II?

America and World War II **Chapter 26** **827**

Section 4 Review

Answers

1. Sentences should use vocabulary words according to their definitions in the section and Glossary.

2. They focused on defeating Hitler because the situation in Europe was desperate.

3. During Operation Overlord, Allied troops invaded and liberated occupied Europe. The invasion led to the defeat of Germany.

4. The "final solution" was the German plan to kill all the Jews in Europe.

5. Fighting on the Western Front: liberated France; Eastern Front: drove the Germans from Russia to Poland to Berlin, led to Germany's unconditional surrender

6. The letter should describe the Nazi persecution of the Jews and urge the government to take action to stop the genocide.

7. First, the Allies drove the Germans out of North Africa. From there, they invaded Italy and forced its surrender. The Soviets endured massive suffering and losses but eventually drove the Germans back hundreds of miles. The Allies then invaded the Normandy coast on D-Day and fought across France. With Soviet troops approaching from the east and British and American troops coming from the west, Germany finally surrendered.

Focus

Bellringer
Daily Test Practice Transparency 26–5

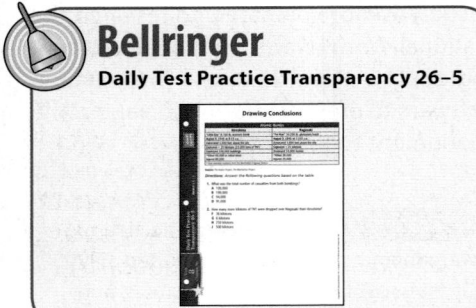

Reading Guide
Answers to Graphic:

March 1945: Americans seize Iwo Jima; **July 1945:** first atomic bomb test in New Mexico desert; **August 1945:** atomic bombs dropped on Hiroshima and Nagasaki; **September 1945:** Japan formally surrenders

Section Spotlight Video

Have students watch the Section Spotlight Video "War in the Pacific" to learn about the Japanese surrender.

Resource Manager

Essential Question
What was the turning point in the war in the Pacific, and what led up to it?

Reading Guide

Content Vocabulary

island hopping   kamikaze
(p. 830)   (p. 830)

Academic Vocabulary

secure (p. 830)   conflict (p. 832)

Key People and Events

Douglas MacArthur (p. 829)
Bataan Death March (p. 829)
Battle of Midway (p. 830)
Guadalcanal (p. 830)
Battle of Leyte Gulf (p. 830)
V-J Day (p. 832)

Reading Strategy

Taking Notes On a time line like the one below, track the important events on the Pacific front in 1945.

| Mar. | July | Aug. | Sept. |
| 1945 | 1945 | 1945 | 1945 |

ILLINOIS STANDARDS
The American Journey

14.E.3 Compare the basic principles of the United States and its international interests (e.g., territory, environment, trade, use of technology).

16.A.3b Make inferences about historical events and eras using historical maps and other historical sources.

16.B.3d Describe ways in which the United States developed as a world power.

17.C.3a Explain how human activity is affected by geographic factors.

War in the Pacific

American Diary

Marine Private Newman Baird was a machine gunner on a tracked landing vehicle. As the Marines hit the beaches on the island of Tarawa, he recalls: "'They [the Japanese] were knocking out [boats] left and right. A tractor'd get hit, stop, and burst into flames, with men jumping out like torches.' Baird's own vehicle was then hit by a shell, . . . killing many of the troops. . . . 'I didn't want to put my head up. The bullets were pouring at us like a sheet of rain.'"

—from Across the Reef

American Marines in battle on the Pacific island of Tarawa, November 21, 1943

R Reading Strategies	C Critical Thinking	D Differentiated Instruction	W Writing Support	S Skill Practice
Teacher Edition • Summarizing, p. 831 **Additional Resources** • Guid. Read., URB p. 99 • Content Vocab., URB p. 73 • Academic Vocab., URB p. 75 • Read. Ess., p. 298	**Teacher Edition** • Making Inferences, p. 829 • Det. Cause & Effect, p. 831 • Analyz. Information, p. 831 **Additional Resources** • Quizzes and Tests, p. 259	**Teacher Edition** • ELL, p. 829 **Additional Resources** • School-to-Home, URB p. 91 • Reteaching Act., URB p. 93 • Differ. Inst., URB p. 83	**Teacher Edition** • Expository Writing, p. 832	**Teacher Edition** • Using Geo. Skills, p. 830 • Visual Literacy, p. 830 **Additional Resources** • Daily Test Pract. Transp. 26-5 • Read. Skills, URB p. 7

The Pacific Front

Main Idea The Allies fought the Japanese for four long years in the Pacific.

History and You Have you ever had to follow a step-by-step plan to finish a project? Read to learn how step-by-step, the Allies pushed back Japan on the Pacific front.

On December 7, 1941, the same day Japan attacked Pearl Harbor, Japanese bombers struck American airfields in the Philippines and on the islands of Wake and Guam—key American bases in the Pacific. In the following days, the Japanese intensified their campaign in the Pacific. They invaded Thailand and Malaya and captured Guam, Wake Island, and Hong Kong.

Japanese troops landed in the Philippines in mid-December and had quickly took the capital of Manila. The defending forces—Filipino and American troops commanded by American general **Douglas MacArthur**—were forced to retreat to the rugged Bataan Peninsula west of Manila and the small island fortress of Corregidor.

The Philippines Fall

After months of fierce fighting, the exhausted Allied troops defending Bataan surrendered on April 9, 1942. The forces on Corregidor held out for another month. The Japanese forced their Bataan prisoners—many sick and near starvation—to march to a prison camp more than 60 miles away. About 76,000 prisoners started out, but only about 54,000 of those on the **Bataan Death March** reached the camp. As survivor Marion Lawton recalled:

PRIMARY SOURCE

"We'd march all day, a continuous plodding along, just trying to keep up. I always tried to stay in the middle of the column rather than on the flanks. That way I was further away . . . and might avoid a . . . beating. I don't know how to explain a typical day except that it was brutal, exhausting, hot, and your feet and legs just ached."

—from *Death March: The Survivors of Bataan*

Two months before the surrender, General MacArthur left for Australia to command Allied forces in the Pacific. MacArthur told the Filipinos, "I shall return."

Island Hopping

With Japan's victories, American morale was low. Then in April 1942, 16 American bombers, launched from an aircraft carrier in the Pacific, bombed Tokyo. This daring raid led by James Doolittle had little military importance, but it lifted Americans' spirits.

Primary Source / **Amphibious Warfare**

The LVT "Amphtrac" In the invasion of Tarawa, only one vehicle—the LVT, or amphibious tractor "amphtrac"—was able to cross hazardous coral reefs and deliver troops onto the beaches. The "amphtrac" is like a boat with tank tracks. A true amphibian is capable of movement afloat and ashore.

Critical Thinking

Making Connections How did physical geography affect U.S. military strategy on the Pacific front during the war?

A Armor-plated pontoon (float)
B Tracks
C Machine guns

Teach

C Critical Thinking

Making Inferences Ask: Why do you think Japan struck American airfields in the Philippines and on the islands of Wake and Guam on the same day as the attack on Pearl Harbor? *(All of the attacks were part of Japan's strategy of disabling the American military in the Pacific.)* **OL**

D Differentiated Instruction

English Language Learners Ask students to list five adjectives to describe the Bataan Death March. *(Possible answers: brutal, violent, cruel, deadly, exhausting)* **ELL**

Primary Source

Critical Thinking Answer
Students should note that because the battles were fought on islands, it was a challenge to transport troops and supplies across a vast ocean area.

Differentiated Instruction

Leveled Activities

BL **Reading Essentials and Note-Taking Guide, p. 298**

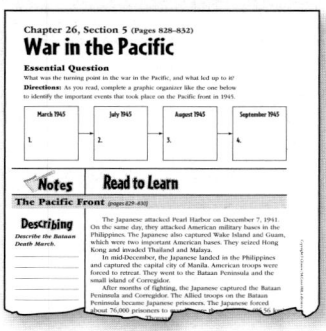

OL **Differentiated Instruction Activity, URB p. 83**

ELL **Reteaching Activity, URB p. 93**

S1 Skill Practice

Using Geography Skills Refer students to the map on this page. **Ask:** After the attacks on Pearl Harbor, what was the first battle fought that is shown on this map? *(the Battle of Coral Sea)* Guam provided a base for launching bombing attacks on what nearby islands? *(Iwo Jima and Okinawa)* **OL**

S2 Skill Practice

Visual Literacy Refer students to the photograph of Iwo Jima on the next page. **Ask:** Why has this image become a symbol of courage and patriotism? *(courage: because the fighting on Iwo Jima was extremely fierce; patriotism: because the men are raising the American flag)* **OL**

✓ Reading Check **Answer:** The Americans were able to destroy four Japanese aircraft carriers and hundreds of airplanes.

Hands-On Chapter Project
Step 5

Recognizing Propaganda

Step 5: Create a Video Students will create a video that encourages people to continue to support the war in the Pacific.

Essential Question: What was the turning point in the war in the Pacific, and what led up to it?

Directions Discuss as a class how video footage can be used as propaganda. Ask

In May 1942 American warships defeated a Japanese fleet in the Battle of the Coral Sea. An even greater victory followed in June 1942. In the **Battle of Midway,** northwest of Hawaii, the navy destroyed four Japanese aircraft carriers and hundreds of airplanes.

The United States was now ready to go on the offensive against Japan. The commanders—General MacArthur and Admiral Chester Nimitz—adopted a strategy known as **island hopping.** This called for attacking and capturing certain key islands. The United States then used these islands as bases for leapfrogging to others, moving ever closer to the Philippines—and to Japan.

Between August 1942 and February 1943, American forces engaged in a campaign for control of **Guadalcanal,** one of the Solomon Islands. The Japanese put up stiff resistance, but the Americans finally **secured** the island.

In June 1944, American forces captured Guam and other islands nearby. Guam provided a base for launching bombing strikes on Japan. In October, American ships destroyed most of the Japanese fleet at the **Battle of Leyte Gulf** in the Philippines.

The Advance on Japan

American forces then closed in on Japan. In March 1945, they seized the island of Iwo Jima and in June the island of Okinawa. The Japanese fought fiercely to defend these islands so near Japan. Thousands of Americans died in the battles, and many thousands more were wounded.

With most of the Japanese air force and navy destroyed, American bombers pounded Tokyo and other major cities of Japan. In desperation, the Japanese unleashed suicide pilots known as **kamikazes.** They crashed planes loaded with explosives into American ships. Kamikaze pilots sank several destroyers during the battle for Okinawa.

✓ Reading Check **Explaining** What is significant about the Battle of Midway?

War in the Pacific NATIONAL GEOGRAPHIC

Honoring Those Who Died Enlisted men from the Naval Air Station at Kaneohe, Hawaii, place leis on the graves of their comrades killed in the Japanese attack on Pearl Harbor. ▼

Midway June 4–7, 1942

Pearl Harbor Dec. 7, 1941

Leyte Gulf Oct. 23–26, 1944

Coral Sea May 4–8, 1942

☐ Japanese Empire, 1936
☐ Japanese occupied territory
— Extent of Japanese control, 1942
← Allied troop movements
✹ Major battle
◎ Atomic bombing

Orthographic projection

830 Chapter 26 *America and World War II*

students to identify techniques that directors might use to promote patriotism, including inspiring images, music, and interviews. Have groups of students research battles fought in the Pacific during World War II. Each group of students should choose one battle and create a video that could be shown to civilians so that they will continue to support the war. When the groups have finished, have them show their

videos to the class. Discuss what the groups did in their videos to get people to continue to support the war, and evaluate whether these methods were effective.

Recognizing Bias Ask: Why is this video a form of propaganda? **OL**

(Chapter Project continued on the Visual Summary page)

The End of the War

Main Idea American use of the atomic bomb brought about Japan's surrender in the Pacific conflict.

History and You What challenges in your life have forced you to make changes? Read to find out how Japanese leaders were forced to make changes as a result of a powerful new weapon.

Although the Japanese faced certain defeat, they continued to fight. Their refusal to surrender led the United States to use a powerful new weapon: the atomic bomb.

In 1939 the German-born physicist Albert Einstein wrote to President Roosevelt warning him that the Nazis might try to use the energy of the atom to build "extremely powerful bombs." Roosevelt then organized a committee of scientists to study the issue. In 1941, the committee members met with British scientists who already were working on a similar bomb. The Americans were impressed with the British research. They then urged Roosevelt to start a program so that the U.S. could develop its own atomic bomb.

President Roosevelt created a top-secret operation, the Manhattan Project. In 1942 scientists at the University of Chicago built the world's first nuclear reactor, a device that splits apart atoms and releases energy. Later, another team of scientists and engineers built an atomic bomb at a secret laboratory in Los Alamos, New Mexico. On July 16, 1945, the first atomic bomb went off in a test near Alamogordo in the New Mexico desert.

Dropping the Atomic Bomb

Even before the bomb was tested, American officials began to debate how to use it. The final decision rested with President Harry Truman. Truman had taken office after President Roosevelt's death on April 12, 1945. Truman did not know the bomb existed until a few weeks before he had to make the decision to use it.

Pearl Harbor Hero

Doris "Dorie" Miller (1919–1943), Mess attendant, USS *West Virginia*
Doris Miller was one of the first heroes of the war in the Pacific. He was awarded the Navy Cross for his actions during the attack on Pearl Harbor. Less than two years later, Miller was killed when the USS *Liscome Bay* was torpedoed and sunk in the Pacific Ocean. A navy ship, the USS *Miller,* was named in his honor in 1973.

Iwo Jima

Ira Hayes (1923–1955), Corporal, 2nd Battalion, 28th Marines
Born and raised on a Pima Indian Reservation in Arizona, Ira Hayes enlisted in the Marine Corps at the age of 19. He was one of the six who raised the flag at Iwo Jima, but Hayes did not feel like a hero:
How could I feel like a hero when only five men in my platoon of 45 survived?

◀ **Raising the Flag at Iwo Jima** Five Marines and one sailor raise the flag on Mount Suribachi on Iwo Jima. For many Americans, the image remains a symbol of courage and patriotism.

Map Skills

Place What strategic importance does the map show for Iwo Jima and Okinawa?

Maps In Motion See StudentWorks™ Plus or glencoe.com.

C₁ Critical Thinking

Determining Cause and Effect Ask: Why did the United States use the atomic bomb against Japan? *(The Japanese refused to surrender.)* **BL**

R Reading Strategy

Summarizing Have students write two or three sentences summarizing the development of the atomic bomb. **BL**

C₂ Critical Thinking

Analyzing Information Ask: What evidence is presented that shows that the Manhattan Project was top secret? *(Even the vice president did not know about it.)* **OL**

War in the Pacific
NATIONAL GEOGRAPHIC

Map Skills Answer
The islands were close to Japan.

Differentiated Instruction

Reading Skills Activity, URB p. 7

Questioning

Objective:	To learn how to ask good questions when reading
Focus:	Remind students that asking questions can help them better understand what they are reading.
Teach:	Have students read the passage about the human cost of World War II, and write two questions to deepen their understanding.
Assess:	Ask students to read their questions aloud to the class.
Close:	List ways in which students can learn unfamiliar words and phrases when reading.

Differentiated Instruction Strategies

BL Ask students to explain the term "human cost."

AL Ask students to use the information in the passage to create a poster about the human cost of World War II.

ELL Have students create a reminder list of the six kinds of questions they can ask themselves while reading.

W Writing Support

Expository Writing Have students write one sentence that identifies the central issue Truman had to consider when deciding whether or not to use the atomic bomb. *(Sample answer: Truman had to determine whether or not it was acceptable to kill large numbers of Japanese citizens in order to save the lives of American troops.)* **AL**

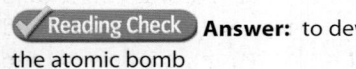 **Reading Check** **Answer:** to develop the atomic bomb

Assess

 History ONLINE

Study Central™ provides summaries, interactive games, and online graphic organizers to help students review content.

Close

Sequencing As a class, create a time line on the board that identifies important events pertaining to the war in the Pacific. **OL**

 Section 5 Review

President Truman later wrote that he "regarded the bomb as a military weapon and never had any doubts that it should be used." His advisers warned him to expect large numbers of casualties if American soldiers invaded Japan. Truman believed it was his duty as president to use every weapon available to save American lives.

The Allies then issued the Potsdam Declaration, warning that if Japan did not surrender, it faced "prompt and utter destruction." The Japanese did not surrender, and Truman ordered the use of the bomb.

Japan's Surrender

On August 6, 1945, an American B-29 bomber, the *Enola Gay*, dropped an atomic bomb on the Japanese city of Hiroshima. Three days later, a second bomb was dropped on the city of Nagasaki. The atomic bombs caused immense destruction. The first bomb leveled Hiroshima and killed between 80,000 and 120,000 people; the Nagasaki bomb killed between 35,000 and 74,000. Thousands more were injured, and many died later from burns and radiation sickness.

Faced with such destruction, the Japanese emperor said that "the unendurable must be endured" and ordered his government to surrender. August 15, 1945, was proclaimed **V-J Day** for "Victory over Japan." All around America, people expressed happiness and relief. Japan signed the formal surrender on September 2 aboard the battleship USS *Missouri*. World War II had finally ended.

In the years immediately after the war, Allied authorities put the top Nazi and Japanese leaders on trial. They were accused of war crimes and crimes against humanity. The Allies held the trials in Nuremberg, Germany, and in Tokyo.

The Cost of the War

World War II was the most destructive **conflict** in history. More than 55 million people died during the war; more than half of these were civilians killed by bombing, starvation, disease, torture, and murder. American casualties—about 322,000 dead and 800,000 injured—were high, but light compared with those of other nations. The Soviet Union suffered more than 22 million deaths. Those who survived faced the huge task of trying to rebuild their lives and their countries.

Reading Check **Describing** What was the goal of the Manhattan Project?

Section 5 Review

History ONLINE
Study Central™ To review this section, go to glencoe.com.

Vocabulary

1. Write a sentence for each key term that demonstrates its meaning: island hopping, secure, kamikaze, conflict.

Main Ideas

2. **Explaining** What was the strategy of island hopping, and what was its purpose?

3. **Describing** What was the Manhattan Project?

Critical Thinking

4. **Comparing** Create a chart like the one below in which you note the reasons for and against using the atomic bomb in World War II.

For	Against

5. **Analyzing** Why were the battles on the islands of Iwo Jima and Okinawa important to the Americans?

6. **Evaluating** What was significant about the cost of World War II?

7. **Answer the Essential Question** What was the turning point in the war in the Pacific, and what led up to it?

Answers

1. Sentences should use vocabulary words according to their definitions in the section and Glossary.
2. Island hopping called for attacking and capturing certain key islands, which could be used as bases to attack others. The purpose was to move closer to Japan.
3. The Manhattan Project was a top-secret operation to develop the atomic bomb.

4. Possible answers: *For:* would prevent the loss of American lives, would force Japan to surrender; *Against:* would kill hundreds of thousands of Japanese civilians, would cause lasting environmental effects
5. The battles were important because the Americans won even though they faced fierce resistance from the Japanese, and the victories brought them closer to Japan.

6. The war was the most destructive in history, costing millions of lives.
7. The turning point in the war was the Battle of Midway in June 1942. The American navy destroyed four Japanese aircraft carriers and hundreds of airplanes, positioning U.S. forces to go on the offensive against Japan.

Visual Summary

1939	
Sept. 1	Germany invades Poland.
Sept. 3	Britain and France declare war on Germany.

▼ Japanese American soldiers fighting in Italy

1940	
June	German troops enter Paris.
July	German air force launches Battle of Britain.
Sept.	Germany, Japan, and Italy sign a pact.

1941	
March	U.S. passes the Lend-Lease Act.
June	Hitler attacks the Soviet Union.
Dec. 7	Japan bombs Pearl Harbor.
Dec. 11	U.S. and Britain declare war on Japan. Germany and Italy declare war on the U.S.

1942	
April	Japan captures Bataan, leading to Death March.
May	United States defeats Japan in the Battle of Coral Sea.
June	U.S. defeats Japan at Midway.

The more WOMEN at work the sooner we WIN!
WOMEN ARE NEEDED ALSO AS...

1943	
Feb.	Germans are defeated at Stalingrad.
July	Allies invade Sicily; Mussolini resigns.
Aug.	Women Air Force Service Pilots is formed.
Sept.	Allies invade mainland Italy; Italy surrenders.

1944	
June 6	D-Day: Allies launch an invasion of Europe.
Aug.	Paris is liberated from German control.

1945			
Jan.	U.S. forces invade Luzon, Philippines.	**June**	U.S. troops capture Okinawa, liberate Philippines.
Feb.	U.S. flag is raised over Iwo Jima.	**Aug.**	Atomic bombs are dropped on Hiroshima and Nagasaki.
April	Franklin Roosevelt dies; Harry Truman becomes president.	**Sept. 2**	Japan signs unconditional surrender, ending World War II.
May 8	Germany surrenders, victory in Europe.		

◄ Raising the flag on Iwo Jima

Tuskegee Airmen ►

STUDY TO GO Study anywhere, anytime! Download quizzes and flash cards to your PDA from glencoe.com.

America and World War II **Chapter 26 833**

Technology Connection Have students visit the Web site for the USS *Arizona* National Memorial. Have them browse through the pictures and other articles on the site. Ask them to write a one-page response paper to their research, describing how the Web site contributes to their understanding of the Japanese attack on Pearl Harbor. **OL**

Formulating Questions Have students work in groups and identify an older person who remembers World War II who is willing to be interviewed. Students should write 10–15 interview questions to find out about his or her experiences during the war. Emphasize that they should write open-ended questions. During the interview, two students should take notes. Have each group prepare a five-minute presentation about the interview. **Ask:** Did you learn anything from the person that you interviewed that surprised you? **OL**

Visual Summary

Hands-On Chapter Project
Step 6: Wrap-Up

Recognizing Propaganda

Step 6: Review and Discussion Students will review their work and discuss how warring nations used propaganda during World War II.

Directions Have students return to their original groups. Have groups make a time line that records important events in the war. Ask students to mark on their time lines when in the war the types of propaganda they created in the chapter project might have been used. When students have finished their group work, lead a class discussion about the propaganda used by both sides in the war.

Making Connections Ask: Can you think of examples of how propaganda is used today? *(Students may identify advertising, political commercials, or slogans created by the government.)* **OL**

Answers and Analyses
Reviewing Main Ideas

1. D Students should remember that dictators took advantage of people's resentment over the terms of the Treaty of Versailles. During the Great Depression, this resentment grew even stronger as unemployment sky-rocketed. This should lead students to choose D. **18.B.3a**

2. C Students should remember that the United States pledged to stay out of the war unless directly attacked. Only choice C was a direct attack on the nation. **16.A**

3. B Students should remember that the war required changes in the nation's economy. For example, automakers shifted from building cars to producing trucks, jeeps, and tanks. This should lead students to select choice B. **15.A**

4. A Students should immediately eliminate the Italians and the Japanese because they were the Axis Powers. The Americans fought the Axis on the Western front, leaving choice A. **16.A.3a**

5. D Remind students that Japan vowed to fight on, even when faced with certain defeat. Only after the massive destruction of Hiroshima and Nagasaki did Japan surrender. Therefore, choice D is correct. **16.A.3b**

Short-Answer Question

6. A possible answer is that no, the American people did not live up to Roosevelt's ideals. For example, even though African Americans and Latinos moved to northern cities to fill jobs in war industries, racial tension and some-times violence resulted. **16.A.3b**

STANDARDIZED TEST PRACTICE

TEST-TAKING TIP

When answering multiple-choice questions, your first answer is usually correct. Do not change the answer unless you are absolutely certain your first answer is wrong.

Reviewing Main Ideas

Directions: Choose the best answer for each of the following questions.

1. One of the factors that contributed to the rise of European dictators was
   A American neutrality.
   B the Nazi-Soviet pact.
   C a policy of appeasement.
   D joblessness and resentment.

2. The United States entered World War II because
   A the Japanese seized Manchuria.
   B German soldiers invaaded Poland.
   C Japanese planes bombed Pearl Harbor.
   D German subs fired on American destroyers.

3. How did the American economy change when the U.S. entered World War II?
   A Many women lost their jobs.
   B Factories shifted to producing tanks.
   C African American workers faced discrimination.
   D The military began drafting workers.

4. Who fought the Axis Powers on the Eastern Front?
   A Soviets   **C** Japanese
   B Italians   **D** Americans

5. The war with Japan ended when the U.S.
   A unleashed suicide pilots.
   B imposed an economic blockade.
   C offered concessions for surrender.
   D dropped atomic bombs on Japanese cities.

Short-Answer Question

Directions: Base your answer to question 6 on the excerpt below and on your knowledge of social studies.

> We Americans will contribute unified production and unified acceptance of sacrifice and of effort. That means a national unity that can know no limitations of race or creed or selfish politics. The American people expect that much from themselves.
>
> —quoted from Roosevelt's fireside chat on February 23, 1942

6. Did the American people live up to Roosevelt's ideals? Give examples to support your answer.

Review the Essential Questions

7. Essay How did the Allies defeat Axis ideas and armies in World War II?

To help you write your essay, review your answers to the Essential Questions in the section reviews and the chapter Foldables Study Organizer. Your essay should include:

- the ideas and acts of aggression by Axis Powers;
- the responses of the Allied Powers to these ideas and acts;
- reasons the Allies were able to cast doubt on fascist ideas and defeat the Axis armies; and
- the costs of the war.

GO ON

Review the Essential Questions

7. If students completed their Foldables correctly, they should be able to describe the responses of the Allied Powers to acts of aggression by the Axis Powers, as well as why the Allies could cast doubt on fascist ideas and defeat the Axis armies. Students should discuss the use of propaganda and military tactics as important components of the Allies' strategy. **16.A**

History ONLINE
For additional test practice, use **Self-Check Quizzes**—Chapter 26 at glencoe.com.

Chapter 26 Assessment

Document-Based Questions

Directions: Analyze the documents and answer the short-answer questions that follow.

Document 1

Gunnar Myrdal wrote the following excerpt in *American Dilemma: The Negro Problem and Modern Democracy* published in 1944.

> Fascism and nazism . . . came to power by means of racial persecution and oppression.

Source: Ronald Takaki, *A Different Mirror*

8. Give two examples from the chapter that support Myrdal's claim.

Document 2

Jan Karski, a leader in the Polish resistance, gave this report to Roosevelt in 1943.

> Our underground authorities are absolutely sure that the Germans are out to exterminate the entire Jewish population of Europe.

Source: Doris Kearns Goodwin, *No Ordinary Time*

9. What events were occurring in European cities that support this statement?

Document 3

For a full week, Allied planes bombed the German city of Hamburg in 1943. Journalist Gwynne Dyer described what the bombing was like.

> Practically all the apartment blocks in the firestorm area had underground shelters, but nobody who stayed in them survived; those who were not cremated died of carbon monoxide poisoning. But to venture into the streets was to risk being swept by the wind into the very heart of the firestorm.

Gwynne Dyer, *War: The Lethal Custom*

10. How much longer did it take for Allied forces to defeat Hitler's army? Describe the effectiveness of the Allied bombing raids using this quote, as well as other facts, to support your opinion.

Document 4

Pearl Harbor was a naval base in Hawaii. The Japanese attacked it early in the morning on December 7, 1941.

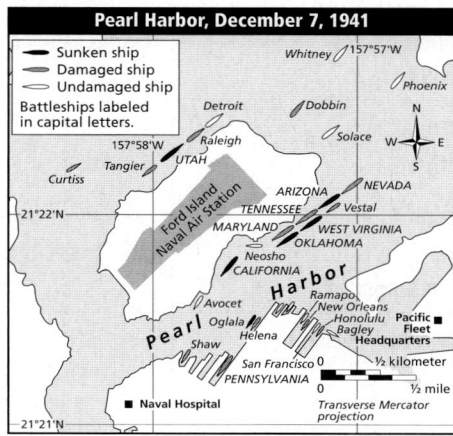

Pearl Harbor, December 7, 1941

11. Using the information shown on the map, explain how the attack on Pearl Harbor impacted the U.S. Navy and American military readiness.

12. Creative Writing Using the information from the four documents and your knowledge of social studies, write an essay in which you:

- create a fictional character—soldier, pilot, diplomat, or leader—who participated in one or more events described in the documents; and
- include details about the person's hardships and reactions.

Need Extra Help?

If You Missed Questions. . .	1	2	3	4	5	6	7	8	9	10	11	12
Go to Page. . .	805	813	815–819	811–823	831–832	817–819	807–812	805–806	825–827	822	813	811–832

---

10. Possible answer: It would be another year and a half before Hitler surrendered. The bombing campaigns were aggressive and extremely damaging to Germany; however, without the destruction of Germany's infrastructure, the Nazis might not have surrendered. **16.A.3c**

11. According to the map, nine ships were sunk, and eight were damaged. Located in Hawaii, the ships and personnel at Pearl Harbor would have been the first to respond to aggression from Japan. The attack at Pearl Harbor found the United States largely unprepared for war. Soon, many big companies were converting their processes to make war materials. **17.A.3b**

12. Students' essays should draw from the chapter, the documents, and personal knowledge to create a fictional character. Students should use descriptive language to describe the events in the documents and the hardships the person faced. **18.B.3a**

History ONLINE
Have students visit the Web site at glencoe.com to review Chapter 26 and take the Self-Check Quiz.

Need Extra Help?

Have students refer to the pages listed if they miss any of the questions.

Document-Based Questions

8. Fascist leader Mussolini consolidated his power and oppressed Italians by banning all parties but his Fascist Party. Hitler and the Nazis rose to power by portraying Germans as being superior to all other people and blaming Jews for Germany's problems. **16.A**

9. Students should include examples of the Nazis' plans to kill all the Jews in Europe. Nazis shot thousands of Jews in the Soviet Union and killed millions of them in camps in Germany and Poland. **16.A.3b**

Unit 9 Planning Guide

UNIT PACING CHART

	Unit 9	Chapter 27	Chapter 28	Chapter 29
Day 1	Unit Opener, Reading History	Chapter Opener, Section 1	Chapter Opener, Section 1	Chapter Opener, Section 1
Day 2		Section 2, Section 3	Section 2, Section 3	Section 2, You Decide
Day 3		Section 4, Geography & History, Visual Summary	Section 3, America's Literature	Section 3, TIME Notebook
Day 4		Chapter Assessment	Section 4, Visual Summary	Section 4, Visual Summary
Day 5			Chapter Assessment	Chapter Assessment

 Teacher to Teacher

Keil Hileman
Monticello Trails
Middle School
Grades 6–8
Shawnee, KS

Developing Visual Literacy Have students skim the chapters in this unit and identify one photograph that they feel is powerful, unusual, or shocking. Then, students should research that photograph using the library or reliable Internet sources. Students should find information about the historical events that are reflected in the photo and possible reasons the photographer took the photo. As students research, they should also look for additional photographs that were taken during the same time period that reflect similar events or themes found in their original photo. Then have students create a visual presentation on the computer that incorporates all of their photographs with music from 1945 to 1975. As part of their presentations, have students provide background information to the class about their original photo and describe the connections between the photographs and the music they selected. Help students by discussing and reviewing their selections and any of the information they want to convey to their audience.

Author Note

Dear American History Teacher,

As you begin to teach this unit, there are themes that recur throughout the chapters that you will want to point out to students.

These two-and-a-half decades represent an era of dramatic change in American history. The Cold War, following World War II, served as the backdrop to many of these events and should be reemphasized as you discuss the social and political upheavals of the 1960s and 1970s. The United States and the Soviet Union emerged from World War II as the two superpowers. The United States, though, was clearly the stronger nation economically and militarily. This fact may help students understand why the United States becomes immersed in so many foreign policy entanglements. Students should gain a sense of how deeply the nation was divided over American foreign policy, especially about the country's involvement in the Vietnam War. The legacy of that war is still being debated by historians, and each of the U.S. presidents in this unit played some role in Vietnam.

The decades of the 1950s and 1960s witnessed some of the greatest social movements of the twentieth century—the civil rights movement, the student movement, the women's movement, and the counterculture movement. New leaders emerged on college campuses, in local communities, and on the national stage. American colleges and universities in particular served as forums for many of the reform movements that you will read about and discuss in these chapters.

These were years of relative prosperity, rising expectations, and the desire to end poverty and suffering among all Americans, as illustrated in President Lyndon Johnson's Great Society. Historians continue to debate the significance of Johnson's presidency and his Great Society programs, but there is little doubt that many of these federal programs—such as Medicaid, Medicare, Head Start, the Child Nutrition Act, and the Clean Water Act—improved the quality of life for millions of Americans.

Albert S. Broussard

Albert S. Broussard

Unit Objectives

After studying this unit, students will be able to:

- Describe the events that led to the Cold War, and discuss the origins, battles, and effects of the Korean War.
- Trace the history of the civil rights movement.
- Describe American involvement in the Vietnam War.

Introducing the Unit

Speculating As students prepare to study the unit, ask them to think of stories they may have heard about life in the United States during the Cold War. **Ask:** How do you think the United States would be different if the Cold War had never happened? *(Students might note that the relationships between the United States and other countries might be different, there might not have been a buildup of nuclear weapons, and that perhaps the Korean War and the Vietnam War might have been avoided.)* Discuss with students that they will learn why the Cold War began and how it influenced the United States's relationship with other countries. **OL**

Unit ⭐9
Challenges at Home and Abroad 1945–1975

Chapter 27
The Cold War Era
1945–1960

Chapter 28
The Civil Rights Era
1954–1974

Chapter 29
The Vietnam Era
1960–1975

Peace movement button, 1970

836

Activity: Why It Matters

Why Study the Civil Rights Movement?
Tell students what they can expect to learn in the upcoming unit. **Ask:** Since the Civil War had freed enslaved people, why do you think the civil rights movement was necessary in the twentieth century? *(Students may answer that the Civil War and Reconstruction did not create a society in which African Americans could exercise their full civil rights. Therefore, the civil rights movement had to work for legal and social changes in order to bring about equality.)* As they study the unit, have students list in their notebooks what changes they think are still needed to achieve equality for all Americans. **OL**

"I had been pushed as far as I could stand to be pushed."
—Rosa Parks

Leaders of March on Washington for Jobs and Freedom, August 28, 1963

837

Connect to Past Learning

Challenges at Home and Abroad In the previous unit, students learned how the Great Depression affected people's lives and how the United States achieved victory in World War II. In this unit, they will learn about the changes the United States experienced after the war, the fight to stop the spread of communism around the world, and the civil rights movement.

More About the Image

Visual Literacy The March on Washington for Jobs and Freedom attracted more than 200,000 demonstrators on August 28, 1963. When organizers began planning the event, there were six goals: meaningful civil rights laws, a massive federal works program, fair employment, decent housing, the right to vote, and integrated education. However, as the date of the march got closer, efforts turned to passing federal civil rights legislation. In this photo, Dr. Martin Luther King, Jr., walks with other civil rights leaders. It was at this event that Dr. King gave his famous "I Have a Dream" speech. As a result of the march, President John F. Kennedy pledged his support to civil rights legislation.

Why Identifying Problems and Solutions Is Important

Identifying problems and solutions is a skill that students will use throughout their lives. Students should realize that it is sometimes difficult, but always important, to identify a problem so that they can work toward a solution.

Learn It!

Create a three-column chart on the board. In the middle column, write: "After lunch period, half the students in the school came down with a stomachache."

Ask students to volunteer possible problems leading to the stomachaches (for example: "The casserole served in the cafeteria was bad," or "Those students were scheduled for tests that afternoon."). Write these examples in the left column. Then ask students to list in the right column several possible solutions to the problem (such as "find a new casserole recipe," "buy new refrigerators for the kitchen," or "practice stress-reduction skills").

Use the exercise to point out that an effective solution can't be derived without first fully understanding the problem. **OL**

Practice It!

Students should list the following:

Problem: People with physical disabilities did not get equal treatment in the workplace.

Solution: A law was passed for removal of barriers to access facilities.

Solution: A law was passed requiring employers to offer more opportunities for disabled workers. **OL**

Reading History

READING SKILL — Identifying Problems and Solutions

Learn It! Textbooks often describe problems that people face and how they try to solve them. Read the passage below. Ask yourself these questions: What is the problem? How did the president try to solve this problem?

> **Problem**
> the nation's economic problems

> **Solutions**
> raise the minimum wage, expand Social Security benefits, increase federal spending to create jobs, build new public housing, and create a system of national health insurance

> —*from Chapter 27, p. 852*
>
> In September 1945, President Truman presented a plan of **domestic**—or home-based—reforms aimed at solving some of the nation's economic problems. Truman later called this program the **Fair Deal.**
> Truman proposed to raise the minimum wage, expand Social Security benefits, increase federal spending to create jobs, build new public housing, and create a system of national health insurance.

Practice It! Read the paragraphs and write down the problem and solution(s) on another sheet of paper.

> —*from Chapter 28, p. 898*
>
> People with physical disabilities also sought equal treatment in the 1960s and the 1970s. Congress responded by passing a number of laws.
> One law concerned the removal of barriers that prevented some people from gaining access to public facilities. Another required employers to offer more opportunities for disabled people in the workplace.

> **Problem**

> **Solution**

Reading Strategy — Outlining

Identifying Problems and Solutions The study of history often addresses how people try to solve problems. Sometimes solutions are complicated and hard to pinpoint (for example, solutions to the Great Depression). Sometimes the root problems are elusive (for example, a large number of people are suddenly admitted to the hospital with an unidentified illness). Ask students to read a subsection of a chapter and outline the problems and solutions they find. The problems often will be the top-level heads, with the solutions as subheads under each problem. **BL**

Academic Vocabulary Preview

Listed below are the academic vocabulary words and their definitions that you will come across as you study Unit 9. Practice It! will help you study the words and definitions.

Academic Vocabulary	Definition	Practice It!
Chapter 27 The Cold War Era		
cooperate (koh · AH · puh · RAYT) p. 844	to work together	**Identify** the term from Chapter 27 that best completes the sentence.
pose (POHZ) p. 845	to present; assert	
stable (STAY · buhl) p. 851	unchanging	**1.** Joseph Stalin believed a reunited Germany would _____ a threat to the Soviet Union.
domestic (duh · MEHS · tihk) p. 852	home-based; internal	
assure (uh · SHUR) p. 858	to promise	**2.** During the war, government controls kept prices _____.
conclude (kuhn · KLOOD) p. 859	to decide	
nuclear (NOO · klee · uhr) p. 862	atomic	**3.** The Federal Highway Act is an example of a successful _____ program.
economy (ih · KAH · nuh · MEE) p. 863	a system of production, distribution, and consumption	
Chapter 28 The Civil Rights Era		
discriminate (dihs · KRIH · muh · NAYT) p. 875	to treat unfairly	**Identify** the term from Chapter 28 that best matches the underlined term or terms.
civil (SIH · vuhl) p. 875	relating to citizens as individuals	
assign (uh · SYN) p. 881	to appoint	**4.** Kennedy and Nixon came from <u>different</u> backgrounds.
consist (KUHN · SIHST) p. 883	to make up	**5.** A new labor movement <u>rose up</u> in the Southwest.
register (REH · juh · stuhr) p. 889	to enroll	
emerge (ih · MUHRJ) p. 890	to rise up	**6.** One <u>goal</u> of the civil rights movement was to include all Americans in the voting process.
aspect (AS · PEHKT) p. 895	a category, feature, or part	
diverse (dy · VUHRZ) p. 896	differing from one another	
Chapter 29 The Vietnam Era		
respond (rih · SPAHND) p. 905	to reply	**Choose** the word that best matches the meaning of each vocabulary term listed below.
occur (uh · KUHR) p. 907	to take place	
trace (TRAYS) p. 911	to follow back to	**7. occur** **9. exclude**
regime (ray · ZHEEM) p. 912	a governing authority	**a.** start **a.** shut out
conduct (KAHN · DUHKT) p. 920	to direct the course of	**b.** disturb **b.** move beside
exclude (ihks · KLOOD) p. 923	to shut out	**c.** happen **c.** invite in
authority (uh · THAHR · uh · tee) p. 927	the power to give orders and make decisions	**8. regime** **10. demonstration**
		a. tool **a.** a failure
demonstration (DEH · muhn · STRAY · shuhn) p. 928	a march in protest	**b.** rule **b.** a protest
		c. plan **c.** an embrace

Academic Vocabulary Preview

Before students begin the Practice It! activities, ask each student to read a vocabulary word and its definition. Make sure they use the phonetic spelling if they struggle with pronunciation.

Then ask students to write a sentence that includes the word. The sentence does not have to relate to the unit content. Next have students find the word in the unit. Students should compare how they used the word to how it is used in the textbook. **ELL**

Practice It!

Answers
1. pose
2. stable
3. domestic
4. diverse
5. emerged
6. aspect
7. c
8. b
9. a
10. b

Reading Strategy Read to Write

Persuasive Writing Ask students to consider a problem they think needs addressing, whether it is an issue in your school, your community, the country, or the world. Tell students to write a persuasive letter to someone who could help (such as their principal or their Congressperson). Students should first clearly define the problem and then offer several solutions. Encourage students to consider actually sending the letter, with your permission, after completing the assignment. Offer help in tweaking the letter as necessary before it is sent. **OL**

Chapter Planning Guide

27

Key to Ability Levels

- **BL** Below level
- **OL** On level
- **AL** Above level
- **ELL** English Language Learners

Key to Teaching Resources

- 📁 Print Material
- 💿 CD-ROM
- 📀 DVD
- 🖨 Transparency

Levels BL	OL	AL	ELL		Resources	Chapter Opener	Section 1	Section 2	Section 3	Section 4	Chapter Assess
					FOCUS						
BL	OL	AL	ELL	🖨	Daily Test Practice Transparencies		27–1	27–2	27–3	27–4	
					TEACH						
	OL	AL		📁	Geography and History Activity, URB					p. 31	
BL	OL		ELL	📁	Time Line Skills Activity, URB		p. 34				
BL	OL	AL	ELL	📁	Writing Skills Activity, URB		p. 23				
BL	OL	AL	ELL	📁	Content Vocabulary Activity, URB		p. 17	p. 17	p. 17	p. 17	
BL			ELL	📁	Academic Vocabulary Activity, URB		p. 19	p. 19	p. 19	p. 19	
BL			ELL	📁	Social Studies Skills Activity, URB				p. 25		
BL	OL	AL	ELL	📁	Differentiated Instruction Activity, URB			p. 27			
BL	OL	AL	ELL	📁	Critical Thinking Skills Activity, URB					p. 29	
BL	OL	AL	ELL	📁	Linking Past and Present Activity, URB			p. 33			
	OL	AL		📁	Primary Source Readings, URB					p. 21	
BL	OL	AL	ELL	📁	School-to-Home Connection Activity, URB		p. 35	p. 35	p. 35	p. 35	
BL	OL		ELL	📁	Guided Reading Activity, URB*		p. 39	p. 40	p. 41	p. 42	
	OL	AL		📁	Economics and History Activity, URB					p. 5	
BL	OL		ELL	📁	Reading Essentials and Note-Taking Guide*		p. 301	p. 304	p. 307	p. 310	
BL	OL	AL	ELL	🖨	Lesson Transparencies		27A, 27B			27C	
	OL	AL		📁	Interpreting Political Cartoons, URB				p. 13		
		AL		📁	Supreme Court Case Studies	pp. 75, 77					
	OL			📁	American Biographies					p. 58	
BL	OL	AL	ELL	📁	Outline Map Resource Book	pp. 6, 41, 43					

Note: Please refer to the *Unit Resource Book: Challenges at Home and Abroad* for this chapter's URB materials.

* Also available in Spanish

Levels					Resources	Chapter Opener	Section 1	Section 2	Section 3	Section 4	Chapter Assess
TEACH *(continued)*											
BL	OL	AL	ELL		NGS US Desk Map		✓	✓	✓	✓	
BL	OL	AL	ELL		American Literature Library		✓	✓	✓	✓	
BL	OL	AL	ELL		Writer's Guidebook		✓	✓	✓	✓	
	OL	AL			American History Primary Source Document Library CD-ROM		✓	✓	✓	✓	✓
BL	OL	AL	ELL		American Music: Hits Through History	✓	✓	✓	✓	✓	
BL	OL	AL	ELL		StudentWorks™ Plus CD	✓	✓	✓	✓	✓	✓
BL	OL	AL	ELL		Section Spotlight Videos		✓	✓	✓	✓	
BL	OL	AL	ELL		Writing Process Transparencies		✓	✓	✓	✓	✓
BL	OL	AL	ELL		Presentation Plus! With MindJogger CheckPoint CD	✓	✓	✓	✓	✓	✓
ASSESS											
BL	OL	AL	ELL		Quizzes and Tests		p. 267	p. 268	p. 269	p. 270	pp. 271, 273, 275
BL	OL	AL	ELL		Authentic Assessment With Rubrics		p. 27				
BL	OL	AL	ELL		Standardized Test Practice						p. 53
BL	OL	AL	ELL		*ExamView® Assessment Suite* CD-ROM*		27–1	27–2	27–3	27–4	Ch. 27
CLOSE											
BL			ELL		Reteaching Activity, URB*		p. 37	p. 37	p. 37	p. 37	p. 37
BL	OL		ELL		Reading and Study Skills Foldables Activity	p. 102	p. 102	p. 102	p. 102	p. 102	p. 102
BL	OL	AL	ELL		*The American Journey* in Graphic Novel					p. 163	
BL			ELL		Reading Strategies and Activities for the Social Studies Classroom		✓	✓	✓	✓	
BL	OL	AL	ELL		Graphic Organizer Transparencies & Strategies		✓	✓	✓	✓	

TeacherWorks Plus
All-In-One Planner and Resource Center

- Interactive Lesson Planner
- Interactive Teacher Edition
- Fully editable blackline masters
- Section Spotlight Videos Launch
- Differentiated Lesson Plans
- Printable reports of daily assignments
- Standards Tracking System

Professional Development Resources

- Strategies for Success
- Building Academic Vocabulary
- Success With English Learners DVD
- Differentiated Instruction Strategies DVD
- Teaching Literacy Strategies in Social Studies DVD
- Assessment DVD
- Standards-Based Instruction DVD

Integrating Technology

27

Using Study Central™

Web Links

Technology Product

Study Central™ helps reinforce and enrich students' under-standing of each section by providing direct links to Internet resources. The Web links

- are customized for each section of a chapter;
- focus on major people, instructions, and concepts;
- are carefully reviewed to make sure they are accurate.

Objectives

The Web links help students

- practice their research and reading skills;
- access useful information on the Internet.

Steps

- Locate the Web page for your textbook on the Glencoe Web site, glencoe.com.
- Click on **Study Central™** under Textbook Resources.
- On the Study Central™ Web site, select a chapter and section using the drop-down arrows and then click **Enter**.
- Click on the **Web Links** tab.
- Click on each link and discuss the information.
- Have the students research different topics on the related Web sites.
- This research information can be used by the students for written reports.

History ONLINE at glencoe.com

	Student	Teacher	Parent
Media Center			
• Student Edition Audio	●		
• Spanish Summaries	●		
• Section Spotlight Videos	●	●	
Social Studies Online Learning Center			
Classroom Tools			
• Multi-Language Glossaries	●	●	●
• Teaching Today		●	
• TIME Current Events	●	●	●
• Beyond the Textbook	●	●	
***The American Journey* Online Learning Center**			
• Study-to-Go™	●	●	●
• Study Central™	●	●	●
• Chapter Overview	●	●	
• Concepts in Motion	●	●	
• ePuzzles and Games	●	●	
• Literature Connections	●	●	
• Online Student Edition	●	●	●
• Self-Check Quizzes	●	●	●
• Student Web Activities	●	●	
• Vocabulary eFlashcards	●	●	
• Web Activity Lesson Plans	●	●	●
• Vocabulary PuzzleMaker	●	●	●

READING SUPPORT FROM JAMESTOWN EDUCATION

- **Timed Readings Plus in Social Studies** helps students increase their reading rate and fluency while maintaining comprehension. The 400-word passages are similar to those found on state and national assessments.

- **Reading in the Content Area: Social Studies** concentrates on six essential reading skills that help students better comprehend what they read. The book includes 75 high-interest nonfiction passages written at increasing levels of difficulty.

- **Reading Social Studies** includes strategic reading instruction and vocabulary support in Social Studies content for ELLs and native speakers of English.

- **Content Vocabulary Workout** (Grades 6–8) accelerates reading comprehension through focused vocabulary development. Social Studies content vocabulary comes from the glossaries of Glencoe's Middle School Social Studies texts.

www.jamestowneducation.com

NATIONAL GEOGRAPHIC

Index to National Geographic Magazine:

The following articles relate to this chapter:

- *"Korea's Dangerous Divide,"* Tom O'Neill, July 2003.
- *"The New Europe,"* T.R. Reid, January 2002.

National Geographic Society Products

To order the following, call National Geographic at 1-800-368-2728:

National Geographic Atlas of the World (Book)

Access National Geographic's dynamic MapMachine Web site and other geography resources at:

www.nationalgeographic.com

www.nationalgeographic.com/mapmachine

Reading List Generator CD-ROM — GLENCOE BOOKLINK 3

Use this database to search more than 30,000 titles to create a customized reading list for your students.

- Reading lists can be organized by students' reading level, author, genre, theme, or area of interest.
- The database provides Degrees of Reading Power™ (DRP) and Lexile™ readability scores for all selections.
- A brief summary of each selection is included.

Leveled reading suggestions for this chapter:

For students at a Grade 6 reading level:
- *I Remember Korea: Veterans Tell Their Stories of the Korean War,* 1950–53, Linda Granfield

For students at a Grade 7 reading level:
- *Harry S. Truman,* Caroline Evensen Lazo
- *The Korean War,* Michael Burgan

For students at a Grade 8 reading level:
- *Joseph McCarthy and the Cold War,* Victoria Sherrow
- *The Chinese Cultural Revolution,* David Pietrusza

For students at a Grade 9 reading level:
- *Mao Zedong,* Jonathan Spence
- *The Cold War: An Uneasy Peace: 1945–1980,* Craig E. Blohm

For students at a Grade 10 reading level:
- *The Collapse of Communism,* Stewart Ross
- *The Cold War,* Britta Bjornlund

The following videotape programs are available from Glencoe as supplements to the chapter:

- **Korea: The Forgotten War** (ISBN 1-56-501540-1)
- **Berlin Airlift: The First Battle of the Cold War** (ISBN 0-76-701166-X)

To order, call Glencoe at 1-800-334-7344. To find classroom resources to accompany many of these videos, check the following home pages:

A&E Television: www.aetv.com

The History Channel: www.history.com

Chapter Objectives

After studying this chapter, students will be able to:

- Explain how and why America aided European nations after World War II.
- Understand the economic, social, and political challenges that Americans faced after World War II.
- Explain how and why America involved itself in the Korean conflict of the 1950s.
- Identify how America's prosperity in the 1950s affected the country's economy and culture.

Motivating Activity

Speculating Within five years of the end of World War II, the United States once again was participating in a military action. This time the fighting was in Korea, and the goal was to stop the spread of Communism. **Ask:** How do you think Americans felt about fighting in another military conflict? Students will form small groups and discuss their speculations. Discussion might include how the recent end of World War II influenced public opinion. Students should evaluate whether their speculations were accurate as they read the chapter.

Chapter 27

The Cold War Era 1945–1960

Beginning in the 1950s, television was the primary source of entertainment.

PRESIDENTS
U.S. Events
World Events

HARRY TRUMAN

1944 — 1948

★ **1945**
Franklin Roosevelt dies

★ **1948**
Marshall Plan is enacted

★ **1945**
Yalta Conference sets plans for postwar world

★ **1948**
- Soviets blockade West Berlin
- State of Israel is created

★ **1950**
Korean War begins

Whatever the weather We only reach welfare **together**

840 Chapter 27

Previewing the Essential Questions

As you begin teaching each section, use these questions and activities to help students focus on the Essential Questions.

Section 1

Cold War Origins Ask: What types of problems existed in Europe after World War II? *(Answers might include establishing and maintaining peace, ensuring stability in Germany, restoring economies, and maintaining democratic societies.)* Point out to students that in Section 1 they will learn how and why America aided European nations after World War II. **OL**

Section 2

Postwar Politics Ask: What challenges might a nation face as it moves from wartime to peacetime? *(Answers might include returning veterans who need jobs and housing, moving from a wartime to a peacetime economy, accumulated debt, and maintaining peace.)* Point out to students that Section 2 discusses the economic, social, and political challenges Americans faced after World War II. **OL**

Section 1: Cold War Origins

Essential Question How and why did America aid European nations after World War II?

Section 2: Postwar Politics

Essential Question What economic, social, and political challenges did Americans face after World War II?

Section 3: The Korean War

Essential Question How and why did America involve itself in the Korean conflict of the 1950s?

Section 4: America in the 1950s

Essential Question How did the American prosperity of the 1950s affect the country's economy and culture?

History ONLINE
Chapter Overview Visit glencoe.com and click on **Chapter 27—Chapter Overviews** to preview chapter information.

FOLDABLES Study Organizer

Organizing Information
Make this Foldable to help you learn about the superpowers.

Step 1 Fold a sheet of paper as shown.

Step 2 Turn the paper and fold it into thirds.

Step 3 Unfold and cut along the two inside fold lines.

Step 4 Label your Foldable as shown.

USA as a Superpower | Both | Soviet Union as a Superpower

Reading and Writing As you read the chapter, describe under the appropriate tabs how the superpowers were similar and how they were different.

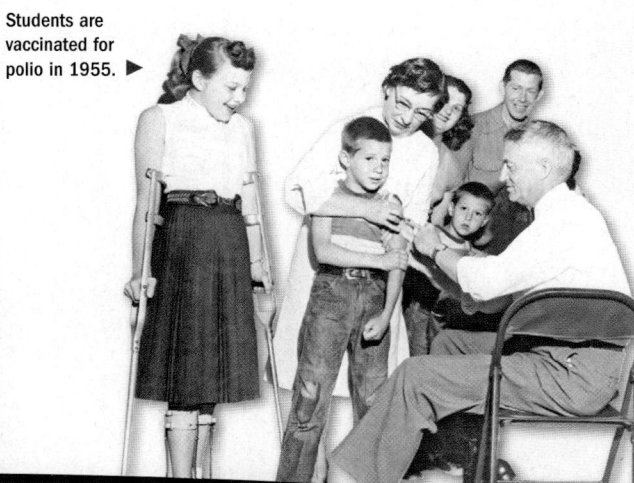

Students are vaccinated for polio in 1955. ▶

DWIGHT EISENHOWER

1954
Senator Joe McCarthy is censured

1955
• Polio vaccine becomes available
• Minimum wage increases to $1 an hour

1956
Federal Highway Act passes

1952 ——————— 1956 ——————— 1960

1954
Roger Bannister breaks the four-minute mile barrier

1957
Soviet Union launches *Sputnik*

Chapter 27   841

Introducing Chapter 27

Time Line Activity

If you have not already done so, have students review the time line. **Ask:** Did the end of World War II lead to a lasting world peace? Explain your answer using the time line. *(No, the Korean War broke out in 1950, just five years after the end of World War II.)*

FOLDABLES Study Organizer **Dinah Zike's Foldables**

Purpose This Foldable helps students understand the similarities and differences between the United States and Soviet Union after World War II.

▭ More Foldable activities for this chapter can be found in *Dinah Zike's Reading and Study Skills Foldables*.

History ONLINE

Introduce students to chapter content and key terms by having them access the **Chapter Overview** at glencoe.com.

Section 3

The Korean War Ask: Do you have a relative or family friend who fought in the Korean War? If so, what has that person told you about the war? *(Students will share their experiences. If possible, invite a Korean War veteran to speak to the class.)* Tell students that Section 3 will present information about the Korean War. **OL**

Section 4

America in the 1950s Ask: What do you know about the 1950s? *(Students may be familiar with television sitcoms such as* Leave It to Beaver, *poodle skirts, the Twist, and Elvis Presley.)* Explain to students that in Section 4, they will learn how the American economy and culture in the 1950s reflected a new prosperity. **OL**

Cold War Origins

Focus

Bellringer
Daily Test Practice Transparency 27–1

Reading Guide
Answers to Graphic:
Truman Doctrine: fight the spread of communism through financial aid; Marshall Plan: lessen the appeal of communism through economic aid

Section Spotlight Video

Have students watch the Section Spotlight Video "Cold War Origins" to learn about the 1945 meeting of Roosevelt, Churchill, and Stalin at Yalta.

Resource Manager

Essential Question ◄
How and why did America aid European nations after World War II?

Reading Guide

Content Vocabulary

iron curtain (p. 844)   espionage (p. 848)
containment (p. 844)   blacklist (p. 848)
airlift (p. 846)   perjury (p. 849)
cold war (p. 846)   censure (p. 849)
subversion (p. 848)

Academic Vocabulary

cooperate (p. 844)   pose (p. 845)

Key People and Events
Harry S. Truman (p. 843)
Mao Zedong (p. 847)

Reading Strategy
Taking Notes On a chart like the one below, record the major purposes of each of these postwar plans.

Plan	Purpose
Truman Doctrine	
Marshall Plan	

ILLINOIS STANDARDS
The American Journey

14.B Understand the structures and functions of the political systems of Illinois, the United States and other nations

14.E.3 Compare the basic principles of the United States and its international interests (e.g., territory, environment, trade, use of technology).

17.D Understand the historical significance of geography.

18.B.3a Analyze how individuals and groups interact with and within institutions (e.g., educational, military).

American Diary

The three most powerful men in the world met in Yalta to discuss the fate of the postwar world. President Roosevelt hoped to promote his vision of postwar cooperation. Prime Minister Churchill spoke elegantly and forcefully. Soviet leader Stalin stubbornly opposed much of what was proposed. Stalin stated to his aides: "They want to force us to accept their plans on questions affecting Europe and the world. Well, that's not going to happen!" As the Allies discovered, Stalin had his own plans.

—quoted in Memoirs by Andrei Gromyko

Churchill, Roosevelt, and Stalin meet at the Yalta Conference.

R Reading Strategies	**C** Critical Thinking	**D** Differentiated Instruction	**W** Writing Support	**S** Skill Practice
Teacher Edition • Outlining, p. 844 • Previewing, p. 846 • Identifying, p. 846 • Questioning, p. 848 **Additional Resources** • Guid. Read., URB p. 39 • Content Vocab., URB p. 17 • Academic Vocab., URB p. 19 • Read. Ess., p. 301	**Teacher Edition** • Identify Central Iss., p. 843 • Predict. Conseq., p. 845 • Analyzing Info., p. 847 **Additional Resources** • Quizzes and Tests, p. 267	**Teacher Edition** • ELL, p. 845 • Aud./Musical, p. 848 • Verbal/Ling., p. 849 **Additional Resources** • School-to-Home, URB p. 35 • Reteaching Act., URB p. 37	**Teacher Edition** • Expository Writ., p. 843 • Personal Writ., p. 846 **Additional Resources** • Writ. Skills, URB p. 23 • Authentic Assess., p. 27	**Teacher Edition** • Using Geo. Skills, p. 844 • Read. a Time Line, p. 847 **Additional Resources** • Daily Test Pract. Transp. 27–1 • Time Line Skills, URB p. 34

Wartime Diplomacy

Main Idea During World War II, the United States, the Soviet Union, and Great Britain worked out plans for the organization of the postwar world.

History and You Have you ever attended a meeting at which there was a lot of disagreement? How were the disagreements handled? Read to learn how the Allies tried to deal with their disagreements about the world's future.

In February 1945, the "Big Three" Allied leaders—Franklin D. Roosevelt, Winston Churchill, and Joseph Stalin—met at Yalta, a Soviet port on the Black Sea. They came to discuss issues affecting the postwar world. Out of this meeting came the Yalta agreement, in which the Soviet Union agreed to enter the war against Japan. In return, the Soviets received some territories in Asia.

Agreeing on other arrangements proved more difficult. Roosevelt and Churchill feared the spread of communism and Soviet control in Eastern Europe. Stalin, on the other hand, wanted this area as a shield to protect the Soviet Union from the West. Germany was a special problem. The Allies finally agreed to divide Germany into four zones, with each zone run by an Allied power.

Stalin agreed to free elections in Soviet-occupied Eastern Europe and to help in planning a new international organization. Roosevelt and Churchill felt encouraged about a peaceful postwar world. Their hopes went unfulfilled.

The United Nations

President Roosevelt died suddenly on April 12, 1945. Vice President **Harry S. Truman** succeeded him. Facing the enormous tasks of the presidency, Truman told reporters, "When they told me [of Roosevelt's death], I felt like the moon, the stars, and all the planets had fallen on me."

Truman decided to go ahead with the formation of the new international organization discussed at Yalta. On June 26, in San Francisco, California, 50 nations signed the charter creating the United Nations (UN). They hoped the UN could settle international disputes and prevent future wars.

Reading Check Describing How did the Allies agree to divide Germany?

Primary Source | **Compromise at Yalta**

Agreement Among the Allies At Yalta, the Allies issued the Declaration of Liberated Europe, which contained the following commitments:

German refugee in Nuremberg, 1945

The Declaration of Liberated Europe

✔ The peoples of Europe can create their own democratic institutions but must rid their societies of Nazism and fascism.

✔ The United States, Great Britain, and the Soviet Union will help the peoples of Europe:

1. Establish peace in their countries.
2. Provide aid to people who need it.
3. Form temporary governments that represent the essentials of a democratic society and hold free elections.

Critical Thinking

Speculating Tensions between the United States and the Soviet Union grew after World War II. Why do you think this happened?

Activity: Why It Matters

Identifying The United Nations today adheres to its original goal of settling international disputes. **Ask:** What disputes are UN forces attempting to settle in today's world? Organize the class into small groups. Each group should read newspapers and newsmagazines for a week and gather articles related to UN activities around the world. Have each group choose one area where UN forces are active and create an informative poster about that mission. Each poster should use text and graphics to answer the questions of where, why, and how the United Nations is attempting to settle the dispute in that area. Have groups share their posters with the class. **OL**

Teach

C Critical Thinking

Identifying Central Issues Ask: What issues did the "Big Three" discuss? *(war with Japan, spread of communism and Soviet control in Eastern Europe, organization of the postwar world, formation of an international organization)* **OL**

W Writing Support

Expository Writing Have students work with a partner to learn more about the organization and goals of the United Nations. Then have them summarize their findings in a one-page report that they share with the class. **AL**

Primary Source

Critical Thinking Answer
Answers might discuss the differing ideologies and economic systems of both countries and the desire to influence other nations.

Reading Check Answer: They divided Germany into four zones, with each one run by an Allied power.

Additional Support

Teacher Tip

Analyzing Primary Sources Students may gather information from local newspapers that include coverage of international events or the online editions of major newsmagazines such as *TIME*.

R Reading Strategy

Outlining To help students understand this subsection, have them create an outline using the headings from the subsection as their outline headings. As students read, have them note important details under each heading. **BL**

S Skill Practice

Using Geography Skills Have students locate Greece and Turkey on the map of Europe at the bottom of the page. **Ask:** How would the location of Greece and Turkey benefit the Soviet Union? *(Greece and Turkey would give the Soviet Union access to the Mediterranean Sea, which was important for shipping and defense.)* **OL**

Primary Source

Critical Thinking Answers
1. "Curtain" refers to a barrier between communism and democracy, and "iron" refers to the barrier's strength and likens it to a shield of Soviet military power.
2. The flowers, the ring, and the formality of knocking suggest a cordial and conciliatory attitude.

Additional Support

R Soviet Expansion in Europe

Main Idea Soviet efforts to spread communism in Europe led to tense relations with the United States, which wanted to contain communism.

History and You Have you ever wanted to stop someone from doing something without having a fight? Read to learn how the United States wanted to stop communism without going to war.

Distrust soon arose between the West and the Soviets. Stalin set up Communist governments and kept Soviet forces in Eastern Europe. Europe eventually split into two armed camps—Communist Eastern Europe and democratic Western Europe.

Winston Churchill believed that the division between East and West was permanent. In 1946 he stated in a speech in Fulton, Missouri, that an **"iron curtain"** had descended on Europe. Churchill meant that the Soviets had cut off Eastern Europe from the West. He warned that the Soviets would eventually try to gain control of other parts of the world.

To halt Soviet expansion, Truman turned to George F. Kennan, an American diplomat. Kennan believed that the United States and the Soviet Union could not **cooperate,** or work together. Therefore, the United States had to be firm. Kennan's policy, called **containment,** stated that the United States had to "contain," or hold back, the Soviets, using military as well as nonmilitary ways.

The Truman Doctrine

The policy of containment soon went into effect. Civil war raged in Greece, as Communists attempted to overthrow the country's **S** pro-Western government. At the same time, the Soviets pressured Turkey to give them naval bases on the straits leading to the Mediterranean Sea.

In March 1947, Truman asked Congress for money to help Greece and Turkey. The Truman Doctrine, as it came to be called,

Europe After World War II
NATIONAL GEOGRAPHIC

Legend:
- Communist countries
- Non-communist countries
- — Iron Curtain

0 — 400 kilometers
0 — 400 miles
Lambert Azimuthal Equal-Area projection

"An iron curtain has descended across the Continent. Behind that line lie all the capitals of the ancient states of Central and Eastern Europe. . . . All these famous cities and the populations around them lie in what I might call the Soviet sphere, and all are subject, in one form or another, not only to Soviet influence but to a very high and in some cases increasing measure of control from Moscow."
—Winston Churchill, March 5, 1946

Critical Thinking

1. **Analyzing Primary Sources** Why do you think Churchill described Soviet domination as an "iron curtain"?
2. **Interpreting** What does the cartoon say about the attitude of Secretary of State Byrnes toward the Soviet leaders?

Activity: Connecting Past and Present

Discussing The "iron curtain" no longer separates Eastern and Western Europe. **Ask:** Have all the former Eastern European Communist nations been able to establish stable democratic governments since the collapse of the Soviet Union? Organize the class into groups, and assign each group one of the following countries: East Germany, Czechoslovakia, Hungary, Romania, Bulgaria, Albania, Poland, and Yugoslavia. To answer the question, ask students to research facts about the government of their assigned country from 25 years ago, 10 years ago, and 1 year ago. Have each group draw its conclusions and summarize them in a one-page report to be shared with the class. *(Answers will vary by country. For instance, Soviet Czechoslovakia split into the Czech Republic and Slovakia in 1989 when the Soviet Union collapsed. Hungary was also under Communist rule and in 1990 held its first elections. Yugoslavia broke apart in civil war fueled by ethnic strife.)* **OL**

provided immediate aid to the Greeks and the Turks. In the long run, the doctrine pledged that the United States would fight the spread of communism worldwide.

The Marshall Plan

In June 1947, George Marshall, the U.S. secretary of state, proposed that the United States give massive economic aid to Western European countries. Their economies were in ruins, and people were starving. After Communists took over the Eastern European country of Czechoslovakia in 1948, Congress approved the plan. From 1948 to 1951, the Marshall Plan pumped $13 billion worth of supplies, machinery, and food into Western Europe. The economic recovery that followed weakened the appeal of communism.

✔ **Reading Check** Summarizing What were the goals of the Truman Doctrine and the Marshall Plan?

▲ U.S. Secretary of State Byrnes calls on Soviet leader Joseph Stalin and government official Vyacheslav Molotov.

Crisis in Berlin

Main Idea The Western Allies successfully resisted Soviet attempts to halt the Allies' plans for uniting West Germany.

History and You Suppose you are trapped on an island without food or water. How might help reach you? Read to learn how the people of West Berlin were helped by the Western Allies when their city was cut off by the Soviets.

· ·

The Allied leaders at Yalta divided Germany into four occupation zones. The Soviet Union controlled the eastern part of the country, while the United States, Britain, and France held zones in the western part. The German capital of Berlin, located deep within Soviet-controlled East Germany, also was divided among the four nations.

President Truman believed that a reunited Germany was essential to the future of Europe. Stalin, on the other hand, feared that a reunited Germany would once again **pose,** or present, a threat to the Soviet Union. He sought to maintain Soviet influence in a divided Germany. Tensions over the German issue led to a serious crisis in 1948.

The Berlin Blockade

On June 7, 1948, the United States, Britain, and France stated their plan to unite their zones to form a new West German republic. Each nation's section of Berlin would be included in this republic as well, even though the city of Berlin lay within Soviet-held East Germany.

The Berlin blockade was Stalin's answer to the West's plans. On June 24, 1948, Soviet troops rushed into position around the edge of West Berlin. Almost overnight they created a blockade, stopping traffic on all highway, rail, and water routes through East Germany to West Berlin. As a result, West Berlin's 2.2 million citizens were cut off from needed supplies. The Soviets hoped this blockade would force the Americans, British, and French to reconsider their plan.

The Cold War Era **Chapter 27 845**

C Critical Thinking

Predicting Consequences Ask: What problems might arise because Allied-controlled Berlin was completely surrounded by Soviet-controlled East Germany? *(Students might predict that Soviet-controlled East Germany could cut off supplies, invade, or stop travel to Allied-controlled Berlin.)* **OL**

D Differentiated Instruction

English Language Learners Have students find two words in the bracketed passage that might be confusing to someone who is learning English. Then have them write questions about the text using each of the words, as well as answers to the questions. Ask students to quiz partners using the questions they have written. **ELL**

✔ **Reading Check** **Answer:** to fight the spread of communism in Europe through financial aid and donations of supplies, machinery, and food

Hands-On Chapter Project
Step 1

Creating a Cover Story About the Cold War

Step 1: Researching the Cold War Small groups of students will learn more about the Cold War in preparation for writing an article for a magazine that examines that era.

Essential Question: How and why did America aid European nations after World War II?

Directions Organize students into small groups. Explain that they will be writing and illustrating a magazine article about the Cold War. Tell students to gather information about the following aspects of the Cold War: (1) American aid to Western European nations; (2) the economic, social, and political atmosphere in the United States; (3) the Korean War; and (4) American prosperity in the 1950s.

Specifying As a class, discuss ways in which America helped Europe after World War II. Which countries were helped? Why did the government feel the aid was necessary in each case? How did the aid support the policy of containment?

(Chapter Project continued in Section 2)

W Writing Practice

Personal Writing Have students read the description of the Berlin Airlift. Ask them to think about how their lives would change if they suddenly had to depend on other countries to deliver their food, fuel, and various supplies. Tell them to write a journal entry in which they describe the changes in their daily lives and how they feel about them. **OL**

R₁ Reading Strategy

Previewing Set a timer for two minutes, and have students preview the section. Remind them to skim the main idea, headings, and text. After they finish, have them complete this sentence: In this section, I will learn about ____. *(Answers might include the Cold War, independence movements around the world, and political changes in China.)* **OL**

R₂ Reading Strategy

Identifying Ask: What was the purpose of the North Atlantic Treaty Organization? *(mutual military cooperation to aid members in containing the Soviet Union)* **BL**

> **Reading Check Answer:** American and British planes airlifted supplies into West Berlin for 10 months.

Additional Support

The Berlin Airlift

Believing that the Soviets wanted the West out of the city, President Truman made U.S. intentions clear: "We stay in Berlin, period." The president, however, did not want to risk war by using military force to end the blockade. Instead he organized a large **airlift** to save the city. American and British planes began flying food, fuel, and other supplies into West Berlin.

The airlift continued day and night for more than 10 months, delivering supplies to West Berlin. In May 1949, Stalin finally ended the blockade, realizing that the West was still intent on uniting their zones. Despite the airlift's success, Berlin and Germany remained divided. By the end of 1949, there were two German states—the Federal Republic of Germany (West Germany), allied with the United States, and the German Democratic Republic (East Germany), a Communist state tied to the Soviet Union.

> **Reading Check** **Analyzing** How did the West respond to the blockade of Berlin?

R₁ Two Armed Camps

Main Idea The United States and the Soviet Union formed rival alliances, and their competition for influence spread to other parts of the world.

History and You Does your school compete with a nearby school in sports or another activity? Read to learn how the United States and the Soviet Union sought support from other nations in their rivalry with each other.

The Berlin crisis showed that the United States and the Soviet Union were locked in a **cold war**—a war in which the two enemies did not actually fight each other. Instead each side began building up its military forces and arms to intimidate the other.

The United States and other Western democracies agreed that military cooperation was the best way to contain the Soviets. In 1949 the United States, Canada, and 10 Western European nations formed the North Atlantic Treaty Organization. Member states agreed to aid any member that was attacked.

Primary Source / Berlin Airlift

Allied Assistance In June 1948, the Soviet Union stopped all land and water traffic from entering or exiting Western-controlled Berlin. The Soviets wanted the Allies to pull out of Berlin, leaving the entire city under their control. Instead, the Allies took to the air. For more than 10 months, British and U.S. cargo planes flew medicine, food, clothing, and even coal to the city's more than 2 million residents. The Berlin airlift involved some 278,000 flights delivering 2 million tons of supplies. Finally in May 1949, the Soviet Union lifted its blockade. Not only did the airlift succeed in stopping the Soviets' European expansion, it created a new bond between the Americans and Germans.

German children wave to a U.S. cargo plane as it flies over Berlin. ▼

▲ Berliners watch as sacks of flour are unloaded.

A 15-year-old girl living near one of the airports where a plane landed every three minutes, said,

"The noise of the planes didn't bother us at all. As a matter of fact, we felt secure. As long as we heard those planes flying, we felt like everything was all right."
—from *Berlin in the Balance*

Fast Facts

The Berlin Airlift The airlift plan called for cargo planes to land and take off from West Berlin every three minutes. At times during the airlift a plane was landing every minute. The cost of the airlift is estimated to have surpassed $200 million.

Cold War Walter Lippmann, writer of the syndicated column "Today and Tomorrow," published some of his columns in a book entitled *The Cold War*. That title brought the term "cold war" into the American vocabulary.

Six years later, West Germany was allowed to form an army and join NATO. In response, the Soviets in 1955 set up a military alliance—the Warsaw Pact—with the Communist governments of Eastern Europe. The formation of NATO and the Warsaw Pact divided Europe into two armed camps.

The United States Rearms

After World War II, some of President Truman's foreign policy advisers in the National Security Council (NSC) argued that America could not rely on other nations to contain the Soviets. Unlike the supporters of the containment policy, these NSC advisers believed the United States needed to take a more active stand against communism everywhere—not just in strategic locations.

In 1950 the NSC released a report, known as NSC-68, which said that the United States must actively "foster the seeds of destruction within the Soviet Union" and fight Communist movements wherever they arose. The United States vowed to combat communist expansion everywhere in the world.

West Berlin, located in the middle of Soviet-controlled Germany, was isolated when Soviet leader Joseph Stalin blockaded all roads, railways, and waterways into the city. All planes were streamed along one of three 20-mile-wide air corridors. ▼

Divided Germany

0   100 kilometers
0   100 miles
Lambert Azimuthal Equal-Area projection

Soviet Zone
British Zone
Berlin
EAST GERMANY
Air corridor
WEST GERMANY
50°N
French Zone
American Zone
N W E S
10°E   15°E   20°E

Critical Thinking

Speculating What might have happened to Germany and other parts of Europe if the Allies had not conducted the airlift?

Independence Movements

As the Cold War deepened, many nations experienced dramatic change. Many areas broke free of colonial rule and became independent. The Philippines gained independence from the United States in 1946. For years afterward, Filipinos struggled with poverty, government corruption, and civil war. In the late 1940s, the South Asian countries of India, Pakistan, and Burma won freedom from British rule. During the 1950s and 1960s, more than 25 African nations gained independence from European powers. The path to freedom in Africa was often bloody. New nations faced the difficult task of building modern societies.

In the Middle East, Jews and Arabs both claimed Palestine, an area the British had controlled. In 1947 the United Nations divided Palestine into independent Jewish and Arab states. The Jews accepted the plan, but the Arabs did not. After declaring independence, the Jewish state of Israel was attacked by the armies of neighboring Arab countries in the first of six major wars between the Arabs and Israelis.

Communism in China

Meanwhile, significant change came to China, Asia's largest country. In 1949 Communist forces under **Mao Zedong** (MOW DZUH·DUNG) defeated armies led by China's leader Chiang Kai-shek (CHAHNG KY·SHEHK). Mao Zedong formed a new Communist state, the People's Republic of China. Chiang Kai-shek retreated with his forces to the island of Taiwan off the southeastern coast of China. The United States recognized the government in Taiwan as the legitimate government of all China.

With Communists ruling mainland China, the Soviet Union had a powerful ally in Asia. It appeared to many people that the entire continent of Asia was in danger of falling to communism.

Reading Check **Evaluating** What do you think was the main cause of the cold war? Why?

C Critical Thinking

Analyzing Information Lead a class discussion about "the difficult task of building modern societies." Have students name aspects of society that are affected by modernization, such as housing, the economy, education, and transportation. **OL**

S Skill Practice

Reading a Time Line Ask: According to the time line at the beginning of the chapter, when was the Jewish state of Israel created? *(1948)* What other world events occurred that year? *(Soviet blockade of West Berlin and the enactment of the Marshall Plan)* **BL**

Primary Source

Critical Thinking Answer
The Soviets might have succeeded in taking over all of Berlin, and eventually, other parts of Europe.

Reading Check **Answer:** Answers might include ideological differences and economic rivalry. Students should defend their answers.

Differentiated Instruction

Writing Skills Activity, URB p. 23

Revising Your Work

Objective: To learn to revise a first draft for clarity

Focus: Ask students to note that the three key parts of revision include looking at paragraphs, sentence structure, and word choice.

Teach: Have students read the practice draft and answer the questions that follow.

Assess: Assess using the Self-Assessment Checklist.

Close: Ask students what they learned that will help them revise their own writing.

Differentiated Instruction Strategies

BL Have students write a paragraph about their favorite sport and assess whether each sentence supports the topic sentence.

AL Ask students to write a one-page review of a movie or TV show using only active voice.

ELL Have students circle words in the activity that they do not understand.

D Differentiated Instruction

Auditory/Musical Have students listen to testimony from blacklisted Americans at HUAC hearings and then to news broadcasts about the hearings, which are available on the Internet. As a class, discuss whether the newscasts are objective and if they describe biases. **AL**

R Reading Strategy

Questioning Organize students into two teams. Have them debate whether there are circumstances when the U.S. government should require members of groups labeled as "subversive" to register and report their members. **OL**

INTERPRETING POLITICAL CARTOONS

Answers

1. McCarthy used unfounded evidence to discredit people.

2. At first, the careers of many innocent Americans were ruined. Later, many turned against McCarthy, and the Congress censured him.

Differentiated Instruction

Primary Sources
INTERPRETING POLITICAL CARTOONS

Cartoonist Herblock comments on the evidence provided by Senator Joe McCarthy for the 1954 Army-McCarthy hearings.

1. **Analyzing Visuals** What does the cartoon imply about McCarthy's tactics?

2. **Evaluating** What were the effects of McCarthyism?

Cold War Fears

Main Idea The Cold War heightened Americans' fears about communism in American society.

History and You Have you ever heard unproven charges made against a friend? How did you react? Read to find out how fear of communism caused some Americans to distrust other Americans in the late 1940s and early 1950s.

· ·

The Cold War increased Americans' fears of communist **subversion,** or sabotage. Many Americans worried that Communists—"Reds"—had penetrated all levels of American society and were weakening the government. This Red Scare led to a massive hunt to uncover Communists. In 1947 President Truman ordered an investigation into the loyalty of all federal employees. Although little evidence of **espionage** was found, many federal workers lost their jobs.

Congressional Investigations

During the Red Scare, both houses of Congress set up investigation committees. In 1947 the House Un-American Activities Committee (HUAC) held hearings on alleged, or suspected, Communist influence in the entertainment industry. As a result, several screenwriters and film directors—the "Hollywood Ten"—went to jail for refusing to answer questions about their political beliefs or those of their colleagues. Reacting to pressure, film companies created **blacklists**—lists of individuals whose loyalty was suspect—that kept people from working in films.

In 1950 Congress passed the McCarran Act, which required all Communist groups to register with the government and to provide lists of members. Truman vetoed the act. "In a free country, we punish men for crimes they commit," he said, "but never for the opinions they hold." Congress overrode his veto.

American Spies Revealed

Meanwhile, stories of spies gripped the country. In 1948 Whittaker Chambers, a magazine editor, told the HUAC that he had spied for the Soviets in the 1930s. He accused Alger Hiss, a former government official, of giving him secret documents to pass on to the Soviets. To support this claim, Chambers showed copies of secret information that he said came from Hiss. Investigators could not prosecute Hiss for spying because too much time had passed since the events occurred. He was

---

Leveled Activities

BL Guided Reading Activity, URB p. 39

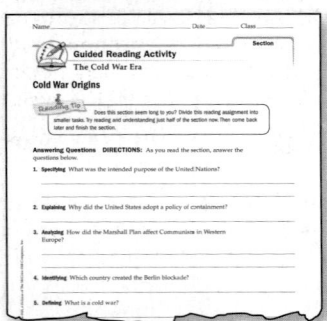

OL Time Line Skills Activity, URB p. 34

ELL Authentic Assessment With Rubrics, p. 27

found guilty, however, of **perjury,** or lying under oath, and sent to prison.

The most dramatic spy case involved the atomic bomb, which the Soviets had acquired by 1949. Julius and Ethel Rosenberg, a New York couple who were Communist Party members, were accused of passing secrets about the atomic bomb to the Soviet Union. The Rosenbergs denied the charges but were sentenced to death for spying. Many people believed that the Rosenbergs were not spies but victims caught up in the Red Scare. Public appeals for mercy failed, however, and the couple was executed in June 1953.

McCarthyism

From 1950 to 1954, the hunt for Communists was led by Republican Senator Joseph McCarthy of Wisconsin. McCarthy claimed that a vast Communist network existed within the government. He called government employees to defend themselves before his committee. His unfounded charges ruined the careers of many innocent Americans. The

word "McCarthyism" emerged to describe "the use of unproven charges to discredit people."

Millions of Americans, however, believed McCarthy. As a result, even the most powerful government officials hesitated to oppose him. In 1954 McCarthy made claims that Communists had infiltrated the U.S. Army. In a series of televised hearings, McCarthy hurled wild accusations at highly respected army officials. Toward the end of the hearings, Joseph Welch, an attorney for the army, said to McCarthy: "Until this moment, Senator, I think I never really gauged your cruelty or your recklessness. . . . Have you left no sense of decency?"

Many Americans now came to view McCarthy as a cruel bully who had little basis for his accusations. Congress also turned against McCarthy. In December 1954, the Senate voted to **censure,** or formally criticize, him for "conduct unbecoming a senator."

✔ **Reading Check** **Describing** What claims did McCarthy make against the U.S. Army?

History ONLINE
Study Central™ To review this section, go to glencoe.com.

Section 1 Review

Vocabulary

1. Write a paragraph using each of the following terms: iron curtain, cooperate, containment, pose, airlift, cold war, subversion, espionage, blacklist, perjury, censure.

Main Ideas

2. **Explaining** Who met at Yalta in 1945, and why did they meet?

3. **Analyzing** Was the Berlin airlift in 1948 successful? Explain why or why not.

4. **Determining Cause and Effect** How did the creation of NATO and the Warsaw Pact eventually affect the relations among European nations?

Critical Thinking

5. **Specifying** On a web diagram like the one below, list some of the direct results in America of the Red Scare.

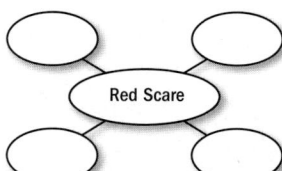

6. **Persuasive Writing** What do you think about the conviction and execution of the Rosenbergs? Write a paragraph that supports your point of view.

Answer the
7. **Essential Question**
How and why did America aid European nations after World War II?

The Cold War Era **Chapter 27** **849**

D **Differentiated Instruction**

Verbal/Linguistic Explain that adding "ism" to the end of a word often refers to a way of thinking or a theory. Ask students to suggest other examples using "ism," and discuss what those words mean. *(Examples include "Buddhism" and "conservatism.")* **OL**

✔ **Reading Check** **Answer:** He accused army officials of being Communists.

Assess

History ONLINE

Study Central™ provides summaries, interactive games, and online graphic organizers to help students review content.

Close

Summarizing Have students write a paragraph summarizing the reasons the United States aided European nations after World War II. **OL**

Answers

1. Students will write paragraphs that use each of the terms correctly.
2. Roosevelt, Churchill, and Stalin; the "Big Three" Allied leaders met at Yalta to discuss how to organize the postwar world.
3. It stopped Soviet expansion in Germany and the rest of Europe, but Berlin and Germany still were divided.
4. It essentially divided Europe into two armed camps.

5. Many federal workers lost their jobs, people in the entertainment industry were blacklisted, and accused Soviet spies were imprisoned or even executed.
6. Students will write paragraphs that support their points of view. All paragraphs should address how the Red Scare influenced American society.
7. America backed the formation of the United Nations to foster peace and settle disputes;

gave Greece and Turkey money to fight off communist influences (Truman Doctrine); gave Western European nations money, supplies, machinery, and food to boost their economies and deter communism (Marshall Plan); participated in the Berlin Airlift to sustain West Berlin during the Soviet blockade; and joined NATO for military cooperation.

Section 2

Postwar Politics

Focus

Bellringer
Daily Test Practice Transparency 27–2

Reading Guide
Answers to Graphic:
Congress limits government spending; labor unions restricted; Truman's Fair Deal promotes more benefits to senior citizens and the poor; desegregation of armed forces; civil rights laws enforced

Section Spotlight Video

Have students watch the Section Spotlight Video "Postwar Politics" to learn more about the United States after World War II.

Essential Question ◄
What economic, social, and political challenges did Americans face after World War II?

Reading Guide

Content Vocabulary
inflation (p. 851)   desegregate (p. 855)
closed shop (p. 853)

Academic Vocabulary
stable (p. 851)
domestic (p. 852)

Key People and Events
Fair Deal (p. 852)
Taft-Hartley Act (p. 853)

Reading Strategy
Taking Notes Create a diagram to describe social and economic change in postwar America.

ILLINOIS STANDARDS
The American Journey

15.A Understand how different economic systems operate in the exchange, production, distribution, and consumption of goods and services.

15.D.3c Explain how workers can affect their productivity through training and by using tools, machinery and technology.

15.E.3b Explain how laws and government policies (e.g., property rights, contract enforcement, standard weights/measurements) establish rules that help a market economy function effectively.

16.C.3b (US) Explain relationships among the American economy and slavery, immigration, industrialization, labor and urbanization, 1700-present.

850

American Diary

When soldiers returned home after World War II, they came back to a nation facing the difficult task of changing from wartime to peacetime. Would the economy collapse again and another depression sweep the country? President Truman was optimistic: "We are having our little troubles now . . . just a blowup after the letdown from war." Public fears, however, forced the nation's leaders into a debate over how best to deal with America's economic problems.

—Harry S. Truman, October 10, 1945

The GI Bill provided many veterans and their families with affordable housing.

Resource Manager

R Reading Strategies	C Critical Thinking	D Differentiated Instruction	W Writing Support	S Skill Practice
Teacher Edition • Questioning, p. 852 • Activat. Prior Know., p. 854 **Additional Resources** • Guid. Read., URB p. 40 • Content Vocab., URB p. 17 • Academic Vocab., URB p. 19 • Read. Ess., p. 304	**Teacher Edition** • Identify. Prob. & Sol., p. 852 • Analyz. Info., p. 853 **Additional Resources** • Quizzes and Tests, p. 268 • Link. Past & Pres., URB p. 33	**Teacher Edition** • Verbal/Ling., p. 855 **Additional Resources** • School-to-Home, URB p. 35 • Reteaching Act., URB p. 37 • Differ. Inst., URB p. 27	**Teacher Edition** • Persuasive Writ., p. 851 • Exposit. Writ., p. 854	**Teacher Edition** • Read. a Chart, p. 851 **Additional Resources** • Daily Test Pract. Transp. 27-2

The Postwar Economy

Main Idea Americans faced rising prices and labor unrest during the late 1940s.

History and You How difficult is it for you to adjust to major changes? Read to learn about how Americans tried to adjust to a peacetime economy after World War II.

After World War II, the United States had to adjust its economy to peacetime life. Industries shifted from producing war materials to making consumer goods, such as cars and appliances. Defense workers had to be retrained to work in consumer industries, and returning soldiers needed jobs.

During the war, government price controls kept the cost of consumer goods **stable,** or unchanging.When the government lifted these controls, prices began to climb. This rise in prices, or **inflation,** also came from a huge increase in consumer demand and spending. During the war years, Americans saved their money because many consumer goods were unavailable or rationed. Now they were eager for new consumer products and services.

Because of inflation, prices rose much faster than wages. During the war, workers had accepted government controls on wages and agreed not to strike. Now they would no longer be put off. When employers refused to raise wages, labor strikes broke out and disrupted the economy. In 1946 a miners' strike raised fears about fewer coal supplies. Meanwhile, a strike by railroad workers led to a shutdown of the nation's railroads.

Alarmed by the labor unrest, President Truman pressured the striking miners and railroad workers to go back to their jobs. In May 1946, he threatened to draft them into the army if they did not return to work. The president insisted he had the right to take such steps to keep vital industries operating.

President Truman finally forced striking miners back to work. He did this by having the government take over the mines. At the same time, he persuaded mine owners to grant many of the workers' demands. Truman also pressured railroad workers to return to work.

Reading Check **Describing** What happened to prices when demand grew after the war?

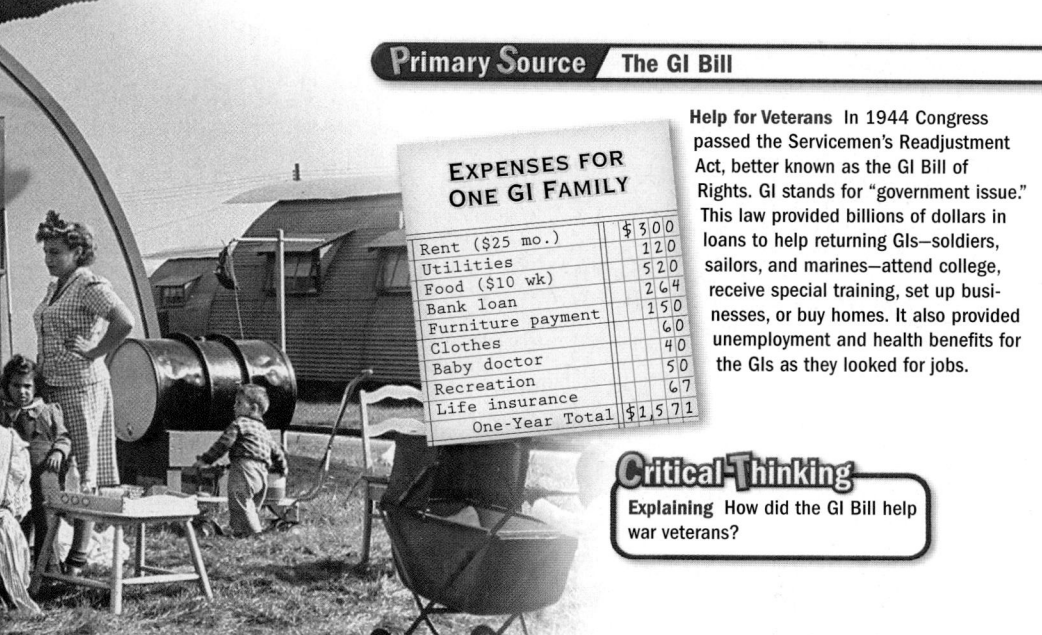

Primary Source / The GI Bill

EXPENSES FOR ONE GI FAMILY

Rent ($25 mo.)	$300
Utilities	120
Food ($10 wk)	520
Bank loan	264
Furniture payment	150
Clothes	60
Baby doctor	40
Recreation	50
Life insurance	67
One-Year Total	$1,571

Help for Veterans In 1944 Congress passed the Servicemen's Readjustment Act, better known as the GI Bill of Rights. GI stands for "government issue." This law provided billions of dollars in loans to help returning GIs—soldiers, sailors, and marines—attend college, receive special training, set up businesses, or buy homes. It also provided unemployment and health benefits for the GIs as they looked for jobs.

Critical Thinking
Explaining How did the GI Bill help war veterans?

Activity: Economics Connection

Comparing and Contrasting President Truman threatened striking miners and railroad workers to keep the country running. **Ask:** What groups today could have the same effect on the economy if they were on strike for an extended period? *(Although few groups today have control over crucial sectors of the economy,* *striking air-traffic controllers, truckers, or longshoremen could disrupt the flow of goods and people.)* **Ask:** What are the main concerns of workers today? *(Answers might include benefits, wages, outsourcing, and job security.)* Have students discuss family members' concerns about their jobs. Remind students to take notes on what they learn so they can share their findings with the class. Write a list of the concerns on the board. Then have students write a paragraph that compares and contrasts workers' concerns today with causes of labor unrest after World War II. **OL**

R Reading Strategy

Questioning Have students change each heading within this subsection into a question. After students read the subsection, have them evaluate whether their questions were answered in the text. **OL**

C Critical Thinking

Identifying Problems and Solutions Have students read about the Fair Deal in the text. **Ask:** What problems did Truman try to solve? What were his solutions? *(Expanded Social Security benefits to help older Americans. Increased federal spending to create jobs and ease the job shortage created by returning soldiers and former defense industry workers. Public housing to help end the affordable housing shortage. National health insurance to provide affordable health care.)* **AL**

This **READING SKILL** (Identifying Problems and Solutions) was introduced in this unit.

R Truman Faces the Republicans

Main Idea President Truman and the Republican-controlled Congress disagreed over how to solve the nation's economic problems.

History and You Have you ever been at a game in which a team that was predicted to lose won a stunning victory? Read to find out how Truman beat the odds in the 1948 presidential race.

In September 1945, President Truman presented a plan of **domestic**—or home-based—reforms aimed at solving some of the nation's economic problems. Truman later called this program the **Fair Deal.**

Truman proposed to raise the minimum wage, expand Social Security benefits, increase federal spending to create jobs, build new public housing, and create a system of national health insurance. However, because of opposition by a coalition of Republicans and Southern Democrats, these measures failed to pass in Congress.

Republicans Control Congress

Many Americans blamed Truman and the Democrats for the nation's problems and called for change. The Republicans seized upon this discontent in the congressional elections of 1946. The slogan "Had Enough?" helped the Republican Party win control of both houses of Congress.

The new Republican Congress set out to limit government spending, control labor unions, and reverse New Deal policies. Conservative Republicans especially favored big business and wanted to limit the power of labor unions.

People IN HISTORY

Hiram Fong
U.S. Senator, Hawaii

On March 12, 1959, Congress voted to admit the territory of Hawaii as a state. One of the two senators elected was Hiram Fong, who had served 14 years in the territorial legislature. As the first person of Chinese descent to hold a seat in the Senate, Fong supported civil rights. He also supported immigration reform that removed discrimination against Asian-Pacific people. Hawaii Senator Daniel Inouye described Fong as *"a legend in his time. He was a patriot . . . a most revered Asian-American leader."*

Margaret Chase Smith
U.S. Senator, Maine

In 1950 Senator Margaret Chase Smith and six other senators issued the Declaration of Conscience condemning "hate and character assassination."

"Those of us who shout the loudest about Americanism . . . are all too frequently those who, by our own words and acts, ignore some of the basic principles of Americanism—The right to criticize. The right to hold unpopular belief. The right to protest. The right of independent thought."

Differentiated Instruction

Harry Truman and Civil Rights

Objective: To learn about Truman's role in the civil rights movement

Focus: Ask students what they have learned so far about Truman's views on civil rights.

Teach: Have students read the excerpt and answer the questions.

Assess: Discuss any answers that vary from the Answer Key.

Close: Ask students to identify any new information they learned about Harry Truman.

Differentiated Instruction Strategies

BL Have students define "discrimination" and explain if they think it exists in their school or community.

AL Ask students to research the civil rights record of a president who served after Truman and compare it to Truman's record.

ELL Ask students if they have experienced discrimination because they came from another country.

Differentiated Instruction Activity, URB p. 27

In the spring of 1947, Republican legislators introduced a measure that became known as the **Taft-Hartley Act.** This measure limited the actions workers could take against their employers. It outlawed the **closed shop,** or the practice of forcing business owners to hire only union members.

The Taft-Hartley Act also allowed the government to temporarily stop any strike that endangered public health or safety. This provision was intended to prevent any future strikes like those of the miners and the railroad workers the year before.

Labor unions sharply criticized the Taft-Hartley Act. They claimed that the measure erased many of the gains that labor had made since 1933. Truman, realizing that the Democrats needed the support of labor, vetoed the act. The Republican-controlled Congress, however, overrode Truman's veto.

Dennis Chavez
U.S. Senator, New Mexico

Dennis Chavez represented New Mexico in the U.S. Senate from May 11, 1935, until his death in 1962. He was the first American-born Latino senator. A lifelong supporter of civil rights, he cowrote one of the first Senate bills to stop discrimination in employment. He declared, *"I have been fighting for the so-called underprivileged all my days because I was one of them."*

CRITICAL Thinking

Speculating If Fong, Smith, and Chavez were in the Senate today, what issues do you think they might be addressing? Why?

Government Reorganization

Truman and Congress agreed on improving the efficiency of the federal government, which had grown considerably since the New Deal. In 1947 Congress passed the National Security Act. It unified the armed services under the Department of Defense. The act also set up a permanent Joint Chiefs of Staff, made up of the heads of each of the armed forces, to coordinate military policy. A National Security Council, located within the White House, would advise the president on foreign and military matters.

The National Security Act also set up another institution, the Central Intelligence Agency (CIA). The CIA aids American foreign policy by collecting information about what is going on in other countries, evaluating it, and passing it on to the president and other foreign-policy decision makers.

Many Americans feared that the CIA would be used to spy on American citizens. Truman, however, promised that the new agency would operate only in foreign lands and would not bring "police state methods" into American society.

The Election of 1948

As the 1948 presidential race neared, Truman seemed to have little chance of winning. Continuing economic problems made the president unpopular with many voters. Truman's failure to get U.S. domestic reforms passed made him look weak and ineffective.

Divisions within the Democratic Party also increased the chances of a Republican victory. At the Democratic national convention, two groups left the party altogether. Reacting angrily to Truman's support of civil rights, a group of Southern Democrats formed the States' Rights Democratic Party, or Dixiecrats. They nominated South Carolina's governor Strom Thurmond for president. At the same time, some Democrats left to form the Progressive Party, with Henry Wallace as their nominee for president. Wallace opposed Truman's foreign policy and called for closer American-Soviet ties.

C Critical Thinking

Analyzing Information Ask: In what ways did the National Security Act attempt to make the federal government more efficient? *(It created the Department of Defense to unify the military and coordinate military policy. The National Security Council was placed in the White House to advise the president. A centralized agency was created to streamline the gathering of intelligence information.)* **OL**

People IN HISTORY

Critical Thinking Answer

Students should point out that the same concerns are addressed today in the Senate, including civil rights, immigration reform, Constitutional rights, and employment discrimination. They would also debate issues related to the war on terrorism.

Differentiated Instruction

Leveled Activities

BL **School-to-Home Connection, URB p. 35**

OL **Reading Essentials and Note-Taking Guide, p. 304**

Chapter 27, Section 2 (Pages 850–855)
Postwar Politics

Essential Question
What economic, social, and political challenges did Americans face after World War II?

Directions: As you read, complete a chart like the one below to list the challenges facing Americans after World War II.

	Challenges
Economic	1.
Political	2.
Social	3.

Notes **Read to Learn**

The Postwar Economy (page 851)

After World War II, the U.S. economy had to adjust to peacetime life. Industries that had made war goods now returned to making consumer goods, such as cars and appliances. Workers had to be retrained, and soldiers needed jobs.

During the war, the government kept the prices of consumer goods from changing. After the war, the government lifted these controls, and prices increased. This increase in prices is called **inflation.** Because of inflation, prices rose faster than people's wages.

Workers had accepted

AL **Linking Past and Present Activity, URB p. 33**

Linking Past and Present Activity
The Cold War Era

National Security

THEN Following World War II, the parts of the federal government related to defense, foreign policy, and national security were reorganized. The National Security Act of 1947 created the National Military Establishment, which was renamed the Department of Defense in 1949. It also created the air force as a separate branch of the military and put the army, navy, and air force under the new Department of Defense.

NOW Following the terrorist attacks of September 11, 2001, another major reorganization related to national security took place. The Homeland Security Act of 2002 created a new cabinet-level department called the Department of Homeland Security (DHS). The purpose of this department is to make the United States more secure from terrorist attacks.

853

W Writing Support

Expository Writing Have students describe the 1948 election to a relative in Europe who knew little about the candidates, issues, or outcome. **OL**

R Reading Strategy

Activating Prior Knowledge Ask: Why did workers, African Americans, and farmers support Truman? (*Truman's Fair Deal would create jobs and improve housing and health care. Truman also supported civil rights.*) **OL**

The Election of 1948 ◻ NATIONAL GEOGRAPHIC

Map Skills Answers
1. the South
2. 114 (Truman: 303; Dewey: 189)

✔ **Reading Check** **Answer:** Polls and experts expected Dewey to win the election; no one expected a Truman victory.

Hands-On Chapter Project
Step 2

Creating a Cover Story About the Cold War

Step 2: Writing the Article Students will write an article about the Cold War.

Essential Question: What economic, social, and political challenges did Americans face after World War II?

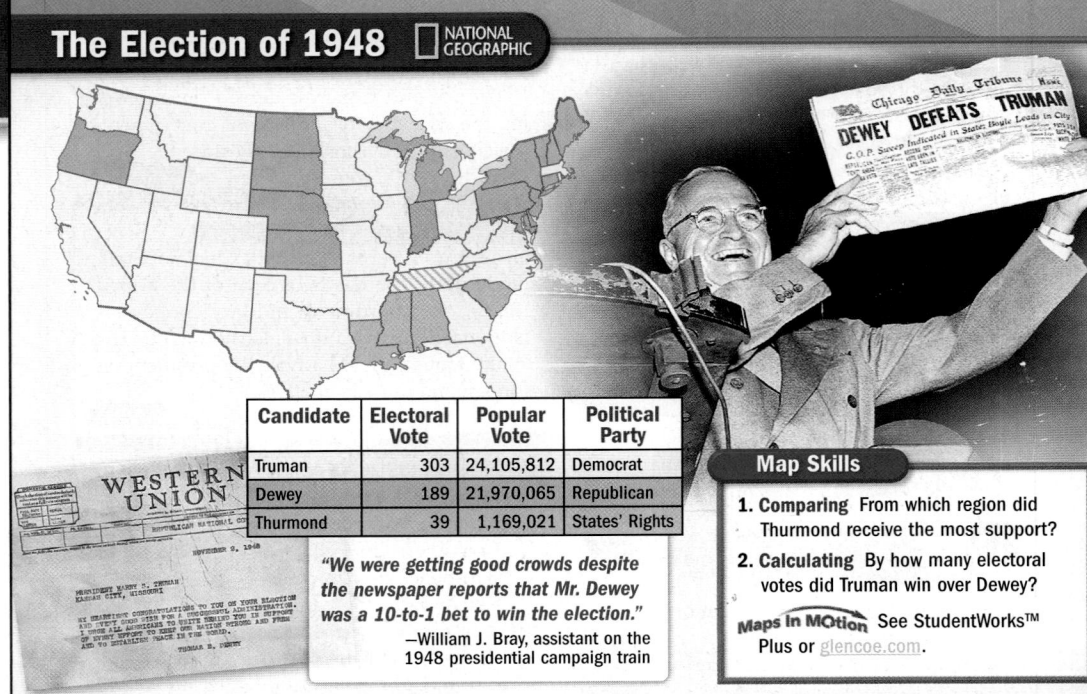

The Election of 1948 ◻ NATIONAL GEOGRAPHIC

Candidate	Electoral Vote	Popular Vote	Political Party
Truman	303	24,105,812	Democrat
Dewey	189	21,970,065	Republican
Thurmond	39	1,169,021	States' Rights

"We were getting good crowds despite the newspaper reports that Mr. Dewey was a 10-to-1 bet to win the election."
—William J. Bray, assistant on the 1948 presidential campaign train

Map Skills
1. **Comparing** From which region did Thurmond receive the most support?
2. **Calculating** By how many electoral votes did Truman win over Dewey?

Maps in MOtion See StudentWorks™ Plus or glencoe.com.

Dewey Leads Polls

With the Democrats badly divided, it looked as though Governor Thomas Dewey of New York, the Republican nominee, would surely win the election. A dignified and popular candidate, Dewey seemed unbeatable. Opinion polls showed him with a huge lead. One pollster remarked: "Mr. Dewey is still so clearly ahead that we might just as well get ready to listen to his inaugural."

Perhaps the only one who gave Truman a chance to win was Truman himself. Ignoring the polls, the determined president poured his efforts into an energetic campaign. Traveling more than 21,000 miles (33,800 km) by train on a "whistle-stop" tour of the country, he gave some 300 speeches along the way. In town after town, he sharply attacked what he called "that do-nothing, good-for-nothing, worst Congress" for rejecting his Fair Deal legislation.

Truman Stages an Upset

On Election Day experts still expected Dewey to win. Expectations for a Republican victory were so great that on the evening of the election—before many votes were counted—the *Chicago Daily Tribune* newspaper issued a special edition announcing "Dewey Defeats Truman."

The nation was in for a great surprise.
W When all the ballots were counted, Truman had edged out Dewey by more than 2 million votes. The president's narrow victory was
R based largely on support from workers, African Americans, and farmers. Almost as remarkable as Truman's victory was the new popularity of the Democratic Party. In the election, Democrats regained control of both houses of Congress.

✔ **Reading Check** **Analyzing** Why was the outcome of the 1948 presidential election a surprise?

Directions Have groups organize their notes into the four categories outlined in Step 1. If they find gaps in their research, have them look for more information. Talk about ways to organize and write an interesting article. Then ask groups to write a three- to five-page article, using this information.

Assessing Have groups trade articles and compare their coverage of the postwar economic, social, and political challenges in the United States. Is any important information missing? Are the facts presented in a clear and interesting manner?

(Chapter Project continued in Section 3)

A Fair Deal for Americans

Main Idea The Truman administration pushed for civil rights reforms.

History and You Have you ever put all your energy into making something important happen? Read to learn why President Truman wanted Congress to pass his legislation.

. . . .

Truman took the election results as a sign that Americans wanted reform. He quickly reintroduced the Fair Deal legislation he presented to Congress in 1945. Some of these reform measures passed, but his plan lacked broad support, and Congress defeated most of the measures. Congress did pass laws to raise the minimum wage, expand Social Security benefits for senior citizens, and provide funds for housing for low-income families.

In a message to Congress in 1948, Truman called for an end to discrimination based on race, religion, or ethnic origins. He tried to persuade Congress to protect the voting rights of African Americans, abolish the poll tax,

and make lynching a federal crime. Despite failing to get these measures passed, the president did take steps to advance the civil rights of African Americans. He ordered federal agencies to end job discrimination against African Americans and ordered the armed forces to **desegregate**—to end the separation of races. The president also instructed the Justice Department to enforce existing civil rights laws.

When Truman proposed his domestic agenda to Congress in 1949, he proclaimed that "every segment of our population and every individual has a right to expect from our government a fair deal." Truman asked for the clearance of slums, government-backed medical insurance, higher minimum wages, and more federal money for public schools. Although much of the president's Fair Deal vision went unfulfilled, he made an important start toward improving the lives of millions of Americans.

✓ **Reading Check** **Analyzing** Why did President Truman call his proposed reforms a "fair deal"?

D Differentiated Instruction

Verbal/Linguistic Write "desegregate" on the board. **Ask:** What does the root word "segregate" mean? *(to isolate or separate)* Explain that "de" means "to do the opposite of" or "to reverse or undo." Thus, "desegregation" is to undo the separation of the races. **OL**

✓ **Reading Check** **Answer:** The reforms were aimed at those whom Truman believed were not treated fairly or equally, including the poor, senior citizens, and African Americans.

Assess

. . . .

History ONLINE

Study Central™ provides summaries, interactive games, and online graphic organizers to help students review content. **OL**

Close

Describing Have each student describe to a partner a challenge that Americans faced after World War II. **OL**

Section 2 Review

History ONLINE
Study Central™ To review this section, go to glencoe.com.

Vocabulary

1. Use each of the following terms in a complete sentence that will explain its meaning: stable, inflation, domestic, closed shop, desegregate.

Main Ideas

2. Explaining What happened to the price of American consumer goods after World War II? Why did this happen?

3. Discussing Why was Truman given little chance of winning the 1948 presidential election?

4. Analyzing What steps did President Truman take to end discrimination and segregation during his term in office? Was he successful?

Critical Thinking

5. Explaining Why was the CIA formed, and why were some Americans suspicious of the organization?

6. Interpreting Create a diagram like the one below that lists the main goals of the Fair Deal.

Fair Deal ⊏⊐

7. Persuasive Writing President Truman threatened to draft striking coal miners into the army. Write a paragraph in which you explain whether you agree or disagree that a president should have this power.

Answer the
8. Essential Question
What economic, social, and political challenges did Americans face after World War II?

The Cold War Era **Chapter 27** **855**

Section 2 Review

Answers

1. Sentences should explain the meaning of each term correctly.

2. Prices rose because the government lifted wartime price controls, and consumer demand and spending increased.

3. His inability to enact domestic reforms made him appear weak; the Democratic Party was badly divided, giving an edge to the Republicans.

4. Truman tried to protect African Americans' voting rights and make lynching a federal crime, but these measures failed. He

ordered the end of job discrimination against African Americans, desegregated the armed forces, and worked to enforce civil rights laws.

5. to gather, evaluate, and transmit information about other countries to foreign-policy decision makers; they thought it would lead to spying against Americans and would create a police state.

6. raise the minimum wage, expand Social Security benefits, expand public housing, offer national health insurance

7. Paragraphs should include information about the president's Constitutional duties.

8. Economic: inflation and job shortages; Social: labor unrest, housing shortages, poverty, discrimination, division over civil rights, lynching, segregation; Political: Republican Congress opposes Truman, federal government growth, divided Democratic Party

Focus

Section 3

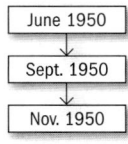

The Korean War

Bellringer
Daily Test Practice Transparency 27–3

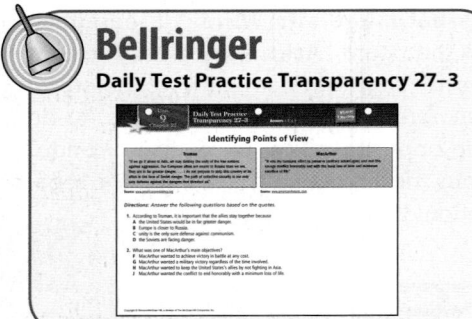

Reading Guide
Answers to Graphic:

June 1950: invasion of South Korea by North Korean troops; **September 1950:** control of most of South Korea by Communists, farthest advance of North Koreans, and UN landing; **November 1950:** farthest advance of UN troops

Section Spotlight Video

Have students watch the Section Spotlight Video "The Korean War" to learn about the Korean conflict of the 1950s.

Essential Question ◄
How and why did America involve itself in the Korean conflict of the 1950s?

Reading Guide

Content Vocabulary
stalemate (p. 858)
demilitarized zone (p. 859)

Academic Vocabulary
assure (p. 858)
conclude (p. 859)

Key People and Events
Douglas MacArthur (p. 857)

Reading Strategy
Taking Notes On a sequencing chart like the one below, list a major event during the Korean conflict in each month and year.

June 1950
↓
Sept. 1950
↓
Nov. 1950

ILLINOIS STANDARDS
The American Journey

14.E.3 Compare the basic principles of the United States and its international interests (e.g., territory, environment, trade, use of technology).

16.B.3d (US) Describe ways in which the United States developed as a world political power.

17.D Understand the historical significance of geography.

18.B Understand the roles and interactions of individuals and groups in society.

American Diary

Twelve U.S. Marines had just led their troops out of a trap. They listened to the words of their commander:
"We will come out as Marines, and not as stragglers. We're going to take our dead, wounded, and equipment when we leave. We're coming out . . . as Marines, or not at all." *Two days of fighting followed. With the arrival of air cover, the Marines pushed back the Chinese and made their escape.*

—*from* Chosin: Heroic Ordeal of the Korean War

A U.S. machine gun crew prepares for combat, November 1950.

Resource Manager

R Reading Strategies	**C** Critical Thinking	**D** Differentiated Instruction	**W** Writing Support	**S** Skill Practice
Teacher Edition	**Teacher Edition**	**Additional Resources**	**Teacher Edition**	**Teacher Edition**
• Summarizing, p. 857	• Predict. Conseq., p. 858	• School-to-Home, URB p. 35	• Expository Writ., p. 859	• Using Geo. Skills, p. 857
• Academic Vocab., p. 858	**Additional Resources**	• Reteaching Act., URB p. 37		**Additional Resources**
Additional Resources	• Quizzes and Tests, p. 269			• Daily Test Pract. Transp. 27-3
• Guid. Read., URB p. 41	• Inter. Polit. Cartoons, URB p. 13			• Soc. Stud. Skills, URB p. 25
• Content Vocab., URB p. 17				
• Academic Vocab., URB p. 19				
• Read. Ess., p. 307				

Conflict in Korea

Main Idea Americans under the United Nations' flag fought a war in Korea during the early 1950s.

History and You How do you deal with people who use force to get what they want? Read to find out how the United States responded to Communist expansion in the Korean Peninsula.

· ·

At the end of World War II, the Americans and the Soviets divided the east Asian country of Korea at the 38th parallel of latitude. The Communists set up a government in North Korea, and an American-backed government took over South Korea.

On June 25, 1950, North Korean troops invaded South Korea in an attempt to take over that country. Poorly armed, the South Koreans were no match for the North. By September, the Communist forces gained control over much of South Korea, including Seoul, the capital city. Only a small area in the southeast around the port city of Pusan was still held by the South Korean army.

Early Phase of the War

President Truman reacted quickly to the Korean invasion, which he believed was supported by the Soviet Union. Without asking Congress to declare war, Truman ordered the use of limited American air and armed forces in Korea. Truman said:

R

PRIMARY SOURCE

"Korea is the Greece of the Far East. If we are tough enough now, if we stand up to them like we did in Greece three years ago, they won't take any next steps."
—from *Presidential Decisions for War*

Truman persuaded the United Nations to send troops. Most of these UN troops were American and under the command of U.S. general **Douglas MacArthur,** a hero of World War II. General MacArthur and the UN forces made a daring landing in the middle of the Korean Peninsula near the port of Inch'ŏn. They took that strategic city and then moved north to push the North Koreans back across the 38th parallel. South Korea now came under the control of UN forces.

S

Primary Source / **The Korean War 1950–1953**

— Truce line, July 1953

SOVIET UNION

PEOPLE'S REPUBLIC OF CHINA

NORTH KOREA
P'yŏngyang

Sea of Japan (East Sea)

P'anmunjŏm
Seoul
Inch'ŏn

SOUTH KOREA
Pusan

JAPAN

0   200 kilometers
0   200 miles
Two-Point Equidistant projection

❶ Farthest advance of North Koreans Sept. 1950
❷ UN landing Sept. 1950
❸ Farthest advance of UN forces Nov. 1950
❹ Farthest advance of North Koreans and Chinese Jan. 1951

Critical Thinking
Analyzing When did UN forces make their farthest advance?

Teach

· · · · · · · · · · · · · · · · · · ·

S Skill Practice

Using Geography Skills Have students look at the Korean War map. **Ask:** What countries are near North Korea and South Korea? *(Soviet Union, People's Republic of China, and Japan)* Which two nations near Korea had Communist governments at the time of the Korean War? *(Soviet Union, People's Republic of China)* **BL**

R Reading Strategy

Summarizing Ask students to write a one-sentence summary explaining why the United States supported sending troops to Korea. *(The United States wanted to stop the Soviet Union from extending its influence into Asia.)* **OL**

Primary Source

Critical Thinking Answer
November 1950

Hands-On Chapter Project
Step 3

Creating a Cover Story About the Cold War

Step 3: Creating the Layout Students will create original drawings and use Internet research to assemble visuals that illustrate their magazine articles.

Essential Question: How and why did America involve itself in the Korean conflict of the 1950s?

Directions Direct students to list the main ideas in their articles and decide key words to use in an Internet search for visuals. In addition, they may draw their own illustrations. Have them write informational captions to accompany the visuals.

Analyzing Ask students to describe how their articles address the Korean conflict and its role in the Cold War.

(Chapter Project continued in Section 4)

The Cold War

Differentiated Instruction

Primary Source — Truman vs. MacArthur

Controversy President Truman relieved General Douglas MacArthur of his command, leading to a storm of controversy. Truman believed in a limited war in Korea, while MacArthur wanted total victory.

GENERAL MacARTHUR FIRED

SEOUL, Korea, April 11, 1951—President Harry Truman fired General Douglas MacArthur, commander of UN troops in Korea. MacArthur and his troops had been forced to retreat over the 38th parallel by advancing Chinese communist troops coming to the aid of North Korea. The General was relieved of duties when he threatened to retaliate with a full-scale attack on China—against orders from Washington. President Truman had called for cease-fire talks hoping to keep the conflict from escalating into war with China.

Critical Thinking

Speculating Why do you think MacArthur remained popular despite being fired?

Taking the Offensive

Encouraged by this success, General MacArthur urged President Truman to order the invasion of North Korea. He **assured,** or promised, Truman that neither China nor the Soviet Union would enter the war, and he pledged that he would have troops "home by Christmas." Truman sought UN approval for an invasion of the North to create a unified and democratic Korea.

After receiving these new orders, MacArthur moved into North Korea and advanced toward the Chinese border. The Chinese Communists saw the advancing troops as a threat. Hundreds of thousands of Chinese troops crossed the border and drove the UN forces back to South Korea. Within weeks, the Communists held Seoul, South Korea's capital.

✔ **Reading Check** **Describing** What line separated North Korea from South Korea?

American Leadership Divided

Main Idea President Truman and General MacArthur disagreed over how to fight the Korean War.

History and You Have you ever been forced to give up something that you liked? Read to find out why General MacArthur had to resign his command of UN forces during the Korean War.

By January 1951, United Nations forces managed to stop their retreat. Launching a counteroffensive, they retook Seoul and pushed the Communists back across the 38th parallel. The war now became a **stalemate,** a situation in which neither side is able to gain much ground or achieve a decisive victory. The stalemate lasted for almost two years, with much bitter fighting along the 38th parallel.

Truman and MacArthur Disagree

As the stalemate continued, Truman thought about negotiating an end to the fighting. MacArthur, however, argued that dropping atomic bombs on Chinese bases and supply lines would bring a quick victory. Truman opposed MacArthur's plan, fearing that it would lead to a larger war with China or develop into another world war.

MacArthur publically criticized the president. In a letter to a member of Congress, MacArthur complained that he was being kept from doing his job. "We must win," he wrote. "There is no substitute for victory."

On April 11, 1951, President Truman relieved General MacArthur of his command in Korea. He **concluded,** or decided, that it was the only action he could take and "still be president of the United States." Truman wrote: "If I allowed him to defy the civil authorities in this manner, I myself would be violating my oath to uphold and defend the Constitution."

MacArthur's firing created a storm of protest in the United States. The general was popular, and polls showed that most Americans supported him against the president. Moreover, MacArthur did not go quietly. He returned home to a hero's welcome. MacArthur also delivered a farewell speech before Congress. "Old soldiers never die," he said, "they just fade away."

Ending the Conflict

The two sides in the Korean War began talks in July 1951. A cease-fire agreement ending the fighting was finally signed in July 1953 during the presidency of Dwight D. Eisenhower. It set up a **demilitarized zone**—a region barring military forces—between the two Koreas. The zone stretched along the border near the 38th parallel.

The Korean War ended with no victory for either side and almost no change in territory. More than 36,000 Americans died, and another 103,000 were wounded. Nearly two million Koreans and Chinese were killed.

By fighting in Korea, the United States 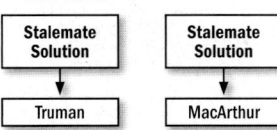 showed the Soviets that it was willing to use force, if necessary, to block the spread of communism. At the same time, the lack of a clear victory led to uncertainty at home about America's foreign policy.

Reading Check Comparing How did Truman's view on Korea differ from General MacArthur's view?

History ONLINE
Study Central™ To review this section, go to glencoe.com.

Section 3 Review

Vocabulary

1. Explain the significance of each of these terms: assure, stalemate, conclude, demilitarized zone.

Main Ideas

2. **Explaining** How did the Korean conflict begin?

3. **Discussing** Why did Truman relieve General MacArthur of his command in Korea?

4. **Identifying** What is a demilitarized zone, and where was it located in Korea?

Critical Thinking

5. **Comparing and Contrasting** Re-create a chart like the one below to compare the stalemate solutions of Truman and MacArthur.

Stalemate Solution		Stalemate Solution
↓		↓
Truman		MacArthur

6. **Expository Writing** Explain in a paragraph the major events that led directly to the stalemate in Korea.

Answer the
Essential Question

7. How and why did America involve itself in the Korean conflict of the 1950s?

The Cold War Era **Chapter 27** 859

W Writing Support

Expository Writing Have students research how Americans in the mid-1950s felt about the way the Korean War ended. Ask them to write a one-page essay summarizing their findings. **AL**

Reading Check Answer: MacArthur wanted a quick victory using atomic weapons, whereas Truman wanted a negotiated end to the conflict to avoid war with China or another world war.

Assess

History ONLINE

Study Central™ provides summaries, interactive games, and online graphic organizers to help students review content.

Close

Explaining Have students write a paragraph that explains why the United States entered the Korean conflict. **OL**

Section 3 Review

Answers

1. Explanations should include the terms in relation to the Korean War.
2. Communist North Korean troops invaded and gained control of South Korea, and the UN sent troops in response.
3. MacArthur and Truman disagreed about how to end the Korean conflict. MacArthur criticized Truman, and Truman asserted his authority by firing the general.
4. an area where military forces are not allowed; along the border of North and South Korea, near the 38th parallel
5. Truman: negotiation; MacArthur: drop atomic bombs on Chinese bases and supply lines to achieve a quick victory
6. Paragraphs should include information about the UN counteroffensive and the 38th parallel.
7. The United States wanted to prevent the Soviet Union from making further gains in Asia and to halt Communist expansion there. President Truman persuaded the UN to send troops after North Korea gained control of most of South Korea in June 1950.

Focus

America in the 1950s

Bellringer

Daily Test Practice Transparency 27–4

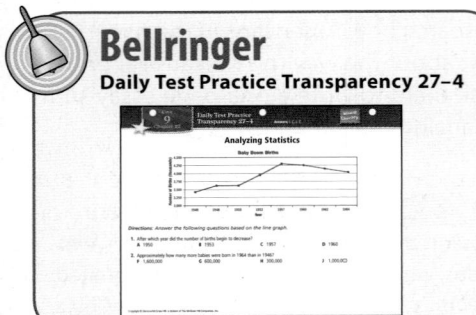

Reading Guide

Answers to Graphic:

1. Seizure of Suez Canal by Egypt and consequent invasion of Egypt by Britain, France, and Israel; the invasion ended due to U.S. and Soviet pressure.
2. Revolt in Hungary aimed at Soviet withdrawal. The crisis ended when the Soviet military crushed the revolt.

Section Spotlight Video

Have students watch the Section Spotlight Video "Problems in a Time of Plenty" to learn about poverty in Appalachia.

Resource Manager

Essential Question
How did the American prosperity of the 1950s affect the country's economy and culture?

Reading Guide

Content Vocabulary

surplus (p. 861)   affluence (p. 863)
arms race (p. 862)   materialism (p. 866)
summit (p. 862)

Academic Vocabulary

nuclear (p. 862)   economy (p. 863)

Key People and Events
Dwight D. Eisenhower (p. 861)
Nikita Khrushchev (p. 862)

Reading Strategy
Taking Notes Re-create a diagram like the one below to identify two Cold War crises that occurred in 1956 and how each was resolved.

○ — (1956 Crises) — ○

ILLINOIS STANDARDS
The American Journey

15.E Understand the impact of government policies and decisions on production and consumption in the economy.

16.B.3d (US) Describe ways in which the United States developed as a world political power.

17.C.3c Analyze how human processes influence settlement patterns including migration and population growth.

17.D.3a Explain how and why spatial patterns of settlement change over time.

American Diary

"Trust was the bedrock of Ike's presidency," one reporter said, adding, "We knew what was in his heart." These words were used to describe Dwight D. Eisenhower, Republican presidential candidate in 1952. Eisenhower's appeal went far beyond party label. His role in World War II made him an unquestioned hero. Above all, his personality made many people feel safe, comfortable, and confident.

—from Hugh Sidey,
TIME *magazine reporter*

Eisenhower supporters in Shreveport, Louisiana, during the 1952 campaign

---

R Reading Strategies	**C** Critical Thinking	**D** Differentiated Instruction	**W** Writing Support	**S** Skill Practice
Teacher Edition	**Teacher Edition**	**Teacher Edition**	**Teacher Edition**	**Teacher Edition**
• Previewing, p. 863	• Determin. Cause & Effect, p. 861	• Intrapersonal, p. 864	• Expository Writ., p. 862	• Using Geo. Skills, p. 861
• Identifying, p. 865	• Draw. Conclus., p. 862	• Auditory/Musical, p. 864	• Personal Writ., p. 864	• Read. a Time Line, p. 863
• Read. Prim. Sources, p. 866	• Identify. Central Iss., p. 865	**Additional Resources**		**Additional Resources**
Additional Resources	**Additional Resources**	• School-to-Home, URB p. 35		• Daily Test Pract. Transp. 27-4
• Guid. Read., URB p. 42	• Quizzes and Tests, p. 270	• Reteaching Act., URB p. 37		• Geo. & Hist., URB p. 31
• Cont. Vocab., URB p. 17	• Econ. & Hist., URB p. 5			
• Acad. Vocab., URB p. 19	• Crit. Think. Skills, URB p. 29			
• Read. Ess., p. 310				
• Pri. Source Read., URB p. 21				

The Eisenhower Years

Main Idea President Eisenhower promoted policies to maintain prosperity at home and to compete with the Soviets abroad.

History and You Have you ever taken part in an exciting contest to win first prize? Read to learn how the United States and the Soviet Union were rivals in a "contest" for world leadership.

In November 1952, Americans elected **Dwight D. Eisenhower** to the presidency in a landslide victory—the first Republican to win the White House since 1928. Eisenhower collected more than 6 million popular votes over Illinois Governor Adlai E. Stevenson, his Democratic opponent, and carried the electoral college 442 to 89. The Republicans also won control of Congress.

Born in Texas and raised in rural Kansas, Dwight D. Eisenhower rose steadily through the army to become supreme commander of the Allied forces in Europe during World War II. People called him "Ike"—and voters trusted him. He won wide support with his pledge to bring the Korean War to an "early and honorable end."

Domestic Policy

During his two terms in office, Eisenhower followed a moderate, or middle-of-the-road, approach to domestic policy. He avoided ambitious new government programs but resisted the pressure to end popular older ones, and sometimes he even expanded them. As he once told reporters: "I feel pretty good when I'm attacked from both sides. It makes me more certain I'm on the right track."

President Eisenhower wanted to make the federal government "smaller rather than bigger." He backed free enterprise, shifted some financial powers to the states, and cut federal spending. When Eisenhower completed his second term in 1961, the federal budget had a **surplus,** or excess, of $300 million.

The greatest domestic program of the Eisenhower years involved building a network of interstate highways. In 1956 Congress passed the Federal Highway Act. The law funded the building of more than 40,000 miles (64,000 km) of highways that tied the nation together. The highway program spurred economic growth, especially in the automobile and oil industries, while improving military mobility in case of an attack.

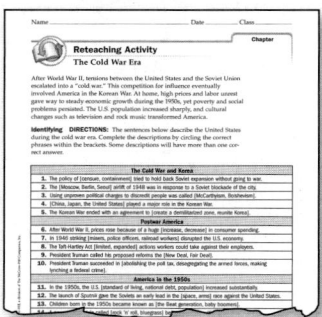

Primary Source / **Election of 1952**

Electoral Vote

83%
17%

■ Dwight D. Eisenhower (R)
■ Adlai E. Stevenson (D)

Popular Vote

0.5% (Other)
55.1% 44.4%

■ Dwight D. Eisenhower (R)
■ Adlai E. Stevenson (D)

Critical Thinking

1. **Interpreting** Which candidate won a majority of the popular vote?
2. **Applying** What is a landslide victory? Would you consider Eisenhower's election a landslide? Explain.

Teach

C Critical Thinking

Determining Cause and Effect Ask: Why was there a budget surplus by the time Eisenhower completed his second term? *(He avoided ambitious government programs, shifted some financial power to the states, and cut federal spending.)* **OL**

S Skill Practice

Using Geography Skills Bring in a road atlas. Organize the class into small groups, and assign each group two cities in the United States. Have groups plan a road trip from city to city using the interstate system as much as possible. **OL**

Primary Source

Critical Thinking Answers
1. Eisenhower
2. an election won by a large majority; it was a landslide because Eisenhower won 83% of the electoral votes, and he received six million more popular votes than his opponent.

Differentiated Instruction

Leveled Activities

BL **Reteaching Activity,** URB p. 37

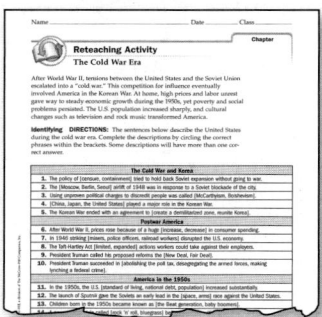

OL **Content Vocabulary,** URB p. 17

AL **Geography and History Activity, URB p. 31**

W Writing Support

Expository Writing Have students work with partners to find out more about the history and importance of the Suez Canal. Then have them write a newspaper article that might have appeared when Nasser seized the canal. Encourage students to include background on the canal, as well as information about the takeover. **AL**

C Critical Thinking

Drawing Conclusions Ask: Why did Eisenhower decide not to intervene in Hungary? *(to avoid war and further tensions with the Soviet Union)* **OL**

✓Reading Check **Answer:** Peaceful coexistence began; the United States and the Soviet Union competed but avoided war.

United States–Soviet Rivalry

During the 1950s, the United States and the Soviet Union engaged in a nuclear **arms race.** Both sides built more and more **nuclear,** or atomic, warheads and guided missiles that could destroy the other side many times over. With the threat of nuclear destruction so great, the United States and the Soviet Union had to act carefully. A crisis, badly managed, could lead to all-out war.

In 1956 two crises tested the superpowers. First, trouble arose in the Middle East when Egypt's president Gamal Abdel Nasser seized the Suez Canal from its European owners. In October, Britain and France joined Israel in invading Egypt. Britain and France hoped to get rid of Nasser, and Israel wanted to end Egypt's military threat. American and Soviet opposition finally forced the three nations to pull out of Egypt.

The second crisis erupted in Hungary, when students and workers demonstrated to demand changes in the government. A new government called for Soviet troops to withdraw. In early November 1956, Soviet leader

Nikita Khrushchev (kroosh·CHAWF) ordered Soviet forces to crush the revolt. President Eisenhower condemned the Soviet crackdown but did not intervene.

By the mid-1950s, the superpowers were interested in easing Cold War tensions. In July 1955, Eisenhower, NATO leaders, and Soviet officials met at a summit conference in Geneva, Switzerland. A **summit** is a meeting of heads of government. The leaders discussed major issues, raising hopes for peace.

After the Geneva summit, a policy of peaceful coexistence emerged. This meant the two superpowers would compete but avoid war. For example, the U.S. and the Soviet Union began competing in a space race. In October 1957, the Soviets sent into space the world's first artificial satellite, called *Sputnik.* The United States set up its own space program headed by the National Aeronautics and Space Administration (NASA).

✓Reading Check **Describing** How did relations between the superpowers change after the Geneva summit?

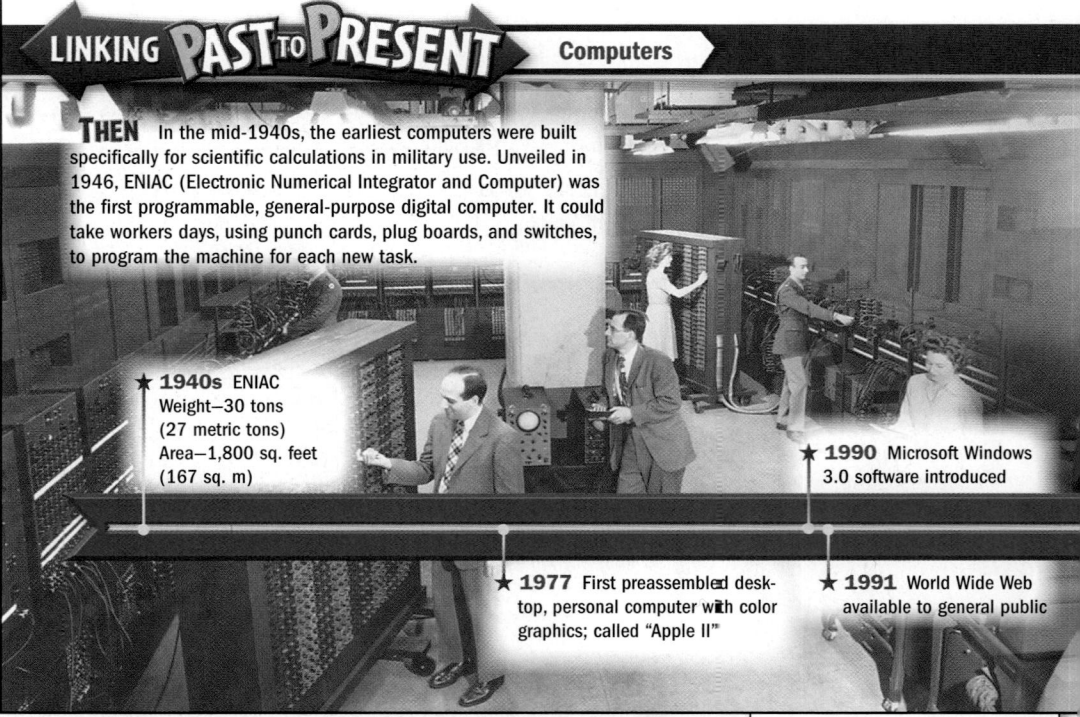

LINKING PAST TO PRESENT — Computers

THEN In the mid-1940s, the earliest computers were built specifically for scientific calculations in military use. Unveiled in 1946, ENIAC (Electronic Numerical Integrator and Computer) was the first programmable, general-purpose digital computer. It could take workers days, using punch cards, plug boards, and switches, to program the machine for each new task.

★ **1940s** ENIAC
Weight—30 tons
(27 metric tons)
Area—1,800 sq. feet
(167 sq. m)

★ **1990** Microsoft Windows 3.0 software introduced

★ **1977** First preassembled desktop, personal computer with color graphics; called "Apple II"

★ **1991** World Wide Web available to general public

Differentiated Instruction

Making Inferences

Objective:	To make an inference using facts
Focus:	Ask students to define "inference" in their own words.
Teach:	Have students answer the questions.
Assess:	Review students' answers and clarify incorrect choices.
Close:	Ask students how making inferences can help them understand what they read.

Differentiated Instruction Strategies

BL Have one student read a question to another and identify which words will help them answer it.

AL Have students quiz each other using questions they create based on inferences in the table.

ELL Have students work in small groups to make a glossary of terms about space exploration.

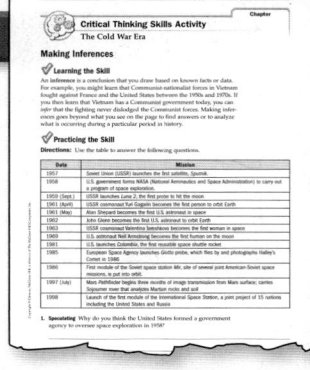

Critical Thinking Skills Activity, URB p. 29

Prosperity and Change

Main Idea A booming economy changed the social and cultural life of Americans during the 1950s.

History and You You probably have heard this expression: "Those were the good old days." For some older Americans, this expression describes the 1950s. Read to find out why the 1950s has this appeal for them.

During the 1950s, the American **economy** —the system of production, distribution, and consumption—grew rapidly. Americans earned higher wages and bought more consumer goods than ever before. As a result, factory production soared. A "baby boom," or increased birthrate, promised even more economic growth in the future.

Many women left the workforce to stay home and raise children. The demand for baby products and services grew. School enrollment soared as the "baby boomers" reached school age, putting a strain on the educational system.

The Consumer Society

Americans of the 1950s went on a buying spree. **Affluence,** the growing variety and quantity of products available, and expanded advertising all played a role in the increased demand for consumer goods. Buying goods became easier, too. Many Americans used credit cards, charge accounts, and easy-payment plans to purchase goods.

Consumers sought the latest products—dishwashers, washing machines, television sets, stereos, and clothes made from synthetic fabrics. The growing market for cars prompted automakers to outdo one another by manufacturing bigger, faster, and flashier cars. New models added stylish features such as chrome-plated bumpers and soaring tail fins.

The advertising and marketing of products on television, on radio, and in magazines created consumer fads and crazes that swept the nation. In the late 1950s, Americans bought millions of hula hoops—large plastic rings they twirled around their waists. Other popular fads included crew cuts for boys, poodle skirts for girls, and a new snack—pizza.

NOW Some 60 years later, personal computers are so small they can be carried in a briefcase or backpack. While the ENIAC could perform about 5,000 calculations per second, the typical home computer works 14,000 times faster, performing about 70 million calculations per second.

★ **2005** 230.4 million personal computers in use in U.S.

Critical Thinking

1. **Differentiating** How have computers changed over time?
2. **Predicting** What do you think computers will look like or be capable of doing in the future?

The Cold War Era **Chapter 27** 863

R Reading Strategy

Previewing Have students read the Main Idea and skim the text of the subsection. **Ask:** What important changes in American culture and society do you think you will be reading about? (*Answers might include family life, purchasing habits, technology, television, and music.*) **OL**

S Skill Practice

Reading a Time Line Have students study the time line at the bottom of the page to learn about the evolution of computer technology. **Ask:** A decade is 10 years. For how many decades have digital computers existed? (*more than 60 years, or six decades—since 1946*) **BL**

LINKING PAST TO PRESENT

Critical Thinking Answers

1. They have become much smaller and faster.

2. Students might speculate that computers will continue to be built even smaller and run faster to fulfill more uses.

Additional Support

Activity: Connecting Past and Present

Analyzing Visuals Advertising can be seen as a reflection of a society. Have students bring in examples of current newspaper and magazine advertisements that depict families. As a class or in small groups, gather examples of consumer advertising from the 1950s. **Ask:** How are families in today's ads different from the families shown in those from the 1950s? (*More minority families are included in ads today, the traditional mother-father-children mix might be more varied, and different activities might be depicted.*) Have students write two or three paragraphs that compare and contrast the activities of families in the 1950s and today as shown in advertising. **Ask:** Do you think today's ads give an accurate view of American families? Do you think the 1950s families were shown accurately? (*Answers will vary, but students should support their answers with examples.*) **OL**

D₁ Differentiated Instruction

Intrapersonal Ask: What do you think it would be like to see television for the first time? How might it change your view of the world? Prompt students to think about how they might feel if their family life did not match the type that was portrayed on television. **OL**

D₂ Differentiated Instruction

Auditory/Musical Bring recordings of rock music from the 1950s to class. As you play each song, ask students if they can hear elements of country music or rhythm and blues. **BL**

W Writing Support

Personal Writing Discuss the concept of a generation gap. Ask students to write a paragraph that explains whether they experience the generation gap in their own lives. **OL**

✔ **Reading Check Answer:** Television created a shared identity and the expectation that Americans should live in happy, middle-class families. It also provided a common source of news and information.

Additional Support

An American Culture

By 1949 more than 900,000 American households had television sets. The sets, in large wooden cabinets, had small screens that displayed grainy black-and-white images. During the 1950s, an average of 6.5 million sets were produced annually. By the end of the decade, most American families had television.

Television changed American life. It became the main form of entertainment as well as an important source of news and information. Millions of Americans gathered to watch weekly episodes of programs such as *I Love Lucy* and *Father Knows Best*. The images shown in many programs—of happy families in neat, middle-class homes—helped shape Americans' expectations for their own lives.

A new form of music—rock 'n' roll—achieved great popularity among teenagers. Rock 'n' roll grew from the rhythm and blues music that African American musicians created years before. It often had some elements of country music. In rock 'n' roll, the tempo was quicker, and electrically amplified instruments—mostly guitars—were used.

One of the first rock hits, reaching number one in 1955, was Bill Haley and the Comets' *Rock Around the Clock*. Adapting the style of African American performers such as Chuck Berry and Little Richard, Elvis Presley burst on the national scene in 1956. Presley quickly became an idol to millions of young Americans. Many young men copied his ducktail haircut and swaggering mannerisms.

For teenagers, the shared experience of listening to the music helped forge a common identity. The differing attitudes of the older and younger generations toward music and other forms of popular culture later came to be known as the generation gap.

✔ **Reading Check** Analyzing How did television change American life in the 1950s?

Economics & History

Bread 180 loaves

Oranges 2 crates

Eggs 131 dz.

Food for a Year *How far would a weekly grocery budget of $25 go to feed a family of four in 1951?*

31 Chickens

Milk 698 qts.

Activity: Collaborative Learning

Creating a Crossword Puzzle Ask students to bring examples of crossword puzzles to class. Discuss some rules for creating these puzzles and writing the clues. **Ask:** How would you describe American culture in the 1950s? (*Answers should reflect the text discussion of television, music, the youth culture, consumerism, poverty, and the Red Scare.*) Organize the class into small groups. Have half the members of each group create a crossword puzzle about American culture in the 1950s. Remind students that they may include television programs, music, literature, other forms of entertainment, attitudes, and political movements. Then have the other half of the group members test the clues to make sure they are accurate and concise. Photocopy the puzzles and pass them out for students to complete as homework. **OL**

Problems in a Time of Plenty

Main Idea Many Americans did not share in the prosperity of the 1950s.

History and You Can you recall hard times in your life? Read on to learn what groups considered the 1950s to be hard times.

. . . .

In the 1950s, more than 20 percent of Americans lived in poverty. Millions more struggled to survive on incomes that were only slightly above the poverty level. Such poverty marred the landscape of the affluent society.

Many farmers did not share in the prosperity of the 1950s. Business enterprises created large profitable farms that used new technology to produce an abundance of food for American and foreign consumers. Small farms, however, could not compete with large farms, so many small-farm families sold their land and migrated to urban areas. Small farmers who continued to farm struggled.

Rural poverty did not always come from agricultural problems. In Appalachia—a region stretching along the Appalachian Mountains—the decline of the coal industry plunged thousands of rural mountain people into desperate poverty. During the 1950s, about 1.5 million people abandoned Appalachia to seek a better life in the nation's cities.

Urban Poverty

As increasing numbers of middle-class Americans moved to the suburbs in the 1950s, they left the poor behind. The inner cities became islands of poverty. Still, people came to cities looking for work. Continuing their migration from rural areas of the South, more than 3 million African Americans moved to cities in the North and the Midwest between 1940 and 1960. For many, however, life proved to be little better in Northern cities. Many poor Latinos—Puerto Ricans in the East and Mexicans in the Southwest and the West—also moved to American cities.

The migration of poor African Americans and Latinos to Northern cities hastened the departure of whites to the suburbs. This "white flight" turned some areas of cities into ghettos—neighborhoods that were inhabited mainly by poor minority groups.

Few good job opportunities existed for the urban poor. Many factories and businesses relocated to suburban areas. In addition, automation—producing goods using mechanical and electronic devices—reduced jobs in the industries that remained. It became more and more difficult for the urban poor to rise from poverty and improve their lives.

The urban poor struggled not only with poverty but also with racial discrimination in employment, housing, and education. Crime and violence often grew out of inner-city poverty, especially among young people who saw no hope for escape from life in the ghetto.

By the Numbers

1951	Comparing by Cost	2007
$0.92	Milk, per gallon	$3.07
$0.75	Eggs, per dozen	$1.54
$0.15	Loaf of bread	$1.15
$0.49	Oranges, per dozen	$1.09
$0.60	Chicken, per pound	$1.03
$0.03	Cost of first-class postage stamp	$0.41
$0.49	Movie ticket	$6.50
$1.45	Average hourly wage	$17.30
$1,995	Average cost of a new car	$27,800
$3,709	Median income for a family of four	$59,000
$299	Television set, 16-inch screen	$299

—from various sources

Critical Thinking

Calculating What percentage of a family's income in 1951 was needed to buy a new car? In 2007?

History ONLINE
Student Web Activity Visit glencoe.com and complete the Chapter 27 Web Activity about life in the 1950s.

The Cold War Era **Chapter 27** 865

R Reading Strategy

Identifying Ask: Which groups of people did not share in the prosperity of the 1950s? *(small farmers, many residents of rural Appalachia, African Americans, Latinos)* **OL**

C Critical Thinking

Identifying Central Issues Ask: What problems did city dwellers face in the 1950s? *(poverty, lack of jobs, racial discrimination, crime, and violence)* Discuss whether the problems city dwellers face today are similar or different. *(Students may say that city dwellers have the same problems, along with pollution, traffic congestion, lack of affordable housing, and so on.)* **OL**

Economics & History

Critical Thinking Answers
about 54% in 1951 and about 47% in 2007

History ONLINE
Objectives and answers to the Student Web Activity can be found at glencoe.com under the Web Activity Lesson Plan for this chapter.

Hands-On Chapter Project
Step 4

Creating a Cover Story About the Cold War

Step 4: Designing the Cover and Putting It All Together Each group will design a colorful, eye-catching front page for its article and assemble the magazine.

Essential Question: How did the American prosperity of the 1950s affect the country's economy and culture?

Directions Instruct students to design an eye-catching cover page that represents the Cold War. Help students plan their covers by discussing elements such as color, fonts, image size, and headlines. Then have each group assemble its cover and article as a magazine issue.

Discussing Ask each group to present its cover page design to the class and explain how it represents the Cold War.

Have the class determine what the cover pages say about American prosperity of the 1950s, and discuss how the Cold War influenced the American economic boom.

(Chapter Project continued on the Visual Summary page)

R Reading Strategy

Reading Primary Sources Invite interested students to read stories and poems by Beat writers such as Jack Kerouac, Allen Ginsberg, and Lawrence Ferlinghetti. Ask them to meet as a group to prepare a program of excerpts from these writers and then present it to the class. **AL**

 Reading Check **Answer:** Corporate and suburban life created the loss of individuality and a focus on money and possessions. Prosperous Americans often ignored the plight of the poor. Women and African Americans were tired of their status as second-class citizens.

Assess

History ONLINE

Study Central™ provides summaries, interactive games, and online graphic organizers to help students review content.

Close

Describing Have students write a paragraph describing what American culture was like in the 1950s. **OL**

 Section 4 Review

Social Critics

Changes in American society in the 1950s caused some people to question the values that were emerging. Some critics charged that the sameness of corporate and suburban life had a cost—the loss of individuality. Others condemned American **materialism**—a focus on accumulating money and possessions rather than an interest in personal and spiritual matters.

Leading social critics examined the complexity of modern society. Many wrote about its effects on individual behavior. William H. Whyte, Jr., studied American business life in *The Organization Man*. He drew a picture of young executives as "organization men" who "have left home spiritually as well as physically." He concluded that businesses discouraged independent thinking and considered the person with new ideas "a threat." Young executives who abandoned their own views were the ones most likely to fit in.

In his book, *The Affluent Society*, economist John Kenneth Galbraith wrote of the prosperous American society of the 1950s. However, not all Americans shared in this prosperity. Galbraith described a suburban family, comfortably installed in an "air-conditioned, power-steered and power-braked automobile, driven through cities that are badly paved, made hideous by litter, blighted buildings, and billboards." Prosperous Americans, Galbraith claimed, often ignored the hardships faced by the rural and urban poor.

Changing Times

A group of writers called the Beats had even sharper criticism of American society. The term "Beat," said novelist Jack Kerouac, meant "weariness with all forms of the modern industrial state." Many young Americans read the works of Kerouac, poet Allen Ginsberg, and other Beat writers. Some adopted Beat attitudes of rebellion against middle-class America.

With American society changing, women and African Americans began questioning their roles. They became increasingly impatient for change and less willing to accept their status as second-class citizens. In the 1950s both groups launched efforts to gain greater freedom and equality.

✓ **Reading Check** **Describing** What criticisms were made about American society in the 1950s?

Section 4 Review

History ONLINE
Study Central™ To review this section, go to glencoe.com.

Vocabulary
1. Write each of the terms and a definition of each in your own words: surplus, arms race, nuclear, summit, economy, affluence, materialism.

Main Ideas
2. **Discussing** While president, what was Eisenhower's greatest domestic achievement, and why was it important?
3. **Explaining** What does it mean to say that Americans became a consumer society in the 1950s?

4. **Summarizing** Why did urban poverty increase during the 1950s?

Critical Thinking
5. **Determining Cause and Effect** On a chart like the one below, identify the direct effects of the 1950s baby boom.

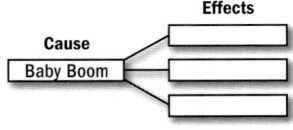

Cause — Baby Boom → Effects

6. **Descriptive Writing** Write a brief description of the types of music that were popular in the 1950s.

Answer the Essential Question
7. How did the American prosperity of the 1950s affect the country's economy and culture?

Answers

1. Students may use their Glossary to help them write their definitions.
2. The interstate highway system was built which connected the country, boosted the automobile and oil industries, and improved military mobility.
3. People began to focus on purchasing and possessions. Americans had more money to buy goods, credit became available, and advertising and marketing increased demand.

4. Middle-class urban residents, factories, and businesses moved to the suburbs, leaving the poor in the cities with fewer jobs. Automation further decreased available jobs. Southern African Americans and Latinos moved to Northern cities, increasing the labor pool.
5. Women left the workforce; baby product and service industries grew; schools became overcrowded.

6. Paragraphs should include information about rock 'n' roll.
7. Americans had money and credit, which fueled consumerism and further economic growth. Consumerism and television led to more products, advertising, and marketing. Conversely, small farmers, African Americans, and Latinos lived in cities with poor job opportunities, while middle-class white people, factories, and businesses moved to the suburbs.

Visual Summary

Visual Summary

Berlin airlift (above);
Senator Margaret Chase Smith (right)

The Cold War

- Soviets occupy much of Eastern and Central Europe
- Truman doctrine proposed
- Congress approves Marshall Plan
- Berlin airlift
- With United Nations, U.S. fights in Korea
- Crisis in the Middle East
- Uprising in Hungary
- War in Southeast Asia
- Troubles in Latin America
- Geneva summit encourages peaceful coexistence
- Space race

Prosperity

- Productivity increases
- Per-capita income and the standard of living increases
- The baby boom increases population
- Suburban housing developments boom
- Car culture grows
- Consumerism grows
- Television viewing increases

Problems and Issues

- Growing competition hurts small farmers
- Decline in coal industry increases poverty in rural areas
- Inner cities decay as businesses and residents relocate
- Social critics question conformity
- Women question their roles in society
- African Americans challenge segregation

Eisenhower's Domestic Policy

- Attempts to limit government spending
- Federal Highway Act
- Extends social programs

◄ Students receive polio vaccine

Study anywhere, anytime! Download quizzes and flash cards to your PDA from glencoe.com.

The Cold War Era **Chapter 27** **867**

Discussing America today supplies military and other aid to foreign nations. **Ask:** What are some countries that America is currently aiding? Why has America chosen to aid each nation? Have students break into small groups. Each group should choose a nation receiving U.S. aid and answer the question. Students will then share their findings. **OL**

Comparing Ask: Do you think American culture today more closely resembles society in the 1940s or the 1950s? Explain your answer. *(The 1950s will be quite familiar to students compared with the 1940s. Similarities include the popularity of television, rock music, a generation gap, the influence of advertising, and consumerism.)* **OL**

Hands-On Chapter Project
Step 5: Wrap-Up

Creating a Cover Story About the Cold War

Step 5: Assessing the Results Students will assess their magazine articles.

Directions Ask each group to write four questions that can be answered by its magazine article. The group should also write the answers. Each group will have another group read its article and quiz the students using the prepared questions. If students find some questions difficult, discuss how the article could present that topic more clearly.

Evaluating Discuss what students have learned about writing. **Ask:** Do you think a magazine article is an effective way to present information about the Cold War? *(Students might answer that the number of pages allows for numerous articles and visuals to be presented.)*

Focus

S Skill Practice

Using Geography Skills Point out to students that the map displays data for both states and specific cities. **Ask:** Which U.S. cities had more than one million people in 1980? *(New York City, Philadelphia, Chicago, and Los Angeles)* **OL**

R Reading Strategy

Identifying Ask: Why are regions of the Northeast and Midwest called the Rust Belt? *(The decline of industry there has left many old, unused buildings and factories.)* **OL**

Have students complete a graphic organizer like the one below that shows the reasons that people moved to the Sunbelt. **OL**

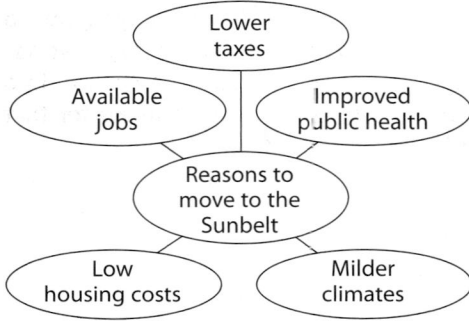

- Lower taxes
- Available jobs
- Improved public health
- Reasons to move to the Sunbelt
- Low housing costs
- Milder climates

Additional Support and Answers

NATIONAL GEOGRAPHIC **GEOGRAPHY & HISTORY**

Changing Settlement Patterns

Shortly after World War II, suburbs sprang up around American cities. By 1960 a majority of Americans lived in suburban areas rather than in cities. Meanwhile, many people were moving from older cities in the Northeast and Midwest toward newer centers in the South and West, the so-called Sunbelt. In most cases, people were going to where the jobs were.

How Did Geography Affect Changing Settlement Patterns?

The open spaces of the Sunbelt were well-suited for population growth. The economy of this area expanded as government defense spending created many jobs. A relatively cheap, nonunion workforce also drew industries from other parts of the nation. Additional factors in the Sunbelt's growth were low housing costs, lower taxes, improved public health, and milder climates. Some of the greatest growth occurred in Florida, Texas, and California.

HISTORIC US 66

Increasing Mobility
Automobiles were essential to the development of the Sunbelt. The Interstate Highway Act of 1956 authorized the construction of a national highway system linking the entire country with roads that were at least four lanes wide. The highways made it easier for Americans to travel west and south.

S Over the past several decades, population growth has been greatest in Southern and Western states.

U.S. Population Growth, 1950–1980

7,700 6,719
3,621 3,005
950 563
915 574 Boston
775 679 San Francisco
Chicago Cleveland New York City Philadelphia
2,968 2,072 1,688
1,970
Los Angeles

249 347
Miami

Change in State Population, 1950–1980
- 200–400%
- 100–199%
- 50–99%
- 0–49%
- Loss

Population Size (in thousands)
2,072 1,688
1950 1980

A Changing Economy In the 1960s, the U.S. economy began to change from a manufacturing-based economy to a service economy or information economy. Many U.S. firms relocated overseas—partly to take advantage of cheaper labor and production costs. Older industrial regions of the Northeast and Midwest started to decline, and these areas came to be known as the Rust Belt, in contrast to the thriving Sunbelt.

Activity: Interdisciplinary Connection

Science Dams serve many purposes. They can control floods, supply drinking water, irrigate crops, serve as recreational areas, and provide habitat for wildlife. Some, like the Hoover Dam, are made to create electricity. Have students research how water creates electricity, in particular the Hoover Dam. **Ask:** What are the components of the Hoover Dam that allow it to create energy with water? How does the dam work? *(The water in the dam flows through a large pipe called a penstock. It then hits and spins a waterwheel called a turbine. The turbine spins and rotates the connecting shaft, which then turns the generator. Magnets inside the generator spin to produce electricity. That electricity flows through wires to the cities where it is used.)* To fully assess your students' understanding of this concept, ask them to create a model of a dam used to create hydroelectric power. They should label the components of the model and write a description of how the dam works. **OL**

Resources As people moved to the dry Southwest, they needed water and electricity. Hoover Dam, on the Colorado River, was built in the 1930s to control flooding and provide electric power. Today, the electricity produced is shared by Arizona, Nevada, and California. **R**

Growing Cities The population of Sunbelt cities such as Las Vegas, Nevada, has exploded in recent decades. Urban sprawl—unplanned development across the landscape—has become common. Destruction of natural habitats and increased traffic and pollution are some effects of urban sprawl. ▼ **W** **C**

Analyzing Geography

1. **Movement** Between 1950 and 1980, which states had the largest percentage of population growth?

2. **Human-Environment Interaction** What kinds of challenges do you think the Sunbelt faces as a result of rapid growth?

Challenges at Home and Abroad **Unit 9** **869**

Teach

R Reading Strategy

Stating Ask: Why was the Hoover Dam built? *(to control flooding and provide electric power to the area)* **BL**

C Critical Thinking

Theorizing Increased traffic is just one effect of urban sprawl, but it leads to another problem—pollution. **Ask:** What are some ways to alleviate traffic problems? *(Sample answers may include using public transportation, adding bike trails to main roads, and carpooling.)* **OL**

Assess/Close

W Writing Support

Expository Writing Have students conduct further research into today's growing cities. Have them choose a city that has undergone growth since 1950, and in a short report explain the reasons for that city's growth. **OL**

Answers

1. Alaska, Nevada, Arizona, and Florida
2. Conserving and regaining natural resources; traffic and pollution control; and providing education, energy, housing, and medical services to the rising population.

STANDARDIZED TEST PRACTICE

Answers and Analyses
Reviewing Main Ideas

1. C The answer is NATO. Students might choose the UN (choice A), but its purpose was to settle international disputes and prevent war, not to halt Soviet influence. **14.E.3**

2. D Truman's Fair Deal included a system of national health insurance. The Taft-Hartley Act (choice B) was during Truman's presidency but was introduced by the Republicans. Truman proposed abolition of the poll tax (choice C), but this measure was to end discrimination rather than solve economic problems. **15.E.3b**

3. C Truman invaded North Korea in an attempt to create a unified, democratic Korea. Choice A is incorrect because Korea was already divided at the 38th parallel. Choices B and D are incorrect because Truman wanted to avoid war with China and the Soviet Union. Truman supported the invasion of North Korea because MacArthur assured him that neither country would join the war. **14.E.3**

4. A The text answers this question, which involves recall. The other answers do not describe NASA but address important topics related to the Eisenhower administration. **16.A**

Short-Answer Question

5. The UN was trying to settle the dispute between Israelis and Palestinians and to prevent future wars. **17.C.3a**

TEST-TAKING TIP

When answering essay questions, organize your thoughts before you begin writing. This will help reduce the time you need to revise.

Reviewing Main Ideas

Directions: Choose the best answers for each of the following questions.

1. Which group formed to stop the spread of Soviet influence in Western Europe?

   A United Nations

   B Warsaw Pact nations

   C North Atlantic Treaty Organization

   D House Un-American Activities Committee

2. What proposal was part of Truman's program to solve the nation's economic problems?

   A the closed shop

   B the Taft-Hartley Act

   C abolition of the poll tax

   D national health insurance

3. Truman tried to contain communism on the Korean Peninsula by

   A dividing Korea.

   B attacking China.

   C defending South Korea.

   D bombing the Soviet Union.

4. Eisenhower established the National Aeronautics and Space Administration (NASA) to

   A conduct U.S. space activities.

   B create jobs for the urban poor.

   C make the federal government smaller.

   D increase demand for consumer goods.

Short-Answer Question

Directions: Base your answer to question 5 on the excerpt below and on your knowledge of social studies.

> More than any single action by the government since the end of the war, this one [the interstate highway system] would change the face of America.... Its impact on the American economy—the jobs it would produce in manufacturing and construction, the rural areas it would open up—was beyond calculation.
>
> —Dwight Eisenhower in *Mandate for Change, 1953–1956*

5. Why did Eisenhower think an interstate highway system was so important to the nation?

Review the Essential Questions

6. Essay How did the economies in the United States and Europe change after World War II?

To help you write your essay, review your answers to the Essential Questions in the section reviews and the chapter Foldables Study Organizer. Your essay should include:

- how and why America gave aid to Europe;
- economic challenges Americans faced;
- how you think the Korean War affected the American economy; and
- how American prosperity affected the economy.

GO ON ➡

Review the Essential Questions

6. Students should use their answers to the Essential Questions and their Foldables to describe how the American and European economies changed after World War II. Essays should include the postwar rivalry between the United States and the Soviet Union as each side tried to gain allies and prove that its system—free enterprise or communism—was superior. Students also should discuss the economic growth that resulted in higher wages and consumerism in the 1950s. **14.E.3**

HistoryⒼONLINE
For additional test practice, use **Self-Check Quizzes**—Chapter 27 at glencoe.com.

Chapter 27 Assessment

Document-Based Questions

Directions: Analyze the documents and answer the short-answer questions that follow.

Document 1

Julius and Ethel Rosenberg were on trial for espionage. The Rosenbergs' lawyer, Emanuel Bloch, made the following plea.

> Through you [Judge Kaufman] the rest of the world will either believe that we are a compassionate nation, a nation built upon the ideals of humanity and justice, or a nation that has been gripped in panic and fear and is embarked upon mad acts.

Source: Emanuel Bloch, NCRRC Letters

7. Was Bloch's plea successful? Explain.

Document 2

President Truman summed up a major economic problem in postwar America during his address to the nation in 1947.

> We all know that recent price increases have denied to many of our workers much of the value of recent wage increases.

Source: Harry S. Truman, *State of the Union Address*

8. What good and bad news did Truman deliver in this excerpt from his speech?

Document 3

President Truman explained why he was relieving General Douglas MacArthur of his command in South Korea.

> The free nations have united their strength in an effort to prevent a third world war. That war can come if the Communist rulers want it to come. This Nation and its allies will not be responsible for its coming.

Source: *Department of State Bulletin*, April 16, 1951

9. What strategy did Truman reject because he thought it could start another world war?

Document 4

This graph shows labor union membership.

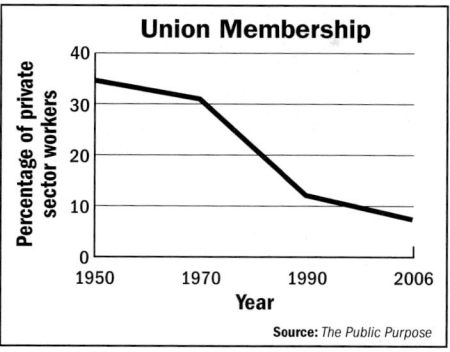

Union Membership

Percentage of private sector workers / Year

Source: *The Public Purpose*

10. Describe the trend in union membership.

Document 5

This excerpt comes from the novel *On the Road*.

> The only people for me are the mad ones, the ones who are mad to live, mad to talk, mad to be saved, desirous of everything at the same time, the ones who never yawn or say a commonplace thing, but burn, burn, burn like fabulous yellow roman candles.

Source: Jack Kerouac, *On the Road*

11. Kerouac uses the term "mad ones." To whom do you think he is referring?

12. Expository Writing Using the information from the five documents and your knowledge of social studies, write an essay in which you:

- describe social and economic changes in the 1950s; and

- describe political changes in the 1950s.

Need Extra Help?												
If you missed questions...	1	2	3	4	5	6	7	8	9	10	11	12
Go to page...	846	852	857	862	861	844–847	849	851	859	852–853	866	845–850

The Cold War Era **Chapter 27** **871**

9. Truman rejected MacArthur's plan to bomb China for a quick victory in Korea. **16.A.3b**

10. Membership in labor unions steadily declined. **16.C.3b (US)**

11. Students may note that Kerouac is describing individuals outside mainstream America who do not blindly accept society's norms but rather think independently. **16.A.3c**

12. Students' essays should reflect an understanding of the documents and how they relate to the chapter material. The essays should be organized to clearly identify groups that were struggling after World War II and the obstacles they faced. Students might include the democratic nations struggling against Communist takeover and nations working toward independence. Groups in the United States might include miners and railroad workers, rural and urban workers, minorities, and small farmers. **18.B.3a**

HistoryⒼONLINE
Have students visit the Web site at glencoe.com to review Chapter 27 and take the Self-Check Quiz.

Need Extra Help?

Have students refer to the pages listed if they miss any of the questions.

Document-Based Questions

7. No, Bloch was not successful; the Rosenbergs were executed in 1953. **18.B.3a**

8. The good news was that wages had risen. The bad news was that prices rose along with wages, so buying power did not increase much. **16.A.3c**

Key to Ability Levels
- BL Below level
- OL On level
- AL Above level
- ELL English Language Learners

Key to Teaching Resources
- Print Material
- CD-ROM
- DVD
- Transparency

BL	OL	AL	ELL		Resources	Chapter Opener	Section 1	Section 2	Section 3	Section 4	Chapter Assess
					FOCUS						
BL	OL	AL	ELL	Transparency	Daily Test Practice Transparencies		28–1	28–2	28–3	28–4	
					TEACH						
	OL	AL		Print	Geography and History Activity, URB				p. 59		
BL	OL		ELL	Print	Time Line Skills Activity, URB				p. 62		
BL	OL	AL	ELL	Print	Writing Skills Activity, URB					p. 51	
BL	OL	AL	ELL	Print	Content Vocabulary Activity, URB		p. 45	p. 45	p. 45	p. 45	
BL	OL	AL	ELL	Print	Academic Vocabulary Activity, URB		p. 47	p. 47	p. 47	p. 47	
BL			ELL	Print	Reading Skills Activity, URB		p. 7				
	OL	AL		Print	Citizenship and Decision-Making Activity, URB					p. 3	
BL	OL		ELL	Print	Social Studies Skills Activity, URB			p. 53			
BL	OL	AL	ELL	Print	Differentiated Instruction Activity, URB			p. 55			
BL	OL	AL	ELL	Print	Critical Thinking Skills Activity, URB					p. 57	
BL	OL	AL	ELL	Print	Linking Past and Present Activity, URB				p. 61		
	OL	AL		Print	Primary Source Readings, URB				p. 49		
BL	OL	AL	ELL	Print	School-to-Home Connection Activity, URB		p. 63	p. 63	p. 63	p. 63	
BL	OL		ELL	Print	Guided Reading Activity, URB*		p. 67	p. 68	p. 69	p. 70	
BL	OL		ELL	Print	Reading Essentials and Note-Taking Guide*		p. 313	p. 316	p. 319	p. 322	
BL	OL	AL	ELL	Transparency	Lesson Transparencies		28A		28B	28C	
	OL	AL		Print	Interpreting Political Cartoons, URB			p. 13			
		AL		Print	Supreme Court Case Studies		p. 73	p. 97			
	OL			Print	American Biographies		pp. 50, 59, 62		pp. 62, 63	pp. 64, 65	
BL	OL	AL	ELL	Print	Outline Map Resource Book	p. 6					

Note: Please refer to the *Unit Resource Book: Challenges at Home and Abroad* for this chapter's URB materials.

* Also available in Spanish

Levels					Resources	Chapter Opener	Section 1	Section 2	Section 3	Section 4	Chapter Assess
BL	OL	AL	ELL								
					TEACH (*continued*)						
BL	OL	AL	ELL	📁	**NGS US Desk Map**		✓	✓	✓	✓	
BL	OL	AL	ELL	📁	**American Literature Library**		✓	✓	✓	✓	
BL	OL	AL	ELL	📁	**Writer's Guidebook**		✓	✓	✓	✓	
	OL	AL		💿	**American History Primary Source Document Library CD-ROM**		✓	✓	✓	✓	✓
BL	OL	AL	ELL	💿	**American Music: Hits Through History**	✓	✓	✓	✓	✓	
BL	OL	AL	ELL	💿	**StudentWorks™ Plus CD**	✓	✓	✓	✓	✓	✓
	OL	AL		📹	**Section Spotlight Videos**		✓	✓	✓	✓	
BL	OL	AL	ELL	🖨	**Writing Process Transparencies**		✓	✓	✓	✓	✓
BL	OL	AL	ELL	💿	**Presentation Plus! With MindJogger CheckPoint CD**	✓	✓	✓	✓	✓	✓
					ASSESS						
BL	OL	AL	ELL	📁	**Quizzes and Tests**		p. 277	p. 278	p. 279	p. 280	pp. 281, 283, 285
BL	OL	AL	ELL	📁	**Authentic Assessment With Rubrics**			p. 28			
BL	OL	AL	ELL	📁	**Standardized Test Practice**						p. 55
BL	OL	AL	ELL	💿	***ExamView® Assessment Suite CD-ROM***		28–1	28–2	28–3	28–4	Ch. 28
					CLOSE						
BL			ELL	📁	**Reteaching Activity, URB***		p. 65	p. 65	p. 65	p. 65	p. 65
BL	OL		ELL	📁	**Reading and Study Skills Foldables Activity**	p. 104	p. 104	p. 104	p. 104	p. 104	p. 104
BL	OL	AL	ELL	📁	***The American Journey* in Graphic Novel**	p. 169					
BL			ELL	📁	**Reading Strategies and Activities for the Social Studies Classroom**		✓	✓	✓	✓	
BL	OL	AL	ELL	🖨	**Graphic Organizer Transparencies & Strategies**		✓	✓	✓	✓	

TeacherWorks Plus
All-In-One Planner and Resource Center

- Interactive Lesson Planner
- Interactive Teacher Edition
- Fully editable blackline masters
- Section Spotlight Videos Launch
- Differentiated Lesson Plans
- Printable reports of daily assignments
- Standards Tracking System

Professional Development Resources

- Strategies for Success
- Building Academic Vocabulary
- Success With English Learners DVD
- Differentiated Instruction Strategies DVD
- Teaching Literacy Strategies in Social Studies DVD
- Assessment DVD
- Standards-Based Instruction DVD

Researching World Book™ Select

Developing Research Skills

Technology Product

World Book™ Select offers thousands of detailed articles chosen from the *World Book Encyclopedia* and covers all curricular areas. World Book™ Select allows students to research national and international topics and issues in social studies and other curriculum areas.

Objectives

After students learn to use World Book™ Select, they will be able to

- develop and expand research and study skills;
- practice reading and writing skills.

Steps

Give students the following directions to use World Book™ Select:

- From the McGraw-Hill Learning Network home page (www.mhln.com), click on **For Students**.
- Choose **World Book™ Select** below **Homework Help**.
- Click the letter for the encyclopedia volume you want to use.
- On the search page for the volume selected:
  - click the title of a featured article on the right side of the page; or
  - click on a topic from the list on the left side of the page; then click on the title of an article of interest.
- Read the article and take notes.

History ONLINE at glencoe.com

	Student	Teacher	Parent
Media Center			
• Student Edition Audio	●		
• Spanish Summaries	●		
• Section Spotlight Videos	●	●	
Social Studies Online Learning Center			
Classroom Tools			
• Multi-Language Glossaries	●	●	●
• Teaching Today		●	
• TIME Current Events	●	●	●
• Beyond the Textbook	●	●	
***The American Journey* Online Learning Center**			
• Study-to-Go™	●	●	●
• Study Central™	●	●	●
• Chapter Overview	●	●	
• Concepts in Motion	●	●	
• ePuzzles and Games	●	●	
• Literature Connections	●	●	
• Online Student Edition	●	●	●
• Self-Check Quizzes	●	●	●
• Student Web Activities	●	●	
• Vocabulary eFlashcards	●	●	
• Web Activity Lesson Plans	●	●	●
• Vocabulary PuzzleMaker	●	●	●

READING SUPPORT FROM
JAMESTOWN EDUCATION

- **Timed Readings Plus in Social Studies** helps students increase their reading rate and fluency while maintaining comprehension. The 400-word passages are similar to those found on state and national assessments.

- **Reading in the Content Area: Social Studies** concentrates on six essential reading skills that help students better comprehend what they read. The book includes 75 high-interest nonfiction passages written at increasing levels of difficulty.

- **Reading Social Studies** includes strategic reading instruction and vocabulary support in Social Studies content for ELLs and native speakers of English.

- **Content Vocabulary Workout** (Grades 6–8) accelerates reading comprehension through focused vocabulary development. Social Studies content vocabulary comes from the glossaries of Glencoe's Middle School Social Studies texts.

www.jamestowneducation.com

NATIONAL GEOGRAPHIC

Index to National Geographic Magazine:

The following articles relate to this chapter:

- **"The Search for PT109,"** Robert D. Ballard, December 2002.

- **"Selma to Montgomery: The Road to Equality,"** Chuck Stone, February 2000.

National Geographic Society Products

To order the following, call National Geographic at 1-800-368-2728:

National Geographic Atlas of the World *(Book)*

Access National Geographic's dynamic MapMachine Web site and other geography resources at:

www.nationalgeographic.com

www.nationalgeographic.com/mapmachine

Reading List Generator CD-ROM

GLENCOE BOOKLINK 3

Use this database to search more than 30,000 titles to create a customized reading list for your students.

- Reading lists can be organized by students' reading level, author, genre, theme, or area of interest.

- The database provides Degrees of Reading Power™ (DRP) and Lexile™ readability scores for all selections.

- A brief summary of each selection is included.

Leveled reading suggestions for this chapter:

For students at a Grade 6 reading level:
- ***Walking to the Bus-Rider Blues,*** by Harriette Gillem Robinet

For students at a Grade 7 reading level:
- ***Rosa Parks: Young Rebel,*** by Kathleen Kudlinski
- ***Just Like Martin,*** by Ossie Davis

For students at a Grade 8 reading level:
- ***Malcolm X,*** by Mark Falstein
- ***Oh, Freedom!*** by Casey King and Linda Barrett Osborne

For students at a Grade 9 reading level:
- ***Linda Brown, You Are Not Alone: The Brown v. Board of Education Decision,*** by Joyce Carol Thomas

For students at a Grade 10 reading level:
- ***Witnesses to Freedom: Young People Who Fought for Civil Rights,*** by Belinda Rochelle

The following videotape programs are available from Glencoe as supplements to the chapter:

- **John F. Kennedy: A Personal Story** (ISBN 0-76-700010-2)

- **Martin Luther King, Jr.: The Man and the Dream** (0-76-701057-4)

To order, call Glencoe at 1-800-334-7344. To find classroom resources to accompany many of these videos, check the following home pages:

A&E Television: www.aetv.com

The History Channel: www.history.com

Chapter Objectives

After studying this chapter, students will be able to:

- Describe the legal and social challenges to racial segregation in the 1940s and 1950s.
- Compare and contrast the presidencies of Kennedy and Johnson.
- Discuss the areas of civil rights that groups tried to improve in the 1960s and the methods those groups used.
- Trace the effects of the civil rights movement on minorities other than African Americans.

Motivating Activity

Visual Literacy Students will learn about the civil rights movement of the 1950s and 1960s. Direct students' attention to the photograph on this page. **Ask:** *What is happening in this scene? (African Americans are marching near the Capitol building in Washington.) How would you describe the appearance of the marchers? (Students may point out how well dressed and dignified the marchers appear.) What do you think the marchers want? (Students may answer that marchers wanted equal rights for African Americans.)* **OL**

Previewing the Essential Questions

As you begin teaching each section, use these questions and activities to help students focus on the Essential Questions.

The Civil Rights Era 1954–1974

March on Washington, August 28, 1963

Linda Brown ▶

PRESIDENTS

U.S. Events

World Events

★ **1954**
Brown v. Board of Education ruling

★ **1955**
Montgomery bus boycott begins

DWIGHT EISENHOWER 1953–1961

JOHN F. KENNEDY 1961–1963

LYNDON JOHNSON 1963–1969

Dr. Martin Luther King, Jr. ▶

★ **1964**
Civil Rights Act passes

1954 — 1959 — 1964

★ **1959**
Fidel Castro seizes power in Cuba

★ **1964**
Nelson Mandela receives life sentence in South Africa

872   Chapter 28

Section ⭐ **1**

The Civil Rights Movement Ask: *How might African Americans challenge racial segregation in the 1940s and 1950s? (African Americans believed they deserved more rights because of their service during the war. They might form groups or hold demonstrations to protest discrimination.)* Tell students that in Section 1 they will learn about challenges to racial segregation. **OL**

Section ⭐ **2**

Kennedy and Johnson Ask: *How might the sudden death of a president affect the policies of his or her successor? (The new president may pursue the same goals as the previous president.)* Point out that differences and similarities between Kennedy and Johnson will be discussed in Section 2. **OL**

Section 1: The Civil Rights Movement
Essential Question What were the legal and social challenges to racial segregation in the 1940s and 1950s?

Section 2: Kennedy and Johnson
Essential Question How were Kennedy and Johnson alike and different as presidents of the United States?

Section 3: The Struggle Continues
Essential Question What areas of civil rights did groups try to improve in the 1960s, and what methods did those groups use?

Section 4: Other Groups Seek Rights
Essential Question How did the civil rights movement affect minorities other than African Americans?

César Chávez was a leading voice for migrant farmworkers. ▶

History ONLINE
Chapter Overview Visit glencoe.com and click on Chapter 28—Chapter Overviews to preview chapter information.

FOLDABLES
Study Organizer

Organizing Information
Make this Foldable to help organize what you learn about how the courts addressed civil rights issues.

Step 1 Fold a sheet of paper in half from side to side so that the left edge lies about 1/2 inch from the right edge.

Step 2 Cut the top layer only to make four tabs.

Step 3 Label the tab as shown.

Civil Rights Act of 1964

Reading and Writing As you read the chapter, list key court decisions about civil rights on the outside of the Foldable. Summarize important details on the inside of the Foldable.

Introducing Chapter 28

Time Line Activity

If you have not already done so, have students review the time line. **Ask:** What years are covered in this chapter? *(1954–1974)* What important events in the civil rights movement occurred during this period? (Brown v. Board of Education *ruling; Civil Rights Act; Martin Luther King, Jr., was assassinated*) What world events might have especially concerned civil rights activists in the United States? *(Mandela's life sentence; British rule of Northern Ireland)*

FOLDABLES
Study Organizer **Dinah Zike's Foldables**

Purpose This Foldable helps students organize information about important civil rights decisions by the courts. The completed Foldable will help them prepare for assessment.

📁 More Foldable activities for this chapter can be found in *Dinah Zike's Reading and Study Skills Foldables.*

History ONLINE
Introduce students to chapter content and key terms by having them access the **Chapter Overview** at glencoe.com.

1968
- Martin Luther King, Jr., assassinated
- Indian Civil Rights Act passes

RICHARD NIXON 1969–1974

1970 Grape workers gain better pay and working conditions

GERALD FORD 1974–1977

1969 — **1974**

1967 First heart transplant performed in South Africa

1972 Britain imposes direct rule on Northern Ireland

1972 Terrorists kill Olympic athletes

Chapter 28   873

Section 3
The Struggle Continues   Ask: What issues might the civil rights movement have addressed? *(Answers may include desegregation of public transportation, desegregation of colleges, and voting rights.)* Tell students that Section 3 will discuss what rights civil rights groups fought for and the methods they used to try to bring about change. **OL**

Section 4
Other Groups Seek Rights   Ask: How might issues facing Latinos and Native Americans have been similar to issues facing African Americans in American society? *(All groups faced prejudice and discrimination, high poverty rates, and poor working conditions.)* Explain that Section 4 will trace how the civil rights movement affected the struggles of other minority groups. **OL**

The Civil Rights Movement

Focus

Bellringer
Daily Test Practice Transparency 28–1

Reading Guide
Answers to Graphic:
1909: founding of NAACP; **1954:** ruling in *Brown* v. *Board of Education of Topeka, Kansas*; **1955:** Supreme Court ruling on integration of public schools; **1957:** confrontation at Central High School in Little Rock, Arkansas

Section Spotlight Video

Have students watch the Section Spotlight Video "The Civil Rights Movement" to learn more about challenges to segregation.

Resource Manager

Essential Question
What were the legal and social challenges to racial segregation in the 1940s and 1950s?

Reading Guide

Content Vocabulary
segregation (p. 875)
integrate (p. 876)
boycott (p. 878)
civil disobedience (p. 879)

Academic Vocabulary
discriminate (p. 875)   civil (p. 875)

Key People and Events
NAACP (p. 875)
Thurgood Marshall (p. 876)
Brown v. *Board of Education of Topeka, Kansas* (p. 876)
Rosa Parks (p. 878)
Dr. Martin Luther King, Jr. (p. 878)

Reading Strategy
Taking Notes Create a time line like the one below to record important events in the early struggle for equal rights.

1909   1954   1955   1957

ILLINOIS STANDARDS
The American Journey

14.C.3 Compare historical issues involving rights, roles and status of individuals in relation to municipalities, states and the nation.

18.C.3a Describe ways in which a diverse U.S. population has developed and maintained common beliefs (e.g., life, liberty and the pursuit of happiness; the Constitution and the Bill of Rights).

16.D Understand Illinois, United States and world social history.

18.C.3b Explain how diverse groups have contributed to U.S. social systems over time.

American Diary

Howard Bailey remembers that when the white high school got new textbooks, the old ones would be dropped off at his African American school. "I can remember that occasionally they would shovel the books out of the pickup trucks with coal shovels and just . . . dump them on the ground outside of the school building. So our teachers and principals would . . . gather them up and tape up . . . the books that were in real bad shape."

—Kentucky Civil Rights Oral History Commission

In *Brown* v. *Board of Education*, the Supreme Court found that segregated classrooms denied children like Linda Brown (first row, far right) equal education.

R Reading Strategies	**C** Critical Thinking	**D** Differentiated Instruction	**W** Writing Support	**S** Skill Practice
Teacher Edition • Summarizing, p. 877 • Inferring, p. 879 **Additional Resources** • Guid. Read., URB p. 67 • Content Vocab., URB p. 45 • Acad. Vocab., URB p. 47 • Read. Ess., p. 313 • Read. Skills, URB p. 7	**Teacher Edition** • Making Inferences, p. 875 • Drawing Conclusions, p. 876 • Analyz. Pri. Sources, p. 878 **Additional Resources** • Quizzes and Tests, p. 277	**Teacher Edition** • Below Grade Level, p. 875 • Kinesthetic, p. 876 • Visual/Spatial, p. 879 **Additional Resources** • School-to-Home, URB p. 63 • Reteaching, URB p. 65 • Differ. Inst., URB p. 55	**Teacher Edition** • Expository Writing, p. 876 • Descriptive Writing, p. 878	**Teacher Edition** • Using Analytical Skills, p. 877 **Additional Resources** • Daily Test Pract. Transp. 28-1 • Soc. Stud. Skills, URB p. 53 • Lesson Transp. 28A

Equality in Education

Main Idea After World War II, African Americans and other supporters of civil rights challenged discrimination in the nation's public schools.

History and You What might it have been like to be told that you could go only to certain schools because of your racial or ethnic background? Read to learn about the struggle to achieve equal rights for African American students in the 1950s.

African Americans had suffered from racism and **discrimination**, or unfair treatment, since colonial times. By the mid-1900s, many African Americans believed that the time had come for them to enjoy an equal place in American life. They fought for equal opportunities in jobs, housing, and education. They also fought against **segregation**—the separation of people of different races.

The Push for Equal Rights

During World War II, African Americans demanded more rights. Their efforts helped end discrimination in factories that held gov-

D ernment contracts and increased opportunities for African Americans in the military.

In Chicago in 1942, James Farmer and George Houser founded the Congress of Racial Equality (CORE). A year later, CORE carried out protests against public places that refused to admit or serve African Americans. CORE protesters successfully ended segregation in many restaurants, theaters, and other public places in Chicago, Detroit, Denver, and Syracuse.

When World War II ended, many African American soldiers returned home hopeful that their country would appreciate their loyalty and sacrifice. In the 1950s, when change did not come as quickly as desired, their determination to end injustices in the United States led to protests and marches—and to the rise of the **civil**(meaning, citizens as individuals) rights movement.

The **NAACP** (National Association for the Advancement of Colored People) had worked on behalf of African Americans since its founding in 1909. In the 1950s, NAACP lawyers searched for cases they could use to challenge the laws allowing the segregation of public schools.

When and **W**here   **School Segregation, 1950**

Regional Differences School segregation was treated differently in various parts of the United States.

Legend:
- Segregated by law
- Local districts decided
- Segregation prohibited
- No specific legislation

Critical Thinking

1. **Identifying** In which category did more states belong: those where the law ordered segregation or those where the law prohibited segregation?
2. **Theorizing** Why do you think segregation was widespread in the South and prohibited in the North?

Teach

D Differentiated Instruction

Below Grade Level Have each student create flash cards testing vocabulary words and important organizations mentioned in this section. Students should exchange their flash cards and quiz one another. **BL**

C Critical Thinking

Making Inferences Ask: Why might African Americans have expected equal treatment in the years following World War II? *(During World War II their efforts helped end discrimination in factories that held government contracts. African Americans also had increased opportunities in the military.)* **OL**

Primary Source

Critical Thinking Answers
1. those where the law ordered segregation
2. Answers will vary but should refer to the tradition of slavery and Jim Crow laws in the South.

Differentiated Instruction

Leveled Activities

D Differentiated Instruction

Kinesthetic Organize the students into two groups based on a superficial difference, for example, by hair color or eye color. Give one group a much smaller portion of the classroom, not enough textbooks, and too few supplies. Give the other group more space, books, and supplies. As a class, discuss students' feelings about the segregated classroom. **OL**

W Writing Support

Expository Writing Have students write an essay in which they answer the following question: Why are separate educational facilities inherently unequal? Allow students to do additional research if necessary. **AL**

C Critical Thinking

Drawing Conclusions Ask: What was the significance of *Brown v. Board of Education of Topeka, Kansas?* (Brown *v.* Board of Education *was significant because it challenged the entire system of segregation by overturning the idea of "separate but equal" established by* Plessy v. Ferguson. *It also convinced many African Americans that it was time to oppose other forms of discrimination as well.*) **OL**

Differentiated Instruction

The *Brown* Decision

D The Supreme Court had upheld segregation laws in the past. In 1896 in *Plessy* v. *Ferguson*, it ruled that "separate but equal" public facilities were legal. **Thurgood Marshall,** the chief lawyer for the NAACP, decided to challenge the idea of "separate but equal." Seven-year-old African American Linda Brown was not permitted to attend an all–white elementary school just blocks from her house. She was told to attend an all–African American school across town. The Brown family sued the school system but lost. Marshall and the NAACP appealed the case all the way to the Supreme Court.

The case of ***Brown v. Board of Education of Topeka, Kansas,*** combined with similar cases, reached the Supreme Court in December 1952. Marshall argued that segregated schools were not and could not be equal to white schools. Thus segregated schools violated the Fourteenth Amendment.

W On May 17, 1954, the Court unanimously ruled in *Brown* v. *Board of Education of Topeka, Kansas,* that it was unconstitutional to separate schoolchildren by race. The *Brown* decision reversed the Court's decision in the earlier *Plessy* v. *Ferguson* case. Chief Justice Earl Warren summed up the Court's new ruling when he wrote:

> PRIMARY SOURCE
>
> "In the field of public education, the doctrine of 'separate but equal' has no place. Separate educational facilities are inherently [essentially] unequal."
> —from *Brown* v. *Board of Education of Topeka, Kansas*

Integrating the Schools

C The Court's decision in *Brown* v. *Board of Education* applied only to public schools. However, it had the much greater effect of threatening the entire system of segregation. The ruling convinced many African Americans that the time had come to oppose other forms of discrimination as well. At the same time, the Court's decision angered many

Primary Source / School Integration

> "In these days, it is doubtful that any child may reasonably be expected to succeed in life if he is denied the opportunity of an education. Such an opportunity, . . . must be made available to all on equal terms."
>
> —*Brown* v. *Board of Education*

The Supreme Court ruled in *Brown* v. *Board of Education* that segregation in public schools was unconstitutional. Some segregated school districts integrated their schools quickly and with no incident. Other attempts to integrate led to anger and opposition. Many schools kept their schools segregated for many years.

◄ Linda Brown was at the center of the *Brown* decision.

white Southerners, who became more determined to defend segregation, no matter what the Supreme Court ruled.

In 1955 the Supreme Court followed up its decision in *Brown* v. *Board of Education* with another ruling. It called on school authorities to make plans for **integrating**—bringing races together—in public schools. The Court also ordered that integration was to be carried out "with all deliberate speed"—as fast as reasonably possible.

Some schools integrated quickly. However, in parts of the South, local leaders vowed to keep African American children out of white schools. A clash between the federal government and these states seemed likely.

Confrontation in Little Rock

In 1957 a federal judge ordered all-white Central High School in Little Rock, Arkansas, to admit African American students. Arkansas governor Orval Faubus opposed integration. In September he called out the state's National Guard to prevent African Americans from entering the high school.

Changing Education

Objective: To understand the *Brown* v. *Board of Education* Supreme Court ruling

Focus: Ask students to briefly explain the background of the *Brown* v. *Board of Education* case.

Teach: Have students read the excerpt and answer the questions.

Assess: Ask for volunteers to read their answers.

Close: Review with students the reasons the ruling radically changed public education.

Differentiated Instruction Strategies

BL Before students answer the questions, have them explain the phrase *inherently unequal.*

AL Have students research and write an essay on whether segregation still exists in America today.

ELL Ask students to give a brief oral summary, in their own words, of the Court's decision.

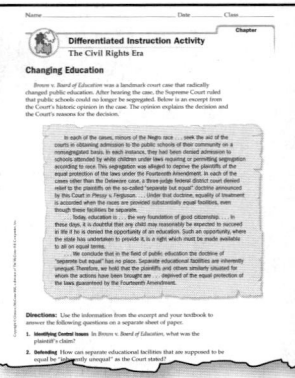

Differentiated Instruction Activity, URB p. 55

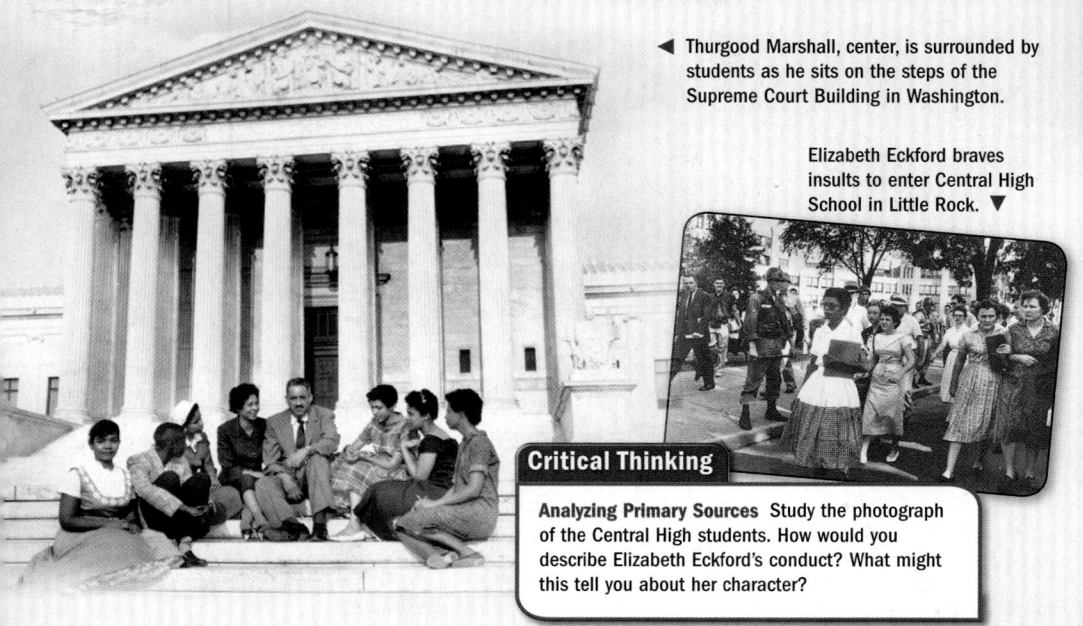

◀ Thurgood Marshall, center, is surrounded by students as he sits on the steps of the Supreme Court Building in Washington.

Elizabeth Eckford braves insults to enter Central High School in Little Rock. ▼

Critical Thinking

Analyzing Primary Sources Study the photograph of the Central High students. How would you describe Elizabeth Eckford's conduct? What might this tell you about her character?

R **Reading Strategy**

Summarizing Tell students to summarize the conflict at Little Rock in two or three sentences. **ELL**

S **Skill Practice**

Using Analytical Skills Ask: What was the significance of the Montgomery Bus Boycott? *(It sparked the mass civil rights movement, which would transform American society.)* **OL**

Primary Source

Critical Thinking Answer
Sample answer: Eckford looks dignified, proud, and brave.

Reading Check **Answer:** *Plessy* ruled that separate facilities were legal as long as they were "equal," providing a legal basis for segregation.

History ONLINE
Objectives and answers can be found at glencoe.com under the Web Activity Lesson Plan for this section.

On the first day of classes, armed members of the National Guard blocked the school's entrance and turned away nine African American students. One of them, 15-year-old Elizabeth Eckford, recalled that when she tried to squeeze past a member of the guard, "He raised his bayonet, and then the other guards moved in and raised their bayonets."

For the first time since the Civil War, a Southern state defied the federal government. Although Eisenhower had doubts about the *Brown* decision, he believed he had to enforce the law. The president warned Faubus that if the students were not admitted, the federal government would act.

When a federal judge ruled that the governor had violated the law, Faubus removed the National Guard. Eisenhower sent hundreds of soldiers to Little Rock to patrol the school and protect the students. Shielded by federal troops, the African American students entered the school.

Reading Check **Explaining** How had the *Plessy* ruling contributed to segregation?

Gains on Other Fronts

Main Idea The success of the Montgomery bus boycott showed that nonviolent protest could help African Americans secure their rights.

History and You Have you ever tried hard to win over someone to your point of view? Read to learn how African Americans convinced officials in Montgomery, Alabama, to end segregation on city buses.
. . . .

While school integration continued, African Americans made other advances in securing their rights. More and more took part in a movement dedicated to securing fair and equal treatment. In 1955, events in Montgomery, Alabama, sparked a chain reaction—the beginning of a mass movement that would change American society over the next 20 years.

History ONLINE
Student Web Activity Visit glencoe.com and complete the Chapter 28 Web Activity about school integration.

The Civil Rights Era **Chapter 28** 877

Hands-On Chapter Project
Step 1

Planning a Civil Rights Campaign

Step 1: Create a Workshop Students will create a workshop to teach methods of peaceful protest to civil rights workers.

Essential Question: What were the legal and social challenges to racial segregation in the 1940s and 1950s?

Directions Organize students into groups of three to four students. Discuss the tactics developed by Martin Luther King, Jr., and others in the civil rights movement. **Ask:** What is civil disobedience? *(the refusal to obey laws that are considered unjust)* Why do you think King believed that nonviolent methods were essential? *(If protesters were nonviolent, they would attract more sympathy for their cause.)*

Have each group create an outline of a five-hour workshop to teach civil rights workers about civil disobedience and nonviolence. Allow students to use the Internet for research. Each group should also create a packet of materials to use in the workshop. Students might include lectures, images from successful protests, role-playing exercises, handouts, and so on.

Identifying Central Issues Ask: What did you conclude was important to teach civil rights workers about civil disobedience and nonviolence? **OL**

(Chapter Project continued in Section 2)

People IN HISTORY

Rosa Parks
1913–2005
Civil Rights Activist

Parks was a civil rights activist as early as the 1940s, but it was her role in the Montgomery bus boycott that ushered in an era of real change for African Americans. Late in life she said: *"I do the very best I can to look upon life with optimism and hope and looking forward to a better day.... [yet] It pains me that there is still a lot of Klan activity and racism."* In 1999 Parks was awarded the highest civilian award in the country, the Congressional Gold Medal.

Dr. Martin Luther King, Jr.
1929–1968
Minister, Civil Rights Activist

In the 1950s, Dr. Martin Luther King, Jr., established himself as one of the main leaders of the civil rights movement. A Baptist minister and stirring speaker, King organized marches, boycotts, and demonstrations that opened many people's eyes to the need for change. In 1964 he was awarded the Nobel Prize for Peace. He said, *"I have the audacity [boldness] to believe that peoples everywhere can have three meals a day for their bodies, education and culture for their minds, and dignity, equality, and freedom for their spirits."* Dr. King was assassinated in 1968 in Memphis, Tennessee.

CRITICAL Thinking

Inferring What do the statements by Parks and King have in common?

W ### The Montgomery Bus Boycott

On the evening of December 1, 1955, **Rosa Parks,** an African American, boarded a bus in downtown Montgomery, Alabama. Parks, a seamstress, was secretary of the local chapter of the NAACP. She found an empty seat in the section reserved for whites.

When white passengers entered the bus, the driver told Parks to move to the rear of the bus. Parks refused. At the next bus stop, she was taken off the bus by police, arrested for breaking the law, and fined $10. The episode could have ended there—but it did not.

Rosa Parks's arrest led African Americans in Montgomery to organize a **boycott**—a refusal to use—the city's buses. The boycott organizers hoped to hurt the city financially and force it to alter its policies. They had strength in numbers—almost 75 percent of the bus company's riders were African American.

At a boycott meeting, a young Baptist minister came forward to speak. Not widely known at the time, **Dr. Martin Luther King, Jr.,** made an impact on the crowd. He declared:

PRIMARY SOURCE

C "We are here . . . because first and foremost we are American citizens and we are determined to apply our citizenship to the fullness of its meaning. . . . And you know, . . . there comes a time when people get tired of being trampled over by the iron feet of oppression."
—from *The Papers of Martin Luther King, Jr.*

The boycott upset many people's daily lives, but the African Americans of Montgomery pulled together to make it work.

Fast Facts

Support for the Boycott African American citizens of Montgomery pulled together during the boycott. Even though they lost money, African American taxi drivers began to charge 10 cents—the regular bus fare—rather than 45 cents to transport African Americans who were boycotting the buses. The Montgomery Improvement Association bought 15 station wagons for transport. Because each car had the name of a sponsoring church on its door, the fleet came to be called "rolling churches." Thousands of boycotters walked. Some white women even smuggled their maids to work. By working together, African Americans dramatically increased the effectiveness of the boycott.

Students hitchhiked to school; workers walked or rode bikes to their jobs. Dr. King helped organize car pools to shuttle people from place to place.

The bus boycott lasted for more than a year. City officials arrested Dr. King and other leaders at different times, but African Americans held firm. The local bus company lost thousands of dollars in fares, and downtown businesses lost customers. Finally, the Supreme Court settled the matter by ruling that the Montgomery bus segregation law was unconstitutional. In December 1956, the boycott ended.

Nonviolent Protest

With the victory in Montgomery, Dr. King became a leader of the civil rights movement. He followed the tactics of A. Philip Randolph, the nation's most prominent African American labor leader. Dr. King was also strongly influenced by Mohandas Gandhi, who used nonviolent protest to help India gain independence from Great Britain. In keeping with his beliefs, Gandhi used protest methods based on **civil disobedience,** or the refusal to obey laws that are considered unjust. Like Gandhi, Dr. King encouraged his followers to disobey unjust laws without using violence. Believing in people's ability to change themselves, he was certain that the American people would eventually convince the government to end segregation.

Dr. Martin Luther King, Jr., was not the only prominent minister in the bus boycott. Many of the other leaders were African American ministers. The boycott could not have succeeded without the support of the African American churches in the city.

In January 1957, Dr. King and 60 other ministers started a new organization called the Southern Christian Leadership Conference (SCLC). SCLC leaders also emphasized nonviolent protest. They showed civil rights workers how to protect themselves from violent attacks. The SCLC also discussed how to identify targets for protests and how to organize people for support. In taking these steps, the SCLC prepared African Americans for the struggle for equal rights.

Reading Check Describing How did the Montgomery bus boycott lead to a change in policy?

CHAPTER 28

Section 1

R Reading Strategy

Inferring Ask: How was Rosa Parks's action an example of civil disobedience? *(Parks disobeyed the law that stated that she must move to the back of the bus if a white person wanted her seat.)* **OL**

D Differentiated Instruction

Visual/Spatial Have students work in pairs to create a flyer to be distributed in African American churches recruiting African Americans to join the civil rights movement. **OL**

Reading Check **Answer:** The Montgomery bus segregation law was declared unconstitutional by the Supreme Court.

Assess

History ONLINE

Study Central™ provides summaries, interactive games, and online graphic organizers to help students review content.

Close

Sequencing As a class, create a time line of events of the civil rights movement in the 1940s and 1950s. **OL**

Section ★ Review

Section 1 Review

History ONLINE
Study Central™ To review this section, go to glencoe.com.

Vocabulary

1. Write a paragraph using each of the following terms: discriminate, segregation, civil, integrate, boycott, civil disobedience.

Main Ideas

2. **Comparing** What was the major difference in the ruling of *Plessy* v. *Ferguson* and *Brown* v. *Board of Education*?

3. **Describing** What impact did the Montgomery bus boycott have on securing equal rights for African Americans?

Critical Thinking

4. **Sequencing** On a time line like the one below, sequence the events that led to integration in Little Rock.

5. **Analyzing** What effect did Dr. Martin Luther King, Jr., have on the growth of the civil rights movement?

6. **Persuasive Writing** Take the role of a newspaper editor. Write an editorial that persuades the residents of your city to reject racial segregation.

Answer the
7. **Essential Question**
What were the legal and social challenges to racial segregation in the 1940s and 1950s?

The Civil Rights Era **Chapter 28** 879

Answers

1. Paragraphs should use words as they are defined in the section and Glossary.
2. *Plessy* found that "separate but equal" was legal. *Brown* found that separate facilities could never be equal, and therefore, segregation was unconstitutional.
3. struck down the bus segregation law in that city and sparked the civil rights movement
4. **December 1952:** Thurgood Marshall argued *Brown* before the Supreme Court;

May 17, 1954: The Court ruled segregation of public schools was unconstitutional; **1955:** The Court ordered public schools to integrate quickly; **1957:** high school in Little Rock, Arkansas, ordered to admit African American students; **September 1957:** Arkansas Guard ordered to keep out African American students, a federal judge ruled this violated the law, and Eisenhower sent soldiers to protect the students.

5. became leader of the civil rights movement, advocated civil disobedience as a way to challenge discriminatory laws
6. Students should include information about racial segregation and the struggle for civil rights in their editorials.
7. CORE founded. Under *Brown* segregation in public schools is unconstitutional. The Court ordered schools to integrate quickly. Rosa Parks challenged bus segregation.

Section 2

Kennedy and Johnson

Focus

Bellringer
Daily Test Practice Transparency 28–2

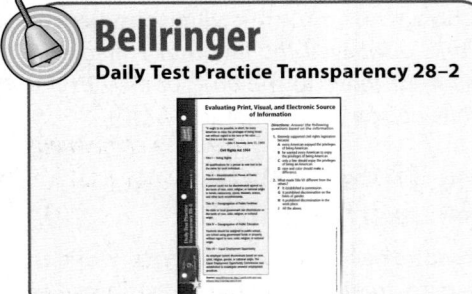

Reading Guide

Answers to Graphic:
New Frontier: federal aid for education; federal aid for the poor; civil rights legislation **Great Society:** programs to reduce poverty (e.g., Head Start, Job Corps, Medicare, and Medicaid); programs to rebuild decaying cities (e.g., HUD and Model Cities); legislation to improve education; and promote civil rights (Civil Rights Act of 1964)

Section Spotlight Video

Have students watch the Section Spotlight Video "Kennedy and Johnson" to learn more about the assassination of President Kennedy.

Resource Manager

Essential Question
How were Kennedy and Johnson alike and different as presidents of the United States?

Reading Guide

Content Vocabulary
poverty line (p. 883)   Medicaid (p. 883)
Medicare (p. 883)

Academic Vocabulary
assign (p. 881)   consist (p. 883)

Key People and Events
John F. Kennedy (p. 881)
New Frontier (p. 882)
Lyndon B. Johnson (p. 882)
Great Society (p. 883)
Job Corps (p. 883)
Civil Rights Act of 1964 (p. 883)

Reading Strategy
Taking Notes On a chart like the one below, list the major aspects of each of these plans.

New Frontier	Great Society

ILLINOIS STANDARDS
The American Journey

14.D.3 Describe roles and influences of individuals, groups and media in shaping current Illinois and United States public policy (e.g., general public opinion, special interest groups, formal parties, media).

15.E Understand the impact of government policies and decisions on production and consumption in the economy.

16.A.3c Identify the differences between historical fact and interpretation.

18.B Understand the roles and interactions of individuals and groups in society.

American Diary

The Democratic nominee for president in 1960 was John F. Kennedy. Some people were concerned that, because of his Catholic faith, Kennedy could be influenced by the Pope. Kennedy confronted this issue openly. "I believe in an America where the separation of church and state is absolute," he said, "where no Catholic prelate [church leader] would tell the president (should he be a Catholic) how to act."

—*from an address to Southern Baptist leaders*

Kennedy campaigns at a July 1960 rally in Los Angeles.

Reading Strategies	**Critical Thinking**	**Differentiated Instruction**	**Writing Support**	**Skill Practice**
Teacher Edition	**Teacher Edition**	**Teacher Edition**	**Teacher Edition**	**Additional Resources**
• Predicting, p. 881	• Making Inferences, p. 881	• Below Level, p. 882	• Persuasive Writing, p. 882	• Daily Test Pract. Transp. 28-2
• Summarizing, p. 881	• Drawing Conclusions, p. 883	**Additional Resources**		
Additional Resources		• School-to-Home, URB p. 63		
• Guid. Read., URB p. 68	**Additional Resources**	• Reteaching Act., URB p. 65		
• Content Vocab., URB p. 45	• Quizzes and Tests, p. 278			
• Academic Vocab., URB p. 47	• Inter. Polit. Cartoons, URB p. 13			
• Read. Ess., p. 316				

Kennedy and the New Frontier

Main Idea John F. Kennedy's presidency appealed to many Americans who wanted change.

History and You Do you think that one person has the power to change things for the better? Read on to learn how many Americans welcomed the election of a young president in 1960.

In 1960 the nation prepared for a presidential election. The Republican candidate, Vice President Richard M. Nixon, pledged to continue the policies of President Eisenhower. The Democratic candidate, **John F. Kennedy,** promised new programs to "get the country moving again."

For much of the campaign, polls showed Nixon in the lead. One reason for this was the fact that Kennedy was Roman Catholic. No Catholic had ever been president, and many Americans feared that if Kennedy won he might show more loyalty to his church than to his country. Kennedy stressed to the country his belief in the separation of church and state.

A War Hero

Kennedy came from one of the country's wealthiest and most powerful families. His father, Joseph P. Kennedy, was a successful business leader and the American ambassador to Britain at the start of World War II.

John Kennedy joined the United States Navy during World War II and was **assigned,** or appointed, to active duty in the Pacific. When the Japanese sank the PT (patrol torpedo) boat he commanded, Kennedy saved the life of a crew member by swimming to shore with the injured man on his back.

Kennedy's political career began in 1946 when he won a seat in Congress from Massachusetts. Six years later, he was elected to the United States Senate. After easily winning reelection to the Senate in 1958, Kennedy ran for the presidency in 1960.

A New President

The turning point in the 1960 election came when the candidates took part in the first televised presidential debates. Nixon, who was recovering from an illness, looked tired and sick. Kennedy appeared handsome and youthful.

By the Numbers / Election of 1960

Candidates	Electoral Vote	Popular Vote	Political Party
Kennedy	303	34,227,096	Democrat
Nixon	219	34,107,646	Republican
Byrd	15	None	Independent

Map Skills

Region In what regions of the country did Kennedy receive the strongest support? In what regions was support for Nixon strongest?

Maps in MOtion See StudentWorks™ Plus or glencoe.com.

Planning a Campaign

Step 2: Create Kennedy Campaign Materials Students will create campaign materials in support of a candidate.

Essential Question: How were Kennedy and Johnson alike and different as presidents of the United States?

Directions Students will create campaign materials for a presidential candidate who strongly supports civil rights.

Have students organize into their groups to choose a candidate and create campaign materials. Each group should create a button, a poster, a bumper sticker, and a newspaper advertisement. When students have finished, display the campaign materials around the classroom.

Evaluating Discuss as a class why people who are committed to civil rights might vote for their candidate. **OL**

(Chapter Project continued in Section 3)

Teach

R₁ Reading Strategy

Predicting Ask: Which candidate do you think won the 1960 presidential election? Why? *(Possible answer: Kennedy won, because he promised change.)* **OL**

C Critical Thinking

Making Inferences Ask: Why did voters fear Kennedy's Catholicism? *(Many Americans feared that Kennedy would be more loyal to his church than to his country.)* **OL**

R₂ Reading Strategy

Summarizing Have students write a few sentences to summarize Kennedy's career prior to running for president. **BL**

Primary Source

Critical Thinking Answer
Kennedy received the strongest support in large northern states and the South. Nixon received the strongest support in the West and the Plains states.

Hands-On Chapter Project
Step 2

W Writing Support

Persuasive Writing Have students write a newspaper editorial backing either Kennedy or Nixon in the 1960 presidential election. **OL**

D Differentiated Instruction

Below Level Have students list the parts of Kennedy's New Frontier program. **Ask:** Was the New Frontier successful? *(no)* Why? *(Congress did not want to fund expensive programs.)* **BL**

Primary Source

Critical Thinking Answer
Johnson wants Americans to view poverty, ignorance, and disease as enemies instead of other people.

✔ **Reading Check** **Answer:** The first televised presidential debate was the turning point, because Kennedy made a better impression than Nixon did.

Primary Source / Civil Rights

Presidential Policies Presidents Kennedy and Johnson expanded civil rights by issuing executive orders and approving laws that affected many areas of African Americans' daily lives.

President Kennedy
- Expanded African American voting
- Increased job opportunities
- Outlawed discrimination in federal housing
- Established Committee on Equal Employment Opportunity

"We are confronted primarily with a moral issue. . . . The heart of the question is—whether all Americans are to be afforded equal rights and equal opportunities. Whether we are going to treat our fellow Americans as we want to be treated."

President Johnson
- Provided funds to poorer states for education
- Gave federal funding to poor African American colleges
- Signed legislation that outlawed discrimination in registering voters

"These are the enemies: poverty, ignorance, disease. They are the enemies and not our fellow men, not our neighbor. And these enemies too, poverty, disease and ignorance, we shall overcome."

Critical Thinking

Analyzing How was President Johnson's quote related to civil rights?

During the debate, he spoke with confidence about the future. Many viewers thought that Kennedy made a better impression.

W In November, nearly 70 million voters turned out to choose between Nixon and Kennedy. The results were extremely close. In the popular vote, Kennedy won 49.7 percent, while Nixon received 49.5 percent. In the electoral vote, Kennedy gained a greater margin over Nixon—303 to 219 votes.

On January 20, 1961, Kennedy was sworn in as the 35th president of the United States. In his Inaugural Address, the young president promised to face the nation's challenges with determination. In closing, Kennedy roused the American people to action: "And so, my fellow Americans: ask not what your country can do for you—ask what you can do for your country."

Domestic Policies

D Kennedy called for a **New Frontier** of social reforms. He backed federal aid for education and the poor. Congress, however, did not want to fund expensive programs.

Kennedy also supported civil rights but feared that moving too quickly would anger Southern Democrats whose support he needed. In 1963 Kennedy's civil rights bill passed in the House but stalled in the Senate.

Kennedy Assassinated

On November 22, 1963, Kennedy arrived in Dallas with his wife, Jacqueline. As the presidential motorcade rode through the streets, shots rang out. Kennedy was shot and later pronounced dead. Vice President **Lyndon B. Johnson** became president.

The assassination stunned the nation. In the midst of the grief, Lee Harvey Oswald, the man charged with the president's killing, was shot and killed as he was moved from one jail to another. A commission, headed by Supreme Court Chief Justice Earl Warren, later stated that Oswald had acted alone. Many people believed that the assassination was a plot.

✔ **Reading Check** **Describing** What was the turning point in the 1960 election?

Differentiated Instruction

The Death of JFK

Objective:	To interpret a political cartoon on the death of John F. Kennedy
Focus:	Review with students why the manner of Kennedy's death was so shocking.
Teach:	Have students study the cartoon and answer the questions.
Assess:	Ask students whether there is anything Mauldin could have drawn differently?
Close:	Discuss with students how political cartoons can influence public opinion.

Differentiated Instruction Strategies

BL Provide students with a photo of the statue in the Lincoln Memorial before they answer the activity's questions.

AL Have students locate other political cartoons on Kennedy's death and compare them with Mauldin's cartoon.

ELL Ask students to come up with a brief title or caption for the cartoon.

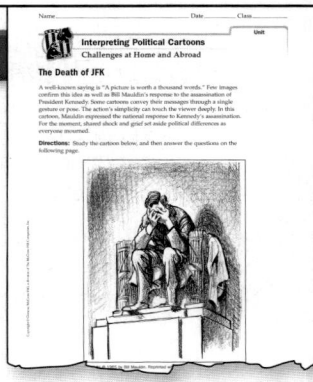

Interpreting Political Cartoons, URB p. 13

The Great Society

Main Idea The Johnson administration expanded Kennedy's domestic plans with far-reaching programs in many areas.

History and You What sort of problems do cities have today? Read to find out about efforts by the federal government to solve these problems.

· ·

President Lyndon B. Johnson outlined a set of programs known as the **"Great Society."** His plan was to reduce poverty, promote equality, improve education, and rebuild decaying cities. Johnson had served 22 years in Congress. He used his legislative skills to persuade Congress to pass these programs.

War on Poverty

In 1964 President Johnson declared the War on Poverty as part of his plan for a Great Society. It **consisted,** or was made up, of programs to help people who lived below the **poverty line**—the minimum income needed to live. For example, Head Start provided preschool education for poor children, and the **Job Corps** trained young people seeking work.

Among the most important laws passed under Johnson were **Medicare** and **Medicaid,** both passed in 1965. Medicare established a health insurance program for all elderly people, financed through the Social Security system. Medicaid provided health and medical assistance to low-income families.

Other parts of the Great Society targeted cities and education. In 1966 the Department of Housing and Urban Development (HUD) was created to fund public housing projects. Another program, Model Cities, provided money to rebuild cities. Schools were helped by the Elementary and Secondary Education Act of 1965.

Although a Southerner, Johnson was not a segregationist and supported civil rights for all Americans. With Johnson's backing, Congress passed the **Civil Rights Act of 1964.** The act banned discrimination against African Americans in employment, voting, and public places. It forbade discrimination not only by race but also by gender, religion, and national origin.

✔ **Reading Check** **Explaining** What was the purpose of the Job Corps?

History ONLINE
Study Central™ To review this section, go to glencoe.com.

C Critical Thinking

Drawing Conclusions Ask: Why do you think Johnson was successful in passing a civil rights bill although Kennedy had not been? *(Johnson had more legislative experience; Congress passed legislation to honor Kennedy.)* **AL**

✔ **Reading Check** **Answer:** to teach job skills to young people seeking work

Assess
· ·

History ONLINE

Study Central™ provides summaries, interactive games, and online graphic organizers to help students review content.

Close
· ·

Comparing and Contrasting As a class, note the similarities and differences between Kennedy's "New Frontier" and Johnson's "Great Society." **OL**

Section 2 Review

Vocabulary

1. Write a sentence for each of the following terms that explains its meaning: assign, consist, poverty line, Medicare, Medicaid.

Main Ideas

2. **Summarizing** What did the Civil Rights Act of 1964 accomplish?

3. **Explaining** What message did President Kennedy send with his Inaugural Address when he said "ask what you can do for your country"?

Critical Thinking

4. **Analyzing** Why do you think John F. Kennedy won the 1960 presidential election over Richard M. Nixon?

5. **Identifying** On a diagram like the one below, list the government plans that were part of Johnson's War on Poverty.

War on Poverty

6. **Expository Writing** Take the role of an adviser to President Johnson. Write an essay that explains which of the president's domestic policies had the most impact on American citizens.

Answer the
Essential Question
7. How were Kennedy and Johnson alike and different as presidents of the United States?

The Civil Rights Era **Chapter 28** **883**

Answers

1. Sentences should use vocabulary words with their correct definitions.
2. It banned discrimination against minority groups in employment, voting, and public places.
3. Kennedy wanted Americans to get involved in making the nation a better place.
4. Kennedy appeared younger and more handsome, and he offered greater hope for the future than did Nixon.
5. Head Start; Job Corps; Medicare and Medicaid; H.U.D.; Elementary and Secondary Education Act of 1965
6. Students should choose one aspect of the Great Society and explain how its programs affected Americans.
7. Kennedy and Johnson had similar ideas for social programs to help Americans (help for the poor, support for education, and civil rights). However, Kennedy was unable to get his initiatives through Congress, while Johnson was highly successful in getting his Great Society programs passed.

Section 3

The Struggle Continues

Focus

Bellringer
Daily Test Practice Transparency 28–3

Reading Guide
Answers to Graphic:

- May 4, 1961: Freedom Riders left Washington, D.C., bound for New Orleans
- Riders beaten in Alabama
- Riders arrested in Mississippi
- In fall 1961, the Interstate Commerce Commission banned segregation on interstate buses and bus stations

Section Spotlight Video

Have students watch the Section Spotlight Video "The Struggle Continues" to learn more about civil rights in the 1960s.

Resource Manager

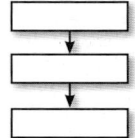

Essential Question
What areas of civil rights did groups try to improve in the 1960s, and what methods did those groups use?

Reading Guide

Content Vocabulary
sit-in (p. 885) interstate (p. 886)

Academic Vocabulary
register (p. 889) emerge (p. 890)

Key People and Events
Ella Baker (p. 885)
Robert Kennedy (p. 885)
James Meredith (p. 886)
George Wallace (p. 886)
Medgar Evers (p. 886)
Voting Rights Act of 1965 (p. 889)
Malcolm X (p. 890)

Reading Strategy
Taking Notes Create a diagram to show the major chain of events for the Freedom Riders in 1961.

Freedom Riders

ILLINOIS STANDARDS
The American Journey

17.D.3b Explain how interactions of geographic factors have shaped present conditions.

18.A Compare characteristics of culture as reflected in language, literature, the arts, traditions and institutions.

18.C.3a Describe ways in which a diverse U.S. population has developed and maintained common beliefs (e.g., life, liberty and the pursuit of happiness; the Constitution and the Bill of Rights).

18.C.3b Explain how diverse groups have contributed to U.S. social systems over time.

884

American Diary

On February 1, 1960, four African American students walked into a store in Greensboro, North Carolina. Sitting down at a "whites-only" lunch counter, they were refused service. The students stayed at the counter until the store closed, then stated that they would sit at the counter every day until they were given the same service as white customers. News of the sit-ins spread rapidly. Other students followed their example. Starting with just four students, a new American mass movement for civil rights began.

Sit-ins, like this one in Greensboro, were nonviolent methods of protest for the civil rights movement.

R Reading Strategies	C Critical Thinking	D Differentiated Instruction	W Writing Support	S Skill Practice
Teacher Edition • Pri. Sources, p. 885 • Visualizing, p. 887 • Act. Prior Know., p. 890 **Additional Resources** • Guid. Read., URB p. 69 • Cont. Vocab., URB p. 45 • Acad. Vocab., URB p. 47 • Pri. Source, URB p. 49	**Teacher Edition** • Ident. Prob., p. 889 • Conclusions, p. 890 • Making Infer., p. 891 **Additional Resources** • Quizzes and Tests, p. 279 • Link. Past & Pres., URB p. 61 • Authentic Assess., p. 28	**Teacher Edition** • Gifted and Talented, p. 886 • Auditory/Musical, p. 888 **Additional Resources** • School-to-Home, URB p. 63 • Reteaching Act., URB p. 65	**Teacher Edition** • Descriptive Writing, p. 886 • Personal Writing, p. 887 • Personal Writing, p. 891	**Teacher Edition** • Using Analytical Skills, p. 885 **Additional Resources** • Daily Test Pract. Transp. 28-3 • Time Line, URB p. 62 • Geo. & Hist., URB p. 59 • Lesson Transp. 28B

The Movement Grows

Main Idea New leaders and groups emerged as the civil rights movement took on new causes.

History and You What do you do if you think you are not being treated fairly? How do you speak out? Read on to learn what actions African Americans took in the 1960s to secure their rights.

A new wave of civil rights activity swept across the nation during the Kennedy and Johnson administrations. Early activity targeted segregation in the South. Segregation existed in the North as well.

In Northern urban areas, African Americans and whites often lived in different neighborhoods; as a result, their children often attended different schools. Soon African Americans expanded their goal to fighting discrimination and racism in the North as well as in the South.

High school and college students staged sit-ins in nearly 80 cities. A **sit-in** is the act of protesting by sitting down. Sit-ins were held throughout the nation against stores that practiced segregation. Store managers wanted to end the disturbances and loss of business. Gradually many stores agreed to integrate.

The sit-ins launched a new civil rights group, the Student Nonviolent Coordinating Committee (SNCC). Civil rights activist **Ella Baker** was a guiding spirit behind SNCC and one of its organizers. Earlier, Baker played major roles in both the NAACP and the SCLC. SNCC was a key player in the civil rights cause for several years.

Freedom Rides

The Supreme Court had ruled in 1960 against segregated bus facilities. Another civil rights group, the Congress of Racial Equality (CORE), decided to see if the ruling was being enforced. On May 4, 1961, a group of African Americans and white CORE members left Washington, D.C., on two buses bound for New Orleans. They called themselves Freedom Riders. The trip went smoothly until it reached Alabama, where angry whites stoned and beat the Freedom Riders.

Television and newspapers reported the beatings. The president's brother, **Robert Kennedy,** the United States attorney general, asked CORE to stop the Freedom Rides for a "cooling-off period." CORE leader James Farmer responded: "We have been cooling off for 350 years. If we cool off anymore, we will be in a deep freeze."

Primary Source | **Birth of the SNCC**

Students Organize As the sit-ins spread, student leaders in different states realized they needed to coordinate their efforts. The person who brought them together was Ella Baker, the executive director of the Southern Christian Leadership Conference (SCLC). At a meeting in 1960, Baker urged students to create their own organization instead of joining the NAACP or the SCLC. Baker told them that students had "the right to direct their own affairs and even make their own mistakes." From this beginning was born the Student Nonviolent Coordinating Committee (SNCC).

Ella Baker ▶

Critical Thinking

Explaining What was the purpose of sit-ins?

Teach

S Skill Practice

Using Analytical Skills Ask: What effect do you think this type of violence might have had on public opinion? *(People might have felt sympathy for the riders and pressured officials to end the violence.)* **OL**

R Reading Strategy

Reading Primary Sources Ask: Did James Farmer agree to the attorney general's request? Why or why not? *(He did not agree, because he argued that African Americans had waited long enough to fight for their rights.)* **OL**

Primary Source

Critical Thinking Answer to integrate stores

Drawing Conclusions Ask: Why do you think sit-ins were effective in challenging segregation? *(Answers should mention the peaceful attitude of protesters, as well as their persistence.)* **AL**

Additional Support

Technology Connection

Freedom Riders Have students do Internet research for three different primary documents about the Freedom Riders. Instruct them to analyze the documents in a two- or three-page paper about the Freedom Riders. Each essay should include an introductory section that answers the following questions: Who (took part)? What (was their goal)? Where (did Riders go)? When (did it take place)? and Why (did it take place)? Each of three remaining paragraphs should analyze one primary document, stating how it contributes to their understanding of the movement. Remind students to include a conclusion. **AL**

D Differentiated Instruction

Gifted and Talented Have students write a chapter for a graphic novel about James Meredith or George Wallace. Instruct them to include information on the person's involvement with the civil rights movement as well as information on how others viewed him at that time. **AL**

W Writing Support

Descriptive Writing Organize students into pairs. Instruct each pair to research and collect images from the Birmingham protests. They should then write a short descriptive newscast to accompany the vivid images from the protests. Have each pair of student newscasters present its report to the rest of the class. **OL**

R Reading Strategy

Reading Primary Sources Ask: Did Kennedy support the civil rights movement? How do you know? *(Kennedy did support the movement, because he stated that it was Americans' moral obligation to support the changes being brought about by the movement.)* **OL**

Hands-On Chapter Project
Step 3

Planning a Civil Rights Campaign

Step 3: Plan a Protest Students will identify a problem in their community, plan a protest, and compare their plan to civil rights protests of the 1960s.

Essential Question: What areas of civil rights did groups try to improve in the 1960s and what methods did those groups use?

886

Violence and Arrests

The Freedom Riders pressed on, only to meet more violence in Birmingham and Montgomery, Alabama. No mobs were waiting for the Freedom Riders in Jackson, Mississippi. However, police, state troopers, and Mississippi National Guard units were everywhere. As the Riders stepped off the bus and tried to enter the whites-only waiting room at the bus station, they were arrested for trespassing and jailed.

Despite the violence and the jail sentences, more Freedom Riders kept coming all summer. In the fall, the Interstate Commerce Commission enforced the Supreme Court ruling, issuing new regulations that banned segregation on **interstate** buses—those that crossed state lines—and in bus stations.

Integrating Universities

African Americans continued to apply pressure to secure their civil rights. They spurred President Kennedy to take a more active role in the civil rights struggle.

In 1962 a federal court ordered the University of Mississippi to enroll its first African American student, **James Meredith.** However, Mississippi Governor Ross Barnett, with the aid of state police, kept Meredith from registering. When President Kennedy sent federal marshals to escort Meredith to the campus, riots erupted. A mob armed with guns and rocks stormed the administration building. The marshals fought back with tear gas and nightsticks. Meredith succeeded in registering, but two people were killed. Federal troops remained at the university to protect him until he graduated in 1963.

Another clash between state and federal power took place in June 1963 in Alabama. Governor **George Wallace** vowed he would "stand in the schoolhouse door" to block the integration of the University of Alabama in Tuscaloosa. President Kennedy, acting on the advice of his brother, Robert, sent the Alabama National Guard to ensure the entry of African Americans to the university. As a result, Wallace backed down.

W Birmingham

In the spring of 1963, Dr. Martin Luther King, Jr., and the SCLC targeted Birmingham, Alabama, for a desegregation protest. Police arrested hundreds of demonstrators, including Dr. King, but the demonstrations continued. During Dr. King's two weeks in jail, he wrote the eloquent "Letter from Birmingham Jail," in which he wrote: "We must come to see . . . that justice too long delayed is justice denied."

National television carried vivid pictures of police setting snarling police dogs on unarmed demonstrators and pushing small children across streets with the powerful impact of fire hoses. President Kennedy sent 3,000 troops to restore peace. On June 11, 1963, in Jackson, Mississippi, **Medgar Evers,** the state field secretary for the NAACP, was murdered. The murder and the events in Alabama forced President Kennedy to make a decision. Appearing on national television, Kennedy spoke of the "moral issue" facing the nation:

PRIMARY SOURCE

"It is not enough to pin the blame on others, to say this is a problem of one section of the country or another, or deplore the fact that we face. A great change is at hand, and our task, our obligation, is to make that revolution, that change, peaceful and constructive for all. Those who do nothing are inviting shame as well as violence. Those who act boldly are recognizing right."
—Kennedy's address to the nation, June 1963

Days later, the president introduced new legislation giving all Americans the right to be served in public places and barring discrimination in employment.

March on Washington

To rally support for the civil rights bill, Dr. King and the SCLC organized a massive march on Washington, D.C., on August 28, 1963. More than 200,000 people of all colors and from all over the country arrived to take part in the event.

Directions Have each student group identify an injustice in their community. **Ask:** How might you protest this injustice? *(Answers may include letters to the editor, protest marches, sit-ins, educational campaigns, and so on.)*

Direct student groups to plan their protests, including how they will protest, how they will recruit protesters, and what their demands will be. Students should create posters detailing their proposals.

Connecting Ask: How do you feel about the possibility of carrying out your protest? *(Students may mention excitement or fear.)* How might your feelings be similar to or different from what civil rights workers felt in the 1960s? *(Civil rights workers faced the possibility of violence and may have felt more frightened.)* **OL**

(Chapter Project continued in Section 4)

Primary Source

Letter from Birmingham Jail

On April 16, 1963, from his jail cell in Birmingham, Alabama, Dr. Martin Luther King, Jr., used the margins of a newspaper and scraps of paper to craft a letter. The letter was in response to criticism from a group of white clergy, who wanted him to stop his nonviolent protests and his desegregation efforts. Dr. King's letter, which has been translated into more than 40 languages, serves as a stirring record of the Civil Rights Movement. **W**

▲ Dr. King in jail

"We have waited for more than 340 years for our constitutional and God given rights. . . . We still creep at horse and buggy pace toward gaining a cup of coffee at a lunch counter. Perhaps it is easy for those who have never felt the stinging darts of segregation to say, 'Wait.' But when you have seen vicious mobs lynch your mothers and fathers at will and drown your sisters and brothers at whim; when you have seen hate filled policemen curse, kick and even kill your black brothers and sisters; when you see the vast majority of your twenty million Negro brothers smothering in an airtight cage of poverty in the midst of an **affluent** society; when you suddenly find your tongue twisted and your speech stammering as you seek to explain to your six year old daughter why she can't go to the public amusement park that has just been advertised on television, . . . then you will understand why we find it difficult to wait. . . . **R**

. . . Let us all hope that the dark clouds of racial prejudice will soon pass away and the deep fog of misunderstanding will be lifted from our fear drenched communities, and in some not too distant tomorrow the radiant stars of love and brotherhood will shine over our great nation with all their **scintillating** beauty.

Yours for the cause of Peace and Brotherhood,
Martin Luther King, Jr."

> Dr. King is referring to the settlers who arrived, in what would become the United States, in the 1600s.

> He was responding to those who said that African Americans needed to move more slowly in their efforts to desegregate.

> Unequal opportunities, when it came to jobs and education, trapped many African Americans in a state of poverty. The frustration was increased by the fact that many whites had opportunities that African Americans were not given.

VOCABULARY
affluent (A•FLOO•uhnt): wealthy
scintillating SIHN•tuhl•AYT•ihng: sparkling, dazzling

Critical Thinking

Interpreting King's letter was seen as a source of hope for African Americans fighting for equality. How does the letter convey that hope? Give examples.

Teach

W Writing Support

Personal Writing Have students take the role of a personal friend of Dr. King's and write a letter to be delivered to him while he is in jail. **OL**

R Reading Strategy

Visualizing Ask: How does Dr. King use descriptive language to help the reader understand the reality of segregation? *(He uses personal examples that people could relate to. For example, to describe the slow pace of segregation, he uses the phrase "We still creep." To show how encompassing and unescapable poverty is, he writes "an airtight cage of poverty.")* **OL**

Answer

Answers will vary, but students might say that King conveys hope that people will gradually begin to see that they are making a mistake in denying rights to African Americans. When he writes that "the radiant stars of love and brotherhood will shine over our great nation," he is implying that instead of working against each other, whites and blacks will one day learn to work together.

Skill Practice

S

Using a Time Line Have students look at the time line. **Ask:** With which events on the time line was Martin Luther King, Jr., involved? *(Montgomery Bus Boycott, Birmingham protests, "I Have a Dream" speech, Selma march)* **OL**

Differentiated Instruction

D

Auditory/Musical Play a recording of Martin Luther King's "I Have a Dream" speech for students. **Ask:** What words and phrases are used over and over again? Why? *(one hundred years later; we cannot be satisfied; I have a dream; let freedom ring; free at last; Dr. King is trying to emphasize his main ideas by repeating them.)* In what other ways does King appeal to listeners' emotions? *(Possible answer: by mentioning the Declaration of Independence)* Ask students to explain how listening to the speech makes them feel. **OL**

The Struggle for Civil Rights, 1954–1965

Sit-in at a lunch counter ▶

★ **May 1954** *Brown* decision declares segregated schools unconstitutional

★ **Sept. 1957** Federal troops escort African American students to desegregate Little Rock's Central High School

★ **December 1955** Rosa Parks is arrested and Montgomery bus boycott begins

★ **Feb. 1960** Sit-in movement spreads after students stage sit-in at North Carolina lunch counter

★ **May 1961** Freedom Riders brave violence to desegregate interstate bus travel

Rosa Parks ▶

Nan Grogan Orrock has served in the Georgia Senate and House of Representatives. As a college student in 1963, Orrock describes how she felt at the march on Washington:

PRIMARY SOURCE

S

"You couldn't help but get swept up in the feeling of the March. It was an incredible experience of this mass of humanity with one mind moving down the street. It was like being part of a glacier. You could feel the sense of collective [united] will and effort in the air."

—from *Like a Mighty Stream*

About 6,000 police officers stood nearby, but they had nothing to do but direct traffic. There was no trouble. Proceeding peacefully through Washington with great dignity and joy, the marchers carried signs urging Congress to act. They sang songs, including the one that became the anthem of the civil

rights movement: "We Shall Overcome." Late in the afternoon, Dr. King delivered a powerful speech. He spoke to the crowd of his desire to see America transformed:

PRIMARY SOURCE

D

"I have a dream that one day this nation will rise up and live out the true meaning of its creed: 'We hold these truths to be self-evident; that all men are created equal.' . . . When we [let] freedom ring, . . . we will be able to speed up that day when all of God's children, . . . [will] join hands and sing in the words of the old . . . spiritual: Free at last! Free at last! Thank God Almighty, we are free at last!"

—from the "I Have a Dream" speech

Freedom Summer

Congress did not pass Kennedy's civil rights bill until after his death. President Lyndon B. Johnson persuaded Congress to pass the bill after he had taken over the office.

888 **Chapter 28** *The Civil Rights Era*

Differentiated Instruction

Marches on Washington, D.C.

Objective: To research historical data about marches on Washington, D.C.

Focus: Ask students to explain why groups would want to demonstrate in Washington.

Teach: Have students research the marches listed and fill in the chart.

Assess: Draw the same chart on the board and ask for volunteers to fill in their data.

Close: Discuss with students whether marches in Washington are effective.

Differentiated Instruction Strategies

BL Have students work in pairs to research the information and complete the chart.

AL Have students write an essay on a Washington, D.C., march they would have liked to attend.

ELL Ask students to explain, in their own words, this sentence: *The goal was to bring about political change.*

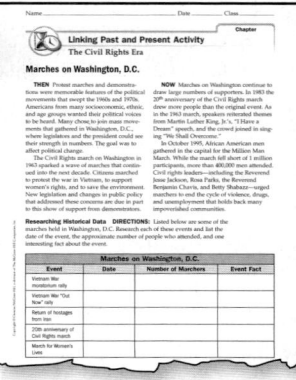

Linking Past and Present Activity, URB p. 61

Birmingham police use hoses to force civil rights protestors to stop their marches. ▶

★ **Sept. 1962** James Meredith tries to register at University of Mississippi

★ **Aug. 1963** King delivers "I Have a Dream" speech during March on Washington

★ **March 1965** King leads march in Selma, Alabama, to build support for new voting rights law

★ **May 1963** Police use force to stop Bir-mingham marchers

★ **July 1964** President Johnson signs Civil Rights Act of 1964 into law

★ **Aug. 1965** Congress passes Voting Rights Act of 1965

◀ National Guard escorts Freedom Riders

Critical Thinking

Analyzing What action did African Americans take in 1960 in the struggle for equal rights?

C Critical Thinking

Identifying Problems and Solutions
Ask: What problem was the Voting Rights Act designed to solve? *(African Americans in the South were being denied the right to vote.)* What other problem did it solve? *(More African Americans held elected office.)* **OL**

This **READING SKILL** (Identifying Problems and Solutions) was introduced in this unit.

The Struggle for Civil Rights 1954–1965

Critical Thinking Answer
They staged sit-ins.

Critical Thinking Practice
Making Connections Ask: How did Meredith's action in 1962 further the civil rights cause? *(by forcing integration of the University of Mississippi)* **OL**

Reading Check Answer: to force buses and bus stations in the South to integrate

---

The Civil Rights Act of 1964 outlawed discrimination in hiring and ended segregation in stores, restaurants, theaters, and hotels. Yet, in many states, poll taxes and other discriminatory laws prevented African Americans from exercising their right to vote.

During the summer of 1964, thousands of civil rights workers spread throughout the South to help African Americans **register,** or enroll, to vote. They called the campaign Freedom Summer, but the workers faced strong, sometimes violent, opposition.

The Right to Vote
The next year SNCC organized a major demonstration in Selma, Alabama, to protest the continued denial of African Americans' right to vote. Police attacked and beat many of the demonstrators.

President Johnson stepped in. On March 15, 1965, in a televised speech, the president urged passage of a voting rights bill. "About this there can be no argument," he said. "Every American citizen must have an equal right to vote." In August, Johnson signed the **Voting Rights Act of 1965** into law. The act gave the federal government the power to force local officials to allow African Americans to register to vote.

The act led to dramatic changes in the political life of the South. In 1966 about 100 African Americans held elective office in Southern states. By 1972 that number had increased 10 times.

After passage of the Voting Rights Act, the civil rights movement shifted its focus. It began to pay more attention to the problems of African Americans trapped in poverty and living in major cities.

Reading Check Explaining What was the goal of the Freedom Riders?

The Civil Rights Era **Chapter 28** 889

Leveled Activities

Primary Source | Malcolm X on Human Rights

"The common goal of 22 million Afro-Americans is respect as human beings, the God-given right to be a human being. Our common goal is to obtain the human rights that America has been denying us. We can never get civil rights in America until our human rights are first restored. We will never be recognized as citizens there until we are first recognized as humans."

—from "Racism the Cancer that is Destroying America"

Critical Thinking

Interpreting What did Malcolm X mean when he said, "We can never get civil rights in America until our human rights are first restored"?

Other Voices

Main Idea Some African American leaders differed with Dr. King's strategy of nonviolent protest.

History and You What causes people to act violently? Read to find out why some African Americans took radical, even violent, stands during the mid-1960s.

By the mid-1960s, the civil rights movement had won numerous victories. Yet a growing number of African Americans grew tired of the slow pace of change and bitter over white attacks.

Malcolm X, born Malcolm Little in Omaha, Nebraska, **emerged**—rose up—as an important new voice for some African Americans. He was a leader in the Nation of Islam, commonly known as the Black Muslims. Malcolm X criticized the civil rights goal of integration, declaring that the best way for African Americans to achieve justice was to separate themselves from whites.

Malcolm X gained increasing support. By 1965, however, he began to change his ideas.

Instead of racial separation, he called for "a society in which there could exist honest white-black brotherhood." Soon afterwards he was killed by a rival group among the Black Muslims. His fiery words and passionate ideas, contained in his writings, continued to influence the civil rights movement after his death.

Black Power

Other African American leaders embraced more radical approaches. Stokely Carmichael, who became the leader of SNCC, advanced the idea of Black Power. This was a philosophy of racial pride that said African Americans should create their own culture and political institutions. Carmichael and other radicals called at times for revolution, a complete transformation of society. Although rejected by groups such as the NAACP, the idea of Black Power had a great impact on the civil rights movement. It became popular in the poor urban neighborhoods where many African Americans lived.

Connecting With Your Community

In Oakland, California, young radicals formed the Black Panther Party. The Panthers symbolized growing tension between African Americans and urban police. Large numbers of urban African Americans felt frustrated about poverty and a lack of jobs. The Panthers demanded reforms and armed themselves. Several clashes with the police occurred.

Violence Erupts

The first major urban riots since the 1940s took place in the summer of 1965 in the Watts section of Los Angeles. In a week of rioting, 34 people died and much of Watts burned to the ground. National Guard troops were called in to end the uprising.

The Watts riot was the first of a series of racial disorders that hit cities in the summers of 1965, 1966, and 1967. In July 1967, five days of protests, looting, and burning in Newark, New Jersey, ended with the deaths of 26 people and more than $10 million in damage. The next week, an uprising in Detroit shut down the city for several days. The governor of Michigan, who viewed the burning city from a helicopter, remarked that Detroit looked like "a city that had been

bombed." President Johnson named a commission to study the causes of the riots and to suggest steps to improve conditions. The report of this group, the Kerner Commission, warned that "our nation is moving toward two societies, one black, one white—separate and unequal."

Dr. King Is Assassinated

On April 4, 1968, racial tension in the United States took another tragic turn. On that night in Memphis, Tennessee, an assassin shot and killed Dr. Martin Luther King, Jr. His murder set off riots in more than 100 cities. Fires burned in the nation's capital, just blocks from the White House.

Thousands of people attended Dr. King's funeral in Atlanta. Millions more watched on television. All mourned the death of an American hero who, the night before his death, said God "has allowed me to go up to the mountain, and I've seen the promised land. I may not get there with you. But I want you to know tonight, that we, as a people, will get to the promised land!"

Reading Check **Explaining** Why did some African Americans criticize integration?

C Critical Thinking

Making Inferences Ask: What effect might the urban riots have had on the progress of the civil rights movement? *(The violence of the riots might have turned people against the movement.)* **AL**

W Writing Support

Personal Writing Have students write a diary entry expressing their feelings about the death of Dr. King. **OL**

Reading Check **Answer:** They believed the best way for African Americans to achieve justice was to separate themselves from whites.

Assess

History ONLINE

Study Central™ provides summaries, interactive games, and online graphic organizers to help students review content.

Close

Identifying As a class, make a list of important people in the civil rights movement. Discuss their differences in strategies. **OL**

Section 3 Review

History ONLINE
Study Central™ To review this section, go to glencoe.com.

Vocabulary

1. Use each of the terms in a sentence that will help explain its meaning: sit-in, interstate, register, emerge.

Main Ideas

2. Discussing What did the organizers of the 1963 march on Washington hope to accomplish?

3. Identifying Who was Malcolm X, and what was his philosophy?

Critical Thinking

4. Analyzing On a chart like the one below, list what each act was meant to achieve.

Civil Rights Act of 1964	
Voting Rights Act of 1965	

5. Speculating How would the civil rights struggle have been different if violence across America had not played a part in it?

6. Descriptive Writing Describe what happened across the nation when Dr. Martin Luther King, Jr., was assassinated.

Answer the
Essential Question

7. What areas of civil rights did groups try to improve in the 1960s, and what methods did those groups use?

The Civil Rights Era **Chapter 28** **891**

Answers

1. Sentences should use vocabulary words according to their definitions in the section and Glossary.
2. They wanted to rally support for passage of Kennedy's civil rights bill.
3. Malcolm X was a leader in the Nation of Islam who initially believed the best way for African Americans to achieve justice was to separate themselves from whites. Later, he called for brotherhood between whites and African Americans. He was murdered by rivals.

4. The Civil Rights Act of 1964 was meant to end discrimination in hiring and segregation in public places. The Voting Rights Act of 1965 was meant to guarantee African Americans everywhere the right to vote.
5. Possible answer: Violence against the protesters helped civil rights workers gain support. Without a violent response, the civil rights movement might have made fewer gains, because their protests would not have been so widely publicized or inspired such public outcry. Later violence

by protesters might have turned people away from supporting the movement.
6. Answers should mention the riots in more than 100 cities and the mourning of millions of Americans.
7. Civil rights groups used civil disobedience and nonviolence to force desegregation of public places, demonstrations to draw attention to the lack of voting rights, and legal challenges to unjust laws.

Focus

C Critical Thinking

Making Inferences Have students read the author biography. Note that the story is not autobiographical but that the characters are composites, or mixtures, of Curtis's family members. **Ask:** Why would an author create characters that are composites of people the author knows? *(It is easier to create characters from people one knows, and it allows the author to combine the personality traits of several people into one character.)* **OL**

R Reading Strategy

Visualizing Read the passage aloud, and have students visualize the action. Ask them if they have ever experienced a sudden noise like that. Did all other noise stop for a few seconds afterward like the author describes? **OL**

Additional Reading

Review suggested books before assigning them.

Meet the Author

Christopher Paul Curtis (1953–) was born and raised in Flint, Michigan, the setting for much of *The Watsons Go to Birmingham—1963*. Though the story is not autobiographical, Curtis admits that the characters are composites of his own family. Curtis was ten years old and living in Flint in 1963, when four African American girls were killed in a Birmingham church bombing.

Vocabulary

bobby pin hair clip

wall socket electrical plug

Building Background

Nine-year-old Kenny and his family have driven from Flint, Michigan, to Birmingham, Alabama, to visit Kenny's grandmother. During their visit, white men bomb an African American church filled with worshippers. After the bombing, Kenny searches for his sister, Joetta, who was attending services that morning. Several days before the bombing, Kenny swam in dangerous waters and was saved from a whirlpool by his brother. In the rubble of the bombed church, Kenny faces the monstrous "Wool Pooh."

THE WATSONS GO TO BIRMINGHAM—1963

Christopher Paul Curtis

I started going to sleep under the tree and thought I was dreaming when the noise came.

R I felt it more than heard it. The giant old magnolia tree shook one time like something had given it a hard snatch by the roots. Then there was a sound like a far-off thunderstorm coming. Except it only thundered one long time.

It seemed like every animal and bird and bug in Birmingham stopped making noise for about two seconds. It seemed like everything that was alive stopped whatever it was doing and was

892

Nonfiction: *The Vietnam War: Life of an American Soldier,* by Diane Yancey, uses photographs and personal quotes from soldiers, nurses, and civilians to describe life during the Vietnam War.

Fiction: *Just Like Martin,* by Ossie Davis, is the story of Isaac Stone growing up in Alabama in 1963. After the bombing of a local church that kills two classmates, Isaac decides to organize a protest march, despite the disapproval of his father.

Fiction: *The Car,* by Gary Paulsen, begins when 14-year-old Terry Anders's parents abandon him. He travels west looking for an uncle, but along the way he meets two Vietnam veterans and has numerous adventures.

For further reading, see **BOOKLINK 3**.

wondering the same thing: What was that noise?

Doors opened in the neighborhood and people came out and looked up in the sky but there was nothing there, not one cloud, nothing to give a clue to what the big hollow sound was, nothing but bright, hot, stupid Alabama sun. . . .

I leaned back against the tree and closed my eyes. I don't know if I got to sleep or not but Momma's scream made me jump nearly to the magnolia's top branch. I'd never heard Momma's voice sound so bad. I felt like I did that time I stuck a **bobby pin** in a **wall socket.**

I ran to the door and into the house and By almost knocked me over running back toward the bedroom.

"What's wrong with Momma?" I asked.

I looked in the living room but Momma and Dad weren't there. I ran back to the bedroom, where Byron was trying to wrestle into a pair of pants.

"By! What happened?"

He got the pants up and said, "A guy just came by and said somebody dropped a bomb on Joey's church." And he was gone, exploding out of the front door trying to zip up his pants at the same time he ran off the porch. . . .

. . . It looked like a river of scared brown bodies was being jerked in the same direction that By had gone, so I followed.

I guess my ears couldn't take it so they just stopped listening. I could see people everywhere making their mouths go like they were screaming and pointing and yelling but I didn't hear anything. I saw Momma and Dad and

Byron holding on to each other, all three of them looking like they were crazy and trying to keep each other away from the pile of rocks that used to be the front of the church. . . .

I got right next to where the door used to be when the guy came out with a little girl in his arms. He had on the same thing Dad did, a T-shirt and pajama pants, but it looked like he'd been painting with red, red paint. The little girl had on a blue dress and little blue frilly socks and black shiny, shiny shoes.

I looked into the church and saw smoke and dust flying around like a tornado was in there. One light from the ceiling was still hanging down by a wire, flickering and swinging back and forth, and every once in a while I could see stuff inside. . . . I could see a shiny, shiny black shoe lying halfway underneath some concrete, then it got covered with smoke, and then the lightbulb flickered out again.

I bent down to pull the shoe from under the concrete and tugged and pulled at it but it felt like something was pulling it back.

All the hair on my head jumped up to attention. The light flickered back on and the smoke cleared and I could see that hanging on to the other end of the shoe was a giant gray hand with cold, hard square fingers.

Oh-oh. . . . The Wool Pooh.

Analyzing Literature

1. **Respond** What descriptions in the scene remind you that the narrator is a child?

2. **Recall and Analyze**
   (a) What is the "red, red paint" on the man's pajamas?
   (b) Who is pulling on the shoe besides Kenny?

3. **Evaluate**
   (a) What does the Wool Pooh symbolize in this scene?
   (b) Why might the author use the Wool Pooh, which almost took Kenny's life in the water, as a symbol at the church bombing?

Teach

R Reading Strategy

Using Context Clues Ask: How did the author feel about Alabama weather? *(He did not like it.)* **BL**

D Differentiated Instruction

Logical/Mathematical Note that the main character progresses from one place to another in this selection. Ask students to list the sequence of events. *(leaning against tree, boom, people looking out, people screaming, and so on)* Next, ask students to list the sequence of Kenny's emotions. *(tired, cranky, surprised, curious, worried, curious, and fearful)* **AL**

Assess/Close

As a class, discuss why the bombed church could be described as a battlefield. *(It was the result of hate; people were killing others.)* Have students reread the selection from *The Red Badge of Courage* from the Civil War and Reconstruction unit. **Ask:** How are these two "battlefield" descriptions the same? *(There is a lot of activity, smoke, and confusion.)* How are they different? *(Curtis includes names; Kenny hears no sounds; in this selection, only one side is trying to hurt the other; in Crane's piece, both sides are shooting; Kenny is acting in the scene.)*

Answers

1. Possible answers: He does not respond as an adult might upon hearing the news. He sees his mother and father upset, and he envisions an inhuman presence at the scene.

2. (a) blood from the girl he is carrying
   (b) the Wool Pooh

3. (a) death
   (b) Kenny is a child and envisions death as a child might.

Focus

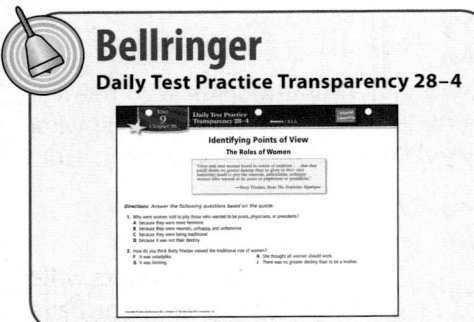
Reading Guide
Answers to Graphic:

more job opportunities; more higher-level jobs open to women; women filled local and state political offices; Sandra Day O'Connor named first female justice of the U.S. Supreme Court

Section Spotlight Video

Have students watch the Section Spotlight Video "Other Groups Seek Rights" to learn more about the struggle for women's rights.

Resource Manager

◄ Essential Question ◄
How did the civil rights movement affect minorities other than African Americans?

Reading Guide

Content Vocabulary

feminist (p. 895)   Latino (p. 896)

Academic Vocabulary

aspect (p. 895)   diverse (p. 896)

Key People and Events

National Organization for Women (p. 895)

Equal Rights Amendment (p. 895)

Sandra Day O'Connor (p. 895)

César Chávez (p. 896)

American Indian Movement (p. 898)

Reading Strategy

Taking Notes In a diagram like the one below, list the early successes of the NOW organization.

NOW Successes

Other Groups Seek Rights

American Diary

By the early 1960s, many women had grown dissatisfied with their roles. Those who worked outside the home had fewer opportunities. Many women were increasingly resentful of a world where newspaper ads were separated into "Help Wanted—Women" and "Help Wanted—Men." Married women could not get credit cards in their own names. Worst of all, women were paid less than men for the same work. As more women entered the workforce, protests for equal treatment grew louder.

By 1960, working women generally held lower-paying and lesser-status jobs. Pilot Jerrie Cobb was an exception.

R Reading Strategies	**C** Critical Thinking	**D** Differentiated Instruction	**W** Writing Support	**S** Skill Practice
Teacher Edition • Predicting, p. 895 • Acad. Vocab., p. 896 **Additional Resources** • Guid. Read., URB p. 70 • Content Vocab., URB p. 45 • Academic Vocab., URB p. 47 • Read. Ess., p. 322	**Teacher Edition** • Comp. & Contrast., p. 897 • Ident. Cent. Issues, p. 898 **Additional Resources** • Quizzes and Tests, p. 280 • Crit. Think., URB p. 57 • Citizen. Skills, URB p. 3	**Teacher Edition** • Gifted and Talented, p. 896 **Additional Resources** • School-to-Home, URB p. 63 • Reteaching Act., URB p. 65	**Teacher Edition** • Expository Writing, p. 895 • Narrative Writing, p. 897 **Additional Resources** • Writ. Skills, URB p. 51	**Teacher Edition** • Using Geo. Skills, p. 896 **Additional Resources** • Daily Test Pract. Transp. 28-4 • Lesson Transp. 28C

Women's Rights

Main Idea The influence of the civil rights movement led many American women to organize and push for greater rights and opportunities.

History and You Policies are supposed to ensure that people are treated fairly. How would you feel about policies that kept women from having the same rights as men? Read to find out how women in the 1960s and 1970s worked for change.

During the 1960s, the movement for civil rights reached women, Latinos, Native Americans, and people with disabilities. Women were the first to benefit. In 1963 Congress passed the Equal Pay Act, which prohibited employers from paying women less than men for the same work.

That same year, in a book called *The Feminine Mystique,* Betty Friedan, herself a wife and mother, described the hopes of many women for greater opportunities in society. In 1966 **feminists**—activists for women's rights—created the **National Organization for Women** (NOW). NOW fought for equal rights for women in all aspects, or categories, of life—jobs, education, and marriage.

In the early 1970s, NOW began a campaign for an **Equal Rights Amendment** (ERA) to the Constitution. The amendment stated that "equality of rights under the law shall not be denied or abridged by the United States or by any state on account of sex." Phyllis Schlafly and other foes of the ERA warned that the amendment would upset traditional social roles and lead to the breakdown of the family. In the end, not enough states ratified the amendment to make it law.

Despite the ERA's defeat, progress was made. Women gained more job opportunities, and more women rose to higher-level jobs in their companies. More women than ever became doctors and lawyers.

Women also filled local and state political offices. Women won seats in Congress and were named to the president's Cabinet. In 1981 President Ronald Reagan appointed **Sandra Day O'Connor** as the first female justice of the U.S. Supreme Court.

✓ **Reading Check** **Explaining** What was the purpose of the Equal Pay Act?

By the Numbers / Women's Pay

Unequal Pay When the Equal Pay Act was passed in 1963, full-time working women were paid 59 cents an hour on average for every dollar received by men. How do these figures compare some 40 years later?

1963 all women	59%
2005 all women	77%
African American women	71%
Latina women	58%

Percentage of Income Compared to That of Men

Source: U.S. Census Bureau, American Community Survey

Critical Thinking

Explaining What challenges did women face in the workforce in the early 1960s?

EQUAL RIGHTS for WOMEN

CHAPTER 28
Section 4

Teach

R **Reading Strategy**

Predicting Have students skim the first paragraph. Then have them predict what they will learn about in this section. **OL**

W **Writing Support**

Expository Writing Have students write an essay on whether women have achieved equality in American society. They should use examples from the text as well as their own knowledge and experience to support their positions. **AL**

By the Numbers

Critical Thinking Answer
Women had fewer opportunities than men, and women were paid only 59 cents for every dollar men made.

✓ **Reading Check** **Answer:** It prohibited employers from paying women less than men for the same work.

Hands-On Chapter Project
Step 4

Planning a Civil Rights Campaign

Step 4: Show Connections Between Civil Rights Groups Students will create a poster showing the connections between the civil rights movement and one other social movement.

Essential Question: How did the civil rights movement affect minorities other than African Americans?

Directions Organize students into their small groups. Instruct each group to choose one group mentioned in this section to research (women, Latinos, Native Americans, or disabled people). Have them research a protest staged by that group. Students should then create a poster about the group and the protest. The poster should highlight any connections between the group and the African American civil rights movement.

Synthesizing Ask: Were there any direct connections between your group and the civil rights movement? Did your group share methods or goals with the civil rights movement? *(Student answers will vary, depending on the group and protest they chose to research.)* **OL**

(Chapter Project continued in the Visual Summary)

S Skill Practice

Using Geography Skills Have students refer to a map or globe to locate countries from which the Latino population has come. **BL**

R Reading Strategy

Academic Vocabulary Have each student write three sentences using the word *diverse*. Have each student read one of their sentences aloud. **ELL**

D Differentiated Instruction

Gifted and Talented Ask: How are food crops harvested in our state? Have students research to learn about work conditions for farm laborers in your state. Students should prepare a report that summarizes the crops, average pay of laborers, and whether the United Farm Workers Union is active in your state and the benefits it provides for laborers. Ask students to imagine how it would feel to do this work day after day, for 10 or 12 hours a day, for low wages. **OL**

Differentiated Instruction

Seeking Greater Opportunity

Main Idea In the 1960s and 1970s, Hispanic Americans, Native Americans, and disabled Americans entered the struggle for equality.

History and You Have you ever refused to buy something in order to protest a certain price or policy? Read to find out how migrant farmworkers, fighting for better wages and working conditions, urged people to use this method.

In the 1960s, the **Latino** (often called Hispanic) population sought equal rights. The term *Hispanic American* refers to Americans who have come, or are descended from others who have come, to the United States from the countries of Latin America and Spain.

Americans of Mexican heritage have lived in the United States since before the nation was founded. In the twentieth century, immigration from Mexico and Latin America rose dramatically. The Latino population in the United States rose from 3 million in 1960 to 42.7 million by 2005. Although they share the heritage of the Spanish culture and language, Latinos are a **diverse** (differing from one another) group with different histories.

Farmworkers Organize

By far the largest Latino group in the United States comes from Mexico. By 2005 more than 21 million Mexican Americans were living in the United States.

The fight for rights started among Mexican American migrant farmworkers, who faced great hardships. The migrant farmworkers did backbreaking work, laboring from dawn until dusk for low wages. When one job ended, they had to travel from farm to farm in search of the next job.

In the early 1960s, migrant workers formed unions to fight for better wages and working conditions. Their leader, **César Chávez**, organized thousands of farmworkers into the United Farm Workers (UFW). The union went on strike and organized boycotts. Consumers across the country supported the UFW by refusing to buy grapes, lettuce, and other farm produce under boycott. The success of the boycotts enabled the UFW to win higher

Primary Source / Protests and Progress

Organizing for Rights From the early 1960s into the 1970s, minorities in America began to organize into groups to voice their concerns to the government over fair treatment and better opportunities. Each group made different demands, but ultimately their goal was the same: a better quality of life.

Beginning in the 1960s, UFW cofounder César Chávez organized successful nationwide boycotts of non-union-picked produce. ▶

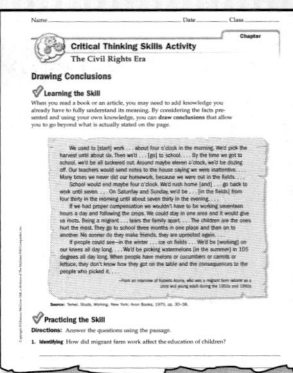
▲
In the 1973 takeover of Wounded Knee, American Indian Movement (AIM) leaders Russell Means and Dennis Banks, along with others, protested the living conditions and treatment of Native Americans.

Differentiated Instruction

Drawing Conclusions

Objective: To learn how to draw conclusions when reading and to go beyond what is stated on the page

Focus: Ask students how they draw conclusions in conducting their daily lives.

Teach: Have students read the excerpt and answer the questions.

Assess: Have volunteers explain how they drew conclusions from the excerpt.

Close: Ask the class to collaborate on a list of guidelines on how to draw conclusions when reading.

Differentiated Instruction Strategies

BL Have students underline sentences in the excerpt that can help them answer the questions.

AL Ask students to write a letter to the editor on the plight of migrant farmworkers, using the excerpt as background material.

ELL Have students circle unfamiliar words in the excerpt and use their dictionaries to define the terms.

Critical Thinking Skills Activity, URB p. 57

wages and shorter working hours for many farmworkers.

After the union boycott, Latinos made other gains. They joined together in an organization called La Raza Unida to fight discrimination and to elect Latinos to government posts. The League of United Latin American Citizens (LULAC) won lawsuits to guarantee Latinos the right to serve on juries and to send their children to integrated schools.

Puerto Ricans and Cubans

Puerto Ricans, another Latino group, come from the Caribbean island of Puerto Rico, a commonwealth of the United States. They are American citizens who have made major contributions to the United States.

In 1970 the first representative to Congress of Puerto Rican origin, Herman Badillo, was elected from New York City. Badillo later served as the city's deputy mayor. Baseball great Roberto Clemente was a hero on and off the baseball diamond. In 1972 he died in a plane crash while delivering relief supplies to earthquake victims in Nicaragua.

▲ Beginning in the 1960s, people with physical disabilities demanded—sometimes through protest—better access to stadiums, restaurants, and other public buildings.

Critical Thinking

Making Inferences How did boycotts and protests help minority groups better their lives?

Because Puerto Rico is not a wealthy island, many Puerto Ricans have migrated to American cities, such as New York City, in search of jobs. As with African Americans, Puerto Ricans have often faced discrimination in the job market.

After Cuba's revolution in 1959, dictator Fidel Castro set up a Communist government. More than 200,000 people opposed to Castro fled to the United States in the 1960s. Thousands more came in the 1980s. These immigrants settled all over the United States. The largest number of Cubans settled in southern Florida, where they have established a thriving community.

Native Americans Organize

After World War II, Native Americans experienced many changes. In the 1950s, the federal government began urging Native Americans to leave the reservations and to work in cities. Federal policy also tried to weaken the power of tribal government.

These efforts did not improve the lives of Native Americans. Many could not find jobs in the cities. Those still crowded on reservations had few jobs or other opportunities. More than one-third of Native Americans lived below the poverty line.

In the 1960s, Native Americans organized to improve their lives. They demanded political power and independence from the U.S. government. Native Americans emphasized their own histories, languages, and cultures in their schools. The National Congress of American Indians (NCAI) sought more control over Native American affairs.

The federal government responded to these issues. Congress passed the Indian Civil Rights Act of 1968, which protected the constitutional rights of all Native Americans. The new law also recognized the right of Native American nations to make laws on their reservations.

Supreme Court decisions in the 1970s reaffirmed the independence of tribal governments. They also confirmed Native Americans' rights to land granted in treaties.

The Civil Rights Era **Chapter 28** **897**

C Critical Thinking

Comparing and Contrasting Ask: How were the goals of the United Farm Workers (UFW), La Raza Unida, and the League of United Latin American Citizens (LULAC) alike? *(All three groups sought to improve the lives of Latinos.)* How were they different? *(The UFW sought to better the lives of Latinos by seeking higher wages and better working conditions. La Raza Unida fought discrimination and sought to elect Latinos to government posts, and the LULAC fought legal challenges to guarantee that Latinos could send their children to integrated schools and serve on juries.)* **OL**

W Writing Support

Narrative Writing Have students write an essay describing the lives of Native Americans in the 1950s and 1960s. **OL**

Primary Source

Critical Thinking Answer
Boycotts and protests focused attention on the inequalities faced by minority groups. Public pressure helped bring about change.

Differentiated Instruction

Leveled Activities

BL Reteaching Activity, URB p. 65

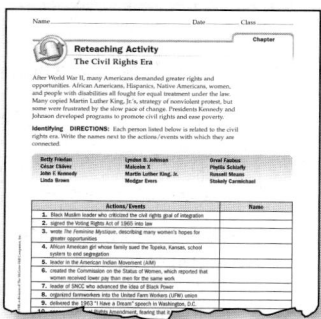

OL Citizenship and Decision-Making Skills Activity, URB p. 3

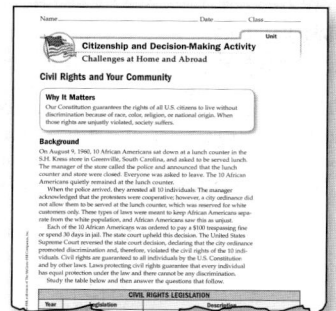

AL Writing Skills Activity, URB p. 51

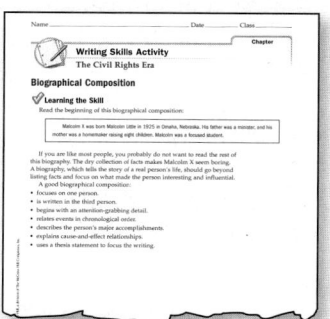

ELL School-to-Home Connection Activity, URB p. 63

C Critical Thinking

Identifying Central Issues Ask: Why was it important for Congress to pass laws for equal treatment of people with physical disabilities? *(People with disabilities have the right to enjoy equal treatment.)* **OL**

 Answer: because some Native Americans believed change was coming too slowly and wanted to take stronger actions

Assess

History ONLINE

Study Central™ provides summaries, interactive games, and online graphic organizers to help students review content.

Close

Making Connections As a class, discuss the connections between the movements for women's rights, Latino rights, Native American rights, and disability rights. **OL**

Section 4 Review

American Indian Movement

Believing change was too slow, some younger Native Americans took stronger actions. In 1968 a group set up the **American Indian Movement** (AIM), which worked for equal rights and improved living conditions. AIM was founded by Clyde Bellecourt, Dennis Banks, and others. Later Russell Means became a leader. AIM carried out several protests. In November 1969, AIM was one of the Native American groups that took over Alcatraz Island, a former prison in San Francisco Bay. AIM wanted the island to serve as a cultural center. The incident ended in June 1971 when the groups surrendered.

In the fall of 1972, AIM occupied the Bureau of Indian Affairs in Washington, D.C. They demanded the lands and rights guaranteed under treaties with the United States. They surrendered the building after officials agreed to review their complaints.

In February 1973, AIM occupied Wounded Knee, South Dakota, the site of the 1890 massacre of Sioux by federal troops. In the early 1970s, Wounded Knee was part of a Sioux reservation. The people there suffered from terrible poverty and ill health.

AIM leaders vowed to stay until the government investigated the treatment of Native Americans. The siege ended, but it focused attention on the conditions under which Native Americans lived.

Americans With Disabilities

People with physical disabilities also sought equal treatment in the 1960s and the 1970s. Congress responded by passing a number of laws.

One law concerned the removal of barriers that prevented some people from gaining access to public facilities. Another required employers to offer more opportunities for disabled people in the workplace. The Education for All Handicapped Children Act (1975) asserted the right of children with disabilities to equal educational opportunity. Schools must also provide special services to meet their needs. As a result of these actions, people with disabilities enjoy more job opportunities, better access to public facilities, and a greater role in society.

 Analyzing Why did the American Indian Movement form?

Section 4 Review

History ONLINE
Study Central™ To review this section, go to glencoe.com.

Vocabulary

1. Use each of these terms in a sentence that tells how it relates to the civil rights movement: feminist, aspect, Latino, diverse.

Main Ideas

2. Discussing What was the Equal Rights Amendment, and why was it challenged by some?

3. Explaining What did César Chávez achieve for Latinos?

Critical Thinking

4. Contrasting Contrast the experiences of Puerto Rican and Cuban immigrants.

5. Sequencing On a time line like the one below, sequence important events of the AIM group in these years.

1968   1969   1972   1973

☐ ☐ ☐ ☐

6. Creative Writing Imagine you are a physically disabled person who has been denied a job because of your disability. Write a letter to your U.S. representative in which you explain how you feel about this situation and what should be done about it.

Answer the
7. Essential Question
How did the civil rights movement affect minorities other than African Americans?

Answers

1. Sentences should use vocabulary words according to their definitions in the section and Glossary.

2. The Equal Rights Amendment promised women equality under the law. Some people fought it because they believed it would upset traditional social roles and lead to the breakdown of the family.

3. He organized the United Farm Workers, which won higher wages and better working conditions for migrant farmworkers.

4. Puerto Ricans have migrated to American cities in search of jobs; Cubans migrated to flee the Communist government. Puerto Ricans face discrimination in the job market. Many Cubans live in a successful and thriving community in South Florida.

5. 1968: AIM founded; **1969:** AIM helped take over Alcatraz Island; **1972:** AIM occupied the Bureau of Indian Affairs; **1973:** AIM occupied Wounded Knee in South Dakota.

6. The letter should describe the discrimination people with disabilities face and propose legislation that should be passed to end discrimination.

7. Women, Latinos, Native Americans, and people with disabilities organized to fight for equal rights. All achieved varying degrees of success in bringing about change, although no group achieved all of its aims.

Visual Summary

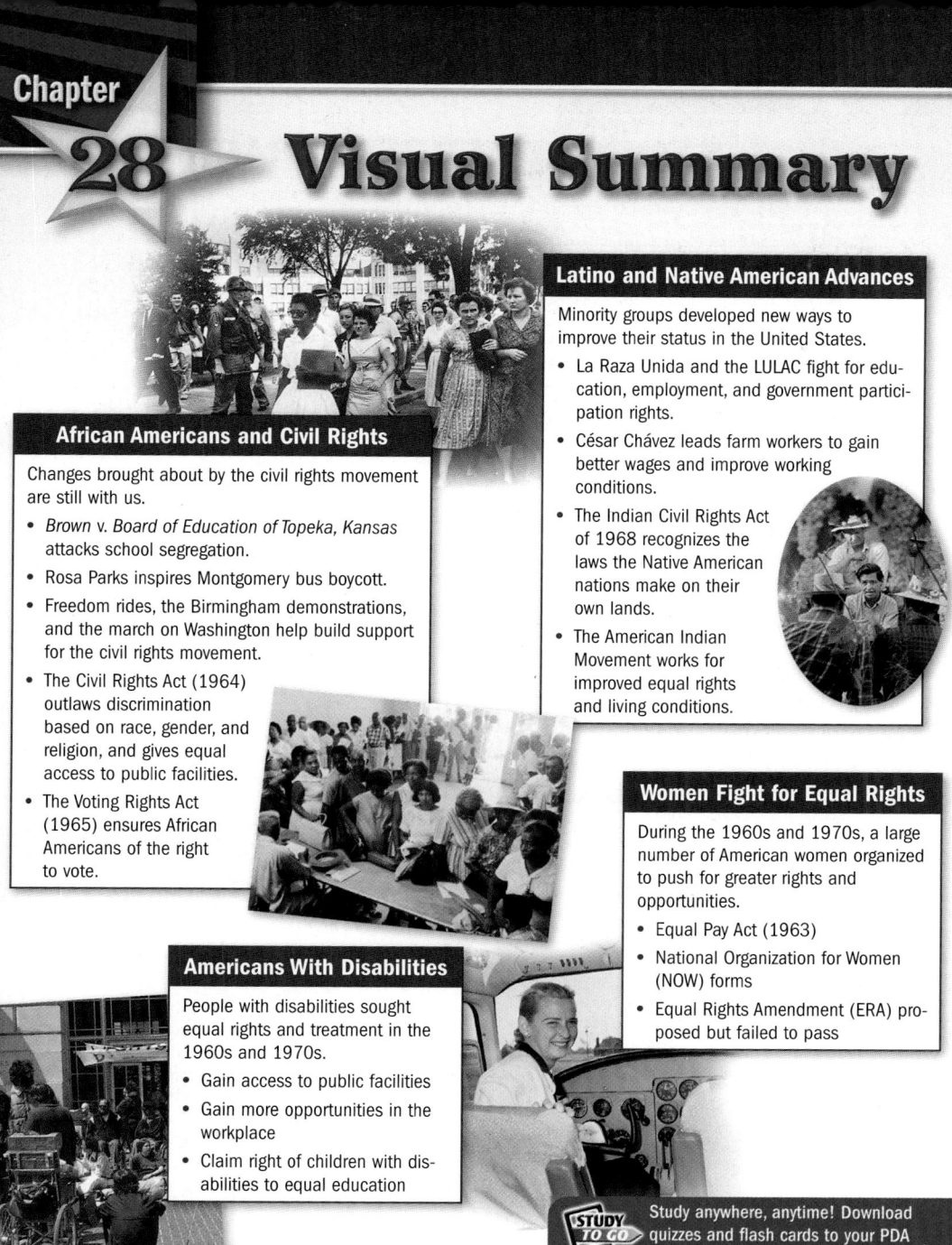

African Americans and Civil Rights

Changes brought about by the civil rights movement are still with us.

- *Brown v. Board of Education of Topeka, Kansas* attacks school segregation.
- Rosa Parks inspires Montgomery bus boycott.
- Freedom rides, the Birmingham demonstrations, and the march on Washington help build support for the civil rights movement.
- The Civil Rights Act (1964) outlaws discrimination based on race, gender, and religion, and gives equal access to public facilities.
- The Voting Rights Act (1965) ensures African Americans of the right to vote.

Latino and Native American Advances

Minority groups developed new ways to improve their status in the United States.

- La Raza Unida and the LULAC fight for education, employment, and government participation rights.
- César Chávez leads farm workers to gain better wages and improve working conditions.
- The Indian Civil Rights Act of 1968 recognizes the laws the Native American nations make on their own lands.
- The American Indian Movement works for improved equal rights and living conditions.

Americans With Disabilities

People with disabilities sought equal rights and treatment in the 1960s and 1970s.

- Gain access to public facilities
- Gain more opportunities in the workplace
- Claim right of children with disabilities to equal education

Women Fight for Equal Rights

During the 1960s and 1970s, a large number of American women organized to push for greater rights and opportunities.

- Equal Pay Act (1963)
- National Organization for Women (NOW) forms
- Equal Rights Amendment (ERA) proposed but failed to pass

STUDY TO GO Study anywhere, anytime! Download quizzes and flash cards to your PDA from glencoe.com.

The Civil Rights Era **Chapter 28** **899**

Visual Summary

Formulating Questions Ask: What else would you like to know about the civil rights movement? Lead a short discussion to generate ideas. Then have students make a list of five questions they have about the movement. When finished, direct them to choose the question they are most interested in. Give them the opportunity to research to find the answer. Ask students to present their findings to the class. Each student should also present one additional question suggested by their research. **OL**

Recognizing Bias Ask students to choose one civil rights protest (for example, the Montgomery Bus Boycott or the Selma marches). Direct students to find two or three newspaper articles from different sources reporting those events. Tell them to bring copies of the articles to class. Then have students highlight statements of fact in the articles with one color and statements of opinion with another. Call on students to share examples with the rest of the class. Lead a discussion about bias in newspaper reporting. **OL**

Hands-On Chapter Project
Step 5: Wrap-Up

Planning a Civil Rights Campaign

Step 5: Review and Discussion Students will review their work and discuss different aspects of the civil rights movement.

Directions Have students return to their original groups. Have groups review their work. As a group, ask them to discuss the different actions and protests their group was involved in.

Differentiating Ask: Did the workshop teaching nonviolent civil disobedience have the same goal as the creation of the campaign materials? *(Possible answer: No; nonviolent civil disobedience has as its goal to* force laws to change; an election campaign has as its goal to get someone elected to enact laws.) What civil rights group's strategies did your protest most resemble? *(Answers will vary.)* How did the protest you studied in step 4 compare to your other civil rights activities in this project? *(Answers will vary.)* **OL**

Answers and Analyses
Reviewing Main Ideas

1. D Students should remember that the NAACP was working to challenge segregation of public schools in the 1950s. Thurgood Marshall was chief lawyer for the NAACP. Students should then select choice D. **18.B.3a**

2. C Students should identify choice A as a program to help senior citizens, choice B as a program to revitalize decaying cities, and choice D as legislation to further African American civil rights. **18.C.3a**

3. A Students should immediately eliminate choice B, because bus desegregation was taken on by the Freedom Riders. Remind students that the goal of Freedom Summer was to register people to vote. **18.B.3a**

4. C Remind students that the United Farm Workers was formed to address working conditions for Latino migrant farm workers; eliminating choice A. NOW worked to earn equal pay for women, choice B. Choices C and D are similar, but students should recall that only choice C was mentioned in the text. **18.C.3a**

Short-Answer Question

5. As students study the graph, ask them how many more Latinos lived in the United States in 2000 than in 1960. This question should help them realize that the population growth of Latino Americans has resulted in increasing political power. **17.A.3b**

TEST-TAKING TIP

Do not wait until the last minute to prepare for a test. Make sure you ask questions in class after you have studied but before you take the test.

Reviewing Main Ideas

Directions: Choose the best answers for each of the following questions.

1. Who argued against "separate but equal" schools before the Supreme Court?
   A Earl Warren
   B James Farmer
   C George Houser
   D Thurgood Marshall

2. How did Johnson expand on Kennedy's plans to help people with low incomes?
   A by establishing Medicare
   B by setting up Model Cities
   C by introducing the Job Corps
   D by pushing through the Civil Rights Act

3. What cause did civil rights workers take on during Freedom Summer in 1964?
   A voter registration in the South
   B enforcement of bus desegregation
   C integration of Southern universities
   D discrimination in employment and housing

4. La Raza Unida was formed to
   A organize farmworkers.
   B demand equal pay for equal work.
   C elect Latinos to government office.
   D extend voting rights to Spanish speakers.

Short-Answer Question

Directions: Base your answer to question 5 on the graph below and on your knowledge of social studies.

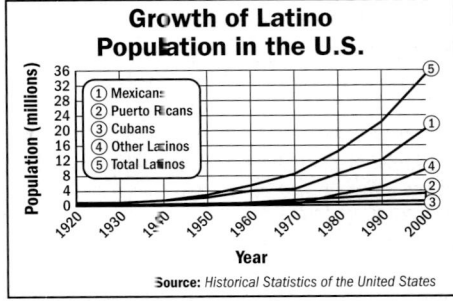

Growth of Latino Population in the U.S.

① Mexicans ② Puerto Ricans ③ Cubans ④ Other Latinos ⑤ Total Latinos

Source: Historical Statistics of the United States

5. Why have Latinos experienced a growing political influence in recent years?

Review the Essential Questions

6. **Essay** How did political, student, and labor leaders respond to different groups' demands for more rights and opportunities?

To help you write your essay, review your answers to the Essential Questions in the section reviews and the chapter Foldables Study Organizer. Your essay should include:
- names of political, student, and labor leaders during the 1940s, 1950s, and 1960s;
- names of organizations formed to meet the demands of struggling Americans; and
- descriptions of the interaction between leaders and organizations.

GO ON

Review the Essential Questions

6. If students completed their Foldables correctly, they should be able to describe responses to the demands of different groups for more rights and opportunities. Students may mention legislation that was passed to address these issues (for example, the Civil Rights Act of 1964), student sit-ins that resulted in the desegregation of lunch counters, and the formation of the United Farm Workers Union to address poor working conditions for migrant farmworkers. **18.C.3a**

History ONLINE

For additional test practice, use **Self-Check Quizzes**—Chapter 28 at glencoe.com.

Chapter 28 Assessment

Document-Based Questions

Directions: Analyze the documents and answer the short-answer questions that follow.

Document 1

James Baldwin wrote about the experiences of African Americans in novels such as *Go Tell It on the Mountain* and *If Beale Street Could Talk*.

> I love America more than any other country in the world, and, exactly for this reason, I insist on the right to criticize her perpetually.

Source: James Baldwin, "Notes of a Native Son"

7. What were two major reasons that Americans like James Baldwin criticized the United States?

Document 2

President Kennedy made the following remark in a speech given on May 18, 1963.

> Liberty without learning is always in peril, and learning without liberty is always in vain.

Source: John F. Kennedy Presidential Library & Museum

8. Which of Kennedy's proposals for the New Frontier addressed the concerns in this quote?

Document 3

Malcolm X explained his view on racism in a speech entitled, "Prospects for Freedom in 1965."

> My religion makes me against all forms of racism. It keeps me from judging any man by the color of his skin. It teaches me to judge him by his deeds and conscious behavior. And it teaches me to be for the rights of all human beings.

Source: John Bartlett, *Familiar Quotations*

9. Compare the views Malcolm X held before 1965 with the view expressed in the quote.

Document 4

> **Voter Registration Before and After the Voting Rights Act**
>
> 7% of African American adults registered to vote in Mississippi before passage of the Voting Rights Act of 1965
>
> ▼
>
> 67% of African American adults in Mississippi registered to vote in 1969
>
> 70% of white adults registered to vote nationwide in 1964
>
> ▼
>
> 90% of white adults registered to vote nationwide in 1969

Source: *TIME* magazine

10. Do you think the Voting Rights Act was strongly enforced in Mississippi? Why or why not?

Document 5

Betty Friedan wrote about the effects of a high birthrate.

> By the end of the fifties, the United States birthrate was overtaking India's. . . . Where once [college women] had two children, now they had four, five, six. Women who had once wanted careers were now making careers out of having babies.

Source: Betty Friedan, *The Feminine Mystique*

11. Did Friedan approve or disapprove of the trend she described in this quote? Explain.

12. Descriptive Writing Using the information from the five documents and your knowledge of social studies, write an essay in which you:

- describe a vision of American life that all the people quoted would approve of; and

- compare this vision with your observations of life in the United States today.

9. Before 1965, Malcolm X wanted to achieve justice for African Americans by separating from whites. In the quote, he expresses a desire to achieve justice for all human beings. **16.A.3b**

10. Students should explain that the act was strongly enforced because the percentage of African Americans registering to vote increased greatly after the act was passed. **16.A.3b**

11. Friedan disapproved of the trend toward more babies. Her book *The Feminine Mystique* focused on women who hoped for career opportunities in order to become more than housewives and mothers. **16.A.3b**

12. Students should use the quotes to describe a vision of American life promising equality and civil rights for all. Their comparisons should be based on their observations of American life today. **18.C.3a**

History ONLINE

Have students visit the Web site at glencoe.com to review Chapter 28 and take the Self-Check Quiz.

Need Extra Help?

Have students refer to the pages listed if they miss any of the questions.

Need Extra Help?												
If you missed questions...	1	2	3	4	5	6	7	8	9	10	11	12
Go to page...	876	883	888	897	896–897	875–879	875	882	890	889	895	884–898

Document-Based Questions

7. Students should note that Baldwin wrote novels about the African American experience in order to expose discrimination. He represents people who valued the United States, but called for an end to racial segregation and discrimination. **16.A.3b**

8. Kennedy proposed federal funds for education. **18.C.3a**

Chapter Planning Guide

29

Key to Ability Levels
BL Below level **AL** Above level
OL On level **ELL** English Language Learners

Key to Teaching Resources
Print Material DVD
CD-ROM Transparency

Levels					Resources	Chapter Opener	Section 1	Section 2	Section 3	Section 4	Chapter Assess
BL	OL	AL	ELL								
				FOCUS							
BL	OL	AL	ELL	Daily Test Practice Transparencies		29–1	29–2	29–3	29–4	
				TEACH							
	OL	AL		Geography and History Activity, URB				p. 87		
BL	OL		ELL	Time Line Skills Activity, URB		p. 90				
BL	OL	AL	ELL	Writing Skills Activity, URB		p. 79				
	OL	AL		American Literature Readings, URB			p. 9			
BL	OL	AL	ELL	Content Vocabulary Activity, URB		p. 73	p. 73	p. 73	p. 73	
BL	OL	AL	ELL	Academic Vocabulary Activity, URB		p. 75	p. 75	p. 75	p. 75	
BL	OL		ELL	Social Studies Skills Activity, URB					p. 81	
BL	OL	AL	ELL	Differentiated Instruction Activity, URB					p. 83	
BL	OL	AL	ELL	Critical Thinking Skills Activity, URB					p. 85	
BL	OL	AL	ELL	Linking Past and Present Activity, URB					p. 89	
	OL	AL		Primary Source Readings, URB			p. 77			
BL	OL	AL	ELL	School-to-Home Connection Activity, URB		p. 91	p. 91	p. 91	p. 91	
BL	OL		ELL	Guided Reading Activity, URB*		p. 95	p. 96	p. 97	p. 98	
		AL		Enrichment Activity, URB			p. 11			
BL	OL		ELL	Reading Essentials and Note-Taking Guide*		p. 325	p. 328	p. 331	p. 334	
BL	OL	AL	ELL	Lesson Transparencies		29A	29A	29A, 29B	29A, 29B, 29C	
		AL		Supreme Court Case Studies					pp. 107, 109	
BL	OL	AL	ELL	Outline Map Resource Book	pp. 6, 24, 30, 52					
	OL	AL		American Art and Architecture Transparencies, Strategies, and Activities					38	

Note: Please refer to the *Unit Resource Book: Challenges at Home and Abroad* for this chapter's URB materials.

* Also available in Spanish

Levels BL	OL	AL	ELL		Resources	Chapter Opener	Section 1	Section 2	Section 3	Section 4	Chapter Assess
					TEACH *(continued)*						
BL	OL	AL	ELL		NGS US Desk Map		✓	✓	✓	✓	
BL	OL	AL	ELL		American Literature Library		✓	✓	✓	✓	
BL	OL	AL	ELL		Writer's Guidebook		✓	✓	✓	✓	
	OL	AL			American History Primary Source Document Library CD-ROM		✓	✓	✓	✓	✓
BL	OL	AL	ELL		American Music: Hits Through History	✓	✓	✓	✓	✓	
BL	OL	AL	ELL		StudentWorks™ Plus CD	✓	✓	✓	✓	✓	✓
	OL	AL			Section Spotlight Videos		✓	✓	✓	✓	
BL	OL	AL	ELL		Writing Process Transparencies		✓	✓	✓	✓	✓
BL	OL	AL	ELL		Presentation Plus! With MindJogger CheckPoint CD	✓	✓	✓	✓	✓	✓
					ASSESS						
BL	OL	AL	ELL		Quizzes and Tests		p. 287	p. 288	p. 289	p. 290	pp. 291, 293, 295
BL	OL	AL	ELL		Authentic Assessment With Rubrics			p. 29			
BL	OL	AL	ELL		Standardized Test Practice						p. 57
BL	OL	AL	ELL		*ExamView®* Assessment Suite CD-ROM*		29–1	29–2	29–3	29–4	Ch. 29
					CLOSE						
BL			ELL		Reteaching Activity, URB*		p. 93	p. 93	p. 93	p. 93	p. 93
BL	OL		ELL		Reading and Study Skills Foldables Activity	p. 106	p. 106	p. 106	p. 106	p. 106	p. 106
BL	OL	AL	ELL		*The American Journey* in Graphic Novel				p. 185		
BL			ELL		Reading Strategies and Activities for the Social Studies Classroom		✓	✓	✓	✓	
BL	OL	AL	ELL		Graphic Organizer Transparencies & Strategies		✓	✓	✓	✓	

TeacherWorks *Plus*
All-In-One Planner and Resource Center

- Interactive Lesson Planner
- Interactive Teacher Edition
- Fully editable blackline masters
- Section Spotlight Videos Launch
- Differentiated Lesson Plans
- Printable reports of daily assignments
- Standards Tracking System

Professional Development Resources

- Strategies for Success
- Building Academic Vocabulary
- Success With English Learners DVD
- Differentiated Instruction Strategies DVD
- Teaching Literacy Strategies in Social Studies DVD
- Assessment DVD
- Standards-Based Instruction DVD

Using the Primary Source Document Library

Searching by Keyword, Author, or Title

Technology Product

Glencoe's *American History Primary Source Document Library CD-ROM* includes more than 200 primary source documents. The documents provide new sources of knowledge that encourage students to think critically about history and historical concepts. *The American History Primary Source Document Library* allows you to

- perform a search based on key words, author names, or titles of documents;
- choose documents from the results list to read and/or listen to;
- utilize **Teaching Strategies, Questions/Answers**, and **Blackline Masters** resources in conjunction with the primary source document to maximize student learning.

Steps

- After launching **Primary Source Document Library CD-ROM**, choose the **Search** button.
- Click on Search icon (binoculars and document) in the toolbar and enter key words.
- Make a selection from the list of documents.
- Review the **Document Overview** and **Guided Reading Questions** at the top of each document.
- Click on the **User's Guide and Teaching Strategies** link. Select **To the Teacher** and **Teaching Strategies** for suggestions on using the primary source documents.
- Select **Questions/Activities** and **Blackline Masters** for worksheets and organizers.

History ONLINE at glencoe.com

	Student	Teacher	Parent
Media Center			
• Student Edition Audio	●		
• Spanish Summaries	●		
• Section Spotlight Videos	●	●	
Social Studies Online Learning Center			
Classroom Tools			
• Multi-Language Glossaries	●	●	●
• Teaching Today		●	
• TIME Current Events	●	●	●
• Beyond the Textbook	●	●	
***The American Journey* Online Learning Center**			
• Study-to-Go™	●	●	●
• Study Central™	●	●	●
• Chapter Overview	●	●	
• Concepts in Motion	●	●	
• ePuzzles and Games	●	●	
• Literature Connections	●	●	
• Online Student Edition	●	●	●
• Self-Check Quizzes	●	●	●
• Student Web Activities	●	●	
• Vocabulary eFlashcards	●	●	
• Web Activity Lesson Plans	●	●	●
• Vocabulary PuzzleMaker	●	●	●

READING SUPPORT FROM JAMESTOWN EDUCATION

- **Timed Readings Plus in Social Studies** helps students increase their reading rate and fluency while maintaining comprehension. The 400-word passages are similar to those found on state and national assessments.

- **Reading in the Content Area: Social Studies** concentrates on six essential reading skills that help students better comprehend what they read. The book includes 75 high-interest nonfiction passages written at increasing levels of difficulty.

- **Reading Social Studies** includes strategic reading instruction and vocabulary support in Social Studies content for ELLs and native speakers of English.

- **Content Vocabulary Workout** (Grades 6–8) accelerates reading comprehension through focused vocabulary development. Social Studies content vocabulary comes from the glossaries of Glencoe's Middle School Social Studies texts.

www.jamestowneducation.com

NATIONAL GEOGRAPHIC

Index to National Geographic Magazine:

The following articles relate to this chapter:

- **"The Heroes, The Healing: Military Medicine From the Front Lines to the Home Front,"** Neil Shea, December 2006.

- **"Weapons of Mass Destruction,"** Lewis M. Simons, November 2002.

National Geographic Society Products

To order the following, call National Geographic at 1-800-368-2728:

National Geographic Atlas of the World (Book)

Access National Geographic's dynamic MapMachine Web site and other geography resources at:

www.nationalgeographic.com

www.nationalgeographic.com/mapmachine

Reading List Generator CD-ROM · **GLENCOE BOOKLINK 3**

Use this database to search more than 30,000 titles to create a customized reading list for your students.

- Reading lists can be organized by students' reading level, author, genre, theme, or area of interest.
- The database provides Degrees of Reading Power™ (DRP) and Lexile™ readability scores for all selections.
- A brief summary of each selection is included.

Leveled reading suggestions for this chapter:

For students at a Grade 6 reading level:
- *Stop the Sun,* by Gary Paulsen

For students at a Grade 7 reading level:
- *Red Scarf Girl: A Memoir of the Cultural Revolution,* by Ji-li Jiang

For students at a Grade 8 reading level:
- *My Life as an Astronaut,* by Alan Bean

For students at a Grade 9 reading level:
- *Fidel Castro: Leader of Cuba's Revolution,* by Tom Gibb

For students at a Grade 10 reading level:
- *The First Moon Landing,* by Sabrina Crewe and Dale Anderson

The following videotape programs are available from Glencoe as supplements to the chapter:

- **Richard Nixon: Man and President** (ISBN 1-56-501742-0)

- **Vietnam: A Soldier's Diary** (ISBN 0-76-700772-7)

To order, call Glencoe at 1-800-334-7344. To find classroom resources to accompany many of these videos, check the following home pages:

A&E Television: www.aetv.com

The History Channel: www.history.com

Chapter Objectives

After studying this chapter, students will be able to:

- Describe the key foreign policy challenges during the Kennedy administration.
- Explain how and why America got involved in the war in Vietnam.
- Discuss the effects of the Vietnam War on the political and social climate of the United States.
- Explain how President Nixon removed the United States from the Vietnam War.

Motivating Activity

Analyzing Students will learn that American public opinion was sharply divided over the Vietnam War. As American involvement increased, so did opposition to the war. When the soldiers returned home, their relatives, like those of Lieutenant Colonel Stirm, were overjoyed to see them. However, the rest of the nation paid little attention. Unlike World War II, there was no hero's welcome for returning Vietnam veterans. **Ask: Why do you think Vietnam veterans did not return to joyous public celebrations?** *(The war had become unpopular, and it did not result in a clear victory.)* **OL**

Previewing the Essential Questions

As you begin teaching each section, use these questions and activities to help students focus on the Essential Questions.

Chapter 29
The Vietnam Era 1960–1975

After spending five years as a prisoner of war in North Vietnam, Air Force Lt. Col. Robert Stirm is reunited with his family.

PRESIDENTS
U.S. Events
World Events

1960 ───── 1964

★ 1961
Berlin Wall erected

★ 1962
Cuban missile crisis erupts

JOHN F. KENNEDY

LYNDON B. JOHNSON

★ 1964
• Gulf of Tonkin resolution passes
• Johnson elected president

★ 1965
U.S. sends troops to Vietnam

1966 ★
Mao Zedong launches Cultural Revolution

902   Chapter 29

Section 1

Kennedy's Foreign Policy Ask: How would you react if you learned that another nation had missiles aimed at the United States? *(Possible responses: shock, fear, desire for government to do something about it)* Point out that in Section 1, students will learn how President Kennedy reacted to Soviet missiles in Cuba and to other foreign policy challenges. **OL**

Section 2

War in Vietnam Ask: Why do you think America's leaders viewed a Communist takeover of Vietnam as a threat? *(They feared that if Vietnam fell to communism, other nations of the region would fall as well, threatening world security.)* Point out that Section 2 explores the reasons the United States became involved in Vietnam and how that involvement grew. **OL**

Section 1: Kennedy's Foreign Policy

Essential Question What were the key foreign policy challenges the United States faced during the Kennedy administration?

Section 2: War in Vietnam

Essential Question How and why did America involve itself in the war in Vietnam?

Section 3: The Vietnam Years at Home

Essential Question How did the Vietnam War affect the political and social climate in the United States?

Section 4: Nixon and Vietnam

Essential Question How did President Nixon remove the United States from the Vietnam War?

History ONLINE
Chapter Overview Visit glencoe.com and click on Chapter 29—Chapter Overviews to preview chapter information.

FOLDABLES Study Organizer

Organizing Information Make this Foldable to help organize what you learn about foreign policy challenges during the Vietnam years.

Step 1 Fold the sides of a piece of paper into the middle to make a shutterfold.

Step 2 Cut each flap at the midpoint to form four tabs.

Step 3 Label the tabs as shown.

Bay of Pigs | Berlin Wall
Cuban Missile Crisis | Vietnam Conflict

Reading and Writing As you read the chapter, list key people, events, and outcomes for each of these foreign policy issues.

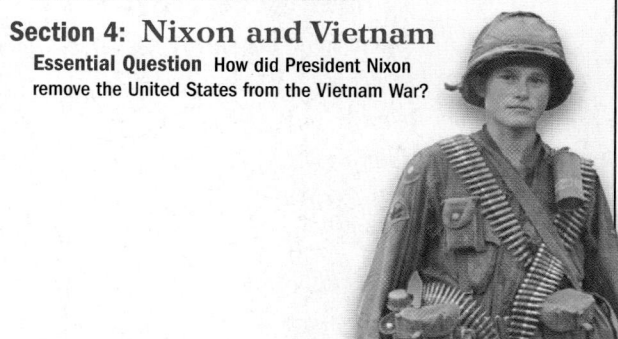

American soldier equipped for battle ▶

Introducing Chapter 29

Time Line Activity

If you have not already done so, have students review the time line. **Ask:** What years are covered in this chapter? *(1960–1975)* Which president sent U.S. troops to Vietnam? *(Lyndon B. Johnson)* Did the Vietnam War end when the American troops left? *(no)* About how much longer did the war last? *(about another two years)*

FOLDABLES Study Organizer **Dinah Zike's Foldables**

Purpose This Foldable helps students organize what they learn about foreign policy challenges during the Vietnam years. The completed Foldable will help them prepare for assessment.

More Foldables activities for this chapter can be found in *Dinah Zike's Reading and Study Skills Foldables.*

History ONLINE
Introduce students to chapter content and key terms by having them access the **Chapter Overview** at glencoe.com.

1968 ★ Martin Luther King, Jr., assassinated

1968 Robert Kennedy assassinated; Nixon elected president

 RICHARD M. NIXON

★ **1969** Neil Armstrong becomes first human on the moon

★ **1973** Last U.S. troops leave Vietnam

1968 — **1972** — **1976**

★ **1967** Arab-Israeli Six-Day War fought

1971 ★ Idi Amin seizes power in Uganda

★ **1972** 11 Israeli athletes killed at Munich Olympic Games

★ **1975** Vietnam War ends after fall of Saigon

Section 3

The Vietnam Years at Home Ask: How would you feel if you were required to go to war while other people your age were excused? *(Students might suggest that this policy is unfair.)* Tell students that in Section 3, they will learn about the military draft and about the growing antiwar protests in the United States. **OL**

Section 4

Nixon and Vietnam Ask: Why would loss of public support for the war influence President Nixon to get America out of Vietnam? *(In a democracy, political leaders serve the people. The party in power must act according to the people's wishes or be voted out of office.)* Explain that Section 4 discusses America's rocky exit from Vietnam. **OL**

Section 1

Focus

Kennedy's Foreign Policy

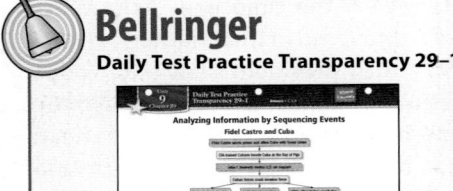

Bellringer
Daily Test Practice Transparency 29–1

Reading Guide
Answers to Graphic:
teachers; health care workers; advisers in farming, industry, and government

Section Spotlight Video

To learn more about challenges in foreign relations during the Kennedy administration, watch the Section Spotlight Video "Kennedy's Foreign Policy."

Essential Question
What were the key foreign policy challenges the United States faced during the Kennedy administration?

Reading Guide

Content Vocabulary
guerrilla warfare (p. 905)   executive order (p. 906)
flexible response (p. 905)   blockade (p. 908)

Academic Vocabulary
respond (p. 905)   occur (p. 907)

Key People and Events
Fidel Castro (p. 906)
Bay of Pigs (p. 907)
Berlin Wall (p. 907)
Cuban missile crisis (p. 908)

Reading Strategy
Taking Notes On a diagram like the one below, note the different areas of work in which Peace Corps volunteers were involved.

Peace Corps Work

ILLINOIS STANDARDS
The American Journey

14.E.3 Compare the basic principles of the United States and its international interests (e.g., territory, environment, trade, use of technology).
16.A.3c Identify the differences between historical fact and interpretation.
17.C.3a Explain how human activity is affected by geographic factors.
17.D.3b Explain how interactions of geographic factors have shaped present conditions.

American Diary

"In the long history of the world, only a few generations have been granted the role of defending freedom in its hour of maximum danger. I do not shrink from this responsibility—I welcome it." Although President Kennedy talked of approaching this responsibility with "energy" and "devotion," events unfolding around the world—in Cuba, Eastern Europe, and Vietnam—would challenge his determination. The new president and the nation soon faced a series of crises.

—from Kennedy's Inaugural Address

President Kennedy called the green beret worn by one of the nation's special military forces "a symbol of excellence, a badge of courage, a mark of distinction in the fight for freedom."

Resource Manager

R Reading Strategies	C Critical Thinking	D Differentiated Instruction	W Writing Support	S Skill Practice
Teacher Edition • Previewing, p. 905 • Inferring, p. 906 **Additional Resources** • Guid. Read., URB p. 95 • Content Vocab., URB p. 73 • Academic Vocab., URB p. 75 • Read. Ess., p. 325	**Teacher Edition** • Making Inferences, p. 905 • Deter. Cause & Effect, p. 906 • Analyzing, p. 907 **Additional Resources** • Quizzes and Tests, p. 287	**Teacher Edition** • Visual/Spatial, p. 907 • Auditory/Musical, p. 908 **Additional Resources** • School-to-Home, URB p. 91 • Reteaching Act., URB p. 93	**Teacher Edition** • Expository Writing, p. 909 **Additional Resources** • Writ. Skills, URB p. 79	**Teacher Edition** • Using Anal. Skills, p. 906 • Reading a Map, p. 908 **Additional Resources** • Daily Test Pract. Transp. 29-1 • Time Line Skills, URB p. 90 • Lesson Transp. 29A

New Directions

Main Idea President John F. Kennedy sought new ways to deal with the challenges and fears of the Cold War.

History and You Have you ever heard the phrase "winning hearts and minds"? It means convincing people to support you rather than just forcing them to obey. Read on to learn how the United States used "good works" to convince the world's poor countries to reject communism.

• •

When Kennedy became president in 1961, America's dangerous rivalry with the Soviets continued to be a major challenge. As a result, the new president had to devote much of his energy in foreign policy to guiding the nation through the deepening Cold War. President Kennedy continued the anti-Communist foreign policy begun under Presidents Truman and Eisenhower. In pursuing that policy, though, Kennedy tried some new approaches.

During the presidential campaign, Kennedy led Americans to believe that the nation had fewer nuclear missiles than the Soviet

Union. As president, Kennedy increased spending on nuclear arms. At the same time, he tried to convince Nikita Khrushchev, the Soviet leader, to agree to a ban on nuclear testing.

Strength Through Flexibility

Kennedy also worked to improve America's ability to **respond**—or reply with action—to threats abroad. In certain areas of the world, Communist groups fought to take control of their nations' governments. Many of these groups received aid from the Soviet Union. They employed **guerrilla warfare,** or fighting with small bands of soldiers who use tactics such as sudden ambushes.

The United States needed a new approach for fighting guerrilla wars. Kennedy introduced a plan called **flexible response,** to provide help to nations fighting Communist movements. This plan relied on special military units trained to fight guerrilla wars. One of these units was the Special Forces, known as the Green Berets. The Special Forces provided the president with troops that were ready to fight guerrilla warfare anywhere around the world.

Primary Source / U.S.–Soviet Relations

In a letter to Premier Nikita Khrushchev of the Soviet Union, President Kennedy expressed the need for direct communication between the leaders. "I think we should recognize, in honesty to each other, that there are problems on which we may not be able to agree."

Kennedy suggested a "hot line" to communicate quickly and directly between the United States and the Soviet Union in times of crisis. The original hot line was a teletypewriter. The hot line today uses two satellite systems and an undersea cable link. The American end of the hot line is located in the Pentagon, the headquarters of the U.S. Department of Defense.

Teletype used for hot line ▶

Critical Thinking

Speculating In what ways might use of the hot line lessen a crisis?

Teach
• • • • • • • • • • •

R Reading Strategy

Previewing Have students read the headings, subheadings, and feature titles in this section. **Ask:** What nations will be part of the foreign policy challenges discussed in this section? *(Soviet Union, Cuba, Germany)* **BL**

C Critical Thinking

Making Inferences Ask: Why do you think Kennedy wanted Americans to believe that the United States had fewer nuclear missiles than the Soviets? *(possibly to gain support for increased spending on nuclear arms, strengthening his negotiating position with Khrushchev)* **OL**

Primary Source

Critical Thinking Answer
The hot line provides a way to make contact quickly in a crisis and to talk things over before a misunderstanding results in war.

Hands-On Chapter Project
Step 1

Broadcasting the News

Step 1: Researching a News Story Students will research an important news story of the Vietnam Era.

Essential Question: What were the key foreign policy challenges the United States faced during the Kennedy administration?

Directions Organize students into small groups. Explain that they are members of a television news station. Have each group select one of these important stories: the Cuban missile crisis, the moon landing, the Gulf of Tonkin Resolution, the Tet offensive, the assassination of Martin Luther King, Jr., or Robert Kennedy, the protests at Kent State or Jackson State, or the Pentagon Papers.

Have students research their story to gather facts and images. Explain that they will prepare the story for a news broadcast.

Determining Cause and Effect As a class, discuss how the Cold War climate led to foreign policy challenges in the 1960s. **OL**

(Chapter Project continued in Section 2)

C Critical Thinking

Determining Cause and Effect Ask: How was poverty in Latin America related to the spread of communism? *(Communist promises of economic equality would appeal to people living in poverty, creating support for a change to a Communist government.)* OL

R Reading Strategy

Inferring Ask: How was the Peace Corps expected to slow the spread of communism? *(by giving aid to the poor around the world)* BL

S Skill Practice

Using Analytical Skills Ask: Why did the rise of Castro seem like a threat to the United States? *(Castro's government was Communist, and Cuba is located close to the United States.)* OL

✓ Reading Check Answer: to aid economic growth in Latin America, which would make Communist promises of economic equality less attractive there

Additional Support

Strength Through Aid

C President Kennedy understood that the poverty in Latin America, Asia, and Africa made the Communist promises of economic equality seem attractive. He decided to provide aid to countries in those areas to counteract the appeal of communism. For example, to help Latin America's economic growth, Kennedy set up a 10-year development plan called the Alliance for Progress.

R In 1961 the president signed an **executive order,** or presidential directive, creating an organization called the Peace Corps. Peace Corps volunteers worked in other countries as teachers, health workers, and advisers in farming, industry, and government. Volunteers spent two years in countries that had asked for assistance. By 1963 some 5,000 volunteers were working in more than 40 countries around the world. Today, the Peace Corps is still active and remains one of Kennedy's most lasting legacies.

✓ Reading Check Describing What was the purpose of the Alliance for Progress?

Cold War Confrontations

Main Idea The Kennedy administration responded to Cold War crises in Cuba and Berlin.

History and You How do you think the U.S. government should deal with threats from other countries? Read to learn how the Kennedy administration dealt with Soviet threats in various parts of the world during the early 1960s.

In 1961, just a few months after taking office, President Kennedy had to deal with a foreign policy crisis in Latin America. That same year, tensions between the United States and the Soviet Union arose in Europe.

Cuba

S The United States faced a new challenge in Cuba, an island country in the Caribbean Sea. This challenge had begun during the last months of the Eisenhower administration. In January 1959, rebel leader **Fidel Castro** seized power and formed a new Cuban government. He soon set up a Communist dictatorship.

Primary Source | Soviet Influence

Footholds and Fences The United States began to see the influence of communism spreading around the world. The U.S. tried to shut down the threat closest to home with the invasion of the Bay of Pigs in Cuba. Half a world away, the U.S. could only watch as Communist East Germany isolated Democratic West Berlin with a cinder block and barbed wire wall.

Invasion of Cuba CIA-trained Cuban exiles landed at the Bay of Pigs on April 17, 1961. Within two days, Cuban President Fidel Castro's troops had captured more than 1,000 of the exiles and stopped the attempt at overthrowing his government.

◄ Exiles taken prisoner

Armed militia of the Castro government ►

The Berlin Wall ►

Activity: Interdisciplinary Connection

Civics Through today's Peace Corps, American volunteers help developing nations around the world. Have students visualize working as a Peace Corps volunteer. Have them go to the Peace Corps Web site, www.peacecorps.gov, and learn about current Peace Corps projects in different nations. Ask students to choose one of these developing nations where they would most like to serve. Then have them write a letter of application to the Peace Corps. In the letter, they should discuss the needs of the country and identify the skills that would qualify them to be of help. OL

Cuba also became an ally of the Soviet Union. These actions worried many Americans because Cuba lies only 90 miles (145 km) south of Florida.

Late in Eisenhower's presidency, the Central Intelligence Agency (CIA) forged a plan to overthrow Castro. The CIA recruited Cuban refugees who had settled in the United States. The plan called for them to land in Cuba and spark an uprising that would overthrow Castro's rule. When Kennedy became president, he learned about the plan and had doubts about it. However, he accepted the advice of military advisers and the CIA and allowed the plan to go forward.

On April 17, 1961, about 1,500 CIA-trained Cuban exiles landed at the **Bay of Pigs** on the south coast of Cuba. Many blunders occurred, and at a crucial moment, Kennedy refused to provide American air support. Within days Cuban forces crushed the invasion and captured the survivors.

The Bay of Pigs embarrassed Kennedy, who took the blame for the failure. The disaster had three effects. First, Kennedy never again completely trusted military and intelligence advice. Second, nations in Latin America lost trust in Kennedy. Third, Soviet premier Khrushchev concluded that Kennedy was not a strong leader and could be bullied.

The Berlin Wall

Although 16 years had passed since the end of World War II, the wartime Allies had still not settled the status of Germany. West Germany became a full member of the Western alliance, and the Soviet Union continued to control East Germany.

The location of Berlin—fully within East Germany—posed special problems. American, British, and French troops still remained in the western part of the city, and they sometimes had difficulty getting into West Berlin and maintaining control there. Meanwhile a steady flow of people fled to West Berlin from Communist East Berlin, hoping to escape economic hardship and find freedom.

At a June 1961 summit conference in Vienna, Austria, Premier Khrushchev told President Kennedy that the West must move out of Berlin, and he insisted on an agreement by the end of the year. Kennedy rejected Khrushchev's demand. To emphasize the West's right to stay in West Berlin, the United States later sent more troops to the city.

Later that summer, a large number of East Germans fled to the West. On August 13, the East German government, with Soviet backing, closed the border between East and West Berlin and built a wall of concrete blocks with barbed wire along it. The Soviets posted armed guards along the wall to stop more East Germans from fleeing to the West. The **Berlin Wall** cut communications between the two parts of the city.

The Western Allies remained in West Berlin. They could do little, however, to stop the building of the wall, which came to symbolize Communist repression.

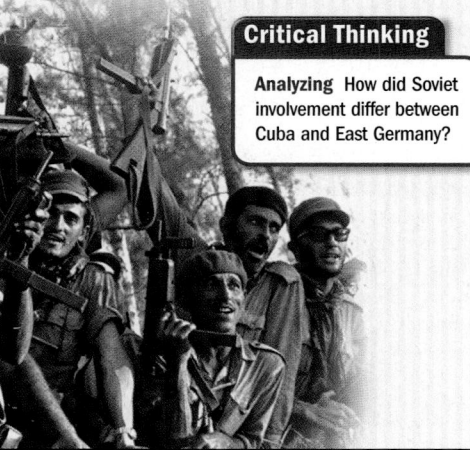

August 1961 To stop the flow of skilled workers, professionals, and intellectuals from leaving East Germany, the Communist country began building the Berlin Wall on August 13. By the 1980s, it had been made taller and wider and stretched 28 miles (45 km) through the middle of Berlin and another 75 miles (120 km) around West Berlin.

Critical Thinking

Analyzing How did Soviet involvement differ between Cuba and East Germany?

Reading Check **Explaining** What kind of government did Fidel Castro establish in Cuba?

The Vietnam Era **Chapter 29** 907

D **Differentiated Instruction**

Visual/Spatial Draw a cause-and-effect diagram on the board, beginning with "Castro seizes power in Cuba" and ending with "Bay of Pigs invasion." Have students identify cause-and-effect relationships during this period. **ELL**

C **Critical Thinking**

Analyzing Ask: How do you think Khrushchev's view of Kennedy after the Bay of Pigs invasion influenced negotiations on Berlin? (*Viewing Kennedy as weak, Khrushchev probably tried to bully him on Berlin.*) **OL**

Primary Source

Critical Thinking Answer
The Soviets controlled East Germany. In Cuba, the Soviets allied with the Castro regime but did not control it directly.

Reading Check **Answer:** Communist

Differentiated Instruction

Leveled Activities

BL **Reading Essentials and Note-Taking Guide, p. 325**

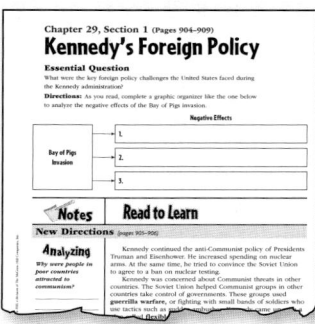

Chapter 29, Section 1 (Pages 904–909)
Kennedy's Foreign Policy

OL **Writing Skills Activity, URB p. 79**

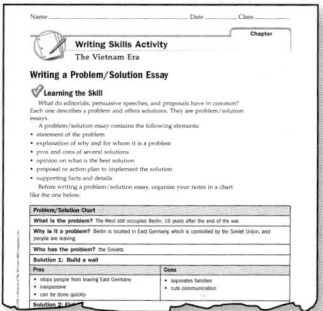

Writing Skills Activity
The Vietnam Era

ELL **Academic Vocabulary Activity, URB p. 75**

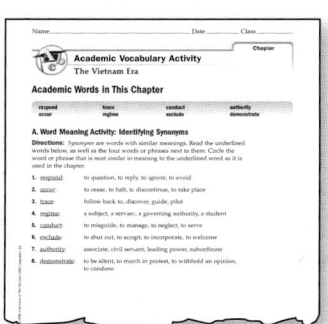

Academic Vocabulary Activity
The Vietnam Era

S Skill Practice

Reading a Map Refer students to the map. **Ask:** What parts of the United States could be reached by missiles launched from Cuba? *(all of the United States except the most northwestern region, Alaska, and Hawaii)* **OL**

D Differentiated Instruction

Auditory/Musical Find Kennedy's dramatic speech from October 22, 1962, on the Internet. Play the 17-minute speech for the class. Then lead a discussion about Kennedy's use of Khrushchev's own words, Kennedy's appeal to the Cuban people, and the emotions Americans must have felt upon hearing this chilling speech. **OL**

Chance & Error in History

Critical Thinking Answer

The United States would have tried to sink Soviet ships and destroy missile sites. Had this effort failed, the Soviets would have established bases for attacking nearly all of the United States. Even if the bases were destroyed, these actions might have set off a war.

Differentiated Instruction

Chance & Error in History

What if the Soviets Had Ignored the Blockade?

Just days after President Kennedy ordered a U.S. blockade to prevent Soviet deliveries of missiles to Cuba, Soviet ships abruptly turned away. When the Soviets offered a deal, Kennedy took it. The Soviets would withdraw their missiles in exchange for a U.S. pledge to never invade Cuba. While it seemed like a victory at the time, it left a Communist government intact just miles from the U.S. coastline. The humiliation of giving in also prompted the Soviets to begin the largest peacetime military buildup in history.

Critical Thinking

Theorizing What might have happened if the Soviets had chosen to ignore the blockade and steamed forward to Cuba?

Maps in Motion See StudentWorks™ Plus or glencoe.com.

The Cuban Missile Crisis

Main Idea The United States forced the Soviet Union to withdraw Soviet missiles that had been placed in Cuba.

History and You Have you ever been in a situation that was so scary, you thought that you would never get through it alive? Read to learn how another crisis in Cuba left Americans and people in many other nations wondering whether the world would survive.

The most dangerous Cold War dispute between the Americans and Soviets came in 1962. Once again the dispute involved Cuba. In mid-October 1962, an American spy plane flying over Cuba made a disturbing discovery. Photographs revealed that the Soviets were building launching sites for nuclear missiles. These missiles could easily reach the United States in a matter of minutes.

For the next week, President Kennedy met secretly with advisers to determine how to deal with the **Cuban missile crisis.** They explored several options, including invading Cuba and bombing the missile sites. New spy photographs showed the bases nearing completion much faster than expected. Kennedy and his advisers needed to reach a decision quickly.

On October 22, President Kennedy, speaking on national television, revealed the "secret, swift, and extraordinary buildup" of Soviet missiles in Cuba. Kennedy ordered the navy to **blockade,** or close off, Cuba until the Soviets removed the missiles. He threatened to destroy any Soviet ship that tried to break through the blockade and reach the island. The president declared: "It shall be the policy of this nation to regard any nuclear missile launched from Cuba against any nation in the Western Hemisphere as an attack by the Soviet Union on the United States."

United States Conflict With Cuba (1959–1962)

Objective: To analyze a time line on United States–Cuban relations

Focus: Review why relations between the United States and Cuba were strained.

Teach: Have students read the background information, review the time line, and answer the questions.

Assess: Ask student volunteers to read their answers aloud.

Close: Discuss why Cuba's location was a critical issue in its relations with the United States.

Differentiated Instruction Strategies

BL Have students circle important time line dates and names before they answer the questions.

AL Stage a debate between students on whether the United States was ethical in its dealings with Cuba.

ELL Ask students to define, in their own words, the following terms: "jeopardized," "confrontation," and "underscored."

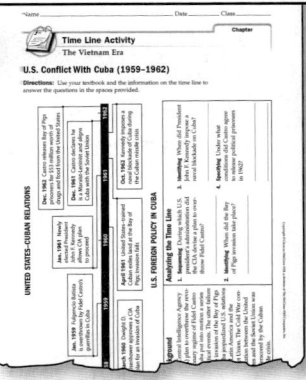

Time Line Skills Activity, URB p. 90

The United States would respond, he warned, with a nuclear attack against the Soviet Union.

As the two superpowers neared the brink of nuclear war, people all over the world waited nervously. After five agonizing days, the Soviet ships turned back. Soviet leaders also agreed to withdraw their missiles from Cuba. The United States agreed not to invade Cuba. Nuclear war had been avoided.

Having come so close to nuclear disaster, the two nations worked to establish better relations. In the summer of 1963, Kennedy and Khrushchev created the hot line between Moscow and Washington to allow the leaders to communicate instantly in times of crisis. That same summer, the two nations signed a treaty banning nuclear tests aboveground and underwater.

Rivalry in Space

Americans and Soviets continued their rivalry in space. In April 1961, Soviet cosmonaut Yuri Gagarin (guh•GAHR•uhn) became the first person to orbit the Earth. One month later, Alan Shepard, Jr., became the first American to make a spaceflight.

Shortly after Shepard's spaceflight, Kennedy committed the nation to the goal of landing a man on the moon by the end of the decade. He asked Congress for more money for NASA (National Aeronautics and Space Administration), which ran the space program. NASA expanded its launching facility in Florida and built a control center in Houston, Texas.

Astronaut John Glenn thrilled the country in February 1962 when he orbited the Earth in a spacecraft, the first American to do so. An even greater triumph for the space program came on July 20, 1969, with the Apollo project. Awestruck television viewers around the world watched the spacecraft *Eagle* land on the surface of the moon.

Hours later, with millions still watching, astronaut Neil Armstrong took the first human step on the moon and announced: "That's one small step for a man, one giant leap for mankind." By the end of the Apollo project in 1972, 10 more Americans had landed on the moon.

Reading Check **Explaining** How was the Cuban missile crisis resolved?

W **Writing Support**

Expository Writing Tell students to log on to the Web site of the Kennedy Space Center, www.nasa.gov/centers/kennedy/home/index.html. Ask them to search for information about past space missions at the center. Have them write a one-page report about a mission that interests them. The report should include the mission's goals and results. **AL**

Reading Check **Answer:** After Kennedy ordered a blockade of Cuba and warned of nuclear retaliation, Soviet leaders agreed to withdraw their missiles and the United States agreed not to invade Cuba.

Assess

History ONLINE

Study Central™ provides summaries, interactive games, and online graphic organizers to help students review content.

Close

Summarizing On the board, list the foreign policy challenges facing the Kennedy administration as the class identifies them. **OL**

Section 1 Review

History ONLINE
Study Central™ To review this section, go to glencoe.com.

Vocabulary

1. Write a sentence that explains the meaning of each of the following terms: respond, guerrilla warfare, flexible response, executive order, occur, blockade.

Main Ideas

2. Describing What was the relationship between guerrilla warfare and Kennedy's flexible response plan?

3. Explaining Why did the Soviet Union build the Berlin Wall?

4. Summarizing What was the responsibility of NASA?

Critical Thinking

5. Analyzing Re-create the diagram below and identify strategies that the Kennedy administration considered to stop the buildup of missiles in Cuba.

Cuban Missile Crisis

6. Expository Writing Take the role of a recruiter for the Peace Corps. Write a speech that describes the creation and mission of the Peace Corps and encourages people to apply.

Answer the
7. Essential Question
What were the key foreign policy challenges the United States faced during the Kennedy administration?

The Vietnam Era **Chapter 29** **909**

Section 1 Review

Answers

1. Students' sentences should correctly explain the meaning of each term.

2. The flexible response plan was a response to the guerrilla tactics of Communist groups. Under the plan, special military units were trained to fight guerrilla wars.

3. to prevent East Germans from fleeing to the West

4. to run the space program of the United States

5. invade Cuba; bomb the missile sites

6. Students' speeches should emphasize the purpose of the Peace Corps and the benefits of joining.

7. spread of communism around the world; arms race; nuclear testing; Communist government in nearby Cuba; Berlin Wall; Soviet missiles in Cuba; rivalry with the Soviets in space

Focus

Section 2

War in Vietnam

Bellringer
Daily Test Practice Transparency 29–2

Reading Guide
Answers to Graphic:

Eisenhower: believed Vietnam was part of the global struggle against communism; sent supplies and advisers to support South Vietnam; **Kennedy:** shared Eisenhower's belief; sent Special Forces to train and advise; **Johnson:** believed Vietnam was not worth fighting for, but couldn't get out; sent American troops

Section Spotlight Video

Watch the Section Spotlight Video "War in Vietnam" to learn more about the deepening conflict in Southeast Asia.

Resource Manager

Essential Question
How and why did America involve itself in the war in Vietnam?

Reading Guide

Content Vocabulary

escalate (p. 913)   napalm (p. 914)
search-and-destroy   Agent Orange
  mission (p. 914)   (p. 914)

Academic Vocabulary

trace (p. 911)   regime (p. 912)

Key People and Events
Ho Chi Minh (p. 911)
Vietcong (p. 912)
Gulf of Tonkin Resolution (p. 913)

Reading Strategy
Taking Notes On a chart like the one below, identify each president's main philosophy about America's involvement in Vietnam.

President	Philosophy
Eisenhower	
Kennedy	
Johnson	

ILLINOIS STANDARDS
The American Journey

14.D Understand the roles and influences of individuals and interest groups in the political systems of Illinois, the United States and other nations.

14.E Understand United States foreign policy as it relates to other nations and international issues.

14.E.3 Compare the basic principles of the United States and its international interests (e.g., territory, environment, trade, use of technology).

17.A Locate, describe and explain places, regions and features on the Earth.

American Diary

American efforts to stop the spread of communism led to U.S. involvement in Vietnam. President Eisenhower believed that "the loss of all Vietnam, together with Laos on the west and Cambodia in the southwest, would have meant the surrender to Communist enslavement of millions." In the late 1950s, President Eisenhower sent military supplies and advisers to pro-Western South Vietnam in support of its fight against Communist North Vietnam. President Kennedy continued this policy.

—*from American Policy Toward Laos*

Vietnamese women work in a rice field.

R **Reading Strategies**	C **Critical Thinking**	D **Differentiated Instruction**	W **Writing Support**	S **Skill Practice**
Teacher Edition • Identifying, p. 911 • Academic Vocab., p. 913 **Additional Resources** • Guid. Read., URB p. 96 • Content Vocab., URB p. 73 • Academic Vocab., URB p. 75 • Read. Ess., p. 328 • Am. Lit., URB p. 9	**Teacher Edition** • Predicting Consequences, p. 914 • Comparing, p. 915 **Additional Resources** • Quizzes and Tests, p. 288 • Enrichment Act., URB p. 11	**Teacher Edition** • Visual/Spatial, p. 911 • Kinesthetic, p. 912 **Additional Resources** • School-to-Home, URB p. 91 • Reteaching Act., URB p. 93	**Teacher Edition** • Persuasive Writing, p. 912 • Expository Writing, p. 913	**Teacher Edition** • Underst. Prim. Sources, p. 911 • Finding the Main Idea, p. 912 • Ident. Prob. and Sol., p. 914 **Additional Resources** • Daily Test Pract. Transp. 29-2 • Lesson Transp. 29A

The U.S. and Vietnam

Main Idea Vietnam became a divided country as a result of conflict between Communist and non-Communist groups.

History and You What would it be like to live in a country where a civil war was raging? Read to learn how a civil war affected the people of Vietnam.

In the early 1960s, the United States became involved in a fight against the spread of communism in Southeast Asia. The war in Vietnam did not unfold as Americans hoped, however. General Maxwell Taylor, who served as U.S. ambassador to South Vietnam, reflected on the problems of the war years after it had ended:

PRIMARY SOURCE

"First, we didn't know ourselves. We thought that we were going into another Korean war, but this was a different country. Secondly, we didn't know our South Vietnamese allies. We never understood them, and that was another surprise. And we knew even less about North Vietnam."

—from *Vietnam: A History*

Origins of the War

The roots of the Vietnam conflict can be **traced**, or followed, back to World War II, when Japanese forces captured the French colony of Indochina in Southeast Asia. Vietnamese forces led by Communist **Ho Chi Minh** (HOH CHEE MIHN) fought against the Japanese.

When Japan surrendered at the end of World War II, Ho Chi Minh declared Vietnam's independence. The French, however, were unwilling to give up their empire. Their Indochina colony—the present-day nations of Cambodia, Laos, and Vietnam—was among the richest of France's colonies, supplying resources such as rice, rubber, and tin. Ho Chi Minh and his forces fought the French in a long, bloody war, finally defeating the French in 1954 at Dien Bien Phu.

The Geneva Accords

That same year, diplomats from the United States, France, Great Britain, the Soviet Union, China, and Vietnam met in Geneva, Switzerland, to work out a peace agreement. According to the Geneva Accords, Vietnam would be divided temporarily.

When and Where / Indochina in 1959

In 1959 North Vietnam began to deliver supplies to its forces in South Vietnam through a network of paths and roads through the countries of Laos and Cambodia. This network became known as the Ho Chi Minh Trail. ▶

← Ho Chi Minh Trail

Critical Thinking

Explaining According to President Eisenhower, why was it important for the United States to help South Vietnam?

CHAPTER 29
Section 2

Teach

D Differentiated Instruction

Visual/Spatial Direct students' attention to the maps on this page. Tell students to refer to them frequently while they read this section's content. **BL**

S Skill Practice

Understanding Primary Sources Ask: According to Taylor, what did Americans lack that hindered their efforts in Vietnam? (*understanding—of themselves, their allies, and their enemy*) **OL**

R Reading Strategy

Identifying Ask: What two nations fought Ho Chi Minh's forces before American troops got involved? (*Japan, France*) **BL**

Primary Source

Critical Thinking Answer
The loss of Vietnam, Laos, and Cambodia would subject millions of people in the region to enslavement by the Communists.

Hands-On Chapter Project
Step 2

Broadcasting the News

Step 2: Writing the Script Students will begin writing their news script.

Essential Question: How and why did America involve itself in the war in Vietnam?

Directions Have students watch television news broadcasts to see how stories are presented. Instruct the groups to review their research and decide how they will present their stories. Each group member should have a role. Roles might include the news anchor, reporters, people being interviewed, the president, and expert analysts. Have them begin writing the script for their story and planning their visuals. Point out that if the issue is controversial, a good news story should present differing viewpoints. Encourage students to write scripts that will hold viewers' interest.

Identifying Key Issues Ask: What event finally brought the United States fully into the war? (*an alleged attack on American ships in the Gulf of Tonkin*) **OL**

(Chapter Project continued in Section 3)

S Skill Practice

Finding the Main Idea Ask: What actions by the leader of South Vietnam contributed to the rise of the Vietcong? *(Diem refused to hold the agreed-upon elections and cracked down on Communists in the south.)* **OL**

D Differentiated Instruction

Kinesthetic To demonstrate the domino theory, bring in some dominoes. Using the map on the previous page, have students label individual dominoes with the names of the nations of Indochina. Ask them to set up the dominoes with North Vietnam in front, followed by South Vietnam, and then the rest of the labeled dominoes. Lengthen the line with several unlabeled dominoes. Then have students knock over the first domino to topple them all. Have students summarize the domino theory in their own words. **BL**

W Writing Support

Persuasive Writing Have students take the role of President Kennedy and write a paragraph stating his policy for American involvement in Vietnam. Paragraphs should include reasons for this policy. **OL**

Differentiated Instruction

The agreement also stated that Ho Chi Minh's Communist nationalists would control the North. Hanoi served as its capital. Non-Communist forces—supported by the United States—would control the South, with Saigon as the capital. Vietnam would be unified in 1956 after national elections.

Neither the United States nor South Vietnam signed the agreement, but they did not oppose its provisions. At the same time, the U.S. emphasized that it would act if Communist North Vietnam moved aggressively against the South.

In 1955 Ngo Dinh Diem (NGOH DIHN deh•EHM), with American support, became South Vietnam's leader. He refused to hold elections and cracked down on Communists in the South. In response the Communists set up the National Liberation Front (NLF), or the **Vietcong.** In 1959 the Vietcong, on orders from Ho Chi Minh, began a war against the Diem **regime,** or governing authority.

A Growing American Role

The United States had replaced the French as the dominant foreign power in the South in 1955. If Communists took South Vietnam, President Eisenhower once said, the other countries of Southeast Asia would fall to communism like a row of dominoes—one right after the other. This domino theory helped shape American policy in Vietnam for the next 20 years.

To support South Vietnam, the Eisenhower administration sent the country billions of dollars in aid. It also dispatched a few hundred soldiers, who acted as advisers to the South Vietnamese government and army.

Like Eisenhower, President Kennedy saw Vietnam as part of the global struggle against communism. Kennedy sent more Special Forces—the Green Berets—to train and advise South Vietnamese troops. Kennedy also pressured Diem to make reforms that would undercut the appeal of communism.

The Vietnam Conflict 1941-1954

Japanese troops advance into Indochina. ▶

Ho Chi Minh ▶

★ **July 1941**
Japan captures French colony of Indochina (Vietnam, Laos, Cambodia)

★ **September 1945**
• Japan surrenders to Allies
• Communist Ho Chi Minh declares Vietnam independent

★ **December 1941**
Japanese bomb Pearl Harbor, Hawaii

★ **Late 1943** Vietnamese battle Japanese

Japanese planes on a bombing mission ▶

An Unpopular War

Objective: To read and analyze a literary selection about the Vietnam War

Focus: Remind students that unlike World War II, the Vietnam War was widely opposed at home.

Teach: Have students read the selection and answer the questions.

Assess: Discuss students' various interpretations of the reading.

Close: Discuss how the Vietnam War might have affected the loved ones of the persons who served there.

Differentiated Instruction Strategies

BL **Have students study the questions first and then read the selection, noting possible answers.**

AL **Ask students to read a memoir of someone who served in the Vietnam War and write a descriptive essay on that person's feelings.**

ELL **Remind students that they should consult the Reader's Dictionary for definitions of unfamiliar words.**

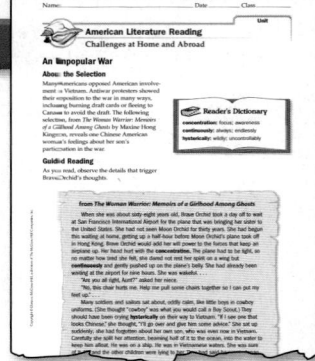

American Literature Reading, URB p. 9

Americans urged him to create a more democratic government and to help Vietnam's peasants. Diem introduced some limited reforms, but they had little effect.

Diem took away rights from the majority Buddhist population and favored Catholics, like himself. Buddhists responded with protests, including Buddhist monks setting themselves on fire on busy streets. As a result of these protests, Kennedy found it difficult to continue to support Diem.

In November 1963, the South Vietnamese army overthrew the government and assassinated Diem. The Kennedy administration had supported the takeover, but not Diem's killing. After President Kennedy's assassination later that month, the question of what to do in Vietnam fell on the shoulders of President Lyndon B. Johnson.

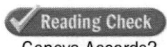 **Reading Check** Analyzing What were the Geneva Accords?

◀ French soldier with Vietnamese prisoner

★ **May 1954**
Vietnamese defeat French

★ **December 1946**
• Beginning of First Indochina War (French vs. Vietnamese)
• U.S. sends aid to France

★ **July 1954**
Peace agreement divides Vietnam into Communist-dominated North and U.S.-supported South

Critical Thinking

Making Connections Why do you think the United States sent aid to France in its battle to keep Vietnam under French rule?

The Conflict Deepens

Main Idea To stop the spread of communism in Southeast Asia, the United States became involved in a war in Vietnam.

History and You What sacrifices must a country make if it becomes involved in a war? Read to learn how the U.S. was affected by its involvement in the Vietnam War.

· ·

At the time of Kennedy's death, the United States had nearly 16,000 American troops in Vietnam as advisers. Secretary of Defense Robert McNamara told the president that South Vietnam could not resist the Vietcong rebels without more help from the United States. In a May 1964 conversation, taped but not made public until 1997, Johnson himself expressed doubts about American commitment. "I don't think it's worth fighting for," he said, "but I don't think we can get out." As Vietcong attacks continued, the United States moved toward deeper involvement in the region.

President Johnson wanted congressional support for expanding the American role in Vietnam. The opportunity to get that support came in August 1964, when North Vietnamese patrol boats allegedly attacked American destroyers in the Gulf of Tonkin near North Vietnam. Congress quickly passed a resolution that allowed the president to "take all necessary measures to repel any armed attack against the forces of the United States." The **Gulf of Tonkin Resolution** gave Johnson broad authority to use American forces.

In 1965 President Johnson began to **escalate**—gradually increase—U.S. involvement in Vietnam. The buildup included both ground troops and an air campaign. United States Marines landed near Da Nang, South Vietnam, on March 8, 1965. During the next three years, the number of American troops in Vietnam rose sharply. About 180,000 U.S. soldiers were in Vietnam by the end of 1965, almost 400,000 by the end of 1966, and more than 500,000 by 1968.

The Vietnam Era **Chapter 29** **913**

Activity: Collaborative Learning

Analyzing Information Have students work with partners to research and write a report about the Gulf of Tonkin Resolution. Ask them to address the following questions in their analysis: What happened in the Gulf of Tonkin incident? What information about the incident did President Johnson withhold from Congress and the American people? What might have been done to prevent the spread of misinformation? How did the resolution affect the future of the United States's involvement in Vietnam? Have students share their findings in a class discussion. **AL**

S Skill Practice

Identifying Problems and Solutions
Ask: What problem did the Ho Chi Minh Trail pose for American troops? *(The enemy used this route to bring equipment south.)* What solution did America's leaders execute? *(intense bombing of the trail)* What new problem did the bombing create because of the trail's location? *(The bombing expanded the war to neighboring countries.)* **OL**

C Critical Thinking

Predicting Consequences Ask: The Vietcong blended with the Vietnamese population. How do you think this fact affected the civilians? *(Many civilians were mistaken for the enemy and killed.)* **OL**

Primary Source

Critical Thinking Answer
In Vietnam, soldiers had to endure biting insects and jungle warfare, a far different environment from Civil War battles fought on American soil.

Exploring Explain to students that the Army and Marine ground troops were called *grunts*. Have them research and report on some of the unique issues faced by these soldiers. **AL**

Differentiated Instruction

Primary Source — A Day in the Life of a Soldier

"My hands are covered with cuts. The jungles have thousands of leeches and mosquitoes of which I think I have gotten bitten almost all over my body.... Actually the fighting is not heavy yet, but the rumor is we're moving south."
—from *Dear America: Letters Home from Vietnam*

◄ American soldier in Vietnam

What would a foot soldier carry?

Typical Gear	Typical Pack
Rifle	Poncho
Web belt with ammo pouches	Poncho liner
Hand grenades	Five C-ration meals
Smoke grenades	Rain jacket
First aid pouch	Sweater shirt
Canteen	Extra canteen
Two bandoliers of ammo	Extra ammo
	Gun-cleaning kit
	Extra smoke grenade
	Extra rifle bolt
	Camera

Critical Thinking

Contrasting How were the experiences of a soldier in Vietnam different from a soldier during the U.S. Civil War?

S In March 1965, the United States unleashed an intense bombing campaign called Operation Rolling Thunder. Some planes attacked the Ho Chi Minh Trail, a network of roads, paths, and bridges that wound from North Vietnam through Cambodia and Laos into South Vietnam. North Vietnamese troops used this route to bring equipment south. Other planes targeted bridges, docks, factories, and military bases in the North.

The bombing increased in intensity from 1965 through 1968. By then American planes had dropped more bombs on North Vietnam than they dropped on Germany, Italy, and Japan during World War II.

Fighting the War

The American troops found fighting a ground war in Vietnam difficult. Dense jungles, muddy trails, and swampy rice paddies hampered troop movement. The South Vietnamese army did not always fight effectively. **C** As the Vietcong guerrillas blended with the population, American soldiers found it hard to tell friends and enemies apart.

The American forces began to conduct **search-and-destroy missions.** The goal was to seek out Vietcong or North Vietnamese units and destroy them. The Americans hoped to eventually defeat the Communists or force them to negotiate. Ground troops coordinated their moves with air support. Patrols on the ground radioed their location, and helicopter gunships roared to the scene to blast the enemy with cannon and machine-gun fire.

Planes bombed areas of South Vietnam in an effort to drive guerrillas from their jungle cover. Both sides used planes to drop **napalm,** an explosive that burned intensely, to destroy jungle growth. North Vietnamese and Vietcong forces also used napalm in flamethrowers, devices that expel fuel or a burning stream of liquids.

To improve visibility, chemical herbicides were sprayed in Vietnam to clear out forests and tall grasses. One herbicide, **Agent Orange,** is believed to have contaminated many Americans and Vietnamese, causing serious health problems.

Leveled Activities

BL Reteaching Activity, URB p. 93

OL Enrichment Activity, URB p. 11

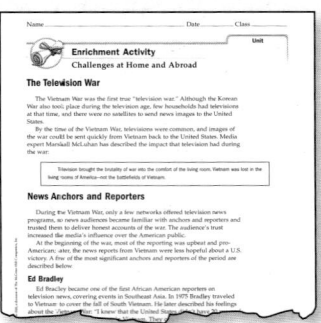

ELL Content Vocabulary Activity, URB p. 73

Frustration Grows

The bombing of the Ho Chi Minh Trail and the North did not stop the constant flow of troops and equipment south. Neither did it break the morale of the North Vietnamese. As one of their leaders later said:

PRIMARY SOURCE

"[We survived] because of our courage and determination, together with wisdom, tactics, and intelligence.... We had to resort to different measures, some of which are quite simple, like hiding in man-holes and evacuating to the countryside. And we fought back with all our forces and with every kind of weapon." **C**

—from an interview with General Vo Nguyen Giap

The search-and-destroy missions killed thousands of North Vietnamese and Vietcong troops—but the troops always seemed to be replaced. What Ho Chi Minh had said to the French became true again: "You can kill ten of my men for every one I kill of yours. But even at those odds, you will lose and I will win."

American troops advanced into rice paddies, jungles, and small villages and killed scores of Vietcong. Yet the next day, the same area often had to be attacked again. American soldiers grew frustrated. Philip Caputo, a young marine lieutenant, recalled the changing attitude:

PRIMARY SOURCE

"When we marched into the rice paddies on that damp March afternoon, we carried, along with our packs and rifles, the implicit convictions that the Viet Cong would be quickly beaten. . . . We kept the packs and rifles; the convictions, we lost."

—from *A Rumor of War*

Debate in the White House

Officials in the Johnson administration saw the mounting Communist losses and believed at first that the United States could succeed. As the war dragged on, however, some officials saw a gloomier situation. Secretary of Defense McNamara began to argue that the ground war and the air attacks had failed and that the war could not be won. Outside the nation's capital, opposition to U.S. involvement in Vietnam grew.

✔ **Reading Check** **Identifying** By what means did President Johnson escalate the U.S. presence in Vietnam?

History ONLINE
Study Central™ To review this section, go to glencoe.com.

CHAPTER 29
Section 2

C Critical Thinking

Comparing Ask: How was the war in Vietnam similar to the war in Iraq? *(Possible similarities: leaders first thought superior firepower would win; enemy used guerrilla warfare; enemy blended with the population; public opposition grew; American leaders began to think the war could not be won)* **AL**

✔ **Reading Check** **Answer:** He used an alleged attack on American ships in the Gulf of Tonkin to win support for expanded involvement.

Assess
. . . .

History ONLINE

Study Central™ provides summaries, interactive games, and online graphic organizers to help students review content.

Close
. . . .

Summarizing Have students identify the key events leading to American involvement in Vietnam. **OL**

Section 2 Review

Vocabulary

1. Write a paragraph using each of the following terms: trace, regime, escalate, search-and-destroy mission, napalm, Agent Orange.

Main Ideas

2. Describing What was the domino theory, and how did it shape American policy in Vietnam?

3. Summarizing How large was the American troop increase in Vietnam between 1963 and the end of 1965?

Critical Thinking

4. Explaining What was the Gulf of Tonkin Resolution, and why was it important?

5. Organizing Information Re-create the diagram below to show the different warfare techniques used in search-and-destroy missions.

Search and Destroy

6. Descriptive Writing Imagine you are an American soldier arriving in Vietnam. In one or two paragraphs, describe the terrain you find yourself fighting in and how it affects your abilities as a soldier.

Answer the
7. Essential Question
How and why did America involve itself in the war in Vietnam?

The Vietnam Era **Chapter 29** 915

Answers

1. Paragraphs should reflect a correct understanding of the terms.

2. The domino theory held that if South Vietnam fell to communism, other countries in the region would also fall like a row of dominoes—one right after another. Based on this theory, American policy committed the United States to involvement in the Vietnam conflict.

3. 180,000 in 1965 – 16,000 in 1963 = 164,000 increase

4. The Gulf of Tonkin Resolution, passed by Congress, gave President Johnson broad authority to use American forces in Vietnam.

5. ground troops coordinate with air support; patrols radio enemy location; helicopter gunships arrive to blast the enemy

6. Students' paragraphs should describe a jungle terrain that poses problems such as limited ability to see the enemy and difficulties in moving troops and equipment.

7. Belief in the domino theory led American presidents to commit to stopping the Communists from taking South Vietnam. Involvement started with sending aid and advisers to South Vietnam. When the South Vietnamese proved incapable of resisting the Vietcong, advisers to President Johnson urged him to expand the American role. An alleged attack on American destroyers in the Gulf of Tonkin provided the excuse that enabled Johnson to get the authority from Congress to send troops.

915

Focus

R Reading Strategy

Activating Prior Knowledge **Ask:** How would supporting the Vietnam War help spread democracy and freedom? *(North Vietnam was a Communist country. When it attacked South Vietnam, it threatened that country's democratic government. Fighting the North Vietnamese was a way of stopping communism.)* **OL**

W Writing Support

Persuasive Writing When Walter Cronkite told TV viewers that Americans have reason to doubt their leaders, his statement was itself a controversial story. He was breaking the unwritten rule that journalists should remain objective and not air their personal views. Even today, some accuse him of betraying the troops in the field. Ask students to write an essay about Cronkite's decision to voice his concerns on the air. Students should explain why they agree or disagree with Cronkite's actions, trying to persuade those with opposing views. **OL**

Additional Support and Answers

Fighting in Saigon during the Tet Offensive, May 1968

916

YOU DECIDE

Should We Be Fighting the Vietnam War?

Building Background

R Government officials urged Americans to support the war's goals of spreading freedom and democracy. President Lyndon B. Johnson responded to criticism of his management of the war by defending the struggle as an idealistic cause.

As U.S. involvement in the war increased, so did opposition to it. The mainstream media, which had tried to remain balanced in their war coverage, now openly criticized the effort. Walter Cronkite, then the nation's most respected newscaster, supported the war effort at first. After traveling to Vietnam to report on the fighting, Cronkite's stories began to include his disappointments with the status of the war.

NO

WALTER CRONKITE,
after the Tet Offensive, February 27, 1968

> *We have been too often disappointed by the optimism of the American leaders, both in Vietnam and Washington, to have faith any longer in the silver linings they find in the darkest clouds. . . .*
>
> *To say that we are closer to victory today is to believe, in the face of the evidence, the optimists who have been* **W** *wrong in the past. To suggest we are on the edge of defeat is to yield to unreasonable pessimism. To say that we are mired[1] in stalemate seems the only realistic, yet unsatisfactory, conclusion. . . . It is increasingly clear to this reporter that the only rational way out then will be to negotiate, not as victors, but as an honorable people who lived up to their pledge to defend democracy, and did the best they could.*

---
[1] **mired** stuck

Technology Connection

Analyzing Visuals Even today, American news coverage of the Vietnam War remains controversial. Many people believe that hard-hitting combat footage on TV turned public opinion against the war. On the other hand, some media analysts claim the coverage was too positive for the first few years of American involvement and that journalists like Walter Cronkite grew skeptical only after the Tet Offensive of 1968. Using the online archives of *TIME* magazine (www.time.com/time/archive), students can evaluate media coverage of the Vietnam War for themselves. Enter "Vietnam" in the Search box, and find the Vietnam-related magazine covers during the war years (1964–1975). Select five or six striking images, and study them carefully. Have students discuss the covers. **Ask:** What messages about the war are communicated in these covers? *(Students should note positive and negative elements in the images and raise questions and draw conclusions about the role of media in history and in their lives.)*

YES

PRESIDENT JOHNSON
Addresses Johns Hopkins University, April 7, 1965

We fight because we must fight if we are to live in a world where every country can shape its own destiny. And only in such a world will our own freedom be finally secure.

This kind of world will never be built by bombs or bullets. Yet the infirmities[2] of man are such that force must often precede reason, and the waste of war, the works of peace. . . .

. . . To abandon this small and brave nation [Vietnam] to its enemies, and to the terror that must follow, would be an unforgivable wrong. . . .

We are also there because there are great stakes in the balance. Let no one think for a moment that retreat from Viet-Nam would bring an end to conflict. The battle would be renewed in one country and then another. The central lesson of our time is that the appetite of aggression is never satisfied.

C

---

[2] **infirmities** weaknesses

DBQ Document-Based Questions

1. **Interpreting** Why does Johnson believe the United States should be fighting the war in Vietnam?
2. **Making Inferences** What does Cronkite believe the result will be if the United States continues fighting in Vietnam?
3. **Analyzing** How do Johnson and Cronkite differ in their views on achieving peace?
4. **Synthesizing** Why might Americans, such as Walter Cronkite, be frustrated with the war?

Antiwar rally at Queens College in New York City

917

Section 3

The Vietnam Years at Home

Focus

Bellringer
Daily Test Practice Transparency 29–3

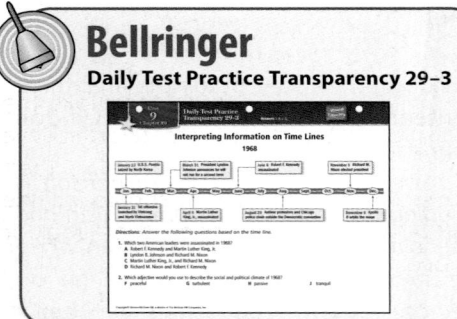

Reading Guide
Answers to Graphic:
rejected traditional American values, wore torn blue jeans and long hair, refused to follow customary social roles of work and family, rejected competition for material goods and personal success

Section Spotlight Video

To learn more about the political and social climate in the United States during the Vietnam War, watch the Section Spotlight Video "The Vietnam Years at Home."

Resource Manager

Essential Question ◄
How did the Vietnam War affect the political and social climate in the United States?

Reading Guide

Content Vocabulary

counterculture (p. 919)

conscientious objector (p. 920)

deferment (p. 920)

credibility gap (p. 921)

Academic Vocabulary

conduct (p. 920)   exclude (p. 923)

Key People and Events

Tet Offensive (p. 921)
Robert F. Kennedy (p. 921)
Dr. Martin Luther King, Jr. (p. 922)
Hubert H. Humphrey (p. 922)
George C. Wallace (p. 923)
Richard M. Nixon (p. 923)

Reading Strategy
Taking Notes On a diagram like the one below, record characteristics of the counterculture in America during the war.

Counterculture

ILLINOIS STANDARDS
The American Journey

14.D Understand the roles and influences of individuals and interest groups in the political systems of Illinois, the United States and other nations.

14.D.3 Describe roles and influences of individuals, groups and media in shaping current Illinois and United States public policy (e.g., general public opinion, special interest groups, formal parties, media).

14.E Understand United States foreign policy as it relates to other nations and international issues.

18.B.3a Analyze how individuals and groups interact with and within institutions (e.g., educational, military).

918

American Diary

As casualties mounted in Vietnam, many people began to protest against the war. Jeff Sharlet was a Vietnam veteran who opposed the war but was disgusted by the attitudes and actions of the protesters. He decided to start a newspaper, *Vietnam GI*, written entirely by veterans and soldiers. The soldiers, whether they supported or opposed the war effort, always knew they could express their views in its pages.

Antiwar demonstration, February 1966

Reading Strategies	**C Critical Thinking**	**D Differentiated Instruction**	**W Writing Support**	**S Skill Practice**
Teacher Edition • Making Connections, p. 921 • Activat. Prior Knowl., p. 923 **Additional Resources** • Guid. Read., URB p. 97 • Content Vocab., URB p. 73 • Read. Ess., p. 331	**Teacher Edition** • Analyzing Information, p. 920 • Analyzing Information, p. 921 **Additional Resources** • Quizzes and Tests, p. 289 • Authentic Assess., p. 29	**Teacher Edition** • Visual/Spatial, p. 919 • Gifted and Talented, p. 919 • Verbal/Linguistic, p. 923 **Additional Resources** • School-to-Home, URB p. 91 • Reteaching Act., URB p. 93	**Teacher Edition** • Narrative Writing, p. 920 • Expository Writing, p. 922	**Teacher Edition** • Taking Notes, p. 921 • Using Inferring Skills, p. 922 **Additional Resources** • Daily Test Pract. Transp. 29-3 • Geo. & Hist., URB p. 87 • Lesson Transp. 29A, 29B

The Youth Protest

Main Idea The war in Vietnam led to sharp divisions between Americans who supported the war and those who did not.

History and You Have members of your family heatedly disagreed over certain issues? Read to learn how the war in Vietnam affected American society.

While fighting raged in Vietnam, the American people disagreed sharply over the war. Pro-war and antiwar groups attacked each other with mounting anger. Antiwar demonstrators called President Johnson and his supporters "killers." Supporters of the war referred to the protesters as "traitors." The war seemed to split America—and much of the division resulted from what people called the generation gap.

As United States involvement in the war increased, so did opposition to it. Some Americans felt that the conflict in Vietnam was a civil war and should not involve the United States. Others were concerned that the cost of America's commitment to Vietnam was hurting domestic programs. Still others

viewed South Vietnam as a corrupt dictatorship and insisted that defending the country was immoral and unjust. All condemned the devastation of the countryside and the lives lost during the course of the war.

Many who opposed the war were part of the **counterculture,** a movement that rejected traditional American values. Some common symbols of the counterculture—torn blue jeans and long hair for males—aroused opposition from parents. Popular music played a role in communicating the ideas of the counterculture.

Other parts of the counterculture represented a more serious challenge to traditional middle-class values. Some young people refused to follow customary social roles of work and family. They aimed to reject aspects of American society such as the competition for material goods and personal success.

Opposition to the Draft

Student protests targeted the selective service system—the draft that supplied soldiers for the war. The law required all men to register for the draft when they reached age 18. Opposition to the draft had two sources.

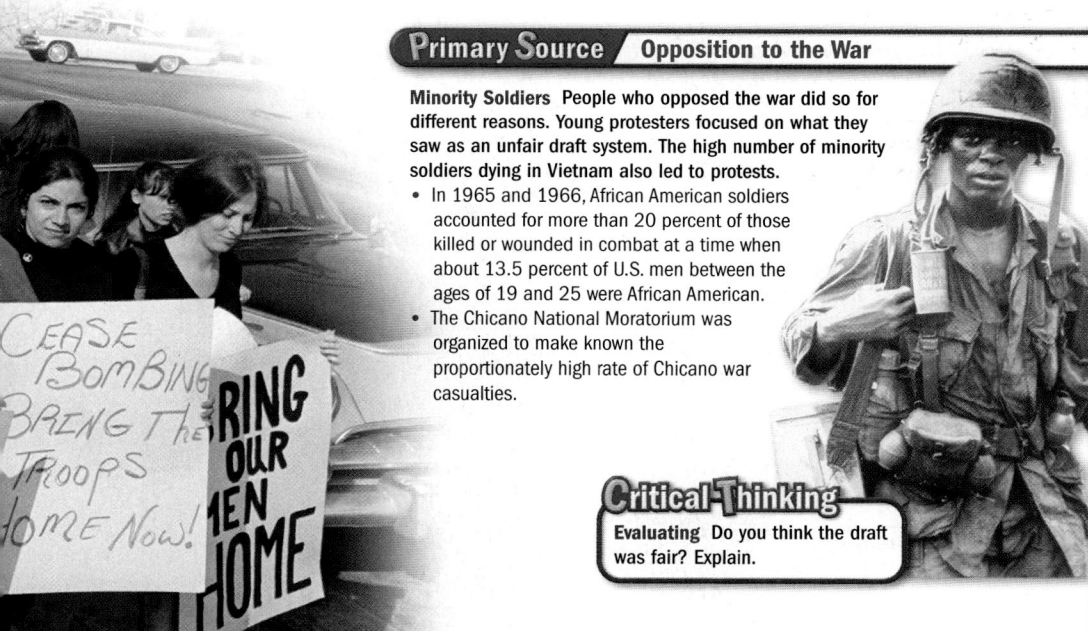

Primary Source / **Opposition to the War**

Minority Soldiers People who opposed the war did so for different reasons. Young protesters focused on what they saw as an unfair draft system. The high number of minority soldiers dying in Vietnam also led to protests.

- In 1965 and 1966, African American soldiers accounted for more than 20 percent of those killed or wounded in combat at a time when about 13.5 percent of U.S. men between the ages of 19 and 25 were African American.
- The Chicano National Moratorium was organized to make known the proportionately high rate of Chicano war casualties.

Critical Thinking

Evaluating Do you think the draft was fair? Explain.

History ONLINE
Objectives and answers to the Student Web Activity can be found at glencoe.com under the Web Activity Lesson Plan for this chapter.

C Critical Thinking

Analyzing Information Ask: How did college deferments discriminate against the poor? *(Men who could not afford to go to college were drafted.)* **OL**

W Writing Support

Narrative Writing Have students work in pairs to write a dialogue between a war protester and a supporter of the war. The dialogue should present points and counterpoints for each viewpoint. Have the pairs perform their dialogue for the class. **OL**

✓ **Reading Check Answer:** became conscientious objectors; burned draft cards

Hands-On Chapter Project
Step 3

History ONLINE
Student Web Activity Visit glencoe.com and complete the Chapter 29 Web Activity about young people and the draft.

Those who were strongly opposed to American involvement in Vietnam believed that by ending the draft, they could halt the supply of soldiers needed to fight there. Others called the draft unfair. Draft boards had the power to give people **deferments** that excused them from the draft for various reasons. Full-time students attending college—mostly from the middle class—received such deferments. As a result, a large percentage of soldiers came from poor or working-class families. Many argued that deferments discriminated against these families.

Some protesters became **conscientious objectors,** claiming that their moral or religious beliefs prevented them from fighting in the war. Other protesters showed their opposition by burning their draft cards—their military registration forms.

Doves and Hawks

Students and other opponents of the Vietnam War came to be called doves. Supporters of the war became known as hawks.

Across the nation more and more Americans came to view the war unfavorably. Some thought the United States should not be fighting in Vietnam. Others opposed the way the government **conducted,** or directed the course of, the war. Both hawks and doves criticized the president for his handling of the war in Vietnam, and his approval rating greatly declined.

As the opposition to the war mounted, the opponents staged larger demonstrations. In October 1967, more than 50,000 people marched to the Pentagon—headquarters of the Defense Department—to protest the war. Of those Americans who supported the war, many openly criticized the protesters for a lack of patriotism.

✓ **Reading Check Describing** How did some Americans protest the draft in the 1960s?

Primary Source / Wounded in War

Rapid Rescue The helicopter ambulance sped up the time in which wounded soldiers received medical treatment. Crews were able to shuttle the injured to a medical facility within one to two hours of a soldier being hurt. And because of the rapid transport, nurses in Vietnam saw more critically injured soldiers. Nurses usually worked 12 hours per day, 6 days per week. The average age of an American nurse in Vietnam was 23.6 years.

A wounded soldier is loaded onto a helicopter. ▶

"Some days you felt you'd lived a lifetime in just a week. Because Vietnam was not John Wayne on the beach at Iwo Jima. It was not ketchup on make-believe wounds. It was more like a grotesque form of 'can you top this,' because each time you thought you'd seen the ultimate, something else would come along."

—Nurse Ruth Sidisin, USAF

Broadcasting the News

Step 3: Preparing the Visuals Students will prepare their images and complete their script.

Essential Question: How did the Vietnam War affect the political and social climate in the United States?

Directions Have the groups prepare the images for their broadcast. Instruct them to include at least one chart, graph, or map, as well as pictures. The images should capture attention and help viewers understand the information in the story. Have students prepare their images for electronic display, for display by overhead projector, or as posters on an easel. Ask them to include informative captions with each image. Have groups complete their scripts, including a discussion of each image presented.

Making Inferences Ask: How might viewers at home react to vivid images of combat? *(Such images might shock viewers.)* **OL**

(Chapter Project continued in Section 4)

1968—Year of Crisis

Main Idea The year 1968 was a turning point in the Vietnam War that greatly affected the nation's political life.

History and You Do you recall a year that is meaningful to you because of the particular events that occurred during that time? Read to learn why 1968 became a significant year for Americans.

- -

The year 1968 opened with a shock for the American people. North Vietnam launched a major series of attacks in South Vietnam. As Americans soon learned, 1968 would be a long, dramatic, and very difficult year.

The Tet Offensive

On January 31, 1968, the North Vietnamese and Vietcong launched a series of attacks, which began on Tet—the Vietnamese New Year. This **Tet Offensive** marked a turning point in the Vietnam War. The Communist attacks targeted American military bases and

Critical Thinking

Speculating How do you think young nurses reacted after working such long hours and seeing such horrific injuries?

South Vietnam's cities. Vietcong troops raided the United States embassy in Saigon, the capital. They also struck in Hue, the ancient capital of Vietnam.

Militarily, Tet turned out to be a disaster for the Communist forces. After a month of fighting, the American and South Vietnamese soldiers drove back the enemy troops, inflicting heavy losses. In the United States, however, the Tet Offensive turned many more Americans against the war—and President Johnson. The American people were shocked that an enemy supposedly close to defeat could launch such a large-scale attack.

Major newspapers and magazines openly criticized the Johnson administration's conduct of the war. Most Americans seemed to agree, believing that the army was losing ground. The Johnson administration developed a **credibility gap**—fewer people trusted its statements about the war.

Political Opposition

As opposition to the war grew, President Johnson faced challenges in his own party. In late 1967, Democratic senator Eugene McCarthy of Minnesota announced that he would run for the party's nomination for the presidency as a protest against the war. Not well known, McCarthy seemed to have little chance of winning. In the March 12 primary in New Hampshire, however, McCarthy surprised everyone by taking 42 percent of the popular vote. Although Johnson won the primary, McCarthy's strong showing indicated widespread opposition to the war.

Later, another antiwar candidate entered the race. **Robert F. Kennedy,** attorney general during his brother's presidency and now a senator from New York, announced that he, too, would seek the Democratic nomination.

The President Responds

Events in Vietnam and the growing antiwar movement disturbed President Johnson. After the Tet Offensive, the American commander in Vietnam, General William Westmoreland, requested still more troops.

The Vietnam Era **Chapter 29** **921**

S Skill Practice

Taking Notes Have students create a three-column chart to take notes as they read. In one column, they should list all Democratic candidates who entered the 1968 presidential race. They should list Republican and independent candidates in the other columns. Then have students subdivide the columns to make room to list each candidate's campaign points. **BL**

C Critical Thinking

Analyzing Information Ask: How did the Tet Offensive help create a credibility gap? *(Government information suggested that the enemy was close to defeat, but the Tet Offensive showed that this information was not true.)* **OL**

R Reading Strategy

Making Connections Ask: Who was Robert Kennedy's brother? *(President John F. Kennedy)* **BL**

Primary Source

Critical Thinking Answer
Students may say that nurses might have developed psychological problems similar to those experienced by combat soldiers.

Differentiated Instruction

Geography and History Activity, URB p. 87

The Election of 1968

Objective: To analyze the results of the election of 1968

Focus: Ask students how President Johnson's decision not to run affected the election.

Teach: Have students read the background information, study the map, and answer the questions.

Assess: Make a transparency of the map, project it, and refer to it as students discuss their answers.

Close: Discuss what effect the violence of 1968 may have had on voters' decisions.

Differentiated Instruction Strategies

BL Have students work in pairs to answer the questions.

AL Have students research and create election posters for the three candidates, stating the campaign positions of each candidate.

ELL Ask students to define the phrases "silent majority" and "law and order" as they related to the election of 1968.

S Skill Practice

Using Inferring Skills Ask: Why do you think President Johnson decided not to send more troops to Vietnam? *(He probably recognized that public opposition to the war was strong and that the war was not going well.)* **OL**

W Writing Support

Expository Writing Have students research, then write a report about the riots that rocked American cities after Dr. King's assassination. Reports should include the cities affected, estimates of the number of participants, and the scope of the destruction. **AL**

A Nation in Crisis NATIONAL GEOGRAPHIC

Critical Thinking Answers

1. the South
2. Disagree; Humphrey won most states in the Northeast.

Skills Practice

Ask: Which column in the chart tells you who won the election? *(Electoral Vote)* **BL**

Additional Support

A Nation in Crisis NATIONAL GEOGRAPHIC

Events of 1968

- President Johnson does not run for reelection.
- Martin Luther King, Jr., and Robert Kennedy are shot and killed.
- Antiwar demonstrations disrupt the Democratic convention in Chicago.
- Demonstrations spread to many college campuses.
- Third-party candidate George Wallace makes a strong showing.
- With Richard Nixon's victory in 1968, Republicans hold a near monopoly on the presidency for the next 20 years.

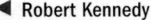
Election of 1968

◀ Robert Kennedy

Richard Nixon ▶

Candidate*	Electoral Vote	Popular Vote	Political Party
Nixon	301	31,785,480	Republican
Humphrey	191	31,275,166	Democrat
Wallace	46	9,906,473	Independent

*One North Carolina elector voted for Wallace

Map Skills

1. **Region** In what area of the nation did Wallace receive the most votes?
2. **Region** Explain why you agree or disagree with the following: The Northeast was Nixon's strongest region in 1968.

Maps in MOtion See StudentWorks™ Plus or glencoe.com.

Instead of agreeing with Westmoreland's request for more troops, the president ordered a reevaluation of the war. He also reevaluated his own campaign for reelection.

On March 31, 1968, President Johnson appeared on television to announce a "new step toward peace"—he would halt the bombing of North Vietnam's cities. He asked North Vietnam for a comparable action so that peace talks could begin. The president concluded his speech with a startling announcement: "I shall not seek, and I will not accept, the nomination of my party for another term as your president."

Violence Erupts

A few days after Johnson withdrew from the presidential race, tragedy struck the nation. On the evening of April 4, a sniper in Memphis, Tennessee, shot and killed **Dr. Martin Luther King, Jr.,** the leading activist in the civil rights movement.

The assassination of Dr. King set off riots across the country. Army troops were called on to control unruly crowds in various cities. Already saddened by Dr. King's death, Americans worried about urban violence.

While the nation agonized over unrest at home and war abroad, the race for president picked up speed. Vice President **Hubert H. Humphrey** joined Eugene McCarthy and Robert Kennedy in seeking the Democratic nomination. Kennedy edged out McCarthy in a number of primary elections, but McCarthy rebounded and scored a victory in Oregon. Humphrey, meanwhile, avoided primaries. He won support among Democratic Party leaders, who in some states chose delegates.

In June 1968, Kennedy and McCarthy faced each other in the primary election in California, the state with the most delegates. That night, after Kennedy won, an assassin shot and killed him. The nation reeled with the shock of yet another assassination.

Activity: Interdisciplinary Connection

Music Print and distribute the lyrics to the moving song "Abraham, Martin, and John," written by Richard Holler and sung by Dion. The lyrics can be found online by searching the John F. Kennedy Library and Museum, www.jfklibrary.org. If possible, also find an audio version and play it for the class.

Ask: Who are Abraham, Martin, and John? *(Abraham Lincoln, Martin Luther King, Jr., and John F. Kennedy)* What does the song say these men have in common? *(They all freed a lot of people—Lincoln freed people from slavery; King and Kennedy worked to free people from discrimination.)*

Who is Bobby? *(Robert Kennedy)* What happened to them all? *(All were assassinated.)* What is the songwriter's view of these men? *(They were good men with admirable values.)* **OL**

The Democratic Convention

By the time the Democrats held their convention in Chicago, Humphrey seemed to have enough votes to win the nomination. As a supporter of civil rights and labor causes, Humphrey had much backing in the party. As a supporter of Johnson's Vietnam policy, however, Humphrey was linked to the party's pro-war wing. Antiwar Democrats felt angry and **excluded,** or shut out, from the convention.

Meanwhile, thousands of antiwar activists flocked to Chicago to protest Humphrey's almost certain victory. Chicago's mayor, Richard J. Daley, feared violence and had the police out in force. When antiwar protesters tried to march to the convention site, police blocked the marchers, who began to pelt the officers with sticks and bottles. The police threw tear gas and charged in, wielding nightsticks. They pursued those who fled, beating some and arresting many.

Humphrey won the Democratic nomination, but the violence—all shown on television—damaged his candidacy. Humphrey admitted, "Chicago was a catastrophe."

The Election of 1968

Most Americans opposed the violence and longed for a return to law and order. As Election Day neared, third-party candidate Governor **George C. Wallace** of Alabama criticized protesters and efforts to integrate schools by busing. His tough stand on law and order and his appeal to racial fears won many voters. Republican nominee, former vice president **Richard M. Nixon,** claimed to stand for the conservative "silent majority" who wanted law and order and did not protest or demonstrate. He also offered "peace with honor" in Vietnam, but gave no details.

In the election, the popular vote was close. Nixon edged Humphrey by about 500,000 votes. In the electoral vote, however, Nixon won a solid majority—301 votes to Humphrey's 191. Nixon became president with the votes of only 43.4 percent of the people, but he and Wallace together won about 57 percent. It seemed that a sizeable majority of Americans wanted the government to restore order.

✓ **Reading Check** **Identifying** What two popular leaders were assassinated in 1968?

D **Differentiated Instruction**

Verbal/Linguistic Have students write two newspaper headlines about the protest at the Democratic convention. The headlines should suggest different views of the incident. **OL**

R **Reading Strategy**

Activating Prior Knowledge Ask: Based on what you know about the civil rights movement, why do you think Wallace won strong support in the South? *(Opposition to integration was strongest in the South.)* **OL**

✓ **Reading Check** **Answer:** Martin Luther King, Jr., and Robert F. Kennedy

Assess

History ONLINE

Study Central™ provides summaries, interactive games, and online graphic organizers to help students review content.

Close

Discussing As a class, discuss the effects of the antiwar protests on the election of 1968. **OL**

Section 3 Review

Section 3 Review

History ONLINE
Study Central™ To review this section, go to glencoe.com.

Vocabulary

1. Use each of these terms in a complete sentence that will explain its meaning: counterculture, deferment, conscientious objector, conduct, credibility gap, exclude.

Main Ideas

2. Explaining What were draft deferments, and who received them?

3. Summarizing What was the Tet Offensive? Why was it significant to the course of the war?

4. Analyzing Why did President Lyndon B. Johnson decide not to seek reelection?

Critical Thinking

5. Identifying On a diagram like the one below, list the major points that Nixon campaigned on in 1968.

6. Analyzing Who were the "silent majority," and how did their votes affect the outcome of the 1968 presidential election?

7. Persuasive Writing Write a short essay to convince the reader to agree with your point of view on this question: *Should America use a draft system with the armed services?*

Answer the
8. Essential Question
How did the Vietnam War affect the political and social climate in the United States?

The Vietnam Era **Chapter 29** **923**

Answers

1. Sentences should reflect a correct understanding of the terms.
2. Deferments were decisions by the draft board to excuse some people from the draft. Full-time students attending college received deferments.
3. The Tet Offensive was a series of attacks launched by the North Vietnamese and Vietcong. Although it was a disaster for the Communist forces, the offensive shocked many Americans, who had been led to believe the enemy was close to defeat. This

caused many more Americans to turn against the war.
4. Widespread opposition to the war eroded Johnson's popularity and gave rise to opposing candidates in his own party.
5. for law and order, against antiwar protests, for "peace with honor"
6. Nixon defined the "silent majority" as conservatives who wanted law and order. These voters helped Nixon win the election of 1968.

7. Students should give reasons to support positions either for or against the draft.
8. As the war dragged on and casualties mounted, public opposition to the war increased. Many people participated in antiwar protests. Nixon campaigned for law and order and for "peace with honor"—promises that helped him win the presidency in 1968.

TIME NOTEBOOK

Focus

R Reading Strategy

Paraphrasing Ask students to write, in their own words, the meaning of the statement "That's one small step for [a] man, one giant leap for mankind." **ELL**

C Critical Thinking

Making Inferences Read aloud the last sentence of the paragraph. **Ask:** Why do you think living in another country made the author appreciate the United States more? *(Student answers should note that the writer was most likely volunteering in an impoverished area where people were facing issues such as lack of food, basic necessities, and poor living conditions.)* **OL**

Teach

W Writing Support

Persuasive Writing Ask students to write a persuasive essay to the store owner that Franklin McCain encountered, suggesting why the store should end the policy to "not serve Negroes." **AL**

Additional Support and Answers

What were people's lives like in the past?

These two pages will give you some clues to everyday life in the United States as you step back in time with TIME Notebook.

Profile

On July 20, 1969, **NEIL ARMSTRONG** *became the first human to walk on the moon. There he spoke the famous words, "That's one small step for [a] man, one giant leap for mankind." Later, Armstrong reflected on his voyage and the "spaceship" we call Earth.*

"From our position here on Earth, it is difficult to observe where the Earth is, and where it's going, or what its future course might be. Hopefully by getting a little farther away, both in the real sense and the figurative sense, we'll be able to make some people step back and reconsider their mission in the universe, to think of themselves as a group of people who constitute [make up] the crew of a spaceship going through the universe. If you're going to run a spaceship you've got to be pretty cautious about how you use your resources, how you use your crew, and how you treat your spacecraft."

—*from the book* First on the Moon

The Peace Corps

Established by President Kennedy in 1961, the Peace Corps sends trained Americans as "goodwill ambassadors" to developing nations. Once there, these volunteers help with agriculture, education, and health projects—as well as with small businesses and rural engineering. Here is what one volunteer said about working with the Peace Corps from 1963–1965:

"I was in college when JFK created the Peace Corps, and I thought it was a great idea. I was inspired by his question, 'Ask not what your country can do for you; ask what you can do for your country.' I wanted to travel and experience a different culture, and I admired President Kennedy's idealism, so I applied. Living in another country, I learned to appreciate my own country more."

924

VERBATIM

WHAT PEOPLE ARE SAYING

❝ We asked for service and the assistant manager came over and said it was a store policy not to serve Negroes....That was primarily local custom, and we said we thought it was a bad custom and something should be done about it. ❞

FRANKLIN MCCAIN,
leader of a sit-in (a nonviolent protest where people sit and refuse to move until their demands are met) at a store in North Carolina in 1960

❝ I was looking to the left and I heard these terrible noises.... So I turned to the right, and all I remember is seeing my husband, he had this sort of quizzical look on his face, and his hand was up. ❞

FIRST LADY JACQUELINE KENNEDY,
recalling the day her husband, President John F. Kennedy, was assassinated in Dallas, Texas, in 1963

❝ It can't happen to this family again! ❞

A BYSTANDER,
in 1968 at the Los Angeles, California, hotel where Senator Robert F. Kennedy, brother to John F. Kennedy, was assassinated

❝ I am the greatest! ❞

BOXER MUHAMMAD ALI,
after he defeated Sonny Liston in the first minute of their 1965 rematch

❝ The people have got to know whether or not their president is a crook. Well, I am not a crook. ❞
PRESIDENT RICHARD NIXON, *1974*

❝ I have a dream that my four little children will one day live in a nation where they will not be judged by the color of their skin but by the content of their character. ❞

REV. MARTIN LUTHER KING, JR.,
August 28, 1963

Fast Facts

The Fighter Who Would Not Fight In 1964, boxer Cassius Clay shocked the boxing establishment by announcing his conversion to the Nation of Islam. Shortly thereafter, Clay took the name Muhammad Ali.

Ali continued to dominate boxing with numerous victories. Then, in 1967, Ali refused induction into the U.S. Army at the height of the Vietnam War, citing his religious beliefs that did not condone violence. Many Americans were opposed to Ali's decision because, at that time, support for the war was strong. He further outraged people by acknowledging that he would be willing to participate in an Islamic holy war, something that seemed in opposition to his anti-Vietnam War position.

Ali was banned from fighting by every state athletic commission in the United States for three and a half years. He was also sentenced to five years in prison; but while he was free on bail, the conviction was overturned by the Supreme Court. Finally, in October 1970, Ali was allowed to return to boxing.

African American Firsts **S**

Many African Americans are making a mark on United States history. Match these famous people with their achievements as the first African Americans to hold these positions.

1. Beverly Johnson
2. Arthur Ashe
3. Constance Baker Motley
4. Shirley Chisholm
5. Thurgood Marshall

a. in 1968, elected to Congress, and in 1972, first woman and first African American to run for United States president
b. in 1964, New York state senator who became a federal judge in 1966
c. in 1975, tennis champ at Wimbledon
d. in 1974, cover model on *Vogue* magazine
e. in 1967, sworn in as justice of the United States Supreme Court

PHOTODISC (BALL)/COMSTOCK

Answers: 1. d; 2. c; 3. b; 4. a; 5. e

MILESTONES
EVENTS OF THE TIME

PUBLISHED. *Silent Spring* by Rachel Carson in 1961, helping to start a new environmental movement in America.

ENROLLED. James Meredith at the University of Mississippi in 1962. The Supreme Court ordered his admission to the previously segregated school.

BROKEN. 25-day fast by César Chávez, labor organizer in 1965. His protest led others to join his nonviolent strike against the grape growers.

TAKEN AWAY. Boxer Muhammad Ali's heavyweight championship title in 1967 after refusing induction into military service. He was found guilty in federal court of violating the Selective Service Act. In 1971 the U.S. Supreme Court overturned his draft conviction.

AIRED. *Sesame Street* for the first time in 1969.

OPENED. Walt Disney World in Orlando, Florida, in 1971.

EVACUATED. The last of American soldiers from Vietnam in 1975.

AL FRENI / TIME LIFE PICTURES / GETTY IMAGES

GIFTED. The Pet Rock was 1975's hot holiday gift. For $3.95 you received a small, obedient "pet" and an owner's manual with housebreaking tips and tricks any rock could learn. A million rocks sold in just a few months.

NUMBERS
WHAT HAPPENED IN 1969

3 Days Duration of the Woodstock Music and Art Fair that attracted hundreds of thousands of young people to a 600-acre (243 ha) farm in New York to celebrate peace and music

7 Baseball player Mickey Mantle's team number, which the Yankees retired when Mantle stopped playing **D**

747 The model number of Boeing's "Jumbo" jet launched this year; the world's largest and heaviest aircraft, it can carry at least 362 passengers, twice as many as an ordinary jet

ANDREAS MANOLIS / REUTERS / CORBIS

250,000 Number of people who marched from the United States Capitol to the Washington Monument in the largest demonstration in Washington's history—all to protest the U.S. involvement in the Vietnam War; President Nixon vowed to ignore the demonstration

CRITICAL THINKING

Making Generalizations How did African Americans who were first in their fields help move the civil rights movement forward?

Speculating What do you think programs such as the Peace Corps and landing a person on the moon did for the image of the United States around the world?

925

Section 4

Nixon and Vietnam

Focus

Bellringer
Daily Test Practice Transparency 29–4

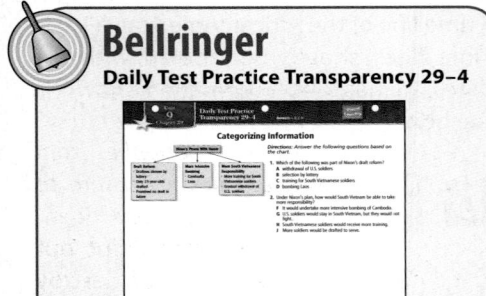

Reading Guide
Answers to Graphic:

reforming the selective service system; giving South Vietnam more responsibility in fighting the war; expanding the bombing campaign

Section Spotlight Video

Watch the Section Spotlight Video "Nixon and Vietnam" to learn more about Cambodia and how the Vietnam War ended.

Resource Manager

Essential Question
How did President Nixon remove the United States from the Vietnam War?

Reading Guide

Content Vocabulary
Vietnamization (p. 928)
martial law (p. 929)
MIA (p. 932)

Academic Vocabulary
authority (p. 927)
demonstration (p. 928)

Key People and Events
Henry Kissinger (p. 927)
Pentagon Papers (p. 930)

Reading Strategy
Taking Notes On a diagram like the one below, list the major points of Nixon's "peace with honor" strategy to end the war.

Nixon Strategy

ILLINOIS STANDARDS
The American Journey

14.E Understand United States foreign policy as it relates to other nations and international issues.

14.E.3 Compare the basic principles of the United States and its international interests (e.g., territory, environment, trade, use of technology).

16.A Apply the skills of historical analysis and interpretation.

16.A.3c Identify the differences between historical fact and interpretation.

American Diary

Speaking to reporters after his election, the new president, Richard Nixon, recalled seeing a young girl carrying a hand-lettered sign at one of his rallies that read: "Bring Us Together Again." This, he promised, would be his chief goal as president. Nixon also vowed to implement his plan to end the Vietnam War. Even though the United States began scaling back its involvement in Vietnam, the American home front remained divided.

Crowds lined the streets for the Inaugural parade following the swearing in of President Richard Nixon, in January 1969.

R Reading Strategies	**C** Critical Thinking	Differentiated Instruction	Writing Support	Skill Practice
Teacher Edition • Read. Pri. Sources, p. 927 • Finding the Main Idea, p. 928 • Identifying, p. 929 **Additional Resources** • Guid. Read., URB p. 98 • Content Vocab., URB p. 73	**Teacher Edition** • Making Inferences, p. 927 • Deter. Cause & Effect, p. 929 • Making Infer., p. 931 • Contrasting, p. 932 • Link. Past & Pres., URB p. 89 • Crit. Think. Skills, URB p. 85	**Teacher Edition** • Intrapersonal, p. 928 • Intrapersonal, p. 932 **Additional Resources** • School-to-Home, URB p. 91 • Reteaching Act., URB p. 93 • Differ. Inst., URB p. 83	**Teacher Edition** • Narrative Writing, p. 929 • Personal Writing, p. 930	**Teacher Edition** • Using Infer. Skills, p. 928 • Using Cause & Effect Skills, p. 930 • Using Infer. Skills, p. 931 **Additional Resources** • Daily Test Pract. Transp. 29-4 • Soc. Stud. Skills, URB p. 81

A New Strategy

Main Idea Nixon took steps to bring American forces home and end the war in Vietnam.

History and You Have you ever worked long and hard on a project and wished that someone could come and replace you so that you could take a rest? Read to find out about a "changing of the guard" during the war in Vietnam.

In his Inaugural Address in January 1969, Richard M. Nixon appealed to the American people for calm: "We cannot learn from one another until we stop shouting at one another—until we speak quietly enough so that our words can be heard as well as our voices."

Nixon had campaigned on a pledge of "peace with honor" in Vietnam. Shortly after taking office, Nixon began taking steps to end the nation's involvement in the war. As a first step, the president appointed Harvard professor **Henry Kissinger** as his national security adviser. Kissinger was given wide **authority**—the power to give orders and make decisions—to use his diplomatic skills to end the conflict. Kissinger launched a

policy he called "linkage." This policy aimed at improving relations with the Soviet Union and China—suppliers of aid to North Vietnam. Kissinger hoped to persuade the two Communist nations to cut back on their aid and help end the war.

At the same time, Nixon wanted to begin pulling American forces out of Vietnam. However, he did not want American withdrawal to be seen as a sign of defeat. Nixon's strategy of "peace with honor" had three parts—reforming the selective service system, giving South Vietnam more responsibility in fighting the war, and expanding the bombing campaign.

Changes in the Draft

Under President Nixon, the selective service system changed. College students could no longer obtain draft deferments, only 19-year-olds could be called for service in Vietnam, and draftees would be chosen by lottery on the basis of their birthdays. Protests against the draft faded with these reforms because the government began calling up fewer young men and because President Nixon promised to eliminate the selective service in the future.

Primary Source — A Changing Foreign Policy

The Nixon Doctrine Nixon and national security adviser Henry Kissinger shared views on many issues. The Nixon Doctrine spelled out a change in the nation's foreign policy. The United States would continue to provide military aid and training to allies. Nixon, however, set limits:

"America cannot—and will not—conceive all the plans, design all the programs, execute all the decisions and undertake all the defense of the free nations of the world."

Critical Thinking

Theorizing Do you think the Nixon Doctrine would change the role of the U.S. in Vietnam? Why or why not?

Teach

C Critical Thinking

Making Inferences Ask: How do you think aid from the Soviet Union and China affected the war? *(Supplies from these nations enabled North Vietnam to resist American firepower almost indefinitely, dragging out the war.)* Point out that American forces could not destroy weapons factories in China and the Soviet Union, as they had in Germany during World War II. North Vietnam could call on its friends to replace equipment that was lost in battle. **AL**

R Reading Strategy

Reading Primary Sources Ask: Why did Nixon call his strategy "peace with honor"? *(He wanted to avoid the appearance of defeat.)* **BL**

Primary Source

Critical Thinking Answer
Students might say yes, because the doctrine stated that America would not take on the entire burden of defending free nations.

Additional Support

Activity: Connecting Past to Present

Interviewing Have students work in small groups to interview someone in their community who was a young adult at the time of the Vietnam War. Each group should prepare questions and make an appointment for the interview. Encourage students to think about what they would like to know and write questions that target this information. Questions might cover the person's feelings about the war then and now, whether the person participated in protests, and any lingering effects of the war for that person. Then have the groups write a magazine article based on their interview. Have interested students combine the articles into a publication. **OL**

R Reading Strategy

Finding the Main Idea Ask: How was Vietnamization supposed to free American troops to come home? *(by having South Vietnamese troops take over the fighting)* **BL**

S Skill Practice

Using Inferring Skills Ask: Why do you think Nixon kept the bombing of Cambodia secret? *(He probably suspected that expanding the war to a neighboring country would be unpopular.)* **OL**

D Differentiated Instruction

Intrapersonal Ask students to visualize being among 300,000 protesters in Washington, D.C., marching with signs and chanting antiwar slogans. As a class, discuss how taking part in this event must have felt to the participants. *(Students might note how crowds tend to feed on one another, intensifying the excitement and sense of empowerment.)* **OL**

Reading Check **Answer:** national security adviser

Differentiated Instruction

Troop Withdrawal

Meanwhile, President Nixon cut back the number of American troops in Vietnam. Known as **Vietnamization,** this plan called for the South Vietnamese to take a more active role in fighting—and for Americans to become less involved. As South Vietnamese soldiers took over, American troops would gradually withdraw from the country. In June 1969, Nixon announced the withdrawal of the first 25,000 American soldiers.

Increased Bombing

In the third part of his Vietnam policy, Nixon expanded the bombing campaign. Hoping to relieve pressure on troops in South Vietnam, Nixon ordered the bombing of enemy supply routes and hideouts in neighboring Cambodia and Laos. Although the president announced the changes to the draft and the troop withdrawals, he kept the bombing of Cambodia secret.

Reading Check **Identifying** To what position did President Nixon appoint Henry Kissinger?

Renewed Opposition at Home

Main Idea As Vietnamization moved forward, a new wave of antiwar protests gripped the nation.

History and You What would make you want to write an angry letter to a newspaper editor, join a protest march, or boycott a film producer? Read to learn why protests against the war in Vietnam resumed in 1969.

A new round of antiwar **demonstrations,** or protest marches, began in late 1969, reflecting the growing sentiment for ending the war. In October more than 300,000 people took part in an antiwar protest in Washington, D.C.

The government also tried to end the war through peace talks with North Vietnam. Henry Kissinger, the president's national security adviser, represented the United States in the Paris talks. The United States had launched the bombing campaign to persuade the North Vietnamese to agree to peace terms.

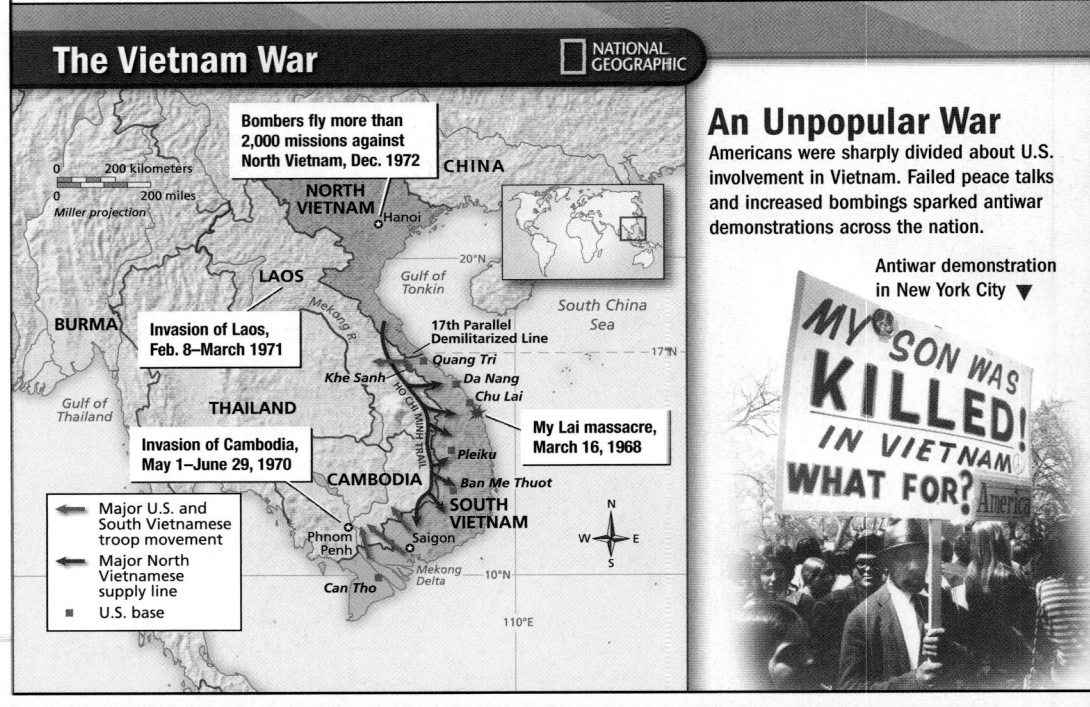

The Vietnam War

An Unpopular War
Americans were sharply divided about U.S. involvement in Vietnam. Failed peace talks and increased bombings sparked antiwar demonstrations across the nation.

Antiwar demonstration in New York City ▼

Leveled Activities

BL Social Studies Skills Activity, URB p. 81

OL Linking Past and Present Activity, URB p. 89

ELL Differentiated Instruction Activity, URB p. 83

The North Vietnamese, however, adopted a wait-and-see attitude. They believed that the growing strength of the antiwar movement in the United States would force the Americans to withdraw.

The new antiwar protests and North Vietnam's unyielding attitude alarmed President Nixon. In a speech in November, he appealed to the "silent majority" of Americans for support for his policy. "North Vietnam cannot defeat or humiliate the United States," he said. "Only Americans can do that."

Expanding the War

Further conflict gripped Southeast Asia when Cambodia plunged into a civil war between Communist and non-Communist forces. In April 1970, Nixon decided to send American troops to destroy Communist bases in Cambodia.

The attack aroused outrage throughout the nation. By sending U.S. troops to Cambodia, critics charged, Nixon invaded a neutral country and overstepped his constitutional authority as president.

Campus Protests

Many Americans viewed the Cambodian invasion as a widening of the Vietnam War. Nixon's action provoked a storm of antiwar protests on campuses across the nation. Most proceeded peacefully. Two protests, however, ended in tragedy.

At a protest at Kent State University in Kent, Ohio, students burned a military building on campus. Ohio's governor declared **martial law**—emergency military rule—on the campus and ordered 3,000 National Guard troops to Kent State.

At noon on May 4, students gathered for a protest rally on the campus lawn. The National Guard, young, inexperienced, and nervous, told the protesters to leave. When some students threw rocks at Guard members, the troops shot tear gas toward the students, and many students ran.

One National Guard unit chased some students between two buildings. Then—for reasons that are unclear—the troops opened fire. Four students were dead, and at least nine more were wounded.

C Critical Thinking

Determining Cause and Effect Ask: How did the antiwar movement affect peace talks? *(It influenced American leaders to seek peace but weakened the American negotiating position.)* **OL**

R Reading Strategy

Identifying Ask: What event set off the protest at Kent State? Why? *(The invasion of Cambodia; it was viewed as a widening of the Vietnam War.)* **OL**

W Writing Support

Narrative Writing Have students conduct research to learn more about the Kent State tragedy. Then ask them to take the role of a Kent State student who was there in May 1970. Have them write a story as a first-person narrative. Stories should describe the unfolding scene and their feelings as witnesses. **AL**

The Vietnam War — NATIONAL GEOGRAPHIC

Graph Skills Answers
1. 30%
2. highest: 1971; lowest: 1966

By the Numbers

United States Troops in Vietnam, 1965–1973

Number of troops (in thousands)

Year

Source: *Statistical Abstract of the United States*

Opposition to the War

Percentage of Americans against U.S. involvement

1965 U.S. escalates involvement
1968 Tet offensive
1969 First withdrawal of U.S. troops
1973 Cease-fire signed

Year

Source: *The Gallup Poll: Public Opinion*

Graph Skills

1. **Identifying** What percentage of Americans were against the war in 1965?

2. **Analyzing** In what year was opposition to the war the highest? The lowest? Why?

The Vietnam Era **Chapter 29** 929

Differentiated Instruction

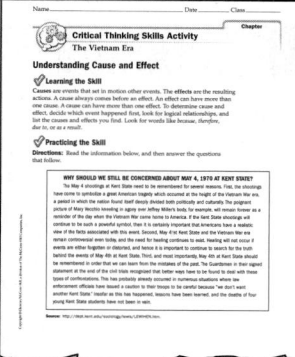

Critical Thinking Skills Activity, URB p. 85

Objective: To understand how to determine cause and effect

Focus: Ask a student volunteer to explain the difference between a cause and an effect.

Teach: Have students read the passage, fill in the chart, and answer the questions.

Assess: Have students compare their charts and answers.

Close: Reinforce with students the process they can use to determine cause and effect.

Differentiated Instruction Strategies

BL Ask students to explain the most important reason the events at Kent State should be remembered.

AL Have students locate the picture referred to in the reading and write a descriptive paragraph about it.

ELL Have students explain "cause and effect" in their own words before they answer the questions.

Violence flared again on May 15 at the nearly all-African American Jackson State University in Mississippi. Following a night of campus protests, two students were shot and killed. Witnesses charged that the police had recklessly blasted a residence hall with gunfire. The police claimed they were protecting themselves from sniper fire. A wave of student strikes followed the tragedies at Kent State and Jackson State. Hundreds of colleges and universities suspended classes.

The Pentagon Papers

In addition to sparking violence on campuses, the Cambodian invasion cost Nixon much support in Congress. Numerous lawmakers expressed outrage over the president's failure to tell them about the action. In December 1970, an angry Congress repealed the Gulf of Tonkin Resolution, which had given the president near-complete power in directing the war in Vietnam.

Support of the war weakened further that year when Daniel Ellsberg, a disillusioned former Defense Department worker, leaked documents to the *New York Times*. These documents, which became known as the **Pentagon Papers,** revealed that many government officials during the Johnson administration privately questioned the war while publicly supporting it.

The documents contained details of decisions that were made by presidents and their advisors without the approval of Congress. They also showed how various administrations acted to deceive Congress, the press, and the public about the situation in Vietnam. The Pentagon Papers backed up what many Americans had long believed: The government had not been honest with them.

Reading Check **Describing** What tragedies occurred at Kent State and Jackson State Universities?

Legacy of the War NATIONAL GEOGRAPHIC

A Monument to the Fallen The war took a heavy toll on America's soldiers and their families. Post-Traumatic Stress Disorder, once called "shell shock," caused hallucinations, nightmares, and depression. In 1982 the Vietnam Veterans' Memorial Wall was dedicated in Washington, D.C. The names of those who were killed or missing in the war are engraved into two black granite walls.

United States . . .

- 58,000 American military personnel were killed
- 75,000 were severely disabled
- 2,338 were listed as Missing in Action (MIA) and 766 were Prisoners of War (POW)
- 725,000 Vietnamese resettled in U.S.
- 6.7 million tons of bombs were dropped on Vietnam (compared with 2.7 million tons dropped on Germany during World War II)

"Dear Michael: Your name is here but you are not. I made a rubbing of it, thinking if I rubbed hard enough I would rub your name off the wall. And you would come back to me. I miss you so."
—from an anonymous note left at the Vietnam Veterans' Memorial

930   **Chapter 29**   *The Vietnam Era*

Peace and the War's Legacy

Main Idea Peace talks led to the withdrawal of all American forces from Vietnam.

History and You Have you ever visited or seen pictures of the Vietnam War Memorial in Washington, D.C.? What effect did the memorial have on you? Read to find out about the end of the war and its impact on Americans.

While antiwar feelings swelled at home—1971 polls showed that nearly two-thirds of Americans wanted the war to end quickly—the Nixon administration negotiated with representatives of the North Vietnamese government. These talks stalled, however.

In March 1972, the North Vietnamese launched another major offensive in the South. Because the United States had few troops left in Vietnam, Nixon resumed bombing. Nixon ordered American planes to bomb targets near Hanoi, the capital of North Vietnam. He also ordered the navy to plant mines in North Vietnamese harbors.

The president, however, stopped insisting that North Vietnam remove all its troops from South Vietnam before a full American withdrawal. Nixon sent Henry Kissinger to negotiate. In the fall of 1972 an agreement seemed ready, but South Vietnam opposed allowing North Vietnamese forces to remain in its territory. As a result the agreement collapsed.

Paris Peace Accords

After his reelection, Nixon unleashed American airpower against North Vietnam. In December 1972, the heaviest bombardment of the war fell on North Vietnam's cities. Nixon stood firm and North Vietnam returned to the talks. Meanwhile, the Americans pressured the South Vietnamese to accept the peace terms. On January 27, 1973, the negotiators signed the peace agreement.

Vietnam . . .
* 1.5 million Vietnamese soldiers and civilians were killed
* 362,000 were severely disabled
* 800,000 children were orphaned
* at least 1 million people fled the country
* 3.5 million acres of Vietnamese land were sprayed with chemicals that could impact the area for up to 100 years

The effects of the Vietnam War still linger. Since the end of the war, more than 40,000 people in Vietnam have been killed by land mines or bombs that did not explode on impact. Agent Orange, a chemical sprayed by Americans to defoliate forests during the war, has been blamed for many birth defects.

"When the war has ended and
the road is open again,
the same stars will course through the heavens.
Then will I weep for the white bones heaped
    together in desolate graves.
of those who sought military honors for their leaders."
—from the diary of an anonymous North Vietnamese soldier

Critical Thinking

Making Inferences Although the countries and soldiers went into battle for different reasons, what did all people involved in the Vietnam War experience?

The Vietnam Era **Chapter 29** **931**

Broadcasting the News

Step 4: Preparing Costumes and Props
Students will plan costumes, make props, and rehearse.

Essential Question: How did President Nixon remove the United States from the Vietnam War?

Directions Have students plan costumes and create props for their roles. Ask the groups to give their news program a name, such as "Action News" or "War Journal," and write a title for their story. Their broadcast should lead with the program name and the story title. Have students rehearse their roles.

Making Inferences Ask: How might Americans at home react to the news that the United States is finally getting out of Vietnam? *(They might be elated that the war is over, but confused by the outcome.)* **OL**

(Chapter Project continued on the Visual Summary page)

D Differentiated Instruction

Intrapersonal Ask each student to write an ending to this statement: "The Vietnam War was tragic because _____." Have students share their responses. **OL**

C Critical Thinking

Contrasting Ask: Why do you think soldiers returning from Vietnam received a different welcome than did the veterans of World War II? *(Most Americans opposed the Vietnam War by its end, and the United States did not achieve a victory in Vietnam.)* **OL**

Reading Check **Answer:** the Communists

Assess
· ·

History ONLINE

Study Central™ provides summaries, interactive games, and online graphic organizers to help students review content.

Close
· ·

Discussing Discuss America's exit from the Vietnam War and the effects of the war. **OL**

Section 4 Review

The War Ends

The United States agreed to pull its remaining troops out of the country. The North Vietnamese agreed to return all American prisoners of war. American involvement in Vietnam ended, but the conflict did not.

The North Vietnamese never gave up their goal of unifying Vietnam under their rule. In early 1975 they began a major offensive. The weakened South Vietnamese army collapsed on all fronts. Within a few weeks, North Vietnamese tanks approached Saigon. As North Vietnamese forces advanced, the last Americans left the country, some by helicopter from the roof of the U.S. embassy. Thousands of Vietnamese who had supported the Americans also fled to the United States. Many more could not escape. On April 30, 1975, Saigon fell to the Communists. Soon after, South Vietnam surrendered. The long war was over.

D The Human Toll

The Vietnam War took a staggering toll. More than one million Vietnamese soldiers and civilians died, and Vietnam lay in ruins with many villages destroyed. More than 58,000 Americans were dead; 300,000 were wounded, many of them permanently disabled. The United States had poured more than $150 billion into the war.

C Impact of the War

About 2.7 million Americans had served in Vietnam. Unlike the veterans of World War II, they found no hero's welcome when they returned home. Many Americans simply wanted to forget the war. They paid little attention to those who had fought and sacrificed in Vietnam.

The relatives of the American soldiers who had been classified as missing in action, or as **MIAs,** continued to demand that the government press the Vietnamese for information. The Vietnamese did allow a number of American groups to search the countryside. As the years passed, however, the likelihood of finding anyone alive faded.

Reading Check **Identifying** Who was in control of Vietnam when the war ended?

Section 4 Review

Vocabulary

1. Write a sentence for each of the following terms, explaining its significance in the Vietnam War era: authority, Vietnamization, demonstration, martial law, MIA.

Main Ideas

2. **Summarizing** What were the results of Nixon's Vietnamization plan?

3. **Explaining** What did Americans realize about the government after the release of the Pentagon Papers?

4. **Discussing** What did the Paris Peace Accords achieve?

Critical Thinking

5. **Categorizing** On a chart like the one below, list the major results from the Vietnam War in each category.

	Numbers of/ Results to
Vietnamese civilians and soldiers killed	
American soldiers killed	
American soldiers wounded	
U.S. cost in dollars	
Vietnamese countryside	

6. **Descriptive Writing** In a paragraph, describe how you feel about Nixon's actions during the Vietnam War and whether they were successful.

Answer the
7. **Essential Question**
How did President Nixon remove the United States from the Vietnam War?

Answers

1. Students' sentences should explain the significance of each term.
2. Nixon withdrew American soldiers; in the end, the South Vietnamese army alone was not strong enough to resist North Vietnamese forces, and South Vietnam fell to the Communists.
3. Americans realized that the government had not been honest with them.
4. The peace agreement got the United States out of the war. The North Vietnamese agreed to return all American prisoners.

5. **Vietnamese killed:** more than 1 million; **Americans killed:** more than 58,000; **Americans wounded:** 300,000; **U.S. cost in dollars:** $150 billion; **Vietnamese countryside:** in ruins; many villages destroyed
6. Students who support Nixon's actions might say that Nixon reformed the selective service system to make it more fair and succeeded in getting the United States out of Vietnam. Students who disagree with Nixon's actions might say that Nixon acted deceitfully, overstepped his authority, and

did not succeed in preventing a Communist takeover of South Vietnam.
7. Nixon expanded the bombing campaign to relieve pressure on South Vietnamese troops so they could take over more of the fighting. Nixon then gradually withdrew American troops. He ordered heavy bombing of North Vietnam to pressure the North Vietnamese to return to peace talks. Meanwhile, he urged the South Vietnamese to accept the terms. When the treaty was signed, the last American troops left.

Visual Summary

1954–1962	
1954	
July	Geneva Accords divide Vietnam
1957	
Oct.	Soviet Union launches *Sputnik*
1961	
April	Bay of Pigs invasion fails
Aug.	Berlin Wall is erected
1962	
Oct.	Cuban missile crisis occurs

▲ Berlin Wall

1963–1967	
1963	
Nov.	John F. Kennedy is assassinated
Nov.	Lyndon B. Johnson sworn in as president
1964	
Aug.	Gulf of Tonkin Resolution passes
1965	
Dec.	U.S. troop levels reach 180,000
1967	
March	War protesters march on Pentagon

Vietnamese village ▶

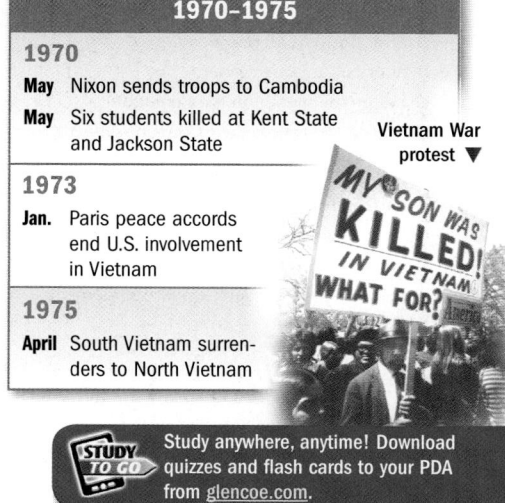

1968–1969	
1968	
Jan.	North Korea captures USS *Pueblo*
Jan.	North Vietnamese launch Tet offensive
April	Dr. Martin Luther King, Jr., is assassinated
June	Robert Kennedy is assassinated
Aug.	Violence erupts at Democratic convention in Chicago
Nov.	Richard Nixon wins presidency
1969	
July	Neil Armstrong walks on the moon

◀ Richard M. Nixon

1970–1975	
1970	
May	Nixon sends troops to Cambodia
May	Six students killed at Kent State and Jackson State
1973	
Jan.	Paris peace accords end U.S. involvement in Vietnam
1975	
April	South Vietnam surrenders to North Vietnam

Vietnam War protest ▼

MY SON WAS **KILLED!** IN VIETNAM WHAT FOR?

STUDY TO GO ▷ Study anywhere, anytime! Download quizzes and flash cards to your PDA from glencoe.com.

The Vietnam Era **Chapter 29** 933

Visual Summary

Analyzing Information Never before had a conflict sparked such widespread and heated protests as did the Vietnam War. **Ask:** Why do you think American opposition to the Vietnam War was so strong? *(Vietnam was a faraway, unfamiliar nation to most Americans. North Vietnam had not attacked the United States and did not seem like an immediate threat to national security. As the death toll and dollar amount rose, the war's goal may not have seemed worth the price.)* Do you think the antiwar movement was good or bad for America? *(Some students might say that the movement pressured America's leaders to end a pointless war. Other students might suggest that such public opposition undercut the efforts of the troops and weakened America's position in peace talks.)* **OL**

Evaluating Lead a class discussion about the goals and legacies of the war. **Ask:** What was the war's main goal? *(to stop the spread of communism)* Did the war accomplish this goal? *(No; the Communists took over South Vietnam.)* Was the war worth fighting? *(Opinions will vary. Have students give reasons for their opinions.)* **OL**

Hands-On Chapter Project
Step 5: Wrap-Up

Broadcasting the News

Step 5: Presenting the Broadcast Students will present their news story.

Directions Have each group present their news story. The rest of the class will serve as the television audience. After each broadcast, have members of the audience describe their reactions. What emotions did the reports bring forth? What did they learn from the story? If possible, videotape the programs and replay the tapes for group self-assessment.

Determining Cause and Effect Vietnam was the first "televised war." Americans were bombarded with a constant stream of war images on the nightly news. **Ask:** How might this televised coverage have influenced public opinion? *(The images made the brutality of war real to Americans at home,* possibly igniting opposition to the war.) Do you think reporters should be allowed to show war footage without restriction? *(Some students might argue for freedom of the press and the public's right to know. Others might say that wartime restrictions are needed to keep information from the enemy and to avoid eroding public support.)* **OL**

Answers and Analyses

Reviewing Main Ideas

1. A Point out the key word "poor" in the question. Students should recognize that choice A is the only action designed to counteract poverty. **18.C.3a**

2. D Remind students that people were attracted to communism by promises of equality. This appeal would be most attractive to people who lacked many of the necessities of life. **17.D**

3. A Remind students that Johnson stopped the bombing as a step toward peace talks. The Tet Offensive was the turning point that prompted this change of policy. **14.E**

4. B Students can immediately eliminate choice D, because protesters wanted peace. They should also eliminate choice A because Nixon would not want the contents of the Pentagon Papers to get out. **14.D**

Short-Answer Question

5. thousands of dead Americans and Vietnamese, and many seriously wounded and disabled young men **16.A.3c**

STANDARDIZED TEST PRACTICE

TEST-TAKING TIP

To understand the questions better, rewrite them in your own words if you have time. Be careful not to change the meaning.

Reviewing Main Ideas

Directions: Choose the best answer for each of the following questions.

1. President Kennedy counteracted the appeal of communism in poor areas of Asia, Africa, and Latin America by
  A creating the Peace Corps.
  B introducing Green Berets.
  C employing guerrilla warfare.
  D spending more on nuclear arms.

2. Communism took root in South Vietnam because
  A President Diem persecuted Buddhists.
  B North Vietnam supported the Vietcong.
  C Eisenhower sent billions in aid to Diem.
  D many Vietnamese lacked land and services.

3. When did President Johnson halt the bombing of North Vietnam's cities?
  A after the Tet Offensive
  B after Nixon's election
  C before the march on the Pentagon
  D during the Democratic Convention

4. Nixon provoked protests on campuses by
  A leaking the Pentagon Papers.
  B sending troops to Cambodia.
  C ending draft deferments for students.
  D having Kissinger seek a peace settlement.

Short-Answer Question

Directions: Base your answer to question 5 on the excerpt below and on your knowledge of social studies.

> He was now in Ward 1-C with fifty other men who had all been recently wounded in the [Vietnam] war—twenty-year-old blind men and amputees, men without intestines, men who limped, men who were in wheelchairs, men in pain. He noticed they all had strange smiles on their faces and he had one too, he thought. They were men who had played with death and cheated it at a very young age.
>
> —Ron Kovic, *Born on the Fourth of July*

5. What was the human cost of the Vietnam War?

Review the Essential Questions

6. Essay What roles did Presidents Kennedy, Johnson, and Nixon play in the Vietnam War?

To help you write your essay, review your answers to the Essential Questions in the section reviews and the chapter Foldables Study Organizer. Your essay should include:

- why and how Americans became involved in the Vietnam War;
- presidential decisions that kept the war going; and
- how citizen protests influenced Johnson's and Nixon's policies.

GO ON

Review the Essential Questions

6. If students completed their Foldables correctly, they should be able to link foreign policy decisions with the progress of the war. Answers should include the following. **Kennedy:** view of Vietnam as part of global struggle against communism, sent Green Berets, supported Diem but removed support when Diem failed to make needed reforms; **Johnson:** used alleged attack on American ships to win congressional approval of Gulf of Tonkin Resolution, increased American involvement with ground troops and air attacks, halted bombing and took first steps toward peace after Tet Offensive; **Nixon:** hired Henry Kissinger to negotiate an end to the war, reformed draft system, began withdrawing American troops under Vietnamization plan, widened the war by invading Cambodia and Laos, concluded the peace accords to get Americans out of the war **18.B.3a**

History ONLINE
For additional test practice, use **Self-Check Quizzes**—Chapter 29 at glencoe.com.

Document-Based Questions

Directions: Analyze the documents and answer the short-answer questions that follow.

Document 1

Four days before the Bay of Pigs invasion, Kennedy responded to press reports of CIA-trained invaders.

> There will not be, under any conditions, any intervention in Cuba by United States armed forces.

Source: Howard Zinn, *A People's History of the United States*

7. Why do you think President Kennedy did not tell reporters about the planned invasion?

Document 2

Madame Nhu, a member of President Diem's family, commented on the monks who protested Diem's policies by setting themselves on fire.

> "Let them burn," she said. "We shall clap our hands."

Source: Stephen Kinzer, *Overthrow*

8. What impact did the monks' protests have on Diem and others?

Document 3

The author of this excerpt talks about the beginning of the Tet Offensive.

> When the assault . . . first began we didn't know what was going on. . . . All the towns of the Delta . . . were full of [Vietcong]. Every town and city in the country was under siege. Every airfield had been hit. Every road cut. They were in the streets of Saigon, in the American embassy. All in one night.

Source: Tobias Wolff, *In Pharoah's Army*

9. Why did Americans criticize the conduct of the war after the Tet Offensive?

Document 4

This political cartoon, titled "Our Position Hasn't Changed At All," appeared in the *Washington Post* on June 17, 1965.

Source: The Herb Block Foundation

10. What does this cartoon say about President Johnson's policy in Vietnam?

Document 5

General James Carroll defended his son's decision to seek conscientious objector status in 1972.

> All I know for sure is this: if human beings don't drastically change the way they resolve their conflicts, we won't survive this century. My son . . . certainly represents a drastic change from the way we were brought up. And that may be just the change we need.

Source: James Carroll, *An American Requiem*

11. What did Carroll's son decide to do? What options did the young man have regarding going to war?

12. Expository Writing Using the information from the five documents and your knowledge of social studies, write an essay in which you:

- explain why the Vietnam War was difficult for Vietnamese and American soldiers and civilians; and
- describe how support for U.S. involvement in Vietnam changed over time.

9. Americans were shocked that a supposedly weak enemy could stage such a strong offensive. Many Americans began to question the war because the offensive made them realize that they could not trust government reports. **16.A.3b**

10. While stating publicly that U.S. policy in Vietnam had not changed, Johnson was increasing U.S. involvement in Vietnam. **16.A.3b**

11. He decided to become a conscientious objector and refused to fight. He could enroll in college to try to get a deferment, he could flee the country, or he could accept prison for refusing to serve. **18.B.3a**

12. The difficulties included the corrupt Diem regime, rugged and swampy terrain, guerrilla warfare, blending of the enemy with the population, aid for the Communist forces from China and the Soviet Union, the Ho Chi Minh Trail through neighboring countries, and the huge loss of life and injuries among civilians as well as soldiers. Support for U.S. involvement eroded over time as the war dragged on and the number of casualties mounted. The Tet Offensive and the Pentagon Papers suggested that government reports were untrustworthy. **14.E.3**

History ONLINE
Have students visit the Web site at glencoe.com to review Chapter 29 and take the Self-Check Quiz.

Need Extra Help?												
If you missed questions. . .	1	2	3	4	5	6	7	8	9	10	11	12
Go to page. . .	906	912	922	929	932	910–932	906–907	913	921	913–922	919–920	910–932

Document-Based Questions

7. He probably wanted the attack to take the enemy by surprise. Also, direct intervention in the affairs of another country would probably be unpopular, if not unconstitutional. **16.A.3b**

8. Members of Diem's regime were unimpressed, but news reports of the burnings horrified the international community and made Kennedy waver in his support for Diem. **18.B.3a**

Need Extra Help?

Have students refer to the pages listed if they miss any of the questions.

UNIT PACING CHART

	Unit 10	Chapter 30	Chapter 31
Day 1	Unit Opener, Reading History	Chapter Opener, Section 1	Chapter Opener, Section 1
Day 2		Section 2, TIME Notebook	Section 2, Section 3
Day 3		Section 3, America's Literature, Visual Summary	Section 4, You Decide
Day 4		Chapter Assessment	Section 5, Geography & History, Visual Summary
Day 5			Chapter Assessment

 Teacher to Teacher

**Laura Tabachnick
Academy School
Brattleboro, VT**

Amending the Bill of Rights Present a role-play scenario for the students to complete in small groups. The groups are members of the National Revision of the Bill of Rights Task Force. They believe that the Bill of Rights is outdated and should be revised. The task force thinks that some of the amendments in the Bill of Rights no longer reflect the needs of most Americans today. The groups should create a document that tries to persuade their state senators to support their cause. They will also make recommendations for changing the Constitution. Students may edit, delete, or add amendments, but the number must remain at 10. For each change, students should explain their rationale and use library sources to find information that supports their argument. Students will then present their proposals to the entire class, who will act as the members of their state legislators' offices. The class should evaluate each group's proposals.

Author Note

Dear American History Teacher,

The concluding unit of a history textbook is never far from today's headlines. Whether students realize it or not, global events exert a powerful influence upon them. For example, global markets affect where students' clothes are manufactured and where their food is grown. A greater awareness of current history will help students better understand and cope with their world.

The United States's international role has dominated its recent history, from the end of the Vietnam War and the Cold War to the war on terrorism. The United States became the world's sole superpower after the collapse of the Soviet Union. As a result, the United States had to extend its responsibilities to maintain world peace and stability. This new role has made the United States a target for those who seek change using violent methods. The shocking attacks on the United States on September 11, 2001, forced a dramatic reconsideration of many American foreign policies and increased the role of the United States military abroad. The legislation that was enacted as a result of the events of 9/11 has also heightened the tension between the demands of national security and the preservation of civil liberties.

Recently, the world has experienced a revolution in communications and information retrieval. In the 1970s, typewriters and the telegraph were still in use, computers were so large that they filled rooms, and just three major television networks dominated broadcasting. Today's students live in a world of personal computers, e-mail, the Internet, cell phones, and multiple-channel cable television. World news travels quickly and is readily accessible to anyone anywhere. The information, though, is more diffuse. These numerous sources of information are often questionable or completely unreliable. To make sense of this complex world and to sort out the verifiable from the dubious, students need a solid foundation of knowledge about their country's recent history.

Donald A. Ritchie

Unit Objectives

After studying this unit, students will be able to:

- Describe the main policy objectives and accomplishments that characterized each of the presidential administrations from the 1970s until the present.
- Evaluate the impact of presidential administrations on American politics from 1970 until the present.
- Discuss the major issues that the United States faces now, such as the war on terror, global warming, and illegal immigration.

Introducing the Unit

Assessing As students prepare to study the unit, ask them to think about how they feel when they find out someone has lied to them. **Ask:** What characteristics are important for a president to have? *(Students might note that a leader should have strong beliefs, have vision for the future, and be honest.)* Discuss with students that they will learn how Americans became more critical and distrustful of the government when they were not told the truth. **OL**

Unit 10 America in a Modern Era 1968 to Present

Chapter 30
America in the 1970s
1968–1981

Chapter 31
New Challenges
1981 to Present

The iPhone is a multimedia mobile phone.

936

Activity: Why It Matters

Why Study Challenges that Face the United States? Tell students what they can expect to learn in the upcoming unit. **Ask:** What should the United States do when other countries violate human rights? *(Students might answer that the United States should withhold aid from or initiate sanctions against those nations. Discuss all reasonab e answers.)* As they study the unit, have students write in their notebooks about how they feel when they hear stories of human rights violations around the world. **OL**

"We have every right to dream heroic dreams. . . . You can see heroes every day going in and out of factory gates."
—Ronald Reagan

Connect to Past Learning

America in a Modern Era In the previous unit, students studied the involvement of the United States in the Cold War, the Korean War, and the Vietnam War. In this unit, they will learn how Americans have responded to terrorism and other challenges by looking for new ways to preserve and protect democratic ideals in a changing world.

Melissa Etheridge performs at Live Earth, the Concerts for a Climate in Crisis, 2007.

More About the Image

Visual Literacy Live Earth was a worldwide concert event that was intended to bring awareness to the global climate crisis. For 24 hours on July 7, 2007, music concerts were held from many locations around the world: Sydney, Tokyo, Shanghai, Hamburg, London, Johannesburg, New York, and Rio de Janeiro, with special broadcasts from Antarctica, Kyoto, and Washington, D.C. The goal was to reach 2 billion people to inform them of the environmental challenges facing humanity. More than 150 musical acts, including Melissa Etheridge, performed that day.

Unit 10 Reading History

Why Monitoring and Clarifying Is Important

Students can use many of the tools discussed in the unit "Reading History" sections to help them better understand their studies. Knowing how to identify inevitable points of confusion and clarify them will help students with comprehension.

Learn It!

Draw the "Monitor/Ways to Clarify" chart on the board.

Have students read a paragraph that may have been difficult for the class. Fill in some of the "Monitor" rows in the table with ideas from students. Continue the exercise, soliciting ways to clarify.

Use the exercise to assure students that everyone gets confused at times, and explain that there are ways to help overcome that confusion. **OL**

Practice It!

Answers will vary, but students may list the following:

Monitor	Ways to Clarify
1. unfamiliar word: *ban*	**1.** dictionary: *to prevent or stop*
2. What is the main idea?	**2.** Nations are working together to make sure that pollution will not harm Earth.
3. What do I already know about nations working together?	**3.** *Globalism* is the idea that different economies and societies are linked together.

READING SKILL — Monitoring and Clarifying

Learn It!

Monitoring is the ability to know whether you understand what you have read. If you do not understand the information, then you must try to identify why you do not understand it. You must *clarify*, or clear up, the parts that are confusing. Read the following paragraph. Use the "Ways to Clarify" for tips about how you can clarify your reading.

Monitor	Ways to Clarify
Are there any words that are unfamiliar?	Use the glossary, a dictionary, or context clues.
What is the main idea of the paragraph?	Try to summarize the information into one sentence to create a main idea.
Is it helpful to use what I already know about democracy to understand the text?	Think about what you have learned about democracy. Then think about how this relates to Iraq.
What questions do I still have after reading this text?	Write the questions and continue to read to find the answers.

—from Chapter 31, p. 994

The United States set out to create a democracy in Iraq. . . . The United States and its allies trained more Iraqis to serve in the police and the military. They also attempted to provide electricity, clean water, schools, and improved health care for Iraq's people.

Practice It!

Read the following paragraph. Draw a chart like the one below to help you monitor and clarify your reading.

—from Chapter 31, p. 1004

Because pollution crosses international borders, many experts believe that nations have to work together to find solutions. In 1987, for example, 23 nations agreed to ban chemicals suspected of harming the ozone layer—a part of the atmosphere that shields Earth from the sun's radiation.

Monitor	Ways to Clarify
1. _____	1. _____
2. _____	2. _____
3. _____	3. _____

938 Unit 10 *America in a Modern Era*

Reading Strategy — Monitoring

Monitoring and Clarifying As students advance in their academic levels, the progressive difficulty of the material can cause some to become frustrated and discouraged. Choose a subsection of a chapter in the unit, or possibly copy and hand out an important document from the era covered, and ask students to read it. Have them create their own "Monitor/Ways to Clarify" table based on the reading. Encourage students to be honest, as they will not be asked to share the table with the class. Consider collecting the tables to assess students' comfort level with the material and their use of monitoring and clarifying tools. **BL**

Academic Vocabulary Preview

Listed below are the academic vocabulary words and their definitions that you will come across as you study Unit 10. Practice It! will help you study the words and definitions.

Academic Vocabulary	Definition	Practice It!
Chapter 30 America in the 1970s		
relax (rih · LAKS) p. 943	to ease	**Identify** the term from Chapter 30 that best completes the sentence.
technology (tehk · NAH · luh · jee) p. 945	scientific tools and material	1. Diplomatic negotiations can dramatically _____ tensions and improve relations between countries.
energy (EH · nuhr · jee) p. 952	sources of usable power	2. The Soviet Union hoped détente with the United States would give them access to American _____.
controversy (KAHN · truh · vuhr · see) p. 954	arguments between opposing viewpoints	3. The 1973 oil embargo forced Americans to conserve _____.
integrity (ihn · TEH · gruh · tee) p. 959	moral character	4. A _____ erupted because Nixon would not give White House tapes to the special prosecutors.
exceed (ihk · SEED) p. 959	to be greater; go beyond	5. Most candidates for public office talk about their personal _____.
Chapter 31 New Challenges		
quote (KWOHT) p. 973	to repeat the words of another	**Identify** the term from Chapter 31 that best matches the underlined term or terms.
theme (THEEM) p. 974	a subject	6. The United States wants to keep its position as a leader in world trade.
retain (rih · TAYN) p. 977	to hold on to	7. Many scientists believe that changes in weather patterns due to global warming are certain.
site (SYT) p. 979	a location	8. Terrorists gave no earlier notice of their attack on the United States.
adequate (A · dih · kwuht) p. 983	enough	**Choose** the word that best matches the meaning of each vocabulary term listed below.
scope (SKOHP) p. 985	a range; area	
prior (PRY · uhr) p. 993	earlier	9. **quote** 11. **decade**
definite (DEH · fuh · niht) p. 997	precise; well-defined	a. comment a. one hundred
decade (DEH · kayd) p. 1001	a period of ten years	b. punctuation b. ten
aware (uh · WEHR) p. 1003	to be mindful; have knowledge of	c. guess c. lifetime
		10. **site** 12. **adequate**
		a. location a. good
		b. vision b. too much
		c. spirit c. enough

Academic Vocabulary Preview

Play the memory game. Before class, make sheets of "cards" for each chapter's terms and definitions. Make a few copies of each chapter's sheets. In class, organize students into pairs, and give each pair a chapter's sheets of terms and definitions.

Have the students cut out the cards, turn them face-down on the desk, mix them up, and play "memory," matching the terms to the definitions. If time allows, have students trade cards with other groups that are working with different chapters and play again. **OL**

Practice It!

Answers
 1. relax
 2. technology
 3. energy
 4. controversy
 5. integrity
 6. retain
 7. definite
 8. prior
 9. a
10. a
11. b
12. c

Reading Strategy   Read to Write

Personal Writing Give students this opportunity to reveal their concerns and frustrations about their school work. Ask them to think about a subject they find challenging and write about how they feel when it is time to go to that class or do that homework. Ask them to then write about how this new tool of monitoring and clarifying makes them feel about that subject (More confident? Hopeful? The same?). Have them conclude by writing down ways in which they could use this new tool in the difficult subject to help them better understand it. **OL**

Chapter Planning Guide

30

Levels BL	OL	AL	ELL		Resources	Chapter Opener	Section 1	Section 2	Section 3	Chapter Assess
					FOCUS					
BL	OL	AL	ELL	Transparency	Daily Test Practice Transparencies		30–1	30–2	30–3	
					TEACH					
	OL	AL		Print	Geography and History Activity, URB				p. 31	
BL	OL		ELL	Print	Time Line Skills Activity, URB				p. 34	
BL	OL	AL	ELL	Print	Writing Skills Activity, URB			p. 23		
BL	OL	AL	ELL	Print	Content Vocabulary Activity, URB		p. 17	p. 17	p. 17	
BL			ELL	Print	Academic Vocabulary Activity, URB		p. 19	p. 19	p. 19	
BL			ELL	Print	Reading Skills Activity, URB		p. 7			
BL			ELL	Print	Social Studies Skills Activity, URB				p. 25	
BL	OL	AL	ELL	Print	Differentiated Instruction Activity, URB			p. 27		
BL	OL	AL	ELL	Print	Critical Thinking Skills Activity, URB			p. 29		
BL	OL	AL	ELL	Print	Linking Past and Present Activity, URB		p. 33			
	OL	AL		Print	Primary Source Readings, URB			p. 21		
BL	OL	AL	ELL	Print	School-to-Home Connection Activity, URB		p. 35	p. 35	p. 35	
BL	OL		ELL	Print	Guided Reading Activity, URB*		p. 39	p. 40	p. 41	
		AL		Print	Enrichment Activity, URB		p. 11			
BL	OL		ELL	Print	Reading Essentials and Note-Taking Guide*		p. 337	p. 340	p. 343	
BL	OL	AL	ELL	Transparency	Lesson Transparencies			30B, 30C	30A	
		AL		Print	Supreme Court Case Studies			pp. 115, 117	pp. 121, 123	
	OL			Print	American Biographies	p. 66				
BL	OL	AL	ELL	Print	Outline Map Resource Book	pp. 27, 28, 30, 43, 45, 49, 50				

Note: Please refer to the *Unit Resource Book: America in a Modern Era* for this chapter's URB materials.

* Also available in Spanish

Levels					Resources	Chapter Opener	Section 1	Section 2	Section 3	Chapter Assess
BL	OL	AL	ELL		**TEACH** *(continued)*					
BL	OL	AL	ELL	📁	**NGS US Desk Map**		✓	✓	✓	
BL	OL	AL	ELL	📁	**American Literature Library**		✓	✓	✓	
BL	OL	AL	ELL	📁	**Writer's Guidebook**		✓	✓	✓	
	OL	AL		💿	**American History Primary Source Document Library CD-ROM**		✓	✓	✓	✓
BL	OL	AL	ELL	💿	**American Music: Hits Through History**	✓	✓	✓	✓	
BL	OL	AL	ELL	💿	**StudentWorks™ Plus CD**	✓	✓	✓	✓	✓
BL	OL	AL	ELL	🔒	**Section Spotlight Videos**		✓	✓	✓	
BL	OL	AL	ELL	🖨	**Writing Process Transparencies**		✓	✓	✓	✓
BL	OL	AL	ELL	💿	**Presentation Plus! With MindJogger CheckPoint CD**	✓	✓	✓	✓	✓
					ASSESS					
BL	OL	AL	ELL	📁	**Quizzes and Tests**		p. 297	p. 298	p. 299	pp. 301, 303, 305
BL	OL	AL	ELL	📁	**Authentic Assessment With Rubrics**			p. 30		
BL	OL	AL	ELL	📁	**Standardized Test Practice**					p. 59
BL	OL	AL	ELL	💿	*ExamView® Assessment Suite* **CD-ROM***		30–1	30–2	30–3	Ch. 30
					CLOSE					
BL			ELL	📁	**Reteaching Activity, URB***		p. 37	p. 37	p. 37	p. 37
BL	OL		ELL	📁	**Reading and Study Skills Foldables Activity**	p. 108	p. 108	p. 108	p. 108	p. 108
BL	OL	AL	ELL	📁	*The American Journey* **in Graphic Novel**					p. 185
BL			ELL	📁	**Reading Strategies and Activities for the Social Studies Classroom**		✓	✓	✓	
BL	OL	AL	ELL	🖨	**Graphic Organizer Transparencies & Strategies**		✓	✓	✓	

TeacherWorks *Plus*
All-In-One Planner and Resource Center

- Interactive Lesson Planner
- Interactive Teacher Edition
- Fully editable blackline masters
- Section Spotlight Videos Launch

- Differentiated Lesson Plans
- Printable reports of daily assignments
- Standards Tracking System

Professional Development Resources

- Strategies for Success
- Building Academic Vocabulary
- Success With English Learners DVD
- Differentiated Instruction Strategies DVD
- Teaching Literacy Strategies in Social Studies DVD
- Assessment DVD
- Standards-Based Instruction DVD

Using TechCONNECT™

Using a Scanner

Technology Product

- Glencoe's TechCONNECT™ is a program that will help students learn how to use a scanner. (For more information or to get a free 30-day trial of Glencoe TechCONNECT™, **visit** techconnect.glencoe.com **and click the Free Trial button**.)

Objective

Students will learn to use a scanner and incorporate scanned images into projects.

Steps

- Log on to TechCONNECT™ and click the **Find your text-book** link.

- After you log on, click **Activity Search**, **Choose Social Studies, Scanners**, and your grade level.
- Have students log on and enter the letters AC and the three-digit activity number.
- Have students read each page and follow the on-screen instructions.
- Have students complete the activity's self-assessment rubric.
- Have students complete the TechCheck, a five-question, multiple-choice quiz, by entering the letters TC and the three-digit activity number.

History ONLINE at glencoe.com

	Student	Teacher	Parent
Media Center			
• Student Edition Audio	●		
• Spanish Summaries	●		
• Section Spotlight Videos	●	●	
Social Studies Online Learning Center			
Classroom Tools			
• Multi-Language Glossaries	●	●	●
• Teaching Today		●	
• TIME Current Events	●	●	●
• Beyond the Textbook	●	●	
***The American Journey* Online Learning Center**			
• Study-to-Go™	●	●	●
• Study Central™	●	●	●
• Chapter Overview	●	●	
• Concepts in Motion	●	●	
• ePuzzles and Games	●	●	
• Literature Connections	●	●	
• Online Student Edition	●	●	●
• Self-Check Quizzes	●	●	●
• Student Web Activities	●	●	
• Vocabulary eFlashcards	●	●	
• Web Activity Lesson Plans	●	●	●
• Vocabulary PuzzleMaker	●	●	●

Reading Support From JAMESTOWN EDUCATION

- **Timed Readings Plus in Social Studies** helps students increase their reading rate and fluency while maintaining comprehension. The 400-word passages are similar to those found on state and national assessments.

- **Reading in the Content Area: Social Studies** concentrates on six essential reading skills that help students better comprehend what they read. The book includes 75 high-interest nonfiction passages written at increasing levels of difficulty.

- **Reading Social Studies** includes strategic reading instruction and vocabulary support in Social Studies content for ELLs and native speakers of English.

- **Content Vocabulary Workout** (Grades 6–8) accelerates reading comprehension through focused vocabulary development. Social Studies content vocabulary comes from the glossaries of Glencoe's Middle School Social Studies texts.

www.jamestowneducation.com

NATIONAL GEOGRAPHIC
Index to National Geographic Magazine:

The following articles relate to this chapter:

- *"Future Power: Where Will the World Get Its Next Energy Fix?"* Michael Parfit, August 2005.

- *"Nuclear Power,"* Charles Petit, April 2006.

National Geographic Society Products

To order the following, call National Geographic at 1-800-368-2728:

National Geographic Atlas of the World (Book)

Access National Geographic's dynamic MapMachine Web site and other geography resources at:

www.nationalgeographic.com

www.nationalgeographic.com/mapmachine

Reading List Generator CD-ROM — GLENCOE BOOKLINK 3

Use this database to search more than 30,000 titles to create a customized reading list for your students.

- Reading lists can be organized by students' reading level, author, genre, theme, or area of interest.

- The database provides Degrees of Reading Power™ (DRP) and Lexile™ readability scores for all selections.

- A brief summary of each selection is included.

Leveled reading suggestions for this chapter:

For students at a Grade 6 reading level:
- *African Women: Three Generations,* Mark Marthabane

For students at a Grade 7 reading level:
- *Jimmy Carter: Beyond the Presidency,* Mellonee Carrigan

For students at a Grade 8 reading level:
- *Jimmy Carter,* Kerry Acker
- *The Great Society to the Reagan Era: 1964-1990,* William Loren Katz

For students at a Grade 9 reading level:
- *The Arab-Israeli Conflict,* Ivan Minnis
- *Apartheid in South Africa,* Sean Connolly

For students at a Grade 10 reading level:
- *Foreign Oil Dependence,* James Haley
- *White House Years,* Henry Kissinger

The following videotape programs are available from Glencoe as supplements to the chapter:

- **Richard Nixon: Man and President** (ISBN 1-56-501742-0)

- **Gloria Steinem: Ms. America** (ISBN 1-56-501518-5)

To order, call Glencoe at 1-800-334-7344. To find classroom resources to accompany many of these videos, check the following home pages:

A&E Television: www.aetv.com

The History Channel: www.history.com

Chapter Objectives

After studying this chapter, students will be able to:

- Explain how Nixon worked to achieve foreign policy goals.
- List Nixon's major domestic challenges in the 1970s.
- Explain how Carter dealt with foreign affairs issues.

Motivating Activity

Identifying Central Issues Both Nixon and Carter addressed foreign relations during their presidencies. Nixon hoped to build a more stable world by improving relations with the Soviet Union and China, and Carter based his foreign policy on human rights. He believed that the United States should not support any countries that violated human rights. **Ask: Which do you agree with? Why?** As you read the chapter, discuss the effectiveness of both presidents' foreign relations policies.

Previewing the Essential Questions

Answering the section-based Essential Questions will help students understand important concepts in the section.

Chapter 30

America in the 1970s 1968–1981

One goal of space exploration was reached on July 20, 1969, when U.S. astronauts set foot on the moon.

RICHARD NIXON 1969–1974

PRESIDENTS
U.S. Events
World Events

1968 — 1971

| 1972 | 1972 | 1973 |
| Nixon visits Beijing | SALT I is signed | Watergate hearings begin |

★ 1967 Six-Day Arab-Israeli War

★ 1971 People's Republic of China is admitted to UN

★ 1973 OPEC imposes embargo of oil to U.S.

Section 1

Nixon's Foreign Policy Ask: What kinds of foreign policy goals might a president have? How could they be achieved? *(A president might want to prevent the spread of terrorism, create a balance of power among nations, and increase trade. The goals could be achieved by visiting countries, forming agreements, and offering aid.)* Point out to students that in Section 1 they will learn about Nixon's foreign policies. **OL**

Section 2

Nixon and Watergate Ask: What types of issues within the United States must the president address? *(The president must address issues such as law enforcement, federal programs, race relations, busing, disability rights, the economy, and unemployment.)* Point out to students that Section 2 discusses how Nixon addressed issues affecting Americans. **OL**

Section 1: Nixon's Foreign Policy

Essential Question What were President Nixon's main goals in foreign policy, and how did he work to achieve them?

Section 2: Nixon and Watergate

Essential Question What were President Nixon's major domestic challenges in the 1970s?

Section 3: The Carter Presidency

Essential Question What major foreign affairs issues did President Carter face during his presidency, and how did he deal with them?

American hostages are paraded by their Iranian captors, 1979. ▼

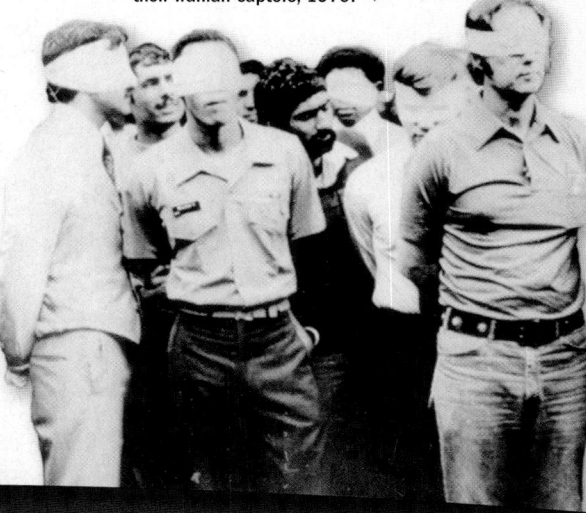

History ONLINE
Chapter Overview Visit glencoe.com and click on Chapter 30—Chapter Overviews to preview chapter information.

FOLDABLES Study Organizer

Organizing Information

Make this Foldable to organize what you learn about the presidents and their policies during the 1970s.

Step 1 Fold a 2 1/2 inch tab along the long edge of a sheet of paper.

Step 2 Fold the paper in thirds.

Step 3 Open the paper pocket Foldable. Staple the ends of the pockets together.

Step 4 Label the pockets as shown.

Reading and Writing
As you read the chapter, summarize key facts on note cards or on quarter sheets of notebook paper. Organize your notes by placing them in your pocket Foldable inside the appropriate pockets.

Introducing Chapter 30

Time Line Activity

Have students review the time line. **Ask:** Which presidents governed during this time period? *(Nixon, Ford, Carter, and Reagan)* Have each student select three events on the time line and write a question about each one. Ask a few students to share their questions with the class. Tell students to look for the answers in this chapter.

FOLDABLES Study Organizer **Dinah Zike's Foldables**

Purpose This Foldable helps students identify the major goals, domestic challenges, and foreign policy issues faced by the presidents during this time. The completed Foldable will help them prepare for assessment.

More Foldables activities for this chapter can be found in *Dinah Zike's Reading and Study Skills Foldables.*

History ONLINE
Introduce students to chapter content and key terms by having them access the **Chapter Overview** at glencoe.com.

★ 1974 President Nixon resigns

 GERALD FORD 1974–1977

 JIMMY CARTER 1977–1981

★ 1979 Iranians take Americans hostages

★ 1980 U.S. boycotts Moscow Olympics

★ 1981 Iranians release U.S. hostages

 RONALD REAGAN 1981–1989

1974 — **1977** — **1980**

◄ Fluctuating prices and supplies of gas meant long lines at gas pumps.

★ 1979 Soviet troops invade Afghanistan

★ 1981 Scientists identify AIDS

Chapter 30 **941**

Section 3

The Carter Presidency Ask: In what ways could a president solve foreign affairs problems without using military force? *(negotiations, treaties, and sanctions)* Tell students that in Section 3, they will learn how President Carter tried to resolve problems without resorting to using military force. **OL**

Focus

Nixon's Foreign Policy

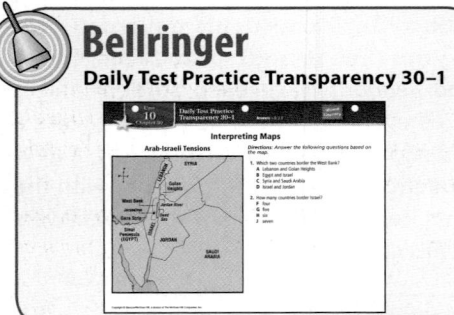

Bellringer
Daily Test Practice Transparency 30–1

Reading Guide
Answers to Graphic:
Answers may include China, Soviet Union, Israel, Egypt and other Arab Nations, and Chile.

Section Spotlight Video

Have students watch the Section Spotlight Video "Nixon's Foreign Policy" to learn more about how President Nixon worked to improve relations with China.

Essential Question ◄
What were President Nixon's main goals in foreign policy, and how did he work to achieve them?

Reading Guide

Content Vocabulary
détente (p. 943)   embargo (p. 946)
balance of power (p. 943)

Academic Vocabulary
relax (p. 943)   technology (p. 945)

Key People
Henry Kissinger (p. 943)
Zhou Enlai (p. 944)
Leonid Brezhnev (p. 945)
Golda Meir (p. 946)
Anwar el-Sadat (p. 946)

Reading Strategy
Taking Notes Re-create a diagram like the one below to show the countries that were the focus of Nixon's foreign policy.

Countries

🔲 **ILLINOIS STANDARDS**
The American Journey

14.E.3 Compare the basic principles of the United States and its international interests (e.g., territory, environment, trade, use of technology).

16.B.3d (US) Describe ways in which the United States developed as a world political power.

17.C Understand relationships between geographic factors and society.

17.C.3b Explain how patterns of resources are used throughout the world.

American Diary

Richard Nixon was long known for his anticommunist views. Thus, many people were surprised when Nixon set out to improve relations with the nation's main rivals—China and the Soviet Union—in the interests of world peace. Nixon announced: "We seek an open world—open to ideas, open to the exchange of goods and people—a world in which no people, great or small, will live in angry isolation."

—from Nixon's Inaugural Address, January 1969

President Nixon's visit to China in 1972 was the first step in establishing better relations between the U.S. and the People's Republic of China.

Resource Manager

R Reading Strategies	**C** Critical Thinking	**D** Differentiated Instruction	**W** Writing Support	**S** Skill Practice
Teacher Edition • Identifying, p. 944 **Additional Resources** • Guid. Read., URB p. 39 • Content Vocab., URB p. 17 • Academic Vocab., URB p. 19 • Read. Ess., p. 337 • Read. Skills, URB p. 7	**Teacher Edition** • Analyzing Info., p. 943 • Identify. Points of View, p. 944 • Making Infer., p. 947 **Additional Resources** • Quizzes and Tests, p. 297 • Enrichment, URB p. 11 • Link. Past & Pres., URB p. 33	**Teacher Edition** • Interpersonal, p. 946 • Below Grade Level, p. 947 **Additional Resources** • School-to-Home, URB p. 35 • Reteaching Act., URB p. 37	**Teacher Edition** • Expository Writ., p. 944 • Persuasive Writ., p. 945	**Teacher Edition** • Using Geo. Skills, p. 945 **Additional Resources** • Daily Test Pract. Transp. 30-1

Easing the Cold War

Main Idea President Nixon sought to ease Cold War tensions by improving relations with the Soviet Union and China.

History and You Have you ever tried to "mend fences" with somebody after a long disagreement? Read to learn about the changing relationships between the United States and Communist nations in the 1970s.

In his Inaugural Address, President Nixon told the American people, "The greatest honor . . . is the title of peacemaker." Many Americans wondered whether Nixon fit the role of peacemaker. During his years in Congress, he gained a reputation as a fierce enemy of communism. Few people imagined that Nixon, the anti-Communist crusader, would introduce policies to improve America's relations with the Communist world.

Behind the Iron Curtain

President Nixon intended to leave his mark on foreign policy. He hoped to build a more stable, peaceful world by reaching out to the Soviet Union and the People's Republic of China. In the summer of 1969, Nixon visited several countries, including Romania—the first time an American president went behind the iron curtain. Nixon wanted to find areas of common interest and cooperation with these Cold War opponents.

Détente

To help him in this task, Nixon appointed **Henry Kissinger,** a Harvard University professor, as his national security adviser. Kissinger and Nixon shared a belief in *realpolitik*—policies based on national interests rather than political beliefs. They believed that peace among nations would come through negotiation rather than through threats or force. Nixon followed a policy of **détente**—attempts at **relaxing,** or easing, international tensions. As détente replaced confrontation, the United States and Communist states could begin working together to resolve issues that divided them.

Nixon realized that détente would work only if a **balance of power** existed. A balance of power is a distribution of power among nations that prevents any one nation from becoming too powerful. "It will be a safer world and a better world," he declared, "if we have a strong, healthy United States, Europe, Soviet Union, China, Japan—each balancing the other, not playing one against the other."

C

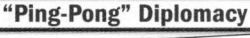

Primary Source — "Ping-Pong" Diplomacy

One of the first steps in improving relationships between China and the United States was the visit of the U.S. table-tennis team to China. *TIME* magazine called it "the ping heard round the world."

Pat Oliphant. *The Denver Post*, 1971.

Critical Thinking

Analyzing Do you think sports can help improve relations between nations? Explain.

Teach

C Critical Thinking

Analyzing Information Ask: What are examples of political beliefs? *(beliefs about democracy, communism, and totalitarianism)* What are examples of national interests? *(increasing trade, cultural exchange among nations, restricting nuclear arms)* How would focusing on *realpolitik* help countries form agreements with each other? *(Realpolitik is practical and doesn't let ideological differences prevent nations from negotiating with each other.)* **AL**

Primary Source

Critical Thinking Answer
Sample answer: Yes, sports can help improve relations between nations because sports provide a common bond between people.

Differentiated Instruction

Monitoring and Clarifying

Objective:	To learn monitoring and clarifying techniques
Focus:	Ask students what they do to understand difficult passages.
Teach:	Have students fill in the first chart. Discuss clarifying methods.
Assess:	Students should read the second excerpt and complete the chart.
Close:	Review methods for clarification.

Reading Skills Activity, URB p. 7

Differentiated Instruction Strategies

BL Ask students to read the first passage and complete the chart.

AL Have students find another challenging passage in this section and create and complete a chart.

ELL Tell students to highlight confusing terms and concepts as they read the second passage, and then create and complete a chart.

Détente in Space

Détente led to the first cooperative space mission between the United States and the Soviet Union. The U.S. *Apollo* and the Soviet *Soyuz* linked up in Earth orbit on July 17, 1975.

▲ Astronauts and cosmonauts share a meal inside the *Soyuz* mock-up during training at the Johnson Space Center in Houston.

▲ A view of the *Soyuz* space capsule from the *Apollo* command module

China

R Détente began with improved American-Chinese relations. Since 1949, when a Communist government came to power in China, the United States had refused to recognize the People's Republic of China. Instead it recognized the anti-Communist Chinese government under Chiang Kai-shek in exile on the island of Taiwan.

C By the time of Nixon's presidency, however, each side had good reasons for wanting to improve relations. China distrusted the Soviet Union. Since the 1960s, disagreements had developed between them that divided the Communist world. Chinese and Soviet troops occasionally clashed along their borders. The United States hoped that recognition of China would help end the war in Vietnam and drive a deeper wedge between the two Communist powers.

The winds of change began to blow in the fall of 1970 when Nixon told reporters that he wanted to go to China. Noting this change in tone, the Chinese responded by inviting an American table tennis team to visit the country in April 1971. A week later the United States announced the opening of trade with China.

"Ping-Pong diplomacy" was accompanied by secret talks between American and Chinese officials about forging closer ties between the two nations. After Kissinger made a secret trip to China in July 1971, President Nixon announced that he would visit Beijing, the Chinese capital, "to seek the normalization of relations."

W In February 1972, Nixon arrived in China for a weeklong visit. Nixon and China's premier **Zhou Enlai** agreed to allow greater scientific and cultural exchange and to resume trade. Although formal diplomatic relations were not established until 1979, Nixon's trip marked the first formal contact with China in more than 25 years.

What Is Détente?

The Nixon administration developed a policy called détente, or relaxation of tensions, between the United States and the Soviet Union and China.

Apollo-Soyuz patch ▲

Goals of Détente
- Reduce risk of nuclear war
- Cut back on military budget
- Forge better relations with rivals

Détente at Work
- President Nixon visits China, Soviet Union
- 1972 SALT I agreement signed
- U.S.-Soviet joint venture in space
- 1975 Helsinki Accords promote rights, trade

Critical Thinking

Analyzing The *Apollo-Soyuz* mission provided an opportunity for scientific research. According to U.S. pilot Vance Brand, the mission also had another goal: "to open the door a little bit between East and West." What do you think Brand meant?

The Soviet Union

Nixon followed his trip to China with a visit to Moscow, the Soviet capital, in May 1972. The Soviets welcomed a Cold War thaw. They wanted to prevent a Chinese-American alliance. They also hoped to buy United States **technology,** or scientific tools and material. Soviet leader **Leonid Brezhnev** remarked, "There must be room in this world for two great nations with different systems to live together and work together."

While in Moscow, Nixon signed the Strategic Arms Limitation Treaty (SALT I). This treaty restricted the number of certain types of nuclear missiles. The United States and the Soviet Union also agreed to work together in trade and science. Nixon—and the world—hoped that a new era of cooperation would bring greater stability to world affairs.

 **Identifying** What is détente?

The Middle East

Main Idea Nixon's foreign policy included easing Arab-Israeli tensions in the Middle East.

History and You Do you think that people of very different backgrounds can live together peacefully? Read to find out how the United States set out to achieve peace between the Arabs and the Israelis.

• •

President Nixon's foreign policy aimed to maintain world stability without being drawn into regional disputes. The president stated that the United States would help other nations but would not take "basic responsibility" for the future of those nations. A crisis soon arose in the Middle East that tested this policy.

Arab-Israeli Tensions

Since the founding of the Jewish state of Israel in 1948, the U.S. had supported Israel in its struggles against its Arab neighbors. Tensions between Israel and the Arab states erupted in war in 1948 and 1956.

In 1967 another war broke out. Fearing an attack from Egypt, Israel bombed Egyptian airfields on June 5. Within six days, Israel wiped out the air forces of its Arab neighbors. Israeli troops moved west into the Gaza Strip and Egypt's Sinai Peninsula and north into the Golan Heights, which were part of Syria. Israel also captured the old city of Jerusalem and the West Bank, the part of Jordan that was west of the Jordan River.

The "Six-Day War" of 1967 left Israel in control of these areas. When the fighting ended, the United Nations asked the Israelis to leave the captured territories. It asked the Arab nations to accept Israel's right to exist. Both sides refused.

The 1967 war also increased the number of Arab refugees, or displaced people. Thousands of Palestinians now lived in Israeli-held territory, and thousands more lived in neighboring Arab states. The Palestinians' demand for their own homeland became another source of instability.

S Skill Practice

Using Geography Skills Show students a map of Israel and its surrounding area. Have them point out the areas mentioned in the text. **Ask:** When Israel moved into the Golan Heights, which country was affected? *(Syria)* When it captured the West Bank, which country did this affect? *(Jordan)* **OL**

W Writing Support

Persuasive Writing Ask students to write a letter from the perspective of the UN either asking the Israelis to leave the captured territories or asking the Arab nations to accept Israel's right to exist. Letters should include at least two reasons the recipients should comply with the request. **OL**

Détente in Space

Critical Thinking Answer

Students may suggest that the mission was intended to relax tensions between the two nations and promote better relations.

Reading Check **Answer:** an attempt to relax international tensions

Additional Support

Teacher Tip

Tell students that a bibliography is a listing of sources, placed alphabetically by authors' last names. A typical entry can look like this: Author Name, *Title of Book,* Publisher, City (where it was published), year (of publication).

Activity: Technology Connection

Creating a Time Line Have pairs of students conduct online research to make a time line. The time line should include events leading up to the signing of the first Strategic Arms Limitation Treaty (SALT I). **Ask:** What prompted the United States to initiate the SALT I talks? *(the proliferation of nuclear missiles)* Have students compile their source information into a bibliography, which will accompany their time lines when they turn it in. Encourage students to print illustrations to add interest. Provide strips of 6" x 18" construction paper, rulers, and tape to help students arrange their entries. Check that dates are spaced appropriately. Provide scissors and glue for students to attach information and illustrations. **OL**

945

D Differentiated Instruction

Interpersonal Ask: Why do you think shuttle diplomacy was more effective than negotiating by telephone or by group meetings? *(People often feel more secure in their home environments, meeting face to face, allows clearer communication, or people on opposite sides of an issue might become angry more easily when meeting in person.)* OL

INTERPRETING POLITICAL CARTOONS

Answers

1. the 1973 oil embargo
2. that very few people would attend church if gas stations closed on Sundays

History ONLINE

Objectives and answers to the Student Web Activity can be found at glencoe.com under the Web Activity Lesson Plan for this chapter.

✔ **Reading Check Answer:** There was an oil shortage, and gas prices skyrocketed.

Hands-On Chapter Project
Step 1

Primary Sources
INTERPRETING POLITICAL CARTOONS

The fuel shortages caused by the 1973 oil embargo plunged the nation into a state of emergency. The Department of Energy considered different plans to save fuel. One plan was to close gas stations on Sundays.

1. **Identifying** What is the event or issue that inspired this cartoon?
2. **Analyzing Visuals** What message is the author trying to convey in this cartoon?

"My text this morning is taken from Paragraph 1: of the President's message in regard to Sunday driving."

Yom Kippur War

Tensions remained high between Arabs and Israelis. As a result, war erupted again in 1973. Egypt and Syria attacked Israel to regain land lost in the 1967 War. Because this attack occurred on Yom Kippur, a major Jewish holiday, the conflict became known as the Yom Kippur War.

Egypt's forces attacked Israel, hoping to recapture the Sinai Peninsula. In early battles, many Israeli planes were shot down. Egypt's troops crossed into the Sinai, and Syria moved into the Golan Heights. With an American airlift of weapons, Israel struck back. The fighting raged until the United Nations negotiated a cease-fire. By this time, the Israelis had regained most of the land lost in the initial Arab advance. Israel also took additional territory from Syria and Egypt.

Angered by the U.S. support of Israel, Arab oil-producing states placed an **embargo**—a

History ONLINE
Student Web Activity Visit glencoe.com and complete the Chapter 30 Web Activity about shuttle diplomacy.

ban on shipments—of oil to the United States and other "non-friendly" nations.

The embargo led to an oil shortage in the United States. Long lines of cars formed at gas pumps as gas prices skyrocketed.

Shuttle Diplomacy

President Nixon sent Kissinger, now secretary of state, to the region to gain Arab trust and to negotiate an agreement between Israel and its Arab neighbors. Kissinger engaged in shuttle diplomacy—traveling back and forth among Middle Eastern capitals trying to resolve the oil crisis and forge a lasting peace.

Early in 1974, **Golda Meir,** the prime minister of Israel, and **Anwar el-Sadat,** the president of Egypt, agreed to separate Israeli and Egyptian forces in the Sinai Peninsula. Then in March 1974, Kissinger persuaded the Arab nations to end the oil embargo. Kissinger also improved U.S. ties with Egypt, the most powerful Arab state, by promising large amounts of foreign aid.

✔ **Reading Check Summarizing** What happened in the United States because of the oil embargo?

Producing a Talk Show

Step 1: Creating a Talk Show Students will learn about political talk shows and organize their own talk show series.

Essential Question: What were President Nixon's main goals in foreign policy, and how did he work to achieve them?

Directions Familiarize students with political talk shows through recorded excerpts of radio and television productions. Explain that they will be playing the roles of interviewers and guests during the project. Guests on the show may be famous people mentioned in the chapter or other American citizens. Organize students into groups of three or four. Ask each group to select a name and host station for its talk show.

Expressing Ask each group to select one event and one guest to interview, based on the content of Section 1. Have each group write five questions to ask its guest, as well as responses that would have been typical from that person at the time. Groups should then choose performers and rehearse. OL

(Chapter Project continued in Section 2)

Latin America

Main Idea The Nixon administration continued the effort to halt the spread of communism in Latin America.

History and You Do you believe one country has the right to interfere in the affairs of another country? Read to find out how concerns about communism shaped the Nixon administration's policies in Latin America.

- -

The Nixon administration sought to prevent the spread of communism in Latin America. In 1970 the country of Chile elected Salvador Allende president. Allende was a follower of Karl Marx, the founder of communism. He became the first Marxist, or supporter of Marx, to rise to power in the Americas through peaceful means.

To boost Chile's economy, Allende's government took over large businesses, gave land to the poor, and raised workers' wages. The economy grew, and the jobless rate declined. Not all of Allende's policies were successful, however. His breakup of large farms led to a decline in food production, which in turn caused food shortages. Also, increased wages led businesses to raise prices.

More important, Allende's policies made him enemies. Wealthy Chileans, frightened by Allende's Marxist views, took their money out of the country and invested it abroad. The United States, angered by Allende's takeover of American companies, decided to undermine the Allende government. It gave money to Allende's political opponents and promoted strikes. It also convinced foreign investors to stop loaning money to Chile. By 1972, Chile's economy was near collapse.

In 1973 Chile's military decided to take action. With the backing of the Central Intelligence Agency (CIA), a group of Chilean military leaders under General Augusto Pinochet overthrew the government and killed Allende. The United States immediately recognized the new military dictatorship and restored foreign aid to Chile.

Reading Check **Explaining** Why did the United States oppose Salvador Allende?

Section 1 Review

History ONLINE
Study Central™ To review this section, go to glencoe.com.

Vocabulary

1. Use each of the following terms in a paragraph about U.S. foreign policy: détente, relax, balance of power, technology, embargo.

Main Ideas

2. **Analyzing** What did the United States hope recognition of China would achieve?

3. **Discussing** What was the purpose of shuttle diplomacy?

4. **Explaining** How did the United States combat President Allende in Chile?

Critical Thinking

5. **Determining Cause and Effect** On a chart like the one below, list a major effect in each country caused by Nixon's foreign policy.

CAUSE: Nixon's Foreign policy → EFFECT: China / EFFECT: Soviet Union / EFFECT: Chile

6. **Expository Writing** In a short essay, discuss Kissinger's achievements during the crisis in the Middle East.

Answer the **Essential Question**

7. What were President Nixon's main goals in foreign policy, and how did he work to achieve them?

D Differentiated Instruction

Below Grade Level Write this cause-and-effect diagram on the board: Allende breaks up large farms → ____ → food shortage. Ask students to fill in the blank. *(decline in food production)* **BL**

C Critical Thinking

Making Inferences Ask: Why did the United States immediately recognize the new dictatorship? *(The U.S. wanted to prevent the spread of communism.)* **OL**

Reading Check **Answer:** Allende was a Marxist, and his government had taken over American companies.

Assess

. . . .

History ONLINE

Study Central™ provides summaries, interactive games, and online graphic organizers to help students review content.

Close

. . . .

Discussing As a class, discuss the main goals of Nixon's foreign policy and how he worked to achieve them. **OL**

Section 1 Review

Answers

1. Paragraphs should use each term correctly in a foreign policy context.
2. The United States hoped to end the war in Vietnam and drive a deeper wedge between China and the Soviet Union.
3. to resolve the oil crisis and forge a lasting peace between the Arabs and Israelis
4. The United States gave money to Allende's opponents, promoted strikes, convinced foreign investors to stop loaning money to Chile, and used the CIA to help overthrow Allende's government.
5. In China—greater scientific and cultural exchange, resumed trade; Soviet Union—SALT I signed, agreed to work together in trade and science; Chile—old government overthrown, foreign aid restored
6. Students' essays should include: separated Israeli and Egyptian forces in the Sinai, helped end the Arab oil embargo, and improved U.S. ties with Egypt.
7. Essays should state that Nixon wanted to build a more stable, peaceful world with a balance of power among nations. He negotiated by visiting nations, implementing shuttle diplomacy, and offering aid.

Nixon and Watergate

Focus

Bellringer
Daily Test Practice Transparency 30-2

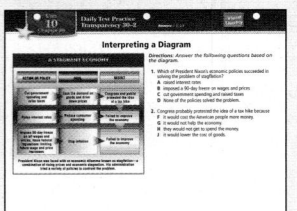

Reading Guide
Answers to Graphic:
federal spending cut; interest rates raised; businesses cut back and production fell

Section Spotlight Video

Have students watch the Section Spotlight Video "Nixon and Watergate" to learn how reporters from the *Washington Post* revealed the president's involvement in Watergate.

Resource Manager

Essential Question
What were President Nixon's major domestic challenges in the 1970s?

Reading Guide

Content Vocabulary
revenue sharing (p. 949)
executive privilege (p. 953)
affirmative action (p. 950)
impeach (p. 953)
tight money policy (p. 950)
amnesty (p. 954)
deficit (p. 951)

Academic Vocabulary
energy (p. 952)
controversy (p. 954)

Key People and Events
New Federalism (p. 949)
Watergate (p. 952)
Sam Ervin (p. 953)
Gerald R. Ford (p. 953)

Reading Strategy
Taking Notes On a diagram like the one below, record the factors that led to stagflation.

1.
2.
Stagflation ← 3.

ILLINOIS STANDARDS
The American Journey

14.F Understand the development of United States political ideas and traditions.

15.B.3b Explain the effects of choice and competition on individuals and the economy as a whole.

15.E Understand the impact of government policies and decisions on production and consumption in the economy.

17.C.3b Explain how patterns of resources are used throughout the world.

American Diary

President Nixon believed that the national government had grown cumbersome and inefficient, and that too many people were dependent on it. In August 1969, he announced a policy called "New Federalism" in a speech to the nation:

"After a third of a century of power flowing from the people and the States to Washington it is time for a New Federalism in which power, funds, and responsibility will flow from Washington to the States and to the people."

—Richard Nixon's address to the nation, August 8, 1969

President Nixon called for stiffer law enforcement measures and more aid for state and local law enforcement agencies.

R Reading Strategies	C Critical Thinking	D Differentiated Instruction	W Writing Support	S Skill Practice
Teacher Edition • Analyzing Text, p. 950 • Identifying, p. 952 • Explaining, p. 954 **Additional Resources** • Guid. Read., URB p. 40 • Content Vocab., URB p. 17 • Pri. Source Read., URB p. 21 • Read Ess., p. 340	**Teacher Edition** • Making Infer., p. 949 • Cause & Effect, p. 950 • Analyzing Info., p. 953 • Drawing Conclus., p. 955 **Additional Resources** • Quizzes and Tests, p. 298 • Crit. Think. Skills, URB p. 29	**Teacher Edition** • ELL, p. 951 • Logical/Math., p. 952 **Additional Resources** • School-to-Home, URB p. 35 • Reteaching Act., URB p. 37 • Differ. Inst., URB p. 27	**Teacher Edition** • Personal Writ., p. 952 • Persuasive Writ., p. 954 **Additional Resources** • Authentic Assess., p. 30 • Writ. Skills, URB p. 23	**Teacher Edition** • Visual Lit., p. 950 **Additional Resources** • Daily Test Pract. Transp. 30-2 • Lesson Transparency 30B, 30C

Nixon's Domestic Program

Main Idea The Nixon administration sought to reduce the role of the federal government in American life.

History and You If you were on a group project and found that you had too much to do, how would you solve the problem? Read to find out how the Nixon administration tried to reduce the federal government's workload by shifting more tasks to state and local governments.

In his 1968 presidential campaign, Nixon pledged to bring back "law and order" to American society. He also vowed to reduce government's role in people's lives.

Nixon's drive to restore law and order involved "cracking down on crime" and imposing stiffer penalties on lawbreakers. To strengthen police powers, Nixon used federal funds to help state and city police forces.

The Courts

Nixon thought the federal courts should be tougher on criminals. "As a judicial conservative," he said, "I believe some Court decisions have gone too far in weakening the peace forces against the criminal forces in our society." During his presidency, four vacancies arose on the Supreme Court. Nixon hoped that the justices he appointed—Warren Burger as chief justice, and Harry Blackmun, Lewis Powell, and William Rehnquist—would shift the Court to a more conservative position. The decisions of the new justices did not fully meet the president's conservative goals, however.

New Federalism

Nixon wanted to reduce federal involvement in people's lives and to cut federal spending. He pledged to "reverse the flow of power and resources from the states and communities to Washington and start power and resources flowing back . . . to the people." To accomplish this goal, he introduced a program called the **New Federalism.** One part of the New Federalism called for giving the states some of the revenue earned from federal taxes for use at the state and local levels. This **revenue sharing** became law in 1972.

Nixon also sought to end or scale back many Great Society programs begun under President Johnson. He promised to "quit pouring billions of dollars into programs that have failed." He abolished the Office of Economic Opportunity, the agency that led Johnson's War on Poverty.

Primary Source / New Federalism

A New Approach President Nixon rejected the idea that "government in Washington, D.C., is inevitably more wise . . . than government at the local or State level." He called for turning over to state and local governments many of the responsibilities of the federal government. New Federalism would make government more effective by:

- reducing big government programs
- restoring political authority to the local level
- directing tax money away from federal bureaucracy
- directing money toward state and local governments

Critical Thinking

Explaining What was the goal of New Federalism policies?

Teach

C **Critical Thinking**

Making Inferences Ask: How would state governors have felt about revenue sharing? *(They were probably glad to get more funding.)* **OL**

Primary Source

Critical Thinking Answer
to make the federal government more effective

Additional Support

Connecting Past and Present

Making Connections Ask: What did Nixon hope to achieve by appointing Warren Burger, Harry Blackmun, Lewis Powell, and William Rehnquist to the Supreme Court? *(to shift the Court to a more conservative position)* Tell students that two Nixon appointees, Clement Haynsworth and G. Harold Carswell, were not confirmed because of their positions on controversial social issues of the time.

Ask: Who is on the Supreme Court now? Have students work in pairs to identify the current justices. Have each pair research one justice and write a one-page summary of the person's political background. Include recent rulings, noting whether they are liberal, moderate, or conservative.

Ask: Are Nixon's conservative hopes still reflected by the current Supreme Court? Have each student respond to this question in a one-page essay. **OL**

S Skill Practice

Visual Literacy Have students study the photograph of the students at the top of the page. **Ask:** Which civil rights policy is evident in the photo? *(busing)* Lead a class discussion on the pros and cons of busing. If students believe busing is effective, ask them why. If they believe it does not work, ask them for alternative methods to desegregate schools. **OL**

R Reading Strategy

Analyzing Text Structure Explain to students that Nixon tried three tactics to cure the nation's economic problems. **Ask:** Why are there four paragraphs in Economic Troubles? *(The first explains the problems. The remaining three outline the ways Nixon tried to solve the problems.)* How does the author help you locate each tactic? *(Each paragraph explains a different approach to solving the economic trouble.)* **OL**

C Critical Thinking

Cause and Effect What were the major causes of the nation's economic problems? *(foreign competition, inflation, increasing cost of oil, slow economic growth, and high unemployment)* **OL**

Additional Support

Primary Source / **New Directions for Equal Rights**

Busing To end segregation in public schools, state courts ordered the busing of children to schools outside their neighborhoods.

Some civil rights leaders and some parents favored the use of busing. Many parents, however, did not want their children attending distant schools.

Diane Joyce kept her job when the Court ruled that gender can be a factor in hiring. ▶

Affirmative Action Opponents of affirmative action argue that merit is the only basis for making decisions on jobs, promotions, and school admissions. Supporters contend that affirmative action programs are needed to encourage the hiring and promotion of minorities and women in fields that were traditionally closed to them.

▲ Columbus, Georgia, students arrive for school, September 7, 1971.

S On civil rights issues, Nixon took a conservative position aimed at appealing to white voters. For example, Nixon opposed busing. Busing was used to promote racial integration by transporting students from mostly white or African American neighborhoods to racially mixed schools.

At the same time, his administration worked to carry out federal court orders to integrate schools. The Nixon administration also promoted **affirmative action,** or preference to minorities in jobs where they previously were excluded. A practical politician, President Nixon did accept new government programs that had popular support. He approved the creation of two new agencies—the Occupational Safety and Health Administration (OSHA) to ensure workers' safety and the Environmental Protection Agency (EPA) to protect the environment.

R Economic Troubles

While attempting to change the direction of government, President Nixon had to deal with serious economic problems. Industry and manufacturing were declining because of foreign competition. Businesses and consumers struggled with inflation—a general rise in the prices of goods and services. This was fueled by international competition for raw materials and the increasing cost of oil. The United States also faced slow economic growth and high unemployment.

C President Nixon tried several approaches to reduce inflation. He began by cutting federal spending. At the same time, he called for a **tight money policy.** Interest rates were raised so that people would borrow less and spend less. With less money in circulation, prices dropped. However, as demand slowed, businesses began to cut back and output fell.

Fast Facts

The Equal Rights Amendment In 1923 Alice Paul and the National Women's Party first proposed the Equal Rights Amendment (ERA). Congress finally approved it in 1972 and sent it to the states for ratification. By the end of 2007, thirty-five states had endorsed it. When and if three more states approve it, the ERA could be added to the Constitution.

Disability Rights Legislation The Disability Rights Section of the U.S. Department of Justice publishes *A Guide to Disability Rights Laws.* The guide summarizes legislation enacted since 1968 to protect the needs of disabled people. It covers a wide range of needs and lists contact information for the agencies that can provide aid.

Affirmative Action The Supreme Court upheld an affirmative action decision allowing race as a factor in college admissions. It said a varied student population offers "educational benefits that flow from a diverse student body."

Disability Rights The Rehabilitation Act of 1973 was the first major legislation to prohibit discrimination against people with disabilities. The act applied to programs that receive federal financial assistance.

▼ Disabled Americans protest for equal rights.

Critical Thinking

1. **Explaining** What were the goals of affirmative action policies?
2. **Speculating** What types of accommodations are available for people with the disabilities shown in the photograph above?

These steps slowed economic growth and led to stagflation—a combination of rising prices and a sluggish economy.

Nixon then switched tactics. He temporarily froze wages and prices and issued guidelines for any future increases. This put a brake on inflation, but the economy remained in a recession.

Later, Nixon tried a third approach—increasing federal spending to stimulate the economy. Although this policy helped revive the economy for a short time, it also created a budget **deficit** in which government spending was greater than government revenue. None of Nixon's policies restored the economy to its previous strength, and economic problems continued to trouble his administration.

✓**Reading Check** **Analyzing** What is the outcome of a tight-money policy?

Reelection and Watergate

Main Idea During his second term, President Nixon was involved in a political scandal that forced him to resign.

History and You What would officials do if someone broke into your school and stole something? Read to learn how an attempted burglary shook the presidency and the nation.

. . . .

As the 1972 presidential election neared, Nixon had doubts about his chances for reelection. The war in Vietnam had not yet ended, and the nation was facing economic problems. The president and his supporters wanted to ensure his reelection. **D**

A Campaign Against Enemies

To carry out his campaign, Nixon relied on a small group of aides, including John Ehrlichman, his chief domestic adviser, and H.R. Haldeman, his chief of staff. In their efforts to win the election, the president and his advisers, it was later revealed, sometimes crossed the boundaries of the law. In 1971, for example, Nixon asked his aides for an "enemies list" of people considered unfriendly to the administration. He then ordered the FBI and the Internal Revenue Service (IRS) to investigate some of these people. Nixon believed that those who opposed his policies posed a danger to the nation's security.

Nixon's campaign committee collected millions of dollars. It used some of this money to create a secret group to stop leaks of information that might hurt the administration. Some campaign money also paid for operations against Nixon's Democratic foes, but that party had many problems of its own.

Landslide Victory

The Democratic Party was split. Candidates seeking the nomination included former vice president Hubert Humphrey, Senators Edmund Muskie of Maine and George McGovern of South Dakota, and former governor of Alabama George Wallace.

America in the 1970s **Chapter 30** **951**

D Differentiated Instruction

English Language Learners Tell students that the prefix "re-" means "again." **Ask:** What does "reelection" mean? *(to elect again)* **ELL**

Primary Source

Critical Thinking Answers
1. to encourage the hiring and promoting of minorities and women in fields that were traditionally closed to them
2. Answers may include wheelchair ramps or bus lifts.

✓**Reading Check** **Answer:** Prices drop because of less borrowing and less spending.

Additional Support

Activity: Collaborative Learning

Making Connections When presidential candidates first began campaigning, television hadn't been invented yet. In 1880 James Garfield used songs to capture the public's interest. One-line messages called "slogans" were also used. Abraham Lincoln campaigned in 1860 with the slogan "Vote Yourself a Farm," and in 1900, William McKinley campaigned with the slogan "A Full Dinner Pail." In 1952, TV ads emerged, and Dwight Eisenhower was able to reach 19 million homes with this new medium.

Arrange students in groups of four and tell them that they will be writing campaign ads for a Democratic candidate in the 1972 presidential campaign. Groups can choose Hubert Humphrey, Edmund Muskie, George McGovern, or George Wallace. Each group should write an ad that showcases its candidate's strengths and/or downplays President Nixon's flaws. They can use a song, a slogan, a TV ad, or all three. Have students present their finished ads to the class. **OL**

Muskie and Humphrey could not gain enough support. Wallace's campaign was cut short in May 1972 by a would-be assassin's bullet that left him paralyzed.

McGovern, the most liberal of the four candidates, won the nomination. Many Democrats and labor union leaders were cool toward McGovern's candidacy.

The Democrats' lack of unity as well as an upsurge in the economy and the prospect of peace in Vietnam led to a landslide victory for Nixon. He won 60.7 percent of the popular vote. The Republican victory in the electoral college was even more lopsided—520 to 17.

The Energy Crisis

During Nixon's second term, severe economic problems confronted the nation. The U.S. economy depended heavily on foreign oil. In 1973 the Organization of Petroleum Exporting Countries (OPEC), placed an embargo on all oil shipments to the United States. As a result, many American companies had to lay off workers, while others raised their prices. Consumers complained about the high prices and the long lines at gas stations.

The president imposed measures to save oil. Nixon also urged Americans to conserve **energy**—sources of usable power—voluntarily. Congress reduced speed limits on highways because a vehicle burns less fuel at lower speeds. To deal with the problem of reliance on imported oil, Nixon urged development of domestic oil, especially in Alaska, which possessed vast, untapped oil reserves.

Watergate

During Nixon's second term, what seemed like a small scandal turned into a presidential crisis. In June 1972, Nixon's reelection committee had five men break into the Democratic Party's office at the **Watergate** apartment-office complex in Washington, D.C. The burglars set out to get information about the Democrats' campaign and to place listening devices—bugs—on the office telephones. A security guard caught them, and the police later arrested the men. Reports soon surfaced that the burglars were linked to the Nixon campaign and were paid from White House funds. The White House denied any involvement.

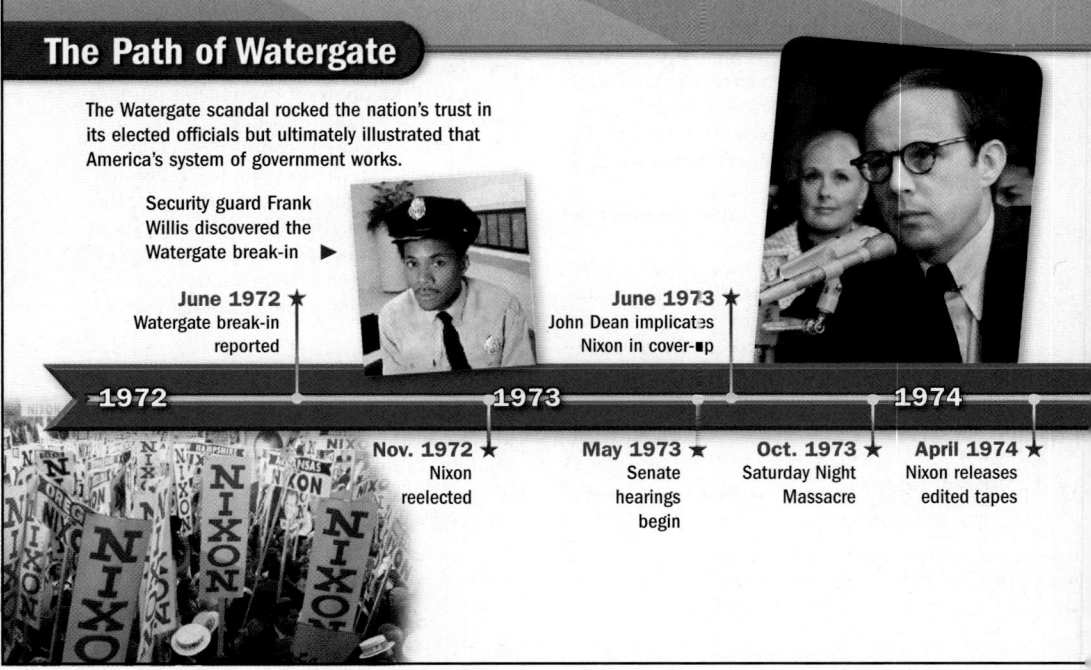

The Path of Watergate

The Watergate scandal rocked the nation's trust in its elected officials but ultimately illustrated that America's system of government works.

Security guard Frank Willis discovered the Watergate break-in ▶

June 1972 ★
Watergate break-in reported

June 1973 ★
John Dean implicates Nixon in cover-up

1972 — **1973** — **1974**

Nov. 1972 ★
Nixon reelected

May 1973 ★
Senate hearings begin

Oct. 1973 ★
Saturday Night Massacre

April 1974 ★
Nixon releases edited tapes

Investigation

Meanwhile, a series of newspaper articles in the *Washington Post* linked the burglary to the Nixon campaign. Eventually, one of the burglars admitted that White House aides had lied about their involvement and had pressured the burglars to plead guilty and remain silent.

In May 1973, the Senate began holding hearings on Watergate. Chaired by Senator **Sam Ervin** of North Carolina, the hearings slowly revealed the inner workings of the Nixon White House. John Dean, a White House official, testified that a cover-up occurred and that Nixon directed it, but he had no evidence to support his claim.

In July investigators learned that a secret taping system had recorded all of the president's office conversations. President Nixon refused to hand over the tapes. He claimed **executive privilege,** the principle that White House conversations should remain secret to protect national security.

Meanwhile, the special prosecutor—someone independent of the Justice Department— requested a court order to get the tapes. Nixon tried to have this official fired, but the attorney general and the attorney general's deputy both refused to carry out Nixon's order. In what became known as the Saturday Night Massacre, Nixon fired these officials and had the special prosecutor removed from office.

In the middle of the turmoil, another scandal struck the Nixon administration. Vice President Spiro Agnew was charged with taking bribes while governor of Maryland. In October 1973, he resigned. **Gerald R. Ford** of Michigan, the Republican leader of the House, became the new vice president.

The President Resigns

To quiet mounting public outrage, Nixon named a new special prosecutor, who was determined to get the tapes. After Nixon had released only edited versions of some of the tapes, the Supreme Court ruled that the president had to turn over all of the tapes, and Nixon complied.

Several days later, the House Judiciary Committee voted to **impeach** Nixon, or officially charge him with misconduct in office. Before the House of Representatives could vote on whether Nixon should be impeached, investigators found clear evidence against the president. One of the tapes revealed that Nixon had ordered a cover-up of the Watergate break-in just a few days after it happened.

With this news, even Nixon's strongest supporters admitted that an impeachment trial now seemed unavoidable. On August 9, 1974, Nixon resigned his office in disgrace. Gerald Ford took the oath of office and became the nation's 38th president.

The Watergate crisis revealed that the system of checks and balances worked to remove a president who had abused his power. Congress passed laws to correct some of the abuses. However, the scandal damaged the public's faith in its political leaders.

✔ **Reading Check** **Explaining** How did Gerald Ford become president?

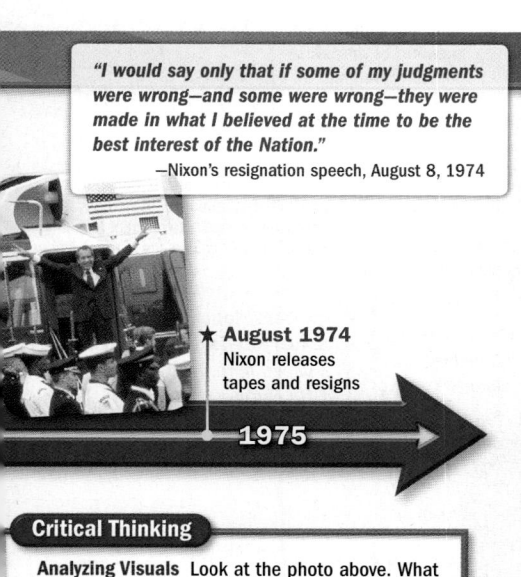

"I would say only that if some of my judgments were wrong—and some were wrong—they were made in what I believed at the time to be the best interest of the Nation."
—Nixon's resignation speech, August 8, 1974

★ **August 1974**
Nixon releases tapes and resigns

1975

Critical Thinking

Analyzing Visuals Look at the photo above. What thoughts or feelings do you think President Nixon was having at the time he left the White House?

C **Critical Thinking**

Analyzing Information Ask: Do you think executive privilege applied to the office tapes? Why or why not? *(No, the situation did not affect national security.)* **OL**

The Path of Watergate

Critical Thinking Answer

Students may say that Nixon looks victorious or powerful but that he might have been acting that way to hide feelings of defeat and rejection.

Skill Practice Ask: Which entry shows that the American system of checks and balances works? *(May 1973; the U.S. Senate took on the case, exerting its power over the executive branch.)*

✔ **Reading Check** **Answer:** Vice President Agnew resigned, so the Republican leader of the House, Gerald Ford, took over the position. When Nixon resigned, Ford became the new president.

Hands-On Chapter Project
Step 2

Producing a Talk Show

Step 2: Selecting an Event Groups will review the section content, select an event, and write an interview for it.

Essential Question: What were President Nixon's major domestic challenges in the 1970s?

Directions Explain to the whole class that the interviewer's role will pass to a different group member for Section 2. Have the groups meet to review the section and select a domestic event they believe was a challenge at the time Nixon was president. They should select the guest(s) to appear on their show.

Identifying Points of View Each group will write interview questions and answers for its guest. Remind groups that their writing must represent the attitudes of the time.

Ask students to consider the issue of equal rights for women. **Ask:** How have attitudes about women in the workplace changed since the 1970s? Encourage students to consider these changes as they compose their interviews. Remind students to include the date and location of the domestic event in the host's introductory remarks. **OL**

(Chapter Project continued in Section 3)

A Time for Healing

Main Idea President Ford set out to unite the nation after the Watergate scandal.

History and You Whom do you turn to for advice when times are difficult? Read to find out how the nation responded to Gerald Ford's leadership.

After becoming president, Gerald Ford assured Americans, "Our long national nightmare is over." To fill the office of vice president, Ford selected Nelson Rockefeller, a highly respected Republican and former governor of New York.

Domestic Controversies

Most Americans welcomed the new president and vice president as a fresh start for the nation. One of Ford's first acts, however, destroyed much of this confidence. On September 8, 1974, Ford granted Richard Nixon a pardon for any crimes he may have committed as president. This meant that the former president could not be prosecuted for his part in the cover-up.

Ford hoped that the pardon would help heal the wounds of Watergate. Instead, the pardon stirred **controversy,** or arguments between opposing viewpoints. Many Americans questioned why Nixon should escape punishment when others involved in the scandal went to jail. Some even accused Ford of striking a bargain with Nixon in advance—the promise of a pardon in exchange for Nixon's resignation. Although Ford defended his action, the new president never fully regained the trust and popularity he enjoyed in his first weeks in office.

Yet another controversy arose when President Ford offered **amnesty,** or protection from prosecution, to men who illegally avoided military service during the Vietnam War.

Primary Source / Congress vs. The White House

The Watergate crisis brought the president into direct conflict with the Congress. Over the course of several months, the Senate Watergate Committee held hearings to investigate the president's staff.

Barbara Jordan was a member of the House Judiciary Committee. ▶

Sam Ervin [1896–1985]
As chair of the Senate committee, Ervin rejected the White House claim of executive privilege as reason to withhold records and evidence.

"Divine right went out with the American Revolution and doesn't belong to White House aides. . . . That is not executive privilege. That is executive poppycock."
—April 1973

Fred Thompson [1942–]
Serving as chief legal counsel to the minority Republicans on the Senate committee, Thompson's team chanced upon critical evidence during an interview with Nixon's appointment secretary, Alexander Butterfield. They called him to testify before the whole committee, and Thompson asked:

"Mr. Butterfield, are you aware of the installation of any listening devices in the Oval Office of the President?"
—July 1973

Barbara Jordan [1936–1996]
Jordan delivered a passionate speech before the House Judiciary Committee on whether to introduce articles of impeachment against President Nixon. It was seen on TV by millions of Americans.

"If the impeachment provision in the Constitution of the United States will not reach the offenses charged here, then perhaps that 18th century Constitution should be abandoned to a 20th century paper shredder."
—July 1974

Counsel Fred Thompson and Senators Lowell Weicker and Sam Ervin during the Senate Watergate hearings ▶

Critical Thinking

Analyzing Why was the Watergate scandal also a constitutional crisis?

Write a Persuasive Essay

Ford promised that these people would not be punished if they pledged loyalty to the United States and performed some type of national service. Although many people approved of amnesty, others thought it was too lenient. Supporters of the Vietnam War argued that draft dodgers and deserters should be punished.

Ford and Foreign Affairs

Ford continued Nixon's foreign policies, relying on Secretary of State Henry Kissinger. Ford and Kissinger extended the policy of détente with the Soviet Union. In late 1974, Ford met with Soviet leader Leonid Brezhnev to discuss arms control. A year later, he traveled to Helsinki, Finland, where he signed the Helsinki Accords with the Soviet Union and other nations. The countries pledged to respect the human rights of their citizens. The accords also set new trade agreements. **C**

The Ford administration also worked to improve relations with China. When Chinese leader Mao Zedong died in 1976, a more moderate government came to power. China's new leaders wanted to increase trade with the United States.

A Troubled Economy

Like Nixon, Ford had to face economic troubles. Inflation and unemployment remained high. By the 1970s, Europe and Japan challenged American world economic dominance. Foreign competition led to factory closings and worker layoffs in the United States. It also contributed to underemployment, people working in jobs that did not fully use their skills. OPEC also kept oil prices high, adding to inflation.

To fight inflation, Ford launched voluntary wage and price controls. He called on Americans to save rather than spend money and to plant their own gardens to counter rising food prices. Despite a small drop in inflation, the economy continued its decline.

Ford also tried to cut government spending to control inflation. When this failed, the president then had Congress pass a tax cut. Some economic growth was achieved, but the cut led to large budget deficits. Despite his efforts, Ford could not solve the nation's economic woes.

Reading Check Evaluating How did Ford attempt to fight inflation? Did the efforts work?

C Critical Thinking

Drawing Conclusions Ask: How do you know that Ford and Kissinger's dealings with foreign nations were successful? *(They extended détente and discussed arms control with the Soviet Union; they signed the Helsinki Accords, pledging with the Soviet Union and other nations to respect human rights; and they improved relations with China, which wanted to increase trade with the U.S.)* **OL**

Reading Check **Answer:** Ford asked for voluntary wage and price controls and for Americans to save money and plant gardens. He cut government spending and had Congress pass a tax cut. The measures did not work.

Assess

History ONLINE

Study Central™ provides summaries, interactive games, and online graphic organizers to help students review content.

Close

Summarizing Lead a class discussion about Nixon's major domestic challenges in the 1970s. **OL**

Section 2 Review

Section 2 Review

History ONLINE
Study Central™ To review this section, go to glencoe.com.

Vocabulary

1. Use each of these terms in a sentence that explains its meaning: revenue sharing, affirmative action, tight money policy, deficit, energy, executive privilege, impeach, controversy, amnesty.

Main Ideas

2. **Explaining** What was Nixon's New Federalism program?

3. **Analyzing** What three things led to Nixon's landslide victory in the 1972 presidential election?

4. **Summarizing** What problems with the economy did President Ford face?

Critical Thinking

5. **Sequencing** On a time line like the one below, note major events that occurred during the Watergate crisis.

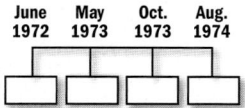

| June 1972 | May 1973 | Oct. 1973 | Aug. 1974 |

6. **Creative Writing** Imagine you write for your school's newspaper. Write an editorial column expressing your opinion of President Ford's plan to offer amnesty to those who avoided the draft.

Answer the Essential Question

7. What were President Nixon's major domestic challenges in the 1970s?

America in the 1970s **Chapter 30** **955**

Answers

1. Students will write sentences using the vocabulary in a context that explains its correct meaning.

2. New Federalism was a plan to return the flow of power and resources to the people by revenue sharing and scaling back federal spending.

3. the Democratic Party was split, an upsurge in the economy, and the prospect of peace in Vietnam

4. inflation, unemployment, foreign competition, underemployment, high oil prices

5. **June 1972:** Watergate break-in reported; **May 1973:** Senate hearings begin; **Oct. 1973:** Saturday Night Massacre; **Aug. 1974:** Nixon releases tapes and resigns; Ford takes office

6. Students' editorial columns should express a personal opinion and support it with details from the text.

7. weakened police, failed federal programs, racial integration, busing, affirmative action, disability rights, stagflation, unemployment

Focus

W Writing Support

Persuasive Writing Have students write a paragraph nominating an influential person, either past or present, to be recognized on the TIME 100 list. **OL**

Teach

C Critical Thinking

Drawing Conclusions After reading the profile of Oprah Winfrey, have students think about what makes a person influential. **Ask:** What qualities do you think the editors of TIME were looking for in a person to be nominated for the TIME 100 list? *(An "influential person" was considered to be someone who had an impact or influence on the lives of many others, whether good or bad.)* **OL**

R Reading Strategy

Using Context Clues Read aloud the quotation from Jimmy Carter in "Verbatim," along with the caption describing the "crisis of confidence." Ask students to use context clues within the quote to determine the meaning of the term "crisis of confidence." **ELL**

Additional Support and Answers

What were people's lives like in the past?

These two pages will give you some clues to everyday life in the United States as you step back in time with TIME Notebook.

ALLSTAR PICTURE LIBRARY / ALAMY

Profile

In 1998 TIME *magazine put together a list called the* TIME 100—*profiles of the 100 most influential people on the planet. It included world leaders, heads of industry—and* **OPRAH WINFREY.** *Here is part of what Oprah's profile said:*

W

"Oprah stands as a beacon, not only in the worlds of media and entertainment but also in many other ways. At 44, she has a personal fortune estimated at more than half a billion dollars. She owns her own production company which creates feature films, TV specials, and home videos. An accomplished actress, she won an Academy Award nomination for her role in *The Color Purple.*

"But it is through her talk show, *The Oprah Winfrey Show,* that first aired nationally in 1986, that her influence has been greatest. When Winfrey talks, her viewers—an estimated 14 million daily in the U.S. and millions more in 132 other countries—listen. Any book she chooses for her book club becomes an instant best seller. When she established the 'world's largest piggy bank,' people all over the country contributed spare change to raise more than $1 million (matched by Oprah) to send disadvantaged kids to college.

C

"Oprah exhorts viewers to improve their lives and the world. She makes people care because she cares. That is Winfrey's genius, and will be her legacy, as the changes she has wrought in the talk show continue to permeate our culture and shape our lives."

FASHION OF THE NATION

The Long & Short of It

In the early 1990s, five college freshmen at the University of Michigan changed basketball fashion. They wore long, baggy shorts instead of the kind with high hemlines like other basketball players wore. Thanks to the "Fab Five," most teams—from high school to the pros—dropped the "high on the thigh" shorts and adopted the long "jams" style.

STOCKDISC CLASSIC / ALAMY

R

Fast Facts

Oprah's Book Club A voracious reader, Oprah started "Oprah's Book Club" on her TV show because she wanted to motivate people to read. She started endorsing books she felt were of literary merit, and when she did, their sales soared. Ten million copies of the first eight selections combined were sold after Oprah's book club endorsements.

Each month, Oprah chose a book and presented it to her audience, then gave them a few weeks to read it. The author of the book would appear on the show to discuss the book. The author, along with a small group of readers, sometimes met in intimate settings such as Oprah's home to discuss the book.

The first book selection was *The Deep End of the Ocean* by first-time author Jacquelyn Mitchard. The publisher initially printed 100,000 copies of the book, but after Oprah's endorsement, an additional 640,000 were printed. Many publishers were caught off-guard by the sudden surge in sales. Oprah later decided to notify publishers of her selections ahead of time, though she asked that publishers, in return, donate 10,000 copies of the selected book to libraries.

TALK OF THE TIMES

"Ten-Four, Good Buddy"

CB radios (or Citizen Band radios) were a huge hit in the mid-1970s. More than 15 million of these two-way devices, which communicate over short distances, were in trucks, cars, and homes. There was even a special radio language. Do you think you have what it takes to chat on the air? Match the CB slang word or phrase with the correct meaning.

1. ten-four	**a.** police officer
2. ten-twenty	**b.** fuel
3. bear	**c.** snowplow
4. saltshaker	**d.** "I heard you"
5. bandage buggy	**e.** user's nickname
6. handle	**f.** location
7. go-go juice	**g.** ambulance

Answers: 1. d; 2. f; 3. a; 4. c; 5. g; 6. e; 7. b

INDEX STOCK / ALAMY

MILESTONES

EVENTS OF THE TIME

In the last quarter of the 1900s, the American people were introduced to inventions, places, and new ideas. Here are just a few examples and when they were introduced:

1976 Call waiting—it is now available for home phones

1979 Rubik's Cube—a habit-forming puzzle created by Hungarian professor Erno Rubik

1979 Susan B. Anthony silver dollar

1980 In-line skates

1983 The computer mouse

1984 PG-13 movie rating

1992 Mall of America—world's largest mall opens in Minnesota

1996 "Dolly"—first lamb cloned from the cell of a fully grown sheep

1999 New heights in trading—the Dow Jones stock indicator breaks 10,000

2000 Census

According to the United States Census, our country's population was 281,421,906 in 2000—having grown by 32.7 million people in the 1990s. Here is how that growth averaged out:

One person was added to the population every 14 seconds

That means 6,300 people were added every day

4,400 of those added were from births (10,600 daily births less 6,200 daily deaths)

1,900 were from immigration

One immigrant was added every 35 seconds

One person left the U.S. to live in another country every 3 minutes

NUMBERS

UNITED STATES AT THE TIME

21 Age of Tiger Woods in 1997 when he set golfing records by winning the Masters Tournament—the youngest and the first of African American or Asian heritage to do so

$229,000,000 Ticket sales from the movie, *E.T., the Extra-Terrestrial,* released in 1982—one of the highest-grossing films ever

0 The number of cases of smallpox reported in 1979; the following year the World Health Organization said the disease had been wiped out thanks to vaccinations

1,920 The number of panels on the NAMES Project Foundation AIDS Memorial Quilt displayed for the first time in Washington, D.C., in 1987—in one weekend more than 500,000 people visited the quilt, which honored individuals who had died of AIDS

HISHAM IBRAHIM / PHOTOV.COM / ALAMY

CRITICAL THINKING

Hypothesizing Why do you think a recommendation from a celebrity (such as Oprah Winfrey) can influence what Americans read or buy? Is this justified? Explain your answer.

Evaluating Rank the items listed in Milestones in importance to you. Have the items impacted your life for better or worse? How?

957

R Reading Strategy

Making Connections Read some of the terms from the box titled "Ten-Four, Good Buddy." Point out that people using CB radios created a unique language. Ask how the slang of CBs compares with the Internet language for instant messaging used today. **OL**

S Skill Practice

Visual Literacy Refer students to the photo of the AIDS Memorial Quilt. **Ask:** Why do you think a quilt was used to honor victims of AIDS? *(Students may say that because a quilt consists of materials that are pieced together, each panel could represent a victim. Joining the panels would represent a "gathering" of all the victims of the disease.)* **AL**

Assess/Close

As a class, discuss what life was like between 1975 and 2000. Ask students if they can recall firsthand any of the milestones or events featured on these pages. Then ask students to predict what events might occur in the next 25 years that will impact the lives of Americans. **OL**

Answers

Hypothesizing Students' answers should demonstrate an understanding of the impact that celebrities and other public figures have on Americans.

Evaluating Students' answers should include an explanation as to whether these items affected their lives.

Section 3

The Carter Presidency

Focus

Bellringer
Daily Test Practice Transparency 30–3

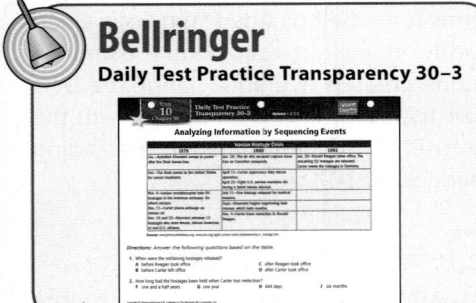

Reading Guide
Answers to Graphic:
create a Department of Energy to oversee energy policy; explore alternative energy sources; collect taxes to further oil production and energy conservation

Section Spotlight Video

To learn more about the election of Jimmy Carter, have students watch the Section Spotlight Video "The Carter Presidency."

Resource Manager

Essential Question ◄
What major foreign affairs issues did President Carter face during his presidency, and how did he deal with them?

Reading Guide

Content Vocabulary
trade deficit (p. 959)   apartheid (p. 960)
human rights   fundamentalist
   (p. 960)   (p. 962)

Academic Vocabulary
integrity (p. 959)   exceed (p. 959)

Key People and Events
Ronald Reagan (p. 959)
Jimmy Carter (p. 959)
Three Mile Island (p. 960)
Camp David Accords (p. 961)

Reading Strategy
Taking Notes On a diagram like the one below, identify the major points of Carter's National Energy Plan.

National Energy Plan

ILLINOIS STANDARDS
The American Journey

14.E Understand United States foreign policy as it relates to other nations and international issues.

15.A.3c Describe the relationship between consumer purchases and businesses paying for productive resources.

15.D.3a Explain the effects of increasing and declining imports and exports to an individual and to the nation's economy as a whole.

15.E Understand the impact of government policies and decisions on production and consumption in the economy.

American Diary

In the 1976 Democratic presidential campaign, James Earl "Jimmy" Carter, Jr., a former governor of Georgia, made a virtue of his lack of experience in the federal government: "We have been shaken by a tragic war abroad and by scandals . . . at home. Our people are seeking new voices, new ideas and new leaders."
Many voters found Carter's down-home style refreshing after the ordeals of the Watergate scandal.

—Jimmy Carter's acceptance speech at the Democratic National Convention, July 15, 1976

Jimmy Carter, with his wife Rosalynn, addresses a crowd following his election victory in 1976.

R Reading Strategies	**C** Critical Thinking	**D** Differentiated Instruction	**W** Writing Support	**S** Skill Practice
Teacher Edition • Identifying, p. 959 • Determin. Import., p. 961 **Additional Resources** • Guid. Read., URB p. 41 • Content Vocab., URB p. 17 • Academic Vocab., URB p. 19 • Read. Ess., p. 343	**Teacher Edition** • Drawing Con., p. 959 • Contrasting, p. 962 **Additional Resources** • Quizzes and Tests, p. 299	**Teacher Edition** • Visual/Spatial, p. 960 **Additional Resources** • School-to-Home, URB p. 35 • Reteaching Act., URB p. 37	**Teacher Edition** • Expository Writ., p. 961	**Additional Resources** • Daily Test Pract. Transp. 30-3 • Soc. Stud. Skills, URB p. 25 • Time Line Skills, URB p. 34 • Geo. & Hist., URB p. 31 • Lesson Transparency 30A

An Informal Presidency

Main Idea President Carter faced a weakened economy and a growing energy crisis.

History and You If you had a choice, would you like to "dress up" or wear casual clothes to an event? Read to find out how Carter wanted to create a more informal presidency.

As the 1976 elections neared, President Ford struggled to gain the Republican nomination. He faced a challenge from the former governor of California, **Ronald Reagan,** who was favored by party conservatives. Ford chose Senator Bob Dole of Kansas as his running mate. **Jimmy Carter** ran as the Democratic candidate, stressing his **integrity,** or moral character, his religious faith, and his standing as an outsider. Senator Walter Mondale of Minnesota ran as vice president.

During the campaign, Ford tried to stress his achievements as president. Carter ran as much against the memory of Nixon and government corruption as against Ford. Carter won in a close election, gaining 50.1 percent **R** of the popular vote. He owed his margin of

victory to support from African American Southern voters.

As president, Carter set a down-to-earth tone. At his inauguration, he wore an ordinary business suit rather than formal clothing. After the ceremony, Carter and his family walked from the Capitol to the White House instead of riding in a limousine, as earlier presidents had done.

Struggling With the Economy

After taking office, Carter cut taxes and increased spending to revive the economy. Unemployment decreased, but inflation rose. Carter then proposed spending cuts and a delayed tax cut. Carter's reversal made him seem weak and uncertain. As an outsider, the **C** president had trouble gaining support in Congress.

Carter made energy policy a priority. High energy costs added to inflation. Also, as American money paid for overseas oil, the nation faced a growing **trade deficit**—the value of foreign imports **exceeded,** or was greater than, the value of American exports. In April 1977, Carter presented a National Energy Plan to resolve the energy crisis.

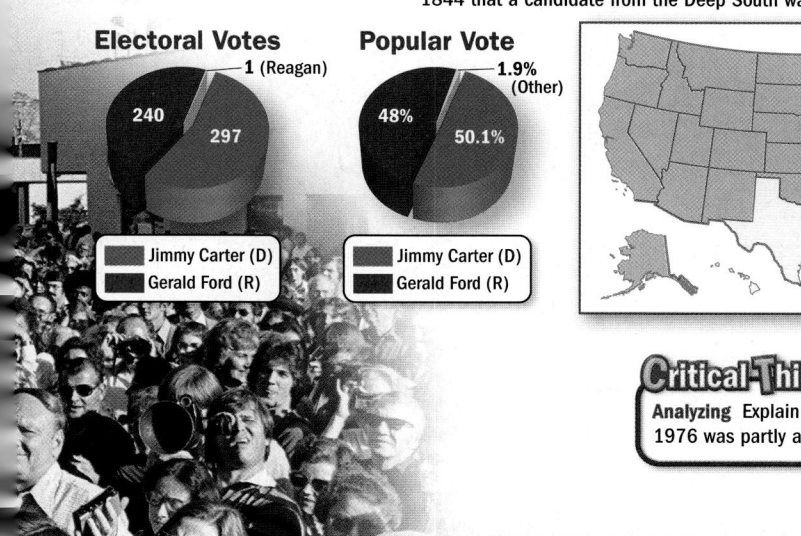

By the Numbers / Election of 1976

A Southern President Jimmy Carter's election marked the first time since 1844 that a candidate from the Deep South was elected president.

Electoral Votes
- 1 (Reagan)
- 240
- 297
- Jimmy Carter (D)
- Gerald Ford (R)

Popular Vote
- 1.9% (Other)
- 48%
- 50.1%
- Jimmy Carter (D)
- Gerald Ford (R)

- Carter (Democratic)
- Ford (Republican)

Critical Thinking
Analyzing Explain how Carter's election in 1976 was partly a result of Watergate.

CHAPTER 30
Section 3

Teach

R **Reading Strategy**

Identifying Ask: Which minority group helped Carter win the presidency? *(African American Southern voters)* **BL**

C **Critical Thinking**

Drawing Conclusions Ask: How did Carter's inexperience on the federal level hurt him? *(He had trouble gaining support in Congress.)* **OL**

Primary Source

Critical Thinking Answer
Ford's association with and pardon of Nixon distanced many voters. Carter's lack of federal experience, his good character, plus his stance against corruption attracted them.

Skills Practice Compare the circle graphs. **Ask:** What effect can the electoral system have on the outcome of a close popular vote? *(It can exaggerate the margin by which a candidate wins.)* **OL**

Differentiated Instruction

Leveled Activities

BL **Reteaching Activity, URB p. 37**

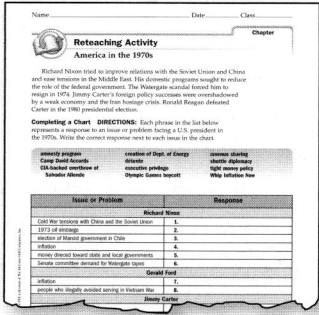

OL **Social Studies Skills Activity, URB p. 25**

AL **Geography and History Activity, URB p. 31**

959

D Differentiated Instruction

Visual/Spatial Organize students into an even number of groups. Half of the groups will represent antinuclear protesters, and the other half will represent people who support nuclear power. Give poster board and art materials to all groups. Have them make signs that the demonstrators would have carried in 1979. Display signs in class and discuss. **BL**

Economics & History

Critical Thinking Answers

1. 2005–2006; 2005–2006
2. Students may find it surprising that the pump price seems to have increased 14 times over since 1950, but when adjusted for inflation, the relative cost has risen by only about one-third. They may also note that the price has fluctuated a great deal in recent years.

Reading Check Answer: unemployment, inflation, high energy costs, growing trade deficit

Differentiated Instruction

Carter's plan included creating a Department of Energy to oversee energy policy, explore alternative energy sources, and collect taxes to further domestic oil production and energy conservation. Congress passed a weakened version of the plan in 1978.

Nuclear Power

In the late 1970s, nuclear power became a major issue. In March 1979, a major accident occurred at the **Three Mile Island** nuclear power plant near Harrisburg, Pennsylvania. An antinuclear protest movement soon spread. President Carter, however, did not want to halt nuclear energy which provided more than 10 percent of the nation's energy. At the same time, supporters of nuclear power argued that, with safeguards, nuclear power did not harm the environment.

Reading Check Identifying What economic problems did Carter face?

Foreign Affairs

Main Idea President Carter had some foreign policy successes but faced a growing crisis in the Middle Eastern country of Iran.

History and You How do you keep from getting discouraged when you fail to reach a goal? Read to find out about the long and difficult effort to release the Americans who were held captive in Iran.

Carter based his foreign policy on **human rights**—a belief that governments ought to respect the human dignity and liberties of their citizens. He proposed that any nation that violated human rights should not receive support from the United States. For example, Carter condemned South Africa for its policy of **apartheid**, racial separation and discrimination against nonwhites.

Carter's human rights diplomacy sometimes caused challenges for the United States.

Economics & History

Average Gas Prices, 1950–2007

Year	Price Per Gallon	Price Per Gallon (adjusted for inflation)
1950	$0.23	$1.91
1955	$0.24	$1.85
1960	$0.26	$1.79
1965	$0.26	$1.68
1970	$0.30	$1.59
1975	$0.48	$1.80
1980	$1.05	$2.59
1985	$1.01	$1.90
1990	$0.97	$1.51
1995	$0.96	$1.28
2001	$1.45	$1.66
2002	$1.31	$1.31
2003	$1.38	$1.52
2004	$1.67	$1.78
2005	$2.20	$2.28
2006	$3.03	$3.09
2007*	$3.26	$3.26

*June 2007   Source: U.S. Department of Energy

If gas cost 23 cents a gallon in 1950, what would be its equivalent price in today's prices? The table to the left shows the price of gas adjusted for inflation.

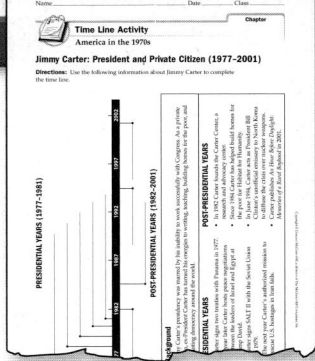

▲ Gas prices in 1991

◄ Gas prices in 2007

Critical Thinking

1. **Calculating** From one year to the next, which year shows the biggest increase in actual price? In price adjusted for inflation?
2. **Analyzing** What, if anything, surprises you about the average price of gasoline over time?

Jimmy Carter: President and Private Citizen

Objective: To complete a time line

Focus: Show students how President Carter's accomplishments continued past his presidency.

Teach: Read the background information, and have students fill in the time line from the events listed.

Assess: Compare students' time lines to the one in the answer key.

Close: Review the chronological order of events.

Differentiated Instruction Strategies

BL Ask students to circle the dates in each accomplishment.

AL Have students create a time line for their own lives, listing their major accomplishments.

ELL Instruct students to rewrite each accomplishment so it is just a simple phrase and a date.

Time Line Skills Activity, URB p. 34

Turbulence to Transformation: The Election of 1980 — NATIONAL GEOGRAPHIC

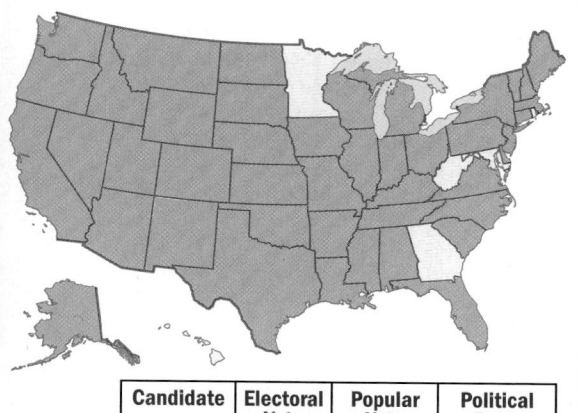

A Landslide for Reagan President Jimmy Carter lost his 1980 reelection bid by a landslide to Republican challenger Ronald Reagan. An important factor was Carter's inability to resolve the Iran hostage crisis. Soon after the inauguration of President Reagan on January 20, 1981, Iran agreed to release the 52 hostages.

Freed American hostages ▶

Critical Thinking

Drawing Conclusions Why would American voters believe Ronald Reagan could negotiate the hostages' release when President Carter was not able to?

Candidate	Electoral Vote	Popular Vote	Political Party
Reagan	489	43,642,639	Republican
Carter	49	35,480,948	Democrat

In 1980 Cuban dictator Fidel Castro allowed thousands of Cubans, including criminals and political prisoners, to leave Cuba by boat for Florida. The United States, however, had trouble absorbing such large numbers of people. By the time Castro ended the boatlift, about 125,000 people entered the United States. Carter had learned that a foreign policy based on a single issue, human rights, had many limitations. Even so, the president continued to speak out on the issue.

The Panama Canal

Carter also acted to end Latin American bitterness over the Panama Canal. Over the years, U.S. control of the canal caused friction between the United States and Panama. Carter signed two treaties with Panama in 1977. The treaties turned the Panama Canal over to Panama by the year 2000 but ensured that the canal would remain a neutral waterway open to all shipping. Some Republicans in the Senate tried to block ratification of the treaties, charging that Carter was giving away U.S. property. The Senate approved the treaties in 1978.

The Middle East

President Carter sought to bring peace to the Middle East. When talks between Israel and Egypt stalled in 1978, Carter invited Israeli prime minister Menachem Begin and Egyptian president Anwar el-Sadat to Camp David, Maryland, for a summit meeting. The three leaders reached an agreement known as the **Camp David Accords.** The agreement led to an Egyptian-Israeli peace treaty signed at the White House in March 1979. The treaty marked the first time that Israel and an Arab nation had made peace.

The Soviet Union

Carter criticized Soviet human-rights abuses, but he also continued talks on arms control. In June 1979, the president signed a second Strategic Arms Limitation Treaty, or SALT II. Critics in the Senate claimed that the treaty gave the Soviets an advantage, and the Senate delayed ratification.

Any hope of Senate approval ended in December 1979, when the Soviets invaded the southwest Asian nation of Afghanistan. Carter ordered sanctions against the Soviets.

America in the 1970s **Chapter 30** **961**

W Writing Support

Expository Writing Have students play the role of a historian who has been asked to write a set of informational cards to be displayed in the Carter Presidential Library. The cards will feature Carter's beliefs about human rights. One card will describe Carter's character, and the others will cover the main foreign affairs challenges he faced. Each card will contain a single paragraph. **OL**

R Reading Strategy

Determining Importance Ask: What was significant about the Camp David Accords? *(It led to the signing of a treaty, marking the first time Israel and an Arab nation made peace.)* **OL**

Turbulence to Transformation — NATIONAL GEOGRAPHIC

Critical Thinking Answer

Carter's human rights' stance made him a weak negotiator against the fundamentalist Muslim leader of Iran. Reagan believed in a strong defense, which would make him a tougher negotiator.

Hands-On Chapter Project
Step 3

Producing a Talk Show

Step 3: Writing the Final Segment Groups will review the section and write a final interview segment for their shows.

Essential Question: What major foreign affairs issues did President Carter face during his presidency, and how did he deal with them?

Directions Have each talk show group review Section 3 and select one foreign affairs issue and a guest to cover in its final interview. Tell groups that they must once again change interviewers to give everyone a chance to play this role. Should a group have more than three students, there may be two interviewers this time.

Issue Resolution Remind students to include the date and location of the event in the host's introductory remarks. **Ask:** Does President Carter's focus on human rights influence foreign affairs today? Discuss how Carter tried to resolve foreign affairs issues. Emphasize that the opinions expressed by guests on the talk shows should be true to the time and to the person interviewed but will not necessarily reflect those of the talk show staff members. **OL**

(Chapter Project continued in the Visual Summary)

C Critical Thinking

Contrasting Draw a two-column chart on the board for everyone to see. Head the columns: "Pahlavi" and "Khomeni." **Ask:** What are some differences between these two Iranian leaders? *(Pahlavi: political ruler, favored the U.S., criticized for allowing Western influences; Khomeni: religious ruler, hostile to U.S., believed in strict obedience to religious law)* **OL**

✓ Reading Check **Answer:** The Soviets invaded Afghanistan.

Assess

History ONLINE

Study Central™ provides summaries, interactive games, and online graphic organizers to help students review content.

Close

Identifying Have the class identify the foreign affairs issues and how President Carter dealt with them. **OL**

Section 3 Review

The United States and other nations refused to take part in the Olympic Games in Moscow.

Crisis in Iran

In the 1970s, Iran was a major U.S. ally in the oil-rich Persian Gulf region. Iran's ruler, Shah Mohammed Reza Pahlavi, built a powerful military with U.S. aid. Many Iranians criticized corruption in his government. Others opposed Western influences, which they felt weakened traditional Muslim values.

In January 1979, Islamic **fundamentalists**—people who believe in strict obedience to religious laws—forced the shah to flee Iran. The new ruler, Muslim leader Ayatollah Khomeini, was hostile to the United States for its support of the shah.

In November 1979, Iranian students, with government support, stormed the American embassy in Tehran, the capital of Iran, and held 52 Americans hostage. The United States was outraged. Attempts to negotiate the release of the hostages failed, and a daring desert rescue attempt ended in tragedy with the death of eight American soldiers. The hostage crisis dragged on and became a major issue in the presidential election of 1980.

The Election of 1980

The months before the 1980 election were difficult for President Carter. Many Americans blamed him for a weak economy and for not gaining the release of the American hostages. Carter's popularity among voters greatly declined.

Despite opposition, Carter gained the Democratic nomination, but the party was deeply divided. The Republicans nominated Ronald Reagan as their candidate. Reagan—a former actor and former governor of California—appealed to many voters with his conservative message of lower taxes, less spending, strong defense, and national pride.

Reagan swept to victory, with an electoral vote margin of 489 to 49. Republicans also gained control of the Senate for the first time since 1954. The election and its aftermath were bitter for Carter. During the last weeks of his presidency, Carter worked to free the hostages. The Iranians finally did release them—after Ronald Reagan took the oath of office.

✓ Reading Check **Summarizing** Why did the United States boycott the 1980 Olympics?

Section 3 Review

Vocabulary

1. Use each of the following words in a paragraph: integrity, trade deficit, exceed, human rights, apartheid, fundamentalist.

Main Ideas

2. **Discussing** What was President Carter's position on nuclear energy?
3. **Explaining** What part did human rights play in Carter's foreign policies?

4. **Analyzing** What were the major reasons Carter lost the election of 1980?

Critical Thinking

5. **Drawing Conclusions** On a chart like the one below, record the major result of each prominent issue of the Carter presidency.

Issue	Result
Panama Canal	
Camp David Accords	
Crisis in Iran	

6. **Persuasive Writing** Write a letter to the editor expressing your opinion about the United States' decision not to take part in the 1980 Olympic Games in Moscow.

Answer the Essential Question

7. What major foreign affairs issues did President Carter face during his presidency, and how did he deal with them?

Answers

1. Students' paragraphs should use all words in an appropriate context.
2. He believed that development should continue because it provided 10% of the nation's energy.
3. Human rights was the focus of Carter's foreign policy.
4. the weak economy, not gaining release of the American hostages in Iran, the divided Democratic Party

5. Panama Canal Control—signed treaties turning over ownership by 2000 and ensuring that the canal would remain open and neutral; Camp David Accords—Egyptian/Israeli peace treaty; Crisis in Iran—failed to negotiate release of U.S. hostages, and rescue attempt failed
6. Students' letters should express one view of the issue and include supporting details from the text.

7. Answers will include: Panama Canal Control—signed treaties turning over ownership by 2000 and ensuring that the canal would remain open and neutral; Middle East Talks—held a summit at Camp David that resulted in an Egyptian/Israeli peace treaty; Afghanistan Invasion—ordered sanctions against Soviets; Crisis in Iran—tried to negotiate release but failed

Visual Summary

Foreign Policy

- President Nixon formulates foreign policy plan of détente, easing international tensions with China and the Soviet Union.
- U.S. signs a treaty limiting nuclear arms.
- War between Israel and its Arab neighbors breaks out in 1973; violence in the Middle East is ongoing.
- U.S. supports the overthrow of Marxist government in Chile.

John Dean testifies during Watergate hearing. ▼

Nixon and Watergate

- Nixon introduces New Federalism.
- U.S. economy suffers under inflation.
- White House involvement with Watergate break-in is revealed.
- Vice President Agnew resigns.
- Nixon appoints Gerald Ford as his new vice president.
- Nixon resigns the presidency.

▲ President Nixon reviews troops during his visit to China.

Ford and Carter

President-elect Jimmy Carter and Rosalyn Carter ▼

- President Ford grants a pardon to Nixon.
- Ford continues détente with the Soviet Union.
- Inflation rises.
- President Carter makes energy policy a priority.
- Carter bases foreign policy on human rights.
- Carter works to bring peace in Middle East.
- Islamic fundamentalists take Americans hostage in Iran.
- Carter loses the 1980 presidential election to Ronald Reagan.

American hostages held in Iran ▼

STUDY TO GO Study anywhere, anytime! Download quizzes and flash cards to your PDA from glencoe.com.

Visual Summary

Clarifying On a sheet of paper, have each student list actions taken during the Nixon administration to explain how his presidency affected the nation. *(Ideas may include: foreign policy, improved trade, lessened threat of nuclear war; New Federalism gave more tax revenues to the states; illegal activities of Watergate affair caused people to lose trust.)* Have students share their ideas with the class and take notes. **OL**

Monitoring Ask: In what ways was the Carter presidency successful, and how did it fail? Organize students into groups of five or six. Pass out several 9" x 3" strips of light-colored construction paper to each group. Have groups write each success and each failure they can think of on a separate strip of paper. Tell groups to arrange all successes as a list and tape together. Have them do the same with the failures. Display the lists and discuss as a class. **OL**

This **READING SKILL** (Monitoring and Clarifying) was introduced in this unit.

Hands-On Chapter Project
Step 4: Wrap-Up

Producing a Talk Show

Step 4: Airing the Talk Shows Groups will present their shows to the class.

Directions Have talk show groups review their work and prepare to present it to the class. Remind them that when they play the role of interviewer, they must introduce themselves, the name of their show, and their host station. Have each group present its talk show to the class.

Analyzing Ask: Which interview included content that taught you something? What was it? Invite class members to offer positive comments about each other's work. **OL**

Focus

R₁ Reading Strategy

Previewing Have students read the paragraph. Ask them to predict the direction they think the story will take. **OL**

C Critical Thinking

Determining Cause and Effect Note that Lincoln has moved from a poor neighborhood to a wealthier one. **Ask:** Why do you think Lincoln's family was able to afford to move? (*Possible answers: They always could have; the parent he lives with remarried or got a different job; the school recruited him as a basketball star; he received a scholarship.*) Have students search the entire selection to support their hypothesis. **AL**

R₂ Reading Strategy

Using Context Clues Ask: What did Lincoln like about his new neighborhood? (*peacefulness, sycamores, neatly piled firewood, flowers, birds building nests, and so on*) Why would Lincoln be having second thoughts? (*School has started, or other events have transpired that we have yet to learn about.*) **OL**

Additional Reading

Review suggested books before assigning them.

Meet the Author

Gary Soto (1952–), the son of Mexican American parents, was born and raised in California. Though much of his writing features Latino boys and girls, young people of all ethnic groups experience many of the same feelings and challenges. Soto's ability to depict real-life situations facing young people makes him one of the country's most influential authors.

R₁ C Building Background

In *Taking Sides*, Lincoln moves from a poor neighborhood, Franklin, to the affluent suburb of Columbus, after his parents' breakup. A star basketball player, Lincoln feels like a traitor when Columbus is set to play Franklin in an upcoming game. As game day approaches, Lincoln struggles with who he is— a Mexican American from the barrio or a student from the suburbs. As you read the excerpt, think about the contrasting social and cultural rules experienced by Lincoln as the new kid in school.

Vocabulary

sycamores trees

scrawny small

stucco hardened sand and cement

opted chose

harangued nagged

splotched stained

Young boys learn the game of basketball on the playground. ▶

TAKING SIDES

Gary Soto

When he had arrived in the new neighborhood, Lincoln had liked the peacefulness of sprinklers hissing on green lawns and the **R₂ sycamores** that lined the street. He liked the splashes of flowers and neatly piled firewood. He liked the hedges where jays built **scrawny** nests and bickered when cats slithered too close. The people seemed distant, but that was fine with him. It was better than the loud cars that raced up and down his old block. It was better than littered streets and graffiti-covered walls that called out "*Con safos*" and "F-14."

Now, three months later, Lincoln was having second thoughts.

* * *

964

Nonfiction: *Revolution in The Valley: The Insanely Great Story of How the Mac Was Made,* by Andy Hertzfeld, is written like a computer blog. The author was part of the team that created the first personal computers. This is his story.

Fiction: *Finding Miracles,* by Julia Alvarez, follows 15-year-old Milly Kaufman as she travels from her adopted parents' home in Vermont to the war-torn Latin American island where she was born. There, she learns what family and heritage really mean.

Fiction: *Juice,* by Eric Walters, tells football-star Moose's story. The school has a new coach who will do whatever it takes to win. But after taking steroids, Moose begins to wonder if winning really is everything.

For further reading, see BOOKLINK 3

Columbus Junior High was a **stucco** group of pink and green buildings and a track the color of rust. The grass, like the grass at other schools, was mostly brown. The trash cans were buckled, but no candy wrappers or potato-chip bags scuttled across the campus. . . .

The kids dressed stylishly. When they smiled, their teeth gleamed with braces. It would never enter their minds to shop at K-mart or tote a bologna sandwich in a twice-used paper bag. Lincoln **opted** to live a simple life. His bologna sandwich, along with an apple and some chips, sat in his backpack, crushed between his geography and math books.

His mother **harangued** him about his clothes, but he wore jeans, busted at the knees, and his coat was a hand-me-down from an uncle. The front of Lincoln's shirt was **splotched** blue where he once let his Bic pen ride in the pocket during a wash.

Lincoln sighed and entered the school grounds. Just two more days to the weekend. . . .

At lunch he ate alone, scribbling out his homework for English, which was mostly recognizing the parts of speech. He thought it was funny how the teacher, Mrs. Baker, said the same things over and over. "A chair is a noun; a beach umbrella is a noun. . . ."

Lincoln bit into his sandwich roughly. He opened his geography book and once again the guy on the camel was smiling his lined face at him. He's like me, Lincoln thought. Brown as earth and no one knows his name. He closed the book when a basketball play came to his mind. . . .

He took another bite of his bologna sandwich and looked up to see James with a girl. Lincoln wiped his mouth, cleared his throat, and said to James, "Hey, homes." To the girl, he said, "Hi.". . .

He's like me, Lincoln thought.
Brown as earth
and no one knows his name.

James said, "This is Monica Torres. Monica, this is Lincoln, ah, let me see. What's your last name, Linc?"

"Mendoza."

"That's right, Linc Mendoza, star basketball player."

Monica smiled as she sat down. "James said you went to Franklin. I used to go there."

"Really?" Lincoln asked, curious, his eyebrows raised. "I don't remember you."

"Well, I did, for two months," she said. "But we moved here. My dad didn't like me going to school in the city."

"But your dad didn't have to go to school."

"It's true. But you know how Franklin is."

"You mean nasty."

"That's one way of putting it."

"That's the only way of putting it."

Lincoln wanted to tell her about the Franklin he knew, but how could he keep the conversation polite?

Teach

C Critical Thinking

Identifying Central Issues Note that Lincoln packs a bologna sandwich and does not dress like his new classmates. **Ask:** Does he care about fitting in? (*Students may say no because if he did, he would listen to his mother about wearing better clothes. Other students may say yes because he hides his sandwich in his backpack.*) **OL**

D Differentiated Instruction

Interpersonal Ask: Have students explain what this sentence means. (*Like the man on the camel, Lincoln is from a different culture and probably believes that others do not see him as a person.*) **OL**

Assess/Close

As a class, discuss the difficulties and advantages in moving to a new school. Ask your students what difficulties Lincoln faces. (*fitting in, loneliness, and so on*) **Ask:** Are there any clues telling us if Lincoln will make friends? (*He is a sports star; James nicknames him "Linc."*)

Answers

1. Possible answers: moving to a new school, disliking one's school, believing that one is alone

2. There is no trash on the ground; the kids at Columbus dress more stylishly; the students have braces and do not shop at K-mart or eat bologna sandwiches from used paper bags.

3. Students may say that Lincoln feels like a loner in his new school and perhaps unimportant.

Answers and Analyses
Reviewing Main Ideas

1. B Choice A is incorrect, as Nixon did not use U.S. aid as a bargaining tool with China. C and D are associated with the Soviet Union. Students should recall that China was interested in resuming trade, choice B. **16.B.3d (US)**

2. A Gas pump lines and strained relations with Egypt resulted from the Yom Kippur War, eliminating choices B and C. Egypt lost the Sinai, eliminating choice D. The answer is A, more Palestinian refugees. **16.A.3a**

3. A Choices B, C, and D are things that happened during Nixon's presidency, but none of them involved reducing the involvement of the federal government. Students should recall Nixon's New Federalism involved revenue sharing. The answer is A. **16.A**

4. C Remind students that Carter ordered sanctions against the Soviet Union, eliminating choice A. Human rights and apartheid played no part in the United States's relations with Iran, eliminating choices B and D. Students should recall that Khomeni was hostile to the United States for its support of the shah and choose answer C. **14.E**

Short-Answer Question

5. Answers will vary, but students should base their answers on their knowledge of Watergate and why Nixon had to resign. Some students may believe that Nixon should not have been given special treatment from Ford and that many other people who have committed crimes do not get pardoned. **16.A.3b**

Chapter 30 Assessment

STANDARDIZED TEST PRACTICE

TEST-TAKING TIP

On a multiple-choice test, remember that you are looking for the best, or most accurate, answer. It might not necessarily be the only answer that applies.

Reviewing Main Ideas

Directions: Choose the best answer for each of the following questions.

1. Nixon improved U.S. relations with China by
   A promising aid.
   B resuming trade.
   C signing SALT I.
   D sharing technology.

2. What was an outcome of the 1967 Six-Day War?
   A more Palestinian refugees
   B long lines at U.S. gas pumps
   C improved U.S. relations with Egypt
   D Egyptian control of the Sinai Peninsula

3. Nixon reduced the involvement of the federal government in people's lives by
   A introducing revenue sharing.
   B promoting affirmative action.
   C approving the creation of the EPA.
   D enforcing orders to integrate schools.

4. Why were the Ayatollah Khomeini and his supporters hostile to the United States?
   A Carter ordered sanctions against Iran.
   B U.S. policies were based on human rights.
   C American leaders supported the shah.
   D Carter condemned the practice of apartheid.

Short-Answer Question

Directions: Base your answer to question 5 on the excerpt below and on your knowledge of social studies.

Finally, I feel that Richard Nixon and his loved ones have suffered enough and will continue to suffer, no matter what I do, no matter what we, as a great and good nation, can do together to make his goal of peace come true.

—President Gerald R. Ford, September 8, 1974

5. Do you think this is a valid reason for pardoning President Nixon? Explain.

Review the Essential Questions

6. Essay Compare and contrast U.S.-Soviet relations in the Nixon and Carter administrations.

To help you write your essay, review your answers to the Essential Questions in the section reviews and the chapter Foldables Study Organizer. Your essay should include:

- an analysis of Nixon's relationship with the Soviets;
- an analysis of Carter's relationship with the Soviets; and
- similarities and differences in the leadership roles the presidents played in an international setting.

GO ON

Review the Essential Questions

6. Students should consult their completed Foldables to find information for their essays. Students' answers will be based on their analyses of the foreign policies of the two administrations. **14.E.3**

History ONLINE
For additional test practice, use **Self-Check Quizzes**—Chapter 30 at glencoe.com.

Chapter **30** Assessment

Document-Based Questions

Directions: Analyze the documents and answer the short-answer questions that follow.

Document 1

Kissinger made this comment about the U.S. role in the overthrow of Chile's elected leader.

> I don't see why we need to stand by and watch a country go communist due to the irresponsibility of its own people.

Source: Tarak Barkawi, *War Inside the Free World*

7. What can you infer about Kissinger's attitude toward communism?

Document 2

In a 1977 interview, former President Nixon was asked about his views on the presidency and the law.

> When the president does it that means that it is not illegal.

Source: Richard Nixon, from an interview with David Frost

8. What does Nixon's statement reflect about how he views the relationship of the president to the laws of the United States?

Document 3

In the following statement, Carter criticized the rise in oil imports during the Ford administration.

> We now import about 44 percent of our oil. . . . We need to shift very strongly toward solar energy and have strict conservation measures.

Source: The First Carter-Ford Presidential Debate, 1976

9. Why was the rise in oil imports a campaign issue in 1976?

Document 4

The graph shows President Nixon's approval rating during parts of 1973 and 1974.

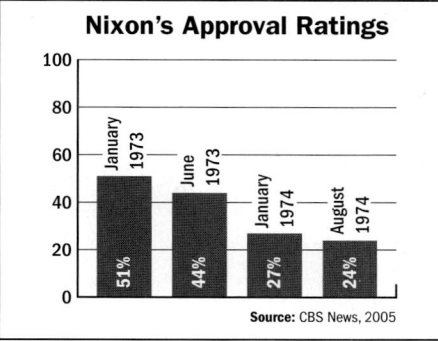

Nixon's Approval Ratings

January 1973	51%
June 1973	44%
January 1974	27%
August 1974	24%

Source: CBS News, 2005

10. What was Nixon's approval rating before he resigned in August 1974? What was the rating in January of that year?

Document 5

Senator William Proxmire objected to billions in military aid authorized by the Camp David Accords.

> The notion that we must provide military assistance to [these] nations . . . is precisely what has led us down this long and bloody and reprehensible road of providing the weapons of death and destruction in the name of peace.

Source: Barbara Hinckley, *Less Than Meets the Eye*

11. What does Senator Proxmire suggest Carter used to persuade Begin and Sadat to sign a peace treaty?

12. Expository Writing Using the information from the five documents and your knowledge of social studies, write an essay in which you:

- discuss the goals of federal policies in the 1970s; and
- discuss how the Watergate scandal affected Americans' view of the presidency.

Need Extra Help?

If you missed questions. . .	1	2	3	4	5	6	7	8	9	10	11	12
Go to page. . .	944	945	949	962	952	943–962	943	953	960	953	961	943–955

9. During Ford's administration, OPEC kept oil prices high, which contributed to inflation and hurt the American economy, but Carter hoped to increase conservation and develop other energy resources. **17.C.3b**

10. 24%; 27% **16.A.3c**

11. Proxmire suggests he promised them both military aid. **16.A.3b**

12. Students' essays should include information about the attempts to normalize relations between nations and cover the increasing mistrust of government caused by the Watergate scandal. **18.B.3a**

History ONLINE

Have students visit the Web site at glencoe.com to review Chapter 30 and take the Self-Check Quiz.

Need Extra Help?

Have students refer to the pages listed if they miss any of the questions.

Document-Based Questions

7. Students should read the question first and seek the answer as they read Document 1. Kissinger seems to believe that the Chileans' right to democratic elections is not as important as stopping the spread of communism. **16.A.3b**

8. Nixon viewed the president as above the laws of the United States. **18.B.3a**

Chapter Planning Guide

31

BL	OL	AL	ELL		Resources	Chapter Opener	Section 1	Section 2	Section 3	Section 4	Section 5	Chapter Assess
FOCUS												
BL	OL	AL	ELL	🖨	Daily Test Practice Transparencies		31–1	31–2	31–3	31–4	31–5	
TEACH												
	OL	AL		📁	Geography and History Activity, URB					p. 59		
BL	OL		ELL	📁	Time Line Skills Activity, URB				p. 62			
BL	OL	AL	ELL	📁	Writing Skills Activity, URB					p. 51		
	OL	AL		📁	American Literature Readings, URB						p. 9	
BL	OL	AL	ELL	📁	Content Vocabulary Activity, URB		p. 45	p. 45	p. 45	p. 45	p. 45	
BL	OL	AL	ELL	📁	Academic Vocabulary Activity, URB		p. 47	p. 47	p. 47	p. 47	p. 47	
	OL	AL		📁	Citizenship and Decision-Making Activity, URB						p. 3	
BL	OL		ELL	📁	Social Studies Skills Activity, URB			p. 53				
BL	OL	AL	ELL	📁	Differentiated Instruction Activity, URB					p. 55		
BL	OL	AL	ELL	📁	Critical Thinking Skills Activity, URB						p. 57	
BL	OL	AL	ELL	📁	Linking Past and Present Activity, URB		p. 61					
	OL	AL		📁	Primary Source Readings, URB			p. 49				
BL	OL	AL	ELL	📁	School-to-Home Connection Activity, URB		p. 63	p. 63	p. 63	p. 63	p. 63	
BL	OL		ELL	📁	Guided Reading Activity, URB*		p. 67	p. 68	p. 69	p. 70	p. 71	
	OL	AL		📁	Economics and History Activity, URB		p. 5					
BL	OL		ELL	📁	Reading Essentials and Note-Taking Guide*		p. 346	p. 349	p. 352	p. 355	p. 358	
BL	OL	AL	ELL	🖨	Lesson Transparencies			31A, 31B			31C	
	OL	AL		📁	Interpreting Political Cartoons, URB						p. 13	
		AL		📁	Supreme Court Case Studies		p. 139		p. 147			
	OL			📁	American Biographies			p. 73				
BL	OL	AL	ELL	📁	Outline Map Resource Book	pp. 42, 43						
	OL	AL		🖨	American Art and Architecture Transparencies, Strategies, and Activities						40	

Note: Please refer to the *Unit Resource Book: America in a Modern Era* for this chapter's URB materials.

* Also available in Spanish

Levels					Resources	Chapter Opener	Section 1	Section 2	Section 3	Section 4	Section 5	Chapter Assess
BL	OL	AL	ELL		**TEACH** *(continued)*							
BL	OL	AL	ELL		**NGS US Desk Map**		✓	✓	✓	✓	✓	
BL	OL	AL	ELL		**American Literature Library**		✓	✓	✓	✓	✓	
BL	OL	AL	ELL		**Writer's Guidebook**		✓	✓	✓	✓	✓	
	OL	AL			**American History Primary Source Document Library CD-ROM**		✓	✓	✓	✓	✓	✓
BL	OL	AL	ELL		**American Music: Hits Through History**	✓	✓	✓	✓	✓	✓	
BL	OL	AL	ELL		**StudentWorks™ Plus CD**	✓	✓	✓	✓	✓	✓	✓
	OL	AL			**Section Spotlight Videos**		✓	✓	✓	✓	✓	
BL	OL	AL	ELL		**Writing Process Transparencies**		✓	✓	✓	✓	✓	✓
BL	OL	AL	ELL		**Presentation Plus! With MindJogger CheckPoint CD**	✓	✓	✓	✓	✓	✓	✓
					ASSESS							
BL	OL	AL	ELL		**Quizzes and Tests**		p. 307	p. 308	p. 309	p. 310	p. 311	pp. 313, 315, 317
BL	OL	AL	ELL		**Authentic Assessment With Rubrics**						p. 31	
BL	OL	AL	ELL		**Standardized Test Practice**							p. 61
BL	OL	AL	ELL		*ExamView® Assessment Suite* **CD-ROM***		31–1	31–2	31–3	31–4	31–5	Ch. 31
					CLOSE							
BL			ELL		**Reteaching Activity, URB***		p. 65	p. 65	p. 65	p. 65	p. 65	p. 65
BL	OL		ELL		**Reading and Study Skills Foldables Activity**	p. 110	p. 110	p. 110	p. 110	p. 110	p. 110	p. 110
BL	OL	AL	ELL		*The American Journey* **in Graphic Novel**					p. 193		
BL			ELL		**Reading Strategies and Activities for the Social Studies Classroom**		✓	✓	✓	✓	✓	
BL	OL	AL	ELL		**Graphic Organizer Transparencies & Strategies**		✓	✓	✓	✓	✓	

TeacherWorks *Plus*
All-In-One Planner and Resource Center

- Interactive Lesson Planner
- Interactive Teacher Edition
- Fully editable blackline masters
- Section Spotlight Videos Launch

- Differentiated Lesson Plans
- Printable reports of daily assignments
- Standards Tracking System

Professional Development Resources

- Strategies for Success
- Building Academic Vocabulary
- Success With English Learners DVD
- Differentiated Instruction Strategies DVD
- Teaching Literacy Strategies in Social Studies DVD
- Assessment DVD
- Standards-Based Instruction DVD

31

Using TechCONNECT™

Create Presentations

Technology Product

Glencoe TechCONNECT™ is an engaging, activities-based online program that enhances comprehension of core subjects while teaching technology skills. (For more information or to get a free 30-day trial of Glencoe TechCONNECT™ for your classroom, **visit** techconnect.glencoe.com **and click the Free Trial button**.)

Objective

Students will create presentations and learn to share information effectively.

Steps

- To see activities correlated to this textbook, log on to TechCONNECT™ and click the **Find Your textbook** link. You can also search for activities.
- After you log on, click **Activity Search**. Choose **Social Studies, Presentation**, and your grade level.
- Have students log on and enter the letters AC and the three-digit activity number.
- Have students read each page of the activity and follow the on-screen instructions.
- Have students complete the self-assessment rubric.
- Students may also complete the activity's TechCheck quiz.
- Review this section with the class.

History ONLINE at glencoe.com

	Student	Teacher	Parent
Media Center			
• Student Edition Audio	●		
• Spanish Summaries	●		
• Section Spotlight Videos	●	●	
Social Studies Online Learning Center			
Classroom Tools			
• Multi-Language Glossaries	●	●	●
• Teaching Today		●	
• TIME Current Events	●	●	●
• Beyond the Textbook	●	●	
***The American Journey* Online Learning Center**			
• Study-to-Go™	●	●	●
• Study Central™	●	●	●
• Chapter Overview	●	●	
• Concepts in Motion	●	●	
• ePuzzles and Games	●	●	
• Literature Connections	●	●	
• Online Student Edition	●	●	●
• Self-Check Quizzes	●	●	●
• Student Web Activities	●	●	
• Vocabulary eFlashcards	●	●	
• Web Activity Lesson Plans	●	●	●
• Vocabulary PuzzleMaker	●	●	●

READING SUPPORT FROM JAMESTOWN EDUCATION

- **Timed Readings Plus in Social Studies** helps students increase their reading rate and fluency while maintaining comprehension. The 400-word passages are similar to those found on state and national assessments.

- **Reading in the Content Area: Social Studies** concentrates on six essential reading skills that help students better comprehend what they read. The book includes 75 high-interest nonfiction passages written at increasing levels of difficulty.

- **Reading Social Studies** includes strategic reading instruction and vocabulary support in Social Studies content for ELLs and native speakers of English.

- **Content Vocabulary Workout** (Grades 6–8) accelerates reading comprehension through focused vocabulary development. Social Studies content vocabulary comes from the glossaries of Glencoe's Middle School Social Studies texts.

www.jamestowneducation.com

NATIONAL GEOGRAPHIC

Index to National Geographic Magazine:

The following articles relate to this chapter:

- **"Urban Sprawl: The American Dream,"** John G. Mitchell, July 2001.

- **"Signs From Earth,"** Tim Appenzeller and Dennis R. Dimick, September 2004.

National Geographic Society Products

To order the following, call National Geographic at 1-800-368-2728:

National Geographic Atlas of the World (Book)

Access National Geographic's dynamic MapMachine Web site and other geography resources at:

www.nationalgeographic.com

www.nationalgeographic.com/mapmachine

Reading List Generator CD-ROM / GLENCOE BOOKLINK 3

Use this database to search more than 30,000 titles to create a customized reading list for your students.

- Reading lists can be organized by students' reading level, author, genre, theme, or area of interest.

- The database provides Degrees of Reading Power™ (DRP) and Lexile™ readability scores for all selections.

- A brief summary of each selection is included.

Leveled reading suggestions for this chapter:

For students at a Grade 6 reading level:
- **Colin Powell: Straight to the Top,** Rose Blue & Corinne J. Naden

For students at a Grade 7 reading level:
- **Global Pollution,** Paul Brown

For students at a Grade 8 reading level:
- **The Challenger Disaster: Tragic Space Flight,** Carmen Bredeson
- **The Haunted Land: Facing Europe's Ghosts after Communism,** Tina Rosenberg

For students at a Grade 9 reading level:
- **Bill Clinton and His Presidency,** Elaine Landau

For students at a Grade 10 reading level:
- **Rain of Troubles: The Science and Politics of Acid Rain,** Laurence Pringle

The following videotape programs are available from Glencoe as supplements to the chapter:

- **Ronald Reagan: The Role of a Lifetime** (ISBN 1-56-501808-7)

- **The Class of the 20th Century: Vol. 6 1976–1990** (ISBN 1-56-501052-3)

To order, call Glencoe at 1-800-334-7344. To find classroom resources to accompany many of these videos, check the following home pages:

A&E Television: www.aetv.com

The History Channel: www.history.com

Chapter Objectives

After studying this chapter, students will be able to:

- Explain how President Reagan's actions and policies reflected his attitude about communism.
- Discuss how President Bush dealt with the domestic challenges facing his presidency.
- Understand how the Clinton presidency altered the U.S. domestic scene in the 1990s.
- Explain how the war on terror changed the way Americans lived.
- Identify ways in which economic and environmental developments led to interdependence among the world's nations.

Motivating Activity

Identifying Limiting pollution and cleaning up the environment are ongoing challenges for the United States and for the entire world. **Ask:** What measures do you think the United States is taking to improve the environment on a global level? Ask students to list environmental initiatives by the United States. Lead the discussion by mentioning cars, electrical usage, water conservation, recycling, and so on. **Ask:** What are you doing at home or at school to help the environment? As you read the chapter, discuss ways in which the list can be changed or expanded. **OL**

Previewing the Essential Questions

As you begin teaching each section, use these questions and activities to help students focus on the Essential Questions.

Chapter 31
New Challenges
1981 to Present

Students take part in a team effort to clean up area near Long Beach, California.

PRESIDENTS
U.S. Events
World Events

1980

★ **1983** U.S. troops invade Grenada

RONALD REAGAN

★ **1986** Space shuttle *Challenger* explodes

GEORGE H.W. BUSH

★ **1990** Americans with Disabilities Act passes

1987

1981 ★ Egypt's president Anwar el-Sadat assassinated

★ **1985** Mikhail Gorbachev becomes leader of Soviet Union

★ **1989** Students protest in Tiananmen Square, China

★ **1990** Nelson Mandela released from South African prison

968   Chapter 31

Section 1

The Reagan Presidency Ask: Have you heard of the Star Wars missile defense plan? Why did President Reagan think it was necessary? *(During the Reagan era, the U.S.S.R.'s nuclear missiles were considered a major threat.)* Point out to students that in Section 1 they will learn how Reagan's policies and actions reflected a commitment to fighting communism. **OL**

Section 2

The Bush Presidency Ask: What challenges did the country face during the presidency of George H.W. Bush? *(President Bush faced international issues such as the fall of communism and war in the Persian Gulf, while the economy was a major issue at home.)* Tell students that Section 2 discusses the foreign and domestic challenges of the Bush administration. **OL**

Section 1: The Reagan Presidency

Essential Question How was President Reagan's attitude about communism reflected in his actions and policies?

Section 2: The Bush Presidency

Essential Question How did President Bush deal with the domestic challenges facing his presidency?

Section 3: A New Century

Essential Question How did the Clinton presidency change the U.S. domestic scene in the 1990s?

Section 4: The War on Terror

Essential Question How has the war on terror changed the way Americans live?

Section 5: Challenges Ahead

Essential Question How have economic and environmental developments led to the world's nations becoming more interdependent?

History ONLINE
Chapter Overview Visit glencoe.com and click on **Chapter 31—Chapter Overviews** to preview chapter information.

FOLDABLES Study Organizer

Organizing Information
Make this Foldable to organize what you learn about the challenges faced by the United States.

Step 1 Place three sheets of paper on top of one another about 1 inch apart.

Step 2 Fold the papers to form six equal tabs.

Step 3 Staple the sheets and label each tab as shown.

New Challenges
1981–Present
- The Reagan Presidency
- The Bush Presidency
- A New Century
- The War on Terror
- Challenges Ahead

Reading and Writing As you read the chapter, record notes, collect terms, note important dates and events, and answer the Essential Questions beneath the tabs.

A family in Mississippi is rescued from flood waters caused by Hurricane Katrina. ▶

★ **1991**
- Operation Desert Storm
- Breakup of Soviet Union

★ **1994**
U.S., Mexico, and Canada found NAFTA

BILL CLINTON

★ **1995**
Bomb kills 168 at Oklahoma City federal building

★ **1998**
President Clinton impeached

1994

GEORGE W. BUSH

★ **2001**
War on terror begins

2001

★ **2004**
Tsunami devastates Indonesia and surrounding regions

★ **2005**
Hurricane Katrina strikes Louisiana and Mississippi

★ **2005**
Terrorists bomb London subway system

★ **2007**
Nancy Pelosi becomes first female Speaker of the House

2008

Woman surveys destruction after hurricane. ▶

Chapter 31   969

Time Line Activity

If you have not already done so, have students review the time line. **Ask:** What disasters did the United States face during the period shown on the time line? *(space shuttle explosion, Oklahoma City bombing, war on terror, Hurricane Katrina)* Discuss as a class how the United States has recovered from these incidents.

FOLDABLES Study Organizer **Dinah Zike's Foldables**

Purpose This Foldable helps students understand the challenges America has faced since 1981. The completed Foldable will help them prepare for assessment.

📁 More Foldables activities for this chapter can be found in *Dinah Zike's Reading and Study Skills Foldables.*

History ONLINE
Introduce students to chapter content and key terms by having them access the **Chapter Overview** at glencoe.com.

Section 3

A New Century Ask: What problems did the country face during Bill Clinton's presidency? *(Students may recall that while the economy rebounded during the Clinton administration, the administration faced serious scandals.)* Tell students that Section 3 will discuss events during the Clinton presidency. **OL**

Section 4

The War on Terror Ask: Why did the United States begin the war on terror? *(The terrorist attacks of September 11, 2001, were the immediate reason, but students should understand that terrorism posed other threats.)* Explain to students that in Section 4, they will learn about the war on terror and the events that led up to it. **OL**

Section 5

Challenges Ahead Ask: What do you believe are the greatest challenges facing America today? *(Answers might include terrorism, pollution, global warming, health care, and so on.)* Explain to students that in Section 5, they will learn about the economic, environmental, and social problems facing America today. **OL**

969

Focus

Bellringer
Daily Test Practice Transparency 31–1

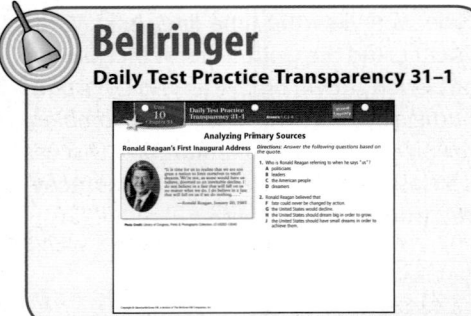

Reading Guide
Answers to Graphic:
fewer rules, lower taxes, less government spending for social programs

Section Spotlight Video

Have students watch the Section Spotlight Video "The Reagan Presidency" to learn about President Reagan's economic policy called Reaganomics.

Resource Manager

Essential Question
How was President Reagan's attitude about communism reflected in his actions and policies?

Reading Guide

Content Vocabulary
deregulation (p. 972)   federal debt (p. 973)
supply-side economics (p. 972)

Academic Vocabulary
quote (p. 973)   theme (p. 974)

Key People and Events
Sandra Day O'Connor (p. 972)
George H.W. Bush (p. 974)
Geraldine Ferraro (p. 974)
Mikhail Gorbachev (p. 975)

Reading Strategy
Taking Notes On a diagram like the one below, identify the building blocks of President Reagan's conservative federal government.

Reagan Conservatism

ILLINOIS STANDARDS
The American Journey

14.E Understand United States foreign policy as it relates to other nations and international issues.

14.E.3 Compare the basic principles of the United States and its international interests (e.g., territory, environment, trade, use of technology).

15.E.3b Explain how laws and government policies (e.g., property rights, contract enforcement, standard weights/measurements) establish rules that help a market economy function effectively.

16.A.3c Identify the difference between historical fact and interpretation.

The Reagan Presidency

American Diary

On March 30, 1981, President Ronald Reagan left a Washington, D.C., hotel after giving a speech. As he passed press photographers and TV cameras, six gunshots rang out. Secret Service agents rushed the president into his limousine and sped toward the hospital. A bullet had punctured his lung and lodged just an inch from his heart. Despite the seriousness of the situation, the president joked on the way into the operating room, telling his doctors, "I hope you're all Republicans."

President Reagan waves to the crowd moments before the assassination attempt.

R Reading Strategies	**C** Critical Thinking	**D** Differentiated Instruction	**W** Writing Support	**S** Skill Practice
Teacher Edition • Set. a Purpose, p. 971 • Questioning, p. 973 **Additional Resources** • Guid. Read., URB p. 67 • Content Vocab., URB p. 45 • Academic Vocab., URB p. 47 • Read. Ess., p. 346	**Teacher Edition** • Predict. Conseq., p. 971 • Identify Central Iss., p. 974 **Additional Resources** • Quizzes and Tests, p. 307 • Econ. & Hist., URB p. 5 • Link. Past & Pres., URB p. 61	**Teacher Edition** • ELL, p. 972 • Logic./Math., p. 973 **Additional Resources** • School-to-Home, URB p. 63 • Reteaching Act., URB p. 65	**Teacher Edition** • Persuasive Writ., p. 972 • Exposit. Writ., p. 975	**Teacher Edition** • Using Geo. Skills, p. 974 **Additional Resources** • Daily Test Pract. Transp. 31-1

The Reagan Revolution

Main Idea President Reagan brought a new conservative approach to government.

History and You What are principles? What principles do you live by? Read to discover the principles that guided the policies of the Reagan presidency.

Ronald Reagan's election to the presidency in 1980 marked a significant conservative shift in America. During the 1970s, the conservative movement had grown throughout the country, most particularly in the South and Southwest.

Many Americans now wanted a return to what Ronald Reagan, a former actor with Illinois small-town roots, called "traditional American values"—an emphasis on family life, hard work, respect for law, and patriotism. They shared the conservative view that the federal government made too many rules, collected too much in taxes, and spent too much money on social programs.

Reagan believed that the key to restoring America's strength and influence was to get Americans to believe in themselves again. He expressed this idea in his Inaugural Address:

PRIMARY SOURCE

"We have every right to dream heroic dreams. . . . You can see heroes every day going in and out of factory gates. Others, a handful in number, produce enough food to feed all of us. . . . You meet heroes across a counter. . . . Their patriotism is quiet, but deep. Their values sustain our national life."

—Ronald Reagan's First Inaugural Address, January 1981

Air Traffic Controllers' Strike

A few months after Ronald Reagan became president, the nation's air traffic controllers went on strike. They refused to go back to work despite the president's orders to do so. President Reagan acted at once, firing the controllers and ordering military staff to oversee air traffic while new controllers were trained to do the work.

Critics of former president Carter felt he lacked leadership and was indecisive. With this action, Ronald Reagan showed that he would stand firm and use his presidency to carry out the policies in which he believed.

Primary Source | The Great Communicator

In His Own Words Ronald W. Reagan was nicknamed "the Great Communicator" because of his extraordinary skill as an orator. He appeared in more than 50 films as a Hollywood actor, which helped him polish his speaking skills.

"Honey, I forgot to duck."
—March 30, 1981, from www.pbs.org (said to Nancy Reagan when she arrived at the hospital following the assassination attempt)

"I've always believed that a lot of the trouble in the world would disappear if we were talking to each other instead of about each other."
—April 11, 1984, from www.reaganfoundation.org

Critical Thinking

Evaluating Why do you think Ronald Reagan was such a popular president?

Teach

R Reading Strategy

Setting a Purpose Have students read the heading and main idea of this subsection. Then ask them to write a one-sentence purpose for reading. *(Sample sentence: I want to learn how Reagan's principles were related to his conservative approach to government.)* **OL**

C Critical Thinking

Predicting Consequences Ask: What would have happened if President Reagan had allowed the air-traffic controllers' strike to continue? *(Air transportation and shipping might have been paralyzed, hurting the economy and angering Americans.)*

Primary Source

Critical Thinking Answer Answers might include Reagan's communication skills, sense of humor, ability to get people to believe in themselves and America, leadership, decisiveness, and optimism.

Additional Support

Activity: Connecting Past and Present

Discussing Ronald Reagan and the conservative movement emphasized family life as a traditional American value. **Ask:** How has American family life changed since the country was founded? Write the following years on the board: 1780, 1820, 1860, 1900, and 1940. Have each student sign up for a year, with the students in each year forming a study group. Have students research American family life during their group's time period. Students should learn about families from all economic levels, focusing on family activities, income, employment, and leisure choices. Have each group prepare a presentation about the American family during its chosen time period, and whether they think family life was better then or now. Have students present their work to the class, and lead a discussion about how each time period might have defined "traditional family values." **OL**

D Differentiated Instruction

English Language Learners Remind students that some words can be understood more easily by looking at the word parts. Write *deregulation* on the board. **Ask:** What does the root word *regulation (regulate)* mean? *(to control by law or authority)* Explain that adding *de* would mean "remove" in this case, so *deregulation* would mean "the removal or taking away of control." **Ask:** Could you use the same reasoning to understand the word *decompress? Department? Defense? Demilitarize? (yes, no, no, yes)* **ELL**

W Writing Support

Persuasive Writing Have the class separate into pairs, read the bracketed text, and decide whether they would support or criticize Reagan's economic policy. Have each pair create an editorial for the newspaper that explains its position on the policy. Remind students to clearly present their points of view and support them with persuasive arguments. **OL**

Deregulation

As part of his promise to reduce government and "get the government off the backs of the American people," Reagan pursued a policy of **deregulation.** This meant cutting the rules and regulations that government agencies placed on businesses. The Department of Transportation, for example, wrote new rules for automobile exhaust systems and safety measures that were easier for car manufacturers to meet.

The Supreme Court

Reagan also put a conservative stamp on the Supreme Court by naming justices to the Court who shared his views. He wanted justices who favored a stricter interpretation of the Constitution. When the president appointed **Sandra Day O'Connor** in 1981, she became the first woman ever appointed to the Court. Reagan later appointed Antonin Scalia and Anthony Kennedy as Supreme Court justices.

Reaganomics

Economic policy formed the core of the "Reagan Revolution." The president believed that lower taxes would allow individuals and corporations to invest in new businesses. Because a tax cut would mean less government income, Reagan also called for less government spending.

Supporters called President Reagan's policy **supply-side economics** because it aimed to boost the economy by increasing the supply of goods and services. Critics labeled the policy "Reaganomics." They held that Reagan's policy would help corporations and wealthy Americans, while only a little prosperity would "trickle down" to average Americans.

In 1981 Congress lowered taxes and reduced federal programs such as student aid, welfare, and low-income housing. Supporters argued that Reaganomics would stimulate the economy, helping everybody in the long run.

People IN HISTORY

Sally Kristen Ride

First American woman in space

In 1983 Sally Ride became the first American woman in space when she orbited the Earth aboard the space shuttle *Challenger.* A strong advocate for improved science education, Ride has written several books for young readers. She says, *"Our future lies with today's kids and tomorrow's space exploration."*

Sandra Day O'Connor

First woman to serve on the Supreme Court

When a Supreme Court vacancy opened in 1981, President Reagan decided to fulfill his campaign promise to name the first woman justice. He chose Sandra Day O'Connor, an Arizona appeals court judge. O'Connor served until 2006. In an interview, she discussed the increased opportunities for women: *"When I went to law school, about 1 percent of all law students were women. And last year, over 50 percent were."*

Differentiated Instruction

Women and the Supreme Court

Objective:	To understand Supreme Court decisions
Focus:	Ask students what kinds of cases the Supreme Court hears.
Teach:	Have students find five interesting Supreme Court decisions and answer the questions.
Assess:	Assess answers according to the Answer Key, and give further guidance if needed.
Close:	Ask students how they will use what they have learned as they read or listen to news reports about Supreme Court cases in the future.

Differentiated Instruction Strategies

BL Ask students to choose a decision and summarize the question before the Court.

AL Ask students to choose a case being argued before the Supreme Court this month and follow its progress.

ELL Ask students to describe a governmental entity in their country of origin that functions like the U.S. Supreme Court.

Linking Past and Present Activity, URB p. 61

While Reagan cut domestic programs, he sharply increased military spending. The president declared that the Soviet threat made a military buildup necessary. With higher defense spending and lower taxes, the government spent more money than it collected in revenue. It had to borrow money to make up the difference. This borrowing increased the **federal debt**—the amount of money owed by the government. Between 1970 and 1980, the federal debt grew from $381 billion to $909 billion. By 1990, the debt had jumped to $3.2 trillion.

President Reagan's economic policy seemed to falter when a recession began early in his first term. However, the economy recovered a year later and began to grow. Businesses expanded, and the high jobless rate declined. Investors showed confidence in the economy with a boom in stock trading.

Reading Check Explaining What caused the federal debt to grow significantly in the 1980s?

Teachers in Space

On January 28, 1986, the space shuttle *Challenger* exploded in space, killing all seven aboard. Among the seven was Christa McAuliffe (below right), a teacher and the first civilian passenger in space. McAuliffe was to teach lessons from space that would be beamed live back to Earth. Barbara Morgan (left) had been McAuliffe's backup in 1986. In 2007 Morgan taught lessons from the space shuttle *Endeavor*.

CRITICAL Thinking

Making Generalizations What special qualities are shared by all these individuals?

Reagan's Foreign Policy

Main Idea The Reagan administration believed that the United States should take strong action to resist Communist influences overseas.

History and You Have you ever heard a politician say that "a strong military helps keep the peace"? Read to learn how President Reagan used the military to check Communist activities abroad.

. . . .

Ronald Reagan pledged in his campaign to wage a tough fight against communism. As president, he adopted a new Cold War foreign policy that rejected both containment and détente. Reagan called the Soviet Union "the focus of evil in the modern world" and an "evil empire." He believed that the United States should use strength to defeat it.

Military Buildup

To carry out his policy, President Reagan launched a massive buildup of the military. He expanded the American arsenal of tanks, ships, aircraft, and nuclear missiles. He defended these actions by **quoting**—repeating the words of—George Washington's advice: "To be prepared for war is one of the most effective means of preserving peace." The Reagan military buildup was the largest peacetime buildup in American history, costing about $1.5 trillion over five years.

Reagan also proposed an antimissile defense system, the Strategic Defense Initiative (SDI). Nicknamed "Star Wars," the SDI would thwart incoming enemy missiles. However, scientists were unable to develop the technology for the SDI.

Latin America

Besides building up the military, Reagan also committed U.S. forces and aid to the fight against communism, especially in nearby Latin America. Late in the Carter presidency, Sandinista rebels overthrew the government in Nicaragua. The rebels set up a socialist system, and accepted aid from both Cuba and the Soviet Union.

New Challenges **Chapter 31** 973

D **Differentiated Instruction**

Logical/Mathematical Ask: By what percentage did the debt grow between 1970 and 1980? *(239%)* Between 1980 and 1990? *(352%)* **AL**

R **Reading Strategy**

Questioning Have students use the Main Idea to create a question, such as "What kind of action did the Reagan administration take to resist Communist influences overseas?" Have pairs of students take turns reading aloud the subsection to find the answer. **BL**

Reading Check **Answer:** More money was borrowed to fund military spending than came in via tax revenues.

People IN HISTORY

Critical Thinking Answer
Answers might include determination, courage, intelligence, and public speaking skills.

BL **School-to-Home Connection, URB p. 63**

OL **Content Vocabulary Activity, URB p. 45**

AL **Economics and History Activity, URB p. 5**

S Skill Practice

Using Geography Skills Have students locate on a globe the following places noted in the text: Nicaragua, Caribbean Sea, Grenada, and Lebanon. **BL**

C Critical Thinking

Identifying Central Issues Ask: What could Reagan include in his speech as examples of a successful first term? *(handling of air-traffic controllers strike, deregulation, business expansion, decline in the jobless rate, stock market boom)* **OL**

INTERPRETING POLITICAL CARTOONS

Answers

1. He is beating on drums, sending his message loudly and continuously.

2. Reagan's message is constant, repetitive, and possibly simple.

✓ **Reading Check Answer:** to protect hundreds of U.S. medical students there and set up an anticommunist government

Hands-On Chapter Project
Step 1

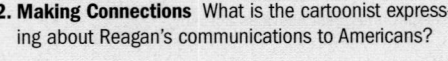

Primary Sources
INTERPRETING POLITICAL CARTOONS

President Reagan held 42 presidential news conferences and gave 47 major presidential speeches during his 2 terms in office. He also made nearly 400 public appearances in the United States outside Washington, D.C.

1. **Identifying** What is President Reagan doing, and what does it mean?
2. **Making Connections** What is the cartoonist expressing about Reagan's communications to Americans?

"CONSTANT DRUMBEAT"

◄ Presidents answer questions from the press at the official podium.

In the early 1980s, Reagan sent aid to the contras, a group battling the Sandinistas. The fighting in Nicaragua sparked disagreement between President Reagan and Congress.

In October 1983, President Reagan took direct military action in the Caribbean. Marxist rebels on the Caribbean island of Grenada staged an uprising. Concerned about the fate of 800 American medical students on the island, Reagan sent troops to rescue them and to set up an anticommunist government.

The Middle East

Reagan's policies were less successful in the Middle East. In 1982 he sent marines to keep the peace in Lebanon. However, a car bomb blast killed more than 60 people at the U.S. embassy in April 1983. Then in October, 241 Americans and 58 French died in attacks on U.S. and French military centers. Rather than deepen U.S. involvement, Reagan withdrew all U.S. forces from Lebanon.

✓ **Reading Check Synthesizing** Why did Reagan take action in Grenada?

Reagan's Second Term

Main Idea During Reagan's second term, the United States continued to act against communism but also held talks with a new Soviet leadership.

History and You What would you do if someone who disliked you decided to change course and become your friend? Read to find out what happened to American-Soviet relations during Reagan's second term.

By 1984, the American economy was booming. In his State of the Union address, President Reagan declared: "America is back—standing tall, looking [toward the future] with courage, confidence, and hope."

President Reagan and Vice President **George H.W. Bush** continued this optimistic theme, or subject, in their campaign for reelection. The Democrats chose Walter Mondale, vice president under Jimmy Carter, and **Geraldine Ferraro,** a member of Congress from New York. Ferraro became the first woman to run for vice president on a major political party ticket.

Writing and Performing a Skit

Step 1: Choosing an Event Students will choose an event for their skit.

Essential Question: How was President Reagan's attitude about communism reflected in his actions and policies?

Directions Organize students into four groups. Assign a president to each group and tell students that they will be writing and performing a three-minute skit about an event that took place during the president's time in office. Have each group choose an event and tell the class why they chose that particular event for its skit.

Identifying Ask students to identify the events in Reagan's presidency that were related to communism. *(military buildup, "Star Wars," sending aid to the Contras, sending troops to Grenada, the INF treaty)* **OL**

(Chapter Project continued in Section 2)

Reagan won the electoral votes in 49 out of the 50 states. It was one of the most lopsided presidential elections in American history. Spurred on by high employment, a strong economy, and low interest rates, Reagan enjoyed high popularity ratings early in his second term.

The Iran-Contra Scandal

Despite his popularity, a scandal cast a shadow over part of President Reagan's second term. Terrorists, with ties to the Iranian government, held Americans hostage in Lebanon. Hoping to secure the hostages' release, Reagan officials made a deal with Iran's Islamic leaders.

Marine Lieutenant Colonel Oliver North and Navy Vice Admiral John Poindexter were both assigned to the White House National Security Council. They arranged for the sale of weapons to Iran in return for help in freeing American hostages. North and Poindexter decided to funnel money from this secret arms sale to help the Nicaraguan contras.

News of these deals—which became known as the Iran-Contra scandal—created an uproar. Critics charged that these deals violated federal laws that barred officials from aiding the contras. Congress held hearings to determine whether the president took part in breaking the law, but no proof of the president's involvement was ever found.

A Changing Soviet Policy

A remarkable shift in Soviet-American relations took shape during Reagan's second term. In 1985 **Mikhail Gorbachev** became the new Soviet leader. Gorbachev was committed to reforming the Soviet government. He called for a policy of glasnost—opening Soviet society to new ideas. Gorbachev also reduced government control of the economy and allowed local decision making. This new policy, perestroika, encouraged the Soviets to seek more changes.

In 1987 Reagan and Gorbachev signed an agreement, the Intermediate-Range Nuclear Forces (INF) Treaty. The treaty aimed to reduce the number of nuclear missiles in each superpower's arsenal. Both nations still held vast nuclear arsenals, but they had taken a major step toward reducing the threat of nuclear war.

Reading Check **Summarizing** What change in Soviet domestic policy took place in the 1980s?

W Writing Support

Expository Writing Have students research the policies of glasnost and perestroika at the library or on the Internet. Ask students to imagine that they were in the Soviet Union when these revolutionary changes were introduced. Have them write a letter to a friend in another country in which they explain some of the changes and how they feel about them. **OL**

 Reading Check **Answer:** The policy of perestroika reduced government economic control and allowed decision making on a local level; it was a step away from communism.

Assess

History ONLINE

Study Central™ provides summaries, interactive games, and online graphic organizers to help students review content.

Close

Listing Have students list three facts about Ronald Reagan's two terms as president. **OL**

 Section 1 Review

Section 1 Review

History ONLINE
Study Central™ To review this section, go to glencoe.com.

Vocabulary

1. Use each of the following terms correctly in a sentence: deregulation, supply-side economics, federal debt, quote, theme.

Main Ideas

2. **Discussing** What did Reagan hope his supply-side economics would accomplish?

3. **Analyzing** What military stand did Reagan take in Nicaragua, and why did he take it?

4. **Explaining** What was the INF treaty?

Critical Thinking

5. **Describing** On a chart like the one below, describe the actions taken by the Reagan administration in the following areas:

Area	Action
Supreme Court	
Domestic Program	
U.S.–Soviet Relations	
Latin America	

6. **Expository Writing** In a paragraph, explain the main philosophy of Reaganomics and what it was supposed to achieve.

Answer the Essential Question

7. How was President Reagan's attitude about communism reflected in his actions and policies?

Answers

1. Students will write sentences using the terms.
2. stimulate the economy by increasing the supply of goods and services, increase investments
3. He aided the contras, who were battling the socialist Sandinista government. He did so to check the spread of communism in Latin America.
4. Intermediate-Range Nuclear Forces Treaty, which was signed by Reagan and Gorbachev to limit nuclear weapons and the threat of nuclear war

5. **Supreme Court:** named conservative justices to the court; **domestic programs:** lowered taxes and reduced federal programs; **U.S.-Soviet relations:** rejected containment and détente, built up military, proposed "Star Wars"; **Latin America:** sent aid to contras, sent troops to Grenada
6. Students' paragraphs should point out that opponents believed Reaganomics would help the wealthy, but not average Americans.

7. Reagan strongly opposed communism, and his policies and actions focused on defeating it. He enlarged the military to discourage the Soviet Union from going to war. When Gorbachev committed to reforming the communist system, however, Reagan cooperated with him to reduce the threat of war. In Latin America, Reagan aided anticommunist forces in Nicaragua and Grenada.

Focus

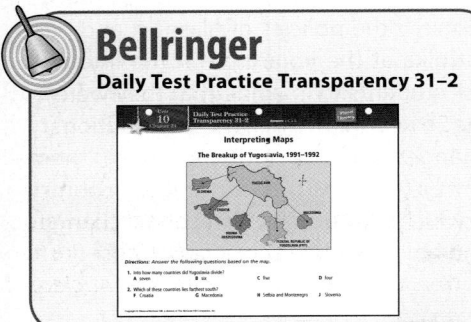
Reading Guide

Answers to Graphic: former Soviet republics gain independence, Soviet Union dissolves

Section Spotlight Video

Have students watch the Section Spotlight Video "The Bush Presidency" to learn how President George H.W. Bush dealt with a serious crisis in the Middle East.

Resource Manager

Essential Question ◀
How did President Bush deal with the domestic challenges facing his presidency?

Reading Guide

Content Vocabulary
coalition (p. 979)   downsize (p. 981)
bankruptcy (p. 981)

Academic Vocabulary
retain (p. 977)   site (p. 979)

Key People and Events
Tiananmen Square (p. 979)
Saddam Hussein (p. 979)
Colin Powell (p. 979)
Norman Schwarzkopf (p. 979)
Operation Desert Storm (p. 979)

Reading Strategy
Taking Notes On a diagram like the one below, determine the effects of the revolt that took place in the Soviet Union at the time of the Bush presidency.

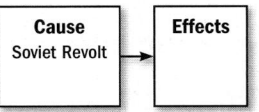

| Cause Soviet Revolt | → | Effects |

ILLINOIS STANDARDS
The American Journey

14.E Understand United States foreign policy as it relates to other nations and international issues.

14.E.3 Compare the basic principles of the United States and its international interests (e.g., territory, environment, trade, use of technology).

18.B.3a Analyze how individuals and groups interact with and within institutions (e.g., educational, military)

The Bush Presidency

American Diary

On September 2, 1944, a young pilot took part in a bombing mission. His plane suffered a direct hit from a Japanese antiaircraft gun. The pilot and his two crew members bailed out into the Pacific Ocean. A U.S. submarine rescued the pilot but the other two men were never found. For his heroism, the pilot—George H.W. Bush—received the Distinguished Flying Cross. More than 40 years later, Bush would become the forty-first president of the United States.

A crowd in Moscow shows its support for the United States, August 1991.

R Reading Strategies	**C** Critical Thinking	**D** Differentiated Instruction	**W** Writing Support	**S** Skill Practice
Teacher Edition • Sequencing, p. 978 • Monitor. & Clarify., p. 979 **Additional Resources** • Guid. Read., URB p. 68 • Content Vocab., URB p. 45 • Academic Vocab., URB p. 47 • Read. Ess., p. 349 • Pri. Source Read., URB p. 49	**Teacher Edition** • Compar. & Contrast., p. 977 • Deter. Cause & Effect, p. 980 **Additional Resources** • Quizzes and Tests, p. 308	**Teacher Edition** • Gift. & Talent., p. 980 • Below Grade Level, p. 981 **Additional Resources** • School-to-Home, URB p. 63 • Reteaching Act., URB p. 65	**Teacher Edition** • Narrative Writ., p. 978	**Teacher Edition** • Using Geo. Skills, p. 977 • Using Geo. Skills, p. 979 **Additional Resources** • Daily Test Pract. Transp. 31-2 • Soc. Stud. Skills, URB p. 53

The End of the Cold War

Main Idea During Bush's presidency, significant global events led to the end of the Cold War.

History and You Why do things change in the world? Do you think people make a difference, or are big events and developments responsible? Read to learn why the Soviet Union collapsed.

In 1988 Vice President George H.W. Bush was elected president. Bush carried 40 states, giving him 426 electoral votes to 112 for the Democratic Party candidate, Michael Dukakis. However, Bush's victory did not extend to Congress. The Democrats **retained,** or held onto, control of the House and the Senate.

A Changing Soviet Union

Bush's presidency was during a time of sweeping change in world affairs. Soviet leader Gorbachev wanted to end the arms race so he could focus on reforms within his country. In 1990 Gorbachev and President Bush achieved a breakthrough with the Strategic Arms Reduction Treaty (START). For the first time, two nuclear powers agreed to destroy existing nuclear weapons. **C**

Most Soviet citizens, however, were more concerned about their own problems than about arms control. For years they had endured shortages of food and basic items such as shoes and soap because of government mismanagement and heavy defense spending. Gorbachev's policies aimed to solve the economic problems, but changes came slowly. With Gorbachev's policy of glasnost, Soviet citizens began to express their dissatisfaction openly.

A Rising Tide of Freedom

With reforms underway in the Soviet Union, the peoples of Eastern Europe felt free to demand change in their countries. In Poland,shipyard workers won the right to form an independent labor union—called Solidarity—in August 1980. Lech Walesa,the leader of Solidarity, emerged as a symbol of resistance to Communist rule. Solidarity forced the government to hold open elections in June 1989.

Elsewhere in Eastern Europe, demonstrators filled the streets of major cities. As public pressure increased and Soviet controls relaxed, long-sealed national borders were opened and Communist governments toppled. **S**

Primary Source | A New Era

Openness As president, Bush continued Reagan's policy of cooperation with Soviet leader Mikhail Gorbachev. Early in his presidency, Bush said, *"a new breeze is blowing across the steppes and cities of the Soviet Union. Why not, then, let this spirit of openness grow, let more barriers come down.*
—from Remarks at the Texas A&M University Commencement Ceremony, 1989

Critical Thinking

Explaining President Bush also called on the Soviet Union to follow policies of "open emigration" and "open airwaves." What did he mean by this?

Gorbachev, President Reagan, and ▲ President-Elect George Bush view the Statue of Liberty after meeting in New York City, December 1988.

Teach

C Critical Thinking

Comparing and Contrasting Ask: How did the arms reduction agreements between Reagan and Gorbachev and between Bush and Gorbachev differ? *(Under Reagan, both the U.S. and the Soviets reduced their nuclear arsenals. Under Bush, both sides agreed to destroy nuclear weapons.)* **AL**

S Skill Practice

Using Geography Skills Have students look at the map of Russia and the independent republics on the next page. **Ask:** Name 10 republics that once were part of the Soviet Union. *(Russia, Belarus, Ukraine, Moldova, Georgia, Armenia, Kazakhstan, Uzbekistan, Azerbaijan, Turkmenistan, Tajikistan, and Kyrgyzstan)* **BL**

Primary Source

Critical Thinking Answer
Bush wanted the Soviets to allow citizens to travel freely across borders and to ease restrictions on the media (including television and radio).

Hands-On Chapter Project
Step 2

Teacher Tip

Preparing Either have a list of possible roles ready to share with groups before this step, or ask a high school drama adviser to visit your class and explain the assignments necessary for putting on a school play.

Writing and Performing a Skit

Step 2: Researching Events Groups will research their events and choose roles for every member of their group.

Essential Question: How did President Bush deal with the domestic challenges facing his presidency?

Directions Have students research their events, then write a description of what their skit will be about and share it with the class. Also have students assign roles to every member of their group: playwrights, prop makers, actors, narrators, costume makers, and so on.

Analyzing Ask students which events reflect ways in which George H.W. Bush handled domestic challenges. *(While Bush was willing to bail out struggling S&Ls, he was not willing to increase federal spending.)* **OL**

(Chapter Project continued in Section 3)

Russia and the Independent Republics
NATIONAL GEOGRAPHIC

Population of the Soviet Union in 1990
289 million

Population of Russia in 1991
148 million

Source: *Encyclopedia of the Nations*

Border of USSR (1990)
Russia after 1991
Independent Republics after 1991

0   800 kilometers
0   800 miles
Lambert Conic projection

Map Skills

1. **Location** Which republics border Uzbekistan?
2. **Calculating** Compare the population of the Soviet Union with the population of Russia after the collapse of the Soviet Union. What is the difference?

Maps in Motion See StudentWorks™ Plus or glencoe.com.

W Writing Support

Narrative Writing Have students research the period and then write and illustrate a children's picture book about two cousins—one in East Berlin and one in West Berlin—who are reunited when the Berlin Wall falls. Students may wish to share their stories with a younger class. **OL**

R Reading Strategy

Sequencing Information Write the following events on the board and have students place them in the correct order: coup defeated, Communist Party outlawed, Soviet Union collapses, Yeltsin defies coup, Communist coup. *(Communist coup, Yeltsin defies coup, coup defeated, Communist Party outlawed, Soviet Union collapses)* **OL**

Russia and the Independent Republics
NATIONAL GEOGRAPHIC

Map Skills Answers

1. Kazakhstan, Turkmenistan, Kyrgyzstan, and Tajikistan
2. Russia's population was reduced by 141 million after the collapse.

 **Answer:** open elections

Additional Support

In late 1989, the iron curtain that had divided Eastern and Western Europe for more than 40 years began to crumble. During this time, Gorbachev encouraged reform.

Freedom also came to East Germany. With protests raging and thousands of citizens fleeing to West Germany, the Communist government opened the Berlin Wall on November 9, 1989. Germans brought hammers and chisels to chop away at the Berlin Wall, long the symbol of the barrier to the West. In 1990 East Germany and West Germany were finally reunited.

Collapse of the Soviet Union

As Eastern Europe was changing, Gorbachev faced opposition from political rivals within the Soviet Union. Some reformers demanded that he move quickly to establish democratic and free enterprise reforms. Hard-line Communists in the military and secret police resisted his changes and feared the collapse of the Soviet empire.

In August 1991, a group of hard-line Communist officials and army generals staged a coup, or an overthrow of the government. They arrested Gorbachev and ordered soldiers to seize the parliament building.

As the world anxiously waited, about 50,000 people surrounded the parliament building to protect it from the soldiers. Boris Yeltsin, president of the Russian Republic and a reformer, stood on top of a tank and declared, "Democracy will win!" President Bush telephoned Yeltsin to express America's support. On August 22, the coup collapsed. Freed, Gorbachev returned to Moscow.

The defeat of the coup brought a tidal wave of democracy. Soon all 15 republics had declared their independence from the Soviet Union. Yeltsin outlawed the Communist Party in Russia. On December 25, 1991, Gorbachev announced the end of the Soviet Union.

Reading Check **Cause and Effect** What did Solidarity accomplish in Poland?

Activity: Collaborative Learning

Writing a Script Gorbachev encouraged free enterprise reforms in a society that was accustomed to daily shortages of consumer goods and a stagnant economy run by a central bureaucracy. **Ask:** How did the free enterprise reforms affect daily life? Lead a class discussion about the meaning of *free enterprise* and how the concept is manifested in students' daily lives. *(Examples might include the ability to choose from several restaurants in their town, the variety of clothes in their closets, and the variety of available television shows.)* Divide the class into small groups, and instruct each group to find descriptions of daily life in the pre-reform Soviet Union. Then have them research what general reforms Gorbachev proposed. Have each group use its findings to write a one-act play in which an American exchange student and a Soviet student meet in a cafe and discuss a typical shopping trip in their hometowns. **OL**

A New Foreign Policy

Main Idea After the Cold War's end, Bush administration officials set out to develop a new foreign policy.

History and You Have you ever had to handle several problems at once? Read to learn about the foreign crises that the United States faced in the late 1980s and early 1990s.

• •

The end of the Cold War brought both hope and new challenges. While redefining U.S. foreign policy goals, President Bush faced crises in various parts of the world.

In 1989 Bush sent U.S. troops to Panama to overthrow dictator Manuel Noriega. Under Noriega's rule, political repression and corruption had become widespread. The troops seized Noriega and sent him to the United States to stand trial for drug trafficking. Panama then held elections and organized a new government.

Bush also was interested in China. In 1974 he had served as the U.S. diplomatic representative to China. During the 1980s, China's Communist government began to reform the economy, but it refused to make political

changes. In May 1989, students and workers in China held protests calling for democracy. On June 4, 1989, troops sent by the government killed several hundred protesters in **Tiananmen Square** in the center of Beijing. Bush and other world leaders condemned the killings.

The Persian Gulf War

President Bush faced perhaps his most serious crisis in the Middle East. In August 1990, Iraq's dictator, **Saddam Hussein** (hoo·SAYN), sent his army into Kuwait, a small neighboring country rich in oil.

Vowing to "draw a line in the sand," President Bush persuaded other nations to join the United States in a **coalition,** or a group united for action. The U.S. forces were commanded by General **Colin Powell,** chairman of the Joint Chiefs of Staff, and General **Norman Schwarzkopf.** Hussein was ordered to withdraw his troops from Kuwait, but he refused.

In January 1991 coalition forces launched **Operation Desert Storm.** Missiles and bombs fell on Iraq, destroying military and civilian **sites,** or locations. Six weeks later, the coalition began a short ground war that freed Kuwait and forced Iraq to accept a cease fire. American troops returned home to cheering crowds.

Primary Source / The Spirit of Freedom

The Barrier Falls In November 1989, crowds tore down the Berlin Wall that had divided Germany and symbolized the "iron curtain" that separated Eastern Europe and Western Europe. ▼

Tragedy in Tiananmen Square In the spring of 1989, Chinese students held demonstrations for democracy. Government tanks and soldiers crushed their protests in Tiananmen Square in Beijing. Many people were killed, and hundreds of pro-democracy activists were arrested. ▶

Critical Thinking

1. **Analyzing** Why was the fall of communism in East Germany significant?
2. **Assessing** How did the United States react to the Chinese government's actions at Tiananmen Square? Was the reaction appropriate? Explain.

D Differentiated Instruction

Gifted and Talented Organize the class into small groups. Each group should choose one of the former Yugoslav republics; make sure each nation is chosen. Groups should research and write a two-page report about their republic's history, natural resources, culture, and government. Then have students conduct a panel discussion in which they explore ethnic conflict in the region. **AL**

C Critical Thinking

Determining Cause and Effect Ask: What caused a civil war to break out? *(The Serbs tried to hold on to parts of Croatia and Bosnia.)* **OL**

Persian Gulf War, 1991 ☐ NATIONAL GEOGRAPHIC

Map Skills Answer

Saudi Arabia was a U.S. ally and borders both Kuwait and Iraq.

✔ **Reading Check Answer:** the crushing of a pro-democracy rally by the Chinese government in 1989

Differentiated Instruction

Persian Gulf War, 1991   NATIONAL GEOGRAPHIC

★ **Aug. 2, 1990** Iraq invades Kuwait

★ **Jan. 12, 1991** U.S. Congress authorizes use of force against Iraq

★ **Feb. 23, 1991** Allied ground war against Iraqi troops begins

★ **Aug. 1990–Feb. 1991** Allied troops move in along Saudi Arabia/Iraq border

★ **Jan. 16, 1991** Operation Desert Storm begins

★ **Feb. 27, 1991** President Bush declares cease-fire

Map Skills

Movement Why do you think Allied troops mobilized their forces from Saudi Arabia?

Maps in MOtion See StudentWorks™ Plus or glencoe.com.

War in the Balkans

Another conflict occurred in Yugoslavia. Yugoslavia had been made up of several republics. After the collapse of Yugoslavia's government, the republics of Slovenia, Croatia, and Bosnia-Herzegovina declared their independence in 1991.

D
C
The people of Croatia and Bosnia included many Serbs—people from the Yugoslav republic of Serbia. These Serbs, backed by Serbia's government, fought to hold on to parts of Croatia and Bosnia. A terrible civil war followed, and thousands died. Reports of killings committed by the Serbs angered world leaders. After NATO took military action, the participants signed a peace plan in 1995 known as the Dayton Accords.

✔ **Reading Check Describing** What political event took place in Tiananmen Square, Beijing?

980 Chapter 31 *New Challenges*

Domestic Issues

Main Idea The federal debt and an economic slowdown were challenges for the Bush administration.

History and You Have you ever come up with a plan to raise money when you wanted to make an expensive purchase? Read to find out how the federal government had to meet financial challenges during the Bush administration.

. . . .

President Bush spent much of his time dealing with foreign policy, but he also faced major domestic challenges. From the Reagan years, Bush inherited a growing federal debt and a slowing economy.

Early in his presidency, Bush faced a serious crisis. During the 1980s, the Reagan administration cut regulations in many industries. New laws eased limits on savings and

---

Using an Electronic Spreadsheet

Objective: To learn how to interpret an electronic spreadsheet

Focus: Ask students to describe spreadsheets and their uses.

Teach: Have students analyze the table and summarize it in two paragraphs.

Assess: Assess the results according to the Self-Assessment Checklist.

Close: Have students share the information they learned with classmates.

Differentiated Instruction Strategies

BL Have students examine and discuss the information in a single row and column of the spreadsheet.

AL Have students create a spreadsheet with the figures shown, then add more columns and rows using fictitious figures and categories.

ELL Carefully explain and demonstrate the use of a formula from the spreadsheet.

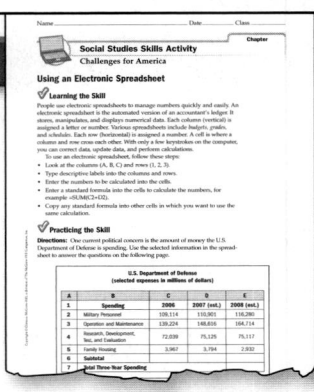

Social Studies Skills, URB p. 53

loan associations (S&Ls)—financial institutions that specialized in making loans to home buyers.

Banking Crisis

The new laws allowed S&Ls to pay very high interest rates to attract deposits and to make far too many risky loans and investments. When many borrowers could not **D** repay their loans and real estate values declined, S&Ls lost millions of dollars. Individual S&L deposits were insured by the government, which now had to pay out billions of dollars to customers of failed S&Ls. To limit the crisis, the government bailed out other struggling S&Ls, a move costing taxpayers almost $500 billion.

Economic Downturn

The heavy borrowing of the 1980s brought trouble to the economy. As the federal debt reached new highs, business and personal debt grew. In 1990 the economy slowed to a recession, partly caused by the end of the Cold War. Cuts in military spending led to job losses in defense-related businesses.

Companies also began to **downsize**—lay off workers—to become more efficient. The nation's debt burden made the recession worse. Individuals and businesses had borrowed heavily and now could not meet loan payments. Some had to declare **bankruptcy,** selling off what they owned to pay debts.

Many people urged the government to stimulate the economy. President Bush refused to increase federal spending. He did agree to extend benefits to the jobless, but he opposed further government involvement.

Accomplishments

Despite disagreements, the president and Congress cooperated on updating the Clean Air Act and pushing forward on civil rights. The Americans with Disabilities Act of 1990 banned job discrimination against people with disabilities. It also opened ways for disabled people to gain easier access to workplaces, transportation, and housing.

Bush also carried out a war on illegal drugs. In 1989 President Bush created the Office of National Drug Control Policy. This department oversees more than 50 federal agencies involved in the war on drugs.

Reading Check Analyzing Why did so many S&Ls fail in the 1980s?

D **Differentiated Instruction**

Below Grade Level Ask: What word describes an institution much like an S&L? *(bank)* Who were the "customers of failed S&Ls"? *(people who had taken out loans with the S&Ls or who had interest-paying accounts with the S&Ls)* **BL**

Reading Check Answer: The S&Ls had paid high interest rates and made risky loans and investments. They failed when many borrowers could not repay their home loans. The S&Ls could not recoup that money because of depressed real estate values.

Assess

History ONLINE

Study Central™ provides summaries, interactive games, and online graphic organizers to help students review content.

Close

Summarizing Ask students to summarize in a few sentences the domestic challenges facing President Bush. **OL**

Section 2 Review

History ONLINE
Study Central™ To review this section, go to glencoe.com.

Vocabulary
1. Use each of these terms correctly in a sentence: retain, coalition, site, downsize, bankruptcy.

Main Ideas
2. **Analyzing** Why was START so important?
3. **Explaining** What action did Bush take in Panama using U.S. troops?
4. **Discussing** Why did the government lose so much money through the failure of S&L banks?

Critical Thinking
5. **Sequencing** Using a diagram like the one below, generally sequence the events that led to the country's deep recession during the 1990s.

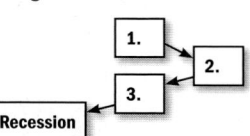

6. **Creative Writing** Take a stand on how you feel about U.S. participation in Operation Desert Storm. Write a short protest or support song about your feelings.

Answer the
7. **Essential Question**
How did President Bush deal with the domestic challenges facing his presidency?

New Challenges **Chapter 31** **981**

Section 2 Review

Answers

1. Students will write sentences using the terms.
2. The United States and the Soviet Union agreed to destroy—rather than merely limit—their nuclear arsenals.
3. The United States overthrew the dictator, after which elections ushered in a new government.
4. The government had insured deposits of individuals in S&Ls and had to repay them.

It also bailed out other S&Ls so they would not fail.
5. (1) Federal debt increases. (2) Business and personal debt increase. (3) Military spending slows as Cold War ends.
6. Students' songs should reflect sentiments about U.S. involvement in Operation Desert Storm.
7. His government bailed out struggling S&Ls to prevent them from defaulting. He chose

not to increase federal spending to stimulate the economy during the recession except to provide benefits to the jobless. He supported measures to fight pollution, job discrimination, and illegal drugs.

Focus

Section 3

A New Century

Bellringer
Daily Test Practice Transparency 31–3

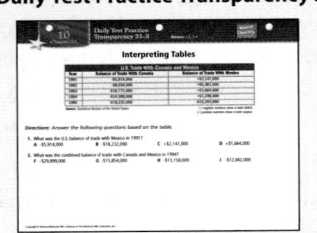

Reading Guide
Answers to Graphic:
Brady Bill, a crime bill banning certain guns and hiring police officers, Family and Medical Leave Act

Section Spotlight Video

Have students watch the Section Spotlight Video "A New Century" to learn about Israeli Prime Minister Yitzhak Rabin.

Resource Manager

Essential Question
How did the Clinton presidency change the U.S. domestic scene in the 1990s?

Reading Guide

Content Vocabulary
grassroots movement (p. 983)
deficit spending (p. 983)
budget deficit (p. 983)
gross domestic product (p. 985)
perjury (p. 985)

Academic Vocabulary
adequate (p. 983) scope (p. 985)

Key People and Events
Bill Clinton (p. 983)
Al Gore (p. 983)
George W. Bush (p. 987)
Richard Cheney (p. 987)
Condoleezza Rice (p. 989)

Reading Strategy
Taking Notes On a diagram like the one below, identify early Clinton-sponsored legislation that passed into law.

Clinton Legislation

ILLINOIS STANDARDS
The American Journey

14.E.3 Compare the basic principles of the United States and its international interests (e.g., territory, environment, trade, use of technology).

15.D.3a Explain the effects of increasing and declining imports and exports to an individual and to the nation's economy as a whole.

17.C Understand relationships between geographic factors and society.

American Diary

At 16 years old, Bill Clinton heard the "I Have a Dream" speech by Dr. Martin Luther King, Jr., for the first time. It inspired him to find common ground in politics for the benefit of all citizens. After becoming president in 1993, he still held his vision of people working together for the common good. He said, "We have got to move beyond division and resentment to common ground. We've got to go beyond cynicism to c sense of possibility."

—from Remarks at Georgetown University, July 1995

Candidate Bill Clinton greets supporters at a campaign rally in 1992.

R Reading Strategies	**C** Critical Thinking	**D** Differentiated Instruction	**W** Writing Support	**S** Skill Practice
Teacher Edition	**Teacher Edition**	**Teacher Edition**	**Teacher Edition**	**Teacher Edition**
• Outlining, p. 983	• Deter. Cause & Effect, p. 986	• Verbal/Ling., p. 983	• Expository Writ., p. 984	• Using Geo. Skills, p. 988
• Identifying, p. 985	• Analyz. Info., p. 987	• Below Grade Level, p. 984	• Persuasive Writ., p. 984	**Additional Resources**
• Summarizing, p. 985	• Identify Central Iss., p. 988	• Intrapersonal, p. 989	• Expository Writ., p. 986	• Daily Test Pract. Transp. 31-3
Additional Resources	**Additional Resources**	**Additional Resources**		• Time Line Skills, URB p. 62
• Guid. Read., URB p. 69	• Quizzes and Tests, p. 309	• School-to-Home, URB p. 63		• Lesson Transp. 31A, 31B
• Cont. Voc., URB p. 45		• Reteaching Act., URB p. 65		
• Academic Vocab., URB p. 47				
• Read. Ess., p. 352				

The Clinton Administration

Main Idea President Clinton struggled with Republicans in Congress and faced impeachment, but he achieved several major economic and social reforms.

History and You Have you ever visited our closest neighbors—Canada and Mexico? Read to find out how the United States and these two nations drew closer together in the 1990s.

After victory in the Persian Gulf War, President Bush's popularity with Americans soared. A troubled economy, however, hurt Bush's reelection chances for 1992 and encouraged challengers to enter the presidential race. The Democrats nominated Arkansas governor **Bill Clinton** to run against President Bush. Clinton chose Tennessee senator **Al Gore** as his running mate. The Clinton campaign focused on the economy and the high unemployment rate.

Unhappy with "politics as usual," many Americans did not want to vote for either Bush or Clinton. A **grassroots movement**—people around the nation organizing at the local level—put Texas business leader H. Ross Perot on the ballot as a third-party candidate.

Perot called for an end to the government's **deficit spending,** or spending more money than it takes in.

Voters elected Clinton, the first president born after World War II. Clinton received 43 percent of the popular vote, Bush 38 percent, and Perot 19 percent. Clinton received less than a majority of the votes because of Perot's strong showing, the highest percentage of popular votes for any third-party candidate since Theodore Roosevelt in 1912.

Domestic Program

One of the new president's goals was reducing the **budget deficit**—the amount by which spending exceeds revenue. Clinton proposed cutting government spending, raising taxes for middle-and upper-income Americans, and providing tax credits to the poorest. Most Republicans in Congress opposed this plan, but it narrowly passed.

Clinton faced even stronger opposition to his plan for health-care reform. His goal was to control rising health-care costs and provide **adequate,** or enough, health insurance for every American. The president named the First Lady, Hillary Rodham Clinton, to head the task force.

By the Numbers / The 1992 Election

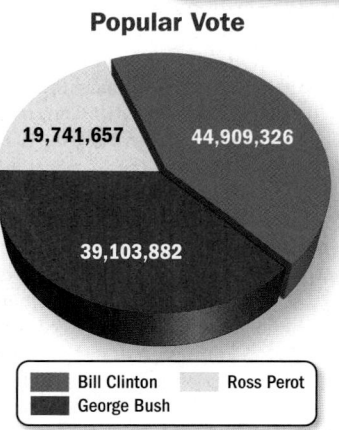

Popular Vote

- 19,741,657
- 44,909,326
- 39,103,882

Bill Clinton — Ross Perot
George Bush

www.presidentelect.org

Three-Way Race Democratic candidate Bill Clinton won the electoral vote by more than a 2-to-1 margin over incumbent President George H.W. Bush. Clinton, however, did not win a majority of the nation's popular vote, but he did beat Bush by six percentage points.

Critical Thinking

Evaluating How can a third-party candidate for the presidency like Perot affect an election?

Teach

R Reading Strategy

Outlining To help students understand this subsection, have them create an outline, using the headings from the section as their outline headings. Have them note important details under each heading using correct outline form. **OL**

For additional practice on this activity, see the Skills Handbook.

D Differentiated Instruction

Verbal/Linguistic Ask: How did the term "grassroots movement" get its name? (*Students may recognize that grassroots are at ground level, which is another way of saying they are local.*) **OL**

By the Numbers

Critical Thinking Answer A third-party candidate can take popular votes from the major-party candidates and thus allow a candidate to win in the Electoral College without having a majority of the popular vote.

Differentiated Instruction

Nobel Peace Prize Winners (1983–2006)

Time Line Activity
Challenges for America

Nobel Peace Prize Winners (1983–2006)

Directions: Use the following information about Nobel Peace Prize recipients to complete the time line.

Time Line Activity, URB p. 62

Objective: To create a time line

Focus: As a class, discuss how time lines can be used to visually order and display events.

Teach: Have students complete the time line using the information supplied.

Assess: Assess answers according to the Answer Key, and give further guidance if needed.

Close: Ask students how they might create and use time lines to study for a test.

Differentiated Instruction Strategies

BL Ask students to find out what other Nobel prizes are awarded in addition to the Peace Prize.

AL Ask students to revise the time line to reflect world events as well as Nobel Prize winners.

ELL Have students choose someone from their country of origin who has worked for peace and report to the class about that person.

W₁ Writing Support

Expository Writing Have the class divide into small groups and conduct research on the Brady Bill. Instruct each group to create a poster that will inform readers how the bill received its name, how it tries to curb gun violence, and the impact it has had on society. Display the posters in the classroom. **AL**

D Differentiated Instruction

Below Grade Level Ask: What is a midterm election? *(an election that occurs two years into a president's term of office rather than at the end of the term)* **BL**

W₂ Writing Support

Persuasive Writing Have students write a speech to be delivered by President Clinton to Congress in 1995 after government had been shut down for the second time. In the speech, the president should outline why compromise is needed and how he feels about the minimum wage and the need for welfare reform. **OL**

Additional Support

Primary Source / **Impeaching a President**

Voting for Impeachment The House of Representatives accused President Clinton of lying under oath and obstructing justice, and voted to impeach him. Now it was up to the Senate to convict and remove him from office. Passionate voices cried out for and against conviction.

For Conviction *"As the youngest member of this body, I believe we must hold firm to the oldest truths. . . . I vote as I do because I will not stand for the proposition that a President can, with premeditation and deliberation, obstruct justice and commit perjury before a grand jury. It cannot be."*

Senator Peter Fitzgerald (R–Illinois) ▲

Against Conviction *"Impeachment is a power singularly lacking any of the checks and balances on which the Framers depended. It is solely a power of the Congress. Do not doubt that it could bring radical instability to American government."*

▲ Senator Daniel Moynihan (D–New York)

Congress rejected the Clinton plan, calling it too expensive and too reliant on government control. Later, Congress did pass measures that provided more health-care protection for the elderly, children, and other groups that were not previously covered.

During his first term, President Clinton won some legislative battles. Despite strong opposition, the president succeeded in passing the Brady Bill of 1993. The law imposed a waiting period and background checks for handgun purchases. The 1994 crime bill banned 19 kinds of assault weapons and provided for 100,000 new police officers.

Another Clinton proposal that became law was the Family and Medical Leave Act of 1993. It permitted workers to take time off from their jobs for special family situations.

Contract With America

Before the 1994 mid-term elections, House Republicans led by Newt Gingrich of Georgia created a new plan. Known as the Contract with America, it called for a "return to the basic values that had built the country: work and family and the recognition of a higher moral authority."

In the contract, the Republicans promised to reduce the federal government, balance the budget, lower taxes, and reform how Congress operates. They also pledged to pass laws to reduce crime, reform welfare, and strengthen the family. The result was a strong Republican victory in the 1994 elections. For the first time in 40 years, the Republicans controlled both houses of Congress. In their first hundred days in office, the Republicans passed much of the Contract with America.

In 1995, however, the Republicans lost ground when they clashed with President Clinton over the new federal budget. This dispute caused the federal government to run out of money. The government shut down nonessential services twice for a total of 27 days. Congress and the president recognized that compromise was needed.

984 Chapter 31 *New Challenges*

Activity: Connecting Past and Present

Assessing In 1994 Newt Gingrich's Contract with America promised Americans a smaller federal government, balanced budget, lower taxes, and congressional reform. **Ask:** Have the goals of the Contract with America been attained? Have the class divide into four groups, and assign each group one of the goals. Each group will research whether its assigned goal has been attained since 1994 and write a short report that explains in what ways the promise has or has not been met. Have the groups share their findings with the class and discuss the overall success and impact of the Gingrich plan. **AL**

The Power to Impeach If a majority of the House votes to impeach, the Senate then has the power to try the official. Only two presidents have been impeached: Andrew Johnson in 1868 and Bill Clinton in 1998. Both were tried by the Senate and acquitted (not removed from office).

Critical Thinking

1. **Analyzing** Why did Senator Fitzgerald believe that the president should be removed from office?
2. **Explaining** What reasons does Senator Moynihan give for his vote not to remove President Clinton from office?

Soon afterward, the Republicans in Congress and President Clinton reached an agreement to balance the budget. The president pushed for an increase in the minimum wage and supported a welfare reform act. This measure set a work requirement for people receiving benefits and put a five-year time limit on benefits.

Clinton Wins a Second Term

The Republicans hoped to regain the White House in 1996. However, the economy was healthy and unemployment was at a 30-year low. President Clinton easily won reelection, beating the Republican candidate, former Senate majority leader Robert Dole.

During Clinton's second term, the economy continued to grow. One measure of economic growth is the **gross domestic product** (GDP), the value of all the goods and services produced in a nation in a year. In 1996 and 1997, the GDP grew by about 4 percent per year—one of the highest rates of growth since the post-World War II boom.

The economy's growth increased the amount of tax money the government received. At the same time, the president and Congress cut back the size of the federal budget. The federal budget is prepared for a fiscal year—a 12-month planning period. The 1998 fiscal year ended with a federal budget surplus—the amount of money remaining after all expenditures—of about $80 billion, the first surplus in three decades.

Scandals and Impeachment

The strong economy kept Clinton's popularity high, but scandals threatened his presidency. Clinton was accused of arranging illegal loans for a real estate company while he was governor of Arkansas. Former judge Kenneth Starr led the investigation. A new scandal emerged involving a personal relationship between the president and a White House intern. Evidence suggested that the president may have committed **perjury,** or lied under oath, about the relationship. Starr widened the **scope,** or range, of the investigation. In September 1998, Starr sent a report to Congress claiming that President Clinton had committed perjury and obstructed justice.

The House of Representatives then began hearings to decide whether to impeach the president. To impeach is to make a formal accusation of wrongdoing against a public official. Despite general agreement that the president had lied, the House was split over whether his actions justified impeachment. Clinton's supporters argued that his offenses did not qualify as "high crimes and misdemeanors," as stated in the Constitution. Clinton's accusers insisted that the president was accountable if his actions were illegal.

In December 1998, the House passed two impeachment articles—for perjury and for obstruction of justice. The case moved to the Senate for trial. A two-thirds majority vote is needed to convict and remove a president from office. In February 1999, the Senate acquitted the president of both charges.

R₁ Reading Strategy

Identifying Ask: Why did Clinton easily win reelection? *(healthy economy and unemployment at a 30-year low)* **OL**

R₂ Reading Strategy

Summarizing Have students write a summary of the Clinton impeachment scandal. Remind students that a summary includes only the most important information from a passage and not every detail. **OL**

Primary Source

Critical Thinking Answers

1. Fitzgerald felt that a president should not obstruct justice and lie to a grand jury.

2. Moynihan believed impeachment is wrong because it is not subject to checks and balances. It would destabilize the government.

Activity: Reporting

Summarizing Ask: What might happen to the country if the government shut down? Have students research newspapers that date from 1996 to find out more about the budget crisis that caused a government shutdown. Have them determine which economic policies and government programs were in dispute and what caused the government to run out of money. Have them look for details about the compromise that allowed the government to begin functioning again. Students should also note public reaction to the shutdowns. Instruct students to tape audio reports about the budget crisis as if they were reporters at the time. Share and discuss the reports in class. **OL**

C Critical Thinking

Determining Cause and Effect

Ask: Why might the elimination of trade barriers among the United States, Mexico, and Canada cause a loss of U.S. jobs? *(U.S. companies would be tempted to manufacture goods in neighboring countries where labor might be cheaper, because they could import the goods without paying tariffs.)* **OL**

W Writing Support

Expository Writing Have students write a report on one aspect of Israeli-Palestinian relations, such as the origins of conflict, the PLO, or peace efforts. **OL**

✔ Reading Check **Answer:** North American Free Trade Agreement (NAFTA)

Hands-On Chapter Project
Step 3

Writing and Performing a Skit

Step 3: Writing the Skit Groups will write their skits and make props and costumes.

Essential Question: How did the Clinton presidency change the U.S. domestic scene in the 1990s?

Foreign Policy

Even as the nation struggled with domestic issues, foreign affairs presented new challenges. Important decisions faced American policy makers on defining the nation's role in the post–Cold War world.

In 1993 Clinton persuaded Congress to ratify the North American Free Trade Agreement, or NAFTA. Under NAFTA the United States, Canada, and Mexico agreed to eliminate trade barriers among the three nations. NAFTA opponents feared a loss of U.S. jobs. Farmers also feared NAFTA, saying that low-priced Mexican produce would undercut American goods. Supporters argued that the treaty would lower prices for American consumers and expand markets.

The Middle East was also a major concern. In September 1993, President Clinton invited Israeli prime minister Yitzhak Rabin and Yassir Arafat, head of the Palestine Liberation Organization (PLO), to the White House for the signing of a historic agreement between the two leaders. Israel recognized the PLO as the representative of the Palestinians, and the PLO recognized Israel's right to exist. The agreement created a plan for limited Palestinian self-government in certain areas.

Opposition to the plan emerged on both sides, and violence in the area continued. In 1995 an Israeli extremist assassinated Prime Minister Rabin. During the remainder of his term, Clinton continued peace efforts, but little success was achieved.

As you read in Section 2, civil war had erupted in the former Yugoslavia. In Bosnia, Serbs engaged in ethnic cleansing—forcibly removing or killing members—of the Muslim population. In 1998 Serbian leader Slobodan Milošević tried to drive Muslims out of the Kosovo region. U.S. and NATO air strikes against Serbia finally forced the Serbs to leave Kosovo and agree to negotiate. Clinton then led peace talks, which produced the Dayton Accords in late 1995.

✔ Reading Check **Identifying** What major trade agreement did Clinton make in 1993?

National Defense, Selected Nations

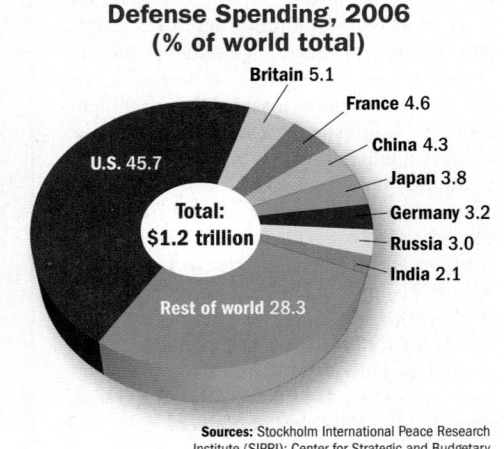

Defense Spending, 2006 (% of world total)

- Britain 5.1
- France 4.6
- China 4.3
- Japan 3.8
- Germany 3.2
- Russia 3.0
- India 2.1
- U.S. 45.7
- Total: $1.2 trillion
- Rest of world 28.3

Sources: Stockholm International Peace Research Institute (SIPRI); Center for Strategic and Budgetary Assessments; International Institute for Strategic Studies

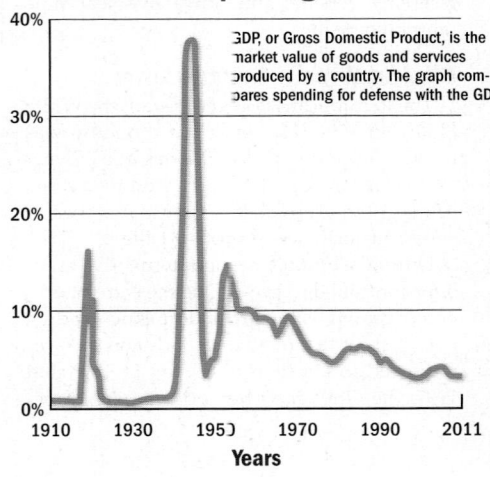

U.S. Defense Spending as % of GDP

GDP, or Gross Domestic Product, is the market value of goods and services produced by a country. The graph compares spending for defense with the GDP.

(Years axis: 1910, 1930, 1950, 1970, 1990, 2011)

986 **Chapter 31** *New Challenges*

Directions Have the playwrights in each group write a skit based on the descriptions and research from Step 2. The skits should last approximately three minutes. While the skits are being written, have other group members create props, prepare scenery, and make costumes. Actors and narrators can help with other tasks.

Analyzing Ask students which event is the most important domestic event from Clinton's presidency. Have them defend their positions. **OL**

(Chapter Project continued in Section 4)

A New President for a New Century

Main Idea As the 2000s began, the United States enjoyed economic prosperity but was deeply divided politically.

History and You Have you seen or taken part in a race in which the outcome was so close that it was difficult to declare a winner? Read to find out how the winner of the 2000 presidential race—one of the closest in American history—was determined.

A s Clinton prepared to leave office, his legacy was uncertain. He had balanced the budget and succeeded in turning around the nation's economy. The impeachment trial during Clinton's second term, however, had left the country divided. Many Americans were pleased with his accomplishments but were disappointed with the president's personal conduct. As the 2000 election approached, the major parties looked for candidates who appealed to a wide cross section of voters.

Comparing the Military, Selected Nations The U.S. military has about 1.5 million personnel on active duty. An additional 1.3 million men and women serve in the reserves.

	Armed forces* in millions	Nuclear warheads, est.	Aircraft carriers
U.S.	1.5	5,163	12
Britain	0.2	200	3
China	2.3	400	0
France	0.3	350	2
India	1.3	50	1
Japan	0.2	0	0
Russia	1.0	5,830	1

*Not including reservists

Graph Skills

Analyzing Explain any trends apparent in U.S. defense spending as a percentage of GDP.

The Candidates

The Democrats nominated Vice President Al Gore for president, hoping that the popularity of Clinton's policies would mean votes for Gore. The large Republican field eventually came down to two men: Governor **George W. Bush** of Texas and Senator John McCain of Arizona. Ultimately, the Republicans chose Bush, the son of former President George H.W. Bush, as their nominee.

Gore made history by naming Senator Joseph Lieberman, from Connecticut, as his running mate. This marked the first time in U.S. history that a Jewish American ran on a national ticket. George W. Bush chose **Richard Cheney** as his running mate. Cheney had served as chief of staff to President Gerald Ford and defense secretary to former President Bush in 1989.

During the campaign, Gore stressed protecting the environment and improving education. Bush also supported educational reform. Calling himself a "compassionate conservative," Bush favored local "grassroots" efforts to help the disadvantaged without large and costly government programs. A major campaign issue was what to do with the budget surplus. Gore and Bush agreed that Social Security and Medicare needed reform, but they disagreed on the details. Both also supported tax cuts and plans to help seniors pay for prescription drugs.

Claiming that there was little difference between Bush and Gore, activist Ralph Nader entered the race. Noting that "too much power in the hands of the few has further weakened our democracy," Nader ran as the nominee of the Green Party, which was known for its strong environmental views.

The Election of 2000

The 2000 election was extraordinarily close between Bush and Gore. For five weeks after the race, the outcome remained undecided. The key state was Florida, where Bush had a slim lead. Without Florida's 25 electoral votes, neither Bush nor Gore had the 270 electoral votes needed to win.

New Challenges **Chapter 31** 987

C Critical Thinking

Analyzing Information Ask: What was George W. Bush's campaign platform? *(educational reform, grassroots programs to help the disadvantaged, Social Security reform, Medicare reform, tax cuts, prescription drug aid to senior citizens)* Then lead a class discussion about which items in the platform were accomplished by his administration. **AL**

National Defense, Selected Nations

Graph Skills Answer

Defense spending as a percentage of GDP peaked during World Wars I and II, then gradually decreased.

Chart Skills Practice

Comparing Ask: What are the three countries with the most nuclear warheads, in order from most to least? *(Russia, United States, China)* **OL**

Additional Support

Activity: Collaborative Learning

Identifying Central Issues Ask: Do similar issues appear from presidential campaign to presidential campaign? Have students form three groups: Republican Party, Democratic Party, and third party. Have each group research its party's platform in the 2000 and 2008 presidential elections. Instruct each group to make a PowerPoint® presentation that clearly states its party's platform for each of the two elections. Have each group choose a representative to present its PowerPoint® presentation to the class while another classmate runs the software. After each presentation, discuss the issues reflected in the platforms. Identify issues that are similar and different in the two elections and write them on the board. Discuss as a class the overall changes in all of the platforms over the years. **OL**

S Skill Practice

S Skill Practice

Using Geography Skills Have students study the map and table at the top of the page. **Ask:** What kinds of information about the 2000 presidential election can you learn from the map and table? *(winner of each state's electoral votes, the number of electoral votes for each candidate, the results of the popular vote)* **BL**

C Critical Thinking

Identifying Central Issues Ask: Why would unity and cooperation be important for an evenly split Congress? *(With neither side in the majority, it would be easy for Congress to get mired in arguments.)* **OL**

Election of 2000   NATIONAL GEOGRAPHIC

Map Skills Answer

Gore won large states with many electoral votes.

Additional Support

Election of 2000   NATIONAL GEOGRAPHIC

Gore and Bush supporters outside the U.S. Supreme Court ▼

Candidates	Electoral Vote	Popular Vote	Political Party
Bush	271	50,456,002	Republican
Gore	266	50,999,897	Democrat
Nader	0	2,882,955	Green

One elector from Washington, D.C., abstained.

Map Skills

Regions Though Gore won less than half of the states, the election was extremely close. Why?

Maps In MCtion See StudentWorks™ Plus or glencoe.com.

Because the results in Florida were so close, state law required a recount of the ballots using vote-counting machines. Gore also asked for hand recounts in several counties, and a battle began over whether and how to conduct them. Lawsuits were filed in state and federal courts. The issue ultimately reached the U.S. Supreme Court.

On December 12, in *Bush* v. *Gore,* the Court ruled that the hand recounts of selected votes in Florida ordered by the Florida Supreme Court violated the equal protection clause of the Constitution. It further held that there was not enough time to conduct a recount that would pass constitutional standards. This ruling left Bush the winner in Florida. The next day, Gore conceded the election.

Bush Becomes President

On January 20, 2001, Bush became the 43rd president of the United States. In his Inaugural Address, President Bush called for "inclusion, not division," saying that America should be united. The need for unity and cooperation was important in Congress as

well. After the election the Senate was evenly split—50 Republicans and 50 Democrats.

In May 2001 Vermont senator James Jeffords left the Republican Party and became an independent. This led to a historic switch in power, transferring control to the Democrats in mid-session. However, in the mid-term elections of 2002, the Republicans regained control of the Senate and increased their majority in the House.

When assembling his cabinet, President Bush sought people from different career backgrounds. He appointed popular retired Army general Colin Powell as secretary of state. He also named Donald Rumsfeld as secretary of defense. Rumsfeld previously served as secretary of defense during the Ford administration. The Bush cabinet also reflected much of the country's diversity, including three African Americans, two Asians, and one Latino.

In addition, five women served in President Bush's cabinet. Elaine Chao, the secretary of labor, was the first Asian American woman to serve in a president's cabinet.

988   Chapter 31   *New Challenges*

Activity: Technology Connection

Evaluating The varied technologies used for voting in the United States added to the controversy over who won the 2000 presidential election. **Ask:** How has new technology affected the voting process? Have students research the various ways in which Americans vote, including the use of levers, punch cards, optical scanners, and touch screens. As a class, discuss the strengths and weaknesses of each method. Then ask students to read about problems caused by voting technology in the 2000 election and to summarize their findings in a short essay that explains the effects of technology on the outcome of that presidential election. **OL**

Other women played leading roles in the new administration. **Condoleezza Rice,** the first woman in history to hold the job of national security adviser, was instrumental in shaping foreign policy. First Lady Laura Bush promoted education. She called attention to the need for recruiting more teachers and improving reading skills.

Domestic Policy

Once in office, President Bush focused on his domestic plans: cutting taxes, improving public education, reforming Social Security and Medicare, and strengthening the nation's defenses. Bush's first task was to carry out his campaign pledge to cut taxes. Some politicians argued that the tax money lost could be used more responsibly, for example, to pay off the national debt. Supporters claimed the cut would help the economy, which had gone into a slump during the election campaign. In June 2001, Congress passed and Bush signed into law the 10-year, $1.3 trillion tax-cut bill.

After passage of the tax-cut plan, Bush proposed reforms in education. He called for public schools to hold yearly tests to measure student performance. He also wanted to allow parents to use federal funds to pay for private schools if their public schools were doing a poor job. Congress refused to give federal funds to private schools, but it did vote in favor of annual testing in public schools for grades 3 to 8. This law became known as the No Child Left Behind Act.

Foreign Policy

In foreign affairs, Bush pushed for new military programs. One was a National Missile Defense System designed to shoot down incoming missiles before they reached the United States. The president argued that missile defense was needed because many hostile nations were developing long-range missiles.

Meanwhile, a horrifying event took place on September 11, 2001,that changed everything. A stunned nation realized that it was not immune to the dangers of a violent world. A new kind of war had begun.

D ✔ **Reading Check** **Summarizing** What was George W. Bush's policy on education?

Section 3 Review

History ONLINE
Study Central™ To review this section, go to glencoe.com.

Vocabulary

1. Write a sentence using each of the following terms correctly: grassroots movement, deficit spending, budget deficit, adequate, gross domestic product, perjury, scope.

Main Ideas

2. **Analyzing** What was Clinton's plan for health-care reform, and who did he name to administer it?

3. **Explaining** What were the main goals of the Contract with America?

4. **Discussing** What caused the confusion over the outcome of the 2000 presidential election?

Critical Thinking

5. **Interpreting** What did George W. Bush mean when he called himself a compassionate conservative?

6. **Identifying** On a diagram like the one below, identify the main goals in Bush's domestic plans.

Bush Domestic Plans ⟩

7. **Persuasive Writing** Decide the answer to this question: *Should a president be protected from impeachment because the presidency is the highest office in America?* Write a one-page persuasive paper describing your opinion on this topic.

Answer the
8. **Essential Question**
How did the Clinton presidency change the U.S. domestic scene in the 1990s?

New Challenges **Chapter 31** **989**

CHAPTER 31
Section 3

D **Differentiated Instruction**

Intrapersonal Have small groups research the No Child Left Behind Act. Instruct them to learn how it affects their school by interviewing a reading and a math teacher. Then have each student write a paragraph about the impact of the act on his or her education so far. **OL**

✔ **Reading Check** **Answer:** He thought parents should be able to direct federal funds to private schools, and he supported annual reading and math tests in public schools to measure student performance.

Assess
. . . .

History ONLINE

Study Central™ provides summaries, interactive games, and online graphic organizers to help students review content.

Close
. . . .
Comparing and Contrasting Have students write a paragraph comparing and contrasting the domestic policies of Bill Clinton and George W. Bush. Remind them that they should summarize their ideas to fit the one-paragraph format. **OL**

Section 3 Review

Answers

1. Students will write sentences using each term.
2. Clinton wanted to control health-care costs and make sure every American had adequate health insurance. He named his wife, Hillary Rodham Clinton.
3. reduce size of the federal government, balance the budget, lower taxes, reform Congress, reduce crime, reform welfare, and strengthen the family

4. The results of the Florida vote were very close, and both Bush and Gore needed the Florida electoral votes to win.
5. He wanted to help those in need while also limiting government spending.
6. cutting taxes, improving public education, reforming Social Security and Medicare, and strengthening defense
7. Students' papers should present an understanding of the purpose of the impeachment process.

8. Nation's economy was healthy with a balanced budget, health-care protection was expanded, handgun purchases became more difficult, some kinds of assault weapons were banned, more police officers were hired, and workers were permitted to take family leave.

The War on Terror

Focus

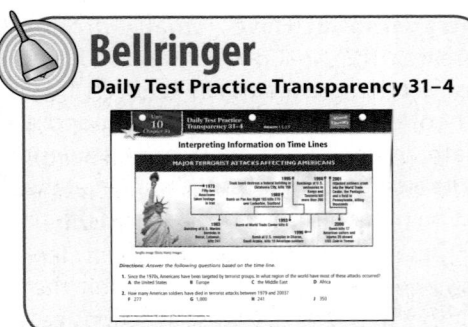

Bellringer
Daily Test Practice Transparency 31–4

Reading Guide
Answers to Graphic:
World Trade Center North Tower, World Trade Center South Tower, Pentagon, plane that crashed in Pennsylvania

Section Spotlight Video

Have students watch the Section Spotlight Video "The War on Terrorism" to learn about the Taliban and the war in Afghanistan.

Essential Question
How has the war on terror changed the way Americans live?

Reading Guide

Content Vocabulary

terrorism (p. 991)   insurgent (p. 994)
fundamentalist   levee
  (p. 992)   (p. 997)
counterterrorism (p. 993)

Academic Vocabulary

prior (p. 993)   definite (p. 997)

Key People and Events

Osama bin Laden (p. 991)
USA Patriot Act (p. 993)
Hurricane Katrina (p. 997)
Nancy Pelosi (p. 997)

Reading Strategy

Taking Notes On a diagram like the one below, identify the American sites of the September 11 terrorist attacks.

```
┌──────┐              ┌──────┐
└──────┘              └──────┘
       ┌─────────────┐
       │ September 11│
       │    Sites    │
       └─────────────┘
┌──────┐              ┌──────┐
└──────┘              └──────┘
```

ILLINOIS STANDARDS
The American Journey

14.C.3 Compare historical issues involving rights, roles and status of individuals in relation to municipalities, states and the nation.

14.D.3 Describe roles and influences of individuals, groups and media in shaping current Illinois and United States public policy (e.g., general public opinion, special interest groups, formal parties, media).

16.A.3c Identify the difference between historical fact and interpretation.

17.D.3b Explain how interactions of geographic factors have shaped present conditions.

American Diary

On September 11, New York City firefighter John Breen had orders to search for trapped people on the top floor of a hotel, nestled between the towers of the World Trade Center. Once inside, Breen felt the hotel begin to sway as the first tower collapsed. "I heard it getting louder and louder like an approaching train. You could hear the floors one on top of each other like dominoes." After the second tower collapsed, it was reported that at least 41 firefighters had been killed inside the hotel.

—from Firehouse Magazine

A man walks amid the rubble of the World Trade Center looking for victims to help.

Resource Manager

R Reading Strategies	C Critical Thinking	D Differentiated Instruction	W Writing Support	S Skill Practice
Teacher Edition • Questioning, p. 992 • Identifying, p. 995 **Additional Resources** • Guid. Read., URB p. 70 • Content Vocab., URB p. 45 • Academic Vocab., URB p. 47 • Read. Ess., p. 355	**Teacher Edition** • Identifying, p. 992 • Analyz. Prim. Sources, p. 994 • Draw. Conclusions, p. 994 **Additional Resources** • Quizzes and Tests, p. 310	**Teacher Edition** • Verbal/Ling., p. 991 • Interpersonal, p. 993 • ELL, p. 995 **Additional Resources** • School-to-Home, URB p. 63 • Reteaching Act., URB p. 65 • Differ. Inst., URB p. 55	**Teacher Edition** • Personal Writ., p. 991 • Expository Writ., p. 994 • Persuasive Writ., p. 996 **Additional Resources** • Writ. Skills, URB p. 51	**Teacher Edition** • Using Geo. Skills, p. 993 • Creat. a Time Line, p. 997 **Additional Resources** • Daily Test Pract. Transp. 31-4 • Geo. & Hist., URB p. 59

The Events of 9/11

Main Idea On September 11, 2001, the United States suffered the worst terrorist attack in its history.

History and You How did people react when they heard about the attacks of September 11, 2001? Read to learn about what effect the attacks had on the nation and the world.

On September 11, 2001, the nation witnessed horrifying acts of terrorism. **Terrorism** is the use of violence against civilians to reach a political goal. Early that morning, terrorists seized four U.S. passenger planes. Two planes were deliberately crashed into New York City's World Trade Center. A third plane was flown into the Pentagon, the U.S. military headquarters in Washington, D.C. A fourth plane was seized, but the passengers heroically fought back. This plane crashed in Pennsylvania. More Americans died in the attacks of September 11, 2001, than died at Pearl Harbor or on D-Day in World War II.

The Spirit of America

The 9/11 attacks shocked Americans, but they responded rapidly to the crisis. Firefighters and medical workers from throughout the nation headed to New York City to help. Across the nation, Americans lined up to donate blood and to collect food, blankets, and other supplies. From coast to coast, people put up flags to show their unity. They held candlelight vigils and prayer services as they searched for ways to help.

The U.S. government also responded quickly to the attacks. The Air National Guard patrolled the skies over major cities. Army National Guard troops were sent to airports to strengthen security. On September 14, President Bush declared a national emergency. Congress approved the use of force to fight whoever had attacked the United States. The U.S. government quickly identified the attacks as the work of a Saudi Arabian man named **Osama bin Laden** and his terrorist organization, al-Qaeda (al KY·duh).

Primary Source / America Is Attacked

World Trade Center

110 floors

110 floors

① 8:45 A.M. American Airlines Flight 11 crashes into North Tower.

② 9:05 A.M. United Airlines Flight 175 crashes into South Tower.

U.S. Customs House 8 floors

WTC 7 47 floors

Marriott Hotel 22 floors

South Plaza Building 9 floors

North Plaza Building 9 floors

Critical Thinking

Analyzing What were some of the obstacles firefighters faced in trying to rescue people from the burning buildings?

Teach

W Writing Support

Personal Writing Ask students to recall where they were on September 11, 2001. If they cannot remember, have them interview an adult about his or her memories of that day. Instruct students to write a paragraph that describes their own feelings on 9/11 or those of the adult they interviewed. Discuss these reactions as a class. **OL**

D Differentiated Instruction

Verbal/Linguistic Ask: What does the word *terror* mean? *(fear, horror, dread, shock)* Is the term *terrorism* appropriate for its definition? Explain. *(Students may respond that violence is terrifying, so the term is appropriate.)* **OL**

Primary Source

Critical Thinking Answer
Answers might include choking dust and smoke, communication problems, and danger of collapse.

Differentiated Instruction

Writing a Bibliography

Writing Skills Activity
Challenges for America

Writing a Bibliography

Objective: To learn how to write a bibliography

Focus: Ask students what a bibliography should include.

Teach: Have students complete the exercises.

Assess: Assess answers according to the Answer Key and Assessment Checklist.

Close: Ask students how they can use bibliographies in books as they read and research subjects.

Differentiated Instruction Strategies

BL Have students identify the elements in bibliographic entries.

AL Ask students to make up five bibliographic entries with incorrect formatting, exchange them, and time how fast students can edit them.

ELL Discuss with students the definitions of the following terms: anthology, editorial, article, transcript, visual media.

Writing Skills Activity, URB p. 51

C Critical Thinking

Identifying Central Issues Ask: Who carries out most terrorist acts against the United States? *(groups from the Middle East)* Why do they have strong feelings against the U.S.? *(because of U.S. support for Israel, and because some Muslims feel that Western culture undermines traditional Muslim values)* **OL**

R Reading Strategy

Questioning Ask students to think of a question about al-Qaeda that they would like to have answered. Students might want to use one of the words *who, why, where, when,* or *how* to help them focus on a specific topic. Then have them read the material under the heading to see if their question is answered there. **OL**

✓ Reading Check Answer: Osama bin Laden formed al-Qaeda in Afghanistan to recruit fighters against the invading Soviet Union. After the Soviet invasion, al-Qaeda became a terrorist group supported by the ruling fundamentalist Taliban; its goal was to drive Westerners from the Muslim world.

Additional Support

Primary Source / Remembering September 11, 2001

"I knew that in an instant we might all be dead. I remember saying the same prayer over and over: 'Oh God, let us escape. Oh God, let me get back to my two boys.'"
—Alison Summers, WTC survivor

"Make no mistake: The United States will hunt down and punish those responsible for these cowardly acts."
—President George W. Bush

"This massive attack was intended to break our spirit; it has not done that. It's made us stronger, more determined and more resolved."
—NYC Mayor Rudy Giuliani

"I told God that I didn't know what I'd done to be in his grace. . . . I just didn't know."
—Michael Benfante, WTC survivor

The Roots of Terrorism

Terrorist groups act on their own and are usually not part of a government. Today, most terrorist acts against Americans have been carried out by groups from the Middle East. Strong feelings against the United States are based partly on U.S. support for the Jewish nation of Israel. In the 1970s, several Middle Eastern nations realized they could fight Israel and the United States by arming and training terrorists. Some Muslims—or followers of Islam, the dominant religion in the Middle East—also feel that Western (American and European) culture undermines traditional Muslim values.

Although the vast majority of the 1 billion Muslims worldwide reject terrorism, some **fundamentalists** like bin Laden do not. Muslim fundamentalists call for a return to traditional Muslim ways. Those who favor bin Laden's methods believe that any action is justified to create a pure Muslim society.

R The Rise of al-Qaeda

Al-Qaeda grew out of the Muslim struggle against the Soviet Union in the Southwest Asian country of Afghanistan. Bin Laden formed al-Qaeda, or "the Base," to recruit new fighters.

When the Soviets left Afghanistan, bin Laden decided that all Westerners should be pushed out of the Muslim world. Bin Laden then turned al-Qaeda into a terrorist group. He won the support of the Taliban, a Muslim fundamentalist group that took power in Afghanistan. Bin Laden's followers set off bombs at U.S. embassies in Kenya and Tanzania in 1998. They also attacked a U.S. navy ship in Yemen in 2000. Then, on September 11, 2001, al-Qaeda struck again, seizing four American passenger planes and carrying out the most deadly terrorist attack in history.

✓ Reading Check Analyzing What caused the rise of al-Qaeda in the Middle East?

992 **Chapter 31** *New Challenges*

Activity: Making Connections

Comparing and Contrasting Ask: When had America experienced extremism and terrorism before 9/11? As a class, brainstorm about events in U.S. history that could be considered acts of extremism or terrorism. *(Ideas include the Oklahoma City bombing, attacks by the Ku Klux Klan, the Eric Rudolph abortion clinic killings, and the activities of the Weatherman faction of the Students for a Democratic Society.)* Have students form small groups. Each group will look up news articles or books about one of these events and its perpetrators. Tell students to focus their research on the national and political responses to each event. Students should try to determine how each event affected the daily life of Americans. To wrap up the activity, have each group summarize its findings and present them to the class in a panel discussion. **OL**

The Victims and Heroes

World Trade Center	
Total Injured	2,261
Total Deaths (ground, including firefighters and police)	2,752
American Airlines Flight 11 Deaths—WTC North Tower	92
United Airlines Flight 175 Deaths—WTC South Tower	65

Washington, D.C., and Pennsylvania	
Total Injured—The Pentagon	76
Total Deaths—The Pentagon (ground)	124
American Airlines Flight 77— The Pentagon	64
United Airlines Flight 93— Shanksville, Pennsylvania	40

Critical Thinking

Evaluating How do you think these acts of terrorism brought Americans together?

Fighting Terrorism

Main Idea After the 9/11 attacks, the United States launched a massive effort to eliminate international terrorism.

History and You What steps does your family take to protect your home from crime? Read to find out what actions the United States and other countries took to fight against terrorism.

After the attacks on September 11, the United States declared war on terrorism. In an address to Congress on September 20, the president demanded that the Taliban in Afghanistan turn over bin Laden and his followers and shut down all terrorist camps. The war against terrorism, President Bush told Americans, would be global in its reach. It would not end quickly, but it was a war the people of the United States were now called to fight: **S**

Protecting America

President Bush took steps to protect Americans from terrorist attacks. On September 24, he issued an executive order blocking the use of funds by individuals and groups suspected of supporting terrorism. The president also created a new federal agency—the Office of Homeland Security—to coordinate **counterterrorism** efforts. Counterterrorism involves military or political activities intended to combat terrorism. In June 2002, President Bush asked Congress to combine all of the agencies responsible for the public's safety into a new department called the Department of Homeland Security.

In late October 2001, Congress passed and the president signed into law new measures to combat terrorism. The **USA Patriot Act** of 2001 gave federal prosecutors and FBI agents new powers to investigate those who plot or carry out acts of terrorism. The law expanded **D** the power of federal agents to tap telephones and track Internet usage in the hunt for terrorists. It also permitted agents to conduct secret searches of a suspect's home or office without giving **prior,** or earlier, notice to the owner of the property.

The War in Afghanistan

The war on terrorism first focused on Afghanistan, where Taliban leaders refused to hand over bin Laden. On October 7, the U.S. military began bombing Taliban and al-Qaeda forces. In December, the Taliban government collapsed, and surviving Taliban members fled to Afghanistan's mountains. Fighting continues between NATO and Taliban forces. Meanwhile, bin Laden remains at large, possibly hiding in the neighboring country of Pakistan.

New Challenges **Chapter 31** **993**

S Skill Practice

Using Geography Skills Have students study the map on the following page. **Ask:** In what countries have terrorist attacks occurred since the U.S. war on terror began? (*Indonesia, Afghanistan, Iraq, Russia, Spain, Saudi Arabia, England, Scotland*) **OL**

D Differentiated Instruction

Interpersonal Ask: What powers does the USA Patriot Act give to federal agents? (*conduct wiretaps, track Internet use, and search homes and offices without prior notice*) Divide the class into small groups to discuss whether they think these powers are effective in the war on terror. **OL**

Primary Source

Critical Thinking Answer
Students might answer that the attacks gave Americans a common enemy. Americans also were united in a feeling of vulnerability and the need to heal a common grief.

Hands-On Chapter Project
Step 4

Writing and Performing a Skit

Step 4: Rehearsing the Skit Groups will rehearse their skits.

Essential Question: How has the war on terror changed the way Americans live?

Directions Have groups print their scripts and make copies for every member of the group. Then have students rehearse their skits, complete with props, costumes, and scenery. Instruct two groups to watch each other rehearse and provide feedback. After the rehearsals, groups should revise their scripts as necessary.

Discussing Ask students how they think each president would have reacted to the war on terror. **OL**

(Chapter Project continued in Section 5)

C₁ Critical Thinking

Analyzing Primary Sources Have students conduct research to locate a primary source written by a U.S. soldier in the Iraq War. Students might find sources in blogs, books, or magazine articles. Ask students to write a summary of their chosen source, describing what life was like for that soldier and some of the challenges he or she faced in Iraq. **AL**

For additional practice on this activity, see the Skills Handbook.

W Writing Support

Expository Writing Ask: Why did support for the war in Iraq decline? Have students write a two- or three-paragraph letter to the editor expressing their views on the lack of support for the war. **OL**

C₂ Critical Thinking

Drawing Conclusions Ask: Why was it more difficult to create a democracy in Iraq than it had been to win the war? *(Insurgents battled U.S. forces, and Iraq was torn apart by disputes among Muslim communities.)* **OL**

Reading Check Answer: weapons of mass destruction

Additional Support

C₁ The Iraq War

The attacks of 9/11 raised fears that terrorist groups might acquire nuclear, chemical, or biological weapons. These weapons of mass destruction could kill tens of thousands of people at a time. President Bush believed that Iraq's government was hiding these deadly weapons and was an immediate threat.

In the summer of 2002, Bush increased pressure on Iraq's dictator, Saddam Hussein. When questions arose over whether Iraq was cooperating with UN weapons inspectors, the president asked the UN to call for the use of force in Iraq. Although some UN members opposed the use of force, the United States prepared for war.

On March 20, 2003, the American military, aided by soldiers from Britain and some other countries, attacked Iraq. The Iraqi army was quickly defeated, and Saddam Hussein was overthrown. He was later captured, tried, and executed for crimes against his people.

The United States set out to create a democracy in Iraq. In 2005, Iraqi voters elected a parliament and approved a new constitution. The United States and its allies trained more Iraqis to serve in the police and the military. They also attempted to provide electricity, clean water, schools, and improved health care for Iraq's people.

These efforts were more difficult than winning the war. **Insurgents,** or rebel groups, battled U.S. forces. Iraq also was torn apart by disputes among Iraq's Muslim communities.

Between 2003 and 2007, more than 3,700 American and British soldiers and 70,000 Iraqis died. As the fighting dragged on, support for the war began to decline. The failure to find weapons of mass destruction also caused many people to wonder if the war in Iraq was a mistake. President Bush, however, was determined to stay the course in Iraq.

Reading Check **Describing** In 2002, what did the U.S. accuse Iraq of hiding?

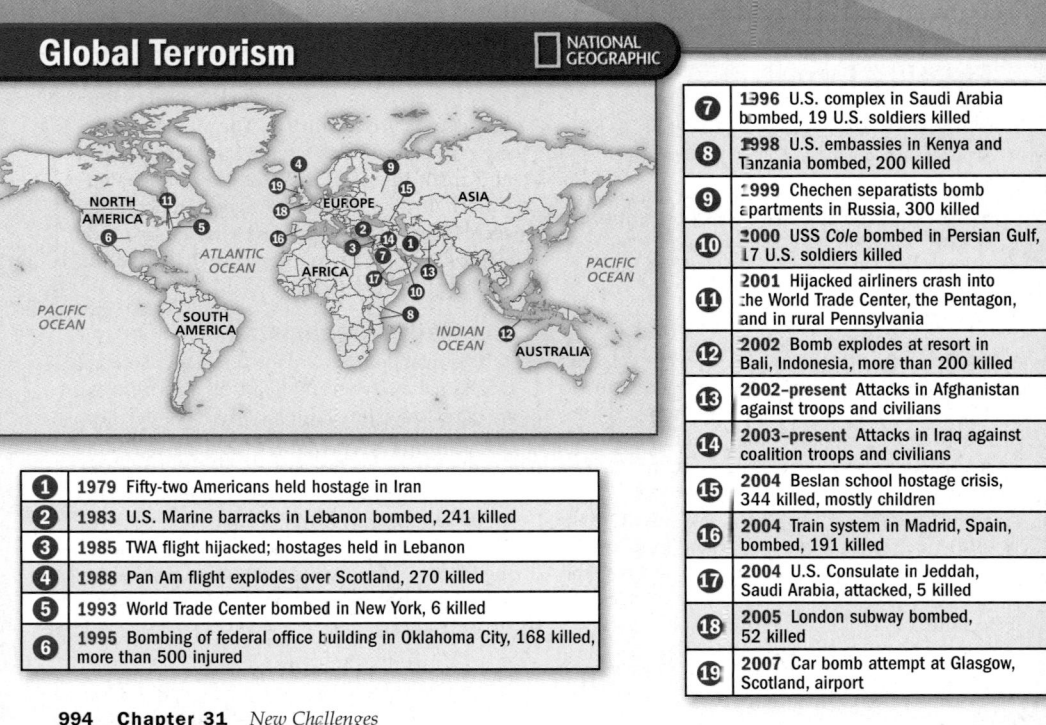

Global Terrorism NATIONAL GEOGRAPHIC

①	1979 Fifty-two Americans held hostage in Iran
②	1983 U.S. Marine barracks in Lebanon bombed, 241 killed
③	1985 TWA flight hijacked; hostages held in Lebanon
④	1988 Pan Am flight explodes over Scotland, 270 killed
⑤	1993 World Trade Center bombed in New York, 6 killed
⑥	1995 Bombing of federal office building in Oklahoma City, 168 killed, more than 500 injured

⑦	1996 U.S. complex in Saudi Arabia bombed, 19 U.S. soldiers killed
⑧	1998 U.S. embassies in Kenya and Tanzania bombed, 200 killed
⑨	1999 Chechen separatists bomb apartments in Russia, 300 killed
⑩	2000 USS *Cole* bombed in Persian Gulf, 17 U.S. soldiers killed
⑪	2001 Hijacked airliners crash into the World Trade Center, the Pentagon, and in rural Pennsylvania
⑫	2002 Bomb explodes at resort in Bali, Indonesia, more than 200 killed
⑬	2002–present Attacks in Afghanistan against troops and civilians
⑭	2003–present Attacks in Iraq against coalition troops and civilians
⑮	2004 Beslan school hostage crisis, 344 killed, mostly children
⑯	2004 Train system in Madrid, Spain, bombed, 191 killed
⑰	2004 U.S. Consulate in Jeddah, Saudi Arabia, attacked, 5 killed
⑱	2005 London subway bombed, 52 killed
⑲	2007 Car bomb attempt at Glasgow, Scotland, airport

994 Chapter 31 *New Challenges*

Activity: Geography Connection

Describing After attacking Iraq in 2003, American leaders vowed to bring democracy and improved living conditions to the citizens of that country. **Ask:** What is daily life like for the people of Iraq? Have students form small groups, and give each group a set of index cards. Tell students to write one aspect of their daily life on each card. *(Examples might include school, shopping, religion, leisure activities, family life, music, sports, and vacations.)* Next, have the students in each group divide the cards evenly among the group members, and ask students to research the aspects of daily life on their cards as they relate to Iraq today. Students will pool their knowledge, and each group will create a mural or large poster about daily life in Iraq. **OL**

Bush's Second Term

Main Idea During his second term, President Bush lost much support as a result of the Iraq war and difficult challenges at home.

History and You Have you ever taken part in an election at your school? Read to learn about the election of 2004, in which more voters turned out than had voted in other recent elections.

....

As the Iraq war dragged on, Bush's popularity began to shrink. The growing national debt fueled by the war sapped the country's economic strength. The failure to find any weapons of mass destruction undermined the president's support. In addition, Bush's standing was hurt by a scandal at the Iraqi prison of Abu Ghraib. There, some Iraqi prisoners of war were abused by their American guards.

Disrupting Terror Plots

Law-enforcement officials such as the officer watching the banks of monitors (above) work to uncover threats from terrorist activity. Highlights of their success:

- **December 2001** Would-be bomber stopped by passengers while on trans-Atlantic flight
- **2003** Disrupted a plot to use hijacked commercial airplanes to attack Heathrow Airport in London
- **2004** Disrupted plot to conduct large-scale bombings in cities in the United Kingdom
- **July 2005** Attempt to bomb the London subway is stopped
- **August 2006** Uncovered plot to smuggle liquid explosives onto trans-Atlantic airline flights
- **June 2007** Vehicles packed with explosives are discovered in London; suspects arrested

> **Critical Thinking**
> **Analyzing** Which attack took place in the U.S. Southwest?

Election of 2004

All of these setbacks gave the Democrats a chance to mount a serious challenge in the 2004 election. The Democratic Party chose Massachusetts senator John Kerry for president and North Carolina senator John Edwards for vice president. The Republicans renominated President Bush and Vice President Cheney.

On domestic issues, the candidates offered the nation a clear choice. Bush pledged to continue to cut taxes while building a strong national defense. Kerry promised to raise taxes on the wealthy to fund wider health-care coverage. Both candidates focused their efforts on a few key states where voters were narrowly divided.

Election Day saw the highest voter turnout since 1968—nearly 61 percent of eligible voters went to the polls. Nationwide, President Bush won a majority of the popular vote. His victory helped increase the Republican hold on Congress.

Security and Civil Liberties

The war on terrorism raised questions about the nation's security and civil liberties. A major issue concerned what to do with captured terrorists. The Bush administration decided to hold them at the U.S. military base in Guantanamo Bay, Cuba. Administration officials claimed that the prisoners were illegal enemy fighters, not suspects charged with a crime. As such, they did not have the right of appeal to an American court.

The U.S. Supreme Court disagreed. In 2004 it ruled in *Rasul* v. *Bush* that foreign prisoners who claimed they were unlawfully held had the right to appeal to a court. In response, the Bush administration set up special military courts to hear each prisoner's case.

However, in 2006, in *Hamdan* v. *Rumsfeld,* the Court struck down this plan. It argued that President Bush's military courts violated U.S. military law and international laws. Bush then asked Congress to pass legislation setting up courts that met the Supreme Court's guidelines.

R **Reading Strategy**

Identifying Ask: Why did Bush's popularity decline? *(growing national debt fueled by the war, failure to find weapons of mass destruction, scandal at Abu Ghraib)* **OL**

D **Differentiated Instruction**

English Language Learners As a class, talk about the meaning of *civil liberties*. *(freedoms of individuals from arbitrary interference by the government, for example, freedom of speech)* **Ask:** In what document are Americans' civil liberties listed? *(the Bill of Rights)* Have students give examples of civil liberties guaranteed by the U.S. Constitution. Then ask them what civil liberties are enjoyed by citizens of their country of origin. **ELL**

Global Terrorism NATIONAL GEOGRAPHIC

Critical Thinking Answer

#6: 1995 bombing of the federal office building in Oklahoma City

Activity: Collaborative Learning

Interpersonal Since 9/11 the debate over the need for security versus the right to maintain civil liberties has intensified in the United States. **Ask:** Do you think the presence of surveillance cameras in your school or town is justified? Begin by instructing each student to determine the number of security cameras he or she encounters in a typical day. Then discuss other nearby places with surveillance devices that students don't experience daily, such as airports, prisons, and office buildings. Students may also research the use of traffic cameras at intersections in some communities. Discuss as a class who these cameras protect and if the cameras violate any personal liberties. Finally, have students form groups and create a poster, skit, or song that expresses how they feel about surveillance in their lives. **OL**

W Writing Support

Persuasive Writing President Bush claimed that monitoring of international telephone calls and e-mails was necessary to deal quickly with terrorist threats. Have students write one paragraph trying to persuade others to agree with their position on this issue. **OL**

DBQ Document-Based Questions

Answers

1. The photos show the devastation and the personal effects of the storm.
2. Students might say the photographer would have a greater impact by showing others the tragedy or argue that helping individuals is always more important.

History ONLINE

Objectives and answers to the Student Web Activity can be found at glencoe.com under the Web Activity Lesson Plan for this chapter.

Differentiated Instruction

Primary Source / Hurricane Katrina

Monday, August 29:

✔ Katrina, a Category 4 hurricane with 145 mph winds, makes landfall near Buras, LA, at 6:10 A.M. CDT (7:10 A.M. EDT).

✔ President Bush makes emergency disaster declarations for Louisiana and Mississippi, freeing up federal funds for aid.

✔ Katrina rips two holes in the Superdome's roof. Some 10,000 storm refugees are inside.

✔ At least eight Gulf Coast refineries shut down or reduce operations.

✔ Airports close in New Orleans, Baton Rouge, Biloxi, Mobile, and Pensacola. Hundreds of flights are canceled or diverted.

◄ Levees in New Orleans failed when the storm surge hit, flooding low-lying areas and trapping many people who did not evacuate.

Hurricane Katrina hit the Gulf Coast as a Category 4 storm with 145 mph winds on August 29, 2005. ▼

DBQ Document-Based Questions

1. **Analyzing Visuals** What do these photographs tell you about the effects of Hurricane Katrina?
2. **Making Decisions** When documenting a tragic event, should a news photographer help a person in need or photograph the scene?

After Bush agreed to protect certain prisoner rights, Congress passed a law stating that anyone declared an illegal enemy fighter by a court could be held indefinitely without trial.

In addition to prisoners' rights, the Bush administration faced challenges about citizens' rights. As part of the war on terror, U.S. security officials had secretly expanded their practice of monitoring, or tracking, international calls and e-mails.

In 2005 word leaked out about this program, creating a controversy. Civil rights groups protested that it would be abused and used to violate citizens' constitutional rights. President Bush argued that he needed to expand this activity without legal approval. In this way, the government would be able to deal more quickly with terrorist threats. After a federal judge ruled the program was not constitutional, Bush officials stated in 2007 that they would carry out the program only with court approval.

Supreme Court Appointments

Early in Bush's second term, he had to fill two vacancies on the U.S. Supreme Court. As a result, the president was able to move the Court in a more conservative direction. First, Bush named federal judge John G. Roberts, Jr., to replace retiring justice Sandra Day O'Connor. Before the Senate could act, however, Chief Justice William Rehnquist died, and the president named Roberts to replace him. Roberts easily won Senate confirmation as chief justice.

Next, Bush tried to fill the O'Connor court vacancy. After Senate opposition to Bush's first nominee, the president named federal judge Samuel Alito, Jr. Although some Democrats expressed concern about Alito's conservative views, the Senate voted 58–42 to confirm Alito.

History ONLINE

Student Web Activity Visit glencoe.com and complete the Chapter 31 Web Activity about America and the war on terror.

Leveled Activities

BL Reading Essentials and Note-Taking Guide, p. 355

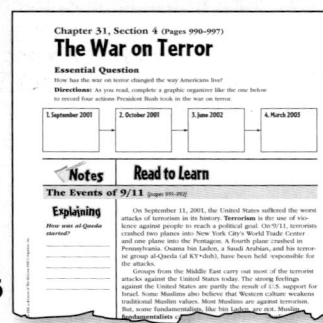

OL Differentiated Instruction Activity, URB p. 55

AL Geography and History Activity, URB p. 59

Hurricane Katrina

A major natural disaster as well as political storms affected Bush's second term. On August 29, 2005, **Hurricane Katrina** struck the Gulf of Mexico coast. Storm conditions raged from Florida to Louisiana. The hurricane destroyed buildings, roads, and electrical lines. Thousands of people were left homeless, and at least 1,800 people died.

The city of New Orleans suffered extensive damage. After the hurricane had passed, rising waters broke through the **levees,** or high walls, that protected the low-lying city. As **S** water flooded neighborhoods, residents who stayed behind during the hurricane were forced to await rescue or to flee. Many waited for days without much food, clean water, or information. Eventually troops and transportation arrived and moved flood survivors to other cities.

News broadcasts of the disaster, however, caused many Americans to wonder why national, state, and local governments were failing to respond more quickly. President Bush fired the head of the federal government's emergency relief agency. He also pledged federal funds to rebuild the city.

The 2006 Midterm Elections

American voters expressed their unhappiness with Bush administration policies in the 2006 mid-term elections. The Democrats won control of both houses of Congress for the first time since 1992. House Democrats then elected **Nancy Pelosi** to be the first female Speaker of the House of Representatives.

The day after the election, Secretary of Defense Donald Rumsfeld—a chief planner of the Iraq war—resigned. Bush chose Robert Gates to replace Rumsfeld and put a new commander—General David Patraeus—in charge of the forces in Iraq. The president then announced a "surge," or rapid increase, of some 20,000 more troops to Iraq.

House Democrats criticized the president's plan. They called for the president to set a **definite,** or precise, timetable for pulling U.S. troops out of Iraq. Whether or not the surge could work was unclear. However, by the autumn of 2007, what was clear was that Americans were divided over the Iraq war and that its outcome remained uncertain.

✓ Reading Check **Summarizing** What did the Supreme Court rule in *Hamdan v. Rumsfeld?*

Section 4 Review

History ONLINE
Study Central™ To review this section, go to glencoe.com.

Vocabulary

1. Use each of these terms correctly in a sentence: terrorism, fundamentalist, counterterrorism, prior, insurgent, levee, definite.

Main Ideas

2. **Describing** How did Osama bin Laden become so strong in Afghanistan?

3. **Explaining** What powers did the USA Patriot Act give to federal officers?

4. **Analyzing** Why was the Supreme Court ruling in *Rasul v.Bush* important?

Critical Thinking

5. **Sequencing** On a time line like the one below, name the events in the war on terror that took place on these dates:

Sept. 2001	Oct. 2001	June 2002	March 2003

6. **Descriptive Writing** In a paragraph, describe how Hurricane Katrina affected specific areas as well as the entire United States.

Answer the
7. **Essential Question**
How has the war on terror changed the way Americans live?

New Challenges **Chapter 31** **997**

S Skill Practice

Creating a Time Line Have students work in small groups to create a time line of Hurricane Katrina and its aftermath. Ask them to use information from the text, as well as outside research. **OL**

✓ Reading Check **Answer:** The special military courts set up by the Bush administration for prisoners of the war on terror were unlawful.

Assess

History ONLINE

Study Central™ provides summaries, interactive games, and online graphic organizers to help students review content.

Close

Assessing Have students write a paragraph stating whether or not they think the war on terror has succeeded, and ask them to defend their position. **OL**

Section 4 Review

Answers

1. Students will write sentences using the vocabulary terms.
2. He gained the support of the Taliban, which ruled in Afghanistan.
3. They could tap telephones, track Internet use, and conduct secret searches of homes and offices without prior notification.
4. The ruling gave foreign prisoners suspected of terrorism who felt they were unlawfully imprisoned the right to appeal to a court.

5. Sept. 2001: terrorist attacks on the World Trade Center and the Pentagon; October 2001: USA Patriot Act signed into law; June 2002: Department of Homeland Security created; March 2003: U.S. defeat of Iraqi army and overthrow of Saddam Hussein
6. Students' paragraphs should accurately describe Hurricane Katrina's local effects, as well as its effect on the nation.

7. Answers might include heightened security at airports and large gatherings, feelings of vulnerability, greater solidarity, heightened suspicion of foreigners, drain on economy from military spending, and heightened debate on the need for security versus protection of civil liberties.

Focus

R Reading Strategy

Questioning The USA Patriot Act, passed just days after the attacks of September 11, 2001, expanded the government's power to obtain personal information about individuals. After reading the passage, have students discuss the significance of these changes, considering the country's past history with personal liberties. **OL**

W Writing Support

Expository Writing Congressperson Slaughter speaks of "national security," a phrase that's very important in modern American history. She identifies two aspects of national security: "protecting our borders," and "protecting our freedoms." Ask students to write a paragraph explaining why Slaughter believes the Patriot Act puts these two goals at odds. **AL**

**Additional Support
and Answers**

YOU DECIDE

Public protests of the Patriot Act

998

Should the Patriot Act Be Reauthorized?

Building Background

The USA Patriot Act gave federal law officials the power to track personal communications and check personal records. Federal officials can tap telephones and computers and get legal access to voice mail and e-mail messages. They could also obtain personal medical, financial, educational, and even library records without proof that a crime has been committed.

Congress passed the USA Patriot Act in 2001 and renewed it in 2006. Americans who supported it said it was an important part of the war on terror. Others, however, argued that the act represents a threat to civil liberties and privacy.

NO

CONGRESSWOMAN LOUISE McINTOSH SLAUGHTER

Mr. Speaker, I rise today in defense of nothing less than our national security, but national security is not just about protecting our borders. It is also about protecting our freedoms.

All of my colleagues understand that the PATRIOT Act has provided the law enforcement agencies with many valuable tools which facilitate[1] their work in the struggle against terrorism. But with these new tools comes a very real danger that the liberty we seek to protect could be easily compromised. . . .

We have evidence which suggests, in contrast to information coming out of the Justice Department, that many of these measures have resulted in the violation of the civil liberties of American citizens. In addition, we understand that some of the extended search and seizure powers used by the law enforcement are apparently not being used for their intended purpose, which is strictly to fight terrorism, and that is unacceptable.

---

[1] **facilitate** to make easy

Technology Connection

Making Connections Ask: How have the privacy rights of international travelers been changed by the need to detect and deter terrorist activities? Have students gather media reports on the changing requirements for international travel. Tell them to check the Web sites of airlines that carry international passengers to review the restrictions on travelers. Then ask them to describe to the class any losses of privacy that have resulted from the need to deter terrorist activity and the movement of terrorists.

YES

ATTORNEY GENERAL JOHN ASHCROFT

Our responsibility was to reorganize our justice system from a backward-looking system focused on prosecution,[2] to a forward-looking system first focused on prevention. Our response was to track down and dismantle highly compartmentalized[3] terrorist networks. To forge new relationships of cooperation with other nations. To mobilize a frightened citizenry. To fight for new and needed tools for law enforcement. To do anything and everything we could under the Constitution to prevent further acts of terrorism. . . .

Congress provided these tools in the USA Patriot Act, . . . and while our job is not finished, we have used the tools provided in the Patriot Act to fulfill our first responsibility to protect the American people. We have used these tools to prevent terrorists from unleashing more death and destruction on our soil. We have used these tools to save innocent American lives. We have used these tools to provide the security that ensures liberty. . . .

America MUST remember. It is my commitment to you that we WILL remember. In the war against terror, we will not falter and we will not fail.

---

[2] **prosecution** the pursuit of legal action
[3] **compartmentalized** divided into separate sections

DBQ Document-Based Questions

1. **Interpreting** What does Ashcroft mean when he states, "We have used these tools to provide the security that ensures liberty"?
2. **Analyzing** What do Ashcroft and Slaughter agree about?
3. **Analyzing** What do Ashcroft and Slaughter disagree about?
4. **Evaluating** Who do you think makes the stronger argument: Ashcroft or Slaughter? Explain your answer.

Firefighter in New York City on September 11, 2001

999

Teach

C Critical Thinking

Analyzing Information Have student groups discuss the distinction Ashcroft is making between a "backward-looking" and a "forward-looking" justice system. Students should discuss why Ashcroft believes such a shift is necessary after the 9/11 attacks. **Ask:** What do you think are the reasons we have had "backward-looking" justice policies? *(To focus on prosecuting those who have actually committed crimes. One major goal of the legal system is to treat citizens as "innocent until proven guilty.")* **OL**

Assess/Close

Benjamin Franklin once said, "Those who would give up an essential liberty for temporary security deserve neither liberty nor security." Ask students to discuss Franklin's words in an age of terrorist threats.

Answers

1. Ashcroft argues that the various laws that are part of the Act have worked to protect the nation.
2. The Attorney General and the Congressperson agree on the importance of fighting crime and terrorism. They also agree that the Patriot Act has made it easier for law enforcement to do its antiterrorist work.
3. Ashcroft views the Patriot Act as a way to protect Americans from the terrorist threat. Slaughter also sees the terrorist threat as serious but asserts that this legislation has led to violations of the liberties of Americans. To her, Americans require protection against both foreign terrorists and abuse of power by their own government.
4. Answers will vary; accept all views supported by the primary-source excerpts.

Focus

Challenges Ahead

Bellringer
Daily Test Practice Transparency 31–5

Reading Guide
Answers to Graphic:
Answers might include Economic Interdependence, Growing Populations, Pollution, Global Warming, and Health Care.

Section Spotlight Video

Have students watch the Section Spotlight Video "The War on Terrorism" to learn about the Taliban and the war in Afghanistan.

Resource Manager

Essential Question ◀
How have economic and environmental developments led to the world's nations becoming more interdependent?

Reading Guide

Content Vocabulary
interdependent (p. 1001)   acid rain (p. 1003)

globalism (p. 1001)   global warming (p. 1004)

trade deficit (p. 1002)   deport (p. 1005)

free trade (p. 1002)   amnesty (p. 1005)

urban sprawl (p. 1003)

Academic Vocabulary
decade (p. 1001)   aware (p. 1003)

Reading Strategy
Taking Notes Complete a diagram like the one below by identifying three global challenges. Then explain why each of these is a problem.

ILLINOIS STANDARDS
The American Journey

14.D.3 Describe roles and influences of individuals, groups and media in shaping current Illinois and United States public policy (e.g., general public opinion, special interest groups, formal parties, media).

15.D.3b Explain how comparative advantage forms the basis for specialization and trade among nations.

16.E.3c (US) Describe the impact of urbanization and suburbanization, 1850–present, on the environment.

18.C.3b Explain how diverse groups have contributed to U.S. social systems over time.

American Diary

In the 1960s, educator Marshall McLuhan used the phrase "the global village" to express the idea that electronic communication would unite the world. The Internet, for example, allows us to communicate with one another regardless of distance. Soon half the people of the world will access the Web, many through wireless devices. Already, more than 25 billion e-mails are sent internationally each day—that adds up to more than 9 trillion e-mails each year!

Students with learning disabilities in Brooklyn, New York, use laptop computers to work on reading skills.

R Reading Strategies	**C** Critical Thinking	**D** Differentiated Instruction	**W** Writing Support	**S** Skill Practice
Teacher Edition • Read. a Prim. Source, p. 1002 • Predicting, p. 1003 • Summarizing, p. 1005 **Additional Resources** • Guid. Read., URB p. 71 • Cont. Voc., URB p. 45 • Acad. Voc., URB p. 47 • Read. Ess., p. 358 • Am. Lit. Read., URB p. 9	**Teacher Edition** • Comp. & Cont., p. 1001 • Pred. Conseq., p. 1004 **Additional Resources** • Quiz. and Tests, p. 311 • Citizen. & Dec. Mak. Skills, URB p. 3 • Inter. Polit. Cartoons, URB p. 13 • Crit. Think., URB p. 57	**Teacher Edition** • Intrapersonal, p. 1001 • Naturalist, p. 1003 • Kinesthetic, p. 1005 **Additional Resources** • School-to-Home, URB p. 63 • Reteaching Act., URB p. 65	**Teacher Edition** • Expository Writ., p. 1002 • Persuasive Writ., p. 1004 • Descriptive Writ., p. 1006 **Additional Resources** • Authentic Assess., p. 31	**Teacher Edition** • Using Geo. Skills, p. 1002 • Read. a Graph, p. 1002 **Additional Resources** • Daily Test Pract. Transp. 31-5 • Lesson Transp. 31C

The New Global Economy

Main Idea Advances in technology now link the United States to a global economy.

History and You Describe something you know about the way people live in another part of the world. How do you know what you know? Read to find out why the world has become more connected during the last 30 years.

In recent years, the United States and other nations of the world have developed a global economy. This means that they are **interdependent,** or rely on one another for raw materials to make goods and for markets in which to sell goods. When the economies of countries are linked, a drought or a war in one region can cause price increases or shortages in another region far away.

The Technology Revolution

A major reason for the rise of the global economy is the technology revolution. Today we take for granted computers, cell phones, cable television, and compact discs. A few **decades**—periods of 10 years—ago, these things had either not been invented or were not widely available.

The invention that drives this revolution is the computer. In the 1960s, scientists developed the integrated circuit, a small electronic device. A decade later, more powerful circuits called microprocessors were developed. They made it possible to make smaller, faster computers that could store a lot of information.

Through their personal computers, people are now able to go on the Internet. This is a huge web of linked computer networks. The Internet has made global communications almost instantaneous.

Global Trade and the U.S.

The technology revolution has tied together people and nations more closely than before. It has contributed to the rise of **globalism.** This is the idea that the world's economies and societies are all part of one big system. Interaction is no longer limited by physical distance.

The United States is a key player in the global economy. Its large, productive economy, based on the free enterprise system, has made it a leader in world trade. The United States exports chemicals, farm products, and manufactured goods, as well as raw materials such as metals and cotton fiber.

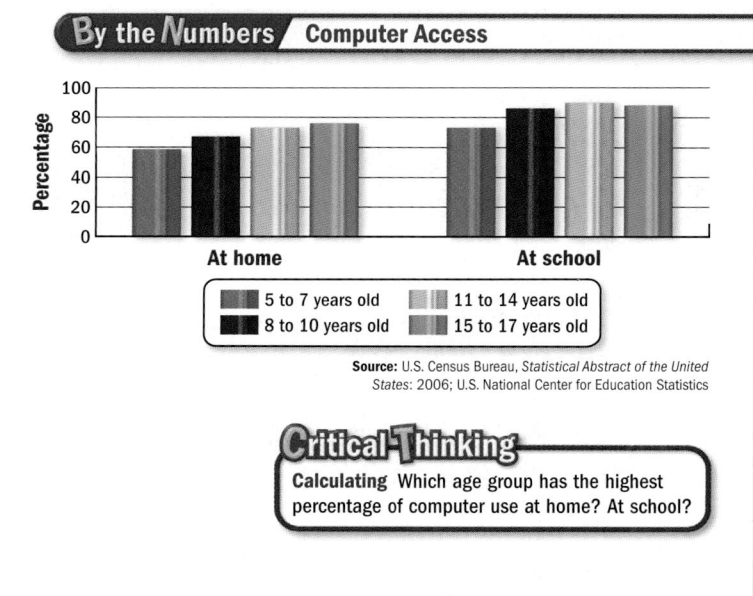

By the Numbers / Computer Access

Percentage

- 5 to 7 years old
- 8 to 10 years old
- 11 to 14 years old
- 15 to 17 years old

At home   At school

Source: U.S. Census Bureau, *Statistical Abstract of the United States*: 2006; U.S. National Center for Education Statistics

Critical Thinking

Calculating Which age group has the highest percentage of computer use at home? At school?

Teach

C Critical Thinking

Comparing and Contrasting Lead a class discussion in which you compare and contrast today's global economy with the economies of the European nations during the Age of Discovery. *(Discussion might center on the lack of economic interdependence at that time; nations were expanding their empires and concentrating on self-sufficiency.)* **AL**

D Differentiated Instruction

Intrapersonal Ask: How would your home life and school experience be different if there were no computers? *(Students should discuss the Internet and the use of computers in many other high-tech devices.)* **BL**

By the Numbers

Critical Thinking Answer At home: 15- to 17-year-olds; At school: 11- to 14-year-olds

Additional Support

Activity: Why It Matters

Evaluating The global economy brings consumer products to the United States from many countries. **Ask:** Should a product's country of origin affect your buying decision? Instruct students to interview family members or other older adults to learn how they felt about foreign-made products when they were in their teens. As a class, discuss these attitudes. Then discuss if and how a product's country of origin influences purchasing decisions today. Divide the class into small groups and debate the pros and cons of buying foreign products. Each group will then write and act out a 30-second television spot that either advocates or argues against boycotting foreign-made consumer products. Groups' views should be supported by facts. **AL**

S₁ Skill Practice

Using Geography Skills Have students locate the countries that supply energy resources to the United States on a world map. **Ask:** Are these suppliers clustered in any one area? *(No; the suppliers are on three continents. Students may point out, however, that many other oil-producing countries are found in the Middle East.)* **OL**

S₂ Skill Practice

Reading a Graph Have students look at the graphs at the bottom of the page. **Ask:** Which countries or entities shown on the graphs experience a trade deficit? *(United States and European Union)* **OL**

W Writing Support

Expository Writing Have students work with partners to research the trade policies of the European Union. Then have them write a one-page paper in which they discuss those policies and whether a similar arrangement would benefit or hurt the United States. **AL**

R Reading Strategy

Reading a Primary Source Ask: Why does President Bush support free trade? *(to help countries out of poverty and to sustain freedom)* **BL**

Additional Support

S₁ The nation imports most of its energy resources, however. The suppliers include Canada, Mexico, Saudi Arabia, and Nigeria.

The United States also buys many additional products from other countries. In fact, the United States spends hundreds of billions of dollars more on imports than it earns from exports. The result is a massive **trade deficit.**

S₂ A trade deficit occurs when a country spends more on imports than it earns from exports. A trade deficit that lasts over a long period can cause economic troubles for a country.

Therefore, selling American-made goods has long been important to the prosperity of the United States. To further American economic growth, Republican and Democratic administrations since World War II have supported **free trade.** This means the removal of trade barriers so that goods flow freely among countries. In 2001 President Bush called for a world trading system that is dramatically open and more free:

PRIMARY SOURCE

R "We know that nations that open their economies to the benefits of trade are more successful in climbing out of poverty. . . . We also know that free trade encourages the habits of liberty that sustain freedom."
—President George W. Bush in a speech to the World Bank

Since its formation in 1995, the World Trade Organization (WTO) has arranged numerous trade agreements and settled trade disputes among the nations of the world. Today, the WTO has more than 140 member countries.

Debate on Free Trade

As the world economy becomes more interconnected, Americans debate whether ending trade barriers helps or hinders the United States. Supporters claim that free trade generally helps the American economy. Those supporters say that American businesses make money selling more goods around the world.

Economics & History

The United States imports many manufactured goods from Japan. Automobiles are the largest single category. ▶

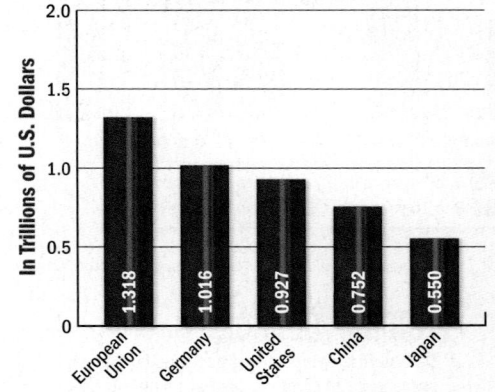

The Five Leading Exporters

In Trillions of U.S. Dollars

European Union	Germany	United States	China	Japan
1.318	1.016	0.927	0.752	0.550

Source: CIA World Factbook, 2006

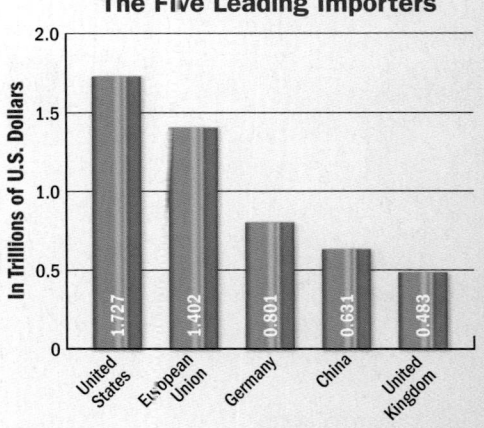

The Five Leading Importers

In Trillions of U.S. Dollars

United States	European Union	Germany	China	United Kingdom
1.727	1.402	0.801	0.631	0.483

Source: CIA World Factbook, 2006

Activity: Economics Connection

Comparing and Contrasting Ask: What is the opposite of free trade? Have students research historical and current ways in which nations have tried to control their trade with others. Students will then work in pairs to create a chart that displays the nation, period of history, and method used to control trade. Post the charts, have students evaluate, then discuss the historical and present-day alternatives to a free-trade system. **OL**

They also claim that American consumers benefit by being able to buy foreign goods that are less expensive than those made in the United States. Supporters of free trade also state that importing low-cost goods keeps inflation and interest rates low.

Opponents, however, charge that free trade has caused manufacturing jobs to move from the United States to nations where wages are low and where there are fewer regulations. They state that having cheap imports available to buy does not help those Americans who can no longer find work because their industries have moved overseas. This transfer of work to other countries is called outsourcing. Because free trade affects jobs—and votes—the debate between supporters and opponents of free trade has become an important part of American politics.

✔ **Reading Check** **Explaining** What does the World Trade Organization (WTO) do?

Proved Oil Reserves by Country, 2006*

Country	Billions of Barrels
Saudi Arabia	264.3
Canada	178.8
Iran	132.5
Iraq	115.0
Kuwait	101.5
U.A.E.	97.8
Venezuela	79.7
Russia	60.0
Libya	39.1
Nigeria	35.9
U.S.	21.4
China	18.3

0 20 40 60 80 100 120 140
Billions of Barrels

Source: *Oil & Gas Journal*; U.S. Energy Information Administration
*Proved reserves are estimated with reasonable certainty to be recoverable with present technology and prices.

Graph Skills

1. **Calculating** What is the difference in dollar amounts between U.S. exports and U.S. imports?

2. **Classifying** Which of the 12 nations shown on this graph are in South America? In Africa?

The Environment

Main Idea Concern about the environment has become a serious political issue in recent years.

History and You Have you seen instances of air or water pollution in your area? Read to learn about challenges to the nation's environment.

Globalism has made people **aware,** or mindful, of issues that affect the world as a whole. In recent years, people have become aware of dangers to the world environment. For example, many people fear that the Earth's resources will soon be unable to support a rapidly rising world population, especially in cities.

Urban sprawl, or the spread of human settlements into natural areas, has created many problems. Urban growth leads to the loss of farmland and wilderness areas. The building of homes and roadways also can produce traffic jams and increase air pollution. Growing populations put strains on water supplies, food supplies, and other resources as well. People in some areas that are growing rapidly want to slow the rate of growth. They fear that having too many people will destroy the wide-open spaces and scenery that attracted them.

Air and Water Pollution

The United States faces several environmental challenges. Air and water pollution remains a problem. Americans burn coal, oil, and natural gas to power their factories and run their cars. Burning these fossil fuels pollutes the air. The pollution mixes with water vapor in the air to make **acid rain,** or rain containing high amounts of chemical pollutants. Acid rain damages trees and harms rivers, lakes, and the stone used in buildings. The United States has acted to reduce the amount of chemicals that are released into the air. Climate experts are particularly concerned about damage to some areas in the eastern United States.

New Challenges **Chapter 31 1003**

Differentiated Instruction

R **Reading Strategy**

Predicting Have students read the Main Idea and answer the following question before reading further. **Ask:** What environmental issues do you think you will be reading about in this subsection? *(Answers might include global warming, water and air pollution, and rising ocean levels.)* **OL**

D **Differentiated Instruction**

Naturalist Have students work in small groups to brainstorm ways in which their school could work to reduce air and water pollution. Each group should make a poster to share its suggestions with the rest of the school. **OL**

Economics & History

Graph Skills Answers
1. $0.8 trillion, or $800 billion
2. In South America: Venezuela; In Africa: Libya and Nigeria

✔ **Reading Check** **Answer:** It arranges trade agreements and settles trade disputes.

Environmental Awareness

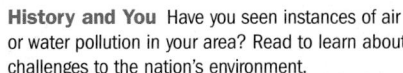

Objective: To learn to interpret political cartoons

Focus: Ask students to discuss the purposes of political cartoons.

Teach: Have students answer the questions.

Assess: As a class, discuss the answers.

Close: Ask students to bring in a political cartoon and analyze it for the class.

Differentiated Instruction Strategies

BL As a class, discuss Native American ideas and beliefs about the Earth.

AL Have students create their own political cartoon about an issue discussed in this chapter.

ELL Have students find a political cartoon that is entirely visual and share it with the class.

Interpreting Political Cartoons, URB p. 13

C Critical Thinking

Predicting Consequences Ask students to list the consequences of global warming given in the text. *(changing weather patterns, droughts, rising oceans, flooding)* Lead a class discussion about how those events might affect students directly. *(Students in coastal or low-lying areas might lose their homes. Some might see increased hurricane activity.)* **OL**

W Writing Support

Persuasive Writing Ask students to work in pairs and choose one alternative energy source, such as wind, solar, or geothermal. Have them research their energy source and write a speech that attempts to persuade the audience that theirs is the best source of energy. Have students give their speeches to the class. **OL**

How Much Do We Recycle?

Critical Thinking Answer

Germany

✔Reading Check **Answer:** It contains chemical pollutants that damage trees, rivers, lakes, and stone used in buildings.

Hands-On Chapter Project
Step 5

Writing and Performing a Skit

Step 5: Performing the Skit Each group will perform its three-minute skit for the whole class.

Essential Question: How have economic and environmental developments led to

---

How Much Do We Recycle?

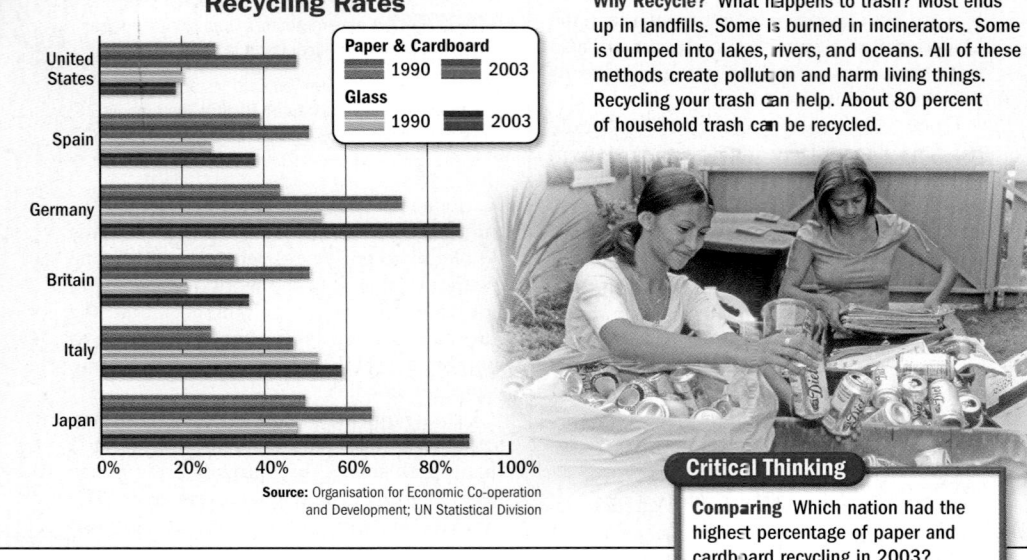

Recycling Rates

	Paper & Cardboard	
	■ 1990	■ 2003
	Glass	
	■ 1990	■ 2003

United States · Spain · Germany · Britain · Italy · Japan

0% 20% 40% 60% 80% 100%

Source: Organisation for Economic Co-operation and Development; UN Statistical Division

Why Recycle? What happens to trash? Most ends up in landfills. Some is burned in incinerators. Some is dumped into lakes, rivers, and oceans. All of these methods create pollution and harm living things. Recycling your trash can help. About 80 percent of household trash can be recycled.

Critical Thinking

Comparing Which nation had the highest percentage of paper and cardboard recycling in 2003?

Because pollution crosses international borders, many experts believe that nations have to work together to find solutions. In 1987, for example, 23 nations agreed to ban chemicals suspected of harming the ozone layer—a part of the atmosphere that shields Earth from the sun's radiation.

Global Warming

Many scientists also think that Earth is getting warmer and are worried that this might be caused by pollution. They claim that the increased burning of coal, oil, and natural gas has released more gases into the atmosphere. These gases have trapped more of the sun's heat near the Earth's surface, raising temperatures around the planet.

Such **global warming**, these scientists claim, will lead to changing weather patterns. For example, a warmer climate could lead to drought conditions in some areas and could melt the polar ice caps. Melting would raise ocean levels and flood low-lying coasts.

The issue of global warming has become very controversial. Critics argue that computer models showing global warming are unrealistic. Many nations, however, are addressing the problem. In 1997, 38 nations signed the Kyoto Protocol promising to reduce pollution that might be causing global warming, but few countries have put the treaty into effect.

The United States has not signed the treaty, believing that it would hurt economic growth. Still, the United States and many other nations are dealing with pollution.

They are trying to use energy more efficiently and burn coal more cleanly. They also have funded research to find new energy sources that are less harmful to the environment. Many countries already have adopted nonpolluting forms of energy such as wind and solar power.

✔Reading Check **Describing** How does acid rain affect the environment?

1004 Chapter 31 *New Challenges*

---

the world's nations becoming more interdependent?

Directions Have each group take turns performing its skit for the entire class. After each performance, lead a class discussion on the event presented in each skit. In particular, encourage students to ask the group members questions about their historical

event and why they decided to portray it the way they did.

Specifying As part of the discussion of each skit, ask students to explain how each of the presidents handled environmental concerns. **OL**

(Chapter Project continued on the Visual Summary page)

A Changing Society

Main Idea As the 2000s begin, immigrants and the elderly make up a larger share of the American population.

History and You Do you remember the reasons why some Americans objected to immigration in the 1800s? Read to find out how the debate on immigration continues today.

. . . .

As America enters the twenty-first century, its population is changing significantly. The number of older Americans has risen. Ways of living and working have changed as a result of new technologies. Above all, changes in U.S. laws and unstable conditions worldwide have led to a dramatic rise in the number of immigrants to the United States.

By 2007, nearly half of all the country's immigrants came from Latin America and Canada, and another third from various parts of Asia. Less than 15 percent came from Europe, the place of origin of most immigrants throughout U.S. history.

Illegal Immigration

Many immigrants have entered the United States legally, but an estimated 12 million of them have arrived without official permission. Today, most Americans view this illegal immigration as a serious challenge to the country. However, people are deeply divided about how to solve the problem.

Some Americans believe that letting illegal immigrants stay in the country undermines respect for the rule of law. They often call for illegal immigrants to be **deported,** or sent out of the country. Others are willing to grant **amnesty,** or a pardon, to people who are already here illegally so that they can take steps toward becoming citizens. To stop further illegal immigration, some people favor allowing potential immigrants to apply for temporary work permits and earn permanent residence if they learn English, pay back taxes, and have no criminal record.

Many Americans on both sides of the issue agree on the need for more border patrols. Some propose building a continuous wall from Texas to California.

U.S. Foreign-Born Population, 1850–2005

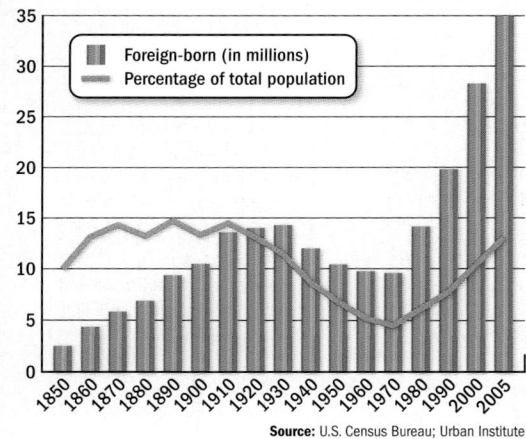

- Foreign-born (in millions)
- Percentage of total population

Source: U.S. Census Bureau; Urban Institute

Three generations of the Solano family from San Antonio, Texas ▶

Graph Skills

1. **Identifying** In what year did the foreign-born population reach its all-time high?
2. **Analyzing** What percentage of foreign-born residents are from Mexico?

Graphs In Motion See StudentWorks™ Plus or glencoe.com.

New Challenges **Chapter 31 1005**

CHAPTER 31
Section 5

R Reading Strategy

Summarizing Have students write a summary of the text describing America's changing society at the beginning of the twenty-first century. To prevent students from repeating the text word for word, tell them their summaries can be no longer than six sentences. **OL**

D Differentiated Instruction

Kinesthetic Ask students to find photos of Americans from as many countries of origin as possible. Have them cut out the photos and glue them onto a poster for a collage titled "America's Diverse Population." Tell students to include names of countries of origin and facts about immigrants in the collage. **BL**

U.S. Foreign-Born Population, 1850–2005

Graph Skills Answer

2005

Differentiated Instruction

Leveled Activities

BL Academic Vocabulary Activity, URB p. 47

OL Critical Thinking Skills Activity, URB p. 57

AL American Literature Reading, URB p. 9

W Writing Support

Descriptive Writing Invite interested students to find first-hand descriptions by illegal Mexican immigrants who journeyed to the United States. Ask the students to write a short story describing the journey of one such illegal immigrant. **AL**

 Reading Check **Answer:** immigration, natural population increase, good health care

Assess

History ONLINE

Study Central™ provides summaries, interactive games, and online graphic organizers to help students review content.

Close

Describing Have each student describe to a partner the ways in which the world's nations are economically interdependent today. **OL**

Section ★ Review

They believe the wall is needed to prevent illegal immigration from Mexico. Critics of the wall-building proposal, however, claim that this would not stop people who are determined to enter the country illegally. Instead, it would force them to take more dangerous risks.

Health Issues

Immigration contributes to population growth. Another factor is natural population increase, or the surplus of births over deaths. Today, the United States has a larger percentage of young people than do other developed countries. Yet, the overall population of the country is aging. This aging is due to a rising birthrate and a declining death rate as well as to the effects of better health care.

Despite health advances, the rates of cancer have risen. Today, cancer and heart disease are the leading causes of death in the United States. This is because of an aging population, pollution, and the unhealthy lifestyle of many Americans who eat high-fat foods and do not exercise enough.

The United States devotes many resources to health care. Still, many Americans are unable to buy health insurance, and others cannot afford health care even with insurance. The high cost of health care also places a burden on businesses that provide health care to employees.

America on the Move

Being mobile, or moving from place to place, has always been a characteristic of American life. Widespread use of the automobile has given people a greater choice of where to live and work.

In recent decades, most of the nation's population growth has taken place in the West and South. These two regions attract residents because of their mild climates and growing industries. Meanwhile, areas of the North, East, and Midwest have lost population. There, heavy manufacturing has declined, although efforts are being made to build more high-tech businesses.

✓ **Reading Check** **Summarizing** What factors have led to population growth?

Section 5 Review

History ONLINE
Study Central™ To review this section, go to glencoe.com.

Vocabulary

1. Use each of the following terms correctly in a sentence: interdependent, decade, globalism, trade deficit, free trade, aware, urban sprawl, acid rain, global warming, deport, amnesty.

Main Ideas

2. **Analyzing** How did international trade change the world economy?

3. **Explaining** What is the goal of the Kyoto Protocol?

4. **Summarizing** What proposals have been made to stop illegal immigration?

Critical Thinking

5. **Organizing** Complete a diagram like the one below to describe the characteristics of the global economy.

6. **Expository Writing** Identify the issue of global concern that you think is the most serious. In an essay, explain why you think it is the most serious problem. Include some possible solutions.

Answer the
7. **Essential Question**
How have economic and environmental developments led to the world's nations becoming more interdependent?

Answers

1. Students will write sentences using the vocabulary terms.
2. International trade linked the economies of the world's nations and helped lead to the growth of globalism.
3. to reduce the pollution that causes global warming
4. deportation of illegal immigrants, allowing potential immigrants to apply for work permits and earn permanent residence, adding more border patrols, building a wall between the United States and Mexico
5. Answers might include dependence on computer technology and instant communication; disturbance in one region can affect prices in another; interaction unaffected by physical distance.
6. Students' essays should accurately describe a global concern and possible solutions.
7. In the global economy, the raw materials and markets of separate nations are interdependent. This globalism contributes to an awareness of the world's shared environment, its problems, and the need for shared solutions. Pollution and global warming are examples of two problems without borders.

Visual Summary

Reagan's Agenda

- Supply-side economics to boost the economy
- Military buildup to fight communism
- Treaty with Soviets to reduce nuclear arms

World Change

- Communism collapses in Eastern Europe and the Soviet Union
- Persian Gulf War/Operation Desert Storm
- Economic recession weakens President Bush's reelection campaign

The Clinton Years

- Clinton and Congress cut spending; reform welfare and health care
- U.S. economy grows; federal budget is balanced
- Scandal and impeachment tarnish the Clinton administration

Bush Takes Office

- Supreme Court resolves 2000 election results dispute; George W. Bush becomes president
- Bush focuses on cutting taxes and reforming education
- Terrorists destroy the World Trade Center and attack the Pentagon
- Bush launches war on terror

Toward the Future

- World trade plays major part in global interdependence
- Global community faces serious environmental problems
- Population increases due to immigration and aging Americans

▲ First section of Berlin Wall torn down, November 10, 1989

Presidential candidate Bill Clinton at campaign rally ▼

California teens clean up trash and litter ▼

▲ Worker walks through the rubble of the World Trade Center, September 11, 2001

STUDY TO GO Study anywhere, anytime! Download quizzes and flash cards to your PDA from glencoe.com.

Visual Summary

Discussing The text mentions several decisions made by the Supreme Court relating to George W. Bush and his administration. As a class, discuss these decisions. *(Decisions include the ruling that left Bush the presidential winner in Florida and led to Al Gore's concession, as well as two decisions on the legal rights of captured terrorists.)* **Ask:** Do you think each Supreme Court decision was in the best interests of the nation? Lead a class discussion about the ramifications of each decision. **OL**

Defending Ask: What do you think is the greatest challenge facing the United States today? Defend your answer in a paragraph. *(Students might include global warming, terrorism, pollution, the global economy, or nuclear war.)* **OL**

Hands-On Chapter Project
Step 6: Wrap-Up

Writing and Performing a Skit

Step 6: Each student will write a one- or two-paragraph review of each skit.

Directions Have students write a review of the other skits. Reviews should be one or two paragraphs long and should take into account such things as historical accuracy, dialogue, props, costumes, scenery, organization, and entertainment value. Have one or two students read a review aloud for each skit.

Synthesizing Ask: Which skit was the most entertaining? Which was the most historically accurate? Students should consider the discussions that arose after the skits and support their answers with specific examples. **OL**

Focus

C₁ Critical Thinking

Making Inferences Ask: Why do you think so many immigrants move from Mexico to the United States? *(Answers may include Mexico's close proximity to the United States, Mexico's poor economy, people looking for a better life, and to move near family members.)* **OL**

C₂ Critical Thinking

Drawing Conclusions Have groups of students discuss what knowledge of U.S. history and government should be required of new citizens. Groups should then write five essay questions they believe could be on a citizenship test for immigrants. **OL**

Have students complete a graphic organizer that shows what immigrants must do to apply to become U.S. citizens. **OL**

To apply for U.S. citizenship
- Offer proof of residence
- Show they have good moral character
- Have knowledge of U.S. history & government
- Usually must have basic knowledge of English

Additional Support and Answers

Immigration

The United States is undergoing its fourth great period of immigration. According to the Census Bureau, the number of foreign-born in the United States increased from 19.8 million in 1990 to 31.1 million in 2000. Never before have so many people immigrated to America.

How Does Geography Affect Immigration?

In recent years, most immigrants to the United States have come from Latin America and Asia. By far the greatest number is from Mexico. While immigration has increased, its effects have not been felt in equal measure throughout the country. Immigrants have tended to settle in the more densely populated areas of the United States: California, Florida, Texas, and the Northeast. The foreign-born population of the United States is growing four times faster than the native-born population. Over the next 50 years, immigrants will account for two-thirds of U.S. population growth.

▼ Mexican American celebration

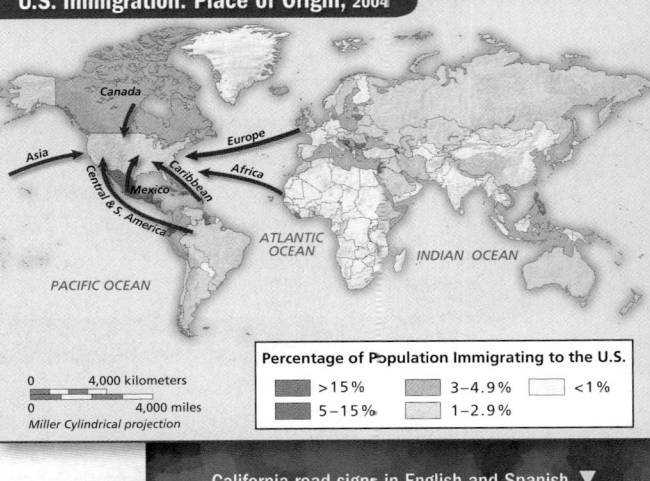

U.S. Immigration: Place of Origin, 2004

Canada · Asia · Europe · Africa · Caribbean · Mexico · Central & S. America

PACIFIC OCEAN · ATLANTIC OCEAN · INDIAN OCEAN

0   4,000 kilometers
0   4,000 miles
Miller Cylindrical projection

Percentage of Population Immigrating to the U.S.
- \>15%
- 5–15%
- 3–4.9%
- 1–2.9%
- <1%

California road signs in English and Spanish ▼

DANGER STAY OUT STAY ALIVE 216 LIVES LOST HERE SINCE 1960

PELIGRO POR FAVOR NO NADE 216 VIDAS PERDIDAS EN EL RIO KERN DESDE 1960

◀ **Becoming Citizens**
Immigrants to America can apply to become U.S. citizens. Applicants must offer proof of residence; evidence of good moral character; and knowledge of the history and government of the United States. In most cases, applicants must have a basic knowledge of the English language. **C₂**

1008 Unit 10 *America in a Modern Era*

Fast Facts

Article II, Section 1 of the U.S. Constitution states that "No person except a natural born citizen, or a citizen of the United States, at the time of the adoption of this Constitution, shall be eligible to the office of President; neither shall any person be eligible to that office who shall not have attained to the age of thirty five years, and been fourteen Years a resident within the United States." The same rule applies to the Vice President. However, a person may run for the House of Representatives after being a U.S. citizen for 7 years and for the Senate after being a citizen for 9 years. Some officials want to change the Constitution to allow anyone who has been a U.S. citizen for 20 years to run for President.

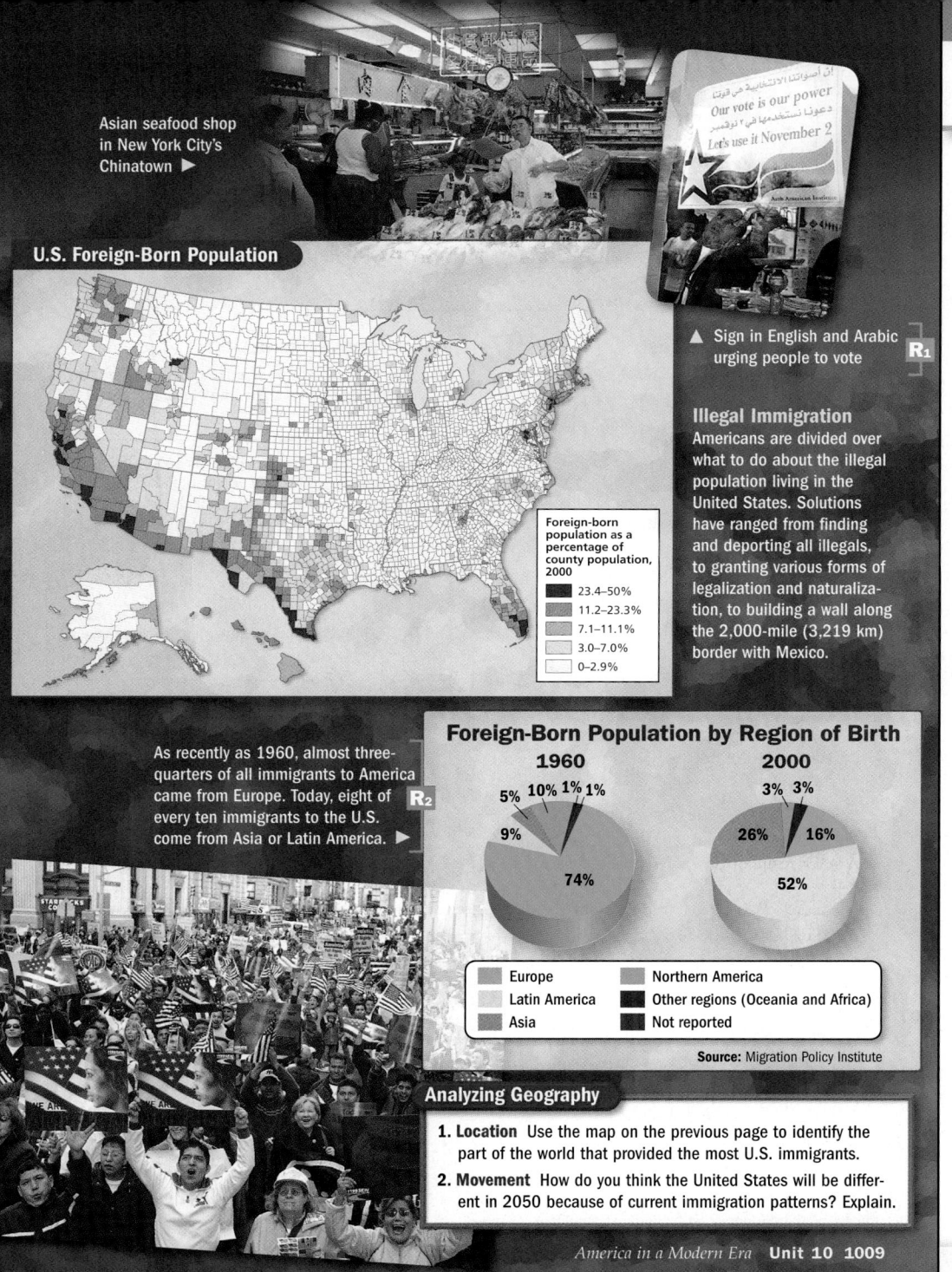

Asian seafood shop in New York City's Chinatown ▶

U.S. Foreign-Born Population

▲ Sign in English and Arabic urging people to vote **R₁**

Foreign-born population as a percentage of county population, 2000

- 23.4–50%
- 11.2–23.3%
- 7.1–11.1%
- 3.0–7.0%
- 0–2.9%

Illegal Immigration

Americans are divided over what to do about the illegal population living in the United States. Solutions have ranged from finding and deporting all illegals, to granting various forms of legalization and naturalization, to building a wall along the 2,000-mile (3,219 km) border with Mexico.

As recently as 1960, almost three-quarters of all immigrants to America came from Europe. Today, eight of every ten immigrants to the U.S. come from Asia or Latin America. ▶ **R₂**

Foreign-Born Population by Region of Birth

1960
- 5%
- 10%
- 1%
- 1%
- 9%
- 74%

2000
- 3%
- 3%
- 26%
- 16%
- 52%

- Europe
- Latin America
- Asia
- Northern America
- Other regions (Oceania and Africa)
- Not reported

Source: Migration Policy Institute

Analyzing Geography

1. **Location** Use the map on the previous page to identify the part of the world that provided the most U.S. immigrants.
2. **Movement** How do you think the United States will be different in 2050 because of current immigration patterns? Explain.

America in a Modern Era **Unit 10 1009**

Answers and Analyses
Reviewing Main Ideas

1. C The federal debt more than tripled between 1980 and 1990. Choice A is incorrect because laws during the Reagan administration favored car manufacturers rather than the environment. Choice B is wrong, as federal programs for low-income housing were cut. Choice D is incorrect because Reagan built up the military rather than reducing it. **18.B.3a**

2. A The government bailed out struggling S&Ls and consumers. This answer is a matter of recall. Choice B, deregulation, was mentioned in the discussion of S&Ls, but it is what caused the crisis rather than its solution. Choices C and D, spending cuts and supply-side economics, are unrelated to the topic. **15.E.3b**

3. D Clinton was unable to pass a universal health care bill. He did pass laws for gun control and family leave (Choices A and C). He also achieved the first federal budget surplus in three decades (Choice B). **16.A**

4. A Bush gained a more conservative Supreme Court. Reading the text will show that he curtailed citizens' rights with the USA Patriot Act, so Choice B is wrong. Choice C is incorrect as the federal debt grew under Bush. Choice D is obviously wrong, as Bush waged war in Iraq and Afghanistan. **14.A.3**

5. C According to the text, scientists believe that global warming will lead to changing climate patterns and melting polar ice caps, which would raise the ocean levels. The terms in the remaining choices are unrelated. **17.B.3b**

Short-Answer Question

6. Students might answer that no records were kept or found, or evidence was destroyed. **16.A.3b**

TEST-TAKING TIP

Answer the questions you know first and go back to those for which you need more time.

Reviewing Main Ideas

Directions: Choose the best answers for each of the following questions.

1. One result of Reagan's approach to government was
   A safe, environmentally friendly cars.
   B more housing for low-income families.
   C a tripling of the 1980 federal debt.
   D a reduction in troop levels.

2. How did the federal government deal with the failures of S&Ls during the late 1980s?
   A bailouts
   B deregulation
   C spending cuts
   D supply-side economics

3. Which of Clinton's goals went unrealized?
   A stricter gun control
   B a federal budget surplus
   C family leave for workers
   D health care for all Americans

4. A major result of George W. Bush's presidency was
   A a more conservative Supreme Court.
   B the expansion of U.S. citizens' rights.
   C federal budget surpluses.
   D improved relations with the Middle East.

5. Which pair of environmental terms has a cause-and-effect relationship?
   A chemicals and urban sprawl
   B acid rain and solar radiation
   C global warming and rising seas
   D water pollution and the ozone layer

Short-Answer Question

Directions: Base your answer to question 6 on the excerpt below and on your knowledge of social studies.

> A few months ago I told the American people I did not trade arms for hostages. My heart and my best intentions still tell me that's true, but the facts and the evidence tell me it is not. . . . [N]o one kept proper records of meetings or decisions. This led to my failure to recollect whether I approved an arms shipment before or after the fact. I did approve it; I just can't say specifically when.
> —from President Reagan's address to the nation about Iran-Contra

6. Why do you think the Iran-Contra hearings never produced any proof of the president's involvement?

Review the Essential Questions

7. **Essay** How are the U.S. economy and environment today linked to the policies of Reagan, Clinton, and the Bushes?

To help you write your essay, review your answers to the Essential Questions in the section reviews and the chapter Foldables Study Organizer. Your essay should include:
- the effects of military spending on the economy;
- the effects of deregulation on the environment;
- the effects of NAFTA on American jobs; and
- the effects of spending on the war in Iraq on the economy.

GO ON

Review the Essential Questions

7. Students should use their answers to the Essential Questions and their Foldables to describe how today's economy and environment are linked to the policies of Reagan, Clinton, and the Bushes. Essays should include the effects of deregulation, military spending, NAFTA, and the war on terror. **15.E.3b**

History ONLINE

For additional test practice, use **Self-Check Quizzes**—Chapter 31 at glencoe.com.

Chapter 31 Assessment

Document-Based Questions

Directions: Analyze the documents and answer the short-answer questions that follow each document.

Document 1

Joseph Hatcher entered army basic training the day before September 11, 2001. Here he comments on his later mission in Iraq.

> There was no mention of a noble cause. At no point through any one of my chain of command was there a noble cause placed on the table. We were given a job, and our job was to go to Iraq for a year and to provide safety and security operations for our area of control.

Source: Trish Wood, *What Was Asked of Us*

8. Explain what Hatcher meant by "a noble cause."

Document 2

The chart shows the value of U.S. imports and exports in two separate years.

U.S. International Trade, 2000 and 2005 (in millions of dollars)		
Exports	**2000**	**2005**
Goods	$771,994	$894,631
Services	$298,603	$380,614
Imports	**2000**	**2005**
Goods	$1,224,408	$1,677,371
Services	$223,748	$314,604

Source: U.S. Census Bureau, *U.S. International Trade in Goods and Services*

9. Based on the chart, how did the value of exports change from 2000 to 2005? During that same time period, how did the value of imports change?

Document 3

This political cartoon comments on present-day election campaigns.

'I'm an American voter and I approve this message.'

10. What does this cartoon say about election campaigns? Why would a voter approve of it?

Document 4

In 2006 New Mexico Governor Bill Richardson urged Congress to help illegal immigrants as well as American businesses.

> Most [illegal] immigrants come to the United States to work low-wage jobs which few Americans want, such as picking crops or cleaning toilets. Our economy creates demand for at least 400,000 new low-skill illegal immigrants per year, but only about 140,000 are allowed to enter legally. When demand and legal supply are so out of line, the pressures for illegal immigration are enormous.

Source: Bill Richardson, speech on comprehensive immigration reform

11. What pressures does Richardson refer to?

12. Expository Writing Using the information from the four documents and your knowledge of social studies, write an essay in which you:

- identify two issues the U.S. faces; and
- explain why the U.S. must address these issues, and what might happen if it does not.

10. The cartoon comments on voters' disapproval of the negative tone of recent political campaigns, which have focused more on personal attacks than on the issues. The voter approves the message because it criticizes the campaigns. **14.D.3**

11. Answers might include the need for low-paid workers and the tendency for businesses to ignore the immigration status of workers they hire. **16.A.3b**

12. Student essays should reflect an understanding of the documents and how they relate to the chapter material. The essays should be organized to clearly describe two important issues in the United States. Issues might include the war on terror, globalism, global warming, communism versus democracy, and so on. Students should explain why the issues need to be addressed and the consequences of not addressing them. **16.A**

History ONLINE

Have students visit the Web site at glencoe.com to review Chapter 31 and take the Self-Check Quiz.

Need Extra Help?

Have students refer to the pages listed if they miss any of the questions.

Need Extra Help?

If you missed questions. . .	1	2	3	4	5	6	7	8	9	10	11	12
Go to page. . .	973	981	984	996	1004	975	970-1005	994	1002	988	1005	1001-1006

Document-Based Questions

8. He was probably referring to bringing democracy to Iraq, an often-cited goal in the Iraq War. **16.A.3b**

9. The value of exports increased, both for goods and services. The value of imports also rose in both categories. **15.D.3a**

Appendix

Using an Appendix

By definition, an appendix is supplementary material attached to the end of a piece of writing. Students can use the appendix to help them understand the material in their textbook. Explain that students may use the appendix to find out what a word means, to find out how to pronounce a word, or to find additional information about a particular topic or document.

Ask: What materials are included in this appendix? *(Skills Handbook, Presidents of the United States, Supreme Court Case Summaries, Documents of American History, English-Spanish Glossary, Index, and Acknowledgments and Photo Credits)* **OL**

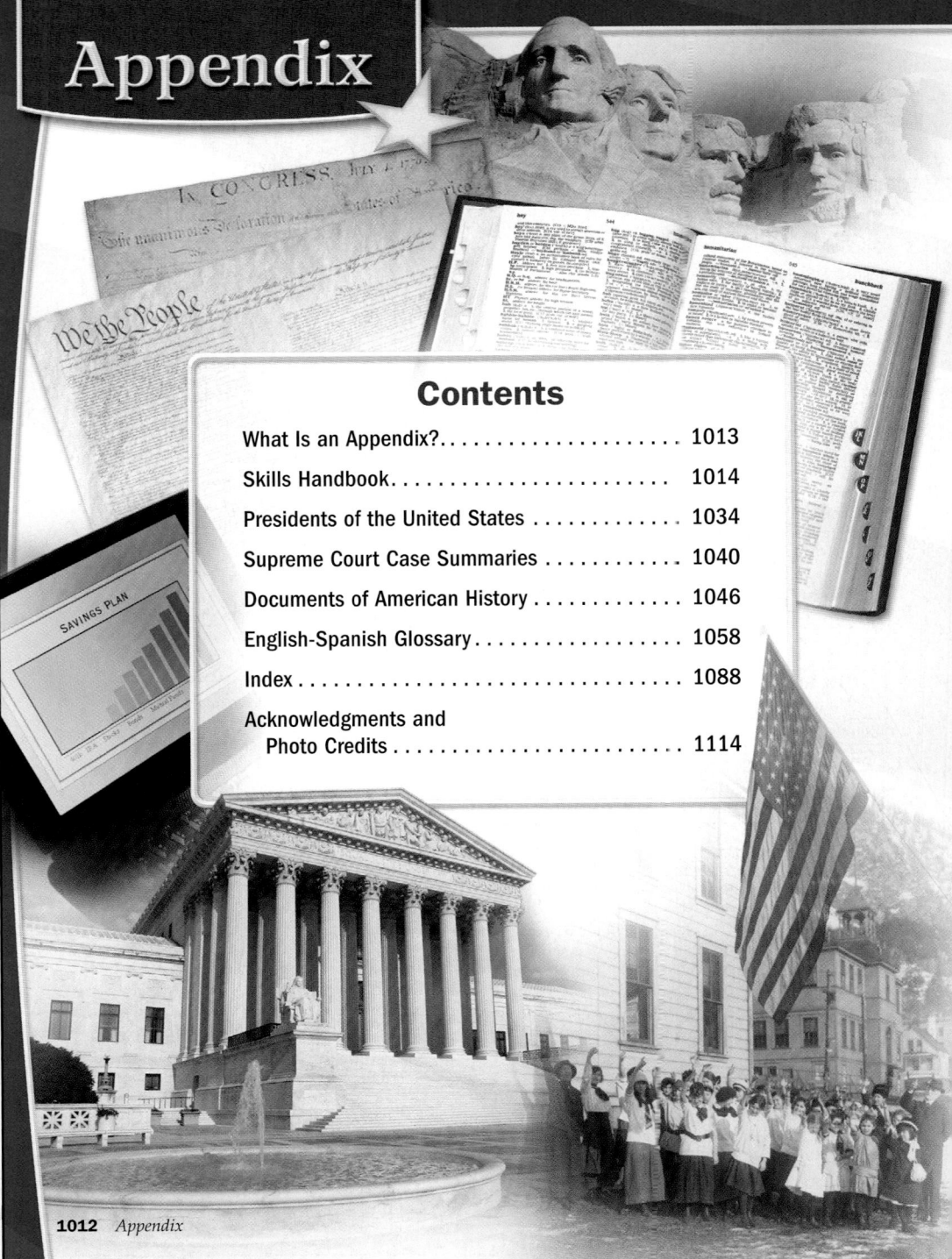

Appendix

Contents

What Is an Appendix?

An appendix is the additional material you often find at the end of books. The following information will help you learn how to use the appendix in The American Journey.

Skills Handbook

The Skills Handbook offers you information and practice using critical thinking and social studies skills. Mastering these skills will help you in all your courses.

Presidents of the United States

The presidents have served as our nation's leaders. In this resource you will find information of interest on each of the nation's presidents, including their term in office, their political affiliation, and their occupations before they became president.

Supreme Court Case Summaries

The Supreme Court Case Summaries provide readable discussions of important Supreme Court cases. The summaries are listed in alphabetical order and include a summary of the facts of the case and its impact.

Documents of American History

This is a collection of some of the most important writings and speeches in American history. Each document begins with an introduction describing the author and placing the selection within its historical context.

English-Spanish Glossary

A glossary is a list of important or difficult terms found in a textbook. The glossary gives a definition of each term as it is used in the book. The glossary also includes page numbers telling you where in the textbook the term is used. Since words sometimes have other meanings, you may wish to consult a dictionary to find other uses for the term.

In *The American Journey,* the Spanish glossary is included with the English glossary. The Spanish term is located directly across from the English term. A Spanish glossary is especially important to bilingual students or those Spanish-speaking students who are learning the English language.

Index

An index is an alphabetical listing that includes the subjects of the book and the page numbers where those subjects can be found. The index in this book also lets you know that certain pages contain maps, graphs, charts, photos, paintings, or cartoons about the subject.

Acknowledgments and Photo Credits

This section lists photo credits and literary credits for the book. You can look at this section to find out where the publisher obtained the permission to use a photograph or to use excerpts from other books.

Test Yourself

Find the answers to these questions by using the Appendix on the following pages.

1. What does *ironclad* mean?
2. Who was the sixth president of the United States?
3. Which section of the Appendix would help you find out about "bleeding Kansas"?
4. What was the purpose of issuing the Seneca Falls Declaration?
5. What was the Supreme Court's decision in *Marbury* v. *Madison*?

Appendix **1013**

Appendix

What Is an Appendix?

Use the descriptions in the student text to explain the sections in the Appendix. Then instruct students to answer the questions at the bottom of the page. Next, discuss the answer to each question. **Ask:** How can the information in each section help you as you read your textbook? **OL**

Tell students to write five questions similar to those in Test Yourself on a sheet of paper. Students should write the answers on the back of the same paper. Then have students exchange questions and quiz each other. Conclude by having students check their responses. **OL**

Answers

Answers

1. It is an armored naval vessel.
2. John Quincy Adams was the sixth president of the United States.
3. Index
4. The purpose was to call for woman suffrage as well as educational and economic opportunities for women.
5. The Supreme Court ruled against Marbury, but it established the Court as the final authority for deciding the meaning of the Constitution. The Court also defined its right to determine whether a law violates the Constitution.

Skills Handbook

Skills Handbook

Teach

The following **Skills Handbook** offers opportunities to practice individual critical thinking and social studies skills. Students can benefit in multiple ways from completing the lessons. First, being equipped with these skills makes students' reading more meaningful and supports the content of the text. Second, the lessons give students practice in using skills they will need to complete standardized tests successfully, as many of these skills are assessed on standardized tests.

You may use the lessons at any point in the text and in any order that you wish. You also can use these lessons as review for students who need extra practice with these skills.

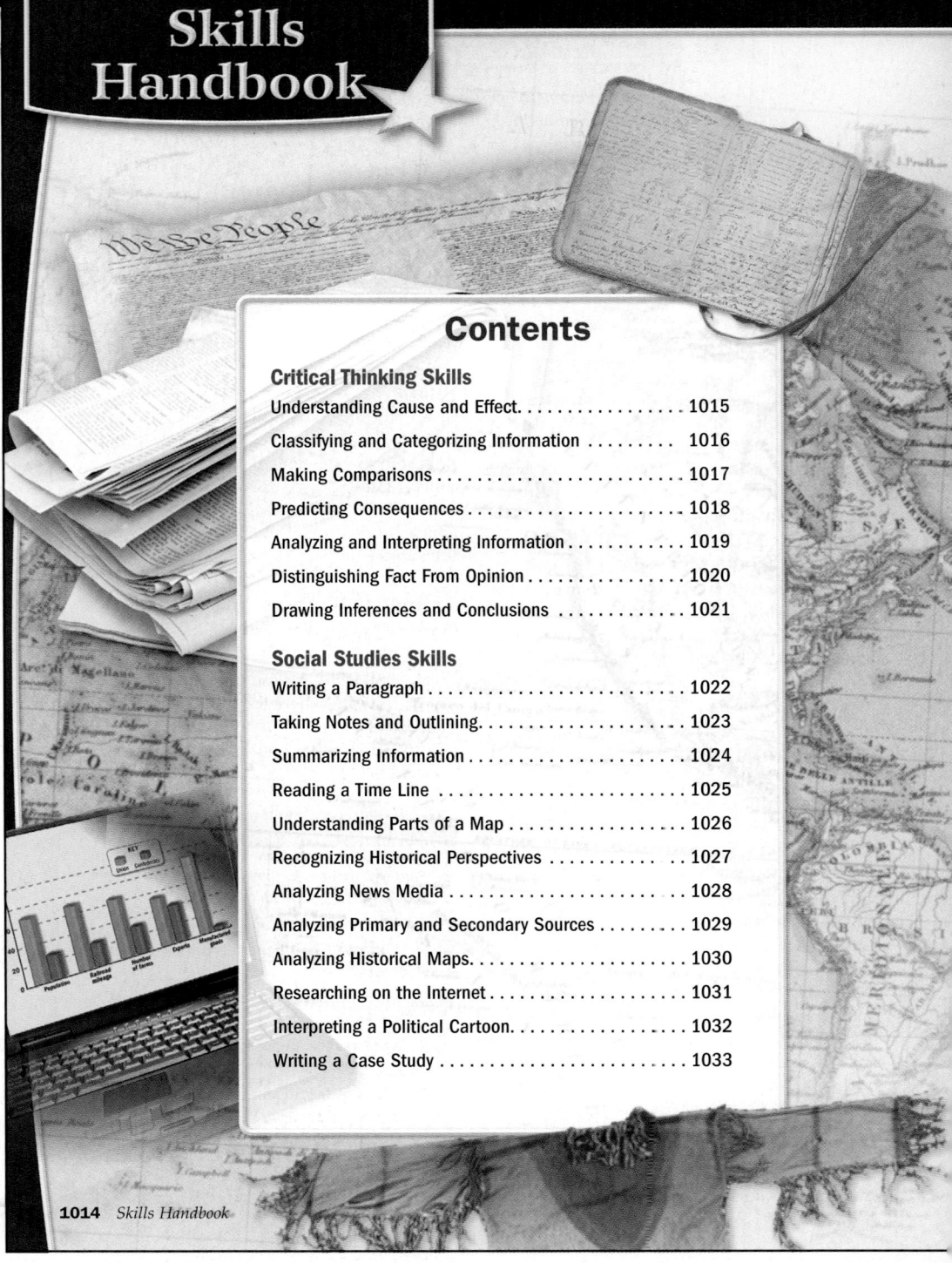

Contents

Understanding Cause and Effect

Why Learn This Skill? C

Cause-and-effect relationships are important in the study of history. To understand cause and effect, consider *why* an event occurred. A *cause* is an action or situation that produces an event. What happens as a result of a cause is an *effect*.

Marco Polo ▶

1 Learn It!

To identify cause-and-effect relationships, follow these steps:

1. Identify two or more events or developments.

2. Decide whether one event caused the other. Look for "clue words" such as *because, led to, brought about, so that, after that, produced, as a result of, since,* or *in the wake of.*

3. Identify the outcomes of events. Remember that some effects have more than one cause, and some causes lead to more than one effect. Also, an effect can become the cause of yet another effect.

> The Crusades brought western Europeans into contact with the Middle East. Arab merchants sold spices, sugar, silk, and other goods from China and India to Europeans. As a result, European interest in Asia grew.
> That interest grew even more after Marco Polo returned from China. In 1296 he began writing an account of his trip. He described Asia's marvels in his book Travels, which was widely read in Europe. Little did Marco Polo realize that 200 years later Travels would inspire Christopher Columbus to sail in the opposite direction to reach the East.

2 Practice It!

Categorize the items below as either *cause, effect,* or *both.*

1. The Crusades brought western Europeans to the Middle East.

2. European interest in Asia grew.

3. Marco Polo wrote *Travels,* an account of his trip to China.

4. *Travels* inspired Christopher Columbus to sail in the opposite direction to reach the East.

3 Apply It!

In a newspaper, read an article describing a current event. Determine at least one cause and one effect of that event, and complete a flowchart like the one below.

Cause → Event → Effect

Skills Handbook **1015**

Answers

Answers

Skills Handbook

Answers

Classifying and Categorizing Information

Why Learn This Skill?

As a student, it is important to know how to organize large quantities of information in an understandable way. *Classifying* helps you to arrange facts into broad groups. *Categorizing* helps you to organize that information into more detailed groups according to common characteristics.

Rudolph Valentino movie poster (left) and King Kong movie poster (right) ▶

1 Learn It!

Follow these steps to learn how to classify and categorize:

1. To classify information, look for topics and facts that have common broad characteristics. In the first paragraph, a broad topic might be *Reasons for Cultural Change in America.* Under this topic, further classifications might be *The Growth of Mass Media* and *Increase in Leisure Time.*

2. Divide the information further into categories, based on more specific characteristics. For example, under *Mass Media,* categories could be *Movies* and *Radio.* Each of those categories could contain more examples and details and could become column heads in a chart.

3. As you read, look for examples that fit into the categories you created.

Cultural changes spread quickly because of the growth of mass media—forms of communication, such as newspapers and radio, that reach millions of people. Laborsaving devices and fewer working hours gave Americans more leisure time to enjoy newspapers, magazines, phonograph records, the radio, and the movies.

In the 1920s, the motion picture industry in Hollywood, California, became a major business. For millions of Americans the movies offered entertainment and escape. The first movies were black and white and silent, with the actor's dialogue printed on the screen. In 1927 Hollywood introduced movies with sound. The first "talkie," The Jazz Singer, created a sensation.

The radio brought entertainment into people's homes in the 1920s. Radio networks broadcast popular programs that included news, concerts, sporting events, and comedies.

2 Practice It!

1. What are two further classifications for the topic *Increase in Leisure Time?*
2. What details/examples from the paragraphs above could you place under the categories *Movies* and *Radio?*

3 Apply It!

Look at the Geographic Dictionary on pages Ref 30–Ref 31. In a chart, list the terms that would fall into the classifications "Landforms" or "Bodies of Water." Can you identify other categories in which to group the information?

Answers

Practice It! Answers

1. print and audio/visual communication
2. Possible answer: Movies—silent movies, "talkies," *The Jazz Singer*; Radio—news, concerts, sporting events, comedies

Apply It! Answers

Students should correctly classify landforms and bodies of water, based on the definitions given in the Geographic Dictionary. Students might divide some landforms into categories such as highlands or lowlands and divide some bodies of water into categories such as inland or coastal.

Making Comparisons

Why Learn This Skill?

When you make comparisons, you determine similarities among ideas, objects, or events. You should also examine qualities that make each of the ideas, objects, or events unique. Making comparisons is an important skill because it can help you to choose among several possible alternatives. **C**

1 Learn It!

To make comparisons, follow these steps:

1. Select the items to compare.

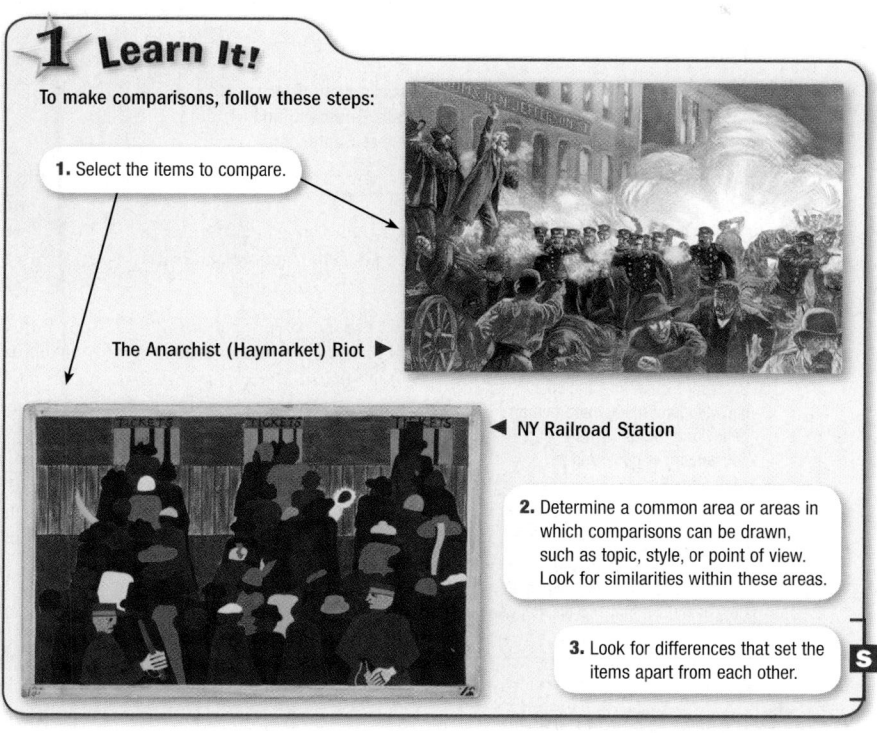

The Anarchist (Haymarket) Riot ▶

◀ NY Railroad Station

2. Determine a common area or areas in which comparisons can be drawn, such as topic, style, or point of view. Look for similarities within these areas.

3. Look for differences that set the items apart from each other. **S**

2 Practice It!

After studying the paintings above, answer the following questions:

1. How are the subjects of the paintings similar?

2. How are they different?

3. What can you tell about the two artists' attitudes toward their subject?

3 Apply It!

Survey 10 of your classmates about an issue in the news, and summarize their responses. Then write a paragraph or two comparing their opinions.

C Critical Thinking

Making Inferences Have students consider a historian who is studying early cultures of North America. Have students brainstorm things that this historian might want to compare. *(Possible answers: use of tools, artwork, methods of worship, structures, food sources)* **Ask:** What knowledge might the historian gain from such comparisons? *(Possible answers: determine which culture was most advanced, understand development trends, learn how one culture might have influenced another)* **OL**

S Skill Practice

Visual Literacy Have students suppose that another painter wanted to create sympathy for the rioters in the Haymarket Riot. **Ask:** How might this painter create the scene differently? *(The painter might show police firing on an unarmed and peaceful crowd of demonstrators.)* **ELL**

Answers

Practice It! Answers

1. Possible answer: Both paintings show dense crowds of people engaged in specific activities. Police officers appear in both paintings.
2. Possible answer: One painting shows a scene of violence and disorder as police battle rioters. The other painting shows the police presiding over an orderly scene. The people in the riot scene are portrayed in a more realistic style than in the railroad station painting.
3. Possible answer: The first painting conveys a sense of chaos and tragedy. The second painting conveys a sense of order and control.

Apply It! Answers

Students should compare the responses of their classmates about an issue in the news. Their paragraphs should note similarities and differences among the expressed opinions.

Skills Handbook

R Reading Strategy

Making Connections Ask students what they think might happen if they played video games the evening before a test instead of studying. *(Students might say that they would not do as well on the test as they would if they had studied.)* **Ask:** On what did you base your prediction? *(Students might point to prior experience, the experience of others, or common sense.)* How might this prediction help you make a good decision before the next test? *(Students might decide to study for the next test to achieve a better outcome.)* **BL**

S Skill Practice

Using Predicting Skills Have students read the first paragraph under a topic heading in their textbooks. Ask them to think about what might happen next. Then have them skim the following paragraphs to see if their predictions are correct. **OL**

Predicting Consequences

Why Learn This Skill?

Predicting future events is difficult, but the more information you have, the more accurate your predictions will be. Making good predictions will help you to make **R S** better decisions. Using these skills can also help you to understand the consequences of historical events.

The assassination of Archduke Franz Ferdinand and Archduchess Sophie ▶

1 Learn It!

To help you make predictions, follow these steps:

1. Gather information about the topic.

2. Use your experience and your knowledge of history and human behavior to predict what consequences could result.

3. Analyze each of the possible consequences by asking yourself: How likely is it that this will happen?

On the morning of June 28, 1914, Archduke Franz Ferdinand, the heir to the throne of the Austro-Hungarian Empire, and his wife Sophie were assassinated while visiting Bosnia, an Austrian province.

Gavrilo Princip, Franz Ferdinand's assassin, belonged to a Serbian nationalist group that had plotted Ferdinand's murder to bring down the Austro-Hungarian Empire and unite the Slavs.

2 Practice It!

Read the excerpt above and answer the following questions:

1. What outcome is most likely to occur between Austria-Hungary and Serbia?

2. On what do you base your prediction?

3. Do you think a situation similar to the one described in the passage is likely to occur again?

3 Apply It!

Analyze three newspaper articles about an event affecting your community or the nation. Make an educated prediction about what will happen, and explain your reasoning. Then write a few paragraphs summarizing your prediction. You may want to check back later to see if your prediction came true.

Answers

Answers

Practice It! Answers

1. Answers might include that Princip will be tried for murder or that Austria-Hungary will declare war on Serbia.
2. Answers might include that in the past, nations have retaliated when attacked.
3. Possible answers: Yes—there are still radical militant groups in the world; No—nationalism and imperialism are not as strong today.

Apply It! Answers

Students should have logical arguments to support their predictions. Encourage them to check later to see if their prediction actually occurred.

Analyzing and Interpreting Information

Why Learn This Skill?

Have you ever heard someone say, "Don't believe everything you read"? To be an informed citizen, you have to analyze and interpret information carefully as you read to make sure you understand the meaning and the intent of the writer. Doing so helps you decide what you think about a subject.

Andrew Carnegie ▶

1 Learn It!

To analyze and interpret information, use the following steps:

1. Identify the topic being discussed.

2. Examine how the information is organized. What are the main points?

3. Think about how reliable the source of the information is.

> [T]he surplus wealth of the few will become, in the best sense, the property of the many. . . . [T]his wealth, passing through the hands of the few, can be made a much more potent [strong] force for the elevation of our race than if it had been distributed in small sums to the people themselves. Even the poorest can be made to see this, and to agree that great sums gathered by some of their fellow-citizens and spent for public purposes, from which the masses reap the principal benefit, are more valuable to them than if scattered among them through the course of many years in trifling amounts.
>
> —Andrew Carnegie, "Wealth"

4. Summarize the information in your own words. Does the information agree with or contradict something you believe?

2 Practice It!

Read the excerpt above and answer the following questions:

1. What topic is being discussed?

2. What is the main point?

3. Summarize the information in this excerpt, and then provide your analysis, based on this information and what you already know about the subject.

3 Apply It!

Select an issue that is currently in the news, such as gasoline prices, global warming, or taxation. Read an article or watch a news segment about the issue. Analyze the information and make a brief statement of your own about the topic. Explain your thinking.

Skills Handbook **1019**

C Critical Thinking

Identifying Point of View Have students find information about Andrew Carnegie in their textbooks. **Ask:** Who was Andrew Carnegie? *(a wealthy industrialist)* How does knowing something about the source help you analyze the quote? *(It helps to determine the reliability of the source and to recognize point of view. This quote reflects a wealthy person's perspective on the accumulation of great wealth.)* **OL**

W Writing Support

Personal Writing Based on their analysis of this quote, have students decide whether or not they agree with Andrew Carnegie. Have them write a response to Carnegie, expressing their position and explaining their views. **OL**

Answers

Practice It! Answers

1. philanthropy by the wealthy
2. Money can better serve the public by being collected by the wealthy and put to use for the public good than if it is distributed directly to some needy people in small sums.
3. Possible analysis: Carnegie is justifying the accumulation of great wealth by a few people. He is saying that by donating surplus wealth to projects that benefit the masses, more people will benefit from the money than if several poor people received small amounts of money directly.

Apply It! Answers

Students should accurately summarize the current issue and its main points and state their positions with supporting details.

Critical Thinking

Analyzing Information Ask: If a statement contains a statistic, can you conclude that the statement is factual? Why or why not? *(No. Statistics can be wrong, can come from an unreliable source, or can be stated in a misleading way.)* **OL**

Critical Thinking

Drawing Conclusions Read students this restatement of an opinion expressed in the excerpt: "The Patriot Act compromises our liberty." Point out that this restatement does not contain the signal word "could" as the original did. **Ask:** Does this restatement reflect an opinion or a fact? Explain. *(Opinion—it still reflects a value judgment.)* What can you conclude about opinions based on this restatement? *(Opinions can be stated without the signal words as if they were facts. Students must be careful not to be fooled by strong statements of opinion masquerading as facts.)* **AL**

Answers

Distinguishing Fact From Opinion

Why Learn This Skill?

To make reasonable judgments about what others say or write, it is important to distinguish facts from opinions. Facts can be checked for accuracy and proven. They answer specific questions such as: What happened? Who did it? When and where did it happen? Opinions are based on people's differing values and beliefs. Opinions often begin with phrases such as *I believe* or *It seems to me.* They also frequently contain words such as *should* or *ought* or judgment words such as *best, worst,* or *greatest.*

Louise Slaughter speaks at
National Press Club June 2007 ▶

1 Learn It!

To learn how to separate facts from opinions, follow these steps:

1. Identify the facts. Ask: which statements can be proved? Where would I find information to verify this statement? If the information is a statistic, it may sound impressive, but you won't know if it's accurate unless you check the source.

2. Identify opinions by looking for statements of feelings or beliefs. Opinions sometimes contain words like *should, would, could, best, greatest, all, every,* or *always.*

All of my colleagues understand that the PATRIOT Act has provided the law enforcement agencies with many valuable tools which facilitate their work in the struggle against terrorism. But with these new tools comes a very real danger that the liberty we seek to protect could be easily compromised in the overzealous pursuit of greater security. . . .

We have evidence which suggests, in contrast to information coming out of the Justice Department, that many of these measures have resulted in the violation of the civil liberties of American citizens. In addition, we understand that some of the extended search and seizure powers used by the law enforcement are apparently not being used for their intended purpose, which is strictly to fight terrorism, and that is unacceptable.

—Congresswoman Louise McIntosh Slaughter,
July 21, 2005

2 Practice It!

The excerpt above is from a speech delivered to Congress by U.S. Representative Louise McIntosh Slaughter concerning the reauthorization, or renewal, of the Patriot Act. Reread the excerpt and answer the questions that follow.

1. Which statements in the passage are factual?

2. Which statements are opinions? Explain.

3 Apply It!

Watch a television interview. Then list three facts and three opinions that you hear.

Answers

Practice It! Answers

1. "We have evidence which suggests . . . that many of these measures have resulted in the violation of the civil liberties of American citizens." ". . . some of the extended search and seizure powers used by the law enforcement are apparently not being used for their intended purpose. . . ."

2. ". . . with these new tools comes a very real danger that the liberty we seek to protect could be easily compromised. . . ." ". . . that is unacceptable."

Apply It! Answers

Students should identify three facts and three opinions from an interview they watched on television. Have them identify key words from the interview that signal opinions.

Drawing Inferences and Conclusions

Why Learn This Skill?

When you make an *inference,* you "read between the lines," or use clues to figure something out that is not stated directly in the text. A *conclusion* is a logical understanding that you reach based on details or facts that you read or hear. By drawing inferences and conclusions you can formulate ideas and make decisions.

Jefferson Davis ▶

1 Learn It!

Follow these steps to draw inferences and conclusions:

1. Read carefully for facts and ideas, and list them.

2. Summarize the information.

3. Consider what you may already know about the topic.

4. Use your knowledge and insight to develop some logical conclusions based on the facts.

> *There can be but little rivalry between ours and any manufacturing or navigating community, such as the Northeastern States of the American Union. It must follow, therefore, that a mutual interest would invite good will and kind offices. If, however, passion or the lust of dominion [power] should cloud the judgment or inflame the ambition of those States, we must prepare to meet the emergency and to maintain, by the final [deciding power] of the sword, the position which we have assumed among the nations of the earth. We have entered upon the career of independence, and it must be inflexibly pursued. . . . As a necessity, not a choice, we have resorted to the remedy of separation; and henceforth our energies must be directed to the conduct of our own affairs, and the [lasting life] of the Confederacy which we have formed.*
> —Jefferson Davis's inaugural speech, February 18, 1861

C1

C2

2 Practice It!

After reading the passage above, answer the following questions:

1. What points does the author make?

2. Which point does your experience contradict?

3. What inference can you make about the Confederate states' reasons for declaring their independence?

4. What conclusions can you draw about Davis' beliefs about a possible war?

3 Apply It!

Read an editorial printed in today's newspaper. What can you infer about the importance of the topic being addressed? Can you tell how the writer feels about the topic? Explain your answer.

Skills Handbook **1021**

C1 Critical Thinking

Making Inferences Ask: What was the South's main economic activity before the Civil War? *(agriculture)* Why, then, should there be little rivalry between the North and South, as Davis stated? *(The North and South did not compete economically. Instead, their economies worked together in "mutual interest.")* **OL**

C2 Critical Thinking

Drawing Conclusions Ask: Did Davis consider the South's decision to separate final, or did he suggest that it might return to the Union under the right circumstances? *(final)* What key words in this speech led you to this conclusion? *("maintain . . . the position which we have assumed," "career of independence," "inflexibly pursued")* **OL**

Answers

Practice It! Answers

1. Possible answer: The South is not seeking conflict with the North; but if forced, it will vigorously defend its cause. The South sees the idea of separation as a necessity, not a choice.

2. Possible answer: The idea of independence for individual states contradicts the idea of unity in today's United States.

3. Students might infer that the South separated in order to maintain its economy and way of life.

4. Davis believes the North's desire to dominate the South will lead to war because he says they "must prepare to meet the emergency and to maintain, by the power of the sword, the position we have assumed."

Apply It! Answers

Students should cite clues in the editorial that led to their inferences about the importance of the topic and the writer's feelings about it.

Skills Handbook

W Writing Support

Descriptive Writing Have students write one paragraph describing their favorite after-school activity. Ask them to underline the topic sentence. Then have them revise the paragraph to place the topic sentence in a different location. Explain that they should revise the wording of the paragraph, as needed, to make the topic sentence work well in its new location. **OL**

D Differentiated Instruction

Verbal/Linguistic Point out that transitional words show relationships between sentences in a paragraph. **Ask:** *What relationships do these transitional words show?* *("Next," "then," and "finally" show sequence. "Also" indicates that the main point in the sentence will be similar to that of the previous sentence. "However" shows a shift in the main point. "Because" and "as a result" show cause and effect.)* **OL**

Answers

Writing a Paragraph

Why Learn This Skill?

W Paragraphs are the building blocks of an essay or other composition. Each paragraph is a unit—a group of sentences about a single topic or idea.

Washington observes Von Steuben drilling troops at Valley Forge ▶

1 Learn It!

Most well-written paragraphs share four characteristics:

At first glance the British had an overwhelming advantage in the war. They had the strongest navy in the world. They also had an experienced, well-trained army and the wealth of a worldwide empire. Britain also had a much larger population than the United States. There were over 8 million people in Britain, compared with only 2.5 million in the United States.

1. A paragraph expresses one main idea or is about one subject. A topic sentence states the main idea, and may be located at the beginning, middle, or end of the paragraph.

2. The rest of the sentences support the main idea. The main idea may be developed by facts, examples, or reasons.

3. The sentences are arranged in a logical order.

4. Transitional words link sentences within the paragraph. Examples include *next, then, finally, also, because, however,* and *as a result.*

2 Practice It!

Use the following sentences to build a paragraph containing a topic sentence and other sentences that give supporting details. Put the sentences in a logical order and add transitional words if you need to. Underline your topic sentence.

1. They were forced to ship soldiers and supplies thousands of miles across the Atlantic.
2. They were fighting on their own ground and fought with great determination to protect it.
3. The Americans possessed some advantages.
4. The British, in contrast, had to wage war in a faraway land.

3 Apply It!

Choose a topic from the era of the Revolutionary War and write a paragraph about it. Then rewrite the paragraph with its sentences out of order. Exchange papers with a classmate. Can he or she find the topic sentence? Does it read logically?

Answers

Practice It! Answers

<u>The Americans possessed some advantages.</u> They were fighting on their own ground and fought with great determination to protect it. The British, in contrast, had to wage war in a faraway land. They were forced to ship soldiers and supplies thousands of miles across the Atlantic.

Apply It! Answers

Each student will assemble a classmate's scrambled sentences into a logical paragraph and identify the topic sentence.

Taking Notes and Outlining

Why Learn This Skill?

Taking notes and outlining are ways of recording important information about what you read. Both methods also help you recall information. Writing down information in a brief and orderly form helps you remember key points and makes it easier to study.

Outlining is similar to sketching a scene. First, you draw the rough shape, or outline, of the picture. Then you fill in the details. Outlining helps you identify main ideas and group related facts.

1 Learn It!

To learn how to take notes, use the following steps:

1. Identify the subject and write it at the top of your page.

2. Select specific details that support the main subject and include them in your notes. Look for topic sentences of paragraphs and words in bold or italics.

3. Paraphrase the information. Putting it in your own words helps you understand the meaning of the information.

4. Condense words into a personal shorthand, such as dropping vowels ("develop" becomes "dvlp"), and use symbols ("and" becomes "+") to save time.

*In 1776 the Second Continental Congress appointed a committee to draw up a plan for a new government. After much debate the Congress adopted the **Articles of Confederation** in November 1777. The Articles, America's first constitution, provided for a new central government under which the states kept most of their power. For the states, the Articles of Confederation were "a firm league of friendship" in which each state retained "its sovereignty, freedom and independence." Under the Articles of Confederation, Congress had the authority to conduct foreign affairs, maintain armed forces, borrow money, and issue currency.*

2 Practice It!

Read the excerpt above. Then, on a separate sheet of paper, take notes on the paragraph. Be sure to consider the following questions.

1. What is the subject of the paragraph?

2. What is the main point of the paragraph?

3. What details are especially important to write down?

3 Apply It!

Read a short article from a local newspaper about a governmental issue. Outline the important information. Write a short summary of the article using only your outline.

Skills Handbook **1023**

Answers

C Critical Thinking

Making Inferences Ask: How do you benefit from describing main ideas in your own words instead of copying word for word? *(shortens the summary but also aids understanding and memory)* **OL**

R Reading Strategy

Visualizing To help students identify the supporting details in this excerpt, create a graphic organizer on the board. Put "new immigrants" in the middle with radiating connectors. Fill in the characteristics of the new immigrants as students identify them in the excerpt. *(from eastern and southern Europe, Catholics or Jews, little English, clustered together in neighborhoods)* **BL**

Summarizing Information

Why Learn This Skill?

Imagine you have been assigned a long chapter to read. How can you remember the important facts? Summarizing information means that you reduce large amounts of information to a few key phrases. Being able to summarize can help you remember the main ideas and key details.

Statue of Liberty ▶

1 Learn It!

To summarize information, follow these guidelines when you read:

1. Read through the selection. Determine the main idea and the most important supporting details.

2. A summary can be a sentence or a short paragraph that includes the main ideas. In your summary, restate the text using your own words. Be brief—do not include many supporting details.

3. For the first paragraph, a summary statement might be: By the early 1900s, immigration patterns were changing and most new immigrants came from southern and eastern Europe.

In the mid-1880s, the pattern of immigration started to change. Large groups of "new" immigrants arrived from eastern and southern Europe. Greeks, Russians, Hungarians, Italians, Turks, and Poles were among the newcomers. At the same time, the number of "old" immigrants from northern and western Europe started to decrease. By 1907, 80 percent of immigrants came from southern and eastern Europe.

Many of these newcomers were Catholics or Jews. Few spoke English. Because of this, they did not blend into American society as easily as the "old" immigrants had. Often, they clustered together in neighborhoods made up of people of the same nationality.

2 Practice It!

After reading the excerpt above, answer the following questions:

1. In a summary of the first paragraph, would you include the statement, "The number of 'old' immigrants decreased"? Why or why not?

2. Write a summary statement for the second paragraph.

3 Apply It!

Read the section titled "Citizen Participation" of the Constitution Handbook of this book. Summarize the information in two or three sentences.

1024 *Skills Handbook*

Answers

Answers

Practice It! Answers

1. Yes, because the statement is a supporting point to the main idea.
2. Summaries will vary but should include the main idea written in the students' own words.

Apply It! Answers

Summaries will vary but should include the meaning of "citizen" and the main duties and responsibilities of citizenship.

Reading a Time Line

Why Learn This Skill?

Knowing the relationship of time to events is important in studying history.
A time line is a visual way to show the flow of dates and events in the correct order that they occurred. On many time lines, the years are evenly spaced. For example, a time line showing 1,000 years might be divided into ten 100-year intervals. Each event on a time line is described beside the date when the event took place.

1 Learn It!

To read a time line, follow these steps:

1. Find the dates on the opposite ends of the time line to know the time span. Also note the intervals between dates on the time line.

2. Study the order of events.

Sojourner Truth ▶

★ **1787** States given authority to decide whether to allow slavery

★ **1831** William Lloyd Garrison begins publishing *The Liberator*

★ **1833** American Anti-Slavery Society founded

★ **1816** American Colonization Society founded

★ **1832** New England Anti-Slavery Society founded

★ **1840s** Sojourner Truth's speeches draw huge crowds

3. Analyze the relationships among events or look for trends. [S]

2 Practice It!

Analyze the time line about the Abolition movement. Use it to answer the questions that follow.

1. What time span is represented?

2. Which occurred first: the founding of the American Colonization Society or the founding of the American Anti-Slavery Society?

3. How many years after states were allowed to decide the issue of slavery did William Lloyd Garrison begin publishing *The Liberator*?

3 Apply It!

List 10 key events that have occurred in your life and the dates on which these events occurred. Write the events in chronological order on a time line.

Skills Handbook **1025**

C Critical Thinking

Identifying Central Issues Point out that sometimes all the events on a time line relate to the same theme. Create a time line on the board using these dates: *1876*—Bell patents telephone; *1879*—Edison invents electric light; *1903*—Wright brothers fly first motorized airplane; *1908*—Ford introduces Model T. Have students identify the relationship between the events and write a title for the time line that reflects its theme. Encourage them to be creative with their title. *(Titles will vary but should reflect the theme of invention or innovation.)* **BL**

S Skill Practice

Reading a Time Line Ask: What trend do you see in this time line? *(The abolition movement appears to be strengthening over time.)* **OL**

Answers

Practice It! Answers

1. about 53 or more years
2. the founding of the American Colonization Society
3. 44 years

Apply It! Answers

Students' time lines should show 10 events with dates in the correct chronological order.

Differentiated Instruction

Visual/Spatial Point out that one use of a map is to get from one place to another. Tell students that a friend is visiting from out of town and wants to ride a bike from home to school. Have students draw a map showing the route their friend should follow, including streets, turns, and any shortcuts. Have them include a key with symbols for traffic lights, stop signs, and landmarks. **ELL**

S **Skill Practice**

Using Map Skills Point out that maps often show lines of latitude and longitude. Latitude lines run east and west. They measure the distance of a place north or south of the equator. Longitude lines run north and south. They measure the distance of a place east or west of a line called the Prime Meridian. Both lines measure distances in degrees. Have students look at the map. **Ask:** What latitude line is close to New York City? *(40°N)* What does it mean? *(New York City is located about 40 degrees north of the equator.)* What longitude line is close to Boston? *(70°W)* What does it mean? *(Boston is located about 70 degrees west of the Prime Meridian.)* **AL**

Answers

Understanding Parts of a Map

Why Learn This Skill?

Maps can direct you down the street or around the world. There are as many different kinds of maps as there are uses for them. Being able to read a map begins with learning about its parts.

1 Learn It!

To understand the parts of a map, follow these steps:

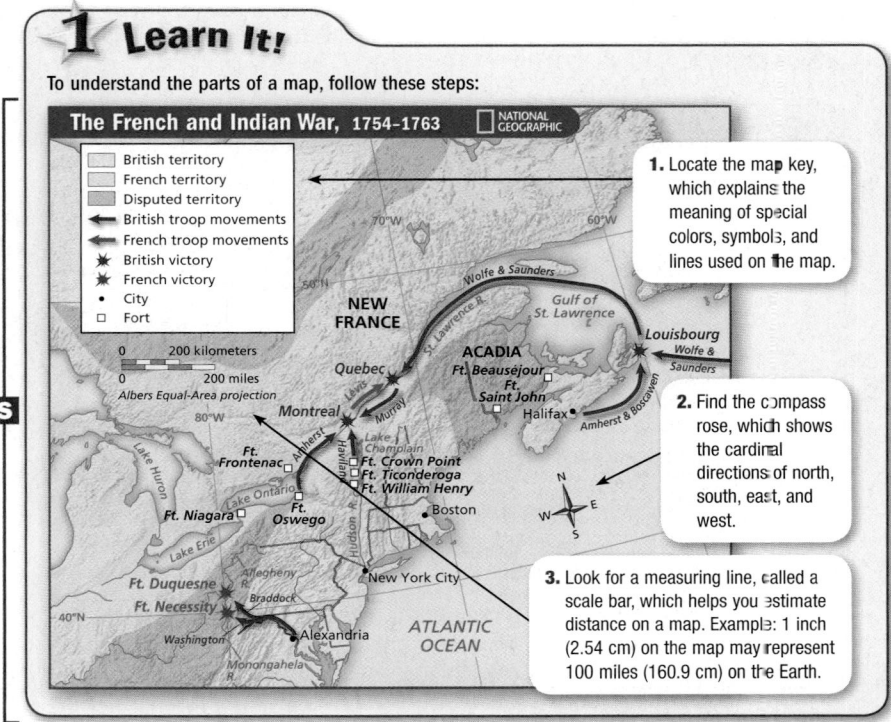

1. Locate the map key, which explains the meaning of special colors, symbols, and lines used on the map.

2. Find the compass rose, which shows the cardinal directions of north, south, east, and west.

3. Look for a measuring line, called a scale bar, which helps you estimate distance on a map. Example: 1 inch (2.54 cm) on the map may represent 100 miles (160.9 cm) on the Earth.

2 Practice It!

The map above shows the territories held by Great Britain and France in North America, as well as the battles between these two countries in their quests to control the North American continent. Look at the parts of the map and then answer the following questions:

1. What color shows the disputed territory?
2. Which direction would you travel to go from Fort Oswego to Boston?
3. About how many miles was it from New York City to Fort Ticonderoga?
4. Who won the battle in Quebec?

3 Apply It!

Create a mental image of your house. Draw a map showing the location of various areas. Include a map key to explain any symbols or colors you use, as well as a scale bar to explain the size of your map compared to the real area. Finally, add a compass rose and title to your map.

Answers

Practice It! Answers
1. purple
2. east
3. about 200 miles (321.87 km)
4. the British

Apply It! Answers
Students' maps should include a key, a scale bar, and a compass rose.

Recognizing Historical Perspectives

Why Learn This Skill?

As you study historical events or read primary sources from the past, you may be surprised by the actions taking place or the beliefs being expressed. To accurately evaluate the event or statement, you must carefully consider the time period and the experiences and viewpoints of the people involved. **c**

1 Learn It!

To learn how to recognize historical perspectives, ask yourself these questions:

1. When was the statement made? To what event or time does the statement refer, and what other related events had occurred before or were occurring at the time?

2. Who is the author or speaker of the statement? What past experiences or current considerations might influence that person's viewpoint?

3. Why is it important to think critically about historical perspectives?

An 1868 treaty was supposed to bring peace, but tensions remained and erupted in more fighting. This time the conflict arose over the Black Hills of the Dakotas. The government had promised that "No white person or persons shall be permitted" to settle on the Black Hills. However, **S** *the hills were rumored to contain gold, and white prospectors swarmed into the area.*

The Sioux protested against the trespassers. Instead of protecting the Sioux's rights, the government tried to buy the hills. Sitting Bull, an important leader of the Lakota Sioux, refused. "I do not want to sell any land. Not even this much," *he said, holding a pinch of dust.*

2 Practice It!

Read the excerpt above and answer the following questions:

1. What conflict is being discussed in the excerpt above?

2. What past events and beliefs may have influenced Sitting Bull's statement? How did white and Native American beliefs about land differ at that time?

3. How does recognizing historical perspectives help you better understand the events and statements related to a historical period?

3 Apply It!

Look in a current newspaper or newsmagazine to find an example of a conflict between two or more groups of people. Write a short summary of how their perspectives of each other have determined their historical and current relationships.

C Critical Thinking

Drawing Conclusions Ask: Why might different people give conflicting accounts of the same event? *(Any historical account reflects the viewpoint of the person telling it. Because no two people have the exact same personal experience, they will communicate different perspectives.)* **OL**

S Skill Practice

Identifying Points of View Ask: How might Native Americans have viewed this promise by the government? *(possibly as a treaty or an agreement entered into by honorable men)* How might white settlers have viewed this promise? *(possibly as a violation of their right to go wherever they wanted)* **OL**

Answers

Practice It! Answers

1. Conflict between white settlers in the Black Hills and Native Americans who lived there

2. Possible answer: Native Americans probably thought the white settlers were bullies who were taking what rightfully belonged to the Native Americans. The white settlers might have thought the Native Americans were not using the land to its fullest advantage.

3. Possible answer: By recognizing the different perspectives, we can see why the conflict between Native Americans and white settlers occurred and eventually influenced the course of history for these two groups.

Apply It! Answers

Students should read a news article that presents a conflict between groups. They should summarize how different perspectives led to the conflicting relationships between the groups involved.

Skills Handbook

Analyzing News Media

Why Learn This Skill?

C Every citizen needs to be aware of current issues and events to make good decisions when exercising citizenship rights. To get an accurate profile of current events, you must learn to think critically about the news.

Herbert Hoover ▶

1 Learn It!

The following steps will help you think critically:

1. Think about the source of the news story. Reports that reveal sources are more reliable than those that do not. If you know the sources, you can evaluate them for reliability and bias.

2. Many news stories also interpret events. Such analyses may reflect a reporter's biases. Look for biases as you read or listen to news stories.

3. Ask yourself whether the news is even-handed and thorough. Is it reported on the scene or secondhand? Does it represent both sides of an issue?

AIM TO PACK COURT, DECLARES HOOVER

President Roosevelt's message to Congress asking for authority to appoint new Federal judges whenever existing ones were over 70 years old was characterized last night by Herbert Hoover, his predecessor in the White House, as a proposal for "packing" the Supreme Court to get through New Deal measures. . . .

"The Supreme Court has proved many of the New Deal proposals as unconstitutional. Instead of the ample alternatives of the Constitution by which these proposals could be submitted to the people through constitutional amendment, it is now proposed to make changes by 'packing' the Supreme Court. It has the implication of subordination of the court to the personal power of the Executive."

2 Practice It!

The excerpt above is from the *New York Times* newspaper of February 6, 1937. Read the passage; then answer the following questions:

1. What point is the article trying to make?
2. Is the article reporting something on the scene or secondhand?
3. Does the article reflect bias or strong opinion about the issue?
4. Is only one side of the issue presented? Explain.

3 Apply It!

Think of a current issue in the news that is controversial or in which public opinion is divided. Read newspaper features and editorials and watch television reports on the issue. Can you identify biases? Which reports more fairly represent the issue and the solutions? Which reports are the most reliable?

Analyzing Primary and Secondary Sources 🄡

Why Learn This Skill?

To determine what happened in the past, historians do some detective work. They comb through bits of written and illustrated evidence from the past to reconstruct events. These bits of evidence are called *primary sources*. They are records of events made by people who witnessed them. Primary sources include letters, diaries, photographs, newspaper articles, and legal documents.

This textbook, like many other history books, is a secondary source. It was written by using primary sources to explain the topics covered. The value of a secondary source depends on how well the author has used primary sources. Learning to analyze secondary sources will help you figure out whether they are presenting topics completely and accurately.

Dr. Martin Luther King, Jr. ▶

1 Learn It!

To analyze a **primary source**, follow these steps:

We have waited for more than 340 years for our constitutional and God-given rights . . . [W]e still creep at horse and buggy pace toward gaining a cup of coffee at a lunch counter. Perhaps it is easy for those who have never felt the stinging darts of segregation to say, 'Wait.'. . . Let us all hope that the dark clouds of racial prejudice will soon pass away.
—Dr. Martin Luther King, Jr.
Letter from Birmingham Jail, April 1963

1. Identify the author, the publication, or the document.

2. Determine when and where the document was written or illustrated.

3. Read the document or study the illustration for its content. Try to answer the five "W" questions:
Whom is it about?
What is it about?
When did it happen?
Where did it happen?
Why did it happen?

2 Practice It!

The primary source above is a small part of a letter written by civil rights leader Dr. Martin Luther King, Jr., while he was in an Alabama jail.

1. When was the letter written?

2. To whom do you think the letter was written?

3. Why do you think Dr. King wrote the letter?

4. How do you know this is a primary source and not a secondary source?

3 Apply It!

Find a primary source and a secondary source related to a single historical topic. In several paragraphs, compare and contrast the information presented in the two sources.

Skills Handbook **1029**

Answers

Practice It! Answers

1. April 1963

2. Students might suggest that the letter was written to white people who said that African Americans should move more slowly toward desegregation.

3. Students might say that it was King's way of expressing his frustration and urging change.

4. The words are a direct quote from Martin Luther King, Jr., and the source lines tell who wrote the words and when.

Apply It! Answers

Students should compare information presented by a primary and a secondary source on the same topic from their past.

S Skill Practice

Using Geography Skills Have students identify the type of map they would consult to find the following information: the location of the Grand Canyon *(physical)*; the average rainfall in the Dust Bowl in the 1930s *(climate)*; the main crops grown in the South in the 1850s *(economic)*. **Ask:** What information would you expect to find on a political map? *(names of nations, national boundaries, cities, large bodies of water surrounding nations)* **OL**

R Reading Strategy

Predicting Ask: What would you expect arrows to show on a map about migration? *(direction of group movements)* On a map about a battle? *(troop movements)* On a map about trade? *(water and overland trade routes)* **OL**

Analyzing Historical Maps

Why Learn This Skill?

S Historical maps show a portion of the world at a specific time in history. These maps can show physical, political, economic, climatic, or cultural information as it relates to that time period. They are useful because of the concise, visual way they present information.

1 Learn It!

To read a historical map, follow these steps:

1. Read the title to see what topic is illustrated. The specific time period is often referenced in the title.

2. Read the legend and any other text.

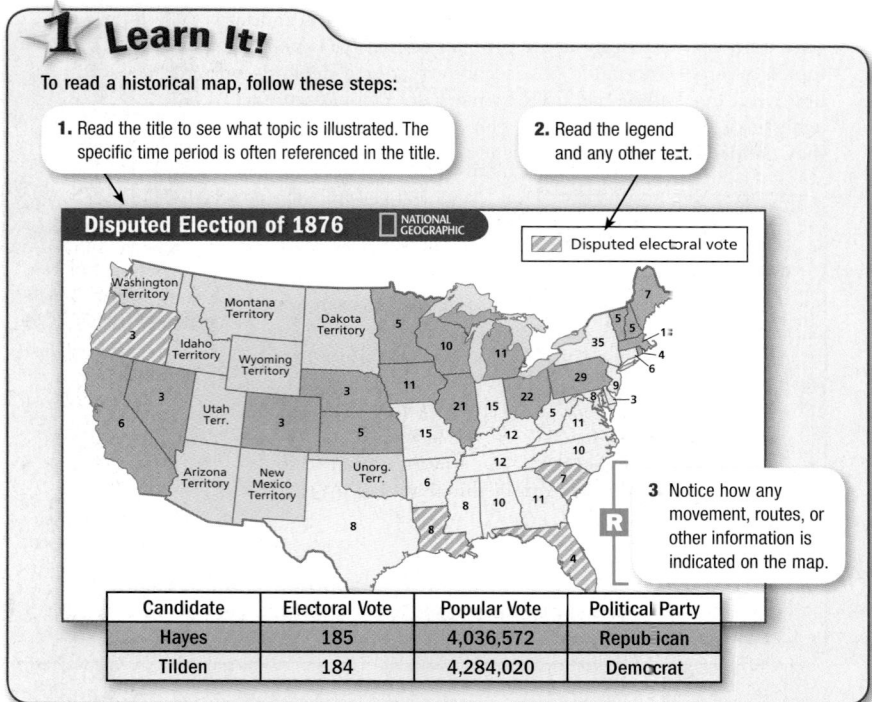

3 Notice how any movement, routes, or other information is indicated on the map.

Candidate	Electoral Vote	Popular Vote	Political Party
Hayes	185	4,036,572	Republican
Tilden	184	4,284,020	Democrat

2 Practice It!

Answer the following questions about the map above:
1. What event and time in history does the map cover?
2. For whom did most Northern states vote?
3. In which states were the electoral votes disputed?
4. Why are there no numbers for electoral votes in the territories?

3 Apply It!

Study the United States Territorial Growth maps on pages Ref 10–Ref 11 in the front of your textbook. Then answer these questions:

1. In which general direction did growth take place?
2. What time period is covered in the last map?

Answers

Practice It! Answers
1. the presidential election of 1876
2. Rutherford B. Hayes
3. Florida, South Carolina, Louisiana, and Oregon
4. People living in the territories could not vote in national elections.

Apply It! Answers
1. from east to west
2. 1850 and beyond

Researching on the Internet

Why Learn This Skill?

Imagine that your teacher has sent you to the Internet to research and write a report about the current makeup of the United States Congress. Knowing how to locate and choose sources that contain accurate and current information will help save you time. You will also be able to write a better and more accurate report.

Joint meeting of Congress ▶

1 Learn It!

Information on the Internet varies widely in its relevance and quality. Not all sources will be useful for your report on members of the Senate and House of Representatives. After choosing a search engine and typing in your topic, follow these steps to help you evaluate and select Internet resources:

1. Locate the author of the Web site and assess his/her qualifications. Is the person or organization credible and legitimate?

2. Evaluate the accuracy of the information. Are the facts on the site documented? Does the site contain a bibliography?

3. Judge whether the information is biased. Does the author present only one point of view?

4. Determine how the information is presented. Are there helpful visuals? Does the text skim the surface or offer in-depth details?

5. Review when the site was last updated. Is the information current?

6. Look for a list of links to other useful resources. Is the information on those sites appropriate and reliable?

2 Practice It!

Look at the following list of sources. Which would be most helpful in writing a report on the United States Congress? Explain your choices.

1. An online encyclopedia written by anyone who wants to contribute

2. www.senate.gov, the home page for the U.S. Senate

3. A student's notes on the Internet about a family trip to Washington, D.C.

4. A government site on Congressional documents drawn up between 1774 and 1785

3 Apply It!

Log onto the Internet to create a bibliography of six sources you might use to write your report. Explain why you would choose each source. Make sure you include information about both the House of Representatives and the Senate, including a breakdown of the membership of each.

Skills Handbook **1031**

Answers

Practice It! Answers

The most helpful choice would be www.senate.gov because it is a credible Web site maintained by the U.S. Senate. The writers of the online encyclopedia may not be screened for proper qualifications. A student's notes would not be authoritative. This government site on Congressional documents covers the wrong time period.

Apply It! Answers

Students should compile a list of six credible and relevant online sources for a report on the current makeup of the U.S. Congress. They should explain why they chose each source.

Answers

1032

Differentiated Instruction

D

Visual/Spatial Ask students to choose an issue that is important to them. They can choose a school, community, or national issue. Have students create two cartoons that portray different points of view about the issue. Display completed cartoons for classmates to interpret. **OL**

S Skill Practice

Interpreting a Political Cartoon

Ask: What symbols appear in this cartoon, and what do they stand for? *(tree: Union; branch of tree: secession; saw: the act of seceding or cutting ties with the Union)* **OL**

Interpreting a Political Cartoon

Why Learn This Skill?

D Political cartoons express opinions through art. The cartoons appear in newspapers, magazines, books, and on the Internet. Political cartoons usually focus on public figures, political events, or economic or social conditions. This type of art can give you a summary of an event or circumstance, along with the artist's opinion in an entertaining way.

1 Learn It!

Follow these steps to interpret a political cartoon:

1. Read the title, caption, or conversation balloons. They help you identify the subject of the cartoon.

3. Examine the actions in the cartoon. Ask yourself: What is happening and why?

S **2.** Identify the characters, people, or symbols shown. Symbols are objects that stand for something else.

4. Identify the cartoonist's purpose; is it to persuade, criticize, or just make people think? What statement or idea is he or she trying to express?

SECESSIONISTS LEAVING THE UNION

2 Practice It!

Study the cartoon above. Then answer these questions:

1. What is the subject of the cartoon?
2. What words give clues to the meaning of the cartoon?
3. What is happening in the cartoon?
4. What message do you think the cartoonist is trying to send?

3 Apply It!

Bring a newsmagazine to class. With a partner, analyze the message in each political cartoon you find.

Answers

Practice It! Answers

1. states seceding from the Union
2. *Union* and *secession*
3. The states are leaving the body of the Union by cutting themselves off.
4. Possible response: The seceding states will fall, not the Union. The cartoonist is predicting a bad outcome for the seceding states.

Apply It! Answers

Students will work in pairs to analyze the message of each cartoon in a newsmagazine.

Writing a Case Study

Why Learn This Skill?

Have you ever wondered what can be done to help keep your community clean? A case study on environmental clean-up and recycling would help define the issue and propose various solutions to the problem.

A case study is an in-depth analysis of a particular situation or problem that could apply to a broader field. It involves thorough research and interviews to gain a better understanding of a problem and to suggest solutions. In this example, a case study might be done on the placement of recycling bins for aluminum cans to determine that action's effect on the community. This type of research tool can help both the writer and reader gain a more extensive understanding of a situation.

1 Learn It!

To learn how to write a case study, follow these steps:

1. Treat the case study like a story: introduce the problem at the very beginning of the study in a manner intended to grab the reader's attention.

3. Use short story writing techniques and plenty of dialogue to keep the narrative interesting.

2. Introduce details about the case including information on the study site, the people involved, and the central issues, in a logical manner.

4. Sum up the issue in the final paragraph. Give the reader the opportunity to come up with various positions that can be taken on the issue.

2 Practice It!

Identify a situation or event described in this book that you think could be investigated as a case study. Write a case study in which you answer the following questions:

1. Is there a problem/issue that could apply to a broader group of people?

2. What are the major issues, and who is involved?

3. What solutions have been attempted and what others could be tried?

3 Apply It!

Research to find two sources of information on the topic of banning teenagers from using cell phones while driving. Create fictional characters that might be affected by a law like this. Use your sources and your imagination to write a one-page case study on the topic.

Skills Handbook **1033**

W Writing Support

Narrative Writing Have students do research on environmental cleanup and recycling. From their research on this broad topic, they should choose a more specific topic as the focus for a case study. Have them write a one- or two-page case study on the topic. **OL**

C Critical Thinking

Identifying Central Issues Point out that a case study can help the writer as well as the reader gain a better understanding of the issues. Have the class discuss what they learned about environmental clean-up and recycling from writing their case studies. **OL**

Answers

Practice It! Answers

Students will write a case study about a situation or an event described in this book. Their case studies should answer the questions posed in this activity.

Apply It! Answers

Students will write a one-page case study on the topic of banning teenagers from using cell phones while driving. Their case studies should include fictional characters and information from two real sources.

Presidents of the United States

In this resource, you will find portraits of the individuals who served as presidents of the United States, along with their occupations, political party affiliations, and other interesting facts.

George Washington ⭐1

Presidential term: 1789–1797
Lived: 1732–1799
Born in: Virginia
Elected from: Virginia
Occupations: Soldier, Planter
Party: None
Vice President: John Adams

John Adams ⭐2

Presidential term: 1797–1801
Lived: 1735–1826
Born in: Massachusetts
Elected from: Massachusetts
Occupations: Teacher, Lawyer
Party: Federalist
Vice President: Thomas Jefferson

Thomas Jefferson ⭐3

Presidential term: 1801–1809
Lived: 1743–1826
Born in: Virginia
Elected from: Virginia
Occupations: Planter, Lawyer
Party: Republican**
Vice Presidents: Aaron Burr,
    George Clinton

James Madison ⭐4

Presidential term: 1809–1817
Lived: 1751–1836
Born in: Virginia
Elected from: Virginia
Occupation: Planter
Party: Republican**
Vice Presidents: George Clinton,
    Elbridge Gerry

James Monroe ⭐5

Presidential term: 1817–1825
Lived: 1758–1831
Born in: Virginia
Elected from: Virginia
Occupation: Lawyer
Party: Republican**
Vice President: Daniel D. Tompkins

John Quincy Adams ⭐6

Presidential term: 1825–1829
Lived: 1767–1848
Born in: Massachusetts
Elected from: Massachusetts
Occupation: Lawyer
Party: Republican**
Vice President: John C. Calhoun

Andrew Jackson ⭐7

Presidential term: 1829–1837
Lived: 1767–1845
Born in: South Carolina
Elected from: Tennessee
Occupations: Lawyer, Soldier
Party: Democratic
Vice Presidents: John C. Calhoun,
    Martin Van Buren

Martin Van Buren ⭐8

Presidential term: 1837–1841
Lived: 1782–1862
Born in: New York
Elected from: New York
Occupation: Lawyer
Party: Democratic
Vice President: Richard M.
    Johnson

William H. Harrison ⭐9

Presidential term: 1841
Lived: 1773–1841
Born in: Virginia
Elected from: Ohio
Occupations: Soldier, Planter
Party: Whig
Vice President: John Tyler

*** The Republican Party during this period developed into today's Democratic Party.
    Today's Republican Party originated in 1854.*

John Tyler 10

Presidential term: 1841–1845
Lived: 1790–1862
Born in: Virginia
Elected as V.P. from: Virginia
Succeeded Harrison
Occupation: Lawyer
Party: Whig
Vice President: None

James K. Polk 11

Presidential term: 1845–1849
Lived: 1795–1849
Born in: North Carolina
Elected from: Tennessee
Occupation: Lawyer
Party: Democratic
Vice President: George M. Dallas

Zachary Taylor 12

Presidential term: 1849–1850
Lived: 1784–1850
Born in: Virginia
Elected from: Louisiana
Occupation: Soldier
Party: Whig
Vice President: Millard Fillmore

Millard Fillmore 13

Presidential term: 1850–1853
Lived: 1800–1874
Born in: New York
Elected as V.P. from: New York
Succeeded Taylor
Occupation: Lawyer
Party: Whig
Vice President: None

Franklin Pierce 14

Presidential term: 1853–1857
Lived: 1804–1869
Born in: New Hampshire
Elected from: New Hampshire
Occupation: Lawyer
Party: Democratic
Vice President: William R. King

James Buchanan 15

Presidential term: 1857–1861
Lived: 1791–1868
Born in: Pennsylvania
Elected from: Pennsylvania
Occupation: Lawyer
Party: Democratic
Vice President: John C. Breckinridge

Abraham Lincoln 16

Presidential term: 1861–1865
Lived: 1809–1865
Born in: Kentucky
Elected from: Illinois
Occupation: Lawyer
Party: Republican
Vice Presidents: Hannibal Hamlin, Andrew Johnson

Andrew Johnson 17

Presidential term: 1865–1869
Lived: 1808–1875
Born in: North Carolina
Elected as V.P. from: Tennessee
Succeeded Lincoln
Occupation: Tailor
Party: Republican
Vice President: None

Ulysses S. Grant 18

Presidential term: 1869–1877
Lived: 1822–1885
Born in: Ohio
Elected from: Illinois
Occupations: Farmer, Soldier
Party: Republican
Vice Presidents: Schuyler Colfax, Henry Wilson

Rutherford B. Hayes 19

Presidential term: 1877–1881
Lived: 1822–1893
Born in: Ohio
Elected from: Ohio
Occupation: Lawyer
Party: Republican
Vice President: William A.
Wheeler

James A. Garfield 20

Presidential term: 1881
Lived: 1831–1881
Born in: Ohio
Elected from: Ohio
Occupations: Laborer, Professor
Party: Republican
Vice President: Chester A.
Arthur

Chester A. Arthur 21

Presidential term: 1881–1885
Lived: 1830–1886
Born in: Vermont
Elected as V.P. from: New York
Succeeded Garfield
Occupations: Teacher, Lawyer
Party: Republican
Vice President: None

Grover Cleveland 22

Presidential term: 1885–1889
Lived: 1837–1908
Born in: New Jersey
Elected from: New York
Occupation: Lawyer
Party: Democratic
Vice President: Thomas A.
Hendricks

Benjamin Harrison 23

Presidential term: 1889–1893
Lived: 1833–1901
Born in: Ohio
Elected from: Indiana
Occupation: Lawyer
Party: Republican
Vice President: Levi P. Morton

Grover Cleveland 24

Presidential term: 1893–1897
Lived: 1837–1908
Born in: New Jersey
Elected from: New York
Occupation: Lawyer
Party: Democratic
Vice President: Adlai E.
Stevenson

William McKinley 25

Presidential term: 1897–1901
Lived: 1843–1901
Born in: Ohio
Elected from: Ohio
Occupations: Teacher, Lawyer
Party: Republican
Vice Presidents: Garret Hobart,
Theodore Roosevelt

Theodore Roosevelt 26

Presidential term: 1901–1909
Lived: 1858–1919
Born in: New York
Elected as V.P. from: New York
Succeeded McKinley
Occupations: Historian, Rancher
Party: Republican
Vice President: Charles W. Fairbanks

William H. Taft 27

Presidential term: 1909–1913
Lived: 1857–1930
Born in: Ohio
Elected from: Ohio
Occupation: Lawyer
Party: Republican
Vice President: James S.
Sherman

Woodrow Wilson ⭐ 28

Presidential term: 1913–1921
Lived: 1856–1924
Born in: Virginia
Elected from: New Jersey
Occupation: College Professor
Party: Democratic
Vice President: Thomas R. Marshall

Warren G. Harding ⭐ 29

Presidential term: 1921–1923
Lived: 1865–1923
Born in: Ohio
Elected from: Ohio
Occupations: Newspaper Editor, Publisher
Party: Republican
Vice President: Calvin Coolidge

Calvin Coolidge ⭐ 30

Presidential term: 1923–1929
Lived: 1872–1933
Born in: Vermont
Elected as V.P. from: Massachusetts; succeeded Harding
Occupation: Lawyer
Party: Republican
Vice President: Charles G. Dawes

Herbert C. Hoover ⭐ 31

Presidential term: 1929–1933
Lived: 1874–1964
Born in: Iowa
Elected from: California
Occupation: Engineer
Party: Republican
Vice President: Charles Curtis

Franklin D. Roosevelt ⭐ 32

Presidential term: 1933–1945
Lived: 1882–1945
Born in: New York
Elected from: New York
Occupation: Lawyer
Party: Democratic
Vice Presidents: John N. Garner, Henry A. Wallace, Harry S. Truman

Harry S. Truman ⭐ 33

Presidential term: 1945–1953
Lived: 1884–1972
Born in: Missouri
Elected as V.P. from: Missouri Succeeded Roosevelt
Occupations: Clerk, Farmer
Party: Democratic
Vice President: Alben W. Barkley

Dwight D. Eisenhower ⭐ 34

Presidential term: 1953–1961
Lived: 1890–1969
Born in: Texas
Elected from: New York
Occupation: Soldier
Party: Republican
Vice President: Richard M. Nixon

John F. Kennedy ⭐ 35

Presidential term: 1961–1963
Lived: 1917–1963
Born in: Massachusetts
Elected from: Massachusetts
Occupations: Author, Reporter
Party: Democratic
Vice President: Lyndon B. Johnson

Lyndon B. Johnson ⭐ 36

Presidential term: 1963–1969
Lived: 1908–1973
Born in: Texas
Elected as V.P. from: Texas Succeeded Kennedy
Occupation: Teacher
Party: Democratic
Vice President: Hubert H. Humphrey

Richard M. Nixon 37 ★

Presidential term: 1969–1974
Lived: 1913–1994
Born in: California
Elected from: New York
Occupation: Lawyer
Party: Republican
Vice Presidents: Spiro T. Agnew,
  Gerald R. Ford

Gerald R. Ford 38 ★

Presidential term: 1974–1977
Lived: 1913–2006
Born in: Nebraska
Appointed as V.P. upon Agnew's
  resignation; succeeded Nixon
Occupation: Lawyer
Party: Republican
Vice President: Nelson A. Rockefeller

James E. Carter, Jr. 39 ★

Presidential term: 1977–1981
Lived: 1924–
Born in: Georgia
Elected from: Georgia
Occupations: Business, Farmer
Party: Democratic
Vice President: Walter F.
  Mondale

Ronald W. Reagan 40 ★

Presidential term: 1981–1989
Lived: 1911–2004
Born in: Illinois
Elected from: California
Occupations: Actor, Lecturer
Party: Republican
Vice President: George H.W. Bush

George H.W. Bush 41 ★

Presidential term: 1989–1993
Lived: 1924–
Born in: Massachusetts
Elected from: Texas
Occupation: Business
Party: Republican
Vice President: J. Danforth Quayle

William J. Clinton 42 ★

Presidential term: 1993–2001
Lived: 1946–
Born in: Arkansas
Elected from: Arkansas
Occupation: Lawyer
Party: Democratic
Vice President: Albert Gore, Jr.

George W. Bush 43 ★

Presidential term: 2001–
Lived: 1946–
Born in: Connecticut
Elected from: Texas
Occupation: Business
Party: Republican
Vice President: Richard B. Cheney

Presidents of the United States

Supreme Court Case Summaries

CONTENTS

Brown v. Board of Education
1954

In *Brown* v. *Board of Education of Topeka, Kansas*, the Supreme Court overruled *Plessy* v. *Ferguson* (1896) making the separate-but-equal doctrine in public schools unconstitutional. The Supreme Court rejected the idea that truly equal but separate schools for African American and white students would be constitutional. The Court explained that the Fourteenth Amendment's requirement that all persons be guaranteed equal protection of the law is not met simply by ensuring that African American and white schools "have been equalized . . . with respect to buildings, curricula, qualifications and salaries, and other tangible factors."

The Court then ruled that racial segregation in public schools violates the Equal Protection Clause of the Constitution because it is inherently unequal. In other words, the very fact of separation marks the separated race as inferior. The Court's decision has been extended beyond public education to virtually all public facilities and activities.

George E.C. Hayes, Thurgood Marshall, and James Nabrit, Jr., were attorneys who argued the case against segregation in *Brown v. Board of Education.*

Bush v. Gore
2000

The 2000 presidential election was hanging in the balance as the state of Florida recounted their disputed ballots. Candidates George W. Bush, Republican, and Al Gore, Democrat, were so close in the polls that there was a manual recount of the votes.

Bush went to the Court to stop the recount, stating that it violated the Fourteenth Amendment. The Court ruled that since the manual recount had no uniform way to judge each disputed vote equally, it did violate the Constitution and had to be stopped. As a result, Bush won Florida's electoral votes and became president.

Dred Scott v. Sandford
1857

Dred Scott was taken by slaveholder John Sanford to the free state of Illinois and to the Wisconsin Territory, which had also banned slavery. Later they returned to Missouri, a slave state. Several years later, Scott sued for his freedom under the Missouri legal principle of "once free, always free." In other words, under Missouri law enslaved people were entitled to freedom if they had lived in a free state at any time. Missouri courts ruled against Scott, but he appealed the case all the way to the United States Supreme Court.

The Supreme Court decided this case before the Fourteenth Amendment was added to the Constitution. (The Fourteenth Amendment provides that anyone born or naturalized in the United States is a citizen of the nation and of his or her state of residence.) The Court held that enslaved African Americans were property, not citizens, and thus had no rights under the Constitution. The decision also overturned the Missouri Compromise of 1820, which

Dred Scott

had outlawed slavery in territories north of 36° 30′ latitude. Many people in the North were outraged by the decision, which moved the nation closer to civil war.

Furman v. Georgia
1972

This decision put a halt to the application of the death penalty under state laws then in effect. For the first time, the Supreme Court ruled that the death penalty amounted to cruel and unusual punishment, which is outlawed in the Constitution. The Court explained that existing death penalty laws did not give juries enough guidance in deciding whether or not to impose the death penalty. As a result, the death penalty in many cases was imposed arbitrarily, that is, without a reasonable basis in the facts and circumstances of the offender or the crime.

The *Furman* decision halted all executions in the 39 states that had death penalty laws at that time. Since the decision, 38 states have rewritten death penalty laws to meet the requirements established in the *Furman* case.

Gibbons v. Ogden
1824

Thomas Gibbons had a federal license to operate a steamboat along the coast, but he did not have a license from the state of New York to travel on New York waters. He wanted to run a steamboat line between Manhattan and New Jersey that would compete with Aaron Ogden's company. Ogden had a New York license. Gibbons sued for the freedom to use his federal license to compete against Ogden on New York waters.

Gibbons won the case. The Supreme Court made it clear that the authority of Congress to regulate interstate commerce (among states) includes the authority to regulate intrastate commerce (within a single state) that bears on, or relates to, interstate commerce.

Before this decision, it was thought a state could close its borders to interstate commerce. The Court affirmed, however, that a state can regulate purely internal commerce, but only Congress can regulate commerce having both intrastate and interstate dimensions.

Gideon v. Wainwright
1963

After being accused of robbery, Clarence Gideon, a poor man, could not afford to hire a lawyer. Gideon defended himself in a Florida court because the judge in the case refused to appoint a free lawyer. The jury found Gideon guilty. Eventually, Gideon appealed his conviction to the United States Supreme Court, claiming that, by failing to appoint a lawyer, the lower court had violated his rights under the Sixth and Fourteenth Amendments.

The Supreme Court agreed with Gideon. In *Gideon* v. *Wainwright* the Supreme Court held for the first time that poor defendants in criminal cases have the right to a state-paid attorney under the Sixth Amendment. The rule announced in this case has been refined to apply whenever the defendant, if convicted, can be sentenced to more than six months in jail or prison.

Hamdan v. Rumsfeld
2006

In 2004 the Bush administration began holding captured terrorist suspects at the American military base in Guantanamo Bay, Cuba. It insisted that these prisoners, as illegal enemy fighters, did not have the right of appeal to American courts. Instead, the president as commander in chief would create special military courts to hear their cases.

In 2006 the Supreme Court struck down this plan in *Hamdan* v. *Rumsfeld*. It argued that Bush's military courts, as they stood, violated both U.S. military law and international law regarding the treatment of prisoners of war. President Bush then asked Congress to pass legislation setting up military courts that met the Court's objections. Prisoners would have the right to see evidence against them, and any evidence obtained by torture would not be accepted in court. However, prisoners could be held indefinitely without trial if the military courts had determined they were being lawfully held.

In 1988 Congress officially apologized for the internment of Fred Korematsu (center) and other Japanese Americans.

Korematsu v. United States
1944

After the Japanese bombing of Pearl Harbor in 1941, thousands of Japanese Americans on the West Coast were forced to abandon their homes and businesses, and they were moved to internment camps in California, Idaho, Utah, Arizona, Wyoming, Colorado, and Arkansas. The prison-like camps offered poor food and cramped quarters.

The Supreme Court's decision in *Korematsu* v. *United States* upheld the authority of the federal government to move Japanese Americans, many of whom were citizens, from designated military areas that included almost the entire West Coast. The government defended the so-called exclusion orders as a necessary response to Japan's attack on Pearl Harbor. Only after his reelection in 1944 did President Franklin Roosevelt rescind the evacuation orders, and by the end of 1945 the camps were closed.

Marbury v. Madison
1803

During his last days in office, President John Adams commissioned William Marbury and several other men as judges. This action by Federalist president Adams angered the incoming Democratic-Republican president Thomas Jefferson. Jefferson then ordered James Madison, his secretary of state, not to deliver the commissions, thus blocking the appointments. William Marbury sued, asking the Supreme Court to order Madison to deliver the commission that would make him a judge.

The Court ruled that the Judiciary Act—the law that gave Marbury his appointment—was unconstitutional. More importantly, the *Marbury* decision established one of the significant principles of American constitutional law. The Supreme Court held that it is the Court itself that has the final say on what the Constitution means. The Court had secured for itself the power to review acts of Congress—the power of judicial review. It is also the Supreme Court that has the final say in whether or not an act of government—legislative or executive at the federal, state, or local level—violates the Constitution.

McCulloch v. Maryland
1819

Following the War of 1812, the United States experienced years of high inflation and general economic turmoil. In an attempt to stabilize the economy, the United States Congress chartered a Second Bank of the United States in 1816. Maryland and several other states, however, opposed the competition that the new national bank created and passed laws taxing its branches. In 1818 James McCulloch, head of the Baltimore branch of the Second Bank of the United States, refused to pay the tax to the state of Maryland. The case worked its way through the Maryland state courts all the way to the United States Supreme Court.

The Supreme Court declared the Maryland tax unconstitutional and void. More importantly, the decision established the foundation for expanded congressional authority. The Court held that the necessary and proper clause of the Constitution allows Congress to do more than the Constitution expressly authorizes it to do. The decision allows Congress to enact nearly any law that will help it achieve any of its duties as set forth in the Constitution. For example, Congress has the express authority to regulate interstate commerce. The necessary and proper clause permits Congress to do so in ways not actually specified in the Constitution.

Minnesota v. Mille Lacs Band of Chippewa Indians
1999

An 1855 Treaty with the United States set aside lands in present-day Minnesota and Wisconsin to several Chippewa bands as reservations at Mille Lacs but made no mention of, among other things, whether it abolished rights guaranteed by previous treaties. Minnesota was admitted to the Union in 1858. In 1990 the Mille Lacs Band and several members sued Minnesota, its Department of Natural Resources, and state officials (collectively State), seeking, among other things, a declaratory judgment that they retained their ownership rights to the land without state interference. The District Court ultimately concluded that the Chippewa retained their claim under the 1837 Treaty and resolved several resource allocation and regulation issues. The State's argument under the "equal footing doctrine," that Minnesota's entrance into the Union in 1855 extinguished any Indian treaty rights, was considered void. The Supreme Court ruled in favor of the Chippewa and the existing 1837 treaty.

In 1963 the arrest of Ernesto Miranda (left) led to a landmark decision.

Miranda v. Arizona
1966

In 1963 police in Arizona arrested Ernesto Miranda for kidnapping. The court found Miranda guilty on the basis of a signed confession. The police admitted that neither before nor during the questioning had Miranda been advised of his right to consult with an attorney before answering any questions or of his right to have an attorney present during the interrogation. Miranda appealed his conviction, claiming that police had violated his right against self-incrimination under the Fifth Amendment by not informing him of his legal rights during questioning.

Miranda won the case. The Supreme Court held that a person in police custody cannot be questioned unless told that he or she has: 1) the right to remain silent, 2) the right to an attorney (at government expense if the accused is unable to pay), and 3) that anything the person says after stating that he or she understands these rights can be used as evidence of guilt at trial. These rights have come to be called the Miranda warning. They are intended to ensure that an accused person in custody will not unknowingly give up the Fifth Amendment's protection against self-incrimination.

New York Times v. United States
1971

In June 1971, the *New York Times* published its first installment of the "Pentagon Papers," a classified document about government actions in the Vietnam War era. The secret document had been leaked to the *Times* by antiwar activist Daniel Ellsberg, who had previously worked in national security for the government. President Richard Nixon went to court to block further publication of the Pentagon Papers. The *New York Times* appealed to the Supreme Court to allow it to continue publishing without government interference.

The Supreme Court's ruling in this case upheld earlier decisions establishing the doctrine of prior restraint. This doctrine protects the press (broadly defined to include newspapers, television and radio, filmmakers and distributors, etc.) from government attempts to block publication. Except in extraordinary circumstances, the press must be allowed to publish.

Plessy v. Furguson
1896

In the late 1800s, railroad companies in Louisiana were required by state law to provide "separate-but-equal" cars for white and African American passengers. In 1890 a group of citizens in New Orleans selected Homer Plessy to challenge that law. In 1892 Plessy boarded a whites-only car and refused to move. He was arrested. Plessy appealed to the Supreme Court, arguing that the Louisiana separate-but-equal law violated his right to equal protection under the Fourteenth Amendment.

Homer Plessy lost the case. The *Plessy* decision upheld the separate-but-equal doctrine used by Southern states to perpetuate segregation following the Civil War. The court ruled that the Fourteenth Amendment's equal protection clause required only equal public facilities for the two races, not equal access to the same facilities. This decision was overruled in 1954 by *Brown* v. *Board of Education of Topeka, Kansas* (discussed previously).

Roe v. Wade
1973

Roe v. *Wade* challenged restrictive abortion laws in both Texas and Georgia. The suit was brought in the name of Jane Roe, an alias used to protect the privacy of the plaintiff.

In this decision, the Supreme Court ruled that females have a constitutional right under various provisions of the Constitution—most notably, the due process clause—to decide whether or not to terminate a pregnancy. The Supreme Court's decision in this case was the most significant in a long line of decisions over a period of 50 years that recognized a constitutional right of privacy, even though the word "privacy" is not found in the Constitution.

Tinker v. Des Moines School District
1969

During the Vietnam War, some students in Des Moines, Iowa, wore black armbands to school to protest American involvement in the conflict. Two days earlier, school officials had adopted a policy banning the wearing of armbands to school. When the students arrived at school wearing armbands, they were suspended and sent home. The students argued that school officials violated their First Amendment right to free speech.

The Supreme Court sided with the students. In a now-famous statement, the Court said that "it can hardly be argued that either students or teachers shed their constitutional rights of freedom of speech or expression at the schoolhouse gate." The Supreme Court went on to rule that a public school could not suspend students who wore black armbands to school to symbolize their opposition to the Vietnam War. In so holding, the Court likened the students' conduct to pure speech and decided it on that basis.

United States v. Nixon
1974

In the early 1970s, President Nixon was named an unindicted co-conspirator in the criminal investigation that arose in the aftermath of a break-in at the offices of the Democratic Party in Washington, D.C. A federal judge had ordered President Nixon to turn over tapes of conversations he had with his advisers about the break-in. Nixon resisted the order, claiming that the conversations were entitled to absolute confidentiality by Article II of the Constitution.

The decision in this case made it clear that the president is not above the law. The Supreme Court held that only those presidential conversations and communications that relate to performing the duties of the office of president are confidential and protected from a judicial order of disclosure. The Court ordered Nixon to give up the tapes, which revealed evidence linking the president to the conspiracy to obstruct justice. He resigned from office shortly thereafter.

Worcester v. Georgia
1832

State officials in Georgia wanted to remove the Cherokee from land that was guaranteed to them in earlier treaties. Samuel Worcester was a congregational missionary who worked with the Cherokee people. He was arrested for failure to have a license that the state required to live in Cherokee country and for refusing to obey an order from the Georgia militia to leave Cherokee lands. Worcester then sued the state of Georgia. He claimed that Georgia had no legal authority on Cherokee land because the United States government recognized the Cherokee in Georgia as a separate nation.

The Supreme Court agreed with Worcester by a vote of 5 to 1. Chief Justice John Marshall wrote the majority opinion, which said that Native American nations were a distinct people with the right to have independent political communities and that only the federal government had authority over matters that involved the Cherokee.

President Andrew Jackson supported Georgia's efforts to remove the Cherokee to Indian Territory and refused to enforce the Court's ruling. After the ruling Jackson remarked, "John Marshall has made his decision. Now let him enforce it." As a result of Jackson's refusal to enforce the Court's order, thousands of Cherokee died on the long, forced trek to Indian Territory, known as the "Trail of Tears."

President Nixon encounters angry protesters in 1974 during the Watergate scandal.

Documents of American History

The Magna Carta

The Magna Carta, signed by King John in 1215, marked a decisive step forward in the development of constitutional government in England. Later, it became a model for colonists who carried the Magna Carta's guarantees of legal and political rights to America.

1. . . . [T]hat the English Church shall be free, and shall have its rights entire, and its liberties unimpaired. . . . we have also granted for us and our heirs forever, all the liberties written out below, to have and to keep for them and their heirs, of us and our heirs:

39. No free man shall be seized or imprisoned, or stripped of his rights or possessions, or outlawed or exiled, or deprived of his standing in any other way, nor will we proceed with force against him, or send others to do so, except by the lawful judgment of his equals, or by the law of the land.

40. To no one will we sell, to no one deny or delay right or justice.

41. All merchants may enter or leave England unharmed and without fear, and may stay or travel within it, by land or water, for purposes of trade, free from all illegal exactions, in accordance with ancient and lawful customs. This, however, does not apply in time of war to merchants from a country that is at war with us. . . .

42. In future it shall be lawful for any man to leave and return to our kingdom unharmed and without fear, by land or water, preserving his allegiance to us, except in time of war, for some short period, for the common benefit of the realm. . . .

60. All these customs and liberties that we have granted shall be observed in our kingdom in so far as concerns our own relations with our subjects. Let all men of our kingdom, whether clergy or laymen, observe them similarly in their relations with their own men. . . .

63. . . . Both we and the barons have sworn that all this shall be observed in good faith and without deceit. Witness the abovementioned people and many others. Given by our hand in the meadow that is called Runnymede, between Windsor and Staines, on the fifteenth day of June in the seventeenth year of our reign.

Illuminated manuscript, Middle Ages

The Mayflower Compact

*On November 21, 1620, forty-one colonists aboard the **Mayflower** drafted this agreement. The Mayflower Compact was the first plan of self-government ever put in force in the English colonies.*

In the Name of God, Amen. We, whose names are underwritten, the Loyal Subjects of our dread Sovereign Lord King James, by the Grace of God, of Great Britain, France, and Ireland, King, Defender of the Faith, etc. Having undertaken for the Glory of God, and Advancement of the Christian Faith, and the Honour of our King and Country, a Voyage to plant the first Colony in the northern Parts of Virginia; Do by these Presents, solemnly and mutually, in the Presence of God and one another, covenant and combine ourselves together into a civil Body Politick, for our better Ordering and Preservation, and Furtherance of the Ends aforesaid: And by Virtue hereof do enact, constitute, and frame, such just and equal Laws, Ordinances, Acts, Constitutions, and Officers, from time to time, as shall be thought most meet and convenient for the general Good of the Colony; unto which we promise all due Submission and Obedience. In Witness whereof we have hereunto subscribed our names at Cape-Cod the eleventh of November, in the Reign of our Sovereign Lord King James, of England, France, and Ireland, the eighteenth, and of Scotland, the fifty-fourth, Anno Domini, 1620.

The Federalist, No. 10

James Madison wrote several articles supporting ratification of the Constitution for a New York newspaper. In the excerpt below, Madison argues for the idea of a federal republic.

By a faction, I understand a number of citizens . . . who are united and actuated by some common impulse . . . adverse to the rights of other citizens. . . .

The inference to which we are brought is that the causes of faction cannot be removed and that relief is only to be sought in the means of controlling its effects. . . .

A republic, by which I mean a government in which the scheme of representation takes place . . . promises the cure for which we are seeking. . . .

The two great points of difference between a democracy and a republic are: first, the delegation of the government, in the latter, to a small number of citizens elected by the rest; secondly, the greater number of citizens, and greater sphere of country, over which the latter may be extended.

James Madison

The effect of the first difference is . . . to refine and enlarge the public views, by passing them through the medium of a chosen body of citizens, whose wisdom may best discern the true interest of their country, and whose patriotism and love of justice will be least likely to sacrifice it to temporary or partial considerations. . . .

Washington's Farewell Address

At the end of his second term as president, George Washington spoke of the dangers facing the young nation. He warned against the dangers of political parties and sectionalism, and he advised the nation against permanent alliances with other nations.

. . . Citizens by birth or choice of a common country, that country has a right to concentrate your affections. The name of American, which belongs to you in your national capacity, must always exalt the just pride of patriotism more than any appellation derived from local discriminations. With slight shades of difference, you have the same religion, manners, habits, and political principles. You have in a common cause fought and triumphed together. . . .

In contemplating the causes which may disturb our union it occurs as matter of serious concern that any ground should have been furnished for characterizing parties by geographical discriminations. . . .

No alliances, however strict, between the parts can be an adequate substitute. They must inevitably experience the infractions and interruptions which all alliances in all times have experienced. . . .

George Washington

The great rule of conduct for us in regard to foreign nations is, in extending our commercial relations to have with them as little political connection as possible. . . .

. . . I anticipate with pleasing expectation that retreat in which I promise myself to realize . . . the sweet enjoyment of partaking in the midst of my fellow citizens the benign influence of good laws under a free government—the ever-favorite object of my heart, and the happy reward, as I trust, of our mutual cares, labors, and dangers.

"The Star-Spangled Banner"

During the British bombardment of Fort McHenry during the War of 1812, a young Baltimore lawyer named Francis Scott Key was inspired to write the words to "The Star-Spangled Banner." Although it became popular immediately, it was not until 1931 that Congress officially declared "The Star-Spangled Banner" as our national anthem.

O! say can you see by the dawn's early light,
What so proudly we hailed at the twilight's last gleaming,
Whose broad stripes and bright stars through the perilous fight,
O'er the ramparts we watch'd, were so gallantly streaming?
And the Rockets' red glare, the Bombs bursting in air,
Gave proof through the night that our Flag was still there;
O! say does that star-spangled Banner yet wave,
O'er the Land of the free, and the home of the brave!

The Monroe Doctrine

In 1823 President James Monroe proclaimed the Monroe Doctrine. Designed to end European influence in the Western Hemisphere, it became a cornerstone of United States foreign policy.

. . . With the existing colonies or dependencies of any European power we have not interfered and shall not interfere. But with the Governments who have declared their independence and maintained it, and whose independence we have, on great consideration and on just principles, acknowledged, we could not view any interposition for the purpose of oppressing them, or controlling in any other manner their destiny, by any European power in any other light than as the manifestation of any unfriendly disposition toward the United States. . . .

Our policy in regard to Europe, which was adopted at an early stage of the wars which have so long agitated that quarter of the globe, nevertheless remains the same, which is, not to interfere in the internal concerns of any of its powers; to consider the government de facto as the legitimate government for us; to cultivate friendly relations with it, and to preserve those relations by a frank, firm, and manly policy, meeting in all instances the just claims of every power, submitting to injuries from none. . . .

James Monroe

Memorial of the Cherokee Nation

The Indian Removal Act of 1830 called for the relocation of Native Americans to territory west of the Mississippi River. Cherokee leaders protested the policy.

We are aware that some persons suppose it will be for our advantage to remove beyond the Mississippi. We think otherwise. Our people universally think otherwise. . . .

We wish to remain on the land of our fathers. We have a perfect and original right to remain without interruption or molestation. The treaties with us, and laws of the United States made in pursuance of treaties, guaranty our residence and our privileges, and secure us against intruders. Our only request is, that these treaties may be fulfilled, and these laws executed. . . .

. . . We have been called a poor, ignorant, and degraded people. We certainly are not rich; nor have we ever boasted of our knowledge, or our moral or intellectual elevation. But there is not a man within our limits so ignorant as not to know that he has a right to live on the land of his fathers, in the possession of his immemorial privileges, and that this right has been acknowledged by the United States; nor is there a man so degraded as not to feel a keen sense of injury, on being deprived of his right and driven into exile. . . .

The Seneca Falls Declaration

One of the first documents to express the desire for equal rights for women is the Declaration of Sentiments and Resolutions, issued in 1848 at the Seneca Falls Convention in Seneca Falls, New York. Led by Lucretia Mott and Elizabeth Cady Stanton, the delegates adopted a set of resolutions that called for woman suffrage and opportunities for women in employment and education. Excerpts from the Declaration follow.

When, in the course of human events, it becomes necessary for one portion of the family of man to assume among the people of the earth a position different from that which they have hitherto occupied, but one to which the laws of nature and of nature's God entitle them, a decent respect to the opinions of mankind requires that they should declare the causes that impel them to such a course.

We hold these truths to be self-evident: that all men and women are created equal; that they are endowed by their Creator with certain inalienable rights; that among these are life, liberty, and the pursuit of happiness; that to secure these rights governments are instituted, deriving their just powers from the consent of the governed. Whenever any form of government becomes destructive of these ends, it is the right of those who suffer from it to refuse allegiance to it, and to insist upon the institution of a new government, laying its foundation on such principles, and organizing its powers in such form as to them shall seem most likely to effect their safety and happiness. Prudence, indeed, will dictate that governments long established should not be changed for light and transient causes; . . . But when a long

train of abuses and usurpations, pursuing invariably the same object, evinces a design to reduce them under absolute despotism, it is their duty to throw off such government, and to provide new guards for their future security. . . .

The history of mankind is a history of repeated injuries and usurpations on the part of man toward woman, having in direct object the establishment of an absolute tyranny over her. To prove this, let facts be submitted to a candid world. . . .

Now, in view of the entire disfranchisement of one-half the people of this country, their social and religious degradation—in view of the unjust laws above mentioned, and because women do feel themselves aggrieved, oppressed, and fraudulently deprived of their most sacred rights, we insist that they have immediate admission to all the rights and privileges which belong to them as citizens of these United States. . . .

Elizabeth Cady Stanton

The Emancipation Proclamation

On January 1, 1863, President Abraham Lincoln issued the Emancipation Proclamation, which freed all enslaved people in states under Confederate control. The Proclamation was a step toward the Thirteenth Amendment (1865), which ended slavery in all of the United States.

. . . That on the 1st day of January, in the year of our Lord 1863, all persons held as slaves within any state or designated part of a state, the people whereof shall then be in rebellion against the United States, shall be then, thenceforward, and forever free; and the Executive Government of the United States, including the military and naval authority thereof, will recognize and maintain the freedom of such persons, and will do no act or acts to repress such persons, or any of them, in any efforts they may make for their actual freedom.

That the Executive will, on the 1st day of January aforesaid, by proclamation, designate the states and parts of states, if any, in which the people thereof, respectively, shall then be in rebellion against the United States; and the fact that any state, or the people thereof, shall on that day be in good faith represented in the Congress of the United States, by members chosen thereto at elections wherein a majority of the qualified voters of such states shall have participated, shall, in the absence of strong countervailing testimony, be deemed conclusive evidence that such state, and the people thereof, are not then in rebellion against the United States. . . .

And, by virtue of the power and for the purpose aforesaid, I do order and declare that all persons held as slaves within said designated states and parts of states are, and henceforward shall be, free; and that the Executive Government of the United States, including the military and naval authorities thereof, will recognize and maintain the freedom of said persons.

And I hereby enjoin upon the people so declared to be free to abstain from all violence, unless in necessary self-defense; and I recommend to them that, all cases when allowed, they labor faithfully for reasonable wages.

And I further declare and make known that such persons, of suitable condition, will be received into the armed service of the United States. . . .

And upon this act, sincerely believed to be an act of justice, warranted by the Constitution upon military necessity, I invoke the considerate judgement of mankind and the gracious favor of Almighty God. . . .

Abraham Lincoln

The Gettysburg Address

On November 19, 1863, President Abraham Lincoln gave a short speech at the dedication of a national cemetery on the battlefield of Gettysburg. His simple yet eloquent words expressed his hopes for a nation divided by civil war.

Four score and seven years ago our fathers brought forth on this continent a new nation, conceived in liberty, and dedicated to the proposition that all men are created equal.

Now we are engaged in a great civil war, testing whether that nation, or any nation so conceived and so dedicated, can long endure. We are met on a great battlefield of that war. We have come to dedicate a portion of that field as a final resting place for those who here gave their lives that that nation might live. It is altogether fitting and proper that we should do this.

But, in a larger sense, we can not dedicate—we can not consecrate—we can not hallow—this ground. The brave men, living and dead, who struggled here, have consecrated it far above our poor power to add or detract. The world will little note nor long remember what we say here, but it can never forget what they did here. It is for us, the living, rather, to be dedicated here to the unfinished work which they who fought here have thus far so nobly advanced. It is rather for us to be here dedicated to the great task remaining before us—that from these honored dead we take increased devotion to that cause for which they gave the last full measure of devotion; that we here highly resolve that these dead shall not have died in vain; that this nation, under God, shall have a new birth of freedom; and that government of the people, by the people, for the people, shall not perish from the earth.

Current day photo of Gettysburg battlefield

I Will Fight No More

In 1877 the Nez Perce fought the government's attempt to move them to a smaller reservation. After a remarkable attempt to escape to Canada, Chief Joseph realized that resistance was hopeless and advised his people to surrender.

Tell General Howard I know his heart. What he told me before I have in my heart.

I am tired of fighting. . . . The old men are all dead. It is the young men who say yes or no. He who led the young men is dead. It is cold and we have no blankets. The little children are freezing to death. My people, some of them have run away to the hills, and have no blankets, no food; no one knows where they are—perhaps freezing to death. I want to have time to look for my children and see how many of them I can find. Maybe I shall find them among the dead. Hear me, my chiefs.

I am tired; my heart is sick and sad. From where the sun now stands I will fight no more forever.

Cheyenne shield

The Pledge of Allegiance

In 1892 the nation celebrated the 400th anniversary of Columbus's landing in America. In connection with this celebration, Francis Bellamy, a magazine editor, wrote and published the Pledge of Allegiance. The words "under God" were added by Congress in 1954 at the urging of President Dwight D. Eisenhower.

I pledge allegiance to the Flag of the United States of America and to the Republic for which it stands, one Nation under God, indivisible, with liberty and justice for all.

Students in a New York City school recite the Pledge of Allegiance.

The American's Creed

William Tyler Page of Friendship Heights, Maryland, wrote The American's Creed. This statement of political faith summarizes the true meaning of freedom available to all Americans. The U.S. House of Representatives adopted the creed on behalf of the American people on April 3, 1918.

I believe in the United States of America as a Government of the people, by the people, for the people; whose just powers are derived from the consent of the governed; a democracy in a republic; a sovereign Nation of many sovereign States; a perfect union, one and inseparable; established upon those principles of freedom, equality, justice, and humanity for which American patriots sacrificed their lives and fortunes.

I therefore believe it is my duty to my Country to love it, to support its Constitution, to obey its laws, to respect its flag, and to defend it against all enemies.

The Fourteen Points

On January 8, 1918, President Woodrow Wilson went before Congress to offer a statement of aims called the Fourteen Points. Wilson's plan called for freedom of the seas in peace and war, an end to secret alliances, and equal trading rights for all countries. The excerpt that follows is taken from the president's message.

. . . We entered this war because violations of right had occurred which touched us to the quick and made the life of our own people impossible unless they were corrected and the world secured once for all against their recurrence. What we demand in this war, therefore, is nothing peculiar to ourselves. It is that the world be made fit and safe to live in; and particularly that it be made safe for every peace-loving nation which, like our own, wishes to live its own life, determine its own institutions, be assured of justice and fair dealing by the other peoples of the world as against force and selfish aggression. All the peoples of the world are in effect partners in this interest, and for our own part we see very clearly that unless justice be done to others it will not be done to us. The program of the world's peace, therefore, is our program; and that program, the only possible program, as we see it, is this:

I. Open covenants of peace, openly arrived at, after which there shall be no private international understandings of any kind but diplomacy shall proceed always frankly and in the public view.

II. Absolute freedom of navigation upon the seas, outside territorial waters, alike in peace and in war, except as the seas may be closed in whole or in part by international action for the enforcement of international covenants.

XIV. A general association of nations must be formed under specific covenants for the purpose of affording mutual guarantees of political independence and territorial integrity to great and small states alike. . . .

Documents of American History

Brown v. Board of Education

On May 17, 1954, the Supreme Court ruled in **Brown** *v.* **Board of Education of Topeka, Kansas,** *that racial segregation in public schools was unconstitutional. This decision provided the legal basis for court challenges to segregation in every aspect of American life.*

. . . The plaintiffs contend that segregated public schools are not "equal" and cannot be made "equal" and that hence they are deprived of the equal protection of the laws. Because of the obvious importance of the question presented, the Court took jurisdiction. . . .

Our decision, therefore, cannot turn on merely a comparison of these tangible factors in the Negro and white schools involved in each of the cases. We must look instead to the effect of segregation itself on public education.

In approaching this problem, we cannot turn the clock back to 1868 when the Amendment was adopted, or even to 1896 when *Plessy* v. *Ferguson* was written. We must consider public education in the light of its full development and its present place in American life throughout the Nation. Only in this way can it be determined if segregation in public schools deprives these plaintiffs of the equal protection of the laws.

Today, education is perhaps the most important function of state and local governments. Compulsory school attendance laws and the great expenditures for education both demonstrate our recognition of the importance of education to our democratic society. . . . In these days,

it is doubtful that any child may reasonably be expected to succeed in life if he is denied the opportunity of an education. Such an opportunity, where the state has undertaken to provide it, is a right which must be made available to all on equal terms.

We come then to the question presented: Does segregation of children in public schools solely on the basis of race, even though the physical facilities and other "tangible" factors may be equal, deprive the children of the minority group of equal educational opportunities? We believe that it does.

. . . We conclude that in the field of public education the doctrine of "separate but equal" has no place. Separate educational facilities are inherently unequal. Therefore, we hold that the plaintiffs and others similarly situated for whom the actions have been brought are, by reason of the segregation complained of, deprived of the equal protection of the laws guaranteed by the Fourteenth Amendment. . . .

Armed guards escort African American students.

John F. Kennedy's Inaugural Address

President Kennedy's Inaugural Address on January 20, 1961, set the tone for his administration. In his address Kennedy stirred the nation by calling for "a grand and global alliance" to fight tyranny, poverty, disease, and war.

We observe today not a victory of party but a celebration of freedom—symbolizing an end as well as a beginning—signifying renewal as well as change. For I have sworn before you and Almighty God the same solemn oath our forebears prescribed nearly a century and three-quarters ago.

The world is very different now. For man holds in his mortal hands the power to abolish all forms of human poverty and all forms of human life. And yet the same revolutionary beliefs for which our forebears fought are still at issue around the globe— the belief that the rights of man come not from the generosity of the state but from the hand of God.

We dare not forget today that we are the heirs of that first revolution. Let the word go forth from this time and place, to friend and foe alike, that the torch has been passed to a new generation of Americans—born in this century, tempered by war, disciplined by a hard and bitter peace, proud of our ancient heritage—and unwilling to witness or permit the slow undoing of those human rights to which this nation has always been committed, and to which we are committed today at home and around the world.

Let every nation know, whether it wishes us well or ill, that we shall pay any price, bear any burden, meet any hardship, support any friend, oppose any foe to assure the survival and the success of liberty.

This much we pledge—and more.

To those old allies whose cultural and spiritual origins we share, we pledge the loyalty of faithful friends. United, there is little we cannot do in a host of cooperative ventures. Divided, there is little we can do. . . .

Let us never negotiate out of fear. But let us never fear to negotiate.

Let both sides explore what problems unite us instead of belaboring those problems which divide us. . . .

Let both sides seek to invoke the wonders of science instead of its terrors. Together let us explore the stars, conquer the deserts, eradicate disease, tap the ocean depths, and encourage the arts and commerce. . . .

And so, my fellow Americans: ask not what your country can do for you—ask what you can do for your country.

My fellow citizens of the world: ask not what America will do for you, but what together we can do for the freedom of man. . . .

President Kennedy speaking at his inauguration

"I Have a Dream"

On August 28, 1963, while Congress debated wide-ranging civil rights legislation, Dr. Martin Luther King, Jr., led more than 200,000 people in a march on Washington, D.C. On the steps of the Lincoln Memorial he gave a stirring speech in which he eloquently spoke of his dreams for African Americans and for the United States. Excerpts of the speech follow.

. . . There are those who are asking the devotees of civil rights, "When will you be satisfied?"

We can never be satisfied as long as the Negro is the victim of the unspeakable horrors of police brutality. . . .

We cannot be satisfied as long as the Negro's basic mobility is from a smaller ghetto to a larger one. . . .

We can never be satisfied as long as a Negro in Mississippi cannot vote and a Negro in New York believes he has nothing for which to vote. . . .

I say to you today, my friends, that in spite of the difficulties and frustrations of the moment I still have a dream. It is a dream deeply rooted in the American dream. I have a dream that one day this nation will rise up and live out the true meaning of its creed: "We hold these truths to be self-evident, that all men are created equal."

I have a dream that one day on the red hills of Georgia the sons of former slaves and the sons of former slaveowners will be able to sit down together at the table of brotherhood.

I have a dream that one day even the state of Mississippi, a desert state sweltering with the heat of injustice and oppression, will be transformed into an oasis of freedom and justice.

I have a dream that my four little children will one day live in a nation where they will not be judged by the color of their skin but by the content of their character. . . .

. . . When we let freedom ring, when we let it ring from every village and every hamlet, from every state and every city, we will be able to speed up that day when all of God's children, black men and white men, Jews and Gentiles, Protestants and Catholics, will be able to join hands and sing in the words of the old Negro spiritual: "Free at last! Free at last! Thank God Almighty, we are free at last!"

Dr. Martin Luther King, Jr.

Glossary/Glosario

Content vocabulary are words that relate to American history content. Words that have an asterisk (*) are academic vocabulary. They help you understand your school subjects. All vocabulary words are **boldfaced and highlighted in yellow** in your textbook.

········· **ENGLISH** ············   ·········· **ESPAÑOL** ············

***abandon** give up (pp. 189, 481)

abolitionist a person who strongly favors doing away with slavery (p. 425)

abstain to not take part in some activity, such as voting (p. 451)

***academy** a private high school; school that provides specialized training (p. 531)

***access** the ability to get to (p. 359)

***accumulate** collect; gather together (p. 256)

***accurate** correct (p. 647)

***achieve** accomplish; gain by effort (p. 380)

acid rain rain containing high amounts of chemical pollutants from the burning of fossil fuels (p. 1003)

***acquire** to come to have as a new or added characteristic, trait, or abilty (p. 31)

***adequate** enough (p. 983)

***adjust** adapt (p. 520)

***advocate** support (p. 790)

***affect** to influence; have an impact on (p. 617)

affirmative action an active effort to improve educational and employment opportunities for minority groups and women (p. 950)

affluence the state of having much wealth (p. 863)

Agent Orange a chemical herbicide used to clear jungle growth in the Vietnam War (p. 914)

***aid** to help (p. 161)

airlift a system of transporting food and supplies by aircraft into an area otherwise impossible to reach (p. 846)

alien an immigrant living in a country in which he or she is not a citizen (p. 269)

***abandonar** renunciar (págs. 189, 481)

abolicionista persona que apoya convincentemente la abolición de la esclavitud (pág. 425)

abstenerse no formar parte de algunas actividades, como votar (pág. 451)

***academia** escuela secundaria privada; escuela que brinda capacitación especializada (pág. 531)

***acceder** capacidad de alcanzar (pág. 359)

***acumular** juntar; reunir (pág. 256)

***preciso** exacto (pág. 647)

***lograr** conseguir; obtener con esfuerzo (pág. 380)

lluvia ácida lluvia que contiene grandes cantidades de sustancias químicas contaminantes provenientes de la quema de combustibles fósiles (pág. 1003)

***adquirir** tener una característica, un rasgo o una aptitud nueva o adicional (pág. 31)

***adecuado** suficiente (pág. 983)

***ajustar** adaptar (pág. 520)

***defender** apoyar (pág. 790)

***afectar** influir; producir un efecto en algo o alguien (pág. 617)

acción afirmativa esfuerzo activo para mejorar las oportunidades educativas y laborales de grupos minoritarios y mujeres (pág. 950)

afluencia estado de poseer mucha riqueza (pág. 863)

Agente Naranja herbicida químico usado para detener el crecimiento de la selva en la Guerra de Vietnam (pág. 914)

***ayudar** asistir (pág. 161)

puente aéreo sistema para transportar alimentos y provisiones con aviones en una zona imposible de alcanzar con otros medios de transporte (pág. 846)

extranjero inmigrante que vive en un país en el que no es ciudadano (pág. 269)

alliance a close association of nations or other groups, formed to advance common interests or causes (p. 109)

alliance system defense agreements among nations (p. 706)

*alter to change (p. 40)

ambush a surprise attack (p. 178)

*amend to alter; improve (pp. 199, 218)

amendment an addition to a formal document such as the Constitution (p. 210)

American System policies devised by Henry Clay to stimulate the growth of industry (p. 324)

amnesty the granting of pardon to a large number of persons; protection from prosecution for an illegal act (pp. 519, 954, 1005)

anarchist person who believes that there should be no government (p. 745)

anarchy disorder and lawlessness (p. 693)

annex to add a territory to one's own territory (p. 371)

*annual yearly (p. 691)

anti-Semitism hostility toward or discrimination against Jews (p. 806)

apartheid racial separation and economic and political discrimination against nonwhites, a policy formerly practiced in the Republic of South Africa (p. 960)

appeasement accepting demands in order to avoid conflict (p. 807)

*approach move toward (p. 135)

appropriate set aside funds for government spending (p. 220)

arbitration settling a dispute by agreeing to accept the decision of an impartial outsider (p. 658)

archaeology the study of ancient peoples (p. 7)

armistice a temporary peace agreement to end fighting (pp. 687, 723)

arms race the competition between the United States and the Soviet Union to build more and more weapons in an effort to surpass the other's military strength (p. 862)

arsenal a storage place for weapons and ammunition (p. 461)

artifact an item left behind by early people that represents their culture (p. 7)

*aspect category, feature, or part (p. 895)

alianza asociación estrecha de las naciones u otros grupos, formada para fomentar intereses o causas comunes (pág. 109)

sistema de alianza acuerdos de defensa entre las naciones (pág. 706)

*alterar modificar (pág. 40)

emboscada ataque sorpresa (pág. 178)

*enmendar modificar; mejorar (págs. 199, 218)

enmienda adición a un documento formal como la Constitución (pág. 210)

Sistema estadounidense políticas creadas por Henry Clay para estimular el crecimiento de la industria (pág. 324)

amnistía otorgamiento del perdón a un gran número de personas; protección para no ser procesado por un acto ilegal (págs. 519, 954, 1005)

anarquista persona que considera que no deberían existir los gobiernos (pág. 745)

anarquía desorden y falta de normas (pág. 693)

anexar agregar un territorio al territorio propio (pág. 371)

*anual cada año (pág. 691)

antisemitismo hostilidad o discriminación hacia los judíos (pág. 806)

apartheid separación racial y discriminación política y económica contra las personas de color, política que se practicaba anteriormente en la República de Sudáfrica (pág. 960)

pacificación aceptación de las exigencias para evitar conflictos (pág. 807)

*acercarse dirigirse hacia (pág. 135)

destinar designar fondos para el gasto del gobierno (pág. 220)

arbitraje resolver una disputa acordando aceptar la decisión de una persona imparcial (pág. 658)

arqueología el estudio de pueblos antiguos (pág. 7)

armisticio acuerdo de paz temporal para poner fin a las guerras (págs. 687, 723)

carrera armamentista competencia entre Estados Unidos y la Unión Soviética para construir cada vez más armas con el fin de superar la fortaleza militar de la otra nación (pág. 862)

arsenal lugar para el almacenaje de armas y municiones (pág. 461)

artefacto artículos provenientes de antiguas civilizaciones que representan su cultura (pág. 7)

*aspecto categoría, característica o componente (pág. 895)

Glossary/Glosario

assembly line a system with machines and workers arranged so that each person performs an assigned task again and again as items pass before him or her (p. 593)

***assign** appoint (p. 881)

assimilate to absorb a group into the culture of a larger population (p. 616)

***assure** to promise (p. 858)

astrolabe an instrument used by sailors to observe positions of stars (p. 31)

***author** writer (p. 421)

***authority** power to decide; power to give orders and make decisions (pp. 283, 927)

autocracy government in which one person has unlimited power (p. 716)

***aware** mindful; to have knowledge of (p. 1003)

línea de ensamblaje sistema con maquinaria y trabajadores dispuestos de tal manera que cada persona realiza una tarea asignada una y otra vez a medida que pasan los artículos frente a ellos (pág. 593)

***asignar** designar (pág. 881)

asimilar absorber a un grupo dentro de la cultura de una población más grande (pág. 616)

***garantizar** prometer (pág. 858)

astrolabio instrumento usado por los marineros para observar las posiciones de las estrellas (pág. 31)

***autor** escritor (pág. 421)

***autoridad** poder para decidir; poder para dar órdenes y tomar decisiones (págs. 283, 927)

autocracia gobierno en el que todo el poder se concentra en una persona (pág. 716)

***conciente** atento; tener conocimiento de (pág. 1003)

B

backcountry a region of hills and forests west of the Tidewater (p. 94)

balance of power the distribution of power among nations so that no single nation can dominate or interfere with another (pp. 706, 943)

bankruptcy the condition of being unable to pay one's debts; one's property is managed or sold to pay those to whom one owes money (p. 981)

barrio a Spanish-speaking neighborhood in a city (p. 668)

***behalf** in the interest of (p. 646)

***bias** prejudice; unbalanced view or consideration (p. 665)

bicameral consisting of two houses, or chambers, especially in a legislature (p. 187)

black codes laws passed in the South just after the Civil War aimed at controlling freedmen and enabling plantation owners to exploit African American workers (p. 523)

blacklist list of persons who are disapproved of and are punished, such as by being refused jobs (p. 848)

blitzkrieg name given to the sudden, violent offensive attacks the Germans used during World War II; "lightning war" (p. 809)

zona rural región de colinas y bosques al oeste de Tidewater (pág. 94)

equilibrio de poderes distribución de poderes entre las naciones de tal manera que ninguna de las naciones pueda dominar a otra o interferir entre sí (págs. 706, 943)

bancarrota condición en la que una persona no puede pagar sus deudas; la propiedad de una persona se vende o administra con el fin de pagar a las personas a las que le debe dinero (pág. 981)

barrio vecindario de habla hispana en una ciudad (pág. 668)

***en nombre de** en beneficio de (pág. 646)

***parcialidad** prejuicio; punto de vista o consideración tendenciosa (pág. 665)

bicameral que consiste en dos cámaras, en especial en una asamblea legislativa (pág. 187)

códigos negros leyes aprobadas en el Sur después de la Guerra Civil que apuntaban al control de los libertos y permitían que los dueños de plantaciones explotaran a los trabajadores afroamericanos (pág. 523)

lista negra lista de personas a las que se rechazaba y castigaba, por ejemplo, al negarles empleos (pág. 848)

blitzkrieg nombre que se da a los ataques repentinos, violentos y ofensivos que los alemanes realizaban durante la Segunda Guerra Mundial: "guerra relámpago" (pág. 809)

Glossary/Glosario

blockade cut off an area by means of troops or warships to stop supplies or people from coming in or going out; to close off a country's ports (pp. 170, 477, 908)

bond a note issued by the government, which promises to pay off a loan with interest (p. 256)

boomtown a community experiencing a sudden growth in business or population (p. 379)

border ruffian Missourian who traveled in armed groups to vote in Kansas's election during the mid-1850s (p. 455)

border state state between the North and the South that was divided over whether to stay in the Union or join the Confederacy (p. 475)

bounty money given as a reward, such as to encourage enlistment in the army (p. 496)

boycott to refuse to buy items from a particular country (p. 125); to refuse to use in order to show disapproval or force acceptance of one's terms (p. 878)

*****brief** short in duration (p. 410)

budget deficit the amount by which government spending exceeds revenue (p. 983)

burgess elected representative to an assembly (p. 61)

bloqueo aislamiento de un área por medio de tropas o barcos de guerra para impedir el ingreso o el egreso de suministros o personas; cierre de los puertos de un país (págs. 170, 477, 908)

bono título emitido por el gobierno con la promesa de pagar un préstamo con intereses (pág. 256)

pueblo en bonanza comunidad que experimenta un crecimiento repentino en los negocios o la población (pág. 379)

rufianes fronterizos hombres de Missouri que viajaban en grupos armados para votar en las elecciones de Kansas a mediados de la década de 1850 (pág. 455)

estado fronterizo estado ubicado entre el Norte y el Sur dividido teniendo en cuenta si formaba parte de la Unión o de la Confederación (pág. 475)

recompensa dinero otorgado como premio, por ejemplo, para incentivar el enrolamiento en el ejército (pág. 496)

boicot negarse a comprar artículos de un país en particular (pág. 125); negarse a usar algo con el fin de demostrar desaprobación o imponer aceptación de los términos de una persona (pág. 878)

*****breve** de duración corta (pág. 410)

déficit presupuestario monto por el cual el gasto del gobierno excede los ingresos (pág. 983)

representante electo representante electo de una asamblea (pág. 61)

C

cabinet a group of advisers to the president (p. 253)

Californio Mexican who was one of the original settlers of California (p. 376)

canal an artificial waterway (p. 315)

*****capable** having the necessary abilities (p. 437)

capital money for investment (pp. 307, 403)

capitalism an economic system based on private property and free enterprise (pp. 307, 745)

carbon dating a scientific method used to determine the age of an artifact (p. 9)

carpetbagger northerner who moved to the South after the Civil War (p. 530)

cash crop farm crop raised to be sold for money (pp. 92, 539)

gabinete grupo de consejeros del presidente (pág. 253)

californio mexicano que fue uno de los primeros pobladores de California (pág. 376)

canal vía artificial de agua (pág. 315)

*****capaz** tener las habilidades necesarias (pág. 437)

capital dinero disponible para inversiones (págs. 307, 403)

capitalismo sistema económico basado en la propiedad privada y en la libre empresa (págs. 307, 745)

datación por carbono método científico usado para determinar la antigüedad de un artefacto (pág. 9)

carpetbagger norteño que se trasladó al Sur después de la Guerra Civil (pág. 530)

cultivo comercial producto agrícola que se vende por dinero (págs. 92, 539)

Glossary/Glosario

casualty a military person killed, wounded, or captured (p. 483)

caucus a meeting held by a political party to choose their party's candidate for president or decide policy (pp. 268, 340)

cede to give up by treaty (p. 377)

censure to express formal disapproval of some action (p. 849)

census official count of a population (p. 313)

***challenge** demanding situation (pp. 465, 479)

***channel** a trench or groove to allow the passage of water (p. 17)

***chart** to map (p. 51)

charter a document that gives the holder the right to organize settlements in an area (p. 60)

charter colony colony established by a group of settlers who had been given a formal document allowing them to settle (p. 101)

checks and balances the system in which each branch of government has a check on the other two branches so that no one branch becomes too powerful (p. 208)

circumnavigate to sail around the world (p. 41)

***civil** relating to citizens as individuals (p. 875)

civil defense protective measures taken in case of attack (p. 817)

civil disobedience refusal to obey laws that are considered unjust as a nonviolent way to press for changes (pp. 421, 879)

civilization a highly developed culture, usually with organized religions and laws (p. 11)

clan a group united by a common interest or characteristic (p. 22)

classical relating to ancient Greece and Rome (p. 30)

***clause** a condition added to a document (p. 191)

clipper ship a fast sailing ship with slender lines, tall masts, and large square sails (p. 390)

closed shop a workplace in which the employer by agreement hires only union members (p. 853)

coalition a group united for action (p. 979)

coeducation the teaching of male and female students together (p. 437)

víctima persona del ejército asesinada, herida o capturada (pág. 483)

caucus reunión celebrada por un partido político para elegir el candidato presidencial de su partido o definir una política (págs. 268, 340)

ceder renunciar por tratado (pág. 377)

censurar expresar la desaprobación formal de alguna acción (pág. 849)

censo registro oficial de una población (pág. 313)

***desafiar** situación difícil (págs. 465, 479)

***canal** fosa marina o surco para permitir el pasaje de agua (pág. 17)

***trazar un mapa** hacer un mapa (pág. 51)

carta de privilegio documento que le otorga al poseedor el derecho de organizar los asentamientos en un área (pág. 60)

colonia con carta de privilegio colonia formada por un grupo de colonos que recibieron un documento formal que establece que pueden establecerse (pág. 101)

controles y balances sistema en que cada rama del gobierno controla a las otras dos ramas, de manera que ninguna de éstas pueda adquirir demasiado poder (pág. 208)

circunnavegar navegar por el mundo (pág. 41)

***civil** relativo a ciudadanos como individuos (pág. 875)

defensa civil medidas protectoras que se toman en caso de ataques (pág. 817)

desobediencia civil rehusarse a obedecer las leyes que se consideran injustas, forma no violenta de exigir cambios (págs. 421, 879)

civilización cultura muy evolucionada, generalmente con leyes y religiones organizadas (pág. 11)

clan grupo unificado por un interés o una característica en común (pág. 22)

clásico relativo a las antiguas Grecia y Roma (pág. 30)

***cláusula** condición anexada a un documento (pág. 191)

velero barco de vela rápido con líneas delgadas, mástiles altos y amplias velas cuadradas (pág. 390)

empresa cerrada lugar de trabajo en el que el empleador contrata, por acuerdo, sólo a miembros del sindicato (pág. 853)

coalición grupo unificado para la acción (pág. 979)

coeducación enseñanza conjunta de hombres y mujeres (pág. 437)

Glossary/Glosario

cold war a struggle over political differences between nations carried on by methods short of war (p. 846)

*collapse break down (p. 775)

collective bargaining discussion between an employer and union representatives of workers over wages, hours, and working conditions (p. 605)

Columbian Exchange exchange of goods, ideas, and people between Europe and the Americas (p. 51)

*commission a group of persons directed to perform some duty (p. 536)

committee of correspondence an organization that spread political ideas through the colonies (p. 128)

*community group of people living in a particular place (p. 396)

*complex complicated; highly detailed (p. 11)

compromise agreement between two or more sides in which each side gives up some of what it wants (p. 200)

*concentrate to focus one's effort on something (p. 821)

concentration camps prison camps used to hold people for political reasons (p. 825)

*conclude decide (p. 859)

concurrent powers powers shared by the states and the federal government (p. 216)

*conduct to direct the course of (p. 920)

Conestoga wagon large, broad-wheeled, canvas-covered wagon used by western settlers (p. 281)

*conflict disagreement (p. 279); war or prolonged struggle (p. 832)

Congress the legislative, or law-making, branch of government (p. 219)

conquistador Spanish explorer in the Americas in the 1500s (p. 43)

conscientious objector person who refuses military service on the basis of moral or religious beliefs (p. 920)

*consent agree to (p. 723)

*consequence result or effect of (p. 402)

conservation the protection and preservation of natural resources (p. 659)

guerra fría lucha por diferencias políticas entre las naciones llevada a cabo a través de métodos no bélicos (pág. 846)

*colapsar derrumbar (pág. 775)

negociación colectiva discusión entre un empleador y los representantes del sindicato de los trabajadores acerca de los sueldos, las horas y las condiciones de trabajo (pág. 605)

Intercambio Colombino intercambio de mercancías, ideas y gente entre Europa y las Américas (pág. 51)

*comisión grupo de personas dirigidas para realizar tareas (pág. 536)

comité de correspondencia organización que divulga ideas políticas a través de las colonias (pág. 128)

*comunidad grupo de personas que viven en un lugar en particular (pág. 396)

*complejo complicado; sumamente detallado (pág. 11)

compromiso acuerdo entre dos o más partes en el que cada una de ellas renuncia a algo de lo que desea (pág. 200)

*concentrar dirigir los esfuerzos a algo (pág. 821)

campos de concentración campos de prisión usados para retener a las personas por razones políticas (pág. 825)

*llegar a una conclusión decidir (pág. 859)

poderes concurrentes poderes compartidos por los estados y el gobierno federal (pág. 216)

*conducir dirigir el curso de (pág. 920)

carreta Conestoga carreta grande de ruedas anchas, cubierta con lona que usaban los colonos del oeste (pág. 281)

*conflicto desacuerdo (pág. 279); guerra o lucha prolongada (pág. 832)

Congreso rama legislativa del gobierno, o rama que dicta las leyes (pág. 219)

conquistador explorador español en las Américas en los años 1500 (pág. 43)

objetor de conciencia persona que se rehúsa al servicio militar por creencias religiosas o morales (pág. 920)

*consentir aceptar (pág. 723)

*consecuencia resultado o efecto de (pág. 402)

conservación protección y preservación de los recursos naturales (pág. 659)

Glossary/Glosario

*consist make up of (p. 883)

consolidation the practice of combining separate companies into one (p. 585)

constitution a list of fundamental laws to support a government (pp. 79, 187)

*consult to seek opinions or information from (p. 681)

*consume to use (p. 726)

containment the policy or process of preventing the expansion of a hostile power (p. 844)

*contrast large degree of difference (pp. 476, 657)

*contribute help to cause an event or situation (p. 305)

*controversy arguments between opposing viewpoints (p. 954)

*convention formal meeting (p. 198)

*convert change religious beliefs (p. 105)

*convince to pursuade (someone) that something is true (p. 523)

convoy a group that travels with something, such as a ship, to protect it (p. 719)

*cooperate work together (p. 844)

cooperative store where farmers bought products from each other; an enterprise owned and operated by those who use its services (p. 575)

corporation a business in which investors own shares (p. 596)

corruption dishonest or illegal actions (p. 530)

cotton gin a machine that removed seeds from cotton fiber (pp. 306, 401)

counterculture a social movement whose values go against those of established society (p. 919)

counterterrorism military or political activities intended to combat terrorism (p. 993)

coureur de bois French trapper living among Native Americans (p. 52)

*create to form; to make (p. 575)

credibility gap lack of belief; a term used to describe the lack of trust in the Johnson administration's statements about the Vietnam War (p. 921)

*credit a form of loan; ability to buy goods based on future payment (p. 530)

*consistir estar compuesto de (pág. 883)

consolidación práctica de combinar diferentes compañías en una (pág. 585)

constitución lista de leyes fundamentales para sostener un gobierno (págs. 79, 187)

*consultar buscar opiniones o infor mación de (pág. 681)

*consumir usar (pág. 726)

contención política o proceso de prevención de la expansión de un poder hostil (pág. 844)

*contraste amplio grado de diferencia (págs. 476, 657)

*contribuir ayudar a provocar un evento o una situación (pág. 305)

*controversia argumentos entre puntos de vista opuestos (pág. 954)

*convención reunión formal (pág. 198)

*convertir cambiar de creencias religiosas (pág. 105)

*convencer persuadir (a alguien) de que algo es verdadero (pág. 523)

convoy grupo que viaja con algo, como un barco, para protegerlo (pág. 719)

*cooperar trabajar en conjunto (pág. 844)

cooperativa tienda en la que los agricultores compraban productos entre sí; empresa que es propiedad de aquellos que utilizan sus servicios y es operada por ellos (pág. 575)

corporación empresa en la que los inversores tienen acciones (pág. 596)

corrupción acciones ilegales o deshonestas (pág. 530)

desmotadora de algodón máquina que sacaba las semillas de las fibras de algodón (págs. 306, 401)

contracultura movimiento social cuyos valores van en contra de aquellos establecidos por la sociedad (pág. 919)

contraterrorismo actividades políticas o militares dirigidas a combatir el terrorismo (pág. 993)

coureur de bois cazador francés que vivía entre nativoamericanos (pág. 52)

*crear construir; confeccionar (pág. 575)

brecha de credibilidad falta de creencias; término utilizado para describir la falta de confianza en las declaraciones de la administración de Johnson acerca de la Guerra de Vietnam (pág. 921)

*crédito una forma de préstamo; capacidad de comprar bienes en función de un pago futuro (pág. 530)

culture a way of life of a group of people who share similar beliefs and customs (p. 9)

*currency metal coins and paper notes used as money (p. 577)

customs duty tax on foreign imported goods (p. 279)

cultura estilo de vida de un grupo de personas que comparten creencias y costumbres similares (pág. 9)

*moneda monedas de metal y billetes usados como dinero (pág. 577)

derecho aduanero impuesto sobre los productos extranjeros importados (pág. 279)

D-Day the day on which the Allied forces invaded France during World War II; June 6, 1944 (p. 824)

*debate discussion by opposing points of view (p. 141)

debtor person or country that owes money (p. 80)

*decade a period of ten years (p. 1001)

*decline descend (p. 774)

decree an order given by one in authority (p. 368)

default to fail to meet an obligation, especially a financial one (p. 775)

deferment an excuse, issued by the draft board, that lets a person be excused from military service for various reasons (p. 920)

deficit the shortage that occurs when spending is greater than income (p. 951)

deficit spending the government spending more money than it takes in (p. 983)

*definite precise or well-defined (p. 997)

demilitarized zone a region where no military forces or weapons are permitted (p. 859)

*demonstration a protest march (p. 928)

*deny not allow access to (p. 664)

deport to send out of a country aliens who are considered dangerous (pp. 745, 1005)

depreciate to fall in value (p. 191)

depression a period of low economic activity and widespread unemployment (pp. 195, 350)

deregulation the act of cutting the restrictions and regulations that government places on business (p. 972)

desegregation ending the practice of separating or isolating people of different races (p. 855)

desert to leave without permission (p. 162)

*design a plan or course of action (p. 106)

Día D el día en que las fuerzas de los Aliados invadieron Francia el 6 de junio de 1944, durante la Segunda Guerra Mundial (pág. 824)

*debate discusión al oponer puntos de vista (pág. 141)

deudor persona o país que debe dinero (pág. 80)

*década período de diez años (pág. 1001)

*decaer declinar (pág. 774)

decreto orden otorgada por una autoridad (pág. 368)

incumplimiento no cumplir con una obligación, especialmente del tipo financiero (pág. 775)

prórroga excusa, emitida por la junta de reclutamietno que le permite a una persona excusarse del servicio militar por diferentes motivos (pág. 920)

déficit carencia que se produce cuando el gasto es mayor que el ingreso (pág. 951)

gastos déficitarios el gobierno gasta más dinero que el que tiene (pág. 983)

*definitivo decisivo o bien definido (pág. 997)

zona desmilitarizada región donde se prohíben fuerzas o armas militares (pág. 859)

*demonstración una marcha de protesta (pág. 928)

*negar no permitir el acceso a (pág. 664)

deportar sacar del país a los extranjeros que son considerados peligrosos (págs. 745, 1005)

desvalorizar reducir el valor (pág. 191)

depresión período de actividad económica baja y desempleo generalizado (págs. 195, 350)

desregulación acción de reducir las restricciones y las regulaciones que el gobierno impone en el comercio (pág. 972)

abolición de la segregación finalización de la práctica de separar o aislar personas de diferentes razas (pág. 855)

desertar abandonar sin permiso (pág. 162)

*diseño plan o instrucciones para realizar algo (pág. 106)

Glossary/Glosario

*detect uncover or discover the true character of (p. 752)

détente a policy which attempts to relax or ease tensions between nations (p. 943)

*device instrument or piece of equipment (p. 759)

*devote to commit by a solemn act (p. 39)

dictator a leader who rules with total authority, often in a cruel or brutal manner (p. 805)

*dimension aspect; one element or factor among many (p. 709)

*diminish to lessen the authority, dignity, or reputation of (p. 222)

disarmament removal of weapons (p. 812)

*discriminate to treat unfairly (p. 875)

discrimination unfair treatment of a group; unequal treatment because of a person's race, religion, ethnic background, or place of birth (pp. 396, 663, 875)

dissent disagreement with or opposition to an opinion (pp. 65, 727)

*distribute give out (p. 493)

*diverse differing from one another (p. 896)

dividend a stockholder's share of a company's profits, usually as a cash payment (p. 596)

dollar diplomacy a policy of joining the business interests of a country with its diplomatic interests abroad (p. 694)

*domestic home-based, internal (p. 852)

downsize the practice of companies laying off workers to become more efficient and to increase their earnings (p. 981)

draft the selection of persons for military service (p. 496)

dry farming a way of farming dry land in which seeds are planted deep in ground where there is some moisture (p. 565)

*dynamic active and energetic (p. 747)

*detectar revelar o descubrir el carácter real de (pág. 752)

détente política que se dirige a distender o aliviar las tensiones entre las naciones (pág. 943)

*dispositivo instrumento o pieza de un equipo (pág. 759)

*dedicarse comprometerse por un acto solemne (pág. 39)

dictador líder que gobierna con autoridad total, en general de forma atroz y cruel (pág. 805)

*dimensión aspecto; elemento o factor entre varios (pág. 709)

*aminorar disminuir la autoridad, la dignidad o la reputación de (pág. 222)

desarme eliminación de las armas (pág. 812)

*discriminar tratar injustamente (pág. 875)

discriminación trato injusto de un grupo; trato desigual debido a la raza, la religión, el origen étnico o el lugar de nacimiento de una persona (págs. 396, 663, 875)

disentimiento desacuerdo con una opinión u oposición a ésta (págs. 65, 727)

*distribuir repartir (pág. 493)

*diverso que difieren entre sí (pág. 896)

dividendo parte de las ganancias de una empresa de un accionista, en general en forma de pago en efectivo (pág. 596)

diplomacia del dólar política que une los intereses comerciales de un país con sus intereses diplomáticos en el extranjero (pág. 694)

*nacional hecho en el país, interno (pág. 852)

reducción de personal práctica de las compañías que despiden trabajadores para aumentar su eficacia y sus ganancias (pág. 981)

llamamiento a filas selección de personas para el servicio militar (pág. 496)

agricultura de secano método de cultivar la tierra seca con el que se plantan las semillas en la profundidad de la tierra, donde reciben humedad (pág. 565)

*dinámico activo y vigoroso (pág. 747)

*economy system of production, distribution, and consumption (p. 863)

effigy rag figure representing an unpopular individual (p. 125)

*economía sistema de producción, distribución y consumo (pág. 863)

efigie figura que representa a un individuo impopular (pág. 125)

Electoral College a special group of voters selected by their state's voters to vote for the president and vice president (p. 207)

*element one part of a larger whole (p. 307)

*eliminate to remove; to eradicate; to end (p. 691)

embargo an order prohibiting trade with another country (pp. 290, 946)

*emerge to become known (p. 205); to rise up (p. 890)

emigrant a person who leaves a country or region to live elsewhere (p. 362)

emigrate to leave one's place of residence or country to live somewhere else (p. 613)

empresario a person who arranged for the settlement of land in Texas during the 1800s (p. 367)

encomienda system of rewarding conquistadors with tracts of land and the right to tax and demand labor from Native Americans who lived on the land (p. 47)

*encounter to come upon; meet (pp. 127, 502)

*energy source of usable power (p. 952)

*enormous huge (p. 760)

*ensure make certain (p. 567)

entrenched occupying a strong defensive position (p. 499)

enumerated powers powers belonging only to the federal government (p. 216)

*environment the complex of physical, chemical, and biotic factors that surround living organisms (p. 605)

*equip furnish; provide with (p. 709)

escalate to increase or expand (p. 913)

espionage spying (p. 848)

*establish to set up (p. 367)

*estate property; land (p. 77)

*estimate approximate number (p. 9)

*ethnic pertaining to a group sharing a common culture (p. 74)

ethnic group a minority that speaks a different language or follows different customs than the majority of people in a country (p. 614); people who share a common language and traditions (p. 705)

*eventually in the end (pp. 374, 689)

evolution the scientific theory that humans and other living things have evolved over time (p. 763)

Colegio Electoral grupo especial de votantes seleccionados por los votantes de su estado para elegir al presidente y al vicepresidente (pág. 207)

*elemento parte de un entero (pág. 307)

*eliminar sacar; erradicar; terminar (pág. 691)

embargo una orden que prohíbe el comercio con otro país (págs. 290, 946)

*surgir hacerse conocido (pág. 205); aflorar (pág. 890)

emigrante persona que abandona un país o región para vivir en otro país (pág. 362)

emigrar dejar el lugar de residencia o el país para vivir en otro lugar (pág. 613)

empresario persona que disponía el asentamiento de la tierra en Texas durante los años 1800 (pág. 367)

encomienda sistema de recompensa a los conquistadores con extensiones de tierra y el derecho de cobrar impuestos y exigir trabajo de los nativoamericanos que vivían en el territorio (pág. 47)

*encuentro topar con; reunirse con (págs. 127, 502)

*energía fuente de alimentación útil (pág. 952)

*enorme inmenso (pág. 760)

*asegurar garantizar (pág. 567)

atrincherado que ocupa una fuerte posición defensiva (pág. 499)

poderes enumerados poderes que pertenecen sólo al gobierno federal (pág. 216)

*medio ambiente complejo de factores físicos, químicos y bióticos que rodean a los organismos vivos (pág. 605)

*equipar abastecer; ofrecer (pág. 709)

escalar aumentar o expandir (pág. 913)

espionaje infiltración (pág. 848)

*establecer instalar (pág. 367)

*propiedad finca, tierra (pág. 77)

*estimación número aproximado (pág. 9)

*étnico que pertenece a un grupo que comparte una cultura en común (pág. 74)

grupo étnico minoría que habla un idioma diferente o sigue diferentes costumbres que la mayoría de las personas en un país (pág. 614); personas con un idioma y tradiciones en común (pág. 705)

*finalmente al final (págs. 374, 689)

evolución teoría científica que sostiene que los seres humanos y otras formas de vida evolucionaron con el paso del tiempo (pág. 763)

Glossary/Glosario

*exceed to be greater; to go beyond (p. 960)

*exclude shut out (p. 923)

executive branch the branch of government, headed by the president, that carries out the nation's laws and policies (p. 207)

executive order a rule issued by a chief executive that has the force of law (p. 906)

executive privilege President Nixon's belief that all White House conversations should be kept secret to protect national security (p. 953)

*expand to increase in size or scope (p. 61)

expansionism a policy that calls for expanding a nation's boundaries (p. 675)

expatriate a person who gives up his or her home country and chooses to live in another country (p. 761)

*expert person with advanced knowledge on a particular subject (p. 755)

*exploit to make use of meanly or unjustly for one's own advantage (p. 682)

export to sell goods abroad (p. 477)

*extract to remove, usually by force (p. 553)

*exceder sobrepasar; ir más allá (pág. 960)

*excluir negar la entrada (pág. 923)

poder ejecutivo rama del gobierno, encabezada por el presidente, que maneja las leyes y las políticas de la nación (pág. 207)

orden ejecutiva regla establecida por un jefe ejecutivo con fuerza de ley (pág. 906)

privilegio ejecutivo creencia del Presidente Nixon acerca de que las conversaciones de la Casa Blanca debían mantenerse en secreto para proteger la seguridad nacional (pág. 953)

*expandir aumentar en tamaño o alcance (pág. 61)

expansionismo política que solicita la expansión de las fronteras de una nación (pág. 675)

expatriado persona que se retira de su país de origen y decide vivir en otro país (pág. 761)

*experto persona con conocimientos avanzados sobre un tema particular (pág. 755)

*explotar hacer uso mezquino o injusto de las cosas para el beneficio propio (pág. 682)

exportar vender bienes en el exterior (pág. 477)

*extraer quitar, en general por la fuerza (pág. 553)

*factor contributing circumstance (p. 563)

factory system system bringing manufacturing steps together in one place to increase efficiency (p. 306)

famine an extreme shortage of food (p. 398)

fascism a political system, headed by a dictator, that calls for extreme nationalism and racism and no tolerance of opposition (p. 805)

fascist a person with extremely nationalistic views (p. 790)

*federal the national or central governing authority (p. 343)

federal debt the amount of money owed by the government (p. 973)

federalism the sharing of power between federal and state governments (pp. 206, 216)

federation a type of government that links different groups together (p. 21)

feminist a person who advocates or is active in promoting women's rights (p. 895)

flapper a young woman of the 1920s who defied conventions in her behavior and dress (p. 759)

*factor circunstancia que contribuye (pág. 563)

sistema de fábrica sistema que reúne las categorías de fabricación en un solo lugar para aumentar la eficiencia (pág. 306)

hambre escasez extrema de alimentos (pág. 398)

fascismo sistema político, encabezado por un dictador, que establece nacionalismo y racismo extremos sin permitir la oposición (pág. 805)

fascista persona con puntos de vista extremadamente nacionalistas (pág. 790)

*federal autoridad del gobierno nacional o central (pág. 343)

deuda federal cantidad de dinero que debe un gobierno (pág. 973)

federalismo posesión conjunta del poder entre los gobiernos centrales y estatales (págs. 206, 216)

federación tipo de gobierno que une a diferentes grupos (pág. 21)

feminista persona que defiende los derechos de la mujer o participa en su promoción (pág. 895)

joven moderna mujer joven de la década de 1920 que desafiaba las convenciones en su conducta y forma de vestir (pág. 759)

flexible response a plan that used special military units to fight guerrilla wars (p. 905)

forty-niner person who went to California during the gold rush of 1849 (p. 379)

***found** establish or set up (p. 46)

free enterprise the freedom of private businesses to operate competitively for profit with minimal government regulation (p. 307)

free trade the absence of trade barriers so that goods flow freely among countries (p. 1002)

frigate small warship (p. 295)

fugitive runaway or trying to run away (p. 451)

***function** operate (p. 75)

***fund** source of money (p. 812)

fundamentalist a person who believes in the literal meaning of religious texts and follows strict obedience to religious laws (pp. 962, 992)

Fundamental Orders of Connecticut the first written plan for a government in America (p. 68)

respuesta flexible plan que usaba unidades militares especiales para pelear en guerras de guerrillas (pág. 905)

hombres del cuarenta y nueve persona que se trasladó a California durante la Fiebre del Oro de 1849 (pág. 379)

***fundar** instaurar o establecer (pág. 46)

libre empresa libertad de los negocios privados de operar de forma competitiva para obtener ganancias con regulación gubernamental mínima (pág. 307)

libre comercio ausencia de barreras comerciales de modo que los bienes circulan libremente entre los países (pág. 1002)

fragata buque de guerra pequeño (pág. 295)

fugitivo persona que huye o trata de huir (pág. 451)

***funcionar** operar (pág. 75)

***fondo** fuente de dinero (pág. 812)

***fundamentalista** persona que cree en el significado literal de los textos religiosos y obedece estrictamente las leyes religiosas (págs. 962, 992)

Órdenes Fundamentales de Connecticut primer plan escrito para un gobierno de Estados Unidos (pág. 68)

G

***generate** create (p. 782)

genocide the deliberate destruction of a racial, political, or cultural group (p. 825)

globalism the idea that the world's economies and societies are all part of one big system (p. 1001)

global warming a steady increase in average world temperatures (p. 1004)

***globe** the planet Earth (p. 51)

***goal** aim or purpose (p. 297)

grandfather clause a clause that allowed individuals who did not pass the literacy test to vote if their fathers or grandfathers had voted before Reconstruction began; an exception to a law based on preexisting circumstances (p. 539)

***grant** special priviledge or authority (p. 43)

grassroots movement people at the local level organizing for political action (p. 983)

greenback a piece of U.S. paper money first issued by the North during the Civil War (p. 497)

***generar** crear (pág. 782)

genocidio destrucción deliberada de un grupo racial, político o cultural (pág. 825)

globalismo idea de que las economías y las sociedades de todo el mundo forman parte de un gran sistema (pág. 1001)

calentamiento global aumento continuo de las temperaturas promedio en el mundo (pág. 1004)

***mundo** planeta Tierra (pág. 51)

***meta** objetivo o propósito (pág. 297)

cláusula del abuelo cláusula que permitía que los individuos que no aprobaban la prueba de alfabetización pudieran votar si sus padres o abuelos habían votado antes de que se iniciara la Reconstrucción; una excepción a la ley basada en circunstancias preexistentes (pág. 539)

***concesión** privilegio o autoridad especial (pág. 43)

movimiento de las bases personas en una comunidad que se organizan para la acción política (pág. 983)

verdes billete estadounidense emitido por primera vez por el Norte durante la Guerra Civil (pág. 497)

Glossary/Glosario

gross domestic product the value of all the goods and services produced in a nation during a one-year period (p. 985)

gross national product the total value of all goods and services produced by a nation's residents during a year, regardless of where production takes place (p. 755)

guerrilla tactics referring to surprise attacks or raids rather than organized warfare (p. 347)

guerrilla warfare a hit-and-run technique used in fighting a war; fighting by small bands of warriors using tactics such as sudden ambushes (pp. 172, 905)

producto interno bruto valor de todos los bienes y servicios producidos por una nación en un año (pág. 985)

producto nacional bruto valor total de bienes y servicios producidos por los residentes de una nación en un año, independientemente del lugar donde se realiza la producción (pág. 755)

tácticas de guerrilla se refiere a ataques sorpresa en lugar de técnicas militares organizadas (pág. 347)

guerra de guerrillas técnica de golpear y huir que se usaba para pelear una guerra; lucha de pequeños grupos de guerreros que usaban tácticas como emboscadas repentinas (págs. 172, 905)

habeas corpus a legal order for an inquiry to determine whether a person has been lawfully imprisoned (p. 495)

headright a 50-acre grant of land given to colonial settlers who paid their own way (p. 61)

hieroglyphics an ancient form of writing using symbols and pictures to represent words, sounds, and concepts (p. 12)

Holocaust the name given to the mass slaughter of Jews and other groups by the Nazis during World War II (p. 827)

homestead to acquire a piece of U.S. public land by living on and cultivating it (p. 563)

human rights rights regarded as belonging to all persons, such as freedom from unlawful imprisonment, torture, and execution (p. 960)

hábeas corpus orden legal para una indagación con el fin de determinar si una persona ha sido arrestada injustamente (pág. 495)

interés concesión de 50 acres de tierra que se les dio a los colonos que pagaron a su manera (pág. 61)

jeroglíficos forma antigua de escritura con el uso de símbolos e imágenes para representar palabras, sonidos y conceptos (pág. 12)

holocausto nombre que se le dio a la masacre de judíos y otros grupos por parte de los nazis durante la Segunda Guerra Mundial (pág. 827)

cesión de tierras adquirir una porción de tierra pública de Estados Unidos al habitarla o cultivarla (pág. 563)

derechos humanos derechos que pertenecen a todas las personas, como la libertad de arresto injusto, tortura y ejecución (pág. 960)

*identify recognize (p. 604)

*impact effect or influence (pp. 171, 487)

impeach to formally charge a public official with misconduct in office (pp. 527, 953)

impeachment charging a public official with misconduct in office; if proven guilty before a designated court, the official is removed from office (p. 953)

imperialism the actions used by one nation to exercise political or economic control over smaller or weaker nations (p. 676)

*identificar reconocer (pág. 604)

*impacto efecto o influencia (págs. 171, 487)

impugnar denunciar formalmente a un funcionario público por mala conducta en el desempeño de su cargo (págs. 527, 953)

impugnación denuncia a un funcionario público por mala conducta en el desempeño de su cargo; si se prueba su culpabilidad ante un tribunal designado, el funcionario es destituido de su cargo (pág. 953)

imperialismo medidas tomadas por una nación para ejercer el control político o económico sobre una nación más pequeña o más débil (pág. 676)

Glossary/Glosario

implied powers powers not specifically mentioned in the Constitution (pp. 218, 266)

import to buy goods from foreign markets (p. 99)

*__impose__ to establish or imply by authority (p. 32)

impressment forcing people into service, as in the navy (pp. 263, 289)

indentured servant laborer who agreed to work without pay for a certain period of time in exchange for passage to America (p. 77)

*__individual__ person (p. 585)

*__inevitable__ unavoidable (p. 455)

inflation a continuous rise in the price of goods and services (pp. 164, 497, 851)

initiative the right of citizens to place a measure or issue before the voters or the legislature for approval (p. 647)

injunction a court order to stop an action, such as a strike (p. 606)

*__innovation__ introduce something new (p. 389)

installment buying a system of paying for goods in which customers promise to pay small, regular amounts over a period of time (p. 756)

*__institution__ an organization (p. 349)

insurgent a person who revolts against civil authority; rebel (p. 994)

integrate to end separation of different races and bring into equal membership in society (pp. 531, 876)

*__integrity__ moral character (p. 959)

*__intelligence__ the ability to understand and use knowledge (p. 651)

*__intense__ exhibiting strong feeling (p. 322)

interchangeable parts uniform pieces that can be made in large quantities to replace other identical pieces (p. 306)

interdependent rely on one another (p. 1001)

*__internal__ within a location such as a nation or state (p. 322)

internment camp detention center where Japanese Americans were moved to and confined during World War II (p. 819)

*__interpret__ to explain the meaning of (pp. 509, 675)

interstate across state lines; connecting or existing between two or more states (p. 886)

poderes implícitos poderes no mencionados específicamente en la Constitución (págs. 218, 266)

importar comprar bienes de los mercados extranjeros (pág. 99)

*__imponer__ establecer o inculpar por autoridad (pág. 32)

requisición captura de personas para el servicio militar, como en la armada naval (págs. 263, 289)

sirviente por contrato trabajador que acepta trabajar sin que le paguen durante un período a cambio del pasaje a Estados Unidos (pág. 77)

*__individuo__ persona (pág. 585)

*__inevitable__ ineludible (pág. 455)

inflación aumento continuo en el precio de los bienes y los servicios (págs. 164, 497, 851)

iniciativa derecho de los ciudadanos de presentar una medida o un problema ante los votantes o la asamblea legislativa para su aprobación (pág. 647)

prohibición judicial orden judicial para detener una acción, como una huelga (pág. 606)

*__innovación__ introducción de algo nuevo (pág. 389)

compra a plazos sistema de pago de bienes en el que los clientes prometen pagar pequeños montos en forma regular durante un período (pág. 756)

*__institución__ organización (pág. 349)

insurgente persona que inicia una rebelión contra la autoridad civil; rebelde (pág. 994)

integrar terminar la separación de diferentes razas e implantar la pertenencia igualitaria en la sociedad (págs. 531, 876)

*__integridad__ carácter moral (pág. 959)

*__inteligencia__ capacidad de comprender y aprovechar el conocimiento (pág. 651)

*__intenso__ que expresa sentimientos fuertes (pág. 322)

partes intercambiables partes uniformes que pueden fabricarse en grandes cantidades para reemplazar otras partes idénticas (pág. 306)

interdependientes que confían unos en otros (pág. 1001)

*__interno__ dentro de un lugar, como una nación o un estado (pág. 322)

campo de internamiento centro de detención donde los estadounidenses japoneses fueron trasladados y confinados durante la Segunda Guerra Mundial (pág. 819)

*__interpretar__ explicar el significado de (págs. 509, 675)

interestatal a lo largo de las líneas estatales; que conecta dos o más estados o se encuentra entre ellos (pág. 886)

Glossary/Glosario

*intervene to involve oneself in the affairs of another (p. 753)

*involve include (p. 221)

iron curtain the political and military barrier that isolated Soviet-controlled countries of Eastern Europe after World War II (p. 844)

ironclad armored naval vessel (p. 483)

Iroquois Confederacy a powerful group of Native Americans in the eastern part of the United States made up of five nations: the Mohawk, Seneca, Cayuga, Onondaga, and Oneida (p. 105)

island hopping a strategy used during World War II that called for attacking and capturing certain key islands and using these islands as bases to leapfrog to others (p. 830)

*isolate cut off or separate (p. 629)

isolationism a national policy of avoiding involvement in world affairs (pp. 675, 753)

*issue point or matter of discussion (p. 165)

isthmus a narrow strip of land connecting two larger land areas (p. 691)

*intervenir involucrarse en los asuntos de otros (pág. 753)

*implicar incluir (pág. 221)

cortina de hierro barrera política y militar que aislaba a los países controlados por la Unión Soviética de Europa Oriental después de la Segunda Guerra Mundial (pág. 844)

acorazado barco naval blindado (pág. 483)

Confederación Iroquesa grupo poderoso de nativoamericanos en la parte este de Estados Unidos compuesto de cinco naciones: mohawk, seneca, cayuga, onondaga y oneida (pág. 105)

ir de isla en isla estrategia usada durante la Segunda Guerra Mundial que consistía en el ataque y la captura de ciertas islas clave y el uso de estas islas como bases para pasar por encima a otras (pág. 830)

*aislar apartar o separar (pág. 629)

aislacionismo política nacional de evitar la participación en asuntos mundiales (págs. 675, 753)

*asunto punto o tema de discusión (pág. 165)

istmo franja angosta de tierra que conecta a dos superficies más grandes (pág. 691)

jazz American music developed from ragtime and blues with African rhythms (p. 632)

joint occupation the possession and settling of an area shared by two or more countries (p. 359)

joint-stock company a company in which investors buy stock in the company in return for a share of its future profits (p. 60)

judicial branch the branch of government, including the federal court system, that interprets the nation's laws (p. 208)

judicial review the right of the Supreme Court to determine if a law violates the Constitution (p. 279)

*justify find reason to support (p. 464)

jazz música estadounidense desarrollada a partir del ragtime y el blues con ritmos africanos (pág. 632)

ocupación en común posesión y asentamiento de un área compartida por dos o más países (pág. 359)

sociedad por acciones compañía en la que los inversores compran acciones en la compañía a cambio de una parte de sus ganancias futuras (pág. 60)

poder judicial rama del gobierno, incluido el sistema de tribunales federales, que interpreta las leyes de una nación (pág. 208)

revisión judicial derecho de la Corte Suprema a determinar si una ley viola la Constitución (pág. 279)

*justificar encontrar razones para apoyar (pág. 464)

kaiser emperor; the leader of Germany from 1871 to 1918 (p. 723)

kamikaze during World War II, a Japanese suicide pilot whose mission was to crash into his target (p. 830)

káiser emperador; líder de Alemania de 1871 a 1918 (pág. 723)

kamikaze en la Segunda Guerra Mundial, piloto suicida japonés cuya misión consistía en estrellarse contra su objetivo (pág. 830)

Glossary/Glosario

*labor to work (p. 585)

laissez-faire policy that government should interfere as little as possible in the nation's economy (pp. 278, 351)

land-grant college originally, an agricultural college established as a result of the 1862 Morrill Act that gave states large amounts of federal land that could be sold to raise money for education (p. 628)

Latino American who has come to the United States from or is descended from people who came from Latin America or Spain (p. 896)

lease to hand over property in return for rent (p. 751)

*lecture talk or speech given to an individual or a group for education or as a gentle scolding (p. 419)

*legal permitted by law (p. 409)

legislative branch the branch of government that makes the nation's laws (p. 207)

levee high walls or an embankment to prevent flooding in low-lying areas (p. 997)

*license to grant official authority (p. 397)

line of demarcation an imaginary line running down the middle of the Atlantic Ocean from the North Pole to the South Pole dividing the Americas between Spain and Portugal (p. 41)

*link join or connect (p. 13)

literacy ability to read and write (p. 412)

literacy test a method used to prevent African Americans from voting by requiring prospective voters to read and write at a specified level (p. 539)

*locate establish (p. 561)

lock in a canal, an enclosure with gates at each end used in raising or lowering boats as they pass from level to level (p. 316)

Long Drive the herding of cattle for 1,000 miles or more to meet the railroad (p. 561)

Loyalists American colonists who remained loyal to Britain and opposed the war for independence (p. 137)

lynching putting to death a person by the illegal action of a mob (p. 540)

*trabajar obrar (pág. 585)

laissez-faire **(dejar hacer)** política que establece que el gobierno no debe interferir en la economía de una nación (págs. 278, 351)

universidad con dotación de tierras federales originalmente, una universidad de agricultura fundada como resultado de la Ley de Morrill de 1862 que le otorgó a los estados grandes cantidades de tierras federales que podían venderse con el fin de reunir dinero para la educación (pág. 628)

latino americano que se trasladó a los Estados Unidos y que es descendiente de personas que provienen de América Latina o España (pág. 896)

alquilar entregar una propiedad a cambio de una paga (pág. 751)

*sermón charla o discurso dirigido a un individuo o grupo con fines educativos o como reprimenda gentil (pág. 419)

*legal permitido por ley (pág. 409)

poder legislativo rama del gobierno que dicta las leyes de una nación (pág. 207)

dique muros altos o terraplén para evitar inundaciones en áreas de baja altura (pág. 997)

*autorizar otorgar autoridad oficial (pág. 397)

línea de demarcación línea imaginaria a lo largo del océano Atlántico desde el Polo Norte al Polo Sur que divide a las Américas entre España y Portugal (pág. 41)

*vincular unir o conectar (pág. 13)

alfabetización capacidad de leer y escribir (pág. 412)

prueba de alfabetización método usado para impedir que los afroamericanos votaran al exigirles a los votantes futuros un nivel específico de lectura y escritura (pág. 539)

*ubicar situar (pág. 561)

esclusa en un canal, un cercamiento con puertas en cada extremo usadas para elevar o bajar barcos al pasar de un nivel a otro (pág. 316)

larga marcha pastoreo de ganado durante 1,000 millas o más hasta llegar al ferrocarril (pág. 561)

partidarios colonos americanos que permanecieron leales a Gran Bretaña y se opusieron a la guerra por la independencia (pág. 137)

linchamiento muerte de una persona por la acción ilegal de una banda (pág. 540)

Glossary/Glosario

*maintain keep or uphold (p. 261)

maize an early form of corn grown by Native Americans (p. 9)

*major greater in size, extent, or importance (p. 621)

majority more than half (p. 337)

Manifest Destiny the idea popular in the United States during the 1800s that the country must expand its boundaries to the Pacific (p. 363)

manumission the freeing of some enslaved persons (p. 197)

martial law the law applied by military forces in occupied territory or in an emergency (p. 929)

martyr a person who sacrifices his or her life for a principle or cause (p. 461)

mass media types of communication that reach large numbers of people, such as newspapers, radio, and television (p. 759)

mass production the production of large quantities of goods using machinery and often an assembly line (p. 593)

materialism attaching too much importance to physical possessions and comforts (p. 866)

Mayflower Compact a formal document, written in 1620, that provided law and order to the Plymouth colony (p. 66)

*mechanism mechanical device (p. 592)

Medicaid a social program that gives the states money to help those who cannot afford to pay for their hospital bills (p. 883)

*medical health; pertaining to the practice of medicine (p. 431)

Medicare a social program that helps pay for medical care for the elderly (p. 883)

mercantilism the theory that a state's or nation's power depended on its wealth (p. 50)

mercenary paid soldier who serves in the army of a foreign country (p. 155)

merger the combining of two or more businesses into one (p. 599)

MIAs soldiers classified as missing in action (p. 932)

*mantener conservar o preservar (pág. 261)

millo forma antigua de grano que cultivaban los nativoamericanos (pág. 9)

*principal de mayor tamaño, grado o importancia (pág. 621)

mayoría más de la mitad (pág. 337)

Destino Manifiesto idea popular en Estados Unidos durante los años 1800 que establecía que el país debía extender sus fronteras al Pacífico (pág. 363)

manumisión liberación de algunos esclavos (pág. 197)

ley marcial ley aplicada por las fuerzas militares en un territorio ocupado o en un caso de emergencia (pág. 929)

mártir persona que sacrifica su vida por un principio o una causa (pág. 461)

medios masivos de información tipos de comunicación que llegan a un gran número de personas, como los periódicos, la radio y la televisión (pág. 759)

producción en serie producción de grandes cantidades de bienes usando maquinaria y a veces una línea de montaje (pág. 593)

materialismo otorgarle mucha importancia a posesiones físicas y comodidades (pág. 866)

Convenio de Mayflower documento formal, redactado en 1620, que le otorgó ley y orden a la colonia de Plymouth (pág. 66)

*mecanismo dispositivo mecánico (pág. 592)

Medicaid programa social que le otorga al estado dinero para ayudar a las personas que no pueden pagar sus gastos hospitalarios (pág. 883)

*médico salud; perteneciente a la práctica de la medicina (pág. 431)

Medicare programa social que ayuda a pagar la atención médica de los ancianos (pág. 883)

mercantilismo teoría que sostiene que el poder de una nación o un estado depende de su riqueza (pág. 50)

mercenario soldado pago que presta sus servicios en el ejército de un país extranjero (pág. 155)

fusión empresarial combinación de dos o más negocios en uno (pág. 599)

MIAs (Desaparecidos en Acción) soldados clasificados como desaparecidos en acción (pág. 932)

Glossary/Glosario

Middle Passage a part of the Triangular trade when enslaved Africans were shipped to the West Indies (p. 91)

migrant worker a person who moves from place to place to find work harvesting fruits and vegetables (p. 788)

***migrate** relocate (p. 788)

migration a movement of a large number of people into a new homeland (p. 8)

militarism a buildup of military strength within a country (p. 706)

militia a group of civilians trained to fight in emergencies (pp. 107, 133)

***ministry** the office, duties, or functions of a minister (p. 438)

***minor** lesser in size, extent, or importance (p. 623)

minutemen companies of civilian soldiers who boasted that they were ready to fight on a minute's notice (p. 134)

mission religious settlement (pp. 46, 82)

mobilization gathering resources and preparing for war (pp. 725, 815)

Model T America's first mass production car made by the Ford Motor Company (p. 593)

monopoly total control of a type of industry by one person or one company (p. 597)

Morse code a system for transmitting messages that uses a series of dots and dashes to represent the letters of the alphabet, numbers, and punctuation (p. 392)

mosque a Muslim house of worship (p. 33)

mountain man a frontiersman living in the mountain wilderness (p. 360)

muckraker a journalist who uncovers abuses and corruption in a society (p. 647)

Travesía intermedia parte del comercio triangular cuando los esclavos africanos se embarcaban hacia las Antillas (pág. 91)

trabajador migratorio persona que se traslada de un lugar a otro para buscar trabajo en el cultivo de frutas y vegetales (pág. 788)

***migrar** cambiar de sitio (pág. 788)

migración traslado de un gran número de personas a una nueva tierra (pág. 8)

militarismo creación de fortaleza militar en un país (pág. 706)

milicia grupo de civiles entrenados para luchar en emergencias (págs. 107, 133)

***clerecía** oficio, deberes o funciones de un pastor (pág. 438)

***inferior** de menor tamaño, grado o importancia (pág. 623)

minutemen compañías de soldados civiles que se jactaban de estar listos para pelear de un momento a otro (pág. 134)

misión asentamiento religioso (págs. 46, 82)

movilización reunión de recursos y preparación para la guerra (págs. 725, 815)

Modelo T primer automóvil estadounidense de producción masiva fabricado por la Ford Motor Company (pág. 593)

monopolio control total de un tipo de industria por una persona o una compañía (pág. 597)

código Morse sistema de transmisión de mensajes que utiliza una serie de puntos y rayas para representar letras del alfabeto, números y puntuación (pág. 392)

mezquita casa de culto musulmana (pág. 33)

hombre montañés colonizador que vive en áreas montañosas naturales (pág. 360)

sensacionalista periodista que revela abusos y corrupción en una sociedad (pág. 647)

napalm an explosive material dropped from airplanes during the Vietnam War (p. 914)

national debt the amount of money a national government owes to other governments or its people (p. 255)

National Grange the first farmers' organization in the United States (p. 575)

napalm material explosivo arrojado desde los aviones durante la Guerra de Vietnam (pág. 914)

deuda nacional cantidad de dinero que un gobierno nacional debe a otros gobiernos o a su población (pág. 255)

Agricultores Nacionales primera organización de agricultores en Estados Unidos (pág. 575)

nationalism intense loyalty to one's nation or group and promotion of its interests above all others (pp. 293, 705)

national self-determination the right of people to decide how they should be governed (p. 729)

nativism the belief that those born in a country are superior to immigrants (p. 762)

nativist a person who favors those born in his country and is opposed to immigrants (p. 399)

*****network** an interconnected system of people or things (p. 453)

neutral rights the right to sail the seas and not take sides in a war (p. 289)

neutrality a position of not taking sides in a conflict (p. 262)

*****nevertheless** however (p. 501)

nomad person who moves from place to place in search of food or grazing land (p. 8)

nomadic moving from place to place with no permanent home (p. 567)

nominating convention system in which delegates from the states selected the party's presidential candidate (p. 340)

nonimportation the act of not importing or using certain goods (p. 125)

*****normal** typical or average (p. 745)

normal school a two-year school for training high school graduates as teachers (p. 420)

Northwest Passage water route to Asia through North America sought by European explorers (p. 51)

*****nuclear** atomic (p. 862)

nullify to cancel or make ineffective (pp. 270, 341)

nacionalismo lealtad intensa a una nación o a un grupo y promoción de los intereses por encima de todos (págs. 293, 705)

autodeterminación nacional derecho de las personas a decidir cómo deben ser gobernadas (pág. 729)

nativismo creencia acerca de que las personas nacidas en un país son superiores a los inmigrantes (pág. 762)

nativista persona que apoya a las personas nacidas en su país y que se opone a los inmigrantes (pág. 399)

*****red** sistema interconectado de personas o cosas (pág. 453)

derechos neutrales derecho a navegar en el mar sin tomar partido en una guerra (pág. 289)

neutralidad no tomar partido en un conflicto (pág. 262)

*****no obstante** sin embargo (pág. 501)

nómada persona que se traslada de un lugar a otro en búsqueda de alimentos o tierras para pastoreo (pág. 8)

nómada trasladarse de un lugar a otro sin hogar fijo (pág. 567)

convención nominadora sistema en el que los delegados de los estados seleccionaban el candidato presidencial del partido (pág. 340)

no importación no importar o usar ciertos bienes (pág. 125)

*****normal** típico o promedio (pág. 745)

escuela normal escuela de dos años para capacitar a los graduados de preparatoria par ser maestros (pág. 420)

Pasaje del Noroeste ruta marítima a Asia a través de América del Norte que buscaban los exploradores europeos (pág. 51)

*****nuclear** atómico (pág. 862)

anular cancelar o hacer inefectivo (págs. 270, 341)

O

*****obtain** to gain (p. 806)

*****occupy** to control (p. 127)

*****occur** to take place (p. 907)

oligopoly market in which a few large companies control prices for an industry (p. 645)

ordinance a law or regulation (p. 190)

*****obtener** lograr (pág. 806)

*****ocupar** controlar (pág. 127)

*****suceder** que tiene lugar (pág. 907)

oligopolio mercado en el que unas pocas compañías grandes controlan los precios para una industria (pág. 645)

ordenanza ley o regulación (pág. 190)

*outcome result (p. 536)

override to overturn or defeat, as a bill proposed in Congress (p. 524)

*overseas across the ocean (p. 817)

overseer person who supervises a large operation or its workers (pp. 94, 408)

*resultado desenlace (pág. 536)

anular revocar o derrotar, como un proyecto de ley propuesto en el Congreso (pág. 524)

*extranjero del otro lado del océano (pág. 817)

capataz persona que supervisa una operación importante o a sus trabajadores (págs. 94, 408)

P

pacifist person opposed to the use of war or violence to settle disputes (pp. 75, 727)

*participate take part in (p. 340)

partisan favoring one side of an issue (p. 265)

*partner associate who agrees to operate a business with another (p. 597)

patent a document that gives an inventor the sole legal right to an invention for a period of time (p. 306)

Patriot American colonist who favored American independence (p. 137)

patroon landowner in the Dutch colonies who ruled like a king over large areas of land (p. 73)

pension a sum paid regularly to a person, usually after retirement (p. 795)

*perceive to recognize; understand (p. 727)

perjury lying when one has sworn an oath to tell the truth (pp. 849, 985)

*personal income money an individual earns from labor or investment (p. 863)

petition a formal request (pp. 140, 190)

*philosophy a set of ideas and beliefs (p. 627)

Pilgrim Separatist who journeyed to the colonies during the 1600s for a religious purpose (p. 65)

pilgrimage a journey to a holy place (p. 33)

plantation a large estate run by an owner or manager and farmed by laborers who lived there (p. 47)

plurality largest single share (p. 337)

*policy plan of action (p. 68)

poll tax a tax of a fixed amount per person that had to be paid before the person could vote (p. 539)

pacifista persona que se opone al uso de guerras o violencia para solucionar conflictos (págs. 75, 727)

*participar formar parte de (pág. 340)

partidista favorece un punto de vista de un asunto (pág. 265)

*socio persona que acepta operar un negocio con otra (pág. 597)

patente documento que le otorga al inventor el derecho exclusivo legal de una invención durante un período determinado (pág. 306)

patriota colono americano a favor de la independencia de Estados Unidos (pág. 137)

patroon terrateniente en las colonias holandesas que gobernaba como un rey en grandes extensiones de tierra (pág. 73)

pensión monto pagado a una persona de forma regular, en general después de su retiro (pág. 795)

*percibir reparar; entender (pág. 727)

perjurio mentir cuando se juró decir la verdad (págs. 849, 985)

*ingresos personales dinero que una persona obtiene de su trabajo o inversión (pág. 863)

petición solicitud formal (págs. 140, 190)

*filosofía conjunto de ideas y creencias (pág. 627)

peregrino separatista que visitó las colonias durante los años 1600 para un propósito religioso (pág. 65)

peregrinación viaje a un lugar sagrado (pág. 33)

plantación propiedad extensa dirigida por un propietario o un administrador y cultivada por los trabajadores que vivían allí (pág. 47)

pluralidad parte mayor (pág. 337)

*política plan de acción (pág. 68)

impuesto de votación impuesto de una cantidad fija por persona que debía pagarse para que una persona pudiera votar (pág. 539)

pool a group sharing in some activity, for example, among railroad barons who made secret agreements and set rates among themselves (p. 587)

popular sovereignty political theory that government is subject to the will of the people (p. 215); before the Civil War, the idea that people living in a territory had the right to decide by voting if slavery would be allowed there (p. 454)

*pose to present (p. 845)

poverty line a level of personal or family income below which one is classified as poor according to government standards (p. 883)

prairie schooner a covered wagon used by pioneers in cross-country travel (p. 362)

preamble the introduction to a formal document, especially the Constitution (pp. 142, 215)

precedent a tradition (p. 253)

prejudice an unfair opinion not based on facts (p. 396)

*previous earlier, coming before (p. 155)

*primary an election in which voters choose their party's candidates (p. 660)

*principal most important (p. 93)

*principle basic or fundamental reason, truth, or law (p. 270)

*prior earlier or before (p. 993)

privateer armed private ship licensed to attack merchant ships (pp. 170, 296)

*proceed continue on (p. 720)

*process prepare (p. 402)

productivity how much work each worker does (pp. 755, 863)

*professional occupations requiring special knowledge or education (p. 651)

*prohibit stop; disallow (p. 123)

Prohibition the nationwide ban on the manufacture, sale, and transportation of liquor in the United States that went into effect when the Eighteenth Amendment was ratified in 1919 (p. 761)

*promote to help advance (p. 782)

propaganda ideas or information designed and spread to influence opinion (pp. 127, 713)

proportional to be the same as or corresponding to (p. 199)

conjunto grupo que comparte una actividad, por ejemplo, los barones ferroviarios que establecían acuerdos secretos y fijaban sus propias tarifas (pág. 587)

soberanía popular teoría política acerca de que el gobierno está sujeto a la voluntad de las personas (pág. 215); antes de la Guerra Civil, la idea de que las personas que vivían en un territorio tenían el derecho de decidir por votación si se permitiría la esclavitud en dicho lugar (pág. 454)

*plantear presentar (pág. 845)

línea de pobreza un nivel de ingreso personal o familiar por debajo de lo que la clasificación es pobre de acuerdo con los estándares del gobierno (pág. 883)

goleta de pradera una carreta cubierta usada por los pioneros en los viajes por el país (pág. 362)

preámbulo introducción a un documento formal, especialmente la Constitución (págs. 142, 215)

precedente tradición (pág. 253)

prejuicio opinión injusta no basada en los hechos (pág. 396)

*previo anterior, que antecede (pág. 155)

*primarias elección en la que los votantes eligen los candidatos de su partido (pág. 660)

*principal más importante (pág. 93)

*principio razón básica o fundamental, verdad o ley (pág. 270)

*previo anterior o antes (pág. 993)

corsario buque privado armado autorizados a atacar a barcos mercantes (págs. 170, 296)

*proseguir continuar (pág. 720)

*procesar preparar (pág. 402)

productividad cantidad de trabajo que realiza un trabajador (págs. 755, 863)

*profesional ocupaciones que requieren conocimiento o educación especial (pág. 651)

*prohibir detener; desaprobar (pág. 123)

prohibición proscripción nacional en la fabricación, venta, y transporte de licor en Estados Unidos que entró en vigencia cuando la Decimoctava Enmienda fue ratificada en 1919 (pág. 761)

*promover contribuir al avance (pág. 782)

propaganda ideas o información diseñadas y difundidas para influenciar la opinión (págs. 127, 713)

proporcional ser lo mismo que o corresponder a (pág. 199)

proprietary colony colony run by individuals or groups to whom land was granted (pp. 74, 101)

*prospect chance for success; outlook (p. 110)

protectorate a country that is technically independent, but is actually under the control of another country (p. 688)

provisional government temporary government (p. 680)

public works projects such as highways, parks, and libraries built with public funds for public use (p. 777)

pueblo home or community of homes built by Native Americans (pp. 17, 46)

*purchase something bought and paid for (p. 283)

Puritans Protestants who, during the 1600s, wanted to reform the Anglican Church (p. 65)

*pursue to continue (p. 177)

colonia propietaria colonia dirigida por personas o grupos que recibían las tierras (págs. 74, 101)

*perspectiva oportunidad de éxito; visión (pág. 110)

protectorado país teóricamente independiente, pero que en realidad está bajo el control de otro país (pág. 688)

gobierno provisional gobierno temporal (pág. 680)

obras públicas proyectos como autopistas, parques y bibliotecas construidos con fondos públicos para uso público (pág. 777)

pueblo casa o comunidad de casas construidas por nativoamericanos (págs. 17, 46)

*compra algo adquirido y pagado (pág. 283)

puritanos protestantes que, durante los años 1600, deseaban reformar la Iglesia Anglicana (pág. 65)

*perseguir perseverar (pág. 177)

Quechua language spoken by the Inca (p. 15)

quipu calculating device developed by the Inca (p. 15)

*quote to repeat the words of another (p. 973)

quota system an arrangement placing a limit on the number of immigrants from each country (p. 762)

Quran the book composed of sacred writings accepted by Muslims as revelations made to Muhammad by Allah through the angel Gabriel (p. 33)

quechua idioma hablado por los incas (pág. 15)

kipu dispositivo para calcular diseñado por los incas (pág. 15)

*citar reproducir las palabras de otra persona (pág. 973)

sistema de cupos un acuerdo que fija un límite en el número de inmigrantes de cada país (pág. 762)

Corán libro compuesto de escrituras sagradas aceptadas por los musulmanes como revelaciones hechas a Mahoma por Alá a través del ángel Gabriel (pág. 33)

*radical extreme (p. 520)

ragtime a type of music with a strong rhythm and a lively melody with accented notes, which was popular in early 1900s (p. 632)

railroad barons powerful and aggressive businessmen who controlled the nation's railroads (p. 585)

ranchero Mexican ranch owner (p. 374)

rancho huge properties for raising livestock set up by Mexican settlers in California (p. 374)

ratify to give official approval to (p. 177)

ration to give out scarce items on a limited basis (pp. 726, 817)

*radical extremo (pág. 520)

ragtime tipo de música con un ritmo intenso y una melodía animada con notas acentuadas, que era popular a principios de los años 1900 (pág. 632)

barones ferroviarios empresarios poderosos y agresivos que controlaban los ferrocarriles de la nación (pág. 585)

ranchero dueño de un rancho mexicano (pág. 374)

rancho vastas propiedades para la cría de ganado establecidas por pobladores mexicanos en California (pág. 374)

ratificar otorgar aprobación oficial a (pág. 177)

ración producir artículos escasos en un período limitado (págs. 726, 817)

Glossary/Glosario

*react respond (p. 289)

realism an approach to literature and the arts that shows things as they really are (p. 630)

rebate discount or return of part of a payment (p. 587)

recall the right that enables voters to remove elected officials from office (p. 647)

recession a downward turn in business activity (p. 755)

Reconstruction the reorganization and rebuilding of the former Confederate states after the Civil War (p. 519)

recruit to enlist soldiers in the army (p. 155)

referendum the practice of letting voters accept or reject measures proposed by the legislature (p. 647)

*regime governing authority (p. 912)

*region an area inside a larger area (p. 314)

regionalism art or literature focused on a particular region of the country (p. 630)

*register to enroll (p. 889)

*regulate to control (p. 450)

*reject refuse to accept (p. 464)

*relax to ease (p. 943)

relief aid for the needy; welfare (p. 776)

relocate to force a person or group of people to move (p. 343)

*rely depend (p. 89)

*remove take away (p. 368)

rendezvous a meeting (p. 360)

reparations payment by a defeated aggressor nation for damages caused by war (p. 730)

repeal to cancel an act or law (p. 125)

republic a government in which citizens rule through elected representatives (p. 188)

republicanism favoring a republic, or representative democracy, as the best form of government (p. 215)

reservation an area of public lands set aside for Native Americans (p. 568)

reserved powers powers retained by the states (p. 216)

*reside to exist or live within (p. 208)

*resistance an opposing force (p. 509)

*reaccionar responder (pág. 289)

realismo enfoque a la literatura y las artes que muestra las cosas como realmente son (pág. 630)

reembolso descuento o devolución de parte de un pago (pág. 587)

llamar a elecciones derecho que le permite a los votantes destituir a los funcionarios electos de sus puestos (pág. 647)

recesión giro descendiente en la actividad comercial (pág. 755)

reconstrucción reorganización y reconstrucción de los antiguos estados de la Confederación después de la Guerra Civil (pág. 519)

reclutar enrolar soldados al ejército (pág. 155)

referéndum práctica que consiste en permitir que los votantes acepten o rechacen medidas propuestas por la asamblea legislativa (pág. 647)

*régimen autoridad del gobierno (pág. 912)

*región área dentro de un área más amplia (pág. 314)

regionalismo arte o literatura que se centra en una región particular de un país (pág. 630)

*registrarse inscribirse (pág. 889)

*regular controlar (pág. 450)

*rechazar negarse a aceptar (pág. 464)

*relajar aliviar (pág. 943)

alivio ayuda para los necesitados; bienestar (pág. 776)

trasladar obligar a una persona o grupo de personas a trasladarse (pág. 343)

*confiar depender (pág. 89)

*quitar arrebatar (pág. 368)

encuentro reunión (pág. 360)

reparaciones pago realizado por una nación agresora derrotada por los daños causados por la guerra (pág. 730)

revocar cancelar una ley (pág. 125)

república gobierno en que los ciudadanos gobiernan a través de representantes electos (pág. 188)

republicanismo a favor de un república, o democracia representativa, como mejor forma de gobierno (pág. 215)

reservación área de tierras públicas reservadas para los nativoamericanos (pág. 568)

poderes reservados poderes conservados por los estados (pág. 216)

*residir existir o vivir dentro (pág. 208)

*resistencia fuerza opuesta (pág. 509)

resolution a formal expression of opinion (p. 125)

*resolve bring to an end (p. 269)

*resourceful creative (p. 361)

*respond to reply (p. 905)

*restriction limitation (p. 291)

*retain hold onto (p. 977)

*reveal show something that was hidden (p. 313)

revenue incoming money (p. 123)

revenue sharing money raised from federal taxes and given to the states for use at the state and local levels (p. 949)

revival a series of meetings conducted by a preacher to arouse religious emotions (p. 419)

*revolution a war to overthrow a government (p. 716)

*rigid firm and inflexible (p. 458)

*route line of travel (p. 430)

royal colony colony run by a governor and a council appointed by the king or queen (p. 101)

resolución expresión formal de opinión (pág. 125)

*resolver poner fin (pág. 269)

*ingenioso creativo (pág. 361)

*responder contestar (pág. 905)

*restricción limitación (pág. 291)

*retener quedarse con (pág. 977)

*revelar mostrar algo que estaba oculto (pág. 313)

ingresos dinero entrante (pág. 123)

participación en los ingresos dinero recolectado de los impuestos federales y otorgado a los estados para gastos estatales y locales (pág. 949)

renacimiento religioso serie de reuniones dirigidas por un predicador para incitar emociones religiosas (pág. 419)

*revolución guerra para revocar un gobierno (pág. 716)

*rígido firme e inflexible (pág. 458)

*ruta línea de viaje (pág. 430)

colonia real colonia dirigida por el gobernador y un consejo designado por el rey o la reina (pág. 101)

saga a long detailed story (p. 38)

scalawags name given by former Confederates to Southern whites who supported Republican Reconstruction of the South (p. 529)

*scheme a plan (p. 795)

*scope range or area (p. 985)

search-and-destroy mission a strategy used in Vietnam in which American forces sought Vietcong and North Vietnamese units to destroy them (p. 914)

secede to leave or withdraw (pp. 285, 341, 451)

secession withdrawal from the Union (p. 463)

sectionalism loyalty to a region (pp. 322, 449)

*secure gain control (p. 830)

sedition activities aimed at weakening established government (p. 270)

segregation the separation or isolation of a race, class, or group (pp. 540, 875)

*select choose (p. 337)

Separatists Protestants who, during the 1600s, wanted to leave the Anglican Church in order to found their own churches (p. 65)

saga historia larga y detallada (pág. 38)

scalawags nombre otorgado por los primeros confederados a los blancos del Sur que apoyaban la Reconstrucción Republicana del Sur (pág. 529)

*esquema plan (pág. 795)

*alcance rango o área (pág. 985)

misión de búsqueda y destrucción estrategia usada en Vietnam en la que las fuerzas estadounidenses buscaban unidades vietnamitas y vietcong para destruirlas (pág. 914)

separarse abandonar o retirarse (págs. 285, 341, 451)

secesión retiro de la Unión (pág. 463)

seccionalismo lealtad a una región (págs. 322, 449)

*seguro que tiene el control (pág. 830)

sedición actividades dirigidas a debilitar un gobierno establecido (pág. 270)

segregación separación o aislamiento de una raza, clase o grupo (págs. 540, 875)

*seleccionar elegir (pág. 337)

separatistas protestantes que, durante los años 1600, deseaban dejar la Iglesia Anglicana para fundar sus propias iglesias (pág. 65)

Glossary/Glosario

settlement house institution located in a poor neighborhood that provided numerous community services such as medical care, child care, libraries, and classes in English (p. 623)

sharecropping system of farming in which a farmer works land for an owner who provides equipment and seeds and receives a share of the crop (p. 531)

shareholder a person who invests in a corporation by buying stock and is a partial owner (p. 596)

*__shift__ to move (p. 816)

siege military blockade (pp. 505, 822)

*__similar__ having common qualities (p. 278)

*__site__ location (p. 980)

sit-in the act of occupying seats or sitting down on the floor of an establishment as a form of organized protest (p. 885)

slave codes laws passed in the Southern states that controlled and restricted enslaved people (pp. 95, 410)

slum poor, crowded, and run-down urban neighborhoods (p. 622)

socialist person who believes industries should be publicly owned and run by the government rather than by private individuals (p. 727)

sodbuster a name given to the Plains farmer (p. 565)

*__source__ a supply (p. 8)

speculator person who risks money in order to make a large profit (p. 112)

sphere of influence section of a country where one foreign nation enjoys special rights and powers (p. 682)

spiritual an African American religious folk song (p. 409)

spoils system practice of handing out government jobs to supporters; replacing government employees with the winning candidate's supporters (p. 340)

square deal Theodore Roosevelt's promise of fair and equal treatment for all (p. 658)

*__stable__ unchanging (p. 851)

stalemate a situation during a conflict when action stops because both sides are equally powerful and neither will give in (p. 858)

standard gauge the uniform width of 4 feet, 8.5 inches for railroad tracks, adopted during the 1880s (p. 586)

casa de beneficencia institución ubicada en un barrio pobre que brindaba diferentes servicios comunitarios como atención médica, atención infantil, bibliotecas, y clases de inglés (pág. 623)

aparcería sistema de agricultura en el que el agricultor trabaja la tierra para un propietario que aporta el equipo y las semillas y recibe una parte de los cultivos (pág. 531)

accionista persona que invierte en una sociedad anónima mediante la compra de acciones y es propietario parcial (pág. 596)

*__cambiar__ transferir (pág. 816)

sitio bloqueo militar (págs. 505, 822)

*__similar__ con las mismas cualidades (pág. 278)

sitio ubicación (pág. 980)

sentada acción de ocupar asientos o sentarse en el piso de un establecimiento como forma de protesta organizada (pág. 885)

códigos de esclavitud leyes aprobadas en los estados sureños que controlaban y clasificaban a los esclavos (págs. 95, 410)

barrio pobre barrios urbanos pobres, superpoblados y destartalados (pág. 622)

socialista persona que cree que las industrias deben ser públicas y estar dirigidas por el gobierno y no por particulares (pág. 727)

rompedor de cesped nombre otorgado al agricultor de Planicies (pág. 565)

*__fuente__ un suministro (pág. 8)

especulador persona que arriesga dinero para obtener grandes ganancias (pág. 112)

esfera de influencia sección de un país donde una nación extranjera goza de derechos y poderes especiales (pág. 682)

espiritual canción popular religiosa afroamericana (pág. 409)

sistema de despojo práctica de repartir puestos gubernamentales a los defensores; reemplazo de empleados del gobierno con defensores del candidato triunfador (pág. 340)

trato justo promesa de Theodore Roosevelt de un trato igualitario y justo para todos (pág. 653)

*__estable__ que no se modifica (pág. 851)

estancamiento situación durante un conflicto en la que una acción se detiene porque ambos lados son igualmente poderosos y ninguno se rendirá (pág. 858)

medida estándar ancho uniforme de 4 pies, 8.5 pulgadas para los ferrocarriles durante la década de 1880 (pág. 586)

standard of living a measure of people's overall wealth and quality of life; a minimum of necessities and luxuries that a group is accustomed to (p. 863)

states' rights rights and powers independent of the federal government that are reserved for the states by the Constitution; the belief that states' rights supersede federal rights and law (p. 464)

state sovereignty the concept that states have the right to govern themselves independent of the federal government (p. 323)

*status rank or position (p. 142)

steerage cramped quarters on a ship's lower decks for passengers paying the lowest fares (p. 614)

stock shares of ownership a company sells in its business which often carry voting power (p. 596)

stock exchange a place where shares in corporations are bought and sold through an organized system (p. 773)

strait a narrow passageway connecting two larger bodies of water (p. 41)

*strategy plan of action (pp. 175, 507)

*stress call particular attention to; emphasize (p. 713)

strike a stopping of work by workers to force an employer to meet demands (p. 396)

strikebreaker person hired to replace a striking worker in order to break up a strike (p. 606)

*structure something that is constructed or built (p. 17)

subsidy grant of money from the government to a person or a company for an action intended to benefit the public (p. 555)

subsistence farming farming in which only enough food to feed one's family is produced (p. 89)

*substitute replacement (p. 496)

suburbs residential areas that sprang up close to or surrounding cities as a result of improvements in transportation (p. 622)

subversion an attempt to overthrow a government by persons working secretly from within (p. 848)

*successor one who follows another in order (p. 99)

nivel de vida nivel de bienestar general y calidad de vida de las personas; necesidades mínimas y lujos a los que un grupo está acostumbrado (pág. 863)

derechos estatales derechos y poderes independientes del gobierno federal que se reservan para los estados a través de la Constitución; creencia acerca de que los derechos de los estados superan los derechos y las leyes federales (pág. 464)

soberanía estatal concepto acerca de que los estados tienen derecho a gobernarse independientemente del gobierno federal (pág. 323)

*estatus rango o posición (pág. 142)

bodega espacio estrecho en la cubierta inferior de un barco para pasajeros que pagan la tarifa más baja (pág. 614)

acciones participaciones de la propiedad de una compañía que en general cuentan con poder de votación (pág. 596)

bolsa de valores lugar donde las acciones en las sociedades anónimas se compran y se venden a través de un sistema organizado (pág. 773)

estrecho pasadizo estrecho que conecta dos masas de agua mayores (pág. 41)

*estrategia plan de acción (págs. 175, 507)

*resaltar poner especial atención en; enfatizar (pág. 713)

huelga cese laboral de los trabajadores para imponerle a un empleador el cumplimiento de las exigencias (pág. 396)

rompehuelgas persona contratada para reemplazar a un trabajador en huelga con el fin de detener la huelga (pág. 606)

*estructura algo construido o fabricado (pág. 17)

subsidio préstamo de dinero del gobierno a una persona o compañía por una acción cuya intención es beneficiar al público (pág. 555)

agricultura de subsistencia agricultura en la que sólo se producen alimentos suficientes para abastecer a una familia (pág. 89)

*sustituto reemplazo (pág. 496)

suburbios áreas residenciales que se extienden cerca o alrededor de las ciudades como resultado de mejoras en el transporte (pág. 622)

subversión intento de derrocar a un gobierno por parte de las personas que trabajan en secreto desde adentro (pág. 848)

*sucesor persona que sigue a otra en orden (pág. 99)

Glossary/Glosario

suffrage the right to vote (p. 435)

suffragist a man or woman who fought for a woman's right to vote (p. 652)

***sum** amount or total (p. 553)

summit a meeting of heads of government (p. 862)

supply-side economics an economic theory that proposes tax cuts as a means of stimulating the economy to produce more goods and services (p. 972)

surplus excess; amount left over after necessary expenses are paid (pp. 93, 861)

***survive** continue to live (p. 347)

***suspend** to prevent or bar from carrying out official duties (p. 526)

***sustain** to suffer or experience (p. 173)

sweatshop a shop or factory where workers work long hours at low wages under unhealthy conditions (pp. 603, 615)

***symbol** an object that represents something else (p. 352)

sufragio derecho a votar (pág. 435)

sufragista hombre o mujer que lucha por los derechos de las mujeres a votar (pág. 652)

***suma** monto o total (pág. 553)

cumbre reunión de los líderes gubernamentales (pág. 862)

economía del lado de la oferta teoría económica que propone recortes impositivos para estimular la economía con el fin de producir más bienes y servicios (pág. 972)

superávit exceso; cantidad que queda después de pagar los gastos necesarios (págs. 93, 861)

***sobrevivir** continuar con vida (pág. 347)

***suspender** detener o prohibir la continuidad de las tareas de un funcionario (pág. 526)

***sufrir** experimentar o sobrellevar (pág. 173)

fábrica donde se explota a los obreros tienda o fábrica donde los empleados trabajan muchas horas por salarios bajos y en condiciones insalubres (págs. 603, 615)

***símbolo** objeto que representa una cosa (pág. 352)

T

***target** an object of attack (p. 809)

tariff a tax on imports or exports (pp. 257, 341)

***technique** skillful method (p. 755)

***technology** the use of science in commerce and industry (pp. 31, 945)

Tejano a Mexican who claims Texas as his home (p. 367)

telegraph a device or system that uses electric signals to transmit messages by a code over wires (p. 391)

temperance the use of little or no alcoholic drink (p. 419)

***temporary** not lasting (p. 449)

tenant farmer farmer who works land owned by another and pays rent either in cash or crops (pp. 81, 407)

tenement a building in which several families rent rooms or apartments, often with little sanitation or safety (p. 622)

***tense** anxious or nervous (p. 823)

terrace a raised piece of land with the top leveled off to promote farming (p. 15)

***objetivo** objeto de ataque (pág. 809)

arancel impuesto sobre las importaciones o las exportaciones (págs. 257, 341)

***técnica** método especializado (pág. 755)

***tecnología** uso de ciencia en el comercio y la industria (págs. 31, 945)

tejano mejicano que reclama Texas como su patria (pág. 367)

telégrafo dispositivo o sistema que usa señales eléctricas para transmitir mensajes mediante códigos y cableado (pág. 391)

templanza consumo de pocas bebidas alcohólicas o ninguna (pág. 419)

***temporal** que no dura (pág. 449)

arrendatario agricultor que trabaja la tierra de otra persona y paga un alquiler en efectivo o mediante cultivos (págs. 81, 407)

inquilinato construcción en la que varias familias alquilan habitaciones o departamentos, en general con escaso saneamiento y seguridad (pág. 622)

***tenso** ansioso o nervioso (pág. 823)

terraza terreno elevado con el extremo superior nivelado para promover la agricultura (pág. 15)

territory an area that is completely controlled by another country as a colonial possession (p. 688)

terrorism the use of violence by groups against civilians to achieve a political goal (p. 991)

*****theme** a subject or topic of a work (p. 974)

theocracy a form of government in which the society is ruled by religious leaders (p. 12)

Tidewater a region of flat, low-lying plains along the seacoast (p. 94)

tight money policy the practice of raising interest rates to slow personal spending (p. 950)

time zone a geographical region within which the same standard of time is used (p. 557)

*****topic** subject of discussion (p. 460)

total war war on all aspects of the enemy's life (p. 507)

totalitarian a political system in which the government suppresses all opposition and controls most aspects of people's lives (p. 806)

*****trace** follow back to (p. 911)

trade deficit the situation when the value of a country's foreign imports exceeds the value of its exports (pp. 960, 1002)

trade union organization of workers with the same trade or skill (pp. 396, 604)

*****tradition** cultural beliefs and practices (p. 205)

transcendentalist any of a group of New England writers who stressed the relationship between human beings and nature, spiritual things over material things, and the importance of the individual conscience (p. 421)

transcontinental extending across a continent (p. 555)

*****transfer** to move from one place to another (p. 155)

*****transform** to change (p. 391)

*****transmit** send from one place to another (p. 589)

*****trend** general direction (p. 599)

triangular trade a trade route that exchanged goods between the West Indies, the American colonies, and West Africa (p. 90)

tributary a smaller river that flows into a larger river (p. 482)

tribute money paid for protection (p. 287)

*****trigger** to start (p. 686)

territorio área controlada completamente por otro país como posesión colonial (pág. 688)

terrorismo uso de violencia contra los civiles por parte de grupos para lograr una meta política (pág. 991)

*****tema** asunto o temática de un trabajo (pág. 974)

teocracia forma de gobierno en la que la sociedad es gobernada por líderes religiosos (pág. 12)

Tidewater región de llanuras planas de baja altura a lo largo de la costa marina (pág. 94)

política monetaria restrictiva práctica de aumentar las tasas de interés para bajar el gasto personal (pág. 950)

huso horario región geográfica en la que se usa la misma hora estándar (pág. 557)

*****tema** objeto de discusión (pág. 460)

guerra total guerra en todos los aspectos de la vida del enemigo (pág. 507)

totalitarismo sistema político en el que el gobierno reprime la oposición y controla la mayoría de los aspectos de las vidas de las personas (pág. 806)

*****rastrear** perseguir (pág. 911)

déficit comercial situación en la que el valor de las importaciones extranjeras de un país exceden el valor de sus exportaciones (págs. 960, 1002)

gremio organización de trabajadores con el mismo oficio o destreza (págs. 396, 604)

*****tradición** creencias y prácticas culturales (pág. 205)

transcendentalista cualquier grupo de escritores de Nueva Inglaterra que enfatizaba la relación entre los seres humanos y la naturaleza, las cosas espirituales en lugar de las cosas materiales; y la importancia de la conciencia del individuo (pág. 421)

transcontinental que se extiende a lo largo de un continente (pág. 555)

*****transferir** llevar de un lugar a otro (pág. 155)

*****transformar** modificar (pág. 391)

*****transmitir** enviar de un lugar a otro (pág. 589)

*****tendencia** dirección general (pág. 599)

comercio triangular ruta comercial que intercambia bienes entre las Antillas, las colonias estadounidenses, y África Occidental (pág. 90)

afluente un río más pequeño que desemboca en un río más grande (pág. 482)

tributo dinero que se paga a cambio de protección (pág. 287)

*****desencadenar** iniciar (pág. 686)

Glossary/Glosario

trust a combination of firms or corporations formed by a legal agreement, especially to reduce competition (p. 597)

trustbuster someone who breaks up a trust into smaller companies (p. 657)

turnpike a road that one must pay to use; the money is used to pay for the road (p. 313)

sindicación combinación de compañías o sociedades anónimas formadas por un acuerdo legal, en especial para reducir la competencia (pág. 597)

destructor de monopolios persona que divide la empresa en compañías más pequeñas (pág. 657)

autopista ruta cuyo uso debe pagarse; el dinero se utiliza para pagar la ruta (pág. 313)

U-boat German submarine in World Wars I and II (p. 709)

unconstitutional not agreeing or consistent with the Constitution (p. 257)

***underestimate** misjudge; disbelieve the abilities of others (p. 295)

Underground Railroad a system that helped enslaved African Americans follow a network of escape routes out of the South to freedom in the North (p. 430)

unemployment insurance payments by the government for a limited period of time to people who have lost their jobs (p. 797)

***uniform** identical; unchanging (p. 255)

***unify** to join together (p. 807)

urban sprawl the spread of human settlements into natural areas (p. 1003)

utopia community based on a vision of a perfect society sought by reformers (p. 419)

***U-boat* (submarino)** submarino alemán en la Primera y Segunda Guerra Mundial (pág. 709)

inconstitucional que no concuerda ni concuerda con la Constitución (pág. 257)

***subestimar** juzgar mal; desacreditar las capacidades de otros (pág. 295)

Ferrocarril Subterráneo sistema que ayudó a los esclavos afroamericanos a seguir una red de rutas de escape del Sur para obtener libertad en el Norte (pág. 430)

seguro de desempleo pagos del gobierno durante un período limitado a las personas que perdieron sus empleos (pág. 797)

***uniforme** que es idéntico; no se modifica (pág. 255)

unificar poner juntos (pág. 807)

expansión urbana expansión de los asentamientos humanos en áreas naturales (pág. 1003)

utopía comunidad basada en una visión de la sociedad perfecta deseada por los reformadores (pág. 419)

vaquero Hispanic ranch hand (p. 562)

vaudeville stage entertainment made up of various acts, such as dancing, singing, comedy, and magic shows (p. 631)

veto to reject a bill and prevent it from becoming a law (p. 349)

Vietnamization Nixon's policy that called for South Vietnam to take a more active role in fighting the war and for Americans to become less involved (p. 928)

vigilantes people who take the law into their own hands (pp. 380, 554)

***violate** disturb or disregard (p. 124)

***vision** an imagined plan (p. 676)

***volunteer** willingly step forward (p. 136)

vaquero dueño de un rancho hispano (pág. 562)

vodevil entretenimiento en un escenario que consta de varios actos, como danza, cantos, comedia y espectáculos de magia (pág. 631)

veto rechazar un proyecto de ley y evitar que se convierta en ley (pág. 349)

vietnamización política de Nixon que sostenía que Vietnam del Sur debía tener un papel más activo en la guerra y que Estados Unidos debía involucrarse menos (pág. 928)

vigilantes personas que toman la ley en sus propias manos (págs. 380, 554)

***violar** alterar o hacer caso omiso (pág. 124)

***visión** plan imaginado (pág. 676)

***voluntario** que tiene voluntad de avanzar (pág. 136)

Glossary/Glosario

***welfare** standard care; well-being (p. 797)

*__widespread__ far-reaching (p. 569)

work relief programs that gave needy people government jobs (p. 781)

writ of assistance legal document that enabled officers to search homes and warehouses for goods that might be smuggled (p. 123)

*__bienestar__ atención estándar; saludable (pág. 797)

*__generalizado__ trascendental (pág. 569)

alivio laboral programas en los que se repartieron empleos del gobierno a las personas necesitadas (pág. 781)

escritos de asistencia documento legal que le permitía a los funcionarios buscar casas y depósitos para almacenar los posibles productos de contrabando (pág. 123)

yellow journalism writing which exaggerates sensational, dramatic, and gruesome events to attract readers, named for stories that were popular during the late 1800s (p. 600); a type of sensational, biased, and often false reporting (pp. 630, 686)

yeoman Southern owner of a small farm who did not have enslaved people (p. 407)

periodismo amarillo escrito que exagera eventos sensacionalistas, dramáticos y atroces para atraer la atención de los lectores, su nombre proviene de las historias populares a fines de los años 1800 (pág. 600); un tipo de información sensacionalista, parcial, y, en general, falsa (págs. 630, 686)

terrateniente menor propietario sureño de una pequeña granja que no tuvo esclavos (pág. 407)

Glossary/Glosario

Index

The following abbreviations are used in the index: m=map, c=chart, p=photograph or picture, g=graph, crt=cartoon, ptg=painting, q=quote.

B

Index

E

Index

Index

Index

Index

Index

Index

T

Index

Acknowledgments

Text Acknowledgments

Grateful acknowledgement is given authors, publishers, and agents for permission to reprint the following copyrighted material. Every effort has been made to determine copyright owners. In case of any omissions, the Publisher will be pleased to make suitable acknowledgements in future editions.

70 From *The Witch of Blackbird Pond* by Elizabeth George Speare. Copyright © 1958 by Elizabeth George Speare, copyright renewed © 1986 by Elizabeth George Speare. Reprinted by permission of Houghton Mifflin Company. All rights reserved.; **130** From *The Journal of William Thomas Emerson: A Revolutionary War Patriot* by Barry Denenberg. © 1998 Reprinted by permission of Scholastic Inc.; **310** Reprinted by permission of Simon & Schuster Books for Young Readers, an imprint of Simon & Schuster's Publishing Division, from *Fever, 1793* by Laurie Halse Anderson. Copyright © 2000 by Laurie Halse Anderson.; **404** From *Day of Tears: A Novel in Dialogue* by Julius Lester. Copyright © 2005 by Julius Lester. Reprinted by permission of Hyperion Books for Children ; **648** From *Counting on Grace* by Elizabeth Winthrop, copyright © 2006 by Elizabeth Winthrop. Used by permission of Wendy Lamb Books, an imprint of Random House Children's Books, a division of Random House, Inc.; **767** "The Negro Speaks of Rivers," from *The Collected Poems of Langston Hughes* by Langston Hughes, copyright © 1994 by The Estate of Langston Hughes. Used by permission of Alfred A. Knopf, a division of Random House, Inc.; **767** "Mother to Son," from *The Collected Poems of Langston Hughes* by Langston Hughes, copyright © 1994 by The Estate of Langston Hughes. Used by permission of Alfred A. Knopf, a division of Random House, Inc.; **892** From *The Watsons Go to Birmingham—1963* by Christopher Paul Curtis. Copyright © 1995 by Christopher Paul Curtis. Used by permission of Doubleday, a division of Random House, Inc.; **964** Excerpt from *Taking Sides*, copyright © 1991 by Gary Soto, reprinted by permission of Harcourt, Inc.

Glencoe would like to acknowledge the artists and agencies who participated in illustrating this program: SettingPace; American Artists Reps Inc.; GeoNova LLC.

Photo Credits

(bl)The Granger Collection, New York; **276** (tr)Private Collection, Peter Newark American Pictures/The Bridgeman Art Library International, (br)Library of Congress, Prints & Photographs Division; **278** (cr)Monticello/Thomas Jefferson Foundation, Inc., (bl)Index Stock; **280** David David Gallery/SuperStock; **282** Brown Brothers; **283** The Granger Collection, New York; **284** (tl)Getty Images, (tr)Clark Family Collection, William Clark Papers/Missouri Historical Society, St. Louis; **286** (tr)Smithsonian Institution; **286–287** (b)Courtesy of the Naval Historical Foundation, Washington, D.C.; **287** (br)U.S. Navy Photo; **288** Private Collection/Photo ©Christie's Images/The Bridgeman Art Library; **289** (tl)The Mariners' Museum, Newport News, VA, (tcr)U.S. Naval Academy Collection, (tr)North Wind Pictures; **290** The Granger Collection, New York; **292** (tl c)The Granger Collection, New York, (tc)Ohio Historica Society, (tr)Getty Images; **294–295** The Granger Collection, New York; **295** (bc)Collection of the New York Historical Society, USA/The Bridgeman Art Library International; **296** Troiani Collection; **297** (cl)Stock Montage/Getty Images, (others)The Granger Collection, New York; **302** (c)Collection of the New York Historical Society, USA/The Bridgeman Art Library, (c)The Granger Collection, New York, (bcr)Hermitage, St. Petersburg, Russia/Bridgeman Art Library; **303** (c)Smithsonian Institution/CORBIS, (bc)Clive Barda/PAL/The Image Works, (br)North Wind Picture Archives; **304–305** (b)Bettmann/CORBIS; **305** (bc)University of Massachusetts Lowell, Center for Lowell History; **306** Smithsonian Institution, Washington D.C., USA/The Bridgeman Art Library; **307** SSPL/The Image Works; **308** The Granger Collection, New York; **310** (tl)Joyce Tenneson, (cr)The Granger Collection, New York; **312–313** The Granger Collection, New York; **314** North Wind Picture Archives; **315** Brand X Pictures/PunchStock; **316** The Granger Collection, New York; **318** (tl br)Bettmann/CORBIS, (c)North Wind Picture Archives/Alamy; **319** (tc)Illustration Works/Getty Images, (c)North Wind Picture Archives/Alamy, (cr)Bettmann/CORBIS; **320** (tr)Bettmann/CORBIS; **320–321** (b)Fourth of July Celebration in Center Square by John Lewis Krimmel, 1819, India ink and watercolor, 31.5 x 46cm, (Bc882 K897), The Historical Society of Pennsylvania; **321** (bc)Gibson Stock Photography; **322** (b)The Corcoran Gallery of Art/CORBIS, (br)Massachusetts Historical Society, Boston, MA, USA/The Bridgeman Art Library; **323** Christie's Images/The Bridgeman Art Library; **325** (cr)Superstock, (others)The Granger Collection, New York; **330** (cl)Historical & Military Archive; **330–331** The Granger Collection, New York; **334** (tc)Woolaroc Museum, Bartlesville, Oklahoma, USA/SuperStock, (bc)Underwood & Underwood/CORBIS, (br)Taxi/Getty Images; **335** (c)Bettmann/CORBIS, (bl)Museum of London/HIP/The Image Works, (br)Houlton-Deutsch Collection/CORBIS; **336** (cr)Archivo Iconografico, S.A./CORBIS; **336–337** CORBIS SYGMA; **338** (c)The Granger Collection, New York, (bl)David J. & Janice L. Frent Collection/CORBIS; **339** (cl)The Granger Collection, New York, (bl)David J. & Janice L. Frent Collection/CORBIS; **340** Bettmann/CORBIS; **342** (tr)James Robinson/Animals Animals/Earth Scenes; **342–343** North Wind/North Wind Picture Archives; **344** Bettmann/CORBIS; **345** (tc)SuperStock, Inc./SuperStock, (cl)Library of Congress, Prints & Photographs Division, [reproduction number, e.g., LC-USZ62-110212], (cr)Buddy Mays/CORBIS; **346** (t)Print Collector/HIP/The Image Works, (tr)North Wind/North Wind Picture Archive; **348–349** The Granger Collection, New York; **350** Collection of the New York Historical Society, USA/The Bridgeman Art Library; **351** (b br)The Granger Collection, New York, (bcr)Ohio Historical Society; **353** (c)Woolaroc Museum, Bartlesville, Oklahoma, USA/SuperStock, (others)Bettmann/CORBIS; **355** National Museum of American History, Smithsonian Institution, Behring Center; **356** (others)Butler Institute of American Art, Youngstown, OH, USA/Gift of Joseph G. Butler III 1946/The Bridgeman Art Library, (cl)Unicorn Productions, (cr)Photo Courtesy of the U.S. House of Representatives; **357** (tr)CORBIS, (c)Alinari Archives/The Image Works, (br)NASA; **358–359** Private Collection/The Bridgeman Art Library International; **359** (cr)Tria Giovan/CORBIS, (tcl)Museum of the Mountain Man, (tcr)Walters Art Museum, Baltimore, USA/The Bridgeman Art Library; **361** (cr)The Granger Collection, New York, (bl)Courtesy National Park Service; **362** The Granger Collection, New York; **364** (l)The Granger Collection, New York, (c)Bettmann/CORBIS; **365** (tr)The Granger Collection, New York, (r)Bettmann/CORBIS; **366 367** The Center for American History, The University of Texas at Austin; **368** (bl)Archives and Information Services Division, Texas State Library and Archives Commission, (bc)The Granger Collection, New York; **368–369** (b)Bettmann/CORBIS; **369** (bl)Bill Heinsohn/Alamy; **370** (cr)Photo Courtesy of Beth Griggs/First Capitol Historical Foundation, (cr)The Granger Collection, New York; **372–373** The Art Archive/Bill Manns; **374** (tcl)Michael T. Sedam/CORBIS, (tr)Painting by William Henry Jackson; William Henry Jackson Collection. Catalog No.SCBL_155. Scotts Bluff National Monument; **375** The Granger Collection, New York; **376** (tc)Library of Congress, (tr)From the collection of the Old State House Museum; **378–379** Bettmann/CORBIS; **380** The Granger Collection, New York; **381** (c)Bettmann/CORBIS, (c)Government Transfer: U.S. DOTT, USM, (bl)Mormon pioneers pulling handcarts on the long journey to Salt Lake City in 1856 (colour litho), American School, (20th century)/Private Collection, Peter Newark Western Americana/The Bridgeman Art Library, (br)Barry Howe/CORBIS; **383** (tr)Bettmann/CORBIS, (cl)From the collection of the Old State House Museum, (bc)Mormon pioneers pulling handcarts on the long journey to Salt Lake City in 1856 (colour litho), American School, (20th century)/Private Collection, Peter Newark Western Americana/The Bridgeman Art Library; **385** The Granger Collection, New York; **386** (t)Museum of the City of New York, USA/Bridgeman Art Library, (cr)The Granger Collection, New York, (bcl)Fritz Polking/The Image Works; **387** (c)The Granger Collection, New York, (bl)SuperStock, Inc./SuperStock, (bcr)Hulton-Deutsch Collection/CORBIS; **388–389** The Granger Collection, New York; **390** (tl)Bettmann/CORBIS, (tc)Private Collection/Peter Newark American Pictures/The Bridgeman Art Library, (tcr)CORBIS, (tr)Mike Simons/CORBIS; **391** (tl)Collection of the New York Historical Society, USA/The Bridgeman Art Library, (tr)Ann Ronan Picture Library/Heritage/The Image Works; **392** (bl)The Granger Collection, New York, (br)The Image Works Archives; **394** (tr)National Park Service Collection; **394–395** Museum of the City of New York, USA/The Bridgeman Art Library International; **396** (others)The Granger Collection, New York, (tr)age fotostock/Superstock; **397** (c)The Granger Collection, New York, (bcl)David J. & Janice L. Frent Collection/CORBIS; **398** The Granger Collection, New York; **400–401** Private Collection, Peter Newark American Pictures/The Bridgeman Art Library International; **402** (tl)SSPL/The Image Works, (tc)The Granger Collection, New York; **404** (tl)Julius Lester, (cr)The Granger Collection, New York; **406–407** Reinhard Eisele/CORBIS; **407** (br)Collection of the New York Historical Society, USA/The Bridgeman Art Library International; **408** The Granger Collection, New York; **409** Carlos Barria/Reuters/CORBIS; **410** (bl)Alabama Department of Archives and History, Montgomery, Alabama, (bc)CORBIS, (br)Louie Psihoyos/CORBIS; **411** (tcl)CORBIS, (tr)The Granger Collection, New York; **413** (tr)Private Collection, Peter Newark American Pictures/The Bridgeman Art Library International, (cl)The Granger Collection, New York, (c)age fotostock/Superstock; **416** (t)City Art Museum, St. Louis, MO, USA/The Bridgeman Art Library, (bc)Masterfile Royalty Free; **417** (c)Bettmann/CORBIS, (bl)Werner Forman/Art Resource, NY, (br)Snark/Art Resource, NY; **418–419** (b)The Granger Collection, New York; **419** (br)National Portrait Gallery, Smithsonian Institution/Art Resource, NY; **420** The Granger Collection, New York; **422** (tl)Photo Researchers, (c)The Natural History Museum/Alamy, (b)TIME; **423** (tl)North Wind Picture Archives/Alamy, (c)Bettmann/CORBIS; **423** (cr)D. Hurst/Alamy; **424** (tl)The Granger Collection, New York, (tr)Library of Congress, Prints and Photographs Division [LC-USZ62-119343]; **424–425** (b)New York Historical Society; **426** (tl)Library of Congress Prints and Photographs Division Washington, D.C., (others)The Granger Collection, New York; **427** Hulton-Deutsch Collection/CORBIS; **428 429** The Granger Collection, New York; **430** (others)North Wind/North Wind Picture Archives, (tl)The Granger Collection, New York; **432** (tr)Bettmann/CORBIS, (bl)The Granger Collection, New York, (br)Louie Psihoyos/CORBIS, Dave King/Dorling Kindersley/DK Images; **433** (others)The Granger Collection, New York, (br)Bettmann/CORBIS; **434–435** The Granger Collection, New York; **436** National Portrait Gallery, Smithsonian Institution/Art Resource, NY; **437** The Granger Collection, New York; **439** (cl)The Granger Collection, New York, (bcl)National Portrait Gallery, Smithsonian Institution/Art Resource, NY; **441** Library of Congress Prints and Photographs Division Washington, D.C.; **446** (t)Library

of Congress, Washington D.C., USA/The Bridgeman Art Library, (cr)Chicago Historical Society, (br)Superstock, (br)Topham/The Image Works; **447** (c)Superstock, (br)Roger-Viollet/The Image Works; **448–449 450** The Granger Collection, New York; **452–453** Smithsonian American Art Museum, Washington, D.C./Art Resource, NY; **453** (br)The Granger Collection, New York; **454** Superstock; **456–457** The Granger Collection, New York; **457** (br)Private Collection, Peter Newark American Pictures/The Bridgeman Art Library International; **458** (tl)David J. & Janice L. Frent Collection/CORBIS; **458–459** The Granger Collection, New York, (c)CORBIS; **459** (cr)Topham/The Image Works, (bl)CORBIS, (bc)Andre Jenny/The Image Works; **460** (tr)Mary Evans Picture Library/The Image Works, (cl)Andre Jenny/The Image Works, (c)CORBIS; **462–463** Mary Evans Picture Library; **463** (br)Lee Snider/Photo Images/CORBIS; **464** The Granger Collection, New York; **465** Topham/The Image Works; **467** (tl)The Granger Collection, New York, (cr)Library of Congress, Washington D.C., USA/The Bridgeman Art Library, (bl)Mary Evans Picture Library/The Image Works; **470** Bettmann/CORBIS; **471** David J. & Janice L. Frent Collection/CORBIS; **472** (br)National Portrait Gallery, Smithsonian Institution/Art Resource, (bkgd)The Granger Collection, New York; **473** (t)Library of Congress, (b)CORBIS; **474** (t bkgd) Bettmann/CORBIS, (c)Historical Art Prints, Inc.; **476** CORBIS; **477** (t)Library of Congress, (b)Military and Historical Image Bank; **478** (l)Library of Congress, (r)MPI/Getty Images; **480–481** Bettmann/CORBIS; **483** (l)MPI/Getty Images, (tr)CORBIS, (br)Hulton-Deutsch Collection/CORBIS; **484–485** Omikron/Photo Researchers, Inc.; **486** (l)CORBIS, (bkgd)PhotoDisc; **490** (t)Courtesy Dennis M. Keesee Collection; **490–491** (b)Medford Historical Society Collection/CORBIS; **491** (b)Royalty-Free/CORBIS, **492** (l)CORBIS, (tr br)Published courtesy of the Trustees of the Boston Public Library, (r)Royalty-Free/CORBIS; **493** The Granger Collection, New York; **494** (l)Dr. Michael Echols, American Surgical Antiques, (bkgd)Library of Congress; **495** (c)Michael Macor/San Francisco *Chronicle*/CORBIS, Eliot Elisofon/Time Life Pictures/Getty Images; **496** (t)David A. Northcott/CORBIS, (b)The Granger Collection, New York; **498** (t)Bettmann/CORBIS; **498–499** (bkgd)MPI/Getty Images, **499** (tr)Old Paper Studios/Alamy, (br)Library of Congress; **500–501** CORBIS; **501** (t)Kean Collection/Getty Images; **502** National Portrait Gallery, Smithsonian Institution/Art Resource; **503** (t)David Muench/CORBIS, (c)The Granger Collection, New York, (b)Military and Historical Image Bank; **504** CORBIS; **506** (t)CORBIS, **506–507** Library of Congress; **508** (l)CORBIS, (r)Royalty-Free/CORBIS; **509** CORBIS; **511** Trish Gant/Getty Images; **513** (tl)Michigan Capitol Committee, photography by Peter Glendinning, (tcl)The Museum of the Confederacy, Richmond, Virginia/Photography by Katherine Wetzel, (c)Royalty-Free/CORBIS, (cr)Creatas Images/Jupiter Images, (b)Library of Congress; **515** (c)The Granger Collection, New York, (c)CORBIS, (bcl)Copyright © 2007 by Robert Frerck and Odyssey Productions, Inc., (bc)Chris Willson/Alamy, (br)Musee Marmottan, Paris, France, Giraudon/The Bridgeman Art Library; **517** (c)National Portrait Gallery, Smithsonian Institution/Art Resource, NY, (bl)Hulton-Deutsch Collection/CORBIS, (bc)The National Archives; **518** (tr)Bettmann/CORBIS; **518–519** (b)Picture History; **519** (br)CORBIS; **520** (tl)CORBIS, (tr)The Granger Collection, New York; **522–523** (b)North Wind/North Wind Picture Archives; **523** (bc)The Granger Collection, New York; **524** (tr)Reuters/Larry Downing/newscom, (others)Bettmann/CORBIS; **525** Bettmann/CORBIS; **526** The Granger Collection, New York; **528** (tr)Courtesy of Special Collections, LSU Libraries, Louisiana State University; **528–529** (b)Bettmann/CORBIS; **529** (bcl)Brooklyn Museum/CORBIS; **530** (tl)Time Life Pictures/Timepix/Getty Images, (tr)Hulton Archive/Getty Images; **532** (c)Photo Researchers, (br)North Wind Picture Archives/Alamy; **533** (tl)CORBIS, (bl)Bettmann/CORBIS, (br)Mary Evans Picture Library/Alamy; **534** (tr)Library of Congress, Prints & Photographs Division; **534–535** (b)North Wind/North Wind Picture Archives; **537** Bettmann/CORBIS; **538** (bl)Bettmann/CORBIS, (bcr)The Granger Collection, New York; **541** (c)The Granger Collection, New York; **542** Bettmann/CORBIS; **543** (tl)Library of Congress, LC-USZ62-104925, (others)CORBIS; **545** CORBIS; **546** (b)Bettmann/CORBIS; **546–547** Museum of the City of New York, USA/Bridgeman Art Library; **550** (t)The Granger Collection, New York, (c)CORBIS, (cr)CORBIS, (bc)Archivo Iconografico, SA/CORBIS, (bcr)The Granger Collection, New York, (br)Joel Page/AP Images; **552–553** CORBIS; **553** (br)Library of Congress, Prints & Photographs Division [LC-DIG-pga-01999]; **554** North Wind/North Wind Picture Archives; **555** L. Berger/SuperStock; **556** The Granger Collection, New York; **558** (tl)CORBIS, (cr)National Archives; **560–561** (b)SuperStock, Inc./SuperStock; **561** (bc)Private Collection, Peter Newark American Pictures/The Bridgeman Art Library International; **562** The Granger Collection, New York; **563** (tl)Private Collection, Peter Newark Western Americana/The Bridgeman Art Library International, (tr)CORBIS; **564** (tcr)North Wind/North Wind Picture Archives, (tr)The Granger Collection, New York, (bkgd)Bettmann/CORBIS; **566–567** The Granger Collection, New York; **569** (cr bcr)The Granger Collection, New York, (bl)Private Collection, Peter Newark American Pictures/The Bridgeman Art Library, (bc)CORBIS; **570** (tl)The Granger Collection, New York, (c)CORBIS; **572** (bl)Private Collection, Peter Newark American Pictures/The Bridgeman Art Library International, (br)Washington *Missourian*, Karen Cernich/AP Images; **572–573** (b)CORBIS, (bkgd)The Granger Collection, New York; **573** (cl)Art Resource, NY; **574–575** (b)CORBIS; **576** (t)CORBIS, (tr)The Granger Collection, New York; **577** The Granger Collection, New York; **579** (tl)SuperStock, Inc./SuperStock, (tr)Library of Congress, Prints & Photographs Division [LC-DIG-pga-01999], (cr)CORBIS, (cr br)The Granger Collection, New York; **581** AP Images; **582** (t)CORBIS, (cr br)The Granger Collection, New York, (b)Charles O'Rear/CORBIS; **583** (others)AP Images, (br)The Granger Collection, New York; **584–585** Private Collection, Peter Newark American Pictures/The Bridgeman Art Library International; **586** The Granger Collection, New York; **588–589** (b)Hulton Archive/Getty Images; **589** (bc)Picture Research Consultants, (br)The Queens Borough Public Library, Long Island Division, Latimer Family Papers; **590** (tl)Underwood & Underwood/CORBIS, (tc)CORBIS, (tr)Bettmann/CORBIS; **591** (tl tc cl)The Granger Collection, New York, (tr)CORBIS, (br)Paul Almasy/CORBIS; **592** (tl)SSPL/The Image Works; **594–595** Roger-Viollet/The Image Works; **595** (br)Bettmann/CORBIS; **596** A'Lelia Bundles/madamcjwalker.com/Walker Family Collection; **597** Bettmann/CORBIS; **600** CORBIS, (cl)Bettmann/CORBIS; **601** (tr)Bettmann/CORBIS, (r)CORBIS; **602–603** CORBIS; **604** The Granger Collection, New York; **605** (tl)Bettmann/CORBIS, (tr)Library of Congress; **607** (tcr)Paul Almasy/CORBIS, (tr)SSPL/The Image Works; **610** (b)The Granger Collection, New York; **610–611** (b)The Granger Collection, New York; **611** (c)Mary Evans Picture Library/Alamy, (br)Hulton-Deutsch Collection/CORBIS, (b)Mary Evans Picture Library, (bl)AP Images, (br)The Granger Collection, New York; **612–613** Library of Congress, Prints & Photographs Division [LC-DIG-ggbain-50437]; **613** (br)CNAM, Conservatoire National des Arts et Metiers, Paris, Archives Charmet/The Bridgeman Art Library International; **614** (t)The Granger Collection, New York, (bc)Royalty-Free, Getty Images, (bcr)Free Agents Limited/CORBIS, (br)Richard Hamilton Smith/CORBIS; **615 616** The Granger Collection, New York; **618** (t)Bettmann/CORBIS, (bl)CORBIS; **619** (t)Bettmann/CORBIS, (cr)Visual Arts Library (London)/Alamy, (bl)Hulton-Deutsch Collection/CORBIS; **620–621** Alvah C. Roebuck/CORBIS; **622** The Granger Collection, New York; **623** (others)The Granger Collection, New York, (bl)Wallace Kirkland/Time Life Pictures/Getty Images; **624** (others)The Granger Collection, New York, (tc)Mary Evans Picture Library/Alamy; **626–627** Mark Rucker/Transcendental Graphics, Getty Images; **628** (cr)Bettmann/CORBIS, (others)CORBIS; **629** (t)CORBIS, (tr)Bettmann/CORBIS; **630** The Granger Collection, New York; **631** Duomo/CORBIS; **633** (cr)Library of Congress, Prints & Photographs Division [LC-DIG-ggbain-50437], (others)The Granger Collection, New York; **635** Bettmann/CORBIS; **636** (bcl)The Granger Collection, New York; **636–637** CORBIS; **640** (t)Paul Thompson/Topical Press Agency/Getty Images, (others)Bettmann/CORBIS, (bc)Hulton-Deutsch Collection/CORBIS; **641** (c)David J. & Janice L. Frent Collection/CORBIS, (bl)Bettmann/CORBIS, (bc)E.A. Kennedy III/The Image Works, (br)Mike Agliolo/Photo Researchers, Inc.; **642–643** The New York Public Library/Art Resource, NY; **643** (cr)The Granger Collection, New York; **644** (t)Bettmann/CORBIS, (tc)The Granger Collection, New York, (tr)Bettmann/CORBIS; **645** Bettmann/CORBIS; **646** (tl)The Granger Collection, New York, (tr)Bettmann/CORBIS, (c)CORBIS; **648** Library of Congress; **651** The Art Archive/Culver Pictures; **652** (tc)CORBIS, (tcr)National Association of

Colored Women Clubs, Inc., (tr)Bettmann/CORBIS, (cl)Library of Congress; **653** The Granger Collection, New York; **654** (tc)Kansas State Historical Society, (others)CORBIS, (cl)Private Collection/Peter Newark American Pictures/The Bridgeman Art Library; **656–657** The Granger Collection, New York; **658** (b)CORBIS, (bl)Private Collection/DaTo Images/The Bridgeman Art Library, (br)The Granger Collection, New York; **658–659** (b)Joseph Sohm/Visions of America/CORBIS; **662–663** The Granger Collection, New York; **663** (bc)CORBIS; **664** The Granger Collection, New York; **665** (tc)Bettmann/CORBIS, (tr)Hulton Archive/Getty Images; **666** (bl)MPI/Getty Images, (br)CORBIS; **667** (bl)Arizona Historical Society, (br)Bettmann/CORBIS; **669** (tr)Private Collection/DaTo Images/The Bridgeman Art Library, (cl)CORBIS, (bl)The Art Archive/Culver Pictures, (br)MPI/Getty Images, (br)Bettmann/CORBIS; **672** (t)Private Collection/Bridgeman Art Library, (bcl)age fotostock/SuperStock; **673** (c)Richard Cummins/CORBIS, (bc)The Granger Collection, New York, (br)Mary Evans Picture Library/The Image Works; **674** (tr)CORBIS; **674–675** (b)Library of Congress, Prints & Photographs Division [LC-DIG-pga-00849]; **676** (cl)Alaska State Archives, (bcr)Holding institution: Alaska State Library, Historical Collections, PO Box 110571, Juneau, AK 99811-0571; mailto:ASL.Historical@eed.state.ak.us; **678–679** U.S. Naval Historical Center Photograph; **679** (br)The Granger Collection, New York; **680** The Granger Collection, New York; **682** (tl)Library of Congress, (tr)The Granger Collection, New York, (tr)Bettmann/CORBIS; **684–685** (b)CORBIS; **685** (bc)ullstein bild/The Granger Collection, New York, (bcr)Lester S. Levy Collection of Sheet Music, Special Collections, The Sheridan Libraries, The Johns Hopkins University; **686** The Granger Collection, New York; **687** (others)The Granger Collection, New York, (c)David J. & Janice L. Frent Collection/CORBIS; **688** The Granger Collection, New York; **690–691** CORBIS; **691** (br)Underwood & Underwood/CORBIS; **693** (others)CORBIS, (cr)CDC, (bl)Lake County Museum/CORBIS; **694** Bettmann/CORBIS; **695** (others)CORBIS, (bc)Library of Congress; **697** (l)Lake County Museum/CORBIS, (tr)The Granger Collection, New York, (cl)Lester S. Levy Collection of Sheet Music, Special Collections, The Sheridan Libraries, The Johns Hopkins University, (bl)Columbus Memorial Library; **698** Columbus Memorial Library; **699** (tr)The Granger Collection, New York, (r)Bettmann/CORBIS; **701** The Granger Collection, New York; **702** (c)The Mariners' Museum/CORBIS, (cr)David Pollack/K.J. Historical/CORBIS, (b)Hulton-Deutsch Collection/CORBIS, (others)Bettmann/CORBIS; **703** (tr)Michael Kooren/Reuters/CORBIS, (others)Bettmann/CORBIS; **704–705** Hulton-Deutsch Collection/CORBIS; **705** (br)Austrian Archives/CORBIS; **706 707** The Granger Collection, New York; **708** (tl)CORBIS, (tc)The Art Archive/Dagli Orti, (tc)The Granger Collection, New York, (cr)The Art Archive/Imperial War Museum; **710** The Granger Collection, New York; **711** (c)Hulton-Deutsch Collection/CORBIS, (bl)Artmedia/Heritage-Images/The Image Works, (br)Sally A. Morgan/Ecoscene/CORBIS; **712–713** The Granger Collection, New York; **713** (br)ullstein bild/The Granger Collection, New York; **715** Topical Press Agency/Getty Images; **716 718–719** CORBIS; **719** (br)Photograph courtesy of the Pocumtuck Valley Memorial Association, Memorial Hall Museum, Deerfield, Massachusetts; **720–721** (b)CORBIS; **721** (br)Alamy; **722** Bettmann/CORBIS; **724–725** CORBIS; **726** (tl)The Granger Collection, New York, (tc)CORBIS, (tcr)David Pollack/CORBIS, (tr)Swim Ink 2, LLC/CORBIS; **728–729 731** Bettmann/CORBIS; **733** (cl)CORBIS, (cr)Alamy, (others)The Granger Collection, New York, (b)Bettmann/CORBIS; **734** (t)Bettmann/CORBIS, (b)VSTOCK/Alamy; **735** (t tc)TIME, (bl br)Bettmann/CORBIS; **737** The Granger Collection, New York; **738** (bcl)The Granger Collection, New York; **738–739** CORBIS; **742** (t)H. Armstrong Roberts/CORBIS, (bl)Bettmann/CORBIS; **743** (t cr)Bettmann/CORBIS, (b)IOC, Olympic Museum/Allsport; **744–745** Hulton-Deutsch Collection/CORBIS; **745** (r)The Granger Collection, New York; **746** (l)MPI/Getty Images, (r)The Granger Collection, New York; **748** (c)CORBIS, (br)The Museum of Modern Art/Licensed by SCALA/Art Resource, NY; **749** (tr)Schomburg Center/Art Resource, (cl)University of Illinois at Chicago, The University Library, Special Collections Department, Arthur and Graham Aldis Papers; **750–751** Library of Congress/Getty Images; **751** (br)David J. & Janice L. Frent Collection/CORBIS; **752** The Granger Collection, New York; **754–755** National Motor Museum/HIP/The Image Works; **755** (bc)Image courtesy of The Toaster Museum Foundation, www.toaster.org; **758–759** Bettmann/CORBIS; **759** (r)Underwood & Underwood/CORBIS; **760** (l)The Granger Collection, New York, (t)CORBIS, (c)Doug Martin; **761** Smithsonian American Art Museum, Washington, D.C./Art Resource, NY, (b)http://www.rootsweb.com/~mobarty/schoolbook/schoolbook2.htm; **762–763** Albert Harlingue/Roger-Viollet/The Image Works; **765** (tl)Hulton-Deutsch Collection/CORBIS, (tr cr)The Granger Collection, New York, (bl)Bettmann/CORBIS; **766** (t)Bettmann/CORBIS, (tl)Miriam Berkley/AuthorPix, (br)Smithsonian American Art Museum, Washington, D.C./Art Resource, NY; **769** Picture Research Consultants; **770** (t)Horace Bristol/CORBIS, (bcr)The Library of Congress; **771** (cr)CORBIS, (bl)National Archives at College Park, Archives II (College Park, MD), (bc)CORR/AFP/Getty Images; **772** (tr)American Stock/Getty Images; **772–773** (b)Bettmann/CORBIS; **773** (b)CORBIS; **774** EFE/CORBIS; **776** Seattle *Post-Intelligencer*; Museum of History and Industry/CORBIS; **777** Arthur Rothstein/Hulton Archive/Getty Images; **778–779** Bettmann/CORBIS; **779** (br)The Advertising Archives; **780** (br)Library of Congress; **780–781** Franklin D. Roosevelt Library; **782** Library of Congress; **784** Bettmann/CORBIS; **785** (cr)Bettmann/CORBIS; **786–787** Bettmann/CORBIS; **787** (br)Marion Post Wolcott/CORBIS; **788** (bl)AP Images, (bc)Library of Congress; **790** (tl)Bettmann/CORBIS, (tl)The Granger Collection, New York; **792** (tl)Dorothea Lange/The Library of Congress, (r)Underwood & Underwood/CORBIS; **793** (t)Lord Price Collection/Alamy, (c)Bettmann/CORBIS; **794–795** Minnesota Historical Society/CORBIS; **796** (b)Library of Congress, (br)Bettmann/CORBIS, (br)Reni Newsphotos, Inc./Library of Congress; **797** (bl)Nicholas Kamm/AFP/Getty Images, (bcr)Time Life Pictures/Getty Images, (br)Hassan Ammar/AFP/Getty Images; **799** (t)Horace Bristol/CORBIS, (tr)Arthur Rothstein/Hulton Archive/Getty Images, (bl)Library of Congress, (br)Franklin D. Roosevelt Library; **801** (tr)The Granger Collection, New York, AP Images; **802** (c)Fox Photos/Getty Images; **803** (cl)U.S. Air Force Museum, (bl)Jack Novak/SuperStock, (bcr)Owen Franken/CORBIS; **804–805** Hugo Jaeger/Timepix/Time Life Pictures/Getty Images; **805** (bc)akg-images/Ernst Kutzer; **806** Bettmann/CORBIS; **808–809** Dmitri Kessel/Time Life Pictures/Getty Images; **810–811** Hulton-Deutsch Collection/CORBIS; **812** (br)Bettmann/CORBIS; **814–815** (b)National Archives; **815** (bcl)Library of Congress, Prints & Photographs Division; **816** (bl)Bernard Hoffman/Time Life Pictures/Getty Images, (bl)Bettmann/CORBIS, (br)National Archives; **816–817** (b)Bettmann/CORBIS; **818** (tc)The Mariners' Museum/CORBIS, (tr)National Archives/Roger-Viollet/The Image Works; **820–821** AP Images; **821** (br)David E. Scherman/Time Life Pictures/Getty Images; **822** Hulton-Deutsch Collection/CORBIS; **823** (c)Bettmann/CORBIS, (cr)AP Images; **824** (bl)Woodfin Camp & Associates, (br)U.S. Signal Corps/Time Life Pictures/Getty Images; **825** (c)Bob Landry/TimePix/Getty Images, (others)Brown Brothers; **826** (tc)ullstein bild/The Granger Collection, New York, (tr)United States Holocaust Memorial Museum, (c)Iian/Alamy; **828–829** The Art Archive/Culver Pictures; **830** (tl)CORBIS; **831** (cl)CORBIS, (cr)National Archives, (bl)AP Images; **833** (b)Hulton-Deutsch Collection/CORBIS, (tr)National Archives, (cl)National Archives/Roger-Viollet/The Image Works, (bl)U.S. Air Force Museum, (cr)Library of Congress, Prints & Photographs Division, (bl)Bettmann/CORBIS, (br)CORBIS; **836** (cl)David J. & Janice L. Frent Collection/CORBIS; **836–837** Robert W. Kelley/Time Life Pictures/Getty Images; **840** (t)H. Armstrong Roberts/Classic-Stock/The Image Works, (br)Swim Ink 2, LLC/CORBIS; **841 through 843** Bettmann/CORBIS; **845** Reprinted from the Des Moines *Registrar*/Jay N. Darling, 1946; **846** (cr)Hulton-Deutsch Collection/CORBIS, (bl)Bettmann/CORBIS; **848** The Granger Collection, New York; **850–851** Ed Clark/Time Life Pictures/Getty Images; **852** (t)Bettmann/CORBIS, (br)Mark Kauffman/Time Life Pictures/Getty Images; **853 854** Bettmann/CORBIS; **856–857** Pfc. James Cox/CORBIS; **858** (tl)CORBIS, (tl)Library of Congress/Getty Images, (tr)Hulton-Deutsch Collection/CORBIS; **860** (tr)David J. & Janice L. Frent Collection/CORBIS; **860–861** (b)Bettmann/CORBIS; **862** (b)Bettmann/CORBIS, (b)Jerry Cooke/CORBIS; **862–863** (b)Erin Patrice O'Brien/Getty Images; **863** (bc)Hugh Threlfall/Alamy; **864–865** Du Pont Company Product Information Photograph Collection. HF197234101. Courtesy of Hagley Museum and Library; **867** (tc bc)Bettmann/CORBIS,

(tr)Mark Kauffman/Time Life Pictures/Getty Images, (cl)Reprinted from the Des Moines *Registrar*/Jay N. Darling, 1946, (br)Swim Ink 2, LLC/CORBIS; **868** (cr)imagebroker/Alamy; **868–869** Charles E. Rotkin/CORBIS; **869** (tl)PictureNet/CORBIS, (bl)Photo by Lynn Betts, USDA Natural Resources Conservation Service; **872** (t cr)Flip Schulke/CORBIS, (bl)Carl Iwaski/Time Life Pictures/Getty Images, (bl)Don Cravens/Time Life Pictures/Getty Images, (bc)Bettmann/CORBIS, (br)Topham/The Image Works; **873** (c)Jason Laure/The Image Works; **874–875** Carl Iwaski/Time Life Pictures/Getty Images; **877** Bettmann/CORBIS; **878** Gene Herrick/AP Images; **880–881** Bettmann/CORBIS; **882** Steve Schapiro/CORBIS; **884–885** Jack Moebes/CORBIS; **885** (br)AP Images; **887** (tr)Bettmann/CORBIS, (tr)Francis Miller/Time Life Pictures/Getty Images; **888** Hulton-Archive/Getty Images; **889** (tc)Charles Moore/Black Star, (cl)Paul Schutzer/Time Life Pictures/Getty Images; **890** (tl)AP Images, (tr)Bettmann/CORBIS; **892** Time Life Pictures/Getty Images; **894–895** AP Images; **895** (bc)Picture Research Consultants; **896** (cr)Collection of David J. & Janice L. Frent, (bc)Arthur Schatz/Time Life Pictures/Getty Images, (br)Bettmann/CORBIS; **897** Bruce Kliewe/Index Stock; **899** (tl)Francis Miller/Time Life Pictures/Getty Images, (others)Flip Schulke/CORBIS, (cr)Arthur Schatz/Time Life Pictures/Getty Images, (bl)Bruce Kliewe/Index Stock, (br)AP Images; **902** (t)Sal Veder/AP Images, (cr)Larry Burrows/Time Life Pictures/Getty Images, (br)Jack Novak/SuperStock; **903** (c)Jack Novak/SuperStock, (bcr)Collection of David J. & Janice L. Frent; **904–905** Horst Faas/AP Images; **905** (r)Bettmann/CORBIS; **906** (cr)Bettmann/CORBIS, (b)Three Lions/Getty Images; **906–907** (br)AP Images; **910–911** Friedrich Stark/Peter Arnold, Inc.; **912** (cr)UPI/Bettmann/CORBIS, (others)Bettmann/CORBIS; **913** Rikli/Roger-Viollet/The Image Works; **914** Vernon Merritt/Black Star; **916 917** Bettmann/CORBIS; **918** (cr)Courtesy of Robert Sharlet; **918–919** (b)Bettmann/CORBIS; **919** (br)Hulton Archive/Getty Images; **920** AP Images; **921** John Olson/Time Life Pictures/Getty Images; **922** (tl)Steve Schapiro/CORBIS, (tr)Bettmann/CORBIS; **924** (tl)NASA, (tr)George Silk/Timepix/Getty Images, (b)Bettmann/CORBIS; **925** (tl)PhotoDisc/Getty Images, (cr)Andreas Manolis/Reuters/CORBIS, (bl)Al Freni/Time Life Pictures/Getty Images; **926** (cr)Wally McNamee/CORBIS, (bl)Al Freni/Time Life Pictures/Getty Images; **926–927** (b)Bettmann/CORBIS; **927** (bcl)CBS/Landov; **928** Charles Gatewood/The Image Works; **930** Steve Raymer/CORBIS; **931** Christian Simonpietri/Sygma/CORBIS; **935** a 1965 Herblock Cartoon, copyright The Herb Block Foundation; **936** (cl)AP Images; **936–937** Justin Lane/epa/CORBIS; **940** (t)CORBIS, (bc)Lawrence Manning/CORBIS; **941** (c)Bettmann/CORBIS, (bl)Black Star; **942–943** (b)OLIPHANT © 1971 Universal Press Syndicate. Reprinted with permission. All rights reserved; **944** (tcr)CORBIS, (others)Bettmann/CORBIS; **945** NASA Stennis Space Center (NASA-SSC); **946** The New Yorker Collection 1973 Alan Dunn from cartoonbank.com. All rights reserved; **948–949** Gerald R. Brimacombe/Time Life Pictures/Getty Images; **950** (tl)Bettmann/CORBIS, (tr)Gary Wagner/Getty Images; **951** Wally McNamee Sygma/CORBIS; **952** (bl)Wally McNamee/CORBIS, (bcl)Dennis Brack/Black Star, (br)Steve Northup/Time Life Pictures/Getty Images; **953** Alex Webb/Magnum Photos, Inc.; **954** (cr)AP Images, (bc)Wally McNamee/CORBIS; **956** (t)Allstar Picture Library/Alamy, (c)NASA, (b)StockDisc Classic/Alamy; **957** (t)Index Stock/Alamy, (bl)U.S. Mint, (br)Hisham Ibrahim/Photov.com/Alamy; **958–959** Bettmann/CORBIS; **960** (cr)Robert Clay/Alamy, (bcr)Aul J. Richards/AFP/Getty Images; **961** Bettmann/CORBIS; **963** (cl)Steve Northup/Time Life Pictures/Getty Images, (cr)CORBIS, (others)Bettmann/CORBIS; **964** (tl)Gary Soto, (br)Michael Newman/PhotoEdit; **968** (c)Jonathan Nourok/PhotoEdit, (cr)Marion Bernstein, (bcr)Sergei Guneyev/Time Life Pictures/Getty Images; **969** (c)Ben Sklar/AP Images, (bc)Mike Greenlar/Syracuse Newspapers/The Image Works, (br)Official White House Photo by Eric Draper; **970–971** CORBIS; **972** (t)Warner Bros./The Kobal Collection; **972** (bl)Bettmann/CORBIS, (br)Wally McNamee/CORBIS; **973** NASA; **974** (tcl)Brooks Kraft/CORBIS, (tcr)a 1983 Herblock Cartoon, copyright The Herb Block Foundation; **976** (cr)Wally McNamee/CORBIS; **977** (br)Bettmann/CORBIS; **979** (bl)Tom Stoddart/Getty Images, (br)Stuart Franklin/Magnum Photos; **980** Jacques Langevin/CORBIS SYGMA; **982** (cr)Steve Liss/Time Life Pictures/Getty Images; **982–983** Cynthia Johnson/Time Life Pictures/Getty Images; **984** (tr)Reuters/CORBIS, (cl)CNN/AFP/Getty Images, (cr)IM SLOAN/AFP/Getty Image; **985** (tl)Library of Congress, (tcl)Najlah Feanny/CORBIS SABA, (tl)The Granger Collection, New York, (tcr)Wally McNamee/CORBIS SYGMA; **988** (tr)Reuters/CORBIS; **990–991** Doug Kanter/AFP/Getty Images; **992–993** Mark Lennihan/AP Images; **995** Matt Cardy/Getty Images; **996** Marko Georgiev/Getty Images; **998** (l)Joseph Khakshouri/CORBIS, (cl)AP Images; **999** (tr)Reuters/CORBIS, (r)Robert McMahan/Bettmann/CORBIS; **1000–1001** Ed Kashi/CORBIS; **1002** Motoring Picture Library/Alamy; **1004** David Young-Wolff/PhotoEdit; **1005** Bob Daemmrich/Photo Edit; **1007** (tl)Tom Stoddart/Getty Images, (cr)Cynthia Johnson/Time Life Pictures/Getty Images, (bl)Doug Kanter/AFP/Getty Images, (b)Jonathan Nourok/PhotoEdit; **1008** (tr)Duane Burleson/AP Images, (cr)Robert W. Ginn/Alamy, (bl)Shannon Stapleton/Reuters/CORBIS; **1009** (tl)V1/Alamy, (tr)Bob Krist/CORBIS, (bl)Shannon Stapleton/Reuters/CORBIS; **1011** Clay Bennett/© 2006 The Christian Science Monitor (www.csmonitor.com). All rights reserved; **1012** (tl)National Archives, (tcl cl)PhotoDisc/Getty Images, (tcr)dynamicgraphics/Jupiter Images, (tr)Joseph Sohm/Jupiter Images, (bl)Brand X/Punchstock, (br)Library of Congress; **1014** (tl)Image Source/Jupiter Images, (tl bl)PhotoDisc/Getty Images, (tr)Clark Family Collection, William Clark Papers/Missouri Historical Society, St. Louis, (bc)The Granger Collection, New York, (bkgd)Fototeca Storica Nazionale/Getty Images; **1015** Roger-Viollet/The Image Works; **1016** (tc)Billy Rose Theater Collection, The New York Public Library for the Performing Arts, Astor, Lenox and Tilden Foundations, (tr)The Gwlection, New York; **1017** (cl)The Museum of Modern Art/Licensed by SCALA/Art Resource, NY, (c)Bettmann/CORBIS, (cr)Oronoz Archivo; **1018** The Granger Collection, New York; **1019** Bettmann/CORBIS; **1020** AP Images; **1021** Topham/The Image Works; **1022** Superstock; **1023 1024** The Granger Collection, New York; **1025** Library of Congress, Prints and Photographs Division [LC-USZ62-119343]; **1029** Bettmann/CORBIS; **1031** (tl)Sandy Schaeffer/Mai/Mai/Time Life Pictures/Getty Images, (cr)Erin Patrice O'Brien/Getty Images; **1032** The Granger Collection, New York; **1033** Jonathan Nourok/PhotoEdit; **1034** Henryk T. Kaiser/Index Stock; **1039** (tl)Official White House Photo by Eric Draper; **1040** (cl)C. Sherburne/PhotoLink/Getty Images, (br)Bettmann/CORBIS; **1041** (bl)Bettmann/CORBIS, (others)C. Sherburne/PhotoLink/Getty Images; **1042** (tr)CORBIS, (others)C. Sherburne/PhotoLink/Getty Images; **1043** (cr)Bettmann/CORBIS, (others)C. Sherburne/PhotoLink/Getty Images; **1044** C. Sherburne/PhotoLink/Getty Images; **1045** (tl)Wally McNamee/CORBIS, (others)C. Sherburne/PhotoLink/Getty Images; **1046** North Wind Picture Archives; **1047 through 1049** Bettmann/CORBIS; **1050 1051** National Portrait Gallery, Smithsonian Institution/Art Resource, NY; **1052** Mark Burnett; **1053** (tcr)Denver Art Museum Collection: Native Arts acquisition funds, 1968.330ab; © Denver Art Museum, (br)CORBIS; **1055** UPI/Bettmann/CORBIS; **1056** Bettmann/Corbis; **1057** Flip Schulke/CORBIS.

Official Presidential Portraits: White House Historical Association.